THE THEME OF THE END PAPERS

1. The early use of fire; 2. The use of the wheel; 3. The development of weaving; 4. The building of the pyramids of Egypt; 5. Moses receives the Ten Commandments; 6. Confucius, one of the great moral philosophers; 7. Hippocrates, the father of scientific medicine; 8. Athens, the cradle of Western culture; 9. Early exploration; 10. The birth of Christ; 11. Medieval culture in Europe; 12. King John signing the Magna Carta; 13. The introduction of gunpowder to European warfare; 14. Gutenberg and the invention of printing by movable type; 15. Copernicus and the modern concept of the universe; 16. The discovery of the new world by Columbus; 17. William Shakespeare; 18. The Declaration of Independence; 19. The Industrial Revolution; 20. Samuel F. B. Morse, inventor of the telegraph; 21. Thomas A. Edison and the first electric light; 22. The Wright brothers at Kitty Hawk; 23. The development of radio communication; 24. The coming of the Atomic Age.

HOW TO USE THE BIBLIOGRAPHY

HOW TO USE THE INDEX

NOTE ON THE PRONUNCIATION SYSTEM

See table of contents,
Page v, Volume 20

The pronunciation of the symbols given below is indicated by the italicized letters in the words that immediately follow them:

ɑ	*f*ather, c*a*r	ə	m*a*ker, *a*go	ŋ	si*ng*ing	t	*t*rot
ɑ̃	(Fr.) él*an, en**	ɜ	f*i*rst, b*u*rn	o	n*o*te, *o*ld	th	*th*irty-*th*ree
ɒ	wh*a*t, n*o*t	f	*f*or*f*eit	õ	(Fr.) b*on*, r*om*pre	t̪h	*o*ther *th*an *th*is
a	*a*sk, *a*nswer;	g	*g*a*g*	ö	(Ger.) sch*ö*n, b*ö*se	u	r*u*le, pr*u*ne
	(Fr.) *a*tt*a*cher	h	*h*ot*h*ouse	ɔ	*o*rb, *a*ll	ü	(Fr.) cr*u*;
æ	h*a*t, b*a*ck	i	*e*ve, benz*i*ne	œ	(Fr.) l*eu*r;		(Ger.) gr*ü*n**
æ̃	(Fr.) v*in*, m*ain**	ɪ	*i*f, st*i*ng		(Ger.) k*ö*nnen**	ʊ	b*u*ll, b*u*sh
ai	cr*y*, sp*i*ne	j	*j*u*dg*e	œ̃	(Fr.) br*un*, l*un*di**	ʌ	b*u*t, s*o*n
au	pr*ow*, l*ou*d	k	ca*k*e	ɔi	t*oy*, p*oi*nt	v	*v*i*v*id
b	*b*o*b*	χ	(Ger.) i*ch*, a*ch**	p	*p*ro*p*	w	*w*ood*w*ork
d	*d*i*d*	l	*l*oya*l*	r	*r*oa*r*	y	*y*ester*y*ear
e	f*a*te, *e*lite	m	*m*i*m*e	s	*s*au*s*e	z	pri*z*es
ɛ	*y*et, sp*e*ll	n	*n*o*n*e	sh	ha*sh*i*sh*	zh	plea*s*ure, a*z*ure

*All symbols marked with a tilde (~) represent nasalized vowels. Thus the French vowels ɑ̃, æ̃, and õ are somewhat like a nasal American pronunciation of the vowels in *pon(d)*, *an(d)*, and *lon(g)* ; by pronouncing these words while holding the nose one may approximate the French sounds.

The symbol ö is roughly equivalent to the vowel of *cu(r)* or *fi(r)*, but with the *r* silent, as in Southern speech. The symbol œ represents the same sound, but shortened, as in *cu(r)tain*, *pu(r)ple*. The nasalized vowel, æ̃, resembles the vowel of *u(r)n*, *chu(r)n*.

The symbol ü represents the sound of *ee* in *fee* pronounced with the lips rounded as for the *oo* in *goose*.

The symbol χ represents the sound of *ch* in Scottish *loch*; it is like the *ck* in *lock*, except that the sound continues.

COLLIER'S ENCYCLOPEDIA

Departmental Advisors

Hubert N. Alyea

Rabbi Morton Mayer Berman

Karl Brown

Rev. Robert I. Gannon, S.J.

John D. Hicks

Robert Earnest Kingery

Katharine F. Lenroot

Rev. Frederick W. Loetscher

William J. Roehrenbeck

Jean C. Roos

Edward L. Smith

COLLIER'S ENCYCLOPEDIA

TWENTY VOLUMES

With Bibliography and Index

WILLIAM T. COUCH

Editor-in-Chief

DAVID CRAWFORD

Managing Editor

Library Consultant and Advisory Editor
LOUIS SHORES

Consultant for Canada
ROBERT H. BLACKBURN

Consultant for Schools
JOSEPH T. GLEASON Jr.

1959

Volume 4

P. F. COLLIER & SON CORPORATION

NEW YORK · TORONTO

COLLIER
BOOKS
SINCE 1875

COLLIER'S ENCYCLOPEDIA

VOLUME FOUR

BRABANT to CÉZANNE

BRABANT [brəba'nt; brɑ'bənt; bra'bā'], the name applied to a province of Belgium, and to a duchy formerly comprising parts of the Netherlands and Belgium.

The Province of Brabant. Brabant, known more properly as South Brabant to distinguish it from the Dutch province of North Brabant, is the central and metropolitan province of Belgium. It covers an area of 1,267 sq. mi., and is bounded by the following provinces: on the north by Antwerp, on the west by Limburg and Liége, on the south and southwest by Namur and Hainaut, and on the west by East Flanders. The province consists of an undulating plateau averaging 400 ft. in elevation, with fertile loamy soils which are intensively cultivated. The principal river is the Dyle; others are the Demer, Senne, and Goethe. Brabant produces an abundance of cereals, fruits, sugar beets, flax, hemp, and tobacco. In the neighborhood of the larger cities, specialization in vegetable growing, particularly chicory, has taken place. Although Brabant is chiefly a region of large farms, many diversified industries flourish along the canals which cross the region. Among the manufactured products are cotton, muslin, velour, lace, and paper. There are also tanneries, refineries, and quarries of porphyry, sandstone, and limestone. The Brabançon horse ranks high among heavy draught breeds. Brussels, capital of Belgium and largest city of the province, is the center of a network of railroads connecting it with all the important cities of the kingdom. Other cities of the province are Louvain, Tirlemont, Nivelles, Hal, Wavre, and Waterloo. The central part of the plateau, in the vicinity of Waterloo and Mont St. Jean, was the scene of Napoleon's defeat in 1815. Other famous battlefields were Ramillies, where Allied forces defeated the French on May 23, 1706, and Quatre Bras, where the French again met defeat on June 16, 1815. The majority of the people of Brabant are Roman Catholics. Flemish is spoken in Brussels and Louvain; French is spoken in Nivelles. Pop. (est. 1953), 1,860,527.

The Duchy of Brabant. The area which comprised the Duchy of Brabant (1190-1430) corresponds roughly to that included in the present Belgian provinces of Brabant and Antwerp, and the Dutch province of North Brabant. This region, forming part of the territory of the Nerviens, was acquired by the Romans, and remained under their domination until the fifth century, when it became part of the Frankish empire and was ruled by the Frank kings until it was united with Lorraine in the ninth century. The countship of Brabant was formed in the tenth century and raised to a duchy under Henry I in 1190. Its rulers were noted for their enlightened policies, such as La Joyeuse Entree, a charter giving popular liberties to the towns and regarded as the Belgian Magna Carta, which was granted by John III and ratified by Duke Wenceslas on his accession in 1356. Philip the Good of Burgundy acquired the duchy in 1430, and it passed to the house of Hapsburg in 1440 by the marriage of his granddaughter Mary to Archduke Maximilian. In 1506, it was transferred to Spain, and was later the center of the revolt of the Netherlands. However, the southern section remained under Spanish rule until the Treaty of Utrecht in 1713. After the union of Belgium with France in 1795, the largest part of the ancient Duchy of Brabant formed the department of the Dyle. In 1815, with the rest of Belgium, it was joined to the Kingdom of the Netherlands. Following the revolution of 1830, which resulted in Belgian independence, the provinces of Brabant and Antwerp became part of Belgium while North Brabant remained with the Netherlands. The title "Duke of Brabant" is conferred on the eldest son of the King of the Belgians.   L. B.

BRABANT, NORTH, the southernmost province of the Netherlands, having an area of 1,920 sq. mi., bounded on the west by the North Sea, on the north by the provinces of South Holland and Gelderland, on the east by the province of Limburg, and on the south by Belgium. The southern part of the North Brabant is the highest, reaching an altitude of 132 ft. The land, consisting of gravel, diluvial sand, and clay, slopes down toward the Hollandsch Diep, the channel on the northwest into which the conjoined Rhine and Meuse rivers empty, along which the land lies below sea level. Into the Meuse, which separates the province from Gelderland on the north, run several small rivers, including the Raam, the Dieze, and the Donge; the Mark, the Dintel, the Steenbergsche Vliet, and the Rozendaalsche Vliet run westward into the sea.

The population of the province is chiefly Frankish. North Brabant was a part of the old Duchy of Brabant, and came under the jurisdiction of the United Netherlands in 1648; since 1795 it has been a separate province of the Netherlands. During World War II the province suffered cruelly in the fighting of 1944. The capital city of the province is 's Hertogenbosch (Bois-le-Duc); other principal cities are Breda, Tilburg, Eindhoven, Helmond, Bergen op Zoom, and Rosendaal. Agriculture, combined with dairying and cattle raising, constitutes the chief occupation of the people, but commerce and industry are also important. The chief products include butter, wool, leather, wheat, barley, and beetroot; hops are also raised. Among the industrial establishments are cigar factories, iron foundries, textile mills, breweries, and shoe factories. Shipping and fisheries are important at Bergen op Zoom. The province is abundantly supplied with railways, canals, shipping, and air services. Pop. (est. 1954), 1,332,033.

BRACCIOLINI, POGGIO. *See* POGGIO BRACCIOLINI, GIOVANNI FRANCESCO.

BRACEBRIDGE, a town in Muskoka District, Ontario, Canada, 120 mi. north of Toronto, from which it is reached by Provincial Highway 11 and the Canadian National Railways. Situated on the Muskoka River, it is a shopping center and supply point for the summer residents and for the many resorts which dot the picturesque Muskoka Lakes region. Manufactures include automotive parts and stainless steel products for the home. Pop. 1956, 2,849.

BRACEGIRDLE, ANNE (c.1663-1748), English actress, was born in the Midlands about 1663. The exact place and date of her birth are not known. She was entrusted to the care of Thomas Betterton and his wife. Her theatrical career began at the age of six, when she played the role of the page in Thomas Otway's *The Orphan* at the Duke's Theatre in Dorset Garden. In 1688 she played the part of Lucia in Thomas Shadwell's *Squire of Alsatia*. She also appeared at the Theatre Royal as Maria in William Mountfort's *Edward III* and as Emmeline in John Dryden's *King Arthur*. In 1693 she appeared for the first time in a William Congreve play, when she took the role of Araminta in *The Old Bachelor*. In 1695 she moved with Betterton and his followers to Lincoln's Inn Fields. It was there that she first played her favorite role, that of Angelica in Congreve's *Love for Love*. She also distinguished herself in such roles as Belinda in Sir John Vanbrugh's *The Provoked Wife* and Almeria in Congreve's *Mourning Bride*. She retired from the stage in 1707 when, in order to decide whether she or Mrs. Oldfield was the more popular actress, they both played Mrs. Brittle in Betterton's *Amorous Widow* on two successive nights. The public decided in favor of Mrs. Oldfield, and that was the end of Anne Bracegirdle's stage career. It was said that she had secretly married Congreve, who left her a legacy. She was noted for her virtue and her charity. She was buried in London on Sept. 18, 1748.

BRACHIOPODA or **BRACHIOPODS.** *See* ANIMAL SYSTEMATICS; LAMP SHELLS.

BRACKEN, JOHN (1883-   ), Canadian political leader, was born at Ellisville, Ontario, June 22, 1883. He was educated at Brockville (Ont.) Collegiate Institute and Ontario Agricultural College at Guelph and received his B.S.A. degree from the University of Illinois in 1906. In the same year Bracken was appointed Manitoba representative for the Dominion Seed Branch, Department of Agriculture, and from 1907 to 1910 was superintendent of Fairs and Farmers Institutes for Saskatchewan. In 1910 he became a professor of field husbandry at the University of Saskatchewan, remaining there until 1920, when he was appointed president of Manitoba Agricultural College. Bracken was elected to the Manitoba legislature in 1922 as a member of the Progressive Party, later the Liberal-Progressive Party, and was re-elected in 1927, 1932, 1936, and 1940. From 1922 to 1942 he served as premier of Manitoba and president of the executive council, and in 1942 became leader of the Progressive-Conservative Party of Canada. In June 1945, he was elected House of Commons leader of the opposition, serving until July 1948, when he resigned from the government. He was also a delegate to the United Nations General Assembly in New York in 1946.   C. W. D.

BRACKEN. *See* BRAKE or BRACKEN.

BRACKENRIDGE, a borough in Allegheny Co., southwestern Pennsylvania, is situated on the west bank of the Allegheny River, 22 mi. northeast of Pittsburgh. Gas and coal are produced near by, and there are truck gardens in the vicinity. This industrial community was incorporated in 1901 and is governed by a burgess and council. Transportation is provided by the Pennsylvania Railroad. Industrial products which contribute heavily to the economy of the borough are bituminous coal, stainless steel, glass, and mirrors. Pop. 1950, 6,178.

BRACKET FUNGI, a large group of tube-bearing fungi, in the family Polyporaceae, which are found on the trunks of trees. Here they form hard, woody, bracketlike or shelflike growths; because of this they are also called shelf fungi. They contribute to the process of decay called dry rot when they grow upon fallen timber and dead underbrush.
                                                        J. C. Wis.

BRACTON, HENRY DE [bræ′ktən] (d.1268), English ecclesiastic and judge, whose real name was Bratton, was born at Bratton Clovelly or Bratton Fleming, Devonshire, and was educated at Oxford University, where he received the degree of Doctor of Laws. In 1245 he was appointed a circuit judge and appears to have been a justice of assize in southwest England after 1248. He is thought also to have served a brief interim appointment as chief justice of England. In 1264 Bracton was appointed archdeacon of Barnstable, but resigned to become chancellor of Exeter Cathedral, an office he held until his death. Bracton's fame rests on his treatise on English law, *De legibus et consuetudinibus Angliae* ("On the Statutes and Common Law of England"), first published by Richard Tottel in 1569. It was the first comprehensive attempt to outline the structure of the common law in England. Bracton died in Exeter in September 1268 and was buried in Exeter Cathedral.   R. T.

BRADDOCK, EDWARD (c. 1695-1755), British soldier, was born in Perthshire, Scotland, probably in 1695. He was commissioned ensign in the Coldstream Guards in 1710; by 1745 he had attained the rank of lieutenant colonel and from 1745 to 1748 served in Holland and at other points in Western Europe. In 1754 Braddock was made a major general and put in command of the British forces in America. Braddock's place in history is the result of his ignorance of primitive warfare, his stupid insistence on his own ideas, and his underestimation of the American Colonial troops, which resulted in stunning defeat, his own death, and the needless death of many of his men.

The new commander arrived in Virginia in February 1755 and found military affairs in much confusion. His mission was to drive the French out of territory on the frontier claimed by Great Britain, on which they had been encroaching. An important point was at the fork of the Ohio River, where the French had erected a palisaded post on the site of what is now Pittsburgh, Pa., and called it Fort Duquesne. As soon as his preparations could be made and a suitable force, to be made up of English regular troops and Colonials, could be assembled, Braddock planned to begin his westward march. In the contingent supplied by Virginia was a young officer, George Washington, who had had considerable experience in Western travel and Indian fighting. Although only twenty-three years of age, Washington had already shown much military ability as a leader. Braddock offered him a subordinate post, which Washington declined, although he accepted appointment as an aide on Braddock's staff. Washington knew the territory over which Braddock's command would travel, and after the troops got under way he attempted to inform Braddock and his officers on methods of fighting

Indians which he had found to be successful. Braddock, however, refused to take his young aide's advice. Instead, the troops moved in close formation with flags flying and music playing. No advance parties were sent out, and there was no scouting of the country through which the troops would pass. On July 9, 1755, at a point south of Fort Duquesne, the column, marching in ordered formations, was suddenly exposed to fire from Indians concealed in ambush. Consternation seized the British. The advance guard recoiled on the main body, adding to the confusion. Braddock, in attempting to hold the troops in ranks, was mortally wounded. Washington and his Colonials saved themselves by breaking ranks and using the protection of the forest. The column was halted, then began a retreat that soon became a rout. Two days later Braddock, after much suffering, reached Great Meadows, a point 20 mi. east of the Monongahela River, where he died July 13, 1755. E. R. A.

BRADDOCK, a borough in Alleghany Co., southwestern Pennsylvania, is situated on the Monongahela River 10 mi. southeast of Pittsburgh. With North Braddock and Rankin, it forms a large steel mill community. Braddock was settled by John Frazier in 1752 and was incorporated as a borough in 1867. A mayor and council governed the community in 1951. The borough was named for Gen. Edward Braddock, who was defeated and mortally wounded there in battle on July 9, 1755, during the French and Indian War. The first Carnegie Library in the United States was established in Braddock. The Pennsylvania, the Baltimore & Ohio, and the Pittsburgh & Lake Erie railroads and river craft supply transportation. Chief manufactures are steel products, machinery, gasoline, wall paper, and plaster. Pop. 1950, 16,488.

BRADENTON [bre'dəntən], a port city and winter resort in western Florida, is the seat of Manatee Co. It lies on the Manatee and Braden rivers, 8 mi. from the Gulf of Mexico and 45 mi. south of Tampa. Hernando De Soto landed on the North American mainland near Bradenton in 1539, an event celebrated annually by the De Soto pageant. The city was settled about 1854 by Joseph Braden, who built Braden Castle, a local landmark. Bradenton was incorporated in 1903 and officially merged with the city of Manatee in 1944. It is served by the Atlantic Coast Line and the Seaboard Air Line railroads. The raising of truck crops and citrus fruits is the principal activity of the surrounding region. Within the city industries include the processing of orange juice and the quarrying and finishing of travertine. Pop. 1950, 13,604.

BRADFORD, GAMALIEL (1863-1932), American biographer, was born Oct. 9, 1863, at Boston, Mass., a direct descendant of Governor William Bradford of Plymouth Colony. Handicapped by a lifelong invalidism which had forced him to withdraw from the class of 1886 at Harvard, Bradford's literary ambitions led him through the writing of many volumes of poetry, fiction, and drama before he found his true medium, the psychograph. With this term, derived from Sainte-Beuve, Bradford described the analysis that, as "a naturalist of souls," he applied to his first successful study, *Lee, the American* (1912). This book launched what was to be a series of seventeen volumes, embracing more than one hundred separate short subjects. Among them are *Damaged Souls* (1923), *Bare Souls* (1924), and *Wives* (1925), as well as three full-length studies, *The Soul of Samuel Pepys* (1924), *Darwin* (1926), and *D. L. Moody, a*

Worker in Souls (1927). A brilliant interpreter of other men, Bradford nevertheless wrote two of his best books about himself, the posthumously published *Journal* (1933) and *Letters* (1934). He died at Wellesley Hills, Mass., Apr. 11, 1932. H. W. Bl.

BRADFORD, ROARK (1896-1948), American short-story writer and novelist, was born Aug. 21, 1896, in Lauderdale County, Tenn. First a journalist in Georgia and Louisiana, after 1926 he devoted himself to fiction. Many times winner of O. Henry Memorial Awards, he published several collections of stories of Negro life in the South: *Ol' Man Adam and His Chillun* (1928)—which provided the basis of Marc Connelly's play, *Green Pastures—Ol' King David an' the Philistine Boys* (1930), and *Let the Band Play Dixie* (1934). In 1931 he published *John Henry,* an account of the folk hero of that name, and in 1939 he dramatized the book. Although best known for stories, he also wrote novels: *This Side Jordan* (1929); *Kingdom Coming* (1933), concerning Negro life in the lower South; and *The Three-Headed Angel* (1937), a chronicle of the white settlement of Tennessee. Bradford died on Nov. 13, 1948, in New Orleans. C. C.

BRADFORD, WILLIAM (1590-1657), governor and a founder of Plymouth Colony, was born in Austerfield, Yorkshire, England. He was baptized Mar. 29, 1590, and was born probably a few days before this date. During his youth he studied history, philosophy, theology, Latin, Greek, and, in later life, Hebrew. He attended Separatist meetings as a child and joined the Separatist Church. In 1607 he and a group of Separatists attempting to go to Holland were arrested and imprisoned in Boston, Lincolnshire. In 1609, Bradford reached Holland with a group of Separatists, and there he studied in Leiden University. He was later apprenticed to a silk dyer. When he reached the age of twenty-one, Bradford sold the farms he had inherited from his family in England, and the next year he became a citizen of Leiden.

Bradford sailed to America with part of the Separatist congregation on the *Mayflower* in 1620. His wife was drowned in Provincetown Harbor before the group landed. They had one son, John. In the spring of 1621, after the first bitter winter in Plymouth, Bradford was elected second governor of the colony. He was re-elected every year until 1656, except for the years 1633, 1634, 1636, and 1644, and in those years he was deputy governor; he was an advocate of rotation in office, and it was at his own request that the office was given to others. His main problems during his terms of office were the disease and famine which afflicted the settlers, hostile Indian attacks, persecution from England, the colony's debts, and rebellions fomented by malcontents.

The land of the colony had originally been held in common, and the colonists had brought the fruits of their labor to a common store, from which they drew supplies. Not enough was produced under this system, and Bradford advocated dividing the land among the colonists, with favorable results. In 1621 a treaty was concluded with Massasoit, chief of the Wampanoag Indians, in accordance with which all the Indian tribes under him made peace with the settlers, and ceded to them the Plymouth region, most of whose Indian residents had been killed by plague. Bradford's firm policy with the Indians prevented a major conflict. The London merchants who had financed the colony sold out to the Plymouth settlers, and in 1626 Bradford and seven others assumed personal responsibility for payment of the debt. Robert Gorges, the son of Sir Ferdinando Gorges, president of the Council for New England, was the first governor general of the council. Bradford was a member of his advisory board. After one winter in Plymouth, Gorges left the colony, which continued to govern itself under Bradford. Bradford ruled firmly but tolerantly. He always viewed the colony as a branch of the Church in Holland, and sought to bring over the remaining members. He married a widow, Alice Carpenter Southworth, in 1623, and they had three children, William, Mercy, and Joseph; the eldest, William, later became deputy governor of Plymouth.

On Sept. 7, 1643, the colonies of Massachusetts Bay, Plymouth, Connecticut, and New Haven formally agreed to a confederation called the United Colonies of America. Bradford served as one of Plymouth's two delegates to the confederation congress four times, during two of which he was elected president of the congress. In collaboration with Edward Winslow, he wrote *Mourt's Relations,* an account of the beginnings of the Plymouth Colony, published in London in 1622. Part of his *Letter Book,* containing copies of letters on colony affairs, was discovered in a Halifax grocery and published by the Massachusetts Historical Society. His *History of Plymouth Plantation,* covering the period 1602-1647, was written between 1630 and 1646. The manuscript was in Boston's Old South Church during the Revolution, and then was regarded as lost until 1855, when it was found in the library of the Bishop of London. The manuscript was returned to the United States in 1897, upon formal request, and placed in the Massachusetts state library. Bradford died in Plymouth, Mass., May 9, 1657.   M. Je.

BRADFORD, a city and a municipal, county, and parliamentary borough in the West Riding of Yorkshire, England, situated 9 mi. west of Leeds, in an important manufacturing and mining district, at the foot of the Pennine Hills. Since Saxon times, Bradford has been a market center; it was listed in the Domesday Book, and laid waste by William I. It was granted by Henry III in 1251 to the de Lacey family, at which time it was already becoming an important wool market. Bradford was incorporated in 1847, was made a county borough in 1888, and became a city in 1897. It returns four members to Parliament. The Parish Church of St. Peter, begun about 1401 on Norman remains, became a cathedral when the diocese of Bradford was created in 1919. Bolling Hall, a restored fourteenth-century building, is a museum, and Cartwright Memorial Hall is dedicated to the inventor of the power loom. Bradford is the seat of numerous technical schools and of the Airdale and United Independent colleges. The city is the chief center in England for manufacturing worsteds and woolens; other goods produced are mohair, alpaca, silk, artificial silk, and velvet. The manufacture of wool in Bradford dates from the sixteenth century and of worsteds from the end of the seventeenth century. There is also some textile machinery manufacturing. Pop. 1952, 288,000.

BRADFORD, a city in McKean Co., northern Pennsylvania, lies in the Allegheny Mountains at an elevation of 1,500 ft. above sea level. It is situated 125 air miles north of Pittsburgh and about five miles from the New York state line. Wells surrounding Bradford produce a high grade of crude oil. New England lumbermen settled the site as Littletown in 1837. The present name was adopted in 1854, and the city was incorporated in 1879. It has the commission form of government. The Pennsylvania, the Erie, and the Baltimore & Ohio railroads and Allegheny Airlines supply transportation. Principal industries include oil refining and the production of oil-well equipment and supplies. Other major manufactured products are face brick, paper goods, cigarette lighters, electronic devices, cutlery, and chemicals. Pop. 1950, 17,354.

BRADFORD-ON-AVON, an urban district, situated 98 mi. southwest of London, in the parliamentary division of Westbury, Wiltshire, England. The district is of ancient origin. In 1945 a burial ground believed to date from 2000 B.C. was discovered. A monastery was founded in Bradford in the eighth century, but the nunnery of Shaftesbury owned the manor from 1001 until the dissolution of monasteries in the reign of Henry VIII. Bradford is listed in the Domesday Book. Among its interesting historical buildings are the Saxon church of St. Lawrence, the medieval tithe barn, and a completely restored Jacobean mansion. The old Flemish cloth-halls are still used as factories. The city's industries include the manufacture of railway springs and tennis balls. The tourist trade is also a source of income. Pop. 1952, 5,525.

BRADLEY, FRANCIS HERBERT (1846-1924), English philosopher, was for nearly half a century the acknowledged leader of British idealism. He was born Jan. 30, 1846, at Glasbury, Brecknock, and educated at Oxford, where, soon after his graduation, he was elected to a research fellowship at Merton College. Here he lived the rest of his life as a secluded bachelor scholar, devoting himself wholly to writing and thinking, and never lecturing, teaching, or appearing at philosophical meetings. From Oxford he occasionally retired to a life of seclusion in France. He was deeply interested in literature as well as in philosophy, and owed no small part of his influence to his mastery of literary style. He was a brilliant and merciless critic of the empiricist tradition in philosophy, and, aided by Green, Caird, and Bosanquet, he decisively broke its hold on the British universities. The government awarded him the rare distinction of the Order of Merit. By general consent he was the foremost figure of his generation in British philosophy. He died in Oxford on Sept. 18, 1924.

The fundamental principles of Bradley's thought correspond to the principles of the two main types of idealism. On the one hand he holds that to be is to be perceived or experienced; "anything, in no sense felt or perceived, becomes to me quite unmeaning." On the other hand, he holds that the real is the rational. The test whether anything is true or real is whether it will satisfy the demands of reason. On the first point he spent little time, for he thought it almost obvious, but to the development of the second he devotes the larger part of his writing.

Bradley recognizes three stages or levels in the life of mind. For each of us experience begins in immediacy, which means that in the early life of the infant nothing is singled out and recognized as such; there is as yet no self or not-self, no explicitly distinguished things or qualities. Little by little, qualities are grouped together to form what we call "things," and these things are related to form the familiar world of common sense and science, which constitutes the second level of mind. Can the philosopher accept this world as fully real? No. He finds, when he examines it, that it is full of contradictions, and what is contradictory must be rejected as unreal. In the first part of his major work, *Appearance and Reality* (1893), Bradley dismisses on this ground the whole world of ordinary experience, including space and time, substance and causality, bodies and selves. In the final part he undertakes a reconstruction. He brings to light the standard he had been using in the first part, namely, satisfactoriness to the intellect, and finds that this lies in logical consistency. But the only knowledge which can own such consistency, he maintains, is a whole that is both inclusive and harmonious, a whole in which nothing is left out and everything is related necessarily to everything else. That the world constitutes a system of this kind, Bradley thought, was an unprovable but unavoidable assumption of philosophy. Such a system is what he means by the Absolute. Its achievement would mark the third and highest level of mind. We shall probably never in fact achieve it, but it may be approximated in degree, and this approximation measures the degree of truth which any system of thought possesses. In his *Ethical Studies* (1876) Bradley devised a corresponding standard for progress in the moral life. His other chief works are *Principles of Logic* (1883) and *Essays on Truth and Reality* (1914). *See also* IDEALISM.   B. B.

BRADLEY, FREDERICK WORTHEN (1863-1933), American mining engineer, was born in Nevada City, Calif., Feb. 21, 1863. He was graduated from the University of California in 1885 and began his mining career on the Mother Lode of California, where he established a record for low mining costs. In 1900 he became associated with the development of the Alaska Juneau Gold Mine, an extensive low-grade gold deposit that appeared unprofitable because of the small gold content of the ore. In spite of many discouragements, he was successful after ten years in bringing this property into profitable production. He established a record for low-cost gold mining on ore averaging less than 90 cents per ton of gold, an unequaled achievement which won him wide recognition in the mining profession. He was also interested in gold dredging in California and development of mercury mines. In 1929 he served as president of the American Institute of Mining and Metallurgical Engineers. He died in San Francisco, Aug. 31, 1933.   W. F. B.

BRADLEY, HENRY (1845-1923), English philologist and lexicographer, was born in Manchester on Dec. 3, 1845. After attending the Chesterfield Grammar School (1855-1859) he went to work, and in 1863 was employed as a corresponding clerk in a Sheffield cutlery firm. Having developed a keen interest in philology, he taught himself a number of European languages, as well as the Classical languages and Hebrew. In 1884 he established himself in London, hoping to support himself by doing literary work. He prepared a review of the *New English Dictionary* that was published in the *Academy* in March 1884. It served to get him an appointment on the staff of that dictionary. In 1889 he was made one of its editors, and in 1915 he was appointed senior editor following the death of Sir James Murray. In 1896 Bradley went to live in Oxford. An Hon. D.Litt. was conferred upon him by Oxford University in 1914. He was president of the Philology Society on a number of occasions (1890-1893, 1900-1903, 1909-1910). He died at Oxford on May 23, 1923. Bradley was the author of *Making of English* (1904), *English Place-names* (1910), and *Spoken and Written Language* (1919). His *Collected Papers* appeared in 1928 with a memoir by Robert Bridges.

BRADLEY, JAMES (1693-1762), English astronomer, was born at Sherborne, Gloucestershire, in 1693, and educated at Balliol College, Oxford. Under the guidance of his uncle, James Pound (1669-1724), who was a skilled astronomer, Bradley made his first astronomical observations. He was elected to the Royal Society in November 1718. In 1719

Bradley took clerical orders on his presentation to the vicarage of Bridstow, but in 1721, when appointed as Savilian professor of astronomy at Oxford, he resigned his ecclesiastical preferments. From 1729 to 1760 he was reader in experimental philosophy in the Ashmolean Museum. Bradley is chiefly remembered for his discovery of the aberration of light, which was communicated to the Royal Society in January 1729. He was appointed astronomer royal in 1742, succeeding Edmund Halley. In 1748 he announced his detection of nutation, having made observations leading up to this discovery during an entire revolution (occupying 18.6 years) of the moon's nodes. A Crown pension of £250 per year was conferred on him in 1752. Broken in health, he retired in 1761 to Chalford, Gloucestershire, where he died July 13, 1762.   L. N. R.

BRADLEY, OMAR NELSON (1893-   ), American soldier, was born in Clark, Mo., on Feb. 12, 1893. He was graduated from the United States Military Academy, West

GENERAL OMAR NELSON BRADLEY

Point, in 1915. He was stationed at various army camps in the United States before he became instructor of mathematics at West Point in 1920. In 1925 he was assigned to a tour of duty in Hawaii. After graduating from the Command and General Staff School in 1929, he was appointed instructor at the Infantry School. In 1934 Bradley graduated from the Army War College, and was again assigned to duty at West Point, where in 1937 he was an instructor in tactics. In 1938 he was transferred to Washington to serve on the Army General Staff, becoming its assistant secretary in July 1939. In 1941 he was appointed commandant of the Infantry School at Fort Benning, Ga., and was promoted to the rank of brigadier general.

After the United States entered World War II, Bradley was made a major general and was sent to North Africa in February 1943, to serve as field aide to Gen. Dwight D. Eisenhower. There he succeeded Gen. George S. Patton as commander of the Second Corps in the Tunisian campaign, which he directed in the capture of Bizerte. Promoted to the rank of lieutenant general, Bradley commanded the Second Corps in the invasion of Sicily, after which he was transferred to England and appointed commander in chief of the American ground forces which were to participate in the invasion of western Europe in 1944. He led the First Army in the invasion of Normandy, and planned the break-through at St. Lo, which precipitated the defeat of the enemy. He was placed in command of the Allied Twelfth

Army Group in western Europe in August 1944, and led it successfully in the operations that culminated in the final German defeat. He remained briefly in Germany with the Army of Occupation, but then returned to the United States, and in June 1945 was appointed to serve as Veterans' Administrator. He was promoted to the temporary rank of general in March 1945, and late in 1947 succeeded Gen. Dwight D. Eisenhower as Chief of Staff of the Army. In January 1949, by special act of Congress, Bradley was appointed to the permanent rank of a full general. In August 1949 he was appointed to the newly created chairmanship of the Joint Chiefs of Staff for a term of two years. He was reappointed to the chairmanship in August 1951, serving until May 1953, when he was succeeded by Adm. Arthur W. Radford. Bradley retired from the army on Aug. 13, 1953, after 42 years of service. In 1956, while chairman of the board of a private company, he was called to head a presidential commission on veterans' benefits. He is the author of *A Soldier's Story* (1951).   S. D.

BRADLEY UNIVERSITY, an accredited, coeducational, privately controlled institution located in the residential district of Peoria, Ill. It was chartered in 1896 as Bradley Polytechnic Institute, and instruction was begun in 1897. In 1920 a four-year program was adopted. Following reorganization in 1946, it became Bradley University. Divisions include the School of Horology, founded in 1897, the Evening School (1910), the College of Liberal Arts and Sciences and the School of Music (1920), the School of Fine Art (1933), the Graduate Division (1944), and Peoria Junior College (1946). Changes in departments resulted in the establishment in 1947 of the Schools of Business Administration, Education, and Engineering. Degrees offered are the B.A., B.S., B.S. in civil, industrial, and mechanical engineering, the Bachelor of Fine Arts, Bachelor of Music and of Musical Education, the M.A., M.S., and the Master of Business Administration. Some schools have co-operative, alternating work-and-study courses which prolong the degree from four to five years.

All nonresident freshmen women must live in dormitories and sophomore and upperclass women in dormitories or in sorority houses under the guidance of a house mother. Exceptions may be made for women who are over twenty-five and in certain other cases. Residential facilities are available for men students. Some scholarship and student loan aid is provided, and more than half of the students earn all or part of their expenses. *For statistics see* COLLEGES AND UNIVERSITIES.

BRADSTREET, ANNE DUDLEY (c. 1612-1672), American poet, was born in England and came to America in 1630. She was the daughter of Thomas Dudley and in 1628 had married Simon Bradstreet; both her father and her husband became governors of the Province of Massachusetts Bay. Her poems were first published in *The Tenth Muse Lately Sprung up in America* (London, 1650), and several fuller editions have appeared since her death. Her longer poems, which include discourses on the four elements, the four humours, the four ages of man, and the four monarchies, show the pervasive influence of Francis Quarles, Sir Philip Sidney, and Edmund Spenser, as well as of Joshua Sylvester's translation of Seigneur Du Bartas' *La Semaine;* but her later and shorter poems, especially her *Contemplations,* are less dependent on stock poetic conventions and contain more original lyric expression. She died in Andover, Mass., Sept. 16, 1672.
L. L.

BRADY, EDWIN JAMES (1869-1952), Australian poet and journalist, was born at Carcoar, New South Wales, on Aug. 7, 1869, and, after spending his youth in the Australian bush, was educated at the University of Sydney and in Washington, D. C. He then entered journalism, becoming the editor of the *Australian Workman* in 1892. In 1901 he became owner of the short-lived newspaper *Grip,* and in 1904 editor of the *Australian Worker*. His best-known book of poems, *The King's Caravan* (1912), brought him widespread recognition as a vigorous singer of Australian themes. Among his other books are *The Way of Many Rivers* (1899), *The Earthen Floor* (1902), *River Rovers* (1911), *Bells and Hobbles* (1912), *Australia Unlimited* (1918), *The House of the Winds* (1919), *The Land of the Sun* (1924), *Wardens of the Seas* (1933), and *Two Frontiers* (1944). He died near Melbourne, July 22, 1952.   R. T.

BRADY, MATHEW B. (c.1823-1896), American photographer, was born in Warren Co., N.Y., about 1823. Introducing Daguerre's methods in New York in 1842, he popularized these photographic innovations with the publication of his successful collection, *Gallery of Illustrious Americans* (1850), and won prizes with his pictures at the London (1851) and New York (1853) world's fairs. After he adopted the wetplate process, his business expanded and he opened a studio in Washington as well. During the Civil War he was official military photographer for the Federal Government and took over 3,500 scenes of battles and soldier life, which he developed in his portable darkroom, thus preserving a monumental collection of war pictures. This unique collection was published as *Brady's National Photographic Collection of War Views and Portraits of Representative Men* (1870), and part of it was acquired by the United States Government in 1875. Brady died in New York City, Jan. 16, 1896.

BRADY, the seat of McCulloch Co. in central Texas, was settled about 1875 as a trading post. It is a shipping point for dressed poultry and processes wool and vegetable oil. Aircraft parts and fabricated metals are also produced. Freightage is supplied by the Gulf, Colorado and Santa Fe Railroad and air service by Trans-Texas Airways. The July Jubilee is an annual race meet, and Richards Park is a recreational area on Brady Creek. Brady is governed by a mayor and city council. Pop. 1950, 5,944.

BRAGA [brɑ′gə], a district and the capital of that district in the province of Minho, in northern Portugal.

The City. The city is situated 700 ft. above sea level, dominating the wide, fertile plains surrounding it, between the Cavado and Este rivers, about 30 mi. northeast of Oporto. It is the terminus of a railroad spur and is a market center for a highly productive farm region. Braga's manufactures include jewelry, felt hats, shoes, cotton textiles, hemp and leather goods, soap, candles, sugar, and cutlery.

Braga is an archiepiscopal see, and its archbishopric contests with Toledo and Tarragona for the ecclesiastical primacy of the Iberian Peninsula. Its position as the head of the Portuguese church was diminished by the creation of the patriarchate of Lisbon in 1716. The city's principal monuments are its churches. The cathedral was originally constructed about 1100, and it was virtually rebuilt in the sixteenth and eighteenth centuries. The west portal is the best part of the structure; the interior contains several interesting tombs, including that of Henry of Burgundy, and some carved oaken stalls. Other important churches are Santa Cruz, with a fine façade, and the pilgrimage church of Bom Jesús do Monte, lying 3 mi. east of the city on Monte Espinho at an elevation of 1,850 ft. The shrine, which is reached by a funicular railway, commands a magnificent view; there are several hotels near by.

The city was probably founded by the Carthaginians in 296 B.C. As Bracara Augusta, it was a Roman provincial center in northern Lusitania, and it remained a commercial point of importance throughout the Middle Ages. The Suevi made it their capital in the fifth and sixth centuries, and under the Visigoths it kept its ecclesiastical primacy. The Moors held Braga from the middle of the eighth century until Ferdinand I reconquered it in 1070. Pop. 1950, 32,153.

The District. The district of Braga has an area of 1,054 sq. mi. and a population density of 177 per sq. mi., the second largest in Portugal after Oporto. It is bounded on the west by the Atlantic Ocean and on the northeast by Spain. There is a coastline of about 15 mi. but no port of consequence. The terrain is mountainous in the interior with rolling plains along the coast and with river valleys. The largest streams are the Cavado and the Ave, both of which are short and seasonal. The district is one of the most fertile in Portugal, the chief agricultural products being wines, oranges, and cereals. Sheep and cattle are also raised. The small mineral resources of the district are only partially exploited. Pop. 1950, 546,302.   R. G. W.

BRAGANÇA [brəgãẽ′nsə], popularly Braganza, a district and the capital of that district in the province of Tras-os-Montes, in the northeastern corner of Portugal.

The Town. The town, which is the see of a bishop, is situated on an outlying hill of the Serra de Nogueira, dominating the upper Sabor River valley, 110 mi. northeast of Oporto and only a few miles from the Spanish frontier. Transportation facilities are furnished by a branch railway line to Tua on the Oporto-Salamanca line that follows the Douro River. Bragança was formerly a flourishing textile center famous for the manufacture of velvet and damask, but the textile industry has deteriorated. It is primarily a market center for the livestock, grain, and olive oil produced nearby. The older part of the town is enclosed within walls. The citadel, built in 1187 by Sancho I, the cathedral, and the church of Santa Maria, with its Baroque façade, are of particular interest.

The town's position near the Spanish frontier has made it strategically important throughout its history. In Celtic times a community existed on the site known as Brigantia, and under the Romans it was Juliobriga. The town suffered from the wars between the Moors and Christians, and it was fortified several times. During the Spanish invasion in 1762 the fortifications were destroyed. The royal family who ruled over Portugal from 1640 to 1910 and over Brazil from 1822 to 1889 derived its name from Bragança. Alfonso, the first of the Braganza family, was the natural son of John I, and he became duke of Braganza in 1442. An heir failed to establish his claim to the throne in 1580 against the superior force of Philip II of Spain, but in 1640, at the end of Spanish rule in Portugal, a Braganza became king as John IV. The latter's successors ruled until the republic was set up in 1910. Pop. 1950, 8,245.

The District. Bragança District, covering an area of 2,527 sq. mi. and bounded on the north and east by Spain and on the south and southeast by the Douro River, is largely mountainous except along the Douro and its two tributaries, the Sabor and the Tua. Between these latter lie the Serras de Bornes, de Nogueira, and de Montezinho, the last not

Stairway to the cathedral at Braga, Portugal

exceeding 5,000 ft. in elevation. For the most part, the soil is not cultivated; on the mountain slopes wooded tracts abound. Pop. 1950, 228,358.   R. G. W.

BRAGANZA or **BRAGANÇA** [brəga′nzə, brəgãẽ′sə], the house of the ruling dynasty of Portugal from 1640 to 1910 and the collateral line of rulers of Brazil from 1822 to 1889. The name was derived from a city and district in the province of Tras-os-Montes, in northern Portugal. The city and the castle were fortified by Sancho I (1112-1185), Portuguese king of the House of Burgundy. In 1442 Dom Pedro, son of John I and regent for Alfonso V, bestowed upon his natural brother Count Alfonso de Barcelos the title of Duke of Braganza.

It was almost 200 years, however, before a member of the Braganza line ascended the throne. The first of the dynasty to rule Portugal was John IV (1640-1656), who was proclaimed king after expelling the Spanish usurpers who had reigned from 1580 to 1640. John, called "the Fortunate," also drove the Dutch out of Brazil in 1654 and during his reign restored Portugal's prestige among the nations. The dynasty's rule from that time until the rise of Napoleon was more or less uneventful. In 1807, however, the French drove the Braganzas and their court into exile in Brazil; the nominal ruler was the insane Queen Maria Francesca, whose son John was acting as regent when he was expelled. In 1821 John returned to Portugal as John VI, having succeeded to the throne during exile on the death of his mother in 1816. A year after his return he declared Brazil an independent country after naming his son, Dom Pedro I, as its first emperor, on Sept. 7, 1822.

When John VI died in 1826, Dom Pedro became king of both Brazil and Portugal; however, he almost immediately abdicated the Portuguese throne in favor of his daughter, Maria da Gloria, who became Queen Maria II. An insurrection in 1828 drove her into exile in Brazil, and her son,

Dom Miguel, whom she had named as regent, usurped the throne. When Miguel was defeated by the British in 1833 his mother was restored to the throne and he was banished.

House of Braganza-Coburg. Upon the death of Maria II in 1853, her consort, Ferdinand of Saxe-Coburg, became regent for their son, Pedro V, and the name of the ruling house became Braganza-Coburg. Pedro died of cholera at the age of twenty-four and was succeeded by his brother, Louis I, who reigned until 1889. When Carlos I came to the throne in that year Europe was entering upon a period of unrest, and the Portuguese ruling family found its position threatened by intrigues. Carlos allowed João Franco to become dictator of the country in 1907, and the bitterness engendered by this action led to the assassination of the king and his eldest son, Louis, in the streets of Lisbon in 1908. His successor, Manuel II, reigned only two years before being deposed by the naval revolt of 1910. After the republic was proclaimed, Manuel lived in exile in England until his death in 1932.

Brazil. Dom Pedro I, first emperor of Brazil, abdicated in favor of his son, Dom Pedro II, Apr. 7, 1831. During his reign he was frequently absent from the country, his daughter Isabella acting as regent during these visits to Europe. On Nov. 15, 1889, Dom Pedro II was dethroned by a revolution and Brazil became a republic. The exiled king died in Paris in 1891.   J. J. Van N.

BRAGG, BRAXTON (1817-1876), American Confederate soldier, was born at Warrenton, N. C., Mar. 22, 1817. He received his early education at home, entered West Point, where he was graduated in 1837 and assigned to the artillery. He saw service in the Seminole War in Florida (1838-1842) and served under General Zachary Taylor in the occupation of Texas (1845-1846). He received the brevet rank of captain, May 6, 1846, for his bravery in the defense of Fort Brown (Brownsville, Tex.); of major for his conduct at Monterey, Mexico; and of lieutenant colonel for his leadership at the Battle of Buena Vista, Feb. 23, 1847. In 1849, after the close of the Mexican War, Bragg became the assistant inspector-general under General E. P. Gaines, and after several years of frontier service resigned from the army Jan. 3, 1856. He became a Louisiana planter and remained so until the beginning of the Civil War, when he was appointed commander in chief of the Louisiana forces. President Jefferson Davis made him a brigadier general in the Confederate Army, Mar. 7, 1861, and he was assigned to command troops in the Pensacola, Fla., area. Soon afterward he was promoted to major general. He was a corps commander and chief of staff under General A. S. Johnston and became a full general after his outstanding work in the Battle of Shiloh, Apr. 6, 1862. On June 20, 1862, he was given command of the Army of Tennessee, and soon afterward began his invasion of Kentucky. After the battle of Perryville, Ky., Oct. 8, 1862, Bragg retreated into Tennessee. Following the engagement at Murfreesboro (Stone's River), Tenn., in December 1862, Bragg retired to positions about 40 mi. south of the town. In the summer of 1863 he was maneuvered southward to and through Chattanooga, taking a position along Chickamauga Creek. Here on Sept. 19-20, 1863, he defeated his opponent, General W. S. Rosecrans, drove his army from the field, and besieged him in the city of Chattanooga. On November 23-25 Grant's relieving Federal Army attacked Bragg's army on Missionary Ridge and forced it to raise the siege of Chattanooga. Bragg halted his army at Dalton, Ga., and was there relieved of his command, Dec. 2, 1863. President Davis called him to Richmond in February 1864 as chief of staff of the Confederate

Army. There he reorganized the War Office. In January 1865 Davis sent Bragg to assist General J. E. Johnston in his attempt to halt Sherman's northward advance through the Carolinas, but to no avail. Both Bragg and Johnston surrendered to Sherman near Durham, N. C., April 27, 1865. Paroled by the Union troops, Bragg went to New Orleans, where he was superintendent of the water works. Later he was commissioner of public works in Mobile, Ala. In 1874 he became chief engineer of the Gulf, Colorado, and Santa Fe Railroad. He died in Galveston, Tex., Sept. 27, 1876. Fort Bragg, N. C., is named in his honor.   W. E. A.

BRAGI [bra′gi], in Scandinavian mythology, the god of eloquence, wisdom, and the art of poetry. He was the son of Odin, and husband of Idun, possessor of the youth-restoring apples. Bragi was thought of as having a long white beard and as being the king of poets, or *skalds*. His name is sometimes linked with the word *bragr,* meaning "foremost" or "best," and also with *bragar-full,* a cup drunk at sacrificial feasts, but this may be coincidental, and have no connection with the mythical Bragi.   C. W. D.

BRAHE, TYCHO [bra] (1546-1601), Danish astronomer born at Knudstrup Manor, then in Denmark, now Sweden, Dec. 14, 1546. He studied at the universities of Copenhagen and Leipzig, and became interested in science. He found that astronomical tables based on the Ptolemaic system were highly erroneous. Soon Tycho began practical observations with crude instruments. In 1572 he observed the brightest nova ever recorded, since called Tycho's Star. Discovery of this star was a blow to the old school, which believed in the immutability of stars. On the island of Hven, Tycho established an observatory and labored for many years. His work on practical astronomy of the sun, moon, comets, and planets was the finest accomplished in pretelescope times. Tycho abandoned the Ptolemaic theory but did not accept the Copernican; he took a halfway position, the result being the "Tychonic system." Tycho's theory was that the earth was stationary, with the moon and sun circling it, but the other planets revolved around the sun. In 1600 he moved to Prague and came to know Johann Kepler. His most important accomplishment was the great series of planetary observations which he left with Kepler. Tycho died at Prague, Oct. 24, 1601. *See also* KEPLER, JOHANN. H. S. R.

BRAHM, OTTO [bra′m] (1856-1912), German drama critic, theatre manager, and stage director, was born Otto Abrahamson in Hamburg, Feb. 5, 1856. He attended universities in Berlin, Heidelberg, Strassburg, and Jena. From 1879 to 1889 he was a dramatic critic in Berlin, becoming a powerful champion of such modern dramatists as Otto Ludwig, Ludwig Anzengruber, Björnstjerne Björnson, and Henrik Ibsen, and of realistic and ensemble acting. In 1889 he helped found the progressive Freie Bühne (Free Stage), and became president, producer, and leading theoretician of this organization, and editor of its weekly magazine. In 1894 he became manager of the Deutsches Theater, enlarged its repertory to accommodate modern plays, and established a realistic style of acting and directing. To this end he created an acting company trained to excel in ensemble playing, and he held this company together for a decade.

Brahm's socially and historically accurate productions became models for the German stage, and "the Brahm style" became synonymous with naturalistic production. Brahm concerned himself primarily with plays as dramatic literature rather than as a springboard for theatrical virtuosity. Although he never claimed credit for directing plays, he was actually co-director of the theatre's modern repertory, planning productions, ruling on all questions concerning presentation, but leaving the technical execution to subordinate directors. Brahm retained managership of the Deutsches Theater until 1905. He died Nov. 28, 1912, at Berlin. *See also* DEUTSCHES THEATER; FREIE BÜHNE.   J. Ga.

BRAHMA or **BRAHMAN** [braˈmə, braˈmən] (Skr., prayer, impersonal spirit, divine essence), a basic term in the Hindu religion, varying in significance at different periods and in different applications. In the Rig-Veda the word means devotion and prayer; subsequently it came to signify the World Soul in contradistinction to the *ātman,* or individual self. In the doctrine of Brahman Atman, the individual soul was identified with this World Soul. The term Brahma also included the conception of the unknown. The deities of the Vedas thus differed from the absolute Brahma of the later Upanishads and the Vedanta.

There are two main concepts of Brahma in the Hindu religion, the neuter and the personal. In accordance with the former, the soul of man joins Brahma when it experiences salvation, and in that union it contemplates ultimate reality. Brahma is imagined, therefore, as without form, name, or sex, as at once transcendent, immanent, and impersonal; it is absolute, moreover, and cannot be described, bounded, or qualified. In the personal concept, Brahma stands at the head of the Hindu triad: Brahma, Vishnu, Siva. As first in the triad, or *trimurti,* Brahma is the creator, the personification of one supreme World Soul, unknown yet knowable, impersonal yet personal. In this view, Brahma is pictured in red with four heads (Siva destroyed one of the original five), and his consort, Sarasvati, or Brahmi, is goddess of speech; thus, to a certain extent, Brahma has been endowed with human attributes. Of the two concepts of Brahma, the neuter and the personal, the first seems more characteristic, and all Hindu groups join in describing it as *sat, chit, ananda* (being, intelligence, bliss), a state of perfect, resigned existence. To the central form of Brahma have attached certain characteristic concepts and institutions—rita (cosmic order), karma (cosmic law threading the events of time), polytheism (the many gods as manifestations of one), and sacerdotalism (priestly orders).

Hinduism in the modern world contemplates Brahma in the Vedic deities, Agni, Vayu, and Indra; in the popular deities of the Puranas, such as Vishnu, Siva, Kali, and Durga; in the philosophic metaphors of the Godhead; and in incarnate form, according to a belief that Brahma was born as a man so that men may realize their divine nature. Rama, Krishna, Buddha, and a number of others are regarded as divine incarnations of Brahma. *See also* HINDUISM; INDIAN PHILOSOPHY.   E. J. J.

BRAHMANISM [braˈmənizəm], the priestly aspect of Hinduism, a religion practiced by more than 260,000,000 Hindus. Coined by the early European travelers and Christian missionaries who found the Brahman caste dominant in Hindu society, the word Brahmanism is the equivalent of what Hindus prefer to call *Sanatana Dharma* (Eternal Religion). Brahmanism is in fact a later development of the Vedic religion of the Aryan invaders of India. More strictly, it was the transformation of the old Vedic faith into a priestly system. Elaborate ceremonies, material offerings, animal sacrifice, and a dominant priestly caste were the outward characteristics of the new faith.

Brahmanism developed its own forms and techniques, its doctrines and institutions. These were set forth in the Vedas, and established and amplified in the Brahmanas (priestly writings), dated about 1000-800 B.C., a group of prose writings which ordained and regulated the rite of sacrifice and presented a variety of religious legends. The Brahmanas stressed a graded caste system, which placed the Brahman on the topmost rung in the social ladder and relegated the low-caste Sudras to the bottom. Inasmuch as Hinduism, for which Brahmanism stood, was a religious system based on priestly hierarchies, it effectually strengthened the caste system and adopted it as a formidable institution. Salvation became increasingly dependent on the sacrifices performed by the Brahman priests. Dietary restrictions, specifically on beef, belong to this stage of India's religious development.

Combined with native pre-Aryan cults, and noted for its pantheistic tendencies, Brahmanism was a distinctive variation on the ancient Vedic themes. Its practitioners gave to Hinduism a new turn, which was expressed in the Upanishads (c. 800-600 B.C.), sacred writings of a philosophic character. An urge toward unity favored the combination of conflicting monotheistic and pantheistic tendencies, and from this compromise arose the conception of Prajapati, the personal creator of the world and the manifestation of the impersonal Brahma. Brahma was conceived as the universal, self-existing World Soul, the keystone of the pantheistic arch of Brahmanism.

Those accustomed to the worship of concrete gods and goddesses did not take kindly to a colorless deity, however, even if the deity was Brahma. To satisfy them Brahmanism was forced to incorporate certain objects of popular devotion, and, accordingly, the three gods Brahma, Vishnu, and Siva were worshipped equally. This triad was a triple impersonation of the divinity responsible for the creation, preservation, and destruction of the universe. Brahmanism thus effected a compromise which satisfied both the esoteric members of the Hindu community and the more popular demands of folk religion. *See also* HINDUISM.   E. J. J.

BRAHMANS, a caste in India, the elite of Hinduism. Brahmans make up about 18,000,000 among the 260,000,000 Hindus in India and Pakistan, or about 7 per cent of the total. For twenty-five centuries Brahmans have enjoyed special rights and privileges among their fellows. Although modern India has had about 3,000 Hindu castes, as subdivisions based upon divergencies of theory and of religious practice have accumulated, there has been for at least 3,000 years a fourfold scheme by which they all are reckoned. It embraces the "priestly" (Brahman), "warrior" (Kshatriya), "vassal" (Vaishya), and "clean" (Sudra) groups, leaving certain primitive, indigenous stocks to fall into an "outcaste" or "untouchable" group. These are known as "pariahs" or "panchamas," and more recently were called *harijans,* or "God's folk," by Mahatma Gandhi, who was himself a Vaishya. Not all Brahmans are or have been priests, nor are the other designations to be taken always literally, as anyone may judge from the numerous subdivisions of the four major groups. Perhaps 1,500,000 Brahmans exercise the priestly office, while another 1,000,000 are religious mendicants, temple attendants, or occupants of minor posts in religious exercises. The majority of Brahmans, those who do not serve directly as religious functionaries, engage in educational, administrative, and other forms of higher public service, or are landowners. Many have become prominent in Indian politics.

Brahmans as a group rate comparatively high in literacy, although Hindus as a mass are at least 85 per cent illiterate, and Brahmans have been the custodians of Hindu learning and interpreters of Hindu religious tradition at its best, however vague and varied this tradition has often been.

Origin. For the origin of Brahmans it is necessary to have recourse more to legend than to history, and Hindu legend makes the Brahman the chief of all created beings, entitled to all honor and respect—in fact, a human god. Actually, the warrior may have been supreme when the Aryans (Indo-Europeans) conquered northern India about 1500 B.C., but as native and alien cultures merged, and as Aryan settlement and rule gradually were extended, the four Vedas were produced as the dominant cultural expression; the chief duty of leading Brahmans came to be the study and the teaching of the sacred Vedas, the regulation of religious ceremonies, and the performance of special sacrifices. Brahmans thus came to be the intellectual aristocracy, their persons inviolable and their prerogatives unchallenged. By the second century B.C., Sanskrit had become a common spoken tongue in the cultured India known then as Aryavarta, or "land of the Aryans," and Brahmans found in it their special medium, while *prakrits,* or vernaculars, were widely spoken by the general populace. Sanskrit literature bulks especially large in philosophical works; examples are the Upanishads and the six "systems" called the *Bhashyas,* or "commentaries." Educated Brahmans have been the authors and expounders of such works. There is a saying that the Brahman who has true knowledge has the very gods in his control, and all Hindus have had for at least 2,000 years a Brahman-consciousness. Southern or Dravidian India came slowly to be Brahmanized in exaggerated form, its cultural history falling subsequently into two instead of four divisions, the non-Brahman and the Brahman. The greatest Indian theologian and philosopher, Shankara, was a Brahman of South India and it is there that "untouchability" has been most pronounced. On the Bengal side there have been five groups of Brahmans, including those who were polygamous (strict Brahmanism is monogamous), and there have been five major kinds of Brahmans in Dravidian India, speaking sometimes mutually unintelligible dialects or languages.

Caste Characteristics. The recognition of the Brahman's status is the central fact of caste. Caste is determined by the operation of karma, and the frequency of rebirth is in accordance with the fruits of karma. Each Hindu is born to his immediate station and to his career; he is and does what his birth determines, the measure of his strict obedience determining his advance in the worldly round. The Brahman believes that he has benefited from previous rebirths and may expect "to come not back to birth." He may have observed the four stages of an orthodox career as the Code of Manu has ordained, namely, as a student of Brahmanical lore, as a householder and family man faithful in every ceremony, as a recluse who has foresworn his family, and last of all as a sannyasi, free of all forms and ceremonies, wandering as a mendicant, heedless of physical conditions, and bent upon release at death and absorption into deity. He seeks release, generally by means of knowledge (*jnana*), from samsara, the "worldly round," into some Great Beyond or Ultimate. Thus the Brahman has held himself in every way to be supreme among the men of earth, and Hindus in general have accorded him this place, each one hoping to come at last into an equal place of preference. The Brahman, at least, could consider caste a garment to be laid aside at death.

The Brahman is peculiarly Indian. He does not represent a single racial stock, although there was something at the very outset of a color line. Varna, or "color," is the term at stake. *Casta,* or "caste," is Portuguese and may be held responsible through false analogy for Western ignorance of the actual Indian scheme. The line was drawn between the Arya, or light color and the non-Aryan darker hue. The Indian natives, whether or not related to the Austronesians, had been deeply darkened by the sun's actinic, burning rays, whereas the "Aryans" had first come from lands where the sun was kindlier. No pure racial stock, however, can be found in India, even though some aryavarna has doubtless been preserved, as among the Rajputs, for example, although they are not Brahmans. The Brahman blood is mixed, and Brahmanism has more of a cultural and religious connotation. It is an institution, or a movement, or a disposition.

Philosophical Beliefs. There is a typical Brahmanical philosophy, to which perhaps a quarter of all Hindus have subscribed. It is monistic and idealistic, and considers the essence of the universe and the soul of man to be one. It is tolerant of things of the world, but seeks an ideal Ultimate. There are, however, different types of Brahmanic philosophy. Many Brahmans of the present day are deeply concerned with politics and are bent upon some transformation of the present world, while there are others who are more theistic than vedantic in their own religion. Most present-day Brahmans do not find it necessary to discard the classical tradition; indeed, they wish to Brahmanize their land anew, instill new breath within her.

The Brahman has been strictly enjoined to refrain from injury to any living thing. He is bidden to speak the truth, never to steal, or to take what is not given, and to be pure, maintaining full control of the human passion: such is the Brahman Code of Manu. A Brahman priest who drinks intoxicating liquor becomes a noxious insect by rebirth; if he steals he may become a snake. And by way of emphasis upon the Brahman's station, he who slays a Brahman becomes in turn a dog, a pig, an ass, and so on, before he may become a Sudra, or "clean" man again. And if a Brahman sins, he is punished all the more because he was a Brahman.

Brahmanism has been the soul of Hinduism, and the Brahman the Hindu spiritual ideal; or at least Hinduism has had its Brahmanical ideal, to which it has made the individual Brahman subject.   J. C. A.

BRAHMAPUTRA [brɑmǝpu'trǝ], a river in Tibet and India. It rises in south central Tibet, 100 mi. south of the source of the Indus, and flows eastward just south of Lhasa, across the Tibetan Plateau. It then makes an abrupt hairpin bend cutting southward across the Himalaya Mountains into the Valley of Assam, India, where it flows westward and then south into the Padma, one of the distributaries of the Ganges, which flows into the Bay of Bengal. The lower part of the river is navigable and forms a valuable inland waterway for flat-bottomed river boats and barges, although the river meanders and has many islands and shoals.   J. E. F.

BRAHMS, JOHANNES [brɑ'ms; brɑ'mz] (1833-1897), a leading German composer of the second half of the nineteenth century, was born May 7, 1833, at Hamburg. His father was a double-bass player in the Hamburg municipal orchestra. His mother, seventeen years his father's senior, was a seamstress and cook. Johannes grew up in the poorest quarter of Hamburg, contributing to the meager family income at an early age by playing in taverns. He received his musical instruction from Eduard Marxsen, who brought him up in the best tradition of the Beethoven era.

At the age of twenty Brahms left his home and went on a concert tour, in the course of which he met the violinist Joseph Joachim, who introduced him to Robert and Clara Schumann. The resulting friendship with these three great artists was of paramount significance in Brahms's life. Fascinated by the Hamburg artist's compositions, Schumann published, in the *Neue Zeitschrift für Musik,* an enthusiastic article about the "young eagle" which made Brahms's name known in all musical circles. From 1857 to 1859 Brahms held a position as conductor and pianist at the German court of Detmold. He then returned to Hamburg in hope of realizing his great ambition to become conductor of the Philharmonic Orchestra in that city. Although a vacancy occurred twice in the following years, Brahms was not chosen. This disappointment, which was responsible for a decided change in the composer's outlook and brought the sarcastic and bitter elements in his nature to the surface, drove him away from Hamburg.

In 1862 Brahms went to Vienna, where he became conductor of the Singakademie (Choral Academy). Although he resigned from this employment after one year, he came, in time, to make Vienna his permanent residence. He even accepted another conducting post there in 1872, when he became artistic director of the Society of Friends of Music. This post he held for three seasons, before deciding that a permanent position interfered too much with his creative work. Henceforth he confined himself to appearing as guest artist in German, Swiss, and Dutch capitals, and was received everywhere with the greatest enthusiasm. Brahms belonged to the comparatively small number of composers whose work has found full recognition during their lifetime. When he died in Vienna, Apr. 3, 1897, the whole musical world mourned the loss of a prince in the realm of music.

Brahms's music shows an interesting mixture of Classic and Romantic elements. If Richard Wagner, the master of the music drama and the greatest contemporary composer in Germany, considered himself as a man to whom the future belonged, Brahms might in some ways be called a composer of the past. His creative output marks an end rather than a beginning. In his works features of the compositions of Palestrina, Bach, Beethoven, and Schumann are revived. Unlike other Romantic composers of his time, Brahms believed in strict musical forms, in clear, logical construction, and in extreme economy of expression. The number of works which he allowed to appear in print is not very large, but each of them is finished to the last detail.

Brahms's works can be divided into four periods. In the early compositions, written before 1855, Brahms shows a marked preference for the piano. These compositions display love for blunt expression and sudden contrasts. They reveal simplicity and a profound tenderness, and the folksong plays an important role in them. The violent eruptions of the earlier works were abandoned in the second period, starting in 1855. The compositions became mellower, softer, more intimate and meditative. It was a period of transition in which youthful vigor was coupled with the symptoms of approaching maturity. The piano no longer seemed adequate for Brahms's compositions; yet the way to the great choral and orchestral works could only be covered step by step. The composer accordingly turned his attention mainly to chamber music. In his third period, starting around the year 1865, Brahms reached his full artistic maturity. The peculiar Brahmsian combination of the spirits of the sixteenth, seventeenth, eighteenth, and nineteenth centuries now reached its highest development, and his great orchestral and choral works were created during this period. The composer expressed himself in as concise and pregnant a manner as possible. Gradually the emotional content became more serious, and we find more of those singularly lusterless pieces full of indefinite melancholy, which forms an essential element in his

work. In the year 1890, after the completion of his G Major Quintet, Brahms felt that his creative powers were exhausted. Henceforth, he planned only to set his older unpublished works in order. But the composer had resigned himself prematurely; before long his creative impulse revived and he began to write again. There are no great orchestral or choral compositions in the fourth period, for Brahms had reverted to the chamber music, the pianoforte compositions, and the songs of his youth. His inspiration had perhaps lost some-

JOHANNES BRAHMS

thing of its freshness, but up to the very last there was no decline, but rather an increase of spiritual and constructive power.

Brahms was active in almost every field of musical composition with the exception of the opera. The work which first made him famous was his *Requiem* (based on words from the Bible, chosen by the composer himself) for soprano and baritone solo, chorus, orchestra, and organ. It was first performed in 1868 in the cathedral of Bremen. Other important works for voices and orchestra were the "Alto Rhapsody" (1869) for contralto and male chorus, words by Goethe; the *Schicksalslied* ("Song of Destiny") (1871) for chorus and orchestra, words by Hölderlin; and *Nanie* (1880) for chorus and orchestra, words by Schiller. Brahms's four symphonies were praised by Hans von Bülow as the greatest orchestral compositions written since Beethoven, and they belong today to the repertoire of every leading orchestra. The dramatic Symphony No. I in C minor (1876) shows a certain similarity to Beethoven's Fifth Symphony in the same key, while No. II in D major (1877) displays a more idyllic character. No. III in F major (1883) and especially No. IV in E minor (1885) are works of epic grandeur, and the Finale of the latter work may be considered as the crowning glory of Brahms's symphonic achievements. To his orchestral works belong the *Variations on a Theme by Joseph Haydn* (1873), a composition as concise in form as it is inspired in content. Of Brahms's four concertos, the lovely Violin Concerto in D major (1878) with its brilliant Finale in Hungarian style, and the serene Second Piano Concerto in B-flat major (1881) ought to be mentioned. There is a large number of outstanding chamber music works, comprising two string sextets and two string quintets, a quintet for clarinet and string quartet, a piano quintet, three piano quartets, three string quartets, three piano trios, a trio for clarinet, French horn, and piano, a trio for clarinet, cello, and piano, three violin sonatas, two cello sonatas, and two clarinet sonatas. Particularly in his younger years, Brahms was a fine pianist and wrote a number of piano compositions which display a very distinctive style of their own. Especially important are his three sonatas, the three sets of variations on themes by Handel, Paganini, and Schumann, and a number of shorter pieces such as capriccios, intermezzi, and rhapsodies. More famous than any of these original compositions are, however, Brahm's arrangements of Hungarian gypsy dance tunes for piano duet. As a composer of songs, Brahms followed the great traditions of the German *Lied,* creating works hardly inferior to those of Schubert and Schumann. He wrote about 300 songs, including numerous arrangements of folksongs, twenty duets, and sixty quartets. Among the best known of these works are: *The Four Serious Songs, Lullaby, Maynight, Eternal Love, Unavailing Serenade,* and *The Smith.* K. G.

BRAHUI. *See* ASIATIC TRIBES.

BRAHUI [brɑhu′i], the language of approximately 127,000 persons in Baluchistan, around Kalat, and of about 80,000 persons in the adjoining part of Sind; the 1931 *Census of India* asserts that "Brahuis" are found in large numbers in western Afghanistan, but without indicating whether they use the same language as the others. The number of Brahui speakers in Baluchistan declined by 18,000 from 1911 to 1931.

The Dravidian character of Brahui is shown by the negative conjugation of the verb, the noun plural suffix -*ḳ,* absence of prefixation and infixation, and some clear etymologies of everyday words (Brahui *nī* "thou," Tamil and Malayālam *nī;* Brahui *iraṭ* "two," Tamil *iraṇḍu,* Canarese *eraḍu;* Brahui *Xan* "eye," Malayālam, Canarese *ḳaṇṇu*). Less decisive evidence for Dravidian kinship lies in the lack of a dual number, of a comparative degree, and of a relative pronoun (Brahui has adopted a relative particle from Balochi, its Iranian neighbor language). Against the theory of Dravidian kinship it may be argued that much of the Brahui vocabulary is of Iranian origin, notably the numerals from four to one thousand, and that Brahui also shares certain grammatical peculiarities with Iranian: it has no gender, and does not have distinct forms for "we" which respectively include and exclude the person addressed.

Brahui has been known to the West only since 1838; it possesses little literature, even in oral tradition. A few texts have been printed, beginning in 1877, in a variety of the Arabic alphabet. Considering the inaccessibility and barrenness of their country, it is unlikely that the Brahui-speakers represent a vanguard of Dravidian migration from southern India; more probably they are a relic of a time when Dravidian was spoken throughout western India, before the Aryan invasions. Their westerly location, however, does not necessarily support the hypothesis that the Dravidians entered India from the west. C. R. Sl.

BRAIDWOOD, THOMAS (1715-1806), British teacher of the deaf and dumb, was born in Scotland in 1715. After graduating from Edinburgh University, he became a schoolteacher. In 1760 he started a school for the deaf and dumb in Edinburgh, the first of its kind in Great Britain and the model for many successors. He followed the system proposed by Dr. John Wallis in *Philosophical Transactions* nearly a hundred years earlier. In 1783 Braidwood's school was given a royal grant and moved to Hackney, near London. Braidwood died in Hackney, Oct. 24, 1806, but his school was continued by his family long after his death. A. W. S.

BRĂILA [brai′la], an important port of eastern Romania and the capital of the department of the same name, on the west bank of the Danube River, 104 mi. from its mouth at Sulina and about 120 mi. northeast of Bucharest, at 45° 20′ N. lat. and 27° 50′ E. long. The port figured in the Turkish Wars of the eighteenth century, and it was taken by the Russians several times during that period. It was burned down in 1770. During World War I Brăila was taken and occupied by the Germans. The Cathedral of St. Michael is the chief building. Brăila is a major grain-shipping port on the Danube, and also a fishing, commercial, and industrial center. Its industrial establishments include steel-rolling mills, flour mills, grain-processing plants, and lumber yards. The chief manufactures are cement, paints, wire products, furniture, leather goods, and food products. Grain is the leading export. The mineral springs of Lake Sarat near by are visited by many for health reasons. The city is connected by rail with Bucharest, Ploești, and Galați. Pop. (off. est. 1948), 95,514. S. A.

BRAILLE, LOUIS [brɑ′i; bre′l] (1809-1852), French educator, originator of the famous Braille touch system by which the blind can read and write, was born in Coupvray, on Jan. 4, 1809. Braille became blind as the result of an accident when he was three years old, and at the age of ten entered the National Institution for the Young Blind in Paris, where he excelled in science and music. In 1826 he worked out his touch system, now in world-wide use, which has as a basis ten fundamental signs expressed by means of perforations. The system is applied also to teaching the blind to read and write music. Braille himself was an expert pianist, organist, and violoncellist. He died in Paris on Jan. 6, 1852. A. S. M. and W. W. Br.

BRAIN, the enlarged anterior end of the central nervous system, primarily a center for the important nerves of the head, which, increasing in complexity and importance in higher forms of life, becomes the central exchange of nervous impulses throughout the body, correlating their messages, originating responses, storing impressions for future use, and finally becoming the seat of the intelligence.

DIVISIONS OF THE BRAIN

The evolution of a complicated exchange system at the head end of the neuraxis is predicated by the existence of important sense organs of sight, hearing, smell, taste and a variety of facial sensations, located in the head and entering this part of the nervous system, together with ascending sensory information from the remainder of the body, demanding mechanisms for analysis, combination and integration. In the lower forms of vertebrated animals (fish, amphibia, reptiles, birds), sensory reactions are relatively stereotyped so that nervous mechanisms are simpler, resulting in a smaller brain. In the mammals, however, a higher level is added to combine all incoming impulses. This is the cerebral cortex and the fibers which serve it. As a result, in mammals, the brain stem, into which the nerves enter, forms only a trunk or stalk for the much-expanded terminal end, which is the cerebrum. In the brain of higher forms, as in man, the shape may be likened to that of a developing mushroom with a stalk. The brain stem is conventionally divided into four segments (bulb, pons, midbrain, thalamus), while the expanded end can be considered as composed of two parts (striatum and thalamus). In addition to these divisions, there is a considerable excrescence to the pons segment of the brain stem: the cerebellum.

The Bulb. The bulb, medulla oblongata (Figs. 1:31, 2:7, 9), is continuous below with the spinal cord and, in addition to relaying the ascending impulses from the cord, contains the connections of the cranial nerves VII-XII. A reference to the chart of cranial nerves in the article on nerve will show that these include such important connections as that to the muscles of the face (VII), to the organs of hearing and the vestibular organ (VIII), the sensory and motor supply to

The Thalamus. The highest segment of the brain stem, the thalamic segment, is extensively overgrown by the cerebrum so that it does not appear at first to be a part of the brain stalk (Fig. 1:24; Fig. 3). In higher brains, this segment is largely a relay center for sensory impulses on their way to the cerebral cortex, so that it is not destined to become very massive. This segment also receives the important optic nerves (Fig. 2:II; Fig. 3:18-20), which partially cross at the

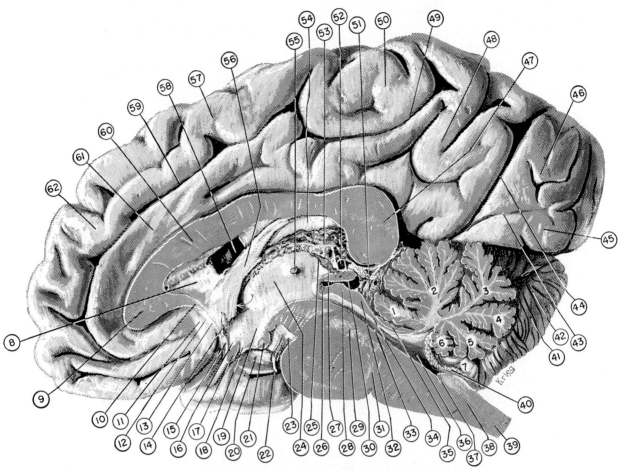

Fig. 1—LATERAL VIEW OF THE MID-LINE SECTION OF THE HUMAN BRAIN

(1) Central lobule of the cerebellum; (2) Anterior quadrate lobule; (3) Posterior quadrate lobule; (4) Superior semilunar lobule; (5) Inferior semilunar lobe; (6) Nodule; (7) Tonsil; (8) Septum pellucidium; (9) Genu; (10) Rostrum of Callosum; (11) Parolfactory area; (12) Post parolfactory sulcus; (13) Subcallosal gyrus; (14) Anterior commissure; (15) Terminal lamina; (16) Optic recess; (17) Optic chiasma; (18) Infundibulum; (19) Hypothalamus; (20) Uncus; (21) Mammillary body; (22) Oculomotor nerve; (23) Interpeduncular fossa; (24) Thalamus; (25) Stria medullaris thalami; (26) Posterior commissure; (27) Habenula; (28) Superior colliculus; (29) Tegmentum; (30) Pineal body; (31) Bulb and pons; (32) Inferior colliculus; (33) Aqueduct; (34) Anterior medullary velum; (35) Lingula; (36) Fourth ventricle; (37) Calamus scriptorius; (38) Central canal; (39) Cord; (40) Chorioid plexus of fourth ventricle; (41) Lateral lobe of cerebellum; (42) Transverse fissure; (43) Calcarine sulcus; (44) Parietooccipital sulcus; (45) Lingual gyrus; (46) Cuneus; (47) Splenium; (48) Precuneus; (49) Marginal part of cingulate sulcus; (50) Paracentral lobule; (51) Subarachnoidal cistern of great cerebral vein; (52) Great cerebral vein; (53) Chorioid plexus of lateral ventricle; (54) Fonix; (55) Massa intermedia; (56) Fornix; (57) Frontal lobe; (58) Lateral ventricle; (59) Cingulate sulcus; (60) Corpus callosum; (61) Cingulate gyrus; (62) Superior frontal gyrus

the organs of the chest and abdomen (IX-X), and to the muscles of the tongue (XII). The roots of these nerves are shown in Fig. 2.

The Pons. The pons (Fig. 2:11) is primarily a continuation of the bulb. It includes chiefly the connections for the general sensations from the face, together with certain motor nerves (V-VI); but it is enlarged ventrally because a massive bundle of fibers to the cerebellum is imposed on it.

Midbrain. Just above the pons is a short segment of the brain stem, the midbrain (Fig. 1:28, 32), which contains reflex centers for vision (superior colliculus) and for hearing (inferior colliculus).

chiasma (Fig. 2:15) and embrace the two sides of the thalamus by means of the optic tract (Fig. 2:3). While most of the thalamus is essentially sensory, its lower, smaller part, the hypothalamus (Fig. 1:19; Fig. 2:14), is regulatory in function, chiefly of the activities of the internal organs.

Cerebrum. The cerebrum in the larger brains forms by far the greatest part of their bulk, particularly in humans. It is extensively convoluted to provide a maximum surface for the cerebral cortex, the center for higher correlations and intellectual activity. A general idea of the relation of the cerebral cortex to the rest of the brain may be gained from an inspection of Fig. 4, where the cortex is represented

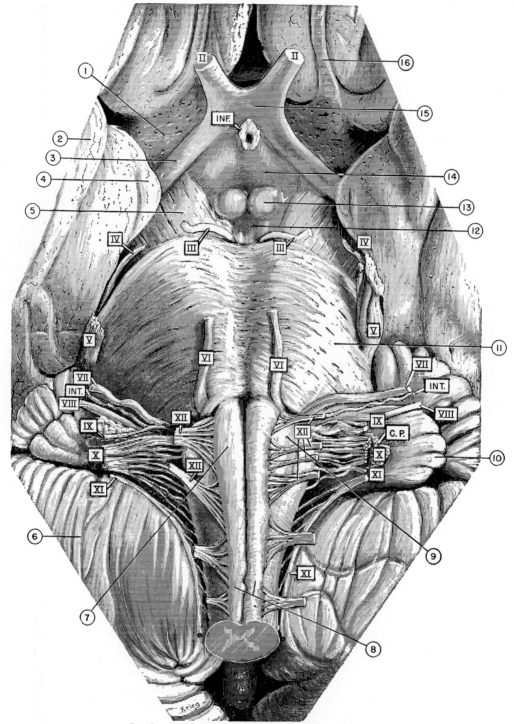

Fig. 2—VENTRAL VIEW OF THE BASE OF THE BRAIN

(1) Anterior perforated substance; (2) Temporal lobe; (3) Optic tract; (4) Uncus; (5) Cerebral peduncle; (6) Cerebellum; (7) Pyramidal tract; (8) Crossing of pyramidal tracts; (9) Inferior olive; (10) Flocculus; (11) Pons; (12) Infundibulum; (13) Mammillary body; (14) Hypothalamus; (15) Optic chiasma; (16) Olfactory tract.

semidiagrammatically as the outer shell. The central core is largely occupied by the multitudinous fibers which serve the cerebral cortex, consisting of sensory nerve fibers passing to it, motor fibers directed downward to the motor cranial and spinal nerves, associative fibers, which connect points on the cerebral cortex, and the massive cross-connection between the otherwise completely divided cerebral hemispheres of opposite sides, the callosum (Fig. 1:60, 9, 47 callosum, genu, splenium). The first of the cranial nerves, that of smell, is the only one entering the cerebrum (Fig. 2:16). Included with the cerebrum, and a part of it, is a group of basally placed masses of nerve cells constituting the striatum, which can be divided, as shown in Fig. 4, into the caudate and lenticular nucleus. Between these two nuclei pass the fibers which connect the cerebrum with the remainder of the brain, the internal capsule. The function of the striatum is poorly understood, but seems to be largely that of regulating certain aspects of motion and of co-ordinating patterns of primitive motor activity.

Cerebellum. The cerebellum (Fig. 1:1-7; Fig. 2:6, 10) is a bulky, oblong, dumb-bell shaped lobe, placed between the brain stem and the hinder part of the cerebrum. It also has a cortex, composed of a lamina of nerve cells and fibers

finds exit to the outer surface of the brain through the fourth ventricle. A disease process which causes obstruction at any part of the ventricular system dams back the cerebrospinal fluid, enlarging the ventricles and precipitating a number of nervous symptoms.

INTERNAL CONNECTIONS

An understanding of the brain is not gained from the recognition of the lobes into which it may be divided, but

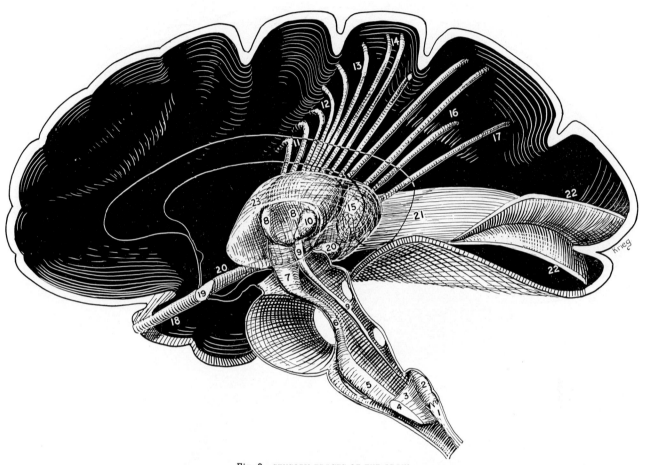

Fig. 3—SENSORY TRACTS OF THE BRAIN

(1) Ascending sensory tract, with (2) its secondary nerve cells, (3) Fibers from the secondary nerve cells, and (4) the crossing of the fibers from the secondary nerve cells; (5, 6, 7) Medial lemniscus; (8) Ventral nucleus of the thalamus; (9) Ascending fibers of the trigeminal nerve; (10) Thalamic nucleus of the trigeminal nerve; (11, 12, 13, 14) Thalmo cortical fibers; (15) Pulvinar; (16, 17) Tracts to the secondary sensory areas; (18) Optic nerve; (19) Optic chiasm; (20) Optic tract; (21) Geniculocalcarine tract; (22) Optic radiations; (23) Anterior nucleus of the thalamus.

whose surface area is increased by being thrown into thin, parallel sheets, or folia, which in cross section have an appearance much like a tiny cedar tree. The cerebellum connects with many parts of the brain stem and cerebrum (Fig. 5). Its function is the regulation and co-ordination of muscular activity.

The Ventricles. The brain develops as a hollow tube and it remains so throughout life, but the cavity becomes much distorted. Within the cerebrum is a paired, horseshoe-shaped cavity, the lateral ventricles. These connect through the interventricular foramina (Fig. 1:arrow) with the median, slitlike third ventricle (Fig. 1:19, 23). This connects below through the narrow, quill-like aqueduct with the pyramidal fourth ventricle, which is placed above the bulb and below the cerebellum. The ventricles are filled with the cerebrospinal fluid which is continuously secreted and

rather from the precise connections which the nerve fibers make within it, just as the hookup diagram of a radio is of more importance than the cabinet. These connections are, for the most part, rather well known, though painstaking and special methods must be applied to ascertain them since they are not demonstrable by simple dissection. They may be grouped as sensory, associative, motor, and cerebellar.

Tracts. The nervous bundles or tracts in the brain show a strong tendency to be grouped according to the functional aspects of sensation which they serve. Thus, though the nervous terminations are indiscriminately mixed on the surface of the body, within the brain pain, touch and temperature pass in distinct tracts, and the bundles of nerve cells to which they connect are also separated into internal masses called nuclei.

Sensory Tracts. The nerve fibers which receive sensations of touch pass up the entire length of the spinal cord as a bundle (Fig. 3:1), synapse, that is, join physiologically, with secondary nerve cells in the bulb (2), arch downward (3), and cross the median plane (4) to ascend the brain stem through the medial lemniscus (5, 6, 7) and end in the ventral nucleus of the thalamus (8). Those from the head, entering through the trigeminal nerve, have a separate ascending tract (9) and a separate nucleus in the thalamus (10).

here to a specialized region on the lateral surface of the cerebral cortex.

Associative Fibers. From these three primary cerebral sensory receptive areas pass many associative fibers to other parts of the cerebral cortex: some of them close by, where the impulses are transformed into perceptions of varying complexity; others intermediate in position between the several areas, where they are combined to produce complex impressions and faculties, such as understanding of speech and

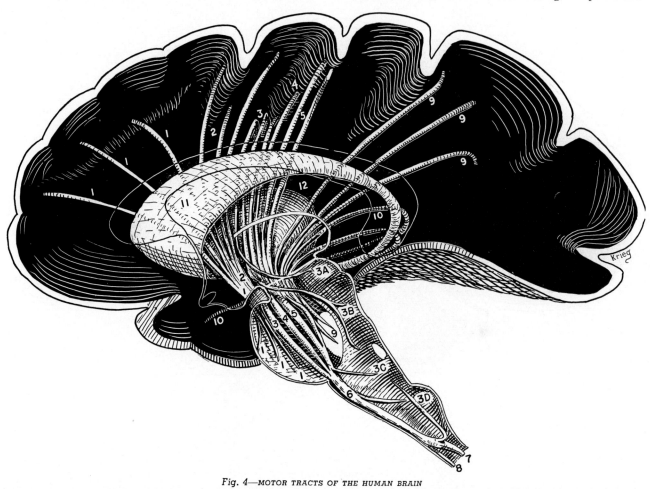

Fig. 4—MOTOR TRACTS OF THE HUMAN BRAIN

(1, 2, 3, 4, 5, 9, 10) Motor fibers of the corona radiata; (3, 4, 5) Fibers from the primary motor area of the cerebrum; (3A, 3B, 3C, 3D) Connections to motor nerves; (6) Pyramidal tracts; (7) Crossed corticospinal tracts; (8) Anterior corticospinal tracts; (11) Caudate nucleus; (12) Lenticular nucleus.

Here all sensory fibers synapse with the tertiary neurons whose fibers continue through the internal capsule to the cerebral cortex chiefly on its dorsolateral surface (11-14). Certain secondary connections are made within the thalamus, chiefly in the pulvinar (15), and these in turn, relay to the cerebrum just behind the main sensory areas of the cortex (16, 17).

Vision. The sensory system for vision enters the brain through the optic nerve (18) and tract (20), synapses in the lateral geniculate body, and thence is relayed through the geniculocalcarine tract (21), which is a broad sheet of fibers running backward in the cerebrum and expanding at its posterior, or occipital, pole to terminate in the cerebral cortex in the vicinity of the calcarine sulcus (22).

Hearing. The central tract for hearing enters through the eighth nerve at the junction of the bulb and pons and is relayed up to the medial geniculate body of the thalamus, where, like other sensations, it is relayed by thalamic cells

reading; and also to the more forward regions of the cerebrum, where they furnish data for motor activity and intellectual processes of various grades. The more complex of these mental processes are located in the forward or frontal region of the cerebral cortex. It is very difficult to understand just what takes place in the frontal cortex, the large size of which is the chief distinction between the brain of man and that of apes. From the results of incising it, a procedure now frequently resorted to in an effort to reduce continuous abnormal states of anxiety, guilt, fear and suspicion, it would seem that its activity is largely to inhibit or prevent free expression of the higher sensory associations, since individuals on whom this operation of frontal lobotomy has been performed may lose these symptoms and tend to develop an easy-going and uninhibited mode of existence and lose higher standards and judgments, intellectual and moral. There are massive regions of the cerebral cortex, particularly on its medial and inferior aspects and in the temporal lobes, whose functions are virtually unknown. Modern brain research is attempting to discover the connections and significance of such areas.

Motor Tracts. While the sensory areas of the cortex are located in the hinder half of the cerebrum behind the central sulcus, the motor regulatory activities proceed from the section in front of the central sulcus. Just as the various segmental levels of the body are represented in a rather precise (but inverted) order in the forward border of the

cortico-bulbar tracts. Other descending fibers are not as strictly motor as the preceding, but connect with the cerebellum through the pons and to relaying mechanisms within the brain stem. There are, of course, shorter circuits of reflex motor activity at lower levels of the brain, formed by way stations along the course of the sensory tracts which connect directly with the cranial and spinal motor nerves.

Cerebellar Connections. The connections of the cerebellum are complex, but may be followed by reference to the legend to Figure 5. *See also* NERVOUS SYSTEM. W. J. S. K.

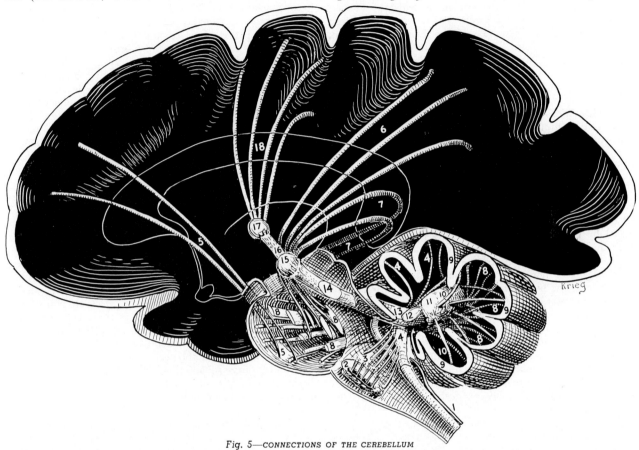

Fig. 5—CONNECTIONS OF THE CEREBELLUM

(1) Dorsal spinocerebellar tract in bulb; (2) inferior olive, sending out (3) olivocerebellar fibers, which cross (1) and join the restiform body (4) which is distributed to the cerebellar cortex, chiefly anteriorly. (5) Pontile nuclei. These are under cerebral cortical influence through (5) frontopontile fibers, (6) parietopontile fibers, and (7) temporopontile fibers, and send (8) pontocerebellar fibers to (9) cerebellar cortex. The cortex, in turn, sends (10) fibers to the (11) dentate and (12) other internal nuclei. These nuclei send a bundle of fibers (13) the brachium conjunctivum forward which cross (14) and terminate largely in the (15) red nucleus; some pass further forward (16) to end in (17) the ventral nucleus of the thalamus, and are relayed (18) to the motor region of the cerebral cortex.

parietal region, the points regulating motor function are arranged in a similar order in the hinder end of the frontal region. It is possible in the exposed brain of a living man to stimulate with a weak electrical current various points in the motor area of the cortex and produce discrete movements, as though they were arranged along this part of the cortex in keyboard fashion. Stimulation of the region farther forward results in bodily movements, but these are more massive and less well marked. In Fig. 4, one sees that the fibers from the motor area pass downward through the central portion of the internal capsule, into the cerebral peduncle (Fig. 2:5) and spread through the pons in the form of large bundles which combine in the bulb as the pyramids (Fig. 2:7, 8). This, the principal motor tract, crosses and takes a new position to pass down the spinal cord as the cortico-spinal tracts. In its course, the motor tract gives off connections to the motor spinal nerves; these are the

BRAINERD [bre'nərd], the seat of Crow Wing Co. in central Minnesota, is located on the Mississippi River, 128 mi. northwest of Minneapolis. Brainerd was founded in 1870 and chartered in 1883. It is a gateway to Minnesota's famous lake region, one of the most popular vacation areas in the United States. Within 25 mi. of the city there are 464 lakes. Discovery of iron ore in 1906 in the Cayuna Range, 15 mi. northeast of the city, has made Brainerd the center of a great iron mining region. The Northern Pacific Railroad and North Central Airlines supply transportation. Industries include creameries and bottling works and a railroad-tie treating plant; manufactures are pulp and newsprint, lumber, and wood products. Brainerd Junior College was established in 1938. Pop. 1950, 12,637.

BRAIN SURGERY. *See* SURGERY (*Neurological Surgery*).

BRAINTREE, a town in Norfolk Co., eastern Massachusetts, is situated 10 mi. south of Boston. It is a residential and industrial community and is governed by the representative form of town meeting. Braintree was settled about 1634. Its first church was built in 1637, and the town was incorporated in 1640. Originally, it included the city of Quincy and the towns of Randolph and Holbrook. The first iron works in New England was established in Braintree in 1644, but nine years later it closed its doors, a failure. The town is the birthplace of General Ebenezer Thayer of Revolutionary War fame and of General Sylvanus Thayer, superintendent of West Point from 1817 to 1833. It is served by the New York, New Haven and Hartford Railroad. Chief manufactures are linoleum, abrasives, and cloth for books. Pop. 1950 (town), 8,337; (township), 23,161.

BRAIN TUMOR. *See* Surgery (*Neurological Surgery*).

BRAIN WAVES, oscillations in electrical potential that are constantly produced by the brain during life. They have a frequency of 3 to 100 per second and a magnitude of 5 to 500 millionths of a volt (recorded from the unopened skull). The study of these waves is known as electroencephalography.

Discovery. As with almost all fundamental discoveries in physiology, brain waves were first discovered in animals. Caton, in England, in 1874 found electrical pulsations produced by the brains of rabbits. Hans Berger reported in 1929 that brain waves could be recorded from the human brain. His work was scorned at first; but later his enemies received greater honor for work on brain waves than did the master. The next development was the invention of the electrical analyzer by W. Grey Walter in the year 1942. This machine reads the brain wave record automatically by collecting the electrical charges at the various frequencies. Thus, the total number of normal 10 per second and abnormal 6 per second waves are counted and the results registered by the analyzing machine. This method is a great improvement over the crude inspection of records by the unaided eye, which easily misses the finer details. Thus, a deep cancer of the brain can be localized by Walter's analyzer but not by crude visual inspection.

Taking of Measurements. Brain waves are measured by means of radio tubes which amplify the current. Salt solution is rubbed on the scalp and electrodes held in place by collodion, wax or tape. The method is painless and no needles are necessary. Electroencephalography is the most harmless of all types of brain examination, but it requires a special training in electrophysiology to interpret the results.

Wave Nomenclature. The alpha waves, 10 per second and from 10 to 100 millionths of a volt, are present on an average of a little over 50 per cent of the time in normal persons. Beta waves are faster, above 15 per second, and are considered normal if the voltage is not over 50 millionths of a volt. When the voltage of these beta waves attains 100 millionths of a volt they become the abnormal waves seen in grand mal epilepsy. The delta waves are abnormally slow, 3 to 7 per second. Some authorities recognize a special type of abnormal wave at 6 per second known as the theta wave (sometimes produced by deep tumors). A special type of abnormal wave, known as a "spike," is an isolated sharp wave lasting only one tenth of a second or less. In major epilepsy or grand mal (violent convulsions) these spikes are found but in minor epilepsy or petit mal (lapse of consciousness lasting a few seconds) each spike is followed by a slow dome-shaped wave. Brain injury, as from a fractured skull, produces abnormally slow waves or sometimes spikes. Cancer of the brain can be localized by slow waves. These brain records are only diagnostic aids and most electroencephalograms are so indefinite that a diagnosis cannot be made without extensive clinical information concerning the other signs and symptoms of the patient.

Normal Waves. The normal electroencephalogram has been neglected for the more easily interpreted pathological records. Study of identical twins showed that the normal pattern is inherited. It is probable that the personality of normal persons is related to their electroencephalogram since extreme personality deviations in delinquent children and psychopaths are associated with abnormal waves in about 60 per cent of the cases. Normal persons with poor personality adjustment, as judged by psychological tests, usually show abnormal brain waves during deep breathing. The deep breathing test which is given by the electroencephalographer to all persons, normal or abnormal, reveals pathological waves not present during quiet respiration, because blood vessels of the brain become narrow during deep breathing and half the normal blood flow to the brain is cut off.

Effect of Drugs. Many drugs affect the brain waves. Acetylcholine and strychnine placed directly on the exposed brain of anesthetized animals increase the voltage and frequency. Dilantin, which is taken to prevent seizures in epileptics, abolishes the abnormal brain waves. Benzedrine accelerates the waves. The low blood sugar produced by insulin gives abnormally slow waves. Abundance of sugar in the blood provides the brain with energy, and some epileptics have normal waves in deep breathing when the blood sugar is high (above 160 milligrams per 100 cc. of blood). Blood sugar has such an important effect on brain waves that it should be determined for every electroencephalogram. In normal persons there is a critical blood sugar level of 130 milligrams per 100 cc. of blood below which level the majority of patients will show abnormally slow waves during deep breathing. In addition to providing energy for the brain, the sugar is converted by vitamin B into acetate and the acetate combines with choline which generates the electrical waves.

Foetal and Infantile Waves. Brain waves can be recorded from the foetus by placing electrodes on the mother's abdomen. The waves of very young babies are slow, about 4 per second. Babies must be put to sleep with pentothal to prevent disturbances of the record by muscular movements. By 10 years of age the waves have the adult pattern. Only about one in seven cases of convulsions in babies is true epilepsy which can be detected by the electroencephalogram.

Origin of Brain Waves. The frequency of brain waves is increased by temperature (as in fever) which indicates they are produced chemically in the brain. The brain produces a very active substance, acetylcholine, which generates a current of negative electricity. An artificial brain wave can be produced by placing acetylcholine on a layer of cholesterol in a test tube. According to this theory the fast waves of major epilepsy are formed by an overproduction of acetylcholine and the slow waves of the minor epilepsy result from a deficiency of acetylcholine in the brain. Another theory postulates that potassium passes out of the brain cells, forming an electrical disturbance. *See also* Bio-electricity.

T. C. B.

BRAKE or **BRACKEN,** a fern, *Pteridium aquilinum,* common to many parts of the world, often covering large areas. It is vigorous and coarse, and sends up many fronds divided into three parts, from underground root stocks. The dried fronds are sometimes used for thatch, litter, and fodder.

This plant is frequently mentioned in literature because of its widespread occurrence, which makes it well known, and because of its reputed magical qualities. On midsummer eve, any person putting "fern seed" from the bracken in his shoe was supposed to become invisible.   G. M. Sm.

BRAKES, devices employed to retard or stop motion by friction or by electromagnetic means. In friction-type brakes, blocks, bands, ropes, cones, disks, and other units are applied

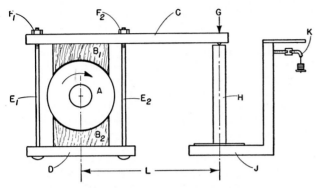

DIAGRAMMATIC SKETCH OF PRONY BRAKE

to the moving member, transforming the mechanical energy of motion into heat energy. In the electric brake, the electric motor is run as a generator, providing braking action through magnetic action. Special-type brakes include the solenoid-controlled friction brake; the water brake, which is a fluid friction brake; the fan brake, which involves air friction in "fan action"; and the Prony brake.

Prony Brake. The Prony brake, used to measure power in a rotating shaft, is typical of the block-type brake and serves to illustrate the braking action of the other types of friction brake. As illustrated, braking action occurs when blocks B_1 and B_2 are pressed against power pulley A by tightening tie rods E_1 and E_2 at nuts F_1 and F_2, respectively. The amount of braking pressure is measured by platform scale J. Knowing the speed of the pulley, the length of the brake arm L, the dead weight (tare) of the arm C and the pedestal H, the power absorbed by the brake is

$$hp = \frac{2\pi LN(W_K - W_0)}{33,000},$$

where hp is horsepower, L is length of brake arm in feet, N is speed of pulley in revolutions per minute, W_K is scale reading at K in pounds, and W_0 is tare in pounds. *See also* Deck Machinery; Dynamometer; Electric Traction; Hoisting Apparatus; Motor Vehicles; Railroads; Street-cars, Electric.   R. C. H. H.

BRAKPAN [bræ′kpæn], a town and mining center in the Union of South Africa, 23 mi. east of Johannesburg, at an altitude of 5,372 ft. in the southern part of the Transvaal. The community was originally laid out as a part of the township of Benoni in 1912. After its founding the town grew rapidly, and in 1919 Brakpan was made a separate community. Iron works are the most important industrial establishments in Brakpan, and gold and silver are mined in the vicinity; there are also brass foundries, jute mills, and electrical equipment works. Brakpan's educational system includes a technical college. The population is about one-third European. Pop. 1951, 85,040.

BRAMANTE [brɑmɑ′nte] (1444-1514), Italian Renaissance architect, whose real name was Donato d'Agnolo or d'Angelo, was born at Monte Asdrualdo (now Fermignano), in the duchy of Urbino, in central Italy. At first he studied painting, probably with such masters as Piero della Francesca and Andrea Mantegna, but later he devoted himself to architecture, becoming one of the great architects of the High Renaissance. He first worked at Milan, where his churches of San Satiro and Santa Maria delle Grazie typify his early manner. After 1499 he lived at Rome, where his deep study of Roman antiquities chastened his style. Patronized by the popes, Bramante had a hand in much of the construction under Alexander VI and Julius II. He was the original architect of the great Basilica of St. Peter, construction upon which was begun by him; it was left for others, however, to bring it to completion. Bramante was responsible for portions of the Vatican Palace, particularly the Court of San Damaso. Other works were the circular Tempietto in the courtyard of San Pietro di Montorio, the cloisters of Santa Maria della Pace, and the masterful Cancelleria, one of the finest of the Roman Renaissance palaces. Bramante died in Rome on Apr. 14, 1514.   R. Ne.

BRAMBLE, MATTHEW, the hypochondriac, gruff, but kindly central character of Tobias Smollett's *The Expedition of Humphry Clinker*. In many ways he expresses Smollett's own opinions and temperament.   R. M. W.

BRAMBLE, a general term for all thorny shrubs of the blackberry and raspberry genus *Rubus,* occasionally indicating specifically the common blackberry of the Old World. *See also* Blackberry; Raspberry; Rubus.

BRAMPTON, the county town of Peel Co., Ontario, Canada, 21 mi. west of Toronto. It was founded in 1834, incorporated as a village in 1852, and as a town in 1873. It was once an important grain market. Brampton is the leading greenhouse center in Canada. The factory output includes boots and shoes, knitted goods, machinery, office furniture, and office supplies. The surrounding area is an important dairy region, supplying milk to the city of Toronto. Pop. 1956, 12,587.   D. F. P.

BRANCUŞI, CONSTANTIN [brɑ′nkush] (1876-1957), sculptor, was born at Pestisani-Gorque in Romania, in 1876. After studying in art schools at Craiova and Bucharest in his native country, Brancuşi went to Paris and entered the École des Beaux-Arts in 1904, but soon left on the advice of Rodin. In a violent revulsion against Realism a few years later, Brancuşi smashed a statue, "The Crossing of the Red Sea," on which he was at work, and began to develop an original style of sculptural abstraction. One of the first sculptors to develop in this direction, he showed much less of the influence of Cubism and other styles of abstraction in painting than did other sculptors, and his work has exerted considerable influence on modern sculpture.

Brancuşi eliminated all realistic detail, reducing the form or concept he was presenting to the simplest geometrical essence he could conceive. He showed great interest in rhythmic repetition, as in his *Endless Column* and his sculptures of *Adam* and *Eve.* He emphasized sensuous qualities of the materials of sculpture, favoring highly polished surfaces of stone or metal, and rough-hewn, cracked or weather-beaten surfaces of wood. He often heightened the effect of material by contrasts, such as laying a smooth, egglike marble "head" on a dark velvet cushion, or poising a highly polished metal or alabaster fish over an oval mirror base. He died Mar. 16, 1957, in Paris.   L. R.

BRANDEIS, LOUIS DEMBITZ [bra'ndais] (1856-1941), American lawyer, was born in Louisville, Ky., Nov. 13, 1856. He graduated from the Harvard University Law School in 1877 and practiced in Boston, Mass., from 1879 until 1916. His liberal ideas caused him to be known as the "people's attorney." Without fee, in 1896 and afterward, he

LOUIS DEMBITZ BRANDEIS

WIDE WORLD PHOTOS

defended the people of Boston against the traction interests, and later defeated efforts to increase the price of gas. During the investigation into the control of the Equitable Life Assurance Society of New York in 1905, he was the attorney for the policy holders and was largely responsible for the drafting of the Armstrong bill, passed in 1906 by the New York state legislature to control the activities of life insurance companies. After this Brandeis formulated the plan of the Massachusetts Savings Bank Insurance Law, enacted in June 1907, which provided workmen with their own organization for handling insurance. Brandeis was an authority on railroad law, and his personal concern with the subject of financial monopoly urged him to undertake a successful campaign in 1908 to prevent the New York, New Haven, and Hartford Railroad from acquiring a monopoly of transportation throughout New England. In 1910, and again in 1913, when he appeared before the Interstate Commerce Commission, he was responsible for preventing increases in freight charges and contended successfully that, on account of their wastefulness and inefficiency, the railroads themselves were responsible for the conditions which led them to ask for the increase. In 1908 he was counsel for the people of Oregon in cases dealing with the ten-hour workday and minimum wages for women. In 1910, during the administration of President William H. Taft, he was a strong defender of Louis R. Glavis in the controversy raised by Glavis' articles in *Collier's Weekly* in November 1909, attacking Richard A. Ballinger, Secretary of the Interior. In 1911 Brandeis was appointed arbitrator in the strike of the New York cloakmakers. Becoming interested in the problems of the Jewish people, he became a leader of the Zionist movement. In 1913 Brandeis was invited by President Woodrow Wilson to enter his cabinet, but, although always willing to offer advice on antitrust laws and banking legislation, he refused to accept. In 1916 he was appointed a member of the United States Supreme Court by President Woodrow Wilson, and despite considerable opposition the appointment was confirmed by the Sen-

ate. During his service on the Supreme Court, Brandeis became famous for his dissenting opinions. During the 1930's, as the membership of the Supreme Court changed from conservative to liberal, Brandeis found himself agreeing more often with the majority; by then his dissenting opinions and the reasoning back of them were adopted by the majority of the court and used in their arguments. He was an outstanding liberal thinker and, as such, was much admired by the people, whose causes he espoused. His book, *Other People's Money,* first published in 1914 and reprinted in 1932, was considered a brilliant analysis of the influence of moneyed interests on the life of the average American. Brandeis died in Washington, D.C., Oct. 5, 1941. Brandeis University at Waltham, Mass., was named for him in 1948.
                                                          R. T.

BRANDENBURG [bra'ndənbɛrg; bra'ndənburχ], formerly a German margravate and an electorate of the Holy Roman Empire and from 1815 to 1945 a province of Prussia. As a province, Brandenburg was divided into the three administrative divisions of Berlin, Potsdam, and Frankfurt, with an area of 15,415 sq. mi. and a population, exclusive of Berlin, of 2,726,025 in 1933. Following World War II Brandenburg was included in the Soviet zone of Germany, and after the establishment of the (East) German Democratic Republic in 1949, the province was federated with it as a state. In 1952 Brandenburg, together with the other historic *Länder* of eastern Germany, was dissolved.

The first known inhabitants of Brandenburg were the Teutonic Semnones, who were succeeded by various Slavonic tribes from the east. Partly subdued for a time by Charlemagne, some of these tribes were later conquered by Henry the Fowler (c. 876-936). For several centuries after this Brandenburg remained partly under Slavic, partly under German rule. The latter gradually prevailed as German colonists pushed eastward during the later Middle Ages. By 1134 Albert the Bear (founder of the Ascanian line which ruled the region until 1320) subdued most of the Slavic inhabitants of the region, and by 1140 Albert was recognized by Pribislav, the childless Slavic duke of Brandenburg, as his heir. As margrave of Brandenburg, Albert did much to Christianize the area and brought in many settlers from the lower Rhineland. After the death of Albert, in 1170, the Ascanian rulers of Brandenburg gradually extended their territories at the expense of Bohemia, Poland, and Pomerania. When the family died out in 1320, the region was held by different dynasties for almost a century; by 1356 recognition of Brandenburg's political importance was indicated by the Golden Bull naming the margraves of Brandenburg as electors of the Holy Roman Empire.

In 1417 Frederick of Hohenzollern, burgrave of Nürnberg, became elector of Brandenburg under the Emperor Sigismund. Primogeniture was introduced in 1473, and for five centuries the power of the Hohenzollerns and of Brandenburg steadily increased. The Hohenzollerns continued to enlarge their territories, build up their economic resources, and develop a large army and efficient administration. The electorate became a leading Protestant state in the sixteenth century. The connection with Prussia began in 1618, when the Elector John Sigismund became Duke of Prussia (part of the Kingdom of Poland) through marriage. In the Thirty Years' War Brandenburg was devastated and its population reduced, but under the guidance of Frederick William, the Great Elector (ruled, 1640-1688), it emerged from the conflict as a considerable military power, enriched by the addition of large territories. Frederick William forced the King of Poland to recognize Prussia as an independent state and applied the doctrines of mercantilism to his domains, building up agriculture and industry and improving transportation. A greatly increased government income was spent on improvements and on an efficient and powerful army. In 1701 the Great Elector's son Frederick won the right to take the title of Frederick I, King of Prussia, in return for agreeing to aid Leopold I in the War of the Spanish Succession. The history of Brandenburg then became merged with that of Prussia.   F. C. H. and W. O. S.

BRANDENBURG, a manufacturing town located in the former Prussian province of Brandenburg, in east central Germany. Brandenburg is situated 40 mi. west of Berlin, astride three branches of the Havel River, on a rolling plain. Once the chief fortress of the Slavic Hevelli, it was taken by Henry I in 927, changed hands again, and was taken by Albert the Bear, who styled himself margrave of Brandenburg. It was an episcopal see from 949 to 1544, joined the Hanseatic League, and became the nucleus of Prussia. It received considerable World War II bomb damage. It was placed in the Soviet Union occupation zone after World War II. The often-restored twelfth-century cathedral occupies an island in the river. There are several other notable buildings, though damaged, including St. Catherine's Church, dating partially from the fourteenth century. Manufactures are bicycles, metal wares, textiles, leather, perambulators, and chemicals. Pop. (est. 1938), 69,200.   C. C. H.

BRANDES, GEORG MORRIS COHEN [brɑ′ndəs] (1842-1927), Danish literary critic, was born in Copenhagen, Feb. 4, 1842, of a well-to-do Jewish mercantile family. After beginning the study of law at the University of Copenhagen, he soon turned to the study of aesthetics and philosophy, and, in 1866, as his contribution to a current intellectual controversy, he published his first book, *Om Dualismen i vor nyeste Filosofi* ("On the Dualism in Our Most Recent Philosophy"). *Æstetiske Studier* (1868) ("Aesthetic Studies") and *Kritiker og Portrætter* (1870) ("Critiques and Portraits") revealed his incisiveness as a critic, his admiration of modern French literature, and, particularly, his adherence to the literary tenets of Hippolyte Taine. In 1870 Brandes obtained his doctor's degree with a thesis, *Den franske Æstetik i vore Dage; en Afhandling om Taine* ("Contemporary French Aesthetics; an Essay on Taine"). Thereupon he went abroad, visiting Paris, Rome, and London and becoming personally acquainted with Taine, Sainte-Beuve, and John Stuart Mill.

Returning to Copenhagen, Brandes began, in 1871, a series of university lectures, later published as *Hovedstrømninger i det nittende Aarhundredes Literatur* (1871-1890), (*Main Currents in Nineteenth-Century Literature,* 1901-1905), a challenge to the intellectual conservatism and stagnation of the time. He stated at the outset that he considered it an honor to be the champion of the principles of free thought and free research. These lectures affected the Danes like a trumpet signal, awakening them from the gentle slumbers of late Romanticism and opening the world of Europe to their somewhat provincial eyes. In 1875 Brandes published a Danish translation of John Stuart Mill's *The Subjection of Women*.

The chair of aesthetics at the University of Copenhagen was vacant, and Brandes was considered the logical successor to the retiring incumbent because of his amply demonstrated ability; but it was feared that his outspoken atheism might not conform with the traditions of the institution, and he was denied the chair. In chagrin he left Denmark (1877) for a sojourn in Germany, where he wrote *Danske Digtere* (1877) ("Danish Authors"), *Esaias Tegnér* (1878), *Benjamin*

Disraeli (1878) (*Lord Beaconsfield,* 1880), and *Det moderne Gennembruds Maend* (1883), (*Creative Spirits of the Nineteenth Century,* 1923), *Ludvig Holberg* (1885), and other important critical and analytical works. In all his writings Brandes proved himself an unflinching champion of realism, as well as an opponent of accepted authority and dogma.

One of Brandes' principal works is *William Shakespeare* (1895-1896); another, *Henrik Ibsen* (1898). During the last two decades of his life he wrote such notable works as *Goethe* (1914-1915), *Voltaire* (1916-1917), *Caius Julius Caesar* (1918), and *Michelangelo Buonarotti* (1921). Of these six biographies, all but the last were translated into English before the author's death. Brandes died in Copenhagen, Feb. 19, 1927.   G. Str.

BRANDING AND OTHER ANIMAL IDENTIFICATION. Cattle branding is the searing of the flesh of cattle with a hot iron to produce an identifying scar. Horses, sheep, pigs, and other animals are also branded for the same purpose. Other forms of animal identification include earmarking, lip marking, metal tags, tatooing, and banding. According to the Oriental Institute of the University of Chicago, branding was customary at least as early as the year 2,000 B.C. Francisco Coronado, a Spaniard who explored the southwestern portion of the United States, had branded cattle with him on the explorations he made about 1540. Throughout the world, wherever there are open ranges, the branding of livestock is employed.

The portions of the animal to which the branding iron is applied vary, but the usual spots are the hind- and forequarters or the buttocks, rarely the ears. Brands are usually placed so that they can be seen readily by persons who tend the stock. Properly done, branding causes only temporary pain, and the wound soon heals. As a rule, horses and cattle are branded when they are very young, still running with their mothers. An unbranded adult animal is termed a "maverick," a name originating in Texas. Just after the Civil War, returning Texan cattle owners found the ranges covered by thousands of full-grown unbranded animals. The custom and rule of the range was that such cattle belonged to the first man who caught and branded them. One John Maverick excelled in this method of appropriating cattle, and so an unbranded adult animal came to be known as a maverick.

Branding has also been employed for the identification of slaves and criminals. At one period in France, prostitutes were branded on the left shoulder with the fleur-de-lis.

Brands of the Arabs. Brand marks of the Arabian tribes are known as *ousoum* or *wusum* (singular— *ousm* or *wasm*). Basic marks and their derivatives form the brands. Some of these basic marks are shown in the illustration.

Early Brands on Staten Island, New York. The early settlers on Staten Island branded their horses, cattle, and other livestock and registered their brands and earmarks as early as 1721. Three of them are illustrated.

Brands of the Western and Southwestern States. Cattle branding in the states of Arizona, California, New Mexico, Texas, and other parts of the Southwest goes back to the time when they were under Mexican rule. Among the missions in California that had extensive cattle herds and lands were those of San Diego, San Gabriel, San Juan Capistrano, and San Luis Rey. Very few of these old brands have remained in use. Some examples of those of early California and mission days are given in the illustration.

In other cattle states, including Colorado, Nebraska, South Dakota, and Wyoming, as well as those in the Southwest,

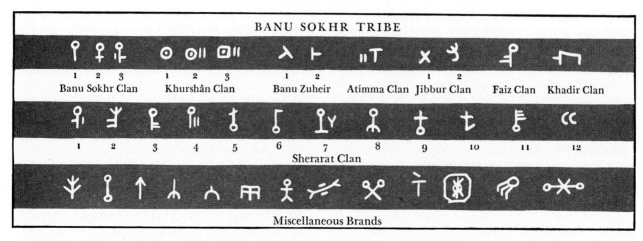

BANU SOKHR TRIBE

1	2	3	1	2	3	1	2			1	2		
Banu Sokhr Clan			Khurshân Clan			Banu Zuheir		Atimma Clan	Jibbur Clan	Faiz Clan		Khadir Clan	

1	2	3	4	5	6	7	8	9	10	11	12

Sherarat Clan

Miscellaneous Brands

EARLY STATEN ISLAND BRANDS

William Macklane, 1721   Justice John Veghte, 1739-1740   Henry Holland, 1760 *(Branded on the off buttock)*

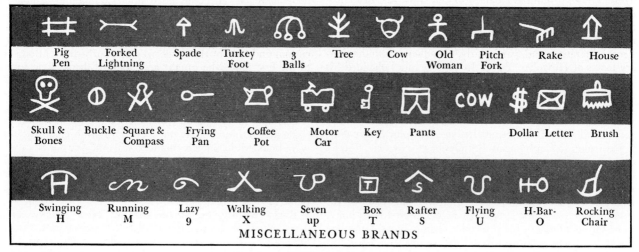

CALIFORNIA AND MISSION BRANDS

Olvera   San Gabriel Mission   San Diego Mission   Bixby Brands   Warner   Forster   Pio Pico   Romulo

Pig Pen	Forked Lightning	Spade	Turkey Foot	3 Balls	Tree	Cow	Old Woman	Pitch Fork	Rake	House

Skull & Bones	Buckle	Square & Compass	Frying Pan	Coffee Pot	Motor Car	Key	Pants		Dollar	Letter	Brush

Swinging H	Running M	Lazy 9	Walking X	Seven up	Box T	Rafter S	Flying U	H-Bar- O	Rocking Chair

MISCELLANEOUS BRANDS

BRANDS

the custom grew up of registering brands with the county or state authorities. The state brand books show many interesting and unusual marks. Duplications of brands under different ownership occur in different states, and even within a state. Some of the old marks date from the early and middle years of the nineteenth century. There are quite noticeable resemblances between many of the brands used in the South and Southwest and those employed by the Arabs. Miscellaneous brands found among those of the western and southwestern states are shown in the illustration.

Marks that were simple in form could be branded over or altered and this was a favorite practice with the "rustlers" who stole horses and cattle. A single circle could have other circles added on either side to form a chain, or a vertical bar could be run across the circle to make a buckle. Similarly, a Swinging H brand might have another rocker added.

Earmarks. In earmarking livestock, the mark is generally made by a cut or slit effected by a gouge or knife. Marks can be made on the upper or under parts of the ear. Those listed in the records of Staten Island from 1678 to

1813 appear to have been predominantly on the under side. Some of the early terms are interesting. They include such words as "hapene" (halfpenny), "swalloe-forke" (swallow-tail), "nicke" (a square cut in the under side), "foor gad," "hind gad," "crope" (crop), "latch," "crabb," "halfe still" and "slitt." The "near ear" was the left and the "off ear" was the right.

Miscellaneous Methods. Lip marks are used on race horses. The tattooing of animals is employed in laboratories for identification and control purposes during experiments and tests. Metal tags have likewise been used for identification. *See also* Birdbanding. D. D. M.

BRANDON, the fourth largest city in Manitoba, Canada, on the banks of the Assiniboine River, 132 mi. west of

50 mi. southwest of Alexandria. As a small trading station during the Civil War, it was the scene of several minor battles. The first, a cavalry charge by Federal troops, took place on Aug. 20, 1860. In the second on June 9, 1863, Federal cavalry under Generals John Buford and Alfred Pleasonton was indecisively defeated by General Jeb Stuart in what proved to be the greatest all-cavalry engagement of the war. It is also known as the Battle of Fleetwood Hill. Other battles were fought here on Sept. 13 and Oct. 11, 1863. The village is provided with transportation by the Southern Railroad. Pop. 1950, 250.

BRANDYWINE, BATTLE OF THE, an engagement between American troops under General George Washington and British troops under Lord Cornwallis, at Brandywine

FROM A PAINTING BY R. C. WOODVILLE
BROWN BROTHERS

THE BATTLE OF THE BRANDYWINE

Winnipeg. The Canadian National and Canadian Pacific railways and Trans Canada Airlines serve the city. The city's name is derived from a post established by the Hudson's Bay Company on the site in 1794. The settlement was incorporated as a city in 1882. Brandon is the center of an excellent agricultural and livestock region of western Manitoba and is known for its annual summer and winter exhibitions. Local industries include meat-packing plants, tanneries, dairies, woolen mills, steel works, and oil refineries. The city is the seat of Brandon College and a radio and television station. Institutions include Brandon Hospital for Mental Diseases, an Indian Residential School, and Brandon Sanitorium. Pop. 1956, 24,796.

BRANDS AND BRAND NAMES. *See* Marketing and Merchandising (*Merchandising*).

BRANDY or BRANDY STATION, an unincorporated village in Culpeper Co., northern Virginia, is situated about

Creek, Pa., Sept. 11, 1777, ending in a British victory. In July 1777, General Sir William Howe left New York and went south by sea to take Philadelphia. He sailed up Chesapeake Bay and landed August 25 at what was known then as Head of Elk, Md., about 50 mi. south of Philadelphia and now near the town of Elkton. Washington marched from Philadelphia to meet Howe and, after preliminary skirmishes, took a stand at Chad's Ford on Brandywine Creek. On September 11, the British army under Cornwallis, moving up the creek to cross it and attack the Americans from the flank, surprised General John Sullivan, whose troops fled. Other sections of the American forces likewise broke and ran. Only those under Washington and General Nathanael Greene held firm. The battle was ended by darkness when the British, instead of pursuing the fleeing Americans, went into camp. Washington gathered his troops, marched northward and encamped near Germantown. The British marched on after breaking camp and occupied Philadelphia, which the Americans had been forced to leave virtually undefended. M. Je.

BRANGWYN, SIR FRANK [bræ'ŋwɪn] (1867-1956), English artist, was born at Bruges, Belgium, May 12, 1867, of English parents. He was apprenticed (1882-1884) to the craftsman-artist William Morris, but soon quit his formal training in favor of the sea, though he continued to paint. Extensive voyaging to many parts of the world gave him an interest in remote places and things, which he later introduced as exotic elements in his paintings. He acquired a taste for intense primary coloring, which, when applied broadly to his canvases or mural surfaces, produced a decorative quality in his art and brought him commissions for mural paintings in England, France, the United States, and Canada. It was, however, Brangwyn's etchings that brought him his greatest fame. In them he shows considerable ability to record dramatically the story of working people and their surroundings, and to depict architectural settings richly and honestly. He also executed designs for various industrial fields, in particular for furniture and tapestry. Brangwyn became a member of the Royal Academy in 1919 and was knighted in 1941. He died on June 11, 1956, in Ditchling, Sussex.　C. P. P.

BRANT, JOSEPH (1742-1807), Mohawk Indian chief, also known as Thayendanegea, was born in the Mohawk country, probably in New York State, in 1742. Sir William Johnson, superintendent of Indian affairs, sent him to Moor's Indian Charity School at Lebanon, Conn., which later became a part of Dartmouth College. There he was educated and converted to the Episcopal Church. In 1774, when Guy Johnson, nephew of Sir William, became head of Indian affairs, Brant acted as his secretary. He fought with the British in the French and Indian War, and later with the white settlers against Pontiac. For his work in organizing and leading Indian tribes in various battles of the American Revolution, he was made a colonel in the English army. After the war he aided United States commissioners in securing peace treaties with western Indian tribes. Brant did Christian missionary work among his people, translated the Prayer Book and St. Mark's Gospel into Mohawk (1787), and with funds collected during a visit to England in 1786 established the first Episcopal church in Upper Canada. On Nov. 24, 1807, he died at his home on Grand River, in Ontario, Canada.　D. R.

BRANT, SEBASTIAN [bra'nt] (1457-1521), German scholar, social critic, and versifier, was born in Strassburg in 1457. He studied in Basel, where in 1484 he secured a license to teach and in 1489 received the degree of doctor of laws. In 1501 Brant became syndic in Strassburg and in 1503 municipal chancellor. He died in Strassburg, May 10, 1521.

Brant composed Latin poems (*Varia carmina,* 1498) and wrote legal compendia, but he is best known for his versified *Das Narrenschiff* (1494) ("The Ship of Fools"), written in German. It castigates the vices and follies of his time, depicting them as the activities of various types of fools. Because of this conceit, carried out with some grim humor, and by virtue of the largely excellent woodcuts, about seventy-five of which are reminiscent of the early style of Dürer, the work became the secular Bible of its age.

The *Narrenschiff* was translated into Low German by Hans van Ghetelen in 1497, and into Latin, in 1497 also, by Brant's pupil, Jacobus Locher. The Latin version led to French (Rivière, 1497; Drouyn, 1498) and English (Alexander Barclay, 1509; Henry Watson, 1509) adaptations, which proved very influential upon the literature and thought of the Renaissance, and this is demonstrated in the works of Robert de Balsac, Pierre Gringoire, d'Adonville, and Bouchet, in the anonymous *Cock Lorelles Bote,* and in the writings of John Skelton, Robert Copland, and Richard Tarlton. Early Flemish (1500) and Dutch (1548) versions were also made. The Strassburg preacher, Geiler von Kaisersberg, delivered 142 German sermons on the *Narrenschiff* in 1498-1499. Editions of the work in various languages were very numerous until the end of the seventeenth century, about thirty being recorded. The *Narrenschiff* contains the first known literary reference, somewhat veiled, to the discovery of America by Columbus, an edition of the Columbus letter having been printed in 1493, perhaps at Brant's instigation, by his Basel publisher Bergmann von Olpe. Erasmus knew Brant and was familiar with his work, and there is evidence that Erasmus' *Encomium moriae* ("The Praise of Folly") was influenced by the *Narrenschiff.*　E. H. Z.

BRANT [bra'nt], a small (24 in.) goose, *Branta bernicla,* breeding on arctic coasts of both the Old and New worlds and wintering on the bays and estuaries of northwestern Europe, the northeastern United States, California, and Japan. The variety of the Atlantic has a black head, neck, and upper breast, with a small white-speckled patch at each side of the upper neck, the upper parts brownish-gray, and the underparts white; the black brant of the Pacific has the underparts mostly black and white speckling on the front as well as the sides of the neck. Brants occur in large flocks on the American coasts, feeding almost wholly on eelgrass; owing to their vegetarian diet they are considered among the finest flavored of the waterfowl.　H. G. De.

BRANTFORD, a city and the county seat of Brant Co., Ontario, Canada, situated on the Grand River, 66 mi. southwest of Toronto. Both county and city are named for Joseph Brant, a noted Mohawk chief, missionary, and leader of the Six Nations, who were given lands along the Grand River in 1784. The descendants of the band still live on a large reserve nearby. Mohawk Church, the oldest Protestant church in Ontario and only Indian Royal Chapel in existence, is located here. White settlement began in 1805. Branford was incorporated as a village in 1830, a town in 1847, and became a city in 1877. It was the home of Alexander Graham Bell, and Bell Homestead and the Bell Memorial are located here. It is also the site of an Ontario government school for the blind. An important industrial center, Brantford has over 100 factories; its chief products include farm implements, machinery, twine, asphalt and abrasive products, paints, varnishes and enamels, wax, textiles, carpets and rugs, electrical equipment, castings, television sets, chemicals, and motor coaches. Pop. 1956, 51,689.

BRANTÔME, PIERRE DE BOURDEILLES, SEIGNEUR DE [brã'to'm] (c. 1540-1614), French historian, son of Baron François de Bourdeilles and Anne de Vivonne, was born in Périgord and was brought up at the court of Marguerite d'Angoulême, later Marguerite de Navarre. He was entrusted with the Abbey of Brantôme by Henry II at the age of sixteen, but did not wish to begin an ecclesiastical career and from 1558 to 1584 traveled extensively in Italy, Scotland, England, Portugal, Spain, and Africa, finally becoming a Gentleman of the King's Chamber of Henry III. He had as friends Filippo Strozzi and François de Guise. A fall from a horse in 1584 forced him to cease his active life and made him a man of letters. Between 1558 and 1584 he engaged in various adventures, missions, and civil, religious, and foreign wars, and knew the great personages of his time in various countries, among whom were Marguerite de Valois, Mary Stuart, Queen Elizabeth of England, Catherine de' Medici, and Soliman II. He died on July 15, 1614.

Brantôme wrote the *Vies des hommes illustres et des grands capitaines français; Vies des hommes illustres et des grands capitaines étrangers; Vies des dames illustres, des dames galantes; Anecdotes touchant les duels,* and *Rodomontades et jurements des Espagnols.* The first edition of his works appeared in 1665-1666.

Brantôme's style is vivid and pleasing, and he does not moralize. He depicts the life of the important people of his time, and he is subjective, inaccurate, superficial, given to telling scandalous stories, and borrowing unscrupulously from other authors, French, Spanish, and Italian, concealing his sources as best he can, often by changing names of characters and places.   P. T.

BRAQUE, GEORGES [braˈk] (1881-   ), French painter, was born May 15, 1881, in Argenteuil, Seine-et-Oise. He began to study painting in Le Havre, going to Paris in 1902, where he worked at the Académie Humbert and the Beaux Arts. Son of a building contractor who specialized in house painting, young Braque early mastered his father's craft, including the graining of wood, and this is evidenced in many of his paintings. Reacting from academicism, he joined *les Fauves* and in 1908 allied himself with Pablo Picasso as one of the pioneers of Cubism. He, with other early Cubists, delighted in breaking apart the elements and objects of nature and reassembling them in new relations. Guitars, mandolins, flutes, and other musical instruments, playing cards, clay pipes, drinking glasses, packages of smoking tobacco and fruits were some materials commonly used by the Cubists, and these are found frequently in Braque's work. He experimented with sand mixed with paint to enrich painting surface, and also with collage, with which Cubists sought to break down the smoothly manipulated illusionistic "skin" of naturalism. His choice of subjects may seem limited until the rich variety of his color is studied. He has painted themes that could be stereotyped: *Reclining Nude; Compotier; Abstract Still Life; Plum, Pear, Nuts and Knife; A Plate of Fruit; A Newspaper; The Blue Guitar; Bowl, Bottle and Guitar; Guitar Player; Peonies; Vase and Fruit*—but these are enlivened by the rich and sensuous, though sober, dignity of his mood, expressed in handsome browns and grays. In 1937 he won first prize of $1,000 at the Carnegie International Exhibition. He is represented in the Luxembourg, the Art Institute of Chicago (with the stunning *Pomona*), the Columbus (Ohio) Gallery of Fine Arts, and the Gallery of Living Art, Philadelphia. Among his book illustrations are wood engravings in color for Erik Satie's *Le Piège de Méduse,* and etchings for Hesiod's *Poèmes.*   E. McC.

BRAS D'OR LAKE [braˈdɔˈr], a large lake which divides Cape Breton Island, Nova Scotia, into two parts. Its northerly extension, St. Andrew's Channel, is separated by Boularderie Island into two inlets: Big Bras d'Or, on the west, and Little Bras d'Or, on the east. At the southern end of the channel Barra Strait, known locally as Grand Narrows, leads directly into Bras d'Or Lake proper, which in turn opens into the Gut of Canso through St. Peter's Canal, thus providing a sheltered route to the markets of Sydney for farmers in the southern part of Cape Breton Island. The lake and canal are 70 mi. long, and the lake is 37 mi. wide at its greatest breadth. Since it is frozen in winter and its

channels and canal are bridged, there is no dislocation of communication among the four counties of Cape Breton, all of which touch upon the lake.

BRASOV (Ger. **KRONSTADT**; Hung. **BRASSÓ**) [braˈshof, kroˈnshtat, brɒˈshsho], the most significant trade and industrial city of Transylvania, in central Romania, at 45° 38' N. lat and 25° 34' E. long. It lies amid the scenic beauty of the Transylvanian Alps, at the northern end of the Predal Pass, about 90 mi. north of Bucharest. Founded in the thirteenth century by the German Teutonic Order of Knights mainly for trade purposes, it accommodated caravans from the Ukraine, Asia, and the cities of central Europe. Wool, skins, and furs seem then to have been the most important local products. Modern means of travel and commerce have brought many industries. Brasov was included in Romania in 1920. The chief center of attraction is the famous Black Church, an Evangelical Lutheran church of late Gothic architecture built in the fourteenth and fifteenth centuries. Other noted buildings are the city hall, built in the fifteenth century and remodelled in the eighteenth, a museum, the citadel, advanced schools, and trade schools. Because of its favorable location, Brasov has an airfield and is an important trade and railroad center. Its beautiful landscape has attracted the tourist trade, and winter sports are popular. Its industrial activity includes the manufacture of airplanes, textiles, metal wares, leather goods, and chocolate and the refining of beet sugar and petroleum. Wood from the Carpathian Mountains provides the material for its furniture industry. Pop. (off. est. 1948), 82,984.   S. A.

BRASSES AND BRONZES. Brasses are alloys consisting chiefly of copper and zinc. They are malleable and ductile, usually yellow in color, and are harder and stronger than copper. Other elements are sometimes added to brasses to give them special properties. The value of brasses is due to their high corrosion resistance, and the ease with which they can be formed and machined.

Bronzes are durable brown alloys consisting chiefly of copper and tin, in varied proportions to suit particular purposes.

BRASSES

A brief discussion of the constitution of brasses will be found in the article on physical metallurgy. Alpha brasses are solid solutions of zinc (maximum about 38 per cent at room temperature) in copper. Beta brass is an intermediate phase of different crystal structure, containing some 46 per cent to 50 per cent of zinc at room temperature, and from approximately 35 per cent to 55 per cent at the highest temperature. Below 450-500° C., it is called beta prime because of a change in the distribution of the two kinds of atoms in the crystal.

Properties of Brasses. The ordinary yellow brasses, unlike steels, cannot be hardened by quenching. Their properties are determined by their composition, and by the amount of cold-working and annealing.

Strength. The strength of alpha brasses increases with increase in zinc content. Beta brass is stronger than the highest strength alpha brass but it is brittle, so mixtures of the alpha and beta phases are used where strength is a primary consideration.

Ductility. Alpha brass has excellent ductility at atmospheric temperatures, its greatest ductility being obtained with about 30 per cent zinc, and in very pure alloys. This composition and purity are used when severe cold-forming, such as in the drawing of cartridge cases, is necessary. While the high-temperature formability of beta brass is excellent, alpha brass has relatively low ductility at elevated temperatures. By keeping its lead content very low, however, commercial hot-working operations are regularly conducted with it.

Cold-working and Annealing. The strength of brass increases when it is cold-formed by rolling at atmospheric temperatures. Cold-working, however, reduces the residual ductility and consequently restricts formability. The effects of cold-working may be removed by heating the brass to some appropriately elevated temperature. Such annealing treatments restore the brass to substantially its original unworked condition. In the production of cartridge cases, each forming operation is followed by an anneal. The annealing temperature is carefully selected to produce a fine-grained, highly ductile metal.

Commercial Brasses. Red brass, which contains 15 per cent or 20 per cent zinc, has good ductility and is used extensively for the manufacture of pipe. Additions of 5 per cent lead and tin yield a corrosion-resistant casting alloy used for valves and fittings. Low brass is a general term used to define mixtures containing less than approximately 20 per cent zinc. It is used for many purposes in which its red to golden color is especially desirable, such as for gold-plated jewelry. Lead is added to all brasses to improve their cutting characteristics, especially in automatic machines.

Cartridge brass, containing 30 per cent zinc, is used for cartridge cases and other products which require severe cold-forming. High brass contains about 35 per cent zinc, close to the maximum amount that can dissolve in the alpha phase. It is a relatively low-cost, highly formable alloy. Admiralty metal contains 29 per cent to 30 per cent zinc plus 1 per cent tin. It retains the excellent cold-working properties of cartridge brass and has excellent corrosion resistance. It is used in condenser tubes and in preheaters for salt-water application. Muntz metal, named for its English inventor, G. F. Muntz, contains 40 per cent zinc. It forms the beta phase at elevated temperatures and therefore is easily hot-formed into rods and tubes.

BRONZES

Bronzes in general contain high percentages of copper, and include tin-copper, aluminum-copper, manganese-copper and silicon-copper alloys. The nickel-copper and the zinc-copper alloys by convention, however, are seldom called bronzes.

Tin Bronzes. The most widely used bronzes are alloys containing principally copper and tin, but most commercial tin bronzes also contain other alloying elements. Phosphorus up to 0.03 per cent is commonly added to deoxidize the melt. It also improves the fluidity of the melt and increases the strength and hardness of the tin bronzes. Small amounts of lead are often introduced in order to improve the machineability of bronzes. In general, tin bronzes are stronger, harder, more corrosion resistant, more expensive, and less formable than the brasses.

The Copper-Tin Phase Diagram. The copper-tin diagram is quite complicated. At 500° C. about 16 per cent tin can dissolve in the lattice of solid copper, forming an alpha solid solution. At lower temperatures, the solubility of tin is limited and bronzes exhibit a tendency to precipitate the hard, brittle, wear-resistant intermetallic compound Cu_3Sn. However, the rate of precipitation is so slow that a supersaturated solution of tin in copper is usually produced under normal conditions of cooling.

Commercial Tin Bronzes. Alpha bronzes are ductile alloys. Those containing low percentages of tin may be commercially hot- and cold-worked, and are used where corrosion resistance and relatively high mechanical properties are re-

quired. The strength and hardness of alpha bronzes increase with tin content and cold-working. Wire products, hardware, stampings and coins are made from alpha tin bronze.

Gun metal is a castable 10 per cent tin bronze containing 2 per cent zinc to permit the production of sounder castings. The as-cast structure consists of a matrix of the ductile alpha solid solution surrounding particles of the hard, wear-resistant Cu_3Sn intermetallic compound. Gun metal is used for bearings, fittings, gears, pump parts and other applications where corrosion- and wear-resistant castings are required.

High-leaded bronze contains various admixtures of lead, even beyond 20 per cent. Lead is insoluble in bronze, therefore cast-leaded bronze consists of a matrix of alpha bronze containing particles of the hard, wear-resistant Cu_3Sn compound and also particles of soft ductile lead. This combination provides excellent bearings for heavy-duty service.

Special Bronzes. *Phosphor bronzes* contain 1 per cent to 11 per cent tin and 0.03 per cent to about 0.3 per cent phosphorus. Usually the phosphorus content is sufficiently high to yield the hard Cu_3P compound. All wrought phosphor bronzes are substantially alpha bronzes. Owing to their high resiliency and endurance strength they are used for diaphragms and springs. Phosphor bronzes having high tin contents are cast; they are used for worm gears, valves, and other applications where wear resistance and corrosion resistance are required.

Aluminum bronzes are copper-aluminum alloys with additions of iron, manganese or nickel. Wrought aluminum bronzes are in general homogeneous alpha solid solutions containing less than 9 per cent aluminum. Cast aluminum bronzes, however, have from 5 per cent to 15 per cent aluminum. The 9 per cent alloy is an alpha solid solution, but higher aluminum contents yield dispersion of one or two hard phases in the alpha matrix, depending upon the heat treatment. Aluminum bronzes have poor casting properties and therefore are more expensive than tin bronzes. Aluminum oxidizes during pouring and induces high shrinkage upon solidification, but aluminum bronzes have excellent strength, corrosion resistance, resistance to oxidation at elevated temperatures, and wear resistance. They are used for gears, dies, propeller blades, and similar applications.

Silicon bronzes are alpha solid solution alloys containing 1 per cent to 4 per cent silicon plus minor amounts of other elements. Silicon bronzes may be wrought or cast. They find major applications in pump parts, valves, and container parts for corrosive brines such as nonoxidizing inorganic acids, sulphite solutions, organic acids, and alkalis.

Manganese bronzes are copper alloys containing about 40 per cent zinc plus varying amounts of tin, iron, aluminum, lead and manganese. They may be cast or hot-worked but their formability is poor at atmospheric temperatures. They have high strength and good corrosion resistance.

Other bronzes make use of beryllium, cadmium, chromium, or a variety of copper-base alloy combinations. The simple brass containing 90 per cent copper and 10 per cent zinc is often called commercial bronze because of its favorable color and because there is a general preference for the name bronze wherever it can be applied. *See also* ALLOYS.   J. E. D.

BRASSICA [bræ′sɪkə], a genus of the plant family Cruciferae, to which many plants of economic value belong. Among them are the cauliflower, cabbage, Chinese cabbage, broccoli, Brussels sprouts, kohlrabi, kale, collards, rape, mustard, rutabaga, and turnip. They are Old World plants whose exact origin is unknown; many are now common weeds throughout the world. They are erect, branching, and may grow to more than 6 ft. tall. The plants are either annuals or biennials. The flowers, which grow in terminal racemes, are from yellow to white. *Brassica oleracea,* a plant native to the west of England, has been developed by cultivation into many varieties: var. *botrytis* is the cauliflower and broccoli; var. *capitata* is the common cabbage; var. *gemmifera* is the

(Left) *Cauliflower,* Brassica oleracea botrytis; (Right) *Cabbage,* Brassica oleracea capitata

source of Brussels sprouts; and var. *italica,* the branching broccoli. There are probably more than forty species of the genus *Brassica.*   R. S. M.

BRASS INSTRUMENTS, the common term for modern Western orchestral and band instruments of the lip-blown type, usually made largely of brass, such as the trumpet and trombone. The French horn is sometimes classed as a brass instrument and sometimes, because of its soft, blending tone and the combinations in which it is used, as a woodwind.   W. Li.

BRATIANU, ION ("IONEL") [brətɪɑ'nu] (1864-1927), Romanian statesman, was born at Florica, Aug. 20, 1864. He was the oldest son of Ion C. Bratianu who had been Romanian premier for thirteen years (1867-1868, 1876-1888). After studying at the Polytechnic School in Paris, Ion, or Ionel, as the son was sometimes called, accepted a position as engineer on the Romanian state railways. Following this he entered parliament (1895) as a Liberal deputy. During the governmental regime of Dimitrie Sturdza he became minister of the interior. In 1909, upon Sturdza's retirement, Bratianu became premier, continuing as leader of the Liberal Party. Like his father, he aimed at the expansion of the urban middle class. After two years in office he resigned, only to return in January, 1914. He continued in office throughout the turbulent World War I years, until Jan. 29, 1918, at which time he resigned rather than accept the terms which Germany imposed after Romania's defeat. In November of that year the Allies were victorious. One month later Bratianu, taking office once again, took this opportunity to denounce the earlier separate peace with the Central Powers. He became Romania's chief delegate to the Paris Peace Conference the following year. Once again, however, he was destined to take the side of the opposition. Protesting the clauses which awarded to Yugoslavia part of the Banat, or frontier province of Temesvar, he refused to sign the treaty, and, after resigning, headed the opposition for several years. In 1922, however, he once again took over the leadership of his country and, save for a brief period in 1926, remained dictator in all but name from 1922 until his death in Bucharest, Nov. 24, 1927. Backed up in his policies by his brother Vintila, Bratianu did much to break up the large landed estates, settle the Jewish question, and extend

universal suffrage in national elections. They opposed the elevation of Prince Carol to the throne. In general they represented the commercial and business interests of Romania but feared the influence of foreign capital and generally discouraged foreign investments and concessions.   W. S. V.

BRATIANU, VINTILA (1867-1930), Romanian political leader, third son of the Liberal leader Ion C. Bratianu, was born at Florica in 1867. Like his brother Ion, Vintila studied in France, returned to Romania to practice his vocation, engineering, then entered politics. At the age of forty-two he became economic and financial adviser to the Liberal Party, of which his brother was the leader. During World War I Vintila became minister of munitions. After the war, in 1922, he became finance minister and held this post for the next six years. Upon the death of Ion in 1927 Vintila became premier in his place, but was forced to resign late in 1928 to make way for the new National Peasant government under Dr. Juliu Maniu.

Like his brother Ion, Vintila Bratianu worked to help the commercial middle class. His aim was to make Romania self-sufficient by fostering home industries and high tariffs. He supported his brother in fighting the growing power of foreign interests. Vintila died at Miraeti, Dec. 22, 1930.
                    W. S. V.

BRATISLAVA (*Ger.* Pressburg) [bra'tɪslɑ'va, prɛsburx], the capital city of Slovakia, in south central Czechoslovakia, located on the Danube River, where the Little Carpathians cross the valley from Austria, opposite the junction of the Hungarian-Austrian-Czech border, about 35 mi. east of Vienna, at 48° 9′ N. lat. and 17° 7′ E. long. The fertile plains of the Danube and Morava valleys and the important industrial districts of Moravia are tributary to the city. Bratislava rivals Vienna as a port and trading center on the Danube River. The founding of the city is obscure. It was an important strategic center in A.D. 1000, served as the Hungarian capital and coronation city when the Turks occupied Hungary, and became part of Czechoslovakia in 1918. As the capital of Slovakia, it was controlled by a German-dominated Slovak group late in 1938. Slovakia was made an autonomous state, controlled and protected by Germany from 1939 until it was liberated by the Soviet Army in 1945. Sabotage was responsible for considerable damage sustained by industrial plants, public utilities, and transportation facilities from 1941 to 1945.

A number of beautiful parks and buildings, a Gothic cathedral, thirteenth- and fourteenth-century churches and municipal buildings, and numerous more modern churches and synagogues grace the city. A modern state-supported hospital, a Slovak university, and other educational institutions, a state insurance headquarters, and numerous banking concerns are centered in the city.

Docking facilities in Bratislava make it potentially the largest port on the Danube. Air lines operate to Vienna, south to Hungary and Yugoslavia, north to Brno and Prague, and east to Kosice and Moscow. Good rail and highway connections extend to Vienna and to cities in Czechoslovakia and Hungary. A variety of industrial plants includes iron and steel works, textile mills, chemical works, food-processing plants, paper and woodworking plants, and an electrical engineering works. The people are mainly Czechs, Slovaks, and Magyars. Pop. 1948, 184,423.   F. Sc.

BRATTLEBORO [bræ'təlbʌro], a village and town in Windham Co., southern Vermont, is situated on the Connecticut River at the mouth of the West, about 55 mi. southeast of Rutland. The community settled by the garrison at Fort Dummer was named for Colonel William Brattle. It was chartered in 1753 and incorporated as a village in 1832. Brattleboro was the birthplace in the 1820's of the Hunt brothers, William M., the painter, and Richard M., the architect. North of the village is "Naulahka," once the home of Rudyard Kipling and his wife, a native of Brattleboro. The author lived here in the 1890's and wrote many of his best works at that time. The village is a winter sports center. It is also the seat of the Austine Institute for the Deaf and the Brattleboro Retreat. Brattleboro is served by the Boston and Maine and the Central Vermont railroads. It is governed by town selectmen. Manufactures include optical goods, maple sugar, paints, flour, and pipe organs. Pop. 1950 (village), 9,606; (town), 11,522.

BRAUCHITSCH, HEINRICH ALFRED HER-MANN WALTHER VON [brɑu'χɪtsh] (1881-1948), German soldier, was born in Berlin, Oct. 4, 1881. He belonged to an aristocratic Prussian family long devoted to military service. In 1900 he was commissioned a lieutenant in the Grenadier Guards and soon afterward was transferred to the artillery. In 1912 he was assigned to the general staff, on which he served throughout World War I. Brauchitsch was discharged after the armistice, but when the German army was reorganized in 1919, in accordance with the requirements of the Peace Treaty, he was commissioned a major. In 1922 he was appointed head of the artillery section in the Ministry of Defense and in 1930 he was made a colonel and placed in charge of military training. He became a major general and chief of the artillery in 1931. Brauchitsch was placed in command of the East Prussia military area in 1933. Because of his admiration for the man and approval of his aims, Brauchitsch had little difficulty gaining the confidence of Adolf Hitler. In 1937 he was placed in charge of the Leipzig military area. In February 1938 Hitler appointed him commander in chief of the German army and a member of the secret council which advised on foreign policy. Brauchitsch personally led his troops in the occupation of Austria in 1938, and later in the occupation of the Sudetenland and Czechoslovakia. When Hitler decided to invade Poland in September 1939, Brauchitsch occupied the country in nineteen days; France and the Low Countries were overrun in the spring of 1940. After these victories Brauchitsch was made a field marshal, July 19, 1940; in 1941 he conducted operations in the Balkans, and later led his troops in the invasion of the Soviet Union. Because of his failure to take Moscow, he was allowed to resign to make way for Hitler, who assumed personal command, Dec. 20, 1941. Brauchitsch was arrested by Allied troops after the invasion of Germany. He died Oct. 18, 1948, in a British military hospital in Hamburg, Germany, where he was being held for trial as a war criminal.

E. B. A.

BRAUN, WERNHER VON [braun] (1912-), rocket engineer, was born in Wirsitz, Germany, on Mar. 23, 1912. He figured prominently in the development of the German V-2 rocket, and in the U.S. Army's Jupiter-C missile which placed the first U.S. satellite in orbit. Von Braun's interest in rocketry was kindled by reading rocket pioneer Hermann Oberth's *Die Rakete zu den Planetenräumen* (1923), (*The Rocket into Interplanetary Space*). He studied engineering, and spent most of his time experimenting with rockets. The German government became interested, for rockets were not restricted under the Treaty of Versailles. In 1932, after receiving his B.S. degree in engineering, von Braun (at the age of 20) was put in charge of the rocket experiment station at Kummersdorf. The final fruit of this project was the V-2 rocket. In 1945, at the end of World War II, von Braun turned himself over to the American military forces. Since 1950 he has been Director of Development Operations Division, Army Ballistic Missile Agency, Huntsville, Ala. In 1955 von Braun became a U.S. citizen.

BRAUNSCHWEIG or **BRUNSWICK** [brɑu'nshvaiχ, brʌ'nzwɪk], an industrial and cultural city in Lower Saxony, one of the states of the (West) German Federal Republic. Once the capital of the former German state of Brunswick, it lies 20 mi. north of the Harz Mountains and 35 mi. east of Hannover on the Oker River, in rolling country. Located near the Weser-Elbe Canal, Braunschweig is a rail junction and a food-transshipment center, noted for its sausages, asparagus, and honey cakes. One of Germany's leading sugar markets, the city also produces canned and dried fruits and vegetables, meat and flour products, and beer. Manufactures include automobiles, bicycles, railroad equipment, radios, and calculating machines, metalware, quinine, furniture, and books. Although the moated old city, with its step-gabled buildings, timbered houses, and many examples of Gothic carving, was heavily damaged in World War II, the town still has many historic buildings and monuments, among which the tomb of Henry the Lion, enclosed in the basilica which he founded in 1173, was only slightly damaged. Also of interest are an art museum, housed in a seventeenth-century château, the heavily damaged Romanesque-Gothic churches of St. Martin and St. Andrew, the Gothic churches of St. Ulric and St. Catharine, the Till Eulenspiegel fountain, and the fourteenth-century town hall, as well as Lessing's grave and the oldest technical school in Germany (founded 1745). Founded in the ninth century, Braunschweig was chartered in the twelfth century by Henry the Lion, Duke of Saxony and Bavaria, whose castle, though gutted by fire in World War II, still stands; later it became an important interior Hanseatic city, reaching its peak between 1450 and 1525. In 1753 the residence of the dukes of Brunswick-Wolfenbüttel was shifted to Braunschweig, which became the capital, in 1918, of the free state of Brunswick in the Weimar Republic. Pop. 1953, 237,000.

BRAURONIA [brɔro'niə], a name given to the moon goddess Artemis. The name was derived from the community of Brauron, in Attica, where a festival in her honor was held every five years at her shrine. Brauronia was also the name given to the festivals. Girls between the ages of five and ten were taken in procession to the goddess and commended to her care as a protectress of youth. Goats were sacrificed, and the rituals demanded that the girls imitate bears. Concerning the origin of the festivals, the Greek lexicographer Suidas recounted that a girl in Attica had been cruel to a domesticated bear, which dismembered her. As a result the animal was killed, but Artemis, to whom it belonged, sent a pestilence to Athens. To placate her, the festivals at Brauron were organized. It was said that the statue of Artemis in her shrine at Brauron was the most ancient of her statues; it was brought from Tauris, where it had been sent from heaven by Orestes and Iphigenia on the advice of Apollo. A precinct on the Acropolis in Athens was dedicated to Artemis Brauronia.

BRAWLEY [brɔ'li], a city in Imperial Co., southern California, is situated 110 mi. east of San Diego. Brawley is the largest city in the Imperial Valley, which was once a desert and which, owing to irrigation, has become a highly productive agricultural district. The city is 119 ft. below sea level, and the rainfall is less than 2 in. annually. Capt. Don Juan de Anza, on his way to establish the *presidio* of San Francisco, was the first white man to cross the valley. Brawley was incorporated as a city in 1908. Irrigation provided by Hoover Dam, through the All-American Canal, has increased the production of lettuce, fruit, vegetables, grains, and cotton. Livestock raising and a sugar-processing plant are other central industries. Of interest are Borego State Park, the Painted Canyon, the Petrified Forest, and the Salton Sea, a lake formed by the 1905-1906 breakthrough of the Colorado River. Brawley is governed by a council, mayor, and city administrator. Pop. 1950, 11,922.

BRAXY [bræ′ksi], also known as bradsot, is an acute, rapidly fatal disease of sheep, due to the invasion of the stomach wall by the bacterium *Clostridium septicum*. It is supposed that the disease results from the eating of contaminated feedstuffs or pasture. Braxy occurs chiefly in northwestern Europe. Affected animals die suddenly without showing symptoms, or death may occur after a few hours of sickness. The walls of the fourth stomach and the upper part of the small intestine are swollen, inflamed (hemorrhagic), and sometimes necrotic. Satisfactory results have been obtained by immunizing sheep with *Clostridium septicum* bacterins and toxoids.   C. R. S.

BRAY, THOMAS (1656-1730), English clergyman, was born at Merton, in Shropshire, in 1656. He was educated at All Souls College, Oxford, graduating in 1678. After being ordained he served as a curate at Bridgworth and then as chaplain to a number of prominent families. In 1690 he became rector at Sheldon. When the Governor of Maryland, in his efforts to establish the Church of England in Maryland and organize its clergy there, wrote to the Bishop of London in 1695, requesting that a clergyman be sent to him to act as the bishop's commissary, Bray was selected. He was unable to proceed to Maryland, however, before the act required for the official establishment of the church was confirmed by the king. Confirmation was delayed, and Bray helped the bishop select missionaries to be sent abroad. Meanwhile, he became involved in a scheme for the establishment of parochial libraries abroad and in England, since he discovered that many clergymen could not afford libraries of their own. In 1699 Bray helped to form the Society for the Promotion of Christian Knowledge, which included but did not limit itself to Bray's library project. On Dec. 16, 1699, though the act had not yet been passed, Bray proceeded to Maryland, arriving the following March. However, he soon returned to England, where it was decided he could be more useful in helping to pass the act that had been twice rejected. The act was finally approved by the king in 1702. In June 1701 Bray founded the Society for the Propagation of the Gospel in Foreign Parts. Thus Bray became the founder of the two oldest church societies. In 1706 he was appointed rector of St. Botolph's in London. He died Feb. 15, 1730, while working on a new project for social service, sending missionaries to render relief and preach to prisoners. Bray wrote extensively in support of his various projects.   E. B. A.

BRAY (*Ir.* Bri Chualaan), a popular holiday resort, in an urban district of the same name, located on the Irish Sea, 12 mi. southeast of Dublin, in County Wicklow, in east central Ireland. The surrounding region is scenic mountainous country. About 1170, Richard de Clare, second earl of Pembroke and Strigul, gave Bray to Walter de Reddesford, who, taking the title of Baron Bray, built a castle there. In the nineteenth century, William Dargan, a railroad promoter, saw Bray's possibilities as a resort and he developed the community, which soon became popular. Bray's chief occupation is catering to visitors; there is also some fishing. Pop. 1951, 12,062.

BRAZEN SERPENT, the serpent made by Moses which Hezekiah destroyed in his desire to uproot idolatry. Hezekiah "broke in pieces the brazen serpent that Moses had

BETTMANN ARCHIVES

MOSES AND THE BRAZEN SERPENT

made: for unto those days the children did burn incense to it: and he called it Nehushtan." (II Kings xviii:4). The name "Nehushtan" could have been derived from *nehosheth,* which meant brass, with the diminutive *an* added to express contempt, so that Hezekiah called it Nehushtan to express his contempt for an idolized object that was merely a piece of brass. The name might also have been derived from *nahash,* which means serpent. Therefore, whether the brazen serpent was worshiped under the name of Nehushtan, or whether it was so called by Hezekiah to express his contempt, is not known.   E. B. A.

BRAZIL, officially the United States of Brazil, the largest republic in South America. With an area of 3,286,111 sq. mi., it occupies nearly half the continent. Among the countries of the world it is surpassed in size only by the Soviet Union, China, and Canada. It is bounded on the north by the Guianas, Venezuela, and Colombia; on the west by Peru; and on the southwest by Bolivia, Paraguay, Argentina, and Uruguay. The Atlantic coast line, which forms the eastern boundary, measures 4,603 mi. from the border of French Guiana to the border of Uruguay.

GEOGRAPHICAL FEATURES

Topography. There is very little flat land in Brazil. The Guiana Highlands and the Brazilian Highlands occupy about 53 per cent of the total area. The largest area of plain is in the lowland basin drained by the Amazon and its major tributaries, the Tocantins, Xingú, Tapajóz, Madeira, Purús, Jurua, Javarí (Yavari), and Negro, an area exceeding 700,000 sq. mi. About 10 per cent consists of river floodplain, which is 50 mi. in width along much of the main stream and in which soils are renewed annually by river-borne silt. The remainder has a gently rolling surface above the level of the highest floods. In the east, where the Amazon passes between the Guiana and Brazilian highlands, the lowland is only a narrow ribbon of floodplain confined between valley bluffs. Above the junction with the Rio Negro and the Rio Madeira, it widens out into a great arc extending some 800 to 1,000 mi. along the base of the Andes Mountains. Downstream from the junction with the Rio Xingú the plain again widens out leaving a broad area of lowland at the mouths of the Amazon, which embraces the huge island of Marajó and extends northward along the Atlantic coast to the Guianas and southeastward into the state of Maranhão.

The Guiana Highlands, extending from the Amazon northward into Venezuela and the Guianas, have a base of ancient crystalline rocks which forms a surface of gently rounded hills covered with a mantle of fine-grained soils. Scattered over these hilly uplands are the stumps of eroded mountains. The most continuous of such areas is the Serra de Tumucumaque, averaging less than 3,000 ft. in elevation, which forms the drainage divide between Brazil and Surinam and French Guiana. In the west, the crystalline base disappears under the stratified formations of the sandstone plateaus of Parima and Pacaraima, of which the highest elevation is Mount Roraima, 9,219 ft., on the British Guiana-Venezuela-Brazil border.

The Brazilian Highlands, likewise composed of crystalline hilly uplands, scattered low mountain knobs and ranges, and interior stratified formations, cover approximately five-eighths of Brazil. The Brazilian Highlands for the most part drop off sharply to the Atlantic. The largest coastal lowlands are the deltas of the Rio Doce and the Rio Paraíba, and the narrow alluvial lowland extending from Santos to Paranaguá, formed of waste material brought down from the highlands by the Iguape. In the southern states of Santa Catarina and Rio Grande do Sul there is a wide coastal zone of alternating sand bars and lagoons, with many sand dunes. The largest of the lagoons are the Lagoa dos Patos and the Lagoa Mirim. The crystalline hilly upland of the northeast rises gradually from the coast to the interior, but from Salvador southward almost to Pôrto Alegre in Rio Grande do Sul the coast is backed by the steep, wall-like slopes of the Great Escarpment, composed of a series of parallel steplike escarpments with deep valleys between. In two places—behind Santos and Paranaguá—it is concentrated in one seaward-facing slope. The average elevation is about 2,600 ft., but in places it is surmounted by mountains rising to 7,000 or 8,000 ft. The crest of the escarpment is broken only by the deep valleys of the Jequitinhonha, the Doce, and the Paraíba. Of these rivers only the flat-bottomed valley of the Doce offers a route of easy gradient to the interior. The Paraíba, above its delta, descends through a narrow rocky gorge; the wide floodplain of its middle course, which lies parallel to the Great Escarpment, provides a route westward to São Paulo. The upland is composed of rounded hills and broad valleys, with scattered ranges of low mountains, most of which are oriented parallel to the line of the coast and the escarpment. Most prominent of the ranges are the Serra da Mantiqueira on the southwest border of Minas Gerais, the Serra dos Orgãos northeast of Guanabara Bay, and the Serra do Espinhaço in the central part of Minas Gerais. The Pico da Bandeira, 9,462 ft. in height and located on the border between the states of Minas Gerais and Espírito Santo, is the highest elevation in Brazil. In the west are vast plateau areas,

formed of a covering of stratified rocks, chiefly sandstones. The eastern limit of the sandstone plateaus of the northeast Brazilian Highlands is a prominent east-facing escarpment or cuesta, which extends southward from Paraíba along the boundary between the states of Piauí and Ceará. The Paraná Plateau in southern and southwestern Brazil is one of the world's largest plateaus built of successive flows of lava or diabase. Both the eastern edge, the Serra Geral, which extends from western São Paulo state to the southern end of the Great Escarpment, and the southern edge, which trends east and west across the state of Rio Grande do Sul, are marked by steep-faced cuestas from which the plateau surface slopes gently westward toward the Rio Paraná. Although most of the rivers which drain the Brazilian Highlands have their sources in the southeast, some on the crest of the Great Escarpment, they flow away from the Atlantic, either westward into the Paraguay-Paraná system or northwestward into the São Francisco or Amazon systems. All the rivers are marked by falls and rapids as they descend over the steep margins of the highlands. At the edge of the Paraná Plateau spectacular falls occur as rivers encounter the resistant diabase formations. Most famous are the Iguaçu Falls of the Rio Iguaçu and the Guaíra Falls, or Salto das Sete Quedas, of the Paraná. In the far west, in Mato Grosso state, is a small portion of the lowlands of the Paraguai, much of which lies under flood-water during the wet season.

In the immense Amazon basin and along the seaward-facing slopes of the Great Escarpment the heavy rainfall and uniformly high temperatures are reflected in tropical rain forest or *selva,* composed of hundreds of varieties of evergreen, broadleaf trees. High overhead the branches interlace in a dense canopy of foliage, so that little sunlight penetrates to the forest floor. Only along the river banks, on steep slopes, or at spots where the foliage has been thinned is there enough light to support the dense growth of underbrush usually termed jungle. Here, intermingled with the forest growth which is usually more than 100 ft. in height, is an immense number of climbing and trailing lianas with strong, cablelike stems, and a profusion of orchids, bromelias, and other epiphytes. Except in the river flood-plains, the soils of the tropical rain forest are generally poor in plant foods, since the heavy rains leach away soluble minerals and under the high temperatures organic matter is destroyed so quickly that little humus is formed. Tropical semideciduous forest is found in areas where rainfall is a little lower and temperatures not quite so high, chiefly along the coast from Cape São Roque to the northern end of the Great Escarpment, along the eastern margin of the highlands south of Salvador, and extending south of the frost line in the valley of the Paraná. The trees are smaller than those of the *selva,* and some species lose their leaves during the dry season. The smaller size and wider spacing of the trees allow enough light to reach the ground to support dense underbrush in some places, but also make the clearing of such a forest easier than the removal of the *selva.* Most of the interior of Brazil is covered with dry savanna and scrub forest. Both are composed of savanna grasses and scattered low scrub trees. Scrub forest or *caatinga* is dominant in the dry northeastern part of the highlands. Savannas with scattered scrub trees or *campo cerrado* cover the vast plateau regions of Goiaz and Mato Grosso in western Brazil. In both scrub forest and savanna areas, stream courses are marked by dense ribbons of *galeria* or tunnel forest, which form a complete arch of foliage across the narrower streams. South of the line of annual frost the tropical vegetation types give way to mixed forests of Paraná pine and broadleaf species, and to the open expanses of tall prairie grasses which extend almost without forest interruption across the southern part of Rio Grande do Sul.

Climate. Many variations of climate are found in the great expanse of Brazil, but there are only a few areas which are either too wet or too dry for agriculture. Most of Brazil receives 40 in. or more of rain annually. There is a small semiarid area in northeast Brazil, in a polygon-

Highland cities of central Brazil, such as Belo Horizonte, have year-round temperatures several degrees cooler than those of the coast. The northern limit of annual frosts is found in southern São Paulo, northern Paraná, and sometimes in Santa Catarina and certain points of Rio Grande do Sul. South of the northern Paraná line, although summers are similar to those in the north, winters are considerably cooler. Frosts occur in the highlands, but only rarely in the deeper valleys.

Rubber workers line up at a latex collection depot on a rubber plantation in Belterra

FISHER · CUSHING

shaped zone extending inland from the coast northwest of Cape São Roque. The problem of this area, which is called the "Polygon of Droughts," is irregularity of rainfall rather than moisture deficiency; although annual rainfall averages 20 to 25 in., fifty years of the hundred between 1835 and 1935 were marked by either floods or drought. Rainfall ranging between 60 and 200 in. a year is found in the upper Amazon basin, along the coast north of Belém, in scattered spots along the Great Escarpment and on the mountain summits of the southeast, and in a small area of the upper Paraná Valley. Summer rains and a winter dry season are characteristic of most of Brazil. The southern states, however, have no real dry season, but rather a winter season of less rainfall.

There is a popular misconception that tropical countries like Brazil have excessively high temperatures. However, at Santarém on the Amazon, only a few degrees from the equator, the highest temperature ever recorded is 96.3° F., and the lowest 65.3°. At Rio de Janeiro the average temperature for the warmest month, which is February, is 79.0°, which is about the same as the average for the warmest month at Raleigh, N. C. The coldest month at Rio de Janeiro, which is July, averages 68.7°, or approximately the same as the coldest month at Miami, Fla. It is the high relative humidity, which averages 78 per cent in Rio de Janeiro, rather than the temperature which causes Europeans and North Americans in Rio de Janeiro and other cities of the southeast coast to complain of heat during the summer months.

Fauna. Among the mammals of Brazil are the sloths, anteaters, agoutis, guinea pigs, pacas, vampire bats, marmosets, porcupines, and spider monkeys. The tapir is the largest land mammal. The marsupials are represented by the opossums. Among the carnivores are the jaguar, yaguarundi, and ocelot. Distinctive rodents, besides the agoutis and guinea pigs, are the capybara and coypu. Armadillos and peccaries are widely distributed. There are several varieties of deer, including the brockets, which are only 19 to 22 in. high. The bird fauna, the most striking and diversified found in any tropical region, contains an immense number of species, most of which, except the migratory forms, do not occur in other regions. Besides some two hundred species of hummingbird, there are other large groups noted for their resplendent plumage. Characteristic of these are the macaws, toucans, cotingas (bellbird, cock of the rock, umbrella bird), manakins, and tanagers. Among the larger game birds are the curassows, guans, and tinamous. The ostrich group is represented by the rheas, who roam in flocks on the dry, open *sertão*. Other birds include the remarkable hoatzin and the jabiru.

The reptiles include the boa, anaconda, bushmaster, fer-de-lance, and various venomous reptiles of the rattlesnake group; also the crocodile, alligator, and the cayman. The fresh-water fishes, which are very numerous, include the arapaima, piranha, angelfish, electric eel, and the lungfish of the Amazon. One of the most striking features of the fresh-water fauna is the number of species of catfish.

P. E. J.

Flora. Brazil, as one of the larger countries of the earth, with great climatic and topographic diversity, possesses probably the most extensive flora of any country. The richness of the floras of tropical forests is well known, and the Amazonian forest is the greatest of all. Local floristic differences and interrelations form such a complex pattern that only with difficulty can any valid generalizations be made.

Relationships. Floristically the Amazonian forest and the forest of the southeast coast are similar, and are related to the rain forests of northwestern South America. Their richness is approximated only in southeastern Asia and Malaysia. Well-known and important members of this flora are the brazil nut, timbo, and Pará rubber. Outstanding families in this forest are Palmae, Leguminosae, Lauraceae, Rubiaceae, Euphorbiaceae, Moraceae, Mytraceae, Lecythidaceae, Voschisiaceae, Meliaceae, and others. Perhaps related to this region are the palm forests of the eastern part of the country. Here *Orbignya, Copernicia,* and *Mauritia* are important genera. The forests of Paraná pine of the south are probably also related to these tropical forests, although the outstandingly dominant tree is one of the scattered southern-hemisphere conifers, relict of a prehistoric austral flora.

The floras of the *campos, cerrados, caatingas,* and other dry regions are mostly related to those of other arid parts of the continent, especially the Paraná and Orinoco basins, though the extreme local endemism in these sections of Brazil almost obscures any external relationships. Prominent families are the Gramineae, Leguminosae, and Palmae. The floras of the flat-topped sandstone mountains of the northern border and those of the high peaks of the southern mountains, although closely related, are so ancient that there seem to be no strong relationships elsewhere.

Economic Plants. The Brazilian flora has yielded many economic plants, including notably the brazil nut, Pará rubber, tapioca, yerba mate, and many outstanding timbers. The name "Brazil" is derived from brazilwood, the earliest export from the country.

Amazonian Rain Forest. The Amazonian rain forest, the largest vegetational region, is by no means uniform. Locally it varies greatly in environmental conditions and in composition. Rainfall is much greater in the upper and lower Amazon than in the central part. Vast areas are flooded annually, and differ in composition from those areas, both away from the river and immediately adjacent to it, which are above high-water level. Vast areas along the rivers, especially in the nonflooded parts, are tangled second-growth forest because of the shifting cultivation practices of the inhabitants. In the immediate vicinity of the rivers, moreover, the changing watercourses cut away areas of forest and build up new land, which is gradually reforested. The succession starts with dense growths of low, reedy grasses, fol-

lowed by giant reeds (*Gynerium*), *Tessaria,* and willows, which are displaced by *Cecropia,* which in turn gives way to *Ficus,* and gradually the primary forest is built up again. This forest is a tall rain forest, complex in composition, with little undergrowth except where light penetrates; it has trees with straight, clean trunks and umbrella-shaped crowns, and a dense canopy of vines. In virgin primary forest the trees are more or less equal in height, while old second-growth can usually be identified by the uneven outline of the canopy. The soils in these lowland forests usually are not very fertile.

Other Forests. Along the southeastern coast is another type of rain forest, growing mostly on the steep slopes of the coastal mountain range. The composition is even more diverse than that of the Amazonian lowlands. Palms are less common, and the broken topography provides habitats for more shrubs. In the states of Maranhão and Piauí, in the northeast, is an extensive area largely covered by palm forest. This is locally called *cocais.*

Savannas, Grasslands, and Scrub. Most of southern Brazil is in the region of the *campos,* characterized by grassland and various formations of scrub and savanna. A curious section of this region lies in the valley of the Rio São Francisco, and is called *cerradão.* It is like savanna in that it is grassland with scattered trees. Owing to the permanently high water table, however, the trees have broad, thin leaves, as would be expected in mesophytic forest. The *campo cerrado* is a thin wood or scrub of varying density and stature, depending on the available moisture.

Paraná Pine. In southern Brazil there is a sizable area dominated by Paraná pine which, with a few secondary species, forms dense forests. This is an important timber-producing region, but the stands are diminishing rapidly.

Mangrove and Strand Plants. The mangrove swamp and strand zones along the coast are similar in aspect to the same formations elsewhere in the tropics. The mangrove formation is made up of trees with conspicuous prop roots or with pneumatophores, organs for aerating the submerged roots, similar to cypress knees. The strand plants are notable for fleshy leaves and other means of existing in spite of extreme salinity. Just back of the strand is a maritime scrub, or low forest, with various semihalophytic and xerophytic shrubs and small trees. The plant life of Brazil was described at great length in Martius' great *Flora Brasiliensis,* which, though many years out of date, remains the greatest of all floristic works on any part of the world. It was written by sixty-five collaborating botanists.   F. R. F.

REGIONAL DIVISIONS

Although Brazil's population has increased rapidly (618 per cent between 1850 and 1950), the total number is still small compared to the vast extent of Brazilian territory. The population is so distributed that three regions of relatively concentrated settlement may be distinguished: (1) the Northeast, between the Cabo de São Roque and a line drawn roughly from the mouth of the Parnaíba to Salvador in Bahia; (2) the Southeast, including the capital, Rio de Janeiro, the rich mining state of Minas Gerais, and São Paulo, the industrial city and its hinterland; and (3) the South, the region of new pioneer settlement in the three southern states. The remaining 75 per cent of Brazil is included in two regions of sparse population: the North, the Amazon basin and the little-explored Guiana Highlands; and the Interior, the vast western pastoral area of the Brazilian Highlands, known to Brazilians as the *sertão.*

The Northeast. The Northeast includes the states of Piauí, Ceará, Rio Grande do Norte, Paraíba, Pernambuco, Al-

SÃO PAULO, BRAZIL

PHILIP GENDREAU

agoas, and Sergipe, and part of Maranhão and Bahia. Along the coast between Natal and Salvador there is a belt occupied by large sugar plantations. The dense population includes a large proportion of Negroes and mulattoes. Plantations of short-staple cotton have been established along the dry in-

Vendors hawking fruits and vegetables on a street in Salvador

BLACK STAR

land margins of the sugar belt. Sugar and cotton grown here are sold on domestic and foreign markets. The small farms of Bahia produce sugar cane, cotton, rice, manioc, and 21 per cent of Brazil's tobacco, while the coastal zone south of Salvador produces 96 per cent of Brazil's cacao. Inland and extending to the coast north of Natal is the dry *caatinga,* with a comparatively sparse population of Portuguese or Portuguese-Indians, and few Negroes. Most of the area is used for grazing, but small agricultural settlements are found in the wetter lands near the Chapada do Araripe, and the Jardim de Seridó, on the Serra de Baturité, and in the São Francisco Valley. Since 1909 the Brazilian government has conducted a program of dam and reservoir construction to meet the problems of alternating drought and flood. In addition to cattle and a little cotton from the irrigated farms, the principal products come from trees growing wild in the scrub forest: long-fiber tree-cotton, carnauba wax, oiticica oil, and castor oil. The principal cities of the Northeast (all seaports) are: Fortaleza, capital of Ceará; Natal, capital of Rio Grande do Norte; João Pessoa, capital of Paraíba; Recife, capital of Pernambuco and Brazil's third largest city; Maceió, capital of Alagoas; Aracajú, capital of Sergipe; and Salvador, capital of Bahia and Brazil's first capital. Coastwise shipping and air service provide connections with the rest of Brazil. Although the railroads of the Northeast do not form a totally integrated system within the area, lines meeting at Monte Azur connect northeast and central Brazil and another line runs from Salvador to Rio de Janeiro.

The Southeast. The Southeast, a zone of concentrated settlement, includes the Federal District with Rio de Janeiro,

the nation's capital; the state of Rio de Janeiro which surrounds the Federal District; the southern parts of Minas Gerais and Espírito Santo; and São Paulo and its hinterland. The pattern of settlement reflects the historical events of the last two hundred years. Gold rushes at the end of the seventeenth century began the penetration of Minas Gerais. In the subsequent cycles of speculative planting of sugar, coffee, rice, and oranges, new agricultural lands were opened up and often later abandoned. The chief concentrations of people are in southern Minas Gerais, in the Paraíba Valley, around the cities of Rio de Janeiro and São Paulo, and in southern Espírito Santo. The Southeast produces 60 per cent of Brazil's sugar, 98 per cent of its coffee, and two thirds of its oranges, as well as jute, and rice for the urban populations of Rio de Janeiro and São Paulo. The rural population consists largely of tenant farmers living in isolated homes or tiny villages scattered over the *fazendas* or large estates. The basic form of land use, however, is pastoral. Much of southern Minas Gerais and parts of Rio de Janeiro state (chiefly the Paraíba Valley) are devoted to the grazing of dairy cattle. In the Serra do Espinhaço of Minas Gerais are located Brazil's great iron ore deposits, estimated to contain about one third of world reserves. Exploitation of these reserves has been limited by lack of smelting coal and by the difficulties of transporting ores and imported coal over the Great Escarpment. Other valuable minerals are manganese, bauxite, zirconium, chromium, molybdenum, nickel, tungsten, beryl, quartz, and industrial diamonds.

Rio de Janeiro, the capital, is the second largest city of South America. Its location on Guanabara Bay, formed by a break in the coastal mountains, gives it one of the finest natural harbors in the world. It is the hub of commercial exchange for all the widely scattered areas of Brazil and is the country's financial center. Famous attractions are Sugar Loaf Mountain (Pão de Açúcar) guarding the harbor entrance, Corcovado peak, and Copacabana Beach on the Atlantic. Other important cities are: Niterói, capital of Rio de Janeiro state; Petrópolis, summer capital of Brazil, located in the Serra dos Orgãos at an elevation of 2,600 ft.; Campos, sugar-refining center on the Paraíba delta; Juiz de Fora, a textile-manufacturing city; and Belo Horizonte, the new and modern capital of Minas Gerais, which was founded in 1898. The principal railroad is the Central do Brasil, which has a main line from Rio de Janeiro to Belo Horizonte and branch lines to São Paulo and numerous smaller cities of the southeast.

São Paulo. São Paulo, only a little more than 220 mi. southwest of Rio de Janeiro, is the focal point of the commercially most prosperous and most rapidly expanding region of Brazil. The hinterland includes the state of São Paulo, the pioneer colonies of northern Paraná, and the westward-moving frontier in the *sertão* of southern Mato Grosso. The crop which has contributed most to the development of São Paulo is coffee. After 1885, coffee planting spread rapidly from the original plantations in the Paraíba Valley westward and northwestward throughout the hilly lands of the state. The expansion of coffee planting was accompanied by immigration into São Paulo of nearly three million persons—Italians, other Brazilians, Portuguese, Spaniards, Japanese, and Germans—about half of whom stayed permanently. São Paulo produces 40 to 50 per cent of Brazil's coffee. Other crops are cotton (over half of the total Brazilian production), sugar cane, oranges, bananas, and rice, as well as the staple crops of maize, beans, and manioc which are grown throughout Brazil.

The city of São Paulo, which had only 64,934 people in

1890 and 579,000 in 1930, increased by 1955 to about 3,000,000 people. It is the principal industrial center of Latin America. The textile industry (cotton, wool, jute, silk, and rayon) is of chief importance, employing about one third of the workers. Others produce metal goods, machinery, clothing, foods and beverages, chemicals, building and construction materials, paper, and rubber goods. Water power has been an important factor in this rapid development. From reservoirs developed on the crest of the Serra do Mar, water is dropped 2,378 ft. to the Cubatão hydroelectric plant, which has an installed capacity of 474,000 kw. São Paulo's

The granite peak of Sugar Loaf Mountain (1,296 ft.) guards the entrance to Guanabara Bay, the basinlike harbor at Rio de Janeiro.

PHILIP GENDREAU

port, Santos, located on the lowland at the foot of the Serra do Mar, is the leading coffee port of the world. Other leading cities of the state are Sorocaba, Campinas, Ribeirão Preto, and Jundiaí. The principal railroad systems are the Mogyana in northeastern São Paulo and southwestern Minas Gerais, the very modern Paulista in central and northern São Paulo, the Sorocabana in southern and western São Paulo, and the Noreste do Brasil crossing southern Mato Grosso to the Paraguay River near Corumbá.

The South. The South, including the three southern states of Paraná, Santa Catarina, and Rio Grande do Sul, is an area of recent pioneer settlement, characterized by small farms worked by their owners. The people are descendants of immigrants from Italy, Portugal, Germany, Poland, Russia, Ruthenia, the Ukraine, and also from other parts of Brazil. Rio Grande do Sul, which has the largest population, includes an area on the southern prairies on which cattle and sheep are raised; a rice-growing area on the floodplain of the Rio Jacuí; an area on the lower slopes of the upland where maize, rye, and potatoes are grown and hogs are raised; and a vineyard area on the higher slopes. The state produces 33 per cent of Brazil's tobacco, 80 per cent of the domestic wines, and 85 per cent of the wheat. The principal cities are Pôrto Alegre, Brazil's fifth largest city; Pelotas; and Rio Grande. The leading industries are meat packing, tanning, textiles, and the processing of foods and beverages. Power is derived from coal from the São Jerônimo and Tubarao mines. The latter mines, in Santa Catarina, also provide coal for the new Volta Redonda steel mill. The agricultural settlements of Santa Catarina produce hogs, milk, butter, rice, tobacco, and wines. The principal towns are Florianópolis, the capital, located on a rocky island off the coast; Joinville; and Blumenau. The

products of the agricultural settlements of Paraná find a market in Curitiba, the capital, which is also a commercial center for the timber, wood pulp, and yerba mate of the western forests. In northern Paraná, coffee growing has increased considerably.

The North. The North, including the states of Maranhão, Pará, and Amazonas, and the federal territories of Acre, Rio Branco, Amapá, and Rondônia, contains 42 per cent of the area of Brazil but only about 4 per cent of the population. The most populous areas are around São Luiz, capital of Maranhão, and Belém, capital of Pará, both near the ocean. A thousand miles up the Amazon is Manaus, capital of Amazonas and the trading center through which all the products of the upper Amazon basin are funneled. Most of the rest of the population is found in thinly scattered groups along the major rivers. Indians inhabit the vast interior forests, but their exact number is not known. The principal products come from the forests of the Amazon: babassu and Brazil nuts, fine cabinet woods, rubber from the wild indigenous rubber trees, and numerous plants used in drugs, dyes, and other chemicals. Cattle are raised on the swampy savannas of the island of Marajó, around São Luiz and Belém, and on the dry savannas far up the Rio Branco north of Manaus. The greatest penetration of the Amazon region occurred during the great speculative rubber boom in the latter half of the nineteenth century. With the establishment of plantations of rubber trees in Sumatra and Malaya, the Amazon after 1910 lost much of its importance as a source of rubber. Rivers are the chief transportation routes. The Amazon is navigable for small ocean-going vessels to Iquitos in Peru, 2,300 mi. from the mouth. Manaus is accessible to the largest ocean-going vessels. The Madeira is navigable for 670 mi., to Pôrto Velho. The tributaries east of the Madeira are all interrupted by falls and rapids within 200 mi. of the main stream. Belém, the principal seaport of northern Brazil, is an important stopover point on international airlines.

The Interior. The Interior, or *sertão,* which extends from the western parts of the eastern states across the vast scrub forest and savanna lands of Goiás and Mato Grosso, has a sparse and widely scattered population. Cattle, grazed on huge ranches, are the principal source of wealth. In the eastern *sertão* there are scattered areas devoted to maize, manioc, rice, beans, sugar cane, and tobacco. Mato Grosso also possesses rich iron-ore and manganese deposits. The principal towns are Uberaba and Uberlândia, both in the Triangulo section of Minas Gerais; Goiânia, the new capital of Goiás; Cuiabá, capital of Mato Grosso; Campo Grande, on the Noroeste railroad; and Corumbá, from which hides and skins, rubber, gold, and ipecac, gathered from a vast territory, are shipped down the Paraguay.

In 1956, preliminary steps were authorized for the transfer of Brazil's capital to the Interior. The new capital, to be called "Brasilia," will be located in the State of Goiás.

P. E. J.

THE PEOPLE

Ethnic Groups. For three centuries Brazil was a Portuguese colony, and its eastern portion was settled by immigrants from Portugal. The language of the country is Portuguese; the traditions, ideals, and social and political standards are inherited from Portugal. The Portuguese language is one of the comparatively few things that Brazilians, with a population half as large as all South America, have in common. From the days of the independent captaincies, into which the coast of Brazil was first divided, Brazil has been more a string of loosely confederated colonies than a cohesive nation. Although it remained nominally a single nation while the Spanish colonies were splitting into a number of countries, each Brazilian community has sought contact with the rest of the world through seaports rather than laterally with its neighbors. Further economic development requires the establishment of communications between the various islands of population. A westward movement, which has been well described as the "moving frontier," was started under the first Vargas administration.

Of the total population (51,973,727 in 1950), about 62 per cent are whites, about 27 per cent are of mixed blood, and abut 11 per cent are Negroes. In the north, people of Negro blood are greatly in the majority. In the states from Rio de Janeiro southward, people who are wholly or nearly white predominate. In the interior, the population is mainly Indian, or a mixture of Indian and white or possibly Indian and Negro. In the southern half of the highland area and conspicuously in the region of São Paulo, European immigrants are numerous.

Brazil is making probably the most interesting experiment in race mixture of any nation in the world. The country is deliberately setting out to absorb by miscegenation all peoples within its borders, which include a large number of Negroes who came as slaves from Africa and an increasing number of Japanese.

The population of Brazil includes various European and Asiatic immigrant groups. One of the first attempts at colonization on a large scale was the introduction of Swiss settlers by John VI of Portugal in 1817. The Germans followed in 1825 and continued coming for half a century. Poles and Russians entered in considerable numbers after 1870, while Japanese immigration began early in the 1900's. The Swiss settled in Nova Friburgo; the Germans later, in the state of Santa Catarina. Italians, the most numerous of any single nationality, have settled in the coffee-growing centers of São Paulo. Extensive settlements of Poles and Russians are found in the state of Paraná. Spanish as well as Portuguese form an important part of the colonization and immigration. The total number of immigrants from 1820 to 1953 was 5,074,471.

Religion. The separation of church and state has been recognized since the establishment of the republic in 1889. The constitution of 1946 makes no reference to the Supreme Being or to any church. The government is forbidden "to establish or subsidize religious sects or embarrass their exercise" (Art. 31). Religious instruction is provided as "part of the teaching schedule of official schools, and shall be administered according to the religious confession of the pupil" (Art. 168); however, "enrollment is optional."

The Roman Catholic Church is the largest religious organization, including about 93 per cent of the people.

RAPHO - GUILLUMETTE

A native displays his pottery in the open market at Belém, chief seaport for Amazonas. The masts are those of Amazon river boats tied at the jetty.

On the discovery of Brazil, Pope Alexander VI designated a dividing line—one hundred leagues west of the Azores—between the territories of Portugal and Spain in South America. The Jesuits and other orders took a leading part in the cultural life of colonial Brazil. The first mass was celebrated by Father Henrique de Coimbra, in Pôrto Seguro, in 1500.

Brazil has three cardinals, and 34 titular bishops and archbishops in all the principal cities. It is divided into 20 ecclesiastical provinces, comprising, within their great circumscriptions, 20 archdioceses, 80 dioceses, 28 prelacies, and two prefectures. In the ecclesiastical provinces there are about 3,500 parishes, 100 curates, and 27 curate chapels. There are about 11,000 Catholic churches.

Protestantism was introduced during the colonial period by the Dutch and French, but failed to prosper after they were driven out by the Portuguese. It was reintroduced by the English and German immigrants in the early part of the nineteenth century and reinforced later by missionaries from the United States. Of the non-Catholics in Brazil, over half are Protestants. The others are, in order of decreasing number, Spiritualists, Buddhists, Jews, and Orthodox Christians.

Occupational Groups. The largest occupational group is that engaged in agriculture, stock raising, and forestry. The second largest is formed by workers in the processing industries. Transportation and communication; public administration and service, law, teaching, national defense, and public security; and the mineral and vegetable extractive industries claim the other important, though much smaller, occupational groups. There is a large number of students and domestic workers.

ECONOMIC RESOURCES AND ACTIVITIES

Economic Development. Sugar, cotton, rubber, coffee, and in a lesser degree, cacao, gold, and tobacco tell the story of the rise and fall of the Brazilian economy. In the seventeenth century Brazil was the greatest supplier of sugar to the world. It lost this supremacy to the West Indies and to

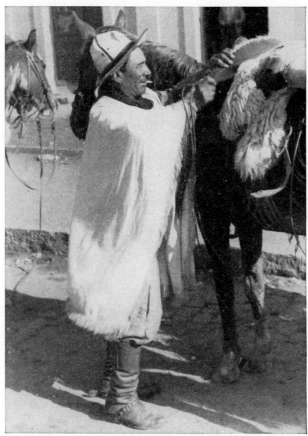

The gaucho's costume includes a broad-brimmed hat, poncho, leather boots, bandana, spurs. These men guard the vast livestock ranges of Rio Grande do Sul where they live out on the pampas.

Europe. During the eighteenth century the world turned to Brazil for newly discovered gold, but the gold rushes to California, South Africa, and Australia surpassed the Brazilian production. Brazilian cotton dominated the London market at the close of the eighteenth century, but the invention of the cotton gin shifted production to the southern United States. Rubber created the miracle city of Manaus, which became almost a ghost town when the British shipped rubber plants out of the Amazon valley to Malaya and introduced scientific cultivation in the Far East. As for coffee, Brazil still provides more than half of the world's supply, but other Latin American countries are also growing coffee, and among them Colombia has become an active rival. World War I brought the first real awareness of the dangers of dependence on monoculture and lack of industrialization, and this led to some action in diversifying crops and erecting factories. The new steel plant at Volta Redonda promised the beginning of an independent industrial life "providing its own most urgent defence and equipment needs." The essential objectives of the program of "economic independence built on steel" suggest that the economy be planned by the state. The constitution of the "new state" in 1937 limited

the exploitation of mines, subsoil wealth, and water power to enterprises composed of Brazilian shareholders, but the 1946 constitution ruled that this development may be carried out by Brazilians or by Brazilian companies with foreign partners. Under the 1946 constitution, foreign-owned deposit banks and insurance companies may operate in Brazil.

When World War II came and Brazil threw in its lot with the Allies, the United States poured in capital, machines, and technicians to hurry the production of rubber, manganese, quartz, and a dozen other fundamental materials. The northern hump of Brazil became an area of airports and shipping centers for Africa, Europe, and Asia.

With peace, the scene quickly changed. Inflation and high prices brought down the standard of living and incited strikes and riots. Wartime accumulation of foreign exchanges bought fewer goods than had been expected. Machinery, railroad equipment, and vehicles of all kinds were worn out, and industry awaited necessary replacements. By 1947 the situation had become serious. Business activity fell as buyers resisted high prices. Speculation in real estate and the building of lavish apartment houses largely took the place of more urgently needed investments in business. The national budget was greatly unbalanced. In spite of this difficult situation, the nation was far from bankrupt. The government rigorously limited imports and national spending. The crisis was met without devaluation of the cruzeiro, the expenditure of the nation's gold reserves, or resort to extensive credit loans. At the same time, the foreign debt, which amounted to $534,914,514 in 1945, was reduced to $300,295,929 as of Dec. 31, 1950.

As at various times in Brazilian history, coffee came to the rescue. A combination of short supply and a marked increase in the use of coffee more than doubled the price of the product which provides more than half of Brazil's exports. This, connected with the restrictive measures mentioned and increased buying by the United States, made 1949 the turning point. According to the Brazilian Government Trade Bureau, 1950 was a record year, with new advances being reached in the principal economic fields. While the country thus escaped from an impending crisis, it had not solved such problems as the low standard of living of

An Indian of the Borobo tribe whittles an arrow deep in the Brazilian jungle. Few outsiders have seen this part of Brazil.

the masses, coupled with the great amount of disease, illiteracy, and insufficient housing.

Until 1950, foreign capital invested in Brazil was preponderantly British, but by that year the situation had changed, with Britain occupying third place, Canada second, and the United States first. In 1955 total gross investments in Brazil amounted to 98,100 million cruzeiros and net investments to 71,800 million cruzeiros. Brazil's leaders insist that the country needs and welcomes foreign private capital, provided that investors obey the law and help to develop the nation's economic and social life. Leading United States concerns already operating in Brazil have continued to expand their operations, while several others keep coming in, especially to set up manufacturing enterprises. In 1955 direct United States capital investments in Brazil exceeded one billion dollars. The largest item was $563,000,000 invested in manufacturing enterprises, represented by packing plants, assembly plants, cotton gins, packaging plants, and drug and toiletry proprietors. United States oil companies have invested $186,000,000 in Brazil, chiefly in storage tanks. Investments in utilities amount to $158,000,000, chiefly by the American & Foreign Power Company. A total of $137,-000,000 is invested in trade, part of which consists of agencies selling United States machinery, movies, and specialties.

Agriculture. Nearly three fourths of Brazil has a tropical climate and about one half is covered by tropical vegetation, which man would have to fight endlessly if he tried to bring the land under cultivation. Only 20 per cent of the country is divided into farms and only about 3½ per cent is under cultivation. Brazil is in no sense a one-crop country, yet one industry, coffee-growing, means more to the international trade of the republic than all other branches of agriculture combined. Coffee, native to tropical Africa, was introduced into Brazil from French Guiana during the eighteenth century, and into the state of São Paulo shortly before 1800. Its cultivation spread, especially in São Paulo, until by 1906 the world market for coffee was saturated. Brazil now produces slightly more than one half the world's supply.

Coffee has been Brazil's principal money crop and gave Brazil the backlog of foreign exchange with which to buy machinery and luxury goods. Coffee planting had been extended to the frost line in the state of Paraná and to the western boundary of the state of São Paulo, and this raised the question of whether production in other sections of the country could be undertaken with profit.

Its ease of production and high degree of utility as food and feed render corn the second crop of the country, the acreage averaging four fifths of that in coffee. Corn combines with rice, beans, and manioc to form the food of the common people. Sugar ranks third among Brazil's crops, with about one third the acreage of corn. Cassava, also called manioc, is a native of Brazil; it grows vigorously in poor soil, yields very heavily with little labor, may be prepared for eating in a variety of ways, and is one of the greatest of all starch-producers. Rice has proved profitable in crop diversification. Although a small production of lowland rice characterizes coastal and river valley districts, upland rice is the larger crop. Cotton has recently awakened much interest as a cash crop. As grown in eastern Brazil, it is superior to most North American upland cotton.

New methods, new knowledge, and new results have recently dominated agriculture. For many years there were only a few scattered agricultural schools with a small number of students. Appreciation of their value has become general,

BLACK STAR

Local fish catch is unloaded at Santos, Brazil, where huge ocean-going vessels also load and unload.

and the number of schools and students is increasing. The state of São Paulo is establishing ten junior agricultural schools where the emphasis is to be on practical farming and there are twelve college-level agricultural schools in Brazil as a whole.

Stock Raising. The raising of cattle is an important industry, providing for the export of hides, wool, and meat. In many regions the grazing of cattle is the keystone of local economy. Three of the most important pastoral districts are those bordering the southern frontier, the northern midlands, and the states of Mato Grosso and Goiás. The great herds in these regions, with subsidiary enterprises, account for the location of great packing plants, as well as the numerous concerns engaged in drying meat for the preparation of jerked beef; many other factories process dairy products.

Improvement of the local breeds is obtained by the importation of foreign livestock. In the frontier region are found Holsteins, the most popular dairy cattle, Hereford, Polled Angus, Shorthorn, and Jersey cattle, and also Romney Marsh, Merino, and Lincoln sheep. In the southern region are Charolais and Dutch cattle; blends of the Indian humped cattle known as the Brahman or Zebu—Gujarat, Nellore and Gir; and Duroc-Jersey, Poland China, and Berkshire hogs. Catalan and Italian asses have also been introduced into this region for breeding purposes.

The Brazilian government is stressing the improvement of livestock and its by-products by every possible means. Breeders are acquiring sound notions of nutrition and animal husbandry. Particular care is paid to the control of disease and insect parasites, under the supervision of the National Department of Animal Production, a division of the Ministry of Agriculture, which has established regional inspectorates in the principal grazing areas.

Forest Products. Because of its proximity to centers of population, the forest strip along the eastern coast has supplied a large part of the lumber cut in Brazil. In the pine forests of the southeast, which cover approximately 100,-

37

000,000 acres, there are large stands of nearly unmixed pine, with mature trees averaging 80 to 100 ft. in height and attaining 4 to 6 ft. in diameter. From 150,000,000 to 250,000,000 ft. of Paraná pine are exported annually to Argentina and Uruguay. Rubber is still of some economic importance, and Brazil is the only American producer of carnauba

Brazilian worker separating coffee beans from twigs and other foreign matter

wax, which is used for electric insulation and phonograph records.

Minerals and Mining. Both placer and vein gold deposits are widely distributed in the highlands of Brazil. Nearly all the gold produced, however, comes from the two very deep mines near Belo Horizonte in Minas Gerais. Coal is so expensive that the mining companies have installed hydroelectric plants to supply power for the mines. Diamonds have been found in Brazil for over 200 years. The importance of this industry has been slight, in part because of the great output from South Africa, but the production was markedly increased during World War II. Manganese is mined in Minas Gerais, 300 mi. north of Rio de Janeiro, and there are also large manganese deposits in the Federal Territory of Amapá. Minas Gerais has iron-ore deposits that are probably the richest and most extensive in the world. Here is a mountain range which is 70 per cent high-grade metal. It is estimated that there are in the area upwards of 12 billion tons of the highest-grade ore and huge additional quantities of lower-grade ore. Most of the ore lies near the surface and forms actual mountains of hematite. The most valuable deposits are about 300 mi. from the coast. Successful exploitation of these deposits has led to highly

increased export of iron ore. Iron-ore deposits in Mato Grosso are estimated at 1.3 billion tons with a 50 per cent ferro-silicate content.

Scattered through the nation are deposits of bauxite, chromium, molybdenum, tin, tungsten, lead, zinc, mercury, platinum, and silver. There are also asbestos, rare quartz crystal, and mica. Brazil is the world's only source of imperial topaz. Petroleum deposits are found in Bahia, Piauí, and other northern states.

Brazil spends $725,000 daily to buy foreign petroleum; yet geologists believe that the nation's petroleum reserves may be among the largest in the Western Hemisphere. The major obstacle to their exploitation at present is the opposition of certain political elements to foreign investment in the petroleum field. A bill for the creation of a company to carry out exploration and development of Brazil's petroleum resources was passed in 1953. The new company, commonly called Petrobrás, comprises both government and private capital and has as its objects prospecting for, extracting, refining, trading in and transporting petroleum and petroleum products. Although its by-laws do not permit any foreigner or even Brazilians married to foreigners to own stock in the company, Petrobrás is free to contract with foreign companies for drilling, prospecting, and other technical jobs. Petrobrás owns a fleet of oil tankers and two refineries. There are also five privately-owned refineries in Brazil, and the expansion of old refineries and the construction of new ones is in progress.

Strategic minerals, in which the United States is especially interested, include iron, manganese, tungsten, beryl, mica, quartz, industrial diamonds, cobalt, nickel, tin, tantalite, and zirconium. Several of these are not mined to a large extent because of transportation difficulties, and funds for their transportation are needed from large industrial and military powers. According to the armament program for the democracies adopted in the early 1950's, the United States began arrangements with Brazil for stockpiling several of these minerals. At the same time Brazil began stockpiling a certain amount in case of future scarcity, and this brought some rivalry between the two countries.

Foreign Trade. Brazil, like all Latin America, depends largely on foreign trade. The federal government watches this trade carefully and adjusts both exports and imports, as well as control of exchange and other economic situations, to keep exports above imports.

The balance of trade with Great Britain for a number of years had been favorable to Brazil, but in 1948 it became unfavorable, with an import balance in 1949 of 950 million cruzeiros. In 1953 an agreement was concluded by Brazil for the liquidation of commercial arrears due Britain on imports, which provided for an application by Brazil to the International Monetary Fund for a drawing of £10,000,000 to be used as a down payment. Payment of amounts due Great Britain has reduced somewhat Brazil's debt to that country.

In 1955 a multilateral trade and payments' agreement was entered into by Brazil, Great Britain, the Netherlands, and West Germany, providing for payment of transactions either in marks, pounds, or guilders, freely transferable within the above area. Other countries such as Austria, Italy, France, and Benelux have since joined the agreement.

Trade with Argentina, with whom political and cultural relations have recently grown more cordial, has developed so that it about equals that with Great Britain. The two neighboring countries supplement each other in many ways although they are rivals in others. Brazil gets a large part of its supplies of extra wheat, as well as other foods and some petroleum, from Argentina; and the latter buys coffee, lumber, textiles, tropical fruits, and rubber goods from its neighbor.

In 1953 the Brazilian government established an import system whereby importers are required to purchase exchange commitment certificates. The total cost of the exchange to the importer is his bid price for the exchange certificate plus the official rate with applicable taxes. Certain items, such as maps and books, are exempt from the import license requirement and from the bidding requirement. There are five categories of import commodities, the first four of which are for items considered essential, while the fifth includes what are termed "non-essential" commodities, including many luxury goods, but also some utilities. The U.S. dollar premium in the fifth category is as high as Cr. 300. The high premiums for U.S. goods in the other categories have discouraged trade with the U.S. to a certain extent, and importers instead buy similar goods from more favorable areas, especially from countries, like Czechoslovakia, with which Brazil has trade agreements. Exchange auctions with such countries are based on trade agreement or covenant "dollars."

Industry. The most important manufacturing industry in Brazil is cotton weaving, followed by the production of rayon goods. Textile production increased by 23 per cent between 1948 and 1953. Brazil also has a large cement industry, ceramic works, refrigerating plants, and metal fabricating plants.

The food processing and plastics industries are also highly significant in Brazil; the latter is expanding rapidly and raw materials, such as bakelite, polystyrene, formaldehyde, and polyethylene, are already being made on a commercial scale in Brazil.

Much progress has been made toward rendering Brazil free from imported items, such as cement, glass, cellulose, tires and tubes, pig iron, iron piping, rails, clothing, household utilities (including sewing machines, refrigerators, and washing machines). The aluminum industry is growing.

The automobile industry is becoming increasingly important. In 1956 a decree was signed for the setting up of a national automobile industry in Brazil. Both Brazilian owned and foreign companies (American, British, German, and Japanese) are engaged in making or assembling automobiles, mostly in the state of São Paulo. An increasing

number of automobile parts are being made wholly in Brazil. It is estimated that by 1964 Brazil should have a fleet of 1,337,000 motor vehicles, of which 643,000 would be trucks.

The Volta Redonda steel mills, completed in 1946 in the state of Rio de Janeiro, form a vital part of Brazil's new industrialization program. The enterprise was financed by a loan of approximately $45 million from the Export-Import Bank of Washington and about the same amount from the Brazilian government. United States machinery and management were used in the construction of the project, which included housing for the 2,500 employees, schools, and community buildings. The enterprise is an important aid in fur-

The rare metal tantalite, secured after several washings at a mine in northern Brazil

nishing material for new railroads, bridges, and construction of all kinds, as well as contributing to a higher standard of living by paying higher wages than are paid to agricultural workers.

By 1950 the steel production capacity of the Volta Redonda plant had risen to 700,000 tons annually. Total eventual capacity is estimated at 1,000,000 tons. Two other important steel mills, both in Minas Gerais, are the Companhia Siderúrgica Belgo-Mineira (a subsidiary of the Luxembourg steel company) which has two plants, and Cia. Acos Especiais Itabira (ACESITA). Another large plant, located at Belo Horizonte, was opened in 1956. The Belo Horizonte plant is capitalized at Cr. 700 million and is already producing seamless tubes; it is jointly financed by German and Brazilian groups and employs German technicians and Brazilian trained personnel.

In order to meet the increasing demand of Brazilian industries for steel and iron, all existing steel mills are expanding their operations and the organization of other steel mills has been announced.

The general lack of fuel in Brazil, in close relationship to

Splitting balls of rubber for grading at Manaus, Brazil

the growing industrialization, gives electric power an overwhelming importance. Fortunately the country is especially blessed with great rivers, ranking sixth among the world's nations in water power. The largest of many power projects is the Paulo Alfonso Project for harnessing the 1,800-mi. Rio São Francisco, which is the sixth largest river in the hemisphere, and traverses five states and drains an area of almost 300,000 sq. mi. Its development was aided by loans from the International Bank for Reconstruction and Development, and the project supplies power to various localities in the states of Alagoas, Bahia, and Pernambuco and is expanding the area to be served.

Transportation. *Water transportation.* The greatest problem of Brazil, with its enormous and scarcely populated territory, is transportation. The cheapest and most widespread means of transportation are the extensive river systems and the 5,000 mi. of sea coast, with the latter reaching practically all the larger cities with the exception of São Paulo. The federal government operates a considerable merchant marine, known as Lloyd Brasileiro, which reaches not only Brazilian ports but also other South American, United States, and European ports. The Amazon system is the largest navigable river system in the world, providing 10,000 mi. of navigable waterways for large steamers and between 20,000 and 30,000 mi. of water usable for at least part of the year by light-draft steamers. The Paraguay-Paraná system connects western Brazil with the neighboring countries of Paraguay, Uruguay, and Argentina.

Railroads. Railroads have been slow in expanding, with a total of 23,016 mi. in 1952, compared to about 27,000 mi. in Argentina which has one third of the territory. Most of the railroads run through the coastal region, with few extending for any considerable distance into the interior except in the states of São Paulo and Minas Gerais. International lines include one running from São Paulo to Montevideo, Uruguay; the Madeira-Mamoré line connecting northeast Bolivia with the Amazon district of Brazil; and the road connecting the port of Santos with the city of Santa Cruz, Bolivia. This important line was fostered by the Brazilian government to open the rich eastern section of Bolivia to a free port on the Atlantic at Santos. About 90 per cent of the railroads are one meter gauge. Federal and state governments own 87 per cent of the railroads in Brazil.

Highways. In recent years the building of highways has made more progress than that of railways. Trucks are taking the place of freight cars in opening up Brazil's great west. The government's goal, to which it is giving much attention, is to make every part of the republic accessible through first-class roads. Total highway mileage in 1953 was 213,149 mi., about 45 per cent of which were municipal roads of poor standards.

Pan American Highway. That part of the Brazilian section which extends for 1,500 mi. from the Uruguayan frontier, via Pôrto Alegre, to Rio de Janeiro has been opened to traffic. Soon it will be possible to drive at all seasons over good paved roads from the capital to the southernmost borders of the country.

Regional Distribution of Railways and Roads. The network of railways in Brazil is concentrated principally in the Southeast where the bulk of the total production of the country is centralized. The same region possesses 40 per cent of all the roads and 66.1 per cent of the total automobiles and trucks. The region known as the South accounts for 17.8 per cent of the total agricultural production of the country and about 30 per cent of the total livestock, while it possesses 29.5 per cent of the total mileage of roads and

only 18.1 per cent of the railways. In the Northeast, there is a distinct predominance of roads. The railway system is about 18 per cent of the total for the country, while the mileage of roads is 20.8 per cent of the national total. The conditions in the Interior are somewhat similar to those of the North. The length of its railways is 4.4 per cent of the total of the country. The state of Minas Gerais is served by three of the longest railroads in Brazil, the Rêde Mineira de Viação, the Estrada de Ferro Central do Brasil, and the Estrada de Ferro Leopoldina.

Aviation. Airplane travel has done more than any other means of transportation to make accessible every section of Brazil, including the tropical jungles of the Amazon, the far west of Goiás and Mato Grosso, mining riches of isolated sections of Minas Gerais, and the cattle ranches of Paraná. It has also placed Brazil within a day's reach of the rest of South America, the United States, and Europe. During World War II, Natal, 1,700 mi. from Africa, developed the longest runways of any airport in the world, where the world's statesmen and military leaders met, and bombers, trucks, tanks, and shells from the factories of the United States were sent on their journey to the Allies in North Africa, Europe, Russia, and China. The airports loaned to the United States during the war were later returned to Brazil to serve her national and international interests. The airplane has eliminated political isolation by transporting a newly elected senator from Amazonas to the federal capital of Rio de Janeiro in a day instead of a month. Passengers, mail, medicine, livestock, machinery, and vaccines to stop epidemics now reach every section of the nation, where people formerly lived weeks away from a doctor or a newspaper. There are eight major airlines in Brazil, wholly owned by Brazilian stockholders. Four of these airlines operate international services, including flights to the United States, and are subsidized by the government. Brazil is one of the leading nations of the world in volume of air traffic.

Telecommunications. Brazil is well served in the telecommunications field: it has international cable, radiotelegraphic, and radiotelephonic facilities. Radio broadcasting is expanding. There are about 600 radio-broadcasting stations in Brazil and six television stations.

GOVERNMENT

On Sept. 18, 1946, Brazil adopted its fifth constitution and returned largely to the conservative document of 1891, modeled on the United States Constitution.

The federated republican form of government is established. Legislative power is exercised by the Chamber of Deputies with the collaboration of a federal Senate. The Senate consists of three representatives from each state and federal district elected by direct suffrage for eight-year terms. The Chamber of Deputies is elected on a proportional basis. Executive power is vested in the president, who is elected by universal suffrage for five years and may not be immediately re-elected for a second term. He is assisted by a military and a civil household and by a cabinet of eleven state ministers. The vice-president takes the place of the president in case of his absence and is also president of the Senate. The court system includes a supreme court, with eleven judges, and various minor courts.

Political Parties. Brazil has never had any well-organized political parties representing definite principles or programs. Parties are loosely organized around individual leaders. During the Vargas regime from 1930 to 1946 political parties were not allowed to function. The Communist Party was outlawed in 1947.

The old port of Bahai, or Salvador, Brazil, is the scene of brisk trading in local products, and here fresh fish, vegetables, and trinkets are sold. At other docks, international trade is carried on.

Monetary Unit. The unit of the monetary system was the milreis until November 1942, when the name was changed to the cruzeiro, equal in value to the old milreis and composed of 100 centavos. The metal money consists of 1 and 2 cruzeiros and 10, 20, and 50 centavos. There is paper money for 1, 2, 5, 10, 20, 50, 100, 200, 500, and 1,000 cruzeiros. One thousand cruzeiros is known as one conto, roughly equivalent (1957) to $15.15 in United States currency.

Finance. In Brazil taxes are levied on income, sales, commercial sales, territorial property, location of property, social security, and excess profits. According to the Brazilian constitution, the budget of the government "shall be one, and shall incorporate all receipts of revenues and provisions of funds, and shall include in detail the expenses and allotments necessary for the payment of all public services." In the United States this type of budget would be called a segregated item budget.

The expenditures of the Brazilian federal government have exceeded revenues for many years. The budget for 1956 was estimated at 71,500,000,000 cruzeiros, with allocations to some of the ministries as follows: military, 26 per cent; communications and public works, 23 per cent; finance, 19.4 per cent; aeronautics, 6.1 per cent; and education, 5.7 per cent. Inflation has been an overpowering problem since the end of World War II, with extremely high prices causing numerous strikes for higher wages.

Armed Forces. The constitution of 1946 designated that there shall be an army, a navy, and an air force and that they are to be used only for defensive action and in keeping the peace of the country, not to wage an offensive war at any time. The president of the nation is the commander in chief of the armed forces. In 1955 the man power of the armed forces was 140,000 men.

All males between the ages of eighteen and forty-five are subject to military duty under a selective service system which provides for one year of service in the first line. In 1942 a decree was signed by President Vargas by which it is possible to increase the size of the army up to 1,200,000. The decree also called for voluntary enlistments. The Brazilian navy is being modernized: two heavy cruisers and two submarines have been purchased from the United States and an aircraft carrier from Britain. The navy arsenal has built several small warships, such as submarine chasers and torpedo-boat destroyers. In 1940 the army and navy relinquished control of air arms to the air ministry, which controls civil and military aviation, but the navy has reestablished its own air force. The independent air force of approximately 22,000 officers and men, the largest in South America, is built around approximately 1,200 planes, about 500 of which were purchased from the United States through the Lend-Lease Program during World War II, while an unspecified number were received from the United States under the terms of a military agreement between the two countries. Sixty per cent of the total number of aircraft is operational. The air defense is organized in four zones (Belém, Rio de Janeiro, São Paulo and Pôrto Alegre), with five air squadrons and one air-transport command. Training establishments are located in Rio de Janeiro, Galeão (at Ilha do Governador), São Paulo and Minas Gerais. Pilots trained in Brazilian flying schools maintain leadership throughout the air force, and technical standards are equivalent to those of the United States. A Joint Brazil-United States Military Commission (JBUSMC) is available to assist in the training of the armed forces of Brazil.

SOCIAL AND CULTURAL CONDITIONS

There are no great fortunes in Brazil, as great fortunes are measured in the United States. Wealthy Brazilian families are classified as those earning over three million cruzeiros

TRIANGLE PHOTO SERVICE

Brazil early developed a characteristic church architecture. A fine example is this eighteenth-century colonial church in Congonhas, Minas Gerais, Brazil, noted for its striking baroque sculpture.

($45,450) annually. According to reports of the division of income tax in 1955 there were 242 persons with a gross income of about $21,200. The increasing prosperity of the upper middle class is shown by the fact that in 1955 there were 25,486 persons with incomes between $4,550 and $15,150, while in the lower middle class there were 65,885 with incomes ranging between $1,800 and $4,550, and in the low-bracket wage class there were 97,409 persons who earned between $750 and $1,800.

For the lower middle class—certain business clerks, private school teachers, and unskilled laborers—life is hard. Even though salaries have been periodically increased, such increases are absorbed by high costs of living, and it is impossible for these people to maintain a healthy diet and decent housing and clothes.

According to a survey conducted by a leading São Paulo newspaper, a Paulista worker spends 43 per cent of the family budget on food, 25 per cent on housing, and about 9 per cent on dress, as compared with 35, 25, and 6 per cent for these items by an American laborer. However, the Paulista need spend less than his American counterpart on fuel, medical aid, and transportation.

The Brazilian labor situation has been characterized by poor pay and the imposition of impossible conditions. President Getulio Vargas introduced new social legislation. From almost nothing he developed enlightened legislation governing relations between labor and capital in such matters as minimum wages, hours, vacations, sanitary conditions, and old-age and sickness insurance. Enforcement of these regulations encountered some resistance, chiefly because management considered such legislation too advanced for a country like Brazil. Progress, however, is steady.

Education. For many years after the establishment of the republic in 1889, education was largely in the hands of the various states and of private schools. A national ministry of education is now making strenuous efforts to advance public education in all parts of the nation. The problem is especially difficult because of the independent spirit of the states and the great distances of many sections from the national capital, where expert help is available. Illiteracy up to the beginning of the Vargas administration in 1934 was approximately 75 per cent. In 1920 there were 1,200,000 children enrolled in primary schools, in 1937 there were 2,700,000 and in 1947 the number had increased to 3,950,000. Great efforts were made in the 1940's and are still being made to reduce illiteracy and to modernize educational methods. In 1946 the Ministry of Education announced plans for 1,000 new rural schools and pledged 66,000,000 cruzeiros for construction of buildings. A concerted plan to develop secondary education, formerly greatly neglected, includes the building of training schools for rural teachers. The campaign against illiteracy in the 1940's brought excellent results, the percentage having been reduced to an estimated 50 per cent in 1946. Some of Brazil's southern states have an illiteracy rate as low as 5 per cent.

The public school system is slowly being federalized. The states control elementary and rural education. By adroit use of small subsidies, the federal government is influencing the state systems to adopt uniform administra-

PHILIP GENDREAU

Former summer palace of Emperor Pedro II, now a national museum at Petropolis, containing the furniture and many private possessions of the Emperor's family as well as the throne and throne room.

tion and curricula. The public system is supplemented by a large number of privately operated secondary schools, *liceos* and *colégios,* and universities whose standards are of a high order. Mackenzie College in São Paulo, organized by New York philanthropists, is one of the most famous privately supported colleges. The administration has encouraged both types of schools and is making an important contribution to further expansion through an intensive program of teacher-training.

The country's 74,892 primary schools had a total enrollment of 4,941,986 students in 1956, and the 2,746 secondary schools reported 619,019 students. In the same year, there were also 206,088 students enrolled in other intermediate schools (commercial, industrial, etc.). As a result of the illiteracy campaign, many thousands of adults enrolled in 1951 to learn to read and write. In 1953, there were 637,289 students enrolled in these special courses, which also include minors, although they consist largely of adults. The illiteracy

BRAZIL

Index to Physical Features and Points of Interest

TOPOGRAPHIC FEATURES

Islands, Peninsulas, Capes, Mountains, Plateaus, Valleys, etc.

Acaraí, mountains . . . . B 1
Açuruá, mountains . . . . E 4
Agamiaure, mountains . . . . B 2
Apiacás, mountains . . . . D 1
Araras, mountains . . . . F 2
Araripe, mountains . . . . D 4
Baleia, point . . . . F 5
Bananal, island . . . . E 2
Bandeira, peak, 9,462′ . . . . G 4
Cachimbo, mountains . . . . D 2
Caiapó, mountains . . . . F 2
Carajás, mountains . . . . D 2
Cassiporé, cape . . . . B 2
Chapada, mountains . . . . F 1
Curumiquara, point . . . . C 5
Desordem, mountains . . . . C 3
Dois Irmãos, mountains . . . . D 4
Dourada, mountains . . . . E 3
Espinhaço, mountains . . . . F 4
Estrondo, mountains . . . . D 3
Formosa, mountains . . . . E 1
Geral de Goáis, mountains . . . . E 3
Gongogí, mountains . . . . E 4
Gradaus, mountains . . . . D 2
Gurupí, cape . . . . C 3
Gurupí, mountains . . . . C 3
Ibiapaba, mountains . . . . D 4
Magoari, cape . . . . C 3
Mantiqueira, mountains . . . . G 4
Maracá, island . . . . B 2
Marajó, island . . . . C 3
Mato, point . . . . D 6
Mato Grosso, region . . . . E 1
Monsaras, point . . . . F 5
Mutá, point . . . . E 5
Norte, range . . . . E 1
Orange, cape . . . . B 2
Parecis, mountains . . . . E 1
Penitente, mountains . . . . D 3
Piauí, mountains . . . . D 4
Roncador, mountains . . . . E 2
Raso, cape . . . . B 3
Santa Catarina, island . . . . H 3
Santa Marta Grande, cape p13
Santo Antônio, point . . . . F 5
São Jerônimo, mountains . . . . F 2
São Roque, cape . . . . D 5
São Sebastião, island . . . . G 4
São Tomé, cape . . . . G 4
Tabatinga, mountains . . . . E 4
Taquara, mountains . . . . F 2
Tocansa, island . . . . C 4
Tombador, mountains . . . . E 1
Tombador, mountains . . . . E 4
Tumucumaque, mountains . . . . B 1
Turí, point . . . . C 4
Veadeiros, plateau . . . . E 3
Xavantes, mountains . . . . E 3

HYDROGRAPHIC FEATURES

Lakes, Rivers, Creeks, Bays, Straits, Seas, etc.

Abacaxis, river . . . . C 1
Aguapeí, river . . . . G 2
Alto Trombetas, river . . . . B 1
Amazonas (Amazon), river . . . . C 1
Anapú, river . . . . C 2
Aporé, river . . . . F 2
Araguaia, river . . . . D 3
Araguaia, river . . . . E 2
Araguarí, river . . . . B 2
Arinos, river . . . . E 1
Balsas, river . . . . E 3
Balsas, river . . . . D 3
Batoui, river . . . . E 2
Brilhante, river . . . . G 2
Camaqua, river q12
Canindé, river . . . . D 4
Canoas, river . . . . H 2
Capim, river . . . . C 3
Cassiporé, river . . . . B 2
Chopin, river . . . . H 2
Contas, river . . . . E 4
Corrente, river . . . . E 4
Corumbá, river . . . . F 3
Cuiabá, river . . . . F 1
Culuene, river . . . . E 2
Curua, river . . . . D 2
Curuá do Sul, river . . . . C 2
Doce, river . . . . F 4
Erepecurú, river . . . . C 1
Fardo, river . . . . F 4
Feia, lake . . . . G 4
Fresco, river . . . . D 2
Grajaú, river . . . . C 3
Grande, river . . . . G 3
Grande, river . . . . E 4
Guamá, river . . . . C 3
Guaporé, river . . . . o 9
Gurgueia, river . . . . D 4
Gurupí, river . . . . C 3
Ibicuí, river p12
Ibiraputa, river q11
Iguaçu, cataracts . . . . H 2
Iguaçu, river . . . . H 2
Iguatemí, river . . . . G 2
Ijuí, river p12
Iriri, river . . . . C 2
Itabapoana, river . . . . G 4
Itacaiunas, river . . . . D 2
Itapecurú, river . . . . C 4
Itapi, river . . . . C 1
Itapicuru, river . . . . E 5
Itararé, river . . . . G 3
Ivaí, river . . . . G 2
Ivinheima, river . . . . G 2
Jacaré, river . . . . E 4
Jacuí, river p12
Jacuípe, river . . . . E 5
Jacundá, river . . . . C 2
Jamachim, river . . . . D 1
Jamundá, river . . . . C 1
Jarí, river . . . . B 2
Javaés, river . . . . E 3
Jequitinhonha, river . . . . F 4
Jurua, river . . . . n 8
Juruena, river . . . . E 1
Longá, river . . . . C 4
Madeira, river . . . . n 9
Maicurú, river . . . . C 2
Manso ou das Mortes, river . . . . E 2
Manuel Alves, river . . . . D 3
Mapuera, river . . . . C 1
Maues Guacu, river . . . . C 1
Mearim, river . . . . D 3
Meia Ponte, river . . . . F 3
Miranda, river . . . . G 1
Mirim, lagoon q12
Mucurí, river . . . . F 4
Negra, river . . . . H 2
Negro, river . . . . F 1
Negro, river . . . . m 9
Norte, canal . . . . B 2
Oiapoque, river . . . . B 2
Pacajá, river . . . . C 2
Pacajá Grande, river . . . . C 2
Palma, river . . . . E 3
Papagaio, river . . . . E 1
Pará, river . . . . C 3
Paracatú, river . . . . F 3
Paraguacu, river . . . . E 5
Paraguai, river . . . . G 1
Paraíba, river . . . . G 3
Paraná, river . . . . E 3
Paraná, river . . . . G 2
Paranaíba, river . . . . F 2
Paranapanema, river . . . . G 2
Paranatinga, river . . . . E 1
Pardo, river . . . . G 2
Pardo, river . . . . G 3
Parnaíba, river . . . . D 4
Parú, river . . . . C 2
Patos, lagoon q12
Paulo Afonso, cataract . . . . D 5
Peixe, river . . . . G 2
Pelotas, river p12
Pequirí, river . . . . F 1
Piauí, river . . . . D 4
Pindaré, river . . . . C 3
Potí, river . . . . D 4
Preto, river . . . . E 4
Purús, river . . . . n 8
Quaraí, river q11
Ronuro, river . . . . E 2
Ribeira, river . . . . G 3
Sangue, river . . . . E 1
São Francisco, river . . . . D 4
São Lourenço, river . . . . F 1
São Manuel ou das Tres Barras, river . . . . D 1
Sete Quedas, waterfalls . . . . G 2
Solimões (Amazon), river . . . . m 8
Sono, river . . . . D 3
Sucuriú, river . . . . F 2
Sul, canal . . . . C 3
Tapajós, river . . . . D 1
Tapirapé, river . . . . E 2
Taquarí, river p12
Taquarí, river . . . . F 1
Tibagi, river . . . . G 2
Tiete, river . . . . G 2
Tocantins, river . . . . C 3
Todos os Santos, bay . . . . E 5
Trombetas, river . . . . C 1
Turiacu, river . . . . C 3
Uatumã, river . . . . C 1
Urucuia, river . . . . F 3
Uruguai, river . . . . H 2
Uruguay, river . . . . H 1
Varzea, river p12
Velhas, river . . . . F 4
Verde, river . . . . E 1
Verde, river . . . . F 2
Verde, river . . . . G 2
Vertentes, river . . . . E 2
Xapecó, river . . . . H 2
Xingú, river . . . . D 2

SPECIAL POINTS OF INTEREST

Parks, Monuments, Ruins, Dams, Sites, Buildings, etc.

Carmo Parish Church, Sabará . . . . F 4
Church of Sebnhor do Bomfim, Salvador . . . E 5
Coffee Exchange, Santos . . . . G 3
Instituto Butantan, São Paulo . . . . G 3
Morro Velho Gold Mine, Nova Lima . . . . F 4
National Museum, Rio de Janeiro . . . . G 4
Opera House, Manaus . . . . m 9
Ouro Preto, national monument . . . . G 4
Sugar Loaf Mountain, Rio de Janeiro . . . . G 4

BRAZIL *Continued*

Carlos Chagas, 4,227...F 4
Carolina, 4,659...D 3
Caruaru, 43,501...D 5
Casa Branca, 7,373...G 3
Cascavel, 2,752...C 5
Castelo, 3,623...G 4
Castro, 6,158...G 3
Castro Alves, 6,479...E 5
Cataguases, 12,837...G 4
Catalão, 6,088...F 3
Catanduva, 21,604...G 3
Caxias, 14,445...C 4
Caxias do Sul, 31,561...p12
Ceará-Mirim, 5,092...D 5
Chapadinha, 1,700...C 4
Cicero Dantas, 1,596...E 5
Clevelândia, 919...p12
Codó, 6,027...C 4
Colatina, 6,451...F 4
Colinas, 1,799...D 4
Conde, 2,953...E 5
Condeúba, 1,440...E 4
Conselheiro Lafaiete, 18,042...G 4
Coreaú, 1,286...C 4
Corinto, 6,678...F 4
Coroatá, 4,970...C 4
Corrente, 1,386...E 4
Correntina, 1,927...E 4
Corumbá, 18,725...F 1
Crateús, 7,391...D 4
Crato, 15,464...D 5
Cristalina, 1,719...F 3
Cruz Alta, 19,375...p12
Cruzeiro, 14,169...G 4
Cuiabá, 23,745...F 1
Curaçá, 1,046...D 5
Curitiba, 141,349...H 3
Curitibanos, 2,059. H 2, p12
Currais Novos, 5,179...D 5
Curuçá, 2,216...C 3
Curvelo, 13,633...F 4
Diamantina, 9,837...F 4
Dianópolis, 804...E 3
Divinópolis, 19,701...G 4
Dom Pedrito, 11,124...q12
Dores do Indaiá, 5,475...F 3
Eldorado, 1,168...G 3
Emílio Meyer, 944...q12
Erechim, 14,418...H 2, p12
Espírito Santo, 9,701...G 5
Estância, 14,051...E 5
Estrela, 3,781...p12
Feira de Santana, 26,559 E 5
Ferros, 1,745...F 4
Floresta, 2,134...D 5
Floriano, 9,101...D 4
Florianópolis, 48,264...H 3, p13
Fordlândia...C 1
Formiga, 11,782...G 3
Formosa, 3,631...F 3
Fortaleza, 205,052...C 5
Foz do Iguaçu, 3,000...H 2
França, 26,629...G 3
Frutal, 2,948...F 3
Gameleira, 3,336...D 5
Garanhuns, 20,550...D 5
Garça, 12,433...G 3
Garibaldi, 3,635...p12
Getúlio Vargas, 2,838...p12
Goiana, 13,744...D 6
Goiandira, 2,652...F 3
Goiânia, 39,871...F 3
Goiás, 5,606...F 2
Governador Valadares, 20,357...F 4
Grajaú, 2,377...D 3

Granja, 3,790...C 4
Gravatá, 10,816...D 5
Guanambi, 2,077...E 4
Guará, 2,570...G 3
Guarabira, 9,425...D 5
Guarapuava, 5,489...H 2
Guaratinguetá, 20,811...G 3
Guaxupé, 9,227...G 3
Guimarães, 1,239...C 4
Ibia, 4,616...F 3
Ibitinga, 6,113...G 3
Icó, 3,953...D 5
Igaraçu, 2,116...D 6
Igarapava, 5,792...G 3
Igarapé Açu, 2,200...C 3
Igarapé Miri, 900...C 3
Iguape, 3,780...G 3
Iguatu, 10,063...D 5
Ijuí, 8,652...p12
Ilhéus, 22,593...E 5
Imperatriz, 1,152...D 3
Inajá, 773...D 5
Inhambupe, 3,245...E 5
Inhuçu, 1,145...C 4
Inhumas, 3,254...F 3
Ipameri, 7,234...F 3
Ipirá, 2,232...E 5
Ipu, 5,874...C 4
Ipueiras, 1,999...C 4
Itabaiana, 5,746...E 5
Itabaiana, 8,670...D 5
Itabaianinha, 2,403...E 5
Itaberaba, 5,896...E 4
Itaberaí, 1,880...F 3
Itabira, 7,357...F 4
Itaboraí, 1,830...G 4
Itabuna, 25,351...E 5
Itacoatiara, 5,867...C 1
Itaguaçu, 838...F 4
Itajaí, 19,797...H 3, p13
Itajubá, 20,627...G 3
Itapecuru-Mirim, 1,871...C 4
Itapemirim, 2,565...G 4
Itaperuna, 8,819...G 4
Itapetininga, 17,475...G 3
Itapeva, 6,072...G 3
Itapipoca, 4,500...C 5
Itaporanga, 3,635...D 5
Itaqui, 8,814...p11
Itararé, 9,177...G 3
Itaretama, 1,559...D 5
Itaúna, 9,254...G 4
Itu, 16,550...G 3
Ituiutaba, 8,002...F 3
Itumbiara, 3,664...F 3
Jaboatão, 34,179...D 6
Jaboticabal, 13,850...G 3
Jacarèzinho, 8,131...G 3
Jacobina, 7,224...E 4
Jaguarão, 9,382...q12
Jaguariaíva, 4,157...G 3
Jaicós, 891...D 4
Januária, 7,023...F 4
Japaratuba, 2,441...E 5
Jaraguá, 2,685...F 3
Jaraguá do Sul, 3,220...H 3, p13
Jardim do Seridó, 1,285...D 5
Jaú, 18,578...G 3
Jequié, 20,652...E 4
Jeremoabo, 2,185...E 5
Jerumenha, 828...D 4
João Pessoa (Paraíba), 89,517...D 6
Joinville, 20,951...p13
Juàzeiro, 15,896...D 4
Juàzeiro do Norte, 41,999...D 5

Juiz de Fora, 84,995...G 4
Júlio de Castilhos, 3,287...p12
Jundiaí, 39,014...G 3
Juquiá, 892...G 3
Juriti, 1,142...C 1
Laguna, 9,459...p13
Lajes, 14,596...H 2, p12
Lapa, 5,381...H 3, p13
Laranjeiras, 4,149...E 5
Laranjeiras do Sul, 962. H 2
Lavras, 12,257...G 3
Lavras da Mangabeira, 2,192...D 5
Lavras do Sul, 2,566...q12
Lençóis, 3,007...E 4
Leopoldina, 10,828...G 4
Lima Duarte, 2,788...G 4
Limeira, 27,552...G 3
Limoeiro, 14,122...D 5
Limoeiro do Norte, 4,647...D 5
Linhares, 2,939...F 4
Lins, 23,737...G 3
Livramento, 29,099...q11
Londrina, 33,095...G 2
Lorena, 16,033...G 3
Luís Correia, 1,450...C 4
Luís Gomes, 1,082...D 5
Luz, 3,255...F 3
Macaé, 10,664...G 4
Macapá, 9,748...B 2
Macau, 7,661...D 5
Maceió, 99,088...D 5
Machado, 6,042...G 3
Mafra, 8,603...H 3, p13
Mamanguape, 6,334...D 5
Manaus, 110,678...m 9
Mandaguari, 6,387...G 2
Manga, 1,525...E 4
Manhuaçu, 6,050...G 4
Marabá, 4,536...D 3
Maracaju, 1,308...G 1
Maragogipe, 9,744...E 5
Maranguape, 5,412...C 5
Marechal Deodoro, 4,999...D 5
Marília, 35,742...G 3
Marquês de Valença, 12,469...G 4
Massapê, 4,601...C 4
Mata de São João, 4,766...E 5
Maués, 1,974...C 1
Miguel Alves, 4,426...C 4
Mineiros, 2,382...F 2
Mirador, 734...D 4
Miranda, 1,593...G 1
Mirassol, 7,620...G 3
Mocajuba, 687...C 3
Mocóca, 7,893...G 3
Mogí das Cruzes, 31,300...G 3
Mogi Mirim, 10,913...G 3
Monte Alegre, 2,768...C 2
Monte Alegre...G 2
Monte Azul, 2,231...F 4
Monte Carmelo, 4,122...F 3
Monteiro, 3,787...D 5
Montenegro, 8,123...p12
Monte Santo, 1,595...E 5
Montes Claros, 20,370...F 4
Morada Nova, 1,496...D 5
Morrinhos, 4,696...F 3
Morro do Chapéu, 1,230...E 4
Mossoró, 19,612...D 5
Muriaé, 11,437...G 4
Natal, 94,812...D 5

Nazaré, 11,205...E 5
Nioaque, 1,279...G 1
Niterói, 170,868...G 4
Nossa Senhora das Dores, 4,091...E 5
Nova Cruz, 5,131...D 5
Nova Friburgo, 28,458. G 4
Nova Granada, 3,316...G 3
Nova Lima, 17,415...G 4
Nova Russas, 3,160...C 4
Nova Soure, 1,286...E 5
Óbidos, 3,419...C 1
Oeiras, 3,748...D 4
Olímpia, 9,245...G 3
Olinda, 38,169...D 6
Oliveira, 7,832...G 4
Orleães, 2,184...p13
Osório, 2,960...p12
Ouricurí, 2,263...D 4
Ourinhos, 13,457...G 3
Ouro Fino, 7,592...G 3
Ouro Prêto, 8,751...G 4
Palhoça, 1,456...H 3, p13
Palmares, 10,055...D 5
Palmas, 2,728...H 2, p12
Palmeira, 3,410...H 3
Palmeira dos Indios, 9,246...D 5
Pao de Açúcar, 3,221...D 5
Pará, see Belem
Paracatu, 5,909...F 3
Paracurú, 1,007...C 5
Paraguaçu Paulista, 6,566...G 2
Paraíba, see João Pessoa
Paraisópolis, 5,341...G 3
Paramirim, 1,271...E 4
Paranaguá, 16,046...H 3
Paranaíba, 1,324...F 2
Paraopeba, 3,889...F 3
Paratinga, 2,741...E 4
Parintins, 5,855...C 1
Parnaguá, 348...E 4
Parnaíba, 30,174...C 4
Passo Fundo, 24,395...p12
Passos, 14,044...G 3
Patos, 13,889...D 5
Patos de Minas, 11,414...F 3
Patrocínio, 6,905...F 3
Patu, 1,531...D 5
Paudalho, 5,360...D 5
Pau dos Ferros, 2,629...D 5
Peçanha, 2,840...F 4
Pedra Azul, 5,589...F 4
Pedreiras, 7,185...C 4
Pedro Afonso, 1,683...D 3
Pedro Avelino, 1,536...D 5
Pelotas, 78,014...q12
Penápolis, 8,832...G 2
Penedo, 14,222...E 5
Pentecoste, 869...C 5
Pesqueira, 13,124...D 5
Petrolândia, 1,971...D 5
Petrolina, 7,478...D 4
Petrópolis, 61,011...G 4
Picos, 4,568...D 4
Pilar, 6,826...D 5
Pindamonhangaba, 13,397...G 3
Pinhal, 10,103...G 3
Pinheiro, 4,477...C 3
Piracanjuba, 2,473...F 3
Piracicaba, 45,782...G 3
Piracununga, 12,546...G 3
Piracuruca, 3,402...C 4
Pirajú, 5,980...G 3
Pirajuí, 5,654...G 3
Piranga, 1,808...G 4
Pirapóra, 8,531...F 4

Piripiri, 4,357...C 4
Pitangui, 5,367...F 4
Planaltina, 1,385...F 3
Poconé, 3,054...F 1
Poços de Caldas, 19,109...G 3
Pombal, 4,867...D 5
Ponta de Pedras, 1,486. C 3
Ponta Grossa, 42,875...H 2
Ponta Pora, 5,152...G 1
Ponte Nova, 15,056...G 4
Pôrto Alegre, 375,049...q12
Pôrto Calvo, 2,309...D 5
Pôrto de Moz, 959...C 2
Pôrto Esperança, 1,174...F 1
Pôrto Feliz, 9,112...G 3
Pôrto Murtinho, 2,806...G 1
Pôrto Nacional, 2,889...E 3
Pôrto Seguro, 1,888...F 5
Pôrto União, 5,405...p12
Pôrto Velho, 10,036...n 9
Posse, 1,109...E 3
Pouso Alegre, 12,509...G 3
Prata, 2,948...F 3
Presidente Epitácio, 2,509...G 2
Presidente Prudente, 26,790...G 2
Princesa Isabel, 3,306...D 5
Propriá, 12,654...E 5
Prudentópolis, 2,823...H 2
Quaraí, 7,358...q11
Queimadas, 2,424...E 5
Quipapá, 2,226...D 5
Quixadá, 5,417...C 5
Quixeramobim, 3,052...D 5
Recife (Pernambuco), 512,370...D 6
Redençao, 1,822...C 5
Remanso, 4,073...D 4
Riacho de Santana, 1,480...E 4
Ribeira do Pombal, 2,769...E 5
Ribeirão Prêto, 63,312...G 3
Rio Branco, 9,371...n 8
Rio Branco do Sul, 715...H 3
Rio Claro, 34,618...G 3
Rio de Janeiro, 2,303,063...G 4
Rio Grande, 63,235...q12
Rio Negro, 7,653...H 3, p13
Rio Pardo, 8,322...p12
Rio Pardo de Minas, 1,069...F 4
Rio Verde, 5,395...F 2
Rosário, 5,316...C 4
Rosário do Sul, 11,992...q12
Rosário Oeste, 1,507...E 1
Russas, 5,531...C 5
Sabará, 9,183...F 4
Sabinópolis, 1,799...F 4
Salgueiro, 3,523...D 5
Salinas, 3,523...F 4
Salinópolis, 1,694...C 3
Salto Grande, 1,893...G 2
Salvador (Bahia), 389,422...E 5
Santa Bárbara, 3,358...F 4
Santa Cruz, 3,197...D 5
Santa Cruz do Rio Pardo, 8,293...G 3
Santa Cruz [do Sul], 13,161...p12
Santa Maria, 44,949...p12
Santa Maria Madalena, 1,101...G 4
Santana, 3,059...E 4

Santana do Ipanema, 3,222...D 5
Santanópole, 1,704...D 5
Santa Quitéria, 1,623...C 4
Santarém, 14,061...C 2
Santa Rita, 12,362...D 6
Santa Rosa, 4,816...H 2, p12
Santa Vitória do Palmar, 5,807...q12
Santiago, 9,469...p12
Santo Amaro, 12,258...E 5
Santo Ângelo, 13,573...p12
Santo Antônio, 2,440...D 5
Santo Antônio de Jesus, 11,417...E 5
Santos, 198,405...G 3
Santos Dumont, 13,599. G 4
São Bento do Sul, 2,712...H 3, p13
São Bernardo [do Campo], 19,960...G 3
São Borja, 11,829...p11
São Carlos, 30,830...G 3
São Cristóvão, 6,742...E 5
São Fidélis, 4,473...G 4
São Francisco, 2,903...F 4
São Francisco [do Sul], 9,825...H 3, p13
São Gabriel, 14,384...q12
São Gotardo, 2,724...F 3
São Jerônimo, 2,848...p12
São João da Barra, 2,777...G 4
São João da Boa Vista, 15,837...G 3
São João Del Rei, 24,560...G 4
São João do Carirí, 1,188...D 5
São João do Piauí, 1,467...D 4
São João Nepomuceno, 6,797...G 4
São Joaquim, 2,097...p13
São José do Rio Prêto, 36,942...G 3
São José dos Campos, 25,892...G 3
São José dos Pinhais, 3,238...H 3
São Leopoldo, 18,380...p12
São Lourenço, 8,692...G 3
São Lourenço do Sul, 4,427...q12
São Luís, 79,731...C 4
São Luís Gonzaga, 7,767...p12
São Manuel, 6,280...G 3
São Mateus, 3,023...F 5
São Paulo, 2,197,360...G 3
São Pedro do Piauí, 1,653...D 4
São Raimundo Nonato, 2,663...D 4
São Sebastiao do Paraíso, 10,532...G 3
São Simão, 3,450...G 3
São Vicente, 28,012...G 3
Senador Pompeu, 5,158. D 5
Senhor do Bonfim, 10,113...E 4
Serra Talhada, 5,353...D 5
Serrinha, 6,602...E 5
Sêrro, 3,746...F 4
Sertânia, 5,170...D 5
Sete Lagoas, 18,438...F 4
Simplício Mendes, 1,243 D 4
Sobral, 22,628...C 4

Sorocaba, 68,811...G 3
Soure, 5,264...C 3
Sousa, 4,555...D 5
Suçuapara, 1,860...F 3
Taguatinga, 1,027...E 3
També, 2,891...D 5
Taquara, 7,274...p12
Tatuí, 13,244...G 3
Tauá, 2,780...D 4
Taubaté, 35,149...G 3
Teófilo Otoni, 19,790...F 4
Teresina, 51,418...D 4
Teresópolis, 14,651...G 4
Tibagi, 1,377...G 2
Tietê, 7,187...G 3
Tijucas, 3,462...H 3, p13
Tocantinopolis, 3,531...D 3
Tôrres, 3,027...p13
Touros, 1,446...D 5
Traipú, 1,866...D 5
Três Corações, 10,025. G 3
Três Lagoas, 7,650...G 2
Triunfo, 2,364...D 5
Tubarão, 11,740...p13
Tucano, 3,039...E 5
Tucuruí, 1,173...C 3
Tupã, 17,946...G 2
Turiaçu, 1,347...C 3
Ubá, 14,022...G 4
Ubaira, 2,217...E 5
Ubaitaba, 2,432...E 5
Uberaba, 42,481...F 3
Ubérlândia, 34,866...F 3
União, 3,198...C 4
União dos Palmares, 6,917...D 5
União da Vitória, 7,628...H 2, p12
Urandi, 1,585...E 4
Uruçui, 1,764...D 4
Uruguaiana, 32,639...p11
Vacaria, 5,516...p12
Valença, 11,492...E 5
Valença do Piauí, 1,886. D 4
Varginha, 13,147...G 3
Veranopolis, 2,637...p12
Viana, 4,995...C 4
Vianópolis, 1,588...F 3
Viçosa, 6,000...D 5
Viçosa, 6,424...G 4
Viçosa do Ceará, 2,534...C 4
Visconde do Rio Branco, 7,357...G 4
Viseu, 1,189...C 3
Vitória, 49,735...G 4
Vitória...C 2
Vitória [de Santo Antão], 15,720...D 5
Vitória da Conquista, 17,503...E 4
Vitória do Mearim, 1,217...C 4
Volta Redonda, 32,143 G 4
Wenceslau Braz, 2,003...G 3
Xique-Xique, 3,844...E 4

STATES

ACRE (Ter.)...n 7
Area...59,139 sq. m.
Pop...114,788
ALAGOAS...D 5
Area...11,016 sq. m.
Pop...1,094,845
AMAPÁ (Ter.)...B 2
Area...53,057 sq. m.
Pop...36,972
AMAZONAS...n 8
Area...614,913 sq. m.
Pop...507,628
BAHIA...E 4
Area...217,669 sq. m.
Pop...4,838,118
CEARÁ...D 5
Area...59,168 sq. m.
Pop...2,706,611
DISTRITO FEDERAL (Federal District)
Area...524 sq. m.
Pop...2,366,372
ESPÍRITO SANTO...G 4
Area...17,089 sq. m.
Pop...860,893
FERNANDO DE NORONHA (Ter.)...*
Area...10 sq. m.
Pop...628
GOIÁS...E 3
Area...240,333 sq. m.
Pop...1,209,368
GUAPORÉ (Ter.)...o 9
Area...98,132 sq. m.
Pop...37,173
MARANHAO...C 3
Area...129,270 sq. m.
Pop...1,577,838
MATO GROSSO...F 1
Area...485,549 sq. m.
Pop...521,316
MINAS GERAIS...F 4
Area...227,310 sq. m.
Pop...7,742,858
PARÁ...C 2
Area...471,010 sq. m.
Pop...1,119,790
PARAÍBA...D 5
Area...21,730 sq. m.
Pop...1,717,160
PARANÁ...G 2
Area...82,823 sq. m.
Pop...2,126,804
PERNAMBUCO...D 5
Area...37,458 sq. m.
Pop...3,395,099
PIAUÍ...D 4
Area...96,261 sq. m.
Pop...1,047,192
RIO BRANCO (Ter.)...k 9
Area...82,747 sq. m.
Pop...17,834
RIO DE JANEIRO...G 4
Area...16,443 sq. m.
Pop...2,300,898
RIO GRANDE DO NORTE...D 5
Area...20,482 sq. m.
Pop...970,348
RIO GRANDE DO SUL...p12
Area...109,066 sq. m.
Pop...4,159,663
SANTA CATARINA...p12
Area...31,329 sq. m.
Pop...1,562,862
SÃO PAULO...G 3
Area...95,453 sq. m.
Pop...9,135,499
SERGIPE...E 5
Area...8,130 sq. m.
Pop...644,255
SERRA DOS AIMORÉS (Disputed Region)...**
Pop...160,915

*** Not shown on map; lies about 225 miles east of Cape São Roque.**

**** In dispute between Minas Gerais and Espírito Santo.**

problem is being fought constantly, and many educational units are being constructed in the various political units of Brazil.

The Minister of Education is aided by a corps of specialists, some trained in the United States. Public instruction throughout the country is provided in establishments supported and maintained by the state governments and by the municipalities, but here highly significant is the contribution of private enterprise towards educational activities. The higher, secondary, commercial, and agricultural courses are all governed by federal legislation fixing the standards under which courses must be carried out in order that diplomas or certificates issued may officially be recognized by the Union. In addition to the supervision of these courses, the federal government also provides directly the higher, secondary, supplementary primary, corrective, and professional instruction. These are ministered through establishments which depend on the Ministry of Education and Culture with only a few exceptions, such as those designed for agronomics, military high and higher grades, and corrective teaching for delinquents and the abnormal, which are subordinate respectively to the ministries of Agriculture, Navy and War, and Justice. The action of the Ministry of Education and Culture is developed through the administrative, co-operative, and executive organs prescribed by Law N. 378 of January 13, 1937, namely, the National Department of Education, comprising Divisions of Primary, Industrial, Commercial, Home Economics, Secondary, and Higher Teaching, and of Extra-school and Physical Education; the National Council of Education; and a number of educational services represented by the University of Brazil, by various distinct institutes of higher education, the Pedro II Colleges (secondary schools), industrial lyceums, the Benjamin Constant Institute for the blind, and the National Institute for the deaf and dumb. Various other organizations, which also constitute agencies for guidance, protection, or operation of educational activities, complete the structure of the Ministry, among these, the National Institute of Pedagogical Services, the National Institute of the Book, the National Institute of Educational Cinema, the Oswaldo Cruz Institute, the National Museum, the National Observatory, the National Library, Ruy Barbosa's House, Historical and Artistic Patrimony Service, the National Historical Museum, the National Fine Arts Museum, the Joaquim Nabuco Institute, the National Theatre Committee, the Imperial Museum, the Radio Education Service, and the National Conservatory of Orpheonic Singing.

The federal government is building the University City at Ilha do Fundão, a small island in the Guanabara Bay. This great project includes a large hospital, a children's institute, and the national schools of engineering and architecture. The University City is planned to house all official colleges and universities now scattered throughout the Federal District.

The statute of the Brazilian universities was promulgated in April 1931, the same date as the decree that reorganized the University of Rio de Janeiro. The latter then embodied the Faculties of Law and Medicine, the Engineering School, the School of Mines, the Faculty of Odontology, the National School of Fine Arts, and the National Institute of Music.

The University of Brazil was legally authorized on July 5, 1937, superseding the old University of Rio de Janeiro, and was provided with administrative, financial, educational and disciplinary autonomy, as well as with a new constitution, on December 17, 1945. The University now includes 14 faculties or schools, comprising pre-existent institutes and others which may eventually be created, the University College for complementary teaching, and the Nursing School, besides 17 scientific institutes.

In 1956 there were 23 universities, comprising 160 schools or faculties, and 188 independent faculties and institutes, bringing the total of higher teaching establishments to 348, which reported 78,659 enrollments.

Art, Literature, and Music. Brazil's contributions to the arts and literature are numerous and notable, which perhaps explains, in some measure, the lively interest of the average educated Brazilian in such pursuits. Machado de Assis, a psychological novelist, and Castro Alves, an epic poet, whose verse aided the successful fight for abolition of slavery, were writers of great distinction. Candido Portinari, realist painter and muralist, and Modestino Kanto, sculptor, have won international reputations. Brazilian music is gaining richly deserved popularity in the United States. Heitor Villa-Lobos, prolific impressionistic composer, and Carlos Gomes, a classicist and composer of the opera *Il Guarany,* have had enthusiastic receptions by United States critics. Guiomar Novaes, described by Ignace Paderewski as a superior pianist, has appeared frequently before United States audiences. Elsie Houston, lyric soprano, was popular throughout the Western Hemisphere; and Bidú Sayão is a leading soprano who has appeared with the Metropolitan Opera Company of New York.

HISTORY

Colonization. Pedro Álvarez Cabral is given credit for the discovery of Brazil in 1500, though others had skirted the northern coast before him. In order to protect the colony from foreign interlopers, John III of Portugal sent out coast patrols in 1526. Rumors of the existence of silver in the south prompted the king of Portugal to dispatch an expedition under a governor, Martim Affonso de Sousa, who in 1532 founded São Vicente, the first formal settlement. Soon after this the king partitioned the region, dividing it into *capitanias,* or captaincies, whose grantees acted as feudal lords. The disadvantages of this decentralized system led to the appointment in 1548-1549 of a governor general, Thomé de Souza, who founded the city of São Salvador, now called Bahia.

In 1555 an expedition of French Protestants under Nicolas Durand de Villegagnon established itself on the bay of Rio de Janeiro. They were ousted in 1567 by Mem de Sá, the third governor of Brazil, who founded the city of Rio de Janeiro in the same year. From 1581 to 1640, during the union of Portugal and Spain, Brazil fell prey to the enemies of Spain. English freebooters harassed the coast. The French settled in Maranhão but were forced out in 1615. The area was separated from the rest of Brazil in 1621 and called the State of Maranhão. The Dutch attacked Bahia in 1624-1625. Being repulsed there, they took Pernambuco in 1630, and until 1654 they controlled much of the territory around and to the north of that city. Count Maurice of Nassau, from 1637 to 1644 the most distinguished of the Dutch governors, introduced Protestantism and many reforms. In 1644 the Brazilians began a successful war against the Dutch, settled by the Hague Treaty of 1661.

The internal development of the colony in the seventeenth century witnessed the struggles of conflicting interests. In 1628 and succeeding years, slave-raiding expeditions of Paulistas, a frontier group of ruffians formed by intermarriage of Portuguese and Indians, destroyed the missions of the Jesuit fathers in the valley of the upper Paraná. The Jesuits appealed to higher authorities, whose decisions were met with derision by the Paulistas. They became noted for their cruelty as they spread through the interior of central and southern Brazil.

During the eighteenth century the excessive taxation imposed by the Portuguese government on gold extraction caused dissatisfaction among the people and led to uprisings. In 1710 fierce fighting broke out between the Paulistas and the Portuguese forces, which did not end until 1714. In 1720 another upheaval occurred, but the government forces defeated the rebels. The propagation of liberal ideas and especially the example given by the thirteen North American colonies, whose constitution was discussed behind closed doors, filled a group of Brazilian intellectuals with dreams of independence. In 1786 a group of Brazilian students in Paris approached the then United States Ambassador to France, Thomas Jefferson, and tried unsuccessfully to obtain his aid. Upon their return to Brazil, some of the students embarked upon a conspiracy with other groups, which spread throughout the country, but the Portuguese government discovered the plot and sentenced the leaders to life-imprisonment or hanging.

In November 1807 the Portuguese royal family and a host of noblemen and officials fled from Lisbon to Brazil before an invading French army; they arrived in Brazil in 1808. The regent, Dom John, set up his court in Rio de Janeiro, opened the ports of the country, established the first press, a medical school, and other institutions. He abolished many of the restrictions on trade and instituted other reforms. In 1815 Brazil was elevated to the status of equality with Portugal. This was one of the reasons why Brazil advanced so much more rapidly than Spanish-speaking countries in America. In 1821 Dom John VI incorporated Montevideo into Brazil as the Cisplatine Province. The transference of the court to Brazil with the vast expenditures involved, and the discrimination against Brazilians in important positions, caused a fruitless effort in Pernambuco in 1817 to set up a republic.

Independence. In 1821, King John returned to Portugal because of a constitutional revolution there, leaving his son Pedro as regent. The efforts of the Portuguese cortes to reduce Brazil to a colonial status irritated the Brazilians. José Bonifácio de Andrada e Silva, a man of extraordinary intelligence and judgment, dominated the situation in the years 1821-1823. A bloodless revolution brought independence from Portugal on Sept. 7, 1822, when Pedro was proclaimed emperor of Brazil. Although a colorful personality, Pedro I fell short of meeting Brazilian standards as an emperor. After his loss of a war with Argentina, his political opponents in the Brazilian parliament forced his abdication in favor of his five-year-old son.

After a ten-year regency, Pedro II, at the age of fourteen, assumed the throne in 1840. He proved to be an amiable and tolerant monarch, of studious tendencies, and he ruled with grace and wisdom for forty-nine years. During his reign the Amazon River territory was opened; rubber and coffee became important commodities; railroads and telegraph lines were built; and immigration was fostered. Education, museums, and libraries also received his attention. In 1850 a law ended the slave trade, and in 1871 the great statesman, Rio Branco, framed a law which freed all Negro children born after that date. Finally, in May 1888, a law of Congress abolished slavery altogether. Many of the planters, disgruntled because they were not indemnified, joined the military, liberals, and republicans in demanding a republic.

On Nov. 15, 1889, a republic was declared, and Pedro II was expelled from the country. An enlightened ruler, moderate, progressive, intelligent, and democratic, he was devoted to the welfare of Brazil. His involvement in wars with the Argentine dictator Rosas and the dictator Francisco Solano Lopez of Paraguay, did not prevent him from initiating an era of internal development aimed at freeing Brazil from its feudalism. But Pedro's refusal to allow army officers to enter political activity aroused their enmity; the large landholders were enraged by the decree ending slavery; and the republicans, whom the emperor had clandestinely en-

EARL LEAF FROM RAPHO-GUILLUMETTE

Jungle river settlement in the interior of Brazil

couraged, turned against him and demanded his abdication. In 1889 Pedro left his country, as he said, "for the good of Brazil."

The Republic. Marshal Deodoro da Fonseca, the military leader of the revolution, became provisional president in 1891, and after the promulgation of a federal constitution, the first constitutional president. He resigned the same year and was succeeded by the vice-president, Marshal Floriano Peixoto. A naval revolt in 1893-1894 was put down with difficulty. The president following Peixoto was Prudente de Moraes Barros (1894-1898), a Paulista, who checked militarism but was unable to solve the financial difficulties although he funded the foreign debt of the country. Manuel de Campos Salles (1898-1902), as president-elect, obtained a loan in Europe to avoid default on the public debt. This eased the financial situation. During his term and later, settlements of boundary disputes were ably negotiated by the great statesmen, Baron Rio Branco and Joaquim Nabuco. Under Francisco de Paula Rodrigues Alves (1902-1906) the beautifying, modernization, and sanitation of Rio de Janeiro took place. Dr. Oswaldo Cruz, noted Brazilian scientist, rid the city of yellow fever. In 1906 the political dominance of the state of São Paulo, which had usually succeeded in filling the presidency, was broken by the election of Affonso Penna, three times governor of Minas Gerais. He died in 1909 and was succeeded by Nilo Peçanha. Marshal Hermes da Fonseca won the election against the distinguished jurist, Ruy Barbosa, and served from 1910 to 1914. During this period a financial crisis, resulting from the fall of coffee and rubber prices, embarrassed the government. In 1917, under the presidency of Wenceslau Braz (1914-1918), Brazil declared war on Germany. Steps toward economic independence and economic progress were results of World War I. In 1919 Epitacio da Silva Pessôa, of Paraíba state, representing Brazil at the Paris Peace Conference, was elected to complete the term of Rodrigues Alves, who died soon after his re-election in 1918. Pessôa lost prestige by failure to develop certain irrigation projects in the northern states. Arthur da Silva Bernardes of Minas Gerais, elected in 1922, had to cope with a military revolution in 1924 and with an economic depression. In 1926, Washington Luiz Pereira de Souza, of São Paulo, known as "the Road Builder," was elected to serve until 1930. In 1930, Julio Prestes of São Paulo was declared elected as president. Getulio Vargas, president of the state Rio Grande do Sul, protested the election of Prestes and led a successful march on the capital at Rio de Janeiro. Vargas governed as provisional president until his election in 1934. Following a *coup d'état* in November 1937, forestalling a regular election in January 1938, Vargas established a dictatorship over Brazil as a corporate state. At a conference of twenty-one American republics held in Rio de Janeiro in January 1942, all the republics but Argentina and Chile voted to sever relations with the Axis nations. On August 22, after repeated submarine attacks on Brazilian ships, Brazil declared war on Germany and Italy. The war years brought a profound change in the economic, social, and international life of the nation. When World War II ended, the people demanded an end of their dictatorship under Getulio Vargas. His resignation was achieved in a bloodless revolution, on Oct. 29, 1945.

The presidential elections of Dec. 2, 1945, were the first held in Brazil in fifteen years and the fairest in all Brazilian history. They were also the largest ever held in Latin America. Of Brazil's 45,000,000 population more than 7,000,000 voters were registered. The principal candidates were two army officers: one mildly liberal on social questions, Brigadier General Eduardo Gomes; the other, a former war minister of President Vargas, General Eurico Gaspar Dutra. General Dutra was elected by a considerable majority. The large vote given to the Communist Party candidate, an unknown non-Communist, Yeddo Fiuza, was a surprise. The former dictator, Getulio Vargas, was himself elected a senator and swung many votes to General Dutra. Thus the conservatives were clearly in power, although the Communist senator, Luis Carlos Prestes, appeared as a strong political force.

Communism and Conservatism. Almost immediately the conservative Dutra administration and the active Communist Party came into conflict. Six months after the elections Brazil received an ambassador from the Soviet Union. When the Vargas control over the labor movement was relaxed by the new administration, the Communists developed their own influence in that quarter. The promotion of a hemisphere defense plan by the United States government aided the Brazilian government in moving against Communist influence. Inflation and high prices brought many strikes and food riots, which the government accused the Communists of promoting. Serious riots in Rio de Janeiro and a stevedores' strike in Santos led to the closing of Communist papers and the jailing of labor leaders. These suppressive measures, however, did not discourage the enthusiasm of large groups for a social revolution. Riots over the high cost of living caused many deaths and imprisonments.

Constitution of 1946. As a result of the work of a constitutional assembly called by President Dutra, a new constitution was proclaimed on Sept. 18, 1946. It mildly reflected the current social structure, but was not socialistic. It authorized congress "to intervene in the economic domain"; but "such intervention shall be based on the public interest and be limited to the fundamental rights guaranteed under the constitution." Foreigners were forbidden to own newspapers or radio stations or to receive government concessions for exploiting the country's mineral resources. Freedom of thought, religion, and expression, without limitation, was guaranteed. The Brazilian Immigration Council announced that the nation was ready to open its doors to at least 100,000 displaced persons of Europe, especially

PHILIP GENDREAU

Trucks at the market place on Rio de Janeiro's waterfront

agricultural workers, artisans, and technicians who would settle in rural sections and develop new communities.

Development of International Relations. Brazil has been noted for its well-trained diplomats and its leadership in international conferences. As the largest country in South America, with frontiers bordering on all but two of the other republics, it has been a strong advocate of settling disputes by arbitration. Brazil appointed its first minister to the United States in 1810, the latter country sending John Graham as minister to Rio de Janeiro. When President Monroe announced his doctrine of "America for Americans," Dom Pedro I, just two years after Brazilian independence, approved the doctrine. He sent a minister to Washington to suggest an alliance with the United States in order to defend the continent. In 1906 a great public building in Rio de Janeiro, which now houses the Federal Senate, was dedicated by United States Secretary of State Elihu Root as the "Monroe Palace." At Pan American conferences, Brazil has always defended the Monroe Doctrine. In both World Wars I and II Brazil followed the lead of the United States.

The great rival of Brazil is Argentina. This rivalry began in colonial days when the Portuguese and Spanish were struggling for dominance in eastern South America. Following independence, these rivalries continued, especially in efforts to control the buffer state of Uruguay, until that country's independence and sovereignty were established.

The prominent part played by Brazil in World War II enlarged its international influence. Brazil's armed forces were also strengthened, and co-operated with the United States and Great Britain in the South Atlantic campaign against German submarines. Brazil began to manufacture its own small warships. A net of landing fields on the "hump" of Brazil, centering at the port of Natal, which is 1,700 mi. from Dakar, Africa, made Natal one of the largest aviation centers in the world. Most of the material flown from the United States for the campaigns in North Africa and the Orient in 1942-1945, was routed via Natal. President Roosevelt used this route to attend his conference with Prime Minister Winston Churchill in Algeria. On his return trip on Jan. 28, 1943, he conferred with President Vargas concerning closer co-operation in winning the war and in the larger industrial development of Brazil.

Brazil has escaped many of the jealousies and fears which other American nations have felt toward each other as fellow members of the Pan American Union, where it has often acted as adjuster of differences between the other republics. Brazil has likewise maintained cordial relations with Europe.

FISHER · CUSHING

Rubber tree seedlings ready for transplanting

Great Britain occupied a pre-eminent place in Brazilian economic life until World War I, and France was Brazil's inspiration in the cultural world. Germany made a great bid for dominance in both realms, especially during the 1930's, but with the coming of World War II it was more than ever clear that Brazil definitely chose to be an American republic and desired to co-operate with the United States and the other American republics. At the same time Brazil entered the United Nations with enthusiasm and appointed its leading statesman to aid in the development of world government. In 1947 Oswaldo Aranha was elected president of the General Assembly of the United Nations.

General Eurico Dutra served his 5-year term as head of a colorless administration. Instead of the period of status quo desired by the landowners, clericals, and military, the country found itself in the midst of inflation, food riots, and communist plotting. In 1950, the old party candidates were swept aside and Vargas was recalled by a large majority, including both the impatient young industrialists and the exploited and poverty-stricken masses.

President Vargas took office again on Jan. 31, 1951, and promised to work under the constitution. But the new and complicated problems found no answer in the old coffee economy and political co-operation with the United States. An overwhelming nationalism and a strong underground communism definitely slowed his program. A surprising anti-American spirit appeared, which alarmed Washington and led to a special visit by Secretary of State Acheson in the summer of 1952. Besides the rapid rise of nationalism, other reasons for suspecting the United States were a feeling that the United States had forgotten its old friend, after exploiting Brazil during the war, and had shifted its attention to Europe, Asia, and even Argentina; the refusal of certain trade concessions and loans; accusations from the U. S. Senate that Brazil had rigged the coffee market; action of certain U. S. firms that seemed to partake of "Yankee imperialism," particularly in relation to contracts for exploiting Brazilian petroleum and aluminum; high-handed methods of collecting Brazilian bonds; and a disregard for Brazilian interests in sending accumulated bank balances to the United States. There was bad feeling on both sides when President Vargas issued a decree, later softened, controlling the export of profits on foreign capital, which led U. S. business to announce the cessation of investment in Brazil.

Especially revealing were the discussions concerning methods to be used in the exploitation of petroleum. While Brazil is supposed to have large deposits of oil, practically nothing has been done about its development for commercial use. Although the nation spends $725,000 a day for foreign petroleum, the state monopoly, Petrobrás, has made little headway in its efforts to explore Brazil's oil resources and thus render it free from imports, chiefly because of lack of adequate technical and financial resources. The fear of foreign trusts is too great, and it will thus be a long time before Petrobrás can finally amass sufficient money with which to carry out a large-scale program in petroleum exploration.

The related problem of the economic development of the country as a whole is constantly being tackled. The Joint Brazil-United States Economic Development Commission, an agency composed of skilled economists and specialists in the fields of agriculture, electric power, mining, transportation, and industry, and a part of the Point Four operations in Brazil, completed its work on Dec. 31, 1953. The Mutual Security Program in Brazil (Point Four) is one of technical co-operation, and its objective is to assist the Brazilian Government through training and demonstration projects that will contribute to the country's own plans for the rational development of its resources. Point Four Operations in Brazil include health and sanitation, agriculture, education, transportation, public administration, community development, minerals investigation, and tourism. The total cost of the Brazilian Government economic development program for the five-year period 1956-1960 is estimated at $2,840 million. The program proposes raising Brazil's electric power capacity to a total of 5.1 million kw. Investment in the oil industry is estimated at $719 million for the expansion of domestic production and the refining and transport of oil. Large sums will also be spent in the railway sector, in the development of air, road, and water transport, as well as in increased production of coal, steel, minerals, paper, and chemicals.

As a result of increasing corruption in the Vargas administration, the opposition party grew stronger. The attempted murder of a journalist who was Vargas' fiercest opponent, in August 1954, and which resulted in the killing of a young Brazilian Air Force officer, gave rise to great turmoil in the country. Having discovered that the attempt had been plotted by his own chief bodyguard, Vargas took his life on Aug. 24, 1954. Vice-President João Café Filho took over the government until Nov. 9, 1955. On Oct. 3, 1955, Juscelino Kubitschek de Oliveira, a former governor of the State of Minas Gerais, was elected president, with João Goulart, who might be termed Vargas' political heir, becoming vice president with the support of labor. Kubitschek was sworn in as president on Jan. 31, 1956, and several members of the former Vargas administration returned to power as a result of political compromises entered into by Kubitschek with the Brazilian Labor Party. Kubitschek has promised that Brazil will make considerable economic progress during his term of office, and has taken some measures envisaged to facilitate the entry of foreign capital into Brazil, especially for the basic industries. The opposition party, UDN (National Democratic Union), has been continuously fighting the government.   S. G. I. and G. A. S.

BRAZIL, a city in western Indiana, the county seat of Clay Co., 16 mi. northeast of Terre Haute, located in a rich coal, shale, and clay area. Brazil, founded in 1843, began as a stopping place for stagecoaches and the covered wagon trade. The discovery of coal fields stimulated the growth of the community at the end of the nineteenth century. As the deep coal mines worked out, the city turned to the production of clay products, manufacturing tile, bricks, ceramic textures, and other clay items. The coal industry has been revived by the development of machinery for opencut mining. Other industries produce tomato products, dairy products, floor finishes, furniture, roofing materials, flour, and domestic animal feeds. Pop. 1950, 8,434.

BRAZOS RIVER [brɑ′zos], one of the large rivers of Texas, flows for about 870 mi. from the junction of the Salt and Double Mountain forks in Stonewall Co. southeastward to the Gulf of Mexico. Its headwaters rise on the Llano Estacado and after cutting their way through an eroded escarpment reach an alluvial coastal plain. The Brazos flows through farm country mainly planted to cotton. It is navigable from 40 to 300 mi., depending upon the season.

The headwaters were probably reached by Coronado in 1541 and by De Soto's successor, Luis Morosco de Alvarado, in 1542; the lower reaches impeded La Salle in his effort to return to the Mississippi in 1687. The first settlement along the Brazos was Stephen Austin's initial colony at San Felipe in 1823. About a year later Josiah Bell established a town downriver which became Columbia; it subsequently became the first capital of the Republic of Texas. Brazoria, near the river's mouth, was established in 1826. The Declaration of Independence (Mar. 2, 1836), launching the Republic of Texas, was proclaimed at Washington, another town on the Brazos. On May 14, 1836 the treaty which concluded the Texas Revolution was signed at the Mexican port of entry of Velasco. This city, located at the river's mouth, had been the scene of a victorious Texan attack in 1832. A town was laid out in 1849 on a site inhabited by the Waco (Hueco) Indians before they were driven out by the Cherokees in 1829. A ferry crossing was established here. In 1870 the ferry was replaced by a single-span suspension bridge, still in use; when built, it was the only bridge across the Brazos and the longest of its type in the United States. The Brazos is used for municipal water supplies, for irrigation, and for

hydroelectric power. The Possum Kingdom Dam (above Mineral Springs) was built in 1940 and the Whitney Dam in 1953. At the river's mouth is the new industrial complex of Brazosport (comprising Velasco, Freeport, and other communities, with a total population of about 25,000). The Brazos River drains about 45,000 sq. mi.   E. A.

BRAZZAVILLE [brɑ′zɑ′vi′l], a river port and the capital of the territory of Middle Congo and of French Equatorial Africa, located on the right bank of Stanley Pool of the Congo River, on the southern border of the country. It is the largest town in French Equatorial Africa and is served by the Ocean Congo Railway. Formerly known as Ntamo, the town was renamed for Savorgnan de Brazza, French explorer, who in 1880 planted the French flag there. Brazzaville has become the governmental and commercial center for the region. The products which pass through for export include rubber, agricultural products, palm oil, cotton, coffee, lumber, and metals. Pop. 1950 est., 83,390.   A. K. D.

BREADFRUIT, an edible tropical fruit, growing on a broad-topped tree, *Artocarpus altilis,* of the mulberry family. The tree, a native of Polynesia, attains a height of about 40

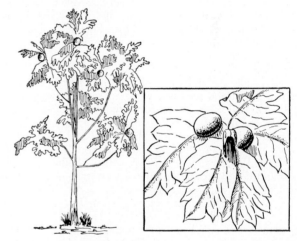

Outline of a Breadfruit tree, showing detail of the fruit and leaf

ft. and bears thick, deeply-lobed leaves, about two feet in length, and large clusters of yellow blossoms. The large, round fruit with a green husk is an essential part of the diet of the Polynesians. They usually bake it, and the resulting taste is like that of wheat bread. They also make flour from the dried slices of the breadfruit. They use the fibrous inner bark for the weaving of cloth and the wood of the tree for clothing and furniture; glue and calking material is derived from the viscous white juice. The jack fruit, *A. heterophyllus,* is used for lumber and has a fruit that is popular in India.

BREAM, a common name applied to various fishes in three different families. One of these, the salt-water bream, *Lagodon rhomboides,* of the porgy family, is often also called pinfish because of the long, sharp dorsal spines. It is found on the Atlantic coast from Cape Cod to Cuba. It attains a length of 10 in.; and it is utilized as a food fish in the south where it is more abundant than in the north.

In southeastern United States, many freshwater sunfishes are called bream or brim, especially the bluegill sunfish, *Lepomis macrochirus.* These are pan fishes of importance, although they seldom exceed a pound in weight.

The golden shiner, *Notemigonus crysoleucas,* a North American fresh-water minnow, is also called bream.

E. C. R.

BREASTED, JAMES HENRY [brɛ'stɛd] (1865-1935), American Egyptologist, archaeologist, and historian, was born in Rockford, Ill., on Aug. 27, 1865. He received his higher education at the Chicago Theological Seminary, Yale University, and the University of Berlin. In 1894 he became an assistant in Egyptology at the University of Chicago and in 1905 was promoted to a professorship in Egyptology and Oriental History. After he had attained competence as an Egyptologist, Breasted accepted a commission from the royal academies of Germany to copy and arrange the Egyptian inscriptions in the museums of Europe in order to facilitate the compilation of the Berlin Egyptian Dictionary. This commission provided him at the same time with the opportunity of gathering the material for his *Ancient Records of Egypt: Historical Documents from the Earliest Times to the Persian Conquest* (1906-1907), which remains a standard work. This work in turn laid the firm foundation for his *History of Egypt* (1905), and this, too, has become a standard text in its field.

Breasted's other works include *Ancient Times* (1916), a textbook on antiquity for high school and college students, *The Conquest of Civilization* (1926), and *The Dawn of Conscience* (1933), which deal with broad humanistic ideas. In the meantime, however, he did not abandon specific problems in his own specialty, and these have proved to be the most lasting products of his pen. His *Battle of Kadesh* (1903) is still a useful study of the world's first well-documented battle; and his finest work, which will probably remain standard after his other writings are superseded, is his monumental *Edwin Smith Surgical Papyrus* (1930).

Breasted, in addition to his philological and historical interests, was also an outstanding archaeologist. In 1905-1907 he directed an expedition to Egypt and the Sudan. In 1919, he founded and became director of the Oriental Institute of the University of Chicago, resumed his archaeological field work, and later organized expeditions in Egypt, Palestine, Turkey, Iraq, and Iran. The Oriental Institute has become the center of Middle East scholarship, archaeology, and publication in the Western Hemisphere. Breasted died on Dec. 2, 1935, in New York City.

C. H. Go.

BRÉBEUF, ST. JEAN DE [brɛ'bœ'f] (1593-1649), Jesuit missionary martyr of North America, was born at Condé-sur-Vire in Normandy, Mar. 25, 1593. After his ordination he went to Quebec, in June 1625, to work among the Huron Indians, and there he experienced great hardships and sharp reversals. Choosing not to flee when the Iroquois attacked the village in which he was working, he was captured, underwent a mock baptism by boiling water, and was tortured to death with hot irons, Mar. 16, 1649. With seven martyred companions he was canonized in 1930, September 25 being assigned as their feast.

W. C.

BRECCIA [brɛ'tshiə], a rock consisting of cemented angular fragments. Breccias differ from conglomerates, which are composed of water-worn, water-deposited pebbles, both in shape of component fragments and in origin. There are several varieties of breccia, each of which is formed by quite different processes. The simplest, and probably the rarest, type is talus breccia, which is created by the cementation of the angular debris (talus) that has accumulated at the foot of a cliff. Another variety is founder or collapse breccia, formed by the collapse of overlying rock into a cave.

Fault or friction breccia is created along a fault plane by movement of one wall of the fault against the other. Cementation of coarse volcanic *ejectamenta* produces volcanic breccia. A pseudobreccia, called replacement breccia, may be produced by irregular replacement, leaving angular masses of unreplaced "host" mineral surrounded by the replacing "guest" mineral.

K. K. L.

BRECHIN [bri'χɪn], a royal municipal burgh and market town in Angus, in the North Angus and Mearns parliamentary division, Scotland, situated on the south Esk River, about 25 mi. northeast of Dundee. David I created a bishopric here in 1150, which was continued as a see of the Episcopal Church of Scotland. The thirteenth-century Holy Trinity cathedral (the parish church, restored), has adjoining it a round tower built in 1000 or earlier. Brechin castle, once used as a fort, is the residence of the earls of Dalhousie. Industries include flax-spinning, linen manufacture, bleaching, rope and paper making, distilling, and iron founding. Pop. 1956 (est.), 7,400.

BRECHT, BERTOLT [brɛ'χt, bɛr'tolt] (1898-1956), German dramatist and essayist, was born in Augsburg on Feb. 10, 1898. He was awarded the Kleist Prize in 1922, an early recognition of his original work as a dramatist. An implacable foe of National Socialism, he went into exile in 1933. After living in the Soviet Union, Sweden, and the United States, he spent the last ten years of his life in East Germany as a strong supporter of the Communist-dominated regime.

At the beginning of his career as a dramatist, Brecht was an Expressionist, as demonstrated in his *Trommeln in der Nacht* (1922; "Drums at Night"), *Baal* (1922), and *Im Dickicht der Städte* (1927; "In the Thicket of the Cities"). His acceptance of Marxian socialism then led to an orientation toward literary realism. But for all his communist convictions, Brecht never ceased to introduce innovations. Most of his plays are supplemented by essayistic notes which explain his esthetic views. Brecht's later plays show four main characteristics: 1, the epic element, by which the plays emphasize pointed presentations of social conflicts and treat dramatic protagonists as mere exponents; 2, the didactic element, by which the plays attempt to educate the audience concerning its social position; 3, music, to provide a greater emotional impact; and 4, adaptation of stories and plays by other writers.

Of this dramatic doctrine, *Die Dreigroschenoper* (1931; *Threepenny Opera,* 1949) is the best example; it also has proved its most successful one. It is an adaptation of John Gay's *The Beggars' Opera* (1728) with music by Kurt Weill. Notable among Brecht's later plays, for which Paul Dessau provided the music, are: *Mutter Courage und ihre Kinder* (1949; *Mother Courage,* 1955), after Grimelshausen; *Der gute Mensch von Sezuan* (1953; *The Good Woman of Setzuan,* 1948); *Herr Puntila und sein Knecht Matti* (1950; "Mr. Puntila and His Servant Matti"), after Wuolijoki; and *Der kaukasische Kreidekreis* (1954; *The Caucasian Chalk Circle,* 1948), adapted from an old Chinese tale. *Furcht und Elend des Dritten Reiches* (1945; *The Private Life of the Master Race,* 1944) is a bitter satire in dramatic form. Brecht died in Berlin, Aug. 14, 1956.

G. L.

BRECKENRIDGE [brɛ'kənrij], the seat of Stephens Co. in north central Texas, is a center for local petroleum production, farming, and livestock raising. Its manufactures include rotary and cable tools, fabricated steel and aluminum, sheet metal, shirts, gloves, and ceramics. Transportation is provided by the Chicago, Rock Island and Pacific Railroad and Continental Air Lines. Founded in 1878 and incorporated in 1919, its population rose to 30,000 after the oil boom of 1920. Breckenridge is governed by a city commission. Lake Daniel, the source of its water, is 8 mi. from the city. Pop. 1950, 6,610.

BRECKINRIDGE, JOHN CABELL [brɛ'kɪnrɪj] (1821-1875), American politician and soldier, was born near Lexington, Ky., Jan. 21, 1821. He was graduated from Centre College (Ky.) in 1838, attended the College of New Jersey, and studied law at Transylvania University. He practiced law at Frankfort, Ky. in 1840; at Burlington, Iowa, from 1841 to 1843; and afterward at Lexington. Breckinridge served in the Mexican War. In 1849 he was elected by the Democrats to the Kentucky legislature and in 1851 to the United States House of Representatives, where he served until 1856. In that year he was elected vice-president of the United States on the ticket headed by James Buchanan. Although Breckinridge was an ardent states' rights man and favored slavery, his presidency of the Senate during the turbulent pre-Civil War period was conducted without partiality. As presidential nominee of the southern Democrats in 1860 he received seventy-two electoral votes. He succeeded John J. Crittenden as United States senator from Kentucky in March 1861, but in December, after he had joined the Confederate Army, he was expelled. Commissioned a brigadier general, he was promoted to major general in August 1862. Breckinridge distinguished himself as a soldier; he fought at Shiloh, Baton Rouge, Chickamauga, and Newmarket, where he defeated Union troops commanded by General Franz Sigel. Jefferson Davis, president of the Confederacy, appointed him Secretary of War in January 1865, a post he held until the collapse of the Confederacy. He escaped to Europe by way of Cuba, but returned to the United States in 1868. He resumed his law practice at Lexington, where he died on May 17, 1875.   D. R.

BRECKNOCKSHIRE [brɛ'knəkshɪr], a border county of South Wales. It is bounded on the north by Radnorshire, on the east by Herefordshire, on the southeast by Monmouthshire, on the south by Glamorganshire, on the southwest by Carmarthenshire, and on the northwest by Cardiganshire and has a total area of 733 sq. mi. The Usk valley divides it into two main parts, with the Mynydd Epynt to the north and the Brecon Beacons to the south. The latter, with peaks of 2,906 ft. (Pen-y Fan) and 2,863 ft. (Corn Du), are the highest mountains in South Wales. East of the Llyfni valley are the Black Mountains, the loftiest being Wann Fach (2,660 ft.). The county slopes east and south, the chief rivers, none of them navigable, being the Wye, which rises in the Plynlimmon Range and forms part of the Radnor border, the Nedd and Taff, which rise in the Beacons, and the Tawe, which rises in the eastern slopes of the Black Forest Mountains. Llyn Safaddan is the largest natural lake in South Wales. The wettest districts are in the south and west. Rainfall varies from 60 to 80 in. in the Beacons region; Bwlch has recorded 135 in. annual rainfall. The average January temperature is between 30° and 40° F.; the average July temperature is 62° F.

Sheep-breeding is the chief industry and most of the wool is exported, although there is a small woolen industry. In the fertile valleys, especially that of the Wye, grains, turnips, and potatoes are grown and butter and cheese are produced. Coal mining and slate-, sandstone-, and limestone-quarrying

are also important industries. A railroad from Hereford to Neath crosses the county via Hay, Talgarth, and Brecknock, with a branch to Merthyr Tydfil, and another crosses it from near Builth to Llanwrtyd Wells. The latter route is the London, Midland & Scottish Railway; all others in the county belong to the Great Western Railway. Brecon, or Brecknock, the county seat, is centrally located on the Usk. Other chief towns are Talgarth, Hay, and Builth Wells. With Radnor, Brecknockshire returns one member to the British Parliament.

The term Brecknock is derived from the Welsh *Brycheiniog,* Land of Brychan, Welsh Prince of Garth Madryn in 400-450. The Silures were conquered by Ostorius Scapula and Julius Frontinus, Roman generals. The Saxons first entered South Wales in 728. The last native prince, overthrown by the Normans about 1091, was Bernard de Newmarch, who governed as Lord Marcher with almost regal powers. Title passed to the Fitzwalter, de Breos, and de Bohun families, the earls of Buckingham, and finally to the crown. The county was formed in 1536, and English law became universal in Wales. Sir Bartle Frere (1815-1884), statesman and colonial administrator, was the most distinguished native. Traces of Roman Bannium (Caer Bannau) remain, as do the keeps of Brecon and Hay castles. Pop. 1952, 56,200.

BRECON or **BRECKNOCK** [brɛ'kən; brɛ'knək], a municipal borough and cathedral and market town and the county seat of Brecknockshire, Wales, situated in the Brecon and Radnor parliamentary division, at the joining of the Honddu and Usk rivers, about 38 mi. northwest of Cardiff. In 1072 the district was conquered by Bernard de Newmarch, who built a castle and abbey here. The castle, around which the town developed, was demolished by the townspeople in the civil wars, to preserve neutrality. Thirteenth and fourteenth century additions to the remains of the Norman church, make it one of the notable cathedrals in Wales. The earliest recorded charter was granted by an earl of Hereford; others were given by Queen Mary in 1536, and later, by Queen Elizabeth. Brecon became a municipal borough in 1835. Industries include cloth weaving and leather working. Pop. 1952, 6,671.

BREDA [breda'], a city in the province of North Brabant, in the southern part of the Netherlands, 24 mi. southwest of 's Hertogenbosch, on the Merk and Aa rivers, at 51° 34′ N. lat. and 4° 48′ E. long. The city has rail connections with Roosendaal and Tilburg, and has good docks, its two rivers having been canalized.

Breda is known to have been a fief of the Holy Roman Empire in the eleventh century and to have received municipal rights in 1252. When Philip, Lord of Breda, died in 1323, his heiress, Alix, sold it to the House of Brabant. Marriage between a member of this house and Engelbert I of Nassau-Dillenburg gave Breda to the House of Nassau in 1404, and thus in the sixteenth century its lord was William the Silent. Spanish forces captured Breda in 1581, but in 1590 Breda was taken by seventy Dutch soldiers hidden in a ship loaded with peat. From 1624 to 1625 the town was subjected to an eleven-month siege, ending in its surrender to Ambrogio di Spinola, Italian general in Spanish service, a scene made memorable in one of Velázquez' most famous paintings. The Dutch under Frederick Henry of Orange retook the town in 1637, and the Treaty of Westphalia, signed in 1648, ceded Breda to Holland. In 1667 the Peace of Breda was signed there, ceding Dutch colonies in North America, including specifically New Amsterdam (New York), to the

English. During the French Revolutionary Wars the town was taken in February 1793 by Gen. Charles François Dumouriez, who was forced to abandon the town in April of the same year; the French under Gen. Charles Pichegru recaptured the town in the winter of 1795. When, however, Russian forces under Gen. Alexander K. Benckendorff approached Breda in December 1813 and the French sallied forth to meet them, the patriotic citizenry shut the city gates and rallied to the defense of their town, thereby preventing the French from returning. The city sustained considerable damage during World War II when it was bombed by the Germans in May 1940. In the fall of 1944, Breda was liberated by Allied troops after the recapture of Antwerp.

Breda, the see of a Roman Catholic bishop, is noted for the Church of Our Lady (now Protestant), a Gothic structure built in the thirteenth century and containing the tombs of Engelbert II of Nassau and of Henry of Nassau, and for its fine town hall and park. It is also the site of the Royal Military Academy, which occupies the ancient Nassau castle, restored in 1696 by William, prince of Orange and king of England.

The city's manufactures include leather goods, matches, paint, textiles, rayon, canned foods, enamel, carpets, furniture, beer, wine, and liquors. It is also a market center. Pop. 1952, 92,731.   B. L.

BREDERO, GERBRAND ADRIAANSZOON [bre′dəro] (1585-1618)

BREDERO, GERBRAND ADRIAANSZOON [bre′dəro] (1585-1618), Dutch poet and dramatist, was born in Amsterdam on Mar. 16, 1585, and died on July 8, 1618. His youth was intemperate in a Bohemian fashion, and he wavered constantly between a full, rowdy enjoyment of life and a sense of remorse and piety. Bredero was the most personal, revealing lyricist of the Dutch poets of the seventeenth century, and his work reveals his problems and personality as very close to those of the sensitive present-day man. He lacked the classical training and scholarship of Pieter Hooft and Joost van den Vondel, but he knew the ways of the humble people of Amsterdam. His poetry has a sweet, charming sentimentality, which is always moving without ever becoming vulgar; it is extremely melodious and supple, and, indeed, most of his lyrics were put to music or written to be sung to known arias. His amorous complaints, which are many and of great beauty, are never hampered by the use of Classical or mythological allusions: he is always straightforward and harmonious.

Several of Bredero's poems describe the rather violent kermises (outdoor festivals) of his countrymen, and he looks at these colorful and often bloody events with the ironic detachment of the city-dweller. He was deeply rooted in his native environment and he imitated nobody.

As a dramatist Bredero wrote one masterpiece, *De Spaansche Brabander* (1618), a biting satire on the bankrupt Antwerp dandies who fled to safety in Holland and who used to look down on the Dutch while imitating Spanish fashions in a hollow display of *grandezza*. Among his other comedies are *De Klucht van de Koe* (1612) and *Moortje* (1615).

J.-A. G.

BRÉGUET, LOUIS [bre′gɛ′] (1880-1955), pioneer airplane designer, was born in Paris on Jan. 2, 1880. He was educated at the Condorcet and Carnot lycées and at the École Supérieure d'Électricité. In 1905 he began work on a gyroplane (helicopter) with flexible wings, in collaboration with Charles Richet and his brother Jacques Bréguet, which lifted itself and its pilot in 1907. His interest in airplanes began shortly after this, and he pioneered, with others, in the construction of metal aircraft before 1914. In his model of

1910, the wing had a single spar consisting of a steel tube of large diameter. His Bréguet-14 day bomber and reconnaissance airplane was made entirely of aluminum except for wooden wing ribs and fuselage fairings and the fabric covering. This bomber was a mainstay of the French Army in World War I and through the 1920's, and was used by sixteen squadrons of the American Expeditionary Force. Bréguet built several military and commercial airplanes and seaplanes, but returned to the gyroplane in 1935, working on a design which flew by a combination of blade flapping and feathering. He continued this work during the German occupation and after World War II. Bréguet also studied bird flight and engine cooling. He never abandoned the large airplane, however, and after World War II has continued the development of commercial transports. He died on May 4, 1955, in Paris.   M. H. Sm.

BREHON LAWS. *See* IRELAND (*History*).

BREITENFELD, BATTLE OF [brɑi′tənfɛlt], an important military engagement of the Thirty Years' War fought Sept. 17, 1631, near Leipzig, Germany, between the joint Swedish and Protestant German forces under Gustavus Adolphus of Sweden and the Catholic forces under the Count of Tilly. The outcome was a victory for Gustavus Adolphus and gave military superiority to the Protestant forces for the first time since the outbreak of the war some thirteen years earlier.   M. K.

BREMEN [bre′mən], a city and an autonomous *Land* (state) in the (West) German Federal Republic. Lying near the mouth of the Weser River, the *Land,* composed of the two cities Bremen and Bremerhaven, has an area of 155.94 sq. mi. and in 1953 had a population of 607,900. In 1871, under the German Empire, Bremen became an autonomous republic, governed by a senate and a lower house. In January 1919, Communists proclaimed it a Soviet state, but were suppressed by government troops; the majority socialists then established a democratic constitution, but in 1933, with the Nazis in power, Bremen was reduced to a purely administrative division. After World War II, Bremen was reconstituted as a state with its boundaries remaining the same as those under the German Republic. The new constitution, adopted in a popular referendum on Oct. 17, 1947, placed the political power in the House of Burgesses. This House appoints the executive body, which is a senate composed of thirteen senators and a president.

Germany's second seaport and capital of the *Land* of Bremen, the city lies on a plain astride the Weser River, 45 mi. above the river's North Sea mouth. Although severely damaged in World War II, most of the city's harbor facilities, particularly those of Bremerhaven, the outer port, were repaired so that the port could be used by American occupation forces, thus restoring some of Bremen's economic life; but recovery since the war was less spectacular than that of Hamburg, Bremen's rival maritime commercial center. The city also has shipbuilding, jute-spinning, oil-refining, and grain-milling industries, and there are food-processing and chemical plants. Other manufactures include automobiles, trucks, and marine equipment. Bremen has long specialized in the shipping and brokerage of cotton, tobacco, and coffee. Former buildings of note that were war-scarred or destroyed include the Gothic town hall, the guild hall, St. Peter's Cathedral, and the Church of St. Ansgarius.

In 788 Charlemagne established a bishopric at the trading village of Bremen, a fact that marks it as the oldest port town of Germany. The archbishopric of Bremen, established in 850, controlled the growing town until the thirteenth century, when the burghers took over the town government and joined the Hanseatic League, in which Bremen subsequently became extremely prominent. In 1522 the city accepted the Reformation, an allegiance still preserved, for the population is predominantly Protestant. The Peace of Westphalia placed the largest part of Bremen under the ducal rule of Sweden in 1648, but in 1741 the town recovered its rights as an imperial free city. Bremen was annexed to France in 1810 by Napoleon as the department of "the mouths of the Weser," but it had joined the German Confederation by 1815, the North German Confederation in 1867, and, as an autonomous state, the German Empire in 1871. Pop. 1953, 483,500.

W. O. S.

BREMERHAVEN [brɛ'mǝrhevǝn; bremǝrhɑ'fǝn], a seaport in the state of Bremen, in northwestern Germany, 39 mi. north of the city of Bremen, on the Weser River where the Geeste joins the estuary. Although much of the city was ruined in World War II when its docks and buildings were bombed, Bremerhaven is still the biggest fishing harbor of the Continent, and, besides its extensive fishpacking and shipbuilding industries, has a heavy passenger traffic, since large liners cannot be accommodated in Bremen. Founded in 1827 on land purchased from Hannover and later enlarged, the city rapidly expanded as a harbor by serving as Bremen's outer port; in 1939 it was absorbed by Wesermünde, a Hannoverian city to the south, but by 1947 the whole municipality, which had been the chief supply port for the American occupation forces, was renamed Bremerhaven and returned to the state of Bremen. Pop. 1953, 124,400.

C. C. H.

BREMERTON [brɛ'mǝrtǝn], a port city in Kitsap Co., western Washington, is located on Sinclair Inlet, an arm of Puget Sound, about 15 mi. southwest of Seattle. It has the commission form of government. Bremerton was incorporated in 1901, and in 1918 annexed the town of Manette. In 1928 it was consolidated with the city of Charleston. Bremerton is the seat of Olympic College, founded in 1946. The Puget Sound naval base and shipyard, located in the city, were extremely active during World War II, a period in which Bremerton's normal population was greatly expanded. The naval base is one of the home ports of the Pacific Fleet, and the city's most important industry is shipbuilding. Bremerton's proximity to the Olympic Mountains and Hood Canal makes it a popular vacation center. Pop. 1950, 27,678.

BRENAU COLLEGE, a privately controlled, accredited, nonsectarian college for women located in Gainesville, Ga., was established in 1878 as the Georgia Female Seminary. The present name was adopted in 1900. The A.B. and B.S. degrees are conferred. Students live in residences or in sorority houses. Scholarship aid is available. *For statistics see* COLLEGES AND UNIVERSITIES.

BRENDAN, ST. [brɛ'ndǝn] (c.484-577) of Clonfert, Irish saint, was born about 484, at what is now Tralee in County Kerry. He was baptized by Bishop Erc, a relative, and nursed by St. Ita. When he was five years old, Bishop Erc took charge of his education. In 512, he was ordained a presbyter. The legend is that Brendan had a vision of a mysterious and delightful land "far from human ken," and an angel appeared to him urging him to go in search of it for God would grant it to him. Brendan is then said to have set out in a small boat covered with hides in search of the promised land. After seven years of wandering, a voice urged him

EWING GALLOWAY

PORT OF BREMEN, GERMANY

to return to Ireland, for there was work to be done there. Five years later he set out again in search of the land of delight, this time accompanied by sixty companions.

The wanderings of St. Brendan were described in one of the most popular of the medieval legends, *The Navigation of St. Brendan.* According to that legend, which mentions only one voyage, Brendan and his companions reached the Terra Repromissionis. People for a long time believed that St. Brendan's Island existed, and a number of expeditions were organized for the express purpose of finding that island described in the legend. The island was often identified with the Fortunate Isles of the ancients. It was variously located by cartographers west of or among the Canary Islands, it was identified with the island of Madeira, and it was even placed as far away as the West Indies. According to Columbus, the inhabitants of the Azores had declared having seen that island. Another theory maintained that the island referred to in the legend disappeared in the Atlantic. According to more recent theories, St. Brendan must have reached the Western Continent. Others merely deny the authenticity of the story.

St. Brendan founded a number of monasteries in Ireland, and it was said that he had more than 3,000 monks under him. The rules of his monasteries were greatly appreciated and were preserved for a long time after his death. He founded notably the monastery of Cluain Ferta (Clonfert) in County Longford. This monastery became the most famous school of Western Ireland. He also founded the monastery at Annaghdown, County Galway, which he placed in charge of his sister Brigh. He died at Annaghdown in 577.

St. Brendan belongs to the second order of Irish saints and is one of the twelve apostles of Ireland. His feast is May 16.

BRENHAM [brɛ'nǝm], the county seat of Washington Co., southeastern Texas, is situated 80 mi. east of Austin. Brenham was founded in 1844 and became a city in 1873. It is a shipping center for livestock, cotton, and grain, and its industries produce machinery, farm implements, cotton, and cottonseed-oil products. Brooms, packed meat, and upholstered furniture are other manufactures. Brenham is the seat of Blinn College. Pop. 1950, 6,941.

BRENNER, VICTOR DAVID (1871-1924), American medalist and sculptor, was born in Shavli, Russia, of American parents on June 12, 1871. In 1890 he came to the United States and worked for several years as a die cutter, but felt the urge to do creative art in metals. He studied in Paris, beginning in 1898 under Louis Oscar Roty, and won prizes for exhibits at the Paris Exposition of 1900 and at the Salon

The Brenner Pass, on the Italo-Austrian border, is the shortest route through the Alps from Italy to Austria.

of the same year. He received awards for his work at the Pan-American Exposition at Buffalo in 1901, and at the Louisiana Purchase Exposition in St. Louis in 1904. Among the prominent museums which have samples of Brenner's medals and sculpture are the Metropolitan Museum of New York, the Paris Luxembourg and the Munich Glyptothek. His portrait medals of Theodore Roosevelt, James Whistler, Carl Schurz, W. M. Evarts, and others are widely known. His best-known work, however, is his design for the United States Lincoln penny. He created the seals of the Fine Arts Federation of New York, and of the New York Public Library. Harvard University possesses his bust of Charles Eliot Norton, in the Fogg Museum in Cambridge. Brenner died in New York, Apr. 6, 1924.

BRENNER PASS [brɛ'nər], an important Alpine pass at 4,495 ft. above sea level and about 25 mi. south of Innsbruck on the Austro-Italian border. It forms a watershed between the Sill River, whose waters flow northward into the Inn River and eventually the Danube River, and the Isarco River, flowing south into the Adige River and the Adriatic Sea. The lowest of the Alpine passes, the Brenner has been traveled since Roman times, and is the shortest route between Italy and central Germany. A carriage road was constructed through the pass in 1772 and a railroad in 1867, using thirty tunnels and sixty large bridges. Both sides of the pass were controlled by Austria for many years, but at the close of World War I, the Italian border was extended northward to it.   S. Van V.

BRENT, CHARLES HENRY (1862-1929), Canadian-American bishop and one of the early leaders in the movement towards the reunion of Christian communions, was born in Newcastle, Ontario, on Apr. 9, 1862. Educated at Trinity College, Toronto, where he took his B.A. in 1884, he was ordained to the priesthood of the Episcopal Church in 1887. After serving in several parishes, he was elected bishop of the Philippines in 1901, serving there until 1918. In the latter year he became Bishop of Western New York and remained in that office until 1926, when he was chosen as the bishop in charge of Episcopal churches in Europe for the next two years. In the period between his election to the Philippines and his death, Bishop Brent developed a strong interest in the reunion of Christian churches; he traveled extensively, attended the so-called "ecumenical conferences" at Lausanne and Stockholm, and was chairman of the committee for the continuation of the conferences. He was also deeply concerned with the problem of narcotics and headed the League of Nations commission on opium control. Bishop Brent died in Switzerland, Mar. 27, 1929.   W. N. P.

BRENTANO, CLEMENS MARIA [brɛnta'no] (1778-1842), German poet, novelist, and playwright, was born at Ehrenbreitstein on the Rhine, Sept. 8, 1778. He was the son of Peter Anton Brentano, a native of Italy, and his wife, Maximiliane, who was a daughter of the novelist Sophie von La Roche. Both mother and daughter were one-time friends of Goethe. Brentano was connected by blood or marriage with several distinguished figures of later German Romanticism, notably his sister Bettina (1785-1859), her husband Achim von Arnim (1781-1831), and the eminent jurist Friedrich Karl von Savigny (1779-1861). After an unhappy childhood and adolescence, followed by a futile attempt at business, he attended the universities of Bonn and Jena. Later he resided in Heidelberg, Vienna, and Berlin. At Heidelberg he was associated with the leading writers of the time, and published, together with von Arnim, an anthology of German folk-poetry, *Des Knaben Wunderhorn* (3 vols., 1806-1808), which was destined to influence widely the development of German lyric poetry and to overshadow Brentano's own remarkable poetic accomplishments.

After the death in 1806 of his first wife, the novelist Sophie Mereau, Brentano contracted a second marriage of brief and unhappy duration. A decade of restless wandering up and down Germany ensued. The brilliant but erratic poet seemed unable to find anchorage, until in 1817 he returned to the Catholic faith, in which he had been born. From then on his life was spent in the service of religion; his most important work was an account of the stigmatic mystic Katharina Emmerich. During his last years his literary activity was limited mostly to revisions of earlier writings. He died at Aschaffenburg, July 28, 1842.

Brentano is at his best in lyric poetry, in which he displays intense emotional power and great grace of form. His purest lyric note is derived from the *Volkslied*. His poetry reflects many moods: wild fantasy, deep piety, irony, humor, and tragedy. He is particularly skilled in blending sense impressions: seeing tones, for example, and hearing colors. His use of imagery is often obscure. As is true of many other Romantics, only Brentano's shorter works can be considered great—a judgment especially applicable to his prose. He wrote the novel, *Godwi* (1800-1802), and a number of plays, but his best works, other than his poems, are three short stories: *Die Geschichte von dem braven Kasperl und dem schönen Annerl* (1817), a realistic tragic tale; *Die Chronika eines fahrenden Schülers* (1818); and *Gockel, Hinkel und Gackeleia* (1838), a fairy tale.   D. F. C.

BRENTANO, FRANZ (1838-1917), German philosopher and psychologist, was born at Marienburg, June 16, 1838. He entered the Roman Catholic priesthood, and in 1866 became docent in philosophy at Würzburg and a professor in 1872. Unable to accept the dogma of papal infallibility, he withdrew in 1873 from the professorship and priesthood, and in 1874 became professor of philosophy at Vienna until 1880. In 1896 he moved to Florence, Italy. He died Mar. 17, 1917, at Zürich, Switzerland. Brentano's fame rests on his *Psychologie vom empirischen Standpunkt* (1874). His psychology was empirical, but not experimental; it dealt not with mental content, but with mental activities and their "intention." He had an important influence upon later German and English psychologists.   F. A. K.

BRENTFORD AND CHISWICK [tshɪ'zɪk], a municipal and parliamentary borough, about 9 mi. west of central London, in Middlesex, England, at the joining of the Brent and Thames rivers, and on the Grand Junction Canal. In 1927, by the Middlesex Confirmation Order, the former urban districts of Brentford and Chiswick were amalgamated, and in 1932 by royal charter they were incorporated under the name of Brentford and Chiswick. For parliamentary purposes the borough forms the Brentford and Chiswick division of Middlesex. There are evidences of prehistoric British and early Roman settlements nearby. In 1016 Edmund Ironside defeated the Danes at Brentford. A toll and market were granted by Edward I to raise funds to build a bridge across the river. Syon House, built in 1547, was later enlarged by Inigo Jones and remodelled by Robert Adam. During the sixteenth and seventeenth centuries the town was a gathering place for London writers, and in the churchyard of St. Nicholas is the grave of William Hogarth, the artist. The Chiswick Press was founded in 1811 by Charles Whittingham. The town is largely residential, but on the outskirts are breweries, soap factories, sawmills, and market gardens. Pop. 1952, 59,970.

BRENTWOOD, a borough in Alleghany Co., in western Pennsylvania, a residential suburb adjoining Pittsburgh. It was incorporated as a borough in 1915 with the merger of the villages of Brentwood, Whitehall, and Point View. Brentwood is governed by a burgess and council. Pop. 1950, 12,535.

BRESCIA [bre'shɑ], a province and its capital in eastern Lombardy, northern Italy.

The City. Brescia is situated 52 mi. east of Milan at the point where the Garza River joins the Po Plain, at an elevation of 475 ft. above sea level. The city lies along the age-old route that skirts the pre-Alpine foothills at the northern edge of the Lombardo-Venetian Plain. It is on the main railway line between Milan and Venice, as well as on several branch lines. Brescia is connected with Milan and Turin by a superhighway.

Brescia possesses numerous industries whose manufactures include iron, steel, aluminum, and glass products, processed foods, and firearms. The city is generally flat and was formerly surrounded by walls, now replaced in part by gardens and boulevards. It is overlooked from the northeast by the imposing Visconti Castle. Among the numerous monuments of interest are the Renaissance Loggia; the Broletto, a palace begun in the twelfth century; various Roman remains, including a statue of the Winged Victory; the old Romanesque cathedral (eleventh-twelfth centuries); and the churches of San Francesco, Santi Nazzaro e Celso, and Madonna della Grazie. Local museums contain interesting archaeological and art works. Many buildings were damaged or destroyed during World War II, including the seventeenth-century Salvadego Palace, of which only the frescoes remain, and Santa Maria dei Miracoli (fifteenth-sixteenth century), whose portico was saved. The modernistic Piazza della Vittoria was built during the Fascist regime.

Known to the Romans as Brixia, the city became an important center under the Roman Empire. In 452 it was sacked by Attila and later became the seat of a Lombard duchy. By the tenth century it was a commune, an outgrowth of the political power of the local bishop. Brescia joined actively in the regional wars and in the Lombard League against imperial pretensions. Beginning in the fourteenth century the city was subject to a succession of overlords—Scala, Visconti, Malatesta, and others. From 1426 to 1797 it belonged to the Venetian Republic, under whose rule there was usually prosperity, if not always peace. After the fall of Napoleon in 1815 it came under Austrian rule. Known as a nationalist revolutionary city, in March 1849 Brescia resisted the Hapsburg troops so forcefully it became known as the "Lioness of Italy." It became part of the Kingdom of Italy in 1860. Pop. 1954, 146,800.

The Romanesque cathedral, called La Rotonda, at Brescia, Italy

LINDSLEY F. HALL

The Province. The province of Brescia has an area of 1,834 sq. mi., comprising 196 communes. It embraces the upper valley of the Oglio River, the piedmont region (Val Camonica) between lakes Leso and Garda, and a section of the northern Po Plain. It ranges in altitude from the Adamello (11,700 ft.) to 125 ft. along the lower Oglio.

In the mountain zone, lumbering is a leading activity; in the intermediate hills, viniculture; and along the two lakes, olive and citrus fruit cultivation. On the plain, forage crops and cereals predominate. Silkworm culture and cattle grazing are also important. Small properties predominate in the mountains, and large estates in the lowlands. Towns of interest in the province, besides the capital, are Chiari, where Eugene of Savoy defeated the French in 1701; Desenzano del Garda and Gardone, resorts on Lake Garda; Sirmione, a health resort; and Salo, temporary capital of Mussolini's last government. Pop. (est. 1954), 871,900.

R. G. W.

BRESLAU, UNIVERSITY OF, since 1946 the University of Wroclaw (Uniwersytet Wroclawin), was founded at Frankfurt-on-the-Oder in 1702. The university church at Frankfurt-on-the-Oder, built by the Jesuits, dates from 1689, and the university buildings, in baroque style, were completed in 1728. At its inception the university included the faculties of Catholic theology and philosophy but to these were added later those of evangelical theology, medicine, and law. In 1741 Frederick the Great favored the university of the Jesuits with his protection, but in 1773 the Jesuit order was suppressed and the university acquired a new temporal status. Because the University of Berlin, founded in 1811, became a strong competitor, the university at Frankfurt-on-the-Oder was moved by Frederick William III to Breslau and merged with the Leopoldina school in that year. A further reorganization under the name University of Wroclaw was made in 1946. In 1948 the university consisted of the faculties of humanistic studies, law and adminstration, sciences, medicine, veterinary medicine, agriculture and soil study, mathematics, physics, and chemistry. The university library contains 492,300 volumes. In 1881 Johannes Brahms wrote his *Academic Festival Overture* on the occasion of receiving an honorary degree from the University of Breslau.

BRESSANONE (*Ger.* Brixen) [brɛ'ssɑno'ne, brɪ'ksən], an historic town in the province of Bolzano, in the Alto Adige region of northern Italy, about 20 mi. north of Bolzano. It is situated picturesquely, 1,650 ft. above sea level, at the confluence of the Rienza and Isarco rivers, in a narrow, verdant valley surrounded on all sides by high mountains. The town is on the international railway between Verona and Innsbruck, Austria, via the Brenner Pass. Because of its moderate climate Bressanone is a popular health and vacation resort. It has a large hydroelectric plant, several industrial establishments, and is a market place for the wine, fruit, wool, and other products of the region. It is the see of a bishop and has several schools and seminaries. Many of the inhabitants speak German.

Bressanone is the most important artistic center in the Alto Adige region (called the South Tirol when it belonged to Austria prior to 1919) and is of special interest for its examples of the fusion of Gothic, Renaissance, and Baroque styles. Among the more notable edifices is the cathedral, originally Romanesque of the thirteenth century but rebuilt in 1754; its cloister, baptistery, and campanile are of particular interest. Adjoining is the episcopal palace, famous for its striking Renaissance courtyard.

The town's history, which appears to go back to early medieval times, has been relatively uneventful of itself. But the town acquired importance as the see of an important prince-bishop, whose temporal domains were secularized by Napoleon in 1803. After the Italian annexation of the South Tirol in 1919, the bishopric straddled the frontier, the larger and more populous part lying in Austria and administered separately. Pop. 1954 (town), 9,100; (commune), 12,800.

R. G. W.

BREST [brɛ'st], a seaport on the westernmost tip of the Brittany Peninsula in western France, 154 mi. northwest of Rennes, in the department of Finistère, at 48° 25′ N. lat. and 4° 30′ W. long. In Gallo-Roman times it was known as Gesocribate, and, in the second half of the Middle Ages, Brest was one of the most important French ports. Its development as the chief naval port of France was accelerated by Richelieu, the statesman and cardinal, in 1631; later by the statesman Jean Baptiste Colbert; and by Sébastien Le Prestre Vauban, the military engineer, from 1680 to 1688. A great majority of the country's naval and merchant marine schools are located at Brest, including the naval school, a hydrographic school, a naval arsenal, and a large naval hospital. Most of the city was destroyed during World War II when the Germans defended it in 1944. Its destruction was so thorough from combat and from the demolition of port installations that, after its capture, it could not be used or repaired as a supply center for American troops. On July 28, 1947, the explosion of a nitrate ship caused further heavy damage to the already war-torn city. As a port, Brest is divided into the naval base at the mouth of the Penfeld River and the commercial port of Porstrein, protected by a long breakwater. Much commerce is carried on with England and Spain, and there are fisheries (mackerel and sardine), distilleries, flour mills, and factories which produce shoes, candles, chemicals, and linens. The city of Brest is also divided in two, Brest proper being on the one side of the Penfeld River and Recouvrance on the other. Pop. 1954, 110,713.

BREST [brɛ'st], a city, formerly called Brest-Litovsk, and the administrative center of the Brest Region in the Byelorussian S.S.R. in the western Soviet Union.

The City. The city is located 110 mi. east of Warsaw and 225 mi. southwest of Minsk. It lies on a height on the right bank of the Bug River at the influx of the Muhavets, and on the Dnepr-Bug Canal, a favorable location for commercial waterway traffic. Brest is also an important rail junction, as well as trade center for timber, grain, and cattle. Its several industries include electrical machinery works, ship and railroad repair shops, and lumber, textile, and food-processing and distillery plants. Pop. (est. 1950), 60,000.

Because of its strategic location, Brest was often besieged —by Mongols in the thirteenth century, Teutonic Knights in the fourteenth, and Tatars in the fifteenth. In 1595-1596 it was the site of the Union of Brest-Litovsk, the act by which six Ruthenian Orthodox bishops brought their clergy and people into communion with the Roman Church. Passing to Russia from Poland in 1795, it became an armed stronghold. It was taken by the Germans and Austrians on Aug. 26, 1915, after a month-long offensive. In 1918 it was the scene of the signing of two peace treaties, one between the Central Powers and the Ukrainians on February 9, and one between the Central Powers and Russia on March 3. Taken by Poland in 1921, it was made capital of the province of Polesie. The city and region were recovered by the U.S.S.R. in September 1939, captured by the Nazis in June

1941, and recaptured by Soviet troops July 28, 1944. Considerable damage resulted from World War II.

The Region. The region (*oblast*) covers an area of approximately 12,000 sq. mi. and occupies the southwestern portion of the Byelorussian S.S.R., bordering on the Ukrainian S.S.R. in the south, and Poland in the west. It lies in the depressions of the Pripet Marshes, a swampy area with poor watersheds. Agriculture is developed mainly in the north, with rye, oats, potatoes, and hemp as the chief crops. Livestock is raised in the forested southern portion. Industries include lumbering and woodworking, food processing, and tanning. The main industrial centers are Brest, Pinsk, and Baranovichi. Of great importance are two canals, the Oginskiy and the Dnepr-Bug Canal which connects the Dnepr Basin with the Baltic Sea through the Pripyat River and provides a cheap waterway between the U.S.S.R. and Poland.

BREST-LITOVSK, TREATY OF, the agreement which was signed on Mar. 3, 1918, between Russia and the Central Powers. This treaty permitted Russia to withdraw from hostilities against Germany in World War I. After the Bolshevik overthrow of the Kerensky government, Nov. 7, 1917, the Bolsheviks demanded a clear-cut statement of Allied war aims, announcing at the same time their policy of "no annexations and no indemnities." On November 28 an armistice and peace were offered to the Germans, and on December 15 an armistice was concluded on the Eastern Front.

Negotiations began at Brest-Litovsk on Dec. 3, 1917. By December 25 the Central Powers had accepted the principle of "no annexations and no indemnities," provided the Allied Powers accepted it in ten days. Appeals from Trotsky, the Russian foreign minister, brought no answer, and the Germans refused to moderate their demands, largely laid down by the military authorities. The conference was suspended, and reopened Jan. 4, 1918. Trotsky refused to recognize the new Baltic states unless a plebiscite were held. On February 10, Trotsky declared the war ended, although no peace had been signed, but on February 18 the Germans began hostilities again. On February 28, at the instance of Lenin, negotiations were resumed, and on March 3, the Treaty of Brest-Litovsk was signed.

Terms. The terms provided for the following: (1) surrender of Karelia, Lithuania, and Poland; (2) evacuation by Russian troops of Latvia, Estonia, Finland, and the Åland Islands; (3) evacuation of the Ukraine and recognition of the treaty between the Central Powers and the Ukraine, which had been signed on Feb. 9, 1918; (4) surrender of Transcaucasia to Turkey; (5) cessation of all Bolshevik propaganda within the territories of the Central Powers. Additional treaties in August forced Soviet Russia to pay six billion gold marks to Germany, grant Germany most-favored-nation treatment in commercial relations, and permit free export of timber.

The Treaty of Brest-Litovsk passed without too much notice in Soviet Russia, which was engrossed with domestic issues, although there was a struggle over its ultimate approval. It gave Germany the possibility of concentrating her waning strength on the Western Front. It served also to steel the nerves of the Allies, since it revealed the essential aims of German imperial policy in eastern and southeastern Europe. H. N. Ho.

BRETHREN IN CHRIST, a sect known also as River Brethren, which arose after the revival of religion among the pietistic Anabaptists of Lancaster Co., Pa., towards the end of the eighteenth century. Although at first they adopted no name, they were called River Brethren because they lived near the Susquehanna and Conestoga rivers and also because they baptized in rivers; the name "Brethren in Christ" was adopted in 1862. About six thousand members of this sect are scattered throughout the United States and Canada but they minister to at least four times as many persons through missions in Africa and India and through evangelistic work carried on in neglected areas by young men of the church. The three orders of the clergy, bishops, elders and deacons, are elected and serve on a volunteer basis. The annual General Conference consists of one delegate for each fifty members. Although there is no printed confession of faith, major practices of the Church include triple immersion for adults, divine healing, the holy kiss, love feasts, feet washing, non-resistance, and scriptural veiling. R. W. A.

BRETHREN OF THE COMMON LIFE, a Christian community founded by Gerhard Groote (1340-1384), born at Deventer, in Gelderland. Its main purposes were the salvation of souls, reformation of the clergy, and spiritual elevation of the laity. Accordingly, it founded schools in the Low Countries and thence throughout Europe. The group was originally united simply by a common ideal; they rejected alms-seeking, modeling themselves after St. Paul. In 1395, Boniface IX approved their rule, which was Augustinian in spirit. Its most famous pupils were Thomas à Kempis, Pope Adrian VI, and Nicholas of Cusa. The Reformation and ensuing upheavals ended this famous congregation. W. C.

BRÉTIGNY, TREATY OF [bre'ti'nyi'] (May 8, 1360), closed the first period of the Hundred Years' War between France and England. Despite their great victory over the French at Poitiers in 1356, when King John II was taken prisoner, the English were too exhausted to continue the war and offered peace. Edward III abandoned his claims to the French crown, but received in return recognition of English sovereignty over Aquitaine, as well as Calais and the northern county of Ponthieu. The French also agreed to pay a huge ransom for the release of King John. The treaty was not well kept, and war broke out again nine years later. F. C. H.

BRETON, JULES ADOLPHE AIMÉ LOUIS [brətɔ̃'] (1827-1906), French painter, was born in Courrières (Pas-de-Calais) on May 1, 1827. Breton has been considered one of the pioneers of open-air painting, and in his works the life of the peasant is idealized. Among his most widely known paintings are *The Return of the Harvesters* (1853), *The Song of the Lark* (1885), and *The First Communion* (1886). His writings include the volumes of verse, *Les Champs de la mer* (1875), and *Jeanne* (1880), the autobiographical *La Vie d'un artiste* (1890), and *Un Peintre paysan* (1896). He died in Paris on July 5, 1906. K. B.

BRETON, NICHOLAS [bre'tən] (c.1555-c.1626), English author, was born in Redcross Street, London. A stepson of George Gascoigne, the poet, Breton studied at Oxford and published about fifty books of fluent but undistinguished verse or prose. His best lyric, "In the merrie month of May," pleased Queen Elizabeth when sung at her window. Breton praised country life in *Wit's Trenchmour* (1597), a prose dialogue between a scholar and an angler, and in *Fantasticks* (1604), an attractive book of prose sketches. A versatile author of pastoral and religious verse, he also wrote prose tales, imaginary letters, essays, and satires. M. E.

BRETON, the Celtic language of Brittany. Breton is spoken by approximately 1,200,000 people west of a line from St. Brieuc to St. Nazaire, in the departments of Finistère, Côtes-du-Nord, and Morbihan. It falls into four main dialects, Léonais in the northwest, Trégorrois in the northeast, Cornouaillais in the southwest, and Vannetais in the southeast. Of these the last differs widely from the other three, notably in the position of the stress, which is on the final syllable of the word in Vannetais whereas in the other dialects it is on the penult as in Welsh. The language is not a survival of ancient Gaulish but was brought to Brittany in the fifth and sixth centuries by immigrants from Cornwall and South Wales. In Modern Breton the nominal and verbal systems are still close to Welsh. The plural formations of nouns correspond; in the verb the chief differences are the loss of the simple preterite tense and the use of the subjunctive as a future. The system of initial mutations, so characteristic of Celtic, is well preserved. But Breton has borrowed an enormous number of words from French, so that the whole vocabulary is threatened. This contrast of vocabulary is probably the most striking difference between Breton and Welsh.

The Middle Breton texts are mostly translations from Latin or French mystery plays, lives of saints, and other works of piety, and the same seems to be true of Modern Breton literature. Only the folk songs and folk tales have independent value, and here the Bretons have a rich heritage. An idea of the form of Breton words may be gained from the Middle Breton text of the Lord's Prayer which follows:

> *Hon tat pe heny so en nefuou, ho hanu bezet sanctifiet. Deuet ho rouantelez. Ho volontez bezet graet en douar efel en nefu. Roit dimp hiziu hon bara pemdeziec. Ha pardonnet dimp hon offansou evel ma'z pardonnomp da nep a'n deueux hon offanset. Ha n'on leset da couezo en temptation. Hoguen hon diliurit uez an drouc. Evel se bezet graet.*

M. Di.

BRETON LITERATURE, the literature of the Celtic-speaking people of the Breton peninsula in France. This peninsula was settled by Britons fleeing from the Saxon invaders in the fifth and sixth centuries of the Christian Era and since that time has been known as Little Britain or Brittany. The Bretons have remained something of a race apart, and many of them still speak a language akin to Welsh. By some fatality no literature in the Breton tongue before 1450 has survived, yet an important oral literature must have existed before this time, at first in Breton and later, as Breton minstrels won popularity abroad, in the French language. As early as 1125 an English chronicler mentioned the fantastic tales of the Bretons about Arthur, and in 1216 the Welsh Giraldus Cambrensis credited "the tale-telling Bretons and their singers" with the legend of King Arthur's being taken to Avalon to be healed.

The influence of these Breton tellers of tales in laying the foundations of Arthurian romance is considerable. By the year 1000 the Bretons had begun to take over from their cousins the Welsh a mass of myth and legend, and this they adapted to French tastes and recited in French prose with dramatic gesture and intonation. In this form the themes of Tristan, the adventures of the Knights of the Round Table, and the mysterious Grail, first fascinated Western Europe. After 1150 French, Anglo-Norman, and German poets were moved to compose romances based on these tales, and the subsequent vast romantic literature centering about Arthur is thus derived more or less directly from the tales of the wandering Breton *conteurs.*

Another important aspect of Breton literature is to be found in the short narrative songs which the Breton singers composed in their own tongue and sang to the accompaniment of harp, fiddle, or lyre. These charming lais were unintelligible outside of Brittany, and in France had to be explained in prose. Neither the original lais nor the prose retellings have survived, but about twenty-five poetic renderings in French couplets, made between 1150 and 1250, have reached us, as well as a few English and Norse translations. Several of these French rhymed lais are coarse and cynical; some deal romantically with the loves of fays and mortals, others treat more realistically of problems of marriage, the testing of wooers, and incognito combats between father and son. A few are laid in the time of King Arthur, and one tells how Tristan arranged a forest meeting with Isolt. If we are to judge the art of the Breton minstrels by the lais of Marie de France (1160-1180), a poetess of the Anglo-Norman court, they possessed the same flair for swift, coherent narrative, dramatic situation, and elfin glamour as do the best English ballads.

The earliest surviving literature written in the Breton language is very different. It consists for the most part of long, ponderous sacred dramas, based either on Latin saints' lives, or on French mystery plays. *The Life of St. Nonn,* dealing with the mother of St. David of Wales, belongs to the late fifteenth century, and this was followed by a Passion Play in 1530, *Le grand mystère de Jésus,* and a mystery play on St. Barbara in 1557, *Le Mystère de Sainte Barbe.* The seventeenth century continued the tradition of pious drama and added farces and romantic subjects, such as new renderings of *The Four Sons of Aymon* and *Huon of Bordeaux.*

The chief glory of modern Breton literature is the large collection of folk tales and folk songs collected in the nineteenth and twentieth centuries. Apart from the spurious publications of Hersart de la Villemarqué, there has been gathered by Souvestre, F. M. Luzel, Anatole le Braz, and others a rich library of ballads, lyrics, and tales which are the genuine products of the peasantry and fisherfolk. These include pious legends of miracles wrought by the saints, explanations of the gray prehistoric stone circles and alignments, fragments of the medieval heritage of the *conteurs,* stories of the spectral Ankou (the personification of death) and his creaking cart, and tales of sirens who enticed sailors into their fatal embraces.

R. S. L.

BRETT, WILLIAM HOWARD (1846-1918), American librarian, was born July 1, 1846, at Braceville, Ohio. After serving in the 196th Ohio Infantry in the Civil War, he attended the University of Michigan and Western Reserve University. Lack of funds, however, prevented him from completing his higher education, and he became a book salesman in a Cleveland store. This experience led, in 1884, to his appointment as librarian of the Cleveland Public Library, a position he held for thirty-four years. In 1894 he organized the Western Reserve School of Library Science, of which he was dean from 1903 until his death. Brett also organized and was the first president of the Ohio Library Association, and in 1896-1897 served as president of the American Library Association. Meanwhile he was responsible for many noteworthy innovations in library science, among them the system of indexing articles in periodicals which remains in use today. Brett promoted the extension of library facilities to schools in the community, and later to branch libraries, churches, settlement houses, factories, and other places where the interested layman could enjoy the advantages of good reading. His work attracted the attention of Andrew Carnegie, the philanthropist, with whom Brett worked in the extension of library facilities to millions of American citizens. Brett also is regarded as one of the forerunners of modern personnel administration in libraries, having devoted much time to the scientific selection of librarians, their professional training, and certification. He was a leading authority on legislation affecting libraries, and was responsible for the passage of laws to protect them from political interference and pressures. In the closing years of his life he was commended by the War Department for his leadership in providing book service to soldiers through camp libraries in World War I. Brett died in Cleveland, Aug. 24, 1918, after being struck by an automobile. N. St.

BRETTON WOODS, a 10,000-acre resort area located in the town of Carroll, Coos Co., in the northern part of New Hampshire. It is set in the White Mountains on the north bank of the Ammonoosuc River, about 25 mi. southwest of Berlin, where there is a commercial airport.

A charter for the land was granted by King George III to Governor Wentworth of New Hampshire, and the region was named for Bretton Hall in Yorkshire. It was the site of the United Nations Monetary and Financial Conference in July 1944. At that time delegates from forty-four nations established the International Monetary Fund and the International Bank for Reconstruction and Development. Its hotel (which is open from May to October), woods, mountain scenery, and near-by Lake Carolyn make Bretton Woods a popular resort.

BRETTON WOODS PLAN, THE, incorporated into law, July 13, 1945, was the result of the deliberation of the International Monetary Conference which met at Bretton Woods, N. H., July 1-23, 1944. This meeting was called to plan for a stabilized world currency by means of an International Monetary Fund and to finance economic reconstruction by means of the International Bank for Reconstruction and Development (also known as the World Bank). Twenty-eight nations, on Dec. 27, 1945, signed the necessary documents to make the plan effective.

BREUIL, HENRI ÉDOUARD PROSPER [brœ'y] (1877-   ), French prehistorian and archaeologist, was born in Mortain (Manche), on Feb. 28, 1877. He was educated at the Collège St. Vincent at Senlis, St. Sulpice, and the Sorbonne. He was ordained a priest in 1900. Breuil served as lecturer in ethnography at the University of Freiburg (1905-1910), became honorary professor of prehistoric ethnography in the Institute of Human Paleontology in 1910, and was made professor of prehistory at the Collège de France in 1929. Breuil's work covered the general field of Paleolithic and Neolithic archaeology, but he is especially noted for his studies of cave art. In 1952 his *400 Centuries of Cave Art* was published, and in 1953 he announced the discovery in a cave in South Africa of a portrait, five or six thousand years old, apparently depicting a woman belonging to a race of white invaders of Africa of the fifth or fourth millennium B.C. G. F. Ek.

BREVIARY [bri'viɛri] (Lat. *breviarium,* an abridgement), the name illogically applied to the single work containing the entire daily office, or public prayer, of the Roman Catholic Church, formerly divided among several books. Its recitation is obligatory for clerics in major orders and for certain religions. It contains chiefly the Psalter, or 150 Psalms; the Proper of the Season, or scripture lessons; hymns and prayers adapted to Advent, Christmastide, Lent, Eastertide, and other periods; and the Proper and Common

MT. WASHINGTON HOTEL, BRETTON WOODS, NEW HAMPSHIRE

of Saints, which give the lessons, prayers, and other formularies for their feasts. The office consists of seven canonical hours: Matins with Lauds, Prime, Terce, Sext, None, Vespers, and Compline. The Eastern churches follow a similar pattern, but generally use separate books. In the Latin Church the most widely used of several breviaries is the *Breviarium Romanum* as restored by Pius V (1568) and reformed by Pope Pius X (1912). Pope Pius XII approved for optional use a new translation of the Psalter (1945). N. J. T.

BREWER, a city in southeastern Maine, situated in Penobscot Co., at the head of navigation of the Penobscot River. It lies opposite Bangor, with which it has bridge connections. Separated from Orrington and established as a separate community in 1812, it was incorporated as a city in 1889. The local government is administered by a manager and council. The principal industries are woodworking and pulp and paper manufacture. Pop. 1950, 6,862.

BREWING. *See* BEER AND ALE.

BREWSTER, WILLIAM (c. 1567-1644), Pilgrim leader, was born in Scrooby, Nottinghamshire, England, probably in January 1567. He attended Cambridge University and was in the service of Queen Elizabeth's assistant secretary of state, William Davison, from 1584 to 1587. After Davison's fall from favor Brewster returned to Scrooby, and in 1607 was imprisoned for trying to escape to Holland. From 1602 he and many of his neighbors had held religious meetings in his manor house and by 1606 had formed the Separatist Church of Scrooby. In 1608 Brewster reached Holland. There he supported himself by teaching English and soon became ruling elder of the Separatists, a position he held until his death. In 1616 he and Thomas Brewer secretly began printing religious books for export to England. Upon the complaint of the English ambassador, the Dutch authorities seized the type and arrested Brewer. Brewster, managing to escape arrest, later went to London, where with Robert Cushman he obtained a land patent for colonization purposes from the Virginia Company. Sailing on the *Mayflower* in 1620, he helped to found the Plymouth Colony in America. Until the arrival in 1629 of Ralph Smith, first pastor of the colony, Brewster acted in that capacity. Although he was never a minister in the official sense, by some authorities he is considered to have been the real leader of the Pilgrim church in the Plymouth Colony. He died at Plymouth, Apr. 10, 1644. D. R.

BREYSIG, KURT [brai'ziχ] (1866-1940), German social and cultural historian, and philosopher of history, was born in Posen, July 5, 1866. He taught at the University of Berlin for twenty-five years as an associate professor and in 1923 was made a full professor. His long tenure at a low rank may be explained by his opposition to the schools of Leopold von Ranke and Heinrich von Treitschke. These schools tended to restrict history to the foreign politics of the Western nations, emphasizing the role of political leaders, and criticizing Breysig along with Karl Lamprecht and others. Breysig felt strongly that history is not the record of one seemingly dominant factor, such as the state, but rather of the interrelationship between all phenomena. He held that it should deal with all peoples, including so-called "primitives" who may appear to lack historical development. Just as the individual passes from infancy through childhood, adolescence, and maturity to senility, every cultural unit, according to Breysig, passes through corresponding historical stages. This theory of cycles was rejected, ridiculed, or ignored by professional historians but was discussed and studied by anthropologists. Oswald Spengler's *Decline of the West* propounded views similar to Breysig's sequence of automatically appearing stages. Breysig died in Berlin, June 20, 1940.   P. H.

BRIAN BORAMHA or **BORU** [bri′n boro′; bri′n boru′] (926-1014), king of Ireland, spent his youth fighting the Danes who were raiding his native Munster. He won his first victory over them in 968 and became King of Cashel by conquest in 978. He subdued all Munster, invaded other parts of Ireland, sometimes in alliance with the Danes, and by 1002 had made himself chief king or *ardri* of Ireland. He won a great victory over the Danes of Dublin at Clontarf on Apr. 23, 1014, but was himself slain.   E. R. A.

BRIANÇON [bri′ā′sɔ̃′], a town in southeastern France, in the department of Hautes-Alpes, 56 mi. northeast of Gap, on a plateau 4,284 ft. high dominating the Durance and Guisanne rivers. Called Brigantio by the Romans, the town had little importance except as a fortress; in 1722 it was fortified by the French. Briançon, which has steep, narrow, winding streets, commands the route of Mont Genèvre between Italy and France; the citadel has a triple wall and a series of ten forts on the commanding heights. Because of its isolation on difficult terrain, most lines of transportation avoid the town, but there is nevertheless a considerable tourist trade. Extensive development of hydroelectric power promises to give Briançon some industrial importance. The two chief industries are processing waste silk and mining talc; cutlery and cotton goods are also produced. Pop. 1954, 6,252.

BRIAND, ARISTIDE PIERRE HENRI [bri′ā′] (1862-1932), French statesman, was born at Nantes, Mar. 28, 1862. After studying law in Paris, he settled in Saint-Nazaire as a lawyer, participating as a journalist in the rising socialist movement. Advocating the general strike as the most effective legal means available to the workers in the peaceful evolution toward their goals, Briand became in the 1890's one of the right-wing leaders of the Socialists. He was an active supporter of Dreyfus, and in 1904 founded, together with Jean Jaurès, the socialist (today communist) daily paper *L'Humanité*. In these years Briand developed his most characteristic trait: the gift of subtle persuasion, aided by an exceptional oratorical ability, used for the sake of reconciling opposing views in the interest of higher ideals. The principle of co-operation based on free consent guided him in all his enterprises.

After his eventual election to the Chamber of Deputies in 1902, Briand took a decisive part in the preparation of the law for the separation of State and Church and, in order to execute this law, four years later he became minister of public instruction in the cabinet of Jean Marie Ferdinand

Sarrien, a post which he kept in the succeeding cabinet of Georges Clemenceau. In carrying out this law without friction, he showed his great statesmanship, although he was excluded from the Socialist Party because of his participation in a bourgeois cabinet. In 1909 he succeeded Clemenceau as head of the government, and successfully handled the railway strike the following year.

As minister of justice in Raymond Poincaré's first cabinet in 1912, Briand became instrumental in Poincaré's election to the presidency of the republic, after which he succeeded the latter as president of the council. In 1914-1915, he was minister of justice in René Viviani's cabinet. During World

ARISTIDE PIERRE HENRI
BRIAND

War I, Briand headed the government from the fall of 1915 to the spring of 1917, and based it on the principle of national unity. During this period, he held for the first time also the post of minister of foreign affairs and his conceptions, despite the weight of the war, slowly shifted from the field of national to that of international co-operation and international peace.

After the fall of his cabinet, Briand remained on the sidelines for three years, although during this period German peace suggestions were transmitted to him (1917). He again became active in 1921 as the head of the government and foreign minister, his efforts being directed toward the execution of the Treaty of Versailles and especially toward peaceful European co-operation. Briand represented France in the Paris and London conferences on German reparations, at the disarmament conference in Washington in November 1921, and at the inter-allied conference at Cannes in the beginning of 1922. In the spring of 1925 he again became foreign minister, a post which he held almost without interruption during the remaining years of his life.

During this period between the two World Wars, Briand became the foremost champion of a Franco-German *rapprochement* and of international co-operation, especially through the League of Nations. He was the architect of the Locarno Conference (October 1925), whose main result was a mutual guaranty of the French and Belgian frontiers, with Germany, Britain, and Italy as guarantors; he was also instrumental in the admission of Germany to the League of Nations in September 1926. Briand and Gustav Stresemann, the German foreign minister, received together in 1926 the Nobel Peace Prize for their common work. Two years later the Briand-Kellogg Pact, providing for the renouncement of war as an instrument of national policy, was signed in Paris by fifteen nations.

Briand was eleven times head of the government and twenty-five times a minister; but despite all detours one straight line led from his advocating co-operation among the workers to his conception of international co-operation and his last ideal of a European federation. He died Mar. 7, 1932, in Paris.   W. Fr.

BRIAR CLIFF COLLEGE, an accredited Roman Catholic liberal arts college for women located on a 65-acre campus in Sioux City, Iowa. It was chartered as a junior college in 1930 and became a senior college in 1937. Its curriculum includes the divisions of letters and fine arts, natural science and mathematics, religion and philosophy, special sciences, and community service. The College confers the following degrees: Bachelor of Arts, Bachelor of Music, Bachelor of Science, and Bachelor of Science in commerce, medical technology, and nursing. Out-of-town students are required to live on campus, unless special permission is obtained to make other arrangements. Scholarships and limited service contracts are available. *For statistics see* COLLEGES AND UNIVERSITIES.

BRIAREUS [braiɛ'əriəs], in Greek mythology, a hundred-handed giant who aided the Olympian gods in their struggle against the Titans. *See also* HECATONCHEIRES.

BRIBERY, at common law, a crime that may be defined as that of giving, offering, or taking of anything of value to influence a person in the discharge of a public or governmental duty. Thus this definition of the crime represents an extension of its original scope, which was limited to the acceptance of a bribe by a judicial officer. At common law, bribery is a misdemeanor; but as codified in the state penal laws of the United States, bribery of public officials is generally constituted a felony. Solicitation of a bribe by an officer is itself denounced as criminal in many bribery statutes, and the crime is considered complete even though no money is paid or promised.

Modern Bribery Legislation. The typical modern bribery statute treats the offense of giving or offering of a bribe apart from the offense of receiving a bribe and deals specifically with bribery relating to particular classes of individuals, such as legislators, judicial officers, voters, witnesses, and jurors.

In the furtherance of fair and free elections, legislation known as Corrupt Practices Acts supplements the bribery statutes by regulating and controlling the activities of political candidates and of persons acting in their behalf. A noteworthy modern development in bribery legislation is the application of concepts of bribery laws to fields, activities, and conduct beyond its traditional limitation to the administration of justice and public or governmental duty. Among such special statutes in some states are laws making it a crime to bribe representatives of labor organizations; to use corrupt influence on agents and employees in relation to the employer's business; to bribe athletes to lose or to try to lose, or to cause their team to lose, a contest or game, or to limit the margin of victory. Corresponding penal provisions are generally enacted for acceptance of bribes in this type of legislation.

Major Principles. The following are a few major principles that have evolved in the main body of bribery law dealing with the corrupt influencing of persons charged with the performance of public or governmental duty.

(a) The offense of bribery on the part of the person seeking to influence the performance of public duty is committed when the offer of a bribe is made, even though the public officer rejects the offer to bribe him. If he accepts the bribe, he himself, of course, has committed bribery.

(b) For a public official to accept a bribe to render a correct decision is as much an offense as his acceptance of a bribe to render an improper decision. "The corruption aimed at is not simply the doing of things which may be improper in themselves, but even the doing of proper things as the result of an improper agreement . . . . the offense is so subtle in its fruits that the law endeavors to lay the axe at its very roots." *People* v. *Furlong* [140 App. Div. 179 (N.Y.)].

(c) The purpose for which a bribe is offered or given to a public officer or solicited and accepted by him must have some relation to his employment or function, although it is not essential that he have actual authority legally to do the act which is the subject of the bribe.

Embracery. Closely identified at common law with the offense of bribery is the misdemeanor of embracery, which consists of the exertion of improper influence upon a juror to influence his verdict, whether by bribery or by other means. In some statutes the offense of embracery is confined to intrusions of this nature upon the juror's responsibilities which fall short of bribery, the latter offense being a separate crime. The juror who has been corrupted by embracery, either at common law or under the statutes, is deemed guilty of bribery if the embracery is tantamount to bribery; of misconduct if embracery in its lesser connotation is involved. *See also* CORRUPT PRACTICES ACTS.   H. Si.

BRICK. *See* ENGINEERING MATERIALS (*Brick and Clay Products*).

BRIDAL VEIL, a broom, *Genista monosperma,* having hanging branchlets of colorless or whitish, pea-shaped, fragrant flowers which suggest a veil. It comes from North Africa and Spain, where it is used to hold sand dunes, and reaches a height of 10 ft. The plant is almost leafless. The flowers, which grow in short, lateral racemes, appear in early spring.   J. C. Wis.

BRIDAL VEIL FALLS, several high and beautiful waterfalls in the Yosemite National Park, in the central part of eastern California. A large tongue or lobe of glacial ice originally scoured out and deepened the Yosemite Valley, through which the Merced River flows. The valley was deepened about 1,000 ft. below the surrounding region, and while ice lay in the valley the tributary streams were either frozen or prevented from cutting their channels any deeper. The result was that when the ice melted and retreated the main stream valley was about 1,000 ft. below the tributary stream valleys, forming a number of hanging valleys. The waterfalls drop from these hanging valleys down to the Yosemite Valley and the Merced River. One of these tributary streams, Bridal Veil Creek, has a vertical fall of 630 ft. over Cathedral Rock, and then falls in a series of cascades for another 300 ft. The falls are called Bridal Veil because the wind blows the water and spray into white swirls resembling a bridal veil.   J. E. F.

BRIDAL WREATH (*Spiraea prunifolia*), a low shrub of the rose family, growing to about 5 ft. Pure white flowers in small clusters line the arching branches in advance of the leaves. The double-flowered form is most often seen. A hybrid, flowering freely in May after the leaves have appeared, is called bridal wreath.   J. C. Wis.

BRIDE OF LAMMERMOOR, THE [læ'mərmur], a novel by Sir Walter Scott, published in 1819 as part of *Tales of My Landlord*. It is the original on which the plot of Donizetti's opera, *Lucia di Lammermoor,* is based.

The Bride of Lammermoor is Scott's version of *Romeo and Juliet*. The setting is East Lothian around 1710, and the interfamily feud is between Edgar, Master of Ravenswood, whose family was ruined helping the Stuarts, and a newly-rich Whig, Sir William Ashton. Marriage between Lucy Ashton and Edgar is prevented by the greed of Lucy's mother and by Edgar's own struggle between his love and his desire for vengeance, the conflict costing Lucy her sanity and leading both lovers to their deaths. Edgar is survived by his faithful, eccentric butler, Caleb Balderstone.   W. Ru.

BRIDGE, a card game. The name is popularly applied to bridge whist, auction bridge, and contract bridge, each of which is related to the parent game of whist. Contract bridge, the most recent member of the whist family of games, calls for the understanding of a variety of factors, giving the game a marked intellectual aspect and possibly contributing to its enormous popularity throughout America and western Europe.

WHIST, BRIDGE WHIST, AND AUCTION BRIDGE

Whist. The parent game, whist, evolved from several older games which succeeded each other under the names of triumph, trump, ruff and honors, whisk and swabbers, whisk, and finally whist. The name whist came to be used late in the seventeenth century. In whist, the dealer turned up the last card as trump. There was no bidding, it being simply a contest to see which side could win the greater number of tricks at the turned trump. In this form of the game there was no dummy. Each player held his cards and played them for himself.

Bridge Whist. Bridge, or bridge whist, was introduced by Lord Brougham in 1894 at the Portland Club in London, and the game remained popular for about ten years, at the end of which time it was supplanted by auction bridge. In bridge whist the last card was not turned up to name the trump suit. Instead, the dealer had the right to choose his own trump. If he wished, he might elect to play the hand without a trump suit at all. If he did not wish to name a trump suit, he could pass or bridge this privilege over to his partner. In such a case, his partner was bound to name a trump or to declare that the hand was to be played without a trump suit. An important new feature of bridge whist was that the dealer's partner put his cards face up on the table immediately after the player to dealer's left had led to the first trick. This exposed or dummy hand was played by the dealer. Bridge whist differed from whist in another important respect, the introduction of the doubling feature. The dealer's opponents had the privilege of doubling the value of the tricks won. The dealer's side then had the privilege of redoubling. If a bid was redoubled, the dealer's opponents could then double again. There was no limit to the number of doubles and redoubles.

Auction Bridge. Shortly after the beginning of the twentieth century, bridge whist was supplanted by auction bridge. The chief new feature of the game was that each player in turn, beginning with the dealer, might bid for the privilege of naming the trump suit. Bidding continued, as at an auction, until no player offered a further bid. Scoring at auction bridge evolved finally into the rubber form. A bonus of 250 points is awarded for winning two out of three games. Game is scored for winning thirty points below the line. And the trick value of the various denominations is six points per trick for clubs, seven for diamonds, eight for hearts, nine for spades, and ten for no trump.

CONTRACT BRIDGE

History. Contract bridge has attained far more widespread popularity than any other member of the whist family. One of its antecedents was a French game known as plafond, which was based on the principle that, in order to gain full reward for tricks taken, a team must first have declared in the bidding its intention to take that specific number of tricks. A game that combined this new principle with the fundamentals of auction bridge was played by a circle of Americans who frequented the Travelers' Club in Paris. In this circle were a number of friends of Harold S. Vanderbilt, noted American yachtsman and card enthusiast. Although they did not have definite or complete rules for the game they played, many of them called their game contract bridge. Eventually, during a steamship voyage from Los Angeles to Havana in November 1925, a small group of players fixed the basic features of the game, features that fundamentally have undergone no important change since then. Vanderbilt has been conceded to be more responsible for creation of the game than anyone else. After the Knickerbocker Whist Club of New York had published the first complete set of laws on the game, with a complete scale of scoring values, Vanderbilt brought out his own set of values which with later variations have become the official scale for the game wherever played.

As compared with auction bridge, the principal new feature of the game was the introduction of the scoring rule that the declaring side could score below the line only for tricks both bid and made. Thus, a player had to bid a game or a slam to get credit for it. In the parent game, auction bridge, a player could score a game at a very low contract, provided he succeeded in winning enough tricks. The new game became instantly popular in fashionable society but was resisted somewhat by staunch adherents of auction bridge. Well-known players wrote books to acquaint beginners with the principles of skillful bidding. A difference of opinion between Ely Culbertson and a group of other experts led to a match between Culbertson and Sidney S. Lenz to test the theories. In this match of 150 rubbers, Mr. and Mrs. Culbertson defeated Lenz, Oswald Jacoby, and Commander Winfield Liggett, Jr. Lenz played throughout, with Jacoby as his partner for the first 103 rubbers and with Liggett for the remaining forty-seven. The match was concluded in January 1932.

In the years preceding World War II, a series of matches was held between teams representing England and the United States. The latter won all of these matches. The International Bridge League, in Europe, held annual tournaments in which teams from many European countries participated. Two teams representing the United States competed in the summer of 1937, when the event was won by a team from Austria.

In the United States, annual tournaments were conducted for some years by two competing associations, the American Bridge League and the United States Bridge Association. These were merged late in 1937 as the American Contract Bridge League. Tournament bridge immediately before World War II was very popular in the United States but suffered a slight slump during the war years due to the restrictions on travel. In the years immediately following the war, all previous attendance records were broken at national and local tournaments. Membership in the American Contract Bridge League has increased at a tremendous rate and is now about 100,000.

An annual feature of bridge competition for many years was the World Bridge Olympic. Hands which required unusually skillful bidding and play were selected in advance by a committee which represented the best bridge players in many countries. These hands were played simultaneously all over the world by thousands of contestants.

International competition was renewed after World War II, and a formal challenge was issued in the latter part of 1950. In a three-way contest held in Bermuda, the United States team defeated England and Sweden and continued to hold the World Title until 1955. In that year they were unseated by England, and subsequently France and Italy have captured the title.

Dealing. Contract bridge is played with the standard deck of fifty-two cards. Generally, unless other arrangements are made, each player cuts a card, and the pair cutting the higher cards play as partners against the two who cut the lower cards. The player who cuts the highest card deals the first hand from a deck that has been shuffled by the player on his left. Thereafter, the deal moves progressively to the left. After the deck has been shuffled, the dealer gives it to the player at his right for the cut. The dealer completes the cut and distributes the cards, one at a time, to each player in turn, beginning with the player at his left. This process is continued until all cards have been dealt.

Bidding. After the deal has been completed, the dealer may bid or pass. The right to bid then passes to the player at the dealer's left, from him to the dealer's partner, who is seated opposite the dealer, thence to the player at the dealer's right, then back to the dealer, and so on. All dealing, bidding, and playing is conducted in this clockwise rotation.

In bidding, a player names the suit he wishes to make trump and the number of tricks that he will undertake to win with his partner's help. A bid by either partner commits the partnership. The number of tricks in excess of the first six is designated in the bid. Thus, a commitment to win seven tricks with spades as trumps would be announced simply as one spade; a commitment to win nine tricks with no trump suit at all would be announced as three no trump.

The bidding proceeds in the style of an auction. At his proper turn a player may bid only if he is willing to bid higher than any previous bid. A bid which calls for a greater number of tricks is automatically higher than any previous bid. In addition, a bid may be higher than a previous bid if it offers to take the same number of tricks in a higher-ranking denomination. The denominations rank in order as follows: no trump (highest), spades, hearts, diamonds, and clubs (lowest). For example, a bid of two no trump outranks a bid of two of any suit.

A player at his proper turn may double the latest bid made by the opposite side. A double, generally speaking, indicates the belief that the opponents cannot fulfill the bid. However, the double has another and perhaps even more important role. This other form of double is used conventionally in the early stages of the auction to announce a rather strong holding hand to force a bid from a silent partner. This is known as the takeout double and is one of the pillars upon which defensive bidding rests. When a contract has been doubled, either player of the contracting side may redouble at his proper turn or make another bid. The effect of a double is to increase the penalties should the contract be defeated. The effect of a redouble is to multiply the doubled penalties by two. The bonuses for making a contract are correspondingly greater if it has been doubled or redoubled.

The auction ends when three successive passes are made. The sole exception to this rule occurs when the dealer and the two next players pass at their first turn to bid. In that case, the last player still has a chance to bid. If the fourth player also passes, the deal is not played, but the next player in proper turn deals a new hand.

Play. When the auction has ended, the play of the cards begins. Of the team winning the final contract, the player who first names the denomination at which the hand is played is the active player or declarer. His partner takes no part in the play of the cards and is known as the dummy. The play is begun by the player at declarer's left. He selects any card from his hand and places it face up on the table. The initial play to any trick is called a lead. The cards of declarer's partner are then placed face up on the table. Declarer chooses one card from this exposed hand, also called the dummy, and plays it on top of the card led. The leader's partner next plays to the trick, and finally the declarer. When a card from each hand has been played, the trick is complete.

A trick containing no trump is won by the highest card of the suit led. When a trick contains a card or cards of the trump suit, it is won by the highest trump. The winner of a trick leads to the succeeding trick. The play consists of thirteen tricks.

Each player is bound to play a card of the suit which has been led. When he holds no card of that suit, the player may choose any card from another suit. There is no compulsion to play a higher card of the suit led or to trump the trick if a blank is held in the suit led.

Scoring. The score is kept on a pad divided into two columns, one column for each team. Roughly midway across both columns a horizontal line is drawn. If the declarer fulfills his contract he scores below the horizontal line the point value of the number of tricks called for in his contract. If he is entitled to additional points for extra tricks made, honors, points derived from setting his opponents, or other premiums, he enters such points in his column above the horizontal line. Points scored below the line count toward game; points entered above the line do not count toward game.

A side scores a game when it amasses a total of one hundred points below the horizontal line. When a side wins two games, it scores a rubber bonus. A game may be scored in a single deal or as the result of several part-score contracts. Whenever either side scores a game in either of these fashions, a line is drawn to signify that previous part scores do not count toward the succeeding game. In such a situation, however, previous part scores are not crossed out; they will be added when the final score is computed. Whenever the rubber is won by either side, a fresh start must be made toward the winning of the next rubber bonus. Whenever a partnership has won one game toward the rubber, it is said to be vulnerable. In this situation, the side is exposed to increased penalties should it fail to make a contract. Likewise, many of the premiums for fulfilling contracts are increased when a side is vulnerable.

The scoring at contract bridge has been altered from time to time. In 1943, the following rules for scoring were adopted:

CONTRACT BRIDGE SCORING

GAME:

One hundred points constitute a game. Only the number of tricks bid and made may be counted toward game. Tricks made over contract count as overtricks. Once a game has been made, partial game scores previously compiled by either team cannot be applied toward the next game.

TRICK SCORE:

	Clubs	Diamonds	Hearts	Spades
Each trick over 6.............	20	20	30	30

No Trump

First trick over 6..............	40
Each subsequent trick..........	30

RUBBER PREMIUM:

If made: in 2 games.................	700
in 3 games.................	500
If unfinished: winner of one game....................	300
winner of part score............	50

SLAMS:

	Not Vulnerable	Vulnerable
Small slam (12 tricks bid for and made)	500	750
Grand slam (13 tricks bid for and made)	1000	1500

OVERTRICKS AND DOUBLED CONTRACT:

	Not Vulnerable	Vulnerable
Undoubled, each trick over contract......	Trick value	Trick value
Doubled, each trick over contract.......	100	200
Redoubled, each trick over contract.....	200	400
For making doubled or redoubled contract	50	50

PREMIUM FOR HONORS IN ONE HAND:

Four (any four of A K Q J 10).......................	100 points
Five (A K Q J 10).............................	150 points
Four aces at no trump............................	150 points

PENALTIES FOR UNDERTRICKS:

	Not Vulnerable		Vulnerable	
	Undoubled	Doubled	Undoubled	Doubled
1 Down...........	50	100	100	200
2 Down...........	100	300	200	500
3 Down...........	150	500	300	800
4 Down...........	200	700	400	1100
5 Down...........	250	900	500	1400
6 Down...........	300	1100	600	1700
7 Down...........	350	1300	700	2000

If redoubled, multiply the doubled values by 2

E. Cu.

Bidding Systems. Because of the great variety of card combinations, it long ago became apparent that standards for hand valuation would have to be adopted. For many years the most widely used standard of valuation was the honor-trick table popularized by Ely Culbertson. Its basis was:

AK = 2 honor tricks
AQ = 1½ honor tricks
A or KQ = 1 honor trick
Kx = ½ honor trick

In the early years of contract, this table was widely employed for both suit and no-trump bidding. But experienced players soon reached the conclusion that in no-trump bidding no pretense at accuracy could be made for the honor-trick table, and the practice developed of assigning point-count value to the high cards. Various tables were resorted to, and attempts at superaccuracy were made by the introduction of fractions, but the only survivor was the 4-3-2-1 scale introduced by Charles H. Goren and now almost universally accepted as the standard system for determining the bidding strength of a hand.

THE POINT-COUNT TABLE
A = 4 points
K = 3 points
Q = 2 points
J = 1 point

Opening Bids. The value of a hand for purposes of opening the bidding is computed by adding the points for high cards to the points assigned for distribution. Distribution points are counted as follows: 3 for a void, 2 for a singleton, 1 for a doubleton.

If a hand contains 14 points it must be opened; if it con-tains 13 points it may be opened if there is a convenient rebid. But all opening bids of 1 in a suit must contain at least two defensive tricks.

An opening bid of 1 no trump is made on an evenly balanced hand with protection in at least three suits and a high-card point-count of 16-18 points.

An opening bid of 2 in a suit is made when a hand is so strong that a game might be achieved even opposite a partner's very weak hand. Such an opening bid is therefore forcing, and both partners are required to continue bidding until they have bid game. The requirements for an opening demand bid are:

with a good 5-card suit..........................	25 points
with a good 6-card suit..........................	23 points
with a good 7-card suit..........................	21 points

Forcing bids may also be made subsequently in the auction. In general, when a player has opened the bidding, any bid by the partnership of exactly one more than is necessary is forcing and acts as a demand for game. In the normal course of bidding, when partner of the opener names a new suit, the opener must bid once more. In other words, a change of suit by responder is forcing for one round.

Responder will usually be in a strategic position to decide how far the partnership may proceed with safety and profit. If the combined partnership assets amount to 26 points (the sum of two opening bids), responder should make a distinct effort to see that a game contract is reached. If the total of partnership assets cannot be fully determined at once, partners should temporize in their bidding, and if it appears that the necessary 26 points are not available, the bidding should be dropped below game.

Not infrequently game may be reached even after an adversary has opened the bidding. Where an opponent of the opener has a hand that he considers to be at least as strong as that of the opener, and if he has hopes of winning the bid and possibly making game if his partner has any values, he makes a takeout double, thus requesting his partner to bid his best suit. The takeout double of 1 in a suit should be based on at least 13 or 14 points (in high cards and distribution) and the double of 1 no trump on at least 16 points or more.

When an adversary has opened the bidding, it may be reasonable to compete with hands of moderate strength by making a simple overcall. While such action does not promise a hand of great general strength, it should be based on possession of a strong suit to avoid the risk of a costly penalty double. Overcalling should be avoided on any hand where, if there is a double, the penalty would exceed 500 points. This means that if the hand is bid, there should be the probability that it will make at least within three tricks of the contract, if the declarer is not vulnerable, or within two, if vulnerable.

Pre-emptive Opening Bids. The modern practice in making opening bids of 3 or 4 of a suit differs widely from that in vogue in the early days of contract. The opening bid of 3 formerly indicated a powerful holding that was based on a solid suit; with experience, however, players discovered that this bid was of doubtful merit and it fell into disuse.

Today, the opening bid of 3 in both major and minor suits is used essentially for obstructive purposes. It is based on a suit of 6 or more cards and in high-card point count is weaker than a conventional opening bid of 1. The pre-emptive bid is not constructive, and the player making it is prepared to take a loss in order to keep his opponents from scoring. To keep this loss within bounds he should have within 3 tricks of his contract when not vulnerable and within 2 when vulnerable.

A pre-emptive bid of 4 in a major suit may be made with a fairly good hand where partner has previously passed and the chances of making a slam appear to be remote.

Slam Bidding. Slam bidding is a key feature of bridge because of the large bonuses involved. In terms of point count, the combined partnership assets should total 33-34 points to produce a small slam and 37 to produce a grand slam. If the slam is to be played at no trump, the required number of high-card points will be sufficient, but at a suit contract a satisfactory trump fit must also be present.

The Blackwood Convention. When it has been determined that a partnership has the proper assets for slam, it then remains to make certain that the opposition cannot take two quick tricks. The most popular method of finding out is the Blackwood Convention, which is a wholesale inquiry for aces and kings. A bid of 4 no trump, after a trump suit has been agreed upon, asks for aces. The responses are as follows:

> With no aces, responder bids 5 clubs
> With 1 ace, responder bids 5 diamonds
> With 2 aces, responder bids 5 hearts
> With 3 aces, responder bids 5 spades
> With 4 aces, responder bids 5 clubs

Observe that the same response is made to show both 4 aces and no aces. In practice, there is not the slightest chance of confusion, for the previous bidding will have made it clear which holding is being described.

If the Blackwood bidder wishes to find out how many kings his partner has, he bids 5 no trump, and his partner responds at the level of 6 in the same way that he has responded to the call for aces.

If the Blackwood bidder decides that there is no slam, he merely returns to 5 of the trump suit agreed upon. Needless to say, he should be very cautious about employing the convention if there is any danger that its use will get the bidding too high.

The Gerber Convention. An outgrowth of the Blackwood Convention is the Gerber 4-Club Convention, which has gained considerable following in certain sections of the country. Some players substitute a 4-club bid for the 4-no-trump bid to ask for aces. The responses follow a similar pattern:

> 4 diamonds shows no aces or 4 aces
> 4 hearts shows 1 ace
> 4 spades shows 2 aces
> 4 no trump shows 3 aces

When the 4-club bidder wishes to inquire for kings, the convention as modified by Charles H. Goren calls for him to bid 5 clubs, and responses are made in the same manner at the level of 5.

A greater number of bridge players retain the 4-no-trump bid to ask for aces but substitute the 4-club call whenever the opening bid has been made in no trump. The reason is that in such bidding the Blackwood bid is not available as an asking bid because 4 no trump is used in its natural sense as a quantitative bid.   C. H. Gor.

BRIDGE, in music, the arched wooden support which keeps the strings of violins and similar instruments stretched taut and which transmits sound vibrations from the strings to the resonant body. A bridge is also a connecting passage between two themes or sections of a composition.   W. Li.

BRIDGEBUILDING BROTHERHOOD (FRATRES PONTIFICES), the name applied to a number of religious fraternities organized in southern France and northern Italy in the twelfth and thirteenth centuries to aid travelers by building bridges and keeping ferries. According to tradition, the movement was started by a shepherd boy named Bénézet, who believed he had received a divine command to build a bridge across the Rhône at Avignon. Aided by the provost, Bénézet began work on the bridge in 1177, but died before it was completed in 1185. Four years later Clement III sanctioned the fraternity, which was organized to carry on the work of bridgebuilding. The movement spread widely, and the brotherhoods did much useful work until they became rich and idle. The order was finally dissolved by Pius II in the second half of the fifteenth century.   F. C. H.

BRIDGEPORT, a port city in southwestern Connecticut and a county seat of Fairfield Co., situated on Long Island Sound, about 17 mi. southwest of New Haven and 56 mi. northeast of New York City. It is served by the New York, New Haven and Hartford Railroad. Bridgeport was founded in 1639; it was incorporated as a borough in 1800 and as a city in 1836. It is essentially a manufacturing city specializing in such products as firearms, brass and bronze items, aircraft, tools, sewing machines, typewriters, drugs, electrical goods, corsets, plated ware, and hardware. During World War II Bridgeport was a center of arms and ammunition manufacture, and the influx of labor greatly increased its normal population. Among the educational institutions in Bridgeport are the University of Bridgeport, Bridgeport Engineering Institute, the Junior College of Connecticut, and the Bullard-Havens Technical School. Pop. 1950, 158,709.

BRIDGEPORT, a borough in Montgomery Co., in southeastern Pennsylvania, situated on the south bank of the Schuylkill River, 17 mi. north of Philadelphia. It is an industrial community surrounded by quarries. Bridgeport was incorporated in 1851, and is governed by a mayor and city council. Manufactures include iron and steel, coke, paper, and cotton and woolen goods. The Reading Railroad provides transportation. Pop. 1950, 5,827.

BRIDGEPORT, UNIVERSITY OF, at Bridgeport, Conn., was chartered in 1947. It began its four-year degree program after 20 years of existence as the two-year Junior College of Connecticut. The junior college, in which are the Weylister Secretarial School and the Fones School of Dental Hygiene, has been retained as a separate division. The University's curriculum is maintained by the colleges of arts and sciences, which includes the divisions of engineering, business administration, and education. Other sections of the university are the Arnold Division of Physical Education and the College of Nursing. *For statistics see* COLLEGES AND UNIVERSITIES.

BRIDGER, JAMES (1804-1881), American fur trapper and scout, was born at Richmond, Va., Mar. 17, 1804. When Jim was twelve his family moved to the vicinity of St. Louis, Mo., where he was apprenticed to a blacksmith. In 1822, he joined a fur-trapping expedition to the headwaters of the Missouri River. During the next twenty years, as an employee or partner in various fur companies, he journeyed constantly over the territory between Canada and the southern boundary of Colorado, and between the Missouri River and Idaho and Utah. He is the first white man known to have seen Great Salt Lake in Utah. On the Oregon Trail in southwestern Wyoming, in 1843, he established Fort Bridger, which served as a hostelry for pioneers migrating to Oregon. In 1853, he was expelled from this post by the Mormons, who wanted a monopoly of the emigrant business. He then retired, but soon entered government service as a scout and guide. He had guided the Stansbury railroad survey party to Utah in 1849, and, in 1857-1858, he conducted A. S. Johnston's army on its Utah expedition. In 1865-1866, he was a guide for the Powder River expedition, and measured the distance on the Bozeman Trail. In 1868 he retired again to his farm near Kansas City, Mo., where he died July 17, 1881.

A. W. Gr.

BRIDGES, (HENRY) STYLES (1898-), American politician, was born in West Pembroke, Me., on Sept. 9, 1898, and received his education at the University of Maine. After working as a county agricultural agent in Maine and New Hampshire and as director of an investment company, he was named a member of the New Hampshire Public Service Commission in 1930, and in 1935 won election as governor of the state. He was elected to the United States Senate in 1936, 1942, 1948, and 1954. As dean of the Senate Republicans after 1954, Bridges is considered one of the most influential of the party conservatives. President pro tem of the 83rd Congress and chairman of the G.O.P. policy committee in the 84th Congress, he also served as a member of the Appropriations and Armed Services committees.   C. W. D.

BRIDGES, ROBERT (SEYMOUR) (1844-1930), English poet laureate, was born Oct. 25, 1844, on the Isle of Thanet, Kent. After being educated at Eton and then Oxford, he studied medicine at St. Bartholomew's and later served on the staffs of various London hospitals; in 1882, however, he abandoned medicine and thereafter devoted himself to poetry. Of his poetic plays *The Return of Ulysses* (1890) is the most important; the most successful of his lyrics, collected in *The Poetical Works* (1914), the year after he was made laureate, are *A Passer-by* and the odes in which he abandoned the particularities of Wordsworth for the generalities of the eighteenth century. These lyrics, which he wrote from 1873 onwards, are characterized by Classical restraint in theme, diction, and image and by experimental prosody. He experimented with quantitative measures and, like his friend Gerard Manley Hopkins, whose works he edited in 1918, with sprung rhythm. Bridges' traditionalism and his decorous experimentation are also shown in his essays on poetry, *Milton's Prosody* (1893) and *Collected Essays* (1927-1936). *The Testament of Beauty* (1929), a long philosophical poem in phonetic spelling and loose Alexandrines, is his most notable work, its theme being his refuge in Platonic beauty from a world grown increasingly tiresome. He died on Apr. 21, 1930, at Chiswell, near Oxford. W. Y. T.

BRIDGES. A bridge is a structure providing passage over a waterway, a valley, a road, or other obstruction or interruption, without closing the way beneath. Bridges are classified (1) by their purpose or function, as aqueduct, viaduct, highway, railway, or footbridge; (2) by their material, as timber, masonry, iron, steel, or reinforced concrete; (3) by their type, as beam, truss, arch, or suspension; (4) by their interspan relations, as simple, cantilever, or continuous; (5) by the relative position of the bridge floor, as deck, through, or suspended; (6) by the method of joining the members, as pin-connected, riveted, or welded; and (7) by the method of providing clearance for navigation, as fixed (high-level), movable, or transporter bridges. Each bridge type is further subdivided on the basis of variations of form, arrangement of parts, or principle of action. A horizontal member simply resting on two supports is a simple beam. A deep, built-up beam, with parts joined to form web and flanges, is a girder. If the beam or girder is replaced by a framed or articulated combination of members, the resulting structural element is a truss. The usual arrangements of truss members employ the triangle as the basic figure resisting distortion. A beam, girder, or truss extending uninterruptedly over more than two supports is termed continuous. An end projecting beyond a support is a cantilever. The span from which it projects is an anchor span. Two cantilever arms from opposite banks or piers, with a connecting span bridging the reduced gap, form a cantilever span; the shorter connecting span is the suspended span. A bridge form in which vertical loading produces a horizontal thrust against the abutments is an arch. A bridge form in which vertical loading produces a horizontal tension or pull upon the abutments is a suspension bridge.

EVOLUTION OF BRIDGES

Primitive Bridgebuilding. Nature fashioned the first bridges. The fallen log, the natural arch formed by erosion, and the stem or vine festooned from tree to tree across a stream were the prototypes of the beam, the arch, and the suspension bridge. Neolithic man, about 5,000 B.C., with his hand-fashioned tools, was ready to imitate the natural structures. The primitive genius who felled a tree so that it dropped across a chasm was the first bridgebuilder. Log beams laid from stone to stone placed across a stream formed the first multiple-span bridge with intermediate piers. To widen his structure, the primitive builder placed two logs side by side. Later, the two tree trunks were separated and branches were laid across them to make the first bridge floor. In the northern glaciated countries, where timber was lacking, man used flat slabs of stone to connect the piers, a type of construction known in a later age as clapper bridges. In the warm southern climates, man fashioned vines or creepers into ropes to form primitive cable crossings. The next step was to string two parallel ropes, with a woven mat resting on the cables to form a floor. For greater comfort and safety, side ropes were later added to this structure, and these were connected to the lower cables by grasses or reeds to form a hammock or cage. With the change from nomadic to community life, bridges were built with more thought for permanence and comfort. As the tree-trunk bridge became inadequate, this type of structure was widened and the logs were adzed and carefully joined. The intermediate piers were made either of stones or of a wickerwork formed of branches and were filled in with earth and stones. The lake dwellers of Switzerland, about 2,500 B.C., built their huts on timber platforms supported on timber piles driven into the bed of the lake—the genesis of the timber pile and trestle bridge. In the warmer climates, the suspension bridge was being developed. The hammock type existed in regions as far apart as China, India, Africa, and South America. The most ancient suspension bridges in China were of the slide-rope or basket type, with a sliding basket or seat transporting the traveler. In India a new idea was born: from two parallel cables, the bridgebuilder hung vertical suspenders of thinner rope which carried the roadway platform at a lower level. This was the real prototype of the modern suspension bridge. India was also the birthplace of the cantilever bridge. Planks of wood, weighted down by the abutment stones, were projected from the two banks, each plank extending a little farther until a single piece was enough to connect the two projections. In Mesopotamia, about 4000 B.C., the true arch was born. It is probable that a Sumerian, in erecting a corbeled arch of horizontal bricks, happened to turn the bricks on end and discovered that the arch ring stayed in place. It took several thousand years for the arch form to develop. There is a vault at Dindereh, in Egypt, composed of three arch rings, which dates from about 3600 B.C. At Babylon a brick arch bridge, built about 1800 B.C. by order of Nimrod to connect two palaces on opposite sides of the Euphrates, was recorded as 30 ft. wide and 660 ft. long. It probably consisted of many short spans carried on intermediate piers. An old arch bridge at Dizful, Persia, built in about 350 B.C., is 1,250 ft. long and consists of twenty voussoir arches which are slightly pointed. About 450 B.C., the Greeks learned to build a voussoir arch, exemplified by one at Pergamum with a bold span of 27 ft.; but by temperament they preferred the post-and-lintel form of structure. The first arch bridges in China appeared after A.D. 100, following contacts with the cultures of Mesopotamia and India. A bridge believed to be the most ancient in the world is the caravan bridge, built about 850 B.C., spanning the river Meles at Smyrna with a single span 40 ft. long. It is said to have been used by Homer who by tradition spent his boyhood on this river, and later by St. Paul when he journeyed to Smyrna.

Roman Bridges. The first Roman bridge of which there is any record was a wooden structure—the Pons Sublicius (Bridge of Piles) over the Tiber, built 621 B.C. This was the bridge Horatius Cocles allegedly defended against the Etruscans in 598 B.C. As a warrior nation, the Romans had to build temporary wooden bridges as aids in conquest. Caesar and Hannibal built pontoon bridges in the same manner as Xerxes had built them four centuries earlier. Caesar has left us the earliest detailed description of a timber trestle, his famous bridge over the Rhine (55 B.C.), of which Vitruvius was probably the engineer. Trajan's historic bridge over the Danube, in Hungary, built A.D. 104, consisted of a series of semicircular timber arches resting on twenty stone piers, 150 ft. high and 170 ft. apart. It was built by Apollodorus of Damascus, the greatest engineer of that period. Not until twelve centuries later was this remarkable span length exceeded. Not satisfied with timber bridges, the Romans sought more permanent forms as enduring monuments of their culture. Many of their magnificent stone arches have endured through the centuries. Over the Tiber, in Rome itself, between 200 B.C. and A.D. 260, they erected eight fine stone bridges, six of which survive, including the Ponte Sant' Angelo. One of the most famous bridges in Italy is the beautiful Ponte di Augusto at Rimini, built about 5 B.C. In Spain, the oldest existing Roman bridge is at Martorell, in the province of Barcelona, built about 219 B.C. It is of hewn stone, with a central arch opening of 121 ft. Another magnificent specimen of Roman bridgebuilding in Spain is the famous bridge at Alcántara, towering a hundred feet above the river Tagus. The six vast semicircular arches of granite cross the gorge in spans of from 92 to 98 ft. It was built by Caius Julius Lacer in A.D. 98 for the Emperor Trajan. Another Spanish example of Roman grandeur is the aqueduct at Segovia, which is 2,500 ft. long and consists of two tiers of arches towering a hundred feet above the houses in the valley below. The greatest of Roman aqueducts is the Pont du Gard, at Nîmes, France, built by order of Agrippa in A.D. 14. It comprises three tiers of semicircular arches. The six huge arches in the first tier include one with an 80-ft. span over the river Gard. The top tier, of thirty-six smaller arches, extends 855 ft. from bank to bank and 155 ft. above the river. All Roman arches were semicircular; and massive piers were used, so that if one span were destroyed, the others would remain standing.

Middle Ages. After Rome crumbled, the remnants of accumulated knowledge were preserved in the half-forgotten religious orders of the Church. Travel was so disordered and dangerous at the end of the twelfth century that groups of churchmen formed a "Brotherhood of Bridgebuilders" to give aid to voyagers and to build bridges. The Altopascio Order, near Lucca in Italy, came to be known as the *Fratres Pontifices*. By decree of Emperor Frederick II in 1244, this hospice undertook to build and maintain, upon the public pilgrims' highway, a bridge for the service of travelers. A group of Benedictine monks in France formed a similar organization—the *Frères Pontiffes*. The beautiful twelfth-century bridge at Avignon was built by St. Bénézet. He was a young shepherd lad when he entered the church at Avignon, interrupted the Bishop's sermon, and declared that God had sent him to build a bridge over the Rhône. The construction required eight years (1177-1185). In honor of this great work, the inspired builder was later canonized. The four arches that remain have spans of from 101 to 110 ft. At the same time a monk in England, Peter of Colechurch, had a similar vision. He proposed the erection of a masonry bridge to cross the Thames at London. Funds were raised by enthusiastic popular subscription. The historic structure, the old London Bridge, was started in 1176 and finished in 1209, four years after the death of its founder. It consisted of nineteen pointed arches, with a drawbridge in one span. For six hundred years this famous bridge, weighted down by shops and dwellings, was the exciting center of London life, until the new London Bridge replaced it in 1831. When the townspeople of Cahors, France, wanted a fine new bridge, they persuaded the bishop of Cahors to direct the work. It took a long time in the building, from 1308 to 1355, but the Pont Valentre is the finest specimen of a medieval fortified bridge in the world. At Toledo, Spain, the Moors erected two bridges of unusual design, the Puente da Alcántara and the Puente de San Martin, over the Tagus. Lucerne, Switzerland, has a famous pair of medieval bridges, the Chapel Bridge (1333) and the "Dance of Death" Bridge (1408). Both are covered timber bridges. The beautiful Ponte Vecchio at Florence, built in 1345 on the design by Taddeo Gaddi, has three spans of 90 to 100 ft. The segmental curve used for the arches was unusual for the time. The famous Karlsbrücke at Prague represents a transition, as it took a century and a half to build, from 1348 to 1507. The piers are medieval, while the gate towers and adorned parapets herald the Renaissance. The medieval builder loaded his bridges with extraneous features, such as decorative and defensive towers, embattled parapets, chapels, statues, shops, and dwellings. Generally the span length of the medieval arch was between 40 and 75 ft. but occasionally spans of remarkable length were achieved. A stone arch built before A.D. 1000 over the Serchio River near Lucca was 120 ft. The first bridge over the Aar at Berne, built in 1204, had a single span of 150 ft. The single granite arch at Trezzo over the river Adda, in Italy, built in 1377 but destroyed in 1410, was 251 ft. The world had to wait five centuries before a masonry arch of longer span was constructed (the Luxembourg Bridge, 278 ft. span, in 1903).

Renaissance. In the Renaissance new ideas were born, but it took hundreds of years for these concepts to reach practical application. Leonardo da Vinci, about 1480, conceived portable military bridges and bascule bridges, but he did not build them. The most significant contribution of the Renaissance to the bridge art was the invention of the truss as a practical span type. Palladio (1518-1580) published his classic treatise in which he applied four different truss systems to bridgebuilding. The Cismone Bridge, employing Palladio's truss design, had a record span of 100 ft. With new advances in theory and technical skill, and as the first real labor-saving machines for construction were evolved, the builders of the Renaissance were able to create bridges befitting the civic spirit of their community, satisfying Palladio's criterion that bridges "should be commodious, beautiful, and lasting." A much admired bridge is the Rialto Bridge over the Grand

KEYSTONE VIEW CO.

RIALTO BRIDGE, VENICE, ITALY

Canal in Venice. In 1587 the Venetian Senate awarded the contract to Da Ponte, who was then seventy-five years of age and who was later also the builder of the famous Bridge of Sighs. The foundation piles were driven with a mechanical pile hammer and, after keeping all the stone-cutters in the city at work for two years, the bridge was completed in 1591. A single opening spans the canal; the arch curve is segmental, with 88½ ft. clear span and 21 ft. rise. The bridge is 75 ft. wide, with shops on both sides of the roadway. A Renaissance bridge even superior to the Rialto in engineering skill and in beauty of design was the Santa Trinità over the Arno in Florence, built between 1567 and 1569 and destroyed in World War II. It had three spans of white marble. The curve of the arches was the most mysterious and the most beautiful characteristic of the bridge. Prior arches had used a ratio of rise to span of ½ to ¼, but the curve of the Santa Trinità arches yielded the extremely radical ratio of ⅐. Bridge construction did its share in transforming Paris from a medieval town to a splendid Renaissance city. The first stone bridge over the Seine, the Pont Nôtre Dame, was built about 1505. The second, the Pont Neuf, started in 1575 and finished in 1606, has been in service more than three hundred years. In the Renaissance period the bridgebuilder was at once engineer, scientist, and artist. People began to regard bridges as civic works of art, and the bridgebuilder became truly a "civil" engineer, a leader in progress and a creator of useful public monuments.

Eighteenth and Nineteenth Centuries. In the eighteenth century, the "Age of Reason," empiricism and convention in bridge design gave way to rationalism and scientific analysis. In 1714 the first treatise on bridgebuilding appeared, written by Hubert Gautier, a French engineer. In 1716, under Louis XV, the Corps des Ponts et Chaussées was founded for the scientific advancement of bridge and road building; and in 1747 there was founded at Paris the first engineering school in the world, the famous École des Ponts et Chaussées. The first teacher and director was Jean Perronet, a brilliant engineer, the "Father of Modern Bridgebuilding." The greatest works of the century came from the inventive genius of Perronet. In his hands the masonry arch reached perfection.

He was the first builder to realize that the intermediate piers bore only the difference between the adjacent thrusts and, accordingly, he reduced the piers to one half their former width. He perfected the arch curve, devised a new pier construction, introduced the balustraded parapet, and invented construction machinery. Perronet's finest bridge, from an engineering standpoint, was the Pont Sainte Maxence over the Oise. The amazing slenderness of the piers was a milestone in bridge design. The bridge stood for nearly one hundred years, until destroyed by the Germans in 1870. For his most famous bridge, the Pont de la Concorde in Paris, Perronet, at the age of seventy-eight, planned an even more remarkable structure, but was forced by ignorant officials to modify his vision; it was too far beyond the grasp of his fellow men. Living in a shack at one end of the work, the old engineer completed the monumental structure in 1791. Perhaps no other bridge in the world has the same quality of civic dignity and nobility. In London the people were clamoring for additional structures over the Thames; the old London Bridge no longer satisfied the needs of the growing city. Money was raised by a government lottery, and between 1738 and 1750 the Westminster Bridge was built. Immediately agitation began for a third structure over the Thames and, between 1760 and 1768, the Blackfriars Bridge was built by Robert Milne, an English engineer who had studied in Italy. The greatest English bridgebuilder of his generation was John Rennie. Apprenticed as a millwright, he studied mathematics, was graduated from the University of Edinburgh, and then toured England on horseback to visit engineering works. In 1785, at the age of twenty-four, he built his first bridge, a three-span elliptical arch bridge across the Waters of Leith, near Edinburgh. In 1809 Rennie was retained to draw up plans for another new bridge over the Thames, later named the Waterloo Bridge. His adopted design consisted of nine semielliptical arches each of 120 ft. span. In 1817 the magnificent bridge was opened with an elaborate celebration, attended by the Prince Regent, the Duke of Wellington, and other notables. The bridgebuilder was offered a knighthood, which he refused, preferring to remain known as John Rennie, engineer of the Waterloo Bridge, which was replaced in 1942 by the present structure. The last of Rennie's great works was the design of the new London Bridge, consisting of five semielliptical arches of 130 to 150 ft. span. After his plans were accepted by Parliament, Rennie died at the age of sixty-one. His son, Sir John Rennie, was selected to build the bridge the father had designed, and in 1831 it was completed. Perronet's segmental and Rennie's semielliptical arch curves brought greater span lengths, more stable arches, and richer beauty. Arch construction had come a long way in its 5,000 years of evolution, from the corbeled vault of ancient Mesopotamia to the arches of the Pont de la Concorde.

Timber Spans and Covered Bridges. Covered wooden bridges may be found in almost all forested countries, among them France, Germany, Norway, England, Austria, Hungary, Switzerland, and Russia. Although Palladio designed and built wooden truss bridges in the sixteenth century, the truss principle had to wait about two hundred years before it was rediscovered. The famous covered bridges of Lucerne undoubtedly inspired the work of the Grubenmann brothers, Johannes and Hans Ulrich, who were village carpenters in the tiny Swiss hamlet of Teufen. Three of their bridges, built between 1756 and 1766, achieved lasting fame, although they are no longer standing, having been destroyed by the French in 1799. The Schaffhausen Bridge over the Rhine in northern Switzerland was a continuous two-span truss resting lightly on an intermediate pier under heavy loads, one span being 193 ft. and the other 171 ft. The bridge at Reichenau was very similar in its truss and arch design, but it had only a single span, 240 ft. in length. The bridge over the Limmat at Wettingen, near Zurich, had a span of 200 ft. (not 390 ft. as traditionally recorded through a historical error). It is believed to have been the first timber span using a true arch — a solid curved arch rib built up of timber layers. By comparison, prior timber spans had used triangular or polygonal tied arches with inclined radiating struts. All

KEYSTONE VIEW CO.

EXTERIOR VIEW OF COVERED WOODEN BRIDGE

three of the Grubenmann bridges combined the arch and truss principles, as did all early wooden covered bridges. The truss, its strength being uncertain, was made to rely somewhat upon the older form of the arch. The first framed timber bridge in America was Colonel Enoch Hale's Bridge over the Connecticut River at Bellows Falls, Vt., built in 1785. The structure was 365 ft. long, but inclined struts and a timber pier on a reef in the middle of the river reduced the length to two spans of about 98 ft. When the bridge was completed, it was heralded as the greatest achievement in American bridgebuilding, and people traveled far to see it. Timothy Palmer, a pioneer bridgebuilder, was among the first to point out the great advantage of covering wooden bridges, insisting that this protection from the weather increased the life of a structure. Between 1804 and 1806 he built a famous timber bridge over the Schuylkill River at Philadelphia, consisting of three arching spans, 150, 195, and 150 ft., carried on stone piers and abutments. It was called the "Permanent Bridge," and carried traffic for fifty years before a fire destroyed it. In 1820 Ithiel Town, a Connecticut architect, took out a patent on a lattice truss. The truss used simple sizes of lumber, and was easy to erect. A typical Town lattice truss was the Tucker Bridge, which succeeded the Enoch Hale structure at Bellows Falls, Vt. Built in 1840, the Tucker Bridge was a continuous truss of two spans; its total length was 262 ft. In 1840 William Howe, an architect in Massachusetts, patented the Howe truss, using timber diagonals with vertical tension rods of iron, representing a transition from the wooden to the iron bridge. In 1844 Caleb and Thomas Pratt invented a truss which was exactly the reverse of the Howe truss; the diagonals, instead of the verticals, were of iron and were in tension.

As late as 1952 there were 1,994 old covered bridges in the United States, 1,919 of them still in service.

Iron Bridges. The first iron bridge was the Coalbrookdale Bridge, over the Severn River in England, an arch of 100-ft. span, built in 1779 by Abraham Darby and John Wilkinson, local iron smelters. The first use of iron in European bridge

construction was for the chain cables of the Wynch Bridge, a suspension footbridge of 70-ft. span over the Tees River in England. It was built in 1741, with the flooring supported directly on the cables in primitive fashion. The suspended level floor, a feature of modern suspension bridges, was invented by an American, James Finley of Fayette County, Pennsylvania. He built the first bridge of this construction in 1801 over Jacob's Creek in his home county, with a span

INTERIOR VIEW OF COVERED WOODEN BRIDGE

of 70 ft. Between 1819 and 1826 Thomas Telford built the Menai Straits Bridge in Wales, a suspension bridge with wrought iron chains, with a record-breaking span of 580 ft. This monumental structure was Telford's crowning achievement, earning for him enduring fame. The most famous of the early railroad bridges is the Britannia Tubular Bridge, built by Robert Stephenson between 1846 and 1850 across the Menai Straits, not far from Telford's suspension bridge. The Britannia Bridge consists of two continuous tubes, placed side by side, carried on two abutments and three towers, forming four spans of 230, 460, 460, and 230 ft. In the 1850's, as wrought iron replaced cast iron in bridge construction for greater safety, many new truss types made their appearance. These were named after their inventors, Whipple, Bollman, Fink, and others. The famous Firth of Tay Bridge in Scotland, completed in 1877, consisted of eighty-four truss spans of wrought iron. On the night of Dec. 29, 1879, thirteen 245-ft. truss spans were blown down by the wind, and a train of six coaches crashed into the waters eighty-eight feet below, with the loss of all passengers. During the 1870's and 1880's bridges on American railroads were failing at a rate of twenty-five a year. Something had to be done. This need inaugurated a new era in bridgebuilding—one of specialization, scientific design, research, specifications, careful detailing, thorough testing and inspection, and a new material, steel. The first all-steel bridge was at Glasgow, S. D., over the Missouri River, built by General William Sooy Smith in 1878. With steel and mathematics, the unsightly iron trusses of the nineteenth century evolved into new bridge forms, forms combining strength and beauty—the modern arch, cantilever, continuous truss, and suspension bridges. The Industrial Revolution had introduced an era of ugly iron bridges, but this necessary period of apprenticeship was brought to an end by the availability of steel.

MODERN BRIDGE TYPES

Steel Arch Bridges. An arch is a structure in which vertical loading produces a horizontal outward thrust which is resisted at the two ends of the span, usually by the abutments. In a tied-arch, the outward thrust is resisted by a horizontal tension member joining the two ends of the arch. Steel arches are three-hinged, two-hinged, or hingeless. Two hinges or rotation points may be provided at the springing points or end bearings, and a third hinge at the crown of the arch. The curved arch rib, corresponding to the arch ring in masonry arches, is the essential load-carrying element. It may be solid-web, as in plate-girder rib arches: or of truss

KEYSTONE VIEW CO.

HELL GATE BRIDGE, NEW YORK CITY

construction, as in truss rib arches. In a deck arch, the horizontal roadway is carried above the arch by means of spandrel columns supported on the arch rib. In a through arch, or arch with suspended roadway, the horizontal roadway is suspended from the arch rib. In a half-through arch, the horizontal roadway line cuts the line of the arch rib. If the full space between the arch rib and the horizontal roadway line above it is utilized for the stiffening construction, the structure is a spandrel-braced arch. Another form of spandrel-braced arch is the Hell Gate Bridge type, in which the top chord is curved for economy, clearance, or aesthetics, and the roadway line is carried at a lower level as a half-through construction. The world's greatest steel arch spans are listed in the following tabulation:

highway, and streetcar loading after more than seventy years of service. The Victoria Falls Bridge over the Zambezi River in Rhodesia, completed in 1907, is a steel arch of 650-ft. span, carrying a railroad over a scenic gorge 400 ft. deep. For erection of the arch, a cableway was used; the first line was sent across the chasm by a rocket. Inspired by the success of the Eads Bridge a generation earlier, the modern era in steel arch construction began with the twentieth century. One of the greatest arches of all time is the Hell Gate Bridge over the East River at New York, with a span length of 977½ feet. Completed in 1917, it was the crowning achievement of Gustav Lindenthal. The roadway is suspended from the arch and carries four railroad tracks on a heavy ballasted floor. The outline of the arch, framed between great masonry towers, produces a monumental composition. Aesthetically, the logi-

THE PORT OF NEW YORK AUTHORITY

KILL VAN KULL BRIDGE, BAYONNE, N. J.

cal form of an arch bridge is the deck type, with the roadway carried in an unbroken line above the arch rib. The Henry Hudson Bridge, carrying the Henry Hudson Parkway over the mouth of the Harlem River at Spuyten Duyvil, New York City, is a deck-arch bridge of 800-ft. span, designed by Robinson and Steinman. The traffic proved so heavy, as

TABLE I. GREATEST STEEL ARCH BRIDGES

Bridge	Span in Ft.	Location	Waterway	Year
Kill Van Kull (Bayonne)	1,652	Port Richmond, N.Y.-Bayonne, N.J.	Kill Van Kull	1931
Sydney Harbor[4]	1,650	Sydney, Australia	Sydney Harbor	1932
Birchenough	1,080	S. E. Rhodesia	Sabi River	1935
Hell Gate Arch[3]	977½	Queens-Bronx (New York City)	East River	1917
Rainbow[1]	950	Niagara Falls, N.Y.	Niagara River	1941
Clifton[2]	840	Niagara Falls, N.Y.	Niagara River	1898
Duisburg-Rheinhausen	838	Germany	Rhine River	1951
Henry Hudson[1]	800	Manhattan-Bronx (New York City)	Harlem River (at Spuyten Duyvil)	1936
Waal River	790	Nijmegen, The Netherlands	Waal River	1939
West End	778	Pittsburgh, Pa.	Ohio River	1931
Croton Lake	750	Westchester Co., N.Y.	Croton Lake	1931
McKees Rocks	750	Pittsburgh, Pa.	Ohio River	1931
Viaur Viaduct[3]	722	France	Viaur Valley	1898
West Bridge	668	Stockholm, Sweden	Lake Mälaren	1936
Victoria Falls[3]	650	Rhodesia	Zambezi River	1907

[1] Hingeless arch. [2] Not standing. [3] Railroad. [4] Railroad and vehicle.

The Eads Bridge, over the Mississippi River at St. Louis, was built between 1867 and 1874 by Captain James B. Eads, the only engineer in the American Hall of Fame. With three arch spans of 502, 520, and 502 feet, it was the largest and boldest arch bridge of its day. This pioneer structure represented the first large-scale use of steel in bridge construction, the first use of pneumatic caissons in the founding of large piers, the first major use of the cantilever method of bridge erection, the first use of hollow tubular chord members, and the first use of high-strength alloy steel as a bridge material. In 1952 the bridge was still standing, carrying heavy railroad,

anticipated by the engineers, that one month after the bridge was opened in December, 1936, the addition of an upper deck was authorized to double the traffic capacity.

Suspension Bridges. A suspension bridge has three essential parts: the towers, the anchorages, and the cables. The cables are the load-carrying and most important element. The trusses or girders serve to stiffen the cables against deformation and to distribute localized load. In America nearly all of the existing suspension bridges are of the wire cable type. In Europe the eyebar or chain type has predominated. The towers of a suspension bridge may be rigid, flexible, or rocker

GEORGE WASHINGTON BRIDGE, NEW YORK CITY

THE PORT OF NEW YORK AUTHORITY

type. In a self-anchored suspension bridge, the masonry anchorages are eliminated and the ends of the cable or eyebar chain are anchored to the structure itself, the stiffening girder acting as a strut for the full length of the bridge.

Between 1856 and 1867 Roebling built the great suspension bridge over the Ohio River at Cincinnati, with a record-breaking span of 1,057 ft.

Brooklyn Bridge. In 1867 Roebling came to New York to

TABLE II. OUTSTANDING SUSPENSION BRIDGES

Bridge	Span in Ft.	Location	Waterway	Year
Golden Gate	4,200	San Francisco-Marin Co., Calif.	Entrance to San Francisco Bay	1937
Mackinac	3,800	Michigan	Straits of Mackinac	1957
George Washington	3,500	New York City-Fort Lee, N.J.	Hudson River	1931
Narrows (Tacoma)	2,800	Tacoma, Wash.	Puget Sound	1951
Transbay (West Bay)	2,310	San Francisco-Oakland, Calif.	San Francisco Bay	1936
Bronx-Whitestone	2,300	Bronx-Whitestone (New York City)	East River	1939
Delaware Memorial	2,150	Wilmington, Del.	Delaware River	1951
Ambassador	1,850	Detroit, Mich.-Windsor, Ont.	Detroit River	1929
Sky Ride[1]	1,850	Chicago (World's Fair)	(Century of Progress Lagoon)	1933
Delaware River[3]	1,750	Philadelphia, Pa.-Camden, N.J.	Delaware River	1926
Bear Mountain	1,632	Bear Mountain-Peekskill, N.Y.	Hudson River	1924
Williamsburg[3]	1,600	Manhattan-Brooklyn (New York City)	East River	1903
Chesapeake Bay	1,600	Sandy Point, Md.	Chesapeake Bay	1952
Brooklyn[3]	1,595½	Manhattan-Brooklyn (New York City)	East River	1883
Lions Gate	1,550	Vancouver, B.C.	Vancouver Harbor	1939
Mid-Hudson	1,500	Poughkeepsie-Highland, N.Y.	Hudson River	1930
Manhattan[3]	1,470	Manhattan-Brooklyn (New York City)	East River	1909
Triborough	1,380	Manhattan-Queens-Bronx (New York City)	East River	1936
Clifton[1]	1,268	Niagara Falls, N.Y.	Niagara River	1869
Cologne[1]	1,240	Cologne-Mülheim, Germany	Rhine River	1941
St. Johns	1,207	Portland, Ore.	Willamette River	1931
Mount Hope	1,200	Bristol, Rhode Island	Narragansett Bay	1929
Florianopolis[2, 3]	1,114	Santa Catharina-Florianopolis, Brazil	Santa Catharina Bay	1926
Deer Isle	1,080	Deer Isle, Maine	Eggemoggin Reach	1939

[1] Not standing. [2] Eyebar cables. [3] Railroad and vehicle.

The first wire suspension bridge was a light footbridge, 408 ft. long and 18 in. wide, over the Schuylkill Falls at Fairmount in Philadelphia, Pa., built in 1816 by White and Hazard, with two cables, each consisting of three brass wires. It collapsed the same year under the winter load of ice and snow. The modern air-stringing method of building parallel wire cables and the stiffening of suspension bridges were developed and perfected by John A. Roebling, who came to America in 1831. Between 1851 and 1855 Roebling built his world-famous Niagara Railway Suspension Bridge, with a span of 821 ft. It was replaced by an arch bridge in 1897.

design and build his crowning work, the Brooklyn Bridge over the East River to Brooklyn. Two years later, after completing his plans and overcoming all obstacles, he died as the result of an accident during the final surveys. His son, Colonel Washington Roebling, carried the work forward and, despite his affliction in 1872 by caisson disease, which left him a helpless invalid, he continued to direct the work to its final completion. On May 24, 1883, the completed bridge, a triumph of engineering, was officially dedicated. It was the first suspension bridge using steel wire for the cables, also steel for the suspended structure. It is undoubtedly the

BROOKLYN BRIDGE, NEW YORK CITY

most famous bridge in the world, and is generally recognized as the most artistically satisfying of the bridges of the age. Roebling taught the world how to build enduring suspension bridges. His bridges stood up when those built by his contemporaries were blown down by the wind. When a later generation of engineers overlooked the fundamental principles Roebling had preached and exemplified, disaster followed. The Brooklyn Bridge held the record as the longest suspension span for twenty years.

Other Suspension Bridge Records. In 1903 the second East River bridge, the Williamsburg, was completed with a span length of 1,600 ft., only 4½ ft. longer than Roebling's span. In 1924 the Bear Mountain Bridge over the Hudson River was completed with a new record span-length of 1,632 ft., only to be surpassed in 1926 by the famed Delaware River Bridge, with a span of 1,750 ft. This in turn yielded to the Ambassador Bridge in Detroit, Mich. (1929), with a span of 1,850 ft. Even this record was soon shattered. In 1931 the George Washington Bridge, spanning the Hudson at New York, was completed, with a span of 3,500 ft., and in 1937 the Golden Gate Bridge at San Francisco eclipsed all records with a span of 4,200 ft. The suspension bridge completely displaced the cantilever as the accepted type for long-span construction.

Later Suspension Designs. The Williamsburg Bridge, designed by Leffert L. Buck, was the first large suspension bridge constructed with steel towers. The stiffening trusses are 40 ft. deep, or ¹⁄₄₀ of the span, the highest depth ratio ever used. Thereafter there was a reversal of trend toward progressively increasing slenderness and grace in the design of suspension bridges, reaching its climax in 1940 in the ill-fated Tacoma Narrows Bridge. The Manhattan Bridge, completed six years after the Williamsburg Bridge, is much more pleasing in design. It was the first application of the flexible design of steel towers. One of the earliest examples of the self-anchored suspension type was the chain bridge of 605-ft. span over the Rhine at Cologne, Germany (1915). Between 1926 and 1928 three bridges of this type were built over the Allegheny River at Pittsburgh, Pa.—the Sixth, Seventh, and Ninth Street Bridges. In 1929 a self-anchored suspension bridge of 1,034-ft. span with wire cables were completed over the Rhine between Cologne and Mülheim, establishing a

new record of span length for the European continent. These bridges set the fashion for the use of stiffening girders, instead of trusses, with resulting simplicity of line and slenderness of proportion. The longest eyebar suspension span in the world is the Florianopolis Bridge, which spans the waters of the Atlantic to carry highway, railway, and aqueduct from the mainland of Brazil to the island city of Florianopolis. It was designed by Robinson and Steinman, and was completed in 1926. With a main span of 1,114 ft., it is the largest bridge in South America. It was the first application of a new form of stiffening truss, yielding a structure four times as rigid as the conventional parallel-chord design while using only two-thirds as much steel. Another novel feature was the use of rocker towers, steel towers designed to rock at the base. Supplementing the eyebar chain and the parallel wire cable, a third type of cable construction is the rope-strand cable, composed of prefabricated, prestressed, twisted rope strands of steel wire, saving the time required for the older air-spinning method. This new type of cable construction was introduced and developed by Robinson and Steinman, commencing with the Grand'mère Bridge in Quebec, Canada (950-ft. span, 1929), and subsequently applied in the Waldo-

TRANSBAY BRIDGE, SAN FRANCISCO-OAKLAND, CALIFORNIA
(West Bay portion)

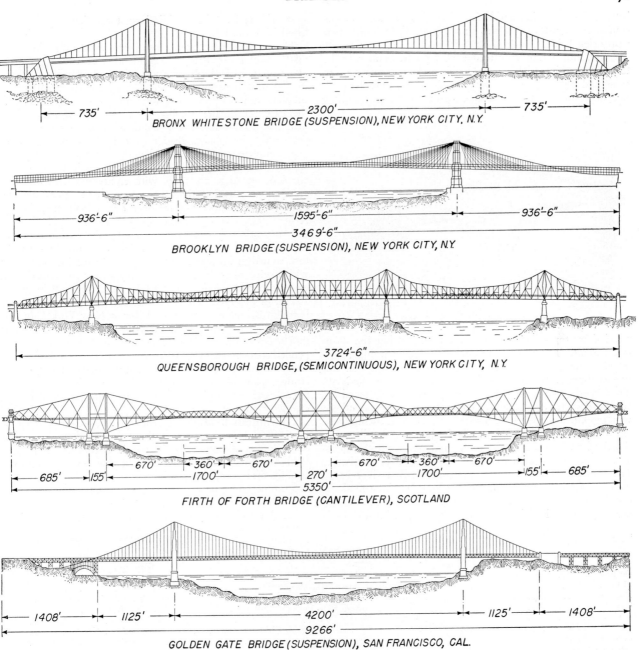

BRONX WHITESTONE BRIDGE (SUSPENSION), NEW YORK CITY, N.Y.

735'   2300'   735'

BROOKLYN BRIDGE (SUSPENSION), NEW YORK CITY, N.Y.

936'-6"   1595'-6"   936'-6"
3469'-6"

QUEENSBOROUGH BRIDGE, (SEMICONTINUOUS), NEW YORK CITY, N.Y.

3724'-6"

FIRTH OF FORTH BRIDGE (CANTILEVER), SCOTLAND

685' 155' 670' 360' 670' 270' 670' 360' 670' 155' 685'
1700'   1700'
5350'

GOLDEN GATE BRIDGE (SUSPENSION), SAN FRANCISCO, CAL.

1408'   1125'   4200'   1125'   1408'
9266'

TYPICAL BRIDGE PROFILES

Hancock Bridge, the St. Johns Bridge, the Thousand Islands Bridge, the Wabash River Bridge, the Deer Isle Bridge, and the Lions Gate Bridge at Vancouver, B.C. (1,550-ft. span, 1939). The George Washington Bridge, spanning the Hudson River at New York with its record-breaking span-length of 3,500 ft., was opened in 1931 at an initial cost of $60,000,-000. It has four parallel-wire cables of 36-inch diameter. Provision was made for eight lanes of highway traffic on the present deck and for the future addition of a lower deck. The record of the George Washington Bridge as the longest span in the world lasted only six years. In 1937 the Golden Gate Bridge at San Francisco was completed with a main span of 4,200 ft. The towers are 746 ft. high, and the span is carried by two cables of 36½ in. diameter. On July 1, 1940, the Tacoma Narrows Bridge at Puget Sound was completed and opened to traffic. Built at a cost of $6,400,000, with a main span of 2,800 ft., it was the third longest span in the world. Four months later, on November 7, 1940, the persistent undulations of the bridge in a 42-mile gale changed to twisting oscillations and increased to destructive amplitude until the main span broke up, ripping loose from the cables and crashing into the waters below. The Tacoma Bridge was by far the most flexible of contemporary suspension bridges. The stiffening girders were only 8 ft. deep, or 1/350 of the span. This yielded entirely inadequate rigidity and energy absorption to counteract the inherent aerodynamic instability of the cross section. The phenomenon is one of self-excited amplification of oscillations, drawing energy from the wind, until the oscillations reach limiting or destructive amplitudes. Future design will emphasize the selection of aerodynamically stable sections and the provision of ample stiffening. The largest bridge project up to 1947, the Transbay Bridge between San Francisco and Oakland, costing $78,000,000, was completed in 1936. The total length is 8 mi., including two suspension bridges, each of 2,310-ft. main span, in the west crossing, and a cantilever bridge of 1,400-ft. main span in the east crossing. This is a double-deck construction for combined highway and railway crossing. A record foundation depth of 240 ft. was reached for one of the piers, using

KEYSTONE VIEW CO.

FIRTH OF FORTH BRIDGE, SCOTLAND

novel dome-topped dredging caissons for sinking the deep foundations. The Bronx-Whitestone Bridge spanning Long Island Sound, with a main span of 2,300 ft., was built in twenty-three months and opened in 1939 in time for the New York World's Fair. In 1946 the bridge was strengthened by adding deep trusses to the stiffening girders and was otherwise modified in order to reduce the aerodynamic oscillations.

Cantilever Bridges. A cantilever span is generally composed of anchored trusses, cantilevered out from the piers and connected by a shorter, suspended span. A cantilever span can be erected without falsework, so that river navigation is not impeded during construction. The first modern cantilever bridge was built in 1867 by Heinrich Gerber across the river Main at Hassfurt, Germany, with a central span of 425 ft. The world's largest cantilever bridges are listed in Table III.

The world's most famous cantilever structure is the colossal Firth of Forth Bridge in Scotland, with two main spans of 1,700 ft. each, built between 1882 and 1890 by Sir John Fowler and Benjamin Baker. The steel truss members are tubular, and the massive towers and trusses are spread at the base for greater stability. The Firth of Forth Bridge held the world's record for length of span for twenty-seven years until the Quebec Bridge over the St. Lawrence River was completed, with a span length of 1,800 ft. The first attempt to build this span ended in disaster in the course of erection, on Aug. 29, 1907, with eighty-two lives lost. Investigations revealed that the collapse was caused by the buckling of a compression member, due to inadequate lacing. A new design was prepared, heavier and more rigid, with the suspended span to be erected by the lifting method. In 1916, when the 5,200-ton span had gone up about twelve feet, something slipped, and the span crashed into the river, with twelve more lives lost. In 1917 a new suspended span was completed and was successfully raised the full height of 150 ft. in ninety-six hours of jacking. In 1909 the Queensborough Bridge over the East River at New York City was completed with two cantilever spans of 1,182 and 984 ft. It differs from other cantilever bridges in that it has no suspended spans so that the structure is semi-continuous. Nickel steel was used for the eyebar tension members. The Howrah Bridge spanning the Hooghly River at Calcutta, built between 1938 and 1943, has a 1,500-ft. span, the third largest cantilever span in the world.

Continuous Bridges. A beam, girder, or truss resting on more than two supports, without intermediate hinges or other interruptions of continuity, is a continuous bridge. With the successful execution of several notable examples around 1917-1918, the continuous truss became established as an important type in American bridge practice. The longest continuous truss spans are listed in Table IV.

The Lachine railroad bridge over the St. Lawrence River,

TABLE III. LONG-SPAN CANTILEVER BRIDGES

Bridge	Span in Ft.	Location	Waterway	Year
Quebec[1]	1,800	Quebec, Canada	St. Lawrence River	1917
Firth of Forth[1]	(2 main) 1,700	Inch-Garvier-Queensferry (Scotland)	Firth of Forth	1889
Howrah	1,500	Calcutta, India	Hooghly River	1943
Transbay[2]	1,400	East Bay Crossing (San Francisco-Oakland, Calif.)	San Francisco Bay	1936
Longview	1,200	Longview, Wash.	Columbia River	1930
Queensborough[2]	(main) 1,182	Manhattan-Queens (New York City)	East River	1909
Carquinez Strait	(2 main) 1,100	Crockett-Vallejo, Calif	Carquinez Strait	1927
Harbor Bridge[1]	1,097	Montreal, Canada	St. Lawrence River	1930
Cooper River	1,050	Charleston, S.C.	Cooper River	1929
East St. Louis	963	East St. Louis, Ill.	Mississippi River	1950
Story Bridge	924	Queensland, Australia	Brisbane River	1940

[1] Railroad.　[2] Railroad and vehicle.

TABLE IV. LONG-SPAN CONTINUOUS TRUSS BRIDGES

Bridge	Span in Ft.	Location	Waterway	Year
Dubuque	845	Dubuque, Iowa	Mississippi River	1942
Duisburg[1]	839	Duisburg-Hochfeld, Germany	Rhine River	1935
Sciotoville[2]	(2 main) 775	Sciotoville, Ohio	Ohio River	1917
Chain of Rocks	699	Near St. Louis, Mo.	Mississippi River	1929
Neuwied[1]	698	Neuwied, Germany	Rhine River	1935
Cincinnati[2]	675	Cincinnati, Ohio	Ohio River	1929
Cape Girardeau	672	Cape Girardeau, Mo.	Mississippi River	1928
Chester	670	Chester, Ill.	Mississippi River	1946
Quincy	628	Quincy, Ill.	Mississippi River	1930
Bourne	616	Buzzard's Bay End of Cape Cod Canal, Mass.	Cape Cod Canal	1934
Sagamore	616	Cape Cod Bay End of Cape Cod Canal, Mass.	Cape Cod Canal	1935

[1] Not standing.　[2] Railroad.

near Montreal, Canada, built in 1888 by C. Shaler Smith with four spans of 269, 408, 408, and 269 ft., was the only continuous truss bridge in America before 1917. The Sciotoville Bridge over the Ohio River, completed in 1917 with two spans of 775 ft., made a new record for span length and established the continuous type in American practice. It is a double-track railroad bridge, built by Gustav Lindenthal with D. B. Steinman as designing engineer. The two spans were necessary to satisfy the navigation requirements, and the continuous truss design afforded an ideal solution, yielding maximum economy of steel, maximum rigidity under railroad traffic, and the important advantage of cantilever erection, leaving the main river channel unobstructed by falsework. Compared with two simple spans, the continuous design saved 20 per cent of the steel required. Around 1927 the application of the continuous type was extended to highway bridges. A more artistic form of continuous truss bridge, with arch outline and suspended roadway in the central span, was developed and applied in a series of effective structures, including the Lake Champlain Bridge (1929), the Bourne Bridge (1934), the Sagamore Bridge (1935) over Cape Cod Canal, and the Mississippi River Bridge at Dubuque, Iowa (1942). The Dubuque Bridge established a new span record, with an 845-ft. central span in the form of a tied arch. Another continuous form, the continuous plate-girder bridge, has received rapid development since 1935. In the United States, three successive records for span-length were established in a brief period: the Thomas A. Edison Bridge at Perth Amboy, N.J., built in 1940, with a main span of 250 ft.; the Lakefront Bridge at Cleveland, completed the same year with a main span of 271 ft.; and the Charter Oak Bridge (1942) over the Connecticut River at Hartford, designed by Robinson and Steinman, with a central span of 300 ft. In 1951 two bridges with continuous girder spans of 375 ft. were built to carry the New Jersey Turnpike over the Passaic and Hackensack rivers. Three new bridges over the Rhine River in Germany established new records for continuous girder spans: Cologne-Deutz (1948), 605 ft.; Bonn-Beuel (1949), 643 ft.; and Düsseldorf-Neuss (1951), 676 ft. A new form of continuous bridge, developed between 1936 and 1940, is the Wichert continuous type, distinguished by the use of linked members forming open quadrilaterals over the intermediate piers. The first bridge of this type was the Pittsburgh-Homestead Bridge (1937) over the Monongahela River, made up of ten semicontinuous arched trusses, including two spans of 533½ ft. In 1938-1941, seven more were built, including the Havre de Grace Bridge (1940) and the Potomac River Bridge at Ludlow Ferry (1941).

Simple Truss Bridges. With the change from timber and iron to steel, the older truss forms (Burr, Town, Howe, Pratt, Whipple, Bollman, Fink, and Warren) have given way to more efficient forms, such as the Baltimore, Parker, and Pennsylvania types, and the K-Truss. The record span lengths are listed in Table V.

Movable Bridges. A movable bridge is one that can be changed in position so as to open a clear passage, or to afford an increased clear height, for ships or boats in navigable channels. The principal modern types are swing bridges, turning about a vertical axis; bascule bridges, swinging upward about a horizontal axis; and lift bridges, moving vertically. Other movable bridge types are retractile bridges, moving longitudinally; transporter bridges, carrying a moving plat-

CAPE COD CHAMBER OF COMMERCE

SAGAMORE BRIDGE, CAPE COD, MASS.

form suspended from an overhead fixed span; and floating pontoon bridges, arranged to retract or swing aside for navigation to pass.

Swing Bridges. A swing bridge (or draw span) is a movable bridge that can turn about a vertical axis to permit shipping to pass. The support on the pivot pier is either center bearing or rim bearing. The two projecting arms act as cantilevers when the bridge is open. When closed, the bridge acts as a continuous truss or girder, resting on three supports if it is center bearing, or on four supports if it is rim bearing. In a bob-tailed swing bridge the two arms are unequal, and a balancing counterweight is usually required on the shorter arm. The combined length, including both arms, is conventionally given as the span length of a swing bridge. A swing bridge requires a large pivot pier in the middle of the channel, rest piers for the open bridge, and long fenders to protect the span when open. It blocks the channel during operation, and full opening is required even for small vessels.

Bascule Bridges. The bascule and vertical lift types of movable bridges offer advantages of rapidity of operation, briefer duration of opening, minimum obstruction of the channel, and greater safety against collision with river craft. In addition, the bascule type offers greater safety to land traffic and unlimited vertical clearance. Since 1919 the record for single-leaf bascule spans has been held by the 260-ft. span of the St. Charles Air Line Railway Bridge at Sixteenth Street, Chicago. The double-leaf bascule had its record span increased to 336 ft. in 1941 by the Canadian Pacific Railroad Bridge over the ship canal at Sault Ste. Marie, Mich. This bascule is unique in that it acts as a simple truss when closed, whereas double-leaf bascules are generally designed to act as two cantilevers locked together at the center.

Vertical Lift Bridges. In a vertical lift bridge the salient feature is the skeleton tower with its suspended counterweight at each end of the lift span. The cables which carry the counterweights pass over sheaves at the top of the towers. The counterweights equal the weight of the lift span, whereas in a bascule bridge heavier counterweights are re-

TABLE V. LONGEST SIMPLE TRUSS SPANS

Bridge	Span in Ft.	Location	Waterway	Year
Metropolis[1]	720	Metropolis, Ill.	Ohio River	1917
Paducah	716	Paducah, Ky.	Ohio River	1929
Tanana River	700	Alaska	Tanana River	1922
Douglas MacArthur[1]	668	St. Louis, Mo.	Mississippi River	1911
Henderson[1]	665	Henderson, Ky.	Ohio River	1933
Louisville	644	Louisville, Ky.-Jeffersonville, Ind.	Ohio River	1919

[1] Railroad.

quired. The first vertical lift bridge was built in 1894 by J. A. L. Waddell at South Halsted Street, Chicago, with a span of 130 ft. The heaviest vertical lift bridge prior to 1919 was the Steel Bridge (1912) at Portland, Ore., with a 220-foot double-deck span, so arranged that the lower or railroad deck could be lifted first for low clearances, after which the entire span could be raised for higher clearances when required. In 1935 the world's longest lift span was completed, the 544-ft. span of the railroad bridge over the Cape Cod Canal. In 1937, the second longest lift span, the 540-ft. Ma-

rope stays, instead of a built-up stiffening truss, to secure rigidity. In the two summer seasons of the exposition, the Sky Ride paid for itself, carrying 4,500,000 passengers without an accident. Including the observation towers, 628 ft. high, the Sky Ride was designed and built in six months at a cost of less than $1,000,000.

Pontoon Bridges. Homer, in the ninth century B.C., mentioned the use of pontoon bridges for the passage of armies. The Persian kings Cyrus, Darius, and Xerxes used pontoon bridges for military purposes between 537 and 480 B.C., cross-

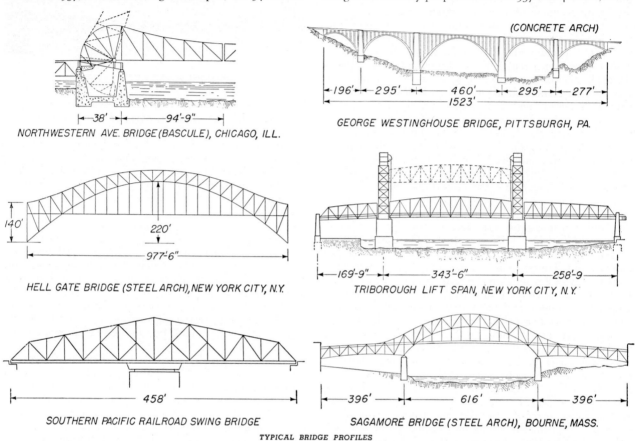

NORTHWESTERN AVE. BRIDGE (BASCULE), CHICAGO, ILL.

GEORGE WESTINGHOUSE BRIDGE, PITTSBURGH, PA.

HELL GATE BRIDGE (STEEL ARCH), NEW YORK CITY, N.Y.

TRIBOROUGH LIFT SPAN, NEW YORK CITY, N.Y.

SOUTHERN PACIFIC RAILROAD SWING BRIDGE

SAGAMORE BRIDGE (STEEL ARCH), BOURNE, MASS.

TYPICAL BRIDGE PROFILES

rine Parkway Bridge between Brooklyn and Rockaway, was completed. The vertical lift bridge has had its chief development in the United States. It has rendered the older movable bridge type, the swing span, practically obsolete. The vertical lift and the bascule are competitive types. The longest double-leaf bascule span is 336 ft.; for longer spans the vertical lift appears to have the field to itself.

Transporter Bridges. A transporter bridge, or aerial ferry, saves the dead weight of a continuous roadway. Unlike a cableway, the span is rigid. The traffic is carried on a moving suspended platform or in suspended cars. It affords an economical crossing where the bridge traffic is light. The aerial ferry over the ship canal at Duluth, Minn. (1904), with a span of 394 ft., was for a long time the only one of its kind in the United States. In 1930 it was converted into a vertical lift span, using the old towers in the reconstructed bridge. The longest transporter span ever built was the Sky Ride at the Century of Progress Exposition at Chicago (1933-1934). This was of the suspension type, designed by Robinson and Steinman, with a span of 1,850 ft. It carried ten 12-ton cars, each holding thirty-six passengers, 215 ft. above the ground. The suspension design was unique, using a system of inclined

ing in this manner the Hellespont (the Dardanelles) and the Danube; and Alexander the Great constructed similar bridges of boats about 330 B.C. To this day pontoon bridges, or "pontons," are an essential part of army equipment. They were effectively used by the Allies in crossing the Rhine in 1945. Nonmilitary pontoon bridges for more permanent crossings, including pontoon draws or floating drawbridges, have been used in various parts of the world. A concrete pontoon bridge across Lake Washington in Seattle, built between 1938 and 1940 at a cost of $8,850,000, is 6,560 ft. long, made up of twenty-four precast cellular reinforced concrete pontoons, with a central opening for ships provided by a sliding, indrawn floating span.

Masonry and Concrete Bridges. The largest stone arch in America is the Cabin John Arch, near Washington, D.C., completed in 1859, a circular arc of 220 ft. span, carrying a water conduit and a carriage-way. For forty-four years this bridge held the record as the largest masonry arch in the world. In 1903, three arches were built, two of which were still the largest in the world in 1952. The largest of these is the Syra Bridge at Plauen, Saxony, with a span of 295 ft. The second largest is the Luxembourg Arch, France, built by

CHAS. R. PEARSON PHOTO

LAKE WASHINGTON "FLOATING BRIDGE," SEATTLE, WASHINGTON

Paul Séjourné, with a span of 278 ft. The third largest masonry arch is a span of 263 ft. built at Montangas, France, in 1909.

In 1903 the art of building great stone arches had reached its climax and apparently neared its end. A new material, concrete, had become available. It was more economical and easier to form and place. Concrete bridges include arches, rigid frames, girder, and slab bridges, and truss and trestle forms. They have been favored for their adaptability to architectural treatment. As a protection against surface deterioration, civic and monumental structures of concrete are often required to be faced with granite or other masonry which will withstand weathering action.

Concrete Arches. Concrete arches have evolved from the earlier solid and closed-spandrel forms to the modern open-spandrel designs, with the roadway carried on spandrel columns supported on concentrated arch ribs. The world's longest arch span of plain concrete is the 280-ft. central span of the Rocky River Bridge at Cleveland, Ohio, completed in 1910. That year marked the climax and end of the brief but rapid development of plain concrete arches. Thereafter reinforced concrete held the field exclusively, permitting new span-lengths to be achieved and completely eclipsing the prior records of stone and plain concrete construction. The world's longest concrete arch spans are listed in Table VI.

In 1916 the great Tunkhannock Viaduct, carrying the Delaware, Lackawanna, and Western Railroad near Scranton, Pa., was completed—a stupendous achievement in its time, with 162,000 cu. yds. of reinforced concrete in the piers and arches. The George Westinghouse Bridge at Pittsburgh (1931) is a fine example of the two-ribbed, open spandrel type. The five arches increase in span length to the great 425-ft. center span—the longest reinforced concrete span in America. The most remarkable of French arches is the Plougastel Bridge at Brest, completed in 1929 with three spans of 612 ft. It was designed and built by Freyssinet, using a method introduced by him for prestressing the arch ribs at the crown with hydraulic jacks to neutralize the stresses from subsequent shrinkage of the concrete. One of the three arch spans was wrecked by the Germans in 1944. The Plougastel Bridge held the world record for reinforced concrete spans until 1940, when the arch at Esla, Spain, was completed with a span of 645 ft. In 1943 the world's greatest concrete arch was completed—the Sando Bridge over the Ångerman River in Sweden, with a record-breaking span of 866 ft. During initial pouring of the concrete in 1939 the centering and forms collapsed with a loss of eighteen lives. European bridges, however, are generally lighter and bolder than American spans, with greater refinements in design and execution. The differences between European and American practice, in both steel and concrete, are explained by the fact

TABLE VI. LONGEST CONCRETE ARCH SPANS

Bridge	Span in Ft.	Location	Waterway	Year
Sando	866	Sweden	Ångerman River	1943
Esla[1]	(main) 645	Spain	Esla River	1940
Plougastel[2]	612	Brest, France	Elorn River	1929
Traneberg	594	Stockholm	Traneberg Sound	1934
La Roche-Guyon	528	France	Seine River	1937
Svinesund	509	Sweden	Svinesund	1946
Bern	492	Switzerland	Aare River	1940
Podolsko	492	Czechoslovakia	Moldau	1942
Castelmoron	470	France	Lot River	1933
George Westinghouse	(main) 425	Pittsburgh, Pa.	Turtle Creek Valley	1931

[1]Railroad. [2]Railroad and vehicle.

that skilled labor is cheaper in Europe and materials relatively more expensive, with greater emphasis on utmost economy.

BRIDGE ANALYSIS

All of the forces acting on a structure, or on any part of a structure, must satisfy the three basic conditions of static equilibrium: (1) the algebraic sum of all vertical forces must equal zero; (2) the algebraic sum of all horizontal forces must equal zero; and (3) the algebraic sum of the moments of all the forces, about any center, must equal zero. Expressed mathematically, the three static equilibrium equations are:

$$(1)\ \Sigma V = 0,\ (2)\ \Sigma H = 0,\ (3)\ \Sigma M = 0.$$

The external forces acting on a structure comprise the applied loads (dead, live, and wind loads) and the reactions at the support. In a statically determinate structure (simple span, cantilever bridge, three-hinged arch, or three-hinged suspension bridge), the static equilibrium equations suffice to determine all external reactions and all primary internal stresses when the applied loads are specified. By applying the equilibrium equations to the structure as a whole, sup-

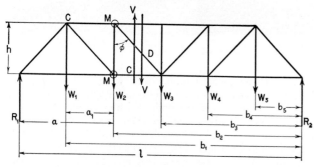

ANALYSIS OF PRATT TRUSS

(W_1, W_2, W_3, W_4, W_5) Weights; (R_1, R_2) Reactions; (V) Vertical shear; (M) Bending moment; (C) Stress in chord member; (D) Stress in diagonal member; (a, a_1, b_1, b_2, b_3, b_4, b_5, l, h) Distances as shown; (ϕ) Angle between diagonal and upright member. Calculations may be made as follows: $R_1 = \Sigma(Wb)/l$; $R_2 = \Sigma W - R_1$; $V = R_1 - (W_1 + W_2)$; $D = V \cdot \sec \phi$; $M = R_1a - W_1a_1$; $C = M/h$

plemented by the condition $M = 0$ at any intermediate hinge, the external reactions are obtained. Then, by applying the equations to any part of the structure, as between one end and any section, the vertical shear and the bending moment at the section are determined, or the stresses in the truss members cut at the section. The accompanying drawing shows the application of this basic procedure to a simple truss with horizontal chords (Pratt type), in determining the reactions R, the vertical shear V at any section, the bending moment M, the stress in a diagonal D, and the stress in a chord member C. In statically indeterminate structures (continuous bridges, rigid frames, two-hinged and hingeless arches, two-hinged and continuous suspension bridges, also trusses with redundant members) the necessary additional relations are supplied by considering the elastic deformations of the structure. Thus, in a continuous girder or truss on three supports, the reaction at the middle support must neutralize the deflection otherwise producible at that point by the applied loading. In an arch or suspension bridge, the end reactions must neutralize the end displacement otherwise producible by the elastic deformation under load. In a truss with redundant members, the elastic elongation of any member must exactly equal the elastic displacement of the two points it connects.

BRIDGE DESIGN AND CONSTRUCTION

The span layout and the type of bridge are determined by the location, the profile of the crossing, the navigation conditions, the clearances required, the foundation conditions, the type and volume of traffic, the materials available, the methods of erection to be employed, and considerations of economy, appearance, and durability. Economic considerations include not only the first cost, but also the future cost of operation and maintenance.

Economic Factors. For a given loading, the weight and cost of a span increase nearly as the square of the span-length. The cost of the spans has to be balanced against the cost of the substructure, consisting of the piers and abutments and their foundations. In a balanced design, where the span-lengths can be varied, the cost of the substructure is roughly equal to the cost of the superstructure. Plate girders are generally adopted as economical up to 100 or 120 ft.; simple trusses for spans up to 300 or 400 ft.; cantilevers, continuous trusses, or steel arches for spans up to 800 or 1,000 ft.; and suspension bridges for spans up to 3,000 or 4,000 ft. Reinforced concrete arches are also used for spans up to 300 or 400 ft. In exceptional cases, these indicated economic limits of span-length are exceeded. For small parkway bridges and grade separations, rigid frames (of steel or reinforced concrete) have come into favorable use.

Loads and Forces. All parts of a bridge have to be designed and proportioned to withstand all of the loads and forces to which they may be subjected, including dead load, live load, impact, wind load, temperature stresses, erection stresses, and (where required) earthquake forces. Live load stresses also include stresses from any lateral and longitudinal forces producible by the moving load. For accurate analysis, the additional secondary stresses (due to deformations of the members) are computed. The live load is usually specified as a wheel-load diagram, giving the weights and spacing of the wheel loads, or as an equivalent uniform load. Bridges are rated by their design loads, as E-60, E-75, H-20, or H-25. An E-60 railroad loading is a conventional engine-load diagram, with a maximum weight of 60,000 lbs. on each driving axle (two wheels). An H-20 highway loading is a conventional loading of 20-ton trucks. Wind load is usually specified at thirty pounds per square foot of exposed surface, but a 50-lb. wind load (as assumed for some bridges) is a safer value. To stiffen a span against transverse forces, lateral bracing is provided in horizontal planes and sway bracing in vertical planes. Adjustment for temperature changes is usually provided by expansion joints, permitting a total movement of one inch per hundred feet of span length. In a simple span, one end rests on a fixed bearing and the other end is supported on an expansion bearing of sliding, roller, or rocker type. In arches, suspension bridges, and other statically indeterminate types, temperature stresses are produced by changes in temperature and are included in the analysis and design.

Floor System. The floor system of a bridge normally comprises transverse floorbeams, framed between the two girders or trusses, and longitudinal stringers, framed between the floorbeams. The bridge floor or deck is carried on the stringers, and (in highway bridges) usually consists of a reinforced concrete slab. To reduce weight, an open-grid floor may be used, or a shallow grid filled with concrete.

Construction Techniques. Early truss bridges (up to 1915) were generally pin-connected, using eyebars or rods for tension members. Riveted construction, heavier and more rigid, has become the prevailing practice. A start has been made in the use of welded connections. Statically indeter-

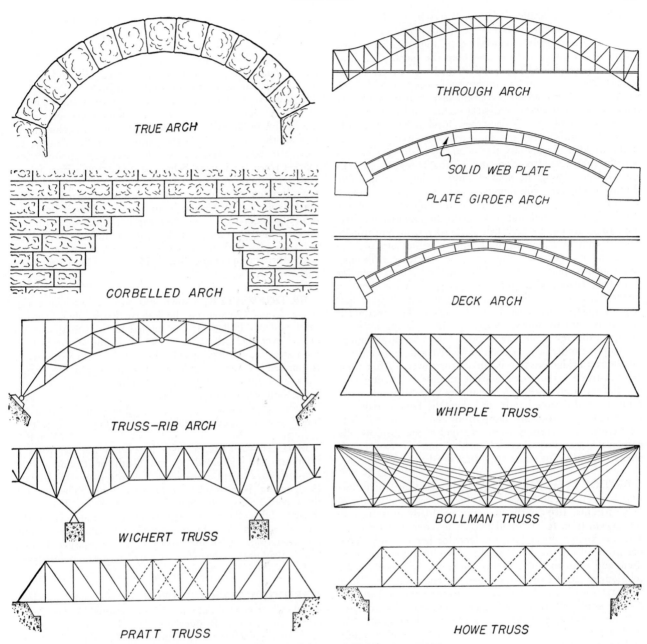

TYPES OF BRIDGE ARCH AND TRUSS CONSTRUCTIONS

minate bridge types, avoided by former generations of bridge engineers on account of the more difficult analysis, have become established as yielding greater efficiency and rigidity. Various high-strength alloy steels have come into use, including nickel steel, silicon steel, and manganese steel. Heat-treated steel, offering increased strength, has been successfully used for eyebars. A start has been made in the use of structural aluminum for bridges.

Bridge Erection. The principal methods of bridge erection are (1) on falsework, (2) by cantilevering, (3) by hoisting into position, (4) by floating into position, (5) by rolling or sliding into position, and (6) by suspension erection. The type of structure and the conditions at the site govern the choice of methods. Erection on falsework is usually the most economical method for a span (such as a truss) composed of numerous members which must be assembled in final position. Favorable conditions are a river bed that will permit the driving of piles, freedom from interference by river navigation, an interval between floods sufficient to allow the span to be assembled and riveted up, and the absence of deep water, swift current, driftwood, and ice. In erection on falsework the floor system is usually erected first and the trusses afterward. The truss connections are riveted up as soon as possible in order that the span may be self-supporting in case the falsework is washed out. For spans of more than 250 ft., a traveler is generally used. This is a framework running on rails carried on the falsework, with hoisting engine and overhead tackle for raising the truss members. Masonry and concrete arches, which require continuous support during placing or pouring, are constructed on specially designed falsework, called centering. The centering must be rigid to resist distortion and settlement. In modern applications, the older form of closely spaced timber-trestle falsework, laid out by rule of thumb, is being replaced by steel bents, scientifically designed. Erection by flotation is used where conditions do not admit the construction of false-work. The previously assembled span, mounted on barges, is floated into place and lowered onto the piers. This lowering is accomplished by means of jacks or by taking on water ballast. Erection by cantilevering dispenses with false-work. Cantilever erection is conveniently used for cantilever spans, continuous spans, and steel arches, and is an important advantage of these bridge types. Steel arches are usually erected by cantilevering out the two halves until they meet at the middle. Temporary ties or anchored holdbacks support the cantilevered portion, and adjustable toggles or jacks are used in making the final closure. In large bridges (including cantilevers, continuous trusses, and truss arches) a creeper traveler is used, riding on the top chords of the panels already erected and picking up the material for erection from cars on the deck below. Girder spans are usually erected without falsework, by simply hoisting into position by means of a gallows frame, gin pole, derrick car, locomotive crane, or floating crane. This method is also used for short truss spans and for other bridge types. A less common method of erection is that of rolling or sliding the span endwise into place after it has been assembled. This method is effectively used in military bridging. In replacing an existing span, the new span may be built alongside (to minimize interruption of traffic) and then moved laterally into position. Suspension bridge erection begins at the towers. After these are constructed, the wires or cable strands are strung over the towers from anchorage to anchorage. Suspenders are hung from the cable bands, and then the floor system and the stiffening trusses are hung from the suspenders. The steel erection, proceeding from each end of the span, usually employs a traveling derrick reaching one or two panels ahead. *See also* FOUNDATIONS; MILITARY ENGINEERING.

D. B. S.

BRIDGET or **BIRGITTA, ST.** [brɪ'jət; bɪrgɪ'tta] (1302-1373), nun and mystic, was born in Sweden in 1302 of noble parents. In 1335 she was appointed lady in waiting to the queen, tried to reform the court without much success, and was known throughout the land for her sanctity. After her husband's death she divided her wealth among her children, and went to Rome in 1349 to secure approval for the religious order of Brigittines which she had founded. There she gave spiritual and material help to the poor, and worked for the pope's return from Avignon to Rome. She revealed that she was frequently visited by Christ and the saints. She died at Rome, July 23, 1373, after a visit to the Holy Land, and was canonized in 1391.

W. C.

BRIDGETON, a city, port of entry, and the seat of Cumberland Co. in southern New Jersey, is located on the Cohansey River, 36 mi. south of Philadelphia. The Central Railroad of New Jersey and the Pennsylvania-Reading Seashore Lines provide freight service. Bridgeton was founded in 1686 by Richard Hancock and incorporated in 1864. It is a trading center for an agricultural region and the canning, freezing, and shipping headquarters for large vegetable and fruit farms. Other manufactures are glass and textile goods, baskets, and machine-shop products. Bridgeton is governed by a mayor and council. A bell cast in 1763 and rung to celebrate the Declaration of Independence is on view at the county courthouse, and the Presbyterian Church (1792) is of historic interest. Pop. 1950, 18,378.

BRIDGETOWN, the capital, port, and largest city of Barbados Island, in the British West Indies, built on a coral-line terrace on the shore of Carlisle Bay, on the southwest coast of the island, at 13° 14' N. lat. and 59° 38' W. long. The city was settled in the late 1600's and has remained continuously in British possession since that time. The mean annual temperature at Bridgetown is 79.6° F., and 62.5 in. of rain falls annually, most of it between June and November. The town is clean and modern and is a West Indian health resort. A bronze statue of Horatio Nelson was erected by the British in Trafalgar Square in 1813, and the chief buildings of the town include the cathedral of the diocese, the church of Saint Mary, the Jewish synagogue, an impressive market place, the Central School, and Harrison's Free School. Although there are few native trees on the island, Bridgetown is noted for its mahogany shade trees. Sugar is the principal export. The harbor is an open roadstead, but ships drawing under 14½ ft. of water can dock. The only railroad on the island terminates at Bridgetown, and air service connects the city with the rest of the British West Indies and with British Guiana and British Honduras. Pop. 1955 (incl. suburbs), 85,000.

J. E. F.

BRIDGEWATER, a town and port in Lunenburg Co., Nova Scotia, Canada, on the Lahave River, about 100 mi. southwest of Halifax. It was named for its situation at the bridge over the Lahave River, which is one of the best salmon streams in Nova Scotia. Founded in 1812, it was incorporated in 1874. Bridgewater is an important lumber shipping center. The divisional headquarters of the Canadian National Railways are located in the town. Industries include the manufacture of diesel engines and building materials and fruit and vegetable canning. Pop. 1956, 4,445.

D. F. P.

BRIDGEWATER, a town in eastern Massachusetts in Plymouth Co., situated 27 mi. south of Boston. Miles Standish in 1649 purchased the townsite from the Indians. Bridgewater is governed by town meeting. The town is the seat of Bridgewater State Teachers College. The Massachusetts State Farm, a large penal institution, is nearby. The New York, New Haven and Hartford Railroad supplies transportation. Dairy and farm produce are marketed in the town. Bridgewater has shoe and nail factories, a brickyard, and a foundry. Pop. 1950, 9,512.

BRIDGEWATER COLLEGE, an accredited, coeducational college of arts and sciences, is sponsored by the Church of the Brethren at Bridgewater, Va. First instruction was given in 1880, when the institution was known as the Spring Creek Normal and Collegiate Institute. In 1882 it was chartered as the Virginia Normal School. Its present name was adopted in 1889 and, following a later change, readopted in 1951. Special features at Bridgewater are a workshop for children's workers, institutes for ministers and church workers, and the Annual Spiritual Life Institute. Degrees conferred are the A.B. and the B.S. in music, home economics, and business administration. Students live in dormitories and approved homes. Generous scholarship and student loan funds are available. *For statistics see* COLLEGES AND UNIVERSITIES.

BRIDLINGTON [brɪ'dlɪŋtən; bɛ'rlɪŋtən], a municipal borough, seaport, and resort situated 31 mi. northeast of Hull, in the East Riding of Yorkshire, England. Bridlington comprises the old town, 1 mi. inland, and Bridlington Quay. It was first recorded in a grant to the Church of St. Mary and St. Nicholas in 1200. The discovery of a mineral spring in the late eighteenth century helped to make it a fashionable health resort. In 1779 John Paul Jones defeated the *Serapis* in Bridlington Bay. In 1899 the community was made a municipal borough. It was intermittently bombed in World War II. The tourist trade is the chief source of income. Pop. 1952, 24,310.

BRIENZ, LAKE OF [brie′nts], in the canton of Bern, central Switzerland, lies east of the Lake of Thun and separated from it by an alluvial fan on which Interlaken is located. Formerly the two lakes were united, but the Lake of Brienz is now 19 ft. higher. It fills the Aare Valley between the ridge of the Brienzer Grat and the Faulhorn group. The Lake of Brienz (elevation 1,860 ft.) is 8¾ mi. long and 1½ mi. wide; its area is 10 sq. mi. and its greatest depth is 860 ft. The town of Brienz, the main settlement along the lake, is located in the east near where the Aare River enters the lake. The light green color of the lake water and the forested mountains that frame it make Brienz a favorite resort for tourists. The town is the center of the wood-carving industry of the Bernese Oberland. A steamer shuttles between Brienz and Interlaken, connecting with the Brünig railway line to Luzern, and calling at Griessbach (near the Falls of the Griessbach, 980 ft. high) and Iseltwald on the south shore, Ringgenberg on the north bank, and Bönigen on the south. The Brünig line, following the north shore of the Lake of Brienz, traverses Brienz, Oberried, Niederried, and Ringgenberg.   S. Van V.

BRIEUX, EUGÈNE [bri′œ′] (1858-1932), French dramatist, member of the Académie Française (1912), was born in Paris, Jan. 19, 1858, the son of a carpenter. He attended only elementary school, but he made up for the inadequacy of his education by omnivorous reading. From 1885 to 1892 he worked as a newspaperman in Rouen and there acquired invaluable experience for his dramatic career.

Brieux's first two plays, *Ménages d'artistes* (1890) (*Artists' Families,* 1918) and *Blanchette* (1892) (*Blanchette,* 1903), produced by Antoine at the Théâtre-Libre, attest to Brieux's preoccupations with social problems, which became the keynote of all his works. *Blanchette,* one of Brieux's best plays, is concerned with the daughter of a tavern keeper who prepares for a teaching position, fails to obtain it, and is constrained to return to her family and work in her father's tavern. Brieux denounces political corruption in *L'Engrenage* (1894), and rails against misguided charity in *Les Bienfaiteurs* (1896). He discusses the questions of marriage without love, celibacy for women, divorce, and the freedom of women in *Les trois Filles de M. Dupont* (1897) (*The Three Daughters of M. Dupont,* 1911), *Le Berceau* (1898) (*The Cradle*), and *La Femme seule* (1913) (*Woman on Her Own,* 1916).

In *Les Remplaçantes* (1901), Brieux criticizes the exploitation of wives by their husbands who send them to Paris to nurse the children of wealthy families. He treats gambling in *Le Résultat des courses* (1893), the inadequacy of human justice in *La Robe rouge* (1900) (*The Red Robe,* 1915), and venereal disease in *Les Avariés* (1902) (*Damaged Goods*). He deals with problems of science in *L'Évasion* (1897) and faith in *La Foi* (1912) (*False Gods*).

Brieux thus brought to the stage a multitude of social problems, some peculiar to his time, some of a more general character. He has no definite philosophy, and his theories are dictated by observation and common sense. His style is without elegance; his plays are loosely constructed. For these reasons, although Brieux has been the most popular French dramatist in England and in the United States, he

has met with considerable criticism in his own country. He died Dec. 6, 1932, in Nice.   F. V.

BRIGHAM CITY [brɪ′gəm], the seat of Box Elder Co. in northern Utah, is situated near the Bear River and Great Salt Lake, 60 mi. north of Salt Lake City. It lies in an agricultural region noted for its peaches, and food processing is its principal industry. The community was settled as Box Elder in 1851 and renamed in 1856 for Brigham Young, who made his last public address here in 1877. It is the seat of the Intermountain Indian School for Navajos, and the Bear River Migratory Bird Refuge is nearby. Chief products of the city are chemicals and rocket propellants. Pop. 1950, 6,790.

BRIGHAM YOUNG UNIVERSITY, an accredited, coeducational, privately controlled university conducted under the auspices of the Church of Jesus Christ of the Latter-Day Saints at Provo, Utah. The institution was founded as Brigham Young Academy in 1875 and enlarged in 1903, when the present name was adopted. Divisions of the university are the Colleges of Biological and Agricultural Sciences, Commerce, Education, Family Living, Fine Arts, Humanities and Social Sciences, Physical and Engineering Sciences, and Recreation, Physical and Health Education, and Athletics; the Graduate School; the School of Nursing; the Division of Religion; the Research Division; and the Extension Division. The main campus is located at Provo, but the L. D. S. Business College and McCune School in Salt Lake City are branches of the university. The Summer Session consists of two five-week terms held on the main campus. This makes it possible to complete a full quarter's work during the summer months. Degrees conferred are the A.B., B.S., M.A., and M.S. Scholarship and student loan assistance is available, and residential facilities are provided for men and women. *For statistics see* COLLEGES AND UNIVERSITIES.

BRIGHT, JOHN (1811-1889), English statesman, was born at Rochdale, Lancashire, Nov. 16, 1811. As a member of an old Quaker family, he was educated at Quaker schools. When later he became a cotton-mill owner, he violently opposed factory laws and simultaneously demanded repeal of the Corn Laws, which were forcing factory owners to pay higher wages. This led to his support of free trade. In 1839 Bright joined Richard Cobden as a spokesman for the Anti-Corn-Law League. He was elected to Parliament in 1843, and in 1846 the Corn Laws were repealed, partly as the result of the Irish potato famine and the consequent need for cheap imported wheat. Thereafter Bright campaigned actively for Irish agrarian and land-law reforms, the disestablishment of the Irish church, parliamentary reform, and limitations on the House of Lords; he strongly disapproved of the Crimean War, and supported the Union in the American Civil War. Bright was a brilliant and powerful orator, always remembering the interests of the factory owner and the value of the middle class. He died at Rochdale, Mar. 27, 1889.

E. R. A.

BRIGHTON, a resort city in southeastern Australia, in Victoria, about 8 mi. south of Melbourne. Located on the east shore of Port Phillip, it is a popular seashore resort and residential suburb of Melbourne. Pop. 1954, 40,450.

BRIGHTON, a municipal, county, and parliamentary borough and seaside resort in Sussex, England, overlooking the English Channel, 51 mi. south of London. The site was occupied by the Romans and the Saxons. Brighton's eleventh century name was Brighthelmstone. When George IV was Prince Regent, he built a pavilion there costing approximately £1,000,000, which the town purchased from the crown in 1850. It was George's patronage of the community that was responsible for its popularity as a fashionable resort. Lord Byron and many of his famous contemporaries were regular visitors to Brighton. During World War I, the townspeople converted the pavilion into a military hospital. In World War II, Brighton suffered heavily from air raids with much loss of life and considerable property damage. It is the seat of Brighton College, an aquarium, and Dyke Road Museum. Brighton became a borough in 1832. Incorporated in 1854, it was made a county borough in 1888. There are many light industries in the area. Pop. 1952, 156,900.

BRIGID, ST. [brɪ'jɪd; bri'ɪd] (c. 451-525), Roman Catholic abbess, was born at Faughart near Dundalk, in County Louth, Ireland. She established a religious foundation at Kildare, which elected her the patroness of consecrated virgins in Ireland. Much of the material provided by the ancient and medieval Celtic hagiographers is legendary. St. Brigid was noted for an extraordinary charity, and her countrymen are profoundly devoted to "the Mary of the Gael." Her right hand is said to be preserved at Lumiar, near Lisbon, Portugal, and another relic is kept at St. Martin's, Cologne. Her body is interred in Downpatrick Cathedral. Her feast is February 1.   W. C.

BRIGITTINES [brɪ'jɪtɪnz; bri'jɪtinz], the members of the Roman Catholic religious order, called also the Order of the Most Holy Redeemer, founded at Vadstena about 1346 by St. Bridget of Sweden. The Order's monasteries were of the type called "mixed," and consisted of a large convent of nuns and a smaller convent of priest monks, who served the common church, both groups being under the government of the superiore. The Order once numbered some eighty monasteries and contributed to the religious, literary, and agricultural improvement of the northern countries especially. Most of its houses disappeared with the Protestant Reformation or subsequently; four, of nuns only, remain in the twentieth century, including the famous Syon Abbey founded in England in 1415, and exiled under Henry VIII and again under Elizabeth, returning in 1861. The Brigittines of the Recollection, founded at Valladolid by Marina de Escobar about 1633, have five convents of nuns. *See also* ABBESS; BRIDGET OF SWEDEN, ST.   W. C.

BRIHASPATI [brihəspʌ'ti], one of the terrestrial gods of Vedic Hindu mythology, prominent in the hymns of the Rig-Veda. He was lord of prayer and devotion (*Brahmanaspati*), and protector of worshipers. Characteristic of the intangible and protean nature of the Hindu deities, he was partly the personification of an abstract idea, and partly an anthropomorphic god with concrete features. Born of heaven and earth, he is described as seven-mouthed, hundred-winged, sharp-horned, blue-backed, and golden-colored. He is armed with a bow, the string of which represents "Holy Order," a golden hatchet, and an iron axe, and stands on a chariot drawn by ruddy steeds. His identity, however, does not always remain distinct. He is often identified with Indra, the god of atmosphere, or "storm," and with Agni, the god of earth, or "fire." This association seems to have taken place in regard to his function as the dispeller of darkness, in which he represents the rays of dawn, and in the story of the release of the cows from their stalls, symbolizing the rending

of the clouds, and the resultant release of the beneficial rains. He was also the priest of the gods, and the inspirer of prayer, or the divine personification symbolizing the magical effect of prayer on the other gods. The myth of Brihaspati was appropriated by the later epic mythology of post-Vedic literature, but many of his qualities are lost, and he is merely represented as a priest and seer, the son of Angiras, and the husband of Tara. He is also the lord of eloquence, and regent of the planet Jupiter. In his earlier capacity as priest of the gods he seems to have been the prototype for Brahma, the priest, and chief god of the Hindu triad.   C. W. D.

BRILL, ABRAHAM ARDEN (1874-1948), psychiatrist, first to introduce Sigmund Freud to the English-speaking world, was born in Kanczuga, Austria, Oct. 12, 1874. Brill came to the United States as a youth, was graduated from New York University in 1901 with a Ph.B., and, in 1903, received his M.D. from Columbia's College of Physicians and Surgeons. After four years at the Central Islip (N.Y.) State Hospital as an assistant physician, he went to Europe, studying in Paris and Zurich, and under Freud. Brill acted as chief of the psychiatric clinic at Zurich, and upon his return to the United States, in 1912, became an outstanding practitioner and teacher of psychoanalysis. He was chief of the clinic in psychiatry and lecturer on psychoanalysis and psychosexual sciences at Columbia University, lecturer on psychoanalysis and abnormal psychology at New York University, and assistant professor of psychiatry at the Post-Graduate Medical School.

His translation of *Freud's Selected Papers on Hysteria*, in 1909, was the first of ten works by Freud translated by Brill into English. Among these were *Three Contributions to the Theory of Sex* (1910), and *Interpretation of Dreams* (1913). In 1909 Brill also translated Carl Gustave Jung's *Psychology of Dementia Praecox*. Brill's original works include *Psychoanalysis—Its Theories and Practical Application* (1921), *Fundamental Conceptions of Psychoanalysis* (1922), and *Freud's Contribution to Psychiatry* (1944). He died in New York City, Mar. 2, 1948.   D. R.

BRILLOUIN, LÉON NICOLAS [bri'ywæ'] (1889-), French physicist, was born in Sèvres (Seine), France, Aug. 7, 1889. He studied physics, chemistry, and mathematics at the École Normale Supérieure, and received his Ph.D. degree from the University of Paris in 1921. In 1919 he was a civilian assistant in military telegraphy, and was also employed in the laboratory of the Centre d'Études in Toulon. From 1920 to 1924 he was secretary-general of the *Journal de Physique*. In 1921 Brillouin lectured at a radio school, and from 1923 to 1928 was assistant director of the physics laboratory at the Collège de France. In 1924 he was awarded the Legion of Honor for his work in theoretical physics and radio. In 1928 he became professor of physics at the Sorbonne, and also lectured at the École Supérieure d'Aéronautique. Brillouin, in 1930, founded the Annales de l'Institut Poincaré. From 1932 to 1939 he was professor at the Collège de France, and for the following two years general director of the French national broadcasting system. He was president of the French Physics Society in 1938. In 1941 Brillouin went to the United States as a visiting professor of physics at the University of Wisconsin, and in 1942 became professor of physics at Brown University. He had previously attended conferences in the United States, Canada, Belgium, the Soviet Union, Germany, and Great Britain. In 1943 he went to Columbia University to conduct research as a member of the Applied Mathematics Group of the National Defense Research Council. From 1946 to 1949 Brillouin taught at Harvard and later entered the field of business machines.

BRILL'S DISEASE. *See* Typhus Fever.

BRINDISI [bri'ndizi], a province and its capital on the Adriatic coast in Apulia (*It.* Puglia), southeastern Italy.

The City. The oldest port in Apulia, Brindisi is located 45 mi. northeast of Taranto. Its harbor provides deep, sheltered anchorage and ready access. The entrance is protected by several islands and fortifications and by a very narrow passage into the inner harbor, composed of two arms that form the peninsula on which the city itself stands. Ships can tie up at the quays bordering the city on its seaward sides. In the older part of the city, on the peninsula, are some interesting monuments: the column marking the terminus of the Appian Way; several medieval churches— San Benedetto, San Giovanni al Sepolchro, and Santa Maria del Casale; and the Hohenstaufen Castle.

The city first acquired importance after the Romans conquered it in 266 B.C., named it Brundisium, and made it a base for operations across the Adriatic. With the decline of Rome, Brindisi experienced a series of foreign rulers, including German, Greek, Norman, Spanish, and French, under whom the city's fortunes fluctuated violently. In the fourteenth century a devastating earthquake ruined the city. After the unification of Italy, the Italian government spent large sums to give Brindisi rail connections, new port facilities, and public buildings.

For a period ending in 1914, Brindisi was the point at which mail and passengers for India were transferred from train to ship. After Brindisi was replaced by Marseille on the India route, it continued to do a thriving business with the Balkans and the Middle East, though Bari tended to take a steadily increasing share of this trade. In the 1930's Brindisi became an important nodal point for civilian air traffic. During World War I Brindisi was of considerable military value to the Allies. In World War II it was occupied by detachments of the British Eighth Army in September 1943, and it was the seat of the Italian government from that date until February 1944. Pop. 1954 (city), 55,500; (commune), 62,500.

The Province. The province of Brindisi, created in 1927, comprises 20 communes with an area of 709 sq. mi. The inland portion of the province lies among the Murgian Hills, where altitudes exceed 1,000 ft. and where vineyards are plentiful and cereals are extensively grown. The rest of the province is Adriatic coastland. Here are found ancient groves of fig, olive, and almond trees, interspersed with vineyards and vegetable gardens. The port of Brindisi is the chief export point for the crops of the province.

Among the other towns of importance in the province are Bari, Lecce, Foggia, Taranto, Ostuni, Francavilla Fontana, Ceglie Messapico, San Vito dei Normanni, Mesagne, and Fasano. Pop. (est. 1954), 326,500. R. G. W.

BRINE SHRIMP, a primitive crustacean of the subclass Branchiopoda which normally lives in water of high salt content. The brine shrimps are fairy shrimps about 0.4 in. long which have become adapted to life in very salty water, such as the Great Salt Lake of Utah and similar salt lakes and ponds throughout the world. They all belong to the genus *Artemia* and possibly to a single species, *A. salina.* The eggs of these crustaceans will withstand drying for long periods and will hatch out in water after being dried for three years or longer. This fact has led to the marketing of brine shrimp eggs on a commercial basis as a source of live food for aquarium fishes. F. A. C.

BRINK, BERNHARD AEGIDUS KONRAD TEN (1841-1892), German philologist and historian of English literature, was born in Amsterdam, Jan. 12, 1841, and studied at Münster and Bonn universities. From 1870 to 1873 he was professor of modern languages at the University of Marburg, and from 1873 to 1892 he served as professor of English at the University of Strasbourg. From 1874 he edited *Quellen und Forschungen zur Sprach- und Kulturgeschichte der germanischen Völker,* one of Germany's most erudite and scholarly publications. His published works include *Geschichte der englischen Litteratur* (1877), which included the study of English literature from Chaucer to Wycliffe. An English translation of this work was published by H. M. Kennedy in 1883. The second volume of Ten Brink's study of English literature covered the period from Wycliffe to the accession of Queen Elizabeth. It appeared in 1896. Ten Brink published *Sprache und Verskunst* in 1884 (English translation, by M. B. Smith, *The Language and Meter of Chaucer,* 1901). Other works by Ten Brink include *Beowulf Untersuchungen* (1888), *Shakespeare, Fünf Vorlesungen* (1893) (English translation, by Julia Franklin, *Five Lectures on Shakespeare,* 1895). Ten Brink died at Strasbourg, Jan. 29, 1892.

BRINTON, DANIEL GARRISON (1837-1899), American ethnologist and archaeologist, who played an important role in the development of scientific anthropology in the United States, was born at Thornbury, Chester County, Pa. He studied at Yale, at Jefferson Medical College, and for one year at Heidelberg and at Paris, his early career being in the field of medicine. During the Civil War (1862-1865), he was a surgeon in the Union Army, serving as medical director of the 11th Corps and later as surgeon in charge of the U. S. Army General Hospital at Quincy, Ill. He then practised medicine at West Chester, Pa., for several years and was editor of the *Medical and Surgical Reporter* in Philadelphia. In 1884 he became professor of ethnology and archaeology in the Academy of Natural Sciences in Philadelphia and in 1886 professor of American linguistics and archaeology at the University of Pennsylvania, a post he held until his death.

An eminent authority and critic and a prolific writer on diverse subjects, including mythology, linguistics, ethnology, and archaeology, he was one of the foremost anthropologists of his day. His principal works include *The Myths of the New World* (1868); *The Religious Sentiment: Its Sources and Aim: A Contribution to the Science and Philosophy of Religion* (1876); *Races and Peoples* (1890). He also edited and published the *Library of American Aboriginal Literature,* 8 vols., 1882-1890. G. F. Ek.

BRISBANE, ARTHUR [bri'zben] (1864-1936), American journalist, was born in Buffalo, N. Y., Dec. 12, 1864, the son of Albert Brisbane, well-known social reformer. He attended public schools in Buffalo and Brooklyn, N. Y., and, from 1877 to 1882, schools in Paris, France, and Stuttgart, Germany. In 1882, on his eighteenth birthday, he was hired by Charles A. Dana as a reporter on the *New York Sun* and later became its London correspondent. His flair for journalism soon won him recognition, and Dana appointed him managing editor of the *New York Evening Sun.* In 1890 he was induced by Joseph Pulitzer to become editor of the *New York World,* and in the rivalry between this paper and William Randolph Hearst's *New York Evening Journal,* Brisbane proved a formidable opponent in the race for increased circulation. In 1897 Brisbane left Pulitzer to become editor of the *Evening Journal,* where he remained for the rest of his life. Although not the originator of "yellow journalism," Brisbane is responsible for many of its characteristics. He invented the large, bold-face headline, and developed many of the tricks of newspaper sensationalism. Under him the *Evening Journal* outstripped the circulation of any other paper, and became known for its lurid reportorial technique. To him, as much as to Hearst, may be attributed this newspaper's policies which encountered severe criticism, notably for the manner in which it helped to foment the Spanish-American War. Brisbane's editorials and his syndicated column *Today* made him famous, and by 1910 he was the highest-paid editor in the United States. In 1912 he

is on a small coastal plain, and the southern extension of the Craig Range lies west of Brisbane. The city has a humid, subtropical climate somewhat similar to that of the eastern Gulf Coast of the United States, and the average annual temperature is 69° F. The coldest month is July, which averages 59° F., while the hottest month, January, averages 77° F. The average annual rainfall is about 45 in. a year. The wettest month is January, having 6 in. of rain, while in August, the driest month, there are only about 2 in. of rain. Agriculture, dairying, and grazing are important activities in the surrounding area; wheat, corn, vegetables, and papayas are grown, and cattle, sheep, horses, and pigs are raised. Dairy products and wool are among Brisbane's major exports.

Queensland has extensive deposits of coal, copper, silver, gold, lead, zinc, uranium, and some tin, all of which are

COURTESY OF THE AUSTRALIAN NEWS AND INFORMATION BUREAU

BRISBANE, CAPITAL OF THE STATE OF QUEENSLAND, AUSTRALIA

bought the *Washington* (D.C.) *Times,* and in 1918 he bought the *Milwaukee Evening Wisconsin.* This transaction, together with his editorial attacks on the British and his antiwar sentiments, brought him before an investigating committee to answer charges of pro-Germanism, but no action was taken, and in 1919 he sold the papers to Hearst. Influenced by the teachings of his Socialist father, Brisbane was earlier known for his radical tendencies, but after he joined the *Evening Journal* his ideas became largely identified with those of Hearst. Brisbane was against the League of Nations. He first supported President Franklin D. Roosevelt, and then repudiated him under the banner of "the Raw Deal." His editorial style was his greatest asset; he was an artist in maintaining his diction and ideas on the simplest level, and was shrewd in sensing the reading habits of his public. He continued to write his editorials almost to the day of his death on Dec. 25, 1936, in New York City. Among his works were *Mary Baker G. Eddy* (1908), *The Book of Today* (1923), *Today and the Future Day* (1925), and several volumes of his editorials.   C. W. D.

BRISBANE, the capital city of the state of Queensland, in northeastern Australia, located at 27° 30′ S. lat. and 153° E. long. in the extreme southeastern part of Queensland, about 500 mi. north of Sydney. Brisbane is about 15 mi. from the mouth of the Brisbane River, which empties into Moreton Bay, in the South Pacific Ocean. Moreton Bay is partially separated from the ocean by Moreton Island. The city

advantageous to the varied business and manufacturing enterprises in Brisbane. The city is connected with the Australian road, rail, telegraph, and radio systems, and has a national and international shipping service. Brisbane also has airline connections with Sydney, Melbourne, and other important Australian cities. The city is the administrative and intellectual center of Queensland, and the University of Queensland is located here. There are numerous parks and recreation areas, Bowen Park and Victoria Park being the largest. Noteworthy buildings include the Queensland Public Library, the Houses of Parliament, the Queensland National Bank, the state Supreme Court, and the City Hall. Among the city's chief institutions are the Queensland Museum, the School of Arts, the Queensland Club, and the large general hospital. Brisbane supports a symphony orchestra and is the seat of Anglican and Roman Catholic archbishoprics.

Brisbane was settled as a convict colony in 1824, and was named after a former governor of New South Wales, Sir Thomas Macdougall Brisbane. It became a free settlement in 1842. It was a city of New South Wales until 1859, when it became the capital of the newly established colony of Queensland, of which it is now the most important port. Pop. 1954, 502,353.

BRISBANE BOX, a large tree, *Tristania conferta,* of the myrtle family, native to Australia. It is often planted in parks and gardens, and occasionally as a street tree. It is evergreen, has large, thick leaves, small, white flowers, and a woody fruit resembling the fruit of some of the species of eucalyptus. The tree reaches a height of 150 ft.   E. McCl.

BRISCOE, ARTHUR JOHN TREVOR [brɪ′sko] (1873-1943), English etcher and painter, was born Feb. 25, 1873, at Birkenhead. He studied first at the Westminster School, then at the Slade School in London. After some six months' study in Paris at the Académie Julien, he began to paint from shipboard the English, French, and Dutch coasts. While at the Slade School, Briscoe had begun to etch, but his first recorded plate is dated 1923. A fellow of the Royal Society of Painter-Etchers and Engravers from 1933, and a member of the Royal Institute of Painters in Watercolours, Briscoe is best known for his etchings of sailing ships— nautically correct to the last piece of rope—and of life at sea. Under the name of "Clove Hitch," he wrote the *Handbook on Sailing* as well as many articles on navigation and technical subjects. Briscoe died on Apr. 27, 1943.   J. S. By.

BRISSOT, JACQUES PIERRE [brɪ′so′] (1754-1793), French Girondin leader, was born in Ouarville, near Chartres, Jan. 14, 1754. Prior to the outbreak of the French Revolution in 1789, he studied law, wrote treatises on penal reform and the philosophy of law, managed a newspaper, and traveled in the United States. His concern for penal reform and emancipation of Negro slaves established him as an eighteenth-century humanitarian. Though he was not a member of the National Assembly, he founded his newspaper, the *Patriote français,* on May 6, 1789, despite official press restrictions. The popularity of this publication helped to secure his election to the Legislative Assembly in 1791 and to the National Convention in 1792. He favored the declaration of war against Austria and Prussia in 1792 as a means of securing the downfall of the monarchy. As leader of the Girondin, or Brissotin, party he was proscribed when the Jacobin Montagnard party executed the *coup d'état* of June 2, 1793. Brissot attempted to elude arrest by flight from Paris, but he was arrested in Moulins and guillotined with the Girondin leaders on Oct. 31, 1793, in Paris.   R. M. Br.

BRISTOL, a port city and a county in itself in southwestern England. It straddles the borders of Gloucestershire and Somersetshire on both sides of the Avon River (the line between the counties), where it joins the Frome, 8 mi. from Bristol Channel, and 118 mi. west of London. Bristol was occupied by Saxons, Danes, and Normans, and Domesday lists it as a royal borough with a mint. The charter of 1373 extended the town and made it a county; this charter was confirmed in 1377 and later in 1488. In 1644 Bristol was incorporated, but it had its first mayor in 1200. Bristol became a market town for wool, and looms were set up in 1337. Its greatest growth was in the fifteenth century under the administration of William Canynges, five times mayor, twice member of Parliament, and founder of the Society of Merchant Venturers, which sponsored the voyages of the Cabots. Canynges rebuilt the thirteenth-century Church of St. Mary Redcliffe, noted for its beauty.

After the founding of Charlestown in Massachusetts, a group of Bristol merchants established a colony in Maine. Thereafter Bristol's history, economically, depended to a large extent upon America. By sending domestic goods to Africa, shipping slaves to America, and returning with cargoes of tobacco and sugar, Bristol became a wealthy port city. With the advent of free trade and the American Civil War ending slavery, the sugar trade declined. This, coupled with the invention of the steamboat, put Bristol in the background, for not only was her port unable to handle the new type of ship, but the heavy dock fees imposed sent most of the shipping to Liverpool. In 1848, however, the city bought the Bristol harbor, cut the dock fees, bought several docks, and extended a new dock to handle the deeper-draft vessels.

In World War II Bristol was severely bombed, with great loss of life and extensive property damage. The docks at Avonmouth and Portishead suffered considerably. Much of the rubble from Bristol, brought to the United States as ballast, was used as fill along New York City's East River to form a dockage area known as Bristol Basin. Extensive repairs were undertaken to restore the water front and the city proper. Aircraft production is the chief postwar industry; others include shipbuilding and the manufacture of prefabricated houses, machinery, foundry products, tobacco, cocoa, and chocolate. Pop. 1952, 443,900.

BRISTOL, a city in Hartford Co., central Connecticut, is situated 17 mi. southwest of Hartford and 28 mi. north of New Haven. It is served by the New York, New Haven and Hartford Railroad. Bristol was settled in 1727 and incorporated as a town in 1785, when it was separated from Farmington. It was incorporated as a city in 1911. The Bristol Clock Museum is the only institution devoted to the horological history of the nation. Famous for its clock making, Bristol is a world center for ball-bearing and precision spring production. Other manufactures include brass and aluminum forgings, printing, archery equipment, and fluorescent lamp parts. Bristol was badly damaged in the floods of August and October 1955. Pop. 1950, 35,961.

BRISTOL, a borough in Bucks Co., southeastern Pennsylvania, is situated on the west bank of the Delaware River, opposite Burlington, N.J., and 20 mi. north of Philadelphia. Bristol was founded about 1681 as Buckingham and incorporated as a borough in 1720, taking its name from the English port. American troops were quartered in Bristol during the Revolutionary War. The town of Harriman, built by the Harriman Shipyard to house its World War I workers, is now part of the borough. Industries include the steel works nearby, a soap plant, zinc and airplane plants, and boatworks. Manufactures are paints and chemicals, leather goods, and parchment paper. Bristol is governed by a burgess and council. Pop. 1950, 12,710.

BRISTOL, the seat of Bristol Co. in eastern Rhode Island, is situated on Narragansett Bay, 10 mi. southeast of Providence. It is on a peninsula in an area devoted to dairying, truck farming, and poultry raising. Originally a part of the Plymouth Colony of Massachusetts, it was incorporated in 1681 and joined Rhode Island in 1747. Bristol has the town meeting form of government. Freight service is provided by the New York, New Haven & Hartford Railroad. Its manufactures are insulated wire, rubber shoes and threads, hydraulic valves, machinery, dresses, and lace. It is also a noted yachting center. Pop. 1950, 10,335.

BRISTOL, an urban unit consisting of two adjoining cities, one in Washington Co. in southwestern Virginia, but politically independent; the other in Sullivan Co. in northeastern Tennessee. Bristol was founded in 1851 and incorporated in 1856. The Southern and the Norfolk and Western railways and Piedmont and Capital airlines provide transportation. Although the two cities are separate politically, they form a single community. The Virginia unit is governed by a

mayor and council; the Tennessee unit by a mayor and commissioners. Sullins and Virginia Intermont colleges are located in Bristol, Va., and King College is in Bristol, Tenn. A point of interest in the region is Unaka National Forest. The region raises beef and dairy cattle, tobacco, and grain. Industries produce machinery, guided missiles, drugs, work clothes, and hosiery. Pop. 1950, Bristol, Va., 15,954; Bristol, Tenn., 16,771.

BRISTOL BAY, a large indentation of the Bering Sea, located north of the Alaskan Peninsula in extreme southwestern Alaska. The shallow bay, which narrows rapidly, is noted for the excellent salmon run. The rivers from Iliamna Lakes, the Katmai (Ten Thousand Smokes) District, drain into Bristol Bay.   J. E. F.

BRISTOL CHANNEL, a shallow inlet of the Atlantic Ocean on the southwestern coast of England, extending between Wales on the north, and Devon and Somerset on the south. Terminating in the estuary of the Severn, it has Lundy Island at its mouth, which flares out into the Atlantic between St. Govan's Head and Hartland Point. With a length of approximately 90 mi. and a width varying from 5 to 50 mi., it is important as a fishing area as well as for commercial reasons. Among the important seaports along its strongly indented coast line are Swansea, Cardiff, Newport, and Avonmouth. Flowing into it are the Carmarthen, Tawe, Taff, Usk, Severn, Avon, Parrett, Taw, and Torridge rivers. Several canals combine with the rivers in permitting ships to travel from the channel far into the hinterland of England.

BRISTOL UNIVERSITY, located at Bristol, England, and founded in 1909, the outcome of a merger of the Bristol

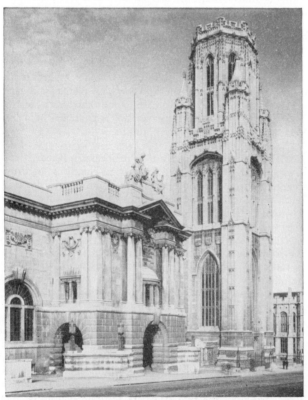

BRISTOL UNIVERSITY, BRISTOL, ENGLAND

Medical School (1832) and the University College (1874), which, in 1893, became the new University College and, in 1909 Bristol University. The faculties in 1948 comprised the departments of art, including a department of teaching; sciences, including a department of agricultural and horticultural research; medicine, associated with the Bristol Royal Hospital; engineering; and law. The university is dedicated to community service. For example, the Colsten Research Society applies academic knowledge to industry, and the department of agriculture is active in the several counties. The main university library, in 1948, contained 155,000 volumes; the medical library, 29,600. The ornithological section is notable. In 1955 the faculty numbered 380 members, and the enrollment (coeducational) was 2,666.
                                                    A. L. H-Q.

BRISTOW, BENJAMIN HELM [brı'sto] (1832-1896), American government official, was born in Elkton, Ky., June 20, 1832. After his graduation from Jefferson College (Pa.) in 1851, he studied law with his father and in 1853 was admitted to the Kentucky bar. Siding with the North in the Civil War, he was commissioned a lieutenant colonel in the Twenty-fifth Kentucky Infantry. He later helped organize the Eighth Kentucky Cavalry, serving as colonel. Having been elected to the Kentucky state senate in August 1863, he resigned from the army and in December took his seat. In 1866 he was appointed assistant United States attorney and on May 4, 1866, he was made United States attorney for the Kentucky district. In 1870 President U. S. Grant appointed him to fill the newly constituted office of United States solicitor general, a post he resigned Nov. 12, 1872, to enter corporation law practice. He was appointed secretary of the treasury in 1874, and in this office he prosecuted and was instrumental in crushing the St. Louis "Whisky Ring," whose members had cheated the government out of millions of dollars in revenue. Prominent among the two hundred or more men indicted was Orville E. Babcock, President Grant's private secretary. (Babcock was later acquitted.) Bristow resigned as secretary of the treasury in 1876, and after his failure to win the nomination for president at the 1876 Republican National Convention, he retired from politics. Until his death, June 22, 1896, he practiced law in New York City.   D. R.

BRISTOW, a city in eastern Oklahoma, is situated in Creek Co., 40 mi. southwest of Tulsa. Bristow was incorporated as a city in 1898 and is governed by a mayor and city council. Transportation for this cotton center is supplied by the St. Louis-San Francisco Railway. In addition to cotton, the chief crop, the district produces corn, alfalfa, and peanuts. Numerous oil fields are located in the vicinity. The region's output is reflected in the city's manufactures: cotton, motor oil, gasoline, cottonseed oil, oil-field machinery, and dairy products. Pop. 1950, 5,400.

BRITAIN. *See* Britannia.
BRITAIN, BATTLE OF. *See* World War II.

BRITANNIA, the Latinized form of Britain. It was the name given in antiquity to the area now covered by England, Scotland, and Wales. Another name for the island was Albion.

The Romans found Britain inhabited mostly by Celtic tribes, which had crossed the channel from the European continent, carrying with them a fully developed culture. It was in Britain that the Celts developed to its highest point the religion called Druidism. Very little is known about

Druidism except that it involved an organized priesthood, which had great influence over the Celts in Britain and Gaul, and that the Druids believed in immortality. It is also known that the religion involved human sacrifice.

Julius Caesar made two expeditions to Britain, in 55 and 54 B.C., but he by no means effected a conquest. As a matter of fact, the Roman occupation of Britain did not take place until after A.D. 43, when the Emperor Claudius landed large forces in the southern part of the island. Londinium (London) and Camulodunum (Colchester) were captured and organized as Roman colonies. Subsequently, the Romans overran the south and pressed steadily northward, despite a temporary setback in A.D. 61, when the revolt of Boadicea occurred. By A.D. 74, Lincoln, York, and Chester were in Roman hands, and the famous Agricola carried the fighting into Caledonia (Scotland) a decade later.

The establishment of a defensible frontier for Roman Britain was a serious problem in the second century. Hadrian, in A.D. 121, ordered the building of the famous wall along the Tyne-Solway line, and twenty years later a similar line was drawn between the River Clyde and the Firth of Forth. Although Septimius Severus, at the beginning of the third century, attempted the conquest of the Picts in Scotland, the Romans eventually had to withdraw behind their walls to the south.

Under the Romans, Britain became thoroughly Romanized and enjoyed a flourishing trade with the rest of the Roman Empire. As time passed, however, with the decline of Roman military power, it became increasingly more difficult for the imperial government to provide protection for Britain. The Romans finally abandoned the island at the beginning of the fifth century.   T. B. J.

BRITANNIA METAL, an antimony and tin alloy, sometimes also containing copper. Britannia metal is most frequently used in manufacturing tableware. The better grades include 10 parts antimony and 90 parts tin; the lower grades, 5 parts antimony, 94 parts tin, 1 part copper.

B'RITH MILAH [brɪ'th mɪ'lə], the Hebrew name for the rite of circumcision practiced by Jews. It is enjoined in the Book of Genesis (xvii: 10-14), in which God commands Abraham to circumcise every man-child on the eighth day after birth, and is one of the basic commandments of Judaism. References to the rite are found in the Bible.

B'rith milah is considered a covenant between God and Israel, and a symbol of the love of the Jew for his people. The rite is performed on the eighth day after birth, no exception being made for the Sabbath and Holy Days, unless postponement is imperative as a health measure. An elaborate ritual takes place on the occasion, the successive steps being called by their Hebrew names *milah, periah,* and *metzitzah.* The circumciser is called in Hebrew *mohel,* and the godfather, who holds the child on his lap, is called the *sandek.* A chair, known as *Kisse shel Eliyahu,* or Elijah's chair (because Elijah, in Malachi iii: 1, is called "messenger of the covenant"), also figures in the ceremony.

The *b'rith milah* is imperative, according to Orthodox Jewish Law, for a male non-Jew who wishes to convert to Judaism. In Reform Judaism the matter was controversial during the nineteenth century, but it was determined in 1892, when the Central Conference of American Rabbis voted to dispense with *b'rith milah* for proselytes.   D. G.

BRITISH BROADCASTING CORPORATION, a corporation, popularly known as the BBC, created in 1927, which has always enjoyed a monopoly of radio sound broadcasting throughout the United Kingdom. Prior to 1954 it also had the exclusive right of broadcasting television programs. An act of Parliament in that year provided for the establishment of an Independent Television Authority which was given the right, under specific limitations, to license private television companies. Competition with the government-sponsored BBC in this field has, however, developed with caution.

The BBC exists by virtue of a charter from the Crown. Its broadcasting rights come from a license issued by the Postmaster-General, a minister of the Crown. The sources of its revenue and the conditions under which it operates are set forth in a separate agreement with this minister, who is also responsible to Parliament for the observance of the terms of agreement. The Corporation consists of nine governors appointed by order-in-council. An appointed Board of Management, with a Director-General at its head, forms the executive. Yet, despite these formal ties with the government, the BBC normally operates without government interference. So slight, in fact, is such interference that criticisms of the Corporation are more frequently leveled at its independence and consequent irresponsibility than at its dependence on the government. Even the monopolistic character of broadcasting in Britain was not seriously opposed until after the advent of the Churchill government in 1951. In the debate that culminated in the Television Act of 1954, practically no voice was raised in favor of replacing the BBC by private broadcasting companies. The British people generally drew a sharp distinction between freedom of the press and freedom of broadcasting.

The revenue of the BBC comes from three main sources: a proportion of the license fees levied on receiving sets; revenue from the sale of BBC publications; and a grant-in-aid from the British Treasury. This last is used exclusively to support the elaborate and world-wide services of the BBC outside the United Kingdom. The annual license fee for radio receiving sets is £1 ($2.80) and for television sets £3. There are over 14,000,000 receiving sets in the United Kingdom, of which about 4,600,000 are for television. The literature published by the BBC includes the *Radio Times* (a weekly with a circulation of about 8,000,000), the *Listener,* and the *BBC Yearbook.* The BBC receives no money from advertisers, except in connection with its publications, because its programs contain no advertising. Even the Independent Television Authority receives a grant-in-aid from the Treasury, and the private television companies that it is permitted to license are strictly limited in the amount of advertising which they may inject into their programs. All sponsored broadcasts are prohibited.

The domestic radio services of the BBC consist of three programs: (1) the regional or "home" services, in which programs are interchangeable throughout; (2) the "light" program, weighted on the side of entertainment; and (3) the "third" program, designed explicitly for cultural and intellectual stimulation. The British public have in the main accepted the principle that the elevation of the standards of taste and discernment is an integral and basic function of this public and publicly supported body. The Corporation conducts a specifically educational program that reaches over 60 per cent of Britain's schools.

The world coverage of the BBC's programs, both radio and television, consists of over 560 hours per week of broadcasting in about 40 languages. Reciprocal relaying of programs with NATO countries is a notable feature of the Corporation's activity.   W. M. W.

BRITISH CAMEROON. *See* CAMEROONS.
BRITISH CENTRAL AFRICA. *See* NYASALAND; RHODESIA.

BRITISH COLONIAL EMPIRE, territories which are under the control of the government of the United Kingdom and have not yet become fully self-governing. They must be distinguished, therefore, from the independent members of the Commonwealth of Nations which possess full internal and external sovereignty, a status toward which the colonial territories are steadily progressing. They must also be differentiated from British-protected states like Kuwait, Bahrein, and Oman in the Persian Gulf which are not considered part of the Empire.

British dependent territories include crown colonies, protectorates, and trust territories. Crown colonies are under the authority of the sovereign, and the British Parliament passes laws for them in any sphere for which their local legislatures and executives have not yet become responsible. Though in practice there is now little difference between crown colonies and protectorates, the latter were originally established by agreement between the British government and local rulers with the intention of protecting the latter from interference in their internal affairs. Trust territories, formerly League of Nations mandates, which were German colonies before 1914, are administered by the Colonial Office under United Nations supervision, which aims at advancing them to self-government as quickly as possible. There are also a very few condominiums which are jointly administered by two or more states; an example of the condominium is New Hebrides, where Great Britain shares control with France.

Position, Population, and Extent. Though British colonies are found as far north as Gibraltar at the entrance to the Mediterranean and as far south as Antarctica (Graham Land), the majority of them are in the tropics. The tropical colonies extend around the world from British Honduras and Jamaica to Gambia in West Africa, to Kenya in East Africa, to Singapore and Fiji Island, but over four fifths of all British colonial territories are now in Africa. The total population of the colonial empire is some 73 million, about 80 per cent of whom are native Africans. There are also Indians, Arabs, and Europeans, especially in East and Central Africa, while the Far Eastern and Pacific dependencies are peopled chiefly by Malayans, Melanesians, and Micronesians. Though English remains the language used by educated groups in the colonies, many languages and dialects are spoken within these territories. There are also sharp differences in religious beliefs and observances.

The colonial empire covers a total area of about 1,823,000 sq. mi. The largest territory within it, with the largest population (33,000,000), is the Federation of Nigeria in West Africa, which comprises 373,000 sq. mi., more than Great Britain, Ireland, and France together. In 1958 the West African colonies as a whole included 35,700,000 people; East and Central Africa, 25,900,000; Mediterranean colonies, 900,000; the Caribbean, 3,500,000; the Atlantic and Indian Ocean colonies, 1,600,000; the Far Eastern colonies, 4,800,000; and those in the Western Pacific, 600,000.

Most parts of the colonial empire confront difficult climatic conditions which have handicapped their development. Some depend heavily on the export of a single crop like cocoa or groundnuts (peanuts), the value of which fluctuates with world demand. But even where most of the people are still illiterate peasants, primarily occupied with growing food for their own use, a steadily increasing number are becoming urbanized and educated and are taking over positions in their territories' advance in self-government. Mining has a key role in such colonies as Tanganyika, the Rhodesias, Borneo, and along the Guinea coast. Manufacturing is increasing, especially in Southern Rhodesia with its dominant white population.

Steep street in Valletta, Malta, named after St. John. This British colony was formerly the property of the Knights of St. John.

A striking feature of the demography of the colonial empire is the presence in a few of the dependencies, notably Kenya and Southern Rhodesia, of a numerically small but politically and economically dominant white group, while a still larger number of colonies have a substantial and sometimes predominant number of nonwhite, non-native peoples. Sierra Leone, which was established as a refuge for freed African slaves, contains a wide variety of peoples from many parts of Africa, who are not assimilated to the indigenous inhabitants of the interior. While Negroes from West Africa form the predominant element in the West Indies, there are also large communities, especially in Trinidad and

COLONIES AND PROTECTORATES OF THE UNITED KINGDOM

TERRITORY	AREA (SQ. MI.)	POPULATION[1]	CAPITAL	STATUS IN 1958
Atlantic and Indian Oceans				
Bahamas	4,400	95,000	Nassau	Colony
Bermuda	21	40,800	Hamilton	Colony
Falkland Islands (excl. dependencies)	4,618	2,250	Stanley	Colony
S. Georgia				
S. Sandwich Is.				
S. Orkney Is.		700–1,400		
S. Shetland Is.				
Graham Land				
St. Helena (civil pop. only)	47	4,760	Jamestown	Colony
Ascension	34	170	Georgetown	Dependency of St. Helena
Tristan da Cunha	38	280	Edinburgh	Dependency of St. Helena
Aden Colony and Perim	80	138,400	Aden	Colony
Aden Protectorate	112,000	650,000	Aden	Protectorate
Mauritius and dependencies	809	585,000	Port Louis	Colony
Seychelles	156	40,400	Victoria	Colony
Far East				
Singapore	224	1,264,000	Singapore	Self-governing state
Brunei	2,226	65,300	Brunei Town	Protected-state
North Borneo	29,387	364,000	Jesselton	Colony
Sarawak	47,071	614,000	Kuching	Colony
Hong Kong	391	2,440,000	Victoria	Colony
Mediterranean				
Cyprus	3,572	526,000	Nicosia	Colony
Gibraltar (civil pop. only)	2¼	25,000	Gibraltar	Colony
Malta and Gozo (civil pop. only)	122	314,000	Valletta	Internal self-government
Caribbean				
British Guiana	83,000	499,000	Georgetown	Colony
British Honduras	8,866	82,000	Belize	Colony
Virgin Islands	67	7,680	Road Town	Colony
West Indies Federation			Port of Spain	Internal self-government,
Barbados	166	229,000	Bridgetown	near dominion status
Jamaica (excluding dependencies)	4,411	1,542,000	Kingston	
Cayman Islands	100	8,160	Georgetown	
Turks and Caicos Is.	166	6,600	Grand Turk	
Leeward Islands:				
Antigua	171	51,900	St. John's	
Montserrat	32	14,300	Plymouth	
St. Christopher, Nevis, and Anguilla	153	53,900	Basseterre Charlestown	
Trinidad and Tobago	1,980	721,000	Port of Spain	
Windward Islands:				
Dominica	305	62,100	Roseau	
Grenada	133	88,200	St. George's	
St. Lucia	238	87,200	Castries	
St. Vincent	150	75,900	Kingstown	
East and Central Africa				
Somaliland	68,000	640,000	Hargeisa	Protectorate
Kenya	224,960	6,150,000	Nairobi	Colony and Protectorate
Uganda	93,981	5,593,000	Entebbe	Protectorate
Tanganyika	362,688	8,456,000	Dar es Salaam	Trust Territory
Zanzibar and Pemba	1,020	277,000	Zanzibar	Protectorate
Fed. of Rhodesia and Nyasaland	487,640	7,260,900	Salisbury	Near dominion status
Northern Rhodesia	288,863	2,181,400	Lusaka	Protectorate
Southern Rhodesia	150,333	2,446,800	Salisbury	Self-governing
Nyasaland	48,444	2,632,700	Zomba	Protectorate
Southern Africa[2]				
Basutoland	11,716	631,396	Maseru	Colony
Bechuanaland	275,000	296,883	Mafeking	Protectorate
Swaziland	6,704	241,865	Mbabane	Protectorate

[1] According to latest available data, compiled chiefly from sources supplied by British Information Services.
[2] These three territories are dealt with by the Commonwealth Relations Office in London and the United Kingdom High Commissioner in Pretoria, South Africa.

(Continued on page 89)

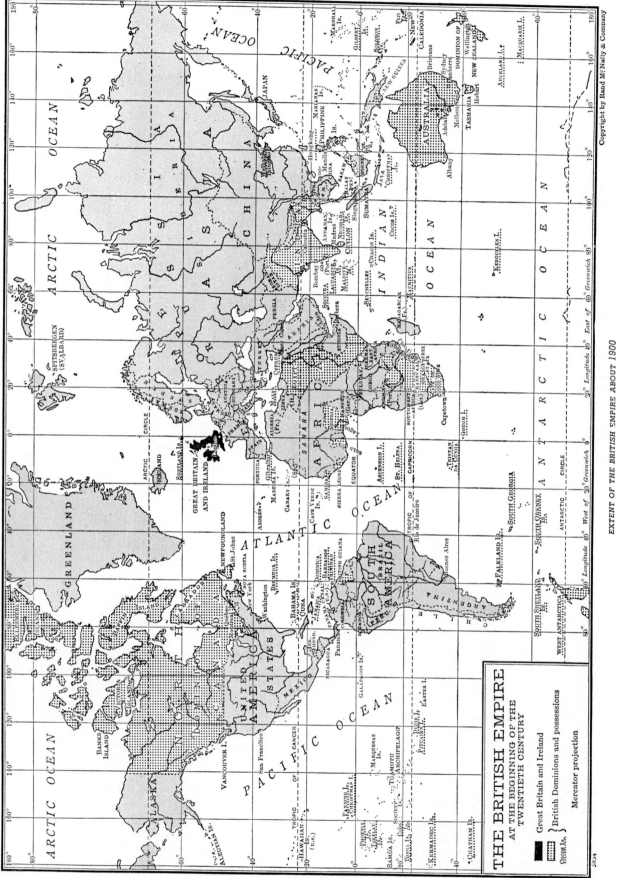

EXTENT OF THE BRITISH EMPIRE ABOUT 1900

Copyright by Rand McNally & Company

THE BRITISH EMPIRE
AT THE BEGINNING OF THE
TWENTIETH CENTURY

Great Britain and Ireland

British Dominions and possessions

Mercator projection

BRITISH COLONIES AND PROTECTORATES (Continued)

TERRITORY	AREA (SQ. MI.)	POPULATION[1]	CAPITAL	STATUS IN 1958
West Africa				
Gambia	4,003	310,000	Bathurst	Colony and Protectorate
Federation of Nigeria: (including Cameroons under U.K. Trusteeship)	373,250	33,278,000	Lagos	Near dominion status
Northern Region (including Northern Cameroons)	281,782	18,128,000	Kaduna	
Eastern Region	29,484	7,640,000	Enugu	
Western Region	45,376	6,402,000	Ibadan	
Lagos (Federal Capital)	27	312,000		
Southern Cameroons	16,581	796,000	Buea	
Sierra Leone	27,925	2,000,000	Freetown	Colony and Protectorate
Western Pacific				
Fiji	7,040	339,000	Suva	Colony
British Solomon Islands	11,500	99,200	Honiara	Protectorate
Gilbert and Ellice Is.	369	40,800	Tarawa	Colony
New Hebrides	5,700	52,900	Vila	Anglo-French condominiums
Pitcairn	2	140	Pitcairn	Colony
Tonga	269	53,800	Nukualofa	Protected state

[1] According to latest available data, compiled chiefly from sources supplied by British Information Services.

British Guiana, descended from people who were originally brought in from India as indentured labor after the abolition of slavery in 1834. Including both Moslems and Hindus, these Indians have retained their distinctive customs and have not merged either with the Negro majority or the small European minority. Indians are also present in substantial numbers in Singapore and along the coast of East Africa and the adjacent islands, and in Mauritius hold a substantial majority over all other groups. There are also many Chinese in Singapore as well as in the colonies of Borneo. Arabs are found along the east coast of Africa from Somaliland to Tanganyika. The presence of these largely unassimilable non-native racial elements complicate the problem of developing representative government in these territories. Still more difficult, however, has been the development of equitable means of representation in the two territories, Kenya and Southern Rhodesia, in which there are substantial white settler groups. Although the Federation of Rhodesia and Nyasaland, which was established in 1953, is based on a concept of the multiracial partnership, native Africans possess relatively little political power. In Kenya, the African position is much stronger but no political arrangement has yet been reached which satisfies both the Africans and the white settlers.

Administration. Each territory in the colonial empire has its own administration which operates with a considerable degree of autonomy within the broad lines of policy laid down by the United Kingdom Government. The Colonial Office, the department of government chiefly responsible for dependent territories, provides them with expert advice and services. Working closely with local administrations, the Colonial Office allocates money for development purposes under the Colonial Development and Welfare Acts. It also provides administrative and professional staffs through the Overseas Civil Service, which serves in the territories abroad in any post not yet transferred to the local inhabitants. The members of this service are paid by the government of the territory in which they serve but can be removed at the discretion of the Colonial Office.

Within each dependency is a governor appointed by the home government. Occasionally, as in Cyprus, the governor rules alone, but ordinarily he is advised by a small appointed executive council of officials, who are known as official members. In most colonies there is a legislature, at least some of whose members are elected by the local inhabitants. As the colony moves toward self-government, the elected representatives become a majority in the legislature and some of these representatives, who are known as unofficial members, are added to the executive council. When the legislature and executive council become composed wholly of representatives of the local inhabitants and particularly when the executive is drawn from the majority party or governing coalition of parties in the legislature, the colony has attained responsible government, with control over most or all of its internal affairs. In the Federations of Rhodesia and Nyasaland, Nigeria, and the West Indies, the executive council is responsible to the legislature but the United Kingdom Government still retains certain authority. In Rhodesia and Nyasaland this authority is exercised over native policy in Northern Rhodesia and Nyasaland, both of which are protectorates, and in Nigeria and the West Indies authority is exercised over external relations. Self-government is advancing so quickly, however, that changes are constantly taking place both in the relations between the home government and the local territory, and in the local constitutional structure.

Finance and Trade. Each territory raises its own basic revenue, but aid is made available by the United Kingdom

A section of the massive dried-stone wall of the Zimbabwe Ruins near Victoria, Southern Rhodesia

EWING GALLOWAY, NEW YORK

government for specific projects, grants-in-aid of administrative expenses, and approved development and welfare schemes. The United Kingdom Colonial Development and Welfare Acts of 1940, 1945, 1949, 1950, and 1955 have assigned £220 million over the twenty-year period to 1960. Since these grants are usually matched by allocations from local funds, welfare and development schemes have been set on foot which involve an estimated expenditure of £600 million ($1,680 million). To provide capital for development projects too risky to attract private capital, the Colonial Development Corporation was set up in 1948 and after some unfortunate ventures is now paying its way with a total in-

ESTABLISHMENT AND ELECTIVE GOVERNMENT OF THE BRITISH COLONIES AND PROTECTORATES

DEPENDENCY	DATE OF ACCESSION	METHOD OF ACCESSION	LEGISLATURE		
			NAME	MEMBERSHIP	
				TOTAL	ELECTED
Mediterranean Area					
Gibraltar	1713	Treaty with Spain	Council	11	5
Malta and Gozo	1814	Treaty with France	Assembly	40	40
Cyprus	1878	Treaty with Turkey	No legislature		
North Atlantic and West Indies					
Bermuda	1609	Settlement	Assembly	36	36
			Council	11	3
Virgin Islands	1666	Settlement	Council	11	6
British Honduras	1638	Settlement	Assembly	15	9
Bahamas	1648	Settlement	Assembly	29	29
			Council	9	
British Guiana	1814	Treaty with Holland	Council	23	14
West Indies Federation			Federal House of Representatives	45	45
Barbados	1627	Settlement	House of Assembly	24	24
			Council	15	
Leeward Islands	1623-1672	Settlement			
St. Kitts-Nevis	1623	Settlement	Council	10	5
Antigua	1632	Settlement	Council	14	8
Montserrat	1632	Settlement	Council	10	5
Jamaica	1655-1670	Conquest and treaty with Spain	House of Representatives	32	32
			Council	15	
Turks and Caicos	1678	Settlement	(Dependency of Jamaica)		
Cayman Islands	By 1750	Settlement	(Dependency of Jamaica)		
Windward Islands	1763	Treaty with France			
Grenada	1783	Treaty with France	Council	14	8
St. Vincent	1763	Treaty with France	Council	14	8
St. Lucia	1814	Treaty with France	Council	14	8
Dominica	1763	Treaty with France	Council	14	8
Trinidad and Tobago	1802; 1814	Treaties with Spain and France	Council	31	24
South Atlantic					
St. Helena	1659	Settlement	No legislature		
Ascension	1815	Settlement	(Adm. from St. Helena)		
Tristan da Cunha	1815	Settlement	(Adm. from St. Helena)		
West Africa					
Gambia	1618-1816	Treaties with native chiefs	Council	23	14
Sierra Leone	1787	Treaties with native chiefs	Council	30	19
Federation of Nigeria	1861-1886	Treaties with native tribes	Federal House of Representatives	194	185
Cameroons	1916-1922	Conquest and mandate	(Adm. from Nigeria)		
Southern Africa					
Basutoland	1868	Treaty with native chief	No legislature		
Bechuanaland	1885	Treaties with native tribes	No legislature		
Swaziland	1890	Treaties with native chiefs	No legislature		
Central Africa					
Federation of Rhodesia and Nyasaland			Federal Assembly	35	35
Southern Rhodesia	1889	Charter and settlement	Assembly	30	30
Northern Rhodesia	1890	Charter and settlement	Council	27	12
Nyasaland	1891	Agreement with Portugal	Council	23	11
Eastern Africa					
British Somaliland	1884	Replaced Egypt	No legislature		
Kenya	1887	Treaty with Sultan of Zanzibar	Council	60	21
Uganda	1894	Treaties with native chiefs	Council	60	30
Tanganyika	1918-1922	Conquest and mandate	Council	60	
Zanzibar and Pemba	1890	Treaties with Germany and sultan	Council	25	

(Continued on following page)

ESTABLISHMENT AND ELECTIVE GOVERNMENT OF THE BRITISH COLONIES AND PROTECTORATES (*Continued*)

DEPENDENCY	DATE OF ACCESSION	METHOD OF ACCESSION	LEGISLATURE		
			NAME	MEMBERSHIP	
				TOTAL	ELECTED
Indian Ocean					
Mauritius	1814	Treaty with France	Council	35	19
Seychelles	1814	Treaty with France	Council	13	4
Aden	1839	Treaty with local sheiks	Council	19	4
Kuria Muria	1854	Treaty with local sheik	(Adm. as part of Aden)		
Perim	1857	Treaty with local sultan	(Adm. as part of Aden)		
Socotra	1886	Treaty with local sultan	(Adm. as part of Aden)		
Kamaran	1915	Settlement	(Adm. as part of Aden)		
Christmas	1888	Settlement	(Adm. from Singapore)		
Southeast Asia					
Singapore	1819	Treaty with Sultan of Johore	Assembly	32	25
Sarawak	1841-1946	Gift to Sir James Brooke from sultan; transferred to U.K.	Council	54	24
Hong Kong	1842	Treaty with China	Council	18	
North Borneo	1846-1881	Treaty with sultan; charter	Council	23	
Brunei	1888	Treaty with sultan	Council	12	
Pacific Ocean Area					
Fiji	1874	Local treaties	Council	33	15
Pitcairn	1790	Settlement	(Adm. from Fiji)		
New Hebrides	1887	Agreement with France	No legislature		
Gilbert and Ellice Islands	1892	Local treaty and settlement	No legislature		
British Solomon Islands	1893	Agreement with Germany	No legislature		
Tonga	1900	Treaty with local king	Assembly	22	14
Canton and Enderbury	1939	Agreement with United States	No legislature		

vestment of £65 million ($182 million). In all, the flow of capital to the colonies from the United Kingdom amounted to between £750 and £1,000 million between 1945 and mid-1956. The United States has also contributed to British African territories under the 1953-1954 Mutual Security Act, the amount totaling £1.7 million by March 1957.

With this stimulus and their own external earnings, the colonial economies have expanded and accumulated substantial reserves. In 1956 their revenues amounted to £542 million compared to £264 million in 1950 and £57 million in 1939. The value of their exports rose from £1,249 in 1950 to £1,445 in 1956 and imports from £1,058 to £1,639. (The 1956 figures exclude Northern Rhodesia and Nyasa-

land.) While the United Kingdom does not dominate their trade, it remains their chief partner, sending the colonies 36.4 per cent of their imports and receiving 24.8 per cent of their exports. Imports from other parts of the sterling area in 1956 amounted to 21.7 per cent, exports to 20.1 per cent. Trade with the dollar area is more limited, amounting in the same year to 10.2 per cent of imports and 13.8 per cent of exports. (Imports in 1956 do not include those to Malaya or Hong Kong.) Of the five major trade areas—East Africa, West Africa, Malay, West Indies, Hong Kong—Malaya was by far the leader in trade, but since Malaya became independent in 1957 the leadership has been shared by Hong Kong and West Africa.

Belize, capital and chief port of British Honduras

A typical village on the island of Antigua, British West Indies

HISTORY OF THE BRITISH EMPIRE

The British colonial system originated in the early seventeenth century; but, except in the West Indies, few of the seventeenth century colonies have remained within the British system and many of those acquired subsequently have either separated from Great Britain or become independent members of the Commonwealth of Nations. Most of the present colonies and protectorates have become so within the last eighty years. Most of them are already well on the way to self-government. It is thus obvious that the British colonial system has undergone radical changes during its long and eventful history.

The Old Colonial Empire 1600-1783. There was little in medieval English history to presage the empire building of the modern period. The English people had shown little liking for the sea, and too often the policy of the king and the interests of the nation had failed to coincide. Only the town of Calais survived into the sixteenth century as a part of the ancient and extensive patrimony of the Crown in France, and that was lost in 1558. Complete failure had attended the efforts to extend English royal control into Scotland; near failure had been the result of a like venture in Ireland. Wales, however, had been pacified and annexed; the Isle of Man had been acquired from Scotland; and the Channel Islands, remnant of the ancient dukedom of Normandy, had been retained.

In the sixteenth century, under the Tudors, foundations were being laid for the subsequent imperial structure, but when Elizabeth died in 1603 little of it was apparent. During that century the interests of monarch and people were united as never before. Englishmen, particularly from Devon and Cornwall, began to take to the sea. Annual voyages of English fishing fleets were made to the Grand Banks off Newfoundland and English merchants were acquiring both capital and experience by conducting speculative overseas enterprises. The activities of the chartered companies for trade to Muscovy (1554), the Levant (1581), Morocco (1585), Guinea (1588), and India (1600), while they did not then result in any permanent acquisitions overseas, did point the way to later expansion. Between 1585 and 1604 the successes of the English in their war with Spain, which at that time included Portugal, gave the nation both confidence and experience in overseas activities. English exploration in the New World went on sporadically throughout the reign of the Tudors (1485-1603), beginning with John Cabot's voyage to the Gulf of St. Lawrence in 1497. Sir Francis Drake in 1577-1580 circumnavigated the globe by way of Cape Horn from east to west and Thomas Cavendish in 1586-1588 circumnavigated the globe from west to east. Martin Frobisher in 1576 explored the coast of Baffin Island in an attempt to discover a northwest passage.

Thus these and other English explorers paved the way for the permanent settlements which were to be established later.

The first stone in the structure of the old colonial empire was laid in 1607 with the establishment in America of Jamestown, just inside Chesapeake Bay. In 1781 with the surrender of Cornwallis to Washington at Yorktown, a dozen

Areas Formerly Under British Imperial Control

Area	Dates of British Control	Subsequent Status
Prior to 1600		
Wales	1277-1536	Integrated with England
Scotland	1173-1314	Independent kingdom
Normandy and other domains in France	1066-1453	Part of France
Calais	1347-1558	Part of France
Seventeenth Century		
Amboina	c.1610-1623	Part of Dutch East Indies
Mocha	c.1620-c.1640	Part of Yemen
Old Providence Isl.	1632-1641	Part of Spanish West Indies
Bandar Abbas	1622-c.1650	Part of Shah's domain
St. Augustine's Bay	1645-1646	Madagascar native rule
Dunkirk	1658-1662	Part of France
Surinam	c.1612-1667	Part of Dutch West Indies
Tangier	1662-1683	Part of Portuguese empire
Darien	1698-1700	Part of Spanish West Indies
Eighteenth Century		
American colonies	1607-1783	Independent republic
Minorca	1713-1783	Part of Spain
Florida, East and West	1763-1783	Part of Spanish West Indies
Senegal and Gorée	1763-1783	Part of French West Africa
Nineteenth Century		
Java	1811-1816	Part of Dutch East Indies
Benkulen	1685-1824	Part of Dutch East Indies
Fernando Po	1827-1858	Part of Spanish Guinea
Mosquito Coast	1630-1859	Part of Nicaragua
Ionian Islands	1814-1864	Part of Greece
Heligoland	1814-1890	Part of German empire
Twentieth Century		
Ireland	1170-1921	Irish Free State (to 1937) or Eire, member of Commonwealth of Nations until 1948; Republic of Ireland
Egypt	1914-1922	Independent kingdom
Weihaiwei	1898-1930	Part of China
Iraq	1922-1930	Independent kingdom
Canada	1670-1931	Member of Commonwealth of Nations
Australia	1788-1931	Member of Commonwealth of Nations
New Zealand	1840-1931	Member of Commonwealth of Nations
South Africa	1814-1931	Member of Commonwealth of Nations
Transjordan	1922-1946	Independent kingdom (Jordan)
India	1639-1947	Member of Commonwealth of Nations
Pakistan	1765-1947	Member of Commonwealth of Nations
Burma	1826-1948	Independent republic
Ceylon	1802-1948	Member of Commonwealth of Nations
Newfoundland	1610-1949	Province of Canada
Anglo-Egyptian Sudan	1899-1955	Independent republic (Sudan)
Gold Coast	1660-1957	United as member of Commonwealth of Nations (Ghana)
British Togoland	1919-1957	
Malaya, Federation of	1786-1957	Member of Commonwealth of Nations

miles from Jamestown, one corner of the imperial structure collapsed. In the interval of almost a century and three quarters since its origin, this empire had come to extend its bounds into five continents. Many of the holdings were acquired by charter-granting and settlement, or by cessions from native rulers; others were gained by conquest from the empires of Portugal, Holland, Spain, and France. Between 1652 and 1674 England fought three maritime wars with Holland to secure free access to India, but it was ousted from the rich islands of the East Indies by 1623.

From 1689 on there was a struggle for empire between England and France that continued, with longer or shorter intervals of uneasy peace, until Waterloo in 1815. The critical wars during this period were the War of the Spanish Succession (1702-1713), which ended in the Treaty of Utrecht; the War of the Austrian Succession (1740-1748); the Seven Years' War (1756-1763), ending in the Treaty of Paris; and the American Revolutionary War (1775-1783), ending in the treaties of Paris and Versailles.

During this period, the possession of dependencies was a secondary consideration to the promotion and protection of trade. This was strikingly illustrated by the pamphlet war which took place in England on the eve of the Treaty of Paris in 1763 on whether the vast French holdings in North America or the small sugar islands of Guadeloupe should be retained. Throughout the period the mercantile theory held sway that national wealth was measured in terms

lows: the chartered company colony of Virginia (1607), the proprietary colony of Newfoundland (1610), the chartered company colony of Plymouth (1620), the chartered company colony of Massachusetts Bay (1629), the proprietary colony of New Hampshire (1629), the proprietary colony of Maryland (1632), the self-governing colonies of Rhode Island and Connecticut (1636), the self-governing colony of New Haven (1638), the proprietary colonies of North and South Carolina (1663), the proprietary colonies of New York and New Jersey (1664), the chartered company colony of Hudson Bay (1670), the proprietary colony of Pennsylvania (1681), the proprietary colony of Delaware (1702), the crown colony of Nova Scotia (1713), the proprietary colony of Georgia (1732), and the crown colonies of Canada, East and West Florida, New Brunswick, Cape Breton Island, and Prince Edward Island (1763). Except in the remote region of Hudson Bay, government by English chartered company proved ineffective and short-lived. It was abandoned for Virginia in 1623 and for Massachusetts Bay in 1630, the latter by the simple device of having the company migrate to Salem, taking the charter with them. Proprietary government appeared to be more suitable and lasted longer. When the American Revolution broke out in 1775, Pennsylvania, Maryland, and Delaware were still under this form of control.

The West Indies. Barbados was permanently occupied in 1627. In the same year the Earl of Carlisle was granted pro-

A Barbadian farmer, clinging to the primitive methods of his ancestors, employs a team of oxen when plowing a sugar cane field.

EWING GALLOWAY, NEW YORK

of the possession of bullion. To secure the favorable balance of trade to increase bullion, trade had to be regulated and protected. This required a mercantile marine and a navy with sea bases to defend it. Important instruments of colonial policy were the Navigation Acts of 1650 to 1697, which sought to promote merchant shipping within the empire, and the empire tariffs and embargoes to direct trade into profitable channels and thus increase the national wealth.

Territorial acquisitions during the period 1600 to 1783 may be divided geographically into the North American mainland, the West Indies region, West Africa, the Indian Ocean, and scattered naval bases.

North American Colonies. The order of founding and original status of the North American colonies is as fol-

prietary rights over all unoccupied islands in the West Indies. After several transfers of this right, the crown took over direct control in 1662. In the Leewards, St. Kitts was occupied in 1623, Nevis in 1628, and Antigua and Montserrat in 1632. The first settlement in the Bahamas was made from Bermuda in 1648. Jamaica was captured from Spain in 1655. The Windwards remained neutral until, by the 1763 Treaty of Paris, St. Vincent, Dominica, Grenada and the Grenadines, and Tobago, all formerly French, were allocated to Great Britain. Although Grenada and Tobago later temporarily changed hands, the former was finally acquired in 1783 and the latter in 1814.

In addition to these islands, which still form part of the British colonial empire in the West Indies, other acquisitions

King Street, main thoroughfare
of Kingston, capital of Jamaica

either of a temporary or partial nature were made. From as early as 1630 English interests were strong along the Mosquito Coast in what is now Nicaragua. British claims to this region were not finally abandoned until 1859. The island of Old Providence, off the Nicaraguan coast, was occupied by English settlers from 1632 to 1641. After 1667, when the Dutch were granted exclusive rights in Surinam, on the Guiana coast, English interests steadily and persistently penetrated into the adjacent territory of Essequibo, in what is now British Guiana. The tragic attempt of the Scots to found a colony at Darien (Panama) began in 1698 and ended in 1700.

West Africa. England's initial interest in Africa was for Guinea gold, but with the growth of its plantation colonies in North America and the West Indies its interest turned almost exclusively to the procurement of slaves. Portugal before 1642, and Holland after that, attempted to monopolize the slave trade, and the early phases of English trade in West Africa had of necessity to be both surreptitious and mobile; its history is, therefore, difficult to trace. In 1618 a temporary settlement was made by the English at the mouth of the Gambia River, but it was only after the first Anglo-Dutch maritime war (1652-1654) that England was in a position to challenge Holland along the Gold Coast. In 1660 the Royal African Company was chartered with a monopoly of English trade along the Guinea Coast. In 1769 James Bruce's successful search for the source of the Blue Nile began the first of English explorations into the interior. But neither accession of territory nor trade followed this initial venture. Soon English humanitarians began vigorous attacks both on the slave trade and on slavery itself. In 1772 Lord Mansfield's verdict made all slaves free on landing in England. Before 1783 William Wilberforce had begun the attack on the slave trade in Parliament and Granville Sharp in the courts.

The Indian Ocean. When, owing to Dutch opposition, trade in the East Indies became first unprofitable and later impossible, the English merchants turned energetically to the development of trade with India. At first content merely to have security for their coastal factories, especially at Surat

(1612) on the west coast and Masulipatam (1611) on the east, they secured something approaching sovereignty at

Directing traffic in Suva, chief city and capital of the tropical
Fiji Islands, a British Crown Colony

Madras in 1639, at Hooghly in 1650, and in 1662 over the island of Bombay, which came as a gift by way of dowry from the King of Portugal. After the British victory at

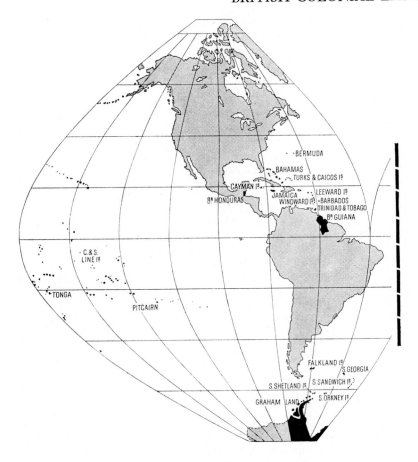

DEPENDENCIES OF
THE UNITED KINGDOM

Colonies in the Western Hemisphere (left) include the islands of Jamaica (with Cayman, Turks, and Caicos), Barbados, Trinidad and Tobago, and the Leeward and Windward islands, all now combined in the West Indies Federation and approaching dominion status. In the Eastern Hemisphere (below), the Federation of Nigeria in Africa is also approaching dominion status.

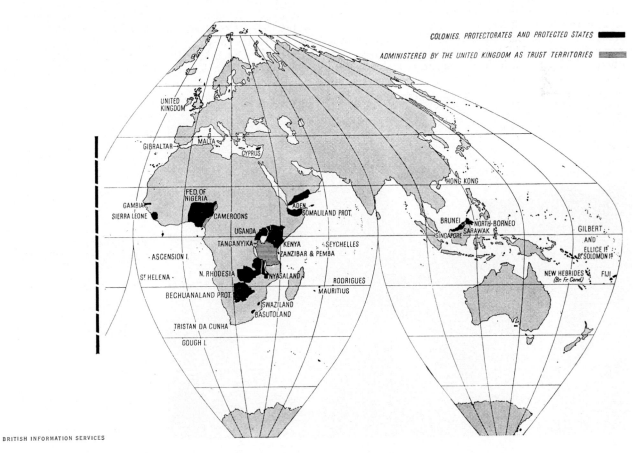

COLONIES, PROTECTORATES AND PROTECTED STATES

ADMINISTERED BY THE UNITED KINGDOM AS TRUST TERRITORIES

Plassey in 1757 the East India Company began to penetrate the subcontinent of India, and Lower Bengal and the Northern Circars came under the control of the company. Lord North's Regulating Act in 1773, however, initiated the process of transferring British interests in India from company to crown control, which was completed in 1858.

Outlying Bases. Hitherto uninhabited, the islands of Bermuda were settled in 1609; before becoming a royal colony in 1684, they were first controlled by Virginia and then by a chartered company of London merchants.

In 1713 Spain was forced to cede Gibraltar to Britain, and at the same time Minorca was also transferred to Great Britain. In 1765 Great Britain laid claim to the Falkland Islands in the far South Atlantic; although formally ceded by Spain in 1771, these islands were not effectively occupied by Great Britain until 1833. In 1790 Pitcairn Island, in the mid-Pacific, was occupied by mutineers from H.M.S. *Bounty,* accompanied by Polynesian women from Tahiti. It was claimed by Great Britain but not formally incorporated into the empire until 1898.

Organization of the Old Colonial Empire. Throughout the seventeenth century the government's machinery for administering the colonies remained simple. Charters were issued, reviewed, renewed, or revoked on royal prerogative and responsibility. Not until the very end of the century did Parliament claim the right to consider such matters as a corollary to the Bill of Rights (1689). Parliament consistently exercised the right to legislate on shipping and trade throughout the empire. Administration of such laws fell to the Board of Customs and Excise, and in 1695 Lords Commissioners of Trade and Plantations, popularly known as the Board of Trade, became the body to administer crown colonies. Both bodies were dissolved in 1782. Within the colonies the most usual form of government was that by governor, council, and assembly, the last regularly elected but with various restrictions on the franchise.

Trade in the Old Colonial Empire. In building an overseas empire, Britain, like her European rivals, at first aimed in its imperial policy at both self-subsistence and monopoly.

The Navigation Act of 1660 required that certain "enumerated" products from the colonies be disposed of only in England, and from time to time the list of such products was extended. By the Act of 1663 almost all goods from continental Europe for the colonies had first to be taken to England. These acts tended to force trade into a simple reciprocal channel between colony and mother country. Trade involving the West Indies, West Africa, England, and New England was more complex in character, and it has been described as triangular though it was, in fact, much more intricate. New England exported timber both to England and the West Indies; New England traders had extensive interests in the African slave trade; and both Old and New England regarded themselves as the apex of a triangle whose other corners were West Africa and the plantation colonies on the American mainland and in the West Indies. India, however, required gold to be sent from England in balance of trade.

The Colonial Empire in Transition, 1783-1858. The American Revolutionary War (1775-1783), in which the colonies were joined by France in 1778, Spain in 1779, and Holland in 1780, was ended by the treaties of Versailles and Paris by which Great Britain recognized the complete independence of the thirteen American colonies, from New Hampshire to Georgia. Tobago in the West Indies and Senegal and Gorée in West Africa were ceded to France, and East and West Florida and the island of Minorca returned to Spain. The British people were profoundly shocked and bewildered by these losses, which came so soon after the glorious victories of the Seven Years' War. But the task of reintegrating what remained and rebuilding a system of empire trade had hardly begun before the French Revolutionary and Napoleonic wars again threw the colonial empire into the crucible. In the Treaty of Paris in 1814 France returned Tobago to Great Britain and also ceded the island of St. Lucia in the Windward Islands, Mauritius and the Seychelles in the Indian Ocean, and the island of Malta and the Ionian Islands in the Mediterranean. By the Treaty of Amiens (1802), the Dutch had already ceded Ceylon to the British, while the Spanish had ceded Trinidad. The Dutch now

One of many volcanic peaks typical of those found on St. Lucia, Windward Islands

SINGAPORE AS VIEWED FROM FORT CANNING IN THE SOUTHWEST PART OF THE CITY

also ceded to the British the western section of Guiana and again ceded the Cape of Good Hope and Malacca. Significant of the temper of British policy following the Napoleonic struggle was the return to the Dutch in 1816 of the rich and populous island of Java.

Between 1783 and 1816 the British dependencies were also being extended by peaceful means. In 1786 the island of Penang in the Malacca Straits was purchased from the local sultan; in 1787 a peninsula at Sierra Leone was similarly acquired; Sydney, Australia, and Norfolk Island, to the east, were occupied in 1788; the province of Wellesley, opposite Penang, was purchased in 1800; Tasmania, to the south of Australia, was occupied in 1803; the islands of Ascension and Tristan da Cunha in the South Atlantic were occupied in 1815, while Bathurst on the Gambia was reoccupied in 1816.

During the remainder of the transitional period (1816-1858), Britain made other acquisitions, most of which were islands: Singapore (1819), the northwestern territories of North America (1821), Lower Burma (1826), Falkland Islands (reoccupied, 1833), Aden (1839), New Zealand (1840), Hong Kong (1842), Natal (1843), British Columbia on the Pacific, and Labuan Island off Borneo (1846), the Danish posts on the Gold Coast (1850), Kuria Muria Islands

in the Arabian Sea (1854), Perim Island at the entrance to the Red Sea (1857), and the Cocos Islands in the Indian Ocean (1857). The nature and location of Britain's acquisitions during the period of transition; the voluntary return of Java; the delay, in spite of repeated urgings, in assuming responsibility for the islands of New Zealand; the refusal to take over the western half of Australia until it appeared as if the French were about to acquire a colony there; and the government's unwillingness to expand in South Africa, all point to a policy of building up bases for trade and defense of the trade routes, and an aversion to territorial expansion. Where large territories were taken over, as in North America and Australia, the motive was mainly that of precluding acquisition by other powers.

In India, which was now administratively separate from the colonial empire, British policy alternated between expansion and retrenchment. The net result was, however, that by 1819 Great Britain was able to declare itself the paramount power in India, and by 1858, when company control was completely abolished, Britain had come to control the whole peninsula, either directly or through treaty agreements with native rulers. Although this Indian empire was not regarded as a part of the colonial empire, the growth of the two empires was inextricably entwined. Beyond the bounds

A view of the town of Aden, held by the British since 1839. Of major strategic importance, it commands the sea route between the Red Sea and the Far East.

East Indian sugar-cane cutters at work on Viti Levu, largest of the Fiji Islands

of India proper the East India Company became responsible for the administration not only of Burma but of outlying British posts all the way from Perim Island, in the west, to Labuan Island, far to the east. In the direction of policy, the two empires were considered together on both parliamentary and cabinet levels, and in the administration of the colonial empire much use was made of military and civil personnel transferred from India.

Several new colonies resulted directly or indirectly from the breakaway of the American colonies. Almost 50,000 American Tories migrated to the remaining British North American colonies, the provinces of Nova Scotia (then including New Brunswick) and Upper Canada (later Ontario) receiving a majority of these "United Empire Loyalists." New South Wales in Australia was established in 1788 for the reception of convicts who in earlier years would have been sent to the southern American colonies. The subsequent rapid growth of these settlement colonies, together with those in South Africa and New Zealand, was the result of the economic dislocation brought to the United Kingdom (so named after the union of Great Britain and Ireland in 1801) by the Industrial Revolution and the simultaneous unprecedented growth of population in both Ireland and Great Britain. These colonies proved as eager for self-government, however, as had the American colonies. In 1837, rebellion broke out in Upper and Lower Canada. This time a satisfactory solution was found in the proposal of responsible government in 1839 in the celebrated *Report* by Lord Durham, who had been advised by reformers in Nova Scotia and Upper Canada, notably Joseph Howe and Robert Baldwin. This proposed a system of government in internal affairs similar to that of the United Kingdom, in which the executive council or cabinet would hold office only so long as it retained the confidence of the lower house of the legislature. Thus while in certain limited fields of imperial concern the governor, responsible to the Colonial Office, would still retain authority; in matters of local concern he would play the role of a purely constitutional monarch. This new and revolutionary system of "responsible" government was first applied in Nova Scotia and in the united province of Canada which had, at Durham's suggestion, been created

in 1841. By 1855 it had also been put into practice in the other provinces of British North America, including Newfoundland, in all the colonies of Australia except Western Australia, and in New Zealand. At first it had been assumed that colonial tariffs were a matter of imperial concern, but in 1859 the Canadian government challenged this view and was not successfully opposed. By 1859, therefore, the basis had been laid for the formation of the later Commonwealth of Nations.

The old colonial empire had been built to promote trade. In the transition period this motive remained predominant, but here, too, a revolution was in the making. In 1776 Adam Smith published his *Wealth of Nations,* which supported the continued control of shipping but denounced the regulation of trade. In 1786 a reciprocal trade treaty was concluded with France; even during the bitter Napoleonic struggles Britain was almost as determined to trade with the enemy as not to have the enemy trade with it. That Napoleon was forced to dress his Grand Army in English woolens was a subject for rejoicing. Nothing was done, however, to free the trade of the colonies until the 1820's, when a small but permanent breach in the old mercantile system was effected: nations which reciprocated were allowed to trade directly with the colonies. In 1830 a similar concession was made for trade between the United States and the British West Indies, but without the reciprocal condition. It was not, however, until the 1840's that the old system of economic imperial monopoly collapsed. In 1846 the Corn Laws were repealed, and by 1850 there were practically no British protective tariffs left. In 1848 many of the colonies were allowed to pass their own tariff laws, provided only that these not be discriminatory. In 1849 the Navigation Acts were repealed, except in regard to coastal trade. Although some of the colonies had been granted local self-government before the new free-trade system was completely established, the new constitutional system was in some measure a corollary of the new economic system. A less welcome corollary of free trade was that colonies that were free to trade were made responsible for their own local defense. The United Kingdom continued, however, to bear the sole burden of defending the sea lanes.

A new motive in the imperialism of the transition period was that of conversion and protection of primitive peoples. The combined attack of religion and humanitarianism on the slave trade resulted in its complete abolition by law throughout the empire in 1807. Sierra Leone was founded in 1787 as a refuge for freed slaves. But, in the main, Britain's interest in tropical Africa dwindled, and in 1828 the government seriously considered a complete withdrawal from the main British bases along the Gold Coast. Even before the abolition of the trade in slaves, British explorers were beginning to penetrate the interior of Africa. Mungo Park in two expeditions, 1795 to 1796 and 1805 to 1806, explored the upper Niger. Between 1816 and 1870 Robert Moffat carried on explorations as well as missionary work in southern Africa. In 1841 David Livingstone, Moffat's son-in-law, entered Bechuanaland and until his death in 1873 did continuous and extensive explorations both north and south of the Zambezi. In East Africa Sir Richard Burton and John H. Speke discovered Lake Tanganyika, and later in the same year Speke discovered Lake Nyanza, source of the White Nile. British trade in tropical Africa came to center in what is now Nigeria, but the British government did not extend its dependent empire in Africa, with the exception of the purchase in 1850 of Denmark's holdings on the Gold Coast of East Africa.

In 1833 the British government passed a law prohibiting slavery throughout the empire as of 1834. The West Indian planters had scarcely recovered from the shock of the abolition of slavery before the British preference on colonial sugar was threatened by the advent of the economic policy of free trade.

It was in South Africa that British policy in this transition period showed the greatest uncertainty and vacillation. It was clear that the chief value of Cape Colony lay in the protection that it afforded to the strategic port of Cape Town. In 1819 British settlers began to arrive, but in such small numbers that, even after the Great Trek beginning in 1836, which led to the founding of the Orange Free State and Transvaal as Afrikaner (Boer) states, the British remained in a minority in the Cape. Only in Natal, founded in 1843, did the British become dominant. In 1848 the British government annexed the Orange Free State, but withdrew in 1854. In 1852 the Transvaal was declared to be independent of British control, but subject to the vague claim of British sovereignty. These clumsy actions contributed to the ultimate conflict of the Anglo-Boer War (1899-1902), precipitated by the rush for gold in the Transvaal and the unsuccessful and bitterly resented attempt culminating in the Jameson Raid to seize control there. This war created divisions within what became South Africa which have never been entirely healed, but it also witnessed the first joint Commonwealth military effort, with Canada, Australia, and New Zealand contributing troops. Moreover the generous peace settlement offered by Great Britain paved the way for a united South Africa to accept dominion status when that became desirable.

Rise and Impact of Commonwealth of Nations, 1858-1914. During the period 1858 to 1914 the settlement colonies that had achieved responsible government in local affairs continued to widen the range of their autonomy, and other colonies joined their ranks. The new status was achieved by Queensland on its separation from New South Wales in 1859, by Cape Colony in 1872, by Western Australia in 1890, by Natal in 1893, by the Transvaal in 1906, and by the Orange Free State in 1907. Although until 1925 the Colonial Office remained the medium of communication between these colonies and the government of the United Kingdom and external relations were largely in the hands of the British, such colonies ceased to be regarded as part of the dependent empire. Their emergence as completely independent states within the Commonwealth of Nations is treated in the article under that head. The unique character

Frederick Street in Port of Spain, the principal city and capital of Trinidad and the West Indies Federation

of their constitutional status and their spectacular growth had, however, an influence on the development of the dependent empire. In particular the success of their intercolonial federations and legislative unions pointed the way to like regional unions among the dependent colonies.

Canada established its federation in 1867, New Zealand its legislative union in 1875, Australia its federation in 1901, and the South African states their legislative union in 1910. On this pattern, the Leeward Islands were federated in 1871, and four of the Malay states in 1895; and similar action of other dependencies followed soon thereafter. From experience with the settlement colonies Britain also learned the dangers of political deadlock and agitation involved in the operation of two-house legislatures, the lower elected, the upper appointed. The constitutions created for the dependent colonies in this period provided, therefore, for unicameral legislatures, and the proportion of official, nominated, and elected members could easily be made adjustable by order in council.

After 1858 India had a secretary of state of its own and was not regarded as part of the colonial empire. But from India, too, valuable experience was available for colonial administration. The Indian Mutiny of 1857 had been preceded, and largely precipitated, by a spate of annexations, by the creation of universities, and by the building of railways. Loyalty to the British connection was to be found largely in the native states, only the external relations of which were controlled by treaty. In the dependent empire throughout this period efforts were increasingly made to retain the services of native rulers in the administration of local affairs. Of the total area added to the colonial empire in this period, much the largest part was given protectorate and not crown colony status. The principle of "indirect rule" as it applied to the dependent empire was given classic statement by Captain (later Lord) Lugard in his *Rise of Our East African Empire* (1893) and later in *Dual Mandate* (1922).

After a short interval (1858-1874) in which government was dominated by anti-imperialists of the Manchester School, the colonial empire began a period of spectacular expansion. Within thirty years both its size and population had more

Part of the diverse irrigation works on the island of Cyprus is this flume cut into the rocky side of a dry gully.

COURTESY OF BRITISH INFORMATION SERVICES

than doubled. This abnormal growth resulted from several causes, but was primarily due to the sudden emergence of rival empire-builders. The situation was made the more critical for the British by the pursuit by these rivals of Britain's earlier policy of imperial monopoly rather than its later policy of free trade. The first in the field was Leopold, King of the Belgians, who in his private capacity inaugurated a scheme in the Congo that at the outset bore the aspect of benevolent humanitarianism, though its mask was removed once the venture was launched. In the early 1880's it became clear that Germany and France, with explorers, missionaries, and traders in the van, were bent on building large monopolistic empires in both West and East Africa, and these nations were shortly joined by Italy. Even somnolent Portugal began to assert transcontinental claims in southern Africa, based on its long association with that part of the continent. Contributing causes for British expansion into Africa were the demands of the missionaries for protection for their wards and themselves against the rising menace of attack by Arab slave traders along the east coast; British protection of Uganda and Nyasaland stemmed directly from this appeal. At the same time, Britain's rising industrial potential created increasing demands for foodstuffs and other raw materials and also for markets for manufactured goods. The improvement in steam transportation and the invention of economic methods of refrigeration added to the urge for overseas trade just as vast territories were being closed to trade by other empire-builders. The same conditions prevailed in southeast Asia and in the southwest Pacific, and here, too, the British, attempting to forestall France, Germany, Japan, and the United States, joined heartily in what has, with little exaggeration, been called the scramble for empire.

Between 1858 and 1874 Great Britain ceded the Mosquito Coast to Nicaragua (1859), and the Ionian Islands to Greece (1864). It acquired only the port of Lagos in what is now Nigeria (1861). In the subsequent period its acquisitions, some assigned to chartered companies, others taken over directly by the Crown as colonies, but mostly given the status of protectorates, were: Basutoland in southern Africa (1868); Dutch posts on the Gold Coast (1872); Perak and Selangor in the Malay Peninsula, and Fiji in the Pacific (1874); the island of Cyprus (1878); North Borneo (1881); British Somaliland (1884); Bechuanaland (1885); Socotra in the Gulf of Aden (1886); Kenya in East Africa; the New Hebrides (a condominium with France) and Pahang and Negri Sembilan on the Malay Peninsula (1887); Brunei (1888); Southern Rhodesia (1889); Nyasaland (1891); Swaziland in southern Africa; Uganda and Zanzibar in East Africa (1890); the Gilbert and Ellice islands in the Pacific (1892); British Solomons in the Pacific (1893); Northern Rhodesia (1890); the Anglo-Egyptian Sudan (a condominium with Egypt) (1898); Tonga in the Pacific (1900); Kedah and Kelantan on the Malay Peninsula (1909); and Johore, also on the Malay Peninsula (1914). In addition to these, the United Kingdom allowed Australia and New Zealand to acquire several strategic areas from New Guinea to the Cook Islands. Especially in Africa and the islands of the Pacific, British acquisitions tended to enlarge quickly, usually by treaty agreements with the native rulers. These additions were particularly striking in Nigeria, which grew from a small enclave about the port of Lagos until it included a territory of 338,593 sq. mi. with a population of more than 20,000,000.

Effects of Two World Wars, 1914-1949. During the quarter century (1914-1939) between the outbreak of World

KOWLOON, HONG KONG'S NAVAL BASE, AS SEEN FROM THE PEAK

War I and the outbreak of World War II, great changes took place in the structure, and some in the extent, of the colonial empire; in the decade 1939 to 1949 these changes were extremely rapid and profound. During the period preceding World War I, the chief function of the British government in its dependencies had been the preservation of law and order. The development of natural resources and the education and social welfare of the native peoples were left largely to private initiative. But between the wars, and particularly after the formation of the coalition government during World War II and the accession to power of the Labour Party in 1945, the British government assumed increasing responsibilities for promoting the economic and social welfare of the peoples in its dependencies. Moreover after 1945 there was a rapid acceleration of the progress towards self-government.

Military operations during World War I had relatively little effect on the colonial empire. Great Britain had built no substantial colonial armies, but such colonial troops as there were saw service beyond their own colonial boundaries. West African troops were employed in the conquest from Germany of Togoland and the Cameroons. A battalion of the West Indian Regiment was despatched to Tanganyika, where units of the King's African Rifles from Kenya were also employed. Other colonial forces were employed in the reduction of Germany's holdings in southeast Asia and the Pacific, or were despatched to the main European theatre of war. The total number of colonial troops employed, however, was small. Except during the brief invasion of Kenya by German forces from Tanganyika, colonial forces were not called upon to defend their own colonies. Despite the German blockade of the United Kingdom, the economic life of the colonies was not seriously affected by the war. More important was the infiltration, during and following the war, of ideas of democratic self-determination, which had been a main issue in the war itself. This was further emphasized by the creation of a Mandates Commission to supervise the administration of territories taken from Germany and Turkey following the war.

Of the mandates assigned to the Allied Powers, Great Britain received from the former Turkish empire Palestine, Transjordan, and Iraq (formerly Mesopotamia). Of the former German Empire it received the minor parts of Togoland and the Cameroons in West Africa and the major part of Tanganyika in East Africa. In the Pacific it received, jointly with Australia and New Zealand, the small phosphate island of Nauru on the equator. Iraq was the first of these mandated lands to be given its independence; this took place in 1930, and two years later it became a member of the League of Nations. Transjordan (since 1949 Jordan) received its independence in 1946, and Palestine, where the situation was much complicated by the internal struggle between Arabs and Jews, in 1948. Thus Britain lost control of its Levantine bastion on its all-important Mediterranean route to India and beyond. Egypt, although not regarded as part of the colonial empire, had provided a base for the defense of the Suez route to the East, but in 1922 Britain's protectorate over that country was also abandoned, and its control of the Suez Canal, though important in World War II, terminated a few years later.

In the period between the wars other changes took place, among them the abolition in 1922 of the British South Africa Company's chartered rights in Northern and Southern Rhodesia; the vote for and receipt of colonial autonomy in the latter, covering all matters except external relations and the regulation of African affairs; and the establishment of legislative councils in Kenya (1919), Tanganyika (1926), and British Guiana (1928). In several of the colonies the elective element in the legislative council was increased. In 1929 Parliament passed a Colonial Development Act which made available for colonial industrial and agricultural develop-

was used for the development of resources or for welfare schemes: improvements in transport facilities were given a high place in the former, and the promotion of education and public health a conspicuous place in the latter, though progress was considerably retarded by the continuing lack of sufficient materials and adequately trained personnel. Colonial territories, notably Malaya and Borneo, also shared in the Commonwealth Colombo Plan for the economic development of south and southeast Asia.

The Royal Palace at Nukualofa, capital of the South Pacific Tonga, or Friendly, Islands, a British protectorate since 1900

ment about $4,000,000 a year, but its aim was somewhat narrowly conceived as the promotion of trade with the United Kingdom. During the same period considerably greater use was made of native inhabitants in the colonial civil service, including their employment in some of the higher positions.

World War II brought economic dislocation to many of the colonies, which had come to rely on the importation of foodstuffs, particularly rice. The scarcity of shipping and the occupation of Burma, from which many of the colonies secured their supplies of rice, also brought hardship. On the other hand, there was an unprecedented demand for certain products, chiefly minerals, and the arrival of Allied troops in many of the colonies in both Africa and the Pacific was financially rewarding. Many more colonial soldiers were enlisted during the World War II than during the previous war. At the beginning of World War II, for instance, the Royal West African Frontier Force numbered less than 7,000; before its end more than 176,000 persons had joined its ranks. Troops from West Africa served in southeast Asia, troops from East Africa in the Ethiopian and North African campaigns. Troops from southeast Asia and the Pacific were employed in campaigns in those regions, and West Indian battalions were used on more than one front. These soldiers, returning to their native villages in Africa, the South Seas, and the West Indies brought with them an intellectual ferment that called for change, and this was speeded by the increasing number of students trained abroad.

In 1940 Great Britain passed the first of several Colonial Development and Welfare Acts, under which, as already indicated, the British exchequer has contributed to economic and social improvements in the colonies. Most of the money

With the end of World War II and the election of the Labour government in Britain in 1945, the tempo of change in the colonies quickened. In many of the colonies audio-visual mass education was inaugurated. Regional colleges with technical and professional branches were established in the West Indies, West Africa, and East Africa to supplement the facilities hitherto provided mostly by missionary organizations. The University of Hong Kong was revived, and a university was established in the Federation of Malaya. Native authorities and regional native councils were encouraged to open vernacular schools. In addition to the secretary of state for the colonies, whose duties usually required his presence in London, a minister of state for colonial affairs was appointed in 1948 as a liaison officer between the colonies and the Colonial Office. Many new constitutions were granted to the colonies, increasing the elective element in local legislative councils and widening the administrative range of native authorities. In 1948 Ceylon became an independent member of the Commonwealth, as India and Pakistan had done the year before. Malta was granted responsible government, in part as a reward for its fortitude during the war. In 1946 the protectorate of Sarawak, after more than a century of rule by the Raja Brooke dynasty, was formally ceded to Britain and became a colony. Also in 1946 the rule in North Borneo of the British North Borneo Company came to an end, and with it the end of chartered company rule in the empire; North Borneo then became a colony. With government support and encouragement, both imperial and intercolonial airway companies were incorporated, and their services rapidly expanded.

Following the war there was a significant movement toward the establishment of regional colonial federations. In 1948 the Federation of Malaya was established and became an independent member of the Commonwealth in August 1957. Though Singapore was not a part of the Malayan Federation, it began to acquire an increasing measure of responsible government. A Central African Council was established in 1945 which paved the way for the Federation of Rhodesia established in 1953 and uniting Southern Rhodesia, Northern Rhodesia, and Nyasaland. In 1957 most of the West Indies islands federated and received responsible government. The same year, the Federation of Nigeria acquired full cabinet government. Both were scheduled to become independent members of the Commonwealth. First of all African colonies territories to graduate to full independence within the Commonwealth, however, was Ghana in 1957.

Less easy was the progress to full self-government of the multiracial territories. Agitation by Africans, especially in Northern Rhodesia and Nyasaland, against a grant of independence to the Federation lest it come under the white domination characteristic of South Africa raised doubts in the minds of British statesmen about the advisability of a full transfer of power. Still more difficult was the situation in East Africa. In 1948, the protectorate of Uganda, the colony and protectorate of Kenya, and the Trust Territory of Tanganyika were united in a loose confederation by the creation of an East African High Commission whose powers extend to such matters of common concern as transportation, research, customs tariffs, currency, and postal services, including telegraph and telephone services. Crucial to its future, however, was the struggle for power within Kenya between the Africans, whose dominant numbers have only recently been reflected in growing political influence, and the minority of white settlers who have long wielded political and economic power within the colonial structure. Unless the Kenya power struggle is resolved in favor of its Africans, Uganda and Tanganyika, both predominantly African territories, will hold aloof from a strengthening of the bonds between the three units.

Most of the British dependent empire was acquired at a time of bitter imperial rivalries. After World War II the trend was toward international co-operation and consultation, not only on the level of the United Nations in the administration of the trusteeship system, but also in the increasing use of interimperial conferences on technical subjects, such as the control of the tsetse fly menace, the prevention of soil erosion, native welfare problems, and the improvement of transport facilities. Africa has been the most conspicuous area of interimperial co-operation, and this is natural in view of the strategic importance and the undeveloped resources of this great continent, in a world that is in need of both resources and security. But increasingly the responsibilities are being assumed by the inhabitants of the territories themselves, and their successful handling will depend not only on the guidance and help being given them from outside but still more on the skill, judgment, and co-operation of their native peoples. *See also* COMMONWEALTH OF NATIONS.　　　　　W. M. W. and G. M. C.

BRITISH COLUMBIA, the most western of the Canadian provinces, bounded on the west as far north as 54° 40′ N. lat. by the Pacific Ocean, and beyond that by the Alaskan panhandle; on the north by 60° N. lat., which is the boundary common to all four western provinces; on the south by 49° N. lat., except where Vancouver Island extends south of the 49th parallel; and on the east by the divide of the Rockies as far north as 54° N. lat., thence by 120° W. long., including a considerable area of Canada's interior plains, which are comprised mostly of the middle Peace and

A small native coasting craft under way in the harbor of Dar es Salaam ("Haven of Peace"), capital and chief port of Tanganyika.

Laird river basins. To the north of British Columbia are Yukon Territory and Mackenzie District of the Northwest Territories; to the east is Alberta; and to the south, in order from east to west, are the states of Montana, Idaho, and Washington. The coast line of the province is about 600 mi. long, excluding the many indentations of the fiorded coast and the approximately 400-mi.-long border along the Alaskan strip. (When the United States purchased Alaska from Russia in 1867, this coastal belt was included in the transaction, since it had been only sparsely settled by Russians.) The province has a total area of 366,255 sq. mi., which is about 10 per cent of Canada's area, and ranks third in size among Canadian provinces, after Quebec and Ontario. Of the total area, 6,976 sq. mi. are inland water areas.

PHYSICAL FEATURES

Geology. The province has a great variety of geological features, with rocks of nearly all geological ages. There have been three widespread periods of mountain formation, which have produced a complicated system of land forms. In Jurassic times, about 140 million years ago, the coastal ranges were initiated, accompanied by the formation of a granite batholith extending for nearly 1,000 mi. from Vancouver to Yukon, and averaging 100 mi. in width. At the same time, a smaller batholith was formed in the Selkirk area in the southeast corner of the province. Later erosion has brought these colossal masses of granite to the surface, and the present ranges have been formed by further elevation. These rocks are the source of many of the valuable metallic ores for which British Columbia is noted.

About the beginning of Tertiary times, about 60 million years ago, a second period of mountain formation

City of Vancouver, British Columbia, showing part of the downtown area, the harbor and docks, and, on the opposite shore, North Vancouver and the Coast Range Mountains.

affected the province. During this period of crustal unrest, which is called the Laramide Revolution, the eastern portion of the province seems to have been pushed bodily to the east, thus forming the Rocky Mountains. In places the older rocks are thrust over the younger rocks, as at Crowsnest Mountain in the far south. There was little igneous action connected with this mountain building; consequently, metallic ores are rare in these eastern mountains.

A third period of mountain formation occurred in late Tertiary or early Pleistocene time, when the Cascade Mountains of Washington State were formed. At this time British Columbia underwent a general uplift of the land, accompanied by outpourings of lava. Much of the province is at an elevation exceeding 3,000 ft., having been raised en masse to that elevation during this Cascadian Revolution. The interior of the province is best described as an elevated basin, rather than an interior plateau. It is a region of uplands, in which the modern rivers have cut deep canyons, which in the southern interior are many hundreds of feet below the general level.

The last phases of change are due to the great ice ages, of which there were probably four, as elsewhere in Canada. Enormous glaciers and ice fields probably covered all of the province. As the ice melted, many of the valleys became lakes, into which fine sands, silts, and clays were deposited.

These deposits now remain as terraces along many valley sides, and they are important for transport lines or for agriculture.

The geology of the province is complicated. Pre-Cambrian rock, such as is found in many of the eastern provinces, does not occur in large areas in British Columbia except in the Columbia Mountain system in the southeast, where they are known as the Beltian Rocks. Cambrian formations are found chiefly in the western Rockies. In the Peace River area rocks of Cretaceous age underlie the plain, but there are older rocks to the westward. Thick deposits of limestone, slate, greywacke, and volcanic rocks of Carboniferous to Jurassic age occur in the interior plateau. The chief Tertiary formations are lake deposits and widespread flows of basic lava in the interior basin.

Topography. British Columbia may be divided into eight topographic regions. The first of these regions comprises the northeast corner of the province and may be called the tramontane district, since it lies beyond the Rockies. It is a region through which the Alaska Highway runs and is quite distinct in structure, climate, and resources. Most of the region is below 3,000 ft., whereas west of the Rockies the province is above this elevation. The western portion of this tramontane region consists of outliers of the Rockies that are wide plateaus about 4,000 ft. above sea level. The Alaska Highway traverses sections at an elevation of 4,000 ft., both to the south and to the west of Fort Nelson. The northern portion of the plain is crossed by the Liard River, and there are hot springs where the highway crosses this river. The Rocky Mountains proper terminate at the basin of the Liard River.

The second topographic region consists of the long rugged ranges of the Rockies proper, which are, for the most part, strongly folded formations. The highest peak is Mt. Robson (12,972 ft.), close to the Yellowhead Pass (3,729 ft.). Among other lofty peaks on or near the Alberta-British Columbia boundary are Mt. Assiniboine (11,870 ft.), Mt. Sir Douglas (11,174 ft.), Mt. King George (11,226 ft.), Mt. Columbia (12,294 ft.), Mt. Lyell (11,495 ft.), and Mt. Joffre (11,316 ft.). From the highest and southernmost pass, South Kootenay or Boundary (7,100 ft.), the passes decrease progressively in elevation toward the north, down to Peace River Pass (2,000 ft.), the lowest of seven principal passes, among which are Athabaska (6,025 ft.), Pine River (2,850 ft.), and Kicking Horse (5,339 ft.). The Peace River rises west of the main range, which therefore does not form the continental divide in the north. The Finlay River, the northern branch of the Peace, rises near the headwaters of the Stikine River.

West of the main range is one of the most striking features of the continent—the Rocky Mountain Trench, extending about 1,000 mi. from Yukon to Montana and varying from a mile to ten miles in breadth. It was formed by crustal movements. Seven important rivers flow through the region, including the Finlay, Parsnip, Fraser, Columbia, and Kootenay, in an almost continous line from the northern British Columbia border to the United States. The union of the Finlay and the Parsnip, flowing southeast and northwest respectively, forms the eastern flowing Peace River, over 150 mi. of its course running through this province. The Kootenay River rises near Kicking Horse Pass, flows

south along the Trench, forms a vast loop through Montana and Idaho, and, re-entering the province, empties into Kootenay Lake. Westward of Nelson it joins the Columbia after a course of 400 mi. The Columbia rises within a mile of the Kootenay, flows northwestward along the Rocky Mountain Trench to a point about 80 mi. north of Golden, where it bends sharply to the south; it then broadens into Upper and Lower Arrow lakes and enters the United States south of Trail.

The third topographic region, in which there is practically no settlement, includes the western half of northern British Columbia. The whole area is mountainous, though none of the peaks reaches 10,000 ft. Four large rivers—the Taku, Stikine, Nass, and Skeena—drain the region to the west. The Stikine is used by small steamers to carry shipments to a drainage divide near the head of the Dease River. From there, cargoes may be conveyed down this river to the Liard and to the settlers near Watson Lake, Yukon. Both the Dease and the southern tributaries of the Liard rise in the Cassiar Range, a north-south inland range that is parallel to the Rockies and extends northward into Yukon. Another north-south mountain chain, the Babine Range, rises between the Coast Mountains and Babine Lake (elevation 2,330 ft.). The highest land east of this region contains the Omineca Range, formed of granite akin to that of the coastal ranges in which valuable minerals have been mined. Broad glaciated valleys covered with coniferous forest are general, but because of a lack of transportation there are only a few small settlements. The large Atlin and Teslin lakes are in the northwest corner of the region, Teslin extending partially into Yukon. The northern coast, most of which belongs to Alaska, is deeply indented and has been drowned to form long, deep fiords, such as Portland Canal which forms the boundary with Alaska; Observatory Inlet; Douglas Channel; and Gardner Canal. The natural outlet is by way of the Skeena Valley, and thereabouts the coastal ranges are lower than to the north or south. The northern transcontinental railway reached the Pacific at Prince Rupert in 1915, and this port serves the northwest region of the province. Across Hecate Strait, 40 mi. wide at its narrowest part, lie the Queen Charlotte Islands, stretching 150 mi. north and south, from just north of 54° N. lat. to slightly south of 52° N. lat. Their extreme breadth is 55 to 60 mi., in the north, and they are separated from the Alexander Archipelago of Alaska by Dixon Entrance. The principal islands of the Queen Charlottes are Graham and Moresby. They are low on the east and have low mountains on the west. Despite its excellent harbors, seams of bituminous coal, abundant timber, and rich fisheries, particularly halibut and herring, the group is sparsely settled. Its area is 3,780 sq. mi. Steamers ply between the mainland and island settlements on the east coast. The natives are Haida Indians.

The fourth topographic region, another almost unpopulated portion of the province, comprises the coastal region south of the Skeena River and north of Vancouver, excluding Vancouver Island. It also is mountainous throughout, though there are a number of broad intermontane valleys with a few Indian villages. The highest mountain entirely in the province, Mt. Waddington (13,260 ft.), is situated in this region in rather inaccessible country about 170 mi. northwest of Vancouver. It carries several long glaciers. The coast is similar to that farther north, deeply penetrated by fiordlike inlets, such as Fitzhugh Sound with its arms, Burke Channel and Dean Channel; and Seymour, Knight, Bute, Toba, and Jervis inlets. The coast is fringed or

B. C. GOV. TRAVEL BUREAU

MT. TRIDENT, KIMBASKET LAKE, BRITISH COLUMBIA

EMPEROR FALLS ON MT. ROBSON IN THE CANADIAN ROCKIES

The sixth topographic region comprises the area in the southeast of the province, known as the Columbia Mountain System. The Selkirks are bounded by the Columbia River and Kootenay Lake on the east, and by the Columbia and the two Arrow lakes on the west, with their southern extremity at the United States border. The Purcell Range is between the Selkirks and the Rockies, and the Monashee Range is west of the Selkirks. The Selkirks, being nearer the moist air of the Pacific, have more snow than do the somewhat higher Rockies. The Selkirks are older mountains and contain many valuable mines. Kimberley has a large lead-zinc mine and its ores are carried to Trail, near the American border, and there smelted with coal from Fernie. There are many deep north-south valleys in this region, and in most cases long narrow lakes such as Okanagan, Arrow, and Kootenay occupy a considerable portion of these depressions. Two very scenic railways cross the region, one through Revelstoke and Kamloops, and the other close to the American border through Nelson to Vancouver. The valleys and uplands are dry, especially in the west where they are utilized by ranchers. In the Okanagan Valley, where the proximity to the Pacific Ocean and the system of mountain ranges produces a climate ideal for fruit raising, are some of the finest apple, cherry, and peach orchards in Canada.

The seventh topographic region is a small area in the southwest corner of the province, comprising Vancouver and the valley and delta of the Lower Fraser River. Three quarters of the population of the province inhabits this area and the southern part of Vancouver Island, which are the sole areas in British Columbia that are warm, well-watered, and level and have good soils. The Greater Vancouver urban area, with more than half a million inhabitants, dominates the province. The Fraser River, which flows westward to Vancouver, has laid down ancient and modern deltas, triangular in shape and about 60 mi. on a side. This delta land, on which many small towns, such as New Westminster, Chilliwack, Mission City, and Ladner are situated, is the most densely settled rural area in the province. The Fraser, although a very rapid river, is navigable up to Yale, 100 mi. upstream from Vancouver. Ocean vessels, however, do not proceed east of New Westminster.

The last topographic region consists of Vancouver Island, the largest island on the west coast of North America, separated from the state of Washington by the Strait of Juan de Fuca, and from the mainland of British Columbia by the Strait of Georgia in the south and Queen Charlotte Strait to the north. It lies parallel to the coast between 48° 20′ and 51° N. lat. and 123° and 128° 30′ W. long., and is 285 mi. long, 40 to 80 mi. broad, and about 12,408 sq. mi. in area. The coast line is precipitous on the west and much indented. The principal inlets, north to south, are Quatsino and Kyuquot sounds, Esperanza Inlet, and Nootka, Clayoquot, and Barkley sounds. Most of the island is mountainous, except the area along the east coast, which has risen from the sea since glacial times. Accordingly, there is very little settlement outside of the southeast coast, except for lumbermen, fishermen, and a few miners. A partially submerged range, the Insular Range, parallels the British Columbia coast, a portion of it forming Vancouver Island and the Queen Charlotte Islands. In general, the mountains of Vancouver Island are between 2,000 and 3,000 ft. in elevation, but several exceed 5,000 ft., notably Mt. Albert Edward (6,968 ft.) and Victoria Peak (7,484 ft.). Nimpkish and Cowichan are among the largest lakes of Vancouver Island. Coal is mined near Nanaimo, and Cumberland on the east coast, and there are also iron and copper deposits on

screened by islands, some of substantial area, such as Princess Royal, King, Banks, Pitts, and Porcher islands. Along the coast are large paper mills, one of which is Ocean Falls, 100 mi. north of Vancouver Island.

The fifth topographic region lies in the central part of the province between the Coast Mountains and the Rocky Mountain Trench and Columbia Mountains. It is sometimes called the interior plateau, though interior uplands is also used. Most of this lies at an elevation of about 3,500 ft. The main river of the province, the Fraser, flows northwest down the Rocky Mountain Trench for 160 mi., rounds the northern end of the Cariboo Mountains, and cuts across the region from north to south. Along its southward course of 400 mi. the river has cut deep canyons, which are especially scenic south of Quesnel and again just north of Hope. The Fraser and its tributaries drain 90,000 sq. mi. Of this area, the basin of the Thompson accounts for 21,800 sq. mi. In the vicinity of Prince George the annual rainfall is about 20 in., but it decreases to the south. A few places near Ashcroft have a rainfall of only seven inches, and semiarid conditions prevail in much of this interior portion of the province. The Cariboo Mountains near Wells were the scene of prosperous gold mining after 1861, when the region was first prospected. The main tributary of the Fraser is the 300 mi.-long Thompson, which enters from the east at Lytton. Both these rivers are bordered by narrow benches, which in many places have produced good crops with the aid of irrigation. Other tributaries are the Stuart, Nechako, Quesnel, Chilcotin, and Lillooet, many of which drain lake areas used for salmon spawning.

The city of Victoria, British Columbia. Above the harbor is the Empress Hotel. At the right are the provincial government buildings.

the island. Dense forests and abundant fisheries are other natural resources. The west coast of the island receives over 200 in. of rain a year, the largest amount of any place on the North American continent. Victoria, the island's largest city with a population of over 50,000, is the capital of British Columbia.

River Basins. About half of the basin of the Liard (100,700 sq. mi.), a small part of that of the Hay (25,700 sq. mi.), and much of that of the Peace River (117,100 sq. mi.) are in northeastern British Columbia, which therefore belongs to the Arctic Basin, since these rivers are tributaries of the Mackenzie. The rest of the province is part of the Pacific Basin, which comprises 387,300 sq. mi. of Canada. To the province belong portions of the basins of the Yukon (35,100 sq. mi.), the Taku (7,600 sq. mi.), the Stikine (20,-300 sq. mi.; 335 mi. long); and the entire basins of the Nass (7,400 sq. mi.; 236 mi. long) and the Skeena (19,300 sq. mi.; 360 mi. long). The Columbia River, of which 460 mi. are in British Columbia, drains an area of 39,300 sq. mi. in the province. Of the drainage area, 15,500 sq. mi. are accounted for by the Kootenay, much of whose 400-mi. course is in the province. The largest and most important river basin of the province is that of the Fraser River (90,000 sq. mi.). Lacking any prominent rivers are the Queen Charlotte Islands, Vancouver Island, some small areas between the major river basins of the northwest coast, and an area (about 100 mi. in width) extending from opposite Pitt Island in the north to the city of Vancouver and constituting a sort of coastal basin.

Climate. Because of its diverse land forms, British Columbia has a great variety of climates. Four main regions may be distinguished: the wet south coast, including Vancouver Island and the southern portion of the Coastal Mountains; the rather arid interior uplands; the Selkirks and Rockies; and finally the tramontane region. The southwest region has the most equable climate in the Dominion and also the wettest in North America. Records of over 300 in. of rainfall a year are known at Henderson Lake, near the west coast of Vancouver Island. Most of the rain of the southwest region falls during the winter and averages more than 100 in. in exposed locations. Along the coast of the mainland the range of temperature between January and July is only 20° F., whereas at Kamloops it is 48° F. Hence, the equable marine condition does not penetrate far inland. During July and August, the warmest months of the year, the average temperature at Victoria is about 60° F., and the average rainfall is less than an inch a month. There, in the coldest months, January and February, the average monthly temperature is only 40° F. These conditions, which are somewhat like those of Mediterranean climates, do not exist, however, in the interior of the province.

In the interior uplands the climate is more continental. April is appreciably warmer than October, and the summers are much less cloudy than the winters. There is as much rainfall in the summer as in the winter. Total rainfall in the southern interior valleys is about 7 to 12 in. a year. Irrigation is required for agriculture.

In the mountain areas of the province the isotherms and rain lines conform to the complex shapes which characterize the contours. In general, the ridges are much colder and wetter than the valleys, and this is especially the case in the Columbia Mountain system of the southeast. Cranbrook, a typical settlement in the Rocky Mountain Trench, has an average temperature of 17° F. in January and 63° F. in July. The average rainfall is only 15 in., with a minimum in April and about one inch in each of the other months. However, at Fernie, higher up in the Rockies, the rainfall increases to 40 in., though it is farther from the Pacific. The average snowfall in this part of the Dominion is very high, amounting to 130 in. at Fernie. Glacier is about the highest station in the Selkirks, and here the average snowfall amounts to 390 in. a year, with over 80 in. falling in December and January.

For the north central part of British Columbia, conditions at Prince George are fairly typical. Here the average temperature is 13° F. in January and 60° F. in July, the range being 47° F., much like that in the southern part of the interior. The average annual precipitation is 20 in., with a minimum in April but evenly distributed during the other months. Of this amount, a good deal falls as snow, there being about 16 in. of snow in each of the two coldest months. At Barkerville, a mining town in the Cariboo Mountains, the average snowfall is 183 in. a year, due to the town's high elevation. Anyox, located on the northwest coast of the province, has a temperature range of only 32°, a condition that results from the proximity of the Pacific. Here, the snowfall is 200 in. a year, although the average monthly temperature falls below 32° F. in only three months of the year.

The climate of the Peace River district in the tramontane region is typified by the conditions near Fort St. John. The temperature in January is 3° F. and in July, 61° F., making a yearly range of 58°. The rainfall is 16 in., with more than 4 in. falling in June and July, the wettest months. The snowfall in the Peace River area is somewhat over 50 in. a year. Since only three months in the year have an average temperature above 56° F., the summer growing season is marginal. This type of climate extends far up the Peace-Liard-Mackenzie downfold, but there is no doubt that with suitable types of grain, and adequate transportation, agriculture could be expanded far north of St. John.

In the Peace River area the climate is moderate for 56° N. lat., with clear, crisp winters and dry, balmy summers. "Chinook" winds descend from the mountains and help to remove the snow in the winter; spring comes early and quickly. Seeding is usually under way in late April, but ice does not break on the river until late April or early May. October brings heavy frosts, but the average frost-free season is about 100 days. Fairly mild weather until Christmas is not uncommon.

Flora. Although the forests of the province constitute the most conspicuous and valuable part of the vegetative cover, British Columbia has grasslands in the valleys of the Peace River region and a parkland coverage in the south-central intermontane area, in which the grasses predominate over the trees. The intermontane grasses are an extension of grasses from more southern climates. Short-grass species predominate in the intermontane region, while both short and prairie grasses are found in the Peace River Valley. The plant life of the province also includes a vast variety of other forms, from the trailing kelps of the fiords, through the ferns, fungi, and mosses of the forest regions and the wild flowers of the open grasslands, to the lichens of the alpine regions.

British Columbia is endowed with the most interesting and extensive forests in the Dominion. There are five main classes of forests: the Boreal Forest, in the northeast or tramontane section of the province; the Sub-alpine Forest, along the Rockies and in all higher elevations of the mountains; the Columbia Forest, in the Columbia Valley; the Coast Forest, in the west; and the Montane Forest, in the semi-arid interior uplands. Since these divisions are closely related to topography and climate, they occur as a series of forest zones more or less parallel to the coast.

In the tramontane region some of the country to the east of the main ridges of the Rockies is at a high level, practically above the tree line. Here, open plateaus with a dwarf or shrubbery vegetation, somewhat akin to the tundra of the north, are characteristic. Below 4,000 ft. is the Boreal Forest, consisting largely of lodgepole pine and black spruce. In the vicinity of the farmlands of the Peace River, the forest is very mixed, consisting essentially of aspen and other poplars, spruce, birch, and balsam fir. Jack pine is common where there is sandy soil.

In the higher levels of most mountains is the Sub-alpine Forest, consisting essentially of Engelmann spruce which reaches up to the tree line. There are many areas of lodgepole pine, especially where fires have been prevalent. Near the treeline, alpine fir is found. Aspens are abundant at the lower edge, and in the south there are small specimens of Douglas fir. This cool-climate forest descends in elevation in higher latitudes and is dominant in the uplands to the north of Prince George, and in the valleys as far north as the Stikine River. In the Nass and Skeena basins, Engelmann spruce mingles with western hemlock, and intrusions of boreal trees, such as black and white spruce, are abundant.

The Columbia Forest has many species characteristic of the Coast Forest, but it is located inland and thus called by a different name. Western red cedar and western hemlock are characteristic trees, but specimens of both grow much smaller than in the wetter coastlands. This forest grows in the valleys south of the Cariboo Mountains and is widest along the southern provincial border. At the lowest levels black cottonwood is common.

The Montane Forest covers most of the Interior Uplands from the Skeena in the northwest as far south as the Okanagan valley. It is widest in the latitude of Prince George, where it extends along the Fraser and Nechako valleys almost from the Rockies to the Pacific. In the south the summer is dry, and the lower levels contain large areas of grasslands with scattered yellow pine. At higher levels, Douglas fir is dominant, with some aspens and lodgepole pine. North of Ashcroft the yellow pine dies out, and a small variety of Douglas fir mixed with aspen is common. Still farther north, near Prince George, aspen is the chief tree, but remnants of the other genera are present also.

The Coast Forest contains the finest stands of large trees left in the entire Dominion. Around the Strait of Georgia, the madrona and the Garry oak are outliers of the forests to the south of the border. The forest extends up to about 4,500 ft. in the mountains, and two genera, the red cedar and the hemlock, are dominant. There are, however, extensive stands of the most valuable of trees, the huge Douglas fir of the coast. Cottonwood, alder, and maple are found in the wet lowlands, and alpine pine and hemlock occur high up near the tree line. In the central coast area the climate is not quite so favorable as in the south, and the trees are correspondingly smaller. Red cedar and hemlock are again dominant. Sitka spruce is found more abundantly than to the south, and Douglas fir and maple occur in the sheltered valleys.

In the vicinity of Prince Rupert, and also in the Queen Charlotte Islands far to the west, Sitka spruce is the dominant tree, with, however, abundant examples of hemlock and red cedar. There are large areas of muskeg in the northeastern part of the Queen Charlotte Islands.

Fauna. The distribution of wild life in British Columbia has been conditioned not only by suitability of locale but also by the barriers to migration set up by the natural features of the province, notably the Rocky Mountains, the Coast Range, and the sea. For many species these barriers have been relative rather than absolute, with the result that many of the faunal differences are merely varietal rather than specific. Several of the mammals found on the mainland are, however, absent from the islands. These include the mountain sheep or big-horn (*Ovis canadensis*), Rocky Mountain

coast. The ducks include the mallard, pintail, wood, canvasback, greater and lesser scaup, eider, goldeneye, greenwinged and cinnamon teal, and the ruddy. The geese include the Canada, lesser snow, cackling, common Brant, and western Canada. Other game birds are the blue grouse, sharp-tailed grouse, and the rock and white-tailed ptarmigan. Other large birds are the horned grebe, the yellow-billed loon, the great blue heron and the snowy owl. Many of the species of smaller birds have varietal differences from similar species farther east.

The northern sea lion and the Alaska fur seal both frequent parts of the coast; the valuable sea otter, practically extinct, may still survive. In the lakes and rivers are various game fish, among which are the Kamloops (rainbow) trout, lake trout, whitefish, pike, inconnu, and grayling. Small fur-bearing animals include the marten, mink, weasel, beaver, red fox, and muskrat.

National and Provincial Parks. Mt. Robson Provincial Park, Yoho (507 sq. mi.), and Kootenay (543 sq. mi.) National Parks, and Mt. Assiniboine Provincial Park extend north and south along the British Columbia side of the divide in the Canadian Rockies. Glacier (521 sq. mi.) and Mt. Revelstoke (100 sq. mi.) National Parks, and Kokanee Glacier Provincial Park are in the Selkirk Mountains. Wells Gray Provincial Park is southwest of Mount Robson

Logs are cut to manageable lengths with a giant saw before passing through a rubber, steel-enforced curtain to the barker at a dissolving pulp plant in Prince Rupert, British Columbia.

goat (*Oreamnos americanus*), moose (*Alces americana*), grizzly bear (*Ursus horribilis*), mountain caribou (*Rangifer montanus*), mule deer (*Odocoileus hemionus*), and coyote (*Canis latrans*). Found on both the islands and the mainland are the black bear (*Euarctos americanus*), wolf (*Canis occidentalis*), lynx (*Lynx canadensis*), elk (*Cervus canadensis*), and coast deer (*Odocoileus columbianus*). The range of the Queen Charlotte black bear (*Euarctos americanus carlottae*) is limited to the islands for which it was named.

There are about 340 known species of birds in the province. Migratory waterfowl are found in great numbers and variety. These follow the rivers and lakes as well as the

and southeast of Quesnel Lake, in the Cariboo Mountains. Manning Provincial Park is situated on the border of the State of Washington, southeast of Hope. Garibaldi Provincial Park (973 sq. mi.) is about 25 mi. north of Vancouver. Strathcona Provincial Park is in central Vancouver Island and includes within its area the highest mountains on the island—Golden Hinde (7,219 ft.) and Mt. Elkhorn (7,200 ft.). Northernmost and largest of the parks is Tweedsmuir Provincial Park (5,400 sq. mi.) east of the Coast Mountains, in the headwaters of the Nechako River. The river is dammed and the scenic lakes of the Park are a reservoir of water-power which is dropped

SMELTERS AT TRAIL, BRITISH COLUMBIA

through the Coast Mountains by tunnel to Kemano. British Columbia contains 1,671 sq. mi. of national parks; its 14,071 sq. mi. of provincial parks constitute more than half the total area of Canadian provincial parks.

ECONOMIC RESOURCES AND ACTIVITIES

Lumbering. British Columbia ranks first among the provinces of Canada in the production of sawmill products, producing about 50 per cent of the value of Canadian lumber. Douglas fir is the chief lumber tree, but western cedar and hemlock (for pulp) are cut on the coast, whereas spruce, larch, and pine are cut in the interior. The Coast Forest, particularly Vancouver Island, supplies about two thirds of the lumber of the province, but increasing amounts are being cut in the interior, especially in the Prince George region. The forest industry, which employs about 20,000 men in the woods, is the primary industry of British Columbia in employment and value. In addition, it supplies the chief raw material for the manufacturing industry. The production of pulp and paper is increasing, partially as a result of integration of the forest industry to make better use of scrap, waste lumber, and broken trees. All of the pulp mills are located on the coast, because of a lack of developed power in the central interior. Most of the lumber and paper is for export. The coast mills ship to the United States and United Kingdom, whereas the interior mills chiefly supply Western Canada.

Fur Trade. Although the province ranges over a widely forested area, its fur trade is relatively minor; in fact, it is less important than in any other Canadian province. Trapping is carried on by Indians in the north, but more than half the value of furs comes from fur-farm production, lo-

cated chiefly in the southwestern corner of the province. Most of the fur-bearing animals of Canada are found in British Columbia, since the habitat of beaver, muskrat, fisher, ermine, marten, and mink extends across Canada in the same latitudes.

Fisheries. The province has the most valuable fisheries in Canada, although the Atlantic provinces have a greater total catch. Salmon accounts for about 70 per cent of the value of fisheries, followed by halibut and herring.

The Pacific salmon belongs to the genus *Oncorhynchus,* and differs somewhat from the true salmon of Europe. There are five species of Pacific salmon, which ascend the rivers of the west in great numbers during the summer and early fall. None of the mature fish returns to the ocean, and the young migrate to the sea when they are over a year old.

Since the Fraser River has the largest drainage basin and most of the interior spawning lakes, it is the chief salmon river. Numerous canneries are located near its mouth. Other smaller canneries are located along the coast, with another concentration near Prince Rupert. The chief center for halibut is at Prince Rupert; these fish are taken on lines instead of nets, since they feed on rough bottom. Herring are very abundant off Vancouver Island and the Queen Charlotte Islands. The inland fishing, except for salmon, is negligible from a commercial standpoint.

Agriculture. The mountainous terrain of British Columbia limits its agricultural industry and provides a good example of the importance of topography as an influence upon industry. This huge province is nearly 200 times the size of Prince Edward Island, but the total amount of cropland is hardly one quarter more. There is an average of one cultivated acre per person in British Columbia, which is not sufficient to feed the province. Only about two per cent of the province's total area is owned as farmland, and only one quarter of that is actually cultivated. Chief crops are hay, oats, wheat, barley, and potatoes. The main value of agriculture comes from the sale of livestock, milk, grain, orchard products, small fruits, and vegetables. The largest areas of cultivation are in the Peace River area in the northeastern part of the province, followed by the Lower Fraser Valley region of the southwest, and then the valleys of the south-central interior.

There are seven agricultural districts, each separated from the others by high mountain ranges. In the far northeast is the Peace River district, in which wheat, feed grains, legume seed, and hogs are produced. All along the northern Canadian National Railway, from McBride through Prince George to Hazelton, are scattered pioneer settlements, where oats, pasture, and legume seed crops are grown. In the center of the rather arid uplands, south and west of the Cariboo Mountains, and in the Chilcotin Plateau, west of the central Fraser River, sheep and cattle are grazed on ranches—sheep in the east and cattle in the west and south. In the extreme southeast of the province in the Kootenay district, the climate is rather arid in the lower valleys, which provide grazing land for cattle. Fruit is grown in this region under irrigation.

The great fruit district is in the southern part of the province in the elongated lake and river valleys, such as Okanagan, Kettle, Arrow, and Kootenay. Extensive irrigation is made possible by damming streams in the upland and diverting water in flumes down to the numerous benches of the main valleys. Penticton, Kelowna, and Vernon are the main fruit-packing centers. British Columbia leads Canada as a fruit-growing province, producing about half of the value of Canadian fruit. Along the shores of Okanagan Lake the chief crops are apples, but apricots, peaches, plums, pears, and cherries are also grown.

The farms are numerous in the Fraser Valley—from Chilliwack to Vancouver—where dairy products, small fruits, vegetables, and poultry are produced. Most of these products are sold in the large city of Vancouver. There is a good deal of farming on the southeast shore of Vancouver Island, where about 50,000 acres are under cultivation. Hay, clover, and oats are the chief field crops. Strawberries are also grown, and there are creameries near Courtenay and Nanaimo. Other farming areas in the province are quite small and are meant only to serve the few small local towns.

Mining. The minerals of British Columbia are associated mainly with deep-seated rocks which were uplifted during several periods of mountain formation. They have a different origin from those which are found in the ancient but very stable rocks of the Canadian Shield. It is not surprising, therefore, that the two provinces with large areas of Shield, i.e., Ontario and Quebec, rank ahead of British Columbia, which produces from 10 to 15 per cent of Canada's mineral wealth. The chief minerals by value are lead and zinc, and of less importance are copper, gold, coal, silver, iron, and tungsten.

The metallic ores are associated chiefly with the enormous batholiths of granite in the Coast, Columbia, and Omineca ranges. Since there was very little igneous activity in the formation of the Rockies, mineral deposits are relatively poor. However, there are large areas of Cretaceous rocks in the Rockies containing valuable coal.

The largest proportion of the lead-zinc production in the Dominion comes from one mine—the famous Kimberley mine in the southeast corner of the province, situated on the eastern slopes of the Purcell Range, about 50 mi. north of the United States border. It is linked by a special branch railway to the Canadian Pacific Railway at Cranbrook, and most of the ore is smelted at Trail about 100 mi. southwest of the mine. This ore deposit was discovered in 1892, but great difficulty was at first experienced in separating the lead and zinc sulphides. This problem was overcome by the flotation process, and after 1910 it became one of the biggest mines in the Dominion. The ore lies under the eastern slopes of Sullivan Mountain, like a vast slab of sulphide, 200 ft. thick in some places, with outcroppings near the upper part of the mountain. Mills and concentrating plants are scattered in the valleys to the east of the mine, and several small communities near the town of Kimberley have been settled as a result of the mining operations. The ore usually contains about 10 per cent of lead and the same amount of zinc, as well as some iron. Silver is also recovered from the ore as are two rare metals—cadmium and bismuth.

Alluvial gold is recovered from the gravels in the rivers of the Atlin region in the far northwest and in the Cariboo district near Quesnel. There is also a good deal of lode gold recovered in many mines, especially around the edges of the interior plateau at Bralorne, Hedley, and Wells. Other gold mines have been operated in other parts of the province, notably in the southeast. During World War II the only mercury mine in Canada operated at Pinchi Lake, northwest of Prince George.

There are many coal fields scattered through the province, two of them being of considerable extent. Near Crowsnest Pass in the southeast corner are several coal-mining towns, of which Fernie is the largest. Near Elk River there are seams as thick as 30 ft. The second field is on Vancouver Island, where somewhat newer Cretaceous coal has been mined for about a century. Many of these mines, near Nanaimo and Courtenay, have been worked out and production is declining. In the interior small coal mines operate near Princeton and at Telkwa, in the Bulkley Valley.

The smelter, refinery, and fertilizer plants at Trail, which are among the largest in the world, smelt other ores beside the lead-zinc from Kimberley. Their power is in part derived from several dams on the Kootenay River just before it joins the Columbia.

Water Power. British Columbia has the second greatest potential water power of all the provinces and ranks third in developed power. The rivers of the coast have the advantages of heavy rainfall and a good drop; however, they are too short, and the rainfall is not sufficient in summer. The Fraser and Skeena rivers are long and have great volume, but they have no natural falls where they cut through the Coast Mountains. Their power may be harnessed by dams. The Columbia river has a great deal of power, much of which is already developed. The northern rivers have potential power, but there is no local demand for its development.

Manufactures. The province ranks third behind Ontario and Quebec in the value of its manufactures. Lumber and other wood and paper products constitute almost 50 per cent of the value of all manufactures. This forest processing industry is concentrated near the forests in the towns and cities of the southwest corner of the province, where sea transport is available. The manufacture of food products is led by fish canneries, which are scattered all along the west coast, but are more numerous in the south. Vegetable canneries are located in the Greater Vancouver area, and fruit packing and processing plants are established in the Okanagan Valley cities. A very large aluminum smelter operates at Kitimat, south of Prince Rupert. The bauxite ore is imported from the Caribbean region, and the great amount of power required is obtained by dropping the backed-up headwaters of the Nechako River through a tunnel in the Coast Mountains.

Finance and Banking. There are almost 300 branches of Canadian chartered banks operating in the province, including the Bank of Montreal, the Bank of Nova Scotia, the Bank of Toronto, the Canadian Bank of Commerce, the Royal Bank of Canada, the Imperial Bank, the Dominion

through routes across the province. The Trans-Canada Highway follows the Fraser and South Thompson route to Banff in Alberta.

Air routes operated by Trans-Canada Airlines run from Calgary and Edmonton to Vancouver and Victoria. Canadian Pacific Airlines run north-south routes from Vancouver to Prince George and the Peace River, as well as trans-Pacific flights to East Asia. Other airlines operate along the coast and run short feeder lines into the interior. American and British airlines stop at Vancouver.

BRITISH COLUMBIA GOVERNMENT TRAVEL BUREAU

PARLIAMENT BUILDINGS, VICTORIA, BRITISH COLUMBIA

Bank, Barclay's Bank (Canada), and the Mercantile Bank of Holland.

Communications. The main line of the Canadian Pacific crosses the Rockies via Kicking Horse Pass (5,339 ft.), cuts through the northern part of the Selkirks, and follows the South Thompson and Fraser Valleys to Vancouver. Its southern line comes through Crowsnest Pass and winds back and forth across southern British Columbia by several interconnecting valleys. Known as the Kettle Valley route, the line continues to the lower Fraser Valley at Hope. In addition, the Canadian Pacific operates ocean vessels and coastal steamers from Vancouver.

The Canadian National main line crosses through the Rockies near Jasper and Yellowhead Pass (3,729 ft.) and then splits. The main line follows the North Thompson and Fraser rivers to Vancouver, whereas the northern line follows the Upper Fraser River to Prince George and thence westward to the port of Prince Rupert. The Canadian National also operates large coastal steamers.

The Pacific Great Eastern, owned by the province, cuts through the Coast Mountains north of Vancouver via Howe Sound, and extends northward on the east side of the Fraser River to Prince George.

Because of the mountainous topography, road construction costs are very high, and the main highway network is still being built. In general, the highways are located in the same valleys as the railways, since these were the best

POPULATION

The population of British Columbia reached 1,398,464 in 1956. At the decennial census of 1951 the population was 1,165,210, an increase of 42.5 per cent since 1941. The rate of growth during the decade 1941-1951 was more than twice that of any other province. In 1951 population density was 3.2 per sq. mi., compared with the Canadian average of 3.6. Half of the population of the province lives in Greater Vancouver, and three quarters of the population is clustered into the southwestern corner of the province, including southern Vancouver Island. The principal cities are Greater Vancouver (530,728 in 1951) and Greater Victoria (104,303). Other urban centers are New Westminster, North Vancouver, Prince Rupert, Trail, Penticton, Kamloops, Kelowna, Nanaimo, and Nelson.

Of the four western provinces, British Columbia has the largest proportion of persons (about 66 per cent) who trace their origin to the British Isles. In 1951 Germans constituted about 10 per cent of the provincial population, followed by Ukrainians, Scandinavians, and French. There were about 30,000 native Indians and about 40,000 Asiatics, chiefly Chinese. Japanese were also numerous in the coast area prior to World War II.

EDUCATION AND CULTURAL FACILITIES

Education. Public school education is free and compulsory from the ages of seven to fifteen. The school system is administered by the Department of Education under the Minister of Education, who is a member of the Executive Council. The Deputy Minister of Education, a member of the Civil Service, is a permanent official. In addition to elementary, junior high, and high schools, there are a number of technical schools where vocational training is given. Correspondence courses in high-school subjects are provided students who cannot attend school regularly. Legislation was passed in 1946 to consolidate the school districts into 74 large administrative areas.

The provincial government supports the University of British Columbia, which has faculties of arts, applied science, agriculture, law, forestry, pharmacy, medicine, and graduate studies. One of the youngest universities in Canada (the first session was opened in 1915), the University enrollment was over 6,000 in 1955. The university has one of the most beautiful campuses in Canada, with a location overlooking the sea at Point Grey, west of Vancouver.

Cultural Facilities. Library facilities include the University Library, the largest in western Canada; the Provincial Library and Archives at Victoria, with over 200,000 volumes; and three Union Libraries, which are supervised by the Public Library Commission and receive aid from the Carnegie Corporation. These Union Libraries are established in the Fraser Valley, Okanagan Valley, and on Vancouver Island. Vancouver has both an art gallery and a symphony society. There are five museums in the province. Nanaimo, Nelson, New Westminster, Prince Rupert, and Trail each have one daily newspaper, Victoria has two, and Vancouver has three. British Columbia publishes more than 50 English-language weeklies.

GOVERNMENT

Government and Politics. British Columbia was named by Queen Victoria in 1858, when a second British crown colony was established on the Pacific northwest coast. The name of British Columbia was retained when the mainland colony was united with the older colony of Vancouver Island in 1866. The area became a province of the Dominion of Canada in 1871.

The titular head of the government is the Lieutenant-Governor, who represents the Crown and is appointed by the Governor-General-in-Council. The premier, who is the leader of the political party with the greatest number of elected legislative members, chooses the members of the Executive Council, who make up the Ministry. The Legislative Assembly is elected for a term not longer than five years. There is no upper house. The province has six representatives in the Canadian Senate and 16 in the Canadian House of Commons.

Political groups in the province did not take labels until 1903. Until recently, the strongest groups have been the old-line parties—Liberals and Conservatives—which appear in federal politics. In the 1930's the Co-operative Commonwealth Federation (C.C.F.) gained considerable strength. In 1952, a fourth party, the Social Credit, which had formed a government for several years in Alberta, took over control of the province's Legislative Assembly and retained control in the 1956 elections.

Outstanding Legislation. In the 1930's the provincial government encouraged the co-operative movement among farmers by passing the Natural Products Marketing Act. The Act permitted the creation of marketing boards to handle the sale and regulate the prices of such natural products as milk, potatoes, and tree fruits. Economic development was also aided by measures for the conservation of the forests, by co-operation with the International Fisheries Com-

mission to regulate methods of fishing, and later by permitting the provincially owned British Columbia Power Commission to enter the public utility field and develop hydroelectric power.

Labor legislation passed in 1946 established 44 hours as the maximum work week. Minimum wage standards are also fixed by law. The Workmen's Compensation Board compensates workmen for injuries received during working hours. In 1947 the Industrial and Conciliation Act made collective bargaining compulsory and prohibited strikes and lockouts occurring before any formal attempt at conciliation.

A Health Insurance Act had been on the statute books since 1936, but was not implemented until about 1950. However, British Columbia has excellent public health and social welfare services available to 90 per cent of the population.

HISTORY

British Columbia was discovered by the Spanish explorer Juan Perez in 1774. His voyage and that of Heceta and Quadra in 1775 bolstered Spain's claim to the Pacific northwest coast. In March 1778, Captain James Cook landed on Vancouver Island at Nootka Sound. His reports of the wealth of furs and of the prospects of a remunerative trade with China induced British traders to come to western shores. In 1788 John Meares, in charge of an expedition under the protection of the East India Company, obtained a grant of land from an Indian chief at Nootka Sound. Spain tried to enforce its rights to the region in 1789 and took steps to plant a colony, but by the Nootka Sound Convention of 1790, Britain obtained trading rights in places unoccupied by Spain. It was not until 1795 that Spain abandoned the coast, although in the meantime Captain George Vancouver had circumnavigated Vancouver Island in 1792 and carried out a survey of the coast in 1793 and 1794.

Exploration was also carried out by overland fur-traders who were partners in the North West Company. In 1793 Alexander Mackenzie crossed the continent by land and reached the Pacific Ocean at Dean Channel, missing Captain Vancouver by a few weeks. Simon Fraser descended the Fraser River in 1808, and David Thompson explored the Columbia River throughout its length between 1807 and 1811.

When the North West Company was joined with the Hudson's Bay Company in 1821, the reorganized company was given the exclusive right of trade west of the Rocky Mountains. The Hudson's Bay Company established a number of trading posts in an attempt to develop the maritime fur trade and to exploit the fur resources of the interior. Fort Vancouver, built on the Columbia River in 1825, was the center of administration of the Columbia District until the Hudson's Bay Company withdrew from Oregon following the settlement of the Oregon question.

In 1849 Britain established a colony on Vancouver Island, to be under the auspices of the Hudson's Bay Company. Victoria, a fur-trading post built in 1843, now became the center of the administration. James Douglas, chief factor of the company, became governor of the colony in 1851, and although an assembly representing the few settlers was set up in 1856, the influence of the company in the government continued.

When gold was discovered on the bars of the Fraser River in 1858 and a gold rush of some 30,000 Americans took place, the British government created a second colony on the mainland. In addition to holding his other office, Douglas was appointed governor of British Columbia. He was forced to sever his connection with the company, however, and the

COURTESY OF BRITISH INFORMATION SERVICES

NILE GORGE, BELOW RIPON FALLS, UGANDA

company's right of exclusive trade was revoked. In 1859, a detachment of royal engineers arrived to build roads and lay out townsites in the mainland colony. In spite of population increase resulting from the Cariboo gold rush in 1862, the colony of British Columbia had no legislative council until 1864. Douglas retired in that year, and the colonies had separate governors until 1866 when they were united under the name of British Columbia.

During the period from 1866 to 1871, the question of entrance into the Canadian confederation was agitated. Finally, on obtaining favorable conditions, including the promise that a railway would be built from the east within ten years, British Columbia became a Canadian province on July 20, 1871.

There followed a period during which British Columbia was discontented with the slow implementation of the terms of union. Secession was threatened on several occasions before relations with the federal government improved with the completion of the Canadian Pacific Railway in 1885. Vancouver was established as the railway terminal and began to grow as a port. Within 20 years it became Canada's fourth city, with 100,000 people in 1911. Settlers arrived in the southeastern section of the province around the turn of the century, primarily as a result of several mining booms and consequent railroad construction. Although irrigation was attempted in south central British Columbia prior to World War I, it was not successful until after 1920, when municipalities generally took over the irrigation works. The north central region was settled after a railroad was built to Prince Rupert in 1915. Settlement in the British Columbia section of the Peace River area remained sparse until rail transportation was extended to Dawson Creek in 1931. With constant improvement of transportation in the interior plateau, the varied resources of the province are being developed and the population is spreading away from its concentration in the southwest.   W. M. W. and J. L. R.

BRITISH COLUMBIA, UNIVERSITY OF, located at Vancouver in the province of British Columbia, Canada. The university was established by the Provincial legislature in 1890, but the university session began in 1915. Temporary buildings existed until 1925, when new buildings were constructed on the 548-acre campus. The library has more than 200,000 volumes. There are faculties of arts and sciences, applied science, education, physical education, commerce, agriculture, and forestry. In addition, the University also includes schools of law, medicine, pharmacy, social work, and architecture. The faculty members number about 350, and, in 1955, the student enrollment amounted to approximately 6,000.

BRITISH EAST AFRICA, a name that prior to 1920 was applied to the region which subsequently became the colony of Kenya. It later came to mean the entire chain of British dependencies along the east side of Africa from the borders of Egypt to those of South Africa, including the inland territories of Uganda, Nyasaland, and the Rhodesias, as well as those along the coast and the island protectorate of Zanzibar. The term is still used in this broad way, but it is increasingly coming to be restricted to three dependencies, the protectorate of Uganda, the colony and protectorate of Kenya, and the trust territory of Tanganyika, because these three, out of a desire for closer economic co-operation, have formed among themselves a constitutional connection that sets them off from Nyasaland and the Rhodesias, which have formed a similar group known as British Central Africa.

As early as 1917 the customs departments of Uganda and Kenya were united under Kenyan administrative responsibility. Currency had already been unified for these two dependencies in 1905. In 1920 an East African Currency Board was established, and Tanganyika and Zanzibar entered the system. In 1926 the Kenya and Uganda railways and inland waterways systems were amalgamated, and the first East African Governors' Conference was held. Meetings of the heads of the three territories became more important with the outbreak of World War II, and after the war further discussions led to the formation of a new interterritorial structure on Jan. 1, 1948.

East African High Commission. The new organization consists of an East African High Commission comprising the administrators of the three territories, an East African Central Assembly, and an executive organization to be supported by certain advisory and consultative bodies. The governor of Kenya is chairman of the High Commission. The assembly consists of twenty-three members, seven of whom were officials appointed by the High Commission, one an Arab similarly appointed, and five chosen from each of the three territories. From Tanganyika and Uganda, one was elected by the unofficial members of the local legislative council, one is a territorial official appointed by the governor, and the governor also appointed three unofficial members to represent European, Indian, and African elements in the population. In Kenya the European and Indian representatives were elected by their respective members in the local council. The administrator to the High Commission, along with other heads of departments, is responsible to the High Commission for the administration of the interterritorial government.

With the inauguration of this central system, postal services, telegraph, and telephone became unified. The government of Tanganyika has already coordinated its customs duties with those of Kenya and Uganda, and during 1948 the customs establishment of Tanganyika was incorporated into that of the other two. On May 1, 1948, the railway system, together with the inland waterway and harbor system of Tanganyika, was similarly amalgamated with the Kenya and Uganda Railways and Harbours Administration. The High Commission is also the East African Air Transport Authority, and as such supervises the operations of the East African Airways whose headquarters are at Nairobi, capital of Kenya. Research and statistical services are also within the competence of the interterritorial organization. In 1955 the International Bank for Reconstruction and Development made a $24 million, 20-year loan to help the East African Railways and Harbour Administration carry out a four-year $100 million development program. From 1945 to 1955 rail traffic in the territories had doubled.

Although the High Commission system was sometimes regarded as a forerunner to closer political union of the three Territories, there were a number of important obstacles to such ties. Tanganyika's status as a United Nations trust territory limited Britain's freedom of action in forming a political link. The outbreak of Mau Mau disorders in Kenya in 1952 was another hurdle for amalgamation. Nevertheless, Britain in 1953 established a royal commission to inquire into economic, social, and racial problems in East Africa as a whole. Reporting on June 9, 1955, the commission recommended the removal of tribal and racial barriers to bring European, Asian, and African into a modern economy working for higher living standards for all.

W. M. W. and W. W. W.

BRITISH EMPIRE, a term used broadly to designate collectively four different political associations: the United Kingdom of Great Britain and Northern Ireland, the Indian Empire, the colonial or dependent empire, and the self-governing Dominions. After 1931 with the enactment of the Statute of Westminster, which gave complete autonomy in both internal and external affairs to the Dominions, the term "Commonwealth" came to be applied to the United Kingdom and the Dominions. With the division of the Indian Empire in 1947 into the two Dominions of India and Pakistan the term "British Empire" came to be restricted to those areas overseas in which the British government continued to exercise any supervisory control. To avoid confusion the term "British Colonial Empire" was substituted to designate these overseas dependencies taken collectively. The trust territories which the British government held for the United Nations were not considered as part of the colonial empire, although usually administered by the British Colonial Office. *See also* BRITISH COLONIAL EMPIRE; COMMONWEALTH OF NATIONS.

W. M. W.

BRITISH GUIANA. *See* GUIANAS, THE.
BRITISH HONDURAS. *See* HONDURAS, BRITISH.

BRITISH ISLES, an island group of Western Europe, consisting of the two main islands of Great Britain and Ireland and about five thousand smaller islands, most of the latter lying to the north and west of Scotland and to the west of Ireland. The British Isles are separated from continental Europe by the English Channel, the Straits of Dover, and the North Sea, and from North America by the Atlantic Ocean. North Channel, the Irish Sea, and St. George's Channel lie between Great Britain and Ireland. At their nearest points the British Isles are 20 mi. from France, about 140 from Norway, 500 from Iceland, and 1,600 from Newfoundland. Politically, they are divided into two sovereign states: (1) the United Kingdom of Great Britain and Northern Ireland, comprising England, Scotland, Wales, the Isle of Man, other adjacent islands, and the six northeasternmost counties of Ireland; and (2) the Re-

public of Ireland, comprising the remainder of Ireland and its adjacent islands. England, Wales, and Scotland each has distinct as well as common political rights, though they and the counties of Northern Ireland all send representatives to the British Parliament. The Isle of Man, off the northwest coast of England, has its own ancient parliament. Manxmen owe allegiance to the British Crown, however, and retain relations with the British Government through the Secretary of State for Home Affairs. The Channel Islands, off the coast of Normandy, are not regarded as part of the British Isles, although their constitutional relation to the British Crown is similar to that of the Isle of Man.

The total area of the British Isles is 120,805 sq. mi., or about that of New Mexico. Inclusive of adjacent islands, the area of England is 50,874 sq. mi., or about that of Alabama; of Wales, 7,466 sq. mi., or about that of Massachusetts; of the Isle of Man, 221 sq. mi.; of Scotland, 30,405 sq. mi., or about that of South Carolina; of Northern Ireland, 5,237 sq. mi., or about that of Delaware; and of the Republic of Ireland, 27,137 sq. mi., or somewhat larger than that of West Virginia. In 1952 the population of England and Wales was 43,940,000 and that of Scotland was 5,114,178. Northern Ireland's population was 1,384,100 in 1953, and the Republic of Ireland had a 1951 population of 2,960,593. *See also* ENGLAND AND WALES; GREAT BRITAIN AND NORTHERN IRELAND; IRELAND; IRELAND, NORTHERN; IRELAND, REPUBLIC OF; SCOTLAND; and WALES. W. M. W.

BRITISH MUSEUM. A national depository in the Bloomsbury district of London, England, housing a collection of exhibits related to art, literature, and science. The Cottonian Library collections of state papers and Biblical and other historical manuscripts of Sir Robert Bruce Cotton (1570-1631), donated to the country in 1702, form the basis of the museum library. The Sir Hans Sloane and Harleian collections were added in 1753, obliging the government in 1759 to house the increasing number of exhibits in Montagu House. In 1772 Parliament was able to obtain title to Sir William Hamilton's collection. It took thirty-two years, from 1823-1855, before work was completed on the central portion of the present structure of Montagu House, the original part of which was built in the form of a hollowed-out square. A façade facing south on Great Russell Street is fronted by an Ionic colonnade of forty-four columns. A circular reading room, established in 1854-1857, was built inside the square of the original structure. A wing, the White Building, was added in 1884 on the southeast side of the main building, while the King Edward VII galleries on the north, with their colonnaded façade facing Montagu Place, were finished in 1914.

Originally the museum was planned to hold natural history objects and manuscripts; however, the increasing number of gifts necessitated more divisions: (1) books, charts, maps, and plans; (2) manuscripts; (3) natural history objects; (4) and (5) Oriental, Greek, and Roman antiquities; (6) medals and coins; (7) medieval and British antiquities; (8) ethnography; and (9) prints and drawings.

In 1881 the natural history department, including zoology, botany, and mineralogy, was moved to South Kensington to the Natural History Museum to allow extra space for manuscripts in the old building. Included among the manuscripts are the *Codex Sinaiticus* and the *Codex Alexandrinus* of the Greek Bible, and the *Lindisfarne Gospels* belonging to the eighth century. Among the antiquities are the Elgin Marbles and the Nereid Monument; the Egyptian collection includes the famous Rosetta Stone.

BRITISH NORTH AMERICA ACT, a statute of the United Kingdom providing for the creation of the Dominion of Canada. It became effective July 1, 1867, with the provinces of Nova Scotia, New Brunswick, Quebec, and Ontario as original members of the Dominion. The act was based largely on resolutions passed by the Fathers of Confederation at the Quebec Conference of 1864. While listing both federal and provincial powers, the act gave the residuum of power to the Federal Government. The Constitution was further centralized by provisions in the act for a federal veto over any provincial act, federal appointment of all provincial governors, who were to be known as lieutenant governors, and right of way for federal legislation over provincial laws in cases of conflict within fields of concurrent jurisdiction. The provinces were given no exclusive field of taxation, and their control over education was to be subject to federal interference in specific cases relating to sectarian schools. Provincial representation in the federal House of Commons was to be based on population; in the federal Senate on equality of sections, not provinces. Originally there were three such sections, Nova Scotia and New Brunswick forming one, Quebec a second, and Ontario a third, each with twenty-four senators. When Prince Edward Island entered the Dominion it received four senators, but Nova Scotia and New Brunswick were each deprived of two. Eventually the four western provinces formed a fourth section, with six senators each. When Newfoundland joined Canada in 1949 it was assigned six senate seats, raising the membership to 102. Senators were to be appointed for life by the Federal Government.

Amendments and Alterations. Amendment to the Federal Constitution, except as it related to provincial government, was not mentioned in the act, and therefore remained by implication within the sole competence of the British Parliament. On Canada's own request this implication was made explicit by the Statute of Westminster in 1931. British acts relating to the Canadian Constitution since 1867 have dealt mostly with minor matters. Some have aimed merely at clarifying the original act, others have provided for representation in the federal legislature of new territorial and provincial areas, still others have merely deleted obsolete sections. Three were temporary acts permitting the Dominion Government to postpone a decennial census, a parliamentary dissolution, and a federal redistribution act, respectively. The Judicial Committee of the British Privy Council, which before World War I had greatly extended provincial powers, granted federal control of radio communication and air transport in 1932. On Canadian request the British Parliament in 1940 extended Canadian federal powers to include unemployment insurance, and old-age pensions were added in 1951. The British Parliament in 1949 granted to the Canadian Parliament the right to amend the Canadian Constitution in a wide range of subjects lying within the field of federal competence. In the same year the Canadian Parliament put an end to appeals in constitutional cases to the Judicial Committee as it had already stopped appeals in cases involving both criminal and civil law. The act of 1867 permitted the provinces to alter their own constitutions except with regard to the office of lieutenant governor. The Federal Constitution itself, even without formal amendment, has been subject to considerable change brought about by the combined effects of custom and judicial interpretation. Most of these changes, except in time of war, have been in the direction of increased provincial powers. These powers had been severely curtailed by the Fathers under the somewhat paradoxical conviction of the aggressive strength of the United States on the one hand, and the inherent weakness of the American federal system on the other. The divisive forces of both geography and history within Canada, however, have persistently tended to pull the Canadian Constitution away from this "more perfect union."

Admission of Colonies. The entire Dominion in 1867 lay within the bounds of the four uniting provinces, the combined area of which was only about one-tenth that of the present Dominion. Lying outside the Dominion to the east were two colonies, Prince Edward Island and Newfoundland with its dependency of Labrador. To the north and west lay the vast holdings of the Hudson's Bay Company, and on the Pacific Coast, the colony of British Columbia. The Act of 1867 established procedures for the admission of these areas into the Dominion of Canada. The Queen in council, on such conditions as she might think fit, was permitted to admit any of the three colonies to the Dominion on addresses from the local legislature and the parliament of the Dominion, and the Hudson's Bay Company holdings on address of the Canadian Parliament alone. British Columbia became a province in 1871, with a one-house legislature and on terms identical with those of the original provinces, except for a complex property and financial settlement. Prince Edward Island entered in 1873 with an anomalous legislature of one house, consisting of both councilors and assemblymen, and again with a peculiar property and financial settlement. Newfoundland continued to stand aloof, but in 1948 voted to become the tenth province in the Dominion. In 1870, after protracted negotiations, Canada secured the entire Hudson's Bay Company holdings between Ontario and British Columbia and between the American boundary and the Arctic Ocean. Anticipating the transfer, the Canadian Parliament had in 1869 passed a North West Territories Act, providing for this entire territorial area a constitution hardly less rudimentary than that previously provided by the Hudson's Bay Company. A sudden and dangerous uprising of half-breeds on the Red River later in 1869 induced the Canadian Parliament to pass the Manitoba Act in 1870 before the territory had actually changed hands. Thus, on the transfer, an area with less than two thousand white settlers along the lower Red River became the "postage stamp" province of Manitoba. It had a two-house legislature and all the trappings of Westminster. Except for the usual *ad hoc* economic settlement, Manitoba entered the Dominion on substantially the same terms as the original provinces. Its governor, however, was given the additional commission of governor of the Northwest Territories. In 1905 the southern portion of the Northwest Territories became the provinces of Alberta and Saskatchewan. An imperial order in council added the Arctic islands north of Canada to the Dominion.

W. M. W.

BRITISH BORNEO. *See* NORTH BORNEO.

BRITISH OCEANIA, a term used to refer to the British island dependencies from the southwest to the eastern Pacific Ocean, including not only the colonies and protected areas of the United Kingdom, but also the possessions and trust territories of Australia and New Zealand. The region extends from the eastern half of New Guinea eastward to Pitcairn and nearby islands, and from the vicinity of New Zealand northward to just beyond the equator, exclusive of two large areas of French sovereignty, centered on New Caledonia and Tahiti, and of American Samoa, a U.S. territory. The British islands spread out over an area of about 15,000,000 sq. mi., but the islands themselves, other than the large Australian holdings in the New Guinea area (183,540 sq. mi.), have an estimated area of only about 27,000 sq. mi. Of an estimated total population of approximately 2,300,000, some 1,700,000 are in the Australian New Guinea territories. Most of the islands are of low coral formation, but a considerable number, including all of the larger islands, are the exposed tops of mountain ridges and peaks, usually having a high volcanic core with a coral fringe.

United Kingdom in Oceania. Apart from occasional exploratory expeditions by naval vessels of the European maritime powers, there was little interest in this vast region before the nineteenth century. The first British colony, however, had been established in Australia in 1788, and Norfolk Island, more than 800 mi. east of Australia, was occupied from there in the same year. Pitcairn Island, in the extreme east of Oceania, was settled by mutineers from the *Bounty* in

ritories in this region was intensified, and partly provoked, by the rise at this time of other empire builders—notably Germany, France, the United States, and Japan. Strong pressures were also brought to bear by the British colonists in Australia and New Zealand, to whom the islands were of strategic importance. The United Kingdom annexed Fiji in 1874. In 1877 it established a High Commission of the Western Pacific, with headquarters in Fiji, to supervise all United Kingdom holdings in Oceania, and also all its subjects outside the organized territories. The Governor of Fiji acted also as High Commissioner. Papua became a protectorate in 1884, though it was later transferred to Australian

Solomon Islanders paddle out to meet a ship anchored off shore. The prows of their canoes are decorated with conch shells.

1790. European and American whalers made extensive use of Pacific Island harbors. Until 1833 the whole area was forbidden territory to all British traders except the East India Company, and it remained uninterested in the South Pacific trade. Even before 1833, however, a lively commerce, much of it based on South America, began to develop. As part of this, liquor and firearms were traded for slaves, and later, with the development of plantations in Queensland, Australia, this notorious labor traffic (blackbirding) spread there, involving especially the western Pacific islands. The situation called increasingly for government intervention.

In the wake of the traders, too, and sometimes ahead of them, had come the missionaries. The London Missionary Society ship *Duff* reached Tahiti in 1797. Protestant and later Roman Catholic missions became established throughout the South Pacific in increasing numbers. Apart from the remoter sections of Melanesia, practically all the inhabitants of Pacific islands are now Christian. Despite calls for intervention, the United Kingdom long remained unwilling to assume any responsibilities in the tropical Pacific islands. Somewhat reluctantly New Zealand was acquired in 1840, when British settlers were moving in. But "little Englanders" continued to dominate British colonial policy until the 1870's.

A wave of expansionism then set in and continued throughout the rest of the century. The urge to acquire ter-

control. In 1887 France and the United Kingdom agreed to a joint protectorate over the New Hebrides, and this, in turn, became a condominium in 1906. The Gilbert and Ellice groups were declared a United Kingdom protectorate in 1892, and the southern Solomon Islands in 1893. The Kingdom of Tonga became a protected state in 1900. The Gilbert and Ellice protectorate, with nearby Ocean Island, became a colony in 1915. The Line Islands, astride the equator in the central Pacific, were annexed in 1916-1917, and the Phoenix group in 1937. Of the latter islands, however, Canton and Enderbury became a condominium of the United Kingdom and the United States in 1939. During World War II the Japanese occupied the Solomons, Nauru, and several of the Gilbert group. Jointly with Australia and New Zealand, the United Kingdom had received a mandate for the island of Nauru from the League of Nations, and this island became a Trust Territory after World War II. In practice, however, the government of Australia has assumed sole responsibility for the administration of the island.

In 1953 the office of High Commission was shifted from Fiji to the British Solomon Islands Protectorate, as part of a development plan for the United Kingdom's holdings in that area, and the High Commissioner became administrator for that protectorate. In addition, the High Commission exercises supervision over the Gilbert and Ellice Islands Colony and United Kingdom interests in the New Hebrides

Condominium, each of which has its own Resident Commissioner under the High Commissioner. The eastern Pacific islands of Pitcairn and the Kingdom of Tonga continue to be supervised by the Governor of Fiji through a "Pito" (Pitcairn-Tonga) office. Fiji remains the hub of sea and air communications for the whole central Pacific.

Australia in Oceania. The interests of Australia are rooted in a complex history of nineteenth century relations of the Australian colonies with the islands to the north and east, variously involving political, commercial, and missionary ties. Since the establishment of the Commonwealth, these interests have become primarily focused in the New Guinea region to the north, that is, the Territory of Papua, and the former German possessions in New Guinea and nearby islands which have become the Trust Territory of New Guinea. Further east it also holds the Trust Territory of Nauru, the federal territory of Norfolk Island, and Lord Howe Island, which is constitutionally a part of New South Wales. During and since World War II, Australia's interest in the Pacific islands became intensified.

The Commonwealth took an active part in the creation in 1948 of a regional advisory and consultative body, the South Pacific Commission, dealing with economic and social welfare and development in the Pacific territories of Australia, France, the Netherlands, New Zealand, the United Kingdom, and the United States. The Commission headquarters is in Noumea, New Caledonia. Australia now administers its two New Guinea territories as a unit under the name Territory of Papua and New Guinea.

New Zealand in Oceania. It was almost inevitable that New Zealand should come to have a primary interest in Oceania. The Dominion owed its own existence to a successful appeal to the United Kingdom to intervene in the Pacific, and New Zealand has often, by itself or in conjunction with Australia, urged the United Kingdom to make greater commitments in the South Pacific; where this has failed, New Zealand has sometimes acted itself.

The Kermadec Islands, about 700 mi. northeast of the Dominion, were annexed in 1887. The Cook Islands, about 1,300 mi. beyond the Kermadecs, were taken over from the United Kingdom in 1901, and in 1903 Niue was separated from the Cook Islands and given a separate administration. At the start of World War I, New Zealand occupied the former German colony of Western Samoa, and in 1920 it became a New Zealand mandate. It is now a trust territory administered by New Zealand for the United Nations. In 1926 the United Kingdom transferred the administration of the Tokelau (Union) Islands, north of Samoa, to New Zealand, and these are administered from Western Samoa. The inhabitants of these islands are chiefly Polynesian.

The Dominion has assumed widespread responsibilities in the central Pacific, in aviation, education, and other services; it is fast becoming the temperate zone for these tropical islands, with communities of islanders living in its cities, notably in Auckland, and increasing interchange by way of trade. The islands are important to New Zealand for security reasons. Interest in the islands also stems from the fact that part of the population of New Zealand is Polynesian (Maori) and closely akin in stock and culture (including language) to the peoples of the Pacific islands, particularly those of Polynesia. For many years New Zealand schools have taught Polynesian Maori music, art, dancing, and folklore, and the Maori language at the university level. The resulting widespread interest in and respect for Polynesian peoples and their traditions has laid a good foundation for a wider trusteeship.   F. M. K. and M. M. K.

BRITISH OCEANIA

Islands	Status	Capital	Area in sq. mi.	Population
United Kingdom				
Fiji Islands	Colony	Suva	7,040	312,678 (1952 est.)
Brit. Solomon Islands	Protectorate	Honiara, Guadalcanal	16,500	100,000 (1954 est.)
Tonga (Friendly) Islands	Protected state	Nukualofa, Tongatabu	269	56,000 (1955 est.)
New Hebrides	Condominium with France	Vila, Efate	5,700	53,000 (1955 est.)
Pitcairn Island	Colony	Adamstown	2	125 (1952)
Gilbert and Ellice Islands	Colony	Tarawa	333	37,272 (1950 est.)
Australia				
Norfolk Island	Federal territory	Kingston	13	942 (1954)
Lord Howe Island	Dependency of New South Wales	Sydney, N.S.W.	5	202 (1951)
Nauru Island	Trust territory	Nauru	8	3,473 (1954)
Papua and New Guinea	Territory	Port Moresby	183,600	1,210,000 (1954 est.)
New Zealand				
Kermadec Islands	Part of New Zealand	. . . . . .	13	11 (1956)
Cook Islands	Part of New Zealand	. . . . . .	88	15,079 (1951)
Tokelau (Union) Island	Part of New Zealand	. . . . . .	4	1,580 (1951)
Western Samoa	Trust territory	Apia	1,133	84,909 (1951)

BRITISH WEST AFRICA, a term used to refer to British dependencies in West Africa—the Federation of Nigeria, attached to which is the British Cameroons; Gambia colony and protectorate; and Sierra Leone colony and protectorate. Formerly included in British West Africa was the Gold Coast, which, together with Ashanti and the Northern Territories, became the independent Republic of Ghana in February 1957, and British Togoland, a former trust territory, which voted to become part of Ghana.

Gambia and Sierra Leone are situated in extreme western Africa, on the Atlantic Ocean, and are separated from each other by French and Portuguese Guinea. Nigeria, by far the largest of the three dependencies, is located on the Gulf of Guinea, east of Ghana and French Dahomey. The dependencies have a total population of over 33,000,000, predominantly Negro, and a combined area of 404,666 sq. mi., distributed as follows: Nigeria, 372,674 sq. mi.; Sierra Leone, 27,924 sq. mi.; and Gambia, 4,068 sq. mi. The economy is basically agricultural, although there are important resources of tin and diamonds. *See also individual articles on each area.*

Ginger, palm kernels, gold, and diamonds are shipped from the port of Freetown, capital of Sierra Leone, British West Africa.

Early History. Only sporadic glimpses of life in West Africa in the pre-Islamic period can be obtained. The empire of Ghana, within the bend of the middle Niger, survived into the Islamic period. It was eventually overwhelmed partly by the rising Songhai Empire to the east and the Mandingo Empire to the southwest. When the Portuguese first arrived on the coast in the fifteenth century, these two rival empires were beginning to disintegrate, and this allowed a Moorish force from the far northwest to become their temporary legatee after 1591. These struggles in the interior had, however, only indirect effects on the life of the Negroes of the coastal region. The Portuguese did some trading in slaves almost from the first and, with the opening up of plantations in the Americas, slaving became the main economic interest of Portugal in West Africa. Isolated English expeditions began to arrive by the mid-sixteenth century, but until 1618 the chief rivals of the Portuguese were the Dutch. French, Danes, Swedes, and even Brandenburgers later established posts along the Guinea coast.

English Establishment. The English attempt to establish a permanent post on the Gambia estuary was unsuccessful, and that region, along with the islands off the Sierra Leone coast, became chiefly the rendezvous of pirates until near the end of the eighteenth century. The chief region of European settlement was along the Gold Coast. English enterprise here took the form of chartered trading companies, the most important of which were the Royal African Company, 1672-1750, and the African Company of Merchants, chartered in 1750. The slave trade came to dominate all other forms of economic activity.

In 1772, Lord Chief Justice William Mansfield ruled that any slave reaching England immediately became free. Following the American Revolution, many of the slaves of American Tories were brought to England where they soon became destitute. In 1787 the Sierra Leone Company was founded by the British Society for the Abolition of Slavery, and received a charter to establish an African colony for the reception of these former slaves. Land was secured from a local chief, and the colony of Sierra Leone was formed.

British Control. In 1807 the slave trade was made illegal throughout the British Empire, and in 1808 the Sierra Leone Company, because of financial difficulties, was forced to abandon control of the settlement it had founded, and Sierra Leone then became a crown colony of the British government. When the trade in slaves stopped, the British government was obliged to take over control also of Gambia in 1816, of the Gold Coast in 1821, and of Lagos in Nigeria in 1861. Dutch and Danish posts along the coasts were abandoned to the British, the Danish by 1850, the Dutch in 1871-1872. Several attempts were made in the nineteenth century to amalgamate the British colonies in West Africa, with administrative headquarters at Freetown in Sierra Leone. But in 1874 the Gold Coast was finally separated from Sierra Leone. Lagos remained under Gold Coast control until 1886. In 1888, Gambia was for the last time separated from Sierra Leone. It may be noted that unification came at a time of uncertainty as to the value of the entire West African venture, and separation came in with a wave of expansionist activity.

Twentieth-Century Developments. During World War I, Great Britain and France occupied Germany's two

Natives of Sierra Leone packing fruit of the oil palm in conical containers, made of sticks and palm leaves, where it will be allowed to ferment.

West African colonies, and at the end of the war Togoland and the Cameroons were divided between them as mandates from the League of Nations. (After World War II the internal boundaries of Togoland and the Cameroons were retained, but the status of these territories was altered to that of trust territories held under the supervision of the United Nations Trusteeship Council.) The war had relatively little effect on British West Africa otherwise. It had been off the main highway to the East ever since the opening of the Suez Canal in 1869, and the war brought no thought of invasion. Some native troops saw service in distant parts of the world, and some ideas of modern nationalism and industrialization came into the region with their return. But, on the whole, the ferment produced was not great.

With World War II, however, the region found itself in a strategic position. Sea and air bases across tropical Africa brought the modern world to its door. Between 1939 and 1945 West African military forces rose from about 8,000 to about 228,000. With ancillary units the number was about 374,000. A large proportion of these forces saw service in regions as remote as Malaya and Europe. The mental impact of this experience as well as the mechanical and technical knowledge and skills obtained were undoubted factors in the ferment that followed the war. The economy of the colonies was also changed by the war: native Africans, who had become increasingly used to imported foodstuffs, especially rice, were forced by the war to be self-sufficient; in Nigeria, tin became of critical importance to the war effort after the Japanese conquest of Malaya in 1942; and trade unions began to be organized.

In the decade following the war Britain's Colonial Development and Welfare acts helped promote increased education, transportation, and government services, while booming markets for West African exports such as cocoa and minerals produced a rapidly rising level of economic activity. Free universal primary education was established in the western region of Nigeria, in 1955, and educational facilities in the area were further increased by the addition of two colleges. Politically, both Sierra Leone and Gambia gained African majorities in their legislatures; the Gold Coast attained independence from Britain in 1957 and became the republic of Ghana; and Nigeria acquired a new constitution and a federal system of government in 1954 and continued to make progress toward its goal of independence from Great Britain.   **W. M. W.** and **W. W. W.**

BRITISH WEST INDIES, the British insular possessions in the Caribbean area. They fall into six groups: (1) the Bahamas, locally regarded as lying outside the West Indies; (2) Barbados; (3) Jamaica, with Turks and Caicos islands; (4) the Leeward Islands; (5) Trinidad, with Tobago; and (6) the Windward Islands. For purposes of historical study, British Guiana in South America, British Honduras in Central America, and Bermuda in the North Atlantic area may be included in this grouping.

Settlement and Expansion. From the middle of the sixteenth century, the English frequented the West Indies to trade with the Spanish colonies in America. Attention, from 1595 to 1625, was concentrated in the southern area, where the English attempted settlement in Guiana and along the Orinoco and Amazon rivers. These early efforts failed, but in 1609 a settlement was made in Bermuda, where Virginian interests soon began the raising of tobacco. The possibilities of this enterprise drew the English southward into the West Indies proper, St. Christopher, or St. Kitts, being settled in 1623. Two years later they were in Barbados, and in the course of the next decade they occupied Antigua, Nevis, and Montserrat. Puritan immigration flowed into the West Indies, as it did into New England, making permanent the possession of the Leeward Islands, the island group southeast of Puerto Rico. In 1655, Jamaica was captured from Spain, the only gain in Oliver Cromwell's vast, abortive "Western Design" of an American empire. Jamaica became the principal English possession in the Caribbean Sea. Its formal annexation in 1670 coincided with the beginning of large-scale growing of cane sugar, which superseded tobacco growing and became the chief asset of the islands for more than two centuries. The excellence of the soil and climate, and the regularity of the prevailing winds, necessary for the operation of the heavy windmills used in the production of raw sugar, made the islands ideal for this industry. Sugar planting was a capitalistic enterprise, conducted on large estates with an extensive labor force. After experimenting with various forms of labor —indentured European servants and prisoners of war—the planters adopted African slave labor, thus effecting a social as well as an economic revolution. The small proprietors disappeared, some drifting to the Bay of Honduras to cut logwood and laying the basis for the future colony of British Honduras, some migrating to the Carolinas on the American mainland, and others joining buccaneers in the Caribbean area.

Early Eighteenth Century. During the early eighteenth century, the West Indies prospered greatly. Sugar growing was extremely profitable, since West Indian sugar had a virtual monopoly of the British market. The planters lived in great splendor on their estates. Two disadvantages later appeared: first, the slave population increased rapidly and discouraged free immigration from Europe; second, absenteeism crept in: the plantation owner resided in the British Isles and managed the estate through an agent, or "attorney." Ultimately, absenteeism proved detrimental to the islands, especially to the older Leeward Islands, causing, among other things, the retardation of education. West Indian residents sent their sons to the mainland for education, Harvard University and the College of William and Mary being the most popular institutions. It was not until 1730 that the West Indies acquired a first-class college of their own in Codrington College, Barbados; prior to that, however, Bermuda had possessed a number of excellent secondary schools, of which one, Warwick Academy, is still in operation. Thus, the West Indies did not follow the strong example of the mainland American provinces in education and in extensive

European settlement. In all the islands, the Church of England enjoyed a position of virtual or actual establishment, so that the parson, along with the planter, dominated the social world. The West Indies were predominantly rural in character; their capitals—St. George's in Bermuda, Bridgetown in Barbados, and Spanish Town in Jamaica—were administrative rather than commercial centers.

As a result of the Anglo-Spanish commercial agreement in the Treaty of Utrecht in 1713, the West Indies found a new source of prosperity as depots for British trade with Spanish America. This growing trade, both legal and contraband, was of great importance to Jamaica, which rapidly outstripped the Leeward Islands and Barbados. Because of its size and its variety of soil and climate, Jamaica was able to

HERBERT LANKS FROM BLACK STAR

Making colorful straw articles in Jamaica, B.W.I.

follow a diversified economy, thus escaping from the position of dependence that sugar growing forced on the smaller islands. Considered collectively, the West Indies played a most important role in the commercial life of the British Empire, supplying a number of tropical products, chief of which was sugar. They purchased from Great Britain almost all of the manufactured goods they needed, thus adding to British fluid capital and directly contributing to the progress of the Industrial Revolution. From the American mainland colonies, the islands drew food, horses, and building material, paying with sugar and molasses, which the New Englanders distilled into rum for use in their own African trade. Finally, as purchasers of slaves, the West Indies helped to maintain the slave trade, one of the main enterprises of the early British Empire. This trade was immensely profitable in itself, as well as the auxiliary to profits from other activities.

Political importance developed from economic preeminence. In local matters, the West Indies were self-governing, most islands possessing a two-house legislature. The planter oligarchy dominated the legislatures and waged a fairly successful warfare with the British government in order to expand their autonomy. In this, they anticipated

most of the constitutional issues which appeared in the early phases of the American Revolution. West Indian governorships were the most desirable posts in the colonial empire, and successful American governors were promoted from Maryland or Pennsylvania to Barbados or Jamaica. The West Indies also maintained a well-subsidized lobby in Parliament and gave a striking example of their power in influencing the terms of the Treaty of Paris in 1763. By this treaty Great Britain returned Guadeloupe to France and Cuba to Spain for Canada and Florida, respectively, because the islands did not wish to endanger the high price of sugar by permitting the introduction of competing areas into the colonial empire; at the same time, however, Great Britain added the smaller Windward Islands, Grenada, St. Vincent, Dominica, and Tobago, whose value was naval rather than commercial.

American Revolution. The West Indies were deeply involved in the American Revolution. Opinion was generally favorable to the American patriot cause, a natural consequence of social and economic intercourse. In December 1774, the assembly of Jamaica adopted a resolution deploring the coercive measures inflicted by the British ministry on the Massachusetts Bay Colony. A year later Bermuda adopted a more active role by selling gunpowder to the Americans; the chief negotiator was Henry Tucker, president of the Bermuda legislative council and administrator of the colony. In the spring of 1776, the heavy guns defending Nassau in the Bahamas were surrendered to Commodore Esek Hopkins of Rhode Island, who hoisted the "grand union flag" of the American Congress and who carried off the royalist governor as hostage, undoubtedly as a means of protecting his island associate. Among the Leeward Islands, sympathy for the American cause was sharpened by business considerations, the islanders engaging in a remarkably lucrative contraband trade. St. Eustatius, the Dutch possession, was the common depot, and its seizure by Admiral George Rodney in February 1781 caused consternation throughout the British West Indies. The islanders took legal action against Rodney, and, while they succeeded in compelling him to make good their losses, their sympathies were alienated further from Great Britain. They made little or no effort to defend themselves but insisted that the British government defend them. The news of Cornwallis' surrender at Yorktown caused general disturbance, as in the case of Barbados, which refused to pay for the provisioning of its garrison. In some of the

St. Lucia is one of the great chain of islands known as the British West Indies. It was formed by volcanic eruption and the extinct cones, known as the Pitons, are in the background.

PHOTO CAROLA

islands an energetic "Gallo-American" party co-operated with the French; it was this group which was largely responsible for the surrender of St. Kitts in February 1782. At one time or another, all of the Leeward Islands, except Antigua, were lost to the French, and Guiana, Honduras, and Florida were overrun by the Spaniards. The sweeping naval victory won by Admiral Rodney over the French under François de Grasse at Les Saintes in April 1782 probably saved the British from being driven completely from the Caribbean.

The West Indies became an asylum for American royalists, despite the hostility which developed between the refugees and powerful local cliques favorable to the patriot Americans. It is possible that the American royalists restored the balance of power in the West Indies. In areas of marginal loyalty, such as Bermuda, they supplied new officials completely devoted to the British crown. In April 1783, a corps of Georgia royalists retook the Bahamas, which had been captured by the Spaniards; this was the final engagement of the Revolutionary War period. The first royal governor of the Bahamas after the Revolution was Lord Dunmore, the last royal governor of Virginia before the Revolution. In spite of the numerous setbacks of the war, the British, by the Treaty of Paris, 1783, suffered only the loss of Tobago. However, the long-range effect of the Revolution was disastrous. American independence deprived the West Indies of their convenient base

War of 1812 with the United States. The expedition which destroyed Washington proceeded from Bermuda; that which failed before New Orleans, from Jamaica. As a result of the peace settlement at Vienna, 1814-1815, the West Indies were consolidated by the annexation of Trinidad and St. Lucia, the reannexation of Tobago, and the extension of Guiana and Honduras. Despite the appearance of stability, however, the overthrow of the traditional economic and social system of the islands was imminent. In 1807, the abolition of the slave trade deprived the West Indies of their former supply of labor, and in 1834 the abolition of slavery struck at the very root of their economy. Although the planters received a sum amounting to over £16,000,000 in compensation for the loss of their slaves, they attempted to hinder the working of the Emancipation Act, thus involving themselves in disputes with the imperial government. Soil exhaustion, absentee ownership, and extravagant financing made it impossible for West Indian sugar to compete with sugar grown on Mauritius, and the adoption of free trade by Great Britain after 1846 completed the ruin of the islands.

In addition to the economic and social revolution caused mainly by emancipation and free trade, there was a further problem. The colonies had had from the beginning a very one-sided type of democracy even for the original settlers and their descendants. Although the legislative assemblies were

The juice of fresh coconuts sold by a street vendor provides refreshment in Port of Spain, Trinidad.

HERBERT LANKS FROM BLACK STAR

of supply, and the remaining British mainland provinces, Nova Scotia and Quebec, failed to fill this essential role. Thus, by the end of the eighteenth century, the great era of West Indian prosperity was drawing to a close.

Emancipation Era. The era of the French Revolutionary and Napoleonic wars brought a temporary resurgence of prosperity to the West Indies. Their products were in demand, and with Great Britain excluded from Europe, they were important markets for manufactured goods. They supplied vital naval bases, especially for the British during the

elected, they represented only a small part of the total population and seldom evidenced any responsibility toward the unrepresented majority. In the end, stalemates between governors and their assemblies, the growing apathy of the voters, and the refusal by the legislatures to improve the conditions of the Negroes and to effect needed reforms led to the loss of representative government. Between 1854 and 1895 all the colonies except Barbados, British Honduras, and the Leeward Islands surrendered their constitutions and became crown colonies.

Twentieth-Century Progress. Twentieth-century developments brought a notable recovery from economic and political prostration. New economic bases were found. Bermuda and the Bahamas capitalized on their tourist attractions. Jamaica developed the production of tropical fruit; Trinidad, the extraction of petroleum and asphalt; and Guiana, the mining of gold and bauxite. The establishment in 1919 of the Imperial College of Tropical Agriculture at San Fernando, Trinidad, made possible extensive research projects. Such projects were especially necessary with the growth of peasant proprietorship, a trend which pointed toward the economic independence of the bulk of the West Indian population. Other encouraging developments included reciprocal trade agreements with Canada and other British Empire countries, which provided outlets for major crops and the extension of a regular Canadian steamship service, furthering contacts between the islands and the American mainland. Nevertheless, as exporters of primary products, the West Indies were vulnerable economically. In the 1930's, as a consequence of the world depression, they suffered severely. Political disturbances followed, commencing in the Leeward Islands in 1935, spreading southward, and reaching a peak in Jamaica and Trinidad in 1937 and 1938. A commission from Great Britain (the Royal Commission of Inquiry) visited the West Indies to examine and report on conditions. The findings, made public in 1940, contained recommendations for greater local production of food, intensified agricultural research, the extension of social services and educational facilities, and the extension of self-government.

World War II. During World War II, the West Indies played a very important part. The defense of the islands devolved largely on local troops. The activities of German submarines and the proximity of French islands, which until 1943 were controlled by a pro-Vichy regime, brought the British West Indies close to the conflict. As well as aiding in local defense, a large number of West Indians enlisted for overseas service, joining the British and Canadian forces or enlisting in the special West Indies battalions authorized in 1944. Enlistments from Jamaica alone amounted to over 5,000. West Indian girls and women joined various women's auxiliary formations, while other West Indians in noncombatant capacities made important contributions to the Allied cause. One of the most interesting of these was the migration of mahogany workers from British Honduras to Great Britain to help man the forestry services there.

In view of the strategic importance of the West Indies in the defense of the Western Hemisphere, naval and air bases for the United States were establishd in Bermuda, the Bahamas, St. Lucia, Antigua, Jamaica, Trinidad, and British Guiana. The West Indian bases played a vital part in the antisubmarine campaigns and in the diplomatic moves which brought the French West Indies to the side of the Allied powers. In 1941, the Anglo-American Caribbean Commission was created to secure co-ordination in carrying out welfare proposals. Thus, in World War II, the West Indies again fulfilled the role of harmonizing relations between the British Empire and the United States.

Development Since the War. In 1946 the French and Netherlands governments joined the Anglo-American Commission, which was then reorganized and renamed the Caribbean Commission. Also following the end of World War II, the advance toward representative and responsible democratic government was accelerated. Universal adult suffrage became general throughout the island group. Full ministerial systems, provided with the powers for a large measure of internal self-government, were established in Trinidad, Jamai-

Paradise Beach, near Nassau, resort capital of the Bahama Islands, B.W.I.

ca, and Barbados. In the latter two islands the lower chambers of the legislatures became elective, and in nearly all the colonies local inhabitants were elected to ministerial posts. Even in British Guiana, where the 1953 constitution was suspended because of fear of Communist subversion, a new constitution became effective in August 1957 under which the legislature again has an elective majority and elected members are appointed to ministries or departments.

The goal of the colonies was a federation with eventual dominion status. The establishment of a federation came closer to actuality when at a London conference of island delegates on Feb. 23, 1956, a final plan of union was approved. The British Caribbean Federation Act was enacted by Parliament in August 1956, and under authority of this law Queen Elizabeth established a federation to be known as The West Indies on July 31, 1957. The West Indies Federation, as it is generally called, consists of a legislature composed of an elected house of representatives and an appointed senate, with a crown-appointed governor general. The Federation consists of Jamaica, Trinidad-Tobago, Barbados, Dominica, Grenada, St. Lucia, St. Vincent, St. Kitts-Nevis-Anguilla, Antigua, and Montserrat, with its capital at Port-of-Spain, Trinidad. In January 1958 Lord Hailes was invested as the first governor general. On Apr. 12, 1958, he appointed the members of the senate. That day also, Princess Margaret, acting on behalf of the Queen, and assisted by Lord Hailes, opened the first Parliament of The West Indies. *See also* WEST INDIES.   J. I. C. and G. Con.

BRITONS, the Celtic-speaking inhabitants living in Britain at the time of the Roman invasions. Celts from the lower Rhine had settled in southern and eastern Britain during the late Bronze Age, about the middle of the 8th century B.C. They were followed about 500 B.C. by other Celts from the Rhone, who brought with them the beginnings of the first Iron Age or Hallstatt culture. In the early 3rd century B.C. fresh waves of Celtic invaders from Brittany spread throughout most of the island. These people represented the late Iron Age civilization, known as the La Tène culture. The last Celtic invaders, the Belgae from northern France, arrived in 75 B.C., and continued to have close connections with their relatives across the Channel. By the time of the Roman conquest Britain was divided among a number of warring tribal kingdoms, including the Belgae of Wiltshire and Hampshire, the Dumnonii of Cornwall and Devon, the Cantii of Kent, the Trinovantes and Iceni of East Anglia, the Silures of Wales, and the Brigantes of Yorkshire. Most probably the original Celtic invaders had amalgamated with a numerous population of more primitive inhabitants, and had imposed their speech and culture on them.

The Britons lived in walled hill forts, in villages of round huts sunk into the ground, in underground chambered houses, or in pile-dwellings in the marshes. At least in the south, however, where trade and town life had begun, the houses must have been of a more advanced type. There was a native Celtic art, derived from the La Tène culture of the Continent, which exhibited great skill, especially in enamelling and bronze products. It was characterized by a love of beauty of form and detail, a free use of geometrical design, and a flamboyant treatment of plant and animal forms, but without human representation. In religion the priesthood of the Druids, with their barbarous rites and sacrifices and secret lore, wielded great influence over the people. Julius Caesar invaded Britain in 55 and 54 B.C., but actual conquest did not come until 43 A.D. under the emperor Claudius. With the collapse of the Western Roman Empire in the 5th century the Romano-British were overwhelmed by the barbarian Anglo-Saxons from the Continent.   F. C. H.

BRITTANY [brɪ'təni], a former duchy and province of the Armorican peninsula, in northwest France, including the modern departments of Finistère, Côtes-du-Nord, Morbihan,

GEIGER · RAPHO · GUILLUMETTE

Preparing sardines for canning at a Brittany sardine factory

Ille-et-Vilaine and Loire-Inférieure. Noted for its beautiful scenery, a large part of Brittany's area of 18,630 sq. mi. is uncultivated, due to rocks and barren soil. In the higher

areas, there is excellent pasture land used for cattle-grazing. Along the coast, however, the dense population is supported by fishing and by an intensive cultivation of fruits and vegetables, fertilized by the abundant harvests of seaweed. A goodly number of the crews and officers of naval and merchant vessels of France have come from Brittany. Brest is a center of naval construction and naval and merchant marine schools. Quimper is noted for its chinaware and lace. Paramé, St. Malo, Dinard, and Concarneau are a few of the fishing ports on the coast; fishing fleets from these ports venture as far as the Newfoundland Banks. The people of Brittany use cider as their principal drink, and many still retain the ancient Celtic language that is closely allied to Welsh. Their distinctive characteristics are due to the fact that the peninsula of Brittany was for centuries separated from the rest of France by forests, and so lived a life apart.

The Celtic tribes of Brittany remained under Roman rule from Caesar's invasion in 56 B.C. until the fifth century, when the Roman troops were withdrawn in the last days of the empire. Throughout the sixth century, many Christian Celts came from Britain to escape the invading Germans, and many petty lordships were established. It was not until the ninth century, under the stress of the Northmen's raids, that these were united under the national hero Nominoë, who at first accepted Frankish suzerainty but later revolted and restored Breton independence. In the second half of the tenth century the chief power of the state was Conan of Rennes, whose son Geoffrey became the first Duke of Brittany. Geoffrey Plantagenet, son of Henry II of England, succeeded to the dukedom in the twelfth century through his marriage to the heiress Constance. Their son, Arthur, was murdered by order of his uncle, King John of England. The defeat of the latter by Philip Augustus, and the marriage of Arthur's sister to the Capetian noble, Pierre de Dreux, brought the duchy under closer French control. In 1341 a disputed succession led to civil war, which ended only in 1364, when Jean de Montfort gained control by the battle of Auray. For more than a century Brittany retained its independence, but in 1491 this was ended, and France became territorially united, when the Duchess Anne, heiress of Brittany, was married to Charles VIII of France. Her daughter Claudia later succeeded to the duchy, but after her marriage to Francis I it was reunited to the Crown by a treaty in 1532, which guaranteed local liberties to the Bretons.   F. C. H.

BRITTEN, EDWARD BENJAMIN (1913-   ), English composer, was born Nov. 22, 1913, in Lowestoft, Suffolk. He studied at the Royal College of Music in London, and between 1938-1942 lived in the United States, where he wrote his *Sinfonia da requiem*, a violin concerto, and a string quartet commissioned by the Elizabeth Sprague Coolidge Foundation. His opera *Peter Grimes* (1945), commissioned by the Koussevitzky Foundation, brought him major recognition. Other works include a piano concerto, *Ceremony of Carols, Les Illuminations, The Rape of Lucretia, Gloriana, Let's Make an Opera,* and *Billy Budd.*
          E. L. F.

BRITTLE STARS, also called serpent stars, marine echinoderms of the class Ophiuroidea, of small or moderate size, common in shallow waters. The body is a central flat disk from which radiate five slender, flexible arms. The basket stars which may grow to about 10 in. across have greatly branched arms. Others are usually less than 6 in. across and unbranched. The mouth, leading to a saclike stomach, is situated in the center of the lower surface of the disk.

The oral surface also bears five pairs of slits leading into genital sacs into which the sex glands discharge their products. The madreporite is on the oral surface. There is no anus. Each arm, supported by an internal row of calcareous ossicles, bears reduced and functionless tube feet. Reproduction is sexual. Swimming larva of the pluteus type are formed. When molested, ophiuroids tend to break off their arms, but they are readily regenerated. L. H. Hy.

BRITTON, NATHANIEL LORD [brɪ'tən] (1859-1934), American botanist, was born in New Dorp, Staten Island, N. Y., Jan. 15, 1859. He received his Ph.D. in 1881 from Columbia University, and for seven years was an assistant in botany to Prof. J. Strong Newberry of Columbia. In 1886 he became an instructor, and in 1891 was appointed professor and head of the department at Columbia. Britton was also a botanist with the New Jersey Geological Survey and a member of the advisory commission on botanical work with the Carnegie Institution of Washington, D. C. He was director of the New York Botanical Garden from 1896 to 1929. During this period it became the third largest botanical garden in the world. Britton conducted botanical expeditions to the West Indies and published works on the flora of New Jersey, the northern United States, Canada, Bermuda, the Bahamas, Puerto Rico, and the Virgin Islands. His insistence on the standardization of botanical nomenclature was of particular importance. He helped organize the Botanical Society of America and was its president in 1898 and 1920. He died in New York, June 25, 1934. C. W. D.

BRIXEN. *See* Bressanone.

BRNO (Ger. **BRÜNN**) [bə'rno, brü'n], the capital of Brno province, Moravia, Czechoslovakia, at the junction of the Svratka and Svitava rivers, 115 mi. southeast of Prague. Fertile agricultural lands are to the south and east, coal mines to the west, and marble quarries to the north of the city. Brno, a Slavic town by the tenth or eleventh century, was an important commercial and trading center for German towns to the north. It was in the Kingdom of Bohemia during the Middle Ages, in the Austrian Empire under the Hapsburgs, and has been in Czechoslovakia since 1918. In 1938 it was the center of a pan-German movement and was a Reich city of Nazi Germany from 1939 to 1945.

Architecturally, Brno is late seventeenth century. It has numerous churches, cathedrals, abbeys, impressive government buildings, and beautiful gardens and squares. The Czechoslovakian government maintains a modern hospital, an accident insurance union, a music conservatory, the Masaryk University, the Polytechnic Institute, a theatre, and an agricultural school. Brno is an important industrial city especially known for its woolen mills, clothing factories, iron and steel mills, chemical works, machinery plants, and a small-arms factory, home of the Bren gun. It is also an important railway center, with main lines leading to Silesia, Prague, Vienna, and to Belgrade, Bucharest, and Istanbul. A major airfield serves air transports between Prague and Bratislava. Pop. 1947, 273,127. F. Sc.

BROACH [bro'tsh], also Bharuch, an old port city of eastern India, in Broach District, northern Bombay State, on the Narbada River, about 15 mi. inland from the Gulf of Cambay, and about 203 mi. north of Bombay. It is the district capital but has declined in importance with the shallowing of the Gulf and the rise of Bombay. About one third of the region is planted in one of the best types of Indian cotton, called "broach." There are textile mills and ginning and processing plants in the city. It is a local market center and a railroad junction. It was taken by the British from the Sindis in 1802. Pop. 1951, 62,729.

BROAD, CHARLES DUNBAR (1887-   ), English philosopher, was born Dec. 30, 1887, in London, and became professor of moral philosophy at Cambridge University in 1933. Broad stresses as basic the distinction between critical and speculative philosophy, which he holds to be distinct subjects requiring different methods of investigation. He maintains that the main task of critical philosophy is to clarify the meanings of such general concepts as cause, change, place, thing. These are constantly used in ordinary life and in science, but nowhere, except in philosophy, do they constitute an explicit subject matter of investigation. Our ordinary understanding of such concepts is "highly confused," as shown by the fact that when we consider them in somewhat unusual situations, we do not know whether to apply them or not. Thus, though we know the ordinary use of "place," we are puzzled by the question, "In what place is the mirror image of a pin?" It is the concern of critical philosophy to make the meanings of such words clear by analysis and definition, so that we shall know how they apply. In addition, critical philosophy subjects to criticism such fundamental assumptions of the sciences as, for example, the assumption that every change has a cause.

The endeavor of speculative philosophy is more ambitious. It is to construct a theory of the universe that will do justice both to the results of the various sciences and to the implications of our moral and religious experience. Broad's skeptical temper, fondness for precision in thought and writing, and demand for careful verification have turned his interest from the problems of speculative to those of critical philosophy. On these latter problems he has written a series of remarkably lucid books, among which are *Perception, Physics, and Reality* (1914), *The Mind and Its Place in Nature* (1925), *Five Types of Ethical Theory* (1930), *Examination of McTaggart's Philosophy* (Vol. I, 1933; Vol. II, 1938), and a book of essays, *Ethics and the History of Philosophy* (1952). M. L.

BROADLOOM RUGS. *See* Carpets and Rugs.

BROCA, PIERRE PAUL [brɔ'ka'] (1824-1880), French anthropologist and surgeon, one of the most distinguished anthropologists of the nineteenth century. He was born at Sainte-Foy-la-Grande, in the department of Gironde, France, June 28, 1824. Trained as a physician, his first successes were in this field. At an early age, Broca began publishing a variety of medical and surgical studies. Among the better known of his works in medicine are a series on the pathology of the articular cartilages (1848-1851) and aneurysms. He was also celebrated for his *Treatise on Tumors*. While still active in his medical career, he became interested in skeletons exhumed from the ancient cemetery of the Church of the Celestines in Paris and published a memoir on them in 1850. From this investigation he developed a keen interest in physical anthropology which absorbed much of his energies in the latter part of his career. He established, with considerable difficulty, the Society of Anthropology of Paris in 1859 and was its guiding force until his death. In 1867 he was named Professor at the Faculty of Medicine and shortly thereafter was admitted to the Academy of Medicine. While continuing his teaching and his organizational efforts, he maintained a steady flow of researches both on the brain and in physical anthropology. His investigation into the seat of articulate language led to his location of the center of speech in the region of the brain which is still known as the "convolution of Broca." His anthropological publications were voluminous and stimulating, and he was particularly fertile in developing the instrumentation that the young science of physical anthropology required. In 1872 he founded the *Revue d'Anthropologie* and in 1876 officially opened the École d'Anthropologie which he had organized. Broca took an active part in French science, was a founder of the French Association for the Advancement of Science, and toward the end of his life received public recognition by his election to a permanent seat in the Senate as a representative of science. He died in the Senate, July 9, 1880.   H. L. Sh.

BROCCOLI, one of the intermediate forms between wild cabbage, *Brassica oleracea,* and cauliflower, of which it is the progenitor. The flower heads, for which it is grown, are smaller, coarser, and slower in maturing than cauliflower or cabbage and are marketed green. Though known for years as a home garden product in Italy and France, broccoli did not become popular in the United States until the early 1900's. Commercially the calabrese type is grown in climates where the winters are mild, as in the West Coast states. Young plants, started from seed in cold frames, should be set out when the leaves are approximately 2 in. in diameter. The plants may be moved from the cold frames early in spring, about one month before the last expected frost. They should be set 9 in. apart. An annual shorter season variety is grown and harvested in early to late fall in the Eastern seaboard states. It requires a well limed fertile soil. Loam soils with plenty of water will produce good yields. The flower buds are cut just before the yellow flowers show. The best quality broccoli is produced in cool weather. Broccoli produces for three months or more and in mild winters may produce all winter. It is high in vitamin content. V. A. T.

BROCK, SIR ISAAC (1769-1812), English soldier, was born in Guernsey, Oct. 6, 1769. In 1785 he entered the army. In 1797 he became a lieutenant colonel and saw service in Holland in 1799 and at Copenhagen in 1801. He took his regiment to Canada in 1802, and in 1810 was given command of the troops in Upper Canada, being promoted to the rank of major general in 1811. In July 1812 he drove back the American general William Hull, who had invaded Canada, and on July 18 received the surrender of Detroit together with Hull's entire army. During an American attack on Queenstown, Ont., near Niagara Falls, Oct. 13, 1812, Brock was killed; a tall column on Queenstown Heights commemorates his death.   E. R. A.

BROCKEN SPECTER. *See* Atmosphere.

BROCKHAUS, HERMANN [brɒ'khɑus] (1806-1877), German orientalist, was born in Amsterdam, Holland, Jan. 28, 1806. He studied at the universities of Leipzig, Göttingen, and Bonn, where he specialized in Oriental languages, and later in Copenhagen, Paris, London, and Oxford, after which he settled in Dresden. In 1839 he was appointed extraordinary professor of the University of Jena, and two years later went to the University of Leipzig. The best-known work of Brockhaus is the *Katha-saritsagata* (English translation, *The Ocean of the Streams of Story,* 1880-1884), a collection of tales compiled by Somadeva Bhatta in the twelfth century, which Brockhaus published in Sanskrit and German. The first parts appeared in 1839. In 1843 the complete German translation of the stories was published and proved of much value in the study of the origin of popular tales. In 1841 Brockhaus published *Ueber den Druck sanskritischer Werke in lateinischen Buchstaben,* a discussion of the reproduction of Sanskrit in the Latin alphabet. In 1845 he published the *Prabodha-Candrodaya* ("The Rise of the Moon of Intelligence"), a philosophical drama by Krishna Misra. *Lieder des Hafis* was published between 1854 and 1860. In 1863 he prepared a new edition of the Persian songs of Hafiz (a fourteenth-century lyric poet), accompanied by Sadi's commentaries. In 1850 he published an edition of the *Vendidad Sade* which included a grammar of the Zend language. In 1852 Brockhaus founded the German Asiatic Society, and in 1856 became editor of the *Allgemeine Enzyklopädie.* He died in Leipzig, Jan. 5, 1877.

BROCKHURST, GERALD LESLIE (1890-   ), English etcher and painter, was born Oct. 19, 1890, in Birming-

GERALD L. BROCKHURST

INTERNATIONAL NEWS PHOTO

ham. In 1902 Brockhurst started attending the Birmingham School of Art, where he worked under E. T. Taylor and Catterson Smith. In 1917 he went to the School of the Royal Academy in London, where he won a traveling fellowship to Paris and Milan. He had etched as early as 1914, but his etchings were not published until 1920. He was elected Fellow of the Royal Society of Painter-etchers and Engravers in 1921, and a Fellow of the Royal Academy in 1937. Brockhurst is best known for his minute craftsmanship, his mastery of technique, and his finish. His etchings of women, for most of which his wife posed, and his portrait of his friend Henry Rushbury, the artist, are among his most popular works. Brockhurst settled in the United States in 1939.   J. S. By.

BROCKTON, a city in southeastern Massachusetts, is situated in Plymouth Co., 20 mi. south of Boston. The site was purchased from the Indians, and the first town was founded in 1700. It was incorporated as North Bridgewater in 1821, renamed Brockton in 1874, and incorporated as a city under that name in 1881. The New York, New Haven and Hartford Railroad serves the city, and there is a municipal airport. Brockton is a trade center for the surrounding region and has long been a center of the nation's shoe manufacturing industry. Electronic equipment, plastics, and clothing are also produced. Brockton supports an orchestral society and monthly art exhibits. Pop. 1950, 62,860.

BROKEN HILL, NEW SOUTH WALES

BROCKVILLE, a city and port in Leeds Co., Ontario, Canada, on the St. Lawrence River at the foot of the Thousand Islands, 125 mi. west of Montreal. Brockville is the county seat of the united counties of Leeds and Grenville. Founded in 1784 and called Buell's Bay, it was a landing place in the 1780's and 1790's for United Empire Loyalists fleeing from the United States. In 1812 its name was changed to Brockville in honor of Sir Isaac Brock, a British general of the War of 1812. A number of skirmishes were fought here in that war between Canadian militia and Americans stationed at Ogdensburg, across the river. In 1832 Brockville became the first incorporated town in Upper Canada (Ontario). The city's manufactured products include marine engines, foundry castings, grinding wheels, hats, patent medicines, milk and cheese products, shoes, and telephones. Pop. 1956, 13,885.

BRODIAEA [brodɪɪ'ə], a genus of the lily family with about thirty species, native to California and the West. From corms (solid bulbs) rise grasslike leaves and straight stems, sometimes to 2 ft., with loose clusters of white, blue, purple, or yellow flowers. Some are in cultivation, such as the spring starflower, *B. uniflora,* from Argentina, with bluish-white flowers.   J. C. Wis.

BRODZINSKI, KAZIMIERZ [brɔji'nyski] (1791-1835), Polish poet, was born in Krolowko, Mar. 8, 1791. He prepared for a military career and entered the artillery in 1809. His first poems, *Pienia Wieskie,* were published in Kraków in 1811. He was garrisoned in Warsaw and Modlin, and participated in Napoleon's Russian campaign in 1812. He returned with remnants of the Polish army to Kraków, and participated in the 1813 campaigns in Austria and Saxony. Made prisoner at the Battle of Leipzig (the Battle of the Nations), he was released on parole and returned to Kraków. Later he was offered a professorship of esthetics and literature at the university of Warsaw, which he accepted. He defended the Romantic genre of poetry, and became a prominent critic, but the suppression of the university by the Russian authorities left him jobless. He contracted a chest ailment and went to Bohemia. His collected poems were published in Vilna in 1842. One of his best-known works is the idyllic narrative poem *Wieslaw,* which helped to focus the attention of Polish poets on national sources for their themes. Brodzinski translated many masterpieces of European literature into Polish, including Walter Scott's novels. The complete works of Brodzinski appeared between 1872 and 1874 in Warsaw. Brodzinski died in Dresden, Oct. 10, 1835.

BROKE, ARTHUR. *See* BROOKE, ARTHUR.
BROKEN CHORD. *See* MUSICAL TERMS.

BROKEN HILL, a silver, lead, and zinc mining center in the extreme western part of New South Wales, in southeastern Australia, located about 250 mi. northeast of Adelaide. The city is situated on the low, hilly upland of the Barrier Range. Immediately east are the plains of the Darling River, which is about 88 mi. to the east. Broken Hill has an arid climate, with only 10 or 12 in. of rain a year. The average annual temperature is about 69° F., and the warmest months are January and February, when high daytime temperatures between 85° and 100° F. are common. The nights cool off considerably. The coldest month is July, which averages around 55° F. The chief vegetation of the surrounding area consists of grass and low bushes, and agriculture is of minor importance, but there is sheep grazing in the area, and the wool industry is important. The city has railroad connections with Sydney to the east and with Port Pirie, Adelaide, and Port Adelaide to the southwest. It also has air service.

The area around Broken Hill was first explored in 1844 by Captain Charles Sturt, and in 1854 the oddly shaped Broken Hill was included in a large sheep ranch controlled by Sir James McCulloch. At Mt. Gipps Station, a few miles from Broken Hill, minerals were found, and in 1883 ore was discovered at Broken Hill. The mine at Broken Hill proved to be one of the greatest silver, lead, and zinc deposits in the world. Blast furnaces were erected, and the site grew into a small city. In 1889 there was an ill-founded and unfortunate boom in property around the mine, and for a short time fortunes were made and lost in worthless mining stock. The Broken Hill Proprietary prospered, but the blast furnaces were shifted to Port Pirie, 200 miles to the southwest, because of a shortage of water. About 1900 the oxidized ore ran out, and it became difficult to process the remaining lead and zinc sulphide ores. By 1902 a flotation process was developed to handle the sulphides. In the meantime the Broken Hill Proprietary was expanding into other ventures, and became a great iron-mining and steel-manufacturing center. Iron ore was brought from Port Whyalla in South Australia, and a steel mill was built at Newcastle, north of Sydney. Since its discovery the Broken Hill mining field has produced 71,000,000 tons of ore. Pop. 1954, 31,387.

BROKER, one who acts as an agent for others in buying, selling, or negotiating contracts, and who receives a commission for his services. Brokers function in many lines of business; there are brokers for various types of commodities and merchandise, for insurance, and for securities. The economic function of a broker is simply to bring buyer and seller together for the conclusion of a transaction. In addition, the broker provides his services as an expert for the principal for whom he acts. Professional brokers are ordinarily very well informed on demand and supply in the market, current prices, and price trends. *See also* MARKETING AND MERCHANDISING.   H. C. S.

BROMBERG. *See* BYDGOSZCZ.

BROME, RICHARD [bro'm] (died 1652), English dramatist, was Ben Jonson's servant in 1614 and was associated with the Queen of Bohemia's company of actors in 1628. During the next fourteen years he wrote his sixteen extant plays. *The Northern Lass* (1632) was praised in verse by Ben Jonson, Thomas Dekker, and John Ford; and Brome collaborated with Thomas Heywood in *The Late Lancashire Witches* (printed 1634). Brome's best plays include *The Antipodes* (1635), a triumph of topsy-turvy humor; *A Jovial Crew* (1641), in which lovers run off to join a troop of gypsies; and *The Sparagus Garden* (1635) and *The Weeding of Covent Garden* (printed 1659), realistic London comedies.   M. E.

BROME GRASS, *Bromus,* the name of a group of grasses both annual and perennial, with about one hundred species native to temperate regions, usually of medium size with large flowering spikelets. About twenty-five species are native to the United States; others have been introduced. Some are cultivated for forage, as Schrader's brome or fescue grass, *B. catharticus,* in the southern states, and Hungarian brome, *B. inermis,* from Montana to Kansas.   J. C. Wis.

BROMELIAS [bromi'liəz], a family, Bromeliaceae, of tropical plants of some nine hundred species. The pineapple, *Ananas sativus,* is the most important species, economically, of this group. Some species grow on dry rocks or in earth, but chiefly they are epiphytes (perching or air plants with or without air roots) which form as characteristic a feature of the American tropics as do the orchids. The bromeliads proper are short-stemmed, with rigid, channeled, often scurfy, spiny leaves, and showy flowers, as in the pineapple. Long or Spanish moss, *Tillandsia usneoides,* is an epiphytic bromeliad that grows on trees, especially live oaks,

in tropical America and the extreme southern United States. Species of *Billbergia* are grown in gardens in warm climates and as house plants.   R. S. Ho.

BROMFIELD, LOUIS (1896-1956), American novelist, editor, and agricultural and political theorist, was born Dec. 27, 1896, at Mansfield, Ohio. He left Columbia University to serve with the American Ambulance Corps in France in World War I. Among the more important of his novels are *The Green Bay Tree* (1924), *Possession* (1925), *Early Autumn* (1926), which was awarded the Pulitzer Prize, *A Good Woman* (1927), *The Farm* (1933), and *Mrs. Parkington* (1943). Visits to India provided the setting for *The Rains Came* (1937) and *Night in Bombay* (1940). Though his early novels received critical acclaim for their honest attempts to portray American society, later works seemed superficial and overly romantic. After long residence abroad, Bromfield returned to the United States in 1939 to live on his Malabar Farm near Mansfield. His strong interest in experimental farming appears in *Pleasant Valley* (1945), *The Wild Country* (1948), *Malabar Farm* (1948), and *Out of the Earth* (1950). *A New Pattern for a Tired Old World* (1954) summarized his political philosophy. Bromfield died Mar. 18, 1956, in Columbus, Ohio.

BROMINE [bro'mɑin; bro'min], symbol Br (Gr. βρῶμos, stench), a nonmetallic chemical element which is a member of the halogen family, Group VII-A in the periodic table. It was discovered by the French chemist Antoine Jérôme Balard in 1826. It occurs extensively as bromides in salt brines, those in Ohio containing up to 4 per cent magnesium bromide; salt deposits, such as those found in Stassfurt, Germany; and in sea water.

Preparation. The methods of obtaining bromine from salt brines depends on the oxidation of the bromide ion to the free element by chlorine. In the process used by the Ethyl-Dow Chemical Company in North Carolina and Texas 150,000 gallons of sea water are stored where they will be warmed by the sun. The sea water is then pumped into a plant, rendered acid with sulphuric acid to prevent reaction between chlorine and water, and finally chlorine is admitted to displace bromine according to the reaction:

$$Cl_2 + 2NaBr \longrightarrow 2NaCl + Br_2 \uparrow .$$

Ninety-seven per cent of the bromine content is liberated, and the spent sea water is discharged into an adjacent river. The bromine-laden air passes into towers where it is absorbed by sodium carbonate to form sodium bromide, $NaBr$, and sodium bromate, $NaBrO_3$. This mixture may be treated later with sulphuric acid to liberate bromine.

PROPERTIES OF BROMINE

Atomic number	35
Atomic weight	79.916
Stable isotopes	79, 81
Density (g./ml.) liq., 20°C.	3.12
Melting point, °C.	—7.2
Boiling point, °C.	58.7
Critical temperature, °C.	302
Solubility (g./100 ml. H$_2$O) 20°C.	3.58
Specific heat (cal./g.) liq., 13-45°C.	0.107

Properties. Bromine is a dark-red, heavy liquid with a disagreeable odor. It irritates the eyes and mucous membranes and, in contact with the skin, produces lesions which heal with difficulty. Chemically less active than chlorine, it combines with both metals and nonmetals. It acts as a bleach and oxidizing agent, displacing iodine from a water solution of iodides. In turn, bromine is displaced from bromides by chlorine and fluorine which are more active.

Uses and Compounds. By far the largest use of bromine in industry is in the form of ethylene dibromide, $C_2H_4Br_2$. Each gallon of leaded gasoline contains about 2 ml. of ethylene dibromide to react with the lead and prevent it from pitting the engine cylinders. Other important bromine compounds are silver bromide in photographic emulsions, sodium and potassium bromides used in medicine as sedatives, and organic halogen derivatives.

Hydrogen Bromide. Hydrogen bromide, HBr, is a colorless gas at room temperature. It is readily formed by direct combination of hydrogen and bromine. The laboratory preparation is the hydrolysis of phosphorus tribromide, in which phosphorous acid is also formed.

$$PBr_3 + 3\,H_2O \longrightarrow H_3PO_3 + 3\,HBr$$

Treating a bromide with concentrated sulphuric acid produces sulphur dioxide and bromine and, therefore, is not a practical preparation method. Like all hydrogen halide gases, hydrogen bromide fumes in contact with moisture. It is very soluble in water (about 500 volumes of HBr dissolve in 1 of H_2O), forming a constant-boiling mixture which boils at $120°C.$ and whose composition is 47 per cent HBr. Anhydrous HBr does not react with metals or with carbonates; neither do its solutions in nonassociating solvents, such as benzene or toluene. In water solution, however, reaction is rapid, even the more electronegative metals, such as mercury, being attacked by HBr in the presence of nitric acid.

Bromides. The preparation of bromides by direct synthesis from the elements is difficult because an oxide layer forms on the metal, preventing further action. Powdered antimony ignites when sprinkled into moist bromine, but in dry bromine the metal remains untarnished for many years. Insoluble halides may be obtained as precipitates by double displacement reactions in aqueous solutions, for example, the formation of silver bromide by the reaction between solutions of sodium bromide and silver nitrate:

$$NaBr + AgNO_3 \longrightarrow AgBr\downarrow + NaNO_3$$

Alkali bromides, such as potassium bromide (KBr), may be prepared by reacting ferrous bromide, made by reaction of free bromine and iron, with an alkali carbonate.

$$FeBr_2 + K_2CO_3 \longrightarrow FeCO_3 + 2\,KBr$$

Anhydrous halides of the tetravalent metals, such as that of tin ($SnBr_4$), are produced only in a dry way, because hydrolysis otherwise occurs. All metallic bromides are solids; most of the nonmetallic bromides are liquids or gases. Bromides are usually soluble in water, except those of heavy metals—silver, copper, lead, platinum. Cupric bromide is a black solid; cobalt bromide, brilliant green; nickel bromide, yellow. The alkali bromides volatilize at high temperatures without decomposition; higher bromides decompose on heating. Under the influence of light, yellowish silver bromide becomes greenish, but it is less light sensitive than the iodide. A number of double salts containing bromine are known, such as cesium zinc bromide, $CsZnBr_2$. Bromides of the tervalent metals, such as aluminum, usually crystallize as hexahydrates containing six molecules of water of hydration, but the hydrate, $AlBr_3 \cdot 16H_2O$, has been obtained. Several tribromides are known, as $CsBr_3$, as are a number of double halide salts, such as $CsIBr_2$ and $CsClBr_2$. The latter are unstable.

Oxides and Oxyacids. Two oxides of bromine, Br_2O and BrO_2, have been prepared, but both are unstable. There are three oxyacids: hypobromous, bromous, and bromic acids. Bromous acid, $HBrO_2$, has been prepared only momentarily. Hypobromous acid, HBrO, and bromic acid, $HBrO_3$, are well known. Pure bromic acid, however, has not been made since its concentrated solutions decompose, giving free bromine and oxygen. If bromine is added to cold dilute potassium hydroxide, potassium hypobromite (KBrO) is formed; with hot solution, the product is potassium bromate ($KBrO_3$). Bromine oxyacids are powerful oxidizing agents useful in industry and analytical chemistry.   H. N. A.

BRONK, DETLEV WULF (1897-   ), American physiologist and biophysicist, was born in New York City, Aug. 13, 1897. In 1920 he was graduated from Swarthmore College where he studied electrical engineering. He received the M.S. and Ph.D. degrees from the University of Michigan. The Ph.D. was granted in 1926, his dissertation being concerned with the electrical properties of the salivary glands. After teaching at Pennsylvania and Michigan universities, he joined the faculty of Swarthmore in 1924, advancing from instructor to professor of physiology and biophysics and serving as dean of men (1927-1929). From 1929 to 1949 he was professor of biophysics and director of the Johnson Research Foundation at the University of Pennsylvania and did most of his major work. He has studied in great detail the nature of sensation, body movement control, the chemical excitation of nerves, nerve impulses and their mechanism, and electrochemical methods of measuring oxygen consumption in nerve fibers. The electrochemical aspects of biological processes have been a major interest of his.

Bronk was co-ordinator of research for the U.S. Army Air Force in World War II and was concerned with the physiological aspects of high-altitude flying. In 1949 he became president of Johns Hopkins University, where he tried to bridge the gap between undergraduate and graduate study, emphasizing the progress of the individual student rather than classroom hours. Since 1953 he has been president of the Rockefeller Institute of Medical Research. Bronk has received many honorary degrees, including the D.Sc. from Swarthmore (1937), Princeton (1947), Northwestern (1948), Pennsylvania (1949), Harvard (1953), and Yale (1955); the LL.D. from Temple (1951), New York University (1951), and Notre Dame (1953); the Eng.D. from the University of Cincinnati (1951); and the D.Med.Sc. from the Women's Medical College of Pennsylvania. He has served as advisor to the U.S. Atomic Energy Commission, the National Bureau of Standards, the Air Force, and the Army. He is a trustee of the Woods Hole Oceanographic Institution, Marine Biological Laboratory, Sloan-Kettering Institute, Rockefeller Foundation, Johns Hopkins University, and the University of Pennsylvania.   A. D. D.

BRONTË [brɒ'nti], the family name of three English novelists, the younger daughters of Patrick Brontë, a clergyman born in Ireland, and his wife Maria Branwell. The three daughters were all born at Thornton, in Yorkshire, Charlotte on Apr. 21, 1816, Emily Jane on Aug. 20, 1818, and Anne on Mar. 25, 1820. When Mrs. Brontë died in 1821, her sister Elizabeth Branwell was called to the parsonage at Haworth, where the family had moved in June 1820, to look after the six children, but since neither she nor their father spent much time with them, they were left free to indulge their fantasies, to invent their own games and imaginary kingdoms, and to read and write as they pleased. Charlotte alone is said to have composed some twenty-three "novels" before she was fifteen. With their sisters Maria and Elizabeth she and Emily entered the new school for clergymen's daughters at Cowan Bridge, later described by Charlotte in *Jane Eyre* as "Lowood," but upon the early deaths of the older girls, allegedly from the rigors of the none too prosperous school, Charlotte and Emily were withdrawn to Haworth. In 1831 Charlotte was sent to Miss Wooler's school at Roe Head, Dewsbury,

COURTESY OF THE METROPOLITAN MUSEUM OF ART

ANNE BRONTË WITH HER SISTERS EMILY AND CHARLOTTE

FROM A PAINTING IN THE LONDON
NATIONAL PORTRAIT GALLERY

where she remained only a year before returning home to supervise the younger children, but in 1836 she again returned to Miss Wooler, this time as governess, and Emily, and later Anne, accompanied her as pupils. By 1839 the sisters were all together again at Haworth, but they were all in precarious health, sorely in need of income, and much troubled by the profligacy of their brother Branwell.

With a school of their own in mind, Charlotte and Emily now decided to study foreign languages in Brussels under the tutelage of Constantin Héger, and though a legacy from their aunt, whose illness and death had recalled them to Haworth, freed them from this immediate necessity, Charlotte accepted an offer to return to the Pensionnat Héger as an instructor and remained there until early in 1844. She then proposed to Emily that they take pupils in the parsonage, but since the two girls met with no encouragement in their search for pupils, they cast about for other means to supplement their income.

In 1846, pooling their poetic compositions, the three sisters published, at their own expense, *Poems by Currer, Ellis, and Acton Bell;* 19 of these poems were by Charlotte, 21 by Emily, and 21 by Anne. The superiority of the more passionate and enigmatic Emily was clearly recognized by the other sisters, but the public was indifferent to all of them alike, and only two copies of the book were sold. Undaunted, the sisters now turned to fiction, and indeed, each had already completed a novel; Charlotte had written *The Professor,* a book based on her experiences in Brussels; Emily had done *Wuthering Heights;* and Anne had finished her *Agnes*

Grey. None of the sisters had as yet found a publisher, however, and it was only with the acceptance and instantaneous success of *Jane Eyre* in 1847 that the way was paved for the publication of the novels of Charlotte's sisters. Charlotte did not have long to relish her literary success, for in 1848 her life was overcast by a series of family misfortunes which by June 1849 left her the sole survivor of the six unusual Brontë children. Branwell died in September 1848 after a disastrous career of intemperance and scandal. Emily followed a few months later, on Dec. 19, and within six months, on May 26, 1849, Anne, whose second novel, *The Tenant of Wildfell Hall,* had appeared in 1848, had also succumbed. Resuming her literary labors, Charlotte nevertheless completed and saw published in October 1849 her novel *Shirley,* which drew on her experiences at Miss Wooler's and on the character of her sister Emily; this she followed in 1853 with *Villette,* which is considered by many her most important book after *Jane Eyre.* In the interval between these two works she had won wide recognition and the friendship of many leading literary figures, notably Mrs. Gaskell, whose *Life of Charlotte Brontë* is still the basic biography of its subject. In 1854 Charlotte was married to her father's curate, Arthur Bell Nicholls, but she did not long survive this event and died of a childbirth illness on Mar. 31, 1855.   H. M. J.

BRONX, THE, the fourth of New York City's five boroughs in population and size, covers an area of 42 sq. mi. It is coextensive with Bronx County, established in 1914 by the State of New York. With the exception of the Borough of Manhattan, which is represented by Marble Hill, a small residential section, the Bronx is the only borough lying in any part on the mainland. It occupies the Y formed by the East and Harlem rivers directly north of Manhattan, from which it is separated by the United States Ship Canal, the Harlem River, and Spuyten Duyvil Creek. The two boroughs are linked by three subways and 14 bridges (the most modern are the Henry Hudson and the Triborough). High Bridge, built between 1839 and 1848, is the oldest span in the city and carries part of Manhattan's piped water supply. The Bronx-Whitestone and Triborough bridges connect the Bronx and Queens. Highways which run northward across the Bronx to Westchester County are the Bronx River, Hutchinson River, and Sawmill River parkways.

Several islands form part of the Bronx. The most important are Riker's Island, which houses the city's model penitentiary; City Island, a beach and boating center; and Hart's Island. Three worn foothills of the Berkshires divide the borough in a northeast-southwest direction. One ridge cuts across Riverdale; the second extends from Van Cortlandt Park to Macombs Dam Bridge, roughly paralleling the Harlem. The Grand Concourse, a tree-lined boulevard, follows its crest. The third lies east of the Bronx River.

History. In 1641 a Scandinavian named Jonas Bronk, or Bronck, acquired 500 acres between the Harlem River and the Aquahung, a stream which became known as Bronk's River, and in this way gave his name to the region. English settlers followed Bronk into the area. Mrs. Anne Hutchinson fled to Pelham's Neck in 1643 to escape from religious prosecution in Boston and Providence. At about the same time John Throgmorton settled at Throg's Neck at the most southeasterly point of the Bronx. In 1646 Adrien van der Donck, a lawyer who became a patroon, acquired a tract of land, extending eight mi. north of Spuyten Duyvil, on which he built a farmhouse. In spite of trouble with the Indians, a permanent community was established. The British colonists were farmers, and the Bronx remained farming country until the

1850's. At that time there were 8,032 inhabitants. By 1860, as the result of an influx of German and Italian immigrants, the population had nearly tripled. In 1874 the townships of Kingsbridge, West Farms, and Morrisania, until then under the control of Westchester County, were absorbed by New York City. In 1895 the entire section east of the Bronx River was also transferred to the city. This area included Throg's Neck, Unionport, Westchester, Williamsbridge, Bronxdale, Olinville, Baychester, Eastchester, Wakefield, and Bartow. In 1898 these towns were merged into the Borough of the Bronx under the Greater New York Charter. The Bronx then had a population of 200,000, but, as the elevated railroads were extended northward and residents of Manhattan began moving to less crowded areas, this number was greatly increased.

Administration. The government of the Bronx, like that of the other four boroughs of New York City, is headed by a borough president whose principal duties are concerned solely with the maintenance of the borough; however, as a member of the Board of Estimate of the City of New York, the city's most important governing body, he exercises one vote in the administration of its affairs.

Higher Education. Among the institutions of higher education in the borough are Fordham University, which occupies a 75-acre campus adjoining Bronx Park and houses the country's leading seismological laboratory; the Bronx Center of Hunter College, a municipally owned, tuition-free college of liberal arts; Manhattan College, a college of liberal arts and technological school in Spuyten Duyvil; the New York State Maritime Academy; and, on University Heights, the College of Arts and Sciences, the College of Engineering, and the Hall of Fame of New York University. Dedication ceremonies of the Albert Einstein College of Medicine of Yeshiva University, planned as a part of a $100,000,000 medical center, were held in October 1955. Although it was founded under Jewish auspices, the new school is non-denominational.

Parks. An area of 5,588 acres in the Bronx has been set aside for recreational and educational purposes. This is the largest percentage of park land in the five boroughs, and of this total Pelham Bay Park accounts for one third. Bronx Park, which lies on both sides of the Bronx River, covers 719 acres of hilly, wooded land and includes a virgin forest of 3,000 hemlocks. The Museum of the Botanical Garden, at the northern end of the park, contains the largest combined horticultural and botanical library in the country. The New York Zoological Garden, usually known as the Bronx Zoo, is situated in Bronx Park and is also the largest of its kind in the country. It houses more than 1,000 species of wild and rare animals, some of which roam freely in a replica of the African veld, separated from the spectators only by a broad moat. In the Children's Zoo, young people may play with domesticated animals. Van Cortlandt Park was given to the city in 1899 by a descendant of the Van Cortlandt family, who owned the land in early colonial times. The Van Cortlandt Mansion, built in 1748 and now a museum in the park, is one of the finest examples of New York's remaining colonial houses. Here, George Washington and General Rochambeau, commander of the French forces who fought alongside the American colonists in the Revolutionary War, were entertained. The park contains a lake, gardens, a forest, golf links, and tennis courts.

Points of Interest. From 1846 to 1849 a small white wooden building, in what is now known as Poe Park, was the home of Edgar Allan Poe. New York University's Hall of Fame is a well-known point of interest. The Yankee Stadium,

home ground of the New York Yankees baseball club, is also in the Bronx. The Bronx County Court is an imposing building of neoclassic design.

Industry. The principal industrial plants of the Bronx, located along the East and Harlem rivers, produce clothing, textiles, chemicals, electrical machinery, furniture, glass, leather, lumber, and paper. Shipbuilding, food processing, and metal working are among the important occupations. Pop. 1950, 1,451,277.

S. D. M.

BRONXVILLE, a residential village, 1 sq. mi. in area, in Westchester Co., New York, is situated on the Bronx River, 15 mi. northwest of New York City. It was incorporated in 1898 and is governed by a mayor and board of trustees, who although elected officials, serve without remuneration. Only the village administrator is a salaried employee. Bronxville is the seat of Sarah Lawrence College, a college of liberal arts for women, and Concordia College Institute, a junior college affiliated with the Lutheran Church. Pop. 1950, 6,778.

BRONZE. *See* BRASSES AND BRONZES.

BRONZE AGE, the second of the three technological stages recognized by Old World archaeologists, one in which bronze had replaced flint and stone as the chief material for weapons and tools. Actually the discovery that copper could be hardened through the addition of tin to form a bronze alloy was secondary to the more fundamental one that moldable metal could be produced from copper ore. Whether standard bronze, having about one part of tin to nine of copper, was used in any particular region depended mainly on the availability of tin and it was possible, for instance, for a complex civilization to flourish in Egypt on a basis of copper. *See also* ARCHAEOLOGY.

J. G. D. C.

BRONZINO, IL [brondzi'no] (1503-1572), Italian painter also known as Agnolo or Angiolo di Cosimo, sometimes referred to as Angelo Allori (actually the name of his best known pupil), was born on Nov. 17, 1503, at Montecelli, near Florence. In 1530 he was commissioned to do some work at Pesaro, but returned in two years to Florence. A pupil of Jacopo da Pontormo, Bronzino typified in his style the height of Mannerism. In his works the picture space is crowded, and organized in formal patterns in layers without real space, with strongly emphasized verticals and crossing diagonals. The proportions of the figures are artificially elongated, the modeling hard and sculpturesque. These characteristics are seen in the *Pietà* and *Christ in Limbo* (both in the Uffizi Gallery, Florence). The literary and theoretical turn of mind typical of the period is reflected in Bronzino's representation of complicated allegorical subjects such as *Venus, Cupid, Folly and Time* (National Gallery, London). In his portraits, notably in the Uffizi *Eleonora di Toledo and Son, Young Man with Lute,* and *Bartolommeo Panciatichi,* he makes a thorough application of the Mannerist aesthetic formula of decorative and formal elegance. Distinctive of his style are the abstractness of characterization, the care and precision of execution, and the reserved, aristocratic types, many of which represent members of the Medici family, to whom Bronzino served as court painter after 1539. He died in Florence, Nov. 23, 1572.

M. C.

BROOK, ALEXANDER (1898-), American painter, was born in Brooklyn, N. Y., July 4, 1898. He studied at Pratt Institute, Brooklyn, and in 1915 at the Art Students'

League, New York, under John C. Johansen, George Bridgman, and Kenneth H. Miller; he later taught at the League and elsewhere. From 1924 to 1927 Brook was assistant director of the Whitney Studio Club; in 1943 he went to Panama and the Caribbean as an artist-correspondent.

Brook is primarily a figure and portrait painter. Though he works in the Naturalistic tradition, he handles his subjects with warm sympathy. Among his works are *Stormy Pastures, Peggy, Raphael Soyer, Georgia Jungle,* which was awarded a $1,000 prize by the Carnegie Institute in 1939, and a portrait of the artist, George Biddle.   E. B. S.

BROOKE, ALAN FRANCIS, 1st VISCOUNT ALANBROOKE [brʊ'k] (1883–   ), British soldier, was born in Bagnéres-de-Bigorre, France, on July 23, 1883.

ALAN FRANCIS BROOKE,
VISCOUNT ALANBROOKE

INTERNATIONAL NEWS PHOTO

He was educated at the Royal Military Academy at Woolwich, England, and in 1902 he was assigned to the Royal Field Artillery. He served in the south of Ireland, was transferred to India in 1906, and was assigned to the Royal Horse Artillery in 1909.

At the outbreak of World War I, Brooke went from India to France, landing at Marseille in September 1914 in command of an ammunition column. He served as an artillery officer during the war and was the originator of the effective barrage map for controlling artillery fire over a wide area, using any number of guns without waste or unnecessary overlap.

He attended the Staff College at Camberly, 1919 and 1923-1927, and was commandant of the School of Artillery, 1929-1932; instructor at the Imperial Defense College, 1932-1934; commander of the Eighth Infantry Brigade, 1934-1935; inspector of Royal Artillery, 1935-1936; director of military training, 1936-1937; commander of a mobile division, 1937-1938; and commander of antiaircraft, 1938-1939. In May 1940, after the outbreak of World War II, Brooke, with the Second Army Corps, British Expeditionary Force, went to France, and by his skill and leadership enabled the British forces to escape encirclement after the Belgian Army ceased fighting. He retired to Dunkerque and was among the last to leave that port for England. In June 1941 Brooke was appointed Chief of the Imperial General Staff, and served until his retirement in 1946. He was made a Field Marshal in 1944. Brooke is regarded as one of Great Britain's experts on mechanization. In 1945 he was created first Baron Alanbrooke of Brookeborough, and the following year received a knighthood and was raised to first Viscount Alanbrooke. He was commander of the parade at the coronation ceremonies for Queen Elizabeth II in 1953.   W. E. A.

BROOKE or **BROKE, ARTHUR** (d. 1563), an English writer who, in 1562, published a verse translation of Matteo Bandello's story of Romeo and Juliet, *The Tragicall Historye of Romeus and Julieit,* which served Shakespeare as the main source for his tragedy. Brooke's poem was released in 1908.

BROOKE, DOROTHEA, the central character in George Eliot's *Middlemarch* (1872). Disappointed and disillusioned in her marriage to the scholar Casaubon, who dies, Dorothea finds fulfillment in marrying Ladislaw, a man of integrity.   G. G. F.

BROOKE, HENRY (c. 1703-1783), Irish author, was born in Raūtavan about 1703. He was educated at Trinity College, Dublin, and studied law in London before returning to practice in Ireland. Subsequently he twice went to England in search of literary fame and there made the acquaintance of Pope, Swift, and Garrick. While he was in London Brooke wrote a philosophical poem, *Universal Beauty* (1735), and a tragedy, *Gustavus Vasa, the Deliverer of His Country* (1739), which was banned from the stage for its supposed references to Walpole; he then retired to Ireland, where he wrote various political pamphlets and a satirical opera. His best work is a novel, *The Fool of Quality* (1765-1770), which describes the Rousseauistic education of a young nobleman. He died Oct. 10, 1783, in Dublin, after a period of mental debility.   F. B. E.

BROOKE, RUPERT (1887-1915), English poet, was born on Aug. 3, 1887, at Rugby School, where his father was a master. Brooke entered Rugby in 1901 and soon distinguished himself as athlete, student, and poet. In 1906 he went to Cambridge, where he deeply impressed his college friends with his talents, charm, and good looks, and where he continued to write much verse, little of which he preserved. After taking his degree in 1909, he spent three years near Cambridge, studying and writing, with occasional visits to London and the Continent. Late in 1911 he published his *Poems.* In 1913 he traveled to the South Seas and spent three happy months at Tahiti, writing poems inspired by the life of the island. He returned to England in June 1914, accepted Winston Churchill's offer of a naval commission at the outbreak of war, and, after short service in the Antwerp expedition, sailed for the Dardanelles. At the Greek island of Skyros he was taken ill with blood poisoning, and on April 23, 1915, he died. A second volume of *Poems* was posthumously published, and in 1918 appeared *The Collected Poems of Rupert Brooke,* with a memoir by Edward Marsh. When Brooke died he was still searching for a poetic manner and style uniquely his own, but he had already achieved poems of genuine distinction and force, the most famous being his sonnet *The Soldier.*   L. A. C.

BROOKE, STOPFORD AUGUSTUS (1832-1916), Irish critic and clergyman, was born in Donegal, Nov. 14, 1832. After completing his education at Trinity College, Dublin, he was ordained in 1857 and attracted large congregations. Later, he acted as chaplain to the Empress Frederick from 1863 to 1865 and was appointed chaplain in ordinary to Queen Victoria in 1872, but as a liberal, he chafed under prevailing conditions and seceded from the Church of England in 1880 to become a Unitarian. Brooke published sermons, theological studies, and controversial writings, but his best books, mostly written after his retirement from preaching in 1894, are concerned with literary criticism. These include *Tennyson, His Art and Relation to Modern Life* (1894), *The Poetry of Robert Browning* (1902), *On Ten Plays of Shakespeare* (1905), *Studies in Poetry* (1907), and *Naturalism in English Poetry* (1920). Brooke died in Surrey on Mar. 18, 1916.　　　　　　　　　　　　W. C. He.

BROOK FARM. *See* COMMUNITIES, CO-OPERATIVE.

BROOKFIELD, a residential village in northeastern Illinois, is located in Cook Co., 11 mi. from Chicago, of which it is a suburb. It is served by the Chicago, Burlington & Quincy Railroad. Brookfield, founded in 1892 and incorporated as a village in 1904, has the council-manager form of government. The Chicago Zoological Gardens, known as the Brookfield Zoo, are located in the village. Pop. 1950, 15,472.

BROOKFIELD, a city in Linn Co., northern Missouri, is situated about 25 mi. east of Chillicothe. It is served by the Chicago, Burlington & Quincy Railroad. Brookfield was founded in 1859 and incorporated in 1868. It is located in the Lafayette coal field region, where shoes and railroad-shop products are manufactured. It has the city manager form of government. Pop. 1950, 5,810.

BROOKHAVEN, the seat of Lincoln Co. in southwestern Mississippi, is 126 mi. north of New Orleans. It is served by the Illinois Central and the Mississippi Central railroads. The district produces livestock, poultry, cotton, corn, sugar cane, peanuts, truck crops, peaches, and pecans. Local industries produce petroleum, lumber, wood pulp, wire cloth, condensers, lawn mowers, brick and tile, clothing, and cottonseed oil. The city is governed by a mayor and council. Pop. 1950, 7,801.

BROOKINGS, the seat of Brookings Co. in eastern South Dakota, is situated near the Sioux River about 50 mi. north of Sioux Falls. It is served by the Chicago and North Western Railroad and by two national air lines at its own airport. Settled in 1870 and incorporated as a city in 1883, it is governed by a commission. Brookings is the seat of South Dakota State College of Agriculture and Mechanical Arts. It is a shipping point for the area's grains and wool and manufactures cleaning and testing equipment, hybrid seeds, and cement blocks. Pop. 1950, 7,764.

BROOKINGS INSTITUTION, THE, a nonprofit corporation organized for scientific and educational purposes and devoted to the public interest. Its objects, as stated in the institution's charter, are "to promote, carry on, conduct, and foster scientific research, education, training and publication in the broad fields of economics, government administration, and the political and social sciences generally . . . without regard to and independently of the special interests of any group in the body politic, either political, social or economic." The reports of its studies are published as books or pamphlets. The institution also advances study in the social sciences by granting research fellowships to specially qualified graduates of leading universities.

The institution had its inception in a group of distinguished citizens, including university presidents, professional men, and business leaders, who were convinced that the success

of democracy depended upon the increase of efficiency in government administration and the broadening of popular understanding of fundamental economic problems. Robert S. Brookings, a St. Louis businessman, who retired in middle life to devote himself and his fortune to the public interest, was largely responsible for the development of the institution which the trustees named in his honor.

The basic income of the institution is derived from its endowment, contributed largely by Mr. and Mrs. Brookings, and also from other gifts. Annual and special grants have been received from various foundations.

Although it has made numerous studies of Federal Government problems, the institution is not in any way connected with the Government and receives no subsidy from it. Likewise, studies dealing with industrial, financial, labor, and agricultural problems have always been carried out with its regular funds. A definite policy of making no investigations on a commercial basis has been maintained.

The economic studies have pertained to both national and international problems. The studies in government have been concerned primarily with public administration. Throughout its history the institution has rendered important direct services to the Federal Government upon request.

Headquarters are in Washington, D. C.　　　M. A. R.

BROOKLINE [brʊ'klain], a residential town in eastern Massachusetts, on the Charles River, 4 mi. southwest of Boston, of which it is a suburb. Until its incorporation as a town in 1705, the community was a part of Boston known as Muddy River Hamlet. Brookline is the largest community in the state governed by the limited town meeting plan. Portions of the residential districts of Chestnut Hill and Longwood and many beautiful homes, including that of Amy Lowell, American poet, are within the town limits. Industries include stone making and the manufacture of automobile bodies, electrical equipment, scientific instruments, boxes and furniture, greeting cards, shades, pottery, and jewelry. Brookline is the seat of Archbishop Cushing and Staley colleges. Pop. 1950, 57,589.

BROOKLYN [brʊ'klɪn], the largest in population of the five boroughs of the City of New York, and the second in area, covers about 81 sq. mi. of southwestern Long Island in the southeastern part of the state of New York. The boundaries of Brooklyn are conterminous with those of Kings County; it is separated by the East River from the borough of Manhattan; by New York Bay from New Jersey and Staten Island (Richmond); and by Rockaway Inlet and Jamaica Bay from the Rockaways. Newtown Creek forms part of the boundary separating it from Queens.

History. The Walloons, who settled in the northwestern section of the present borough of Brooklyn, were the first to buy land in the area. William A. Bennet and Jacques Bentyn purchased 930 acres of land from the Indians in Gowanus, in the southwest portion of Long Island, in 1636; in the following year Joris Jansen de Rapelje obtained a grant of land and settled north of Gowanus, near Wall-boght (Wallabout Bay) with his wife, who became known as the "Mother of Brooklyn." In 1640 the first English settlers arrived at Gravesend (named for the English city of Gravesend), on the southwest coast of Long Island, which included present-day Coney Island. In 1642 a ferry service from Long Island to New Amsterdam (Manhattan) was instituted. In 1643 Lady Deborah Moody and her followers settled at Gravesend after having been expelled from the Puritan Church in Massachusetts. On May 7, 1654, the residents obtained a release of the territory of "Gravesend Nec" and "Conyne Island" from the Canarsee Indians. In 1645 the Dutch established Brueckelen (named for a village in Holland), in the area between Wallboght and Gowanus, and in the following year it was granted local officers. In 1661 Peter Stuyvesant laid out Boswyck (Bushwick), and in the same year the first free public school in the area was opened. By 1664, when the English assumed control of the area, the villages of Midwout (Flatbush), New Ameersfoort (Flatlands), Gowanus, New Utrecht, Bedford, Williamsburg, and Rood Hoek (Red Hook) had been established, the whole area being part of the province of New Netherlands. During the Revolutionary War the British held Long Island, and there were several skirmishes in the area which is today Brooklyn. The Battle of Long Island, considered one of the decisive battles of the Revolution, was fought on Aug. 27, 1776, in the area now known as Brooklyn Heights and Prospect Park.

While the residents of Dutch descent farmed inland, those of British descent who had settled in Manhattan built slaughter houses and tanneries along the waterfront. The busiest section was that surrounding the ferry landing at Wallabout Bay, where a market had been established for the local farm produce. In 1816, when this district, in the vicinity of what is now Hoyt and Fulton streets, was incorporated as the village of Brooklyn, it had an estimated population of 4,000 and an area of 1 sq. mi., and had been known at different times as Breuckelen, Brookland, Brocklin, and Brookline. In 1834 Brooklyn was chartered as a city, absorbing twenty-five outlying villages. Each village retained its original name, as have the other communities since merged with the city. Industries developed rapidly following the chartering of Brooklyn as a city, but its prosperity received a severe setback in the disastrous fire of 1848, which destroyed large portions of the city. In 1855 the town of Bushwick and the city of Williamsburg were merged with Brooklyn. Communications with Manhattan were greatly facilitated after 1883 when the famous Brooklyn Bridge, designed by John A. Roebling, and constructed by his son Washington A. Roebling, was completed. In 1896 Brooklyn was made co-extensive with Kings County. Ever since its incorporation as a city Brooklyn had fought against losing its "independence" by a merger with New York; but commercial and industrial interests made such a merger highly desirable, and in 1898 Brooklyn became a part of the City of New York, with the status of a borough. Communications between Manhattan and Brooklyn were further improved with the opening of the Williamsburg Bridge in 1904 and the Manhattan Bridge in 1909.

Borough Administration. The Borough of Brooklyn is governed in common with the other four boroughs comprising the City of New York by a mayor and city council. Its internal administration, like that of the other boroughs, is headed by a borough president, who is elected for a four-year term and whose duties are primarily concerned with the maintenance of the borough. The borough president is also a member of the New York City Board of Estimate, a municipal governing body. The presidents of Manhattan and Brooklyn have two votes each on the board; those of the other three boroughs, one each.

Notable Buildings. The large Brooklyn Civic Center, a $25,000,000 project, covers an extensive area surrounding Borough Hall, a white marble structure begun in 1835 and completed in 1850. Also important are the American Red Cross Building, the Transit Authority Building, the Domestic Relations Court, a Welfare Center, and the War Memorial. The Supreme Court, Cadman Plaza Park, and a City Prison and Remand Shelter are other structures. East

of Borough Hall are the Kings County Courthouse, with its marble facade, Corinthian portico, and iron dome over 100 ft. high, and the Municipal Building and Hall of Records. Buildings of historic interest include those of Erasmus Hall High School which opened as a private school in 1787; the Flatbush Dutch Reformed Church, built about 1794; the Lefferts House in Prospect Park, built about 1777. Ebbets Field, the home of the former Brooklyn Dodgers baseball team for many years, was built in 1913 in the Flatbush section of the borough. The team transferred its franchise to Los Angeles after the 1957 season.

Education and Culture. Brooklyn's public schools comprise over one third of the schools of New York City. Its institutions of higher learning include Brooklyn College (one of the four branches of the municipal College of the City of New York), Brooklyn Law School, St. John's University, Pratt Institute, Long Island University, The Polytechnic Institute of Brooklyn, and St. Joseph's College for Women. The Long Island College of Medicine, which is located in the borough and which became part of the University of the State of New York in July 1947, is affiliated with eleven hospitals in the borough: the Long Island College, Kings County, Methodist, Greenpoint, Kensington Avenue, Brooklyn Eye and Ear, Maimonides, and Jewish hospitals, the Brooklyn State Hospital for Mental Disease, and the House of St. Giles the Cripple. The college is also affiliated with the Red Hook-Gowanus Health Center, which functions as a clinic.

Brooklyn has maintained a cultural life separate from that of Greater New York but yet integrated with it. Famous musicians and orchestras appear regularly at the Brooklyn Academy of Music and the borough has its own symphony orchestra. The borough's museums include the Brooklyn Museum and the Children's Museum, both units of the Brooklyn Institute of Arts and Sciences, and the Long Island Historical Society. The Brooklyn Public Library is notable for its modern central (Ingersoll) building, its business reference library, and 47 branches.

Parks. There are 5,238 acres of land devoted to park areas. Marine Park, located near Jamaica Bay, comprises 1,822 acres and is the largest. Prospect Park, the second largest, contains a zoo, playing fields, a lake, Lefferts House, and numerous statues and monuments commemorating noted people and events in United States history. On Lookout Hill stands a shaft honoring the soldiers who defended the rear of the American army at the Battle of Long Island (Aug. 27, 1776). At one of the main entrances to the park is the Grand Army Plaza with the Soldiers' and Sailors' Memorial Arch. Bordering Prospect Park, but not a part of it, is the Brooklyn Botanic Garden. The garden is famous for its horticultural exhibits, its rose garden, and Japanese cherry trees.

Beaches. Much of the Brooklyn shore along the Lower Bay is devoted to bathing and amusement facilities. Coney Island, known throughout the world, is the borough's most popular beach and amusement area. Among the other beaches are Brighton, Manhattan, and Sheepshead Bay.

Residences. Brooklyn is popularly called the "Borough of Churches" and the "Borough of Homes." There are more than 400 churches within the borough. Except for the north and northwestern waterfronts, which are highly industrialized, and the downtown business areas, Brooklyn is a residential city. The borough contains approximately 62,000 one-family houses, 201,200 two-family houses, and 551,000 apartment houses.

Military Installations. The United States Navy Yard, popularly known as the Brooklyn Navy Yard, was established in the Wallabout Bay area in 1801 and is one of the largest naval installations in the country, containing extensive shipbuilding and ship-repair yards, dry docks, a naval hospital, and other naval facilities. In 1930 New York City's first municipal airport, Floyd Bennett Field, was opened on the southern tip of the borough, on former Barren Island, in Jamaica Bay. A United States Naval Reserve unit occupied part of the field in 1938, and a naval station was commissioned there in 1941. In the latter year the navy purchased the field outright. The coast guard maintains installations in Brooklyn, and the chief army installations are Fort Hamilton, guarding the entrance to New York Harbor, and the Brooklyn Army Base.

Transportation. Brooklyn has transportation facilities linking it with all of the boroughs of New York City. The Brooklyn, Manhattan, and Williamsburg bridges connect it with Manhattan, and three subway systems supply transportation to Manhattan, the Bronx, and Queens. Ferry service is available to Staten Island (Richmond). The Brooklyn-Battery Tunnel, New York's longest tunnel, extends for 1.7 mi. from Battery Park in Manhattan under the East River to Hamilton Avenue in Brooklyn, where it joins the Belt Parkway, a 33-mi. network of parks and highways encircling Brooklyn and Queens. The Brooklyn Heights-Gowanus Parkway, a continuation of the Belt Parkway, and a part of the projected Brooklyn-Queens Expressway, was completed in 1951. This triple-deck parkway is an outstanding engineering feat: its top lane forms a pedestrian promenade, including parks, overlooking New York Harbor; the two lanes under the Brooklyn Heights cliff are for motor vehicles traveling in opposite directions. The parkway is designed to carry traffic from the Brooklyn Battery Tunnel, part of the way in sunken roadways, through the Borough Hall district and on to New England. In 1956 the New York State Legislature approved construction of a bridge connecting Brooklyn with Staten Island across the Narrows in New York Bay. Approximately 70 steamship freight lines use the borough's port facilities, and 14 trunk railroads provide freight facilities to the docks and the borough's industrial establishments. The only direct passenger rail service available in Brooklyn is supplied by the Long Island Rail Road, which connects the boroughs with communities on Long Island. Brooklyn's own airport, Floyd Bennett Field, serves mainly military and noncommercial traffic.

Commerce and Industry. The Borough of Brooklyn is a great maritime, industrial, and commercial center, ranking fifth in the United States as a manufacturing center. Clothes, shoes, textiles, chemicals, electrical machinery, typesetting equipment, lumber, glass, leather, metal, paper, transportation equipment, and foodstuffs are among the leading products of its highly diversified factory output. The borough is one of the chief spice markets in the world. Approximately 40 per cent of the commerce leaving New York City for foreign ports clears from Brooklyn's extensively developed waterfront. A series of huge shipping terminals, among them the New York Dock, Erie Basin, the Atlantic Basin, and Bush Terminal, line New York Bay and the East River. Bush Terminal on the bay is an industrial city in itself. A large international traffic in grain is maintained at Brooklyn, rendered possible not only by the local port facilities but by the availability of grain elevators. Approximately 80 per cent of the grain shipped from the metropolitan area is shipped from Brooklyn docks. In July 1955 the Port of New York Authority began a seven-year project to modernize the Brooklyn piers along the two-mile section from the Brooklyn Bridge to the Atlantic Basin. Brooklyn also has large areas devoted to its wholesale and retail trade. The

chief retail shopping area of the borough is located in the Borough Hall section. Pop. 1950, 2,738,175. S. D. M.

BROOKLYN, POLYTECHNIC INSTITUTE OF, an accredited, privately controlled technological school for men, is situated in Brooklyn, New York. The Institute was chartered as a preparatory school and college of liberal arts and engineering in 1854, and first instruction was offered in 1855. In 1889 the charter was amended to include a school of science and engineering. Undergraduate afternoon and evening courses were established in 1904, and graduate evening sessions were begun in 1925. The B.S. in chemistry, mathematics, and physics, bachelor degrees in chemical, civil, electrical, mechanical, metallurgical, and aeronautical engineering, the Master of Engineering, master in various engineering curricula, the M.S., and the Ph.D are conferred by the Institute. Options in plastics and nuclear engineering are allowed. The Institute operates the Polymer Bureau, the Microwave Research Institute, and the Aeronautical Research Laboratory.

There is a student loan fund, and undergraduate scholarship aid can be obtained. Graduate fellowships in substantial amounts are also available. There are no dormitories or dining-hall facilities. *For statistics see* COLLEGES AND UNIVERSITIES. W. L. McC.

BROOKLYN COLLEGE, an accredited, coeducational, publicly controlled college supported by New York City, located in the borough of Brooklyn on 42 acres of land. The institution was established in 1930 by combining the Brooklyn centers of City College and Hunter College. Divisions added later include courses for teachers, 1931; graduate work, 1935; and adult education, 1947. Degrees offered are A.B. and B.S. in liberal arts; B.S. in home economics, education, physical education, and health education; and the Master of Arts. In 1948 a five-year teachers education program, underwritten by the state of New York and leading to the Master of Arts degree, was established and opened to state residents. The diploma of Associate in Arts is offered, especially in evening sessions, in a two-year curriculum. Diplomas are also available for occupational training in accounting, banking and finance, civil service, and journalism. The adult education program was instituted in 1947 to reach local communities. Courses are given at the college, at libraries, and at other public buildings throughout the borough. Tuition is free to candidates for the baccalaureate degree. United States citizenship and residence in New York City are required for matriculation. There are no residence facilities, since most students live at home. A few scholarships are available to New York City residents. *For statistics see* COLLEGES AND UNIVERSITIES. J. R. To.

BROOKS, PHILLIPS (1835-1893), American Episcopalian minister, was born in Boston, Mass., Dec. 13, 1835. He was educated mainly at Harvard, where he later became a powerful religious influence. His first rectorate was in Philadelphia, where he remained from 1859 to 1869; his second, at Trinity Church, Boston, lasted until he became Bishop of Massachusetts in 1891. At Yale in 1877 Brooks delivered the Lyman Beecher *Lectures on Preaching,* probably the most influential work on the subject; here he defined preaching as "the bringing of truth through personality." In the pulpit he stressed the Incarnation of Christ and the brotherhood of man, always in the spirit of radiant optimism. He is known to later generations chiefly through his collected *Sermons* (ten vols., 1910), his Christmas hymn, *O Little*

Town of Bethlehem, and the biography by A. V. G. Allen, *Life and Letters of Phillips Brooks* (1901). Brooks had a nobility of character which places him in the forefront of American pastors. He died on Jan. 23, 1893, in Boston.

A. W. B.

BROOKS, ROBERT CLARKSON (1874-1941), American political scientist, was born in Piqua, Ohio, Feb. 7, 1874. He was graduated from the University of Indiana in 1896 and later studied at Cornell University and at Halle and Berlin universities in Germany. Brooks became professor of economics at Swarthmore College in 1904, was professor of political science at the University of Cincinnati from 1908 to 1912, and in the latter year returned to Swarthmore as Joseph Wharton professor of political science, a position he held until his death. His intense interest in practical politics was reflected in his works *Corruption in American Politics and Life* (1910) and *Political Parties and Electoral Problems* (1923). He favored a realistic approach to political science and had a deep respect for democracy. His admiration for the Swiss people and their government led to his *Government and Politics of Switzerland* (1918) and *Civic Training in Switzerland* (1930). As a result his work gained recognition in Switzerland as well as in this country and he was awarded an honorary doctorate by the University of Berne. In his last book, a more popular one, *Deliver Us from Dictators!* (1935), he again expressed his democratic convictions. An outstanding teacher and scholar, he was elected president of the American Political Science Association for the year 1940. Brooks died in Chester, Pa., Feb. 2, 1941.

J. R. P.

BROOKS, VAN WYCK (1886-), American critic and editor, was born Feb. 16, 1886, at Plainfield, N. J. After graduating from Harvard University in 1908, he traveled abroad, worked on editorial assignments, and published a first book, *The Wine of the Puritans* (1909). Brooks taught English for two years at Leland Stanford University before producing in *America's Coming of Age* (1915) and *Letters and Leadership* (1918) so incisive an analysis of the condition of American literature that he was recognized almost at once as an important critical voice. In these books, as in *The Ordeal of Mark Twain* (1920, 1933) and *The Pilgrimage of Henry James* (1925), Brooks charged that the acquisitive elements in American society had vitiated the native literature, and called for a social revolution which should bring thought into closer relation with life. In later books he turned to an exploration of the American literary past, most notably in the five-volume *Makers and Finders: A History of the Writers in America, 1800-1915,* which included *The Flowering of New England* (1936), *New England: Indian Summer* (1940), *The World of Washington Irving* (1944), *The Time of Melville and Whitman* (1947), and *The Confident Years: 1885-1915* (1952). Other volumes, such as *The Opinions of Oliver Allston* (1941) and *Essays Old and New* (1946), are more strictly in the critical tradition. Brooks was an editor of *The Freeman* (1920-1924), and helped to found *The American Caravan,* an anthology of experimental writing.

H. W. Bl.

BROOKS–BAXTER WAR, in the reconstruction of Arkansas, an episode growing out of the attempt of Joseph Brooks to oust Elisha Baxter from the governorship. In 1872, amid a confused riot of partisanship, Baxter, the candidate of the "regular" Republican Party, won the governorship by a majority of 3,000 over Brooks, who was supported by "reform" Republicans, Liberal Republicans, and Democrats. As governor, Baxter conciliated Democrats and won

their support but angered his own followers. Brooks obtained a court decision favoring his claim to the governorship, and in April 1874 seized the capitol, ousted Baxter, and proclaimed himself governor. The reconciled Democrats rallied to Baxter's support, while the disgruntled "regular" Republicans transferred their adherence to Brooks. Both sides appealed to Washington, and both armed their supporters. The Federal Government ordered the United States troops to Little Rock, Ark., to prevent bloodshed, and the Grant administration sought a compromise. Meanwhile, the state supreme court supported Brooks and the legislature upheld Baxter. On May 13, 1874, President Grant issued a proclamation sustaining Baxter as governor and ordering his opponents to disperse. Brooks surrendered the capitol, and the state transported the troops of both factions to their homes.

W. B. H.

BROOKS RANGE, formerly called the Endicott, or the Brooks-Endicott Range, is the extreme northwestern extension of the Rocky Mountains in Alaska. The Brooks Range is about 550 mi. long, and trends in an east-west direction, from the Richardson Mountains on the western side of the delta of the Mackenzie River, in northwestern Yukon Territory of Canada, across northern Alaska almost to Cape Lisburne on the Arctic Ocean. The Brooks Range separates the Arctic slope province on the north from the Yukon Basin on the south. The range is practically uninhabited and little known, but the eastern half of the range is much higher and more of an unbroken barrier than the western half, which is a hilly upland region. The Brooks Range is covered by snow for much of the year, and gives rise to the southwesterly flowing Koyukuk River and some smaller tributaries of the Yukon and Porcupine rivers. The largest river that drains northward is the Colville. It is possible to make an overland crossing of the Brooks Range from the vicinity of Bettles or Wiseman on the Upper Koyukuk to Barrow on the Arctic Ocean, but the trip is extremely arduous and seldom attempted. In 1885 the Range was named Endicott by Gen. H. T. Allen, but the name was changed to honor the geological work of A. H. Brooks.   J. E. F.

BROOM, *Cytisus,* a large group of spring-flowering plants of the pea family, mostly shrubby, rarely treelike, all native to the Old World. Several species and hybrids are grown in gardens. The flowers are yellow, white, or occasionally purple. Scotch broom, *C. scoparius,* native to Europe, is now naturalized in the United States, especially in California. It has erect, slender branches to 10 ft., small leaves, and profuse light yellow pealike flowers. Spanish broom, *Spartium junceum,* a European shrub of a closely allied genus, is cultivated in mild areas. The large yellow flowers are fragrant. Butcher's broom, *Ruscus aculeatus,* an evergreen shrub grown in Florida and California, belongs to the lily family. Members of the genus *Genista,* very similar to *Cytisus,* are also called broom.   J. C. Wis.

BROOM CORN, *Sorghum vulgare technicus,* is a close botanical relation of kafir, durra, and the syrup sorghums. It is a sturdy annual grass, with the seed borne in loose panicles on the ends of long straight branches, which constitute the brush for which the crop is grown. Standard varieties grow 10-15 ft. high, with brush 18-30 inches, mainly used for carpet brooms. Dwarf varieties grow 4-6 ft. with brush of 12-24 inches, which is used for whisk brooms. Well-colored brush can be obtained only when there is dry weather during the ripening season. The crop is therefore unprofitable wherever autumn rains occur, but is widely grown in

Oklahoma, Kansas, the Panhandle section of Texas and the central Mississippi Valley. Any soil suitable for maize is good for broom corn, and the preparation is the same, although the ground is harrowed several times before the crop is sown. This is usually done in late May or June when the ground is warm. Harvesting is usually done when the blooming season closes, as the ripening of the seed makes the brush brittle. The cut brush is hauled to sheds where the crop is threshed, the worthless parts removed, and the rest dried rapidly in the shade in order to avoid bleaching. When completely dry, the brush is baled for shipment in bales of 300-400 lbs. When broom corn grows until seed is produced, it is threshed and fed to hogs and chickens.

Figures for 1940 report 300,000 acres of broom corn grown in south central United States, which produced 40,000,000 tons of brush.

BROOM CORN PRODUCTION IN THE UNITED STATES
(10-Year Average, 1930-39)

	Acreage	Production (Tons)
United States (total)	324,000	41,260,000
Leading States:		
Oklahoma	132,000	15,050,000
Illinois	38,000	9,460,000
New Mexico	47,000	5,380,000
Colorado	49,000	4,540,000
Texas	25,000	3,630,000

C. K. H.

BROOMRAPE, *Orobanche,* low parasitic herbs of the Orobanchaceae family found in Europe and North Amer-

STANDARD OIL CO., N. Y.

Broom-corn field near San Antonio, Texas

COURTESY OF THE AMERICAN MUSEUM OF NATURAL HISTORY

Pale or naked broomrape, Thalesia uniflora

ica, which attach themselves to the roots of various plants. They have no leaves or chlorophyll. The numerous two-lipped yellow or purplish flowers are borne on sticky stems.
J. C. Wis.

BROTHERHOOD OF ST. ANDREW, an organization throughout the Anglican communion for the purpose of spreading Christ's Kingdom among men, especially young men and boys. It was founded in St. James' Church, Chicago, on St. Andrew's Day 1883, under the leadership of the rector, Rev. W. H. Hibbert, and Mr. James L. Houghteling, a Chicago banker. It has two rules, one of daily prayer for the extension of Christ's Kingdom among men and the other of service; obedience to the second rule obliges a member to make at least one earnest effort each week to lead some man nearer to Christ through his church.
L. C. L.

BROTHERS KARAMAZOV, THE [kɑ'rɑmɑ'zɔf], a Russian novel, by Fyodor Dostoyevsky, first published in 1880 with the title *Bratya Karamazovy*. It is one of the most profound psychological and philosophical novels of the nineteenth century, although the author regarded it as only a prelude to a second part. It deals with the old roué, Fyodor Karamazov, and his three sons, Dimitry, a sensualist with an appreciation of Christian morals and a willingness to suffer, the cynical Ivan, the greatest of Dostoyevsky's intellectual doubles, and Alyosha, the future hero and a believing Christian, but still a Karamazov. No modern work of fiction presents a more forceful discussion of the existence of God and the reasonableness of atheism and amorality than does this, the last work of its author. Dostoyevsky hoped to solve the problem of faith and unbelief, but the magnitude of the task, as well as his own unresolved and conflicting inclinations, prevented him from reaching his goal, though they perhaps aided him in attaining the terrible drama and the deeply suggestive symbolism of the characters and the events of the book.
C. A. M.

BROUGHTON, HUGH [brɔ'tən] (1549-1612), English theologian and Hebrew scholar, was born at Owlbury, Bishop's Castle parish, in Shropshire. He entered Magdalene College at Cambridge in 1569 and became a fellow at St. John's and Christ's colleges. In London, he became a preacher and published *A Concent of Scripture* (1588), a work mainly concerned with scriptural chronology, in which he protested his belief in the integrity of the New and the Old Testaments. It was severely attacked and he was called upon to defend it in a series of lectures. In 1589 he left for the Continent where he was involved in many religious discussions with men of other faiths who held him in even higher esteem than those of his own faith. Except for short trips to England, he remained on the Continent until the death of Queen Elizabeth. In 1599 he published his *Explication on the Article of Christ's Descent into Hell,* expressing the view that Hell was not a place of torment, but a state of departed souls. Broughton felt the urgent need of preparing a better translation of the Bible than those available. In 1593 he had written a letter to the Queen drawing her attention to the matter. In 1597 he published, while in Holland, *An Epistle to the Learned Nobilities of England touching translating the Bible from the Original.* When King James finally appointed a committee of 54 translators for the preparation of a revised translation of the Bible, however, Broughton was not included. Later he severely criticized the King James version, and published his own corrections, but his critics dismissed these as the labors of a disappointed man. The dramatist Ben Jonson satirized Broughton in *Volpone* and again in *The Alchemist.* In 1611 he returned home from another journey to the Continent, and died at Tottenham, Aug. 4, 1612.

BROUN, (MATTHEW) HEYWOOD (CAMPBELL) [bru'n] (1888-1939), American journalist, was born Dec. 7, 1888, in Brooklyn, N.Y. Leaving Harvard in 1910, he became a sports reporter for the New York *Morning Telegraph.* As a member of the staff of the *Tribune* (1912-1921) he reviewed plays and began his widely read column, "It Seems to Me." This he took with him to the New York *World* in 1921 and continued it in the Scripps-Howard newspapers after 1928 when he left the *World* over a dispute about his liberal views concerning Sacco and Vanzetti. After 1935 he contributed also to *The Nation* and *The New Republic* and edited his own weekly newspaper, *Broun's Nutmeg,* from his home in Stamford, Conn. Several collections of his newspaper pieces have been published.

A many-sided man, Broun also wrote novels (*Gandle Follows His Nose,* 1926) and collaborated on a satiric biography of Anthony Comstock (1927) and a study of anti-Semitism, *Christians Only* (1931). In 1930 he ran unsuccessfully for Congress as a Socialist and in 1931 produced and acted in his own musical comedy, *Shoot the Works.* He was a founder and the first president (1933-1939) of the American Newspaper Guild. His writings show his devotion to the many liberal causes he upheld. Though he wrote too rapidly and too much, his fluent, persuasive, and humorous style assured him of a wide popularity in his own time. Broun died Dec. 18, 1939, in New York City. *Collected Edition* (1941) is a selection of his writings edited by his son, H. H. Broun.   R. W. D.

BROUWER, ADRIAEN [brau'wər] (c.1606-1638), Flemish genre and landscape painter, was born at Oudenaarde probably in 1606. His earliest instruction in painting he probably received from his father, who executed sketches for tapestries. Running away to Antwerp when he was sixteen years old, Brouwer came under the influence of Pieter Brueghel the Younger, and at this stage he painted canvases that are archaistic and Flemish in their color and execution. After a brief stay in Amsterdam from 1625 to 1626 he settled in Haarlem, as an accomplished master of his art. Brouwer's residence in Holland is marked by a modification of his scale of colors, reflecting the powerful influence of Frans Hals, to whose circle he belonged. He also began to paint landscapes during this period. Returning to Antwerp in 1632, he revealed his maturity in the greater plasticity of his figures and stronger characterization of his subjects. His subject matter is generally that of the tavern, showing scenes of drinking, smoking, and peasant merriment. Brouwer was buried at Antwerp, Feb. 1, 1638.   D. R. C.

BROWALLIA [browæ'liə], a genus of the potato family, having about ten species native to South America. They are annual plants bearing numerous white, violet, or blue flowers, several of which are cultivated as ornamentals. The amethyst browallia, *B. americana,* is a slender, branching, erect plant reaching a height of 24 in. It bears numerous small blue, white, or lavender flowers over a long period. *B. speciosa,* shrubby at base, sometimes reaches a height of 5 ft. It bears larger, deep blue flowers, and is cultivated by florists as a pot plant; it is also grown in gardens.
    J. C. Wis.

BROWDER, EARL (RUSSELL) [brau'dər] (1891-), American Communist leader, was born at Wichita, Kans., May 20, 1891. Because of difficult circumstances he quit public school at the age of nine, and in later years taught himself law. Browder worked with the Farmers' Co-operative, and when he was fifteen he joined the Socialist Party. In 1912, after a split with that organization, he joined the Syndicalist League of North America and became editor of the League's magazine, *The Toiler.* Believing the United States was being swayed by imperialist propaganda in World War I, Browder organized the League for Democratic Control to "disseminate the idea that the people of America should have a voice as to whether or not they wished to go to war."

During World War I, under a charge of conspiracy against the government, Browder was tried, convicted, and imprisoned at Fort Leavenworth until 1920, during which time he studied communism and joined the Communist Party in the United States. He became a member of the central committee of the Communist Party in the United States in 1921, and continued in that capacity until he was expelled in 1946. He traveled in Europe and Asia to study the labor movement and was secretary of the Pan-Pacific trade union secretariat at Shanghai and Hankow, 1927-1929. In 1930 he was chosen general secretary of the Communist Party in the United States. As Communist candidate for president of the United States in the 1936 and 1940 campaigns, he based his platform on maintaining what he believed to be democracy in the United States.

As a consequence of his militant pro-Communist, pro-Russian attitude and the agitation in the United States against Nazi Germany, and then against Nazi Germany and Communist Russia after the formal alliance of the two countries, Browder was brought to trial on an unlawful passport charge, and in February 1940 was sentenced to four years in the Atlanta Federal prison. He was released in May 1942 when President Roosevelt commuted his sentence.

At intervals during the period from 1930 to 1944, Browder acted in an editorial capacity on *The Daily Worker* and from early 1944 to the fall of 1945 was nominally editor-in-chief.

On May 22, 1944, the Communist Party transformed itself into the American Communist Political Association, with Browder as president, but on Jan. 14, 1946, reverted to its former status. Because of accusations by the French Communist leader, Jacques Duclos, and others, denouncing

Browder and other American Communist leaders for swerving "dangerously from the victorious Marxist-Leninist doctrine," Browder early in 1946 was replaced in his office and authority by William Z. Foster, and was expelled from the party. Subsequently, he acted as American agent for Soviet publishers. In 1948, he was accused by *The Daily Worker* of "openly peddling his wares of anti-Communism" under the pen name of "Americus," and of being "Wall Street's apologist." He wrote numerous political tracts and *War or Peace With Russia* (1947). W. E. A.

BROWN, SIR ARTHUR WHITTEN (1886-1948),

British aviator, was born in Glasgow, Scotland, in 1886, of American parentage. He was educated in Manchester, England, and then served an apprenticeship with the Westinghouse Electric and Manufacturing Company of Manchester. In 1914 he enlisted in the British army and the following

(Left) *Sir John Alcock and* (Right) *Sir Arthur W. Brown*

year obtained a transfer to the Royal Flying Corps as an observer. He was shot down over enemy territory and spent eighteen months as a prisoner of war in Germany. After his repatriation in 1917 he was employed in the Ministry of Munitions on production of aeroplane engines. In 1919 he met John William Alcock, a World War pilot who was making preparations for a flight across the Atlantic in an attempt to win the prize of £10,000 offered by the London *Daily Mail*. Brown joined him as aerial navigator and they took off from St. John's, Newfoundland, on June 14, 1919, in a twin-engine Vickers-Vimy biplane; 16 hours and 12 minutes later they landed in Clifden, Ireland, becoming the first men to make a nonstop flight from America to Europe. They were both knighted by King George V that same year. Sir Arthur died Oct. 4, 1948. C. W. D.

BROWN, CHARLES BROCKDEN (1771-1810), born

in Philadelphia, Pa., Jan. 17, 1771, was America's first professional author. Precocious son of a Quaker merchant, he was early influenced by the French Revolution and the current rationalistic faiths in human progress, benevolence, and the power of education. In 1793 he gave up study of the law to devote his time to liberalistic writing. In the first two years of a short residence in New York he published the four novels on which his fame rests: *Wieland* (1798), *Ormond* (1799), *Arthur Mervyn* (1799-1800), and *Edgar Huntly* (1799). Although unpolished and often stilted, these Gothic romances were important for their imaginative and yet rational use of sensational material, their realistic description of American scenes, their keen plot suspense, and especially their fine understanding of human reactions to powerful emotions. Brown's other writings, which include treatises, essays, translations, and minor works of fiction, are largely

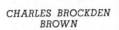
*CHARLES BROCKDEN
BROWN*

FROM AN ENGRAVING BY
H. B. HALLS SONS FROM
THE PORTRAIT BY
JAMES SHARPLES

COURTESY OF THE NEW YORK
PUBLIC LIBRARY

forgotten. His health, which had been delicate since childhood, failed in 1809, when his lungs became gravely affected. He died Feb. 22, 1810, in Philadelphia. E. Sh.

BROWN, ERNEST WILLIAM (1866-1938), American

astronomer, was born at Hull, England, Nov. 29, 1866. He was educated at Cambridge University and became professor of mathematics at Yale in 1907. Brown spent nearly a lifetime studying the celestial mechanics of the moon. His *Tables of the Moon* is the leading authority on the subject. Brown showed the existence of changes in the earth's rotation, and extended his researches to planetary theory, asteroids, resonance, and the famous three-body problem. He died July 22, 1938, in New Haven, Conn. H. S. R.

BROWN, FATHER, the hero of a series of detective

stories (published 1911, 1914, 1926, 1927), by G. K. Chesterton. The little priest, modelled on Chesterton's friend, Father O'Connor, owes his success in solving crime mysteries primarily to his observation of facts so obvious and familiar as to be generally overlooked. F. A. L.

BROWN, FORD MADOX (1821-1893), English painter,

was born Apr. 16, 1821, at Calais, France, of English parents. He was closely associated, in mid-century, with the Pre-Raphaelite Brotherhood, as the first instructor and the friend of two of its leaders, Dante Gabriel Rossetti and William H. Hunt. Brown exhibited great variety in his art, but also unevenness of quality. His student days were spent in Belgium, under several masters, and there he emerged as a vigorous painter given to romantic subjects, theatrical and even melodramatic. In 1845, at Rome, he observed the work of Johann Friedrich Overbeck and Peter von Cornelius, who were often referred to as the "German Pre-Raphaelites," and discovered, in consequence, that his own style was much too florid. Accordingly he simplified it, and it lost in the process much of its robustness. Occasionally he rediscovered his old power, as in *Christ Washing Peter's Feet* (London, National Gallery). This painting, done in striking but harmonious colors and lines, and imaginatively composed, dates from 1852, but it was altered several times before 1890. Brown died in London, Oct. 11, 1893. C. P. P.

BROWN, GEORGE (1818-1880), Canadian journalist and statesman, was born near Edinburgh, Scotland, Nov. 29, 1818. In 1838 his father, Peter Brown, migrated with his family to New York, becoming a journalist and founding the *British Chronicle* in 1842. Dissatisfied with conditions in the United States, the Browns moved to Toronto in 1843. There they founded first the *Banner,* a Presbyterian weekly, and then, in 1844, replaced it with the *Globe,* which under George Brown's editorship became the most influential political newspaper in Canada. Brown was already of importance in the Reform Party before he entered the Assembly in 1851. Within a few years, he had become the party's leader in Upper Canada. Canada's major political problem in that period was the relationship between the French Roman Catholics of Lower Canada and the English Protestants of Upper Canada, who had been in uneasy union under one government since 1840. Brown's vigorous advocacy of the extreme Upper Canadian viewpoint contributed to increasing the friction between the two, to the extent of virtually deadlocking the machinery of government by 1864. Meanwhile, among others, he had become convinced that the solution lay in the creation of two separate provinces and their federal union, either alone or along with the rest of British North America. Although inclined to favor the smaller federation, Brown saw that the larger offered certain advantages, particularly if it should include the Hudson's Bay Territory, in which he was greatly interested. To advance such a scheme, Brown, at considerable sacrifice of personal wishes and political advantage, in 1864 joined a coalition dominated by his rival, John A. Macdonald, whom he disliked intensely. He played a prominent part in the confederation conferences at Charlottetown and Quebec, and in the debates of 1865, when confederation was approved in the Canadian Assembly. Although disagreement with Macdonald brought about his resignation before the task was completed, Brown's statesmanlike attitude in 1864 had already won him a place as a pioneer of Canadian confederation. His subsequent influence was exercised mainly as editor of the *Globe,* but was by no means negligible. He was shot by a disgruntled employee and died May 9, 1880, in Toronto.   D. G. G. K.

BROWN, HENRY KIRKE (1814-1886), American sculptor, was born at Leyden, Mass., Feb. 24, 1814. His most important work is the equestrian statue of George Washington in Union Square, New York City, and though he won many commissions for public monuments none of them approach the Washington statue in style and distinction. Brown followed the fashion of his time and went to Italy to study sculpture, but he remained there for only four years and was one of the first American sculptors to maintain that study in Italy was not a necessity. He died in Newburgh, New York, July 10, 1886.   A. Ten E. G.

BROWN, JACOB JENNINGS (1775-1828), American soldier, was born on May 9, 1775, in Bucks Co., Pa., of Quaker parentage. Self-educated, he taught school in New Jersey, and later was a surveyor, working near Cincinnati. He returned east in 1798 to teach school in New York City, and later was Alexander Hamilton's private secretary. His fortunes improved, he bought several thousand acres of land, and founded the town of Brownville, N. Y., becoming a county judge. In 1811, he was appointed a brigadier general in the state militia. When the War of 1812 began, Brown was put in command of the defense of Ogdensburg and Sackett's Harbor. His strategy of harassing and checking the

enemy caused the British finally to withdraw (Mar. 29, 1813) from the Lake Ontario region. Brown became a brigadier general in the regular army on July 19, 1813, and on Jan. 24, 1814, was made a major general. He was placed in command of western New York, with Winfield Scott and E. W. Ripley as brigadiers. On July 3, 1814, Brown captured Fort Erie, and on July 5 he crushed the British force under General Phineas Riall at Chippewa. On the following July 25, with General Winfield Scott, he routed General Gordon Drummond at the Battle of Niagara (Lundy's Lane). He defeated Drummond again in a second engagement (Sept. 17, 1814)

GENERAL JACOB
JENNINGS BROWN

FROM AN ENGRAVING BY
J. WOOD

COURTESY OF THE NEW YORK
PUBLIC LIBRARY

which ended the northern campaign. In 1815, when the army was reduced and reorganized, Brown became the senior officer on the active list, and on Mar. 10, 1821, became general in chief of the United States Army, a position he held until his death in Washington, D. C., on Feb. 24, 1828.
    W. E. A.

BROWN, JOHN (1800-1859), American abolitionist, was born in Torrington, Conn., May 9, 1800. At the age of five he moved to Hudson, Ohio, with his father, a Pilgrim descendant with abolitionist sympathies. At eighteen Brown chose the ministry, but after a short period of study became a land surveyor. He had been engaged in various business ventures, including sheep raising and tanning, before he went bankrupt in 1842 in Akron, Ohio. He lived in Pennsylvania and Massachusetts before he settled in 1849 at North Elba, N. Y., where he farmed a tract in a Negro farming settlement set up by the abolitionist Gerrit Smith.

In 1855 Brown joined five of his sons, who had preceded him to Kansas. The passage of the Kansas-Nebraska Act had turned the dispute between the "free state" and "proslavery" settlers of the region into anarchical warfare. Brown's belief that he had a divine mission to destroy slavery was shared by his family. (Twice married, he was the father of twenty children.) His sons participated actively in all of his fanatical abolitionist plans. Brown became a leader of the "free state" settlers in Kansas, and on the night of May 24, 1856, he led the Pottawatomie Massacre, in which five "proslavery" settlers were murdered in retaliation for the previous murder of five "free state" settlers. Brown's subsequent success in several skirmishes between the two factions increased his confidence in his ability to abolish slavery through revolutionary acts.

In 1858 he left Kansas to establish a mountain stronghold in Virginia for runaway slaves. At Chatham, Canada, with forty-six associates (thirty-five of whom were Negroes), Brown set up a "provisional constitution and ordinance for the people of the United States." He and his fellow conspirators elected themselves to offices of the provisional government, which included a congressional legislative body. Then, without their knowledge but with funds he had obtained from Gerrit Smith and other abolitionists of his acquaintance, and with arms he obtained from the Massachu-

COURTESY OF THE METROPOLITAN MUSEUM OF ART

LAST MOMENTS OF JOHN BROWN

FROM A PAINTING BY THOMAS HOVENDEN

setts-Kansas Committee, Brown took a force of twenty-two men to Harper's Ferry, Va. On Oct. 16, 1859, he captured the federal arsenal and sixty leading citizens, whom he planned to use as hostages. Two days later Colonel Robert E. Lee, with a small force of United States Marines, recaptured the arsenal. Brown and his associates were arrested, tried, and convicted on various charges, including treason, at Charlestown, Va. (now W. Va.). Brown was found guilty, sentenced to death, and hanged, Dec. 2, 1859.   D. R.

BROWN, ROBERT (1773-1858), Scottish botanist, born at Montrose, Dec. 21, 1773. He attended Marischal College, Aberdeen, and was graduated from Edinburgh University in 1795. Serving in the north of Ireland as assistant surgeon in the Forfarshire regiment, he met Sir Joseph Banks, who in 1801 appointed him the naturalist of Capt. Matthew Flinders' expedition. The expedition circumnavigated Australia, visited New South Wales and Van Diemen's Land, and made exhaustive studies of the flora. Upon his return to England with more than 4,000 plant specimens in 1805, Brown was appointed librarian of the Linnaean Society. In 1810, he was appointed librarian to Sir Joseph Banks and that same year published his *Podromus Florae Novae Hollandiae et Insulae Van Diemen.*

Brown discovered and named the nucleus of the cell, and observed and depicted nuclei in surface layers of tissue. He pioneered in microscopical examinations of fossils and in observation of the nature of the sexual process (pollination) in higher plants. Because of his attention to detail in microscopic research, Brown made his most important discovery in 1827. He observed pollen grains darting here and there in zigzag fashion. He then tried other substances and found that they possessed this motion when the particles were sufficiently small. From these experiments he concluded that this motion, now known as Brownian Movement, was due to the activity of suspended particles caused by collision with the molecules of the surrounding solution.

On his death in 1820 Sir Joseph Banks bequeathed his library and collections to Brown for life. These Brown transferred to the British Museum in 1827 when he became keeper of its new botanical department, a position he held until his death in London, June 10, 1858.

Among Brown's honors were: Fellow of the Royal Society, 1811; Foreign Associate of the French Academy of Science, 1833; Copley Medal, 1839; president of the Linnaean Society, 1849-1853; and member of the Prussian order *Pour le Mérite.* The Royal Society reprinted his complete writings, except the *Prodromus,* in 1866.   D. D. M.

BROWN, THOMAS EDWARD (1830-1897), British poet and schoolmaster, was born at Douglas, Isle of Man, on May 5, 1830, and was educated at home, at King William's College, and at Oxford University. He taught at various secondary schools, longest at Clifton College near Bristol, 1863-1892. His popularity as a poet is based on his narrative and lyric poems composed in an artificial Manx dialect and based on knowledge of his native island home. His first volume, *Betsy Lee,* appeared in 1875. Other collections were *Fo'c's'le Yarns* (1881); *The Doctor* (1887); *The Manx Witch* (1889); *Old John* (1893). His collected poems appeared in 1900, 1908, and 1930, and his *Works and Letters* were edited by S. T. Irwin in 1900. Brown died while on a visit to Clifton College on Oct. 29, 1897.

BROWNE, CHARLES FARRAR (1834-1867), American humorist, better known by his pen name Artemus Ward, was born April 26, 1834, near Waterford, Maine. After working as printer and contributor to newspapers in the East and in Ohio, Browne in 1857 became city editor of the Cleveland *Plain Dealer,* where he became nationally famous as the creator of Artemus Ward, supposedly a traveling exhibitor of waxworks. In 1859 he left Cleveland for New York and in 1861 became editor of *Vanity Fair,* leaving this post in April 1862, to tour the country for three years as a humorous lecturer. Appearances in England and contributions to *Punch* occupied him from 1866 until his death from tuberculosis at Southampton, England, on Mar. 6, 1867. Browne's whimsical humor featured comic misspellings, barbaric grammar, and the salty manner of backwoods characters. His chief books are *Artemus Ward: His Book* (1862), *Artemus Ward: His Travels* (1865), *Artemus Ward in London* (1867), and *The Mormons* (1868).   H. C. Ca.

BROWNE, ROBERT (c. 1550-c. 1633), English religious reformer, leader of the first Separatists, was born at Tolethorpe, in Rutlandshire. The Congregationalists regard him as the first exponent of the basic tenets of their doctrine. Little is known of his early life. He came of a good family and is said to have entered Corpus Christi College in Cambridge in 1570. He graduated in 1572 and became a schoolmaster, probably in London. In 1578 Browne returned to Tolethorpe, then to Cambridge, where he met a clergyman, Richard Greenham, who encouraged him to preach in the neighboring villages. He was soon given charge of a parish in Cambridge. He resigned a few months later, for he was finding more and more things to criticize in the existing state of affairs of the Church of England. He was against ordination and also the parochial system, for he wished to make the church an exclusive organization open to the worthy alone. "The Kingdom of God was not to begin by whole parishes, but rather of the worthiest, were they never so few," he said. Browne stood for a complete separation of church and state. He left Cambridge and stayed with a friend, Robert Harrison, at Norwich. There a number of people adhered to his doctrines and separated themselves from the official church. They came to be known as the Brownists. On several occasions the Bishop of Norwich, attempting to destroy this dissident movement, ordered that Browne be imprisoned, but Lord Burleigh, a distant relative of Browne, intervened each time in his behalf. The situation became so unpleasant, however, that in 1581 Browne's followers decided to migrate to Middelburg, in Holland. While in Holland, Browne wrote *A Treatise of Reformation without Tarrying for Anie; A Book which Showeth the Life and Manners of all True Christians,* and *A Treatise upon the 23d of Matthew.* These were circulated in England. In 1583 a royal proclamation was issued against the Brownists, and two men who were caught distributing Browne's writings were condemned to be hanged. During the same year a schism occurred within the group at Middelburg, and Browne, leaving behind Harrison and the majority of his followers, sailed to Scotland with a few devotees. There he failed to arouse interest in his movement and was forced to leave for England. He returned to Rutland and continued to preach until, it is said, he was finally excommunicated by the Bishop of Peterborough. Then occurred the sudden change which has baffled so many since, for Browne suddenly ceased to be a nonconformist. In 1586 he became Master of the Stamford Grammar School. He became rector at Achurch-cum-Thorpe Waterville, in Northamptonshire, in 1591. Except for ten years, which cannot be clearly accounted for, it is known that he quietly served at Achurch for the rest of his life. He died in prison at Northampton, where he had been incarcerated for having struck the parish constable in a sudden fit of temper. The exact date of his death is unknown.   E. B. A.

BROWNE, SIR THOMAS (1605-1682), English physician and writer, was born Oct. 19, 1605, in London. He was educated at Winchester and Broadgates Hall, Pembroke College, Oxford, receiving his B.A. degree in 1626 and his M.A. in 1629. He studied medicine and practiced in Oxfordshire. He traveled on the Continent, pursuing medical studies at the universities of Montpellier, Padua, and Leiden, receiving from Leiden the degree of M.D. (1633). He returned to practice medicine near Halifax, where he wrote *Religio Medici,* which circulated in manuscript for several years. In 1637 Dr. Browne removed to Norwich. In 1641 he married Dorothy Mileham, whose delightful postscripts to her husband's letters are cherished by his admirers.

The appearance in print of *Religio Medici* ("The Religion of a Doctor") (1642), written some years previously, spread Browne's renown as author, although he disavowed the publication, bringing out a corrected edition the next year. It was the subject of *Observations* by Sir Kenelm Digby (1643) and was immediately translated into Latin. For its contemporaries the book carried a paradox in its title; modern readers are struck by its mixture of faith and skepticism, scientific acumen and credulity, even as they are charmed by

its humanity and eloquence. In 1646 appeared *Pseudodoxia Epidemica,* commonly known as *Vulgar Errors,* Browne's longest work, one in which he examined the sources of human error generally and made particular inquiries into certain beliefs erroneously held. This work emphasizes the transition between the age of authority and the new scientific era. Browne was of both worlds, a disciple both of Bacon and Aristotle. The curious erudition with which he expatiates on a variety of subjects gives the book an odd attractiveness, even when it is strangest to modern ways of thinking.

SIR THOMAS BROWNE

The unearthing of a group of burial urns near Norwich gave Browne occasion to compose one of the noblest of meditations on death and immortality, *Hydriotaphia, Urn-Burial* (1658). With it was published *The Garden of Cyrus,* a curious work which begins with a reference to the lozenge arrangement for planting trees, and proceeds by pursuing the lozenge figure and the mystical number 5 throughout the cosmos and microcosm. At his death Browne left in manuscript a tract entitled *Christian Morals,* which was published in 1716.

Although his uncritical erudition and highly Latinized vocabulary, which influenced Samuel Johnson, lend a certain characteristic denseness to his writing, Browne holds a high place among English prose masters by the eloquence of his periods, to which he made the sounds of words contribute no less than did Milton, and by the loftiness of the Christian Platonic speculation which was his natural medium.

Browne was a royalist, but during the civil wars and the Commonwealth period he went his way without any sign of political zeal. The collection of curiosities in his house in Norwich was famous. He corresponded with scientists and antiquarians, including John Evelyn, and made reports to the Royal Society, but he never became a member of the organization. That honor came to his eldest son, Edward (1644-1708), also a physician and president of the Royal College of Physicians. On a royal visit to Norwich in 1671, Charles II knighted Thomas Browne; the mayor, who otherwise would have received the title of knight, yielded it to the town's first citizen. Browne died on Oct. 19, 1682, his seventy-seventh birthday, in Norwich.   T. H. E.

BROWNE, WILLIAM (c.1591-c.1645), English poet, was born at Tavistock, Devon, and educated at Oxford and the Inner Temple. An admirer of Edmund Spenser and Sir Philip Sidney, he idealized English country life in *Britannia's Pastorals* (Book I, 1613; Book II, 1616; Book III, unfinished).

The Shepherd's Pipe (1614) contains seven eclogues by Browne. His *Inner Temple Masque,* acted in 1615, dramatizes the story of Ulysses and Circe. Browne left in manuscript sonnets to Caelia and the famous epitaph on "Sidney's sister, Pembroke's mother," wrongly attributed to Jonson.

M. E.

BROWNELL, HERBERT, JR. [brauneʹl] (1904-   ), American lawyer and government official, was born in Peru, Nebr., Feb. 20, 1904. He was educated at the University of Nebraska and Yale Law School and joined a New York law firm in 1929. From 1932 to 1937 he was a Republican member of the New York State Assembly. Brownell managed Thomas E. Dewey's first successful campaign for governor in 1942, and in 1944 and 1948 managed Governor Dewey's campaigns as a presidential candidate. He was also chairman of the Republican National Committee from 1944 to 1946. He played a leading role as campaign strategist for Dwight D. Eisenhower in 1952, in recognition for which he was named United States Attorney General in the new Republican Administration, taking office on Jan. 21, 1953. Brownell's charge in November 1953 that Harry Dexter White had been appointed to high government office in 1946 although he "was known to be a Communist spy by the very people who appointed him" touched off a bitter political controversy. His anti-Communist program as head of the Justice Department included additions to the Attorney General's subversive list and proposals for more stringent statutes, including the death penalty for peacetime espionage. He resigned his office on Oct. 23, 1957, and returned to private law practice.

C. W. D.

BROWN-EYED SUSAN, *Rudbeckia triloba,* also called coneflower, a coarse, alternate-leaved biennial herb, to 5 ft. high, of the family Compositae, native from New Jersey to Georgia and Louisiana. It is commonly grown as a summer-blooming flower in gardens. The showy flowers, to 2½ in. across, have deep-yellow rays, sometimes tinged orange or brownish at the base, radiating from a blackish-purple disk, or cone.

J. C. Wis.

BROWNIAN MOVEMENT. *See* KINETIC THEORY AND STATISTICAL MECHANICS (*The Methods of Statistical Mechanics*); SURFACE PHENOMENA.

BROWNING, ELIZABETH BARRETT (1806-1861), English poet, the wife of Robert Browning, was born Mar. 6, 1806, in Coxhoe Hall, near Durham, the eldest of the eleven children of Mary Graham Clarke and Edward Barrett Moulton. The surname Barrett was later added when Mr. Moulton inherited Barrett property in Jamaica. Miss Barrett's girlhood was spent at Hope End, near the Malvern Hills, but in 1832 the family went to Sidmouth, Devon, and in 1835 they removed to London, living first at 74 Gloucester Place and thereafter at 50 Wimpole Street. Her education was unusually liberal; she read widely, studied Greek and Latin with her brother's tutor, and was deeply influenced by the blind scholar, Hugh Boyd, who discussed Greek and other literatures with her. At the age of thirteen she composed an epic, *The Battle of Marathon* (1820), and at eighteen, *An Essay on Mind* (1826), which showed some little learning. Her next substantial work, an excellent translation of Aeschylus' *Prometheus Bound* (1833), was followed by *The Seraphim and Other Poems* (1838), a romantic and visionary volume which was well received, though not widely popular, and served to extend her literary acquaintance.

For a number of years Miss Barrett was an invalid, suffering from an injury to her spine and weakness of the lungs; she was also for a time prostrated by shock and grief over the drowning (1838) of her favorite brother, Edward, in an accident at Torquay, where they had gone for the benefit of her health. Nevertheless, her uncertain health did not interrupt her literary life, and in her secluded room in London she wrote numerous letters to her friends Mary Mitford, Harriet Martineau, Mrs. Anna Jameson, Hugh Boyd, Richard Hengist Horne, B. R. Haydon, and others. She also contributed verse and prose essays to *The Athenaeum* and some

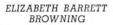

ELIZABETH BARRETT
BROWNING

FROM A PAINTING BY
FIELD TALFOURD

COURTESY OF THE MENTOR
ASSOCIATION

poems to American journals. In 1844, two volumes of her poems appeared which so deeply impressed Browning that he wrote to the author and initiated a correspondence. This was punctuated by later regular visits which ended, Sept. 12, 1846, in their secret marriage at St. Marylebone Church, the secrecy being necessitated by the fanatical feudal rule of Miss Barrett's father over his children.

Presently established in an apartment in the Casa Guidi, in Florence, near the Pitti Palace, the Brownings wrote, read, and received many visits. After the birth of their son, Robert Wiedeman Barrett (d. 1913), they spent some summers at Siena or Bagni di Lucca, passed their winters in Rome, and also visited Paris and London. *Casa Guidi Windows* (I, 1848; II, 1851) showed Mrs. Browning's passionate sympathy with the Italian struggles for freedom. *Poems* (1850) contained not only a revised translation of *Prometheus Bound* but also the memorable *Sonnets from the Portuguese,* the series of poems addressed to her husband which she had not shown to him until 1849 at Bagni di Lucca. Her next important work, the verse novel *Aurora Leigh* (1857), expressed her opinions on various social questions. *Poems before Congress* (1860) and *Last Poems* (1862), chiefly on political themes, were written when her health was failing. She died rather suddenly during an attack of bronchitis, June 29, 1861, and lies buried in the Protestant Cemetery in Florence under a tomb designed by Frederick Leighton. A memorial tablet was soon placed on the wall of Casa Guidi by the Florentines.

As a poet Mrs. Browning was much more famous than was her husband during her life, both in England and in America, and when Wordsworth died, in 1850, some of her admirers wished her to be made Poet Laureate. Her special traits were her spiritual elevation and insight, her intense sincerity, her keen judgment, and her sympathy with all who were oppressed or suffering; but poetic technique meant less to her than did spontaneity, and she has been justly criticized for carelessness in composition, and also for a too learned allusiveness. Among her most enduring poems are *The Cry of the Children, Cowper's Grave, The Deserted Garden, Work, The Dead Pan, A Musical Instrument,* and *Sonnets from the Portuguese,* which is considered her greatest work. Her *Letters* contain many fine passages of criticism, description, and philosophy.   M. H. Sh.

BROWNING, JOHN MOSES (1855-1926), American firearms inventor, was born in Ogden, Utah, Jan. 21, 1855. He was the son of Jonathan Browning, a frontier gunsmith, who had moved to Ogden from his birthplace in Tennessee. Young Browning was issued his first patent, for a breech-loading single-shot rifle, in 1879. He secured patents on many of his designs and improvements for a long line of sporting and military firearms, including auto-loading and repeating rifles and shotguns. In 1890 the United States Army adopted the Colt machine gun designed by him, and later his automatic pistol. With the advent of World War I, Browning submitted to the United States Government a recoil-operated, .30-caliber heavy water-cooled machine gun, and a gas-operated light automatic rifle. These were adopted as the Browning Machine Gun, Model 1917, and the Browning Automatic Rifle, Model 1918. His .50-caliber version of the machine gun in a larger size became basic United States aircraft armament in World War II. He also invented a 37-mm. automatic cannon which was adopted by the United States armed forces, and designed a new over-and-under double-barreled shotgun. He died of a heart attack at Herstal, Belgium, Nov. 26, 1926.   C. T. H.

BROWNING, ROBERT (1812-1889), English poet, was born at Camberwell, a suburb of London, on May 7, 1812. His father, also named Robert Browning, and his grand-

ROBERT BROWNING

FROM A PAINTING BY
FIELD TALFOURD

father were both employed in the Bank of England; his mother, Sarah Anna Wiedemann, was of German and Scottish parentage. From his father Browning learned to love books and to delight in grotesque rhymes and drawings, and from his mother he acquired much of his nervous sensitiveness, his love of music, and his strong religious instincts. The youthful Browning was treated with some indulgence; until he was fourteen he attended local schools, but after that age he received little formal education, though he read voraciously in his father's extensive library and had tutors in music, French, and Italian. Under this training he grew

to be a self-willed youth, conscious of his abilities in music, poetry, and drama, and eager to excel in all these fields.

Although Browning had composed verses even before he had learned to write, it was probably not until his discovery of Shelley and Keats in 1826 that he became confirmed in his intention to become a poet. Under the influence of Shelley he became temporarily an atheist and a vegetarian and composed his first poem, *Pauline; A Fragment of a Confession,* published anonymously in 1833. This work was hardly noticed by the reviews, and not a copy was sold, but John Stuart Mill made notes for a review, in which he ridiculed the young poet for his confession of real and fancied sins and for his even more imaginary claim that he was cured, and these notes were sent to Browning. This reception of *Pauline* marked a turning point in Browning's poetry. Hitherto he had worn his heart upon his sleeve, but now he resolved that henceforth his poetic utterances should be "dramatic," that is, put in the mouths of dramatic characters, rather than in his own. His next important work, *Paracelsus* (1835), was dramatic in form. Like *Pauline,* it was autobiographical in spite of its supposed use of the life of the medieval physician. Also, like *Pauline* and *Sordello* (1840), *Paracelsus* was deeply indebted to Shelley. Few copies of *Paracelsus* were sold, but the poem brought Browning into the literary and artistic circles of London and won him the friendship of Macready, Forster, and others. *Sordello,* the last of Browning's long autobiographical poems, was incomprehensible to the public and did much to destroy the small reputation which he had begun to enjoy. Part of the reason for *Sordello's* failure was that in his exposition of the psychological intricacies of his hero, Browning neglected to inform his readers of external events. The failure of *Sordello* concluded the first phase of his literary career.

The second phase was a dramatic one. In 1837, at Macready's request, Browning wrote the play *Strafford,* and in May of that year it was presented five times at Covent Garden. Its success was slight but it was sufficient to keep the poet trying, and in the next ten years he wrote six plays for the stage. The most notable of these were *A Blot on the 'Scutcheon* (1843), and *Luria* (1846). None of these plays was successful on the stage. Each contains passages of poetic power and beauty, but Browning's habit of putting elaborate analyses of motive into the mouths of his characters was not calculated to induce theatrical success.

As a natural development for his disappointing experiences with dramas and long psychological poems, Browning now devoted increasing attention to the dramatic monologue. This was a new form which was better suited to his talents and was closely related to the short dramatic scene that had served as an excellent vehicle for his ideas in *Pippa Passes* (1841). Early examples of his skill in handling the form appeared in a group of poems called *Dramatic Lyrics* (1842), which formed the third part of *Bells and Pomegranates,* a serial collection of Browning's poetic and dramatic works; of these, two of the most notable are *Porphyria's Lover,* which was originally published in 1836 in the *Monthly Repository,* and *My Last Duchess. Dramatic Romances and Lyrics* (1845), which formed the seventh part of *Bells and Pomegranates,* contained a further development of the form in *The Bishop Orders His Tomb at St. Praxed's Church.* Then followed, in 1855, the remarkable collection entitled *Men and Women,* in which Browning exploited the dramatic monologue magnificently in such poems as *Saul, Andrea del Sarto,* and *Fra Lippo Lippi.* Besides these triumphs, the volumes of Browning's middle years also contain numerous and unforgettable lyrics, many of them dealing with the intimate relationship in love between men and women. Among the poems that appeared in *Men and Women* are *The Last Ride Together, Love among the Ruins, One Word More, A Toccata of Galuppi's, A Grammarian's Funeral,* and *"Childe Roland to the Dark Tower Came."* The poems of *Dramatis Personae* (1864) are more reflective than dramatic or lyrical, but among them are such notable works as *Rabbi Ben Ezra* and *Abt Vogler.* After the publication of the collections *Dramatic Lyrics, Dramatic Romances and Lyrics,* and *Men and Women,* Browning radically altered the distribution of their contents. As a result, the grouping of individual poems in subsequent editions bears only a slight resemblance to their original grouping and seriously obscures the order of their composition.

Browning's genius entered a particularly flourishing period after his marriage to Elizabeth Barrett, in 1846, and their subsequent removal to Italy. Florence was their chief home until Mrs. Browning's death in 1861, and here and elsewhere in Italy Browning reviewed and reshaped his poetic career, made new friends, often painters, sculptors, and writers, and prepared his *Men and Women.* His wife influenced him to deal with religious and moral questions more than he had heretofore done, and his preoccupation with such topics shows itself in *Dramatis Personae* (1864), published after her death and his return with their son to England. The poet's residence in Italy was the golden period of his life and of his genius, although a full recognition of his place among English poets did not come until the publication of *The Ring and the Book* (1868-1869).

The poet found the materials for *The Ring and the Book* in Florence in 1860 in a bound collection of legal papers now called "The Old Yellow Book," after Browning's own description of it. They concerned the seventeenth-century trial of Count Guido Franceschini for the murder of his wife, and from these sordid materials Browning made his masterpiece. In 21,000 lines he told the story ten times over, adopting different points of view in ten dramatic monologues. It was a bold and successful experiment, though hardly good history, and with this achievement Browning took his place among the great poets of England.

The rest of Browning's life may be briefly told. He wrote several long poems dealing with the psychology of dubious characters and two in defense of Euripides. He also wrote much speculative verse upon religious topics and some excellent ballads and lyrics. He became a social lion and a great diner-out, but his chief care was for his son. In success, as in adversity, his aggressiveness and impatience were occasionally apparent, but these qualities were merely the darker side of his power. In 1881 a society was founded in his honor in London, and in America he was held in even higher esteem. Browning died in Venice on Dec. 12, 1889, and was buried in the Poet's Corner in Westminster Abbey.

Since his death Browning has maintained his place as a major poet in the Romantic movement. His particular gift to literature was his development of the dramatic monologue, and into that form he managed to fit his dramatic sense, his psychological insights, his speculative vein, and his vigorous powers of expression. A number of his lyrics and short poems have also found a permanent place in literature. His effect upon later writers in form and diction has been considerable, but as yet this effect has not been fully estimated. *See also* BROWNING, ELIZABETH BARRETT; PIED PIPER OF HAMELIN, THE; PIPPA PASSES; RING AND THE BOOK, THE.

W. C. DeV.

BROWNSBURG, a village in Argenteuil Co., Quebec, Canada, situated on the West River, 4 mi. west of Lachute, on Highway 31, and served by a spur of the Canadian Pacific Railway. It was incorporated as a village in 1935. Explosives, which were first manufactured here in 1880, and plastics are manufactured. Pop. 1956, 3,412. D. F. P.

BROWN-SÉQUARD, CHARLES ÉDOUARD [braʊ'n seˈkaˈr] (1817-1894), French physiologist and physician, was born in Port-Louis, Mauritius, Apr. 8, 1817, of an American father and French mother. He later adopted French citizenship. In 1837 he went to Paris to study medicine and obtained his M.D. in 1846. His subsequent career was a restless mixture of research, lectureships, and the practice of medicine in France, the United States, England, Mauritius, and other countries. Brown-Séquard was head of a hospital for epileptics and paralytics in London from 1859 to 1863, lectured on physiology at Harvard University from 1864 to 1867, practiced medicine in New York and Paris, and in 1878 was appointed professor of physiology at the Collège de France. His reputation was launched in 1846 by his M.D. thesis on the pathology and physiology of the spinal cord, and he continued important research on the nervous system, the spinal cord, blood, animal heat, epilepsy, paralysis, and the character of the brain. In his later years Brown-Séquard received some unfavorable publicity for advocating a sheep-hormone injection to prolong human life. He founded and edited the *Journal de Physiologie de l'Homme et des Animaux,* was president of the Biological Society, and founded the Archives de la Physiologie for the collection of his numerous publications. He died in Sceaux, near Paris, Apr. 2, 1894. C. W. D.

BROWNSON, ORESTES AUGUSTUS (1803-1876), American author and clergyman, was born at Stockbridge, Vt., on Sept. 16, 1803. He was self-educated. In 1822 he joined the Presbyterian Church and in 1824 the Universalist, becoming a minister of the latter denomination in 1826 and preaching in Vermont, New Hampshire, and northern New York. Brownson hoped to aid the laboring class by moral, not political, means. He advocated the socialistic ideas of Robert Owen, was a corresponding editor of the *Free Enquirer,* and in 1828 helped found the Workingmen's Party. In 1828 he edited the *Gospel Advocate,* published in Auburn, N. Y. His increasingly liberal views estranged the Universalists, so he withdrew from the denomination. In 1832 he became a Unitarian and acted as minister at Walpole, N. H., from 1832 to 1834 and at Canton, Mass., from 1834 to 1836. In 1836 he formed his own church, the Society for Christian Union and Progress, and published his first book, *New Views of Christianity, Society, and the Church,* which condemned both Catholocism and Protestantism. In 1838 Brownson founded the *Boston Quarterly Review,* which was merged with the New York *Democratic Review* from 1842 to 1844. In 1844 Brownson resumed its publication in Boston under the name of *Brownson's Quarterly Review,* which continued until 1865 and from 1873 to 1875. Following his return to Boston in 1844, Brownson was closely associated with William Henry Channing, Henry David Thoreau, George Bancroft, and George Ripley, the founder of Brook Farm. His conversion to Roman Catholicism in October 1844 astonished the public, who identified him with New England liberalism, and cost his *Review* many subscribers. On the other hand, his immoderate pro-Catholic zeal made the Catholics distrust him, and an invitation to become professor of philosophy at Dublin University was withdrawn. His publications included *Charles Elwood, or the Infidel Converted* (1840) and *The Spirit-Rapper: an Autobiography* (1854), both novels; *The*

Convert: or, Leaves from My Experience (1857), his autobiography; *The Mediatorial Life of Jesus* (1842); and *The American Republic: its Constitution, Tendencies and Destiny,* which appeared as a series of articles in the *Democratic Review* and was published in book form in 1865. Brownson died at Detroit, Mich., on Apr. 17, 1876.

BROWNSON DEEP, a trough believed to be the deepest in the Atlantic Ocean. It is a tremendous east-west extending submarine valley located in the Atlantic Ocean, north of Puerto Rico and the Virgin Islands. The average depth is about 20,000 ft., while in its Milwaukee Depth it descends 30,246 ft. below sea level.   J.E.F.

BROWNSVILLE, an industrial borough in Fayette Co., southwestern Pennsylvania, is about 30 mi. south of Pittsburgh on a slope above the Monongahela River. The town was founded in 1785 by Thomas and Basil Brown, who set up an Indian trading post on the site of Old Fort Redstone, an early Indian fortification chosen in 1758 by Col. James Burd of the British forces for a stockade. Brownsville played a part in the Whiskey Rebellion when a group of men gathered here on July 27, 1791, to protest the four pence per gallon impost placed on whiskey by the Federal Government. In the nineteenth century the town became a landmark for westbound pioneers. The difficult journey over the Allegheny Mountains ended at Brownsville, and the travelers continued inland on the Monongahela River. Brownsville was an early boatbuilding center. The *Comet,* built in 1813, was the first steamer to navigate the Monongahela, Ohio, and Mississippi rivers, and it made a successful trip to New Orleans in 1814. Brownsville is reputed to be the site of the first iron bridge, the first nail factory, and the second paper mill built west of the Alleghenies. The Brownsville Iron Bridge, built of iron forged locally in 1836, continues to stand. It was erected at the instigation of Henry Clay, whose carriage overturned at this point, throwing him into Dunlap's Creek. He is supposed to have said, "Clay and mud shall not be mixed in this place again." The order for the bridge followed his return to Washington, D. C. In 1933 the borough of South Brownsville was merged with Brownsville. Rail facilities are furnished by the Pennsylvania, Monongahela, and the Pittsburgh & Lake Erie railroads. Located in the midst of a rich coal-mining country, Brownsville has large coke ovens. Railroad shops, machine shops, a distillery, and the building of diesel-powered towboats comprise its other industries. Pop. 1950, 7,643.

BROWNSVILLE, a port of entry in the southernmost tip of Texas and the seat of Cameron Co., is situated on the Rio Grande, about 20 mi. from the Gulf of Mexico, opposite Matamoros, Mexico. Two international bridges cross the Rio Grande at Brownsville, which is located in a rich agricultural area producing cotton, citrus fruits, and vegetables. The site was settled in 1772 when land was granted by Spain to José Salvador de la Graza. In 1846 Gen. Zachary Taylor took possession of the settlement and built a fort, first named Fort Taylor. The fort was attacked by the Mexicans and gallantly defended by Maj. Jacob Brown, for whom the city and the fort, an active army post in World War II, were named. General Taylor defeated the Mexicans at the Battles of Palo Alto and Resaca de Palma in 1846. During the Civil War the port was a busy base for Confederate blockade runners, and the Confederates won what is said to have been the Civil War's last engagement at Palmito Hill on May 12, 1865, a month after Gen. Robert E.

Lee surrendered. Vacationists at Brownsville are offered salt-water fishing and game hunting. A beach resort on Padre Island is reached by a causeway across Laguna Madre. Annually, just before Lent, Brownsville holds a colorful, four-day Charro Days fiesta, a costumed celebration dedicated to the preservation of Mexican customs.

The city is an important transportation junction. Its inland deepwater harbor is visited by coastwise and foreign ships, and its airport is a connecting point between Mexico and the United States with service by Braniff International, Pan American World, and Eastern airlines and Aero Transportes. The Missouri Pacific and the Southern Pacific provide rail transportation. Brownsville is the financial and commercial center of the lower Rio Grande valley. Its industries include shrimping, cotton compressing and warehousing, vegetable and fruit processing, and the manufacture of palm-leaf hats and petrochemicals. Texas Southmost College was established here in 1926. A city manager heads the government. Pop. 1950, 36,066.

BROWN-TAIL MOTH, *Nygmia phaeorrhea,* a white moth having the abdomen broadly tipped with brown and a wing expanse of about 1½ in. It was imported into North America from Europe, being discovered in New England in 1897. There have been other accidental introductions, and the moth became established in the maritime provinces of Canada. During the twentieth century there have been numerous interceptions of larval nests on nursery stock imported from Europe. The eggs are laid in marshes, and the young larvae build nests of silk and leaves on twigs, in which to pass the winter. Both adults and larvae bear poisonous hairs, which cause "brown-tail rash," and also respiratory disorders when inhaled. Destruction of the nests and spraying have practically exterminated this pest in North America, but the fight against the gypsy moth has been less successful.

C. H. Cu.

BROWN UNIVERSITY, an accredited, privately controlled, nonsectarian institution, is located on a campus of 40 acres in Providence, R. I., at the head of Narragansett Bay. Its coordinate for women, Pembroke College, has its own campus nearby. The graduate school is coeducational.

The charter granted in 1764 to Rhode Island College by the Colonial Assembly provided for absolute liberty of conscience and prohibited religious tests. The following year the college was started in Warren, R. I., by the Baptists. The move to Providence was made in 1770. From 1776 to 1782 the college was closed, its property being put into use as a hospital and barracks for American and French troops. In recognition of a gift from Nicholas Brown, the present name was adopted in 1804.

The elective principle was introduced into the curriculum in 1850, and in the same year courses in applied science were introduced. The medical school was established in 1811 but was discontinued in 1828. Graduate work was introduced in 1887 and was established as a special department in 1903; the graduate school dates from 1927. Women's College was formed in 1891, and in 1928 its name was changed to Pembroke College in Brown University. The degrees of A.B. in liberal arts, Sc.B. in applied mathematics, chemistry, engineering, and physics, M.A., Sc.M., and Ph.D. are conferred. A curriculum adopted in 1946 is designed to provide basic knowledge in a variety of fields and an introduction to the several methods of thinking during the first two years and a concentrated study in a particular field during the last two years. A program to encourage independent thinking was initiated in 1953. Open to students in the upper half of the entering class, it places emphasis on the analysis of ideas expressed in great works of art and literature. Classes are limited in size (25 students), formal lectures are held to a minimum, and each student is expected to participate freely in the round-table discussions.

Notable buildings include University Hall, the original "College Edifice" built in 1770, the Metcalf Research Laboratory for graduate work in physical chemistry, the Wriston

University Hall, Brown University, seen through the Van Wickle Gates, quartered French and American troops during the Revolutionary War.

Quadrangle, which provides student housing, the John Carter Brown Library, which contains the foremost collection of Americana published before 1801, the Annmary Brown Memorial with its collection of fifteenth-century books, the University Library with more than 830,000 volumes, and the Ladd Astronomical Observatory.

Substantial scholarship and student loan aid is available. There are dormitory facilities for men at Brown, and at Pembroke for women. *For statistics see* COLLEGES AND UNIVERSITIES.   J. R. To.

BROWNWOOD, the seat of Brown Co. in central Texas, is situated 142 mi. southwest of Fort Worth in a fertile agricultural area. Extensive oil fields and limestone and shale deposits are located in the vicinity. Brownwood is an agricultural community with diversified manufacturing interests ranging from food products to farm machinery. Lake Brownwood, covering 8,000 acres, furnishes an unlimited supply of water for municipal, industrial, and irrigational purposes. The government of the city is headed by a manager and council. Brownwood is the seat of Howard Payne College. It handles and ships large quantities of cotton, grain, poultry, dairy products, pecans, wool, cattle, and oil. Transportation is provided by the Gulf, Colorado and Santa Fe Railway. Pop. 1950, 20,181.

BROZ, JOSIP (TITO) [brɔ′z] (1892-   ), Yugoslav soldier and dictator, was born in Kumrovec, near Zagreb, Croatia, May 25, 1892, of peasant stock. He had little formal education and began life as a metalworker. When World War I broke out he was drafted into the army of Austria-Hungary, of which Croatia was then a province. In 1915 he was slightly wounded and captured by Tsarist troops. The Slavs under Hapsburg rule were then struggling for inde-

pendence, and Broz recruited South Slav units from among prisoners taken by Russia. In the midst of this work the Russian Revolution occurred and Broz, a young soldier with strong radical ideas and aspirations for Croat freedom, joined the Russian Bolshevists. He later became a member of the Communist Party.

After the close of World War I, Broz returned to his home in Croatia, then a part of the newly formed Yugoslav kingdom, and resumed his trade as a metalworker. By this time he had become a trained labor organizer and Communist agitator, and in this dual capacity he began organizing the Zagreb railway workers for the Moscow Comintern. The Yugoslav secret police soon arrested him, and Broz served intermittent prison sentences during the next few years. In 1937 he became secretary general of the Yugoslav Communist Party. When the Germans entered the Balkans in 1941 Broz did not oppose them, but went about the country organizing underground Communist groups. When Hitler attacked his Russian ally, June 22, 1941, Broz openly opposed the Germans. He and his partisans for a time co-operated with his rival, Draža Mihajlović, and together they liberated Užice, in central Yugoslavia, and made it their headquarters. Broz's alliance with Mihajlović was ended soon afterward both because of the intense personal rivalry between the two leaders and because of their different objectives. Broz followed Russian Communist partisan strategy; Mihajlović sought to preserve power for King Peter and the Yugoslav *émigré* government and to be prepared for co-operation with Allied troops when they should enter the Balkans, meanwhile doing little actual fighting except against the partisans.

At this period of his life little was known about Broz. His movements and operations, however, developed such importance that Great Britain sent a mission to discuss co-operation and collaboration. As his success and influence increased, and as it became clear that the Soviet Union would be allowed a sphere of influence in the Balkans, Mihajlović was dropped by the Allies and Broz became the most important leader in the Balkans. He accepted military supplies and food from the United States and Great Britain but held fast to the Russians. In November 1942, using the pseudonym "Tito," he organized the Yugoslav Anti-Fascist National Liberation Council, and late in 1944 he visited Marshal Joseph Stalin in the Kremlin and was acclaimed a hero.

In the first months of 1945 all Yugoslavia was liberated from German control, and on Mar. 7, 1945, Tito, who had already appointed himself a marshal, became prime minister and dictator of Yugoslavia. He was the political and military ruler of the country, with Soviet support. From this time until June 28, 1948, Tito was a Kremlin protégé, but on this date he was denounced by the Cominform for following "an incorrect line in the basic question of foreign and domestic policy" and for carrying out "a hateful policy in relation to the U.S.S.R." Tito had visited Moscow in April 1945; he had paid a state visit to Warsaw and Prague in March 1946; to Sofia in November 1947; and to Budapest and Bucharest in December 1947. On each occasion he had signed a bilateral treaty of friendship and mutual aid. As time passed, however, it became evident that Tito's brand of patriotism was not acceptable to Moscow. On Apr. 13, 1948, Tito had written Stalin: "Even though we love the U.S.S.R., we cannot love our own country less." Because he thus evinced a primary loyalty to his native country, he was subjected to bitter criticism by the Russians, but he held to his decision to do what he could for Yugoslavia as a free independent nation, securing capital loans and executing foreign trade agreements helpful to his country. After breaking with the Cominform, Tito embarked on a program of increasingly close relations with the West, at the same time liberalizing the internal dictatorship and building up the strongest European army outside the Soviet bloc in order to be able to resist possible aggression from the Soviet Union or its satellites. He arranged for American financial assistance to Yugoslavia during the food crises in 1950 and 1951 and for American equipment and services to build up his army.

Tito was elected president of Yugoslavia on Jan. 14, 1953, and in the same year paid a state visit to Britain. The unsettled Trieste dispute continued to place a strain on Yugoslav-Italian relations, but in 1954 Tito moved closer to the Western nations by laying the groundwork for a formal military alliance with Greece and Turkey, both members of the North Atlantic Treaty Organization.   T. R. H.

BRUAY-EN-ARTOIS [brü'ε'ɑ̃na'rtwa'], a city in the northeast of France, on the Lawe River, in the department of Pas-de-Calais, 6 mi. from Béthune. Its importance lies in the fact that it has some of the most important coal mines of the Pas-de-Calais area. The coal is excellent for coking and for the extraction of gas. Large breweries are also located there. Pop. 1954, 31,923.

BRUCE, ROBERT. *See* ROBERT I, THE BRUCE.

BRUCELLOSIS. *See* INFECTIOUS ABORTION; UNDULANT FEVER.

BRUCE OF MELBOURNE, 1st VISCOUNT (STANLEY MELBOURNE BRUCE) (1883-   ), Australian prime minister and political leader, was born at Melbourne, Australia, on Apr. 15, 1883. He was admitted to the bar in 1907, but did not enter politics until his election to the Australian House of Representatives in 1918. His leadership in the Australian delegation at the Assembly of the League of Nations in 1921 and his tenure in the office of Commonwealth Treasurer (1921-1923) gave him valuable training. Bruce became Prime Minister and Minister for External Affairs upon the fall of the government of William Morris Hughes in 1923. In general, he continued the policies of the previous government, and attempted to strengthen the consultative machinery of the British Commonwealth. Because of failure to receive adequate preference in British markets at the Imperial Conference of 1923 his government gave special attention to the marketing of Australian products elsewhere. In 1929 he attempted to secure repeal of Australian Commonwealth legislation for industrial arbitration and to return the problem to state jurisdiction. A bitter fight resulted and the ministry fell when Hughes proposed vital amendments to the bill.

Bruce was returned to the Australian parliament in 1931 and served as minister without portfolio, 1932 to 1933. He represented Australia at the Ottawa Conference in 1932 and at the World Economic Conference in London in 1933. He was Australian High Commissioner in London, 1933 to 1945, and was president of the Montreux Conference called in 1936 to revise the Straits of the Dardanelles question. From 1942 to 1945, he represented Australia in the United Kingdom war cabinet and on the Pacific War Council. During the same period he was minister for Australia to the Netherlands government (in exile) domiciled in London on account of German occupation of the Netherlands. In 1946 and 1947, he served as chairman of the Preparatory Commission on World Food proposals and after 1947 served as chairman of the Finance Corporation for Industry. He

was created a viscount in 1947. In 1951 Lord Bruce became the first Chancellor of the Australian National University, Canberra.   R. V. S.

BRUCH, MAX [bru'χ] (1838-1920), German composer, was born Jan. 6, 1838, at Cologne. A pupil of Ferdinand Hiller, Karl Reinecke, and Ferdinand Breuning, the young composer soon began to produce the choral works which were to contribute to his fame during his lifetime. After several musical posts in Germany and England, he succeeded Heinrich von Herzogenberg as director of composition at the Berlin Hochschule in 1892. He died at Friedenau, Oct. 2, 1920.

The only works of Bruch which have survived as concert pieces are the first two of his three concertos for violin and orchestra, and his *Kol Nidrei* for violoncello. His many vocal compositions have sunk into oblivion.   P. G. G.

BRUCITE, a naturally occurring magnesium hydroxide, $Mg(OH)_2$, named after the pioneer American mineralogist, Archibald Bruce, who first described this mineral in 1814. It is white or light green in color and is foliated with one direction of perfect cleavage and with characteristic pearly luster on the cleavage faces. It occurs in low temperature hydrothermal veins in serpentine, and in crystalline limestones and dolomites as a replacement or as a decomposition product from other magnesium minerals. Brucite is used in making basic refractories. It is mined at Gabbs, Nev., and in Quebec and Ontario.   K. K. L.

BRÜCKNER, ALEXANDER [brü'knər] (1856-1939), Polish writer, historian, philologist, and linguist, was born at Tarnopol in Galicia on Jan. 29, 1856. He studied at Lwów (Lvov) and became in 1881 professor of the University of Berlin. He devoted most of his time to the study of the history and the language of his native Poland, but he had also a profound knowledge of other Slavic nations, especially Bohemia and Russia. Among his most important works are the *Böhmische Studien* (1887-1892), devoted to medieval Czech literature; *Średniowieczna poezja lacinska w Polsce* (1902-1904) ("Medieval Latin Poetry in Poland"); *Dzieje polskiej literatury w zarysie* (1908) ("Sketch of the History of Polish Literature"); *Dzieje języka polskiego* (1914) ("History of the Polish Language"); and *Słownik etymologiczny języka polskiego* (1916) ("Etymological Dictionary of the Polish Language"). He died in Warsaw in 1939.   G. B.

BRUCKNER, ANTON [bru'knər] (1824-1896), Austrian composer, was born at Ansfelden, Upper Austria, Sept. 4, 1824. The son and grandson of village school teachers, he developed his musical talents with unusual slowness. He was forty years old when he wrote his first work of primary importance, fifty before he found any recognition, and sixty when at last he became famous. Bruckner was, at first, organist of the cathedral in Linz, and later on a professor of organ and composition at the Conservatory of the Gesellschaft der Musikfreunde in Vienna. He died there on Oct. 11, 1896.

Bruckner's compositions are for the greater part symphonies and choral works, influenced by the Austrian Baroque music of the seventeenth and eighteenth centuries, with its antiphonal dialogues between the different choruses of voices and instruments. Bruckner's orchestration reveals him as an accomplished organist and a student of older keyboard music. The symphonies are typically Austrian, closely related to the works of Haydn, Beethoven, and Schubert, but the deep admiration Bruckner felt for the works of Richard Wagner is also unmistakable. Basically they follow the Classical form in four movements without any concession to the programmatic tendencies of the Berlioz-Liszt school, but Bruckner's symphonies are on a larger scale than those of the earlier composers of Vienna. They are longer and make greater use of the brass section. Bruckner is a mystic, and the visionary power of his musical language secures him a place of his own among the instrumental composers of the nineteenth century. On the other hand, the similarity existing between the different symphonies—together with certain mannerisms and a lack of formal concentration in their composer's style—has stood in the way of their full success. Only Austria and parts of Germany have been completely won to Bruckner, while the English-speaking countries have displayed only a limited interest in his compositions.

Bruckner's main works are his nine symphonies (especially No. III, D minor, dedicated to Wagner; No. IV, E-flat major, "Romantic"; No. V, B-flat major, "with choral"; No. VII, E major, one of his most beautiful works; No. VIII, C minor; No. IX, D minor, unfinished, in three movements) and a single chamber music work, the String Quintet, F major. His church compositions include the beautiful *Te Deum* and three masses, especially No. II in E minor, for chorus and wind instruments only, and No. III in F minor, a magnificent work.

A strange controversy about Bruckner's symphonies started more than thirty years after his death. The composer had made a practice of showing each work before publication to friends and pupils, among them Arthur Nikisch, Hermann Levi, the two Schalk brothers, and Johann Loewe. These men advised him to make cuts and to use a more Wagnerian technique of orchestration. Bruckner followed his advisers in many cases, and the original manuscripts, mostly preserved by the National Library, Vienna, reveal how different his original intentions were from the versions he presented in print. It remains an unsettled question whether the "Urfassung" (the original version) or the one engraved during the composer's lifetime is preferable.   K. G.

BRUEGEL, PIETER, THE ELDER [brɜ'gəl] (c.1520-1569), Flemish painter and designer of prints, was one of the foremost artists in the history of Flemish painting. His family came probably from one of the two towns in Flanders named Bruegel; the Bruegel in North Brabant is near 's Hertogenbosch, where Hieronymus Bosch was born and worked many years before, and in early pictures by Bruegel there are strange creatures similar to inventions by Bosch. According to Karel van Mander, Bruegel was a pupil of Pieter Coeck van Aelst, who died in 1550. The following year he became a member of the painters' guild in Antwerp, and in 1563 he married Coeck's daughter. In 1552 and 1553 he traveled in Italy, recording in many exquisite drawings of Alpine and southern landscapes how deeply the scenery of the trip impressed him. Returning to Antwerp, he made a business arrangement with the engraver Hieronymus Cock, and for a number of years turned out remarkable drawings which Cock and his assistants engraved and published. Moving to Brussels in 1563, Bruegel continued to make drawings for Cock, many of them satirical and showing keen perception, but most of his time during the six years that remained of his life was apparently devoted to painting.

Nearly all of Bruegel's important works are signed and dated. His superb *Tower of Babel,* now in Vienna, was painted in 1563. The following year saw the production of two of his rare religious paintings, the *Adoration of the Magi* (National Gallery, London) and the *Way of the Cross* (Vienna). In 1565 Bruegel completed his series representing the months of the year, of which five paintings are preserved, three in Vienna, one at Castle Roudnice in Bohemia, and one in the Metropolitan Museum in New York. Five important signed paintings bear the date 1568. Bruegel died in Brussels, Sept. 5, 1569.

Bruegel's works influenced his followers deeply and there are numerous copies and free versions. In his technical ability and his solution of artistic problems he has no rival. In his subject matter, with its perceptive account of life in the Flemish villages and on the farms, he is always fresh and interesting. His art provides a remarkably instructive and ironic picture of the occupations, amusements, superstitions, and weaknesses of his contemporaries, and vividly presents the Flanders of his day, torn by religious strife and suffering from Spanish oppression. Bruegel's son Pieter the Younger (c. 1564-c. 1638) was also a painter, as were numerous other members of the Bruegel family in succeeding generations.

M. Sa.

BRUENING, HEINRICH. *See* BRÜNING, HEINRICH.

BRUGES (Flem. Brugge) [bru'zh, brü'zh; bru'gə], a city in western Belgium, the capital of the province of West Flanders, about 60 mi. northwest of Brussels and 50 mi. west of Antwerp. It is situated about 6 mi. from the North Sea, to which it is connected at Zeebrugge, Blankenberghe, and Ostend by a series of canals. The city is surrounded and intersected by canals which are crossed by 54 bridges. Bruges derives its name from its numerous bridges, for *brug* in Flemish means bridge. The canal linking the city with Zeebrugge was begun in 1896 and completed in 1907. It is over 6 mi. long, 72 ft. wide at the bottom, 229 ft. wide at the surface, and 28 ft. deep. It runs at sea level throughout its course. Ships drawing 25 ft. can use the canal to reach the city wharves.

More than any other city of Belgium, Bruges has retained the characteristic appearance of the Middle Ages. After the seventh century Bruges developed rapidly as a trade center of importance. In the ninth century it became the residence of the counts of Flanders, and Count Baldwin II fortified the community in 837. By 1180 Bruges was the recognized capital of Flanders. Under the rule of the Flemish counts until the fifteenth century it achieved its greatest prosperity and wealth. It became one of the chief commercial centers of northern Europe and was a leading member of the Hanseatic League. Its wool manufactures grew and flourished, and a brisk wool trade was carried on with England. During the fourteenth century it was considered the northern twin of Venice. In this period its Bourse regulated the rate of exchange in Europe, and the city became a cultural center and the residence of many noted artists, including Jan van Eyck. Bruges declined rapidly after its access to the sea was stopped by the silting of the Zwijn, which was complete by 1490, and its trade and importance were assumed by Antwerp. Another factor in its decline in the fifteenth century was the rebellious conduct of its citizens against the Austrian dynasty, which punished them severely for disobedience. Some of its trade revived in the sixteenth century when it became a market for Spain's trade with the New World. But in the seventeenth century the city suffered from the religious persecutions and atrocities of Philip II and the Duke of Alva. Both the Dutch and French laid siege to the city during the wars of the Spanish and the Austrian successions. The French captured it in 1794, and it was in Dutch hands from 1814 to 1830. During World War I Bruges was occupied by the Germans after 1914, and along with Zeebrugge it was an important base for the fitting out of submarines. In World War II it was also occupied by German forces. Most of the city's buildings suffered little damage by World War II action, but some damage was caused by the destruction of nearby bridges, and three of the four city gates were damaged.

The city has many interesting and beautiful landmarks. The Cathedral of St. Sauveur and the Church of Nôtre Dame date from the thirteenth and fourteenth centuries and are examples of early Gothic architecture. The Church of Nôtre Dame contains many famous and valuable paintings and sculptures, including a marble group of the *Virgin and Child* attributed to Michelangelo, and the tombs of Charles

EWING GALLOWAY

View of a canal in Bruges, Belgium, "The City of Bridges"

the Bold and Mary of Burgundy, his daughter. On the night of Sept. 7-8, 1940, the Germans stole many of Nôtre Dame's art treasures, including Michelangelo's *Madonna,* Pieter Pourbus' *Adoration of the Shepherds* and the *Last Supper,* and Anthony van Dyck's *Crucifixion.* These were returned in August 1944. The Halles, a sixteenth-century market hall on the Grande Place, contains Bruges' famous belfry, 350 ft. high, which is celebrated for its forty-eight chimes. The principal paintings by Hans Memling are found in the old Hôpital St. Jean. The Chapelle du Saint-Sang (Chapel of the Holy Blood) is a two-story building on whose site it is said that Theodoric of Alsace deposited some drops of the blood of the Savior brought from Palestine. The museum contains a great collection of early Flemish paintings. The vistas of the old quays, the canals with their stone bridges, and the numerous ancient houses attract many tourists and artists. The sixteenth-century houses of the Beguinage were damaged slightly in World War II.

The women of Bruges are known for their lacemaking. The chief manufactures include linen, damasks, woolens, cottons, rope, jewelry, railroad equipment, and beer. Shipbuilding is important. The city serves as an export port for agricultural produce, coke, and manufactured articles, and it is an importing center for wine, oil, and raw materials from the Belgian Congo. Pop. 1952, 51,924.   S. D. M.

BRUGMANN, KARL [bru′gmɑn] (1849-1919), German linguist, was born at Wiesbaden, Mar. 16, 1849. With the exception of a few years at Freiburg in Baden, he was professor of Indo-European linguistics at the University of Leipzig from 1882 until his death, thirty-seven years later.

The most famous representative of the school of so-called "Neogrammarians" (German *Junggrammatiker*), Brugmann systematized all Indo-European grammar that was known in his time in the monumental but dogmatic and rigid trea-

tises *Grundriss der vergleichenden Grammatik der indogermanischen Sprachwissenschaft* (1886-1900) and *Griechische Grammatik* (1885), works which remained for decades the bible of many linguists. His learning and his capacity for organizing material was enormous, and they gave him for a long time the reputation of being the leading figure not only among Indo-Europeanists but even among all linguists. His theoretical principles, summarized in *Zum heutigen Stand der Sprachwissenschaft* (1885), were strongly attacked by his own professor and former friend, Georg Curtius, with whom he quarreled in 1878, and by the Italian linguist G. I. Ascoli. Faithful to the doctrines of his youth, however, Brugmann remained indifferent to the new linguistic trends of the twentieth century and showed no sign of modifying his methods. He died at Leipzig on June 25, 1919.   G. B.

BRULÉ, ÉTIENNE [brü′le′] (c.1592-1633), French explorer, was born at Champigny about 1592. He went to Canada in 1608 and was one of the first settlers of Quebec. In 1612, while living with the Hurons in the vicinity of Georgian Bay, Brulé probably saw that part of Lake Huron and was thus the first European to see one of the Great Lakes. He may also have discovered Lake Ontario in 1615. Brulé's other explorations, which are difficult to trace accurately, carried him to Lakes Erie and Superior as well, and on one mission for Champlain he followed the course of the Susquehanna River to its outlet in Chesapeake Bay. In 1629 he deserted to the English and piloted the fleet of Sir David Kirke from the Saguenay to Quebec. He later returned to live among the Hurons, who killed him in 1633.

BRUM, BALTASAR [bru′m] (1883-1933), Uruguayan statesman and journalist, was born in Artigas, June 18, 1883. He became Uruguay's youngest president and South America's most brilliant advocate of an American League of Nations. As a university student he was a disciple of the social reformer, Batlle, and spent his life fighting for ideals which made Uruguay one of the world's most democratic nations. As minister of education, a post that he assumed in March 1913, Brum completely reorganized Uruguay's educational system. During World War I, as minister of the interior and of foreign affairs, he established Uruguay's foreign policy of arbitration on all points of dissension, including those which concerned national honor. He urged, too, that the National Council of Administration share the president's executive power. At the close of the war Brum became president of Uruguay. He held this post until 1923. His term is notable for its widesweeping reforms within the country, for its leadership in the solidification of the Pan-American movement, and for the "Brum doctrine" proposing an American League of Nations. Two of Brum's outstanding writings are *La Paz de America* and *La Doctrina del arbitraje amplio.* Brum died in Montevideo on Mar. 31, 1933.   S. G. I.

BRUNEI [brunɑi′], a British protectorate on the north coast of the island of Borneo, on the South China Sea. It consists of two separate lobes of territory, the eastern part about 55 mi. wide and the western section 7 to 15 mi. wide, each with a sea front but otherwise enclosed within the British colony of Sarawak. Brunei has an area of 2,226 sq. mi. and a population estimated at 43,000 in 1947. Except for a narrow coastal plain the country is rugged, with altitudes increasing toward the south but seldom reaching 4,000 ft. Precipitation varies with altitude from about 100 in. in the lowlands to over 200 in. on some of the highlands. Most of the rainfall comes between November and May, but there is no dry season. The annual mean temperature is 80° F. Heat and moisture combine to produce a heavy forest cover. There are valuable hardwoods, but difficulties of transport have limited lumbering operations. Agricultural production includes cassava, pineapples, bananas, rice, sugar cane, savo, and livestock. Plantation rubber regularly accounts for about 10 per cent of the value of exports. Other forest products exported are native Jelutong rubber and cutch, a tanning material from mangrove bark. Oil, however, is Brunei's predominant export, accounting for about 80 per cent of the total value of exports. Seria is the center of oil production. Brunei produces about 5,000,000 metric tons of oil a year, exceeding that of any other British possession. Shipbuilding and fishing are of minor importance.

The people of Brunei are mostly of Malay stock. There are about 1,500 Chinese, but their position in the economic life of the protectorate gives them an importance out of proportion to their numbers. There is an inconsiderable number of Indians and Europeans. Most of the people are Mohammedan, although there are pagans in the more remote interior. The administration is in the hands of the British resident and a body of civil servants mostly seconded from the Sarawak civil service, formerly from the civil service of Malaya. The British resident is assisted by a state council, which consists of the sultan, who presides, the resident, and ten others. The British resident is responsible to the governor of Sarawak, who also holds the title of High Commissioner for Brunei. The governor is, in turn, responsible to the Commissioner General for the United Kingdom in South-East Asia. The capital is Brunei Town.

Prior to the fifteenth century the state of Brunei was a feudal dependency of the Hindu Kingdom of Java. With the breakdown of that kingdom and the conversion of many of the Brunei people, including its ruler, to Mohammedanism in that century, an independent sultanate was established. In the ensuing centuries the sultan was able to hold off successive attempts of Portuguese, Spanish, Dutch, and British and even to extend his domain to include not only the entire north coast of Borneo (whose name was merely a corruption of the name of his state) but also some of the adjacent Philippine Islands. In the nineteenth century, however, this once mighty principality was tottering under the combined attack of pirates from without and enemies within. In 1841 the sultan, in gratitude for aid received in putting down an insurrection in the southwest, ceded to James Brooke, an adventurous Englishman, the territory of Sarawak and made him its rajah. From time to time thereafter the dynasty of the "white rajahs" succeeded in securing further cessions, until Sarawak surrounded Brunei. In 1847 the British government, anxious to put an end to piracy along the coast, secured special rights in the island of Labuan in Brunei Bay. In 1881 the British North Borneo Company received a royal charter, and from time to time it, too, was able to whittle away the domain of the sultan. In 1888 the British established a protectorate over the sultanate itself, and in 1906 secured the right to administer both its internal and external affairs, except in regard to Malay customs and Islamic religious affairs. In 1931 oil began to be produced in Brunei and the economy of the country underwent a sudden transformation. Between 1942 and 1945 the territory was under Japanese control, and much damage was done both to oil wells and rubber plantations. In 1946 British civil administration was restored, and in 1948 the British resident was placed under the supervision of the governor of Sarawak. The latter territory had become a crown colony in 1946 with the cession to the British government of the land which

for over a century had been at once the state and the estate of the Brooke family. Relations between Brunei and Sarawak have always been close.   W. M. W.

BRUNELLESCHI, FILIPPO [bru'nelle'ski] (c. 1377-1446), generally acclaimed the first great architect of the Italian Renaissance, was born in Florence. His early training was in the field of sculpture and bronze founding. After his defeat by Lorenzo Ghiberti in the competition for the design of the bronze doors of the Baptistery of San Giovanni at Florence, Brunelleschi went to Rome, where for four years he applied himself to a careful study of Classical Roman architecture. In 1420 he entered a competition for the design and erection of the dome for the unfinished cathedral of Florence. This dome was an original and unique contribution to the evolution of architectural forms and the forerunner of such domical masterpieces as those of St. Peter's in Rome and St. Paul's in London.

But Brunelleschi's fame rests on no single achievement. He was the architect of other important structures, each of which is characterized by masterful construction and elegant form. Among his better-known examples are the charming Pazzi Chapel in the cloister of Santa Croce, the churches of San Lorenzo and Santo Spirito, and the central portion of the robust Palazzo Pitti—all in Florence. He died in Florence in 1446.   R. Ne.

BRUNETIÈRE, FERDINAND [brü'nətyɛ'r] (1849-1906), French literary critic and orator, was born at Toulon, July 19, 1849. He contributed to the *Revue bleue,* became director of the conservative and aristocratic *Revue des deux mondes* (1893), and was the leader of the fight against Naturalism with his book, *Le Roman naturaliste* (1883). In 1886 he was appointed professor at the École Normale Supérieure, to which he had been refused admission as a student.

The influence of evolutionist ideas is apparent in Brunetière's theory of literary criticism. According to this theory, literary genres have developed in a way comparable to the evolution of natural species, from original confusion to divisions and distinctions, as described in Brunetière's books: *L'Évolution de la critique* (1890), *Les Époques du théâtre français* (1892) (*The Law of the Drama,* 1914), and *L'Évolution de la poésie lyrique* (1894). Brunetière's *Études critique sur la littérature française* (1880) (*Essays in French Literature,* 1898), and his studies on individual authors, among them *Honoré de Balzac* (1906) and *Bossuet* (1914), are splendid examples of scientific investigation. In them Brunetière applies a form of objective and dogmatic criticism derived partly from Sainte-Beuve and Hippolyte Taine, but he separates himself from his masters when he seeks in literature a moral and social value. His critical works are remarkable for the wealth of biographical and chronological information that they contain. He has revealed the importance of periods of transition in literature and of secondary, but nevertheless influential, authors, heretofore neglected.

Brunetière was converted to Roman Catholicism in 1890 and became an indefatigable champion of his new faith in scores of lectures, articles that were published for the most part in the *Revue des deux mondes,* and books, such as *La Science et la religion* (1897), *Discours de combat* (1900-1907), *Sur les chemins de la croyance* (1904), and *Études sur le XVIIIe siècle.* He was an original and conscientious scholar, a vigorous polemist, and an orator of great talent to whom modern theories of the history of literature owe much. Brunetière died in Paris, Dec. 9, 1906.   F. V.

BRUNHILD or **BRÜNNEHILDE.** *See* Brynhild.

BRUNHILDA [brunhɪ'ldə] (Brunechildis) (d. A.D. 613), Visigothic princess. Daughter of Athanagild, Visigoth king, Brunhilda married Sigebert, King of Austrasia, in 566; her sister, Galswintha, married Chilperic, King of Neustria. When Chilperic murdered Galswintha in order to return to his mistress, Fredegund, a bitter feud arose between him and Sigebert. As a result, Sigebert was killed. After her husband's death, Brunhilda continued the fight and was at last victorious over Chilperic. Aspiring to the rule of Austrasia and Burgundy, she aroused the enmity of the nobles of those lands, and in her old age was delivered by them into the hands of King Clotaire II, of Neustria, son of Fredegund. In A.D. 613 she was bound by her own hair to the tail of a horse and dragged to her death. *See also* Brynhild (Brunhild, Brünnhilde).   T. B. J.

BRUNI, or **BRUNO, LEONARDO** [bru'ni, bru'no] (1369-1444), Italian humanist, one of the earliest of the Renaissance scholars, was born at Arezzo in 1369. He studied law and philosophy in Florence and later, under the influence of Jean de Ravenne and Chrysoloras, he became absorbed in the study of the Classics. In 1405 he was appointed secretary at the Papal Chancery, and he served in that capacity under popes Innocent VII, Gregory XII, Alexander V, and John XXIII. In 1415 Bruni established himself in Florence, where he devoted himself to literary work. From 1427 until his death, he was chancellor of the republic of Florence. He wrote a twelve-volume *History of Florence* in Latin (1415), which was translated into Italian by Donato Acciajuoli in 1473. Despite his preference for the Latin language, Bruni wrote the lives of Dante and Petrarch in the Italian vernacular. He also translated into Latin several of the works of Aristotle, Plato, Demosthenes, and Aeschines. He died in Florence on Mar. 9, 1444.

BRÜNING, HEINRICH [brü'nɪŋ] (1885-   ), German politician, was born in Münster, Westphalia, Nov. 26, 1885. Brüning received his early training in law at the University of Munich, in history and literature at Strasburg, and in political science at Münster and Bonn universities. During World War I, from 1915 to 1918, Brüning served as an officer on the Western Front. At the close of the war he became a Catholic social worker at Dr. Sonnenschein's Welfare Institute. Brüning's next post was that of secretary to Adam Stegerwald, the man who was the founder of the influential Federation of Christian Trade Unions movement. In 1921 when Stegerwald became the prime minister of Prussia, Brüning succeeded him in the management of the Catholic trade unions and retained that position until 1930. In 1921 also, Brüning founded and partly edited the union daily, *Der Deutsche.*

The political career of Heinrich Brüning began with his election as member of the Reichstag in 1924. There he soon became a prominent member of the taxation committee and in 1925 promulgated the so-called "Lex Brüning" dealing with tax reforms. In 1929 he succeeded Stegerwald as head of the parliamentary Zentrums-Partei or Catholic Centrist Party. After the resignation of Müller in 1930, Brüning was appointed reich chancellor and charged with forming a ministry which was not to be based upon a parliamentary coalition. When the Reichstag rejected his emergency measure he procured a dissolution and new elections in September 1930. In March 1931, when the need for drastic governmental economy became evident, Brüning assumed the power of governing Germany by emergency measures issued by the president of the Reich.

During 1931 Brüning conferred with foreign envoys on war debts, and visited London, Paris, and Rome in the interests of international co-operation to lessen economic difficulties. The proposed Austro-German customs pact found an advocate in the Reich Chancellor, who held that it did not violate the Geneva Protocol of 1922 and was therefore no concern of the League of Nations. In 1932 Brüning headed the German delegation to the Disarmament Conference at Geneva. Ascetic and scholarly, lacking the fiery appeal of his chief opponent, the Nazi Führer Adolf Hitler, Dr. Brüning as a political figure nevertheless gained the confidence of the German moderate parties. Brüning failed because he could neither form a coalition of parties to support his labor and agricultural programs, nor control the Nazis, Communists, and Nationalists. He was overthrown by a conspiracy instigated by militarists, reactionaries, and opportunists. Von Hindenburg forced Brüning's ministry to resign May 30, 1932, to be followed first by Fritz von Papen and then by Hitler. Brüning for a time was leader of the Center Party, but later came to the United States and from 1939 to 1952 he was Littauer professor of government at Harvard University. In 1952 he accepted a teaching post at Cologne University in Germany.   R. H. L.

BRÜNN. *See* Brno.

BRUNO, GIORDANO [bru'no] (c. 1548-1600), Italian philosopher, was born in Nola. He attended school in Naples, where he entered the Dominican order at the age of fifteen. Charged with heresy in 1576, he fled and began a wandering life that took him to Geneva; to Toulouse, where he taught for two years; to Paris (1582); to London (1583), where he lived for two years in the household of the French ambassador; again to Paris; hence to Marburg, Wittenberg, Prague, Helmstedt, and Frankfurt. In 1591 he was denounced by the Venetian nobleman, Giovanni Mocenigo, and delivered to the Inquisition (1592). Bruno was imprisoned and tried, first in Venice, and subsequently in Rome. The numerous charges against him included blasphemy, immoral conduct, and heresy in matters of dogmatic theology, and involved some of the basic doctrines of his philosophy and cosmology. Upon his refusal to recant, he was sentenced to death and burned at the stake on the Campo dei Fiori in Rome, Feb. 17, 1600.

Bruno's early writings include an Italian comedy (*Il Candelaio,* 1582), and several treaties on the theories of Ramon Lull and on artificial memory. Most important for his philosophy are the Italian dialogues written in England, and the Latin poems written in Germany. In the dialogue *Degli eroici furori,* Bruno follows the traditions of Renaissance Platonism in praising the "heroic" love of the infinite. His metaphysical doctrine is found in his dialogue *Della causa,* in which he maintains that God (the Infinite) includes or combines all attributes, whereas particular phenomena are nothing but particular manifestations of the one infinite principle. A single universal matter and a single universal form, or soul, are said to be the immediate principles of all particulars; but it is not completely clear whether or not form and matter are ultimately identical with each other or with the Infinite. Bruno's cosmology is contained in his dialogue *Del infinito.* In this work he refutes the traditional Aristotelian cosmology and states that the physical universe is infinite and includes an indefinite number of worlds each consisting of a sun and several planets. The earth, no longer the stable center of the universe, becomes thus a small star among the others in an infinite universe.

In his metaphysics, Bruno provided a connecting link between Cusanus and Spinoza and also exercised a direct influence on classical German idealism. In his cosmology, Bruno followed Lucretius and Copernicus, but he developed the implications of the Copernican system much further than Copernicus himself had done. More than the other Italian philosophers who were his contemporaries, Bruno deserves to be called a forerunner, if not a founder, of modern science and philosophy. In his thinking as well as in his writing he is bold and imaginative rather than precise or careful, yet his agreement with later scientific and philosophical theories that were unknown in his own time is often surprising. His tragic end has made him a martyr of philosophical liberty, if not of science. P. O. K.

BRUNO OF COLOGNE, ST. (c.1030-1101), founder of the Roman Catholic order of Carthusians, was born in Cologne about 1030 and ordained there in 1057. His early years as a priest were given to teaching and administration. Having inveighed against the dubious practices of an archbishop, he was deprived of his offices. The Carthusian order was founded in 1084, when Bruno retired with six companions to the desert of Chartreuse. After six years Pope Urban II called him to Rome for consultation. Later Bruno established two other monasteries in Calabria. He wrote commentaries on the Psalms and the Pauline Epistles. His feast is October 6. W. C.

BRUNO OF QUERFURT, SAINT (c. 970-1009), German missionary and martyr, belonged to a noble family of Saxony. He was related to Emperor Otto III. Bruno received his education at the Cathedral school of Magdeburg, where he was placed under the care of Archbishop Adalbert. He was later summoned to the imperial court, where he was appointed chaplain to Holy Roman Emperor Otto III. In 996, Bruno accompanied Otto to Rome for the Emperor's coronation. In Italy, he left the Emperor to enter the monastery of Pereum, near Ravenna. When, in 997, Bruno received news of the murder of Adalbert, Bishop of Prague, who lost his life while serving as a missionary to the Prussian heathen, he decided to replace the Bishop. After preparing himself for his projected missions, he was appointed archbishop over the heathen by Pope Sylvester II. Bruno was consecrated by the Archbishop of Magdeburg in 1004. Unable to proceed to Poland because of war, he went instead to Hungary, where he found time to complete a life of St. Adalbert (*Vita S. Alberti*). Not too successful in his work among the heathen of Hungary, Bruno then proceeded to Russia in 1007, where he successfully brought Christianity to the heathen living between the Danube and the Don. In 1008 he was finally able to go to Poland, where he heard of the murder of five monks who had preceded him there. He then wrote *Vita Quinque Fratrum Poloniae* as a memorial to those martyrs. On his mission to convert the heathen, Bruno began in Prussia and gradually moved toward the borders of Russia, where he and his party were murdered by hostile heathens on Feb. 14, 1009. His body was bought from the heathens and brought back to Poland by Duke Boleslav.

BRUNOT, FERDINAND [brü'no'] (1860-1938), French linguist, was born at Saint-Dié (Vosges) in 1860. From 1900 onward he taught the history of the French language at the Sorbonne. His first work was *La Doctrine de Malherbe d'après son commentaire sur Desportes* (1891), an examination of the stylistic and grammatical doctrine of Malherbe. His lifework is the admirable *Histoire de la langue française,* of which the first volume appeared in 1905, and the tenth and last in 1943, after his death; it carries the history of the French language from its origins to 1900 and is one of the best existing descriptions of any language. Brunot shows in it a fine feeling for the close interrelationship between language and literature, as well as for the impact of social and historical events of every kind on the development of the language. Among his other important works are *La Pensée et la langue; méthode, principes et plan d'une théorie nouvelle du langage appliquée au français* (1922) and *Précis de grammaire historique de la langue française; avec une introduction sur les origines et le développement de cette langue* (1887). In 1932 he published his salty and amusing *Observations sur la grammaire de l' Académie Française* (1932). Brunot died in Paris, Jan. 30, 1938. G. B.

BRUNSWICK (BRAUNSCHWEIG) [brʌ'nzwɪk, brɑu'nshvɑiχ], the name of a ruling family and of a former duchy and state in north central Germany. Brunswick proper had an area of 1,418 sq. mi. and a population (1939) of 599,208. A disjointed state of three main sections and several enclaves (districts lying entirely within foreign territory), lying between the Harz Mountains and the Aller and Weser rivers, Brunswick was bounded on all sides by the Prussian provinces of Hanover and Saxony, except where Lippe touched one of the western borders and where Anhalt was contiguous with a southeastern border. The principal cities were Hildesheim, Holsminden, Goslar, Helmstedt, Wolfenbüttel, and Braunschweig (Brunswick), the capital. The entire region is now included within the autonomous state of Lower Saxony in the (West German) Federal Republic.

Brunswick was established in 1235 from the ancestral lands of the Guelph duke, Henry the Lion, Duke of Saxony and Bavaria (1129-1195). In 1181 after a conflict with Emperor Frederick I (Barbarossa), Henry lost his possessions in Saxony and Bavaria, retaining only Brunswick and Lüneburg. Not until 1235, however, was Henry's grandson Otto the Child (1204-1252), proclaimed the first Duke of Brunswick-Lüneburg by Emperor Frederick II. In 1237 the Duchy was divided again when Otto's sons succeeded him, John establishing the House of Lüneburg and Albert, the house of Brunswick. For the next five hundred years the power of the duchy and of the ruling family declined because of further territorial divisions and domestic conflict, which resulted, eventually, in the establishment of seven separate branches of the Brunswick family. Of the seven, the two most important were the Brunswick-Wolfenbüttel and the Brunswick-Lüneburg lines. After the latter branch obtained control of Hanover, Duke Ernest Augustus, the first Elector of Hanover, married Sophia, granddaughter of James I of England, in 1658. Under the British Act of Settlement in 1701, the English Crown was settled upon Princess Sophia, and her son, George Louis of the Brunswick-Lüneburg-Hanoverian line, became George I of England upon the death of his cousin, Queen Anne, in 1714.

For eight years, from 1806 to 1814, Brunswick was included in the Kingdom of Westphalia which Napoleon created for his youngest brother Jérôme Bonaparte, who became its king in 1807. In 1814, however, the Congress of Vienna restored the duchy to its original rulers, represented at that time by Duke Frederick William, who died in 1815. His son Charles, an unpopular ruler, was forced to leave the country for good during the revolutionary upheavals of 1830, and in 1831 Charles was formally replaced by his brother William, who proved an able and popular ruler. In 1884, after the death of William, the last member of the Brunswick-Wolfenbüttel line, Brunswick was claimed by the Duke of Cumberland (son of the King of Hannover, which had been annexed to Prussia). However, his refusal to recognize the constitution of the German Empire, the provisions of which required that he formally renounce his claim to Hanover in order to succeed Duke William of Brunswick, prompted Bismarck, in the same year, to appoint Prince Albert of Prussia as regent. After the latter's death in 1906, the Brunswick diet elected Duke John Albert of Mecklenburg-Schwerin to the regency of the state, and finally, in 1913, the question of succession was settled when the duchy was awarded to Ernest Augustus,

BRUNSWICK, a town in Cumberland Co., southwestern Maine, is situated on the Androscoggin River, 28 mi. northeast of Portland. Founded in 1628, Brunswick was incorporated as a town in 1719. It is the site of Bowdoin College, the alma mater of Longfellow, Hawthorne, Franklin Pierce, and Robert E. Peary. Harriet Beecher Stowe wrote *Uncle Tom's Cabin* in Brunswick. Local industries include pulp, paper, textiles, and canning. Pop. 1950, 7,342.

BRUNTON, DAVID W. (1849-1927), mining engineer, was born in Canada and received his technical education at the University of Michigan. His first mining work was in Colorado in 1875. Later he became consulting engineer for

BRUNSWICK (BRAUNSCHWEIG), GERMANY, AS IT APPEARED BEFORE THE EXTENSIVE DAMAGE SUSTAINED IN WORLD WAR II

PRESS ASSOCIATION, INC.

second son of the Duke of Cumberland, who had renounced his claim to Hanover and married Princess Victoria Louise, only daughter of Emperor William II. After World War I, Brunswick, like all other German states, became a part of the Weimar Republic.

In 1934, with the reorganization of the Reich under Hitler, Brunswick became merely an administrative unit. In 1946, after World War II, Prussia was dissolved, and, in the resulting redistribution of territory, most of Brunswick was incorporated in Lower Saxony. *See also* BRAUNSCHWEIG.

R. H. L.

BRUNSWICK, the seat of Glynn Co. in southeastern Georgia, is situated on a landlocked harbor in Oglethorpe Bay, 8 mi. from the Atlantic Ocean, and about 65 mi. south of Savannah. The Oglethorpe area was first visited by Spanish missionaries in 1568. In 1736 General James Oglethorpe built Fort Frederica, established as a national monument in 1945. The English defeated the Spaniards in the Battle of Bloody Marsh on nearby St. Simons Island in 1742. Brunswick was founded in 1771 by order of the Colonial Council; it was incorporated as a city in 1856 and has the commission-manager form of government. Brunswick's proximity to the sea makes it a center in which much sea food is processed and shipped. A winter resort itself, the city is also a gateway to such nationally known vacation spots as Sea Island, St. Simons Island, and Jekyll Island. Local manufactures include naval stores, boilers, tools and dies, lumber and pulp, and garments. Pop. 1950, 17,954.

Marcus Daly in Butte, Mont., where he remained until the copper properties were sold to the Anaconda Copper Mining Company. He then returned to Denver, where he won wide recognition as a consultant in tunnel work. He developed the principles and practice of accurate ore sampling by cutting through the whole stream of particles at the same time. He started the system of using mine geologists to follow continuously all workings and to record precisely the geological indications that had escaped the operating men. He is best known for the invention of the Brunton mining compass for rapid underground surveys, an instrument used by mining engineers and military men. He died Dec. 17, 1927.

W. F. B.

BRUSH, CHARLES FRANCIS (1849-1929), American inventor and industrialist, was born in Euclid, Ohio, Mar. 17, 1849. He attended public schools in Cleveland, Ohio, and received his M.E. degree from the University of Michigan in 1869. After his graduation he worked as a public chemist, and from 1873 to 1877 maintained a small business as an iron dealer. He had shown remarkable mechanical ingenuity from early youth, and his experiments with electrical machines led to the invention of a dynamo in 1876 for the production of high-tension current of constant voltage, which became the parent of the modern generator. He also developed the arc-light which bears his name, and the fundamental storage battery. These contributions greatly speeded the growth of the electric lighting industry. In 1879 Brush demonstrated the first street lighting in Cleveland, and by 1882 the "Brush lights" had spread over a large part of the United States and to some countries in Europe. Brush formed the Brush Electric Company in 1880, and though he had some difficulty in protecting his patents, he was able to merge his company with the Edison Company and several lesser companies in 1891 to form the General Electric Company. In his later years he became interested in other scientific developments, and in 1905 formed the Linde Air Production Company for the production of oxygen from liquid air. Brush also designed a new type of vacuum gauge, and wrote several works on the results of his researches in metallurgy. In 1910 he published *A Kinetic Theory of Gravitation*, in which he maintained that gravitation was caused by the absorption of isotropic ether waves of short length, and a year before his death he founded the Brush Foundation for the Betterment of the Human Race to promote research in eugenics. Brush was the recipient of many honors, among which were the Rumford Medal in 1899, and the Edison Medal in 1913. He died in Cleveland, Ohio, June 15, 1929.

C. W. D.

BRUSH, GEORGE DE FOREST (1855-1941), American portrait painter, was born at Shelbyville, Tenn., Sept. 28, 1855. He studied at the National Academy of Design, New York; under Gérôme at the École des Beaux Arts, Paris; and in Florence, Italy. After six years abroad, he painted Indians in the American West. Brush's notable Indian paintings include *The Silence Broken, Before the Battle, Mourning Her Brave,* and *The Indian Hunter.* Between 1901 and 1913 he painted eleven *Mother and Child* canvases. Among his outstanding paintings are *In the Garden*, Metropolitan Museum, New York; *Mother and Child*, Boston Museum; *Mother and Children*, Pennsylvania Academy, Philadelphia; *Mother and Child*, Corcoran Gallery, Washington, D.C.; *Portrait of a Young Woman*, Smith College; *The Young Violinist*, Worcester Museum; and *Family Group*, Art Institute of Chicago. Brush won gold medals at the Paris (1900), Buffalo (1901), and St. Louis (1904) expositions. He became a charter member of the National Institute of Arts and Letters, 1898; a National Academician, 1906; and a member of the American Academy of Arts and Letters, 1910. Brush died at Hanover, N. H., Apr. 24, 1941.

COURTESY OF THE NEW YORK ZOOLOGICAL SOCIETY

BRUSH TURKEY OF AUSTRALIA

BRUSH TURKEY, a fowl like bird, *Alectura lathami,* of eastern Australia, typical of the family known as megapodes or mound builders. It is the size of a small turkey, with a yellow wattle (in the male) and the head naked and neck rose-red; its plumage is brownish-black above and brownish-gray below. The brush turkey and its relatives have unique breeding habits: the males, with their large feet, collect a huge mound of vegetable matter, and in this mass the enormous eggs are buried by the females, to be incubated by the heat generated by decay. The young may never know their parents, coming from the eggs fully feathered and able to fly the day they are hatched.

H. G. De.

BRUSILOV, ALEKSEI ALEKSEEVICH [brusyi'lɔf] (1853-1926), Russian soldier, son of a general, was born in Kutais, in the Caucasus, Aug. 19, 1853. Soon after entering the Russian cavalry he served in the Russo-Turkish War, 1877-1878, and thereafter rose steadily to the command of the Second Cavalry Division of the Guard in 1906. Five years later he was placed in command of an army corps in Podolia. At the outbreak of World War I, from this vantage point, Brusilov invaded Galicia. In April 1915 he was placed in command on the Carpathian front, and there received the brunt of General August von Mackensen's offensive to reconquer Galicia. In the face of great odds Brusilov conducted a skillful withdrawal. In April 1916 he was placed in command of the Southwestern Army Group, and successfully led his troops in a drive to reconquer Galicia and Bukovina. But for the failure on the part of the Russian government to supply him with necessary equipment when he had almost cut off the retreat of the Austrians, he might have achieved the greatest single victory of the war. After the abdication of Tsar Nicholas II in 1917, Brusilov tried to maintain discipline and carry on the war. He resigned his command in May 1917, but his resignation was refused and he was appointed commander in chief of all Russian armies. Soon afterward the Kerensky government fell, and Brusilov was arrested by the Bolshevists. For two months he was imprisoned in the Kremlin, but then he sided with the Bolshevists and was placed in command of a militia organization. He fought in Poland and was later appointed cavalry inspector. Brusilov retired in 1924 and died in Moscow, Mar. 17, 1926.

BRUSSELS (Fr., **BRUXELLES;** Flem. **BRUSSEL)** [brʌ'səlz, brü'sɛ'l, brʌ'səl], the capital of Belgium and of the province of Brabant. It occupies a central location in the country, at 50° 50' N. lat. and 4° 20' E. long., about 26 mi. south of Anvers, on the Senne River, a tributary of the Scheldt, and on the canal connecting the port of Antwerp with Charleroi, center of the industrial region. It is also at the crossroad of the main international transportation lines.

History. Remains of an important Roman villa and Frankish cemeteries have been discovered in the area included in the oldest section of the city. Islands among the marshes of the Senne were good defensive sites where the early inhabitants sought refuge. Brussels thus probably took its origin from Brockzele, "the village of the Marshes." The main island on which St. Géry founded an oratory in the late sixth or early seventh century continues to be known as Ile St. Géry. The islands were fortified at the fall of Charlemagne's empire. During the period of security and prosperity which followed the Norman invasion in the tenth century, and because of privileges given by the city's counts, Brussels developed rapidly. Commerce and industry flourished; an important road connecting Cologne on the Rhine to the Flemish cities of Ghent and Bruges crossed the city bringing many travelers and much business to the city. An important market was created, which continues to be called the Grande Place. The city expanded first on the alluvial plain of the river forming what is called the "low-town," which remains as the commercial and business center of the city. Later, a duke of Brabant built a castle on the eastern edge of the plateau bordering the Senne Valley, and the Abbey of St. Jacques on the Coudenberg was erected near by. A new settlement grew there, the "high-town," which continues as the aristocratic district of the city. In the first half of the thirteenth century, new ramparts comprising eight gates and twenty-four towers were built to protect the old primitive center and the new growing suburbs.

The city had its charter confirmed in 1356. Under the charter the citizens were granted the most extensive rights: equality of all the citizens before the law, individual freedom, and the right to resist the prince.

Brussels became the most important city of the Duchy of Brabant, and in 1383 the dukes transferred their capital from Louvain to Brussels. The city acquired new municipal rights in the defense of which it fought bitterly against the dukes of Burgundy into whose hands it fell in 1430. It was brought by Marie de Bourgogne to her husband Maximilian I. Charles V lived in Brussels often and abdicated there in 1555. Brussels was at that time the court residence in the Netherlands.

While numerous noble families built their castles on the eastern slope and on the plateau bordering the valley, the industrial and commercial districts of the city expanded gradually along the river itself. In 1561 a canal was built parallel to the river, connecting Brussels to the Scheldt. In this period the city was described as one of the "finest, largest, and best-situated cities in Europe." But it was also the scene of political troubles under Philip II who ruled from 1556 to 1598. Atrocities were committed by the Duke of Alva in 1567 and 1568 in his suppression of the Dutch nobles who had set up a government in 1566. It was in Brussels that Count Lamoral Egmont and Count Philip de Montmorency Horn were executed as traitors. Their execution is usually taken as the date of the beginning of the famous revolt of the Netherlands from Spain. In the war of Spain against Louis XIV, Brussels suffered much and was severely damaged by the French bombardment under Villeroi in 1695, which destroyed many houses of the Grande Place. Later it suffered in the war of Austria against Louis XV, but under the mild rule of Maria Theresa, Brussels flourished and many of its institutions and public buildings were founded. Chief town of the department of the Dyle during the French period from 1794 to 1814, it was one of the residences of the king of the Netherlands from 1815 to 1830. After the revolution of 1830 which gave Belgium its freedom, Brussels became the capital of the kingdom.

The demolition of the ramparts which were replaced by boulevards started new improvements in the urban development of Brussels. The city extended outside of its former limits and gradually the surrounding villages were included in the urban district. Especially under the reign of Leopold II, great improvements were made: the Quartier Léopold and Quartier Louise were built, the broad Avenues de Zervueren and Louise were created to connect the city with the Forêt de Soignes and the Bois de la Cambre with the purpose of leading the population to the most beautiful part of the surrounding countryside. Also many improvements were achieved in the downtown area. The Senne was covered and the broad boulevards du Nord, Anspach, du Hainraut and du Midi, replaced the slums.

Brussels was occupied by the Germans during World War I from August 1914 to November 1918. Philippe Baucq, Edith Cavell, and many others accused of being Allied agents were executed by the Germans in Brussels. The burgomaster, Adolphe Max, and numerous citizens were held in captivity. After the war the American Relief Commission helped greatly to restore many institutions of the city.

In World War II Brussels fell to the Nazis in May 1940 and was subjected to harsh terms of occupation. The burgomaster and many citizens were removed from office, and some were sent to concentration camps in Germany. Only a few quarters of the city were affected by bombardments and flying bombs. Just before the Germans evacuated the city, they deliberately destroyed the Palais de Justice. On Sept. 3, 1944, Allied forces liberated Brussels.

Monuments. The Church of Sts. Michael and Gudule, begun about 1220, is one of the best examples of pointed Gothic architecture. Its stained glass is famous. The Church of Notre Dame des Victoires is also celebrated for its wonderful decoration. Notre Dame de la Chapelle is constructed partly in the Roman style and partly in Roman-ogival style.

The Grande Place, which is considered one of the most interesting public squares in Europe, contains the famous Hôtel de Ville and, on the opposite side, the Maison du Roi, masterpieces of Gothic secular architecture. The Hôtel de Ville was begun in 1401, and it is topped by a 360-ft. tower, which is crowned by a golden copper statue of St. Michael. The Maison du Roi was almost entirely rebuilt after 1695.

Other buildings of note include the king's palace, the Palais de la Nation or House of Parliament, the Bourse, the Column of Congress with the Tomb of the Unknown Soldier of World War I, the royal library, and the Ancient and Modern Arts Museum. The Parc Royal, the Garden of the Petit Sablon, and the botanical gardens are noted for their grounds and exhibits. The Palais des Beaux Arts has become the chief intellectual and artistic center of the city.

Education. The city's university was founded in 1834 by Theodore Verhaagen without the co-operation of the state or church. It continues to be supported primarily by private subscription. In the 1920's the buildings erected for the university's use were partly financed by American funds of the Commission of Relief in Belgium. Although the Germans closed the university in 1941 and took captive the presidents of the various schools, several departments went underground and maintained classes. Other educational facilities in the city include a royal conservatory, technical schools, and horticulture schools.

Transportation and Industry. Brussels is connected by air and rail with Berlin and Paris and other major European cities. In addition, it has air connections with London, New York City, Cairo, Teheran, Tripoli, Leopoldville, and Johannesburg. Although the Senne River is not navigable, the city is connected by canals with Charleroi, Mechlin, Antwerp, and the Atlantic Ocean. These canals give access to the Rupel and the Scheldt rivers.

Formerly famous only for its laces and carpet manufactures, Brussels in the twentieth century became a diversified industrial community. In addition to the lace and carpets, local industries include in their output furniture, clothing, chemical products, soap, curtains, and electrical equipment. Pop. 1952, 180,771; (including communes) 1,140,000.

L. B.

BRUSSELS, UNIVERSITY OF, at Brussels, Belgium, founded in November 1834. This institution has always been a "free university," meaning that it was not established as a state-supported and state-controlled institution. Its founders had in mind a school which would be an offset to the Catholic university founded in 1834 at Mechlin and moved, in 1835, to Louvain. Among the professors of the University of Brussels have been eminent leaders of the

Liberal Party. Unlike the University of Louvain, where instruction is given alternately in French and Flemish, the University of Brussels is predominantly French, though some instruction is given in Flemish. The Belgian government always grants liberal subsidies to this institution amounting to about two-thirds of the sums given to the

MARCUS JUNIUS
BRUTUS

FROM AN UNFINISHED
BUST BY MICHELANGELO

three state universities, at Liège, Ghent, and Groningen. Attached to the university is the School of Applied Sciences (the Polytechnical Institute). Brussels is much larger than either Liège or Ghent or Groningen, and its student population larger than the others; student enrollment in the years after World War II averaged 4,000. The Nazis, at the beginning of their occupation of the country during World War II, marked this university as the center of liberal culture, for which reason they decided to replace the professors with those selected by them in Germany. The students, then numbering about 2,000, promptly went on strike, and so the university remained closed during the rest of the war. Located in the capital, and having at its disposal the rich treasures of the Royal Library, as well as access to the city's fine institutions, the university rivals older and more famous schools.

A. Hy.

BRUSSELS GRIFFON. *See* Dog.

BRUSSELS SPROUTS, one of the seven distinct vegetables developed from the wild cabbage, *Brassica oleracea,* native to the northwestern shores of Europe. Seedlings and young plants of brussels sprouts, *B. oleracea gemmifera,* can be distinguished only with difficulty from those of cabbage, cauliflower, broccoli, kale, collard, and kohlrabi, by the shape of the leaves, but as the plants reach maturity, buds form at the bases of the leafstalks like miniature, globular cabbage heads. The buds grow to 1 or 2 in. in diameter when conditions are favorable. Brussels sprouts do best in rich, moist, but well-drained and well-limed soil. Seed is sown about midsummer; the seedlings are transplanted 30 to 36 in. apart each way, and kept cleanly cultivated until the sprouts begin to form in the fall. When the sprouts are about 1 in. in diameter they may be cut for use. Brussels sprouts are an exceedingly hardy, long term, cold weather crop. They are able to stand snow and freezing temperatures. In cold climates they may be stored by lifting entire plants and storing them in mounds on the ground. They should be covered to prevent alternate freezing and thawing. In the South, they may remain in the garden, and may be harvested all winter. V. A. T.

BRUTUS, MARCUS JUNIUS (c.79-42 b.c.), one of the principal assassins of Julius Caesar. As the son-in-law of the younger Cato and the descendant of Lucius Junius Brutus, who had driven Tarquin the Proud from Rome, Brutus had reason to be a defender of the Roman Republic. Despite the fact that he sided with Pompey, Julius Caesar pardoned Brutus after the Battle of Pharsalus (48 b.c.) appointing him governor of Cisalpine Gaul. It was rumored that the reason for this unusual clemency was that Caesar was the father of Brutus, but this can not be substantiated. However, Brutus did not long remain loyal to Caesar. He joined with Gaius Cassius, Casca, and the other conspirators in assassinating Caesar on Mar. 15, 44 b.c. Then, when the Roman mob, led by Mark Antony, turned on Brutus and Cassius, they fled to the East. In 42 b.c., the forces of Antony and Octavian met those of Brutus and Cassius on the battlefield of Philippi in Macedonia. Here, a double battle was fought; in the first engagement, Cassius committed suicide when he thought that the army of Brutus had been overwhelmed. About three weeks later, Brutus came to grips with Antony and Octavian in a second battle. He was defeated and took his own life.

T. B. J.

BRYAN, ELMER BURRITT (1865-1934), American educator, was born in Van Wert, Ohio, Apr. 23, 1865. After graduating from Indiana University in 1893, Bryan studied at Harvard and Clark universities. He was professor of social and educational science at Butler College (1896-1897), assistant professor (1897-1899), and associate professor of pedagogy at Indiana University (1899-1901). He went to the Philippine Islands as a normal school principal in 1901 and in 1903 became general superintendent of education for the territory. He returned to the United States as professor of educational and social psychology at Indiana University (1903-1905) and was president of Franklin College (1905-1909), of Colgate University (1909-1921), and of Ohio University (1921-1934). He wrote *Nascent Stages and Their Pedagogical Significance* (1900) and *Fundamental Facts for the Teacher* (1911). He died in Detroit, on Oct. 15, 1934.

M. Sr. and W. W. Br.

BRYAN, KIRK (1888-1950), American geologist, was born in Albuquerque, N. M., Jan. 22, 1888. He was educated at the University of New Mexico and Yale University. He joined the U.S. Geological Survey in 1912, becoming senior geologist in 1926. Bryan lectured on geology at Yale and at Harvard universities from 1926 to 1950. He served in the U.S. Army during World War I. Bryan was geologist for the Columbia Basin project, the National Geographic Society's Chaco Canyon expediton, the Middle Rio Grande Conservancy District, the San Juan project, and the Valsequillo project. He studied especially the behavior of ground water and the engineering geology of reservoirs and dams. Bryan died on Aug. 22, 1950, in Cody, Wyo.

BRYAN, WILLIAM JENNINGS (1860-1925), American political leader, was born in Salem, Ill., March 19, 1860. He graduated from Illinois College in Jacksonville, Ill., in 1881, and from the Union College of Law in Chicago in 1883. After legal practice in Jacksonville from 1883 to 1887, he moved to Lincoln, Neb., where he entered politics. In 1890 he was elected to Congress and served two terms, but was defeated for the Senate in 1894. As a congressman, Bryan won attention by his marked oratorical abilities, particularly in speeches opposing the tariff and the repeal of the Sherman Silver Purchase Act. By the time the Democratic National Convention met in 1896, he had become known throughout the South and West as a champion of the free coinage of silver. He served on the Convention's platform committee, and his famous "cross of gold" speech, delivered at a critical moment, won him the presidential nomination. He was nominated also by the Populist Party. Bryan made a spectacular 18,000-mile campaign, appealing to the discontented farmers and workers against the sound-money, high-tariff policies of William McKinley and the Republicans. He was defeated by a popular majority of less than 600,000 out of a total vote of 13,600,000. He had become the dominant figure in the Democratic Party and remained so until the rise of Woodrow Wilson. Bryan opposed American expansionist policy at the conclusion of the Spanish-American War, but used his influence with Democratic senators to secure ratification of the controversial treaty with Spain. His apparent purpose was to build up the issues of imperialism and Philippine independence as campaign material for the 1900 election. He was again nominated for President by the Democrats, but McKinley, stressing the nation's prosperity, defeated him more decisively than in 1896.

Bryan did not participate actively in the 1904 presidential election, when conservatives controlled the Democratic Convention. However, he was nominated for the third time in 1908, but lost to William H. Taft. At the 1912 Convention Bryan urged the nomination of a progressive and finally threw his support to Wilson. In recognition of his outstanding position in the party, Wilson appointed him Secretary of State. As Secretary of State, Bryan's influence with Democratic congressmen was invaluable in carrying through the administration's domestic reform program. He negotiated arbitration treaties with thirty nations. A believer in the strictest neutrality, Bryan, with the coming of World War I, became critical of Wilson's policy toward Germany. Consequently, rather than dispatch Wilson's second *Lusitania* note, which he considered unduly provocative, Bryan resigned his office June 9, 1915. Bryan's influence in the Democratic Party was waning rapidly; his last appearance at a national convention was in 1924, when he favored William G. McAdoo for President and opposed any party stand against the Ku Klux Klan.

Bryan used both the newspaper and the lecture platform to further his views; he published the weekly *Commoner* from 1901 to 1913, and for thirty years was a popular Chautauqua lecturer. A strong fundamentalist in religion, he took part in campaigns for state legislation prohibiting the teaching of evolution in the public schools. When a Dayton, Tenn., teacher, John T. Scopes, was tried, in 1925, for violating such a law, Bryan joined the prosecution. The high light of the trial was the cross-examination of Bryan by Clarence Darrow, one of the defense counsel. On July 26, 1925, five days after the conclusion of the trial, Bryan died in his sleep at Dayton.

R. E. N.

BRYAN, the seat of Williams Co. in northwestern Ohio, is situated 50 mi. west of Toledo in an agricultural area producing principally grains and alfalfa. Founded in 1840, Bryan was incorporated as a city in 1849. It is governed by a mayor and council. The New York Central System supplies rail transportation, and air service is available at Bryan-Defiance Airport. Local manufactures include washing machines, furnaces, air-conditioning units, pharmaceuticals, spark plugs, and lubricating equipment. Bryan is also noted for its advertising novelties, display tables, metal toys, and candy. Pop. 1950, 6,365.

BRYAN, the seat of Brazos Co. in east central Texas, is 97 mi. northwest of Houston. It is served by the Missouri Pacific and the Southern Pacific railroads. Bryan was founded in 1855 and incorporated in 1886. It has the city manager form of government. Allen Academy, a junior military college, and Bryan Air Force Base for jet pilot training are located here. Manufactures are furniture, shoes, and cottonseed oil. Pop. 1950, 18,102.

BRYANSK [brya'nsk], an *oblast* (region) and its capital, in the Russian Soviet Federated Socialist Republic, in the western Soviet Union. The city, founded in the twelfth century, is on the navigable Desna River and is an important rail junction. It has large iron works, and manufactures chiefly machinery, cement, artificial slate, rope, and clothing. The *oblast,* which has a temperate climate, covers an area of 13,400 sq. mi. on the forested western slopes of the central Russian upland and the northeast Dnieper Valley. The chief crops are rye, oats, hemp, potatoes, and some wheat and tobacco. Hog raising and cattle breeding are carried on extensively, and peat, phosphorite, and quartzite are mined. Lumbering and the manufacture of matches, paper, and wood products are very important. Besides Bryansk city, other industrial communities are Bezhitsa, Klintsy, and Unecha. Pop. city (est. 1950), 90,000; *oblast* (est. 1954), 1,850,000.

G. A. T.

BRYANT, WILLIAM CULLEN [brai'ǝnt] (1794-1878), American poet and journalist, was born Nov. 3, 1794, at Cummington, Mass. His father early encouraged him to rhyme in imitation of Alexander Pope and published the boy's Federalist satire on Thomas Jefferson, *The Embargo, or Sketches of the Times* (1808). In the fall of 1811 Bryant wrote the first draft of *Thanatopsis,* in which he rejected his mother's Calvinism for a faith shaped from the stoicism of the ancients, his father's Unitarianism, and the deism of certain of his classmates during his one year at Williams College (1810-1811). Bryant studied law, practiced near Cummington in the hamlet of Plainfield (1815-1816), and then removed to Great Barrington, Mass.

At Great Barrington Bryant labored hard for a small salary in the civil courts, was elected to minor town offices, and married Frances Fairchild, "fairest of the rural maids" (1821). Meanwhile he won recognition as a poet with *Thanatopsis,* which was submitted to the *North American Review* by his father in 1818, and also with his Phi Beta Kappa poem at Harvard, a slender volume of *Poems* (1821), and his contributions to the *United States Literary Review* of Boston (1824-1825). Now completely emancipated from his father's literary classicism, Bryant, both as poet and critic, attempted to reinterpret in American terms the attitudes of the English Romantics.

Leaving the law and the Berkshires in 1825, Bryant moved to New York to edit the *New York Review* and to do hack writing. He joined the staff of the *New York Evening Post* as assistant editor in 1827 and remained, later as editor and part owner, until his death. In the *Post* he defended free trade, free speech, free soil, and free men—not only on the plantation but in the factory. Bryant presided when Lincoln spoke in Cooper Union (1859), helped organize the Republican Party, and aggressively supported the Northern cause during the Civil War. The *Post* backed so many minority causes that it never brought Bryant a large income, but what he earned he invested shrewdly in real estate and in his last years he was a wealthy man. Even though he lacked the color of his more famous fellow-editors, he was nevertheless respected as "the grand old man of the *Post.*"

Poetry, never a vocation with Bryant, occupied little of his time in New York. He wrote an occasional review or a

BRYCE CANYON NATIONAL PARK, UTAH

lecture and a little poetry (*Poems,* 1832; *The Fountain and Other Poems,* 1842; *Thirty Poems,* 1864) which never surpassed his earlier work. For a half century he was generally ranked with the chief American authors, an honor to which literary historians now generally agree he was entitled from the early 1820's to perhaps 1835 or 1840. He died on June 12, 1878.

Bryant combined a Calvinist's sense of man's evil nature with a Classicist's sense of man's mutability, a deist's faith in the goodness of God, a humanitarian's devotion to freedom and reform, and a Romantic's belief in the beauty and joyousness of the external world. All this he expressed in elevated prose and in equally sober yet simple and technically skillful poetry.   T. McD.

BRYCE, JAMES (1838-1922), Viscount Bryce of Dechmont, English statesman, historian and political scientist, born in Belfast, Ireland, May 10, 1838, the son of James Bryce, a Scottish schoolmaster. He was graduated from Trinity College, Oxford, in 1862, and continued his studies at Heidelberg University. He was admitted to the bar in 1867, and became regius professor of civil law at Oxford in 1870, serving until 1893. Elected to the House of Commons for the first time in 1880, he served in several Liberal party governments, as under secretary for Foreign Affairs, 1886-1892; chancellor of the Duchy of Lancaster, 1892; president of the Board of Trade, 1894; and chief secretary for Ireland, 1905-1907. Bryce made the first of a number of visits to America in 1870, and as British ambassador to the United States, 1907-1913, devoted his efforts to promoting diplomatic relations between Great Britain and Canada, and the United States. He was singularly successful. In 1913, Bryce was elevated to the peerage. He devoted his remaining years to his writings.

Combining the life of a scholar with that of a practical statesman, Bryce traveled most widely in the United States, South America, Europe and the British Dominions, and his experiences encouraged the use of comparative and observational methods in his political and legal writings. *The Holy Roman Empire* (1864), his initial essay, written while he was professor at Oxford, is a valuable study in the history of political institutions. His best known work, *The American Commonwealth* (1888), was the first important study on the subject and remains today a classic treatise. His *Modern Democracies* (1921) is one of the best appraisals of the leading democracies of the early twentieth century. Among his other works, *Study in History and Jurisprudence* (1901) is recognized for its importance in the field of comparative jurisprudence. He died at Sidmouth, Devonshire, Jan. 22, 1922.
                                                                D. G. H.

BRYCE CANYON NATIONAL PARK, 56 sq. mi., in the central part of southern Utah, 26 mi. southeast of the town of Panguitch. The park actually is not a canyon as it is formed by a large U-shaped amphitheatre 3 mi. long and 2 mi. wide, formed by erosion of the limestone Paunsaugunt Plateau. Wind erosion has left many weird forms and spires, temples, and organ-like formations. Even more amazing than the rock shapes, however, are their colors, which range from brilliant red to pink and shades of yellow to white. A distinctive feature is the lack of erosion by streams on the relatively flat surface on either side of the canyon. However, below the rim, erosion has produced the famous forms of Bryce Canyon. This erosion has been accomplished mainly by rain, snow, and frost, prying off fragments of the cliffs, and by chemical agencies decomposing the rock. The streams do not flow into the canyon, but away from it across the level plateau.

The park is named for Ebenezer Bryce whose home was on the site in 1875. A description of the canyon was first written by T. C. Bailey in 1876. The park originally was established as a national monument in 1923; in 1924 Congress changed the name to Utah National Park. In 1928 it was proclaimed Bryce Canyon National Park and thousands of acres were added to the original monument area.   J. E. F.

BRYENNIOS, PHILOTHEOS [brie′nios] (c.1833-1917), Greek ecclesiastic and incunabulist, was born in Istanbul in 1833. First educated in Istanbul, he went to the theological school of Halki (an island near Istanbul), and continued his higher education in philosophy and history at the universities of Leipzig, Berlin, and Munich. He was appointed professor of church history and exegetics at the theological school of Halki in 1861, becoming director of the school in 1863. In 1865 he attended the Old Catholic Conference at Bonn, where he was informed that he had been appointed metropolitan of Seres, Macedonia. In 1875 he became metropolitan of Nicomedia in Asia Minor. In 1873, working in the library of the monastery representing the Jerusalem patriarchate in Istanbul, he discovered among others a manuscript which contains a synopsis of the Old and New Testaments, the First and Second Epistles of Clement of Rome to the Corinthians, and the only known manuscript of the *Teachings of the Twelve Apostles (Didachē)*. A vast literature has since grown up around this manuscript. Bryennios prepared an edition of the *Epistles of Clement* in 1875. His edition of the *Teachings of the Twelve Apostles* was published in 1883. He died in Halki in 1917.   S. D.

BRYENNIUS, NICEPHORUS [braie′nios] (c. 1062-1137), Byzantine soldier and historian, was born in Orestias, Macedonia, towards the middle of the eleventh century. He was the son of another Nicephorus Bryennius, a famous general who usurped the throne in 1071 but was deposed ten years later by Alexius Comnenus. The young Bryennius became the personal confidant of Alexius, and was given the titles of "Caesar" and "supreme commander." He defended Constantinople against Godfrey de Bouillon during the First Crusade, and distinguished himself in the war between Alexius and Bohemund, prince of Antioch, negotiating the peace of 1108. He was renowned for his learning and military prowess, and married Anna Comnena, daughter of Alexius. In 1118 he was involved in a plot to overthrow John, Alexius' son and successor, but either because of alleged cowardice or perhaps an unwillingness to betray his benefactor's son, the plot proved abortive, and he was banished to Oenoe on the Black Sea. He was later reinstated and went to Antioch, Syria, in 1137 to aid in the war against the Crusaders, but ill health forced him to return to Constantinople, where he died shortly after. Bryennius also wrote a history of the period, covering approximately the years 1057 to 1081, which is considered one of the best histories of its time. It is written in a clear narrative style, reveals a good sense of judgment, and profits from the author's ability to draw on much eye-witness material.   C. W. D.

BRYMNER, WILLIAM [brī′mnər] (1855-1925), Scotch-Canadian landscape painter, was born at Greenock, Scotland, Dec. 14, 1855. He went to Canada in 1857. In 1878 he commenced five years' study at the Académie Julien, Paris, under Adolphe William Bouguereau and Robert-Fleury. Brymner was director of advanced classes at the Art Institute of Montreal from 1886 until 1921. He was elected to the Royal Canadian Academy in 1886, to its vice-presidency in 1907, and was its president from 1909 to 1917. In the National Gallery, Ottawa, are his *Dolly at the Sabot Maker's, Early Moonrise in September, Evening, Fog on the Coast, Nude,* and *A Wreath of Flowers.* Brymner's influence upon all Canadian painting was great. He died at Chester, England, June 18, 1925.

BRYNHILD (BRUNHILD, BRÜNNHILDE) [brü′nhilt, bru′nhilt, brünhi′ldə], mythical heroine, who first appears in several lays of the Old Norse poetic *Edda.* In them Brynhild does not emerge as a consistent or identical personality, nor as part of a single story, but the following different elements are discernible: she is a mortal woman fond of war; she is one of the Valkyries, daughter of King Budli, and has supernatural powers; the hero awakens a fire-girt maiden sunk in a magical sleep by Odin as punishment (the "sleeping-beauty" motif); Sigurd wins Brynhild for Gunnar by deceit; and she causes Sigurd's death from motives of jealousy and revenge. These elements are combined in their most satisfactory form in the Icelandic *Volsunga Saga.* Sigurd, the heroic slayer of dragons, breaks through the encircling fire and awakens the Valkyrie, Brynhild, sunk in a magical sleep. They pledge eternal love. He later weds Gudrun, an enchanted spell causing him to forget Brynhild, and, disguised as Gunnar, wins Brynhild for the latter. She subsequently instigates the murder of Sigurd, and finally, throwing herself on his funeral pyre, is united with him in death. In the later *Nibelungenlied* much of this story is lost. Brunhild (Brynhild) remains a superhuman Amazonian woman, who will wed only the man who surpasses her in athletic trials involving strength and fleetness of foot (at the cost of his head if he does not), but she is now queen of "Issland," living in the castle "Isenstein." The main plot centers around the winning of Brynhild for Gunther (Gunnar) by deceit. There seems to have been no original meeting between her and Siegfried (Sigurd), nor does she instigate his death, or die with him. This story clearly lacks the passion, appeal, and power of the earlier version, and Brynhild loses most of her color. Richard Wagner's characterization of Brünnhilde and the main lines of his plot for the four operas of the *Ring* cycle are drawn from the *Volsunga Saga* version of the legend. Brynhild is not to be confused with the historic Visigothic princess Brunhilda. *See also* NIBELUNGENLIED.   C. W. D.

BRYN MAWR COLLEGE [brī′n maˈr], an accredited, privately controlled, nonsectarian, liberal arts college for women, on a 60-acre campus in Bryn Mawr, Pa., 5 mi. west of Philadelphia. Related originally to the Society of Friends, Bryn Mawr was chartered by the State of Pennsylvania in

1880 and opened in 1885. The degrees conferred are A.B. in liberal arts, M.A., M.S.S., and Ph.D. Since 1937 the Graduate School has been open to men and women.

Interdepartmental courses have been developed in philosophy, economics, politics, English, and history, biology, physics, geology, chemistry, and mathematics. Graduate and undergraduate study has been promoted in borderline research fields such as geophysics, biophysics, and biochemistry.

The library contains many notable collections of Classical archaeology and literature, Old French and Germanic works,

The M. Carey Thomas Library at Bryn Mawr College

and incunabula consisting of philosophical and theological works of the fifteenth century. A Far Eastern collection contains material from Korea. Available also to students are the libraries of the colleges, municipalities, and learned societies of the surrounding area. Reciprocal arrangements exist with two neighboring Friends' colleges, Haverford and Swarthmore, making possible three-way exchanges of faculty and sometimes of students. Substantial scholarship and loan aid is available to graduate and undergraduate students. There are 10 residence halls for undergraduate students and a center for women graduates. *For statistics see* COLLEGES AND UNIVERSITIES.

BRYONY [brɑi' əni], the common name of various Old World climbing perennials. *Bryonia dioica,* a member of the gourd family with yellow flowers and red berries, is a rapid grower. The black bryony, *Tamus communis,* a member of the yam family, has shining, heart-shaped leaves, yellowish flowers, scarlet fruit, and black roots.   J. C. Wis.

BRYOPHYTA [brɑɪɒ'fɪtə], a small group of green plants including the Musci (mosses) and Hepaticae (liverworts). Approximately 14,000 species of mosses and 9,000 species of liverworts are recognized. All bryophytes are small plants usually 1-5 cm. long except for some aquatic species which may become 30 cm. long. The plant itself is either a leafy stem or a flat thallus.

Occurrence. Bryophytes can grow in almost any habitat. The majority grow in moist places on soil, rotting logs, and bark of living trees. Some are adapted to live, however, in extremely dry places, in deserts or on exposed rocks, where they grow only in the moist seasons. A few species are aquatic, growing submerged in bogs, ponds, streams, or lakes; none is marine. In the moist tropics, bryophytes form a conspicuous part of the vegetation, sometimes making long festoons from branches, or thick mats over the tree trunks and ground. The vegetation of arctic bogs and tundra is composed chiefly of bryophytic species.

Economic Value. Because of their ability to grow on bare rocks and soil, bryophytes are important in plant succession. Certain species of bryophytes and lichens are the first plants to appear on exposed rocks, and aid in fragmentation of the stone to begin the accumulation of soil and humus. They have little other economic value except for the moss genus *Sphagnum,* which, as peat, is used for fuel, packing, and in gardening, and has been used for

·BRYOPHYTA

(Left) Marchantia polymorpha, one of the most widely found liverworts; (Center) Riccia natans, the only totally aquatic liverwort; (Right) Preissia commutata

surgical dressings. Sphagnum inhabits bogs throughout the world. Because the moss itself is acid, bacterial and fungal decay does not occur in sphagnum bogs, and dead organic matter is preserved intact. The dead sphagnum is compressed by the weight of the living plants above it and becomes peat. The compact peat is cut in blocks and used for fuel in parts of the British Isles and elsewhere. Less compact peat is used for packing. Because of its acid condition, peat is useful in gardening to combat excessive alkalinity in the soil and to create an artificial acid environment to meet the requirements of certain ornamental shrubs. In addition to the acid and therefore sterile condition of the sphagnum, it has phenomenal absorptive powers which make it useful in surgical dressings. Sphagnum can absorb sixteen to twenty times its weight of water, whereas cotton absorbs only five to six times its own weight.

Asexual Reproduction. In addition to their sexual reproduction, most bryophytes have mechanisms for asexual or vegetative reproduction. Merely by growth and branching of the plants, mosses and liverworts can multiply and spread over large areas. Other methods include fragmentation and the production of specialized bodies for vegetative reproduction. In some species the tips of the leaves break off and produce new plants. In others, leafy buds or groups of cells, gemmae, regularly appear and are capable of propagating the plants. Almost any vegetative cell or group of cells, if isolated from the parent plant, can regenerate into a new plant.

MUSCI

The moss plant consists of a central axis or stem with spirally arranged leaves. The spiral arrangement, however, is not always apparent, and some mature moss plants appear dorsiventrally symmetrical by rearrangement of the parts. Many moss plants grow erect and unbranched in dense tufts or cushions; others are branched many times and may grow creeping on the substratum.

Rhizoids. Bryophytes produce no true roots; instead, multicellular branched filaments of cells called rhizoids, anchor the plant to the substratum. When young, the rhizoids absorb moisture and dissolve nutrients from the soil, but this function is lost when the rhizoids reach maturity.

Stems. The stem tissue of many mosses consists of undifferentiated cells, whereas in others there is a central strand of thick-walled cells. These undoubtedly give me-

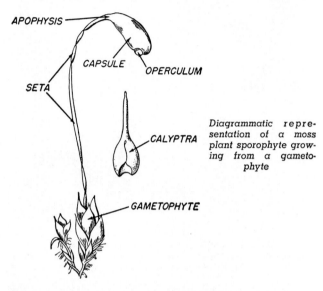

Diagrammatic representation of a moss plant sporophyte growing from a gametophyte

chanical support but are not comparable to the vascular system found in the ferns and flowering plants. There is no evidence that this central strand acts in conduction. Most of the water and dissolved substances used in the life processes of mosses and liverworts rise on the outside of the plant in the crevices between leaves and stem by capillary action. The leafy plants of some species are especially adapted for this type of conduction. The species of *Sphagnum* produce leafy branches in groups. One or more of these branches is pendant close to the stem, producing a continuous leafy sheath along the stem in which water and solutes rise by capillary.

Leaves. Leaves of mosses vary widely in shape and form. They are usually only one layer of cells thick; however, leaves of a few species are bordered by several thicknesses of cells. If a midrib is present it may be single, several cells thick, and extend to the apex of the leaf, or it can be short and double. Some species are characterized by plate or column-like outgrowths on the midrib. The margin may be smooth or toothed by single or double teeth, flat or variously rolled. Leaves vary in shape from round through oval and lanceolate to long and linear. Each species, however, is fairly constant, so that leaf characters are useful in identification.

Reproduction. The sex organs or gametangia are produced terminally on the main or lateral shoots. The male and female organs may be produced together on the same branch or on different branches and are always associated with sterile multicellular filaments, paraphyses. The male organ, antheridium, is a globose or cylindrical multicellular sac which contains many cells, each of which at maturity produces two biciliate motile sperm. The female organ, archegonium, is flask-shaped and also multicellular; the base of the flask or venter contains the egg cell and the neck contains canal cells which disintegrate on maturity to pro-

duce a substance that attracts the sperm. Moisture in the form of a drop of rain or dew is necessary in order that the sperm may reach the archegonium and fertilization take place. The antheridial sac breaks irregularly and the sperm escape, swim to the neck of the archegonium and down the neck canal, where one sperm unites with the egg to form the zygote.

Sporophyte. This process results in doubling the chromosome number, produces a diploid plant, the sporophyte, and ends the gametophyte or haploid phase of the life history. The zygote begins divisions within the archegonium, and for a time the archegonium grows with the developing embryo sporophyte. By the time the young sporophyte is visible to the naked eye three parts are apparent: the foot, which is embedded in the base of the archegonium; the stalk or seta; and the capsule which, when mature, will con-

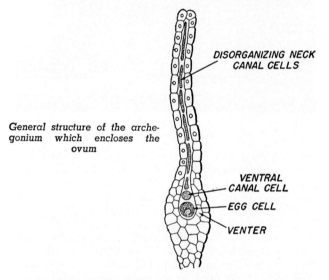

General structure of the archegonium which encloses the ovum

tain the spores. The growing sporophyte soon breaks the archegonium circularly at the base and carries it as a covering, the calyptra, over the capsule until maturity. The mature capsule is a beautifully intricate structure. The typical capsule opens by means of a lid or operculum, which falls at maturity by the dehiscence of a specialized row of thick-walled cells, the annulus. This exposes a mouth which may be naked or protected by one or two concentric rows of teeth, the peristome. The teeth of the peristome may be simple plates of tissue or may bear transverse, hygroscopic thickenings; they vary in number from four to sixty-four, the usual number being sixteen.

Reduction Division. Spores are produced in the capsule in large numbers. Generally there is in the capsule a sterile central cylinder, the columella, and around this, the spore sac. One of the last two divisions producing the spores reduces the chromosome number by one-half, bringing about a return to the haploid or gametophyte chromosome number and ending the sporophyte phase. When the spores are mature, the columella and other tissues within the capsule break down, leaving only a mass of loose spores.

Gametophyte. The spores fall or are shaken from the capsule and may be carried long distances by wind, water, or animals. If a spore falls in a moist place it germinates into a branched, many-celled filament, the protonema. The protonemal filaments which remain on the surface of the ground contain chloroplasts and develop straight cross walls. The branches which grow into the soil lack chloroplasts, develop oblique cross walls and become the rhizoids. At intervals along the filament, lateral leafy buds appear and develop into leafy moss plants. Thus one spore may produce a whole colony of moss plants. In some species, the green protonema is persistent and may cover several square feet of ground; in most species it is evanescent and disappears after the appearance of the leafy plants.

HEPATICAE

Liverworts have, with a few exceptions, a distinct upper and lower surface and are of two types, thalloid and leafy. The typical leafy liverwort consists of a central axis or stem which bears two opposite rows of similar leaves and often a third row of smaller underleaves. The liverwort leaf may be entire, variously lobed, toothed, or fringed. The leaves

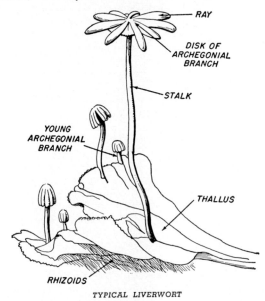

TYPICAL LIVERWORT

of some species are folded, forming two lobes equal or unequal in size and with either the dorsal or ventral lobe larger. The ventral lobe may give rise to an inflated sac, as in the genus *Frullania.* These sacs are often filled with water and may be inhabited by colonies of small animals such as rotifers.

The thalloid liverworts consist of flat expanded tissues several layers of cells thick, and vary in complexity of structure. The most elaborate thallus is that of *Marchantia,* in which three regions are differentiated: a compact colorless ventral tissue, a green dorsal tissue with air chambers, and an epidermis with pores. The pores of the epidermis open into the air chambers equipped with short branched filaments of chlorophyllose cells which manufacture all the food for the plant. Scales and unicellular unbranched rhizoids are produced from the ventral surface of the thallus.

As in the mosses, water and solutes are carried to the various parts of the plant by capillarity on and between the leaves and stems or the scales, rhizoids, and thallus. In the stem of leafy liverworts and in the midrib region of the thalloids, a central strand is usually developed and contributes some support to the plant body.

Reproduction. The structures and mechanism of sexual reproduction in the liverworts resemble those found in mosses. The antheridia and archegonia are produced in the axils of special leaves along the leafy stem, or embedded in the thallus, or on special receptacles produced by some of the thallus liverworts. A tubular leaf, involucre or perianth, protects the archegonium and developing sporophyte. The

antheridia produce many biciliate sperm, and fertilization takes place within the archegonium. The sporophyte develops immediately within the venter of the archegonium, the calyptra. The mature sporophyte is simple, consisting of a foot embedded in the gametophyte, a seta, and capsule. The capsule is composed of a wall, one to seven layers of cells thick, and contains many spores and sterile hygroscopic filaments, the elaters. When the spores are mature the seta

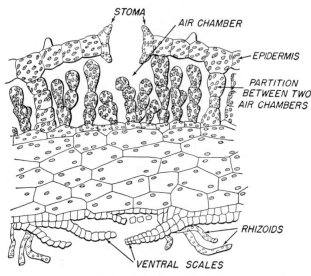

SECTION OF A LIVERWORT LEAF

elongates and the capsule is pushed through the calyptra and beyond the perianth or involucre. The capsule of the leafy liverworts opens by splitting longitudinally into four valves; that of the halloid ones opens irregularly. When the archegonium is embedded in the thallus, as in *Riccia,* the sporophyte develops in the thallus and the spores are released only on decay of the gametophyte plant. The spores germi-

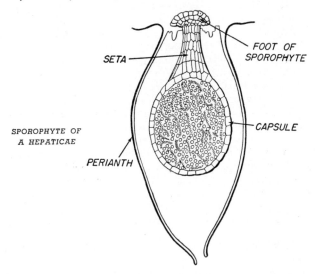

SPOROPHYTE OF A HEPATICAE

nate to produce a filamentous or thalloid protonema which in turn produces directly the mature gametophyte plant.

ALTERNATION OF GENERATION

The bryophyte plant itself is haploid; it is the gametophyte or gamete-producing plant. It is green, manufactures its own food, and is therefore independent. The sporophyte (spore-producing plant) is the diploid plant, contains little or no chlorophyll, and is attached to and largely dependent upon the gametophyte. The opposite condition occurs in the other common woodland plants. The ferns, conifers, and flowering plants are sporophytes; the gametophyte of these plants is reduced to either a minute evanescent green plant or to a few cells contained within the tissues of the sporophyte. Therefore, the bryophytes fit into the evolutionary picture as a specialized group with obscure origins in the simpler green plants, the algae. Their specialized gametophytic and sporophytic structures apparently have not evolved directly into any of the higher plants.   F. E. W.

BRYOZOA [brai'ozo'ə], also known as Polyzoa, a phylum consisting of a group of invertebrates which bud to form colonies. Some of them are mosslike, whence the name Bryozoa, but most of them are encrusting or nodular. Their nearest relatives are probably the Brachiopoda, but the two groups have been separated since early Paleozoic time and were both abundant in the Ordovician. They are important to the geologist as index fossils. It is estimated that there are about three thousand living species. Bryozoa sometimes become a nuisance by encrusting ship bottoms and buoys, or by clogging water pipes.

The individual Bryozoa is usually less than a millimeter long, but is rather highly organized: it has a U-shaped gut, a pharynx, an esophagus (sometimes a gizzard), a stomach, and an intestine; a simple nervous system; several sets of muscles, and ciliated tentacles for the apprehension of microorganisms for food. The skeleton is the chitinous body wall, which is usually heavily calcified; in a few fresh-water species, the wall is gelatinous. The body wall is known as the zooecium, and the movable internal part as the polypide or zooid. The tentacles are extended in feeding, and withdrawn when at rest, by means of muscles, the aperture being closed by sphincter muscles or by an operculum like a trap door.

Bryozoa are bisexual; the eggs may be discharged, but usually the egg is withheld in the body cavity, or in a special brood chamber, or ovicell, until the larva, the Cyphonautes, is formed and metamorphosed into the ancestrula or first individual of a new colony. It is freed through a birth opening or through disintegration of the parent.

Some remarkable features of the Bryozoa are: polymorphism, there being several types of modified individuals, including avicularia, radicles, stolons, and gonoecia; degeneration and regeneration of the polypide; communication pores in the walls of adjacent individuals; self-fertilization, in many species; and profuse and rapid budding.

There are two classes of Bryozoa: (1) Endoprocta (Kamptozoa), which is recent; and (2) Ectoprocta. A subclass of the latter consists of the Gymnolaemata, of which there are five orders: Trepostomata, a fossil; Cryptostomata, a fossil; Cyclostomata, a fossil and recent; Cheilostomata, a fossil and recent; and Ctenostomata, also a fossil and recent. A second subclass, Phylactolaemata, is fresh-water and recent.   R. C. O.

BRYUSOV, VALERY YAKOVLEVICH [bryu'sɔf] (1873-1924), Russian poet, novelist, dramatist, and critic, father of Russian symbolism, was born in Moscow on Dec. 13, 1873, the son of a well-to-do merchant. He started writing verse in 1881 and, while still a student at the University of Moscow, published his poetry in an anthology, *Russian Symbolists,* in 1894. In the same year he published his translation of Paul Verlaine's *Romances sans paroles.* Before graduating in 1899, Bryusov published his first two books, *Chefs d'oeuvres* (1895) and *Me eum esse* (1897); thereafter, he published a new book almost every year. From the start

Bryusov tried to astound his readers, as when he published a so-called poem consisting of one line: "Oh, cover thy pale legs." For ten years he was the *enfant terrible* of Russian literature, finally gaining recognition for his masterful technique and great erudition. In 1904 he founded the famous symbolist review, *The Scales.* From 1910 to 1912 he was literary editor of the influential monthly, *Russian Thought,* discovering and encouraging many new writers. He traveled extensively abroad, where he met almost all the outstanding poets and writers of his time, including Émile Verhaeren, who exercised a great influence on his poetry. In 1913 Bryusov started the publication of his collected works in twenty-five volumes. Besides poetry, these contained his two novels, *The Altar of Victory* (a story of Rome in the fourth century) and *The Fiery Angel* (a story of sixteenth-century Germany), his short stories, and works of literary criticism. His numerous translations of the poetry of Verlaine, Verhaeren, Maeterlinck, Oscar Wilde, and Edgar Allan Poe were not included. As a dramatist Bryusov was not highly successful, his one outstanding play being *The Earth* (1904). During World War I, he was a war correspondent and after the Bolshevik revolution joined the Communist Party. He died in Moscow on Oct. 9, 1924.
    L. I. St.

BUANSU. *See* DHOLE.

BUBASTIS [bubæ'stɪs], an ancient city, in northeastern Egypt, situated near modern Zagazig. In ancient history the city appears under several names, the most important being "Pa-Bast," "Bast," and "Pibeseth." "Bubastis" is Greek for the name of the Egyptian feline goddess Ubasti, who derives her name from the city Bast. "Ubasti" means "she of Bast." Bast was better known as "P-ubasti," meaning "the place of Ubasti." The Greeks called both the place and the goddess "Bubastis" ("Bubastos"). Bubastis remains as a collection of mounds which were excavated in 1886 and 1887. These mounds, called "Tell Basta," date back to the fourteenth Egyptian dynasty, established in 1788 B.C., and to the Eighteenth Dynasty, established in 1580 B.C. Ubasti is represented with the head of a lioness, and she frequently appeared as a cat-headed woman. In the cat cemetery located amidst the ruins are large brick chambers packed with mummies, some of them in cat-shaped wood or bronze containers. In ancient times multitudes of the people attended the great festivals at Bubastis. Rameses II is said to have built the canal near the city which went from the Tanitic branch of the Nile River to the Bitter Lakes. About 1000 B.C. Shashaq I, a Libyan adventurer and founder of the Twenty-second, or Bubastite, Dynasty, made Bubastis his capital city. About 350 B.C. Bubastis was captured and destroyed by the Persians.
    W. S. V.

BUBONIC PLAGUE. *See* BLACK DEATH; GREAT PLAGUE.

BUCARAMANGA [buka'rama'ŋga,] the capital of the department of Santander, Colombia. It is located on the Lebrija River, about 185 mi. northeast of Bogotá, in the center of Colombia's rich coffee and tobacco district. The city lies in a mountainous terrain about 3,000 ft. above sea level and has a mean temperature of 70° F. and an annual rainfall of about 63 in. Founded in 1622, it is a beautiful city with many fine parks and monuments; among its most prominent buildings are the government houses; the twin-towered cathedral; and the chapel of Los Dolores, where Simon Bolívar once took refuge. The city's industries include cigar and cigarette factories, and gold, silver, and iron are mined in the surrounding region. Air service connects Bucaramanga with the chief cities of Colombia. Pop. 1951, 102,887.

BUCER, or **BUTZER, MARTIN** [buˈtzər, buˈtzər] (1491-1551), German Protestant reformer, born at Schlettstadt (Sélestat), near Strasbourg, Nov. 11, 1491. His name originally was Kuhhorn, Bucer or Butzer deriving from the Greek for "cow horn." In 1506 he became a Dominican, but at Heidelberg in 1521 he heard Martin Luther and was converted to Protestantism. He left the Dominican order and became chaplain to the Elector Palatine. After preaching a while at Wittenberg, he went in 1523 to Strasbourg, where he became one of the principal leaders of the German Protestants. He tried to reconcile the differences between the opposing schools of Protestant thought of Zwingli and Luther and in 1540 and 1541 attempted to bring about a reconciliation between Catholics and Protestants, but he refused to sign the Augsburg Interim in 1548. Consequently he was forced to leave Strasbourg. He accepted the invitation of Thomas Cranmer, archbishop of Canterbury, to go to England, where Edward VI commissioned him to prepare a Latin translation of the Bible. Later he became Regius Professor of Divinity at Cambridge. He died at Cambridge, Feb. 28, 1551.   S. D.

BUCHAN, JOHN (1ST BARON TWEEDSMUIR OF ELSFIELD) (1875-1940), Scottish novelist, historian, and statesman, was born on Aug. 26, 1875, in Perth, Scotland, the son of a clergyman. After studying at Glasgow University and Oxford, he became a lawyer in 1901 and in the same year secretary to Lord Milner, head of the High Commission in South Africa. In 1907 he joined the publishing firm of Thomas Nelson & Sons. During World War I he served on the headquarters staff of the British Army in France and in 1917 became Director of Information for the government. From 1927 he represented the Scottish universities in Parliament, but in 1935 he was appointed Governor-General of Canada and elevated to the peerage. In 1937 he was made Chancellor of the University of Edinburgh.

Buchan's chief literary distinction was won as a novelist; among his more memorable works are *Prester John* (1910), *The Thirty-nine Steps* (1915), and *Greenmantle* (1916). These and other novels are distinguished as adventure-romances by their action, their style, and their evocation of atmosphere. Buchan was a prolific historical writer as well; among his works in this field are *Sir Walter Raleigh* (1911), *The Battle of Jutland* (1917), *A History of the Great War* (4 vols., 1921-1922), *Julius Caesar* (1932), *Oliver Cromwell* (1934), and *Gordon at Khartoum* (1934). He died in Montreal, Canada, on Feb. 11, 1940.   J. C.

BUCHANAN, FRANKLIN [byukæˈnən] (1800-1874), Confederate naval officer, was born in Baltimore, Md., Sept. 17, 1800. He became a midshipman in the United States Navy in 1815. He was in the Mediterranean, then fought piracy in the Caribbean, becoming a lieutenant in 1825. In 1833 he was first lieutenant on the *Delaware,* which carried the United States minister, Edward Livingston, to France. Buchanan saw service in the Pacific from 1839 to 1840. After being promoted to commander in 1841, he conceived the plan for organizing a naval school at Annapolis and was appointed its first superintendent Oct. 10, 1845. Later asking for active service, he was assigned the sloop *Germantown* in 1847, and was active during the Mexican War. He was placed in command of Commodore M. G. Perry's flagship

Susquehanna in the expedition to Japan in 1853 and is believed to have been the first United States naval officer to set foot on Japanese soil. He became a captain Sept. 14, 1855. After returning to the United States he was made commander of the Washington Navy Yard. Assuming Maryland would secede from the Union, he resigned from the Navy, Apr. 22, 1861. He later attempted to withdraw his resignation, but was dismissed from the service May 14. He joined the Confederate Navy, Sept. 5, 1861, with the rank of captain, became chief of the Bureau of Orders and Detail, and was placed in command of the Chesapeake Bay fleet, Feb. 24, 1862. Buchanan destroyed the U.S.S. *Congress* at Hampton Roads, Mar. 8, 1862. Because he received a wound there, he did not participate in the famous fight of the *Monitor* and the *Merrimac* on Mar. 9. Buchanan was promoted to admiral Aug. 26, 1862, and was appointed commander of the naval forces at Mobile. He surrendered his flagship *Tennessee* in the Battle of Mobile Bay, Aug. 5, 1864, after his ship had been put out of commission by gunfire from Admiral D. G. Farragut's fleet. Buchanan remained a prisoner until he was exchanged in February 1865. He returned to his home in Talbot Co., Md., and became president of Maryland Agricultural School, a position which he held for the year 1868-1869. He died at his home, "The Rest," in Talbot Co., May 11, 1874.   W. E. A.

BUCHANAN, GEORGE [byukæˈnən] (1506-1582), Scottish scholar, historian, and controversial political figure, was born in Killearn, Stirlingshire, February 1506. He spent more of his life in France, however, than in Scotland. He was a tutor to the natural son of James V, professor at Bordeaux (where Montaigne was among his pupils), prisoner of the Inquisition (1549-1551), satirist and bitter critic of the Franciscans and Mary, Queen of Scots. His best works were written in Latin, but he also composed several political pamphlets in English. Buchanan has been termed the Scottish Ascham in style, although he is certainly more pedantic. Headstrong and naïve, he was an active reformer with a passion for education and a strange mixture of personal traits. His chief Latin works are the *Detectio Mariae Reginae* (1571), *De sphaera,* and *Rerum Scoticarum historia* (1582). He is also the author of an elegy describing the privations of a student in Paris. Buchanan died on Sept. 28, 1582, in Edinburgh, Scotland.   M. W. St.

BUCHANAN, JAMES (1791-1868), fifteenth President of the United States, was born near Mercersburg, Pa., Apr. 23, 1791. His father and mother were both of Scotch-Irish descent, the father having emigrated from northern Ireland in 1783. Buchanan attended the local schools and Dickinson College, in Pennsylvania, from which he was graduated in 1809. He was admitted to the bar in 1812.

Public Life. In 1814 Buchanan was elected by the Federalists to the House of Representatives in the Pennsylvania Assembly and for the rest of his life combined public service with practice of the law. During the War of 1812, which he first opposed and then supported, Buchanan was saddened by the death of the young lady whom he had planned to marry. He remained a bachelor for the rest of his life. In 1820 Buchanan was elected to the United States House of Representatives, where he remained for ten years. When the Federalist Party dissolved, he found it relatively easy to join the Jeffersonian Democrats; and when the followers of Jefferson divided between the Clay-Adams faction and the Jacksonians, Buchanan identified himself with the latter. Upon his retirement from the House in 1831, President Andrew

Jackson persuaded him to become minister to Russia, where he served for two years. Returning to the United States, he was elected in 1834 to the Senate, where he remained until 1845. Buchanan became the unquestioned leader of the Democratic Party in Pennsylvania. In the state convention of 1844 the delegates, supporting James K. Polk for president, endorsed Buchanan for secretary of state, a position to which he was appointed after Polk's victory over Henry Clay. For the next four years Buchanan was occupied with diplomatic

COURTESY OF THE NEW YORK PUBLIC LIBRARY

JAMES BUCHANAN

FROM AN ENGRAVING BY H. B. HALL JR.

questions concerning Texas annexation, the Mexican War, and the discussions with Great Britain relative to Oregon boundaries. Buchanan loyally supported Polk's imperialist doctrines and himself proposed to purchase Cuba from Spain. After the defeat of the Democrats in 1848, Buchanan retired to his home near Lancaster, Pa., and there laid plans for his presidential campaign in 1852. He was a leading candidate for the presidency, but was defeated on the forty-ninth ballot by the dark horse, Franklin Pierce, who after his inauguration appointed Buchanan minister to Great Britain. Buchanan's connection with the Ostend Manifesto was followed with the opinion that though slavery was a bad institution, the Federal Government had no legal right to interfere with it where it then existed. His refusal to adopt a positive position made him a compromise candidate, and in 1856 he won the Democratic nomination on the seventeenth ballot. Supported by the South and by five northern states, he was elected over John Charles Frémont and Millard Fillmore, receiving 174 electoral votes.

The Presidency. Two days after Buchanan's inauguration the Dred Scott decision was handed down by the Supreme Court, and it was hoped that this would settle the controversy with respect to slavery, as Buchanan had predicted it would in his inaugural address. Hardly had the decision been announced, however, than the controversy broke forth

with renewed vigor and intensity. Buchanan proposed to control the situation by preventing agitation and by enforcing the Fugitive Slave Law. At the beginning of his administration Buchanan announced his intention of adhering to the popular sovereignty principle so far as it affected the situation in Kansas, where the slavery and the antislavery forces were engaged in a bitter struggle to control the state. He drew away from his original determination, however, by using his influence to secure the admission of Kansas into the union under the proslavery Lecompton Constitution. He charged that the antislavery forces had used unfair methods in the election of their candidates; they retorted that unfair methods were used not only to advance the Lecompton bill and the compromise English bill, but also to prevent the re-election of Stephen A. Douglas as senator from Illinois. Whatever the truth of these charges, the result was chaos and uncertainty. Buchanan lacked the moral courage, the self-reliance, and a soundness of judgment that would have made it possible to view the controversy dispassionately and realistically. Always the situation controlled the President rather than the reverse. Buchanan, a strong advocate of states' rights, believed in the right of each state to decide for itself whether it should be slave or free. Throughout his term he sought to divert attention from the issue—slavery and its background—that was on everyone's mind. He urged the acquisition of Cuba, he favored railroad building and development in the West and Southwest, he hailed the discovery of gold in the Pike's Peak area as an outlet for pent-up energy and emotion, he approved of the Pony Express and the extension of the telegraph, but the discovery of oil in northwestern Pennsylvania was hardly noticed.

John Brown's raid, his trial, and execution helped to crystallize sentiment, both north and south. Buchanan was not considered as a candidate for re-election, but the split in the Democratic Party created by the break with Douglas made the party division and the sectional alignments definite. It is uncertain how Buchanan could have prevented the events of the three months between Lincoln's election and his inauguration. Many of the problems that faced him originated, perhaps, as much in the failure to make an appraisal of his probable conduct as in the need of the action or measure proposed as an aid in solving the problems that faced the sections, both individually and collectively. The secession of South Carolina posed a situation with which Buchanan was not willing or able to cope. His conduct of affairs following this action has been much criticized, but even at this date it is not possible to say just what should have been his policy. The North and the South were evenly divided as to what action to take, and the attitude of the West was uncertain. The events of the next ninety days created an alignment of forces that made possible Lincoln's firm action after he was inaugurated. Efforts at compromise had proved unavailing; as the probable consequences of disunion became more evident, the North and the West closed ranks, and the political sentiment in the South became more evident. No legislation that would enable him to deal with the situation was forthcoming, and when Buchanan turned the government over to Lincoln and a new party came to power, the measures that would have to be enacted if the Union was to survive had become more evident. It is worth noting that for several weeks after he took office Lincoln made little change in the policy Buchanan had followed.

Retirement. After Buchanan turned over his office to Lincoln on Mar. 4, 1861, he retired to his home, "Wheatland," near Lancaster, Pa. He supported Lincoln's administration. He was accused of being a traitor and of cowardice and weakness of character. Buchanan, the strict constructionist, could hardly have acted otherwise than he did. He was a man of high character, unimpeachable honesty, patriotism and considerable ability. He died at "Wheatland," June 1, 1868. G. E. M.

BUCHAREST (Rom. Bucureşti) [byukərɛ′st, bu′kʊrɛ′sht], the capital city of Romania, located in southern Romania on both banks of the Dâmboviţa River, a tributary of the Danube, at 44° 25′ N. lat. and 26° 10′ E. long. The city suffers extremes of climate, being very hot in summer and bitterly cold and windy in fall and winter. The city lies in a strategic focal position on the Walachian plains of the lower Danube, where it commands important trade routes to Bulgaria, Hungary, and the U. S. S. R.

History. In the sixteenth century, Bucharest was a walled city, and was probably founded on the site of a Roman fortress. After being destroyed by the Turks in 1595, a new, larger wall was built, and a century later the city became the capital of the principality of Walachia. During the eighteenth and nineteenth centuries it frequently changed hands, being ruled in turn by Turks, Russians, and Austrians. In 1861 the city became the capital of the newly created kingdom formed by the union of Walachia and Moldavia. By 1910 the city had expanded beyond its wall, and several suburbs were in the early stages of development. In 1916 after German and Bulgarian armies under August von Mackensen invaded and captured the city without a struggle, the government transferred its seat to Iasi in Moldavia. Upon the capitulation of the Central Powers in 1918, Bucharest again became the capital, this time of a much enlarged Romania.

Buildings and Streets. Since 1918 the city has shown a phenomenal growth; the walls have been removed, and it is the center of a network of at least eight railroads, and is the principal terminus of the Romanian air lines. The center of the city is attractively and substantially built of stone and brick above the flood level, but around the center there are primitive buildings, poorly constructed. Wide boulevards cross the city, the principal one being the Calea Victorei. Among notable buildings are the royal palace, the palace of justice, and the cathedral of the metropolitan of Romania. Some damage was inflicted on the city by both Axis and Allied bombings during World War II. On Aug. 23, 1944, Romania withdrew from the war and accepted the armistice terms of the United States, Great Britain, and the U. S. S. R. The next day Nazi bombers raided Bucharest, and the royal palace was severely damaged. This action was followed by a formal declaration of war against Germany on Aug. 25, 1944. Most of the Allied bombings were confined to the great Malaxa locomotive works east of Bucharest, resulting, however, only in slight damage.

Education and Culture. As the education center of Romania, Bucharest has a large university; high schools for technical studies, forestry, agriculture; business administration schools; and an academy of music and dramatic art. It is the site of the Romanian Academy, founded in 1866, and of the Academy of Science, founded in 1865. Among the many libraries is the Library of the Romanian Academy, containing old Romanian and Slavonic documents concerning Romania's history and language. Many other schools, libraries, museums, theatres, a broadcasting station, a music conservatory, and an astronomical observatory give Bucharest a high rank among the educational centers of central Europe. As a religious center, it is the site of the National Museum of Religious Art, established in 1931, which contains inter-

esting frescoes, carpets, censers, reliquaries, crucifixes, icons, tombstones, and chalices. The city is the headquarters of the Orthodox archbishop of Romania.

Commerce and Industry. Besides being the political, cultural, and educational center of the country, Bucharest is the financial and industrial nucleus as well. Its favorable location in the midst of a densely populated fertile plain, and its proximity to abundant supplies of petroleum, salt, and water, facilitate the manufacture of chemicals and textiles. Its citizens also manufacture furniture, bricks, soap, metal wares, paper, and army supplies. Its distilleries, breweries,

BURTON HOLMES FROM EWING GALLOWAY
BUCHAREST, CAPITAL OF ROMANIA

flour mills, meat-packing plants, foodstuff industries, and railroad repair shops employ a large number of its inhabitants; its refineries produce oil products and beet sugar. Many institutions are centralized there, including the National Bank of Romania, the country's only bank of issue; the telegraph system; the postal system; and the chief commercial, legal, and insurance houses. Possessing a large cosmopolitan population, Bucharest dominates the intellectual, social, and political life of Romania. Pop. 1948, 1,041,807. S. A.

BUCHAREST, TREATY OF, an agreement signed Aug. 10, 1913, ending the Second Balkan War and sealing the defeat of Bulgaria by its former allies, Serbia and Greece, which had been joined by Romania and Turkey. The Treaty of Bucharest marked a fundamental change in the Balkan balance of power in favor of Serbia. Serbia obtained central Macedonia, a part of southern Macedonia and one-half of the Sanjak of Novibazar, the other half going to Montenegro. Greece received the island of Crete, and most of southern Macedonia, including the city of Salonika. Romania obtained northern Dobrudja, from Turtukaia on the Danube to Erkene on the Black Sea. Bulgaria was forced to restore eastern Thrace, with Adrianople (Edirne), to the Ottoman Empire. The result was that Bulgaria, having lost Monastir and Ochrid to Serbia and Salonika and Kavalla to Greece, retained only a small part of Macedonia. On the Aegean coast Bulgaria retained only the strip of territory between the Mesta and Maritsa rivers, with the port of Dedeagatch (Alexandroupolis).

The balance of power in the Balkan region definitely favored Russia and the Triple Entente as against Germany and Austria-Hungary. The reduction of Turkish territory in Europe to the Enos-Midia line was not welcome in Germany, now posing as the friend of the Sublime Porte and contending strongly for political influence in Constantinople. The Balkan states were also dissatisfied as a result of the Treaty of Bucharest, despite their acquisitions of territory. Serbian feeling was strong against both Austria-Hungary and Italy, while Bulgaria had not gained coveted territory in Macedonia and Thrace, and had lost in Dobrudja to Romania. The Ottoman Government looked abroad for redress of its own losses. All in all, the Treaty of Bucharest helped to set the stage for the outbreak of World War I.

H. N. Ho.

BUCHENWALD [bu'χǝnvɑlt], a German concentration camp in World War II, in central Germany, near Weimar. When the camp was liberated by Allied forces in April 1945, 20,000 emaciated prisoners, little more than living skeletons, were all that remained of the 82,000 who had been registered on the camp records the previous month. Evidence of wanton brutality and wholesale slaughter was clear. Corpses of men and women littered the grounds of the camp, and in some places bodies were stacked like cordwood. American troops discovered incredible facilities for torturing and killing the slave laborers and political prisoners of Buchenwald. Huge furnaces existed for purpose of mass cremation, and it has been ascertained that 32,705 lives were taken by so-called "scientific" processes.

BUCHMAN, FRANK NATHAN DANIEL [bu'kmǝn] (1878-   ), American spiritual leader, founder of the world movement known as Moral Re-Armament (M.R.A.), was born at Pennsburg, Pa., June 4, 1878. He graduated from Muhlenberg College in 1899 (M.A. 1902; Honorary D.D. 1926) and later studied at Cambridge University (1921-1922).

From 1909 to 1916 he was secretary of the Y.M.C.A. at Pennsylvania State College, and during World War I was with a flying squadron caring for prisoners. As professor for the Hartford Theological Foundation from 1916 to 1921, he traveled widely in Europe, Asia, and the Far East. In 1921 he began to devote full time to a program of "world-changing through life-changing." He aimed to develop in every country groups of leaders trained in the four moral standards, "absolute honesty, purity, unselfishness, and love" and "the guidance of God." In 1921 Dr. Buchman visited Oxford, and seven years later a group of students that he had trained traveled to South Africa where they were christened by the press "The Oxford Group," a name which spread with the development of the work to more than 60 countries. In 1938 on the foundation of this world network of trained leadership, he launched the program of Moral Re-Armament which sought to become the ideological spearpoint of Christian democracy. From 1946 on he presided at the annual M.R.A. world assemblies at Caux, Switzerland. He was knighted by King Paul of Greece (1948), was made a member of the French Legion of Honor (1950), received the Grand Cross of Merit from the West German government (1952), and was decorated by the governments of Japan, China, the Philippines, and Thailand (1956).   DuB. M.

BUCHNER, EDUARD [bu'χnǝr] (1860-1917), winner of the Nobel prize in chemistry for 1907 for his "chemical-biological investigations in cell-less fermentation," was born in Munich on May 20, 1860, and was killed in World War I on Aug. 24, 1917. He became a professor of chemistry at Berlin in 1898, at Breslau in 1909, and at Würzburg in 1911. In 1903 he had corroborated J. Traube's theory that fermentation by yeast was not caused by the cell but by zymase, an enzyme which was present therein, and which, extracted from the cell, would still cause fermentation.   H. N. A.

BUCHU [byu'kyu; bu'ku], the name given to the bitter, leathery, heathlike leaves of species of *Barosma,* especially *B. betulina,* low, heavy-scented evergreen shrubs of the rue family from South Africa. Buchu leaves were formerly used medicinally.   R. S. Ho.

BUCK, CARL DARLING (1866-1955), American linguist, was born Oct. 2, 1866, at Orland, Me. He studied at Yale, where he received his doctoral degree in 1889, at Athens, 1887-1889, and at Leipzig, 1889-1892. Buck taught Sanskrit and Indo-European linguistics in the University of Chicago from 1892 to 1933. He published numerous works, especially in the fields of Greek dialectology and Osco-Umbrian; his excellent *Grammar of Oscan and Umbrian* (1904, expanded 1928) and his *Introduction to the Study of the Greek Dialects* (1909, revised 1927) remain essential tools for every scholar working in those languages. He also wrote a *Comparative Grammar of Greek and Latin* (1933). He died in Chicago, Ill., on Feb. 8, 1955.   G. B.

BUCK, FRANK HOWARD (1884-1950), American jungle explorer, was born Mar. 17, 1884, near Gainesville, Tex. After being educated in Dallas public schools, he traveled in the Midwest, finally settling in Chicago where, at the age of twenty-one, he married the drama critic, Amy Leslie. Her acquaintances aided Buck in becoming a theatrical agent. Buck's first trip away from the United States was in 1911, to the South American jungles, where he sought birds and returned to New York to sell them. Before World War I he went to Singapore and later returned to the San Francisco Exposition, and was engaged in administrative work. As a result of his explorations and travels which took him across the Pacific Ocean more than forty times and around the world more than a dozen times, Buck compiled his book *Bring 'Em Back Alive* (1930), the title being drawn from his own record of never having willfully harmed any form of wild life. Buck brought many "firsts" in animals to United States zoological gardens, such as the man-eating tiger, the largest king cobra ever captured alive, the pigmy water buffalo (anoa) of Celebes, and the babirusa, rarest of wild swine. He owned what is probably the largest private zoo in the world, at Amityville, L. I., N. Y. Buck collaborated with Edward Anthony in the writing of *Wild Cargo* (1932) and with Ferrin L. Fraser on *Fang and Claw* (1935), *Tim Thompson In the Jungle* (1935), and *On Jungle Trails* (1937). Buck's autobiography, *All In a Lifetime,* appeared in 1941. He died in Houston, Tex., Mar. 25, 1950.   W. E. A.

BUCK, PEARL SYDENSTRICKER (1892-   ), American novelist, was born in Hillsboro, W. Va., June 26, 1892. Her parents, missionaries, returned to China a few months later, and that country was her home until 1933. She attended boarding school in Shanghai, and graduated from Randolph-Macon Woman's College, Lynchburg, Va., in 1914. She received M.A. degrees from Cornell, 1926, and Yale, 1933. She was married to John Lossing Buck, an American missionary, in 1917. Mrs. Buck taught English literature at the University of Nanking, 1921-1931; Southeastern University, Nanking, 1925-1927; and Chung Yang University, Nanking, 1928-1930. Among her early works were *East Wind: West Wind* (1930); *The Good Earth* (1931), which won a Pulitzer Prize in 1932 and was translated into almost 20 languages, dramatized, and filmed; *Sons* (1932); and *A House Divided* (1935). The last three novels were published in one volume in 1935, under the title *House of Earth. The Exile* (1936) and *Fighting Angel* (1936) are biographies of Mrs. Buck's parents and were published together as *The Spirit and the Flesh.* She also translated a Chinese classic by Shui Hu Chüan as *All Men Are Brothers* (1933). In 1935 her first marriage ended in divorce, and she married her publisher, Richard J. Walsh. She was elected to the American Institute of Arts and Letters in 1936 and won the Nobel Prize for literature in 1938. Mrs. Buck's many later writings include: *The Chinese Novel* (1939); *Other Gods* and *Dragon Seed* (1942); *The Promise*

PEARL SYDENSTRICKER
BUCK

JOHN GLIDDEN

(1943); *Portrait of a Marriage* (1945); *China in Black and White* (1946); *Peony; Pavilion of Women; Big Wave* (1948); *Kinfolk* (1949); *American Argument* (with C. Robinson, 1949); *Imperial Woman* (1956). She has been president of the East and West Association since 1941. Her residence in China, study of Chinese classics, and thorough knowledge of Chinese character exceptionally qualified her to make Oriental civilization understandable and significant to Western readers. *The Good Earth* is the most effective portrayal of Chinese peasant life in American fiction. In 1958 she revealed that she had published five novels on American subjects between 1945 and 1953 under the name of John Sedges. She has also written plays for television. W. Lin.

BUCKBEAN, *Menyanthes,* a genus of the gentian family with two species native to north temperate regions, found in bogs and shallow water. It has basal leaves and a flower stalk to 18 in., bearing white or purplish five-parted flowers in clusters covered with a heavy white beard.   J. C. Wis.

BUCKEYE, common name of several North American species of the genus *Aesculus,* a group of shrubs and trees of the horse chestnut family. They are often cultivated for their handsome palmate leaves and white, red, or yellow flowers in conspicuous pyramids. The large fruiting capsules are often prickly; the brown, shiny seeds are inedible.

The Ohio buckeye, *A. glabra,* with prickly fruit and greenish-yellow flowers, rarely exceeds 30 ft. It is found in great numbers along the Ohio River, hence the nickname, Buckeye State. The yellow buckeye, *A. octandra,* of the east central region of the United States, a rather tall tree reaching a height of 90 ft., has five leaflets, yellow flowers, and smooth fruits. It is cultivated as an ornamental. The white buckeye, *A. parviflora,* also called bottlebrush buckeye, is a large spreading shrub of the southeastern United States, covered in midsummer with bristling spikes of white flowers. The California buckeye, *A. californica,* has white to rose-colored flowers. The red buckeye, *A. pavia,* has dark-

red flowers and smooth fruits, while the painted buckeye, *A. neglecta,* a shrub or small tree, has yellow flowers, red-veined at base. The last two are natives of the south-eastern United States. The red horse chestnut, *A. carnea,* a popular, cultivated, small tree, with handsome clusters of red flowers, is a hybrid of the horse chestnut, *A. hippocastanum,* and the red buckeye.

Buckeye lumber is furnished by both the Ohio buckeye and the yellow buckeye, but chiefly by the latter, because of the larger size of the tree. Buckeye wood is light in weight, white in color, soft, and weak. It is used principally for furniture, boxes, crating, caskets, and artificial limbs. *See also* HORSE CHESTNUT.   A. H. Gr.

BUCKEYE BUTTERFLY, the common name of *Junonia coenia,* one of the four-footed butterflies of the family Nymphalidae. It is distributed over most of the United States and Central America, and is characterized by the presence of one large and one small, bluish-centered eye-spot on each wing. The larvae feed on plantains (*Plantago*), are dark in color, paler below, and with branched spines above.   C. H. Cu.

BUCKINGHAM, 1ST DUKE OF (GEORGE VILLIERS) [bʌ'kiŋəm; vɪ'lərz, vɪ'lyərz[(1592-1628), English courtier, was born in Leicestershire on Aug. 28, 1592. He appeared at court in 1614 and was made cupbearer to James I. He was championed by the many courtiers who desired to oust the Earl of Somerset, the current favorite. In 1615

FIRST DUKE OF
BUCKINGHAM
(GEORGE VILLIERS)

FROM AN ENGRAVING BY
H. GARNIER FROM A
PAINTING BY C. JOHNSON

COURTESY OF THE NEW YORK
PUBLIC LIBRARY

he became Gentleman of the Bedchamber and was knighted and granted a pension. When Somerset fell from favor, Villiers took his place. In 1616 he was appointed Master of the Horse and was created Viscount Villiers; in 1617 he was made an earl and in 1623 Duke of Buckingham. At first he took little part in politics, devoting his time to strengthening his own position at court by acquiring control of the royal patronage and by arranging good marriages for his brothers and sisters. He married a daughter of the Duke of Rutland, and by 1619 he was driving the great Howard family from political power. He secured the position of lord high admiral for himself and even tried to do something to correct abuses in the navy. In affairs of state, however, he followed no consistent policy either in regard to the proposed Spanish marriage of Prince Charles, later Charles I, or to the question of aiding the Palatinate. By 1622 Buckingham had acquired as much influence over Prince Charles as he had over his father, and in 1623 he succeeded in persuading King James to allow the Prince and himself to go incognito to Madrid to demand the Spanish infanta in marriage with Charles. The journey was a failure and Buckingham urged war with Spain. By this he hoped to gain popularity as a patriotic leader. The war, too, was a failure which led to his first impeachment, and after Charles I succeeded to the throne in 1625 Buckingham persuaded the King to declare war on France as well. In the war Buckingham gained none of the glory he expected, for his naval expedition to La Rochelle in 1627 was a fiasco. He was looked upon as the backbone of the King's resistance to the wishes of the Commons. Parliament was dissolved to save him, but in 1628 he was again impeached. He was assassinated at Portsmouth by John Felton, a discharged officer, on Aug. 23, 1628.   E. R. A.

BUCKINGHAM, 2ND DUKE OF (GEORGE VILLIERS) (1628-1687), English statesman and author, second son of the first duke of Buckingham, was born at Westminster, Jan. 30, 1628. He was brought up with the children of Charles I and went to Trinity College, Cambridge. He fought for the king in the two civil wars, escaping in 1648 to Holland. There he joined the Prince of Wales, who in exile took the title of Charles II when his father was beheaded. Buckingham accompanied Charles to Scotland in 1650 and shared in the defeat at Worcester in 1651. Again he escaped to Holland, but disagreeing violently with Charles's other advisers, especially Hyde and Nicholas, Buckingham returned to England in 1657 to marry the daughter of the parliamentary general, Lord Fairfax, and so regain his estates. Cromwell regarded this as the beginning of a Presbyterian plot against the government, and Buckingham was imprisoned in the Tower from August 1658 to February 1659. With Charles's restoration in 1660, Buckingham was soon returned to favor. He intrigued against Hyde, who had become Earl of Clarendon, and was partly responsible for his fall in 1667. For a time thereafter he was the king's chief adviser and a member of the so-called Cabal. He favored religious toleration and an alliance with France, but was deceived over the secret Treaty of Dover by his astute rival, Lord Arlington. Attacked for his scandalous life and his supposed popery, Buckingham joined the parliamentary opposition and became a champion of Protestant dissenters. He died at Kirkby Moorside in Yorkshire, Apr. 16, 1687. Though witty, generous, and of great natural accomplishments, he was unstable, vain, and unscrupulous. A poet of some merit, he is still remembered for his popular play, *The Rehearsal,* first performed in 1671. The butt of this satire on the heroic tragedies of the day was John Dryden, who retaliated in *Absalom and Achitophel* with a brilliant satirical portrait of Buckingham in the character of Zimri.   E. R. A.

BUCKINGHAM, a town in Papineau Co., Quebec, Canada, situated on Rivière du Lièvre 5 mi. above its confluence with the Ottawa River and 18 mi. northeast of the city of Ottawa. It is on Provincial Highway 35 and is served by a Canadian Pacific Railway spur line. The first sawmill in Buckingham was built in 1823, and for many years the town was important for lumber. The town was incorporated in 1890. Pulp mills were built in 1902 and a paper mill at nearby Masson in 1929. Power sites on the river develop over 250,000 h.p. Pop. 1956, 6,781.

BUCKINGHAM MEMORIAL FOUNTAIN, located in Grant Park, Chicago, Ill. The fountain was made possible by Miss Kate S. Buckingham as a memorial to her brother,

Clarence Buckingham. Funds used in its design and construction totaled $700,000. Dedication ceremonies were held in 1927. Constructed of reinforced concrete faced with pink Georgia marble, the fountain is located in a garden about 600 sq. ft. Its main pool, 280 ft. in diameter, has four large segmental portions interrupted by square angles. The fountain's 133 jets, when operating at full capacity, spout 14,000 gallons per minute. Sometimes referred to as the Colonnades, it is the largest illuminated fountain in the world.   R. W. C.

BUCKINGHAM PALACE, a London palace at the west end of St. James's Park, originally built by Sir George Goring (later Earl of Norwich) during the reign of James I. It was

COURTESY OF BRITISH INFORMATION SERVICES

BUCKINGHAM PALACE, LONDON, ENGLAND

rebuilt in 1674 and 1703 by John Sheffield, Marquess of Normandy (created Duke of Buckingham in the latter year), and in 1761 was acquired by George III. It was remodeled in 1825 by Sir John Nash as architect, and since 1837 has been the London residence of the British sovereigns. The east wing by Edward Blore was added in 1846, giving the palace the plan of a great quadrangle. However, in 1912 and 1913 Blore's façade toward St. James's Park was removed and the present façade by Sir Aston Webb was erected. The great ballroom dates from 1856. The palace contains a considerable collection of art objects, among them some three hundred paintings, including royal portraits. The gardens cover some forty acres, a part of them occupying the site of Mulberry Garden, built by James I in 1609 and a favorite resort of literary men of the seventeenth and eighteenth centuries.   R. Ne.

BUCKINGHAMSHIRE (*abbr.* Bucks), an inland county of England, covering an area of 749 sq. mi. in the south midlands. It is bounded by Northamptonshire on the north, Bedfordshire, Hertfordshire, and Middlesex on the east, Surrey and Berkshire on the south, and Oxfordshire on the west. The county is intersected by the chalk range of the Chiltern Hills. There is good grazing land and heavy arable land in the county; dairy farming and market gardening are both important. A large railway works has developed near the town of Bletchley, and other industries have moved into the county, along with housing developments for London workers. Beech forests supply the chair-making industry of High Wycombe. North of High Wycombe is Hughenden Manor, home of Benjamin Disraeli. Pop. 1952, 394,700.

BUCKLE, GEORGE EARLE (1854-1935), English editor, was born on June 10, 1854, at Twerton-on-Avon, near Bath. He was educated at Winchester and at New College, Oxford, and from 1877 to 1885 was a fellow of All Souls College. In 1880 he was admitted to the bar but did not practice, for in the same year he became a member of the staff of *The Times* of London. When Thomas Chenery, the editor, died four years later, Buckle was selected to fill the vacancy. He chose as his assistant another young editor, John B. Capper, and it was then said that the *Times* was being run by "two boys." Buckle believed in a policy of sane imperialism, and encouraged the economical and political development of India. However, he opposed home rule for Ireland. During his tenure as editor, the *Times* in 1887 published forged letters of Charles S. Parnell, believing them to be authentic, and the resultant embarrassment led to the reorganization of the paper under Alfred Harmsworth, Lord Northcliffe. Buckle resigned as editor in 1912, and upon the death of William F. Monypenny that same year, undertook the completion of the last four volumes of *The Life of Benjamin Disraeli, Earl of Beaconsfield* (6 vols., 1910-1920). Buckle also edited *The Letters of Queen Victoria,* second series (3 vols., 1926-1928); and third series (3 vols., 1930-1932). He died in Chelsea, London, on Mar. 3, 1935.

C. W. D.

BUCKLE, HENRY THOMAS (1821-1862), English historian, was born at Lee, in Kent, Nov. 24, 1821. He was a delicate child and had little formal education, but since he had inherited a considerable fortune he was able to travel and devote himself to historical studies. In 1857 he published the first volume of his *History of Civilization in England,* which won him an immediate reputation as a scholar; the second volume followed in 1861. Shortly after its appearance he went for an extended tour of Egypt and Palestine, but was stricken with a fever and died at Damascus, May 29, 1862.

E. R. A.

BUCKMINSTER, JOSEPH STEVENS (1784-1812), American clergyman, was born May 26, 1784, in Portsmouth, N.H. His father, a clergyman, educated him at home. Later he attended Phillips Exeter Academy and Harvard College, where he graduated at the age of sixteen. He returned to Phillips Exeter to teach, and in 1803 became a tutor at Waltham. While at Phillips Exeter and Waltham he studied theology, and on Jan. 30, 1805, was ordained and installed as pastor of the Brattle Street Church in Boston. In 1806 he went to Europe and returned with a valuable collection of 3,000 books. Buckminster is mainly credited with introducing Bible scholarship in the United States. He was a member of the Anthology Club, a literary society in Boston, and frequently contributed to its monthly anthology. In 1807 he founded the Boston Athenaeum. He died in Boston, June 9, 1812.

BUCKNELL UNIVERSITY [bʌknɛ'l], an accredited, privately controlled, coeducational institution related to the Baptist Church. It was established on a 321-acre campus at Lewisburg, Pa., and chartered as the University of Lewisburg in 1846. In 1886 the present name was adopted in honor of William Bucknell, a benefactor. The degrees conferred are the A.B. in liberal arts and the B.S. in business administration, engineering, education, and science. Professional degrees are offered in chemical, civil, electrical, and mechanical engineering, and graduate degrees are the A.M. and M.S. in biology, commerce and finance, education, and chemical engineering.

A far-reaching study of educational objectives and the curricular program is in progress. The interdepartmental integration course at senior level is designed to assemble all the student has learned and to graduate him with a working philosophy. All first-year courses in modern languages are on a five-hours-a-week basis, instead of the traditional three-hours-a-week basis. Language majors are required to live in language houses. Humanistic studies in the engineering program have been increased, new emphasis being given for engineering students to the study of languages, literature, and general humanistic subjects. Limited scholarship and student loan aid is available. Dormitory residence is required for all women and for freshman students. *For statistics see* COLLEGES AND UNIVERSITIES.

BUCKNER, SIMON BOLIVAR, JR. (1886-1945), American soldier, was born near Munfordville, Ky., on July 18, 1886, the son of a general in the Confederate army. He entered the Virginia Military Institute in 1902, and in 1904 was appointed to the United States Military Academy, West Point, from which he graduated in 1908 and commissioned a second lieutenant of infantry. From 1910 to 1912, and again from 1915 to 1917, Buckner served in the Philippines. In 1917 he was transferred to the aviation section of the Signal Corps, and was assigned to train fliers at Kelly Field in Texas. In August 1918 he was transferred to Washington, D. C., where he served in the operations section of the air service and studied at the Army War College. From 1919 to 1923 Buckner was an instructor in infantry tactics at West Point, after which he attended the Infantry School, the Command and General Staff School, and the Army War College. From 1929 to 1932 he served as executive officer of the Army War College, and in 1932 he was again on duty at West Point. In 1933 he became commandant of cadets there, serving until 1936. In 1940 Buckner became a brigadier general in the regular army and chief of staff of the Sixth Division, and in July 1940 he was appointed commander of United States troops in Alaska. In 1941 he was promoted to the rank of major general. Buckner later commanded defense troops who drove off Japanese forces which had succeeded in gaining a foothold in the Aleutians. In 1943 he was promoted to the rank of lieutenant general, and in June 1944 was transferred to the South Pacific area, where he was placed in command of the Tenth Army. His troops invaded Okinawa in April 1945. Buckner was killed in action toward the end of the Okinawa campaign, on June 18, 1945.

S. D.

COURTESY OF THE AMERICAN MUSEUM OF NATURAL HISTORY

BUCKTHORN, RHAMNUS CATHARTICA

BUCKTHORN, the common name of a large genus, *Rhamnus,* of the buckthorn family with almost one hundred species of spiny shrubs, rarely trees. They are native chiefly to temperate regions, with about twelve species in North America. Some are valuable as ornamental, medicinal, or dye shrubs. They have smooth leaves, greenish flowers, and berrylike fruits. The purging buckthorn (*R. cathartica*) and the alder buckthorn (*R. frangula*), native to the Old World and planted for ornament, are sparingly naturalized in eastern North America. These and others yield cathartic drugs and dyes. The lance-leaved buckthorn (*R. lanceolata*) and the swamp buckthorn (*R. alnifolia*), native to the eastern United States, are small shrubs; the Indian cherry (*R. carolinianum*), growing to 40 ft., is native to the South. The better known species of the Pacific slope are: the cascara sagrada (*R. purshiana*), yielding the well-known drug; the coffee berry (*R. californica*); and the redberry (*R. crocea*).

J. C. Wis.

BUCKWHEAT, *Fagopyrum esculentum,* a member of the buckwheat family, is an annual plant, grown for food and also as green manure. Native to Siberia and Manchuria, it has been grown extensively in China from prehistoric times. It is an important crop in Japan and Russia from where it was introduced into Europe. It is not a true cereal, but is usually classed as such in market reports. The name seems to be a corruption of beech-wheat, the German *Buchweisen,* for the seed in form resembles beechnuts but has the food characteristics of wheat. The plant is branching and erect, with many heart-shaped leaves and white flowers whose nectar makes a much desired dark honey. The luxuriant foliage gives the crop ability to smother weeds; and the fact that, when plowed under, it decays quickly makes it desirable as a green manure. Its chief value is, however, its grain used as stock feed and as flour by the poorer classes of the Old World. In America buckwheat flour is largely used for griddle cakes. Rutin, a valuable drug in the treatment of hardening of the arteries, is extracted from buckwheat meal. Buckwheat is tender and must be sown after danger from frost is past. It takes only 8-10 weeks from sowing to maturity. Its seed will germinate well in dry soil, but the crop grows best in moist cool climates. It thrives in many kinds of soils which are suitable for cereals. It is grown on a number of farms in the hilly sections of the country, and in the north is a popular crop because it can be sown up to midsummer. The three varieties used are the common or dark-colored grain, the silver held with light-colored grain, and the Japanese. In recent years, buckwheat crops in the United States have been only about half as large as those in the first quarter of the century, the average acreage harvested between 1937 and 1946 being 416,000. The acreage harvested in 1948, one of the smallest of record, was only 337,000, with a yield of 6,324,000 bu.

C. K. H.

BUCOLICS. *See* Eclogues.

BUCOVINA [bu'kovi'nɑ], a region of east central Europe, formerly a Romanian district having an area of 4,030 sq. mi., divided in 1944 between Romania and the Soviet Union. Physically, the Bucovina region is part of the northern Carpathian Foreland, with its southwestern half rising up slopes of the Carpathian Mountains and the northeastern half extending across a rolling, dissected plain. Northeast of the Siretul River are horizontal sandy marls and alluvial deposits, while on the southwest are the Carpathian sandstones with ridges of conglomerates. Mineral wealth is not great, although considerable salt and some petroleum are produced, and Soviet geologists claimed discovery after World War II of commercial deposits of manganese, iron, and copper. Mineral springs are numerous, while brownstone is quarried for architectural purposes.

The climate is typically middle-eastern European, with severe winters, as shown by a January mean temperature of 25° F. on the lowlands, and warm summers, with a July mean of 70° F. Precipitation is mostly in summer, averaging 25 in., when westerly winds bring Atlantic moisture. Soils are very productive, since the northeastern portions are loess-covered and support a large agricultural population. Soils of the Carpathian slopes are thinner and are not generally plowed. A well-watered land, Bucovina possesses numerous small rivers, many of them rising on the northern Carpathian watershed. Chief streams include the Dnestr, Prut (Pruth), Suceava, Siretul, and Moldova. One of the great natural resources is the extensive forest coverage. Beeches predominate in the lower areas, and give the area its name, since Bucovina means "Land of the Beeches." Conifers are the principal trees on the higher elevations, giving the name Waldkarpathen or "Forested Carpathians" to the mountains. Although forests cover 60 per cent of its area, Bucovina has extensive farm land, meadows, and pastures; it is both an agricultural and timber-producing region.

From 1918 to 1940 Bucovina was a district of Romania, in the northern part of the country, adjoining Poland and the Soviet Union on the north. Its population was officially estimated in 1937 at 910,997. Prior to World War II the Ruthenians comprised 38 per cent of the population, and the Romanians, 34 per cent; minority groups included Jews, 13 per cent; Germans, 8 per cent; Poles, 4 per cent; and a small number of Magyars, Russians, and Armenians. About 70 per cent of the inhabitants were of the Orthodox faith, and 11 per cent, Roman Catholic. Cernăuți (Russian, Chernovtsy; Austrian, Cernowitz), the capital of the district, had a population of 110,357 in 1937. Situated on the Prut River and on the important railway line connecting Bucharest (Bucuresti) with Lvov (Lwow), the city was the seat of a university founded in 1875 and of the Orthodox religious head for the district.

Northern Bucovina, including the city of Cernăuți, which became Chernovtsy, was incorporated by the Soviet Union into the Ukrainian S.S.R. in 1940, following cession of the area by Romania. The important cities within southern Bucovina, which remains a part of Romania, are Rădăuți (Radautz), Suceava (Suczawa), Campulung Moldovenesc (Kimpolung), and Siret (Sereth).

History. Bucovina was a part of the Roman province of Dacia. In the fourth century it was overrun by the Huns. The Slavs settled the district in the course of the sixth century. In the fourteenth century Bucovina became a part of the Moldavian Principality. The first reference to the district by the name of Bucovina appeared in the agreement concluded in 1412 between the Polish king, Jagellon, and the Hungarian king, Sigismund. In 1512 Moldova (Moldavia), including Bucovina, submitted to the Turks. It was occupied by the Russians in 1769 and evacuated in accordance with the Treaty of Kutchuk-Kaindardji in 1774. Under pressure, the Turks ceded Bucovina to Austria in 1775. In 1786 it was incorporated into Galicia as the district of Czernowitz; in 1849 it became a crown land of Austria, and it remained in this position until the end of World War I. The Treaty of St. Germain in 1919 gave only the southern portion of Bucovina to Romania, but the subsequent Treaty of Sèvres (July 10, 1920) assigned the whole district to Romania. On June 27, 1940, Romania accepted a Soviet ultimatum for the cession of northern Bucovina, an area of about 2,035 sq. mi. with 717,500 inhabitants. The district was reincorporated into Romania after the Romanian attack on the Soviet Union in 1944, but was lost again to the Russians by the armistice agreement of Sept. 13, 1944.

W. S. V.

BUCUREŞTI. *See* BUCHAREST.

BUCYRUS [byusɑɪ′rəs], a city in northern Ohio, the county seat of Crawford Co., situated on the Sandusky River, 60 mi. north of Columbus. It is served by the New York Central and the Pennsylvania railroads. Bucyrus, first settled in 1819, was founded in 1821 and incorporated in 1886 as a city. Farms in the vicinity produce livestock, incubator chicks, grain, and hay. Local industries are largely devoted to the production of power shovels and cranes for heavy construction and mining work. Other activities are the manufacture of road-surfacing, brick, and tile machines; castings; burial vaults; lamps; rubber; roller-bearings; and farm implements. Pop. 1950, 10,327.

BUDAPEST [bu′dəpɛ′st; bʊ′dɒpɛ′sht], the capital and largest city of Hungary, on both banks of the Danube River, in the north central part of the country, situated at 47° 30′ N. lat. and 19° 5′ E. long. Budapest was incorporated as a single city in 1873 when four towns, Buda, Pest, O-Buda, and Köbánya, of which Buda and Pest were the largest, united. Buda, on the high west bank of the Danube River, is the center of the administrative, artistic, and intellectual life of the country. Pest, which is on the plains to the east, is the industrial and commercial heart of the city. It faces the plain at the point where the Danube passes through the Bakony Hills. The city has accordingly been a gateway through which have poured the civilizing influences of the West.

History. The Romans established a frontier post called Aquincum near Great Island on the Danube. With the invasion of the northern and eastern barbarians this outpost fell. Later, in the tenth century, the Magyars built a defensive town, Old Buda, adjacent to the Roman ruins. The initial foothold of the Magyar tribesmen appears to have been downstream.

Because of its strategic position, Buda has been the spearhead for invasions of the plains, and the last defensive outpost against aggression from the plains. Consequently, the city has changed hands many times. In the mid-fourteenth century it became the capital of Hungary. During the reign of Matthias Corvinus, 1458-1490, the city expanded and became a capital of great splendor known throughout the continent. Lying at the junction of the East and West, Buda benefited artistically and culturally from both civilizations. But in the sixteenth century the Turks swept across the Danubian plains and captured and sacked Pest in 1526. They were forced to lay siege to Buda for fifteen years before finally occupying it in 1541. For 140 years the Turks made Buda their administrative and military outpost, until they were routed by the Austrians in 1686. During the Turkish rule all the accumulated treasures of art, and all scientific acquisitions within the city were destroyed, and the Austrians found nothing but ruins in both Buda and Pest. The restoration was the work of centuries, and the rapid development of the two communities did not begin until the second half of the nineteenth century.

Pest does not share the antiquity of Buda. It was destroyed by the Mongols in 1241, but it revived and grew thereafter as a trading post serving the great plain. In the nineteenth century it surpassed Buda in growth and development. The flat site, having unlimited room for expansion, permitted Pest to become a nucleus for incoming railroads and industrial development, and it became, as a consequence, the capital of modern life in the dual city.

After World War I the Communists gained control of the city for a short time, 1918-1919, and in 1919 the Romanians occupied and looted it. With the conclusion of the peace treaty it became the capital of independent Hungary. It was sought out as the refuge point for unemployed government officials and refugees from the lost Hungarian lands. Conditions in the city were further aggravated by the virtual standstill of the milling industry after the war, as this industry was the mainstay of Budapest's economic life. In addition, the financial structure of the great city was in a state of collapse, and it did not improve until after financial reconstruction was undertaken in 1924 as a result of international action. During World War II Budapest was a major battleground. For almost fourteen weeks, from Nov. 1, 1944, when the Red Army reached the outskirts of the city, until Feb. 13, 1945, the German garrison was under continuous siege. Stalingrad alone offered a more stubborn resistance. Pest suffered less damage than Buda as the Germans took advantage of Buda's defensive position. Budapest was one of the most completely ruined cities of central Europe as a result of the war. Nearly three fourths of its buildings were damaged or destroyed, including the royal palace.

General Description. The city has had numerous sieges and fires, so that many of its edifices are not as old as those of most other European cities. Standing on St. Gerard's Hill (Gellérthegy), almost 400 ft. above the Danube, all of Pest and a significant part of Buda are in full view. In Pest, directly across the river, is the Inner City (Belváros), which, because of avenues radiating out from its own encircling boulevard, appears as the hub of a wheel. Directly on the river is the Francis Joseph Quay, and farther north, the park, Corso, of Pest. Above the shopping-district buildings rise the city hall, the university and its library, and several large churches, among them the Evangelical and the Greek.

To the north is the Leopold quarter (Lipotváros), extending from the river for three quarters of a mile inland. In a setting of beautiful parkways and fine hotels along the river bank are the parliament buildings. This late Gothic group

EASTFOTO

SZABADSAG SQUARE IN BUDAPEST

has a background of Renaissance and modern style buildings, including the Palace of Justice, and the agriculture and other departmental edifices. Other prominent features in this quarter are the stock exchange, the Academy of Science, and St. Stephen's Cathedral. To the northeast is Theresa quarter (Terezvaros), whose notable aspects are the western railroad depot and yards, the telephone building, a 1,000-acre city park, the Opera House, the Music Academy, and several museums. The beautiful Andrassy Avenue crosses lengthwise through the area to the city park.

To the east and south of the Inner City are the Elizabeth (Erzsebetvaros), the Joseph (Jozsefvaros), the Francis (Fere-

Bastion, a remnant of the old city wall on the west river bank. Farther uphill is the ancient and beautiful Gothic Church of St. Matthias, where once the Ottoman Sulieman Pasha stabled his horses. Three other prominent buildings near by are the Finance Ministry, the official residence of the prime minister, and the Renaissance-style palace of Archduke Joseph. The constricted, ancient, winding streets of the remainder of the hill are lined with residences of Hungary's old families. The Christian quarter (Krisztinavaros) has the large military hospital and the southern railroad station.

In addition to the steep, round Sun Hill (Naphegy), a residential section near the Taban quarter, many villas are

Budapest as seen from Gellerthegy, some one thousand feet above the Danube

nezvaros), and the Köbánya quarters, which, aside from the National Museum, National Theatre, large synagogues, and public buildings, such as markets, hospitals, and churches, are characterized by the radial street pattern. The streets are lined with factories that are serviced by the eastern railroad depot and yards. Most of the damage to Pest during the siege of World War II was caused by German artillery fire from Buda.

The six bridges across the Danube connecting the city were destroyed in 1945 during the retreat of the Germans. The famous Lancz-Hid suspension bridge was one of the largest in Europe. It was completed in 1849, and was 1,230 ft. long and 39 ft. wide. Its chain hung from two pillars 160 ft. high. When it was opened in 1849 it was called the World's Eighth Wonder. Margaret Bridge, the work of the famous French engineer Alexandre G. Eiffel, had three arms and connected the city with Margaret Island. The destruction of these bridges collapsed the internal transportation of the city, but by 1947 several of them had been temporarily replaced.

Margaret Island divides the river. Once a refuge for an order of nuns, it has become both a summer and winter playground, possessing extensive and beautiful grounds, a sulphur spring, a hotel, a swimming pool, a skating rink, and provisions for other sports. Farther in the distance, on the west bank, is O-Buda (Altofen). Just at the north edge of O-Buda is Aquincum (many baths), a Roman colony whose antiquities are preserved in a museum among ruins of an amphitheatre, a cemetery, and an aqueduct. South of Margaret's Island is the Watertown quarter (Vizivaros), on the small terrace at the north foot of the Var (Fortress) Hill. Noteworthy features of this quarter are schools, colleges, scientific institutions, and offices. Fortress Hill has Fisher

visible in the hilly upland to the west. A second glance at the west riverbank shows two parks near Margaret Island containing the Emperor and the St. Luke baths. Farther south is the Gothic-style, red-brick Calvinist Church, and close by are the ruins of the Lancz-Hid Bridge.

South of this point are the royal gardens, extending to the Elizabeth Bridge. South of Francis Joseph Bridge is the Polytechnical University, adjoining the new Clayfields quarter (Lagymanyos). Numerous sulphur and mineral spring establishments are at the south foot of St. Gerard Hill. Very few of these famous buildings of Buda escaped the ravages of the seven-week siege of Budapest in January and February of 1945. Among those totally destroyed was the Royal Palace built by Maria Theresa in 1749-1771, restored in 1849 after a fire, and greatly extended in 1894-1906 in the Baroque style. It had a 1,000-ft. facade facing the Danube, and was crowned by a central dome 203 ft. high. Of the palace's 860 rooms, one of the most spectacular was the Hapsburg room, under the central dome.

The destructive effects of the siege aggravated the housing situation in the city. It was estimated that 4 to 5 per cent of the dwellings were totally destroyed, 23 per cent badly damaged, and 47 per cent damaged. Ten per cent of the 1,800 factories of the city were damaged so badly that they were forced to close.

Economic Activity. Budapest recovered rapidly after the cessation of hostilities of World War II. It remains the focal point of Hungarian trade, gathering most of the country's stock, wool, hides, cereals, and wine for final processing and redistribution. Budapest is connected by air and rail with all large European centers. It is the chief rail center of the country and the focal point for Danube shipping. Pop. (off. est. 1948), 1,073,000.   H. J. R.

BUDAPEST, PÉTER PÁZMÁNY UNIVERSITY OF,

was originally founded in Nagyszombat, Hungary (now Trnava, Czechoslovakia), in 1635 by Archbishop Péter Pázmány. It was an outgrowth of a former Jesuit College established in 1561. Queen Maria Theresa transferred the institution to Buda in 1777 and gave it university status. Shortly after this time Emperor Joseph II moved it to Pest, where it is located today. Latin was spoken until 1848 when it was displaced by the native tongue. The institution was renamed in 1921 in honor of its founder. In the early years there were only faculties of philosophy and theology, but faculties of law were added in 1668 and of medicine in 1748. The library was established in 1635 and in 1948 had 802,915 volumes. After World War II, the student enrollment totaled over 10,000 and the faculty numbered about 125. Architecturally the university buildings express the Renaissance style, but the main building, completed in 1900, is baroque, as is the university church, erected from 1715 to 1756. The ceiling of the church was painted by Johann Bergh.

BUDAUN

[budau'n], a city in the west central, or Rohilkhand, section of the United Provinces of north central India, center of the Budaun district, located at 28° 2′ N. lat. and 79° 10′ E. long. on the Sot River. Budaun is in a well-watered, almost level section of the Upper Ganges Plain, and the city is the market center of an agricultural district. The rainfall varies between 30 and 50 in. a year, almost all of which falls during the summer season. The winters are clear, cool, and dry, and the spring is unusually hot and cloudy, while the summer is warm and wet. Indigo factories exist in the town. The principal agricultural products of the surrounding area are grains, and wheat is the major product. Corn, barley, grain, millet, rape, mustard, sesame, linseed, and a little sugar cane are also grown.

The city was founded about A.D. 900-910, and was developed around a now ruined fort. In 1196 it fell to the Moslems, who constructed a large mosque in 1296 from the ruins of a Hindu temple. In 1571 the community was burned and rebuilt. In 1801 Budaun was ceded to the British by the Nawab of Oudh. The British established a post at Budaun in 1838. Pop. 1951, 53,521.   J. E. F.

BUDDENBROOKS

[bu'dənbroks], a German novel by Thomas Mann, first published in 1901; it appeared in English translation in 1924. First conceived as a study in child psychology, *Buddenbrooks* was to be the story of a frail, sensitive, highly musical boy, Hanno Buddenbrook, who can cope neither with the exigencies of everyday life, nor, in particular, with the monotony and harshness of uninspired school regime. Mainly under the influence of the Naturalistic theory, with its strong emphasis upon heredity and environment, Mann decided to describe in detail the family background of his hero and ended by giving a comprehensive chronicle of four generations of wealthy grain merchants in a North German city. In such a context, the suffering and the premature death of young Hanno finally became nothing but the concluding chapter of a long process of slow but relentless decay. This process, however, offers a double aspect: the gradual loss of vitality and robustness which the Buddenbrooks undergo is at the same time the decisive basis of their growing refinement, differentiation, and artistic creativeness. The road from the bourgeois to the artist leads through the experience of disease.

In spite of the apparent morbidity of its theme, *Buddenbrooks* is not a morbid novel. Through its wealth of material, its vivid and realistic descriptions of life with its weddings and funerals, family dinners, and business transactions, and its host of sharply delineated characters, it has gained general recognition as the classical representation of German middle-class life in the nineteenth century. The Buddenbrook family is supposedly modeled after Mann's father's family.
B. Bl.

BUDDHAGHOSA

[bu'ddəgo'sə] (early fifth century), Indian Buddhist commentator, whose name signifies "the voice of Buddha," is called "the Great" to distinguish him from others of the same name. He was born a Brahman, not far from the Great Bo-Tree at Buddh Gaya in northern India. Revata, his teacher, converted him to Buddhism. At Revata's suggestion Buddhaghosa went to Ceylon, where he wrote *Vissuddhi Magga* ("The Path of Purity"), described as the encyclopedia of Buddhism; and commentaries on the *Nikayas,* the *Abrudhamma,* and the *Vinaya.* The Sinhalese texts used by Buddhaghosa have been completely lost. He returned to Buddh Gaya and died there.   S. D.

BUDDHISM

[bu'dizəm]. Both as a religion and as a philosophy, Buddhism grew out of the teachings of Gautama Buddha in the sixth century B.C. Over a billion people of virtually all of Asia have been under its influence. It has two broad divisions, Southern Buddhism in India, Ceylon, Burma, Cambodia, and Thailand, called "Hinayana," or Small Vehicle, because it emphasizes individual salvation, and Northern Buddhism in China, Korea, and Japan, called "Mahayana," or Great Vehicle, because it emphasizes universal salvation. Besides these, there is Lamaism in Tibet and Mongolia, which is a mixture of Mahayana Buddhism and the animistic Bon religion of Tibet.

Buddhism has an elaborate pantheon, headed by the One Buddha in Hinayana and the Many Buddhas in Mahayana. A Buddha is an Enlightened One who possesses Supreme, Universal, and Perfect Wisdom, known by various names, notably Sakyamuni, Amitabha, Locana, Vairocana, according to the various aspects of the One Buddha. In Mahayana, the Buddha is usually represented by the Three Bodies, a triad corresponding to the Body of the Law, the Body of Bliss, and the Body of Transformation, or other threefold aspects, such as the Past, Present, and Future, or Wisdom, Discipline, and Compassion. These Buddhas are followed by many *arahans* or Worthy Ones, and *bodhisattvas* or saints. The most popular among the latter are Maitreya, Manjusri, and Avalokitesvara, the Goddess of Mercy, as the deity is known in the West.

Buddhist temples are among the most highly ornamented and colorful buildings in Asia, and they are always associated with beautiful pagodas in which are kept the supposed relics of the Buddha. Buddhist literature is vast, both in size and in variety of ideas. The Canon exists in Hinayana, Tibetan, and many Mahayana versions, the Mahayana edition of 1924 containing 13,520 parts in 100 volumes of 1,000 pages each. Buddhist ceremonies, music, and festivals are most elaborate, and Buddhist painting and sculpture represent fine examples of oriental art.

There are 12,000,000 adherents and 125,000 monks in Burma; 47,000,000 adherents, 78,000 temples and 8,000 churches in Japan; 200,000 monks in Thailand; 750,000 monks and nuns, 27,000 temples and 3,500,000 "home disciples" in China; 1,000,000 priests and followers in Tibet. In addition, there are an untold number of Asians who accept Buddhism along with other religions as a part of their syncretic religion.

As a philosophy, Buddhism developed in diverse directions immediately after Gautama's death. By the fourth century B.C., Gautama's followers had split into two schools, with the liberal Mahasanghikas opposing the conservative Theravadas. A century later, the two schools further split into eighteen, the most orthodox and influential being the Sarvastivada School, which insisted that all elements of existence were real, although the self was unreal.

In the first century A.D., Asvaghosha taught the doctrine that all reality was created by a universal consciousness; thus he laid the foundation of Mahayana Buddhism. Later, Nagarjuna (c. A.D. 100-200) furthered the development of Mahayana by advocating the doctrine that reality was void, in the sense that it was an absolute devoid of all particular qualities.

The Hinayana School of realism, the Abhidharmakosa School (Chú-she), taught that "all exists." The Hinayana School of nihilism, the Satyasiddhi School held that neither the self nor the dharmas exist. The Hinayana Disciplinary School (Vinaya, Lu, Ritsu) emphasized discipline. All these were introduced into China and Japan from India. At the same time, many Mahayana schools developed in China, on the basis of certain Indian texts. Of these, the Three-Treatise School (Madhyamaka, San-lun, Sanron) regarded reality as Void. The Idealistic School (Yogacara, Wei-shih, Hosso) asserted that both the self and all elements of existence were mere ideation. The Avatansaka School (Hua-yen, Kegon) treated all elements in the universe as a "Grand Harmony," one element involving all the rest. The Mystical School (True Word, Shingon) considered both the static world and the dynamic world as the mystical manifestations of the Buddha himself. The T'ien-t'ai School (Tendai), indigenous to China, held that the Void, temporary existence, and the Mean were identical. The Meditation School (Ch'an, Zen) believed in salvation by contemplation and intuition. The Pure Land School (Ching-t'u, Jodo), also purely Chinese, advocated salvation by faith.

This highly organized and stratified religion developed from a humble beginning. Gautama taught only a simple and practical way of life, rejecting the two extreme doctrines of his time, asceticism and hedonism, and taught instead the Middle Way or the Noble Eightfold Path, namely, right views, right intention, right speech, right action, right livelihood, right effort, right mindfulness, and right concentration.

To support his doctrine, he enunciated in his First Sermon the Four Noble Truths: (1) existence is suffering, because it is bound in the chain of births and deaths; (2) the cause of suffering is craving, which is generated in the Twelvefold Chain of Causation, namely, ignorance, aggregates, consciousness, names and forms or body and mind, the six sense-organs, contact, sensation, desire, grasping, coming into existence, birth, and old age and death, one leading to the other; (3) the cessation of suffering is Nirvana, negatively the state of extinction of passions, and positively the state of bliss; and (4) the way to remove suffering is the Noble Eightfold Path.

Elaborating on the Four Noble Truths, the Buddha taught the doctrine of Impermanence and Non-Ego. He declared that both the self and things were only compounds of elements and, as such, had no permanent identity, but were always in the processes of Production, Stagnation, Deterioration, and Extinction. On the practical side, he taught the Threefold Learning, that is, Discipline, or a highly developed moral consciousness, Meditation, and Wisdom, or insight into the Supreme Truth. He promoted the traditional doctrine of Karma, the doctrine according to which every act has a definite moral influence which determines the nature of one's future existence. He urged the removal of the Ten Fetters, especially the delusion of the self, doubt, and the belief in the efficacy of ceremonials; the Four Intoxications—bodily passions, becoming, delusions, and ignorance; the Five Hindrances—desire for worldly advantages, the corruptions arising out of the wish to injure, torpor of mind, fretfulness and worry, and instability of mind. For the novice he taught the Ten Precepts (abstinence from taking life, from theft, from impurity or sensuality, from lying and harsh speech and foolish talk, from intoxication, from irregular eating, from dancing and similar entertainments, from garlands and ornaments, from high and broad couches, and from accepting gifts of gold and silver) as the minimum requirements for a mendicant's moral life. For a fuller life, whether for the monk or layman, he taught virtue, kindness, love, compassion, noninjury in the broadest sense, liberality, the Golden Rule, and the sense of duty.

After the death of the Buddha, a series of Councils were held (c. 483 B.C., c. 383 B.C., c. 240 B.C., and A.D. 70) to discuss and fix the Buddhist canon. Buddhism as a philosophy and a religion was fast growing, and, thanks to the efforts of the Indian King Asoka (c. 240 B.C.), it spread over India and Ceylon. In the fifth century A.D., it began to assimilate Hindu elements. Because of its emphasis on the monastic order and its neglect of the layman, it declined in the seventh century, and, by the time of the Mohammedan invasion in the twelfth century, it had lost its vitality. However, before it had very much declined in India, it spread southeastward to Burma and beyond, and northward to China.

Buddhism entered China about the time of the beginning of the Christian era. There it existed as a primitive religion of charms and spells, along with, and often mixed with, native Taoism. Soon, however, great masters arrived from India, with new ideas, and for eight hundred years the interchange of religious talents between India and China was not interrupted.

Although Hinayana was first transplanted to China, it was Mahayana that bloomed there. The Hinayana ideal of achieving individual salvation at Nirvana was supplanted by the Mahayana ideal of universal salvation of all sentient beings. The Hinayana goal of becoming an *arhat,* or "the Worthy One," was replaced by the ideal of the *bodhisattva,* the Buddha-to-be or Saint, who, although ready to attain Buddhahood in Nirvana, prefers to remain in the world to work for the salvation of all. The idea of sudden enlightenment supplemented that of gradual enlightenment, and faith and devotion were added to wisdom as means of salvation. Buddha-nature was considered to be inherent in all people and Buddhahood attainable at once and in "this very body," the layman thus becoming as important as the clergy. Interpretations of scriptures and rules became much more liberal, and the Hinayana doctrine of the One Buddha gave way to the doctrine of Many Buddhas, or, rather, the Buddha in many aspects and, therefore, appearing in different forms. Philosophy tended toward idealism, culminating in the theory of "mere consciousness" and the doctrine of Thusness or Void.

Buddhism in China reached its zenith in the ninth century, both in religion and in philosophy. Because it renounced the family, it was never accepted by the Confucianists, though it was generally tolerated. Since the eleventh century, it has been fading out, and at present it plays only a minor rôle as an outmoded religion, though its influence on Chinese thought and art in the past was considerable.

In the fifth century A.D., Buddhism went to Japan from

China, by way of Korea, and all the ten Chinese schools were introduced. Eventually, the Pure Land School gave rise to four sects—Jodo, Shin, Yuzunembutsu, and Ji—and out of the Tendai School grew the nationalistic and aggressive Nichiren Sect, which, unlike all other Buddhist sects, centers on its founder Nichiren (1222-1282). Fortunately, in the history of Japanese Buddhism there were really great men, notably Prince Shotoku (573-621), Kobo Daishi (774-835), and Dengyo Daishi (767-822), and it is due to them and their followers that Japan has yet today the most profound Buddhist scholars, the finest Buddhist universities, the most important Buddhist publications, and the most valuable Buddhist art treasures.   W.-T. C.

BUDDING, a method of plant propagation. In this form of grafting, the bud of one variety is inserted beneath the bark of another variety so that the cambium tissues of each

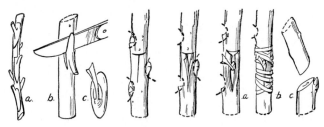

BUDDING

Budding is generally done in midsummer when the bark peels easily. (a and b) Leaf buds are taken from the present season's growth. (c) A sliver of wood is left on the bud when it is cut. Center: The stock (the rooted plant on which the new variety is to be budded) is disbudded and a T-shaped cut is made; the bud inserted in the cut (a) and bound in place (b). The top of the stock is cut away above the bud the following spring when growth starts (c) and disbudded below it to enable all growth to come from the inserted bud.

are held firmly together. If the union is successful, the bud grows and bears flowers, foliage, and fruit of its own variety, not that of the plant to which it was transferred. *See also* GRAFTING.   H. Wd.

BUDDINGTON, ARTHUR FRANCIS (1890-   ), American geologist, was born in Wilmington, Del., Nov. 29, 1890. He received his Ph.B. degree in 1912, his Sc.M. in 1913, from Brown University, and his Ph.D. from Princeton University in 1916. From 1917 to 1919 he was an instructor in geology at Brown University, in 1920 a petrologist with the geophysical laboratory of the Carnegie Institution, and in the same year was appointed assistant professor of geology at Princeton. Buddington became a professor in 1932, and chairman of the department in 1936. He was also associated with the United States Geological Survey and the New York State Museum. During World War I he served with the Signal Corps and the Chemical Warfare Service. Buddington was president of the Geological Society in 1943, and has contributed articles on the geology and mineral deposits of Alaska and the Adirondack Mountains, as well as on the findings of geological surveys in Newfoundland and the Cascade Mountains of Oregon. After World War II Buddington resumed his work at Princeton. He has been adjudged sixth among the hundred geologists in the United States.   C. W. D.

BUDÉ, GUILLAUME [bü'de'] (1467-1540), French scholar, often known under his academic name, Budaeus, was born in Paris in 1467. He began to study law at Orléans,

but soon gave it up. A few years later he developed an interest in Greek, which he proceded to master, and he returned to the study of law as well as to the study of mathematics, history, theology, medicine, and the natural sciences. Budé became one of the most learned men of his age. He translated a number of treatises by Plutarch (1502-1505), published his *Annotationes in XXIV libros pandectarum* (Paris 1508), an epoch-making work in the study of law, and in 1514 appeared his *Libri V de asse et partibus ejus* (Paris), his well-known work on ancient coins and measures. He prepared a French summary of this work in 1522 at the request of Francis I. In 1520 was published Budé's *De contemptu rerum fortuitarum libri tres,* a treatise on morals and philosophy. This was followed by his *Commentarii linguae graecae* (Paris 1529-1548) and his *De philologia* (Paris 1530), all of the preceding constituting his most important works. His complete works were published in four volumes at Basel in 1557. Budé was acquainted with Desiderius Erasmus, Sir Thomas More, François Rabelais, and others.

Budé's vast erudition served to gain him an appointment as secretary to King Louis XII. He was sent on a mission to Rome in 1515. When he returned, he became the constant companion of Francis I. He used his influence with the king to help establish the *Collegium Trilingue* in Paris. This college was finally established in 1530. It later became the Collège de France after changing its name on several occasions. Budé also founded the Royal Library at Fontainebleau, which was later moved to Paris and still later became the Bibliothèque Nationale. He died in Paris on Aug. 22, 1540.

BUDĚJOVICE, ČESKÉ. *See* ČESKÉ BUDĚJOVICE.

BUDENNY, SEMYON MIHAILOVICH [bʊdjɔ'nɜɪ; bʊdɛ'ni] (1883-   ), Soviet military leader, was born in Koziurin in the Salsk District of the Don Oblast, Apr. 25, 1883. He received no formal education until he entered military service, being mobilized in the Russo-Japanese War, 1904-1905, during which he served as a private in a cavalry regiment. After the war he returned to his farm, but was recalled to service at the beginning of World War I, and rose to the rank of sergeant-major by 1917. After the March 1917 revolution, he was a member of a divisional soldiers' soviet. Following the Bolshevik revolution in November 1917, he became active in organizing Red cavalry units in the Don region. He rose quickly in rank during the Civil War, commanding a cavalry division in January 1919, a cavalry corps in June 1919, and the First Cavalry Army in November 1919. It was only in that year that he became a member of the Communist Party. His exploits during the Civil War are almost legendary. In April 1920 during the Russo-Polish War he led his army all the way from the Caucasus to the gates of Warsaw.

In September 1920 he helped in the last assault against the White army under General Wrangel. In 1924 he was made a member of the central executive committee of the U.S.S.R. Between 1928 and 1932 he attended the Moscow Military Academy, and in 1935 was created Marshal of the Soviet Union. In 1937 he was appointed commander of the Moscow military district, and during the war against Finland, 1939, he commanded an army. In August 1940 he was appointed first vice-commissar of defense. After the German invasion, he was appointed, on July 11, 1941, commander in chief of Soviet armies on the southwestern front, but was not able to check the German advance. It was he who, in August 1941, ordered the destruction of the Dnepr River dam.

On Oct. 23, 1941, he was relieved of active command and charged with the recruiting and training of new armies. Since then, though appearing regularly on state occasions, he has been a mere figurehead. Budenny was awarded the Order of Lenin in 1953.   L. I. St.

BUDGE, SIR ERNEST ALFRED WALLIS (1857-1934), British orientalist and archaeologist, was born in Cornwall, England, July 27, 1857. He was educated at Christ's College, Cambridge, studying Semitics, and from 1885 to 1920 he was Keeper of the Department of Egyptian and Assyrian Antiquities of the British Museum. He was knighted in 1920. Budge supervised excavations at Nineveh and Der, in Mesopotamia, and at Assuan and Gebel Barkal, the ancient capital of Ethiopia, in Africa. He died in London, Nov. 23, 1934.

Budge's many writings reveal the great breadth of his interests in the ancient world; many will remain standard in the reference field. His Ethiopic contributions alone, listed in *Aethiopica Revue Philologique* (July 1935, pp. 134-136), consist of about two dozen books of texts and translation, besides numerous articles; among the most important of these works is *The Book of the Saints of the Ethiopian Church.* Budge's Syriac texts include *The Book of Paradise* (1904), republished under the title, *Stories of the Holy Fathers* (1934). Other texts of the early Church include his *Coptic Homilies* (1910), and *Coptic Martyrdoms* (1914). The Egyptian texts include: *The Book of the Dead* (1899, revised 1909), *The Papyrus of Ani* (1913), *The Egyptian Heaven and Hell* (the book of Am-tuat, 1925), and *The Teachings of Amen-em-àpt, Son of Kanekht* (1924). In the Assyrian groups are *Assyrian Texts* (1880) and *Tell el-Amarna Tablets* (autotype facsimiles, 1892). Among his many works on history, religion, and general culture are: *The Literature of the Ancient Egyptians* (1914), *By Nile and Tigris* (1920), and *The Dwellers on the Nile* (1926).   G. D. Y.

BUDGET, BUREAU OF THE, an agency through which the president of the United States discharges one of his most important functions, that of preparing annually the national budget for presentation to Congress. Created by the Budget and Accounting Act of 1921, the bureau was first located in the Treasury Department, but was responsible directly to the president. Under Reorganization Plan I of 1939, the bureau was transferred to the Executive Office of the president, where it is co-ordinate with the White House staff and the Council of Economic Advisers. The Budget Bureau is, however, much more extensively staffed than either of the two latter.

The primary task of the bureau is preparation of the Annual Budget for presentation by the president to the Congress in January of each year, and implications inherent in this responsibility give the bureau a role of major significance. The bureau is also charged with supervising and controlling the administration of the budget, conducting research to improve administrative management, encouraging governmental efficiency and economy, clearing and co-ordinating department advice on proposed legislation, assisting in the co-ordination, clearance, and preparation of proposed executive orders, co-ordinating the statistical services of the government, and reporting upon the progress of the work and activities of all agencies of the government. The bureau was handicapped in the discharge of its duties by lack of commensurate appropriations until 1938. Since then its staff and resources have been expanded.

The bureau is headed by a director appointed by the president without confirmation by the Senate. There are four offices of the bureau: Budget Review, Legislative Reference, Management and Organization, and Statistical Standards; and five divisions: Commerce and Finance, International, Labor and Welfare, Military, and Resources and Civil Works. The bureau also maintains a field service.
          R. F. S.

BUELL, DON CARLOS [byu'əl] (1818-1898), American soldier, was born near Marietta, Ohio, Mar. 23, 1818. He graduated from the United States Military Academy, West Point, in 1841 and was assigned to the infantry. Buell became a first lieutenant, June 18, 1846, and was brevetted captain for distinguished service during the Mexican War. He was assistant adjutant general in Washington during most of the period from 1848 to 1861, with the rank of lieutenant colonel. At the outbreak of the Civil War, Buell was appointed brigadier general of volunteers, May 17, 1861, helped organize the Army of the Potomac, and in November succeeded to the command of the Department of the Ohio. Buell occupied Bowling Green, Ky., Feb. 14, 1862, and entered Nashville on February 25. He became major general of volunteers Mar. 21, 1862. After being driven out of Lexington and Frankfort, Ky., by General Braxton Bragg in the summer of 1862, Buell engaged Bragg's army at Perryville, Ky., on Oct. 8, 1862, in an indecisive battle. Because of his tardy pursuit of Bragg's forces withdrawing through Cumberland Gap, Ky., Buell was relieved of his command on October 24 by General W. S. Rosecrans. After being investigated by a government commission, which rendered an adverse though unpublished report, Buell resigned his commission June 1, 1864. After the war he became president of an iron foundry. He died Nov. 19, 1898, in Rockport, Ky.
          W. E. A.

BUENA PARK, a residential city in Orange Co., southern California, situated 22 mi. southeast of Los Angeles. It was incorporated in 1953 and operates under the council-manager form of government. It is in the midst of a large industrial area served by the Santa Fe, Southern Pacific, and Pacific Electric railroads. The leading manufactured goods include paint, heating equipment, food supplements, and tomato products. Pop. 1957, 26,551.

BUENAVENTURA [bwe'naventu'ra], the most important Pacific port, and the third most important seaport, of Colombia. The city is built on Cascajal Island on Chocó Bay and is in the department of Valle del Cauca. It is approximately 210 mi. southwest of Bogotá and is linked by road, rail, and air with Bogotá, Cali, and other cities of Colombia. Buenaventura has a warm, rainy climate, with a mean temperature of 86° F. With its modern harbor, it is primarily important as an export point, especially for the coffee, gold, platinum, sugar, and hides of the rich interior. Industries include tanneries and alcohol distilleries.

A city of crooked streets and unpaved lanes lined with primitive huts, Buenaventura has some modern office buildings and a sizable hotel. Founded in 1545 by Juan Ladrilleros, Buenaventura was destroyed by Indians in the sixteenth century. Reconstructed, it suffered from an earthquake, a tidal wave, and in 1931 was razed by fire, so that none of the original settlement remains. Pop. 1951, 35,087.
          S. G. I.

BUENA VISTA, BATTLE OF [bwe'na vi'sta] (Feb. 22-23, 1847), an engagement in the Mexican War. The battle was won by General Zachery Taylor's American army of 4,759 men over Mexican forces three times as large. On February 20, Taylor occupied an exposed position at Agua Nueva.

When he learned that the Mexican general Santa Anna was approaching, General Taylor retreated along a road 12 mi. toward Saltillo. Halting near the northern end of a mountain pass at the hacienda of Buena Vista, Taylor enfiladed with artillery the deep gullies that creased most of the pass. When skirmishing began on February 22, it became apparent

BROWN BROTHERS

GENERAL ZACHARY TAYLOR AT THE BATTLE OF BUENA VISTA

that Taylor lacked sufficient strength on the American left, where the Mexicans were able to approach along the shallow end of lateral ravines and on the slopes of the adjoining mountains. The next morning the Mexican thrust pushed back the American left flank as if it were a swinging door. As Santa Anna's troops poured through to the hacienda, Taylor appeared, threw in his reserves, and with the invaluable aid of Jefferson Davis' Mississippi Rifles regiment, checked the retreat. Artillery batteries of Braxton Bragg, J. M. Washington, and Thomas W. Sherman cut down

further attacks of the Mexican reserves. Taylor then reorganized his line toward the east, and by nightfall had recovered the lost ground. During the night the Mexican army began its retreat to San Luis Potosí. Taylor's victory later helped him to win the presidency. The American losses in officers and men were 746; reported Mexican losses (including prisoners and deserters) were 3,494.   G. W. S.

BUENOS AIRES [bwe′nos ɑi′res; bo′nəs ɛ′əriz], the capital and chief port of Argentina, and also a province of Argentina.

THE CITY

The city of Buenos Aires, capital of Argentina, comprises a federal district, having been separated from the province in 1880. Situated on the west bank of the Plata Estuary, Buenos Aires is about 125 mi. west of Montevideo, Uruguay, 171 mi. from the Atlantic Ocean, and 5,870 mi. from New York City. The city's climate is moderate, the temperature ranging from a high of 96° F. in January or February (the seasons being reversed below the equator) to a low of 27° in July or August. Rains and windstorms are frequent; the average rainfall is 33 in. annually.

History. Buenos Aires was founded in February 1536 by Pedro de Mendoza, Spanish colonizer, who landed on the site with a large expeditionary force. Continual battles with the Indians led to the abandonment of the settlement in 1540, when it was burned. The settlers retreated to Asunción, in present-day Paraguay. In 1580 the city was reestablished by Juan de Garay, a Spaniard who had arrived in the area about 1532 in the train of Blasco Nuñez Vela, the viceroy who ruled the Spanish colonial empire in South America from Lima, Peru. Buenos Aires prospered despite attacks made in the second half of the seventeenth century by French, Portuguese, and Danish forces, and by 1770 the city ranked fourth in size in the Peruvian viceroyalty. Dissatisfaction developed among the Porteños (citizens of Bue-

Buenos Aires, capital of Argentina, as seen from the air

COURTESY OF MOORE McCORMACK LINES

The British Clock Tower dominates the Plaza Brittania

nos Aires) over being ruled from Lima by aristocratic ecclesiastical-minded landowners, and Charles III of Spain, fearing a revolt which might lead to independence from Spain, established the independent viceroyalty of Río de La Plata in 1776, including areas which were later to become Argentina, Uruguay, Paraguay, and Bolivia. Buenos Aires was named the capital of the new viceroyalty. Attracted by the growing prosperity of the region, the British in 1806, then at war with Napoleon and his ally, Spain, attacked and seized Buenos Aires, but they were soon expelled. An attempted invasion made the following year by the British also failed. Emboldened by this success, and stimulated by thoughts of revolt and freedom infiltrating from France and from the newly established republic of the United States in North America, a great gathering of armed people in Buenos Aires on May 25, 1810, demanded and achieved the resignation of the Spanish viceroy and the formation of a representative government. However, formal declaration of independence from Spain of the "United Provinces of Río de La Plata" was not made until July 9, 1816, and actual independence was achieved by force of arms in 1817. (May 25, known as "Revolución de Mayo," has become a national holiday in Argentina and July 9 is Argentina's "Independence Day.")

A period of anarchy and dissension followed in the former viceroyalty. The area that was to become Paraguay had broken away and formed an independent regime in 1811. Bolivia declared its independence in 1825, and in the same year war broke out with Brazil over possession of Uruguay, resulting in the formation of an independent Uruguayan republic in 1828. In 1852 Paraná, on the left bank of the Paraná River, was made the federal capital, and a constitution for the new republic was formulated the following year. In 1861 Gen. Bartolomé Mitre assumed power and transferred the capital to the city of Buenos Aires, pending his

election in 1862 as president of the republic of Argentina. Continued dissension between the city and the province of Buenos Aires was not alleviated until 1880, when the federal district of Buenos Aires was created and separated from the province. A new city, La Plata, was built as the province's capital. Since then the city of Buenos Aires has developed rapidly. The introduction of railways (the first being opened in 1857) in the latter half of the nineteenth century stimulated industrialization, which was augmented by increased shipping trade following substantial British and American investment in developing the economy of the country. By 1940 Buenos Aires ranked among the ten largest cities of the world and had become the second most important port in the Western world, surpassed only by New York City.

Administration. The municipal government of Buenos Aires is composed of two branches: the legislative (city council) and the executive. The former is composed of 22 councilmen elected by the taxpayers for four years, half retiring in rotation every two years. They serve without pay. The head of the executive is the *intendente municipal,* or mayor, appointed by the president of the republic with the consent of the Senate. He holds office for three years and is eligible for reappointment. He is the liaison officer between the municipal and the federal governments. The federal government has control of, and pays for, the police and fire departments. Certain branches of education and sanitary regulations for the city as a port are also responsibilities of the federal government. The municipal government is responsible for all other regulations, and it has the power to impose taxes and fees of several kinds to maintain itself. In local matters the municipal government regulates sanitation. Building regulations are rigidly enforced.

General Description. Buenos Aires is an exceedingly cosmopolitan city, not only because of its European culture and its large admixture of European population but also because of its general appearance. Although essentially a European city, it maintains its own distinctive air. The city was originally planned on a "chessboard" pattern in blocks 400 ft. square. In general this plan has been adhered to, and narrow old streets have been wiped out to create wide, tree-shaded boulevards. Many palm trees not indigenous to the area have been planted, giving the city a semitropical atmosphere. Avenida de Mayo, a mile in length and 120 ft. wide, is the principal business thoroughfare. It stretches from Plaza de Mayo, where the Casa Rosada (the government house) is located, to the Plaza del Congreso, overlooked by the national capitol, the Palacio del Congreso, or Congress Hall. Lining it are many of the city's chief buildings. Avenida Santa Fe, running north to Palermo and the suburbs, and Calle Florida, in the center of the city, contain many luxurious shops. The Avenida Nueve de Julio, commemorating the date of Argentina's declaration of independence, is 160 ft. wide, and underneath it is parking space for 1,000 cars. The Avenida General Paz is a wide and handsome highway, 15 mi. long. Calle Rivadavia is called by the Porteños the longest street in the world, for it extends well beyond the city limits, practically dividing the city into two equal parts. The streets crossing it at right angles have different names north and south.

At the Parque Palermo, on the Avenida del Libertador General San Martín, are situated the Hipodromo Argentino Palermo, one of the handsomest racetracks in the world; the Argentine Polo Association grounds; and a public golf course. The principal Argentine livestock exhibition, which takes place every July, is held in the grounds of the Argentine Rural Society facing the Plaza Italia. The Parque 3 de Febrero, Buenos Aires' most popular park, is about 3 mi. from the center of the city. Not far from it is the zoological garden, containing a large collection of animals and birds. In the municipal botanical gardens, facing the Plaza Italia, are specimens of plants from all sections of the world. The municipal swimming pool, located on the river front, is surrounded by beautiful gardens. In all, Buenos Aires has six public gardens, 16 parks, and 83 plazas, which provide the public with approximately 3,400 acres of trees, flowers, shrubs, and recreational areas.

Throughout the city there are statues of famous men in Argentine and South American history. A statue of George Washington was erected in 1913 in the Parque Palermo in celebration of the centenary of 1910. It was donated by citizens of the United States living in Buenos Aires.

The city's principal buildings include, in addition to the Casa Rosada and the Palacio del Congreso, the Cabildo, formerly a government administration building, erected in 1711 and now a national museum commemorating the revolution of 1810; the old Congress Hall, built in 1863, containing the official archives; the law courts, four large buildings in the neo-Greek style; the Banco Central; the Banco de la Nación; the mint; the War Ministry; and the Stock Exchange. The world-famous Jockey Club was destroyed by fire in 1953 by followers of Perón.

The archbishop's residence flanks the Roman Catholic cathedral on the Plaza de Mayo. The cathedral, constructed on the site of the first church in Buenos Aires, dates from the second half of the eighteenth century. It contains the tomb of José de San Martín, Argentine military hero. The Church of San Ignacio de Loyola has occupied the same site since 1722. Two paintings reputed to be by Michelangelo are found in the Church of San Francisco. St. John's Pro-

Cathedral, an Anglican church, was opened in 1831. The American Church, built in 1863, was the first Methodist Episcopal church established in South America.

Education and Culture. The University of Buenos Aires is the country's leading institution of higher learning. The city has an institute for secondary schoolteachers, an institute of modern languages, a school of social work, an institute of physical education, and a school specializing in the training of teachers in methods of visual study and nature study. The city's primary schools are splendid examples of architecture. Noted institutions of scientific research include the Atomic Energy Commission, the Institute of Experimental Medicine for the Study and Treatment of Cancer, the Institute of Physiology, and the Mission of Regional Pathology, the latter two being units of the University of Buenos Aires.

Buenos Aires is one of the chief centers of Latin-American culture. The opera house, opened in 1908, can seat 3,750 people and is municipally operated. The open-air theatre in the Parque Centenario, seating 8,000, offers opera, ballet, and symphonic concerts in the summer. Also of note are the National Conservatory of Music and Declamation, the School of Plastic Arts, the Mitre Museum and Library, the National Library, the Natural Science Museum, the Municipal Museum, the Museum of Fine Arts, the National Historical Museum, the Colonial and Historical Museum, and the Postal, Telegraphic, and Philatelic Museum. The city has a television station and 12 broadcasting stations.

Suburbs. Greater Buenos Aires (pop. 1947, 4,618,255) takes in the surrounding suburbs. The social and economic life of these communities is that of the capital's, but they are not part of the federal capital, being administered locally under the jurisdiction of the provincial government. They in-

EWING GALLOWAY, NEW YORK

In the center of Plaza de Mayo is the Piramide de Mayo, commemorating the independence of Argentina.

Bright lights on Avenida Corrientes, Buenos Aires

clude Ramos Mejía, Flores, Lomas de Zamora, Temperley, Quilmes, and Avellaneda to the west and south, and Belgrano, Tigre, San Isidro, and Hurlingham to the north. Avellaneda, a city in itself, is the most heavily industrialized. Tigre, part of which is on an island, is particularly noted for its beauty. Transportation to the capital is provided by buses, trains, and motor vehicles. Within Buenos Aires these facilities are supplemented by five subway systems.

Transportation. Much of the importance of Buenos Aires as Argentina's foremost transportation center stems from its favorable geographical location. It is the focal point for the country's rail, air, ship, and highway traffic. From it fan out the approximately 27,700 mi. of main rail lines to Paraguay, Bolivia, Chile, the Andean lake region, and all other sections of Argentina. A branch of the Pan American Highway connects Buenos Aires and Chile; another branch goes to Bolivia through Rosario and Córdoba. International air lines link Buenos Aires to the Americas, Great Britain, Continental Europe, Africa, and the Orient. The Argentine air lines exclusively serve the country. When Ezeiza Airport was opened in 1949 it was the largest in the world. Three of the 12 runways are 300 ft. wide and 10,000 ft. long. On the river front, near the center of the city, is the "Aeroparque," an airport used by planes connecting Buenos Aires with the interior and with Uruguay and Paraguay. A flying boat service operating from the New Port links Buenos Aires with many other river cities.

Buenos Aires' harbor, through which passes more than half of the nation's commerce, is man-made. Channels were dredged through the silt of the river that blocked entrance to large vessels. The main channel and its northern branch are 31 ft. deep. A southern branch of the main channel is approximately 27 ft. deep. The port of Buenos Aires comprises the older section, which includes four docks and the north and south basins, and the New Port, which contains six docks. Because of the congestion at Buenos Aires during the busy months, the city has lost some of its export trade, but it has retained its supremacy as a receiving port and the gateway to the regions, including Paraguay and Bolivia, served by the Plata, Paraná, and Uruguay rivers. River craft, as well as ships from all corners of the world, dock at Buenos Aires, one of the world's major ports.

Industry. Greater Buenos Aires is the core of Argentine industrial life. Industries other than those concerned with meat packing and refrigeration and flour milling were of little importance prior to 1914. Until then numerous articles for domestic consumption were produced on a small scale. Since World War I the growth of manufacturing has been tremendous, and Buenos Aires disputes first place in industrial development in South America with São Paulo, Brazil. As before World War I, the *frigoríficos,* the meat-packing houses, are the city's most important plants. In 1949 the largest refrigerating plant in the world was located in the Buenos Aires district. It can handle 5,000 cattle and 10,000 sheep daily. Flour milling continues as one of the leading industries. Others include shipbuilding, printing and publishing, tanning, and the manufacture of chemicals, pharmaceuticals, foodstuffs, textiles, furniture, perfumes, soap, paints, aircraft, machinery, vehicles, electrical equipment, and pneumatic tires. Pop. (city) 1947, 2,981,043; est. 1956, 3,609,000; (federal district, including Isla Martin García) 1947, 2,982,-580; est. 1956, 3,611,000.

THE PROVINCE

Buenos Aires Province, in east-central Argentina, is the nation's most important province and its largest in land area and population. It has a total area of 116,322 sq. mi. and surrounds the federal district, which has an area of 77 sq. mi. and comprises the city of Buenos Aires. The province, considered the heart of Argentina, is bounded on the north by the provinces of Córdoba, Santa Fe, and Entre Ríos, the Paraná River separating it from the latter. The Plata River separates it on the east from the Republic of Uruguay, and the Atlantic Ocean bounds it on the east and south. The extreme southern portion of the province is cut off from Río Negro Province by the Negro River, and La Pampa Province forms its western boundary. The province is made up largely of the famous pampa, the rich prairie which is generally flat and practically treeless. There are two ranges of low mountains in the southern section of the province, one in the vicinity of Mar del Plata and the other in the vicinity of Bahía Blanca. Buenos Aires Province is well supplied with lakes and rivers, and many of the navigable rivers flow into the Atlantic Ocean. The Salado River is the largest river that flows within the province and does not form one of its boundaries. It enters Buenos Aires near the northwestern boundary and flows southeast to the Atlantic Ocean. The Colorado River is another of the country's large estuaries that crosses the province, in the southern section; it empties into the Atlantic Ocean. The other principal rivers, the Paraná, the La Plata, and the Negro, form the province's boundaries.

The soil of the Humid Pampa, the section of the pampa in which the province lies, is extremely rich. The fertility of the soil plus the abundant rainfall and mild, temperate climate have made agriculture very productive. Cattle raising has been a very important industry since its introduction by the Spaniards, and though the great *estancias,* or cattle ranches, no longer dominate the country's economy they remain an important source of income. Sheep grazing is also important. Large-scale farming developed at the end of the nineteenth century, and the province is a leading producer of Argentina's major crops: corn, wheat, and linseed and sunflower seed, used to make oil. Fruit, barley, oats, rye, and vegetables are also grown.

Argentine industry is concentrated in the province, the federal district, and Greater Buenos Aires. The leading industrial cities in the province include Avellaneda, Bahía Blanca, and La Plata, and the chief industries are meat-packing plants, flour mills, tanneries, cheese factories, creameries, foundries, shipyards, textile mills, and plants producing household appliances and electrical equipment.

BUFFALO'S CIVIC CENTER, WITH McKINLEY MONUMENT IN THE CENTER AND CITY HALL IN LEFT CENTER

Although Buenos Aires has a large water frontage, there is a paucity of good harbors. The principal ports are La Plata in the north, the chief export point for the cereals and meat products of the vicinity, and Bahía Blanca in the south, the chief outlet for the agricultural products of south-central Argentina. The development of an important commercial harbor at Mar del Plata, the country's most famous seashore resort, was begun in the 1930's. About one-third, 8,247 mi., of the total railroad mileage in the country is located within Buenos Aires Province, and air service supplements rail transportation at many points.

After the federal district of Buenos Aires was created in 1880, La Plata was founded as the provincial capital. It is the province's second largest city and is noted for its university, its meat-packing plants, and the modern harbor. It is also the capital of the La Plata district. Avellaneda is the largest and chief industrial city in the province, and Bahía Blanca is the third largest city. Pop. 1947, 4,272,337; est. (1956), 5,059,000.　　　　　　　　　　　　S. G. I.

BUENOS AIRES, UNIVERSITY OF. *See* LATIN AMERICA (*Universities*).

BUFFALO, second largest city in New York State and in 1950 the fifteenth in the country, is one of the Great Lakes' vital commercial ports. It is the seat of Erie Co. and is situated at the eastern tip of Lake Erie and along the Niagara River. Spanning the river at Buffalo are two international bridges (U.S.-Canadian): the railroad bridge, opened to traffic in 1873, and the Peace Bridge, opened to motor traffic in 1927. Niagara Falls is 18 airline mi. northwest of the city.

Transportation. Buffalo is a transportation center served by 10 trunk (U.S. and Canadian) railroad systems and three passenger terminals. Buffalo Airport, 9 mi. from City Hall, provides facilities for four passenger-mail and two freight airlines. The Port of Buffalo serves the Great Lakes and is connected with the Atlantic Ocean by the Welland Canal and the St. Lawrence River and by the New York State Barge Canal (replacing the historic Erie), the Hudson River, and New York Harbor. The bulk of traffic handled consists of raw materials for Buffalo's steel mills and iron foundries and grain for its flour mills and grain elevators.

History. The settlement of Buffalo originated at the point where Buffalo Creek enters Lake Erie. The first white settler was Daniel Chabert Joncaire, a fur trapper, who set up a farmstead in 1758. The French established a fort on the Lewiston Heights above the mouth of the Niagara River as early as 1727. Falling to the British, and renamed Fort Niagara in 1759, it passed to the United States after the Revolutionary War, when it became a U.S. military post. During the War of 1812 Buffalo was the center of much frontier activity and was raided and burned by the British and Indians.

Work was begun on the western end of the Erie Canal near Buffalo in 1823 and was completed in 1825. This provided the city with a shipping outlet to the East and transformed Buffalo into a growing city. In 1843 the first grain elevator in the world was built in Buffalo by Joseph Dart. Since then the city has become one of the greatest distribution points of the eastern United States for the great supplies of western grain. In 1896 Buffalo received its first electric current generated by hydroelectric power at Niagara Falls. Prior to the Civil War the city was an important terminal station on the underground railroad for the escape of Negro slaves from the United States into Canada. Two Buffalo men went to the White House, Millard Fillmore in 1850 and Grover Cleveland in 1884 and 1892. President William McKinley was assassinated while attending the Pan American Exposition held in Buffalo in 1901. Theodore Roosevelt, McKinley's successor, took the oath of office in a Buffalo residence. Mark Twain lived here at the time he was editor of the Buffalo *Express.* The Prince of Wales, later King Edward VIII, participated, in 1927, in the dedication of the Peace Bridge. Buffalo, incorporated as a village in 1816 and as a city in 1832, has the mayor-council form of government.

Streets and Parks. Most of Buffalo is laid out on the rectangular street plan. There are, however, a few circles with radiating streets, the most notable being Niagara Square (Civic Center), around which are located the City Hall, the State Office Building, and the United States Court House. The principal streets are Main Street, running north and south a quarter mile east of the Civic Center; Delaware Avenue, running north; and Genesee Street, running northeast from the Civic Center. Industry is concentrated in the harbor area, along the Niagara River, and around the railway terminals on the East side. The northern and southern sections and parts of the eastern and western sections are residential. There are ten municipal and four county parks. Noteworthy monuments are the McKinley Memorial in Niagara Square; the Soldiers and Sailors Monument (Civil War) and the "Hiker" statue (Spanish-American War) in Lafayette Square; the Commodore Perry Monument in the Front Park; and the Abraham Lincoln statue in the Rose Garden in Delaware Park. The Memorial Auditorium, on South Main Street, is dedicated to the dead of World War I.

Education and Culture. Institutions of higher education include the University of Buffalo, the State University College for Teachers, Canisius, D'Youville and Rosary Hill colleges, Mt. St. Joseph Teachers College, and the Erie County Technical Institute. Among the city's cultural institutions are the Kleinhans Music Hall, housing the Buffalo Philharmonic Orchestra; the Albright Art Gallery; the Historical Society Museum; the Museum of Natural Sciences; and the Erie County Library, a system which includes the Buffalo Public and Grosvenor libraries.

Commerce and Industry. The area's principal industries are iron and steel, grain milling and storage, chemicals, meat packing, electric and electronic products, and machinery. Pop. 1950, 580,132.   N. Car.

BUFFALO, a popular name which is used indiscriminately for several widely differing members of the wild ox family. It was applied first to the black water buffalo, *Bubalis bubalis,* of India. This animal has been domesticated for centuries, and is used widely for draft and milking purposes throughout most of the warmer sections of Asia and Africa. In the Philippines, a small variety goes by the name carabao. The wild water buffalo, which still roams the Indian forests, is a magnificent animal and is rated by many sportsmen as one of the most dangerous of all big game

animals. A large bull stands 6½ ft. high at the shoulders and measures 14 ft. from the nose to the tip of the tail. The horns are triangular in cross section and curve out and back from the head in a great arc as much as 12 ft. 2 in. from tip to tip. A small black buffalo, the timarau, *Anoa mindorensis,* inhabits the Philippine island of Mindoro. It stands 3½ ft. tall. A slightly smaller animal, the anoa, *Anoa,* is found in the Celebes. Several varieties of Cape buffaloes, *Syncerus caffer,* and of Congo buffaloes, *S. nanus,* live in southern and western Africa, respectively. The horns of the

YLLA

WATER BUFFALO OF INDIA

big Cape species are flattened, and expand at the base until they meet in the center of the forehead. By common usage, buffalo has become the accepted popular name of the high-humped American bison, *Bison bison,* and to some extent of the European bison or wisent, *B. bonasus. See also* ANOA; BISON; WISENT.   V. H. C.

BUFFALO, UNIVERSITY OF, an accredited, coeducational, privately controlled institution at Buffalo, N.Y. Except for the School of Law, the Chronic Disease Research Institute, and the Albright Art School, all of the university's divisions are housed on the 175-acre main campus, on which are 21 buildings, including a Medical-Dental School and four residence halls. The University was founded in 1846, and first instruction was begun in the School of Medicine. Millard Fillmore, the thirteenth President of the United States, was the first Chancellor. Other divisions were founded or affiliated in the following order: School of Pharmacy, 1886; School of Law, 1891; School of Dentistry, 1892; College of Arts and Sciences, 1913; Summer Session, 1915; Millard Fillmore College (Extension and Adult Education), 1923; School of Business Administration, 1927; School of Nursing, 1930; School of Education, 1931; School of Social Work, 1936; Graduate School of Arts and Sciences, 1939; School of Engineering, 1946; Division of General and Technical Studies, 1950; Chronic Disease Research Institute, 1950; Albright Art School, 1954.

The degrees conferred are the B.A., A.A., A.A.S., B.S. (engineering, nursing, business, pharmacy), Ed.B., B.F.A., M.A., M.S. (nursing, engineering), M.S.S., LL.B., D.D.S., M.D., Ed.D., and Ph.D. The College of Arts and Sciences allows the student to have a wide choice in electives. However, in the beginning of the third year, the student is expected to select a field of concentration. A comprehensive examination, in addition to regular course examinations, must be passed. Special advance-credit examinations are given to students entering with superior proficiency in certain subjects.

The Chronic Disease Research Institute maintains a department of physical medicine and rehabilitation and a respirator center, partially financed by the National Foundation for Infantile Paralysis. Special programs are conducted in hearing and speech therapy, occupational therapy, and physical therapy.

The Lockwood Memorial Library contains the Wickser collection of books and manuscripts of James Joyce, and a collection of twentieth century poetry, manuscripts, and books. The Museum of Comparative Anatomy is in the Medical-Dental School.

The Schools of Medicine and Nursing are affiliated with the Buffalo General, Children's, Meyer Memorial, Millard Fillmore, Deaconess, Gowanda State, Buffalo Veterans, J. N. Adair Memorial, and Wyoming County hospitals and the Roswell Park Memorial Institute.

Student scholarships and loan funds are available, and there are assistantships and teaching fellowships for graduate students. *For statistics see* COLLEGES AND UNIVERSITIES.
N. Ca.

BUFFALO BERRY, *Shepherdia argentea,* a shrub of the oleaster family native to the Rocky Mountain region and the plains eastward to Kansas. Thorny stems growing to 18 ft. bear silvery leaves, small yellowish flowers, and red or yellow edible berries which make excellent jelly. It is often grown as a hedge plant in the Northwest. A smaller species, *S. canadensis,* is thornless with tasteless fruit.
J. C. Wis.

BUFFALO BUR, *Solanum rostratum,* a very spiny annual of the nightshade family, sometimes called sandbur or prickly potato. Native to the prairies from South Dakota to Mexico, it has spread as a weed to the east coast. Erect to 2½ ft., it is much branched with leaves like those of the potato and showy yellow flowers. Its many seeds are enclosed in a very prickly, burlike calyx. It is the original host plant of the destructive potato beetle. *See also* SOLANUM.
J. C. Wis.

BUFFALO CARPET BEETLE is the common name of *Anthrenus scrophulariae,* of the family Dermestidae. The larvae feed on feathers, woolens, and hair, and are frequently serious pests: carpets are often badly damaged, but probably the greatest damage is to stored woolen goods and furniture.

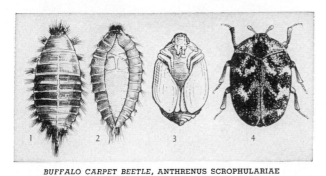

BUFFALO CARPET BEETLE, ANTHRENUS SCROPHULARIAE
(1) Larva; (2) Pupa, within the larval skin; (3) Pupa, ventral view; (4) Adult

The eggs are laid on or near the larval food, often in lint-filled cracks in a floor. The full-grown larvae are short, stout, and thickly covered with long hair; at the tail end is a heavy brownish brush. The adults are black with a varied white and orange pattern, and feed on the pollen of plants. The varied carpet beetle, *Anthrenus verbasci,* has very similar habits, but is more prone to attack cereals and other seeds. The black carpet beetle, *Attagenus piceus,* is fully as injurious as the others named, and like them, has been widely distributed by commerce. In all, the life cycle re-

quires about one year, but may be considerably less in warm climates.
C. H. Cu.

BUFFALO FISH are large suckers, of the family Catostomidae. The name refers to the hump on the back of old fish. The largemouth buffalo fish, *Megastomatobus cyprinella,* and the black and smallmouth buffalo fishes, *Ictiobus,* are found in the Mississippi Valley and Great Lakes region. They are partial to large rivers and lakes and are the largest suckers, some reaching a length of 3 ft. and a weight of 50

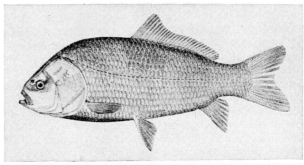

COURTESY OF U.S. FISH AND WILDLIFE SERVICE
SMALLMOUTH BUFFALO FISH

lbs. Carplike in appearance, they possess a deep body with a long dorsal fin and an inferior mouth. Food is obtained in the mud and consists of insect larvae and small mollusks. Breeding occurs in April near the edge of backwaters. While buffalo fish is taken commercially, especially in the Mississippi Valley, its flesh is not highly regarded. E. C. R.

BUFFALO GRASS, *Buchloe dactyloides,* a low perennial grass with strong fibrous roots, native to plains and prairies from Minnesota and Saskatchewan to Texas and Mexico. When unmixed with other grasses, it forms a close, soft, grey-green turf and a tough sod. In large areas on the uplands, known as the short grass country, it is the most important grazing grass, and is also valuable for fodder. The sod houses of the early settlers were built chiefly from its sod.
J. C. Wis.

BUFFER STATE, an independent state or autonomous region whose independence serves as a geographic barrier between major states or major areas. It is one of the traditional instruments of power politics, and its role was most prominent in the period between the Congress of Vienna in 1815 and the Paris Peace Conference of 1919. The purpose of a buffer state is to act as a barrier for the contiguous major states, protecting them against sudden unexpected attack from a potential neighbor enemy. It has the further purpose of preventing friction and incidents which are likely to arise on a common frontier between states during periods of stress in foreign relations. Some classic illustrations of buffer states are Afghanistan, between Russia and India; Czechoslovakia, between Germany and Austria; Austria, between Germany and Hungary; Manchuria, between Russia, China, and Japan; and Holland and Belgium, between France and Germany and the United Kingdom. The value of a buffer states was far more evident in the days of nonmechanized warfare. In the modern era of airplanes, motorized units, guided missiles, and atomic weapons, a buffer state's value is considerably less. The tendency of modern diplomacy appears to be that of translating the nineteenth-century buffer state into a twentieth-century satellite state.
S. L. W.

BUFFLEHEAD or **BUTTERBALL,** a small duck, *Bucephala albeola,* breeding in subarctic America and wintering at suitable localities throughout much of the United States and northernmost Mexico. The male, only slightly larger than a teal, is mostly white, but boldly marked with black; the back of the head and upper neck is beautifully glossed with purple and green. The female is brown and white, with a white cheek patch. In each sex the head is covered with unusually dense, fluffy plumage that increases its apparent size out of proportion to the tiny body; for this reason it was originally called the buffalo-headed duck.

H. G. De.

BUFFON. GEORGES LOUIS LECLERC, COMTE DE BUFFON [bü'fɔ̃'] (1707-1788), French naturalist, was born in Montbard (Côte d'Or), Sept. 7, 1707. He studied mathematics at the Collège de Dijon, but a trip to Italy turned his interests to natural history. He also spent a year in England learning the language and translating Sir Isaac Newton's *Fluxions* and Stephen Hales' *Vegetable Statistics.* In 1739 Buffon was appointed superintendent of the Jardin du Roi and the Royal Museum, and the remainder of his life was devoted to scientific study and the compilation of his *L'Histoire naturelle* (44 vol., 1749-1804). The first three volumes of this work, written in collaboration with L. J. M. Daubenton, were brought out in 1749 and met with instant acclaim. Another twelve volumes appeared in 1767, ten more in 1786, a supplement of seven volumes in 1789 (the fifth of which was the celebrated *Époques de la nature* [1779] on the formation of the earth), and the final twelve volumes, completed by B. G. E. de Lacépède, were published posthumously in 1804. This monumental work was written in a pleasing style and did much to popularize the study of natural history. Buffon was admitted to the Académie Française in 1753, his inaugural address being the famed *Discours sur le style,* in which he set a new standard for literary style. He died in Paris, Apr. 16, 1788.   C. W. D.

BUG [bʊg'], two rivers in eastern Europe. The northern Bug rises in Soviet Galicia east of the city of Lvov, marking the eastern border of Poland for over 100 mi. to Brest-Litovsk, below which it turns westward through Polish territory to join the Vistula 25 mi. below Warsaw. It is 450 mi. long and is navigable as far as Brest-Litovsk.

The other Bug is a stream in the southwestern Ukrainian S.S.R. and southwestern Soviet Union, usually called the Southern Bug to distinguish it from the Bug River in Poland, a Vistula tributary. The Southern Bug rises in swamps near the village of Sholodez, in the western Ukraine, and flows southeasterly in a winding course. Its mouth at Nikolaev on the Black Sea is a drowned valley or Liman, part of the great Dnepr Liman. While the upper course of the stream is on the crystalline rocks and southward-dipping sedimentaries of the Podolian-Azov upland, the lower course is southwest of the upland, between the Dnepr Hills and Bug Hills. As a result, there are several rapids, especially at Pervomaisk, in the uplands and many sandbanks in the lower reaches. With a length of 465 mi., the system drains approximately 26,225 sq. mi., and has a width up to 528 ft. in its lower course. Its mouth in the Bug Liman is several miles wide. Tributaries are small and unimportant, but include the left-bank affluents of Sinyukha and Ingulets, the latter entering at Nikolaev. Because of its rapids, the stream is practically useless for navigation. Cities along the banks of the Bug include Vinnitsa, Pervomaisk (formerly Ol'viopol), Voznesensk (formerly Konstantinovka), and Nikolaev.   C. C. H.

BUG [bʌg'], a term often applied to many kinds of insects, although in its true application it refers only to members of the orders Hemiptera and Homoptera. The bugs are characterized by an incomplete metamorphosis, only egg, nymph, and adult stages occurring. The nymphs and adults are rather similar in appearance, the adult characters being attained after three or more molts. They have sucking mouth parts, and feed upon the juices of plants, on the blood of animals, and upon other insects.

The Hemiptera may be recognized by the way they hold their wings—flat over the back; and by their antennae, which, except in some aquatic families, are moderately long. Wings are usually present in the adults, but in some they may be reduced in size or entirely absent, as in the bedbugs. The classification is based on all parts of the body and appendages, but wing venation is most important in distinguishing the families.

The largest bugs belong to the family Belostomatidae, the giant water bugs, of which the giant fish killer, *Lethocerus indicus,* of Asia and the East Indies is one of the largest. It has a length of four in., and is eaten by the natives. The South American *L. grande* attains a length of 4½ in. The Notonectidae or back swimmers, and the Corixidae or water boatmen, are other large families of aquatic bugs. The hind legs of the insects belonging to these three aquatic families are especially adapted for swimming. The back swimmers as their name implies swim on their backs. The lace bugs of the family Tingidae are easily identified by their wings which are lacelike in appearance.

Many of the Hemiptera are of economic importance. The chinch bug of the family Lygaeidae attacks corn and other cereals. *Blissus leucopterus* has been especially destructive to grain in the United States. The stinkbug (Pentatomidae) contains both beneficial and injurious forms; it gives off a

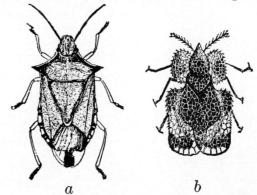

Stinkbug (a) and lace bug (b)

most unpleasant odor when disturbed. The leaf bugs (Neridae) are injurious to plants. The squash bugs (Coreidae) and the grass bugs (Corigidae) are generally injurious, while the assassin bugs and kissing bugs (Reduviidae) may be beneficial or injurious. The bedbugs (Cimicidae) are not known to transmit disease, but are pests that live on warm-blooded animals, including man.

The Homoptera, which are distinguished by possessing wings of almost uniform texture, held rooflike over the back when at rest, are almost all injurious to vegetation, and many of them transmit plant diseases. The leaf hoppers, aphids, scales, and cicadas are some of the familiar members of the order.   C. H. Cu.

BUGENHAGEN, JOHAN [bu'gənha'gən] (1485-1558), German Protestant reformer (sometimes called Pomeranus), was born near Stettin, in Pomerania, June 24, 1485. Ordained in 1509, Bugenhagen became vicar of the Marienkirche at Treptow. In 1521 he went to Wittenberg, where he became professor of theology. Becoming involved in the controversy over the Sacrament, he gained prominence by his *Interpretatio in Librum Psalmorum* (1523). Bugenhagen helped unite the Protestant Free Cities with Saxony, and introduced the Lutheran faith into northern Germany, about 1530. He was a friend of Martin Luther and assisted him in his translation of the Bible. Bugenhagen translated the Bible into Low German in 1553. He wrote a *History of Pomerania* and collaborated with Phillip Melanchthon in writing *The Interim of Leipzig.* Bugenhagen died in Wittenberg, Apr. 20, 1558. M. Sr.

BUGGE, ELSEUS SOPHUS [bu'ggə] (1833-1907), Norwegian linguist and philologist, was born at Harwik, Jan. 5, 1833. He taught linguistics and Old Norse in the University of Christiania (now Oslo) from 1866 until his death, July 8, 1907, at Tonset. Bugge's main interest centered on Norse language and legends, and from 1891 onward he worked on the monumental edition of the oldest runes, *Norges Indskrifter med de aeldre Runer,* which was completed after his death. Bugge also contributed to other fields of linguistics, such as Etruscan, Osco-Umbrian, Lycian, Armenian, and pre-Greek Anatolian. G. B.

BUGI. *See* INDONESIAN PEOPLES.

BUGLE, a genus, *Ajuga,* of the mint family, comprised of ten or more species native to Europe. These plants are small, hardy, perennial herbs growing as high as 12 in., having coarsely-toothed leaves and dense spikes of bluish-purple, or occasionally rosy and white, flowers. Bugles will stand considerable shade. The species *A. genevensis,* which grows as tall as 8 in., and bears blue flowers in May or June, has several garden forms. The carpet bugle, *A. reptans,* is a fast-growing species reaching a height of 4 in.; it bears shiny leaves and deep purple flowers. J. C. Wis.

BUGLE, a lip-blown, brass-constructed musical instrument distinguished from the trumpet by its shorter, wider, more conical bore, and its more cuplike mouthpiece. Originally a hunting horn, in the seventeenth century the bugle came to be made of metal and to serve as the chief signal instrument of European military regiments. In the nineteenth century, its musical capacities were increased by the application of keys and valves which furnished a full chromatic scale, but the military instrument, virtually obsolete in radio-directed warfare, is restricted to its natural harmonic series of notes. *See also* TRUMPET; OVERTONES. W. Li.

BUICK, DAVID DUNBAR [byu'ik] (1854-1929), American pioneer automobile builder, was born in Scotland, Sept. 17, 1854. Buick's first business venture was the formation in Detroit, Mich., in 1884, of the company of Buick and Sherwood, manufacturers of plumbing supplies. At that time Buick had already shown his inventive turn of mind by developing a new method for bonding porcelain and metal. Early in 1900 he began experimenting with gasoline engines for marine and farm use, and in 1901 formed the Buick Auto Vim and Power Company in Detroit. The following year he adapted his engine to the "horseless carriage," changed the name of his company to the Buick

Manufacturing Company, and in 1903, with the financial help of Frank and Benjamin Briscoe, produced his first automobile. Buick was the originator of the valve-in-head engine and the windshield. He ran heavily into debt, however, and the Briscoes sold their interest to James Whiting of the Flint (Mich.) Wagon Works, for $3,500, the amount of Buick's indebtedness to them. Under Whiting the Buick Motor Car Company produced fifty-three cars in two years, but made no profits, and in 1905 the company was taken over by William C. Durant. Durant introduced better business methods and gradually made the company profitable. After the reorganization Buick left the company, having lost his entire savings, and went to California, where he engaged in the oil business. At first he prospered, but because of costly litigation he withdrew from the field and went to Florida, where he tried real estate, but again failed. He finally returned to Detroit, and for a period was director and chief engineer of the Detroit School of Trades. Buick died in Detroit, Mar. 5, 1929. C. W. D.

BUILDING AND EQUIPMENT SELECTION. *See* INDUSTRIAL PRODUCTION (*Production Facilities*).

BUILDING CONSTRUCTION, the art of erecting structures consisting of walls, floors, and roofs to provide quarters for such uses as residence, business, manufacturing, education, worship, entertainment, hospitalization, and storage. Many types of construction and a great variety of materials are used, specific selections depending on numerous factors which include character of occupancy, climate, location, land cost, local materials, and funds available.

Outstanding Buildings. Buildings may be outstanding because of religious significance, historic association, architectural merit, structural features, floor area, height, or other notable characteristics. Buildings notable for their floor areas are the Merchandise Mart in Chicago and the Pentagon Building, Arlington, Virginia, which provides quarters for the Department of Defense. Each has a floor area of nearly 100 acres. The tallest building in the world is the Empire State Building in New York City, which has 102 stories, and a height of 1,472 ft. The tallest buildings in each of a number of American cities are shown below:

City	Building	Stories	Height, Ft.
New York	Empire State	102	1,472
Cleveland	Terminal Tower	52	708
Chicago	Board of Trade	44	612
Pittsburgh	Gulf	44	582
Cincinnati	Carew Tower	48	574
Detroit	Penobscot	47	564
Columbus	Am. Ins. Union	46	555
Philadelphia	City Hall		548
Baltimore	O'Sullivan	35	500
Seattle	L. C. Smith	42	500

Other well-known structures notable for height are:

Name	Location	Height, Ft.
Eiffel Tower	Paris	984
Washington Monument	Washington, D.C.	555
Ulm Cathedral	Germany	528
Cologne Cathedral	Germany	515
Pyramid of Cheops	Egypt	481

Building Costs. Because of the magnitude of the expenditures on new buildings, the building industry is an important factor in the economic life of the country; but because of the wide fluctuation in these expenditures, there is often either widespread unemployment or an acute shortage of building labor.

Marked increases in the dollar cost of building have occurred since the outbreak of World War I. According to the index published by *Engineering News-Record,* which is based on a value of 100 for the year 1913, costs rose rapidly after 1917, reaching a peak of 207 in 1920. By 1922 the index had dropped to 155. After increasing to 186 in 1923, it remained at about that value until 1930. By 1932 the index had dropped to 141. From this low value it climbed steadily until the end of World War II, in 1945, when it reached 239. Because of the substantial increases in wages and material costs accentuated by labor and material shortages, which occurred when there was great need for additional building space, the cost index showed a marked upward trend, reaching 289 by the end of 1946 and 327 at the end of 1947. During the next decade, it increased steadily to 500 and gave no indication of pausing in its upward trend. In 1913 a finished fireproof multistory office, apartment, or educational building of average quality cost about $5 per sq. ft. of floor area; in 1946 such a building cost about $15 per sq. ft. of floor area, and this cost was doubled by 1957 when prices continued to show a definite upward trend.

Design Loads. Loads considered in the design of buildings may be divided into three groups: dead loads, live loads, and lateral loads. Dead load includes the weight of all parts of a building, such as the walls, permanent partitions, floors, roof, and fixed equipment. Live load includes the weight of

Apartment house construction of poured concrete

BLACK STAR

all furniture, movable equipment, occupants, stored material, temporary or movable partitions, and snow and ice that may accumulate on the roof. Lateral load includes wind pressure, earth pressure against foundation walls, and earthquake shock. If the basements extend below ground-water level, hydrostatic pressures which act laterally against the foundation walls and upward against the lower basement floor must be considered.

Floor Load. Allowances for live loads may be as little as 40 lb. per square foot for dwellings and the rooms of hospitals and hotels. For offices and rooms with fixed seats such as auditoriums, schoolrooms, and theaters, a live floor load of

FAMOUS TALL STRUCTURES
(a) Empire State Building, New York City, 1,472 ft.; (b) Chrysler Building, New York City, 1,046 ft.; (c) Eiffel Tower, Paris, France, 984 ft.; (d) Woolworth Building, New York City, 792 ft.

about 50 lb. per square foot is used. For areas where people may be crowded close together, such as aisles, corridors, lobbies, assembly halls without fixed seats, and gymnasiums, a live floor load of 100 lb. or more per square foot is provided for. Live floor loads used for commercial, industrial, and storage buildings depend on the use which is to be made of a building and vary from 75 lb. per square foot for salesrooms handling light merchandise to 250 lb. per square foot for general storage and up to 500 or 600 lb. per square foot for heavy storage such as machinery, canned goods, and barreled oil. It is commonly required by building codes that allowable floor loads for commercial, industrial, and storage buildings be posted conspicuously in the parts of a building to which they apply.

Snow and Ice Load. Provision for accumulations of snow and ice depends on climatic conditions and varies from zero to about 30 lb. per square foot.

Wind Load. The actual wind load to which a building may be subjected at any instant during a severe windstorm varies greatly from point to point on the windward side, and there is a tendency for partial vacuums to form on the leeward side. In order to make provision for wind, a uniformly distributed horizontal force of 20 lb. per square foot area of the surface exposed to the wind is commonly used in design. The wind is assumed to have any direction that may be critical. Since wind velocities increase with the height above the ground surface, the upper portions of high buildings may be designed for greater wind loads than the lower 300 ft. or so. In regions subject to hurricanes and tornadoes, higher wind loads should be used.

Earthquakes. In many parts of the world earthquakes have had disastrous effects on buildings. Practically no part of the United States has been free from earthquakes during the rather brief period covered by records. Experience has shown that the probability of severe earthquakes in certain sections is so great that provisions should be made to cope with earthquake shocks. A regulation applying to all public buildings is in effect in California. The common provision for earthquake shocks is to design buildings for forces acting in any horizontal direction on every portion of a building and the live load it carries, equal to from 2 to 10 per cent of the weight of that portion. Such a provision usually depends on the character of the foundation material, minimum value applying to buildings on rock foundations and maximum to buildings on soil foundations with low bearing capacity. Actually, earthquake phenomena are much more complex than would be indicated by the above provisions. Also, the proportioning of the mass of a building and the type and details of construction, such as the ties between the individual elements, are of great importance in its resistance to earthquake shocks. Buildings with steel and reinforced skeleton construction resist earthquakes far better than those with masonry construction.

Parts of a Building. The part of a building above ground is called the superstructure and the part below ground the substructure. The load-carrying portions of a building consist of bearing walls, beams, columns, trusses, and arches.

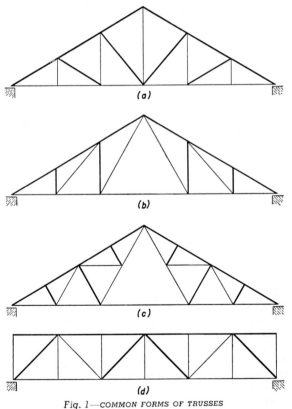

Fig. 1—COMMON FORMS OF TRUSSES

(a) Howe; (b) Pratt; (c) Fink or French; (d) Warren

The walls of a building are the vertical portions that enclose the building or subdivide it into rooms; the subdividing walls are commonly called partitions. A beam is a relatively long slender member supported at one or more points along its length and designed to carry loads acting perpendicular to its length. Beams are usually in a horizontal position and the loads are usually vertical. They transfer floor and roof loads to bearing walls or partitions, to columns, or to trusses, arches, or other beams called girders, which in turn transfer the loads to bearing walls or columns. A slab is a flat mem-

ber, usually of reinforced concrete, which spans the space between beams and girders to form a floor or roof. A column is a relatively slender vertical member which transfers floor, roof, and other loads to the foundations. A truss (*see* Fig. 1) is a framed structural element consisting of members so arranged as to form groups of triangles lying in a single plane. The common type of arch is a curved member which is con-

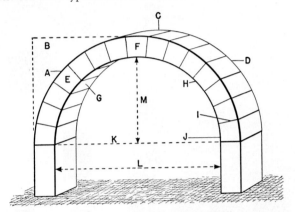

Fig. 2—TYPICAL ARCH CONSTRUCTION

(A) Extrados; (B) Spandrel; (C) Keystone; (D) Voussoir; (E) Haunch; (F) Crown; (G) Soffit; (H) Intrados; (I) Skewback; (J) Springer; (K) Springing line; (L) Span; (M) Rise

vex upward and spans an opening (*see* Fig. 2). An arch exerts lateral thrusts as well as vertical reactions at the end supports when carrying vertical loads. It need not necessarily be curved but may be a small member of brick or stone spanning a window or door opening in a masonry wall, or a large member of steel, wood, or reinforced concrete with a long span which, with other arches, supports a roof covering a large area (*see* Fig. 3).

In bearing-wall construction, loads are transmitted to the foundations primarily by walls, whereas in skeleton construction all loads are transmitted to the foundations by a rigidly constructed framework or skeleton made up of beams, girders, and columns. The roof, floors, walls, and partitions, together with their loads, are carried by this skeleton. The exterior walls are called curtain walls. Bearing-wall construction is usually more economical for buildings less than four stories high. Skeleton construction is advantageous for tall buildings; skyscrapers are always of skeleton construction. Until 1884 the height of buildings was limited to about 16 stories, because, with increased height, the bearing walls in the lower stories had to be made excessively thick. Skeleton construction, first used in the Home Insurance Building, Chicago, in 1884, removed structural restrictions on height. This form of construction was devised by William L. Jenney, a Chicago engineer, who is commonly credited with being the father of the skyscraper. An earlier restriction on the height of occupied buildings was the stair-climbing ability of the tenants. Development of the elevator, beginning about 1860, removed this limitation. During recent years, the automatic elevator, operated by the passengers, has come into extensive use in office buildings and apartment houses.

Building Planning. The use to be made of a building largely determines its interior, which, in turn, determines its form and mass. Since there is usually no single plan that will satisfy the conditions imposed by use, the plan and the exterior form can be considered together to produce an efficient and attractive structure. A manufacturing plant should be so planned that the raw material to be processed can be delivered at a point near where the manufacturing starts and then proceed through the building with a minimum of lost motion to the area where the finished product is stored or delivered. Office buildings, hotels, and apartment buildings

PHILIP GENDREAU. N.Y.

Frame construction of a dwelling house

are designed to produce the largest possible proportion of rentable floor area and still give suitable corridors, elevators, stairways, and exits. The window area and direction of exposure are important factors determined by special uses. Protection against noises, both interior and exterior, is especially important in planning modern buildings. Air conditioning is provided in many new office buildings, hotels, hospitals, assembly rooms, restaurants, and, to a considerable extent, in industrial buildings, and dwellings. The requirements of building codes have marked effects on plan and structural features of new construction.

Building Codes. Each city has a code to which buildings must conform. Code requirements depend on the police power of government for enforcement. Unless a code requirement can be shown to be necessary for safety or health, it may not be supported by the courts. The fact remains, however, that the thousands of separate building codes tend to perpetuate the use of traditional building materials and construction practices.

Building codes are concerned with such factors as types and quality of construction, quality of materials, loads to be provided for, allowable stresses in structural materials, window areas, ventilation, fire-resisting features of construction,

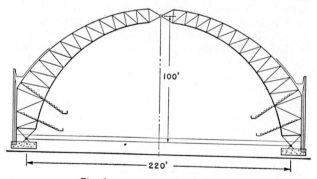

Fig. 3—THREE-HINGED STEEL ARCH

fire-extinguishing equipment, heating appliances, elevators and stairways, electrical installations, plumbing requirements, maximum building heights, and portion of lot occupied by a building.

Classification According to Use. Buildings are classified according to use as public buildings, such as courthouses, schools, colleges, libraries, churches, and theaters; institutional buildings, such as hospitals, firehouses, police stations, and jails; residence buildings, such as dwellings, apartments, hotels, and dormitories; business buildings, such as office buildings, stores, restaurants, and factories; and storage buildings, such as warehouses, grain elevators, freight depots, garages, hangars, and barns.

Classification by Relative Fire Resistance. Building codes also classify buildings according to type of construction into fireproof, semifireproof, slow-burning, ordinary, and frame construction. The most important factor in this classification is resistance to fire exposure. In classifying buildings, it is necessary to have some measure of the performance of walls, columns, floors, and other members when they are exposed to fire. This need has resulted in the standard fire test, which consists of exposing, in the laboratory, a sample of a material or a building member to a fire of specified intensity and ordinarily to a water stream from a fire hose when the samples or members are hot. Performance is defined as the number of hours of resistance to standard exposure elapsing before the first critical point in behavior is observed. For example, a material is given a two-hour rating if it successfully withstands the test for that period. Various codes differ in their requirements, but the following will serve as illustrations:

Fireproof. In fireproof construction, walls are of masonry or reinforced concrete. The bearing walls, columns, and wall-supporting girders have a four-hour rating; and other walls, beams, girders, floors, and roofs have a three-hour rating.

Semifireproof. Semifireproof construction is similar to fireproof except that the ratings are reduced by one hour.

Slow-burning. In slow-burning construction, the walls are of masonry or reinforced concrete. The columns, floors, and roof construction consist of heavy timbers with smooth flat surfaces assembled to avoid thin sections, sharp projections, and concealed or inaccessible spaces. Wall-supporting girders and structural members, if of steel or reinforced concrete instead of timber construction, have fire-resistance ratings of not less than three hours. This type is also called heavy timber construction and mill construction.

Ordinary. In ordinary construction, exterior walls are of masonry or reinforced concrete. Interior structural members are wholly or partly of wood of smaller dimensions than are required for slow-burning construction or of steel that is not protected against overheating, as required in fireproof or semifireproof construction.

Frame. In frame construction, exterior walls and interior construction are wholly or partly of wood of small dimension. It includes buildings with brick or stone veneer, stucco, or sheet metal over wood exterior walls. Most dwellings are of the frame type.

Factors Against "Fireproofness." No building is wholly fireproof. Fire-exposure may cause considerable damage to the highest type of construction. The term "fire-resistive" or "fire-resistant" is more correct. Structural damage caused by a fire in a fireproof building may not be severe, but loss of life due to heat exposure, suffocation, or other causes may be great. The chief cause of such damage is the burning of combustible contents such as furniture.

The capacity of structural-steel members to carry stresses is considerably reduced at the high temperatures which may prevail during a severe fire. Therefore it is necessary to surround steel beams, columns, and reinforcing bars in reinforced construction with fire-resistant materials, such as brick, concrete, hollow tile, or gypsum blocks. The thicknesses required vary from 2 to 4 in. For reinforced-concrete construction, it is required that the reinforcement be placed from $1\frac{1}{2}$ to 2 in. from the surface of columns and beams and $\frac{3}{4}$ in. from slabs.

Walls and Partitions. Exterior walls, except those of frame buildings, are usually constructed of brick, stone, hollow-clay tile, concrete blocks, or combinations of these materials laid up with mortar joints (*see* Fig. 4). The minimum thickness permitted is 8 in. for one-story residences and 12 in. for other buildings. For bearing walls, thickness is determined largely by the number of stories, the thickness increasing, by stories, from the top of a wall downward. Exterior walls are also made of reinforced concrete, with a minimum thickness of 6 in. for bearing walls.

After World War II, the construction of exterior curtain walls with self-supporting structural frames, especially for office buildings, increased. These walls are constructed of

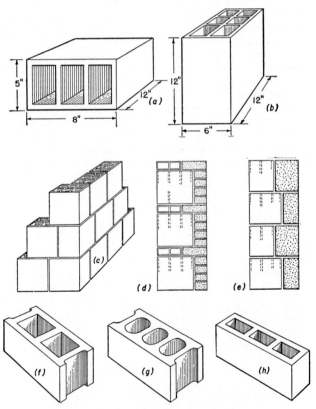

Fig. 4—TYPES OF BUILDING BLOCKS

(a) Standard tile for side construction; (b) Standard tile for end construction; (c) Hollow tile wall; (d) Brick facing; (e) Stone facing; (f) Wall block; (g) Wall block; (h) Partition block

various materials which permit a decrease in the weight and thickness of the wall. The load to be carried by the structural frame is thereby reduced, and the usable floor area is increased. Such walls consist of an exterior facing of sheet aluminum, stainless steel, porcelain enameled steel, bronze, or other sheet materials. To increase resistance to external fires, a concrete or other masonry backing about 4 in. thick is required by many, but not all building codes;

this is followed by an insulating layer and vapor seal and some form of finished surface, such as sheet metal or asbestos-cement board, on the interior. Because the wall is formed of several layers of materials, this type is called sandwich construction. It is usually arranged in prefabri-

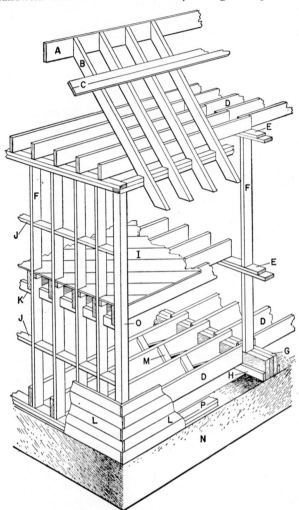

Fig. 5—FRAME BUILDING CONSTRUCTION

(A) Ridge; (B) Rafter; (C) Roof sheathing; (D) Joists; (E) Plates; (F) Studs; (G) Girder; (H) Ledger strip; (I) Rough flooring; (J) Bridging or firestopping; (K) Ledger board or ribbon; (L) Sheathing; (M) Cross bridging; (N) Foundation wall; (O) Corner post; (P) Sill

cated panels, called sandwich panels, which can be erected rapidly under almost any weather conditions.

Interior walls and partitions are constructed in the same manner as outside walls, except curtain walls. When they are nonbearing, the usual materials are hollow tile, concrete blocks, or gypsum blocks. Nonbearing walls may be thinner than bearing walls.

Exterior walls of frame buildings (*see* Fig. 5) are usually constructed of 2- by 4-in. vertical wooden members called studs, spaced 16 in. apart and covered on the outside with 1-in. wood sheathing, placed horizontally or diagonally, and on the inside with lath and plaster. Sheathing paper tacked to the outside of the sheathing reduces air leakage. A finishing material is placed outside of the sheathing. This may be wood siding placed horizontally, shingles, or a 4-in. veneer of brick or stone anchored to the studs. Insulation is commonly placed between studs to reduce heat transfer. Interior walls and partitions are similar to exterior walls except that sheathing and insulation are omitted and lath and plaster surfaces are placed on both sides of the studs.

Beams. The various classes of beams, including girders, joists, purlins, and rafters, may be rolled steel sections, reinforced concrete, or wood. Rolled steel members are I-shaped in cross section and are available in depths from 3 to 36 in. They usually support timber floor construction or roof decks, or reinforced concrete slabs. Bar joists, constructed of steel bars or other light steel sections arranged in the form of Warren trusses, as shown in Fig. 1d, but without the vertical member shown there, are extensively used.

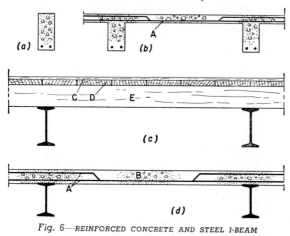

Fig. 6—REINFORCED CONCRETE AND STEEL I-BEAM
CONSTRUCTIONS

(a) Reinforced concrete beam; (b) Reinforced concrete floor on reinforced concrete beams; (A) Steel reinforcing rods
(c) Wood floor on steel I-beams, shown for comparison;
(C) Finished wood floor; (D) Wood sub-floor; (E) Wood floor joist
(d) Reinforced concrete floor on steel I-beams; (A) Steel reinforcing rods; (B) Concrete slab

Reinforced-concrete beams (*see* Fig. 6a) are usually formed in one piece, with a slab spanning the space between beams and supported by them. The portion of the slab on each side of the beam, together with the rectangular beam, forms a T-shaped cross section (*see* Fig. 6b). Concrete will withstand large compressive stresses but is weak in tension. Hence, steel reinforcing bars are placed where tensile stresses exist. By using high-strength reinforcing in concrete subject to flexure, and by introducing tensile stresses into these bars before the member is loaded, material can be saved. However, the cost of labor usually more than offsets the reduction in the cost of materials. For this reason, prestressed concrete is not used as extensively in building construction in the United States as in other countries.

Wood beams are rectangular in cross section. In slow-burning construction, timbers are of a minimum size of 6 by 10 in. spaced about 4 ft. apart. They usually support wood subfloors or roof decks at least 3 in. thick (*see* Fig. 7a). In ordinary and frame construction, roof and floor beams are usually planks 2 in. thick and from 4 to 12 in. deep, spaced 16 in. apart and supporting a 1-in. subfloor or roof deck (*see* Fig. 7b).

Columns. Steel columns are usually rolled members which are H-shaped in cross section, with depths from 6 in. to 18 in. Columns of similar shape are built up from steel plates and angles fastened, riveted, or welded together (*see* Fig. 8a). Reinforced-concrete columns may be square, round, or octagonal in cross section (*see* Fig. 8b), with longitudinal bars supported by small, closely spaced

spirals wound around them to give lateral support. Ties spaced farther apart may be used instead of spirals.

Trusses. Trusses are constructed of rolled-steel members of various cross sections riveted or welded together, or of wood members bolted together or fastened with special connectors (*see* Fig. 1.). Reinforced-concrete trusses are rare.

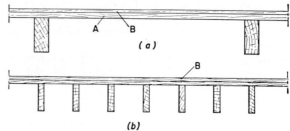

Fig. 7—WOOD BEAM CONSTRUCTION

(a) Heavy timber construction; (A) Wood sub-floor; (B) Finished wood floor or roofing
(b) Frame construction; (B) Finished wood floor or roofing

Arches and Rigid Frames. Simple arches may be constructed of brick or stone to span openings in masonry walls (*see* Fig. 2). They also may be made of steel, reinforced concrete, or timber in complicated forms, with spans as great as 300 ft. to support the roofs of hangars, auditoriums, and gymnasiums (*see* Fig. 3). Rigid frames are special forms of arches, usually with vertical sides, which are used to support roofs over large floor areas in such structures as have been mentioned. They may be constructed of steel, reinforced concrete, or wood.

Thin-Shell Roofs. The construction of reinforced-concrete thin-shell roofs has increased markedly in recent years. This form of construction is used for hangars, field houses, sports arenas, auditoriums, and other buildings with large unobstructed floor areas. The most common form is the barrel type which consists of a reinforced concrete shell, 3-6

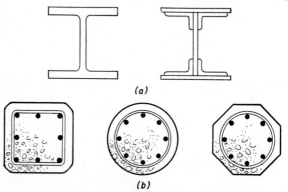

Fig. 8—STEEL AND REINFORCED-CONCRETE COLUMNS

(a) Steel columns: (Left) Rolled steel columns; (Right) Built-up steel columns (b) Reinforced-concrete columns: (Left to right) Square, round, octagonal

in. thick and built monolithically. The under side is constructed of reinforced-concrete arches which are curved in the form of a segment of a circle, ellipse, or parabola. The shell spans the distance between the arches, providing the structure with stiffness to resist unbalanced loads. Thin-shell reinforced-concrete domes without stiffening members are also built.

Domes. Domes are also constructed with structural frames of steel, wood, and occasionally aluminum. These frames are covered with various materials which, in turn, are covered with some form of roofing material.

Structural Subfloors and Roof Decks. The space between beams, joists, rafters, and purlins is spanned by subfloors or roof decks, to provide surfaces to receive the flooring and roofing materials.

If the supporting members are heavy, widely spaced timber beams, the subfloor or roof deck is usually made of planks 2

ally they may be connected by various forms of joints cut in the timbers themselves. Steel members are riveted or welded together, or bolts may be used for minor connections. During recent years, high-strength bolts have been extensively used instead of rivets. This greatly reduces the noise, which is an important advantage in business and hospital areas,

In the construction of a modern office building, the concrete floor is laid soon after each floor of the structure is raised.

in. or more in thickness or of pieces 2 in. thick and from 2 to 8 in. wide placed on edge and spiked together to form a laminated slab. If planks laid flat are used, either tongue-and-groove or splined lumber is employed, to prevent differential vertical movement.

If the supporting members are light, closely spaced wood joists, the subfloor is usually of 1-in. boards laid diagonally on them. Roof decks, supported by light, closely spaced rafters, are constructed in the same manner but laid perpendicular to the direction of the rafters.

If the supporting members are steel I beams, the subfloor or roof deck may be of heavy planks as described above or may be a reinforced-concrete slab.

If the supporting members are reinforced-concrete beams, the subfloor or roof deck will usually be a reinforced-concrete slab.

Framing and Forms. Assembling the various beams, girders, and trusses which enter into the construction of a building is called framing. The members that are to be framed together must be of appropriate materials. Wood, steel, and reinforced-concrete beams are used with masonry walls. Wood beams are used with wood columns and with steel columns. Steel beams are used with steel columns, and reinforced-concrete beams are used with reinforced-concrete columns. Wood subfloors and roof decks are used with steel and wood beams and columns, whereas reinforced-concrete floor slabs and roof decks are used with reinforced-concrete beams and columns.

Light wood construction of 1- and 2-in. material is held together by nails and spikes. Heavier timbers are bolted together with various metal connecting devices, or occasion-

and simplifies construction procedures. Plain- and reinforced-concrete members are formed in place by pouring freshly mixed concrete into forms of wood or steel. It is necessary to make joints to allow for changes in the concrete's dimensions because of temperature changes. Because of the joints, the structure is not in one piece. Such concrete construction is, nevertheless, called monolithic (one-stone). After the concrete has set and hardened sufficiently, the forms are removed.

The cost of forms is an important part of the cost of concrete construction. As a result, buildings are designed so that some, or all, of the structural elements can be cast in forms which can be used over again many times. To be advantageous, several identical items must be used in a building. The casting may be done on the job or at a central casting yard serving many jobs. Some types of members, such as joists, have been standardized and are carried in stock. The various elements are designed so that they can be fastened together on the job to produce a stable structure. This procedure is called precast construction. Prestressed members are usually precast.

Another procedure for reducing form costs is known as lift-slab construction. In carrying it out, the ground floor is constructed in the usual manner. Steel columns are then erected, and the upper floors and roof slabs are successively cast on top of the ground-floor slab and on top of each other, with a membrane or film between them. Each slab is lifted to its final position, beginning with the roof slab which is on top of the pile, by jacks fastened to the tops of the columns. Once in position, the slab is connected to the columns so that it will remain in place. This type of construction has been used only for buildings up to six stories in height.

Stairways and Elevator Shafts. Open stairways constitute a fire hazard, since they serve as flues that direct the fire upward. This has caused great loss of life and property damage. Building codes require the enclosing of stairs. A typical requirement is that buildings exceeding 30 ft. to the floor of the topmost story or occupied by more than 40 persons above or below the first story, and multifamily houses more than 2 stories high, must be enclosed with specially constructed fire partitions. No openings except outside windows and the necessary doorways are permitted in stair enclosures, and self-closing fire doors must be used in such openings. Stairways must be constructed of noncombustible materials. The number and width of exit stairways is determined by the number of persons to be provided for. Series of openings

EWING GALLOWAY

Thin aluminum sheets are lighter, cheaper, and more rapidly installed than conventional facings.

from floor to floor for elevators, ventilation, light, or other purposes must be enclosed to form shafts in a manner similar to stairways.

Flooring Materials. In general concrete floor slabs and wood subfloors are covered with wearing surfaces. Among the significant properties of a flooring material are appearance, durability, comfort, noiselessness, fire resistance, ease of cleaning and maintenance, and resistance to acid, alkali, grease, oil, and dampness. Cost is also an important factor.

Flooring materials may be divided into rigid and resilient types. Rigid materials include concrete, terrazzo, clay tile, marble, and flagstone. Resilient types include linoleum, cork carpet, cork tile, rubber tile, asphalt tile, vinyl plastic film, and wood. The more common species of wood used are yellow pine, fir, oak, maple, and birch.

The type of subfloor also affects the selection of the flooring material. All flooring materials may be laid over concrete

floor slabs. Concrete and terrazzo require no special adhesive. Clay tile, marble, and flagstone are bedded in cement mortar. The resilient types are held in place by special adhesives. It is desirable first to cement a bituminous-saturated felt paper to the concrete and then to cement the flooring to the paper. Wood flooring may be fastened in this manner, or wood nailing strips to which the floor boards are secured may be embedded in or anchored to the concrete.

Concrete floor slabs may be given a finish that will serve as a wearing surface. Such surfaces may be made more attractive and their tendency to dust may be avoided by painting with special concrete paints.

Only the resilient types of flooring materials can be laid over wood subfloors, unless concrete slabs are interposed. Resilient types (except wood) are cemented to wood subfloors by adhesives, with an intervening felt paper, as for concrete subfloors. Wood flooring is nailed to wood subfloors by blind nailing so as to eliminate nailheads from the surface.

Roofing Materials. Factors that influence the selection of a roofing material are the slope of the roof, durability, initial cost, maintenance cost, resistance to fire, weight, type of roof construction, and appearance. Types of roofing materials suitable for sloping roofs are wood, asphalt, and asbestos shingles; clay, cement, and metal tile; copper, zinc, aluminum, and tin-plated steel sheet metal; aluminum and plain or galvanized steel corrugated sheets; and bituminous-saturated roll roofing.

The type of roofing most appropriate for flat or gently-sloping roofs comprises several layers of asphalt- or tar-saturated felt cemented together with asphalt or tar roofing cement and usually covered with gravel. Copper, zinc, or tin-plated steel sheet metal and roll roofing are also used. Flat roofs that must withstand foot traffic may be covered with built-up roofing on top of which clay flooring tile, slate, or flagstone is bedded in bituminous cement.

Interior Wall Surfaces. Industrial buildings, warehouses, gymnasiums, and many other classes of buildings may not require special finishes on interior wall and ceiling surfaces. In finished buildings, however, interior wall surfaces and ceilings are usually coated with plaster. This is a mortar, generally with gypsum cement as the cementing material, though lime or Portland cement may be used. The cementing material, mixed with sand and water, is laid with a trowel and other tools to give a rough or smooth surface, and hardens by chemical action. A thin finish coat may be placed on the plaster after it has set.

The walls of corridors and certain rooms of more costly buildings are often covered with clay tile or thin slabs of stone. This covering may extend the entire height of the wall or only from 4 to 8 ft. above the floor, in which case it is called a wainscot. Brick or facing tile with plain, glazed, or enameled exposed faces may be built into masonry walls to form finished surfaces.

Paneled or plain surfaces of decorative woods are used extensively. Veneered plywoods are well adapted to this purpose. Wood surfaces are not permitted in the highest type of fireproof building. Various types of sound-absorbing acoustical materials may be used on walls and ceilings. Plywood and various types of fiberboard may be nailed directly to wood studs to form finished wall and ceiling surfaces.

Windows and Doors. Frames are provided in window and door openings to hold the window sash and doors. Casings and other trim, usually wood, are applied to give a finished appearance. If greater fire resistance is required, wood members covered with sheet metal, called kalamein construction, are used. Hollow-metal members are used in the most fire-resistant construction. The windows of industrial buildings are often made of light rolled-steel sections so formed that their edges can be built directly into masonry walls without special frames.

Glass for use in window sash and doors is of many types. Wire glass, which consists of wire mesh embedded in glass, is used in metal windows and doors to increase their fire resistance and often in other windows and doors to reduce breakage. Special kinds of glass have been developed to reduce the amount of radiant heat from the sun ordinarily absorbed by glass. This is also accomplished by the use of panes consisting of two sheets of glass with a small space between them which is filled with dry air and sealed. The dry air prevents condensation between the sheets. During recent years, the glass area has been greatly increased in many types of buildings. On the other hand, many windowless buildings have been constructed to secure better control of lighting and for safety and other reasons.

The Settling Problem. The problem of preventing or lessening the settling of buildings is one of the major problems encountered in building design. The upper portion of the earth's surface consists of solid rock called bedrock, which is exposed or is overlaid with unconsolidated material formed by weathering of rock and called soil or earth. Buildings

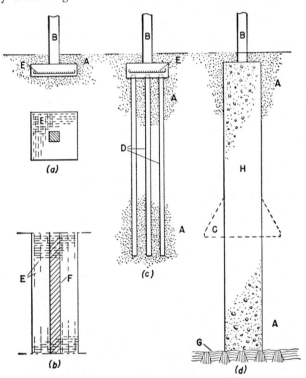

Fig. 9—VARIOUS FORMS OF FOUNDATIONS
(a) Spread foundation; (Above) Front view; (Below) Top view; (A) Soil; (B) Column; (E) Reinforced concrete footing
(b) Running-slab foundation; (E) Reinforced concrete slab; (F) Wall
(c) Pile foundation; (A) Soil; (B) Column; (D) Piles; (E) Reinforced concrete footing
(d) Pier foundation; (A) Soil; (B) Column; (C) Belling-out of pier on firm clay when pier is not carried to bedrock; (G) Bedrock; (H) Concrete pier

founded on rock do not settle, but those founded on soil settle by amounts varying from a fraction of an inch to 2 ft. or more. If an entire building settles uniformly, the consequences may not be serious except with relation to sidewalks and paved streets. Uneven settling, however, causes walls to

crack; columns, walls, doors, and windows to be out of plumb; floors to crack, to be out of level, and to be uneven; machinery to get out of adjustment; and many other objectionable results.

Settling is due primarily to squeezing together of the soil grains by the building load, reducing the void space between them. If the proportion of voids is relatively small, as in dense sands, settling will be relatively small, whereas, if the proportion of voids is large, as in most clays, settling will be relatively large. Also, if the voids of sands are filled with water, it will be squeezed out rapidly, because sands are very permeable, and any settling that is to occur will take place as soon as the load is applied. In contrast, the voids of clays are nearly always filled with water, regardless of the position of the ground-water level; and, since clays are almost impermeable, settling takes place slowly but continues for many years. The type of settling problem anticipated by the designer greatly influences his choice of the type of foundation he will use.

Foundations. Foundations for buildings may be divided into three types: spread, pile, and pier. The type selected for a specific building depends on the magnitude of the wall and column loads, the character of the underlying soil, the depth to bedrock, the position of the ground-water level, the amount of settling permissible, and other factors.

Spread Foundations. Most buildings are founded on spread footings because of their lower cost. These usually are rectangular slabs of reinforced concrete placed under columns, as shown in Fig. 9a, or long slabs of reinforced concrete running continuously under walls, as shown in Fig. 9b. The entire area occupied by a building is sometimes covered with a reinforced concrete mat or raft, from 2 to 8 ft. thick, on which all walls and columns of the building rest. The widths of wall footings and the areas of column footings are so proportioned as to make settling of all parts of a building as nearly uniform as possible and prevent the pressure of the footings on the soil from exceeding the safe bearing capacity of the soil.

Pile Foundations. Piles are long, slender, closely spaced vertical members of timber, concrete, steel shells or pipes filled with concrete, or structural steel H sections driven or otherwise placed in the soil and on top of which reinforced concrete pile caps are placed to support the walls and columns of a building, as shown in the column footing in Fig. 9c. Such foundations are called pile foundations. The piles may be placed in two or more rows under a wall, or else in a cluster under a column. The pile cap transmits the wall or column load to the heads of the piles. A pile may, in turn, transmit the load to the surrounding soil by skin friction along the length of the pile, by bearing at its point, or by a combination of these effects. If the deposit into which the pile is driven is fairly homogeneous, most of the load will be transmitted by skin friction, but if a pile is driven through a soft deposit to rock or into a firm deposit all or most of the load will be transmitted by point bearing. Pile diameters are usually about 12 in. at the head and taper to a smaller tip, though the cross section may be uniform. They are spaced from 2½ to 3 ft. center to center, depending on the diameter, and vary in length from a few feet to 40 or 50 ft. In exceptional cases they may approach 200 ft. in length. Timber piles are usually made of tree trunks with the branches trimmed off. To avoid decay, they must be entirely submerged below the ground-water level or impregnated with decay-resisting chemicals.

Pier Foundations. The columns of most very tall buildings are supported on cylindrical piers of concrete, from 3 to 15 ft. in diameter, carried to bedrock as shown in Fig. 9d, or belled out in hardpan or firm clay, as shown by the dotted line, to increase the bearing area of the base. Such foundations are called pier foundations. The excavation of the wells for the piers involves difficult and costly operations.

In downtown districts of New York, Chicago, Philadelphia, Pittsburgh, and St. Louis, bedrock is less than 125 ft. from the surface. In Cleveland the piers supporting the tower columns of the Union Terminal Building are carried down 262 ft. below the ground surface to bedrock. These are the deepest foundations in the world. In New Orleans and many other cities the depth to bedrock is too great to be reached by foundations.

CONSTRUCTION PROCEDURE

All except the simplest buildings are constructed according to plans and specifications prepared by architects and engineers. A building may be erected by individuals or organizations employing the laborers and buying the materials and equipment directly, but normally the work is done by a contractor who agrees, in a written bid or proposal, to complete the building according to the plans and specifications for a given price called a lump sum or for whatever amount it costs him plus a fixed fee or a percentage of the actual cost to him. He may do all or a large part of the work under a general contract, but he usually makes use of subcontractors who agree to do certain parts of the work, such as painting, plastering, or plumbing, for a lump sum, either cost plus a fixed fee, or cost plus a percentage of the cost. The contractor usually employs a superintendent, who is on the job at all times to co-ordinate the work of the various trades and to have general supervision of the job for the contractor. The architect also has a superintendent, or clerk of the works, who makes certain that the plans and specifications are carried out. If the owner makes changes in the plans and specifications, the architect issues a change order to the contractor. If the change involves an increase in cost, the additional amount, called an extra, is agreed upon before the work is done. If there is a reduction in cost, the owner is credited with this amount.

It is usually important that an office building, hotel, or other business building be completed by a certain date, so that leases beginning on that date can be made to prospective tenants, that orders can be accepted for manufactured articles for delivery on a fixed date, and that other activities can be scheduled in advance. To co-ordinate the various operations involved and to schedule the ordering and delivering of materials and equipment, a time schedule, usually in chart form, is prepared before construction starts. This schedule gives the starting date, the required rate of progress, and the date of completion for the many classes of work involved, such as excavation, structural frame, masonry, and plumbing. As soon as work begins, a progress chart is started. This chart shows the actual starting time for each class of work and the progress up to the close of the daily, weekly, or monthly periods adopted for reporting. By comparing the time schedule and the progress chart, which are usually combined, the status of each class of work can be determined at the close of each reporting period. Since various classes of work are interdependent, a delay in one class may result in a corresponding delay in completing the entire building. Operations which the progress chart indicates are lagging are speeded up to avoid such a delay. W. C. H.

BUILDING MATERIALS. *See* ENGINEERING MATERIALS.

BUISSON, FERDINAND EDOUARD [büi's5'] (1841-1932), French educator, was born in Paris, Dec. 20, 1841. His early education was at the Lycée Bonaparte, and for a time he earned a meager living as a tutor in Paris. He then took the state teacher's examination in the field of philosophy, but on refusing to give the required oath of allegiance to the Emperor was forced to go into political exile in 1866. He was able to secure a temporary appointment as a professor at the University of Neuchâtel in Switzerland, where he remained from 1866 to 1870. He returned to France in September 1870, and in 1871 he was appointed an inspector in the ministry of education under Jules Simon. While in Switzerland Buisson attended the first Congress for Peace and Liberty in 1867 with Giuseppe Garibaldi, and also the second Congress at Lausanne in 1869 under Victor Hugo. He was the French representative at educational expositions at Vienna in 1873 and at Philadelphia in 1876, and published valuable reports on his missions. In 1878 Buisson was appointed inspector general and in 1879 director of the primary instruction division of the French Ministry of Education, and collaborated with Jules Ferry in the formulation of laws directed toward free, secular, and compulsory elementary education. From 1896 to 1901 he occupied the chair of Science of Education at the Sorbonne, and during 1902-1914 and 1919-1923 was a Radical-Socialist member of the Paris Chamber of Deputies. In this capacity he supported proportional representation, woman suffrage, and a compulsory system of free, secular education. Buisson was an early advocate of a League of Nations, and in 1927, together with Ludwig Quidde of Germany, won the Nobel Prize for being "the world's most persistent pacifist." From 1916 until 1926 he was also president of the League for the Rights of Man. Among his writings the *Dictionnaire de Pédagogie* (1882-1884) is foremost. Buisson died in Oise, February 16, 1932. C. W. D.

BUITENZORG [bɔi'tənzɒrχ], also Bogor, the capital city of the residency of the same name in West Java, in Indonesia, about 40 mi. south of Batavia. The residency is predominantly mountainous country with numerous volcanoes. It also has many fertile plateaus on which large crops of coffee, beans, tea, rice, and spices are grown. Located about 800 ft. above sea level, the city has a mild climate averaging 77° F. Its climate and its beautiful surroundings were the major factors in its selection by Governor General van Imhoff as his residence in 1745 instead of Batavia where malaria was rife. The native community, known as Bogor, that van Imhoff found on the site, is presumed to have been the seat of the native princes of Padjadjaran. Van Imhoff named his estate Buitenzorg, meaning "without care," and the community which grew up around the estate adopted the name. In 1780 Buitenzorg became the official residence of the governor general of the Netherlands East Indies, and numerous government departments were moved to the city from Batavia because of the healthier conditions. The city soon became the social capital of Java. The palace of the governor general is situated in a beautiful park which forms a section of Buitenzorg's world-famous botanical gardens. The palace is built on the site of van Imhoff's original residence. The entire city is dotted with beautiful public and private gardens and has a number of impressive public and private buildings. It has a racetrack, insane asylum, a police training school, and a veterinary school. The city is connected with Batavia by rail, and its rail yards and rubber factories are its chief industries. Pop. (est. 1941), 65,000, including approximately 5,000 Europeans. B. L.

BUKHARA or **BOKHARA** [bʊkɑ′rɑ, bokɑ′rɑ], a city in the Uzbek S. S. R., in the central southwestern Soviet Union, and a former khanate in central Asia.

The City. Bukhara, a commercial city, lies in an oasis about 142 mi. west of Samarkand among several branches of the Zeravshan River, which loses itself in the desert sands to the southwest. The new town of Kagan, mainly a Russian community, is located on the Trans-Caspian Railway a few miles southeast of Bukhara and is sometimes referred to as New Bukhara. Founded in 830 on the site of an older settlement, Bukhara was pillaged by Genghis Khan in 1220, was rebuilt, and was looted again by his successors in 1273 and 1276. During the sixteenth and seventeenth centuries it was a flourishing Mohammedan holy city, a center of Islamic culture and learning, with numerous schools. It became capital of the Khanate of Bukhara in 1561, remaining independent until 1868, when it became a Russian vassal state. There was fighting in the city in the revolution after World War I, and Bukhara became part of the Soviet Union in 1924. The city has a definitely Eastern appearance. It is surrounded by a crumbling mud-brick wall, possesses narrow, crooked streets crossing many canals, and has scores of mosques. The chief mosque is Mir-Arab, with a colorful 100-ft.-high cupola, presenting a contrast with the town's low, flat-roofed mud houses. Near the Mir-Arab is the 203-ft. minaret from which state criminals were thrown until 1871. There are numerous bazaars and an old slave market. Bukhara is connected by a spur line to the Trans-Caspian Rail-

sixth century of the Christian Era, giving it its Turkish character. Conquest in the eighth century by Arabs and Persians made it Mohammedan, and Bukhara became a leading center of Islamic culture. Seljuk Turks conquered it in the twelfth century, and Genghis Khan overran it in 1218, completing his conquest in 1220 when he sacked the city of Bukhara. Timur the Lame (d. 1405) made this province the center of his Asiatic empire and Samarkand his resplendent capital. Both Bukhara and Samarkand remained for several decades thereafter foremost centers of art and learning. Upon the breakup of Timur's empire Bukhara emerged in 1405 as a separate khanate, with the khanate of Samarkand usually subject to it. By 1500 it had come under the control of the Uzbeks, a branch of eastern Turks, who ruled the khanate from then on. Until modern times it retained a medieval atmosphere and the military-like organization established by Genghis Khan; its rulers were Oriental despots, often cruel and fanatical Mohammedans.

The major ethnic groups in Bukhara were the Uzbeks, who constituted the peasantry and rank and file of the armies, and the Tadzhiks, who formed the merchant, intellectual, and priestly classes. Kirghizes, Turkomans, Arabs, Persians, Jews, and Turks made up the rest of the population.

Most of the territory of the Khanate of Bukhara is desert, but several large oases and rivers of mountain source, notably the Amu Darya and Zeravshan, enabled an agriculture productive enough to support a population of a million and a half. Mohammedan law assured equitable distribution of

Outside an old mosque in the central Asian city of Bukhara tradesmen vend fruit and water jars.

SOVFOTO

way. An old caravan city, it continues as a trading center for central Asia, dealing in rugs, textiles, karakul, and manufactured wares. Pop. (est. 1950), 60,000.   C. C. H.

The Khanate. The Khanate of Bukhara existed in central Asia from 1405 to 1920, occupying 83,000 sq. mi. north of the Amu Darya River between the Pamir Mountains and the Khanate of Khiva. The city of Bukhara was its capital after 1561.

The country has a long history of foreign invasion and internal struggles. Originally inhabited by Aryans, it was conquered by Cyrus the Persian (540 B.C.) and Alexander the Great (327 B.C.). Altai Turks overran the country in the

water for irrigation, if not reasonable rents. Grains, fruits, cotton, and other crops were grown. At the same time Bukhara and Samarkand became the crossing points of caravan routes from China, India, Persia, Russia, and Siberia, attaining their greatest prosperity in the fifteenth and sixteenth centuries. Russia invaded the Khanate in 1866 and in 1868 imposed a protectorate upon it. Russian overlordship mitigated some of the harsher features of native rule, slavery and torture being abolished. After their conquest of central Asia the Russians built the Central Asian Railway (Caspian Sea-Bukhara-Tashkent) and the Orenburg to Tashkent railways, which opened this region to Russian colonial exploitation and trade. Cotton growing was increased to supply Russian textile mills, and the city of Bukhara became a market for Russian textiles and other manufactures. Little was manufactured in the city except coarse fabrics. Nevertheless, by the end of the nineteenth century it was the leading trade center of central Asia. During the Russian Revolution and Civil War an agrarian movement arose against the emir, feudal landowners, and clergy, which Bolshevik agents used to overthrow the emir in September 1920 and declare the Bukhara People's Soviet Republic (not Socialist until October 1923), ostensibly independent. In September 1924 the Bukharan republic joined the Khivan and Turkestan republics to reform as the Uzbek, Turkoman, and Kirghiz (later Kazakh) republics.   R. H. F.

BUKHARI, MOHAMMED IBN ISMĀ'ĪL AL- [æ'l buχɑ'ri] (810-870), Arabic scholar, was born of a Persian family at Bukhara on July 21, 810. He studied the Islamic traditions at the age of eleven, and at sixteen he made a pilgrimage to Mecca. Al-Bukhari then proceeded to Egypt, and from there to Asia. In the course of his travels, which lasted sixteen years, he collected more than 300,000 traditions concerning the acts and sayings of the Prophet Mohammed and his companions. These he proceeded to sift, separating the true ones from the false. His most famous work was *El Djami el-Sahih* ("Collection of the True"), in which more than 7,000 genuine traditions were collected and arranged in an elaborate chapter scheme. This book was meant to serve as the basis for a complete system of jurisprudence. The *Sahih* came to be regarded as one of the most sacred books of Islam. Al-Bukhari died at Kartank, near Samarkand, on Aug. 31, 870. His grave became a place of pilgrimage for the faithful of Islam.

BUKHARIN, NIKOLAI IVANOVICH [buχa'ryin] (1888-1938), Russian revolutionary and Marxist theorist, was born in Moscow, Oct. 9, 1888. While in secondary school he started his revolutionary activity and was a leader of a student strike during the revolution of 1905. For a while he attended the University of Moscow, where he studied philosophy. In 1906 he joined the Bolshevik branch of the Russian Social-Democratic Workers Party and worked as a propagandist and organizer during the next five years, serving two terms in jail for revolutionary activity. In 1911 he emigrated to Germany. The following year he met Lenin and started to work with him in the editorial committee of *Pravda*. Late in 1912 he moved to Vienna, where he remained until the outbreak of World War I. Soon afterward he was jailed by the Austrian authorities as a Russian spy but released upon identification by Austrian Socialists and expelled to Switzerland. In 1915, provided with a false passport, he went to Sweden, but there was arrested by the police as an undesirable revolutionist and expelled to Norway. In 1916 Bukharin went to Denmark and from there to New York, where he edited the Russian daily *Novy Mir (New World)*. After the March 1917 revolution, he returned to Russia via Japan and Siberia. He was elected member of the executive committee of the Moscow soviet and of the Moscow committee of the Bolshevik Party. In December 1917 he became editor of *Pravda*, the official organ of the Communist Party, which office he occupied until 1928. In 1926 he replaced Zinoviev as president of the Communist International but was removed from this office and expelled from the party in 1928, having been accused of falsifying Marxism. A year before, the Great Soviet Encyclopedia had characterized him as one of the leading participants of the October revolution,

an outstanding theorist of communism, economist and sociologist. In 1929, after confession of his errors, Bukharin was readmitted to membership in the Communist Party and to all his high offices, with the exception of that of editor of *Pravda*. In February 1934 he became editor of *Izvestia*, the official organ of the Soviet government, but in March 1937 he was once more removed from all offices and expelled from the party, having been accused of being a Trotskyite. He was a defendant, together with twenty other prominent Old Bolsheviks, at the last of the famous "purge" trials, held at Moscow from March 2 to 13, 1938, before the military tribunal of the Soviet Supreme Court. Accused of high treason, he was found guilty, condemned to death, and executed on Mar. 13, 1938.   L. I. St.

BUKOVINA. *See* BUCOVINA.

BULAWAYO [bu'ləwɑ'yo], a city in southwestern Southern Rhodesia, the capital of a district of the same name, in Matebeleland, situated approximately 4,410 ft. above sea level, about 230 mi. southwest of Salisbury, in a veld region bordered by savanna grasslands. Although there are gold reefs in the district and coal in the vicinity, farming and livestock raising are the principal occupations of the region. A major railroad junction and headquarters of the Southern Rhodesia Railways, Bulawayo is an important industrial and distribution center. Its established industries consist of iron and steel works, flour mills, iron and brass foundries, breweries, a large sugar refinery, and soap, automobile-assembly, farm-implement, and mineral-water factories. The sugar for the refinery is obtained chiefly from the sugar plantations at Sena, in Mozambique, on the Zambezi River, but raw sugar is also shipped from the Triangle Sugar estates in the southeastern corner of Southern Rhodesia. About 8 mi. northeast of Bulawayo is the railroad town of Cement, the town being named after its chief manufacture. The cement is made from limestone obtained from quarries at Colleen Bawn about 70 mi. southeast of Bulawayo.

Bulawayo was founded in 1893. Its name, a Zulu word meaning "the place of killing," commemorates the mass execution on the site of the city of some rebellious natives by a native general named Mogilikatse who crossed the Transvaal to Matebeleland in 1837 and 1838. The present city is about 2 mi. from Government House, where the *indaba* tree remains. It was under this tree that Lobenguela, head chief of the Matebeles, held his court in the nineteenth century. The hut occupied by Cecil Rhodes in the early days of Rhodesian history also stands near the city. Of additional interest in the vicinity is Rhodes' grave in the Matopo Hills, 20 mi. southwest of Bulawayo. The hills and dam, popularly called World's View, are favorite excursion points, as are the Khami Ruins.

An important educational center, Bulawayo has missionary primary and secondary schools, a large government primary school, several preparatory schools, and a government technical and mining school. The government schools are nonsectarian. Sites of interest within the city include the public library, the bronze statue of Rhodes, and the National Museum of Southern Rhodesia, which contains a good geological collection and relics from the Zimbabwe and other Rhodesian ruins. Pop. (est. 1951, including suburbs), 125,000.   A. K. D.

BULB, in botanical definition a thickened subterranean bud with fleshy scales or coats, usually able to grow roots from its lower side. Its function is to carry the plant over the season, when it cannot grow, as in winter or a dry season. The word is, however, commonly and commercially used to describe, in its dormant condition, the large group of flowering plants which grow from such thickened underground buds. In this state, they can readily be dug, stored, shipped, sold, and replanted. This use of the word includes, in addition to true bulbs, corms which are solid, not scaled—such as crocus, gladiolus tubers which are succulent with eyes near the surface, dahlias, potatoes, and even fleshy roots such as ranunculus. It is in fact widely used for such fleshy underground roots in which, after the upper growth dies, new stems, leaves, and buds are stored. Bulbs are often classified as hardy or tender, depending on their ability to withstand frost; or as spring, summer, or autumn bulbs depending on their season of bloom. Bulbs for the American market were once almost entirely imported, chiefly from Holland. Today many are grown in the United States.

J. C. Wis.

BULBUL [buˈlbʊl], a large assemblage of small to medium-sized songbirds combined in the family Pycnonotidae. Most of them occur in the tropical and subtropical regions of Africa and Asia, but one species is Japanese and another has reached extreme northwestern Africa. They form a fairly homogeneous group, having in common short wings, a relatively long tail, a slender, slightly curved bill, small feet, and a remarkably soft, fluffy plumage, especially thick on the lower back. Most species have a few almost invisible hairlike feathers springing from the hind crown and nape. Their plumage is generally simple olive or brown, although black and white and also yellow occur. All are arboreal, feeding on insects and fruits, and many are familiar residents of gardens. The name is of Persian or Arabic origin and is ill-applied, since the bulbul of the Oriental poets is believed to have been a nightingale.

H. G. De.

BULFINCH, CHARLES (1763-1844), sometimes referred to as the first American architect, was born in Boston, Mass., Aug. 8, 1763. After graduating from Harvard in 1781, he traveled and studied in Europe. On his return in 1786 he was commissioned to design the Tontine Crescent in Boston, the first solid block of residences in New England. At this time he designed a number of houses which are still standing on Beacon Hill in Boston. When he was thirty-two, Bulfinch designed his most famous structure, the new State House in Boston. He also designed the Maine Capitol at Augusta and the Connecticut State House at Hartford. President James Monroe was so impressed with his Boston State House that he appointed him to succeed Benjamin Henry Latrobe as supervising architect of the National Capitol in 1818, where he was mainly concerned with rebuilding parts of the Capitol which were burned by the British in 1814. In 1830 he returned to Boston, where he died on Apr. 15, 1844. Bulfinch's style, achieved by a skillful and original combination of Renaissance and Adam detail, was so personalized that architectural historians still refer to the Bulfinch front as a distinct type of façade.

F. J. R.

BULGANIN, NIKOLAI ALEXANDROVICH (1895-), Soviet statesman, was born in Nizhni-Novgorod (now Gorkiy), Russia, June 11, 1895. He received a good secondary education and joined the Communist Party in 1917, serving as a member of the secret police from 1918 to 1922. He then joined the party bureaucracy and helped direct the national economy. In 1927 Bulganin was named manager of the most important Soviet electrical equipment factory, and four years later he became mayor of Moscow.

Retaining this office for six years, he helped to modernize the city and to make it a propaganda showplace of the Soviet Union. He joined the top rank of government administrators in 1937, heading the State Bank and becoming a deputy premier. With the Nazi invasion of Russia in June 1941 he was named one of the top political commissars of the army and, although without any previous personal

NIKOLAI ALEXANDROVICH BULGANIN, SOVIET STATESMAN

SOVFOTO

military command experience, he continued to be associated with the military until 1955, largely in the role of political overseer. He was named a marshal during the war, and shortly after the war became a member of the Politburo. From 1947 to 1949 and from 1953 to February 1955, he was minister of defense and titular head of the Red Army. He then became premier, holding office from Feb. 8, 1955, to Mar. 27, 1958, when he resigned in favor of Nikita S. Khrushchev. Following this event, he returned to his former position as head of the State Bank.

C. W. D.

BULGARIA [bʌlgɛˈəriə], a country of southeast Europe, lying between 44° 12' and 41° 14' N. long. and between 22° 21' and 28° 36' E. lat. and covering an area of 42,796 sq. mi. Its boundary line is 1,397 mi. long and is divided as follows: with Romania in the north, across the Danube, 377 mi.; with Turkey on the southeast 145 mi.; with Greece on the southwest 302 mi.; and with Yugoslavia on the west 325 mi. On the east Bulgaria has a coast line of 248 mi. on the Black Sea.

GEOGRAPHIC FEATURES

Topography. Bulgaria is mainly a mountainous country. Mountain ranges and hills occupy over 56 per cent of its area, the remaining 44 per cent consisting of fertile plains and plateaus. The main topographic feature of the country is Stara Planina, or the Balkan Mountains, from which the whole Balkan Peninsula derives its name. Like an enormous dachshund, whose head and front legs touch the frontier with Yugoslavia in the west and whose hind legs stretch as far east as the Black Sea, Stara Planina extends for 370 mi. across the country and divides it into two separate regions, northern and southern. The range is 12-30 mi. wide and rises up to 7,793 ft. at majestic Botev Peak. Most of the summits are of an alpine character and well-rounded. They provide rich pastures during the summer when, for long months, the shepherd shares the solitude of the mountain with only his flock and faithful dog. The shepherd, his flock, and his dog and their life on the mountains have figured prominently in the national folklore from time immemorial. Twenty highway passes, including the famous Ship-ka Pass, and several railway lines traverse the mountains.

Between the Danube River, which forms the greatest part of the Bulgarian frontier with Romania, and Stara Planina lies the Danubian Plain, the main grain-growing district of Bulgaria. It slopes gently from the Balkan Mountains toward the Danube River, where it ends abruptly in a steep cliff. Geologically, the Danubian tableland is a plateau of nearly horizontal strata, with the underlying rocks displaying roughly south to north fault lines. Along these lines run the tributaries of the Danube in Bulgaria: the Iskar, or Isker, rising in the Rila Mountains, and the Osam, Yantra, and Rusenski Lom, having their sources in the Balkan Mountains.

Topographically, southern Bulgaria is much more complex and contains a whole system of mountains. The southwestern part is almost entirely occupied by the Rhodope Mountains system, which consists of the Rhodopes themselves and the Pirin and Rila mountains. In the Rila Mountains is the highest peak in Bulgaria and the second highest in the Balkans, Musala (called Stalin Peak for some years after 1949), 9,592 ft., from which it is possible to obtain a magnificent vista of vast coniferous forests, lakes, alpine meadows, and torrential streams. The Rhodope system is rich in minerals and forests. Sheltered among the mountains lie the valleys of the Struma and Mesta rivers. East of the Rhodope Mountains is the Thracian Plain, consisting of the valleys and basins of the Maritsa River system and extending to the Black Sea coast. It is noted for its fertility. The fields, in many cases well-irrigated, are planted with wheat, corn, tobacco, rice, sunflowers, medicinal herbs, truck-garden crops, and mulberry trees. Two smaller mountain ranges occupy the southeastern part of the country. One of the most beautiful and most famous regions of Bulgaria is the Valley of Roses, situated between the Balkan Mountains and a parallel west to east range of mountains called Sredna Gora. In this valley during the month of June, unique plantations of white and red roses extend as far as the eye can see. Bulgaria produces about two thirds of the attar of roses used in the perfume industry of the world.

If one flies over the country, the main impression is one of variety, a continuously changing panorama; in the north, the Blue Danube, with small passenger boats and tugs, lazily chugging along; in the central part, long mountain ranges, some of them snow-capped all year round, and forests with many varieties of trees, but with pine, oak, and beech predominating; in the south, large fertile basins devoted to crop growing; and in the east, the Black Sea with extensive sandy beaches. Little villages are dotted here and there on the sides of the mountains, while larger towns have grown up in the valleys, by the larger rivers, and along the Black Sea coast. Ancient monuments of different ages and different origins are found all over the country, testifying to the fact that Bulgaria lies on one of the ancient crossroads of the world and that many invaders and several civilizations have left their mark here.

Climate. The large mountain systems, the altitude, and the atmospheric pressure determine the regional variations of climate in Bulgaria. The continental type of climate prevails in northern Bulgaria, and the whole of the Danubian Plain is exposed in winter to severe northern winds from Russia. The Balkan Mountains stop their progress southward, but, at the same time, the mountains do not allow the Mediterranean influence, which pervades southern Bulgaria, to penetrate into the northern part of the country. The Black Sea coast has a marine climate.

The average annual temperature of the country is about 55° F. but is subject to wide variations according to region and altitude. The town of Lom, on the Danube in extreme northwestern Bulgaria and situated only 131 ft. above sea level, enjoys an average annual temperature of 53° F.; the town of Samokov in the Rhodope Mountains at an elevation of 3,116 ft. has an average annual temperature of 46° F.; and Musala Peak, 9,592 ft., has an average annual temperature of 27° F. The valleys and basins are protected against devastating storms and frosts by the mountain ranges. Even so, frosts in the winter often cause considerable damage to crops. The length of the frost-free season varies between 180 and 260 days. Droughts sometimes occur in the lowlands, while the higher mountains have high annual precipitation: a fall of 75 in., mostly snow, has been recorded in the Rila and Pirin mountains. The average annual precipitation is 25 in.

Natural Resources. The rivers of Bulgaria, which originate mostly in the Balkan Mountains and flow either north to the Danube, the only navigable river, or south to the Maritsa River and the Aegean Sea, are used for irrigation or power supply. The latest estimate of the hydroelectric potential of the country is in the neighborhood of 25 billion kw-hr per annum.

The soils of the country vary considerably as a result of the interplay of climate, flora, and relief characteristics. The Danubian tableland is covered mainly with loess, the chernozems of which possess porous structure, fine texture, and high water-holding capacity and humus, all elements of high fertility. Brown soils predominate in the Thracian Plain, while the mountains have a mixture of brown and gray podzols and mountainous meadow soils. In the river valleys and some coastal districts are alluvial soils. Diluvial soils northeast of the Rhodopes are used mainly for the production of tobacco. The natural high fertility of the soils has been somewhat reduced by extensive deforestation in some parts of the country and by the insufficient use of natural and chemical fertilizers.

The country's mineral resources are relatively unimportant in its economy. Extensive research has been done in an attempt to locate further deposits, and oil has been discovered recently, but not in sufficient quantity to justify exploitation. The main mineral resource is coal. There are some twenty coal basins scattered in different parts of the country. Although a certain amount of anthracite is available, the main variety is brown coal, mined in the vicinity of Sofia, the capital. The total coal reserves of Bulgaria have not been definitely established, but estimates run between 5 and 10 billion tons. In recent years uranium has been discovered in the Sofia district and in Sredna Gora, but information on it is not available. While the country's total reserves of iron ore run to only 10 million tons, there are good deposits of ferroalloy metals, such as manganese, chromium, and molybdenum. Of no less importance are the lead, zinc, and copper deposits of the country. The lack of minerals for fertilizers is felt badly by a country that is primarily agricultural.

Bulgaria has a wealth of mineral springs. About 70 thermal springs, with temperatures ranging between 100° F. and 187° F. and with alkaline, sulphurous, and carbonaceous characteristics, have been used for medicinal purposes since the time of the Roman Empire and are visited today not only by Bulgarians but also by people of many other lands.

Natural Vegetation and Wildlife. The plant varieties in Bulgaria belong mainly to two vegetation zones: the middle-latitude forest and steppe zone and the Mediterranean woodland zone. In the northeast corner of the country, the

VIEW OF SOFIA, CAPITAL AND LARGEST CITY OF BULGARIA.   IN THE BACKGROUND IS ONE OF THE PEAKS OF THE VITOSHA MOUNTAINS.

plain of the Dobrudja exhibits the typical characteristics of the steppe zone. Westward but still north of the Balkan Mountains, the Danubian Plain bears similar characteristics, but with more forests and smaller clusters of trees than the Dobrudja. Much of it has been cleared of deciduous forests to open up the land for cultivation of grain, corn, and industrial crops. Further south, in the Balkan Mountains and their foothills, are deciduous forests, in the lower altitudes, followed further up by conifers and by alpine meadows near the top. The Mediterranean type of vegetation is found in the Thracian Plain together with the middle-latitude forest. The climate here favors the cultivation of cotton, tobacco, mulberry trees, vines, and vegetables of all sorts. Along the Turkish and Greek borders are species of typically Mediterranean vegetation, such as citrus fruit trees, fig trees, and rhododendrons.

Forests occupy about one third of the land, and about half of them consist of brushwood. Of the other half, 73 per cent are deciduous forests, with beech, oak, and hornbeam predominating; and the rest are coniferous forests.

The wildlife of the country, including wild game, has been greatly depleted with the reduction of the forested area, but the bear, wild boar, elk, wolf, chamois, and the wildcat still roam proudly through the forests. Almost every winter, when food becomes scarce in the mountains, packs of wolves descend at night to harass the animals of some isolated village. Sometimes they carry away a sheep or a calf and on rare occasions they have been known to kill a human being. During hard winters organized expeditions of local hunters try to exterminate wolf packs prowling in the neighborhood of villages.

ETHNOLOGY AND POPULATION

Ethnic Origins. The Bulgars were a people of Asiatic origin who founded states between the Volga River and the Ural Mountains about the fifth century A.D. In the seventh century some moved westward along the Black Sea, then on to the Danube, which they crossed to conquer the local Slavs and establish the first Bulgarian Kingdom in the region of the present Bulgarian state. A second group pushed north to the central Volga region, where their capital, Bulgar, flourished as a trading center until the rise of Kazan in the fifteenth century. The Volga Bulgars, like the Chuvash and Khazars, spoke a language related to primitive Turkic. Those who founded the Bulgarian state south of the Danube were soon assimilated by the local Slav population, which they had conquered. They acquired the language and, to a great extent, the way of living of the rural Slavs, and they gave to the Bulgarian state their name, occasional traces of their physical characteristics, some of their vigorous spirit, and a few words of their original language.

Early Bulgarian society developed under two main influences: Byzantine and Turkish. The Byzantine influence has remained most marked in the Black Sea coastal areas and in certain districts along the present Bulgarian-Greek frontier. The Turkish influence has left a strong imprint on the population inhabiting the southern sections of the country and in the Dobrudja. In more modern times, the influence of Russia and the Western nations, especially France, England, and America, was added. Russian literature and music came easily to the Bulgarian student and intellectual because of the similarity of language and the Slavic bond. On the other hand, since the nineteenth century, the classical writers and the philosophical thought of the West have inspired some of the most prominent writers and politicians of the country. The ideas of the American and the French revolutions inspired the Bulgarian fighters for liberation from the Ottoman Empire.

Language. The Bulgarians speak a language akin to a number of other Slavic languages, especially Serbo-Croatian and Russian. They use the Cyrillic alphabet, composed in the ninth century by the brothers Cyril and Methodius and carried to the other Slav countries by Bulgarian missionaries. With one or two minor exceptions the same alphabet is in use today by the Russians, Serbs, and Macedonians. The spelling was simplified in 1945 through the elimination of three archaic letters from the alphabet.

Minorities. More than 90 per cent of the population is Bulgarian. The leading minority groups are the Turks, estimated at about 6 per cent, followed by gypsies and Jews, and a few Romanians, Russians, Armenians, and Greeks. There is also a sprinkling of Tatars, Germans, Gagaouzes, Tsintsars, and Serbs.

Religion. Almost all Bulgarians are members of the Bulgarian Orthodox Church, which has a long and significant history. The first autocephalous Bulgarian patriarchate was established in 925 at Ochrid, Macedonia. It was abolished a century later and was turned into a Greek archbishopric under the direct jurisdiction of Constantinople. In the thirteenth century it was re-established as a patriarchate in Tirnovo, only to fall under Greek jurisdiction again when Bulgaria became part of the Ottoman Empire. In 1870 its independence was again granted by the Turks, but in 1872 the ecumenical patriarch at Constantinople declared the Bulgarian Church schismatic because it had been established by non-Christian authority. The schism was healed in February 1945 as a result of intervention of the leaders of the Church in the Soviet Union with the ecumenical patriarch in Constantinople.

In spite of all its trials through the centuries and in spite of the land-reform law of 1946 and the law of 1945 recognizing civil marriage which considerably reduced its power, the Bulgarian Orthodox Church has represented an unbroken link of continuity and has not only been a source of religious devotion, but has also played an important part in preserving cultural values and the national spirit through the long years of foreign domination.

The most important non-orthodox citizens are the Turks and the Pomaks, a small group of converted Bulgarians who are Mohammedans. The next most important non-orthodox group consists of Jews. There are negligible numbers of Roman Catholics and Protestants, the latter converted by American missionaries, who have been active in Bulgaria since about the middle of the nineteenth century.

Population. Population developments in Bulgaria are marked by two principal trends: a rapid increase and a movement from the rural to the industrial districts. Bulgaria has an area slightly larger than Tennessee but has more than twice as many people. According to census figures announced early in 1957, the country has a population of 7,629,-254 and a density of population of 178.5 per sq. mi., compared to 6,090,215 and a density of 149.7 in 1935. Of the total population, 66.5 per cent live in the agricultural villages and 33.5 per cent in the towns and cities, compared to 80.7 per cent and 19.3 per cent, respectively, in 1935.

Bulgaria and Albania are the only Balkan countries which have more males than females. In 1955 the number of males to 1,000 females was estimated at 1,005. The economically active group embraces two thirds of the population. During the period 1948-1952, the birth rate was 23.2 per thousand of the population; the death rate, 11.2.

Cities. The capital and largest city, Sofia, has grown from 287,976 inhabitants in 1935 to nearly 700,000 in 1957. Other large cities are Plovdiv, Varna, Dimitrovgrad (Rakovski), Ruse, and Burgas. Smaller cities include Dimitrovo (Pernik), Pleven, Stara Zagora, Sliven, Tolbukhin (Dobrich), Kolarovgrad (Shumen), Yambol, Pazardzhik, and Khaskovo.

Migrations. There were large movements of population both into and out of Bulgaria after World War I. About 250,000 Bulgarians from Thrace moved from Greece into Bulgaria, while 40,000 Greeks left Bulgaria for Greece and 200,000 Turks emigrated to Turkey. More Turks, about 30,000, left Bulgaria for Turkey between 1939 and 1945. In September 1940 the district of South Dobrudja, with a population of 300,000, was incorporated into Bulgaria from Romania. Some 38,226 Jews left Bulgaria for Israel during the period 1947-1954. Between 1947 and 1951, 1,800 refugees entered Yugoslavia, while during 1947 about 1,000 persons were repatriated to Soviet Armenia. There are no official figures of the number of political refugees who have fled from the oppression of the Communist regime to Greece, Turkey, and other Western countries, but their number is considered to run into thousands. Altogether it is estimated that about 1,000,000 Bulgarian nationals are out of the country, most of them in Yugoslavia, Romania, Greece, Russia, and other European countries. The number of Bulgarian immigrants to the United States is small, with about 700 Bulgarian settlements, mostly in the industrial urban centers in the north.

GOVERNMENT AND POLITICS

Constitutional Structure. The current Bulgarian Constitution dates from Dec. 4, 1947, when it replaced the old Tirnovo Constitution and established the present "People's Republic" of Bulgaria. The Tirnovo Constitution had regulated the political life of Bulgaria, with only small interruptions, since Apr. 16, 1879. It was based largely on the Belgian Constitution and provided for a hereditary constitutional monarchy with unicameral parliamentary government, based on the principle of the separation of powers. The Tirnovo Constitution was one of the most democratic constitutions in the world, but its letter and spirit were sometimes abused because the country was relatively young as an independent nation, and because of a number of devastating wars, sharp inter-party struggles, and interventions by the king.

When the Communist-dominated Fatherland Front first obtained power in 1944, it proclaimed its full adherence to the Tirnovo Constitution, but this proved to be only a tactical step on the road to a constitution based on the theory and practice of modern Communism as demonstrated by the Soviet Union. In fact, the constitutional organization of the new Communist state of Bulgaria was entirely dominated by the Soviet Union. Hence, the new Constitution is for all practical purposes a copy of the Soviet "Stalin" Constitution; it was approved under the name of the "Dimitrov Constitution," after the Communist leader Georgi Dimitrov, on Dec. 4, 1947, the anniversary of the "Stalin" Constitution. It consists of 11 Chapters and 101 Articles and contains the usual Communist phraseology—"people's republic," "people's democracy," "all power belonging to the people," "truly representative organs," "political freedoms," etc.—calling the structure of government "democratic centralism." In reality, behind these exercises in Communist semantics, the Constitution establishes a system of highly centralized dictatorship, exercised by the Communist Party.

The social and economic principles on which the Constitution is based are enumerated in a special chapter. Most of the means of production are owned collectively, by the state or the state-controlled co-operatives, private ownership being strictly controlled and subject to expropriation. The state can nationalize any sector of the nation's economic activity. The land "belongs to those who cultivate it," but land property is restricted and can also be expropriated by the state. All economic activity is directed by the state on the basis of state economic plans, and social welfare is the exclusive interest and responsibility of the state. The "supreme organ" of state power is the National Assembly, which is "the only legislative organ" of the Republic. It elects a presidium and appoints the cabinet, amends the Constitution, decides on peace and war, territorial changes, budgets, and economic plans, and appoints the Supreme Court and the State Prosecutor. It is elected for a term of four years by "free and secret ballot" on the basis of universal suffrage for all citizens over 18 years of age.

The Constitution further regulates the system of local government. The country is divided into the following administrative units: the capital, Sofia, and its wards; 12 regions; 95 districts; 26 large cities with the status of district;

A copper mine and smelter plant on the upper Isker River in the Balkan Mountains north of Sofia

and 2,056 rural and urban communes. All of these units are governed by the "People's Councils," elected for three-year terms.

The judicial system is centered in the Ministry of Justice. The Constitution calls the judges "independent and subordinate to the laws of the country."

The Constitution in Practice. The practical application of these provisions during the years since their adoption has built up an exact replica of the Soviet form of government. The familiar pyramid has emerged of political, administrative, economic, judicial, and cultural units, closely interwoven and each of them subordinated to a higher unit, with the leaders of the Communist party on top of it, wielding complete direction and control of all the sections of national life. This is freely admitted, if not in the Constitution itself, in the numerous Party declarations in accordance with Communist doctrine. The state is "a dictatorship of the proletariat" and the implementation of this dictatorship is entrusted to the Communist Party as "the *avant garde* of the proletariat." The Party is the supreme repository of power, guided by one ultimate principle: "the building of socialism." Anything else, including the interpretation of constitutional clauses, is of secondary importance. The principle of checks and balances that underlies the American Constitution does not exist. Elections are called "free and

secret," but they are conducted under moral, economic, and police pressure and there are no real ways of independently checking the results. Besides, there is only a single list, which is composed and controlled by the organs of the Communist Party. In Bulgaria, as in the Soviet Union, the Communist leaders adhere strictly to the one-party system. Thus, a true expression of the people's will cannot be obtained. Public opinion has no way of making itself felt since the government has established an absolute monopoly of the press, radio, and publishing industry. The intellectuals have either been silenced or turned into agents of the Party, helping to propagate the Communist creed, and extolling the methods, deeds, and leading personalities of the government. Professors, students, writers, poets, journalists, and scientists are forced to adhere strictly to the Party line, which, in the field of the arts, goes under the name of "socialist realism." Any deviation meets with legal punishment or loss of livelihood.

"Socialist justice" operates in the same totalitarian manner. While the Constitution contains a clause stating that "judges are independent," in actual fact they have been turned into organs serving the aims of the Communist Party. As a Bulgarian Communist jurist, Stefan Pavlov, wrote in *Penal Procedure and Court Organization,* published in Sofia in 1950, "the independence of judges is not to be understood as independence from the people's democratic state . . . this independence does not place judges above the working class, the Party, or the political policy of the Party."

Political Parties. Ostensibly, the government is in the hands of a coalition, the Fatherland Front, under whose title the ballots are presented to the electorate. In actual fact, however, the Fatherland Front is only a façade; its operations are conducted entirely by the Communist Party with the help of a few members of the other political parties, whose free and independent existence has been banned. The Fatherland Front originated during the Second World War to conduct the resistance movement against the Germans. It united at that time with the Communist Party, the Agrarian

Party, and other Bulgarian democratic parties. From the very moment, however, that the Fatherland Front came to power in 1944 with the help of Russian troops, the Communist Party occupied the key positions in the government and began a systematic process of displacing the coalition government with a purely Communist one. Pressure, intimidation, imprisonment, and murder were employed in the course of the transformation. Among those killed was the Agrarian leader Nikola Petkov, a man of great integrity and courage, who was executed on Sept. 23, 1947. The voices of other democratic leaders were silenced by internment or

reality political commissars, has been established and all military units have these commanders.

The Bulgarian army is a formidable force because it is well-trained and suffered few losses in World War II. Although, under the Paris Peace Treaty of 1947, the Bulgarian army was reduced to 65,000 men, it is believed that it now numbers about 200,000. The army's former German equipment has been supplanted with equipment from the Soviet Union, which considers Bulgaria of foremost military importance to it. To strengthen the military ties with the Soviet Union, a network of first-class highways and railways, a

Chemical-plant workers in Dimitrovgrad, an industrial city in southeast central Bulgaria

imprisonment, and the Communist Party became the supreme ruler of the country.

The origins of the Communist Party in Bulgaria go back to 1891 and the foundation of the Bulgarian Social-Democratic Party. In 1903, following the trend of world communism, it split into two factions which later became the Communist and Socialist parties. In 1919 the Communist Party joined the Third International, which was led in the 1930's by the Bulgarian Communist Georgi Dimitrov. In 1923 the Communists staged an uprising but were crushed and pushed underground. In 1927 they re-emerged on the political scene as the Workers' Party but became illegal again in 1934 when the Constitution was suspended and all parties temporarily abolished. In 1938 the Workers' Party was re-established. After Yugoslavian Marshal Tito's expulsion from the Comintern, the new Communist Party was purged of Tito sympathizers and those guilty of "left-wing sectarianism." Whether as a legal party or underground, the Bulgarian Communists consistently plotted for the forcible overthrow of democratic government and the establishment of a Communist dictatorship. That became possible only after Russian troops invaded Bulgaria in September 1944 and imposed the Communist regime upon the people.

Armed Forces and Security Police. The militia (security police) is under the control of the Communist Party and all important army posts—intelligence, supplies, personnel, and the war ministry—are also controlled by the Party. There are also a certain number of Soviet officers and instructors in all army formations. A military school for political training of the so-called assistant commanders, in

large bridge across the Danube between Russe and Giurgiu, Romania, and at least ten airfields for jet planes have been built. Black Sea ports have been turned into efficient naval bases, the Bulgarian naval forces increased, and shipyards built to turn out naval craft for Russia.

International Relations. The Bulgarian government conducts its international policy on the basis of "eternal Soviet-Bulgarian friendship," close relations with the other Communist countries, and friendship with other nations, great or small. Translated into practical terms, this has meant backing Soviet international moves at every stage. When Soviet policy has required it, as in the case of Yugoslavia, the Bulgarian government has made several reversals of its policy. Although it has professedly sought improved relations with its Greek and Turkish neighbors, mutual distrust remains. Bulgaria is a member of the United Nations and of the Communist-controlled Warsaw Pact. The Bulgarian representatives in the United Nations invariably vote with the Soviet delegation.

ECONOMIC LIFE

Before World War II. Bulgaria is basically an agrarian country, and before World War II the backbone of the country's economy was the Bulgarian peasant. He was not rich, but he was industrious, proud, and independent. He owned his own plot of land and worked it with the help of his family. There were very few hired hands on Bulgarian farms. Gradual improvements of agricultural methods were carried out with the help of agrarian co-operatives, and enough agricultural goods were produced to feed the whole population of Bulgaria and to export increasing quantities in order to be able to import industrial necessities. The industrial development of the country went at a slow pace, with emphasis on light industry—consumer goods and food processing—since the country did not possess sufficient mineral wealth to justify building up heavy industry. The general standard of living was low, compared to Western standards, and many economic problems faced both the government and private enterprise: overpopulation of the villages, the necessity of providing cheap money for farm improvement and industrial development, and the need to shift the direction of foreign trade, which was going mainly to Germany and was thus creating economic dependence on a greater power. Progress in meeting these problems was interrupted by the war.

The Government in Control. After securing for itself control of the political, police, and military apparatus of the country, the Communist government took sole charge of its economic life. It established the Supreme Economic Council, which controls all aspects of the country's economy—imports, exports, banking, raw materials, distribution of goods, prices, profits, and labor. The economic plans of the government are based on the theory of Marxism as practised by the Soviet Union and have developed according to the general strategy of Soviet economic policy. The Bulgarian Communist leaders, who have remained faithful to Stalin's ideas and practices, particularly in regard to forced industrialization as the basis of the economy, adopted the "Soviet example" and set about applying it to conditions in Bulgaria, even though these differed from those in the Soviet Union. The idea of being able to reshape the whole economic structure of the country with the aid of two or three five-year plans was to them fascinating in itself. But more important was the need to co-ordinate the Bulgarian economy with the economy of the whole Communist camp, led and controlled by the U.S.S.R. Bulgaria was to produce goods that the Soviet Union needed for home consumption or for export, according to the general policies of the Soviet leaders.

Industrial Development. Accordingly, in 1949, the government announced its plan to launch an ambitious program of building heavy industry; its first five-year plan laid full emphasis on heavy industry: 5,600,000,000 leva were budgeted for investment in heavy industry and only 1,200,-000,000 leva for light industry. The plan disregarded practical difficulties, such as the scarcity of raw materials and trained hands, and it disregarded the consumer needs of the people to whom present hardships were excused on the basis of future gains. The plan prescribed a 350-per-cent increase in heavy industry and a 120-per-cent increase in light industry during the five years of its duration. The industries which were to be developed first were metallurgy, the electrotechnical industry, machine-building, chemicals, and building materials. In 1952 the government announced that industrial output had risen four times as compared to 1939 and that the number of men employed in industry had risen by 100,000.

When considering the statistical figures of the government, two peculiarities are met with: one is, that, starting almost from scratch as far as heavy industry is concerned, figures like a 350-per-cent increase are not too difficult to attain; the second is that Communist figures are seldom absolute and the percentages are designed not so much to give information as to present a picture that is desirable from the point of view of the government.

The second five-year plan (1953-1957) again laid stress on heavy industry. It envisaged an investment of 11,200,-

000,000 leva in heavy industry and 2,840,000,000 leva in light industry. Industrial production was to be increased by 60 per cent and the production of foodstuffs and consumer goods by 30 to 52 per cent. Coal output was to reach 14,000 metric tons and power production, 2,732,000 kw-hr. After Stalin's death in 1953, the Bulgarian Communists, following the example of Georgi Malenkov in Russia, promised to give greater attention to consumer needs, but the building up of heavy industry was continued in the same relentless manner. Large investments in heavy industry also proceeded in spite of signs of popular dissatisfaction. The money came first from appropriating a large slice of the national material production. Personal consumption in the 1950's represented only 60 per cent of the net material product as against 80 per cent during the years before the war. A second source of investment funds was borrowing from the Soviet Union. Although the exact terms of the trade and loan agreements between the two countries have never been made public, it was believed in the mid-1950's that Bulgaria's indebtedness to Russia had become so great that a large part of the country's exports to the Soviet Union went for meeting loan payments. This might be one of the explanations why, while it was claimed that production had gone up by 500 per cent, the standard of living of the people remained low.

A woman mechanic in a cement plant in Dimitrovgrad

Reorganization of Agriculture. In order to control the peasant population and its produce, to free manpower for industry, and to acquire more means to build up industry, the government undertook a thorough reorganization of Bulgarian agriculture. During the first period (1945-1947) farmers were advised to form co-operatives. As inducement, the co-operatives were treated more favorably than the independent farmers, both in being provided with cheap credit and machinery and in being compelled to make smaller deliveries to the state at a low price. Since the majority of the peasants preferred the status of independent farmers, the government decided to employ other means of persuasion. A drive was begun for compulsory collectivization, the task being placed in the hands of Communist Party functionaries and the police, who used promises and threats, intimidation and economic sanctions, imprisonment and persecution of whole families of reluctant peasants, and even murder. In 1953 several peasant riots in northern Bulgaria were severely suppressed. Gradually, greater and greater numbers of peasants were forced into what were still euphemistically called "farm co-operatives" but which were in fact collective farms. By the end of 1955 Bulgaria had gone further than any of the other satellite countries on the road to land collectivization. At that time, 51 per cent of the agricultural land had been collectivized. While the leaders of other Communist-controlled countries, particularly Yugoslavia, Poland, and Hungary, had, by the mid-1950's, begun to realize that the peasants dislike collectivization and a trend had set in towards reducing the collectivization drive and even towards a return to private farming, the Bulgarian government went on unhesitatingly with its collectivization plans. In March 1956 it was announced that 80 per cent of the land had been collectivized. Considering that the 20 per cent remaining in private hands is mostly in the mountainous regions and consists of poor, marginal land, Bulgaria can be said to have completed land collectivization. In some respects Bulgaria has gone even further than the Soviet Union, where large amounts of meat and dairy produce are still supplied by private sectors of the economy. This forcible collectivization has caused a number of difficulties, among them disappointing production figures and deepening antagonism between the peasants and the government.

Finance. A series of laws passed since the end of World War II has transferred all private banks to the state. Other credit institutions and insurance companies were also nationalized, and the banking system centralized under the National Bank. In 1947 a law was passed by which old currency was exchanged for new, enabling the government to stabilize the lev and discourage inflation. A highly artificial rate of exchange is maintained toward the Soviet Union and its satellites, on the one hand, and the Western countries, on the other. It favors the Soviet bloc and makes commerce with the West almost impossible.

Foreign Trade. The political and economic dependence of Bulgaria on the Soviet Union is clearly seen in its import-export figures. Before World War II Bulgaria traded mostly with her neighbors and the countries of central and western Europe, mainly Germany. Trade with the Soviet Union was on a very small scale. Today the situation is reversed. According to figures published by the ministry of foreign trade in 1956, 82.4 per cent of Bulgaria's foreign trade in 1949 was with Communist countries, mainly Russia; 92.3 per cent in 1951; 85.5 per cent in 1953, and 87.9 per cent in 1955. The main export items are tobacco, ores and concentrates, fresh and processed foods (including vegetables, meat, and eggs), nonferrous metals, minerals, cement, calcinatory soda, sulphuric acids, metal-processing machines, lathes, electric motors, fabrics, and plywood. The chief items of import are machines and tools, ferrous and nonferrous metals, asbestos, rubber, cellulose, newsprint, and cotton. Relations with the Soviet Union are based on trade and loan agreements which are continuously renewed. A 1957 agreement stipulated that Bulgaria would be supplying mainly agricultural goods to Russia until 1970. An important provision was the arrangement by which uranium ore from Bulgaria was pledged to the Soviet Union.

SOCIAL AND CULTURAL LIFE

Social Security and Public Health. Before World War II Bulgaria was one of the most advanced countries in the field of social security. All workers and employees were members of a state-controlled social-security system, which embraced all aspects of social aid—for unemployment, accidents, and sickness, as well as old-age benefits. The Communist government retained this system in its general lines but introduced many modifications. The social-security system is now operated by the trade unions under government control, with the exception of old-age pensions, which are administered directly by a government department. Today, social security in Bulgaria has been turned into a political and economic weapon. It discriminates against all anti-Communists, against non-members of the trade unions, and against the small private economic sector. At the same time, it grants larger benefits to shock-workers, to those who have worked longer, and to those who have contributed to the Party's struggle for power. Thus, an anti-Communist can have no job and no unemployment benefits and a young expectant mother may not have full maternity benefits if she has not completed a minimum of work. On the other hand, a former revolutionary gets full pension payments and benefits even if he is not gainfully employed. The Communist Party utilizes the social-security system to strengthen itself politically and to extract greater effort from the workers.

In the field of public health, government figures indicate that significant progress has been made. Before the war, the Bulgarians, sturdy by nature, lacked adequate medical attention. There was a shortage of hospitals, doctors, nurses, and medicine. In 1938 there were 3,098 physicians, or approximately one physician to every 2,000 persons. Today the public health system has been remodelled and expanded. By a law of 1951 the state supplies free treatment to the entire population. It was claimed in 1955 that the country had 351 general hospitals, 29 tuberculosis hospitals and sanatoria, 711 maternity hospitals and homes, and 1,500 dental offices. There were also 8,300 physicians, or one to every 900 persons.

Education and Youth Organizations. The thirst for education has been a characteristic feature of life in Bulgaria since her liberation from the Ottoman Empire in 1878. Great strides were made in that respect, especially in eradicating illiteracy. Although the 1934 census showed an illiteracy rate of 19.5 per cent, it was mainly among the aged, and Bulgaria was ahead of her Balkan neighbors in that respect. Schools for national minorities were established where children were permitted to use their own language. Several foreign-controlled schools were opened, the most important being the American colleges at Simeonovo, near Sofia, and at Lovech. Primary education was provided free by the state and was compulsory. Students continued their education either in Bulgarian universities and academies or in foreign universities, particularly in Germany, France, Austria, Yugoslavia, and Czechoslovakia.

When the Communist Party took over in Bulgaria after World War II, it introduced Communist indoctrination in all educational establishments. The Party believed that if it could indoctrinate the minds of youth, the future would belong to Communism. With great care and energy, the educational system was directed toward that end. The basis of all education became the Communist theory of dialectical materialism. The old text-books were destroyed and history and science rewritten to serve the aims of Communist indoctrination. Educational facilities were greatly expanded. Many new schools and universities, especially technical colleges, were opened. Today the government claims that there is no illiteracy in the age group under 50, that over 84 per cent of grammar-school graduates continue their studies in the middle schools and universities, and that Bulgaria occupies first place in the world in the percentage of college graduates relative to her population. On the other hand, the authorities are displaying alarm at the failure to capture youth for Communism. There are positive signs that while there are more educated people in Bulgaria now, the majority of young men and women have turned a deaf ear to Communist propaganda. The regime's press and radio periodically launch campaigns designed to attract youth. They often complain of "hooliganism" amongst youth, lack of interest in Marxist doctrines, and leanings towards the "degenerate" Western way of life. On many occasions, students have been expelled for political unreliability.

All youth organizations are under the direct control of the Communist party. Here again the virtues of the new "Socialist Man" are extolled, but, as in the schools, the results have been far below the expectations of the Communist regime. This failure to win over the rising generation is the source of the most serious apprehension on the part of the Communist leaders.

Religion and the Family. As mentioned elsewhere, the Bulgarian Orthodox Church has a long history and is closely connected with the struggles of the Bulgarians for national and spiritual freedom. To the Communists in Bulgaria, the Church is "the opiate of the people" and Communism's deadly enemy. When the Communist government came to power it declared open war on religion, using ideological

who visits the churches and attends Church rites bears, in the eyes of the Communists, moral and political stigma. In spite of this, religion is still a vital force in the lives of the people, and for great Church ceremonies, unprecedented numbers of people turn out to worship and pray.

The family institution has also become more resilient than the Communists expected. In some instances damage has been wrought upon the family unit by the principle that the Party has the prior claim to the allegiance of the individual. But most often parents and children have come together in the family as a haven against the intimidations and insecurity of Communist society. Men and women have been forced to develop a dual personality: using compliance and subterfuge in their relations with the regime, and being themselves and truthful among their own kin and friends.

There is no possibility of individual expression and initiative in any social activities, as all societies and organizations have been taken over by the Communist Party which controls and leads the Women's Union and the youth, sports, and all other organizations.

Literature and the Arts. Bulgaria is in a sense the cradle of Slavic culture. With the adoption of Christianity in 865 by Saints Cyril and Methodius, the basis was laid for the beginnings of religious literature. Bulgarian missionaries carried the alphabet to all Slav lands, and the Russians and the Serbs trace the origins of their cultural life to Bulgaria. During the five centuries of Ottoman domination, the cultural traditions of Bulgaria were maintained mainly by the Bulgarian Church. The Bulgarian religion and language safeguarded the national consciousness for nearly five cen-

DANCING AT A BULGARIAN
VILLAGE WEDDING

TRIANGLE PHOTO SERVICE

and administrative means. Brutal repressive measures were employed. Mock trials of priests were staged. Some Church leaders were killed and others imprisoned, over 200 priests being sent to forced labor camps. Church lands were confiscated, churches and monasteries were desecrated. After the purges and intimidation, the regime effected a reorganization of the Church, promoting to its leadership people who were prepared to collaborate with it. Today, although religion is considered by the authorities as doomed in the long run, religious activities are legally free. Yet, anyone

turies of Turkish rule, during which many valuable libraries and historical documents were destroyed. In the latter part of the eighteenth century, there began a Bulgarian national renaissance. In 1762, Father Paisii, a Bulgarian monk of Macedonian origin, wrote a history of Bulgaria in which he urged the Bulgarian people to retain full use of their language and learn about their glorious past. The publication of this history marks the beginning of a strong popular movement for education and for religious and political freedom. Since the second half of the nineteenth century, the country has undergone a complete cultural renaissance. During this period Bulgaria has produced a number of outstanding writers (*see* BULGARIAN LITERATURE), poets, artists, scholars, and scientists. Although few Bulgarian works have been translated into Western European languages, a considerable number have been available in other Slav tongues.

In the past, Bulgarian literature was marked by the characteristic of all free creative art, the search for individual expression. Instructive, realistic, romantic, and symbolic schools were represented. Today the picture is different.

TRIANGLE PHOTO SERVICE

The Monastery of St. Michael the Archangel, near Dryanovo, Bulgaria, probably built during the Second Bulgarian Kingdom

Bulgarian literature now bears the uniformity which is characteristic of all Communist literature and art. The government has established complete monopoly and control over all communications media: books, newspapers, radio, theatre, art, and the film. Most of the old authors have been denounced. Purges and trials were employed to remove all independent thinkers and writers, and their books were destroyed or banned. In some places, every book written before the Communists came to power was burned, as in the town of Lom in 1944. Writers are directed to produce books which are in accordance with Communist ideology, that is, books that would be useful to the regime as indoctrination weapons. The writers are controlled and censored by the Union of Writers, which in turn is controlled and guided by the Communist party. The prescribed method is "Socialist realism" under which writers must praise the class struggle, the achievements of the regime, and

the Soviet Union as the workers' paradise and protagonist of peace; attack the "remnants of the bourgeoisie" and the democratic powers, especially the United States, as imperialists and warmongers; and, in general, follow the example of Soviet literature. According to the Communist leader Chervenkov, "the heart of the writers must belong to the Party." It has gradually been discovered that the heart of the writers cannot belong simultaneously to the Party and to the readers. The writing is dry, doctrinaire, dogmatic, uniform, and uninspired and fails to attract readers. This points up the dilemma of the writer, or of any artist, in a Communist society: if he does not follow the Party line he is not allowed to write; if he does follow it, he fails to gain an audience.

Historical Monuments. Scholars and admirers of Roman, Byzantine, and Turkish culture and civilization find Bulgaria a fertile field for study. Roman engineering works, churches and monasteries of Byzantine architectural patterns, and Turkish villages and mosques are the chief attractions. The outstanding historical monument is the Rila Monastery, built in the tenth century high in the Rila Mountains. The Alexander Nevsky Cathedral in Sofia, dedicated to the great Russian hero, is the finest in the Balkans. Hagia Sofia Cathedral, the oldest Bulgarian cathedral, was built in 1329. The Shipka Monastery was built in the Shipka Pass in memory of the thousands of Russians and Bulgarians who lost their lives defending the pass against the Turks from 1877 to 1878. Turnovo, the medieval capital of Bulgaria, along with Pliska and Preslav, antedating Turnovo, are also of considerable interest to students of history. Baba Vidin, a medieval fort on the Danube, is still in use.　　N. P.

HISTORY

The Bulgarians, one of the Central Asiatic tribal conglomerations, settled during the fifth century along the northern shores of the Black Sea, particularly in the northern Crimea. They consisted of two ethnic subgroups: the Kutriguri and Utiguri. From the Crimea and the adjacent areas they gradually moved toward the Danube and the Byzantine Empire. At first they were used by the Byzantine authorities to combat the Gothic efforts to conquer the Balkans. In 551 the Kutriguri attacked Thrace, penetrated to the Aegean in the south and the Adriatic in the west, and contributed to a general weakening of the Byzantine Empire. At the same time the eastern Bulgarian branch, the Utiguri, were organized under Byzantine sponsorship in a loose tribal confederation, which was used by Constantinople as a buffer against various Turkic peoples. In the seventh century the Khazars pushed the Bulgarians into present-day Bessarabia and Dobruja, whence they made frequent attacks on the Byzantine lands. These attacks were particularly successful during the periods of Byzantine wars with the Persians and the Saracens.

The First Bulgarian Kingdom. In 679 the militarized Utiguri-Bulgarian tribes crossed the Danube to the vicinity of Varna and founded their first Balkan state, whose territory was demarcated by an agreement between the Bulgarian ruler Asparukh (643-701) and Emperor Constantine IV. The latter's successor, Justinian II (685-711), tried to reimpose Byzantine dominations, but his efforts proved to be fruitless.

The military failure of Justinian II caused discontent in Constantinople, and he was imprisoned but soon escaped. Through extensive help received from the "Bulgarian and Slav" forces of Asparukh's successor, Tervel (702-719), Justinian defeated his enemies and reassumed the emperorship. In return he granted Tervel several territories and referred to him as "Caesar" (King), thus signifying the independent status of the Bulgarian state. The renewed Byzantine efforts to defeat the "barbarians" added new victories for Tervel, and the peace of 716, recognizing Bulgarian achievements, was in force for thirty years.

During the next century the Bulgarians consolidated their rule over the local Slav population, which outnumbered them but was unable to marshal any resistance to the superior military organization of the Bulgarians. As conquerors, the Bulgars imposed their name on the local Slavs, but as a minority they gradually accepted the Slav language and became a Slav ethnic group. The process of Slav-Bulgar amalgamation lasted for several centuries and was not fully completed before the tenth century. Although the Bulgars became a Slav ethnic group, their social organization manifested elements drawn from Slav agricultural communities and Turko-Tatar military organization. Bulgarian society was dominated by military nobility, which was divided into higher nobility (*boliades, boliare*) and lower nobility (*bagains*).

During the seventh and eighth centuries the Bulgars waged continuous wars against various Slav groups and Byzantium. Many Slav groups were forced to migrate to Asia Minor. In an effort to reinforce their boundaries the Byzantine authorities brought to the Balkans large groups of Armenians and Syrians.

During the reign of Krum (802-814) Bulgaria developed a consolidated state structure, and its army became a serious threat to the independence of Byzantium. In 809 Krum's forces captured Sofia, in 811 they killed Byzantine Emperor Nicephorus (802-811), and in 813 they captured Adrianople. In the west Krum extended his rule to present-day Banat and thus became a neighbor of the Frankish Empire. Krum was an able administrator and made efforts to regulate the internal social and economic relations by codified law. He was succeeded by Omortag (814-831), who moved the capital to Preslav (821), a city built under his supervision. In 824 he conquered the Slav tribes Timochani and Branichevtsi and extended his state to Srem; he held the cities of Sirmium and Singidunum, the latter acquiring the Slavic name Belgrade. These regions were occupied by the Bulgarians until 1018. Omortag's son Malamir (831-836) consolidated the new state and fought the spread of Christianity.

During the reign of Presyam (836-853) the Bulgarian forces attacked Rashka, the embryonic Serbian state headed by Vlastimir, but their efforts bore no fruit. Presyam's successor Boris (853-888) adopted Christianity (865) and oscillated in his loyalty between Rome and Constantinople. The adoption of Christianity was effected primarily for political reasons: it was calculated to enhance the international prestige of the new state. Boris appealed to the Pope to recognize an organization of the Bulgarian patriarchate as an independent body and to place the leading ecclesiastic positions in the hands of Bulgarians. However, in 870 Constantinople recognized the independence of Boris' church, a fact which cemented co-operation between Byzantine and Bulgarian ecclesiastic authorities. Christianity was particularly strengthened with the arrival in Bulgaria of Kliment and Naum, the pupils of the Slav missionaries Cyril and Methodius, who translated the principal passages from the Scriptures and Byzantine religious works into Slav and who laid the foundation of Slav literature. Boris' son Vladimir (888-893) made an abortive effort to suppress Christianity. His father left the monastery to which he had retired and, ending Vladimir's rule, established the latter's younger brother Simeon on the throne.

Simeon (893-927), who was educated in Constantinople, is generally considered the greatest of all Bulgarian rulers. His lifelong ambition was to conquer Constantinople, and he fought against the Byzantine forces in 894, 896, 904, 913, and 920 to 924. As a result of these continuous wars the possessions of the Bulgarian state included the territory from the Adriatic in the west to the Black Sea in the east. Between the Lim and Ibar rivers Simeon organized a Serbian state which was dependent on him and which a few years before his death acquired full freedom. In 895 the Byzantine authorities made an alliance with the Magyars in an effort to check the rising power of the Bulgarian state. In 925 Simeon proclaimed himself "Tsar of the Bulgarians and Greeks," and at the same time he elevated the Bulgarian archbishopric to a patriarchate. During his reign Sofia became a great center of learning and the cradle of Slav literature. Many Byzantine legal and theological books were translated into Slav. According to some Slav scholars, it was under Simeon's sponsorship that the first compilation of Slav legal customs was made. His state was a highly centralized structure: he replaced the hereditary rulers of provinces by men responsible to him.

After Simeon's death the Bulgarian empire began rapidly to deteriorate. His son Peter (927-969) had neither ambition nor capacity to carry on further military conquests. His country was internally torn by the rise of the Bogomil heresy, basically a social movement in reaction to the parasitic life of military and ecclesiastic nobility. Among Macedonian Slavs several rebellions took place, and the Serbian ruler Chaslav succeeded in eradicating the last traces of Bulgarian domination in Rashka. In 968 the forces of Russian Prince Svyatoslav crossed the Danube and established themselves in Bulgarian territory.

Peter was succeeded by Boris II (969-972). During the first year of his reign Svyatoslav made his second invasion of Bulgaria and penetrated as far as the Bulgaro-Byzantine frontier. This forced the Byzantine Empire to undertake concrete measures for the protection of its territory. Emperor John Zimisces attacked Svyatoslav and defeated his army in 972, gaining a victory which opened the door for Byzantine penetration into Bulgaria. John Zimisces immediately proclaimed Bulgaria a Byzantine province, abolished the Bulgarian patriarchate, and established Byzantine garrisons throughout the country.

Byzantine authorities imposed their rule exclusively in eastern Bulgaria. The western regions, with the capital first in Sofia and then in Ohrid, continued to enjoy independence of both their state and patriarchate. Samuel (980-1014), a nobleman of the Shishman family, consolidated the new state and became *de facto* ruler of Bulgaria. In 1014 Samuel's forces were defeated at Balasitsa by the army of Emperor Basil II, who acquired the name "Murderer of Bulgarians." Basil took 14,000 prisoners and blinded 99 out of each 100. In 1021 the Byzantine army conquered Srem, the last independent Bulgarian territory.

Under Byzantine rule Bulgaria was divided into districts ruled by Byzantine officials. Outstanding among these officials were Constantine Diogenes, archont of Srem, Nicephorus Proteron, and Constantine Comnenus. The new rulers preserved and developed the feudalist institutions.

The Second Bulgarian Kingdom. The second Bulgarian state was founded in the twelfth century by two brothers, Peter and Ivan Asen I, of the Bulgarian nobility (*boliare*). At the end of the twelfth century, the combined Magyar and Serbian armies attacked the Byzantine Empire and conquered Sofia. This stimulated the northern Bulgarians to rise against their Byzantine rulers. Assisted by the Vlachs and Cumans, the Bulgarians succeeded in liberating their country in 1186. In 1187 the Byzantine Empire was forced to conclude a peace treaty with Bulgaria and to recognize its independence. Ivan I was crowned in Turnovo as a "Tsar of the Bulgars and the Vlachs." Peter ruled the eastern provinces and had his capital in Preslav. Ivan died in 1196; Peter was killed in 1197 by dissident nobles. Their younger brother Kaloyan (1197-1207) became the new ruler. He fought successfully against the Magyars and re-established friendly relations with the Roman Church. He had hoped to be made an emperor, but Pope Innocent III had him crowned in Turnovo in 1204. His successor Boril (1207-1218) lost his throne in 1218, and the new ruler became Ivan Asen II (1218-1241), who received Russian assistance. During his rule Bulgaria was internally consolidated. In 1230 the Bulgar forces defeated Theodore Angelus, the ruler of Epirus and Salonika, and became the chief power in the Balkans. The new Bulgarian empire included, in addition to its ancient territory, Macedonia and a large section of Albania. After the defeat of Theodore Angelus, the latter's influence in Serbia was weakened, and his son-in-law Radoslav was forced to transfer the royal prerogatives to Vladislav, a brother-in-law of Ivan Asen II. Asen made an unsuccessful effort to organize an Orthodox coalition against the Latin Empire at Constantinople. He died during the Tatar invasion in the Balkans, the result of which was that the Bulgars were compelled to pay an annual tribute to the Tatar ruler.

Asen's successors could not preserve the state intact and establish their control over the feudalistic leaders who dominated individual provinces. Michael Asen (1248-1257) lost Macedonia to Byzantium. In 1256 he attacked Serbia, and his forces penetrated as far west as the Lim River, but they were unable to incorporate the new territory into the Bulgarian state. Michael was assassinated by his cousin, Kaliman II (1257-1258). The Bulgarian state continued to disintegrate, and the Tatars, Greeks, and Magyars tried to form their own factions in the country. The decline of the state was not prevented by Ivailo (1277-1279) or Ivan Asen III (1279-1280). In 1281, George Terter (1281-c.1292), a Cuman, became the supreme ruler. He waged several wars against the Tatars and maintained friendly relations with Milutin, King of Serbia. In 1292 he was forced by the nobility to flee to the Byzantine Empire, where he was imprisoned. His disappearance unleashed new contending forces in Bulgaria, which became an arena of many internal clashes. During this period King Milutin of Serbia established his influence in Branichevo and defeated Shishman, the ruler of the Vidin area.

Terter's son, Svetoslav (1295-1321), succeeded in his effort to improve the internal political situation and to liberate the country of the last remnants of the Tatars. His son George II (1322-1323) did not leave any male successors, and after his death Michael III Shishman (1324-1330), son of Shishman and brother-in-law of King Milutin of Serbia, became the new ruler. With Byzantine help and encouragement he attacked Serbia, but in 1330 his army was annihilated at Velbuzhd, and he was killed. This opened the door to the development of a strong Serbian influence among the ruling circles of Bulgaria and to the growing consolidation of Serbian rule in Macedonia. Michael was succeeded by his wife Neda, but in 1331 the throne was occupied by Ivan Alexander (1331-1370) who maintained friendly relations with Serbia. His sister Yelena was married to Dushan, the powerful ruler of Serbia. During

Ivan's reign Bulgaria was subject to frequent attacks by the Turkish forces. During his life Ivan divided Bulgaria into two provinces ruled by his two sons Stratsimir (1371-1396), who ruled Vidin and northwestern Bulgaria, and Ivan Shishman III (1371-1393), who ruled in central Bulgaria. Northeastern Bulgaria (Dobruja) became an independent state. While Stratsimir's domain was continuously attacked by the Magyars, that of Shishman was forced to fight the Turkish penetration into the Balkans. Frequent fratricidal wars contributed largely to a rapid weakening of Bulgarian statehood. A large-scale development of various ascetic movements and religious sects also contributed to the internal weakening of Bulgaria. The outstanding literary figure of the fourteenth century was Theodosius Tirnovski, whose work was concentrated on the popularization of the basic theological tenets of Byzantine Orthodoxy.

The Turkish Domination. In 1393 the Turks conquered Turnovo, the capital of Bulgaria, and took Shishman to Philippopolis (Plovdiv), where he was executed in 1395. In 1394 northeastern Bulgaria was occupied by the Turks, and in 1396 the Vidin area. Thus, after 208 years of existence, the Second Bulgarian Kingdom came to an end. Many Bulgarians fled to Serbia, where some, like Constantine the Philosopher and Gregory Tsamblak, became renowned men of letters. The Turkish regime was somewhat more tolerant than the medieval rule of native *boliare*. However, this was a dark age in the cultural development of the Bulgarian people. Some Bulgarians adopted Mohammedanism, which gave them special privileges in the Turkish feudal system. Since the Turks were interested primarily in holding the towns, the peasant masses were isolated and able to preserve their ethnic individuality. The Bulgarian Church was fully subordinated to the Greek Patriarch of Constantinople, who entrusted the leading ecclesiastical positions to Greek clergy.

During the fifteenth century the Bulgarian territory became on several occasions a theatre of Turko-Magyar wars, which caused heavy losses in population as well as a general economic deterioration. In 1598 a small Bulgarian uprising took place in Turnovo, and a descendant of the Shishman family became the ruler, assuming the name Shishman III. The uprising was immediately put down by the Turks, and Shishman III fled to Russia while Metropolitan Dyonisius and 50,000 Bulgarians retreated to Walachia.

During the seventeenth century the Vidin area was for a short period occupied by the Austrian forces. During the end of the eighteenth and the beginning of the nineteenth century this area was a *de facto* independent state ruled by Ottoman renegades.

During the Russo-Turkish War of 1828 a Bulgarian liberation movement crystallized. Educational work and general cultural activities during the nineteenth century were instrumental in the growth of Bulgarian national consciousness. The foundations for the Bulgarian cultural movement were laid by the monk Paisii, who lived in Mount Athos and who, in 1762, wrote a book glorifying the past kings and church leaders. Sofroni Vrachanski wrote at the beginning of the nineteenth century several books in Bulgarian recording the current events and having a didactic and nationalist tendency, the first books to be printed in Bulgarian. He used the language spoken by the peasants, and he criticized the monastic isolation of Bulgarian clergy. Vrachanski laid the foundation for a secular cultural movement. In 1750 Bulgaria had 21 elementary schools, of which 2 were in towns and 19 in villages. Eighty years later the total number of schools was 189. The first Bulgarian primer was written by Beron and was printed in 1824.

Turnovo, on the banks of the Yantra River, was Bulgaria's capital and cultural center during the Middle Ages.

The Greek War of Independence served as a call to arms to various Bulgarian nationalist organizations, and during the following decades several abortive uprisings took place. Important to the development of the movement for national independence were the appointment of an archbishop of the Bulgarian Uniate Church by the Pope, and, particularly, the Turkish establishment of a Bulgarian exarchate in 1870.

Liberation and Independence. In 1876 a large-scale revolt against the Turkish rule was organized in Bulgaria. The center of the uprising was the Philippopolis sanjak. Inadequately armed and lacking sufficient unity the rebels were ruthlessly massacred by the Turkish forces. The British statesman Gladstone condemned this massacre, and he was greatly responsible for winning the Western European countries to the side of Bulgaria. The next year Russia declared war on Turkey, and Russian forces penetrated into the Balkans. On Mar. 3, 1878, victorious Russia compelled Turkey to sign the Treaty of San Stefano whereby Bulgaria became an autonomous principality of 4,000,000 inhabitants. The new state included Rumelia and the largest sections of Macedonia and Thrace. However, the Congress of Berlin of July 13, 1878, decided that Bulgaria be limited to the area between the Danube River and the Balkan Mountains, that Rumelia be organized into an autonomous province, and that both of these units be dependent on Turkey.

The Constitutional Assembly, in which radical trends predominated, convened on Feb. 22, 1879, in Turnovo and drew up the first constitution of modern Bulgaria. On Aug. 29, 1879, the assembly elected Prince Alexander of Battenberg, a member of the family which ruled the grand duchy of Hesse-Darmstadt, to the Bulgarian throne. He pursued conservative policies, though the country was largely in favor of a liberal government. However, since the Liberals were outspokenly anti-Russian, Prince Alexander received support from the Russian government.

On Sept. 18, 1885, Bulgaria and Rumelia were united. Two months later Serbia declared war on Bulgaria. The Serbian army was routed at Slivnitsa on October 18 and 19, and peace was concluded at Bucharest on Mar. 3, 1886, on direct intervention by Russia and Austria-Hungary. On Sept. 7, 1886, Prince Alexander was forced by the Russians to abdicate. After protracted negotiations Prince Ferdinand of Saxe-Coburg (1887-1918), an Austrian choice, was selected to be the new ruler. Russia refused to recognize him.

In 1908, following the Austro-Hungarian annexation of Bosnia and Herzegovina, Bulgaria proclaimed its full independence, and Ferdinand assumed the title of Tsar.

In 1912 Bulgaria, Serbia, Greece, and Montenegro, at the instigation of the Great Entente states, particularly Russia, founded a Balkan Alliance with the original purpose of forming a wall against the eastward expansion of Germany and Austria-Hungary. Prompted by an internal crisis in Turkey and encouraged by the outcome of the Italo-Turkish War of 1911-1912, the Balkan allies attacked Turkey in October 1912. The Turkish forces were soon defeated, and, by the London Peace Treaty, Turkey was forced to surrender her territories west of the Enos-Midye line. In the meantime the Balkan allies could not agree on the partition of the newly liberated territories, particularly Macedonia. During the night of June 29-30, 1913, the Bulgarian army made an unexpected attack on the Serbian and Greek garrisons in Macedonia. In this war Turkey and Romania also participated. The Bulgarian army was defeated, and Bulgaria suffered considerable territorial losses. By the Bucharest Treaty of Aug. 10, 1913, almost the whole of Macedonia was divided among Serbia and Greece, and Dobruja was given to Romania. Serbia also acquired the Bosilgrad and Tsaribrod districts. By the Constantinople Treaty of Sept. 29, 1913, the city of Adrianople (now Edirne) and the surrounding territory were returned to Turkey.

After the military catastrophe and heavy territorial losses the Bulgarian liberal parties (the Liberal Party of Vasili Radoslavov; the Party of Young Liberals, headed by Dimitri Tonchev; and the National-Liberal Party of N. Gennadiev) organized a common movement that fought for the substitution of close co-operation with Austria-Hungary for traditional Russophilism. On July 17, 1913, Radoslavov formed a Liberal cabinet, and this was the beginning of the incorporation of Bulgaria into the system of the Central Powers.

On Oct. 15, 1915, the Bulgarian army, as an ally of the Central Powers, invaded Serbia. As a result of World War I Bulgaria lost its Aegean outlet to Greece, and the Strumitsa district to Yugoslavia. Tsar Ferdinand was forced to abdicate, and the throne was given to Boris III (reigned 1918-1943). The champions of Bulgarian militarism lost their hold on the country, and the Agrarian Party came to power. Agrarian leader Alexander Stamboliski formed a cabinet on Oct. 3, 1918. Stamboliski gave his country new orientation. At home he sought to develop a "peasant democracy." Abroad he worked to establish friendly relations with Balkan states, especially Yugoslavia. But the nationalist and conservative elements opposed his ideology, the I.M.R.O. (Internal Macedonian Revolutionary Organization) resented his policy of peace with the neighboring states, and the Communists saw in Stamboliski's movement a serious rival. A group of conspirators, backed by Colonel Volkov, of the Officers' League, Alexander Tsankov, future leader of a fascist party, and the I.M.R.O. leaders, seized Stamboliski on June 9, 1923, and murdered him.

The period of "Democratic Experiment" was followed by a period of "Democratic Entente," a coalition formed by Tsankov. The influence of the Army and the I.M.R.O. was paramount, and a vigorous drive against the Agrarians and Communists was launched. There were assassinations on the streets of Sofia. In September 1923, Communists attempted an uprising but were crushed and dispersed. Meantime there were frontier skirmishes with Greece and increasing tension between Bulgaria and Yugoslavia. Relations with Turkey were bad, whereas the Italian influence grew. Within Bulgaria, a conflict between the more democratic "Federalist" and conservative "Bulgarophile" wings of the I.M.R.O. developed. The leader of the former (Protogerov) was assassinated in 1928, and the leader of the latter (Ivan Mihailov) emerged as a powerful revolutionary. Andrei Liapchev headed the government from 1926 to 1931, when Democrats and Agrarians won the elections. But government crises continued and even intensified in the period 1932-1934. In May 1934, a coup was staged by Kimon Georgiev of the "Zveno" group and Damian Velchev of the Military League. They represented the middle-class and intellectual elements, opposed the I.M.R.O., favored friendship with Yugoslavia, and had a political program that was influenced by fascist corporate principles. In 1935 King Boris freed himself of the Georgiev-Velchev regime and appointed the more amenable Kiosseivanov as premier. All political parties were disbanded. On Jan. 24, 1937, a Pact of Eternal Friendship was signed with Yugoslavia, and a few months later an agreement was signed with the Balkan Pact countries, permitting Bulgaria to rearm. Thereafter the German influence became very strong and there was much opposition to the government; despite the ban on political parties, the opposition bloc won 56 out of 160 parliamentary seats.

World War II. On Mar. 1, 1941, at a ceremony at Vienna, Prime Minister Bogdan Filov signed the Tripartite Pact allying his country with Germany, Italy, and Japan. In April 1941 the German army entered Bulgaria to use it as a springboard for an attack on Yugoslavia and Greece. Bulgaria was allowed, in the wake of the German armies, to occupy Yugoslav and Greek Macedonia, Greek Thrace, and parts of Serbia, where she was compelled to wage a constant struggle with the organized native resistance.

After the German attack on Russia in June 1941, Bulgaria refused to enter the war, but when Germany declared war against the United States in December 1941, Bulgaria followed suit and on Dec. 13, 1941, declared war on the United States and Great Britain.

On Aug. 23, 1943, King Boris died in circumstances that have not yet been explained, and was succeeded by Simeon II. Since Simeon was a minor, royal authority was vested in a Council of Regents consisting of Prince Kiril, General Mikhov, and Bogdan Filov. The Regents continued the policy of full loyalty to the Axis. In 1943, as the political situation worsened, Dobri Bozhilov succeeded Filov as prime minister. In December 1943 and March 1944 the Allies bombed Sofia and the government was thus further weakened. In June 1944 Ivan Bagrianov formed a cabinet, declared Bulgaria's neutrality, spoke openly of peace, and sent envoys to Cairo to meet with representatives of the United States and Great Britain, the only nations with which Bulgaria was at war. On September 2 a new government was formed under Konstantin Muraviev, representing moderate democratic elements. It was unwilling to incorporate representatives of the Fatherland Front coalition or to renounce some of the territories annexed from Yugoslavia and Greece. To "legalize" its intentions of conquest the Soviet Union, without informing the Allies, declared war on Bulgaria on September 5, at a time when Bulgaria was under a democratic and pro-Ally administration and was eager for peace. On September 9 a coup d'état was effected by the Fatherland Front, and a pro-Soviet government, headed by Kimon Georgiev, was formed. The Fatherland Front included the representatives of various democratic parties but was dominated by the Workers' (Communist) Party. During the month of September the Red Army occupied Bulgaria, and the Bulgarian government declared war on Germany. The new regime concentrated its attention on the elimination of all Axis collaborators and on discrediting political leaders who refused to accept Communist domination. During the early months of the new regime the Communists established their full control over the press, radio, labor movement, co-operative organizations, internal affairs (police), and the judiciary system. The electoral law drawn up by the new cabinet did not provide sufficient guaranties for a free election of parliamentary representatives. The United States and Great Britain had repeatedly protested against the Bulgarian electoral law and conditions which precluded fair elections, as provided by the Yalta and Potsdam agreements. The first protest, in August 1945, brought some changes; the opposition parties and their newspapers were recognized, and a degree of free expression was authorized.

Bulgaria Under Communist Rule. In an effort to strengthen the Workers' (Communist) Party, the Soviet Union established diplomatic relations with Bulgaria on Aug. 14, 1945. In December 1945 the Moscow Conference of Foreign Ministers resolved that the Bulgarian government be advised to include in the cabinet two representatives of democratic opposition parties, and that the recognition of Bulgaria be contingent on her fulfillment of this advice. The recognition was soon put into effect.

During the pre-election campaign Georgi Dimitrov, the former head of the Comintern, arrived in Bulgaria from the

U.S.S.R. He became prime minister and took direct part in the election campaign. The election for the Grand National Assembly, Oct. 27, 1946, gave the pro-Russian Fatherland Front coalition 364 of the 465 assembly seats. The Communist Party alone won 277 seats. The strongest of the opposition parties, the Agrarian Union, under the leadership of Nikola Petkov, won 90 seats. Although the opposition took part in the parliamentary elections of October 1946, it complained that Communist Party intimidation and underhand methods had made free elections impossible. On Nov. 22, 1946, the new Fatherland Front government was sworn in, with Georgi Dimitrov, veteran revolutionary and top-ranking Bulgarian Communist, as prime minister. H. K.

Beginning in 1946 Bulgaria faithfully followed the Communist Party line as dictated by Moscow. The first part of the decade was marked by a ruthless struggle against all non-Communist elements in Bulgaria and by bitter hostility to the non-Communist outside world, especially Bulgaria's neighbors, Greece and Turkey. Under the slogan of "liquidating fascists," the Communists removed all potential

Foreign relations during this period followed a simple line: what Moscow said and did was right and what the democracies said and did was wrong. In neighboring Greece, when a Communist insurrection broke out, the Bulgarian authorities, in line with Moscow, declared that the Greek government was "monarcho-fascist" and gave every possible help to the Communist rebels. Turkey was treated as a "reactionary country, agent of the Western imperialists."

With Yugoslavia, on the other hand, relations were very close until June 1948. The Bulgarian dictator Georgi Dimitrov visited Marshall Tito in August 1947, and at the end of November Tito returned the visit. At that time, the two Balkan dictators were considering a federation of Bulgaria and Yugoslavia, an idea which Stalin rejected, either because he already suspected that Tito might prove difficult to manage or because he did not want, on principle, to see any of the satellites change their status of direct dependence on Moscow.

Relations between Bulgaria and Yugoslavia changed radically when Stalin ordered the Cominform denunciation of

The city of Pleven, in northern Bulgaria. The mausoleum in the background was erected in memory of Russian troops who liberated the city during the Russo-Turkish War in 1877, after nearly 500 years of Turkish rule.

sources of opposition. Many anti-Communists were put to death without a trial, some after trumped-up charges heard in Communist courts. The most famous trial was that of Nikola Petkov, the leader of the Agrarian Party and one of the most heroic figures of Bulgarian democracy. In spite of world-wide protests, in which the U.S. and British governments participated, Petkov was executed on Sept. 23, 1947. Thousands of other anti-Communists were sent to prisons and concentration camps. All leaders in the political, cultural, and social life of the country were replaced by trusted Communists, and the country's intellectual élite was destroyed. The number of anti-Communists who perished during the first decade of Communism in Bulgaria has not been revealed, but it is estimated in tens of thousands. The Agrarian and Socialist parties were suppressed. The courageous Socialist leader Kosta Lulchev was sentenced on Nov. 15, 1948, to 15 years of imprisonment for articles critical to the regime. The field was thus cleared for the full tide of Communism. The whole constitutional structure of the country was rebuilt in accordance with the Communist creed and forced industrialization and collectivization were launched in earnest.

Tito's brand of Communism in June 1948. Bulgaria joined in the denunciation and purged its own Titoists, among them Traicho Kostov, second secretary of the Bulgarian Communist Party and one of its most famous stalwarts, who was tried for conspiracy and espionage in the fall of 1948 and hanged on December 16.

When Georgi Dimitrov died in July 1949, his position as prime minister was inherited by Vasil Kolarov, while Dimitrov's brother-in-law Vulko Chervenkov, who had spent most of his mature life in Moscow, became Dimitrov's successor as secretary of the party and the most powerful man in Bulgaria. The change of dictator brought no change in policy, as Chervenkov remained a faithful follower of the Moscow line. When Kolarov died on Jan. 23, 1950, Chervenkov became prime minister as well as secretary of the Communist party. From all indications, it appeared that of all the Russian satellites, Bulgaria was most faithfully following the Stalinist pattern and was at the same time the most hermetically closed to the outside world.

After Stalin's death, when Moscow's policy toward Tito changed, the Bulgarian leaders followed the same line and made overtures of rapprochement to Tito. As relations be-

RULERS OF BULGARIA

Dates of Reign	Name of Ruler	Succession
–562	Candich	Khagan (Khan) of the Utigurs
562–568	Baian	Khagan; subdued by Turks
568–584	Kubrat or Kurt the Liberator	King of Old, or White, Bulgaria; a Hun
584–642	Kurt or Crobatus	Of the family of Dolo; his uncle, Organa, regent during earlier part of reign
642–643	Beznur (Batbian)	

THE FIRST BULGARIAN KINGDOM

Dates of Reign	Name of Ruler	Succession
643–701	Asparukh (Asperuch, Isperikh, Eshberuch)	Origin unknown
702–719	Tervel	Son (or grandson) of Asparukh
724–740	Sevar	Khan of the family of Dolo (Dulo)
740–756	Kormisosh (Kormisos)	A boyar of the family of Vokil or Ukil
756–762	Vinek (Vineh)	Son of Kormisosh; massacred with family
762–765	Telets	A boyar of the house of Ugain; murdered
765–767	Sabin	Son-in-law of Kormisosh
767–772	Toktu	Brother of Baian; both killed
772–772	Pagan	Deposed; killed by slaves
772–777	Telerig	Forced to flee
777–802	Kardam	
802–814	Krum (Crummus, Crumn, Keanus Magnus) the Legislator	Perhaps descendant of Kubrat
814–831	Omortag	Son of Krum
831–836	Malamir	Son of Omortag
836–853	Presyam (Pressian)	
853–888	Boris I (Michael) the Christener	Nephew of Malamir; abdicated in favor of son Vladimir to go into a monastery
888–893	Vladimir the Apostate	Son of Boris; deposed by father and blinded
893–893	Boris I restored	Nephew of Malamir; ousted Vladimir
893–927	Simeon (Symeon)	Younger son of Boris I
927–969	Peter I	Younger son of Simeon; George Sursubul, maternal uncle, regent
969–972	Boris II	Son of Peter I, deposed by Eastern Emperor John Zimisces
980–1014	Samuel	Son of Nicholas Shishman, a noble
1014–1016	Gabriel Radomir	Son of Samuel, murdered by Vladimir, a cousin
1016–1017	John Vladimir	Cousin of Gabriel; usurped throne
1017–1018	Maria	Wife of John Vladimir; took over government; abdicated
	Under Eastern Roman Empire (1018-1186)	

THE SECOND BULGARIAN KINGDOM

Dates of Reign	Name of Ruler	Succession
1187–1196	Ivan Asen I	Boyars (nobles); brothers; re-established Bulgarian state
1187–1197	Peter	
1197–1207	Kaloyan (Yoannitsa, Calo Joannes)	Younger brother of Ivan and Peter; assassinated
1207–1218	Boril (Boris)	Nephew of Ivan
1218–1241	Ivan Asen II	Greatest Bulgarian ruler; son of Ivan Asen I
1241–1246	Kaliman I (Kaloman, Caloman)	Eldest son of Ivan Asen II; poisoned by stepmother
1248–1257	Michael Asen	Half brother of Kaliman; assassinated by cousin, Kaliman II
1257–1258	Kaliman II	Cousin of Michael Asen; killed
1258–1277	Constantine Tykh	Elected; assumed name of Asen
1277–1279	Ivailo	
1279–1280	Ivan Asen III	
1281–c.1292	George Terter	
1295–1321	Svetoslav	Son of Terter
1322–1323	George II	Son of Svetoslav
1324–1330	Michael III Shishman	
1330–1331	Neda	Wife of Michael III
1331–1370	Ivan Alexander	
1371–1396	Stratsimir	Son of Ivan; ruled northwestern Bulgaria
1371–1393	Ivan Shishman III	Son of Ivan; ruled Central Bulgaria; captured 1393; executed 1395
	Under Turkish (Ottoman) Empire (1396-1878)	

MODERN BULGARIA

Dates of Reign	Name of Ruler	Succession
		Bulgaria liberated by the Treaty of San Stefano, Mar. 3, 1878; through British pressure on Russia, the Treaty of Berlin, July 13, reduced the boundaries of new Bulgarian state, requiring it to remain part of the Turkish Empire
1879–1886	Alexander of Battenberg (1857-1893)	Second son of Prince Alexander of Hesse-Darmstadt and nephew of Tsar Alexander II of Russia, appointed prince of Bulgaria; forced to abdicate by Russians
1886–1887	Stambulov, Karavelov, Mutkusov	Regency appointed by Prince Alexander; resigned when Prince Ferdinand was elected.
1887–1918	Ferdinand of Saxe-Coburg (1861-1948)	Son of Prince August of Saxe-Coburg-Gotha; bore title of Prince to 1908, when he declared Bulgaria independent of Turkey and called himself Tsar; abdicated on defeat in World War I
1918–1943	Boris III (1894-1943)	Son of Ferdinand; died mysteriously
1943–1946	Simeon II (1937-)	Only son of Boris III and Queen Ioanna (Princess Giovanna, daughter of Victor Emmanuel III of Italy); lost throne on referendum
	Bulgarian People's Republic (1946-)	

tween Moscow and Belgrade changed, so did relations between Belgrade and Sofia. When Khrushchev launched the
de-Stalinization campaign in February 1956, the Bulgarian
leaders hesitated for a long time before adopting any liberalizing measures, but in April a half-hearted effort was made
to conform to the new "softer" line of Moscow. Vulko
Chervenkov was subjected to mild criticism in Parliament as
an exponent of the "personality cult" and, as a result, relinquished his post of prime minister to Anton Yugov, though
remaining a strong influence in the background. Former
Communist leader Traicho Kostov, who had been executed
in 1948 for alleged "Titoism," was posthumously rehabili-
tated. In the months that followed, certain economic concessions were granted to workers and peasants. But politically there was no liberalization. The regime kept tight control over the political and intellectual life of the country.
Police terror returned at the time of the Hungarian revolt in
October 1956: suspected persons were imprisoned or sent
out of the large cities, students were expelled from the universities, and potential opponents were threatened with
drastic measures. In spite of the continuous boasting of the
regime that the economy was growing fast, by the summer
of 1957 unemployment had become so serious a problem
that thousands of Bulgarian youths had to be sent to the
Soviet Union and Czechoslovakia to relieve the situation.
Bulgarian Communist leaders became alarmed when, in July
1957, Khrushchev carried out a purge of pro-Stalinists in the
Soviet Union, for they had pursued, on the whole, a Stalinist policy and their future existence seemed to depend on
whether or not the new Soviet leaders could trust them.

N. P.

BULGARIAN, the language of the Bulgarians, spoken in
Bulgaria, in the neighboring regions of Yugoslav and Greek
Macedonia, and in Greek and Turkish Thrace. There are
also Bulgarian colonies in the Dobruja, in Walachia, and in
Bessarabia. The total number of speakers of Bulgarian dialects is approximately 6,570,000 of whom some 5,275,000 are
in Bulgaria, 111,000 in the Soviet Union, 364,000 in Romania, 646,000 in Yugoslavia, 75,000 in Turkey, and 99,000 in
Greece. Bulgarian is a Slavic language of the Southern
group, like Serbo-Croatian and Slovenian; but it has entered
with other non-Slavic Balkan languages, Greek, Romanian,
and Albanian, into a linguistic alliance which has entirely
changed its structure. As a result, it now may be said to be
the most modern or "Western" of the Slavic languages.

The main characteristics of the Balkan group to which
Bulgarian belongs are the following: (1) the creation of a
postposed article, as in Bulgarian *selo-to,* "the village"; (2)
the loss of declension, which is replaced by the use of prepo-
sitions, as in English and the Romance languages; (3) the
loss of the infinitive, which is replaced by the conjunction *da*
with the finite verb in the indicative; (4) an enormous use
of parataxis instead of hypotaxis; and (5) the use of countless
idioms, proverbs, and expressions of every kind. In other
words, Bulgarian is essentially an analytical language,
whereas all other Slavic languages are synthetic, like Latin,
Old Greek, and Sanskrit. Most of these Balkanic innovations
seem to have started from Middle or Modern Greek. The
main phonological difference between Bulgarian and the
other Slavic languages is that proto-Slavic *ty* and *kt* become
št, and **dy* becomes *žd;* thus, **svetya,* "light" is Bulgarian
svešta, *noktis is *nošt* (Russian *noč'*), and **widyo* is *viždam.*

Bulgarian may be divided into three main periods: Old
Bulgarian (also called Old Church Slavic), from the ninth
to the eleventh century; Middle Bulgarian, from the twelfth
to the fifteenth century; and Modern Bulgarian, from the

sixteenth century onward. The main transformation of Bulgarian into an analytic language started in the Middle Bulgarian period.

The Bulgarians were orginally not Slavs, but an Asiatic
people speaking an Altaic language akin to modern Chuvash
(the name Bulgarian means Volga-people). The Altaic element has completely disappeared from their speech, however, unless it is true, as some believe, that they preserve a
residue of less than a dozen Altaic words. As a result of the
long Turkish domination, Bulgarian naturally received many
Turkish words and even a few suffixes, including *-če, -lj,* and
-lek. It has also absorbed many Greek words and, mainly
through Greek, many Italian ones. Bulgarian is written in
Cyrillic characters. *See also* LINGUISTIC ALLIANCE; OLD
CHURCH SLAVIC; SLAVIC.   G. B.

BULGARIAN LITERATURE. Old Bulgarian literature was written in Old Church Slavonic by the disciples
of Saints Cyril and Methodius who were settled by Tsar
Boris (reigned 853-888) in Ohrid and Preslav. Their work
in translating the Church books and the Fathers was continued with translations of the Chronicles and with original sermons and lives of Bulgarian saints. The Turkish conquest
put a stop to this work, and under the rule of the Ottoman
Empire and the Greek Patriarch of Constantinople, literature was reduced to mere collections of religious and proverbial writings, the so-called *Damascenes.*

The revival started with the *History of the Slav Bulgarians*
(1762) by Father Paisii of the Monastery of Hilendar on
Mount Athos (1722- ?), which called attention to the
glorious past of the Bulgarian Empire and revived the long-
forgotten aspirations of the people. For the next century,
the writers were more interested in developing the modern
language, teaching the people, and preparing the movement
of national liberation than in literature in the narrow sense
of the word. Petko Rachev Slaveykov (1827-1895) was
the first important poet. Before the liberation, the great poet,
however, was Hristo Botev (1848-1876), who died in an
ill-fated attempt to free his country. His 22 poems marked
the high point of lyric and patriotic verse.

Once independence was won, in 1877, literature developed rapidly and Ivan Vazov (1850-1921) was long the
acknowledged leader. During more than fifty years of
activity, he created all forms of literature—poetry, novels,
short stories, and dramas. His greatest novel was *Under the
Yoke* (1894), on the war for liberation, but his works reflect
all the changing fortunes of the Bulgarian people. He was
seconded by the other writers of prose, Konstantin Velichkov
(1855-1907), Todor G. Vlaykov (1865-1943), Anton Stras-
himirov (1872-1937), Stoyan Mikhaylovski (1856-1927), and
Aleko Konstantinov (1863-1897).

The next generation, led by such poets as Pencho Slaveykov
(1866-1912), Peyo Kracholov Yavorov (1876-1914), and
Petko Yu. Todorov (1879-1916), drew for their inspiration
on European literatures as well as on their native scene.
Pencho Slavey Kov, Petko's son, became the leader of the in-
dividualist school. He reached perfection in his lyrical poems.

With the Balkan Wars of 1912 and 1913, misfortune
came upon the Bulgarian people, who again and again paid
the price of joining the defeated side in an endeavor to
recover what they felt were their natural boundaries. A new
mood of disillusionment and often of mysticism appeared
along with a growing sense of artistic refinement and bor-
rowings from the European symbolists. Among the poets
of this period are Dimcho Debelyanov (1887-1916), Nikolay
Raynov (1889-   ), Todor Trayanov (1882-1944), Nikolay

Liliyev (1876-), and Elizavyeta Bagryana. In prose the leading authors were Yordan Yovkov (1884-1938) and Georgi Raychev (1882-).

After World War I, and the ensuing period of political unrest, two tendencies developed. The one was the peasant and provincial story as exemplified by the *Brothers* of Dobri Nemirov (1882-) and stories by Angel Karaliychev (1902-). The other was the rise of the historical novel with an often crude glorification of the Bulgarian past. The life of the cities has been relatively neglected as a subject for literature. Dimitar Shishmanov (1889-1945) with his *Shadows on the Acropolis* was the chief writer to develop a really cosmopolitan and yet patriotic outlook on the world.

In criticism, Bulgarian literature has been grouped around such periodicals as the symbolist *Hyperion* and the *Zlatorog* with its search for artistic perfection. Yordan Badev is, perhaps, the leading critic who seeks to evaluate the authors for their work and skill without regard to the theories of the different schools. World War II has introduced a new period, stressing those Communist elements which had previously been rejected by the Bulgarian people, and these will undoubtedly be an important factor in the future development of the literature.   C. A. M.

BULGE, BATTLE OF THE. *See* WORLD WAR II.

BULKELEY, MORGAN G. (1837-1922), insurance executive, legislator, and first president of the National Baseball League, was born at East Haddam, Conn., Dec. 26, 1837. Bank president, lawyer, and Civil War veteran, Bulkeley was president of the Hartford (Conn.) Charter Oaks Baseball Club when the National League was organized in 1876. Named the league's first president, he placed it on a firm basis with his dynamic leadership. After one year as league president, he was made president of the Aetna Life Insurance Company. He became mayor of Hartford (1880), and was governor of Connecticut (1888-1893), and United States senator (1905-1911). Bulkeley served on the commission that authenticated the origin of baseball, and in 1937 was named to the Baseball Hall of Fame for meritorious service to the sport. He died Nov. 6, 1922, at his home in Hartford.
M. Bg.

BULL, JOHN (1563-1628), English composer and organist, was born in Somersetshire in 1563. He became one of the most important composers of the Elizabethan Age, an age characterized by the excellence of its music. After a period of training at the Chapel Royal, he was made organist of Hereford Cathedral in 1582. In 1585 he was appointed Master of the Children at the Chapel Royal, and in 1591 became its organist for Queen Elizabeth. On the recommendation of Queen Elizabeth, he was appointed professor of music at Gresham College in 1596. Not knowing Latin, he was granted special permission to lecture in English. In accordance with the school regulations, Bull was forced to resign from this institution when he married in 1607. In 1611 he was in the employ of the Prince of Wales as musician. Soon after he proceeded to Belgium where, in 1613, he was appointed organist in the Archduke's Chapel at Brussels. In 1617 he accepted the post of organist at Antwerp Cathedral. While in Belgium, John Bull made the acquaintance of Jan P. Sweelinck. He and Sweelinck greatly affected the development of contrapuntal-keyboard music. Bull is credited with more than two hundred compositions for the organ, virginal, and voice. Most of these have remained in manuscript form. The difficulty of many of his compositions demonstrate that Bull must have been an

extremely good performer. He died at Antwerp on Mar. 13, 1628.   E. B. A.

BULL, OLAF (1883-1933), Norwegian poet, was born in Oslo, Nov. 10, 1883, the son of a popular novelist, Jacob Breda Bull. His life included an unconventional, unsettled existence, some of it spent in Copenhagen, Rome, and Paris, where he received deep impressions from the French symbolists and Henri Bergson. His first collection of poems appeared in 1909, his last in 1930; together they fill two slender volumes, in which he creatively and movingly elaborates such themes as the coming of spring, the passing of love and beauty, the meaning of life, and the mystery of death. Through his symbolism and subtle assonances he created a form that appealed more to the few than the many; reflective, though not always melancholy, he emphasized the power of remembrance to recreate beauty out of the past in a way that is reminiscent of John Keats. He died on June 23, 1933.   E. H.

BULL, in the financial or commercial sense, is one who anticipates an upward movement of prices. It may also be used to describe such a movement, e.g., a rise in prices may be termed a "bull movement" and a rising market a "bull market."   H. C. S.

BULL, PAPAL (from Lat. *bulla,* a leaden seal), the most solemn form of papal document, until the eleventh century written on papyrus, thenceforth on parchment, and invariably since the ninth century describing its papal author as "bishop, servant of the servants of God." Its name derives from the leaden seal, attached by laces of hemp or silk and bearing the pope's name on one side, with the heads of Sts. Peter and Paul on the other. The oldest papyrus bull extant is dated Jan. 22, 788, although extant seals from lost documents are two centuries older. A distinction between "great bulls" and "little bulls" dates from the eleventh century. The latter were less solemn; some of them embodied, for example, the administrative decretals upon which the science of canon law was later constructed. From them also developed the simpler papal document known since 1431 as a "brief." The rare *bullae aureae* (golden bulls) were those for which golden seals were used, instead of lead, in token of exceptional solemnity. A famous example is the bull conferring the title of "defender of the faith" upon King Henry VIII. Until 1878 bulls continued to be written as in medieval times, in archaic Gothic script, characterized by manifold contractions and with no punctuation; because this script was so difficult, it became customary to issue an accompanying copy in ordinary handwriting. However, since the pontificate of Pope Leo XIII from 1878 to 1903, bulls have been written in clear Roman script and, for greater facility in transmission by mail, the leaden seal is often replaced by a red stamp bearing the same device.   J. J. B.

BULLARD, ROBERT LEE [buʼlərd] (1861-1947), American soldier, was born on Jan. 15, 1861, in Youngsborough, Ala. He graduated from the Alabama Agricultural and Mechanical College in 1880, taught school at Opelika, Ala., and in 1881 he was admitted to the United States Military Academy at West Point from which he graduated in 1885. Commissioned a second lieutenant, he participated in operations against the Apache Indians in Arizona and served in the Southwest until the Spanish-American War. In 1898 he was chosen colonel of the Third Alabama Volunteers and in 1899 was appointed colonel of the Thirty-ninth

United States Volunteer Infantry. In 1902, as a major, he was transferred to the Twenty-eighth Infantry in the Philippines, where, in central Mindanao, he established the first Moro government. From 1907 to 1908 he was attached to the American provisional government of Cuba; in 1911 he was promoted to the rank of colonel in the Regular Army. He attended the Army War College in Washington, D. C., graduating in 1912, having served on the Mexican border in 1911; he served there again in 1917. With the entry of the United States into World War I, Bullard was sent to France in command of the Second Brigade, First Division. Shortly thereafter he was promoted to major general and placed in command of the First Division, which was to be the first American division to take its place in the front lines. In 1918 he was appointed commander of the Third Army Corps, and in October of the same year promoted to lieutenant general in command of the United States Second Army. He distinguished himself in the battle for the reduction of the Marne salient, and in the Meuse-Argonne offensive, acquiring the nickname of "Counterattack Bullard" for his refusal to halt attacking operations. In 1919 he returned to the United States and assumed command of the Second Corps Area, where he remained until his retirement in 1925. He then became president of the National Security League, an organization devoted to the promotion of peacetime military preparedness. Bullard died at Governor's Island, N.Y., on Sept. 11, 1947. He published *Personalities and Reminiscences of the War* (1925), *American Soldiers Also Fought* (1936), and *Fighting Generals* (1944).

BULLDOG. *See* DOG.
BULLDOZER. *See* EXCAVATORS.

BULLFIGHTING, the custom of holding public contests between bulls and men. It is an ancient custom, not confined to any particular age or ethnic group. Early historical records tell of bullfighting being practiced in Korea, China, Egypt, Greece, and Rome in the pre-Christian era. Its origin

EWING GALLOWAY, NEW YORK

At a bullfight at Quito, Ecuador, the matador executes a veronica in maneuvering the bull around the ring.

apparently is to be sought in some form of nature worship—as a ritual intended to promote agricultural fertility. As a modern custom, bullfighting is the national pastime of Spain. It is also practiced in Mexico, the largest arena in the world being located in Mexico City, and in Central and South American countries. Portugal also has bullfights, but, unlike those in Spain, they are bloodless and are chiefly tests of horsemanship.

Development in Spain. In Spain, the country most commonly associated with the custom, bullfighting was introduced by the Moors and was a favorite sport during their long occupation. The Moorish chieftains interested the Spanish nobility in bullfighting, and a keen rivalry developed. In the middle of the eleventh century the great Cid, Don Rodrigo Díaz de Bivar, is said to have been the first

EWING GALLOWAY, NEW YORK

The matador thrusts his estoque into the bull in an attempt to kill him.

Spaniard to kill a bull in the ring. This he did, with a lance.

For six hundred years, the toreador, mounted on a horse and armed with a long lance, played the chief role in bullfighting. The first unmounted professional to fight a bull in the arena was the Spaniard, Francisco Romero, of Rondo, Andalucia, in about 1700. He was the first matador to employ the sword as a weapon for killing the bull; and he also introduced the muleta, a red flag attached to a short staff, used in "playing," or maneuvering, the bull around the ring.

Since then the mounted toreador has become obsolete, and the matador ("killer of the bull"), who fights entirely on foot, has played the chief role in the Spanish bullfight (*corrida de toros*). The matador's assistants in the fight include three or four *banderilleros* and two or three *picadors*. The function of the *banderilleros* is to "play" the bull with their capes and to plant the *banderillas,* which are slender shafts about 30 in. long, trimmed with colored streamers and having at one end a harpoon-shaped steel point. The *picadors,* mounted on old and worn-out horses, wound the bull, but not mortally, with their long, steel-pointed lances. A matador serves a long apprenticeship before participating in a major *corrida.* Frequently gored in fighting, he leads a hazardous life. A noted performer may receive a fee (out of which he pays his assistants) as high as $10,000 for a single afternoon's fighting; he is also given a place in the public esteem similar to that of an outstanding baseball player in the United States. Among the great matadors of Spain are Rafael Molina y Sánchez (1841-1900), known as Lagartijo; Salvador Sánchez (1842-1898), known as Frasculeo; José Gómez Ortega (1895-1920), known as Joselito or El Gallito; Rafael Ortega Gómez (1916-1940); Manolete (1917-1947); and Juan Belmonte y Garcia (1892-   ).

Bullfighting spectacles are held in a *plaza de toros,* a special arena enclosed by a wooden barrier (*barrera*) about 4 ft. high.

There are over two hundred of these arenas in the larger towns and cities of Spain, with seating capacities ranging from a few hundred to 12,000, as in the large arena at Madrid. More than 1,000 bulls and 5,000 horses are slain annually in Spain. The bulls are of a special breed raised in the provinces and known for fighting qualities. Fighting bulls must weigh not less than 542 kilos, or 1,194 lb.; they must be from four to five years old, free of physical defects, and armed with sharp horns.

The bullfighting season in Spain begins about the first of March and continues until the middle of November. The fights are held on Sunday afternoons and on festive holidays. Usually, in each *corrida,* six bulls are killed by three different matadors, who account for two bulls apiece according to a formalized sequence of maneuvers designed to display the skill and the courage of the matador and the power and bravery of the bull.

Sequence of Spanish Bullfight. The spectacle of bullfighting presents a series of acts culminating in the killing of the bull. As a prelude, mounted arena officials (*alguacils*) and all those who will take part in the subsequent bullfights parade around the arena in brightly colored costumes. Then the bull is released from a darkened pen where he has been held for some hours. Once in the open, goaded by a beribboned metal spike planted in his shoulder just before entering the arena, the bull faces the *banderilleros,* who, on foot, flaunt their capes before him, playing the animal so that the matador can observe its fighting characteristics, its manner of charging, and its way of hooking its horns. The matador also takes his turn with the *capa,* or fighting cape, executing difficult "passes" such as the *veronica* to demonstrate his skill and his mastery of the bull.

Following these preliminary maneuvers, aimed at wearing down the bull, comes the actual bullfight, which is divided into three parts (*suertes*). The first act (*suerte de picar*) begins when the signal is given to the *picadors* to enter the arena on decrepit horses. Since 1927 the law has required that the belly of the horse be protected by mattress armor, and that the picador wear leg armor. It is the function of the picador to make a gash with his lance between the shoulder blades of the bull as the animal charges the horse. The wound must not be too deep, and should serve as an aid to the matador when he gives his final *coup de grâce.* In case a horse is gored, the *banderilleros* with their capes stand ready to distract the bull from the fallen *picador.*

For the second act (*suerte de banderillear*) the *banderilleros* put aside their capes. Each *banderillero* takes up instead, in either hand, two *banderillas,* which he attempts to plant in the massive neck muscles of the bull, around the wound made by the picador. If successfully placed, the six or eight *banderillas* aid the matador by causing the bull to lower its head and by checking any tendency of the animal to hook with its horns.

In the last act (*suerte de matar*) the matador is alone with the bull. He is now familiar with its fighting characteristics, and is ready for the death blow. His reputation as a slayer of bulls is at stake. He is armed with a sword, which he holds in his right hand; in his left hand is the muleta, with which he manipulates the bull into a favored position. The death thrust with the sword must be made from in front and must be placed between the bull's shoulder blades, according to rules and long-standing custom. After the bull has been killed, its carcass is dragged from the arena by a team of three mules. The arena is then scraped, and sawdust is spread over the bloody patches in preparation for the next fight.

Portuguese Bullfighting. In Portugal, the toreador, mounted on a horse, is still the chief figure in bullfighting. His aim, however, is merely to evade the rushes of the bull. Should the bull barely touch the horse with its horns, the tips of which have been covered protectively, the crowd in the stands loudly voices its disapproval. The fight terminates when the bull has become exhausted. The animal is then driven from the arena by the toreador's team of assistants.   L. C. S.

BULLFINCH, any one of several species of small, heavy-billed Old World finches of the genus *Pyrrhula.* The best-known form is *P. pyrrhula* of Europe and western Asia. The male has the face, crown, nape, wings, and tail blue-black; the mantle blue-gray; the rump white; and the sides of the head and neck and the under parts deep rose-pink. The female is similar, but its mantle is gray-brown and the under parts are brown with a pinkish tinge. The bullfinch feeds mainly on insects, weed seeds, and berries; at certain seasons it is destructive to gardens by eating the young buds of fruit trees. It is popular as a cage bird, both for its pleasing colors and for its ability to learn to whistle simple airs.   H. G. De.

BULLFROG, *Rana catesbiana,* the largest frog in North America, ranging from Canada to Mexico east of the Rocky Mountains, and named from the loud, bellowing call which

COURTESY OF U.S. FISH AND WILDLIFE SERVICE

BULLFROG, RANA CATESBIANA

may be heard half a mile. Some specimens are 8 in. long, with another 9 in. of stretched hind leg. The frog's back is blotched, drab or blackish-green, while the under parts are yellowish white. Solitary in habits, it is one of the most aquatic of frogs. The tadpoles often attain large size, and remain as larvae for more than two years before metamorphosis. Very voracious, grown bullfrogs often eat small birds, other frogs, and salamanders, in addition to insects. In turn, man considers the large hind legs a delicacy. Attempts have been made to farm frogs, but most of the frogs acquired for eating purposes are caught from the wild.   A. Sv.

BULLHEAD, any of several species of catfish of the genus *Ictalurus* (*Ameiurus*), found in ponds and streams of the middle and eastern United States and Canada. They are catfish of the family Ictaluridae. The common species are the brown bullhead, which is the horned pout of New England; the yellow bullhead; and the black bullhead. They are easily recognized by the naked body, the small adipose or fleshy fin on the back near the tail, and the four pairs of long fleshy barbels surrounding the mouth. Strong, pointed, pectoral and dorsal spines make it difficult to remove a fishhook. Bullheads are a highly regarded food fish in some areas. They seldom exceed a foot in length. During the breeding season the sticky eggs are laid in a circular nest near shore. The male bullhead guards first the eggs and later the young fish, as long as they stay in schools. E. C. R.

BULLINGER, HEINRICH [bʊ'lɪŋər] (1504-1575), Swiss Protestant reformer, born at Bremgarten in Aargau, Switzerland, July 18, 1504. The son of a Roman Catholic priest, Bullinger was sent to the Brothers of the Common Life school at Emmerich in Westphalia and entered the University of Cologne in 1519. He read the works of Martin Luther and Melanchthon (Philipp Schwarzert) and was converted to Protestantism, later becoming a disciple of Huldreich Zwingli. He was appointed teacher at the Cistercian monastery of Kappel, Switzerland, in 1523, but he accompanied Zwingli to a conference with the Anabaptists at Zürich in 1525 and to one with the southern German theologians at Bern in 1528. In 1529 he was appointed pastor of the Reformed Church at Bremgarten. He witnessed the battle of Kappel, Oct. 11, 1531, at which Zwingli was killed and the Catholic cantons defeated Bern and Zürich, but Bullinger escaped to Zürich, where he was appointed pastor of the Gross Münster as successor to Zwingli. He corresponded

is effectively defined in terms of gold but gold is not coined, the country is said to have a gold-bullion monetary standard. Advantages of this standard include economy in the use of gold and a higher degree of concentration of monetary reserves. After World War I gold-bullion standards became prevalent in the leading nations. S. E. B.

BULL KELP, *Nereocystis luetkeana,* a gigantic seaweed with long, cablelike stem, solid at the lower end, but hollow at the upper end, terminating in a large bulb, beyond which the leaves are borne. It occurs in the Pacific coastal waters from California northward. J. C. Wis.

BULL ROARER, a flat, oval, wooden slab, tapering at either end, which is whirled around on a string to produce a roaring noise as it rotates through the air. Among primitive peoples the bull roarer was usually associated with magic or religion. In Australia, New Guinea, and elsewhere it was employed in initiation rites, where it represented the voice of spirits. Among the Indians of the southwestern United States its booming symbolized thunder, and it was used in ceremonies to produce rain. H. T.

BULL RUN or **MANASSAS** [mənæ'səs], two important engagements (July 21, 1861, and Aug. 30, 1862) of the Civil War, called the battles of Bull Run after a stream in northeastern Virginia near which the battles were fought, or,

BATTLE OF BULL RUN
A desperate struggle on a bridge during the retreat of the Union Army from Manassas during the American Civil War

EWING GALLOWAY, NEW YORK

widely with Protestant leaders, attempting to reconcile the theological differences among them. In 1549 Bullinger and John Calvin brought about the unification of the churches of Geneva and Zürich, the *Consensus Tigurinus* on the Lord's Supper sealing the accord. Bullington also wrote the second Helvetic Confession, made public in 1566. This united the Evangelical Reformed Churches. He died in Zürich, Sept. 17, 1575. S. D.

BULLION, precious metals when held uncoined, as in the form of bars; also the commodity value of coins. Standard bullion in the United States contains nine-tenths pure gold and one-tenth copper alloy. When a nation's monetary unit

by the Confederates, the battles of Manassas, after the town.

1. The First Battle of Bull Run was a preliminary test of strength between the opposing sides, as the Union and the Confederacy rapidly organized their forces for war. Lincoln's call for troops had brought thousands of untrained militia into Washington, and Northern enthusiasm demanded a movement "On to Richmond" before the ninety-day enlistments expired. Yielding to popular pressure, General Winfield Scott outlined a plan of campaign. The Union forces in Virginia consisted of 35,000 men along the Potomac River opposite Washington, under General Irvin McDowell; 20,000 under General Robert Patterson in the Shenandoah Valley, and 10,000 at Hampton Roads under General B. F. Butler. A

Confederate army of 43,000 men under General P. G. T. Beauregard was at Manassas Junction; 10,000 men under General John B. Magruder were near Hampton Roads, Va.; and 10,000 under General Joseph E. Johnston were watching Patterson in the Shenandoah Valley. Scott proposed that McDowell attack Beauregard, while Butler retained Magruder and Patterson prevented Johnston from joining Beauregard. Patterson, however, retreated, and Johnston hastened to join Beauregard. McDowell, uncertain as to the changed situation, attacked Beauregard on the morning of July 21. Advancing across Bull Run Creek and storming the plateau of Manassas, the Union forces pushed the Confederates back more than 2,000 yd. before a stand, led by General T. J. Jackson, thereafter called "Stonewall" Jackson, halted the retreat. From noon until 3 P.M. the two armies fought desperately. In midafternoon the advance contingent of Johnston's force, 2,000 men under General E. Kirby Smith, began to reach the battlefield. The Federal troops were forced into a slow retirement from the field, which then turned into a confused rout. The Confederates, as inexperienced in warfare as their opponents, failed to follow up their advantage. The Union casualties were 460 killed, 1,124 wounded, and 1,312 captured or missing; the Confederates lost 1,982 killed and wounded. The battle convinced the North that the war was not to be a "ninety-day picnic," and that there was urgent need for drastic military, economic, and other measures.

2. The Second Battle of Bull Run, on Aug. 29-30, 1862, was fought over approximately the same ground as the first. General R. E. Lee's army, in two corps commanded by Generals James Longstreet and Stonewall Jackson, drawn up along the Rappahannock, faced a Federal army under General John Pope, who had just been called from the West and placed in command of the Army of the Potomac. Hoping to defeat Pope before reinforcements could arrive, Lee sent Jackson with 25,000 men around Pope's army to cut off the railroad over which Union supplies came. After several days of maneuvering, on August 29 Pope turned on Jackson, who with difficulty held his ground. By noon Longstreet had joined Jackson; Pope's men also received reinforcements. Pope ordered General Fitz-John Porter to turn Jackson's right. But Porter, realizing the odds against him, refused to sacrifice his men. Pope attacked elsewhere and was repulsed. By nightfall the Confederates were in position, and Pope's army had suffered reverses in the day's attacks. On August 30, Pope sent Porter against Lee's center, but Porter failed to make headway. Then Lee's whole line, 4 mi. long, made a general attack. The Union forces, not in proper alignment to meet the assault, were driven back. The main objective of the Union forces was to hold two elevated points, Bald Hill and Henry House Hill. They succeeded in holding the latter, while the main body of the Federal forces withdrew across Bull Run Creek in orderly retreat. Heavy rain delayed the pursuit and made possible the retreat of Pope's army into the protection of the Washington defenses. Panic struck the city, and the government called all available troops to its defense. In the battle the Federals had about 63,000 men and the Confederates 54,000. The casualties from August 16 to September 2 were about 9,100 men for the Confederates; Pope's losses totaled about 14,500 men. Pope was relieved from his command as a consequence of his defeat.   W. B. H.

BULLSNAKE, broadly any snake of the North American genus *Pituophis*, but most frequently *P. Catenifer sayi*, is one of the largest (growing to 7 ft. 8 in.), best-known, and best-liked American serpents. Like its close relatives the pine and gopher snakes, its snout is designed for bur-

rowing and its epiglottis is modified for loud hissing. From Wisconsin to Alberta and south to Mexico these prairie snakes consume so many destructive rodents that they are generally protected by landowners. Large numbers are killed by automobiles, however, on the highways of the Great Plains. Large, docile, and brightly patterned, bullsnakes are used in many "snake-charming" shows.   M. G. N.

BÜLOW, PRINCE BERNHARD VON [bülo] (1849-1929), German diplomat, was born at Klein-Flottbek, Holstein, May 3, 1849. Although educated for the law, he chose diplomacy as his career, and after filling subordinate posts in Athens, Paris, and St. Petersburg he was appointed minister to Romania in 1888 and ambassador to Italy in 1894. In 1897 Bülow was appointed secretary of state for foreign affairs and in 1900 became chancellor of the German Empire, heading the government from 1900 to 1909. Bülow's conduct during and after the *Daily Telegraph* interview in 1907, revealing Kaiser Wilhelm II's policy toward England, embittered the Kaiser, who in July 1909 dismissed his former favorite. Early in World War I he was again sent to Rome as ambassador, but his special mission proved fruitless when, in May 1915, Italy joined Germany's enemies. Besides his *Deutsche Politik* (1914), a defense of his policy, Bülow wrote *Imperial Germany* and later dictated four volumes of indiscreet but well-written *Memoirs,* which were published posthumously. After living for fifteen years in retirement, he died in Rome, Oct. 28, 1929.   R. H. L.

BÜLOW, HANS VON [bü'lo] (1830-1894) (full title: Hans Guido, Freiherr von Bülow), German pianist, composer, and conductor, was born in Dresden, Jan. 8, 1830, the son of Eduard von Bülow, a well-known author. In early youth Hans showed no interest in music but at the age of nine he began to study piano with Friedrich Wieck, father of Clara Schumann, who laid the foundation for his later superb technique. From 1841 to 1845, he studied with Adolf Friedrich Hesse, Moritz Hauptmann, Louis Plaidy, and Max Karl Eberwein, making constant progress. In 1848 he entered the University of Leipzig to take up law, and in 1849 he attended the University of Berlin. Soon thereafter Bülow renounced the study of law for a musical career. At Zürich, under Wagner's direction, he did some theatrical conducting. Bülow began to study pianoforte under Liszt at Weimar in June 1851, and in 1853 made his first concert tour, visiting Vienna, Budapest, Dresden, Karlsruhe, Bremen, Hamburg, and Berlin. From 1855 until 1864 he was principal master of pianoforte at the Berlin conservatory of Professors Stern and Marx. On concert tours through Germany, the Netherlands, and Russia, he won new laurels as a conductor and virtuoso. In 1857 he married Liszt's daughter Cosima who in 1869 left him and married Richard Wagner. Bülow became principal conductor of the Royal Opera at Munich in 1864, and director of the Munich Conservatorium in 1867. At the former he conducted the now historic first performances of *Tristan und Isolde* and *Die Meistersinger.* After his divorce in 1869 he left Munich; for some years concert tours become his main occupation. In 1878 Bülow was appointed *Kapellmeister* of the Hoftheater at Hannover and in 1880 become *Hofmusikintendant* to George, Duke of Saxe-Meiningen. For the next five years, the latter's orchestra was among the finest in Europe. Ill health in later life sent Bülow to the dry climate of Egypt. He died in Cairo, Feb. 12, 1894. In playing and conducting, Bülow's mastery of detail, analysis of effects, and warmth and spontaneity merited the highest praise. His symphonic compositions have not lived. The most interesting include

Op. 20, *Nirwana, symphonisches Stimmungsbild;* Op. 10, music to *Julius Caesar;* Op. 16, *Des Sängers Fluch;* Op. 23, *Vier Charakterstücke für Orchester;* and Op. 21, *Il Carnoväle di Milano.*

BULRUSH, *Scirpus,* a large genus of grasslike plants native the world over. The great bulrush (*S. lacustris*) grows to 9 ft. in shallow, quiet water in North America, Europe, and Asia. The green pithy stems are sometimes used for mats or chair bottoms. Other tall forms are the river bulrush (*S. fluviatilis*) and the California bulrush (*S. californicus*). The common rush (*Juncus effusus*), also used

pots in which both honey and pollen are stored. Mating takes place in the fall, the females alone surviving the winter. In the tropics, reproduction takes place throughout the year. Bumblebees of the genus *Psithyrus* are parasites of species of the genus *Bombus,* or *Bremus.*   C. H. Cu.

BUMPPO. *See* NATTY BUMPPO.
BUNA RUBBER. *See* RUBBER (*Synthetic Rubber*).

BUNAU-VARILLA, PHILIPPE JEAN [bü′no′ va′-ri′ya′] (1860-1940), French engineer and diplomat, was born in Paris, July 26, 1860. After his graduation from the École

BOTTOM RIGHT. P. J. VAN HUIZEN FOR U.S. FISH AND WILDLIFE SERVICE: OTHERS, W. F. KUBICHEK FOR U.S. FISH AND WILDLIFE SERVICE

(Top left) *Bulrushes, important food and cover plants for wildlife, are taken from an area of abundance for transplanting in areas of sparseness and along dikes (top right) to control erosion.* (Bottom left) *The result of bulrush plantings after a few years.* (Bottom right) *Closeup of snow geese rising from the bulrushes*

for weaving mats, is sometimes called bulrush, and in England the name is sometimes used for cattails (*Typha*). The bulrush of Egypt mentioned in the Bible was the papyrus.
                                                        J. C. Wis.

BULWER-CLAYTON TREATY. *See* CLAYTON-BULWER TREATY.

BULWER-LYTTON, EDWARD GEORGE EARLE LYTTON. *See* LYTTON, FIRST BARON (EDWARD GEORGE EARLE LYTTON BULWER-LYTTON).

BUMBLEBEE, the name given to members of the family Bombidae, of the order Hymenoptera. In England they are frequently called humblebees, in France *bourdons.* Bumblebees usually build their nests in the ground, the queens excavating the nest and caring for their offspring until workers are produced. The workers then take care of the developing offspring, and the colony grows rapidly. Instead of honeycombs, the bumblebees build round or oval honey

Polytechnique in 1880 he worked in Algiers and Tunis on government projects for the improvement of railroads and harbors. In 1884 he became associated with the Panama Canal enterprise of Ferdinand de Lesseps, and was appointed chief engineer in 1885. Besides suggesting many improvements in the original plans, he developed new engineering methods, such as his invention of an electric dredge for increased speed and greater economy of operation. Bunau-Varilla remained with de Lesseps until 1888, and when work on the canal later came to a standstill he was active in urging the United States to continue the project. He fought against the proposed canal through Nicaragua, and in 1902 he engineered the revolution which separated Panama from Colombia and permitted resumption of work on the canal. In 1903 he was appointed minister of the new republic of Panama to Washington and negotiated the treaty by which the United States acquired the rights to the Canal Zone. In 1904 he returned to Europe to become manager of the Madrid-Cáceres railroad. He also built the Congo railroad in West Africa, improved the navigable waters of Romania, and submitted designs for the first Paris subway system, which were later adopted. Bunau-Varilla died in Paris, May 18, 1940.   C. W. D.

BUNCHBERRY, *Cornus canadensis,* a low herb of the dogwood family, native in woods of northern North America. In the spring it grows small, greenish, sometimes purple

COURTESY OF THE BROOKLYN BOTANIC GARDEN

BUNCHBERRY, CORNUS CANADENSIS

flowers, in a dense head surrounded by four white bracts, giving the appearance of one large single flower. They are produced above the whorl of leaves at the top of the upright stem. Bright red berries borne in a bunch provide the plant with its most common name. It is also called dwarf cornel.
                                                    G. M. Sm.

BUNCHE, RALPH JOHNSON (1904-   ), American educator, political scientist and United Nations mediator, was born in Detroit, Mich., on Aug. 7, 1904. He was educated at the University of California and at Harvard and became dean of the political science department of Howard University in 1937. During World War II he served with the Office of Strategic Services and the State Department. In 1946 he joined the United Nations, and when Count Folke Bernadotte, United Nations mediator in Palestine, was assassinated in September 1948, Bunche was appointed to succeed him and was chiefly responsible for restoring peace in the Holy Land in 1949. He then returned to the United States to resume his duties as senior director of the United Nations Trusteeship Division. For his achievements as United Nations mediator, Bunche was named winner of the 1950 Nobel Peace Prize, becoming the first Negro to win the award. In 1950, he was appointed to the faculty of Harvard University as professor of government but was given an indefinite leave of absence immediately to work with the United Nations.   W. A. W.

BUNCHFLOWER, *Melanthium,* a group of showy plants in the lily family, native to the eastern United States. The small, whitish flowers are borne in large numbers in a single, erect, pyramidal panicle, topping the coarse, leafy stem. *M. virginicum,* which favors wet situations, has been brought into cultivation. The linear leaves may become 12

in. long; the plants, from 2½ to 5 ft. high, growing from a stout rhizome.

BUNIN, IVAN ALEXEYEVICH [bu′nyɪn] (1870-1953), Russian novelist and poet, was born in the town of Voronezh on Oct. 10, 1870, to a noble family. Bunin was graduated from the Yelets Gymnasium and attended the University of Moscow for one year. His first book, a volume of verse, was published in 1891. In 1903 he was awarded the Pushkin Prize for literature largely for his translations of poetry, including that of Longfellow's *Hiawatha.* In 1909 he was elected an honorary member of the Russian Academy. He fled from Russia following the Revolution, and lived in western Europe until his death in Paris on Nov. 8, 1953.

In 1910-1911 Bunin wrote a novel, *The Village,* in which he vividly described the dying patriarchal life of the Russian peasantry, and this work placed him immediately in the forefront of Russian novelists. There followed the short stories, *The Gentleman from San Francisco, Brothers, Mitia's Love, The Affair of Cornet Yelagin,* and many others. His last full-length novel was *The Life of Arseniev.* More recently there appeared a book of his short stories, entitled *The Dark Alleys.*

Bunin cannot be fully identified with any one school of literature. He cannot be classed with the Russian Symbolists or the Decadents, because of the importance he attaches to realistic detail in depicting the life and psychology of his characters. Nor, on the other hand, can he be identified with the Social-Realists, because of the extreme individualism and the aestheticism that he brings to bear in the treatment of realistically drawn characters. The combination of these traits establishes him closest to the Neo-Realists, those Russian writers of the beginning of the twentieth century who attempted to combine in their art the traditions of Russian classical realism with the new point of view very close to symbolism. The underlying theme of Bunin's art is the contrast of beauty and the eternal life of nature with transitory human life. Bunin humbly accepts the inevitable end of every individual personality, saying that it is only love that is capable of sustaining man in these circumstances; love is the last straw at which he clutches, but love itself and its beauty are doomed to die as a result of the conditions prevailing on earth.

Bunin is one of the finest of Russian stylists. His language is remarkably clear and precise. In his description of nature and his psychologically realistic approach to human characters, he can be considered the successor of Leo Tolstoy, though his sense of irony is more profound. He was awarded the Nobel Prize for literature in 1933.   M. T.

BUNKER HILL, BATTLE OF (June 17, 1775), one of the earliest engagements of the American Revolution. Actually the battle was fought on Breed's Hill, somewhat nearer Boston, but the general impression at the time was that it took place on the more strategically valuable Bunker Hill. The British general, Thomas Gage, was besieged in the town of Boston by American troops during the summer of 1775. The Americans had failed, however, to occupy and fortify Bunker Hill, to the north, and Dorchester Heights, to the south—the two elevations which commanded the town. It was rumored that General Gage planned to take them; anticipating this move, the Americans decided to forestall him. On the night of June 16 more than 1,000 American troops, under the command of Colonel William Prescott, marched over Charlestown Neck, beyond Bunker Hill, and up Breed's Hill. Their fortifications were completed by dawn

THE BATTLE OF BUNKER HILL
FROM AN ENGRAVING BY S. N. GIMBREDE FROM A PAINTING BY JOHN TRUMBULL

of June 17. The American general, Israel Putnam, then moved the trenching tools to Bunker Hill and began fortifying it. The British vessels in the Charles River cannonaded the Americans during the morning, and the British began moving troops across from Boston to the east side of Breed's Hill. American reinforcements were slow in arriving because Colonel Prescott and the other American commanders, not being certain which of their positions would come under attack first, held their troops in check. At least two generals, Putnam and Joseph Warren, were on the same field without troops. Some 3,000 British troops, led by General Sir William Howe, started the march up Breed's Hill, covered by fire from British ships in the river. They were met by withering volleys from the Americans and driven back. This happened twice, but the third time the British were successful, for American powder was running out. General John Stark, one of the American commanders, had kept an escape route open, and the Americans were able to retreat over Charlestown Neck. The British dead amounted to more than one-third of their 3,000 men; the Americans lost about 400. The battle was hailed as a moral victory for the Americans, incredibly bad though their tactics had been, for they had inflicted heavy casualties on the best of British regulars. It resulted also in the recall of General Gage and his replacement by General Sir William Howe, who had personally led his men up the hill.   M. Je.

BUNKER HILL MONUMENT, an obelisk erected on Breed's Hill in Boston, Mass., to commemorate the Battle of Bunker Hill. The cornerstone of the monument was laid by the Marquis de Lafayette on June 17, 1825, on the fiftieth anniversary of the battle between the British, under General William Howe, and the Americans, led by Colonel William Prescott. Daniel Webster delivered the dedicatory oration. Completed in 1843, the monument was dedicated, on June 17, by President John Tyler. Daniel Webster again was the principal speaker. Standing near the spot where General Joseph Warren of the American forces fell, the granite shaft is 221 ft. high, 31 ft. square at the base, and 15 ft. square at the top. A winding flight of 295 steps leads to a chamber at the monument's summit. Four windows in this outlook offer a complete view of the surrounding Charlestown district of Boston. The monument is located on an eminence 110 ft. high, in the center of the ground included in the old breastwork which was stormed by the British. *See illustration on following page.*   R. W. C.

BUNNER, HENRY CUYLER (1855-1896), American author and editor, was born in Oswego, N. Y., on Aug. 3, 1855. He attended private school in New York and prepared for but did not attend Columbia. After contributing to a short-lived weekly called the *Arcadian,* he became assistant editor in 1877 of *Puck,* the earliest American comic weekly, and shortly thereafter became its editor-in-chief, a position he held for the rest of his life. He often wrote half of the material in early issues of *Puck,* and continued to contribute prose and verse, jokes, parodies, lyrics, stories, character sketches, and editorials. He excelled in the writing of light verse and parodies, and had short stories published in *Century, Scribner's* and *Harper's.*

His volumes of poems, *Airs from Arcady and Elsewhere* (1884) and *Rowen* (1892), with later lyrics and "Ballads of the Town," were collected after his death as *The Poems of H. C. Bunner* (1896). Two novels, *The Midge* (1886) and *The Story of a New York House* (1887), draw upon his beloved New York City for scenes and characters, as does much of his writing. Bunner's skill and urbanity are apparent in the stories collected in *Short Sixes* (1890), *Zadoc Pine* (1891), and *More Short Sixes* (1894). "Love in Old Clothes," "Zadoc Pine," and "As One Having Authority" are stories which can stand with the best produced in America. His skillful adaptations of De Maupassant stories in *Made in France: French Tales Retold with a United States Twist* (1893) were so authentic in tone that one entirely original story by Bunner escaped detection by the critics.

that in English practice 80 per cent of the heat escaped with waste gases, completely revised gas analysis. He invented the carbon-zinc electric cell in 1841. Five years later he studied the volcanic rock formations and geyser action in Iceland, doubtless laying thereby the foundation of modern petrology. He introduced iodometry into volumetric analysis in 1852, and carried out photochemical researches with Sir Henry Roscoe from 1855 to 1863. Meanwhile, in 1859, with G. R. Kirchhoff, professor of physics at Heidelberg, Bunsen embarked on problems of spectroscopic analysis, discovering by this means the elements rubidium and cesium. Bunsen also had a gift for dextrous manipulation. Among the many pieces of laboratory apparatus invented by him are the Bunsen valve, the filter pump, the ice calorimeter, the vapor calorimeter, and the hydrogen chloride photometer. His invention of the Bun-

BUNKER HILL MONUMENT

FROM AN OLD ENGRAVING BY
E. A. BOWLE

COURTESY OF THE NEW YORK
PUBLIC LIBRARY

In 1887 Bunner settled in Nutley, N. J. There and in New York City he was the center of a brilliant social circle, distinguished for his superlative memory, broad sympathies, and never-failing verve and wit. He died in Nutley on May 11, 1896.   E. Sh.

BUNSEN, ROBERT WILHELM EBERHARD VON

[bu′nzən; bʌ′nsən] (1811-1899), was born at Göttingen on Mar. 31, 1811, and died in Heidelberg on Aug. 16, 1899. From 1828 to 1838 he studied at the University of Göttingen, where his father was librarian, receiving his doctorate for a thesis on hygrometers. Subsequently he studied in Paris, Berlin, and Vienna. He then became lecturer at Göttingen in 1834, succeeded Friedrich Wöhler at the Polytechnic Institute of Kassel in 1836, and went to Marburg from 1839 to 1851. Following one year at Breslau, from 1852 until his retirement in 1889, he was professor at Heidelberg where he resided until his death.

His accomplishments were great. In 1837, while at Kassel, Bunsen investigated arsenic compounds, discovering cacodyl, but he lost the sight of one eye from an explosion of cacodyl cyanide and nearly lost his life by inhaling its poisonous fumes. Thenceforth Bunsen worked exclusively in the inorganic field. His studies of blast-furnace gases, which showed

sen burner is questionable, since adjustable burners utilizing this same principle had already been designed by Michael Faraday and by Peter Desdga. Aside from his extensive researches, Bunsen was a great teacher, with an abounding sense of humor and a fatherly interest in his students, many of whom later became famous chemists. A statue was erected to him in the Bunsenstrasse in Heidelberg. Only one book was written by him: *Gasometrische Methoden,* a valuable reference work on gas analysis.   H. N. A.

BUNTING, a name most properly applied to a large number of heavy-billed Old World finches in the genus *Emberiza.* They breed throughout the temperate regions of Europe and Asia, and some species reach the tropics in winter. They are distinguished from other finches by a bony knob on the palate. Their plumages are combinations of black, white, brown, yellow, olive, and chestnut. They feed on weed seeds, grains, fruits, and insects. In the New World their name is loosely used for a variety of birds, of which some are not even of the same family, although others are not too distantly allied. Among the latter group are the snow bunting or snowbird, which breeds in arctic regions but visits the northern United States in severe weather; the lark bunting, *Calamospiza melanocorys,* a black bird with white wings that inhabits the Great Plains; and the brilliantly colored members of the genus *Passerina,* exemplified by the indigo and lazuli buntings.   H. G. De.

BUNYAN, JOHN (1628-1688), English religious writer, was born November 16, 1628, at Elstow, Bedfordshire. He learned reading and writing in a village school and worked with his father, a tinsmith or brazier, until his mother's death in 1644, at which time he took up arms in the civil wars. In 1647 he returned to Elstow and married. His growing religious feeling was nurtured by two devotional books that constituted his wife's dowry. Influenced also by the Puritan enthusiasms of the age, he became fearfully conscious of his own sinfulness. He gave up swearing, dancing, bellringing, and playing tipcat, yet continued to feel that he had forfeited salvation.

Not until Bunyan had joined a nonconformist church in Bedford did he begin to enjoy spiritual peace. Soon after he moved to that city in 1655, his wife died, leaving him with

JOHN BUNYAN

FROM AN ENGRAVING BY
W. HOLL FROM A
DRAWING BY DERBY

COURTESY OF THE NEW YORK
PUBLIC LIBRARY

four small children; in 1659 he remarried. Since for several years he had been an unlicensed preacher to nonconformist groups throughout the district, at the Restoration in 1660 he was arrested and imprisoned. His stay in Bedford jail could have been short, but he would not promise to desist from preaching; he was therefore kept in custody most of the time until released by Charles II's Declaration of Indulgence in 1672. His jailers were far from strict, and he had freedom to make thread laces for a living, to preach to fellow prisoners, to study the Bible and John Foxe's *Book of Martyrs,* and to write.

Much of his writing during this time was in the form of controversial pamphlets, but he also produced *Grace Abounding to the Chief of Sinners* (1666), an intimate revelation of his own spiritual struggles, in which, however, he exaggerates the depravity from which he rose. Apparently it was during a short imprisonment in 1675 that he wrote *The Pilgrim's Progress,* his most famous work. This allegory of a Christian's progress toward salvation, told in terms of romantic adventure, seemed to some of Bunyan's pious friends much too entertaining to be effective moral teaching, but Bunyan felt sure that there was no harm in making truth and goodness attractive. Upon its publication in 1678, the book became immediately popular among religious people of the lower classes, although it was not accepted as a literary classic until the middle of the nineteenth century. Since then, critics have pointed out that its direct, clear style was an important

influence on the development of modern prose and that its simple story and realistic detail give it a place in the early history of the novel.

None of Bunyan's other works achieved equal fame, excellent though some of them were. *The Holy War* (1682) is an elaborate allegory of the strife between Emanuel and Diabolus for the possession of the town Mansoul. *The Pilgrim's Progress, Part II* (1684), telling how Christian's wife and children followed after him, has less doctrine and more human characters. *The Life and Death of Mr. Badman* (1680) gives, in dialogue form, a concrete picture of life in a provincial town, with emphasis on the folly, roguery, and wickedness to be found there. In his last years, Bunyan was a respected religious leader over a wide territory and preached part of every year in London. There he died Aug. 31, 1688, and was buried in Bunhill Fields.   H. B. W.

BUNYAN, PAUL, mythical hero of the lumber camps of the American Northwest, a giant superlumberjack credited with digging Puget Sound and the St. Lawrence River and with excavating the Grand Canyon. It is said that the legend originated during the Papineau rebellion in Canada, in 1837. By 1860, the legend had spread throughout the Northwest. One authority, Esther Shephard (*Paul Bunyan,* 1924), holds that evidence points to Quebec or northern Ontario as the original source of the legend, but other evidence assigns Michigan, Wisconsin, or Minnesota as its cradle. It may be that the mythical John Henry, in the South, is an adaptation of Paul Bunyan. Elsewhere, Scandinavian and American Indian modifications of such a hero have been noted.

A famous myth is Bunyan's discovery of the blue ox. This ox, as a calf, broke down the timber standing in its path over the mountain. Its tail brush was a dark blue, like cypress in the twilight; its footprints were so large that to see across them three men must needs stand close together. The distance between these hoof prints was so great that none but the hero himself could follow them. The width between the eyes of the bright blue ox varied from twenty-four axe handles and a plug of tobacco to forty-two axe handles. A crow accustomed to roost on the left horn of the ox undertook one winter a flight to the right horn. The bird was lost from view in its passage, but with the first spring thaw it alighted safely on the tip of the other horn. Paul Bunyan's ability in tracking animals was unique. Coming across the carcass of a bull moose that had died of old age, he followed its tracks back to the place where it was born. These legends are the familiar hero sagas of the *Nibelungenlied* and the stories of Ulysses in the *Odyssey* of Homer, told in the spirit and environment of the American north woods.

A statue of Paul Bunyan stands on the lake front in Bemidji, Minn.   A. W. Gr.

BUPHAGUS [byu′fəgəs], in Greek mythology, the son of Iapetus and Thonax, an Arcadian hero. A river in Arcadia was named for him. He nursed Iphicles when the latter was wounded in the battle against the Molionides. In spite of Buphagus' care, however, Iphicles died, and Buphagus was later killed by Artemis.

BUR, the name applied to seed cases covered with spines, such as the chestnut bur, or with prickles, such as the burdock. To aid seed dispersal, various plants have seeds equipped with hooked prickles which become easily attached to the wool or hair of animals. Often the word forms a characteristic part of a name, such as sandbur, cocklebur, burdock, and bur marigold.   J. C. Wis.

BURA [byu′rə], in Greek mythology, the daughter of Ion, ancestral hero of the Ionians, and Helice. Bura, or Buris, one of the twelve original Achaean cities which stood on the Bay of Corinth, was named after her. The city was destroyed by an earthquake and later rebuilt a short distance inland.

BURBAGE, JAMES [bɜ′rbɪj] (c. 1530-1597), English actor and builder of what was at once the first Elizabethan theatre and the first regular theatre in London, was born of Hertfordshire stock. He at first earned his livelihood as a joiner, but finding this occupation unprofitable, he turned to acting. By 1572 he was a leading member of the Earl of Leicester's Men, the company with which, as player, he was principally associated. He married Helen (or Ellen) Brayne and by her had five children, of whom the most famous was his actor son, Richard (1567-1619). After about 1576 the family lived in or near Halliwell Street, Shoreditch, which was for a time the center of theatrical activity.

Anticipating that profit might be made from speculation in an actual theatrical structure, Burbage in April 1576 leased from Giles Allen property adjacent to Finsbury Field, which constituted part of the dissolved priory of Holywell, and erected there a wooden building, adapted architecturally from the inns where professional companies frequently played. This was called simply the "Theatre." Since Burbage had no more than a hundred marks of his own, he financed the venture principally by inducing his brother-in-law, John Brayne, a well-to-do grocer, to invest in it; by borrowing money; and by pawning the lease. Though the Theatre was profitable and was used by the principal London companies, Burbage was frequently involved in litigation, and Allen refused to renew the lease. The building later passed to Burbage's older son, Cuthbert, who with the help of his brother, Richard, began to demolish it in 1598 and used the timbers to build the Globe Theatre.

In 1585 James Burbage, along with John Brayne, began a seven-year affiliation with the adjacent theatre, the Curtain, built in 1577, but in 1596 he took a more important step, when he purchased certain rooms in the precinct of Blackfriars and made them over into an indoor theatre. This became the playhouse for various companies of children and later a winter home for the King's Men, but Burbage lived to see none of this. Shortly after he had made his alterations at considerable expense, the aristocratic residents of the precincts petitioned the Privy Council to forbid the public use of a "common playhouse" in their neighborhood. The compliance of the council shattered Burbage's plans. He made over his interest in Blackfriars to Richard, died soon after, and was buried at Shoreditch on Feb. 2, 1597.

From the perhaps biased evidence of the various lawsuits in which Burbage was engaged, it appears that he was a man of irascible temper, violent expression, and doubtful integrity. At the same time, his courage and enterprise left their mark in the development of three of the most important theatres of his time and were directly responsible for the building of the first theatre of Elizabethan London.   R. H. Ba.

BURBAGE, RICHARD (1567-1619), famed English Elizabethan actor, was born in 1567, perhaps at Stratford-on-Avon. Son of James Burbage, who erected the first professional theatre in England, Burbage inherited the Blackfriars Theatre and, with Shakespeare, John Heming, and Henry Condell as partners, erected the Globe Theatre, using the timber frame of his father's old playhouse, the Theatre. He became the leading actor for the Lord Chamberlain's Men, which was also Shakespeare's company, and besides creating, in all probability, all of Shakespeare's major tragic roles, he also played the leads in Ben Jonson's *Every Man in His Humour, Volpone,* and *The Alchemist.*

Shakespeare left Burbage a memorial ring in his will, and it is plain that the bond between the two men was close. It is probable that the playwright was guided in his choice of material and in his characterizations by Burbage's acting personality and talent. Burbage was something of a painter in oils as well as an actor, and the Chandos portrait of Shakespeare is attributed to him. He died in London and was buried at St. Leonard's, Shoreditch, Mar. 16, 1619.

                                                  J. Ga. and T. G. R.

BURBANK, LUTHER (1849-1926), American naturalist, experimental biologist, and plant breeder, was born at Lancaster, Mass., Mar. 7, 1849. He was educated at local schools and at Lancaster Academy. Always devoted to the study of nature, particularly plant life, he purchased some land at Lunenburg and started experimenting with plants. Here in 1873 he developed the Burbank potato. On account of poor health he moved to California and at Santa Rosa established Burbank's Experimental Farms. One of his early experiences is interesting. A fruit grower wanted 20,000 young prune trees for delivery within ten months, and nurserymen said this was impossible. Burbank accepted the order, planted almonds, and carefully tended them. He then secured thousands of prune shoots and when the almond trees were sufficiently grown he budded the prune buds into them. The order was delivered ahead of the specified time limit. Burbank's scope of activity covered a wide range of plant improvement: flowers, fruits, grains, grasses, trees, and vegetables. He not only improved existing varieties but created new ones. Besides the Burbank potato, he was the originator of the rapid-growing edible thornless cactus; a wide variety of plums, prunes, and other fruits; roses and many other flowers. In his development work he employed both selection and cross-breeding. With marked success he applied Mendel's laws of heredity to produce new varieties of plants. He was a firm believer in the theory of the inheritance of acquired characteristics and in that of the constant mutability of species. He grew more than a million plants annually for testing purposes and at times had several thousand experiments under way. He was a special lecturer on evolution at Leland Stanford University and held membership in many scientific and horticultural societies in both the United States and Europe. His chief publications were *Luther Burbank, His Methods and Discoveries* (12 vols., 1914-1915), *How Plants are Trained to Work for Man* (8 vols., 1921), and *The Training of the Human Plant* (1907). He died at Santa Rosa, Apr. 11, 1926.

                                                           D. D. M.

BURBANK, a city adjoining Los Angeles and Glendale in Los Angeles Co., southern California. It is served by the Southern Pacific Railroad and several scheduled and non-scheduled airlines. In 1867 Dr. David Burbank, a pioneer from New Hampshire, bought the land on which the city was built. Burbank was incorporated in 1911 and is governed by a city manager. Its principal industries are the manufacture of aircraft and aircraft equipment and the production of motion pictures. Factory output also includes cosmetics, soap, household appliances, small tools, jewelry, and electronic equipment. Pop. 1950, 78,577; 1957, 90,966.

BURBOT [bɜ′rbət], *Lota lota,* is the only freshwater representative of the cod family, Gadidae. It is found in cool, deep waters of the lakes and larger streams of northern North America and Siberia. Somewhat eel-shaped, with long dorsal and anal fins, it has a fleshy barbel on the chin, and numerous, minute scales embedded in the skin. In the Great Lakes region, burbot reach a length of 2 ft. and in Alaska they attain 5 ft. and a weight of 60 lbs. Spawning during the winter, the large females produce as many as 670,000 eggs. It is a very predacious fish feeding mostly on other fishes, especially commercially valuable white-

COURTESY OF U.S. FISH AND WILDLIFE SERVICE

BURBOT, LOTA MACULOSA

fishes and ciscoes. It is a competitor for food with the more desirable lake trout. Burbot has been unappreciated as a food fish but may become popular because it has excellent flesh. Also its liver is a rich source of vitamins.   E. C. R.

BURCHFIELD, CHARLES EPHRAIM (1893-   ), American painter, was born in Ashtabula Harbor, Ohio, Apr. 9, 1893. His training and earliest encouragement came from Henry G. Keller at the Cleveland School of Art. In 1921 Burchfield moved to Buffalo, where he was a wallpaper designer; in 1925 he moved to Gardenville, N. Y.

While he uses oil occasionally, Burchfield's major medium is water color, in which he has painted scenes of Ohio and upper New York State. At first predominately imaginative, his style has since contained varying proportions of Romanticism and Realism, with a strong emphasis on mood and bold decorative pattern. Among his works are *Country Blacksmith Shop* (1928) (oil), *Sulphurous Evening* (1930) (water color), *Burning Muckland* (1932) (water color), and *In a Deserted House* (1939) (oil).   E. B. S.

BURCKHARDT, JAKOB [buʹrkhɑrt] (1818-1897), Swiss historian and writer on art, was born in Basel, May 25, 1818. At the universities of Berlin and Bonn (1839-1843) he studied general history with the German historians, Leopold von Ranke and Johann Gustav Droysen, and art history with Franz Kugler. Burckhardt first visited Italy in 1838, and returned to Basel in 1843. He published *The Age of Constantine the Great* in 1852 and *The Cicerone, a Manual to the Enjoyment of Italian Works of Art,* in 1855. In 1845 Burckhardt became professor of history in the University of Basel, and from 1855 until 1858 he taught at the Zurich Polytechnic School, after which he returned to the University of Basel as professor of history and of art history, remaining until his retirement in 1893. His masterpiece, *The Civilization of the Renaissance in Italy* (1860), was the first comprehensive survey of its type. Burckhardt was both a capable historian and an inspiring teacher. His later works include *The History of the Renaissance in Italy* (1867) and the posthumously published *The Culture of the Greeks* (1898-1902) and the lectures *Reflections on History* (1906). Burckhardt died at Basel, Aug. 8, 1897.

BURDEN. *See* MUSICAL TERMS.

BURDETT-COUTTS, BARONESS ANGELA GEORGINA [bɜrdɛʹt kuʹts] (1814-1906), English philanthropist, was born in London, Apr. 21, 1814, the youngest daughter of Sir Francis Burdett. In 1837 she inherited the banking fortune of her grandfather, Thomas Coutts, and added his surname to her own. She then devoted her life to philanthropic causes, which she personally administered and supervised. Her many philanthropies included churches and schools, housing projects, and a host of lesser private charities for the relief of the poor and suffering. She endowed three colonial bishoprics and donated large sums for the exploration and internal development of Britain's expanding colonial empire. She also generously assisted the areas of famine and distress in Ireland and in 1869 built the Columbia market in order to supply cheaper fish and vegetables in a poor district of London, but it proved abortive because of the opposition of vested interests. In 1871 she was created Baroness Burdett-Coutts of Highgate and Brookfield, Middlesex, by Queen Victoria in gratitude for her services to humanity and the following year became the first woman to be presented with the freedom of the City of London. She was decorated by the Sultan of Turkey in 1878 for her contribution to relief work during the Russo-Turkish War, and at the age of 67 married William Lehman Ashmead-Bartlett, an American by birth, who assisted his wife in the administration of her philanthropies and later became a Unionist member of Parliament. Her many friends included Charles Dickens, Benjamin Disraeli, Tom Moore, Samuel Rogers, and Michael Faraday. She died in London, Dec. 30, 1906, and is buried in Westminster Abbey.   C. W. D.

BURDOCK, *Arctium lappa* and *Arctium minus,* two very similar biennials of the family Compositae, native of Europe and Asia, which have spread widely as weeds over the

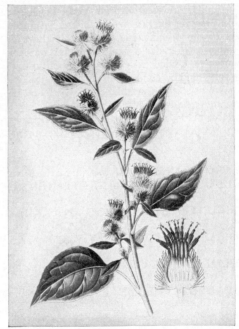

THOME—DR. LASCOFF

BURDOCK

United States and Canada. *A. lappa* grows to 9 ft. with coarse leaves, sometimes 18 in. long, and purplish florets compressed in bur-like heads. *A. minus* is somewhat smaller. The burs, sticking to clothing or to animals, carry the seeds far afield. In Japan the roots and young growth are used in soups.   J. C. Wis.

BURDWAN [bʌrdwɑ'n], a city in the central part of West Bengal, India, located on the Banka canal of the Damodar River, 67 mi. northwest of Calcutta by rail. It is the administrative center of Burdwan District. The city is an important railroad junction and is the marketing and small-products manufacturing center of the District, which produces rice, potatoes, and sugar cane. The eastward shift of the Ganges has left part of the area suitable for very rich winter crops and the region of the Damodar River is especially known for its fine watermelons. During the wet monsoon, floods of the Damodar and its tributaries used to destroy property and wash out roads and bridges almost every year. The Damodar Valley Project, started in 1949, has been designed to alleviate these conditions by controlling floods, irrigating more than a million acres of land, supplying hydroelectric power, and feeding a multi-lock navigation canal connecting the industrial areas of Asansol and the agricultural tracts of Burdwan with the port of Calcutta.

The chief places of interest in Burdwan are the palace and garden of the Maharaja of Burdwan; the palace contains a fine museum and library. Burdwan also has a few interesting temples, several ancient tombs, and some very large artificial lakes. Pop. 1951, 75,376.   M. R.

BUREAUCRACY [byurɒ'krəsi], derived from bureau, a government office transacting public business. It may be defined as a system of organization or administration characterized primarily by (1) a sharp delineation of functions and powers assigned each member, (2) the maintenance of certain standards of competence for each job or position, and the appointment to the jobs or positions of persons who presumably have such competency, and (3) the principle of hierarchy, that is to say, the placing of each person (below the top executive or executives) on graded levels of titles and duties. In practice, the principle of hierarchy means that the members of the organization are combined in larger and larger units, each under a superior officer or boss. In the organization of United States governmental administration, for example, employees and officers are combined in small units known as sections and branches, which are recombined in larger units known as divisions and bureaus, which in turn are recombined in the largest units—departments, agencies, and corporations—responsible to the president and Congress.   D. W.

BUREAU OF CUSTOMS. See CUSTOMS, BUREAU OF.

BUREAU OF INTERNAL REVENUE. See INTERNAL REVENUE.

BUREAU OF STANDARDS, NATIONAL. See COMMERCE, DEPARTMENT OF.

BUREAU OF THE BUDGET. See BUDGET, BUREAU OF THE.

BUREAU OF THE CENSUS. See CENSUS, BUREAU OF THE.

BUREAU OF THE MINT. See MINT, BUREAU OF THE.

BURGAS [bʊ'rgɑ's] (Bourgas), a Black Sea port in eastern Bulgaria, about 140 mi. northeast of Plovdiv, on the Gulf of Burgas, at 42° 30′ N. lat. and 27° 30′ E. long. It is the capital of the district of Burgas. The city is located on a low tongue of land bounded on the north and the west by two large lagoons known as Ludza and Kara Yunus. Quays south of the city provide berthing facilities in water deep enough for large vessels. After World War I the importance of Burgas as a port increased notably, its volume in some years sur-

passing that of Varna, until then the most important Black Sea port in Bulgaria. The city is linked by rail from Paris to Istanbul, and has rail connections with Ruschuk by way of Stara Zagora. Burgas handles most of Bulgaria's important export trade in tobacco and much of the country's exports of grain, manufactured wood articles, attar of roses, dairy products, eggs, fruits, and oil cake. An important part of Bulgaria's imports of iron and steel, machinery, petroleum and petroleum derivatives, chemicals, and vehicles enter through the port. Factories for metal goods, sugar, soap, flour, and other products are located in the city. The Gulf of Burgas is the principal center for Bulgaria's sea fishing and for the preservation of fish by salting, drying, and smoking. Production of salt from sea water is another industry for coastal towns near Burgas, especially at Pomorje, northeast of the city, and at Sozopol, to the southeast. Pop. 1945, 43,684.
                E. St.

BURGENLAND [bʊ'rgənlɑnt], a province in eastern Austria, with an area of 1,532 sq. mi. It is bounded on the north by the province of lower Austria, on the east by Hungary, and on the south and west by Styria. Some foothills of the Alps lie in the western region. The northern half of Burgenland slopes from the Leitha Mountains, 1,560 ft. through a terraced landscape to the reed flats of the western shore of the Neusiedler See, Austria's largest lake, beyond which stretches a plain used for pasturage. The southern half of Burgenland is more undulating terrain, watered by the Raab River. Wheat, rye, barley, oats, sugar beets, and potatoes are the most important crops in this mainly agricultural province. Lignite, antimony, sulphur, and limestone are worked to some extent, but there are no industries of importance. Minor industries are weaving, matchmaking, and sugar refining. Eisenstadt, the capital, with a population of about 5,000, is the largest town.

Under the Carolingian rulers, settlers from the dukedom of Franconia migrated to the area now known as Burgenland, the name dating only from 1918-1921. Originally Austrian, the region was turned over to Hungary in 1647. Until the end of World War I the area comprised Burgen or the townships of Ödenburg, Wieselburg, Eisenburg, and Pressburg. The Treaty of St.-Germain (1919) gave Austria Ödenburg, Wieselburg, and Eisenburg. Slavic-speaking Pressburg went to Yugoslavia. When Austria tried to take possession, Hungarian armed bands resisted. On Oct. 13, 1921, guided by the Inter-Allied Commission, Austria and Hungary agreed to hold a plebiscite, which resulted in Hungary's retention of Ödenburg (Sopron), while the other districts went to Austria. Until 1938 Burgenland remained a federated province of the Austrian Republic; between 1938 and 1945 it formed part of Greater Germany. After World War II it was included in the Soviet zone of occupation until the signing of the Austrian peace treaty on May 15, 1955. Pop. 1951, 276,136.

BÜRGER, GOTTFRIED AUGUST [bü'rgər] (1747-1794), German poet, was born near Halberstadt on Dec. 31, 1747. He studied theology at Halle and law at Göttingen. After twelve years as a district magistrate, he became a lecturer in aesthetics at Göttingen and later an assistant professor. His first marriage was complicated by his love for his wife's sister (the "Molly" of his poems), whom he married after his wife's death. The last years of his life were made wretched by an unhappy third marriage, continuing poverty, ill health, and a severe critical attack on his poetry by Schiller. He died at Göttingen on June 8, 1794.

Bürger is known chiefly for his ballads, which elevated the

popular German ballad to a work of art. *Lenore* (1773), his most famous ballad, was imitated by Walter Scott in *William and Helen,* and enjoyed immense popularity all over Europe. In a setting of the Seven Years' War it recounts the story of the gruesome ride of a ghostly lover and his bride, and it is given unsurpassed vividness and suspense by the skillful use of onomatopoeia, refrain, and dialogue. Bürger's later ballads, whose high moral tone contrasted strangely with his life, did not equal *Lenore* in quality or popularity. Among the best-known are *Das Lied vom braven Manne* (1777), *Der wilde Jäger* (1778), and *Des Pfarrers Tochter von Taubenhain* (1781).

Bürger's lyrics enjoy a high critical reputation, if less general popularity than his ballads. His translations include *Macbeth, Munchausen, Benjamin Franklin's Youth,* and parts of the *Iliad* and *Aeneid.* W. W. P.

BURGESS, CHARLES FREDERICK. *See* PERKIN MEDAL.

BURGESS, GIOVANNI ERNEST WATSON (1886-), sociologist, was born in Tilbury, Ont., Canada, May 16, 1886. He received his B.A. degree from Kingfisher College in Oklahoma in 1908 and his doctorate from the University of Chicago in 1913. He taught sociology at Toledo (Ohio) University from 1912 to 1913, and was successively assistant professor of sociology at the University of Kansas, 1913-1915, at Ohio State University, 1915-1916, and at the University of Chicago, 1916-1921. Since 1927 he has been professor of sociology and since 1945 chairman of the department of sociology at the University of Chicago. His doctoral dissertation, *The Function of Socialization in Social Evolution* (1913) was followed by two community surveys: *The Belleville Survey,* with J. J. Sippy, in 1915, and the *Lawrence Social Survey,* with F. W. Blackmar, in 1916. In association with Robert E. Park, he initiated the pioneer studies in human ecology and the urban community at the University of Chicago, in the course of which new methods of empirical investigation emphasizing the ecological base of human social life were perfected. Among the studies embodying the new techniques for the more precise and comparative analysis of social phenomena which were carried out under his direction, were those on delinquency and crime, family disorganization, mental disorder, and community organization. These have not only given Chicago the reputation of being the most thoroughly studied city in America, but have also led to the formulation of a comprehensive theory of city structure and growth, based on the principle of concentric zones differentiated by intensity of land use, type of occupancy, and the incidence of problems of human adjustment. An important by-product of this research program was the accumulation of a body of more reliable basic social data by census tracts and local communities which, aside from its scientific value for the accurate depiction of the characteristics of types of natural areas, proved to be of great practical importance in administration of social institutions and public services and in city and regional planning. Burgess' work, in addition to his research in human ecology and the urban community, is outstanding in two other fields: (1) studies in the changing structure and modes of adjustment of the family, and (2) the development of a theory and ingenious techniques for the prediction of human behavior. In the latter field Burgess applied actuarial methods to social data for the prognostication of the success or failure of prisoners on parole. He subsequently adapted these prediction techniques to other areas of social adjustment, especially engagement and marriage.

While these novel contributions promised to be of great practical significance, their prospective contribution to the discovery of the basic factors underlying human behavior and their role in the development of a more adequate theory of social causation make them of utmost importance in the effort to construct a truly empirically founded science of sociology.

Other important works of Burgess are *Introduction to the Science of Sociology* (with Robert E. Park, 1921), *Predicting Success or Failure in Marriage* (with Leonard S. Cottrell, Jr., 1939), and *The Family* (with H. J. Locke, 1945). He was president of the American Sociological Society in 1934 and of the Sociological Research Association in 1942, and editor of the *American Journal of Sociology* from 1936 to 1940. L. W.

BURGESS, JOHN WILLIAM (1844-1931), American historian and professor, was born in Giles Co., Tenn., Aug. 26, 1844. His family were Whig Unionists, and this background was fundamental for Burgess' lifelong support of American nationalism. He served in the Union army, and then enrolled at Amherst College, graduating in 1867. After practicing law in Massachusetts, and teaching briefly at Knox College, Ill., Burgess went to Germany to study law and government. There he came under the influence of some of the greatest European scholars. He returned to the United States in 1873 and joined the teaching staff at Amherst College, there instituting the seminar method. In 1876 he went to Columbia University where he remained for the rest of his life. He was instrumental in establishing the Faculty and School of Political Science, 1880, which marked the transformation of Columbia College into a university. Many famous scholars began their studies in history and political science in Burgess' seminars. His publications included *Political Science and Comparative Constitutional Law* (1890-1891), two vols., and *The Reconciliation of Government with Liberty* (1915). His works on the subject of history centered on the Civil War and its aftermath and included *The Middle Period* (1897); *The Civil War and the Constitution* (1901), two vols.; and *Reconstruction and the Constitution* (1902). Burgess died in Brookline, Mass., Jan. 13, 1931. M. K.

BURGH, HUBERT DE [bɜ'rg] (d. 1243), chief justiciar of England, was chamberlain to King John in 1201, but it is doubtful if he was ever custodian of Arthur of Brittany (see Shakespeare's *King John,* Act 4). He fought bravely for John in France, and it was on his advice that the King granted the Magna Charta in 1215. He was appointed justiciar in the same year, and in 1216 defended Dover Castle against the attack by Louis VIII of France. With ships from the Cinque Ports in 1217 he decisively defeated the French fleet commanded by Eustace the Monk, off Dover, bringing reinforcements for the French, and the invasion of England was abandoned. From 1219 Hubert held almost supreme power in England, but had, however, to meet the hostility of the Poitevin, Peter des Roches, and a body of English nobles jealous of Hubert's influence and wealth. King Henry III finally turned against him and in 1232 he was dismissed from his offices. He took refuge in the sanctuary at Bury St. Edmunds, but was forcibly removed and kept in strict confinement until released on sureties tendered by the King's brother and three earls. In 1233 he was again imprisoned, but in 1234 was reinstated in his possessions. He died May 12, 1243. E. R. A.

BURGHLEY, BARON [bɜ'rli]. *See* CECIL, WILLIAM, BARON BURGHLEY.

BURGLARY, at common law, the crime of breaking and entering the dwelling house of another in nighttime with intent to commit a felony therein. Unless all of the six elements—(1) breaking, (2) entering, (3) dwelling-house character of the premises, (4) occupancy of another, (5) nighttime, and (6) intent to commit a felony within the dwelling—appear, at common law the crime of burglary has not been committed. However, the lesser offense of "housebreaking" under the English statute of 1861, might have been perpetrated, even though the premises unlawfully broken and entered was not a dwelling house, and the breaking and entry occurred in the daytime. Likewise, entering into a dwelling house in the nighttime, without breaking, but with intent to commit a felony therein, although not burglary, constitutes a felony under the same statute.

In the United States the definitions of burglary appearing in the modern penal codes of the several states are disparate. Typical state statutes approximate a composite of common-law burglary and the English crime of housebreaking or else set up different degrees of burglary with the lesser degrees akin to variant aspects of housebreaking; some dispense with the element of intent to commit a felony and substitute intent to commit a crime, felony, or misdemeanor. In a number of American jurisdictions, laws are in force that make it a crime to possess tools or implements commonly used for the commission of burglary under circumstances

evincing an intent to use them or permit their use for purpose of burglary.

The word "breaking" as employed in the law of burglary does not necessarily require that any damage be done to any part of the house. Among the acts which have been construed as constituting breaking are the lifting of a door latch, the opening of an unlocked closed window or door, and the removing of a wire screen over an open window. A guest in a hotel who opens with requisite unlawful intent the closed door of a room occupied by another guest is deemed to be guilty of breaking. Moreover, if entrance to a house is obtained by fraud or threats, the premises are generally deemed to have been broken. A number of state penal codes expressly make breaking out of a building equivalent to breaking into it.

The term "entering" as known in the law of burglary does not require that the burglar's body be completely within the house. It suffices that some part of the body, for example a hand or finger, protrude into the interior. Indeed, a tool or implement inserted in the house to detach or remove property may be deemed a burglarious entry.

Although burglary is generally associated with larceny, the requisite breaking and entering of a house, accompanied by an intent to commit other crimes of given degree, is likewise generally held to be burglary. However, it is not necessary that any crime actually be committed within the house, since the breaking and entry with criminal intent, itself consummates the offense of burglary.   H. Si.

BURGLARY INSURANCE. *See* INSURANCE.

BURGOS [bu′rgos], the name of both a province and its capital in Old Castile, in north central Spain.

The City. The city is situated on the shallow and unruly Arlanzón River, at 2,785 ft. above sea level, about 130 mi.

The Casa del Cordón, in Burgos, was built toward the end of the fifteenth century.

THREE LIONS

north of Madrid. The city is in a position to dominate the land routes leading from the upper Ebro River Valley to the *meseta* of Castile. Burgos has a climate marked by long, cold winters and hot summers, with an average annual rainfall of 22 in. It is the see of an archbishop and during the Spanish Civil War (1936-1939) was headquarters for General Francisco Franco's rebel regime. Burgos is primarily an administrative center and market place for the fertile region in which it lies. There are a few small industries producing foods, textiles, and paper. It is on the main railway line from Madrid to Bilbao, and is also a highway junction.

The city is dominated to the north by a hill, Cerro de San Miguel, on the brow of which is the massive castle. The older portion of town, between the castle and the river, presents a medieval appearance. To the south and east are newer quarters. The most notable building is the Gothic cathedral, begun in 1221 and completed in the latter part of the sixteenth century, with its magnificent nave and choir and several richly decorated chapels, a golden staircase, and a cloister. The façade is marked by two delicate spires. The edifice is built of white limestone. The ancient colored-glass windows were almost wholly destroyed by an explosion in the castle in 1813. Other interesting religious structures are the Gothic churches of San Nicolás and San Esteban. The castle, largely in ruins, once served as the residence of the Castilian kings, and it was the scene of the marriage of Edward I of England to Eleanor of Castile. Though the interior was badly damaged by fire in 1736, the French were able to defend it against the Duke of Wellington in 1812.

The medieval quarter contains several interesting secular buildings, including the town houses of various noble families, such as the Casa de Miranda and the Casa del Cordón. In several places there are reminders of the eleventh-century hero, the Cid Campeador, whose remains lie in the Casa Consistorial. A mile west of town is the Convent de las Huelgas, originally a summer palace of the Castilian kings, converted in 1187 to a Cistercian nunnery for noblewomen, with vast properties and privileges. It contains the tombs of several historic personages. Also in the vicinity are the Carthusian monastery of Miraflores, founded by John II, with several valuable architectural and monumental features; the convent of San Pedro de Cardeña; and the monastery of Silos, with its beautiful Romanesque cloisters, founded before the Arab conquest.

The origin of Burgos dates back to the ninth century, when it was ruled by counts whose task it was to defend the eastern border of the Asturian kingdom against the Moors. In time, as the "Reconquest" progressed, these counts freed themselves from the control of León and other neighboring monarchies and set up a kingdom of their own—Castile—with its capital at Burgos, the first monarch being Fernando I (1035-1065). Several Cortes were held in the city, which grew in political and economic importance. In the thirteenth century Valladolid, more centrally located in the expanding kingdom, became a serious rival, as did Toledo later on. Burgos' downfall came with the city's participation in the *comunero* revolt against Charles V in 1520, and after that it declined in political and economic importance. Early in the Spanish Civil War it was seized by the Rebels, and from here Franco organized the offensives against Madrid, Barcelona, and the Basque Provinces. Because of its interesting medieval structures, Burgos is becoming increasingly popular with tourists. Pop. 1950, 61,789.

The Province. The province of Burgos has an area of 5,481 sq. mi. On the north it reaches the Cantabrian Range and extends southward beyond the Duero River. Its eastern boundary cuts through the Sierra de la Demanda. The enclave of Treviño, though a part of this province, is entirely surrounded by the province of Alava. Most of the terrain consists of foothills and the rolling plains of the Castilian *meseta*. The northern zone is drained by the upper reaches of the Ebro River; the center by the Pisuerga and Arlanzón; and the south by the Duero.

The climate—cold winters and hot, dry summers—is not propitious for intensive agriculture. Cereals are grown widely but by primitive methods; cattle and sheep are raised in large numbers. The countryside is sparsely populated. A large part of the area is forested with pine and deciduous trees, giving rise to local lumber and furniture industries. Minerals are of little importance. The province is inadequately provided with railways, there being none from north to south. Miranda de Ebro and Aranda de Duero are the only large centers besides the capital. Pop. 1950, 390,058.   R. G. W.

BURGOYNE, JOHN [bɜrgɔi'n] (1722-1792), English general, politician, and dramatist, was born in London on Feb. 24, 1722. Educated at Westminster School, he entered the army in 1740, but because of his debts he sold his commission in 1746 and retired to France. When the Seven Years' War broke out in 1756 he re-entered the army, served in the expeditions against Cherbourg and St. Malo, and was sent to Lisbon as a brigadier general in 1762 to aid England's ally, Portugal. He had entered Parliament in 1761 and from 1768 to 1774 showed ability as a speaker and a politician. He tried his hand at writing, and in 1775 his first play, *The Maid of the Oaks,* was produced in London by Garrick. In 1774-1775 he served under General Thomas Gage at Boston and in 1776 under Sir Guy Carleton in Canada, and in 1777, as major general, he was given command of a British force to advance south from Montreal against the American revolutionaries. He captured Ticonderoga, July 6, 1777, but was forced to surrender to the Americans under General Horatio Gates at Saratoga Oct. 17, 1777, owing in some measure at least to the failure of General Sir William Howe to advance from New York to meet him. Burgoyne's surrender was instrumental in bringing France to the aid of the Americans and thus contributed greatly to the cause of American freedom. Few battles in history have had such great ultimate influence as did the Battle of Saratoga. From 1782 to 1783 Burgoyne was commander in chief in Ireland but soon afterward withdrew from public service. He wrote a number of satiric attacks upon the government and several plays, of which *The Heiress* (1786) achieved a great success. He died in London on June 4, 1792.   E. R. A.

BURGOYNE'S CAMPAIGN (1777). The Benedict Arnold-Richard Montgomery invasion of Canada in 1775-1776 had caused the British to send part of their army to Quebec. In 1777 they proposed to reunite their forces at New York and to split the Americans into two groups of states. Gen. Sir John Burgoyne was ordered to move southward from Canada by way of Lake Champlain and the Hudson River to Albany. There he was to be joined by Lt. Col. Barry St. Leger, who was to march eastward from Oswego down the Mohawk Valley. Gen. Sir William Howe was to send troops up from New York, while he personally was to take Philadelphia. Burgoyne started south and soon captured Fort Ticonderoga, and later moved slowly southward to Fort Edward on the upper Hudson. From there he sent out a raiding party to the east to capture stores that were supposed to be at Bennington, Vt.

The British force of German, loyalist, and Indian troops did not get to the Vermont line. John Stark, who had quit the main army because Congress had not made him a brigadier general, gathered the local militia and marched westward and met the British on Aug. 16, 1777, about 3 mi. northwest of the town of Bennington, Vt., in Hoosick Township, N. Y. He attacked from all sides, driving the Indians away. The German commander, Friedrich Baum, was killed, his soldiers exhausted their powder, and their cannon were

SURRENDER OF GENERAL BURGOYNE AT SARATOGA, NEW YORK, OCTOBER 17, 1777

BETTMANN ARCHIVE

FROM A PAINTING BY COLONEL TRUMBELL

seized and turned upon the reinforcements sent out by Burgoyne. The Battle of Bennington ended with the close of day, the British losing perhaps 800 men.

St. Leger had laid siege to Fort Stanwix (now Rome, N.Y.). The relief of the fort had first been undertaken by local militia under the leadership of Nicholas Herkimer who, on the morning of August 6, had been ambushed at Oriskany by troops from St. Leger's command and Indians under Joseph Brant. Many of Herkimer's troops deserted, but Herkimer, though mortally wounded, held his position until nightfall, when the British and Indians withdrew. Soon afterwards Benedict Arnold led a force of 2,000 men up the Mohawk River to relieve the fort. On Arnold's approach St. Leger's Indians deserted and he gave up the siege, returning to Oswego and thence to Canada.

Burgoyne, constantly harassed and undecided as to just what course to follow, finally got his troops in motion, accompanied by his thirty wagons of private baggage, and by many of the wives and children of his soldiers. The Americans were gaining reinforcements steadily. Gen. Horatio Gates replaced Gen. Philip Schuyler in the command, and Benedict Arnold was irked by supposed bad treatment at Gates's hands. An effective American force faced Burgoyne. The first clash occurred at Freeman's Farm on September 19. The result was indecisive. On October 7 Burgoyne attacked the American position unsuccessfully and then retreated to Saratoga. His soldiers were deserting; the roads were impassable. On Oct. 17, 1777, he surrendered to Gen. Gates with his entire army.

The surrender at Saratoga was one of the decisive events in world history in its ultimate consequences. The victory brought France into the war on the side of the Americans. A formal alliance, the dispatch of an expeditionary force and a fleet, and the establishment of financial credit for the purchase of munitions and supplies, soon followed.   M. Je.

BURGUNDIANS, a German tribe which originally lived in northern Germany between the Oder and Vistula rivers. They were early enemies of the Alamanni, and eventually moved toward the Rhine frontier during the reign of Diocletian. Under their king, Gundicar, the Burgundians entered the Roman empire in the fifth century A.D. and were settled as colonists in the Rhône valley. As allies of Rome they fought against Attila in A.D. 451, but in the troubled years toward the end of the century they appear to have established an independent kingdom along the Rhône. The famous Burgundian king, Gundobad (d. 516), though an Arian, allowed his son to be educated as a Roman Catholic. Gundobad is chiefly remembered for his codification of Burgundian laws, *lex Gundobadia*. With the rise of the Franks under Clovis, the independence of the Burgundians declined. The conquest of the Burgundians was completed by Clovis' successors in 534, and the Burgundians were absorbed by the Franks. *See also* BURGUNDY; CLOVIS; FRANKS.   T. B. J.

BURGUNDY (Fr. BOURGOGNE) [bɜ'rgəndi, bu'r-gɔ'ny], a name first applied to an early Teutonic kingdom founded by the Burgundii (or Burgundiones) in the valleys of the Saône and Rhône rivers in southeastern France during the fifth century of the Christian Era. Admitted to the region by the Romans, they soon accepted Christianity. They were conquered by the Franks in 534 and were thus absorbed into what later became the Carolingian empire. The second kingdom of Burgundy, or Jurane Burgundy, was founded in the ninth century after the division of the Carolingian empire by the Treaty of Verdun in 843. After its union with Provence it included western Switzerland and, in what is now France, the Free County of Burgundy (Franche-Comté), Savoy, the Lyonnais, Dauphiné, Vivarais, and Provence. It extended from the Mediterranean Sea north as far as Basel, Switzerland, and from the Rhône Valley eastward to the Italian Alps. From the thirteenth century until its disappearance it was called the kingdom of Arles. Physiographically, it was divided into two sections: the lowlands of the Saône and Rhône river valleys, and the mountainous section, containing some of the highest peaks in Europe, of the Alps and Jura mountains. The commercial routes between Italy, France, and Switzerland crossed the level areas of Burgundy, and its command of the mountain passes gave it military routes into those countries. This kingdom became more dependent on the Holy Roman Empire until, at the death of its ruler, Rudolph III, in 1032, it became a fief of the Emperor Conrad II of Germany. Arles continued to be a separate kingdom in the Holy Roman Empire, and many emperors bore the title of king of Arles, but their authority over the territory was only nominal except for short intervals under stronger emperors. Frederick Barbarossa, by his marriage to Beatrix, the heiress of Franche-Comté in 1156, asserted his authority over the kingdom. But as the imperial authority continued to weaken, French influence over the country became stronger. Provence, Lyonnais, Vivarais, and Dauphiné were successively acquired by France. The Swiss Confederation acquired the eastern section. In 1378 the Emperor Charles IV ceded imperial rights over the kingdom of Arles to the dauphin, later Charles VI of France, and the kingdom ceased to exist as a separate state.

The name "Burgundy" came to be restricted to the Free County of Burgundy, or Franche-Comté and the Duchy of Burgundy, created by Charles the Bald, grandson of Charlemagne, in the ninth century. This was the portion of the original kingdom of Burgundy which had remained French. A line of Capetian dukes held the duchy from the eleventh century, and also secured the Free County as an imperial fief, but with the death of Duke Philip of Rouvres the line died out in 1361, and the duchy became part of France. John II of France granted the duchy to his younger son, Philip the Bold. Through his marriage with the heiress of Flanders, widow of the last duke of Burgundy of the old line, Philip added the Free County of Burgundy and the countship of Flanders to his domain.

Under Philip the Good, grandson of Philip the Bold, and son of John the Fearless who was murdered in 1419, the Burgundian power grew through the acquisition of the Netherlands and other territories. During the period of the Hundred Years' War Philip allied himself with the English and made possible their control of northern France. His son, Charles the Bold, inherited the ducal crown in 1467, fought with Louis XI of France, and conceived the plan of uniting his scattered lands by seizing Lorraine, and thus building up a new and powerful monarchy. He was defeated and killed by the Swiss at the battle of Nancy in 1477, leaving as his heiress his daughter Mary. As her guardian, Louis XI claimed possession of her lands. However, she was married to Maximilian, son of the Holy Roman Emperor. They succeeded in obtaining Franche-Comté and Artois as the inheritance of their daughter Margaret, although the Treaty of Arras in 1482 confirmed Louis in his possession of the duchy of Burgundy and it became a province of France. It was a *pays d'états,* with the estates meeting at Dijon. Louis

XIV later conquered the Free County of Burgundy, and kept it by the Peace of Nimeguen in 1678.

Climatically the region has cold winters and hot summers, being moist on the mountain sides and dry in the valleys. Chablis, Côte d'Or, Beaujolais are among the famous wines derived from the Burgundy vineyards. The fertile river valleys are planted in wheat and corn; the Montceau and Epinac coal basins are the basis of the many industries of Burgundy. After the French Revolution Burgundy was divided into the departments of Yonne, Saône-et-Loire, Ain, and Côte d'Or.

H. M.

BURGUNDY GATE or **BELFORT GAP,** located in eastern France. To the north rise the spurs of the Vosges Mountains: the Ballon d'Alsace, 4,000 ft.; Baerenkopf, 3,500 ft.; and to the south the Jura Mountains of 1,700 ft. elevation. Between the two mountain areas is the entrance of Valdieu or Burgundy Gate. Climatically the winters are rigorous, with strong winds blowing through the gap. The summers are hot. This area is one of the industrial regions of France, the principal cities being Belfort, Valdoie, and Danjoutin, which make use of the iron ore of Châtenois and coal from the Vosges region of Ronchamp. The fame of the Burgundy Gate lies in the fact that it is a route of invasion into France. Belfort was ceded to France at the Treaty of Westphalia in 1648. First fortified by Sébastien Le Prestre Vauban, French military engineer, it withstood three sieges, in 1814, 1815, and 1870. In 1870 it was bombarded for 73 days and capitulated only after orders were given by the national government after the armistice. The French troops marched out retaining all military honors and France was permitted to keep the city. A monument, the Lion of Belfort, was carved from the rock of the citadel by Frédéric A. Bartholdi to commemorate the siege.

BURHANPUR [bu'rhanpu'r], a city in the western part of central India, located at 21° 17' N. lat. and 76° 16' E. long., on the Tapti River in the Nimar District of Madhya Pradesh State. Burhanpur is about 310 mi. northeast of Bombay and is in a broad river valley at an elevation of about 1,200 ft. The Satpura Range is about 10 mi. to the northwest of the city, and the Gawilargh Hills are about 15 mi. to the southeast. Burhanpur receives between 20 and 40 in. of rainfall a year, almost all of which falls during the summer season. The winter months are cool, clear, and pleasant, averaging about 50° F., but the summers are hot. The surrounding region is an agricultural district, and grain and cotton are processed in the city, which has railroad connections with Bombay and the rest of India.

Burhanpur was founded in A.D. 1400 and became the administrative center of Khandesh. The city was held by the Moslems for two centuries, when it became part of the empire of Akbar. Until 1635 it was one of the important administrative centers of the Mogul Empire. The city is noted for two ruins: that of Akbar's Red Fort, built about 1600, and that of a mosque built by Ali Khan in 1588. Pop. 1951, 70,066.

J. E. F.

BURI [bu'ri], in Scandinavian mythology, the father of Borr, and grandfather of Odin, chief god of the Eddic myths. His name figures in the story of the creation of the world and the origin of the frost giants. Buri, "fair of feature, mighty and great," was said to have appeared when the mystic cow, Andhulm, licked the ice-bound salt rocks.

C. W. D.

BURIAL MOUNDS. *See* MOUNDS.
BURIAL RITES. *See* DEATH CUSTOMS AND RITES.

BURIAT MONGOLIA. *See* BURYAT-MONGOLIA.

BURKE, EDMUND (1729-1797), British statesman and author, was born in Dublin, probably on Jan. 12, 1729. He graduated from Trinity College, Dublin, in 1748, and entered the Middle Temple, London, in 1750 to study law, but soon abandoned it and turned to letters. In 1756 he published two short works that gained him considerable reputation: *Vindication of Natural Society,* a satirical imitation of the writings of Lord Bolingbroke, and *The Philosophical Inquiry into the Origin of our Ideas on the Sublime and the Beautiful.* For nearly thirty years Burke also contributed to the *Annual Register.* From 1759 to 1765 he was private secretary to William Gerard ("Single Speech") Hamilton, and in 1765 became private secretary to the Marquis of Rockingham, the prime minister, who assisted Burke in his campaign for election to Parliament. He proved a tower of strength to the Rockingham Whigs as a debater and as an adviser on matters of policy and reform. In 1770, in his *Thoughts on the Present Discontents,* he stated the principles upon which he felt the Whigs should act, accusing the government of strangling public opinion. As a result, he incurred the wrath of some of the powerful Whig leaders. On Mar. 22, 1775, in the House of Commons, Burke delivered what is considered by some his greatest speech, *Conciliation with America.* As agent for the colony of New York, beginning in 1771, Burke supported the cause of the American colonists with vigor. He was appointed paymaster of the forces under Rockingham in 1782 and under Portland in 1783, and introduced substantial reforms in the auditing of accounts. In 1783 he drafted the India Bill presented by Charles James Fox to reform the East India Company, and from 1786 to 1790 he concerned himself with the impeachment of Warren Hastings for his actions in India, making several of his best speeches in behalf of the prosecution; Hastings was acquitted, however, in 1795. In the meantime Burke had broken with his reformist friends, Charles James Fox, Richard Brinsley Sheridan, and others, and had adopted a bitterly conservative point of view, being accused of "loving liberty only in the guise of order." In 1790 his *Reflections on the Revolution in France* appeared; it had enormous success in creating an anti-French party in England, but Burke failed to conciliate his old Whig friends in the *Appeal from the New to the Old Whigs* in 1791. He had attained political respectability and popularity, and in 1796 resumed his attack on the French Revolution in his *Letters on a Regicide Peace.* He died in Beaconsfield, July 9, 1797. Burke's speeches read well, but he was not a great orator. Especially in his later years, his style was too florid, his language too involved and often too violent, and his speeches too long, as well as being delivered in a heavy Irish accent.   E. R. A.

BURLEIGH, BARON. *See* CECIL, WILLIAM, BARON BURGHLEY OR BURLEIGH.

BURLEIGH, HARRY THACKER [bɜ'rli] (1866-1949), American singer and composer, was born in Erie, Pa., on Dec. 2, 1866. He sang in Erie church choirs, and obtained a scholarship at the National Conservatory of Music in New York, where he remained four years as a student, for two of them as an assistant in teaching pianoforte and solfeggio. He studied harmony with Rubin Goldmark and counterpoint with Max Spicker. Burleigh played double bass and timpani in the Conservatory Orchestra, and became its librarian. In 1894, St. George's Episcopal Church, in New York City, chose him baritone soloist from among sixty competitors. His first solo there was Fauré's *The Palms,* on Palm Sunday, 1895, which he later sang for fifty-two consecutive Palm Sundays. In 1900, Burleigh commenced twenty-five years' service in the choir of Temple Emanu-El, New York, one of the nation's largest synagogues. He was the first Negro member of that choir. He made several concert tours of the United States and Europe, singing before numerous notables, and in a command performance for King Edward VII. Burleigh pioneered in introducing spirituals to the concert stage, publishing Negro folk songs, and arranging them for singing with accompaniment. He arranged over a hundred spirituals, including *Deep River, Nobody Knows the Trouble I've Seen, Couldn't Hear Nobody Pray,* and *Were You There?* He composed over 250 songs, mostly semi-classical ballads. He was musical editor for G. Ricordi & Sons, New York music publishers. He was a charter member and, since 1941, a director of the American Society of Composers, Authors and Publishers. In 1917 he received the Spingarn Medal, given annually for a major contribution to Negro life, for his distinguished achievement in music. After his retirement from St. George's choir in November 1946, he devoted himself to composing. Burleigh died in Stamford, Conn., Sept. 12, 1949.

BURLESQUE, a native form of entertainment exploiting broad humor, created about 1865 by Mike Leavitt. Burlesque shows, often called burleycues, were built for many years on the same pattern. A featured comedian headed the show, and he worked with three or four lesser comedians who wore comic make-up, drooping trousers, putty noses, and ludicrous wigs. The first part of the show consisted of ensemble singing and dancing, comedy sketches, or "bits." The middle part, or olio, was made up of variety acts. The second part was largely a repetition of the first, with illustrated songs, monologues, a comedy finale by the entire company, and an "Extra Added Attraction," a pugilistic bout or suggestive dance. About 1920 the strip tease, a disrobing number of uncertain origin, became the chief attraction. The "bits" were adaptations of humorous anecdotes in the tradition of the *Gesta Romanorum,* later to be known as smoking-car jokes. They relied almost entirely on *double entendre* and slapstick apparatus. Expurgated "bits" became, eventually, the revue "blackout" of the 1920's.

Burlesque, though largely a disreputable amusement, was the training school for many famous stars of musical comedy, revue, motion pictures, and radio. Among them were Al Jolson, W. C. Fields, Fannie Brice, Sophie Tucker, Jack Pearl, James Barton, Leon Errol, Bobby Clark, Willie Howard, Bert Lahr, and Weber and Fields. Among the popular companies and stars were Rentz-Santley, Sam T. Jack's, "Bozo" Snyder, Billy Watson's "Beef Trust," "Wine, Women and Song," "Sliding Billy" Watson, and Rose Sydell's "London Belles." The "wheels," or circuits, were touring companies under rival managements. Except for the inclusion of occasional travesty skits, the entertainment bore no relation to classic burlesque. *See also* SATIRE.   B. So.

BURLEY, the seat of Cassia Co. in southern Idaho, is situated on the Snake River at 4,100 ft. above sea level. It lies about 35 mi. east of Twin Falls in an agricultural area where livestock is raised. Founded in 1905, Burley has the mayor-council form of government. Sites of interest nearby are the Minidoka National Forest and the City of Rocks. Transportation is furnished by the Union Pacific Railroad. Local industrial products are potato flour, sugar, and bricks. Pop. 1950, 5,924.

BURLINGAME, ANSON [bɜ'rlɪŋgem] (1820-1870), American legislator and diplomat, was born in New Berlin, N. Y., Nov. 14, 1820. He lived in Ohio and Michigan in his youth and attended one of the branches of the University of Michigan. He was graduated from Harvard Law School in 1846. While practicing law in Boston, Burlingame became prominent through his campaign speeches for the Free Soil Party. The American ("Know Nothing") Party elected him to the Massachusetts state senate in 1853-1854 and in 1854 to the United States House of Representatives. He was re-elected to Congress by the Republicans, serving there until 1861, when President Lincoln appointed him minister to Austria. On account of his advocacy of Hungarian independence, he was not received by the Austrian government, and in June 1861 he was appointed minister to China. His ambassadorial work greatly influenced the Chinese toward a more modern reaction to the Occidental world. In November 1867 he resigned to become minister plenipotentiary of a Chinese diplomatic mission to the United States and the principal countries of Europe. As such he negotiated a series of articles supplementary to the Reed Treaty (later called the Burlingame Treaty) which gave China and the United States reciprocal privileges, including freedom of worship and the mutual exchange of the privilege of placing consuls in Chinese and American ports, respectively, in the interests of improved trade. As a representative of China, he had concluded similar treaties for China with Holland, Denmark, Prussia, and Sweden, and was in St. Petersburg to arrange a treaty with Russia when he died, Feb. 23, 1870.   D. R.

BURLINGAME [bɜ'rlɪŋgem], a city on San Francisco Bay in San Mateo Co., west central California, is situated 15 mi. south of San Francisco. It was founded in 1868 as a planned residential community and named for diplomat Anson Burlingame. Burlingame was incorporated as a city in 1908 and is governed by a mayor, council, and city manager. Its principal industries produce rubber tiles, loose-leaf binders, insulated trollies, baked goods, and commercial dryers. Pop. 1950, 19,886; 1957, 21,985.

BURLINGTON, a city in southeastern Iowa, the county seat of Des Moines Co., located on the Mississippi River, 170 mi. southeast of Des Moines. It is served by the Chicago, Burlington & Quincy, and the Chicago, Rock Island & Pacific railroads. In 1829, Zebulon Pike, explorer of Pike's Peak, established a trading post on the townsite. The first settlers came in 1833 and named the community Flint Hills. It was later named after Burlington, Vt. In 1838 it was chartered as a city and became the capital of Wisconsin Territory. The surrounding farming region produces livestock and grains. Local industries supply engines, furniture, caskets, chemicals, leather goods, boxes, soap, wearing apparel, mattresses, biscuits, and candy. Burlington (Junior) College was founded in 1920. Pop. 1950, 30,613.

BURLINGTON, a city and port of entry in west central New Jersey, is situated in Burlington Co. on the Delaware River, 18 mi. southwest of Trenton. It lies in a rich agricultural area, for which it is a trade center. Founded by Quakers in 1677, it was originally called New Beverly, and later Bridlington. It was incorporated as a town in 1693, re-incorporated in 1733, and incorporated as a city in 1784. It has the mayor and council form of government. Burlington was the capital of New Jersey under the colonial government and until 1790 under the state. Sites of historical interest are the birthplaces of James Fenimore Cooper

and Capt. James Lawrence and a residence of Gen. U. S. Grant. Burlington supports a junior college and a library chartered by George II in 1758. Transportation is provided by the Pennsylvania Railroad, and manufactures include textiles, spark plugs, fences, cast iron piping, typewriter ribbons, storage tanks, and shoes. Pop. 1950, 12,051.

BURLINGTON, a city in Alamance Co., in northern North Carolina, about 20 mi. east of Greensboro. It is served by the Southern Railroad. The city was founded in 1845 and incorporated in 1887. The Battle of Alamance was fought 9 mi. from the site of Burlington in 1771. Elon College is within 2 mi. of the city. Dairying, tobacco growing, and truck farming are the principal activities of the region. Textiles, hosiery, and furniture are the city's chief manufactured products. Pop. 1950, 24,560.

BURLINGTON, the largest city in Vermont, a port, and the seat of Chittenden Co., is situated in the northwestern part of the state on Lake Champlain, about 40 mi. northwest of Montpelier. The surrounding Green Mountain country is a noted winter and summer vacation area. Burlington was granted a charter in 1763 but not settled until 1773, and it was incorporated in 1865. Government is by a mayor and council. Notable persons associated with Burlington include Ethan Allen; his brother, Gen. Ira Allen, who founded the University of Vermont; Edward Everett Hale, the writer; and John Dewey, the philosopher. The city is the seat of the University of Vermont, the State Agricultural College, and Trinity College for women. Fort Ethan Allen is 3 mi. away. The city is served by the Central Vermont and the Rutland (freight) railroads, by ferry to Port Kent, N.Y., and by Colonial and Northeast airlines. Burlington is the manufacturing center of the state. Its output includes structural steel, woolen goods and sportswear, maple products, venetian blinds, paints, ovens, kitchen tools, brush fibers, breakfast foods, mattresses, electrical goods, and beverages. There is also a meat packing plant and a distillery. Pop. 1950, 33,155.

BURMA, UNION OF [bɜ'rmə], the largest independent republic of continental southeast Asia. It occupies the northwestern third of the Indochinese peninsula, covering an area of 261,610 sq. mi., slightly less than that of the state of Texas. Shaped like a kite with a long tail, it is bounded on the northwest by East Pakistan and the Indian state of Assam, on the north and northeast by China, and on the east by Laos and Thailand (Siam); the remainder of its perimeter forms part of the coast line of the Bay of Bengal. The country is divided into two well-defined regions known as Upper and Lower Burma. The latter includes the plains and deltas of the Irrawaddy, the Sittang, and the Lower Salween rivers; the littoral of Arakan; and the Tenasserim region, which is the long tail of the kite extending down the western side of the Malay Peninsula. This lower region is the principal agricultural section of Burma. Upper Burma includes the upper Irrawaddy Valley, with extensive irrigated areas, and the wild hill country, a mining region and the home of the native tribesmen.

GEOGRAPHICAL FEATURES

Geology and Relief. Burma is composed of a north-south-trending central basin, which is occupied by the Chindwin, Irrawaddy, and Sittang rivers. This central valley is surrounded on all sides except the south by high mountains. To the west, on the Indian and Pakistan borders, are the Naga, Manipur, and Chin hills, ranges with a core of ancient crystalline rock and peaks reaching elevations of over 8,000 ft. These ranges may be the extreme southern extension of the Himalaya Mountains, which make a sharp right-angle curve to the south around the head of the Assam Valley. Composed of numerous folded ridges, they form an effective barrier to east-west overland transportation.

In the extreme north, just north of Putao, the boundary of Burma is in the peaks of the Patkai, part of the Hump, ris-

stream, debouches to the east near Moulmein. In the dry zone of central Burma are some low, isolated volcanic hills.

The northern part of the west coast of Burma, called the Arakan, is a narrow strip with many small offshore islands. The largest of these are the Akyab, Ramree, and Cheduba islands. The mountains, called the Arakan Yoma, rising to more than 6,000 ft., are close to the coast, and small streams carry sediment down to the Bay of Bengal to form a low, swampy area. The southeastern panhandle of Burma is formed by the long, narrow Tenasserim section. The mountain backbone is composed of a range of granite rising from 3,000 to 4,000 ft., and some sedimentary rocks. There are a few peaks with an elevation between 6,000 and 7,200 ft. The coast is very narrow and swampy, and there are many offshore islands, forming the Mergui Archipelago.

Climate. With the exception of some of the high plateaus, mountain-tops, and the dry Mandalay Basin, Burma is a hot, humid country, and all of it is under the influence of the monsoon winds. The average annual temperature at Rangoon is 81° F., and the average monthly temperatures vary between 77° F. in January, the coldest month, and 88° F. in April, the warmest month. Mandalay, in the central region, has an average annual temperature of 82° F., but the average in January is 70° F., and in April, 90° F.

The amount of rainfall varies tremendously within the country because of the differences in elevation and exposure to monsoon winds. Rangoon receives about 100 in. of rain a year; most of it falls from May to September during the period of in-blowing, or wet, monsoons, with July alone averaging about 22 in. The Arakan and Tenasserim coasts receive as much as 200 in. of rain yearly, but the basin of Mandalay, in a rain shadow, receives only 35 in.

Soils. The soils of Burma may be divided into four classes which correspond generally to the physiographic regions: the river deltas of the south, the river valleys farther north, the rolling uplands of the interior basin, and the mountains on the periphery. The depth, organic content, and fertility of these soils decline in this same sequence. Crop failures are unknown in the extensive deltaic regions where the natural acidity of the local soil is being constantly neutralized by deposits from the more alkaline uplands. The abundance of moisture on the rich, deep soil makes it especially suitable for the cultivation of rice. Although the soil in the flood plains of the rivers farther north is less deep, it is equally fertile, but irrigation is needed to supplement the sometimes erratic rainfall and the unpredictable river levels if security in agriculture is to be assured. The soils of the rolling and sometimes rugged uplands vary greatly from place to place, and irrigation is often impossible. But there are various areas of marked fertility. The soils in the mountainous regions have suffered great depletion through erosion and are for the most part either sterile or incapable of cultivation. This is particularly true in the far north. The sterility would have been even greater had the region been subject to more extensive deforestation. Roving tribesmen inhabiting hill regions burn off cultivable areas (*taungya*) which can produce crops for a year or two out of eight or ten.

Flora. Over half of the area of Burma is still forested. Some of it is impenetrable jungle. The most conspicuous tree, as well as the most economically valuable, is the teak, which accounts for almost 98 per cent of the total value of timber exports. Other valuable trees are the *Acacia catechu*, whose heartwood, catechu, provides an extract used in dyeing; the India-rubber tree; the ironwood of Pegu (*Xylia xylocarpa*), and the cinchona, from whose bark quinine is extracted. The forests contain a wide variety of arboreal spe-

ing to heights between 15,000 and 18,000 ft. East of the central valley are the Kaolikung Mountains, separating Burma from southwestern China, and attaining an elevation of 13,000 ft. South of the Kaolikung range is the Shan Plateau of central and eastern Burma, with a rolling and dissected surface rising from 3,000 to 4,000 ft. above sea level, through which the Myitnge and Salween rivers have cut deep valleys. A steep escarpment, from 3,000 to 4,000 ft. high, marks the western border of the plateau. Along the Thai-Burma border run the High Tanen-Taunggyi Mountains, which extend southward into the Tenasserim range.

The central valley is a broad area of alluvium and sediments that slopes gently to the south. The extreme southern part is formed by the swampy compound delta of the Irrawaddy and the Sittang, with a low mountain range, the Pegu Yoma, dividing the two rivers. The Salween, a swifter cies, both evergreen and deciduous. In much of the drier interior the vegetative cover consists mostly of thorn scrub and grasses. In the mountains the forest often gives place to open fen and grassland. On the lower levels of the mountains oak and pine are widespread. Higher up these give place to the rhododendron. Of the cultivated plants rice easily holds first place, especially in the south. In the north the crops raised are of great variety including, along with rice, corn, millet, sesame (for its seed oil), tobacco, cotton, sugar cane, legumes, and tea.

Fauna. The northern part of the country is particularly rich in game animals. These include the elephant (domesticated in the south); tiger; leopard; Himalaya and Malaya bears; one- and two-horned rhinoceroses; wild pigs; various species of deer including the barking deer (*Muntjac*), thameng (*Cervus eldi*), and the sambar (*Cervus unicolor*); two goat antelopes, the goral and the serow; the banteng (*Bibos sondaicos*); the gaur (*Bibos gaurus*); the flying fox; two species of gibbons; and several species of monkeys. Among the birds are the green peafowl (a pheasant), several species of small parrots, the paddy bird, and the ubiquitous house crow. Conspicuous among the snakes are the python and the cobra. There are also crocodiles, lizards (including the familiar gecko), and turtles. Edible fish are plentiful both along the coast and in the rivers.

ETHNOLOGY AND POPULATION

Ethnic Groups. The population of Burma was officially estimated at 19,045,000 in 1953. The Burmese-speaking people, two thirds of the total population, constitute the largest ethnic and linguistic group. Other important groups are the Karens, numbering approximately 1,500,000; Tai (Shans), 1,300,000; Kuki-Chins, 500,000; Mons, 400,000; Palaung-Was, 225,000; and Kachins, 200,000. Before World War II there were over a million Indians in Burma but they are fewer now. There are also some 300,000 Chinese.

Burmese. Originally, the Burmese came from the highlands of eastern Tibet and western China, pushing southward until they reached the central plains, where they are now settled. Burmese is a polytonic, monosyllabic language related to Tibetan. Although the language has a simple grammar, it is difficult for Europeans to understand because of its tonal inflections and complicated word order. The Burmese alphabet, adopted from the Pali of India, has ten vowels and thirty-two consonants and a characteristic rounded form. Ethnically, the Burmese are Mongoloid, showing the characteristic features of short stature, straight black hair, high cheekbones, and the eye-fold.

Karens. The Karens, originally a hill people, are heavily concentrated in the Tenasserim, Pegu, Bassein, Salween, and Toungoo divisions of Lower Burma. They are the dominant group in the Kayah State (formerly Karenni States) and in the Karen State, the latter constituted only in 1954 after the pacification of the rebel Karens. Both states are represented in the Union cabinet and have considerable autonomy. The Sgaw Karens of the plains have been particularly receptive to Western culture and many have adhered to the Christian faith.

Shans. In the northern hill region, known as the Shan State, are the Shans, related to the Thailanders and to the Thai of southern China. They have a written language of their own which, however, has declined because of the scant number of books and periodicals being produced. They feel cultural bonds with the Thai of Thailand. The Shan peoples as a group are less westernized than the Burmese of the plains, but their Sawbwa princely rulers are often well

BY BOB LANBACH, FROM BLACK STAR

SHWE DAGON PAGODA IN RANGOON

educated along Western lines. Numerous tribal hill peoples live intermingled with the valley-dwelling Shans.

Chins. The Chins are related to the Lushai and Kuki peoples of Assam; they occupy the hill tracts north of the Arakan Yoma in western Burma. The so-called Chin Hills reach from the Bassein district in the south, northward to the upper reaches of the Chindwin River. A warlike people, the Chins presented a considerable problem to the British in their settlement of Upper Burma. They make excellent soldiers. Some of the Chins have become converts to the Christian faith.

Mons. The Mons are related to such people as the Khmer of Cambodia, the Moi of Assam, and the Lawa of Thailand, and their language has affinities with the Malayo-Polynesian and Melanesian languages of Oceania. At one time the Mons occupied all of Lower Burma, but they have since become concentrated in the delta regions of the Irrawaddy, Sittang, and Salween rivers. They are being rapidly absorbed into the Burman ethnic and linguistic group. Many of the leaders of modern Burma have been Mons.

Kachins. The Kachins are a primitive hill people who predominate in the relatively unsettled northern corner of Burma north of the city of Bhamo and along the Chinese border. They were animists in religion and tribal in social organization, but many are now Baptists. Each village is controlled by a hereditary chief. Contact with the outside is maintained by the government railway which extends to Myitkyina, some 90 mi. directly north of Bhamo, and by river boats between these centers during the season of high water on the Irrawaddy. Some Kachins have moved south, and substantial numbers of Chinese refugees have recently moved into the Kachin Hills region. The Kachins, organized in the Kachin State, have local autonomy. The elimination of slavery in the more isolated villages has been a persistent problem for the government of Burma, but may now be said to have been accomplished.

Religion. Buddhism is the religion of about 85 per cent of the people of Burma. It is known as Theravada or Hinayana Buddhism and is akin to that practiced in Thailand, Cambodia, and Ceylon in contrast to the northern Mahayana form practiced in Tibet, China, and Japan. Hinayana Buddhism employs Pali as its sacred language, while Sanskrit is used in Mahayana Buddhism. Burmese Buddhism lacks the organization and elaborate hierarchy usually associated with formal religion. Each village has a monastery, *pongyi kyaung,* presided over by a monk, called *pongyi.* While a very small village will have only one monk, the larger cities will have several monasteries and numerous monks. The city of Mandalay, for example, has 20,000 monks. Near the monastery is a pagoda, which is not a temple but a spire of concentric circles of solid masonry. Three of the largest pagodas in Burma are the Shwe Dagon in Rangoon, the Shwesandaw in Prome, and the Arakan of Mandalay. Other religious groups represented in Burma are the Animists, Moslems, Hindus, and Christians.

Distribution of Population. Burma is a rural country. Only three cities, Rangoon, Moulmein, and Mandalay, have over 100,000 population. Rangoon, Burma's capital and most important port, is on the Rangoon River of the Irrawaddy Delta, 25 mi. from the Bay of Bengal. Moulmein, to the southeast, is a port at the mouth of the Salween. Mandalay is in the heart of Upper Burma, 350 mi. north of Rangoon. Other important towns are the port of Akyab, the rail and trading centers of Prome, Myitkyina, and Lashio, and Toungoo in the Sittang Valley.

GOVERNMENT

The constitution of the Republic of Burma provides for a president, a cabinet, and a two-house legislature. The president is elected for five years by the two houses of parliament sitting in joint session. His powers are largely nominal since all his acts must be countersigned by a responsible minister. Although he may delay the signing of bills for not more than seven days, he has no veto on legislation. He is a member neither of the legislature nor of the cabinet. The cabinet consists of the prime minister, several department heads, and ministers of the Shan, Kachin, and Kayah states and of Karenni and Chin affairs. Following the British principle the cabinet as a whole can retain office only with the confidence of the lower house of the legislature. The prime minister selects his ministers. He himself is appointed by the president, but only after nomination by the lower house of the legislature. This lower house is called the chamber of deputies. Its numbers, which may be altered by ordinary legislative enactment, are approximately double those of the upper house or chamber of nationalities. Deputies represent single-member constituencies which may not contain more than 100,000 nor less than 30,000 persons. The franchise in parliamentary elections is extended to men and women alike. Money bills must originate in the chamber of deputies, and the upper house is prevented from amending such bills. The chamber of nationalities consists of 125 members. Of these, only 53 represent Burma proper. Shans, Karens, and Kachins each have a council of state consisting of their respective representatives in the Burmese parliament. Constitutional privileges guaranteed to minority states of the Union can be altered only with the consent of the state council concerned. The councils have limited legislative jurisdiction in the fields of agriculture, education, and justice. Each of the states also has an administrator appointed by the central government.

ECONOMIC RESOURCES AND ACTIVITIES

Agriculture. Burma is predominantly an agricultural country. Agriculture is concentrated in the deltas and valleys of the Irrawaddy, Chindwin, and Sittang rivers. The main crop is rice, grown on two thirds of the cultivated land of the country. Burma is one of the leading rice-producing countries of the world, and normally the country with the largest rice surplus, her prewar exports being more than the combined total of her two chief rivals, Indochina and Thailand. While this level was not reached in the early postwar years, Burma's economy depended on rice exports and suffered from declining markets. On the small farms of Upper Burma other important crops are grown, principally sesame, cotton, peanuts, sugar cane, legumes, and tobacco. The Shan State produces a surplus of draft cattle.

Mining. Burma's extensive mineral wealth is still largely undeveloped. The production of petroleum has been the most important mining development, with a considerable output attained under the British. The oil fields are in the central part of the country, extending along the Irrawaddy River Valley; Yenangyaung and Chauk are oil-producing regions. There are also oil fields on the Shan Plateau. Silver and lead are mined, principally at Bawdwin in the Shan Plateau, and the Tenasserim section has valuable deposits of tin. Tungsten is produced in the Kayah State. Gold is found in stream gravels in north Burma. There are also some deposits of lignite, iron, copper, zinc, and nickel. Burma is also famous for rubies from Mogok on the Shan Plateau, and most Chinese jade comes from the Mogaung and Myitkyina districts.

Industry. Burma has made little progress industrially. The milling of rice, whereby this important product is prepared for export, is by far the most important industrial activity and employs the greatest number of laborers. Lumber milling and oil refining are also of considerable importance. Minor industries include the manufacture of cotton goods, tanning of leather, and rubber processing. The average number of workers per factory in Burma prior to World War II was less than 100.

The government of Burma has launched a development program by which it plans by 1959-1960 to increase gross domestic production by 31 per cent, per capita production by 4 per cent, national consumption by 38 per cent, and per capita consumption by 8.7 per cent. The program will require an investment of 7,900 million kyats (one kyat = about 21¢). Lack of administrative experience and the persistence of disorder have hampered the economy.

Transportation and Communications. Burma's railway system includes 2,000 mi. of meter-gauge track connecting all of the important cities. However, there are no railway connections across the frontiers. The main arteries of travel and trade in Burma are the Irrawaddy River and its tributaries. Road construction has lagged in Burma, principally because the river and rail facilities have been adequate in the direction of the main flow of traffic. Only three roads cross the border: the Burma Road, starting at the Lashio railhead and going eastward to China; one through the Shan State into Thailand; and the Ledo Road, built under the stress of war, which starts in Assam, India, and crosses northern Burma to Yünnan province in China.

Through its capital, Rangoon, Burma maintains communication with Calcutta and Singapore by submarine cable. It also has radio connection with these ports and through them with world services. The British Overseas Airways Corporation connects Rangoon with Calcutta, London, Shanghai, and Auckland. Rangoon is a regular stop for globe-circling flights of Pan American World Airways. Despite internal disorders in Burma the Union of Burma Airways was inaugurated on Sept. 11, 1948, with initial services between Rangoon and Bassein, Anisakan, Magwe, Toungoo, and

Meiktila. There are internal systems of telegraphic and telephonic communication.

Commerce. Before World War II, when Burma was a part of the British Empire, fully three fourths of her foreign trade was within the empire. India and Ceylon are now Burma's best customers, while India, the United Kingdom, and Japan supply most of her commercial needs. Her chief exports are rice, petroleum, timber (teak), cotton, hides, metals and ores, beans, rubber, and lac. The principal imports are cotton goods, machinery, hardware, coal, silk, and sugar. Approximately 90 per cent of Burma's foreign trade goes through the port of Rangoon. Other leading ports are Bassein, Akyab, Moulmein, Tavoy, and Mergui.

SOCIAL AND CULTURAL ACTIVITIES

Health Problems. Despite a relatively high standard of living and considerable progress in public health services and socialized medicine, Burma still has serious health problems. The most serious is that caused by malaria, which accounts for two fifths of all deaths. Tuberculosis is also an important cause of death; it has been said that Rangoon has the second highest death rate from this disease in the world. Venereal disease is common. Other prevalent sicknesses which sap the vitality of the people are trachoma, leprosy, beriberi, cholera, dengue fever, dysentery, and sprue.

Social Customs and Standards. The typical Burmese house has side walls of bamboo matting, a thatched roof, and a floor of sawed boards. It is usually erected on posts some 5 ft. above the ground. In the cities the homes of the wealthier people are of European-type construction. The principal article of diet in Burma is rice, to which is added a curry of meat, vegetables, and fish paste, all highly seasoned. The national costume, worn even by city-bred Burmans, is the *longyi,* a cylinder of cloth one yard or more in diameter, which is wrapped around the hips and folded over in front to form a sort of skirt reaching to the ankles; a jacket is worn over the upper part of the body. The *gaungbaung,* a pastel-colored silken kerchief covering a bamboo frame, is worn on the head. Stockings are seldom worn, but most people wear leather toe-strap sandals.

The social structure of Burma is democratic, with no caste as in India. The women are freer and have a higher status than in any other Oriental country. The age of marriage is the same as that in Western countries,

and there is reasonable freedom of choice, both for men and women. Women retain their maiden names after marriage; there is no objection to remarriage of widows or divorcees. Polygamy is permitted but rarely occurs. Large families are not usual.

Education. Primary education in Burma is provided in part by the ubiquitous monastery schools, in part by secular schools, most of which are maintained by the state. These total approximately 5,000, including some above the primary grades. The medium of instruction is Burmese, with English a compulsory second language above the fifth grade. The apex of Burma's educational system is Rangoon University, with faculties of arts, science, engineering, law, education, medicine, and forestry. There are also colleges at Mandalay and at Moulmein, and a school of fine arts, music, and drama at Rangoon. Except in the monastic schools coeducation is the common practice in Burma, from primary grades through the university. With the exception of Japan, Burma has the highest percentage of literacy among the Oriental nations.

HISTORY

Early Peoples and Dynasties. Little is known of Burma's early history. It is believed that the Negritos who inhabit the Andaman Islands in the Bay of Bengal are the survivors of a group which was at one time scattered over Burma. The peoples of modern Burma are the descendants of various Mongoloid tribes who at an early period pushed southward down the Irrawaddy and Salween rivers from Tibet and western China. Authentic history of Burma dates from the reign of King Anawratha, founder of the dynasty with its capital at Pagan, in the Irrawaddy in central Burma, in the eleventh century A.D. From this period until the overthrow of King Thibaw by the British in 1886, the history of Burma is one of various small kingdoms and dynasties attempting to establish control. The historic rivals of the Burmese were the Mons of Lower Burma.

British Rule. British influence began when the East India Company sent agents to Burma in the seventeenth century. Beginning in 1825, British influence and control were gradually extended until, at the close of the third Anglo-Burmese War in 1886, the country was annexed and became a part of British India. In 1937, Burma was separated from India and given its own constitution. While this constitution provided for a government elected by the people of Burma, Great Britain, through a governor, still retained control of defense, finance, and foreign affairs, as well as administration of frontier areas. Burma, with an elected legislature and a cabinet of Burmese ministers, was not a colony, but had the status of a self-governing unit of the British Commonwealth. The period from 1931 to the outbreak of World War II was characterized by intermittent disorders and strong discontent with British rule, as well as conflict between the Burmese and Indian residents of the country over economic and religious matters.

World War II. Burma was quickly overrun by Japan in the early days of World War II and became a puppet state of that power. On Aug. 1, 1943, amid great pomp and ceremony, Burma was granted a fictional independence by Japan, with Ba Maw, the puppet premier, as head of the government. On the day independence was granted, Ba Maw declared war on the Allies and simultaneously signed a pact of alliance with Japan. This was the beginning of a difficult period for Burma. Cut off from her world markets, and with Japan unable either to buy her surplus or to supply her import needs, Burma was reduced to dire economic straits. The country also suffered from

EWING GALLOWAY, NEW YORK

On a farm in Upper Burma water buffalo thresh grain by trampling it.

Street scene in Rangoon, capital of the Union of Burma

inflation, black market operations, and a Japanese army of occupation which ignored the Burmese government and appropriated whatever it needed or wanted. As a result of all these factors, Burma's youthful nationalist leadership turned against the Japanese in 1945.

Independence and Early Struggles. In May 1945, Great Britain issued a White Paper announcing a new plan which definitely promised dominion status for Burma after a period of reconstruction. This, however, did not satisfy the Burmese, and on Oct. 17, 1947, British Prime Minister Clement R. Attlee and Burmese Premier U Nu signed a treaty in London, effective Jan. 4, 1948, granting Burma independence outside the Commonwealth as the Republic of the Union of Burma.   G. G. C. and W. M. W.

The first president of the Burmese republic was Sao Shwe Thaik, a Shan Sawbwa prince, and the first prime minister was U Nu. The latter had assumed the leadership in the independence movement after the assassination on July 19, 1947, of U Aung San with six of his executive councillors by U Saw of the Myochit or rightist party. U Nu was the leader of the Anti-Fascist People's Freedom League (AFPFL), the dominant party, with strong socialist proclivities. Many factors contributed to the almost complete breakdown of government during the first year of the republic's existence. The British had granted local autonomy to the Burmese in 1937. There had, therefore, been little time for the training of responsible leaders before the collapse of the government with the coming of the Japanese. These had left in their wake not only economic dislocation but political confusion. Rivalry among political leaders and subversive Communist propaganda aggravated disorderly conditions. Within the country the absence of adequate lines of communication and the presence of several nationalities with different languages made national unity difficult. Such nationalism as there was tended to separate rather than unite, but the government enjoyed one considerable advantage. If intransigent national and ideological groups could not be induced to support the government, they also could not be brought to co-operate with each other in attacking the government. Near anarchy prevailed for the better part of two years. The Karen nationalist rebellion, which started almost a year after that of the dissident leftist

groups, almost ended the career of the new republic. During the spring of 1950, the government managed to win back some of the extensive territory from which it had been forced to withdraw and began to police the principal routes of transportation. Disorder continued to be widely prevalent throughout the countryside, so that economic recovery was nevertheless slow. Government revenues were derived during the ensuing years very largely from the proceeds of monopoly sales of rice surpluses abroad.

During the concluding months of 1950, the AFPFL excluded dissident pro-Communist elements. At the same time, the government supported the United Nations defense of South Korea and moved to accept American technical assistance in the economic sphere. The first general elections, held in 1952, resulted in an overwhelming victory for the AFPFL, which captured more than two thirds of the seats in the chamber of deputies. U Nu continued as prime minister and a former Burman chief justice, U Ba U, became the new president.

International Relations. Even before the last ties with the British Commonwealth of Nations were cut, Burma had established diplomatic relations with the government of the United Kingdom by the mutual exchange of high commissioners. Following the separation these high commissionerships were raised to embassies. The new Union of Burma established early diplomatic relations with the United States and India. Burma also was the first non-Communist country to recognize Communist China (in December 1949), and Rangoon's established policy has been to preserve friendly relations with Peking. Eventually diplomatic relations were established with the U.S.S.R. as well.

Burma is firmly committed to the support of the United Nations, of which it became a member on Apr. 19, 1948. This was demonstrated by Burmese support of the UN defense of South Korea in 1950 and by Rangoon's condemnation of the Soviet Union's intervention in Hungary in 1956. But in general Burma's foreign policy has been closely integrated with the neutralist, or third force, policy championed by India's Premier Nehru. In May 1954 Burma's Socialist party sponsored the convening in Burma of an Asian Socialist Conference, including parties extending as far afield as Israel and

Japan. A second session, meeting in Japan later in 1954, also found a Burmese acting as chairman. Burma was an enthusiastic official participant in the Bandung Conference in 1955, which affirmed general opposition to imperialist pressures from whatever direction they might come.

Having been victimized in World War II, Burma avoided becoming entangled in the cold war alignment or in any future conflict growing out of prevailing world tensions. Difficulties with some 12,000 refugee Chinese Nationalist troops, who were occupying sections of eastern Burma, and whose presence constituted a possible invitation to Communist Chinese intervention, caused Burma's abrupt termination of American economic aid in 1953, in the belief that Washington had failed to restrain its Nationalist Chinese ally on Formosa from sending American arms to the Kuomintang rebels in Burma. U Nu was one of five Asian prime ministers who agreed at Colombo in 1954 to reject membership in the Southeast Asia Treaty Organization. American economic assistance on a modest basis was resumed in 1957.

Internal Affairs. Burma's principal domestic difficulties developed in the area of administration and the handling of industrial projects connected with the officially planned program of economic development. Lawlessness and rebel resistance continued to hamper efforts at economic recovery. Mismanagement of the rice surpluses—careless handling of stored rice, monetary defalcations, barter deals with Communist countries—caused much embarrassment and serious losses in 1956-1957. U Nu resigned in favor of his deputy, Ba Swe, in June 1956 but resumed his office in March 1957 after general elections again returned a safe majority for the AFPFL coalition; but rifts began to appear and the nonrebel Communist opposition scored fairly impressive gains. U Win Maung, a Karen, became president in 1957.   J. F. C.

BUR MARIGOLD, the common name of a large genus (*Bidens*) of the family Compositae, with about ninety widely distributed species of which perhaps thirty occur in North America. Many are widely diffused as weeds. They grow to 2 ft., with divided leaves, yellow or white small flowers, and numerous flat seeds armed with two to four hooks, which cling to animals or clothes. They are also known as tickseed, sticktight, or beggar's tick.   J. C. Wis.

BURMESE [bɜrmi′z; bɜrmi′s], the official language in the Union of Burma, uncontested in the Irrawaddy Valley, and superimposed in the mountain region on the tribal dialects of the Shans, Kachins, Karens, and Chins. Burmese is part of the Tibetan-Burmese sub-group of the Sino-Tibetan family of languages. Native simple nouns and verbs in Burmese are monosyllabic. Often they are distinguished from each other only by intonation; but to express an idea a combination of several such syllables is often necessary. Some syllables are purely formal, without any meaning by themselves. While sharing these general characteristics and also the absence of gender and number with other members of the Sino-Tibetan family, Burmese may be distinguished from these languages by virtue of the fact that it shares still more characteristics with Austronesian and that, as a result of having accepted Buddhism from India, it has taken in many Pali words and features.

The oldest known inscription in Burmese is found on an eleventh-century stone pillar in Myazedi, written in Burmese, Pali, Mon, and Pyu. There are also very old translations of Indian Buddhist texts. The Burmese alphabet is an adaptation of the old Pali alphabet of India, the origin of which is traceable to the Phoenician alphabet.   P. F.

BURNAP, DANIEL (1759-1838), Connecticut clockmaker, was born in Coventry Township, Conn., on Nov. 1, 1759, in what is now Andover. He learned clockmaking as an apprentice to Thomas Harland at Norwich, Conn. About 1780 he settled in East Windsor, Conn., and there started his own clockmaking business. His clocks, still extant in fair numbers, are among the most interesting American examples of the late eighteenth and early nineteenth centuries. He specialized in eight-day brass movements in tall cases, though he may have made a few wooden movements after the style of the Cheneys. Eli Terry learned from Burnap many of the methods he later put to good use in clockmaking. Burnap may well have been the first to use interchangeable parts and mass production, since from his records it appears that he built more than one clock at the same time. However, Harland also may have followed this practice. Sometime after 1800 Burnap moved back to Coventry and by 1805 built a house in which he lived for the rest of his life. As justice of the peace, he held courts on the ground floor. In his shop he continued to make clocks and also brass hardware, surveyors' instruments, and silver spoons and buckles. Few of his clocks are dated after 1815, at which time he turned his shop over to an apprentice and, from his attic, carried on the less taxing work of engraving and watch repair. He died in Coventry on Sept. 26, 1838.   B. P.

BURNE-JONES, SIR EDWARD (1833-1898), English painter and designer, was born at Birmingham, Aug. 28, 1833. His career ran parallel to that of his Oxford contemporary, William Morris, with whom he traveled after leaving the university and with whom he studied painting under Rossetti. Several trips to Italy brought Burne-Jones in touch with the work of fifteenth-century Italian artists, from whom he borrowed many decorative elements. His works are most effective when part of a decorative scheme, as, for example, his tapestries, stained-glass windows, or mosaics. His style sometimes deals in broad decorative areas rather than lines, as in *The Mill* (1870-1872), at the Victoria and Albert Museum in London; or his linear treatment may depend upon eccentricity, as in the *Perseus* series, or upon sweeping vertical motion, as in *The Days of Creation.* The influence of Rossetti is unmistakable, whether it expresses itself in the effeminate character of Burne-Jones' stock faces or in the decorative allover pattern of many of his works. Burne-Jones died in London, June 17, 1898. (*See illustration on following page.*)   C. P. P.

BURNET, *Sanguisorba minor,* a perennial herb of the rose family, native to Europe and Asia and naturalized in North America. It grows from 1 to 2½ ft. tall, bearing 6 to 10 pairs of small leaflets and greenish flowers. The fresh young leaves are used in salads.   J. C. Wis.

BURNEY, FANNY (MME. D'ARBLAY) (1752-1840), English novelist and diarist, was born June 13, 1752, at King's Lynn, Norfolk, daughter of the composer and music historian Charles Burney. An unusually sensitive observer, she recorded her experiences and feelings with candor and charm in diaries begun during May 1768. Published, after her death, as *Early Diary* (1889, 1907) and *Diary and Letters, 1778-1840* (1842-1846, 1904-1905), they are admired as highly as her best novels. Their substance is valuable and fascinating. She was attached to the English royal household from 1786 to 1791 and was acquainted with many prominent figures of the late

CHANT D'AMOUR

FROM A PAINTING BY SIR EDWARD BURNE-JONES

eighteenth and early nineteenth centuries, among them Samuel Johnson, David Garrick, and Benjamin Disraeli. She also met many French notables (1801-1812) when her husband, the exiled General Alexandre d'Arblay, whom she had married in 1793, returned to France to recoup his fortunes.

Mme. d'Arblay's best novel is *Evelina,* published anonymously in 1778. *Cecilia* (1782), though wordy and not uniformly convincing, still holds interest by its quick perceptions, its characters, and its reflection of the times. Awkward pomposity marred the author's other novels, and only one of her four plays was produced. Her *Memoirs of Dr. Burney* (1832), although incredibly affected in style, contains valuable historical material. Mme. d'Arblay's last years were saddened by the death of her husband and only son. She died in London, Jan. 6, 1840. *See also* EVELINA.

R. M. W.

BURNHAM, DANIEL HUDSON [bɜ'rnəm] (1846-1912), American architect and city planner, was born at Henderson, Jefferson County, N. Y., on Sept. 4, 1846. He was educated in Chicago and at Waltham, Mass. In 1871, he joined John W. Root (1850-1891) in the practice of architecture in Chicago. To this firm were entrusted many important commissions, among them the general architectural superintendence of the World's Columbian Exposition of 1893. In order to take care of their large commissions, Burnham and Root developed the large departmentalized type of

architectural office later found in many American cities. Burnham and Root were important in the development of the steel-skeleton building frame which made possible the American skyscraper. Among their Chicago buildings which were milestones in this development may be named the Rookery Building, the Rand-McNally Building, and the Masonic Temple, which for a time was the highest building in existence. Burnham's Flatiron Building in New York has become a famous landmark. His practice extended from coast to coast and to foreign lands, as in the development of the city plan for Manila. He prepared plans also for San Francisco, Baltimore, and Chicago, the last with E. H. Bennett. He had much to do with the development of Washington, D. C., and his firm designed the Union Station in that city. Burnham was president of the American Institute of Architects in 1894 and received many honors. He died June 1, 1912, in Heidelberg, Germany.

R. Ne.

BURNHAM, SHERBURNE WESLEY (1838-1921), American astronomer, was born in Thetford, Vt., Dec. 12, 1838. He graduated from Thetford Academy and migrated to Chicago, where he became a court reporter. However, his main interest was in astronomy, and in Chicago he set up a private observatory with a 6-in. telescope. He became the world's leading observer of double stars. For a few years Burnham was on the staff of the Lick Observatory, on Mt. Hamilton, Calif., and later was astronomer at Yerkes Observatory of the University of Chicago, at Williams Bay, Wis. In 1874 Burnham was made a Fellow of the Royal Astronomical Society of England and received the gold medal in 1894 for his discovery and measurement of double stars. In 1904 the Paris Academy of Sciences awarded him the Lalande prize in astronomy. He published several catalogs of double stars, and his most important work was the *General Catalogue of Double Stars within 121° of the North Pole* (1906). Burnham himself discovered more than 1,300 double stars. He died in Chicago, Ill., Mar. 11, 1921.   H. S. R.

BURNING BUSH, the common name of diverse plants, including the wahoo (*Euonymus atropurpureus*) and the strawberry bush (*E. americanus*), North American shrubs with bright-red fruits. Dittany or gas plant (*Dictamnus*), an old-fashioned garden perennial, is sometimes called burning bush.   J. C. Wis.

BURNLEY, a municipal, county, and parliamentary borough situated in Lancashire, England, at the junction of the Brun and Calder rivers, and on the Leeds and Liverpool Canal, 212 mi. northwest of London, in a coal-mining and manufacturing district. Roman remains have been discovered in Burnley, but the borough's development is modern. Incorporated in 1861, it was made a parliamentary borough in 1867 and a county borough in 1888. The American Civil War stopped the import of cotton and caused a severe depression during which men on relief were engaged on public works. In 1902 the municipality bought Towneley Hall and Park, converting the mansion into a museum and art gallery. Industries include cotton weaving, iron founding, and the manufacture of worsteds, sanitary wares, and brick. Pop. 1952, 83,860.   A. W.

BURNOUF, EUGÈNE [bü'rnu'f] (1801-1852), French Indologist, was born in Paris on Aug. 12, 1801, the son of the philologist, Jean Louis Burnouf. Burnouf started his career as a lawyer, but he soon left this profession, attracted by the newly opened field of Oriental studies. He followed the courses of Antoine Chézy and Abel Rémusat and cultivated the friendship of Christian Lassen. In 1829 Burnouf became professor of grammar at the École Normale; in 1832 he succeeded Antoine Chézy in the chair of Sanskrit at the Collège de France and J. F. Champollion at the Académie des Inscriptions, of which, at the end of his life, he was elected perpetual secretary.

Burnouf may be said to have founded Indology and Iranology in France, and to have given, with some help from Franz Bopp, the first serious interpretation of the Avesta, the manuscripts of which A. H. Anquetil-Duperron had first brought to the West in 1762. He died in Paris on May 28, 1852.   G. L. D.V.

BURNS, JOHN (1858-1943), English labor leader, popularly known as "Honest John," was born in London on Oct. 20, 1858. He attended a Battersea elementary school, worked at various jobs, and in 1872 was apprenticed to an engineer. While following his trade he became a very successful outdoor speaker and labor agitator. He read widely, had a powerful voice, and was deeply convinced of the merits of labor socialism. In 1884 he joined the Social Democratic Federation, became an executive of the Amalgamated Society of Engineers, and in 1889 was a Progressive member of the London County Council, supported by a weekly allowance subscribed by the Battersea workingmen. With Ben Tillett he organized the London Dock Strike in 1889 and

did much during this time to put life and vigor into the trade union movement. In 1892 he became Labour M.P. for Battersea, serving until 1918, and from 1905 to 1914 was in the Liberal cabinet. In 1914 he was made president of the Board of Trade, from which post he resigned in August 1914, as he disagreed with his colleagues' attitudes toward the French alliance, though not on the need for curbing Germany. Soon afterward he retired from public life, largely on account of the death in action of his only son. In 1918 he thought to stand for Parliament from Battersea, but as he was unable to secure local support he retired permanently to private life. He died in London on Jan. 24, 1943. An honest and vehement man, Burns had real power as a speaker on behalf of labor and freedom.   E. R. A.

BURNS, ROBERT (1759-1796), the most famous of Scottish poets, was born at Alloway, Ayrshire, Jan. 25, 1759, the eldest son of William Burnes, a tenant farmer, and his

ROBERT BURNS

FROM A PAINTING BY CHAPPEL

BETTMANN ARCHIVE

wife, Agnes Broun. Despite his poverty, William Burnes managed to provide his sons with a brief schooling in standard English literature, and although Agnes Broun was illiterate, she had a large store of traditional songs, ballads, and folk sayings which, with his later intensive reading of such material, were to be of great influence on her son's poetry. By the age of twelve, Burns was doing a man's work on the farm, frequently with inadequate food, to the permanent detriment of his health; and his efforts to better his condition, first by studying surveying and later by engaging in flax-dressing, were abortive. With his father's death, Feb. 13, 1784, Burns was left as head of the family, and he and his brother Gilbert leased Mossgiel Farm, near Mauchline.

Burns had written verses as early as 1781, but in 1784 he discovered Robert Fergusson's poems, which, he said, roused him "to emulating vigor." The first products of this new inspiration were satires on local ecclesiastical squabbles; these delighted the laity but angered the clergy, and before long the Kirk was able to retaliate by disciplining Burns for his liaison with Betty Paton, a farm servant. When this affair was succeeded, late in 1785, by a more embarrassing one with Jean Armour, the poet resolved to emigrate to Jamaica, delaying only to publish by subscription his *Poems, Chiefly in the Scottish Dialect* (Kilmarnock, July 1786). This volume presently reached the attention of Dugald Stewart, the Earl of Glencairn, and of other influential persons, and they persuaded the poet to remain in Scotland and to try a new edition of the poems in Edinburgh. This second edition (May 1787) brought Burns a profit of more than £500, of which he lent part to his brother, and invested most of the rest in renting and stocking a new farm, Ellisland, near Dumfries.

During his stay in the capital, and during tours of the Border and the Highlands, Burns was lionized by fashionable society. Some of the aristocracy, however, were displeased by the poet's forthright utterances, and by his occasional social gaucherie. His second winter (1787-1788) in Edinburgh was something of an anticlimax, although it included a casual flirtation with Mrs. Agnes M'Lehose. During the spring of 1788 Burns received instructions for qualifying as an excise officer, acknowledged Jean Armour as his wife, and began work at Ellisland. The farming venture was unsuccessful, and Burns now took up excise work, moving into Dumfries in November 1791; from then until his death, excise pay was his sole support. A third edition of his *Poems* appeared in 1793, but without profit to him, since he had sold his copyright. Nor did two other literary projects give him any profit commensurate with his efforts. In Edinburgh, Burns had met James Johnson, an engraver who had undertaken to publish *The Scots Musical Museum,* a collection of traditional Scottish songs, with their music, and to this work Burns devoted most of his poetical energy during the remainder of his life, collecting songs and music, and writing or adapting lyrics for the airs which lacked suitable words. In the *Museum,* and in the later *Select Collection* of an Edinburgh dilettante named George Thomson, Burns published more than three hundred songs. His only other major work during the post-Edinburgh years was *Tam o' Shanter,* his "standard performance in the Poetical line," composed in 1790 for Captain Francis Grose, who had asked for a witch story to accompany the engraving of the ruins of Alloway Kirk in his *Antiquities of Scotland* (1791).

Despite his outspoken sympathy with the French Revolution, which almost cost him his excise post in 1793, Burns was in line for promotion in the service when his health failed. He died, July 21, 1796, of a disease diagnosed as endocarditis, leaving his wife and five surviving children in poverty. A subscription was started for their relief, and the task of editing the poems and writing a biography was entrusted to Dr. James Currie of Liverpool. The subscription accomplished its financial purpose, but Currie's interpretations of the poet's weaknesses of conduct fostered a legend of dissipation and decadence not borne out by the full facts now available. It has been said of Burns that he was not so much conspicuously sinful as that he sinned conspicuously. *See also* JOLLY BEGGARS, THE; COTTER'S SATURDAY NIGHT, THE.

DeL. F.

BURNSIDE, AMBROSE EVERETT (1824-1881), American politician and businessman, was born at Liberty, Ind., May 23, 1824. He graduated from the United States Military Academy, West Point, in 1847 and became a lieutenant of artillery. Burnside took part in the final stages of the Mexican War as escorter of mails in the frontier country. He resigned his commission in October 1853. For five years he manufactured firearms, inventing a breech-loading rifle, and then became associated with the Illinois Central Railroad.

At the outbreak of the Civil War, Burnside was appointed colonel of the First Rhode Island Infantry and commanded a brigade in the First Battle of Bull Run, July 21, 1861. He was promoted to brigadier general on August 6. Starting in October, he organized the Coast Division of the Army of the Potomac, which sailed for North Carolina in January 1862. Burnside's capture of Roanoke Island in February and of New Bern in March marked the first important Union victory in the East. He was promoted to major general on

Mar. 18, 1862, and soon thereafter commanded reinforcement troops of the Army of the Potomac. He achieved the victory of South Mountain on September 14, and commanded the left wing of the Army at Antietam on September 16-17. Burnside was commander of the Army of the Potomac on December 13, during the Battle of Fredericksburg, a Confederate victory; after the battle he tendered his resignation to Lincoln, who refused it. Feeling that his subordinate officers were hindering a capable command, Burnside dismissed several of them on Jan. 23, 1863. Lincoln then relieved him of his command and replaced him with General Joseph Hooker.

In March, however, Burnside was appointed to the command of the Department of the Ohio. In the late summer and fall of 1863 he conducted a campaign in eastern Tennessee, driving southward from Kentucky. This, his most notable military achievement, greatly aided the late Federal victory at Chattanooga. Burnside captured Knoxville on September 2 and succeeded in repulsing the superior Confederate forces under General James Longstreet, who besieged the city from Nov. 16 to Dec. 4, 1863. Burnside was reassigned to command the Ninth Corps in Grant's army. He participated in the battles of the Wilderness and Spotsylvania Court House. Outside of Petersburg, in what is now Crater Park, Burnside conducted the laying and detonation of a mine beneath the Confederate troops. Although the Confederates were momentarily routed, they quickly recovered and disastrously defeated the Northern troops, July 30, 1864. Burnside was blamed by a court of inquiry for the defeat, and he resigned his commission.

After the end of the war Burnside held executive positions with various railroads. He was elected governor of Rhode Island in 1866, 1867, and 1868. In Europe during the Franco-Prussian War, Burnside acted as mediator between the Prussians and the besieged Parisians during 1870 and 1871. In 1874 he was elected United States senator from Rhode Island on the Republican ticket, serving until his death, which occurred on Sept. 13, 1881, in Bristol, R. I. His style of facial adornment—short side whiskers joining a mustache but with the chin clean-shaven—originated the colloquial nouns "burnsides" and "sideburns." W. E. A.

BURNT NJÁL. *See* NJÁLS SAGA.

BURR, AARON (1756-1836), American soldier and statesman, was born in Newark, N. J., Feb. 6, 1756. His father, the Reverend Aaron Burr, was president of the College of New Jersey (later Princeton University), when he died in 1757. Burr's mother, daughter of the noted Calvinist theologian, Jonathan Edwards, died shortly afterward. Burr graduated from the College of New Jersey in 1772 and was attending Tapping Reeve's law school when he joined Washington's army in Cambridge at the beginning of the American Revolution. Burr later served with Arnold on the march to Quebec, with General Richard Montgomery, and again with Washington. At Valley Forge he was made a lieutenant colonel. In 1779 he renewed his study of law, was admitted to the bar in 1782, and in 1783 began practice in New York, where in the following ten years he became prominent professionally and socially. He was elected to the New York state legislature in 1784 and in 1789 became state's attorney general. In the 1791 election for the United States Senate he defeated Alexander Hamilton's father-in-law, General Philip Schuyler, and in the presidential election of 1800 he ran on the same party ticket with Thomas Jefferson. During the campaign, Burr organized the Tammany society and negotiated so effectively that he received as many electoral votes as Jefferson, which threw the decision to the House of Representatives. Burr remained away from Washington, D.C., during the voting and on the thirty-sixth ballot Jefferson—chiefly through the support of Alexander Hamilton—was elected, Burr being chosen vice-president. The hostility between Burr and Hamilton came to a climax during Burr's campaign for governor of New York in 1804. Hamilton made derogatory remarks about him, which finally provoked

AARON BURR

FROM A PAINTING BY
JOHN VANDERLYN

CHARLES PHELPS CUSHING

Burr to challenge him to a duel with pistols at Weehawken, N. J., on July 11, 1804, in which Hamilton was mortally wounded.

Burr's political future in the East was ended and he went west, returning in 1806 with a plan to colonize a large tract of land in Louisiana. His ambiguous remarks on his colonization plans created suspicion, and President Jefferson, informed that Burr intended to separate the western states from the Union, had him arrested on a charge of treason. Although he was exonerated in his trial, which ran from April to October 1807, Burr never regained the confidence of the people. In June 1808 he went to Europe, where he lived for four years, returning in June 1812 at the request of his daughter, Theodosia Alston. He again practiced law in New York and in July 1833 was married to Eliza Jumel, widow of a rich merchant, whose colonial mansion on the Harlem River, in what is known as Washington Heights, is now a New York City museum. The marriage failed, and shortly afterwards, on Sept. 14, 1836, Burr died at Port Richmond, Staten Island, New York.   D. R.

BURRILLVILLE [bʌ'rɪlvɪl], a township occupying the northwestern corner of Rhode Island, in Providence Co., about 23 mi. northwest of the city of Providence. Burrillville comprises the villages of Pascoag, Bridgetown, Harrisville, Oakland, Mapleville, Glendale, Nasonville, and Tarkiln. The township is administered by a mayor and council. Within its boundaries are the Clear and Chepachet rivers, Sucker Pond, Herring Pond, Wilson Reservoir, and Pascoag Reservoir. Freight transportation for the township is provided by the New York, New Haven and Hartford Railroad. Wools and worsteds are the chief local manufactures. Pop. 1950, 8,774.

BURRO FAT, *Isomeris arborea,* a shrub of the caper family, native to southern California, growing to 4 ft., with large yellow flowers which are conspicuous in the coast veg-

etation. The bitter, pealike seeds are held in prominent inflated pods, and the bruised foliage has a strong, unpleasant odor.   J. C. Wis.

BURROUGHS, GEORGE [bʌ'roz] (c. 1650-1692), American clergyman, was born about 1650 in Massachusetts. Graduated from Harvard College in 1670, he became a preacher at Casco (now Portland), Me., in 1674. In August 1676 the town was destroyed by Indians. Burroughs accepted a call to become preacher at Salem Village (now Danvers), Mass., in 1680, but his ministry in that town was not a happy one; both the townspeople and other ministers were hostile to him. Assailed by debts, and having failed to gain the sympathy of his congregation, he was compelled to leave Salem Village in March 1683. In June 1685 he returned to Casco, where he was well liked. On May 20, 1690, the town was again destroyed by the French and Indians. Burroughs then became a preacher at Wells, where people he had known at Salem fought him and accused him of being a confederate of the devil. He was arrested in May 1692 and appeared before magistrates and ministers for examination before trial. He was jailed in Boston and tried at Salem on August 5. At the trial some persons who claimed to have been bewitched accused him of responsibility for their miseries. Others, who had confessed being witches, accused him of being the chief actor at their ceremonies. Still others declared that they had seen him display such feats of strength as could not have been achieved without the help of the devil. Furthermore, though he had acknowledged the existence of witches before, and even accused them of being responsible for the miseries of the country, he persisted in denying the existence of witches at his trial. Although no "witch marks" were found on him, he was convicted at Salem and executed on Aug. 19, 1692.

BURROUGHS, JOHN (1837-1921), American author and naturalist, was born in Roxbury, N. Y., on Apr. 3, 1837. He was brought up and educated in the country on his father's farm, spending one term each at the Ashland and Cooperstown seminaries. From 1854 to 1863 he taught in a country school, and in 1863 received an appointment as a clerk with the Currency Bureau of the Treasury Department in Washington, D. C. He remained there until 1873, when he became a government bank examiner, and then moved to a fruit farm at West Park, N. Y., where he built a secluded cabin, known as "Slabsides," and spent the remainder of his life writing popular works on nature themes. As a young man he had made the acquaintance of Walt Whitman, who influenced him greatly, and Burroughs' first book, *Notes on Walt Whitman as Poet and Person* (1867), was dedicated to him. Burroughs commenced writing nature essays for the *Atlantic* in 1865, and his first nature book, *Wake-Robin,* appeared in 1871. Although not a naturalist in the strict scientific sense of the term, he was a keen student of nature and wrote voluminously in praise of its beauty. His works include *Birds and Poets* (1877), *Locusts and Wild Honey* (1879), *Leaf and Tendril* (1908), *Time and Change* (1912), *The Summit of the Years* (1913), *The Breath of Life* (1915), and *Under the Apple-Trees* (1916). He died on Mar. 29, 1921.   C. W. D.

BURROUGHS, WILLIAM SEWARD (1855-1898), American inventor of the adding machine, was born in Auburn, N. Y., Jan. 28, 1855. His father was a model maker for castings and new inventions, and Burroughs received a limited education in local schools in Auburn and in Lowell,

Mich. He commenced work at the age of fifteen and was employed in banks, stores, and lumber yards. From 1877 to 1881 he was a clerk at the Cayuga County National Bank in Auburn. He also worked in his father's shop and other machine shops in St. Louis, Mo. Having worked in a bank and being interested in machinery, Burroughs sought to develop a machine that would overcome inaccuracies and save time in bookkeeping. He completed his first crude adding machine in 1885, but due to its many imperfections, it met with no success. In 1886 he organized the American Arithmometer Company in St. Louis, with Thomas B. Metcalf, his financial backer, as president, and by 1888 he had sufficiently improved the machine to obtain his first patent. Burroughs had the greatest difficulty in obtaining sufficient funds to continue experimenting on the machine, but by 1892 he perfected it and commenced producing the first practical adding and listing machine ever devised. He was awarded the John Scott Medal of the Franklin Institute in 1897. Burroughs died in Citronella, Ala., Sept. 14, 1898. In 1905 the name of his company was changed to the Burroughs Adding Machine Company.　　C. W. D.

BURRO WEED, *Allenrolfea occidentalis,* a member of the goosefoot family, is a shrub growing to 4 ft., native to alkaline marshes from Texas to Utah and California. It is much branched, with scalelike leaves and small flowers in crowded spikes and, although much larger, closely resembles samphire, to which it is related. It is also called pickleweed and iodine bush.

BURSA or **BRUSA** [bu′rsa, bru′sa], a city in northwestern Turkey and the capital of the vilayet of the same name, located 18 mi. southeast of its port, Mudanya, on the Sea of Marmara, and 267 mi. by highway west of Ankara. It is on the terraced slopes of Ulu Dag (8,343 ft.) and has a mild climate. January, the coldest month, averages between 45° and 50° F., while July averages between 75° and 80° F. Annual rainfall averages between 25 and 35 in. Long famous for its silk, the city's chief industries are silk-spinning and the making of carpets and richly embroidered prayer rugs. The city has excellent rail, road, and air connections with other important Turkish cities. Agriculture is the main occupation of the vilayet, which lies in a very fertile plain. Vegetables, cereals, cotton, tobacco, opium, olives, and mulberries are grown; olive oil is one of the region's major products. Chrome is mined at Ulu Dag, and the city is the center of the mining activities. The mountain is also popular as a skiing center in winter.

The city is identical with the Prusa of Classical times. It was reputedly founded by the Bithynian King Prusias at the suggestion of Hannibal, who took refuge here after his defeat in North Africa. The capital of Bithynia in the second and first centuries B.C., it flourished under Roman and Byzantine rule and escaped the Arab invasions. The city became the capital of the Ottoman empire in 1326. In the early fifteenth century it was sacked by Tamerlane. It was the scene of much fighting during the Graeco-Turkish war of 1919-1922 and during the Turkish war of independence between the nationalist forces of Mustafa Kemal (later Kemal Ataturk) and the troops of Sultan Mohammed VI.

The city is a beautiful one, with its many mosques and minarets, kiosks, gardens, and modern buildings. There are numerous tombs of sultans and other Moslem notables. Traces of the city's illustrious past can be seen on several mosques, where the craftsmanship of the Byzantines and

Persians is displayed. Outstanding are Yesil Cami, or the "Green Mosque"; Yesil Medesse, formerly a school and now the museum of antiquities; Yesil Turbeh, a tomb with fine tiles; Yildirim Cami od Sultan Bayezid, with its sculptured marble panels; and Ulu Cami, or the "Grand Mosque," with its many-domed ceiling, all of the fifteenth century; and the Yeni Kaplica bath of the sixteenth century. This and other baths and the hot iron and sulphur springs have long made the city a popular health resort. Pop. 1950, city, 100,007; vilayet, 541,987.

BURSE (Gr. βύρσα, skin or hide, whence bag or purse), in ecclesiastical usage, the receptacle for carrying the folded corporal to and from the altar in the Roman Catholic Church. Introduced at a late date, its use spread from the fourteenth century onward and is now mandatory. It is made of two pieces of cardboard, covered with linen or silk and fastened on three edges; the upper side is of the same color as the vestments.　　N. J. T.

BURT, SIR CYRIL LODOWIC (1883-　　), English psychologist, was born in London, Mar. 3, 1883, and educated at Oxford and Würzburg (1908). After teaching at Liverpool and Cambridge universities, he became psychologist for the education department of the London County Council, in 1924 professor of education, and then, in 1931, professor of psychology at the University of London, where he remained until 1950. He revised and standardized the Binet and other intelligence tests, worked on quantitative methods to measure temperament, delinquency, and mental retardation, and was interested in the use of factor analysis in research. Burt was a member of the British War Office's committee on personnel selection, and in 1953 became editor of the British *Journal of Statistical Psychology*. Among his best known books are *Mental and Scholastic Tests* (1921), *The Young Delinquent* (1925), *The Backward Child* (1937), and *Factors of the Mind* (1940). He was knighted in 1946.　　F. A. K.

BURT, MAXWELL STRUTHERS (1882-1954), American writer, was born in Baltimore, Md., Oct. 18, 1882. He was reared in Philadelphia, educated in private schools, and before entering college worked for two years as a reporter on the Philadelphia *Times*. He graduated in 1904 from Princeton University, where he had been editor of the *Tiger,* then studied in Munich and at Oxford University. After two years as instructor in English at Princeton, he moved to the Jackson Hole region of Wyoming in 1908 to take up ranching, and in 1913 he married the novelist Katherine Newlin. In World War I he served in the Air Force, and thereafter continued his literary career. His works include *The Delectable Mountains* (1924) and *Festival* (1931) (novels); *Chance Encounters* (1921), *John O'May and Other Stories* (1918), and *They Could Not Sleep* (1928) (short stories); *In the High Hills* (1914) and *When I Grow Up to Middle Age* (1925) (poetry); *The Other Side* (1929) and *Escape from America* (1936) (essays); *Powder River* (1939) (history); *The Diary of a Dude Wrangler* (1924) (autobiography); *Philadelphia; Holy Experiment* (1942), and *Along These Streets* (1945). Burt died Aug. 28, 1954, in Jackson, Wyo.

BURTON, SIR RICHARD FRANCIS (1821-1890), English explorer and orientalist, was born in Torquay, Devonshire, Mar. 19, 1821. A childhood on the Continent fostered a love of travel and a fluency in languages which remained with Burton throughout his life. After a year at Oxford, in 1842 he joined the East Indian army. In Sind, mingling with natives, he mastered Gujarati, Marathi, Hindustani, Persian, and Arabic. In 1853, disguised as a Pathan, he made the journey to inner Arabia described in *Pilgrimage to Al-Medinah and Mecca* (1855). He was the first white man to penetrate Somaliland and to discover Lake Tanganyika (1858); these and other explorations are described in his later books, which include *First Footsteps in East Africa* (1856), *Lake Regions of Equatorial Africa* (1860), *The Highlands of Brazil* (1869), *Unexplored Syria* (1872), and *Ultima Thule* (1875, dealing with Iceland). Burton served as consul at Fernando Po, Santos, Damascus, and Trieste; he was nominated for knighthood in 1885. His best-known work is a faithful colloquial translation of the Arabian Nights, published as *The Thousand Nights and a Night* (1885-1888). He died in Trieste, Oct. 20, 1890.   J. O. B.

BURTON, ROBERT (1577-1640), English writer, was born in Lindley, Leicestershire, Feb. 8, 1577. After attending school at Sutton Coldfield and Nuneaton, Warwickshire, he entered Brasenose College, Oxford, as a commoner in 1593 and in 1599 was elected a student of Christ Church. He took the degree of B.A. in 1602, M.A. in 1605, and B.D. in 1616, and after graduation served as tutor and college librarian. Later, he held three benefices in the church, being made vicar of St. Thomas's, Oxford, in 1616, rector of Walesby, Lincolnshire, in 1624, a living which he resigned in 1631, and rector of Segrave, Leicestershire, some years later. Burton's life in Christ Church was that of a scholarly recluse, devouring the books of the Oxford libraries and particularly devoting himself to the studies of medicine, mathematics, astrology, and geography, but that he was not altogether cut off from worldly affairs is indicated by his service as clerk of the Oxford market in 1615, 1616, and 1618. During these years he contributed Latin and English verses to a score of Oxford publications.

Burton's first extended work was a Latin comedy, *Philosophaster,* written in 1606 and acted at Christ Church eleven years later, but the work to which he in an almost literal sense devoted his life was *The Anatomy of Melancholy,* whose first edition appeared in 1621. The author signed himself "Democritus Junior," after the Greek philosopher Democritus, who made anatomical studies seeking the source of the black bile, or melancholia. Burton declared that he wrote the book in order to escape the ravages of this disease, which he may have inherited from his mother and her family, and it is likely that he was also influenced by her interest in medicine. The *Anatomy* is a vast compendium of learning on the subject of melancholia, drawn from all available sources, ancient and modern, and ordered in a carefully systematized presentation. In spite of the waywardness of the style and the writer's uncritical acceptance of authority, it is a work of serious scientific merit which has been characterized by Sir William Osler as the greatest medical treatise written by a layman. Its wealth of curious learning, salty wit, and hearty common sense has commended it to readers in search of rich mixed feeding. Constantly revised and enlarged, it passed through five editions during the author's lifetime, and several more thereafter. Burton died in his Christ Church rooms, Jan. 25, 1640, near the date which he had predicted by casting his own horoscope. His brother William (1575-1645), an antiquarian and translator, erected a monument to him in Christ Church Cathedral. Valuable collections of Burton's books are preserved in the library of his college and in the Bodleian Library at Oxford.   T. H. E.

BURTON, THEODORE ELIJAH (1851-1929), American lawyer and legislator, was born at Jefferson, Ohio, Dec. 20, 1851. He was graduated from Oberlin College in 1872, was admitted to the bar in 1875, and began the practice of law in Cleveland. Burton became a member of Congress in 1889, serving until 1891. He was again a member of the House of Representatives from 1895 until 1909, when he resigned to become a United States senator, holding this office until 1915. In 1921 Burton returned to the House of Representatives and in 1928 was elected to the Senate. President Theodore Roosevelt appointed him chairman of the Inland Waterways Commission in 1907, and on the reorganization of this body in 1909 as the National Waterways Commission, he continued as chairman. He also served on the National Monetary Commission, 1908-1912. From 1904 until 1914 Burton was a member successively of the executive council and committee of the Interparliamentary Union, and appeared as the United States delegate of the Union at many international congresses. In 1922 he was appointed by President Warren G. Harding a member of the Debt Funding Commission. He was chairman of the United States delegation to the Conference for the Control of International Traffic in Arms at Geneva in 1925. A convinced pacifist, and president from 1911 to 1915 and again in 1925 of the American Peace Society, Burton made many speeches in Congress opposing the Navy's efforts to obtain larger appropriations. He was a prominent figure in the campaign which led to the nomination of Herbert Hoover as Republican candidate for the presidency in 1928. Burton was the author of *The Life of John Sherman* (1906), *Corporations and the State* (1911), and *The Constitution, Its Origin and Distinctive Features* (1923). He died in Cleveland, O., on Oct. 28, 1929.   R. T.

BURTON, WILLIAM MERIAM. *See* PERKIN MEDAL.

BURTON-ON-TRENT, a county borough in Staffordshire, England, situated on the Trent River, about 122 mi. northwest of London. The Trent and Mersey Canal provides additional water transportation facilities for the community, which is an important railroad and industrial center. The town's first charter was granted in the twelfth century, and it was incorporated in 1878 as a part of the Burton parliamentary division of Staffordshire. Mary, Queen of Scots, shortly before she was beheaded, was imprisoned in a nearby castle, the ruins of which remain. Some fragments of a Benedictine abbey dating from 1002 are embodied in the eighteenth-century Church of St. Mary and St. Modwen. Because of abundant sulphate of lime in the water, Burton has been one of Europe's chief ale-brewing cities since 1708. Ale brewing dates from the time of the abbey in Burton. Coal, potter's clay, and gypsum are natural resources of the region. Pop. 1952, 48,800.

BURTON PROCESS. *See* PETROLEUM (*Thermal Cracking*).

BURU [bu'ru], an island in the Molucca group of East Indonesia (3° 27' S. lat.; 126° 36' E. long.), included in the commune of South Moluccas. The island is about 90 mi. long and 50 mi. wide. It has an area of nearly 3,500 sq. mi., or slightly less than that of Connecticut. The interior is mountainous, the highest peak rising to an elevation of 7,967 ft. The climate is rather warm and humid, and much of the island is clothed with tropical forests containing some teakwood and ebony. Grass-covered hills and plains, with occasional sago-palm swamps, characterize much of the northern part.

The native tribes of Buru, known as Alfuros, are closely related to other groups of aborigines throughout the Moluccas. They depend largely upon subsistence agriculture for a living with some supplementary gathering and hunting in the forests and fishing near the coast. The inland tribes are mostly pagan, while many of those near the coasts, owing to external influences, are at least partly converted to Mohammedanism or Christianity. There has been a limited influx of Arabs, Chinese, and Indonesians from other islands to some of the coastal areas. The estimated population of the island in 1930 was 27,000. A local export industry of some importance is the manufacture of oil of cajuput from the leaves of an East Indian tree, *Melaleuca leucadendron,* which is used mainly as an application for skin diseases. The island was at one time claimed by the sultan of Ternate, but this claim was repudiated by the Dutch in 1683. The Japanese occupied Buru early in World War II and subsequently used it as an advance air base for attacks against Allied bases in Halmahera and western New Guinea. Following the cessation of hostilities the island was returned to Netherlands control. It was incorporated into independent East Indonesia in 1946 and in the Republic of Indonesia in 1949.

R. G. B.

BURUJIRD [bu′rūji′rd], a city in western Iran, 33° 55′ N. lat. and 48° 55′ E. long., on the motor road from the Persian Gulf to Tehran. The altitude is 5,420 ft. The town, formerly the capital of Lurestan, is the capital of Burujird Province. It is situated in a pleasant and fertile valley where water is plentiful and crops are irrigated. Burujird has wide, level streets and presents an attractive appearance. It is a center for nomadic tribes, who drive their herds of sheep, goats, and cattle to the mountains for the summer season and descend to the plains for the winter. They live largely in black tents of a cloth made from goat's hair. Opium is being replaced by other crops. Rugs are also made in the city and the surrounding district. Handwork made from nickel is a noted product of the place and may be purchased in the bazaars. The city has banking, telephone, telegraph, postal, and railway facilities. Pop. 1944, 45,710.　　　J. C. Wi.

BURUSHASKI [bu′rushæ′ski], a language spoken in northern India, in the states of Hunza and Nagir. It had about 20,000 speakers in 1931, while the closely related Werchikwār dialect, spoken in the Yasīn district to the westward, had about 7,500. Being an unwritten language, Burushaski is known only in the form in which it has been spoken since about 1877, when Occidental investigators began to give it serious attention; hence nothing can be said of its history. A considerable body of texts has been recorded in phonetic transcription and translated into English, especially by D. L. R. Lorimer. Some interesting features of the language are the following: the use of aspirated stop consonants and of post-alveolar consonants; the grammatical division of nouns into four classes, one denoting male human beings, a second denoting female human beings, a third denoting animate nonhuman beings and certain inanimate objects, and a fourth denoting all other inanimate objects; and the vigesimal basis of the numerical system. No kinship of Burushaski with any other language or language family in the world has been established. Possibly it is the modern representative of some prehistoric language community of interior Asia, crowded almost out of existence by the spread of the great language families, Turkish, Tibeto-Chinese, and Indo-European.　　　C. R. Sl.

BURY, JOHN BAGNELL (1861-1927), British historian and classical scholar, was born on Oct. 16, 1861. He was educated at Trinity College, Dublin. Though a fine Greek scholar, he decided to study history, and in 1893 he was appointed professor of modern history at Trinity College; in 1898 he was also made Regius professor of Greek. In 1902, he became Regius professor of modern history in the University of Cambridge, and he reluctantly severed his connection with Dublin. His finest historical work was concerned with the history of the later Roman Empire, especially in the Near East. Between 1896 and 1900 he edited an edition of Edward Gibbon's *Decline and Fall of the Roman Empire,* equipping it with an excellent introduction and notes; this has been the standard edition. On the same subject, he published *History of the Eastern Roman Empire* (1912), *History of the Later Roman Empire* (1923), and *The Invasion of Europe by the Barbarians* (1928); these represent a very real contribution to historical scholarship. He also wrote a *Life of St. Patrick* in 1905 which evoked considerable controversy, a *History of Freedom of Thought* (1913), and *The Idea of Progress* (1920). Bury died in Rome on June 1, 1927.

E. R. A.

BURY [bɛ′ri], a municipal, county, and parliamentary borough, situated in Lancashire, England, on the Irwell River, 196 mi. northwest of London, in a densely populated coal-mining and manufacturing district. Bury was the site of a Saxon fort, and the Church of St. Mary, rebuilt in 1876, was mentioned in Domesday. Until 1846, Bury was governed by three constables, chosen annually; it was incorporated in 1876 and made a county borough in 1888. The borough sends one member to Parliament. John Kay, inventor of the flying shuttle, was born in Bury, and Sir Robert Peel, whose grandfather founded the calico-printing industry in 1770, was born in a neighboring town. Industries include bleaching, dyeing, and weaving of cottons and woolens, calico printing, manufacture of paper, and iron founding. Pop. 1952, 58,310.

BURYAT. *See* ASIATIC TRIBES.

BURYAT-MONGOL AUTONOMOUS SOVIET SOCIALIST REPUBLIC [bʊrya′t mɒ′ŋgəl], a territorial division in southern Siberia. It is bounded on the north by the Irkutsk Oblast, on the east by the Chita Oblast, on the south by the Mongolian People's Republic, and on the west by Lake Baykal, the Irkutsk Oblast, and the Tuva Autonomous Oblast. The Aga National Okrug and Ust-Orda Buryat-Mongol National Okrug lie nearby, to the southeast and the west, respectively. Buryat-Mongolia, which became an Autonomous Soviet Socialist Republic (A.S.S.R.) within the Russian Soviet Federated Socialist Republic in 1923, occupies an area of 135,600 sq. mi. and had an estimated population of 650,000 in 1956. It has forested mountains in the north and intermontane steppes in the south. Its climate is severe, continental, and dry. The short summers have much sunshine, although two thirds of the low annual precipitation (8 to 13 in.) falls in that season.

The principal ethnic groups are Buryats (about 35 per cent) and Russians (about 60 per cent). The Buryats, whom many ethnologists believe to be related to the American Indians, are Mongols who emigrated to the Baykal region during the twelfth and thirteenth centuries. Originally pagan hunters and fishers, later they became pastoral nomads and adopted Lamaism, a Tibetan form of Buddhism, as their religion. They resisted the Russian advance for a century (from 1628 to 1727) before submitting completely. Early in the Soviet regime, the Buryats acquired a national alphabet devised by Russian scholars, and a national literature has begun to develop. The literacy rate has been raised to 70 per cent. The prerevolutionary dominance of ecclesiastics has been curbed by the Soviet authorities; the legions of monks (lamas), which included about a third of the male Buryat population, have been reduced to a comparatively small number. Buryat-Mongolia is represented by eleven deputies in the Soviet of Nationalities, one of the two supreme legislative organs of the U.S.S.R.

Buryat-Mongolia is considered one of the most prosperous areas of Siberia. Since the Buryat-Mongol A.S.S.R. was founded, the Buryats have largely abandoned their nomadic life and have made great progress in agriculture. Under strong government encouragement and assistance, the land under cultivation has increased threefold. Most of the peasant holdings have joined the collective farms (the *kolkhozy*). In cattle breeding, still the major occupation, Buryat-Mongolia occupies a leading place in the Soviet Union. The region is also known for excellent horses and sheep, and there is an average of three head of livestock per inhabitant. In the northern section gold is mined; in the south, tungsten and molybdenum are mined at Gorodok and coal at Gusinoozersk. There are a number of modern fisheries on Lake Baykal, and a woodworking industry is developing in this section. Throughout the area, there is an estimated sixty million acres of virgin timber. The export trade in sable furs is important.

Ulan-Ude, formerly called Verkhne-Udinsk, is the capital and industrial center. In it are a huge locomotive and car works for the Trans-Siberian Railway, the largest Siberian meat-packing plant, a glass factory, kilns, flour mills, and power plants. The population increased from 29,000 in 1926 to 158,000 in 1956. *See also* ASIATIC TRIBES; ULAN-UDE.

W. S. V. and T. Sh.

BURY ST. EDMUNDS [bɛ'rɪ], a municipal borough in the parliamentary division of the same name, West Suffolk, England, is situated on the Lark River, 87 mi. northeast of London, in a farming area. A monastery founded on this site in 633 became the burial place of the martyred King Edmund in 903, and from this event the place, in the tenth century, took its present name.

About 1024 Canute destroyed that monastery, erected a new one for the Benedictines, and freed the town of bishops' rule, though the bishops had made it a borough. In 1214, the barons met there secretly and vowed to force King John to restore the laws of Edward the Confessor and to ratify the Magna Charta, which he signed in 1215. The town was incorporated in 1606-1607. In World War II, a Royal Air Force airfield was constructed there. Bury St. Edmunds is a market center for agricultural produce and implements. Pop. 1952, 20,240.

BUS. *See* MOTOR TRANSPORT; MOTOR VEHICLES; TROLLEY BUSSES.

BUSBY, RICHARD [bʌ'zbi] (1606-1695), English scholar, was born in Lutton, Lincolnshire, Sept. 22, 1606. Educated at Westminster School and Oxford University, he received his B.A. in 1628 and his A.M. in 1631. He became tutor in his college, then served as rector of Cudworth in Somersetshire. Busby was headmaster of Westminster School from 1638 until his death. Among his pupils were Robert South, John Dryden, and John Locke. His publications were mainly grammars and expurgated editions of the Classics for school use. Busby died on Apr. 6, 1695, and is buried in Westminster Abbey. A. W. S.

SOVFOTO

An audience on a collective farm in Buryat-Mongolia witnesses a performance of the local theatrical group.

BUSEMANN, ADOLPH [bu'zəman] (1901-), German specialist in high-speed air flow and high-speed aircraft design, was born Apr. 20, 1901, in Lübeck, and received the engineer's diploma in general machine design from the Technische Hochschule in Brunswick. In 1925 he went to the Kaiser Wilhelm Institute for Flow Research in Göttingen, under Professor Ludwig Prandtl. He carried out investigations on supersonic air flow, and published the section on gas dynamics in the *Handbuch der Experimentalphysik* in 1931. In 1931 he accepted an appointment to the faculty of the Technische Hochschule in Dresden. In 1936 he became chief of the Institute for Gas Dynamics in the Hermann Göring Foundation for the Encouragement of Air Flight, in Brunswick, and was in charge of supersonic wind tunnels there. After World War II he was sent to the United States, where he was assigned to the National Advisory Committee for Aeronautics at Langley Field, Va., in the compressibility research division. His contributions to research have been numerous, including earlier studies in strength of materials and elasticity and, since 1929, in the field of aerodynamics at high subsonic and supersonic speeds, on thermodynamics, swept wings, drag, boundary layer, and compressibility effects. In 1933 Busemann published in Berlin a study of the molecular nature of heat. M. H. Sm.

BUSH, VANNEVAR (1890-), American scientist, was born Mar. 11, 1890, at Everett, Mass. He graduated from Tufts College in 1913 and, after continuing his studies at Massachusetts Institute of Technology, became an assistant professor of electrical engineering at that institution. While at Massachusetts Institute of Technology, he built, with Samuel H. Caldwell, the famous differential analyzer which, by means of electronic tubes and circuits, calculates twenty-five different sets of data in a few minutes. During World War I, Bush was with the United States Government, working on a submarine detector and a magnetic cable capable of guiding ships into harbors at night. Bush received his doctorate in engineering in 1916. In 1928 he won the Levy Medal of the Franklin Institute for his work in the field of mathematical instruments, and in 1932 he became vice-president of the Massachusetts Institute of Technology. In 1939 he became president of the Carnegie Institution of Washington, D. C.

In June 1940, President F. D. Roosevelt appointed Bush chairman of the National Defense Research Committee which directed United States armament research. Bush had also been named head of the National Advisory Committee for Aeronautics in 1939, which, in 1941, became part of the Office of Scientific Research and Development, with Bush as its director. After mobilizing the country's scientists and co-ordinating their efforts to produce the atomic bomb, Bush

245

was appointed by President Harry S. Truman in 1947 as chairman of the Research and Development Board. He resigned Oct. 14, 1948, to return to the presidency of the Carnegie Institution of Washington.

Bush believes that scientific progress is essential to the national welfare, and he has advocated the foundation by the government of a research organization to aid schools in the preparation of students for work in the sciences. Bush is also credited with modifications of the vacuum tube and improving the design of four-engine bombers. He is the author of *Endless Horizons* (1946), *Modern Arms and Free Men* (1949), and other more technical works.   W. E. A.

BUSHEHR. *See* BUSHIRE.

BUSH HONEYSUCKLE, the common name of the several North American species of *Diervilla,* small deciduous shrubs of the honeysuckle family, closely allied to weigelas. The common bush honeysuckle (*D. lonicera*) is a low-spreading shrub with yellow flowers, found from Canada south to North Carolina and west to Wisconsin.

Bush honeysuckle is applied also to shrubby species of *Lonicera,* widely-planted, vigorous bushes bearing masses of pink, white, or yellow flowers, followed by red, yellow, or black berries.   J. C. Wis.

BUSHIDO [bushi′do], a Japanese word meaning "chivalry," originally applied to the code of the feudal *samurai,* or warrior. It consisted of *gishi,* loyalty, and *giri,* justice, implied courage and truthfulness, and borrowed from the ethics of Confucianism. As an ethical standard for all Japanese, the term dates from the end of the nineteenth century. Propagated by the War and Education departments, *bushido* was the core of Japanese militarism and solidarity. After the Russo-Japanese War, in 1905, the word gained currency abroad as descriptive of the morale of the Japanese army.
                                                                      A. W. Bu.

BUSHIRE [bushi′r], also known as Bandar Agu Shehr or Bushehr, a port and air station in southwestern Iran, on a peninsula on the northeastern coast of the Persian Gulf, at 28° 59′ N. lat. and 50° 49′ E. long. The city is a passport examination port and a quarantine station, and it is the seat of government for the Persian Gulf region of Iran; the Iranian governor general of the ports of the gulf is resident there. The peninsula affords inner and outer anchorage, but ocean-going steamers discharge their cargo several miles offshore. The climate is exceedingly hot most of the year.

Bushire became virtually an English port about the time that the American colonies asserted their independence, and the British Resident in Bushire became the most powerful official on the Persian Gulf. England maintained a fleet of gunboats in the gulf to keep pirates from molesting shipping on the route to India, and also to maintain peace in the region. Following the discovery of oil in southern Iran, ports farther north in the gulf became more important. During World War I the peninsula was occupied for a time by British forces.

The verdure of the region consists largely of palm trees; many dates also are cultivated and exported, largely to the United States. Tobacco, hides, carpets, and opium are also exported from Bushire. Aside from routes along the coast, the chief motor road from Bushire winds up to the plateau, the two important passes on the road being known as the Pir Zan and Dokhtar; both have very steep curves. The distance by this road to Shiraz, former capital of Iran, is a little more than 170 mi.

Bushire is a regular port of call for British airlines and for steamers of several lines. Both steamer and air connections are made at the port for Karachi and Bombay. Pop. 1944, 27,317.   J. C. Wi.

BUSHMAN. *See* AFRICAN PEOPLES.

BUSHMASTER, the longest New World poisonous snake, *Lachesis mutus,* occasionally exceeding 11 ft. It is unique among American pit-vipers in laying eggs; a 7-ft. to 9-ft. female may lay about ten eggs; she coils about them.

COURTESY OF THE AMERICAN MUSEUM OF NATURAL HISTORY
BUSHMASTER, LACHESIS MUTUS

The bushmaster occurs sporadically in forested areas, from Costa Rica to Brazil, often lurking in mammal burrows. It has a rasplike skin and a black and pinkish pattern. It is delicate in captivity, so is rarely seen.   M. G. N.

BUSHNELL, HORACE [bu′shnəl] (1802-1876), American clergyman and theologian, was born at Bantam, Litchfield County, Conn., Apr. 14, 1802. A graduate of Yale College (1827), he taught at Norwich, Conn., and later was associate editor of the New York *Journal of Commerce.* He enrolled in the Law School at Yale, becoming a tutor in Yale College, but in 1831 he entered the Divinity School. From 1833 to 1859 he was pastor of the North Congregational Church in Hartford, Conn. He wrote *Christian Nurture* (1847), *God in Christ* (1849), and *Christ in Theology* (1851), the last expressing his theory that language is inadequate to express or define spiritual things; it can only suggest them. An attempt was made to try him for heresy, but the charges were dismissed. He died in Hartford, Feb. 17, 1876. Bushnell Park and the Bushnell Memorial Theatre in Hartford are named after him.   S. D.

BUSH PIG or **RED RIVER-HOG,** a mammal, *Potamochoerus,* of forested Africa. It is bright red, although adults in eastern Africa become black. From 2 to 2½ ft. high at the shoulders, it measures about 4 ft. from its nose to the end of its short tail. Its tusks are 6 or 7 in. long. Found south of northern Ethiopia and the Sudan, it ranges from sea level to the upper limits of brush or tree growth. Bush pigs are nocturnal and are seldom seen. They sometimes do considerable damage to crops.   V. H. C.

BUSH TIT, either of two species of small American songbirds in the genus *Psaltriparus,* allied to the chickadees. The common species of the western United States, *P. mini* *mus,* is gray with a pale-brown cap; *P. melanotis* of Mexico and Guatemala has the cap gray, the mantle pale brown, and the sides of the head black. Except when breeding, they

NATIONAL AUDUBON SOCIETY

BUSH TIT

travel in flocks and in all their actions they show their relationship to the chickadees. Their purse-shaped nests, about ten inches long and closely woven of vegetable fibers and moss, are suspended from the swaying ends of slender branches. H. G. De.

BUSINESS AND INDUSTRY, HISTORY OF. Business, the art of combining labor, natural resources, and capital in a process that leads to the sale of goods and services, and business administration, which consists of policy formulation, management, and control have undergone an immense evolution since they first appeared in the days before recorded history. But many of the business institutions that are commonplace today already existed in the ancient world, although obviously on a much smaller scale and in a much cruder form. Agriculture was then the chief economic activity, but in the stronger and more flourishing centers, commerce (or business) followed closely behind. Even before 3000 B.C., business was a respectable occupation in the Middle East, not so much for its own value but because it was closely connected with religion. Sumerian and Babylonian temples were the first countinghouses, and their priests operated an intricately planned economy. As bailiffs of the gods they controlled commerce and trade and regulated the activities of a thriving merchant class. Much later, Phoenicians from widely scattered cities like Tyre, Sidon, and Carthage and Greeks from Miletus, Corinth, and Alexandria were very busy traders. Often regarded with great disdain by their contemporaries, they sailed the seas and roamed three continents during the Hellenic, Hellenistic, and Roman civilizations, exporting and importing goods and accumulating and spreading culture as part of the never-ending search for profit and adventure.

The Rise of Business Institutions in the Ancient World. *The Use of Money.* These far-flung and daring trading ventures would hardly have been possible without the development of three extraordinarily important business institutions: the use of money, the keeping of accounts, and

the creation of formal business organizations. Quite early in their history, Sumeria and Babylonia initiated a money system. Merchants used the precious metals as a medium of exchange, and priests carried on a crude banking business by loaning money out at interest, although they did not create deposits—the essence of modern commercial banking. It is from Mesopotamia that we have inherited the expressions "grains" and "shekels" to designate specific amounts of gold and silver, for the money units in that ancient country were not coins, but quantities weighed out for each transaction according to approved standards of weight. Coins did not appear until shortly before 700 B.C., when Lydia began minting them, but by 500 B.C. they were common in Greece, as were money-changers. The final step in the evolution of money and banking came in the late years of the Roman Republic when deposit banking (i.e., the creation of money in excess of cash holdings) appeared.

The Introduction of Business Records. Mesopotamia was also the birthplace of business records. Quite logically the priests, who were stewards of the temples and transacted a volume business, found it expedient to keep records and render accounts of tax payments, stocks of goods, and so forth. We have a multitude of such records going back beyond 2000 B.C. They are the oldest intelligible writings that have been discovered, and it seems reasonable to conclude that writing and the literature that followed originated with these business records. But the records of the ancients, numerous as they were, were rather simple, even though the Phoenicians appear to have used a crude form of double-entry bookkeeping.

The Rise of Formal Business Organizations. The form of business organization used by the ancients was much more complicated. Mesopotamian merchants, for instance, conducted relatively complex partnerships and even formed companies. They maintained representatives in widely dispersed cities and transacted business with letters of credit. They sent to distant places commission salesmen who were required by law to keep and submit strict accounts of their sales and activities. The Greeks added further sophistication to business organization; and the Romans, who otherwise contributed little to business in general, devoted some of their great legal talents to giving the modern corporation its start. In the late years of the Republic, they created the *universitas,* a corporate body possessing a common treasury and a legal personality separate and distinct from that of its owners.

The Nature of Ancient Business. These business organizations of the ancients were mainly confined to trade. The Greeks did some large-scale mining, and Egyptian and Roman construction work is still a source of amazement, but manufacturing remained a small-scale operation, with most establishments having only a handful of workers. To be sure, an Athenian shieldmaker employed 120 men, and in Rome there were some large units in baking, fulling cloth, brickmaking, pottery, mining, and smelting. Nevertheless, the ancient world was, on the whole, a world of far-flung commercial ventures and entrepreneurs who engaged in trading, exchange, land ownership, and tax collecting. And this was the way the business world continued to look, except, of course, on a much larger and more efficient scale, until relatively modern times. From 1200 on, it is true, the legacy of the ancient world was greatly expanded, but the changes that occurred, vast as they were, were more a matter of degree than of kind.

Rise of Business in the Middle Ages. *The Italian Cities.* After the fall of Rome, trade, commerce, and industry continued in the East under the Byzantine Empire and later under the Saracens. In the West, on the other hand, big business did not function again until approximately the thirteenth century, when it reappeared in the Italian cities. From the twelfth to the fourteenth century, Amalfi, Venice, Florence, and Genoa were the dominant business communities, with essentially the same characteristics. By far the most important businesses were trade and commerce and their complements, banking and exchange.

Types of Business Enterprise. Most manufacturing was in the homespun and handicraft stages, offering little oppor-

most common. The merchant princes ordinarily used the partnership, of which there were essentially three types. The first, which had been well known in ancient times, was prominent in the Italian cities around 1100 and still exists in the modern world in the form of sharecropping. Under it, one partner contributed all the capital and took three quarters of the profits; the other did all the work for one quarter of the profits. Under the second arrangement, one partner contributed most of the capital; the other contributed a little capital and all the work; and the profits were divided evenly. Under the third form, all the partners contributed

Goose merchants of ancient Egypt, as shown in an Old Kingdom tombstone painting at Saqqara.

tunity for practicing business administration or for gathering profits. Some handicraft manufacturing, such as cloth-making and glass blowing, did turn out a large product, and in fifteenth-century Florence, these industries used relatively advanced machinery and division of labor, although the emphasis was usually on human energy, and few capital goods were used in production. The one outstanding exception was shipbuilding, which was a large-scale operation using considerable capital equipment. Mining offered a somewhat broader field for business acumen than manufacturing, and by the late Middle Ages there were several extensive mining enterprises in Sweden and central Europe.

Types of Businessmen. In every large medieval city, there were two groups of businessmen. The first group consisted of what may be called "petty capitalists": the traveling merchants, the shopkeepers, hucksters, and peddlers who served a small local market; and the artisans who manufactured goods, either within or outside a guild. The second group was composed of the large entrepreneurs, the "sedentary merchants," who sat in their countinghouses supervising their varied trading and banking interests. Their tentacles stretched all over the world and their powerful influence seeped into every nook and cranny of every household in every large city.

Development of the Partnership. In organizing their ventures, businessmen used various forms of organization. Among the small businessmen the sole proprietorship was

both capital and work. This was usually a family partnership and was most prominent in the heyday of the Italian cities. It was capable of raising impressive amounts of capital, but occasionally there were ventures that required even more capital than the partners were willing or able to risk. In such cases, shares were sold to individual investors. Throughout the Middle Ages, this device was occasionally used in shipbuilding and in single large-scale trading ventures. Late in the Middle Ages, it was used to raise the large capital required in the major mining enterprises.

The Era of Traveling Merchants. *The Champagne Fairs.* During most of the medieval period, at least until the end of the thirteenth century, the petty capitalist traveling merchant handled most of the trading. Like that of most small businessmen before and since, his lot was not too enviable. He covered enormous distances and faced frightful dangers. Total turnover of goods was much too small, and the rate of profit much too meager; nevertheless, the number of active merchants was disproportionately great. Picking up goods here and there, they covered all of Europe, constantly going from one of the numerous fairs to another. The most famous and best-attended fairs were those that were held in Champagne, in northern France. To Champagne, which lay across the main trade routes in easy access to northern Europe, came merchants from the Levant, Italy, the northern countries, and the Low Countries. For 32 weeks in every year for more than 100 years, they bought and sold textiles, furs, drugs, food, and other commodities, made loans, collected debts, and changed money. Then the fairs suddenly faded away, for a trading system centered on fairs and operated by petty capitalists no longer served an expanding and increasingly complex economy.

The Hanseatic League. As cities grew, they inevitably became the centers of trade, and the merchants who lived in the cities did more and more of their trading at home. As early as the twelfth century, traveling merchants in some of the larger cities in the North were beginning to band together in a loose federation of local guilds (hanses), which

they also had a better comprehension of the entire business situation than their rivals had. They operated under more or less permanent partnerships instead of under a loose federation such as the Hanseatic League used. They covered a much wider area and had more efficient administrative control. The great Italian merchant, Francesco Datini (1335-1410), for example, operated in all the Italian cities as well as in Spain, France, England, Africa, and the Levant. He kept in close touch by letter with his many agents and commission merchants, some of whom, like Andrea Barbarigo, later became great merchants in their own right.

SHOPS OF ANCIENT ATHENS

BETTMANN ARCHIVE

in 1300 became known as the Hanseatic League. Composed of associations of independent merchants from more than 70 German towns with posts stretching from London to Russia, the League long commanded the commerce of the whole Baltic and North Sea area. It threatened the traveling merchant, though not fatally, for most of the hanse members were themselves small traveling merchants.

Expansion of the Italian Sedentary Merchants. Meanwhile, the Italian sedentary merchants, who had been constantly gaining strength, were eager to expand even at the expense of the small merchants. When, at the end of the thirteenth century, the Count of Flanders offered them the freedom of the strategic port of Bruges in the heart of the Flemish cloth area, they immediately forsook Champagne, sent their agents and partners to Flanders, and thereby reduced the traveling merchant and the fairs to unimportance. Only a short time later, they had control of all foreign trade except in Germany and the Baltic. These remained for some time longer the monopoly of the Hanseatic League, even though by 1370 the latter had already entered a period of stagnation and decline. This decline, incidentally, was one of the longest in the annals of economic history, for it lasted almost 300 years until 1669, when the last Hanseatic diet was held. After that date only Lübeck, Hamburg, and Bremen remained of the once-great Hanseatic League.

There were many reasons why the sedentary merchants triumphed over the traveling merchants and superseded the Hanseatic League, but the chief reason was their superior efficiency as businessmen. Quick to adopt new methods,

Contributions of the Italian Merchants. *Accounting.* The Italian sedentary merchants also excelled their rivals in the use of business tools. They made wide use of the bill of exchange (known as early as 1156) and of marine insurance (originated in Genoa in the early fourteenth century). Above all, they made great strides in accounting, without which the development of capitalistic business would be impossible. They introduced modern double-entry bookkeeping, and a Venetian, Luca Pacioli, wrote the first treatise on bookkeeping in 1494. It was the Italians who taught accounting to the rest of the world and set the stage for its later refinement.

The Use of Credit. The Italians also led in credit and banking techniques. To be sure, credit was not a new thing. It had been common in the ancient world, and it permeated the whole economy even in the early Middle Ages when the Jews, largely because of the Church's strictures against interest, were the busiest moneylenders. But Christians quickly learned how to circumvent the rules against interest and soon supplanted the Jews. First were the Knights Templars, who loaned to kings from 1182 until their suppression in 1312. But like the Jews, the Templars were moneylenders, not bankers. The Italians were the first since the Romans to operate deposit banking, that is, to create money on the basis of fractional reserves.

The Rise of Private Banks. *The Power of Banking Families.* Long before the first public banks were formed in Barcelona (1401) and in Genoa (1407), the family partnerships of the sedentary merchants were conducting thriving private banks. By 1250, every major Italian city had a dozen or more important trading and banking firms; Florence alone had 80. By the fourteenth and fifteenth centuries, the fascinating business of banking had attracted men from all

Open-air shop of a seller of bread, as shown in a wall painting at Pompeii

countries, but the Italians were the leaders and, contrary to popular opinion, there were few Jews. Shylock, the type of the medieval usurer, was a figment of the imagination. The beau ideal was the Florentine or South German banker. Families like the Medici and the Fuggers were wealthier than the states in which they lived, and they wielded more power than kings. Indeed, they elected kings and made popes and became noblemen themselves. Members of the Medici family became counts and queens and popes; and the Fuggers supported the Hapsburgs, paying the bribes that made Charles V Holy Roman Emperor. The secret of their power was simple: they had money, and money was desperately needed to finance political intrigue, war, and luxurious living. The demand for money was so great that bankers were able to charge interest rates of from 10 to 100 per cent, and often much more.

Banking Hazards and Failures. But despite their prodigious power, medieval bankers led uneasy lives. Most of the populace feared and hated them; their rivals incessantly plotted against them; and their financial risks (as evidenced by their high interest rates), especially in the unproductive business of making loans to kings, were even greater than their fabulous rewards. Since they lived dangerously and were never too far removed from financial disaster, many of them, including the most successful, eventually failed. In the panic of the early fourteenth century, before the rise of the Medici, bankruptcy befell the Peruzzi, the Macci, the Scali, the Frescobaldi, and the Bardi, all glamorously wealthy Italian banking families. Jacques Coeur (1395-1456), the colorful French banker who was said to have been worth $9 million, failed in 1455. The Fuggers of Augsburg, who had their thumbs in every business pie and were at one time the

wealthiest house in Europe and one of the wealthiest families that ever lived, went bankrupt in 1607. It was much safer to retain a trading business along with banking than to put all one's eggs in the banking basket, even if the basket were secured, as it often was, by human hostages. Thus the Italian firms which, like the Medici, maintained various manufacturing enterprises along with banking, survived and prospered better than those who went all out for banking. But despite fluctuations, Italian businessmen maintained their power well into the sixteenth century, long after the political and military power of the Italian cities themselves had begun to decline.

Decline of Italy. Italy's decline began when the discovery of new trade routes and new worlds caused the commercial center to shift from the Mediterranean to the Atlantic Coast. Slowly the center of business activity moved north, stopping for a brief time in Augsburg, that citadel of moneyed merchants that lay on the trade route from Venice to the North, before reaching Antwerp, the new center of the Flanders cloth district, around 1500.

The Rise of Amsterdam in World Commerce. A century later Amsterdam, the hub of the intensely business-dominated Dutch civilization, was the world's commercial capital. Most of the Western world's trading took place in its Bourse, and from its shores the Dutch burghers sent out the finest ships to bring back wealth for them and, for the Netherlands, the glory of being the world's most advanced economy. But from 1550 on, the English economy, guided by the Tudors, the experience of Italian bankers, and the

Medieval bankers and financiers discussing business matters. Even in these early times the businessman relied upon the advice of the financial expert.

astuteness of the British banker Sir Thomas Gresham, had also grown rapidly and by 1650 it was ominously threatening the Dutch supremacy.

The Dutch and the English. *The Joint Stock Company.* In building their business institutions, both the Dutch and

the English profited greatly from the Italians; but they also made their own solid contributions by greatly expanding the regulated trading company and greatly refining the joint-stock company, which was the immediate ancestor of the modern corporation. The essence of the regulated company was that each member traded on his own in a centrally directed enterprise. In a joint-stock company, on the other hand, each owner contributed a share of capital to a common pool and shared profits and losses in proportion to ownership. In other words, there was no common stock of capital in a regulated company as there was in a joint-stock company. Although both the regulated company and the joint-stock company were known in medieval times in such institutions as the Hanseatic League and the Merchant Adventurers' Company and in Italian shipping and southern German mining, the Dutch and the English were the first to make frequent use of the devices, especially the joint-stock company. The Muscovy Company, founded in 1551, and the Africa Company, founded in 1555, were the first, but they were not successful and the Muscovy Company quickly changed to a regulated company.

The East India Companies. By far the most famous of the joint stock trading companies were the English East India Company (1600) and the Dutch East India Company (1602). The latter is usually considered the first stock company in the modern sense, for it was more or less permanent, instead of being organized for a single venture. Although its charter was originally granted for only 21 years, it was renewed over and over again for almost two centuries. Moreover, its capital was permanent from the beginning, whereas the English East India Company did not have a permanent capital until 1657.

No other companies in business history have been more colorful than the East India companies. Granted great powers by their charters, they were veritable nations in themselves. They coined money and passed laws, maintained armies and navies, waged war, and signed peace treaties. The English company sent Robert Clive to India and for years governed that vast domain very much as it pleased. The Dutch company sent its East Indiamen to Java Head and Japan and was the absentee landlord for much of Oceania. Riddled with bureaucracy, both companies seemed clumsily inefficient; by today's standards their management

would be condemned as worse than inept. Yet they made huge profits. The English company paid its owners 400 per cent between 1683 and 1692, and throughout the rise and fall of the Dutch Empire, the Dutch company, co-operating with two other great business institutions—the Amsterdam Bank and the Amsterdam Exchange—produced profits which averaged 18 per cent a year for almost 200 years.

Development of Manufacturing. The Dutch East India Company and its counterparts marked the zenith of the sedentary merchant, but even at the time they were formed there were already at work economic forces that resulted in

Seventeenth-century shoemaker's establishment

the eclipse of the merchant. All through the sixteenth and seventeenth centuries, especially after 1650, population grew considerably, new markets were opened and old ones were made more accessible, mass consumption became a possibility, and the putting-out system of manufacture began to displace handicraft. It was a great time for a petty capitalist artisan to be alive, for after centuries of humble living he had his opportunity to rise to power. With the introduction of machinery, steam power, and heavy capital equipment in the Industrial Revolution, manufacturing supplanted commerce in business importance, and a new group, the industrialists or industrial capitalists, replaced the merchants as the dominant force in the business community. But this great flowering of manufacturing business, unlike mercantile enterprise, was confined to a very limited area, Western Europe and Japan. The rest of the Far East until recent

Later studies covering the origins of American business leaders from 1870 on revealed that the self-made man was more the exception than the rule, despite the emphasis on the Horatio Alger theme in American culture.

The Manufacture of Interchangeable Parts. The industrial businessman's chief ability was to increase production, and when an industrial society was first evolving or when a specific industry was new, this talent was immensely valuable. Then the problem was to turn out the goods to cover a virgin market, and this was the industrialist's great forte. By the second half of the eighteenth century, individualistic

A marketplace of about 1560, showing a stationer's shop and a shoemaker's shop at the right, and, on the left, a spectacle store

times has not gone beyond the stage of the merchant, and Russia until the Revolution was a land of landed aristocrats and small-scale manufacturing.

From Petty Capitalists to Giants. In some parts of the world, notably in the United States, where the transition took place later than in Great Britain, sedentary merchants were able to adjust themselves to the business of mass production manufacturing, and men like Francis Cabot Lowell, Patrick Tracy Jackson, and Nathan Appleton dropped their shipping and trading enterprises and began to manufacture textiles. But the most famous industrialists as, for example Sir Richard Arkwright, the textile baron; Josiah Wedgwood, the potter; Matthew Boulton, who helped make James Watt's steam engine a success; Alfred Krupp, the German ironmaster; Andrew Carnegie, the steel tycoon; and the so-called American "robber barons"—Jay Gould, John D. Rockefeller, Cornelius Vanderbilt, and John Jacob Astor—were petty capitalists grown big.

This is not to say that they were all self-made men. Josiah Wedgwood (1730-1795) came from four generations of potters; Matthew Boulton (1728-1809) inherited a thriving business; and Alfred Krupp (1812-1887) inherited a small ironworks. But Richard Arkwright (1732-1792) was a barber turned textile manufacturer; Andrew Carnegie (1835-1919) was an immigrant bobbin boy; and Henry Ford (1863-1947) was a farm boy. In support of the self-made thesis, an investigation made about 1910 concluded that 88 out of 139 cotton manufacturers in one English town were self-made.

industrial entrepreneurs had installed the machinery supplied by the Industrial Revolution and were mass producing consumer goods like textiles, china, and novelties. But heavy machinery and precision goods were still manufactured to order by hand. These could not be mass produced until the appearance of interchangeable parts, which in turn required complicated machine tools.

Before the end of the eighteenth century, the French were experimenting with interchangeable parts manufacture, but these experiments were not successful and were soon abandoned. Not long after, however, American businessmen, led by Eli Whitney (1765-1825) and the Connecticut arms makers, also began experimenting with interchangeable parts, and by the War of 1812 they had demonstrated that the idea was practical. In fact, they were so successful that, by 1850, the whole process of mass producing standardized articles with interchangeable parts became known, throughout the world, as the "American System." By then armaments, clocks, farm equipment, and other metal goods were being manufactured with interchangeable parts. Meanwhile, the appearance of the railroads not only broadened the market area, but also created a demand for heavy goods, thus further accelerating mass production. One more step—the development of scientific management—was required to bring mass production up to date. Here, too, the French did the spadework early in the Industrial Revolution. But once more it was Americans, particularly Frederick W. Taylor (1856-1915) and Henry L. Gantt (1861-1919), who put the idea into effect near the end of the nineteenth century, and some of whose methods were already in use in the steel, automotive, and other heavy manufacturing industries around the turn of the century.

The Development of Mass Production. Mass production greatly accelerated the growth of big business. Not that big business was a completely new phenomenon; there had been some relatively large businesses in the Middle Ages and a great many more just before the Industrial Revolution; but what made "big business" a household word was the expansion of railroads and the appearance of mass production in the heavy goods industries. These required enormous capital and necessitated widespread ownership of Gargantuan plant and equipment. As early as 1853, for example, the New York Central Railroad had 2,500 stockholders and the Delaware and Hudson had 4,200 employees. By the end of the nineteenth century, some manufacturing firms had grown to a size that dwarfed what had been considered huge at the beginning of the century. Boulton's factory had employed 1,000 workers and Arkwright's 300, but by 1899, although the average manufacturing firm in the United States employed only 22 workers, Carnegie steel employed 40,000. Fifty years later, this figure in turn seemed small when General Motors employed over 600,000.

Portrait of the Businessman. Although strong in production, the industrial businessman had many serious weaknesses. He was a "rule-of-thumb" businessman, although one authority, in speaking of the American scene, suggests that the "informed" businessman was becoming more and more common, especially after 1860. The "sophisticated" businessman, described as one who has a real knowledge of what is going on inside and outside the business, and who uses permanent administrative staffs and ancillary business agencies, was rare indeed before 1900 and most likely did not exist at all. Most industrialists were not concerned with what was not intimately associated with their business. Few

of them had a labor policy, and those who did were heavily paternalistic. In a widely-quoted statement that was in many respects reminiscent of medieval business opinion, George F. Baer, the coal and railway magnate, said in 1902: "The rights and interests of the laboring man will be protected and cared for . . . by the Christian men whom God, in his infinite wisdom, has given control of the property interests of the country . . . ."

The Businessman as Seen by the Public. Such statements did not endear the industrialist to the public; but then most industrialists were completely oblivious of public relations. One of the greatest failures of American industrialists was the failure to achieve a dominant position in the country's social life, even though the United States was considered a business civilization. True, the American businessman was never held in contempt as businessmen had been in Greece and Rome, and there was no native aristocracy to treat him patronizingly as his colleagues were treated in England. Neither was he omnipotent as his predecessors had been in Babylonia, Phoenicia, and Holland. The public regarded him with the same fear and antagonism that was demonstrated toward the Italian merchants and the South German bankers. As popularly portrayed, the industrialist was an uncouth, avaricious, ruthless, antisocial money grubber. To the agrarians, he and his activities were responsible for the sinful metropolitan centers and the luxurious living to which they always ascribed the decay and fall of civilization.

Cultural Contributions of the Businessman. Yet historically the centers of culture have always been the urban centers where business flourished. The things that characterize culture and civilization—music, painting, literature, science, education, and philanthropy—have always flowered in the business centers, such as Ionia, Alexandria, Florence, Amsterdam, London, and New York, and very often it was because of the business class that the arts thrived. The

Court of the West India Company's House in Amsterdam, Holland. This building was first occupied by the company in 1674.

Medici and other Italian bankers subsidized the superb art of Renaissance Florence, and the painter Giotto was actually a member of the business class. The Dutch burghers, crass as they were, had their portraits painted by Rembrandt, and Rubens was a businessman in art. From the fortunes of Peabody, Carnegie, and Rockefeller came the original huge foundations that subsidized hospitals, health, and education. The cynical Nobel left his dynamite fortune as a memorial to peace and idealism. The miserly Russell Sage financed social work. The brewer Matthew Vassar endowed a

equally adroit in a market in which replacement demand was more important than new demand. Even in the United States, where salesmanship and advertising were to reach their fullest development, there were only about 1,000 traveling salesmen in 1860; the first deliberately planned national advertising campaign did not occur until 1899, and the first book on advertising as a business force was not published until 1913. Industrial businessmen relied heavily on price competition. From an internal view this practice was often disastrous, for when business activity declined, price-cutting

Workshop of a carriage builder in the late eighteenth century

women's college. The imperialist Cecil Rhodes left a fortune to cement international amity, and the Englishman James Smithson endowed the utterly American Smithsonian Institution. The list could be lengthened indefinitely, without even mentioning the indirect influence of businessmen on the life of their times.

Early Business Shortcomings. Despite their prodigious growth, businesses often failed to develop a long-range policy. This weakness prevented the industrialists, for example, from diversifying their operations, so that they remained specialists to the end. Nor did they develop or take advantage of new business tools and techniques in management, marketing, and finance. They failed, for example, to take advantage of the corporate form of business organization even after governments had liberalized the law by extending limited liability and by passing general corporation acts (New York, 1811; Connecticut, 1817; the United States in general after 1850; and Great Britain, 1844 and 1855) that permitted corporations to be formed without a special act of legislation.

Many industrialists continued to use the sole proprietorship and the partnership long after their businesses had grown huge. Consequently their organizations were often awkward and unwieldy (the Carnegie Company, for example, at one time had 40 partners). They also tended to run their businesses as one-man shows and did not give their associates a free hand in administration. Similarly, the industrialists made no spectacular progress in marketing. At times, of course, businessmen, like Wedgwood and Boulton, traveled the territory to stimulate a desire for a new product; but although adept at tapping a new market, they were not

resulted in widespread bankruptcy and often left the victors crippled.

Financial Weaknesses. But even more than in management and marketing, industrial businessmen were weak in finance. They were heavy in fixed capital but light in working capital and consequently did not maintain adequate reserves to tide them over periods of depressed business. Even the greatest industrialists found themselves at one time or another desperately short of cash. Their difficulties stemmed mostly from their obsession with production, but were also caused by their extreme prejudice against bankers and the financial trappings which bankers emphasized. Moreover, for most of them, accounting was in the infancy in which the Italians had left it 400 years before. Some firms, it is true, were practicing cost accounting of a sort shortly after the Civil War, but the advanced techniques were not adopted until the twentieth century. The first controller of an American industrial enterprise did not appear until 1892; the theory and practice of cost accounting did not become widespread until 1910; and it has only been in the last 25 years that the income statement has taken precedence over the balance sheet.

Business Remedies. The weaknesses in the business structure did not go unheeded. Gradually business techniques improved, and the "sophisticated" businessman replaced the "informed" businessman in the leading firms. There were three main causes for this gradual evolution: the general process of economic growth, which produced ever-larger business units; the changes in economic and social institutions, such as the growth of labor unions and the increased importance of government, which presented businessmen with a whole set of new problems; and the actions of businessmen themselves in attacking the problems of price competition and weak financial policy.

Development of Trusts and Cartels. The last quarter of the nineteenth century witnessed a great wave of business consolidations which was repeated in the 1920's on a larger

AN EIGHTEENTH-CENTURY WHEEL FACTORY

CULVER SERVICE

scale, and in the 1950's on a smaller scale. The consolidation movement followed different lines in the different centers of business activity. In Great Britain mergers and holding companies were most popular. The Nobel Dynamite Trust, the first holding company and the first international cartel, was formed in 1886, and J. & P. Coats had a virtual monopoly in thread by the late 1890's. Consolidation reached its peak in Britain in the 1920's with the formation of such colossi as Imperial Chemicals (1926) and Unilever (1929). In Germany, unlike England and the United States, the government encouraged cartels, and they began to appear after the industrialization of the 1870's. Then in the 1920's, numerous holding companies, including I. G. Farben (1925) and Vereinigte Stahlwerke (1926), were formed under the aegis of commercial bankers who were always very influential in German business.

The Rockefeller and Morgan Empires. In the United States, John D. Rockefeller (1839-1937) (and his associates in Standard Oil) and investment bankers like J. P. Morgan (1837-1913) pioneered in business consolidation. Standard Oil in 1879 formed the first of many American trusts, and Standard Oil (New Jersey) in 1899 was one of the first American industrial holding companies. Morgan, previously concerned with important railroad consolidations, became involved in manufacturing in the 1890's; and in 1901 his banking firm was responsible for the formation of the United States Steel Corporation, presumably the first billion-dollar enterprise in history.

New Management Techniques and Personnel. Rockefeller and Morgan also pioneered in adopting new financial and management techniques. Rockefeller, wrote Ida Tarbell, had the soul of a bookkeeper; unquestionably he had a genius for cost accounting. He also had a bent for co-operative management, and almost from its beginning, Standard Oil used the committee system in making important business decisions. Morgan, whose interests were unusually diversified even for an investment banker, relied heavily on managers such as Elbert H. Gary of United States Steel. In time, these and other similar arrangements gave rise to a large group of professional administrators, the management men,

who soon became the most influential individuals in so-called "big business." Indeed, in some areas of the world, notably West Germany, no one knows exactly who owns some of the largest business enterprises, which are nevertheless very efficiently conducted by professional managers.

The Professional Manager. The professional administrator is highly sophisticated. Relying heavily on his administrative aides and ancillary agencies, he is an almost anonymous personality, far removed from yesterday's heroic captain of industry. Yet he is concerned with all the problems that have always confronted businessmen, as well as with a few additional ones of recent vintage—labor, public, and government relations. It seems probable that he is more

BETTMANN ARCHIVE

Rolling sheet iron in an iron plant in the late nineteenth century

efficient, if less spectacular, than the nineteenth century industrialist.

The Chance for Business Survival. If profit is the measure, then from the days of Sargon the Magnificent to the General Motors Corporation and the petty capitalist corner drugstore of today, a snap judgment would conclude

Carding, drawing, and roving in a cotton textile mill in 1839. Note the presence of child labor.

that there have been some spectacular successes and some-what fewer cataclysmic failures; but most businesses have hovered about the line between success and failure, with more falling below the line than surviving above it. At the height of a business boom the profit rate for all American corporations varies between 9 and 12 per cent of sales. During great depressions, such as that of the 1930's, corporations in the aggregate lost money. Even at the height of prosperity, the rate of business failure is high, and it is stupendous in panics and depressions.

Since the days of ancient Babylon, the pages of economic history have been colored by the accounts of the great financial and economic cataclysms that brought thousands to ruin. The repudiation of royal debt and the subsequent breakdown in the money market that occurred in 1345 brought great hardship to many smaller citizens of Florence as well as to the great banking houses. The tulip craze in Holland in the early seventeenth century culminated in the crash of 1637, again bringing financial ruin and economic hardship to all citizenry, and to small business as well as large. Almost a century later the maniacal frenzy to buy shares resulted in the explosion of the South Sea Bubble in 1720. Another financial panic after the Napoleonic wars brought wholesale financial ruin. The "Great Depression" of the 1870's carried into bankruptcy firms in all parts of the world, a situation that was repeated in the 1890's and once again in the 1930's. In between the major panics and depressions, less significant business recessions occurred with discouraging frequency, killing off a great many more business firms. Of those who survived major and minor depressions, many eventually retired voluntarily and another large number was absorbed in merger and consolidation. Because of one thing or another, therefore, but mostly because of bankruptcy, few firms survive for very long. Indeed, four out of five companies disappear within ten years of formation. Yet there

are some very old business firms, American as well as European.

Old European Firms. Of course, no American firm approaches the antiquity of some European enterprises. German breweries, French wine cellars, and Danish and Scotch distilleries go back long before the Declaration of Independence; and some predate the discovery of America. Some European public banks are very old. The Bank of Amsterdam, founded in 1609, was the first public bank north of the Alps. The Bank of England was founded in 1694, Sun Insurance, Ltd., in 1710, the Royal Exchange Assurance in 1720, and the Norwich Union in 1797. The Hudson's Bay Company (1670) still survives from the days of the chartered companies. Crosse and Blackwell handled spices in 1706, long before they came to the Colonies, and Revillon Frères was founded in 1723, long before it opened a branch in America. The Wedgwoods still operate the very prosperous business that Josiah Wedgwood founded in 1759. The Creusot iron-works in France bought one of Watt's steam engines only six years after America declared its independence. By that time, however, America had a few established firms of her own.

Old American Firms. Of the approximately 4,250,000 businesses in the United States, about 100 date back to before 1800. A surprisingly large number of these—fifteen —have remained in the same family, but not one of them is large or famous. Eleven, including the Perot Malting Company (1687), reputedly the oldest company in the United States, are located in Philadelphia and the surrounding area. The other ten are: Rhoads and Sons, tanners (1702); Skillman Express Storage and Furniture Exchange, Princeton (1743); Demuth Tobacco Shop, Lancaster (1770); Pugh Inc., augers and bits (1778); Nathan Trotter, metal merchants (1787); Warner Company, building materials (1794); Rowland, Inc., spring manufacturers (1795); McIlvan Company, lumber (1798). Three firms are in New England: D. L. Slade, Boston, spices, (1734); Dexter and Sons, Windsor Locks, Conn., paper specialties (1767); and Bird and Sons, building materials, Walpole, Mass. (1795). One firm is in Baltimore: Jenkins and Company, undertakers, founded in 1799.

About 160 American firms are over 150 years old; 36 are in banking and insurance, 35 print newspapers and books, and 85 are in manufacturing and trade, although predominantly in the latter. Here again few, even among the banks, insurance companies, and newspapers, are very large or very well known. The Bank of New York (1784) is the oldest surviving public bank. *The Saturday Evening Post* (1728) is the oldest periodical. The Presbyterian Ministers Fund (1717) is the oldest life insurance company, and the Philadelphia Contributionship (1752) is the oldest fire insurance company. The Taylor-Wharton Iron and Steel Company of High Bridge, N.J. (1742) is the oldest manufacturer of durable goods. The oldest well-known manufacturing company is Devoe and Raynolds (1754), followed by a handful of other famous names before 1808, including P. Lorillard (1760), Revere Copper and Brass (1801), Scovill Manufacturing (1802), and E. I. Du Pont (1802). Between 1810 and 1820 appeared Lukens Steel (1810), Saco-Lowell Shops (1812), J. P. Stevens (1813), Consolidated Gas of Baltimore (1816), Owens-Illinois Glass (1818), Merck and Company (1818), and Brooks Brothers (1818).

It would appear that, in the world of business, the best way to survive and grow old was to stay small and to produce consumer goods with an inelastic demand. Heavy goods brought fortune and fame and offered an opportunity to become an industrial giant, but it was a "prince and pauper" game in which the chances for survival were far less favorable than in small business.   H. E. K.

BUSINESS CYCLES, a term denoting the irregular alternations of business activity from peaks of prosperity to the low points of depressions. Prior to the crisis of 1929, which precipitated the depression of 1929-1939, the length of business cycles averaged about four years from boom to boom in the United States, and a little more in other leading nations. The length varied, however, from one to twelve years. Business activity in major booms, measured chiefly by productive activity, commonly rose as high as 15 per cent above the general average of current business. Depressions sank 15 to 20 per cent below. On the whole, a typical cycle, disregarding a number of very small ones, may be pictured by a wave with a length of four years. Certain ordinary terms used in describing the business cycle have somewhat technical meanings. The crest, as the term implies, is the highest point reached in the boom, usually determined after minor irregularities are rounded off. The trough, similarly, is the bottom of the wave. The crest is usually marked or followed by a crisis, or a distinct turn downward, analogous to the crisis of a fever. The crisis may develop a panic, with ruinous sales of securities and runs on banks. An analysis of the cycle distinguishes certain phases such as the expansion and contraction phases. It will also involve consideration of other concurrent aspects of business variations, the numerical influences of which are removed, when possible, from index numbers representing the cycle. These influences include the so-called secular trend, or average rate of growth of business over the decades, and the seasonal factor, the influence of weather and custom on such things as the sale of fuel or the holiday trade. Accidental factors, such as strikes and earthquakes, are also noted.

Cyclic Irregularities. Though the business cycle centers about industrial production and gross national product, it does not affect all phases of business alike. Livestock marketings, for example, though strongly influenced by prosperity and depression, are thrown out of phase largely because it takes time to build up herds and flocks. In somewhat the same way, a multiplicative effect is carried over from the shifting demand for certain factory products to the producers of machines and machine tools. Building construction, also, though sometimes a major phase of the cycle, often merges into longer cycles. Producer goods reflect the cycle to a greater degree than consumer goods. In fact, the cycle may plausibly be regarded as successive pulsations of active capital investment.

Some activities tend to precede the main features of the business cycle. This was formerly true of the stock market. On the average, but with wide variations, the crest of the stock market has preceded the crest of business activity by about six months. Those who are in touch with the plans of business leaders naturally anticipate profits. On the other hand, some aspects of business have tended to follow the most obvious features of the cycle.

Not many types of business activity have tended to run directly counter to the cycle; in fact, gold production is perhaps the only one. And this was true only of the days when the gold standard was allowed to operate relatively freely. In earlier times, notably in the nineteenth century after the Napoleonic Wars, price inflation in the boom put a damper on gold production, since the price of gold was fixed at the mint and costs of production were increased. On the other hand, the cost of producing gold fell with other costs during depressions; hence its production was stimulated, and the search for new gold fields was intensified. Of course, accidental discoveries of new ores, or new methods of processing the ores, in turn inflated prices. This was particularly true of the South African gold boom near the end of the nineteenth century. The increased production of gold, finding its way into the channels of world trade, was perhaps the chief factor changing the declining price trend prevailing after the Civil War into the rising trend which prevailed in the years from 1896 to the beginning of World War I.

Social Aspects. The business cycle has been closely related to various social phenomena. In earlier decades, for example, marriage and divorce rates, and the consumption of luxuries, varied more or less closely with the cycle. Church activities varied somewhat in reverse order. Crime rates also responded to the cycle, but in several different ways, depending on the nature of the crime. In general, the cycle was definitely correlated with many activities and moods other than those directly expressed in business data.

The Physical Environment. It has been argued that there has been a measurable relationship between business cycles, particularly the more severe ones, and the cycles observable in nature, such as weather and sunspots. The matter is debatable, but the evidence points to some degree of concurrence in the past. Weather cycles with alternations stressing favorable and unfavorable crop years, extending over periods ranging from a decade to a generation, have been noted. In earlier times, when farming was the principal occupation, weather was obviously a determinant of prosperity, and it still is in certain cases. But the cycle, as it has been known in recent years, has more and more departed from this simple relationship to agriculture. Man has, of course, developed in a natural environment, and in a limited sense has been wholly conditioned by it. Yet he has partially freed himself from the tyranny of nature, and his ambitions point to still greater freedom. Hence it is obviously an exaggeration to picture him as a victim of depressions and wars arbitrarily caused by nature.

Credit and Gold. The business cycle is closely related to the expansion and contraction of money and its substitutes, the chief substitute in the cycle, as we have known it, being credit. This is nothing new, for in ancient times, credit was likewise used to augment the precious metals, and booms and depressions were familiar incidents. The trader often yielded priority to the dictator or fighting noble, who sometimes brought a forced and temporary stability to the gyrations of prices, but the cure was in many instances worse than the disease. During the nineteenth century, under the leadership of Great Britain, gold became the sole monetary standard of the leading nations, so that, in effect, international trade had a single standard currency. The dollar, pound, franc, and mark were merely comparable weights of gold. The cycle centered about British manufacturing and financial ascendancy, and its nature was modified as management entered into central banking in an endeavor to curb the gyrations of the cycle. This feature of the development of the cycle may best be described in the words of Allan Sproul, former president of the Federal Reserve Bank of New York (cf. *Monthly Review Supplement,* Federal Reserve Bank of New York, January 1947). Discussing the gold standard, Mr. Sproul wrote: ".... it flourished with London as the acknowledged financial center of the world, with Great Britain as the great exporter of capital and the great importer of raw materials, and with the rest of the trading world largely revolving about the center. In essence it was an adjustment between one economy and the rest of the world. . . . [As] it became necessary to cope with . . . cyclical depressions, elements of management crept into the gold standard even while it was still referred to and considered to be automatic. Central banks became more and more aware of their powers and responsibilities." Mr. Sproul goes on to explain the reason why the public is so ignorant of the important functions of central banks by saying: "Central bankers have long been known as members of the silent service. We have preferred, traditionally, to let our acts speak for us and not to explain them."

Causes of Cycles. The causation of alternate booms and depressions is a question concerning which there are various schools of thought. The reasons for the wide differences of opinion seem to be the extreme complexity of the subject and the prejudices and interests that are involved. It is not possible, therefore, to be dogmatic concerning causes. Perhaps the most that can be done is to call attention to certain factors which distinguished economists have emphasized in explaining business instability. In a sense, perhaps, all the varying authorities are right in that each calls attention to one or more of the innumerable factors involved. For example, one authority argues that successive booms are initiated by profitable inventions. Another emphasizes variations in bank credit. Still others find that the blame for business instability should be placed on overproduction, on underconsumption, on excessive speculation, on misplaced investment, on extravagance, on "psychology," or, in the opinion of extreme radicals, merely on "capitalism." The controversial literature on business cycles leads the reader to react against an attempt to find a "cause" and to accept the philosopher's dictum that current happenings can be explained only by all the past. It is no accident that one of the best-known recent works on business cycles is in reality

a complete system of theoretical economics, with historical references. It may, therefore, be advisable to approach the problem of causation by attempting to characterize American cycles, and particularly the so-called Great Depression (1929-1939) which preceded and was closely related to World War II.

The Great Depression. Before this depression the typical cycle had varied as previously described. The most outstanding characteristic of the boom had been an intensification of business activity, marked by a rise in both production and prices. The initiative seems generally to have been taken by the heavy industries related to investments, and the stimuli obviously centered about an anticipation of profits. With the outlook favorable, banks extended credit. Management bid excessively for the means of production and created surplus jobs, thus increasing costs. But sooner or later an excess of bank credit jeopardized reserves, and high prices caused, or threatened to cause, an outflow of gold as business increasingly bought relatively cheaper goods abroad. Consequently banks restricted credit. Business contracted, failures increased, and a surplus of unemployed means of production forced costs and prices down. Though the Great Depression was four or five times as deep and as long as would normally be expected, it followed the traditional pattern, though with certain notable exceptions. To begin with, it was preceded by a postwar boom which was stimulated by the need of repairing the wastes of war. But the price level was brought under some degree of control, chiefly as a result of the enlightened policies of Benjamin Strong, governor of the Federal Reserve Bank of New York. This was one of the first serious attempts to maintain a reasonable degree of business equilibrium.

Fiscal Controls. The Great Depression and World War II stimulated a demand for fiscal reform. Laws designed to stabilize the stock market were put into effect. Federal Reserve leadership openly assumed responsibility for influencing the supply of money with a view to stabilizing price levels. Consequently business opinion tentatively assumed that inflation and deflation beyond an innocuous minimum had become impossible. That extremes were less likely was generally conceded, but doubt persisted. Fear engendered by heavy taxation, government debt, and foreign relations threatened to disrupt controls. On the other hand, the application of modern science to production and finance supported confidence.

Historic Cycles. It should be noted that in contrast with the business cycle as here discussed, less definite cycles of longer duration have been postulated. For example, after World War I the Russian economist, N. D. Kondratieff, aroused an animated discussion by suggesting that in European experience cycles of about half a century could be traced. And irregular historic epochs of relative economic advance and retreat have been studied. Currently, attention is focused on cycles which prevail under business conditions today.   G. R. D.

BUSINESS EDUCATION, or, more properly, education for business, is concerned with the relationships, techniques, attitudes, and knowledge necessary for an individual to understand the social institution of business, and the economic environment, and to adjust himself to it. Accordingly, education for business is as important for persons who are consumers of the goods and services of business as it is for individuals who intend to produce those goods. Historically, business education has been concerned with preparing students for jobs in business. Since the middle

1920's, there has been recognition of the personal use and social values of business education for all persons. More recently it has taken on a broader significance involving an understanding of the American economic system.

History. The beginnings of business education are found in the apprenticeship system. Formal school training for business, including bookkeeping, penmanship, and arithmetic, was given in the Latin grammar schools and in the academies. There were also many private teachers of bookkeeping and penmanship. A few early high schools in the United States included courses in bookkeeping in the curriculum. It was not, however, until private business schools developed that business education can be said to have become a recognized part of education in America. Developing slowly after 1820, and limiting instruction principally to bookkeeping, arithmetic, and penmanship, business colleges, as they were known, grew rapidly after the Civil War, in response to the needs of the nation's expanding economy. Invention of the typewriter and the consequent increase in the business use of shorthand also stimulated the development of business education. Since then, business education has been introduced into practically every type of school: university, college, junior college, high school, night school, and even elementary school. Until after World War I, the private business school provided the dominant form of business education in the United States. The public secondary school has since exceeded other types of institutions in enrollment, in the number of teachers, and in public concern and interest.

Collegiate Schools of Business. The function of collegiate instruction in business, including the granting of degrees, is preparation for business careers on a professional or executive level. The occupations for which preparation is given and the curricula offered vary widely. However, all include a more or less extensive foundation in economic theory and basic business background, and some background of general education. The curricula most commonly offered are accountancy, banking and finance, business administration, management, and marketing. Other curricula offered include retailing and sales management, industrial relations, insurance, secretarial administration, office management, transportation, hotel administration, foreign trade, business teacher education, and public administration.

About 150 collegiate institutions have separate schools or colleges of business administration or commerce. Another 600 institutions, including liberal arts colleges and teachers colleges, offer major programs in some phases of business. Business curricula leading to graduate degrees are found in approximately 150 institutions. Several collegiate schools of business are now offering a doctor's degree in business administration (D.B.A.). This is in response to demands for a greater knowledge of theory and for experience in business research, along with a greatly increased demand for teachers of business on the collegiate level.

Enrollments in collegiate schools consist mainly of men, although the introduction of secretarial administration and office management has increased the number of women enrolled. Many collegiate schools of business maintain research bureaus designed to furnish various kinds of current business information to businessmen. Close relations between the college or university and the business community are maintained by these schools.

Private Business Schools and Junior Colleges. The function of private business schools and junior colleges, which give business training on a post-high-school level, is preparation for semiprofessional business occupations: jobs which require greater maturity, more seasoned judgment, and longer preparation than are required for routine or general clerical jobs. Curricula usually offered are those in accountancy, business administration, merchandising, and secretarial training. Some schools specialize in one curriculum, such as secretarial training or accountancy.

In private business schools offering courses of less than a year in length, the study is intensive, and is confined to the essentials needed to secure and hold a business position. Junior colleges generally, and business schools in increasing numbers, offer business background work and a functional type of general education. Junior colleges usually offer, in addition to terminal or semiprofessional business training, introductory courses for collegiate training, and also, occasionally, basic business courses as part of the general education program.

Since World War II, there has been a trend, first noticeable in the late 1930's, toward upgrading terminal vocational business education into intensive curricula offered by public schools in the thirteenth year, by technical institutes, and by area or regional vocational schools, all of which require high-school graduation for admission.

Enrollments, varying from institution to institution, are divided almost evenly between men and women.

High Schools. Two functions are recognized by high schools: (1) basic business education for all pupils without regard to their probable occupational training, and (2) vocational business training for stenographic, general clerical, and retail-store or distributive occupations. The extent of the courses depends on the size of the school and the nature of the community. Generally, the smaller high schools confine their offerings to basic business and preparatory vocational training. On the other hand, high schools in metropolitan areas may offer, in addition to basic business, a number of specialized vocational programs, including co-operative part-time classes as part of the federally aided vocational education program.

From two thirds to three fourths of the high schools give education for business, and more than 50 per cent of high school pupils are enrolled in one business subject.

BUSINESS LOANS. *See* BANK LOANS AND CREDIT (*Bank Loans*).

BUSINESS MACHINES AND EQUIPMENT. Business machines and modern business equipment handle dozens of clerical tasks which, before the twentieth century, had to be performed almost wholly by hand. It is difficult to exaggerate the saving in time and manpower effected by the development of the modern systems. For example, an electronic punched-card sorting and tabulating machine, one of the most complex mechanisms ever constructed, can handle in one hour a volume of work that formerly required a dozen bookkeepers a week or more to perform—and with no possibility of error. Some of the machines and systems in use today were invented before 1900, but they were of crude design and construction and could not compare in performance with their modern counterparts.

Addressing Machines. The first record of the invention of an addressing machine dates back to 1870, when a patent was issued to James McFatrich of Lens, Ill., for a machine called the McFatrich Mailer; as far as is known, this was the first addressing machine. It was limited, at first, to use in newspaper offices only, but was later adapted to mercantile and manufacturing concerns.

The first addressing machines used parchment paper with

the name and address cut into the paper by needlepoint type, with which the early stencil-cutting typewriters were equipped. The stencils were then fed through the addressing machines. Later, brass strips were employed and welded together to form a long continuous strip, which was run off a drum on a high-speed addressing machine and automatically wound on another reel after printing. Individual aluminum plates were later substituted for the brass strips. These could be detached and removed when the address became dead. The capacity of this type of machine has been

ELLIOTT ADDRESSING MACHINE CO.

AUTOMATIC ADDRESSING MACHINE

developed so that by printing names and addresses from huge drums on magazines and circulars, a rate of 15,000 addresses an hour can be maintained.

Modern equipment in a large publishing house often combines several types of office machines to produce results unobtainable from one unit. This complex equipment bears little resemblance to earlier models which were hand fed and hand selected. Today addressing machines are equipped with controls to enable them to recognize tabs on plates, causing them automatically to select or omit certain codes, and to duplicate, triplicate, or quadruplicate any item. The machines are available with cut-offs, daters, listers, numbering attachments, skipping devices, signals, spacers, tag feeders, and multiplicators. Attachments can be procured to feed envelopes, mail strip lists, and set up town and route markers as well as feed the publications being addressed.

Autographic Registers. The autographic register was developed through the adaption of carbon paper to reproduce a copy of an original transaction and provide a means of filing the record. This type of equipment was first developed in 1883 by James C. Shoup, who founded the Autographic Register Company. The basic principle of providing a locked compartment that would contain a copy in duplicate or triplicate and still allow the original copy to be removed is still incorporated in autographic registers today. Continuous forms made in duplicate or triplicate, interleaved with carbon or backed with carbon, are used. By means of pinfeed platens, or rollers, and the use of a crank, each form is turned into place for writing and then cranked out of the unit. The carbon copy is fed into a receptacle as the original is ejected and a new form is fed into place. Accurate alignment is assured and a complete record of all transactions is maintained in the locked machine. Forms can be constructed so that only that portion which is necessary is registered on the copy. Machines are also equipped so that only a summary need be retained in the unit. This total summary register is designed so that the

summary sheet remaining in the machine travels only a portion of the distance traveled by the ejected form. The equipment may also be used to eject multiple copies of forms while retaining a complete copy of the transaction, or set up as a manifolder which will release all copies of a form for distribution. Automatic registers are manufactured in various sizes and forms, being combined with cash registers in some instances so as automatically to open the cash drawer when a transaction is recorded, or to open it by the pressure of a key, or plunger, on completion of the transaction.

Cash Registers. In 1879 James Ritty, an American, developed the first cash register. This machine consisted of a wooden cabinet containing a paper roll ruled in columns. Each column was provided with a key which when pressed, punched a hole in the corresponding column on the roll, rang a bell and indicated the amount that had been registered for the customer to see. In order to total the business transactions, the proprietor unlocked the cabinet and removed the paper, which was perforated with holes in the various columns. By counting these holes, multiplying each number by the denomination of the columns, and cross-footing, a total of the amount of business could be obtained. In 1884 John H. Patterson invented a cash register in a more complex form. He developed the application of a cash drawer and wheels that would automatically total the dollars and cents as they were rung up. The first machines recorded cash only, and were not provided with a printed tape.

Modern machines are equipped with tapes as well as separate checks that can be handed to the customers as receipts. The basic principle involves the use of keys which are depressed for amounts to be rung up, and other keys for types of classifications. Levers also are provided to show type of sale, department charged, or sales person. They are electrically operated, and upon depression of a total key automatically classify, register, print a sales slip, visually indicate the amount rung up, and open a cash drawer, which may be selected from a multiple of drawers, to receive the payment. Many varieties of cash registers are manufactured. Basically they perform the same function, but are composed of different variations and combinations of features according to individual requirements.

Coin Changers and Counters. The first coin changer was invented by William H. Stoats in 1890. It provided

JOHNSON FARE BOX CO.

AUTOMATIC COIN COUNTER

for the automatic release of one coin at a time from a rack in which the coins were held. This was effected by the depression of a lever controlling the channel. Today coin changers are made in various forms. Those used in restaurants, banks, and stores are equipped with rows for the stacking of all denominations of fractional coins and a complete set of keys that may be depressed to eject the exact change for a dollar or a half-dollar transaction.

In 1902 J. M. Johnson secured a patent on a machine to count coins. Records show that a Mr. Bonsano in 1856 previously had obtained a patent on a coin handler, but had never developed it. A coin counter as used today is an electrically operated device that can sort into denominations mixed coins, ranging in value from pennies to half dollars and automatically count and wrap individual types of coins by a single adjustment of the stacking mechanism. Such machines are used primarily where a large volume of cash business occurs, as in factory payrolls, restaurants, banks, and coin-operated vending machine concessions.

Dictating Equipment. In 1887 the first development of a dictating machine became known to the general public as the Graphophone. This machine was developed by Chichester A. Bell and Charles Summer Tainter. The machine recorded sound by means of a wax cylinder on which was engraved a continuous spiral groove. It provided a means of permanently recording and reproducing sound. The early Graphophone was a cumbersome piece of equipment that was operated by a treadle motor and fly-wheel. The cylinder, made of paper, was coated with a thin layer of wax, which was engraved by means of a steel needle.

The only basic change in this original principle has been along the lines of using a magnetized tape or wire that can be re-employed after the message has been "wiped off." Most firms still employ the principle of engraving on wax cylinders, although cylinders are now supplemented in some cases by flat records similar to phonograph recordings. Modern machines are small and compact. All are equipped with automatic stop and start buttons, repeat mechanisms, and indicating devices to record last dictating position. All are electrically operated and easy to use.

Employed with the dictating machine is a unit called a transcribing machine. This machine embodies the principles of the dictating machine but is constructed to reproduce the dictated sound. The typist or secretary places the tape, cylinder, or wax record in her unit and plays back the recording. Typewriters are hooked up automatically with the dictating machine, allowing the operator to turn the dictating off and on according to the speed with which she

can type. Units are so compact that they actually take up less space than a typewriter.

A shaving machine, electrically operated, is employed with the cylindrical type of wax recorder. The cylinder is placed on a mandril, just as it is on the dictating and transcribing machines. A knife is so adjusted that as it moves along the rotating cylinder it shaves off a very fine layer of wax. The

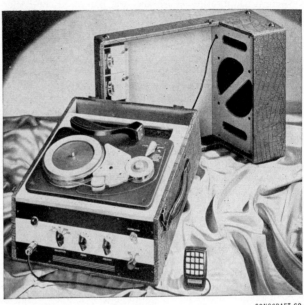

SONOCRAFT CO.

WIRE SOUND RECORDER

surface is left perfectly smooth so that it can again be used for dictation. This process can be repeated as many as 100 times with each wax cylinder.

Duplicating Machines. Probably the first practical duplicating machine for making a large number of copies was built in this country in 1887 by A. B. Dick and called a Mimeograph. This machine used a stencil, and the impression paper was placed in a set frame. Ink was then applied to the stencil which was in position over the paper. A machine utilizing the gelatin process was originated in Germany in 1880 by Alexander Shapiro. This machine duplicated by means of a glue and glycerin coated roll. The original copy was laid on this substance and when removed the ink impression was left on the damp surface. Blank sheets were then run over the roll, receiving a copy of the original impression.

Various makes of both the ink and gelatin duplicators are on the market today. Some are hand fed and some completely automatic. Hand-fed machines are used for frequent changes and few copies; automatically fed machines will produce thousands of legible copies from one master impression, and can turn out from 5,000 to 10,000 copies an hour. All are simple to operate.

A specialized type of duplicating machine is one developed to print from type or from etched zinc plates by the lithographic or offset printing method. During the early part of 1900 a flat-bed machine consisting of two parallel flat plates, joined by four rocker arms and held in position by a spring, was invented to produce duplicated letters with type through carbon-paper impressions. Later this machine was further developed by a Mr. Gamneter, who originated the idea, into the rotary principle in use today. Inked ribbon, and later printer's ink, was used to produce the copy. The principle remains the same today, even though metal plates

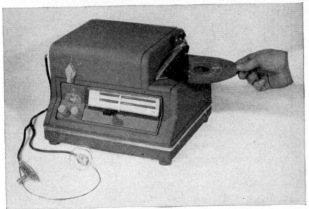

THOMAS A. EDISON CO.

DESK-TYPE DICTATING MACHINE

and paper mats are used instead of set type. An engraved, flexible, zinc plate can reproduce a photograph on the printed paper. This is called the Multilith process. Multigraph machines, which use type and a ribbon of page width, are capable of producing work in very fine tolerances. They are operated at the rate of 5,000 printed forms per hour.

Modern duplicating machines are automatic and electrically operated, and may be set to stop when the required number of copies has been run off. They require a minimum of time and experience to operate, and are used frequently to take the place of a printing press in business establishments.

Figuring Machines. Modern figuring machines come in thousands of different models and sizes. They can generally be classified as adding, billing, bookkeeping, calculating, posting, and listing machines. Many have some of the characteristics of each.

Adding Machines. Probably the oldest known type of device for adding mechanically is the abacus. Calculations are made on this primitive instrument by sliding beads along rods. The abacus and the suanpan, which are based on the same general principles, were the earliest adding machines. During the 1600's various attempts were made to construct successful adding machines, but not until 1820, when Charles Xavier Thomas developed his automatic calculator in London, was any progress made. The best machines are electrically operated, especially those classified as bookkeeping, billing, and posting machines. Other units are normally operated by a lever pulled by the operator. The machines range in size from small portable table models to large units containing many counters. Many are capable of performing subtraction, multiplication, and division. Adding machine patents were granted to E. D. Barbour in 1872, Frank S. Baldwin in 1875, Henri Pattin in 1883, Dorr E. Felt in 1887, A. C. Lundlum in 1888, and William S. Burroughs in 1888. As improvements were made during the early 1900's, more patents were granted and continual studies were made in the development of new machines. Machines today carry the names of some of the original patent holders, but for the most part all of the modern units are equipped with the same features, except for small variations in design and attachments.

Adding machines are equipped with two distinct types of keyboards: the full keyboard and the ten-key type. The full keyboard has the keys arranged in rows of nine keys each from 1 to 9. The number of these rows determines the total amount that can be figured. All machines are equipped with counters that accumulate the amounts. The number of columns varies with the type of machines and the application. Full keyboard machines run up to a capacity of 999,999,999. Specially made machines can be had for larger totals. The keyboard of this type of adding machine is equipped with additional keys, such as total, subtotal, nonadd, error, repeat, and separate column-release keys. Shuttle, automatic or semiautomatic, and crosstabulating carriages are available. Printing capacities vary from a full ledger sheet to the small tapes used in balancing accounts. Most units are equipped with visual counters which indicate the amount in the machine so that it may be read before printing.

Both the full keyboard model and the ten-key type are made as duplex machines. A duplex machine has two sets of adding dials and carries two totals simultaneously. Individual totals are accumulated in one counter and a grand total in another. The work performed by these machines

represents a different type of application. They are more expensive and consequently should be used only where the job requires either proof totals or other applications relative to dual controls. Machines are used for proving daily postings, balancing, checking deposit slips, recapitulating sales, figuring discounts, computing commissions, and so on.

Calculators. Calculating machines differ from adding and listing machines in that they do not print. They are used where quick calculations must be made and for analysis of

UNDERWOOD CORP.

TYPICAL ACCOUNTING MACHINE

payroll reports, fractional calculations, figuring percentage, formulas, and other types of mathematical problems. Trained operators are necessary for efficient operation, as many calculations depend on the use of levers and depression of certain keys not found on adding machines.

Basically there are two types of calculators, the key-driven and the crank-operated. The key-driven models have a full keyboard and visible counters at the top or bottom of the keyboard. They are usually equipped with a lever on the side to clear out the totals. Some machines are made with a key to permit subtraction, although most models depend on the use of complements to effect this. Models weigh from 6 to 15 lb. Crank-operated calculators employ the use of keys and levers to calculate. The amount is first set up on the keyboard and turned into the machine. These machines are electrically operated, and employ the use of a motor bar to perform what is done by key depression on the key-driven calculator. A movable carriage which is located above the keyboard has two sets of visible counters. One of these registers the result in any problem, such as the sum in addition, the product in multiplication, the minuend in subtraction, and the quotient in division. Each type of machine is set up to clear the dials by the depression of a key upon the completion of a problem. The machine effects multiplication by consecutive addition. Division is consecutive subtraction. Machines are made in varying sizes; the smallest have 6 keyboard columns, 6 upper dial positions, and 12 lower dial positions. The larger models have from 10 to 12 keyboard and upper dial positions and twice as many lower dial positions. Variations from any standard type of machine are available and can be planned by a trained specialist.

Billing, Bookkeeping, and Posting Machines. Billing, bookkeeping, and posting machines are all variations of adding machines and typewriters. Some incorporate a typewriter keyboard; others merely have various keys set up to indicate a particular type of transaction. These machines are manufactured by most writing-machine companies, adding machine manufacturers, cash-register companies, and other companies specializing in billing, bookkeeping, and posting machines.

Noncomputing machines resemble typewriters, and are designed to post on continuous-form bills or forms that are fed through the platen in multiple copies from specially designed feeding-racks. Carbon paper is sometimes interleaved and sometimes part of the continuous form design. They may be electrically or manually operated.

Computing machines may or may not have a typewriter keyboard. They are mostly used for bookkeeping and posting machines, being equipped with counters to pick up old balances and post the new balance after the transaction is entered into the mechanism. A typical model today is electrically operated, posts statement and ledger simultaneously or individually, has 42 typewriter keys and 81 amount keys, and has complete visibility at the printing line. Debit and credit balances are computed and printed automatically. Proof totals are accumulated and printed automatically. There are an injector for speedy form insertion, tally tape for checking, a double spacing device, and original printing appears on both tapes and form. Keys are provided to meet the customer's need and can be set up to indicate whatever is necessary for the particular type of application involved.

DIEBOLD CO.

ROTARY CARD FILE SYSTEM

Filing Systems. A filing system is a part of office routine and has its general applications. There are several filing systems on the market that make use of notched or punched cards. Cards vary in size according to the amount of information necessary or size of the file. Rods or needles are employed to locate the particular types of cards needed. Sorting can also be accomplished by this process. Automatic sorters sort cards by electrical and mechanical means in connection with complete systems of accounting.

Intercommunication Equipment. The uses of the telephone, interoffice phone, loud speaker, telephone system, and automatic call system have been developed and specialized for each particular type of job. Teletypewriters may be hooked up to send and receive messages at branch plants, as well as at various departments located in different parts of a building. The pneumatic tube is used in some large buildings to carry messages or money from given points to a centrally located receiving station. Automatic conveyors made of rubber or rubberized material are often employed in shipping departments, but their office application is limited.

Miscellaneous Equipment. Various attachments are used in connection with operations performed by other office appliances.

Burster. Bursters are used to cut one form away from another. Continuous forms that have been prepared on billing equipment or tabulating machines are fed into a burster either by means of pressure-feed rolls or pin-feed platens. Bursters cut individual forms from 3 to 20 in. in length. Multiples can be burst, but they usually require machines employing a knife. The operation involved is to feed the form between two sets of rollers. The second set, located by an adjusting screw so that it is spaced approximately the length of the form away, turns at a faster rate of speed and so "bursts" the form.

Decollator. A decollator is used to separate multiple copy forms after printing. Stationary types, depending on gravity feed, may be set up behind the printing machine and as the form is fed out, it automatically separates it and decollates the carbon paper. Other units are motor-driven and decollate the various copies by means of pin-feed platens and corresponding punches in the continuous forms.

Imprinter. An imprinter is used to imprint title headings or lines on previously printed forms. It can be had in hand-operated or motor-driven models to print on single sheets or on continuous forms.

Endorser. Endorser units are used for signing or endorsing pay orders, drafts, checks, and other legal documents. Hand stamps and automatic machines are both employed, the hand stamp being used for individual pieces of paper while the automatic devices are attached to bursters that handle continuous forms. Most endorsers, check certifiers, signers, and cancelers are equipped with both a locking device and a counter to protect the machine from being employed illegally. Endorsers are also made to feed individual forms through a motor-driven unit which will date and sign forms at a rate of 12,000 to 15,000 an hour.

Folder. Folding machines have been developed to a high degree of efficiency and are used where a large amount of mail or circular material is handled. Insurance companies have their own machines for policy-folding. There are many different models, all following the same principle. The paper is placed on a rack and fed automatically through a series of rollers and knives that fold and press the form as many as five times. Speeds up to 20,000 an hour are obtained.

Sealer, Gluer, and *Stamper.* Although sealer, gluer and precancelling stamp are office appliances, they usually are classed as mail-room equipment. They are essentially parts of other machines. Automatic units can feed, stamp, seal, and glue envelopes at speeds up to 20,000 an hour.

Scales. There are three general types of scales for office use: the computing postal scales, the merchandise scale, and the heavy-capacity scale. The computing postal scale is made in capacities up to 70 lb. First, second, and third class matter, both domestic and foreign, parcel posts, and express matter may be weighed and the postage computed. The face of the scale is usually a cylinder dial, fan-type dial, or clock-face dial. The same principle, however, is employed by all scales. The postage required is automatically computed as the material is weighed. The modern computing merchandise scale was developed from the old counter computing scale. This scale is equipped with a chart which automatically indicates weight and computes value. The heavy-capacity scale for office use is made in both beam and dial models. They are variously used, especially the dial models, not only for weighing, but also for counting, testing, and other special purposes.

Tabulating Machines. There are two basic types of tabulating equipment. Both use the principle of automatically actuating machines to add, subtract, multiply, and divide in various combinations, and in the same operation prepare finished reports showing alphabetic descriptions as well as the calculated results.

In the latter half of the 1880's Dr. Herman Hollerith, employed by the United States Government in the compilation of the census, felt that the methods then employed would soon necessitate an overlapping period between the compilation of one census and the start of another. Consequently, the first statistical machines were invented by Dr. Hollerith about 1887. The experience gained in the development of the fundamentally simple system of actuating counters by means of holes punched in pieces of paper or cards has resulted in the tremendously complicated units which prepare completed reports with a minimum of effort on the operator's part.

I. B. M. Punched Card Equipment. Some of the newer units developed by the International Business Machines Corporation make use of electronic tubes for instantaneous calculations. A tabulating card of 80 columns is used to actuate the machine. It is divided from top to bottom into 12 equal spaces. The card is 3¼ by 7⅜ in. and is punched with rectangular holes which permit electrical contacts to be made. The card itself is a nonconductor of electricity. Alphabetic punching is accomplished by a combination of a hole in either the 12, 11, or 0 positions at the top of the card and a numeral from 1 to 9. For example A is punched by 12 and 1, B by 12 and 2, etc. A keyboard controls an electrical punching mechanism to cut the holes in the card. A speed of 10,000 punches an hour is average. The tabulating card, once prepared, becomes the basis of actuating the other machines used in the electric accounting machine system. The machines are capable of addition, subtraction, multiplication, and division. Speed of operation depends on the type and complexity of operations. Some 6,000 multiplications per hour may be handled by electronic machines.

Various sorters are used to arrange cards in different sequences, both alphabetically and numerically. Machines sort on one column of the card at a time. Up to 38,400 sorts per hour are possible on an electronic sorter. Cards are interfiled, merged, or selected from one or two files at the same time by means of a collator. This machine operates on one or multiple columns at the same time. It is capable of passing from 14,000 to 28,000 cards per hour through its two feeds. Actual operations determine speed. Cards also can be put in an interpreter, which will print across the top of the card the punched information. Information can be deleted or repeated according to the wiring.

The largest types of I.B.M. printers, or electric accounting machines, are made in hundreds of different models to meet

the requirements of the job. The basic machines list and accumulate at the same time that they add, subtract, and print answers showing net balances where necessary. Eighty counters are controlled by plugboard wiring on the side of the machine and can be made to operate in various groupings. Each machine has 43 alphabetical type bars and 45 numerical type bars. The alphabetical type bars also print numerical information. This machine will operate at the rate of 4,800 to 9,000 cards an hour. An automatic carriage is used to space continuous forms used in the preparation of various

RALPH C. COXHEAD CORP.

OFFICE COMPOSING MACHINE

A special adaptation of the typewriter, providing a selection of type faces by means of removable curved segment type plates. Spacing between letters can be "justified" to produce lines of typing of equal length.

reports. This carriage operates in conjunction with both the tabulating cards passing through the tabulator and the tabulator itself in spacing the forms being printed.

Remington Rand Punched Card Equipment. Remington Rand, Inc., manufactures a line of tabulating equipment formerly called the Powers accounting machines. Powers machines are mechanical. They pick up their impulses from cards by push rods, commonly called rods or Boden wires, which are flexible steel cables with movable centers. The actuating of the adding and printing mechanisms are through latches, gears, panels, etc., so that the entire machine depends upon mechanical movement for its operation.

The tabulating card has 90 columns, 45 in the upper and 45 in the lower half, and is divided into an upper and lower half, each comprising 6 positions from top to bottom. These 6 positions are numbered 0, 1-2, 3-4, 5-6, 7-8, and 9. The card is 3¼ by 7⅜ in. A ⅛-in. round hole punched in the cards is the means of transcribing the information. Punches are made in various styles and models. Keys are depressed by hand to set up the information in the machine. The holes are all cut at the same time automatically. Punches are made with both numerical and combination numerical-and-alphabetic keyboards similar to that of a typewriter. Other automatic punches transfer information from one card to another and operate by means of translators, which are wired to perform some fixed operation and placed in the machine to control its functions. The speed of punching cards depends to some degree on the kind of key punch used. An average speed of 10,000 key depressions an hour is standard.

A multiplier is used to extend factors up to 6 x 6 digits and to punch a product of 12 digits into a tab card. It is capable of being used as a normally operated calculating machine in conjunction with multiplication, and produces a printed tape of the calculations performed as a by-product of the extension operations.

Sorters are used to arrange cards in different numerical sequences for reports. The machine sorts on one column of the card at a time. Its speed is 25,200 sorts per hour. Cards are filed by means of a "multicontrol reproducing punch" after they have been arranged in numerical sequence by a sorting machine. This unit operates at 6,000 cards per hour.

Cards, once punched, can be put in on the interpreter and the complete 90 columns of the cards interpreted in one operation. Information can be deleted according to the interpreting unit used.

The largest type Remington Rand tabulator operates at a constant speed of 6,000 cards per hour. It will list and accumulate at the same time, printing totals according to the setting of its accumulators. All 90 columns of information on the card, alphabetical and numerical, can be listed on one line of the report. One hundred type bars are provided, giving any combination of alphabetical and numerical information. The machines are equipped with a variable spacing carriage which allows continuous forms to be used, and provides for the automatic spacing of the forms as the machine prints the reports.

Time Recorders. In 1871 John C. Wilson developed the first practical time recorder. It contained a clock with a block foundation supporting brass discs and printing indicators. A ribbon was part of the removable unit which did the printing on an indexed cylinder. In 1888 W. L. Bundy developed an employee time-register, and in 1892 E. S. Phelps was granted a patent on a recording door-lock.

The modern time-recording devices are similar in general characteristics. In order to account for employees' time, clocks are used to register the start and stop time on individual cards. These clocks are electrically operated and run off electrical impulses sent out from a master clock once every minute. Other clocks are set up to operate independently according to the system installed. Where a master clock is installed, any number of secondary clocks both for time-telling and registering employees' time can be located throughout the plant and office area, and can be controlled by the master clock. The time register used to record employees' time can either be "trigger tripped" or made to print automatically when the card is inserted into the slot. The printing mechanism and throat are so designed that "lates," out early or overtime, can be registered on separate parts of the card. These clocks automatically shift for each day of the week and need little adjustment other than to change the ribbon.

Time stamps, which record receiving time and start-and-stop time on various jobs, are made so that it is necessary only to bring the head down upon the paper beneath it. The stamp automatically changes the date, hour, minute, and meridian, and may also be set up to record seconds if necessary. The job recorder, which is a variation of time stamp, will show the start-and-stop time and department.

Recording locks, used on doors, are both sold and leased. They contain a printing mechanism which not only records the time but also the individual code letter or number assigned to an employee. This is printed on a control tape which is locked in the mechanism and can later be removed and checked. These locks are impossible to open and close without making a record on the tape.

Writing Machines. The first known attempt to invent a writing machine was in 1714, when a patent was issued to Henry Mills, an English engineer. In 1829 William Austin Burt was granted the first American patent. However, the first successful manufacturing was not undertaken until 1873, when E. Remington and Sons, gunmakers of Ilion, N.Y., went into production.

Modern machines are all manufactured on the same fundamental principles. The steel type-bars are so arranged that they print at a common center; the step-by-step escapement mechanism provides for letter spacing; the paper is fed around a cylinder called the platen; a lever at the sides moves the paper for line spacing and, in most cases, serves as a carriage-return mechanism On most machines the type-

RECORDAK CORP.

MICROFILM READER

Page shown is an enlargement of the 35 mm. (or 16 mm.) micro-film carried in the spools above the reading window.

bars are arranged in front of the carriage, so that they strike on the front of the platen when the corresponding keys are pressed. The arrangement of letters on the typewriter keys has, with minor variations, been standard since the invention of the first writing machine. The typewriter keyboard is composed of four banks of keys. The top row consists of figures, special characters, and punctuation marks. Usually there are 42 keys writing 84 characters. Machines are made with 38, 44, and 46 keys, but are not considered standard. Shift keys are used to print capital letters and certain symbols or punctuation marks. Special keys are also found on various types of machines.

Machines are made in all sizes and combinations, with platens available up to 20 in. in length for special ledger printing. Various kinds of type can be used with either 10 or 12 characters to the inch. Machines are equipped with two-color ribbons (red and black) for special reports. By the use of special platens as many as 20 copies can be made. Electrical machines have key-operated carriage returns. The writing machine itself is also often combined with an adding machine for billing, posting, and bookkeeping operations.   F. W. J.

BUSINESS MANAGEMENT. *See* BUSINESS ORGANIZATION AND MANAGEMENT.

BUSINESS ORGANIZATION AND MANAGEMENT. The term business organization may be applied to two separate kinds of activity. The first is concerned with methods of creating the various types of commercial and industrial enterprises. The second deals with their administrative structures and management methods.

FORMS OF BUSINESS ORGANIZATION

Single Proprietorship. The single proprietorship is a form of business organization in which one person is the sole owner. The proprietor assumes unlimited liability for business debts and usually full responsibility for management. However, he may employ someone else to manage the business either for a salary or for a share of the profits. The proprietor usually supplies a large part of the cash or other assets necessary to establish the business, and additional sums may be borrowed on short-time or long-time loans.

The legal formalities necessary to establish a single proprietorship consist only of the procurement of business permits, the payment of local license fees, and possibly the trans-

An example of single proprietorship is the general store which serves small communities.

fer of title to real estate. The proprietor also establishes his credit with banks and vendors of merchandise by submitting certain financial information to them.

The single proprietorship is important in farming, local service enterprises, retail and wholesale trade, many professions, and some branches of manufacturing. Industries in which the single proprietorship is important are characterized by the small amount of capital per establishment, the need for rendering a personal service to customers, and frequent style changes in the case of some manufacturing industries. The single proprietorship is also likely to be successful in industries which produce heavy, bulky products and highly perishable commodities which must be made near the place where they are to be consumed.

General Partnership. The Uniform Partnership Act defines a partnership as an association of two or more persons to conduct a business as co-owners for profit. The partnership is formed by oral, written, or possibly implied agreement between the members. In most states the partners must be natural persons, though a few states permit corporations to be members. The partnership is not considered a separate legal person in the sense that a corporation is a person. It is only an association of persons. To constitute a partnership,

the purpose must be profit. If the purpose is not profit but something else, such as the mutual benefit of the members, the organization is not a partnership but an unincorporated association.

Characteristics. The attributes of the general partnership are as follows: (1) it is based upon a contract rather than a state franchise or charter; (2) the partners are personally liable for the debts of the business in case the assets are insufficient to pay them; (3) suits are brought against the partners individually rather than against the partnership; (4) real estate required by the business may be owned by the partners individually and held in trust for all of the members; (5) the partnership is dissolved when one partner withdraws, dies, becomes bankrupt, or goes insane; (6) each partner is authorized to act as agent in making contracts for the conduct of the business; (7) ordinary business affairs are decided by majority vote of the partners, and the general nature of the business may be changed only by unanimous consent.

Rights of the Partners. The members of a general partnership have the following rights: (1) Each member is entitled to a share of the profits. In the absence of other agreement, profits are shared equally. (2) Partners are entitled to full information concerning the affairs of the business. They may examine the partnership books of account and any other records. (3) All partners share in the management unless they agree otherwise. However, the partners by agreement may permit a senior partner to have the deciding vote in certain matters, and they may deny voting rights to any member, provided such an arrangement is unanimously agreed upon at the time the partnership agreement is made. A partner who does not participate in the affairs of the business is called a dormant partner. (4) A partner who incurs expenses in the conduct of partnership affairs is entitled to reimbursement from the other partners. (5) When the business is terminated and the assets are disposed of, each partner is entitled to a share in the proceeds after all outside liabilities have been paid, provided the original capital contribution of the partner exceeded his share of the losses.

Methods of Dividing Profits. Partnership profits are divided equally unless the partners agree otherwise. Partners may not assume that division will be made in the ratio of capital invested by each, because the contributions of the partners include time, labor, skill, and management capacities. Some of the methods by which profits may be divided are: (1) interest on capital contributions and the balance equally or in some agreed ratio; (2) salary allowances to the partners and the balance equally, or in some agreed ratio; (3) interest on capital, salary allowances, and the balance equally or in some agreed ratio; (4) any arbitrary ratio which may be agreed upon.

Procedure at Dissolution. When a partnership is dissolved, the business may or may not be terminated. If the business is continued as a new partnership, it is necessary to record: (1) the changes in the values of the assets employed in the business as agreed upon by the partners; (2) payments made to a retiring partner; and (3) the contribution of cash or other assets made by an entering partner. In the case of an incorporation of a business formerly conducted in partnership, the assets and liabilities are legally considered to have been sold to the corporation for its capital stock. The original capital contributions of the partnership are repaid by distributions of the stock of the new corporation.

When a partnership business is liquidated, the assets may be sold separately or as a unit. Gains and losses are shared by the partners in accordance with the partnership agreement. Distributions of the cash proceeds are made in the following order: (1) liabilities to creditors are liquidated; (2) loans from partners are repaid; (3) original capital contributions of the partners are returned to them; (4) the balance, representing profit, is distributed in accordance with the agreement for sharing profits and losses. In case of a loss rather than a gain, the share of the loss to be borne by each partner is deducted from the amount of his capital contribution to determine the balance due him. If the share of the loss to be borne by a partner exceeds his capital contribution, he is required to pay into the business the amount of the excess.

Limited Partnership. The limited or special partnership differs from the general partnership in that one or more partners may have a liability limited to the amount of the original capital contribution. Limited partners share profits, but they may not be assessed for losses, even though the assets of the business are insufficient to meet the claims of creditors. Limited partners are not permitted to act as agents for the partnership or to participate in any manner in the management. Limited partnerships are required to have one or more general partners to assume responsibility for the management and liability for the debts. General partners in a limited partnership have unlimited liability.

The origin of the limited partnership is found in the Roman laws which permitted a master to supply the capital for trading enterprises conducted by a slave without liability on the part of the master. It was extensively used by the merchants of the Italian cities after the eleventh century. The French copied it from Italy, and in turn introduced it in America in their colony of Louisiana. The limited partnership is regulated by law, which usually requires that the agreement limiting the liability of any partner be made a matter of public record. The usual requirement is that a copy of the partnership agreement be filed with the recorder of deeds in each county in which the business is to be transacted.

Mining Partnership. In many states, a special form of the partnership is used in the petroleum, lead, zinc, and other extractive industries. Shares in the mining partnerships are transferable, and the partnership is not dissolved by the death, bankruptcy, or insanity of a member. Partners are not permitted to make contracts for the business unless expressly authorized to do so. The management is delegated to a board, the powers of which are fixed by the partnership agreement. Mining partnerships are organized by common law contract and not by charter. They are not recognized in all of the states.

Partnership Association. Partnerships in which all of the members have limited liability may be organized in a few states, among them Pennsylvania, New Jersey, Ohio, Virginia, and Michigan. The business of such a partnership, called a partnership association, is managed by a board of directors and designated officers. The capital is divided into shares which may be transferred, subject to approval of the purchaser of the shares by the other members. Property is owned and suits at law may be brought by the firm. Partnership associations cannot be organized in a state unless authorized by statute.

Joint Venture. A partnership which is limited in scope of business transactions and in duration is called a joint venture or joint adventure. A venture is formed for a specific purpose, such as the making of a single shipment to market or the purchase of property for resale. It is characterized by a limitation upon the rights of members to act as agents. The arrangement terminates upon the completion of the business of the venture. In most states corporations may participate in joint ventures, provided their charters authorize them to do so. Usually corporations may not be members in general partnerships.

Joint Stock Company. This form of business organization is a common-law association with continuous existence, transferable shares, and unlimited liability of the members. It is formed by contract, which is called articles of association. Management is delegated to a board of directors or governors. Members of the board are elected by the members. The board appoints a president and other officers, who make contracts and transact the ordinary business of the company. Shares are represented by stock certificates, as in the corporation. However, the joint stock company is not a legal entity, and therefore has no right to own property or to bring suits at law in its own name. The officers act in their own names for the benefit of the company. The joint stock company is regulated by law in some states. Many courts regard it as a form of the partnership. It is not a common form of organization in the United States, but is well-known in Great Britain, where it originated and where the taxes on the corporate form are so heavy as to make another form of organization preferable in many enterprises. Its principal advantage in the United States is lower taxes, since it does not pay the general incorporation tax or the annual corporate franchise tax. It is also exempt from some other taxes, such as the fee for amendment to the articles of association. For purposes of the income tax and the stock transfer tax, the joint stock company is regarded as a corporation. From about 1500 to 1650 the joint stock company was a common form of business organization in England. Many of the trading enterprises of that day took this form of organization. The best-known were the East India Company and the Hudson's Bay Company, though many others were organized. Still other companies, such as the London Company and the Plymouth Company, were organized for colonizing purposes. Many joint stock companies were organized in the American colonies for business purposes, particularly for commerce on the sea.

Business Trust. A form of organization variously known as the business trust, Massachusetts trust, associations under deed of trust, or the common-law business trust, is formed by contract between the creators of the trust or the settlors and other persons who agree to act as trustees. The creators of the trust transfer to the trustees certain cash, securities, or property to be managed for the benefit of other persons who are known as beneficiaries or *cestui que trust*. The assets of the trust are known as the trust principal or corpus. The income of the trust principal is paid to the beneficiaries according to the provisions of the trust agreement. Some individuals may hold all three positions in relation to the trust, namely, creators, trustees, and beneficiaries. However, the three groups may not be identical. If that situation should exist, the element of trust would disappear and the business would be a partnership.

Position of Trustees. The trustees have the right and the responsibility to manage the trust principal, subject to any limitations contained in the trust agreement. They may be removed from office only in case they are guilty of gross mismanagement or fraud. Their term of office is usually for the life of the trust, which may be for the life of certain designated persons in being at the time of the agreement, plus twenty-one years. Vacancies in the board of trustees caused by the death or resignation of a trustee are filled by the remaining trustees. The board may choose a president and other officers to manage the business and to make contracts in the name of the trust. Trustees are not liable for the debts of the business, provided all contracts are made in the name of the trust estate. They are entitled to compensation for their services, even though the trust agreement makes no provision for compensation.

Position of Beneficiaries. Trust beneficiaries hold a position in relation to the trust much like that of the stockholders of a corporation, though legally their position is very different. Their equity in the trust principal is represented by trust certificates, which are readily transferable, and are bought and sold in the securities markets. Dividends from earnings are payable on the trust shares when such payments are declared by the board of trustees. At the termination of the trust, the beneficiaries share ratably in the corpus after all liabilities have been paid. If the assets are insufficient to pay the liabities, the beneficiaries are not liable to assessment. The trust may issue both preferred and common shares, and the groups of certificate holders have such rights in the dividends and the trust principal as may be specified in the trust agreement. Holders of preferred shares may be entitled to receive a stipulated rate of dividends before any payments are made to the holders of the common shares, and also to a stated amount at the termination of the trust before any payment is made on the common shares.

Holders of trust shares have no right to vote at annual meetings, as do holders of shares of stock in a corporation. Trustees have full authority to fill vacancies in the board. If trustees should be made subject to the will of the shareholders, the element of trust which characterizes this form of organization would not exist.

Use of the Business Trust. The trust is a fairly common form of organization for such enterprises as investment companies and public utilities. It is used to a limited extent in manufacturing enterprises. Its advantage is its freedom from incorporation taxes, annual franchise taxes, and fees for do-ing business in other states than the state in which it was formed. For purposes of property taxes and income taxes, it is taxed like a corporation. Transfers of its shares are subject to the usual stock transfer taxes. The principal disadvantage of the trust is that some states treat it as a partnership, and therefore make the holders of trust shares liable for the debts of the business. Businesses which operate in many states usually consider that this form of organization involves too much risk for the holders of the trust shares. A further social disadvantage is that the trustees are beyond the control of the beneficiaries. The lack of control lends itself to abuse.

Corporation. The best-known definition of the corporation is that which was given in 1819 by Chief Justice John Marshall in the famous Dartmouth College case. He defined it as "an artificial being, invisible, intangible, and existing only in the contemplation of the law." The law regards the corporation as a legal person capable of making contracts, holding title to property, bringing suits at law, being made the defendant in such suits, and maintaining a continuous existence separate and distinct from that of its shareholders, directors, or officers.

Corporations may be either stock or non-stock. Stock is issued by corporations which need to raise a part of their invested capital through the sale of securities. Many enterprises, both governmental and private, are organized as corporations. Institutions which receive a large part of their capital by taxation or by gifts may be organized as non-stock corporations. Examples are colleges and universities, endowed research or philanthropic institutions, municipalities, various other governmental units, such as drainage districts, college fraternities, and many co-operatives.

Origin of the Corporation. The beginnings of the corporation are found in antiquity. Some writers consider the Greek city-states to have been the first corporations, because they borrowed money and assumed obligations for which later generations became liable without a specific agreement on their part. Other authorities credit the Romans with having created the corporation as a device for organizing the affairs of religious societies as well as business enterprises. Roman corporations held title to real estate and other property, and in many other respects acted as separate entities.

After the fall of Rome commerce and business languished, and the corporation was for many centuries used only as a device for organizing religious orders, schools, and municipalities. The modern business corporation is believed to have evolved from the joint stock company between 1600 and 1688, when the Stuart rule came to an end in England. Since the joint stock company had transferable shares and a continuous existence, the principal change necessary for the evolution of the corporation was based upon the theory that the corporation is a separate legal person with the right to act in its own name. This change was achieved by gradually including in the charter such attributes as the following: (1) the right to possess a seal to designate official acts and contracts, (2) the right to own real property, (3) the power to bring action in the courts in the name of the entity itself, (4) the right to sue its own shareholders, (5) continuous existence regardless of changes in the officers or shareholders, and (6) limited liability of the shareholders.

Early Corporations in America. During the Colonial era, the corporate form was used principally by colleges and municipalities. Business corporations, so far as is known, were then only six in number. These were a fishing company (1675), two trading companies (1682 and 1732), an insurance company (1768), and two wharf companies (1760 and 1772). Most of the corporate charters came from Parlia-

A bustling industrial center along the Passaic River in New Jersey. Harrison is at the upper left; Newark on the right.

ment or the colonial legislature. Some were granted by the king or queen, and others by the governors of the Colonies. From 1776 to 1800 the number of charters granted to private enterprises totaled 335, of which 219 were for toll roads, toll bridges, and canals. The early corporations were formed by special incorporation, that is, by separate legislation enacted for each corporation organized. After 1811 this practice was gradually abandoned; an officer in the office of the secretary of state, usually the commissioner of corporations, was authorized to issue charters as an administrative act. Special incorporation was prohibited by most state constitutions adopted after 1850. With the growth of transportation, manufacturing, and commerce after 1865, the corporation increased in importance until it became the prevailing form of organization in many lines of activity, particularly banking, transportation, and the heavy manufacturing industries.

Legal Concepts of the Corporation. The legal entity concept of the corporation is generally accepted by the courts. This concept is that the corporation is a legal person with a continuous existence which is separate from that of the directors, officers, and stockholders. The concept affords a logical explanation of such attributes as limited liability of the stockholders, the denial to stockholders of any right to act as corporate agents, and other features of the corporation. However, the corporation cannot be considered a person for many purposes, such as voting, serving on a jury, serving a jail sentence for commission of a crime, and taking the oath required of trustees. The courts have also found it necessary to disregard the corporate personality or "to pierce the corporate veil," as jurists sometimes say, where the fiction of the corporation is used for antisocial purposes. To illustrate: if a person who owns all of the stock of a corporation sets fire to the corporate property, the courts treat the stockholder and the corporation as one and the same, and they hold in such cases that the corporation cannot collect the insurance. The courts generally regard the corporation and the stockholders as identical if the "notion of legal entity is used to defeat public convenience, justify wrong, protect fraud, or defend crime." (*United States* v. *Milwaukee Refrigerator Transit Co.,* 142 Fed. 247, 1905.)

A second concept of the corporation is defined as an association of persons endowed by law with certain legal powers and privileges. According to the association theory, the corporation is a useful collection of legal relations. It is a union of persons operating under the authority of the state for the accomplishment of certain purposes. This concept makes unnecessary the disregard of the legal entity, because the purposes for which the corporation is organized are limited to those objectives which are considered by the law to be justifiable.

A third concept regards the corporation as a legal unit or a legal agency endowed by the state with certain rights and attributes (*Clarke* v. *Bennett,* 284 N.W. 876, 1939.) This concept also limits the initial grant of rights and powers to the corporation instead of conferring a broad group of attributes and then denying certain of them when the occasion requires. However, the legal unit concept has not been generally accepted by the courts.

Procedure for Incorporation. The method of incorporating a business varies with the state, but in general the following steps are required:

(1) Plans for the corporation are made. The purposes of the business, the capitalization, kinds of stock to be issued, and duration of the corporation are agreed by promoters or others concerned.

(2) Subscriptions for the number of shares required by law are received. The requirement varies with the state.

(3) The charter is drawn for submission to the proper state officer.

(4) Application for the charter is made by the incorporators to the state officer, usually the commissioner of corporations. The incorporation fees are paid when application is made.

259

(5) Application for the charter is approved by the commissioner.

(6) The incorporators meet to accept the charter formally. The commissioner of corporations is notified of acceptance. At this same meeting, by-laws of the corporation are adopted and the first board of directors is elected.

(7) The board of directors meets, authorizes the issue of stock in exchange for property or for cash, elects officers, and transacts such other business as the situation requires.

(8) The stock is paid for and is issued in accordance with the subscription contracts. The corporation is now organized and functioning.

The Corporate Charter. Legally, the charter is a contract between the corporation and the state. It confers certain privileges and imposes certain obligations upon the corporation. The corporation is not in existence when the charter is issued and therefore cannot be a party to the contract at that time. It becomes bound by the contract when it formally accepts the charter through the action of the incorporators acting as stockholders.

The charter contains the following provisions: (1) The corporate name. (2) Powers of the corporation. (3) Total authorized stock. If more than one class of stock is authorized, the rights of the various classes are described. (4) Duration of the corporation. In some states duration may be in perpetuity. (5) Number of directors and the method of their election. (6) Powers of the directors. Certain limitations upon their powers, such as that of borrowing money, may also be stated. (7) The location of the principal office, which must be in the state of incorporation. (8) The names and addresses of the incorporators and the number of shares subscribed by each. (9) The signatures of the incorporators.

Capitalization. The stock of a corporation, in most states, may be issued for cash, property, labor, or services. When assets are transferred to the corporation, they become corporate property and are intermingled with other assets owned. Thereafter each share of stock outstanding represents an equity or part ownership in the net assets of the corporation (total assets less liabilities) but not in any specific assets or property. The assets belong to the corporation, and the stockholders have certain claims or rights which flow from the ownership of the stock. A share of stock is therefore a group of rights in relation to the corporation. In the absence of specific provision in the corporate charter, all stock issued by a corporation is alike and has the same rights. The charter may give the holders of some stock special rights, or it may deny certain rights to some stock. The charter may provide for two, three, or even more classes of shares. The various classes may differ in their rights to receive dividends, to share in the assets at dissolution, to vote, or to convert the shares into another kind of security.

Common Stock. Stock which has no special rights or privileges is called common stock. If a corporation has only one class of outstanding stock, all of the shares have the same rights and all are common. Stock may be assigned an arbitrary value called par value. If it is not assigned a value, it is known as no-par stock. The par value assigned is not necessarily related to the price of the stock in the market. The market value depends upon the prospective earnings and dividends of the corporation and other factors. The holders of common stock usually have the following rights: (1) Stockholders are entitled to receive dividends when declared by the board of directors. The directors are not ordinarily required to declare dividends, even though the corporation has made profits. (2) Stockholders may vote at meetings of stockholders. This right includes also the right to be notified of meetings and to vote by proxy if the stockholder cannot be present. (3) The right to a share in the corporation assets at dissolution, after creditors have been paid, is inherent in the stock. If the assets are insufficient to pay the corporate debts, stockholders receive nothing. They usually are not subject to assessment to pay the debts, but in some states they may be assessed to pay taxes or to pay wages of employees. (4) Stockholders have limited rights to inspect the corporate records. In many cases only the stock records are available to stockholders, and in many states the directors by unanimous vote may deny to stockholders the right to inspect any of the records of the corporation. In some states stockholders must own a specified percentage of the stock and must have been stockholders for six months or more before they may examine the stock records. (5) Stockholders usually have the right to buy new issues of stock before the stock can be offered for sale to others. This right is subject to various restrictions by charter or by vote of the stockholders themselves, such as the reservation of certain shares for sale to employees. (6) The owner of corporate stock has the right to sell the stock and to have it transferred on the books of the corporation. Co-operative organizations using the corporate form frequently restrict the right to sell by requiring that the stock be sold to persons acceptable to the co-operative.

Preferred Stock. When a corporation wishes to raise additional capital, it may then issue preferred stock. The holder of preferred stock usually has no right to vote at stockholders' meetings. He has, however, two advantages over the holder of common shares: (1) he is entitled to receive dividends at a fixed rate of return before any are paid on common stock, and (2) his claim to a proper share in the assets of the corporation, in case of liquidation, has priority over that of the common stock holder. Preferred stock may be cumulative; if lack of funds prevents the payment of dividends for one or more years, these back dividends must be forthcoming in their entirety before a dividend may be declared on the common stock. Like common stock, preferred stock may be par or no-par. Participating preferred stock is entitled to share with the common in any extra dividends which may be declared after each class has received dividends at a stipulated rate. The conditions under which the classes of stock participate vary with the corporation.

Corporation Bonds. A bond is a long-term corporate debt represented by an engraved document and issued in a series. Each bond is part of a group. Bonds are issued in accordance with an agreement between the issuing corporation and a trustee. The agreement, which is called a trust indenture, prescribes the rights of the bondholders, the obligations of the corporation, and the duties of the trustee.

Bonds are classified according to security as first mortgage, second mortgage, general, or debenture bonds. Debenture bonds have a claim upon the income of the corporation which ranks ahead of any stocks, but are unsecured so far as assets are concerned. According to methods of paying interest, bonds are classified as coupon or registered bonds. Other classifications indicate methods of repayment of the principal or the uses to which the funds are to be applied at the date of issue, such as refunding or bridge bonds.

LEGAL CONTROLS

State Legislation. Numerous state laws relate to the form of business organization. Every state has a law prescribing the procedure for forming corporations; the capitalization permitted; the powers of corporations; and the duties, liabilities, and rights of stockholders and directors. State laws also prescribe the conditions under which corporations from other states may enter to do business. A majority of the states have enacted a uniform partnership act defining the relations of partners to each other and to creditors. Some states have enacted special legislation for the regulation of business trusts and joint stock companies.

State Securities Legislation. The laws of the states regulating the issue and sale of securities are commonly referred to as blue-sky laws. The first state to enact such legislation was Kansas in 1911. Within two years, eighteen other states had such laws. Subsequently all of the states enacted securities legislation except Delaware and Nevada. The constitutionality of such legislation was upheld by the United States Supreme Court in 1917. In its decision the court gave the laws their common name by stating that many securities are of no more value than a piece of the blue sky. Of older origin, however, is the Western expression "blue-sky man," for a person selling title to lands not his own. The state laws vary considerably in their details, but they may be grouped into four classes: (1) The fraud type merely defines fraud or deception in the sale of securities and provides penalties. It authorizes the state attorneys to bring prosecutions in cases of fraud, provides for the issuance of injunctions by the courts to prevent fraudulent sales, and prescribes penalties for violation. (2) The inspection type of law provides that all securities sold in the state must be registered with the securities commissioner, who is authorized to prevent the sale of fraudulent securities. The securities permitted to be sold must meet certain requirements as to prospectus and information supplied to purchasers. These requirements vary with the state and also the security. (3) The licensing type of law requires that dealers in securities must be licensed. A dealer who is found guilty of selling fraudulent securities or using fraudulent sales methods may be denied a license. (4) The licensing and inspection type of law requires that dealers be licensed and that all securities be registered. This type of law is the most common and also the most effective.

State Antitrust Laws. Almost all of the states now prohibit combinations in restraint of trade, whether such a combination takes the form of pool, trust, association, partnership, holding company, or otherwise. Usually the state prohibition is statutory, though some states have included the provisions in their constitutions. Penalties are sometimes a stated fine for each day of violation and sometimes a fine for each transaction or sale, in addition to prison sentences. The state antitrust laws have been partially successful in preventing purely local combinations. They have had little effect on large corporations which operate across state boundaries or on pooling agreements of nation-wide scope.

State Price-Control Legislation. Price legislation is designed principally to control the growth of chain stores and to protect independent retailers. The laws are of two types. State unfair practices acts prohibit sales by retailers below cost. State fair practices acts permit manufacturers to prescribe the minimum prices at which their products may be sold to consumers. In other words, they make legal the practice of resale price maintenance.

The first state to prohibit sales below cost was California in 1913. Other states did not enact similar legislation until about 1935, when the price controls embodied in the National Industrial Recovery Act and its codes were made invalid by the United States Supreme Court (55 Sup. Ct. 837). By 1940 a majority of the states had enacted almost identical legislation. Cost, as defined in the law, includes invoice price plus a pro rata amount of rent, heat, and light, and numerous other expenses. The law has not been effective because of the difficulties of determining cost.

Resale price-maintenance legislation is permissive in character. It permits a manufacturer to prescribe the price below which his branded product may not be sold. Retailers are bound by the contract, even though the contract is with the wholesaler or other distributor and not with the retailer directly. California also led the way in this legislation by enacting such a law in 1931. Most of the states later enacted similar laws. Price-maintenance laws have not hurt chain stores but have resulted in some increases in prices.

Federal Legislation. The United States Government left much of the regulation of business organization to the states until 1933. With the advent of the New Deal there was increased federal regulation of business organization, and a number of laws were enacted during the years 1933 to 1940 concerning governmental control of business.

Securities Act of 1933. The federal Securities Act of 1933 requires that any issue of stocks or bonds of any industrial corporation or foreign government to be sold in interstate commerce be registered with the Securities and Exchange Commission. To register securities, the issuer must file a registration statement containing specified detailed information concerning the business, the financial condition of the issuer, and the terms of the security. Copies of the prospectus to be used in selling the security must also be filed. Each purchaser must be supplied with a copy of the prospectus. The registration statement at the office of the commission is available to the public for inspection. The prospectus must contain all information which is material to the issue and also all information necessary to make the facts as stated not misleading. Persons who sign incorrect or misleading statements are liable to investors who purchase the securities without knowledge that the statements are false. The Securities and Exchange Commission does not commend any securities as investments or any statements filed with it. It may require that statements be amended to provide additional facts or to clarify the information given. If an issue is found to be fraudulent, the commission may issue an order prohibiting its sale. Although highly speculative securities may be sold, their sale may be made difficult by the requirement that all unfavorable facts be stated in the prospectus.

Securities Exchange Act of 1934. Securities exchanges are now required to register with the Securities and Exchange Commission, except for certain small exchanges which are not of national importance. To register with the commission, an exchange must file copies of its constitution and its regulations, which must have the approval of the commission. The exchange must agree to comply with the provisions of the Securities Exchange Act of 1934, to prevent the manipulation of security prices, and to take such measures as are necessary to insure that all transactions on the exchange are fairly and honestly conducted. No trades in a security may be effected unless the security has also been registered with the commission. This provision brings all securities traded on exchanges within the commission's control. The act requires that detailed financial and other information must be available to investors.

Public Utility Act of 1935. The Public Utility Holding Company Act of 1935 was designed to correct numerous abuses which had been practiced by such companies during the period preceding the crisis of 1929, and which had been exposed by investigations and reports of the Federal Trade

Commission between 1929 and 1935. Some of the more significant provisions of the law are as follows:

1. Holding companies are not permitted to purchase the securities of local utilities unless the Securities and Exchange Commission has given its consent.

2. Holding companies must have the approval of the Securities and Exchange Commission to issue securities, and the commission is not authorized to approve issues of no-par stock, nonvoting stock, or preferred stock. Bonds of holding companies must be secured by physical properties or first mortgage bonds of subsidiary corporations.

3. The commission is authorized to regulate dividend payment of holding companies, purchases and sales of stock of subsidiary corporations, and the methods of soliciting proxies for meetings of stockholders.

4. Contracts for the performance of various services by one subsidiary for another, such as purchasing, construction, and income-tax computation, are subject to review and control by the commission.

5. Holding-company systems must be simplified. Intermediate holding companies beyond the third stage must be eliminated. That is, an operating company may be controlled by a holding company which in turn may be controlled by another holding company. The pyramid cannot be carried further. In no case may a holding company control various subsidiaries which do not constitute an integrated system.

Chandler Act of 1938. Prior to 1933 the reorganization of large corporations requiring a readjustment of their debt structure was accomplished by receivership and the sale of corporate assets at receivers' sales. The method, which was in accordance with the provisions of the Bankruptcy Act of 1898, was to organize a new corporation to purchase the entire assets of the old corporation. The plan for such a sale required the approval of the court in charge of receivership and also of the holders of securities. One feature of the plan usually was a reduction of the bonded debt of the old corporation. In 1933 Congress amended the Bankruptcy Act by adding Section 77, which provided for the reorganization of railway corporations under the supervision of the court without a receiver's sale. A similar amendment in 1934, known as Section 77B, authorized the same procedure for industrial corporations. The Chandler Act of 1938 repealed Section 77B and made new provisions for corporate reorganizations.

The Chandler Act continues the plan of reorganization without a receiver's sale. It places increased authority in the hands of the court and the Securities and Exchange Commission. An independent trustee must be appointed to manage the corporation during the period of reorganization. The trustee is required to formulate a plan of reorganization which is submitted to the court for approval. The court submits the plan to the Securities and Exchange Commission for its opinion as to the feasibility and fairness of the plan. A copy of the opinion of the commission is supplied to each security holder, and the holders of securities then vote upon acceptance of the plan. Unanimous consent is not required, but all must accept if the court so orders. The act is intended to reduce the cost of reorganizations, increase the power of the government over corporate affairs, and protect the interests of security holders.

Investment Company Act of 1940. Investment companies were made subject to control by the Securities and Exchange Commission by the act of 1940. The law prohibits many former financial practices of investment companies. These included excessive borrowing, speculation in the stock market, certain questionable accounting practices, changes in control of investment companies by brokers and other interests, and changes in investment-company management without stockholder consent.

Trust Indenture Act of 1939. This law requires that the trustee under a bond issue be independent of the issuer corporation and also of trustees under other bond issues of the same corporation. It sets forth the action which a trustee is required to take when a corporation defaults in the payment of interest or principal of a bond issue. The purpose of the act is to assure that trustees represent the interests of bondholders rather than of the corporation which issues the securities.

Federal Antitrust Legislation. The first federal antitrust law was the Sherman Act of 1890, declaring illegal monopolies and combinations in restraint of trade in the form of trusts or otherwise. The Clayton Act of 1914 prohibited interlocking directorates among industrial corporations with assets of $1,000,000 or more. It prohibited interlocking directorates between two or more national banks or between national banks and state banks with capital and surplus of $5,000,000 or more. The Clayton Act also made illegal the acquisition by one company of the stock of another where the acquisition substantially lessens competition. The Federal Trade Commission was created in 1914 to enforce certain provisions of the Clayton Act. The Federal Trade Commission Act, passed in 1914, prohibits the use of unfair methods of competition in commerce.

Robinson-Patman Act of 1936. This law amended the Clayton Act of 1914 to render illegal a discrimination in prices by a manufacturer as between his customers. Quantity discounts are permitted only to the extent that the manufacturer saves in his selling and other expenses by selling in large quantities. The law also prohibits fake brokerage fees and other indirect forms of price discrimination. The act was designed to place independent retailers in a better competitive position as against chain stores.

MANAGEMENT AND ADMINISTRATIVE ORGANIZATION

Nature of Organization. Organization in a business enterprise is the breaking down of the major purpose or activity into its related component parts. Each principal part of the major activity is further subdivided. This process is continued until the detailed jobs are defined and organized. At each stage in the division of functions and subfunctions, a person may be placed in charge of the work. Three types of industrial administrative organization have been developed, namely, the line, the functional, and the line and staff.

Line Organization. The pure line organization is characterized by control over individuals. Authority descends from one level in the administrative organization to the next, and each person likewise reports only to the person directly above him. Each person has complete control over his subordinates subject only to that control over himself which is exercised from above.

Functional Organization. A function is an activity or a group of related activities. Organization by functions therefore means that executives and subexecutives are in charge of activities rather than of persons. Thus an executive might be made responsible for time studies, repairs and maintenance of machines, or problems of shop discipline. All of the workers report to each boss or supervisor for purposes of a particular activity. The bosses are responsible for activities rather than workers. This system was devised

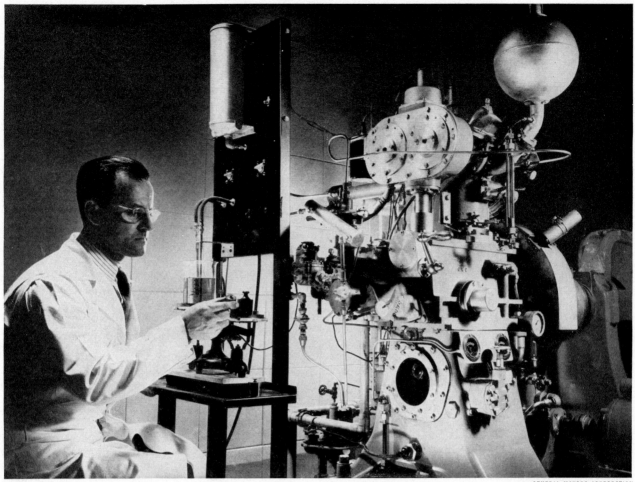

GENERAL MOTORS CORPORATION

Research is an important factor in modern industry. Shown here is a single cylinder engine used for basic fuel research by scientists at General Motors Corporation.

by Frederick W. Taylor in his well-known work at the Midvale Steel Company in Philadelphia about 1880. It has the advantage of developing specialists. Its disadvantages are that it confuses the worker and makes difficult the placing of definite responsibility for job failure.

Line and Staff Organization. The third type of organization combines the principles of the line organization with those of the functional. It organizes the principal activity, such as manufacturing or retail selling, by the line method and provides staff officers or specialists who perform services for the line. The line officers retain complete control over their departments and their subordinates. The staff officers are not regarded as bosses or supervisors. They act only in an advisory capacity.

Multiple Management. The system of organization known as multiple management is designed to utilize fully the capacities of all persons in the organization. It is not a separate type, but is superimposed upon the line and staff organization. The plan was developed by the McCormick Company of Baltimore during the 1930's, and it was subsequently adopted by many companies. It provides for a junior board of the executives of middle management for the purpose of making suggestions relating to any phase of management. The recommendations of the junior board must be approved by top management before being put into effect. The junior board is self-perpetuating. Each six months, members of the board rate each other as to their

value on the board. Members with the lowest ratings are dropped from the board, and the remaining members fill the vacancies. Boards which operate in a similar manner have been organized for salesmen, foremen, and other executives.

Principles of Administrative Organization. Most administrative organizations originally were designed for small enterprises and were gradually expanded as the businesses increased in size. As a business grows, the tendency is to place new departments or divisions directly under the general manager rather than under a subordinate. Minor changes here and there throughout the organization are also made without the knowledge of top management. The result of these two developments is that many undesirable relationships are established which must be reviewed and corrected from time to time. Some of the principles which should be observed in reorganization are indicated in the following paragraphs:

Definite Responsibility. Each executive or supervisor should know the precise limits of his authority. He should know what persons are under his supervision and what decisions he is to make. He must know what questions are to be referred to higher levels. This problem is usually met by the development of an organization manual describing the duties of each position.

Centralization of Authority. All authority at each successive level should be centralized. Final responsibility for all policies and decisions should rest with one person or board.

Definite Lines of Communication. Each executive should have channels of communication for reaching all persons under his supervision. Orders and instructions should flow down from the top of the organization, and reports of accomplishment and questions concerning new situations requiring clarification on policy should be submitted from below. The organization will not function properly if information concerning difficulties at the lower levels is suppressed and reports of failures are delayed for fear of criticism.

Lines of Promotion. Every business should have a definite policy as to promotion. The lines of promotion should be made known to all members of the organization. Each person should know the lines of promotion which are open to him. Some lines of promotion are indicated on the organization chart, though such charts usually indicate only the major positions. They are not sufficiently detailed to show all possibilities. Employees find it impossible to rise from one level to another at some places in the organization. This is especially true of the staff departments where technical training is required of persons holding the higher positions.

Relation to Personnel. The organization chart should be adapted to the capacities and interests of the executives who are to perform the duties. Ideally, the chart is drawn without regard to individuals who are to perform the duties in each position. In practice, recognition usually must be given to the fact that capacities vary.

Balance. An organization is well balanced when every department is properly developed in relation to every other department and no undue emphasis is placed upon any one of them. Employees throughout the organization should be able to perform the duties of their positions with comparable expenditures of time and effort and with no extraordinary pressure at any point.

Vertical Co-ordination. The successive levels in the organization should function smoothly through a proper division of duties and responsibilities, the development of an understanding between persons, and an adequate communication system.

Horizontal Co-ordination. Co-operation between the various departments, and particularly between the line and the staff departments, is very desirable but difficult. One reason is that the success of the staff departments is measured by the extent to which they can reduce costs through such measures as motion and time studies, work simplification, improved layouts, accident prevention, and the settlement of worker grievances. Frequently, the line executives object to outside interference, seek to avoid changes and interruptions, and dislike suggestions for improvements which might subject them to criticism for their own failure to originate proposals.

Management Policies. The policies of management depend to some extent upon the individual, the company, and the industry. However, the following policies are applied generally:

Problems of Top Management. The chief officers of the company should devote their attention to such problems as the expansion or contraction of the activities of the enterprise, the direction of expansion, public relations, financing through banks and the securities markets, dividend policies, and other such general problems. Top management should not try to supervise directly the detailed operations and activities of the enterprise.

Delegation of Authority. Management must delegate authority to handle many of the details of the enterprise. This practice sometimes results in a divergence in point of view, which makes it difficult for executives at one level to understand the problems and the decisions made at another level. The lower levels in the organization are concerned with the pressure of the work and are not consulted in changes of methods and policies.

Promotion from Within. Most organizations have an established policy of filling positions by promotion. This policy encourages persons throughout the organization to strive for promotion and to attempt to merit it. Frank B. Gilbreth and Lillian M. Gilbreth devised a three-position plan which pictured every person throughout the organization as having three positions: a worker in his present job, a student of the job ahead, and a teacher of the person in the job below him. Objections to such a policy are that transfers from one department to another create difficulties, that some will be disappointed if they fail to obtain promotion, and that the occasional employment of some executives from outside the organization would be desirable for the purpose of developing a new point of view within the organization.

Promotions on Merit. Persons promoted to executive positions should have demonstrated their ability to perform the duties of their new positions. Promotion always carries a risk for the person promoted, and for the organization, because new administrative positions usually require capacities which the incumbent did not have an opportunity to demonstrate in a position of lesser responsibility. Frequently a capable employee becomes a poor supervisor or other type of executive.

Judgment by Standards. Executives should judge their subordinates by standards which should be understood by all persons concerned. Standards by which a manager may judge his subordinates are financial standards and performance standards. A financial standard makes use of monetary figures. An expense budget is such a standard. Performance standards are based on work done, such as production, number of items rejected by inspection, attendance, and safety record. Some standards attempt to measure subjective qualities, such as co-operativeness, loyalty, job attitude, and judgment in meeting new situations.

Transfers and Demotions. Persons who are placed in positions for which they are unsuited may be transferred. A more severe action is demotion or discharge. Persons who have reached the top in a department or line of promotion may be given additional opportunity by transfer. The possibility of demotion may be reduced by giving a person a trial period in the higher position before permanent promotion. This may be done during the absence of the regular incumbent because of illness or vacation. Another expedient is the creation of a position with a higher salary or pleasing title to which an unsuccessful executive may be promoted. This is the policy commonly referred to as "kicking the person upstairs."

Position of Foremen. The line between men and management has usually been drawn between foremen and men. Foremen have been excluded from most labor unions to which workers belong. During World War II the movement for the unionization of foremen gained impetus. After the war the question of recognition of separate unions for foremen became acute. Foremen demanded greater security in their jobs, a procedure for settling their own grievances, exact descriptions of their jobs and their authority, more liberal vacations, and many other privileges. Top management contended that a union of foremen was inconsistent with the position of foremen as a part of management. They also held that foremen's unions would create a gulf within the organization, impeding the flow of communications and reports. The Labor Management Relations Act of 1947 provides that supervisors are not employees and that the employer is not legally required to bargain with such a union.

Business Reports. In a manufacturing enterprise periodical reports are prepared showing the results of operations and the financial condition of the business. Persons requiring various kinds of reports are stockholders, directors, top management, supervisors at various levels, banks, bondholders, tax authorities, and governmental regulating agencies.

Reports required by stockholders, directors, and creditors include balance sheets, profit and loss statements, and statements of surplus. In addition, a budget for the next year, half-year, or month may be submitted to banks, general creditors, and directors. Reports for supervisors and foremen include: (1) a budget of departmental expenses, (2) a comparison of budget with actual figures at the end of each month, and (3) reports of labor costs, repairs, and other expenses, spoilage, accidents, production, and idle machine time.

Reports used for judging the efficiency of various executives and the performance of equipment include: (1) accounts of customers written off as uncollectible; (2) performance of machines or equipment; (3) cost of production, classified as material, labor, expenses; (4) proceeds of sale of scrap; (5) inventory figures for various materials; (6) tool inventories, purchases, and breakage; (7) production orders completed on time and not completed on time; and (8) additions to property and machinery accounts each year.

Reports are also necessary to check the performance of individual workers. Some of these are: (1) number of days worked; (2) amount of production; (3) wages earned, including bonus; (4) bonus for quality, or items rejected by inspection; (5) deductions from wages for income tax, social security, insurance, and union dues; and (6) accidents.

Business Records. Reports are prepared from records. The information which pertains to the business as a whole is derived from the general or financial accounting records. Such records consist of the following: (1) Vouchers, which include sales tickets, purchase invoices, receipts for disbursements, authorizations for writing off uncollectible accounts, and other business papers. (2) One or more journals in which business transactions are first recorded to show what accounts are affected, that is, debited and credited. (3) A general ledger to which transactions are transferred or posted from the journals. The ledger accounts provide space for entering the date of each transaction, an explanation, and two money columns, one for debits and another for credits. The general ledger supplies the information from which the balance sheet and the profit and loss statement are prepared. (4) Other ledgers or records which show information in more detail than can be shown in an account in the general ledger. These records are called subsidiary ledgers. Examples are: accounts receivable and accounts payable ledgers, inventory records, and cost records.

Internal Audit. To audit accounting records means to inspect or check them to verify their correctness. The volume of business transactions in a large enterprise is so great as to require a continuous verification, in addition to an annual audit. This is usually accomplished by having the records of one employee verified by comparison with the work of another. For example, the accounts with customers

may be kept by one bookkeeper, while the general ledger accounts are kept by another. The general ledger account shows the amount due from all customers, which should agree with the total balances as shown in the detailed records. Checks of this kind are made each day in the offices of a large business. Errors are discovered and corrected immediately. This kind of verification is called internal check or internal audit.

External Audit. An external audit is made by an accountant who is not on the regular accounting staff of the company. The public accountant should be independent of the company whose accounts he audits. The Federal laws now require that the financial statements of any corporation whose securities are sold on a registered stock exchange, or which sells a new issue of securities in interstate commerce, must be audited by an independent accountant. To be independent, an accountant should not own a substantial amount of stock in the corporation, should not be an officer or other employee, should not be related by blood to any of the officers, and should not be paid a fee which is contingent upon the results of the audit. The extent to which an independent accountant examines or checks the accounting records depends upon the extent and the effectiveness of the internal audit. Independent accountants may inspect the books monthly, or they may wait until the end of the year to begin the annual audit.

Industrial Research. Industrial development has proceeded at an accelerated rate since the beginning of the Industrial Revolution, which is usually dated from about 1775. The changes in materials, design of product, machinery and equipment, and methods of production within a decade now exceed in magnitude the changes in many decades or even in a century during the era of handicraft or cottage production. The application of science to industry, the division of tasks into repetitive operations, the development of national and international markets, and the increasing specialization as between businesses have combined to create a need for industrial research. This research is of three types: pure research, corrective research, and developmental research.

Pure Research. Pure research attempts to discover new scientific principles and properties of matter without regard to the possibilities of using the information. Research of this kind is conducted in industry in such fields as chemistry, physics, botany, and related sciences. Most businesses do little research of this kind, but leave the work to universities, endowed institutions, and the governmental laboratories. The information is usually made available to all scientists in scientific journals.

Corrective Research. Some research is directed at the correction of defects in products, machines, or methods of manufacture. It is designed to perfect the results of earlier research which may have been made inside or outside the organization. Most research departments prefer not to spend a large amount of their time and money in this kind of work. For this reason, they prefer to work in a building which is entirely separate from the factory, or may even be located at some distance from the plant.

Developmental Research. Developmental research relates to the development of new methods of manufacture, new machines, new products, new types of packages, or new styles and designs. Industrial research is usually developmental in nature.

Use of Pilot Plants. A plant which is organized to try out new methods or to manufacture a new product on an experimental basis is called a pilot plant. Many corporations use pilot plants to test ideas with a relatively small investment for the purpose of perfecting a product or a method before they embark upon a broad expansion program that might be disastrous financially.

Organization for Research. The research department may be a major department in an enterprise or it may be a division of the manufacturing department. In either case, its expenditures should be subject to careful scrutiny by top management. This is done through the use of a budget. The expenditures are subject to two types of control:

1. The total amount to be spent is budgeted. This amount is subject to monthly, semiannual, annual, or other periodic review.

2. The amount to be spent on each major research project should be approved in advance by a committee of top

ers, of accident costs, and of materials spoilage. (4) Fluctuations in employment increase overtime pay during busy seasons. (5) Variations in production result in an inefficient use of plant and equipment because of idle time during slack seasons.

Methods of Stabilization. The planning of corrective measures requires attention to the causes of instability. The most significant of these are: (1) personal maladjustment or mental and physical limitations of the worker, (2) seasonal fluctuations in sales and production, (3) cyclical fluctuations in sales and production, (4) technological improvements, and (5) long-term changes in demand.

Each of these causes requires its own corrective measures. Personal maladjustment may be reduced by better methods of selection and placement, education and training, follow-

PILOT PLANT

Large-scale demonstration of fluid retorting of oil shale is being made at this pilot plant. The raw shale feed hoppers are in the upper left section of the structure; in the upper right is the vessel in which a portion of the spent shale is burned to provide heat necessary for the retorting operation. Within the jacket, in the right central portion of the photograph, is the retort.

STANDARD OIL CO. (N.J.)

management. If a proposed program is to extend over a period of more than one year, the budget committee should have some assurance as to the total cost and not merely the cost for the ensuing year. Projects which prove impractical should be abandoned as soon as further expenditures appear to be unprofitable. Such projects should be fully reported for the records to prevent a repetition of similar research at a later period.

Stabilization Programs. Employers are becoming increasingly concerned with the possibilities of stabilizing employment and production. This problem is significant to management for several reasons. (1) Many companies pay a worker the amount of his wages for an agreed period when he is discharged or laid off. These payments, called severance pay, can be reduced if fluctuations in employment can be minimized. (2) State unemployment compensation laws assign merit ratings to employers on the basis of their success in stabilizing employment. A high rating reduces the cost of unemployment insurance. (3) Fluctuations in employment increase the cost of selecting and training work-

up and counseling, and transfer of misplaced workers. Seasonal fluctuations in sales have been reduced by some companies by promoting sales in slack seasons, persuading customers to place orders in advance by offering special discounts, bringing out new products and new designs in dull seasons, and developing new markets which dovetail with the old. Even though sales fluctuations are not entirely eliminated, production and employment may be stabilized partially by producing for stock in the off season and by using the production force for maintenance and construction work. Other successful policies are the transfer of employees from one department to another (as in a large retail store), the development of new products for introduction in slack seasons, and the planning of employee vacations for the dull season.

Few companies have been able to stabilize employment during periods of prosperity and depression. The measures suggested for the elimination of seasonal unemployment have met with limited success in controlling the larger fluctuations. The construction, railway, and steel industries can stimulate neither off-season sales nor produce for stock. Thus far, the government has been compelled to assist with make-work projects, construction, public works projects, and relief programs.

The introduction of labor-saving devices and methods has for its objective the realignment of certain workers and their jobs. An expanding industry or company can transfer displaced workers to other jobs. Other companies usually retain workers whose jobs are superfluous by providing make-work employment until normal turnover creates places for them. This frequently means that they must take lower-rated jobs at less pay. Many union contracts require employers to give notice to workers six months in advance of their displacement and to train them for other jobs. This policy may be a solution to the problem so far as the individual worker is concerned, but it is not a complete solution for the community when fewer new workers are taken into the organization.

A gradual decrease in the demand for a product may in some cases be met by plans for a shift to the production of some other commodity, such as a change from wagons to automobiles. This solution is not possible for many industries, such as railroads, hotels at a declining summer resort, or businesses dependent upon a waning lumber supply. The problem in such industries is not so difficult for the worker, since normal turnover affords a partial solution and some workers may be able to transfer to another locality. *See also* CORPORATION LAW; INDUSTRIAL PRODUCTION; INDUSTRIAL RELATIONS; INDUSTRIAL TECHNIQUES; MARKETING AND MERCHANDISING; RESTRAINT OF TRADE LAWS. R. N. O.

BUSINESS TAXES. *See* TAXATION.

BUSINESS TRUST. *See* BUSINESS ORGANIZATION AND MANAGEMENT.

BUSIRI, MUHAMMAD [busi'ri] (1213-c.1296), Arabic poet of Berber origin, was born at Abusir, Egypt, on Mar. 7, 1213. He lived at Beilbeis in Egypt under the patronage of the Vizier Ibn Hanna, writing religious poetry that was very popular in the Islamic world. He was the author of the famous "Poem of the Mantle" (*Al kawakib al-durriya fi madh khair al barriya*) popularly known as the *Burda*. In it the poet praised the Prophet, who cured him of paralysis by appearing to him in his sleep and wrapping him in his cloak. The poem soon came to be regarded as sacred. Verses from the *Burda* were used as charms. It also was used in the services for the burial of the dead. More than ninety commentaries of the *Burda* have been written in various Oriental languages. Busiri died about 1296; the exact date given differs in the various accounts of his life.

BUSIRIS [byusai'ris], according to Greek legend, an Egyptian king, the son of Poseidon and Lysianassa. Apollodorus, an Athenian grammarian of the second century of the Christian Era, relates that Busiris, king of Egypt, when the land had suffered from famine for nine years, was counseled by Phrasius, a seer from Cyprus, to offer up an annual sacrifice of a foreigner to Zeus. The king follows this advice, commencing with the seer. When Heracles (Hercules) arrives in Egypt he is likewise led to the altar for sacrifice, but, bursting his bonds, slays Busiris and his sons. Several pictorial commemorations of the legend have been found on vases and other objects. There is, however, no indication that such a king ever existed, and the invention of the story by the Greeks probably has a two-fold origin, from the notorious hostility of the Egyptians towards foreigners and the obvious connection with the Egyptian myth of the slaying of Osiris. It was said that at Per-Asar, Osiris' temple-city in the Delta, in which was located the temple of Isis, the Egyptians offered up human sacrifices, said to be red-headed men (that is, foreigners). It seems likely that Busiris is a Greek corruption of Per-Asar, the "tomb" or "home" of Osiris. There are several other kings of the same name mentioned in various accounts, one of whom was a distant successor to King Menas and was also the founder of the city of Zeus (or Thebes). C. W. D.

BUSONI, FERRUCCIO BENVENUTO [buso'ni] (1866-1924), Italian composer, transcriber, pianist, and conductor, was born Apr. 1, 1866, at Empoli, which is near Florence. Busoni's reputation rests primarily on his powers as an interpretive artist, combining a superlative technic with musicianship of the highest order. He was also a prolific composer; but his music, which makes no concession to popular taste or fashion, has never received general recognition. His works include operas, orchestral compositions, concertos for piano, violin, and clarinet, choral pieces, chamber music, songs, piano compositions, and many transcriptions which are often creations in themselves. He died July 27, 1924, in Berlin. E. L. F.

BUSTAMANTE Y RIVERO, JOSÉ LUIS [bu'stama'nte i rive'ro] (1894-   ), Peruvian political leader and writer, was born in Arequipa, Jan. 15, 1894. He graduated from the University of Arequipa and began the practice of law with considerable success. He participated in the revolution against Leguia in 1930, and has been a consistent liberal. Bustamante entered diplomacy when he was appointed minister to Bolivia, serving from 1934 to 1939, after which he served in the same capacity in Uruguay, 1939-1942. He was elected president of Peru in June 1945 for a term of six years in one of the warmest political battles in the history of Peru. His support came from a combination of the liberal Aprista party, under the direction of Victor Raul Haya de la Torre, and other Leftist organizations. After a stormy three years in office, during which he found it necessary to move more and more to the Right, he was forced to resign on Oct. 29, 1948, by a Rightist military coup, General Manuel Odría becoming provisional president. Bustamante was forced into exile and went to Buenos Aires. He is a distinguished writer. S. G. I.

BUSTARD, any one of a number of medium-sized to large Old World birds, allied to the rails and cranes. They are combined in the family Otididae. They inhabit Europe, Africa, and temperate and tropical Asia; one species is isolated in Australia. They live on open lands, in Europe breeding in fields of grain, in Asia and Africa haunting desert or semiarid plains. Many, if not all of them, have elaborate courting displays. Their diet consists chiefly of vegetable matter, but small forms of animal life are devoured when obtainable. A characteristic species, *Otis tarda,* is the largest European land bird; a fully developed male may measure 4 ft. in length, have a wingspread of 8 ft., and weigh as much as 32 lb. It is much sought as a game bird and in some districts, notably the British Isles, has been exterminated. (*See illustration on following page.*) H. G. De.

BUTADIENE. *See* PETROLEUM (*Polymerization*).
BUTANE. *See* PETROLEUM (*Natural Gas*).
BUTANOL. *See* FERMENTATION INDUSTRIES (*Acetone and Butanol*).

Rothesay, on the island of Bute, from which the county of Buteshire, Scotland, takes its name, is a prominent yachting center.

BUTE, 3RD EARL OF (JOHN STUART) [byu't] (1713-1792), Scottish politician and amateur botanist, was born in Edinburgh on May 25, 1713. He was educated at Eton and succeeded his father as earl in 1723. His political importance began in 1747 when he became a friend of Frederick Louis, Prince of Wales, and after the latter's death in 1751 he remained as adviser to the Princess and the confidant of the young Prince George. When the prince succeeded to the throne as George III in 1760, Bute was made privy councilor, groom of the stole, and first gentleman of the bedchamber. He exercised so much political influence that in March 1761 he was given the high office of secretary of state. He brought about the elder Pitt's downfall in October and succeeded him as prime minister in May 1762. George III had placed him in office to break the power of the Whig oligarchy and bring about a peace with France. He succeeded in both objectives and the Peace of Paris was signed in February 1763. In April he resigned, partly because he was not overfond of political responsibility, partly because he was unpopular both as a Scottish favorite and as the man who had ousted the Whigs. He retained influence with the King until 1765 and in 1766 opposed the government policy toward the American Colonies. He was elected a representative peer for Scotland in 1768, but after 1774 took no further part in politics. He was a patron of literature and gave Dr. Samuel Johnson a pension of £300 a year. After leaving active political life he traveled incognito on the Continent. He was passionately devoted to botany and in 1785 published his *Botanical Tables* in nine volumes. He died in London on Mar. 10, 1792.   E. R. A.

Eastern Great Bustard, Otis tarda dybowski

BUTE, an island in the Firth of Clyde, one of a group of islands which form the county of Buteshire in southwestern Scotland. It is separated from Argyllshire by the Kyles of Bute, a channel less than one mile wide. Bute is 15½ mi. in length and has an average width of 3½ mi., with an area of 46 sq. mi. Although the soil is light and gravelly, Bute produces excellent crops, and two thirds of the area is under cultivation. Herring fishing and stock raising are the chief occupations. The climate is one of the mildest in Scotland, and there is an important tourist trade. The ancient castle of Mt. Stuart, the seat of the Marquis of Bute, chief landowner of the island, is located near Rothesay, a popular summer resort. The remains of Rothesay Castle date from the fourteenth century. Pop. 1952, about 10,070.   S. Van V.

BUTENANDT, ADOLF FRIEDRICH JOHANN

[bu'tənɑnt] (1903-   ), German biochemist, was born Mar. 24, 1903, in Wesermünde-Lehe. He was educated in Marburg, and studied at Göttingen (1924-1927). Butenandt was assistant in chemistry at Göttingen from 1927 to 1931, director of the organic medical biochemical section of the Chemical Institute at Göttingen from 1931 to 1933, and subsequently professor in the Technical High School at Danzig. He is noted for his work on the sex hormones, notably for the preparation of testosterone and androsterone, the latter from kidney secretions. He has also investigated the chemical structure of the progestins, substances that make the lining of the womb ready for implantation of the fertilized ovum. Butenandt and Leopold Ružička were jointly awarded the Nobel prize in chemistry in 1939 for their independent researches on sex hormones, but the Nazi government forced Butenandt to decline it. He was professor of physiological chemistry at the University of Tübingen from 1945 to 1956.

H. N. A.

BUTESHIRE

[byu'tshɪr], an insular county of western Scotland, comprises the seven islands of Bute, Inchmarnock, Great Cumbrae, Little Cumbrae, Arran, Holy Island, and Pladda, all within the Firth of Clyde. Its maximum length is 35½ mi., extreme width 11⅓ mi., and area 225 sq. mi. The county's population in 1952 was 18,624. In the north, Bute is separated from Argyllshire by the narrow Kyles of Bute, and in the southeast from Ayrshire by the Firth of Clyde. To the west is the peninsula of Kintyre, to the southwest Arran, on the east the Cumbraes and the Ayrshire coast. Bute is 15½ mi. long, averages 3½ mi. in width, and, with Inchmarnock off its west coast, has an area of almost 50 sq. mi. The irregular coast is deeply indented by Rothesay, Kilchattan, St. Ninian's, and Ettrick bays. Three valleys traverse the island from northeast to southwest, terminating in bays: the northernmost from Kames to Ettrick Bay, the middle from Rothesay to Scalpsie Bay, and the southernmost from Kilchattan to Stravanan Bay. The northern part is hilly, culminating in Kames Hill (911 ft.). Glenmore Burn is the principal stream, and there are a number of fresh-water lakes, among them lochs Fad, Quien, and Ascog. Inchmarnock, 2 mi. long, is rather flat, fertile, and well-wooded in the south. Its greatest elevation is 165 ft.

Arran is bounded on the southwest and northwest by Kilbrannan Sound, separating it from Kintyre in Argyll; on the northeast by the Sound of Bute; and on the east by the Firth of Clyde, between the island and Ayrshire. Pladda lies south, and Holy Island east, of Arran. Arran is 19⅓ mi. long north and south, with an extreme width of about 10½ mi., and its area exceeds 165 sq. mi. The northern and southern portions of Arran are very dissimilar in character. In the north are lofty, rugged, granite mountains, with scanty vegetation, separated by gorges and glens radiating outward from the center. Principal summits are Goat Fell (2,866 ft.), Caisteal Abhail (2,735 ft.), and Ben Tarsuin (2,706 ft.). Seven others exceed 2,000 ft. in elevation. Southern Arran is an undulating tableland with a general elevation of 500 ft. to 800 ft., traversed by a series of east to west ridges, a somewhat bleak region. Ard Bheinn (1,676 ft.), A' Chruach (1,679 ft.), and Beinn Bhreac (1,649 ft.) are the highest elevations. Arran has fine coastal cliffs. The great central granitic area of northern Arran is almost equally divided by the glens of Iorsa Water and Easan Biorach which meet at Loch na Davie. The former stream, 8 mi. long, the longest in Arran, flows southwest to its mouth at Dougrie. Easan Biorach flows north to the sea at Loch

Ranza. In southern Arran are many lesser streams. Most of the lochs are on the west side; the most notable are Loch Tanna, the largest, 1 mi. long, at 1,065 ft. elevation, and picturesque Loch Carrie an Lochain, 1,080 ft.

Great Cumbrae lies off the southeast coast of Bute. With a rocky coast line it is quite similar to Bute in topography: hilly in the interior, rising to 417 ft. above sea level, 3¾ mi. in length, 2 mi. in width, 10½ mi. in circumference, and 3,120½ acres in area. Little Cumbrae, somewhat over a mile distant to the south, consists of volcanic rocks (Lower Carboniferous) forming a series of gently sloping terraces upon a substratum of Old Red Sandstone. The surface

COURTESY OF BRITISH INFORMATION SERVICES

Heather-clad hills rolling down to the edge of one of the many lochs of the Firth of Clyde create a typical Buteshire scene.

is moorland, with a high point of 409 ft. It is 1¾ mi. in length, and has an area of 723 acres.

Buteshire is essentially a portion of the mainland. The great Highland boundary fault cuts across Arran and Bute; it has been traced from Dougrie on the northwestern shore of Arran across the Sound of Bute, thence to Rothesay Bay and to Toward Point on the mainland. Arran and Bute north of the fault belong geologically to the Highlands, south of it, to the Lowlands. Northwest of the line are the crystalline schists of the Highlands, best seen in Bute; to the south are the younger Palaeozoic rocks, notably the Arran Triassic sandstones. Much of Bute and Great Cumbrae are formed of Upper Old Red Sandstone, separated from the schists by the fault. Moraines are abundant in the Arran glens. A 25-ft. raised beach exists along Scalpsie Bay, Bute, and is prominent all round Great Cumbrae. In the large islands there are traces of a 100-ft. raised beach.

The suggested derivations of Bute are various: from Irish *both,* "cell" (an allusion to St. Brandon's cell, sixth century); from British *buth* or Gaelic *bhiod,* "corn" (an allusion to the island's comparative fertility); or from Norse *böta,* "lights" (allusion to beacons). Buteshire early in the Christian Era was inhabited by the Picts. In the fifth century, Fergus Mor, son of King Erc of Dalriada (in Ireland), brought his Christian tribe, the Cinel Gabran, to Kintyre,

Arran, and Bute. The Cumbraes, closer to Strathclyde or Cumbria, were peopled by the British. From this time until the eighth century there was almost continual strife between the Scots of Argyll, the Picts, and the Strathclyde Britons. Rothesay Castle is reputed to have been begun in 1098 by Magnus Barefoot, a Norwegian chieftain. In 1263 King Haakon of Norway appeared with a fleet of 160 ships, captured Rothesay Castle, and occupied Bute and Arran. The Scots offered to relinquish the Hebrides to him in exchange for the present Buteshire and the surrounding mainland. He refused, but was defeated by storms and in battle at Largs on the Ayrshire coast. The islands passed to the High Stewards of Scotland. Robert Bruce captured the castle in 1312. It was a favorite residence of Kings Robert II and III. The latter, Robert III, in 1398 made his eldest son David the Duke of Rothesay, a title still held by the heir apparent to the throne, the Scotch counterpart of the Prince of Wales. Robert III died there in 1406. In 1498 the castle became the seat of the Stuarts of Bute, who resided there until 1685 when the Earl of Argyll rendered it uninhabitable during the course of his futile demonstration in favor of the Duke of Monmouth. The troops of Cromwell had previously damaged it. John Bute was sheriff of Bute (including Arran and the Cumbraes) in 1388.

Arran has steamer connection with Greenock, Campbeltown, Ardrossan, and Ayr on the mainland. Rothesay on Bute is reached by steamers from Glasgow, Greenock, Gourock, and Craigendoran. A carriage road 56 miles long runs around Arran, which is crossed by roads from Shiskine to Brodick and Lagg to Lamlash. Most of Bute has good roads, and a road encircles Great Cumbrae. On Arran the villages are on the coast, but Bute has farms in the interior. Major crops are oats, turnips, and potatoes. Horses, sheep, and cattle are raised. Rothesay exports the agricultural produce of Bute. It is estimated that one third of the county cannot be cultivated; only one sixth is under cultivation. The main activity, apart from agriculture, is catering to tourists and holiday trade.

Major towns are Brodick and Lamlash, resorts on Arran; Millport, a resort and fishing port on Great Cumbrae; and Port Bannatyne and Rothesay, the county capital (pop. 10,145 in 1951), on Bute.

Arran has an annual rainfall of 40 to 50 in., as does the southern part of Bute. Central Bute has 50 to 60 in., and the northern part, 60 to 80 in.

Holy Island owes its name to the cave cell of an anchorite, St. Molios. Loch Ranza, Brodick, and Kildonan Castles are on Arran, while Bute has Rothesay and Kames Castles and Mount Stuart, built by the second marquis of Bute in 1877. In 1750 the second lighthouse in Scotland was erected on Little Cumbrae.

John Stuart, Earl of Bute, was prime minister of Great Britain 1761-1762. The mathematician, Dr. Matthew Stewart, father of Dugald Stewart the philosopher, was born in Rothesay. Daniel Macmillan, a founder of the publishing house, was born in 1813 on Arran. David Robertson of Glasgow, eminent marine biologist, removed to Rothesay in 1860, dying there about 1896. The marine station there owes its being to his researches and efforts.   S. VanV.

BUTLER, ALBAN (1710-1773), English Roman Catholic hagiographer, was born in Northampton, Oct. 24, 1710. He early became interested in biography. He was educated at the English College of Douay, where he became professor of philosophy and divinity. In 1735 Butler was ordained a priest. While at Douay he published his *Letter on the History of the Popes*. In 1745 he took a trip with the Earl of Shrewsbury and two other companions through France, Italy, and the Netherlands; his account of the trip was published in 1803 by his nephew in Edinburgh. On his return to England he was appointed to a mission to Staffordshire, then became chaplain to the Duke of Norfolk. His next residence was at Norwich. He accompanied a pupil on a trip to the Continent, and it was in Paris that he was able to complete his *Lives of the Saints,* which he had long been preparing. Its four volumes were published anonymously in London (1756-1759). The second edition, which included notes that had been omitted from the first, was published in twelve volumes in Dublin (1779-1780). Butler was appointed president of the English College at St. Omer, France, and later also became vicar general to the bishop in that region. He died at St. Omer, May 15, 1773. He also wrote *Life of Mary of the Cross, Life of Sir Tobie Matthews,* and a number of sermons and discourses. His unfinished work, *Moveable Feasts and Fasts,* was published posthumously.

BUTLER, BENJAMIN FRANKLIN (1818-1893), American soldier, politician, and lawyer, was born at Deerfield, N.H., Nov. 5, 1818. He graduated from Waterville (now Colby) College in 1838 and returned to Lowell, Mass., to which he had moved when quite young. Butler studied law and was admitted to the bar in 1840. As a Democrat, he was elected to the Massachusetts House of Representatives in 1853 and to the state senate in 1859. At the outbreak of the Civil War he was appointed brigadier general in the state militia and proceeded to Washington with the Eighth Massachusetts Regiment. He was placed in command of the region including Annapolis and Baltimore. Butler was appointed a brigadier general of volunteers in the United States Army, May 16, 1861, and placed in command of Fortress Monroe and eastern Virginia. He was defeated by the Confederates at Big Bethel, Va., in June, and afterward was relieved of his command; however, he was put in charge of an expedition which succeeded in capturing Forts Hatteras and Clark, on the North Carolina coast, Aug. 27 and 28, 1861. Butler returned to Massachusetts and organized a brigade which was to act as the land complement to a naval invasion of New Orleans. He occupied that city May 1, 1862, and remained there until the following December 16, when he was removed by the United States government for having conducted a censurable administration of the city. His famous Order No. 28 threatened that any New Orleans woman who should insult any member of the Federal forces would be treated as "a woman of the town plying her avocation," an action which earned him the local epithet "Beast Butler." At the end of 1863 Butler was placed in charge of the Department of Virginia and North Carolina, being simultaneously commander of the Army of the James and commissioner of prisoner exchanges. Butler was defeated at Bermuda Hundred, south of Richmond, and in December 1864 he was relieved of his command by General U. S. Grant. He returned to Lowell. In 1866 he was elected by the Massachusetts Republicans to Congress, where he served until 1875 and again from 1877 to 1879; during this time he was conspicuous as a Radical Reconstructionist. After two unsuccessful attempts to gain the governorship of Massachusetts, Butler was finally elected Democratic Governor of Massachusetts in the state electoral race of 1882. But he tasted political failure again, as the unsuccessful Anti-Monopoly and Greenback Party presidential candidate in 1884. He died in Washington, D.C., Jan. 11, 1893.   W. E. A.

BUTLER, JAMES GLENTWORTH (1821-1916), American clergyman, was born Aug. 3, 1821, in Brooklyn, N.Y. After graduating from Yale University he prepared himself for the ministry, first at the Union Theological Seminary, then at the Yale Divinity School. He was ordained in 1852, and served at the Walnut Street Presbyterian Church in Philadelphia from 1852 to 1868. In 1868 he became editor of the *American and Foreign Christian Union,* a post he retained eleven years. He then proceeded to prepare his monumental commentary, *The Bible Work.* This task occupied him for twenty years (1874-1894) and the work was translated into many languages; Butler's fame chiefly rests upon it. He also wrote *Topical Analysis of the Bible* (1897); *Vital Truths Respecting God and Man* (1904); and *Present-Day Conservatism and Liberalism* (1911). He died in Boonton, N.J., Dec. 28, 1916.

BUTLER, JOSEPH (1692-1752), English divine, moralist, and writer, was born on the outskirts of Wantage in Berkshire, May 18, 1692. Though he came from a family of dissenters, he was ordained in the Church of England shortly after receiving his B.A. from Oxford University in 1718. Best known as Bishop of Durham, Butler held many important and influential positions in the Church, being at one time rector of Stanhope and dean of St. Paul's. At the philosophical evenings of Queen Caroline he came into close contact with many of the outstanding figures of his period, such as Bishop Berkeley, Alured Clarke, Benjamin Hoadly, and Thomas Sherlock. As an author, Butler is chiefly known for his contributions to the field of ethics and religion. Deploring the narrow self-regard and the decline of religious interest and belief in his time, Butler sought in his *Fifteen Sermons* (1726-1729) to make clear the demands incumbent upon men to observe the claims of benevolence and conscience which he considered as integral to human nature. In his *Analogy of Religion Natural and Revealed to the Constitution and Course of Nature* (1736), considered by many to be an answer to the deism of Matthew Tindal, Butler aimed to show the plausibility of revealed religion and the obligations it imposed upon men to follow. These two works, taken together with his *Six Sermons Preached Upon Public Occasions,* also make evident Butler's attitude toward the major philosophical issues of his day. He died at Bath, June 16, 1752.   W. J. N.

BUTLER, NICHOLAS MURRAY (1862-1947), American educator and publicist, was born at Elizabeth, N. J., Apr. 2, 1862. Graduating from Columbia University (1882), he took his Ph.D. there (1884) and studied in Berlin and Paris (1884-1885). For the next sixteen years he was associated with Columbia University in the following capacities: assistant professor of philosophy, tutor, adjunct professor, dean of the faculty of philosophy, and professor of philosophy and education. During this period he organized and was first president of Teachers College (1889-1891). He became acting president of Columbia University in 1901 and president in 1902.

He was president of the National Educational Association (1895), became a trustee of the Carnegie Foundation for the Advancement of Teaching (1905), and of the Carnegie Corporation (1925). Butler was active in national politics and received the Republican electoral votes for vice president of the United States in 1912 after the death of the regular nominee. In 1889 Butler founded the *Educational Review* and was its first editor. He became chancellor of the American Academy of Arts and Letters in 1924 and served as its president (1928-1941). He was also president of the Carnegie Endowment for International Peace (1925-1945) and chairman of the Carnegie Corporation in 1937. In 1931 he shared with Jane Addams the Nobel Prize for peace. Butler's works include *Education in the United States* (1910), *The Meaning of Education* (1915), *The Faith of a Liberal* (1924), *Across the Busy Years* (2 vols., 1939, 1940), *Liberty, Equality,*

NICHOLAS MURRAY BUTLER

COURTESY OF COLUMBIA UNIVERSITY

Fraternity (1942), and *The World Today* (1946). He retired from the presidency of Columbia University in 1945 and died in New York, N.Y., on Dec. 7, 1947.

M. Sr. and W. W. Br.

BUTLER, PIERCE (1866-1939), American jurist, was born in Dakota County, Minn., Mar. 17, 1866. He graduated from Carleton College, Northfield, Minn., in 1887, was admitted to the Minnesota bar in 1888, and commenced the practice of law in St. Paul. Butler was appointed assistant county attorney of Ramsey County, Minn., in 1891 and became county attorney in 1893, serving until 1897. From 1899 until 1905 he was general counsel for the Chicago, St. Paul, Minneapolis, and Omaha Railroad. His specialty was the legal aspects of railroad administration and valuation, and in both he was employed by the United States and the Canadian governments as an expert and arbitrator. In 1910 Butler was counsel for the United States in the prosecution of the meat-packing companies under the Sherman Anti-trust Act. In December 1922 the Senate ratified his appointment by President Warren G. Harding as an associate justice of the United States Supreme Court. In this position he delivered his best-known written decision, dealing with the Teapot Dome case, in 1927. A conservative in virtually all of his decisions, Justice Butler was an outspoken opponent of the New Deal policies of President Franklin D. Roosevelt. He died in Washington, D.C., Nov. 16, 1939.   R. T.

BUTLER, SAMUEL (1612-1680), English satirist, author of *Hudibras,* was baptized Feb. 8, 1612, at Strensham, Worcestershire. He had little formal education, but increased his learning while in the employ of several important families. After the Restoration he became secretary to the Earl of Carbery, and in 1661 steward of Ludlow Castle. Soon after, he married and moved to London. In 1663 he published the first authorized edition of *Hudibras,* Part I. The second part appeared in the following year, and the third in 1678. The poem was very popular, and Butler is said to have received some temporary recognition from the court. He died Sept. 25, 1680, and was buried in the churchyard of St. Paul's, Covent Garden, London.

Much of Butler's writing remained in manuscript until the publication in 1759 of *The Genuine Remains in Verse and Prose,* which contained *The Elephant in the Moon,* a satire on the Royal Society, and a series of biting *Characters* in prose. *Hudibras* remains, however, his most important work. It is a burlesque heroic poem ridiculing the Puritans, as represented in the characters of Hudibras, a quixotic, hypocritical knight, and his squire, Ralph. Disconnected episodes also satirize astrology, lawyers, and chivalric love. For his impudent verse Butler developed a distinctive treatment of the iambic tetrameter couplet, ever since known as Hudibrastic style.   H. B. W.

BUTLER, SAMUEL (1835-1902), English author, was born Dec. 4, 1835, at his father's rectory, Langar, near Bingham, in Nottinghamshire. Educated first at Shrewsbury, he graduated from St. John's College, Cambridge in 1858. It has been understood that he would then follow his father and grandfather into the ministry but when he came to prepare for ordination he found that his faith did not admit the efficacy of infant baptism, and he refused to be ordained. An altercation with his family ensued, and in 1859 he emigrated to establish a sheep run in New Zealand. There he read Charles Darwin's *The Origin of Species* and was immediately captivated by the theory of evolution. His earliest sketches, concerned with Darwin's ideas, were contributed to local newspapers. The sheep run prospered, and in 1864, having doubled his original capital, Butler returned

Samuel Butler, English writer of the nineteenth century

BETTMANN ARCHIVE

to England financially independent. Thereafter, he devoted his next few years to a study of painting and to reworking his earlier articles. These he included, together with realistic reminiscences of his New Zealand days, in his first important work, *Erewhon,* published in 1872. The book was immediately popular and brought Butler some fame; it was his only publication to show a profit. *Erewhon* was followed in 1873 by *The Fair Haven,* which purported to be a defense of the miraculous element in Christianity, but was, by implication, a statement of Butler's own rationalistic views. His interest in evolution had steadily grown, but further study had convinced him that Darwin, in stressing evolution as a mechanistic process, had slighted individual intelligence; and Butler now turned for confirmation to the writings of the earlier teleological evolutionists, such as Comte de Buffon,

Chevalier de Lamarck, and Erasmus Darwin. Their theories and his own concept of heredity as the unconscious memory of previous habits he put forth in *Life and Habit* (1877), *Evolution Old and New* (1879), *Unconscious Memory* (1880), *Luck or Cunning?* (1886), and *The Deadlock in Darwinism* (1890). During his later years Butler made prose translations of the *Odyssey* and *Iliad,* and he brought forth in *The Authoress of the Odyssey* (1897) the theory that the *Odyssey* was written by a woman. His last important works were *Shakespeare's Sonnets Reconsidered* (1899) and *Erewhon Revisited* (1901). He died in London on June 18, 1902. His autobiographical novel, *The Way of All Flesh,* was issued in 1903. Other published writings include: *Alps and Sanctuaries* (1881) and *Ex Voto* (1888), concerning the art of north Italy; *Essays on Life, Art, and Science* (1904); and *Note-Books* (1912). *See also* EREWHON; WAY OF ALL FLESH, The.   J. V. R.

BUTLER, SMEDLEY DARLINGTON (1881-1940), American soldier, was born at West Chester, Pa., on July 30, 1881, of Quaker family. He attended Haverford School, leaving in April 1898 to accept a commission in the United States Marine Corps. He was with Admiral W. T. Sampson's fleet at the battle of Santiago in July 1898, served in the Philippine insurrection, and was promoted to captain in 1900. During the Boxer Rebellion in 1900, he participated in the fighting at Tientsin and in the march of the international expedition from Tientsin to Peking to relieve the beleaguered civilians in the capital. Butler served with United States Marines in Panama, Honduras, and Nicaragua, reaching the rank of major. His health suffered in the tropics, and he resigned to manage a West Virginia coal mine, but soon afterwards was reappointed without loss of rank. He participated in the capture of Veracruz, Mexico, in 1914, during the American intervention in Mexico and won the Congressional Medal of Honor. In 1917, as a lieutenant colonel, he led United States Marines in the storming of Fort Rivière, Haiti, stronghold of the Cacos bandits, organized a native constabulary, and was awarded a second Congressional Medal of Honor. During World War I Butler commanded at Camp Pontanezen, Brest, France, from Oct. 15, 1918, until July 31, 1919. He was promoted to colonel in March 1919, to brigadier general in March 1921, and received the Distinguished Service Medal in 1919. On leave from the Marine Corps, he was Director of Public Safety of Philadelphia from January 1924 until December 1925. In 1926 he commanded the San Diego Marine Barracks. He was promoted to major general in July 1929 and retired on Oct. 1, 1931. Butler was outspoken in his criticism of public officials and in 1930 barely escaped court martial for his criticism of Italian Premier Benito Mussolini, after the Premier's car had run over a child in Rome. Butler was nicknamed "Old Gimlet Eye" and "Old Duckboards." His bravery and aversion to red tape made him popular with enlisted men, despite his strict discipline. As an administrator, he was impartial, courageous, and incorruptible. He published his autobiography, *Old Gimlet Eye* (1933), and *War Is a Racket* (1935). He died in Philadelphia, Pa., on June 21, 1940.

BUTLER, a city in western Pennsylvania, the county seat of Butler Co., situated 30 mi. north of Pittsburgh. It is bisected by Conoquenessing Creek and is the center of a rich coal, limestone, gas, and oil region. Livestock, poultry, potatoes, and truck crops are raised in the vicinity. Butler was settled about 1800; three years later it was incorporated as a borough and received its city charter in 1917. It had the commission form of government in 1951. Butler is built on hills originally owned by Robert Morris of Philadelphia, the financier of the Revolutionary War, and is named for Maj. Gen. Richard Butler of the Revolution. Transportation is supplied by the Pennsylvania, the Baltimore & Ohio, and the Bessemer & Lake Erie railroads. Chief industrial products are railroad cars, refrigerators, plate glass, oil-well and plumbing supplies, machinery, engines, metal products, rubber goods, clothing, dairy products, packed meat, and flour. Pop. 1950, 23,482.

BUTLER UNIVERSITY, an accredited, coeducational, privately controlled institution, is related to the Disciples of Christ Church and affiliated with the John Herron Art Institute. It is situated on 256 acres of land adjoining the residential section of Indianapolis, Ind., 5 mi. from the center of the city. Butler was chartered as Northwestern Christian University in 1850, and first instruction was given in 1855. In 1877 the present name was adopted in honor of Ovid Butler, a benefactor and one of the founders. The School of Religion was added to the original College of Liberal Arts and Sciences in 1924, the College of Education in 1930, the College of Business Administration in 1937, and the University College and the College of Pharmacy in 1945. In 1951 the Jordan College of Music was merged with Butler.

The degrees conferred are the B.A. and B.S. in liberal arts and sciences; the B.S. in business administration, pharmacy, and education; the B.Mus.; the B.D., M.R.E., M.Th., and M.S.M. in the School of Religion; and the M.A. and M.S. in

earliest capital of Lower Egypt. The goddess Buto was represented both in human form and as a serpent, but in all her forms she bore the scepter and crown of the Lower Kingdom. She was the nurse of the sun god, Horus, and of Bast, the cat goddess. The Greeks identified her with their own goddess, Leto.

BUTT, DAME CLARA (1873-1936), English contralto, was born at Southwick, Sussex, on Feb. 1, 1873. She entered the Royal College of Music on a scholarship, and there studied under Henry Blower. She made her debut at Albert Hall on Dec. 7, 1892, singing the part of Ursula in the *Golden Legend* by Arthur Sullivan. In 1895, she left for Paris to complete her musical training. There she studied with Jacques Bouhy, and later with Mme. Etelka Gerster. She won great renown as a concert singer and was especially sought for the singing of oratorios and at festivals. She visited America in 1899 and 1913. In 1913 and 1914 she toured the world with her husband, R. Kennerley Rumford, a baritone. She was created a Dame of the British Empire in 1920. Numerous compositions were written especially for her, notably Edgar Elgar's *Sea Pictures,* Herbert Bedford's *Romeo and Juliet,* and Frederick Cliffe's *Triumph of Alcestis.* She died at North Stoke, Oxford, on Jan. 23, 1936.

BUTTE [byu't], an important mining city in southwestern Montana, the county seat of Silver Bow Co., situated 65 mi. southwest of Helena. It is served by the Butte, Anaconda and Pacific, the Great Northern, the Northern

Bird's-eye view of the city of Butte. The Butte-Anaconda Copper plant is at the left.

the Graduate Division. Courses are available in teacher training, journalism, library science, and home economics, and preprofessional instruction in dentistry, engineering, law, medicine, medical technology, optometry, dietetics, religion, pharmacy, and nursing are given.

There is a men's dormitory which houses 282 students and a women's dormitory for 236. *For statistics see* COLLEGES AND UNIVERSITIES.

BUTO [byu'to], Egyptian goddess who was the personification of Lower Egypt. She founded the city of Buto on an island of a lake in the Nile Delta, and it became the

Pacific, the Union Pacific, and the Chicago, Milwaukee, St. Paul & Pacific railroads. The Northwest Airlines and the Western Air Lines also supply transportation. Butte was founded in 1864 and incorporated as a city in 1879. It has the mayor-council form of government. The city is located on the western slope of the Rocky Mountains and is 5,755 ft. above sea level. The mining of silver was the leading interest of the region until the price fell in 1893. The rich copper deposits were first tapped extensively in about 1882, and by 1900 nearly half the world's copper supply was produced in the district. Other important metal deposits are lead, manganese, zinc, and gold. The latter was discovered near Silver Bow Creek in 1861. Ranches in the vicinity of Butte raise livestock and supply the extensive stockyards and packing interests in the city. Chemicals are also produced. Hot springs and the Lewis and Clark Cave are located nearby. The city is the seat of the Montana State School of Mines and Butte Business College. Pop. 1950, 33,251.

BUTTE, a geological term for a flat-topped mountain or hill formed by the erosion of a plateau, mesa, or level area. Only a portion of the former surface, which has had a more resistant cap of rock, stands as an isolated hill or mountain. Sometimes the material underlying the hard, horizontal surface rock is softer than the surface, and so the sides of the mountain are very steep and, in some cases, undercut. This situation occurs when horizontal beds of lava have overlain soft sandstone or other sedimentary beds. Buttes are a common erosional form in mountainous areas in a semiarid to arid climate. Many buttes occur in the southwestern United States.   J. E. F.

BUTTER AND EGGS, common name of the toadflax, *Linaria vulgaris,* a familiar plant of the figwort family. Of European origin, it has spread throughout the United States. The seed is said to be dispersed widely on shipments of coal. Bright spikes of yellow and orange-tipped flowers are abundant throughout the summer.

BUTTERCUP, the common name of numerous species of *Ranunculus,* of the crowfoot family. Many have a wide range as weeds. The shining yellow flowers of the meadow

Bulbous Buttercup, Ranunculus bulbosus

or tall buttercup (*R. acris*), native to Europe and Siberia, are familiar throughout the northern United States and Canada. The creeping buttercup (*R. repens*) has a similar range. Two native American species, the marsh buttercup (*R. septentrionalis*) and the California buttercup (*R. californicus*), are especially conspicuous in bloom. The double-flowered form of *R. repens* is seen occasionally in gardens. More striking in greenhouse and garden is the turban or Persian buttercup (*R. asiaticus*), the cultivated form of which produces globular double flowers in many colors.   G. M. Sm.

BUTTERFISH, *Poronotus triacanthus,* a deep-bodied, compressed fish with a row of pores on the upper side above the lateral line. They are classified in the family Stromateidae, together with a large number of small fishes, including

the harvest fish, *Peprilus.* The butterfish is a rather common shore species along the Atlantic coast. Although it seldom grows larger than 8 to 12 in., or weighs more than a pound, it is commercially important. The annual catch averages about 12,500,000 lb. Butterfish eat plankton, small fishes, and squid. Their buoyant eggs are laid in June and July. The young may often be seen in the shelter of large jellyfish.
                                                                    E. C. R.

BUTTERFLY. Butterflies, with the moths, form the large order of scaly-winged insects, the Lepidoptera. Butterflies differ from the moths structurally in having their antennae clubbed or at least swollen at the end, and in lacking the frenulum, a spinelike device which connects the front and hind wings of most moths. In general, butterflies have slender bodies, are brightly colored, and fly in the daytime, while moths have stout bodies, are dull-colored, and fly at dusk or in the nighttime. There are, however, some brightly colored, slender-bodied moths, and conversely, there are butterflies, especially those in the family group known as "skippers," that are stout-bodied and rather dull-colored, and that may be active at night.

Structure. The body of an adult butterfly is divided into three regions—head, thorax, and abdomen. The most prominent features of the head are the large, almost hemispherical, compound eyes, and a pair of long, jointed antennae or "feelers" which project from the forehead between the eyes. On the underside of the head is the coiled proboscis, an extensible tube formed by the grooving together of paired concave organs (the two halves of the proboscis may be easily separated with a pin) through which the insect draws nectar by means of a bellowslike sucking pump. On either side of the proboscis is a three-segmented, heavily scaled sensory organ, the labial palp. The thorax consists of three segments, the pro-, meso-, and metathoraces. Each bears one pair of legs, and the last two thoracic segments (the meso- and the metathoraces) each bears a pair of wings. As in other insects, the wings of butterflies are supported by a system of tubular struts from the abdomen called veins. The type of venation is a valuable aid in studying the relationships of the various groups of butterflies. The abdomen is a roughly tubular structure made up of 10 segments, the last two or three of which are modified into secondary reproductive organs, the external genitalia. These organs are very variable and have been used extensively in the classification of the butterflies, especially in differentiating species.

The entire adult butterfly, with the usual exception of the compound eyes, is covered with hairs. Some of these hairs are very flattened and are called scales. On the wing these scales are arranged very much like shingles on a roof: they are easily detached, and therefore the specimens must be handled with care in order to avoid giving them a rubbed or worn appearance.

Pigmentation. The colors of butterflies may be divided into two classes, those caused by the pigments which are deposited in the scales, and those caused by interference with, or diffraction of, light due to the nature of the construction of the scales, the so-called "structural colors." A large part of the structural colors in butterflies, such as the iridescent and metallic colors that are found in the wings of morpho butterflies are caused by superimposed layers of very thin transparent plates which interfere with the reflection of light of certain wave lengths. Although some of the most beautiful butterflies are known to display structural colors, pigmentary colors are by far the most commonly seen in the butterfly group.

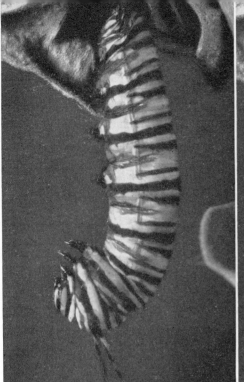

METAMORPHOSIS OF THE BUTTERFLY

Above Left. Caterpillar attaching itself to a plant.

Above Center. Beginning of cocoon formation.

Above Right. Two thirds of the cocoon completed.

Above Left. Completed cocoon.

Above Right. Cocoon showing crack before butterfly emerges.

Right. Butterfly just emerged from its cocoon.

LIFE HISTORY

After mating, the female butterfly lays her eggs, sometimes singly, sometimes in clusters, on the food plant of the larva or caterpillar. On hatching, many larvae devour the empty eggshell before beginning to feed on the plant. The larvae grow very rapidly, shedding their old skin or exoskeleton four or five times before they are fully grown. Most caterpillars feed on the leaves of plants. A few, such as those of some skippers, live as borers in the stems and roots of plants. The larvae of a number of lycaenids (Lycaenidae family) display cannibalistic habits, and a very few are predators, for example, the North American harvester which feeds on plant lice or aphids. Although most butterfly larvae are solitary, a few are gregarious, such as those of the Baltimore checkerspot which live together in a web, and the Mexican pierid in which the caterpillars live in a gourdlike nest, going out at night to feed, and pupating together head downward in the nest.

When the caterpillar attains its full growth, it undergoes a transformation into the quiescent pupa or chrysalis stage during which its larval organ systems are dissolved and rebuilt into the structures of the adult butterfly. The caterpillar usually spins a small button of silk from which it hangs head downward during the molt which transforms it into a pupa. While grasping the shed larval skin between the edges of its abdominal segments the pupa fastens itself to the button of silk with a hooked structure, the cremaster, at the end of its abdomen. In two groups, the swallowtails and their allies, and the whites, sulphurs, and orange tips, the pupa is held in an upright position by a silken girdle around its middle. In a few butterflies, principally certain parnassians and the majority of the skippers, the larvae pupate in crude cocoons. After a period ranging from a week to several years the butterfly emerges from the chrysalis and expands its wings by pumping fluid into them from the body cavity. When the wings have dried the butterfly is ready for flight.

The length of the complete life cycle varies greatly and many factors are involved. In the Arctic, where the growing season is short, it may commonly take two or more years, with the larva hibernating during the cold periods. In contrast, many temperate or tropical forms, such as the alfalfa butterfly, may have four or more generations a year. Butterflies may hibernate in any stage of the life history. The vast majority hibernate as larvae or pupae.

GEOGRAPHICAL DISTRIBUTION

Many factors influence the distribution of butterflies. Important among these are 1) geographical barriers, both past and present, that is, oceans, deserts, glaciers, and so on; 2) food plant distribution and preference—species which can feed on only one plant are restricted to the area occupied by that plant; 3) strength of flight—powerful fliers such as the swallowtails have broader ranges than relatively weak fliers such as orange tips; and 4) degree of tolerance to the various physical factors of the environment.

General Geography. With the exception of Antarctica, butterflies are found on all the continents. They may be found within a few hundred miles of the North Pole, far above the treeline on mountains, in deserts (especially in the spring or after a rainstorm), in thick forests or jungles, and even far out at sea during migrations. Some butterflies, such as the cosmopolites, are nearly world-wide in distribution, while others are restricted to very small areas; for example, the White Mountain butterfly is limited to the summit of Mt. Washington and a few nearby peaks.

Butterflies have their greatest development and diversity in the tropics, where a great many species can often be taken in one locality. Despite the large numbers of species in the tropics, however, only a few individuals of any one species can usually be collected at a given time. To find vast numbers of one species it is best to go to the Temperate Zones, or even to the Arctic, where one may come across fields or tundra areas which are literally swarming with individuals. The bog copper has been seen in such vast numbers in the cranberry bogs around Lakehurst, New Jersey that 15 to 20 could be taken with a single sweep of the net almost anywhere in the huge bogs.

Habitats. Butterflies vary widely in their flight habits and habitat preferences. The fritillaries are usually found coursing rapidly over open fields or feeding at thistles. The falcate orange tip is found in deciduous woods early in the spring, flying with a peculiar, weak, windmilling motion. The satyrs have a characteristic slow, jerky flight, and are nicknamed "bouncing browns."

In the tropics one can find glassy-winged ithomiines flitting lazily through the forest, or vast assemblages of swallowtails and giant sulphurs (as well as other butterflies) gathered to sip moisture around puddles. Seemingly always in a hurry, giant morphos flit along with a powerful yet deceptively leisurely-looking flight. One Mexican species of white morpho has been described as looking like a "flying pillowcase."

Although some butterflies such as the monarch are powerful fliers and are found almost everywhere, most species are characteristically found in a specific type of habitat. Some butterflies such as the bog copper and the jutta arctic are found in acid bogs, while others such as the Baltimore checkerspot and the two-spotted skipper are inhabitants of fresh water marshes. The hoary elfin and the common sooty wing seem to prefer relatively dry areas, while Edwards' fritillary has been taken in numbers around the scattered flowers of the South Dakota Bad Lands. The northern metalmark, the pearly eye, and the Compton tortoise shell are species found mostly in wooded areas, as is the banded purple which is often seen flying up and down along shaded watercourses.

Even in the relatively uniform environment of the Arctic tundra butterflies show habitat specificity. On Southampton Island in northern Hudson Bay the Hecla orange butterfly and Ross' Alpine prefer the low, moist sedge meadows, while Booth's sulphur, the nastes sulphur and the melissa arctic prefer the higher dry tundra ridges. The lesser fritillaries are found mostly between these two habitats, along the bases of the ridges.

Some butterflies patrol a regular territory, often defending it pugnaciously against other butterflies of the same or different species, and even sometimes against birds! Among butterflies for which this type of activity has been recorded are the pearl crescent and the American copper.

Zebra butterflies sometimes gather in numbers in the evening and spend the night roosting in groups in trees. Other butterflies, such as the tiger swallowtail, have been observed traveling in one direction (from woods toward open fields) in the morning and in the opposite direction in the evening. Swallowtail butterflies are also frequently observed flying in numbers around hilltops. It has been suggested that they are carried there by the wind, but no detailed observations have ever been made.

Migration. Migration of butterflies is a subject which has attracted considerable attention in recent years. An effort has been made in North America to study the migra-

1, 2. Painted Lady (Vanessa cardui), worldwide, except South America. 3. Peacock Butterfly (Vanessa io), Europe. 4, 5. Callithea optima, Peru. 6, 7. Tiger Swallowtail (Papilio glaucus), United States. Two color variations. 8, 9. Owl's Face (Caligo atreus), Southern Mexico. 10. Bhutanitis thaidina, China. 11. Dead Leaf (Kallima tribonia), Sumatra. 12. Dead Leaf, seated, with closed wings. 13. Monarch (Danaus plexippus), North America. 14. Viceroy (Limenitis archippus), a mimic of the Monarch. 15. Agrias claudianus, underside, Peru. 16. Morpho (Morpho anaxibia), Brazil. 17. Sulphur (Phoebis avellaneda), Cuba. 18. Bird Wing (Ornithoptera priamus), Queensland, Australia.

PHOTOGRAPH BY NICK LAZARNICK. MOTH SPECIMENS FROM THE AMERICAN MUSEUM OF NATURAL HISTORY

1. and 2. Spice-Bush Silk, male (1) and female (2), Atlantic Coast to Rocky Mountains. 3. Polyphemus, Canada into Mexico. 4. and 5. Io, male (4) and female (5), Canada to Florida; Texas and Mexico. 6. Pandora, Montana to Mexico; Rocky and Cascade Mountains. 7. Beautiful Pinkwing, Atlantic Seaboard. 8. Virgin Tiger, northeastern United States and Canada. 9. Great Tiger, northern United States and Canada. 10. Small Tiger, northern North America. 11. Darling Underwing, Appalachian Region. 12. Yellow Emperor, United States and Canada. 13. Green Sphinx, New Mexico to Brazil. 14. Royal Walnut, Appalachian Region. 15. Green Wing Saddle-back, New England to Texas. 16. Luna, Canada to Mexico, east of Rockies. 17. Joker, Pacific States. 18. Cecropia, Canada to Mexico, east of Rockies. 19. Thisbe Clearwing or Clearwing Sphinx, New England to Florida; Texas. 20. Cynthia, eastern North America.

ROSS E. HUTCHINS

Migration patterns of the monarch butterfly in the United States.

tion of the monarch butterfly, probably the most famous migrant, by marking specimens and releasing them. Results so far have been inconclusive. The monarch normally moves southward in swarms in autumn, and northward individually in the spring. Presumably, few if any individual butterflies make the complete round trip, the journey being completed by the offspring of the original migrants. Another well known migrant is the cloudless sulphur, which usually migrates northward at the end of the summer. Many other butterflies have been recorded in swarming or migratory flights. The snout butterfly has been known to darken the sky in some areas and vast swarms of the West Coast lady have been recorded in California. Flights of large sulphur butterflies have been recorded by ships far out at sea. Much information is still needed concerning the phenomenon of migration.

INTERRELATIONSHIPS WITH OTHER ANIMALS

Of all the groups of butterflies, the members of the Lycaenidae family seem to show the greatest departures from "normal" larval habits. Aside from the already mentioned predatory activities of the larvae of the harvester butterfly and others, the larvae of a number of species of the family live mutualistically with ants, the ants tending them and protecting them from enemies in return for sweet glandular secretions or "honeydew." The larvae of other lycaenids, such as an Australian species, are predators on ant larvae. These larvae have very tough hides, which protect them from the assaults of the ants defending their brood. They pupate enclosed by the cast larval skin which serves as a protective puparium. Certain pierids also enter into an association with ants, giving off a sugary liquid through tubular setae which connect with honeydew producing glands.

Parasites of Butterflies. Butterflies are attacked in all stages of their life history by assorted parasites. Tiny wasps lay their eggs in the eggs of butterflies. The wasps pass through the larval and pupal stages within the butterfly egg, and adult wasps emerge from the egg instead of butterfly larvae. The female wasps fly in searching patterns which are often typical of the individual species, darting in to lay the eggs when a suitable caterpillar victim is discovered. The eggs may be either injected under the cuticle by the ovipositor, or laid on the surface of the caterpillar's skin. In the latter case the grubs eat their way into the caterpillar after hatching from the egg.

Various flies, largely of the family Tachinidae, also parasitize butterfly larvae. The habits of the tachinids are variable. The female fly may deposit either eggs or newly hatched grubs on the surface of the caterpillar's skin or (rarely) inject the eggs under the skin. Tachinids may pupate within the host chrysalis, or the grubs may leave the doomed caterpillar and pupate in the ground.

Predators of Butterflies. Predators which attack butterflies range from other insects to man himself. Certain wasps attack caterpillars, paralyzing them and carrying them to their burrows to serve as food for their larvae. Various other wasps feed chewed-up caterpillars to their young. Compared to their larvae, adult butterflies are subject to the attacks of relatively few arthropod predators. Dragonflies, mantids, and robberflies, among other insect species, and spiders, take their toll.

Birds are doubtless the most important vertebrate predators of butterflies. They attack larvae, pupae, and adults. Caterpillars often are the principal food of nestlings. Various rodents, lizards, and frogs also feed on butterflies. Both larval and adult butterflies are eaten by man in various parts of the world. In the Philippines the abdomens of bird-wing butterflies are eaten, and caterpillars of certain skippers are fried and canned in Mexico.

Protective Mechanisms. To protect themselves from their numerous enemies the butterflies have evolved a large variety of defensive mechanisms.

Disagreeable Taste. Some, such as the monarch whose larvae feed on the milkweed, and the pipe vine swallowtail whose larvae feed on *Aristolochia* plant reputedly have body juices which are acrid and distasteful to predators. The butterfly-feeders presumably learn to avoid them.

Mimicry. Natural selection has permitted other species to take advantage of the immunity enjoyed by the disagreeable butterflies. Any variant individual of another species which resembles an unpleasant tasting (model) butterfly would have a selective advantage, being relatively more protected from predation than others of its kind. Natural selection has in this way slowly adapted various butterflies to mimic protected species, thus avoiding the attacks of birds and other predators which have learned by experience to avoid the model. The most widely known North American model-mimic pair is that of the monarch and the viceroy. The monarch, which is the model, belongs to the subfamily Danainae. The viceroy, the mimic, belongs to a different subfamily, the Nymphalinae. In Florida there exists a darker cousin of the monarch, the queen butterfly, which is also mimicked by a dark geographical variety of the viceroy butterfly.

Coloration. Many butterflies that are neither mimetic nor foul-tasting resort to various types of protective coloration to escape from their enemies. The chryxus arctic occurs in two forms in the Sierra Nevada of California; a dark form in areas of dark basaltic rock, and a light form in areas of light granitic rock. Many larvae and pupae show this background resemblance, being the same shade of green as their food plants. Adult angle-wing butterflies closely resemble dead leaves when they have their wings folded. However, the most amazing of this type of protective resemblance is that of the oriental leaf or dead leaf butterflies whose remarkable similarity to a dead leaf when in the resting position is shown in the color plate.

Some butterflies, such as many morphos, are very brightly colored on the upper surface and very dull beneath. This device gives some protection from birds or other aerial predators. Other butterflies employ a different kind of camouflage, having their outlines broken up by bold, contrasting patches of color. Certain species have bright markings which tend to draw the attention of the predator away from the vital areas of the body. This device may explain the eye-spots of many satyrines and morphines and the bright patches of the orange tips.

Other Protective Devices. Many butterfly larvae are spiny, which may give them some protection. The larvae of the family Papilionidae have a Y-shaped eversible scent gland just behind the head. The gland is protruded whenever the caterpillar is disturbed, and the resultant powerful odor probably has some protective value.

ECONOMIC IMPORTANCE

Useful Aspects. Butterflies are useful to man in several ways. Besides being a source of food, they help to pollinate many plants and are highly prized for their esthetic value. So many morpho butterflies were collected in Brazil for use in making ornamental trays and pictures that the Brazilian government had to intervene for the protection of the butterflies.

Butterfly Pests. A number of butterflies may be classed as economic pests, although they are of minor importance when compared to their distant cousins such as the codling and gypsy moths. The imported cabbageworm, the larva of the cabbage butterfly, does a tremendous amount of damage to the cabbage crop every year. This species was imported into the United States from Europe in the middle of the last century and spread rapidly over all of North America. The caterpillar of the alfalfa butterfly is a very important pest of alfalfa in the western states. The larva of the giant swallowtail may sometimes be a pest on citrus crops in the southeastern United States, where it is known as the "orange dog." Two species of satyrs known as the "rice butterflies" are pests of rice in Asia. One of them also attacks sugarcane, bamboo, and barley.

MAJOR BUTTERFLY GROUPS AND THEIR DISTRIBUTIONS

Superfamily Papilionoidea (true butterflies)
  Family Papilionidae (swallowtails, parnassians)
    Subfamily Papilioninae (swallowtails and their allies)
      Worldwide in distribution but mainly tropical, reaching greatest diversity in Old World tropics.
    Subfamily Parnassiinae (parnassians and their allies)
      Holarctic and oriental in distribution with greatest diversity in Asia.
    Subfamily Baroniinae (one species only)
      Southwestern Mexico.
  Family Pieridae (whites and sulphurs)
    Subfamily Pseudopontiinae (one species only)
      West Equatorial Africa
    Subfamily Dismorphiinae (dismorphiines)
      Primarily Neotropical in distribution, with one Palearctic member.
    Subfamily Pierinae (whites, cabbage butterflies, orange tips)
      Cosmopolitan, with greatest variety in tropics.
    Subfamily Coliadinae (yellows and sulphurs)
      Cosmopolitan, with greatest variety in tropics.
  Family Nymphalidae (four-footed butterflies)
    Subfamily Danainae (monarchs, milkweed butterflies)
      Cosmopolitan in distribution, with greatest development in tropics, especially in the Old World.
    Subfamily Ithomiinae (ithomiines, glassy-wings)
      Neotropical except for one member found only in Papua.
    Subfamily Satyrinae (satyrs, wood nymphs, grass nymphs)
      Cosmopolitan in distribution, well represented in temperate regions and Arctic.
    Subfamily Morphinae (morphos, caligos)
      Indomalayan and Neotropical in distribution.
    Subfamily Calinaginae (one species only)
      Himalayas.
    Subfamily Charaxinae (charaxines, leaf-wings)
      Tropicopolitan in distribution, sparsely entering temperate regions.
    Subfamily Nymphalinae (fritillaries, checkerspots, angle-wings, admirals, and others.)
      Cosmopolitan, with greatest variety in tropics.
    Subfamily Acraeinae (acraeines)
      Indomalayan, Ethiopian, and Neotropical in distribution, with greatest diversity in Africa.
  Family Libytheidae (snout butterflies)
    Cosmopolitan in distribution.
  Family Lycaenidae (blues, coppers, hairstreaks, metalmarks)
    Subfamily Styginae (one species only)
      Peruvian Andes.
    Subfamily Lycaeninae (blues, coppers, hairstreaks)
      Cosmopolitan.
    Subfamily Riodininae (metalmarks)
      Tropicopolitan in distribution, a few Nearctic and Palearctic; by far most diversely and abundantly represented in Neotropical region.
Superfamily Hesperioidea (skippers and giant skippers)
  Family Hesperiidae
    Subfamily Megathyminae (giant skippers)
      Southern United States and northern Mexico.
    Subfamily Hesperiinae (true skippers)
      Cosmopolitan in distribution.
    Subfamily Euschemoninae (one species only)
      Australia.

P. R. E.

BUTTERFLY BUSH, *Buddleia,* a group of shrubs of the logania family, the individual flowers of which somewhat resemble lilacs. The species most commonly planted in the north, *B. davidi* (formerly often called *B. variabilis*), is sometimes known as summer lilac. Discovered in China in the latter half of the nineteenth century, *B. davidi* has been a highly favored hardy shrub since early in the twentieth century, when nurserymen began introducing improved, larger-flowered forms with a color range from white through delicate orchid-pink to deep purple. The gracefully tapering spikes of fragrant flowers sometimes reach more than 1 ft. in length. Butterflies hover around them in great numbers. The shrubs are tall, with slender, often arching stems; the leaves are slender, toothed, dark green above, and whitish beneath. If the stems are cut in winter, new ones will sprout from the roots in spring. Other species are less hardy and though a few will stand frost, some are suited only to greenhouse culture. They are grown from seed or cuttings, and do best in spacious quarters in sun, in a rich, well-drained soil. Flowers may be white, orange, or lavender.

C. H. Wo.

BUTTERFLY FISH, family Chaetodontidae, are deep-bodied salt-water fishes of small size and brilliant coloration. The small mouth is edged with brushlike teeth, and the dorsal fin is scaled at the base. They are found in pools in coral reefs, and are exceedingly quick of movement. Many kinds are found in the West Indies, but the center of their abundance is Polynesia.

The fresh-water butterfly fish, or chiseljaw, *Pantodon buchholzi,* belongs to a much more primitive family and is limited to the brooks and swamps of West Africa. The pectoral fins are large and expanded, much as in the salt-water flying fish. It is able to make rather erratic flights of about 6 ft. The pelvic fin rays separate to form long filaments. It is also characterized by an enormous mouth and silvery colored body. This fish makes an interesting aquarium pet. E. C. R.

BUTTERFLY LILY or **MARIPOSA LILY,** *Calochortus,* and globe tulip, small, gaily-flowering plants of the lily family, native to western North America. The blossoms vary greatly in color and form. J. C. Wis.

BUTTERFLY PEA, *Clitoria mariana,* a perennial, often twining, of the pea family, growing on dry soils from New Jersey south. It grows to about 3 ft., with smooth leaves of three leaflets and light blue, showy, fragrant pea-shaped flowers in early summer. J. C. Wis.

BUTTERFLY WEED, *Asclepias tuberosa,* called also pleurisy root, a perennial belonging to the milkweed family. It is a brilliant flower of midsummer, growing in dry, sandy places from Maine to Florida and Arizona. Heads of intense red-orange bloom, very attractive to butterflies, are carried at the top of leafy branching stems to 3 ft. The seed pods are long and hairy. J. C. Wis.

BUTTERNUT, *Juglans cinerea,* the common name of a tree of the walnut family native to moist land from New Brunswick to Georgia and west to Arkansas and South Dakota. Often 100 ft. tall, it is widely branched, with smooth, gray bark, small clusters of four-ribbed nuts and, coarse-grained, light-brown wood, which is used for furniture and interiors. Sugar may be made from the sap, and the inner bark has cathartic properties. In Colonial times the green husks of the nuts were used to dye homespun fabrics yellow, whence the term "butternut jeans." J. C. Wis.

BUTTERWORT, *Pinguicula,* a genus of the bladderwort family with about thirty species, chiefly native to damp northern regions in both hemispheres, called also bog violet. These are insectivorous plants with succulent greasy leaves covered with sticky hairs growing in a basal rosette. When an insect is caught in these hairs, the margins of the leaves roll in and exude a fluid which dissolves the insect, permitting the leaves to absorb it, after which they unroll. The single flowers, borne on a long stem, are spurred and usually purplish. *P. lutea,* the only yellow-flowered species, is native to pine barrens from North Carolina to Louisiana.

J. C. Wis.

COURTESY OF THE AMERICAN MUSEUM OF NATURAL HISTORY

Butterfly Weed, Asclepias tuberosa, *with detail of flower and seed*

BUTTONBUSH or **HONEYBALLS,** *Cephalanthus occidentalis,* a summer-flowering shrub of the madder family, native to swampy places throughout the United States and southern Canada. The leaves are smooth, glossy, and pointed; the flowerheads, fragrant, creamy-white balls, are one inch in diameter. In the Southwest, the buttonbush resembles a small tree. J. C. Wis.

BUXTORF, JOHANNES (THE ELDER) [buˈkstɔrf] (1564-1629), German Protestant authority on Hebrew and rabbinical literature, was born at Kamen, Westphalia, Dec. 25, 1564. He was the first of a notable family which for four consecutive generations occupied the chair of Hebrew at the University of Basel. He was educated at Marburg and Herborn. While at Herborn he helped Piscator, professor of theology at that university, prepare a Latin translation of the Old Testament. He later pursued his studies of Oriental languages and rabbinical literature at the universities of Heidelberg, Basel, Zürich, and Geneva. In 1589 he was placed in charge of Hebrew studies at the University of Basel and was formally installed as professor of Hebrew there in 1591. He was recognized by Protestants as the foremost authority in his field. Buxtorf regarded the original text of the Old Testament to be free from error, since he considered it divinely inspired. His works include *Manuale Hebraicum et Chaldaicum* (1602) and *Juden Schül* (1603). The latter work was translated into Latin as *Synagoga Judaica* (1604); in it he described the beliefs and religious practices of the Jews. He also wrote *Lexicon Hebraicum et Chaldaicum cum breve lexico rabbinico philosophico* (1607), *De abbreviaturis Hebraicis* (1613), *Biblia Hebraica cum paraphrasi Chaldaica et commentariis rabbinorum* (4 vols., 1618-1619), and *Tiberias, sive commentarius masorethicus* (1620). Buxtorf devoted twenty years of his life to the preparation of a Chaldaic, Talmudic, and Rabbinic dictionary. Before he could complete it he died in Basel, Sept. 13, 1624, but this work and others were completed by his son, Johannes Buxtorf the Younger.

BUXTORF, JOHANNES (THE YOUNGER) (1599-1664), son of Johannes Buxtorf, the Elder, and also a Hebraist, was born in Basel, Aug. 13, 1599. He was educated at the University of Basel, obtaining his master's degree at the age of sixteen. He also pursued studies at the universities of Heidelberg, Dort, and Geneva. Like his father, he established a solid reputation in the field of Oriental languages and rabbinical literature. In 1622 he published his *Lexicon Chaldaicum et Syriacum*. He was offered the chair of logic at the University of Lausanne, but declined it. In 1624 he became deacon of a church at Basel, and in 1630 was appointed to succeed his father to the chair of Hebrew at Basel. In 1654 he was also appointed to the chair of Old Testament Exegesis. The younger Buxtorf spent ten years completing his father's dictionary, published as *Lexicon Chaldaicum Talmudicum et Rabbinicum* (1632-1639), and also his father's *Concordantiae Bibliorum Hebraicae*. He also published Latin translations of Maimonides' *Guide of the Perplexed* and ha-Levy's *Cuzari,* and numerous original works. He died in Basel, Aug. 17, 1664, and was succeeded in the chair of Hebrew by his son, Jakob Buxtorf (1645-1704), who was in turn succeeded by a cousin, Johannes Buxtorf (1663-1732).

BUZZARD, any of a number of species of medium-sized to large hawks combined in the genus *Buteo.* They occur in temperate and tropical regions throughout the world, excepting Australasia. They are heavily built, with short, broad wings, able to soar but slow in flight. Of a somewhat sluggish disposition, they feed almost entirely on small rodents, reptiles, frogs, and crayfish, but are often unjustly accused of attacking domestic fowls. The best-known American species are the red-tailed and red-shouldered hawks. The so-called turkey buzzard of the United States is actually a New World vulture.   H. G. De.

BUZZARDS BAY, an arm of the Atlantic Ocean on the southern coast of Massachusetts. It is about 30 mi. long, and varies in width from 5 to 10 mi. with the greatest breadth at the line of Woods Hole. The village, now the headquarters of a famous oceanographic institution, was once a whaling port, as were Falmouth, Wareham, and New Bedford. The last was once the world's greatest whaling port. With the decline in whaling after 1855, traffic in the bay almost ceased until the Cape Cod Canal, connecting Buzzards with Cape Cod Bay, was finished in 1914. Private craft frequent the bay, which is bordered by many estates, including those on the Elizabeth Islands which separate the bay from Vineyard Sound. The Acushnet, Weweantic, and Wareham rivers empty into the bay on the northwest shore.   E. A.

BYDGOSZCZ [bɪ′dgoshtsh] (*Ger.* Bromberg), a city in the province of the same name in Pomerania, north central Poland, about 150 mi. northwest of Warsaw near the Vistula River. Lying in the midst of a large agricultural area, its industries are principally connected with agriculture. It is a leading railroad junction and has trade largely in timber, wool, flour, leather, and coal. Bydgoszcz, which lies on a canal connecting the Vistula with the Oder-Warta river systems, was originally a trading settlement on the border between Pomerania and Poland. It declined because of raiding carried on by the Teutonic Knights, but revived under Casimir III, king of Poland, during the latter half of the fourteenth century. However, its commerce declined again in the seventeenth century. In 1807, by the Treaty of Tilsit, the city was annexed to the grand duchy of Warsaw. Prussian forces occupied it in 1813, and Prussia held it until 1918, when the city was returned to Poland after World War I. Pop. 1946, 134,614.   L. M. A.

BYELORUSSIAN SOVIET SOCIALIST REPUBLIC

[byɛ′lorʌ′shən], the third largest Slavic state among the fifteen constituent Republics of the Union of Soviet Socialist Republics. Byelorussia, also known as White Russia, has an area of 81,000 sq. mi. Its capital is Minsk.

The Byelorussian Republic lies on the Baltic to Black Sea river route and extends from 51° 14′ to 56° 10′ N. lat. and from 23° 11′ to 32° 45′ E. long. It is bounded on the west by Poland, on the east by the Smolensk and Bryansk oblasts, on the south by the Ukrainian Soviet Socialist Republic, and on the north by the Pskov Oblast. The most important of the rivers transversing the republic are the Western Dvina, Berezina, Dnepr, Pripyat (Pripet), and the Sozh. These rivers drain into the Baltic Sea and Black Sea, thus making Byelorussia a portage ground and watershed for the river routes leading north and south. There are 4,000 lakes in the republic. The climate, affected by the Baltic Sea and the Atlantic Ocean, is cold in winter and warm in summer. The average temperature is 63.5° F. in July and 19.7° F. in January. Precipitation ranges from 27.3 to 21.5 in. annually.

Resources. More than a third of the land is covered with peat and other swampy soils, especially in the Pripet Marshes in the south. A huge swamp-drainage program is under way which will make more land available for cultivation and regulate the flow of the rivers. Peat is the leading mineral resource, with reserves estimated in billions of tons. It is used as fuel in several large electric power stations, as fertilizer, as livestock litter, as a raw material for the chemical industry, and for the generation of household gas. Limestone, chalk, quartz sand, and clay are the only other minerals found in the republic. There are large deposits of potassium chloride and sodium chloride northeast of Mozyr.

Byelorussia lies in the mixed forest zone, and forests cover about 29 per cent of the total area. Coniferous trees (Scotch pine and spruce) predominate in the north, and to the south are found the birch, alder, aspen, oak, and hornbeam. Scotch pine is used for building timber; spruce, for pulpwood; birch, alder, and oak, for plywood and veneers; and aspen, for matches. The Republic shares with Poland the Belovezha (Bialowieza) wildlife preserve, which contains the last of the almost extinct European bisons (aurochs).

Agriculture. Most of the soil of Byelorussia is podsolic, with clayey loam on uplands and morainal hills and sandy loam and sand on hill slopes and in depressions. This podsolic soil requires the application of fertilizers and lime before it can be used for agriculture. Less than a third of the acreage is cultivated, and 20 per cent of all the land is in pastures and hay fields. Because the cultivable area is so limited, and there is a surplus of rural manpower, efforts are made to increase crop yields and to promote farm activities which require many workers and yield valuable products. Ten per cent of the Soviet Union's flax acreage is in the Republic. Hemp, low-grade *makhorka* tobacco, and sugar beets are also grown. Byelorussia is one of the leading hog-raising areas in the Soviet Union. Hog farms are associated with potato fields. Potatoes provide much of the hog feed, as well as being a staple food and a raw material for alcohol and starch industries. The chief food grain is rye; wheat and buckwheat are also grown, but some grain must be imported from other parts of the Soviet Union.

Industry. Byelorussia was one of the most backward sections of European Russia prior to the Bolshevik Revolution. Since the inception of the Soviet regime, great stress has been placed on industrial development. Machine building is the leading industry, and the plants concentrated in Minsk, Gomel, Mogilev, and Vitebsk manufacture trucks, tractors and other farm machinery, tools, road-building machinery, motorcycles and bicycles, radios, and motors. Other leading industries are the manufacture of such wood products as plywood, matches, paper, artificial fibers, furniture, and prefabricated houses; linen, cotton, and woolen textiles; and clothing and shoes.

Population and Religion. The population in 1956 was estimated at 7,992,000, or slightly over 4 per cent of the total population of the Soviet Union. Approximately 80 per cent speak the Byelorussian (or White Russian) language, a Slavic tongue related to Russian; the other 20 per cent are Russians, Jews, Poles, and Ukrainians. The population was increased from over 5,000,000 to 9,200,000 in 1939 by the addition of territory acquired from Poland. As a result of losses in World War II, the population was greatly reduced. After the war there was some exchange of people with Poland. Most of the population is Orthodox. Other religious groups are Roman Catholic, Uniate, and Jewish.

History. The Byelorussian derives his name from the traditional white homespun garments he wore. He is generally brown-haired, and brown-eyed. Although he has escaped intermixture with the Tatars and Turks, there has been some admixture with the Lithuanians and Poles, who formerly ruled Byelorussia.

Byelorussia fell under Polish domination in 1386 when Grand Duke Jagellon of Lithuania married Queen Jadwiga of Poland. The Russian rulers, Ivan III, who reigned from 1465 to 1505, and Basil III, who ruled from 1505 to 1533, wrested most of the Byelorussian territory from Poland. By the Treaty of Vilna (1656), Poland ceded practically all White Russia to Moscow. The three partitions of Poland (1772, 1793, and 1795) saw the restoration of the rest of the Byelorussian territories to Russia. Byelorussia again became a battleground in 1812 when Napoleon traversed it to reach Moscow. The most famous battle was fought at the Berezina River on the retreat from Moscow.

In 1916, during World War I, the Germans invaded the country; by 1918 they reached Minsk, but retreated in November of that year. In 1919 the Soviet Union waged war with Poland, which aspired to dominate all White Russia, and by the Treaty of Riga (1921) the western part of Byelorussia was ceded by a weakened Soviet Union to Poland. At the Paris Peace Conference in 1919 the so-called Curzon Line was proposed as the frontier between Poland and Byelorussia. This was an attempt to fix the eastern frontier of Poland on a racial rather than a political basis. In 1939 the Russians again restored these lands to the Byelorussian Republic. However, in June 1941, during World War II, the Germans occupied the area and held it until July 1944 when the Russians recaptured it. The German occupation reduced Byelorussia to a virtual desert. Minsk, Gomel, Mogilev, and Orsha were completely destroyed. Over 3,000,000 people were left homeless. At the Yalta Conference in February 1945 the United States and Great Britain agreed with the Soviet demand that the eastern frontier of Poland should be substantially the Curzon Line. On Aug. 16, 1945, the Soviet Union and Poland agreed by treaty to fix their common frontier on the Curzon Line except for some deviation of from three to nineteen miles in favor of the Poles.

In October 1945 the Byelorussian S.S.R., the Ukrainian S.S.R., and the U.S.S.R. became the three Soviet members of the United Nations. R. J. K. and T. Sh.

BYELY, ANDREI [bye'l31] (1880-1934), Russian novelist, poet, philosopher, and literary theorist, was born in Moscow, Oct. 14, 1880. His real name was Boris Nikolayevich Bugayev. The son of an eminent scientist, Professor N. Bugayev, Byely was graduated from the School of Science of the University of Moscow in 1903, and at that time was already known in Russian literary circles.

Byely's four books of *Symphonies* (1902-1907) were his first major prose work. They were a daring experiment in prose based on laws of musical construction and on the emotional values of rhythm and sound, and they brought him recognition as an unusual artist and a leading symbolist. In *The Silver Dove,* a novel published in 1910, Byely masterfully linked the devices of symbolism with realism and combined rich humor with profound psychological analysis. *The Silver Dove* and *Petersburg* (1913) were his great achievements in point of literary merit and sociological significance.

The most important of Byely's works in prose during the Revolutionary and post-Revolutionary periods were his memoirs and autobiographical novels. The first novel of this group of works, *Kotik Letayev* (1917), is a brilliant work of experimentalism somewhat reminiscent of Joyce; among other works of this series are *The Crime of Nicholas Letayev* (1921), *The Journal of a Crank* (1923), and several volumes under the general title, *Moscow.*

In three volumes of his memoirs Byely told powerfully and realistically the story of his life, his philosophical wanderings, and the cultural and sociological upheaval of his time.

In poetry as in prose Byely explored new aesthetic and formal possibilities. Among his books of poems are *Gold in Azure* (1898-1904), *Ashes* (1909), *Urn* (1909), *The First Meeting* (1921), and *After the Parting* (1922), and his theses on the theory of symbolism and prosody, together with some of his philosophical essays, make up a volume entitled *Symbolism* (1910). But it is Byely's prose, with its bold and original revolutionary innovations, that constitutes his greatest contribution to literature. Byely died in Moscow on Jan. 8, 1934. N. D.

BYNG OF VIMY, 1ST VISCOUNT (JULIAN HEDWORTH GEORGE BYNG) [vi'mi] (1862-1935), British soldier, was born probably in or near London, Sept. 11, 1862. He joined the Tenth Hussars in India in 1883, served in the Sudan (1884), afterwards in the Boer War (1899-1902), and in 1912 commanded the British army in Egypt. By 1909 he had been promoted to major general, and in 1914 was assigned to command the Third Cavalry Division in France. In 1915 Byng was sent to the Dardanelles and, in command of the Ninth Army Corps at Gallipoli, showed considerable skill in withdrawing his troops when the British attack failed. From May 1916 to June 1917 he commanded the Canadian Corps in France, where it played a major part in the capture of Vimy Ridge. From 1917 to 1919 Byng commanded the Third British Army, with the rank of full general, and gained fame for his leadership in the "battle of the tanks" at Cambrai, in November 1917. In October 1919 he was made a baron, and served as governor general of Canada from 1921 to 1926, when he was elevated to a viscountcy. In 1932 he became a field marshal. Byng was commissioner of the London Metropolitan Police from 1928 to 1931. He died at Thorpe-le-Soken, Essex, June 6, 1935.   E. R. A.

BYRD, HARRY FLOOD [bə'rd] (1887-   ), American politician, brother of Rear Adm. Richard Byrd, was born at Martinsburg, W. Va., on June 10, 1887, of an old Virginia family. He attended public schools in Winchester, Va., studied at the Shenandoah Valley Academy, and at the age of fifteen, became publisher of the Winchester *Star*. He soon acquired another newspaper, took up farming in Virginia, and developed a successful business in apple orchards. He served in the Virginia Senate from 1915 to 1925 as a Democrat and was chairman (1922-1925) of the Democratic State Committee. Byrd was elected governor of Virginia in 1925 and immediately sponsored the introduction of state government organization and administrative reforms which previously had been repeatedly defeated. He increased appropriations for the University of Virginia, initiated a state highway construction program, and secured enactment of the first antilynching law in the United States.

Upon retirement from the governorship in 1930, Byrd, holding no political office, became one of the most influential members of the Democratic National Committee. He was proposed by the state of Virginia at the 1932 Democratic National Convention as a presidential nominee, and in March 1933 he was appointed to complete an unexpired term in the United States Senate. He was elected in 1934 and re-elected in 1940, 1946, and 1952. He opposed work relief in 1935 because he believed it to be a state function, and opposed many New Deal measures. He supported Lend-Lease and revision of the Neutrality Act.

Byrd has always exercised a strong conservative influence, both in state and national affairs, and has consistently urged economy in the government administrative organization, particularly in cases of overlapping and duplicating agencies and of excessive personnel. He was instrumental in securing the setting up of the Hoover Commission on economy in government. He also urged sole United States trusteeship of the Pacific islands formerly mandated to or occupied by the Japanese. Senator Byrd became a leading opponent of the Supreme Court's desegregation decision.   W. E. A.

BYRD, RICHARD EVELYN (1888-1957), American naval officer, explorer, and scientist, brother of Sen. Harry Flood Byrd, was born in Winchester, Va., on Oct. 25, 1888. His education included training at Shenandoah Valley Military Academy, Virginia Military Institute, and at the University of Virginia. He graduated from the United States Naval Academy in 1912. He was assigned to sea duty and later was stationed at Guantánamo, Cuba. In 1918 Byrd took up aviation and was appointed commander of the United States Air Forces in Canada. He was one of the first in 1918 to fly an NC-1 flying boat, prototype of the first airplane to cross the Atlantic. In 1925 he made the first of five explorations of the Arctic and Antarctic as commander of the aviation unit of the MacMillan Polar Expedition; in 1926 he and Floyd Bennett made the first successful flight over the North Pole. In 1927, soon after Lindbergh's trans-Atlantic flight, he flew from New York to France. During 1928-1930,

he made his first expedition to the Antarctic, established his base at Little America, on the Bay of Whales, and flew for the first time over the South Pole. On his second expedition (1933-1935) he discovered and named the Edsel Ford Mountains and Marie Byrd Land, and spent five months alone, 123 mi. south of Little America, making scientific observations. In 1939, as commander of the United States Antarctic Expedition, he made numerous flights over the area to substantiate United States claims to the region, and mapped mineral deposits. During World War II he did confidential work in connection with air bases outside the United States. In January 1945 President Roosevelt awarded him the Legion of Merit. On Dec. 2, 1946, Byrd, in command of a large, elaborately equipped expedition, left the United States for the Antarctic to make a geological survey of the South Pole area, study weather conditions, test personnel and equipment, and search for possible uranium deposits. After exploring 1,700,000 sq. mi., the expedition returned to the United States in April 1947.

In 1954 Byrd was appointed head of the U.S. Navy's Operation Deepfreeze I, part of the government's contribution to the International Geophysical Year of 1957-1958. Byrd was also placed by President Eisenhower in charge of all Antarctic activities of the United States and was responsible for the preparation and execution of Antarctic policy. He visited the Antarctic from December 1955 to February 1956 to superintend the Deepfreeze operation but was prevented by illness from seeing the conclusion of the program. Byrd died in Boston, Mass., on Mar. 11, 1957.

Byrd invented several instruments for use in aerial navigation, including a bubble sextant, a sun compass, and a drift indicator. His books include *Skyward* (1928), *Little America* (1930), *Discovery* (1935), and *Alone* (1938).
          S. Van V. and W. Lin.

BYRD, WILLIAM (c. 1543-1623), English composer, was born probably in Lincolnshire in 1543. One of the most important of all English musicians, he is particularly remembered for his sacred choral music, although his string, keyboard, and secular vocal compositions are significant in the development of the musical forms of the period. No reliable information on the first twenty years of Byrd's life has been discovered, but it is believed that he was probably a pupil of the famous Thomas Tallis. He occupied the post of organist at Lincoln Cathedral from 1563 to 1572, but in the latter year, or thereabouts, he began sharing the position of organist for the Chapel Royal with Tallis. He was active in the music of the chapel until his death, probably in Essex, July 4, 1623.

Byrd's sacred music, written partly for the Roman Catholic Church, of which he was a member, and partly for the Anglican, is similar in style to that of Palestrina and Orlando di Lasso, but it is especially characterized by unusual and often harsh harmonies. Byrd was one of the founders of the English school of madrigalists and contributed compositions to numerous published collections of the day. His instrumental works are original enough to justify his being called an important pioneer in the instrumental forms of the seventeenth century.   R. M. K.

BYRD EXPEDITIONS. Rear Admiral Richard Evelyn Byrd, United States Navy, explored or directed the exploration of more previously unseen areas of the earth's surface than any individual in the twentieth century. He pioneered in the early development of long-range, transoceanic, and high latitude flights, and was first to fly over both the North and the South poles. He led numerous private and

United States Government expeditions for the combined purpose of exploration, technical development, training, and scientific observation.

Byrd's interest in exploration was heightened by several historic airplane flights which he planned and directed. After World War I he was in charge of the navigational preparation for the first successful transatlantic flight made by the Navy in 1919. The flying boat *NC4,* a pusher-type biplane, reached Lisbon by way of Newfoundland and the Azores. Later that year, as part of the Navy's plan to acquire the *ZR2,* which was then in England, Byrd was assigned to this hydrogen-filled dirigible. An explosion over the Humber River destroyed the craft, killing 45 out of the 48 men and officers aboard. Admiral Byrd had reported for duty the previous day, and only by chance had not been aboard. In 1927, after his early polar expeditions, Byrd flew from New York to France in a trimotor Fokker plane. Unfavorable visibility was encountered over the French coast, but the plane was successfully brought down a short distance offshore without loss of life. The flight was most notable for the fact that the plane carried for the first time over the Atlantic a payload of 800 lb. and a passenger, foreshadowing the use of planes in regular transoceanic commercial traffic. The account of this flight and of Byrd's earlier Arctic work is given in his first book, *Skyward.*

Arctic Expeditions. *Navy-MacMillan Expedition.* Byrd began to plan his first polar expedition in 1925. This was the first successful effort to use airplanes to explore the Far North. For expedience Byrd joined forces with Donald MacMillan as commanding officer of the naval unit of the Navy-MacMillan Arctic Expedition. Byrd used two Loening amphibian planes for aerial reconnaissance in the vicinity of Cape Sabine and over the ice caps of Ellesmere Island and northwest Greenland. He made an important flight northwest from Etah over a portion of the Arctic Ocean searching for the "appearance of land" reported by Peary. This was a record high latitude for airplanes at that date. During these flights Byrd was able to demonstrate the utility of the sun compass as a navigating instrument in regions where the magnetic compass was subject to wide errors.

Flight over North Pole. In 1926 the Byrd Arctic Expedition, with the ship *Chantier* and a trimotor Fokker monoplane, made Kings Bay, Spitzbergen, its base. From this point, using ski landing gear, the plane flew north, and in Byrd's own words, "at 9:02 Greenwich Civil Time on May 9, 1926, our calculations showed us to be at the Pole." Thus Byrd and Floyd Bennett, his companion, were the first persons to reach the North Pole by plane. Successful navigation was attributed to the sun compass, Byrd being supplied with two such instruments, a fortunate precaution since the bubble sextant he also carried was accidently damaged during the flight. With this proof that airplanes were capable of flying anywhere, he turned his attention to new areas of pioneering.

Antarctic Expeditions. Byrd next turned his attention to the Antarctic, where his greatest achievements were to be made. No American expeditions had gone to the South Polar regions in nearly 100 years. Here lay a great continent almost completely unknown. Byrd painstakingly prepared a series of expeditions, each larger and more important than the last. Again he pioneered with the use of airplanes for aerial reconnaissance mapping, and took along a large staff of scientists for detailed observations.

Expedition of 1928-1929. In 1928 the Byrd Antarctic Expedition with two ships, the 500-ton *City of New York* and the 800-ton *Eleanor Bolling,* and three planes, a trimotor

Ford, a single-motor Fokker, and a single-motor Fairchild folding-wing monoplane, set up a base called Little America on the Ross Ice Shelf at the Bay of Whales. A full complement of over 106 men and nearly 100 dogs accompanied this expedition. Valuable aid was also obtained from Norwegian whaling ships, which helped transport men, dogs, and equipment a part of the way and which towed the *City of New York* through the ice pack fringing the entrance to the open Ross Sea. After wintering at Little America, Byrd took off in the ski-equipped Ford plane, and on Nov.

WIDE WORLD PHOTOS

The Antarctic region showing new discoveries made by the Byrd expedition. (1) The Knox coast area, site of the land of lakes, and (2) the Queen Mary coast where aerial observers discovered islands of rock jutting above the surrounding ice.

29, 1929, circled the vicinity of the South Pole and returned safely to his base. This was the first plane to reach the South Pole. Byrd thus became the first person to have flown over both poles. Other flights took Byrd over unknown territory, to discover what he named the Rockefeller Mountains, the Edsel Ford Mountains, and Marie Byrd Land, the latter designating that part of the Antarctic east of the 155th Meridian west of Greenwich.

A geological party led by the second in command, Dr. L. M. Gould, traveled by dog teams to explore a portion of the Queen Maud Mountains. Scientific work was achieved also in the fields of physics, meteorology, geomagnetism, electronics, radiowave propagation, glaciology, oceanography, and zoology. Admiral Byrd wrote a full account of this expedition, entitled *Little America.*

Expedition of 1933-1934. In 1933 Byrd took a second expedition to the Antarctic, using two ships, the 700-ton *Bear of Oakland* and the 4,000-ton freighter *Jacob Ruppert;* four airplanes, a Curtis Condor, a Kellett autogyro, and two single-motor monoplanes. With a total complement of more than 130 men and 150 dogs, plus six over-snow vehicles, it set up a base, called Little America II, at the Bay of Whales. Fifty-five men remained here throughout the year 1934.

During the polar night Byrd himself manned an advance base alone for five months at 80° S. lat. This was the first inland station ever to be established in Antarctica to study the meteorology of the region. Byrd's hazardous and lonely experience is told in his book *Alone*. Aerial reconnaissance from Little America extended Marie Byrd Land, and defined the Ruppert Coast, Rockefeller Plateau, and Edsel Ford Range, as well as the Hal Flood and William Horlick Mountains. Several field parties traveling by dog sleds and snowmobiles made surveys, and geological, glaciological, magnetic, seismic, and biological studies in the Rockefeller, Edsel Ford, and Queen Maud Mountains. Dr. Thomas C. Poulter, second in command, directed the scientific research of this expedition, which made important contributions in geophysics, geomagnetism, cosmic radiology, seismology, meteorology, meteoric and auroral phenomena, glaciology, zoology, botany, and oceanography. A full account of the expedition is given in Byrd's book *Discovery*.

Expedition of 1939-1940. In 1939 the United States Antarctic Service Expedition under Byrd's supervision, using the *Bear of Oakland* and the Coast Guard cutter *North Star* with four planes, a Beechcraft, two Condors, and a Barkeley Grow seaplane, established two bases. One for thirty-three men was set up at the Bay of Whales as Little America III, or West Base; the other for twenty-six men, at Marguerite Bay, Palmer Land, as East Base. For this expedition a snow cruiser had been built, 55 ft. long, 20 ft. wide, and 15 ft. high, with balloon-tired wheels 10 ft. in diameter. The snow cruiser was unloaded at the Bay of Whales, but through faulty design was found unusable.

Flying in the Barkeley Grow seaplane from the *Bear of Oakland*, Byrd made the important discovery of the coastline comprising the southern limit of the Pacific Ocean. These were hazardous flights over an area previously considered unapproachable by earlier explorers. The Ruppert Coast was extended for nearly 500 mi. to the 15,000-ft. coastal Mount Ruth Siple, and continued with a small gap for another 750 mi. to define the Walgreen coast and Thurston Peninsula. After the 1939-1940 Antarctic summer field season, Byrd returned to the United States to direct his bases by radio while he turned his attention to problems connected with World War II.

From West Base, which was commanded by Dr. Paul A. Siple, a veteran of both previous Antarctic Expeditions, exploratory work was conducted by air and on the surface, resulting in further description of Marie Byrd Land, the Antarctic cordillera and the Ross Ice Shelf. From East Base, under the command of Richard B. Black, planes flew farther along the Andean-Palmer Peninsula range for about 400 mi., and the southern shore of the Alexander I Island and King George VI Sound was delineated primarily by a two-man sledging party led by Finn Ronne, covering over 1,250 mi. in its ground survey. The scientific results of the United States Antarctic Service Expedition, primarily directed by Dr. F. Alton Wade, embracing findings in geography, geology, glaciology, geophysics, biology, physiology, nutrition, and many other fields, constituted a wealth of highly valuable data, and was published in the *Proceedings* of the American Philosophical Society, Vol. 89, No. 1.

Expedition of 1946-1947. After World War II the Navy Operation Highjump, with Rear Admiral Byrd as officer in charge, made extensive exploratory investigations, in the Antarctic summer of 1946-1947, encompassing all but a small portion of the entire Antarctic circumference. This operation was conducted by a naval task force which included a complement of 4,000 personnel, and thirteen naval vessels

operationally commanded by Rear Admiral Richard Cruzen, U.S.N., from the airplane carrier *Philippine Sea* and the ice breakers *North Wind* and *Burton Island* to the submarine *Sennett* and about twenty aircraft of various types. The expedition operated as three groups. A base was established at the Bay of Whales, in the vicinity of the former Little Americas, from which reconnaissance and photographic flights were made. About seventy over-snow vehicles, including trailers, were used in the construction of the 197-man base camp, with its air strip for planes equipped with ski-wheel landing gear.

Much modern equipment was used, including jet assistance in airplane takeoff from carriers or snow fields, electronic surveying devices, trimetrogon photo mapping cameras, radar, electronic landing devices, and airborne magnetometers. As reported by Byrd, about 5,400 mi. of coastline was photographed as well as about 340,000 sq. mi. of previously unseen territory. The expedition was not without fatalities, as was the misfortune of all of Byrd's previous expeditions; four men were killed accidentally, a loss which might have been greater had not the survivors of a plane crash off Thurston Peninsula been rescued after an intensive search. Considerable scientific research was accomplished in addition to geographic exploration, particularly in meteorology, oceanography, glaciology, and material testing.

Expedition of 1955-1956. In December 1955 the Navy launched Operation Deepfreeze, with Rear Admiral Byrd as officer in charge. Laden with prefabricated buildings and over 9,000 tons of supplies, the expedition prepared for U.S. scientific studies in Antarctica during the International Geophysical Year, July 1957 to December 1958. Byrd was responsible for setting up a permanent administration unit of the U.S. antarctic undertakings. Operation Deepfreeze sent 1,800 men and seven ships, which included the icebreakers *Glacier*, *Edisto*, and *Eastwind*, the cargo ships, *Greenville Victory*, *Nespelen*, and *Wyandot*, and the freighter *Arneb* headed by Rear Adm. George J. Dufek, operations commander.

Byrd's flagship *Glacier*, of 8,625 tons displacement and 21,000 horsepower, landed at Ross Island on December 18. The expedition planned the establishment of two main bases, 447 mi. apart; in March, 166 Seabees and Navy specialists were left behind to build and man the bases. One, erected on the Ross Ice Shelf in the Little America region, is the chief U.S. scientific station. The other, on land far back in McMurdo Sound on the southern tip of Ross Island, is the Williams Air Operating Facility, named for a Seabee lost when his tractor broke through ice into 600 ft. of water. The Sound's thick ice provides runways for the heaviest planes. In December the *Glacier* reconnoitered an ice air strip which could receive the eight multi-engine planes waiting in New Zealand for a hazardous 2,400-mi. overwater flight. A helicopter team headed by Comdr. Gordon K. Ebbe took off from the *Glacier*, and red-flagged an 8,000-ft. strip along frozen McMurdo Sound, 35 mi. to the south near Hut Point. On December 20 four planes, two twin-engine Neptune P2V's and two four-engine Skymaster R5D's, successfully made the 2,400-mi. nonstop flight from New Zealand to McMurdo Sound. The two Skymasters were the first four-engine planes ever to fly in Antarctica and the first to land there on wheels alone. The four smaller aircraft, ski-wheel DC-3's and Grumman Albatross triphibians, had been forced to return to New Zealand because of adverse winds.

In ten spectacular survey flights from the McMurdo Sound ice strip between January 3 and January 14, U.S. Navy long-range planes of the Air Development Squadron Six observed approximately 800,000 sq. mi. of unknown territory—a sixth of Antarctica. These flights over the "area of inaccessibility," Antarctica's remotest region, revealed the highest area yet discovered; the polar plateau rises gently toward a level of roughly 14,000 ft.

On January 8, 1956, Byrd made his third flight to the South Pole, accompanied by his deputy, Dr. Siple; they flew in a four-engine Navy Skymaster R5D. Byrd and Siple discovered two ranges of mountains west of the Victoria Land peaks, and other ranges inland from Weddell Sea. They also noted evidence of slight glacial withdrawal, in such features as the bare mountains over broad areas and the ponds and bowl-like mountain cirques free from ice.

But for the Byrd Expeditions, knowledge of how to cope with extremes of cold would be far less advanced. Besides vast scientific knowledge, Byrd brought to the world the realization that the airplane is an important factor in exploration; with it he has unveiled most of the mysteries of the great continent of Antarctica within a generation. The training value of the expeditions is reflected in the fact that, not counting the purely military or naval personnel, well over 90 per cent of the men associated with them have put their specialized knowledge to the service of their country, many in positions of great responsibility. P. A. S.

BYRNES, JAMES FRANCIS [bɜ'rnz] (1879-), American politician and lawyer, was born in Charleston, S. C., on May 2, 1879. He left school at the age of fourteen, became a court reporter, studied law, and was admitted to the bar in 1903. In that year he bought and for four years edited the Aiken (S. C.) *Journal and Review,* and in 1908 he was elected solicitor, Second Circuit, South Carolina. He was later elected to Congress and served in the United States House of Representatives from 1911 until 1925. He ran unsuccessfully for the United States Senate in 1924, but was elected in 1930 and 1936. During President Franklin D. Roosevelt's second term, Byrnes allied himself actively with the group of moderate senators who opposed many New Deal domestic policies. Byrnes was appointed an associate justice of the United States Supreme Court in June 1941, but resigned in October 1942, to assume direction of the new Office of Economic Stabilization. He was appointed director of the Office of War Mobilization in May 1943, serving until April 1945, and attended the Yalta Conference in February 1945. Byrnes was appointed Secretary of State on June 30, 1945, accompanied President Harry S. Truman to the Potsdam Conference, and participated in the Big Three foreign ministers' councils in the fall of 1945. In 1946, he attended the United Nations Security Council sessions in London and New York. Later in the year he was an important figure at the peace conference held in Paris, at which peace treaties were negotiated and eventually signed, on Feb. 10, 1947, with Italy, Bulgaria, Hungary, Romania, and Finland. Byrnes resigned as Secretary of State on Jan. 7, 1947, and resumed his law practice. In 1950 he was elected governor of South Carolina, taking office on Jan. 10, 1951. He took a strong stand in favor of racial segregation in public schools, and in the 1952 Presidential campaign gave his support to the Republican candidate, Dwight D. Eisenhower. Governor Byrnes was named a delegate to the eighth United Nations General Assembly in September 1953. His term as governor expired in 1955. He is the author of *Speaking Frankly* (1947).

BYRON, GEORGE GORDON, 6th BARON BYRON [bai'rən] (1788-1824), English poet, letter-writer, traveler, and political figure, was born in London, Jan. 22, 1788. His father was Captain "Mad Jack" Byron, who died in France

in 1791 and whose daughter, Augusta, by a first marriage, was destined to play a crucial role in the poet's life. Byron was brought up partly by his eccentric mother, Catherine Gordon of Gight, and also at times by her London lawyer, John Hanson. A lame right foot, ignorantly treated, was a life-long embarrassment to Byron; but it did not prevent him from riding or from becoming a good swimmer, and it probably increased the notoriety of such later adventures as his swimming of the Hellespont in imitation of Leander. At Harrow, which he attended from 1801 to 1805, Byron took a definite part in school affairs, cricket, swimming, and orations, and for hours a day he lay dreaming on a slab in the churchyard, now pointed out as "Byron's Tomb." It was Harrow that educated him in the Classical studies that were to lend charm to his famous later pilgrimages in Italy and Greece. After leaving Harrow, Byron attended Trinity College, Cambridge, from 1805 to 1808, receiving the M.A. degree by peer's privilege after an irregular course. He had inherited the Byron title and the estate of Newstead Abbey from his great-uncle, the fifth baron, in 1798.

In 1809 Byron took his seat in the House of Lords, printed his first significant poem, *English Bards and Scotch Reviewers,* and began with his best friend, John Cain Hobhouse, the Mediterranean tour that produced the first two cantos of the autobiographical *Childe Harold's Pilgrimage* in March 1812. For a time, the success of this book made Byron the idol of London society, a romantic figure who looked and acted the moody character of his pilgrim. This dramatic quality also appeared in the darker and more mysterious heroes of a succession of eastern tales that now followed: *The Giaour* and *The Bride of Abydos* in 1813 and *The Corsair* and *Lara* in 1814. John Murray, Byron's London publisher and his faithful adviser, sold 10,000 copies of *The Corsair* on the day of publication. All of these works seem to reflect aspects of Byron's own life, whether in its actual events or in terms of Byron's inner emotions: *The Bride* is concerned with the tragic love of a brother and sister; *The Corsair* has a hero with a hidden past; *Lara* is also darkly piratical, and Byron liked to hint that he himself had known something of piracy. These romantic narratives surpassed in popularity those of Scott. Byron was by this time firmly established in the literary scene, and by 1816 his friends included Scott, Rogers, Moore, Leigh Hunt, Sheridan, and John Murray, as well as an array of lords and ladies at whom he was to laugh in the later cantos of *Don Juan.*

If Byron longed for relief from what had now become a dissipated life and from financial worries over Newstead Abbey, he found it suddenly in mixed fashion in the love, suggested above, that developed between him and his half-sister Augusta, now Mrs. Leigh, in 1813. This relationship became for him both a deep distress and a great inspiration; it apparently explains the fact that his marriage, in January 1815, to Miss Annabella Milbanke, a charming, well-educated girl and an heiress, was a failure and ended in separation a year later, shortly after the birth of a daughter, Ada. In 1816 Byron left England forever, torn by remorse and driven by social ostracism which his separation from his wife and his unpopular political position had called down upon him. Byron now resumed work on *Childe Harold's Pilgrimage.* A sense of fatality, the "star of his destiny," appears as the new Childe Harold, older in ideas and in experience, resumes his travels. In magnificent stanzas he describes the battlefields of Waterloo and the Rhine castles, surveys European war and literature, and dwells on the characters of Napoleon, Rousseau, Voltaire, and Gibbon, and on the grandeur of mountain and sea. This third canto owes much to the influence of Shelley, whom Byron now joined near Geneva, and to Shelley's introducing him anew to the poetry of Wordsworth. Byron and Shelley circumnavigated the lake, read Rousseau's *Nouvelle Héloïse,* and explored the castle of Chillon. A brief liaison with Claire Clairmont, a connection of Mary Shelley's, resulted in the birth of Byron's daughter Allegra, who died in an Italian convent at the age of six. Before the end of 1816 Byron, once again accompanied by Hobhouse, went on to Venice. Shelley took the manuscripts of the third canto of *Childe Harold* and *The Prisoner of Chillon* to London, where they were immediately published.

In Venice Byron wrote *Manfred* and *The Lament of Tasso,* accepting six hundred guineas for the two works. This was the first money he had taken for himself from a publisher. The fourth canto of *Childe Harold* begins in Venice on the Bridge of Sighs and views the history and art of Italy. In Venice Byron spent two years of utter debauchery and dissipation, living in a palace on the Grand Canal with an assortment of animals and a succession of common prostitutes. In April 1819 he met the young and beautiful Teresa, Countess Guiccioli, who immediately fell in love with him and soon afterward became his mistress. Byron, faced with the prospect of another serious liaison, had the choice of staying where he was, of fleeing from Teresa back to England, or of following her and her elderly husband to their palace in Ravenna, a city that was, in 1819, the center of revolutionary fervor against Austria. First he impulsively packed for England; the gondola and his goods were at the door. Then he decided on Ravenna. Teresa succeeded in understanding him in their ensuing relationship, and in his mixed career she was one of the few effective influences for his good.

Byron lived in Ravenna for two years till October 1821, a period of great social and literary activity. He had begun his vast satiric epic, *Don Juan,* in 1818, and was to write sixteen cantos of it by the time of his death six years later. The poem is uncompleted, but it remains Byron's most substantial and impressive achievement. Among other works of this last period in Ravenna, Pisa, and Genoa, are *The Prophecy of Dante* (1821), *Marino Faliero* (1821), *Cain* (1821), *The Vision of Judgment* (1822), and *The Island* (1823). In Ravenna, which he enjoyed more than any other city he lived in, he took the part of Teresa's family, the Gambas, in revolutionary agitation. The Gambas were ousted from the city, however, and Byron went on to Pisa, following Teresa, who was now separated from her husband by papal decree. In Pisa Byron and Shelley invited Leigh Hunt to come from London and edit a journal for their writings, *The Liberal,* but only four numbers appeared. In Pisa, too, Byron met E. J. Trelawny, an adventurer more Byronic than Byron, with whom Byron and Pietro Gamba were soon to depart for the revolution in Greece.

Early in 1823 Byron acceded to the call of the London Greek Committee, sold his yacht *Bolivar,* chartered a 120-ton brig, sailed from Genoa in July, and after various delays was received at Missolonghi with full military honors by the head of the Greek staff, Mavrocordato, who was to be three times prime minister of liberated Greece. But Byron's health was failing. He died, either from meningitis or an epileptic seizure, Apr. 19, 1824. His body was carried to England on a warship and buried in Hucknall Torkard Church, near Newstead.   R. A. R.

BYTOM [bi′tɔm] (*Ger.* Beuthen), a city in the Upper Silesian district of southwest Poland, located among low hills on the former German-Polish border, about 160 mi.

southwest of Warsaw, in the center of the Upper Silesian iron and coal industry. It is an important industrial city in which machinery is produced. Originally Bohemian, it became Prussian in 1742. After World War II it was ceded to Poland, and its name was changed from Beuthen to Bytom. Its population is now entirely Polish. Pop. 1946, 93,277; est. 1954, 121,000.   L. M. A.

BYZANTINE ARCHITECTURE [bɪza′ntɪn; bɪ′-zəntɪn; bɪza′ntɑɪn; bɪ′zəntɑɪn], the first of the great domical styles of architecture. It had its development in the large area dominated politically and culturally by Byzantium, later Constantinople (now Istanbul), capital of the East Roman Empire. Its active period extended from the sixth to the fifteenth centuries, preceded by a formative period and followed by a long period of derivative work. The origin of Byzantine style is the subject of deep controversy. F. A. Choisy, French archaeologist (1841-1909), and Josef Strzygowski, Austrian art critic (1862-1941), argued for a Near-Eastern origin, while G. T. Rivoira, Italian art critic (1849-1919), and his followers supported the cause of Roman influence. The fact remains that elements common to each area are ingredients of the developed Byzantine procedure in building. These may be defined as a color-incrusted domical style with the structural fabric composed of arches, vaults, and domes supported on massive piers by means of pendentives or squinches. The Byzantine is the first and only occidental style to join a dominant richness of color to vital, rationally controlled, structural forms of high functional integrity.

Development. At the time of its development, there already existed in the Mediterranean region the essential elements of the Byzantine style. The basilican plan occurred throughout the entire region in the multicolumned, timber-roof type of the Early Christian church, and in various examples of the Roman basilica with vaults supported on a few widely spaced massive piers, buttressed by barrel vaults, as the Basilica of Maxentius (312), Rome. The central-type plan was to be found in a variety of forms, as Minerva Medica, built in the third century, Rome; St. Costanza (or Tomb of Constantine) built between 326 and 329, in Rome; the Orthodox Baptistry, built in the fifth century, in Ravenna; and St. Stefano Rotondo, fifth century, in Rome. The cruciform plan existed in simple form in the Tomb of Galla Placidia, fifth century, in Ravenna. The domed-cross-in-square plan was found in a Roman tomb (second century A.D.) at Kusr-en-Nêuijîs in Palestine. In this instance, the central area was covered by a dome continuous with the pendentives and buttressed by barrel vaults, while the re-entrant angles of the cross each contained a small chamber.

The pendentive, which allowed the structural development of the style, was also known from at least the second century. It was used in the middle of the fifth century in Hagia Sophia, Salonika, but in a tentative form, without true spherical triangles.

The coloristic richness of Byzantine work and its plastic emphasis were known in Asia Minor, and the boldness of its engineering was preceded by the daring of Roman work during the empire. Yet, it must be acknowledged that the Byzantine builders used these elements primarily as a point of departure and developed them with a new artistic and rational discernment, which, by the sixth century, had fused them into a definitely new style of marked individuality and great structural integrity. In the process, they succeeded in perfecting the arcuated principle of construction in Hagia Sophia, Constantinople, as the Greeks, a thousand years earlier, had perfected the post-and-lintel principle of construction in the Parthenon.

Periods. The K. J. Conant chronology divides Byzantine architecture into seven periods: (1) period of gestation (395-527), Proto-Byzantine architecture experimentation in Italy, Egypt, Syria, Anatolia, and Macedonia; (2) First Golden Age (527-726), a period of great political power and marked architectural activity; (3) Iconoclastic Age (726-867), period of internal strife and political instability, little architectural activity; (4) Second Golden Age (867-1204), period of renewed political power and architectural activity; (5) Latin domination (1204-1261), period of great national disaster and loss of sovereignty, no architectural activity; (6) Byzantine Renaissance (1261-1453), weak, but stately revival, architectural activity largely in the Balkans; (7) period of derivations (1453 to present), end of Byzantine Empire

layers in turn. This produced a dome economical to build (in an area where wood for centering was scarce) and of greatly reduced outward dome thrust, owing to its almost monolithic character when completed.

Structure. The structural ease and efficiency of the Byzantine method of constructing vaults and domes did not in itself permit the perfection of a domical style of architecture. Previously, great domes had been built on circular plan units. If a great national style was to develop, essentially domical in principle, it was necessary that it be flexible enough to meet the requirements of complex buildings containing apartments of a wide variety of shapes and sizes. Consequently, other means of support for the dome had to be found to permit it to rest on a square plan unit.

Roman precedent did not supply the answer, since it used the domical method of construction in confusion with the

Citadel (to rear of Mameluk Tombs) at Cairo, Egypt

but continuation of architectural influence in Russia, the Balkans and Mohammedan areas.

Materials. Although stone was used in eastern Russia, Armenia, Syria, Crete, and Cyprus, the predominant structural material in the area dominated by Constantinople was large, flat, hard-fired brick (approximately 16 in. by 21 in. by 1½ in.) held together with mortar of a markedly strong and adhesive quality that permitted wide joints to be used with safety. Three or four courses of brick frequently alternated with a course of cut stone or marble to add strength or enhance the decorative effect.

Architectural details, such as columns, capitals, inset panels, grills, wall veneers, and paving, were of various marbles or porphyry. Vaulted members and vertical surfaces in the upper zones of the interiors were covered with rich mosaics of precious glass tesserae, carefully set in layers of specially prepared mortar.

Vaults and domes were mainly constructed of brick, laid in courses radiating to the spring line of the opposite side of the dome or vault, rather than to its center, thus making the courses flatter in slope. The strongly adhesive mortar largely eliminated wood centering as used by the Romans. It permitted each course of a dome to be constructed, allowed to set, and then form the support for each of the next

post-and-lintel method without achieving the pendentive on a grand scale; its domical structures neither departed from the circular plan, nor ever quite forsook the principle of the lintel in construction. Consequently, application of the Roman method failed to solve the problem of a complete domical system.

It was the Greek intellect working in Constantinople, under the stimulus of the past engineering triumphs of Imperial Rome, that first scientifically comprehended the full significance of the pendentive, previously used in only a tentative fashion.

In Hagia Sophia, Constantinople, built between 532 and 537, the pendentive was perfected, providing with mathematical accuracy perfect structural support for a great dome over a square plan unit. The designers fully grasped the significance of their achievement, and proceeded to apply the same logic to the development of pure arcuated principles throughout Hagia Sophia. The arch, vault, semidome, and dome, all supported on piers, were made the structural determinants. The column itself was relegated to secondary importance to serve as a colonnaded screen between great piers, or utilized in other minor ways as a scale-giving element. The classic orders were abolished, and a plastic conception of design in plan, section, and elevation took definite

Hagia Sophia at Istanbul, Turkey, an impressive example of a dome on pendentives.

form, justly expressing in all its parts an arcuated emphasis. Engineering was daring, yet controlled by strict functional design, so that the whole fabric became a fixed or predetermined mass yielding a closed organism as incapable of expansion or contraction as a Vermeer painting or a Brahms symphony, thus satisfying the requirements of completeness of form conception.

Exterior Design. In general, the external effect was dominated by the dome, or domes, which sprang from the massive bulk of the church proper, buttressed by one or more apses capped by an exposed semidome, and buttressed by vaulted aisles of one or two stories. Fenestration was arched and fitted with grilles or perforated slabs. Doors were frequently of bronze with applied reliefs, bosses, and borders.

The effect was one of compact power and strength as opposed to the soaring lightness of the Gothic cathedral. Walls were of brick and stone, or entirely of stone in regions where that building material was readily available. In early work, little exterior enrichment was used, and domes tended to be low in mass. In later work, the dome was often set on a drum pierced with windows, or with the windows projecting into its base. The late churches were taller, and the whole effect somewhat more vertical. Likewise, more elaboration was general in the use of marble veneer, blind and open arcades, engaged columns, groups of windows, niches, molded string courses, and cornices. A projecting foreporch and an appended chapel were frequently found

in late work, which may be said to be smaller in scale than early work, but still most skillfully designed on rhythmic and plastic principles.

Interior Design. The Byzantine builders dispensed with the classic orders, as such, and produced in their place columnar supports, capitals, cornices, moldings, and friezes more suited to the spirit of their architecture. It was usual to have a stilted arch spring directly from the capital in Byzantine work, contrary to classic practice. To express this new use, the designers: (1) redesigned the classic Corinthian and Ionic capitals with a more compact and solid mass, reducing undercutting and projecting motifs to make them more structural; (2) inserted the pulvino or dosseret (a strong truncated wedge-shaped block of marble) between the base of the arch and the capital, to transfer the weight carried through the wider arch to the narrower capital and shaft below; and (3) united pulvino and capital into a single functional design, of great variety and expressive beauty, called a pulvinated capital.

In general, capitals were of white marble, sculptured by the drill technique and enriched with gold; bases were likewise of molded white marble in contrast to the richly colored marble or porphyry shafts (often red, blue, or green). It should be noted that the column was used in a protected position, as in an arcade connecting the structural piers; the combination of pier, arch, vault, and dome was the structural signature of the arcuated style. Throughout a Byzantine church, this plastic conception is constantly expressed, with the dome proving the dominant—indeed the controlling—element in design.

The general interior effect was of great aesthetic distinction. Granting the structural achievement of Byzantine architecture, its great glory lies in the splendor of its controlled and functional decoration, that was at once supremely logical and vibrantly emotional. In its fusion of the mind and senses, it stands unequalled in the whole range of architectural history, with the possible exception of the thirteenth-century French Gothic cathedral.

With almost an Oriental sense of privacy, the Byzantines concentrated their decoration within the building, rather than on its exterior. It was here that the great lessons in the use of controlled decoration were stated. There are four main component parts to this structural decoration. They are: (1) mosaics or tempera wall painting; (2) varied marble veneers, columns, carved capitals, carved or inlaid friezes, panels, and the like; (3) the plastically expressive architectural forms that control the first two; and (4) the carefully calculated use of light as an active ingredient in the over-all decorative effect.

These four component parts are so integrated that separate analysis is never complete. Floors were paved with marble in geometric designs. It was usual to veneer the lower part of the walls on the interior with panels of different richly colored marbles so cut that the veining

jewellike material, with roughly fractured edges, to catch the light. Gold and silver tesserae were formed by fusing a thin sheet of the precious metal between two layers of glass. Each tessera varied in size, and the surface was purposely kept irregular so that the light would reflect from it in various points of light.

In preparing a surface for mosaics, a scratch coat of fairly coarse lime was applied to the masonry and a second, finer coat followed. When this had dried, the designs were sketched on it, and the mosaicist then spread the area to be covered, immediately, with a coat of special mortar. Finally, the squares of precious glass were firmly pressed into it, following the designs previously applied. In this way, a certain spontaneity was possible, a permanence assured, and the finished mosaic literally became a part of the building structure.

Backgrounds were generally of shimmering gold mosaics, studded with silver tesserae. Occasionally, vibrant blue or green was used for the background in the early work. The pictorial designs were strategically placed against the background and included Biblical incidents, saints, court personages, symbols, floral motifs, and borders—all designed with a hieratic reserve and abstract in spirit, as opposed to the naturalism of Classic art.

As in the case of painting, region and time affected the designs in a definite degree. In a single mosaic, as many

Interior view of Hagia Sophia

had a design interest. These were banded with a different colored marble either plain or sculptured, to draw the whole series together. Occasional use was made of inset panels carved in low relief with stylized linear decoration such as vines and peacocks. A marble string course, cornice, or frieze, either plain, molded, carved, or inlaid, separated the marble wall treatment from the curved and vaulted upper areas, usually on a line with the springing of the vaults. These upper zones were reserved for the mosaics; in late work, tempera wall painting was used as a substitute.

Mosaics. The mosaics were composed of small pieces of

as fifty different colors or shades of colors were used. When seen against the curving surfaces of the architectural forms, and from the floor level, illuminated by the ever changing shafts of light, they took on strangely moving effects of beauty. Indeed, the whole interior of a Byzantine church thus decorated presents a color-charged richness that is unequalled in any other style, and remains one of the chief glories of our architectural heritage. St. Mark's, Venice; St. Luke of Stiris at Phocis, Greece; Church of the Chora, Constantinople; Tomb of Galla Placidia, Ravenna; and parts of many others are leading examples of this art.

St. Mark's, Venice, Italy

Church Furniture. The four main elements of church furniture were: the altar, iconostasis (choir screen), ambo (pulpit), and the baptismal font. These varied in degrees of richness, most being of plain, inlaid, or sculptured marble. Special examples were remarkably lavish, such as the gold, jewelled and enamel altar frontal, and the sculptured silver iconostasis that old accounts report at Hagia Sophia, Constantinople. Lighting fixtures were in the form of bronze, silver, or gold candelabra, and chandeliers holding glass bowls for oil and floating wicks, as recorded in Procopius.

PLAN TYPES

There are five main types of Byzantine church plans. Each varies somewhat according to region and date.

Basilican Plan. The basilican type was early introduced in Constantinople, as in the reported plan of the first church on the site of Hagia Sophia, and as still evidenced there in St. John the Baptist of the Studion, begun 463. Since this plan type was not utilized in the metropolis after the fifth century, it should be observed that it was largely Early Christian of the Roman school in structural character.

It was a three-aisle, timber-roofed basilica, with arcaded side aisles supported on marble columns with Corinthianesque capitals, and approached through a wide narthex and atrium. Variation from the Roman type occurred in its having second story aisles (*gynacaeum,* or women's gallery), the

apse being expressed polygonally on the exterior, and in being broad for its width.

In contrast to the Constantinopolitan area, the basilican plan continued to be used in Greece in both the simple and more developed form, involving barrel or groin vaulting of nave and side aisles, and use of the prothesis and diaconicon. Examples of this are: St. Philip in Athens and the church at Calabacca (both sixth century and with timber truss roofs); St. Anargyre and St. Stephen at Castoria (both barrel vaulted and from the eleventh century); and the church of Hagia Sophia at Ochrida, Yugoslavia (tenth century), with barrel vaults and superimposed side apses at the east end. The simple basilican plan, however, did not prove a useful vehicle for developed Byzantine design.

Simple-Central Plan. In either round or polygonal form, the central type was used throughout Byzantine architecture. The simpler form (baptistry of Hagia Sophia, Constantinople) stems from Roman mausolea or circular plan units found in the Roman Baths. The more complex type (SS. Sergius and Bacchus, Constantinople) has a closer plan connection with Minerva Medica, Rome; the Constantinian Church of the Holy Sepulchre, Jerusalem; or St. Stefano Rotondo, Rome. St. Vitale (built 526-547), Ravenna, with central nave and eight radiating apses was useful in establishing the essentially domical nature of Byzantine architecture, although the pendentive was neither employed here nor in the related church of SS. Sergius and Bacchus (527). Both these churches used semidomes as abutments to the central dome, and thus contributed to the major development of this procedure on a grand scale in Hagia Sophia, Constantinople, and likewise to the later churches built on the quatrefoil plan. Choisy believed that the domed octagonal church (SS. Sergius and Bacchus) likewise influenced the plan type of such monastery churches as Daphni and St. Luke of Stiris in Phocis, Greece.

While aesthetically successful, the simple central plan, in either of its forms, lost favor owing to its relatively large amount of waste space and its somewhat restricted nave area.

Domed-Basilica Plan. The domed-basilica plan features a domed, longitudinal nave and absence of projecting transepts. Side aisles extend the length of the nave and support a women's gallery that frequently continued across the west end of the church.

Hagia Sophia, Constantinople, is the classic example of this plan type at its best. It is marked by complete sanity of structural articulation, except for visible means of opposing the diagonal thrust of the dome. With its extended nave, it provided an ideal solution, from both practical and aesthetic points of view, for the functioning of the church ritual. St. Irene (532, with eighth-century alterations) and the Church of the Chora (527, with remodelling in seventh, ninth, and eleventh centuries), both at Constantinople, are other examples of this important plan type.

While Josef Strzygowski (1862-1941) gave it Eastern origin, this plan type must acknowledge some dependence on Roman precedent as evidenced in the Basilica of Maxentius, Rome. A less significant variant of the domed-basilica plan is found in Greece (Church of the Panaghia of the late thirteenth century), in the Brontochion monastery at Mistra. According to Strzygowski, this latter type stems from Asia Minor and Syria as evidenced by the fifth-century church at Miriamlik, near Seleucia. Its fault lies in its lack of structural clarity, since the dome appears casually suspended over two bays of a uniformly arcaded nave, without functionally expressing, by means of piers, the added support necessary for the dome.

Cross-of-Domes Plan. While a recognized Byzantine type, the cross-of-domes plan found scant usage. It is identified by its exposed cross plan formed by the nave and broad transept. The crossing and the four arms of the cross are marked by exposed domes, supported on massive piers, through which the aisles penetrate (St. Mark's, Venice).

Both the interior and exterior present effects of great plastic beauty, but it is the single important exception to the Byzantine concept of church planning on the theory of the fixed or predetermined mass, yielding a closed organism, since it is capable of expansion without destroying its organic unity. Since the re-entrant angles of the plan are left open, there is little abutment to the diagonal thrust of the central dome. There is reference to a church of this type at Gaza, on the site of the temple of Marnas, which was destroyed in 402.

The Church of the Holy Apostles, Constantinople, as extended by Justinian, was a famous example and served as the prototype for the remodeled St. Mark's, Venice, which is the outstanding extant Byzantine example of the cross-of-domes plan. Its influence may be traced in such Romanesque churches as St. Front, Périgueux, and the cathedral at Angoulême.

Domed-Cross-in-Square Plan. In its developed form, the domed-cross-in-square plan is a frequent and beautiful type, primarily used in relatively small churches. It is characterized by the cross-inscribed-within-a-square plan, the use of five domes—central dome and one over each of the four corner bays formed between the re-entrant angles between nave and transept; hence, differently placed than in the cross-of-domes plan—a vertically emphasized mass, and effects of symmetry about the horizontal and vertical axes of the plan. This type is doubtless a development from the domed basilica.

The first important example was the Church of the Nea, Constantinople (now destroyed), built by Basil I, between

THE BASILICA OF SAN VITALE, RAVENNA, ITALY

867 and 886. Other examples are: St. Mary Diaconissa (ninth century) and SS. Peter and Mark (ninth century), in Constantinople; the church of the Panaghia (eleventh century); the smaller church of the Monastery of St. Luke of Stiris in Phocis; and, St. Theodore (twelfth century), Constantinople. Among the many variations in this plan type are those with composite, trefoil additions at the east end as found in several instances on Mt. Athos (Vatopedi of the eleventh century and Chilandari of the thirteenth century).

Other Types of Buildings. As in church architecture, the work prior to the age of Justinian bore the closer resemblance to Roman building. Slowly, adjustments in design came in that more fully reflected the changed climate, the different materials available, and closer contacts with Asia Minor. Unlike Diocletian's palace at Spalato, Dalmatia, or the palace at Antioch, the Byzantine palace became a complex assembly of more or less separate, incredibly lavish, one- and two-story structures set in a vast parklike area, somewhat resembling the Kremlin. Scant remains exist of private dwellings.

Monasteries originated in the retreats of the hermits, and developed through a grouping of relatively independent units into the coenobium for a religious community. This finally evolved into a developed monastic plan of a walled enclosure with the church in the center and the abbot's residence, cells, refectory, and offices on the periphery, as at Chilandari on Mt. Athos.

Town planning acknowledged some dependence on Rome with principal thoroughfares marked by commemorative arches, columns, and statuary. Fountains were important features, and streets were often arcades with shops opening directly into the arcades, somewhat as in Bologna. The forum was a center of public life, and entertainment was provided by theatres, hippodromes, and baths that were less complex than Roman examples. Public buildings were imposing.

Fortifications were well developed with triple lines of defense in city walls, or by chains of forts. Bridges, highways, aqueducts, reservoirs, and vaulted cisterns were well developed and engineered.   J. G. Van D.

BYZANTINE EMPIRE, the name which is generally applied by the majority of historians to the Eastern Roman Empire, but more particularly to that portion which still survived at the beginning of the seventh century of the Christian Era. After Justinian's death in 565 his successors were unable to defend the dominions they had inherited. Much of reconquered Italy fell to the Lombards, and the advance of the Avars and Slavs into the Balkans destroyed the Latin civilization of Illyria. In this period the Eastern Roman Empire lost most of its ties with the West and became essentially a Greek kingdom, with only a slight Roman character. Centered about Constantinople, which was originally called Byzantium, the empire gained the fitting name of Byzantine. This centralization was furthered by the Arab conquests of the seventh century, which took from the empire the provinces of Syria, Egypt, and Africa, and the control of the southern Mediterranean.

HISTORY OF THE EMPIRE

Formative Period. *Reforms of Diocletian and Constantine.* The separation of the eastern and western halves of the old Roman Empire in A.D. 395, with their ethnic and cultural differences, had begun with the administrative reforms of Diocletian, who reigned from A.D. 284 to 305.

When Constantine established the capital of the empire at Byzantium (Constantinople) on the Bosporus in A.D. 330, it was a recognition of the economic and political importance of the eastern half. Even before this time the old Roman Empire of the first century, with its city-state system of government, had become a highly centralized monarchy under a divinely constituted emperor. With the economic decay of the Roman Empire, barter took the place of a money economy. The free peasant cultivators became servile, and the cities fell into financial difficulties and lost their local independence to the growing bureaucracy of the central government.

Under Diocletian and Constantine a caste system was instituted in which the people became virtually slaves of the state. With the decadence of the West and its classical culture, Eastern influences grew stronger, politically, in the divine-right monarchy, as well as in philosophy, art, and religion. Constantine accepted Christianity as the favored religion, and his successors made it the religion of the state, outlawing the pagan cults. The eastern provinces of the Roman Empire, which had been superficially Romanized, remained more vigorous culturally and economically than those in the West. More and more they tended to become the center of a new theocratic monarchy.

Barbarian Invasion of West. In the latter part of the fourth century the barbarians began to break into the weakened Roman Empire, but it was the western half which crumbled before them. A century later imperial rule had disappeared throughout the western provinces. Britain had long since been abandoned to the native Romanized Celts and to the heathen Angles and Saxons, who soon invaded from the south and east. Spain had fallen to the Visigoths, Italy to the Ostrogoths, northern Africa to the Vandals, and Gaul to the Franks and Burgundians. The eastern part of the empire survived partly because the barbarians were mainly attracted to the western provinces, but also because of its greater vitality and the strength and wealth of Constantinople. Unlike Rome, which had been a political center, Constantinople by the end of the fifth century had become a great commercial metropolis.

Reconquests of Justinian. In the sixth century a series of vigorous and capable emperors appeared, to maintain the Roman law and administrative system, and to defend and even to expand the Eastern Roman Empire. The greatest of these was Justinian, who reigned from 527 to 565. Justinian's administrative reforms, codification of Roman law, and building of the great church of St. Sophia at Constantinople were matched by his military exploits. Imbued with the idea of restoring Roman rule over the lost provinces of the West, Justinian engaged in a long series of wars which reconquered northern Africa, Italy, and a part of southern Spain. Belisarius was his outstanding general.

Struggle for Survival. But the conquest was only temporary. The empire was not strong enough to hold these distant possessions. Soon after Justinian's death the Lombards invaded Italy and left to the empire only scattered parts of the coast. In Spain also, the imperial possessions were soon reduced by the Visigoths to a few seaports. The policy of reconquest had been unwise, exhausting the financial strength of the empire while the Sassanid Empire in Persia and the Avars and Slavs on the Danube made ready to move across the frontier. While his attention was fixed on regaining territories in the West, Justinian had to neglect what he already possessed.

Wars of Heraclius. Under Justinian's successors a prolonged war was waged with the Persians, and the Balkans were ravaged repeatedly by hordes of Avars and Slavs. It was not until Heraclius secured the throne in 610 that a worthy successor to Justinian appeared. But for a dozen years his enemies advanced, the Avars penetrating even to the walls of Constantinople, and the Persians conquering Syria and most of Asia Minor and invading Egypt. By 619 the situation was so desperate that Heraclius bought off the Avars and devoted everything to the preparation for war against the Persians. In a great offensive lasting from 622 to 628 Heraclius defeated the Persians and restored the frontier as it had existed under the emperor Maurice, who reigned from 582 to 602.

Arab Invasions. The triumph of the empire again was short-lived. Within a decade all of Heraclius' reconquests were lost to the new Arab Moslem power. Both Persia and the empire were exhausted by war and could not withstand the advance of the fanatical Arabs. The Persian empire was overrun, and the Moslems were stopped in their sweep around the eastern Mediterranean only when they reached the gates of Constantinople. Although they were later driven from Asia Minor, the Arabs retained Syria, Egypt, and Africa, due as much to general discontent in those lands over taxation and religious strife as to the Arabs' fighting ability. When the last attack on Constantinople was repulsed in 718 by Leo III, the empire was left with only the Balkans—where the Bulgarians had already entrenched themselves—Asia Minor, Sicily, and scattered portions of the coastal areas in Italy.

Religious Strife. But the empire had enough vitality to live on for more than seven centuries. Leo III and his Isaurian dynasty had brought a revival of strength which held the Moslems and the Bulgarians in check. He began the long campaign against the use of images and pictures in Christian worship, which produced much internal strife and furthered the separation between the eastern and western parts of the Church. The struggle came to an end in 843 with an imperial edict which formally restored the use of images. During this period imperial rule almost ended in Italy and Sicily, and the state was threatened by the rise of a feudal, landed aristocracy and the continued growth of an overcomplex bureaucracy.

The Macedonian Dynasty (867-1081). After the passing of the Moslem danger, the Byzantine government became increasingly incompetent, filled with palace intrigues in which evil women played a large part. The Empress Irene (797-802) gained the throne after blinding and deposing her own son, but she lost it by one of the insurrections which thereafter became common. The worst of a long line of decadent rulers was Michael III (842-867), "the Drunkard," whose favorite was a former Macedonian horse-trainer named Basil. Rising from chief equerry to co-emperor, Basil eventually murdered Michael and became sole emperor (867-886), thus founding the great Macedonian dynasty, which was in control during the most brilliant period of later Byzantine history.

Era of Progress. Basil I issued some law books to supplement Justinian's code, reformed the finances of the state, and called a general council in an attempt to settle various ecclesiastical disputes between the Pope and the Patriarch of Constantinople. It was not until 898, after the death of Basil I, that a temporary settlement was made between the two churches. The son and grandson of Basil were scholars who wrote important books dealing mainly with administration, and they did much to encourage learning in the empire. But the morality of the court continued to decline. In the later tenth century it was dominated by the Empress Theo-phano, who was accused of a number of murders, including those of her two husbands and a father-in-law.

Military Victories. Her second husband was the great general, Nicephorus Phocas, who carried on a triumphant campaign against the Moslems, extending the empire into the northern part of Syria. He was assassinated by his nephew, John Zimisces, with the connivance of Empress Theophano. John succeeded him as emperor, but had to leave the war in Asia to fight against the Russians, who under Prince Vladimir occupied Bulgaria and demanded tribute from the empire. The campaign of John Zimisces in mid-tenth century ended in a great victory against the Russians, who were driven beyond the Danube. The eastern part of Bulgaria became a Byzantine province. Under Basil II (976-1025), John's successor, the rest of the Bulgarian kingdom was conquered and added to the empire. Friendly relations were established with Prince Vladimir, and arrangements were made for trade between the two states. The Russians accepted Christianity and ecclesiastical rule from Constantinople, which paved the way for the penetration of Byzantine cultural influences into Russia.

Turkish Invasion. After the death of Basil II in 1025 the Byzantine Empire suffered another relapse. The second of Basil's daughters died unmarried in 1056, ending the Macedonian line. Generally incompetent rulers followed, who secured the throne through palace intrigue, since no orderly system of succession had been established. Under them the last vestiges of imperial rule in Italy ended, an open breach developed between the papacy and the Church at Constantinople, and a fresh Moslem offensive endangered imperial possessions in Asia. This last was caused by the expansion of the power of the Seljuk Turks throughout the Saracen state. In 1071 they annihilated the army of Romanus IV at Manzikert. At one stroke the military power of the empire was destroyed, and all Asia Minor was lost except for a few places on the coast. At the same time the Normans from southern Italy were threatening attack from the west.

The Comneni and the Angeli (1081-1204). The Emperor Alexius Comnenus, who came to the throne in 1081, was able to recover the possessions on the Macedonian coast which had been lost to the Normans, but had to appeal to the Pope and the western princes for aid against the Turks. Thinking to secure a force of mercenary adventurers, Alexius was embarrassed by the great crusading armies led by land-hungry nobles.

Crusades. The Crusaders warded off the menace of the Turk, but in the end they caused the ruin of the empire. The Fourth Crusade was diverted from Egypt to Constantinople mainly through the influence of the Venetians, who wished to obtain a better trading position in the Aegean and Black seas. Since the Crusaders were in debt to them for transportation and supplies, and were chiefly adventurers interested more in plunder than fighting the Turks, the Venetians were able to gain their way. The excuse for the attack was that Emperor Isaac Angelus had been deposed and blinded by his brother, Alexius III, and that Isaac's son, Alexius IV, had sought aid to gain the throne. Alexius IV was the brother-in-law of King Philip of Swabia, who supported the project. Pope Innocent III did not act too decisively to block the attack on Constantinople, possibly because he hoped to gain control over the schismatic Greek Church.

Decline and Collapse. Constantinople fell to the Crusaders in the fall of 1203. Isaac and Alexius were restored, but when they refused to fulfill the impossible demands of the Crusaders, the city was stormed again in 1204 and given over to plunder. Most of the empire was divided up among the leaders of the expedition and the Venetians, who got trade concessions and most of the islands. A small part of the Byzantine Empire continued to exist in Asia Minor. Count Baldwin of Flanders became the Emperor of the new Latin Empire of Constantinople. It lasted until 1261, when Greek rule was restored at Constantinople under the Palaeologue dynasty; but much of Greece remained in the hands of French nobles, and the islands and coasts of the Peloponnesus were kept by Venice.

The great days of the Byzantine Empire were past, and it was gradually reduced by the advance of the Slavs and Bulgars from the north, and the Ottoman Turks from the south. The Slavs and Bulgars eventually fell back exhausted, but by 1355 the Turks held all of Asia Minor. They began plundering expeditions across the Dardanelles into Thrace. The weakness of the empire encouraged the Turks to conquer the Balkans. Constantinople was left isolated for a long time, with only a few remaining outlying possessions. In 1453 the new Ottoman sultan, Mohammed II, besieged the city and forced it to surrender.

BYZANTINE CIVILIZATION

The Byzantine Empire, at the crossroads between the East and West, was subjected to racial and cultural influences from both directions. The population was distinctly cosmopolitan, a mixture of many races, but unity of culture was achieved through the use of the Greek language and the supremacy of the Greek Orthodox faith. Elements of strength resulted also from the efficient administrative organization inherited from the late Roman Empire, and from the economic prosperity, which was at its height from the eighth to the eleventh centuries. Constantinople was in a strategic position as a commercial metropolis, with a network of trade routes connecting it on the west with Italy and Greece, on the north with Russia, and on the east with Egypt, Syria, Persia, and the Far East. In addition, the highly skilled craftsmen of Constantinople and other cities of the empire produced in their workshops a variety of luxury goods for the trade.

Occupying this strategic and almost impregnable position, Constantinople was one of the most splendid and magnificent cities of the Middle Ages, and was the vital center of the Byzantine world. In the field of literature and learning Byzantine civilization was distinctly conservative. The Greek classics were the basis of education, and an excessive veneration for them prevented the development of a creative spirit. Except in the field of historical writing, where vitality existed, the main contribution of Byzantine literature was in the important task of preserving the Greek classics by copying texts, and in the production of encyclopedias and commentaries.

It was in the field of art that Byzantine culture achieved its most original and creative expression. Great churches, such as the Church of St. Sophia, and the decorative arts of mosaics, frescoes, sculpture, and ivory and jewel carvings express the spirit of Byzantine culture. From Constantinople the cultural influences spread westward to Italy, especially to Ravenna and Rome, and northward into the Slavic world. In the ninth century the Bulgar khan accepted the Greek Orthodox faith and the civilization accompanying it. The Russian Slavs in the tenth century also accepted this faith, similarly acquiring the Greek culture. *See also* BYZANTINE ARCHITECTURE; PAINTING (*Byzantine Painting*). F. C. H.

BYZANTIUM. *See* İSTANBUL.

C

C. Unlike most of the letters of the alphabet, *C* does not appear among the more ancient letter forms. It is derived directly from the classical Latin. Its corresponding third place in the alphabet of the original Semitic and of the Greek derivatives is known as ⅃ *gimel* and Γ *gamma*, respectively (hard *G*). The Etruscans, from whom the Romans adapted their alphabet, retained *K* for a time as the sign of *Kh* (from *kaph-kappa*), but around 400 B.C. they abandoned the sign for this sound; and because they made no distinction between the unvoiced and voiced *k* and *g* and discarded *k* and *q* in their spelling, they adopted *C* as the symbol for *g* and *k*. In the Latin, ⟨ or *C* was retained to represent such abbreviations as *C* for Gaius and *CN* for Gnaeus. The Etruscans chose *C* (as *k*) to be used only before *e* and *i; K* before *a;* and *Q* before *u*, there being no *o* in the Etruscan alphabet. The Latin alphabet adopted all three of these letters with these sound values, but eventually dropped the *K* except as the initial of well-known or official words (for example, *Kalendae*), using *C* for both the sounds of *g* and *k* and retaining *Q* for the *k* sound when followed by *u*. During the third century (around 250 B.C.), *C* was changed to *G* for the sound of hard *g*, and was given sixth place in the alphabet. Note the development of the C form in the accompanying table.

Pronunciation. Because of its palatalization in front of the palatal vowels *e* and *i*, Latin *c*, which had once only the value of *k*, has taken over new values, all palatal or dental: *ce, ci* are pronounced *če, či* in Italian and Romanian; *se, si* in French, English, Andalusian, and Spanish-American; and *þe, þi* in Castilian Spanish. German received from the French schools in Carolingian times the Old French articulation *tse, tsi*, which it still preserves, as in *Cicero, Accent;* but it frequently writes also *z: Akzent* (but not *Zizero*). The sign *c* has the same value in the Latin alphabets adopted by Western Slavic languages (Polish, Czech, Slovak, Lusatian, Croat, Slovenian); the other Slavs use the Cyrillic alphabet. For the sound *č* (English *ch*) these alphabets introduced the new sign *č* or (in Polish) the digraph *cz.*

The palatalization of Latin *c* in *ce, ci*, which started during the early centuries of the Christian Era, has had on all Western Latin alphabets the undesirable effect of giving a different value to *c* in the two groups *ce, ci* and *ca, co, cu*. Inversely, these same alphabets are confronted with the problem of finding a fitting representation for the sound *k* in front of *e* and *i*: Italian has *ch(e), ch(i)*; Spanish and French, *qu(e), qu(i)*, since the Latin groups *que, qui* had come to be pronounced *ke, ki;* English and German, more reasonably, *k(e)* and *k(i)*. Old French adopted the digraph *ch* for the (new) French *č* in *chanter, chambre,* preserved in English *chant, chamber.* In French this *č* became *š*, whereas the English *ch* preserved the older articulation. However, the digraph *ch* is sometimes pronounced *k* in English words of Greek origin (*echo, chaos, archaeology*) and *š* (*sh*) in some French words of recent importation: *champagne, chic, machine, chauffeur, chaise* (the same word as the older *chair* with *ch = č*). Spanish also adopted (from France) *ch* as *č*, whereas Italian used *ch* for *k* before *e* and *i* (*see above*); and German, following a Latin usage, adopted it for its new as-

pirate *ch* (also as in Scottish *loch*). The ancient Latin value of *c* as *k* even in front of *e* and *i* is still preserved in Irish and Welsh. In German and English the letter *c* could well be suppressed, except in the digraph *ch*, for other letters are capable of performing its functions with less ambiguity.

Uses. Because of its third position, *C* is generally the sign of fair or average quality, as in school marks. In footwear, it indicates an average width. In algebra, *c* denotes the third

Origin	Form
Cretan Hieroglyphic	⌐
Semitic	⌐ ⌐
Early Phoenician	⌐ ⌐
Cypro-Phoenician	∧ ⌐
Early Hebrew	⌐ ⌐
Greek Ninth Century B.C.	⌐ ⌐
Greek Eighth Century B.C.	⌐
Crete Seventh Century B.C.	∧
Boeotia Eighth-Seventh Century B.C.	⌐
Etruscan	⌐ ⟨ ⟨ ⟩ ⌐
Latin Fourth Century B.C. Capitals . .	⟨ C
Latin Third Century A.D. Uncials . .	⟨ C
Slavic Cyrillic	Γ
German	ℭ
English	C

known quantity, as in $(a + b + c)$, and in Roman numerals C denotes 100. In the Elizabethan system of numerology, it represented 3. In outlining, it may denote the third co-ordinate item or the third subordinate entry. In music, C occupies the unique position of being the keynote of the most fundamental of the scales, known as "natural" because it requires no accidentals. On the piano keyboard all the keys of this scale are white. C represents also notes on the treble and bass scores. Middle C is the central key of the piano and organ keyboard. Together with F and G, the note C indicates one of the three clefs. A short clarinet is voiced in C. In design, C is used to denote objects approaching this curved form, as in C clamp, C spring. Because of its being easily confused with *G* as a letter design and more likely because many scientific symbols are based upon the Greek alphabet and C does not appear therein, C is rarely used in scientific symbolism. In chemistry, however, C is the symbol for carbon. *See also* ABBREVIATIONS; ALPHABET; SIGNS AND SYMBOLS; WRITING.   O. W. H-Q.

CABALA [kæ′bələ; kəbɑ′lə], Jewish esoteric philosophy and theosophy concerned primarily with the mysteries of God, the universe, and all of creation. The name is derived from the Hebrew verb *ḳabel* ("to receive") and implies that the Cabala was received, in the form of special revelations, by a few of the elect, who were especially chosen for the privilege because of their saintliness. Those who received the esoteric doctrine in turn transmitted it likewise only to a selected few capable of receiving and understanding the mystic lore and using it properly.

Cabala is divided into two systems, the one theoretical and the other practical. Theoretical Cabala, which borders on dogmatic religion, consists of theosophical speculations and has for its principal thesis the idea that the world is an emanation of the spiritual essence of God. According to this thesis, God, termed *en sof* ("endless one"), is infinite, and he made his existence manifest in the world through ten *sephiroth*—spheres or emanations of radiance—which are called Crown, Wisdom, Intelligence, Greatness, Strength, Beauty, Firmness, Splendor, Foundation, and Sovereignty. Theoretical Cabala contains elements from ancient Egyptian, Babylonian, and Greek philosophies and from the philosophic mysticism of Philo and the early Christian Gnostics. The doctrines of reincarnation and transmigration of souls, and of reward and punishment after death, figure in Cabalistic teachings.

Practical Cabala deals with the theurgic elements in mystic and esoteric doctrines. It is based on the belief that these doctrines can be translated into action, and specifically, that they can be applied for the performance of miracles and to speed the coming of the Messiah. It is concerned with the use, to achieve particular ends, of divine names and words, talismans, amulets, ascetic practices, and theosophic arithmetic. According to Cabala, angels may be conjured up by sainted Cabalists to do their bidding, and spirits and demons may be silenced by prayer and the use of amulets.

Cabalists ascribed the transmission of the esoteric doctrine from God through the angels to Adam, Noah, Moses, David, Solomon, and finally to the reputed mystic sage, Rabbi Simeon ben Yohai, who committed it to writing during the first century of the Christian Era. This legendary theory of the origin of Cabala points to its great antiquity. Critical scholarship maintains, indeed, that Cabala was the outgrowth of the consciousness of the Jewish people in ancient days of the nearness of God and his sovereignty. Allusions to esoteric teachings are found in the Apocrypha and Pseudepigrapha (Ecclus. iii:22; Esdras xiv:5-6). The Talmud refers to the mystic speculations of some of the sages and to the esoteric studies of *maaseh bereshith* ("story of creation"), based on Genesis, and *maaseh merkabah* ("story of the divine chariot"), based on the visions described by the prophet Ezekiel in the first and tenth chapters of his book. Esoteric literature, however, did not appear before the Gaonic period of Babylonia (sixth to eleventh century of the Christian Era). In that period there appeared the mystic books *Sefer Yetzirah* ("Book of Creation"), *Shiyur Komah* ("Measure of Heights"), and *Hechaloth* ("Halls"), the first of which was attributed to Abraham, the others to Rabbi Ishamel, who suffered martyrdom during the Hadrianic persecutions. In the thirteenth century appeared the work that became the Bible of the Cabalists, the *Sefer Hazohar* ("The Book of Splendor"); this was compiled by Moses de León in Spain and ascribed to the authorship of Rabbi Simeon ben Yohai.

Cabala found its way from Babylonia to Italy and thence to Provence and Spain. In Spain it flourished during the time of the Inquisition, serving as an antidote to the sufferings of the Jews at the hands of the Holy Office. After the expulsion of the Jews from Spain (1492), Cabala entrenched itself in Safed, Palestine, where a group of great Cabalists, among them Solomon Alkabetz, Isaac Luria, and Hayyim Vital, were gathered. The Cabala of Isaac Luria, which was largely of the practical type, found its way to Poland, where it played an important part in the founding of Hasidism. Many Christian scholars took up the study of Cabala, some of them finding in it the concept of Trinity. One of the outstanding Christian Cabalists was Pico della Mirandola (1463-1494). Pope Sixtus IV, a contemporary of Mirandola, had a number of Cabalistic works translated into Latin.   M. A. G.

CABALLERO, FERNÁN [kɑ′bɑlye′ro] (1796-1877), the pseudonym of the Spanish novelist Cecilia Böhl von Faber. Daughter of the famous Hispanist Johan Nikolas von Faber and of an Andalusian mother, Fernán Caballero was born Dec. 25, 1796, in Morges, Switzerland, and educated in Germany. Her father became a consul at Cádiz and she lived for the rest of her life in Spain. She survived three husbands: Captain Planells, who died in 1818; the Marquis del Arco Hermoso, who died in 1835; and Don Antonio Arro de Ayala, who died in 1853.

Fernán Caballero began her literary career rather late in life. She wrote mostly novels, some of them composed originally in French or German. Although the foreign element is not apparent in the Spanish translations, it is quite clear that she wrote from an alien viewpoint. Her descriptions of fiestas and villages reveal the foreigner's sense of discovery rather than the living experience of the Spaniard in his own scene. Nevertheless, through her love for Spain, Fernán Caballero was able to give a convincing picture of Andalusian life, its folklore, and its peculiarities. Her best novel is *La Gaviota* (1849). Many critics consider it the first modern Spanish novel, chronologically speaking, and in style as well as focus it represents a transition from Romanticism to *costumbrismo,* a literary movement specializing in scenes of local color. Although Fernán Caballero intentionally idealized the society of her time, she employed the colloquial language of the common people; the novel is not an invention, she maintained, but a direct copy of reality. Yet her work is transitional, and one finds in it many Romantic traits, especially certain images which reveal her sharp sensitiveness. She died in Seville, Apr. 7, 1877.   J. A. L. M.

CABANATUAN [kɑbɑ′nɑtwɑ′n], a municipality with an administrative unit and 18 districts in the Republic of the Philippines, the capital of Nueva Ecija Province, in central Luzon. It is a transportation center 60 mi. north of Manila and has rail connections on the Manila-Dagupan line, shallow draft water transportation via the Pampanga River, and highway connections to other towns of central Luzon. There is an airport 6 mi. east of town which lies on the southeast bank of the Pampanga River in the fertile central plain of Luzon. The famous death march from Bataan in 1942 terminated at Camp O'Donnell near Cabanatuan. On Jan. 30, 1945, United States Rangers and Filipino guerrillas made a daring rescue of the 513 prisoners, most of them survivors of the death march. Cabanatuan has a hospital, several small hotels, schools, theatres, rice mills, and a soap factory. Buildings are principally two-story frame structures with galvanized iron roofs and native nipa shacks. Nueva Ecija, a fertile agricultural district, was in the area of agrarian unrest in

Picking cabbages on one of the truck farms near Vineland, New Jersey

1945-1948 and within the realm dominated by the Hukbalahaps during those years. Rice and sugar cane are the principal crops of the region. The population of the town of Cabanatuan was 15,691 in 1948.   A. Cu.

CABANO [kəba'no], a village in Témiscouata Co., Quebec, Canada, situated on the western shore of Lake Témiscouata, about 35 mi. southeast of Rivière-du-Loup, on Highway 2 and the Canadian National Railway. Cabano is a center for the lumbering industry of the region. Pop. 1956, 2,350.   D. F. P.

CABBAGE, the oldest and most widely grown vegetable of the *Brassica* group, belonging to the mustard family. The other members of this group include broccoli, Brussels sprouts, cauliflower, Chinese cabbage, kale, kohlrabi, and turnips. Cabbage is distinguished from them by the short, petioled leaves and later development of a compact head, by compressed stem and leaves, the latter developing from within but swelling outward. Selective breeding has produced several distinct types of cabbage: early, midseason, and late; green and purple; large and small heads; flat, oval, conical, and globular; savoy types; and those with either smooth or crumpled leaves.

Cabbage may be grown in almost any type of well fertilized soil; however, it is a heavy feeder and must be given plenty of organic matter if it is to do well. It is a cool-season crop, and seed may be sown indoors in sandy soil about two months before planting-out time. When the plants are about two inches high they may be set out in the garden. A second transplanting, though not necessary, usually is beneficial. Cultivation should be very light, as cabbage roots grow near the surface.

Chinese Cabbage. Chinese cabbage is a member of the *Brassica* group, grown in China for centuries but only recently introduced into the United States. Chinese cabbage usually is handled as an autumn crop, and seed should be planted in late July. The seed may be sown directly in the ground where it is to grow. Seedlings should be thinned to stand about eight inches apart. The plant produces an elongated, loose head. It may be used as a salad green or cooked in the same manner as cabbage. Chinese cabbage is notably stronger in flavor than any of the other members of the cabbage group.

CABBAGE BUG, the name given to one of the stinkbugs, *Murgantia histrionica,* of the family Pentatomidae. It is a black and red species, often marked with orange, yellow, and white. It attacks a wide variety of plants, but is particularly fond of cabbage and other crucifers. The eggs are laid in batches on the leaves, and the young begin sucking the juices of the plant shortly after they are born. The adults survive winter under debris of various kinds, emerging from their hibernation quarters upon the advent of warm weather.   C. H. Cu.

CABBAGE BUTTERFLY, the common name of *Pieris rapae,* a white butterfly having black tips on the front wings, with one black spot in the male and two in the female. The hind wings of both sexes have a single black spot. It is a native of the Old World and first appeared in Canada in 1858, whence it spread to the whole of temperate North America, reaching San Francisco about 1886. Its green larvae feed on cruciferous plants of various kinds, and are particularly destructive to cabbages and turnips. In Europe it is called the turnip butterfly; the cabbage butterfly of that region is *Pieris brassicae,* a larger species, but fully as destructive to cabbages there as *P. rapae* is in America. The cabbage butterfly is now found in most temperate areas of the world.   C. H. Cu.

CABELL, JAMES BRANCH [kæ'bəl] (1879-1958), American novelist, poet, and critic, was born on Apr. 14, 1879, at Richmond, Va. After graduating in 1898 from the College of William and Mary, he successively taught Greek and French, worked on the staffs of various newspapers, and engaged in coal mining. During this period he also began to publish the sophisticated, pseudoarchaic, and highly mannered ironical romances and short stories concerning the mythical medieval country of Poictesme, for which he is best known. His works include *The Line of Love* (1905), romanticized tales of medieval life; *The Cords of Vanity*

JAMES BRANCH CABELL

FROM A PORTRAIT BY
WILLIAM L'ENGLE

(1909), concerned with modern Virginia; *The Rivet in Grandfather's Neck* (1915), cynically portraying Southern idealism; *The Cream of the Jest* (1917), telling of a modern author's search in the dream world for the "ageless, lovable, and loving woman"; *Jurgen, A Comedy of Justice* (1919), his most famous book, telling the erotic pilgrimage of a skeptic in search of his wife; *Figures of Earth* (1921), showing the unconventional Dom Manuel in various amours; and *The Silver Stallion* (1926), a narrative of the legends concerning Manuel that arose after his death. According to the author, the critical works, *Beyond Life* (1919) and *Straws and Prayer-Books* (1924) are the prologue and epilogue to the Poictesme series. His later works appeared under the name of "Branch Cabell" and include the trilogy, *Smirt* (1934), *Smith* (1935), and *Smire* (1937), reasserting his theory of fiction as an allegorical interpretation of the dream of life; and *The St. Johns* (1943), a social history of the Florida river's region, *There Were Two Pirates* (1946), a novelette, and *The Devil's Own Dear Son* (1949), which form another trilogy called *It Happened in Florida*. Cabell died on May 5, 1958, in Richmond, Va.

CABINET GOVERNMENT, a system of responsible government, of English origin, operating in conjunction with a legislature and a titular head of state, in which a council of ministers or cabinet acts as the real executive authority in the administrative branch, and provides the parliamentary leadership in the legislative branch.

Major Features. The principles of cabinet government include the legal supremacy of the legislative over the executive branch; dominance in a bicameral legislature of one house, usually the popularly elected one; selection of the cabinet from among the members of the party or coalition of parties which enjoys a majority in the legislature; and cabinet tenure of office during the will of the legislature.

Origin and History. As a product of evolutionary development, cabinet government was not consciously created. It originated out of the practical experience of several centuries, so that its history is the entire constitutional history of England. Generally speaking, Anglo-Saxon and Norman kings of England combined legislative and executive authority in their own hands, but even these feudal monarchs depended on a Great Council of the nobility and a Curia Regis, the latter the forerunner of the modern Privy Council and cabinet, to advise them. In the thirteenth century the Great Council took shape as a Parliament, soon divided into two houses, Lords and Commons. Forced to obtain parliamentary assent to collect sufficient tax money, English kings were increasingly obliged to consult Parliament in making laws and choosing ministers of the crown. The Tudors' insistence on absolutism was followed by Stuart claims to rule by divine right, but two popular revolutions, that against Charles I in 1642 and that against James II in 1688, firmly established the supremacy of Parliament.

Another prerequisite to the development of cabinet government was the establishment of parliamentary control over the king's ministers. Charles II began the practice of selecting a committee or cabinet to assist him, a custom continued by William of Orange. The first Hanoverian king, George I, unable to speak English and with little interest in politics, chose his prime minister from the majority party which controlled the House of Commons. He rarely attended cabinet meetings, and let parliamentary majorities and the cabinet formulate government policy, a practice continued by George II. Sir Robert Walpole, who directed the government during this period, from 1721 to 1742, established the custom of cabinet leadership. When his party lost its Commons majority in 1742 he resigned, recognizing the principle of cabinet or ministerial responsibility to the House of Commons.

Organization and Function in England. After the resignation of a prime minister and his cabinet, or after a parliamentary general election, the sovereign commissions the leader of the majority party to form a government. The leader, who assumes the position of prime minister himself, selects a ministry of some 60 members, each of whom fills a responsible administrative position and retains his seat in Parliament. From among these ministers, the prime minister chooses a smaller body, numbering 20 to 25, the members of which are invited to attend cabinet meetings. These cabinet ministers are also appointed members of the Privy Council, a body of some 350 persons which never meets for administrative purposes, but in whose name the cabinet officially acts.

As the link between the executive and the legislature, the cabinet has a dual function. First, its members individually direct the affairs of the various major departments, such as the Foreign Office, Treasury, War Office, etc., and collectively determine and co-ordinate executive policy. Second, the cabinet formulates a legislative program, drafting, introducing, and advocating the passage of the main bills which provide funds and authority for the government. The cabinet is collectively responsible before Parliament for its policies and the character of governmental administration. In the face of a defeat in the House of Commons, it resigns in a body, unless the prime minister can obtain the sovereign's dissolution of Parliament and can win the resulting general election.

Cabinet Government Elsewhere. Cabinet government has been widely adopted over the world. It has been most effectively transplanted in form and spirit, however, to the Scandinavian countries and to the British Dominions. The prime exponent of cabinet government on the European continent has been France under the Third Republic, 1871-1940, and under the Fourth Republic, 1946-1958. Italy after 1861 likewise modeled its political institutions after the English cabinet system, though cabinet government operated with much less success and was discarded after Mussolini came to power in 1922. Cabinet government was restored in Italy with the establishment of the republic in 1946. In most of central and eastern Europe cabinet government was only imperfectly adopted. After World War I it enjoyed a temporary popularity, particularly with its adoption by the Weimar Republic in Germany, 1919-1933. Soon thereafter it declined in most states and gave way to the forces of dictatorship or resurgent absolutism.   D. G. H.

CABINET MOUNTAINS, a part of the northern Rocky Mountains located in extreme northwestern Montana. These mountains extend in a northwest-southeast direction roughly paralleling the Idaho-Montana boundary line. They are composed of Pre-Cambrian sediments which have acquired their present form through faulting, folding, erosion, and glaciation. The southeastern ranges are higher than the northwestern, but the highest elevation is 8,712 ft. at Snowshoe Peak, in the northwest.   J. E. F.

CABLE, GEORGE W[ASHINGTON] (1844-1925), American author and reformer, was born Oct. 12, 1844, in New Orleans. At the age of fifteen he began work as a clerk, later served two years in the Confederate Army as a cavalryman, and finally started his literary career writing for newspapers and magazines. His first stories, published in *Scribner's Monthly,* were collected as *Old Creole Days* (1879), and his novels *The Grandissimes* (1880) and *Dr. Sevier* (1884) also drew upon the rich material of early Louisiana culture. Others of his books are largely historical, such as *Strange True Stories of Louisiana* (1889), *The Creoles of Louisiana* (1884), and *Bonaventure* (1888), while still others, such as *The Cavalier* (1901), reflect his experiences in the Civil War. Cable was a successful platform reader and lecturer, and in the 1880's he lectured and wrote effectively in support of prison reform and fuller rights for Negroes. Later, as an editor and through cultural organizations, he engaged in less controversial programs for general betterment. Cable moved to Connecticut in 1884 and lived there the rest of his life. This had the effect of removing him from his material

GEORGE W[ASHINGTON] CABLE

CULVER SERVICE

and there is a falling off of inspiration in his later works. His last book was *The Lovers of Louisiana* (1918). Cable died in St. Petersburg, Fla., on Jan. 31, 1925.   A. Tu.

CABOT, GEORGE (1751?-1823), American merchant and politician, was born in Salem, Mass., Dec. 16, 1751 (according to his biographer, Henry Cabot Lodge). He was educated in Salem local schools and in 1766 entered Harvard but left after two years to go to sea as a cabin boy.

At the age of eighteen he became captain of his brother's schooner, which was engaged in trade between the Colonies and Bilbao, Spain, and in 1777 he left the sea to enter his family's shipping business. The Cabots' privateers and armed merchantmen continued to trade with Spain throughout the Revolutionary War and thus built up a flourishing business which permitted George Cabot to retire in 1795 with a considerable fortune. He was also a director of the Bank of Massachusetts, the first bank in the state. Cabot became active in politics as early as 1778 in connection with a group of Essex County merchants and lawyers who later formed the nucleus of the Federalist Party and were known as the "Essex Junto." He was elected United States Senator from Massachusetts in 1791. The following year he submitted a bill which was passed "to regulate the capture and delivery of fugitives from justice." It was passed with little comment, but reappeared more than half a century later in the portentous form of the Fugitive Slave Law. A strong Federalist, Cabot was a close friend and adviser of Alexander Hamilton. Cabot resigned from the Senate in 1796 and two years later, when the office of Secretary of the Navy was created, President John Adams appointed him to the post with the Senate's approval. When notified, Cabot declined to serve, but nominally retained the office pending the appointment of a successor; thus his name stands on the records as the country's first Secretary of the Navy. In 1814 Cabot was chosen president of the Hartford Convention, on the radical tendencies of which he exerted a unionist and moderating influence. He died in Boston, Apr. 18, 1823.   C. W. D.

CABOT, JOHN [kæ′bət] (1450-1498), Italian navigator and explorer, was born Giovanni Caboto in 1450, probably in Genoa. He migrated to Venice in 1461, became a citizen there in 1476, and made trading voyages in the eastern

Mediterranean Sea. Cabot moved to England about 1484, where he joined the shipping community at Bristol. He received letters patent from King Henry VII, granting him authority to claim for England any islands or mainland he might find, and giving him the right to colonize and organize trade with these colonies. He sailed from Bristol, May 2, 1497, in the *Mathew,* and landed on June 24 at Cape Breton Island, which he mistook for the northeastern coast of Asia. Cabot cruised along the coast east of the Gulf of St. Lawrence, taking his departure from Cape Race homeward. He

JOHN CABOT

BROWN BROTHERS

undertook a second voyage in 1498, in which he explored the east and west coasts of Greenland, and reached Baffin Land, Labrador and Newfoundland. He followed the coast as far south as 38° N. lat., but found no signs of the Eastern civilization he had envisioned. Lack of supplies forced Cabot to return to England, where he died soon after his arrival.
                                                        S. Van V.

CABOT, SEBASTIAN (c. 1476-1557), Venetian navigator, was born in Venice, Italy, in about 1476. He accompanied his father, John Cabot, on the second (1498) voyage to America and is credited with a voyage about 1509 in search of a northwest passage to the Orient. In 1512, Cabot made a map of the provinces of Gascony and Guyenne for King Henry VIII of England, and from that year until 1516 was map maker to King Ferdinand II of Aragon. He held the important post of pilot major to Emperor Charles V from 1519 to 1526 and again from 1533 to 1544. In 1526, Cabot commanded a Venetian expedition from Seville in search of the fabled riches of Ophir and Cathay. Determined to find a strait to the Pacific Ocean, he reached the Río de la Plata, Argentina, encountering members of the Juan de Solis expedition, who told him of the riches of the country. In search of these, he ascended the Uruguay River, entered the Paraná River to the rapids at Apipé, and descended the Paraguay River to the Bermejo River. He returned in 1530 to Seville, whence he was banished to Oran, Africa, for three years. He published an engraved map of the world in 1544. Upon the accession of King Edward VI in 1547, Cabot moved to England, where he was granted a pension. In 1551, he founded in London and became governor of the Muscovy Company of Merchant Adventurers, which sent expeditions in 1553 and 1555 in search of a northeast passage to the Orient. He died in 1557.   S. Van V.

CABRAL, PEDRO ÁLVARES [kəbra'l] (c. 1460-c. 1526), Portuguese navigator, was born about 1460. He was sent by King Emanuel I of Portugal in command of a fleet of thirteen ships to establish trade with the East Indies, sailing Mar. 9, 1500, on a route west of that which was in his orders. The equatorial current carried him even farther westward, and caused his accidental discovery of Brazil on April 22. Unknown to Cabral, Vicente Yáñez Pinzón had reached the South American coast below Cape St. Augustine earlier in 1500; he separated a ship from his fleet, and sent it to Portugal to announce his discovery, for which he was given full credit. Regarding the easternmost part of South America as a region which had been assigned to Portugal, by a papal bull of Alexander VI, and by the Treaty of Tordesillas in 1494, Cabral took possession of it in the name of the Portuguese king. From Brazil, Cabral resumed his voyage, now eastward to India. He lost four of his vessels in a storm off the Cape of Good Hope, but continued to Calicut, where he attempted to found a trading post, before returning to Portugal in June 1501.   S. Van V.

CABRILLO NATIONAL MONUMENT [kɑbri'lyo], a half-acre park located on Point Loma, San Diego Bay, in southwestern California. This park, established Oct. 4, 1913, marks the point of land first seen by the Portuguese navigator Juan Rodríguez Cabrillo, on Sept. 28, 1542. He is credited with discovering San Diego Bay, Santa Monica Bay, the Santa Lucia Mountains, and Monterey Bay.   J. E. F.

CABRINI, ST. FRANCES [cɑbri'ni] (1850-1917), Roman Catholic saint, the first American citizen to be canonized, was born in Lombardy, Italy, on July 15, 1850. In

SAINT FRANCES XAVIER CABRINI

CHARLES PHELPS CUSHING

1880 she founded the Missionary Sisters of the Sacred Heart with the intention of laboring in China, but Pope Leo XIII sent her to aid the neglected Italians in America by conducting schools, orphanages, and hospitals, and by offering religious instruction. The work expanded to Central and South America, Paris, Spain, and England, with such success that Piux X approved the institute in 1907. St. Frances died in Chicago, Dec. 22, 1917, was beatified Nov. 13, 1938, and canonized July 17, 1946.   W. C.

CACAO [kəkɑ'o; kəke'o], the source of chocolate and cocoa, is prepared from the seeds of *Theobroma cacao,* a member of the cola family. The Spanish word "cacao" is a variation of the original Aztec *cacauatl.* The name chocolate is derived from the Mexican Indian words *choco,* meaning "foam," and *atl,* meaning "water." "Cocoa" is an English-language corruption of "cacao." The plant and its chief product are known as cacao throughout the rest of the world. Chocolate is one of the most nutritious of all beverages; it also contains theobromine, a stimulating alkaloid closely related to caffeine and theophylline. *Theobroma,* meaning "food for the gods," supplies most of the substances required for human nutrition. Unlike coffee and tea, chocolate is a food as well as a beverage. The roasted nibs contain approximately 50 per cent fat, 20 to 25 per cent carbohydrates, 15 to 20 per cent proteins, up to 1.5 per cent theobromine, 5 per cent moisture, and 3.5 per cent ash, including such minerals as calcium, iron, magnesium, potassium, sodium, and a little cacao red coloring matter.

Botany. Cacao is an American tree native to coastal Mexico, Central America, and South America. The tree reaches 40 ft. in the wild state, but is kept pruned to 15 to 25 ft. under cultivation. Leaves, reddish when young, are thin, evergreen, glossy, elliptic-oblong, and up to one foot long. Flowers are very small, pinkish white, waxlike in appearance and inconspicuous; they grow in a most unusual manner directly from the main trunk and branches. Fruits are pods 8 to 15 in. long which ripen fully in four months. They are the size of large cucumbers or elongated, furrowed melons. The semiwoody rinds, which pass through several color stages, have a leathery appearance. The red variety turns carmine to vermilion to orange or reddish-brown. The yellow variety changes from green to yellow. Pods contain 20 to 50 seeds enveloped in a gummy liquid which coagulates into a soft whitish pulp when exposed to air. Each almond-shaped seed (bean) is enclosed in a parchment shell with two oil lobes.

History. Cacao beans, discovered during the Spanish conquest of Mexico and also by Pizarro in Peru, once were used as money, serving as a currency medium as well as a source of food and beverage. The beans were first brought into the United States for chocolate manufacturers when Gloucester, Mass., fishermen accepted them as money for goods exchanged in tropical America. One hundred and thirty years after cacao beans reached Spain, the first European country to use chocolate, they were introduced into England, and in 1657 the beverage was advertised in London. Chocolate, coffee, and tea were introduced into England at about the same time. Chocolate became popular, however, only after the addition of vanilla. Serving chocolate, as serving coffee and tea, has always been a symbol of welcome and sociability and has been significant in the customs of many people. Spaniards reported that the Aztec Emperor Montezuma would drink no other beverage from the golden ceremonial goblets.

The first chocolate mill in North America was operated in 1765 in Milton Lower Mills, a part of Dorchester, Mass. In 1780, Dr. James Baker acquired it and founded Walter Baker and Co., Ltd. By 1790, 500,000 lb. of cacao beans were imported annually. By 1900, 20,000,000 lb. were imported and the estimates for 1950 were over 700,000,000 lb.

Agriculture. Of the nine species of *Theobroma,* only *T. cacao* and its varieties are cultivated widely. Cacao plants are very sensitive to drought, frost, and wind; they require a rich but well-drained soil at an altitude not exceeding 2,500 ft. Seeds are planted four or five to each hole in rows 5 yd. apart. Sometimes they are germinated in bamboo joints or palm leaf baskets and transferred later, basket and all, to the plantation. Seedlings are grown for the first 2 to 4 yr. under the shade of banana, breadfruit, mango, or rubber trees. The blossoms are destroyed until the fifth year. Full maturity is reached by the eighth year and maximum yield by the tenth to twelfth year. Fruits are produced for thirty to eighty years. Two major fruiting periods occur each year, although flowers and pods may be seen on the same tree at all seasons.

Production. Three main types of cacao are produced, and most plantations grow a mixture. *Criollo,* meaning "native-born," is the finest. Much of it is from Venezuela and Nicaragua. *Forastero,* meaning "stranger," has three subtypes and is the source of more than 80 per cent of the world's crop. *Calabacillos,* meaning "little pumpkin," because of the shape of the pods, is the poorest quality. Annual world production of all cacao exceeds 1,700,000,000 lb. The Gold Coast of West Africa accounts for over one third of the world's cacao exports. In Brazil it was first cultivated in 1740 in the state of Pará. The state of Bahia now produces 90 per cent of the Brazilian crop, which amounts to nearly one fifth of the cacao world exports. Cacao ranks third in value of all Brazilian exports.

Until 1900, 80 per cent of all cacao was produced in its native home, tropical America. By 1949 it was estimated that 32 per cent was coming from the Western Hemisphere and 68 per cent from the Eastern Hemisphere.

Harvesting and Processing. Careful choice in picking is essential, because high-quality chocolate is obtainable only from mature fruit. Skilled male pickers, *tumbadores,* cut fruit from the trunks with machetes and from the branches by means of mitten-shaped knives at the ends of long poles. Women fill baskets with pods, carry them to a clearing, and pile them on the ground. Men open the pods by two to four blows of a long knife; experts open 500 per hour. Girls separate the beans from pulp by hand or, sometimes, by an instrument fashioned from a beef rib. The beans are spread on trays or banana leaves or in sweating boxes, for fermentation by the beans' own enzymes and wild yeast for two to nine days. The beans then are dried on concrete drying grounds by exposure to the sun for several days, after which they are graded and bagged.

Processing begins by machining and sieving the beans to break and remove the parchment shells, the stony hard radicle, and other extraneous matter. These shells, formerly sold for a very poor beverage, are discarded or used as fuel in the roasting furnaces. Uniform roasting of clean beans is accomplished in revolving drums. Crisp roasted beans are broken up by a machine which also fans out shell fragments and separates the broken beans (the nibs) into relatively uniform sizes by passing them over a series of sieves.

Roasted nibs are crushed between grinding stones to produce a thick plastic liquor which solidifies upon cooling and forms bitter chocolate. Cocoa is the sifted, powdered press cake formed by hydraulic pressure during the removal of fat from the chocolate liquor. Cocoa possesses only 18 per cent fat. Chocolate, sweetened with sugar and flavored with vanilla, is sweet chocolate. If powdered milk is added, it is known as milk chocolate. Extra cacao butter is added to chocolate if it is used to coat confections. The chocolate liquor-paste is placed in a warm compartment, mixed thoroughly, and deposited in molds to give the familiar commercial forms.

In cocoa manufacture, the original fat content is reduced to much less than half of that of the original chocolate; also, sugar and dried milk are added to the sifted cocoa powder. Dutch-type cocoa is cocoa powder treated with alkali to darken the color and to give a slightly different flavor.

Other Uses. Most chocolate products are blends of ordinary and fine grades. The United States imports, without duty, over 40 per cent of the world's crop. Cocoa butter is the chief by-product of the chocolate industry and is very useful in pharmaceutical preparations because of its freedom from rancidity and its blandness. Basic chocolate products manufactured in the United States are valued annually at nearly $100,000,000. The per capita consumption of chocolate in the United States exceeds 5 lb. and is increasing constantly.
R. H. C.

CÁCERES [kɑ'theres], the name of both a province and the capital city of that province in the Estremadura region, in west central Spain.

The City. The city is situated about 150 mi. southwest of Madrid, on a hill overlooking the valley of the Tajo, or Tagus, River, which flows 15 mi. to the north. It lies on a branch rail line from Mérida to Malpartida, where it connects with the Madrid-Lisbon line. The city has regional importance as a commercial center, and its industries produce leather goods and cheap textiles. The phosphate deposits at nearby Las Minas are exploited.

The upper and older part of Cáceres is partly enclosed within walls of Roman and Arabic origins in which some of the towers and gates, including the Arco de Estrella, remain. In this quarter are the Gothic churches of Santa María la Mayor and San Mateo. The latter was built on the emplacement of a mosque, and its tower dominates the city. Among the secular structures are the mansions of several families noted in Spanish history, such as Ulloa, Carvajal, and Saavedra. The city still preserves the flavor of the Spanish Reconquest as well as of Arab rule and the Middle Ages.

The Romans created camps in the vicinity, but little is known of the town until the eleventh century. Cáceres was taken from the Arabs several times and then lost, in 1142, 1171, and 1184, and only in 1229 was it captured and held by Alfonso IX of León, who conferred many rights on it and aided in its reconstruction. Some authorities hold that the Military Order of Santiago was founded at Cáceres. The city was occupied by Nationalist forces early in the Civil War. Pop. 1950, 40,009.

The Province. The province of Cáceres has an area of 7,705 sq. mi. It is bounded on the north by León, on the east by Castille, on the south by the province of Badajoz (also in Estremadura), and on the west by Portugal. Along the northern border lie the Sierra de Gata, Tras la Sierra, and the Sierra de Gredos, where elevations exceed 6,000 ft. In the south are the lower Sierras de San Pedro, de Montánchez, and de Guadalupe. The latter lies entirely within the province; hence the southeastern corner of the sierra falls within the Guadiana watershed. Most of the province, however, is drained by the Tajo, or Tagus, River, of which the chief tributaries here are the Alagón and Tiétar to the north, and the Ayuela, Salor, and Almonte to the south.

The Tajo, flowing from east to west through a deep and inaccessible trench, divides the province into two distinct parts. To the north the mountains and their outlying extensions are forested and well watered. Property is widely distributed and the population tends to live in small centers or on the land. Grain, fruit, olives, and vegetables are the chief crops of the district. To the south of the river the terrain is flatter, rainfall is lower (below 30 in. a year), and summers are hotter. The land is held by large owners who prefer to raise livestock rather than cultivate cereals, and the population is thus sparse and poorer than in the north. Droughts are not uncommon, and rivers generally dry up in the summer. Cáceres shares with the other Estremaduran province of

CHARLES PHELPS CUSHING

Giant cactus plants in the Arizona desert near Phoenix

Badajoz the distinction of being first as a livestock producer, goats, sheep, and swine being the principal stock.

All of Spain's phosphates come from the mines of the province, and limestone is quarried near the capital. Food processing, tanning, flour milling and the making of chemical fertilizers are provincial industries, though large-scale industrial development is lacking. Rail and highway communications are inadequate.

Important cities and towns in the province, in addition to Cáceres, are Plasencia, a cathedral town founded in the twelfth century by Alfonso VIII and surrounded by a double circuit of walls; Arroyo de la Luz, a market place and industrial center; Valencia de Alcántara, frontier station and a former fortress, with a Roman aqueduct; Trujillo, of Roman origin (Turgalium) and with Moorish remains, the birthplace of Francisco Pizarro, who erected palaces with the spoils of Peru; and Alcántara, a picturesque town on the south bank of the Tagus (Tajo) River near the Portuguese border, deriving its name (*al-Kantara*, Arabic for "bridge") from a high, six-arched Roman bridge built in the time of Trajan. Alcántara is the original home of the knightly Order of Alcántara, created to fight the Moors.

Although the province of Cáceres is the second largest in area in Spain, it has one of the lowest population densities in the country, with approximately 72 persons per sq. mi. Pop. 1950, 548,256. R. G. W.

CACOMISTLE [kæ′komɪ′səl], a mammal, *Bassariscus astutus,* of the order Carnivora, related to the raccoon. Found in Central America and as far north as Oregon, the cacomistle is the most primitive of the raccoon family, Procyonidae. Although its skull and dentition are remarkably doglike, its limbs are modified in accordance with its arboreal habits to resemble those of other procyonids. The cacomistle is a slender, graceful animal a little smaller than a domestic cat; it has a long cylindrical tail marked with black and white rings. Known also as the ring-tailed cat, cat squirrel, or mountain cat, its proper name is derived from the Aztec word *cacomixtl.* G. M. C.

CACTUS, a family, the Cactaceae, of succulent plants of more than 1,300 species characterized by prickles, spines, or thorns on stem or body. They are indigenous to the Western Hemisphere from Canada to Patagonia; and while they are generally considered desert plants, some are from high mountains and others grow in the warm, humid tropics. They are adapted to drought by an apparent absence of leaves, by the root structure, and by the usually swollen stems, which have tremendous water-storage capacity.

The cacti have a bewildering variety of forms, such as *Pereskia,* a leafy plant considered to be close to the ancestral form. Some, like the mescal button, are very small, an adult form being no more than 3 in. in diameter. Others are epiphytes, growing in trees and having aerial rootlets and whiplike stems. The forms known as night-blooming cereus climb, clinging tightly to a wall or trunks of trees by means of aerial roots. A striking contrast in size and shape is that of the saguaro, *Cereus giganteus,* with columnar branches growing to 50 ft. in height and weighing tons, compared with the tiny thimble-sized cactus, *Mammillaria fragilis.*

Cacti are not important as stock food, although in parts of Mexico there is little else during drought. The use of spineless forms of the prickly pear for this purpose, as developed by Luther Burbank, led to their introduction into the Mediterranean regions, China, and Australia, where they have become pernicious weeds. The edible berrylike body of the fruit of such species as the prickly pear and Indian fig is widely used in tropical regions; these species are grown commercially in southern California and are used in some countries as fencing and fuel.

Cacomistle, Bassariscus astutus

Many cacti have value as ornamentals, and a vast interest in them has developed in the United States. The flowers are generally quite showy, with white, yellow, and brilliant shades of red of satiny texture. Many are grown purely for their weird, fantastic shapes in a desert garden. Others, such as the Christmas cactus, have long been known as house plants. R. S. Ho.

CACUS [keˈkəs], in Roman mythology, a giant, the son of Vulcan, who lived in a cave on Mount Aventine. When Heracles came to Italy with the cattle of Geryon, Cacus dragged some of the cattle into the cave by their tails, but their lowing betrayed their whereabouts, and Heracles killed the thief. Cacus was probably a primitive Roman deity of fire. G. E. D.

CADALSO Y VÁZQUEZ, JOSÉ DE [katɑˈlso i vɑˈthketh] (1741-1782), Spanish author and soldier, was born at Cádiz, Oct. 8, 1741, and received his education at a Jesuit school in Paris. During his youth he traveled extensively in western Europe and acquired the familiarity with French and English literature which later exerted an influence on his work.

On his return to his own country, Cadalso proceeded to join the army and ultimately rose to the rank of colonel. While stationed in Madrid, he fell in love with the actress María Ibañez, and her sudden death left a lasting effect on his work. At this point, however, he was transferred to Salamanca, where he became a member of the Salamancan School of poets and exercised an influence upon the most notable of them, Meléndez Valdés. When Spain declared war against Great Britain in 1778, Cadalso joined his regiment in the siege of Gibraltar. He was killed in action there, Feb. 27, 1782.

In some of his work, Cadalso may be classed with the precursors of Romanticism. His melancholy and elegiac collection of prose dialogues, *Noches lúgubres* ("Melancholy Nights"), which dramatized the death of his beloved and his attempts to disinter her body, shows the influence of Edward Young's *Night Thoughts*. Caldalso's dependence on French Classicism is shown in his somewhat inferior plays, the most notable of which is *Don Sancho García, conde de Castilla* (1771), an historical drama, which suggests the work of the great nineteenth-century romantic dramatist, José Zorrilla. Cadalso's poetry is of little greater value; his *Ocios de mi juventud* (1773) ("Diversions of My Youth") has some inspiring moments and in form shows the influence of Quevedo. In prose Cadalso frequently employed satire, and *Los Eruditos á la violeta* (1772) ("The Learned on the Violet") is an amusing take-off on pedantry and superficial knowledge. Of all his works, however, the posthumous *Cartas Marruecas* (1793) ("Moroccan Letters") is the most important. This series of fictitious letters, although it is modeled on Montesquieu's *Lettres persanes,* is a highly original handling of the problem of Spain's decadence. In this work Cadalso shows himself to be an essayist of unusual ability and one of the most important Spanish prose writers of the eighteenth century. J. A. L. M.

CADDICE FLY or **CADDIS FLY,** any insect belonging to the order Trichoptera. They are rather mothlike in appearance, but differ in having hairs instead of scales on the wings, and their larvae are aquatic. There are more than 3,000 known kinds, and the larvae of most, soon after hatching from the eggs, build cases or nets in which they spend their underwater life. In some primitive forms the case is not constructed until the larva is well grown. In several of the families that live in running water, the larvae build silken nets in which food is caught; beside the net, or beneath it, they build a silken case in which they live. If dislodged, they spin a silken thread and later crawl back along it to their cases. The best known of the caddice flies are those that build cases which they carry about with them, enlarging them as occasion arises; these may be four inches long. Some species utilize the hollow stems of grass or reeds, but the majority build cases of specific design and of

Typical Caddice Flies

varied materials. In all, the materials are held together by silk. When the larva is mature, it makes a cocoon within the case or sometimes merely closes the ends. The emerging adult is able to fly as soon as it reaches the surface of the water. C. H. Cu.

CADDO. *See* INDIAN TRIBES, NORTH AMERICAN.

CADDO LAKE, an irregularly shaped body of water situated on the boundary line between northwestern Louisiana and eastern Texas. The lake is 17 mi. northwest of Shreveport in Caddo Parish, La., and extends into Texas between Marion and Harrison counties. It was formed by the backing up of the waters of Cypress Creek, a tributary of the Red River, and is about 20 mi. in length. Caddo Lake communicates with Soda Lake, adjacent to Shreveport, and is navigable by river boats which can pass into the Red River. J. E. F.

CADENCE [keˈdəns] (Lat. *cadere,* to fall), in music, a sequence of tones or chords, habitually occurring at the end of a musical phrase or section and conveying the idea of conclusion. The derivation of the word is a reminder of the fact that in earlier centuries, before the break-up of the modal system about 1600, the chief cadence formula was the falling of the melody to the keynote from the note above. Since the seventeenth century, however, cadences have been characterized by harmonic rather than melodic aspects. The two final cadences common today are the authentic and the plagal or "Amen" cadences:

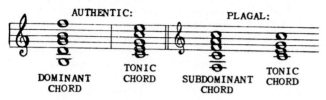

AUTHENTIC: PLAGAL:

DOMINANT   TONIC   SUBDOMINANT   TONIC
CHORD   CHORD   CHORD   CHORD

Other cadences, less emphatically final, are called "deceptive" or "imperfect" cadences.   W. Li.

CADENZA [kədɛ'ntsə; kədɛ'nzə], a term in music referring to: (1) a free and virtuosic flourish, usually in rapid notes, found chiefly in Italian opera and in nineteenth-century instrumental solo music; or (2) a more extended passage in the same improvisatory style. In the latter sense, the cadenza occurs near the close of a concerto movement and affords the soloist a maximum opportunity for the display of his technical skill. The flourish type of cadenza was developed to the utmost in seventeenth- and eighteenth-century opera, in which it provided an opportunity for the display not only of vocal techniques but also of creative ingenuity, the soloist being expected to improvise a new cadenza at each opportunity. The longer cadenzas in instrumental concertos, in which the soloist rhapsodizes upon preceding thematic material with much use of trills, arpeggios, and scales, were also improvised until the beginning of the nineteenth century; at that time, however, Beethoven, in his Piano Concerto No. 5 (the "Emperor" Concerto), led the way in writing out the exact cadenza to be performed at each point in the score, thus insuring an adherence to the particular style of the work as a whole.   W. S. N.

CADILLAC [kæ'dɪlæk], the county seat of Wexford Co. in western Michigan, is a resort city situated on Lake Mitchell, 97 mi. north of Grand Rapids. It is also a shipping center for the farm and dairy products yielded by the surrounding country. Cadillac was founded in 1871 as Clam Lake. It was incorporated as a city in 1877 and renamed in honor of Antoine de la Mothe Cadillac, founder of Detroit. It has the commissioner-manager form of government. The city is well known as a center for winter sports, and numerous lakes and streams provide sportsmen with excellent fishing. Freight transportation is supplied by the Pennsylvania and the Ann Arbor railroads. Local industries include the manufacture of lumber, malleable iron heaters, chairs and tables, veneers, boats, automobile accessories, road machinery, cement blocks, and rubber goods. Timber is a natural resource of the region. Pop. 1950, 10,425.

CÁDIZ [ke'dɪz; kɑ'ɵith], one of the chief seaports of southwestern Spain and the province of which the city is the capital.

The City. Cádiz, the city, is situated on a fairly flat limestone promontory at the end of a narrow five-mile peninsula that forms the Bay of Cádiz on the Atlantic coast of Andalucía at the point where the Guadalete River empties into it, at 36° 29' N. lat. and 6° 18' W. long. This sandy peninsula extends in a roughly northwest direction from the mainland, or rather from the Isla de León, which itself is separated from the mainland by the Canal of Sancti Petri. The climate is generally moist and warm. Dry winds from the land frequently blow in the winter, but during the rest of the year off-sea breezes bring in moisture.

Cádiz owes its importance over the centuries to its harbor and to the ready defensibility of its highly strategic position. The bay is divided into two parts, divided by the narrow waist formed by the promontories of Puntales, a spur on the isthmus leading to Cádiz, and the Trocadero, jutting out from the mainland just south of the mouth of the Río de San Pedro. Both promontories are well fortified. The outer bay to the north, though less protected, is deeper and more spacious, and the entrance to it from the open sea is also guarded by fortifications and by the rocky islets and shoals of Los Cochinos and Las Puercas. The inner bay is shallower. On its southern shore is the important naval base and arsenal at San Fernando.

The port of Cádiz lies on the east side of the city and has more than two miles of docks, shipyards, and other waterfront facilities, including railway sidings. The port is regularly used by several oceanic shipping lines and by coastal services from nearby ports on the Atlantic and the Mediterranean. The volume of traffic declined in the early twentieth century but was somewhat aided by the re-establishment of a free port in 1914. The establishment of American military bases in Spain after World War II increased shipping, construction, and storage activity in Cádiz and the vicinity. Exports include sherry and other wines, salt, fruit, olives, sugar, minerals, and cork; imports, foodstuffs, coal, manufactured goods, and lumber. There are several small factories in Cádiz and nearby cities on the bay, and its fishing industry employs several thousand workers.

Though very ancient in its origins, Cádiz presents a generally modern appearance, having straight, if narrow, streets and freshly whitewashed edifices. The only quarter having a medieval aspect is the section surrounding the cathedral. The restricted area has left room for few open spaces and has obliged the residents to build their flat-roofed houses several stories high, surmounted in many instances by minaret-like *miradores,* or galleries. Despite the air of brightness and cleanliness, the city is very poorly drained, and its sewage tends to collect in the adjacent sea. There are no springs; drinking water must be brought in from Puerto Santa Maria, across the bay, over a 30-mi. aqueduct; water is also collected in cisterns from the run-off of rain on the roofs.

The city is surrounded by walls except on the side toward the port. The only landward entrance to the city is at the Puerta de Tierra on the isthmus. On the western side of the promontory are the castles of Santa Catalina and San Sebastián, the latter built on a tongue of rock jutting three fourths of a mile out into the sea on Phoenician foundations. Along several portions of the circumvallation are promenades and parks, and beyond the walls there are some popular bathing beaches.

The principal monuments in the city, which is the see of an archbishop, include the Old Cathedral, built in 1265, destroyed in 1596, and rebuilt in 1602; the New Cathedral, a Neoclassical structure dating from the late eighteenth and early nineteenth centuries; the Capuchin Chapel of Santa Catalina, mid-seventeenth century, containing many works of Murillo, including his last painting, *The Marriage of St. Catherine;* the Oratorio of San Felipe, built in 1671, which contains several works of art and was used as the seat of the Cortés during the siege of 1811-1812; the Picture Gallery; and the Archaeological Museum. Cádiz possesses the oldest medical school in Spain, attached to the University of Seville and founded in 1748. Suppressed in 1843, it was later revived. Cádiz is also the seat of the Academia Hispano-Americana de Ciencias y Artes, founded in 1910. Pop. 1950, 98,754.

The Province. Cádiz, the southernmost province in

PORT OF CÁDIZ, SPAIN

COURTESY OF THE SPANISH TOURIST OFFICE

Spain, has an area of 2,827 mi. This figure does not include the Ceuta enclave on the north coast of Morocco, which for administrative purposes is attached to the province of Cádiz. The province is bounded on the north by the provinces of Huelva and Seville, and on the east by that of Málaga. The coastline of the province extends from the mouth of the Guadalquivir River southward past Cape Trafalgar and Point Marroquí, past the Bay of Algeciras and Gibraltar to Cape Sardina, which is just beyond the mouth of the Guadiaro River. The western half is coastal lowland and rolling plain, as is also the district behind Gibraltar in the southeast. Higher ground is encountered in the center and in the northeast, where elevations exceed one mile. The chief rivers are the Guadalquivir, Guadalete, Barbate (an outlet for the Laguna de la Janda), and Guadiaro.

The climate is generally mild, but varies with altitude and other physiographic features; rainfall is sometimes deficient, with damaging effects on crops and vineyards. Much of the higher zones are forested, producing cork. In the lowlands grain, wine, fruits, and olives are produced. The evaporation pans around the Bay of Cádiz produce considerable salt, and fishing thrives. Manufacturing is of minor importance. The area is lacking in adequate railway transportation, the chief lines being those running to Cádiz and Algeciras. Near Cádiz and Jerez are several local lines and tramways.

Other important cities in the province are Jerez de la Frontera; La Línea; Algeciras; San Fernando, a naval base and headquarters on the south side of the Bay of Cádiz; and Sanlúcar de Barrameda, known to the ancients as Luciferi Fanum, a beach resort and center for the export of manzanilla wine. From this city's port at Bonanza, on the nearby Guadalquivir, Columbus sailed on his voyage in 1498, and Magellan on his circumnavigation of the globe in 1519. Among the smaller cities of note in the province are Puerto Santa María, at the mouth of the Guadalete, which has a Moorish castle and a fine bathing beach and exports excellent wines; Chiclana de la Frontera, noted for its sulphur springs; Puerto Real, known to the Romans as Portus Gaditanus, reconstructed under Isabella I in the midst of salt marshes; Arcos de la Frontera, situated in an easily defensible position in the upper Guadalete Basin, called Arco-

briga by the Romans and Medina Arkosch by the Moors; Vejer de la Frontera, with its distinctly Moorish flavor, situated a few miles inland from Cape Trafalgar, where the famous naval battle took place on Oct. 21, 1805; Medina Sidonia, a crumbling town still showing traces of its glory in former times, when it was the principal residence of the powerful family founded by Alonso Pérez de Guzmán, progenitor of the dukes of Medina Sidonia; and Rota, seaport and military air base, the ocean terminus of a pipeline extending across Spain from Zaragoza. Pop. 1950, 693,267.

History. Gadir, as the city of Cádiz was called by the Phoenicians, was the oldest Phoenician colony in Spain. It was reputedly founded by settlers from Tyre about 1100 B.C. and was later (c. 500 B.C.) taken over by Carthage when it occupied the southern part of the Iberian Peninsula. The Carthaginians made Gadir their principal base in Spain until the founding of New Carthage (now Cartagena), and it was employed by Hannibal in his campaign across Spain and France into Italy. Jealous of Carthage, the city became a Roman ally in 206 B.C. and was renamed Gades. It acquired Roman citizenship and flourished under the empire, holding much of the commerce of the fertile valley of the Baetis (Guadalquivir). It began to decay in the fourth century and was virtually destroyed by the invading Visigoths; hence almost nothing remains of the ancient city. It was one of the first Spanish cities to fall (711) to the Arabs, who called it Jezirat-Kadis. The Arabs ruled the city until 1262, when it was captured by Alfonso X, "the Learned," of Castile. The city was of minor importance under the Moors, and its early medieval history is largely unknown.

When the Spanish captured Cádiz they were obliged to completely rebuild and repopulate the city; they also provided it with extensive fortifications. The city's real prosperity began after the discovery of the New World, when it became the home port for the "silver fleets" bound to and from the Americas. All this concentration of wealth naturally invited attacks by Spain's enemies, including the Barbary pirates (notably in 1553 and 1574), who were repelled. In April 1587 Sir Francis Drake suddenly appeared in Cádiz harbor, burned a score of ships, and harried the coast as far north as Lisbon. This action, however, did not prevent the "Invincible Armada" from sailing the next year to its destruction in the English Channel. In June 1596, another English force under Robert Devereux, Earl of Essex, and Admiral Charles Howard appeared at Cádiz and surprised a fleet Philip II had assembled to carry aid to the rebellious Irish. The English destroyed 13 men-of-war and 40 galleons and sacked the town after taking its forts, but soon retired because of discord among the leaders. The city had to be largely rebuilt, and it enjoyed two more centuries of great prosperity, successfully repelling subsequent English attacks, as in 1625, 1656, 1702, 1797-1798, and 1800. The attack of 1800 was led by the British naval hero Horatio Nelson. During this era the value of gold and silver passing through Cádiz from America exceeded 100,000,000 pesos a year

The Napoleonic Wars were the undoing of Cádiz. The British assaults between 1797 and 1800 were a prelude. In 1808 a French fleet in the inner bay was captured by the men of Cádiz. The city was besieged by the French from February 1810 to August 1812, when it was relieved by Arthur Wellesley, Duke of Wellington. During this time the Cortes took refuge in Cádiz, and in 1812 it adopted a liberal constitution, later repudiated by the returning King Ferdinand VII. On Jan. 1, 1820, an insurrection in favor of the restoration of this constitution was started by army officers at Cádiz, but in 1823 a French army under Charles de Valois, Duke of Angoulême, captured the forts of the Trocadero across the bay and liberated Ferdinand, who had been brought, as a prisoner of the Cortes, to Cádiz. The city has since been noted for its espousal of revolutionary causes. Meanwhile, its commerce was greatly diminished by the defection of the Latin American republics, whose trade had been a monopoly of Spain. Rebel forces under Francisco Franco took Cádiz very early in the Civil War of 1936-1939.   R.G.W.

CADMAN, CHARLES WAKEFIELD (1881-1946), American composer, was born Dec. 24, 1881, in Johnstown, Pa. During his career he was at various times a composer, a music critic, an organist, and a conductor. He also lectured on American Indian music and used Indian themes in some of his works. Cadman wrote in many forms but he is best known for his songs, the most popular of which are *From the Land of the Sky Blue Water* and *At Dawning*. He died in Los Angeles, Dec. 30, 1946.   R. Mo.

CADMAN, SAMUEL PARKES (1864-1936), Anglo-American Congregational leader of Wesleyan antecedents,

DR. SAMUEL PARKES
CADMAN

EWING GALLOWAY

was born on Dec. 18, 1864, in Wellington, Shropshire, England. He graduated from Richmond College in 1889 and came to the United States in the following year. Most of his active ministry was spent in Brooklyn, mainly as pastor of the Central Congregational Church (1901-1936), President of the Federal Council of the Churches of Christ in America (1924-1928), and National Radio Preacher for the Federal Council (1928-1936). He also often preached at universities and lectured at theological seminaries on various aspects of the ministry and of the humanities. He wrote fourteen scholarly books, including *Ambassadors of God* (1920) and *The Three Religious Leaders of Oxford* (1916), the latter including studies of Wycliffe, John Wesley, and John Henry Newman. S. Parkes Cadman became known for his breadth of culture and charm of style and was considered perhaps the leading pulpit orator of his day in America. He died in Plattsburg, N. Y., July 12, 1936.   A. W. B.

CADMIUM [kæ′dmiəm], symbol Cd, element number 48, at. wt. 112.41, density 8.6, m.p. 320.9° C., b.p. 765° C. Cadmium is in Group II-B of the periodic table, being intermediate between zinc and mercury. Its atomic structure shows that there are two valence electrons which are quite a distance from the nucleus, and so are easily lost. As a result, cadmium shows only metallic properties, and in its compounds it has a valence of 2.

Cadmium was discovered in 1817 in zinc ore, practically its only source, in which it averages less than 0.5 per cent. The rare mineral greenockite is cadmium sulphide, occurring as a yellow incrustation on zinc blende. Since cadmium is more volatile and more easily reduced than zinc, these metals are obtained together and separated by fractional distillation, or selective electrolytic deposition. Because zinc will displace cadmium from its solutions, zinc shavings are sometimes used for the displacement of cadmium from mixed solutions of the salts of the two metals.

Properties. Cadmium is a white metal with a bluish tinge resembling zinc in appearance and behavior. It is slightly harder and heavier than zinc and is more malleable and ductile. It dissolves readily in nitric acid, but it requires heat to effect solution in hydrochloric and sulphuric acids.

Uses and Compounds. For nearly a century after its discovery, no uses were found for cadmium, and it was sometimes referred to as "the unwanted stepchild of zinc." The automobile developed a demand for cadmium, first as a rustproof coating for nuts, bolts, and other small parts. Later the demand for cadmium increased greatly because of its use in bearing metals. During World War II cadmium ranked high among critically short metals, and its uses were rigidly controlled. In 1944 nearly 9,000,000 lb. were produced in the United States. Cadmium is still used mainly in electroplating as a protective coating for iron and steel, particularly in automobiles and aircraft. The molten metal is sometimes sprayed on steel in gasoline storage tanks, where it is useful in preventing corrosion and sludge formation. Cadmium alloys are also used for solders and low-melting fuse metals.

About 3 per cent of the total supply of cadmium is used for making compounds, which closely resemble those of zinc. The most important difference comes from the fact that cadmium forms no compounds which are acidic like the zincates. Cadmium forms some double salts like $Cd(CN)_2 \cdot 2KCN$, used in electroplating, and $CdI_2 \cdot 2KI \cdot 2H_2O$, used in testing alkaloids. The simple iodide CdI_2 and the other halides are used in photography, engraving, and lithographing. Cadmium sulphide, CdS, is known as cadmium yellow. It is a brillant yellow pigment which is very permanent, used by artists and in coloring soaps, glass, textiles, paper, rubber, printing inks, glazes and fireworks. Cadmium "sulphoselenide" is a mixture of cadmium sulphide and selenium. It is known as cadmium red, the shade of which varies with the amount of selenium contained. Its uses are similar to those of cadmium sulphide.   B. S. H.

CADMUS [kæ'dməs], in Greek mythology, a Boeotian hero and the founder of Thebes. The son of Agenor, king of Phoenicia, Cadmus was also the brother of Europa, who was beloved by Zeus in the form of a bull. When Europa was carried off to Crete on the back of the god in this disguise, Cadmus was sent in pursuit by his father with instructions not to return without her. Unable to find his sister, Cadmus was directed by an oracle to end his quest and instead to follow a cow and build a town where she should lie down exhausted. The cow led him to the site of Thebes, where a dragon, sacred to Ares, guarded a fountain. Cadmus slew the dragon and, following the instructions of Athena, sowed its teeth in the ground. From these teeth a race of armed men presently sprang forth and fell to fighting each other; all but five were killed, but these assisted Cadmus in building the Cadmeia, or citadel of Thebes. After Cadmus had done eight years' penance for slaying the dragon, he was finally permitted to marry Harmonia, daughter of Ares and Aphrodite. Harmonia received as a bridal gift a beautiful necklace made by Hephaestus, but it brought nothing but misfortune to the family. Cadmus and Harmonia had four daughters, Semele, Ino, Autonoe, and Agave, and one son, Polydorus; Semele and Ino among these, and also Actaeon, son of Autonoe, and Pentheus, son of Agave, all suffered violent deaths. The necklace was later given to Eriphyle, who was slain by her son Alcmaeon. Cadmus and Harmonia later withdrew from Thebes to Illyria, where they were transformed into serpents, their souls being taken to Elysium. Cadmus was said to have introduced into Greece the Phoenician alphabet. *See also* TAURUS.   G. E. D.

CADORNA, COUNT LUIGI [kado'rna] (1850-1928), Italian soldier, was born in Pallanza, Sept. 4, 1850. He was the son of General Raffaele Cadorna, another famous Italian general, and was given a military education, receiving his first army commission in 1868. Cadorna was on his father's staff when the general captured Rome in 1870. He rose steadily in the army, meanwhile achieving renown as a brilliant writer on military strategy. In 1915 he became chief of the Italian general staff, and when Italy entered World War I in May 1915 he was made supreme field commander. Cadorna conducted the campaigns in the Trentino and along the Isonzo River against the Austrians with comparative success, but paid little attention to the condition and morale of his troops. In the disastrous Caporetto retreat of Oct. 24, 1917, one of the greatest Allied reverses of the war, Cadorna lost his Second Army and more than 100,000 men. Despite the Austrian break-through, however, he was able to extricate the remainder of his forces and halt the enemy at the Piave River by the first week in November. He was succeeded in command, Nov. 8, 1917, by General Armando Díaz, and thereafter served for several months on the Supreme Allied War Council before retiring. Under the Fascist regime he was given the rank of marshal in 1924. Cadorna died in Bordighera, Dec. 21, 1928.   H. McG. S.

CADOUDAL, GEORGES [ka'du'da'l] (1771-1804), French royalist leader of the Chouan resistance to the first French Republic, was born Jan. 1, 1771, in the village of Kerléano, Brittany. Like many others in western France, he joined the loyalist forces in La Vendée in 1793. Taken prisoner, he escaped and became active in the faction known as the Chouans ("Screech Owls"), a royalist underground movement which derived its name from the owl-like cry which its members used for a signal. Until 1800 Cadoudal was one of the most resourceful leaders of the group, attracting even the admiration of Napoleon; but after the Battle of Pont-de-Loch in January of that year he ceased his activities and journeyed to Paris for a conference with Napoleon, then First Consul. Napoleon was reported to have offered Cadoudal strong inducements to join his army, but the royalist leader declined and sought refuge in England in 1801. In 1803 he returned to France, having plotted meanwhile with General Charles Pichegru, Jean Victor Moreau, and others to assassinate Napoleon and overthrow the government. The conspiracy was discovered and Cadoudal was arrested in March 1804. He was guillotined in Paris, with eleven associates, on June 25, 1804.   W. Fr.

CAECILIANS [sisɪ'liənz], a group of limbless Amphibia belonging to the order *Gymnophiona.* Resembling earthworms, they inhabit swampy places in almost all tropical countries except Madagascar. They are mud-burrowers and seldom are seen, although sixty or seventy species are known. On their bodies are transverse folds in the grooves of which tiny hidden scales are found in some genera. Midway between the eye and nostril is a peculiar sensory tentacle which is protruded for the purpose of feeling about, for the lidless eyes are practically functionless. In some species, the female lays large-yolked eggs about which she coils until the larvae hatch and enter the water. Other forms have no aquatic larval stage and only a few species have external gills. Members of the genus *Typhlonectes,* which inhabit the rivers of South America, resemble eels and often measure eighteen inches long. They are wholly aquatic and produce live young, an unusual procedure, for only a few Amphibians are ovoviviparous.   A. Sv.

CAECILIUS STATIUS [sisɪ'liəs ste'shiəs] (c.219-c.166 B.C.), Roman comic poet, was born an Insubrian Gaul, but was captured during a Gallic war in north Italy about 200 B.C. He was brought to Rome as a slave but later received his freedom and took his name from his patron. Like Plautus and Terence, Caecilius adapted Greek plays to the Roman stage, his favorite Greek model being Menander. Some forty titles and three hundred lines of his work survive. The youthful Terence is said to have read his *Andria* aloud to Caecilius, being eager for his encouragement, and ancient critics speak highly of him, Volcacius Sedigitus ranking him first among Roman comic poets. Horace and Varro also extol his work, although Cicero and Quintilian, however, are less enthusiastic.   G. McL. H.

CAECUM. *See* COMPARATIVE ANATOMY.

CAEDMON [kæ'dmən] (seventh century of the Christian era), the shepherd-poet and later monk of the abbey of Whitby, Northumbria, whose name is associated with the earliest Christian poetry in English literature, flourished about A.D. 675. Caedmon's life is described by Bede in his *Ecclesiastical History of the English People* (completed in 731). Caedmon, then an old man and without skill in reciting verse, seeing the harp approaching him at an evening's entertainment, slipped away to the stable and fell asleep among his cattle. There he dreamed that a shining figure appeared to him and said, "Caedmon, sing me something." "I cannot sing," said the shepherd, "that is why I came away." "But you can," said the visitant. "What shall I sing?" "Sing the beginning of Creation." Then, says Bede, Caedmon began to sing. Next morning, remembering his verses, he was taken to the Abbess, and she had Bible stories read to him which he, "ruminating like a clean beast," turned into verse.

Caedmon, according to Bede, sang first the earth's creation, the story of Genesis, the departure of the Children of Israel from Egypt, the Incarnation, Passion, and Ascension of Christ, and the Last Judgment, and he gives a prose paraphrase, in his Latin text, of the hymn which Caedmon first sang. This has been preserved in its original Northumbrian form and in a West Saxon translation of Bede's *History*. A special interest attaches to this hymn, for it is the earliest English poem of which the date and authorship are known, and it is the only specimen of Caedmon's verse that can definitely be ascribed to him. The following translation into modern English alliterative verse conveys a sense of the form and content of Caedmon's verse:

> Now hymn we aloud the Lord of Heaven,
> Praise His wisdom and wonderful power,
> The glorious work of the great Creator,
> How the Father Eternal founded this world.
> First He set for the sons of men,
> Heaven to roof them. The Holy Ruler,
> The King of mankind, then cast the foundations
> Of earth in the midst, and made thereafter
> Land for the living, the Lord Almighty.

This fragment is a brief hymn of praise and does not conform to the type of Biblical narrative ascribed by Bede to Caedmon. The extant narrative poems of a manuscript dating from about the eleventh century, the so-called Junian

CAEN, NORMANDY, FRANCE

Manuscript, long known as "Caedmon's Paraphrase," have been demonstrated by modern scholarship to belong to a later period and different authors, and are no longer ascribed to Caedmon. Though Bede's account of Caedmon is colored by the legendary accessions characteristic of his time, there is undoubtedly a core of historic truth in his story. J. D. S.

CAELUM [si'ləm], the Graving Tool, a small, elongated, inconspicuous southern constellation of modern record, centered at right ascension, 4 hr. 40 min.; declination, —38°. It includes no stars brighter than those of fourth magnitude.
J. H. P.

CAEN [kã'], the capital city of the department of Calvados in Normandy, in northwestern France, about 9 mi. south of the mouth of the Orne River and approximately 125 mi. northwest of Paris, at 49° 12′ N. lat. and 0° 18′ W. long. Caen lies in the middle of a fertile plain and is a noted market, trading, and commercial center. It achieved importance as early as the tenth century, and flourished under William the Conqueror and other dukes of Normandy, of which principality it became the capital. English forces headed by Edward III took the city and plundered it in 1346. The English took Caen again in 1417, and occupied it until 1450, when French troops recaptured it. In the religious wars during the Reformation, Caen suffered much damage. Protestant forces under Admiral Gaspard de Coligny seized the city in 1562. The industries of the town were almost ruined by the revocation of the Edict of Nantes in 1685, as Huguenot workers of the mills and factories left the city seeking safety, many embarking for England. In 1795 Caen became the headquarters of the Girondist opposition to the national Convention held in Paris in 1793. The city escaped damage during World War I, but during World War II most of it was destroyed or badly damaged; only the western section and the periphery of the town escaped bombardment. Among the monuments destroyed were the Church of Saint-Gilles, dating from 1082; the Escoville Mansion, an excellent example of French Renaissance civic architecture built in 1532-1542; the spire of the Church of Saint Pierre, built by William the Conqueror, who was buried in the building; the City Hall, built in the eighteenth century; and the portal of the Castle, the only portion which remained of the extensive fortifications around the building begun by William the Conqueror. Points of interest which survive include the Church de la Trinité, formerly the Church of the Abbaye-aux-dames, a fine specimen of Norman-Romanesque architecture, construction of which was begun in 1066 by Matilde, wife of William the Conqueror; the prefecture; the palace of justice; the university; the public library; two excellent hospitals; and several museums. The broad streets of the city are laid out regularly, and there are many fine open squares. Charlotte Corday, who was born near the city, set out from Caen in 1793 to assassinate Jean Paul Marat, a leader in the French Revolution. Daniel F. E. Auber, the composer, and François de Malherbe, the poet, were born at Caen. George Bryan Brummel, the English dandy known as Beau Brummel, lies buried at Caen, where he served as a British consul.

The importance of Caen as a trading center is augmented by a canal which connects the city with the sea. Coal, timber, dairy products, fruit, grain, coal, and iron ore are among the chief articles of trade; another is the famous Caen building stone excavated from quarries to the south and west of the city. Local manufactures include textiles, lace, metal and leather goods, cutlery, rope, and beverages. The city contains sawmills, shipyards, distilleries, dyeworks, and foundries. Pop. 1954, 67,851.

CAERLEON [karli'ən], a village in the southern parliamentary division of Monmouthshire, England, on the Usk River, situated about 150 mi. east of London. It is known as the site of the Roman fortress Isca Silurum, founded and garrisoned by Augustan Legion II. In 1926, when money was raised to buy and excavate the area, remains of Roman and British buildings and stone paved roads were found, built on ruins of wooden structures. The discoveries did not support the legend that King Arthur held his round table in the community. In the eighth and ninth centuries Danes plundered and sacked Caerleon. Welsh and Mercians contested its possession until the Norman Conquest, when the struggle was transferred to the Welsh and Normans between 1113 and 1174. Alfred Tennyson spent several months in Caerleon while preparing his *Idylls of the King*. Pop. 1952, 4,887.

CAESAR [si'zər], the cognomen of the Julian family (Gaius Julius Caesar, for example) which was retained by the early Roman emperors, the Julio-Claudians, to emphasize their family relationship with the great Julius. Beginning with the Flavian dynasty of Vespasian, this family relationship no longer existed. Nevertheless, "Caesar" was retained by the Flavians and their successors as a title, and thus it survived into modern times in the titles kaiser and tsar. From the third century onward, the Roman emperors employed the title Augustus, and gave the title of Caesar to subordinates whom they wished to make their successors. T. B. J.

CAESAR, GAIUS. *See* CALIGULA.

CAESAR, GAIUS JULIUS (100-44 B.C.), Roman general and statesman, was born July 12, 100 B.C. The family background of Julius Caesar was sufficiently aristocratic to insure his early entry into Roman politics. However, his progress toward the higher offices was slow because he lacked financial backing and because the party with which he identified himself soon fell from power. After first marrying—and soon divorcing—an heiress, Caesar married the daughter of Cinna. He thus became a member of the Marian (the popular) party which lost its influence in politics after the victories of Lucius Sulla and the senatorial party (83 B.C.). Caesar lost all his property and narrowly escaped execution when he refused to divorce his second wife and break off his Marian connections. Influential friends persuaded Sulla to spare Caesar's life, but Sulla warned them that he saw in this young man "many a Marius."

During the next decade, while his political fortunes were in eclipse, Caesar lived in the East. He spent some time at the court of Nicomedes of Bithynia and also studied oratory at Rhodes. When the tide turned against the senatorial party during the consulship of Pompey and Crassus (70 B.C.), Caesar returned to Rome to resume his career in politics. He served as quaestor in Sicily in 68 B.C. and as curule aedile in Rome three years later. As aedile, with financial aid from Crassus, Caesar gained great popularity through lavish personal expenditures on the public games. In 63 B.C., he became Pontifex Maximus, a lifetime appointment which made Caesar the head of the state religion.

Caesar became the partner and political manager of Crassus, the wealthiest man in Rome. The principal object of their numerous intrigues during this period was to destroy the prestige of Pompey, who had won new laurels in his wars against the pirates and Mithridates. Although Caesar did become praetor in 62 B.C., earlier schemes of

Crassus and Caesar to gain power were not so successful: Catiline had to be repudiated after Cicero defeated him for the consulship, and a plan for the annexation of Egypt also failed. A religious scandal which involved Clodius and Caesar's third wife, Pompeia, in 62 B.C., made it necessary for Caesar to divorce Pompeia since "Caesar's wife must be above suspicion."

When Caesar returned to Rome in 61 B.C., after serving as propraetor in Spain, he found that the senatorial party

GAIUS JULIUS CAESAR

COURTESY OF THE NEW YORK
PUBLIC LIBRARY

had become fearful of Pompey's great popularity and political power, which they resolved to diminish by refusing to compensate his veterans or to ratify the settlements which he had made in the East. Pompey, Crassus, and Caesar, opposing the existing system of government, formed the private political coalition known as the First Triumvirate (60 B.C.). By combining their resources in this manner, the triumvirs were able to elect Caesar to the consulship for 59 B.C. As consul, Caesar secured the enactment of laws which fulfilled Pompey's desires, provided Crassus with a contract to collect the taxes of the province of Asia, and gave Caesar himself a proconsulship in Gaul.

When Caesar first went to Gaul, only the southern portion of the territory was claimed by the Romans, but in a decade of campaigning he overran all of present-day France and crossed the Rhine into Germany. He also claimed the conquest of Britain, but his campaigns there were indecisive. Nevertheless, in Gaul Caesar was successful in building up a strong and efficient army, and he amassed a fortune in plunder.

During Caesar's absence in Gaul, the First Triumvirate fell apart. Crassus was killed by the Parthians in 53 B.C., and Pompey renewed his old connections with the senatorial party. Open conflict between Caesar and Pompey was precipitated in 49 B.C. when the Senate ordered Caesar to give up his command in Gaul and return to Rome as a private citizen. Instead, Caesar led his army across the Rubicon, a river between Cisalpine Gaul and Italy, and marched upon Rome. He drove the Pompeian adherents from Italy to the Greek peninsula, where he defeated them overwhelmingly at Pharsalus in 48 B.C. Pompey fled to Egypt, where he was killed at the order of the reigning Ptolemy, the brother of Cleopatra.

Caesar also went to Egypt as a conqueror; there he became involved with Cleopatra and put her on the throne in place of her brother Ptolemy. He pacified the East and wiped out the remnants of the senatorial armies at Thapsus in Northern Africa (46 B.C.) and Munda in Spain (45 B.C.).

Caesar was at the height of his power. Although the real bases of his strength were his popularity with the army and the fact that he had wiped out his principal opponents, he also had a stronger constitutional position than any Roman leader who had preceded him. He was dictator and Pontifex Maximus for life; in 45 and 44 B.C. he also held the consulship and combined with this the authority of a tribune. By virtue of his censorial powers as Prefect of Morals, he could control the membership of the Senate. Special laws gave him the right to make peace and war in the name of the Roman state, the command of all troops, and the right to nominate and appoint the magistrates.

After he had destroyed all organized opposition, Caesar began a program of reconstruction and reform. This involved an extension of Roman citizenship to provincial areas, the founding of Roman colonies at advantageous commercial sites (present-day Seville, Arles, and Corinth), the granting of municipal charters to a number of provincial cities (present-day Lisbon, Toulon, and Vienna), the adoption of the Julian calendar, and a reform of the currency. Plans he did not live to carry out included a codification of Roman law, the construction of a canal through the Isthmus of Corinth, and an expedition against the Parthians.

The autocratic character of Caesar's rule aroused fears that he might destroy the Roman republican system and set up a monarchy. The presence of Cleopatra in Rome fostered rumors that Caesar intended to make her his queen. Although Caesar publicly refused an offer of kingship, suspicion was not allayed, and a group of senators led by Marcus Brutus and Gaius Cassius began to plot his overthrow. In the Senate, on Mar. 15, 44 B.C., the conspirators attacked Caesar and stabbed him to death.

The genius of Caesar had many facets. He was more than a great general, comparable and perhaps superior to Alexander the Great. The Romans recognized Caesar's ability as an orator, no mean distinction in the days of Cicero and Hortensius. As a writer of prose, the clarity of Caesar's style is evident from a reading of his *Commentaries*. Caesar also had administrative capacity, and his nonpolitical reforms and innovations showed breadth of vision in economic, legal, and cultural matters. Caesar correctly diagnosed the inevitable trend of the Roman government toward autocracy, but he made the mistake of attempting to transform the republic into an Oriental monarchy in one generation.

Actually, it is not definitely known, but only suspected, that Caesar's goal was monarchy. The Romans thought it was, but the available facts show only that Caesar thought autocracy the immediate solution for Rome's political ills. In view of the poverty of ancient methods of transportation and communication, it is probable that autocracy provided a more efficient government for a large empire than would have been possible with a more liberal form.   T. B. J.

CAESAREAN SECTION. *See* OBSTETRICS.

CAGAYAN DE ORO, the capital of the province of Misamis Oriental on northern Mindanao in the Republic of the Philippines. It is a port of entry on Macajalar Bay off Mindanao Sea. The national airport is 3 mi. from the city. The soil of the surrounding region is very rich, and coconuts are the main crop, with corn interplanted among the palms. Rice and pineapples are also raised. Lumbering and fishing are also important. Cagayan de Oro is the seat of the Catholic Archdiocese of Mindanao. Pop. 1948, 46,266.

CAGLIARI [kɑ′lyɑri], a city on the island of Sardinia and the capital of Cagliari Province and of the island.

City. Cagliari, situated on the southern coast of Sardinia at the head of the Gulf of Cagliari, lies on sloping ground between two hills over 300 ft. high. The coast is low in both directions, and toward the west there are extensive marshes interspersed with shallow ponds. The climate is mild; snow is rare, and the average annual precipitation is about 17 in., most of it falling in the winter.

Cagliari is the southern terminus of the cross-island railway running to Sassari and Olbia; and steamship and air service connect it with the Italian mainland, Sicily, and other Mediterranean countries. The city is the commercial center for southern and central Sardinia. There are shipyards and a variety of industries producing ceramics, chemicals, cement, foodstuffs, wine, and machinery. Quantities of salt are produced in the saltworks in the marshlands, and salt, wine, and minerals are exported. Fishing is also a source of income.

Among the city's monuments are the Phoenicio-Punic cemetery on the hill of Bonaria, the Roman amphitheatre, the Pisan cathedral, the royal palace, occasionally a residence of the former royal family, the university (founded in 1606), and the National Museum. Most of the old walls have been torn down to allow for expansion, but a few towers remain.

Cagliari has been inhabited since the Neolithic Age, and nearby are several of the enigmatic *nuraghi* (prehistoric towers). After being a Phoenician colony, Cagliari prospered under the rule of Carthage. The Romans took the city in 238 B.C. and populated it with Roman colonists. When the Arabs came, after interludes of Vandal and Byzantine rule, Cagliari became a mere village; those inhabitants not taken into slavery sought refuge in the island's interior. In the thirteenth century the Pisans built a castle and made Cagliari one of the strongest points in the western Mediterranean. Early in the fourteenth century the Catalans drove out the Pisans and established their own colonies. Charles V sought to make Cagliari a well-defended base against Turkish incursions. In 1708 the city was bombarded by a British fleet on behalf of Austria's pretensions to Sicily. In the Treaty of London of 1718 it was given over to the House of Savoy which, during the Napoleonic era, occupied the city, protected by the British fleet. During World War II, as the military headquarters of Sardinia, the city was heavily bombed until the Allies occupied the island in the spring of 1943. Pop. 1954, 148,500.

The Province. The province of Cagliari comprises 160 communes and covers an area of 3,590 sq. mi. The terrain is in part hilly and in part consists of plains through which flow several of the island's rivers, including the Tirso, Flumendosa, and Flumini Mannu. The soil is generally good, but until recent decades malaria was a serious problem. Living conditions have been improved, hydroelectric power is being developed, and more land is being brought under cultivation by draining projects and reclamation works started under the Fascists and vigorously pushed after World War II. The province has granite and limestone quarries and is one of the richest in Italy in mineral resources, notably coal, lead, silver, zinc, and iron.

Important towns in the province include Iglesias, an industrial and mining center; Carbonia, founded in 1938 as the center of the coal-mining industry; and Oristano, a food-processing center. Pop. (est. 1954), 711,900.   R. G. W.

CAGLIOSTRO, ALESSANDRO, COUNT (1743-1795), Italian alchemist and imposter, whose real name was

Giuseppe Balsamo, was born in Palermo, Sicily, in 1743, of poor parents. Escaping from Sicily after a series of petty crimes, he traveled through Greece, Egypt, Arabia, Persia, Rhodes, and Malta, assuming the title of count and marrying Lorenza Feliciani, the daughter of a high-born Roman family. He continued his travels in Europe, posing as a physician, alchemist, necromancer, and freemason. He sold miraculous philtres and potions, alchemistic powders, and elixirs of youth and posed as the founder of an occult branch of freemasonry. Through the daring and ingenuity of his enterprises he gained great wealth and an amazing reputation among the best society of Europe. In 1785 he was implicated in the Affair of the Diamond Necklace and was imprisoned in the Bastille. Banished from France, he went to Rome, where he was arrested for heresy in 1789 and condemned to death. The sentence was later commuted to life imprisonment and he died in the prison of San Leo in 1795. Alexander Dumas's novel, *Memoirs of a Physician,* is based on Cagliostro's adventures. *See also* DIAMOND NECKLACE, AFFAIR OF THE.   C. W. D.

CAGUAS [ka'gwas], a city and judicial district, about 20 mi. south of San Juan, Puerto Rico. It was founded in 1775 in a fertile interior valley of the island and named for Caguax, a famous Indian chief. It is one of the four largest cities on the island and one of its most prosperous industrial and agricultural centers. Caguas was chartered as a city in 1812 and the government is by a mayor and municipal assembly. It is the birthplace of many famous Puerto Ricans, one of them being José Gautier Benítez, one of the outstanding poets of Latin America. The city supports two high schools, four schools of commerce, and two broadcasting stations. In the fertile soil of the region sugar, vegetables, and fruits are raised. Caguas is also one of the chief tobacco centers on the island. Manufactures include clothing, radio and television parts, ice, optical parts, bed springs, mattresses, buttons, trophies, leather articles, and furniture. Pop. 1950, 33,759.

CAHOKIA [kəho'kiə], the largest prehistoric group of artificial earth mounds in America north of Mexico. It is located near East St. Louis, Ill., in Madison County. The mound site was named after an early eighteenth century tribe of the Illinois Confederacy which lived in the area but did not build the mounds. The largest Cahokia mound measures approximately 1,000 by 720 ft. at the base and 100 ft. in height. It is a rectangular, flat-topped pyramid constructed with four separate lower terraces and a probable ramp. This great mound is sometimes known as "Monks Mound" after a colony of Trappists who lived on the mound summit in the nineteenth century. Besides the great mound, from 45 to 85 lesser pyramidal mounds have been reported from the site. Many of these, however, have since disappeared as the result of modern cultivation. The area covered is between 3 and 4 sq. mi. of rich river bottom land. Two archaeological cultures are represented at Cahokia. Both belong to the Mississippian Pattern. The earlier is sometimes referred to as the "Old Village" Focus (c. A.D. 800-1250); the latter has been known alternatively as the "Beanpot" or Trappist Focus (c. A.D. 1250-1450). *See also* ARCHAEOLOGY (North America).   G. R. W.

CAICOS ISLANDS [kai'kəs], also called the Turks and Caicos Islands, a group of 30 or more small islands with an area of 165 sq. mi., which form the extreme southeastern end of the Bahama Chain. These low islands are 108 mi.

north of Hispaniola. The Turks and Caicos Islands belong geographically to the Bahamas, but politically they were a dependency of Jamaica until April 1958, when they formed their own government, remaining outside the new West Indies Federation. Grand Caicos, the largest island, is 25 mi. long and up to 10 mi. wide. Grand Turk Island is 7 mi. long and 2 mi. wide. Sponge fishing and saltmaking are the chief occupations. Pop. (est. 1955), 6,600.

J. E. F. and G. Con.

CAILLAUX, JOSEPH MARIE AUGUSTE [ka'yo'] (1863-1944), French politician, was born in Le Mans, Mar. 30, 1863. In 1888, after a brilliant academic career, he entered the ministry of finance, where he rose rapidly. He gained additional political experience by his election in 1898 to the Chamber of Deputies as representative for Mamers. As an expert in the field of taxation, Caillaux was chosen minister of finance when Pierre Waldeck-Rousseau formed his ministry in 1899. Caillaux held this portfolio for three years, during which he effected a number of financial reforms. After Georges Clemenceau became premier late in the fall of 1906, Caillaux again became minister of finance for three years. In 1911, at the time of the Agadir crisis, Caillaux himself was premier. Distrustful of professional diplomats, he conducted private negotiations with the German embassy in Paris in an effort to arrive at a Franco-German understanding. When the secret of these negotiations became known, he was forced to resign. In retirement he published his version of the incident in a book, *Agadir: ma politique extérieure* (1919).

In January 1914, when Caillaux was again in office at the finance ministry, a series of newspaper attacks upon him ultimately led to the fatal shooting of Gaston Calmette, the editor of *Figaro,* by Mme. Caillaux. The trial became a *cause célèbre* of the time. Mme. Caillaux, ardently defended by her husband, who had resigned from public office, was eventually acquitted.

During World War I, Caillaux was scornfully critical of the conduct of affairs and continued to believe in the possibilities of an early and honorable peace between France and Germany. In January 1918 he was arrested and early in 1920 was brought to trial before the Senate, acting as the High Court of Justice, charged with having plotted against the security of the state. He was sentenced to pay the costs of the trial, to imprisonment for three years (considered as having been served during his period of detention), and to loss of civic rights for ten years.

Once more in political oblivion, Caillaux retired to Mamers, where he wrote *Où va la France? Où va l'Europe?* (1922) (*Whither France? Whither Europe?,* 1923), a critical review of the war. In 1924 he was granted amnesty and in 1925 became minister of finance in the Paul Painlevé government. The crisis of the franc, however, forced him out of office. He then resumed work as a legislator, having been elected to the Senate. In 1932 he was chosen president of the finance committee of the Senate, and in 1935 he returned to the cabinet as minister of finance in the short-lived Bouisson government. Thereafter Caillaux's political influence steadily declined, although he retained the chairmanship of the finance committee of the Senate until the World War II collapse of France in 1940. He took no part in political activity during the German occupation. Caillaux died at Mamers, Nov. 21, 1944.   B. C. W.

CAIMAN [ke'mən], sometimes called South American alligator, any of seven tropical American alligatorlike crocodilians of three genera (*Caiman, Melanosuchus, Paleosu-*

chus); generally under eight feet in length, although the black caiman (*M. niger*) of Brazil and the Guianas reaches fifteen. Unmolested caimans are unlikely to attack man, but the capturing of large specimens is a hazardous task. *See also* CROCODILE.　　　　　　　　　　　　　M. G. N.

CAIN, in the Old Testament, the oldest son of Adam and Eve. He was a tiller of the soil by occupation (Gen. iv:2), and when God accepted the offering of his shepherd-brother Abel in preference to his, his wrath and jealousy were aroused and he killed Abel. In punishment, Cain was condemned to wander, protected only by the mark of God, which was to prevent any one from slaying him. Cain wandered to the land of Nod—wanderland—where he married and built a city (Gen. iv:17). He was finally slain by an arrow from the bow of Lamech. In the New Testament, Cain is referred to as an antithesis to Christian faith and brotherly love (Heb. xi:4; I John iii:12; Jude 11).　　　　M. A. G.

CAIN: A MYSTERY, a dramatic poem in three acts, by Lord Byron, published in 1821. *Cain* is a bold dramatization of the Old Testament story in sociological terms. The British clergy and most of the reviewers condemned the play as impious and atheistical.　　　　　　　　　　　　R. A. R.

CAINE, SIR THOMAS HENRY HALL [ke'n] (1853-1931), English novelist and playwright, was born in Runcorn, Cheshire, May 14, 1853, and died on the Isle of Man,

COURTESY OF THE NEW YORK PUBLIC LIBRARY

SIR THOMAS HENRY HALL CAINE

Aug. 31, 1931. After studying architecture, Caine entered journalism in Liverpool; from there, he moved on to London where he was a close friend of the poet, D. G. Rossetti. He began writing novels in 1885; after some years his novels sold in enormous quantities, and his stage adaptations of his works played extensively in the English-speaking world. Caine was a man of great energy, and he traveled widely, not only to further his own literary interests but as a propagandist

for the English cause in World War I. His piety is indicated by the fact that during all his adult life he planned and worked on his *Life of Christ,* which was published posthumously in 1938.

In Caine's novels, piety is effectively combined with the melodramatic, as may be observed in *The Christian* (1897) and *The Eternal City* (1901). Most critics prefer, among the novels, those that give a picture of life on the Isle of Man: *The Deemster* (1887), *The Manxman* (1894), and *The Woman of Knockaloe* (1923).　　　　　　　H. H. Wa.

ÇA IRA [sa' i'ra'] (*"We Will Succeed"*), one of the earliest and most popular songs of the French Revolution, said to have been sung for the first time during the Parisians' march on Versailles on the night of Oct. 5-6, 1789. The original words are attributed to one Ladré, a popular street singer of the day, but several later variants seem to have arisen anonymously in folk song fashion. The music to which these verses were sung was an already popular contredanse tune called *Le carillon national,* composed by a Parisian orchestra violinist named Bécourt. The song soon became popular in England, both with and without its French words, and also in the United States, where during Washington's second administration (1792-1796) it became the party song of the Jeffersonian Democrats.　　　　W. Li.

CAIRNGORM [kɛ'rngɔrm], or smoky quartz, a dark yellow-brown variety of quartz, which chemically is silicon dioxide, SiO_2. It has a hardness of 7 on Mohs' scale and a density of 2.65. Cairngorm crystallizes in the hexagonal system. It was named for Cairngorm, Scotland, where the finest specimens of this mineral are obtained. Clear, gem-quality specimens of cairngorm are not common. When very dark, it is called morion, which is also a semiprecious gem stone. *See also* QUARTZ.　　　　　　　A. E. A.

CAIRO [kai'ro], the capital of Egypt, the largest city in the Arab world, and the political and cultural center of Egypt. It is situated on the Nile River, about 100 mi. from its mouth on the Mediterranean, and 12 mi. south of the apex of the delta, at 31° 13' E. long. and 30° 2' N. lat., approximately that of Houston, Tex., and Jacksonville, Fla. Cairo extends for 5 mi. along the east bank of the Nile, stretching north from the old Roman fortress of Babylon, and covering an area of more than 80 sq. mi. It is built on the alluvial plain of the Nile Valley, depending on the Nile for its water supply. The city, at an altitude of 95 ft., is in a desert region having an average annual rainfall (in the winter months) of 1.27 in. The winters are moderate, and the summers are hot and dry, except in August, when the Nile floods and causes very high humidity. The average temperature range from December to March is 49° F. to 61° F.; from March to July 71° to 88°. July and August temperatures are in the high 90's, occasionally rising to 114°. A daily drop in temperature of from 5° to 30° occurs at sunset.

Cairo is essentially a market city. The most important articles of trade are gum, ivory, hides, and ostrich feathers from the Sudan; cotton, sugar, and grain from upper Egypt; indigo and shawls from India and Iran; sheep and tobacco from Asiatic Turkey; and European manufactures, such as machinery, hardware, glass, and cotton and woolen goods. The local industries include textile factories, paper mills, a sugar refinery, and cigarette factories. Cairo is also the center of the Arabic film industry, supplying motion pictures to the entire Arab world.

General Description. The Arab section of the city and the quarters of the Copts, who adopted Christianity in the third century and claim direct descent from the ancient Egyptians, lie in the eastern portion of the city, known as Old Cairo; the government offices, other modern public buildings, and the European residential quarters are almost all in the western or modern half. To the south are remains of the old walled city and the Roman Fortress, Babylon, which according to Strabo, was founded by emigrants from that famous Mesopotamian city. About 14 mi. north of the city lie the ruins of Memphis, the Pharaonic capital, and 5 mi. to the north of it is the ancient city of Heliopolis, near which a modern suburb has been built with the same name. Adjoining Heliopolis are the airfields of Almaza and the Cairo International airport (formerly Farouk Airport and during World War II the United States Army Air Force's Payne Field), terminals of many airlines serving the Middle East and continuing to the Far East and Australia. The suburb of Gezira (Arabic *Gezira,* "island") is an island in the Nile, largely residential and containing polo fields, tennis courts, swimming pools, a race-course, cricket grounds, a golf course, and a country club. Sailing (in native *feluccas*) is also a favorite sport, as is horseback riding. The suburb of Zamalek is on the island, while Dokki, Maadi, and other suburbs surround the city. To the west, across the Nile, is Giza, whence runs a modern highway, the Mena Road, leading to the village of et-Talibiya. Here are found the world-famous Great Sphinx and the pyramids of Cheops, Khefren, and Mycerinus.

Modern Cairo. The modern section of Cairo proper, dating from the French occupation (1798-1801), is well laid out and has broad thoroughfares, handsome stone residences and apartment houses, and fine squares. This attractive section centers about the Ezbekieh Gardens, which cover about 20 acres. Near the Kasr al-Nil Bridge, connecting Cairo with Gezira, stands the famous National Museum, housing, among other treasures, the noted Tutankhamen collection, with its solid-gold sarcophagus and other treasures. In this section are modern stores, restaurants comparable to those of Paris, theatres, night-clubs, and large de luxe hotels.

Old Cairo. The older portion of the metropolis is one of the world's most picturesque Oriental cities, with more than 400 mosques and minarets and several ancient *souks* (bazaars), the most important of which is the Khan al-Khalili. Most of the streets in the old section are winding lanes, narrow and crooked, and few of them are paved. The stone houses, several stories high, have window lattices of wrought iron; humbler residences on the outskirts of the city are mud huts and in marked contrast with those of the modern section. An outstanding landmark of Old Cairo is the citadel, al-Kala, which was built by Saladin about 1177 on the Mokkatam Hills, the city's eastern limits. The citadel contains a palace, five mosques, and a well, sunk 270 ft. deep in solid rock. The oldest mosque is that of Amr Ibn al-As, founded in the seventh century; the next oldest is the mosque of Ibn Tulun, begun in 876 and completed three years later. Perhaps the most interesting is the al-Azhar, founded in 972, a combined mosque and university. This institution, the chief theological seminary in the Islamic world, is attended by students from all Moslem lands. Also interesting as excellent examples of Islamic art are the mosques of Sultan Hasan (1356), Barkuk (1384), and Kait Bey (1475). The skilled use of stone filagree, faience, alabaster, and exquisite mosaic makes these edifices masterpieces of their kind. The tombs of the Mamelukes, sometimes inaccurately referred to as the tombs of the caliphs, lie to the east of the city. These

Fortified gate to the city of Old Cairo

tombs, dating from the fifteenth century, are of great architectural interest. Near these tombs stood the stylites known as Cleopatra's Needles, one of which now stands in Paris and the other in New York's Central Park.

Cultural and Educational Institutions. In addition to the University of al-Azhar, the city of Cairo contains the University of Fouad (Fuad) I, the American University, and the People's University. Other higher schools include the Institute for Agriculture, the Institute of Finance and Commerce, the School of Applied Arts, the School of Fine Arts, the Institute for Women Teachers of Arts, the School of Applied Engineering, the Institute of Education, and the Institute of Education for Women. There are many learned societies and research institutions, a number of cultural societies, twelve museums, and thirty libraries.

History. Cairo was founded by Jauhar al-Kaïd, conqueror of Egypt for the Fatimid caliph Al-Moïz, in A.D. 968. According to tradition, the planet Mars (also known in Arabic as "the conqueror") crossed the meridian of the area at the same time. Hence the city was called "Al-Kahira," (its present Arabic name) meaning "the conqueror," corrupted in English to Cairo. The city grew and prospered until 1517, when the Turks captured it, after which it declined. In 1798, however, it was taken by the French, who initiated its modern development. British and Turkish forces recaptured Cairo in 1801, and the city was handed over to the Turks. Mohammed Ali, originally the Turkish viceroy and later undisputed master of Egypt, made Cairo the capital of his virtually independent kingdom. Thereafter the city continued to flourish, and after the British occupation in 1882 it remained the most important center in Egypt. During World War II it became the headquarters of the Allies in the Middle East; the Cairo Conference was held here from Nov. 22 to Nov. 26, 1943. Pop. 1947, 2,090,654.

CAIRO, a city in southern Illinois, the county seat of Alexander Co., located at the junction of the Ohio and Mississippi rivers, about 150 mi. southeast of East St. Louis. The site of Cairo was first explored by the French in the latter part of the seventeenth century. The first permanent community was established in 1818, and Cairo was incorporated as a city in 1857. During the Civil War it became a strategic position for campaigns in the South, for Fort Defiance at Cairo Point commanded river operations. For several months in the first two years of the war General Ulysses S. Grant used the city as a headquarters. Cairo has the commission form of government. Its position at the juncture of the Ohio and Mississippi rivers has made its survival dependent upon the maintenance of a system of levees. The first of these projects was begun in 1857, and subsequent improvements have assured the security of the city. Factories, mills, and grain elevators handle the agricultural products and timber from the surrounding rich valleys. Cottonseed oil products and hardwood flooring are the chief manufactured products. Pop. 1950, 12,123.

CAITHNESS [ke'thnəs], a maritime county of Scotland, with an area of 686 sq. mi. Its water boundaries are the Atlantic Ocean on the west, Pentland Firth on the north, and the North Sea on the east. It forms the northeastern extremity of the mainland of Scotland and has but one land boundary, Sutherland, on the southwest. Dunnet Head Promontory is the northernmost point of the British mainland. John o' Groat's House is nearby. The Orkney and Shetland islands, to the northeast, are separated from the mainland by Pentland Firth, an arm of the Atlantic. The northern coast of Pentland Firth is bold and precipitous from Wick to the Ord of Caithness; on the southeast the coast is low and sandy. There are many small streams. A considerable portion of the land is in deer forests. The flagstone quarries and the coast fisheries are the main industries. Although it is in the north, Caithness-shire is not Highland in character or customs, and Gaelic is scarcely spoken. The Norse invasions of the tenth century are recalled by many Norse place names. Wick, mentioned in Norse sagas as early as 1140, is noted as a herring fishery town. Caithness and Sutherland together send one member to Parliament. Pop. 1952, 22,926.   S. Van. V.

CAIX, NAPOLEONE [ka'iks] (1845-1882), Italian linguist, one of the founders of Romance linguistics in Italy, was born at Bozzolo (Mantua), Aug. 17, 1845. During his distinguished career in teaching at the University of Florence, he directed his main effort toward tracing the origin and the formative influence of literary Italian, finding both in the language of poetry. Of his many works his most important is *Le Origini della lingua poetica italiana* (1880). Caix died in Bozzolo on Oct. 22, 1882.   G. B.

CAJEPUT TREE [kæ'dzhəpət], a conspicuous (60 ft.) creamy-white-flowered Australian tree, *Melaleuca leucadendron*, one of the bottlebrushes. It has been planted in warm temperate regions and in the cypress swamps of southern Florida it has gone wild. It is also known as cajuput or punk tree. *See also* BOTTLE BRUSH.   J. C. Wis.

CAJETAN, JACOPO TOMMASO DE VIO [kæ'jɪtæn] (1468-1534), Italian churchman, was born in Gaeta in 1468. He entered the Dominican order in 1484 and studied and taught theology and philosophy at various universities in Italy. Cajetan became general of the Dominicans in 1508. He was made a cardinal in 1517 and bishop of Gaeta in 1518. As papal legate in Germany, 1518-1519, he attempted to reconcile Martin Luther with the Church. Throughout his life Cajetan was a disciplined student and his published works

include St. Thomas Aquinas' *Summa* with commentaries, a translation of parts of the Bible with the assistance of Hebrew scholars, and his *Opera omnia,* which were published in 1639.

CAJORI, FLORIAN [ka'zhɔ'ri'] (1859-1930), American mathematician, was born in St. Aignan, near Thusis, Switzerland, Feb. 28, 1859. At the age of sixteen he went to the United States, where he graduated from the University of Wisconsin and then did graduate work at Johns Hopkins University. He became professor of applied mathematics at Tulane University in 1887 and was professor of physics at Colorado College in Colorado Springs, Colo., from 1889 to 1918. Cajori's outstanding reputation in the field of mathematics secured him a unique appointment in 1918 to the chair of history of mathematics at the University of California, where he remained until his death, Aug. 14, 1930. Cajori was noted for his works on the history of mathematics, the most important of which were *Teaching and History of Mathematics in the United States* (1890), *The History of Mathematics* (1894) and *The History of Mathematical Notations* (1928-1929). He also wrote biographies of William Oughtred (1916) and Ferdinand Rudolph Hassler (1929).
                    C. W. D.

CALABAZILLA [kæləbəsi'lyə], a plant also known as the Missouri gourd or the wild pumpkin. It is a perennial of the gourd family, *Cucurbita foetidissima,* native to North America. Calabazilla is a prostrate, long-running vine, the fruit of which is inedible. The long-stalked leaves are somewhat heart-shaped, and their lower surface is rather silvery. The smooth fruit is of the same shape and size as an orange, and its color is green with irregular areas of yellow. Calabazilla withstands heat well and grows in sandy waste land. It is found wild from Missouri west to California and south to Mexico. In the northern part of its range the fruit frequently does not mature. The blossoms are similar to those of the pumpkin. The root, which may be 6 in. or more in diameter, is often as long as 6 ft. It has a characteristic odor suggesting decay, which accounts for the specific name, *foetidissima.* The plant is sometimes used on arbors, but since it is coarse and has a peculiar odor, it is not popular. R. S. M.

CALABRIA [kalɑ'briɑ; kəle'briə], a region occupying the southernmost peninsula, or toe, of the Italian mainland. The name originally applied to the heel of Italy (the Salentine Peninsula) and the instep (Lucania), as well as to the land of *ager Bruttium.* Since medieval times Calabria has designated only the latter, which, since Bourbon rule, has comprised the provinces of Cosenza, Catanzaro, and Reggio di Calabria.

Topography. Calabria, covering an area of 5,821 sq. mi., is 175 mi. long and varies in width from 72 to 20 mi. The coast is devoid of islands; there are no good natural harbors, and only two mediocre ones at Reggio Calabria and Croton. The peninsula is subject to frequent and violent seismic disturbances; thirty disastrous earthquakes have occurred since the twelfth century. In recent geologic ages the Calabrian coasts have been rising, as evidenced by clearly visible terraces, especially on the Tyrrhenian coast. The region is generally mountainous, with elevations of from 6,000 to almost 8,000 ft., and there are narrow coastal plains. However, in some places the mountains seem to rise from the sea. Elsewhere there are a few fairly level river valleys extending inland for some distance.

Climate. The climate depends on the altitude, with typically Mediterranean conditions prevailing in the lower and middle zones. Summers are hot, winters cool; rainfall in the winter varies from 20 to 35 in. On the plateaus, however, winters are cold with much snow, and the annual precipitation averages over 55 in. The water dissipates rapidly, and most Calabrian streams are trickles in the summer. The natural vegetation is controlled by the altitude and climate —from subtropical at sea level to alpine pastures and woodlands in the Sila.

Population. The population has increased rather slowly in modern times because of the slow development of natural resources, the former prevalence of malaria and other endemic diseases, the frequency of earthquakes, poor communication facilities, and the resultant emigrations. This latter trend was pronounced from the end of the nineteenth century until after World War I. Between 1901 and 1914 some 675,000 Calabrians migrated abroad, primarily to the United States, Argentina, Brazil, and France. Some of these emigrants later returned with savings which enabled them to acquire property or businesses in their native villages; others sent remittances to aid their families. The population is distributed unevenly. About 30 per cent of the inhabitants live in the coastal zone up to 800 ft., most of these living in scattered dwellings. The balance of the population dwells in communities, 60 per cent between 800 and 2,500 ft., and the rest at 2,500 to 3,250 ft. There are few towns with a population over 10,000. Ethnically the inhabitants are fairly homogeneous, despite infusions of African, Arab, Greek, and Albanian blood during the Middle Ages. Pop. (est. 1954), 2,107,500.

Economic Life. Until recent times the general economic life of Calabria has been backward, with primitive housing and hygienic conditions, although certain towns and districts have been exceptionally progressive and prosperous. The region's isolation from national and world markets, its lack of political significance, and the archaic land-owning system were in part responsible. Efforts to improve conditions have been going on for several decades, and the plains of Croton and Caulonia are part of recent land-reclamation programs. More homes are being built in the lowlands, which are now safe from malaria; water is being provided; and road and rail communications improved. The land is fertile, and most of the people are engaged in agriculture, although fishing and lumbering are important, and as hydroelectric plants are built more industries have been established. Thus, the harnessing of water power in the Sila made possible the erection of chemical plants in Croton. Half of the land is cultivable, and figs, wheat, citrus fruits, chestnuts, and olives are grown; and silkworms are raised. Cattle and sheep are grazed. Rock salt and sulphur are mined.

The city of Reggio Calabria is the terminus of the two principal railway lines of Calabria; one hugs the Tyrrhenian coast north to Naples; the other follows the Ionian shore to Taranto and Brindisi. There are also a few branch and narrow-gauge feeder lines. The highway network was improved following World War I because of Reggio Calabria's position as the chief supply point on the mainland for Sicily, which is only 2 mi. from the mainland across the Strait of Messina.

Calabria is picturesque and is noted for its scenic beauty, particularly on its west coast, but unlike other parts of Italy is not well known to tourists, because until recent years roads were inadequate, many places were inaccessible, and the living conditions were very poor, with a lack of adequate tourist facilities.

History. The eastern coast of the Calabrian Peninsula formed part of Magna Graecia, and such Greek colonies as Sybaris, Crotona, Locri, and Rhegium played important roles

in the history of Hellenic politics and culture. Their influence, however, was confined largely to the coast, for inland were the Bruttii, who blocked Rome's expansion southward. Following the disintegration of the Empire, Byzantine rule was asserted after a confused period of Gothic and other Germanic invasions. In the tenth century Calabria was united in a *theme* under the Byzantine Emperor Nicephorus Phocas II. Constantinople, however, was unable to promote prosperity or offer protection against Arab raids. Commerce declined, malaria spread over the lowlands, and the large estates (*latifundia*) gripped the land in their social and economic tentacles. In the eleventh century the Normans drove out the Byzantines, and under Norman and Hohenstaufen feudal rule the region enjoyed peace if not liberty, whereas decay set in under the successive Angevin, Aragonese, and Hapsburg houses. The Spanish and Austrian rulers took little interest in Calabria and allowed the feudal barons to reassert some of their power, to the detriment of peasants and citizens alike.

When the Bourbons assumed power early in the eighteenth century, they at first enlisted the strong support of the people. Later on, however, after the Napoleonic era, the Masonic, Carbonari, and other liberal and republican movements gained warm adherents in Calabria; and in 1860 the region fell to Garibaldi's forces. Following unification, the Italian government undertook to stamp out brigandage, illiteracy, malaria, and other age-old problems, but the region's backwardness and poverty hindered these efforts.

ITALIAN STATE TOURIST OFFICE

Buildings along the sea in Reggio Calabria, seaside resort, chief industrial city, and provincial capital, in the region of Calabria

On Sept. 3, 1943, during World War II, the British Eighth Army crossed the Strait of Messina to land in Calabria along a coastal strip stretching from Reggio Calabria to Cotrone. Little opposition was encountered. By September 8 it had reached Locri and Palmi. A second landing above Palmi resulted in the capture of Vibo Valentia. Cosenza fell on September 14. The capture within less than a fortnight of three seaports and ten airfields in Calabria and Apulia enabled the Allies to launch large-scale operations against Naples and other major Italian cities.   R. G. W.

CALADIUM [kǝle′diǝm], a genus of the anthurium family, with perhaps a dozen species native to tropical America. They are herbaceous perennials, growing from large rhizomes, with lance-shaped leaves about 2 ft. tall, beautifully marked or mottled in shades of red, pink, violet, green, and white. Many garden forms have been developed. Caladiums are sometimes used in gardens in mild climates but are chiefly grown by florists as winter pot plants.　　J. C. Wis.

CALAHORRA [kɑ'lɑo'rrɑ], an episcopal see of the archbishopric of Toledo, in the province of Logroño in Old Castile, northern Spain. It is situated on a slope overlooking the Cidacos River about three miles from the latter's confluence with the Ebro, and lies on the Zaragoza-Bilbao railway. Calahorra serves as a market for a fertile district in the upper Ebro Valley, producing grain, fruit, olive oil, wine, and vegetables. Several small food-canning and fertilizer plants are also found there.

The town presents a medieval appearance, with winding, narrow, and steep streets and many old houses. The principal monuments are the modified Gothic cathedral, restored in the late fifteenth century, and the Casa Santa, containing the bodies of the two saints, Emeterius and Celedonius, beheaded on the spot about 300. The principal remains of the Roman city are the circus and aqueduct.

The Iberians held this point against Pompey in 76 B.C. but gave it up four years later after a heroic resistance marked by prolonged and intense famine. Later known as Calagurris Nassica, it was the birthplace of Marcus Fabius Quintilianus, famous master of eloquence and rhetoric. It fell to the Arabs, who fortified it, but was retaken by Don Garcia, King of Navarre, in 1054. Pop. 1950, 13,183.
　　　　　　　　　　　　　　　　　R. G. W.

CALAIS [ka'lɛ'; kæ'le; kæ'lɪs], a seaport and the largest city of the department of Pas-de-Calais, in northwestern France, located on the Strait of Dover, about 186 mi. north of Paris, at 50° 58' N. lat. and 1° 50' E. long. Until the eleventh century Calais was little more than a fishing village. Its strategic location as the point in France nearest England, about 20 mi. across the strait, then required its fortification, a task accomplished by Philip Hurepel, Count of Boulogne. After the victory of English troops headed by Edward III over French forces at Crécy, Aug. 26, 1346, Calais was besieged by the English for nearly a year before it was taken. The city, which became a great trading center under English occupation, was retaken in 1558 by French forces under Francis, Duke of Guise. Thereafter Calais remained in French hands until 1595, when it was captured by Spanish troops. Spain held it until 1598; then the city was returned to France by the Treaty of Vervins. Calais was severely damaged by bombardment from 1914 to 1916 in World War I, and in World War II a large part of the city again suffered destruction.

The older part of the city, surrounded by docks and waterways, is the northwest section; the eastern and southern parts comprise the larger, modernized, industrialized section of St. Pierre. Calais' chief points of interest are the Church of Notre Dame, dating from the fourteenth and fifteenth centuries; the ancient Hôtel de Ville, rebuilt in 1740; and the Hôtel de Guise. Most of the streets are broad and well paved. A sculptured group by François Rodin of the six citizens who offered their lives in 1347 to save Calais after the English siege is one of the city's most notable monuments. The principal industrial establishments are lace and tulle factories; mills also produce hosiery and wool, cotton, and silk products, as well as hats and gloves. In addition, there are salt refineries, distilleries, and shipyards. Herring and cod fisheries are extensive. The port accommodates the largest oceangoing vessels, and the city is an important trading center, with good rail and air connections. Pop. 1954, 60,340.

CALAIS [kæ'lɪs], a city and port of entry in Washington Co., in northeastern Maine, situated on the west bank of the St. Croix River at the head of navigation, 136 mi. northeast of Bangor and opposite St. Stephen, New Brunswick, Canada, with which it is connected by a bridge. It is a tourist and trade center for eastern Maine. Calais was chartered as a city in 1851 and is governed by a manager and council. It was settled by lumbermen in 1778 and for many years was called Township No. 5. In 1806 it was named Calais in honor of the French port. It is on the Maine Central Railroad. Dairying, poultry-raising, and berrying are important activities in this region. Sawmills were established in 1802. The industrial output of the city includes pulpwood, shoes, knitted goods, and canned blueberries. Pop. 1950, 4,589.

CALAIS, SIEGE OF, a beleaguerment of the French city of Calais by the English during the Hundred Years' War. The siege began in the summer of 1346, after the English victory at Crécy. Edward III invaded France earlier in the year, plundered parts of Normandy, and then laid siege to the seaport of Calais, on the English Channel. Despite the use of artillery by the attackers, and the suffering of the besieged, the city held out until 1347. Furious at the obstinate resistance, Edward was with difficulty dissuaded from putting the inhabitants to the sword. Six of the citizens, with ropes around their necks, offered their lives in return for those of the rest. They were spared through the intercession of Edward's consort, Queen Philippa. Calais was strongly fortified by the English and remained an important commercial and military outpost for England until 1558, when it fell to Francis of Lorraine, Duke of Guise.　　F. C. H.

CALAMONDIN [kæləmɒ'ndɪn], a hybrid citrus fruit, one of the hardiest known, believed to have arisen naturally in China through insect pollination of a sour, loose-skinned mandarin orange (one of the tangerine group) and a kumquat. In flavor it has more contrast than the kumquat, the thin, deep orange-colored skin being sweeter and the tender, juicy, orange-colored pulp more acid. The ripe fruit is nearly spherical, slightly flattened, 1 to 1¼ in. high, containing from 7 to 10 segments and only a few small seeds. Widely cultivated in the Philippines, it is also grown in Hawaii and the United States. It was introduced into Florida as the "Panama orange" and into Hawaii as the "Philippine orange." It is believed to be the same as an orangequat and has been given the botanical name of *Citrus mitis,* though it is a probable bigeneric hybrid, not a true species. The fruits are used for marmalade and beverage, besides being eaten raw and whole.　　J. C. Wis.

CALAMUS [kæ'ləməs], *Acorus calamus,* a perennial herb of the arum family commonly called "sweet flag" because of the aromatic quality of the horizontal rootstocks. It grows in moist places in Europe and North America. *See also* Sweet Flag.

CALCAREA. *See* Animal Systematics; Sponge.

CALCEOLARIA [kæ'lsiolɛ'əriə], a genus of the figwort family containing about two hundred species, both herbs and shrubs, native chiefly to South America, some to Mexico and New Zealand. Many herbaceous varieties are grown by florists because of their showy and curiously inflated flowers, somewhat resembling those of the lady's-slipper, which are usually spotted and of various rich colors.　　J. C. Wis.

CALCITE [kæ′lsait], a widespread mineral composed of calcium carbonate, $CaCO_3$. Calcite crystals tend to be prismatic and pointed, in which case the mineral is known as dogtooth spar. Clear, colorless, and flawless crystals are also known as Iceland spar. Far more abundant is the granular calcite that composes various rock species such as chalk, limestone, marble, and tufa. The word "calcite" comes from the Latin *calx,* meaning "burnt lime." When calcite is heated, carbon dioxide is driven off, and the resultant material, quicklime, CaO, has the property of setting when mixed with water and allowed to harden. Throughout historic time, and probably before, mankind has heated (burned) calcite-bearing rocks in order to obtain mortars and cements. Iceland spar is used in optical instruments to polarize light; calcite has the property of splitting light into two rays, each vibrating at right angles to the other, and the Nicol polarizing prism is so constructed that only one of these rays emerges from the prism.

Calcite crystallizes in the rhombohedral class, whereas the other calcium carbonate mineral, aragonite, is orthorhombic. The commonest form is the scalenohedron which gives the "dogtooth" effect. Cleavage is perfect in three directions, producing six-faced rhombs. The hardness of calcite is 3, which is much softer than another common glassy mineral, quartz, possessing a hardness of 7. Furthermore, calcite effervesces vigorously in dilute acid. Calcite is usually, but not necessarily, white or colorless. It occurs in drusy crystals, in massive beds, in cave deposits, in veins, as a hot-spring deposit, and even in microscopic crystals cementing grains of sand together into a sandstone.

The most abundant occurrence of calcite is as the sole essential constituent of limestone. This calcite originally accumulated on the floor of an ancient sea in three possible ways: (1) through the secretion of calcium carbonate by organisms, especially shell-builders; (2) by chemical precipitation; and (3) as detrital grains resulting from the erosion of older limestones. Calcium carbonate is a common compound in solution in circulating ground (underground) waters. It is picked up through the solution of calcite in veins and limestones, and through percolation through zones where primary calcium minerals are undergoing decomposition. This calcium carbonate may be redeposited as calcite in caves, in veins and vugs, as a cement between grains in rock, and as calcareous tufa around hot springs and geysers. Calcite also occurs as a hydrothermal vein mineral and even as an accessory mineral in pegmatites. It is second only to quartz in its wide range of geological occurrences. Marble is a calcitic rock resulting from the recrystallization of limestone during metamorphism. As a result of this recrystallization the calcite individuals are coarser than they were before, and the crystals are interlocking.   K. K. L.

CALCIUM [kæ′lsiəm], symbol Ca, a metallic chemical element in Group II-A of the periodic table. Calcium is the first, most important, and most abundant member of the "triad" that the alchemists called the alkaline earths, the other members being strontium and barium. Calcium is the third metal in abundance in the crust of the earth.

Properties. Silvery white when freshly cut, calcium soon becomes dull gray because of the formation of an oxide coating. The metal is crystalline, harder than lead, malleable, and ductile. It may be sublimed below its melting point when heated in a vacuum; it reacts moderately with water and slowly with alcohol. Calcium burns when heated in air, forming the oxide, CaO, and nitride Ca_3N_2; hot, it also unites directly with the halogens.

PROPERTIES OF CALCIUM

Atomic number	20
Atomic weight	40.08
Stable isotopes	40, 44, 42, 43, 46, 48
Density (g./ml.)	1.54
Melting Point, °C	851
Boiling Point, °C	1487
Specific Heat, 0-20° C.	0.145
Electrical Resistivity (microhm-cm.) 20° C.	4.6
Hardness (Mohs' scale)	1.5

Uses. The main use of calcium is as a deoxidizer for metals, especially nickel, copper, and stainless steel. Both the metal and hydride are employed in preparing metals, such as chromium, thorium, and uranium, which are difficult to reduce. Calcium-lead alloys find limited use in battery plates and bearing metals. Calcium pellets are also useful in removing the last traces of air from vacuum tubes and tungar rectifiers.

Compounds. The compounds of calcium are numerous. In contrast to the limited usefulness of the metal, they have been widely used since primitive man took refuge in limestone caves. Calcium is always bivalent.

Calcium Oxide. The most important manufactured compound of calcium, it is a starting point for making other useful calcium products. The oxide, which has the formula CaO, has several commercial names, such as lime, burnt lime, unslaked lime, quicklime, and stonelime. It is prepared by expelling carbon dioxide from limestone in some sort of a lime kiln in which wood, coal, oil, or gas may be used as a fuel. Pure lime is white, porous, very resistant to the effects of heat, but brilliantly luminous (hence, the "limelight") at high temperatures. On exposure to moist air, it absorbs carbon dioxide and moisture and crumbles to a powder known as air-slaked lime. When a little water is added to calcium oxide, much heat is liberated and the oxide slakes, becoming calcium hydroxide or slaked or hydrated lime. When calcium oxide is heated with silica or silicates, a reaction takes place forming calcium silicate, which is known as slag in the winning of metals from their ores or as glass when the product is transparent. Lime is extensively used in preparing plaster and mortar in building operations, and in the manufacture of bleaching powder (chloride of lime), leather, and various medicinal and food products where a safe and inexpensive basic material is needed.

Calcium Hydroxide. A white powder formed by slaking lime, it is sparingly soluble in water; a saturated solution is known as limewater. If an excess of calcium hydroxide is suspended in water, the white mixture is known as milk of lime. Calcium hydroxide, $Ca(OH)_2$, is alkaline and absorbs carbon dioxide from the air. It is used in medicine, mainly as an antacid, and in making plaster, mortar, cements, and water paints and for dehairing hides in the manufacture of leather. Mortar is prepared by mixing slaked lime with sand and enough water to make a plastic mixture. When put in place in a wall, the slaked lime reacts with carbon dioxide of the air, forming calcium carbonate as the wall hardens; moisture is set free as this reaction takes place. Plaster is like mortar; sometimes hair is added to help it stay in place. Cement is made by igniting an intimate mixture of calcium carbonate (limestone, chalk, or marl) with a silicate such as clay, shale, or blast-furnace slag. When cement is mixed with sand and gravel or crushed rock and enough water to form a plastic mass, concrete is formed. This sets and hardens without contact with carbon dioxide, thus furnishing an artificial stone of great usefulness.

Calcium Carbonate. Calcium carbonate, $CaCO_3$, the most abundant mineral that does not contain silicon, is known as limestone or marble. It also is found in such crystalline forms as calcite, and in chalk, coral, eggshells, and shells of sea animals; dolomite is a double carbonate of calcium and magnesium. Calcium carbonate is insoluble in pure water, but it dissolves in water containing carbon dioxide, being transformed into the soluble calcium bicarbonate, $Ca(HCO_3)_2$. When a solution of calcium bicarbonate is boiled, carbon dioxide is expelled and the insoluble calcium carbonate is precipitated. Such reactions explain the formation of boiler scale when hard water is used in a teakettle, service pipe, or boiler. Similar reactions take place on a large scale in nature, resulting in the formation of limestone caves and the growth of stalactites and stalagmites. Hard water contains such salts as calcium or magnesium bicarbonate or sulphate, which, in addition to forming a deposit as boiler scale when the water is boiled, prevent ordinary soap from functioning as a dirt remover.

Calcareous deposits near Pamukkale, Turkey

Calcium Sulphate. Calcium sulphate, $CaSO_4$, is found in nature as the mineral anhydrite; its hydrate, $CaSO_4 \cdot 2H_2O$, is the important commercial mineral known as gypsum, alabaster, mineral white, or satin spar. Gypsum is added to cement to prevent too rapid setting; it is used in the manufacture of blackboard crayon, land plaster in agriculture, filler in paint, as a glaze in paper, and as a polishing powder. When gypsum is heated at 165 to 200° C. it loses about 75 per cent of its combined water and forms plaster of Paris. When this material is moistened it absorbs water and sets to a solid mass. As the setting takes place, the mass expands slightly, so that plaster of Paris can be made to reproduce the fine lines of any object. It is extensively used in making statuary, surgical casts, dental casts, and stucco and wallboard for the building industries. When gypsum is heated until it loses all its combined water, it is used for making floor plaster or hard-finish plaster. The drying agent known as Drierite, a specially prepared anhydrous calcium sulphate, is efficient in removing moisture from gases and organic liquids. It is sometimes colored with a dye that changes color as the drying agent approaches exhaustion. It is regenerated by heating.

Other Sulphur Compounds. Calcium sulphite, $CaSO_3$, and bisulphite, $Ca(HSO_3)_2$, are used for bleaching wood pulp in the manufacture of paper, for preventing souring in fermentation, and as an antichlor in bleaching fabrics.

Calcium sulphide, CaS, is made by igniting a mixture of calcium sulphate and carbon or calcium carbonate and sulphur. It is used as a depilatory and in luminous paints.

Halides. Calcium chloride, $CaCl_2$, is obtained from natural brines or as a by-product from such chemical processes as the manufacture of soda by the Solvay process. It may also be obtained by treating calcium oxide or calcium carbonate with hydrochloric acid. When a solution of calcium chloride crystallizes at ordinary temperatures, the colorless deliquescent hexahydrate, $CaCl_2 \cdot 6H_2O$, is obtained. When these crystals are heated, the dihydrate, the monohydrate, or the anhydrous salt is obtained. These compounds absorb moisture readily and are used as drying agents, to melt snow and ice, and to dissipate fog. Their solutions are used to keep down dust on highways and in mines, as an antifreeze, as the cooling brine in refrigeration plants, and in the manufacture of cement, fire extinguishers, and fireproof fabrics. The medicinal grade finds many uses, such as the checking of hemorrhage and increasing the coagulability of the blood.

Calcium bromide, $CaBr_2$, and iodide, CaI_2, resemble the chloride. They are used in photography and medicine.

Calcium fluoride, CaF_2, is the native mineral fluorite or fluorspar. It differs from the other halides in being highly insoluble. It is the main source of fluorine.

Bleaching Powder. This compound is ordinarily called chloride of lime or chlorinated lime. Its composition is somewhat variable, but the formula $CaCl \cdot OCl$ represents its approximate composition. It is prepared by passing chlorine through a rotating cylinder so constructed that a continuous shower of slaked lime falls through the stream of gas. Bleaching powder is a whitish powder with a strong odor of chlorine. On exposure to air it absorbs moisture and carbon dioxide, with the liberation of chlorine. The usual commercial product yields about 35 per cent "available chlorine." Bleaching powder has been extensively used in bleaching fabrics, soap, and wood pulp, and in laundering; also in disinfecting drinking water, sewage, and in such localities as a damp cellar. In recent years its use in bleaching has declined because liquid chlorine and calcium hypochlorite are more convenient and efficient.

Calcium Hypochlorite. The hypochlorite, $Ca(ClO)_2$, called high-test hypochlorite or perchloron, is a white nonhygroscopic powder having the odor of chlorine. It yields about 99 percent "available chlorine" and hence is more than twice as strong as bleaching powder. It handles easily and does not deteriorate from standing.

Phosphates. Tribasic calcium phosphate, $Ca_3(PO_4)_2$, is found in the mineral phosphorite or phosphate rock. It is also the main mineral component of the bones of animals. The main source of phosphorus and its compounds, it is used in manufacturing porcelain, enamels, and milk glass, and in the production of other phosphates. Dibasic calcium phosphate, $CaHPO_4$, is used in animal feeds, in dental powders and pastes, in fertilizers, and in table salt to prevent the caking which is due to moisture. Monobasic calcium phosphates, $Ca(H_2PO_4)_2$, is the familiar calcium "superphosphate" or "superphosphate of lime." It is more soluble in water than either the tribasic or dibasic salt and hence is available for immediate use as plant food.

Calcium Carbide. This compound, which has the formula CaC_2, is prepared by heating calcium oxide and coke, charcoal, or anthracite coal in an electric furnace. When water is added to calcium carbide, acetylene is produced. When calcium carbide is heated in an atmosphere of nitrogen, calcium cyanamide is formed.

Calcium Cyanamide. Calcium cyanamide, $CaCN_2$, formerly important in the fixation of atmospheric nitrogen, is now used mainly as a fertilizer and in the casehardening of steel. When calcium cyanamide is hydrolyzed in an autoclave with steam, ammonia is produced; when fused with salt and carbon, it forms sodium cyanide, $NaCN$, which is extensively used in the winning of gold from its ores.

Calcium Arsenate. This white powder has the formula $Ca_3(AsO_4)_2$ and is made by a reaction between calcium chloride, calcium hydroxide, and ammonium arsenate. Calcium arsenate is used extensively as an insecticide, especially in the dusting of cotton fields to destroy the boll weevil and of trees to remove destructive insects.

Calcium Silicate. This substance, $CaSiO_3$, is found widely distributed in nature as wollastonite. Slag, formed in metallurgical processes by the reaction of lime and sand, SiO_2, is considered to be calcium silicate. If the ore being treated contains excess limestone, which yields lime in the furnace, sand is added; if an excess of sand is to be removed, limestone is added. The resulting slag is usually much lighter than the molten metal being won from the ore and rises to the surface from which it is drawn off while still liquid. Other calcium silicates of complex composition are found in nature.

B. S. H.

CALCULATOR. *See* BUSINESS MACHINES AND EQUIPMENT; MATHEMATICAL MACHINES.

CALCULUS, DIFFERENTIAL AND INTEGRAL,

two related branches of mathematics, also known as the infinitesimal calculus, which constitute a method of dealing with magnitudes in a state of change or growth, such as the height of a growing individual, rates of population increase or decrease, the acceleration and deceleration of a bullet, and the motion of a heavenly body. One application is in finding the area of curved surfaces, which was done by Archimedes (third century B.C.) by adding together (integrating) a large ("infinite") number of straight lines following the outline of the curves and thus making the curved shape a many-sided polygon; the greater the number of approximately equal straight sides, the less the difference between their sum (integral) and the length of the arc desired. Nearly two thousand years later, early in the seventeenth century, Johannes Kepler devised improvements on this Archimedean method of exhaustions. Finally, late in the same century, two rival geniuses, Isaac Newton in England and Gottfried Wilhelm von Leibniz in Germany, independently developed a calculus capable of general application.

The chief concern of differential calculus is with the problem of the rate of change of a function in relation to a variable quantity on which it is dependent. In mechanics, to cite an important application, the differential calculus is used to investigate the motion of objects acted upon by forces. Newton used it to prove that the orbit of the earth, a body acted upon by the (gravitational) force of the sun, is an ellipse. The idea of instantaneous rate of change is used in pure geometry, as in the construction of tangents to curves.

The integral calculus deals chiefly with processes inverse to those treated in the differential calculus. Among its applications are the determination of plane areas bounded by curves, as discussed above, and of the bounding areas and the volumes of solids. In physics and engineering, such quantities as pressure, work, and moments of inertia, and the location of the center of gravity, are determined by the integral calculus.

DIFFERENTIAL CALCULUS

Limit of a Variable. The notion of a variable approaching a limit will be explained by referring to the elementary geometry problem of finding the formula for the area of a circle. The area of a regular polygon of n sides inscribed in the circle is studied. While n is permitted to increase indefinitely, the increasing area of the polygon approaches a limit, and this limit is defined as the area of the circle. If u is the variable area of the polygon, and a the area of the circle, as n increases, the difference $(a-u)$ decreases, until ultimately it is less than any preassigned number, however small.

The above relation is expressed mathematically by $u \rightarrow a$, meaning "u approaches a as a limit."

When a variable approaches zero as a limit, it is called an infinitesimal. In the above example, $(a-u)$ is an infinitesimal, because $\lim (a-u) = O$. The infinitesimal is not necessarily a small quantity, but a quantity which becomes indefinitely smaller. For example, when the polygon inscribed in the circle in the problem above is a triangle $(n = 3)$, the difference in the areas of the circle and the polygon is considerable, but $(a-u)$ is nevertheless an infinitesimal.

Derivatives. The notion of derivative is basic. It may be interpreted geometrically as follows: consider a point $P(x,y)$

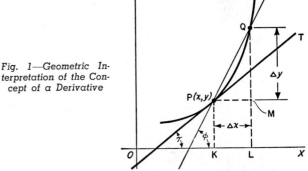

Fig. 1—Geometric Interpretation of the Concept of a Derivative

on a curve (Fig. 1) having an equation $y = f(x)$. Draw a secant (SQP) through P and through a nearby point $Q(x + \Delta x, y + \Delta y)$. Let point Q move along the curve and approach P. The secant through P and Q will then pivot about P, and its limiting position as P and Q coincide is the tangent line (T)

Now, since $y = f(x)$.

Then $y + \Delta y = f(x + \Delta x)$.

In Fig. I. $y + \Delta y$ is represented by the distance LQ. Substituting $f(x)$ for y, and solving for Δy,

$$\Delta y = f(x + \Delta x) - f(x)$$

represented by the distance MQ. Therefore

$$\frac{\Delta y}{\Delta x} = \frac{f(x + \Delta x) - f(x)}{\Delta x} = \frac{MQ}{PM} = tan \angle QPM = tan \Phi$$

which is the slope of the secant line SQP. As Δx approaches zero as a limit, the ratio $\frac{\Delta y}{\Delta x}$ is represented by the symbol $\frac{dy}{dx}$, which is read as "the derivative of y with respect to x."

Thus, $$\frac{dy}{dx} = \lim_{\Delta x \to 0} \frac{f(x + \Delta x) - f(x)}{\Delta x} = tan \tau$$

where τ is the angle the tangent line (T) makes with the X-axis.

The derivative of the function at any point is given by the above basic formula, and is defined as the slope of the tangent at any given point. The distances Δx and Δy are merely taken as being "reasonably small," as indicated by the statement that Q lies nearby P.

The derivative of y with respect to x, is written variously as

$$\frac{dy}{dx}\ ,\ \frac{df(x)}{dx},\ f'(x),\ \text{and}\ y'.$$

Rules have been developed whereby the derivatives of functions can be obtained without direct recourse to the definition.

For example, if $y = x^n$, then $\frac{dy}{dx} = nx^{n-1}$;

if $y = sin\ x$ (x measured in radians), $\frac{dy}{dx} = \cos x$; if $y = \log_e x$ (e being the base of natural logarithms), $\frac{dy}{dx} = \frac{1}{x}$.

Rules have also been developed for differentiating sums, differences, products, and quotients of functions.

Higher Derivatives. The derivative of a function $f(x)$ is another function of x, which in general can be differentiated again. This is called the second derivative of y with respect to x, and is denoted by $\frac{d^2y}{dx^2}$ or y'', etc. It may be possible to differentiate the second derivative, and obtain a third derivative, etc. The symbol for the nth order derivative is $\frac{d^ny}{dx^n}$.

Maxima and Minima. A function $y = f(x)$ has a relative maximum value y_1 at $x = x_1$ if $f(x) < y_1$ for all values of x near x_1. At such a point x_1, $\frac{dy}{dx} = 0$ for most functions commonly dealt with in practice; hence the derivative plays an important role in the discussion of maxima (and minima). Let it be required to lay a rope 100 ft. long, in a rectangular shape, so as to enclose a rectangle of maximum area. If x is the length of a rectangle of perimeter 100, the width must be $50 - x$. The area y will be given by

$$y = x(50 - x) = 50x - x^2.$$

Let us imagine that the function y is graphed. Evidently, at the point on the graph that has the greatest y, the tangent to the graph is horizontal. This is a geometric counterpart of the physical fact that as one approaches the top of a smooth hill, one finds the hill less and less high. There is still an ascent just before the top; immediately after, there is a descent. The top is horizontal. Thus we have to find a value of x for which the derivative of y with respect to x is zero.

In this case $$\frac{dy}{dx} = 50 - 2x,$$

so that for a maximum y, x must be 25. Since each side turns out to be equal to 25, the rectangle is a square, and the maximum area is 625 sq. ft.

A similar discussion would hold for a minimum-value problem. At those values of a function $f(x)$ for which $f(x)$ is either a maximum or a minimum, $f'(x) = 0$. Tests exist whereby a maximum can be distinguished from a minimum. These tests are essential to all maxima and minima problems because $f'(x)$ may vanish at a point and yet that point may yield neither a maximum nor a minimum value of the function involved.

Straight-Line Motion. Various problems in kinematics can be solved by the use of differential calculus. If a particle moves along a straight line so that, at any time t, the distance y from some fixed point, called the origin, is given by $y = f(t)$, then the velocity of the particle is given by $dy/dt = f'(t)$ and the acceleration by $d^2y/dt^2 = f''(t)$. As an example, let the height y ft. after t sec. of a certain body projected vertically upward be given by $y = 100 + 80t - 16t^2$. Upon differentiating once, it is found that the velocity v at any time t is given by $v = dy/dt = 80 - 32t$; another differentiation yields the acceleration $d^2y/dt^2 = -32$. It is noted that the maximum height is 200 ft. and occurs when $t = 5/2$ sec. These ideas can be extended to curvilinear motion, where velocity and acceleration become vector quantities.

Related Rates. Suppose that a relation exists between two variables y and z, each of which is a function of time t. Then the derivatives of y and z with respect to t are related and represent, respectively, the rates of change of y and z with respect to time t. The specific relations involved may be used to solve many types of problems.

Suppose that water escapes through a conical filter at the rate of 3 cc. per second. Let the filter be in the shape of a cone 2 in. in radius and 4 in. deep. We wish to find how fast the level of the water is falling when the depth of the water is $1\frac{1}{2}$ in. Let the depth of the liquid at time t be h, and let r be the corresponding radius of the surface of the liquid. Then $r/h = \frac{2}{4}$, or $r = \frac{1}{2}h$. We want dh/dt. Now, for a circular cone the volume, V, is given by the formula

$$V = \tfrac{1}{3}\pi r^2 h = \tfrac{1}{12}\pi h^3, \qquad \frac{dV}{dt} = \tfrac{1}{4}\pi h^2 \frac{dh}{dt} = -3$$

Using 1 in. = 2.54 cm., we get

$$-3 = \tfrac{1}{4}\pi\left[\ 1.5(2.54)\ \right]^2 \frac{dh}{dt},$$

whence $dh/dt = -0.26$. Therefore the water level is falling at the rate of 0.26 cm./sec.

Approximate Formulas. Consider a ring formed by two concentric circles of radii x and $x + \Delta x$, respectively, where Δx is small. The area of the ring will be the amount Δy by which the area y of a circle of radius x will increase when the radius is increased by Δx. Now, when Δx is small, $\Delta y/\Delta x$ is practically the derivative of the area y with respect to x. The area $y = \pi x^2$, and $dy/dx = 2\pi x$. Hence an approximate formula for the area of the ring is $2\pi x\ \Delta x$. In general, since $dy/dx = \lim_{\Delta x \to 0} \Delta y/\Delta x$, $\Delta y/\Delta x = dy/dx$ approximately, so that for small Δx, $\Delta y = dy/dx\ \Delta x$ approximately.

In order to prove that the above approximation is a fair one, the following is the actual formula for the area of a ring bounded by two circles of differing radius:

Area $= \pi(\text{radius}_1 + \text{radius}_2)\ (\text{radius}_1 - \text{radius}_2)$.
So,

$$\Delta y = \pi(x + \Delta x + x)\ (x + \Delta x - x)$$
$$= \pi(2x + \Delta x)\ (\Delta x)$$
$$= 2\pi x\Delta x + \pi(\Delta x)^2$$

When Δx is very small, the term $\pi(\Delta x)^2$ can be ignored. Hence, one can see that the original approximation was justifiable.

Similarly, for a spherical shell of inner radius x and outer radius $x + \Delta x$, the approximation $4\pi x^2\ \Delta x$ is found for the volume. This method of approximation is continually used in engineering work.

The differential calculus is of great importance in many other fields of application. The whole theory has been generalized to n dimensions.

INTEGRAL CALCULUS

Integrals. Here the notion of integral is basic. Let $dy/dx = f(x)$ be given. Then, $y = \int f(x)dx$ is that function which, when differentiated, yields $f(x)$. It is called the integral of $f(x)$. The details of integration are much more involved than those of differentiation, but systematic methods have been devised that reduce to a minimum the necessary labor in some cases. These are integration by parts, integration by transformations, and integration by partial fractions. The first two are general methods, whereas the last is specially designed for the quotient of two polynomials. Tables of integrals have been prepared, and the usual problem in integration is to reduce a given integral to one of known type.

Indefinite Integral. The integral $\int f(x) \, dx$ is called the indefinite integral of $f(x)$ and is a unique function $F(x)$ only to within an additive constant, since the derivative of a constant is zero. Generally it is written as $\int f(x) \, dx = F(x) + c$.

Definite Integral. In many problems involving integration it is necessary first to calculate the indefinite integral and then to evaluate this between certain limits. This process corresponds, in differential calculus, to finding first the derivative of a function and then evaluating it for a specific value of the variable. The definite integral of $f(x)$ evaluated between two limits of x is written $\int_a^b f(x) \, dx$ and equals $F(b) - F(a)$, where $dF/dx = f(x)$. For example, suppose it is desired to find the area of a circle. Let the equation of the circle be $x^2 + y^2 = r^2$. The area is given by $\int y \, dx$. Hence, by using symmetry, we find

$$A = 4 \int_0^r \sqrt{r^2 - x^2} \, dx$$

$$= 4 \left[\frac{x}{2}\sqrt{r^2 - x^2} + \frac{r^2}{2} \arcsin \frac{x}{r} \Big|_0^r \right] = \pi r^2$$

Integration as a Process of Summation. Up to this point we have treated integration as the inverse process of differentiation. By this process it is possible to derive the formula for area used above. Consider the graph whose equation is $y = f(x)$. We wish to find a formula for the area between this curve, the x-axis, and the ordinates erected at $x = a$ and $x = b$ (*see* Fig. 2). Erect an ordinate y at a

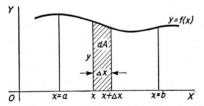

Fig. 2—Integration as a process of summation

general point x. If x is increased by an amount Δx, the area will be increased by an amount ΔA. If Δx is small, ΔA will be approximately equal to $y \, \Delta x$. That is, $\Delta A/\Delta x = y$ approximately. In the limit, as $\Delta x \to 0$, we get $dA/dx = y$ exactly. From this, by integration, we find that the general formula for area is $A = \int y \, dx$. The specific area, between a and b, will be $\int_a^b y \, dx$ as in the preceding paragraph, y being substituted for $f(x)$.

But it is also possible to derive this formula for area by the process of summation. To this end we consider the curve $y = f(x)$ in the interval (a,b) and divide the interval into

n regions by the $n + 1$ points: $x_1 = a, x_2, \ldots, x_{n+1} = b$. We erect the corresponding ordinates y_i and set $\Delta x_i = x_{i+1} - x_i$. We now form the sum

$$f(x_1) \Delta x_1 + f(x_2) \Delta x_2 + \ldots + f(x_n) \Delta x_n.$$

This sum is usually denoted by the symbol

$$\sum_{i=1}^{n} f(x_i) \Delta x_i$$

It seems geometrically evident that the limit of this sum, as the number of points becomes infinite and as each $\Delta x_i \to 0$, will be equal to the area between the curve, the x-axis, and the ordinates $x = a$ and $x = b$. It is a fundamental theorem in the integral calculus that

$$\lim_{\substack{n \to \infty \\ \Delta x_i \to 0}} \sum_{i=1}^{n} f(x_i) \Delta x_i = \int_a^b f(x) \, dx$$

We may shorten this process by reasoning that the area of one infinitesimal strip is $y \, dx$, and the total area is the sum of all such, or $\int y \, dx$.

Length of a Curve. Returning to the circle whose equation is $x^2 + y^2 = r^2$, it can be shown that the length of the circumference of this circle will be given by

$$4 \int_0^r \frac{r \, dx}{\sqrt{r^2 - x^2}} = 4 \arcsin \frac{x}{r} \Big|_0^r = 2\pi r$$

Volumes and Surface Areas. If the area under $y = f(x)$ is revolved around the x-axis, a volume will be generated. The area of a circular cross section cut by a plane perpendicular to x is πy^2. If this is multiplied by the thickness dx of an infinitesimal slice, the differential volume will be $dV = \pi y^2 \, dx$; whence $V = \int \pi y^2 \, dx$. Since $y = f(x)$ is a known function, the integration of $\int_a^b \pi [f(x)]^2 \, dx$ yields the volume between a and b.

More generally, if the cross-sectional area of a solid perpendicular to the x-direction can be expressed as a function of x, say $A(x)$, then $\int_a^b A(x) \, dx$ gives the volume. For ex-

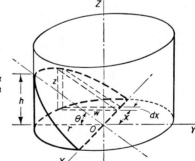

Fig. 3—Calculation of a volume by integration

ample, suppose a wedge is cut from a cylinder of radius r by a plane passing through a diameter and making an angle $\theta = \arctan h/r$ with the Δ base. Then, as in Fig. 3,

$$\frac{h}{r} = \frac{z}{w}, \quad \text{or} \quad z = \frac{h}{r} w,$$

and
$$w^2 + x^2 = r^2.$$

The volume element is

$$dV = \tfrac{1}{2}wz \, dx = \tfrac{1}{2}\frac{h}{r} w^2 \, dx = \tfrac{1}{2}\frac{h}{r}(r^2 - x^2) \, dx.$$

From this we compute

$$V = \tfrac{1}{2}\frac{h}{r} \int_{-r}^{r} (r^2 - x^2) \, dx = \tfrac{2}{3}hr^2.$$

The curve $y = f(x)$, when revolved about the x-axis, generates a surface area

$$S = 2\pi \int y \, ds = 2\pi \int_a^b y \sqrt{1 + y'^2} \, dx.$$

Approximate Integration. One of the serious difficulties encountered in the theory of integration is the impossibility, in many cases, of expressing the indefinite integral $\int f(x) \, dx$ in terms of the elementary functions. Methods of approximate numerical integration aid in the computing of definite integrals. Rules such as the trapezoidal rule, Simpson's rule, and others, and mechanical and electronic computers, are used extensively in approximate integration.

Again, the integral calculus has been generalized to n dimensions.

See also CALCULUS OF VARIATIONS; FUNCTION; MATHEMATICAL INSTRUMENTS; CALCULUS OF OPERATIONS.

C. O. O.

CALCULUS OF OPERATIONS, that branch of calculus which is primarily concerned with subjecting symbols of operation (transformation) and of magnitude to algebraic operations.

Operator Theory. Many of the problems of mathematical analysis concern themselves with situations in which a point in one space goes into a point in the same or a different space. With a sufficiently broad approach, the designation "point" may refer to a function. The correspondence between the first and second points is said to be accomplished by a transformation or operation. Operator theory is devoted on the one hand to the cataloguing and classifying of various types of transformations and their properties, and on the other to the formulation of symbolic methods whereby computations can be minimized. In customary usage, operator theory is restricted to situations for which the space admits of addition or multiplication of points, that is, to linear spaces, groups, rings, fields, and so on.

Problems and Applications. Let D and R be real linear or vector spaces, not necessarily distinct. That is, the elements are vectors, so that the sum of two elements and the product by a scalar are defined and satisfy the usual vector conditions. There need be no finite set of base vectors. Let a vector r in R correspond to d in D. This correspondence is denoted by $T(d) = r$. T is referred to as an operator of the domain D to the range R. (Other algebraic structures may replace the real linear space, for instance groups or rings or nonreal linear spaces. Moreover, the correspondence need not be single-valued.) An operator is distributive if

$$T(\lambda d + \lambda' d') = \lambda T(d) + \lambda' T(d'),$$

where λ, λ' are any real numbers, and d, d' are any elements of D. If D and R are also topological spaces of such a nature that d and $d + d'$ are continuous operations, then a distributive continuous operator is called a linear operator. If Q contains D and R, then $T^2(d)$ is defined as $T(Td)$ and similarly for $T^n(d)$, provided these relations have meaning.

The contribution of the field of operational calculus is the abstract formation and generalization of such topics in classical mathematical analysis as differential equations or integral equations. The modern developments in quantum theory have furnished a powerful stimulus to research in operator theory. The most complete studies refer to distributive operators on so-called Hilbert space. The interest is in large part in the representation of such operators by integral transforms.

Two important distributive operators are those of differentiation, p, and integration p^{-1}. Here the elements of D and

R are functions of a variable x. Then

$$p^{m+n} = \frac{d^{m+n}}{dx^{m+n}} = p^m p^n, \quad p^0 f(x) = f(x),$$

for m, n nonnegative integers. Since integration involves an arbitrary constant, p^{-1}, then p is not necessarily the identity operation p^0. Formal rules for combining these operators date back to George Boole (1815-1864); e.g., formally.

$$e^{-hp} f(x) = \sum (-1)^n h^n \frac{d^n}{dx^n} f(x)/n! = f(x-h).$$

The Heaviside calculus restricts D to be the domain of functions $f(x)$ vanishing for negative x (or for $x < x_0$). The function $1(x)$, which is 0 or 1 depending on whether x is negative or nonnegative, plays a dominant role. Some of the "rules" developed are

$$p^{-n} 1(x) = \frac{x^{n-1}}{n!} 1(x), \quad (p+a)^{-1} 1(x) = e^{-ax} 1(x),$$

$$a \geqq 0, \quad \frac{d}{dp} F(p) 1(x) = -x F(p) 1(x),$$

and on replacing $n!$ by $\Gamma(n+1)$ an association valid for nonintegral n is obtained.

A central result is the composition or convolution theorem that if $F_1(p) 1(x) = f_1(x)$ and $F_2(p) 1(x) = f_2(x)$, then

$$F_1(p) F_2(p) 1(x) = F_2(p) F_1(p) 1(x) = \int_0^x f_1(x-t) f_2(t) dt.$$

For instance, applied to p^α, $\alpha \neq 0$, -1, -2, a fractional integration or differentiation is defined. For example, consider

$$\sum_1^N a_i \cdot \frac{d^i}{dx^i} \cdot y(x) = g(x),$$

where $y(x)$ and its first $n-1$ derivatives vanish for $x = 0$. Suppose $y(x) = Y(p) 1(x)$, $g(x) = G(p) 1(x)$. Write

$$F(p) = \sum_1^N a_i p^i.$$

Suppose $\phi(x) = F(p)^{-1} 1(x)$. Then

$$y(x) = Y(p) 1(x) = G(p)/\phi(p) 1(x) = \int_0^x g(t) \phi(x-t) dt.$$

Various algorithms connected with partial fraction expansions of rational functions, of asymptotic series, and so on, are included in the standard rules. In practice, $y(x) = Y(p) 1(x)$ is often written $y(x) \sim Y(p)$ or $y(x) \doteq Y(p)$.

A different viewpoint leading to the same general results is that of Vito Volterra's (1860-1940) functions of the closed cycle. Somewhat similar theories can be built for operators of the same type, for instance for $x(d/dx)$, and so on, and for most general situations where several operations are introduced by Volterra, Pincherle, and others. The significant feature of the Heaviside calculus for the applied mathematician is that transcendental problems of x are reduced to algebraic problems in functions of p. The methods find their greatest practical use for constant-coefficient differential equations, difference equations, and integral equations with kernel $K(x,t) = K(x-t)$. In general, extension to more recondite equations involves loss of the "pure algebraization" character.

In the modern approach, the correspondence $F(p) 1(x) = f(x)$ is given a rigorous representation, usually by the Laplace or Fourier integral, or abstractly in terms of operators in certain linear topological spaces such as the so-called Hilbert space. In this way, conditions for the validity of the heuristic rules are established.

D. G. B.

CALCULUS OF VARIATIONS, a branch of the infinitesimal calculus in which the variation of a curve is fundamental. A general problem of the calculus of variations in the plane is that of finding, among all continuous arcs $y = y(x)$ which join two points $P_1(x_1, y_1)$ and $P_2(x_2, y_2)$ and have continuously turning tangents, one certain arc for which a well-defined integral

$$J = \int_{x_1}^{x_2} f(x, y, y') \, dx \qquad \left(y' = \frac{dy}{dx} \right)$$

takes on an extreme value.

Isaac Newton considered a problem of this type when he determined the shape of a surface of revolution which would encounter minimum resistance when moved through a resisting medium. His results are stated in his *Principia* (1686). In 1696, Johann Bernoulli proposed the brachistochrone, or shortest-time, problem: to determine the path down which a particle will fall from one fixed point to another in the shortest possible time. The path is a cycloid, as was proved by Johann Bernoulli and his brother Jakob by different methods. In 1744, Leonhard Euler published a theorem that is fundamental in the theory of the calculus of variations: every function y that minimizes or maximizes the integral J must satisfy the differential equation $\frac{d}{dx} f_{y'} = f_y$. Further necessary conditions were discovered by Adrien Marie Legendre in 1786, Karl Gustav Jacob Jacobi in 1837, and Karl Weierstrass. Then in 1879 Weierstrass established a set of sufficiency conditions that would determine whether or not a particular arc would cause J to have an extreme value.

The problem of determining the surface of revolution of minimum area, one of the earliest problems studied, is a good illustration of the general theory of the calculus of variations in the plane. An arc $y = y(x)$, which joins two points P_1 and P_2 in the xy plane, generates a surface of revolution about the x axis whose surface area is

$$J = 2\pi \int_{x_1}^{x_2} y \sqrt{1 + y'^2} \, dx.$$

A minimizing arc must be a member of the two-parameter family of catenaries:

$$y = \frac{b}{2} \left[e^{\frac{x-a}{b}} + e^{\frac{-x-a}{b}} \right],$$

which is the general solution of the Euler equation. The Weierstrass sufficiency theorem is then applied to determine whether or not a minimum exists. This minimal surface may be exhibited mechanically. Construct a wire frame in which the x axis is a wire joining the centers of two circular rings of radii y_1 and y_2, respectively, each ring being in a plane perpendicular to the x axis. When this frame is dipped into a soap solution and removed, the soap film remaining on the frame will be the minimal surface generated by a catenary, provided the circular rings are not too far apart.

Various modifications of the simplest problem in the plane have been discussed. The end points of the arc, one or both, may be allowed to vary, as in the problem of finding the shortest distance between two curves in the plane. The problem of finding an arc $y = y(x)$ for which the integral J takes on an extreme value while at the same time another integral

$$\int_{x_1}^{x_2} g(x, y, y') \, dx$$

remains constant, has been studied extensively. The problem of determining a plane curve of given length that encloses

the greatest area is of this type. The curve is a circle, but a rigorous proof of this result is not simple.

In 1806, Joseph Louis Lagrange published a generalization of the problem of the calculus of variations to a space of $n + 1$ dimensions. The problem of Lagrange is to find, among the arcs $y_i = y_i(x)$, where $i = 1, \ldots, n$, those which are continuous with continuous first derivatives; join two points $P_1[x_1, y_1(x_1), \ldots, y_n(x_1)]$ and $P_2[x_2, y_1(x_2), \ldots, y_n(x_2)]$; and satisfy a set of independent equations $\phi_\alpha(x, y_1, \ldots, y_n) = 0$, $(\alpha = 1, \ldots, m < n)$, one for which a well-defined integral

$$J = \int_{x_1}^{x_2} f(x, y_1, \ldots, y_n, y'_1, \ldots, y'_n) \, dx$$

takes on an extreme value. This problem has many applications in physics and mechanics. Modern mathematicians have discussed further generalizations of the problem and have produced an extensive literature. — A. O. H.

CALCUTTA [kælkʌ'ta], former capital of India and present capital of the state of West Bengal. It is the largest city and leading port in India, located in the southern part of the state, in eastern India at 22° 34′ N. lat. and 88° 24′ E. long. The city is on the Hooghly River, one of the major tributaries of the Ganges, about 80 mi. north of the Bay of Bengal. Calcutta is built on a low, flat, swampy delta, a few feet above sea level, and has a warm monsoon climate with cool, clear weather in January and February; a hot, cloudy, humid season from March to June; a hot, rainy season from June to September; and a warm, dry season from September to December. The mean annual temperature is 78° F., with an average of 86° F. in May, the warmest month, and 65° F. in January, the coolest month. The rainfall is from 60 to 100 in. annually, 12 in. of the total falling during July. The flora and fauna of the vicinity are tropical.

Calcutta is a metropolitan center for a group of districts and suburbs that extend about 20 mi. north and south along the Hooghly River, on the west bank of which is the large industrial area of Howrah. The city centers around the Maidan, a large park along the Hooghly containing the Victoria Memorial and the present Fort William and bounded by Chowringhee Road, a broad, tree-lined avenue of hotels, theaters, restaurants, and shops. North of the Maidan is Government House, executive mansion of the governor of West Bengal, and the site of the original Fort William (built in 1696) which contained the guardroom known as the "black hole" of Calcutta's most notorious legend. The city is one of the most colorful and varied in the world, and aside from its large commercial and industrial developments contains the famous Kali Ghat and temple, a pilgrimage center around which the city originally developed, the University of Calcutta, the National Library, containing more than 700,000 books and rare manuscripts and now housed in the former viceregal palace, the celebrated Jain temple, a large mint on the city's outskirts, and all kinds of markets, bazaars, and places of outdoor entertainment. Further notable institutions include the Bose Research Institute, the School of Tropical Medicine, and the Institute of Rubber Industry, as well as numerous museums, botanical and zoological gardens, hospitals, parks, cricket and polo fields, race tracks, and every kind of temple and shrine.

Although Calcutta is still the world's largest jute-milling and export city, shipment volume has diminished since the partition of Bengal assigned the jute-raising Brahmaputra valley to Pakistan. Calcutta also exports tea, shellac, and vegetable oil, and imports rice, sugar, and manufactured

THE BEAUTIFUL JAIN TEMPLE AT CALCUTTA, INDIA

goods. One of India's most important industrial centers, Calcutta has the heaviest concentration of the country's jute mills and presses, as well as being a leading city in textile (cotton, silk), printing, and bookbinding industries. Other manufactures include chemicals, glass, paper, soap, cigarettes, paint, shoes, rubber and leather goods, pottery, bricks, and cement. The major shipping outlet for the mineral resources (mica, iron, manganese, coal, and limestone) of the Chota Nagpur Plateau and Damodar Valley, Calcutta is an important transport and communications center. Besides a network of rail and highway connections, the airport outside the city at Dumdum is one of the busiest in Asia, for most of the freight moved between Calcutta and the hill states is carried by air, and there is commercial and passenger service not only to other points in India, but also to Europe, the Middle East, America, and the rest of Asia. The Hooghly River, which is 27 ft. deep at Calcutta and has a tidal bore 11 ft. high in the spring, follows a winding course with many sandbars, making it difficult to navigate, particularly for ships of more than 1,200 tons. Large ships must anchor and wait for high tide to cross two separate bars, so that the trip from the bay to Calcutta is frequently a long one. Some ships must be backed down the river if conditions are not favorable for turning at Calcutta, but in spite of these difficulties the city is India's most important and busiest port.

Founded in 1690 at the former village of Sutanuti by Job Charnak of the East India Company, Calcutta (originally Kalikata) developed a thriving trade with the pilgrims to the temple of Kali, and grew steadily in size and importance,

serving as the transport outlet for the rich rice-growing region as well. Captured in 1756 by the nawab of Bengal, who stifled most of the garrison in the "black hole," Calcutta was recaptured by Clive, who defeated the Bengalese ruler the following year. In 1833 Calcutta became the capital of British India, remaining so until 1912, when New Delhi was made the capital because of its more central location. During World War II the city was the nearest port to the China-Burma-India theater of operations, and a vital supply and transport center. Pop. 1951, 2,548,677.

CALCUTTA, UNIVERSITY OF, one of India's leading institutions of higher learning, established at Calcutta, Jan. 24, 1857. The university adopted in its constitution the form, government, and regulations of the University of London. The university was limited by the act of 1857 to giving examinations to persons who had acquired proficiency in the different branches of literature, science, and art, and did not offer instruction. At first its authority over educational standards included all of northern India, but this authority was lessened by the establishment of the University of the Punjab in 1882 and the University of Allahabad in 1887. In 1904 the university was empowered to provide instruction and to maintain libraries, laboratories, and museums. The faculties of arts, science, law, medicine, and engineering were instituted. The language of instruction is English. The university senate has power to make and alter by-laws and regulations subject to the approval of the government of Bengal. A certain amount of higher instruction is directly under university supervision, but most of it is given in the 105 affiliated colleges. The Medical College of Bengal, at Calcutta, was founded in 1835 and became affiliated with the university on its establishment in 1857. Since then other colleges have progressively gained affiliation status, and the most recent additions to the university have been the Institute of Nuclear Physics, established in 1951; the Institute of Jute Technology; and a school of social work.

The central library of the university contains over 222,750 volumes and includes a large collection of Bengali and Tibetan manuscripts, rotographic copies of rare Arabic and Persian manuscripts, and 593 books of the Chinese Sung Dynasty Tripitaka (collection of Buddhist scriptures). There are laboratories in the departments of physics, chemistry, mathematics, and experimental physiology, and museums attached to the departments of anthropology and ancient Indian history and culture. The Asutosh Museum of Indian Art, opened in 1937, contains coin collections, a folk-art gallery, sculpture, paintings, textiles, and metal and ivory exhibits illustrating the different phases of Indian art. The university press publishes specialized lectures delivered by the university staff, theses of successful candidates for doctorate degrees, and a number of periodicals; many standard works on Indian culture and history have also been published. Enrollment, 1955: 78,940.

CALDER, ALEXANDER (1898-   ), American sculptor, was born in Philadelphia, Pa., on July 22, 1898. His father was Alexander Stirling Calder, the sculptor, and his mother was a painter. Young Calder received a formal education in mechanical engineering at Stevens Institute of Technology, Hoboken, N.J.; after graduating in 1919 he worked for four years in various apprenticeships. In 1922 Calder began to study drawing in a public night school, and from 1923 to 1926 he studied at the Art Students League in New York and did free-lance work for the *National Police Gazette*. He first exhibited his paintings in 1926, at which time he also took up wood carving. Going to England and then Paris, he made his first animated toys and did his first wire sculptures, among them his well-known "Circus." Following a successful Paris exhibition in 1927, he had his first United States one-man exhibition in New York the following year, showing wire sculptures. He began to work with jewelry in 1929. In 1930, influenced by leaders of the *de Stijl* group such as Mondriaan, Calder experimented briefly with abstract painting, then with abstract "stabiles," stationary free-form sculptures contrasting with the freely moving "mobiles" for which he is best known. He married Louisa James in 1931 and returned to Paris, where he held his first exhibition of mobiles. After two years in Europe he bought a farm at Roxbury, Conn., which has been the Calders' home since then, though they have spent much time in France and other foreign countries. In 1935 he designed settings for Martha Graham's *Panorama,* and in 1939 he designed a water ballet for the New York World's Fair. New York exhibitions include a one-man exhibit of his jewelry in 1940 and, at the Museum of Modern Art in 1943, a large retrospective exhibit of his work in painting, graphic art, wire sculpture, stabiles and mobiles, and jewelry. In 1948 the ministry of education in Rio de Janeiro, Brazil, sponsored an exhibition there; and in 1950 *The New York Times* termed Calder "one of the ten best illustrators of children's books of the past fifty years."   E. McC.

CALDER, ALEXANDER STIRLING [kɔ'ldər] (1870-1945), American sculptor, was born in Philadelphia on Jan. 11, 1870. He studied at the Pennsylvania Academy of Fine Arts in Philadelphia, and in Paris under Henri Michel Antoine Chapu and Jean Alexandre Joseph Falguière. Calder was a member of the National Academy and executed many famous statues, including that of George Washington on the west side of the arch in Washington Square, New York City, and those of John James Audubon and William Penn in the American Hall of Fame. Other works by Calder can be seen in the Metropolitan Museum of Art in New York City, in the St. Louis Art Museum, in the Pennsylvania Academy of the Fine Arts, and in other museums throughout the United States. His style was distinguished for its monumental simplicity. He died in New York City on Jan. 6, 1945.

CALDERÓN DE LA BARCA, PEDRO [ca'lderɔ'n de la ba'rka] (1600-1681), Spanish dramatist, was born at Madrid, Jan. 17, 1600. The son of an hidalgo from the Montaña district of Asturias, Calderón was sent to a Jesuit school and later studied canon law at the universities of Alcalá and Salamanca. He left the latter university in 1620 and soon made his literary debut. His life, unlike that of his great predecessor, Lope de Vega, was largely uneventful except for a few years of foreign travel and military service. Perhaps the only incident now remembered that gives an indication of the passionate depths that underlay his poetic impulse is his daring armed entry into a convent in pursuit of a certain Pedro de Villegas, who had wounded his brother. Calderón's production of *comedias* for public performance ceased when he was ordained as a priest in 1651. He continued to write *autos* (religious plays), however, and special pieces for the court. After service as a chaplain in Toledo, he returned to Madrid in 1666, where he lived quietly until his death, May 25, 1681.

Style and Technique. Calderón wrote little that was not dramatic and created a group of literary disciples in his distinct manner of Spanish *comedia*. His innovations were in style and technique. He retained the *comedia's* traditional three acts, the characteristic and almost operatic variation of verse types, and the representation of character in terms of such national values and channels of conduct as honor, but the sense of his poetry and of his dramatic structure was his own. Calderón's dramas are Baroque. He adopted the soaring "cultist" metaphor employed by Luis de Góngora, but bound its expansive force within the iron cage of the Neo-Scholastic logic; consequently there resulted a conflict of freedom and imprisonment, of verbal passion and repression, that is typically Baroque. One of Calderón's frequent poetic devices is to pile one splendid metaphor upon another, and then to join them in a final listing in order to accentuate the logical tension of their disparity. His style twists and writhes in an effort to free itself from the bonds of necessity, and it is interesting to note that imprisonment and freedom themselves are among Calderón's favorite dramatic themes. Not only are there physical prisons; even man's stay on earth is seen as closed in by walls of death, an imprisonment for which the only alleviation lies in dogmatic conformance. Thus Calderón is not only a stylist but a dramatist of rebellion, and, beyond rebellion, of forced submission to Catholicism and social values. In *El Médico de su honor* ("The Doctor of His Own Honor") the protagonist is forced to kill his wife despite her innocence because she was suspected publicly and because the code of honor demands such retribution. The structure of Calderón's plays is equally rigid, and beneath the rush of event and surprise can be traced a detailed logical planning, an inevitable causality which holds the straining scene together. As in El Greco's paintings, there is a basic symmetry beneath the immediately evident color and movement. Calderón's contributions to the *comedia,* then, consist of a treatment of style, theme, and structure that is not less original for being profoundly Baroque.

Works. Altogether Calderón composed some 111 *comedias* and about 70 *autos,* most of them extant. Of his *comedias* the best known are *El Alcalde de Zalamea* ("The Mayor of Zalamea"), *El Mágico prodigioso* ("The Prodigious Magician"), which in many ways parallels the Faust legend, and the famous *La Vida es sueño* ("Life Is a Dream"). This last play has often been termed the Catholic reply to tragedy. Its hero, Segismundo, a prince of Poland, has been imprisoned by his father in a deserted tower because of an astrological prediction, and he is impotently rebellious against his chains. The King decides to test Segismundo's behavior and has him drugged and transported secretly to the palace. He awakes in the role of prince, and his arrogance and misconduct are such as might be expected. When subsequently he is returned in the same manner to his prison, Segismundo becomes convinced that life is indeed a dream and that mundane desires and problems are therefore of little account; he has been trained in the way of submission. It is a striking dramatic device, and the poetry and presentation of the play are breathtaking in their power. Calderón's position as one of the great Catholic dramatists is further confirmed by his *autos sacramentales.* These are perhaps best defined as representations of dogma, and are often allegorical in substance. Their abstract nature gave free rein to Calderón's mastery of Scholastic logic, and they were presented usually in connection with the celebration of the Eucharist. Perhaps the most read at present is *El gran teatro del mundo* ("The Great Theatre of the World").

Calderón's position as the last great Golden Age dramatist of Spain, and the Baroque intensity of his thematic approach and style, have contributed to his importance in the history of European literature. When Schlegel and other German critics were trying to break French Neoclassic molds for the drama, they looked equally to Calderón and to Shakespeare for inspiration from the past. Calderón had more or less defined the Spanish drama for Europe, and his influence on Romanticism was extremely important. Shelley was very fond of his dramas, and Calderón's influence is still recognizable in so late a writer as Hugo von Hofmannsthal.

S. G.

CALDERÓN GUARDIA, RAFAEL ÁNGEL [kɑ'lderɔ'n gwɑ'rθhyɑ] (1900-   ), Costa Rican political leader, was born Mar. 10, 1900, at San José. He received his early education in the San José public schools, then attended the University of Louvain and University of Brussels, receiving his M.D. degree from the latter in 1927. After practicing for some years in San José, he was elected president of the faculty of medicine in the National University of Costa Rica. Calderón served as vice-president of the Costa Rican Congress, 1935-1937, and president of the Congress, 1938-1939, then was elected president of Costa Rica for the term 1940-1944. He ran for president again in 1948, but was defeated. Charging fraud, Calderón asked Congress to declare the election invalid and bar the president-elect from office. The election was annulled, but on Dec. 15, 1948, the governing junta declared Calderón a traitor for having furnished ammunition to invading rebels in an attempted *coup d'état* against the provisional president, José Figueres. He was interned when he entered Nicaragua in March 1949, but by 1951 he was in Mexico. From this distance he directed his followers, who were allied with the Communists in their hostility toward President

Ulate, in demonstrations, bombings, and even alleged attempts on the life of the minister of foreign affairs.

S. G. I.

CALDWELL, ERSKINE PRESTON (1903-   ), American novelist, short-story writer, and social commentator, was born Dec. 17, 1903, at White Oak, Ga. He began his literary career with the "hard-boiled" novel, *Poor Fool* (1930). From this he moved to the fiction of regionalism combined with horror, comedy, and an undertone of social criticism. The title of his book *Tobacco Road* (1932) has become the common term for a way of life and, dramatized by Jack Kirkland, was a highly successful play. *God's Little Acre* (1933) has been enormously popular, and short stories

ERSKINE CALDWELL

like *Daughter* and *Kneel to the Rising Sun* are anthology favorites. From 1935 to 1942 Caldwell produced several volumes concerned with economic conditions in the United States and Russia, where he went in 1941 as war correspondent. Three of these books, *You Have Seen Their Faces* (1937), *North of the Danube* (1938), and *Say! Is This the U.S.A?* (1941), are illustrated with photographs by Margaret Bourke-White, who was then his wife. Caldwell's short stories have been collected in *Complete Stories* (1953). Between 1944 and 1949 Caldwell again wrote of the poor of his native state in *A House in the Uplands* (1946), *The Sure Hand of God* (1947), *This Very Earth* (1948), and *Estherville* (1949). His other works include *Episode in Palmetto* (1950), *Call It Experience* (1951), an autobiography, and *A Lamp for Nightfall* (1952).

G. C. K.

CALDWELL, FRANK WALKER (1889-   ), American aeronautical engineer, was born at Lookout Mountain, Tenn., Dec. 20, 1889. After graduating from the University of Virginia, in 1908 he entered the mechanical engineering course at the Massachusetts Institute of Technology, where he helped build and fly several gliders between 1910 and 1912. After graduating in 1912, he became a process engineer, in 1916 taking charge of the propeller department of the Curtiss Aeroplane and Motor Company at Buffalo, N. Y.

Sent to the Mexican border to solve problems connected with propellers of Army planes there, Caldwell established a small factory and developed a successful method for treating propeller wood. In 1917 he was made chief of all propeller engineering work in the Army Air Service at Dayton, Ohio, retaining this position until his resignation in August 1928.

After a short period as a consulting engineer, he became chief engineer of the Standard Steel Propeller Company on June 1, 1929, and its successor companies, including the Hamilton Standard Propeller Division of the United Aircraft Corporation. He became director of research of the latter corporation in 1940.

While responsible for the design of all aircraft propellers used by the army in World War I, Caldwell assisted with the design of a number of navy propellers. In 1918 he developed the Micarta propeller, the first to be successfully made of material other than wood, which was used in a number of record flights. He developed various controllable-pitch and reversible propellers, made of wood, Micarta, or steel, and steel adjustable-blade propellers which in the 1920's were used widely by the navy and army and by such fliers as Lindbergh, Earhart, Byrd, and Wilkins. He played a leading part in the development of the Hamilton Standard two-position controllable propeller and its constant-speed propeller, and received special mention when the Collier Trophy was awarded this company in 1934. He received the Sylvanus Albert Reed Award of the Institute of the Aeronautical Sciences in 1935 for his propeller work, and was president of the Institute in 1941.

Caldwell's contributions to fundamental aeronautical engineering have included a number of successful laboratories built under his supervision. His apparatus for propeller testing established at the Westinghouse Electric and Manufacturing Company in 1917, the large propeller testing laboratory at McCook Field and its successor at Wright Field, Dayton, Ohio, and the later research installations at the United Aircraft Corporation in East Hartford, Conn., were some of these. His high-speed wind tunnels at McCook Field led to the first photographs of the vortices over the tips of airfoils, and to the first tests showing the losses in lift-drag ratio, because of the change in air flow over airfoils at high speed. He has written a number of reports and articles on propeller research and manufacture and wrote the section on propellers in *Aircraft Power Plants,* by Edward T. Jones, Robert Insley, and F. W. Caldwell (1926).　M. H. Sm.

CALDWELL, the county seat of Canyon Co. in southwestern Idaho, is situated on the Boise River, 30 mi. west of Boise, at an elevation of 2,367 ft. The city is governed by a mayor and council, and is the seat of The College of Idaho. The Union Pacific Railroad supplies transportation. Caldwell is the trade and shipping center for the surrounding agricultural district. The local industries include flour and planing mills, dairies, food processing and seed-corn plants, stockyards, and a fishing tackle factory. Pop. 1950, 10,487.

CALEB, in the Old Testament, head of the tribe of Judah, was one of the twelve princes whom Moses sent to spy out the land of Canaan and to learn whether it was practical for the Israelites to attempt to conquer it at that time (Num. xiii ff). Caleb, supported by Joshua, another of the spies and later the successor to Moses, maintained that, in spite of the strength of the Canaanites, the Israelites would succeed in conquering the land because of a divine promise. The Israelites, however, were discouraged by the pessimistic reports of the other ten, and, according to tradition, they continued to wander in the desert for forty years. At the end of this period Caleb was rewarded for his faithfulness by receiving Hebron and the neighboring hill country as his share, after the conquest of the land was completed by Joshua. (Jos. xiv:6-15).　M. A. G.

CALEB WILLIAMS, ADVENTURES OF, a novel by William Godwin, first published in 1794. The work was intended to illustrate "the tyranny . . . exercised by the powerful members of the community against those who are less privileged than themselves." Melodramatic, occasionally powerful, it describes the cruelty of a country squire, Falkland, to his poor but faithful secretary, Caleb Williams, who suspects him of murder. Hounded by Falkland and his agents, Williams eventually confronts Falkland with the charge and wins a confession from him.　H. M. J.

CALEDONIA, the name given in Roman times to the northernmost part of Britain, the area north of the Firth of Forth–Clyde line, which was the stronghold of the Picts and Scots. It is still used as a poetic synonym for Scotland.

CALEDONIAN CANAL, a ship canal in the counties of Inverness and Argyll in northern Scotland, connecting Moray Firth to Loch Linnhe. It is formed by uniting a chain of lakes, Lochs Ness, Oich, Lochy and Eil, by navigable canals. The entire system is 60½ mi. long, but the canal proper is 22 mi. long, the rest of the length being in the lochs. The average depth is 18 ft. James Watt, inventor of the steam engine, prepared designs for the canal in 1773, but his estimates were too high for the contractors, and the project was postponed for thirty years. Telford and Jessop prepared new estimates, and work was begun in 1803. The canal was opened when it was two-thirds finished, in 1822, and was completed in 1847. The cost, up to May 5, 1849, was £1,311,270.　S. Van V.

CALENDAR (from *calendae* or *kalendae,* "calends," the first day of the Roman month), a system of establishing the relations between the year and its divisions in such manner that, for one important result, the seasons occur at approximately the same day every year. The chief functions of the calendar are (a) to establish dates and (b) to measure equal time intervals. Under (a), dates to be established may be those of physical phenomena such as equinoxes, eclipses, tides, and other periodic occurrences, or nonperiodic phenomena such as earthquakes. Also, historical and civil events are thus recorded in exact chronology. A third kind of dating is that of ecclesiastical events and movable feasts, including the date of Easter. Under (b) the calendar is used in the commercial field and at home, where salaries, accounts, and business relations need to be based on intervals of time. The many statistical and scientific uses of time intervals come under this heading.

TYPES OF CALENDAR

There are three main types of calendar: (1) the lunar, (2) the solar, and (3) the lunisolar.

Lunar. The lunar calendar preserves the length of the lunar or synodic month (29½ days) and disregards the length of the solar year. The Mohammedan calendar is a good example. Most of the cultural groups using a lunar calendar reckoned the months as having 29 and 30 days alternately, thus averaging 29½ days. In using the lunar calendar, the lunar year has been taken as (12 × 29½) or 354 days. A lunar year of 12 synodic months actually has 354.367056 days; the decimal here is unaccounted for in the calendar and amounts to 11.012 days in 30 lunar years. By intercalating (inserting) 11 days in every 30 lunar years, this calendar becomes very accurate with respect to the moon. The main difficulty with it is that its year is about 11 days shorter than the solar year, causing the seasons to occur at earlier and earlier dates through the years; hence it is impracticable in civil affairs.

Solar. The solar calendar holds to the length of the solar year as nearly as possible, but it disregards the lunar month and assumes a set length of month. The Julian calendar is an excellent example; others are the old Mayan and Egyptian calendars. The solar calendar commonly has four crucial points—the two equinoxes and the two solstices. It appears to be convenient to have the vernal equinox fall on or about March 21; and in order to accomplish this result, an intercalation must be effected. The solar year being 365.2422 days in length, the decimal (0.2422) of a day must be provided for. This discrepancy amounts to nearly 1 day in 4 years. However, the adding of 1 day every 4 years, with no exceptions, would cause the seasons to become earlier and earlier in the calendar by about 0.0078 day a year or nearly 1 day a century. In 400 years the March equinox would occur 3.12 days earlier than on March 21. Hence, to keep the seasons in line, 1 day is added every 4 years, except on century years not divisible by 400; i.e., the year 2000 will be a leap year, but 2100, 2200, and 2300 will not. This scheme is used in the Gregorian calendar.

Lunisolar. In the lunisolar type of calendar there is an attempt to keep the lengths of lunar month and tropical year in harmony by periodic adjustments. Thus, the lunar month of 29½ days is made into a 29-day or 30-day month alternately, and 12 of these give 354 days; additional months are added at times, to bring the number of calendar days to the number of days in a solar year. Commonly this is done by intercalation of a 13th lunar month every 2 or 3 years. Such an expedient is required in order to have the agricultural seasons occur at about the same calendar day each year. The Jewish calendar is an example of the lunisolar type.

MEASUREMENT OF TIME

The measurement of time, certain units of which are recorded by the calendar, is based on periodic movements of natural phenomena. The rotation of the earth on its axis measures the day, the revolution of the moon around the earth gives the lunar month, and the revolution of the earth around the sun makes a solar year.

Solar Day. The earth's rotation being essentially very uniform, an apparent solar day is the interval between two successive passages of the sun over the lower meridian. Apparent solar days are not uniform in length, so that for time-keeping purposes the mean sun is used, and a mean solar day (used in civil life) is thus the interval between two successive transits of the mean sun over the lower meridian. Mean solar days are all of constant length. The beginning of a new day is at 0 hr. (zero hour) or midnight, at least in most countries. This has not always been so, for in Biblical and old Greek, Jewish, and other times, the day was often held to begin at evening. The Romans had their day commence at different times during different periods of their history.

Lunar Month. The month was based originally on the period of the moon's revolution around the earth, that is, the synodic period, or interval between two successive new moons or full moons. The mean synodic month, called a lunation, is 29 days, 12 hr., 44 min., 2.8 sec. in length. In Biblical times a lunation was taken as 30 days, but the Romans, Greeks, and others standardized on 29½ days. A lunar month appeared to be a convenient unit of time for human affairs that was somewhere between a day and a year. Indeed, in early times much stress was put on the use of the moon as a time measurer, probably because of the ease of

observing the satellite in its phases. But a lunation has been connected with religious matters and so has had perhaps an overimportant part in calendar making.

Year. The kind of year used for ordinary purposes, including the calendar, is the tropical year ("year of the seasons")—the interval between two successive returns of the sun to the vernal equinox. In 1950 its length is 365 days, 5 hr., 48 min., and 45.7 sec., and it is decreasing at the rate of about 0.5 sec. per century. Very early civilizations used this seasonal year; and the records of the Egyptians, Chinese, and others show that its length was taken originally as 360 days. Still, at a comparatively early time the solar (tropical) year had begun to be known more accurately, first as 365 days; then the Egyptians established 365¼ days; and Hipparchus, famous ancient astronomer, diminished the ¼ day by a few minutes. The civil year has not, by any means, always begun on January 1. The time of the spring equinox seemingly was the beginning of the year with many of the earliest civilizations, though the Egyptians began their year with the autumnal equinox.

HISTORIC CALENDARS

Greek. The old Greek calendar had normally a year of 354 days. Because of the 11¼ extra days needed to match

NEW YORK PUBLIC LIBRARY

ANCIENT SCANDINAVIAN CALENDAR

this with the solar year, they added 90 days (11¼ × 8) every 8 years. These 90 days were split into 3 embolismic (30-day) months, and the cycle of 8 years was called an octaeteris. After about 432 B.C., the Greek calendar was based on the Metonic cycle, then on the Callippic cycle. These are discussed later in this article under Cycles and Eras.

Roman. The original Latin calendar (about eighth century B.C.) comprised 10 months or 304 days, according to the old historians; 5 months having 31 days each, 4 months having 30, and 1 month having 29 days. The year began on March 1, thus giving the month names—*Octo*ber, for example, for the eighth month; and the day began with the midnight hour. The Roman calendar underwent a number of changes. By tradition, King Numa Pompilius added two months, Januarius and Februarius, about 713 B.C. Numa's calendar had 7 months of 29 days, 4 months of 31 days, and Februarius with 28 days, making 355 days. About 451 B.C., a group of 10 magistrates, the Decemvirs, rearranged the months, giving them the present order; that is, they changed the year's beginning from Martius to Januarius. Later, the College of Pontiffs, with the Pontifex Maximus as chief, was founded and took complete charge of the calendar.

Julian. By 46 B.C., when Julius Caesar was made Pontifex Maximus, calendar dates had come to be decidedly out of step with natural events. So many complaints had been lodged that Caesar had the opportunity to effect radical changes. To restore the calendar to its former relation to the seasons, Caesar extended the year 46 B.C. to an extraordinary length, upon advice of Sosigenes, an Alexandrian astronomer. He added 23 days of an intercalary month after Februarius, and he added two months of 34 and 33 days between November and December, so that the year contained 445 days and was called the year of confusion. Caesar's next move was to fix the normal length of the year as 365 days, with one day intercalated every 4 years, after February 24, to make up to 365¼ days, the supposed true length of the tropical year. Caesar deliberately abandoned the lunar year entirely and adopted a solar year. Except for leap year all intercalation became unnecessary. He settled on exactly 365 days 6 hr. as the length of the year, and an approximation of this value has been used ever since. He had a series of 3 common years and a fourth, a leap year. Caesar also altered the month lengths again (*see* Table I), giving Februarius 29 days in common years and 30 in leap years. This, then, was the Julian calendar, now frequently called Old Style, introduced on Jan. 1, 45 B.C. In 44 B.C. the name of Quintilis was altered to Julius in honor of Julius Caesar, and the vernal equinox was moved to its original date of March 25.

Augustan. The pontifices after Caesar's death seem to have misinterpreted the leap-year precepts, because for 36 years they had a leap year every third year instead of every fourth. Augustus Caesar, the first Roman emperor, rectified the mistake by omitting three intercalations, from 8 B.C. to A.D. 8. Since A.D. 8, the system of leap years occurring on only the years that are multiples of 4 has been in operation. Sextilis was renamed Augustus in honor of the new emperor. Also, the days in this month were increased from 30 to 31. As if to make up for this, one day was omitted from Februarius. September and November were shortened from 31 to 30 days, and October and December were lengthened from 30 to 31, supposedly in order to balance the calendar. Thus the present scheme of months and days was evolved. Some authorities hold that Julius (not Augustus) Caesar introduced the present sequence.

Table I summarizes the differences between the three latest Roman calendars.

Calends, Ides, and Nones. The Romans used the plural forms "calendae" (calends), "ides," and "nones" as reference points in designating the days of the month. The calends were the first day of the month. The ides were the 15th day of Martius, Aprilis, Julius (Quintilis), and October, and the 13th day of the other months. By modern reckoning, the nones came on the 8th day before the ides. The Romans, however, included the ides themselves, making the nones the 9th day, whence the term (from *nonus,* "nine"). The ides of Martius (March) were March 15, or loosely, this day plus the 7 days preceding it—March 8 to March 15, inclusive. The nones of Martius, Aprilis, Julius, and October fell on the 7th day of these months, and on the 5th day of the other months. The days of the month were counted backwards—from the

TABLE I. THE MONTHS IN THREE ROMAN CALENDARS
(In Days)

Name of Month	Calendar of the Decemvirs, c. 414 B.C.	Calendar of Julius Caesar, 45 B.C.	Calendar of Augustus, 8 B.C.
Januarius	29	31	31
Februarius	28	29-30	28-29
Martius	31	31	31
Aprilis	29	30	30
Maius	31	31	31
Junius	29	30	30
Quintilis*	31	31	31
Sextilis†	29	30	31
September	29	31	30
October	31	30	31
November	29	31	30
December	29	30	31

* Called Julius in the calendars of Julius and Augustus.
† Called Augustus in the calendar of Augustus.

ides and nones for the first half of the month and from the calends of the following month for the second half of the month.

Gregorian. The Julian year, being 365 days 6 hr. long, exceeds the true solar year by 11 min. 14 sec., so that dates of physical phenomena came to occur earlier and earlier according to the Julian calendar. The season dates, and notably the Easter date, assumed a growing discrepancy which became annoying. In A.D. 325 the Council of Nicaea instituted the decree that Easter was to be uniform at the Christian churches. Various proposals were introduced in succeeding years. Finally, those of Aloysius Lilius (Luigi Lilio Ghiraldi), a Neapolitan astronomer and physician, and of Christopher Clavius, a Bavarian Jesuit, were adopted by Pope Gregory XIII. On Feb. 24, 1582, he issued a bull containing two chief alterations of the Julian calendar: (1) 10 days were to be dropped from the calendar of 1582, the day after October 4 become October 15; this change was to restore the vernal equinox date to March 21, which was presumably the date of the vernal equinox in A.D. 325. (2) Three out of every four century years were to be common years, rather than leap years; only the century years evenly divisible by 400 were to be leap years. Thus, 1582 the first year of the Gregorian calendar. This calendar, often called New Style, was adopted by France in that year, some other Catholic countries following in 1583. Other countries adopted the Gregorian calendar at various times, Great Britain beginning in 1752. By A.D. 1700, a leap year under the Julian calendar, the discrepancy was 11 days, so in Great Britain the day after Sept. 2, 1752, became September 14. Also in 1752, the beginning of the year in England was changed to January 1; formerly it had been Annunciation Day, March 25. The retrospective feature of the correction has caused much confusion for many years. Gregory XIII made the correction refer back to the Nicene Council date. If he had not insisted on this point, probably alteration (2) alone would have eliminated the confusion. The Gregorian calendar is the one in use today in the United States and most other countries, including the Soviet Union, which abandoned the Eastern (Julian) calendar shortly after the "October" (actually November) Revolution led by the Bolshevists in 1917. The Gregorian calendar is not absolutely correct, the calendar year being 26 seconds longer than the tropical year. This difference will not amount to 1 day until 3,323 years have elapsed. Instead of omitting 3 leap years in every 400 years, leap years omitted every 128 years would rectify the calendar so that 100,000 years would elapse before it became out of step with the solar year by 1 day.

Jewish. The Jewish calendar, typically lunisolar, is of very ancient lineage. It has months of 29 and 30 days alternately, with a month intercalated every third year. The intercalation of an extra month (Veadar) is introduced every 3rd, 6th, 8th, 11th, 14th, 17th, and 19th year of a 19-year cycle, just before the month of Nisan. Originally the Jewish year began with the month Tishri at the autumnal equinox, and this is now the beginning of the civil year, although the church year commences at Nisan, at the vernal equinox. The intercalations have the effect that the lunation during Nisan is regularly the one in which the vernal equinox occurs. Whereas the Gregorian calendar has two kinds of years— common years and leap years—the Jewish calendar has common years of 12 lunations and embolismic years of 13 lunations. In the embolismic year the 30 days intercalated before Nisan are composed of 1 day belonging to the 6th month (Adar), which normally has 29 days, and 29 days making up the month Veadar. The Jewish lunisolar calendar is actually more complicated than described here. Though it is fairly adequate for time measuring, it is not an efficient modern instrument for its purpose, because it has to use the lunar month.

Mohammedan. Before the time of Mohammed, who died in A.D. 632, the Arabs had a lunisolar calendar, using lunar months with intercalations something like those of the Jewish calendar. It is believed that abuse of the old calendar led Mohammed to eliminate the added months and use a typically lunar calendar. In this, whose year one is A.D. 622, the day and the synodic period of the moon are the only natural units used, the seasons not being taken into account. The lunar month was used as 29½ days and the year had 12 months of 29 or 30 days alternately. In a cycle of 30 years the final month had 29 days in 19 of the years, and 30 in the other 11. The Mohammedan calendar is used extensively throughout the Near East and Middle East, though in 1925 Turkey abandoned it in favor of the Gregorian calendar.

Egyptian. The very early Egyptian calendar was of the lunar kind, as is evidenced by the crescent-moon hieroglyph for "month." Later the Egyptians made much of the annual flooding of the Nile, which acted as a time reference for them; indeed, it even assisted in establishing a solar calendar. According to James Harvey Breasted, this calendar was first set up in 4236 B.C. and this is called the earliest known date. The solar year had 12 months of 30 days each, and at the end of the last month 5 epagomenal (additional) days were introduced, giving 365 days. Because the civil year was short ¼ day, on the solar year, the calendar and the seasons showed an ever-widening discrepancy with the years. By means of the heliacal rising of the star Sirius, the Egyptians discovered that 1,461 Egyptian years of 365 days equal 1,460 solar years of 365¼ days. This interval was known as the Sothiacal period. For a long time the clergy prevented any change in the calendar; finally, in 238 B.C., King Ptolemy III decreed the addition of 1 day every 4 years, in a similar manner to our leap-year day. Thus the solar calendar as now used was begun. The Egyptians' day began at sunrise, and their week was of 10 days, with 3 weeks in each month.

Chinese. The earliest or prehistoric Chinese calendar was lunar. Around 2357 B.C. the Emperor Yao became dissatisfied with the lunar type of calendar and asked his astronomers to determine the equinoxes, to use intercalary months, and set up the seasonal calendar, for agricultural reasons. In order to reconcile the 354 days of the lunar year with 365 days in the astronomical year, intercalation had to be effected, and so 7 months were added in every 19 years, with carefully expressed precepts for their use. Although the solar and the lunar year were reconciled, the lunisolar discrepancy remained and was corrected when it reached particular values. The calendar was still insufficient; the years were of unequal length and the equinoxes were not fixed in the calendar. The Chinese year had 24 half months. Jesuit missionaries were given the problem of dealing with this calendar in the seventeenth century. They corrected it, but further errors were made by the Chinese people. The calendar had a cycle of 60 years, with stems, branches, and repetitions of each, to which amusing names were attached. The first cycle began in 2637 B.C. After the Western penetration of China during the nineteenth century, the Gregorian calendar became necessary in commerce, and in 1911 it was adopted by the new Chinese Republic. The people continued to use the ancient lunar calendar, but since 1930 its use has been forbidden.

Mayan. The ancient Mayas had a remarkable knowledge of time measurement, as the Spaniards found upon exploring Mexico and near-by areas in the sixteenth century. The accu-

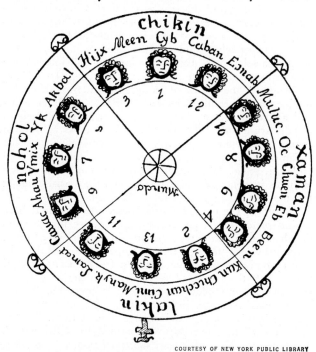

COURTESY OF NEW YORK PUBLIC LIBRARY

MAYAN CALENDAR WHEEL
FROM BOOK OF CHILAM BALAM OF KAUA

racy of their calendar was amazing. The only discrepancy between the Mayan calendar and the Julian canceled out when the Gregorian correction was added to the Julian calendar. The old calendar of Mexico had 360 days arranged in 18 months of 20 days each. There was a name for each month and each day, and there were 5 extra days belonging to no particular month. The calendar showed 28 weeks, each of 13 numbered days, or a total of 364 days, so that there was one day left over. A reformation occurred by A.D. 1091. Apparently the calendar had become unsatisfactory to the priests.

so they devised another one of 13 months, likewise numbered, each of 20 days. The marvel of the calendar of the Mayas is that the ancient Mexicans should have hit upon the true length of the tropical year. Probably a long and precise series of observations was made in order to achieve this result.

A generalized and restored reproduction of the Aztec calendar stone, executed by V. Foscato in terrazzo, is inlaid in the floor of the Solar System Room of the Hayden Planetarium, New York City. The original (shown on p. 130 of Vol. 2) was discovered in Mexico by Cortes' troops in 1519 and was rediscovered in 1790 after having been re-buried. It is a huge basaltic block 12 ft. in diameter, for the design alone. This curious carving is enormously complicated. The face in the center represents the sun. The four large rectangles adjacent to the sun contain heads symbolizing dates of the four former epochs of the world, called suns by the Aztecs, and four other shapes between these rectangles represent the four directions. The bulging curved shapes at the left and right of this second circle show claws belonging to a fire serpent grasping a human heart. The heads and conventionalized symbols in the rectangles of the next band are symbols representing the 20 days of the month. Outside of these are bands portraying eagle feathers, jades, and ceremonial symbols. The large triangular figures represent the sun's rays, and at the bottom of the outer circle are two fire serpents supposedly representing the heat of the sky.

CYCLES AND ERAS

Dominical Letter. The Dominical (or Sunday) Letter is a scheme showing the relation between the day of the month and the day of the week for any given year. It determines particularly the Sundays, and from this the entire calendar year may be constructed. A table of weekday letters may be made as follows:

```
       A   B   C    D    E   F    G
Jan.   1   2   3    4    5   6    7
       8   9   10   11   12  13   14
       15  16  (and so on to end of year)
```

Thus every day except February 29 of leap year has a letter. A certain day of the week has always the same letter for the entire specified year, except in leap years, so that whatever letter represents the first Sunday represents all Sundays in the year. Knowing the Dominical letter (A to G) of a year gives the entire order of days of the week in that year. The following tabulation will prove useful:

When Jan. 1 Is:	Dominical Letter Is:
Sunday	A
Monday	G
Tuesday	F
Wednesday	E
Thursday	D
Friday	C
Saturday	B

To determine the order of weekdays and to set up an entire calendar for any year, one needs (a) a table of the Sunday letter of every year and (b) a table giving the calendar arrangement for any year, when the Sunday letter is known.

In Table II, the place of intersection of the century-year column with the line showing the last two digits in the year desired gives the Dominical letter. *Example:* Find the Sunday letter for 1950. Intersection of the 1900 column with the 50 line gives A, the Sunday letter. Leap years have two letters; and the century years, such as 1900, are in the top row.

Metonic Cycle. The Metonic cycle expresses the relation between a lunation and a tropical (solar) year, and it has been the basis of the Greek, Jewish, and some other calendars. This cycle, of 19 years of 12 months each, has 7 months intercalated. It is named after the Greek astronomer Meton, who discovered it independently about 432 B.C., though it is held to have been known to the Chinese as far back as 2269 B.C. Meton observed that a period of 19 solar years is composed of 235 lunations. He used exactly 365¼ days for the

TABLE II. DOMINICAL (SUNDAY) LETTERS FOR ANY YEAR FROM A.D. 1600 TO A.D. 2800

(After Alexander Philip)

Last Two Digits in Year				Century Years, A.D.			
				1700 2100 2500	1800 2200 2600	1900 2300 2700	1600 2000 2400 2800
00				C	E	G	BA
01	29	57	85	B	D	F	G
02	30	58	86	A	C	E	F
03	31	59	87	G	B	D	E
04	32	60	88	FE	AG	CB	DC
05	33	61	89	D	F	A	B
06	34	62	90	C	E	G	A
07	35	63	91	B	D	F	G
08	36	64	92	AG	CB	ED	FE
09	37	65	93	F	A	C	D
10	38	66	94	E	G	B	C
11	39	67	95	D	F	A	B
12	40	68	96	CB	ED	GF	AG
13	41	69	97	A	C	E	F
14	42	70	98	G	B	D	E
15	43	71	99	F	A	C	D
16	44	72	..	ED	GF	BA	CB
17	45	73	..	C	E	G	A
18	46	74	..	B	D	F	G
19	47	75	..	A	C	E	F
20	48	76	..	GF	BA	DC	ED
21	49	77	..	E	G	B	C
22	50	78	..	D	F	A	B
23	51	79	..	C	E	G	A
24	52	80	..	BA	DC	FE	GF
25	53	81	..	G	B	D	E
26	54	82	..	F	A	C	D
27	55	83	..	E	G	B	C
28	56	84	..	DC	FE	AG	BA

year and had 19 Julian (solar) years equal to 6,939 days 18 hr., and 235 lunations equal to 6,939 days, 16 hr., and 31 min. He had to intercalate 7 embolismic months in this cycle, since 19 years of 12 lunar months each totals only 228 months. Certain authorities hold that Meton's intercalations were made in the 3rd, 6th, 8th, 11th, 14th, and 19th years of the cycle. In accordance with this scheme, the years other than those just enumerated contained 12 lunar months of 29 and 30 days used alternately, while the 7 years mentioned had 13 months of the same length, with the embolismic month of 30 days for 6 of its years and of 29 days for its 7th. The first Metonic cycle is said to have begun in July of the year 432 B.C. The moon's phases recur on the same days, within a few hours; therefore, if new-moon dates are recorded for a cycle, they become known for the next cycle.

Callippic Cycle. Callippus, another Greek astronomer, improved upon Meton in 330 B.C. by establishing a cycle of 76 years (19 × 4). The Callippic cycle invariably included

TABLE III. A CALENDAR FOR ANY YEAR (JULIAN OR GREGORIAN)

(Revised from Alexander Philip)

COMMON YEARS — Dominical Letters and Initial Days

Dominical Letters	Sun.	Mon.	Tue.	Wed.	Thu.	Fri.	Sat.
A	Sun.	Mon.	Tue.	Wed.	Thu.	Fri.	Sat.
G	Mon.	Tues.	Wed.	Thu.	Fri.	Sat.	Sun.
F	Tue.	Wed.	Thu.	Fri.	Sat.	Sun.	Mon.
E	Wed.	Thu.	Fri.	Sat.	Sun.	Mon.	Tue.
D	Thu.	Fri.	Sat.	Sun.	Mon.	Tue.	Wed.
C	Fri.	Sat.	Sun.	Mon.	Tue.	Wed.	Thu.
B	Sat.	Sun.	Mon.	Tue.	Wed.	Thu.	Fri.

Month	Days in Month							
Jan. / Oct.	31 / 31	1, 8, 15, 22, 29	2, 9, 16, 23, 30	3, 10, 17, 24, 31	4, 11, 18, 25	5, 12, 19, 26	6, 13, 20, 27	7, 14, 21, 28
Feb. / Mar. / Nov.	28 / 31 / 30	5, 12, 19, 26	6, 13, 20, 27	7, 14, 21, 28	1, 8, 15, 22, 29	2, 9, 16, 23, 30	3, 10, 17, 24, 31	4, 11, 18, 25
Apr. / July	30 / 31	2, 9, 16, 23, 30	3, 10, 17, 24, 31	4, 11, 18, 25	5, 12, 19, 26	6, 13, 20, 27	7, 14, 21, 28	1, 8, 15, 22, 29
May	31	7, 14, 21, 28	1, 8, 15, 22, 29	2, 9, 16, 23, 30	3, 10, 17, 24, 31	4, 11, 18, 25	5, 12, 19, 26	6, 13, 20, 27
June	30	4, 11, 18, 25	5, 12, 19, 26	6, 13, 20, 27	7, 14, 21, 28	1, 8, 15, 22, 29	2, 9, 16, 23, 30	3, 10, 17, 24
Aug.	31	6, 13, 20, 27	7, 14, 21, 28	1, 8, 15, 22, 29	2, 9, 16, 23, 30	3, 10, 17, 24, 31	4, 11, 18, 25	5, 12, 19, 26
Sept. / Dec.	30 / 31	3, 10, 17, 24, 31	4, 11, 18, 25	5, 12, 19, 26	6, 13, 20, 27	7, 14, 21, 28	1, 8, 15, 22, 29	2, 9, 16, 23, 30

LEAP YEARS — Dominical Letters and Initial Days

Dominical Letters	Sun.	Mon.	Tue.	Wed.	Thu.	Fri.	Sat.
AG	Sun.	Mon.	Tue.	Wed.	Thu.	Fri.	Sat.
GF	Mon.	Tue.	Wed.	Thu.	Fri.	Sat.	Sun.
FE	Tue.	Wed.	Thu.	Fri.	Sat.	Sun.	Mon.
ED	Wed.	Thu.	Fri.	Sat.	Sun.	Mon.	Tue.
DC	Thu.	Fri.	Sat.	Sun.	Mon.	Tue.	Wed.
CB	Fri.	Sat.	Sun.	Mon.	Tue.	Wed.	Thu.
BA	Sat.	Sun.	Mon.	Tue.	Wed.	Thu.	Fri.

Month	Days in Month							
Jan. / Apr. / July	31 / 30 / 31	1, 8, 15, 22, 29	2, 9, 16, 23, 30	3, 10, 17, 24, 31	4, 11, 18, 25	5, 12, 19, 26	6, 13, 20, 27	7, 14, 21, 28
May	31	6, 13, 20, 27	7, 14, 21, 28	1, 8, 15, 22, 29	2, 9, 16, 23, 30	3, 10, 17, 24, 31	4, 11, 18, 25	5, 12, 19, 26
Feb. / Aug.	29 / 31	5, 12, 19, 26	6, 13, 20, 27	7, 14, 21, 28	1, 8, 15, 22, 29	2, 9, 16, 23, 30	3, 10, 17, 24, 31	4, 11, 18, 25
Mar. / Nov.	31 / 30	4, 11, 18, 25	5, 12, 19, 26	6, 13, 20, 27	7, 14, 21, 28	1, 8, 15, 22, 29	2, 9, 16, 23, 30	3, 10, 17, 24, 31
June	30	3, 10, 17, 24	4, 11, 18, 25	5, 12, 19, 26	6, 13, 20, 27	7, 14, 21, 28	1, 8, 15, 22, 29	2, 9, 16, 23, 30
Sept. / Dec.	30 / 31	2, 9, 16, 23, 30	3, 10, 17, 24, 31	4, 11, 18, 25	5, 12, 19, 26	6, 13, 20, 27	7, 14, 21, 28	1, 8, 15, 22, 29
Oct.	31	7, 14, 21, 28	1, 8, 15, 22, 29	2, 9, 16, 23, 30	3, 10, 17, 24, 31	4, 11, 18, 25	5, 12, 19, 26	6, 13, 20, 27

19 leap years, whereas the Metonic cycle had a variable number of leap years.

From Table III, any Julian or Gregorian calendar year may be constructed. *Example:* Find the day of the week of Aug. 10, 1908. The Dominical letters, obtained from Table II, are ED. From the leap-year section of Table III, the Sunday letters ED give the row of weekdays, from which it is found that the column containing August 10 intersects the ED row at Mon. Hence the given day was a Monday. Jan. 1 in Table III corresponds to Wed. (*see* ED row), Feb. 1 to Sat., Mar. 1 to Sun., and so on.

Golden Number. The years of the Metonic cycle bore the numbers 1 to 19, the number of the year therefore showing the relation of the year to the particular cycle. The position of any year in the cycle is given by its number, known as the golden number because in Classical times the phases of the moon were inscribed in gold on public monuments. In modern times the golden number has served only to indicate the position of the year in the cycle as an aid to determining the date of Easter.

The golden number of any year is easily found by the use of Table IV. *Example:* Find the golden number for 1950. First find 1900, which is in the first horizontal line under "Century Years." Follow this horizontal line to the left until the vertical colum containing 50 in the "Last Two Digits of Year" section is reached. The golden number for 1950, which appears at this intersection, is 13.

Solar Cycle. The solar cycle of 28 years was designed to show the relation between the day of the week and the day of the month. If there were no leap years, the day of the week and the day of the month would show a regular correspondence in a series lasting 7 years, because there are 7 different weekdays and the year may begin with any one, and moreover, the common year is 1 day longer than 52 weeks. But leap year every 4th year has the result that 28 years are needed to exhibit all the possible calendars in the

TABLE IV. GOLDEN NUMBERS FOR A.D. 1 TO 4000
(Julian or Gregorian)

Century Years			Last Two Digits of Year																		
			00	01	02	03	04	05	06	07	08	09	10	11	12	13	14	15	16	17	18
			19	20	21	22	23	24	25	26	27	28	29	30	31	32	33	34	35	36	37
			38	39	40	41	42	43	44	45	46	47	48	49	50	51	52	53	54	55	56
			57	58	59	60	61	62	63	64	65	66	67	68	69	70	71	72	73	74	75
			76	77	78	79	80	81	82	83	84	85	86	87	88	89	90	91	92	93	94
			95	96	97	98	99														
			Golden Numbers																		
0	1900	3800	1	2	3	4	5	6	7	8	9	10	11	12	13	14	15	16	17	18	19
100	2000	3900	6	7	8	9	10	11	12	13	14	15	16	17	18	19	1	2	3	4	5
200	2100	4000	11	12	13	14	15	16	17	18	19	1	2	3	4	5	6	7	8	9	10
300	2200	....	16	17	18	19	1	2	3	4	5	6	7	8	9	10	11	12	13	14	15
400	2300	....	2	3	4	5	6	7	8	9	10	11	12	13	14	15	16	17	18	19	1
500	2400	....	7	8	9	10	11	12	13	14	15	16	17	18	19	1	2	3	4	5	6
600	2500	....	12	13	14	15	16	17	18	19	1	2	3	4	5	6	7	8	9	10	11
700	2600	....	17	18	19	1	2	3	4	5	6	7	8	9	10	11	12	13	14	15	16
800	2700	....	3	4	5	6	7	8	9	10	11	12	13	14	15	16	17	18	19	1	2
900	2800	....	8	9	10	11	12	13	14	15	16	17	18	19	1	2	3	4	5	6	7
1000	2900	....	13	14	15	16	17	18	19	1	2	3	4	5	6	7	8	9	10	11	12
1100	3000	....	18	19	1	2	3	4	5	6	7	8	9	10	11	12	13	14	15	16	17
1200	3100	....	4	5	6	7	8	9	10	11	12	13	14	15	16	17	18	19	1	2	3
1300	3200	....	9	10	11	12	13	14	15	16	17	18	19	1	2	3	4	5	6	7	8
1400	3300	....	14	15	16	17	18	19	1	2	3	4	5	6	7	8	9	10	11	12	13
1500	3400	....	19	1	2	3	4	5	6	7	8	9	10	11	12	13	14	15	16	17	18
1600	3500	....	5	6	7	8	9	10	11	12	13	14	15	16	17	18	19	1	2	3	4
1700	3600	....	10	11	12	13	14	15	16	17	18	19	1	2	3	4	5	6	7	8	9
1800	3700	....	15	16	17	18	19	1	2	3	4	5	6	7	8	9	10	11	12	13	14

same order. As a table of identical calendars shows, the interval separating years with identical calendars varies from a minimum of 6 to a maximum of 28 years.

Dionysian (Paschal or Easter) Cycle. The Dionysian cycle of 532 years has as components the lunar cycle of 19 years and the solar cycle of 28 years. It is said to have been established by Dionysius Exiguus in A.D. 532. A lunar cycle began, according to his ruling, with that year, the first period of a new Easter cycle, which places the birth of Christ in the year A.D. 1. (This date has been in dispute and is frequently given by reliable authorities as 4 B.C.) The Dionysian cycle contains a complete range of Easter dates.

Epact. The epact is the number of days in the age of the moon on January 1 of any year. Thus each year has an epact number. The epact was constructed by Lilius and put into operation by Clavius, a priest under Pope Gregory XIII, in preparing the new calendar tables to show Easter and other dates. For the Easter date a lunar almanac is used, and opposite the epact concerned that new moon is located by which the first full moon after the vernal equinox is found. The Sunday following is Easter. The epact was supposedly an improvement over the golden number. It allowed dates of all new and full moons throughout the year to be calculated, from the age of new moon on January 1. A complete table of epacts covers 7,000 years; after this, the whole series is repeated. Epacts run in cycles of 19 numbers per cycle. The rule for finding the epact number is to add 11 to the epact of the year before; if the sum is over 30, subtract 30. The rule is not very exact, for 30 is only the approximate figure, and the astronomical data sometimes varies about a day from the results of the rule. The epact was not used until the Gregorian calendar was invented. A cycle beginning with epact 11 is reputed to have commenced with 1 B.C. Description

and precepts regarding the epacts appear very complex until one has mastered the detail.

Roman Indiction. The Roman Indiction is a cycle introduced by Constantine I, the first Christian Roman emperor, for use in connection with commercial affairs and tax collecting. The whole sequence of year numbers was divided into 15-year intervals, each interval being an indiction. The cycle was counted as beginning Jan. 1, A.D. 313. The year A.D. 1 would therefore have been the 4th year of an indiction. The rule to find the number of year in the current indiction is, add 3 to the date, and divide by 15, the remainder being the number. For 1950 the number of the year in the present Roman Indiction is 3.

Julian Period. The Julian period, a general and universal cycle or period used in chronology, was invented by Joseph Scaliger, French chronologist, in 1582. ("Julian" here has nothing to do with Julius Caesar or the Julian calendar.) A Julian period is composed of 7,980 years, and is a multiple of the solar cycle (28 years), the Metonic cycle (19 years), and the Roman Indiction (15 years). The year and day of the beginning of the Julian period, as established by Scaliger, are Jan. 1, 4713 B.C., since the three cycles all began together on that date. The cycle is not completed until the end of A.D. 3267. To find the number of a year in the Julian period, add the year to 4713; the sum is the number sought. The year 1950 is number 6663 of the Julian period. Individual days in the period are indicated by the days elapsed since the beginning of the period, and every day has its own Julian-day number. Thus, Jan. 1, 1950 (beginning at Greenwich mean noon) is known as J.D. 2,433,283. Tables of Julian-day numbers are given in government ephemerides to facilitate turning any date into its J.D. number, for astronomical calculations involving large time intervals.

Roman Era. The Roman Era was the era by which the Romans reckoned historical events. They numbered the years consecutively beginning with the year of the founding of Rome, traditionally 753 B.C. The year number was preceded by the initials A.U.C., an abbreviation for *anno urbis conditae* (in the year of the founding of the city). The year 1950 of the Gregorian calendar corresponds to 2703 of the Roman Era.

Olympic Era. The Olympiads, the 4-year intervals between the Greek games held at Olympia, were used in an-

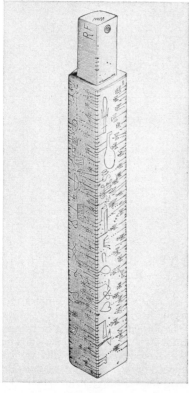

ANGLO-SAXON CALENDAR
The notches on the corners indicate days, while the devices attached to the lines extending from the notches denote days of special observance.

NEW YORK PUBLIC LIBRARY

cient Greek chronology. The time of the games was governed by the first full moon after the summer solstice, in the month Hecatombeon, nearly the same as the present July. The first Olympic games were held on July 17, 776 B.C. The calendar and months used were lunar, and the Metonic cycle intercalations were in operation. In the fourth century of the Christian Era, on the abolishment of the Olympic Games by Theodosius I in A.D. 392, the use of the Olympiads was abandoned in favor of the Roman Indiction. The term "Era of the Olympiads" often occurs in chronology.

Era of Nabonassar. The Era of Nabonassar, one of the first eras to become established, is named after King Nabonassar of Babylon. It is of particular interest to astronomers because it was used to express dates by Hipparchus and also by the Alexandrian astronomer Ptolemy in his *Almagest*. Moreover, the study of modern astronomy seems to have commenced with this era and in Babylonia. The beginning of the era was Feb. 26, 747 B.C. (Julian calendar), the first year of Nabonassar's reign. Ptolemy began his day with mean moon of the meridian of Alexandria, and the year used was the Egyptian year of 365 days with 12 months of 30 days and with 5 epagomenal days added. Whether or not the Babylonians used the era near the time of its beginning is uncertain, but the later Babylonians probably did. April 23, 1950, Gregorian calendar, is the first day of the year 2699 of the Era of Nabonassar.

Jewish Era. The Jewish Era starts from the assumed date of creation—or in 3761 B.C.—and was used with the Jewish calendar, whose civil year begins near the September equinox. September 11, 1950, Gregorian calendar, starting at sunset, is the first day of the year 5711 of the Jewish Era.

Mohammedan Era. The Mohammedan Era (Era of the Hegira) began on July 16, A.D. 622, after the flight of Mohammed from Mecca. October 12, 1950, Gregorian calendar, beginning at sunset, is the first day of the year 1370 of the Mohammedan Era.

Christian Era. The Christian Era began on Jan. 1, A.D. 1. As has been noted, the cycle of the Christian Era is supposed to have been started by Dionysius Exiguus in A.D. 532 and to run contemporaneously with the Dionysian cycle. He designated the beginning of the year A.D. 1 to have been March 25, and therefore Dec. 25, A.D. 1, was called the birth date of Christ. Pope Gregory XIII altered the beginning of the year to January 1. Historians and chronologists for a long time have adopted Dec. 25, 1 B.C., as the day of the Nativity. Much discussion and disagreement on this important point has taken place, and modern research has generally established Dec. 25, 4 B.C. as the date. A point of confusion regarding dates like these is that astronomers often call the year of the birth of Christ the zero year or A.D. 0, the year preceding being 1 B.C. However, other astronomers as well as most historians and chronologists have no year 0, but instead have A.D. 1 following the end of 1 B.C. Allied to this question is the unending dispute as to whether years such as 1800 and 1900 are the last of the old century or the first of the new one. Astronomers commonly prefer to use the '00 (century) years as the beginning of a new century.

The Easter date is notoriously one of great oscillation; it may occur on any day between March 22 and April 25, inclusive. The rule is that Easter must fall on the first Sunday after the full moon following the vernal equinox, March 21. And according to the English Book of Common Prayer, "... if the full moon happens upon a Sunday, Easter-day is the Sunday after." The date has been subject to much strife and argument. It has, naturally, great historical meaning. The Gregorian correction is now followed by most churches; but since Easter is based on the moon, it is still necessarily out of adjustment with the sun.

CALENDAR REFORM

Although the Gregorian calendar is very accurate and as a whole conforms to the natural phenomena, yet internally its present arrangement into component parts makes it a somewhat inadequate instrument for certain features of civil life. Improvement has long been agitated, and various associations for this purpose have been formed.

Defects of Gregorian Calendar. The Gregorian calendar has perhaps a dozen defects of differing degrees of seriousness. In general, the chief weakness is in the uneven division into half years, quarter years, months, and weeks. The quarters now contain 90, 91, or 92 days. Four main defects are the following:

(1) Theoretically, the civil or calendar year should be of the same length as the astronomical (tropical) year, but this is impossible because the tropical year does not contain an even whole number of days. Because of the need for intercalation of an extra day on leap year, there are two types of year (common year and leap year). A year may begin on any one of the days of the week, giving 7 types of common year and 7 types of leap year, or 14 kinds of year. Nor is this pattern repeated every 14 years; 28 years are needed for the cycle of one series to be repeated in order.

(2) The lengths of the months are unequal: there may be 28, 29, 30, or 31 days, an irregularity causing difficulty in accounting and statistics.

(3) The year does not have an integral number of weeks, either in common years or leap years. The weeks are uneven in number in the quarter year, the half year, and in the months except February.

(4) Dates or days from week to week or month to month, or even year to year, do not correspond, so that it is difficult to locate specific events. For example, Thanksgiving Day is always a Thursday, but the day of the month is variable; Christmas is always December 25, but the day of the week varies.

Suggested Improvements. Many proposals for a reformed calendar have been made, of which the three discussed below have emerged as taking the lead.

International Fixed Calendar. The international fixed calendar (13-month calendar) is a revised version of a new calendar proposed by Auguste Comte (1798-1857), French founder of Positivism, in 1849. It was designed by Moses Bruines Cotsworth (1859-1943), English statistician, who in 1942 founded the Internal Fixed Calendar League. The calendar consists of 13 months of 28 days each, the months being identical and beginning on Sunday. The 7th month, Sol, is interposed between the two sets of 6 that have the usual names. This gives 365—(13 × 28), or 1 day left over, to be called Year Day, following December 28. When there is a leap year, as in the present calendar, this would be observed as Leap Day, following June 28. These two "stabilizing" days would have no weekday names. Cotsworth suggested that the month names be dropped and Roman numerals be used instead. The month VII, or Sol, would begin on what is now June 18. As will be noted in Table V, the 13-month calendar is extremely uniform and easy to use. The year is an exact multiple of the month and the week, and the month is an exact multiple of the week. If the month were used as a standard for statistical purposes in place of the half year and quarter year, this calendar would be of considerable value. The difficulty is that 13 months cannot give even quarters and halves. Although this is true, the fact that equal quarters of 91 days each are available (Leap Day and Year Day are never counted) would seem to blunt this criticism. The most important criticism is that the calendar is so different from the present one that the change necessary for its inauguration would be too drastic to enlist the support of important groups devoted to tradition.

TABLE V. SAMPLE MONTH OF THE 13-MONTH INTERNATIONAL FIXED CALENDAR

Sun.	Mon.	Tue.	Wed.	Thu.	Fri.	Sat.
1	2	3	4	5	6	7
8	9	10	11	12	13	14
15	16	17	18	19	20	21
22	23	24	25	26	27	28

World Calendar. The world calendar of 12 months, in its present form, has been urged by many adherents, especially Miss Elisabeth Achelis. According to her, the calendar "gradually evolved from Switzerland as a result of a study made at the request of the International Congress of Commerce in 1914." She established the World Calendar Association in 1930 and started the *Journal of Calendar Reform* in 1931. The basic unit is the quarter year. Beginning January 1 on Sunday, the first three months have 31, 30 and 30

days, respectively. The month names are the same as at present. Each of the other quarters is identical with the first 3 months. Leap-Year Day (June W) would occur after June 30, and the Year-End Day (December W) would follow December 30. Opponents of the World Calendar suggest as its disadvantages that each month extends over parts of five weeks, and each month of any quarter begins on a different day of the week. Its advocates consider it an advantage that the calendar in many respects resembles the calendar now in use.

Perpetual Calendar. Another proposed calendar, similar in many respects to the World Calendar, was proposed by Willard E. Edwards of Honolulu, Hawaii. The delegate to the United States Congress from Hawaii has several times proposed its adoption and reports that it has been endorsed by the legislatures of Hawaii and Massachusetts. Like the World Calendar, it has four three-month quarters. They begin with Monday, January 1; the first two months of each quarter have 30 days, the last 31 days. Monday is the first day of each week, and the fact that every "quarter day" (1st of January, April, October) falls on a Monday is held to be beneficial to business. Another advantage cited is the elimination of Friday the 13th from the calendar. Between December 31 and January 1 falls the Day Apart, a holiday, and every four years Leap-Year Day falls between June 31 and July 1. A three-day holiday inevitably accompanies Christmas and New Year's.

TABLE VI. 12-MONTH FIXED CALENDARS

World Calendar							Perpetual Calendar						
	S	M	T	W	T	F	S	M	T	W	T	F	S	S

World Calendar:

	S	M	T	W	T	F	S
Jan. Apr. July Oct.	1	2	3	4	5	6	7
	8	9	10	11	12	13	14
	15	16	17	18	19	20	21
	22	23	24	25	26	27	28
	29	30	31				
Feb. May Aug. Nov.				1	2	3	4
	5	6	7	8	9	10	11
	12	13	14	15	16	17	18
	19	20	21	22	23	24	25
	26	27	28	29	30		
Mar. June* Sep. Dec.†						1	2
	3	4	5	6	7	8	9
	10	11	12	13	14	15	16
	17	18	19	20	21	22	23
	24	25	26	27	28	29	30

Perpetual Calendar:

	M	T	W	T	F	S	S
Jan. Apr. July Oct.	1	2	3	4	5	6	7
	8	9	10	11	12	13	14
	15	16	17	18	19	20	21
	22	23	24	25	26	27	28
	29	30					
Feb. May Aug. Nov.			1	2	3	4	5
	6	7	8	9	10	11	12
	13	14	15	16	17	18	19
	20	21	22	23	24	25	26
	27	28	29	30			
Mar. June* Sep. Dec.†				1	2	3	
	4	5	6	7	8	9	10
	11	12	13	14	15	16	17
	18	19	20	21	22	23	24
	25	26	27	28	29	30	31

* Leap-Year Day follows June 30 (or 31) every 4 years.

† Year-End Day (Day Apart) follows December 30 (or 31) of each year.

H. S. R.

CALENDAR, CHURCH, also called the ecclesiastical or liturgical calendar, the systematic correlation of recurrent religious observances, such as feasts and fasts, with measures of time based on periodic natural phenomena, such as the day, the lunar month, the seasons, and the solar year. For the Jewish Passover the first Christians substituted the annual commemoration of Christ's Resurrection (Easter), and for the Jewish Sabbath, a weekly commemoration of the Resurrection (the Lord's Day or Sunday). The difficulties of harmonizing the Jewish lunar reckoning with the solar calendar of the Romans occasioned the prolonged paschal controversy, the eventual settlement of which determined the characteristic form of the Christian church calendar.

Upon Easter is centered the oldest Christian liturgical cycle, its elements dating from the first century to (presumably) the fourth century. Before Easter come the fast of Lent (40 days, variously reckoned) and the commemoration of the Passion on Palm Sunday and during Holy Week; 40 days after Easter comes Ascension Day, and 10 days later Pentecost (Whitsuntide). To this cycle the medieval Western Church added Trinity Sunday (the first after Pentecost) and Corpus Christi (Thursday after Trinity Sunday). A second ancient cycle begins with Advent, culminates in Christmas and the Epiphany, and ends between January 18 and February 21, when the Sunday called Septuagesima begins the preparation for the next Easter. The early Christians observed also the anniversaries of the martyrs, to which were eventually added the feasts of other saints.

The calendar for a given year represents the harmonizing, in accordance with gradually evolved rules or rubrics, of three elements: first, the civil calendar (in the East generally the Julian Calendar, in the West the Gregorian); secondly, the two liturgical cycles of Easter and Christmas; and thirdly, the list of saints' days and fast days observed in the particular church, rite, or order. *See also* CALENDAR.

N. J. T.

CALENDULA [kələ′ndzhulə], a genus of the family Compositae, with about twenty species of annual and perennial herbs, native to the Mediterranean region. The pot marigold, *C. officinalis,* is a popular annual. It is sometimes used in cooking. This flower was called marigold by William Shakespeare.

CALEXICO [kələ′ksɪko], a port of entry and border city in Imperial Co., southern California, is 125 mi. southeast of San Diego. It is separated by a fence from Mexicali, Baja California. Calexico was incorporated in 1908 and has the commission form of government. Farming and cattle raising are its chief occupations. Money crops are lettuce, sugar beets, tomatoes, melons, flax, and alfalfa. Water for irrigation is brought from the Colorado River by the All-American Canal. The Southern Pacific Railroad provides freight service, and Bonanza Airlines operates from Calexico Airport. Supporting industries are food packing and the manufacture of fertilizers. The Southwest Outdoor Pageant, held annually at Calexico, is sponsored by the state of Baja California, Mexico, and Imperial Co. Pop. 1950, 6,433.

CALF DIPHTHERIA, also known as necrotic stomatitis, gangrenous stomatitis, ulcerative stomatitis, necrotic laryngitis, malignant stomatitis, or sore mouth, an acute, infectious, highly fatal disease of calves.

Cause. Calf diphtheria is reported to be caused by the organism *Actinomyces necrophorus,* a fungus which invades injured mucous membranes of the mouth and throat, sometimes when the calf is cutting its first teeth.

Symptoms. The common symptoms include slobbering, nasal discharge, sometimes wheezing and coughing, depression, weakness, and loss of flesh. Extensive ulceration of the mouth may be observed, and swellings may appear on the side of the cheek or in the region of the throat.

Control. Sick animals should be isolated promptly, and their housing quarters thoroughly cleansed and disinfected. The ulcerated areas of the mouth should be treated with an antiseptic such as potassium permanganate or dilute tincture of iodine. The mouth should also be washed frequently with warm salt water. Sulphonamides have been used successfully in treatment.   C. R. S.

CALGARY [kæ′lgəri], a city in southern Alberta, Canada, at the junction of the Bow and Elbow rivers, 180 mi. south of Edmonton, at 51° 5′ N. lat. and 114° 5′ W. long. It was founded in 1875 as a station of the Royal North West Mounted Police. Calgary was incorporated as a town in 1884 and as a city in 1893. It grew rapidly during the opening of the West. The magnificent Canadian Rockies, 50 mi. to the west, form a striking background for the city. Three of Calgary's educational institutions are Mount Royal College, a branch of the University of Alberta, and the Provincial Institute of Art and Technology. A rodeo called the Calgary Stampede is a famous annual summer event. Calgary is an important center for the Canadian Pacific Railway; the city is also served by the Canadian National Railways and the Trans-Canada Air Lines. It is an important retail and wholesale distribution center; it is also the center of a rich cattle-ranching, wheat-growing, and oil- and coal-producing region, and an oil-refining center of importance. Meat-packing plants, railroad shops, flour mills, petroleum plants, and factories producing acids, alkalis, and salts are the city's chief industries. Pop. 1956, 181,780.

CALHOUN, JOHN CALDWELL [kəlhu′n] (1782-1850), American vice-president, legislator, and political leader, was born on Calhoun Creek, in Abbeville County, S. C.,

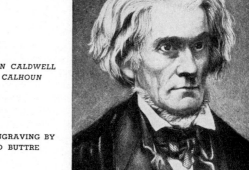

JOHN CALDWELL
CALHOUN

FROM AN ENGRAVING BY
RICE AND BUTTRE

Mar. 18, 1782. After home study and brief schooling at Waddell's Academy in Columbia County, Ga., Calhoun entered the junior class at Yale College, from which he was graduated in 1804. He then studied law at Litchfield, Conn., and Charleston, S. C.; he was admitted to the bar in 1807 and began law practice in Abbeville, S. C.

Early Career. Calhoun took an early interest in politics. He was elected to the South Carolina legislature in 1808 and to the national House of Representatives in 1811. When he entered Congress the country was engaged in constant disputes, particularly with Great Britain, on the subject of impressments and neutrality growing out of the Napoleonic conflict in Europe. President James Madison, following the lead of his predecessor, Thomas Jefferson, but with less skill, was insistent that the United States remain at peace, whatever the cost. A group of the younger Congressmen known as the "War Hawks" did not agree with this policy of appeasement and clamored for war. Calhoun joined their ranks without hesitation and soon was one of the leaders. When war with Great Britain finally came in June 1812, he was unremitting in his efforts to speed military success—so much so, in fact, that he was called "the young Hercules who carried the war on his back." After the war he plunged into the problems of peace and expansion, and was known as "the most elegant speaker in the House." In October 1817, President James Monroe appointed Calhoun secretary of war, and he served in that capacity until March 1825. His conduct of the office was characterized by notable improvements in the organization and administration of the army. Calhoun in 1822 announced himself as a candidate for president, but withdrew in favor of Andrew Jackson. When John Quincy Adams was elected president in 1824, Calhoun was elected vice-president.

Sectional Leadership. The period which followed was a critical one: it marked the transition of the country from an old era to a new one, an era in which the old Revolutionary leaders were giving way to a new generation, of which Calhoun was one of the most forceful leaders. The period also marked a change in Calhoun. From being a nationalist "above all sectional and factious prejudices," he became an ardent states' rights advocate and an outstanding sectional leader. The growing alliance between the expanding free West and the industrial North was upsetting the political balance that had existed between the free North and the slave South. The Missouri Compromise was the first important move in the struggle to maintain equilibrium in the relationship. At the same time, the tariff issue began to assume national importance, and the South became alarmed lest the protectionist program of the North be pursued too far. In the *South Carolina Exposition and Protest* of 1828, Calhoun set forth Southern objections to the tariff and embodied the doctrine of recourse which became famous as "nullification." He followed the *Exposition* with his "Fort Hill letter" of July 26, 1831, which in effect was a revision of the *Exposition* to serve as his personal manifesto. The Fort Hill letter was followed by a long letter to Governor James Hamilton of South Carolina, dated Aug. 28, 1832, on "state interposition"; this document is considered by many to be Calhoun's masterpiece among his several expositions.

Clash with Jackson. The next five years were momentous in American history. Calhoun, re-elected vice-president in 1828, found President Andrew Jackson opposed to his views, and the two men clashed on several occasions. Jackson accused Calhoun, while secretary of war, of interfering with his policy in Florida in a secret and underhanded manner. The President gave his support to Peggy Eaton as much to humiliate Calhoun as to honor Senator John H. Eaton and his wife, and he opposed Calhoun's political dialectics with his own forthright military acts. Jackson could exercise authority; Calhoun could only acquiesce or disagree. The arguments of Daniel Webster in his historic debate, the last week of January 1830, with Senator Robert Y. Hayne of South Carolina were Jackson's answer to Calhoun's doctrine of nullification. Hayne viewed the Union as "a compact between the states" that could be altered or broken, but Webster conceived "Liberty and Union, now and forever," as "one and inseparable." The breach between Calhoun and Jackson deepened, each accusing the other of ulterior motives. The enactment of the tariff of 1832 was the signal for an Ordinance of Nullification by South Carolina. Jackson's supporters countered with the so-called Force Act, empowering Jackson to use force to support federal legislation. Calhoun resigned as vice-president in 1832 and was elected to the Senate. Together, he and Henry Clay secured enactment of the compromise tariff of 1833, and the Nullification Ordinance was repealed. "Thus the olive branch and the rod were bound up together."

Senatorial Career. The next ten years of Calhoun's life were devoted to an attempt to reconcile his separatist doctrine of "a compact" with the broader doctrine of a federal union.

He faced the slavery controversy with reluctance, and labored incessantly to avoid the issue of the "irrepressible conflict" toward which his theories were leading him and his section. In 1843 he resigned from the Senate and began an active campaign to obtain the presidential nomination in 1844; however, he withdrew from the contest in January 1844, and in March became secretary of state in President John Tyler's cabinet. In this capacity he favored the annexation of Texas. At the end of Tyler's administration Calhoun refused the mission to England tendered him by President James K. Polk and again returned to private life, though his friends at once started a campaign to secure him the presidential nomination in 1848. The turn of events after the annexation of Texas and the Oregon Dispute with Great Britain caused him to return to the Senate in November 1845, and three months later, on Mar. 16, 1846, he assumed leadership in the Oregon controversy with a speech in which he contended that there must be no compromise with Great Britain or there would be war.

Political Philosophy. During this latter period, 1845-1849, Calhoun composed and completed his *Disquisition on Government,* describing the nature and purpose of government as he conceived them and the restrictions that must be imposed on it in the interest of otherwise helpless minorities. He also virtually completed his *Discourse on the Constitution and Government of the United States,* which in effect gave specific application to the thesis set down in his *Disquisition on Government.* But the current crisis could not be solved by dissertations. In the face of the debate on the Wilmot Proviso and other questions growing out of the Mexican War, Calhoun proposed an address on the slavery issue, but insufficient support was forthcoming. Before the end of 1849 an irregular convention in California applied for statehood with a constitution excluding slavery. Henry Clay prepared his celebrated omnibus bill, later largely enacted into what came to be known as the Compromise of 1850. Calhoun, though approving the purpose of the bill, criticized the text as failing to provide adequate guarantees for the South. On the theme "How can the Union be preserved?" Calhoun set forth his views in his last formal speech, which he was too ill to deliver. It was read to the Senate on Mar. 4, 1850, by Senator J. M. Mason of Virginia. Calhoun died in Washington, D. C., Mar. 31, 1850.

W. E. A.

CALI [ka'li], capital of Valle del Cauca department, in southwestern Colombia, located on the Cali River, approximately 105 mi. southeast of Buenaventura, at 3° 25' N. lat. and 76° 30' W. long. It is situated 3,327 ft. above sea level at the foothills of the Western Cordillera. The city's average temperature is 77° F. The valley surrounding the city between the Central and Western Cordilleras is very picturesque. Rain is abundant, and the fertile soil yields large crops of sugar cane, cotton, cacao, coffee, tobacco, and corn. Cali was founded by the Spaniards in 1536. After the opening of a railroad in 1914 to the port of Buenaventura, the city boomed. Its importance increased rapidly because nearly all the traffic bound for Buenaventura, the country's only important Pacific port, passes through Cali. By the 1940's Cali was Colombia's fourth largest city. In addition to rail facilities, the city has air and highway connections with other cities in the country and is an important commercial and manufacturing center. Its industrial products include alcoholic beverages, cotton textiles, soap, perfumes, pharmaceuticals, shoes, clothing, and tobacco products.

Like many other cities in South America, the metropolis has suffered damage from earthquakes throughout its his-

GOLDEN GATE BRIDGE, SAN FRANCISCO, CALIFORNIA, THE WORLD'S TALLEST AND LONGEST SINGLE-SPAN SUSPENSION BRIDGE

tory, and as a consequence its churches, including the Cathedral of San Pedro and the Church of La Merced, and other public buildings dating from the colonial period have required restoration, which has altered their original architecture. Most of the city's important buildings are modern edifices, including the Hermitage, a chapel of modern construction in the Gothic style. The city was severely damaged in August 1956 when an explosion wrecked eight blocks in the downtown commercial area, killing over 1,000 persons.

Cali is the seat of the University of Valle, noted for its medical school. Near the city is the Hill of Los Cristales, named for its abundant deposits of quartz and marble. Pop. 1951 (city), 241,357; (metropolitan area), 270,000. S. G. I.

CALIBAN [kæ'lɪbæn], a misshapen monster, son of the witch Sycorax, in Shakespeare's comedy *The Tempest*. Nursing a bitter grudge against Prospero, who has enslaved him and taken possession of the island he considers his own, Caliban makes a ludicrous and unsuccessful attempt to have his master murdered by two shipwrecked drunkards, Stephano and Trinculo. The language of Caliban, which he uses principally to curse his teacher Prospero, is remarkable for its vivid, natural imagery.

CALICO BASS. *See* CRAPPIE.

CALICUT [kɑ'lɪkʌt], now officially Kozhikode, a seaport on the southwestern or Malabar coast of India, located in the Malabar District of Kerala State. It is situated on the low coastal plain and has a high temperature throughout the year, with about 15° F. difference between seasons. The rainfall is unusually high, ranging between 100 and 150 in. annually; most of it occurs during the summer monsoon, and in the month of June about 30 in. fall. Coconut palms are the major product of the Calicut area, with about half the land devoted to their growth. Calicut is also famous as a spice center, exporting ginger, pepper, and cinnamon. The

city became known to Europeans in 1498 when Vasco da Gama, the Portuguese explorer, stopped there. Because of its spices and other commodities, the port was highly prized and was plundered several times. About 1514 Affonso de Albuquerque, another Portuguese explorer, built a fort to protect the valuable trade center, but in 1792 Calicut was ceded to the British and became a part of British India. Because of the rise of Bombay, Cochin, and other ports, Calicut has decreased in international importance, but it remains the fourth largest city and the second largest business center of Kerala State. Pop. 1951, 158,724.

CALIFORNIA, popularly known as the Golden State, is the third largest state in the United States. It comprises a total area of 158,693 sq. mi., including 1,953 sq. mi. of inland water area. Only the new state of Alaska, and Texas, are larger. California's land area is larger than that of the British Isles. New York, Delaware, Ohio, New Jersey, and all the New England States together could be put within the boundaries of California. The state is bounded on the west by the Pacific Ocean, on the north by Oregon, on the east by Nevada and Arizona, and on the south by Mexico. The Colorado River forms the dividing line with Arizona. The state is about 780 mi. long, extending in a general direction of northwest to southeast from 42° N. lat. at the north to 32° 45′ N. lat. at the south. Its most westerly point, Cape Mendocino, is at 124° 26′ W. long. and its most easterly point, on the Colorado River, is at 114° 9′ W. long. The general coast line of the state of California comprises a total length of 913 mi. California varies in width from approximately 150 to 375 mi.

California entered the Union on Sept. 9, 1850, as the 31st state. The capital is Sacramento and there are 58 counties in the state, including the nation's largest, San Bernardino (20,160 sq. mi.). The state motto is *Eureka* (I Have Found It!); the state flower is the golden poppy; the state trees are the California redwoods; the state bird is the

California Valley quail; and the official state song is "I Love You, California."

GEOGRAPHIC FEATURES

Topography. The topography of California is extremely varied, ranging from the second highest point in the continental United States, Mt. Whitney (14,495 ft.), to the lowest, the sink of Death Valley (282 ft. below sea level). Between these extremes exist almost every variety of surface feature. Most conspicuous is the great central valley and its bordering mountain ranges. This valley, made up of the valleys of the Sacramento and San Joaquin rivers, is bounded on the east by the magnificent towering Sierra Nevada. On the west it is bordered by the lower Coast Range.

California's largest river, the Sacramento, runs in a southward direction for 382 mi. from its source in Siskiyou County to its outlet in Suisun Bay. About 225 mi. of its length is navigable during high water seasons. Its principal tributaries are the McCloud, Feather, Pit, Yuba, and American rivers. The San Joaquin River, running in a generally northward direction from its headwaters in the mountains of Fresno County, is 350 mi. long from the junction of its south and middle forks in Madera County to its outlet in Suisun Bay. It is navigable all year around at least as far as Stockton. Into it drain the Fresno, Merced, Tuolumne, Stanislaus, Calaveras, Mokelumne, and Cosumnes rivers. The San Joaquin Valley makes up more than three fifths of the total area of the great valley, which is approximately 18,000 sq. mi.

The valley itself, California's principal agricultural area, is protected on all sides by mountains, except at Carquinez Strait, which, breaking the Coast Range near its center, serves as the single drainage outlet for the entire valley and empties its waters into the sea through the Golden Gate. The Coast Range runs roughly parallel to the western shore of the state from a point near Mt. Shasta, where it joins with the northern end of the Sierra Nevada, to the Tehachapi Mountains, where it again converges with the Sierra. It is made up of many vaguely defined smaller ranges. The principal small valleys running through it north of San Francisco are the fertile Sonoma, Santa Rosa, and Napa valleys, and south of San Francisco the Santa Clara Valley of the north, the Salinas, and the Pajaro valleys. The Coast Range varies in width from approximately 20 to 40 mi., and in altitude from 2,000 to 8,000 ft. above sea level.

The Sierra Nevada, meaning "snow-covered mountain range," extends for some 430 mi. near the eastern border of the state, dropping off sharply on its eastern slope but comparatively gently toward the west, about 200 ft. to the mile. More than 50 peaks of the Sierra Nevada reach an elevation above 13,000 ft., with the peak of Mt. Whitney attaining an altitude of 14,495 ft. Passes through the Sierra Nevada are from 7,000 to 10,000 ft. above sea level. Glacial lakes like Lake Tahoe and great canyons like Yosemite Valley are among the most notable scenic wonders of this spectacular mountain range. North of the great valley, mountains reach to the Oregon border. The northeastern corner of the state comprises volcanic plateaus which are largely arid, while northwest section is made up of wooded mountains, notably the Klamath and Siskiyou ranges.

The natural dividing line between the northern and southern sections of the state runs from Point Conception, south of which the coast line turns abruptly eastward, through the Tehachapi Mountains to the northeast. The southern section, roughly a third of the total area of the state, is characterized by numerous small mountain ranges running in various directions with valleys between. There is one large coastal plain, the Los Angeles Plain. Fertile valleys include the Santa Clara Valley of the south, the San Fernando Valley, the Coachella Valley, the San Gabriel Valley, and the reclaimed Imperial Valley. The San Gabriel, San Bernardino, San Jacinto, and Chuckawalla mountains are among the ranges forming barriers between the valley areas.

East of the southern Sierra Nevada are the arid valleys: Owens Valley, once potentially agricultural but now relatively barren; Death Valley, between the Panamint and Amargosa ranges, which contains the lowest elevation in the continental United States, 282 ft. below sea level; the Mojave Desert which was originally an arid wasteland; and the Colorado Desert where more than a half million acres of Imperial Valley land have been reclaimed. Chief among the rivers of southern California are the Owens River, the waters of which are drawn by aqueduct into Los Angeles; the Mojave; and the Colorado. There are many other streams which flow only part of the year, drying up in the arid season. The mountains of southern California do not for the most part reach elevations above 3,000 to 5,000 ft., although in the northeastern section of the area Telescope Peak attains 11,045 ft. and White Mountain 14,242 ft.

The California coast line is for the most part rugged. There are only two natural harbors of primary importance, San Francisco Bay and San Diego Bay. To these has been added the man-made harbor of San Pedro. Secondary harbors are Humboldt Bay, on which lies Eureka, and Monterey Bay, the harbor for Santa Cruz and Monterey. Coastal islands are relatively few. The principal ones are the Farallon group, small, bare, rocky islands lying west of San Francisco Bay; the San Luis Buttes near San Luis Obispo, of which the best known is Morro Rock; and the Santa Barbara Islands, a group of nine lying between Santa Barbara Channel on the north and San Diego on the south, of which the most famous is Santa Catalina. Within San Francisco Bay are Angel Island, Yerba Buena (or Goat), and Alcatraz, and within San Pablo Bay is Mare Island.

THE GREAT SEAL OF THE STATE OF CALIFORNIA

Climate. In general, two distinguishing features of the California climate are the relatively small variations in temperature and the two-season rather than four-season year. Average temperature for the state during the coldest month in the year is 51° F.; during the warmest, 70°. The two seasons are the wet and the dry, and rains are usually confined to the months between October and May, with heaviest precipitation between November and March. Nevertheless, there is almost as great a variation in climate throughout the state as there is in topography. Death Valley has had the highest temperature ever recorded in the United States,

134° F., while a reading of −56° F. has been taken at the top of Mt. Lassen.

The coastal area from the northern boundary of the state to Point Conception is characterized by a moderate and invigorating climate, varying only slightly from winter to summer. Coastal currents warm the area, while fogs and breezes cool it. Average temperature in the San Francisco section during the coldest month in the year is 50° F., and during the warmest, 61°. The climate of the coastal strip between Point Conception and the Mexican border is warmer and drier than that of the northern coast, but there is greater variation between the seasons. In the Los Angeles area, average temperature during the warmest month of the year is 71° F.; during the coldest, 55°.

The great interior valley has wider variations in temperature. August temperatures at Stockton and Sacramento usually range from 57° F. to 87°. At the southern end of the valley, the average August range is from 62° to 98°, and the mercury often rises above 100° at Fresno and Bakersfield. Sierra Nevada temperatures vary sharply above the 2,000-ft. level. Heavy rain- and snowfalls are common in the winter. This mountain range protects northern California from the weather fluctuations of the area to its east, as the southern ranges protect southern California. Similarly, the Coast Range protects the northern part of the state from cold northwest winds. The southeastern section of the state, made up principally of the desert areas, is arid, warm in winter, and hot in summer. Rainfall throughout the state varies from more than 100 in. annually in the northwest corner to 3 in. or less in the southeast.

Earthquakes occur at irregular intervals, the most destructive having been that of 1906 in the San Francisco area and that of 1933 in the Long Beach area.

Soils. The soils of California have been the subject of analytical study since the early 1850's. As early as 1857 a soil map grading the lands by quality was made at Mission San Gabriel. By dividing the state's soils into sandy loams,

View of Death Valley, California, with clay hills and a dry wash in the foreground, the Panamints in the background.

loams, clay loams, and clays, the following differentiations are made: the Sierra Nevada, the deserts, and most of the state south of Los Angeles have predominantly sandy loams; a large part of the Coast Range and the northeastern mountain section have predominantly clay loams; the great valley has at its eastern border a broad strip of loam, while its cen-

tral section is predominantly clay. Scientists, analyzing the soils from another point of view, have found that acid soils predominate in California's regions having high precipitation, while basic soils predominate in dryer areas. The larger proportion of the agricultural lands are transported soils, which fall into two groups: the recent and the old transported soils. The recent ones are of highest quality and form about three fifths of the arable land of the state.

Forests. Forest lands cover about 42,500,000 acres in the state, about 17,300,000 being commercial forest land and nearly 20,000,000 being national forests administered by the United States Forest Service. Extensive cutting of timber began in the 1850's, and by the middle 1930's approximately

Heavy redwood logs are stacked in huge piles preparatory to sawmill operations in Humboldt County, California.

7,700,000 acres had been logged over and approximately 500,000 acres reclaimed for use as agricultural land. Today, the volume of saw timber on commercial forest lands in the state is about 360,000,000,000 bd. ft. The principal commercial species are pine, redwood, and Douglas and other varieties of fir.

Flora. In general, the vegetation of California can be classed as forest, woodland, scrub, grassland, marsh, and strand. The forest is a dense type of tree growth and requires an annual precipitation of at least 30 in. Along the northern and central portions of the coast is found the forest with the largest trees. The climate is cool and foggy, with a rainfall of from 30 to 100 in.; the winters are mild. The redwood, *Sequoia sempervirens;* madrona, *Arbutus menziesii;* tan oak, *Lithocarpus densiflora;* Douglas fir, *Pseudotsuga taxifolia;* canoe cedar, *Thuja plicata;* and Lawson cypress, *Chamaecyparis lawsoniana,* are among the tallest trees known anywhere, many of them reaching heights of over 200 ft., or, in the case of the redwood, over 300 ft. The tallest individual redwood on record is 364 ft. tall; it is known as the Founders Tree and stands near Dyerville, in the north coast region. This type of forest extends from the Oregon state line in canyons and on seaward slopes to the Santa Cruz Mountains. The floor of such a forest abounds in ferns, mosses, and many beautiful herbs.

The coastal marshes and strand vegetation of California are interesting. The saline swampy areas have many rather fleshy plants, of relatively few families, such as the pigweeds (Chenopodiaceae), as well as some grasses. The beaches, sand dunes, and other strand types tend to have herbs of the creeping or prostrate habit that help bind the loose soil. These include: sand verbenas, *Abronia;* grasses and sedges; tansy, *Tanacetum; Artemisia;* beach burs, *Franseria;* and strawberry, *Fragaria.* At most, such areas are a very narrow strip along the immediate coast.

Farther inland than the forests mentioned above and away from the immediate coastal fogs, the tree growth is less dense and with more broad-leaved trees, such as madrones, *Arbutus;* various oaks, *Quercus Kelloggii, Q. Garryana, Q. chrysolepis,* and *Q. Wislizenii;* big-leaved maple, *Acer macrophyllum;* and California bay, *Umbellularia californica.* Still farther away from the coast this type of forest passes into open oak woodland with the grassy spots between the trees turning brown during the summer. Up to about 5,000 ft. these forests and woodlands are typical of the Coast Range, Above 5,000 ft. the forest is largely of the yellow-pine type, *Pinus ponderosa*—an open coniferous forest.

The Great Valley has been considerably changed by cultivation, but originally it was largely an open grassland with various perennial bunch grasses, *Stipa, Poa,* and *Aristida,* which have mostly been replaced by annual weedy grasses because of overgrazing or by agricultural crops. Along the streams are willows, *Salix,* and cottonwoods, *Populus;* and in many open places occur peculiar depressions of the "hog-wallow" type, which catch and hold water during the wet season and become extremely dry in the summer. They contain several local and endemic species: *Downingia, Brodiaea,* and *Plagiobothrys.* In wet springs, the vast grassy plains and rolling hills support great numbers of annuals, which, since they are not concealed by any woody or taller plants, display tremendous masses of color. These include: California poppy, *Eschscholzia;* owls-clover, *Orthocarpus;* sunshine, *Baeria; Monolopia* and many other composites; *Lupinus;* and thistle sage, *Salvia carduacea.*

The western foothills of the Sierra Nevada have open oak woodlands with intermediate areas which are grassy and flowery in the spring; at elevations of from 2,000 to 3,000 ft. they begin to show either chaparral or yellow pine forest. The California chaparral is a low, dense woody growth of broad-leaved species that maintains its harsh foliage throughout the year. Many of the species are able to stump-sprout after a fire. This formation also covers great areas in the Coast Range, particularly in the southern part of the state. It inhabits a region with mild winters, hot, dry summers, and total annual rainfall of from 14 to 25 in. Often this low scrub is almost impenetrable and grows to a height of from 3 to 6 or even 10 ft. It consists of various species of *Quercus, Adenostoma, Ceanothus, Cercocarpus, Rhamnus, Prunus, Fremontia,* and *Arctostaphylos.* Like other woody covers, the chaparral is of inestimable value in preventing erosion and in conserving water largely through the duff of leaves that accumulate under it. Chaparral is sometimes called elfin forest and is rather distinctively Californian, most of the species involved and even some of the genera being endemic. They are largely plants whose ancestors migrated long ago from the Mexican highlands, later dying out in the intermediate regions as these became desert.

On the lower western slopes of the Sierra Nevada, chaparral may be present, reaching elevations of almost 5,000 ft., or it may scarcely occur. In either case, the yellow pine forest occurs as the next formation above oaks or chaparral. Mixed with other pines and oaks, firs and incense cedar, this forest tends to be rather open, with many fine tall trees. It is found also in the northern Coast Range and in the mountains of southern California, occupying a region with an annual pre-

EWING GALLOWAY

YOSEMITE FALLS, YOSEMITE NATIONAL PARK, CALIFORNIA

cipitation of from 25 to 80 in., part of which is snow. The growing season is from four to seven months, and temperature extremes run from below zero to over 100° F.

Above the yellow pine is a more northern forest made up of red and white fir, *Abies magnifica* and *A. concolor;* mountain hemlock, *Tsuga mertensiana;* lodgepole pine, *Pinus contorta* var. *murrayana;* and Jeffrey pine, *Pinus Jeffreyi.* Here, in scattered groves, is found the giant sequoia, *Sequoia gigantea,* with the most massive trunk of any known tree. The giant sequoias are among the oldest living things in the world. They are not as tall as the redwoods but have greater diameters, sometimes exceeding 30 ft. One of the largest trees in the world is the giant sequoia called the General Sherman, in Sequoia National Park; it is 272 ft. high and has a maximum diameter of 36.5 ft. Still higher in this area, the forest becomes more boreal and at about 11,000 ft. is replaced by alpine summits bare of tree growth and covered with various arctic herbs, such as certain buttercups, *Ranunculus;* sedges, *Carex;* grasses, *Poa, Agrostis,* and *Festuca;* and paintbrush, *Castilleja nana.* The growing season is very short and snow remains throughout the year in sheltered spots.

One other forest of low elevation in the area west of the Sierra Nevada should be mentioned. This is the closed-cone pine forest that occurs in interrupted stands near the coast from Mendocino County to Santa Barbara County. It is best known on the Monterey Peninsula, where it surrounds the towns Carmel, Pacific Grove, and Monterey. Growing in regions of cool climate and rather barren soils, it is made up of such species as *Pinus radiata, P. muricata, P. contorta, P. remorata,* and various cypresses, *Cupressus macrocarpa, C. Goveniana,* and *C. pygmaea.* These species are often quite local; the pines are closely related to each other, as are the

337

cypresses. Both are relics from the past, representative of a forest that is dying out. On the pines, the cones remain closed and hang on the trees for many years, in some cases not discharging their seeds until after heat from fire. With them is a characteristic shrubby population of certain species of California lilac, *Ceanothus;* manzanita, *Arctostaphylos;* and huckleberry, *Vaccinium.*

East of the Sierra Nevada and the more southern mountains, rainfall is very slight, the clouds having discharged their water content on the mountain summits. Humidity is low and summer temperatures are high. In this desert area, many of the woody plants have very interesting arrangements for retaining their moisture, such as mucilaginous or resinous sap, and leaves which are reduced or lacking entirely in the dry season or, if persistent, are covered with wax or hair or with deeply embedded stomates. In some cases they curl, and the stomates become covered. Some herbaceous plants live over as underground bulbs; others are short-lived annuals that carry out their complete span of life in a few weeks, the species living during the dry months only as seeds. Much of the desert area consists of land-locked basins into which drain waters from the surrounding hills, and in which a salty or alkali deposit, extremely inimical to most plant growth, gradually accumulates. Such is the case in Death Valley, Owens Valley, and Salton Sink. In such areas the species are fleshy and of comparatively few groups. On better-drained slopes and open spaces are creosote bush, *Larrae;* burro weed, *Franseria;* and various cacti. Since the rainfall scarcely, if ever, wets the ground to any considerable depth, the roots of such shrubs spread out in the shallow topsoil and the plants are widely spaced. Along the washes and water courses are deep-rooted shrubs and small trees, such as mesquite, *Prosopis;* ironwood, *Olneya;* and desert willow, *Chilopsis.* Partly in the protection of bushes and partly in loose soil, such as along washes, occur the spring annuals, which even on the desert may make great masses of color in an occasional wet spring.

In the somewhat higher altitudes of the desert mountains the rainfall increases enough to support low arborescent species, such as Joshua tree, *Yucca;* juniper, *Juniperus;* and piñon, *Pinus;* as well as sagebrush, *Artemisia,* and more shrubby types. In general, the southern deserts of the state have a Sonoran affinity, while the more northern are like those of the Great Basin, of which they actually are the western portion.

Fauna. The range of California's fauna is as wide as that of its topography and climate. There are more than 400 identified species of mammals and almost 600 identified species of birds within the borders of the state. Of all the North American life zones, only the tropical is not represented. Among the mammals are the rabbit, cougar, opossum, raccoon, deer, elk, bear, beaver, otter, and badger. Birds include the jay, hummingbird, magpie, quail, sparrow, thrush, and grouse. Lake and stream fish include numerous varieties of trout and salmon and some sturgeon. Marine fish include salmon, bass, tuna, pilchard, barracuda, and swordfish. The grunion is found nowhere in the world except off the shores of California. Notable among California's shellfish is the abalone. Reptiles include the rattlesnake, tortoise, and the horned toad.   P. A. M.

ECONOMIC RESOURCES AND ACTIVITIES

Minerals and Mining. Mining is California's primary industry from an historical point of view, for the gold of the Mother Lode belt brought the state's first large population influx in 1849. While there had been earlier discoveries, not until January 1848 was the strike made which began the gold rush. Maximum production was reached in 1862 with 3,932,631 fine oz. Since that time production has dropped to an average today of about 220,000 fine oz. yearly. In little more than a century of gold mining California has produced over 100,000,000 fine oz. Silver production reaches about 760,000 fine oz. annually.

Mining as a whole ranks third among California's basic industries, and California ranks second (after Texas) among the nation's mineral-producing states. The total annual value of California's mineral production is about $1,500,000,000. Some 60 different mineral commodities are produced, the most important being petroleum, natural gas, and natural gasoline.

Maintenance crew works on pipe road leading to oil storage tanks at large refinery in Martinez, California.

California's oil fields, the first of which was discovered in the 1860's, gradually increased in production until in 1914 they produced a total of 104,000,000 bbl. Early in the 1920's many new fields were discovered, and 1923 production was 264,000,000 bbl. Production was stabilized at above 200,000,000 bbl. yearly thereafter until World War II, when it increased to 300,000,000 bbl. annually. Recently production has reached approximately 350,000,000 bbl., and California is the second highest (next to Texas) petroleum-producing state in the nation. The state also ranks next to Texas in the production of natural gasoline, with an output of almost 30,000,000 bbl. annually, and next to Texas, Louisiana, and Oklahoma in the production of natural gas, with an output of about 500,000,000,000 cu. ft. annually. In the production of Portland cement California ranks second to Pennsylvania in the nation, producing about 35,000,000 bbl. yearly.

Agriculture. *Crops.* Historically, California agriculture begins with the Spanish missions, for the indigenous Indians of the state had virtually no regular cultivated crops. There was continued cultivation of crops by the Spanish and Mexican settlers, and later, in the 1840's, by European settlers. But it was not until the 1850's that extensive land cultivation began. Even during the height of the gold rush certain men suggested that the real wealth of California lay not alone in its mines but in its crops as well. The first state constitution, adopted in 1850, contained a provision for the encouragement of agriculture, and by the mid-1850's a state agricultural society and many local agricultural groups had been formed. As early as 1854 the first issue of the *California Farmer and Journal of Useful Sciences* was published, and in 1862 the state legislature passed the first act toward implementing the formation of a state agricultural college.

Wheat production was for a time the most important of the state's agricultural industries. Beginning in the 1850's, it developed so rapidly that in 1878-1879 the crop had a cash value of about $40,000,000, more than twice the cash value of the annual gold production. By 1890 California was the leading wheat-producing state in the nation, with output at more than 40,000,000 bu. At the turn of the century, however, production started declining, and in 1913 it stood at only 4,200,000 bu. Today, production of wheat averages less than 9,000,000 bu. annually, and barley has become the leading grain crop. California is the leading state in the production of barley, having an annual output averaging more than 70,000,000 bu. California also ranks among the first states in the nation in the production of hay, with an output of over 6,000,000 tons annually; potatoes, with over 1,000,000 tons; and rice, with about 10,000,000 bags (of 100 lb.). Production of cotton and cottonseed has become important in recent years, with about 1,500,000 bales (of 500 lb.) of cotton and about 550,000 tons of cottonseed produced annually.

It is for the production of fruits and truck crops that California agriculture is most famous. Among truck crops the state leads the nation or ranks next to first in the production of artichokes, honeyball melons, asparagus, lima beans, broccoli, Brussels sprouts, cantaloupes, carrots, cauliflowers, celery, garlic, honeydew melons, lettuce, onions, spinach, and tomatoes. California leads the nation in the production of peaches, pears, grapes, lemons, prunes, walnuts, apricots, strawberries, almonds, prunes, olives, figs, avocados, cherries, and dates, and ranks high in the production of oranges and grapefruit. Cash receipts from all farm marketings total over $2,500,000,000 annually.

Farms and Farm Lands. About 30 per cent of the total area of the state is in cropland, pasture, and rangeland. There are about 123,000 farms, with an average size of about 307 acres, and an average value for land and buildings of $59,144. The total cash farm income of over $2,500,000,000 annually is the highest in the nation, and the average farm income is well above the national average.

Irrigation. The California pattern of wet winters and dry summers had early brought about the necessity for irrigation which was begun on a small scale in the eighteenth century by the mission fathers. In southern California especially, need for irrigation was felt, and throughout the state local irrigation projects were established. What is generally considered the first commercial organization formed for irrigation purposes was started in Yolo County, in Sacramento Valley, in 1856.

In the early 1870's Congress ordered a survey for an irrigation project embracing the entire great valley. Finally in the 1930's the long-desired $360,000,000 Central Valley Reclamation Project was started. This project aimed at preserving the existing agricultural developments of the southern San Joaquin Valley by diverting the surplus waters of the Sacramento basin to the dry areas of the San Joaquin basin. Today, over 7,000,000 acres throughout the state are irrigated.

Animal Industry. California is one of the leading states in the value of livestock and produces more than 40 per cent (by value) of the nation's sheep and lambs. It leads the nation in number of turkeys raised and is a major producer of chickens, commercial broilers, and eggs. Cash receipts from livestock and livestock products are almost $1,000,000,000 annually.

Before the gold rush, California's economy was based principally upon trade in hides and tallow, largely to the exclusion of agriculture and industry. The California Mexican cattle were of poor quality compared to American-bred cattle. Their meat was extremely inferior, and when Americans demanded American-bred cattle, large herds were driven in from the Midwest and Texas. In 1848 there were fewer than 300,000 head of cattle in the state; by 1860 there were some 3,000,000. By 1870 there were only 670,000, entire herds having been decimated by the disastrous drought of the years 1862-1864. Since that time, however, the industry has steadily advanced, stimulated by the study and improvement of breeds, and demand for dairy products. Today there are over 3,800,000 head of cattle in the state.

The 1850 census showed a total of only 17,514 head of sheep in California. They were principally of an inferior grade. By 1876, however, there were more than 6,000,000 sheep in the state, and the average quality had been raised by the introduction of improved breeds. In the 1880's and 1890's, however, the price of wool dropped, and the increased use of land for agricultural purposes encroached upon the sheep ranges. Flocks fell off markedly, but increased again after the end of the nineteenth century. Today the sheep industry represents more than $70,000,000 of invested capital, and the total number of sheep and lambs is about 2,000,000.

The poultry industry, as an industry, did not start until the 1870's. Largely centered around the town of Petaluma, it developed so rapidly that by 1890 it had grown from a few flocks to a total estimated 500,000 fowl in the area. In 1900 shipment of California eggs to the east began. In 1930 there were about 4,500,000 birds in the Petaluma area. Today there are about 29,000,000 chickens in the state, and Los Angeles County has become the leading producer, with the Petaluma area ranking second.

A segment of the Santa Ana Freeway, with a view of suburban areas about 30 mi. out of Los Angeles

Manufacturing. Manufacturing in California increased rapidly during World War II, when the demand for ships and airplanes was at its height, and has steadily continued to increase. In 1943 wage-earner pay rolls stood at a total of $2,244,200,000, of which $1,385,700,000 went to workers in aircraft and shipbuilding. In 1957 there were more than 1,200,000 people employed in manufacturing in the state earning wages totalling over $6,500,000,000 annually. Value added by manufacture for the state is more than $12,000,-000,000 annually.

During the Spanish and Mexican period, only simple ranch and mission industries existed. The gold rush, however, stimulated local manufacture, and, although at first the population was for the most part too busy mining to turn to manufacturing, gradually lumber mills, flour mills, tanneries, wagon factories, foundries, and even billiard table manufactories were established. The Civil War stimulated production of manufactured goods, as did the wealth and interest of Californians like William Ralston, who fostered such enterprises as a furniture factory, a woolen mill, and a beet-sugar mill. The completion of the transcontinental railroad in 1869, bringing in eastern goods at prices lower than those manufactured in the West, retarded California manufacturing, particularly coming as it did on the eve of the country-wide depression of the 1870's. However, in 1899 value of manufactured goods was $257,000,000, and by 1925 it had increased to $2,443,000,000. In 1939 it stood at $2,798,180,-000, and California ranked seventh in the nation in value of manufactured products.

In value added by manufacture the transportation equipment industries rank first in the state, especially for the production of aircraft, missiles, automobiles, and ships. Second in value are the food industries which supply one third of the nation's processed fruits, vegetables, and fish, and nearly all of its wine. The electrical machinery industries, including the relatively new electronics industry, are third in importance. Fourth are the non-electrical machinery industries supplying machinery for oil fields, house-holds, and food processing plants, as well as computing machines. Fifth in value are the fabricated metal industries. Other important industries include the lumber and wood-working, primary metal, printing and publishing, petroleum refining, apparel, paper, furniture, and stone, clay, and glass industries.

Commerce and Trade. California's ocean ports, principally Los Angeles Harbor and the San Francisco Bay area, handle about 8,000,000 short tons (of 2,000 lb.) of imports annually and ship about 8,000,000 short tons of exports. In coastwise commerce, California's ports receive about 22,-000,000 short tons and ship about 32,000,000 short tons.

Trade. The number of wholesale establishments in the state almost tripled between 1929 and 1954, and sales increased from $4,000,000,000 to over $18,000,000,000. Similarly, the number of retail establishments increased from 80,000 in 1929 to more than 130,000 in 1954, and sales advanced from $3,000,000,000 to over $15,500,000,000. The Los Angeles, San Francisco-Oakland, and the San Diego metropolitan areas are the leading retail centers in the state.

Banking. Prior to 1848, California had had no banking as such, but when gold production began, demand rose for the means of handling and transporting the treasure. This service was first rendered by tradesmen and saloonkeepers, who held the miners' gold dust and nuggets in safekeeping. Gradually banking operations developed, often first as a side line to merchandising as in the case of I. W. Hellman, who, starting as a Los Angeles merchant, became one of the state's most influential bankers. Express companies also went into banking, first merely transporting treasure, then issuing exchanges, and finally offering all banking services. Banks were not allowed to print paper money, provision being made against such practice in the state constitution, and even as late as the 1920's there was little paper money in circulation in the state. The Comstock Lode silver mines in Nevada brought more wealth into California in the 1860's and 1870's than had the gold rush. California money developed the Nevada mines, California interests controlled them, and their profits were released through California. The period was one of generally wild speculation in mining stocks, but from it came California's first great fortunes.

Branch banking in California was first successfully organized under the leadership of A. P. Giannini. His Bank of America had its beginning in the early 1900's in a small Italian savings and loan society. Today it has over 600 branches, with total deposits of over $10,000,000,000.

Transportation. Transportation to California in the earliest period was principally by water. The first group to travel overland through the state was a part of the Portola-Serra party, which walked north from La Paz in Mexico to San Diego Bay in 1769, and later went on to San Francisco Bay. However, not until the gold rush period, when immigrants began coming into the state from the East, did overland travel become common, and not until the establishment of the Overland Stage route did it become of importance commercially.

Early trade with California was carried on by means of sailing ships which traveled from the east coast around Cape Horn. In 1849 the Panama route was initiated; the United States Mail Steamship Company and the Pacific Mail Steamship Company started operating steamships from the east coast of the United States to Panama, and from Panama up the west coast to California. At first all goods had to be taken across the Isthmus of Panama on pack trains, but in 1855 the Panama Railroad was completed. In 1858 Congress gave the Butterfield Overland Mail a subsidy which made possible the operation of the first regular overland mail service to California. The stagecoaches traveled the distance between St. Joseph, Missouri, and San Francisco, at first via the Santa Fe trail, in about 23 days, and later through Utah and Nevada, in an average of 17 days. This was an improvement over ocean service, which took some three months from coast to coast. The next step in shortening communication time was the Pony Express, which covered the 1,900 mi. between Missouri and California in an average of 10 days. Initiated in 1860, it was terminated in 1861 with the completion of the transcontinental telegraph line. California's first railroad was the 22-mi. Sacramento Valley line completed in 1856. In 1869 completion of the transcontinental railroad was observed by the dramatic driving of the last spike at Promontory, Utah. In 1887 the Atchison, Topeka and Santa Fe completed its line into Los Angeles, later extending it northward to San Francisco. In 1887 the Southern Pacific Company completed its line north from San Francisco into Oregon, and in 1901 it completed its southern line to Los Angeles. In 1910 the Western Pacific brought its tracks into San Francisco through the Feather River Canyon route.

California's internal transportation had originally been by Indian canoe, later by horse and Mexican cart, and still later by river boat, stagecoach, and railroad. In 1909 the creation of the California State Highway Commission signaled the beginning of the automobile age. Today California has about 135,000 mi. of state, county, and city roads. Almost 20,000 mi. of the California total constitute freeways and expressways which are part of a highway system which is continually being expanded.

The state has over 450 airports, the largest ones being in the San Francisco and Los Angeles areas, which receive both trans-Pacific and transcontinental flights, and in the San Diego area, which receives transcontinental flights.

GOVERNMENT AND POLITICS

Constitution. California's first constitution, ratified on Nov. 13, 1849, almost a year before the establishment of statehood on Sept. 9, 1850, was revised and a new constitution drawn up and ratified, on May 7, 1879. This constitution has since remained in force, although, by 1958, 308 amendments had been added to it. It does not differ radically from those of most other states. Literacy is a requirement for suffrage; cross-filing by candidates in primary elections is allowed; and a candidate may be nominated by two or more parties provided he has won his own party nomination first.

Government. The governor, lieutenant governor, state controller, secretary of state, state treasurer, and superintendent of public education are elected for four-year terms midway between national presidential elections. The legislature consists of a senate of 40 members, elected on the basis of counties or larger areas for four-year terms, and an assembly of 80 members, elected from districts of nearly equal population for two-year terms. The legislature meets annually to adopt a state budget and meets in odd years to consider other legislation. California has the initiative and the referendum. Residence requirements for voting are one year in the state, 90 days in the county, and 30 days in the precinct. The local unit of government is the county, usually established by charter and administered by boards of supervisors.

The state supreme court consists of a chief justice and six associate justices, appointed by the governor, confirmed by a judicial commission, and approved by the voters.

California is represented in the United States Congress by two senators and 30 representatives.

Politics. The Republicans have held the preponderance of party power in California since about 1898, and all governors between that year and 1936 were Republican. However, the Democratic presidential candidate carried the state in the elections of 1932, 1936, 1940, and 1944 (President Roosevelt's terms) and 1948 (President Truman's). In 1952 and 1956 President Eisenhower carried the state.

In the decade of the 1850's California was governed by Democratic factions. William M. Gwin was the leader of the southern branch, with David C. Broderick leading the so-called Tammany Democrats against him. In 1860 there

Old Spanish Lighthouse in San Diego stands on the site of the Cabrillo National Monument, which commemorates the discovery of California by Juan Rodriguez Cabrillo in 1542.

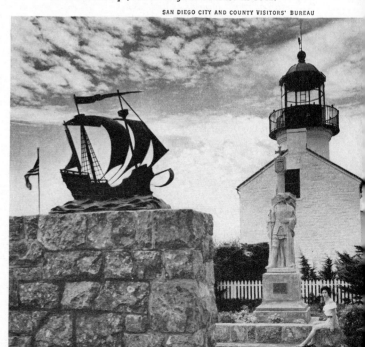

SAN DIEGO CITY AND COUNTY VISITORS' BUREAU

J. ALLEN HAWKINS

THE HUNTINGTON LIBRARY, SAN MARINO, CALIFORNIA

was a swing toward the Republican party, the state's electoral votes going to Abraham Lincoln. During the Civil War the opposing factions were the Republicans and the Secession party. Such leaders as Governor Leland Stanford, Colonel E. D. Baker, and Reverend Thomas Starr King threw their support behind the Union cause and prevented the Secessionists from controlling the state.

In the 1870's the Workingmen's Party, centered in San Francisco and led by Denis Kearney, aimed toward excluding Chinese immigration, weakening the power of the capitalistic monopolies, and raising the position of labor. Although the party never achieved dominance, its power was felt. Anti-Chinese labor legislation finally went into effect, the power of the railroad was broken, and California became a leader in labor legislation.

In 1907 a progressive Republican group was formed. Its candidate, Hiram W. Johnson, who was elected governor in 1910 on his promise to "kick the Southern Pacific Railroad out of the Republican Party and out of the state government" succeeded in breaking the railroad's hold.

Outstanding Legislation. California's most important era of constructive legislation was from 1911 to 1916, when the Republican platform under the leadership of Hiram W. Johnson was being enacted. Initiative, referendum, and recall were provided for. Social legislation included provision for old-age pensions and for teachers' pensions. Labor legislation included bills prohibiting child labor, establish-

ing employers' liability, providing for a minimum wage, and limiting hours of labor for women. Civil service laws were passed, the franchise was extended to women, and a "blue-sky" law was enacted.

SOCIAL AND CULTURAL ACTIVITIES

Education. The first state constitution provided for the establishment of a free public school system, and in 1866 the legislature adopted a revised school law which fixed state and county school taxes at adequate levels and established the basic elements of what has become one of the most advanced state systems of free public education. State support was extended to high schools in 1903, and in 1916 junior colleges were recognized by law as part of the state's secondary school system. There are now nearly 70 junior colleges with a total enrollment of over 100,000.

Today more than 2,750,000 pupils attend California's approximately 5,000 public kindergartens, grammar schools, and high schools annually. There are more than 100,000 teachers in the public schools drawing average annual salaries of $5,750. Education is also extended to disabled and handicapped children. Adult education, in which California was a leader, is also provided for.

The University of California was established in 1868, the oldest branch being at Berkeley. Later extensions included the University of California at Los Angeles, the college at Santa Barbara, and the agricultural college at Davis. Other

HOLLYWOOD BOWL, CALIFORNIA

state-supported institutions of higher learning are the state colleges of Chico, Fresno, Long Beach, Sacramento, San Diego, San Francisco, and San Jose, the California State Polytechnic College at San Luis Obispo, and Humboldt State College at Arcata. Private institutions of higher education include the California Institute of Technology, Claremont College, The Claremont Graduate School, Claremont Men's College, the College of the Pacific, George Pepperdine College, Golden Gate College, Loyola University of Los Angeles, Mills College, Occidental College, Pomona College, Stanford University, the University of Redlands, the University of San Francisco, the University of Santa Clara, the University of Southern California, and Whittier College.

Cultural Features. Art, literature, and the theatre have long been important in California life. The California theatre started probably in Monterey in 1847, when a company of soldiers produced a play titled *Putnam, or the Lion Son of '76,* and became very active in San Francisco and the mining regions during the 1850's and 1860's, when almost every noted American and British actor played in the state. Later southern California became the center of the motion picture industry. Stimulus to the arts in California was given by the Panama Pacific International Exposition of 1915 and the Golden Gate International Exposition of 1939 and 1940. Opera has been popular in California since the 1850's, continued in the modern period by the San Francisco Opera Association's annual season. Both San Francisco and Los Angeles have first-rate symphony orchestras.

Recreational Areas. State and nationally owned areas in California are used as recreation grounds by millions of people yearly, and serve conservation purposes as well. There are 18 national forests, covering about one fifth of the state's area, 4 national parks, and 8 national monuments. Notable are Yosemite National Park, Lassen National Forest, Lassen Volcanic National Park, and Death Valley and Muir

Woods National Monuments. The state system includes about 150 parks and monuments totaling more than 600,000 acres. Among them are the site of Marshall's gold discovery near Coloma, the old mining town of Columbia in Tuolumne Co., and the William Randolph Hearst estate at San Simeon.

POPULATION

California is second (next to New York) in population among the states. The total population of the state, according to the 1950 census, was 10,586,223, a 53.3 per cent increase over 1940, and the 1957 estimate was well over 14,-000,000. Between 1940 and 1945 the population increased by almost 2,000,000 as the result of the influx of production workers during World War II, and since then the population of the state has continued to increase. In 1950 urban population was 8,539,420; rural nonfarm, 1,478,572; and rural farm, 568,231.

Cities. The chief centers of population are the Los Angeles metropolitan area (with 4,367,911 in 1950; 1,970,-358 in the city proper) and the San Francisco-Oakland metropolitan area (with 2,240,767; 775,357 in the city of San Francisco and 384,575 in Oakland proper). Other leading cities are San Diego (334,387), Long Beach (250,-767), Sacramento (137,572), Berkeley (113,805), Pasadena (104,577), Richmond (99,545), Glendale (95,702), San Jose (95,280), and Fresno (91,669).

Racial and Ethnic Groups. Of the total population, 84.4 per cent are native white, according to the 1950 census; 9.3 per cent, foreign-born white; 4.4 per cent Negro; and 1.9 per cent, Japanese, Chinese, and other races. The total foreign-born population of 985,333 included 162,309 from Mexico, 110,754 from Canada, 104,215 from Italy, 78,728 from England and Wales, 70,791 from Germany, and 66,552 from the U.S.S.R.

Occupational Groups. The estimated 5,638,000 employed persons in the state in 1957 included 1,287,000 engaged in manufacturing; 1,227,000 in retail and wholesale trade; 876,000 in service occupations; 381,000 in transportation, communication, and other public utilities; 354,000 in construction; 488,000 in agriculture; 244,000 in finance, insurance, and real estate; and 741,000 in government.

STATE CAPITOL, SACRAMENTO, CALIFORNIA

HISTORY

Exploration and Settlement. The name of the state probably had its origin in a sixteenth-century Spanish romance by Garcia Ordoñez de Montalvo, titled *Las Sergas de Esplandian,* which described a mythical island inhabited by Amazons and called California. The name was first applied to Baja California, the peninsula extending south of what is now the Mexican border. Later the name was applied to Alta California, which became the state of California. Hernando de Alarcón, searching with Coronado for the fabled Seven Cities of Cíbola, was the first explorer to set foot on California soil in 1540. Credit for California's discovery, however, is usually given to the navigator Juan Rodríguez Cabrillo, who on Sept. 28, 1542, sailed into San Diego Bay, and later made explorations northward past the Golden Gate. The next year Bartolomé Ferrelo, who succeeded to the command of Cabrillo's ships after his death, explored the coast as far north as southern Oregon. Other explorations followed at intervals. In June 1579 Sir Francis Drake sailed past the Golden Gate, anchored near Point Reyes, and christened California New Albion. In 1602 Sebastián Vizcaíno anchored in San Diego Bay and then continued his explorations as far north as Monterey Bay.

Colonization of Baja California was started in 1697 when, under the order of the Society of Jesus, a mother mission was dedicated at Loreto and the establishment of a chain of mis-

sions northward begun. In 1767 the Jesuit order was suppressed and later the work of establishing Alta California missions was given to the Franciscan order. Spain's plan was to colonize Alta California with missions, presidios (military garrisons), and pueblos (civilian towns) simultaneously. In 1769 Don Gaspar de Portolá, Governor of the Californias, Father Junípero Serra, president of the projected missions, and Captain Fernando Rivera y Moncada, military commander, arrived at San Diego Bay. Here was established the first in a chain of installations. In the years following, a series of 21 missions was established, the last a few miles north of San Francisco Bay. The mission fathers brought to the California Indians, notably poor in culture, a measure of learning and practical experience in construction and agriculture, in addition to spiritual guidance. Pueblos were established at locations that became Los Angeles, San José, and Santa Cruz, and presidios at San Diego, Santa Barbara, Monterey, and San Francisco. One reason for Spanish colonization of Alta California was the threat of the Russians, who held Alaska and in 1812 established a settlement north of San Francisco Bay at Fort Ross. In 1822 Mexico became independent of Spain, and California became a Mexican province. The next year the last of the missions was founded, and ten years later a decree was issued ordering secularization of the missions.

European settlers began to arrive in small numbers. In 1814 the first Englishman, John Gilroy, had come to California. In 1839 John Augustus Sutter, German-born Swiss, arrived and the next year began building his agricultural empire on the Sacramento River. In 1841 he purchased from the Russians all of their property at Fort Ross, and their withdrawal the following year ended the threat of Russian domination in California. In 1843 Thomas Oliver Larkin was appointed United States consul at Monterey.

Political Development. Great Britain and France indicated interest in California, and at the same time feeling grew in the United States that its logical western border was the Pacific Ocean. By the 1840's California was a focal point of international interest. There was conflict between the American settlers and the local Mexican officials. In May 1846, war between the United States and Mexico was declared. A group of English-speaking settlers raised the Bear Flag at Sonoma on June 14, 1846, declaring California a sovereign state. The Bear Flag Republic was short-lived, however, for on July 7, Commodore John D. Sloat of the United States Navy raised the American flag at the Mexican capital of Alta California, Monterey, and two days later Captain John B. Montgomery raised the flag at San Francisco. Not until February of 1848, however, was the treaty of Guadalupe–Hidalgo signed, ending the war.

Because the gold rush, which began in 1848, accelerated its early growth and because of the political conflict which developed in the discussion over slavery and its extension into the newly acquired Mexican territory, admission of California to the Union became one of the important enactments of the Compromise of 1850, and California became a state without having first served its apprenticeship as a territory. In fact, so anxious were Californians for statehood that they organized their government many months before statehood was granted.

On Aug. 1, 1849, California elected 48 delegates who met the following month in Monterey to draw up the state's first constitution. It was modelled basically upon the constitutions of New York and Iowa, but several provisions were the result of long debate. It was decided that California was not to become a slave state, and free

Negroes were not to be barred; the eastern boundary of the state was drawn where it has remained; and proposals to divide the state into two parts, north and south, were defeated. On Nov. 13, 1849, the constitution was ratified by a vote of the people and Peter H. Burnett was elected the state's first governor. On Sept. 9, 1850, nearly a year later, President Millard Fillmore signed the bill admitting California to the Union as the 31st state.

Statehood. The state capital was first at San José, and later at Vallejo and Benicia before being permanently located at Sacramento in 1854. California during the 1850's was a raw, unregimented section. In order to maintain law and order and suppress criminal activities, in 1851 and again in 1856 San Francisco resorted to vigilante committees. In the mining sections, lynch law was not uncommon.

During the Civil War, California remained in the Union

this warm body of water is about 64,000 sq. mi. and the coast on both sides is irregular and much indented. There are numerous small islands in the Gulf; the largest ones, Angel de La Guarda and Tiburon, are in the northern part. The southern part of the Gulf is about 6,000 ft. deep, but it shallows to the north where, at the head of the Gulf, the Colorado River deposits great amounts of sediment. During recent geologic time the Gulf extended northward into southern California and the Salton Sea occupies the former head of the Gulf of California. Both sides of the Gulf are rugged and the shores are sparsely populated. This body of water is noted for its pearl fishing.   J. E. F.

CALIFORNIA, UNIVERSITY OF, an accredited, coeducational, nonsectarian state university with eight campuses: Berkeley, Davis, La Jolla, Los Angeles (U.C.L.A.),

THE BERKELEY CAMPUS OF THE UNIVERSITY OF CALIFORNIA

despite early efforts to bring about secession. Many Californians fought in the Confederate Army, however, although a larger number were in the Union forces. At the end of the 1860's, California's isolation was ended by the completion of the Central Pacific transcontinental railroad. The 1870's saw the rise of the Granger movement in California, as elsewhere, and of the comparable Workingmen's Party among urban laborers. In the 1880's southern California underwent a land boom, and the greatest migration into the state since the gold rush took place. The principal development of the southern part of the state dates from that movement. World War I saw an increase in the state's population and industry which, however, was far exceeded by the great influx of population and increase of industrialization during and following World War II. In the decade from 1947 to 1957, California led all states in construction of new industrial plants and expansion of existing ones, with a total investment of more than $5,000,000,000.   R. Te.

CALIFORNIA, GULF OF, an arm of the Pacific Ocean separating the peninsula of Lower California or Baja California on the west from the states of Sonora and Sinaloa on the mainland of Mexico on the east. The Gulf, which is 740 mi. long and from 50 to 130 mi. wide, occupies the southern part of the great Pacific Coast downfold. The total area of

Mount Hamilton, Riverside, San Francisco, and Santa Barbara. A full-time enrollment of more than 37,000 students (in addition to 100,000 part-time extension students) and approximately 2,500 faculty members make it one of the largest universities in the world. The University was chartered by the state in 1868, and instruction began a year later in Oakland. Teaching facilities were moved to Berkeley in 1873. The Davis and Riverside campuses were established by legislative and regental action in 1905. The La Jolla campus, site of the Scripps Institution of Oceanography, became a part of the University in 1912, and in 1919, when the Los Angeles State Normal School was transferred to the University, a southern branch was established. In 1927 this campus was renamed the University of California at Los Angeles and two years later was moved to its present site in the Westwood Hills. The Mount Hamilton campus, home of the Lick Observatory, was presented to the University in 1888, and the San Francisco Medical Center was opened in 1873 following the acquisition by the University of Toland Medical College. Santa Barbara College became part of the University in 1944, also by legislative and regental action.

The Berkeley campus, oldest of the eight in the state-wide system, covers more than 900 acres in the foothills east of San Francisco Bay. Here are colleges of Letters and Science, Agriculture, Architecture, Chemistry, and Engineering and schools of Business Administration (graduate and undergraduate), Criminology, Education, Forestry, Law, Librarianship, Medicine (first year of curriculum), Nursing, Optometry, Pharmacy (first year of curriculum), Public Health, and Social Welfare. Also at Berkeley are research institutes and bureaus in such fields as Slavic studies, public administration, experimental biology, engineering research, child welfare, East Asiatic studies, and international relations. International House, one of four such organizations in the world, is designed to promote acquaintanceship between foreign and American students.

The Davis campus, 13 mi. west of Sacramento, covers 3,000 acres in the heart of California's fertile Central Valley. About two thirds of the campus acreage is devoted to crops and farm animals for use by the College of Agriculture in teaching and research. The campus also maintains a School of Veterinary Medicine and a College of Letters and Science.

Oceanographic research carried on at La Jolla by the Scripps Institution of Oceanography includes studies in ocean currents and waves, submarine geology, marine physics and chemistry, and marine plants and animals. Instruction and research training for graduate students is provided.

On the Los Angeles campus, second largest in student enrollment, are colleges of Letters and Science, Engineering, Applied Arts, and Agriculture and schools of Business Administration (graduate and undergraduate), Education, Pharmacy, (first year of curriculum), Law, Medicine, Nursing, Public Health, and Social Welfare. Institutes and bureaus are those of governmental research, transportation and traffic engineering, industrial relations, and business and economic research. The Senator William Andrew Clark Memorial Library, a famous collection of books, pamphlets, and manuscripts concerning the history of Montana and English culture from 1600 to 1900, is nearby.

Mount Hamilton (4,209 ft.), in the Santa Clara Valley near San José, is the site of the Lick Observatory which does research in astronomy and instructs and provides research facilities for advanced students. A new 120-in. telescope, second largest in the world, has been installed.

For more than half a century the Citrus Experiment Station for research and graduate instruction in subtropical horticulture has been in operation on the 1,000-acre Riverside campus. A college of Letters and Science, which offers a four-year liberal arts curriculum in the humanities, social sciences, physical sciences, and life sciences, was established here in 1949.

The San Francisco campus is devoted exclusively to the medical and health sciences. Instruction and research is carried on in the schools of Medicine, Nursing, and Pharmacy and in the College of Dentistry. Special research facilities are maintained in the fields of radiology, tropical diseases, experimental surgery, experimental oncology, and ophthalmology. Also located in San Francisco are the affiliated Hastings College of the Law and the California School of Fine Arts.

Santa Barbara College, situated on a 408-acre seashore campus a few miles from Santa Barbara, offers four-year undergraduate programs in such fields as education, home economics, industrial arts, mathematics, music, physical education, physical sciences, psychology, and speech. Some graduate instruction, leading to the master's degree, is given.

The University's library contains more than 3,630,000 volumes, the largest collections being at Berkeley (more than 2,000,000 volumes) and at Los Angeles (more than 1,100,000). Special libraries are maintained in city and regional planning, mathematics-statistics, mineral technology, landscape architecture, biochemistry, agricultural economics, biomedicine, meteorology, theatre arts, and industrial relations.

Administration of the University is entrusted, under the state constitution, to a corporate body titled "The Regents of the University of California." It is composed of 24 members—16 of whom are appointed by the state governor for 16-year terms, while eight are ex officio. The corporation has "full powers of organization and government, subject only to such legislative control as may be necessary to insure compliance with the terms of the endowments of the University and security of its funds."

The Regents select a president who is responsible to the board for the administration of all eight campuses. To assist him, there are chancellors on the Berkeley and Los Angeles campuses, provosts on the Davis, Riverside, and Santa Barbara College campuses, directors on the La Jolla and Mount Hamilton campuses, and statewide vice-presidents for business affairs, agricultural sciences, medical and health sciences, and University Extension.

To facilitate the administration of academic matters, the Regents have established an Academic Senate, divided into two sections, Northern and Southern, and faculty organizations at Santa Barbara College and Riverside. Subject to regental approval, these groups, in general, determine the conditions for admission, authorize courses of instruction, and exercise general supervision of the discipline of students. *For statistics see* COLLEGES AND UNIVERSITIES.   G. A. P.

CALIFORNIA INSTITUTE OF TECHNOLOGY, an accredited, privately controlled college of enginering and science, graduate school, and research institute for men at Pasadena, Calif., known originally as Throop Polytechnic Institute, a preparatory and manual arts training school. The move to the present campus was made in 1910, and the present name was adopted in 1920. Instruction and research are carried on chiefly in Pasadena on a 32-acre campus. The Institute also maintains an experimental farm in Arcadia, a marine biological laboratory on the coast at Corona del Mar, and an astrophysical observatory site on Palomar Mountain in San Diego County; these add more than 2,000 acres to the land owned by the Institute. Facilities of the Mount Wilson Observatory, the Pacific Aeronautical Library in Hollywood, and the Huntington Library and Art Gallery are available for study and research.

No degrees are offered in liberal arts, but there are many liberal arts courses; every student is required to devote one quarter of his class time to arts, letters, and the social sciences. The B.S. is conferred in engineering and in science. Various professional degrees and the graduate degrees of M.S. and Ph.D. are offered. The divisions include biology, chemistry and chemical engineering, geological sciences, physics, mathematics, electrical, civil, and mechanical engineering, and aeronautics and meteorology.

The buildings house laboratories for instruction and research in hydraulics, soil mechanics, plant physiology, high-voltage power equipment, aeronautics, nuclear physics, and other technical subjects. The geology laboratory contains a museum of geological and paleontological materials, and for astrophysical study there are the 200-in. telescope on Palomar Mountain and the 100-in. telescope on Mount Wilson.

Freshman scholarships are awarded on a competitive basis, and some half and full tuition scholarships are available to upper classmen. Loan funds are limited, but there is opportunity for students to earn part of their expenses. The administration cares for needy cases. Dormitory facilities are provided. *For statistics see* COLLEGES AND UNIVERSITIES.

CALIFORNIA LILAC, several western North American species, and varieties of *Ceanothus,* woody plants of the buckthorn family. They are valued in gardens for their clusters of blue, white, or pink flowers. *C. thyrsiflorus,* with blue flowers, grows on canyon walls from Monterey to Oregon, sometimes reaching a height of 25 ft. It is also called blue blossom and blue myrtle.   J. C. Wis.

CALIFORNIA MISSIONS, a group of twenty-one ecclesiastical establishments organized between 1769 and 1823 by monks of the Franciscan order for the Christianization and education of the American Indians in California. The first was established at San Diego under the direction of Father Junípero Serra, who was a Spanish missionary in America.

Originally situated about a day's journey apart, these missions, as the Franciscan program expanded, developed into a continuous chain of great landed estates reaching from San Diego on the south to Sonoma, beyond San Francisco, on the north. The monks became not only the spiritual leaders of the country, but also farm managers, merchants, and the virtual rulers of the Indians. Since the Indian population at a single mission at times reached 2,000 neophytes, the program required extensive lands for the mission grain fields, orchards, and pastures; a group of buildings including the church, priests' quarters, shops, and storehouses; a cemetery; and a water-supply system. The buildings were generally situated near the center of the mission estate and had to be capable of defense in the event of an attack by hostile Indians.

In general, the arrangement, following that of monastic institutions in Mexico and Spain, featured a central cloister-enclosed patio. Surrounded by buildings and guarded by a double gate, the patio furnished a place large enough to accommodate the Indian population and movable property in case of trouble. This patio, the focal point of work-a-day activities, usually had a fountain at its center, as at Santa Barbara. The church building stood away from this courtyard but dominated the mission group. Usually a plaza containing arcaded walks fronted the roadway. The missions of Santa Barbara, San Juan Capistrano, and San Juan Bautista are surviving examples of the more elaborate of these establishments.

The prosperity of the missions and the corresponding backwardness of other institutions in California led to dissatisfaction, not only among the settlers in California, but also among officials in Mexico and Spain. By these officials the missions were regarded as a priestly feudal system, the priest playing the part of the lord, the Indians becoming the serfs. In spite of frequent criticism, however, matters went well for the priests until 1813, when the Spanish Cortes ordered that all lands which had been in the hands of the priests for ten years or more be returned to the Indians. Ferdinand VII repudiated this law in 1814, and for a time the priests were safe.

With Mexican independence came an order to "liberate" the Indians, suspend the annual stipends of the priests, form the mission establishments into villages, and make land grants to such Indians as were able to support themselves. This order was not carried out, however, and a decree in 1828 provided that the mission properties should not be colonized until some disposition could be made of those Indians unable to shift for themselves. Here matters stood until Apr. 16, 1834, when a secularization law was passed. In a very short time, as a result of this law, the splendid system of mission establishments was ruined. Ten of the missions were secularized in 1834, six more the next year. By 1836 only an eighth of the Indians remained and, without care, the mission properties rapidly depreciated. Under Governor Pio Pico the lands and buildings were sold to defray the expenses of administration. Thus the great properties passed into private hands, except for the churches and small adjacent lands which were returned to the ecclesiastical authorities by the United States courts after American occupation. The picturesque ruins of the churches are today the principal reminders of this historic missionary project. Insofar as funds have permitted, church officials have repaired and restored the interesting old structures. Good examples of this restoration are the missions of San Diego de Alcalá, San Juan Capistrano, Santa Barbara, La Purisima Concepción, and San Carlos Borromeo at Carmel.   R. Ne.

CALIFORNIA NUTMEG, the common name for one of the tumion trees, *Torreya californica.* It is a coniferous evergreen tree of the yew family. *See also* CONIFER; TORREYA.   C. H. Wo.

CALIFORNIA POPPY, *Eschscholzia californica,* a member of the poppy family, is a perennial about 12 in. high, native to California. Its handsome, pale yellow to orange, four-petaled flowers may be 3 in. across, with a brilliant sheen. The foliage is bluish green and finely divided. It is much cultivated as an annual in gardens, and grows wild in Australia and India. It is the state flower of California.   J. C. Wis.

CALIFORNIA STATE POLYTECHNIC COLLEGE, an accredited institution for men and women specializing in the study of agriculture, engineering, and arts and sciences, occupies 3,823 acres of land, of which 2,850 are located in San Luis Obispo, 157 acres in the Voorhis unit in San Dimas, and 816 acres in the Kellogg unit in Pomona, Calif. Established by the Legislature of the state of California in 1901, the institution opened as a state vocational high school and was the forerunner in California of vocational education along agricultural and industrial lines. California Polytechnic raised its level of instruction to that of a junior college in 1927. In 1933 it was changed from a junior college to a two-year and three-year technical college. Authority to award the B.S. degree for completion of the four-year curriculum was granted in 1940. The college is dedicated to the principle that students need to know the technical and manual processes in agriculture, engineering, and other occupational fields, as well as the theories which govern these processes, and further, that students who intend to become teachers in these and related subjects should master the practical techniques of the subject.

The B.S. is now offered for completion of the four-year curriculum in the following majors: agriculture (agricultural engineering, mechanized agriculture, agricultural inspection, animal husbandry, field crops, fruit crops, dairy husbandry and manufacturing, farm management, ornamental horticulture, poultry husbandry, soil science, agricultural management and sales); engineering (aeronautical, air conditioning and refrigeration, architectural, electrical, electronic, mechanical, printing, and industrial); and arts and sciences (agricultural journalism, biological sciences, education, English and speech, home economics, mathematics, physical education, physical sciences, social sciences, agricultural chemistry). The college grants the M.S. in agriculture, biological science, education, English, mathematics, health and physical education, physical science, and social science. Graduates are recommended for the general secondary teaching credential in any of the following majors: social studies, mathematics, physical science and general science, life science and general science, agriculture, physical education, and English.

In 1938 a completely equipped school and farm near San Dimas, in Los Angeles County, was deeded to California Polytechnic College by its owners, Charles B. Voorhis of Pasadena and his son, former Congressman Jerry Voorhis. This gift was put to use as a plant-industries branch of the college. In 1949 the Kellogg Arabian Horse Ranch near Pomona was donated to the college by the Kellogg Foundation for the advancement of practical education and for the perpetuation and improvement of the Arabian horse breeding program in America. The state of California is now building a complete college facility on this property to accommodate 3,000 students by 1960.

Dormitories and cafeterias are provided, and there is a completely equipped and staffed infirmary. Freshman and advanced scholarships are offered by many industrial concerns, and student loan funds are administered on a basis of need. Generous opportunity for self-help is made available by the college's policy of giving students experience by employing them to operate the campus and farm. *For statistics see* COLLEGES AND UNIVERSITIES.

CALIGULA (GAIUS CAESAR) [kəlɪ′gyulə] (A.D. 12-41), Roman Emperor from A.D. 37 to 41, was the son of Germanicus and grand-nephew of Tiberius (Emperor, A.D. 14-37). As a child, Gaius had been the favorite of the legionaries in the Rhineland where he had followed his father, Germanicus, about the camps wearing the army boots from which his nickname Caligula (Little Boots) was derived. As Emperor, Gaius made a good beginning when he suppressed the informers employed by Tiberius and entertained the Roman populace with gladiatorial shows and festivals. Within a short time, however, Gaius became insane, and henceforth the members of his court were the victims of a reign of terror which has no parallel in history. During his meals he caused criminals, and even innocent persons, to be stretched on the rack and beheaded; every day saw the execution of one or more of the most respectable citizens of Rome. At a distance of nineteen centuries, the mad pranks of Caligula have their comic side. There was the German campaign in which, failing to find the enemy, the emperor dressed up half the army as Germans and pursued them with the other half. Then there was the "invasion of Britain" when the army was marched to the Gallic shore of the English Channel where helmets were filled with sea shells to be carried back to Rome as the spoils of the campaign. At Rome, Caligula's horse had an ivory stable with a golden manger, and the noble animal once held the consulship. It was perhaps amusing to watch a Roman emperor making horrible faces at himself in a mirror, but the laughter of the courtiers must have been a bit forced at the famous banquet where Caligula shared with them the highly entertaining thought that he could have all their heads cut off. In A.D. 41 he was assassinated by a conspiracy of the praetorian cohorts.

T. B. J.

CALIPH [ke′lɪf; kæ′lɪf], from Arabic *khalifah* (successor), the title formerly given to an Islamic ruler in his capacity as commander of the believers and as successor to Mohammed. As supreme head of the world-wide Islamic community, a caliph administered the spiritual and secular departments of the faith.

Most of the caliphs were of the Sunnite branch of Islam, which includes the majority of orthodox Moslems. The Sun-

nities believed that Mohammed was a prophet called by divine command and that he was therefore unable to bequeath his priestly office to any successor. According to this belief, Mohammed's successors were the heirs of temporal, secular authority only.

The schismatic Shiites took a different view of the caliphate. They insisted that Allah had provided for both the spiritual and secular leadership (imamate) of the Moslem community. The Shiites recognized the descendents of Ali, cousin of Mohammed and husband of Fatima, his daughter and only survivor, as the legitimate imams of Islam, to the exclusion of all Sunnite caliphs. The Fatimid Caliphate (c. 909-1171) was the only major Shiite caliphate in Islam.

Other dissenting dynasties, such as the Idrisids of Morocco (788-974) and the Safawids of Iran (1502-1736), also claimed the caliphal title. After World War I the collapse of the Ottoman Caliphate threatened to put an end to the caliphate in Islam. Conferences held in Cairo and Mecca failed to settle the future of the office, and the trend toward the secular state, initiated by modern Turkey, has gained slow momentum in the rest of the Moslem world. A list of the caliphates follows.   E. J. J.

Orthodox Caliphate (632-661). The Orthodox Caliphate refers to the period of the first four caliphs. These orthodox caliphs ruled Islam from Medina, and during their rule the office was elective and theocratic. They were Abu-Bakr, 632-634, the father-in-law of Mohammed; Omar, 634-644, actually the first to be called caliph; Othman, 644-656; and Ali, 656-661, husband of Fatima, the favorite daughter of Mohammed. During this period Arab forces conquered Syria, Palestine, Armenia, Persia, and Egypt; Cyprus, Crete, and Rhodes also fell into their hands.

Ommiad Caliphate (661-750). The Ommiad Caliphate was ruled by the followers of Othman, called Ommiads. The capital was Damascus in Syria; Mecca and Medina were sacked and Arabia was subjugated. Ommiad power extended from Syria westward to the Pyrenees Mountains and eastward to the Indus River. During this caliphate the office of caliph became hereditary and a bureaucratic machinery was created to meet the demands of the vast Moslem Empire.

Abbasside Caliphate (750-1258). The Abbasside Caliphate took its name from Abbas, the uncle of Mohammed. It had its center at Baghdad, and Persia became the dominant country. Harun al-Rashid (786-809) patronized a luxurious and brilliant court, described well in *The Thousand and One Nights*. His successor, Mamun (813-833), was also a patron of culture, giving great encouragement to the translations of the ancient Greek classics. The Abbasside Caliphate and the city of Baghdad were destroyed by the Mongol Tatars in 1258.

Ommiad Caliphate in Spain (756-1031). This caliphate was founded by the sole refugee from the Ommiad massacre at Damascus in 750. Córdoba was the capital, but Toledo, Granada, and Seville became centers of learning frequented by Moslem, Jewish, and Christian scholars.

Fatimid Caliphate in Egypt (909-1171). The Fatimid Caliphate actually began in Tunis in 909, but was shifted to Egypt in 969. Its caliphs claimed descent from Ali and Fatima. The caliphate was conquered by Saladin in 1171, and subjected to the Abbassides.

Ottoman Caliphate (1517-1924). Between 1258 and 1517, Abbasside caliphs served as puppets under the Mameluke control in Egypt, but in 1517 the Ottoman Sultan Selim I, according to tradition, captured the last Abbasside caliph and usurped the title of caliph for the Ottoman dynasty. The

Ottoman caliphate was abolished in 1924 by the Turkish National Assembly.   H. C. K.

CALISTHENICS. *See* GYMNASTICS.
CALIXTUS. *See* CALLISTUS.

CALLA [kæ′lə], *Zantedeschia aethiopica,* the calla of gardens, also called lily of the Nile, a member of the arum family, not a true lily. It is a perennial herb native to Africa, much grown as an ornamental outdoors in warm climates, and by florists and occasionally as house plants in cold climates. The leaves are lance-shaped, glossy and handsome; what is usually considered the flower is, in reality, a white spathe, or leaf, surrounding the spadix, or spike, on which the many tiny true flowers are crowded. California supplies the rest of the United States with roots, which are brought to flower under cool conditions and with ample water and rich soil. The golden calla is *Z. elliottiana.*   J. C. Wis.

CALLA, WILD, *Calla palustris,* a perennial of the arum family, a handsome aquatic herb sometimes called water arum, native to northern Europe, Asia and northeastern North America. It has heart-shaped, glossy leaves about 8 in. high, and a white flowering spathe, or bract, surrounding the short spike of yellow flowers, which develop into showy red berries.   J. C. Wis.

CALLAO [kɑyɑ′o], the chief seaport of Peru and a constitutional province on the central coast of the republic at 12°

pered, and during the sixteenth century it was frequently sacked by buccaneers, including Francis Drake. In 1746 a tidal wave following an earthquake flooded the city; the ruins of this community remain under water. Callao was rebuilt three quarters of a mile from the original site. Heavily fortified, it withstood several sieges by Spanish forces in the Peruvian struggle for independence. In 1881, during the War of the Pacific, it was taken by Chilean forces. By the Treaty of Ancón in 1883 the Chileans returned the port to Peru.

Callao has one of the best harbors on the west coast of South America. More than half of the foreign trade of Peru passes through the port. The inner harbor, covering an area of 655 acres, is protected from the sea by breakwaters; its entrance and channels have a depth of 37 ft. In 1935 Callao's modern maritime terminal was opened, and in 1938 the shipping facilities were further improved by the completion of a drydock approximately 570 ft. long. A naval arsenal was also completed in 1938. Callao is not only the republic's chief port, but in conjunction with Lima forms Peru's chief industrial and commercial district. Its industrial establishments include breweries, flour mills, foundries, lumber mills, soap and candle factories, and a meat-packing plant. Pop. (est. 1947), city, 82,608; province, 97,600.   S. G. I.

CALLES, PLUTARCO ELÍAS [kɑ′yes] (1877-1945), Mexican statesman, was born in Guaymas, Sonora, Sept. 25, 1877. Little is known of his childhood, but at the age of 17 he became teacher of his primary school and there developed concern over the economic and political conditions of Mex-

SEAPORT OF CALLAO, PERU

EWING GALLOWAY, NEW YORK

2′ S. lat. and 74° 4′ W. long. The province covers an area of 14 sq. mi. and comprises the port of Callao; its suburbs, Bellavista, La Punta, and Chucuito; and a number of islands including San Lorenzo, Las Palominas, and Frontón. The city is the gateway to Lima, 8 mi. to the northwest. Callao was founded in 1537 and became an important shipping point for the riches taken by the Spanish conquerors. The port pros-

ico. He supported General Venustiano Carranza's campaign against the government of Victoriano Huerta and when Carranza was elected president, was appointed minister of commerce, labor and industry. He served as secretary of the interior under President Álvaro Obregón from 1920 to 1924. Elected president in 1924, Calles continued Obregón's progressive and democratic policies. He became involved in a bitter conflict with the Roman Catholic Church in Mexico when the episcopate took a positive stand against the religious and educational provisions of the Mexican Constitution. It was during this time that the privilege of saying Mass was denied priests of the Church. With the aid of United States Ambassador Dwight W. Morrow, Calles worked out a settlement of the disputes with foreign countries over titles to petroleum lands. His term expired in 1928, but his tremendous influence over the Mexican people and his dominance of national politics led his successor, President Lázaro Cárdenas, to send him in exile to the United States in 1936. He later returned to Mexico, where he died, Oct. 19, 1945.　　　　　　　　　　S. G. I.

CALLICRATES [kəlɪ'krətiz] (fl. fifth century B.C.), Greek architect, was one of the Athenian artists who carried out Pericles' plans for making Athens the cultural center of Greece. He and Ictinus were the architects of the Parthenon, built between 447 and 438 B.C., as a new temple to Athens' patron goddess, Athena, and it has stood ever since as the crowning achievement of Greek architecture. The Doric order is handled in perfect proportion, and the Ionic is adapted effectively for interior use and combination with Doric.

The Ionic details may have been Callicrates' contribution to the joint design of the Parthenon, if we may judge from his mastery of the Ionic order in the little Temple of Athena Nike, built about 426 B.C., high on a bastion at the entrance to the Acropolis. The close similarity of both plan and details of the Nike Temple and the Temple on the Ilissus makes it probable that Callicrates designed the latter also. He showed a particular skill in adapting the plan of the Nike Temple to its difficult location.

Official state building accounts, which record his work on the Parthenon and on the Nike Temple and its altar, show that he completed also the middle long wall of the fortifications between Athens and its harbor town, Piraeus, in 443-442 B.C. Callicrates was one of the chief state architects of Athens.　　　　　　　　　　　　　　　L. T. S.

CALLIMACHUS [kəlɪ'məkəs] (fl. c. 250 B.C.), Greek poet, grammarian, and critic, was born at Cyrene in Africa. After teaching school at Eleusis in Egypt, a suburb of Alexandria, he attracted the attention of Ptolemy II, probably by his politically inclined *Hymn to Zeus* (c. 285), and was summoned to Alexandria. Here under the patronage of Arsinoë, sister-wife of Ptolemy, he rose to be leader of the literary world, though his poetic theory was opposed by several poets, including Apollonius. This position he maintained under Ptolemy III, but no work of his can be dated certainly after 240 B.C.

According to Suidas he was an indefatigable writer and composed more than eight hundred works. Many of these were prose works, now lost, of a typically Alexandrian, encyclopedic nature—for example, treatises on *Names of Races, On Birds, Names of Months, Foundations of Cities,* and *On the Rivers in the World.* His most important prose work was the *Pinakes,* a critical and biographical catalogue, in 120 volumes, of the authors whose works were preserved in the Alexandria Museum. In spite of his extensive work in the Museum, however, it is improbable that he was ever chief librarian. The poetry of Callimachus was known until 1910 only by six *Hymns,* about sixty *Epigrams,* and reputed translations of his writings like Catullus' *Lock of Berenice* and Ovid's *Ibis.* Many of the epigrams are exquisite gems; the hymns are modifications of the Homeric hymn type, not

always successful. Since 1910, papyrus discoveries have revealed large, if mutilated, parts of the *Aetia* ("Origins" of cults, customs, and cities), the *Iambics,* and the *Lyrics.* Scraps of a short epic poem, the *Hecale,* have also been found. One of the most valuable papyrus discoveries is the *Diegeseis* (a partial digest of several of the *Aetia,* the *Iambics, Lyrics,* and *Hecale*).

Several passages in Callimachus' poems indicate that he had formulated a specific theory of poetic composition. Avoidance of genres where perfection had already been attained (the Homeric epic, for example), novelty, brevity, and a finished technique are among his stipulations. His own works fulfill these conditions admirably and justify Ovid's dictum that he is weak in inspiration but strong in technique.　　　　　　　　　　　　　C. M. D.

CALLINUS [kəlɑɪ'nəs] of Ephesus, Greek elegiac poet, flourished probably in the middle of the seventh century B.C. It was disputed by the ancients whether he or Archilochus invented the elegiac distich, i.e., made it a poetic form of literary importance, but it seems likely that Callinus was slightly earlier than Archilochus. How much he wrote is unknown; only one fragment of twenty-one lines is now extant. In this the poet urges his fellow countrymen to rouse themselves from their lethargy and meet the invading Cimmerians. The language of his poem demonstrates the close dependence of early elegy upon Homeric epic, while the poet seems to anticipate the later convivial elegies in addressing his words of exhortation to a group reclining at their ease.
　　　　　　　　　　　　　　　　　　C. M. D.

CALLIOPE [kəlɑɪ'əpi], a musical instrument developed during the nineteenth century in America, named after the muse of epic poetry. Several octaves of organ-like pipes are blown by pressure from a steam boiler controlled through a keyboard. Designed to attract people from great distances to showboats and circuses, the calliope is distinguished by its loud, wheezing tone.　　　　　　　　　　W. Li.

CALLISTUS I, SAINT [kæl ɪ'stəs] (died 222), pope, whose name was written by such Latins as Augustine, Optatus, etc., as Calixtus or Calixtus, was a former slave of the Christian Carpophorus. Callistus was banished on the complaints of the Jews to the mines of Sardinia and was liberated under Pope Victor I. Under Pope Zephyrinus, Callistus became deacon in charge of the community cemetery on the Appian Way which still bears his name. Callistus acquired great influence in the Church and was an outspoken opponent of the Monarchians. Elected successor of Zephyrinus, he showed himself an energetic pontiff (217-222). He excommunicated Sabellius, the most prominent champion of modalism, and accused Hippolytus of ditheism. In the meantime, Hippolytus set himself up as antipope. The struggle was extended to embrace the field of morals when Hippolytus espoused rigoristic teachings. That Callistus was a martyr is very doubtful.　　　　　　　　　　　　E. A. R.

CALLISTUS II [kəlɪ'stəs] (c. 1060-1124), pope, born Guido, son of Count William of Burgundy, was a relative of the imperial family. Becoming archbishop of Vienne in 1088, he showed himself an uncompromising foe of lay investiture and an outspoken opponent of the concessions made under duress by Pope Paschal II to Emperor Henry V. Pope from 1119 to 1124, he maintained this attitude, but in 1122 was able to come to an agreement with the emperor in a Diet at Worms. Callistus granted that the election of bishops and abbots might take place in the presence of the emperor or his agents and that the emperor should have the right to invest them with the scepter, i.e., with their dignity as princes of the empire. Henry agreed to give up investiture with ring and staff, i.e., with spiritual functions; to allow free elections; and to aid in the restoration of church property which had been confiscated during the long struggle. The settlement was in the nature of a compromise, but the papacy came off the better. The concordat was announced at the Lateran Council of 1123, at which the decrees against simony and the marriage of priests were renewed.

E. A. R.

CALLOT, JACQUES [ka′lo′] (1592-1635), French printmaker, was born in Nancy of parents attached to the court of Charles III, Duke of Lorraine. From 1608 to 1621 he passed his apprenticeship in Florence and Rome. The *Temptation of St. Anthony* (1617) and the *Fair at Impruneta* (1619) already show him to be master of his own style of fantastic realism. Combining the pointed elegance of mannerism with his own cold intensity, he worked out a new style and a new technique of hard-ground etching admirably suited to portray the new fields of subject matter that he explored. His plates of the Commedia dell' Arte, gypsies, court of manners of Lorraine, or the incidental bestialities of war are characteristic of his interest.

Callot returned to France in 1622 and worked in Paris, where he made prints illustrating various sieges of Louis XIII and presenting views of the city and its life. Returning finally to Nancy in 1630, he produced the great *Martyrdom of St. Sebastian* (1631). Nancy was besieged in 1632 by Cardinal Richelieu and the King, and in the following year, as a patriot of Lorraine, Callot produced the first atrocity pictures of war in his impressive series, *The Miseries of War*. Especially memorable in these plates are the tree ripe with corpses in *The Hanging* and the murder and rape depicted in *The Raid*. Callot died in Nancy on Mar. 24, 1635.

S. M.

CALORIMETER. *See* Gas Calorimetry; Steam.

CALTANISSETTA [kɑ′ltɑnissɛ′ttɑ], the name of both a province and its capital city, in central Sicily.

The City. The city is about 62 mi. southeast of Palermo and is located on a branch railway connecting it with Palermo, Catania, and Agrigento. It is the center for the agricultural and mineral products of the province and has a technical institute and a school of mines. The city became prominent under Norman rule in the eleventh century, but there are few medieval remains. It prospered during the period of Spanish rule, in the sixteenth and seventeenth centuries. During World War II it was the scene of heavy fighting. Pop. 1954 (city), 46,800; (commune), 60,900.

The Province. The province of Caltanissetta consists of 22 communes with an area of 812 sq. mi. Except for the coastal plain around Gela on the southern shore of Sicily, the terrain is hilly. Almost 30 per cent of the adult population is engaged in agriculture, with mining next in importance. Cattle are raised, and the principal agricultural products are cereals, wine, almonds, olives, and fruit. Caltanissetta is the only province in Italy where cotton is grown in any quantity. Rock salt is mined, and, as the result of the expansion of the sulphur-mining industry in recent decades, the province accounts for two fifths of Sicily's total sulphur output. As the center of these operations, the capital has also grown. The illiteracy rate in the province has been as high as 50 per cent, but it is being decreased as a result of Sicily's land-reform program. Most of the people live in large

villages and towns, such as San Cataldo, Gela, Niscemi, and Mazzarino. Pop. (est. 1954), 308,900.

R. G. W.

CALUMET CITY [kæ′lyʊmɛt], a city on the Calumet River in Cook Co., Illinois, adjoining Chicago on the southwest and Hammond, Indiana, on the east. The city was incorporated in 1925 and is administered by a mayor and council. Calumet City was called West Hammond until 1924, when the present name was adopted. The principal industrial activities are canning, bottling, meat packing, and the manufacturing of fertilizers and chemicals. Pop. 1950, 15,799; 1954, 19,066.

CALUSA. *See* Indian Tribes, North American.

CALVADOS [ka′lva′dɔ′s], a department in northwestern France, with an area of 2,197 sq. mi., bounded on the north by the English Channel, and by the departments of Eure on the east, Orne on the south, and Manche on the west. The name of the department is derived from an extensive ledge of rock along the coast, between the mouths of the Orne and Vire rivers, on which one of the vessels of the Spanish Armada, the *Salvador,* corrupted into "Calvados," was wrecked. The surface of the department is hilly and undulating, with extensive plains and fertile valleys. The navigable rivers are the Orne, Tougue, Vire, and the Dives. The department has broad, rich pastures, and many horses, cattle, sheep, and hogs are reared. Excellent butter and Camembert and Pont l'Evêque cheese are made. The cider and apple brandy of Calvados are considered among the best. Cereals are produced but are secondary in importance. There is coal mining at Caen, Trouville, and Honfleur, and iron smelting at Saint-Rémy, Saint-André, and Jurques. Bayeux, on the Aure River, 5 mi. from the sea, is an old Norman town, famous for its Bayeux Tapestry, a strip of embroidery on coarse linen depicting Norman life and the conquest of England. Napoleon had it exhibited in the chief towns of France to win support of his projected English invasion. Bayeux now manufactures porcelain and stained-glass windows. Caen, the prefecture, is a center for the study of Norman art. Often called "Norman Athens," it became important around 1070, when William I of England and Normandy and his wife Matilda built two abbeys there, the Abbaye aux Hommes and Abbaye aux Femmes, which are still standing. This act represented a penance by the pair, who, as first cousins, had ignored a papal prohibition of their marriage two decades previously. William's body is buried there. Caen manufactures lace, linen, cotton goods, gloves, and hosiery. Stone, minerals, horses, butter, cheese, cider, and brandy are exported. Calvados was formed from part of Lower Normandy in 1790. Pop. 1954, 442,991.

S. Van V.

CALVARY [kæ′lvəri]. (1) The place where Jesus Christ was crucified. The Latin *calvaria* is a translation of the Greek *kranion,* meaning skull, which is an interpretation by the Evangelists of the obscure Hebrew word *Golgotha* (Matt. xxvii: 33). The common opinion places Calvary on the west side of Jerusalem, now within the city walls. During the Crusades this hillock was included under the roof of the Church of the Resurrection, where it remains today. Others place the site above Jeremiah's grotto outside the Damascus Gate. This latter site is known as Gordon's Calvary.

(2) A representation in the open air of the crucifixion, or a series of representations of the various scenes of Christ's Passion.

W. C.

CALVÉ, EMMA (EMMA DE ROQUER) [ka′lve′, də rɔ′ke′] (1858-1942), French operatic soprano, was born in Décazeville, department of Aveyron, France, Aug. 15, 1858. The first seven years of her life were spent in northern Spain and at the age of ten she entered a convent in Montpellier, France. In 1873 she moved to Paris, where she studied singing under Jules Puget, a retired tenor of the Paris Opera. She then toured France, giving concerts, but met with no particular success until her operatic debut in 1882 as Marguerite in *Faust* at the Théâtre de la Monnai in Brussels. Her first appearance at the La Scala Opera in Milan in 1887 as Ophelia was disappointing and she was hissed by the audience, but she studied diligently and later triumphed in the same role. Thereafter she sang at the Opéra Comique in Paris and in leading opera houses all over the world. She made her American debut at the Metropolitan Opera House in New York in 1893 and met with sensational success as Carmen. Calvé was considered by many critics the finest of all Carmens, and was also outstanding as Santuzza in *Cavalleria Rusticana,* a role which she sang at the first French performance of that opera in 1892. She sang for thirteen consecutive seasons at the Metropolitan Opera House and in 1910 virtually retired from the stage, confining herself to occasional concert appearances. The remainder of her life was spent at the Château de Cabrières in France, where she taught singing. She died in Millau, France, Jan. 6, 1942.

                                       C. W. D.

CALVERLEY, CHARLES STUART [kæ′lvərli] (1831-1884), English poet and humorist, was born at Martley, Worcestershire, on Dec. 22, 1831. He was educated at Harrow School and proceeded to Balliol College, Oxford, where he remained from 1850 to 1852. Following an undergraduate scrape, he transferred to Christ's College, Cambridge, where he graduated, receiving his M.A. in 1859. Calverley was called to the bar in 1865, but an injury sustained a year later while ice-skating kept him from practicing law. Although this accident clouded the rest of his life, he continued to write light verse of the type which, in *Verses and Translations* (1862), had already brought him a reputation. His other books include *Theocritus Translated into English Verse* (1869) and *Fly Leaves* (1872). His poems, which are lightly satirical, have often been imitated by later humorists and are included in many anthologies of humorous verse. Calverley died in London on Feb. 17, 1884.

                                       R. T.

CALVERT, GEORGE. *See* BALTIMORE, LORD GEORGE CALVERT.

CALVIN, JOHN [kæ′lvin; ka′lvæ′] (1509-1564), French theologian and reformer, was born Jean Chauvin, or Caulvin, in Noyon, about fifty miles north of Paris, on July 10, 1509. He was reared in a cultured environment, was educated at the universities of Paris, Orléans, and Bourges and at the Collège de France, and in his first work, a commentary on Seneca's *De clementia* (1532), showed himself to be a cultured humanist, well versed in both the Latin and the Greek classics. His later work also demonstrated his thorough mastery of patristics. About the year 1533 Calvin was suddenly converted and devoted himself promptly and sincerely to God. Almost at once he was accepted as the outstanding scholar and spokesman of the Protestant movement in France, and as such he wrote opposing the doctrine of the soul's sleep, shared in the production of the Protestant Manifesto which Nicholas Cop proclaimed in his rectoral address to the University of Paris in 1533, and then stated the French Protestant faith in his *Institutes of the Christian Religion*

(first published in Latin at Basel in 1536, and later expanded and translated into French).

Compelled by persecution to flee France, Calvin was retained at Geneva to organize the Reformed Church and labored there first as lecturer on the Holy Scriptures and later as pastor. Calvin's program was for all the citizens of Geneva to accept a comprehensive confession of the Reformed faith and to swear to live accordingly, to nurture their children in this faith by catechetical instruction, and to watch over the lives and morals of the people by means of godly elders appointed in each part of the city. Because of

JOHN CALVIN

FROM AN ENGRAVING BY
CONGUY

his stand for the sanctity and the independence of the Church, Calvin was expelled from Geneva in 1538, but his recall in 1541 was an authorization to resume his labors where they had been interrupted.

During his exile Calvin was pastor of a congregation of French refugees in Strasbourg. While there he learned much from Martin Bucer and also from Melanchthon, whom he met at the reunion conferences of 1539-1541, and developed his program of worship, pastoral care, congregational singing of the psalms, and popular preaching. During this period also he married Idelette de Bure, "the excellent companion of his life," defended the Reformed Church in Geneva in a magnificent *Reply to Sadoleto,* published his commentary on Romans, and enlarged and translated the *Institutes* from Latin into French.

During the last twenty-three years of his life, Calvin made Geneva the center of militant Protestantism. He founded and lectured daily in the academy which later became the University of Geneva, preached in the Cathedral of St. Pierre, wrote commentaries on most of the books of the Bible, corresponded with persons of all ranks throughout Europe, and received and provided for the Protestant refugees. Until his death in Geneva, on May 27, 1564, he governed the turbulent city by his ministry of the Word of God in the pulpit, in the Venerable Company of ministers, and in the Consistory which disciplined the people. Since Calvin held no civil office, it has been denied that he set up a theocracy, but with all the fervor of his being and all the power of his logic he insisted that the citizenry live according to the Word of God. On Calvin's instance, Servetus, who had escaped the Inquisition at Vienne, was charged with heresy and blasphemy and was thereafter tried and executed in 1553 by the civil court of Geneva. Such persecution was the practice of every established church in the sixteenth century, but the spiritual descendants of Calvin have erected a "monument of expiation" at the place where Servetus was executed.

As a churchman, Calvin was the organizer of modern Presbyterianism. For him the Church invisible is the whole number of God's elect and the Church visible is the mother of the faithful. Wherever the Word is truly preached and the sacraments of baptism and the Lord's Supper properly administered, there is the Church. She is governed by Christ, her Head and King, through His Word and Spirit and by the ministry of men. Her officers are teachers, pastors, elders to administer discipline, and deacons to minister to the poor and needy. Calvin's work changed Geneva from a profligate city into what John Knox called "the purest school of Christ since the days of the Apostles."

As a commentator, Calvin discarded medieval exegetical methods and brought out the historico-grammatical sense of Scripture, giving it a practical application to life. The permanence of this work is evident in a recent remark by Karl Barth that Calvin's commentaries are still "better than most." The *Institutes* started as a little catechism of six chapters and grew through successive editions into a large textbook of systematic theology. This Reformed guide to the understanding of the Scriptures uses the Apostles' Creed as the plan for its four books: (1) on God the Father, or the knowledge of the Triune God, creation, and Providence; (2) on God the Son, or man's fall and redemption through Christ; (3) on God the Holy Spirit, or the saving application of Christ's atonement to God's elect; (4) on the Church, the sacraments, and civil government. The *Institutes* are a determined effort to present in orderly form the teaching of the Holy Scriptures, particularly as they had been clarified by Augustine and Luther. Calvin laid special emphasis on the self-existent deity of each Person of the Trinity; on the threefold office of Christ as Prophet, Priest, and King; on the work of the Holy Spirit; and on the place of ethics and of prayer in theology. For Calvin, God is "Father and Lord," sovereign Father and fatherly Sovereign. Controversies with Jerome Bolsec and Albert Pighius led Calvin to develop his doctrine of predestination, by which the rule of faith denies all human merit, to the end that God may have all the glory of saving sinners and that men may rejoice in the glory of His free grace as given in Jesus Christ.

W. C. Ro.

CALVIN COLLEGE AND SEMINARY, an accredited, privately controlled, coeducational college of arts and sciences at Grand Rapids, Mich., affiliated with the Christian Reformed Church in America. It is located in the city's residential district, occupying about 17 acres. Calvin College was chartered in 1876 to train men for the ministry and was expanded into a general college in 1900. The A.B. degree is offered in the preseminary course, in education, or in the general college course, and the B.S. degree is optional for students who include 60 hours in sciences and mathematics in their programs. Students who complete three years of preprofessional work and one year in professional school are entitled to the bachelor's degree on the combined curriculum plan. Scholarship and student loan aid is available in small amounts. Some dormitories are available. *For statistics see* COLLEGES AND UNIVERSITIES.

CALVINISM, the system of theology and ethics constructed by John Calvin, which constitutes the basis of modern Presbyterianism. Calvin was born in Noyon, France, in 1509, and was educated at the University of Paris, but he spent his most productive years in Geneva, Switzerland. Be-

ginning as a humanist and becoming a reformer involuntarily, he made a profound and lasting impression on his own and subsequent generations by the clarity of his mind, his deep religious devotion, and his organizing and administrative genius.

Calvin was the author of a forty-volume commentary on the Bible, and he constructed his theological system upon the basis of Holy Scriptures. The system is set forth in a work of two volumes, each of more than six hundred pages, called *The Institutes of the Christian Religion* (1536). This study covers the entire compass of the Christian faith as expressed in doctrine and dogma, liturgy, sacraments, ecclesiastical organization and discipline, and the relation of Church and State.

The central principle of Calvin's theological thought is the sovereignty of God. In summarizing his ideas, some scholars emphasize only the rather imperious logic by which he derives from the principle of sovereignty of God the doctrine of absolute predestination and unconditional election—an aspect of his thought that has often been called fatalism. A more careful study of Calvin proves that he regarded free will and human responsibility and accountability as possessing an importance equal to that of predestination. It may be said, indeed, that no reformer emphasizes Christian ethics and conduct more strongly than he. He believed that salvation is the result of faith in Christ, and that the genuineness of this new life in Christ is attested by the conduct and attitudes which exemplify it.

Calvin also may be called, by virtue of his ideas on the sources of political power, the architect of democracy. In his view, kings derive power from the people over whom they rule; the State is ordained of God, but it is accountable to God; the people are justified in overthrowing a ruler or government which defies God. Believing that the whole of life must be under the domination of God, Calvin took a deep interest in its political aspects. He became, in effect, the power behind the Geneva city council, and, in the twenty-five years that he spent in Geneva, he made it a city of God.

M. J. H.

CALVO, CARLOS [kɑ'lvo] (1824-1906), Argentine diplomat and historian, was born in Buenos Aires, Feb. 26, 1824. His fame rests principally on his authorship of the doctrine, bearing his name, that persons living in a foreign country should settle their complaints through local courts and not by demands made through their diplomatic representatives. The Calvo Doctrine, first advanced in 1902, gave his name historical importance. Because of a certain similarity, the Calvo Doctrine is often confused with the Drago Doctrine, which claims that foreign nations have no right to use force in the collection of debts from the debtor country. Calvo was ambassador to Germany, Great Britain, and France, and in 1884, was one of the founders of the Institut de Droit International. The publication in 1863 of his principal work, *Derecho internacional teórico y práctico de Europa y America,* made him a prominent authority on international law. His fifteen-volume collection of Latin American treaties and diplomatic papers, published between 1862 and 1867, is also a monumental work. Between 1864 and 1875 he also published a five-volume set, *Annales historiques de la révolution de l'Amérique latine.* Calvo died in Paris, May 4, 1906.

S. G. I.

CALYCANTHUS [kæ'lɪkɑ'nthəs], a small genus of aromatic North American shrubs of the family Calycanthaceae, often planted as ornamentals. These bushy shrubs, which may attain a height of 9 ft., have opposite leaves and bear reddish-brown flowers in spring. Because of its highly fragrant flowers, *C. floridus* is the most-prized species. The calycanthus is also called sweet shrub, strawberry shrub, and Carolina allspice, though *C. occidentalis* grows in California. *See also* ALLSPICE, CAROLINA.

CALYDONIAN HUNT, THE [kæ'lɪdo'nɪən], in Greek mythology, a famous episode centering about the life and death of Meleager, the son of Oeneus, king of Calydon, and Althaea. When Meleager was born, the Fates declared that he would live only until a certain brand on the hearth had burned to ashes. Althaea consequently snatched the brand from the fire and carefully preserved it while her son grew to manhood and took part in the Argonautic expedition. After his return, his father, who had incurred the wrath of Artemis by failing to offer her a sacrifice, was plagued by a huge boar sent by the goddess to ravage the land, and Meleager called together a band of heroes to hunt the boar. Among those in the hunt were Theseus, Jason, Peleus, Telamon, Castor and Pollux, Nestor, Atalanta (daughter of Iasius), and Althaea's brothers, Plexippus and Toxeus. The boar rushed upon its pursuers, but after Atalanta had first wounded it, Meleager was able to deliver its death blow. He gave the head and hide of the boar to Atalanta as a token of her prowess, and when Althaea's brothers objected and tried to take them from her, a fight ensued in which Meleager killed his two uncles. Althaea, eager to avenge the deaths of her brothers, threw into the fire the brand upon which Meleager's life depended; when it was consumed, Meleager died, and Althaea killed herself in remorse.

According to an earlier version, related by Phoenix in *Iliad* IX, the quarrel over the spoils was between the Calydonians and the Curetes, their neighbors, who were led by Althaea's brothers. After the slaying of Plexippus and Toxeus, Meleager, cursed by his mother, withdrew from the fight and the Curetes besieged Calydon. Meleager refused to enter battle until his wife Cleopatra persuaded him, but Homer does not describe Meleager's death.   G. E. D.

CALYPSO [kəlɪ'pso], in Homer's *Odyssey,* a nymph, the daughter of Atlas. She lived on the island of Ogygia, where Odysseus was shipwrecked, and influenced him to remain there for seven years. *See also* ODYSSEUS; ODYSSEY, THE.
G. E. D.

CAM, or CÃO, DIOGO [kãu] (fl. 1481), Portuguese explorer, was an esquire in the king's household when he was commissioned, in 1481, to make a voyage of discovery beyond Cape Catherine, on the west coast of Africa 2° south of the equinoctial line, the most southerly point which had been reached at that time. He sailed from Lisbon early in 1482, taking with him several *padrões,* or granite pillars surmounted with crosses and having the royal arms carved on them. Cam was ordered to add duplicate inscriptions in Portuguese and Latin, with his name and the date, when he placed these pillars in territories he discovered, signifying that the territories belonged to Christendom and Portugal. He placed one at the mouth of the Congo River in 1482. He traded with the natives of the Congo kingdom, and sent some Christian Negroes inland to its ruler, taking hostages for their safety. Cam continued south as far as Cape St. Mary, 13° 28′ S. lat., where he erected another *padrão.* He returned to Lisbon in 1484, and was promoted to the rank of cavalier and given an annuity and a patent of nobility in recognition of his services. In 1485 he returned to the Congo. He sent presents to its king, and returned the hostages.

He sent delegates to ask the natives to become Catholics, and they were subsequently converted. Cam continued south to Cape Cross, 21° 50′ S. lat., where he erected another *padrão.* His fleet returned to Portugal before August 1487. There are conflicting reports of his death, some sources saying he returned to Lisbon, others saying he was killed at sea off Cape Cross in 1486.   S. Van V.

CAMACHO, MANUEL ÁVILA [kamɑ'tsho] (1897-1955), Mexican statesman, was born on Apr. 24, 1897, in Teziutlán, state of Puebla. He was educated in public schools, and at the age of 17 he joined the ultimately successful revolution against Victoriano Huerta, whose excessive cruelties had prevented U.S. recognition of his regime. Camacho was skilled in negotiation and a moderate social reformer. He served as minister of national defense, 1937-1939, and was then elected to the presidency to succeed the more radical Lázaro Cárdenas. Camacho resolved Mexico's former troubles with the Catholic Church and with foreign investors, and negotiated settlements of nearly all the difficulties which had estranged the United States and Mexico. During World War II he co-operated closely with the United States and its Allies. He was defeated for re-election in 1946 by Miguel Alemán, and then retired to private life. He died Oct. 13, 1955, near Mexico City.

CAMAGÜEY [kɑ'mɑgwe'], formerly Puerto Príncipe, the capital and principal city of Camagüey Province, located in east central Cuba. Located 45 mi. southwest of the port of Nuevitas and 300 mi. southeast of Havana, Camagüey is Cuba's largest inland city. It lies in the center of a productive cattle, lumber, sugar cane, and fruit region. The city's industries include sawmills, distilleries, tanneries, and plants for processing dairy products. Camagüey is also an important rail and air center. Founded in 1514 by Diego Velásquez, Spanish soldier and administrator, it is noted for its Spanish colonial charm, with narrow streets, balconied homes, and many churches, including the cathedral, rebuilt in 1617. In the center of the city is the Plaza Agramonte. Pop. 1953, (city), 110,388; province, 618,256.

CAMALDOLESE ORDER [kəmæ'ldoli'z], a Roman Catholic brotherhood, was founded by St. Romuald in 1012 at Camaldoli, Italy, and was approved by Pope Alexander II in 1072. For six centuries the order grew steadily as one body, but in the course of time it became divided into five separate congregations, of which only two remained in 1946. One of these, the Congregation of Cenobite Hermits, which then numbered 117 professed members, dates back to 1012. The other, the Congregation of Mount Corona, was begun in 1523. The Cenobites, who daily chant the Divine Office in choir, live according to a strict interpretation of the rule of St. Benedict. To the practices of the Cenobites the hermits add continual contemplation, strict fasts, seclusion in their cottage-like cells, and silence that is broken only two or three times a week. Among the members of this order were the great canonist Gratian (twelfth century) and Bartolommeo Cappellari, who in 1831 became Pope Gregory XVI.
W. C.

CAMBACÉRÈS, JEAN JACQUES RÉGIS DE, DUKE OF PARMA [kã'ba'se'rɛ's] (1753-1824), French jurist, was born in Montpellier, Oct. 18, 1753. In 1792 he was sent by the department of Hérault as a deputy to the National Convention, where he concentrated on legislative work, and in 1795 became president of the Committee of Public Safety. In 1799 he was made minister of justice and second consul after the *coup d'état* of Brumaire. He gave substantial aid to Napoleon in his seizure of power. After Napoleon had become emperor, Cambacérès was made arch-chancellor and president of the Senate for life, as well as a prince of the empire. In 1808 he received the title of Duke of Parma. Although he was also active in the diplomatic field, Cambacérès was especially concerned with the codification of the civil law in the Code Napoléon of 1804. After the first downfall of Napoleon in 1814, Cambacérès retired to private life but reluctantly accepted his former duties during the Hundred Days. After Napoleon's final defeat he was exiled from France, but his civil rights were restored in 1818. Cambacérès died in Paris, Mar. 8, 1824.   W. Fr.

CAMBAY, GULF OF [kambe′], a cornucopia-shaped body of water, formed by an extension of the Arabian Sea into the northwestern coast of peninsular India. The gulf separates the Kathiawar peninsula from the Indian mainland. It lies northwest of Bombay, and it is 125 mi. wide at its mouth. The city of Cambay at the head of the gulf, once famous as one of the two great trading ports of India (mentioned by Marco Polo in 1293), is now nearly cut off from the sea by the silting up of the gulf. On its eastern side the gulf receives the discharge of the Narbada and Tapti rivers, and on the north that of the Sabarmati and the Mahi and its tributaries. Surat, at the mouth of the Tapti, declined in importance because of silt deposit. Bhavnagar, on the east coast of Kathiawar is a deep-sea port which has become a rival of Bombay. Railways serve the area. The gulf also is notable for the "bore" or rushing tide in the north. High spring tides rise and fall as much as 33 ft., and run at a velocity of 6-7 knots, causing great damage to shipping. The average depth of the channel is from 4 to 6 fathoms, and shoals shift constantly, with river inundations. The soil of the area between the Mahi and Sabarmati rivers is so impregnated with salt that the subsurface water is brackish.   J. E. F.

CAMBODIA [kambo′diə], a kingdom of southeast Asia, located on the lower Mekong River between Thailand and South Vietnam on the Indochinese peninsula. Much of the country, which has an area of 53,668 sq. mi., is marshy and is flooded by the Mekong during the October-April rainy season. The climate is tropical. Rice is the chief crop; cotton, pepper, sugar cane, kapok, castor beans, coffee, tea, and silk are also produced. There are a number of deposits of iron ore.

The Cambodian people are an ethnic mixture with Indian, Mongoloid, and Malaysian elements, more closely related to the Thais than to the Annamese. Phnom Penh, the capital and chief city, had a population of 123,883 in 1948 and about 375,000 in 1953. The predominant religion of Cambodia is a tolerant Buddhism with a trace of Brahmanism. Pop. (1948), 3,227,000; (1953), 4,073,967.

History. Indian culture was brought to Cambodia in the early centuries of the Christian Era by successive Indian immigrations. The Khmer nation arose in the fifth century and reached the zenith of its development about 900. The Khmers developed a remarkable architecture, the most notable example of which is the temple of Angkor Vat dating from the early twelfth century. The ruins of this temple were rescued from the jungle in the middle of the nineteenth century. For several centuries, Cambodia was the victim of aggressions from Siam and Annam, and it was for this reason that the king placed his country under French protection in 1863, but it was not until 1884 that Cambodia came under French administration. In 1907, Siam ceded the

DEANE DICKASON—EWING GALLOWAY

THE ANGKOR VAT, A TEMPLE OF THE KHMER DYNASTY ERECTED IN NORTHWESTERN CAMBODIA IN THE EARLY TWELFTH CENTURY

Cambodian provinces of Battambang and Angkor to France.

Cambodia, like the other Indochinese protectorates, was formerly governed by a French resident superior, under whom a native administration functioned. After the Japanese occupation in World War II, France granted Cambodia a degree of autonomy. On May 6, 1947, a constitutional monarchy with an elected legislature was set up, and on Nov. 8, 1949, an agreement with France called the Kingdom of Cambodia an independent state within the French Union. Complete sovereignty was recognized by an agreement signed in Paris on Dec. 29, 1954. King Norodom Sihanouk attempted to change the electoral provisions of the 1947 constitution, but, meeting with disapproval from the International Control Commission supervising the Geneva Agreement which terminated the war in Indochina, the king abdicated in favor of his father, Norodom Suramarit, on Mar. 2, 1955. Norodom Sihanouk then organized a political party, the Popular Socialists, which was approved overwhelmingly in the September 1955 elections. As premier, the former king adopted a policy of neutralism in the "cold war," rejecting protection on the part of the Southeast Asia Treaty Organization, and severed all ties with the French Union. Cambodia was admitted to the United Nations in December 1955. Despite the resignation of Norodom Sihanouk as premier in March 1956, Cambodia continued its neutralist role, accepting aid from the Communist Chinese as it had previously accepted aid from the United States.

CAMBRAI [kã′brɛ′], a city in the department of Nord, in northern France, 39 mi. south of Lille on the canalized Schelde River. The city was originally a fortification of the Nervii, a Gallic tribe. The Romans called it Camaracum. In 445 it became one of the Frankish capitals. Ravaged by the Normans in 870, it revived and flourished, becoming a commune in 1076. The town was famous for its manufacture of the fine linen fabric called cambric, invented there in the thirteenth century, probably by Baptiste of Cambrai. Louis XI of France occupied Cambrai in 1477, but during the following year the town passed under the control of the Holy Roman emperor, Maximilian I. Since 1677 it has been in the sole possession of France.

Cambrai was extensively damaged in World War I; it was the site of the Battle of Cambrai in 1917. In 1940, during World War II, Cambrai was captured by the Germans in their early drive to the sea and was not recaptured until September 1944, when it was yielded by the Germans with little resistance. The nineteenth-century cathedral at Cambrai is a monument to François de Salignac de La Mothe-Fénelon (1651-1715), French prelate and author who labored in Cambrai and died there. The principal local industry is the manufacture of textiles; the confectionary industry is important to a lesser degree; and there is some trade in sugar, coal, grain, and cattle. Pop. 1954, 29,567.

CAMBRAI, BATTLE OF, a British-German engagement of World War I, notable for the success with which tanks were employed. It failed to achieve permanent results because of the almost complete lack of reserves to follow and exploit the initial successes.

On Nov. 20, 1917, the tanks supported by the infantry, all under the immediate command of General Sir Frederick Byng, moved forward, achieving important gains. The attack had achieved a complete surprise and the ground over which the advance had taken place was comparatively unmarked. There had been no preceding heavy artillery bombardment to create as many obstacles for an attack as it destroyed. After the first day, the advance slowed down considerably and by the end of a week of fighting any advance movement had ceased, as the troops engaged were wearied from fighting without relief. On November 30 the Germans counterattacked, and by December 7 the British, with only slight gain, had been forced back to their starting position. Losses on both sides had been about equal.

The Battle of Cambrai was the last of the great blows of attrition in the west. It demonstrated the mobility and striking power of the tank, but emphasized the necessity for prompt and effective re-enforcement with fresh reserves to follow up and exploit initial gains. Instead of being a mobile machine-gun nest, the tank had demonstrated its value as an offensive weapon of power and mobility. It rendered wire entanglements useless as a protection against surprise and eventually converted a war of fixed position into a war of movement.

The Battle of Cambrai ended about where it began, but it had taught both sides a valuable lesson.   M. K.

CAMBRIAN PERIOD. *See* GEOLOGY.

CAMBRIDGE [ke'mbrɪj], a municipal and parliamentary borough and university town, 57 mi. north of London, England; it is the county seat of Cambridgeshire. It is situated on the Cam River, formerly known as the Granta. The name Cambridge is probably a corruption of the Saxon *Grantebrycge*. There is evidence to support the belief that it was occupied by the Romans, Saxons, and Normans and pillaged by the Danes. The charter of Henry I refers to Cambridge as a borough and grants it rights to impose tolls and regulate traffic. Richard II held a parliament at Cambridge in 1388, and during the time of the Civil War Oliver Cromwell represented it in Parliament. In addition to Cambridge University, one of the most famous British universities, educational institutions include three theological schools, Westminster College, Ridley Hall, and St. Edmund's House; and the Perse grammar school. Among its churches are Great St. Mary's, the university church; St. Benet's, with its pre-Norman tower; and the Church of the Holy Sepulcher, one of the four round churches in England. The town returns one member to Parliament. Cambridge's economic life centers primarily in the university, but the city is also an important agricultural marketing center. Pop. 1952, 90,740.

CAMBRIDGE, a port town and the seat of Dorchester Co. in eastern Maryland, is situated on the Choptank River, near Chesapeake Bay, 40 mi. southeast of Annapolis. The town is served by the Pennsylvania Railroad and is a shipping center for oysters, oyster shells, and fish. Its chief manufactures are lumber, canned goods, wire, brick, boats, animal feed, and fertilizer. Crab packing and garment manufacturing are other industries. Pop. 1950, 10,351.

CAMBRIDGE, a city in eastern Massachusetts, the county seat of Middlesex Co., situated on the north bank of the Charles River, opposite Boston. It is an educational, industrial, and residential community originally known as New Town, a fort established about 1632 by the courts of assistants, meeting in Boston. A direct tax on the wooden palisades encircling the settlement led to the first protest in the colonies against taxation without representation. It was incorporated as a town in 1636 and renamed in honor of the English university. Stephen Daye's printing press, the first brought to the colonies from England, was set up in Cambridge in 1639. Published in that year was *An Almanack for New England,* followed by *The Bay Psalm Book*. George Washington took command of the Continental Army on July 3, 1775, in Cambridge. It was also the meeting place of the convention that framed the state constitution in 1779 and 1780. The city was incorporated in 1846 and is governed by a council and city manager.

Since the founding of Harvard College, in 1636, Cambridge has been a cultural and literary center. It was the birthplace of Oliver Wendell Holmes and James Russell Lowell. Craigie House, headquarters of General Washington until the British evacuated Boston, was later the home of Edward Everett and Henry Wadsworth Longfellow. Among the many noted residents of Cambridge were Elbridge Gerry, John Fiske, and Louis and Alexander Agassiz. The city includes among its numerous educational institutions the Massachusetts Institute of Technology, Radcliffe College for women, which is affiliated with Harvard University, and Cambridge Junior College, a private institution. The Boston and Maine and the Boston and Albany railroads furnish transportation facilities. The principal industries are the manufacture of bakery goods, confectionery, electrical apparatus, furniture, foundry products, rubber goods, and soap. Printing and publishing are also leading activities. Pop. 1950, 120,740.

CAMBRIDGE, a city in east central Ohio, the county seat of Guernsey Co., situated in the heart of the lake region of Ohio, 85 mi. northeast of Columbus. The area is rich in natural resources, which include coal, oil, gas, timber, building stone, and pottery clay. The site was plotted and settled in 1806 by pioneers from the Isle of Guernsey, after which the county was named. Cambridge was incorporated as a city in 1837 and has the council-mayor form of government. The community sponsors a theatre group and a symphony orchestra. The city is the site of Cambridge State Hospital for the feeble-minded. Transportation is supplied by the Pennsylvania and the Baltimore & Ohio railroads. A wide variety of industries located here include metal and tool and die works, pharmaceutical plants, glassworks, railroad shops, and furniture and automobile parts factories. Pop. 1950, 14,739.

CAMBRIDGE PLATONISTS, THE, a group of seventeenth-century English religious philosophers at Cambridge University. During the religious controversy between the

Puritans and the Anglicans they exhibited a spirit of reasonableness, moral earnestness, and idealism which, with their frequent references to Platonic writers, has gained them the name of Platonists. Their central idea was that essential religious truths are few and clear, ascertainable almost completely by human reason, but fully revealed and confirmed in Christian gospel. Religion they conceived to be primarily the practice of so living according to these truths that the fundamentally good nature of man is assimilated more perfectly to the divine. In emphasizing morality, reason, and the simplicity of essential Christian doctrine, they stood apart from both the harsh theology of Calvinism and the ceremonialism of William Laud's episcopacy.

All save one of the Platonists were graduates of Emmanuel College. The eldest, Benjamin Whichcote (1609–1683), was influential as a tutor and preacher from 1633 until the Restoration. His philosophy first clashed openly with Calvinism in 1651, when an exchange of letters with a former tutor shows that Whichcote was then regarded as the leading spirit of a group imbued with unorthodox thought. His *Sermons*, unpublished until 1698, stress the function of reason in religion and the idea that religion is the tuning of man's spiritual nature into a harmonious temper. Not especially indebted to Plato himself, Whichcote is said to have set his students to reading Plato, Cicero, and Plotinus. His pupil John Smith (c.1616–1652) continually quotes Plotinus in his *Discourses*, published in 1660, in elaborating his mystical conception of religion as the "intellectual sensation" of God.

Nathanael Culverwel (c.1618–1651) attempted in *The Light of Nature* (1652) to ground the ideas of the group in a systematic philosophy of moral law, but the most famous of the Platonists are Ralph Cudworth (1617–1688) and Henry More (1614–1687). Cudworth's *True Intellectual System of the Universe* (1678) is a vast refutation of materialism, particularly of Hobbes, and an unfinished exposition of a philosophy combining Cartesian elements with a theory of a "plastic Nature." More, of Christ's College, was a prolific writer now best known for his *Philosophical Poems* (1647) and *Divine Dialogues* (1668). A mystic, an investigator of spiritualism, and a frequent visitor at Lady Conway's philosophic retreat at Ragley, he is most interesting of all. The Cambridge Platonists stated impressively the idea of personal religion and developed the principle of tolerance in an age favorable to neither.   F. B. E.

CAMBRIDGESHIRE, an inland county in eastern England, with an area of approximately 492 sq. mi. It is bounded by the counties of Norfolk and Suffolk on the east, Essex, Bedfordshire and Hertfordshire on the south, Huntingdonshire, Northamptonshire, and Lincolnshire on the west, and Lincolnshire and Norfolk on the north. There are low chalk hills in the southern part of the county. The highest elevation, in the Gogmagog Hills, is 220 ft. The northern section of the county, including the Isle of Ely and part of the Great Bedford Level, is in the Fen District. It is flat country, and originally was mostly fen and marsh, but it has been drained, and its now fertile soil produces good crops. Agriculture is the leading industry, with grain the main crop. Brewing and malting are also important. Cambridge, the county town, on the Cam River, is the seat of Cambridge University, which grew up around the religious establishments of the twelfth century. The Isle of Ely was the last stronghold of the Saxons against the Norman conquerors. The county sends one member to Parliament. Pop. 1952, 176,300.

CAMBRIDGE UNIVERSITY, one of England's oldest and foremost institutions of higher learning, located at Cambridge, Cambridgeshire. It comprises numerous colleges dating from the thirteenth, fourteenth, fifteenth, and sixteenth centuries.

History. From the eleventh century the town of Cambridge has been known as a center of learning because of the monasteries which developed there. As a university Cambridge may be said to have originated about 1200. By 1226 its chancellor had been recognized by the king and the pope, and a papal bull officially founding the university was issued in 1318. This act, however, merely gave formal sanction to an institution already a century old. The history of the university contains little of note until the fifteenth century, when the institution became a center of orthodoxy largely through the presence of the mendicant religious orders which at that time made Cambridge an important center of their educational activities. The first of the university's organized colleges was Peterhouse, founded in 1284. It was followed by University Hall, 1326, which became Clare Hall in 1336; Pembroke, 1347; Gonville and Caius College, 1558, an expansion of Gonville Hall, established in 1349; Trinity Hall, 1350; Corpus Christi, 1352; King's, 1441; Queen's, 1475

A view of Dunster House, Harvard University, and the Weeks Memorial Bridge, spanning the Charles River in Cambridge, Mass.

Trinity Library and St. John's College, Cambridge University, England

(originally St. Bernard's, 1446); St. Catherine's, 1475; Jesus, 1497; Christ's, 1505 (which absorbed God's House, 1441); St. John's, 1511; Magdalene, 1542; Trinity, 1546; Emmanuel, 1584; Sidney Sussex, 1588; Downing, 1800; and Selwyn, 1882. In addition to these colleges for men, Girton, 1873, and Newnham, 1875, were established for women.

Outstanding among the university's teachers have been Desiderius Erasmus (1466-1536) who taught Greek; Sir John Cheke (1514-1557), regius professor of Greek; and Thomas Linacre (1460?-1524), eminent humanist. Famous alumni include Thomas Bilney (1495?-1531), martyr and heretic; Robert Barnes (1495-1540), also a martyr and heretic; William Tyndale (1492?-1536), translator of the New Testament and the Pentateuch; Martin Bucer (1491-1551) who also served as professor of theology; and Thomas Cramer (1489-1556), reformer and archbishop of Canterbury.

Administration. Cambridge, like all British universities, is a corporate, autonomous institution, controlled by a voluntary society, having its own government, regulating its own finances, and exercising the right to appoint its own staff and to control all university affairs. In no sense is Cambridge a national or state university. In this connection one writer has stated that "the British universities are the creation of the British nation, not of the British state." It is true that Cambridge is financially aided by local governing authorities and by the national treasury, but such aid does not infringe upon the autonomy of the institution. The governing bodies of Cambridge have always been the resident bodies; in other words, the faculty controls the entire life of the university. Moreover, each college within the university is autonomous. The Cambridge colleges are small, averaging about 270 students each. The central university unit, however, has expanded in more recent years, particularly in science. Cambridge is a residential and tutorial university. The faculty consists of approximately 300 members, and the student enrollment is usually about 5,000.

Curriculum and Facilities. The curriculum for the university as a whole is broad and modern, placing strong emphasis upon philosophy, science, ancient and modern languages, and mathematics, and giving increasing recognition to the importance of engineering, agriculture, medicine, and law. History and psychology, likewise, have well-developed departments.

The scientific laboratories include the famous Cavendish Laboratory for physical research; the chemical laboratory; the laboratories in engineering, psychology, physiology, biochemistry, and biophysics; and the pathological laboratory.

There are several museums, among them an archaeological and an ethnological museum, and the Fitzwilliam Museum. The Molteno Institute of Animal Parasitology, the Captain Scott Polar Research Institute, and the solar physics observatory are notable university units. Two theological seminaries also are included within the university.

The Cambridge library of more than 1,000,000 volumes is distributed among the many colleges. It dates from the early part of the fifteenth century. There are many notable collections in theology, law, the classics, topography, and medicine. More than 10,000 manuscripts are catalogued, among them the Codex Bezae of the four Gospels and the Acts. Trinity College alone has more than 100,000 volumes and 2,000 manuscripts, including the Capell Collection of Shakespearean literature, German theology, and philosophy. Clare College owns the George Ruggle collection of early Italian and Spanish plays. The Gonville and Caius College library contains numerous ancient manuscripts, and King's College possesses numerous oriental manuscripts. Magdalene College owns the Pepysian collection and Peterhouse has a unique collection of manuscript music. Semitic literature is featured in the Queen's College library, and St. John's has large numbers of early printed books on English history.

Architecturally, Cambridge University is notable particularly for the buildings of King's College, the chapel of which is famous for its stained glass windows and fan vaulting. Among the museums, the Fitzwilliam has noteworthy architecture.   A. L. H-Q.

CAMBYSES II [kambai'siz], king of Persia from 528 to 521 B.C., succeeded to the throne on the death of his father, Cyrus the Great. He is chiefly remembered for his conquest of Egypt in 525 B.C. Aided by Phanes, a mercenary soldier who had deserted the Egyptian army, Cambyses was able to overcome the feeble resistance offered by Psammetichus III at Pelusium in 525 B.C. and captured Memphis. After the outlying provinces in the west, Cyrene and Libya, had recognized his authority, Cambyses sent a strong force to take the oasis of Sivah in the Libyan desert, but the entire force is said to have perished in a sandstorm. A subsequent campaign against the Ethiopians to the east was equally unsuccessful. Soon afterward Cambyses became insane, and his death occurred in 522 B.C.; it is uncertain whether he committed suicide or died of blood poisoning.   T. B. J.

CAMDEN, WILLIAM (1551-1623), English antiquary and historian, was born in London on May 2, 1551, and was educated at St. Paul's School and Oxford. At an early age he started to accumulate the great mass of antiquarian material necessary for his great work, *Britannia, sive florentissimorum regnorum Angliae, Scotiae, Hiberniae, et insularum adjacentium ex intima antiquitate chorographica descriptio* ("Britannia; or A Geographical Description from Remote Antiquity of the Most Excellent Kingdoms of England, Scotland, Ireland, and the Neighboring Isles"), a work which was first published in 1586. Meanwhile he earned his living as a schoolmaster at Westminster School, using the long holidays to travel over England and study the relics of its past. *Britannia,* a topographical and historical survey, achieved great success at home and abroad; six editions appeared in Camden's lifetime, and it was first translated into English in 1610. In 1597 Camden was relieved from financial anxiety by being appointed Clarenceux King-of-Arms, one of the three members of the Herald's College. In 1605 he published his *Remains,* containing material left over from the compilation of *Britannia.* The first volume of his more famous *An-*

nales rerum Anglicarum et Hibernicarum regnante Elizabetha, a history of the reign of Queen Elizabeth down to 1588, appeared in 1615; the second volume, bringing the account down to the accession of James I in 1603, was published posthumously in 1625. In 1622 he founded what is today the Camden Professorship of Ancient History at Oxford. This simple, honest, and remarkably industrious man was one of the founders of English historiography. He died at Chislehurst, Nov. 9, 1623.   E. R. A.

CAMDEN, a city in south central Arkansas, the county seat of Ouachita Co., at the head of navigation on the Ouachita River, located 98 mi. south of Little Rock. It is served by the St. Louis Southwestern, the Missouri Pacific and the Chicago, Rock Island and Pacific railroads, and by river craft. A mayor and board of aldermen head the city government. Camden is a shipping center for cotton, livestock, poultry, truck crops, and fruit. Local industries produce paper products, furniture, art pottery, and asphalt roofing. Wood working, cotton ginning, machine shop and foundry work are also activities of the city. Natural resources of the area include lumber, oil, and lignite. Pop. 1950, 11,372.

CAMDEN, a city in southwestern New Jersey, a port of entry, and the county seat of Camden Co., is situated about 26 mi. south of Trenton. It is located on the Delaware River opposite Philadelphia, Pa., with which it is connected by rail, a suspension bridge, and the Walt Whitman Bridge. The site was discovered in 1631 by Commander DeVries, a Dutchman, and in 1638 was settled by a Swedish colony. In 1681 William Cooper built a home on a point of land below Cooper River and named it Pyne Poynt. From here he ran a ferry to Philadelphia. In 1773 Jacob Cooper, a descendant of William Cooper, laid out a town site and named it after the Earl of Camden. The city was first incorporated in 1828 and in 1844 was made the seat of Camden Co. Camden was reincorporated under a revised charter in 1871 and has the commission form of government. During the Revolutionary War the city was the scene of considerable fighting and was occupied alternately by American and British troops. Camden was the home of the poet Walt Whitman and his homestead is maintained by the city as a museum. Whitman's body is buried in Harleigh Cemetery. Camden is also the seat of the College of South Jersey and the South Jersey Division of the School of Law, both of which are units of Rutgers State University. The city's products include soups, pens, linoleum, leather goods, pharmaceuticals, phonograph records, steel, and textiles. As a shipping center it became an important factor in the nation's efforts to maintain a huge merchant fleet during World War II. Pop. 1950, 124,555.

CAMDEN, the seat of Kershaw Co. in north central South Carolina, is situated on the Wateree River about 30 mi. northeast of Columbia. It lies in the heart of the sandhills or long-leaf pine belt and is the state's oldest inland community, having been settled as early as 1733. In 1758 it was permanently settled by Irish Quakers and named Pine Tree Hill. In 1768 a charter was granted by George III, and about 1774 the name was changed to honor Lord Camden, a champion of colonial rights. Camden was incorporated in 1791 and has the mayor-manager-commission form of government. The agricultural area for which the city is a trade center produces cotton, tobacco, and grain as its principal crops. Camden is unusually rich in historical associa-

tions. Lord Cornwallis made it the principal British garrison in the state, and fourteen battles of the Revolutionary War were fought within a radius of 30 mi. Most important were the Battle of Camden (Aug. 16, 1780), in which the Americans were defeated, and the Battle of Hobkirk Hill (Apr. 25, 1781), in which the British captured the town. A "Little Declaration of Independence," drawn up at Camden on Nov. 5, 1774, was a forerunner of those of Mecklenburg and Philadelphia. As an active Confederate storehouse in the Civil War, the city was virtually burned to the ground by General Sherman's troops in February 1865. Camden's industries manufacture textiles, synthetic fibers, pulpwood, lumber, veneers, cottonseed oil and meal, farm and textile machinery, corn and meat products, and iron castings. Pop. 1950, 6,986.

CAMDEN, BATTLE OF (Aug. 16, 1780), a British victory in the Revolutionary War. After the capture of General Benjamin Lincoln and his American army in Charleston in May 1780, General Horatio Gates, who had rightly or wrongly won much glory as the conqueror of General John Burgoyne at Saratoga, was sent with Continental troops under General Baron de Kalb to oppose the British drive from the south. They went slowly, gathering reinforcements of local militia. The British had collected stores at Camden, S.C., which was on the main road from Charleston into the interior. Gates and Cornwallis, on the same day, planned surprise attacks, and the two forces met midway between Gates' camp and Camden. When the Americans saw the British, the militia ran without making a stand. The regular troops fought but were killed or captured almost to a man. Baron de Kalb was among those mortally wounded.

                                                                M. Je.

CAMEL, a ruminant, *Camelus,* domesticated in Arabia, northern Africa, and most of Asia. For centuries, domesticated camels have proved indispensable in the deserts of

KEYSTONE VIEW CO.

BACTRIAN CAMEL

Asia and Africa for riding and draft purposes. Their flesh has provided meat; their hair, cloth; and their bones, ivory. The milk is extremely rich and nutritious.

One of the animal's three stomachs contains "water-cells" which can store as much as 1½ gal. of water, enough to last for about three days. In the one or two humps on the animal's back, reserve food is stored in the form of fat.

Two species of camels are recognized. The single-humped

dromedary, *C. dromedarius,* is a native of Arabia, but has existed for some time only in captivity. It has short hair, long legs, and is 6 to 7 ft. tall at the shoulder. It can maintain a swinging trot at 9 mi. an hour for many hours, and can cover 100 mi. in a day. It is used mostly as a saddle animal. The two-humped camel, *C. bactrianus,* has long hair, shorter legs, and larger feet. It is slower, but a much better pack animal than the dromedary. It can carry 500 to 1,000 lb. 25 to 30 mi. in a day. One of the two races of this species still occurs in Chinese Turkestan and Mongolia.

                                                        V. H. C.

CAMELLIA [kəmiʹliə; kəmɛʹliɑ], a genus of evergreen shrubs or small trees (40 ft.) of the tea family, native to Asia. These are tender plants much grown as ornamentals

COURTESY OF NEW YORK BOTANICAL GARDENS

CAMELLIA, CAMELLIA SASANQUA

outdoors in mild climates and in greenhouses in the north. *C. japonica,* usually a shrub, may reach 40 ft. It has glossy broad leaves, dark above, light below, and flat, many-petaled, waxy flowers, red to white, with pink and striped varieties. *C. sasanqua* is more straggly, with smaller flowers and *C. reticulata* is larger, with crimson-rose flowers sometimes 7 in. across. The many beautiful varieties of *C. japonica* are increasingly popular for gardens in mild parts of the United States. Camellias often are called japonicas.   E. R. C.

CAMELOPARDALIS [kæʹmələpɑʹrdəlɪs], the Giraffe, a northern constellation, named in recent times, between Ursa Major and Cassiopeia. It includes an extensive area of the sky extending from about declination 52° almost to the north celestial pole. In it are no stars brighter than of the fourth magnitude, and relatively few even of these.

                                                        J. H. P.

CAMELOT [kæʹmələt], the traditional and legendary capital of King Arthur's realm. Authorities disagree as to its actual location in Britain. Caxton, in his Preface to Sir Thomas Malory's *Morte d'Arthur,* refers to Camelot as a town in Wales, yet Malory himself identifies it several times with Winchester. In the French romances upon which Malory drew there was no attempt to associate Camelot with a definite place. It was described simply as an "adventurous" and delightful city, or as a place which the Saracens held in Britain. It is sometimes identified with Cadbury in Somersetshire, where a space on a hilltop, surrounded by a trench, is known locally as "Arthur's Round Table." There are other suggestions that the center of King Arthur's activities

may have been in the north of Britain. All of these nebulous associations bear out Tennyson's lines in the Epilogue to the *Idylls of the King* when he speaks of Arthur as

> . . . that gray king whose name, a ghost,
> Streams like a cloud, man-shaped, from mountain peak,
> And cleaves to cairn and cromlech still.

Whatever and wherever Camelot was, there is no disputing its central place in the Arthurian legend as the capital of the kingdom and the home of the Round Table. There Arthur was married to Guinevere in the church of St. Stephen's "with grete solempnité"; there the Grail was brought into the presence of the assembled knights; there many tournaments and high festivals were held. Most of the romances say nothing of the city after Arthur's death. However, in the *Mort Arthur* of the prose cycle long attributed to Robert de Boron, King Mark of Cornwall, hoping to absorb the fallen Arthur's kingdom, lays waste most of the city of Camelot and destroys the Round Table.   N. C. S.

CAMENAE [kəmiʹni], in Roman mythology, fountain nymphs who had the power of prophecy and were identified with the Greek Muses. The most important of the Camenae was Carmenta.   G. E. D.

CAMEO [kæʹmio], a term used to denote engraved art work in relief on precious or semiprecious hard stones, on glass imitation stones (known as "pastes"), or sometimes on the shells of mollusks. Cameo engraving on gems, rings, or other ornaments is the obverse of intaglio engraving, in which the design is incised below the surface. Cameos are therefore purely decorative and, unlike intaglios, do not have a secondary function as seals or signets. Introduced in Greece in the Hellenistic period, about the fourth century B.C., cameos later became very popular in Rome, where portraits and mythological or historical scenes were favorite subjects with the engravers.   C. W. D.

CAMERA (Latin *camera,* chamber), an enclosed box, tube, or bellows chamber with an aperture or opening through which the image of an object is recorded on a light-sensitive material. In all but the pinhole camera the aperture is fitted with a lens, by which the rays of light are directed to the recording material. The several types of cameras, in their approximate order of development, are as follows:

(1) *Pinhole.* The simplest type, without a lens.

(2) *Fixed-Focus.* So called because their lenses cannot be adjusted for picture taking at various distances. Available in box, folding, twin-lens reflex, and miniature styles; used almost exclusively for picture taking outdoors in sunshine.

(3) *Folding.* With adjustments for focusing and exposure; the most popular "family type" camera.

(4) *Single-Lens Reflex.* In the past, used principally for outdoor press photography and heavy-duty snapshooting; the first camera to offer a full-size preview up to the instant of snapping the shutter.

(5) *Twin-Lens Reflex.* One of the most popular types; used for both professional and amateur photography.

(6) *35-Millimeter.* Used principally by photojournalists and amateur photographers and for the making of 2- × 2-in color slides.

(7) *Miniature.* A precision instrument, with up to 2¼- × 3¼-in. negative. Extremely popular in fields where versatility and portability are important; can be used with roll film, film packs, or sheet film.

(8) *Press.* A heavy-duty type, taking pictures 2¼ × 3¼ in., 3¼ × 4¼ in., or 4 × 5 in.; employed extensively in newspaper and general publication photography.

(9) *View.* Intended primarily for studio work; used extensively for portraiture, commercial photography, architectural photography, and other fields in which large negative size and multiple adjustments are particularly helpful.

(10) *Motion Picture.* Used for movie making in both amateur and

professional sizes; attachments for recording sound on film available in the professional types.

(11) *High-Speed Motion Picture.* Intended specifically for scientific and industrial use; takes as many as 8,500 pictures a second; used to study the motion of high-speed machines and other objects where the action is too fast for the eye to follow.

(12) *Microfilm.* Used to reduce and record documents on film; particularly helpful where a large mass of reference material must be stored in a small space.

In addition to the types mentioned above, there are more or less specialized cameras, including television, aerial, recording, spectroscopic, and photomicrographic.

All cameras are constructed on the same basic principles as were the first crude, wooden, box cameras made over a century ago. The essential parts of a camera are: (1) a light-tight box or bellows, (2) a lens to form the image on the film, (3) a shutter to measure exposures when light is admitted to the film in the camera, (4) a negative holder or carrier to hold films in position during exposure, and (5) a view finder or ground glass to determine picture area. These component parts fulfill the requirements for the simple box camera or the view camera.

By the addition of special accessories and other refinements, the utility and scope of the camera may be extended to meet almost any photographic requirement. Note, for example, the expensive miniature cameras, the complicated recording cameras used in high-speed testings, and the huge astronomical cameras. Refinements in cameras include focusing scale; coupled range finder; adjustable lens diaphragm; focusing lens; variable shutter speeds; reflex, eye level, and wire view finders; depth-of-field index; swing adjustments to correct perspective; film counters; mechanism to prevent double exposure; built-in flash synchronizers; extensions for close-up photography; a tripod socket; and interchangeable backs for films or plates.

Camera design has kept pace with the many improvements. The first Daguerre camera was a crude wooden box with a lens at one end and a place to insert the sensitized plate at the other. New cameras appeared with changes on the original pattern. But it was not until the beginning of

Typical box camera with flash attachment

EASTMAN KODAK PHOTO

the twentieth century that important camera changes started coming from the manufacturers in the United States, England, France, and Germany, where the most important advances were made. Up until 1890 the view camera, which used glass plates, was the standard equipment. Then with the perfection of the roll film by the Eastman Kodak Company a radical change took place in camera design. This new film made possible the development of the modern box camera, the folding camera, miniature cameras, and even the amateur and professional motion picture industry. Today the camera-manufacturing business runs into millions

of dollars annually with over 35 million camera owners in the United States alone. Most of these use the average snapshot type, which is not complicated in its operation.

PRINCIPAL TYPES

There is no one camera which can be used for every photographic purpose. Photography is more than just making

Typical folding camera with f/3.5 lens, coupled range finder, and between-the-lens shutter with 9 speeds to 1/500 sec.

ANSCO PHOTO

snapshots. The average amateur likes a simple, easily operated camera; the news photographer requires a press-type camera, with larger film size and fast shutter speeds up to 1/1,000 sec.; a commercial photographer needs an 8 × 10-in. view camera when making architectural or industrial pictures; the laboratory technician may use a complicated recording camera; the advanced amateur and publication photographer may use a reflex or 35-mm. camera. Obviously, the selection of a camera depends on its later use.

The hundreds of different cameras fall into nine main classifications. When the photographer is familiar with these groupings, it is much easier to choose the camera suited to his particular requirements. Many photographers have two or more cameras in order to meet their needs.

Fixed-Focus and Box Cameras. The box type of camera is one of the simplest cameras made. It actually consists of a light-tight box, a lens set at a fixed distance from the roll film, and a reflecting view finder. Millions of people have taken their first pictures with this type of camera. There are no focusing adjustments or lens-speed settings. The camera is simply loaded, aimed at the subject by using the reflecting view finder, and the shutter released to make the exposure. This type of camera usually has a very simple lens designed to give good average results. Its relative aperture of the lens may be from f/11 to f/16. Those box cameras which have built-in flash synchronization can be used indoors as easily as they are used outdoors in daylight.

Folding Roll-Film Cameras. The important features of the folding camera are compactness, a collapsible bellows between the lens and the camera body, adjustable diaphragm and shutter speeds, focusing scale, usually a better lens than those on box cameras, and several types of view finders. The folding feature of this camera makes it very desirable when traveling as well as for ordinary use when the camera is packed in a suitcase or carried over the shoulder. There is no ground-glass back for focusing in the folding camera, which uses roll film instead of cut-sheet films or plates. The average lens apertures are around f/3.5 and f/6.3. Of late years the folding cameras have been improved by adding a built-in range finder coupled to the lens. With it, the photographer can eliminate inaccuracies when judging distances between object and camera. Coupled range finders were first introduced on the 35mm. miniature cameras.

Miniature Cameras. The development of miniature cameras started with the first introduction of the Leica camera by Ernst Leitz of Wetzlar, Germany, in 1923. This camera was a real precision instrument, which used 5-ft. lengths of standard perforated 35mm. motion picture film. It also had a focal-plane shutter, speeds up to 1/500 sec., optical view finder, accessory range finder, anastigmat lens in collapsible mount, a film exposure counter, and a mechanism to prevent double exposures on the same film area. Photographers were slow to realize the advantages in using such a small camera which could be carried in the coat pocket. After 1930 the real miniature-camera boom started when the term "candid photography" was popularized by the use of many unposed photographs which began to appear in the magazines. A few years later the Contax camera, similar to the Leica, was made by Zeiss in Germany.

The better-made 35mm. miniature cameras offer many important features. There is a wide choice of film available because these cameras use the same films manufactured for the professional 35mm. motion picture cameras. One loading is sufficient to make about 36 $1 \times 1\frac{1}{2}$-in. exposures. When this film is developed in a fine-grain developer, excellent enlargements exceeding 11×14 in. may be made. The original cost of film per picture is negligible. Focal-plane shutter speeds up to 1/1,000 sec. are possible. The built-in lens-coupled range finders give accurate automatic focusing. Interchangeable lenses make it possible to use the 35mm. miniature cameras for ordinary snapshots or for long-focus photography when photographing objects at a distance.

35mm. Miniature camera with interchangeable lens feature, coupled range finder, rapid-wind film advance, double-exposure prevention, exposure counter, and shutter speeds from 1 to 1/1000 sec.

E. LEITZ PHOTO

Wide-angle lenses are available for photographing scenes which cannot be obtained with the regular lenses.

With the introduction of 35mm. Kodachrome film in 1935, followed by Anscocolor, miniature cameras really came into their own. Photographers now had the opportunity of photographing in natural colors and then using the finished color positives for projection when mounted in 2×2-in. lantern slides. Fine color reproductions from 35mm. color film could also be made for illustrations in publications. Color was only one of the applications for the 35mm. camera. It has also been used for making fast-sequence pictures, for important industrial recording work, in photomicrography, in all types of close-up copying, and in medical and stereoscopic photography. The versatility of 35mm. cameras has grown with each new development in films, flash equipment, lenses, and other accessories.

After the development of the 35mm. cameras the term "miniature camera" was also applied to cameras using larger roll films. These larger cameras adopted some of the original miniature-camera features, such as coupled range finder, interchangeable lenses, film counters, and new designs. To-

day the term miniature camera may be applied to cameras which make negatives up to $2\frac{1}{4} \times 3\frac{1}{4}$ in.

Twin-lens reflex camera

BURLEIGH BROOKS, INC.

Reflex Cameras. There are two types of reflex cameras: twin-lens and single-lens. These cameras are designed on the principle of the simple reflecting view finder. The image formed by the taking or auxiliary lens is reflected onto a mirror which directs the image to the viewing ground-glass surface at the top or back of the camera. The advantage of this reflecting principle is that the image seen on the ground glass will be exactly the same as on the film at the instant of exposure. The photographer has the added advantage of seeing this full negative-size image right up to the instant of exposure.

The twin-lens reflex cameras have two matched lenses, one for taking the picture and the other for use as an extremely accurate reflecting view finder. The image is reflected upon the viewing glass by means of the auxiliary lens. The camera user cannot see the actual depth of field when the diaphragm of the taking lens is closed to smaller openings. There is usually a depth-of-field scale available on a card or on the camera for checking on the nearest and farthest sharp images produced by the taking lens.

The single-lens reflex camera, made in various negative sizes from 35mm. to 5×7 in., has a reflecting mirror which picks up the image from the taking lens and projects it to the

Single-lens reflex camera

ground glass at the top or back of the camera. A light-excluding hood surrounds the image on the ground glass. A late refinement is an automatic diaphragm release which is synchronized with the shutter release lever. In use, the lens diaphragm is set at any smaller stop from the full opening; then at the instant of exposure the diaphragm closes automatically to the predetermined opening as the picture is made. The single-lens reflex cameras in the larger negative sizes are usually quite bulky and heavy, lacking the versatility of the lighter twin-lens reflexes. However, they give larger negatives which may ensure sharper images for big enlargements.

Cut-Sheet Film-Pack Cameras. Cut-sheet film-pack cameras are related to the folding cameras but with the additional feature of having a ground-glass back for focusing and a holder for sheet films or plates. With an adapter, they accept roll film. Other refinements may include longer bellows extension and provision for attaching a lens-coupled range finder. Press-type cameras are of this classification.

Studio and View Cameras. These have been the main cameras used in professional and commercial photography since the camera was first made. They represent the simplest type of equipment: lens, bellows, and a rigid back to hold the ground glass for focusing and also the film or plate holders. A tripod is essential for holding the view camera in a fixed position while in use. The 8 × 10-in. view camera is the average size used for most commercial photography. But there are larger sizes and also smaller ones with negative dimensions down to 3¼ × 4¼ in. Larger view cameras produce negatives for contact printing and enlarging.

VIEW CAMERA WITH MONORAIL BED

GRAFLEX PHOTO

Motion Picture Cameras. The introduction of color films has stimulated interest in 8mm. and 16mm. motion picture cameras among amateur photographers.

8mm. Cameras. The 8mm. cameras are compact instruments accepting either a roll or magazine of 16mm. (double 8mm.) film. The film is inserted in the film chamber and, after being run through the camera once, is removed, turned over, and reloaded for a second run through the camera. This results in two strips of exposures on the single 25-ft. length of 16mm.-wide film. After processing, the film is slit down the middle and the two pieces spliced together end-to-end to give one 50-ft. length of 8mm. film. Those who select 8mm. movie cameras do so primarily for reasons of economy. While many 8mm. movie cameras cost as much as some 16mm. cameras, film cost is greatly reduced.

16mm. Cameras. The serious amateur movie maker generally works with a 16mm. camera since the larger picture area (four times) on the film gives better image quality on the screen. Amateur 8mm. movie cameras range from single-lens, fixed focus, magazine-loading types to multiple-lens,

turret models with such built-in professional features as frame counters, reverse-wind, variable shutter, synchronous motor (electric) drive, and sound recording.

Amateur motion picture cameras are generally powered by a hand-wound spring motor which drives sprockets and a take-up spool in the film chamber or magazine to transport the film across the picture aperture. Simultaneously, the

TYPICAL PRESS-TYPE CAMERA

GRAFLEX PHOTO

motor drives a pulldown claw which thrusts into a sprocket hole of the film, pulls the film down into place behind the exposure aperture, withdraws and moves into position again to draw down the next frame of film. While the film intermittently passes the exposure aperture, a revolving shutter blade permits light to enter so that an image focused by the lens is recorded. This action continues to expose a series of pictures so long as the release button is held down. Most 8mm. and 16mm. motion picture cameras permit the photographer to shoot at different rates of speed for certain effects; speeded-up motion, 8 frames per second (fps); normal speed (silent), 16 fps; normal speed (sound), 24 fps; slow motion, 32 or 64 fps. Many 16mm. movie makers work at 24 fps to get steadier pictures and to add sound to their films.

Sound Films. Sound may be added to 16mm. films in four ways: (1) by recording an optical tract on a "print" of the originally exposed film; (2) by synchronizing projection with specially recorded discs that carry narration and a musical and sound effects background; (3) by synchronizing projection with a tape-recorded sound track; and (4) by use of a magnetic sound track on the film. In the last a stripe

TYPICAL 8MM. AMATEUR MOTION PICTURE CAMERA

REVERE CAMERA CO.

of magnetic oxide is permanently bonded along one edge of the processed and edited film. With a 16mm. projector having a magnetic recording-playback head or accessory attachment, a sound track of near professional quality can be recorded on the magnetic oxide stripe as the film is projected. After rewinding, the film with sound is ready for showing. Errors and even the entire sound track can be erased, and corrections or a new track can be re-recorded with ease. Reasonably good lip synchronization is possible. Few amateurs, however, use this technique because of the high cost of the equipment necessary.

16mm. amateur motion picture camera with triple lens turret, reverse wind, frame counter, focusing finder, and single-frame exposure mechanism

Magnetic striping on 8mm. film has not been practical because the slow speed of film through the projector does not allow satisfactory sound fidelity. In 1956, 8mm. projectors with synchronous motor drives were marketed, making good synchrony of the projector with a tape recorder possible and allowing 8mm. movie makers to show films with synchronized narration, plus musical and sound effects background.

Stereo Cameras. The introduction of the Stereo Realist 3-D camera by the David White Co., of Milwaukee, Wis., in 1947, revived the popularity of three-dimensional photography, which had fallen off in the 1920's. The Stereo Realist was designed for use by the beginner, the amateur, and the professional photographer. It and competitive cameras marketed by other manufacturers used 35mm. color film and produced two alternately spaced transparencies with a single exposure. With variable shutter speeds of up to 1/300 sec. and lenses of f/2.8 maximum aperture, 3-D cameras can take pictures under almost all conditions. They generally incorporate such other features as coupled range finders, bubble (spirit) levels, exposure counters, and flash-synchronized shutters. After processing, the matching pairs of color transparencies are mounted in slides for viewing.

TYPICAL 35MM. STEREO CAMERA

Adapting Conventional Cameras to 3-D. With the use of accessory lenses and lens attachments, conventional 35mm. cameras can take stereo pictures. A beam splitter has been made available for cameras with noninterchangeable lenses, and twin lenses in a single mount have been marketed for cameras with interchangeable lenses. Both enable the con-

ventional 35mm. camera to take two matching pictures simultaneously on a single $1 \times 1\frac{1}{2}$-in. frame of film.

Viewing Stereo Pictures. Stereo slides are looked at through hand viewers or by projection. The hand viewer has two eyepieces, a slot in which the slide is placed, and either AC- or battery-powered illumination. To ensure even illumination, light is passed through a diffuser before it reaches the slide. Adjustments for interocular spacing, as well as focusing, are provided.

To project stereo pictures, the slide is placed in the path of two beams of polarized light. The two polarized images thrown on the screen are viewed as a single three-dimensional picture through spectacles having polarized lenses.

Polaroid Land camera showing dry, positive print which is removed from back of camera one minute after the exposure is made

Polaroid Land Camera. These folding-type cameras are capable of producing positive prints within one minute after the picture has been snapped. Four models have been introduced. Three give $3\frac{1}{4} \times 4\frac{1}{4}$-in. pictures; one gives $2\frac{1}{2} \times 3\frac{1}{2}$-in. pictures. The Model 110 "Pathfinder" has a between-the-lens shutter with speeds up to 1/400 sec., a coupled range finder, and an f/4.5 lens; the others have an interconnected shutter and diaphragm system which sets the lens opening and the shutter speed simultaneously when a dial is turned to a number. Maximum and minimum lens apertures on these models range from f/8.8 to f/50, while shutter speeds vary from 1/8 sec. through 1/100 sec. The back from a Polaroid Land camera can be used in place of the conventional film holder on certain press- and view-type cameras.

Special Cameras. With new photographic applications being developed every year, the requirements for more specialized cameras grow rapidly. In the medical field there are the eye camera, the endoscopic camera, and a camera which takes flash pictures of the stomach interior. The United States Navy with Douglas Winnek has developed a trivision camera for making stereoscopic pictures which are viewed direct, without the usual stereo viewer.

Another specialized camera is an automatic camera which takes up to 100 ft. of 70-mm. film and makes $2\frac{1}{2} \times 2\frac{1}{2}$- or $2\frac{1}{2} \times 3$-in. negatives. This camera is used for portrait and baby photography. It can also be used for instrument recording where the larger negative size is desired. A fluoro-record camera makes records directly from the X-ray fluorescent screen. A special camera was used for recording the atomic-bomb tests at Bikini in the summer of 1946. It has also been used to photograph action scenes, from the take-off of a jet-propelled plane to the finish of horse races. A camera has also been developed for photographing the radar-screen image during the flight of an airplane.

There are many types of specialized recording cameras for industrial use. The astronomer has adapted a camera for use on the huge telescopes for recording distant stars and planets. At important sporting events, political conventions, or other occasions which draw huge crowds, Big Bertha cameras are used by press photographers for taking long-distance action pictures. The Big Bertha is similar to a 5 × 7-in. camera, but with a lens of 40- or 60-in. focal length and additional focusing controls and frame.

The publication photographer may also use a camera which records up to 120 action pictures per second. This camera is useful when photographing the successive motions of a baseball pitcher in action or the brilliant run of a football player. After development the best negatives in the series are selected for enlargement and use in the magazine or newspaper.

Aerial Cameras. Aerial cameras serve in war and peace. These cameras were the aerial reconnaisance eyes of the military forces during World War II and recorded strategic enemy moves and locations. In peace the aerial camera may serve for charting new polar regions, surveying a coast line, or photographing a city. There are many types of aerial cameras, ranging in negative size from 4 × 5 to 9 × 18 in. Many of them operate automatically from the pilot seat of the airplane. There are five-lens and nine-lens aerial cameras designed for use on large mapping projects where speed and economy are required. The nine-lens camera has a tremendous area coverage on its 23 × 23-in. negative. One negative can cover an area of over 120 sq. mi.

ROLLEIFLEX CAMERA IN
ROLLEIMARIN HOUSING
FOR UNDERWATER PHO-
TOGRAPHY

BURLEIGH BROOKS. INC.

Underwater Cameras. Although specialized cameras are available for underwater photography, several conventional cameras may be used by enclosing them in watertight housings designed for the purpose. With such equipment, pictures can be taken at depths as great as 180 ft.

Miniature vs. Larger Cameras. The smaller cameras make negatives too small for the usual contact prints. The larger cameras give good-quality negatives from 2¼ × 3¼ in. up. These larger negatives make good-sized contact prints. Equipment for making contact prints is much simpler and cheaper than the apparatus required for enlargements.

CAMERA PARTS

Familiarity with some of the mechanical parts helps in selecting and operating the camera. Types of shutters are described subsequently in this article. The following parts should also be considered.

Diaphragm. The amount or quantity of light which passes through the shutter is measured by the diaphragm. The majority of lenses have the adjustable iris type of diaphragm. The simpler cameras have a movable slide with fixed apertures. A greater range of adjustments is naturally available with the adjustable type.

Lens. The familiar axiom that a camera is as good as its lens has a great deal of truth. A good accurate shutter is also important for the best results. Lens and shutter are one of the most important combinations of the camera. A lens must be actually used to determine its quality for the photographer. A responsible manufacturer will endeavor to produce the best lenses possible for the various price classes.

Focusing. All cameras except the fixed-focus types have provision for focusing the lens to make the image sharp on the film or plate. Usually there is a focusing scale mounted on the bed of the camera for making the proper adjustments. Some lenses have a focusing scale on the lens mount. The lens-coupled range finder is still another accurate means of adjusting the lens when focusing upon an object. The focusing adjustments on a camera are important and should be checked occasionally for accuracy.

Film Holder. The film holder keeps the roll or cut-sheet film in one plane at the back of the camera during exposure, an important factor in obtaining a sharp image. In the roll-film cameras the film is advanced from the supply spool over protective rollers, past the image-plane opening, to the winding or take-up spool. The film is held flat by the rear pressure plate of the camera and under tension. Some cameras use cut-sheet film holders that hold one or two sheets of film, magazine-type holders for six exposures and/or film packs containing a dozen film sheets. These film holders are inserted at the back of the camera when ready for use.

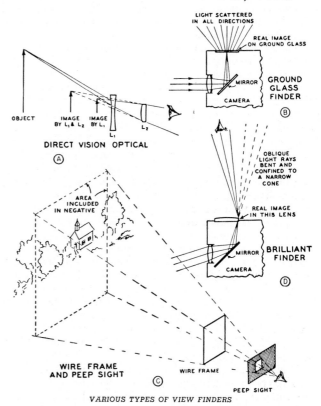

VARIOUS TYPES OF VIEW FINDERS

View Finders. A view finder shows the photographer just what the camera sees. There are various types (see illustration), such as the reflecting ground-glass finder (B), used on the box type of cameras; the reflecting brilliant finder (D), which has a second lens to receive the image collapsible direct-vision wire-frame finders (C), which have a front-wire negative-size frame above the lens and a rear peep sight at the image plane; and the direct-vision optical view finder (A), which is like a miniature telescope in reverse to give a reduced image of the scene to be photographed.

The reflecting finders are used below eye level, whereas the direct view finders are used at eye level during the picture-taking process. These finders come in various forms and refinements. Some have parallax adjustments which correct for any error between the finder position on the camera and the lens. A few cameras have the view finder combined with the built-in range finder for additional convenience in operation.

There are also other parts and refinements, such as the bellows which excludes light, the tripod socket, the depth-of-field scale, and the self-timer; and special adjustments such as rising front, swing back, and a double-extension bellows.

W. D. M. and E. E. H.

CAMERA SHUTTERS

The camera shutter is a mechanical device which permits, for a controlled time interval, the passage of light from outside the camera to the light-sensitive material inside.

Early Shutters. In pioneer photography, the "shutter" was a cap which fitted over the lens. To make an exposure, the photographer simply removed the lens cap for the minute or more which was required to record an image on the light-sensitive materials of those days. With the introduction of the wet collodion process (about 1850) and subsequent improvements in the sensitivity of photographic emulsions, a number of different types of mechanical shutters were invented. One of the first of these was the simple drop or guillotine shutter, consisting of an opaque screen with a cutout aperture. As the screen was dropped or passed rapidly before the lens, the aperture in the screen allowed light to pass through for a brief interval. Among other types developed were the rotary, roller-blind, single-flap, double-flap, and multiple-flap shutters. W. D. M. and E. E. H.

By far the most common types of shutters are those found on the popular box cameras. While these shutters may vary from one camera model to another, practically all of them are adaptations or refinements of the rotary shutter. They consist of one or two plates which rotate in an arc around an axis located outside the circumference of the lens opening. Their shapes may vary; they may be crescent-shaped or rectangular, with a circular hole cut out of the rectangle at a point which passes over the lens opening. Some double-action rotary shutters have two of these rectangular plates, mounted so that they swing in opposite directions. In passing each other, the holes of the two plates are simultaneously aligned with the lens opening. Box-camera shutters usually give an exposure of about ⅟₃₀ or ⅟₄₀ sec. On some cameras there is a "bulb" setting, at which the shutter remains open as long as the shutter-release lever is held down, permitting manual synchronization of the shutter operation with the firing of flash lamps. This manual synchronization is called the open-flash technique.

With the exception of box-camera shutters, the majority of shutters on modern amateur and professional still cameras are either the between-the-lens or the focal-plane type.

Between-the-Lens Shutters. Most modern between-the-lens shutters consist of a number of thin metal blades which are placed between two lens elements so as to overlap and prevent light from passing through the lens while the blades are at rest. By means of springs, the blades may be made to separate for the desired time interval, after which they are returned to the overlapped position. The time interval is controlled by cams and a chain of gears.

Self-setting. Between-the-lens shutters are further classi-fied as either self-setting or presetting. The self-setting or automatic shutters, with which most of the simpler folding cameras are equipped, do not require cocking. Spring tension is set up by the shutter-release lever during the first part of the shutter tripping motion. Such shutters are usually capable of only a limited range of slower speeds.

Presetting. Presetting or cocking shutters can operate more accurately at a greater range of speeds—often from as slow as one second to 1/400 second or faster. In this type of shutter, the necessary spring tension is produced by the separate action of cocking before the shutter can be tripped. Some roll-film cameras incorporate interconnected shutter-locking and film-advance devices which automatically cock the shutter as the film is advanced.

Speeds. When a between-the-lens shutter is tripped, the shutter blades start separating at the center of the lens aperture and move outward far enough to clear the maximum lens aperture, where they dwell for a controlled period before returning to the overlapped position. Even though the thinnest, lightest-weight material practical is used in their manufacture, a slight amount of time is needed for the blades to overcome friction and inertia in moving. The amount of light that passes during the opening and closing operations is therefore constantly changing, as shown in Fig. 1.

The shutter speeds which are marked on a shutter housing or elsewhere on a camera are not usually intended to corre-

Fig. 1—VARYING AMOUNT OF LIGHT PASSED BY SHUTTER OPENING

spond exactly with the total time during which the shutter is open. Instead, the markings indicate effective exposure time, which is defined as a theoretical time which would be required for the quantity of light actually transmitted through the shutter during one cycle of operation to be transmitted if the shutter were fully open for the indicated period. By stating a shutter speed in terms of effective exposure time, a definite amount of light at a given lens aperture is specified. The total open time is significant as far as motion-stopping characteristics are concerned, but it cannot be an accurate indication of the amount of light actually passed, due to the constantly changing size of the aperture during opening and closing. The concept of basing shutter-speed markings on effective exposure time is relatively new and has been adopted as the American standard.

Efficiency. Efficiency of a between-the-lens shutter is defined as the ratio of the quantity of light actually transmitted at a given shutter setting and lens opening to the amount which would be transmitted if the shutter were fully open for total open time. An efficiency of 100 per cent is impossible to achieve because of the factors of inertia and friction. Fig. 2 shows diagrammatically the efficiency of a hypothetical shutter operated at ⅟₁₀₀ sec. and maximum lens aperture; ⅟₁₀₀ sec. and ¼ maximum lens aperture; and ⅟₁₀ sec. and maximum lens aperture.

The top diagram shows that out of 12.5 milliseconds, about 2.5 are used for the blades to open fully, and about the same amount of time is spent by the blades in closing. The shutter permits light to pass the instant the blades begin to open, and starts reducing the amount of light the instant the blades begin to close. This action is compensated for by taking the half-open position as a basis for measuring shutter efficiency, since area (a), which represents exposure, equals area (b), which represents no exposure. The same relationship exists between areas (d) and (c). On this basis the efficiency of the hypothetical shutter illustrated is about 78 per cent.

The lower diagram shows that shutter efficiency is greater with slower speeds, since the time required to open and to close the blades constitutes a smaller percentage of the total open time than it does at faster speeds. At 1/10 second and with a fully open lens aperture, the efficiency is about 97 per cent.

Flash Shutters. Most between-the-lens shutters provide for automatic synchronization of the shutter opening with the firing of flashlamps without the use of an external accessory flash synchronizer. Operation of the shutter-release lever closes electrical contacts which are built into the shutter and connected to a battery and flashlamp holder outside the camera. For use with Class M lamps having 20 milliseconds time lag before reaching peak intensity, provision is made for delaying the opening of the shutter so that it is not fully open until the peak of the flash is reached. Class F flashlamps, having only 5 milliseconds time lag, are synchronized by reducing the delay interval, or by by-passing the shutter-delay mechanism—in which case only the slower shutter speeds can be used.

Fig. 3 shows a between-the-lens flash shutter. Flash discharges with no time lag (high-speed flash) are synchronized with shutter-blade action by an electric circuit formed through connector post (k) and closing it at (l) through part (m) which moves upward as blades open. Photoflash lamps with five milliseconds time lag are synchronized by sliding the letter F on the limiting stop (n) opposite index (o). Clockwise movement of lever (p) sets up spring tension through gear train (q) and moves cam (r) upward. Down-

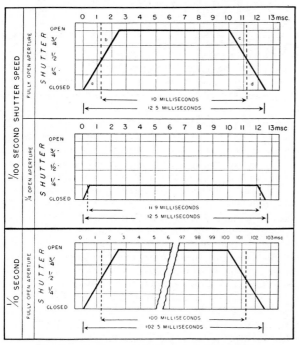

Fig. 2—SHUTTER OPERATION AT VARIOUS SPEEDS

ward pressure on lever (h) now allows its extension (s) to move sideways to cam (t). Lever (u) follows, and opposite end closes contacts (v). This releases gear train which, through downward movement of step between cams (r and t), actuates lever (s) and releases shutter so that blades are fully opened about five milliseconds after electric circuit has been closed. Synchronized flashlamps with 20 milliseconds'

time lag are accomplished similarly. Limiting stop (n) at letter M (o) permits extended movement of lever (p) which, in addition to the action described above, engages oscillating pallet (w). The pallet's action slows down counterclockwise travel of "step," and shutter is released so that the fully open position is reached about 20 milliseconds after contacts (v) have closed.

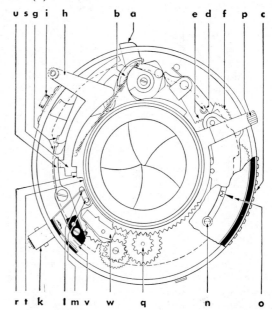

Fig. 3—BETWEEN-THE-LENS SHUTTER WITH FLASH SYNCHRONIZER
(a) Shutter preset; (b) Spring; (c) Shutter speed selector; (d) Cam; (e) Gear sector; (f) Gear train; (g) Time and bulb exposure levers; (h) Release lever; (i) Cable release socket; (k-w) See text

Focal-Plane Shutters. These are curtain-type shutters that operate immediately in front of, and parallel to, the light-sensitive materials in the camera. Unlike between-the-lens shutters, which expose all portions of the film or plate simultaneously, they expose one portion after another. Two variations are the fixed-slit and variable-slit shutters.

Fixed-Slit Shutters. These have a single opaque curtain operating between two rollers located on opposite sides of the picture area. Spaced at intervals along the length of the curtain are slits of varying widths. In operation, part of the curtain is carried from one roller to the other, motivated by spring tension on one of the rollers. Enough of the curtain is wound onto the take-up roller to permit one of the slits to pass before the film or plate. Exposure is selected by winding into position a slit of the desired size and adjusting the amount of spring tension.

Variable-Slit Shutters. These have two curtains close to each other, operating on separate pairs of rollers. One of the curtains has an aperture approximately the same size as the picture area. When a shutter speed is selected, the second curtain is partially drawn over this aperture, forming a slit, the size of which can be varied with the several different exposure settings. When the shutter is released, the two curtains are wound onto their respective take-up rollers, keeping the same relative position to each other so that the slit is not covered. Variable-slit shutters are especially adapted for use in miniature cameras, which cannot conveniently accommodate the longer curtain or the variable spring-tension mechanism required by fixed-slit shutters.

In operation, the curtains move from left to right, shutter speeds from 1/50 to 1/1000 second being determined by width of the curtain opening. Acceleration is compensated for by widening of slit as it travels across film plane. The difference in the diameters of the coaxial rollers at left accomplishes this. Speeds from 1 to 1/25 second are controlled by varying the delay of the lower curtain after the top curtain has completed its run. At bulb setting, the top curtain moves across when the shutter-release button is depressed, and the lower curtain follows when the button is released.

Speeds. Because of inertia, friction, and the increasing diameter of the take-up roller as the curtain is wound onto it, the slit tends to accelerate. This change during travel ends in inequalities of effective exposure over the distance covered by the slit, unless provision is made for counteracting the acceleration. In fixed-slit shutters, a retarding device is sometimes used; in variable-slit shutters the slit is sometimes made to enlarge slightly during its travel.

Effective exposure time at any point along the path of the shutter is equal to $\frac{w}{vs}$, in which w is the width of the shutter slit and vs is the linear velocity of the shutter slit. Exposure times marked on the camera usually are about halfway between the effective exposure times at the beginning and at the end of the slit travel.

The efficiency of a focal-plane shutter depends on the width of the shutter slit, the lens stop used, and the distance between the shutter slit and the light-sensitive material. As a general rule, focal-plane shutters have greater efficiency than between-the-lens shutters at the shorter exposure settings.

Distortion may result when very fast-moving objects are photographed with cameras having focal-plane shutters. If the object image moves across the focal plane in the same direction as the shutter slit, the object in the final photograph may have the appearance of being stretched out. If the image moves in the opposite direction to the shutter slit, the object may appear compressed in the photograph.

Synchronized flash contacts are built into many focal-plane shutters. Connected to an outside battery and flashlamp holder, they close when the shutter is actuated. Time is allowed for the lamp to reach its peak intensity before the shutter slit passes before the film or plate. Special flash lamps having a flash of comparatively long duration must be used, since focal-plane shutters require more time to expose the entire area of the film or plate than do between-the-lens shutters.   D. W. McK.

FLASH EQUIPMENT

Flash photography was used in 1865 when Charles Piazzi Smyth made interior photographs of the Great Pyramid in Egypt by burning strips of magnesium for intense illumination. The use of magnesium flash powder followed, and continued until the invention of the noiseless and smokeless flashlamps in 1929. At first, these marvelous new flashlamps were used for open flash exposures similar to the flash powder methods. The photographer would open the camera shutter, fire the flash, and then close the shutter. The new lamps were a great improvement over the fire hazards and burns of the flash powder. However the open-flash method restricted photography to still objects. The news photographers wanted photographs of action scenes. The next logical step was the development of the synchronizer. With this electrical timing equipment mounted on the camera, the flashlamp burned during the full opening of the camera shutter, which could be set at the faster speeds up to about 1/200 second.

Synchronizers. The flashlamps reached their peak of intensity in about 20 milliseconds while the camera shutter took only 5 milliseconds to reach its full opening. A synchronizer

was essential for correct timing. Such a flash synchronizer included a battery, case with flashlamp socket, reflector, and the synchronizing mechanism which is commonly attached on or near the camera shutter.

Mechanical Synchronizer. Out of the early pioneering stages, two types of flash synchronizers were developed, and are now in common use. One is the mechanical synchronizer, first developed by Morris and Hy Schwartz in 1930-1931. In operation, the mechanical synchronizer is set in motion by pressing a wire cable release mounted on the battery case. This release closes an electrical contact which sends the battery current directly to the flashlamp to ignite the combustible material a fraction of a second before releasing the shutter. By the time the flashlamp is at its full burning peak the camera shutter has reached its full opening.

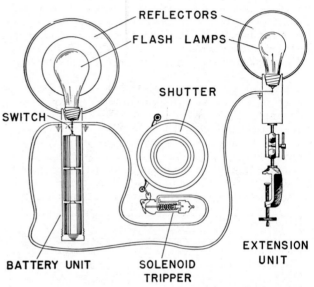

COURTESY OF WILLARD D. MORGAN

Component parts of a typical synchronized flashlamp assembly

Electrical Synchronizer. The all-electrical unit is the other type of synchronizer. It has a solenoid tripper attached directly to the release of the shutter. When the release button on the battery case is pressed, the electric current passes to the flashlamp to give it a head start, and then the mechanism closes the circuit to the electric tripper on the shutter.

Built-in Synchronizer. Cameras were produced in 1942 with built-in flash synchronizing equipment. This eliminated the customary outside synchronizer. An innovation was that adjustments from 0 to 30 milliseconds were provided for use with the electronic speedlamps (0 milliseconds), the midget gas-filled flashlamps (5 milliseconds), and the regular flashlamps (20 to 30 milliseconds). With all these mechanical improvements in synchronizers the lamp manufacturers produced flashlamps of constant firing periods and with various sizes to meet most photographic demands.

Flashlamp. In 1929 J. Ostermeier constructed the first flashlamp, which was filled with aluminum foil and oxygen. From then on photography entered a new era. The photographer was now completely independent of sunlight.

With the use of the flashlamp, containing such an intense light output, it is possible to use smaller diaphragm openings and obtain greater depth of field in the resulting photograph. This is especially true when using the larger cameras with longer focal-length lenses.

Multiple and Remote Lighting. Still another important

feature in the development of flash photography has been the use of multiple and remote lighting. Flashlamps on extension wires attached to the camera synchronizer can be placed in any position around the subject to improve the illumination. In this way natural room illumination can be duplicated, or possibly a complicated machine in a factory is skillfully illuminated from the sides and rear to give a natural effect. It is even possible to use a remote control for tripping the camera.

PRESS-TYPE CAMERA EQUIPPED FOR FLASH PHOTOGRAPHY

This is especially valuable for close-up photography of birds and for night photography of animals. The use of extension flashes can be used when photographing a long banquet table, a street or market scene at night, or a simple Christmas scene when the extension lamp is placed behind a log in the fireplace. Remote flash pictures have even been made of the ocean bottom for scientific studies.

High-Speed Flash Photograhy. Flash photography entered the field of ultra-speed action with the development of the speedlamp by Harold E. Edgerton, at the Massachusetts Institute of Technology just before World War II. With this equipment the photographer could make exposures up to 1/30,000 second. Again, a completely new photographic camera range was open for exploration. A golf ball was "stopped" in flight, the wings of a hummingbird were recorded in action, and even a bullet was "stopped" in flight and recorded on the photographic film. The speedlamp is used at sports events to reveal previously unseen action. This new electronic flash source has also proved invaluable for photographic studio work in photographing the actions of children.

The speedlamp consists of a power unit for operating the flash tube in a reflector. The power unit of the first speedlamp, known as the Kodatron, converts the ordinary 115-volt house current to 2,000 volts by means of a transformer. This current passes through a rectifier and the resulting direct current charges a condenser. The charging cycle takes about 10 seconds. When the release is closed by a synchronizer on the camera the energy stored in the condenser is discharged through the flash tube, causing the xenon gas within the tube to flash. Up to 100,000 flashes have been made with the same flash tube. Late developments in electronic flash equipment provide a flash duration of less than one millionth of a second, as well as compact, inexpensive, portable units for the amateur. The latter are powered by conventional dry batteries, by rechargeable wet cells, or by nickel-cadmium batteries. Their flash durations are usually of the order of 1/500–1/2,000 sec.

B-C (Battery-Capacitor) Flash Photography. B-C flash photography, which has come into wide use, was made possible with equipment first produced by the Kalart Company in 1935. It has been used successfully since that time by professional photographers; however, the original equipment was too bulky for general use. Popular use of this technique had to await improvements in the electrical components. With the small powerful batteries and capacitors now available, various manufacturers have been able to produce small, compact, and lightweight B-C flash equipment, which provides a more positive firing result for single and multiflash circuits. The flashlamps in the B-C system are not fired by the batteries but rather by the capacitor, which draws current from the battery, stores it until the instant of flashing, and then releases it to the lamps with a strong rapid surge.

W. D. M. and E. E. H.

PHOTOGRAPHIC LENSES

Photographic lenses are essentially curved pieces of glass or other transparent materials, used to refract rays of light emanating from an object to form an image on a sensitized surface.

Lens Aperture and Field. A photographic objective lens is well corrected for a high aperture and also for covering a wide field. This is in contrast to telescope or microscope objectives, for example, which give good definition only over a small region close to the lens axis.

Aperture. The aperture of a photographic lens is always expressed as a fraction of the focal length, thus $f/4.5$ or $f/16$, because it can readily be shown that the photographic exposure required does not depend on the actual linear aperture or on the actual focal length of the lens, but only on the ratio of these quantities. Hence a 2-in. $f/2$ lens has the same photographic speed as a 6-in. $f/2$ lens, even though the diameter of the latter lens is three times as great as that of the former lens.

Portable electronic flash unit, consisting of (right) power pack holding dry batteries and (left) flash head and mounting bracket

Field. All photographic lenses must form a sharp image on a flat plate or film, the extent of which depends on the requirements. Thus the angular field to be covered by a lens will be dependent on the film size and on the focal length. Most normal camera lenses cover a 53-deg. field, which means that the picture diagonal is equal to the focal length of the lens. However, motion picture cameras usually cover a field of only about 28-deg., the focal length of the lens being about twice the picture diagonal. This is done deliberately, in order to allow the camera to be set well back from the subject. Many miniature cameras have interchangeable lenses of various focal lengths; in this case, since the picture size is the same for all lenses, the angular field to be covered by each lens varies inversely as the focal length. In cameras equipped with a rising front, the angular covering power of the lens must be great enough to cover the film at the extreme limit of the rising front.

Wide-angle lenses are lenses which cover an angular field much greater than normal, even up to and sometimes exceeding 90 deg. The focal length of a wide-angle lens is thus much shorter than normal for a given camera.

Depth of Field. The range of acceptable object distances, within and beyond the focused plane, is called the "depth of field" of the lens. The usual formulae for computing it are:

$$\text{Far depth} = \frac{s^2 c}{d s' - s c} = \frac{s c}{m d - c},$$
$$\text{Near depth} = \frac{s^2 c}{d s' + s c} = \frac{s c}{m d + c}.$$

In these formulae, s is the distance of the focused plane from the camera lens, s' is the distance from lens to image mathematically expressed as: $s' = f (1 + m)$, c is the acceptable diameter of the "circle of confusion" upon the film, d is the linear clear aperture of the lens, f is its focal length, and m is the magnification, equal to the ratio of image size to object size. The value of d is conveniently found by dividing the focal length of the lens by its f-number. The usually accepted magnitude of c is $1/250$ in. ($1/10$ mm.) for ordinary cameras, $1/500$ in. ($1/20$ mm.) for miniature cameras, $1/1000$ in. ($1/40$ mm.) for 16mm. cinecameras, and $1/2000$ in. ($1/80$ mm.) for 8mm. cinecameras.

The Miniature Camera. Quite apart from its obvious advantage of portability, the miniature camera has many real optical advantages. For, provided the final prints are of the same size, it can readily be shown that the depth of field of any camera varies as the square of the object distance divided by the diameter of the lens aperture. Hence a miniature camera with a 2-in. f/2 lens (aperature = 1 in.) will have the same ultimate depth of field as a 6-in. f/6 lens (aperture = 1 in.), provided of course that the miniature film negative is enlarged three times in printing to bring the picture size up to that made with the larger camera. The miniature camera thus has the same depth of field as the larger camera and nine times the photographic speed. On the other hand, it must be added that because the miniature negative must be enlarged three times as much as the larger negative, graininess, scratches, and all other photographic imperfections become three times as conspicuous in the miniature negative, and so do errors in focus and the effects of unsteadiness or vibration in the camera.

Depth of Focus. An important factor to be considered, particularly in miniature cameras, is the permissible error in focusing within the camera itself. This is entirely distinct from depth of field, which is the acceptable range of object distances in front of the camera.

If one is unable to distinguish between a circle of confusion c on the film and a true image point, and if the lens has an f-number N, then one will be unable to detect an error in focus equal to the product of $N \times c$. This fact will cover errors due to buckling or curvature of the film, and to incorrect setting of the focusing adjustment of the camera lens itself. The product $N \times c$ is known as the depth of focus of the lens.

Lens Coating. It was mentioned above that the speed of a lens depends only on the ratio of aperture to focal length. This is not, however, quite correct as no lens transmits all of the light that falls upon it. The glass itself absorbs light to a very slight extent, and each glass-air surface reflects about 5 per cent of the light incident upon it. Thus each surface transmits only 95 per cent, and the resultant transmission of a lens with 8 glass-air surfaces will be only $(0.95)^8 = 66$ per cent.

If this were all, it would not be particularly serious, as the photographer would merely have to increase the exposure time somewhat. However, the light reflected from the inner surfaces must find its way out of the front of the lens again, and in doing so it suffers another 5 per cent reflection from each surface. The doubly reflected light then finds its way back into the camera, where it either fogs the film uniformly or forms some kind of a definite ghost image or flare spot.

To eliminate this undesirable doubly-reflected light, it has become customary since about 1942 to coat all the glass-air surfaces of a lens with a microscopically thin layer of magnesium fluoride. If this is of the correct thickness, it has the property of reducing the surface reflections from its normal value of about 5 per cent to about 1 per cent, thus entirely eliminating all trouble from ghosts and flare spots, and substantially increasing the over-all light transmission of the lens.

Focusing a Lens. The simplest method of focusing a camera is to move the lens, as a whole, back and forth until the sharpest possible definition is obtained. However, in folding cameras it is a considerable mechanical problem to move the front-board and at the same time keep it rigidly parallel to the film plane. Consequently, folding cameras are now commonly equipped with lenses of the triplet or Tessar type, in which focusing is done by moving only the front element of the lens, the shutter and the remaining lens elements remaining fixed. As the front element of such a lens is generally two or three times as strong as the complete objective, the longitudinal focusing motion required for the front element alone is very much less than the movement which would be necessary if the entire lens were moved. The focusing scale is then conveniently placed around the front element mounting.

Principal Types of Photographic Lens. Simple box cameras, and some low-priced folding cameras, are usually equipped with a single meniscus landscape lens. This lens is made from one piece of glass, and gives surprisingly good definition at an aperture not greater than about f/14. By combining two such meniscus lenses, one in front of and one behind a central diaphragm, a periscopic lens can be constructed which will give satisfactory definition for amateur purposes at an aperture of about f/11.

By making both components into spherically corrected cemented doublets, with relatively strong cemented interfaces, the famous Rapid Rectilinear or Aplanat lens is obtained. This lens gives good definition at apertures of f/7.7 or slightly higher, and the diagonal of the film is about equal to the focal length of the lens, representing a 53-deg. field. However, since about 1925, this lens has been superseded by some type of anastigmat.

Anastigmat Lenses. The simplest possible anastigmat lens is the so-called Cooke triplet lens, comprising two nearly plano-convex positive lenses spaced apart, with a biconcave lens situated between them. This type of lens can be made to give entirely acceptable definition at apertures of f/4.5 or less over the usual 53-deg. field, and at apertures of f/3.5 or even f/2.9 over restricted fields. When made as a high-aperture, narrow-field lens, the length of the lens is considerably longer than the diameter, this type being commonly used for projection lenses, to project either standard or 2x2-in. miniature slides on a screen. It is also frequently used for 8 and 16mm. motion picture cameras. By achromatizing one or more of the elements in a Cooke triplet, a whole family of fine lenses can be designed. Literally hundreds of different types of modified triplets have been made, typical examples being the Tessar, Xpres, Heliar, Pentac, Hektor, and Ektar f/3.5. By splitting the back element into two closely-spaced lenses, an even higher aperture can be obtained, such as in the f/2.5 Speedic or Tachar. Another line of lenses has been derived from the simple triplet by splitting the middle negative element into two with a central air space. These quadruplet lenses can be made to give excellent definition at apertures as high as f/3.5, examples being the Celor, Aviar, Dogmar, Unofocal, and Lustrar.

Double Lenses. Between 1890 and 1905, most photographic anastigmats were of the symmetrical or almost symmetrical double lens type, the two halves of which contained three, four or sometimes five lenses cemented together into a solid meniscus-shaped group. Many of these, by careful design, were convertible, i.e., each half could be used alone, or two halves of any focal length could be combined together to make a compound lens of shorter focal length. This type of lens is excellent for a tripod camera equipped with a ground-glass focusing screen, but the aperture seldom exceeds f/6.3, and with the coming of the compact roll-film camera, it has largely disappeared. Typical examples of double lenses are the Dagor, Collinear, Orthostigmat, Holostigmat, Angulon, Double-protar, and Turner-Reich. In some instances, the inner elements of the two triplet combinations are separated to give the designer greater degrees of freedom for the correction of aberrations. This type of construction is employed in the Euryplan, Plasmat, Orthometar, and wide-angle Xpres lenses.

True wide-angle lenses, covering a field of 90 deg. or more, are generally either of very low aperture, such as the f/18 Protar (Fig. 3), or they consist of four strongly meniscus elements surrounding a central stop, such as the Aristostigmat and Topogon. The latter covers a 90-deg. field at f/6.3, and is much used for aerial surveying. An extreme example is the Hypergon, which covers a 130-deg. field at a very low aperture (f/40).

Telephoto Lenses. At the opposite end of the scale from a wide-angle lens is the telephoto lens. This is of a very special type of construction, comprising a positive front member widely separated from a negative rear member. By this means the over-all distance from the front of the lens to the film plane can be made considerably less than the focal length, with obvious advantages in respect to portability and compactness. Unfortunately it is not possible to design a good telephoto lens of aperture much higher than about f/4, nor covering a field greater than about 25 deg. to 30 deg., and it is generally preferable to use a lens of normal type rather than a telephoto if compactness is not an important consideration.

Sometimes a lens of the reversed telephoto type is employed. This consists of a large negative lens in front, followed by a small and compact positive rear lens, and it has the opposite property to a telephoto lens: viz., there is a large clearance between the back of the lens and the focal plane. This is of use in some special types of camera such as the Technicolor camera, in which a beam splitter must be inserted between the lens and the film.

Large-Aperture Lenses. In recent years, lenses of large

aperture have been developed. About 1920 H. Lee designed the Opic lens—a 6-element system, of meniscus construction, which was the first to give satisfactory definition over a 50-deg. field at f/2. It has been extensively imitated and modified, notable examples being the f/2 Biotar, Summar, Ektar, and Xenon. By reducing the angular field to 28 deg., the aperture has been increased to f/1.4 for 16mm. motion picture cameras. Since about 1932, the same construction has been applied to professional motion picture cameras in the Speed Panchro and Baltar lenses, and to theatre projectors in the Super Cinephor lens.

The construction of the Zeiss Sonnar lens represents an extreme modification of the Cooke triplet in which the middle negative component has been replaced by a thick,

A KEY TO LENS ABILITY

Relative Sizes of Various Lenses	Relative Exposure Times Required	Approximate Relative Speeds	Glass Elements Used in Lenses
MENISCUS		1	
DOUBLET		1½	
ANASTIGMAT· f/9.8		3	
ANASTIGMAT f/6.3		6	
ANASTIGMAT f/4.5		11	
ANASTIGMAT SPECIAL f/3.5		18	
EKTAR f/1.9		62	

COURTESY OF EASTMAN KODAK CO.

Comparison of various types of lens, showing relative performance, size, and component parts

meniscus-shaped, cemented triplet, and the rear positive component has been replaced by a cemented doublet or triplet also. A modified form has been adopted by other manufacturers. Examples are the Ernostar, Retina-Xenon, and Fluro-Ektar. Apertures of f/1.5 can be achieved with this form of lens, over fields as great as 42 deg.

Zoom Lenses. A special type of motion picture lens is the so-called zoom lens. This is a complicated unit containing some means for varying the focal length without throwing the image out of focus. Thus during a zoom, the size of the picture steadily grows or shrinks, giving the effect of moving the camera toward or away from the subject. The difficulties of designing a zoom lens are great, and only a very few successful designs have ever been completed. The best-known zoom lens for 35mm. cameras is the Varo, and for 16mm. cameras the Zoomar.

Portrait Lenses. Historically, the oldest large-aperture lens is the portrait lens, which was designed by J. Petzval in 1840. This lens consists of two widely spaced doublet lenses, and it is characterized by a high aperture, excellent central definition, and a rather narrow field. The original Petzval lens covered a 20-deg. field at f/3.5. It is now manufactured mainly as a motion picture projection lens at apertures of f/1.6 to f/2.0 and covering a 10-deg. field. Some modern 2-in. f/1.6 projection lenses for use with 16mm. film are equipped with a field flattener, which is a negative lens close to the film plane. This device greatly extends the useful angular field without affecting the central definition.

Apochromatic Lenses. A special lens that is of great importance, even though the number manufactured is relatively small, is the apochromatic process lens used in photoengraving. These lenses are generally of f/10 aperture and about 18 in. or more in focal length, and the image is exceptionally well corrected for a range of magnifications from two times magnification to three times reduction, most work

excellent definition over a field of 9 x 9 or 9 x 18 in. for use in automatic aerial cameras. By the end of World War II, telephoto lenses of 40-in. focus and f/5 aperture were just coming into production, and the difficulties of manufacture may well be understood when it is realized that such a lens is over 8 in. in diameter, and contains about seven separate elements. The lens barrel must be equipped to hold the lens at a constant temperature while the atmospheric temperature may drop from 120° F. down to perhaps —60° F.; and means must be provided to keep the image constantly in focus over a range of atmospheric pressures from the normal 760 mm. at sea level to perhaps 150 mm. at 40,000 ft. For night aerial photography by flashlight, 12-in. f/2.5 lenses have been manufactured, covering a 9x9-in. picture. For aerial survey work, the favorite lens is the f/6.3 metrogon, which covers a 9 x 9-in. picture at a focal length of only 6 in., representing an angular field of 90 deg.

Lens Attachments. The most familiar lens attachments are weak positive lenses to enable the user to focus sharply

Use of filters to obtain desirable sky effects. (Left) Blue light of sky, to which film is especially sensitive, causes overexposure of sky and loss of cloud detail. (Center) Addition to lens of moderate filter absorbs some blue light, providing some cloud detail. (Right) Heavier filter overcorrects blue sky, producing darkened sky and sharp cloud detail, as shown.

being done at about unit magnification. Since many halftones are now being made in color, it is absolutely necessary that a process lens should give the same image size in all colors, and that all the colored images should fall into a common focal plane. When these two requirements are realized, the lens is called "apochromatic." Typical examples are the Alethar, Apo-Planar, Apo-Tessar, Apo-Xpres, Apo-Eikonar, Artar, Metra Scienar, Apo-Ektar, and Apo-Lustrar.

Enlarging Lenses. Lenses intended for use on photographic enlargers must be corrected for near objects so as to give their best definition and the flattest possible field at a magnification between 1:1 and 5:1, since that is the range most commonly used. Ordinary camera lenses are often used for enlarging, but better results are obtained by using lenses designed for the purpose. These are frequently of an almost symmetrical construction and cover a 40-deg. field at about f/4.5. Their color correction must be such as to bring into a common focal plane both the yellow light, which is most visible to the eye, and blue light, for which bromide paper has its maximum sensitivity.

Microfilming. Some very fine lenses of 2- to 2½-in. focus and f/8 aperture are manufactured for microfilming documents. They must give an actual resolving power on film of more than 100 lines per mm. (2,500 lines per in.)

Aerial Photography. During wartime, there is always a great demand for lenses for aerial photography. These must be of long focus and moderate aperture, but they must give

on objects too close to be covered by the normal focusing range of the camera. These are known as "portrait" or "close-up" attachments. The Zeiss Proxar, Enteco, Tiffen, and the Kodak Portra lenses are of this type. The power of attachment lenses is often designated in diopters, the diopter being the reciprocal of a meter, hence a lens of three diopters power has a focal length of 33 cm.

Negative attachment lenses are sometimes used to increase the focal length of the camera lens in order to obtain a somewhat larger picture. As it is necessary to rack the lens out to a considerable distance beyond the normal focusing position, when such an attachment is used, a double-extension camera bed is generally required. The Zeiss Distar and the Kodak Telek lenses are of this type.

Cinecameras are sometimes equipped with Galilean-telescope attachments, which increase or reduce the effective focal length, and hence the picture size, without altering the distance of the main lens from the film or affecting in any way the f-number of the system. Thus a reversed Galilean telescope with a magnifying power of 0.5 will halve the focal length of a cinecamera lens and double the angular field. Examples are the Ampli-cinor, the Hyper-cinor, and the Morton telephoto and wide-angle attachments.

Other attachments include diffusing devices, color filters, or polarizing material, for special photographic effects. Examples of useful filters are the K1, K2, X1, G, and 23A.

R. Ki. and E. E. H.

CAMERINO [ka'meri'no], the highest and one of the most picturesque cities in the Marches of east central Italy. Camerino is in the province of Macerata, about 30 mi. southwest of the city of Macerata, over 2,000 ft. above sea level. The winters are cold, and the average annual precipitation exceeds 40 in. Little remains of the ancient and early medieval city, and the principal monuments date from the fourteenth to the sixteenth centuries. In the vicinity are the ruins of several castles and fortresses which formerly served to defend the city and its state.

The University of Camerino was created in 1727 by papal decree. In 1861 it became a "free" institution. It gives degrees or diplomas in law, chemistry, and pharmacy. Attached to the university are the Valentinian Library, a meteorological observatory, and a botanical garden.

Ancient Camerinum was an early ally of Rome and became a *municipium* after the Social War. Following the decay of the Roman Empire, it fell in turn to the Goths, Greeks, and Lombards, the latter including it in the Duchy of Spoleto. Charlemagne made it the capital of the March of Camerino. In 1198 Innocent III subjugated it to the church, without depriving the city of its autonomy and its prosperity. Camerino was involved in the conflict between the papacy and the empire, and under Manfred it was completely destroyed in 1259. It was rebuilt through the initiative of the Varano family, which ruled, with two brief interludes, until 1545, when it became an integral part of the Papal States. Pop. 1954 (city), 4,200; (commune), 11,500.   R. G. W.

CAMERON, SIR DAVID YOUNG (1865-1945), British painter and etcher, was born in Glasgow, June 28, 1865. He started on a mercantile career, studying at the same time at the Glasgow Art School and later at the Edinburgh School of Art. He began to etch in 1887. The influence of Seymour Haden, Charles Méryon, J. M. Whistler, and Rembrandt is apparent in his early prints, but he developed his own style, which emphasized design and austerity of feeling in architecture and landscape. *Five Sisters* (1907), portraying in rich tones the famous York Minster windows, is a splendid example of his architectural prints. A characteristic landscape is *Ben Ledi* (1911), which, though reminiscent of Claude Lorrain, is superb in its strength of design, and in its mood, expressive line, and rich dry-point shadows. Cameron is one of the most important etchers of the early twentieth century. He was elected Associate of the Royal Academy as engraver (1911), as painter (1916), and as Academician (1920). He is represented in American print collections and in the British Museum. Many of his paintings are in European museums. Cameron died at Perth, Scotland, Sept. 16, 1945.
G. Von G.

CAMERON, SIMON (1799-1889), American politician, was born at Maytown, Pa., Mar. 8, 1799. He became an orphan at the age of nine. At fifteen he was employed as a printer in the office of the *Northumberland County Gazette,* and at nineteen he was appointed assistant editor of the *Harrisburg Republican.* Cameron began making money through investments in banking and railroads, and successively became publisher of the Doylestown, Pa., *Bucks County Messenger, Doylestown Democrat, Bucks County Democrat,* and *Pennsylvania Intelligencer.* In 1824 he began to participate actively in politics in support of John C. Calhoun, then secretary of war, who later became vice-president. In 1826 Cameron was appointed adjutant general of Pennsylvania and also obtained the lucrative post of state printer. He quit journalism in 1827 and began building a state-wide political machine in Pennsylvania. In 1845 Cameron won the United

States Senate seat vacated by James Buchanan; he was again elected to the Senate, this time as a Republican, in 1857, and in 1860 he became a presidential candidate at the Republican national convention. President Abraham Lincoln was subsequently persuaded to appoint him secretary of war, but within two years Cameron's malfeasance in that office had compelled his resignation at the request of the president, who sent him abroad as minister to Russia. After resigning from that post in November 1862, Cameron was returned to the Senate by the Republicans in 1867, and was repeatedly re-elected until 1877, serving as chairman of the Committee on Foreign Relations from 1872. In 1877 he retired and was succeeded in the Senate by his son, James D. Cameron.

Simon Cameron is regarded by many historians as the first state boss in American politics. During his political life numerous charges of corruption were made against him, but his widespread influence maintained him in office. His mishandling of funds entrusted to him as a commissioner for the settlement, under treaty, of claims made by relatives of the Winnebago Indians became a national scandal. Cameron died in Donegal, Pa., June 26, 1889.   D. R.

CAMERON, the seat of Milam Co., in east central Texas, is situated about 130 mi. southeast of Fort Worth in an area devoted to diversified farming and the raising of cattle, poultry, melons, and cotton. It was founded about 1830. The government is by mayor and city council. Transportation is supplied by the Atcheson, Topeka and Santa Fe and the Southern Pacific railways. Cotton ginning and compressing, and oil refining are its chief industries. Other important trade items are cottonseed oil and creamery products. Pop. 1950, 5,052.

CAMEROONS, THE [kæmǝru'nz], that part of the Kamerun, formerly a German colony in west Africa, which comprises two trust territories administered by Great Britain and France. The Cameroons are bounded on the northwest by Nigeria, on the east and south by French Equatorial Africa and Spanish Guinea, and on the southwest by the Bight of Biafra and Gulf of Guinea, extensions of the Atlantic Ocean. The southern boundary is two degrees north of the equator and the northern apex extends into Lake Chad. All but a relatively narrow strip along the northwestern boundary, which for British administrative purposes is attached to Nigeria, is under French trusteeship.

The total area of the two trust territories is about 200,500 sq. mi. In 1953 it had an estimated population of 4,561,000, including about 15,000 non-Africans. Bantu Negroes predominate in the south and west; to the north and east are Negroid Sudanese with a considerable admixture of Hamitics, notably the Fulani. A few of the earlier pygmy inhabitants are still to be found in the more inaccessible and heavily forested regions. Not now included in the Cameroons is a large area of 107,270 sq. mi., lying southeast of the French trust territory, which was ceded by France to Germany in 1911 but reincorporated into French Equatorial Africa after its capture by British and French forces in 1916. After World War I the present territory of the Cameroons was divided into French and British mandates under the League of Nations. The new trusteeship areas under the United Nations have the same boundaries as the former League mandates.

Geographical Features. The land rises gradually westward to mountain ranges running from south of Lake Chad southwestward to the sea, terminating in the Great Cameroon Peak, about 13,353 ft. high and the highest peak in west Africa. The Cameroon Mountains are greatly denuded ancient ranges which have gained in elevation by great volcanic upheavals and comparatively recent lava outflow, as was made evident by the volcanic activity of Mount Cameroon in 1909 and 1922. The country is well watered by numerous rivers flowing toward the Atlantic Ocean, Lake Chad, and the Congo Basin. Rio Del Rey, in the extreme north of the coast, an important estuary open to ships, is formed by the meeting of five streams which rise in the mountains bordering Nigeria and the Cameroons. Other rivers are the Sannaga, which enters the sea a little farther south, and the Nyong entering the sea north of the port of Kribi. The Cameroons have a tropical climate with heavy rainfall and high temperatures on the coast, which is swampy and unhealthful. The seaward side of the Cameroon Mountains receives the heaviest rainfall (about 400 in. annually at Great Cameroon

COURTESY OF BRITISH INFORMATION SERVICES

Native village in the British Cameroons

Peak). However, from the southwest monsoon, even on the French side (4,000-6,000 ft.), the precipitation is very heavy, and in many places it is over 100 in. Inland, rainfall decreases rapidly.

The soil in the coast region is fertile. Numerous vegetable products of great commercial value are grown, mainly on plantations controlled by Europeans. Chief products are palm oil, palm kernels, cacao, rubber, and bananas. The mangrove swamps of the coast are succeeded by imposing forests, including mahogany, ebony, teak, and other valuable trees, followed by a lighter form of tropical forests on the highlands. Above them is a grassland plateau suitable for cattle.   S. Van V.

German Kamerun (1884-1916). The first German annexation of territory in this region took place in 1884. It was preceded by, and to a large extent resulted from, the increasing activities of German missionaries, explorers, and traders. The area first taken over lay along the coast and was limited in extent. Subsequent German policy in the Kamerun was characterized by three elements: territorial expansion, national monopoly of trade and resources, and establishment of a plantation system. As a result of the first, the Kamerun by

1911 had come to include an area of 307,840 sq. mi. and extended to the Congo River in the south, the Ubangi River in the east, and Lake Chad in the north. Restrictions on international trade in the Kamerun naturally intensified the international struggle for African domain. Even during World War I there was much agitation in Germany for the eventual building of a transcontinental German *Mittel-Afrika* in which the Kamerun would form an essential bastion. The development of plantations in the Kamerun proved unexpectedly difficult and unremunerative. Most of them were located not far from the coast and many were in what is now the British Cameroons province; but even there, with relatively easy transport facilities, only 48,000 acres were under cultivation by 1914. Some of the plantations belonged to commercial companies, some to individual Germans, none to the government. Douala, at the mouth of the Vuri River, was the capital. This port, now in French territory, was also the center of a small railway system radiating north and east.

French Cameroons. The Anglo-French campaign against the Kamerun in World War I ended in the capitulation of the German forces and the division of the country into provisional zones of military occupation. In preparation for the establishment of civil administrations, an internal boundary agreement was reached in 1919, and in 1920 a beginning was made in actual boundary marking. In sections of the north this work is still incomplete. In 1922 France was assigned as the mandatory power for the area already in French occupation, and in 1946 the same territory became a trust territory when the United Nations replaced the League of Nations as the supervisory power. Exclusive of the area reabsorbed into French Equatorial Africa, the French section of the Kamerun, which then became known as the Cameroons, was about 166,500 sq. mi. in extent. By decrees of 1921 and 1925 the French Cameroons was completely separated from other French African territory and its high commissioner was placed directly under the French minister for overseas territories. There was considerable confusion in the territory during World War II as the Vichy and the Free French governments contended for control. With the establishment of the fourth French Republic in 1946 the government of the Cameroons was reorganized. In 1955 it included a high commissioner with an advisory council, a territorial representative assembly, and municipal and rural councils. The territory has a representation of five in the assembly of the French Union, of four in the French National Assembly, and of three in the Council of the Republic. Voters are divided into two classes: French citizens and enfranchised Africans. The franchise has been progressively extended so that those who read French or Arabic, who hold drivers' and hunting licenses, or who are mothers or heads of families can cast their votes. The territorial assembly is composed of 50 members. It has the power to consider proposed legislation presented to it by the high commissioner; one of its most important tasks is the approval of the budget. Education throughout the territory is conducted in the French language. The criminal law is based on the French penal code, although many disputes are settled extraofficially by local chiefs. In general, the French policy here, as elsewhere throughout its overseas domain, has been the assimilation of the native peoples to French ways of life. Yaoundé is the capital, and Douala and Kribi are important commercial centers. Douala is connected with France by air. There is a customs union between the French Cameroons and French Equatorial Africa. In 1946 the French government inaugurated an elaborate plan for the economic and social development of the Cameroons. Since 1947 the French government has spent $91 million for expanding ports and rail facilities and for roads, hydroelectric projects, and other services.

British Cameroons. The area of the former German Kamerun under British administration between 1916 and 1922 was formally assigned in the latter year to the United Kingdom as a mandatory power. This area consisted of two strips of territory, both contiguous to the eastern boundary of Nigeria but separated from each other by a gap of about 45 mi. astride the Benue River, where Nigeria and the French Cameroons have a common border. This lack of territorial compactness, coupled with the wide divergences in social organization, especially between the predominantly Moslem region to the north of the gap and the essentially pagan region to the south of it, induced the British government not to attempt a political separation of the Cameroons from Nigeria. From the beginning, therefore, the British Cameroons have been administered as a part of Nigeria, each district or province of the former being integrated with adjacent districts or provinces of the latter. The total area of the British Cameroons is about 34,080 sq. mi. Of this total only about 6,900 sq. mi. lie to the north of the gap. Under Nigeria's 1954 constitution, the northern Cameroons is represented in the House of Assembly and the House of Chiefs of the Northern Region and shares in the representation of this division in Nigeria's federal House of Representatives. The Southern Cameroons, on the other hand, is a quasi-federal territory, with a legislative council of its own. This latter area elects six members to the Nigerian House of Representatives. The population of the British Cameroons in 1953 was 1,441,000.

Whereas the French have followed an overseas policy of assimilation to France, the British in their sector have followed the policy known as "indirect rule." Throughout the British Cameroons, native authorities have either been retained or actually created, and the range of their power in legislative, judicial, and executive matters has steadily extended. In the Moslem northern region these authorities exercise power over much larger areas than in the pagan south. The most northern district, Dikwa, with a population of 219,300, is under the Emir of Dikwa, whereas the district Bamenda in the southern section is divided among more than 20 native authorities. Elected village councils, both in the southern area and in the Dikwa emirate and other parts of the north, were established after World War II, bringing increasing political education and experience to all parts of the trust territory. One of the leading parties was the Kamerun National Congress, which elected all six of the Southern Cameroon's delegates to the Nigerian House of Representatives in 1954.

During World War I the German plantations in the British Cameroons were held by the custodian of enemy property. After the war an attempt was made to sell these properties, but with slight success. In 1924, therefore, their former owners were permitted to reacquire their former holdings, and by 1939 only one plantation was not so occupied. In that year, however, the plantations were again expropriated, and after World War II the Cameroons Development Corporation was created by the British government to operate these holdings on a nonprofit basis, all net production and trading revenues to be at the disposal of the governor of Nigeria and to be applied for the benefit of the African population of the Cameroons. In addition to this, the imperial Colonial Development and Welfare Act of 1945 placed substantial sums at the disposal of the government, the largest Cameroons item being that allocated to road communications, for the twofold purpose of opening up the hinterland and improving the connections between the Cameroons and Nigeria. The estimated cost of the entire ten-year plan for the Cameroons is about $6,600,000. The territory has no railways. The chief ports of the territory are Victoria and Tiko. Tiko is connected by the West African Airways with Lagos, Nigeria, and through this airport with British Overseas Airways.

W. M. W. and W. W. W.

CAMILLE. *See* DAME AUX CAMÉLIAS, LA.

CAMILLUS, MARCUS FURIUS (d. 365 B.C.), Roman general of the early Republican period. In the crisis precipitated by the long siege of Veii, the Romans made Camillus dictator in 396 B.C. He brought about the capitulation of Veii, but was forced into exile when he was accused of having kept a large part of the booty for himself. In 390 B.C., after the Gauls had captured most of Rome, Camillus was recalled from exile and again made dictator. He maintained his reputation as a successful general by driving the Gauls from Rome. Camillus is reputed to have driven off the Gauls again when they reappeared in 367 B.C. Actually, many of the stories which gathered about his almost legendary figure can not be fully accepted as fact. Of his existence there can be no doubt, but it is difficult to reconstruct his career. The Romans, however, cherished his memory and called him "a second founder of Rome."   T. B. J.

CAMISARDS [ka'mi'zɑ'r], term applied to the Protestant peasantry of the Cévennes, which revolted against the government of Louis XIV during the early years of the eighteenth century, defying particularly the religious policies of the Crown. Louis XIV's revocation of the Edict of Nantes in October 1685 was one of the major underlying reasons for the uprising. The appearance of various types of prophetic and apocalyptic literature, denunciatory of Rome, also provided an important background for the revolt. The writings of Pierre Jurieu, French Huguenot publicist and ecclesiastic, who lived in exile in Holland, were particularly significant in this respect. Jurieu's *L'Accomplissement des prophéties,* which appeared in 1686, even predicted the imminent fall of Roman Catholicism.

The name given to those engaged in the revolt is said to be derived from the obsolete French word *camisade,* which was used to refer to those nightly expeditions in which the participants wore a shirt (*chemise*) over their armor. The scene of conflict was particularly the eastern part of the province of Languedoc, and the fact that this insurrection was in large part contemporaneous with the War of the Spanish Succession caused considerable anxiety to the government. The revolt began in July 1702, with the assassination of the Abbé du Chayla, a veteran missionary, inspector of missions in the Cévennes and a noted persecutor of Protestants. Both sides carried on the conflict with great cruelty, sparing neither age nor sex. Although sometimes defeated in fixed encounters, the Camisards were highly successful in night raids and in ambuscades.

Among their outstanding leaders was Jean Cavalier, who displayed a gift for military leadership and who defied successively three marshals of France sent against him. In May 1704, Claude Louis Hector de Villars, the marshal who suppressed the movement, held a conference with Cavalier at Nîmes, and there induced the insurrectionist leader to surrender by the offer of a commission in the king's army and the promise of certain religious guarantees. Later, however, Cavalier fled from France and joined the Allies, finally dying in 1740 in the British service as a major general. By 1710 the last of the Camisard leaders had been hunted down, but Protestantism still continued secretly to linger in remote sections of the Cévennes.   B. C. W.

CAMMAERTS, ÉMILE [kɑ'marts] (1878-1953), Belgian poet, was born in Brussels, Mar. 16, 1878. He was educated at the University of Brussels and in 1908 moved to England, although he retained his Belgian citizenship. In 1914 Cammaerts became professor of Belgian studies at the University of London. He achieved popularity with his poems of World War I, in English translation entitled *Belgian Poems* (1915), *New Belgian Poems* (1916), *Through Iron Bars* (1917), and *Messines* (1918). A collection of his verse, *Poèmes Intimes,* appeared in 1922. Other works, mostly historical and political, are *History of Belgium* (1921), *Treasure House of Belgium* (1924), *Discoveries in England* (1932), *Rubens* (1932), *Albert of Belgium, Defender of Right* (1935), *The Laughing Prophet; the Seven Virtues and G. K. Chesterton* (1937), *The Keystone of Europe: a History of the Belgian Dynasty* (1939), *The Flower of Grass* (1944), *The Peace That Was Left* (1945), *Principalities and Powers* (1947), and *The Devil Takes the Chair* (1949) an allegory. Cammaerts also translated Ruskin and Chesterton into French, and in 1917 wrote two plays, *Les deux bossus* and *La Veillée de Noël.* He died in Radlett, England, on Nov. 2, 1953.

CAMÕES or CAMOËNS, LUIZ VAZ DE [kamoĩ'sh; kæ'mɔɛnz] (c.1524-1580), considered the greatest Portuguese poet, lived during the reigns of three kings, John III, Sebastian, and the Cardinal-King Henry. His entire life was deeply rooted in the national existence, and its very essence was transmuted into his poetry. During this span Portugal plunged from the illusory splendor of the days of Manuel the Fortunate to the ignominy of defeat and servitude.

Camões was born in Lisbon, or possibly Coimbra, presumably in 1524. All Portugal at this time was acutely conscious of the heroic maritime explorations and conquests of the recent past, of the creation of an opulent empire

LUIZ VAZ DE CAMÕES

FROM AN OLD ENGRAVING

CULVER SERVICE

overseas, and of aspirations to hegemony in world affairs. It was, furthermore, an epoch in which material splendor was becoming more and more intensified by the spirit of the Renaissance. Camões studied in Coimbra, first at the College of All Saints and then at the university until 1542 and soon thereafter made his way to Lisbon. The next ten years he spent on the turbulent fringes of the royal court. At the outset he was well received in Lisbon, but apparently

as a result of his intemperate conduct he fell into difficulties and disgrace. Perhaps the most celebrated phase of this period of his life is his passion for a lady traditionally identified as one of the queen's attendants, Caterina de Ataide, whose name can be read in the anagram "Natercia," found in Camões' love poems. Possibly the reality of this affair has been exaggerated, for the examples of Dante and Petrarch made almost obligatory the fiction of concentrating the generalized Neoplatonic spirit of love upon some specific person.

Camões incurred the active disfavor of the court, doubtless, as he himself said, because of the intrigues of envious courtiers, but also in some degree because of his indiscreet conduct, which added to the offense he had already given by his play *El Rei Seleuco* ("King Seleucus"), whose plot recalled King John's loss of his bride to his own father, Manuel. Camões found it necessary to spend the better part of a year away from Lisbon and then enlisted for military service in North Africa, where he remained in the vicinity of Ceuta from 1547 to 1549. There he lost his right eye in a skirmish. Returning to Lisbon, Camões failed to obtain rewards for his services, and in his disappointment he engaged in a series of brawls and scandals that culminated in his seriously wounding one of the king's retinue, Gonçalo Borges, during the feast of Corpus Christi. The penalty was an imprisonment from which he was released only on the recovery and magnanimous forgiveness of his victim. Camões received the king's full pardon by enlisting for service in India, and on Mar. 24, 1553, he set sail for Goa for a sojourn destined to last seventeen years.

In the Orient Camões met with ever increasing disappointment. His duties took him westward from Goa to the Red Sea and eastward as far as Macao on the Chinese coast, where he remained two years, only to be deported to stand trial for alleged irregularities in handling funds. The vessel bearing him back to Goa was wrecked in the Gulf of Tonkin, where the picturesque tradition has it that he swam ashore carrying in one hand the unfinished manuscript of his great epic poem, *Os Lusíadas.* In Goa he underwent further imprisonment. Finally he began his homeward journey with the aid of Pedro Barreto, who in 1567 took him as far as Sofala, on the east coast of Africa; but he remained there for two years, lacking sufficient funds to proceed farther, and succeeded in reaching Lisbon only in 1570. His homeland gave him a sorry welcome. The country was ravaged by plague; his remaining friends were few and his means fewer; and "Natercia" had died in 1556 during his stay in the Orient. He had completed his epic, however, and after its publication in 1572 received a three-year pension from King Sebastian. This, despite a lapse in payment, was renewed and continued for his lifetime. Camões' last days were clouded by the disastrous defeat and death of King Sebastian at al-Qasr al-Kabir, and he died in misery June 10, 1580, only shortly before the vacant throne of Portugal was annexed by Philip II of Spain.

Os Lusíadas. Camões' greatest creation is his epic *Os Lusíadas* (1572). No single hero, no abstraction or symbol of his nation, had sufficient amplitude to encompass his heroic vision of Portugal; he therefore proposed, as he himself tells us, to transform into one song, mighty enough to reach every corner of the universe, all of the martial heroes of Portugal. These men he saw as the heroic individual incarnations of a single virility whose superhuman force had launched them into uncharted seas, spreading afar the true Faith and erecting the edifice of a vast empire. Hence for his title, Camões chose a newly coined word meaning "The Men of Portugal," for the nation, which had been known since ancient times as Lusitania, was supposedly named for its mythical founder Lusus, son of the god Bacchus. This title has not infrequently been misinterpreted as "The Lusiad" by analogy to the titles of such classical epics as the *Aeneid* or the *Iliad*.

To his task Camões applied a talent which, being quintessentially Portuguese, was primarily lyrical. His poem, although cast in the conventional Vergilian mold, is a vast paean rather than a heroic narrative. The framework of the poem is simple, being merely successive stages of the voyage of Vasco da Gama, a distant kinsman of Camões and the first Portuguese navigator to reach India and return by rounding the Cape of Good Hope, a voyage in whose wake the poet himself sailed. Around this framework Camões worked the substance of his poem, expanding it to ten cantos, or 1,102 stanzas of eight lines, known in Portuguese as *octavas*. In imitation of Classical models, the destinies of the human adventurers were interwoven with the machinations of the gods. Bacchus, seeking to prevent the Portuguese from eclipsing his own martial feats in India, strove to thwart the Lusitanians; Venus assumed the role of their protectress, regarding them as the true heirs to the imperial destiny, the valor, and even the speech of her cherished Romans. This device and, on the same artistic plane, a mythological treatment of cosmography afforded Camões the opportunity for magnificent pictorial passages, such as his description of Triton with its curious reminiscences of Manueline sculptural decoration. It also encouraged his use of rich poetic imagery, sonorous concatenations of names which evince a sensuous delight in the sheer music of syllables, and Arcadian scenes like the description of the Isle of Love. Such devices even modify the structure of the epic, as when, after the banquet on the Isle of Love, a nymph foretells the triumphs of heroes who came after Vasco da Gama. Above all, by the artifice of integrating the adventures of mortal Portuguese men with the rhythm of existence of the immortal gods, Camões expressed in effective symbols his deep conviction of the epic destiny of his nation.

Into the slight framework of his epic Camões worked the names and feats of all the traditional national heroes, from the semilegendary Viriatus to the ill-starred Sebastian. With more than mere ingenuity he contrived to instill into these fragments of history a glow of patriotic feeling by putting them into the mouths of individuals speaking in moments of heightened emotion. Thus two entire cantos, the second and third, presumably the original nucleus of the poem, are a recital of heroic national deeds made to the African King Melinde by Vasco da Gama himself at the flood tide of patriotic fervor inspired by the first and safe arrival of Portuguese vessels at the borders of the enigmatic Indian Ocean. In a different but no less intense mood, the tale of the Twelve of Portugal draws together in a patriotic bond the Portuguese mariners huddled on a lonely deck surrounded by the immensity of a tropical Oriental night. Yet again, to impress a haughty Indian potentate, the emblems on the national banners are translated by Paulo da Gama, Vasco's brother, into a drama of the stirring deeds they symbolized.

Camões derived much of his descriptive material from experience and observation, but he transformed it into poetic images with the sense of the beauty and wonder imminent in earthly things which was the special heritage of the Renaissance mind. Thus he painted the towering bulk of a waterspout, or the white sands of a tropical beach strewn with scarlet sea shells, or the ominous Cape of Good Hope, a malignant giant lying athwart the coveted passage to the Orient. Or, turning within himself, he put into his epic poignant expressions of his own troubled spirit. In the technical execution of the verses critics have pointed out flaws, but viewed in its totality the poetry is magnificent. The generations of poets since the days of Sá de Miranda had perfected the imported octave as a genuinely Portuguese poetic form. Camões handled this stanza masterfully, adapting it to the many moods of the poem, from martial and heroic to intimate and lyrical, varying its internal rhythms, or building up an unbroken flow from stanza to stanza. In short, Camões had absorbed and assimilated the art of general Classical and Renaissance poetry at the same time that he had steeped himself in the specific poetic tradition of his own nation; he was endowed to a unique degree with the power of transmuting the world about him and his own inner vision into the splendor of poetic images; and, sustained by his lofty, heroic vision of Portugal, he created a poem which ranks as the masterpiece of Portuguese literature.

Other Works. Passing mention must be made of Camões' three dramatic works: *Auto dos Anfitriões*, in mixed Spanish and Portuguese, as was often the way of Gil Vicente; *Auto d'el Rei Seleuco*, which gave offense to King John III; and *Auto de Filodemo*. The first two were based on Classical themes and the third upon tales of knightly adventure. None is particularly noteworthy, except for the competence of the verse.

Camões expressed himself, perhaps even more characteristically than in his great epic, in his shorter lyrical poems, his odes, elegies, eclogues, songs, and, above all, sonnets. His Coimbra days, filled with the reading of Classical and Renaissance poetry, his years in Lisbon, his loves, his banishment and days of soldiering in Africa, the sea voyage to India, his exile in Goa and Macao with its shipwreck and miserable hours in prison, the death of "Natercia," all had emotional significance for him in terms of passion, nostalgia, resignation, bitterness, and patriotic fervor. All took form in both the native songs and in the *dolce stil nuovo* not long since naturalized by Sá de Miranda. To be sure, his extensive output, even discounting probably apocryphal lyrics, is uneven; but at his frequent best he is unsurpassed by any other national poet. Such poems as the sonnet on the death of "Natercia," *Alma minha gentil* ("My Beloved"), or the exquisite octosyllables, *Sobolos rios que vam,* whose nostalgic opening lines paraphrase Psalm CXXXVII ("By the rivers of Babylon") are among the most beautiful in the language.
R. S. Ws.

CAMOMILE [kæ′momai′l], *Anthemis,* the common name for low, daisylike, heavy-scented, many-branched plants of the family Compositae, native to the Old World. There are annual, biennial, and perennial species. The clustering flowers are single or double and have white or yellow rays. Some species have become weeds. Several of the perennials, such as the golden marguerite, *A. tinctoria,* are excellent ornamentals. The Roman or English camomile, *A. nobilis,* growing to 1 ft. with aromatic foliage, is used medicinally and, when grass seed was hard to get, was popular for lawns and paths. The German camomile, *Matricaria chamomilla,* is also used medicinally.

False camomile, *Boltonia,* a genus of the family Compositae, has about six species native to the United States and eastern Asia. They are stemmed, herbaceous perennials growing to about 3 ft., with delicate asterlike flowers of white, purple, or pink blooming in late summer. Several are grown as ornamentals.
E. R. C.

CAMORRA [kɑmɔ'rrɑ], a secret criminal group in the Kingdom of Naples which survived after the unification of Italy. Its origins are obscure but its existence was well known by 1830. It had its own laws, hierarchy of officers, and courts; it exacted tribute from vice, gambling, theft, begging, and smuggling; its power rested on intimidation. The society had its agents throughout the country, in the army, within the prisons, even in the courts; but its greatest hold was in the underworld of the city of Naples. Like the Mafia of Sicily, it flourished because of an unhealthy society and widespread distrust of the government of the restored Bourbons. After 1848 some leading *camorristi* espoused the national cause, and for a brief period after Garibaldi's conquest in 1860, the Camorra was even entrusted with police power. It is said to have disappeared by the end of the nineteenth century, but only after a protracted campaign against it by the government of united Italy.   H. McG. S.

CAMOUFLAGE [kæ'mʊflɑʒ], any measure which aims to mislead by misrepresenting the existence or the true identity of installations, equipment, or activities. Camouflage is a two-edged weapon. It provides passive protection in its phase of concealment, and offers a field for offensive action in its facet of deception.

Defensive Camouflage in Nature. Many animals have been endowed with a coating of protective coloration which enables them to blend into the background of their natural habitats. The zebra's pattern makes the animal less visible in its natural surroundings; the polar bear is difficult to see against the ice fields; the walking-stick insect can hardly be observed among the twigs of a bush. The color of a chameleon varies with the reptile's background and mood, and the markings of the flounder change, enabling the fish to blend with its background.

Aggressive Camouflage. *Early Uses.* In the twelfth century B. C. the Greeks are said to have used aggressive camouflage in the capture of Troy. The deception they employed was the Trojan Horse. Made of wood and filled with Greek soldiers, it was placed outside the walls of Troy as a gift. After it had been hauled inside the walls, the Greek soldiers came out under cover of darkness to open the city gates, allowing the Greek army to take the city.

Sun Tzu, in the oldest known military book (500 B.C.), said, "All warfare is based upon deception. Hence when we are able to attack we must seem unable; when we are maneuvering our forces, we must seem to be inactive; when we are near we must make the enemy believe we are far away; and when we are far away the enemy must believe that we are near."

World War I. During World War I, camouflage measures entered into plans for operations, as well as those for precautionary defense. Examples of camouflage caught the public eye; the word became common. The most notable use of camouflage was an antisubmarine measure. Merchant vessels were disguised by spectacular painting designed to confuse enemy calculations of an intended victim's course and speed. Q-boats further dramatized camouflage; fitted to look like merchant ships, they were instead vessels equipped with high-caliber guns.

World War II. Camouflage was of even greater importance in World War II because of the effectiveness of aerial reconnaissance. Particularly in combination with photography, aerial observation made concealment and confusion of targets a prime necessity. Camouflage was used: to protect against aerial observation, photography, or bombing; to decrease the risk of a ship's being sighted by submarines; to impede the determination of correct data about a ship's speed and course, necessary for accurate firing of torpedoes; to reduce the visibility of submarines or aircraft; to conceal concentrations of troops, guns, camps, and military installations; to protect landing fields and the planes using them; to conceal or to disguise industrial installations; and to protect the individual fighting man.

Elements of Camouflage. *Role of the Observer.* To form some idea of the elements involved in camouflage, it may be useful to think of an observer's behavior under particular conditions. The eyes of the aerial observer, for example, give him a mental image of what lies before him, and he draws inferences as to what he sees. If he takes photographs, the inferences are made by skilled examination of the pictures. The conclusions in either case may be correct, or they may be an illusion. The process may be considered to involve three steps: detection, recognition, and identification. If a dummy battery, which has been "carelessly" disguised by screens, is identified as an actual enemy battery, camouflage is successful by illusion. If a PT-boat, thoroughly covered by tropical foliage at the bank of a jungle river, is not seen by an air observer, camouflage is successful because there is no detection.

Specific Factors. Successful camouflage requires a study of visibility under varying conditions. The elements to be considered are illumination, the transparency of the space between the observer and the object, and the contrasts. Variations of these elements control what the observer sees. In haze he may not see what his infrared camera will expose; in fog nothing may be detected, even if there are great contrasts and direct illumination. During World War II landing operations were constantly carried out under smoke screens which rendered observation ineffective and foiled air attacks. Camouflage can fall short of concealment, but, by confusing observation, it can be extremely effective under many conditions.

Methods. *Reduction of Visibility.* The methods used in camouflage seek the absolute concealment of objects. Usually, however, they achieve only reduced visibility. This is accomplished by matching the color and especially the tone of the surroundings. The planting of trees and the simulation of foliage by the use of net screens covered with actual foliage or artificial garnishing are also employed. The handling of shadow is extremely important. It may be done by the use of screens to eliminate the shadow. Sometimes, horizontal screens are placed at various heights on a chimney to distort the shadow by making the chimney appear like a tree or other object.

The blackout is a form of camouflage which, by preventing local illumination, avoids the outlining of buildings, installations, or cities by contrast. Reduction of visibility may be accomplished by painting ships and planes. Ships are generally painted gray or a combination of blue and white; mottling over the upper surface, with counter-shading on the under surface, is employed for planes.

Minimizing Eye-catching Features. Another method of camouflage is avoidance of features which attract attention. This involves the changing of large shapes within areas of smaller ones and the elimination of straight lines in otherwise irregular terrain. A long, straight highway, for example, should be broken into segments by cover or coloring and should not terminate abruptly. Regularity in shapes, such as tank forms, or regularity of spacing within installations should be avoided. Since recognition follows detection, the *camoufleur* gives particular attention to the disguise of conspicuous, large objects, such as crossroads or bridges, which serve as landmarks for the observer. The control of texture and the elimination of shine require close attention, as these qualities affect reflection.

Dispersion. Dispersion involves the separation of units to take advantage of the location and makes the entire activity more difficult to detect. It also renders the units more easily treated by camouflage and more susceptible to concealment by natural tree growth or by planting.

Applications. Over the years, a body of systematized knowledge about camouflage has been built up. Thus, camouflage may be considered to be a science, but the application of this knowledge in war is an art which includes discipline, imagination, and aggressiveness. Camouflage, to be effective as a defense measure, must be perfectly maintained, for a single flaw that has been overlooked may destroy the entire effect.

In the use of camouflage in war, there is a battle of wits between the camouflage planner and the observer. The latter seeks detection, recognition, and correct interpretations. The *camoufleur* does his best to prevent these, or to prevent or delay recognition when detection cannot be avoided. If the observer is in a bombing plane, for example, detection must occur before continuing to the attack, and recognition must be sufficiently ahead of the point of bomb release to allow the bombsight to be effectively used. Camouflage seeks to prevent this.

A classic example of the use of defensive camouflage is illustrated by the screening of a German dock area during World War II. Barges in the end of the dock supported stretched canvas which was painted to simulate a continuation of the surrounding structures. An actual bridge was thus made to appear as the end of the water area, and a dummy bridge was constructed at the proper distance from it to appear as the real bridge in its normal position.

Problems. Camouflage of important land installations in urban areas is difficult. Rivers, roads, and large conspicuous structures, such as stadiums, cannot be concealed, and these landmarks serve as guides to enemy bombers. For vital installations the solution of the problem is dispersal and separation from telltale localities. The basis of effective camouflage for such installations is precautionary design, made before the installations are erected.   P. L. C.

CAMP, WALTER CHAUNCEY (1859-1925), American sportsman, father of American football and originator of the annual All-America team, was born Apr. 7, 1859, at New Haven, Conn. Entering Yale University in 1876, he helped organize an intercollegiate football team in his freshman year, when the game was simply a rough variation of English rugby. In 1877 he was Yale's representative at the first intercollegiate football conference and was a member of every subsequent convention and of the rules committee until his death. He is credited with inventing the scrimmage—a lineup of players on opposing sides at the start of each play—which he called the distinguishing feature of the American game. It enabled the development of football strategy, which was Camp's chief contribution to the sport. Although he never officially held the position of head coach, he was chief football adviser, "coach of the coaches," for thirty years at Yale, and as treasurer of the Yale Field Association he was responsible for the general management of all Yale athletics until his resignation in 1910.

The first All-America football team was selected by Camp in 1889. Five Princeton University players were named and three each from Yale and Harvard universities. Eventually hundreds of assistants throughout the country sent him recommendations for the mythical eleven. Until his death the selections were published in *Collier's* magazine, to which Camp contributed a regular column, "Outdoor America," for many years. Meanwhile he worked through the ranks to become president of the New Haven Clock Company, eventually becoming chairman of the board. Always an ardent believer in physical conditioning, he devised a setting-up routine which he named the "Daily Dozen," a term destined to become part of the language. Camp taught the drills to the Navy's physical education instructors in World War I and himself led President Wilson's war cabinet through the exercises for a time. He died in New Haven, Mar. 14, 1925.
                                                                    R. E. Le.

CAMPAGNA, GEROLAMO [kampa′nya] (c.1549-c.1626), Italian sculptor, was born at Verona about 1549 and studied under Danese di Michele Cattaneo at Verona, Venice, and Padua. Upon the death of his master in 1573 he finished the reliefs for the Cappella del Santo in Padua. His most important works are to be found in Venice and include the early statue of the Doge Leonardo Loredano, on the Doge's tomb in Santi Giovanni e Paolo; the altar of San Giorgio Maggiore; and the statue of St. Anthony in San Giacomo di Rialto. Campagna is noted for the sensitive but firm modeling of the heads of his figures. He died, probably in Venice, some time around 1626.   R. T.

CAMPAGNA DI ROMA. *See* ROME.

CAMPANELLA, TOMMASO [kampane′lla] (1568-1639), Italian philosopher, was born at Stilo, in Calabria, Sept. 5, 1568. He became a Dominican at fifteen, studying scholastic philosophy at Dominican schools. On reading Telesio's *De rerum natura* he turned against Aristotelian philosophy and published a defense of Telesio entitled *Philosophia sensibus demonstrata* (1591). Arrested in 1599 for conspiring against the Spanish regime at Naples, he was imprisoned for a term of twenty-seven years, during which his chief philosophical works were written. He died in Paris on May 21, 1639.

Campanella's philosophy attempts a scientific proof of the doctrines of Christianity on the basis of sense perception and the mind's knowledge of itself. The universe is constituted by the mixture of being with nonbeing, change arising from the contrary principles of love and strife. All things possess soul and feeling on various levels; all strive for self-preservation, but in rational beings this is ultimately achieved only through union with God.

The political philosophy in his *Città del sole* (*City of the Sun*) advocates a communistic, eugenically controlled society, ruled by a priest-king and three ministers of state. This utopian picture reflects Campanella's dream of converting all mankind to Catholicism through his philosophy and of establishing an authoritarian world state under the leadership of the Papacy.   E. A. M.

CAMPANIA [kampa′nya], a region in the southern part of Italy, comprising the area on the west coast of the peninsula along the Tyrrhenian Sea between the Garigliano River on the north and the Gulf of Policastro on the south. Campania extends inland to the easternmost range of the Apennines and includes a large proportion of mountainous country. Also within the region are the islands of Capri, Procida, Ischia, and the Pontine Islands. The modern Campania thus refers to a much wider area than did its ancient counterpart, *ager Campanus*, which was confined essentially to the plain behind Naples. Campania comprises the provinces of

SORRENTO, ITALY, OVERLOOKING THE BAY OF NAPLES

Avellino, Naples, Salerno, Benevento, and Caserta. It covers an area of 5,248 sq. mi.

Topography. Economically and historically the coastal plains are the most important part of the region and contain a large part of the population in spite of the presence of Mount Vesuvius. The soil of the Campanian Plain which lies between the mountains and the sea is extremely fertile, particularly where it is of volcanic origin. The Campi Flegrei, located in the western part of the province of Naples, forms a zone of hot springs and extinct volcanic matter, while Vesuvius is still active. The Plain of Paestum, along the Gulf of Salerno in the south, is composed of material deposited by the Sele River and its tributaries.

The mountainous zones comprise the interior and also the peninsula of Sorrento, projecting into the Bay of Naples, and the Cilento Peninsula, which is situated between the Gulf of Salerno and the Gulf of Policastro. Several roughly parallel chains or massifs provide the backbone of the mountainous zone. In the north is the Matese (6,300 ft.); in the center, the Monti Picentini (6,000 ft.); and in the Cilento Peninsula, several isolated peaks of which the highest is Monte Cervati (6,200 ft.). Except for its easternmost edge, Campania lies within the Tyrrhenian watershed. Its chief rivers are the Sele, Volturno, and Garigliano, with their tributaries.

Climate. The wide variation in topography results in similarly marked differences in climate within the region. The coastal regions and the adjacent plains enjoy hot summers and moderately cool winters, as is evident from the palms and other subtropical vegetation found there. The highlands are not only colder in winter, but receive much more rain, as much as 75 in., compared with 40 or 35 along the coast. The rainy season comes in late fall and early winter; the summers are generally dry.

Flora. The natural vegetation, in turn, reflects topographic and climatic conditions. Up to 1,300 ft., thickets, shrubs, and plane trees are found. On the middle slopes of the mountains, there are oak and other deciduous trees; and higher up, above the timber line, are beech and fir, interspersed with pasture lands.

Population. Approximately 85 per cent of the population of Campania (estimated at 4,515,700 in 1954) lives in urban centers. However, the proportion of those in scattered dwellings rises to nearly one third in the province of Benevento. About two dozen cities have a population of over 15,000, and nearly all of these are on the Bay of Naples and in the fertile Campanian Plain.

Only in recent decades has the population of Campania increased to any extent. The census records from 1861 to 1921 showed only a small increase, while the record for 1911 even showed a decrease over previous censuses. The emigration after the unification of Italy was the primary reason for the slow rate of population growth in the region, but the malarial conditions of the coastal lowlands and the unproductivity of the mountain areas were contributing factors. During the first fifteen years of the twentieth century the number of emigrants, most of whom went to the United States or Argentina, reached 1,000,000. The number dropped during World War I, but mounted again in 1920 to 82,779. Later the Fascist regime discouraged and eventually forbade emigration, and the rate dropped sharply.

Economic Activities. Of the four principal agricultural regions, there is first the very fertile central and southern parts of the Campanian Plain and the district around Salerno, where wheat, corn, tobacco, olives, vegetables, fruit, and grapes for wine are produced in large quantities. The holdings in this area tend to be rather small. Secondly, there are plains where cultivation is extensive and the raising of livestock is very important, such as in the lower valleys of the Garigliano, Volturno, and Sele. As reclamation work goes on in this area where malaria had always been a danger, and as more land is brought under cultivation, economic conditions here are improving. The third region comprises the hills and mountain slopes up to about 2,000 ft. and is characterized by an expanding grain culture as well as orchards and vineyards. In the highest, fourth zone, woods and pastures intermingle with cultivated fields of hardy grains and vegetables. Sheepherding is common in this area, which is, in general, the poorest of all the zones.

Fruit canning, food processing, fishing, and the making of wine, olive oil, cheese, and hemp are also important industries. There are sulphur mines in the province of Avellino. The tourist industry is of major importance in Naples and its environs. The chief industrial cities are Naples and Salerno. Among the most important manufactures are cotton textiles, machinery, iron and steel, at the Ilva plant west of Naples, and such luxury and export items as gloves, cameos, laces, and statuary. Naples, a great port and railway center, is the hub of Campania's communications system. Smaller ports are Salerno, Torre Annunziata, and Castellammare di Stabia. The latter city has diversified industries, naval yards, and an arsenal; and its mineral springs have made it a health resort since Roman times. The region's highway network has been improved and expanded.

History. The coastal area of Campania, especially around Naples, was colonized by the Greeks, whereas the mountainous interior was occupied by the Samnites and other Italic tribes. Campania was one of the early conquests of Rome, and as an important coastal and seaport area it played an important part in the expansion of her empire. After the disintegration of the Roman Empire, however, Byzantine rule was established along the coast. Lombard rule was established over the principality of Benevento and later over the principalities of Salerno and Capua in the interior. As the Byzantine power waned, Naples, Sorrento, and Amalfi became largely self-governing. This politically fragmented condition made the conquest of Campania by the Normans fairly easy. Starting with the county of Aversa in 1030, they expanded in all directions until, by 1139, even Naples fell to them. Thenceforth, the region was governed by the Normans, and by the Hohenstaufens, Angevins, Aragonese, Spanish, and Bourbons as part of the Kingdom of Naples, or the Two Sicilies. In 1860 Campania joined united Italy. The Campania region was heavily bombed and damaged during World War II.

CAMPANILE [ka′mpəni′li; Ital. kɑ′mpɑni′le], a bell tower, frequently detached from the church, cathedral, or town hall to which it belongs. Originating after bells were adopted by the Christian Church during the sixth century, the campanile, serving both as a belfry and a watchtower, became an important feature in Italian architecture.

Lombardic Examples. Lombardy, in northern Italy, produced the finest of these towers. Perhaps no feature of the Lombard Romanesque has more completely disseminated itself beyond the limits of the Lombard style than has the bell tower. Unlike the round towers of Ravenna, among the earliest of their kind, Lombard towers were square in plan and, in the earlier examples, unadorned until the open-belfry stage was reached. A low pyramidal roof of tiles generally crowned these structures. The campanile of the cathedral at Torcello is an excellent unadorned specimen. Soon, however, the lower walls were relieved by pilaster strips and engaged (partly embedded) shafts, knitted together by bow-shaped corbel tables (flat raised surfaces) which marked the various stages. The next step was to pattern the walls with superimposed blind arcades and eventually to pierce the walls with openings that increased in area as the top was approached. The tower at Pomposa illustrates this fenestration, or window treatment. Earlier and later types of Lombardic campaniles are illustrated by the towers that flank the Church of Sant' Ambrogio at Milan and by the campanile of the cathedral at Cremona.

Roman Examples. Curiously, the earliest extant square towers are to be found adjacent to churches at Rome. Dating from the seventh century are the campaniles of Sts.

Giovanni Paolo, San Lorenzo in Lucina, St. Agnes Outside-the-Walls, and San Giorgio in Velabro. One of the tallest and most graceful in Rome is the terraced clock and bell tower of Santa Maria in Cosmedin. The tower at Terracina is particularly interesting in having its four stages adorned with pointed blind arcades with occasional openings left for light.

San Gottardo, Milan. A particularly beautiful campanile is the octagonal belfry of San Gottardo at Milan, all that remains of this venerable church. Of brick, it is ornamented with marble corner columns which ascend the principal shaft to be united by blind arcades at the top. Above this stands an open octagonal belfry, of smaller diameter, crowned by a tall conical roof. The tower is excellent in composition, ornament, and coloring, which is of a deep rich brick red with inserts of terra cotta. Other interesting examples are the campaniles of San Zenone at Verona, San Abbondio at Como, and San Pietro at Bologna.

San Marco (St. Mark's), Venice. The graceful tower of San Marco, begun near the opening of the tenth century, retained its original form until about the middle of the twelfth century, when it was largely rebuilt in the form approaching that of recent centuries. This tower collapsed in 1902 but was reconstructed (1905-1912) according to its time-honored design, which has been much admired and copied by architects. It presents a square shaft of brick

CAMPANILE OF ST. MARK'S, VENICE, ITALY

RAFFIUS · CUSHING PHOTO

topped by a belfry of white Istrian stone and a steep roof ornamented in blue with gold stars. The magnificent loggia at its entrance does not belong to the original construction but is the work of the Renaissance master Jacopo Sansovino (c. 1486-1570).

Leaning Tower, Pisa. The Campanile (Leaning Tower) of Pisa, begun in 1174, is a circular structure of superimposed white-marble arcades some 52 ft. in diameter and 179 ft. high. During its erection, the foundations settled on one side, causing the tower to lean 13 ft., 10 in. from the vertical. Its decorative arcades, enhanced by the bright Italian sun, form a spectacle both unique and beautiful. The belfry is reached by a ramp within the tower.

Creeping, or European bellflower, Campanula rapunculoides

COURTESY OF THE AMERICAN MUSEUM OF NATURAL HISTORY

Giotto's Tower, Florence. One of the most famed and beautiful of all Italian church towers is the campanile of the Cathedral of Florence, popularly known as Giotto's Tower. Giotto (c.1266-1337) did not live to finish its construction, but Andrea Pisano and Francesco Talenti completed it, with some changes in Giotto's original design, in 1387. The general mass is that of the traditional Lombard campanile. Its exterior has a veneer of rich white and green panels with inserted strips of colorful mosaics by the brothers Cosmati. The openings, of Gothic design, blend beautifully into the mural adornment of the walls; and the sculptural figures, canopies, and groups of small twisted columns are among the decorative triumphs of the era. The general effect produced, described as a "union of strength and delicacy, of simplicity of design with richness of ornament," places Giotto's Tower well toward the top in campanile design. Giotto himself personally sculptured two of the bas-reliefs which ornament the tower.

Communal Towers. Campaniles attached to churches or cathedrals were not the only belfries erected by medieval Italy. In the category of communal towers, erected both for defense (watchtowers) and alarm (belfries), are such towers as those at San Gimignano and Bologna, the Palazzo dei Signori at Verona, and the brilliant alarm tower on the Palazzo Vecchio at Florence. The Palazzo rises to a height of 300 ft. from the face of the crowning gallery of the palace, itself terminating in an embattled cornice bearing the open belfry. This tower, greatly admired by architects, was the prototype of many a firehouse tower during the Eclectic period of American architecture, near the close of the nineteenth century. Other edifices like the

Bargello at Florence, Palazzo Pubblico at Siena, Palazzo del Podestà at San Gimignano and Palazzo dei Priori at Volterra furnish comparable examples.

Though western Europe has towers and belfries attached to churches and cathedrals, usually they are such integral parts of the design as not to stand apart as separate entities, except in the civic towers of the Low Countries. Such towers as that on the Halles at Bruges, Belgium, are comparable to Italian examples, as are certain of the carillon towers of Holland and Belgium. Here, as in the Italian towns, towers were erected as symbols of power or as civic commemorative monuments.

In Great Britain and the United States, campaniles have been erected as civic projects or as commemorative monuments, the Cabot Tower at Bristol, England, for example, and the campaniles on certain American college campuses.

R. Ne.

CAMPANULA [kampǽ'nyulɑ], a large genus of plants of the bellflower family, chiefly native to the Northern Hemisphere. They are herbs with bell-shaped flowers, white, violet-blue, or deep violet. Among the twenty species found in the United States are the tall bellflower, *C. americana*, 6 ft. tall with dull blue flowers in long clusters; the harebell or bluebell, *C. rotundifolia*, low (1.5 ft.) with drooping flowers; and the dainty (1-3 ft.) California bellflower, *C. prenanthoides*. Bellflowers are easy to grow, and many, both tall and dwarf, are cultivated. *See also* BELLFLOWER; HAREBELL.

J. C. Wis.

CAMPBELL, ALEXANDER (1788-1866), Irish-American editor, preacher, college president, and religious reformer, was born at Ballymena, County Antrim, Ireland, on Sept. 12, 1788, the son of Thomas Campbell, a Seceder Presbyterian minister. After a year in the University of Glasgow he came to America in 1809 to join his father in Washington, Pa., and in 1811 settled at Bethany, in what later became West Virginia. Both father and son broke with the Presbyterian Church in 1812, adopting baptism by immersion at this time, and together embarked on a program of reform. This program was designed to end sectarian divisions and to unite Christians by granting them liberty in all matters of opinion and by prescribing no other conditions of fellowship than those which were applied in the primitive church.

Alexander Campbell soon assumed the leadership of this movement. He founded, edited, and published a magazine, the *Christian Baptist* (1823-1830), while he was associated with the Baptists, but when the movement which he led became a separate religious body, the Disciples of Christ, in 1830, he began publication of the *Millennial Harbinger,* which continued until 1870 and under his editorship until 1863. Campbell was a voluminous writer, made many lecture and preaching tours, engaged in five public debates, one with the social philosopher Robert Owen and one with the Roman Catholic Archbishop Purcell of Cincinnati, was a member of the Virginia Constitutional Convention of 1829, conducted a large and profitable farm, and was for twenty years the president of Bethany College, which he founded in 1840. Before his death on Mar. 4, 1866, in Bethany, the religious movement which he initiated had attained a membership of more than 300,000.

W. E. G.

CAMPBELL, BEATRICE TANNER, known on the stage as Mrs. Patrick Campbell (1865-1940), English actress and wit, was born in London on Feb. 9, 1865. She was married twice, in 1884 to Patrick Campbell, who died in 1900, and in 1914 to George West. Her appearance in 1893, under Pinero's direction in the leading role of his then revolutionary play, *The Second Mrs. Tanqueray,* put her immediately into the forefront among English actresses. She is remembered along Broadway as the temperamental star of Shaw's *Pygmalion,* whose manager, A. H. Woods, once carpeted the street in front of the Selwyn Theatre with tanbark to quiet the street noises while she was playing. In her later days she made a cult of rudeness, and she may be remembered as much for her excessively frank *mots* as for her acting talent, which dimmed as she grew older. She died in Pau, France, Apr. 9, 1940.   D. T.

CAMPBELL, SIR COLIN, BARON CLYDE (1792-1863), British soldier, was born in Glasgow on Oct. 20, 1792, as Colin Macliver. He entered the army as an ensign in 1808 and served with great bravery in the Peninsula War from 1810 until 1813, when he had already reached the rank of captain. After nearly three decades of garrison duty, from 1842 to 1846 he served in China, being promoted to brigadier general in 1844. In 1846 he was sent to India, took part in the second Sikh War, and was put in command of the North West Frontier from 1849 to 1852. He was knighted in 1849. He returned to England in 1853, was made a major general in 1854, and played a distinguished part before Sevastopol (1854-1855) during the Crimean War. In July, 1857, on the outbreak of the Sepoy Mutiny, he was appointed commander in chief in India. He organized a small army, subdued lower Bengal, and fought his way to the relief of Lucknow and the evacuation of its garrison. In 1858 he recaptured Lucknow, subdued Oudw, and brought peace to northern India. For his distinguished services as a military organizer and as a fighter, he was promoted to the rank of general and was made Baron Clyde in 1858, and field marshal in 1862. In 1860 his failing health forced him to leave India. He died at Chatham, England, on Aug. 14, 1863.   E. R. A.

CAMPBELL, SIR MALCOLM (1885-1949), British sportsman, the first man to go five miles a minute in an automobile, was born in Kent, England, Mar. 11, 1885. He served in the Royal Air Force in World War I. Campbell set his first record in the first of his several speed cars named *Bluebird* when he drove 146.16 m.p.h. in Wales in 1924. Several times in the next thirteen years he set new one-mile speed marks on courses at Daytona Beach, Fla., and the Bonneville, Utah, salt flats. Campbell broke Major H. O. D. Segrave's record with a 206.956-m.p.h. run at Daytona Beach in 1928 and beat his own mark with 245.735 m.p.h. on the same course on Feb. 5, 1931, a feat for which King George V knighted him. At Bonneville, on Sept. 3, 1935, Sir Malcolm became the first man in history to drive more than 300 m.p.h., being timed at 301.129. In 1937 he retired from auto racing and turned to motor boats. He set a world record for unlimited hydroplanes when he piloted his *Bluebird* 141.7 m.p.h. at Lake Coniston, England, Aug. 19, 1939. After World War II, Campbell experimented with jet-propelled boats. He died Jan. 1, 1949, at his home in Surrey.

R. E. Le.

CAMPBELL, THOMAS (1777-1844), Scottish poet, was born July 27, 1777, in Glasgow. He was educated at the University of Glasgow, where he distinguished himself in classical studies. After a period of indecision as to his professional life, he turned to literature and in 1799 produced *The Pleasures of Hope,* an unusually successful didactic poem in couplet form. After nine months' stay in Ratisbon he returned to London, and on Oct. 10, 1803, married his cousin

Matilda Sinclair. In 1809 appeared his poem *Gertrude of Wyoming,* a highly colored account of the destruction of Wyoming, Penn., which took place in 1778. His extensive anthology, *Specimens of the British Poets* was completed in 1819. From 1820 to 1830, he acted as editor of the *New Monthly Magazine,* but he found his work uncongenial and performed it poorly. In 1825 he wrote his important communication to the London *Times* suggesting the establish-

THOMAS CAMPBELL

FROM AN OLD ENGRAV-
ING OF A PAINTING BY
SIR THOMAS LAWRENCE

ment of the University of London; with the aid of Lord Brougham (1778-1868) this project was brought to a successful completion in 1828.

Campbell's declining years were largely given over to the writing of inferior biographies of Mrs. Siddons (1834) and of Petrarch (1840). He visited Algeria in 1834 and published his *Letters from the South* in 1837. His two narrative poems *Theodoric* (1824) and *The Pilgrim of Glencoe* (1842) disappointed early admirers. Campbell's fame rests chiefly upon his martial poems, *Ye Mariners of England, The Battle of the Baltic,* and *Hohenlinden,* all published early in his career. Acclaimed in his lifetime as a "living classic," praised by Byron and Francis Jeffrey, Campbell enjoyed a very high reputation, especially during the early years of the nineteenth century. He died at Boulogne, June 15, 1844. C. D.

CAMPBELL, WILLIAM WALLACE (1862-1938), American astronomer, was born in Hancock Co., Ohio, Apr. 11, 1862. He graduated from the University of Michigan in 1886, and for the next two years taught mathematics at the University of Colorado. He returned to the University of Michigan in 1888 to teach astronomy. In 1891 he went to the Lick Observatory, Mount Hamilton, Calif., as an astronomer, becoming director in 1901. Campbell's principal work was the determination of stellar radial velocities by high-precision spectrographic means. One of his leading researches was the determination of solar motion and the "sun's way." Campbell discovered many spectroscopic binaries and was particularly interested in solar eclipses. He conducted eight eclipse expeditions from 1898 to 1923. In 1923 Campbell became president of the University of California, resigning in 1930. He wrote *Elements of Practical Astronomy* (1900), and *Stellar Motions* (1912). Campbell died in San Francisco, Calif., June 14, 1938.   H. S. R.

CAMPBELL, a city in Mahoning Co., Ohio, located on the Mahoning River, adjacent to Youngstown. Campbell was known as East Youngstown from 1909, the date of its incorporation, until 1926 when the city council changed the name. The city is administered by a mayor and council. Transportation facilities are supplied by the major air and rail lines serving near-by Youngstown. Campbell is known for its steel products, particularly sheet and tubing. Wood patterns, sash, and storm windows are also manufactured. Pop. 1950, 12,882.

CAMPBELL-BANNERMAN, SIR HENRY (1836-1908), British politician, was born in Glasgow on Sept. 7, 1836, and was educated at Glasgow High School, Glasgow University, and Trinity College, Cambridge. He entered Parliament in 1868 as Liberal member for Stirling Burghs, a seat he represented until his death. From 1871 to 1874 and from 1880 to 1882 he was financial secretary to the War Office; in 1882 he became secretary to the Admiralty and in 1884 Chief Secretary for Ireland. He entered the cabinet as Secretary for War in 1886, but the government was defeated and it was not until 1892 that he returned to this office, which he held until 1895. Throughout he had supported Home Rule for Ireland, the great issue of the day. The divisions that had arisen in the Liberal Party because of this question led, in 1899, to the election of Campbell-Bannerman as its leader in the House of Commons, not because he was particularly distinguished but because he was the man least likely to offend any interest. In this position he opposed tariff reform (i.e., the imposition of duties on imports). He became Prime Minister in December 1905; and in the parliamentary elections held the following month, the Liberals gained an overwhelming victory over the Unionists (Conservatives and Liberal-Unionists). His greatest achievement was the grant of responsible government to South Africa. Early in 1908 his health became poor, and he resigned on April 4. He died in London on Apr. 22, 1908.   E. R. A.

CAMPBELLFORD, a town in Northumberland Co., Ontario, Canada, is situated on the Trent River, 95 mi. northeast of Toronto. A village since 1876, it became a town in 1906. The surrounding countryside is devoted to dairying, and the production of cheese is of major importance. Power developments on the Trent are utilized for the manufacture of lumber and wood products, shoes, and woolens. Pop. 1956, 3,425.

CAMPBELLTON [ka′mbəltən], a town and port in Restigouche Co., New Brunswick, Canada, situated on the Restigouche River, 180 mi. north of Saint John, on Provincial Highway 11. Rail transportation is furnished by the Canadian National Railways. An important sawmilling center, the town was incorporated in 1888. About 55 per cent of its people are of French origin. Pop. 1956, 8,389.
     D. F. P.

CAMPECHE [kampi′tshi; kɑmpe′tshe], a city and a state on the west coast of the Yucatán Peninsula in southeastern Mexico, on the Gulf of Campeche.

The City. Campeche, a seaport and the capital of Campeche state, is situated about 95 mi. southwest of Mérida and about 600 mi. east of Mexico City. It is a rail and air junction, with connections to Mérida, Mexico City, and Veracruz, and a trading center, exporting sugar, fine woods, cigars, hides, chicle, and sisal. The harbor is shallow; vessels anchor outside the port. Campeche's industrial products include cigarettes, cigars, copra, coconut oil, cordage, tortoise-shell articles, leather goods, hats, and liquors. The prosperity which the city enjoyed as one of the three open ports operating under the Spanish regime in the sixteenth and seventeenth centuries is reflected in its many shaded squares, old citadel, university, museum, hospital, market, and handsome theatre. Historically, Campeche is noteworthy as the spot where the Spaniards first set foot on Mexican soil, in 1517. The city was founded 23 years later by Francisco de Montejo on the site of an old Indian village. In 1659 the city was sacked by the British and in 1678 and 1685 by buccaneers; ruins of walls 8 ft. thick are relics of defenses erected against such raids. During the revolution of 1842 several battles between Mexicans and Yucatán natives took place in Campeche. There are a number of picturesque caves near Bolonchenticul, 40 mi. east. Pop. 1950, 31,279.

The State. Campeche state, organized in 1862, has an area of 19,672 sq. mi. It is bounded on the west by the Gulf of Campeche, on the north by Yucatán, on the east by Quintana Roo, on the southwest by Tabasco, and on the south by Guatemala. The climate is hot and the rainfall frequent and heavy. The state is largely a sandy, unproductive plain, but there are tracts in the north, where elevations occur, which are suited to cattle-grazing; bananas, cotton, corn, tobacco, sugar cane, rice, and coconuts are also grown here. Fishing is carried on along the coast and in the Laguna de Términos, which is enclosed by the sand bar of Carmen Island. The southern part of the state is heavily forested, yielding, in addition to medicinal plants, cedar, lignum vitae, mahogany, and other valuable woods, including the *palo de campeche,* a logwood for which the state is named. Logwood and chicle, extracted from the *zapote chico* tree, are among the chief exports. There are a number of navigable rivers in the south, and the principal railway

Old city wall with tower fortress built at Campeche in the time of Spanish rule

crosses the state from Tabasco to Mérida. Carmen is the chief city and seaport after Campeche; other important centers are Calkini and Hecelchakán. Pop. 1950, 122,098.

S. G. I.

CAMPER, PETER [kɑ′mpər] (1722-1789), Dutch naturalist, was born at Leiden, the Netherlands, May 11, 1722. His father, Florent Camper, was a clergyman and other members of his family had long been distinguished in the local government.

Camper combined a deep aesthetic sense and interest in the arts with a love for natural history. It was this combination that led to some of the work for which he is still remembered. Educated in medicine, he received his degree at Leiden in 1746. After visiting England and various scientific centers on the continent, where he came into contact with the leading scientists of his day, he returned to the Netherlands and settled at Franeker in 1749 as professor of medicine and surgery. In 1755 he was called to Amsterdam where he was appointed professor at the Athenaeum. In 1761 he retired from Amsterdam, returning once more to Franeker. In 1763 he was appointed professor at Groningen. He died at The Hague, April 7, 1789.

Although Camper wrote on medical subjects, his best-known contributions lay in the field of natural history, a subject to which he was deeply devoted and which he approached primarily as a comparative anatomist. He dissected and reported exhaustively on orangutans, elephants, birds, and other animals. He described fossils that came to his attention and wrote about a considerable range of subject matter. He is an important historical figure in anthropology because of his discovery of the usefulness of the facial angle for determining not only differences between animals but also racial differences between the varieties of man. This represented one of the first attempts to bring measurement and objective observation to the problem of racial classification. Camper was widely known and respected. He received many of the highest honorary distinctions in science and also served his country in a political capacity.

H. L. Sh.

CAMPERDOWN, BATTLE OF (Oct. 11, 1797), a naval engagement off the coast of the Netherlands between a British squadron commanded by Admiral Adam Duncan and a Dutch fleet under Admiral Jan Willem De Winter. Holland had been invaded a short time earlier by the French, and a Batavian Republic had been organized in close alliance with France. The Dutch fleet thus became a definite threat to British supremacy of the seas, and its destruction was eagerly sought by the British Admiralty. This objective was substantially achieved by the English victory at Camperdown.

M. K.

CAMP FIRE GIRLS, INC., a national American youth agency for girls from 7 to 18, founded in 1910 by a group of educators headed by Dr. and Mrs. Luther H. Gulick. It was incorporated in 1912. About 400,000 girls in over 300 councils throughout the United States are engaged in the organization's leisure-time program. Members govern themselves by the Law of the Camp Fire Girls: Worship God, Seek Beauty, Give Service, Pursue Knowledge, Be Trustworthy, Hold on to Health, Glorify Work, Be Happy. The organization's primary purpose is to perpetuate the spiritual ideals of the home and to stimulate and aid in forming good health and character habits. Through its Seven Crafts: Home, Creative Arts, Outdoors, Frontiers of Science, Business, Sports and Games, and Citizenship, girls learn by doing, and earn honors in four ranks: Trail Seeker,

Wood Gatherer, Fire Maker, and Torch Bearer. Ceremonials, known as council fires, are held in observance of special occasions: awarding of honors, taking of rank, welcoming new members, or celebrating anniversaries. Recognizing that the interests of young girls vary with their growth, the organization provides programs for three age groups—Blue Birds, from 7 through 9; Camp Fire Girls, from 10 through 14, and Horizon Clubbers, from ninth grade through high school. In supplementing training at home, church, and school, Camp Fire directs girls' recreational activities into wholesome channels by redirecting interests to worthwhile causes and challenging creative imagination.

E. McS.

CAMPHOR. *See* ORGANIC CHEMISTRY.

CAMPHOR TREE, *Cinnamomum camphora,* a member of the laurel family native to China and Japan, is a dense-topped tree growing to 40 ft. It has shining thick leaves, small yellow flowers, and berrylike fruits. All the juices of the tree contain camphor, and from these gum camphor is made. It is much planted for ornament, especially along roads in Texas, southern California, and Florida, where it has sometimes run wild. The wood, which retains its aroma a long time, is much used for chests and cabinets.

J. C. Wis.

CAMPI, GIULIO [kɑ′mpi] (c.1502-1572), Italian painter and a member of a family of painters, was born in Cremona about 1502. He studied in the city of his birth under his father, Galeazzo Campi, and later, from about 1540, in Mantua, under Giulio Romano. He was the founder of the school of Cremona. Among his works are a portrait of his father in the Uffizi, Florence; the altarpiece for the high altar at San Abbondio; and a series of frescoes in the church of Santa Margherita, Cremona. He died in Cremona in 1572.

R. T.

CAMPIN, ROBERT [kɑ′mpɪn] (c.1418-1444), Flemish painter formerly known as the Master of Flémalle and Master of the Mérode Altarpiece. Campin, an artist in Tournai, is known from documents to have been a teacher of the famous Rogier van der Weyden and of Jacques Daret, who were enrolled as his apprentices from 1427 to about 1432. In 1909 Hulin de Loo suggested that Campin might be the painter of an important group of pictures whose origin had long been unknown. The style of these paintings shared so many characteristics with that of an altarpiece known to have been painted by Jacques Daret, and also with early works of Rogier, that de Loo reasoned they might have been painted by the early master of the two painters. Certain modern critics have even attempted to ascribe Campin's works to Rogier in his early period. But these works of Campin's are coarser in technique, stronger in modeling, and less noble in conception than Rogier's. They include four startlingly powerful panels, fragments of dismembered altarpieces, which are now in the Städel Institute in Frankfurt-am-Main. Three of them, which are supposed to have come from the Abbey of Flémalle, gave Campin the name Master of Flémalle; a triptych formerly belonging to the Countess Mérode at Tongerloo, Belgium, accounts for the name Master of Mérode. This altarpiece is now in The Cloisters, New York City. There are also by Campin a *Nativity* in the Museum at Dijon, two wings from the so-called Werl altarpiece in the Prado, and about twenty additional paintings, some of them only parts of larger works or contemporary copies of pictures which have long been lost. Campin died on Apr. 26, 1444.

M. Sa.

CAMPINAS [kəmpi′nəs], a city on the Piracicaba River, in the state of São Paulo, in southeastern Brazil, located at 22° 50′ S. lat. and 47° 5′ W. long. The city is connected with Santos, 115 mi. to the southeast, by railroad and highway, the latter route passing the beautiful waterfalls of Salto d'Itu. Campinas, which is 2,000 ft. above sea level, lies in a shallow valley of the central plateau of Brazil. The temperature ranges from 60° F. to 82° F. Campinas is a leading market for agricultural products, especially cotton and corn. The city has an excellent agricultural school. Among the local industries are sugar refineries, tanneries, foundries, food-processing plants, textile and paper mills, and drug, soap, and cosmetic factories. Pop. 1950, 99,156.

CAMPING, an activity which, in general terms, involves temporary outdoor living. The word comes from the Latin *campus* meaning field. Camping, as a mode of living, is as old

Campers at Schroon Lake in the heart of New York's Adirondack Mountains cook at an outdoor fireplace.

as man and was probably the earliest form of living of the human race.

History. In primitive times, man's endeavors were largely centered about food, clothing, and shelter; and oftentimes were characterized by wandering from place to place in quest of better living conditions. Most organized groups, ranging from tribes to nations in their earliest stages of development, lived as nomads. The Bible has many examples of camp life, such as the wandering of the Israelites in the wilderness. The present concept of camping comes largely from the American Indians. Not only did they obtain their food, clothing, and shelter directly from nature through highly developed outdoor skills, but, in addition, had an aesthetic sense of appreciation of the outdoors. Their skills included hunting, fishing, handling of canoes, living in the woods, crafts, and fighting. In the United States seventy-five per cent of the population before 1880 were farmers or pioneers, and the children received most of their training through blazing trails, clearing the land, and other outdoor activities closely associated with camp life.

Thus, the human race has lived in camp situations—sleeping, eating, and working in the outdoors—for hundreds of thousands of years, while the modern indoor mode of life is only a few centuries old. Man's physical, mental, and spiritual characteristics were developed in a vigorous outdoor environment. The urge to be out-of-doors and to camp is thought by some to be a biological characteristic of man.

The advent of an industrialized society with its changed mode of living, congestion, specialization, and mass education, prompted a "return to nature" movement of many patterns, camping being one of the most popular. By the time three decades had elapsed in the twentieth century, and half the population of the United States lived in cities of eight thousand or over, most of the city dwellers and many in the rural areas had little knowledge of the woods, birds, animals, and flowers, and the skills that would enable them to enjoy the outdoors. Consequently, modern camping developed, designed to supplement modern living and provide opportunities for the development of outdoor skills, appreciations, and attitudes that are the birthright of any child.

CAMPING FOR PERSONAL RECREATION

Camping as a means of personal recreation may apply to a night's outing in a pup tent in one's back yard or to several weeks of outdoor living on a secluded lake or mountain. In any case the camper employs a minimum of primitive but functional equipment that furnishes almost all of civilization's basic conveniences. The essential purpose of camping, on any level, is to get out of doors and enjoy the experience of living close to nature.

Today's camper may travel by foot, horse, motorcar, or plane to the spot where he plans to camp, but once he arrives there, he usually supplies his own accommodations, or has, at the most, a bare wooden shelter or lean-to to live in.

The ideal campsite should be on rather high dry ground that drains easily. It should be away from thick tree-growths but near a good supply of firewood and water. Sleeping on the bare ground is made far more comfortable by the use of an air mattress which is inflated as used. If this type of equipment is not available, small pine boughs or other leafy branches may be piled into a fairly comfortable mattress. In the event that none of these sleeping aids is obtainable, a shallow trough may be dug to fit the hips and heels and the sleeper will pass a more restful night.

Ordinarily a party of two can be fairly well sheltered by using the standard pup tent. Larger parties require the taller and warmer wall tents that have floors and screening of suitable fabric to make them insect-proof.

Light sleeping bags of good quality are worth while under all circumstances since they take the place of several woolen blankets and provide a waterproof outer cover as well. Additional fundamental equipment necessary for a comfortable campsite includes a small gasoline stove for emergency or wet-weather cooking, a canvas water bucket or covered water storage bag, a sheath knife, a small hand axe, a waterproof flashlight, a set of aluminum cooking utensils, a set of eating utensils of the same material, a waterproof match box, and an adequate first-aid kit. Very useful but not essential are a large metal or canvas wash basin and a gasoline lantern.

Personal clothing should be durable, plain, and comfortable. Shoes should be at least high enough to cover the ankles and of roomy, soft, waterproof construction with heavy soles. It is best to wear only white woolen socks, particularly if any extensive hiking is planned. Trousers, for both men and women, offer the best protection when worn full-length and are most comfortable when made of tightly woven cotton poplin for warm weather and of worsted wool in colder seasons. At any time of the year shirts and short jackets are most useful when made of woolen material. A rough hat and leather gloves are good protection articles of clothing to take along on a camping trip.

A camper's fire must serve any one or all of three purposes: cooking, heating, and illumination. It thus requires some practice to build and control a fire for all of these functions, and at the same time avoid bad personal burns or destructive forest or brush fires. Campers often build too large a fire for efficient cooking. The proper use of very green forked sticks and large fore- and back-logs for supporting the cooking utensils allows full use of the heat from small cooking fires. After all cooking has been completed, the same fire may be built along different lines for either warmth or light. It is always convenient to heat the hot water for dishwashing during the consumption of the meal, before extinguishing or altering the cooking fire.

Experienced campers make wide use of dried or concentrated foods and juices. Fruits, vegetables, soups, eggs, and milk are among the staple food products that are available in this easy-to-carry form. Smoked or canned meats are practical when no hunting or fishing is possible to supply fresh meat. Packaged cereals and prepared mixes can be used as a basis for all camp meals. Also available are canned butter and jams for use with crackers, bread, or camp-made biscuits. To add tastiness to the often rather dull camp meals, a mild condiment such as ketchup, mustard, or tomato sauce is worth using. Purification tablets for drinking water make it unnecessary to boil water from unknown sources.

ORGANIZED CAMPING IN THE UNITED STATES

Development. The growth of organized camping in the United States commenced during the last half of the nineteenth century. The first organized camp was a school camp, founded by Frederick William Gunn in the summer of 1861 and located in Connecticut on Long Island Sound. It was for boys, and the program centered around military activities common to the Civil War period. The first recorded private camp was established in 1876 near Wilkes-Barre, Pa., by Joseph Trumble Rothrock, a physician. Twenty boys spent four months at the camp, participating in a program designed to provide experiences in healthful living. The camp established by Rev. George W. Hinckley at Wakefield, R. I., was probably the first church camp.

The period of greatest expansion in number and kinds of camps came from 1910 to 1930. By this time there were many youth agencies that included camping in their programs. National and state parks, equipped for camping and available to both youths and adults, developed rapidly. Such facilities are often free to the public or may be secured for minimum fees. A number of industries have also provided camping facilities for employees and their families. Another interesting development is the purchase and operation of camps by labor organizations.

Types of Camps. There are in the United States more than thirty distinct types of organized camps under the direction of agencies such as the Y.M.C.A., the Y.W.C.A., churches, Boy Scouts, Girl Scouts, Camp Fire Girls, Federation of Girls Clubs, Woodcraft League of America, newspapers, and magazines. Camps were also established by civic organizations including Rotary, Lions, Kiwanis, Exchange, Optimists, and others.

There were also educational, family, travel, ranch, health, tutoring, work, and music camps and special camps for undernourished, crippled, and cardiac cases.

Boys' and girls' summer camps, both private and institutional, are most common. Private camps usually extend for a period of about eight weeks, with fees of from $100 and upwards, while institutional camps have shorter sessions, often for only a two-week period, with fees ranging from nothing to $15.00 a week.

School Camping. School camping is an extension of the academic curriculum into the out-of-doors to provide those learning experiences that can be accomplished best outside the classroom and away from the immediate school environment. The areas of learning to which the camp makes a unique and important contribution include: social living, healthful living, work experience, science, and outdoor recreation.

There are many patterns of camping and outdoor education used by schools, such as year-round camping, weekend camping, outpost camping, travel camping, and day camping. Some schools that have facilities are operating camps so that children and teachers of selected grades, usually beginning with the elementary school, may spend two or more weeks camping during the school year. Usually a group of schools provide for a camp staff and use common facilities. Costs are paid from regular school funds, in addition to those contributed by community agencies. The cost of food, usually covered by a fee, is paid by the parents. Large numbers of schools that do not have camps suitable for year-round use provide opportunities for summer camping and occasional camp trips throughout the school year.

Today some states have legislation enabling school districts to purchase and operate camps as a part of the regular school program. Not only can camp counselors be trained through camps, but classes in human growth and development, psychology, and social work find it an excellent laboratory in which to study the behavior and learning of boys and girls.

Camping Associations and Agencies. Effort has been made to improve and extend camping by voluntary associations throughout the United States. Chief among them is the American Camping Association, an organization made up of representatives from private camps, institutional camps, and public camps. The Association has developed standards for the improvement of program and facilities. Many states have camping associations which serve similar purposes. State agencies also have a part in the development of camping, since several of the states have laws requiring approval or licensing of all camps.

Summary. The rapid increase in the number of camps of all kinds; the ability of the public, through better communication facilities, to reach the woods, lakes, hills, and streams; the provision by governmental agencies of public lands and facilities for outdoor recreation; and the more recent inclusion of camping in many schools and colleges point toward the continued growth of camping in America. Leaders in the field believe that camping is perhaps the most significant social trend toward strengthening the physical and mental fabric of an industrial society and renewing the spirit of man. Camping and outdoor activities are considered by some to be the "common mooring" of modern society. J. W. Sm. and A. Pe.

CAMPION, EDMUND [ka'mpiən] (1540-1581), English Jesuit, was born in London, Jan. 25, 1540, the son of a bookseller of the same name. He was educated at Christ

Church Hospital and at St. John's College, Oxford, and remained at St. John's to become a noted orator and tutor. Although raised as a Catholic, he took the Oath of Supremacy and the order of deacon in the Anglican Church. Repenting, he left Oxford in 1569 for Ireland, where he came under suspicion as a proselytizer for the ancient faith. Returning to England for a short time, he finally crossed to Douai and entered the seminary there. In 1573 Campion was admitted into the Society of Jesus and was ordained in 1578 in Prague. Assigned to the English Mission, he returned to England with Robert Parsons to win back Catholics who were wavering in their faith. On July 17, 1581, he was arrested as a traitor. Efforts to force him to recant failing, he was brought to trial in November and hanged at Tyburn on Dec. 1, 1581. His principal literary work was the tract, *Decem rationes*. He was beatified by Leo XIII in 1886.   W. J. R.

CAMPION, THOMAS [ka′mpiən] (1567-1620), English poet and composer, was born Feb. 12, 1567, in Chancery Lane, London, and studied at Cambridge and Gray's Inn. After serving as a soldier in Normandy in 1591, he published Latin epigrams and elegies in 1595. He wrote both words and music for *A Book of Airs* (1601), with his friend Philip Rosseter, and in *Observations in the Art of English Poesie* (1602) he gave examples of classical quantitative meters in English verse. Having qualified as Doctor of Medicine at Caen in 1605, he practiced medicine in London until his death on Mar. 1, 1620, in St. Dunstan's in the West. Campion wrote three wedding masques produced at court. His Latin verse, collected in 1619, was admired during his lifetime, but his modern fame rests on the beautiful poetry and music in his several books of songs, which have rarely been equaled in English lyric poetry.   M. E.

CAMPOAMOR Y CAMPOOSORIO, RAMÓN DE [ka′mpoamɔ′r i ka′mpooso′rio] (1817-1901), Spanish writer, was born in Navia, Asturias, Sept. 24, 1817, and was orphaned in early childhood. While still quite young, Campoamor considered becoming a Jesuit, but rejected the idea and went to Madrid, where he began the study of medicine. He soon abandoned this career in favor of literature and politics. A distinguished speaker of mildly conservative opinion, he was elected a deputy of the Cortes as well as being appointed provincial governor and secretary of the treasury. As a writer Campoamor explored all literary fields, from philosophy, in works such as *El Personalismo* (1855) and *Lo Absoluto* (1865), to tragedies such as *Guerra a la guerra* (1868). Yet he was particularly interested in poetry, and his renown among his contemporaries was such that he was compared to the greatest poets of humanity. Critics in later times have considered his work to be of little value from an aesthetic point of view, but interesting in so far as it reflects the tastes and ideas which characterized Spain just before the end of the nineteenth century. Although most of his works were written before the time of the Restoration (1874-1898), Campoamor anticipates and clearly represents this later period, known in Spain as "the foolish years." He died Feb. 11, 1901.

In his *Poética* (1883) Campoamor maintains that only rhythm should separate poetry from prose. His verses accord with this prosaic conception of poetry and represent a reaction against the excessive pomposity of the Romantic period. Indeed, Campoamor carries the reaction so far that at times he seems to identify poetry with platitude. His theory which holds that there is a relation between poetry and prose, how-

ever, foreshadows a prevalent twentieth-century conception of poetry.

Campoamor's poetry is sometimes extensive and pretentious, sometimes brief and simple. An example of his more elaborate style is *El Drama universal* (1869), in which he tried "to embrace all the passions and realities of life." It was a distinct failure. His briefer poems, often satiric, are more interesting, especially as documents of the time. Campoamor was the poetic echo of the society of his period; his value lies in his portrayal of an entire epoch.   J. A. L. M.

CAMPOBASSO [kɑ′mpo bɑ′sso], a province and its capital and chief city in the Abruzzi e Molise region, in south central Italy, situated on the Adriatic slope of the Apennines, some 40 mi. from the sea at an elevation of 2,620 ft. Because of its inland and mountainous position, the city experiences cold winters, when most of the rain falls, and cool summers. Campobasso is the market place for a considerable area of fertile farmlands producing wine, olive oil, fruit, and livestock, chiefly swine. The manufacture of cutlery is a leading industry of the city; other products are macaroni, flour, and furniture. The city has a technical institute. Although it is one of the less accessible provincial capitals of Italy, off the main tourist routes, Campobasso has railway connections with the Bari-Ancona line at the Adriatic port of Termoli, and with the Naples-Foggia line at Benevento. Overlooking the city is a hill crowned with the Monforte Castle, built in the fifteenth century. Pop. 1954 (city), 22,900; (commune), 30,000.

The province of Campobasso has an area of 1,714 sq. mi. and is crossed by the Apennines. The chief economic activities are agriculture, stock raising, and fishing, off the Adriatic coast. There is also some manufacturing. Pop. (est. 1954), 407,100.

CAMPO FORMIO, TREATY OF [kɑ′mpo fɔ′rmio] (1797), the settlement concluding the war which had been in progress between France and Austria between 1792 and 1797. As a result of Napoleon's campaigns in Italy in 1796 and 1797, the Austrian government was compelled to sign preliminaries of peace on Apr. 18, 1797, at Leoben. The final treaty was signed on Oct. 17 of the same year at Campo Formio. There were three main provisions. (1) The Austrian Netherlands and the Ionian Islands were ceded to France outright. (2) By a secret clause, the Austrian emperor consented to use his good offices to secure for France a great part of the left bank of the Rhine. A congress of the Holy Roman Empire was to be assembled at Rastatt to bring this clause into effect. (3) Austria agreed to recognize the two Italian states recently founded under French sponsorship: the Ligurian Republic and the Cisalpine Republic. The former was composed of Genoese territory, and the latter of Milan, Modena, a portion of Venetia, and a strip of papal territory. By the treaty French policy achieved an objective it had been pursuing since Richelieu's time: France finally reached her "natural" boundaries. The Rhine and the Scheldt were now her frontiers, and her influence in Italy was paramount. These newly won gains, however, proved far from secure. Great Britain was unreconciled to the new state of affairs, and Austria had by no means relinquished hope of regaining her lost possessions and with them her prestige.   M. K.

CAMPOS [kã̃′mpus], a city in the state of Rio de Janeiro, in southeastern Brazil. It is the state's leading industrial city, located on the south bank of the Paraíba River, about 23 mi.

from the coast and 198 mi. (by rail) northeast of Rio de Janeiro. The city is situated on a low-lying alluvial plain and has a warm and humid climate; the coldest month, July, averages between 50° and 68° F. The average annual rainfall is about 50 in. Campos, founded in 1730, is the center of a fertile region producing sugar, tobacco, cotton, rice, coffee, and tropical fruits. The principal industrial establishments are sugar refineries, alcohol distilleries, and canneries. Coastal lakes and canals afford adequate transportation. Pop. 1950, 52,677.

S. G. I.

CAMROSE, a town on Stony Creek, in Alberta, Canada, 50 mi. southeast of Edmonton. Founded as a planned railway village with the name of Sparling in 1904, it was incorporated as a town with its present name in 1907. It is the site of a Lutheran college and a normal school. The town is a distributing center for a rich agricultural area. Some lignite is mined on the outskirts. Pop. 1951, 4,131.

CAMS, profiled machine members which produce an intermittent motion, usually a reciprocating movement. The manner in which typical cams operate is described in the following illustrations.

Fig. 1 illustrates two common forms of cam action. In (a), shaft 1 turns at constant speed and cam 2 acts against

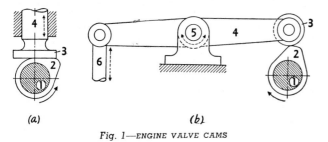

Fig. 1—ENGINE VALVE CAMS

flat foot 3 to lift follower 4 once each revolution of the shaft, as the high point of the cam passes under the follower foot. In (b), the cam acts against a roller 3, instead of a flat face as in (a), and the follower 4 is pivoted at 5 to give a downward push of rod 6. Cam arrangements of these types are used in gasoline engines to actuate the combustion-chamber valves. The valve remains closed for nearly three quarters of the revolution of the camshaft, opening quickly under cam action

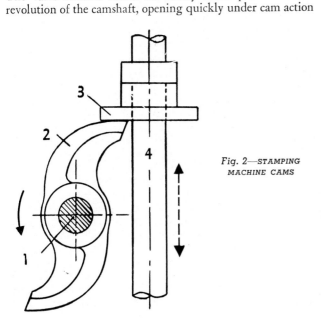

Fig. 2—STAMPING
MACHINE CAMS

and closing equally fast under spring action. The duration of valve opening depends upon the amount of cam dwell, or relative length of the high point of the cam face. Note that the dwell in (b) is longer than that in (a).

Cam designs for special services are shown in Figs. 2 and 3. Figure 2 represents a stamping action where cam 2 on constant-speed shaft 1 lifts follower shaft 4 twice every revo-

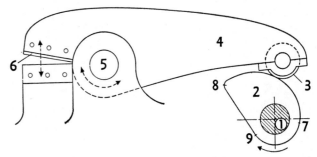

Fig. 3—SHEARING-MACHINE CAMS

lution through flat face 3. The resultant motion of the follower shaft produces pounding or stamping at regular intervals. Heavy-duty shearing action is depicted in Fig. 3. Cam 2 on constant-speed shaft 1 operates follower 4 through roller 3 in a specific manner to produce the desired shearing action at 6. A follower pivot is provided at 5. The specially designed shape of the cam causes the jaws of the sheer to approach each other with decreasing speed as the roller contact of the follower moves from points 7 to 8 on the cam face. Then, the shear rapidly returns to its open position under cam action from points 8 to 9, and the jaws of the shear remain open from points 9 to 7. Cams of these and similar types are widely used in automatic machinery to simulate hand motions and controls.

R. C. H. H.

CAMUS, ALBERT [ka'mü'] (1913-   ), French novelist and journalist, was born Nov. 7, 1913, in Mondoni, Algeria. During the German occupation of France he founded the resistance newspaper *Combat* and emerged from World War II as one of the intellectual leaders of the younger school. His works include *Noces* (1939) ("Wedding Feasts"), *L'Étranger* (1942) (*The Stranger,* 1946), *Le Mythe de Sisyphe* (1942) (*The Myth of Sisyphus,* 1955), *La Peste* (1947) (*The Plague,* 1948), *Le Minotaure* (1950), *Actuelles* (1950), *L'Homme revolté* (1951) (*The Rebel,* 1954); and four plays, *Caligula* and *Le Malentendu* ("The Misunderstanding"), both produced in 1944, *L'État de Siège* (1948) ("The State of Siege"), and *Les Justes* (1950) ("The Just"). Later works include *La Chute* (1956) (*The Fall,* 1957) and short stories, of which six were translated in *Exile and the Kingdom* (1958). Camus frequently writes on the theme of modern conscience, and he has sometimes been identified with the Existentialists. He received the Nobel Prize for literature for 1957.

R. J. N.

CANAAN [ke'nən], in the Old Testament, the son of Ham and grandson of Noah (Gen. ix:22; x:6), was traditionally the ancestor of the Canaanites, who occupied the lowlands of Palestine. The word *Canaan* comes from the root designating "to bow down" and was the name by which the land west of the Jordan, including Syria and the mountainous districts inhabited by Amorites, were known in early Biblical times. According to tradition, Abraham was bidden by God to leave his native Chaldea, and go to Canaan, which became the land of his descendants.

M. A. G.

CANAANITE [keˈnənɑit], a term designating a group of Semitic languages of ancient Syria and Palestine, embracing Hebrew, Phoenician, and other closely related dialects. Phoenician included the ancient dialects of the maritime city-states along the coast of what is now the Lebanese Republic; Hebrew speech fell into two main categories: the northern, or Israelite, and the southern, or Judean, branches. Other near-by nations also adhered to the Canaanite speech belt, among them the Moabites, who have left us a royal inscription so close to Hebrew that it can be interpreted on the basis of an Old Testament grammar and lexicon. Doubtless other neighbors, like the Edomites and Ammonites, used Canaanite, but the direct evidence is sketchy.

The earliest evidence of Canaanite dialects is shown in Canaanite words inserted into the Babylonian tablets found at Tell el-Amarna and dating from the early fourteenth century B.C. These words show that the Canaanite shift of $\bar{a}$ to $\bar{o}$ had already taken place; they also attest *bad*, "in the hand," as against Hebrew *ba-yad*. Far to the north, the Ugaritic documents of the Tell el-Amarna age, though they do not have the shift from $\bar{a}$ to $\bar{o}$, also use the form *bad*. Such indications as the latter have led most scholars to classify Ugaritic as Canaanite; but the fact remains that it is the only one of the alleged ancient Canaanite dialects that cannot be read, with minor adjustments, on the basis of the Old Testament grammar and lexicon.

The most distinctive feature of Canaanite is the inverting temporal use of the conjunction *wa*. When *wa* is prefixed to a verb at the beginning of a clause, it often gives the past, or "perfect," tense a future meaning, and the future, or "imperfect," tense a past meaning.   C. H. Go.

CANADA, a federated state occupying a large portion of the North American continent north of the United States. The word "Canada" is of Indian origin but of doubtful derivation. Its use was first noted by Jacques Cartier in 1535 as applied by the Indians of the village of Stadacona (now Quebec) to their tribal holding in that vicinity. The French extended its use to their St. Lawrence colony with its undetermined northwestern boundary. The British retained the name for the same area (although the St. Lawrence colony was officially known as Quebec) and in 1791 designated as "Lower" and "Upper" Canada what are now Quebec and Ontario respectively. In 1867 the name was given to the new federation. The term "Dominion of Canada" is not strictly accurate and is being replaced by the simpler designation "Canada." Canada is a limited monarchy and a parliamentary democracy, in association with other members of the Commonwealth of Nations. It consists of ten provinces, two federal territories, and the Labrador dependency of the province of Newfoundland. It is somewhat larger than either continental Europe or the United States.

Boundaries. Continental Canada is bounded on the east by the Atlantic Ocean, on the north by the Arctic Ocean, on the west by Alaska and the Pacific Ocean, and on the south by the United States. The Canada-Alaska boundary follows the 141 meridian from the Arctic to within 30 mi. of the Pacific, thence southward by a sinuous line about 30 mi. inland from the Pacific to the Portland Canal and 54° 40' N. lat. The Canada-United States boundary follows 49° N. lat. from the Pacific to Lake of the Woods, thence by connecting rivers, lakes, and portages to Lake Superior, through lakes Superior, Huron, Erie, and Ontario and their connecting waters, and down the St. Lawrence River to 45° N. lat., roughly along that parallel to the Connecticut River, thence by an irregular line bearing northeast to a line due north

from the source of the St. Croix River, and down that line and river to Passamaquoddy Bay. The length of the Canada-Alaska boundary is 1,540 mi. and of the Canada-United States boundary 3,987 mi. The main islands belonging to Canada in the Atlantic are Newfoundland, Cape Breton, Prince Edward, and Anticosti; and in the Pacific, Vancouver and the Queen Charlotte group. Also belonging to Canada is the Arctic Archipelago, bounded on the west and east respectively by 141° and 60° W. long.

Area. The total area of Canada on the accession of Newfoundland and its Labrador dependency on Mar. 31, 1949, was 3,845,774 sq. mi. The total area of the ten provinces is 2,333,795 sq. mi., that of the federal territories is 1,511,979 sq. mi., and that of Labrador about 110,000 sq. mi. In thousands of square miles the provinces, arranged in order of magnitude, are: Quebec, 595; Ontario, 413; British Columbia, 366; Alberta, 255; Saskatchewan, 252; Manitoba, 247; Newfoundland, 43; New Brunswick, 28; Nova Scotia, 21; and Prince Edward Island, 2. The area of Quebec exceeds twice the area of Texas by the area of Oklahoma. Prince Edward Island is only slightly larger than Delaware. Of the federal territories the Yukon has 207,076 sq. mi. and the Northwest Territories 1,304,903 sq. mi. The latter is divided into districts as follows: Mackenzie, on the mainland north of 60° N. lat. between the Yukon and 102° W. long., with 527,490 sq. mi.; Keewatin, between Mackenzie and Hudson Bay, with 228,160 sq. mi.; and Franklin, which consists of the Arctic Archipelago, with 549,253 sq. mi.

GEOLOGIC MOVEMENTS

The geologic structure of Canada consists of three major continental land forms: (1) a shield, (2) young mountains, and (3) downfolds.

The Canadian Shield. The Canadian Shield, which occupies about half the area of the Dominion, is a billowing crust of ancient rocks, geologically important because it does not yield at all readily to the vast earth forces involved in mountain building. This area, extending from Labrador to Lake Winnipeg, Lac la Ronge, the western end of Lake Athabaska, and Great Bear Lake, is characterized by expanses of granite rock, small lakes, and widespread woods of spruce and pine. Geologists know that its ancient rock formations date back before the Cambrian Period, five hundred million years ago. These formations show evidences of great crumpling as a result of the earth movements of the Pre-Cambrian Period, but the shield has been too stiff to yield to the pressures which elsewhere have produced mountains since the Cambrian Period. Though largely granite and gneisses, the shield also contains large areas of altered sediments, schists, and lavas.

Young Mountains. Along the Pacific coast the young mountains are found in crustal folds paralleling the coast line. It seems probable that another shield, even larger than the Canadian Shield, builds up the floor of the eastern Pacific Ocean and that these young mountains resulted from a contraction of the earth's crust and squeezing of the weaker crustal folds between the unyielding masses of the two shields.

Jurassic Period. A "lost continent," sometimes called Cascadia, aided, it seems, in the creation of the Canadian Coastal Ranges and of the more eastern Selkirk Range. Sixty million years ago, in the Jurassic Period, a wide continental area, which later sank into the ocean, hung along the margins of the Pacific. In much the same location as the modern Canadian Shield, there stretched a huge undulating surface of granite rock, called Laurentia. Between Cascadia and Laurentia lay a wide inland sea slowly being filled with Jurassic deposits. Beneath the surface of this sea vast bulges of granite rock were hurled up by earth forces of unknown origin. These bulges, known as batholiths, pushed up the earth's crust to form mountains.

Cretaceous Period. Later, about forty-five million years ago during the Cretaceous Period, silts filled up much of this inland sea, which had come to cover an even larger area. These silt deposits became Canada's central prairies.

Alpine Storm. Another phase of crustal movement, referred to as the Alpine Storm, followed the Cretaceous Period at the dawn of the Tertiary Age, thirty million years ago. Canada experienced only the earliest part of the Alpine Storm, the part called the Laramide Revolution, during which the Rocky Mountains that reach from Alaska to the United States were formed. The western floor of the Cretaceous sea buckled up into a broad fold, the rising crust pushing over to the east. When the crust cracked along a gigantic fault or fracture, the western fold was bodily pushed over the lower portion to the east, forming the famous overthrust and steep scarp which characterize the Rockies in southern Canada. The classic example of this overthrust is Crows Nest Mountain, where ancient Paleozoic rocks can be seen lying horizontally on top of much younger Cretaceous rocks. Younger and less eroded than the Coastal and Selkirk ranges, and containing no granite batholiths, the Rockies are largely devoid of the valuable minerals which characterize the older mountains.

Downfolds. Downfolds, which form the third major feature of the structure of Canada, are created when the earth's crust buckles to form young mountains. Since the earth's thick crust will not bend at right angles, young mountains are invariably paralleled with corresponding downfolds. On the western side of the Canadian Rockies, for example, is the long, broad basin downfold of interior British Columbia, called the Rocky Mountain trench. On the eastern side lies a wide depression in which are found one of the most remarkable strings of huge lakes in the world and some of the largest rivers, such as the Mackenzie, the Slave, and the Red. The floor of the Cretaceous sea had been raised above sea level during the Tertiary Period, and although large lakes and even small seas developed, this area gradually became part of the single great land mass stretching from the Pacific to the Canadian Shield.

Old Mountains. In the southeast corner of the Dominion, the Maritime Provinces and the St. Lawrence River region form a complex geologic structure which is of different origin from the main portion of Canada. Here are what are known as old mountains, created in an early period of world-wide mountain building, the Acadian Storm of the early Devonian Period. The Acadian Storm tossed up giant mountains across the Maritimes and Newfoundland in the same manner as the more recent Alpine Storm created the Rockies, but in the thirty million to forty million years which followed the Acadian Storm these high mountains were worn down to mere stumps. These stumps or roots of young mountains are called old mountains. In the Maritimes, later storms struck these old mountains and raised them en masse often a thousand feet or more. The rounded ridges which cross the Maritimes from southwest to northeast are the relics of the Acadian Storm. The Appalachian Storm in the Permian Period, about one hundred and fifty million years ago, also created a set of young mountains rising parallel to the Acadian mountains. These young mountains were, in turn, worn down by the ages, then lifted, to 4,000 ft. in some cases, by the Alpine Storm. Their plateaulike elevations form the Shickshock and Notre Dame mountains of Quebec.

Ice Age. The Great Ice Age, which endured for the greater part of the last million years and is known to geologists as the Pleistocene Period, left perhaps the most marked impression on the Canadian landscape. Moving down from the north, successive mammoth icecaps covered North America as far south as the Missouri and Ohio valleys. After they thawed, glacial debris or till, fragments torn from the underlying rock upon which the glacier had rested, was strewn across the Dominion. Almost all Canadian agriculture is based upon soils derived from this till. Although granite ripped from the Canadian Shield is commonly found as far south as the Ohio Valley, the bulk of the glacial till in any area results from the area's own rock formations.

With the passing of the last icecap, perhaps some twenty thousand years ago, a number of interesting features developed in the Canadian landscape. As the vast ice load disappeared in the St. Lawrence River area, the sea rushed inland, reaching well into the bed of Lake Ontario. Later the earth's crust, responding to the lighter burden upon it, rose, elevating above sea level large areas of marine silt in the Montreal and Quebec regions and creating the good soil in this section of the Dominion. The slow removal of the giant icecap also caused remarkable changes in the direction of flow of such major rivers as the Red, the Nelson, and the St. Lawrence. The drainage of the upper Great Lakes has only comparatively recently followed the path over Niagara Falls instead of the older path through the Trent River, the Mohawk Gate, and the Hudson River.

GEOLOGIC FORMATIONS IN CANADA

Age	Period	Began Millions of Years Ago	Type, Distribution, and Economics
Recent		(Last 40,000 Years)	Lake silts, marine clays of Quebec
Tertiary	Pleistocene	1	Glacial tills, moraines, etc.
	Pliocene	4	Some lake silts in Rockies
	Miocene	15	Volcanic lavas in British Columbia
	Eocene	30	Sandstones and coal, southern prairies
Mesozoic	Cretaceous	50	Vast areas in western prairies
	Jurassic	70	Granite batholiths of Selkirks, etc.
	Triassic	100	Lavas and sandstones, west Nova Scotia
Paleozoic	Permian	150	Red rocks of Prince Edward Island
	Carboniferous	250	Coal measures in the Maritimes
	Devonian	300	Limestones S. W. Ontario; Mackenzie Basin
	Silurian	350	Niagara Cuesta and vicinity
	Ordovician	400	Rocks between Toronto and Kingston
	Cambrian	450	Core of the Rockies
Pre-Cambrian	Keeweenawan		All in shield: Great Slave Lake, Lake Superior
	Animikie		Thunder Bay, Sudbury, slates, etc.
	Huronian		Cobalt quartzites, etc.
	Algoman		Porcupine granites, etc.
	Sudburian		Sudbury schists and quartzites
	Laurentian		Vast areas of granite in shield
	Grenville		Limestones near Ottawa River
	Keewatin		Michipicoten lavas, etc.

Classification of Geologic Formations. The foregoing table classifies geologic formations in Canada, indicating geographic distribution, some economic contributions, and approximate age as determined by investigations of the radioactive properties of the minerals in their deposits.

TOPOGRAPHY

Each of the three major structural divisions of Canada has a direct and distinct effect upon the welfare and interests of the people. Since the Canadian Shield accounts for approximately 58 per cent of the land in the Dominion; the downfolds and associated level formations, 24 per cent; and the rugged mountains of the far west, 18 per cent, the shield is dominantly responsible for surface conditions affecting human endeavor.

Surface of the Shield. As the slow-weathering granites of the shield in themselves require ages to form soil, Canada owes a debt to the ancient icecap which covered the shield with a blanket of glacial debris, usually a foot or two thick and often having a depth of many feet in depressed areas. Actually less than 10 per cent of this great land structure consists of barren rock and lakes. The characteristic feature is badly drained muskeg, with a close-set cover of coniferous forest growing in poor soil, which also nourishes great areas of sphagnum moss. In the drier portions of the shield this forest is valued for its production of woodpulp and construction timber. Also it is believed that in the future some valuable use will be found for the immense areas of low-grade spruce and fir growing in the poorly drained, colder sections of the shield.

Structural Gates. The main structural corridors or gates of the Dominion, through which the traffic important to man's activity passes, linking together the various sections of the huge country, are also of major importance in a survey of the topography of Canada. There are four chief gates of this nature. One of these provides a corridor for traffic from the vicinity of Sorel, slightly northeast of Montreal, across the St. Lawrence depression, up through the Richelieu and Lake Champlain to New York. This corridor was probably formed by one of the graben or depressed areas characteristic of the surrounding region.

The second of the four main gates of the Dominion joins the lowlands around Hudson Bay with the St. Lawrence corridor. This one is in part occupied by the Ottawa River. Probably formed by one of the northwest-to-southeast warps which are evident in the Hudson Bay area, this gate lies only about 1,000 ft. above sea level.

The third important gate is along the valley of the Red River, which flows north into Lake Winnipeg in the province of Manitoba, approximately midway across the country. Originally this valley was occupied by a huge river by which the waters of a lost glacial lake called Lake Agassiz flowed into the Mississippi River. Today there is a very low but important river divide at Traverse Lake in South Dakota. Down the Red River thousands of immigrants reached the prairies, and along it American railroads were able to reach Emerson and so make rail connection with Winnipeg from the south before the Canadian Pacific Railway arrived at this point in its western extension.

Near Finlay Forks in the heart of the Rocky Mountains in British Columbia is the fourth great gate, joining the main low-level area of Canada with the Pacific coast. At only 2,000 ft. above the sea, the Peace River cuts through the main mass of the mountains, near Finlay Forks. The river was here before the mountains were uplifted, and through the ages it has managed to saw its way through the rocks at the same rate at which the mountains were elevated.

The Northeast. The northeast portion of Canada consists of the most elevated section of the whole mammoth granite shield, in the area known as the Coast of Labrador, part of the province of Newfoundland. Here in the Torngak Mountains the shield has been raised to heights approaching 5,000 ft. Subjected to the frosts of the ice ages for much longer periods than the southern section of the shield, the plateaus of this region have been carved into numberless peaks and semicircular depressions or cirques. Farther inland in this region there is some evidence of warps and depressions in the shield, with the deep folds running northwest to southeast, following the dominant direction of the structural grain of the greater portion of the Dominion.

Northern Quebec. In the center of northern Quebec is an extensive plateau reaching over 3,000 ft. high. Situated in the vicinity of Lake Attikonak on the borders of Labrador, this may be called the Attikonak Plateau. It is bounded on the north by the Hamilton River and on the west by the Manikuagan River. No elevation of equal height is found between it and the slopes of the Rocky Mountains, 2,000 mi. to the west.

The Maritime Provinces. The dominant direction of the surface folds becomes more evident in the western sections of the shield, but in the extreme southeast of the Dominion, in the Maritime Provinces and Newfoundland, the dominant direction of the crustal folding is different, turning definitely southwest by northeast. This shift in direction is caused by the presence of the old mountains whose flattened summits date back before the mountain-making earth movements of the adjoining regions. Highest among the old mountains, the Shickshock Range and Notre Dame Mountains in the Gaspé region of Quebec reach an elevation of 4,350 ft. Other examples of the worn-down folds of old mountains are found in Nova Scotia and New Brunswick, but in these provinces the stubby peaks barely reach a height of 1,500 ft.

St. Lawrence Basin. Undoubtedly the most interesting feature of the topography of southeastern Canada is the much disturbed portion of the earth's crust which is drained by the St. Lawrence River. Here the ancient folds of the Appalachian Mountains run parallel to the southern margin of the shield, and in the intervening depression the faultings and crumplings of the earth's crust in the past are still evident. Indeed, mild earthquakes occur here more frequently than in any other part of Canada, testifying that the earth crust is still slipping and yielding along this ancient line of weakness.

Reversing Falls at Saint John, New Brunswick, are produced by the strange action of the waters of the St. John at the point where the river empties into the Bay of Fundy. At high tide the water flows up-river, tumbling over rocks in the river bed; at low tide the river resumes its normal flow, and the water pours over the same obstructions into the bay.

COURTESY CANADIAN PACIFIC RAILWAY

Below the terrace of the Banff Springs Hotel is the narrow, winding ribbon of the Bow River, overshadowed by the steep-sided, pyramid-shaped mountains of the Canadian Rockies.

Quebec Valleys. Some of the most interesting topographical districts of Quebec have developed where small portions of the earth's surface have slipped below the general level of the area. These depressions are called graben and account for the valleys in the vicinity of the city of Quebec and for the area containing Lake St. John at the head of the Saguenay River.

Hudson Bay Area. The lowest sections of the entire Dominion are to the westward of Hudson Bay. Here in the distant past the ocean invaded a depressed area of land which lies in the familiar northwest-southeast direction. Evidences of northwest-to-southeast warps in the geologic structure are also found far to the north in Fox Basin, Baffin Island, and Smith Sound. Hudson Bay itself is quite shallow for such a large expanse of water, and its shores are correspondingly flat, especially in the southwest.

Great Lakes. The Great Lakes include the largest areas of fresh water in the world and are not paralleled as a phenomenon elsewhere except in Africa. Their paradox is that they have only very small rivers draining into them. Their basins, areas which drain into the lakes, are small because river divides run quite close to the lakes on the north and south, especially near Longlac, Ont., and Erie, Pa.

Most of these lakes rest in deep valleys, partially scooped out by the great ice masses of the past. Lake Superior, however, lying along the margin of the Canadian Shield, seems to be in part a cuesta lake, with the edge of the younger,

horizontal earth formations on top of the ancient shield standing up like a wall or cuesta and restraining the waters along the southeastern side of the lake. A similar explanation to this can be given for Georgian Bay, which lies on the Canadian Shield and is dammed on the western side by the nearly complete cuesta of Bruce Peninsula and Manitoulin Island.

Northwestern Ontario. No part of the world has more small lakes and devious rivers than the northwestern section of the province of Ontario. Built upon the southern reaches of the Canadian Shield, the terrain here is a curious geologic combination of old and new. The shield itself exhibits a surface more than five hundred million years old, while upon it has been dumped the glacial debris of the last icecap, forming a veneer only some fifteen thousand years old.

In this region the glacial till has been deposited quite haphazardly on the undulating surface of the shield, permitting the rains to collect in small depressions, forming lakes and twisting rivers. Geologists believe that a more economical and regular river pattern will eventually develop and most of the lakes will be filled up or completely drained. Without waiting for these relentless, time-absorbing processes of nature, however, human enterprise has already effected one change in the drainage system of this area. Just north of Lake Nipigon, a large dam has been erected, deviating the headwaters of the Ogoki River from their former pathway into Hudson Bay to a channel into Lake Superior, a diversion which may substantially explain the subsequent rising of water levels on the Great Lakes.

Manitoba. Lake Winnipeg, in the province of Manitoba, is at the western margin of the shield where the vast mass of granite trends to the northwest. Some few thousand years ago the whole of southern Manitoba was flooded by a large glacial lake known as Lake Agassiz, which for hundreds of years was dammed on the north by the giant wall of its icecap creator. The silt which formed on the floor of the lake during this period constitutes today part of the rich soil of the province. Lake Agassiz drained to the south

places along this northwest margin of the shield, water has accumulated and is held back by the overlying cuesta. This explains the long arm on the north of Great Slave Lake, and part of the structure which retains Great Bear Lake. The Canadian Northwest Territories have numerous examples of northwest-southeast depressions, among which the Mackenzie Valley is the most important.

Alberta. To the west of the Missouri coteau, the land gradually ascends to 3,000 ft. among the foothills of the Rocky Mountains in Alberta. Here there is a rather abrupt rise where ancient rocks thrust out over the marine deposits of the former Cretaceous sea.

COURTESY OF MANITOBA BUREAU OF TRAVEL AND PUBLICITY

A COPPER MINE AND SMELTER AT FLIN FLON, MANITOBA

through the valley which forms one of the four main structural gates of the dominion, but when the icecap melted, removing the north wall of the lake, the waters flowed off to the north, as do the present lakes of this area, Lake Winnipeg, Lake Winnipegosis, and Lake Manitoba.

Saskatchewan. All along the western edge of the Canadian Shield is a scarp formed of the younger structure overlying the ancient granite of the shield. Known as the Paleozoic cuesta, this formation includes such elevations as Riding Mountain, Duck Mountain, and Porcupine Mountain. To the west of these extends a moderately level portion of the prairies which cover most of the province of Saskatchewan. These prairies are the elevated floor of the ancient Cretaceous sea which once covered this area. Along a line stretching northwest from southwest Saskatchewan, again following the dominant structural direction of the dominion, the prairie level rises to a height of over 2,000 ft. in a second great cuesta, the Missouri coteau.

Northwest Territories. The Paleozoic cuesta continues to the northwest from Porcupine Mountain and ultimately reaches the Arctic Ocean north of Great Bear Lake. In

British Columbia. The province of British Columbia, in broad topographical outline, consists of a great basin 300 mi. wide and about 3,000 ft. high, lying in the usual direction and guarded on the east and west by mountains towering 10,000 ft. or more. The Selkirk Mountains between these ranges complicate this pattern somewhat in the southeast section of the province as they reach west to join the Coast Range near the town of Penticton and form a closed rim to the south of the basin. Into the floor of the basin, rivers have cut deep canyons which are most evident along the Fraser River. The forces which produced the surrounding mountains also gave rise to parallel mountain ranges with deep fold-valleys which have been occupied by the main rivers, such as the Fraser, the Columbia, and the Kootenay. This region has also been covered with icecaps on several occasions and, in addition, has been raised en masse by earth movements of the past. As a result the region exists as one of the most complicated glacial topographies in the world.

Among the bordering mountains, the highest peak is Mount Waddington, rising to 13,260 ft. and dominating the

Coast Range. It is about 180 mi. northwest of Vancouver. The highest peak in the Canadian Rockies is Mount Robson, 12,972 ft. Many others in this group reach a height of 10,-000 ft. Similar heights are found in the Selkirk Mountains, and several lengthy glaciers flow down the valleys to the Homathko and Klinaklini rivers.

Along the great barrier of the Rocky Mountains there are a number of passes such as Kicking Horse Pass (5,339 ft.), where the Canadian Pacific Railway crosses the divide, the Yellowhead Pass (3,729 ft.), and Crows Nest Pass (4,461 ft.). Lowest but least used of the main passes is the one by the Peace River (2,000 ft.). The central portion of British Columbia also has an opening to the sea through a relatively low section of the Coast Range. This wide gap contains

does in general bear out the expectation that places at equal distance from the equator will exhibit similar temperatures, the presence of mountains and large bodies of water connected with tropical oceans also has distinct effects upon different locations within the same latitudes. The presence of mountains makes a region colder at the rate of approximately 3° F. to every 1,000 ft. of mountain elevation, so that polar climates are created in the mountainous areas when they receive no counteracting warmth from bodies of water with tropical currents. Hudson Bay is largely frozen over in January and does not warm the surrounding land, while the southwestern corner of the Dominion, near Vancouver, is the only area of the country which remains above freezing during that month.

White Horse, Yukon, is the starting point for river boats heading north for Dawson and the Klondike region.

the Skeena River, which is the natural outlet of this portion of the province.

Yukon Territory. On either side of the Prince Rupert River, to the south and to the north along the panhandle of Alaska, the Coast Range starts ascending to greater heights. The highest section of the entire Dominion is reached at the southwest corner of the Yukon Territory where Mount Logan towers to a height of 19,850 ft. and Mount Elias near by, on the border of Alaska, reaches 18,008 ft. The northern prolongation of the Rocky Mountains in these latitudes, the Pelly Range and the Mackenzie Mountains, have only a few peaks rising to 9,000 ft.

CLIMATE

Temperature. The temperature of so large a country as Canada is dependent not only upon the region's position relative to the equator but also upon the topographical features. The areas along the coast have low temperature variations or a so-called marine climate, while high variations of temperature or a continental climate prevail among the inland regions, especially in the north. Furthermore, the west coast of Canada may be observed to have a milder climate than the east.

Summer temperatures in the Dominion do not differ greatly, whereas temperatures in coastal and inland areas in the winter vary almost 60 degrees. This fact indicates that the extreme continental climates are caused by bitter winters rather than by any substantial change in summer temperatures.

Although the actual temperature pattern across Canada

In summer the temperature zones follow relatively the same pattern as in winter, but there is not so wide a variation between northern and southern regions. Except for the ice-covered land of some Arctic islands, all Canada remains far above the freezing point in summer, most of it registering warmer than 50° F., permitting the spread of vegetation over the whole of the Dominion. An average summer temperature of 57° F. extends northward in a limited area across the Arctic Circle as far as Victoria Island, and is an important factor in establishing the northern limit of various crops.

The area of the Dominion which has a variation of 64 degrees in temperature between January and July includes most of the north central section. This is the area with a very marked continental climate. The zone affording a range of 50 degrees between summer and winter temperature is even larger and determines the areas with a continental climate, as contrasted with a marine climate. Nearly all of Canada except British Columbia and the St. Lawrence regions can be described as having a marked continental climate.

Rainfall. There are also radical differences in amount in the rainfall in the four typical localities. The presence of warm oceans provides the good rainfall in the west and southeast, the only areas of Canada which have the advantage of abundant rains. The cold oceans along the north and northeast coasts are not of much value in producing rain. The rainfall in the St. Lawrence region is also increased by rain formed when the polar air masses sweeping down from the north across the Hudson Bay area and the tropical air masses moving up into Canada from Florida or the Gulf of Mexico meet above the southeast corner of the Dominion. This is perhaps the commonest source of rain in the St. Lawrence region.

Much the same phenomena occur on the Pacific coast, where the rainfall is very heavy. In general a total of 60 to 80 in. of rain is received annually all along the Pacific coast, and in parts of Vancouver Island the fall reaches over 200 in. This fall is rapidly reduced as the warm moist air passes inland, and in the long, north-south valleys characteristic of British Columbia there are areas of desert flora. The inland mountain ranges such as the Selkirks and the Rockies precipitate rain, but the rainfall here never reaches the level of the Coast Range because by the time the warm air reaches them a good deal of its water content has already been lost. Associated with the meeting of polar and tropical air masses, which causes the heavy rainfall on the Pacific coast near the southern border of the Dominion, are revolving eddies of air called cyclones or lows. When such a cyclone is formed, it moves eastward at a rate of about 500 mi. a day

and by drawing in cold air from the north and warm air from the south produces plentiful rains.

Canada has two large dry regions. One is in the extreme north, by coincidence in the area of the Magnetic Pole; the other, in the prairie southwest. Of more significance, however, are the areas with a moderate rainfall, between 12 and 15 in. annually. While this rainfall would be too low for agriculture in very hot countries where evaporation is great, in Canada it is usually sufficient for crops. As a result, except for the very dry areas, hardly any part of the Dominion is without sufficient rainfall for some crops. Farming is difficult, however, in limited areas where low rainfall is very erratic, as in those receiving 12 in. one year and 5 the next.

One of the most interesting features of the Canadian climate is the belt of rather good rainfall, averaging about 15 in., which extends from Lake Winnipeg northwest toward the city of Edmonton, Alberta, and the Rocky Mountains. Unlike the desert and semidesert land which separates the Pacific coast of the United States from the well-watered eastern section of that country, this belt of adequate rainfall

Long-Term Temperature and Precipitation Data for 35 Representative Stations in Canada

Station	Height Above Sea ft.	Length of Record yrs.	TEMPERATURES (Fahrenheit) Annual	Jan.	July	Highest On Record	Lowest On Record	Heating Factor Day-Degrees[1]	Killing Frost Average Dates Last in Spring	First in Autumn	PRECIPITATION (inches) Annual Total	Annual Snow	Jan.	Apr.	July	Oct.	Number of Days Rain	Total
Gander, N'f'ld.	482	11	39·3	19·2	62·3	91	−16	9,477	May 29	Oct. 2	38·24	121·0	2·81	2·32	3·65	3·87	129	199
St. John's, N'f'ld. ...	296	67	40·9	23·5	59·6	93	−21	8,876	June 2	Oct. 10	53·78	101·1	5·31	4·16	3·54	5·27	147	208
Charlottetown, P.E.I. ...	186	65	41·7	17·8	65·6	98	−27	8,263	May 13	Oct. 22	39·47	113·0	3·76	2·78	2·98	4·07	119	162
Annapolis Royal, N.S. ...	10	25	44·4	24·4	64·4	89	−13	7,665	May 20	Oct. 6	41·41	74·8	4·20	2·77	3·40	4·19	115	140
Halifax, N.S.	83	75	44·0	23·6	64·7	99	−21	7,380	May 11	Oct. 14	55·74	70·8	5·40	4·54	3·79	5·42	130	156
Sydney, N.S.	48	69	42·3	22·1	63·6	98	−25	7,896	May 29	Oct. 13	50·24	97·9	5·16	4·03	3·37	4·70	127	165
Chatham, N.B.	98	50	40·2	12·2	66·6	102	−43	8,887	May 19	Sept. 29	40·74	107·3	3·38	3·02	3·91	3·97	107	151
Fredericton, N.B.	164	67	40·7	13·5	66·1	101	−35	8,663	May 20	Sept. 24	42·80	95·5	3·87	2·94	3·53	4·11	108	149
Saint John, N.B.	119	56	41·4	19·3	61·0	93	−21	8,081	May 4	Oct. 16	42·26	71·1	4·28	3·22	3·03	4·01	134	168
Arvida, Que.	335	10	36·4	3·6	65·0	95	−42	10,585	May 19	Sept. 19	38·93	116·1	2·90	2·53	4·81	3·53	112	176
Fort McKenzie, Que.	250	9	22·4	−12·5	54·2	91	−60	15,695	July 8	July 26	22·04	82·4	1·24	1·02	3·67	1·77	77	167
Lennoxville, Que.	498	24	40·3	12·8	66·2	99	−48	8,996	May 28	Sept. 9	39·56	89·4	3·46	2·60	4·12	3·63	104	150
Montreal, Que.	187	55	42·8	13·8	69·8	97	−29	8,284	Apr. 28	Oct. 17	40·80	112·3	3·76	2·60	3·74	3·42	112	164
Kapuskasing, Ont.	752	19	32·4	−1·7	62·4	101	−53	11,374	June 14	Sept. 1	27·59	91·0	2·00	1·82	3·43	2·50	95	182
Ottawa, Ont.	260	65	41·5	11·9	69·6	102	−35	8,674	May 7	Oct. 2	34·23	82·0	2·93	2·70	3·39	2·93	98	139
Port Arthur, Ont.	644	62	36·2	6·7	63·0	104	−41	10,045	May 26	Sept. 20	23·66	42·9	0·91	1·49	3·56	2·45	78	129
St. Catharines, Ont.	347	21	47·8	26·0	71·1	104	−12	6,607	May 7	Oct. 20	27·03	37·7	2·30	2·39	2·39	2·18	99	132
Toronto, Ont.	379	105	45·1	22·6	68·9	105	−26	7,236	May 2	Oct. 14	32·18	61·9	2·71	2·48	2·95	2·43	109	145
Churchill, Man.	43	30	17·8	−19·0	53·7	96	−57	15,735	June 28	Aug. 26	15·96	56·9	0·48	0·89	2·19	1·43	52	101
The Pas, Man.	890	27	30·6	−8·7	64·6	100	−54	12,160	May 30	Sept. 7	15·44	44·9	0·61	0·81	2·22	1·16	59	102
Winnipeg, Man.	786	66	35·0	−3·1	66·9	108	−54	10,841	May 27	Sept. 14	21·19	53·6	0·92	1·37	3·08	1·49	67	118
Prince Albert, Sask.	1,414	54	32·9	−4·3	63·4	103	−70	11,337	May 30	Sept. 10	16·11	51·5	0·74	0·93	2·18	0·84	62	116
Regina, Sask.	1,884	55	34·5	−0·7	64·8	111	−56	10,891	June 6	Sept. 10	14·70	28·8	0·51	0·74	2·38	0·86	59	109
Beaverlodge, Alta.	2,484	31	35·3	5·6	59·8	98	−54	10,950	June 4	Sept. 4	17·19	70·1	1·27	0·78	2·21	1·11	76	127
Calgary, Alta.	3,540	55	38·4	13·1	61·5	97	−49	9,111	June 1	Sept. 6	16·65	50·0	0·51	0·99	2·51	0·69	57	101
Edmonton, Alta.	2,219	56	36·6	5·9	61·6	99	−57	9,826	May 30	Sept. 6	17·38	46·4	0·88	0·88	3·32	0·75	73	133
Medicine Hat, Alta.	2,365	55	41·9	12·0	69·3	108	−51	8,495	May 12	Sept. 19	12·81	35·6	0·63	0·77	1·68	0·62	56	100
Cranbrook, B.C.	3,014	35	40·7	16·7	63·2	102	−41	8,760	June 10	Aug. 28	14·41	56·7	1·80	0·68	1·14	0·89	69	106
Nelson, B.C.	2,235	39	45·2	24·4	66·4	103	−17	7,278	May 13	Sept. 30	27·77	89·3	3·47	1·57	1·62	2·35	102	131
Penticton, B.C.	1,121	32	47·8	26·8	68·3	105	−16	6,346	May 7	Oct. 3	10·85	24·0	0·98	0·68	0·79	0·83	83	102
Prince George, B.C.	2,218	27	38·5	12·9	59·6	102	−58	8,996	June 18	Aug. 22	19·98	62·7	1·81	0·84	1·63	1·99	123	162
Victoria, B.C.	228	54	49·5	38·7	60·0	95	−2	4,935	Mar. 18	Nov. 27	27·13	13·4	4·49	1·18	0·44	2·81	141	144
Dawson, Y.T.	1,062	41	22·8	−21·0	59·6	95	−73	14,620	June 4	Aug. 16	12·83	56·2	0·87	0·51	1·53	1·17	63	117
Coppermine, N.W.T.	13	13	11·3	−18·9	50·1	87	−54	19,710	June 25	Aug. 22	10·72	57·0	0·57	0·84	1·33	1·16	40	103
Fort Good Hope, N.W.T.	214	31	17·0	−23·6	59·3	95	−79	17,520	June 15	Aug. 6	10·63	50·0	0·53	0·49	1·55	1·09	46	106

[1] Day-degrees represent the difference in temperature between the mean temperature of the air and the temperature of 65°F. multiplied by the number of days during which the outside temperature was lower than that figure, computed for the period Sept. 1 to May 31. Fuel consumption for heating purposes will be proportional to these totals.

Source: *Canada Year Book, 1954.*

provides Canada with a bridge of good agricultural land connecting the eastern and western sections of the country.

Seasonal Rainfall. Since rainfall is generally associated with the movements of warm moist air, it is not unnatural that the continental area of Canada should receive its maximum rainfall during the summer months. It is interesting to note, however, that around Hudson Bay the ice and cold waters retard the warm period. In the Hudson Bay region the maximum rain falls in August and September, while inland the maximum is received in June and July.

The heavier rainfall in winter on the southwest coastal area is due to the apparent movement of the sun. Because of the inclination of the earth's axis in its orbit around the sun, in summer the sun is right over Havana, Cuba, while in winter it is over Rio de Janeiro, Brazil. The three main rain belts of the earth change position according to the position of the sun. The Canadian rain-producing polar belt of air spreads south over the Dominion in the winter and increases, in a somewhat complicated fashion, the rainfall along the British Columbian coast.

Classes of Canadian Climate. The following table summarizes the classes of Canadian climate.

CLASSES OF CANADIAN CLIMATE

	Marine or Coastal	Continental or Inland
Temperature	Small range, with moderate winters, as in Vancouver and Halifax	Large range, with cold winters, as in Dawson and Winnipeg
Rainfall	In west: heavy, much in winter. In east: heavy, more uniform	In north: light, most in summer. In south: moderate, most in summer

Arctic Summer. The effect of the long day of the arctic summer is of great importance to the development of the northern regions of Canada. Near the Arctic Circle, in the vicinity of Great Bear Lake, the schedule of daylight hours extends from 24 hours on June 21 to none on December 21. Further south, in such pioneer regions as those along the Peace and upper Mackenzie rivers, this means that during the growing period of important crops such as wheat, oats, and

HEAT RECEIVED IN 24 HOURS DURING MIDSUMMER
(*Gramcalories per Square Centimeter*)

Latitude	40	50	60	70	80	90 (Pole)
Heat Units	490	510	480	470	450	340

Source: *The Canadian Climate*, C. E. Koeppe, Bloomington, Ill.

potatoes in the warm months of May, June, July, and August, the sun shines from 15 to 20 hours a day. This long daily period of sunlight in the summer compensates a good deal for the bitter cold conditions of winter when, fortunately, many plants are out of ground. The foregoing table, recorded for June 21 at various Canadian latitudes, illustrates the important fact that during midsummer there is no substantial difference in the heat units received during twenty-four hours by crops planted at Toronto, latitude 43°, and at Aklavik, latitude 66°, north of the Arctic Circle. In winter the temperatures of these locations vary by some 43 degrees.

Snowfall. To Canada snow is less important than rain. Snow, nevertheless, protects the young winter-wheat plants in Ontario, provides highways for lumber camps, and has helped to make Canada a center for winter sports.

In general, Canada does not receive a heavy snowfall. As the amount of snow depends upon the supply of moist air just as much as upon low temperature conditions, and as the air in north central Canada is fairly dry, this region receives less than 40 in. of annual snowfall. For this same reason, the Selkirk Range receives more snow than the higher Rockies because it is nearer the moist winds of the Pacific Ocean. The heaviest snowfall is in the mountains near Alaska, but over 120 in. usually fall in northern Newfoundland and also in Quebec northwest of Anticosti Island.

SOIL

The settlement of a country eventually follows to a large degree the distribution of its soil and climate. Although the essential features of a soil depend to some extent upon the character of the underlying rock, the major factor in establishing the quality of a soil which has been in place for a considerable length of time is the climate to which it has been subjected, especially the amount of rainfall and heat. Various soil zones of Canada, therefore, are controlled by such prominent features of the climate as the cold temperatures of the northern sections, the dryness of the inland areas, and the increased rainfall on the coasts.

Podsol. The most widespread type of soil in the Dominion is called podsol. An ashy layer, from several inches to a foot or more thick along the Canadian coasts where the rains are heaviest (over 60 in.), podsol exists where the soils have been washed by constant rains for countless years. Unfortunately, as the soluble elements of the soil are drained away, the most fertile portions, those upon which plants depend for their growing and fruiting, are lost. Where the rainfall is heavy and the climate cool, extensive growth of moss also takes place. This in turn gives rise to beds of peat, a characteristic feature of the muskeg bogs of northern Canada.

Podsol is the dominant soil of the treeless areas of the tundra and also of the great spread of coniferous forest. In the forest a thin layer of leafy material covers the soil, but beneath this leafy surface the ashy layer of the podsol is almost invariably found. Washed deeper into the soil, soluble iron contents and fine clays often accumulate a foot or less beneath the surface. In warm countries a layer of reddish gravelly material called laterite results from this concentration of iron, but this is rarely found in cool Canada. The layer of clay beneath the podsol is, however, very common in the Dominion.

Black Earth. In areas where the rainfall is lighter, especially where there is a seasonal summer rainfall, some of the best soils in the world are found. In these areas the conifer forest gives way to wide grasslands, called savannas or prairies. Here continual heavy rains have not leached from the soil the valuable soluble salts, and the gradual decay of grass roots slowly adds rich, black humus to the surface layers. Called black earth by English soil experts and *chernozem* by the Russians, this valuable type of soil creates a belt of fine farmland country, extending in a crescent from Winnipeg to Saskatoon, to Edmonton and Calgary.

Chestnut Earth. Where the rainfall is less than 13 or 14 in., conditions are too dry for the development of much humus, and the soil takes on a chestnut color. Though not equal in fertility to the black earths, this dark brown earth is very good soil and provides a zone of valuable farmland on the drier side of the black-soil belt.

With still lower rainfall and hot summers, the soils take on a gray hue. Salt, lime, and gypsum tend to accumulate in the lower layers where they are carried by the rains, and then during the dry seasons partially rise to the uppermost layer, creating the glistening surfaces of salt and gypsum which are characteristic of hollows in really dry countries. Canada has no widespread areas of dunes or desert and very little of this semidesert terrain. It is found, however, on the southern edge of Saskatchewan and Alberta where the rainfall is very low and the rivers end in salt lakes or playas.

The following table summarizes the main soil zones of the Dominion, indicating their relationship to rainfall and the prevalent vegetation.

DISTRIBUTION OF SOIL CLASSES

Rainfall in Inches	Vegetation	Surface Soil	Lower Layer
100	High moor	Peat, Podsol	Laterite, Clay
60	Forest	Podsol	
40	Savanna, Woodland	Podsol	
30	Savanna, Prairie	Black earth, Chestnut earth	
20	Savanna, Prairie	Black earth, Chestnut earth	Salt, Gypsum
10	Desert	Dune, Gray earth	Salt, Lime, Gypsum

FLORA

The vegetation of Canada follows, as do the soils, the general dominant controls of climate. The bleak, northern, treeless zone called the tundra, and the vast region of coniferous forest known as the taiga, form the largest divisions of the Dominion plant-cover.

Tundra. This area, comprising the northern coasts and all the islands of the Canadian Archipelago, is often referred to as the Barren Grounds, but this gives an incorrect impression of its vegetation. For example, in the area around Tukoyaktuk, 250 mi. north of the Arctic Circle, the ground in summer is completely covered with a thick growth of many different types of herbs and tiny trees. On the tundra, dwarf willows up to 3 ft. high are abundant in the gullies, and dwarf birch about 6 in. in height are also common. Large patches of flowering lupin, a variety of Shasta daisy, betony, and smaller patches of buttercups, shineleaf, and dryas may also be seen. Primulas, fireweed, Labrador tea, and cranberries, together with many sedges and grasses, make up the rest of the cover. It is this type of vegetation that supports the large herds of caribou which graze in the region; and since the snow cover is light in the winter, the animals find no difficulty in grazing during the cold months of the year.

Taiga. South of the tundra is the taiga, a Russian name generally adopted to describe the coniferous forest-land which comprises the largest portion of the mainland of the Dominion. The taiga stretches across Canada from the northwest to the east, forming a zone about 700 mi. wide and over 2,500 mi. long. Along the southwest margin of the large central portion in which black spruce is the most abundant tree, the aspen outnumbers the spruces slightly, but most geographers include this aspen belt as part of the taiga. Also generally included in the taiga is the northwest extension of the spruce forest among the broad low valleys of the Yukon Territory.

The ragged edge of stunted spruce which forms the northern boundary of the taiga stretches farther north along river valleys than on the rounded uplands between the rivers. It reaches to 69° N. lat. along the Mackenzie, Anderson, and Coppermine rivers, cuts south to about the Arctic Circle along the uplands around Great Bear Lake, and falls back to about 55° N. lat. near James Bay and again in Labrador. The major determining factor is the July temperature. Where

this is above 50° F., there is enough heat in summer for the growth of trees.

Somewhat different climate factors control the southern boundary of the taiga, which runs approximately from Edmonton to Winnipeg and Quebec. It has been found that if an area has more than five and a half months a year of temperature over 43° F., the climate is too warm for the coniferous trees of the taiga. South of this temperature line the vegetation consists primarily of the deciduous type of tree like the maple and oak. If the rainfall in these higher temperature areas is below 20 in. annually, as it is in the center of the continent, however, then leaf-shedding trees give way to grassland or prairie vegetation. Thus Winnipeg occupies a key position in the vegetation of Canada. To the north is the taiga; to the southeast it is wet enough for the sugar maples, hemlocks, and oaks of the lake forest; and to the west stretch the drier areas of the prairies. While the spruces are the dominant trees of the taiga and even straggle north into the tundra, in the denser forests a short distance to the south tamarack or larch and white birch are fairly plentiful. The balsam poplar also reaches the extreme northern limits of the taiga except in central Quebec. The jack pine, the balsam fir, the mountain ash and cedar, and the white and red pine all are found in the northern taiga but are limited in their northern pioneering by varying requirements of higher temperatures.

The poplars are the most widespread trees of the southwest taiga. The aspen extends throughout the taiga, while the cottonwood remains mainly in the warmer southwest portions. In the east where the rainfall is heavier, the southern edge of the taiga is marked by increasing numbers of sugar maples, hemlocks, and oaks. These become dominant as the lake-forest area is reached.

Lake Forest. The lake-forest area is mixed in character, with sugar maple widely distributed, and birch, hemlock, and white pine abundant in the northeast in the Ottawa region. In the district north of Lake Huron, birch, spruce, and aspen are perhaps more abundant than maple. In the vicinity of Toronto, sugar maple and beech dominated until most of this area was cleared for farmland. In the eastern townships of south Quebec, spruce, fir, maple, and birch are all well represented.

The small forest region on the north shore of Lake Erie is characterized by natural vegetation entirely different from the taiga. This forest represents the northern limits of many of the trees common to the United States. Among these are chestnut, tulip tree, hickory, black gum, magnolia, papaw, red bud, and sassafras. There are also many of the trees of the lake-forest zone, but there are very few coniferous trees in the region.

Acadian Forest. In the extreme east of the Dominion the coniferous trees reappear in dominant numbers in the Acadian forest, which has cooler summers than the lake forest. In the Acadian forest, balsam fir and black and red spruce are the most common. Cedar and tamarack are more abundant in the extensive swampy areas of the Maritime Provinces. Maple is most common in Prince Edward Island, but yellow birch, red spruce, and beech are also prevalent. Red pine as well as black spruce represent the conifers. The balsam fir is particularly abundant in Cape Breton Island, while near Halifax red spruce is equally prevalent.

Prairie Zone. In the prairie zone in the southwest of Canada, where the long, dry periods prevent the growth of trees, the natural vegetation may be subdivided into the long-grass area and the drier short-grass area. Typical among the long grasses, which occur when the rainfall is over 14 in.

annually, are the *Agropyron* and *Bromus*. Chief among the short grasses are grama, June, and spear grass.

British Columbia. The rugged topography of British Columbia has led to the spread of a forest cover which in general is quite different from that found in the rest of the Dominion. The Rocky Mountains mark the western limits of such widespread trees as the jack pine and the tamarack, while the black and white spruce extend westward only as far as Prince George. In the forests of the Rockies, Engelmann spruce, hemlock, and lodgepole pine are found.

The montane forest of the inland basin of British Columbia contains yellow pine and Douglas fir, but other pines and aspens are also common. Here the rainfall is so low that cactus and other plants of desert variety exist.

Some of the finest trees of Canada are found along the west coast in the Columbia forests. Here the Douglas fir occasionally grows to a height of 300 ft. and is one of the Dominion's chief sources of lumber. Here also is the red cedar and the western hemlock. To the north another valuable conifer, the Sitka spruce, becomes quite abundant, while in the warm wet corner to the south, around Vancouver, are found the sole representatives of two warm-climate trees, the madrona and the Garry oak. The latter is the only oak native to the Pacific coast of Canada.

FAUNA

There are half a dozen main faunal regions in the Dominion. The Arctic zone is the habitat of the polar bear, musk ox, barren-ground caribou, arctic fox, and arctic hare. Among the distinctive birds are the snowy owl, gyrfalcon, and willow ptarmigan. The Hudsonian zone includes the northern portion of the taiga, where the July temperature is below 57° F. Here are found the wolverine, great gray owl, and the rough-legged hawk.

The higher portions of the western regions are grouped in an Alpine zone. Here are found the Rocky Mountain goat, mountain sheep, hoary marmot, and Franklin grouse. The Algonquin zone lies to the south of the Hudsonian zone, and its typical animals are the lynx, porcupine, and star-nosed mole. Among the birds are the white-throated sparrow, junco, and Canada jay. The Assiniboian zone corresponds to the prairies, and here are found the pronghorn, coyote, prairie hare, and badger. The Alleghanian zone is in the far southeast on the borders of the United States. It is the northern limit of such birds as the snow thrush, bluebird, catbird, and bobolink.

POPULATION

Statistics. The total population of Canada, according to the 1951 census, was 14,009,429, an increase of 21.8 per cent over 1941. Excluding Newfoundland, which was not a part of Canada until 1949, the increase amounted to 2,141,358, or 18.6 per cent, compared with a population increase of only 10.9 per cent in the previous decade. The percentage increases during the first four decades of the twentieth century were 34.2, 21.9, 18.1, and 10.9. The populations of the provinces and territories in 1951 were: Ontario, 4,597,542; Quebec, 4,055,681; British Columbia, 1,165,210; Alberta, 939,501; Saskatchewan, 831,728; Manitoba, 776,541; Nova Scotia, 642,584; New Brunswick, 515,697; Newfoundland, 361,416; Prince Edward Island, 98,429; Northwest Territories, 16,004; and Yukon Territory, 9,096. The census figure of June 1, 1956, showed a total Canadian population of 16,080,791.

Distribution. Most of the people of Canada live in an area which hugs the long boundary between the Dominion and the United States. This populous zone forms an elongated and irregular strip across the base of the Dominion as it juts and bulges northward at intervals to include areas where the natural environment is favorable. Its pattern offers additional evidence that it is the natural features of a country, such as topography, temperature, rainfall, and soil, which control the population distribution and that man lives most successfully in areas where nature has prepared a suitable environment for his occupation.

In the eastern section of the Dominion the populous zone has a depth of about 300 mi. in the Maritime Provinces, and in eastern Quebec along the Saguenay River. Here a wide depression or graben in the sterile rocks of the Canadian Shield has filled up with good soil for farming. A drop to 150 mi. occurs behind Montreal, but above Toronto the zone bulges again to a depth of 400 mi. in the clay belt formed

LAND AREA AND DENSITY OF POPULATON, BY PROVINCES AND TERRITORIES, CENSUS YEARS 1921-1951

Province or Territory	Land Area in Sq. mi.	Population, 1921		Population, 1931		Population, 1941		Population, 1951	
		Total	Per sq. Mile	Total	Per sq. Mile	Total	Per sq. Mile	Total	Per sq. Mile
Newfoundland	147,994[1]	....	....	....	....	....	....	361,416	2.44
Island	40,559	....	....	....	....	....	....	353,526	8.72
Labrador	107,435[1]	....	....	....	....	....	....	7,890	0.07
Prince Edward Island	2,184	88,615	40.57	88,038	40.31	95,047	43.52	98,429	45.07
Nova Scotia	20,743	523,837	25.25	512,846	24.72	577,962	27.86	642,584	30.98
New Brunswick	27,473	387,876	14.12	408,219	14.86	457,401	16.65	515,697	18.77
Quebec	523,860	2,360,510	4.51	2,874,662	5.49	3,331,882	6.36	4,055,681	7.74
Ontario	348,141	2,933,662	8.43	3,431,683	9.86	3,787,655	10.88	4,597,542	13.21
Manitoba	219,723	610,118	2.78	700,139	3.19	729,744	3.32	776,541	3.53
Saskatchewan	220,182	757,510	3.44	921,785	4.19	895,992	4.07	831,728	3.78
Alberta	248,800	588,454	2.37	731,605	2.94	706,169	3.20	939,501	3.78
British Columbia	359,279	524,582	1.46	694,263	1.93	817,861	2.28	1,165,210	3.24
Canada (exclusive of the Territories)	2,118,379	8,775,164	4.14[2]	10,363,240	4.89[2]	11,489,713	5.42[2]	13,984,329	6.60[3]
Yukon Territory	205,346	4,157	0.02	4,230	0.02	4,914	0.02	9,096	0.04
Northwest Territories	1,253,438	8,143	0.01	9,316	0.01	12,028	0.01	16,004	0.01
CANADA	3,577,163	8,787,949[4]	2.46[5]	10,376,786	2.90[5]	11,506,655	3.22[5]	14,009,429	3.92[3]

[1] Includes Labrador. [2] Calculated on the basis of 2,003,319 sq. mi. which excludes the land area of Newfoundland. [3] Includes Newfoundland. [4] Total includes 485 members of the Royal Canadian Navy recorded separately in 1921. [5] Calculated on the basis of 3,462,103 sq. mi. which excludes the land area of Newfoundland.

Source: *Canada Year Book,* 1954.

by a bygone glacial lake known as Lake Ojibway. Further westward, in the conifer forest along the northern shore of Lake Superior, the zone completely disappears for a space penetrated only by small lumber camps. This section is so barren of natural resources that almost no settlement has developed since the territory was first explored. At the western end of the lake where the two large cities of Fort William and Port Arthur are located, the populous zone picks up again and grows steadily in the western half of the Dominion. In the meridian of the city of Edmonton in central Alberta, the zone is at its widest in a large northern bulge which includes the farmland along the Peace River. These farmlands are made possible by the abnormal northern extension of warm air in summer.

In British Columbia the topography is such a controlling feature in the population distribution that the zone breaks up into a number of irregular belts surrounding rugged mountain areas which do not permit dense population. While the greater part of British Columbia has a topography sternly limiting the population, in the vicinity of Vancouver at the mouth of the Fraser River there is a very large delta of deep alluvial soils where some 70 per cent of the population of the entire province lives.

Another feature of the population distribution of Canada is the result of the shift from an agricultural to an industrial economy. There are several very dense clusters of population which are explained by the necessities of industry. The cluster on the east coast of Cape Breton Island results from the presence of abundant coal in that area. Large steel works have been developed here near the city of Sydney. Other rather dense clusters of population occur in the neighborhood of Montreal and Hamilton, resulting in part from the abundance of hydroelectric power available in the area.

The presence of plentiful power or mineral resources is responsible for the division of the Dominion into so-called urban and rural areas. Since the start of World War I, Quebec, Ontario, and British Columbia have been definitely more urban than the other seven provinces. In 1951, 67 per cent of the population of Quebec was urban; Ontario had a somewhat smaller percentage; and British Columbia had an urban population of about 55 per cent. On the other hand, during the same period, Prince Edward was 72 per cent rural, and New Brunswick had the next highest rural population with 67 per cent. The fact that Quebec, which has a predominantly French population, and British Columbia, which is the most predominantly English of all the ten provinces, are leading urban provinces would seem to indicate that it is environment rather than linguistic groupings or cultural background that causes the variation between rural and urban population in the Dominion.

Cultural Groups. As very little is known of the precise racial identity of the immigrants to Canada, much error is usually involved in attempting a racial classification. Very likely many of the French and English immigrants share the same Nordic racial background, having emigrated from Normandy and the northern coasts of France, and from eastern England, respectively. The term cultural groups may be used with accuracy, however, in referring to British, French, and other population elements. Some of the largest of these are indicated, by province, in the accompanying table.

Excluding the Negroes, who total only 22,000, the entire population of Canada belongs to one or other of the worldwide races of Alpine broadheads or Mediterranean narrowheads. Few other primitive races ever reached America from northeastern Asia, and the Nordics, who later emigrated to Canada, are usually accepted as a blond variant of the Mediterranean race.

The population of the Dominion also includes about 155,000 Indians and only about 9,000 Eskimos. The aboriginal tribes entered the continent by the Bering corridor, mostly within the last 12,000 years. The Indians spread widely over the continent, the earlier Mediterranean narrowheads being pushed to the east, while the later Alpine broadheads settled in the west near the main route by which all peoples traversed the continent. The arrival of the Eskimos cannot be dated at all accurately, but in many ways they represent a variant of the earlier narrowheads and are not very different from some of the adjacent Indians.

The current home of the few Eskimos of Canada is in the mainland tundra, and on Baffin Island and the islands of Hudson Bay. The Indians have retreated before the European colonists or have merged with them. There are, however, some large Indian reserves, such as the one near Brantford, Ontario. Ontario has over 37,000 Indians, mostly in the northern sections, and British Columbia has about 28,000. There are also approximately 17,000 to 21,000 in each of the provinces of Quebec, Saskatchewan, and Alberta, and only a few, about 5,000, live in the marginal lands of the Northwest Territories and the Yukon.

The French in Canada are almost entirely descended from the original, preconquest settlers, who left France a century before the French Revolution. They represent a survival of the earlier French culture, which has little in common with that of post-Revolutionary France. In 1760 there were about 60,000 French settlers in Canada. This small population has grown to approximately 4,300,000, occupying a continuous

POPULATION BY CULTURAL GROUPS IN 1951
(in thousands)

	B.C.	Alta.	Sask.	Man.	Ont.	Que.	N.B.	N.S.	PEI	Nfld	Total[xx]
British	766	452	352	363	3,082	492	295	483	81	338	6,710
French	42	56	52	66	478	3,327	198	74	15	10	4,319
German	55	108	136	54	222	12	3	29	..	..	620
Ukrainian	23	87	78	99	94	13	..	1	..	..	395
Russian	22	15	19	8	17	8	..	..	..	..	91
Polish	16	30	26	38	90	17	..	2	..	..	220
Dutch	33	29	30	42	98	3	6	21	..	..	264
Scandinavian	66	71	62	33	37	5	3	3	..	..	283
Jewish	5	4	3	19	75	73	1	2	..	..	182
Italian	17	6	1	3	88	34	..	2	..	..	152
Indian and Eskimo	28	21	22	21	37	17	2	3	..	1	166
Total[x]	1,165	939	832	777	4,598	4,056	516	643	98	361	14,009

[x] Includes less important cultural groups. [xx] Includes Yukon and Northwest Territories.
Source: *Canada Year Book,* 1954.

strip of territory from Sudbury, Ontario, to Moncton, New Brunswick. The Catholic Church is powerful in French Canada and encourages the slow spread of the French settlers, as compared with the far-distant migrations of the Anglo-Saxons. Also the birth rate in essentially French Quebec is approximately 7.7 higher per thousand than in British Columbia which is predominantly English.

A great number of Loyalists poured into Canada at the time of the American Revolution, settling for the most part in Nova Scotia, New Brunswick, and southern Ontario, at a time when the French were mainly concentrated in Quebec and Acadia, now Nova Scotia.

Descendants of German stock colonized the region near Halifax, Nova Scotia, and about the middle of the nineteenth century Mennonites of German origin founded Berlin, now Kitchener, in Ontario. In 1873 another group of Mennonites settled in the empty lands south of Winnipeg.

The great influx of settlers to Canada occurred, however, after the Canadian Pacific Railway crossed the prairies in 1883 and especially when new lines developed the lands of the northern black-soil areas at the close of the century. The opening up of these new lands and the extensive advertising campaigns which accompanied it in the early 1900's resulted in thousands of immigrants pouring into Canada. From about 1907 to 1912, over 200,000 Europeans, mostly Germans and Slavs, were emigrating to the Canadian prairie lands each year.

The Ukrainians and the Russians, although speaking essentially the same language and varying slightly in cultural characteristics, settled more or less independently of each other. Dukhobors, a Russian religious sect, settled in Saskatchewan in the vicinity of Saskatoon and east of Verigin. Later, the more extreme of this sect moved into the new lands of southeast British Columbia. As the accompanying table indicates, in 1951 the Russians were more abundant in Saskatchewan than in the adjacent provinces, while the Ukrainians had their largest settlement in Manitoba but were almost as numerous in Alberta, Saskatchewan, and Ontario.

The Polish groups are found chiefly in Ontario and in the

United Church), Baptist, Lutheran, Jewish, Ukrainian (Greek Catholic), Greek Orthodox, and Mennonite.

G. T.

GOVERNMENT AND POLITICS

Canadian Constitution. The Canadian form of government is based both on statute and custom. The written constitution consists of the British North America Act (1867) and its amendments as these have been interpreted by the courts. These British statutes set the upper and lower limits within which centralization and decentralization in Dominion-provincial relations can be effected. In the creation of the written part of the Canadian constitution much use was made of the experiences of the United States, both by way of example and warning. Several provisions of the original statute aimed to prevent provincial rights from jeopardizing national unity. The federal government, for example, was given a blanket right of veto of provincial statutes, of appointment and dismissal of provincial governors, and of all judicial appointments. Federal statutes were to take precedence over provincial statutes in fields of concurrent jurisdiction. Criminal law and all residual powers were declared to lie within federal control. Nevertheless, custom and judicial interpretation have tended to strengthen the powers of the provinces, except in wartime.

If Canadian federalism can best be understood against an American background, Canadian legislative procedures and the relation of the legislative and executive branches of government have borrowed heavily from British experience. This part of the Canadian constitution is almost wholly unwritten. Canada is a limited monarchy, and at the head of its government is the governor general. He is appointed by the Crown, which he represents. The appointment is, however, made only on the advice of the Canadian government, and communication in this procedure takes place between the Canadian prime minister and the private secretary to the Crown. The functions of the governor general in Canada are similar to those of the Crown in the United Kingdom. He signs all federal statutes and orders in council, appoints government officials, opens, prorogues, and dissolves parlia-

BANFF NATIONAL PARK, NEAR LAKE LOUISE, ALBERTA

CANADIAN PACIFIC RAILWAY CO.

three prairie provinces. The Jewish groups tend to concentrate in the larger towns and, hence, are found almost entirely in the industrial provinces of Ontario and Quebec.

Religion. The three leading religious denominations in Canada, according to the 1951 census, are as follows: Roman Catholic, 43 per cent; United Church (Methodist, Presbyterian, and Congregational), 20 per cent; and Anglican, 15 per cent. Other denominations include Presbyterian (non-

ment, calls for general elections, and in general represents the state. His actions, however, are taken only on the advice of his ministers. Whether in emergency the governor general retains any residual power of independent prerogative action and, if so, what the nature and basis of this power is, remains a matter of uncertainty. In any case, care is taken by all concerned to avoid having the question emerge in practical form.

Cabinet. Legally, the cabinet is merely the executive

committee of the privy council, whose rulings bear the title of orders in council. Practically, the council does not exist and the cabinet alone is privy to the Crown. At the head of the cabinet is the prime minister, who is appointed by the Crown on advice of the outgoing prime minister. The prime minister is the leader of the dominant party in the House of Commons. The other cabinet ministers are likewise appointed by the Crown, but on advice of the existing prime minister. The cabinet as a whole remains in office only so long as it retains the confidence of the House of Commons. Lack of confidence may be indicated either by a direct no-confidence vote or by the defeat of an important government measure in the House. In anticipation of such defeat, a government may advise a dissolution of Parliament, hoping for more adequate support in the newly elected House. It is this cabinet responsibility to Parliament that makes it necessary for cabinet ministers to have seats in Parliament. Since the responsibility is to the lower, not to the upper house, it is in the former body that most of the cabinet ministers have seats. If a minister without a seat is appointed, he must secure one without delay or resign his portfolio. The cabinet is a corporate body, and a vote of censure on one of its members involves the downfall of all.

Senate. The federal upper house consists of 102 members appointed for life by the Crown on nomination of the federal cabinet. Instead of provincial equality of representation, however, there is a regional equality. The regions are (1) the four western provinces, each with 6 members, (2) Ontario and (3) Quebec, each with 24 members and (4) the Atlantic provinces of Nova Scotia and New Brunswick, with 10 members each and Prince Edward Island with 4 members. In 1949 Newfoundland, on joining Canada, was given 6 senatorial seats. Unlike the United States Senate, the Canadian upper house has no special executive functions; unlike the British House of Lords, it has no special judicial functions. Cabinet responsibility to the Commons has undoubtedly lowered the prestige of the Senate. Although the Senate must pass all money bills before they are signed, it may not initiate such measures. Otherwise Senate and Commons stand legally on a par in matters of legislation. In practice, however, the Senate has become chiefly a reviewing body. Appointed for life, usually after long service to their party, the members of the Senate are normally older than their counterparts in the Commons. Both the method of appointment and the basis of representation have prevented the Senate from becoming a defender of provincial rights— a function largely taken over by the cabinet, the members of which are always carefully selected on the basis of geographical distribution.

House of Commons. After the entry of Newfoundland membership in the House of Commons totalled 265. The old basis of representation was changed in 1952 to a complicated arrangement, by which all the provinces were given a flexible representation determined by the ratio of their population to the total population of Canada. Through this new system Quebec is assigned 75 seats, Ontario 85, and so down the list to the smallest province, Prince Edward Island, which has 4 seats. In addition, the Yukon Territory has one representative, as does the Mackenzie district of the Northwest Territories. Unlike the Senate, whose speaker is appointed by the federal government, the Commons elects its own speaker, who is nominated by the Prime Minister. Although provinces are represented in the Commons on the basis of population, constituencies vary greatly in size. All but two constituencies return only one member each. The maximum length of life of a parliament is five years, but a

dissolution may be effected at any time within that period. Such dissolution does not affect the Senate. There is no provision for joint sessions of House and Senate. In the case of a persistent deadlock, the Crown may appoint two additional senators from each region, but such action has never been taken.

Courts. There are two federal courts in Canada, the Supreme Court and the Exchequer Court. The former sits at the capital and is the final court of appeal in both civil and criminal matters. The Exchequer Court hears cases in which the government is financially involved. It also exercises admiralty jurisdiction, and in this capacity it acts as an appeal court for district admiralty courts. Except for certain semi-judicial bodies such as the Board of Transport Commissioners, all other Canadian courts are provincial. The law enforced in criminal courts is, however, federally enacted, and the prerogative of pardon is exercised only by the governor general, acting on advice of the federal minister of justice. All Canadian judges are appointed by the governor general in council for life, except Supreme and Exchequer court judges, who must retire at the age of 75. Any judge may be removed by the Crown on joint address of both houses of Parliament.

Civil Service. The Civil Service Commission is responsible for examining and recommending the appointment of civil servants below the rank of deputy minister. A notable exception is that of postal officials in the outside service. Civil servants enjoy the federal franchise, but are precluded by law from sitting in Parliament and by practice from taking an active part in political campaigns. The growth in governmental activities in Canada has been reflected in a large increase in the federal civil service, which increased from 46,106 in 1939 to 131,646 in 1952.

The Provinces. At the head of each provincial government is a lieutenant governor who has the same relation to his ministers in executive council as has the governor

PRIME MINISTERS OF CANADA SINCE CONFEDERATION

Ministry	Prime Minister	Length of Administration
1	Sir John MacDonald	July 1, 1867–Nov. 5, 1873
2	Alexander Mackenzie	Nov. 7, 1873–Oct. 16, 1878
3	Sir John MacDonald	Oct. 17, 1878–June 6, 1891
4	Sir John Abbott	June 16, 1891–Nov. 24, 1892
5	Sir John Thompson	Dec. 5, 1892–Dec. 12, 1894
6	Sir MacKenzie Bowell	Dec. 21, 1894–Apr. 27, 1896
7	Sir Charles Tupper	May 1, 1896–July 8, 1896
8	Sir Wilfrid Laurier	July 11, 1896–Oct. 6, 1911
9	Sir Robert Laird Borden	Oct. 10, 1911–Oct. 12, 1917 (Conservative Admin.)
10	Sir Robert Laird Borden	Oct. 12, 1917–July 10, 1920 (Unionist Administration)
11	Arthur Meighen	July 10, 1920–Dec. 29, 1921
12	W. L. Mackenzie King	Dec. 29, 1921–June 28, 1926
13	Arthur Meighen	June 29, 1926–Sept. 25, 1926
14	W. L. Mackenzie King	Sept. 25, 1926–Aug. 6, 1930
15	Richard Bedford Bennett	Aug. 7, 1930–Oct. 23, 1935
16	W. L. Mackenzie King	Oct. 23, 1935–Nov. 15, 1948
17	Louis Stephen St. Laurent	Nov. 15, 1948–June 21, 1957
18	John George Diefenbaker	June 21, 1957–

general to his cabinet. He is, as stated, a nominee of the federal cabinet, but in law he is as fully a representative of the Crown, within the province, as is the governor general in his larger sphere. His term of office is four years, but his tenure may be either lengthened or shortened. His executive council, like the Canadian cabinet, sits in the legislature and is responsible to it. In 1867 all the provinces except Ontario had two-house legislatures. Only

GOVERNORS GENERAL OF CANADA

Name	Date of Assumption of Office	Date of Departure
Viscount Monck	July 1, 1867	Nov. 14, 1868
Lord Lisgar	Feb. 2, 1869	June 21, 1872
Earl of Dufferin	June 25, 1872	Oct. 19, 1878
Marquis of Lorne	Nov. 25, 1878	Oct. 27, 1883
Marquis of Lansdowne	Oct. 23, 1883	May 25, 1888
Lord Stanley of Preston	June 11, 1888	July 15, 1893
Earl of Aberdeen	Sept. 18, 1893	Nov. 14, 1898
Earl of Minto	Nov. 12, 1898	Nov. 18, 1904
Earl Grey	Dec. 10, 1904	Oct. 12, 1911
Duke of Connaught	Oct. 13, 1911	Oct. 7-9, 1916
Duke of Devonshire	Nov. 11, 1916	July 19, 1921
Lord Byng of Vimy	Aug. 11, 1921	Sept. 29, 1926
Viscount Willingdon	Oct. 2, 1926	Jan. 14, 1931
Earl of Bessborough	Apr. 4, 1931	Sept. 26, 1935
Lord Tweedsmuir	Nov. 2, 1935	Feb. 11, 1940 (died in office)
Earl of Athlone	June 21, 1940	Mar. 16, 1946
Viscount Alexander of Tunis	Apr. 12, 1946	Jan. 28, 1952
Vincent Massey	Feb. 28, 1952	......

CANADIAN NATIONAL RAILWAYS

An exact replica of a gate in the ancient city wall of Quebec. Tours by caleche are popular with tourists.

Quebec now retains its legislative council. It is clear that a two-house legislature is not essential for responsible government. Canadian experience, however, seems to indicate that a two-party system reduces the need for gubernatorial intervention.

Federal-Provincial Relations. There is no constitutional machinery in Canada expressly designed for the conduct of either interprovincial or federal-provincial affairs, such as exists for diplomatic action in external affairs. The remoteness of most of the provincial capitals from the Dominion capital at Ottawa has accentuated the difficulty of consultation and co-operation in the development of harmonious and effective policies in matters of common concern. The ever-increasing complexity of the financial relations between the federal and the provincial governments as federal revenues rise and provincial educational and welfare expenditures increase, have placed an added strain on the administration of the Canadian federal state.

Franchise and Civil Rights. There are three levels of franchise in Canada: municipal, provincial, and federal. The first two are based on provincial legislation and vary somewhat from province to province in the minority groups that are excluded from the right to vote. The Federal Elections Act of 1938, with its successive amendments, extended the federal franchise to all British men and women who are 21 and have the necessary residence qualifications, except the following: judges and district election officers, criminals and the mentally incapable, those disqualified by corrupt election practices, treaty Indians except those with war service, Eskimos, and all Doukhobors resident in British Columbia. The act of 1948 removed the ban on granting the franchise to those of Japanese ancestry.

Citizenship in Canada is determined by the Citizenship Act of 1946, which took effect Jan. 1, 1947. It prescribes the conditions under which citizenship may be acquired and lost, providing for the retention of British nationality by Canadian citizens and repealing the previous rule by which a woman, on marrying, acquired her husband's status. Non-Canadian British nationals may vote after a residence of one year, but may not acquire Canadian citizenship until they have completed five years' residence. Alien residents may acquire both citizenship and the franchise after five years. They are required to take the oath of allegiance and also must swear that they will fulfill their duties as Canadian citizens.

Canada's written constitution is concerned with the limitation of the powers of governmental bodies in relation to each other, not with the limitation of the powers of government in relation to human rights. Such limitation in Canada is self-imposed, and has its basis either in custom or political expediency. Occasionally it takes the form of ordinary statute law. After World War II the governments of Canada and several of the provinces took action with regard to certain minority groups, which was widely regarded as infringing on the natural rights of native-born Canadians. A resultant attempt to have a bill of rights written into the Canadian constitution was not supported in Parliament, and without such action the British Parliament would, of course, refuse to amend the British North America Act. There were also doubts expressed as to whether a bill of rights would effect any marked improvement in the situation, since to define an individual's rights might be to limit them. Most Canadians preferred to approach the question of preserving civil liberties in the empirical and *ad hoc* manner traditionally used in Canada and throughout the Commonwealth.

Political Parties and Policies. The four leading parties in Canada are the Liberal, Conservative, Co-operative Commonwealth Federation (socialist), and Social Credit. The Liberal Party traces the main line of its party ancestry back through the Canadian Reform Party to the English Whigs; the Conservative Party goes back to the English Conservative Party. The Socialist Party (popularly known as the C.C.F.) has two roots: agrarian reform and the labor movement; it has drawn most of its strength from the former and has its chief center in Saskatchewan. The Social Credit Party drew from the radical monetary reform movement of England in its early years but has lately neglected this influence in favor of a more orthodox approach to provincial administration. It can now be considered a conservative party. Its chief center is in Alberta. The Union Nationale is usually classified as conservative; maximum home rule for Quebec is its distinctive policy. A more detailed examination of these parties and their policies is given in the article dealing with Canadian political parties. The Liberal

Party was dominant in the House of Commons in Ottawa from 1935 until 1957 and thus formed the Federal executive during that time. Its greatest electoral victory was obtained in the contest of June 17, 1949, when the party secured an absolute majority in the House of Commons. The party standing after that election was: Liberals, 193; Conservatives (including the Union Nationale), 42; C.C.F., 12; Social Credit, 10; and independents, 5. However, in the 23rd general election, June 9, 1957, the Liberals fell from power with the advent of an unexpected Conservative victory. The new House of Commons was made up of 109 Conservatives, 105 Liberals, 25 C.C.F., 19 Social Credit, and 5 independents. An anomalous feature of Canadian election results has been the disparity between the various parties' strengths in certain provinces in the federal and provincial legislatures. Ontario, for example, has supported the Conservatives for the provincial government since the end of World War II, while just as consistently electing Liberals to a majority of the province's seats in the federal House of Commons. In Quebec the Union Nationale (Conservative) party is firmly entrenched in the provincial field, while in federal elections it can make no headway against the Liberal ascendancy in the province.

Provincial elections since 1952 have served to strengthen the control of the Socialist government in Saskatchewan and of the Social Credit government in Alberta. The hold of the Union Nationale on Quebec has been slightly weakened. In British Columbia the coalition government was decisively defeated in 1952 and replaced by a Social Credit government which, in subsequent elections in 1953 and 1956 managed to secure comfortable majorities over the Socialist opposition. In the Maritime Provinces and Newfoundland there existed little real opposition to Liberal provincial administration, except in New Brunswick where the Conservatives have been in control since 1952.

Public Finance. Federal revenue for the fiscal year 1953-1954 was $4,396,319,583, or a per capita earning of $297. Federal expenditure amounted to $4,350,522,378 or a per capita outlay of $294. The income tax provided over half the total revenue of the Dominion—$2.4 billions. Other sources of revenue, in order of importance, were the sales tax, customs import duties, non-tax revenue, and miscellaneous taxes and excise duties. Over $1.8 billions of this revenue in 1954 were spent on national defence; other large sums were devoted to paying the interest on the public debt, to provincial subsidies and tax rental payments, and to family allowances and health grants, etc.

Provincial and municipal revenues for 1951 were $1,596,-214,000; the provinces collected 17.7 per cent of the country's total revenue, and the municipalities 12.2 per cent, leaving the federal government with the balance (70.1 per cent). Provincial revenues are obtained from liquor control and sales, gasoline taxes, payments from the federal government, and revenues from the public domain. Provincial expenditures for 1951 were $1,039,370,000, while municipalities spent a total of $772,817,000. These figures amounted to a total of 35.6 per cent of the expenditures of Canadian governments in that year. Provincial and municipal expenditures were devoted to public welfare services, old age pensions, highway construction and maintenance, education, and debt charges. Education has been by far the largest item of municipal expenditure since World War II.

Federal subsidies to the provinces are based on the complex financial provisions of the British North America Act of 1867 and many later adjustments, some of which have involved only a few of the provinces while others have changed the system of grants for Canada as a whole. The situation having remained unsatisfactory, with rising federal revenues and rising provincial obligations, a royal commission in 1940 advocated the withdrawal of the prov-

One of the world's largest grain elevators is situated on a point of land jutting into Lake Superior at Port Arthur, Ontario. Lake freighters carry the grain to United States and Canadian seaports designated as overseas transshipment points.

AIR VIEW OF NEATLY PATTERNED FARMLANDS IN WESTERN CANADA

inces from certain areas of the field of direct taxation and a corresponding increase in the obligations of the federal government to support the welfare services. Only temporary adjustments in this direction could be made during World War II, and the federal-provincial conference of 1946 failed to secure a general agreement. By 1952, however, all the provinces except Quebec had agreed to withdraw from the fields of personal and corporation income tax in return for a substantial federal compensation adjusted to the changes in the Canadian economy.

FEDERAL AND PROVINCIAL FINANCES IN CANADA, 1911-1951

	1911	*1921*	*1931*	*1941*	*1951*
Federal Finance—					
Customs revenue ....$	71,838,089	163,266,804	131,208,955	130,757,011	295,721,750
Excise revenue ....$	16,869,837	37,118,367	57,746,808	88,607,559	241,046,174
Income tax ....$	....	46,381,824	71,048,022	248,143,022	1,513,135,510
Sales tax (net).........................$	....	38,114,539	20,783,944	179,701,224	460,120,405
Total receipts from taxation.............$	88,707,926	368,770,498	296,276,396	778,175,450	2,785,349,899
Per capita receipts from taxes...........$	12.69	43.10	29.02	68.37	203.13
Total revenue ....$	117,780,409	436,292,185	356,160,876	872,169,645	3,112,535,948
Revenue per capita......................$	16.87	50.99	35.04	76.63	226.99
Total expenditure ....$	122,861,250	528,302,513	440,008,855	1,249,601,446	2,901,241,698
Expenditure per capita..................$	17.58	61.75	43.26	109.80	211.58
Gross debt ....$	474,941,487	2,902,482,117	2,610,265,699	5,018,928,037	16,923,307,028
Assets ....$	134,899,435	561,603,133[1]	348,653,762[1]	1,370,236,588[1]	5,489,992,080[1]
Net Debt ....$	340,042,052	2,340,878,984	2,261,611,937	3,648,691,449	11,433,214,948
Provincial Finance—					
Gross general revenue....................$	40,706,948	102,030,458	179,143,480	404,791,000[2]	1,260,943,000[2]
Gross general expenditure................$	38,144,511	102,569,515	190,754,202	349,818,000[2]	1,344,456,000[2]

[1] Active assets only. [2] Fiscal year ended nearest December 31 of the year stated.

Source: *Canada Year Book,* 1954.

THRESHING MACHINE IN OPERATION ON A LARGE FARM IN PRINCETON, ONTARIO, CANADA'S RICHEST AGRICULTURAL AREA.

The national debt in 1914 was $544,000,000, and had largely been incurred on revenue-producing projects. By 1939 the debt had risen to $3,711,000,000 and by Mar. 31, 1948, to $17,197,000,000 or $964 per capita (net debt). By March 31, 1954, the gross debt of the Government of Canada was $14,576,000,000, a significant decrease from the year before. Ninety-seven per cent of this debt was payable in Canada, the balance in New York and London. The total of outstanding provincial debts at the end of the 1952 fiscal year was $3,372,766,000. The total of municipal debts at the end of the 1952 fiscal year was $1,831,899,000, much of it acquired in school expenditures.

From the end of World War II to the end of the 1948 fiscal year the Canadian dollar increased in terms of United States currency from about 90 cents to 95 cents. When, in September 1949, the British pound was devalued by one-third the Canadian dollar was devalued to 90 cents.

In 1950 the Canadian dollar was allowed to reach its own level without government control, and before the end of the year it had reached par with the United States dollar for the first time since 1934. By mid-summer of 1952 it was at a premium of four per cent, the rise being caused chiefly by the extensive investment of American capital in rapidly expanding Canadian enterprises. Since then this percentage has fluctuated, but the Canadian dollar has generally been at a premium.

One of the distinctive features of the Canadian economy is the existence side by side, within the same enterprise, of both public and private ownership and operation. This is true on both federal and provincial levels. Most conspicuous, perhaps, is the federal ownership and operation of the Canadian National Railways, with 22,437 mi. of track, which competes with the privately owned and operated Canadian Pacific Railway, with 16,564 mi. of track. Jointly they operate the Alberta Railway in the west and several "pool" trains in the east. Both are equally subject to the ruling of the Board of Transport Commissioners. Both share in government business; but while the private line has always been a source of profit to its owners, the national line has usually been a liability. Deficits incurred by Canadian National Railways have, however, sprung in whole or in part from the insolvent character of the lines that were taken over to form the system. They have also been attributed to the fact that some of the amalgamated lines were originally constructed with government aid for non-economic national purposes. The federally owned Trans-Canada Air Lines and the private Canadian Pacific Airways are similarly under the regulatory control of the Air Transport Board. The Canadian National Steamships Company, government owned and operated, is subject to the Canada Shipping Act of 1934, as are the privately owned ships of the Canadian Pacific Steamship Company and other private Canadian shipping companies. In radio the system of the Canadian Broadcasting Corporation is in competition with many other Canadian systems and stations, some privately, some provincially owned. This dual system of public and private ownership calls for restraint on the part of government. The specialized functions of the National Film Board and the Bank of Canada have made them less competitive with private enterprise. Several federal wartime Crown corporations have been liquidated.

Provincial governments are also in varying degrees the owners and operators of public utilities. As is to be expected, the socialist government of Saskatchewan has proceeded farthest in this direction. This province owns and operates telephones, highway buses, and electric generators; it also insures automobiles, makes and sells boxes, and fillets and sells fish. Most of the provinces, with Ontario in the lead, have acquired and constructed elaborate hydroelectric systems. Ontario and British Columbia own and operate railways; Alberta owns a railway which is jointly operated by the Canadian Pacific Railway and Canadian National Railways. Some provinces operate savings banks; all but Prince Edward Island sell liquor; some operate radio stations. Unlike federal ownership, however, the provinces tend to move toward government monopoly in many of the fields in which they first operated in competition with private enterprise.

Defense. With the end of World War II there was a rapid demobilization of most of the personnel of the armed services and a dismantling of war plants or their transformation to peacetime use. After the war the three service ministries were replaced by a single minister of National Defense, under whom the chiefs of staff of the three services operate. The minister of National Defense is advised by a Defense Council. National defense headquarters are at Ottawa. Interservice organizations also include the Defense Research Board and the Department of Defense Production. Defense policy aims at building up large, part-time reserve forces and much smaller but more highly trained permanent forces. Re

dian Air Force, as reorganized in 1947, has an authorized permanent establishment of 40,423 officers and men, with a tactical wing of 3 squadrons, an interceptor wing of 5 squadrons, and 2 photographic and 2 transport squadrons. There is also an auxiliary force whose authorized strength is 15 squadrons. The navy has a permanent establishment of 15,546. The Royal Canadian Navy (Reserve) has an authorized complement on its active list of about 5,000 officers and men. In 1953 the ships of the Canadian navy consisted of an aircraft carrier, 2 cruisers, 8 destroyers, 9 minesweepers, 3 frigates, and many smaller auxiliary vessels.

In addition to defense headquarters, each service has its

PRODUCTION OF FIELD CROPS[1], 1911-1951

Crop	1911[2]	1921[2]	1931	1941	1951
Wheat ....bu.	132,077,547	226,508,411	321,325,000	314,825,000	552,657,000
Oats ....bu.	245,393,425	364,989,218	328,278,000	305,575,000	488,191,000
Barley ....bu.	28,848,310	42,956,049	67,382,600	110,566,000	245,218,000
Corn ....bu.	14,417,599	10,822,278	5,449,000	12,036,000	15,915,000
Potatoes ....bu.	55,461,473	62,230,052	52,305,000[3]	39,052,000[3]	48,355,000
Hay and Clover...................ton	10,406,367	8,829,915	14,539,600	12,632,000	19,484,000

[1] Exclusive of the Territories. [2] Figures are for 1910 and 1920 respectively. [3] Cwt.

Source: *Canada Year Book,* 1954.

search is stressed, and an attempt is made to have civil and military investigations promote their mutual development. The strategic co-ordination of defense plans, particularly with the United States and the United Kingdom, is a distinctive feature of postwar development. This applies particularly to the defense of Canada's northland.

There has been a rapid expansion of defense educational and training facilities, and a co-ordination of these with special courses provided in universities and colleges. The National Defence College at Kingston, Ont., established in 1948, is limited to senior civil and military officers and examines particularly the relation of civil and military

own headquarters under its chief of staff. All are located at Ottawa. The army is organized in five commands; the air force in two; and the navy in two.

ECONOMIC RESOURCES AND ACTIVITIES

Production. The conventional picture of Canada as a land of farms, flanked to the north by interminable forests, is hardly indicated by production figures. Since the turn of the century Canada has been steadily expanding her industrial productivity, with the result that a largely rural society of fifty years ago has now become a heavily industrialized and urban society, producing consumer and

DAIRY PRODUCTION AND TOTAL VALUE OF DAIRY PRODUCTS, 1911-1951

	1911[1]	1921[1]	1931	1941	1951
Total milk production...........'000 lb.	9,806,741	11,897,545	14,339,686	16,549,902	16,423,582
Cheese, factory[2] ....lb.	199,904,205	162,117,000	113,956,639	151,866,000	94,261,000
Butter, creamery ....lb.	64,489,398	128,745,000	225,955,246	285,848,196	257,165,000
Butter, dairy ....lb.	137,110,200	107,379,000	98,590,000	82,796,000	46,727,000
Other dairy products.................$	35,927,426[3]	110,623,000	109,262,600	159,363,878	412,938,000
Total Values, Dairy Products..........$	103,381,854	222,775,000	192,384,173	301,673,472	638,018,000

[1] Figures are for 1910 and 1920 respectively. [2] Figure for 1951 represents cheddar and other cheeses made from whole milk; prior to 1941 figures included other cheeses for Quebec only. [3] Does not include skim milk and buttermilk.

Source: *Canada Yearbook,* 1954.

policies. Royal Roads at Esquimalt, B.C., although administered by the navy, provides training leading to commissions in any of the armed services. Royal Military College, Kingston, is a similar institution administered by the army, as is the Collège Militaire Royal de Saint-Jean in Quebec. Training for staff appointments in the army is given at the Canadian Army Staff College at Kingston, and in the air force at the Royal Canadian Air Force Staff College at Toronto. The army conducts twelve specialized training schools.

The army has an active force with an authorized strength of 48,458 officers and men, and a reserve force, which is liable for active service, of about 180,000. The Royal Cana-

capital goods for an international market. Canada is now one of the great trading nations of the world and its people enjoy a standard of living second only to that of the United States, whose spectacular economic developement in the twentieth century Canada is now matching, although on a more limited scale. By mid-century the products of manufacturing accounted for over 25 per cent of the national income of Canada and realized a figure over twice as large as that produced by agricultural activity, which until 1900 had been the country's primary industry. Mining, forestry, and fishing followed in this leading group of Canadian industries, although far behind the value of the production set by the two giants of the Canadian economy—manufacturing and farming. The national income of Canada in 1952 stood at $18,221 millions and had increased four-fold since 1939. Undoubtedly the consequences of World War II, calling forth a tremendous expansion of productive capacity, two-thirds of which was found to be adaptable to peacetime uses after 1945, and the effect of the rearmament program associated with NATO and the Korean War, had been mainly responsible for this new condition of the Canadian economy.

Agriculture. The Canadian prairies are the most important region of agricultural production in the Dominion. Here are grown the basic food crops, like wheat and other cereals, which are shipped to world markets and form such a distinctive part of Canadian foreign trade. The prairies are also noted for stock raising (in the drier, western parts) and for specialized farming, like the growing of sugar beets on irrigated land. British Columbia has only a small proportion of its area suitable for farming but within these sections are the Okanagan valley, the center of a large fruit-growing activity, and the lower mainland and southern Vancouver Island district, which supply vegetables and dairy

poultry farming are carried on over most of the area. In general, farming in the Maritime provinces exists to serve the local market, with the exception of these specialized aspects of it. Following general trends, there has been a tendency in Canada toward specialized agriculture. Specialization is most noticeable in the production of wheat, dairy products, beef cattle, poultry, fruits, sugar beets, tobacco, and furs, and it has been both the cause and effect of expansion in agricultural education and research. Much of Canadian agriculture remains highly diversified, however, and some approaches the self-subsistence level. In parts of the country it is even integrated with such nonagricultural pursuits as forestry or fishing. Field crops are the most important farm products. The gross value of these crops in 1953 amounted to about 40 per cent of the value of all agricultural products—$2,741 millions. Wheat remains Canada's outstanding field crop. Its production in 1953 reached 13 million bushels, of which about half were exported by the Canadian Wheat Board under the International Wheat Agreement. Although Canada regularly produces only about one-third the amount of wheat raised in the United States, its export of

MINERAL PRODUCTION IN CANADA, 1911-1951

		1911	1921	1931	1941	1951
Gold	oz t.	473,159	926,329	2,693,892	5,345,179	4,392,751
Silver	oz t.	32,559,044	13,543,198	20,562,247	21,754,408	23,125,825
Copper	lb.	55,648,011	47,620,820	292,304,390	643,316,713	539,941,589
Lead	lb.	23,784,969	66,679,592	267,342,482	460,167,005	316,462,751
Zinc	lb.	1,877,479	53,089,356	237,245,451	512,381,636	682,224,335
Nickel	lb.	34,098,744	19,293,060	65,666,320	282,258,235	275,806,272
Pig Iron	long ton	819,228	593,829	420,038	1,528,053	2,552,696
Coal	short ton	11,323,388	15,057,493	12,243,211	18,225,921	18,586,823
Natural Gas	M cu. ft.	....	14,077,601	25,874,723	43,495,353	79,460,667
Petroleum, crude	bbl.	291,092	187,541	1,542,573	10,133,838	47,615,534
Asbestos	short ton	127,414	92,761	164,296	477,846	973,198
Cement	bbl.	5,692,915	5,752,885	10,161,658	8,368,711	17,007,812

Source: *Canada Year Book*, 1954.

products to Vancouver and Victoria. Considerable stock raising takes place in the interior Cariboo area. Ontario, especially the southern part of the province, has extensive mixed farming, dairying, and truck gardening to serve the needs of its large industrial centers. The Niagara district is famous for its fruit and berry crops, while most of Canada's tobacco is grown in the district north of Lake Erie in southwestern Ontario. Quebec also has a mixed type of agriculture, with many regions specializing in crops suited to local conditions—e.g. the gathering of maple sugar and syrup in the Eastern Townships. In the Maritimes pota-

that commodity is usually about two-thirds of the American export. Other important Canadian field crops in 1953 were: oats; hay and clover; barley; rye; mixed grains, and potatoes. Livestock production normally amounts to about 40 per cent of the value of field crops. Cattle, hogs, sheep and lambs are the chief animals raised. The gross value of dairy products was $413 millions in 1953, but a proportion of this accrued from factory processing.

Less than 20 per cent of Canada's gainfully employed males are farmers. Recent estimates put the value of capital invested in about 660,000 Canadian farms at nearly $10

FOREST PRODUCTION AND VALUE OF LUMBER PRODUCTION, 1911-1951

		1911	1921	1931	1941	1951
Primary forest production	$	....	168,054,024	141,123,930	213,163,089	782,525,015
Lumber production	M ft. b.m.	4,918,202	2,869,307	2,497,553	4,941,084	6,948,697
	$	75,830,954	82,448,585	45,977,843	129,287,703	507,650,241
Total sawmill products	$	....	116,891,191	62,769,253	163,412,292	591,551,749
Pulp and paper products	$	....	151,003,165	174,733,954	334,726,175	1,237,897,470
Exports of wood, wood products and paper[2]	$	56,334,695	284,561,478	185,493,491	387,113,232	1,399,076,131

[1] Fiscal years. [2] Years ended Mar. 31 prior to 1931.

Source: *Canada Year Book*, 1954.

toes are grown extensively for seed and table consumption in central New Brunswick and Prince Edward Island, apples are produced in the Annapolis valley and dairying and

billions at the mid-century. Only about 16 per cent of Canada, however, is suitable for agriculture, and only about 7 per cent is actually under cultivation. Farms vary greatly

Loggers use a power saw to fell a giant tree. The forests of British Columbia, in which are found Douglas fir, Sitka spruce, Engelmann spruce, hemlock, lodgepole pine, and, in the warmer sections of the south, madrona and Garry oak, provide the raw material for one of the province's most important industries—the lumber mills of Vancouver.

STEFFENS·COLMER STUDIO: LTD.

Armed with a pike pole, a logger works on a log boom in Vancouver, British Columbia.

STEFFENS·COLMER STUDIO. LTD.

in size, from the small truck farm of the east to the cattle ranches of the west.

Mining. Of all Canadian primary industries, mining has had the most striking development during the past half century. Between 1896 and 1954 the value of the annual **mineral** output increased from $22 millions to $1,454 mil-

lions, and the per capita value from $4.42 to $96.93. This all-time high was reached through spectacular gains in the value of crude petroleum production, copper, nickel, and asbestos. Gold output also remained high, although the price per ounce dropped in 1954. Petroleum, with a value of over $245 millions in 1954, had surpassed gold as the most valuable mineral that is extracted in the Canadian economy by mid-century.

Minerals in Canada are widely scattered over the Dominion. Coal is found on both coasts: in British Columbia in both the coastal regions and in the mountainous interior; and in Cape Breton Island and Nova Scotia on the Atlantic coast. It is also found in the Rocky Mountain foothills in Alberta. Canada's chief supplies of petroleum and natural gas come from Alberta, in the Edmonton area, where about half the oil requirements of the country are now being produced. Metals are found chiefly in the rocks of the Canadian Shield, with the consequence that Manitoba, Ontario, and Quebec, the three provinces largely covered by the Shield, constitute the most important mineral producing region in Canada. Gold comes primarily from the Porcupine and associated fields in northern Ontario, as does nickel and copper. The Flin Flon ore bodies on the border of Manitoba and Saskatchewan are also important copper and gold producers. Ontario produced all of Canada's cobalt, mag-

in the process comes from British Guiana. Important deposits of base metals like lead and zinc have recently been discovered in the Bathurst area of New Brunswick. There have been producing mines of this type in Newfoundland for many years. The largest silver-lead-zinc mine in Canada, however, is at Kimberley in southeastern British Columbia. Nova Scotia has important deposits of non-metallic minerals like salt and gypsum. Radium is mined at Great Bear Lake in the Northwest Territories, and uranium at Beaverlodge Lake near Lake Athabasca in Saskatchewan. Structural minerals are distributed very widely over Canada and are extensively used in local areas.

Several recent developments in Canadian mining warrant special mention. Canada's lack of iron has been a conspicuous feature of its economy. During World War II a beginning was made in the development of iron resources in northern Ontario, in the Michipicoten region north of Sault Ste. Marie, and at Steep Rock west of Port Arthur. Since the war the iron resources on the Quebec-Labrador bound-

Collecting lobster pots in Nova Scotia, the world's largest lobster-exporting region

nesium, calcium, and platinum metals at the mid-century. Iron ore is also mined in western Ontario—at Steep Rock and in the Algoma area—and in the neighborhood of Marmora, north of Lake Ontario. Quebec's iron ore deposits

ary, first discovered in 1895, have been favorably reported on both as to quality and extent. In 1947 air transportation to the region was provided, and subsequently a railway company constructed the 360 mi. of track from Seven Islands

MANUFACTURING IN CANADA, 1911-1951

	1911[1]	1921[1]	1931[2]	1941[2]	1951[2]
Employees ....No.	515,203	438,555	528,640	961,178	1,258,375
Capital ....$	1,247,583,609	2,697,858,073	3,705,701,893	4,905,503,966	....
Salaries and wages..................$	241,008,416	497,399,761	2,587,566,990	1,264,862,643	3,276,280,917
Values of material used in............$	601,509,018	1,365,292,885	1,221,911,982	3,296,547,019	9,074,526,353
Products—					
Gross[3] ....$	1,165,975,639	2,488,987,148	2,555,126,448	6,076,308,124	16,392,187,132
Net[3] ....$	564,466,621	1,123,694,263	1,252,017,248	2,605,119,788	6,940,946,783

[1] Figures are for the preceeding year. [2] Statistics are exclusive of construction hand trades, repair and custom work but include non-ferrous metal smelting not included in earlier years. [3] For 1931, 1941, and 1951 net value of production is computed by subtracting the cost of fuel and electricity, as well as the cost of materials, from the gross value of the products. Source: *Canada Year Book*, 1954.

in Ungava stand at the threshold of development. The province of Quebec produces copper, zinc, gold and silver, titanium and asbestos. Aluminum smelting on a large scale is carried on at Arvida in Quebec but the bauxite ore used

on the St. Lawrence to Burnt Lake which would make major mining operations possible. The first shipments of iron ore were brought out by rail in 1954 from what appears to be one of the richest deposits of iron ore in North Amer-

Synthetic-rubber plants, such as this, near Sarnia, Ontario, help maintain Canada's place in world industry.

Paper making in northern Ontario, representative of a group of industries which owe their growth to the development of the province's forest resources.

ica. The efficient development of this resource is closely connected with the completion of the St. Lawrence Seaway. In 1949 Canada, by securing the adhesion of Newfoundland, came into direct control of the iron resources on Bell Island, in Conception Bay, from which 1,634,500 tons of iron were exported in 1952, mostly to Canada. Since World War II new sources of oil have been discovered and their exploitation begun. Wells have been drilled in several widely separated parts of central and northern Alberta. As the Turner Valley wells, from which Canada had previously secured almost all of its local oil, had begun to decline, these new sources were welcomed. By 1952, Alberta produced 96 per cent of Canadian crude oil and 90 per cent of Canadian production of natural gas. Deposits of uranium have been discovered and are being developed in the Northwest Territories and Saskatchewan.

Canada's leading minerals are crude petroleum, nickel, copper, gold, coal, asbestos, zinc, lead, and iron. The country also has a substantial industry in clay products, cement, sand and gravel, and building stone. Canada has regularly been the chief producer of platinum and its associated metals; it also produces about 80 per cent of the world's nickel.

Forestry. About 42 per cent of Canada is forest-clad. Some of the forest belt across Canada, especially along the tundra fringe, is unsuitable for development and other areas have been inaccessible; however, exploitation is possible over about 578,000 sq. mi. or 70 per cent of the productive forest area of Canada. Of this forest, approximately 63 per cent is comprised of softwood, 25 per cent mixed wood, and 12 per cent hardwood. There are 150 species of trees in Canada.

coast salmon, herring, and halibut are caught; on the Atlantic shore cod, haddock, hake, herring, lobster and other shellfish are the principal fish taken. Whitefish and trout are also caught in inland waters by commercial fishermen.

Of the $24 millions worth of furs produced in 1952, 58 per cent came from trapping and the remainder from fur farming. Mink and fox were the most important types of fur-bearing animals kept, although the chinchilla was gaining in popularity. In the wild state mink, muskrat, marten, fox, and beaver were important species for the trapper. Fall-

The waterfront at Toronto, second largest city in Canada and the industrial capital of Ontario. In the background (left) is the Royal York Hotel, largest in the British Commonwealth; (right) the Bank of Commerce Building.

PHILIP GENDREAU

New uses have increasingly been found for wood previously regarded as useless. In 1950 the leading items in Canadian forest production, by value, were logs and bolts, pulpwood, fuel wood, railway ties, poles, mining timber, fence posts, and wood for distillation purposes. Over 90 per cent of the total output of forest products was used in Canada. Output in 1952 was over $800 millions in value.

Fish and Furs. The long association of the fisheries and the fur industry with the early history of Canada is noted in the historical section. The fishing grounds kept both English and French interested in North America throughout the sixteenth century. The fur trade gave economic worth to Canada throughout the French regime and in the early period of British rule. In the first half of the nineteenth century the primacy of furs was replaced by the primacy of timber, and in the second half by the primacy of agriculture. Fish are still of great importance, however, in the economies of both Nova Scotia in the east and British Columbia in the west. In Newfoundland, Canada has acquired a new province in which the fisheries have dominated the economic life of the people for 350 years. Only in the Northwest Territories has the fur trade remained dominant.

Canada is one of the main fish-producing and fish-exporting countries of the world, with a yearly catch of about 1,900 million lbs., 90 per cent of which is exported. The United States takes most of the exports, but markets are also found in the Mediterranean countries, in Great Britain, in the West Indies, and in South America. On the Pacific

ing prices, however, resulted in farm sales, both in the form of live animals and of pelts, of only $10 millions. Fur farms are widely distributed across the country, with Ontario leading in the value of pelts and Quebec in the number of farms. Prince Edward Island, original home of the fur-farm industry, had dropped to eighth place in the value of fur-farm animals in 1952.

Manufactures. Among Canadian cities Montreal and Toronto have a large and varied manufacturing activity, ranging from the production of iron and steel goods to the innumerable processes of light industry. Hamilton, at the western end of Lake Ontario, specializes in the making of iron and steel and the products fabricated from these materials. Other important manufacturing centers in Ontario are London, Brantford, Peterborough, Windsor, and Oshawa. Most of the Dominion's textile industry is located in Quebec and in eastern Ontario in the Ottawa valley, and in the neighborhood of Winnipeg. Winnipeg is also a major center for agricultural products, being the site of the largest stockyards in Canada and the home of many flour mills. British Columbia specializes in the processing of wood products and in mineral smelting, but it also has a varied light industry in the Vancouver area. The Maritime provinces have a major iron and steel mill at Sydney, together with old-established industries in various centers, like the sugar refinery at Saint John, shipbuilding and repairing at Halifax, and textile, boot and shoe factories in several towns in Nova Scotia and New Brunswick. Newfoundland has produced pulp and paper for many years, but since the end of World War II the province has embarked on an ambitious industrialization program, the success of which it is as yet too early to foretell.

The total gross value of manufactures in 1953 was over $17 billions, and the net value over $8 billions, the latter figure including gross value, less costs of fuel, electricity, and materials. The manufacture of pulp and paper has been the leading industry of the country for many years and has not lost this position even with the great expansion of manufacturing in Canada since 1945. By the mid-century the pulp and paper industry stood first among all industries in value of production, in exports, in wages paid, and in capital in-

centers for the production of hydroelectric power and extensive construction work is planned to enable existing hydro facilities to supply the needs of the expanding industrial activities of these provinces. The Niagara River, Ottawa River, the St. Lawrence River, the Severn River, the Shipshaw River, the Saguenay River, and many others have been harnessed to provide power for the central provinces. In Manitoba a great deal of hydroelectric power is produced from the Shield in the area east of Lake Winnipeg; and in British Columbia large power plants are in operation north of Vancouver, on Vancouver Island, on the Bridge River, on Lower Arrow Lake and on the Columbia River. In the Maritimes power sites are limited but those that are

Royal Bank of Canada and the City Hall, Winnipeg, Manitoba

vested. Together with sawmilling, furniture-making and other industries based on the use of wood, it accounted for 20 per cent of the value of manufactures in Canada.

Slaughtering and meat-packing stood second among Canadian industries in 1953, and with the processing of other products coming from Canadian farms—butter and cheese, flour, and other food products—constituted 12 per cent of the total value of manufacturing shipments. Non-ferrous metal smelting and refining ranked third among the industries in value of factory shipments. Almost all the ore used in this activity came from domestic sources except for the aluminum industry, which imported ore from South America. The making of motor vehicles was Canada's fourth industry in value of production and the refining of petroleum was fifth. Both these activities had gained rapidly in importance since 1945. After them came the manufacture of iron and steel, men's clothing, motor vehicle parts, rubber goods, etc. The aircraft industry, though not among the first ten industries in Canada, was one of the fastest-growing activities in the national economy. Ontario was the most industrialized province, producing almost half the nation's manufactures. Behind it came Quebec, specializing in pulp and paper, and British Columbia.

Hydroelectric Power. The major hydroelectric power sites in Canada are found where the flow of water from the Canadian Shield or the Cordilleran mountains offers a source of hydraulic power to large urban and industrial areas nearby. Thus, Ontario and Quebec are today the chief

available, such as on the St. John River, for instance, have been developed for local needs. Newfoundland and Labrador appear to have a very large hydroelectric power potential, of which only a fraction is being used at the present time.

In 1955 hydroelectric installation in Canada had a capacity of 17,000,000 hp. Almost 50 per cent of the available power was located in Quebec, and 27 per cent in Ontario. With the absence of known coal resources in either of these provinces, and with the increasing cost and uncertainty of coal from the United States as a source of power, this development of "white coal" has been of prime importance, especially in the two central provinces, which between them account for 80 per cent of Canada's total net production values. That even this supply of electricity was still inadequate was dramatically demonstrated by the blackout in Toronto late in 1947. New construction of hydroelectric facilities, however, particularly those associated with the development of the International Rapids section of the St. Lawrence Seaway, should go far to meet this deficiency. The per capita installation of hydroelectric power in Quebec and British Columbia was the highest in the world, although the figure for the whole of Canada was below that of Norway. Canadian power was very low in price; residential consumers paid about half the United States rates for similar forms of power. Although all the provinces except Newfoundland and Prince Edward Island have government power commissions, privately owned electric stations still produce somewhat more power than those publicly owned.

Trade. *Foreign.* Canada ranks after the United States and the United Kingdom as one of the world's leading trading nations. In 1953 its exports were valued at $4,069 millions and its imports at $4,832 millions. The total gave it a per capita external trade of $630, or three times that of the United States. Although the relative extent of this trade has been consistent through many years, the nature of the trade has lately been undergoing a radical change. Instead of being solely an exporter of primary products and an importer of manufactured goods, Canada now exports mostly goods that have gone through at least some stage of manufacture or processing. Only 7 per cent of all forestry exports are unmanufactured. Much of Canada's wheat is exported in the form of flour; processed meat, rather than cattle, is exported. The imports of raw materials for manufacture, as in the case of the aluminum industry, of oil and coal for power and heat, and the increasing demand for citrus fruits, have combined with other factors to change the nature of imports as well.

Of the twenty leading export commodities in 1954, four forest products accounted for 45 per cent of the value, seven minerals for 25 per cent, and three agricultural products for 19 per cent. Farm implements, machinery, and whiskey were the leading manufactured goods exported from Canada.

The principal imports in 1954, in order of value, were machinery and parts, petroleum, electrical goods, automobile parts, aircraft parts, rolling mill products, fuel oil, coal, and automobiles.

After a series of surpluses in its trading accounts, Canada has, in the postwar period, begun to incur large deficits. These deficits are not obtained from commodity trading so much as from the "invisible transactions," such as interest and dividend payments to foreign investors, international travel obligations, costs of shipping services, etc. In most

Along the Cabot Trail, a scenic highway encircling the entire northern coastline of Cape Breton Island.

years this debt is more than offset by large inflows of foreign capital for direct investment in Canadian enterprises.

Domestic. Domestic trade remained at a high level after the war. The limits placed on trade arose from short supply rather than from purchasing power. Retail sales in 1954 amounted to $11,928 millions or almost $800 per capita. Ontario accounted for over 30 per cent of retail sales, with Quebec, British Columbia, and the Maritime Provinces following in that order. Since 1941 the rise in the volume of domestic business has greatly exceeded the rate of population growth in Canada.

Banking. The banking system of Canada consists of the federal Bank of Canada, with headquarters in Ottawa and an agency in each province, and ten chartered banks with a total of 3,500 branches or subagencies throughout Canada and 100 branches or subagencies abroad. The chartered banks are the Bank of Montreal, Bank of Nova Scotia, Toronto-Dominion Bank, Provincial Bank of Canada, Canadian Bank of Commerce, Royal Bank of Canada, Banque Canadienne Nationale, Imperial Bank of Canada, and Barclays Bank (Canada). Savings-bank services are provided by the Federal Government and some of the provinces, and trust companies have limited banking functions.

The Bank of Canada, established in 1935, is owned and operated by the Federal Government. Federal finances must be handled by this bank, and provincial finances may be. The bank issues and controls Canadian currency; bank notes formerly issued by the chartered banks are gradually being called in. Under certain conditions the Bank of Canada may make advances either to the federal or provincial governments and accept deposits from them. It may buy coin or bullion, but in 1940 its gold holdings were transferred to the Foreign Exchange Control Board. A subsidiary of the Bank of Canada is the Industrial Development Bank, whose president is the governor of the Bank of Canada. The Industrial Bank on Mar. 31, 1953, had over $37 millions in loans outstanding to a wide variety of Canadian industries.

The total assets of the chartered banks in 1952 were over $9,700 millions, and the deposits were over $8,800 millions. The chartered banks are under inspection by the Federal Government, and their operations regulated by the Federal Bank Act, which is reexamined by Parliament at decennial intervals, following which all bank charters are reviewed.

Transportation and Communications. *Railways and Steamships.* Railways are of primary importance in the Canadian economy. The vast size and difficult topography of the country has made the building of railways at once expensive and essential. One result has been the consolidation of several bankrupt lines and the building of others by the Canadian government in the national interest. The government-owned and operated Canadian National Railways has over 50 per cent of the total trackage of 43,133 route miles. This line has its operating headquarters at Montreal and its main eastern terminus at Halifax, N.S. In Nova Scotia there is a spur to North Sydney, where connection is made by ferry to Port aux Basques, Newfoundland, whence a railway runs to St. John's, the capital. In 1949 the Canadian National Railways took over both ferry and railway when Newfoundland entered the federation. In the west the termini are at Vancouver and Prince Rupert, both in British Columbia. The C.N.R. also operates the government railway to Churchill on Hudson Bay. On the Pacific the Canadian National Steamships operates a service connecting these termini and continuing north to Ketchikan, Alaska. On the Atlantic the West Indies branch of the C.N.S. operated a regular service between Canada and the

West Indies until 1952. The Canadian National Railways also operates a railway express and a telegraphic service, as well as a number of hotels along its lines from coast to coast.

The Canadian Pacific Railway has its main eastern terminus at Saint John, N.B., but it also maintains a ferry from that port to Digby, N.S., whence it has running rights to Halifax. Its western terminus is at Vancouver, B.C., but it operates a ferry to Victoria on Vancouver Island. The Canadian Pacific also possesses a coastal service from Victoria to Skagway, Alaska. In the Atlantic this steamship line connects Canada with the United Kingdom, using the port of Montreal in the summer and Saint John in the winter. The C.P.R. has its own steamers on the upper Great Lakes, with a regular summer service between Port McNicoll and Fort William. Here as elsewhere it is in competition with the government-owned system which, through the Northern Navigation Co., operates between Sarnia and Fort William. The C.P.R. also has a chain of hotels along its main line, and has subsidiary express and telegraph services. The

lines connecting with the T.C.A., the C.P.A.L. in 1949 added two trans-Pacific services, one from Vancouver to Hong Kong, the other from Vancouver to Sydney, N.S.W. A new service, from Vancouver to Holland across the polar regions, has just been approved by the Air Transport Board. There are also many small companies still serving the occasional needs of the mining enterprises of the north.

Inland Waterways. Navigation on Canada's inland waterways is largely limited to the St. Lawrence-Great Lakes and to the Mackenzie River of the far north. Both of these systems suffer by being closed during the winter months. The Mackenzie River is navigable for vessels of shallow draft without the need of canal construction, but the St. Lawrence-Great Lakes system is not so fortunate. Navigation is blocked by the rapids in the St. Lawrence between Montreal and Prescott, by Niagara Falls, and by the St. Marys River between Lakes Huron and Superior. Since the beginning of the twentieth century the canal system on the St. Lawrence has been able to take vessels of only 14 ft. draft.

OCCUPATIONAL GROUPS IN CANADA, 1911-1951

	1911	1921	1931	1941	1951
Labour force[1] ....No.	....	....	4,105,000	4,417,000	5,255,000
Gainfully Occupied—[2]					
Agricultural occupations ....No.	933,735	1,035,283	1,127,682	1,083,816	826,759
Other primary occupations ....No.	139,877	115,737	150,276	203,586	196,996
Manufacturing occupations ....No.	372,234	406,677	495,842	709,181	973,982
Construction occupations ....No.	150,567	162,275	203,056	213,493	319,065
Transportation occupations ....No.	158,926	199,568	289,030	311,645	492,986
Trade and finance occupations .....No.	221,805	293,334	352,414	370,617	520,761
Service occupations ....No.	322,895	420,173	616,953	725,456[3]	919,922
Clerical occupations ....No.	106,351	217,937	258,684	314,051	541,713
Labourers occupations ....No.	317,244	306,215	426,242	252,093	323,829
Not stated occupations ....No.	....	7,149	1,654	11,413	63,600
Totals, Gainfully Occupied.......No.	2,723,634	3,164,348	3,921,833	4,195,951[3]	5,179,613[5]
Wage-earners[4] ....No.	1,628,273	1,972,089	2,570,097	2,816,798[3]	4,006,466

[1] Exclusive of persons in institutions, remote areas, Indians on reservations, and the Armed Forces. [2] Exclusive of the Territories. [3] Exclusive of persons on active service on June 2, 1941. [4] Figures for occupational groups include labor force 14 years of age and over. [5] Exclusive of Newfoundland with a labour force of 106,540 persons. Source: *Canada Year Book,* 1952-1953, and 1954.

Pacific Great Eastern Railway is owned and operated by the government of British Columbia. The Northern Alberta Railway into the Peace River country is owned and operated jointly by the C.N.R. and the C.P.R. The Ontario government both owns and operates the Ontario Northland Railway from North Bay to Moosonee on James Bay. In 1952 there was still some railway building in both east and west. Mining interests were constructing a 360-mile line north from Seven Islands on the north shore of the St. Lawrence to tap the rich iron deposits on the Quebec-Labrador boundary, and the Canadian National was running a spur from Terrace on its main Prince Rupert line to the aluminum refinery being built at Kitimat on Douglas Channel.

Air Lines. Air services in Canada are also closely affiliated with the two great railway lines. The Trans-Canada Air Lines, like the C.N.R., is government-owned. It operates a service from Vancouver to Halifax, with a branch in the west from Lethbridge, Alta., to Edmonton, and two branches in the east from Toronto to Windsor, Ont., and from Toronto to New York. In the east the line extends beyond Halifax to Sydney, N.S., Gander, Nfld., and across the Atlantic to the United Kingdom. During World War II the Canadian Pacific Air Lines began by absorbing small lines flying into the remote north. To this series of north-south

The Welland Canal, which circumvents the Niagara River, was deepened in 1931 to take vessels of 30 ft. draft. The Sault Ste. Marie Canal between Lake Huron and Lake Superior on the Canadian side of the St. Marys River has a draft of 25 ft.; an American canal parallels it on the opposite side of the river. Other Canadian canals, such as the Rideau, Trent Valley, Chambly, Carillon, and St. Peters, are of minor importance. In 1952 the cargo tonnage through the Welland Ship Canal was 17,910,756, more than half of which originated in the United States. The figure for the St. Lawrence canals was 9,836,395 and for Sault Ste. Marie, 3,295,423. The Canada Steamship Company operates both passenger and freight services on the St. Lawrence and the Great Lakes. In 1951 the president of the United States assured the Canadian government that if the U.S. Senate did not shortly endorse the St. Lawrence Seaway agreement of 1941 he would approve of Canada proceeding alone to deepen the international section of the St. Lawrence for navigational purposes. After reaching an agreement with Ontario regarding the development of hydroelectric power along the Seaway, the Canadian government secured the passage of a federal act empowering the government to appoint a St. Lawrence Seaway Authority to proceed with the enterprise. This board was duly appointed early in 1952.

In 1953 the New York State Power Authority was designated as the United States agency to co-operate with Ontario in the construction of the power phase of the project, and later the United States declared its intention of participating in the navigational aspect of the Seaway. Construction was therefore begun in 1954.

Highways. The total road mileage in Canada is 568,774, of which about 75 per cent is unsurfaced; of the total of 173,232 mi. of surfaced roads, 87 per cent is gravel. The Northwest Highway System, known in the United States as the Alaska Highway, between Dawson Creek, B.C., and Fairbanks, Alaska, is about 1,600 mi. in length and is open to civilian travel. In 1949 the Federal Government agreed to share equally with the provinces in the construction or improvement of a trans-Canada highway. Much construction is necessary in the rough country north of Lake Superior in order to make this road a reality.

Communications. Telegraphic services are largely in the hands of the two railway systems. About 58 per cent of the telephones of Canada belong to Bell Telephone Company in Ontario and Quebec. There are, however, no less than 3,114 telephone systems in Canada. Large systems are operated by the provincial governments of Alberta, Saskatchewan, and Manitoba. There are 2,354 co-operative systems, almost half of them in Saskatchewan. The Federal Government operates an extensive system of both telephone and telegraph services to the more remote settlements, especially in the north.

The government-owned Canadian Broadcasting Corporation operates both long-wave and short-wave systems for local and overseas receivers respectively. It is supported by government grants and by revenues from advertising. There are in addition both provincially and privately owned broadcasting systems throughout the country. On some of the private systems all of the programs, and many of them on the C.B.C., are given in French. In 1952 there were over 2,300,000 receiving sets in Canada.

Television, under the auspices of the Canadian Broadcasting System, was introduced in the Toronto area in 1952 and since that time has spread to most of the principal cities of the Dominion. A national network system is envisaged when facilities are available. As in radio, privately-operated television stations were in existence, all in areas not served by the public corporation.

The communication services of the Post Office have been materially aided by air mail, particularly in view of the great distances to be covered. There are 12,254 post offices in Canada, and the gross postal revenue in 1953 was $119,567,922.

The press in Canada consists of 82 daily newspapers with a total circulation in 1952 of 2,961,901, and 736 weekly newspapers with a circulation of 2,533,978. Of these, 12 dailies with a circulation of 608,597, and 127 weeklies with a circulation of 1,521,684, were in the French language.

There were also several weeklies in other languages, the largest in both numbers and circulation being in Ukrainian.

Labor. The labor force in Canada, consisting of all civilians in the country over 14 years of age who had jobs or were seeking work, totalled over 5,300,000 at the beginning of 1955. Males represented about 75 per cent and females 25 per cent of the total labor force. Average weekly earnings and salaries continued to rise and in industrial occupations had reached the rate of $56 per person by early 1953. There were over 1,200,000 trade union members in Canadian labor at that time. Over 500,000 of these belonged to the Trades and Labour Congress of Canada, whose international unions are affiliated with the American Federation of Labor. A total of 350,000 belonged to the Canadian Congress of Labour, established in 1940, whose international unions are affiliated with the Congress of Industrial Organizations. As in the United States, a merger of these two large unions is being effected. The remaining groups of the Canadian labour movement are either members of the Canadian and Catholic Confederation of Labour, or, like the railway brotherhoods, are in independent organizations.

In 1940 a constitutional amendment permitted the Federal Government to enter the field of unemployment insurance; benefits were first paid by the Federal Government in 1942. All the provinces have workmen's compensation acts, providing benefits to certain classes of workers. The time lost by strikes in Canada was only .06 per cent in 1944. In 1946 it rose to .5, but by 1952 it had dropped to .29.

SOCIAL AND CULTURAL CONDITIONS

General Characteristics. Scattered along the American border from coast to coast, the populations in the various regions of Canada display in their social pattern a somewhat greater similarity to their counterparts to the south than to their compatriots to the east or west. The pattern of southern Saskatchewan more closely resembles that of Montana than that of Nova Scotia, as the pattern of New Eng-

EDUCATION IN CANADA, 1911-1951

Item		1911	1921	1931	1941	1951
Education—						
Total Enrollment	No.	1,361,205	1,880,805	2,264,106	2,131,391	2,880,043
Average Daily attendance[2]	No.	870,532	1,349,256	1,801,955	1,802,300	2,123,184
Teachers[2]	No.	40,516	56,607	71,246	75,308	89,534
Public expenditure on	$	37,971,374	112,976,543	144,748,823	129,817,268	454,139,000[3]

[1] All types of educational institutions. [2] Provincially controlled ordinary and technical day schools. [3] 1950 figure. Source: *Canada Year Book,* 1954.

land more closely resembles that of Nova Scotia than that of Wyoming. This is not to imply that Canadian life has been patterned on American. There is almost no contact, for instance, between Saskatchewan and Montana. Much of the similarity is simply due to the effects of similar circumstances on society on both sides of the border. There is not only the similarity of soil and climate, sea, mountain, and treeless plain, which inevitably condition or help to condition ways of thinking and living together. There is also much similarity of age-long tradition and of racial stocks, especially from northern Europe. It is fascinating to search for differences, but minutiae may well be magnified to distortion.

Differences there are across the border, differences which seem to stem chiefly from more recent political tradition. To the south is the glory of the American Revolution; to the north the glory of loyalty to old traditions. To the south institutions are for the convenience of those who have them;

THE CHÂTEAU FRONTENAC, QUEBEC'S MOST FAMOUS HOTEL, ON CAP-AUX-DIAMANTS, WAS BUILT IN 1892.

to the north institutions transcend the individual, as they outlive the generations. The difference in attitude comes out most clearly in relation to law, but it can also be seen in the more personal affairs of social life. Tradition, religion, and even climate conspire to give a cohesion to family life. Such a fundamental difference is as easy to recognize as it is difficult to prove.

The province of Quebec has usually been regarded as differing from the rest of Canada not only in language and tradition but also socially. The most outstanding change which has affected Canada in more recent years, however —namely, the urbanization of the Canadian people—has had its most rapid and most profound effect on the province of Quebec. Quebec now ranks as the province with the highest proportion of urban dwellers; this is 67.3 per cent, compared with the Canadian average of 56.7 per cent, according to the census of 1951, and recent years have continued to add to this urbanization of the French Canadians. What effect this may come to have on the traditionally simple piety of a settled and conservative people, with their love of the soil, their devotion to family and local community, and their high birthrate, is impossible to foresee.

Education. In Canada, as in the United States, education has been constitutionally placed beyond the reach of federal jurisdiction. Both the Federal Government and Parliament have, however, been given the special role of defending religious denominational rights in regard to education as these were in effect when the provinces entered the federal union. Without any constitutional amendment, the Federal Government and Parliament have also assumed certain duties in the promotion of agricultural and technical education, fields in which, presumably, religious interests are not in-

volved. Finally, the Federal Government is responsible for the education of Indians, which has, in practice, come to mean education in Indian reserves. In the territories the federal power in education is unchallenged. In these vast areas, however, the government has come to lean heavily on the missionary societies, particularly those of the Anglican and Roman Catholic churches, and they in turn lean on the Fed-

James McGill, Scottish-born Canadian businessman, founder of McGill University at Montreal, Canada

eral Government for financial support. The educational systems, as set up by the provinces, may be divided into two quite separate areas; that of Quebec and that of the rest of Canada. The widely varying systems established are treated in some detail in the articles on the various provinces. With the end of World War II the Canadian Government, like that of the United States and some other countries, inaugurated an elaborate plan to provide funds for the continued education of demobilized service personnel. This it did, not by developing federal schools but by granting allowances to veterans as well as to the institutions serving them.

COMMONWEALTH AND FOREIGN RELATIONS

In 1956 Canada was represented abroad by 30 ambassadors, 7 high commissioners, 7 ministers, 4 permanent delegations and missions, and several consuls and trade commissioners exercising semidiplomatic functions. These officials are

States are in good relations with each other. Canada's thinking, therefore, like Canada's trade and, in fact, Canada's whole history, is fundamentally triangular. Except for the relations with the United States and the United Kingdom, Canada's closest contacts, although almost wholly on the economic level, are with the West Indies, in which Canadian banks operate twenty-eight branches. Although there is as yet no thought of closer political ties with this region, the complementary character of their products is likely to lead to increasing commercial relations. Canada had also had close relations with Newfoundland, which, on Mar. 31, 1949, became

Fishermen sorting the day's catch on the Gaspé Peninsula. In the background, across the water, is Percé Rock and the village of Percé.

all under the Minister of External Affairs, who is a member of the cabinet and of Parliament. In most of the British Commonwealth countries Canada is represented by a high commissioner, and most of the Commonwealth countries are similarly represented in Ottawa. Canadian tariffs are levied on other Commonwealth members' imports, and conditions under which other Commonwealth citizens may be admitted are determined by law. Conditions under which they may be deported are similarly determined. Canada has voluntarily retained the British Parliament as the only body which may legally amend the Canadian constitution. This it does, of course, only on advice; there is some doubt, however, as to whose advice is necessary. Holders of the so-called "treaty" theory of federation claim that since federation was a pact of all the provinces, all of them must agree on any change. Others hold that a simple request from the Federal Parliament should suffice. In 1949 the Canadian Government announced its intention of seeking some way of amending the constitution in Canada. In 1950 the Federal Parliament was given authority to amend those parts of the Canadian constitution relating to purely federal functions. Only the inability of the federal and provincial governments to agree on a method for amending the federal-provincial aspects of the constitution stood in the way of complete Canadian independence of the United Kingdom's Parliament. Otherwise Canada is as free in its Commonwealth as it is in its foreign relations.

The chief cornerstone in Canada's external policy is the cultivation of good relations with the United Kingdom and the United States. It is clearly realized that such a condition is possible only if the United Kingdom and the United

Canada's tenth province. Canada was an active member of the League of Nations and has joined the United Nations. On the other hand, its economic growth has been considered the result of its persistent economic protectionism. Canada also became a charter member of the North Atlantic Treaty Organization and has increased its military commitments in Western Europe.

HISTORY

Aboriginal Peoples. The first Canadians were Asiatic Mongoloids. Evidence has recently been concentrating on the conclusion that these ancestors of Canada's present Indian and Eskimo population began coming to Canada from northeast Asia at about the end of the last glacial period. At least one early migration route across Canada can be traced fairly accurately by linking the points between Alaska and New Mexico at which artifacts of a characteristic pattern have been discovered, sometimes in conjunction with the bones of animals long since extinct in North America. This route lay across the Yukon Territory, much of which had remained unglaciated, and along the high plains to the east of the Rocky Mountains, between the alpine glaciers retreating to the west and the Keewatin Glacier retreating northeastward. This pioneer migration seems to have taken place in a series of separate movements over a protracted period, with the Eskimo migration possibly the latest.

The fundamental differences in language and the substantial differences in physical type between Indian and Eskimo and among the Indian tribes themselves may be attributed in large part to divergences before the migration to North America took place. Differences in material culture may be attributed chiefly to adjustments to local geographical conditions in Canada. So completely had these adjustments been made that when the French first settled in Canada, it was the white man who had the most to learn and the red man the most to teach. French Canada's dependence on the fur trade throughout the century and a half of French rule brought a lively realization to both races of their mutual dependence. This gave to the Canadian Indian a place in Canadian life strikingly different from the position of the Indians farther south.

Viking Voyages. The first Europeans known to have reached Canada were the Vikings. Leif Ericson's North American landfall in about A.D. 1000 has come to be regarded as authentic historical fact, even if the precise location of the landing cannot be determined. Subsequent Norse voyages to the Canadian coasts, covering a period of more than two centuries, may also be regarded as substantially proved. But these extended voyages left no certain influences on either Indian or Eskimo. Indeed, it is still a matter of doubt whether the *Skraeling* of the Icelandic sagas were Eskimo or Indian. The sagas themselves, however, may have helped to provide a foundation for the persistent European legends of land to the west.

First European Explorations. In 1497, John Cabot, a Genoese in the service of England, with eighteen men in a small ship, the *Matthew,* headed west in search of a passage to China. He reached the eastern coast of Canada, possibly Labrador or Cape Breton Island, thus laying the basis for England's claim to have anticipated the Spaniards in the discovery of the American mainland. The more practical result of the voyage, however, came from Cabot's report of the presence of codfish off the south coast of Newfoundland in such numbers that they could be taken in baskets. Fishing fleets from England, France, Portugal, and Spain were soon frequenting the Grand Banks and the lesser banks stretching from Newfoundland to Cape Cod. At first little or no use was made of the adjacent coasts by the fishermen on the banks because of the employment of the "green" fishing technique. Later in the sixteenth century, first the English fishing fleets and then the fleets of the other nations began to turn to "dry" fishing, which necessitated the construction of platforms ashore on which to dry the fish. The result was that before the end of the century, and before any permanent settlements had been effected, the entire northeast coastline of North America had become well known. This inevitably brought the fishermen in contact with the Indian inhabitants and resulted in the growth of a secondary enterprise, the fur trade.

English expansion in the sixteenth century concentrated on the search for a passage to Asia to the northwest of Newfoundland, and the prosecution of the fisheries to the southeast. France, which was late in entering the field, attempted to unify its efforts by limiting exploration, fishing, and the fur trade to the region about the Gulf of St. Lawrence. In 1535, Jacques Cartier reached Hochelaga (now Montreal) at the head of navigation on the St. Lawrence. He was in search of a passage to Asia, but was not above acquiring a cargo of furs from the Indians. By the end of the century the fur trade had become well established at Tadoussac, at the mouth of the Saguenay River.

FRENCH COLONIAL PERIOD IN CANADA

Acadian-Nova Scotian Colony. France made its first relatively permanent settlement in North America in 1605 with the establishment of Port Royal in western Nova Scotia, then called Acadia. A previous settlement on an island at the mouth of the St. Croix River had only survived the winter of 1604-1605. The Port Royal community endured, but its site was not well chosen: it was on the wrong side of Nova Scotia for easy access to the fisheries and on the wrong side of the Bay of Fundy to serve as a center for the fur trade. Moreover, its ice-free port left the settlers constantly exposed to attack from the sea. In addition, its

BETTMANN ARCHIVE

Jacques Cartier, French explorer of the sixteenth century who navigated the St. Lawrence River

FROM AN ENGRAVING BY J. GANDON

fertile hinterland, the long and narrow Annapolis Valley, was more of a liability than an asset as long as it remained unsettled; and after more than sixty years of attempted settlement the entire colony numbered less than four hundred persons. As early as 1613, Port Royal was destroyed by a force from the infant colony of Virginia. In 1621 the peninsula of Nova Scotia, together with the islands of the Gulf of St. Lawrence and the mainland of what is now New Brunswick, were granted by King James I to Sir William Alexander (later Earl of Stirling), and in 1628, Port Royal was occupied and Scottish colonization begun. But Charles I, anxious to conciliate France, renounced the grant, and the region was again occupied by France in 1633. Under Cromwell, Acadia in 1654 again became Nova Scotia and remained such until 1667. Again occupied by the English in 1690 and again awarded to France by the Treaty of Ryswick in 1697, it was finally taken by the British in 1710 and remained in British hands by the Treaty of Utrecht in 1713. This treaty, however, returned the Gulf islands, notably Cape Breton Island and Prince Edward Island (then known as Île Royale and Île St. Jean, respectively), to France, and left the status of the New Brunswick area undetermined.

At the time of the cession of Nova Scotia to Great Britain the permanent Acadian population of the peninsula probably numbered less than 2,000. Already some of these colonists had moved from the lower Annapolis Valley to the Minas Basin area and the Isthmus of Chignecto, both farther up the Bay of Fundy. With the establishment of the British government based on Port Royal, then renamed Annapolis Royal, this movement up the bay was naturally accelerated. The British government thus found itself isolated from its new subjects, and for thirty years it had no other subjects to govern. As long as peace continued, this arrangement

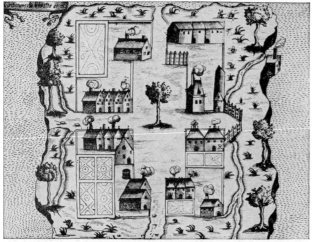

COURTESY OF THE NEW YORK PUBLIC LIBRARY

Île Ste. Croix, established in 1604, was the earliest French settlement in Acadia.

proved satisfactory, but when war broke out between France and Great Britain in 1744, difficulties began to arise. In 1720 the French had erected a fortress at Louisbourg, on Cape Breton, and had urged the Acadians to join their compatriots on the islands of the Gulf of St. Lawrence, but few complied. With equal intransigence, they refused to take the oath of allegiance to their new ruler. Long accustomed to changes in international status and to slight control by any government, they claimed the status of neutrals.

In 1745, Louisbourg fell before a joint attack of British naval and Massachusetts militia forces. In 1748, to the great annoyance of the New Englanders, it was returned to France, and in 1749 the British attempted to neutralize this French "Gibraltar" of the Gulf of St. Lawrence by the establishment of a naval base at Halifax. This also became the colony's capital and at once began to attract a miscellany of settlers—Rhinelanders, New Englanders, and Irish. The final struggle for the control of North America was at hand. Fighting began unofficially farther west in 1755 and quickly spread east. The Acadians still refused the oath of allegiance, and in that year Gov. Charles Lawrence caught and dispersed more than 6,000 of them among the other British colonies; a larger number escaped to the forest. After the end of the Seven Years' War in 1763, many of the Acadian exiles returned to Canada and settled along the south shore of the Bay of Fundy and in the northern districts of New Brunswick. Their influence in the life of the Maritime Provinces and the nation as a whole has become increasingly important since then.

When the Acadians were moved out, the New Englanders moved into their abandoned settlements. To these newcomers, political articulation was the very breath of life. Hardly had the first of them unpacked when they began to agitate for the establishment of a representative assembly, and they were so successful that by 1758 such an assembly was actually in session at Halifax. These second founders of

Nova Scotia brought with them not only a lively political sense but other distinctive features of New England life. Like the Acadians, they have left a permanent mark on Nova Scotia which no subsequent migration has been able to obliterate. The year 1758 was marked not only by the establishment of representative government in Nova Scotia, but also by the fall of Louisbourg, and with it the complete collapse of French power in the Acadian region. British control of the entire Maritime region was confirmed by the Peace of Paris, 1763. Throughout the first century and a half of Acadian history, divisive forces had been too much for both French and British colonial administrators. Particularly had the French failed in their attempts to establish close relationships within their Acadian holdings and between them and their larger colony on the St. Lawrence.

Founding of Quebec. In the summer of 1603, the French explorer Samuel de Champlain visited Tadoussac, on the St. Lawrence, with a fur-trading expedition. He spent the period from 1604 to 1607 in Acadia helping the Huguenot Sieur de Monts to establish his trading company at Port Royal, and then, realizing the superior advantages of the St. Lawrence over the Acadian region, he founded Quebec in 1608. Despite the brighter prospects, however, many of the ills that beset the Acadian venture also retarded the growth of Quebec; and the latter suffered from some ills

BUREAU OF INFORMATION, GOVERNMENT OF NOVA SCOTIA

The main gate of Port Royal Habitation in Lower Granville, Nova Scotia, is a replica of the original building erected by Samuel de Champlain in 1605 as his headquarters and capital of Acadia.

peculiar to itself. Defense from the sea appeared much easier at Quebec, but, actually, unless the colony could become self-contained, it remained exposed to attack by any power that could control the sea lanes to the Gulf of St. Lawrence. Land defense required the maintenance of cordial relations with neighboring Indian tribes. Unfortunately, these neighbors were in deadly conflict with each other, and Champlain, who only vaguely understood the situation, felt obliged to take sides and, in doing so, chose the weaker. Finally, the French government was unwilling, during the first half century of Quebec history, to assume responsibility for colonial administration, preferring to grant the necessary powers to a trading company that should meet administrative costs out of monopolistic trading profits. But promotion of settlement was expensive, while the fur trade was remunerative, and a succession of companies lost their monopolistic rights because of their unwillingness or inability to bring out colonists. Out of these circumstances arose most of the difficulties encountered by the colony on the St. Lawrence during its first half century.

Champlain's Policy and Explorations. From the first, Champlain realized that Canada, as the colony came to be known, would have to pay its own way if it were to survive. He realized equally that only the fur trade could keep the company, and therefore the colony, solvent. Success of the fur trade, in turn, would depend on maintaining good relations with the Indians who procured the furs in the interior and brought them to Quebec. Along the lower St. Lawrence Valley and to the north of the Ottawa River were nomadic bands of Indians of Algonquian speech; beyond the Adirondacks, to the south of the St. Lawrence, were the Iroquois-speaking Five Nations; and to the north of Lake Ontario were other tribes, also of Iroquois speech but bitterly hostile to the Five Nations. The Huron confederacy to the south of Georgian Bay formed the core of this resistance to the Five Nations. It is significant that Champlain, in his first expedition into the interior in 1609, was in search not of furs but of Mohawks. On the lake which has since borne his name he encountered the dreaded Iroquois and shot two chiefs. The Five Nations were thereafter the enemy, and, as events turned out, many historical developments were to stem from Champlain's decision to side with the primitive Algonquin bands and the Huron confederacy. Later in the same summer Henry Hudson, in the service of the Dutch East India Company, sailed up the Hudson River toward Albany, which was only 70 mi. from Lake Champlain. This event meant that the Five Nations also would soon find a source of muskets.

Champlain's more constructive work, however, lay in the explorations which he made and which he encouraged others to make. As early as 1610, one of his young men, Étienne Brulé, was exploring the Ottawa route to the west. He spent several years living with the Indians of the upper country. He came to know the Huron country well, and may even have penetrated beyond Sault Ste. Marie into Lake Superior. Champlain himself explored the upper Ottawa River in 1613, and Lakes Huron and Ontario and the region between them in 1615 and 1616. The desire to find a route through the continent to the Pacific Ocean still lured him, but in later years he concentrated on the expansion of the fur trade to the exclusion of the grander project.

Coming of the Missionaries. Despite the emphasis on the fur trade, however, the Indians were to Champlain not merely a source of revenue. Along with encouraging young men to live among the Indians of the upper country in their own communities in order to expand the fur trade, he was also urging missionary organizations in France to send out other young men to convert the Indians to Christianity. In 1615 he was successful in securing the services of the Franciscan Récollets. These gentle clerics immediately proceeded into the upper country to work principally among the Huron tribes, which were largely sedentary. A few attempts were made to follow wandering bands of

hunting Indians through the forest, but for the most part the Récollets concentrated on the Hurons. Not for long, however, did this order enjoy its missionary monopoly in Canada. In 1625 members of the more militant Jesuit order arrived, and by 1628 the last of the Récollets had left Canada. The Jesuits showed equal diligence and courage and were backed by a much more powerful organization. But their

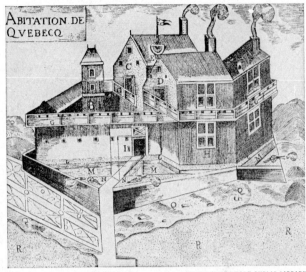

COURTESY NEW YORK PUBLIC LIBRARY

Samuel de Champlain's sketch for the original fort and residence at Quebec, below Cap-aux-Diamants, in what is now the Lower Town of Quebec

work with the Hurons was hardly begun before it was disrupted by the capture of Quebec by the English in 1629. When Quebec was again returned to the French in 1632, it was largely through aid of the Jesuit order that Champlain was able to bring about an attempt at re-establishment of the trading settlement. Champlain returned to Quebec in 1633 but died two years later.

Reorganization of Quebec Control. Meanwhile, the fur-trading interests in France had been reorganized. During the first twenty years of Quebec history various trading companies had successively enjoyed a trade monopoly in return for administering the affairs of the colony. In 1627 these weak and transient companies had been replaced by a strong company headed by the king's prime minister, Cardinal Richelieu. This Company of New France, or Company of One Hundred Associates, sent out its first convoy to Canada in 1628. It was captured in the Gulf of St. Lawrence by an English force under the Kirke brothers, operating under letters of marque and reprisal from the English government. An even larger convoy suffered a similar fate in 1629, and this time the colony capitulated. It was not until 1633 that the French government at Quebec was re-established. The company, despite its strength, never quite recovered from this blow, and because of the growing danger of Iroquois attack on the fur convoys on the Ottawa River, decided in 1645 to sell its trade monopoly to a local Canadian company known as the Compagnie des Habitants. The old company, however, retained its rights to the soil of Canada, as well as to the appointment of government officials.

The Huron Massacre. Hardly had the Company of New France abandoned its trading rights when the Five Nations invaded the Huron country in force. In 1648 and 1649 they destroyed the settlements of both the Hurons and their neighbors, the Tobaccos, slaughtering men, women, and children and scalping Jesuit priests. A small remnant of Hurons escaped eastward to the protection of their friends, the French, at Quebec; more crossed Lake Huron but, being pursued, were forced to cross Lake Michigan, where the Hurons and Tobaccos merged under the name of Wyandots. In their new Wisconsin home they eventually helped to promote both French missionary enterprise and the Canadian fur trade by spreading among neighboring tribes good will toward the French and hatred of the Five Nations and their Dutch supporters. But the immediate result of the Huron massacre for the French was disastrous enough. The Ottawa region, as well as the upper St. Lawrence, was practically closed to the fur trade, and reports of the massacre circulated in France and brought the already small stream of immigration to a virtual stop. The Jesuits attempted to snatch victory from disaster by sending missionaries to the Five Nation settlements. Meeting with great opposition, they attempted to persuade some of the Indians to move north of the St.

strengthened by the creation of a small appointed council to assist the governor.

Establishment of the Church. In 1659, Bishop François Xavier de Laval-Montmorency arrived at Quebec. As a secular priest with Jesuit training, he was ideally fitted to build up a parish system among the settlements without discouraging the Indian missions in the upper country. Earnest in the promotion of his faith, his contentious and theocratic tendencies brought him into constant conflict with the secular power, but he succeeded in putting an indelible mark of piety on the settlements along the St. Lawrence. Bishop Laval's precepts contrasted sharply with the outlook of the other characteristic group in French Canada—the *coureurs de bois.*

Expansion in Wilderness. While Champlain had encouraged his young men to live with the Indians, later governors not only urged them to remain in their parish-seigneuries, but prohibited them from leaving unless they secured

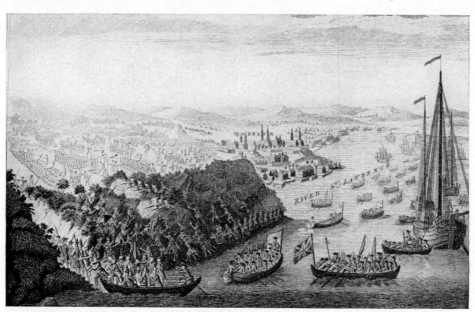

An old print showing the English forces attacking Quebec. The assault was made under General Wolfe on Sept. 13, 1759.

Lawrence and within the French sphere. In this they were eventually somewhat more successful, although their protégés were immediately expelled from the confederacy.

Montreal, which had been founded by Sieur de Maisonneuve in 1642 as a frontier missionary and fur-trading post, was particularly exposed. For a time following the massacre, furs were brought out of the upper country by the devious route of the upper Ottawa and St. Maurice rivers to Three Rivers, which had been founded in 1634; but soon a new system of convoyed brigades down the Ottawa to Montreal was devised. The French settlers, however, particularly those in the fertile Montreal area, remained in constant danger. Close settlement under local leaders was essential to survival, a circumstance which not only favored a revival in Canada of the French feudal system but made it virtually imperative. The New World, in fact, was reproducing with considerable exactness those conditions in early France out of which the feudal system had evolved—a central government too weak to protect its people, and the menace of barbaric and hostile forces. On the St. Lawrence, it was the Mohawks and Onondagas who took the place of the ancient Huns and Vandals. Seigneur and habitant (a French settler) each realized that the other was essential to his continued existence. In 1647 the central government at Quebec was

a trader's license. These were rigidly limited. Nevertheless, an increasing number of young French Canadians went west, and, to escape the penalties imposed, they frequently took their furs to Albany rather than to Montreal. Some of them returned in old age to Quebec; others married Indian wives and remained in the western forests. Their descendants, known as *métis,* became a distinct element in French expansion in North America. Their departure from the French settlements along the St. Lawrence was undoubtedly hastened by the addition of spiritual to feudal regimentation as Laval energetically expanded the parish system throughout the French settlements. Here, too, Laval's success and failure were closely related. Most of the *coureurs de bois* were without formal education and left no records of their "voyages" into the interior. This was not true of the brothers-in-law Pierre Radisson and Sieur de Groseilliers, who, throughout the 1650's and into the 1660's, were pushing into the unknown west. Much of their time was spent in the region to the south of Lake Superior, but they also visited the Cree Indians to the north of that lake, acquiring considerable knowledge about the country draining into Hudson Bay. On their return to Montreal, expecting to be honored for their exploration, they were fined for having gone "up country" without permission. In disgust, they offered

Waterfront at Lunenburg, Nova Scotia, first settled in 1753. In its shipyards was built the Bluenose, Nova Scotia's champion racing schooner.

their services to the English, and as a direct consequence the Hudson's Bay Company was chartered by Charles II in 1670. Their departure from Canada coincided with Louis XIV's determination to revoke the charter of the Company of New France and to make Canada a direct dependency of the crown (1663). Louis also enlarged the governor's council and created a new office, that of intendant, responsible for finance, police, and the administration of justice.

Although the French venture on the St. Lawrence had been discouraging so far, the main features of French-Canadian life had already taken shape. Little that was new was added in the next century of French rule. The colony grew in numbers and in stability, but it kept its earlier form. The real change came, not in either spiritual or secular institutions, but in a fundamental shift in the attitude of the people toward themselves and toward the world outside.

CANADA AS A FRENCH CROWN COLONY

Policy of Louis XIV. In 1663, Louis XIV, with the able assistance of his minister, Jean Colbert, attacked the problem of Canada with vigor. A census was taken, and it showed that the entire Canadian population, after more than fifty years of attempted colonization, was just over three thousand. Canada was at once made a royal colony. The most pressing needs were obviously population and security against attack. Realizing that the great preponderance of men over women in Canada had been one of the reasons for so many of the younger men escaping from the settlements and becoming *coureurs de bois,* Louis determined that women as well as men should be induced to emigrate to the colony. This policy was energetically pursued for the next twenty years. The migration during this period was probably under 8,000. Compared with the migration that had been going on to the English colonies to the south, this was insignificant, and, compared also with the population of France, which was several times larger than that of England, it was trifling. Compared with the handful of settlers who had come to Canada in the previous period, however, it was phenomenal. Had the stream of French immigration into Canada continued, the outcome might have been very different. But in the 1680's Louis was forced to decide between having his young men go to the New World to help to make Canada a rival of England's colonies, and keeping them in France for use in securing what he regarded as France's natural eastern boundary. He decided in favor of his European policy.

In 1665, to secure Canada against attack, Louis sent out one of his regiments of the line, the Carignan-Salières. In 1666, Marquis Alexandre de Tracy, the new commander of the

French Canadian hunter on snowshoes

FROM AN OLD WOODCUT

413

forces in North America, led an expedition into the Iroquois country beyond the Adirondacks. Although this force, made up of French regulars, Canadian militia, and Indians, failed to come to grips with the enemy, it burned vast stores of food and several settlements. In 1667, a peace agreement was reached. For the next eighteen years Canada was undisturbed, a condition which not only promoted the expansion of settlement but encouraged exploration. Both the Ottawa and the upper St. Lawrence rivers were reopened.

Westward Movement. At this stage, emphasis in the westward movement was divided between northwest and southwest. Economic policy lured the fur traders toward the northwest, while political policy was soon centered on a grand project of linking the Gulf of St. Lawrence with the Gulf of Mexico by a series of forts. This latter plan lies largely outside the field of Canadian history, although the voyage of Louis Jolliet and Father Marquette down the Wisconsin and Mississippi rivers to the mouth of the

Monument of Samuel de Champlain, seventeenth-century French explorer, fur trader, and first governor of Quebec, which was erected in his honor at Orillia, Ontario

Arkansas River in 1673, and La Salle's more famous voyage down the Illinois River and the Mississippi to the latter's mouth in 1682 did have considerable effect on the morale of the Canadian people. Less spectacular progress was made in the opening up of new fur country to the northwest. In the drive to the southwest, the governor, the Comte de Frontenac, erected a fort in 1673 at the lower end of Lake Ontario, where Kingston now stands. Another fort was erected at Niagara in 1679, and later, in 1701, one at Detroit. To the northwest, the most strategic point was Sault Ste. Marie, between Lakes Huron and Superior. Here, in 1671, the French staged an impressive ceremony attended by many Indian tribes, and in one sweeping gesture, the entire region from the Sault to the Pacific was taken over in the name of France. This assertion of sovereignty in the northwest was followed by the establishment of trading posts.

In the late 1670's and early 1680's Sieur Du Lhut (Duluth) established posts on Lake Nipigon, north of Lake Superior; at Kaministiquia, which later became Fort William; and at the junction of the Kenogami and Albany rivers only 150 mi. from James Bay. He also explored the rugged country to the northwest of Lake Superior, proceeding by way of the Lake of the Woods almost to the edge of the prairies.

The French by this time had established themselves well within the area claimed by the Hudson's Bay Company, and the stage was set for the final struggle for control in that region. During the 1680's Canada sent several expeditions by sea to Hudson Bay, and sporadic fighting took place while England and France were still at peace. In these encounters, Pierre Radisson, French Hudson Bay explorer, fought at times with the English and again with the French. Eventually, after posts on the bay had been taken and retaken during King William's War, 1689-1697, and Queen Anne's War, 1702-1713, the Hudson Bay region was awarded by the Treaty of Utrecht in 1713 to the British.

In 1731, Gilles Hocquart came to Canada as intendant. As such, he was responsible for the solvency of the colony, and he realized the importance of expanding the fur trade. That same year Pierre Gaultier de La Vérendrye, his three sons, and a nephew, began a long fur-trading career in the northwest. They eventually reached the prairies and established posts on the Assiniboine and Saskatchewan rivers. In 1748, however, the far-sighted Hocquart was replaced at Quebec by the last and worst of Canada's intendants, François Bigot. The Vérendryes were recalled from this promising penetration in the northwest and repudiated. After one weak attempt to follow up the work of the Vérendryes, French expansion to the northwest was abandoned and the fur trade in that region collapsed.

Growth and Alienation of Colony. Meanwhile, in the French settlements along the St. Lawrence, life had been going on uneventfully. Neighboring colonies on the Hudson River had changed masters in 1664, but Charles II was on friendly terms with Louis XIV. The Iroquois had ceased to be a menace, and the St. Lawrence colony was being greatly enlarged by new settlers from the mother country. However, with the substitution of William and Mary for James II on the English throne in 1689, matters appeared less propitious. In anticipation of attack by both the Iroquois and the English, Governor Frontenac, who had been recalled in 1682, was again dispatched to Canada. The Iroquois were again pacified and, in 1690, Sir William Phips was obliged to lift a naval siege of Quebec. During the remainder of King William's War, and throughout Queen Anne's War and King George's War, the French Canadians, in contrast to their Acadian compatriots, enjoyed comparative immunity.

Beneath the quiet surface, however, a fundamental change was taking place. Without further aid of immigration, the population of Canada steadily increased. By 1763 the French-Canadian population was 65,000. Ties with the mother country became less and less important, and for most Canadians life came to be circumscribed by the parish-seigneury. Even Quebec was far away, and its society, seeking to imitate the grandeur of Versailles, was regarded without affection. The French government had ceased to be vitally interested in the welfare of the Canadians, and this was reflected in the lower caliber of the colonial officials, who came to be looked upon as outsiders. Throughout, the colony was uniform in having one language (no longer identical with the language of France), one religion, and one social system. There were no pockets of nonconformity or even differences, such as marked the English colonies to

DEATH OF GENERAL JAMES WOLFE

the south. Slowly but inevitably a separate people, no longer Frenchmen away from home but solely *Canadien,* had been developing along the St. Lawrence. Even before the fleur-de-lis was lowered from its staff on Cape Diamond in 1759 a new nation had arisen in the New World. Like the Acadians by the sea, they asked only to be left alone, but unlike the Acadians, they were in a position to bargain about the price.

French and Indian War. In the conflict known as the French and Indian War, 1755-1763, the Canadians for the most part were mere onlookers. Quebec fell in 1759 and Montreal capitulated in 1760. The Peace of Paris was signed in 1763, but British military government continued until the following year. In spite of a certain bewilderment at their automatic change of allegiance from French to British, Canadian reaction to the new regime was mainly one of relief that the fighting was over. The titanic struggle for world empire had raged from the Ganges to the Mississippi, and yet Canada, lying directly in the path of conflict, had remained in relative calm. Canadian militia had fought alongside French regulars, but they had been fighting for Canada instead of an empire.

EARLY BRITISH RULE IN CANADA

Policies of New Government. As far as Canada was concerned, the war ended in 1760 with the capitulation of Governor Philippe de Rigaud, Marquis de Vaudreuil. With the fighting over, it was easy for James Murray, the first British governor, to be less exacting than the last French governor could have been. By the terms of the capitulation, the Canadians had been granted freedom of religious worship, the right to return to France if they chose, and security in their property. They were content to have things remain as they had been, and the new governor proved equally set against change. The governor was a soldier and the son of a Scottish nobleman, while the people had a long heritage of autocratic rule in Canada and in France. Consequently, democratic institutions made no appeal to either. Particularly distasteful to both was the New England variety of democracy.

The home government, however, had ideas of its own as to the role of the new colony in an enlarged empire. Already events were pointing toward the American Revolution, and the English colonies were still the heart of the overseas empire. Following the Peace of Paris of February 1763 came the British Royal Proclamation of October of that year. It decreed that the entire region beyond the Appalachian ranges was to remain Indian territory. Also, to permit expansion southward into newly acquired Florida and northward into Canada, it required that the respective governors should, as soon as circumstances allowed, establish representative forms of government on the model of the older royal English colonies. Meanwhile, new settlers coming to Canada were to be assured that they might enjoy the benefits of the laws of England. The chief difficulty with this "blueprint" for the enlarged American empire was that the English colonists to the south continued to push westward and could not be induced to move north or south. The few who did come to Quebec and Montreal were not settlers but traders, and when they found that the colony was not likely to be assimilated to the southern type, many of them returned home. In Canada they were known as *Bastonaise,* and were heartily disliked by both British officials and Canadians.

Reactions of French Colonists. Few Canadians took advantage of the British offer of transportation to France. Probably less than five hundred left the New World, including a few seigneurs, mostly those who had rank as *noblesse;* a few of the leading merchants, chiefly those representing French mercantile establishments; and a few professors from Quebec. The remaining Canadian society was, of course, far from being classless. A fairly sharp line, both social and geographic, separated the settlers on the St. Lawrence from the *coureurs de bois* of the "up country," and within the parish-seigneury system there were the seigneurs, the priests, and the habitants. The *coureurs de bois* were at first the least enamored with the new order of things; they feared for their means of livelihood, the fur trade, and some of them were not long in finding an instrument of attack. An indeterminate proportion of them found in the Pontiac conspiracy of 1763 a means of attempting to cut off the western country from the east in anticipation, apparently, of the return of French power to North America. But with the defeat of that Indian uprising, they soon came to accept the situation and shortly were enthusiastically at work in the interests of the Montreal fur trade. In fact, they found the trade at first more to their liking than it had been, for the British refused to give a monopoly to any company. Free trade in furs appealed to the *coureurs de bois.* They and the Montreal traders alike faced the threat of competition from the fur trade based on Albany to the south and on Hudson Bay to the northwest. This cordiality increased as control of the Montreal fur trade gradually shifted from New Englanders to Scotsmen, owing in part, perhaps, to the age-long good will between France and Scotland. The practice of Scotch "wintering partners" of sharing with the French the rigors of frontier life was a contributing factor.

The Quebec Act. For nearly two centuries there have been conflicting opinions about the purpose of the Quebec Act passed by the British Parliament in 1774. One point of view is that its aim was to promote the welfare of Canada and so insure the friendship of the king's new subjects; another is that it was intended to thwart the rebellious ambitions of the king's old subjects farther south. Still another view is that Parliament had both aims in mind. What the statute did, in effect, was to give legislative authority to a state of things that had already largely come about. The purpose apparently was to insure, as far as this could be done by legislation, that the situation would remain unchanged.

The civil law in Canada during the French regime had been based on the *coutume de Paris.* Neither Governor Murray nor Guy Carleton, who had succeeded him in 1766, had wanted any change in this law, and the Canadians were more than content to abide by their ancient usages. On the other hand, English criminal law, which affected fewer people than the civil code, was easily substituted for the more rigorous French criminal code. The Quebec Act provided for the retention of Canadian civil law and the establishment of English criminal law. The French Canadians had been enjoying complete freedom of worship; the new act confirmed this right. The only settlements in the region between the Ohio and the Mississippi rivers had been French, and the only trade had been the fur trade based on Montreal; the act simply gave legal political recognition to this existing situation by annexing this region to what became known officially as the Province of Quebec. The government, both before and after the conquest, had been completely in the hands of a governor and his appointed council; this was continued by the Quebec Act, with the collateral opinion that the colony was not yet suited to the establishment of representative institutions. The council was to have the right not only to administer the laws but to pass new ordinances which should have the force of law throughout the colony. This was aimed at allowing a modernization of commercial law. The council was not given the power to tax, except that it could permit parishes to raise funds for local improvements. Lands might, at the discretion of the Quebec government, be acquired on English tenure. The way was thus left open to some change, but at the discretion of the governor and council. With the exception of the holdings of the religious orders, Church property was to be left in the possession of the Church. Most of the property of the orders, however, was that of the Jesuits, and since this order had been suppressed by the pope in 1773, this decision was far from drastic in its effect upon the Church. The Church also was given the right to levy on its members all of its accustomed dues. This part of the act caused a friendly disposition on the part of the Church authorities toward the British government, but, conversely, it somewhat cooled the ardor of the habitants for the new order. The enthusiasm of both the seigneurs and priests for the British cause during the American Revolution, and the contrasting lukewarm attitude of the habitants, stemmed in part from the terms of the Quebec Act.

Effects of American Revolution. The American Revolution began in April 1775. On May 1 the Quebec Act went into effect, and on May 10 an American force was on Lake Champlain heading toward Canada. Lack of experience and a divided command hampered this incursion throughout the summer. The invasion of Canada was preceded in 1774 by an appeal to the Canadians to join the Continental Congress. The virtues of English liberty were extolled and the political philosophy of John Locke commended. The result might have been more effective had the American propagandists not also appealed to the British people for support, referring to the Roman Catholic religion as having "dispensed impiety, bigotry, persecution, murder, and rebellion throughout every part of the world." Copies of the document addressed to the British reached Canada via England well in advance of the military invasion of Canada by the Americans. From the start, therefore, the Canadian clergy denounced the Revolution as "impious and treasonable." The seigneurs also rallied to the support of Sir Guy Carleton, the British governor of Quebec, and offered their services as militia officers. All that was lacking was men to serve under these officers, but pitifully few habitants joined the British forces, and, as a further disappointment to Carleton, some joined the American forces. In the main, however, the people were content to look on and to sell their produce impartially to either side. The merchant class in Montreal and Quebec was also divided in its sympathies, making the conquest of Montreal late in 1775 comparatively easy. By the end of the year, Quebec itself was under siege, but greater loyalty and determination, along with superior defense advantages, saved the city. The year 1776 saw the last American soldier off Canadian soil. Danger again threatened momentarily in 1778, when the Frenchman, the

Marquis de Lafayette, proposed that he be allowed to invade Canada. When this suggestion was vetoed by General George Washington of the American forces, the last menace to Canada was removed and the center of conflict remained in the colonies to the south.

In the transitional period of North American history between the British conquest and the American Revolution, the region between Maine and the Gulf of St. Lawrence had undergone relatively little change. After the fall of Louisbourg in 1758, New Englanders had arrived in increasing numbers and given a New England cast to the entire area, particularly along the northwest coasts of the peninsula from the head of the Bay of Fundy to Annapolis Royal. On the other hand, a close relationship existed in Nova Scotia between army and navy officials, Anglican clerics, and government officials; and between this group and the New Englanders there was inevitable friction. This dissension was fully revealed by the American Revolution.

Following the Seven Years' War, Great Britain had decided at first to consolidate its maritime area holdings to the northeast of Maine. At the close of the war, Prince Edward Island, Cape Breton Island, and the mainland (now New Brunswick) between the isthmus of Chignecto and the St. Croix River had been annexed to Nova Scotia. This unification had been more a consolidation of territory than a consolidation of peoples, for in 1763 there had been almost no settled areas beyond the peninsula. But no sooner had the union been effected than British policy began to swing in the opposite direction.

In 1764, Prince Edward Island had been surveyed; and in 1767 the entire island, with the exception of some small areas of lands reserved for use of the government, was granted to military and naval officers and others in favor with the home government. At one stroke, therefore, this "garden of the gulf" had become a land of absentee landlords, a second Ireland; and it was to remain such for more than a century. In 1769, at the request of these absentees, Prince Edward Island had been formed into a separate colony, and in the following year its first governor, Walter Patterson, arrived and was sworn in. The new colony was naturally slow in acquiring settlers, since contact with the mainland was always difficult, and sometimes impossible, during the winter months. Political and geographical separation combined to create an intense insularity among its people.

During the American Revolution the Nova Scotian outposts were exposed to Yankee privateers, but Halifax remained impregnable. The American commander, Washington, firmly refused to sanction an attempt to acquire the area, despite the known presence in Nova Scotia of a considerable number of sympathizers with the Americans. Fort Cumberland, on the isthmus, was for a time in local revolutionary hands. In fact, some issues of the government newspaper issued in Halifax had appeared in late 1765 and early 1766 bearing a skull and crossbones where the stamp of George III should have been. It was Halifax and the fleet that probably kept Nova Scotia from becoming a fourteenth colony. Of course all the inhabitants outside of Halifax were not New Englanders. In the early 1770's there had been some small settlements of Scotch settlers in the Pictou region, and some Irish and Yorkshire settlements on the isthmus, but the predominant element in the colony was still undoubtedly that from New England.

Tory Migrations. The American Revolution had another effect on this maritime region. It was directly responsible for bringing to this area a great wave of new settlers, anti-Revolutionaries from the thirteen colonies. A few came following the British retreat from New England, but many more came with the eventual evacuation of New York in 1783. The total migration could hardly have been less than 35,000; the majority came to the peninsula of Nova Scotia, a few went to Prince Edward and Cape Breton islands, and some 10,000 settled in the virgin wilderness of the lower St. John Valley to the north of the Bay of Fundy, while almost 7,000 frontiersmen passed overland into upper Quebec (later Ontario). A consequence of this migration was the separation from Nova Scotia of both Cape Breton Island and the region beyond the isthmus, later known as New Brunswick, in 1784. This increased the number of the Maritime Provinces to four. The divisiveness inherent in the life of this region from the very beginning of French rule had been supplemented by the determination of the British government to divide and rule. Consolidation of this maritime area has remained an unrealized dream.

Not all of the Loyalists who went to the maritime area remained. Some, especially those who brought their slaves, later joined the other stream of refugees who went from south of the Mason-Dixon line in the United States to the British West Indies; others, principally those who were not American-born, eventually returned to England; a few later joined those who had already gone to the upper St. Lawrence region; and a large number returned to the United States. But the majority remained in the Maritime Provinces. Although they greatly outnumbered the earlier pre-Revolutionary Americans from New England, the latter were still strong and highly articulate. It is significant that in the later struggle for colonial autonomy in the Maritime Provinces some of the outstanding advocates of the new order were descendants of the Tories of 1783. Undoubtedly, however, the union of American Tory Anglicans with English officialdom in the army, navy, government, and church, did temper whatever radicalism survived among the pre-Revolutionary Americans in Nova Scotia. There was to be nothing in the history of the Maritime Provinces remotely resembling the Canadian Rebellion of 1837.

One peculiar aspect of this Tory migration was that it stopped as suddenly as it had started. In fact, the movement had hardly reached its peak before the stream began to flow in the opposite direction; and, in varying degrees, it has continued to flow out of the maritime area and into the United States ever since. The Tory migration was a movement, not from the bottom, but from the top of American society. Not only was it a predominantly urban group which moved north; it was a group made up of an altogether disproportionate number of professional and business men. Adjustment to the wilderness was for them particularly difficult, which helps to explain not only why so many of them later left the area, but also why so many of those who remained became leaders in church and state.

The Loyalist migration to the Maritime Provinces might be regarded as the flight of American "Cavaliers" driven out of their homeland by triumphant American "Roundheads." The record of Tory gentlemen and their ladies hewing out new homes for themselves in the New Brunswick forest became one of the foundation stones of Canadian tradition. They and their direct descendants were permitted by the British government to style themselves "United Empire Loyalists." This was as near as English Canada ever came to establishing an hereditary aristocracy.

The Loyalists who proceeded overland to what became Ontario were of a different variety—in fact, several different varieties. They included most of the Mohawk tribe and others of the Five Nations, many Germans, and some Huguenots, as well as the predominant Scotch, Irish, and English. Many had fought on the British side. Few of them were city-bred. In fact, they came mostly from the western frontiers of New York and Pennsylvania and were, therefore, experienced in pioneering. In their new home, however, they found themselves within the province of Quebec—which had never known any of the institutions of democracy. Consequently, their first move was to agitate for separation from Quebec. This was granted to them in 1791. The new province became known as Upper Canada, while the remaining French section received the name of Lower Canada. Both sections were accorded representative institutions.

There was another major difference between the Loyalist migration to New Brunswick and that to Upper Canada. Whereas the former had been sudden both in its beginning and end, that to Upper Canada became a continuing process. This was because Upper Canada, unlike New Brunswick, lay directly in the path of American westward migration. The total Loyalist migration to Upper Canada was under 7,000, but in the next twenty years, many times that number of Americans settled in the province. On the outbreak of the War of 1812, Upper Canada was inhabited almost wholly by Americans, but the post-Loyalists outnumbered the Loyalists by at least five to one. This was one of the main reasons why the American government regarded the conquest of this fertile province as likely to be merely a matter of marching.

Status of French Canadians. The American Revolution and the subsequent Loyalist and post-Loyalist migrations to the east and west of them had lasting effect on the French Canadian people. The failure of the habitants to respond to the call of the seigneurs for military service had lowered the prestige of that aristocratic group whose standing had already been materially affected by the British conquest of Canada. The Roman Church had survived, but the French state had fallen, and the seigneurs were the local representatives of the latter. The position of the priests, on the other hand, had been strengthened, and the Church became the great defender of French-Canadian survival. With the English-speaking Protestants pouring into the regions both to the east and west of the French settlements

on the St. Lawrence, the need for French-Canadian vigilance became more urgent than ever before.

Revision of Colonial System. The communities remaining to Great Britain after the American Revolution were still mainly dependent on British colonial policy, and were to remain so for at least another half century. This policy was largely confused, but the dominant note was one of subdued hope that the lesson to be learned from the Revolution might make it possible for the British to try again in this new British North America. What this lesson was, exactly, became the subject of more confusion of thought. In the main, however, the tendency was to believe that in the thirteen colonies the executive under the crown had been too weak and divided, and that the popular legislatures had been allowed to become too strong.

In 1786, Guy Carleton, who had formerly been governor at Quebec and subsequently commander-in-chief of the British forces in North America, was created Baron Dorchester and commissioned as captain-general and governor-in-chief not only of Quebec but also of each of the Maritime Provinces. Each province was also to have a lieutenant-governor, but Dorchester was to have the general oversight. Shortly, the British government asked the British Parliament to pass a constitutional act which would provide for the separation of Quebec into Upper and Lower Canada. Both the act and the order of separation became law in 1791. The act provided for the division of Canada into two provinces, Upper and Lower Canada. These provinces were to have separate governments, each headed by a governor and lieutenant governor appointed by the crown; separate legislative councils appointed for life by the governor; and elective assemblies of very limited powers. This act marked the first statutory grant of representative government to a British colony. It also made provision for the endowment of the Church of England in both provinces by the allocation to its use of one seventh of all the crown lands, and legalized the creation in both provinces of an hereditary aristocracy. The act also gave to the British government the right of veto, and to the local governor the right either to reserve or veto any provincial legislation. Although the provinces were to have limited rights to levy customs duties, the British government retained the same right. This was, it

*"INDIANS PORTAGING FURS"
BY CORNELIUS KRIEGHOFF,
1838.*

is true, limited by the terms of the Declaratory Act of 1778, which had provided that the British Parliament would not levy duties merely for the purpose of raising revenue but continued the right to levy duties for the purpose of regulating trade. Nor did this affect the customs duties that had already been imposed before 1778. Some eighteenth-century imperial revenue acts were, in fact, retained in Canada until the mid-nineteenth century.

Boundary Dispute with United States. The confusion in British minds following the Revolutionary War was seen also in the negotiation of the treaty of peace. It was necessary to draw a boundary for the new republic. The extension of the boundary of Quebec in 1774 had been one of the grievances set forth in the Declaration of Independence, and the American negotiators insisted that this boundary be altered. The result was a compromise line between the western boundary of Quebec as set forth in the royal proclamation of 1763 and that given in the Quebec Act. The disputed area lay to the west of the point where 45° N. lat. intersects the St. Lawrence River. The line of 1763 had excluded from Quebec all of what is now Ontario except a narrow strip to the south of the Ottawa River; the line of 1774 included in Quebec not only all of Ontario but all of the country to the southwest of the Great Lakes between the Ohio and the Mississippi rivers. The line of 1783 was run up the St. Lawrence and through Lakes Ontario, Erie, Huron, and Superior. At the moment the chief significance of this decision was that the Montreal fur trade had its territory cut in two.

The full force of this blow to Canada's most remunerative industry was not immediately felt. Because of what the British regarded as the American nonfulfillment of treaty agreements, British garrisons continued to occupy strategic posts in the American northwest, and fur trade based on Montreal continued to be pursued on a reduced scale within American territory. But in the following decade this trade within American territory was virtually stopped by the negotiation of Jay's Treaty in 1794, providing for the withdrawal of all British forces from American territory by 1796. There were, it is true, certain special provisions favorable to the prosecution of the Canadian fur trade within American territory. Indians were to be permitted to pass freely across the international boundary in either direction, and goods used in the fur trade were to be given a privileged position in respect to custom duties. Nevertheless, the position of the Canadian fur trade in American territory was bound to be affected by other regulations. Wayne's defeat of the Indians at Fallen Timbers in 1794 adversely affected the trade, and the persistent belief on the American side of the line that Canadians were responsible for the arming of the Indians kept local officials from administering the terms of the treaty in a liberal spirit. Canadians and Indians did continue for a time to co-operate in the prosecution of the fur trade in the remoter Wisconsin area, but it was evident that before long the fur trade based on Montreal would have to confine its activities to the British side of the boundary.

Competition in Fur Trade. The Montreal trade, in fact, had suffered from a long series of difficulties: the Seven Years' War, the Pontiac uprising, and the Revolution. These hazards forced the independent Montreal traders into a monopolistic union initiated in 1783-1784 with the organization of the North West Company. The fur country now lay to the north and west of Lake Superior. Thus the new Montreal company merely escaped from American restrictions by moving into the heart of the Hudson's Bay Company's preserves. Deadly rivalry between these two British fur companies soon developed, and, while urging both companies on to tremendous expansion efforts, it brought both to the verge of bankruptcy.

This struggle for supremacy between two companies, one based on Montreal and the other on London, had far-reaching effects upon the subsequent history of the entire northwest quadrant of North America. For more than a century, the Hudson's Bay Company had pursued its conservative way, sending ships from England and trading with the Indians at various posts on Hudson Bay. The new westward thrust of the Montreal traders forced the ancient company to adopt a more aggressive policy. In 1774, even before the union of the Montreal traders into a single organization, the Hudson's Bay Company established its first interior post, Cumberland House, on the lower Saskatchewan River. But the initiative remained with the "Montrealers," whose energetic and sometimes ruthless Scottish business heads and tireless voyageurs extended the North West Company's lines farther and farther into the remote north and west. In 1789, Alexander Mackenzie led an expedition to the mouth of the Mackenzie River on the Arctic Ocean, and in 1793 he reached the Pacific by a river route which included going up the Peace, down part of the Fraser, and down the Bella Coola. In 1808, Simon Fraser went down the Fraser River to its mouth, near the present city of Vancouver, B. C.; David Thompson traversed the entire length of the Columbia River to the Pacific in 1811. Meanwhile, the company was establishing posts on both sides of the Rocky Mountains. Only to the east of the mountains did the Montreal company come into direct competition with the Hudson's Bay Company, but it paid heavily in transportation costs for its virtual monopoly of transmountain trade.

The maritime fur trade on the Pacific was still being claimed as a monopoly by the British East India Company. In the far west of British North America, therefore, the rival claims of Calcutta, London, and Montreal met, not to mention the additional claims of the United States, Spain, and Russia. Consequently, much more was involved than the mere matter of taking sea otter or seal. The acquisition of Louisiana by the United States in 1803 left a thousand miles of undetermined boundary between British and American claims from the Lake of the Woods to the Rockies, and beyond the mountains was another five hundred miles of undetermined boundary between British and Spanish claims. The Spanish claims were soon removed by the Nootka Sound Convention in 1790, but while Spanish ships were moving out, New England vessels were moving in. It was both the strength and the weakness of the North West Company that its contact with the Pacific coast was not by sea but by land. Its position was more secure, but its trade was economically more hazardous by reason of the enormous costs of transportation of trade goods and furs by canoe from the Pacific Ocean area to Montreal.

War of 1812. Upper Canada was the chief battleground of the War of 1812. A few of the recent American settlers in that province joined the invading armies and a somewhat larger number joined the Canadian militia, but the great majority remained onlookers. This did not, however, detract from the feeling of pride which the inhabitants derived from the success of British arms in ridding the province of all the invading forces. Except for considerable and inevitable economic dislocation, the war, on the whole, was of some economic advantage to the Upper Canadians. The presence of some 25,000 British regulars considerably improved the province's monetary situation. The province had already begun to develop its first cash crop—timber—and this had come into demand in Great Britain as the result of the long Napoleonic struggle. Squared timber had become for the Upper Canadian economy what beaver had long been in the economy of Lower Canada, and fish in the economy of the Maritime Provinces.

A by-product of the War of 1812 in both Upper and Lower Canada was a temporary mitigation of the rising political asperities in both provinces. The constitutions, almost identical, which had been given to these provinces in 1791 by the Constitutional Act had provided for governors appointed by the home government, and for executive and legislative councils also appointed by the home government on the governor's nomination. Along with these appointees were the members of the legislative assemblies, who were to be elected by the people. This system was an invitation

groups: the urbanites in Quebec and Montreal, the rural inhabitants of the Eastern Townships, and a very small enclave of settlers far to the east on the Gaspé peninsula. The settlement in the Eastern Townships was in reality a post-Revolutionary northern projection of Vermont. Not until the 1830's was this region given any representation in the assembly, and even then the Vermonters did not feel drawn to the Tory politicians of Montreal and Quebec. The Gaspé settlement, begun as a Loyalist refuge, was too remote to affect matters at the capital one way or the other. The struggle, therefore, was narrowed down to one between the business and governmental groups in Lower Canada's two chief cities and the great majority of the French Canadians, who were still predominantly rural and entirely French-speaking and Catholic.

The spearhead of the French opposition to the government clique was the agitation of local lawyers and journalists.

The Château de Ramezay in Montreal, home of early governors of Canada, was built in 1705 by the French governor for whom it is named. Now a museum, in 1775 it served as headquarters for an American Revolutionary army.

to deadlock, and the same situation existed under the constitutions of the Maritime Provinces. Only Cape Breton Island had been refused a representative assembly. However, when that island was reannexed to the province of Nova Scotia in 1820, all the British provinces had substantially the same forms of government; and in the struggles that ensued, and which became increasingly bitter, many parallel situations emerged. These struggles dominated the entire period between 1814 and 1846.

CONSTITUTIONAL CONFLICT IN THE PROVINCES

Lower Canada. It was in Lower Canada that the struggle over constitutional rights developed an element of hatred not paralleled elsewhere, since it became increasingly a struggle, not of parties or of classes, but of nationality and religion. Some of the province's governors were more sympathetic to the predominant French-Canadian majority than others, but on the whole the governors were, or were regarded as being, the leaders of the English group. Actually, the power of the executive at Quebec was usually wielded not by the governor, but by a small group of English-speaking officials who came to be known as the "chateau clique." Against them, even the most sympathetic governor was usually powerless to improve relations between the two dominant nationalities in his province. The English-speaking inhabitants were divided into three quite separate

The French clergy feared the extremists on both sides: English Toryism was too closely associated with Anglicanism, and French-Canadian radicalism eventually showed some distinct signs of having imbibed some of the doctrines of the anticlerical radicalism of France. That actual civil war was averted was attributed largely to this intermediate position of the French-Canadian Catholic Church. On the whole, the Catholic Church in Lower Canada had, as was natural, tended to favor the French-Canadian political agitators in the struggle with the English-speaking oligarchy, being more convinced that Canadian patriots could be insulated from Parisian radicalism than that a wedge could be driven between the Toryism and the Anglicanism of the English-speaking group. Anticlerical radicalism of the French Revolutionary type had, in fact, been successfully kept out of Canada by the joint efforts of both the church and the government of Lower Canada. During the French Revolution many refugee French clerics had found a home in Canada and had intensified the hatred among the Canadian clergy for the new regime in France. The revolutionaries of France, it is true, had attempted, through such agents in the United States as Genêt and Adet, to secure the adhesion of the French Canadians to the French Revolutionary cause, but their efforts had only heightened the determination of the French-Canadian clergy to insulate their people. There was considerable spiritual affinity between Catholic and Tory but none between the Catholic and French radicalism.

French-Canadian opposition to the rule of an English oligarchy was a curiously paradoxical movement, fundamentally different from the seemingly similar movements in the other provinces. Insofar as the opposition to British rule at Quebec in the first half of the nineteenth century received any wide support—and at first support was almost universal—it was because it represented itself as a radical attempt to acquire power so that life in Lower Canada might be kept essentially as it had always been. It was radically conservative. Its leaders argued that, to ensure economic and cultural stabilization in the face of efforts of the English oligarchy to intensify the province's life by promoting immigration and urbanized big business, the legislative assembly should have the upper hand over the executive, and that the legislative council should be made elective so that it, too, might be an instrument of French-Canadian determination to resist change.

It was both the strength and the weakness of the patriot movement that it fell so completely under the spell of its one great leader, Louis Joseph Papineau. He was an aristocratic seigneur and a staunch supporter of seigneurial rights. At first his political affinities had been with English liberalism; but after the British attempt to force the reunion of Upper and Lower Canada in 1822, he became increasingly anti-British and fell under the influence of the radical movement in France. As his preachments became increasingly violent, he provoked the growing displeasure of the church. After the promulgation in 1834 of the Ninety-two Resolutions by the assembly, of which he was speaker and unchallenged leader, Papineau began to lose not only church support but also that of many of the moderate French-Canadian Reformers.

The rebellion in Lower Canada broke out in 1837. Except for some fighting within a short radius of Montreal, Lower Canada refused unconditionally to ally itself with armed opposition against the established government, and the Roman Catholic Church gave its endorsement to the moderates by roundly denouncing the Papineau movement. The establishment on the St. Lawrence of a republic along lines eventually demanded by Papineau would, it was felt, almost inevitably draw Lower Canada within the ambit of the greater American republic to the south. The Catholic leaders at Quebec were no more enamored of such a prospect in 1837 than their predecessors had been in 1775.

The weapons employed in the constitutional struggle in Lower Canada from 1791 to 1837 did not differ essentially from those employed in the other provinces during the same period. But the fact that in Lower Canada the lines were increasingly drawn on a basis of nationality and religion gave the contest in that province a peculiar bitterness. Lord Durham hardly exaggerated the situation in Lower Canada when he later described it as "two nations warring in the bosom of a single state." The specific reforms advocated did not differ essentially from province to province as long as the fight remained on the constitutional level. In each there was an attempt to secure control of the public revenues, and thus the control of administrators of the government. In each there was an attempt to have the legislative council made elective. The irresponsible executive was strengthened in his fight to retain power by his independent control of several sources of revenue, notably the returns from the sale or leasing of crown lands, the customs revenues arising from imperial statutes, and in extremity the funds that might be made available on loan from the imperial military chest. With direct taxation virtually unknown in British North America, almost the only source of revenue at the disposal of the legislature was that arising from provincial customs duties, and even this source was not available without the concurrent assent of the appointed legislative councils. It was undoubtedly this vulnerable position of the assemblies that drove both Upper and Lower Canada into the Rebellion of 1837. That none of the Maritime Provinces went beyond the limits of constitutional warfare was due chiefly to the difference in political background of the people in the two areas.

New Brunswick. New Brunswick remained what it had been from the beginning, a Loyalist province. Unlike the struggle in the other provinces, constitutional difficulties in New Brunswick were settled in two distinct stages. In 1837, at the suggestion of the Colonial Office, the provincial legislature undertook responsibility for meeting a permanent civil list in return for legislative control over the revenues of the crown. But it was not until 1854 that the first Reform cabinet took over executive control as a result of that party's victory in a general election.

Nova Scotia. There was more violent agitation for constitutional change in Nova Scotia, where the people were highly politically conscious and articulate. But political thinking in Nova Scotia never went beyond the precedents of British constitutional usage. There was some slight influence from the mellowing democratic ideas of New England, with which Nova Scotia was always in close touch, but for the most part, Joseph Howe and his Reform party drew their inspiration from English Liberalism.

Prince Edward Island. On Prince Edward Island, the land question tended to eclipse all other problems, and the struggle for colonial autonomy was a dependent issue. This connection was due to the fact that the absentee landlords had been able to win the staunch support of powerful officials at the Colonial Office.

Upper Canada. Only in Upper Canada was political opinion strongly affected by the rising tide of democratic radicalism in the western United States. The geographic proximity of Upper Canada to the areas in the United States where this movement was dominant, and the proximity of the Maritime Provinces to New England and sources of influence from England were primary reasons for the different course taken by the constitutional struggle in these two areas. However, even in Upper Canada the principles of English Liberalism prevailed over the ideas of Jacksonian Democracy. Even before the outbreak of the Upper Canadian Rebellion, the strength of the moderate Reformers under Egerton Ryerson and Robert Baldwin was increasing; that of the rebellious William Lyon Mackenzie, declining.

Trend Toward Colonial Autonomy. The Earl of Durham, who was appointed governor general and high commissioner of Canada in 1838, was undoubtedly a powerful influence in this critical period, but there were others equally determined to follow the path of colonial autonomy rather than that of republican separation from Great Britain. Increasingly, after the Upper and Lower Canadian rebellions of 1837, the goal of the reformers in all the provinces became the establishment of the British principle that the executive council should hold office only as long as it retained the confidence of the representatives of the people in the provincial assembly. At first, application was sought only in local matters, but out of the principle was later to grow full-fledged dominion status and eventually the Commonwealth of Nations, a form of political association hitherto unknown to political science.

What was new in this experiment was not, of course, that an executive should be dependent on the good will of a popular legislature. That had been a fairly well-established principle of the government of the United Kingdom for several decades. What was new was that such a system should be applied to a colonial dependency without destroying the imperial tie. It was the faith that this could be done that gave significance to colonial leaders like Joseph Howe in Nova Scotia and Robert Baldwin in Upper Canada, and to imperial statesmen like the Earl of Durham, the third Earl Grey, and the Earl of Elgin. This faith, of course, did not emerge in a constitutional vacuum, nor was it nurtured solely by political theory; it grew and matured in an empire that was in the process of discarding

most important state paper in British imperial history. Lord Durham belonged to the radical wing of the Whig Party. He was the son-in-law of the second Earl Grey, of Reform Bill fame, and came to Quebec in 1838 armed not only with a great reputation but also with a sheaf of royal commissions such as none of his predecessors at Quebec had ever enjoyed. Like Baron Dorchester and his successors, he held commissions as captain-general and governor-in-chief over all the provinces severally. However, these governorships had never given to their holders any actual administrative control outside of Lower Canada. Each province, except Lower Canada, had been administered solely by a lieutenant-governor; only if the governor of Lower Canada should actually go to some other province

An old print of Bytown, now Ottawa, the capital of Canada, about 1840. The view is from Parliament Hill overlooking the Ottawa River and shows the Chaudière Falls in the background.

its ancient economic theory and practice of mercantilism. In part, at least, the new political freedom was a natural corollary of imperial free trade. Some significance, therefore, must be attached to the correlation of political and economic events as the new order was appearing.

The first distinct break in the old colonial system on its economic side had come in the early 1820's when the British government, which was still Tory, had first permitted foreign countries to trade directly with the colonies under certain rather strict reciprocal conditions. In 1830, in the dying days of the Wellington regime, the United States had been admitted to the British West Indian trade, without reciprocal stipulations. The latter act had been inimical to the important Maritime Province shipping interests, but there had been no loosening of imperial control of revenue arising in the Maritimes. On the other hand, control over crown revenues in Upper Canada had been transferred in 1831 from executive to legislative hands. The Whig administrations of Grey and Melbourne in the 1830's did practically nothing to liberalize either the economic or constitutional systems of the old colonial regime. In 1838, however, after the outbreak of the rebellions in 1837, Melbourne's colonial secretary, Lord Glenelg, sent Lord Durham to the seat of trouble to investigate.

Lord Durham's Report. Durham's "Report on the Affairs of British North America" in 1839 is, perhaps, the

and there be sworn in, did he exercise any authority in that other province. Thus the original intention of the British government that one governor should exercise a supervisory authority throughout British North America had been thwarted from the beginning. Durham, therefore, was given two additional commissions. One made him the king's high commissioner in both Upper and Lower Canada simultaneously, and entitled him, in fact required him, to investigate the situation in both areas and suggest remedies for the obviously distressing and dangerous conditions which prevailed. The other commission made him governor-general of all the provinces, including even Newfoundland, and presumably, therefore, enabled him to exercise authority throughout the entire area of British North America.

Thinking of his problem in these large terms, Durham, even before he left England, determined to aim at a grand federation of all the British provinces. However, when he reached Quebec and called for delegates to be sent from the various provinces to confer with him on this scheme, he soon discovered that separation, based on both geographical and historical factors, was too powerful to make this plan a possible answer to the immediate problems. In his report, therefore, the over-all federation was relegated to the position of an ultimate objective. On the other hand, a speedy reunion of Upper and Lower Canada seemed to Durham to be an urgent necessity. He regarded the French Canadians as an amiable but backward people and believed that union of the two Canadian provinces would help in their assimilation to more progressive English ways. The two provinces he saw as eternally united by nature, with one great waterway, the Great Lakes and the St. Lawrence River, extending the entire length of both. His report strongly recommended their complete political unification. Although the population of the Lower province was the larger, Durham urged that representation in the united assembly be based solely on population, counting upon the immigrant tide, still flowing strongly into the Upper province, to give to it the ultimate advantage.

Durham's chief remedy for the constitutional ills that were so adversely affecting all the provinces was the establishment of a system of government by which executives held office at the discretion of the representative assemblies. There were, of course, several fields of government which could not safely be entrusted to such an executive because their control would involve the power to thwart and perhaps destroy British imperial unity. These fields would, he thought, include such matters as the power to alter provincial constitutions, to administer crown lands in the interest of immigration and settlement, and to regulate external trade and external relations generally. Durham's other recommendations included the promotion of education, the extension of representative municipal institutions, and the development of intercolonial transportation facilities. In January 1839, his report was presented to the British Parliament.

Union of Upper and Lower Canada. The first overt act based on Durham's report was the union of Upper and Lower Canada in 1841 by the imperial statute of 1840, under the name of the Province of Canada. But if Durham's advocacy of this union received prompt acceptance, his insistence that each of the two sections, now to be known as Canada East and Canada West, should have representation in the new assembly strictly in proportion to population was set aside in favor of absolute equality of representation for the two sections. This feature of the act of union served to accentuate the existing differences between the two areas. The result was that, while the obvious intent of the statute was to make a real and organic union of the two former provinces, the constitution, in practice, more and more gave the union the appearance of a dual state. It was to take a quarter of a century, however, to bring the realization that deadlock was inherent in such a system.

Just prior to the outbreak of the Canadian rebellions, Lord John Russell had secured the passage through the British House of Commons of ten resolutions, one of which denied the possibility of the application to the colonies of the principle of so-called responsible government. Russell, however, was aware of the need on the part of colonial governors to secure the services of local executive officers who could retain good relations with their local assemblies. He therefore insisted that such local executive officers could henceforth expect to retain office on the basis of political expediency only, not, as heretofore, merely on good behavior. The governors were to be free to appoint and dismiss officials at their discretion, requiring only approval from the Colonial Office. This plan, Russell expected, would make it possible to keep executive and assembly in harmony as much as was possible under imperial supervision. The act of union itself made no mention of the relation that should exist between executive and legislative power in the new province. In one respect, however, the act looked forward to a new incidence of responsibility. This was in the matter of revenue control, all crown revenues being made subject to legislative disposal. Imperial customs duties continued, however, to be imposed in the province, and the actual administration of the crown lands remained an exclusively executive responsibility.

Intermediate Governmental Practice. Charles Poulett Thomson was sent to Canada to be first governor of the united province and to put the act of union into effect. In England he had been distinguished chiefly for his business acumen and had risen to be president of the Board of Trade. For his new role he was ennobled with the title of Baron Sydenham of Kent and Toronto. His chief policy was to distract attention from the constitutional problem by concentrating the attention of the people on economic development. He was greatly aided in this by being able to announce, at his first meeting with the united legislature, the promise of the British government of a guaranteed loan of £1,500,000, to be used for reducing the public debt and for local improvements. The issue of responsible vs. irresponsible government he attempted to side-step by having his provincial secretary, S. B. Harrison, secure passage through the united assembly of a series of resolutions which deftly refrained from either opening or closing the door to the system which the Reformers were determined to obtain. In practice, Sydenham chose the middle way; he selected popular men for his executive councilors, but indicated that he himself would preside at all council meetings, and that he had the right to appoint and dismiss members on his own sole authority.

Sydenham died later in 1841 before he had been able to demonstrate the workability of his intermediate system. His successor, Sir Charles Bagot, came near to the realization of complete cabinet responsibility to the legislature, but he, too, died within fifteen months after his arrival in the province. He was succeeded by Sir Charles Metcalfe, governor from 1843 to 1845. Metcalfe, in sharp contrast to Bagot, was vigorous, outspoken, and determined to rule. Having served in India, he seemed at times to forget that Canada was on the St. Lawrence and not on the Ganges. The result was a rising tension and an increasing determination on the part of the Reformers to have responsible government without cavil and without reservations. Matters once again seemed to be heading toward a crisis.

The Corn Laws. In the meantime, the British government was steadily approaching a virtual revolution in its imperial economic policies. With the return of a Tory government in 1841, a general overhauling of the imperial economic system took place. In regard to wheat, the chief export of Upper Canada, pressure both from British consumers and Canadian producers led the government in 1843 to secure passage of a bill for a substantial increase in the preference for Canadian wheat and flour entering Great Britain. American wheat milled in Canada was rated as Canadian.

This action resulted in a spurt of milling activity along the St. Lawrence, stimulated also by construction of a St. Lawrence canal system between Prescott and Montreal capable of taking vessels of 9-ft. draft. But, while mills were still being erected and shipping facilities improved, the Corn Laws were repealed in 1846, and the Canadian farmer and businessman alike faced apparent disaster. No sooner had the Corn Laws been repealed than the Robert Peel government fell, and the Liberals came into power under Lord John Russell, who shortly chose the third Earl Grey as colonial secretary.

Establishment of Responsible Government. In 1847, the Earl of Elgin was sent to Canada as governor, having been advised by Grey to establish the principle of responsible government. At the same time Grey sent dispatches with similar instructions to the lieutenant-governors of Nova Scotia and New Brunswick. The governors were given to understand that, in the event of any disagreement between themselves and their legislatures in matters of purely provincial concern, they need no longer look to the Colonial Office for support. In January 1848 a responsible government was set up in Nova Scotia, and two months later a responsible ministry was established in the province of Canada. Thus, without any imperial statute, order in council, or any other formal document, a new and altogether revolutionary change in colonial constitutions was effected. Even in the informal instructions no attempt was made to draw up any list of imperial or provincial fields. It was stressed that this would have to be left to the judgment of the governor himself, since the same type of subject might under some circumstances be purely local and under others of vital imperial concern. This new system required considerable ability on the part of the governor, for he had to be a constitutional monarch in local matters, a servant of the British government in imperial matters, and a judge as to which role he should play from one issue to another.

For a time the provincial Tory parties, having strenuously opposed the establishment of the new system, remained hostile. They regarded the system as having given perpetual power into the hands of their opponents. Economic distress and political hostility combined in 1849 to cause rioting in Montreal, which was then the Canadian capital. The signing of the Rebellion Losses bill by Elgin in the spring of that year was the signal for an especially violent outbreak. The Parliament building was burned, and the governor subjected not only to abuse but to physical attack. In October of the same year many of Montreal's influential Tory businessmen and politicians signed an Annexation Manifesto advocating the union of Canada and the United States. The Loyalist tradition seemed in eclipse. But the crisis had hardly been reached before the situation began to improve. The Tories had not only shocked their opponents, but had astounded themselves. When it was seen that neither the governor nor the Colonial Office was to be frightened into a return to the old system, the Tories began to look about for new objectives and new political platforms. These they soon found in the field of economic development.

Effects on Political Parties. Before turning away from constitutional matters, several other aspects of the struggle over provincial autonomy should be noted. Back of the interminable bickering and jockeying that had gone on in all of the provinces prior to the establishment of the new constitutional system, there was on the side of the British government much confusion of thought both as to the nature and the purpose of empire, and on the provincial side a growing sense of provincial unity despite increasing political-party differences. Perhaps the most notable instance of the emergence of a sense of nationality was in Nova Scotia, where geography and history together had hitherto seemed to conspire to keep the various communities of the province from merging into one social whole. During the first half of the nineteenth century the seemingly impossible had been achieved, and in this achievement the constitutional struggle itself had played a notable part, concentrating attention on the rights of the province to manage its own affairs. In Upper Canada, the constitutional issues were chiefly regarded as instruments for economic change. Upper Canada society tended to split on economic policy, descendants of the older settlers along the St. Lawrence and on the lower lakes being opposed by the more recent settlers in the rugged interior regions. The former had come to have a creditor mentality; the latter, a debtor; the former, a predominantly urban outlook; the latter, a purely rural one.

Religious as well as economic issues became inextricably identified with the central constitutional struggle in all the provinces. In each of them the Anglican church was closely identified with the Tories, and in all provinces the non-Anglican bodies were predominantly on the side of reform. The religious cleavage was particularly evident in Upper Canada, where the clergy land reserves which were still being set apart for the promotion of Anglicanism became at once a religious and an economic grievance. The Roman Catholic church in come of the provinces tended to side with the Reformers.

Economic, religious, and political factors thus entered into the constitutional issue throughout British North America. In the first half of the nineteenth century two political parties were taking form, and this early matrix remained clearly evident in party conflict in later decades, regardless of changing issues. The names Tory and Reformer were shortly to be altered to Conservative and Liberal, but much of the old tradition was to remain in them.

INTERNAL DEVELOPMENT FROM 1814 TO 1860

Road Construction. Although the boisterous political warfare that led up to the granting of responsible government had tended to distract colonial attention from economic development and in some instances to retard it, the first half of the nineteenth century was one of marked progress. Trunk highways were completed, both parallel to the main waterways and connecting them. The Kingston Road between Toronto and Montreal, which throughout its length ran along the river bank, made connection at Toronto with Georgian Bay by way of Yonge Street, with London and Sandwich by Dundas Street, and with Niagara by way of Hamilton. It connected at the Montreal end with roads to Quebec north and south of the St. Lawrence, the south road extending down the Gulf of St. Lawrence to Metis. By 1830 Montreal was also connected by tolerably good roads with New York and Boston, and Quebec was also linked with Boston. The Talbot Road between St. Thomas and Delhi had been extended east and west to connect the Niagara and Detroit frontiers. Various attempts had been made to open an all-year road betwen Quebec and the Atlantic ports of Halifax and St. John, but difficulties in co-ordinating plans of the provinces and uncertainty as to whether such a road should be built primarily for economic or strategic advantage had combined to thwart the project. The route via Metis, the Matapedia River, and the Gulf shore of New Brunswick was favored by the strategists because of its distance from the United States; the route via Rivière du Loup, and the Madawaska and St. John rivers was obviously preferable economically. By making the upper St. John a part of the American boundary, the Webster-Ashburton Treaty of 1842 had rendered the St. John route useless as a military road. By mid-century, Nova Scotia had a highway system radiating from Halifax, making provincial communications by sea of secondary importance. Throughout all Canada, colonization roads opened up the back country to the limit of settlement. The stage coach came into increasing use on the main highways after the War of 1812, particularly at points where there were breaks in navigation, such as the rapids sections of the St. Lawrence.

Canal Building. The 1840's were eminently Canada's canal-building era. Already, in 1829, a private Canadian company, under W. H. Merritt's energetic leadership, had, with considerable government assistance, constructed the Welland Canal between Lakes Ontario and Erie to circumvent the Niagara River. The Welland Canal was later taken over by the government and enlarged to conform with the 9-ft. depth of the St. Lawrence canals, completed in 1848. At the same time canals were being constructed in other parts of Canada, but they were of less economic importance. In Canada, canal construction followed the introduction of steam navigation. The first steamer in Canada operated between Montreal and Quebec in 1809. In 1816 the first steamer appeared on Lake Ontario. On the Great Lakes the steamship was many decades in effectively supplanting the schooner, but on the St. Lawrence between Montreal and Quebec the transition was much more rapid. This aided Montreal in its rapid overtaking of Quebec as Canada's commercial center. The construction of a system of canals on the St. Lawrence between Montreal and Prescott was Canada's answer to the challenge of the Erie Canal, which had been completed in 1825. Unfortunately the completion of the Canadian canals coincided not only with the abolition of British preference for Canadian grain and flour but also with the construction of a railway between Albany and Buffalo which gave all-year transportation facilities. This new challenge could only be met by a Canadian railway to parallel the St. Lawrence.

Railway Construction. In the decade of the 1850's attention centered in railway construction. In 1854, Sir Allan MacNab, Canada's Tory premier, declared that railways were his politics, and in this attitude he was by no means alone. In railways, as in canals, there was a very close connection between private and governmental promotion. Whereas in 1849 there were only 66 mi. of railways in all of British North America, by 1860 there were over 2,000 mi. By the latter date the railways in Nova Scotia, linking Halifax with Truro and Windsor, had been completely taken over by the government. The longest and most important line in New Brunswick—the European and North American, between St. John and Shediac, on the Northumberland Strait—had also been taken over. In Canada, the Grand Trunk, between Rivière du Loup, 115 mi. below Quebec, and Sarnia, on the St. Clair River, had become so closely associated with the government that the question was frequently asked whether the government ran the railway or whether the railway ran the government. Substantial government support was also received by the other main lines, notably the Great Western, between the Niagara River and the Detroit River; the Northern, between Toronto and Georgian Bay; and the St. Lawrence and Atlantic, between Montreal and Portland, Me. The smaller colonization and lumber lines received support from municipalities.

For many years there had been strong advocacy of a railway that would link the Maritime ice-free ports with the St. Lawrence Valley. This was represented as a work of imperial concern and essential for Canadian defense. Unfortunately for the project, the British government felt unable to give it the necessary support, and the separate provinces were unequal to the task. With painful slowness, the St. Andrews, New Brunswick, and Quebec line was pushed northward, and by 1860 it was just approaching the St. John Valley, less than 70 mi. from its initial point on Passamaquoddy Bay. The boundary decision of the Webster-Ashburton Treaty of 1842 had made it necessary, if the road were to be of any use for defense purposes, to take a circuitous route, first due north and then southwest, to reach Quebec. This meant that the line would have to follow the upper St. John River, which actually became the international boundary. This, of itself, was enough to preclude the possibility of securing aid from the British government.

This railway-building era in British North America ended as abruptly as it had begun. The depression of 1857 dried up the sources of capital and by 1860 railroad building had come to an almost complete stop, not to begin again until after the union of the provinces in 1867.

Population Changes. The revolutionary changes taking place in imperial constitutional and economic policies in the 1840's tended to distract Upper Canadian attention from another important change, population. Between 1831 and 1851 Upper Canada's population increased by over 400 per cent. Apart from natural increase, this was due almost wholly to immigration from the United Kingdom. Scottish agricultural settlers were a conspicuous element in this growth in the 1830's, as well as Irish farmers, following the potato famine of 1846; English farmers came during the whole period. A substantial reason for the victory of the Upper Canadian reformer Robert Baldwin, whose ideas were based on British Liberalism rather than on the more radical political philosophy emanating from the United States, was the added strength given to him by these new arrivals. The continued growth of Lower Canada's population was due almost entirely to natural increase. In 1850 Upper Canada's population overtook that of Lower Canada and has remained in the lead ever since. The Maritime Provinces were hosts to large numbers of immigrants from the United Kingdom until about 1825, and their population continued to grow rapidly for another decade. After 1835 the growth of the Maritime population slowed down noticeably, except between 1846 and 1854 in New Brunswick, where Irish immigrants accounted for a large increase.

Political Shift to Conservatism. In the promotion of railways, the Conservatives had taken a more enthusiastic part than the Liberals, particularly in Canada. The urge toward such promotion, therefore, had not a little to do with the return to power of the Conservative Party in most of the provinces in the middle 1850's. The Liberals appeared to have dissipated their strength in the constitutional struggles of the previous decade. Only in New Brunswick did their hold on the province continue into the middle 1860's, but at the expense of their reforming zeal. Once the Liberals had firmly established those reforms for which they had been agitating they, at least for a time, seemed to have little more to offer.

A general election was held in Canada in July 1854. When the Liberal government under Hincks and Morin met the legislature in August, it was found that they did not have the necessary support of the assembly, and in September they resigned and were replaced by what was nominally a coalition. In reality, however, it was soon found that the Conservatives in the new government, under the leadership of John A. Macdonald, were in actual control. In January 1855, this government was reorganized, most of the Liberals being dropped and Conservatives put in their places. Notable among the new members was George Étienne Cartier. Macdonald and Cartier remained the dominant Canadian political leaders until after the outbreak of the American Civil War, the Liberals returning to power for only three days, in August 1858. Macdonald's great power lay in his skill in political manipulation; Cartier's contribution was the winning of the Catholic church in Quebec to the side of Conservatism.

Not all of the early achievements of this party are to be credited solely to Conservative initiative. Had the Liberals been able to retain their power, they might have reaped where they had sown. It was, however, the Conservatives who received the credit for abolishing the seigneurial system in Quebec and the clergy reserves throughout the province in 1854. But equally important was the securing of a trade agreement with the United States.

The Reciprocity Treaty. The Reciprocity Treaty was negotiated with the United States in 1854 and became effective in 1855. By this agreement between the British American provinces and the United States most of the natural products of each were admitted without duty into the other; the St. Lawrence River and the government canals of each were thrown open to the other; and the inshore fisheries of the North Atlantic were made reciprocally available to both.

The Maritime Provinces and Newfoundland were included in the terms of the Reciprocity Treaty and all of them acceded to the agreement. The initiative in securing the treaty, however, was with the Canadians. The British negotiator was Lord Elgin, governor of Canada. Although this international agreement was regarded by Elgin as one of distinctly imperial concern, and therefore not within the working orbit of responsible government, he kept in close touch with his Canadian ministers throughout the negotiations. Not only did this procedure irk the other provinces, but they also regarded the opening of their fishing grounds to Americans as the price which they were asked to pay for the free entry of Canadian produce into American markets. In short, the Reciprocity Treaty was a grievance. Nor did the free entry of Maritime timber into the United States please the important shipbuilding industry in the Maritime Provinces, although these provinces profited by the agreement.

It was Canada, however, that undoubtedly reaped the richest rewards. Trade with the United Kingdom declined temporarily, but trade with the United States almost doubled. This, in turn, stimulated both shipping on the Great Lakes and railway traffic. The prospect of trade in this new area was one of the forces behind the extensive railway building undertaken at this time. However, the shift from export to the United Kingdom to export to the United States required less reorienting of Canada's railway systems than might have been expected. Only below Montreal was the rerouting of traffic severely felt. It was in the political rather than the economic aspects of the new alignment that Canadians found cause for increasing concern, fearing that the flag might follow the trend of trade. Imminence of civil war in the United States turned attention in British North America toward a closer linking of the provinces, both economic and political.

Trade Changes. Agriculture had long been the leading occupation of the Canadian people, but not until the 1850's did the export of agricultural products exceed the products of the lumbering industry. With the union of the North West Company of Montreal and the Hudson's Bay Company in 1821, the new company, which retained the name of Hudson's Bay Company, decided to abandon Montreal as a center for the western fur trade. As a consequence the export of furs from Canada fell to insignificant proportions, and Montreal's contact with the vast hinterland beyond the

Great Lakes was severed for the next fifty years. The export of potash and pearlash, which occupied a conspicuous place in Canadian trade figures in the early years of the nineteenth century, also fell as a result of the competition of European mineral potash. By the midcentury sawed lumber was beginning to overtake squared timber as an export item, with white pine accounting for about half of the total product. In New Brunswick lumbering provided much the largest export product. Nova Scotia still relied on fish and fish products for its main exports. In Prince Edward Island lumbering had by 1850 dwindled to insignificance. Agricultural products had become the leading items of export, as they have since remained. Newfoundland exported only fish and fish products. In Nova Scotia and New Brunswick the manufacture and sale of wooden ships continued at a high level throughout the 1850's.

CREATION OF THE DOMINION OF CANADA

Origin of the Union Movement. The movement to unite the British North American provinces into a national government was slow in getting under way. Prior to 1849 attention in the provinces had been centered in the provincial-imperial relation, not in the intercolonial. In the efforts to secure provincial autonomy there had been little or no co-operation among the several provincial Reform parties. Even the more violent efforts of the rebels of 1837 had been seriously weakened by the inability of the Upper and Lower Canadians to act in unison. The very nature of the goal of the Reformers had tended to stress provincial loyalties, and it was only to be expected that those who had fought the hardest to give their provinces control over their own affairs would not respond to the prospects of handing over power wrested from the mother country to any extraprovincial body. Provincial loyalties were not easily transformed into a larger British North American loyalty, and in the same sense that the winning of responsible government by the several provinces can be credited chiefly to the Reformers, the creation of the Dominion of Canada can be regarded as distinctly a Conservative achievement.

In 1857 the ten-year rule of the Reformer Joseph Howe in Nova Scotia came to an end with the defeat of his party in a general election. J. W. Johnstone succeeded to the premiership. Hardly had he taken office when a Nova Scotia deputation was sent to London with instructions to confer with the British government on the subject of a general union of all the provinces. The main object of the deputation, however, was to secure aid for an intercolonial railway between Halifax and Quebec. The failure of the railway negotiations, therefore, inevitably led to the temporary setting aside of the union proposal. Although Johnstone had been known as a supporter of the general union of the provinces from as early as the Durham conference at Quebec in 1838, there is little historical evidence that, in 1857, he had given it his determined adherence.

In Canada, following the three-day rule of the Liberals in August 1858, the Conservative government was reorganized. Alexander Galt was the most notable addition. In the cabinet he represented the English-speaking population of Lower Canada, and in particular its Montreal business interests. Before agreeing to join the government, he secured the promise of Macdonald, Cartier, and their colleagues that the federation of all the provinces would be made a plank in the Conservative platform. Galt's conversion of Cartier to the cause of federation was of particular importance to the eventual success of the union movement. A resolution favoring consideration of federation was duly presented to the Canadian legislature and passed. When this became known in London, however, the governor, Sir Edmund Head, received a sharp rebuke for having allowed such a subject to have been brought to this stage without the prior consent of the Colonial Office. The project then mysteriously died, or went underground. It seems doubtful whether Macdonald favored such a proposal at this time, even though he might have regarded its advocacy as a useful device for diverting the increasing demands of the Liberals of Upper Canada for representation by population in the existing union of Upper and Lower Canada.

Prior to the American Civil War a general union of all the provinces had been regarded in the main as a possible result that might be expected to follow from the completion of an intercolonial railway. The war had hardly begun before the *Trent* affair in December 1861 threatened hostilities between the United States and the United Kingdom. Had that come about, British North America, as in the War of 1812, would probably have been the area of conflict, and this threat caused the Colonial Office to propose an executive union of the provinces for defense only. This project aroused little interest in the provinces. At a conference in Quebec in 1862 the proposal was flatly rejected. The Colonial Office at this time was, in fact, under the influence of "little Englandism," and there was some thought of allowing Canada to cut adrift if it cared to do so, and of retaining the Maritime Provinces for their strategic importance in naval defense of the North Atlantic. However, while the British were inclining toward imperial devolution, the provinces were becoming increasingly aware of the value of the British connection, and this reversal of roles eventually produced a reversal of policies. Prior to 1864 the Colonial Office, fearful of the possibilities arising from a strong provincial confederation, had continued to favor a union of the Maritime Provinces alone and had looked with disfavor upon any scheme that would also include Canada in a real federal union.

Charlottetown Conference. With secret Colonial Office backing, the Maritime governors worked for the smaller union, and in September 1864 a conference of Maritime delegates was held at Charlottetown, Prince Edward Island. It was immediately discovered that the project lacked popular support. The ostensible purpose of the whole project was to increase the efficiency of government and to reduce the expense. Obviously, this would require a close legislative union, with the elimination of the three separate provincial governments. This, in turn, would have involved the abandonment of at least two, and possibly all three, provincial capitals. Colonial autonomy in the Maritimes was too deeply rooted thus to be directed by gubernatorial behest, even when backed by the Colonial Office.

Meanwhile, in Canada, the constitutional machine had been operating with more and more difficulty, and in 1864 was on the point of collapse. Upper Canada, whose population had now become decidedly greater than that of the lower province, had become increasingly insistent upon representation by population. Lower Canada was correspondingly set against it. The avowed policy of the Liberals of Upper Canada was to solve the deadlock by re-establishing the two Canadas as separate but federated provinces; failing that, to dissolve the union completely. As the deadlock persisted and all constructive legislation became impossible, George Brown, editor of the influential Toronto *Globe* and leader of the radical wing of the Upper Canadian Liberals, pro-

posed a coalition with the Conservatives, which was accepted in June 1864. The primary objection of this coalition was to seek a solution of Canada's impasse in a general federation of all the provinces of British North America; short of this, the coalition government would attempt to reorganize the province of Canada into two federated provinces. It was at this juncture that word came of the proposed Maritime union conference. The Canadian government asked for permission to send an unofficial deputation to Charlottetown to discuss the possibility of this larger federation. The

EDITORIAL ASSOCIATES PHOTO

Fort Garry, built as Fort Gibraltar in 1805 by the Northwest Company as a fur-trade post, was renamed Winnipeg in 1835 and became the nucleus of a settlement which was incorporated as the city of Winnipeg in 1873.

permission was granted, and on the day that the Maritime conference convened the Canadian delegates arrived. The result was that the Charlottetown Conference, originally called to consider the smaller union, spent its time in discussing the larger union.

The Quebec Resolutions. Enough progress seemed to have been made at Charlottetown to warrant a formal conference to consider the larger union, and, accordingly, this was convened at Quebec in October 1864. Without the previous consent or even knowledge of the Colonial Office, thirty-three of the delegates, who later came to be known as the "Fathers of Confederation," drew up a series of seventy-two resolutions. In 1867 these resolutions were, with a few minor alterations, written into the British North America Act.

Only in Upper Canada did the Quebec Resolutions receive an enthusiastic reception, being accepted by Conservatives and Liberals alike. The Lower Canadian section of Canada's coalition government had not included a single Liberal, since Cartier considered their support unnecessary, and the result was that cleavage over federation in Lower Canada was on straight party lines. In New Brunswick, the nominally Liberal government which had given its warm support to the federation scheme was soundly beaten in the general election of 1865 by an avowedly antifederation party.

In Nova Scotia, the scheme was saved from defeat by the simple device of not having it introduced. The legislatures of Prince Edward Island and Newfoundland defeated it overwhelmingly. Federation might well have ended there had it not been for two external circumstances that strangely combined to bring it about.

One of the most startling results of the Quebec Conference was the sudden conversion of the British government to the plan for a general union of all the provinces. This appears to have been brought about by the simultaneous arrival in London of George Brown and Lieutenant-Colonel Jervois, R. E. The former explained to the Colonial Secretary, Edward Cardwell, that in no sense was an interprovincial federation to be regarded as an attempt to weaken the imperial tie. On the contrary, one of its chief merits was seen to be the strength that it would give to the British provinces to resist any movement from the south to draw them within the orbit of the United States. Jervois was able to supplement this by reporting the weakness of provincial defense because of the complete lack of coordination among the provinces. From that time forward,

the Great Lakes, be forthwith abrogated. Others went further and urged that the British provinces be annexed to the United States as soon as the war was over. Consequently, in the British provinces there was a growing conviction that a political union was an urgent necessity if British North America was to survive.

Economic Grounds for Union. The movement to unite the provinces received considerable support from those whose interests were mainly in economic development. Such a union would at once remove all tariff barriers among the provinces, and make possible the erection of a tariff wall about the Canadian nation as a whole. It would not only encourage but necessitate the construction of intercolonial railways, and if, as the Quebec Resolutions envisaged, the union came to include the entire region to the Pacific Ocean, such construction would be on a colossal scale. The advocates of union, therefore, included railway promoters and dreamers as well as those who wanted union chiefly for safety's sake. During the American Civil War the American tariff had been raised to unprecedented heights. When the Reciprocity Treaty was abrogated in 1866, the

Meeting of the "Fathers of Confederation" at Quebec in 1864. The series of resolutions drawn up at this conference became the basis for Canadian union which took place in 1867.

the Colonial Office did not waver in its support of the federation movement. In fact, it threatened to recall at least one colonial governor who, having determined upon Maritime union, seemed to find it difficult to change his mind.

Effect of American Civil War. A critical factor was the American Civil War and its implications for British North America. By 1864 there was no longer any doubt as to which side would win. If the Southern Confederacy feared defeat, British North America feared a Northern victory, since the war had produced an increasingly anti-British feeling in the North, particularly against Canada. This province had been used by Confederate agents to attack the North in the rear, and the Canadian government had been none too energetic in handling the situation. This was 1837 in reverse. The spearhead of opposition to Canada came from the growing numbers in the Fenian Brotherhood. But as the war progressed, anti-Canadian feeling throughout the North became more and more widespread. Influential Americans were calling for the abrogation of the Reciprocity Treaty at the earliest possible date, which was 1865. There were even those who urged that the Rush-Bagot agreement of 1817, which limited armaments on Lake Champlain and

full weight of this protective system was turned against trade with the British provinces. On the economic side, as on the political, union seemed urgent.

British North America Act. The British North America Act was passed by the British Parliament and came into force in 1867 on July 1, a date since observed as the Dominion's national holiday. As the establishment of responsible government had affected the relations between the imperial government and the provinces without altering the relations of the provinces to each other, so, conversely, did this act affect the relations of the provinces without altering the imperial relationship. The act bore, and still bears, unmistakable evidence of the circumstances of its origin. Considering the long separate existence of the provinces, their diverse origins, and the geographical obstructions to communication, the act called for an extraordinary degree of centralization. Only fear of external aggression could have produced such a document.

The federal executive was given the sole power to appoint for life all senators, to appoint all judges for both civil and criminal courts, and to appoint all governors of provinces, whose title was to be only that of lieutenant-governor. It was given a blanket right to disallow any provincial legislation. The federal legislature also was given a wide range of power. Unlike the American constitution, the Canadian document placed criminal law among federal subjects. The federal legislature was given both a general taxing right and the exclusive right to indirect taxation. The provinces were given no exclusive tax field; instead, they were to be heavily subsidized from the federal exchequer under an elaborate series of agreements. This was the great compromise of the Canadian constitution. From the Quebec Conference to modern times, it has not ceased to cause friction between the federalists and the provincials. Lower Canada, of course, insisted that education be a provincial responsibility. The act made it so, but subject to federal intervention in case of provincial interference with existing minority rights to denominational schools. At one step the provinces moved from a separation which was almost complete, to the status of a highly centralized federal state.

Provincial organizations were to be retained, except in the case of Canada, which was to be divided into Ontario and Quebec, with the same boundary that formerly separated Upper from Lower Canada. In one respect the provinces received more power than the federal government; they were given the right to alter their own constitutions, except for provisions affecting the office of governor. (In 1949 the Dominion Parliament was given the right to change the constitution, but only with regard to federal matters.) Had provision been made to have federal senators appointed not only from but by the provinces, and had each province been given equal representation in the Senate, that body might have become a bulwark of provincial rights. But senators were to be federally appointed, and representation was based on sections, not provinces. In the original act there were three sections, each having an equal number of senators: the Maritime Provinces, Quebec, and Ontario. This arrangement placed Senate representation on a basis which was much nearer to equality according to population than to equality by provinces. Macdonald, the outstanding figure in the negotiations, advocated reducing the provinces to municipal status; the act seems to have reflected his views.

It was Macdonald who headed the new government in 1867. His cabinet, although nominally a coalition, was predominantly Conservative, and defections from the Liberals and additions from the Conservatives shortly made it unquestionably a Conservative regime. The appointments to the first federal Senate were also made from both parties. But this equality did not last long after the birth of the Dominion.

TERRITORIAL AND PROVINCIAL EXPANSION

The Northwest Territories. The act of 1867 had set down the procedure by which new areas might be added to the dominion, and within the next four years physical expansion was the most conspicuous aspect of development of the new dominion. Organized colonies were to be admitted by imperial order in council on request from the colony and the Canadian Parliament; territories were to be admitted by imperial order on request of the Canadian Parliament alone. The first area added was the vast region held by the Hudson's Bay Company between Ontario and the Rocky Mountains. Of this region, that part draining into Hudson Bay had been held by the company in proprietary ownership since 1670 under the name of Ruperts Land. Between Ruperts Land and British Columbia lay the Northwest Territory, in which the company had secured exclusive trading rights at the time of the amalgamation of the North West Company with the older company

in 1821. In consideration of a Canadian payment of £300,000 and grants of land including one twentieth of all the area south of the north branch of the Saskatchewan River, the company surrendered its proprietary and monopolistic rights in both regions, and in June 1870 the British government ceded the entire area to Canada.

In anticipation of the transfer, the Canadian Parliament passed the Manitoba Act providing for the immediate creation of a province out of a tiny segment of this great domain, an area about 100 mi. square directly to the north of the American border and astride the Red River. Another act set up a rudimentary form of government for all of the new area beyond Manitoba. This entire area beyond Manitoba, extending northward to the Arctic and westward to British Columbia and Alaska, was to be called the Northwest Territories. From the Lake of the Woods westward to the Rockies the British-American boundary had already been fixed by treaty in 1818 at 49° N. lat.

Province of Manitoba. Manitoba at the time of its creation contained some 14,000 Indians, only 558 of whom were sedentary; 5,757 French half-breeds or *métis;* 4,083 Scotch half-breeds; and only 1,565 white settlers. The haste with which this small area, with an insignificant population almost wholly unlearned in the ways of self-government, was made into a Canadian province was due to conditions both within and without the area. Within, there had just been rebellion; and Louis Riel, French *métis* leader of the uprising, was still in control on the Red River. He continued to hold power for about two months after the province had come into being. There was real danger that these *métis,* unless they were appeased, might succeed in their threat to rouse the Indians. At the same time, just across the American border, only 60 mi. from the capital, Fort Garry (later Winnipeg), a Fenian group was gathering under W. B. O'Donoghue.

The real danger, however, was not in these two movements, which were menacing enough. Farther up the Red River, in Minnesota, a great wave of American migration was heading toward the international border. In 1850, while still a territory, Minnesota had had a population of only 6,077, but by 1870 this had increased to 439,706. Moreover, behind the pioneers were the western Republican politicians, calling loudly for the annexation of all of western Canada. This was one of the reasons for the annexation of the Hudson's Bay Company holdings to Canada and the sudden creation of Manitoba as a curious addition to the provinces of the dominion. The situation was made more difficult by the fact that in 1821 the amalgamated Hudson's Bay Company had abandoned all trade contacts between the West and Montreal. Silence had descended on the region to the north of the Great Lakes, and it remained unbroken between 1821 and 1870. Manitoba, midway between the Atlantic and the Pacific, was tragically isolated from the other provinces.

Province of British Columbia. Events were also quickening in the extreme west on both sides of the international border. The end of the American Civil War in 1865 released expansionist energies that naturally turned westward. Alaska, with its panhandle running down the coast to 54° 40' N. lat., was purchased by the United States from Russia in 1867. The Canadian federation of that same year also turned British-American attention westward, since most of the good land and considerable submarginal land in the eastern Canadian provinces had already been taken up. In 1869, California had been linked with the eastern United States by rail. The Oregon Treaty of 1846 had run the international boundary through to the Pacific along 49°

N. lat., but the situation had become so fluid that it was unrealistic to rely too heavily on paper lines. British Columbia had come into existence as a colony in 1858 and had been united with the neighboring colony of Vancouver Island in 1866. Although the gold rush to the Fraser River area had subsided from the heights reached between 1858 and 1860, many of the people who remained were Americans from California, and thus in this district, as in the Red River area, there was danger of annexation. In 1871, therefore, British Columbia entered the Dominion as the sixth province. It entered, however, only on the Canadian promise that within ten years a railway would be built through Canadian territory to link the Pacific area with the eastern provinces. Like Ontario, British Columbia entered the Dominion with a one-house legislature. The Dominion now extended from the Atlantic to the Pacific, and from 49° N. lat. to the Arctic. With the entry of Prince Edward Island in 1873, only Newfoundland, with its Labrador dependency, remained outside.

POLITICAL DEVELOPMENTS FROM 1870 TO 1896

The Washington Treaty. The end of the American Civil War had not improved relations between the United Kingdom and the United States. In 1871 the Washington Treaty was negotiated, settling the Alabama claims and other disputes which had endangered their peaceful relations. Some of the terms directly concerned Canadian-American affairs, and the generally improved relations between the two major powers helped to lessen the undoubted tension between the new dominion and the older republic. Of particular concern to Canada were the terms regarding navigation and the fisheries. The United States was to have permanent use of the St. Lawrence River. The United Kingdom undertook to urge on Canada the admission of American shipping to the Welland and the St. Lawrence canals; the United States undertook to urge a like admission of British shipping to state canals adjacent to the border. Under the treaty, the boundary line between Vancouver Island and the mainland was to be determined by the emperor of Germany, whose arbitral decision, rendered in 1872, upheld the American claim that the line should follow Haro Strait.

Several articles in the Washington Treaty were to be in effect for ten years from ratification. After that, either side could terminate these temporary provisions on two years' notice. These included reciprocal facilities for each nation to bond goods proceeding through the other in overseas trading and limited admission to coastal trade in inland waters. Also included were provisions for the admission of fishermen of both nations to the inshore fisheries of the Atlantic Ocean north of 39° N. lat., and the free admission into each country of fish taken in such waters. A commission meeting at Halifax in 1877 to determine the amount which the United States should pay in consideration of the greater value of the Dominion fisheries set this advantage at $5,500,000. Payment was made, but at the earliest possible time, in 1883, the United States served notice of its intention to end the agreement in regard to fisheries and the reciprocity on fish imports. The agreement therefore ended in 1885.

The Washington Treaty broke new ground and set a precedent in Canadian-British relations. A Canadian, Prime Minister Sir John A. Macdonald, was one of the five British negotiators. Later, in the Canadian Parliament, he urged the acceptance of the treaty terms, while admitting that his British colleagues had secured imperial advantage at Canadian expense. He had been unable even to place the matter of Fenian depredations in Canada on the agenda. The Liberal opposition profited by Macdonald's embarrassment, but was not yet strong enough to defeat him.

In 1871 the population of the Dominion stood at 3,689,257. The British North America Act had required the new dominion to complete a railway from Halifax to Quebec without delay, and the imperial order admitting British Columbia had required that a railway be built from eastern Canada to the Pacific by 1881. These were colossal tasks for a nation so limited in population to undertake, even under the Conservative Party, which had previously won a reputation for railway building. However, Macdonald's opinion was that, if the government was prepared to help the railways, the railways should help the government. The result of this attitude was the "Pacific scandal" and the defeat of the Conservative party in 1873.

Victory and Failure of Liberals. This political reversal brought Alexander Mackenzie, another Scot, to the premiership. Mackenzie, however, was different from his predecessor, Macdonald. Whereas Macdonald's strength lay in pliability, Mackenzie's strength was his capacity for hard work and his determined rigidity. Both men knew what they wanted but differed greatly in their methods of achieving results. Mackenzie, who was not too venturesome and who stubbornly advocated free trade, was unfortunate, however, in coming into control at the time of the onset of the depression of 1873. In 1876 the Intercolonial Railway was finally completed between Halifax and Quebec, but the Pacific railway was quite beyond the range of Mackenzie's, or possibly of Canada's, abilities at this time. A few links in the water route to the Red River were completed before 1878, and also a short line south from Winnipeg to the American border, but the real task of linking east with west still remained.

Some notable advances were made in the Mackenzie period in the development of Canadian autonomy. Edward Blake became minister of justice in 1875 and immediately began negotiations for the loosening of restrictive imperial ties. This was in the best Liberal tradition. In 1876 the Canadian Supreme Court was established, although the attempt to eliminate an ultimate appeal to the imperial Judicial Committee of the Privy Council was frustrated. In 1878, on Blake's insistence, the imperial instructions to Canadian governors-general were substantially altered. The right of pardon thereafter was to be exercised, except in certain exceptional circumstances, only on advice of a Canadian minister. Canadian acts on a substantial list of subjects had previously to be submitted by the governor for imperial assent; this requirement was eliminated. Reservations, where such were still called for, were to be inserted by the Canadian Parliament in its own acts. These changes represented a step in the direction of Dominion autonomy, but much still remained to be done. Liberal advocacy of such autonomy was handicapped by the fact that, although in imperial relations the Liberals were on the side of Canadian self-government, in the field of Dominion-provincial relations they were usually to be found struggling against federal centralization.

Macdonald's "National Policy." Macdonald was returned to the premiership by an overwhelming vote in the general election of 1878. The issue was what Macdonald called the National Policy. The avowed aim of this policy was to build the Dominion into an economically self-sufficient nation. The platform's chief plank was a protective tariff for the development of eastern Canadian industry, but the policy also included the promotion of immigration into the

*(Top) Quebec's cannon-topped Citadel commands a fine view of the turreted Château Frontenac. Both overlook the St. Lawrence River.
(Bottom) The fishing village of Rivière-au-Renard is typical of the picturesque northern coast of the Gaspé Peninsula.*

(Top, left) A clean broad parkway fronts the beautiful Peace Tower and East Block of Houses of Parliament at Ottawa. The tower's four huge clock dials each measure 16 feet in diameter.

(Top, right) The Canadian Memorial, impressive monument to World War I soldiers, is situated on the spacious plaza facing the turreted Chateau Laurier, one of Ottawa's luxurious hotels.

(Center, left) The Parliament Buildings of Quebec City are among the most beautiful structures in Canada. Alcoves in the façade of this building house statues of prominent Canadians.

(Center, right) In Victoria, the British Columbia provincial Parliament Buildings are brightly lighted at night. They house the Natural History Museum, the Mineralogical Exhibit, the Connaught Library, and the provincial archives.

(Left) St. James Cathedral, Montreal, is viewed from the Windsor Hotel, overlooking Dorchester Street and Dominion Square. The tall building in the distance is the great Royal Bank Building.

(Right) The Ontario Parliament Buildings are situated in Queen's Park, civic and cultural center of Toronto. Here too is found the Royal Ontario Museum with its famous Chinese art collection.

new West and the energetic prosecution of railway construction to the Pacific. Actually, there was nothing new in these proposals beyond the combination and the emphasis, but the Conservative appeal had the additional advantage of the failure of the Liberals in the depression years. As for tariffs, the latter had pinned their hopes on being able to secure from the United States a renewal of the reciprocity agreement of 1854, and had failed. American tariffs were still at their wartime height and showed no signs of being lowered, so that Canadians in general turned sadly but decidedly from reciprocity to retaliation.

In 1879, Canada became protectionist, and it has remained so ever since. Although the 1879 tariff schedule was high, it was still considerably lower than that of the United States. The central Canadian provinces received most of the advantages of the new order while the Maritime Provinces suffered most of the hardship. Consequently, it was only natural that from this time forward the Maritime Provinces should become predominantly Liberal. Their difficulties were increased when, in 1885, the products of their fisheries were no longer admitted free into the United States. Furthermore, the inability of the Maritime shipbuilding industry to shift from wooden ships to iron added to their burdens, and dissatisfaction with the federal union deepened into a chronic sense of grievance.

The construction of a railway to the Pacific strained to the limit both the political resources of Macdonald and the economic resources of the country. After considering government ownership, Macdonald returned to the earlier Canadian policy of government aid and private ownership. In 1880 the Canadian Pacific Railway Co. was formed, receiving with its charter a gift of $25,000,000 and 25,000,000 acres of fertile prairie land. Construction was begun in 1881, and in 1885 the line was completed from Montreal to Vancouver, B.C. This vast enterprise faced huge obstacles in its later stages. The difficulties were noticeably increased by the depression in Canada in 1883, which did not lift until after the line was completed. Several times the government had to give additional assistance.

Securing immigrants proved to be the hardest part of the National Policy to effect. The completion of the Canadian Pacific Railway failed to bring the anticipated rush of settlers to western Canada. The second Riel rebellion, this time on the North and South Saskatchewan, gave the Canadian prairies unfavorable publicity. In this second attempt to overthrow Canadian rule in the west, Riel was able to secure considerable assistance from the Indians. Although the immediate danger of Indian attacks was over as suddenly as it developed, fear of raids on frontier settlements remained throughout the century, combining with economic and social isolation and the rigors of climate to cause a withdrawal from the area that in some years assumed alarming proportions. The Canadian homestead laws were even more liberal than those in the United States, but as long as good free land was available south of the border there was little chance for western Canada to grow. In Ontario, as well as farther west, there was some immigration, particularly from the United Kingdom; but as these newcomers entered, native-born Canadians were leaving for the United States. This drain on Canadian population had a serious effect on Canadian morale. In general, the first thirty years of the dominion's history were predominantly a depression period which was all the more discouraging when compared, as it constantly was, with the spectacular expansion of the United States.

Decline of Conservatives. Macdonald died in 1891,

after winning the general election of that year but before the meeting of the new Parliament. From his death to the defeat of the Conservatives in the election of 1896 there was a succession of four prime ministers. This period of Conservative decline coincided with a third depression. The party had been the staunch advocate of national consolidation, and recurrent depressions frequently played into the hands of provincial rights' advocates. Despite the centralizing features of the constitution, the provinces had retained their virility, and their efforts were increasingly aided by the effects of judicial interpretation upon the Canadian constitution. The decisions of the Judicial Committee of the Privy Council steadily narrowed the range of the Dominion's general power in matters of "peace, order, and good government," while they extended the field of provincial control over "property and civil rights." Macdonald and his Conservatives had achieved conspicuous success in the establishment of the Dominion and the completion of the Canadian Pacific Railway. Their outstanding failure had been their inability to secure national consolidation.

The outstanding issue in the election of 1896 was the right of the federal government and Parliament to interfere in Manitoba's school legislation. Wilfrid Laurier, the Liberal leader, was against such interference. He was also opposed to the federal veto power, which he thought should not be used in nonconstitutional matters, and in constitutional issues should be left to the courts.

In general, the period from 1867 to 1896 had appeared discouraging, but it had not been static. In regard to railways, on which the Canadian economy was particularly dependent, the mileage increased from 2,278 mi. in 1867 to 16,270 mi. in 1896. In addition to the Intercolonial and the Canadian Pacific which together linked Halifax and Vancouver, southern Ontario and southwestern Quebec had been covered with a close network of railways. The Grand Trunk had absorbed the St. Lawrence and Atlantic (1854), the Northern (1881), and the Great Western (1882), as well as many smaller lines, and it had constructed others. The Canadian Pacific, after completing its main line between Montreal and Vancouver, had steadily increased its coverage, and by 1890 had extended its line from Montreal to Windsor, Ont., to the southwest, and to Saint John, N.B., to the east. The center of both systems was Montreal. In Nova Scotia, Halifax had been connected with both the east and west ends of the peninsula, and in New Brunswick the line from Shediac, opposite Prince Edward Island, to Saint John had been extended to the Maine border, where it connected with an American line to Boston.

Export trade, although not commensurate with railway development, had been substantial during this period. In 1868, Canada's exports were valued at $52,701,720; in 1896 they had reached a value of $116,314,543. Between 1871 and 1901 Canada's population increased from 3,689,257 to 5,371,315, and the native-born element increased from 3,003,035 to 4,671,815. During the same period, however, Canadian-born residents of the United States increased from 493,464 to 1,179,922, or by 139 per cent.

CANADIAN PROSPERITY FROM 1896 TO 1917

Liberal Regime. A new era in Canada's development began in 1896 after the victory of the Liberals over the Conservatives. Opposition to the long Conservative rule at Ottawa had come from several sources. In the Maritime Provinces it sprang mainly from a desire for freer trade and greater provincial autonomy; in Ontario and Quebec it had developed largely from a religious root. Before 1885

Macdonald had been able by his exceptional skill to keep his team of Quebec Catholics and Ontario Orangemen together, but his decision in 1885 that Riel must hang had aroused the bitter resentment of Quebec, where Riel was regarded as a Catholic martyr. His decision in 1888 to resist the insistent clamor from Ontario for the vetoing of the Quebec Jesuit Estates bill had equally alienated Ontario. It took the Manitoba school question to defeat the Conservatives, but economic retardation might have been a more effective force if the Liberals had been able to propose any remedy that would have been acceptable both to protectionist Ontario and Quebec and the free-trade Maritime Provinces. As events developed, however, the Laurier regime from 1896 to 1911 was one of unparalleled prosperity, during which the value of Canadian exports jumped from $116,000,000 to $290,000,000.

Population Growth. This increase was not immediately reflected in immigration, but by 1903 three streams of new population had begun to converge on Canada: one from the United Kingdom, one from the United States, and one from continental Europe. By 1911 more than 300,000 were entering Canada annually, and the Dominion's population had increased from 5,371,315 in 1901 to 7,206,643, a gain of 34.17 per cent.

However, the distribution of this increase was very unequal. During that decade, Prince Edward Island actually lost almost 10 per cent of its population, while Saskatchewan, which became a province in 1905, increased from 91,279 to 492,432, or by 439.49 per cent. In Ontario and Quebec, the immigrants went almost entirely to the cities. During the decade, Ontario's urban population increased by 42 per cent and its rural population by only 4 per cent; Quebec's urban population increased by 47 per cent and its rural population by only 4.4 per cent. The greatest part of this urban increase was due to immigration from the United Kingdom and from southern and eastern Europe. The spectacular growth of population on the Canadian prairies came almost equally from the three main sources. American immigration into western Canada was almost wholly agricultural, and came from the western fringe of the Middle West. Some of the newcomers were descendants of earlier immigrants from Ontario to the United States; a considerable number were European-born Americans, but the predominant element was American-born. They added at once numbers, experience in subhumid agriculture, and exuberance. There was, of course, a fourth element in western Canada's growing population, migrants from eastern Canada. It was from this last group that political leadership at first came, but increasingly those from the United Kingdom and the United States took part in western political life, particularly in the two new provinces, Alberta and Saskatchewan, which were created in 1905. They were separated by the meridian of 110° W. long.

This unprecedented growth under Laurier was only in part the result of government action. Clifford Sifton, Laurier's efficient minister of the interior, did much to advertise Canada, and particularly western Canada, abroad. But good times and rising agricultural prices, coupled with the end of good free land in the United States and the disturbed conditions in Europe, were the chief driving forces. Both Canada and the United States, in fact, reflected the attraction of North American prosperity in this period. Canada, with free western land, secured about 1,500,000 immigrants from 1901 to 1910, while the United States, without the attraction of free land, increased its population by 8,800,000 immigrants.

Development of Transportation. Improved transportation facilities were another achievement of the Laurier regime. By 1903 the St. Lawrence canals throughout the rapids section between Prescott and Montreal had been deepened to accommodate vessels of 14-ft. draft. In 1887 the Welland canal had been similarly improved. But the most important development was in railway construction. William Mackenzie and his partner, Donald Mann, had received munificent aid in the building of the Canadian Northern from Quebec to Vancouver through Edmonton, Alberta, and the Yellowhead Pass. This line was well on the way toward completion by 1914. In 1903 the government decided on a third transcontinental line to run from Moncton, New Brunswick, to Prince Rupert, British Columbia. The section east of Winnipeg was built by the government and the section west of Winnipeg by a subsidiary of the Grand Trunk, the Grand Trunk Pacific. This line was also nearing completion when World War I began. By 1915, Canada had three transcontinental lines; one was credited to the Conservatives, and the other two were claimed by the Liberals. The first line was paying good returns; the latter two were headed for insolvency.

External Problems. The Laurier regime brought to Canada not only prosperity but a constant series of imperial and international problems. In 1896, Laurier rejected his former policy of reciprocity with the United States. A few token reductions were made, but in the main the Canadian tariff remained distinctly protective. In 1897 a preference on British imports was established, and in 1898 it was increased to 25 per cent. But this had little or no effect on Canadian imports from Britain. Whereas in 1896 these had represented 31 per cent of Canada's total imports, by 1911 the proportion was only 24 per cent. During the same period Canada's imports from the United States increased from 51 per cent to 61 per cent. Despite the Dingley tariff of 1897, there was only a slight and temporary decline in Canada's export trade with the United States, and a corresponding increase in exports to the United Kingdom. From 1900 to 1911 the proportion of Canada's exports to the two countries remained constant, the United Kingdom absorbing slightly more than 50 per cent, and the United States about 35 per cent.

In 1897, Laurier attended a colonial conference in London, and in the same year the discovery of gold in the Canadian Yukon brought another international problem. In London, Laurier stoutly rejected Chamberlain's project for an imperial federation. The gold rush to the Yukon raised the question of Canada's Alaska boundary, for the only access to the Canadian gold fields lay through disputed territory. It was not until 1903, however, that Laurier was able to secure a British-American treaty defining the boundary. This decision completely cut off northern British Columbia and the Yukon from the Pacific Ocean. Although two of the three British negotiators were Canadian, they were outvoted. Laurier decided that Canada should become independent in matters of treaty negotiations in which its interests were primarily concerned.

Laurier, however, was no mere French-Canadian nationalist. He dexterously guided Canada through the trying period of the Boer War, 1899-1902, maneuvering between Quebec isolationism and Ontario imperialism. The government sanctioned the voluntary enlistment of a limited number of Canadian soldiers to fight in South Africa under imperial officers. Most of the imperial troops were withdrawn from Canada and replaced by Canadians, while the naval bases at Halifax and Esquimalt were taken over by Canada in 1905. Meanwhile, in 1904, Laurier had dismissed Lord Dundonald, the British officer commanding the Canadian Militia, who had publicly criticized the Canadian government. Laurier also dealt with the problem of naval defense, and in 1910 was able to secure from Parliament an appropriation for the operation of two light cruisers. The Conservative alternative was a Canadian donation to the United Kingdom for the construction of dreadnoughts. This was the main issue in Quebec in the Dominion elections of 1911.

After 1903, President Theodore Roosevelt's "big stick" was laid aside in the dealings of the United States with the United Kingdom and Canada, and relations that had been severely strained noticeably improved. President William H. Taft continued this conciliatory policy when he assumed office in 1909. In 1907, James (later Lord) Bryce became British ambassador to the United States and pursued a policy of keeping in close touch with the governments of all three countries. In 1908 he concluded a general arbitration treaty with the United States, and also a treaty for the precise demarcation of the Canadian-American boundary from ocean to ocean. In 1909 he negotiated a treaty for the establishment of a permanent International Joint Commission that would have final jurisdiction in all cases of claims of injurious uses of international waters along the boundary; this commission might also, with mutual consent, be used in any arbitral proceedings. In 1909 he also negotiated with the United States a treaty providing for the arbitration of the long-standing dispute about fishing rights along the North Atlantic coast. The award was duly made in 1910, and accepted by both sides in 1912. Thus the fisheries problem, which had first arisen in 1783, was finally settled, but not before radical changes in fishing techniques had made the problem largely academic. On the whole, the award supported the British and Canadian claims.

In 1911, United States President Taft secured congressional approval of a reciprocal trade agreement, subject to Canadian acceptance. Since the end of the previous Reciprocity Treaty in 1866, Canadians had made repeated journeys to Washington to seek its renewal until, finally, loss of hope coupled with national pride had stopped these appeals. But Taft's action had reopened the door, and Laurier chose this auspicious time to call for a general election. His campaign, however, was ill-fated. Taft and his supporters made speeches which were widely interpreted in Canada as implying that they regarded reciprocity as a step toward political union. Consequently, the Conservatives under Robert Laird Borden were able to make the issue one of loyalty to Canada and the Empire. Even free-trade Manitoba turned against the Liberals. In Quebec the main issue was Laurier's naval defense program, and a curious alliance between Borden and Henri Bourassa, fiery French-Canadian nationalist, made it possible for the Conservatives to appeal to imperialists in Ontario while attacking imperialism in Quebec. Laurier was decisively beaten and his defeat doomed reciprocity. Political allegiance had won over economic advantage.

Borden's Conservative Administration. Borden, who later was knighted, won the election of 1911 with Quebec nationalist support. He found that his associates in "war" must continue to be his companions in peace. Quebec had opposed Laurier's navy, but certainly not because it favored Borden's scheme for supporting the imperial navy. Faced with Quebec opposition in the country and Liberal Senate opposition in Parliament, Borden's naval policy was still only on paper when World War I broke out in 1914.

In tariff, Borden retained the Laurier preferential schedule. This, in 1907, had been elaborated into a "three-decker"

scale, with British imports at the bottom, certain favored nations in the middle, and the United States and other unfavored nations which made no concessions to Canada on the exposed upper "deck." Some of the tariff tension was relieved in 1913 when the American Congress adopted the milder Underwood Tariff.

Actually, the change from Laurier to Borden produced even less change in government policy than had the shift from Tupper to Laurier fifteen years before. In railway construction, as many miles of rails were laid in the first five years of Borden's administration as in the previous fifteen years; and Canada in the years immediately before World War I was for the first time building railways faster than the United States. The chief urge was to secure added outlets for western Canadian wheat. Whereas in 1900 the Canadian prairie had produced 17,000,000 bushels of wheat, in 1915 it produced 378,000,000 bushels. New settlements in the west also stimulated manufacturing in the east. The net value of Canadian manufactures increased from $215,000,000 in 1900 to $1,410,000,000 in 1917, when, for the first time, it equalled the value of Canada's field crops. Canada almost doubled its mineral production between 1905 and 1915. In the same period the development of water power for hydroelectric installations increased sixfold, and the value of newsprint exported jumped from $2,612,243 in 1910 to $53,640,122 in 1920.

In the first years of Borden's administration immigration continued at a steady pace. The peak year was 1913, when 402,432 settlers entered Canada. World War I brought migration from the Old World to a halt, but settlers continued to come from the United States to the Canadian west even after the United States entered the war.

To Borden must go the credit for the first extension of the federal franchise. Macdonald's Dominion Franchise Act of 1885 had aimed rather to restrict than to extend the right to vote in federal elections. It had been repealed under Laurier in 1898, and the right to vote in Dominion elections had again been based on provincial franchise acts. For the federal election of 1917, women who were close relatives of service personnel were given the franchise. In 1918 a permanent federal franchise act gave women equal franchise rights with men, although the requirements for both were still determined by provincial acts. But property qualifications were no longer required in any of the provinces except Nova Scotia and Prince Edward Island. In 1920 a Dominion franchise act completely eliminated provincial franchises for federal elections, and women were given equal rights with men. Already, however, all of the provinces except Quebec and Prince Edward Island had extended the franchise to women. Under the new Canadian act, the federal franchise was limited only by qualifications of British birth or naturalization and Canadian residence, but restrictions in naturalization continued to disfranchise certain national and racial groups. By the end of World War II all of the provinces had adopted woman suffrage.

CANADA IN WORLD WAR I

Conscription and Participation. It was, of course, World War I that gave distinction to the Borden administration. The difference between the imperial policy of Laurier and that of Borden was at first rather one of emphasis than of principle. Both were staunch supporters of complete Canadian autonomy in matters that concerned Canada; but where Laurier was fearful of imperial domination, Borden chiefly feared Canadian isolation. This corresponded with Borden's strength in Ontario and Laurier's support in Quebec. When World War I broke out in 1914, both leaders advocated Canadian participation, but when, in 1917, Borden became convinced that voluntary enlistment would not suffice, the two were sharply at odds over conscription. Borden was able to secure passage of a measure through Parliament in June of that year. The government was strengthened in October by the adhesion of several proconscription Liberals, and in the general election of December this coalition government secured a decided victory. The cleavage between Quebec and the rest of the Dominion deepened during the remainder of the war, becoming a wound that has never healed.

With a permanent militia in 1914 of less than 4,000, the Canadian army by 1918 had enlisted over 600,000 soldiers, of whom about 425,000 served overseas and more than 60,000 died in service. Canada's naval contribution was less significant, although, despite sinkings, there was a phenomenal increase in merchant tonnage. In 1920 the Canadian Government Merchant Marine had 30 ships in commission and 62 under construction; ships were operated as a subsidiary of the government railways. The Canadian Pacific Steamships, Ltd. also increased its tonnage and extended its services on both the Atlantic and Pacific oceans. The Canada Steamship Lines, operating on inland waterways, also profited by wartime trade. Most of Canada's aid to Great Britain's air defense took the form of enlistments in the Royal Flying Corps, of whose personnel Canadians came to account for one third. Toward the end of the war, Canada formed its own Canadian Royal Flying Corps. In food, money, and munitions the per capita contributions of the Dominion were very large.

In 1917 an imperial war cabinet was formed in London, and Borden, with the prime ministers of the other dominions, helped to direct imperial war strategy on the highest political level. It was natural, therefore, that Canada should be given an official, if minor, part in the peace negotiations. The Covenant of the League of Nations being an integral part of the Versailles Treaty, Canada became a charter member of that organization, eligible to election to its council. This gave to the country an international status it had never hitherto possessed.

Postwar Problems. The task of restoring Canada to the ways of peace seemed even heavier than the previous task of putting the nation on a war footing. Agrarian revolt was growing in the west. Economic dislocations, labor agitation, and the difficulties of demobilization added to the burden. In 1919 a general strike in Winnipeg threatened to paralyze that key to the west and to spread to other centers. In 1920, Canada experienced a depression, and Borden was forced through ill-health to resign, leaving the formidable tasks facing the government to be assumed by Arthur Meighen, a staunch Conservative protectionist and the leading supporter of conscription.

DOMINION AFFAIRS FROM 1921 TO 1939

Election of W. L. Mackenzie King. In 1921, William Lyon Mackenzie King, grandson of the Mackenzie of rebellion fame, won the premiership in a decisive victory of the Liberals over the Conservatives under Meighen. King assumed office on Dec. 29, 1921. In the federal Labour Department he had been deputy from 1900 to 1908, and minister from 1909 to 1911. As an advocate of reciprocity he had been decisively defeated in the general election of 1911; as an opponent of conscription he had again been defeated in 1917. On the death of Laurier in 1919 he had been chosen at a national convention to lead the Liberal Party. During most of the war years he had been engaged in industrial research in the United States.

When King faced Parliament in 1922 he had need of all his skill. More than half of his party came from the one province of Quebec, which had been the black sheep of the Canadian family during the war years. West of the Great Lakes the Liberals had returned only six members. The newly organized Progressive Party under T. A. Crerar secured one seat in New Brunswick, none in Quebec, but 24 in Ontario and 39 in the west. Free trade and the nationalization of railways were conspicuous features in the Progressive policy. The party refused to coalesce with the Liberals, and King was left in a weak position.

Amalgamation of Railways. Canada's railway problem had to be faced. During the last years of the Borden regime the government had been forced to take over the Canadian Northern, the Grand Trunk, and the Grand Trunk Pacific. The original agreement with this last company when it was chartered in 1903 was that it should lease from the government the National Transcontinental Railway from Winnipeg to Moncton. But financial embarrassments had made this impossible, and the entire line from Moncton to Prince Rupert had come into government hands. In 1923 all of these government-owned rail lines, together with the Intercolonial Railway, were formally amalgamated into a single system under the name of Canadian National Railways, with Sir Henry Thornton as president. This system, with 22,545 mi. of rails in 1924, proved to be a serious drain on the Dominion treasury, which was already overburdened with carrying charges on the national debt and war pensions. These latter items had increased between 1914 and 1921 from $13,205,405 to $176,972,271. The C.N.R. system was faced with rising wages and material costs along with declining revenues due, in part, to increasing diversion from rail to highway transportation in the 1920's. As an economy measure, the government pursued a policy of selling ships of the Canadian Government Mercantile Marine. War luxury taxes and the income tax (first levied in 1917) were retained and the Dominion sales tax (levied in 1920) was increased. None of these measures added to the government's popularity. In 1923 the preference on imports from British countries was slightly increased; otherwise the tariff was left substantially undisturbed, further provoking the restive Progressives.

Second Victory for King. Following the general election of 1925 the position of the Liberals was more precarious than before. Although the Progressives held only 25 seats, the Conservatives had increased their number from 50 to 116. The Liberals had only 101 seats and were therefore still dependent on Progressive support, ever more grudgingly given. In January 1926 the new Parliament met. In June, King advised the governor-general, Lord Byng, to dissolve the House. The advice was rejected, King promptly resigned, and Meighen again became prime minister. But if the Progressives had found it hard to support the Liberals, they found it impossible to aid the Conservatives. Meighen, therefore, advised a dissolution, and his advice was accepted. In September the new general election was held, and the right of the governor to refuse a dissolution was made a prominent issue of the campaign. In the new House, the Liberals had 116 seats, the Conservatives 91, and the Progressives had almost disappeared. King was at last in a position to adopt a more constructive course.

New Dominion Status and Relationships. Later in 1926, King attended an imperial conference in London, where a formula descriptive of the dominion-imperial relationship was agreed upon. Great Britain and the dominions alike were "autonomous communities within the British Empire, equal in status, in no way subordinate one to another in any aspect of their domestic or foreign affairs, though united by a common allegiance to the Crown, and freely associated as members of the British Commonwealth of Nations." In 1920, Borden had secured British approval for the establishment of Canadian legations, and in 1923, for the first time, Canada had both negotiated and signed on its own behalf, without United Kingdom intervention, a treaty with the United States—the "treaty for securing the preservation of the halibut fishery of the North Pacific." King appointed a minister to Washington in 1926, to France in 1928, and to Japan in 1929; these governments reciprocated by establishing legations at Ottawa. In 1927, Great Britain sent a high commissioner to Ottawa, and the diplomatic status of the Canadian high commissioner to London was regularized. Since 1924, Canada had had a permanent advisory officer at Geneva, seat of the League of Nations. It also had permanent representation in the International Labor Organization, and in 1926 was elected to a nonpermanent seat on the League of Nations Council. At the imperial conference in 1930 it was agreed that dominion governors-general might henceforth be appointed by the Crown on advice of the cabinet of the dominion concerned. It remained only to base this new dominion status on law. This was accomplished in 1931 by the Statute of Westminster. Although King was no longer in office, having been defeated in the election of 1930, this imperial act was the culmination of negotiations in which he, as minister of external affairs, had played a distinguished part. The Department of External Affairs had been created by Laurier in 1909, and since 1912 the portfolio had been held by successive prime ministers.

Bennett's Conservative Administration. It was obviously the depression, beginning in 1929, that defeated the Liberals in 1930, bringing Richard B. Bennett to the premiership. Law was Bennett's profession; business, his avocation. Born in New Brunswick, he had moved to Calgary, Alberta, in 1897, and had grown up with the west. He became not only prime minister, president of the privy council, and secretary of state for external affairs, but also assumed the arduous task of minister of finance. He also kept close personal supervision over the other ministries.

It was by raising the tariff that Bennett proposed to restore Canadian prosperity. The American Hawley-Smoot tariff of 1930 had raised additional barriers against Canadian lumber and farm products, but even without this, Canada's trade balance with the United States had become decidedly adverse. In 1931 and 1932, Bennett, therefore, further raised the Canadian protective tariff. At the same time some concessions were made to British imports. But Canada continued to buy predominantly from the United States and to sell chiefly to the United Kingdom, although imports and exports with both nations kept falling off.

The abandonment by the United Kingdom of both the gold standard and free trade in 1931, and the determination of France and Germany to become agriculturally self-sufficient further hampered Canada's export trade. Since a protective tariff obviously was not enough, Bennett turned to an old remedy, freer Commonwealth trade. In 1932 an imperial economic conference met at Ottawa. But Great Britain, although no longer a completely free-trade country, was not prepared for so drastic a solution as free trade within the Commonwealth and protection against all foreign nations. A few bilateral trade agreements were made, but the essential tariff structure throughout the Commonwealth remained unaltered. By 1934, Bennett was ready to consider another earlier panacea, a trade agreement with the United States. He had appointed his brother-in-law, Major Herridge, as minister at Washington. Herridge and President Franklin D. Roosevelt were on friendly terms, and the latter was known to be well disposed toward the establishment of more cordial relations with Canada. Negotiations, however, had not been concluded when Bennett was defeated in the general election of 1935.

Meanwhile, the depression which had started in Canada in 1929 was intensified by the coincidence of a long series of drought years in the west. In Ontario and Quebec, where agriculture was still rather diversified, there was a distinct back-to-the-land movement in the 1930's. Saskatchewan and Alberta also had population shifts, but they were chiefly from land in the south to land in the north. Some, particularly those who went into the Peace River country, found good land and prospered; others in the stampede pushed into the wooded country of northern Saskatchewan, where fertile soil was scarce. Relief expenditures were a heavy drain on provincial and federal treasuries as poverty and, especially in the industrial areas of the east, mass unemployment became widespread in the Dominion. It was the first Canadian depression in which refuge could not be sought in the United States. Migration was prevalent within Canada, but both immigration and emigration had practically stopped.

Return of King and Liberals. In January 1935 Bennett announced a radically new policy which startled both his opponents and his supporters. Its obvious model was the American "New Deal." He pushed through Parliament measures relating to wages, hours of labor, marketing, farm credit, and unemployment insurance. On these he went to the country in October and was decisively defeated by the Liberals. The Conservatives retained only 39 seats, while the Liberals secured 171. There were, however, two new groups: the Social Credit party under William Aberhart, which in the same year had swept Alberta in a provincial election; and the Co-operative Commonwealth Federation, which had been organized by J. S. Woodsworth in 1932 by a union of labor and farmers. The Social Credit party secured 17 seats at Ottawa; the Co-operative Commonwealth Federation, seven. In October 1935 William Lyon Mackenzie King was again Canada's prime minister.

Thereafter, except for a serious drought in the west in 1937, Canada made progress toward recovering from its depressed state. External trade had already begun to show distinct signs of improvement. Negotiations with the United States for the amelioration of trade restrictions had been pushed to completion in 1935. At the same time Bennett's "new deal" legislation had been referred to the courts for a ruling on its constitutional validity. In 1937 the imperial judicial committee declared almost the entire series of acts to be invalid, and this led to the opinion that if the British North America Act constituted a barrier to social reform that Act ought to be re-examined. Thus a royal commission was appointed in 1937 to report on the Act as it affected Dominion-provincial relations, and to suggest changes. The commission did its work well but slowly, and by the time its report was presented in 1940, Canada was at war and in a poor position to consider structural changes within the Dominion; consequently, action was indefinitely delayed. The commission recommended the abandonment by the provinces of income tax and succession dues and the assumption by the Dominion of the provincial debts. It advocated that the federal government be responsible for some of the social services carried by the provinces, notably unemployment insurance and relief, and that a national adjustment grant be provided for equalizing the abilities of the provinces to carry on the work of education and other social services. Later, after the end of World War II, King's attempts to secure provincial approval for the adoption of certain health and welfare proposals met with failure. Meanwhile, the provinces had surrendered their rights to levy income and corporation taxes and accepted a rent from the Dominion for the exclusive use of these fields.

WORLD WAR II AND AFTER

Canadian Entry into War. The third King administration had hardly begun when war threatened and external relations became ever more absorbing. Japan had invaded Manchuria in 1931, and Canadian opinion had been unmoved. Nor was there much serious concern shown when Hitler rose to power in 1933. When Italy invaded Ethiopia in 1935 and the League of Nations had been called upon to apply economic sanctions, the Conservatives had approved in principle the application of such pressure against Italy. With the change of government at Ottawa in October 1935, Dr. W. A. Riddell, Canadian representative at Geneva, after attempting in vain to secure instructions from the new government, proceeded on the assumption that the policy had not been altered. The Liberal government, always hesitant about involvements in European affairs, repudiated Riddell's action, and he was later recalled and sent to New Zealand as a trade commissioner. The French-Canadians, with Rome as their spiritual center, were averse to weakening Italy.

In 1936, King attended the League Assembly in person, and there roundly condemned the use of force in securing peace, saying that the League should confine its efforts to conciliation. King was an advocate of appeasement, an attitude growing out of his determination to maintain Canadian unity at any cost.

Thereafter events began to quicken. Hitler occupied the Rhineland in 1936, Austria and the Sudetenland in 1938, and the remainder of Czechoslovakia and eventually Poland in 1939. On Sept. 3, 1939, two days after the invasion of Poland, Great Britain declared war on Germany. On September 10, with approval of the Canadian Parliament, the Canadian government declared war.

Wartime Economic Improvement. Before Canada was actually at war, a Wartime Prices and Trade Board was established by an executive order based on the War Measures Act, which had been passed in the early days of World War I and forgotten in the interval of peace. Thereafter and throughout the war, orders, boards, and regulations followed each other in rapid succession. The result was that the Canadian economy was kept under control while the war effort was gaining momentum. In fact, it was only with the coming of the war that the last vestiges of the depression were swept away. Canada was able to finance participation in the war by increased taxation and internal borrowing alone, and, despite the diversion of almost a million men into the fighting services, the value of exports increased from $838,000,000 in 1938 to $3,440,000,000 in 1944. The outstanding increase was in manufacturing, where the total value of output increased from $3,338,000,000 in 1938 to $8,733,000,000 in 1943. In mining there was a notable increase in the production of aluminum and a decided drop in gold production. Increased shipbuilding, both naval and mercantile, was an outstanding phase of Canadian development. Between 1939 and 1945 Canadian vessels suitable for foreign trade increased from 37 to more than 200; and whereas Canada entered the war with

6 destroyers and 11 smaller craft, this number was expanded during the war to 378 warships and more than 400 smaller vessels, most of these being built in Canada. Aircraft showed a similar unprecedented development. War and prosperity also combined to give the two great railway systems of Canada, the Canadian Pacific Railway and the Canadian National Railways, a profit balance unique in Canadian history; in fact the publicly owned system for the first time ceased to burden the Canadian taxpayer. But the very magnitude of the wartime development made all the greater the later problems of adjustment to peacetime economy.

Military Participation in War. The problem of stimulating and sustaining Canada's wartime production was, however, less difficult than the political problem of steering a course between the increasingly divergent views of French-speaking and English-speaking Canadians. The major issue, as in World War I, was that of conscription. Under the War Measures Act of 1914, the government already had enough authority to call for voluntary recruits for the army, and during the relatively quiet winter of 1939-1940 this proved sufficient. King's Minister of Justice, Ernest Lapointe, gave his support to this, while assuring the government and the country that he would never support conscription. In 1940, with the European situation assuming an ever more alarming aspect, Parliament passed a National Resources Mobilization Act, which gave the government power to organize both the economic and man-power resources of the country. In August a national registration of man power was made. It was not, however, until June 1941, that a proclamation ordered men between 21 and 24 to report for compulsory military training. Their term of service was to be two years, and they were not to be called to serve outside of North America. From time to time the age group was enlarged. In April 1942, a plebiscite was taken in Canada as to whether the government should be relieved of its earlier promise not to limit conscripts to home service. The verdict was strongly in favor of releasing the government, but French Canada voted almost unanimously in the negative.

Meanwhile, two Canadian armies were emerging, a conscript one at home and a volunteer one on active service abroad. In 1944, King's Minister of National Defense, Colonel James Layton Ralston, resigned because of the government's unwillingness to send conscript troops overseas to provide adequate reinforcements in view of the heavy casualties being suffered in Europe. The government redoubled its efforts to secure overseas recruits voluntarily from among the home-service troops, but before the end of the war in 1945 it sent about 16,000 conscripts to the European theatre to reinforce the volunteers already there. In all Canada sent 411,502 troops overseas.

Canada entered the war with about 4,500 permanent militia. During the war about 700,000 entered the army. War dead numbered 22,910, equivalent to about 39 per cent of the World War I toll. The personnel of the Canadian navy rose from 3,604 in 1939 to 96,705 during the war; the dead numbered 1,978. The Royal Canadian Air Force was increased from a prewar strength of 4,606 to 215,200; fatalities in this branch were 17,130. Late in 1939 an agreement had been reached among Great Britain, Canada, Australia, and New Zealand for the establishment in Canada of the British Commonwealth Air Training Plan for the training of air crews. Half of the cost and all of the administration was assigned to Canada; the program made a notable contribution to British air power, training 131,551 aircrew men.

Wartime Co-operation and Relations. The United States and Canada were drawn together both in prewar defense measures and in the conduct of the war. In August 1938, President Roosevelt, in a speech at Kingston, Ontario, had said that Canada could be assured that "the people of the United States will not stand idly by if domination of Canadian soil is threatened by any other Empire." In August 1940, an agreement was reached at Ogdensburg, N. Y., for the establishment of a Permanent Joint Board on Defense. In the same year negotiations were begun looking toward the construction of a St. Lawrence Seaway, and in March 1941 an agreement was signed. Running into both sectional and constitutional difficulties, this agreement became a political issue on both sides of the boundary throughout the war years and those that immediately followed. In 1942 an agreement was reached for the construction of an Alaska highway between Dawson Creek, B.C., and Fairbanks, Alaska, and the road was completed with amazing rapidity. Another joint defense project was the construction of an oil pipeline between Norman Wells, Northwest Territories, and Whitehorse, Yukon Territory; this was completed in 1944. In the pooling of resources, war planning, and organizational interlocking, each year of the war brought the two countries more closely together.

The extension of Canada's external relations was one of King's major policies. In addition to the raising of the Canadian high commissionership in London to diplomatic status and the establishment of the legations in the United States, France, and Japan already mentioned, many permanent trade commissions were established in different parts of the world. On the eve of World War II the tempo of this expansion began to be quickened. Just before the outbreak of war, legations were established in Belgium and Holland. During the war, high commissioners were sent to Eire, the Union of South Africa, Australia, New Zealand, and Newfoundland. Legations or embassies were established in Argentina, Brazil, Chile, China, Cuba, Czechoslovakia, Greece, Mexico, Norway, Peru, Poland, and the U.S.S.R. In the postwar period diplomatic services were extended to Denmark, Luxembourg, Sweden, Switzerland, Turkey, and Yugoslavia; and official diplomatic missions were sent to Japan and Germany. A permanent delegate was also sent to the United Nations, and a high commissioner to newly independent India. In 1943 the legation to the United States was raised to ambassadorial rank. Canada established its first consular office in 1940; and by 1956 it had consular services in Brazil, the Philippine Republic, and in the United States where there were nine consular offices. However, it was not from this far-flung expansion of Canada's external contacts that Canadians derived the most satisfaction, but rather from the unusually close relations of Canada, the United States, and the United Kingdom in the prosecution of the war and in the postwar period. Canadians have long realized that good relations between these three great English-speaking nations are essential to their very existence as a nation. Many have thought of Canada's role as that of interpreter between these two other powers. In the complex international atmosphere that characterized the postwar period, this role was to become significant.

Postwar Developments and Outlook. Early in 1948 King, having reached the age of 74 and having been prime minister for 22 years, announced that in August 1948 a national Liberal convention would be held to choose his successor. It chose Louis St. Laurent, Mackenzie King's Minister of Justice during the war, and from 1946 to 1948 Minister of External Affairs. St. Laurent immediately became the leader of the Liberal Party, but King retained the premiership until Nov. 15, 1948. A federal general election on June 27, 1949, returned 193 Liberals to the Commons out of a total of 262. Conservative strength dropped from 66 in 1945 to 42, Cooperative Commonwealth Federation from 29 to 12, and Social Credit from 13 to 10.

A few months before the elections of 1949 another event of importance took place. This was the transformation of Newfoundland, with its dependency Labrador, into a Canadian province. Newfoundland had refused in 1867 to join the Canadian federation. In the deep depression of the early 1890's Newfoundland had been willing to consider terms of entrance, but the Canadian conditions had seemed unacceptable. In 1933 it had chosen to seek refuge from bankruptcy by abandoning its constitution, under which it enjoyed an autonomy similar in principle to that of Canada, and again became a mere British dependency, governed by an appointed commission. In 1948 Newfoundland held two referendums. In the first, a plurality voted in favor of union with Canada in preference to the other two possibilities: a return to colonial autonomy or the retention of the existing commission form of government. In the second, held on July 22, a small majority voted in favor of union with Canada. On July 30 Prime Minister King announced that, despite the size of this majority, Canada would accede to Newfoundland's request. Later in the year detailed terms of union were drawn up and signed by the two governments. Having secured the approval of the Newfoundland Commission and the Canadian and British parliaments, Newfoundland became the tenth province of Canada on Mar. 31, 1949. It was given six seats in the Senate and seven in the House of Commons. Newfoundland and Labrador added 152,734 sq. mi. to Canada's territory and approximately 327,000 people to its population, but the addition of the new province did not meet with the whole-hearted approval of Canadians, many of whom were troubled about the cost of confederation. It was estimated that during the first few years the obligations undertaken in the confederation agreement would cost the Canadian treasury some $50 million a year. Nevertheless, the prospect of an increase in trade through the removal of previous heavy duties on Canadian imports, the discovery of vast iron deposits in Labrador, and the strategic location of both Labrador and Newfoundland on the airways to Europe made the new province a valuable acquisition to the nation.

While the negotiations with Newfoundland were in progress, Canada was also preparing to launch a new era in foreign affairs by signing the North Atlantic Treaty in April 1949. It had been Canada's policy previously to refrain from direct commitments with foreign nations during peacetime. One of the results of the North Atlantic Treaty was to draw the political, military, and economic ties of the United States and Canada closer together, chiefly through joint military planning by the two countries, the establishment of a joint industrial-mobilization committee, and the exchange of officers to work on mutual defense problems. On June 5, 1949, Canada and the United States announced a new air agreement. Newfoundland's union with Canada had made some new arrangements necessary since the United States had maintained important air bases on that island under an agreement with Great Britain during the war. The new agreement provided for continued American rights at the Gander airfield and for the opening of Stephenville and Argentia bases to Canadian and other commercial traffic. Under the agreement Canada also gained four important new routes into the United States, and the Trans-Canada Air Lines gained a new competitive route across the Atlantic.

Port Radium, near the Arctic Circle on Great Bear Lake in the Northwest Territories, where the Eldorado Mines produce pitchblende, from which radium and uranium are derived.

Advances in air transportation were also made within Canada itself, principally on north-south routes which had previously been neglected in favor of east-west routes. Northern Canada has become increasingly important with the discovery of iron in northwestern Ontario and northern Quebec, uranium in western Canada, especially in the Goldfields-Beaverlodge region of northwestern Saskatchewan, titanium in the Lake Allard district of Quebec, and oil and rare minerals in Alberta and the Northwest Territories.

The postwar period also witnessed an increase in immigration to Canada. Between 1931 and 1945 immigration had been at a virtual standstill. With the end of World War II, in addition to European displaced persons and British war brides, Canada began to receive a substantial number of immigrants, especially from the United Kingdom. The average annual immigration during World War II was about 10,000; in 1946 it was 71,719, and more than this number arrived in Canada during the first eight months of 1948. By the summer of 1951 the total postwar immigration to Canada had reached half a million persons.

By mid-1952 the Canadian economy was expanding at an unprecedented rate. Defense appropriations were higher than they had ever been except during wartime. In 1952 a greatly enlarged federal-provincial pension scheme was in operation, providing grants for low-income persons between the ages of 65 and 69 and for all persons over 70. Despite these defense and welfare expenditures the federal surpluses have continued to rise in the years since World War II. The country's expanding economy, together with its increasing population, seem to presage a new period of material growth and national assurance for Canada. To many Canadians, the decision in 1953 to undertake the St. Lawrence Seaway, with or without U.S. participation, symbolized this new and confident maturity of the nation. The unexpected Conservative victory in the 1957 elections may be taken as a further indication of Canada's role, since the Conservative Party stood for closer Commonwealth ties and less economic inter-dependence with the United States.

W. M. W. and D. M. L. F.

CANADA BALSAM (Canada turpentine), a liquid oleoresin from the balsam fir, *Abies balsamea* of the northeastern United States and Canada. The balsam is pale yellow or greenish-yellow, transparent and viscous, dries very slowly but becomes harder with age. It has little medicinal value, although it is popular as a cough remedy in the region it inhabits. Its chief uses are as a cement for lenses, in the manufacture of fine lacquers, and for mounting specimens in microscopy.

J. A. Bo.

CANADA COMPANY, the only land company of any magnitude to operate in Upper Canada (Ontario), was formed in 1824 to colonize the crown and clergy reserves of the province. A royal charter was granted on Aug. 19, 1826. The venture was opposed by the clergy, who had an interest in the clergy reserves. A large tract of land, called the "Huron Tract," amounting to 1,000,000 acres in the southwestern part of the province was substituted for the reserves. For this tract, located largely in Huron and Perth counties, the company paid approximately £300,000. The first secretary of the company was John Galt, the Scottish novelist, whose inquiries in Upper Canada had played a large part in setting up the organization.

The company quickly began settlement. The town of Guelph was founded in 1827 and Goderich, Stratford, and St. Marys followed. A road was built from the head of Lake Ontario to Goderich, and by 1834 there were about 2,500 settlers in the Huron Tract. The company faced many difficulties in competition with the free grants made by the province. Galt was not practical and was soon superseded, but the territory opened by the company proved to be rich farm land and became one of the most prosperous regions in the province.

J. J. T.

CANADA EXPEDITION (1775-1776), a military operation in the Revolutionary War. On May 10, 1775, troops commanded by Ethan Allen (1738-1789) and Benedict Arnold (1741-1801), on orders from the American Revolutionary leaders, captured Fort Ticonderoga and Crown Point on Lake Champlain. Following this capture a plan was formulated to invade Canada, where it was believed the French inhabitants would revolt because of the unrest and discontent brought about by the enforcement of the Quebec Act of

1774. The movement involved a two-pronged attack: one column, under General Richard Montgomery (1738-1775), went up the Hudson River-Lake Champlain route and captured Montreal on Nov. 12, 1775. Ethan Allen, who accompanied Montgomery as a volunteer, was captured, Sept. 5, 1775, near Montreal. The other column, under Arnold, went up the Kennebec River through Maine and down toward Quebec, where it arrived after many hardships on Nov. 13, 1775. On December 31 Arnold and Montgomery made a joint attack on the fortress of Quebec, but it failed. Arnold was wounded and Montgomery killed. Arnold then besieged and captured Quebec, and held it until June 1776, when British reinforcements under Sir Guy Carleton (1728-1808) arrived. Arnold withdrew southward, followed by the British. After a series of delaying engagements, including a naval battle on Lake Champlain on Oct. 11, 1776, which prevented Carleton from joining General Sir William Howe on the lower Hudson River, Arnold united with the American troops near Ticonderoga. Carleton returned to Canada, and Howe to New York. Canada remained firm in its allegiance to Great Britain.   M. Je.

CANADA FIRST MOVEMENT, a political movement originated in Canada in 1868 to promote national interests beyond the scope of newly achieved confederation. The group grew out of a chance meeting in Ottawa of a handful of enthusiasts who were inspired by the success of the confederation project as set forth in the British North America Act. The five founders, H. J. Morgan, Charles Mair, R. J. Haliburton, G. T. Denison, and W. A. Foster, were joined by others. The term "Canada First" apparently was first employed by Foster in a lecture entitled, "Canada First, or our New Nationality."

In the federal general election of 1874, Canada First entered candidates under the name of the Canadian National Association, presenting its aims in the *Nation,* a weekly newspaper. The political program of the Canadian National Association called for the establishment of a protective tariff, the right to negotiate treaties, and so forth. For a brief period, it appeared that Canada First had attracted Edward Blake, a leading member of the Liberal Party, but the conversion was only temporary and the movement failed to develop into an organized political body. Important elements in its program were taken over by the two major parties, the Conservatives, for example, appropriating the protective tariff. The fundamental weakness of Canada First was its total inability to state its program in terms acceptable to French Canadians; it remained throughout its career an Anglo-Canadian movement.   J. I. C.

CANADIAN-AMERICAN RECIPROCITY. The policy of mutual trade concessions between the United States and Canada was initiated partly as a result of the repeal of the British Corn Laws in 1846. This action had resulted in curtailment of Canadian exports to Great Britain, and Canada was impelled to seek easier access to the American market. The first move in the direction of reciprocity had been made in 1818 in the British-American agreement covering American fishing rights in Canadian territorial waters. The interpretation of this treaty, however, engendered frictions which threatened hostilities.

The mounting Crimean crisis spurred the British in 1854 to conclude a new agreement, the Elgin-Marcy Treaty, greatly extending American use of the inshore fisheries and opening American territorial waters to British subjects south to 36° N. lat. The new treaty established virtual free trade in natural products; it was to run for ten years and was to remain effective thereafter until denounced on twelve months' notice by either party. The United States terminated it in 1866, despite its economic advantages, for various reasons; one of them was the ill feeling which had arisen during the American Civil War.

The newly constituted Dominion of Canada in 1867 and afterward made several moves to renew reciprocity. Growing Canadian industry, however, generated sentiment for protectionism, both as a makeweight to induce the United States to restore reciprocity and as an end in itself. The latter aspect soon dominated, abetted by repeated American rebuffs of Canadian overtures. In 1897 Prime Minister Wilfrid Laurier announced that there would be "no more pilgrimages to Washington," but he left the door open for a possible agreement later.

President William Howard Taft, forced by circumstances to present a positive achievement to the people prior to the Congressional elections of 1910, made the first move. Especially burdensome among many problems was the Payne-Aldrich Tariff of 1909 which, belying Republican promises of tariff reform and particularly failing to reduce the rates on newsprint, evoked general disapprobation in the press. Taft, anxious to preserve the principle of protection while gesturing toward tariff reform, saw limited reciprocity as an answer to his difficulties and approached Laurier. The latter, also a prey to domestic pressures including renewed demands for reciprocity, responded favorably. Negotiation produced agreement, Jan. 26, 1911, providing (1) mutual free entry of most natural products; (2) lowered and identical rates on numerous manufactures; and (3) a loophole whereby free newsprint might be obtained. Two vigorous campaigns were thus launched. Defection of standpat party leaders and insurgent tariff reformers, plus his own easily misinterpreted statements, hampered Taft's effort. He triumphed in July 1910 through the aid of the Democratic opposition and a vocal press, pleased at the prospect of duty-free newsprint—a certainty regardless of Canada's action. Laurier's opposition, momentarily disconcerted, staved off adoption by an early vote and, forcing long discussion, eventually drove the Prime Minister to take the question to the country. The ensuing campaign rallied diverse forces of protectionism, Quebec racialism, patriotic devotion to Great Britain and thinly veneered anti-Americanism to defeat both Laurier and the agreement.   L. E. E.

CANADIAN-AMERICAN RELATIONS. The relations between Canada and the United States, and the influences of their people upon each other, have been conditioned both by geography and history. Within the historical field, however, political, diplomatic, economic, social, and intellectual factors have been so dependent upon each other that they are best considered within a single chronological framework. Also, since influences of the United States on Canada have been greater than those of Canada on the United States, it is necessary to give special emphasis to the former.

GEOGRAPHIC FEATURES AFFECTING RELATIONS

Inland Waterway Region. One of the conspicuous aspects of population distribution in North America is the concentration of people to the north and south of the Great Lakes-St. Lawrence waterway. To the north, about 60 per cent of Canada's population lives within 100 mi. of the waterway; to the south, within 300 mi. are more than half of the people of the United States. This concentration around interlinking bodies of water through which runs the international boundary has been a prime factor in determining Canadian-American relations. From the earliest days of colonial expansion, this great inland waterway has acted as a powerful magnet on both nations. Much of Canadian life, in fact, has come to revolve about a Montreal-Windsor axis. Both of these cities are located on this waterway, the former on the St. Lawrence, about 40 mi. from the international boundary; the latter on the Detroit River, only a mile from American territory. In the United States, the New York-Chicago axis has been hardly less dependent on the Great Lakes system. New York secured its eastern supremacy not so much from its port as from its principal river, the Hudson, which gave it easy access to Montreal by the Hudson-Richelieu gap, and to Lake Ontario and the west by the Hudson-Mohawk route. From Lake Ontario westward, the natural New York-Chicago route lay by the north (Canadian) shore of Lake Erie. Three American and two Canadian railway systems later connected Buffalo with Detroit across southwestern Ontario, despite the fact that two crossings of the international boundary were involved. In this area, therefore, the New York-Chicago axis actually coincides with the Canadian axis between Montreal and Windsor. The advantage derived by Chicago from its strategic position on the lakes is obvious.

Between Toledo and Quebec this inland waterway consists of Lake Erie, Lake Ontario, and the St. Lawrence River, which lie almost parallel with the Atlantic coast and from which they are separated by a land area ranging from 500 to 300 mi. in width. The rivers entering the Atlantic Ocean between Maryland and Maine flow mostly from the northwest, so that early settlers ascending their alluvial valleys moved toward Canada.

Close to the Great Lakes, in a broad arc from northern Minnesota to eastern Pennsylvania, vast resources of coal and iron have been developed. The very lack of corresponding coal deposits and, until lately, of iron ore in Canada has served to interlock Canadian and American industry in a unique way. In short, the Great Lakes boundary region has been a standing invitation to intercourse between the two nations. However, the concentration of population in this region has been due not merely to the rich resources of the area and the commercial advantages of the waterway. The so-called Canadian Shield, with its inhospitable soil and climate, has crowded the Canadian population southward against the American border. In the United States, on the other hand, the prevalence of the slave-operated plantation system, coupled with the northwesterly to southeasterly flow of rivers already noted, tended to direct American westward migration to the north of the Mason-Dixon Line and thus into the Great Lakes region. Old Virginia, under slavery, was at one point less than 90 mi. from Lake Erie.

The Remaining Boundary. To the east and west of this central section the international boundary region was quite different. To the east, the terrain between the centers of population in the Canadian maritime provinces of Nova Scotia, New Brunswick, and Prince Edward Island and the New England centers was, and still is, difficult and largely unproductive. Early contacts were possible only by sea. However, since Nova Scotia's Atlantic harbors are close to the great circle between American Atlantic ports and the ports of northern Europe, it was the sea, with its commerce and its fisheries, that drew the maritime provinces within New England's ambit.

With the exception of the Red River Valley no great concentrations of populations occur along the international boundary between Lake of the Woods, north of Minnesota,

and the Rocky Mountains. The sparseness of population in the boundary region between eastern Saskatchewan and western Alberta is particularly noticeable, this being the region where the northern lobe of what formerly was called the "Great American Desert" protrudes into Canada. On the Pacific Coast, however, lies Canada's third largest city, Vancouver. Less than 20 mi. from the American border, Vancouver's life is closely tied to the populous and fertile Puget Sound area by easy land and sea communications. Farther up the coast the Alaska panhandle landlocks the Canadian Yukon, so that all access to the Klondike gold fields from the Pacific is across American territory.

HISTORY OF RELATIONS

Early French-English Hostility. For the first century and a half of English and French settlement in North America the disposition toward intercolonial relations was conspicuously lacking. Between the English and French settlements lay a broad belt of rugged Appalachian highlands inhabited by Indians determined to resist encroachment from either side. Trade between the two groups was difficult, since the rigid mercantilist restrictions of both English and French empires made it illegal. Sometimes *coureurs de bois* brought furs surreptitiously to Albany, but in so doing they tended to ostracize themselves at Montreal and so were unable to act as go-betweens. The far-faring French missionaries did not even go to Albany. English traders, on the other hand, avoided the interior, so that the Hudson-Richelieu gap was effectively closed at both ends. To these barriers to intercourse were added those of language, economic and political institutions, and religion. Economic and social contacts between the two groups did not exist.

Although England and France were at peace with each other throughout most of the seventeenth century, England occupied Quebec from 1629 to 1632, and Acadia in 1613 and again from 1654 to 1670. However, with the accession of William III to the English throne in 1689, there began a succession of devastating wars, in all of which the American colonies were involved. These were, to give them their American names, King William's War, 1689-1697; Queen Anne's War, 1702-1713; King George's War, 1744-1748, and the French and Indian War, 1755-1763. During this era the English settlements had been slowly but steadily pushing inland, while the French pursued an active and grandiose policy of encirclement of the English settlements by building a line of forts to the southwest, from the St. Lawrence to the Gulf of Mexico. The persistent use by both sides of Indian allies frequently made the fighting cruel and bitter. The struggle became increasingly the vital concern of the colonists themselves as the fate of the warring colonies was equally involved with the fate of the rival empires. In fact, the last great struggle broke out not in Europe but in Pennsylvania, while Great Britain and France were still at peace.

By the Treaty of Utrecht in 1713, Great Britain acquired the peninsula of Nova Scotia from France. Far from ending the struggle in the Acadian region, this only served to intensify it by bringing the contestants closer to each other. Events during the next half-century were to show that New England was perhaps even more concerned than England with the outcome in Acadia. New Englanders gave vital aid in the reduction of the French fortress of Louisburg on Île Royale (now Cape Breton Island) in 1745, and in 1758, ten years after the island had been returned to the French by the Treaty of Aix, they helped to take it again. Meanwhile, in 1755, the mounting bitterness of the Acadians in Nova Scotia had been circumvented by the simple device of removing the Acadians. Their fertile dike-land farms were speedily taken over by New England immigrants, and Nova Scotia became "New England's out-post." In 1758 it acquired representative institutions.

Two notable results developed from the first hundred and fifty years of English-French relations in North America. The more conspicuous was the abiding dislike of the two groups for each other; the more significant was the feeling of cohesion within each of these groups resulting directly from the dangerous proximity of the other. The Albany Convention of 1754, even if unsuccessful, had been a clear sign that the English colonists, under the growing French and Indian menace, had taken the first step toward American union, and by 1763 the French Canadians were already on the threshold of a national entity. By 1763, therefore, two distinct peoples had emerged in North America. The French Canadians were, and have remained, foremost in insisting that the boundary between them and the United States remain international.

Effect of British Rule in Canada. With Great Britain's acquisition of Canada and the rest of Acadia by the Peace of Paris in 1763, one flag flew from the Gulf of Mexico to the Hudson Bay. This change, however, had surprisingly little effect upon the relations of the two colonial groups. The old hostility remained, as did also the old French imperial policy, to which the British fell heir. This policy had two main objectives: the strengthening and consolidation of French settlement along the St. Lawrence, and expansion from the St. Lawrence toward the southwest. Already in 1763 the American Revolution was casting a long shadow across Great Britain's path to empire, and it seemed advisable to insulate the French from the English colonists, the "new subjects" from the old. It also seemed desirable to set bounds to the expansion of the latter. The French language, the French civil law, and the Roman Catholic religion were given official recognition by the Quebec Act of 1774. This act also made new territorial provisions. The British Proclamation of 1763 had set aside the trans-Appalachian region as Indian country; the Quebec Act annexed to Quebec the entire northeastern quadrant of Louisiana, between the Ohio and Mississippi rivers. To the English colonies along the Atlantic, this action was merely a new phase of the old French menace, and for Canadians, also, an old danger simply assumed a new guise; the less sinister did British conquest appear, the more dangerous seemed the threat of American expansion.

Developments After the American Revolution. The first major change in Canadian-American relations came as a by-product of the American Revolution. Some 40,000 "Loyalists" streamed from the revolting colonies into British North America at the close of that struggle. About 7,000 went into the wilderness west of the French seigneuries, where later, in 1791, they founded the province of Upper Canada (now Ontario); the rest settled along the St. John River and on the peninsula of Nova Scotia. Those along the St. John River secured the separation of New Brunswick from Nova Scotia in 1784, and those going to the peninsula of Nova Scotia rapidly submerged the earlier New Englanders. The Loyalists, except the few who went to western Upper Canada, were predominantly Tory and Anglican, so that the second major contribution of the United States to Canada was Toryism. In this faith the provinces of Ontario and New Brunswick were founded.

The effect of the coming of the Loyalists on Canadian his-tory was obvious and profound. It meant that English-speaking Canadian traditions were to be grounded in a rugged and determined conservatism, and that French Catholic Canadian conservatism was henceforth to be at once reinforced and threatened from three sides. For the young American republic to the south, this mass exodus of so many of its most stalwart conservatives also had meaning. The going of these refugees helped in the process of converting the doctrine of the right of revolution from the tenet of a minority into a national credo, of which the form, more than the content, was later to be altered by the American Civil War.

The period following the American Revolution was one of uncertainty on both sides of the international line. Hatred of British imperialism had united the colonies during the war, but more was needed to unite them in peace. Although the United States acquired by the Treaty of Paris in 1783 the entire region east of the Mississippi, British forces continued to be stationed in the old Northwest, and Canadian traders continued to operate there. Indian attacks on American frontier settlements were regularly attributed to British-Canadian support. The complete withdrawal of British control in this Ohio-Mississippi area was provided for in Jay's Treaty of 1794 and was completed by 1800. The base for this British control had, of course, been Quebec. Nor did the attempt of the British to tap the trade of the old Northwest cease with the withdrawal of British troops.

War of 1812 and After. In British North America, and particularly in Upper Canada, the situation became confused by the steady stream of pioneering American immigrants pouring into the provinces in the wake of the Loyalist migration. By the outbreak of the War of 1812 these later American migrants had come to outnumber the Loyalists in Upper Canada by at least five to one. Upper Canada was still completely American in population, but it now contained two kinds of Americans. Neither group, however, gave any substantial support to the American invasion in 1812, both disapproving of this new phase of American westward expansion. But neither did they give much support to the 25,000 British regulars, and total enlistment in the militia in both Upper and Lower Canada was under 5,000. The tradition of Canada's successful repulsion of American invasion has persisted, however, and has powerfully reinforced the earlier Loyalist tradition, which was distinctly anti-American.

After the Treaty of Ghent in 1814 attention in both countries became increasingly drawn to economic development. While British engineers, at United Kingdom expense and in the interest of Upper Canadian defense, were building the costly Rideau Canal to circumvent the St. Lawrence between Montreal and Kingston, Upper Canadians were building the Welland Canal at their own expense to lure western American traffic into the Great Lakes-St. Lawrence channel. The Welland Canal was completed in 1829, but already it had been anticipated by the state of New York, which had completed its Erie Canal in 1825. The completion of the St. Lawrence canals was still beyond the powers of the two separate Canadian provinces. With the 1840's, however, came three events of good import for Canadian trade with the American West. In 1841 the two provinces were united under the name of United Canada, and in the same year the British provided a large loan for Canadian internal improvements. This fund enabled Canada to complete its St. Lawrence canal system for use of vessels up to a nine-foot draft by 1850. In 1843 the British Parliament passed an act admitting into the United Kingdom, as Canadian, all flour ground in Canada whether from American or Canadian grain. However, these moves to divert American trade into Canadian channels were countered by the American Congress, which in 1845 and 1846 passed acts providing for the free bonding of all goods passing between British North America and Europe across American territory. Shortly after this the last links in a railway chain between New York and Chicago were completed, giving these two centers easy access to each other in winter as well as summer. Meanwhile, the British had abolished their Corn Laws in 1846, and their Navigation Acts in 1849. All of Canada's economic advantage from imperial connection seemed to be suddenly at an end. In despair at the collapse of their elaborate and costly plan, the leading Montreal Tory businessmen signed in 1849 an "Annexation Manifesto" urging union with the United States. Economic frustration demanded action. Two other solutions offered hope: one was railway building, the other was reciprocity of trade with the United States. In the 1850's both of these closely integrated solutions were attempted.

New Trend in Political Relations. Meanwhile, also, new patterns had been emerging in the political relations of the two countries. In 1817 the Rush-Bagot Agreement to limit naval armaments on Lake Champlain and the Great Lakes had been signed. This agreement still stands and has become the symbol of peace between the two countries. In 1818 the boundary between the Lake of the Woods and the Rocky Mountains had been fixed along the forty-ninth parallel; joint occupancy had been provided for west of the Rockies. In the same year, far to the east, an agreement had been reached on American fishery rights along the British North American coasts. These settlements had substantially lessened the international tension resulting from the War of 1812. On the other hand, the effect of the steady penetration of radical American political ideas into the British provinces, particularly Upper Canada, during the 1820's and 1830's had not been so conducive to harmony. Jacksonian Democracy, in fact, had become one of the mainsprings of the Canadian Rebellion of 1837, and considerable encouragement and even some armed help had come from the United States. But the rebellion had failed dismally, and radicalism in Canada had received a heavy blow. The anti-Americanism of the Tories had been intensified, but the Reformers had emerged as the real legatees of the rebellion; they drew their inspiration, not from American democracy, but from British liberalism.

In the 1840's, along both eastern and western ends of the international boundary, dangerous tensions arose. The "Aroostook War" led to the signing of the Webster-Ashburton Treaty, 1842, settling the undetermined part of the eastern boundary. In the West, the Oregon Treaty, 1846, ended the joint occupancy of the region west of the Rockies by continuing the line along the forty-ninth parallel to the Pacific Ocean. Settlement of the boundary question was necessitated by the threat involved in the Democratic Party's slogan in the American presidential campaign of 1844 of "fifty-four forty or fight."

Relations from 1850 to 1861. In the 1850's American attention became distracted from the Canadian border by growing internal difficulties in the South. Nevertheless, Canada's governor-general, James Bruce, Earl of Elgin, secured in 1854 the signing of the Elgin-Marcy Reciprocity Treaty, which was duly ratified by the American Senate and the legislatures in Canada and the Maritime Provinces, and came into operation in 1855. This agreement granted shipping of both the United States and the British provinces free use of the St. Lawrence and the Great Lakes, together with all of the canals owned by the governments involved. It gave Americans access to all inshore fishing grounds of the British provinces. It also provided for the complete removal of import duties on all of the chief natural products of each country on entering the other. Trade between the British provinces and the United States quickly responded to the new stimulus, soon doubling in volume and remaining at this high level until the outbreak of the American Civil War in 1861.

Partly in anticipation of this speeding up of trade, the British provinces had already begun extensive railway building programs. Whereas, in 1849, there had been only 66 mi. of railway in all of the provinces, by 1860 there were more than 2,000 mi., mostly in the province of Canada. Four main lines were constructed in this province: one from Rivière de Loup, below Quebec, to Sarnia, opposite Port Huron, Mich.; another from Montreal to Portland, Me.; a third from Toronto to Collingwood, on Georgian Bay; and a fourth from Fort Erie, opposite Buffalo, to Windsor, opposite Detroit. The international purposes behind the building of these lines were evident enough.

Effects of American Civil War. The outbreak of the American Civil War in 1861 caused only a temporary decline in trade between British North America and the United States, and before the end of the war in 1865 this trade had reached an all-time high. But as trade increased, good relations declined. Early in the war this was mostly the indirect result of deteriorating Anglo-American relations, at once reflected in and aggravated by Queen Victoria's neutrality proclamation, the North's blockade of the South, the Trent Affair, and other incidents. Also, as the war progressed, there were an increasing number of irritating border incidents that affected the relations of the United States and British North America directly. These, for the most part, were connected on the one hand with the persistent attempt to force men in British North America into service in the Northern armies, and on the other hand with the failure of Canada to prevent Confederate agents from using provincial bases for raids into the United States, notably the St. Albans raid of 1864. Before the war was over, feeling in the United States had reached such a height that some leading American newspapers were making threats not only of abrogating the Reciprocity Treaty but also of annexing British North America as soon as the war was over. The first of these threats was carried out in 1865, bringing the Reciprocity Treaty to an end in 1866. The second, that of annexation, was a real menace to the very existence of British North America until the signing of the Treaty of Washington in 1871.

The American Civil War had resulted in a decided rise of the American tariff scale from its previous moderately protective levels. The imminent prospect of the end of the reciprocal trade agreement of 1854 had brought the British provinces to an economic impasse. In casting about for an alternative trade outlet, provincial leaders were led to consider the improvement of interprovincial trade, which so far had been of inconsiderable proportions. A mere customs union might have sufficed, but a close political union seemed to offer the double advantage of offsetting not only the economic threat of the United States but the threat of political extinction as well. The Quebec Conference of 1864 and the resultant British North America Act of 1867 were direct results of this feeling. The Dominion of Canada came into existence under the ominous shadow of a victorious North.

Not only did the American Civil War help to precipitate

the creation of the dominion, it was also a prime determinant of the form of the dominion constitution. Fear of American aggression, which was heightened by the Fenian movement, seemed to demand a union as closely knit as the centrifugal forces within the provinces would permit. Paradoxically enough, the fear of American strength was coupled in British North American minds with the apparent weakness in the United States Constitution shown by the fact of the Civil War. The United States Constitution thus served as both model and warning in the drafting of the Canadian Constitution. The Canadian federal government was given power to appoint all provincial governors, all federal senators, and all judges; it was also given a blanket right of veto on provincial legislation. The federal Parliament was given the residuum of power. In general, the aim was to make Canada a more perfect union.

Tense Relations of the New Dominion. The formation of the dominion did little immediately to relieve the international tension. Fenian raids continued. What did eventually alleviate the strain was the negotiation in 1871 of the Treaty of Washington, which settled most of the outstanding grievances on both sides. The rights of the United States in the British Atlantic fisheries were restored to what they had been under the Reciprocity Treaty; fish and fish products were again to have free entry from one country to the other; and the St. Lawrence River was to be perpetually free to the shipping of both countries. Unfortunately for good Canadian-American relations, the problem of reparations to Canada for Fenian depredations was left untouched. The strain between the new dominion and the older republic was thus alleviated but not removed.

The tension was further increased by the failure of the United States to lower the tariff schedule which had been in effect during the American Civil War. With minor deviations, the tariff remained at a threateningly high level throughout the rest of the nineteenth century. At first Canada attempted to circumvent this barrier by securing a renewal of the reciprocity agreement of 1854. Failing in this, it erected a frankly retaliatory tariff wall in 1879, following the adoption of a "National Policy" in 1878. This new policy in turn required a reorientation of Canadian railway policy. It was on British insistence that the Intercolonial Railway, completed in 1876, had been circuitously and expensively constructed along the north shore of New Brunswick. It was by Canada's own decision that the Canadian Pacific Railway between Montreal and Vancouver, completed in 1885, was run less circuitously but much more expensively to the north of Lake Superior. Thus, Canada's persistent railway problems have grown by implication out of the National Policy, which in turn resulted from strained Canadian-American relations.

By 1867 the Dominion of Canada extended only from Nova Scotia to Ontario. By 1871 it reached from the Atlantic to the Pacific. This sudden and spectacular expansion was also in large measure the result of conditions in the United States. In 1850, Minnesota had had a population of only 6,000; by 1870 its population had reached 440,000. The most attractive part of this new state was the upper Red River Valley. The lower Red River Valley, which lay across the international boundary and was still part of the property and the exclusive domain of the Hudson's Bay Company, contained in 1870 less than 2,000 white inhabitants. It thus became apparent that if this part of the valley were not to be overwhelmed by the wave of American migration, its political status would have to be altered radically and quickly. At any moment rebellious half-breeds under Louis Riel might be joined by the Fenians already massing just across the border, only 60 mi. up the river from Fort Garry (now Winnipeg). In 1870, therefore, the whole of the Hudson's Bay Company preserves were annexed to Canada, and simultaneously the handful of white settlers on the lower Red River found themselves in the tiny but full-fledged province of Manitoba. Similar danger of absorption into the United States hastened the entry of the colony of British Columbia into the Dominion in 1871.

Direct American influence on western Canada did not end with the establishment of these provinces. The Canadian western homestead system was based largely on the American Homestead Act of 1862, and even reproduced the American rectangular survey method, with its meridians, thirty-six-mile-square townships, and mile-square sections. Slightly less use was made of American experience in the administration of territorial areas. In the development of western agricultural techniques, the borrowing was, and has remained, substantial and mutual.

Interlocking of Railways. Despite the determination of American and Canadian authorities to keep their economic policies aimed at national self-sufficiency, the two policies became increasingly intertwined during the last decade and a half of the nineteenth century. This was at once the cause and effect of increased railway interlocking. The Canadian Pacific Railway had no sooner completed its expensive line north of Lake Superior than it began to acquire possession, or at least control, of lines in the United States that would short-circuit its own north shore route. Thus the Soo Line was acquired in 1890, and by 1893 was extended to tap the main Canadian Pacific line at Moose Jaw, Saskatchewan. By 1903 the Canadian Pacific had direct connection between Winnipeg and St. Paul, and by 1909, by acquiring both the South Shore line and a dominant interest in the Wisconsin Central Railway, it had secured two alternative routes to the east in addition to its main north shore line. Meanwhile, in 1889, it had, by purchase and construction, completed connection between Montreal and Saint John, New Brunswick, across the state of Maine. The Great Northern and the Northern Pacific railways were, in turn, building energetically into the western Canadian area, and further interpenetration was taking place in the Montreal area and in southwestern Ontario. There was, in fact, a brief interval toward the end of the nineteenth century when railways were being built for economic rather than for political reasons. The spectacular development of motor highway construction eventually brought an end to the era of railway construction, first in the United States, later in Canada. By this time, however, Canadian railways had come to own or control over 7,000 mi. of trackage in the United States, and American lines over 1,500 mi. in Canada. In all, there were about 50 rail gateways between the two countries. When, following World War II, the expansion of mining in northern Canada called for renewal of railway construction, this too was closely linked with the American market.

Mass Migrations and Their Effects. The Dominion of Canada had been born in 1867 in fear, but also in hope. Subsequent events in the United States had soon dissipated the fear, but other conditions had helped to destroy the hope. On both sides of the boundary there was a tendency in newly settled areas to equate progress with population growth. Unfortunately for Canadian morale, there was also a natural tendency to measure the growth of Canadian population by comparing it with growth in the United States. After 1867, Canada's population had grown with distressing slowness, and even the opening up of the West and the costly construction of the Canadian Pacific Railway had produced meager results. Canadian economy did not show resilience to the cyclic depressions of 1873, 1882, and 1893. European immigrants showed a decided preference for the United States, and many of those coming to Canada later moved south. But the most distressing fact was that throughout the period from 1867 to 1896 Canada was losing to the United States an alarming proportion of its native-born population, and that these expatriates were going from all sections of the dominion, even from the new West. Between 1861 and 1901, while Canada's native-born population increased by only 86 per cent, the Canadian-born element in the United States increased by 372 per cent. By the end of the century no less than 20 per cent of all of Canada's native-born people were living in the United States. This condition could scarcely be matched by any European country, with the possible exception of Ireland.

The effect of this mass migration on Canada was obvious; its influence on American life is more difficult to gauge. Except for the French Canadians, these migrants adapted themselves to their new environment more easily and quickly than other American immigrant groups. In the cities near the border to which most of them went they shortly became indistinguishable from the American native-born. Undoubtedly, however, their net influence was in the direction of conservatism and stability.

Relations from 1896 to 1938. In 1896 a Republican president was elected in the United States, and in that same year a Canadian general election brought the Liberals into power, with Wilfrid Laurier, a Roman Catholic and French Canadian, as prime minister. More significant, perhaps, was the simultaneous upswing of economic life in both countries. Despite the double defense of American and Canadian protective tariff walls, trade between the two countries grew amazingly, with only slight recessions in the 1920's and a major recession in the depressed 1930's. Canadian imports from the United States increased from $54,000,000 in 1896 to well over a billion dollars during World War II. Canadian exports in the same period grew from $38,000,000 to over $900,000,000. Following the reciprocal trade agreement of 1935, Canada was for the first time able to replace the United Kingdom as the United States' best customer. Canada became increasingly dependent on American products, e.g., petroleum and citrus fruits; the United States on Canadian wood pulp, nickel, and asbestos.

The course of political relations after 1896 was not at first so propitious. Again, as in the American Civil War period, this was partly due to deteriorating Anglo-American relations. The Venezuela boundary dispute, the Boer War, and rising American imperialism played their part, but the low point in Canadian-American relations was reached in the Alaska boundary dispute. After 1903, however, relations began slowly but steadily to improve. The creation in 1909 of a department of external affairs at Ottawa, and the establishment in the following year of a permanent International Joint Commission considerably improved the machinery for handling the relations of the two countries. In 1910 the North Atlantic fisheries award finally laid to rest an old source of irritation. The Canadian rejection of the United States' offer of reciprocity in 1911 was only a temporary setback, somewhat offset by the favorable American (Underwood) tariff of 1913. Differing attitudes toward World War I between 1914 and 1917, and following 1918, helped indirectly to establish American recognition of Canada's independent national existence.

Canada's growing national consciousness after World War

I, coupled with the increase in international trade, the rising volume of tourist traffic passing across the border in both directions, and the multitude of problems involved in the enforcement of prohibition in the United States, united in 1927 to produce the first direct diplomatic contacts between the two countries, marked by the establishment of United States and Canadian legations at Ottawa and Washington, respectively. Already, of course, Canadians had been taking an increasing part in support of the United Kingdom diplomatic service, and in 1923 Canada had actually signed the North Pacific Fisheries Treaty on its own behalf, accepting no aid from the mother country except the use of its seal. The Statute of Westminster of 1931 left Canada in exclusive control of its own external affairs.

World War II and After. Hardly had Canada secured from Great Britain the right to stand on its own feet than it began to receive the offer of a helping hand from the United States. At Kingston, Ontario, in 1938, President Franklin D. Roosevelt assured Canada that the United States "would not stand idly by" if Canada were threatened. World War II already was threatening the world's peace. In 1940 the Ogdensburg Agreement was published, envisaging the co-ordination of Canadian and American defense policies and administration. The Alaska highway (Alcan) was one conspicuous result. Construction of a deep-sea waterway linking the St. Lawrence and the Great Lakes and providing further economic and defensive ties between the two countries was the goal of an agreement signed in March 1941. In 1957 this giant hydroelectric and navigation international project was nearing completion.

Meanwhile, after 1896 the former migration pattern, with a steady movement southward and no corresponding movement northward, had come to an end. Partly as a result of the construction of two additional transcontinental railways across Canada, the Grand Trunk Pacific and Canadian Northern, the West had begun to attract immigrants, particularly a rising volume from the American West. By 1913 this American migration had reached an annual total of 140,000, but the volume remained substantial until 1921. After 1931 it fell to insignificant proportions. Unlike the Canadian southward movement, which also continued in substantial volume until the depression of the 1930's, this American migration was almost wholly agricultural. In the Canadian West, the Americans made a valuable contribution to agriculture, particularly in relation to dry-farming technique; they also added an infectious buoyancy to western Canadian life. Their presence was more slowly noticeable in the field of Canadian politics.

Following World War II, Canadian migration to the United States speedily resumed substantial proportions. This time, in addition to the disproportionate number of professional men and women, the movement included a large proportion of skilled technicians and craftsmen. The reverse movement of Americans to Canada remained insignificant. Canada, however, became of increasing interest to Americans, and the tourist trade became one of the country's major industries. American capital investments in Canada, which by 1923 had come to exceed the total investment of all other countries in Canada, continued to mount. Despite Canada's large adverse trade balance with the United States, Canadian currency had by 1957 reached a premium of about 5 per cent over the American dollar. But most significant, perhaps, was the fact that in a profoundly troubled world Canada had come to be viewed by Americans as a country whose destiny had become inextricably interwoven with their own.   W. M. W.

CANADIAN ASSOCIATION FOR ADULT EDU-CATION, a group founded in 1935 to serve as a national co-ordinating body and general clearinghouse of information for agencies and individuals working in the field of adult education in Canada. The Association publishes a magazine, *Food for Thought,* conducts a study and research program, sponsors demonstrations, experiments, training projects, and institutes, and carries on an extensive publications program. Three times a year it brings together various national organizations through its Joint Planning Commission. It sponsors jointly with the Canadian Broadcasting Corporation a radio and television public affairs program, *Citizens' Forum.* It has been especially active in advancing the educational use of mass media, including films, radio, and television. Funds are provided by member organizations, individuals, departments of government, and foundation grants.

G. Bu.

CANADIAN LITERATURE. The development of a significant body of Canadian literature has been impeded by many factors lying beyond the control of the individual artist. The English-speaking reading public in Canada has always been small and, until recently, subject to the strong pull of overseas ties. For the greater part of the nineteenth century native critics and most native writers seem to have shared Matthew Arnold's view that talk of a distinctive English-Canadian literature was absurd; and English writing in Canada was generally characterized by close adherence to the literary models and ideals of the mother country. Toward the end of the century the colonial spirit tended to give way to one equally obstructive to the development of a good literature, a shrill-voiced nationalism that demanded that the writer be aggressively "Canadian," that he "paint the maple" and employ only Canadian themes. Happily, there are evidences in contemporary literature that the colonial spirit is almost wholly dead and petty nationalism no longer a significant force. The concern of contemporary writers to achieve universal effects, and the steady growth of an increasingly independent reading public, suggest that a Canadian literature worthy of international recognition may be developing.

ENGLISH-CANADIAN LITERATURE

Poetry. The Canadian poetry written in English in the years immediately following the fall of New France was in no sense native literature. The heavy-handed political satire of Jonathan Odell (1737-1818) and his fellow loyalists reflects nothing of the new environment. The loyalist poets were concerned only with affirming their fidelity to the king and attacking, in labored heroic couplets, the country from which they were exiles. The first poem that may correctly be called native literature was not written until early in the nineteenth century. In 1825 Oliver Goldsmith (1781-1861), a native of Nova Scotia, published *The Rising Village,* a professed imitation of *The Deserted Village* of his illustrious granduncle. Written in smooth-flowing monotonous heroic couplets, *The Rising Village* is of little intrinsic worth, but it is to be remembered as the first English-Canadian poem that shows unmistakably the influence of the local environment.

During the nineteenth century the influence of old-country models was marked in Canadian poetry. In the pre-Confederation period the prevailing models were neoclassic. The first poet to exhibit traditional Romantic characteristics in his work was Charles Sangster (1822-1893). Sangster records his impressions of the native scene in two volumes of lyrics, which, though written long after Romanticism was a spent force in England, are imitative in spirit and technique of the poetry of Wordsworth and Byron. Sangster was the first of the long line of Canadian poets who have found their inspiration almost wholly in nature.

Charles Mair (1838-1927) extended the range of native poetry to include themes drawn from Canadian history. His most ambitious work, *Tecumseh: A Drama,* is an attempt to describe in chronicle verse form the western movement of the white man. Charles Heavysege (1816-1876) is remembered as the author of a lengthy closet drama, *Saul,* which won high praise from many contemporary men of letters including Emerson, Hawthorne, and Coventry Patmore; and in recent years there has been some revival of interest in Heavysege's work. He was neither slavishly imitative of conventional models nor aggressively national in spirit. In his best poems he achieved a degree of universality seldom attained by any of his contemporaries.

In the history of English-Canadian literature the greatest formative influence has been exerted by the "Group of the Sixties." Its leading members were Charles G. D. Roberts, Bliss Carman, Archibald Lampman and Duncan Campbell Scott, all of whom were born in Canada between 1860 and 1862. For good or ill these writers stamped Canadian poetry with a distinctive design that impelled wide imitation. Of the group, Roberts and Carman enjoyed until recently the greatest reputation; but the trend of contemporary taste and criticism suggests that there is more of permanent value in the work of their less flamboyant associates, Lampman and Scott. Archibald Lampman (1861-1899), born and educated in Ontario, was by profession a civil servant. He published two volumes of poems, and in 1900, the year after his untimely death, his collected verse was issued with a sensitive memoir by his friend Duncan Campbell Scott. The influence of Keats is apparent in much of Lampman's work; he is a poet of sensations rather than ideas. His best poems are a happy blend of appropriate traditional techniques and native themes. Lampman was the first Canadian poet to show that effective treatment of native materials does not involve the rejection of Classical form. Charles G. D. Roberts (1860-1943) was for over half a century a colorful dominant personality in Canadian literature. Born in "the cradle of Canadian poetry," Fredericton, New Brunswick, Roberts was at his best when recording his sensitive appreciation of the beauties of his native province. But his interests were not merely regional; he was the first Canadian poet by whom the note of national self-consciousness was unmistakably sounded. *Canada* and *An Ode for the Canadian Confederacy* voice almost stridently a citizen's pride in his native land. Most of his poetry written after 1900 was vaguely transcendental in spirit, but Roberts was not a profound thinker, and his philosophical poems are almost uniformly superficial. It seems likely that, except for a few early nature pieces, Roberts will be remembered not as a poet but as the author of some of the best animal stories ever written. Bliss Carman (1861-1929), like his cousin, Charles G. D. Roberts, was born in Fredericton. He was the most fluent of Canadian poets, and once the most popular, but not much of his work is remembered today. At his best Carman wrote some fine lyrics, for he was unusually sensitive to the impressions of nature and the music of words. But the adolescent neo-paganism and pseudophilosophical pretentiousness that mar much of his later poetry have made Carman unpalatable to present-day tastes, and his reputation has suffered the most marked decline of all the members of the group. But it is likely that a few of his earlier lyrics such as *The Ships of Yule* and *Low Tide On Grand Pré* in which his lyric note is at its purest, will continue to be read. Duncan Campbell Scott (1862-1947) was born in Ottawa. Like Lampman he entered the civil service, where he had a distinguished career, becoming head of the Department of Indian Affairs. His poems have been published in nine volumes, including the *Collected Poems* (1926). Much of Scott's poetry is a recording of the impressions of natural scenery, but unlike his fellows of the Group of the Sixties, Scott was inspired by nature in its wilder aspects. Nor was Scott wholly preoccupied with nature themes. His work in the Department of Indian Affairs enabled him to study thoroughly the Indian character and customs, and these are recorded in his poetry more accurately and effectively than anywhere else in Canadian literature. Scott's reputation now stands higher than that of any other of the group, though he was for long overshadowed by the swashbuckling personalities of Roberts and Carman, and it seems likely that he will be enduringly remembered as the author of several of the finest poems written on the American continent, notably the long ballad, *The Piper of Arll*, which profoundly influenced John Masefield, and the deeply moving elegy, *The Closed Door*, inspired by intense personal bereavement.

The work of Isabella Valancy Crawford (1850-1887), the author of some unorthodox lyrics of fine intensity, and of George Frederick Cameron (1854-1885), whose poetry, like that of Heavysege, was neither self-consciously national nor slavishly derivative, also deserves mention.

The poetry of the early twentieth century continued, in the main, to be traditional in form and spirit. Francis Sherman (1871-1926), a native of Fredericton, New Brunswick, was strongly influenced by the Pre-Raphaelites; and Marjorie Pickthall (1883-1922) came under the spell of the Celtic Twilight. At her best Miss Pickthall wrote lyrics of a pure singing quality unsurpassed in Canadian literature, and she made effective use of local character and environment.

Since World War I Canadian poetry has made some progress towards a greater maturity. Contemporary writers are concerned, as their predecessors seldom were, with intellectual content, and much of their poetry is in a cosmopolitan rather than a national tradition. Such writers as Robert Finch (1900-   ), A. J. M. Smith (1902-   ), Earl Birney (1904-   ), Leo Kennedy (1907-   ), and A. M. Klein (1909-   ) have done much to dispel the widely held conception of Canadian poetry as being almost wholly concerned with celebrating the beauties of local scenery in orthodox verse forms. Of these poets A. M. Klein is a truly international figure. Indicative, too, of the existence in Canada of an enlarged conception of the nature of poetry is the fact that the most popular of living Canadian poets, E. J. Pratt (1883-   ), is little concerned with facets of national life or scenery. Pratt, a native Newfoundlander, is a poet of the sea and the most original voice in Canadian literature. His themes include storm and shipwreck and seal hunting and underwater battles in the deep. He is a superb narrative poet, unconventional in style, unorthodox in subject matter; and his work is infused with an exuberant delight, which is expressed in words reminiscent of the great Elizabethans.

Prose Fiction. The development of the novel in Canada, like that of poetry, has been hindered by the timidity of native writers who until rather recently had been satisfied to imitate established old-country and American models. In fairness to the novelist it must be said that he, even more than the poet, has been handicapped by the lack of a large reading public in Canada. In trying to reach readers outside his own country, he has not unnaturally tended to imitate the best-seller in the United States and abroad.

The first novel written in Canada was the work of Frances Brooke (1724-1789), a talented English bluestocking of Dr.

Johnson's circle, who, as wife of a military chaplain, lived in Quebec city for a few years after the fall of New France. Quebec was the scene of some of the action of her most popular novel, *The History of Emily Montague*. But Major John Richardson (1796-1852) was the first truly native novelist. His most successful work, *Wacousta* (1832), which has for its subject the conspiracy of Pontiac, is the pioneer English-Canadian historical novel, the first of a long and undistinguished line. Writing in emulation of James Fenimore Cooper, Richardson exhibits all the defects and few of the virtues of his model. In *Wacousta* the background is at times adequately realized, but the dialogue is stilted and unconvincing and most of the fictitious incidents palpably absurd.

Thomas Chandler Haliburton (1796-1865) was the most important Canadian writer of fiction in the nineteenth century. A celebrated figure in the early life of Nova Scotia, Haliburton won literary renown through his creation of the character of Sam Slick, the smart Yankee, who wins his way by "soft sawder" and his knowledge of human nature. According to Justin McCarthy, the sayings of Sam Slick once rivaled in popularity those of Sam Weller. Haliburton had little sense of form, and his Sam Slick sketches cannot be said to constitute a true novel; but he was the creator of the most memorable character in Canadian fiction, one who provoked wide imitation in the United States.

In spite of Haliburton's excellent use of local types and situations, the historical novel remained the form dearest to the English-Canadian fiction writer. William Kirby (1817-1906) drew his inspiration from Dumas, and his one novel, *The Golden Dog*, which has for its background "the death agony of New France," is a faithful and highly popular imitation of Dumas at his most melodramatic. Gilbert Parker (1862-1932), though born in Ontario, spent the greater part of his life in England, where for eighteen years he was a member of the House of Commons. In *The Seats of the Mighty* (1896), *When Valmond Came to Pontiac* (1895), and other works, Parker followed the tradition established by Richardson and Kirby. These novels for a time enjoyed great vogue on both sides of the Atlantic, but Parker's reputation has suffered a great decline. Like his predecessors, Parker inclined too often to melodrama, and his characters were seldom more than puppets.

The most popular of all Canadian novelists is Charles W. Gordon (1860-1937), who wrote under the pseudonym, "Ralph Connor." For a time a missionary in the west, Gordon was the first writer to realize the literary possibilities in the material provided by the settlement of the Canadian frontier. First and always a preacher, he dramatized his message with skill and sincerity, bringing to life a score of types—the prospector, the remittance man, the mountie—which are now commonplaces in American literature. His best-known works include *Black Rock* (1898), *The Sky Pilot* (1899), *The Doctor* (1906), which are in part autobiographical, and two stirring tales of the Northwest Mounted Police, *Corporal Cameron of the Northwest Mounted Police* (1912) and *The Patrol of the Sundance Trail* (1915). Gordon was the first Canadian novelist who, employing purely Canadian themes, was able to make a substantial living from his pen. His books have sold over five million copies and even today are rarely out of print.

In spite of occasional earlier evidences of talent among Canadian novelists, it was not until the 1920's that the Canadian novel showed some signs of maturity. The novelists of the 1920's took their artistic responsibilities more seriously than their predecessors and wrote a few books with claims to distinction. Laura Goodman Salverson (1890-   ), a Canadian of Icelandic descent, told the story of Icelandic emigrants to Canada in *The Viking Heart,* a novel which has been many times reprinted. Robert J. C. Stead (1880-), put to excellent use his knowledge of western ranch and farm life in several novels, at least one of which, *Grain,* is an undeviatingly faithful record of life on a western wheat farm. Alan Sullivan (1866-1947), whose book of tales of the far north, *Northern Lights,* has become a textbook, wrote many plays, novels, and poems on Canadian themes, notably *The Great Divide* and *Three Came to Ville Marie,* as well as religious and other plays, including *And From That Day* and *The Jade God.* Frederick Philip Grove (1871-1948), who came to Canada from Sweden in young manhood, brought to the contemplation of the prairie scene a cultured and philosophical mind. The best of Grove's novels, *Our Daily Bread* and *Fruits of the Earth,* are reminiscent of Hardy in their evocation of somber sentient landscape; but Grove is hardly likely to live as a novelist, since, in spite of his great literary gifts, he was unable to create believable characters.

The writings of Mrs. Salverson, Stead, and Grove give promise, as yet unfulfilled, of the development in western Canada of a vigorous regional culture. In eastern Canada Mazo de la Roche (1885-) came into prominence with the publication in 1927 of the first of the "Jalna" series, of which there are now fourteen volumes. There is nothing distinctively regional or national about Miss de la Roche's work. Her appeal is international, her novels distinguished not by a faithful recording of the native scene but by a remarkable ability to evoke her characters. Of all present-day English-Canadian writers Miss de la Roche enjoys the widest reputation abroad. Of the other Canadian novelists who established themselves in the 1920's, Morley Callaghan (1903-), is outstanding. His novels, such as *Strange Fugitive* (1928) and *They Shall Inherit the Earth* (1935), are the first in Canadian literature to reveal a strong vein of social consciousness. Callaghan's style is at times strongly imitative of that of his master, Ernest Hemingway; but his best work is characterized by a degree of artistic sophistication seldom equaled by his contemporaries. Unfortunately, Callaghan has never secured in Canada either the recognition or the sales that his unusual talents merit.

Callaghan is the forerunner of the novelists who within the last few years have sounded, though not always clearly, a new note of seriousness. Although the historical novel continues to be popular and has found its finest native exponents in Frederick Niven (1878-1944) and Thomas Raddall (1903), the "social problem" novel has also been most vigorously developed and has received popular approval. Gwethalyn Graham (1913-) has achieved international reputation through her romantic treatment of the problem of anti-Semitism in *Earth and High Heaven;* and Hugh MacLennan (1907-) deals impressively in *Two Solitudes* with the duality of the Canadian people. Among western Canadian writers Sinclair Ross (1908-) deserves special mention. His one novel, *As For Me And My House,* portrays realistically life in a small prairie town during the hungry 1930's.

The short story has never gained an important place in Canadian literature, possibly because of the lack of sufficient periodicals in Canada to make its cultivation financially worthwhile. The animal stories of Charles G. D. Roberts are among the first and best of the genre; but Roberts has had no successors of equal competence. In the 1930's Morley Callaghan wrote some fine stories, which, like his novels, are sophisticated in technique and infused with a strong sense of social consciousness; and Sinclair Ross in a few short dramatic tales has caught superbly the spirit of contemporary prairie life. The most successful of contemporary short-story writers is Thomas Raddall, who writes in the tradition of Stevenson and Quiller-Couch.

Essays and Literary Criticism. The dearth of good literary journals in Canada has led to the discouragement of the essay. Most English-Canadian literary periodicals have been short lived, and writing for them usually has been a labor of love. The first literary journal of consequence, *The Nova Scotian,* was founded by one of Canada's most distinguished statesmen, Joseph Howe (1804-1873). While ostensibly a newspaper, *The Nova Scotian* found room in its columns for Haliburton's Sam Slick series, and Howe's own essays, *The Nova Scotian in England, Eastern Rambles,* and *Western Rambles.* Howe's essays are generally rhetorical in tone, and the best of them reflects a good deal of their author's colorful and vigorous personality.

W. H. Blake (1861-1924) is best known for his superb translation of Louis Hémon's *Marie Chapdelaine;* but his descriptive essays, *Brown Waters and Other Sketches* and *A Fisherman's Creed,* are among the best ever written in praise of angling and the country life. Sir Andrew MacPhail (1864-1938) edited *The University Magazine,* the most distinguished of Canadian literary periodicals, and was himself a frequent contributor to it. MacPhail's keen mind and vigorous style are admirably exemplified in his three volumes of collected essays, *Essays in Puritanism, Essays in Politics, Essays in Fallacy.*

The most original essayist in Canadian literature, and certainly the most popular, was Stephen Leacock (1869-1944). Many of Leacock's essays, sketches, and burlesques belong to the ephemera of literature; but his *Sunshine Sketches of a Little Town* (1912), a wholly delightful evocation of the atmosphere of an Ontario small town at the turn of the century, seems likely to be an enduring classic of humor. *My Discovery of England* (1922), *Nonsense Novels* (1911), an admirable burlesque of popular literary styles, and *Behind the Beyond* (1913) are others of Leacock's volumes which have won wide and deserved popularity. There is nothing subtle about Leacock's technique; his work abounds in situations conceived in the most outrageously slapstick spirit, but in one or two of the "Sunshine Sketches," at least, he has created characters worthy of a place in the great English comic tradition.

Literary criticism has so far achieved little stature in Canada, although some competent work has appeared in such contemporary literary journals as the *Canadian Forum* and the university publications, *The Dalhousie Review, Queen's Quarterly,* and *The University of Toronto Quarterly.* A few volumes of criticism have appeared that are worthy of note, including *A History of English-Canadian Literature to the Confederation* (1920), by Ray Palmer Baker; *Headwaters of Canadian Literature* (1924), by Archibald MacMechan; *The White Savannahs,* by W. E. Collin; and *On Canadian Poetry* (1943), by E. K. Brown. E. A. McC.

FRENCH-CANADIAN LITERATURE

French Canadians are descendants of the *habitants* or peasants who stayed on in Quebec after the conquest. The peculiar complexion of their literature is due to their racial spirit and to tensions inherent in their political and geographical situation, the main factor of which is the close proximity of a powerful alien culture.

French-Canadian literature, properly speaking, began with the introduction of a printing press and the founding of the *Quebec Gazette* in 1764. The important literary movements did not, however, grow out of journalism, but out of the spiritual awakenings occasioned every now and then by the alarming nature of the historical situation.

Nineteenth Century. The first such awakening took place after the abortive rebellion against the rule of the English bureaucrats in 1837. Lord Durham, in his *Report,* offended the sensibilities of the French Canadians by referring to them as a people without a history and a literature. It has been said that it was Durham's words that inspired the young lawyer F. X. Garneau with the desire to demonstrate to his compatriots and the world that they had a glorious history. His *History* (1845) was a record of the glorious deeds of the ancestors of his people as he had found them recorded in the voyages of Cartier and Champlain, in the histories of Lescarbot and Charlevoix, in the "relations" of the Jesuit martyrs, and in the letters and mystical writings of the Ursuline nun, Marie de l'Incarnation. But Garneau's *History* had a significance far beyond its historical importance. If, for the last hundred years, French Canadians have been a self-conscious ethnic or racial unity engaged in a fight for survival, determined not to allow their personality to be lost in the ocean of industrialism that threatens to engulf them, it is due in no small measure to lessons they learned from Garneau. Garneau discovered that the strength of the French spirit lay in its power of cohesion and its power of resistance, and he prophesied that his people would continue to survive, provided they continued to be themselves, ethnically and spiritually. Our destiny, he told them, is linked up with the preservation of our religion, our language, and our laws. Garneau is still known as the "national" historian.

A little later, in 1866, Bishop Laflèche taught the French Canadians other lessons which they have not forgotten. They were charged, he said, with a mission to spread Catholicism and French culture throughout North America. And he held up before their eyes an ideal form of government which he had found in the early history of the Jewish people, a form which recognizes God as the head and source of power: theocracy. The idea of the theocracy is expressed concretely in the educational institutions known as Catholic universities and classical colleges, in which the students learn to think of theology as the "queen" of the sciences. The lessons of Bishop Laflèche helped to give to the French-Canadian soul its special temper.

The peasant way of life is characterized by a feeling for the land, a feeling that it is a precious thing to which a man's life is bound in a holy bond of unity; this is a feeling handed down from father to son in an unending sequence. It expresses itself in the conception of social life based upon the family as the primary and central institution in the social pattern, a pattern which in French Canada is fundamentally religious: families are grouped along the river bank and along the back road in a parish, of which the church is the symbol of union and togetherness. In conformity with the theocratic idea, which recognizes God as head, the father is a patriarch. His holiness is recognized in many ways. On New Year's Day he extends his blessing to the family, the bread is crossed before it is broken, the members cross themselves before beginning their labors, which are broken at intervals by prayers. All the traditional sacraments fall into this pattern of life: feast days and vital celebrations, birth, baptism, marriage, death, Mid-Lent, All Souls' Day, the Feast of the Dead. What it gives is a sense of permanence, peace, security, harmony, order, respect for ancient sanctities, wisdom born of millenniums of human experience. In literary history the patriarchal way of life produced what might be called the classical tradition of the French-Canadian novel, examples of

which are Chauveau's *Charles Guèrin* and Gérin-Lajoie's *Jean Rivard.*

The most important group of writers in the nineteenth century, the Group of 1860, claimed Garneau as their prophet. They met in a bookshop run by the poet Crémazie in Quebec city and dedicated themselves to heroic and patriotic poetry, legends of pioneer days, and the study of history. Besides Crémazie there were the historian Abbé Casgrain and J. C. Taché, known for his legends and his stories of woodsmen and *voyageurs.* It was Taché who drew these writers together with the magazine *Les Soirées Canadiennes* (1861-1865), in which his stories first appeared. It was during this literary awakening that the best-known French-Canadian novel appeared— Gaspé's *Les anciens Canadiens,* a tale of "seigneurial" life immediately before and after the conquest. The Garneau tradition in historical writing was continued in the twentieth century by Canon Lionel Groulx and Professor Guy Frégault, although its supremacy was not uncontested. Canon Groulx developed the racial and peasant thesis until it became a principle of separation. The Abbé Maheux opposed him with the idea that Anglo-Canadians and French Canadians have Norman blood in common and are separated by nothing more than prejudice. Other twentieth-century historians may be classified as scientific historians; the chief of these are Gustave Lanctot and Léon Gérin, whose studies of social types and changing economies anticipated the work of such American sociologists as Miner and Hughes by at least a generation. One of the outcomes of historical study in Quebec has been the development of the historical novel, the best of which are the work of Marmette, Laure Conan, and L. P. Desrosiers.

Near the end of the nineteenth century a group of poets known as "regionalists," of whom Blanche Lamontagne was the best representative, were inspired by the beauties of the Quebec landscape and the arts and crafts inherited from their grandparents. One of the best of the poets, Alfred Des Rochers, felt he was a "fallen" son of ancestors whose vitality and courage he tried to recapture among the wilder aspects of nature in the north country. About 1898 to 1900, the Montreal School, in opposition to the regionalists, extolled and illustrated the aestheticism of the French parnassians and symbolists. Émile Nelligan was a victim of melancholia and spent half of his life in an asylum. Paul Morin, whose image of perfection was the peacock, was pained at the sight of factory chimneys along a river bank.

Twentieth Century. The wars of the twentieth century were occasions for revivals of nationalism. In 1900 Mgr. Camille Roy, cleric, educationist, and literary critic, called for a "nationalization" of literature. Most of the influential newspapers of the present day were founded in the early 1900's. Again, in 1917, certain writers, historians, economists, and journalists grouped themselves round a magazine, *L'Action française,* determined to save the cultural values and to take stock of and protect the natural resources of their province— in short, to preserve their inheritance. Out of this movement grew the historical writings of Canon Groulx, the social and political philosophy of M. Edouard Montpetit (continued by M. Esdras Minville), the work of Marius Barbeau, the celebrated folklorist, which has been continued by M. Luc Lacoursière, and the work of the "small" historians interested in all the local crafts of woodcarvers and goldsmiths and the domestic arts of weaving, lace-making, bookbinding, bakery, and confectionery.

Another spiritual awakening occurred in 1934 when Robert Charbonneau, novelist and publisher, François Hertel and St. Denys Garneau, poets, began to publish a review with the suggestive title *La Relève*. These men had a deep sense of religious values and a sense of the grandeur of the Christian *mystique*. Garneau died in his early thirties. Hertel went to Paris. Charbonneau remained in Montreal, writing and publishing. The poetry of this group is metaphysical. Through their fiction runs a consciousness of the debased condition of man's soul, a sentiment which raises their work above the regionalism of many of their compatriots. Anne Hébert, poetess, expresses her lament for the lost world of childhood in ways that are reminiscent of her cousin Garneau. Alain Grandbois, who has traveled the world and met with disappointments and ghostly reminders everywhere, is the most brilliant, while the most serious, French-Canadian poet of today. His metaphysical anguish is more existential than Catholic. He is haunted by the thought of death, which to him is an essential constituent of life. He pictures a dark ocean over which his boat is drawn inexorably towards a rendezvous with death.

A foreign element, present in Chauveau, which was born of the economic and geographical situation, must be noted in tracing the development of the classical tradition that stems from Chauveau. This alien culture is industrialism. The industrial spirit flourished in the atmosphere of Puritanism, which favoured rational and scientific enquiry, and, as a consequence, happiness came to be represented in terms of money and possessions. As early as the nineteenth century streams of French-Canadian immigrants flowed from Quebec to the textile cities of New England. In search of higher standards of living they went as far as California and the Klondike. Some returned older and wiser men; those who remained suffered from homesickness; some died in the service of Anglo-Saxon gods. One of the best of recent novels, Ringuet's *Trente Arpents* (*Thirty Acres,* 1940), pictures a French-Canadian farmer ending his days in the service of gasoline, engaged as a night watchman in a garage.

The "national" solution of the problem of the lure of the United States is to choose to remain on the land in Quebec, and this choice has been best expressed in literature by Louis Hémon's novel *Maria Chapdelaine*. Maria turns from the United States, represented by Surprenant, and chooses to remain on the land in Quebec with Eutrope Gagnon. In the silence after her mother's death Maria listens to the voice of Quebec, the voice of her race, saying: "Three hundred years ago we came . . . and we have remained. . . . We are people of a race that knows not how to perish." Other variations of the tradition are found in the novels of Antoine Savard, L. P. Desrosiers, and Mme. Guèvremont. Savard's novels of "colonization" are twentieth-century versions of *Jean Rivard,* except that Savard's inspiration is far more lyrical. Mme. Guèvremont pictures the decay of the patriarchal way of life, while Desrosiers has created a "new order" within the peasant tradition, portraying farm life in the Laurentian mountains and speaking of the "mysticism" of the farm.

Gabrielle Roy was the first to explore the field of industrial realism. Not a native of Quebec, she stands outside the Quebec tensions and her art has a universal reach. Her theme in *Bonheur d'occasion* is poverty, the soul-destroying slavery of industrial life temporarily relieved by the artificial prosperity born of war. Roger Lemelin in his novels, *Au Pied de la Pente Douce* and *Les Plouffe,* has drawn pictures of life in working-class homes of Quebec's Lower Town against a background of shabby orthodoxy, popular superstitions, and "nationalist" demagogy. Jean Jules Richard's *Le Feu dans l'amiante* is a story, in the Zola tradition, of asbestos workers during the strike of 1949. The tone is vicious, sullen; the feelings are rather coarse.

Other evidence of social revolt is found in the works of Andre Langevin who attacks social injustice with the weapons of existentialist thought in the novels *Evadé de la nuit, Poussière sur la ville,* and *Le Temps des hommes*. Eugene Cloutier and Jean Filiatrault attempt to show what it is to be an artist. For Cloutier (*Les Témoins* and *Les Inutiles*), it is to be a fragmented personality always being tempted to kill, to commit suicide, or to escape. In Filiatrault's world (*Terres stériles* and *Chaînes*), man kills the thing he loves, is bound by the filial law of hate, and is mentally alienated in order to live. W. E. C.

CANADIAN NATIONAL LEAGUE, a party formed in Quebec in June 1903, for the purpose of securing maximum autonomy for the provinces within Canada, and for Canada within the British Empire. Known as La Ligue Nationaliste, it was inspired by Henri Bourassa, French Canadian journalist and politician, who was disappointed by the cautious trend of Liberal Party policies in both federal and provincial politics. In 1910 the safeguarding of minority rights was added to the original aim. The League favored nationalization of public utilities, selective immigration, and social reforms similar to those sponsored by progressive groups in the United States.

Politically, the League was first active in the province, where, in 1908, Bourassa won a personal victory over Sir Lomer Gouin in the St. James division, Montreal. The League was drawn into national politics in opposition to the naval policy of Prime Minister Wilfrid Laurier, which it considered likely to involve Canada indiscriminately in British wars. In a by-election in 1910, a Nationalist won in Laurier's old home constituency. In the general election of 1911 the League won twenty-seven of Quebec's sixty-five seats, contributing materially to the Liberal Party's overthrow. This achievement virtually ended the League as an organized political force. A conspicuous feature of League activity was the maintenance of two newspapers: *Le Nationaliste,* in 1903 and *Le Devoir,* in 1910. J. I. C.

CANADIAN NATIONAL PARKS, areas of scenic beauty, recreational appeal, or historic interest which have been set aside by the Canadian government to be preserved in perpetuity as national playgrounds for the enjoyment, recreation, and education of the public. All national parks are also wild-life sanctuaries, but in addition to those having pronounced scenic or historic appeal certain others have been set aside especially as game preserves. With one exception all national parks are located in provinces, and are under the administration of the Federal Government functioning through the National Parks Bureau at Ottawa.

Origin of the Park System. Canada's system of national parks owes its origin to the discovery of hot sulphur springs on the eastern slopes of the Rocky Mountains in what is now the Province of Alberta. The discovery was made in 1883 by engineers surveying the route for the Canadian Pacific Railway, and as pronounced medicinal qualities were attributed to the waters, the government of the day was confronted with the choice of allowing the springs to pass into private ownership or retaining them as part of the public domain under an administration to be set up for that purpose. The latter course was adopted, and in 1885 a reservation of ten square miles was set aside in the area of the springs. Presently, however, it was decided to enlarge greatly this area, and to set up the beginnings of a system of national parks. In 1887 Rocky Mountains National Park, which included the hot springs reservation and contained an area of

THE NARROWS IN WATERTON LAKES NATIONAL PARK, ALBERTA

260 square miles was established by Act of Parliament. As the name conflicted with that of one of the national parks in the United States it was subsequently changed to Banff National Park, and under that title the park has become known as one of the great mountain playgrounds of the world. Its area, changed from time to time, now consists of 2,585 square miles. It lies wholly within the Province of Alberta, reaching westward as far as the Great Divide—the crest of the Rockies marking the boundary between Alberta and British Columbia. Its administrative center takes the name of the park, Banff, which is located on the main line of the Canadian Pacific Railway 84 mi. west of Calgary.

Administration. In the administration of the national parks it is the policy of the Canadian government to combine public ownership with private initiative. The parks belong to the people as a whole, held in trust for them by the government; land in the parks is not sold but is leased for long periods on favorable terms to corporations or others for business purposes, and to private citizens for home sites. The government, through the National Parks Bureau, lays out town sites, provides roads and streets, public camping grounds, sites for cabins, bathhouses, sanitation, golf courses, tennis courts and other sports grounds, fish hatcheries for the maintenance of fish in the lakes and rivers; in some of the parks maintains museums and examples of wild animal life; has its own system of wardens for protection against fire and enforcement of regulations; and, in short, conducts the general administration of the area. Schools are under the control of the government of the province in which the park is located; churches are established by the religious denominations which they represent; hotels and business places are operated by private enterprise subject to the regulations made by the National Parks Bureau. All buildings must harmonize with a general type of architecture, and plans must be approved by the Bureau. The aim is to afford the greatest extent of personal liberty along with a centralized control in those matters which relate to the public as a whole or to the welfare of the park. Each park has its local superintendent and administrative staff, but general direction is from Ottawa. The national parks are not operated by the government with a view to making profit. Many of the services are free to the public, and others, such as the use of golf courses, tennis courts, and bathhouses, may be had for a nominal charge. There is no charge for the admittance of individuals to the parks, although fees ranging up to two dollars for the season are charged for automobiles using the park highways. The main purpose of the parks is conservation; while small areas around the headquarters and other special spots may be landscaped and otherwise improved, thousands of square miles are maintained in their natural condition, and it is planned that for all time these areas shall be available to the public in their natural wilderness state.

Scenic and Recreational Parks. Banff National Park has mountains rising to 10,000 ft. and higher, glaciers, lakes, rivers, and mountain valleys, of which the most important is the valley of the Bow River, affording as it does an **easy**

route by both rail and motor car up to and beyond the Great Divide. Its principal centers are Banff and Lake Louise, where luxurious tourist hotels are operated by the Canadian Pacific Railway. Under other ownership are less expensive places for tourist accommodation. A paved road, the Banff-Jasper highway, crosses the park from east to west, with its western end in Vancouver. It has two main branches, one swinging southerly through Kootenay National Park and connecting with the highway system of the United States, and the other swinging northwesterly along a great trench in the Rocky Mountains and connecting with Jasper National Park.

Amusements in Banff National Park, as in other national parks in the Canadian Rockies, consist of motoring over the park highways, hiking or horseback riding along trails penetrating remote areas not yet reached by motor roads, canoeing and boating on the lakes and rivers, mountain climbing with experienced guides, fishing, bathing in hot water pools, photography, and enjoying the grandeur of the scenery. Among the man-made attractions are golf courses, tennis courts, picnic grounds, and camping facilities. The Banff School of Fine Arts, which holds sessions each summer, provides cultural opportunities combined with outstanding recreational attractions. At present the popularity of Canada's national parks is mainly limited to the summer months, but the season is gradually being extended to make them year-round resorts. Winter sports include ice carnivals, curling bonspiels, and similar amusements. Skiing, although essentially a winter sport, may be enjoyed in some of the parks in all months of the year. The flora and fauna are interesting and varied, and the visitor who has a flair for geology finds in the exposed mountain sides many opportunities for study.

After the passing of the legislation which set up Banff National Park the idea of a whole system of national parks for Canada quickly seized the public imagination. In 1886 two other parks were established; Yoho, in British Columbia on the western slope of the Rockies immediately adjoining Banff on the east; and Glacier, also in southeastern British Columbia but located on the summit of the Selkirk Range. Yoho, well named from an Indian word expressing surprise or delight, contains within its 507 sq. mi. some of the most rugged mountain scenery to be found in any part of Canada. The visitor, entering the mountains from the east with ease via the Bow River Valley in Banff National Park, is confronted with an almost precipitous drop a few miles west of the Great Divide. To drive a railway through the obstacles of this area called for engineering skill and daring of the highest order. From an altitude of 5,337 ft. above sea level at the point where the railway passes from Banff to Yoho National Park and to Field, B.C., there is in less than 15 mi. a drop of 1,265 ft. Even this distance of 15 mi. was achieved by driving two tunnels into neighboring mountains and describing an almost complete circle in each, thus lengthening the route by more than 6,000 ft. and easing the gradient accordingly. These Spiral Tunnels, as they are called, are as interesting to the visitor as any of the magnificent scenery with which they are surrounded.

From the height of land, railway and highway plunge into the Kicking Horse Pass, through which the Kicking Horse River has cut its precipitous route. At Field the gradient levels out somewhat, and after dropping another 1,500 ft. the Kicking Horse merges with the Columbia River. Field is the administrative center of both Yoho and Glacier national parks. Glacier National Park (521 sq. mi.) is located about 25 mi. west of Field in a very mountainous area and, until recent years, could be reached only by rail. It is noted particularly for its vast ice fields, glaciers, canyons, and valleys.

Next in the series was Waterton Lakes National Park, an area of 204 sq. mi. in the southwest corner of Alberta. In conjunction with Glacier National Park (U.S.) it constitutes the Waterton-Glacier International Peace Park, dedicated to perpetual peace between the United States and Canada. It is particularly noted for its beautiful lakes and exceptional coloring. There is a permanent townsite at Waterton Lakes with all the usual park conveniences and commercial places of business, and a fine hotel is operated by the Great Northern Railroad.

Jasper National Park, on the eastern slope of the Rockies in west central Alberta, was established in 1907. Its area of 4,200 sq. mi. makes it the largest scenic and recreational national park in Canada. It is served by the main line of the Canadian National Railways, by highway from Edmonton on the east and by the Banff-Jasper highway connecting with the Trans-Canada Highway to the southeast. Although essentially a scenic park it also has historic interest. It was through the region's passes that the early explorers, traders, and missionaries found their way to the Pacific Coast. Through it flows the Athabasca River, named from the Athabasca Trail, the route followed by the traders long before rail connection had been established across the mountains. Jasper, too, has its medicinal hot springs and various attractions and facilities similar to those in Banff. The administrative headquarters are at the town of Jasper, the principal center in the park. Four miles from the town, on the shores of beautiful Lake Beauvert, is Jasper Park Lodge, a luxurious hotel operated by the Canadian National Railways. In the town and elsewhere are other accomodations for tourists, some of them open the year round. Like all other national parks in Canada, Jasper is a wild-life sanctuary where

Ice crevasses in Illecillewaet Glacier, Glacier National Park, add to the thrill of mountain climbing.

The South Gate of Riding Mountain National Park, Manitoba, established in 1929.

CANADIAN NATIONAL FILM BOARD PHOTO

game is strictly protected, but it is extensively used as a base and outfitting point for hunting expeditions penetrating the wild country to the north and west.

The Banff-Jasper highway, opened to the public in 1940, connects the towns of Jasper and Banff, 184 mi. apart, and traverses some of the finest scenery in the Rockies. The route is marked by high mountains, glaciers, rivers, waterfalls, and lakes. Its most outstanding feature is the Columbia Ice Field, estimated to be 150 sq. mi. in extent, resting at an altitude of 11,000 ft. on the very dome of the mountain system of the continent. Waters from its melting ice, 600 ft. thick, find their way to three oceans—the Pacific, the Arctic,

ALBERTA FALLS, JASPER NATIONAL PARK

COURTESY CANADIAN NATIONAL RAILWAY

and the Atlantic. Throughout its course the highway is at all times within a national park, either Jasper or Banff; it crosses from one to the other at Sunwapta Pass at an altitude of 6,675 ft.

In 1914 Mt. Revelstoke National Park, an alpine plateau of 100 sq. mi., was added to the system. By this time, however, the parks movement had spread to eastern Canada, and in that same year St. Lawrence Islands National Park, a mainland landing spot and group of 12 islands in the St. Lawrence River, was established. Its total area is only 172 acres, and it has not been greatly developed, but it is popular for camping, fishing, and bathing. Four years later Point Pelee National Park, the most southerly mainland point in Canada (in the same latitude as the northern boundary of California) was established with an area of slightly more than six square miles. It has fine beaches and is a popular summer resort, being close to the cities of Windsor in Canada and Detroit in the United States. It is famous also for its flora and as a resting place for migratory birds. Georgian Bay Islands National Park, in Georgian Bay near Midland, Ontario, consists of 30 islands with an area of 5.37 sq. mi., and is a recreation center used extensively by outing organizations not only from Canada but also from the United States. It was established in 1929.

Kootenay National Park, in southeastern British Columbia, was established in 1920. It has an area of 543 sq. mi. and is entered by the Banff-Windermere Highway, which at its northern end connects with the Trans-Canada Highway and at its southern end links up with highway connections in the United States. It has famous hot springs and fine scenery. Tourist accommodation is furnished mainly at Radium Hot Springs, at the southern end of the park.

The national parks movement extended to the so-called "prairie provinces" in 1927 with the establishment of Prince Albert National Park in central Saskatchewan, north of the city of Prince Albert. It is a forested lakeland covering an area of approximately 1,869 sq. mi. marked by extensive waterways and fine beaches. Two years later Riding Mountain National Park was established in southwestern Manitoba on a plateau rising more than 1,000 ft. above the level country to the east and north. Its area of 1,148 sq. mi. contains some beautiful lakes and much fine forest. It is a popular summer resort frequented by the residents of the provinces of Manitoba and Saskatchewan and of many states of the Mississippi Valley.

Banff Springs Hotel, in Banff National Park, Alberta, is a world famous winter and summer resort.

HERBERT LANKS FROM BLACK STAR

Cape Breton Highlands National Park was established in the northern part of Cape Breton Island, in the Province of Nova Scotia, in 1936. It has an area of 390 sq. mi. and presents striking examples of rugged Atlantic and Gulf of St. Lawrence coast lines against a mountainous background. The following year Prince Edward Island National Park was established in the Province of Prince Edward Island. It consists of a strip some 25 mi. long on the sand beaches of the northern shore backed by the beautiful rural scenery of the "garden province."

The latest addition to Canada's national parks system is an area of 79.5 sq. mi. on the Bay of Fundy eastward from St. John, New Brunswick. Proclaimed in April 1948, this park has been developed along the same lines as the others, with a golf course, tennis courts, heated salt-water swimming pool, and other amusement facilities in addition to the advantages afforded by nature.

Animal Parks and Reserves. The national parks so far described are of the scenic and recreational type. There are also certain parks intended essentially for the preservation of game animals and other wild life. Both types of parks come under the administration of the National Parks Bureau at Ottawa, and the distinction between them is not absolute; for example, the scenic parks are also game sanctuaries having considerable populations of bison, elk, moose, deer, bears, beavers, and other wild animals, and the animal parks have certain scenic and other recreational attractions. The first of them was called Buffalo National Park and was established in 1908, occupying 197.5 sq. mi. near Wainwright, in eastern Alberta. It was planned mainly as a buffalo reserve, but is not now used for that purpose. Five years later Elk Island National Park was established in central Alberta near Edmonton. It had been an animal reservation since 1906 but was not given national park status until 1913. It consists of a fenced area of 75 sq. mi. containing usually more than 1,000

head of plains buffalo as well as large numbers of deer, elk, and moose. It has been developed also as a recreational park equipped with golf course, tennis courts, bathhouses, tourist accommodations, and camping facilities.

The largest park in Canada, if not in the world, is Wood Buffalo National Park, which has an area of 17,300 sq. mi., most of it in northern Alberta but also partly in the Northwest Territories. It contains many thousands of bison and other animals and waterfowl indigenous to that part of the country. It is as yet undeveloped, and is administered, not by the National Parks Bureau but by the Bureau of Northern Affairs, also at Ottawa.

Historic Parks. Another type of national reservation in Canada includes those set aside to be preserved because of the historic associations connected with the areas in which they are located. Few of them are more than 100 acres in extent. They include Fort Anne in Nova Scotia on the site of the early Acadian settlement of Port Royal, now equipped with a fine museum and library; Fort Beauséjour in New Brunswick, the site of a French fort erected about the middle of the eighteenth century, and now containing an important museum; Fortress of Louisbourg on Cape Breton Island, Nova Scotia, the site of an old walled city and a key position in the struggles between the British and French, destroyed in 1760, now marked by a museum; Port Royal, near Annapolis Royal, Nova Scotia, where a reproduction of the Habitation erected by DeMonts and Champlain in 1605 has recently been built; Fort Chambly, at Chambly Canton, Quebec, a French fort built on the Richelieu River in 1665 and rebuilt in 1711, now housing a museum and including a military cemetery; Fort Lennox, near St. Johns, Quebec, a military post built by the British to command the Richelieu River from the south and containing well-preserved stone buildings and earthworks; Fort Wellington, near Prescott, Ontario, on the St. Lawrence River, built by the British to protect com-

453

munication between Montreal and Kingston, and maintained in a good state of preservation; Fort Malden, at Amherstburg, Ontario, on the Detroit River, at one time an important military post, now famous mainly for its museum; Fort Prince of Wales, near Churchill on Hudson Bay in northern Manitoba, a British post which was captured by the French in 1782; Woodside, at Kitchener, Ontario, boyhood home of the late W. L. Mackenzie King, former Canadian Prime Minister; Lower Fort Garry, on the Red River about 20 mi. north of Winnipeg, Manitoba, a stone fort built by the Hudson's Bay Company between 1831-1839; and Fort Battleford, 4 mi. south of North Battleford, Saskatchewan, a Northwest Mounted Police Post built in 1877 in Cree Indian territory, whose original buildings house a museum and are surrounded by a log stockade. There are also several hundred National Historic Sites, marked with cairns or plaques or otherwise, which are not given the status of national parks but are preserved as landmarks in the history of the nation.

Value of Parks. The national parks of Canada constitute a public property of much scenic and historic interest, and have conservation features of great present and future value. Their total area is approximately 29,000 square miles and they are visited each year by more than 3½ million tourists, many of them from the United States. As tourist business is a large contributor to the Canadian economy, the parks, in addition to their aesthetic, historic, and conservation value, have an economic significance which ranks them among the important national assets of Canada. R. J. C. S.

CANADIAN POLITICAL PARTIES.

The political history of Canada divides at 1849. Up to that time party differences had centered in the struggle for responsible government, but after achieving that goal with the signing of the Rebellion Losses Bill in 1849, they tended to follow economic and financial rather than constitutional and political lines.

Clear Grits and Rouges. The two extreme parties which fell outside the moderate central group were the Clear Grits in Canada West (Ontario), and the Parti Rouge in Canada East (Quebec). These two groups, though both radical, had little in common. The Clear Grits expressed the agrarian discontent of the then western part of Canada, advocating extension of the franchise, annual parliaments, easier credit, and acquisition of additional western territory. Although unsympathetic at first, George Brown, editor of the Toronto *Globe,* became the leader of this party. The Rouges, led by A. A. Dorion, supported the political ideas of Louis Joseph Papineau, French-Canadian leader. They were anticlerical and followed the radical principles of European and American liberals of that time.

The two groups were united in opposition to the central Liberal-Conservative group. However, friction developed when the Clear Grits, who mistrusted Roman Catholic Canada East, adopted a slogan of "rep. by pop.," or representation by population. This would have given Canada West a majority in the legislature and, consequently, was objectionable to the Rouges, who benefited from the equal representation provided by the Act of Union. The two reform parties also divided on the question of separate Protestant and Roman Catholic schools.

Liberal-Conservatives and Liberals. In 1854 the government of Canada was a Liberal-Conservative coalition led at first by Allan McNab and A. N. Moran. Later, Sir John A. Macdonald steadily increased his power and influence, and in 1856 he replaced McNab and established a control which dominated the Canadian politics, except for short

periods, until 1891. Sir George Étienne Cartier, later prime minister, represented the French-Canadian element in the coalition during the earlier years. Government was complicated by the presence in Canada of two nationality groups with different languages, creeds, and social customs. The Liberal-Conservative group was not actually a party, since it was composed of supporters with varying political convictions. Far to the right was McNab, a Tory, while Cartier, in the other direction, was a reformer.

Many factors, internal and external, combined to force the British North American colonies to discuss union. The Rouges under Dorion were opposed to union, while Brown, the Clear Grit leader, supported the movement long enough to assure its success. On July 1, 1867, Canada (what is now Ontario and Quebec), New Brunswick, and Nova Scotia, were united as the Dominion of Canada. Manitoba, British Columbia, and Prince Edward Island soon were added. Following confederation, party divisions were at first not clearly defined. Macdonald continued governing by means of the Liberal-Conservative group which had brought about confederation. The opposition was divided between the Clear Grits, the Rouges, and the supporters of Joseph Howe in Nova Scotia, who opposed confederation. As ministers retired, Macdonald replaced them with Conservative supporters, with the result that the government became predominantly Conservative. Opposition was carried on by the remnants of the Clear Grit or Reform Party, which after confederation became the Liberal Party. Brown, using the Toronto *Globe,* was spokesman for the party.

In 1873 the Liberals (popularly called Grits), under Alexander Mackenzie, took over the government and remained in office until 1878. This period also was marked by the rise and decline of the Canada First Party, a nationalist group which advocated, among other things, a protective tariff. Goldwin Smith, historian and editor, and Edward Blake were leaders in this movement. The party disappeared but most of the planks in its platform were taken over by the major parties. For example, Macdonald's high tariff program, called the "National Policy," with which he won the election of 1878, was very similar to the Canada First protection policy.

The Liberal-Conservative and Liberal parties have alternated in power in Canada since confederation. The principal leaders of the Liberal-Conservatives have been Macdonald, Sir Robert Borden, Richard B. (later Viscount) Bennett, and Arthur Meighen. In 1942, when John Bracken was chosen as leader, the name of the party was changed to Progressive-Conservative. The most influential Liberal party leaders have been Alexander Mackenzie, Sir Wilfrid Laurier, William Lyon Mackenzie King, and Wilfred St. Laurent.

Other Parties. At various times since confederation third parties have sought power. In the early years of the twentieth century Henri Bourassa launched a nationalist party in Quebec which opposed imperial entanglements and fostered French-Canadian nationalism. After the election of 1911 the party held the balance of power, but it was quickly absorbed into the Conservative government.

In 1919 a newly organized party, the United Farmers of Ontario, called the U. F. O., swept into power in Ontario, where E. C. Drury became prime minister. The success of this agrarian movement encouraged rural leaders, and in 1920 the National Progressive Party was organized, with T. A. Crerar as its leader. In 1921 sixty-five members of the party were elected to the Canadian Parliament, but later the party declined and by 1926 had disappeared.

During the depression of the 1930's many economic remedies were proposed. In Alberta, a "soft money" party following the doctrines of a Major Clifford Hugh Douglas, British engineer and social economist, was organized under the leadership of William Aberhart. Called the Social Credit Party, it swept the province in 1935 and subsequently returned some members to the Canadian Parliament.

In 1932 the Co-operative Commonwealth Federation, a Socialist Party commonly called the C.C.F., was organized. J. S. Woodsworth, labor member of Parliament for a Winnipeg constituency, was the first leader; he was succeeded by M. J. Coldwell. The party's platform advocates: (1) the establishment of a planned system of social economy for the production, distribution, and exchange of all goods; (2) socialization of the banking, credit, and financial systems of the country, with social ownership, operation, and control of public utilities and natural resources; and (3) security for workers and farmers; equal opportunity for all without regard to religion, race, or color; social security; and the development of co-operative enterprises.

In Canada, labor has not organized on party lines. The C. C. F. claims to speak for labor.   J. J. T.

CANADIAN PROVINCIAL PARKS. Provincial parks in Canada differ mainly from national parks in that they come under the control of the provincial legislatures rather than that of the Federal Government. The same general purposes and principles of conservation apply, with such modifications as may be required by local conditions. On the whole, less development has been done in the provincial than in the national parks, and they are a smaller factor in the tourist business of the country, although some of them are generously patronized by the population of adjacent cities and towns and also by visitors from other lands.

British Columbia Provincial Parks. Provision has been made for provincial parks in British Columbia on a larger scale than in any other province except Quebec, 12, 496 sq. mi. of scenic territory having been reserved for this purpose. Individual parks range from small areas suitable for local recreational centers to great wilderness reserves with an area of 5,400 sq. mi., such as Tweedsmuir Park, the largest scenic park in Canada. It lies inland from the Pacific Coast between Vancouver Island and Prince Rupert, and has historic significance from the fact that it was on the route traveled by Sir Alexander Mackenzie when, in 1793, he made one of the first overland crossings of North America. The park is famous for its spectacular Rainbow Mountains, its fine timber, abundant wild life, and its great profusion of flowers. Still with few local improvements, it is best approached by way of Bella Coola, an inlet on the Pacific. Other British Columbia provincial parks, although not so extensive in area as Tweedsmuir, are marked by fine mountain scenery, good fishing and big-game areas, glaciers, rivers, lakes, waterfalls, mountain valleys, and heavily forested terrain. Garibaldi Park of 973 sq. mi., not far from the city of Vancouver, is famous for its peaks and glaciers, and for its wild flowers and strange geological features. Wells Gray Park includes part of the Cariboo Mountains and also some of the best fishing and big-game areas in the province. Mt. Robson Park features Mt. Robson, highest mountain in the Canadian Rockies, 12,972 ft. Tourist possibilities which may develop along the Alaska Highway have been recognized by setting aside Liard River Park in that area for future development. Of the 69 parks under provincial administration about half are of the community type, designed mainly as vacation spots for the communities which they serve.

Alberta Provincial Parks. Although Alberta has a

larger area of national parks than any other province, this has not deterred the provincial government from setting aside a large number of parks, most of them small, to be operated under provincial administration. They are not designed to compete with the great scenic attractions of the national parks, but mainly to provide convenient vacation places for the local and surrounding population. Most of them are

CANADIAN NATIONAL FILM BOARD

View from the top of the skyline ski trail in Garibaldi Provincial Park, British Columbia, with Diamond Head mountain in the background

located on attractive lakes where good picnic and camp sites are available. Aspen Beach Park, on the shore of Gull Lake, west of Lacombe, in central Alberta, is one of the most popular, and provides good bathing, boating, and canoeing. It has a considerable community of summer cottages. Gooseberry Lake Park, on Gooseberry Lake, has its sports ground and a number of cottages; Lundbrek Falls Park, west of Macleod, attracts its quota of fishermen, and Sylvan Lake Park, on Sylvan Lake west of Red Deer, about halfway between Calgary and Edmonton, is a popular bathing place. Among the larger provincial parks is Ghost River Park, on a beautiful artificial lake on the Ghost and Bow rivers between Calgary and Banff. Its 535½ acres provide an excellent summer vacation spot with beautiful views up the Bow River Valley to the Rocky Mountains. Bad Lands Reserve has been established north of Drumheller to preserve the fossilized remains of prehistoric animals for which the Red Deer River Valley is famous, and Saskatoon Lookout Reserve preserves a fine lookout point in the Grande Prairie district. Throughout its length and breadth the province is liberally spotted with areas of this kind designed to save for present and future generations the natural beauty of the landscape or places of outstanding interest, and at the same time provide suitable opportunity for camping and outdoor recreations. Many of them are in the prairie country, long distances from the mountains, and serve to correct the impression that the beauty of the Canadian West is limited to its mountain areas. There is a charm about the lakes and rivers of the prairie

DON COLTMAN—CANADIAN PACIFIC PHOTO

Elks Falls, one of the most spectacular sights on Vancouver Island, British Columbia, has given its name to the Provincial Park established there.

country, and about the very landscape itself, which is not less attractive than that to be found in more spectacular surroundings.

Saskatchewan Provincial Parks. The provincial parks of Saskatchewan are evidence that the province is not merely a vast area of fertile but treeless prairie with nothing to break the vision but the distant and level horizon. Seven permanent park reserves in the southern part of the province are all well forested and contain many beautiful lakes where there are good opportunities for camping, fishing, bathing, and general outdoor summer vacation life. Cypress Hills Park, a few miles north of the United States boundary, is in the heart of the heavily forested Cypress Hills area, and is equipped with bungalow, lodge, cabin, and auto-camp accommodation. It has abundant spring water, and wood for fuel. Moose Mountain Park occupies part of another elevation farther east, and it also is not far from the United States border. It is heavily forested with poplar and birch and liberally studded with pleasant lakes. The famous Qu'Appelle Lakes, in the equally famous Qu'Appelle Valley, afford the setting for Katepwe Park, about 60 mi. northeast of Regina. It is equipped with camp kitchens, bathhouses, and other holiday conveniences. Good Spirit Lake Park, 20 mi. west of Canora, is similarly equipped, and provides good fishing and bathing. A 35-sq.-mi. block, consisting largely of virgin forest north of Kelvington, has been preserved as Greenwater Lake Park. Adjoining Lake Manitou, famous for its medicinal waters, the provincial government has set aside an area of about 4 sq. mi. for park purposes, known as Little Manitou Park and equipped with modest accommodation. Madge Lake, with its shore line of 47 mi., densely wooded and with fine sandy beaches, is the setting for Duck Mountain Park, about

15 mi. northeast of Kamsack. All these parks are in the southern half of Saskatchewan. The northern half, heavily wooded and parklike by nature, is served mainly by the national park north of Prince Albert.

Manitoba Provincial Park. The Whiteshell Forest Reserve in eastern Manitoba, although originally preserved for forest protection purposes, is also extensively utilized as a provincial park. It was set aside in 1930, and contains an area of 1,088 sq. mi., mostly rugged rock-land of the Pre-Cambrian formation. Several rivers and more than 200 lakes give it special appeal to the canoeist, camper, and fisherman. The northern part of the area is still mostly in its primitive state, covered with a heavy growth of pine, spruce, birch, tamarack, and poplar. In the southern part a number of lakes have been developed as summer resorts. The principal fish available are lake trout, pickerel, northern pike, bass, and perch, and fishing is the outstanding attraction. A large fish hatchery assures replenishment of the supply. Wild animals include moose, caribou, deer, beaver, muskrat, and fox. The southern part of the park is a game reserve, but in the northern part hunting in season is permitted. Great numbers of waterfowl frequent the wild rice beds in some of the lakes. The Whiteshell area also has its historic background; in 1734 La Vérendrye traveled the Winnipeg River, which skirts the northern edge of the reserve. The park may be reached from Winnipeg via the Trans-Canada Highway, a distance of about 85 mi.

Ontario Provincial Parks. Five provincial parks in Ontario are dedicated mainly to the preservation of the forests and the wild life which they shelter; a sixth is devoted only to summer camping and summer sports. The largest, Algonquin Provincial Park, 2,750 sq. mi., lies between Georgian Bay and the Ottawa River, and may be said to mark the division between southern and northern Ontario. It was established in 1893, and while still essentially wilderness territory, has been made accessible by modern highway from Ottawa to Huntsville, by two lines of railway, and by numerous landing places for amphibious aircraft. Good fishing is available, but other game is strictly protected. A fish hatchery provides for the re-stocking of lakes and streams. Cabins and cottages are for sale or rent; there are several modern hotels, and those who really want to "get back to nature" may bring their tents and camp by any of the beautiful lakes and streams. The next largest park in Ontario is Quetico, 1,720 sq. mi. of virgin wilderness lying along the north side of the International Boundary between Fort William and Fort Frances, in the far western part of the province. This park is inaccessible by automobile except from the neighboring state of Minnesota. In it the conditions of 300 years ago have practically been preserved to this day. Lake Superior Provincial Park, 540 sq. mi., provides good fishing, but is a wilderness area with little in the way of modern conveniences; Sibley Provincial Park, 63 sq. mi., is also a wilderness area without camping facilities. Rondeau Provincial Park, 8 sq. mi., is a triangular-shaped peninsula on the northern shore of Lake Erie and at almost the extreme southern point of Canada. It has fine playground facilities such as tennis, golf, archery, shuffleboard, and dance pavilions, and is an excellent base for boating on Lake Erie. Ipperwash Beach Provincial Park is on the shore of Lake Huron. Its extent is only 109 acres but it includes a fine sandy beach and woodland area with good camping facilities, and is easily reached by highway.

Quebec Provincial Parks. Laurentides is the outstanding park in the Province of Quebec. Located 25 mi. north of the city of Quebec, and comprising an area of 3,613 sq. mi., it is one of the largest parks in Canada and one of the most attractive. Its altitude of about 3,000 ft. above sea level assures a clear and pleasant summer climate. There are more than 1,500 lakes in the park which serve as headwaters of many rivers and streams, some of them draining northward into Lake St. John and the Saguenay River, while others flow southward into the St. Lawrence. Two good highways lead into the park, and the more remote regions may be reached by well-kept trails. Lodges for tourists are maintained by the provincial government, which supervises the service and rates. Only one variety of game fish is found in the waters of the park, but it is the coveted brook trout. Wild animals include bears, wolves, moose, deer, and smaller fur bearers, but as the park is a game sanctuary all are strictly protected by law. La Vérendrye or Mont Laurier-Senneterre Park, 4,747 sq. mi., is located in the southwestern part of the province, and is conveniently approached by highway from Montreal. It has many lakes and rivers and a large variety of fish, which includes brook trout, black bass, pickerel, and northern pike. Cabins and boats may be rented from the Game and Fisheries Department of the Quebec government. Mt. Orford Provincial Park is located on Mt. Orford, in the southern part of the province. It has an area of about 16 sq. mi. and an altitude of 2,860 ft. It has a golf course, and its slopes are well adapted to skiing. Gaspesian Provincial Park, in the Gaspé Peninsula, 514 sq. mi., was established mainly to preserve its native caribou herds. Like other parks in Quebec, it provides fine scenery, good fishing, and the special charm of a French-Canadian background.

Parks of the Atlantic Provinces. Provincial park land in Newfoundland covers 48 sq. mi. and includes Serpentine Park on the west coast of the province and an area on the Upper Humber River. New Brunswick, Nova Scotia, and Prince Edward Island have many civic parks but none that come within the provincial classification.   R. J. C. S.

CANADIAN RIVER, a stream about 906 miles long, one of the major tributaries of the Arkansas River, in the southwestern United States. The Canadian River rises in Colfax County, northeastern New Mexico, and the headwater streams come from the Sangre de Cristo Mountains of the southern Rockies, as well as from the Raton district, which is immediately south of the Colorado-New Mexico boundary line. The headwater streams join near Taylor Springs in the southeastern part of Colfax County. The Canadian River flows generally southward into San Miguel County, New Mexico, where it turns eastward, flowing across the panhandle of Texas into Oklahoma. Crossing almost the entire width of Oklahoma in a series of large bends and meanderings, it turns northeast to join the Arkansas River on the boundary of Muskogee and Haskell counties, in east central Oklahoma. The Canadian River has no major tributaries except the North Canadian River, 760 mi. long, which joins it near Eufaula, McIntosh County, Oklahoma, flowing just north and approximately parallel with the Canadian River. Among its larger headwater creeks and streams are the Mora, Conchas, and Ute, all of which are in New Mexico.

Because the Canadian River crosses a semiarid region, it is, for most of the year, a shallow, muddy stream, filled with sand bars and flowing between broad banks. During the spring and early summer, when water from melting snow and sudden thunder showers swells the river, it occasionally becomes a raging torrent. Along the headwater streams in New Mexico there are some piñon and juniper forests, and at its confluence with the Arkansas the Canadian flows through a small region of oaks and hickories. For most of its course it flows across the cattle- and wheat-producing short-grass country of New Mexico and Texas and the tall-grass region of Oklahoma. The Canadian has cut a course across the high plains to form the boundary line between these plains, to the north, and the Llano Estacado, to the south.

The Canadian River is one of the major sources of water for a large semiarid region. Among irrigation projects is the Conchas Dam near Tucumcari, N. M., completed in 1939. In 1949 the U.S. Congress approved a plan to spend $85,000,000 for a development and irrigation program for the Canadian River watershed district. The river passes near Tucumcari, N. M., and Amarillo, Texas. Oklahoma City, Okla., is on the North Canadian River.   J. E. F.

CANAIGRE [kəne'gər] *Rumex hymenosepalus,* a perennial herb of the buckwheat family, native in sandy soil from Texas to California. It grows to three feet, has large docklike leaves, and clusters of greenish flowers. Because the stems are sometimes used like rhubarb it is often called wild rhubarb or California pie-plant. It has some ornamental value, and tannin is produced from the tuberous roots.

          J. C. Wis.

CANALETTO, born **GIOVANNI ANTONIO CANALE** [kanale'tto; kana'le] (1697-1798), Italian painter and engraver, was born in Venice on Oct. 18, 1697. He worked first under his father, who was a theatrical scene painter, and then for a short time in Rome, where he studied perspective and painted architectural remains. When he returned to Venice, his pictures became so successful that he was twice invited to London, once in 1746 and again in 1751. The best of his many views of Venice, which include the *View of the Grand Canal* (Liechtenstein Gallery, Vienna), the *View of the Salute* (Louvre, Paris), and the *View of the Carità* (National Gallery, London) are accurately rendered in terms of perspective but are saved from mere topographic exactitude by a fine sense of color and atmosphere. In Canaletto's late style there is a sacrifice of pictorial freedom to greater precision, and his work tends to lose some of its richness of tone and linear fluency. He died in Venice on Apr. 20, 1768.   M. C.

CANALS, artificial watercourses built for drainage, for water supply, including power and irrigation, or for navigation.

Drainage Canals. Drainage canals are often built in lowlands to provide more efficient runoff of surface water, thus permitting such lowlands to dry and to be put to better agricultural or industrial use. Because of irregularity of slope in the natural topography and in order to maintain a uniform slope of canal from the source to the mouth, it is sometimes necessary to build sections of such canals by placing raised banks so that the canal bottom will be as high as or, in some cases, higher than, the surrounding land.

Water-Supply Canals. Water-supply or irrigation canals serve primarily to transport water from the reservoir, or place of accumulation and storage, to the land to be irrigated, or to a water-supply distribution system. In the case of a power plant the canal carries water from the storage reservoir to a pressure conduit, or pipe to a turbine wheel, through which it drops to the elevation of the tailrace, or outlet; in so doing it imparts energy to the turbine. Canals of this type are also built with a sloping bottom to produce flow of the water. Since the quantity of flow increases with an increase in slope, it is in the interest of economy to make this slope as great as practicable. The steepness of slope is

ONTARIO DEPT. OF TRAVEL AND PUBLICITY

RIDEAU CANAL LOCKS, ONTARIO, CANADA

limited, however, by the tendency of higher velocity of flow to scour the canal.

Navigation Canals. Navigation canals serve as channels through which vessels may be propelled or towed. Such canals are often constructed within approximately level reaches of rivers by placing dams at intervals so that the intervening reaches thus created are filled with still water. Vessels pass upward and downward at the dams through locks, which are boxlike watertight chambers large enough to contain one or more barges. Locks are provided with intake valves that permit filling the lock to the level of the upper reach of the canal. Discharge valves lower the water in the lock to the level of the lower reach of the canal. Closure at the lower and upper ends is effected by pairs of swinging gates set in recesses so as to provide a smooth wall surface for the lock when they are swung open. The gates are made a little wider than the width of the canal and are mitered so as to act as an arch and to withstand the water pressure from the upper level. To ascend from one level to another, a barge or vessel floats into the lock with the lower gates open and the upper gates closed. The lower gates are then closed and water is admitted through filling valves. The water, and with it the floating vessel, rises in the lock to the level of the upper pool. Then the upper gates are opened and the vessel floats out of the lock at this level. For a downward-bound vessel, the procedure is reversed. Other devices to accomplish the transfer of vessels between different levels include the inclined lift, the vertical lift, and other special apparatus, the principal purpose of which is to avoid the use of the very considerable quantity of water passed from the upper level to the lower level with each "lockage," or passage of a vessel through the ordinary lock.

Early History. Many references to navigation canals are found in the ancient records of Assyria, Babylonia, China, Egypt, Greece, India, Persia, and Rome, and in the writings of medieval England, France, Germany, Holland, and Russia. In China, the Grand Canal built in the thirteenth century to join the Pei-ho and the Yangtze Kiang was used for irrigation and for navigation. It seems to have contained no locks, so that portage of cargo was probably necessary between different levels of the canal.

Definite reference to the use of navigation canals with locks is found in Italian history of the Renaissance. In 1481 the two Domenico brothers of Viterbo constructed a lock chamber with gates, and Leonardo da Vinci built six locks to join the canals of Milan. In England, Foss Dyke built during the Roman rule was deepened in 1121 to make it navigable. In 1761 the Duke of Bridgewater completed a canal between Manchester and Worsley. In France, the Languedoc canal between the Bay of Biscay and the Mediterranean was completed in 1681. It was 148 mi. long, 6½ ft. deep, and had 119 locks, rising to 620 ft. above sea level. In Russia, the construction of a system of canals to connect St. Petersburg (now Leningrad) with the Caspian Sea began in the eighteenth century. In Sweden a canal from Ekilstuna to Lake Mälaren was completed in 1606.

In Canada, the first lock canal, the Lachine, was built between 1779 and 1783 to by-pass the rapids in the St. Lawrence between Montreal and Lake St. Francis. The locks were less than 40 ft. long and 6 ft. wide and had a depth of 2½ ft.

In the United States, the first canal was built at South Hadley, Mass., between 1792 and 1796. This canal, built with private funds, marked the beginning of an era of active canal construction, first by many corporations formed during this period and later by the several states. These new waterways were intensively used for transportation of goods until the introduction of steam railroads in the 1830's. During the next seventy years, more than half of these canals were abandoned because of the competition of the railroads for commerce.

Notable Canals. Among the canals remaining in active use today are the canalized system of the Mississippi River and its tributaries, the Ohio, Missouri, and Tennessee; the connection with the Great Lakes system through the Illinois River; the New York State Barge Canal system, which succeeds the famous Erie Canal completed in 1825; the Gulf Intracoastal Waterway and the Atlantic Intracoastal Waterways; the Cape Cod Ship Canal; the St. Marys Falls Canal between Lake Huron and Lake Superior; and the Lake Washington Ship Canal from Puget Sound to Lake Washington. The Cape Cod Canal, built by private capital in Massachusetts during 1909-1915 to connect Cape Cod Bay and Buzzards Bay, a distance of about 7⅔ mi. in the land cut, was later purchased by the Federal Government and has since been deepened and widened to provide a channel 500 to 700 ft. wide at the bottom.

Depths dredged and maintained in these waterways are 6 to 9 ft. in the Mississippi, 12 and 14 ft. in the New York State Barge Canal system, 27 ft. in the Cape Cod Ship Canal, 25 ft. in the St. Marys Falls Canal, 12 and 16 ft. in the Intracoastal systems, and 25 ft. in the Lake Washington Ship Canal.

Canada's system of canals connects Montreal with the westernmost Great Lakes. The head of ordinary ocean-going navigation on the St. Lawrence River is at Montreal, approximately 1,000 mi. above the mouth. Above this point, vessels pass westward around rapids into Lake Ontario, through the following canals: Lachine, Beauharnais, Soulanges, Cornwall, and Williamsburg. These canals were under construction or enlargement from about 1820 until the end of the nineteenth century. Their minimum lock dimensions are 270 ft. for length, 43.67 ft. for width, and 14 ft. for depth; some are much larger. The Welland Ship Canal, successor to earlier canals connecting Lake Ontario and Lake Erie, was under construction from 1913 to 1932. It is 27.6 mi. long, and its eight locks, all 80 ft. wide and 30 ft. deep over the sills, range from 859 to 1,350 ft. in length. The Canadians completed a canal between Lake Huron and Lake Superior as early as 1798. Its greatly enlarged successor, the Sault Ste. Marie Canal, skirts the rapids around the St. Marys River and provides for the passage of vessels of 25 ft. draft. Its single lock is 900 ft. long and 60 ft. wide. An alternate canal on the United States side is called the St. Marys Falls Canal.

The Panama Canal, across the Isthmus of Panama, is 51 mi. in length. It provides a channel of 300 ft. minimum width and 41 ft. depth through Gatun and Miraflores lakes and Gaillard (Culebra) Cut. The locks are 1,000 ft. long, 110 ft. wide, and 41 ft. deep over the sills.

A great network of barge canals is found in Great Britain, the Netherlands, Belgium, France, and Germany, with depths of 6 to 10 ft. Ship canals include the North Sea Canal between the North Sea at IJmuiden and the IJsselmeer, length 18 mi., depth 40 ft.; the Kiel Canal between the North Sea and the Baltic Sea, 61½ mi. in length and 36 ft. deep; the Kronstadt Canal, joining the roadstead in the Gulf of Finland with one of the deltaic mouths of the Neva River at Leningrad, length about 28 mi., depth 28 ft.; the Manchester Canal in England, connecting Manchester with the River Mersey at Eastham near Liverpool, length about 35½ mi., depth 28 ft.

The Bruges Ship Canal connects Zeebrugge Harbor, an artificial harbor on the North Sea coast of Belgium, with the city of Bruges; the length is about 6 mi., the depth 28 ft. The Ghent-Terneuzen Canal connects the city of Ghent with the River Schelde at Terneuzen; the length is 18 mi., the depth about 28 ft. *See also* KIEL CANAL; PANAMA CANAL; RIVER ENGINEERING; SUEZ CANAL.   J. M. Bu.

CANAL ZONE. *See* PANAMA.

CANANDAIGUA [kænənde′gwə], the seat of Ontario Co. in northwestern New York, is situated at the north end of Lake Canandaigua, 28 mi. southeast of Rochester. It is an agricultural, industrial, and resort community in a farming area of the Finger Lakes region. The city is governed by a mayor and council. Canandaigua is on the site of Gandundagwa, an ancient Seneca settlement which was second in importance among the villages of the Six Nations. Canandaigua was settled in 1789 and became a town about 1791. Canandaigua Academy, founded in 1795, and Ontario Female Academy, a pioneer in women's education established in 1825, are among the city's institutions for learning. A U.S. Veterans' Hospital is also located here. The New York Central and the Pennsylvania railroads provide transportation. Chief products include chemicals, knit goods, building blocks, sauerkraut, fishing tackle, fire alarm systems, and hardware specialties. Pop. 1950, 8,332.

CANANDAIGUA LAKE [kænənde′gwə], one of the long, narrow Finger Lakes of west central New York State. It is situated in Ontario County and extends southward to form the northwestern border of Yates County. The lake is 15 mi. long and up to 2 mi. wide; it has a surface elevation of 668 ft. above sea level. The lake basin was formed by a lobe of the continental glacier which deepened and enlarged a river bed. The terminal moraine deposited by the glacier dammed the river and turned it into a long, narrow lake. Canandaigua Lake is drained by Clyde Creek, a tributary of Seneca River. The region is noted for its summer resorts and vineyards. The town of Canandaigua, the site of a veterans' hospital, is at the northern end of the lake.   J. E. F.

CANANEA [kɑnɑne′ɑ], a town in the state of Sonora, in northwest Mexico, situated in the Sierra Madre Occidental, at an elevation of about 5,200 ft., about 135 mi. northeast of Hermosillo and 48 mi. by highway southwest of Douglas, Ariz. It is one of the largest copper-producing centers in the world. Silver, lead, and zinc mining and cattle raising are also important occupations. To the south lies Old Cananea, an interesting Indian village. Pop. 1950, 17,914.   S. G. I.

CAÑARI. *See* INDIAN TRIBES, SOUTH AMERICAN.
CANARIE. *See* MUSICAL TERMS.

CANARY, a name applied to the serin finch, *Serinus canarius,* inhabiting the Azores, Madeira, and the Canary Islands, and to the numerous domesticated breeds derived from it. In its natural state it has upper parts of olive-green and gray with dark streaks and under parts of yellow and white with dark streaks on the flanks. It was first imported into Europe early in the sixteenth century; from there it has been carried to every part of the world and has become the best-known and most popular of all cage birds. Many cultivated varieties have been developed which differ considerably from the wild ancestor in shape and color; the commonest of these is wholly of the clear yellow now known as canary yellow. Careful selection has at the same time brought about a great improvement of its singing powers. The breeding and care of canary birds has in some places given a livelihood to numerous persons, and the culture of the canary is in many countries fostered by clubs and shows. Caged birds seldom survive when released, although on one of the Pacific islands a flourishing colony has developed from a few liberated pairs.   H. G. De.

CANARY GRASS, *Phalaris,* a genus of temperate-zone grasses, native in Europe and America. *P. canariensis,* a 4-ft. annual of the Mediterranean region, is grown commercially for canary seed. Ribbon grass or gardener's garters, *P. arundinacea* var. *picta,* a tall (6 ft.) perennial with white striped leaves, is grown in gardens.   J. C. Wis.

CANARY ISLANDS, a Spanish archipelago off the northwest coast of Africa. The Canary Islands comprise an area of 2,807 sq. mi. There are seven islands covering an arc of some 250 mi., with six uninhabited islets at the archipelago's eastern extremity. The principal islands are Tenerife, Grand Canary, Fuerteventura, and Lanzarote. All the islands are mountainous and of volcanic origin. The Pico de Teide on Tenerife is 12,162 ft. high, and on Palma and Grand Canary there are peaks of 7,770 and 6,400 ft., respectively.

The climate is mild and pleasant and has long attracted visitors from northwestern Europe, notably Britain. The rainfall is negligible near sea level, being 11 in. at Las Palmas, but it increases at higher altitudes. The Pico de Teide is snow-covered much of the year. Altitude also determines the types of vegetation, both natural and cultivated. At an elevation of 1,000 ft. agricultural products

Camels are used to pull a crude plow on a field in Lanzarote, Canary Islands.

are tropical, including bananas, coffee, sugar cane, citrus fruit, and date palms. At a still higher altitude cereals, tobacco, tomatoes, and grapes are grown. At an elevation of 3,000 to 6,000 ft. are forests, chiefly pine. On the highest slopes only stunted shrubs are found.

The economy of the islands is essentially agricultural. In the early days of Spanish rule, sugar cane was grown extensively on large slave-worked plantations. When West Indian competition made sugar less profitable, early in the nineteenth century, wine became the great export. The cochineal insect, valuable in dye production, was also introduced, and its export became very profitable. Later on, the vineyards were destroyed by a fungus, and aniline dyes have largely replaced those made from cochineal. Early in the twentieth century, bananas became the most important article of export, both in value and in volume. The other chief exports are tomatoes, potatoes, dried fish, tobacco, and embroidered goods. The women of the Canaries are noted for their fine lace and embroidery work. In 1951, exports from the islands were valued at 125 million dollars, and imports, 137 million.

The principal ports are Las Palmas and Santa Cruz de Tenerife, both of which are important fueling and communications centers for ocean liners and cargo ships on transatlantic routes. Both ports are connected by air with Seville and Madrid, and by steamship service with Barcelona, Cádiz, Marseille, and Casablanca. Inter-island transportation is available by boat, and there are daily flights between Tenerife and Great Canary.

The Canary Islands, with a population in 1950 of 807,773, are administered as an integral part of Spain. In 1927 they were divided into two provinces: Las Palmas, consisting of the islands of Lanzarote, Fuerteventura, and Grand Canary; and Santa Cruz de Tenerife, consisting of Tenerife, Palma, Gomera, and Hierro. The 1950 population of Las Palmas province was 379,977, and that of Santa Cruz de Tenerife, 427,796. They are thus among the most densely populated provinces of Spain.

The original inhabitants of the Canaries, the Guanches, were in large part exterminated, the rest being absorbed by the Norman and Spanish settlers. A certain amount of Negro blood has been introduced into the islands from near-by Africa. The universal language is Spanish.

History. The Canaries, possibly known in ancient times as the "Fortunate Isles," were probably known to the Phoenicians and certainly to the Romans. Arab sailors stopped there in the twelfth century. Portugal claimed the islands in 1341, but Castile took possession of them in 1402, thereby ushering in a confused period of claim and counterclaim, finally resolved by the Treaty of Alcacova (1479) by which Portugal surrendered her claims to the Spanish crown. Several bloody campaigns were required before the Guanches, the aboriginal inhabitants, were subjugated. Columbus stopped at Las Palmas en route to America on his first voyage, and thereafter the islands were much used by vessels in the trade with Spanish America. The Spanish government at one time used the islands as a place of political exile, and in 1936 the Canaries served General Franco as the first base for the nationalist rebellion against the Republic.

CANASTA. *See* CARD GAMES (*Rummy*).

CANBERRA [kæ'nbɛrə], the capital city of Australia, in the federal district officially known as the Australian Capital Territory, in the southeastern part of the country. It is 155 mi. southwest of Sydney and 280 mi. northeast of Melbourne. Canberra is beautifully situated in a basin surrounded by flat-topped and pyramid-shaped hills; the northern foothills of the Gourock Range are to the east, and the northern extension of the Australian Alps to the west. A short distance to the east is the upper course of the Murrumbidgee River. The city has a dry, subtropical type of climate, with warm summers. January averages 69° F., while July, the coldest month, averages 42° F., and there are occasional frosts. The average annual rainfall is 24 in., and fall (April) is the wettest season. The area around Canberra is not developed economically. There is a little farming for local needs, and an increasing tourist trade. But the major activity is the administration of Australia.

The city and federal district owe their existence to the rivalry between Sydney and Melbourne. Since neither of these cities could agree on the site of a permanent capital, the location was chosen in 1908, and in 1909 New South Wales surrendered title to the area. A contest held to secure suitable city plans was won by Walter Burley Griffin of Chicago in 1913, and the city was founded in that year. Griffin planned a city based on two concentric circles: one circle to contain the government buildings and the other commercial buildings; smaller circles connect the larger circles. Canberra had a difficult beginning. First, World War I interrupted both plans and construction. The cornerstone of the capital was laid in 1920 by Edward, Duke of Windsor, then Prince of Wales. On May 9, 1927, King George VI, then Duke of York, opened the first parliamentary session in the new Parliament House. The depression halted construction in 1929 and, finally, World War II interfered with completion of the buildings.

Parliament House, Canberra, in the Australian Capital Territory, is surrounded by parks and gardens. Facing the entrance is the King George VI Memorial.

COURTESY AUSTRALIAN NEWS & INFORMATION BUREAU

The city is connected by railroad, highway, and airline with Adelaide, Brisbane, Melbourne, Perth, Sydney, and other important Australian cities. It is the seat of Canberra University College and the Australian National University, established in 1946 for post-graduate research in medicine, physical and social sciences, and Pacific studies. Tourist attractions include the Australian-American Memorial, the Australian War Memorial, Parliament House, and the Church of St. John the Baptist (1841). Located here also are the Royal Military College, the Royal Australian Air Force base, and the Royal Australian Navy communications center. There are parks in the center of Canberra, which is often called the "garden" city. Pop. 1954 (city), 28,277; (Australian Capital Territory), 30,000.

CANBERRA AGREEMENT, THE, between Australia and New Zealand concluded at Canberra, Australia, Jan. 18, 1944, was the first step toward the formation of a united political, military, and economic front between the two countries. It provided for a continuous means of consultation on the control of territories, native welfare, and air communications in the South Pacific area and proposed a South Seas regional commission, to be composed of Australia, New Zealand, Great Britain, France, and the United States, to consider postwar development and native welfare in the islands adjacent to the two dominions.

CANCAN [ka′nkan; kã′kã′] (also known under the name of *chahut*), a wild and indecorous French dance of the nineteenth century in fast double time, imitating the Spanish fandango. Originally a slow and decorous dance, the cancan gradually developed suggestive movements which excluded it from high society. The comedian Masarié is credited with having popularized the cancan when, in 1830, as "Joco" he

introduced the *chahut* to the French. According to other sources the cancan was originally a dance imitating monkeys. Offenbach inserted one into his *Orpheus in Hades,* and transferred from this work it has more recently become popular as a part of the ballet suite *Gaîté Parisienne* (1938), arranged by Manuel Rosenthal. P. N.

CANCER, the Crab, a constellation whose symbol ♋ is the fourth sign of the zodiac, which the sun enters on June 22. Its center is at right ascension, 8 hr. 40′; declination, +20°. This is an inconspicuous group, including no stars brighter than of the fourth magnitude. It is historically important, for around 125 B.C. Hipparchus found that the sun at the summer solstice was among the stars of Cancer and therefore stood at noon over locations at 23½° N. lat., and this parallel was named the Tropic of Cancer. Precession of the equinoxes has since moved the summer solstice westward about 30° into Gemini, but the old geographical term still stands. Cancer includes many interesting telescopic doubles. Especially attractive is Praesepe, or the Beehive (M 44), an open cluster of over 300 faint stars. To the unaided eye, this appears as a dim, hazy spot.

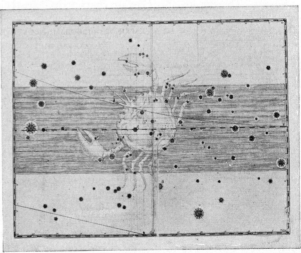

COURTESY OF AMERICAN MUSEUM OF NATURAL HISTORY

Cancer, "The Crab"

In Classical mythology, the Crab pinched Heracles' foot when he was fighting the Hydra. Heracles crushed the Crab, but Juno later placed it in the skies.   J. H. P.

CANCER. *See* Tumors.

CANCERROOT, a common name applied to parasitic herbs of the broomrape family which bear scales in place of leaves and are yellowish or brownish in color. The beech-drop, *Epifagus virginiana,* the squawroot, *Conopholis americana,* and the one-flowered broomrape, *Orobranche uniflora,* are common throughout most of the United States.

        J. C. Wis.

CANCIONEIRO [kã'syʊne'ru]. The Portuguese word *cancioneiro* denotes in general any collection of songs, but in particular the term designates three great compilations of medieval poetry in the Galician-Portuguese language, known as the *Cancioneiro da Ajuda, C. da Vaticana,* and *C. Colocci-Brancuti,* now *C. da Biblioteca National.* Both the *Vaticana* and the *Colocci-Brancuti* are copies of originals now lost, made in Italy during the Renaissance; and their contents are substantially alike, since the former, with 1,205 poems, duplicates all but 442 of the 1,567 lyrics in the latter. An index of a lost codex compiled in the sixteenth century by Angelo Colocci contains 1,675 entries, roughly corresponding to the contents of the Vatican and the Colocci-Brancuti manuscripts, and allusions exist to still other similar collections which have dropped from sight. The *Cancioneiro da Ajuda,* although fragmentary and containing but 310 poems, many of which occur in the other two *cancioneiros,* is much more ancient, and may well be an unfinished and mutilated original compilation dating from the late thirteenth or early fourteenth century. The three *cancioneiros,* which thus complement one another and preserve over 1,500 different lyrics of the twelfth, thirteenth, and fourteenth centuries, together with the names of many of their composers, point to the existence of a lost general *cancioneiro,* and thus warrant the use of the term to designate the corpus of medieval Galician-Portuguese lyric poetry. Often coupled with the three Portuguese collections is the thirteenth-century compilation made by King Alfonso X of Castile, composed in Galician, and known as the *Cantigas de Santa Maria.* Not to be confused with the medieval *cancioneiros* is the collection of Portuguese poems made in the sixteenth century by Garcia de Resende and known as the *Cancioneiro Geral.*

Forms. The *cancioneiro* poets are characterized by their lyrical grace and technical virtuosity. The framework within which they operated was narrow, for they limited themselves to three attitudes: that of the lover expressing the mortal pangs of unrequited love in a *cantiga d'amor* (lay of love); that of the lovelorn maiden singing a plaint about her absent loved one in a *cantiga d'amigo* (lay of a lover); or that of an individual heaping caustic, ribald abuse and taunts on some victim in a *cantiga d'escarneo e maldizer* (lay of mockery and vilification). By another method of classification, the lyrics may be divided according to subject or occasion as village dance songs (*bailadas*), mountain songs (*serranilhas*), boat songs (*barcarolas*), dawn songs (*alvoradas*), pilgrim songs (*cantigas de romaria*), or, when in the form of a poetic duel, as *tençoes.*

The hundreds of *cantigas d'amor*—in the *Cancioneiro da Ajuda* alone, 304 of the 310 poems are of this type—reflect more strongly than the other types the spirit of palace and court. Kings, nobles, knights, and professional poets vied with one another and in their compositions refinement, artifice, and convention reached their apogee. Their lyricism, which is subjective both conventionally and genuinely, is purely static, the only intimation of movement being a yearning for death. Courtly love achieved the ultimate polish: the lady was, with rare exceptions, unidentified; her physical traits were etherealized to a mere assertion of the fact of her beauty. The singer's love was never consummated. The expression was distilled into the volume of only a few stanzas at most, and the poetic beauty consists in the verbal arabesques spun around the simple theme, in repetition, with or without modulations, in artful linking, and occasionally in the use of a refrain.

The *cantigas d'amigo* are courtly expressions of the innate lyricism and melancholy of the Portuguese people. These poems are redolent of the forest, field, river, and sea, or their rhythms may pulse with the measures of the village dance. It is noteworthy that the sea, the ever-present highway to glory and adventure, appears in this poetry purely as a lyrical motif, the cause for the separation of lovers, or the death of a loved one, and its waves and beaches are melancholy consolations to the bereft maiden. Characteristically the stanzas of these poems are short, with strongly marked parallelism of content and rhyme, and in them the refrain is frequent.

The *cantigas d'escarneo e maldizer,* on first impression so radically different in conception and spirit, are in fact implicit in the very nature of the *cancioneiro* poetry. Displaying all the ingenuity and poetic artifice of the other types, they give vent to a vein of mockery, ribaldry, savage satire, and a raffish delight in the coarse and obscene which, without paradox, could be fully cultivated only in the highly refined, poetic atmosphere of the court.

Origins. The poetry preserved in the *cancioneiros* is the product of a school that flourished for some 150 years in Portugal, especially during the thirteenth century, and whose art was practiced elsewhere in the Iberian Peninsula. The lyrics are extant, the authors are for the most part identified, and the poetic art is thoroughly explored; but the genesis of this poetry still poses a puzzle. The problem is to evaluate the respective roles of at least three antecedents: the poetry of Provence; the Arabic lyric of the Moslem regions of Spain and Portugal; and an indigenous poetry whose existence, formerly a matter of conjecture, has been attested by the discovery of brief lyrics termed *harjas* in Arabic, which are couched wholly or in part in a Hispano-Romance tongue. A fourth possible factor to consider is the medieval Latin lyric poetry of Europe, although its influence has been disputed.

Beyond doubt the influence of the poetry of Provence was important. The French blood and ties of the Portuguese kings, the sojourns of princes and nobles in France, the influx of French warriors aiding in the warfare against the Moslems in the Iberian peninsula, the commercial intercourse, and travel along the pilgrimage route to Santiago de Compostela in northwestern Spain can account for the infiltration of the poetry of Provence into Galicia and Portugal. The similarity of the native language to that of Provence undoubtedly favored the naturalization of the poetry. And there is positive evidence of the presence of Provençal troubadours in Portugal. Furthermore, the indebtedness is evident in the poetic forms and devices, the terminology, and the vocabulary; and the imitation is explicitly avowed, as for example by the poet-king Denis.

On the other hand, the Provençal poetry itself did not spring into being out of a vacuum, and it has been demonstrated that the Spanish Moslems developed and cultivated, before the flowering of Provençal poetry, a type of lyric which undoubtedly was disseminated into Romance-speaking territory, and which in strophic form, imagery, and spirit is demonstrably similar to the poetry of Provence and Galicia-Portugal, not only in the amatory but also in the defamatory mood. Given the deep interpenetration of the Moslem and Christian cultures, the influence of the Arabic poetic art and spirit on the *cancioneiro* poetry can be debated only in respect to degree.

In the third place, it can no longer be doubted that the courtly *cancioneiro* poetry flourished on the subsoil of an indigenous poetic element, this being a body of Hispano-Romance verse antedating the influx of Provençal poetry and exemplified by the *harjas,* the oldest of which are certainly earlier than the first dated *cancioneiro* poems. A good proportion of the extant *harjas,* wherein a maiden complains of her lover, bear a striking resemblance to the *cantigas d'amigo* in tone, theme, and even wording; and the Mozarabic dialect in which they are expressed is linguistically akin to Galician-Portuguese.

King Denis. Denis, sixth king of Portugal, who reigned from 1279 to 1325, is the most distinguished, although not the only author of royal blood among the *cancioneiro* poets. Literary influence upon his life was strong. He was tutored by the French ecclesiastic and man of letters Aymeric d'Ebrard, afterwards Bishop of Coimbra. His grandfather, whom he visited in his youth, was Alfonso X of Castile, renowned patron of learning and letters. Emulating his grandfather, King Denis fostered learning in his own kingdom, commanding the translation into Portuguese of learned works in other tongues and establishing the center of studies which became the University of Coimbra. Even more enthusiastically than his father, Alfonso III, he welcomed to his court *trobadores, jograis,* and *segreis,* composers and singers by occupation, and he himself practiced the poetic art. No separate anthology of his verse has survived, but 138 of his poems have been preserved in the *cancioneiros,* from which they have been abstracted and edited as a separate collection. With King Denis the poetic movement neared its end, and it survived his death only a brief time, but in the King's hands the lyric attained some of its most nearly perfect expressions. Denis cultivated all three types, *cantigas d'amor, cantigas d'amigo,* and *cantigas d'escarneo e maldizer,* composing with exquisite technical skill and remarkable charm. At times, notably in the *cantigas d'amor,* he affected what he termed the "Provençal manner;" but on the other hand he implied that there was another less conventional and more sincere manner, one which is exemplified in his *cantigas d'amigo,* whose fresh bucolic and popular quality reflect the side of the King's genius which manifested itself in activity to promote the well-being of his people and earned him the title of *Rei Lavrador.* R. S. Ws.

CANDIA. *See* IRÁKLION.

CANDIDA [ka'ndɪdə], one of the "pleasant" plays in G. B. Shaw's *Plays, Pleasant and Unpleasant* (1898). *Candida* is a well-made play, constructed according to Classical standards and possessing unity of time, place, and action. The Classical obligatory scene of the "auction" suggests Ibsen's *Lady from the Sea,* but the two plays have independent inspirations. The conflict in *Candida* is presented as a clash between the ideologies of Christian Socialism and the Pre-Raphaelite Movement. Eugene Marchbanks, a young aristocrat and poet, falls in love with Candida, the wife of the devoted vicar of St. Dominic's, Victoria Park E., Rev. James Mavor Morell. Candida, the incarnation of the "mother" woman, divining Eugene's infatuation, decides to draw him out and then explain to him the true nature of love. She is not interested in the platitudinous sermons of her husband, who is intoxicated with his own oratorical phrases. At the climax she places herself at "auction" before Marchbanks and her husband and, as both auctioneer and slave, ironically listens to the bids of her "masters." Although Eugene makes the more poignant and poetic bid, Candida accepts her husband's offer because he is weaker and needs her more than Marchbanks does. The play is Ibsen's *A Doll's House* in reverse. Eugene rises above the bourgeois interpretation of love as contentment, and goes out into the night to larger hopes and greater deeds. This is the "secret in the poet's heart" and the justification of the play's subtitle, *"A Mystery."* A. H.

CANDIDE [kɑ̃'di'd], a philosophical tale by Voltaire, written in 1758 and published in 1759 (definitive version 1761), 42 editions appearing in Voltaire's lifetime. The work ridicules contemporary foibles, such as pride of rank, religious and political intolerance, and complacent optimism (as derived from Alexander Pope and the philosopher Leibniz). Candide, an unsophisticated youth, goes through many adventures; he loses his home because he loves above his rank, is forced into military service, sees the horrors of war, witnesses material and moral destruction during the Lisbon earthquake (1755), suffers from the Inquisition, flees to South America, visits Jesuit-ruled Paraguay and the wonderland Eldorado, returns to Europe, and finally settles with his companions near Constantinople to "cultivate his garden," i.e., to gain his life by the work of his hands, for "work alone makes life bearable, keeps away boredom, vice and need." The sarcastic picture of the intolerable abuses that fill the world and the satire on the placid attitude that accepts them are of timeless significance. Voltaire's criticism conveys to the reader an appeal to fight oppression and to strive for the enlightenment of mankind. H. D.

CANDIRU, or **CARNERO** [kandɪ'əru, kɑrnɛ'əro], *Vandellia cirrhosa,* a parasitic South American catfish of the family Pygidiidae. A small species, usually not exceeding 2 in. in length, it has a long slim body, sharp teeth on the jaws, and jagged spines on the gill. It slips under the gill cover and fastens onto the gills of large fishes, usually catfish, where it regularly lives. The blood which flows from the wound is sucked up. In addition, the gill cover serves as a shelter from its enemies. The candiru is dreaded in many parts of Brazil because of its habit of entering the urethra of bathers. Having entered and set its opercular spines, it causes terrible pain, and death may ensue if it reaches the bladder. It may be removed successfully by a surgical operation. When in the water native bathers use special fiber sheaths to protect themselves. Some other small species of the same family may pierce the skin of fishes or other animals and suck the blood of their victims. E. C. R.

CANDLEBERRY. *See* BAYBERRY; WAX MYRTLE.

CANDLEMAS [ka'ndəlməs] (O.E. *candelmaesse*), is the feast of the Purification of the Virgin Mary, which commemorates the Presentation of the child Jesus in the Temple and the ritual purification of his mother forty days after his birth (Luke, ii, 22-38), celebrated February 2. By the Greeks it is called the *Hypapante Kyriou,* or Meeting of the Lord, in reference to the meeting of Christ and his mother with Simeon and Anna. Attested in the East in the fourth century, the feast spread slowly in the West. The blessing of candles for liturgical and devotional use, prescribed by the Roman Missal for this feast, came into common use from the eleventh century onward. The priest, in purple cope, recites five prayers over the beeswax candles, sprinkles them with holy water, incenses them, and distributes them to those present as the choir sings the *Nunc dimittis* or Canticle of Simeon (Luke ii, 29-32). The procession symbolizes the entry of Christ, "Light of the World," into the temple.   W. C.

CANDLENUT, a Malayan tree, *Aleurites moluccana,* of the spurge (euphorbia) family, widely cultivated and somewhat naturalized in tropical countries, where it is grown for its oil-yielding seeds; it reaches a size of 60 ft. The rough, roundish, black-shelled nuts, marbled in grayish-white, 1 to 2 in. in diameter, are edible and highly nutritious if roasted about twenty minutes. The oil from the seeds has commercial use in varnishes and native use as a natural candle.
     J. C. Wis.

CANDLES. Candles and tapers are primarily wax-impregnated wicks and papers. Candles have been important since ancient times as sources of light, and although they were replaced first by kerosene lamps and later by the incandescent electric lamp, their use has actually expanded because of their ornamental value. In spite of progress in lighting, the term "candle power" is used as a unit for measuring the brilliance of any given light.

Ingredients. Ancient candles as well as modern varieties were manufactured by molding a blend of fats and waxes around a wick prepared from flax or cotton. Machines have replaced hand labor, and new wax formulations have been introduced for decorative effects. The first waxes used were mutton tallow and beeswax. The latter is still prescribed for candles used in the Roman Catholic Church. Spermaceti, obtained from whales, was introduced into candles during the American Revolution. During the middle of the nineteenth century, paraffin wax was added to the list of waxes recommended for candle manufacture. Later, stearic acid was found to impart greater illuminating power than tallow and other glyceride fats.

Candle-Wax Formulation. Wax formulations suitable for candles utilize paraffin wax, stearic acid, hydrogenated vegetable oil, beeswax, carnauba wax, candelilla wax, and ozocerite, in that order. Standard candles contain paraffin wax (60 per cent), stearic acid (35 per cent), and beeswax (5 per cent). Pure beeswax candles vary from the pure insect wax to those containing as much as 50 per cent paraffin wax and 10 per cent stearic acid. Depending upon conditions of finished-candle storage, the wax blend may be stiffened with carnauba or candelilla or softened by using amorphous paraffin waxes. Suitable oil-soluble dyes may be used as coloring.

Wicking is braided from good quality cotton or linen and is then pickled by soaking in solutions of borax or ammonium chloride, sulphate, or phosphate. This treatment facilitates proper burning of the wick and prevents afterglow when the candle is extinguished. Porosity or capillarity of the wick must be so regulated as to burn all of the wax formula melted by the wick flame.

Modern candle plants are equipped with wax-melting kettles for blending the wax formulas and with candle-molding machines equipped with a series of molds whose temperatures can be controlled. Each cylinder mold contains a hollow piston through which the wick is fed. The wax formula is cooled as low as possible without solidifying and is pumped into the molds. Cooling water is then cir-

culated until solidification is complete. The finished candles are automatically ejected and the wicks are cut. The cycle is then repeated. Finishing operations include cutting to standard length and polishing with buffers.

Numerous special candles are molded in almost any desired shape, size, or color. Some are perfumed so as to impart a desired odor when burned. Candles burning with colored flames have been patented but do not contain appreciable quantities of wax and have not been successful because of their tendency to smoke.   H. H. Y.

CANDLEWOOD, or **CANDLEWORT,** the name given to any finely split wood of a resinous nature that may be used for torches or as a substitute for candles. The rhodeswood, *Amyris balsamifera,* of tropical America, and the ocotillo of the southwestern United States are examples.
     J. A. Bo.

CANDY. *See* Kandy.

CANDYTUFT, *Iberis,* a genus of the mustard family with about thirty species native to the Mediterranean region, including annuals, perennials, and some shrubs, all low-

COURTESY OF N.Y. BOTANICAL GARDENS

Candytuft (Iberis), of the mustard family, is native to southern Europe and western Asia.

growing (6-24 in.). *I. sempervirens,* widely grown in gardens, is woody, with small evergreen leaves and white flowers in spring. The rocket candytuft, *I. amara,* and globe candytuft, *I. umbellata,* are popular annuals, the first with heads of fragrant white flowers, the second with flowers not fragrant, in shades from white to pink and purple.
     J. C. Wis.

CANE, the common name of two species of bamboo, the only ones native to the United States. They are large grasses, forming dense thickets, known as canebrakes, along rivers in the southern states. The large cane, *Arundinaria gigantea,* grows to 30 ft., the small cane *A. tecta,* to 14 ft.   J. C. Wis.

CANEA. *See* Khania.
CANELLA. *See* Indian Tribes, South American.

CANELLA [kənɛ'lə] *Canella alba,* a tree growing to forty feet, a member of the canella family, native to the West Indies and Florida. It is highly aromatic, with leathery leaves, fragrant purple flowers, and black berries. An infusion of the orange colored inner bark has a spicy odor and bitter taste, and is locally used as a spice. It is sometimes called wild cinnamon.   J. C. Wis.

CANELLO, UGO ANGELO [kɑnɛ'llo] (1848-1883), Italian linguist and philologist, was born at Guia (between Treviso and Belluno), on June 21, 1848. He studied first medicine and then letters in the University of Padua, where he received his doctor's degree in 1869. He then went to Bonn to study with the founder of Romance studies, Friedrich Diez, and may be credited with having implanted in Italy, where it was to prosper greatly, the severe linguistic method favored by Diez in the study of Romance languages. Canello taught German language and literature in the Accademia Scientifico-Letteraria in Milan (1874-1875), and then he was called to Padua to occupy the first Italian chair of Comparative History of Romance Literatures, created for him by Minister Bonghi on the suggestion of G. I. Ascoli. There he taught until his death, which resulted from a traffic accident in Padua on May 29, 1883.

Although he yielded in some measure to the general Darwinian and positivistic trend of his times, which tended to assimilate linguistics and literature to the natural sciences, Canello introduced daring new concepts, which went beyond that frame and announced new times. In dealing with words he constantly tried to discover life behind them, to understand the person who used them, and so to interpret history. His etymological as well as his literary studies show therefore a fine artistic penetration and a definite interest in semantic and cultural problems. The great *History of the Italian Language,* which he had carefully planned, was interrupted by his death. Among his most important works are the following: *Il Vocalismo tonico italiano,* published in *Rivista di filologia romanza,* I (1874), and in *Zeitschrift für romanische Philologie,* 1 (1877); *Gli allòtropi italiani,* in *Archivio glottologico italiano,* III (1879), a model of research, which presents a study of linguistic doublets of the type seen in the English words *loyal: legal; La Vita e le opere del trovatore Arnaldo Daniello* (1883), which was highly praised by Karl Bartsch; and several other works on Provençal poetry. Canello also translated with fine taste several poems of the troubadours. G. B.

CANE SUGAR. *See* Sugar Cane; Food Industries.

CANES VENATICI [ke'niz vinæ'tɪsai], the Hunting Dogs, a modern constellation located immediately under the handle of the Big Dipper. Its brightest star, Cor Coroli, of the third magnitude, is an interesting telescopic double. The group contains the globular cluster M 3 and abounds in nebulae.

Mythology pictures this group as the two dogs of Boötes eagerly chasing the Big Bear around the celestial pole, the North Star. J. H. P.

CANFIELD. *See* Card Games.
CANFIELD, DOROTHY. *See* Fisher, Dorothy Canfield.

CANISIUS, ST. PETER [kəni'shəs] (1521-1597), Jesuit, leader in Germany of the Counter Reformation, called "the second apostle of Germany," was born at Nijmegen, the Netherlands. He entered the Society of Jesus in 1543, founding the first German house of the Order at Cologne in 1544, and serving as its first German Provincial from 1556 to 1569. He attended the Council of Trent as theologian of Cardinal Otto Truchsess in 1547 and as papal theologian in 1562. He labored with effective energy to restore and preserve the Catholic faith in central Europe. Traveling tirelessly through Germany, Poland, Austria, and Switzerland, he preached, founded schools, and published countless books and pamphlets, including the famous triple *Catechism* which had over two hundred editions in twelve languages before his death at Freiburg in Switzerland, Dec. 21, 1597. He was canonized and named a doctor of the church in 1925, September 26 being assigned as his feast. W. C.

CANISIUS COLLEGE, an accredited college of arts and sciences and graduate school occupying 12 acres in a residential area of Buffalo, N.Y., was founded in 1870 by the Fathers of the Roman Catholic Society of Jesus. Day sessions of the College are for men only; evening sessions and all graduate classes are coeducational. The College confers the A.B. and B.S. in liberal arts and sciences, the B.B.A., and the B.S. in business and in accredited pre-engineering, predental, and premedical studies. The Graduate School offers the A.M. in English and history, the M.S. in chemistry, and the M.Ed. An accredited program for secondary school teacher training leads to permanent New York State teacher certification. A basic liberal arts curriculum, embracing English literature, modern languages, history, speech, sociology, natural sciences, mathematics, philosophy, and theology, at least 80 semester hours, is required in every undergraduate program. Canisius has an active chapter of the National Jesuit Honor Society, Alpha Sigma Nu. Liberal undergraduate scholarships and graduate fellowships are awarded, and grants-in-aid and student loans are available. On-campus dormitory accommodations are not provided, but economical boarding facilities exist in the immediate neighborhood. *For statistics see* Colleges and Universities.

CANIS MAJOR [ke'nɪs], the Greater Dog, the prominent constellation centered at about right ascension, 6 hr. 40 min.; declination —22°. It includes the brightest star in the

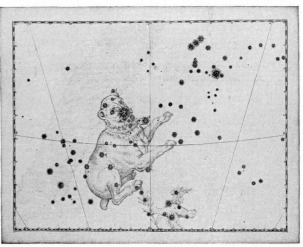

COURTESY OF THE AMERICAN MUSEUM OF NATURAL HISTORY

CANIS MAJOR, "THE GREATER DOG"

sky, Sirius, and four stars of the second magnitude. These with some fainter ones outline fairly well the figure of a dog. The group may be seen from any part of the world except in high northern latitudes. The Milky Way crosses its eastern part. The constellation includes some interesting double stars and two clusters.

In mythology, Canis Major was the larger of the two dogs that were constant companions of Orion, the Hunter. *See also* Sirius. J. H. P.

CANIS MINOR, the Lesser Dog, the small constellation located immediately north of the celestial equator at right ascension 7 hr. 30 min., and therefore visible from almost any part of the world. Aside from the bright star Procyon and a third-magnitude star, there is nothing in the group but dim objects. The faint star designated 14 is an interesting telescopic triple. In mythology, Canis Minor was the smaller of Orion's dogs. *See also* Procyon. J. H. P.

CANKERWORM, the name given to the caterpillars of the geometrid moths. They are also known as inchworms, spanworms, and measuring worms because of the loop formed by their bodies as they crawl. The six true legs are present in front, but only two pairs of false legs are present at the rear. In walking, the hind legs are pulled up close to the front ones, and when they secure a firm grip, the body is stretched forward. More than 2,000 different kinds are known, and many are serious pests. In both the spring cankerworm, *Paleacrita vernata,* which normally lays its eggs in the spring, and the fall cankerworm, *Alsophila pometaria,* the females are wingless. Pupation takes place in the ground, the females crawling up the trunks of trees to mate and lay their eggs. The larvae of both species often occur together. The larvae have the habit, when disturbed, of dropping, spinning a silken thread as they go, and climbing up it when danger is past. When numerous, cankerworms may defoliate large areas of forest. The adults are medium sized moths usually about 1 in. across the wings, and a few species 2 in. They do not generally fold their wings over their backs, as do other moths, but leave them spread and extended while at rest.   C. H. Cu.

CANNA [kæ′nə], the only genus of the canna family, with about fifty species native to tropical regions, with many species in Mexico and South America. They are handsome herbaceous plants, 4 to 10 ft. high, with broad, striking leaves, often bronze, and red or yellow flowers in large irregular clusters. Cannas were used chiefly for their foliage until about 1860, when a new race of dwarf hybrids with superior foliage appeared and from these, crossed with other species, varieties, often with fine, soft-colored flowers have been developed. After the countries where much hybridizing has been done, some are called Italian, and others French varieties. Cannas are used largely in civic plantings where bold, strong effects are needed. Cannas are of easy culture, but the roots must be dug and stored over winter. Starch is procured from the roots of *C. edulis,* native to tropical America and widely cultivated for this purpose. Indian shot is a common name for canna.   J. C. Wis.

CANNAE, BATTLE OF [kæ′ni] (216 B.C.), one of the great battles of the Second Punic War. At Cannae, in southeastern Italy, Hannibal encountered a Roman army much larger than his own. Depending upon his cavalry to destroy the enemy's wings, Hannibal formed his infantry in a hollow crescent and gave ground at the center as the Romans advanced. In the meantime his cavalry routed the Roman flankers and then fell upon the Roman rear. The trap was closed as Hannibal's infantry surrounded the enemy on the remaining three sides. The Roman losses were 25,000 killed and 10,000 taken prisoner; Hannibal's loss was 5,700.   T. B. J.

CANNAN, EDWIN (1861-1935), British economist, was born in 1861. He was educated at Balliol College, Oxford University, and began lecturing at the London School of Economics in 1897. From 1907 to 1926 he was professor of political economy at the University of London, and was dean of the university's faculty of economics from 1900 to 1904. His *History of the Theories of Production and Distribution in English Political Economy from 1776 to 1848* (1893) established him as an authoritative historian and a penetrating analyst of British economic thought. In his *History of Local Rates in England* (1896) he compared equity with economy as criteria of taxation, "economy" being used in the sense of

the best utilization of available means. He concluded that, of the two, the principle of equity was the weaker, because that which is just and equitable may prove no longer economical. An uneconomic basis of taxation, he held, leads to an uneconomic distribution of population. In *Money* (1918) Cannan stated that "marginal utility plays the same part with regard to gold (both for ordinary purposes and for currency) as it does with other commodities." On the supply of money, he said that increased demand for currency does not always cause "an exactly proportional rise in the value of currency and a reciprocal fall of price." Cannan also contributed a valuable clarification and modernization of Adam Smith's theory of supply and demand. Among his other works are *Elementary Political Economics* (1888), *Coal Nationalization* (1919), *An Economist's Protest* (1927), *A Review of Economic Theory* (1929), *Balance of Trade Delusions* (1931), and *Economic Scares* (1933). Cannan died at Bournemouth, Apr. 8, 1935.   E. W.

CANNES [ka′n], a popular resort city on the Mediterranean coast of southeastern France, in the department of Alpes-Maritimes, about 19 mi. southwest of Nice. Cannes lies on the pleasant Golfe de la Napoule, noted for its excellent beaches and its agreeable climate. The average temperature is 50° F. during the winter; rain falls about seventy days in the year. The resort is situated on a slope backed by a range of hills, a fertile and picturesque region in which flowers, citrus fruit, olives, figs, peaches, and grapes grow in abundance. Cannes is supposed to have been an ancient Roman settlement, but little is known of its early history. Tobias George Smollet, the British novelist, described it as a mere fishing village in 1763. Napoleon landed near Cannes on escaping from Elba in 1815. In 1834 Henry Peter Brougham, British chancellor and baron of Brougham and Vaux, became attracted to the place and built a villa there, establishing its vogue as a fashionable resort. A meeting of the Supreme Council of the Allies, the Conference of Cannes, was held at the resort from Jan. 6 to Jan. 13, 1922, to consider modifying reparations which were being exacted from the defeated nations after World War I. In World War II the town was held for a short time by Italian forces, following the Italian invasion of southern France in June 1940.

Magnificent boulevards are a feature of Cannes and of its environs. Some sections of the town contain steep streets and picturesque flights of steps leading from one level to another; the older part of the town is built on Mont Chevalier, a height jutting out into the sea, while the newer sections lie along the lower coastline. Points of interest include the Hôtel de Ville; the Musée Rothschild, exhibiting engravures, paintings, and sculptures; the Church of Notre Dame d'Espérance; the tower, 70 ft. high, and other remains of the ancient Château des Abbés de Lerins, constructed between 1070 to 1385 on the summit of Mont Chevalier; the Musée Lycklama, containing, among other exhibits, a notable collection of Classical antiquities; the great Casino Municipal; and statues of Lord Brougham, of Edward VII, and of Frédéric Mistral, the Provençal poet; and a memorial to the war dead. Excursions to the Lerins Islands attract many visitors. On one of these islands, the Island of Ste Marguerite, the Man in the Iron Mask was imprisoned in the seventeenth century. Achile Bazaine, the French marshal courtmartialed in 1873, escaped from his prison on this island the following year and fled to Spain. A famous monastery dating from the fifth century and a castle built in 1088 stand on the Island of St. Honorat. Cannes has a good harbor, and oils, anchovies, and fruit are among the principal exports. Local manufactures include

The yacht basin and beach, dotted with gay cabanas, in a setting of luxuriant growth at Cannes, a fashionable resort on the French Riviera

soaps, ceramics, and perfumes, and fishing remains an important occupation. Air and rail services connect Cannes with other parts of Europe. Pop. 1954, 50,192.

CANNIBALISM, the practice of eating human flesh, derives its name from *canibi,* a native variant of Carib (West Indies), the tribe among whom Spanish discoverers first noted the custom. The more formal and earlier term was anthropophagy, or "man-eating." Cannibalism is usually associated with savage tribes of the West Indies, adjacent South America, the South Seas, and west and central Africa, but was also met with less commonly in other quarters of the world. It may have existed among Europeans in pre-Christian times. There is some evidence of it in the Bronze Age of Bohemia and Austria, among the early Neolithic people of Switzerland, and even in the much earlier Aurignacian stage of central Europe. It may have been one of the earliest of human traits.

Primitive peoples so frequently equated men and animals in their thinking that it is possible that human flesh was not considered significantly different from other foodstuffs. There is probably no instinctive aversion to eating it; the horror shown by civilized and many primitive peoples was developed by convention, parallel to the aversion to eating other foods considered unorthodox, unclean, or unfit for human consumption, just as the pig and dog are unclean foods for all Semitic peoples. The abhorrence of such foods is an extraordinarily deep emotion, not dictated by biological necessity. Cannibalism has often been a resort under stress of extreme famine, or, as with castaways, when there were no other resources. But it was very unusual for cannibalism

as an accepted practice to include eating one's own fellow tribesmen.

Human flesh was never a component of everyday foodstuffs, though some tribes of New Guinea and west Africa indulged frequently. The aims of the practice were sometimes religious, in connection with sacrifice; or even more widely, the flesh of an enemy was devoured in order to secure his qualities of bravery or magic power. In some instances the complete destruction of the corpse by eating it was thought completely to destroy a lodging place for the ghost. Without doubt mere savage revenge and bloodthirstiness were motives.

Cannibalism varied widely in occurrence and character. In the New World it was concentrated in the Antilles-Amazon area. In Aztec ceremonial sacrifices large numbers of human victims were eaten. In North America cannibalism centered along the Gulf Coast and was an incidental rite of frenzied ceremonialists on the north Pacific Coast, but elsewhere on the continent was little more than devouring an enemy's heart to acquire his virtues. African instances show the same variation: the practice was common in the Congo and westward north of the Gulf of Guinea, but it appears to have been wholly absent on the upper Nile and of little consequence in southern Africa. In western Africa members of the important Leopard Society, who dressed in leopard skins and thought themselves transformed into beasts, killed their victims for ceremonial eating. Among Bagesu and their neighbors of the lake region, in cannibal feasts to honor their dead, there was the unusual feature of eating their own clansmen's corpses. Victims' bodies were eaten at shrines in central Nigeria and as a rite among the

Ovimbundu of southwest Africa before the departure of a caravan. In the equatorial forests cannibalism was of considerably more consequence. The Banyanzi of the middle Congo, according to one observer, "were not ashamed of cannibalism and expressed a preference for human flesh." The Fang of Gaboon, celebrated cannibals, offered human flesh in markets, and in the Congo slaves were expressly fattened for the purpose. Cannibalism seems to have been uncommon in Malaysia, though it was reported to be a limited custom of the Batak of Sumatra. There was extensive man-eating in eastern New Guinea and in Melanesia, adjacent to the East, where warfare and hostility to strangers were dominant traits. While in some regions ritual imposed curbs, such as forbidding a man to eat one he had himself killed, in the Fly River district of south New Guinea cannibalism was unrestrained and the flesh served as common food. Here extermination was the fate of weak tribes, looked on as a legitimate source of food supply by stronger neighbors. The flesh was highly esteemed, especially parts of female corpses, but usually the whole body was eaten after roasting with sago. On the other hand, cannibalism was relatively rare in Micronesia and in central Polynesia, where Hawaiians and Society Islanders professed a horror of it, although they practiced human sacrifice. It was a prevailing practice in westernmost Polynesia, in Fiji, Tonga, and New Zealand, which were near cannibal-ridden Melanesia, and it was common as far east as the Marquesas, Easter Island, and the Cook group. Fijians were notorious cannibals; not only was the flesh of enemies customarily eaten, but commoners also were sacrificed for the purpose. The flesh was cooked apart from other foods and eaten with wooden forks, which were taboo for other uses. The Maori of New Zealand held the flesh of enemies one of the most desirable ends of warfare. Throughout Polynesia revenge motivated the practice, for to devour an enemy was to express extreme contempt.   L. S.

CANNING, GEORGE (1770-1827), English statesman, was born in London on Apr. 11, 1770. His uncle, a wealthy banker, took charge of his education and sent him to Eton and Christ Church, Oxford. Though his relatives and early friends were Whigs, he entered Parliament in 1793 as a Tory supporter of the younger Pitt, whose ministry he defended with brilliant oratory and pungent wit. From November 1797, to July 1798, he was the most successful contributor to *The Anti-Jacobin,* a paper founded to ridicule the French republicans. In 1796 he had been made Undersecretary for Foreign Affairs. He held minor offices from 1799 to 1801, when he resigned with the fall of Pitt's ministry. When Pitt returned to office in 1804, he became Treasurer of the Navy, an office he held until Pitt's death in 1806. From 1807 to 1810 he was Secretary of State for Foreign Affairs in the Portland ministry; during this period his most brilliant achievement was the seizure of the Danish fleet at Copenhagen and the consequent frustration of Napoleon's efforts to dominate the Baltic. In 1809, finding his vigorous war policy opposed by his colleague Viscount Castlereagh, the Secretary for War, he suggested to Portland that Castlereagh be removed. Castlereagh heard of the proposal, challenged Canning to a duel, and wounded him in the thigh.

Castlereagh and Canning became bitter political opponents, and Canning acquired a reputation for trickery which was not wholly deserved but which kept him in minor offices until 1822. In that year Castlereagh, then Marquis of Londonderry, committed suicide, and Canning succeeded him as Secretary of State for Foreign Affairs and leader of the House

of Commons. His reputation rests largely on the policy he pursued in this office, one of general nonintervention in the affairs of other countries, though he showed sympathy with, and sometimes supported liberal and national movements abroad, as in Greece and Latin America. He also gave security to Portugal. In 1823, Great Britain, unlike the United States, had not recognized any of the Latin American states, some of which were still fighting for their independence from Spain. However, Canning's policy was to prevent intervention in the Western Hemisphere on the part of the Holy Alliance, to whose pretensions as upholder of the *status quo* Great Britain was opposed. The Monroe Doctrine, announced by President Monroe on Dec. 2, 1823, which stated that the United States could not "behold such interposition, in any form, with indifference," was actually inspired by a suggestion made by Canning to Richard Rush, United States Minister to Great Britain. Canning, however, had desired a joint statement by the two governments, and he especially disapproved the sentences of the Monroe Doctrine that discouraged future European attempts to establish any new colonies in Latin America. Even with these reservations, he had a basis for his later boast, "I called the New World into existence to redress the balance of the Old." In domestic issues, Canning favored abolishment of civil disabilities for Catholics (so-called Catholic Emancipation) and repeal of the corn laws. In April 1827 he succeeded Lord Liverpool as Prime Minister, but died at Chiswick on August 8 of that year.
                                                        E. R. A.

CANNING INDUSTRY. One method of preserving food is to place it in a hermetically sealed container and sterilize it by heat. Heating the food at scientifically prescribed times and temperatures destroys or inhibits all spoilage micro-organisms (bacteria, molds, and yeasts) present on the raw food; the hermetic seal of the container prevents infection by spoilage organisms in the atmosphere. If not rendered sterile, these organisms would utilize the food to support their own life cycles, just as man does, and would alter the natural characteristics of the food chemically or physically, or both.

The effectiveness of this method of preserving food has been demonstrated by foods canned over long periods of time. For example, cans of roast veal and of carrots and gravy left on the Arctic ice by William Parry, the English Arctic explorer, on his third expedition in search of the Northwest Passage in 1824, were opened by English scientists 114 years later (in 1938) and found in excellent condition. The investigators reported survival of vitamin D in the canned veal, and little effect on the carotene content of the original carrots. Canned pea soup and canned beef from the same source, opened in 1911, 87 years after being packed, were eaten and found to be fresh and palatable.

History. In 1795 the armies of England, Prussia, Austria, Spain, and Sardinia were fighting France, where a revolution was in progress. French forces were winning battles, but were losing lives, not only on the battlefield but also by scurvy and other forms of malnutrition. Some method of carrying food stores to soldiers abroad, and for sailors at sea, was direly needed; foraging was not a sufficient expedient. The five-man French Directory offered a prize of 12,000 francs to the patriot who would devise some new and successful method of preserving food so that it would remain fresh and wholesome over long periods of time.

Appert. Nicolas Appert, an obscure citizen who had been a chef, pickler, preserver, wine maker, brewer, confectioner, and distiller, entered upon a fourteen-year period of experimentation and in 1809 was awarded the prize by Napoleon

Bonaparte, then emperor of France. Appert's method was explained by its discoverer in a treatise published the following year and first translated into English in 1811. This book, *L'Art de conserver, pendant plusieurs années, toutes les substances animales et végétales* (*The Art of Preserving,* 1920) was the first treatise in a long line of subsequent works on canning technology, although a previous reference to preserving food in a sealed container by applying heat had been made by Lazzaro Spallanzani, the Italian naturalist, in 1765. By repeated and painstaking tests, Appert had demonstrated that heat, applied to food sealed in an airtight container, in some manner prevented the food from spoiling. He had used widemouthed glass bottles, which he filled with the food, corked carefully, and heated in boiling water. It was not until fifty years later, about 1860, that Louis Pasteur, the French chemist, scientifically demonstrated that spoilage was caused by micro-organisms. Appert's treatise revealed that he had successfully preserved more than fifty kinds of food. He did not know why his methods were successful, but many of his recommendations are valid and are still followed, particularly his realization of the necessity for complete cleanliness and sanitation in commercial canning, which reduces the load of spoilage organisms on the raw food that must be killed by the heat process, and his realization of the absolute need of permanently sealing the container to exclude air.

Durand, Donkin, and Hall. After the publication and translation of Appert's methods, commercial canning, though not then so designated, spread from France to England, where in 1810 Peter Durand had obtained a patent covering the use of iron and tin to make canisters for preserving foods. John Hall, founder of the famous Dartford Iron Works, and his associate, Bryan Donkin, recognized a promising outlet for their metals if tin-coated iron containers could be used to hold foods processed by the Appert method. They added food preservation to their enterprises and, after many trials, began to receive a favorable response from British army and navy commanders, including Arthur Wellesley, Duke of Wellington. By 1818 the Donkin and Hall products were being delivered in considerable quantities to the Admiralty Victualling Depot and were attracting the attention of explorers of those times, including Sir John Ross, Otto von Kotzebue, and Parry.

Kensett and Underwood. The new food preservation method reached the United States in 1819, and there began its spectacular growth into one of the important industries of the world economy. Thomas Kensett in New York, in 1819, and William Underwood in Boston, at about the same time, were putting up foods by the Appert method, using glass jars and bottles, sealed with cork stoppers wired tight, but in 1839 both these American pioneers began packing their growing list of preserved products into metal canisters. They used a crude, handmade canister, and it is that word, from the Greek original *kanastron,* meaning basket of reeds, that gave the currently accepted name of canning to the process of sterilizing foods by heat and sealing them hermetically. England in the early nineteenth century was accustomed to using reed baskets for tea, coffee, spices, fruits, and vegetables. Hence Durand, patenting his metal container, called it a tin canister. Underwood's Yankee bookkeepers and salesmen abbreviated canister to "can," and the word got into the vernacular. The word "can" was an early example of American slang adopted into accepted terminology. Can, and from that word "canned" and "canning," came into recognized usage and became part of the official, legal, and scientific definitions of the container, the product, and the process.

The canning industry has taken a leading role in developing automatic harvesting machinery, such as this corn picker.

Development in the United States. American inventive and business ability is largely responsible for the rapid and extensive growth of commercial food canning, which has been more marked in the United States than elsewhere. This fact was made evident first in a series of inventions and improvements in containers and in the machinery and equipment to handle and fill them. Later it was demonstrated in the application of scientific principles to canning, until research and scientific procedure became the basis of practically all canning operations, from cultivation and harvesting in the field and orchard to sealing of the package that reaches the consumer.

Containers. Appert's stout glass jars with their crude, wired and waxed cork stoppers were difficult to handle and to seal. Glass blowing by mouth was their method of manufacture. Kensett and Underwood found them expensive and suffered financial losses from breakage. The American glass container industry was slow in developing, fruit jars not being available in quantity until 1870; consequently early canners in the country naturally turned to containers made of metal.

Metal Containers. Kensett and Ezra Daggett, his partner, received a patent, signed by President James Monroe, granting them "rights to an improvement in the art of preserving" and referring to "vessels of tin." The early Durand container, and later versions of it, was as crude an article in many ways as the first glass jars and bottles used for canned foods. The canisters were heavy. British Navy victualling lists of 1818 cite vegetable soup in 4-pound canisters, as contrasted with the common 10½- to 11-oz. can at present in use for that product. The smallest canister shown in the 1818 lists was 1 lb. 6 oz., and the majority of canned items were delivered in packages of 2 lb. or more. Pioneering canners of America imported tin-plated sheet iron, which Yankee tinsmiths cut into cylinders by hand. Circular tops and bottoms were cut out of the sheet, and the can bodies, tops, and bottoms were joined manually and soldered along the side seam and end sections. A hole was left in the top end through which the food could be forced. After filling, this hole was

469

closed by soldering on a tin disc. A small hole was left in this cap to permit air to escape when the contents were heated, and after the canned food had been processed, this hole in the cap was tipped with solder. Known as the "hole-in-top" can, this article would be made by an industrious workman at the rate of about 60 cans in a ten-hour day. In contrast, one assembly line in a modern can-making factory can produce as many as 1,000 cans a minute.

The turn of the century brought about a revolutionary change in the fabrication of the tin can. Although the open-top and hole-in-top cans by this time were being cut out partially by foot presses and other semiautomatic tools rather than by hand shears, there had been practically no change in

COURTESY OF NATIONAL CANNERS ASSOCIATION

Automatic pitting machine, into which peaches are being fed, removes kernels and cuts fruit in half.

the architecture of the can. The bodies and ends were still being joined by the application of solder. This method was displaced by the introduction of the modern "sanitary" can, so made that its parts are joined and locked by crimping of the metal. Sealing compounds are used in the end seams, and solder only on the outside of the body seams, the entire operation being accomplished by automatic machinery. This is the type of can which has since come into universal use.

The term "tin can," so commonly used, is a misnomer, because tin cans are actually steel sheets coated with tin, either by dipping or electroplating, and consist of about 98.5-99.75 steel and 0.25-1.5 per cent tin. The modern American canning industry uses over 37 billion individual tin containers. The use of such containers increased so rapidly during the nineteenth century that it led to the establishment of a special branch of the steel industry for the production of tin plate, a mild steel suitable for coating with pure tin. Improvements in the dipping or coating techniques were made in the tin plate mills until, today, the finished food can is made by one of two methods: hot-dip tinning or electrolytic tinning. The latter is a rapid, nearly continuous process.

Glass Containers. Improvements in glass food containers and in metal and cork closures also have been achieved. There has been a trend toward the use of lighter-weight

glass, toward refinements in annealing methods, and toward the sealing of liners for the closures, as well as toward wider-mouthed bottles and jars, with a resultant increase in the number and variety of canned food products that are packed in glass. The use of glass containers was greatly expanded during World War II, when Japan's seizure of the tin-producing areas of Asia shut off tin shipments to the United States. Glass containers in later use were made by automatic machinery, rather than blown by mouth. Sealing closures also were made by machine, and the filling and sealing of foods in glass containers were done by automatic machines in the cannery. Modern glass jars are highly uniform and resistant to mechanical and heat shock, and have found increased acceptance among commercial canners.

Automatic Canning Machinery. Inventiveness in developing processing methods and automatic machinery and equipment has also contributed greatly to the phenomenal growth of canning in the United States. In 1850 canners were boiling filled cans of foods for long periods of time. Sir Humphry Davy, an English chemist, had disclosed the fact that the boiling temperature of water could be raised from 212° F. to 240° F. by adding calcium chloride to the water in the cooking kettle. Isaac Solomon, a Baltimore canner, adopted this procedure in 1861 and thus reduced the time necessary for sterilization from five or six hours to a half hour. A first-class cannery whose kettle capacity would produce 2,500 cans of food daily was thus enabled to turn out 20,000 cans. This innovation proved timely, because the Civil War had increased the demand for canned foods. Production increased sixfold in a decade. In 1874 a closed steam-pressure kettle, or retort, was patented by A. K. Shriver of Baltimore. With pressure indicated by a steam gauge and regulated by a steam cock, controlled high temperatures became possible, and the time necessary for effective processing was brought to a new minimum. Before the end of the nineteenth century automatic devices for removing peas from the vines, and for husking and cutting corn, had been perfected and were in use. Important inventions accelerated and made automatic the peeling of apples, pineapples, and peaches, and the butchering and cleaning of salmon. These developments resulted in immediate increases in the volume of such foods being canned.

Mechanical improvements are continually being made in all the basic operations of typical commercial canneries: in the harvesting and handling of the raw product at the factory; in soaking, washing, sorting, and grading; in blanching (a precooking process); in peeling and coring; in filling and exhausting (expelling air and gases); in sealing, processing, and cooling the hot cans as they come from the cook; in labeling; and in the final warehousing and packing of the goods into shipping containers. Moreover, the development of efficient conveying systems between the machines that carry out these operations has made fruit, vegetable, fish, meat, milk, and specialty canning almost completely automatic.

Research. *Establishment of Laboratories.* Louis Pasteur's theory of fermentation, announced in 1860, brought no particular change in the canning technique developed by Appert, but it supplied the scientific explanation of the principle that had been lacking. Another thirty-five years elapsed before scientific work was directed specifically to canning. In 1895 Dr. Samuel C. Prescott of the Massachusetts Institute of Technology, and William L. Underwood, grandson of the pioneer Boston canner, first traced spoilage of certain lots of canned corn to inadequate sterilization. This work was soon followed by similar studies on peas by H. L. Russell of the University of Wisconsin. Organized research on canned foods was begun later by the United States Department of Agriculture. An investigation by Bronson Barlow of the University of Illinois in 1913 disclosed that certain thermophilic (heat-loving) bacteria, capable of living at temperatures as high as 150° F. to 160° F., are potent causes of spoilage in canned foods. This discovery began a new chapter in the bacteriology of canning.

The tools of science began to be applied to canning. Important research laboratories were created by the American Can Company and by the National Canners Association, the trade association of the industry, which had been founded by Frank E. Gorrell at Bel Air, Md., and had moved to Washington, D. C., in 1913. For the first time a research labora-

ducing troublesome bacteria into cannery equipment, standards of bacteriological purity are worked out, and special grades are produced to meet the exacting needs of the canner.

Development of C-Enamel. Formerly canners had trouble with certain products, particularly canned corn, due to "corn black," a black discoloration of the contents. Although harmless to health, this made the food unsalable and resulted in much economic loss. Solution of the problem was found in the National Canners Association laboratories through development of a special enamel lining for cans which absorbed and held traces of material responsible for discoloration. This "C-Enamel" is generally used for such products.

Nutritive Value of Canned Foods. Although it has been found that certain critical vitamins and minerals are partly

Sardine canning is carried out with automatic machinery, using production-line techniques.

COURTESY OF MAINE SARDINE INDUSTRY

tory had been set up by a trade association to study the scientific problems of an industry. A staff of four technologists was assembled under the direction of Dr. W. D. Bigelow and Dr. A. W. Bitting. As the programs and the staff expanded, branch laboratories of the association were created in Seattle in 1919 and in San Francisco in 1926.

Processing Studies. Until the new laboratories began their intensive studies of time and temperature requirements for processing canned foods in 1918, this critical step had been based on rule-of-thumb practice. Research now brought about modern sterilization procedures based on scientific knowledge of the flow of heat through each product and the amount of heat required to kill spoilage bacteria.

Finding and Eliminating Sources of Bacteria. Sterilization by canning is made easier and more reliable by keeping spoilage bacteria out of the product or by holding it to a minimum. Constant field investigations among the canneries are conducted by technologists of the National Canners Association to determine sources of bacterial infection and the correct practices for eliminating them.

Checking of Ingredients. Because common ingredients such as sugar and starch are sometimes the means of intro-

dissolved during all types of food cooking, one important characteristic of canning is that each individual can serves as a pressure cooker and concentrates the dissolved nutrients into a small amount of liquid that may be further reduced in volume, and may be served with the solid food in such a way as to conserve the food values to a maximum extent. Modern research into the nutritional values of foods dates from about 1900, and was instigated by the belief that other factors besides protein, carbohydrate, fat, and mineral content of food might be involved in the nourishment of the animal body. By 1923 research into the subject was well under way in this country and abroad. In that year a fourteen-year collaborative program of the National Canners Association and Columbia University was initiated. In 1942 the National Canners Association and the Can Manufacturers Institute of New York City jointly sponsored a program involving research grants to a number of well-known universities and colleges. The laboratory findings, as disclosed in a series of bulletins and technical papers, have revealed that high ratios of vitamins, minerals, and calories are retained in foods canned for standard commercial use. The reports disclosed the content of principal canned foods in terms of calories, proteins, carbohydrates, fats, vitamins A and C, four of the B-vitamins (thiamin, niacin, riboflavin, and pantothenic acid), and such minerals as iron, phosphorus, and calcium.

PRODUCTION OF CANNED GOODS IN THE UNITED STATES
(in millions of standard cases)

	1938	1940	1945	1950	1955
Fruits	40	49	52	77	92
Juices	39	55	111	109	99
Vegetables	122	133	177	166	197
Specialties	67	79	83	113	128
Milk	49	58	90	68	60
Fish	17	19	19	30	26
Meat[1]	7	12	43	27	33
Total	341	405	575	590	635

[1] Excluding meat soups and canned poultry.

Source: National Canners Association

Other Problems. *Waste Disposal.* Large-scale canning operations result in much waste from unused portions of raw material; food-laden wash water is an example. Disposal of this waste without creating nuisances or polluting streams is the subject of continuing research, and workable methods are being found and followed by canners. One of the most novel of these methods is that of applying the liquid wastes to large areas of land by means of spray irrigation. Under proper conditions this does not produce objectionable odors, nor does it pollute ground waters.

Cannery Sanitation, Lighting, and Safety. In their efforts to maintain the high quality of canned foods, canners carry out research in industrial laboratories to determine the most effective tools and methods for efficiently producing canned foods under highly sanitary conditions.

Effects of Exposure to Atomic Bomb Explosions. In May 1955 at the Nevada test site of the U.S. Atomic Energy Commission 25,000 samples of more than 60 major canned foods were exposed to a 30-kiloton atomic explosion. Tests on the samples showed that no significant toxic by-products were formed, and that there was little or no loss of the food's vitamin content. Chemical changes were minor, as were changes in the flavor and texture of the foods.　N. H. B.

CANNIZZARO, STANISLAO [kɑ'nniddzɑ'ro] (1826-1910), Italian chemist, discoverer of the Cannizzaro reaction and champion of Avogadro's hypothesis, was born in Palermo, Sicily, July 16, 1826. He studied medicine at Palermo, which he left in 1845 for Pisa, where he investigated salicin, $C_{13}H_{18}O_7$, while acting as assistant in chemistry to Rafaelle Piria during 1845-1846. During the revolutionary year 1848 he left a similar position in Turin to participate in an unsuccessful insurrection in Sicily. He escaped to Paris in 1849, where he studied under M. E. Chevreul and, with F. S. Cloëz, prepared cyanamide. He also investigated santonin, $C_{15}H_{18}O_3$. From 1851 onward until his retirement he was professor of chemistry at Alexandria, Geneva (1855), Palermo (1860), and, finally, Rome (1871).

In connection with his discovery of benzyl alcohol, in 1852, Cannizzaro first described a reaction, since known as the Cannizzaro reaction, to the effect that an aromatic aldehyde is decomposed by alcoholic potash into a mixture of the corresponding acid and alcohol.

$$2C_6H_5CHO + H_2O \xrightarrow[\text{potash}]{\text{alcoholic}} \underset{\text{alcohol}}{C_6H_5CH_2OH} + \underset{\text{acid}}{C_6H_5COOH}.$$

In 1858 Cannizzaro wrote a pamphlet, *Sunto di un corso di filosofia chimica* ("Summary of a Course in Chemical Philosophy") in support of the hypothesis which Count Amedeo Avogadro, a fellow countryman, had postulated in 1811: that equal volumes of all gases at the same temperature and pressure contain the same number of molecules. There was great hostility toward this basic hypothesis among many scientists, and the controversy became so intense that a convention was called to Karlsruhe in 1860 to clarify the issue. A heated discussion took place there, participated in by F. A. Kekulé, J. B. A. Dumas, C. A. Wurtz, and other famous chemists. Cannizzaro distributed his pamphlet, which insisted on the difference between molecular and atomic weights, among those present. His clear style and his incontrovertible arguments won him immediate acceptance, and Avogadro's law thereafter became a maxim among chemists. In 1891 the Royal Society (London) bestowed the Copley Medal on Cannizzaro in recognition of his contribution to chemistry at this conference.

In 1858 also, Cannizzaro developed a reliable method of determining the atomic weight of an element from the percentage compositions of its pure compounds.

Cannizzaro also took an active part in public service. In 1871 he became a member of the Italian Senate and later its vice-president, and as a member of the Council of Public Instruction he furthered scientific education in Italy. He died in Rome on May 9, 1910. *See also* AVOGADRO, AMEDEO; AVOGADRO'S NUMBER.　H. N. A.

CANNON, JOSEPH GURNEY (1836-1926), American legislator, was born at New Garden, N. C., May 7, 1836. At Bloomington, Ind., he attended school until he was 14

Joseph Gurney Cannon

CULVER SERVICE

and then, while clerking in a country store, read law. He completed his studies at the Cincinnati Law School, Cincinnati, O., and was admitted to the bar at Terre Haute, Ind., in 1858. That year he moved to Shelbyville, Ill., and thence to Tuscola. The following year he practiced law at Danville. He served as state's attorney from 1861-1868. In 1873 he was elected to the U.S. House of Representatives from Illinois, and served there, except for the terms of 1891-1893 and 1913-1915, until 1923 when he retired. He was a member of the House Appropriations Committee for 22 years. As Speaker of the House (1903-1911) his control of procedure, described as arbitrary and partisan, became known as "Cannonism." He was largely responsible for the low rate on second-class mail and the admission of packages to the mail, beginning the parcel-post service. Personally popular with most of his colleagues, he was affectionately referred to in later years as Uncle Joe. He died in Danville, Ill., on Nov. 26, 1926.   D. R.

CANNON. *See* ARTILLERY.

CANNON-BALL TREE, *Couroupita guianensis,* a tall, soft-wooded timber tree of the lecythis family, native to Guiana and sometimes planted in warm climates. Large clusters, 2 to 3 ft. long, of showy flowers, yellow and red on the outside, and crimson-lilac inside, are borne on the trunk and larger branches. They are followed by round reddish fruits 6 to 8 in. in diameter with woody rinds.
                                                       J. C. Wis.

CANO, ALONSO [kɑ'no] (1601-1667), Spanish painter, sculptor, and architect, known as El Granadino, was born at Granada on Mar. 19, 1601. He studied at Seville and went to Madrid in 1637, where he became friendly with Velázquez who was responsible for his appointment as a court painter two years later. In 1644, under suspicion of having murdered his wife, he fled from Madrid to Valencia, but he later decided to return to the capital, where he was tortured on the rack. His accusers failing to wring a confession from him, he was adjudged innocent, and, leaving the city, he settled in Granada. He was appointed canon of Granada in 1651 and was the architect of Granada Cathedral, which was begun in 1667. During his lifetime he was acclaimed as the Spanish Michelangelo, but later critics have not rated him so highly. Among his works are the bust of St. Paul in Granada Cathedral, the *Conception of the Virgin* in San Diego, Granada, and the paintings of the *Seven Joys of the Virgin,* which are, with most of his works, in the Prado, Madrid. He died at Granada on Oct. 5, 1667.
                                                              R. T.

CANOEING [kənu'ɪŋ], a form of water transportation employing a long, narrow craft made of skin, bark, metal, plastic, or wood. The first canoes, created in the pre-Stone Age, were keelless, only slightly stable, had extremely shallow draft, and could easily be carried for portage. The crew faced forward and propelled them by means of paddles. Sails also provided propulsion in oceanic canoeing, and the long push-pole supplemented the paddles for navigating bayous and swamps in the tropics, as well as rapids of fast-water streams farther northward. While canoeing still serves as a means of transportation the world over, during the past 100 years it has also become popular as a recreational and competitive sport. John MacGregor, a British lawyer, is credited with popularizing it. Between 1849 and 1869 MacGregor's books, recounting his experiences on long European cruises, created widespread interest in canoeing in England and America.

Early Organizations. MacGregor was the guiding spirit of a group of enthusiasts who, in July 1865, organized the Royal Canoe Club on the Thames River near London. He was the Royal's first captain, and the Prince of Wales, later Edward VII, was its first commodore. Among the early members whose books also contributed to growth of the sport were Warington Baden-Powell, and a nobleman who wrote under the pen name "Tiphys." In the summer of 1871 the increasing number of enthusiasts in America led to the founding of the New York Canoe Club at St. George, Staten Island, N. Y., and by 1880 other clubs of this type were formed along the eastern seaboard; many are still flourishing. As in England, these early canoeists wrote extensively of their travels and the art of building and handling their light craft. Prominent among them were Nathaniel Holmes Bishop and Charles Ledyard Norton.

American Canoe Association. By August 1880 cruising and competition between the clubs had reached a peak indicating the need for a national organization to set standards and to exchange information with the canoeing fraternity abroad. The American Canoe Association thus was formed at a meeting at Crosbyside Park, Lake George, N. Y. W. L. Alden of the N.Y.C.C. was elected commodore and

PHILIP GENDREAU, N. Y.

Canoeing in Fish Creek Pond, a New York State public camp site off Saranac Lake

Nathaniel H. Bishop secretary-treasurer. Summer headquarters of the A.C.A. was at Grindstone Island, in the Thousand Island group of the St. Lawrence River, and through resultant contacts with Canadian clubs the Canadian Canoe Association likewise developed. Some years later, in England, the British Canoe Union was organized. Since its inception the A.C.A. has annually published a yearbook and sponsored a canoeing magazine. Its earliest publication was *The American Canoeist,* published from 1882 through 1887 by Arthur Brentano, an ardent canoeist, with Norton, C. Bowyer Vaux, William Whitlock, and C. K. Munroe as editors. Since June 1941 the editor has been Charles E. Burns, assisted by such prominent canoeists as Oscar S. Tyson, Emmett S. Lundbeck, and Theodore D. Alteneder, past commodores of the Association, aided by many volunteer contributors. Growth of the A.C.A. was steady, and soon made necessary regional divisions for administrative purposes. Thus the Atlantic Division, comprising the metropolitan New York area, came into being; the Central Division functioned with members from upper and western New York state; the Eastern Division covered the New England area and later absorbed a small group known as the New England Canoe Racing Association; the Western Division centered around Chicago and Milwaukee, and absorbed the Western Canoe Association; the Middle States Division centered at Philadelphia and Washington, D. C., and absorbed the Middle States Canoe Racing Association; the Northern Division provided liaison with the Canadian Canoe Association; the Dixie Division functioned in the southeastern states; the Rocky Mountain Division (admitted in 1955) comprised the states of New Mexico, Colorado, Wyoming, and Montana; and the Pacific Division operated on the west coast.

Activities. Activities comprise the encouragement of cruising, which ranges from week-end springtime "white-water" runs on freshet-swollen streams to more ambitious trips, such

Indians fishing from a handmade bark canoe on the Pend Oreille River, Washington.

as the circumnavigation of the eastern half of the United States via the Great Lakes, Mississippi River, Gulf of Mexico, and Atlantic intracoastal waterway. National paddling championships and sailing championships are held annually after divisional qualification trials. The quadrennial selection of the United States Olympic canoe team follows the same pattern. Both paddling and sailing competition is carried on with the Canadian Canoe Association. Trophies, some dating back to 1880, are awarded the winners. Seniority classifications in racing are determined by past performance in competition, and the craft used are grouped into classes ranging from stock-model pleasure canoes to the very highly specialized racing types.

International Competition. After World War I canoeing gained impetus in continental Europe and national associations developed to unite the many clubs that came into existence. Activity principally took the form of cruising and racing in craft closely resembling the Eskimo kayak, although the open canoe of the American Indian had many devotees. With such widespread activity it was natural that an international federation should develop, and that the sport should seek recognition in the Olympic Games. The Internationale Representationschaft des Kanusport (I.R.K.) therefore was successfully formed in 1924 at a meeting in Copenhagen, with a membership of 21 national canoeing associations. In the same year a demonstration of canoeing was arranged on the program of the Olympiad at Paris. The Washington Canoe Club, of Washington, D. C., entered a four-man team which, with teams from four other nations, staged the demonstration. In 1936 the sport was formally admitted to the program of the Olympiad at Berlin. Nine nations, including the United States, sent teams. Nine events were held on the River Spree at distances of 10,000 m. and 1,000 m. for one-man and two-man crews in various categories of rigid racing kayaks, folding kayaks, and racing canoes. With the opening of World War II the I.R.K. dissolved, although competition within national limits, and even internationally in middle Europe, continued. After the cessation of hostilities in 1945 the old federation was reorganized as the International Canoe Federation (I.C.F.), with 17 member nations. Canoeing competition is a fixture at the Olympic Games. Canoeists from all over the world meet in nine events. Men compete in single and double kayaks over distances of 1,000 and 10,000 meters, and in single and double canoes over the same distances. There is one event for women, a 500-meter race in single kayaks. Contestants use special canoes and kayaks built to I.C.F. specifications.

Unorganized Activities. No description of canoeing would be complete, however, without mention of the unorganized activity in the United States and Canada. In unattached status the canoeists of these countries number hundreds of thousands, and range from the merest tyro to the capable professional guide. Each segment of this multitude indulges in its phases of unofficial competition. In scouting groups and private children's camps canoeing, canoe sailing, wilderness canoe cruising, and novice canoe racing are major activities. At summer resorts and along nearly every stream and lake in the country individual canoeists are to be found, and even groups organized into small local clubs which never have affiliated with the national association. At the more than 35 national aquatic schools conducted annually by the American Red Cross Water Safety Service, with a total of more than 3,000 students, canoeing skills and the administration of camp canoeing programs constitute an integral part of the curriculum of training for volunteer Water Safety Instructors.

American Racing Events. Most colorful of unofficial activities are the professional and semiprofessional marathon racing events which take place annually about the country. By far the most gruelling of these is the 450-mi. Minneapolis Aquatennial Canoe Derby from Bemidji, Minn., down the Mississippi River to Minneapolis, annually sponsored by a group of local sportsmen and newspapers. Entry lists consist heavily of professional guides, woodsmen, trappers, and Indian residents of the region, using their own canoes of varying sizes and design. The course of this race is over part of the river made famous by early Mississippi explorers such as Father Louis Hennepin, General Lewis Cass, Henry Rowe Schoolcraft, Jean Nicolas Nicollet, and Captain Willard Glazier. Next in colorful appeal is the three-day downstream "white-water" race of Canadian guides and Indians, on the St. Maurice River to Trois-Rivières, Quebec, Canada. Each year there is a locally sponsored Bayou Barrataria pirogue race, which draws its entry list almost exclusively from among the Cajun muskrat hunters and trappers of the bayou country in the Mississippi delta region near New Orleans, La.

Outstanding Canoe Journeys. Still another impressive phase of unofficial canoeing activity is the many solitary journeys that have been made in quite modern times, either as true pioneering ventures or retracing the routes of early explorers. Many of these cruisers never have published the stories of their trips. About 1903 a Canadian, using a typical Peterborough canoe, made a round-the-world cruise alone. In 1910 a German manufacturer of folding-kayaks sponsored a trans-Atlantic cruise by Captain Roemer. The captain coasted from Hamburg, Germany, to Santander, Spain, and thence to the Canary Islands off the coast of Africa. From this point he successfully made a 58-day crossing to one of the islands of the Lesser Antilles. His destination was New York City, but he was lost when unexpectedly caught in a Carribean hurricane during a 40-mi. run between islands. June to September 1934 saw the pioneer cruise of two high school boys, Arnold Sevareid and Walter C. Port, from Minneapolis, Minn., to York Factory, on Hudson's Bay. From July 1935 to July 1936 Hardy Nurmsen, an Estonian boy residing in New York City, circumnavigated the eastern half of the United States. Two canoeists, Geoffrey Pope and Sheldon Taylor, both of New York City, successfully cruised from New York to Nome, Alaska, between April 1936 and August 1937. Much of their route covered that of Sir Alexander Mackenzie's explorations of 1789 to 1793, and included the Grand Portage of the fur-trading voyagers of that day. From April 1946 to November 1947, two separate and almost parallel transcontinental cruises were made, using Mackenzie's Peace River route.

Dr. Hannes Lindemann of Hamburg, Germany, sailed

and paddled a 17-ft. canoelike craft across the Atlantic Ocean from the Canary Islands to St. Martin, W.I. He made the crossing in 72 days late in 1956. *See also* SMALL BOATS.

W. Van B. C.

CANON, in music, is, as its name (derived from the Greek word meaning "law") implies, the strictest and most circumscribed form of musical composition: a melody begun by one voice or instrumental part is imitated, echo-like, by another part beginning anywhere from one note to several measures later. This imitation may be identical, interval for interval, as in strict canon, or slightly altered, as in free canon; it may be in unison with the first part, or at the octave, the fifth, or some other interval. The imitation may also be in shorter notes (diminution) or longer notes (augmentation), and it may even be turned upside down (inversion) or sounded backwards (as in the crab canon). These and other similar devices, scattered through two or a great many more parts heard simultaneously, result in a complicated pattern of sound often more intriguing to the eye than to the ear. Certain seventeenth-century canons contain forty-eight parts, and in such compositions the ear cannot follow all the diverse imitations of the melody though it may find pleasure in the total effect.

The canon was a favorite form among composers during the contrapuntal epoch, or roughly from the thirteenth to the early eighteenth century, and in an elementary form, called canonic imitation, has been used in larger works by many later composers. (It appears, for example, in the first movement of Schubert's *Unfinished Symphony.*) The round, a vocal canon in which a simple melody is repeated ad infinitum by voices beginning at different intervals as in the familiar *Row, row, row your boat,* has been a pleasantly sociable form of music-making since at least the early fourteenth century when the famous *Sumer is icumen in* was written. In seventeenth- and eighteenth-century England rounds enjoyed great popularity under the name of "catches," famous for their punning and often salacious humor.

W. Li.

CANON CITY [kæ'nyən], the seat of Fremont Co. in south central Colorado, is situated on the Arkansas River at 5,343 ft. above sea level. It lies about 38 mi. northwest of Pueblo in a fruit- and truck-farming area. Gold, coal, and silica are regional resources, and numerous hot and cold mineral springs are nearby. Founded by Anson Rudd about 1860, Canon City was incorporated in 1872. The municipal government is administered by a city manager. During the local gold rush of 1859 and 1860 the town underwent a boom. In the early period of the town Joaquin Miller, the poet, was mayor, judge, and minister in Canon City. Features of special interest are the municipal museum containing a fine archaeological and wildlife collection; the "Oldest House," a log-and-adobe cabin built by Anson Rudd; and the site of Pike's Blockhouse, camping ground of Lieutenant Zebulon Pike (Pikes Peak) who camped at this point while exploring the Grand Canyon of the Arkansas River and the Royal Gorge. A 1,500-ft. suspension bridge, 1,050 ft. above the river, spans the Gorge near the city. The magnificent scenery of this territory draws many sightseers to the city. The Colorado State Penitentiary is in the city. Transportation is supplied by the Denver & Rio Grande Western and the Atchison, Topeka and Santa Fe railroads. The city's industries include bottling and cement works and creameries. Pop. 1950, 6,345.

CANONESS [kæ'nənəs], in the Middle Ages a member of a group of women who were bound by rule to chastity and obedience, though not to poverty, but who did not take perpetual vows. They gave instruction to girls and worked at the making of vestments and of liturgical books. Their communal life was freer and more secular than that of nuns.

L. C. L.

CANONICAL HOURS [kənɒ'nɪkəl], a series of religious devotions appointed for stated hours of the day, observed sometimes by the laity, frequently required of the clergy, and almost invariably in use in monasteries. In the Jewish religion three periods a day were designated for prayer. In the Christian Church in the East these three periods developed into eight by the end of the fourth century. By the sixth century six periods were observed in the West, Vigil or Matins, Lauds, Terce, Sext, Nones, and Vespers; the sixth century added Prime (between Lauds and Terce) and Compline. Of these, Matins and Vespers early became public services said in church. The canonical hours are contained in the Breviary.

S. B.-S.

CANONIZATION [kæ'nənɪze'shən] (from late Latin *canonizare,* "to put in the catalogue of the saints"), in canon law, the authoritative declaration that a person is among the saints.

Several substantial differences distinguishing canonization and apotheosis tell against a common origin. For several centuries public ecclesiastical honors were accorded martyrs and confessors of the faith on the authority of bishops or patriarchs, but only within their respective territories. This episcopal authority was restricted by the popes after the late eleventh century, and in 1634 Pope Urban VII formally reserved to Rome both canonization and beatification. There have been few canonizations in Churches not in communion with Rome. In the Roman Catholic Church canonization is now accorded only to those already formally or equivalently beatified, the chief additional requirement being the proving of two (or three) miracles wrought through the intercession of the Beatus. Canonizations are usually accompanied by splendid ceremonies in St. Peter's at Rome. *See also* BEATIFICATION.

N. J. T.

CANON LAW, THE CODE OF, the collection of canons or laws effective in the Latin Church (the Western patriarchate of the Roman Catholic Church) as of Pentecost, May 19, 1918. Begun by Pope Pius X in 1904 to codify, render uniform, and modernize ecclesiastical law, it was prepared under the direction of Cardinal Pietro Gasparri, submitted for comment to all prelates legitimately invited to ecumenical councils, and published (1917) by order of Benedict XV. Besides the Profession of Faith of Pius V and Pius IX, a detailed constitution regulating the election of the pope, and other documents, it contains 2,414 canons in five books: I (1-86) General Norms: relation of the Code to particular laws; II (87-725) Persons: clerics, religious, laics; III (726-1551) Things: sacraments, sacred places and times, divine service, teaching authority of the Church, benefices, Church property; IV (1552-2194) Ecclesiastical Procedure: trials, beatifications and canonizations, special procedures against clerics; and V (2195-2414) Crimes, Punishments, and Special Offenses.

A preface was prepared, summarizing the history of earlier canonical collections and of the compilation of the present Code. In 1917 was established the Pontifical Commission for the Authentic Interpretation of the Code of Canon Law, and in 1935 another commission was appointed to prepare a code of Eastern canon law. *See also* LAW.

N. J. T.

CANON OF SACRED SCRIPTURE, a collection or list of books received as sacred and inspired. A smaller and a larger Old Testament were handed down by the Jews, the former by Palestinian, the latter by Alexandrian, or Hellenistic, Jews; the Alexandrian Canon became the first Old Testament of Christendom. The Canon of the New Testament, now universally received, was recognized by synods at Rome in 382 and at Carthage in 397. In the first edition of Luther's Bible (1534), and in subsequent Protestant Bibles, books of the original Christian Canon not in the Palestinian or Hebrew Bible were relegated as Apocrypha to a separate place between the two Testaments; after 1826, publication in English of these Apocrypha in Protestant Bibles almost entirely ceased. In answer to Luther's innovation, the Council of Trent in 1546 explicitly declared that all the books of the original Christian Bible were canonical, and the Roman Catholic Church accepts them as such today, designating as deuterocanonical the books that Luther called Apocrypha. In the Greek Orthodox Church, a tendency on the part of Russian theologians and authorities to reject the deuterocanonical books began early in the eighteenth century. The Monophysites, Nestorians, Armenians, and Copts admit the larger catalogue and several books of doubtful authenticity besides. *See also* Apocrypha; Bible; New Testament, The; Old Testament.　　　　　W. C.

CANONSBURG [kæ′nənsbɜrg], a borough in southwestern Pennsylvania, oldest borough in Washington Co., situated in a fertile farming area, 19 mi. southwest of Pittsburgh. Natural resources of the region are coal and gas. Canonsburg was founded in 1787 and incorporated as a borough in 1802. South Canonsburg was admitted into the borough in 1911. The community was a center of action in the Whiskey Rebellion in 1794. Freight service is supplied by the Pennsylvania Railroad. Local industries include potteries and steel mills. Other products are chemicals, electrical equipment, radio and television sets, and fabricated wire products. Pop. 1950, 12,072.

CANONS REGULAR OF THE HOLY SEPULCHRE, a medieval order of canons, established in Jerusalem early in the twelfth century, who lived according to the Rule of St. Augustine. The older view that the order goes back in its history to a group of clergy on Mount Sion, ruled over by St. James the Less in apostolic times, is not held by modern scholars. By a papal decree issued in 1143, the Canons held possession of the Church of the Holy Sepulchre in Jerusalem; they also served other churches in the environs of Jerusalem and held property in the chief countries of Europe. The order was weakened by Moslem attacks in the early years of its existence, and upon the fall of Jerusalem, in 1187, the Canons fled from the Near East to their European properties. In 1489, Pope Innocent VIII suppressed the Canons in Italy and transferred their property to the Knights of Malta. The Order survived in the rest of Europe until the French Revolution.　　　　　L. C. L.

CANOPUS [kəno′pəs], also designated Alpha (α) Carinae, the star, the second in apparent brightness in the entire heavens, with a magnitude of −0.86. It lies in the southern constellation Carina, and cannot be conveniently seen north of lat. 32° N. Rated a supergiant, its intrinsic luminosity is extremely high—2,000 times that of the sun—but its distance of 98 light-years reduces its apparent brightness to less than that of the relatively near-by, but less luminous, Sirius. In color, Canopus is whitish-yellow. At one time

Canopus was considered 650 light-years distant and the most luminous of all naked-eye stars, about 80,000 times that of the sun; but as a result of measurements in 1947 its distance was thought to be considerably less. *See also* Carina.
　　　　　J. H. P.

CANOVA, ANTONIO [kanɔ′va] (1757-1822), Italian sculptor, was born Nov. 1, 1757, at Possagno, in the province of Treviso. When he was twelve, the Venetian senator Giovanni Falier took him to study under Toretti in Venice. A marble group of *Daedalus and Icarus* (1779), the outstanding work of his early Venetian period, is in the naturalistic and sensuous Rococo style. After a trip to see the antiquities of Rome and Naples, Canova in 1781 settled permanently at

ANTONIO CANOVA

EWING GALLOWAY, NEW YORK

Rome, where he joined a group of artists and scholars whose studies were engendering a new style strongly imitating the antique.

Theseus and the Minotaur, Canova's first work in this restrained, Neoclassic manner, was followed by the tomb of Clement XIV, which made the artist famous and assured the triumph of Neoclassicism in sculpture. Among the many other tombs by Canova the most significant are those of Clement XIII (finished 1792), of the Archduchess Maria Christina in Vienna, and of the poet Vittorio Alfieri in Florence.

Pre-eminent among Canova's sculptured portraits of the illustrious—including Napoleon Bonaparte and George Washington—is his exquisite and daring likeness of Pauline Bonaparte as *Venus Victrix* (1807). His antique themes, such as the two versions of *Cupid and Psyche,* were so popular that he and his pupils made several replicas.

Long before his death at Venice on Oct. 13, 1822, Canova's renown was international. Princes and kings vied for his services. Venice and the papacy granted him liberal pensions, and in 1817 Pope Pius VII named him Marquis of Ischia.
　　　　　G. H. Hu.

CANT, in linguistic science, a vocabulary developed by members of a particular class of society for purposes of secret communication. The fact that cant is intended to be understood only by a restricted group distinguishes it on the one hand from slang, a set of expressions that is essentially intended for general dispersion, and on the other from jargon, which although the special language of a given trade or profession, is not intentionally restricted to a special group.

Origins. The origins of cant are, in the nature of things, obscure and subject to controversy. All European cants show some common features, Mediterranean cants in particular sharing the words *arto* for "bread," *lenza* for "water," and *bisto* for "priest," among other common elements. The question of whether monogenesis or polygenesis is the more valid explanation of this phenomenon has been warmly debated. The monogenesis thesis was defended by George Borrow, the polygenesis thesis by G. I. Ascoli, the latter being accepted, with some reservations, by nearly all later scholars. The origin of particular cant words is often indeterminable, largely because the vocabulary of cant changes with extraordinary rapidity and may reflect occasional events that were little known and are now no longer remembered.

Formation. The main processes by which cant is formed are the usual ones associated with language changes, but a special frequency attaches to inversions, metathesis, and the use of suffixes. These processes bring cant into close relation with the important linguistic phenomenon of taboo. In both cant and taboo there is manifest a deliberate effort to change the form of a word in order to hide its meaning—from human understanding in cant, and from some supernatural intelligence in taboo. Thus, by an inversion of syllables, Italian *presto* becomes in cant *stopre;* by the addition of a suffix, English *dark* becomes *darkmans.*

Among other processes that play a part in the formation of cant, an important one is the employment of casual assonances or rhymes. Thus, *twist and twirl* may be used in cant for "girl," *storm and strife* for "wife," and *lump o' lead* for "head"; in Italian cant, *mandare in Piccardia* means "fare impiccare"; in French cant, *aller à Rouen* means "se ruiner." Such expressions, many of which have a distinct flavor of folk etymology, exist in every colloquial language, but they are especially common in Italian, where puns and plays on words are of frequent occurrence. Another process that figures in the formation of cant is the replacement of the personal pronoun by a word in common use, as in Italian one finds *manello* or *mamma* for the first person singular pronoun, and *tua madre* for the second person singular pronoun. Other phenomena of change, such as antonomasia and poetic metaphor, are of general occurrence in language, but they are found more frequently than elsewhere in cant, which is dependent for its effectiveness on a rapid replacement of terms. The use of images and descriptive words in cant is often strikingly poetic, as in such coinages as *ice* or *sparklers* for "diamonds," *rod* for "revolver," *convict* for "zebra," *gazers* for "Federal agents," and in Italian, *espina* for "suspicion," *secreto* for "dagger," *bruna* for "night," and *perpetua* for "soul."

An important characteristic of modern cant is its brevity. It consists almost exclusively of monosyllabics, whereas it once used heavy, long words such as *clapperdogeon, hankstelo, holwendods, jobbernoll, jockungage, nigmenog,* and the like. The substitution of *broad* for "woman," *law* or *bull* for "policeman," *eye* or *dick* for "detective," *clown* for "village constable," and *poke* for "pocketbook" clearly illustrates the current tendency to be short, concise, and effective.

History and Distribution. Cant exists among all European nations. The *Donat proensal* in the thirteenth century mentions the word *gergons* as "vulgare trutannorum." In Italy cant is called *furbesco* (from *furbo* "sly," "astute"); in France, *argot*; in Spain, *caló*; in Portugal, *calão*; in Germany, *Rotwelsch*; in Romania, *limba cârâitilor*, or "thieves language." There are moreover many provincial or dialectal cants, such as the *mourmé* in Savoy, the *montmorin* in the Alps, the *bellau* in the Jura, the *lingua zerga* in Venetia.

The most ancient text of European cant is found in two unpublished sonnets in manuscript, exchanged before 1460 by Giovanni Francesco Soardi and the humanist Felice Feliciano. Feliciano's sonnet begins in good Italian, with the line *Non può quanto bisogna alto volare;* it contains, however, several words of *calmone,* a northern cant which is very close to the Venetian type and has, among other substitutions, *pelosa* for "soul" and *verbare* for "to speak." Other traces of cant are found in a letter of the poet Luigi Pulci to Lorenzo the Magnificent in 1472, and in the famous "profession of faith" put by Pulci in the mouth of his scoundrel hero Margutte in the eighteenth canto of *Il Morgante Maggiore;* these are the oldest records of a Tuscan cant. The Venetian cant, which is much more diffused and important than the Tuscan, is known especially through the *canzoniere* of Andrea Michieli called Strazzola, who was born around 1450 and died in 1510. An even more extensive use of cant for literary purposes was made by Antonio Brocardo, who lived in the first part of the sixteenth century, and then by Giovan Francesco Ferrari and Bartolomeo Bocchini called Zan Muzzina, both of whom used the Venetian cant. A precious dictionary, *Modo novo da intendere la lingua zerga,* was published in 1549 and reissued many times thereafter.

French cant was made famous in the fifteenth century by the poet François Villon, some of whose ballads are so studded with cant words as to be in great part incomprehensible. The first documents of the Spanish *germanía* are contained in Juan Hidalgo's *Romances de germanía* (1609). The first mention of German *Rotwelsch* or *Rotwälsch* dates from the thirteenth century, but the first vocabularies are the work of Gerold Eslibach, dated 1490, and the *Liber vagatorum* first printed in High German in 1510 and later in Low German and in the dialect of the Lower Rhine. This *Rotwelsch* is mostly distorted German, with many Hebrew and Italian words; such formations as *bregan,* from *pregare,* and *barlen,* from *parlare,* may be compared with *kapieren,* from *capire,* in Modern German student slang.

English cant is first known through R. Copland's *The Hye Waye to the Spyttel House* (1517). Other early examples may be found in John Awdelay's *Fraternitye of Vacabondes* (first edition 1561), Thomas Harman's *Caveat for Commen Cursetours* (1567), the anonymous *Groundwork of Connycatching* (1592), and several other works.

Cant in the United States. In the United States, a cant has been developed by a number of different groups, having in common a need or a desire for a vocabulary that is not generally understood.

The cant of American criminals was mainly derived from England up to the time of the Civil War. Sir Robert Peel's reform of the London police system, in 1829, drove many criminals from London, and a number of them took refuge in the United States, bringing their vocabulary with them. Many escaped convicts went to California in the 1850's, and a large part of their cant is still used there. During the Civil War, however, American criminals started original creations of their own, and from 1870 onward they became leaders in the field, exporting their terminology, which was more varied and picturesque than that of their English brothers, to England and to other countries. The prohibition era of the 1920's brought to American bootleggers and gangsters great prosperity and even a certain prestige, and the motion-picture industry, by mass production of gangster films, gave to the cant of this underworld a great and perhaps excessive publicity all over the world.

American cant is, like English and unlike Continental cant, essentially national, but there are exceptions to this rule; a few German words, for example, such as *spiel, fin,* and *gelt,* and a few Yiddish words, such as *ganov* and *kibitzer,* have come into the language, mainly by way of New York channels. There are, of course, many logical differences, especially between the cant of the eastern and of the western states. Thus, a forger may be called a *scratcher* on the Pacific coast, a *paperhanger* on the Atlantic coast; a jewelry store may be called a *slum-joint* in the East and *icehouse* in the West.

Special varieties of criminal cant have arisen from time to time in response to special circumstances. The drug peddlers who started their activity in 1915 called the physicians who supplied drugs, *ice-tong doctors*, the addicts *junkers*, and the Federal agents *whiskers* or *gazers*. The powerful racketeers of the Prohibition era introduced *big shot, triggerman, hideout, heat, to take for a ride, to put on the spot*, and many other terms that have now become slang or even colloquial American and may soon be standard.

Prisons have a cant of their own. In this vocabulary, bread is *punk*, sugar is *sand*, a judicial sentence is a *bit*, prison is the *big house*, a reformatory is a *college*, and *to burn* or *to fry* means "to be electrocuted."

The cant of American hoboes and tramps, reflecting as it does the migratory lives of these classes, is closely related to the jargon of railroadmen. Thus, a locomotive is a *hog*, a conductor is a *con*, a Pullman sleeper is a *snoozer*, and a passenger car is a *cushion*. Among other curious coinages, a tramp has a *moniker* for a name, and the boy he takes along for small services is his *lamb, guntzel,* or *purshun*.

The carnival, the circus, and the burlesque have likewise a cant of their own, which was once, though less now than formerly, close to that of the hoboes. In this cant, clowns are *white-faces*, a tamer is a *trainer*, elephants are *bulls*, zebras are *convicts*, camels are *humps*. Theatrical men also speak a special language, and H. L. Mencken, in *The American Language*, reproduces a long dialogue heard on Broadway which is practically incomprehensible to people outside of show business. In show business in general, however, the line between cant and jargon is too nebulous to be clearly defined.

G. B.

CANTABILE. *See* MUSICAL TERMS.

CANTABRIAN MOUNTAINS, a chain of mountains forming a western ramification of the Pyrenees, in northern Spain. They extend for about 300 mi. along the Bay of Biscay from the western Pyrenees to Cape Finisterre, traversing the Basque Provinces, Asturias, and Galicia. They consist of a series of parallel chains sloping abruptly on the north to the sea, while the southern sides descend more gently toward the meseta. The chain culminates in the Torre de Cerredo (8,786 ft.). Highway passes are few and relatively high. There are several railroads crossing from Castile to Lugo, Oviedo, Santander, and Bilbao. The mountains are rich in minerals, especially coal and iron. N. C.

CANTAL [kã'ta'l], a department in south-central France, with an area of 2,229 sq. mi., bounded by the departments of Puy-de-Dôme on the north, Haute-Loire on the east, Lozère and Aveyron on the south, and Lot and Corrèze on the west. The department, entirely mountainous, is occupied by the great volcanic massif of Mont du Cantal and its contreforts, one of the groups which constitute the Auvergne Mountains, culminating in the Plomb de Cantal, 6,096 ft. high. The navigable rivers are the Dordogne and the Allagnon. The soil is not fertile, except in the valleys, some of which are 3,000 ft. above sea level; in the low cantons rye, oleaginous plants, hemp, flax, and buckwheat are grown. The declivities of the mountains, however, afford good pasturage, and grazing is an important industry. About 20,000

tons of cheese are produced. At Pleaux, Aurillac, and Champagnac 130,000 tons of coal are mined a year. Aurillac, the prefecture, located on the Jordanne River, 269 mi. south of Paris, is known for its cattle market and as a center for the manufacture of umbrellas and slippers. Chaudes-Aignes, a small watering place in the valley of a tributary of the Truyère River, has five thermal springs, the hottest in France, reaching a temperature of 180°. The water is used for all purposes, even for heating the houses in winter. Mauriac, an ancient town in the northwestern part of the department, has a Romanesque church of the twelfth century, containing a black image of the Virgin. The exports of the department are horses, cheese, leather, and wax. Cantal was formed from the southern part of the old province of Auvergne. Pop. 1954, 177,065.

CANTALOUPE [ka'ntəlup; ka'ntəlop], *Cucumis melo cantalupensis*, a variety of muskmelon obtaining its name from Cantaluppi, Italy, where it has long been grown. Originally derived from southwest Asia, the cantaloupe has a hard rind, often rough or furrowed. In the United States and Canada the name is applied, incorrectly, to all muskmelons.

CANTATA [kəntɑ'tə], a choral composition consisting of solos, recitatives, and choruses with instrumental accompaniment. The cantata may be either a sacred work, similar to an oratorio but on a smaller scale, or it may be a secular story or drama adapted to music but not intended to be acted. With the rise of instrumental music in the seventeenth century, the term "cantata" (from the Italian *cantare*, "to sing") was applied to a composition to be sung, in contrast to a sonata (from the Italian *sonare*, "to sound"), a piece to be played on an instrument. J. S. Bach's cantatas for the Lutheran service represent the highest development of the form.

D. L. E.

CANTERBURY [ka'ntərbɛri; ka'ntərbəri], a city and county borough, situated in the Canterbury parliamentary division of Kent, England, 62 mi. southeast of London, on the Stour River, at the head of a beautiful valley of the North Downs. It is the archiepiscopal see of the Primate of the Church of England. Canterbury was the Roman-British Durovernum, flourishing at a junction of roads from Kentish ports to London. In 560 it became the capital of Kent. In 597 after St. Augustine converted the Saxon King Aethelbert to Christianity he established himself in Canterbury as the first archbishop, and the church became the first cathedral with a monastery in England. The famous cathedral, originally Augustine's undertaking, was repeatedly gutted by fire and rebuilt during the Norman and subsequent eras. It is an outstanding example of the blending of Norman and Perpendicular styles. Archbishop Thomas à Becket was murdered in the cathedral in 1170, and after his canonization in 1172 thousands of pilgrims visited his shrine until it was dismantled by Henry VIII in 1538. Geoffrey Chaucer's *Canterbury Tales* have immortalized these pilgrimages.

Henry III in 1256 sold the city and the right to elect bailiffs to the inhabitants, and during the reign of Henry VI the community was incorporated. Canterbury sent two members to Parliament from 1283 to 1885, then one until 1918 when it was disfranchised. The city suffered considerably from bombing in World War II. It is a railroad junction and has a large agricultural trade. Pop. 1952, 29,600.

CANTERBURY BELLS, the common name for *Campanula medium*, a favorite garden biennial blooming in late spring, a 4-ft.-tall spike of pink, blue, violet, or white bell-shaped flowers 2 in. long. Developed into many horticultural forms, some varieties of Canterbury bells have a flaring, corolla-like calyx surrounding the large bell. *See also* CAM-PANULA. J. C. Wis.

CANTERBURY CATHEDRAL, an English Gothic cathedral located in Canterbury, near the southeast coast of England. Established by St. Augustine in 603, the cathedral later became the ecclesiastical center of Britain. It is mainly Perpendicular (fifteenth century) in style, although fragments of Norman work remain and the choir is late twelfth century. Canterbury was a Benedictine monastery, and its guest houses, granaries, and other monastic buildings once extended north to the city walls. Only the rebuilt cloister and the rectangular chapter house remain.

The cathedral is incredibly long and low, with a roof line broken by the soaring central tower and the lower western towers. These latter are suggestive of France, though the immense Perpendicular window between them is typically English. Entrance is through the richly decorated porch on the south side. The present nave is that seen by Chaucer's Canterbury pilgrims. Though stripped of its rich furnishings and resplendent colors under Henry VIII and later under Cromwell, it is still splendid, and is characteristic in its great length and its division into areas of activity.

The separating screen between nave and choir is a reminder that laymen were restricted to the naves of these monastic cathedrals whose primary purpose was to serve as worship centers for the cathedral chapters. Only on festival occasions were the people admitted to the eastern arm to gaze upon the glorious shrines of the holy dead. The choir of Canterbury was built after the burning of the earlier choir in 1174. Its irregularities are due to the use of parts of the older walls. Beyond the choir lay the goal of the pilgrim thousands who visited Canterbury, the shrine of Thomas à Becket, ablaze with gold and glowing jewels. This was removed and his body destroyed in the reign of Henry VIII, but the cathedral itself remains his shrine. A. K. L.

CANTERBURY TALES, THE, the most famous work of Geoffrey Chaucer, begun about 1387 and worked at intermittently, presumably until his death in 1400. It is a collection of stories offering a wide variety of theme and spirit, all but two of them in verse, supposed to have been told by a varied company of pilgrims as they ride along the road to Canterbury. A Prologue describes and characterizes the individual pilgrims, and links between the tales deal with episodes of the journey. There are tales of high seriousness and tales of ribald mirth. Though unfinished, it is regarded as Chaucer's masterpiece. *See also* CHAUCER, GEOFFREY. R. K. R.

CANTICLES. *See* SONG OF SOLOMON.
CANTILENA. *See* MUSICAL TERMS.

CANTILLON, RICHARD [kã'ti'yɔ̃'] (c. 1680-1734), Irish merchant and economist, was born in County Kerry about 1680. His early life is obscure. He carried on business as a merchant in London and later as a banker in Paris, becoming wealthy through financial dealings. He was living in London again at the time of his death. Cantillon's fame rests on his *Essai sur la nature du commerce en général*, published posthumously in London in 1755. It was popularized about 1880 by the British economist, William Stanley Jevons, who called it the "cradle of political economy" because it was a systematic treatment of almost the whole field.

CHARLES PHELPS CUSHING

Through the 16th-century Christchurch Gate is caught a glimpse of the west entrance of Canterbury Cathedral and, above it, the great west window noted for its fine medieval stained glass.

The first part of the book defines wealth, resolving it into the elements of land and labor. It states that the time, expense, and difficulty of learning a type of work, the risk involved in the work, and the capacity and responsibility required of the worker account for the variations in wages. This is the germ of Adam Smith's theory of wages. Cantillon contrasted real value, which arises from the cost of production, with market value, which depends on supply and demand. Currency, either paper or coin, was not the true measure of a nation's wealth, he said; land was the source of wealth. This was the basis of the Physiocratic doctrines, and François Quesnay, founder of the Physiocratic school, acknowledged it as such.

Land returned three kinds of income, Cantillon said, paying first the expenses of the cultivator, then the profits of the operator, and third the owner. He stated that non-agricultural enterprises did not offer any equivalent of the third kind of income. Cantillon's book discusses such topics as barter, market prices, circulation of money in amount and rapidity, credit, interest and its causes, the rise and fall of interest rates, foreign trade, and banking. His treatment of some subjects clearly anticipates later ideas, such as the Malthusian theory of population. Cantillon wrote: "Men multiply like mice in a barn, if they have the means of subsistence without limit; and the English in the colonies become proportionally more numerous in three generations than they would in England in thirty; because in the colonies they find new lands to cultivate." Cantillon was the first to use the phrase "real or intrinsic value" (called "normal value" today) and showed its whole relation to market value. His treatment of these and other topics, such as the effect of an increase in money supply on the general price level, and his treatment of bimetallism, show that he was far ahead of his time. Cantillon died May 14, 1734, apparently murdered by a former servant, who had set fire to his house.   E. W.

CANTON [kantɒ′n] (Chin. Kwangchow), the capital city of Kwangtung Province and the largest commercial center in southern China. It is on the Pearl, or Canton, River, 80 mi. from the South China Sea, at 23° 7′ N. lat. and 113° 15′ E. long. The river flows through the northern section of the city and enters the delta through the Bocca Tigris (Tiger's Mouth), about 20 mi. south of the city. The climate of Canton is uncomfortably hot and humid in summer, the temperature rising as high as 100° F. in July and August; the average winter temperature is about 55°. Between 60 and 80 in. of rain fall annually; as much as 12 in. fall during August. According to the 1953 census, Canton had a population of 1,598,900.

History. Modern Canton was founded in A.D. 1053, when the Chinese drove the Tai peoples from the site. It was the earliest seaport of China opened to foreign trade. The Portuguese, who were the first foreigners to visit Canton, arrived in ships in 1516. The Spanish arrived in 1575, the Dutch in 1604, the English in 1637, and the Americans in 1784. At first foreign merchants were allowed to live only in designated areas of the city during the trade seasons. All business with foreign traders was monopolized by Co-hong, the guild of licensed merchants engaged in foreign trade, which consisted almost entirely of the exportation of tea and rhubarb. In the early 1800's, however, opium from India and Persia began to be imported, a development which led to the "Opium War." On June 3, 1838, Lin Tse-hsü, commissioner for the suppression of opium, demanded the surrender of stocks of opium held by British and American ships. Several hundred chests of opium were burned publicly by city officials, precipitating a temporary occupation of Canton by British forces in 1841. The city was formally opened to trade under the Treaty of Nanking signed the following year on August 29.

Canton, the scene of an abortive revolutionary attempt made by Sun Yat-sen against the Manchus in 1895, was the cradle of the Chinese Revolution. The most memorable day in the year to Cantonese is March 29, a national holiday commemorating an attack made in 1911 on the Manchu viceroy's yamen (official building), under the leadership of Gen. Hwang Hsin, in which 72 revolutionaries met martyrdom. These heroes lie buried in one grave at Hwang Hwa Kang (Yellow Flower Cliff), which has become a suburban scenic shrine. The uprising of March 29, 1911, was suppressed by an imperial officer, Admiral Li Tsuen. Later in the same year, the new Manchu viceroy appointed to Canton was assassinated and an attempt was made on the life of Admiral Li. In October the boisterous revolutionary sentiment became overwhelming, and the Manchus gave up Canton, the whole province of Kwangtung declaring itself independent. In 1913 a revolt broke out in Canton against the dictatorship of Yuan Shih-kai, and an expedition was formed against him, but this uprising was suppressed by Gen. Lung Chai-kwong of Kiangsi Province. Three years later, when Yuan Shih-kai attempted to make himself emperor of China, revolutionary forces proclaimed him a traitor and pushed their way into the city. A fierce battle ensued, terminated only by the removal of General Lung from his post. In 1917 a republican government was established in Shanghai by the Kuomintang, which later moved to Canton with the intention of maintaining a parliamentary regime in the south while attempting to conquer the north. Dr. Sun Yat-sen became president of the regime, but China did not become

unified until 1926, when the North Expedition, headed by Gen. Chiang Kai-shek, set out from Canton and accomplished its mission within the same year.

At the high tide of the Nationalist Revolution in 1925, British residents in Shameen, the foreign-settlement area of Canton, became the target of an anti-imperialist movement. On May 30 a strike of Chinese laborers was organized against a Japanese cotton mill in Shanghai. In support of the strikers, Shanghai students paraded in the Shanghai International Settlement. The settlement police, under command of a British officer, fired upon the demonstrators, causing some casualties among the students. The anti-Japanese hostility immediately became anti-British, and a student demonstration was staged in Canton proper and in Shameen. Again the students were fired upon, and more casualties resulted, the incident becoming known as the "Shameen massacre." Consequently, a nationwide boycott was instituted against Hong Kong and against British trade in general which lasted eighteen months.

In the Sino-Japanese War, which broke out in 1937 following the occupation of Manchuria by Japan in 1931 and subsequent encroachments on Chinese territory by Japanese forces, the Japanese seized Canton on Oct. 21, 1938, and held it until Sept. 12, 1945. The British settlement at Shameen was returned to China in 1943 when Great Britain surrendered its extraterritorial and treaty-port rights in China, but the actual taking over was not effected until the end of World War II. In the Kuomintang-Communist civil strife which followed the conclusion of World War II Canton was named the provisional capital of Nationalist China in early 1949, but the city was abandoned in October of that year as Communist forces pushed southward. The Communists entered the city unopposed on October 14.

General Characteristics. Canton is a city of paradoxical appearance and culture. The older north and central parts of the city contain a maze of narrow streets, one- and two-story houses, and overcrowded tenements. A striking feature of the city is the swarm of houseboats on the river on which many of the people live. The southern section of the city has broader paved streets and many modernized buildings. Yut Sau Shan, a famous hill near the southern section, is the site of a public park. On the summit of this hill stands a famous five-story pagoda, housing a museum. On this hill is also the Sun Yat-sen obelisk, and just below it is the beautiful Sun Yat-sen Memorial Hall, which has a curved roof of bright purple tiles. The Flower Pagoda, built in the sixth century, is 270 ft. high, has nine stories, and is octagonal in shape. Near it is the Five Fairies Temple, a Taoist center.

Much of the population of Canton has become Westernized through contact with foreigners. Despite this fact, ancient customs and superstitions are practiced to a large extent. The city is the center of a special Chinese dialect. Canton is renowned for the great variety and delicacy of its food. Chop suey is a westernized version of Cantonese food. Small steamed pies, cakes, buns, and raviolis are served from morning till late in the afternoon in the hundreds of tea houses found throughout the city.

The most modernized part of the southern section of Canton is Shameen, an island formerly comprising the British, French, and other foreign settlements. Formerly a muddy flat on the Pearl River bank, Shameen was set apart for the British and the French in 1859 after their residences in Canton were destroyed during the Opium War of 1841. The British and the French together built a concrete embankment along the southern and southeastern bank of

Shameen, where the main current of the Pearl River passes. A canal was dug to separate Shameen from the southern part of Canton. Only at two places was the concession area connected by bridges with the city, and at ten o'clock at night the bridges were closed, turning Shameen into an isolated island. The British settlement occupied an area of about 90 acres; the French settlement, about 44 acres. In this westernized community, intersected by broad avenues shaded by banyan trees, are located the foreign consulates, banks, big trading firms, and many modern residences and churches, including a Roman Catholic cathedral.

Educational Institutions. Many schools in Canton have been founded with funds sent home by the city's thousands of emigrants. Higher institutions of learning include the missionary-founded Lingnan University and the National Sun Yat-sen University, the latter having one of the finest college buildings in all China.

Communications. Canton is well served by three railway lines: the Canton-Peking Railway, which forms a main artery northward; the Canton-Kowloon Railway, which goes southeast to Kowloon, opposite Hong Kong across the strait; and a third line which goes westward to Samshui on the West River (Si Kiang). While Canton scarcely begins to rival Hong Kong as a port, since it is located comparatively inland on an estuary, it is nevertheless an important river port. There are extensive dock and shipyard facilities on the banks of the Pearl River. The main channel from Canton to Whampoa, 10 mi. to the south, was dredged in 1949, and since then Canton has been accessible to deep-draught, ocean-going vessels. Hong Kong can be reached in three hours by rail or overnight by water. Airlines connect Canton with other large Chinese cities. Since the Communists came to power, Canton has become China's chief port of entry from Hong Kong.

Economy. Manufacturing and trade hold important places in the city's economy. Local plants include silk filature and piece-goods establishments, tanning and leather works, cabinet works, matting and fan factories, textile, hosiery, and embroidery plants, match factories, brick kilns, cement factories, and ice plants. The processing of food and essential oils is important; there are marine engine, shipbuilding, and sail yards, and, in addition, a well-developed fishing industry. Rubber soles for shoes, bristles, mother-of-pearl inlay, jade and ivory carving, firecrackers, and porcelain and china are also produced. As part of the Communist industrialization drive, an industrial district has been built up on the eastern outskirts of Canton. The large plants in this area include a cannery, a textile mill, a cotton bleaching and dyeing mill, and factories producing newsprint, cane sugar, glass, plastics, and insecticides.

A. C. T. and T. Sh.

CANTON [ka'ntən], a city in western Illinois situated in Fulton Co., 25 mi. southwest of Peoria, in an agricultural area marked by diversified farming. Natural resources of the region are coal and clay. Founded in 1825, Canton was incorporated as a city in 1854 and has the mayor and council form of government. Transportation is provided by the Chicago, Burlington & Quincy and the Toledo, Peoria & Western railroads. Industries include the manufacture of agricultural implements and machinery, toilet preparations, cigar boxes, bricks, concrete blocks, overalls, and livestock feed. Woodworking and creamery products are also trade items. Pop. 1950, 11,927.

CANTON, a town and village in Norfolk Co., eastern Massachusetts, situated on the north bank of the Neponset River, 14 mi. south of Boston. It is an industrial community, settled in 1630 and incorporated in 1797. It is governed by a town meeting. Before its incorporation Canton was a part of Stoughton. The town is the seat of the State Hospital School for Crippled Children. Canton is the site of Paul Revere's foundry, the first copper-rolling mill in the country, where the copper for the State House dome in Boston and Fulton's first steamboat was rolled. Revere's powder mill, which operated during the Revolution and the War of 1812, was also located in the community. John Eliot preached to the Indians at the foot of Blue Hill, site of Harvard Meteorological Observatory. The New York, New Haven & Hartford Railroad supplies transportation. Canton's principal products are textiles, rubber goods, and technical and radio apparatus. Pop. 1950 (village), 4,739; (town), 7,645.

CANTON, a city in central Mississippi, the county seat of Madison Co., situated in a farming area, 20 mi. north of Jackson. Founded in 1824, it was incorporated in 1834 and is governed by a mayor and board of aldermen. Clothing, tent, and lumber manufacturing are the principal industries. Pop. 1950, 7,048.

CANTON, a city in western North Carolina, situated in Haywood Co., on the Pigeon River, 2,609 ft. above sea level, 20 mi. southwest of Asheville, in the Great Smoky Mountains area. Diversified farming marks the surrounding territory, with tobacco, corn, and wheat among the leading crops. Timber is a natural resource of the region. Canton was incorporated as a city in 1893; its government is administered by a mayor and board of aldermen. Transportation is provided by the Southern Railway. The principal industry is centered in Canton's pulp, paper, and tannin plant, one of the largest in the world and in connection with which a reforestation program is carried on to insure future raw materials. Lumber is also milled. Pop. 1950, 4,906.

CANTON, a city in northeastern Ohio, the county seat of Stark Co., situated on Nimishillen Creek, about 20 mi. southeast of Akron. It is a large industrial community in a rich farming area. Coal mines, limestone quarries, gas wells, and clay pits are found in the vicinity. Canton was settled in 1805 and became the county seat in 1809. Incorporated as a village in 1822, it became a city in 1854 and is governed by a mayor and council. President William McKinley lived in the city and is buried on Monument Hill. The Baltimore & Ohio, the Pennsylvania, and the Wheeling and Lake Erie railroads and United, Eastern, Capital, and American airlines provide the city with transportation. Industrial products include alloy, open hearth, and stainless steels, roller bearings, electric cleaners, gas and diesel motors, street lighting standards, and brick, clay, and tile products. Canton is the home of one of the largest roller bearing factories in the world. Pop. 1950, 116,912.

CANTON, a territorial division in Switzerland and France. Twenty-two cantons, three of which are divided into demicantons, comprise the member states of the Swiss Federation. Two representatives for each canton and one for each demicanton, or 44 representatives in all, sit in the Council of States.

The French cantons, created at the time of the French Revolution, are territorial subdivisions of the *arrondissements* and comprise an average of about twelve communes. They numbered 3,031 in 1954. Each canton is the seat of a justice of the peace and elects one member to the general council of the department.   M. B. W.

CANTON ISLAND, the most northerly of the Phoenix group of atolls, in the north-central Pacific Ocean, under joint United Kingdom and United States control, and a stop-over point on the air route between Hawaii and the South Pacific. It lies at 2° 50′ S. lat. and 171° 43′ W. long. and is of typical atoll formation. The roughly diamond-shaped lagoon is about 9 mi. by 4½ mi. and is almost completely ringed with a narrow ribbon of barren land up to 12 ft. above sea level. A major airstrip and a seaplane base were in extensive use here during World War II, and the former now services the various commercial airlines flying between North America and Australia and New Zealand.

The island has no indigenous inhabitants. In 1937, when its potential use for aviation came to be realized, United States and British parties established settlements on the island. A subsequent agreement placed this island and another of the Phoenixes, Enderbury, under joint control, and both the United States and British governments maintain small establishments. The island is named for the New Bedford whaling vessel *Canton* which was wrecked there in 1857. Pop. 1950, 272.   F. M. K. and M. M. K.

CANTOR, GEORG (1845-1918), German mathematician, was born Mar. 3, 1845, in St. Petersburg, Russia. He is noted for clarifying the basic notions inherent in the modern real number system. For more than 2,000 years, since the time of the Pythagoreans, the character of irrational numbers was not fully understood. Zeno's paradoxes (problems dealing with infinitesimals and continuity in motion) had withstood all attempts at explanation. Explanations were forthcoming in the fundamental researches of Cantor and of Julius Dedekind in the theory of infinite sets. Cantor died at Halle, Jan. 6, 1918.   C. O. O.

CANTÙ, CESARE [kɑntu′] (1804-1895), Italian writer, politician, historian, was born at Brivio, Italy, Dec. 5, 1804. He was educated at Milan, abandoned an early intention of entering the priesthood, and went into the teaching profession. The Italian spirit of his writings led to a year's imprisonment by the Austrian government (1833-1834) and the loss of his teaching position. His *Universal History,* published at Turin in twenty volumes, was repeatedly revised and served several generations of Italians. In 1848, Cantù joined those urging Charles Albert to grant a constitution to Lombardy and make war on Austria, but he favored a republic for Lombardy rather than annexation to Piedmont. After 1849, he returned to Milan and wrote a comprehensive *History of the Italians* and *History of Ten Years.* He served for a short time as member of the Italian parliament, but spent most of his life, after the liberation of Lombardy, in writing and as director of the *Archivio di Stato.* He died in Milan, March 11, 1895.   H. McG. S.

CANTUS FIRMUS. *See* MUSICAL TERMS.

CANUTE or **CNUT** [kənu′t, knu′t] (c. 994-1035), King of England, Denmark, and Norway, was the second son of Sweyn, King of Denmark, who conquered eastern and central England in 1013 and died in 1014. Harold, the younger son, succeeded him in Denmark, and Sweyn's warriors proclaimed Canute ruler of England. The English almost immediately drove him off, but he conquered the whole country between 1015 and 1017. Canute had been baptized before 1013, and he became an ardent Christian, making the arduous pilgrimage to Rome in the year 1026-1027. He succeeded to the throne of Denmark on Harold's death in 1018, and in 1028 he reconquered Norway from its native king. Though ruling such an extensive empire, he showed great affection for England, making it his home and placing Englishmen such as Earl Godwin in positions of trust and importance. He was an able ruler; and though crafty and violent in temper, he showed self-control and understanding toward his subjects. There is probably no factual basis for the story that he rebuked his courtiers' flattery by commanding the tide to cease its advance. He died at Shaftesbury on Nov. 12, 1035.   E. R. A.

CANVASBACK, a 24 in. duck, *Aythya valisineria,* allied to the redhead, from which it is most easily distinguished by its forehead, which is low and sloping down to a long bill that is about three times longer than it is wide. It is found throughout North America, breeding in the northwestern regions where it nests near the water among the reeds or grasses. It winters in the more suitable places throughout the United States and Northern Mexico. It is found occasionally as far south as the West Indies and Guatemala. The head and neck of the male are reddish brown, the breast black, the under parts white, and the upper parts white, very finely barred with gray; the female is gray and brown in color. The canvasback feeds on a variety of water plants, but its favorite food is wild celery, and it formerly occurred in enormous rafts on lakes and bays where the plant is abundant. It is well known for the distinctive flavor its flesh acquires because of this spicy plant on which it feeds. The slaughter resulting from its fame as an epicurean dish has greatly diminished its numbers.   H. G. De.

CANYON, a valley with precipitous sides. The term, derived from the Spanish, *cañón,* is widely used in southwestern United States, where early Spanish explorers found many large canyons. A canyon is similar to but larger than a gorge. Canyons are formed by the vigorous erosive action of a river, generally in a semiarid region where surface wash and slump do not destroy the vertical walls. The canyons of the Yellowstone River in Wyoming, the Snake River in Idaho, and the Columbia River in Washington and Oregon are good examples. Probably the most famous canyon in the world is the Grand Canyon of the Colorado River in Arizona; in some places the walls of this canyon rise more than a mile above the river in successive cliffs of brilliantly colored rock. Submarine canyons are not uncommon and some rival in depth the deepest canyons on the earth's surface. These submarine canyons are found on the coastal shelf off the mouths of large rivers, such as the Hudson River in New York and the Congo River in Africa.   J. E. F.

CANYON DE CHELLY NATIONAL MONUMENT [də she], a scenic attraction located in Apache Co., northeastern Arizona, about 50 mi. northwest of Gallup, N. M. It is between the northern and southern Navajo Indian Reservations. The canyon has been formed by the headward erosion of Chinle Creek, which is a tributary of the San Juan River. The Chinle has cut a deep canyon into the Colorado Plateau, and the park includes a 20-mi.-long box canyon and beautiful 700- to 1,000-ft. cliffs of brilliant red sandstone. There are numerous cliff dwellings and ancient ruins in this park. Canyon de Chelly National Monument has an area of 83,840 acres and was proclaimed on Feb. 14, 1931.   J. E. F.

CANZONA or CANZONE. *See* Musical Terms.

CANZONE [kɑntso'ne] (Italian, from Latin *cantio,* "song"), a type of lyric suitable for singing, consisting of stanzas which are, with the occasional exception of the final one, identical in metrical structure. Dante, in *De vulgari eloquentia,* gave rules for the canzone and called it the noblest form of vernacular poetry, superior to ballata and sonnet.

The typical canzone-stanza consists of two similar sections of two or more lines each, followed by a third section which may be divided into two parts; if it is so divided, the stanza is quadripartite like a sonnet. The final stanza, sometimes shorter than the others, frequently addresses the poem itself as an envoi. A collection of lyrics, such as those of Petrarch, is called *canzoniere.*

The canzone was developed in the first half of the thirteenth century by the earliest Italian poets, in imitation of the *canso* of the Provençal troubadours. Whereas the troubadours usually kept the same rhymes in all the stanzas of a poem, and repeated over and over a few metrical schemes, the Italian poets generally used different rhymes in each stanza and showed originality in devising variations of form. Many canzoni were composed by Dante and his contemporaries, and by Petrarch, who established the style of lyrics for the fifteenth and sixteenth centuries. In the nineteenth century the canzone was revived by several of the leading Italian poets, among them Giacomo Leopardi.   K. McK.

CÃO, DIOGO. *See* Cam, Diogo.

CAPACITORS. *See* Electricity and Magnetism; Electric-Power Transmission; Insulating Materials, Electrical.

CAP-DE-LA-MADELEINE [ka'p də la ma'dlɛ'n], a city in Champlain Co., Quebec, Canada, adjoining the city of Trois-Rivières. It is 81 mi. southwest of the city of Quebec, on the east bank of the St. Maurice River at its confluence with the St. Lawrence. Granted to the Abbé de la Madeleine by Louis XIV, it contains the celebrated Catholic shrine of Notre Dame du Très-Saint-Rosaire, built in 1714. Incorporated as a town in 1918, it became a city in 1922. An industrial town, its manufactures include newsprint, aluminum foils, paper bags, clothing, adhesives, and lumber. Power for these industries is supplied by the Shawinigan Falls development. Its people are of French descent. Pop. 1956, 22,943.   D. F. P.

CAPE ANN, a rocky promontory of Essex County, in northeastern Massachusetts, situated approximately 31 mi. northeast of Boston. The cape is about 14 mi. long and 10 mi. wide at its base and includes the city of Gloucester and the town of Rockport. Annisquam harbor forms a large indentation on the northern side and Gloucester harbor on the southern side of the cape. Cape Ann is noted for its rocky coastline, fishing fleets, artist colonies, and many summer resorts.   J. E. F.

CAPE ANTEATER. *See* Aardvark.

CAPE BRETON HIGHLANDS NATIONAL PARK, a scenic and recreational park in Nova Scotia, situated in the northern part of Cape Breton Island, between the Gulf of St. Lawrence and the Atlantic Ocean. Canada's first seacoast park, it was established by the Canadian government in 1936 and comprises an area of about 390 sq. mi. Its interior is a high plateau bordered by heavily forested hills which descend to a rugged coast broken by deep bays and inlets and the green valleys surrounding the lower stretches of many mountain streams. The landing place of John and Sebastian Cabot, who claimed the region for Henry VII of England, in 1497, is located in the park. In their honor a spectacular scenic highway which almost completely encircles the park has been named the Cabot Trail. The Nova Scotia government maintains a luxurious hostelry—Keltic Lodge—on Middle Head Peninsula, near the park headquarters. *See also* Canadian National Parks.   R. J. C. S.

CAPE BRETON ISLAND. *See* Nova Scotia.

CAPE CHARLES, the southern tip of the Delmarva Peninsula, which separates the southern end of Chesapeake Bay on the west from the Atlantic Ocean on the east. It is situated at 37° 5′ N. lat. and 75° 58′ W. long. in Northampton County, Va., about 26 mi. northeast of Norfolk. The area produces sweet and white potatoes, melons, beans, peas, and tomatoes, and many fish and shellfish are caught. Much of this produce is transported to Norfolk and the mainland by small boats. The town of Cape Charles is on the southwestern side of the peninsula about 10 mi. northwest of the cape.   J. E. F.

A view of Canyon de Chelly from the Rock Window. In the middle distance is one of the several small farms in the canyon.

THE CAPE COD SHORELINE AT NORTH TRURO, MASS.

CAPE CHESTNUT, *Calodendrum capense,* a southern African evergreen tree of the rue family growing in subtropical regions. It is a large (70 ft.) and striking flowering tree with dark green foliage and a great number of rose-lilac flowers. The fruit is round, woody, and somewhat larger than a walnut. It is covered with conspicuous tubercles and contains three large black seeds.   E. McCl.

CAPE COD, a 65-mi.-long, narrow, hook-shaped peninsula that extends into the Atlantic Ocean from southeastern Massachusetts. It is from 1 to 19 mi. wide and was made into an island by the completion of the Cape Cod Canal in 1914. The cape, which comprises Barnstable County, Mass., juts eastward and then bends to the north. It is bordered on the west by Cape Cod Bay, on the east by the Atlantic Ocean, on the south by Nantucket Sound, and on the southeast by Buzzards Bay and Vineyard Sound.

Cape Cod was formed by the continental glacier, which deposited a sand, gravel, and clay moraine on top of coastal plain deposits. The hook shape and the recurved spit at Provincetown are the result of ocean currents reorganizing the loose material. The eastern side of the cape is being carried away at the rate of three feet a year. Cape Cod is an area of dunes and low, sandy hills covered by pine and oak. It has many miles of fine beaches and a number of interesting little harbors. There are also many fresh water ponds on the cape. The climate is tempered by the surrounding ocean and is cool and pleasant during the summer; the winters are mild but windy. The cape is a humid region, but practically no snow falls during the winter. Deer, rabbits, quail, pheasant, and ducks are the most common fauna. The cape and its surrounding waters have large numbers of fish, lobsters, and clams; the cape was named after the large number of cod found there.

Cape Cod is a popular summer tourist attraction, and it is also a center of cranberry and strawberry production as well as commercial fishing. There are many small towns. The largest towns are Provincetown, where the Pilgrims landed in 1620; Chatham; Hyannis; Woods Hole; Falmouth; and Sandwich.   J. E. F.

CAPE COD CANAL, a 7.6-mi.-long channel in southeastern Massachusetts connecting Buzzards Bay on the southwest with Cape Cod Bay on the northeast. The canal reduces the New York-to-Boston water route by 75 mi. This sea-level channel cuts through sand and gravel hills across the base of Cape Cod in Barnstable County. The approach channel in Buzzards Bay is 4.5 mi. long and in Cape Cod Bay is 0.5 mi. long; the minimum width is 100 ft. and it is 25 ft. deep. The canal has a strong tidal current. The project was started by private capital in 1909 and finished in 1914; it operated under a toll system until 1928, when the United States Government purchased the canal for $11,500,000. It is now toll free and more than 5,000,000 tons of cargo pass through it every year. A large part of the freight is coal, oil, and other bulky products. The canal makes Cape Cod an island which is connected to the mainland by a railroad and a vehicle bridge at Bourne and the Sagamore Bridge at Sagamore.   J. E. F.

CAPE COWSLIP, *Lachenalia,* a genus of attractive, small (12 in.), bulbous plants in the lily family, native to South America. The flowers, which are similar to lily-of-the-valley, appear in a variety of colors. In northern greenhouses they may be brought into bloom early in spring by control of temperature and water.

CAPE FARO. *See* FARO POINT.

CAPE FEAR, the southeasternmost point of North Carolina, located at 33° 50′ N. lat. and 77° 57′ W. long. on Smith Island, off the mouth of the Cape Fear River in Brunswick County. The island was formed by the breaking up of a barrier beach that extends along much of the North Carolina coast. The seaward side of the low, sandy island is shaped almost like a right angle, and the point of the angle is called Cape Fear. The cape received its name because navigators feared the strong coastal current and dangerous, shifting sand bars along this part of the coast. Cape Fear is marked by a lighthouse.   J. E. F.

CAPE FEAR RIVER, the longest river entirely within the state of North Carolina. It is about 200 mi. long and drains an area of approximately 8,310 sq. mi. The headwater streams, the Deep and Haw rivers, rise in the piedmont belt just east of Winston-Salem and join near the edge of the coastal plain at Haywood, on the border of Chatham and Lee counties in the central part of the state, to form the Cape Fear River. The river flows generally southeastward and empties into the Atlantic Ocean just north of Cape Fear. The largest tributaries are the South River and the Northeast Cape Fear River.

The headwaters of the Cape Fear River flow through a tobacco-growing region, while the lower part of the river is in a cotton, corn, vegetable, and sorghum area. Part of the drainage basin is covered with longleaf and loblolly pine forests, and along the bottom lands are cypress, tupelo, and gum trees. Some lumbering is carried on, and turpentine and resin are extracted from the pine trees. The most important cities on the river are Fayetteville in Cumberland County, Elizabethtown in Bladen County, and Wilmington in New Hanover County. Wilmington is a port situated at the head of a broad estuary, and Fayetteville is the headwater for small-boat navigation.   J. E. F.

CAPE GIRARDEAU [dzhɪ′rɑrdo], the largest city and agricultural trade center of southeastern Missouri, is located on the Mississippi River in Cape Girardeau Co. about 100 air mi. south of St. Louis. It was founded in 1735 as an Indian trading post by Ensign Sieur Jean B. Girardot, a French naval officer, and was occupied by the Spanish in 1793. Cape Girardeau was chartered as a town in 1806 and incorporated as a city in 1843. Its principal manufactures are cement, shoes, food products, electrical appliances, limestone, furniture, and clothing. Cape Girardeau is the home of Southeast Missouri State College, St. Vincent's Academy, and Cape Office Training School. Pop. 1950, 21,589.

CAPE HATTERAS [hæ′tərəs], a point of land located just off the central part of the coast of North Carolina. It is situated at 35° 15′ N. lat. and 75° 32′ W. long. on the sea-

Bridge across the northern entrance of the Cape Cod Canal, Massachusetts

ward side of a long, low, narrow island. The whole northern part of the North Carolina coast is fringed by a barrier beach which has been shaped by wind and tides into a cuspate foreland, and Cape Hatteras is the name of the sharp eastern point of this barrier beach. Numerous inlets have been cut through the beach, dividing it into a series of long, narrow islands which partly enclose Albemarle Sound on the north and Pamlico Sound on the south. Kitty Hawk, site of the first heavier-than-air flight by the Wright brothers, is on one of these islands east of Albemarle Sound.

Cape Hatteras is east of Pamlico Sound, and the Cape Hatteras region is a dangerous zone for navigators because of the shifting sand bars and strong currents. Many ships have been wrecked in this district, particularly during storms that carried them too far inshore. Hatteras Island is inhabited and there are a few small settlements on the island, among them Hatteras, Frisco, Buxton, Avon, and Rodanthe. The cape is guarded by two beacon lights.   J. E. F.

CAPE HONEYSUCKLE, *Tecomaria capensis,* a South African climbing shrub of the bignonia family. It is often planted in frost-free regions as a hedge plant. It has dark green pinnate leaves and large handsome orange-red flowers. Its fruit is bean-like and contains many seeds.   E. McCl.

CAPE HORN, the rocky southern headland of Horn Island, Chile, which marks the southern tip of South America at 56° S. lat. and 67° W. long. Although continuously storm-swept, the route around the Horn provided easier navigation for sailing vessels than the Strait of Magellan. It was named by the Dutch navigator Willem Schouten in 1616 for his birthplace, Hoorn, Holland. Antarctic weather conditions prevail at the cape, and it has been the scene of many shipwrecks.   P. E. J.

CAPE HUNTING DOG, a long-legged, large-eared animal, *Lycaon pictus,* suggesting a cross between a wolf and a hyena. Although it is a true dog and a member of the family Canidae, the Cape hunting dog has also been called the hyena dog. In color it varies greatly, its coat consisting of very irregular patches of black, white, and yellow. Unlike other members of the dog family, the Cape hunting dog possesses only four toes on each foot. Like the dhole, large packs of these animals hunt together and are able to run down even the fleetest of antelopes. The Cape hunting dog is a native of South Africa.   G. M. C.

Cape Cowslip, Lachenalia

CAPE JASMINE, a popular evergreen shrub, *Gardenia jasminoides,* which grows to about 6 ft. in height. It has dark, thick, shiny leaves and bears large, double, waxy, white, fragrant flowers from 1 to 3 in. in diameter, which are favorite flowers in corsages.

ČAPEK, KAREL [tsha′pɛk] (1890-1938), Czech journalist, novelist, and dramatist, was born Jan. 9, 1890, in Malé Svatoňovice, Bohemia. He studied philosophy in Prague, Berlin, and Paris and received a degree of Doctor of Philosophy in 1915. From 1917 forward he was on the editorial staff of various newspapers in which many of his short stories and essays first appeared. In 1935 he married Olga Scheinpflugová, noted Czech actress and writer. He died on Dec. 25, 1938.

Čapek was an adherent of pragmatism. He won world renown as the author of plays that have been produced all over the world, his popularity springing from his ability to treat serious themes with a generous dose of humor. The best known of the plays is *R. U. R.* (1921), a satire on mechanized civilization. *The Insect Comedy* (1921), written in collaboration with his brother Joseph, portrays greed, parasitism, egocentrism, and militarism. *The Macropoulos Secret* (1922) is an amusing argument against everlasting life. *Power and Glory* (1937) and *Mother* (1938) deal with dictatorship and war, but, being written in the shadow of World War II, lack the humor of the previous works.

The social problems underlying Čapek's dramas are expressed in some of his novels. *Krakatit* (1924) deals with the invention of an explosive capable of world destruction. In *The War with Newts* (1935) sea monsters, educated by man, threaten his existence. In his famous trilogy, *Hordubal* (1934), *Meteor* (1934), and *Ordinary Life* (1934), Čapek deals with the problems of individuals. A man is what he thinks he is, what he might have been, and what others believe him to be; good or bad, all men are brothers.

Letters from Italy (1923), *Letters from England* (1924), *Letters from Spain* (1930), *Letters from Holland* (1932), and *Travels in the North* (1936), are humorous travel stories. *Fairy Tales* (1932), *Dashenka, or the Life of a Puppy* (1933), and *I Had a Dog and a Cat* (1939) are delightful stories for children. The remaining works translated into English are *Adam the Creator* (1927), *The Absolute at Large* (1922), *President Masaryk Tells His Story* (1930), *The First Rescue Party* (1937), *The Cheat* (1938), *Intimate Things* (1925), *Tales from Two Pockets* (1929), *Gardener's Year* (1929), and *How They Do It* (1938).

J. B. K.

CAPE LEADWORT, *Plumbago capensis,* a climbing or upright straggling shrub of the plumbago family, often grown out of doors in frost-free climates, in groups or rows where a large mass effect is desired. It has medium-sized, evergreen leaves and very showy, azure blue, tubular flowers.

E. McCl.

CAPELLA [kəpɛ′lə], also designated Alpha (α) Aurigae, the bright star in the constellation Auriga. North of 44° N. Lat., Capella becomes circumpolar and never sets. Slightly farther south, it dips for a short time below the northern horizon, and 12 hr. later is almost at the zenith. Capella is the same type of star (yellow) as the sun. It is rated sixth in brightness in the entire sky, is approximately 40 light-years distant, and in intrinsic brightness is over 100 times greater than the sun. *See also* AURIGA.

J. H.P.

CAPE MAY, a peninsula, 17 mi. long and 11 mi. wide, that forms the extreme southeastern section of New Jersey.

The Atlantic Ocean is on the east, and Delaware Bay is on the west of the peninsula. The whole peninsula lies within Cape May County, and in the central part of the low, flat, sandy and pine-covered peninsula is the town of Cape May Court House. At the extreme southern tip are the towns of Cape May Point, West Cape May, and Cape May. The peninsula is a resort area as well as a truck-gardening and poultry-raising region. Belleplain State Forest and Great Cedar Swamp are both located on the peninsula. The eastern side of the peninsula has a series of off-shore islands which almost enclose long narrow bays.

J. E. F.

CAPE OF GOOD HOPE, formerly Cape Colony, a province of the Union of South Africa, lying at the southern end of the African continent. It is bounded on the west by the Atlantic Ocean, on the north by Southwest Africa and Bechuanaland, on the east by Transvaal and Orange Free State, on the northeast by Orange Free State, Basutoland, and Natal, and on the southeast and south by the Indian Ocean. It is the largest province of the Union of South Africa, comprising an area of 277,113 sq. mi., extending 450 mi. in length and 600 mi. in breadth, with a coastline of about 1,300 mi.

Geographical Features. *Topography.* Parallel to the lowlands of the south coast are several granite and sandstone mountain ranges rising in terraces toward the north. Between these ranges are large plateaus, the greatest of which form seven eighths of South Africa. The heights of the principal mountains average 6,000 to 7,000 ft.; starting on the northwest coast and going inland and southward are Vogel Klip, Lange Berg, Bokkeveld, Rokkeveld, and Roggeveld; going eastward are the Nieuwveld, Little and Great Zwartberg, and Lange mountains. At Capetown, in the southeast, Table Mountain reaches an elevation of about 6,000 ft. In the northeast, in Griqualand, are the Asbestos Mountains. Compass Berg in the northeast is over 8,000 ft. high. There are few inland rivers and streams and most of these are not navigable. Although there are no natural harbors on the coast, there are many bays, the principal ones being Saint Helena, Saldanha, Table, False, and Walker on the Atlantic Ocean, and Mossel, Plettenbergs, Saint Francis, and Algoa on the Indian Ocean.

Climate. The climate of the province is moderate, healthful, and dry, particularly in the western areas. Extremes of heat and cold are rare. The mean annual temperature over most of the country is over 60° F. except in the higher regions, where it is colder; but the dry climate characteristic of the southern area also prevails in the north as a result of the elevation and the proximity of the ocean.

Flora. In the southwestern region, where vegetation has to withstand long droughts, the plants consist of low brushes and shrubs from 2 to 8 ft. high and are characteristic of the coastal districts and mountain slopes. In the inland valleys there also grow bulbous and tuberous plants and along the riversides grow the typical palmiet and pig lily. The evergreen forests on the seaward slopes of the mountain ranges included yellow woods, stinkwood, and black ironwood, and climbing plants are abundant. There are also some soft oaks, pines, gums, and wattles. Because of the increasingly dry climate farther inland on the west coast there is no vegetation except for the typical sparse desert grasses, succulents, and low bushes. Before the rains the inner plateau is scrubby and barren, but afterward bulbous plants and annuals bloom for a few weeks. In the northwest and coastal area beyond Algoa Bay vegetation is largely grassland, the trees consisting mostly of acacia. On mountain slopes in this region patches of forest occur up to 6,000 ft. and include yellow woods, ironwood, and lemonwood. Along the coast belt below 1,000 ft. the palm predominates, with climbing plants such as the Natal cherry and wild grape.

Fauna. Lions and giraffes are dying out, but the African elephant still roams the southern forests, and the buffalo, leopard, jackal, hyena, antelope, baboon, and aardvark are still plentiful. Birds include vultures, eagles, pelicans, flamingoes, and ostriches. There are snakes of the large species, as well as venomous varieties, including the *cobra di capello*. Whales and seals abound in the coastal waters; both salt-water and fresh-water fish are plentiful.

Economic Resources and Activities. Sheep raising is the most important industry and wool is the chief export. These are surpassed in value only by diamonds, which are the chief mineral wealth of the province, produced at Kimberley and in the Barkley West districts. Other industries are mining, farming, stock raising, forestry, and fishing. The principal minerals, other than diamonds, are coal, copper, gold, asbestos, salt, and tin. In the southwestern and eastern parts of the province large quantities of wheat, oats, and barley are grown. The raising of steers, sheep, horses, goats, and ostriches is extensive. The vineyards are famous for their fine wines. Flour milling is also important. Considerable revenue is obtained from the transportation of goods to and from Rhodesia, the Transvaal, and the Orange Free State; there are over 5,000 miles of railway in the province—mostly government owned and operated—and there are extensive postal, telephone, and telegraph facilities.

Government. The province has 22 members in the Senate of the Union of South Africa, and 57 members in the House of Assembly. The franchise is granted to native-born or naturalized South Africans over 21 years of age who are literate and have been resident in the province for 12 months. Voters must possess property worth £75 or receive annual wages totaling at least £50. Persons of non-European descent are not eligible for election to a seat in either house. In the provincial government of the province there is a provincial council of 57 members, elected for a three-year term. Europeans and non-Europeans may sit in the provincial council, and the qualifications for voting are the same as those for the Union elections. All ordinances of the council must be approved by the Union government. The council has the power to impose direct taxation upon the province for provincial purposes. An administrator of the province is appointed by the Union government for a five-year term, and there is an executive committee composed of the administrator and four persons elected by the provincial council. Romano-Dutch law forms the basis of the judicial system. There are three superior courts in the province under the Supreme Court of the Union of South Africa, and there are a number of lower courts that hear cases in local magisterial districts. Local government in the Cape is administered by divisional and municipal councils and village-management and local boards. These are under the legislative control of the provincial council.

Education. The province possesses an excellent system of primary education. The demands for higher education are taken care of by the University of Capetown and by several colleges. In 1952 there were 950 primary schools for Europeans and 239 secondary schools, as well as a number of special schools. There were seven teacher-training colleges. For colored (of mixed race) pupils there were 1,020 denominational primary schools and 31 secondary and high schools, one teacher-training college, and a number of other schools. For the Africans there were 2,301 denomin-

ational primary schools, 64 secondary and high schools, and some other institutions.

Population. The province is the most densely populated area of the Union. The total population at the 1951 census was 4,421,704, including about 2,484,000 Bantus, 982,000 persons of mixed racial descent officially classified as "colored," 936,000 Europeans, and the remainder Asians and other groups. Agricultural pursuits employ the largest number of people, but manufacturing and commerce in the growing factories of Capetown, Port Elizabeth, and East London have gained an increasing portion of the working population. The principal cities, with their 1951 census populations are: Capetown, 440,925; Port Elizabeth, 169,277; East London, 90,606; Kimberley, 58,777; Uitenhage, 38,709; and Paarl, 29,987. Other smaller centers are Grahamstown, Queenstown, De Aar, Beaufort West, Graaff-Reinet, Upington, Mafeking, George, Worcester, and Kingwilliamstown.

History. The Cape of Good Hope was discovered in 1488 by the Portuguese explorer Bartholomeu Dias. Dutch settlers arrived at Table Bay in 1652 and formed the Dutch East India Company. They became the nucleus of the colony and in 1685 invited settlers, obtaining 150 from among the French Huguenots driven from France by the revocation of the Edict of Nantes. These intermarried with the Dutch and by 1691, because of the absence for a time of further immigration, were regarded as the parent stock of the colony. Their descendants are called Afrikaners. In 1795 the British captured the Cape; they returned it to the Dutch in 1803, but seized it again three years later. By the terms of the Convention of London of 1814 and the Vienna peace settlements of 1815, the Cape region was annexed by Great Britain.

In 1835, because of the long-standing grievances of the Dutch farmers (or Boers) toward the attitude of the British with respect to the Kaffirs, from 7,000 to 10,000 started the "Great Trek" (1835-1845) from Cape Colony eastward to the lands which eventually became the Transvaal and Orange Free State republics.

Meanwhile Cape Colony remained a separate colony under a governor, council, and house of assembly. In spite of years of native wars, depressions, and Boer hostility, British power was steadily extended north of the Cape. In 1867 diamonds were discovered along the Orange River and the Vaal, and in 1871 the blue clay of Kimberley yielded an unsuspected harvest; diamond hunters swarmed into the region from many nations.

In 1858 Sir George Grey proposed the federation of all the colonies and states of South Africa. After responsible government was granted to Cape Colony in 1882, several voices, including those of the Fourth Earl of Carnarvon and James Anthony Froude, were raised to favor the creation of a British federation in South Africa; such movements were nourished by commercial interests throughout the region. The Boer hostility to Great Britain, however, was rising in the latter half of the nineteenth century; the Afrikaner Bond was organized with the avowed purpose of expelling the British from all South Africa. In 1881 a war broke out between the British of the Cape and the Boers of Transvaal and Orange Free State. This war was a chapter in the years of Boer-British hostility that ended in the Boer War of 1899-1902. After the Boer War the British South African states speeded the development of their own resources, but Cape Colony, the Transvaal, the Orange Free State, and Natal were confronted by native difficulties, serious economic disturbances, and several other problems. In a convention held in 1907-1908 they decided upon unification. The result was the creation of the Union of South Africa in 1910. *See also* UNION OF SOUTH AFRICA. G. Sm.

CAPERBUSH, *Capparis spinosa,* a low (3 ft.), straggling, spiny shrub from Mediterranean regions, grown there over rocks and in dry walls for the greenish flower buds, from which the pickles known as capers are made. It is grown in greenhouses, and infrequently outdoors in California, for the flowers, with purple filaments etched against wavy white petals. R. S. Ho.

CAPERCAILLIE [kæ'pərke'lyi], a species of grouse, *Tetrao urogallus,* the largest of the Old World forms. It occurs in a number of closely related groups, chiefly in coniferous forests, from the British Isles to Kamchatka. The male, which is almost three feet long, is blackish, with deep metallic green on the breast and a brown tinge on the wings, and has a bright red wattle over the eye; the female, only two feet long, is red-brown, mottled with buff, whitish, and black. The polygamous cock struts before the hens with tail spread fanwise like a turkey. The bird feeds in summer on insects and berries, but in winter on pine and fir needles, which give its flesh a strong and unpalatable flavor. The name, which has a Gaelic derivation, means "horse of the woods"; it is also spelled capercailye, capercailze, or capercally.

CAPET, HUGH [ke'pɪt; kæ'pɪt; ka'pɛ'] (c.939-996), first Capetian king of France, was born about 939, the son of Hugh the Great, Count of Paris and Duke of the Franks. He succeeded to his father's titles and powers in 956. When Louis V, the last Carolingian ruler of France, died in 987, Hugh was elected king with the support of the powerful churchmen, Adalberon and Gerbert, as well as the Duke of Normandy and the Count of Anjou. His suzerainty was readily recognized by the great barons of the kingdom, but they rendered neither homage nor service, and his authority was mainly theoretical. In an attempt to purchase their allegiance Hugh had given them large grants of royal lands, thus weakening his own position. Such power as he had was based on his own feudal domain, the Île de France, which was smaller than many of the fiefs belonging to the lords. During his nine-year reign Hugh did little more than maintain himself against Charles, Duke of Lower Lorraine, the Carolingian claimant. Nevertheless he was able to retain his hold on the throne, and insured the succession by associating his son Robert with him as king. He avoided submission to the emperor, and quarreled with the pope, but he was otherwise a devoted son of the Church. He was lay abbot of the abbeys of St. Martin at Tours and St. Denis, was interested in clerical reform, and was careful to maintain control over the archbishopric of Tours and the great bishoprics and abbeys of the Île de France. He died in Paris, Oct. 24, 996. F. C. H.

CAPETIAN DYNASTY [kəpi'shən] (987-1328), a line of French kings named after the founder, Hugh Capet. With the death of King Louis V, the last direct descendant of Charlemagne, the French throne became vacant. Upon the advice of Adalberon, Archbishop of Rheims, the nobility offered the crown to Hugh Capet, Count of Paris, in 987. He thus became the founder of a dynasty which converted the loose feudal monarchy into a centralized government, and laid the foundations of the modern French state. The first four Capetians are not especially notable, but with the accession of Louis VI (1081-1137) the royal power began to assert itself over its feudal rivals. Under Philip Augus-

tus (1165-1223) the annexation of Normandy and other English fiefs in France nearly doubled the royal domain, while the establishment of Paris as the seat of government marked the beginning of an administration directly under royal control. The growth of a national government, as opposed to feudal claims, was continued by Louis IX (1214-1270) and reached its climax under Philip IV (1268-1314). Under this monarch, the institutions of the French state, such as the Parlement of Paris and the Estates General, assumed the forms they were to maintain until the French Revolution. Additional annexations of territory increased the royal domain. With the death of Charles IV in 1328, the direct line of Hugh Capet came to an end. The crown then passed to Philip of Valois, a nephew of Philip IV. The Valois kings, who were thus a branch of the Capetian house, continued to reign until 1589, when they were succeeded by the Bourbons, who traced their ancestry back to a younger son of Louis IX. With the exception of the Bonapartes, all the monarchs of France since 987 have been descendants of Hugh Capet. *See also* CAPET, HUGH.

J. F. R.

CAPE TOWN, [Kaapstad in Afrikaans], the capital of the Cape of Good Hope Province and the legislative capital of the Union of South Africa, is located near the southern tip of Africa, on Table Bay, at the foot of Table Mountain. It is an important port and many steamship lines use its wharfage, drydock, and other facilities. It is served by railroads and airlines. Local agricultural products, such as dried and fresh fruits, and gold and diamonds from the Transvaal are its chief exports. The principal industries are the manufacture of asbestos products, bricks, tiles, cement, wood products, metal and engineering products, foodstuffs, condiments, paper, wine, spirits, tobacco, clothing, boots and shoes, textiles, furniture, bedding and upholstery, chemicals, drugs, cosmetics, fertilizers, paints and varnishes, brushes, leather goods, soaps, jewelry, electrical and radio products, wire, and fencing. Diamond cutting, shipbuilding, process engraving, and printing are also important. Agricultural products include dairy products, grain, fruits, and vegetables.

Cape Town is the oldest European settlement in South Africa. The Dutch East India Company's representative, Jan Van Riebeeck, colonized it in 1652. A fortress known as the Castle, begun in 1666 and completed in 1679, still stands. English, Dutch, and Portuguese ships stopped there for supplies on their way around the Cape of Good Hope. From 1795 to 1803 the British held all of the Cape Colony in the name of the Prince of Orange, who had taken refuge in England after the French seizure of Holland. Cape Town and the colony were returned to Holland under the Treaty of Amiens in 1802, when Holland was a dependency of France. After Great Britain won command of the sea by defeating the French and Spanish forces at Trafalgar, Sir David Baird was sent to South Africa with a fleet and took possession of the city and colony in 1805. In 1814, after Napoleon's downfall, Holland formally ceded the colony to Great Britain. In 1820 four thousand British settlers were sent to the west side of the Fish River, and from that time the British population of Capetown and the colony grew steadily.

The South African Public Library in Cape Town was founded by Lord Charles Somerset in 1818. The South African Museum, established in 1825, has natural history, geology, and archaeology collections. The University of Cape Town was the earliest institution of higher learning in South Africa. The university's new buildings are on the grounds of Groote Schuur (Big Barn), the former residence of Cecil Rhodes and now the official residence of premiers of the Union of South Africa, at Rondebosch, 5 mi. outside the city. The South African National Gallery, the Michaelis Gallery, the Municipal Botanic Gardens, the House of Parliament, the Government House, the City Hall, the Dutch Reformed Groote Kerk, and the Anglican cathedral are other points of interest. An observatory is located 3 mi. from

the school. Other departments of the university include arts and education, physics and mathematics, botany and zoology, psychology, fine arts and architecture, law, music, and social sciences.

The student body numbers about 4,000 and there is a faculty of 330. Dormitory facilities accommodate about 1,000 students. There are five separate libraries with a total of

GOVERNMENT HOUSE AT CAPE TOWN, IN THE SHADOW OF TABLE MOUNTAIN

PHILIP GENDREAU

the city. Cape Town has a municipal orchestra and English and Afrikaans theaters. Pop. (prelim. 1951), 440,925; metropolitan area, 577,211. H. M.

CAPE TOWN, UNIVERSITY OF, a coeducational institution of higher learning located in and near Cape Town, Union of South Africa. The oldest university in the country, it was founded in 1829 as the South African College. Until 1879 it was maintained by a group of private individuals, but in that year a company was formed to direct its affairs. Between 1911 and 1916 the college included the postmatriculation classes of the Diocesan College at nearby Rondebosch, and the teacher training classes of the Cape Town Normal College.

In 1918 it was chartered as a university with the present name. Bequests from Sir Julius Wernher and Alfred Beit together with a large loan from the government assured the new university of an adequate initial endowment. The land for the main campus at Rondebosch, a suburb of Cape Town, is part of the huge Groote Schuur estate, bequeathed to the nation by Cecil Rhodes, where the main units of the university moved in 1925.

Research facilities available to students include the South African Museum, the Bolus Library and Herbarium, the School of African Studies, the Anthropological Museum, the Marine Biological Laboratory, and the National Botanic Gardens at nearby Kirstenbosch.

The medical school adjoins the site of the $5,000,000 Groote Schuur Hospital which is the teaching hospital for

250,000 volumes. The university also offers ample opportunity for postgraduate study.

CAPE VERDE ISLANDS (ILHAS DO CABO VERDE) [ke′p vɜ′rd, i′lyəzh dʊ kɑ′bʊ vɛ′rthə], an archipelago of fourteen islands, an overseas territory of Portugal, lying 350 mi. off Dakar, French West Africa, which is on the Cape Verde Peninsula. The four smallest islands are uninhabited. The total island area is about 1,557 sq. mi. Although the islands are of volcanic origin, the only crater still occasionally active is one with an elevation of 9,000 ft. on Fogo (Fire) Island. Also mountainous are São Tiago, São Vicente, São Nicolau, and Santo Antão. The easternmost members of the group, Maio, Boavista, and Sal, are less rugged.

In general the higher areas and the coasts are bare, the natural vegetation being confined to the valleys; the hot, generally dry climate is partly responsible. Rainfall is irregular and its failure has caused famines. At Praia, the capital, the average precipitation is 11 in. The rainy season, such as it is, runs from August to November, the hottest part of the year. To make matters worse, the hot, dry harmattan wind blows from the Sahara. Tropical diseases are prevalent. It should be pointed out, however, that conditions vary from island to island and within the individual islands, depending on the local topography.

The flora is tropical and in general resembles plant life on the near-by continent, although several species are peculiar to the islands. The Portuguese have introduced a number of trees as well as the cultivation of coffee, sugar cane,

Praça Alexandre de Albuquerque in the city of Praia

various vegetables and fruits, and several of the cereal grains. The native fauna shows little variety, but the Portuguese settlers introduced cattle, horses, asses, and goats, of which there are about 100,000 head in all.

The islands' principal exports are oilseed, fish, spirits, coffee, sugar, fruit, vegetables, hides, and salt. Bunker coal and fuel oil comprise a large part of the islands' imports, thus raising the imports to the point where they exceed the exports. Many Cape Verde workers migrate seasonally to South America, bringing back accumulated wages and increased spending power.

The territory of Cabo Verde, administered by a governor resident at Praia, has autonomy in fiscal and administrative matters. Before 1951 it was a colony, and before 1878 it was administered as part of Portuguese Guinea. Praia, on São Tiago, is the capital and largest city (pop. 9,880). Although its harbor is wide and deep, it is not so well protected as that of Mindêlo on São Vicente, an important coaling station on the route from Europe to South America. Transatlantic aircraft are serviced at the airport of Espargo on Sal Island. Small steamers ply between the islands. There are about 350 mi. of roads.

In the 1950 census, the population was 147,328, of whom 3,034 were Europeans; 101,726, mulattoes; 42,475, Negroes; and 93, other. São Tiago, with over 70,000 inhabitants, is the most populous island. Next in order are Santo Antão (28,000), Fogo (20,000), São Nicolau (15,000), and Brava and São Vicente (10,000 each). None of the few towns has more than 10,000 inhabitants. The prevailing languages are Portuguese and a patois compounded of Portuguese and African dialects.

When they were discovered by Italian navigators around 1460, the islands were uninhabited. Shortly thereafter, the Portuguese took possession and began to settle the islands one after another, importing Negro slaves from the African mainland. In the sixteenth century the islands were used as a penal colony. Despite its strategic location, the Cape Verde group has enjoyed a generally tranquil history and has never passed from Portuguese control except for the period of Spanish rule over the homeland, from 1580 to 1640. The harbor of Nossa Senhora da Luz on Maio was occupied by the British until the end of the eighteenth century.   R. G. W.

CAPE VERDE PENINSULA (*Fr.* Cap Vert), on the coast of the French colony of Senegal, has at its tip the westernmost point of Africa and the nearest to South America, Cape Almadies (17° 33′ W. long.). The rocky peninsula, some 20 mi. from east to west and up to 7 mi. across, affords the only natural shelter along the otherwise sandy coastline. It was first seen about 1445 by a Portuguese navigator, João Fernandes, and was given its name, meaning "green cape," because the native baobab trees formed a verdant contrast to the bleak desert background. The Portuguese settled on the island of Gorée in the bay which forms the concave southern shore of the peninsula. Gorée was taken by the Dutch in 1588, by the French in 1677, and several times by the British for brief periods, and was a center of the slave trade. In 1857, on the mainland opposite Gorée at the southern tip of Cape Verde Peninsula, the French built the fort of Dakar, which became the capital and major community of French West Africa.   E. A.

CAP-HAÏTIEN [ka′pa′i′syã′], a port and city on the north, or Atlantic, coast of Haiti, at 19° 47′ N. lat. and 72° 13′ W. long., about 110 mi. north of Port-au-Prince, the capital. The city is the most picturesque in Haiti and recent renovations and the building of a waterfront boulevard have not destroyed the French colonial charm of its pastel houses with their elaborate balconies, its short, narrow streets, and its old fountains. Cap-Haïtien was founded about

1666 by Bertrand d'Ogeron de la Brouère, French voyager and colonizer, and became a leading port and city of the Plaine du Nord, at one time a region of large plantations and homes. It was captured and burnt in 1791 by Pierre Dominique Toussaint L'Ouverture, Haitian general and liberator, and suffered a disastrous earthquake in 1842. Cap-Haïtien became the capital of Henri Christophe, who ruled as king of North Haiti from 1811 to 1820. Inland from the city is Sans Souci, Christophe's famous palace, and on top of the mountain behind the palace stands the boat-shaped Citadel Laferrière which Christophe built to withstand a possible French seige. The rather dry region east of Cap-Haïtien produces some sisal; west of the city lies an area which produces bananas and tropical fruit for export. Cap-Haïtien has a small tourist trade. Pop. (prelim. 1950), 24,423.

CAPILLARIES, the delicate, almost transparent blood vessels which are the terminal ramifications of the vascular system, from the term *capilla* meaning hairlike. The capillaries are offshoots of the arterioles, the smallest unit of the arterial system, each arteriole having as many as ten to twenty of these branches. The capillaries are an integral part of all tissues, forming a freely intercommunicating network of vessels in close contact with the cellular structures which they keep supplied with nourishment, and from which they remove the waste products of cellular activities. The distal continuations of the capillaries join with one another to form the collecting venules, which return the blood from the tissues to the heart. The vessels between the arterioles and the venules are collectively referred to as the capillary bed, an organic unit whose function is to regulate the local blood supply in accord with the requirements of the tissues. The capillary branches of the arterioles possess in their junctional region a well-defined collar of muscle cells, whose arrangement permits these structures to act as sphincters controlling the flow of blood into the network of capillaries. Under normal conditions only a small proportion of these so-called precapillary sphincters are open so that blood flows through a fraction of the available channels. A characteristic feature of the circulation through the capillary bed is the presence of periodic, spontaneous cycles of contraction and dilation of the muscle cells surrounding the arterioles and precapillaries, producing a discontinuous and intermittent blood flow through the capillaries. The capillary wall, which consists of a patchwork of closely joined, extremely thin cells (endothelium), has no muscle cells surrounding it and does not appear to be contractile, except in certain lower forms such as the frog and fish. The capillary endothelium is sufficiently porous to permit ready interchange of materials between the blood and tissues. Normally only water and dissolved substances pass through freely in both directions, the blood cells and proteins being retained inside the vessels. In certain organs such as the liver, spleen and adrenal glands, the typical capillaries are replaced by sinusoids, which are abrupt enlargements of the vessel forming a cavernous pocket through which the blood trickles slowly and often serve for the temporary storage of blood. B. W. Z.

CAPITAL. *See* ARCHITECTURAL TERMS.

CAPITAL, a term used in business and economics to denote either an income-producing fund or the concrete instruments of production, such as buildings and machinery. In the former sense the term "money capital" is sometimes used. The instruments of production often are called capital goods.

Capital Goods. Early economists were inclined to emphasize the definition of capital as capital goods, and to speak of capital as wealth devoted to the production of more wealth. When the term is used in this sense, it is apparent that the accumulation of capital becomes highly significant as a factor in the growth and development of a country. The process of capitalistic production is time-consuming and roundabout. Under typical modern conditions it involves elaborate equipment, extensive use of mechanical power, and complicated productive procedures and techniques.

Capital goods, as one of the major factors of production, are the result of men's past efforts, whereas land is a gift of nature; but when a money value is placed upon either, it may be called capital in the broader sense of the word. Businessmen often use the term, sometimes meaning the capital goods themselves, but more often it refers to the goods measured in terms of money. The capital goods wear out and are replaced, but capital, as the businessman uses it, is more permanent. To the extent that prices are stable and efficiency of production is maintained, the money equivalent of the aggregate of capital goods changes little, if at all.

Fixed and Circulating. A distinction sometimes is made between fixed and circulating capital. Fixed capital is relatively durable and may be used over a long period of time, whereas circulating capital is nondurable and may be used up in a single process. The power plant of a factory is an example of fixed capital; the coal that it burns is a form of circulating capital.

Ownership Claims. Capital in the financial sense is an ownership concept, representing the present values of income claims against intangible wealth, such as good will, patents, credits, and other sources of income, as well as claims against tangible capital goods (production goods). Thus, in ordinary business usage the capital of an enterprise consists of the amount invested, the surplus, and the undivided profits.

The distinction between capital as production goods and capital as a financial and ownership concept has given rise to similar differences in the definitions of capitalism. Those who emphasize the capital-goods concept think of capitalism as a system of economic organization characterized by the use of elaborate labor-saving equipment. Those who emphasize the financial and ownership aspect consider the essential feature of capitalism to be the private ownership of the capital. All modern industrial countries, including the Soviet Union, are capitalistic in the sense that great importance is attached to the use of capital goods, but Russia is not a capitalistic country in the sense that private ownership of major forms of capital goods is permitted. *See also* CAPITALISM; LAND; INDUSTRIAL PRODUCTION. M. C. M.

CAPITAL, EXPORT OF. *See* INTERNATIONAL EXCHANGE, CREDIT, AND CURRENCY.

CAPITALISM, a term popularly applied to that type of economic system which is characterized by private ownership of property, freedom of enterprise with its accompanying profits and competition, and freedom of choice by the individual consumers. No satisfactory definition of this elusive expression exists, nor in all probability will any ever be generally agreed upon, since capitalism means different things to different men with different ethical standards.

Evolution. Forms of capitalism have been in evidence since the beginning of recorded history. Ancient Egypt, Babylonia, Carthage, Greece, and Rome afford abundant examples of societies based on private property and individual enterprise, including the most extreme instance of private property, slavery. In general, however, the history of mankind is the history of power and despotism, of the subjection of the masses to the whims and caprices of individual dictators and the ruling classes. It was only in the latter part of the medieval era in Europe that outstanding rudiments of capitalism as a system began to appear; and, roughly, it is only in the years since 1800 that *laissez faire* and capitalism have supplanted feudalism and mercantilism as an economic system in many parts of the world. By a process of evolution the capitalism of commerce and trade in early modern times gave way to the industrial capitalism generated by the Industrial Revolution, which in turn has been succeeded by what may all too loosely be termed finance or mass production capitalism.

To Adam Smith, author of one of the most influential works on economics ever published, *The Wealth of Nations* (1776), the term "capitalism" was apparently unknown. He wrote, rather, of the "natural order" of liberty, standing in the forefront of the first important organized movement to liberate the productive forces of the individual man from the shackles of public authority. Relying upon the theory of natural harmony in economic matters, he maintained, with fellow liberals of his day, that if economic laws, as he viewed them, were allowed to operate unchecked under a common standard of ethics, maximum production and a general state of well-being would be the result. Based upon this all-important doctrine of individual self-interest and free enterprise, the liberalism of Adam Smith's time has become the cardinal doctrine of modern capitalism.

It was with the onset of the Industrial Revolution in the eighteenth century, however, that modern capitalism indicated maturity. In the span of a lifetime, 1770 to 1840, developments occurred which replaced the practice of previous centuries with the rush and roar of contemporary civilization. Many early civilizations had been built upon the labor of exploited human beings. Modern civilization has been built, in great part, upon man's inventions and mechanical power. The productivity of human hands with tools has been increased enormously throughout the world, primarily under the stimulus provided by free individuals and private enterprise.

Defects of Capitalism. Critical supporters of a capitalistic economy or free enterprise are aware, however, that within the virtues of capitalism lie also its evils and dangers as a by-product of human frailties. Uncontrolled free enterprise and free competition in many instances lead to excessive individualism and aggressiveness, stimulated by the prospect of large monetary returns or profits which are regarded as just returns for superior intelligence, for the expenditure of managerial time and effort in supplying goods and services, and for taking the risks that usually attend free enterprise and free competition. The individual producer and trader in the past faced dangers and responsibilities that only the courageous and ingenious would dare to meet. Production and trade were not only ventures but adventures. The latter term, indeed, was the title applied to the activities of those who risked their financial security in purchasing stock in companies which promoted English colonization in the Western Hemisphere during the seventeenth century. In protecting their investments, individual producers or traders often resorted to means which led to exploitation and gross injustice. Industry and business, under the then approved regimes for privateering and buccaneering, were forced to employ acquisitive characteristics of strategy and tactics similar to those essential in military warfare. The story of capitalism is to a large degree the drama of conflict by free producers, free traders, and free individuals for survival.

Cumulatively the effects of exploitation and injustice led to organized efforts by the victims of the abusers of free enterprise, with the result that various kinds of laws and controls arose, avowedly in behalf of those who were wage or salary earners. Actually, however, collectivistic controls also invoked exploitation and injustice, for under various forms of the socialistic system control of the individual, of free enterprise, and of free competition was taken over by the state which, in turn, evolved some form of a capitalistic dictatorship by an individual or by a tyrannical party in power.

Nature of Modern Capitalism. In the early days of the Industrial Revolution the *laissez-faire* policy of Adam Smith was adopted in England, cradle of individual liberty, common law, and free economy. The intolerable industrial conditions which developed as a result of social changes under this policy, conditions which gave rise in socialist literature to the coinage for the first time of the term "capitalism," made necessary the intervention of the government in the interests of individuals and workers. Since then the ever-growing integration, interdependence, and complexity which the age of invention has thrust upon national economies have seemingly produced an order in the United States which perhaps may best be designated as controlled and regulated free enterprise. The so-called free enterprise system in reality has become a hybrid system, a cross between eighteenth century liberalism and modern socialistic controls. American capitalism is a mixture of government ownership, control and operation of large segments of business, joint government ownership and private operation of certain small segments, and private ownership and government control on a prodigious scale of much of the American economy. That this has come to pass is largely the result of the excesses of business men themselves, of social reformers, and of the activities of organized labor. Though competition in its various manifestations is a basic rule, monopoly control in some businesses and labor organizations has grown apace in recent years. Monopoly prices, as well as government-controlled prices, tend not only to be high but also unresponsive to changes in economic conditions. Both long-term and installment debts of the people had mounted by 1957 to unprecedented levels. Maldistribution of wealth and income have worked to the detriment of social standards for the majority of the population. A multitude of corporate and other devices, such as the holding company, trusteeship, and the public agency, has in some instances made a mockery of the theory of competition.

Government Controls. The trend toward centralization in government, furthermore, has piled control upon control. Few things have seemingly a greater capacity for growth than government agencies and bureaus. Each sector of established government controls tends to become a dynasty and automatically to erode the remaining area of free economy.

One understandable factor, however, is the circumstance that every country must somehow organize itself in order to cope with its economic problems. In some way or other decisions must be reached as to how people, available labor, and resources shall be best employed. What, for instance, shall be produced, and how much, and where, and by what methods, are questions that press for answers by free individuals themselves or planners. Under socialism and other isms these decisions are made by government decrees and appointed planning committees; under fascism, by dictators.

Under free enterprise or capitalism, on the contrary, these decisions are left, in the main, to the free choice of individuals and groups. Socialism and fascism represent planning by government authority; capitalism represents planning by free individual authority through the instrumentality of free exchange and productive capacity in harmony with law and order.

The crucial difference between socialism and fascism, on the one hand, and capitalism, on the other, here manifests itself. Capitalism may use as much of a planned economy as its rival economic systems, but with one vital distinction: that production and consumption are not completely controlled by authority imposed from above, but also by the interaction of individual relations and prices in a free market place according to law. Consumers make their wants known to producers by their purchases. In general, all producers including wage earners tend to adjust their output to the consumer market and to produce whatever can be sold to the best advantage. Consumer demand, at times influenced by advertising, determines which of several purposes shall be served by management, labor, land, buildings, and materials available for production.

In this manner economic activity under the capitalist exchange and price system is automatically regulated. Of such significance, in fact, is the role of individual judgment in the making of most fundamental decisions that capitalism is correctly known as the system of free enterprise and, in the United States, as the American system of free enterprise. Such a description, however, is not wholly accurate. There always have been, and there are today, some services which either cannot or should not be left to the workings of private enterprise. Nothing is more obvious, in a survey of economic history, than the conclusion that among individual enterprisers are those who at times threaten the foundations of private enterprise if they are left free to do as they wish. Nothing is more demonstrable than the tendency of some business men, and labor leaders and employees as well, to engage in practices designed to stifle competition and freedom of action. Capitalism is in no way a thing exclusive of government; it is, and necessarily must be, subject to the government. J. M. F.

CAPITALIZATION,

CAPITALIZATION, a term used most generally in reference to the security issues of a corporation. It has a variety of meanings. Most commonly, capitalization refers to the sum of the outstanding securities of a corporation, including the outstanding stocks, both common and preferred, bonds, and long-term notes. In law, capitalization generally refers to the par value or stated value of the stock, whether issued or not issued and outstanding. In this latter view, bond issues or other certificates of indebtedness are not encompassed within the meaning of capitalization. Where par-value stocks, that is, those having a designated face value, are used, the stock capitalization may be indicated in terms of the number of par-value shares or in terms of the gross amount of dollars at which the shares are recorded on the books. Where no-par-value stocks are employed, the stock capitalization is expressed generally in terms of the number of shares, especially when the no-par stocks are recorded on the books at a nominal value.

Capitalization of Income. Capitalization may also refer to the process of determining the present capital value of assets on the basis of their income-yielding power. The process, more commonly termed the capitalization of income, involves the determination of the future annual income to be secured from the assets employed in the business and the selection of a rate of capitalization. Thus an expected annual income of, say, $100,000 is capitalized by a fair rate of return on the investment, say 5 per cent, and a capital value of $2,000,000 is determined——$100,000 ÷ 0.05 = $2,000,000. This is the equivalent expression of saying that $2,000,000 invested on the expectation of a 5 per cent return should yield $100,000 annually. In capitalizing income there are two major considerations, namely, the proper estimation of future annual income and the selection of a proper rate of capitalization. Neither of these is easily determined, and both involve estimation and the exercise of judgment. The capital value of assets is apt to be overstated or understated, and hence the securities issued on the basis of the estimated value of the assets may be too generous in amount or less than might be warranted. The terms overcapitalization and undercapitalization often are used to refer to the relationship between actual earnings and the expected fair and reasonable rate of earnings on the permanent capital obligations. If the actual earnings are insufficient to provide for the regular payment of interest on outstanding bonds and for a reasonable rate of return on the stockholders' commitment, then the corporation is said to be overcapitalized. If the earnings are high and in excess of fair and reasonable rates of return on the investments of the security holders, the corporation may be said to be undercapitalized. "Overcapitalization" is also used to refer to a situation where more face value of securities is issued than the value received in exchange for them. Thus when securities are issued for services or intangibles of dubious worth or for overvalued property, a condition of overcapitalization arises. N. L. S.

CAPITAL MARKET. *See* BANKING, INVESTMENT.

CAPITAL PUNISHMENT. *See* PENOLOGY AND PRISONS.

CAPITAL UNIVERSITY, founded in 1830, is owned and maintained by the American Lutheran Church on a 30-acre campus at Bexley, Ohio, a suburb of the city of Columbus. Capital is coeducational and has an undergraduate enrollment of 1,100 students. It is accredited by the North Central Association. The Conservatory of Music is approved by the National Association of Schools of Music, the Theological Seminary by the American Association of Theological Schools. The standard liberal arts and sciences curriculum is provided. Preprofessional preparation is carried on in 30 fields, among which are dentistry, engineering, forestry, law, medicine, and theology; and the Conservatory offers training in all areas of music. The University confers the Bachelor's degree in the arts, education, music education, music, nursing, science, and theology.

Notable collections in the fields of history, religion, and music, including musical, literary, and religious recordings, are contained in the University library. Students also have the use of the facilities of the Ohio State Library, the Ohio State University Library, the Ohio State Archaeological and Historical Society Library, and the public libraries in the city and suburbs.

Competitive scholarships, awards for leadership and special proficiencies, grants-in-aid, student loans, and part-time work opportunities are available. Resident students live in university-supervised accommodations. There are no fraternities or sororities. *For statistics see* COLLEGES AND UNIVERSITIES.

CAPITOL, UNITED STATES, actually, several stone buildings joined together, is the meeting place of

THE CAPITOL, WASHINGTON, D.C.

the United States Congress. It has served this purpose since 1800, with one interruption from 1814 to 1819 to repair the ravages of a fire set by the British during the War of 1812. The buildings total 750 ft. in length and are 121 to 140 ft. in depth. The height to the top of the statue of Freedom is 287 ft., 5½ in. The building area is nearly 4 acres, and the surrounding grounds are more than 116 acres. The site, an 88-ft. plateau dominating Washington, was chosen by Major Pierre Charles L'Enfant, who laid out the city in 1791.

A competition for the plans of the Capitol was announced in 1792. The design of an amateur architect, Dr. William Thornton, was selected, and the cornerstone was laid on Sept. 18, 1793. Thornton collaborated with James Hoban, the designer of the White House, which is at the other end of Pennsylvania Avenue. As a result there is a considerable stylistic relationship between the two structures, in spite of attempts by Étienne Hallet and George Hadfield, both temporarily in charge of the erection, to change Thornton's plans. The north wing was finished in 1800 and the south wing seven years later, under Benjamin H. Latrobe, supervising architect from 1803 to 1818. The section between the wings, where the dome now stands, was completed in 1824 under the direction of Charles Bulfinch of Boston. The original flat dome was modeled after that of the ancient Pantheon in Rome. The present hemispherical cast-iron dome, designed by Thomas U. Walter of Philadelphia,

was finished in 1863. On it stands a 19½ ft. bronze statue of Freedom, by Thomas Crawford. This later dome, though somewhat too large for the structure that supports it, has become, in the eyes of most Americans, the outward symbol for legislative bodies. As a consequence, most state capitols built since the Civil War have similar domes. The Capitol has undergone some additions and remodelings, although the central section is essentially as it was originally planned. During the 1850's wings were added at either end for the House of Representatives and the Senate. The House and Senate office buildings were completed in 1908 and 1909, respectively. Steam heat was introduced in 1865, elevators in 1874, and electric lighting in 1882.

Most of the sculpture inside and on the building dates from the nineteenth century. It is artistically undistinguished, although of considerable interest because of its patriotic subject matter. Some good paintings are housed in the building, including portraits by Gilbert Stuart, John Trumbull, Rembrandt Peale, John Vanderlyn, and Thomas Sully.

F. J. R.

CAPIZ [kɑ'pis], a municipality with 34 barrios, or districts, in the Philippine Republic, the capital and most important commercial center of Capiz Province, in northern Panay Island, on the Sibuyan Sea. Capiz, 265 mi. southeast of Manila, has narrow-gauge railway connections with Iloilo, across the island 60 mi. to the south. It is not far from a copper mine, near Pilar, which began production in 1936.

The town of Capiz lies along both banks of the Panay River about 2 mi. above its mouth. A large plain extends east and southeast from the town, but there are hills immediately to the south and southwest. Port Capiz, 5 mi. by road or river northwest of the old town, can accommodate vessels of 1,000 to 1,500 tons. Sugar, rice, and nipa thatch are exported. Corn, abaca, bananas, and tobacco are also grown in Capiz Province. Fishing and the weaving of cotton, abaca, and piña are the town's leading industries. Principal buildings are a large Roman Catholic church, a Protestant church, the provincial capitol, provincial high school, trade school, and a hospital. Manuel Roxas, Philippine independence leader and first president of the Philippine Republic, was a native of Capiz; and the town was renamed Roxas in his honor. Pop. 1948 (town), 11,673.

A. Cu.

CAPONSACCHI, GIUSEPPE [kɑ'ponsɑ'kki], the chivalrous young priest of Browning's *The Ring and the Book* (1868-1869), who assists Pompilia to escape from her husband, Guido Franceschini. Later, after Guido has fatally wounded Pompilia, Caponsacchi eloquently defends her before a court of justice in Rome. W. C. DeV.

CAPORETTO, BATTLE OF [kɑ'poreʾtto], an engagement of World War I fought at Caporetto, Italy, between Italian and German forces, Oct. 24, 1917, ending in defeat of the Italians by the Austrian and German armies. During the early part of 1917, the Italians had made many advances. The end of that year found the Russians in revolt with a resultant decrease in the number of German troops needed on the Eastern Front. Many of these soldiers were sent to help the Austrians on the Italian battlefield. A large amount of artillery was also sent to the Italian theatre by the Germans. These preparations were successfully kept secret from General Cadorna, the commander of the Italian army. General Cadorna also ignored the weak defenses along the Caporetto sector where the Italians had far fewer troops than elsewhere. The German command, however, did not ignore the weakness of this area and, Oct. 24, 1917, a powerful infantry and artillery attack against this region sent the Italian troops reeling back. They had to retreat to the Piave River where they were able to hold. At this point, General Diaz took over the command from General Cadorna. Other Allied troops came in to help but they were too late to prevent the Italian defeat which greatly weakened the already tired Italian forces. Allied reinforcements, however, helped the Italians prevent the Germans and Austrians from moving farther into Italy. All told, during this important battle, the Italians lost about 600,000 men and all the ground they had gained in the early months of 1917.

M. K.

CAPPADOCIA [kæ'pədo'shiə], an ancient region of Asia Minor with boundaries which varied at different times in ancient geography. The Greek historian Herodotus (fifth century B.C.) stated that the province extended from Mount Taurus to the Euxine. Later in the century the Persians divided the province into two satrapies; the interior one was called Cappadocia and the coastal one was commonly referred to as Pontus. After the fall of the Persians the name Cappadocia was applied only to the former. Cappadocia then was bounded on the north by Pontus, on the south by the ranges of Mount Taurus, on the east by the Euphrates, and on the west by Lycaonia. The geographer Strabo, writing at about the beginning of the Christian Era, stated that there were only two cities in the province: Mazaca, the capital, and Tyana, about 10 mi. southwest of Nigdeh. Archelaus

Sisines, the last king of the country, founded the city of Archelais (now Akserai), which became an important Roman colony after the subjection of the province by Tiberius in A.D. 17. In A.D. 70 Cappadocia was joined to Armenia Minor by Vespasian. After 395, upon the final division of the Roman territory into eastern and western domains, Cappadocia remained part of the Eastern Roman Empire until it was overrun by the Seljuk Turks in 1074; by that time it had become predominantly Armenian. In the fourteenth century it became part of the Ottoman Empire. The mountainous pastures of Cappadocia were a grazing ground for fat-tailed sheep and a special breed of horse. R. T.

CAPPER, ARTHUR (1865-1951), American journalist and politician, was born July 14, 1865, at Garnett, Kan., where he graduated from high school. Beginning as a compositor, 1884, on the *Topeka Daily Capital,* he filled many

ARTHUR CAPPER

INTERNATIONAL NEWS PHOTO

positions and became the publisher in 1892. He also published many farm journals; *Capper's Weekly,* the best known of these, attained a large circulation throughout the Middle West. Entering political life, Capper was Republican governor of Kansas from 1915 to 1919, and senator for five terms, from 1919 to 1949. He was the leader of the farm bloc from 1920 to 1923, and his book *Agricultural Bloc* (1922) is a record of his leadership. Capper died in Topeka, Kan., on Dec. 19, 1951.

CAPRERA [kɑprɛ'ərɑ], an island a few miles off the northeast coast of Sardinia, near the eastern outlet of the Strait of Bonifacio, and famous as the chosen residence of Giuseppe Garibaldi, Italian revolutionary leader. Caprera's six square miles are granitic. A drawbridge and a 2,000-ft. causeway connect the irregular coast of Caprera with Maddalena Island, site of an important Italian naval base (demilitarized after World War II by the peace treaty of 1946). The highest point on Caprera is Monte Teialone, 700 ft. in elevation. Pop. 1951, 114.

Roman remains, particularly a bust of Maximian, were found on the island. Garibaldi bought land in Caprera in 1855 and there he and his sons built a small dwelling . Although the stirring events of the years 1855-1871 frequently drew Garibaldi back into the arena of Italian and European politics, he always returned to Caprera, which became a place of pilgrimage for republicans and liberals from many lands. He died on Caprera on June 2, 1882. In 1907 the Italian Government declared the island a national monument. Garibaldi's former home is now a museum.

One of the many beaches on the Isle of Capri. In the background the Faraglioni rocks rise out of the Bay of Naples.

CAPRI [kɑ'pri], a rugged limestone island three mi. southeast of the Sorrentine Peninsula, in the province of Naples, Italy, separating the Bay of Naples from the Gulf of Salerno. The steeply inclined island measures about 4 by 2 mi. Capri's low humidity and sunny, mild climate (mean temp. 50° F.) have attracted visitors since ancient times, and the tourist trade is the principal source of income. Among local products are olives, fruit, fish, and, especially, wine. The annual rainfall of only 35 in. necessitates importation of water. Geologically, the island is a continuation of the Sorrentine Peninsula, and its highest point, Monte Solaro, exceeds 1,900 ft.

The town of Capri strides a saddle about 400 ft. above sea level, between two higher spurs. There are two ports, neither well protected: one at Marina Grande on the north side and a seldom used one at Marina Piccola on the south. The former is a half mile from the town of Capri, with which it is connected by a funicular railway. Steamships touch Sorrento, Naples, and Salerno on the mainland. Two and a half miles west of the town of Capri is the smaller town of Anacapri, situated 900 ft. above sea level. The island contains famous subterranean caves, notably the Blue, Green, and White grottoes, which are reached by boat. There are numerous interesting structures on the island, including the remains of several Roman villas.

Capri has been occupied since the Stone Age and at various times was inhabited by Phoenician and Greek colonists. Under Roman rule it acquired fame as the residence of emperors, including Augustus and Tiberius. During the Dark Ages it was attacked by the Vandals and by North African Corsairs. After periods of Lombard and Amalfitan rule, it was acquired by the Normans.

Thereafter, although it was often the subject of dispute and conflict, Capri shared the political fortunes of Naples. When the French took Naples in 1806, they dispatched a force to occupy and fortify Capri. They were dispersed by the British, who held the island for Ferdinand IV of Naples until Oct. 4, 1808, when they were overcome and were obliged to surrender to French troops under Murat. In 1815 it was restored to Italian control, where it has remained, except for German occupation during World War II. Pop. 1954, 9,900.

R. G. W.

CAPRICE or **CAPRICCIO** [kəpri's, kɑpri'ttsho], a form of instrumental music similar to but usually shorter than the fantasia, implying no particular structural design and allowing the composer's imagination free rein. Caprices composed in the sixteenth and seventeenth centuries for organ or other keyboard instruments are largely contrapuntal in texture and quick in tempo. Nineteenth-century caprices are mostly short piano pieces of whimsical character. Rimsky-Korsakov's popular *Spanish Caprice* is a well-known example of this musical form. W. Li.

CAPRICORNUS [kæ'prɪkɔ'rnəs], the Goat, a constellation in the southern celestial hemisphere. Its symbol ♑ is the tenth sign of the Zodiac, which the sun enters on Dec. 22. At the time of Hipparchus (about 125 B.C.) the sun was among the stars of this group at the winter solstice. Accordingly, on this shortest day of the year the sun at noon was directly overhead at all places $23\frac{1}{2}°$ south of the terrestrial equator, and the parallel of $23\frac{1}{2}°$ S. Lat. was named the Tropic of Capricorn. Since that time the precession of the equinoxes has moved the solstice westward about 30° into Sagittarius, but the geographical term still stands. Capricornus is centered approximately at right ascension, 21 hr.; declination, —20°. Although it includes no stars brighter than the third magnitude, its large, roughly right-triangular shape is quite conspicuous on a clear, moonless night. Alpha Capricorni, the most northerly star of the triangle, is a naked-eye double.

In mythology, Capricornus represented the god Pan, who in fright jumped into the water and was curiously transformed: the part above the water into a goat, the submerged part into the tail of a fish. J. H. P.

CAPSIAN [kæ′psiən], a name given by prehistorians to an Upper Paleolithic culture of blade and burin tradition after Gafsa in Tunisia. At one time the Capsian culture of north Africa was regarded as a possible source of the European Chatelperronian culture, but recent research has suggested that cultures of this tradition reached the African continent comparatively late. J. G. D. C.

CAPTAIN. *See* MILITARY PERSONNEL.

CAPTAIN BALL, a simple team game of throwing and catching played with a basketball. The game, originally called center ball, was invented about 1890 by Dr. E. A. Poos, of Cincinnati, Ohio. The rules show numerous variations in detail, but are essentially as follows. A rectangle thirty by sixty feet is divided into two square courts by a center line. In each court are six four-foot circles, one at the center, the others near the boundaries. The game is played by two teams of twelve men each, of which six must remain in the circles in one court; the player in the center circle is the captain, the others basemen. The remaining players of each team, called guards, move at will in the other court. After a center jump, as in basketball, the players of each team try to secure the ball and to pass it among themselves. A point is scored whenever a captain catches the ball thrown to him by one of his basemen. In general, players are restricted according to the rules of basketball. A frequent variation is to allow a score when the guards of one team all catch the ball in turn. D. A. H.

CAPTIVI (THE CAPTIVES) [kæptai′vai; kæpti′vi], a comedy by Plautus, written between 207 and 184 B.C., with an unusually serious tone and elevated theme. It presents the devotion of Tyndarus, a slave, who changes places with his master, allowing him to escape from captivity to arrange for an exchange of prisoners of war. Tyndarus is finally revealed as the long-lost son of his captor, having been stolen in infancy. The play is rich in dramatic irony, and many adaptations have been made, of which Ariosto's *I Suppositi* is the most famous. G. E. D.

CAPUA [kɑ′pwɑ; kæ′pyuə], a town and archiepiscopal seat in the province of Naples, in Campania, southern Italy,

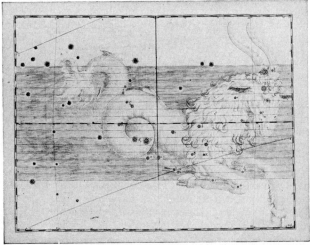

AMERICAN MUSEUM OF NATURAL HISTORY

CAPRICORNUS, "THE SEA GOAT"

about 21 mi. northeast of Naples. It is situated on the Volturno River, in level country. The town lies on the Rome-Caserta-Naples rail line and is a market center for the products of the region, chiefly cereals, grapes and other fruit, hemp, olives, and livestock. The manufactures include wine, cheese, macaroni, and farm machinery.

The walls of modern Capua, several times enlarged, remain as they were in 1732. There are a few remnants

PHOTO BY BROWN BROTHERS

Ruins of an early Roman amphitheatre near Capua, Italy

of the Lombard period, fewer from the Byzantine and Roman eras. The Volturno is crossed by a Roman bridge (on the Via Appia) of five arches and protected on the south bank by a turreted gate built by Frederick II and in part demolished by the Spanish in 1557. Destroyed in World War II, the bridge has been rebuilt. The cathedral, built in the eleventh century and reconstructed in the eighteenth and nineteenth centuries, has a massive eleventh-century campanile and contains interesting tombs and mosaics. The provincial museum possesses important archaeological finds. The palace of the Norman princes goes back to the late eleventh century, and the Fieramosca Palace, constructed in the fourteenth century, shows a mixture of Gothic and Saracen styles. Nine miles to the east is the basilica of Sant' Angelo in Formis, rebuilt in the eleventh century and interesting for its style and frescoes.

Though the town bears the name of ancient Capua, it actually rests on the site of ancient Casilinum. The latter was the port for Capua, which was 3 mi. southeast, where stands the modern city of Santa Maria Capua Vetere. Modern Capua was built along the Appian Way on the site of Casilinum when the residents of old Capua evacuated their city after it was destroyed by the Arabs about 840. In the ninth century the Lombard counts of Capua, previously vassals of the dukes of Benevento and then Salerno, became in effect independent. For a brief period early in the tenth century the counts held the Beneventan domain. Then followed a period of dynastic quarrels, contested successions, revolts, and imperial interference, with Capua as the focal point. The last Lombard prince was expelled from Capua in 1062 by the count of Aversa. The latter's state soon fell apart, and in 1134 Capua submitted to Roger II of Sicily, becoming part of the Norman domains. It then followed the fortunes of the Neapolitan kingdom until it became part of unified Italy. Pop. 1954 (city), 13,200; (commune), 16,600. R.G.W.

CAPUANA, LUIGI [kɑpwɑ′nɑ] (1839-1915), Sicilian critic and novelist, was born May 28, 1839, in Mineo, Sicily.

His family was well to do and young Capuana was enabled to exercise his talents to the full. His life was one of varied activities: he was dramatic editor of *La Nazione* in Florence; he taught at the Magistero in Rome and in the University of Catania (1902); he was interested in politics and served as mayor of his home town; and he found time for many other interests. He is best remembered as a proponent of *Verismo,* of which he was a more articulate and less faithful disciple than his friend Verga, and as the author of *Il Marchese di Roccaverdina* (1901), a well-constructed and competent novel of the naturalist school, and a number of good short stories, notably those included in *Le Paesane* (1894). Of his numerous critical works *Studi sulla letteratura contemporanea* (first edition, Milan, 1879; second edition, Catania, 1882) may be cited as best exemplifying his easy style and sound critical judgment.   T. G. B.

CAPUCHIN, or **SAPAJOU** [kæ′pyutshɪn, sæ′pəju], of the genus *Cebus,* a tropical American monkey, well known in the northern countries as the curl-tailed, organ grinders' monkey as well as for its antics in zoological parks, where it is often kept in large numbers. The capuchin is a robust monkey with limbs of moderate length and a prehensile tail, which is, however, not naked beneath and is usually carried in a spiral curl over the back. The brain case is well developed, and the face largely bare. The thumb is well developed. The pelage is hairy, rather than furry. There are many species of capuchin monkeys, their combined ranges extending from Costa Rica to Paraguay. The largest species has a body 24 in. long, with a tail of about 20 in. Capuchins travel in large bands in the forest, living at a medium level in the trees, and rarely descending to the ground. They eat a wide variety of foods, including fruit, insects, and birds' eggs. As pets capuchins are quite satisfactory for they are quick, vivacious, and intelligent. They are easily kept and readily adapt to varied climates.   R. T. H.

CAPUCHINS [kæ′pyutshɪnz; kæpyushi′nz] (Ital. *cappuccini,* hooded), members of the Roman Catholic Order of Friars Minor Capuchin, one of the three independent branches of the Franciscans, dating from 1525. At that time the Franciscans were divided into two distinct families, of which one, the Conventuals, accepted revenues by papal dispensation. The other, the Observants, adhering strictly to the primitive ideal of Franciscan poverty, refused fixed revenues and lived on casual alms. In practice the Observants relaxed their principle of poverty. Father Matteo di Bassi (c. 1495-1552), a member of the Observants of Fermo, urged a strict interpretation of the Franciscan poverty. He secured permission from Rome and initiated the Capuchins. Capuchins wear a beard, a coarse brown habit girded with a cord, a long pointed hood, and sandals. Their community life is strict; the lay-brothers have to beg, and their churches are plain. The Capuchins were among the most effective preachers and missionaries of the sixteenth and seventeenth centuries. They numbered about 14,000 professed, of whom some 700 are in the United States, where the first establishment was made in 1857. The Capuchins conduct parishes, and labor in the foreign missions.   W. C.

CAPULETS AND MONTAGUES. *See* ROMEO AND JULIET.

CAPULIN MOUNTAIN NATIONAL MONUMENT [kəpyu′lɪn], a park in Union Co., northeastern New Mexico, near the source of the Cimarron River, between the small towns of Folsom and Capulin and near the Chicago, Burlington, and Quincy Railroad tracks connecting Trinidad, in southern Colorado, and Dalhart, northwestern Texas. Capulin Mountain is a recently extinct volcano with an almost perfect cone. This symmetrical cinder cone rises 1,500 ft. above the plain and the base of the mountain is 1½ mi. in diameter. The crater of the volcano is 1,500 ft. wide and 75 to 275 ft. deep. Because the mountain is a perfect example of a conical extinct volcano, it was made a national monument by presidential proclamation on Aug. 9, 1916. The monument, containing 680 acres, is in a semiarid area.   J. E. F.

CAPYBARA [kæ′pɪbɑ′rə], a rodent of the genus *Hydrochoerus.* It is the largest living rodent, sometimes weighing 150 lbs. Its length is over 40 in.; its height 20 in. or more. It is found from Central America to northern Argen-

YLLA

CAPYBARA, HYDROCHOERUS CAPYBARA

tina and from the Atlantic to the foothills of the Andes. Capybaras are gregarious, herds of fifty or more occasionally being seen, though they usually travel in family groups of from three to ten. Capybaras move at a slow, lumbering pace on land, and are poor runners, but are good swimmers, being able to stay under water for perhaps seven or eight minutes. They usually stay within a hundred yards of water, to which they retreat whenever threatened. Their food consists of water plants or the bark of trees and occasionally cultivated crops. Hoofs are present on all toes, of which there are four on the front foot and five on the hind, though the first and fifth toes of the hind foot are very small. Extinct forms, from the Pleistocene epoch, were as large as black bears. There is a single litter per year consisting of five or six young.   A. E. W.

CAQUETIO. *See* INDIAN TRIBES, SOUTH AMERICAN.

CARACAL [kæ′rəkæl], a lynx, *Lynx caracal,* found in the warmer parts of Asia and in Africa. A little larger than a fox, it is about the same height. It is pale brown in color, tinged with red, and has black ears tipped with long black hairs. The under parts are paler in color, and are lightly sprinkled with black or chestnut spots. The caracal is active and muscular, although it is not especially fleet, like most other predaceous cats. Smaller in size than the common lynx, it is thoroughly at home among the branches of trees. The headquarters of the caracal are Arabia, Egypt, South Africa, Persia, and the greater part of India.   G. M. C.

CARACALLA (MARCUS AURELIUS ANTONINUS) [kærəkæ′lə] (A.D. 188-217), Roman emperor. Caracalla, the son of Septimius Severus, is chiefly remembered as the author of the famous Antonine Constitution of A.D. 212, an edict which extended Roman citizenship to all free men within the borders of the Roman Empire. As to the purpose of the edict, there is no general agreement. Some scholars have characterized it as a triumph of statesmanship which helped to unify the imperial population, while others have pointed out that it broadened the tax base and simplified criminal jurisdiction. Other actions of Caracalla were less statesmanlike. In 212 he murdered his brother, who was joint-emperor with him, resorted to a disastrous inflation of the imperial currency, and tried to persuade the Romans that he was Alexander the Great reborn. After victories over the Alamanni and the Goths, Caracalla embarked upon an unpopular war against the Parthians in A.D. 216. He was assassinated by his own officers the following year.   T. B. J.

CARACARA [kɑ'rɑkɑ'rɑ], any one of three species of raptorial birds in the genus *Polyborus,* intermediate between the falcons and the New World vultures. They are restricted to the New World, and one species, *P. cheriway,* occurs in North America as far north as Arizona, Texas, and Florida. The bird is a large, long-legged, naked-faced hawk, mainly black, but with the throat buffy, the nape, mantle, and breast barred with black and buff, and the tail white, barred and tipped with black. The caracaras share many habits with the vultures, and often associate with them to feed on carrion, but are capable also of capturing such creatures as frogs, lizards, and small snakes. Perched or walking, they have a peculiarly stiff, wooden appearance, but their flight is strong, rapid, and direct, in the manner of a true falcon.
                                                      H. G. De.

CARACAS [kɑrɑ'kɑs], the capital city of Venezuela, situated 8 mi. inland from the north central Caribbean coast and about 7 mi. from La Guaira, the city's port, at 10° 30′ N. lat. and 60° 55′ W. long. Caracas lies on the slopes of the outer cordilleras, 3,035 ft. above sea level, and has a pleasant, equable climate, the temperature only occasionally going below 60° F. in December, the coldest month, or above 80° F. from June to September. The city was founded in 1567 by Diego de Losada as the city of Santiágo de León de Caracas, Caracas being the name of the Indian tribe then inhabiting the region. The city prospered, but in 1595 was sacked and laid in ruins by the English. The French pillaged the town in 1766. Simón Bolívar, who liberated the country from Spain, was born there in 1783, and Francisco Miranda, another great Venezuelan patriot, was also born in Caracas, about 1750. Caracas became the first settlement in South America to achieve independence from Spain. Much damage and loss of life was suffered by the city during the war of liberation, and in 1812, Caracas was almost destroyed by an earthquake which buried nearly 12,000 persons in the ruins of the city. Another tremor in 1900 also caused much destruction.

Modern Caracas is an exceedingly attractive city, symmetrically planned and having numerous parks, plazas, and wide boulevards. Much of its architecture is colonial Span-

Air view of Caracas, Venezuela. In the foreground is the new development, "Centro Bolívar," which houses government departments. Caracas has experienced remarkable growth, in large part a result of the development of oil resources at nearby Lake Maracaibo.

INTERNATIONAL NEWS PHOTO

ish. The principal square, the Plaza Bolívar, occupies the center of the city and contains an equestrian statue of Bolívar the Liberator. Around this plaza are grouped the cathedral, the Capitolio, the palace of justice, the archbishop's palace, the Casa Amarilla, the Bolívar Museum, the general post office, the National Pantheon, the Central University, and the principal hotel. The Museum of Fine Arts is situated in Los Caobos, an eastern residential section. Essentially an Old World city in many ways, Caracas nevertheless has much modern elegance. There are many examples of the most advanced architecture, including modern apartment houses and public buildings. Chief among these is the new "Centro Bolívar," on Avenida Bolívar, a $300-million development, with twin towers, 27 stories high. Most of the building is occupied by government offices; on the ground level are shops and restaurants.

Much of the recent development and modernization of Caracas has been due to increased revenue from the exploitation of oilfields in the vicinity. The city is also important as a communications hub, for highways, railroads, and airlines, as a banking and commercial center, and as an industrial metropolis. Its industries include meat-packing and automobile-assembly plants, sugar refineries, breweries, tanneries, sawmills, and factories manufacturing a variety of products, including clothing, paper, tobacco, glassware, and pharmaceuticals. Pop. 1950, 495,064.

CARACCI, ANNIBALE. *See* CARRACCI, ANNIBALE.

CARAJA. *See* INDIAN TRIBES, SOUTH AMERICAN.

CARAVAGGIO, MICHELANGELO DA [kɑ'rɑvɑ'd-jo] (c. 1565-1609), Italian painter, was born in Caravaggio near Bergamo c. 1565. In 1584 he was sent to Milan as a painter's apprentice, and after 1589 he was in Rome, employed for a time in the studio of Giuseppe Cesare d'Arpino, before he ultimately attracted the favor of a number of wealthy patrons. His undisciplined character involved him in numerous criminal processes of law and he was forced to flee from Rome several times. In 1606, finally, charged with murder in a tavern brawl, he fled to Naples. After brief periods of activity in Naples, Malta, and Sicily, he was eventually granted a papal pardon, but died of malaria in Porto Ercole on his way back to Rome in 1609.

Caravaggio's art represents a reaction against the decorative superficiality and theorizing abstraction of Mannerism, as well as against academic eclecticism. With a contempt for conventional formulas, he effected a naturalistic reform, based on an essentially visual and dramatic realism and an effort to interpret religious themes in terms of human and everyday experience. The style developed during his comparatively brief but productive career is serious and thoughtful, shunning the pretty and trival, and marked by a handling of light and shade which was both technically and imaginatively new and inventive.

The lyrical realism of his early style is rooted in his raining in the North Italian tradition. The distinctive elements are structural equilibrium, a restricted palette of light, cool color and delicate chiaroscuro, and a tenderness of sentiment which by its sincerity and restraint is isolated from the expressional traditions of both Mannerism and the later Baroque. These qualities distinguish *Rest on the Flight into Egypt* and the *Magdalene* at the Galleria Doria, Rome, and the *Fortune Teller* at the Louvre. In later paintings, *St. Matthew and the Angel*, Berlin, *Supper at Emmaus*, National Gallery, London, and *Conversion of Paul*, Santa Maria del Popolo, Rome, the dynamic replaces the static in

conception and arrangement, realizing a forceful directness of expression and increased dramatic coherence. The color becomes dark and glowing, and a concentrated light, falling diagonally from above, isolates the figures in striking relief against a dark background, unifying the picture both visually and dramatically, and intensifying the psychological interpretation of the theme. The rigorous chiaroscuro of this period of Caravaggio's work provided the source for the superficially imitative style of the Tenebrists, so called from their use of dramatic contrasts of light and shade.

Caravaggio's last period, representing a transition to spatial chiaroscuro, with the plastic emphasis tempered by a new conception of space as an enveloping medium, is exemplified in *Death of the Virgin*, at the Louvre, and *Madonna del Rosario*, in Vienna. The chiaroscuro is organized in terms of area contrasts, masses of deep shadow against masses of strong light, frequently with a classical, predominantly horizontal organization. Subject matter is presented with compelling actuality, the mystical and supernatural translated into terms of the earthly and everyday, in a serious and soberly personal interpretation.

Caravaggio's style, variously interpreted, had enormous influence not only in Italy, but also on Vouet, La Tour, Valentin, and the Le Nains in France, and on Honthorst, Terbruggen, and Hals in Holland. His principle of dynamic chiaroscuro, in which forms are dissolved and surfaces unified, found its logical development in Rembrandt.

M. C.

CARAVANSARY or **CARAVANSERAI** [kærəvɑ'n-səri, kærəvɑ'nsərai] (Persian *kārwānsarāī*, caravan inn), a large building, generally surrounding a court, where caravans rest at night.

Relay stations were constructed along the well-maintained carriage roads of the Persian Empire as early as 500 B.C. Such structures were the forerunners of the caravansaries, which survive throughout the Moslem lands of the Near and Middle East and North Africa. They are located at intervals of a day's journey, about twenty miles for a camel caravan, along main trade routes. Many are in desolate surroundings but others are at the gates of towns or within the towns. These structures offered facilities for the essential needs of man and beast: a well for water, a place for the animals to rest, a sheltered area for the unloaded baggage, rooms for sleeping, and a kitchen.

The caravansary is normally rectangular in plan, with covered areas of one or more stories around the sides of a very large open court. The bare exterior walls, built of brick or stone, were pierced by a single gateway, so that the structure offered considerable protection against marauding bands.

Thousands of such caravansaries were built from the tenth century almost to the present day, but they are falling into ruin as freight is carried by more modern means. They were erected by kings; Shah Abbas of Persia (Iran) is said to have ordered the construction of 999 caravansaries in the early seventeenth century. They were built also by local governors, by pious Moslems who provided funds for their upkeep, or by the innkeepers themselves. The several Moslem lands display regional variations in plan forms and constructional materials. In Turkey, dressed stone was the usual material, and because of the comparatively severe climate the court area was sometimes vaulted over. In Iran, most of the caravansaries were of brick. This country shows a special interest in plan; one of the finest structures is octagonal in form.

The term "khan" was often applied to the caravansaries in Turkey, Syria, and Egypt, but in these countries the khan was also a structure erected in the towns, similar to the caravansary in plan, used either as a wholesale warehouse or as a food market.   D. N. W.

CARAWAY [kæ′rəwe], *Carum carvi,* a biennial herb of the parsley family native to the Old World and sparingly naturalized in the United States. It has finely divided leaves, slender stems 1 to 2 ft. high, and umbels of small white flowers. It is widely cultivated for the aromatic seeds, used in cakes, confectionery, cordials, and soap.   J. C. Wis.

CARBINE. *See* FIREARMS.
CARBOLIC ACID. *See* POISONS.

CARBON, (Latin *carbo,* "coal" or "charcoal") symbol C, a solid nonmetallic chemical element, found in Group IV-A of the periodic chart. It occurs free in nature as coal, diamond, and graphite and, combined, in all organic materials, both animal and vegetable, in carbon dioxide, and as calcium carbonate in chalk, marble, limestone, and pearls. Despite its wide distribution, carbon constitutes only 0.19 per cent of the earth's crust.

Properties. Carbon is unreactive at ordinary temperatures; that is why charcoal drawings by cave men are still preserved. Heated in the air, it burns, combining with oxygen to form carbon dioxide, CO_2; in a limited supply of air, carbon monoxide, CO, is formed. At high temperatures carbon combines with sulphur to form carbon disulphide, CS_2, and with silicon and certain metals to form carbides, such as silicon carbide, SiC, and calcium carbide, CaC_2. In the electric arc, carbon combines with hydrogen to form acetylene; in the blast furnace it unites with iron to form the carbide, Fe_3C, or cementite, a material that cements the iron particles (ferrite) together. At high temperature, carbon is an excellent reducing agent and as such is used extensively in metallurgy.

PROPERTIES OF CARBON

Atomic number		6
Atomic weight		12.010
Stable isotopes		12, 13
Density (g./ml.)	Diamond	3.51
	Graphite	2.25
Melting point, °C.		3,500
Boiling point, °C.		4,830
Specific heat, 20°C.	Diamond	0.12
	Graphite	0.17
Linear coefficient of thermal expansion, 40°C.	Diamond	1.18
	Graphite	7.86
Electrical Resistivity, (microhm-cm.)	Diamond	5×10^{-8}
	Graphite	1,375
Hardness (Mohs' scale)	Diamond	10
	Graphite	0.5–1.0

Allotropes. *Diamond.* Diamonds were first obtained from India; for this reason, the metric carat (0.2 g.) used in weighing them is the weight of a bean of the carob, an Asiatic evergreen. In 1727 Brazilian deposits were opened, and in 1867 the enormous South African diamond fields started production and South Africa has since become the chief producer of diamonds. Diamond cutting is an art which engages experts who are clever in eliminating flaws and obtaining maximum brilliance from a given rock. At one time the diamond-cutting industry was centered in Amsterdam, the Netherlands; Antwerp, Belgium, has been a diamond-cutting center for many generations.

It is believed that the diamond has been formed at vast depths as a result of high temperatures and great pressures,

crystallizing from a magnesium silicate lava. Henri Moissan attempted to produce diamonds artificially in 1893 after he developed the electric furnace; in 1955 synthetic diamonds were produced in the laboratories of the General Electric Co. by subjecting a heated carbonaceous compound to pressures of 1,500,000 lb. per sq. in.

N. W. AYER & SON
AMERICAN MUSEUM OF NATURAL HISTORY
Two allotropes of carbon: diamond (left) and coal (right)

X-ray crystallographic studies have shown that diamond is of the regular or isometric system, the carbon atoms fitting in the corners of a tetrahedron with a fifth atom at the center. A high index of refraction causes diamond to scatter light and glitter. The rarer blue, red, and green stones are valuable. The black variety, known as carbonado or bort, is useful industrially for boring and cutting and grinding, but not as a gem.

Diamonds resist the action of most chemicals, including acids; but upon being heated to 1,900° C. in the absence of air, they are transformed into a black graphite. Heated in air or oxygen, diamonds burn to form carbon dioxide. This was first demonstrated in an experiment carried out by Antoine Lavoisier in 1772; Sir Humphry Davy in 1814 proved that carbon dioxide is the sole product.

Graphite. Graphite occurs in nature. It may be prepared synthetically in the electric furnace by the Acheson process in which anthracite or coke is heated with ferric oxide or silica. Graphite was known to the ancients; the word comes from the Greek *graphein,* to write. The Romans confused graphite with lead (*plumbum*) and with molybdenum sulphide, MoS_2, calling the latter and graphite *plumbago.*

Graphite is a soft, shiny, gray-black substance. It is greasy to the touch and leaves a black mark when drawn across white paper. It is not attacked appreciably by chemical agents or even by oxygen at high temperatures. X-ray analysis shows graphite to consist of layers of hexagonal rings of carbon atoms. This structure accounts for the greasy feel of graphite, the layers sliding over one another. Graphite is used as filler in dry-cell batteries, as a lubricant, in silver polish and glazing powder, and for electrodes.

Coke. About 200,000,000 tons of coke are produced each year by the destructive distillation of soft coal. Of this total, some 70 per cent is used in pig-iron blast furnaces and the remaining 30 per cent in melting nonferrous metals and in manufacturing water gas for foundries and domestic heating. Very little coke is now made in the once-important beehive oven. Gas carbon, a hard iron-gray deposit formed in the upper portion of the towers during the distillation of coal, is used for electrodes. Carbon black is formed by burning a flame in an insufficient supply of air. It is almost entirely used in compounding rubber for automobile tires.

Lampblack, used in printer's ink, is made by the incomplete combustion of petroleum.

Charcoal. When wood is heated in the absence of air,

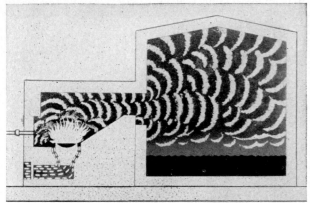

NATIONAL CARBON COMPANY, INC.

Lampblack production furnace in which oil is burned in a deficiency of air, forming soot (lampblack), which can be collected

it chars, forming charcoal; volatile by-products include wood alcohol, acetone, and acetic acid. At one time this variety of carbon was thought to be amorphous, but X-ray analysis has shown it to have a crystalline structure. Although its density is 1.9, it floats on water because it contains absorbed air. Heating in steam for long periods renders charcoal highly absorptive. It is then known as active charcoal and is used in the sugar industry to decolorize brown sugar, forming pure white crystals. Bone black or animal charcoal, made by heating the bones of animals in iron retorts, is particularly useful as a decolorizing agent. Gas-mask charcoal for World War I was prepared from coconuts and other shells, but the technique of making it from sawdust and other woody materials was developed later. Activated carbon is also used as a catalyst, in chromatographic analysis, and to produce a high vacuum at liquid-air temperatures by absorbing gases.

COMPOUNDS OF CARBON

Carbon Dioxide. *History and Occurrence.* In the seventeenth century van Helmont distinguished between carbon dioxide and ordinary air. In 1754 Joseph Black obtained carbon dioxide by heating calcium and magnesium carbonates and also by treating them with acid. Carbon dioxide, CO_2, occurs in the air, in the soil, and in subterranean waters. It escapes through fissures in the earth, as in the Grotta del Cane near Naples. It is a product of combustion, decay, fermentation, and respiration. It is a by-product of coke-oven operation and is purified by scrubbing the off-gases through sodium carbonate, Na_2CO_3, to form a solution of the bicarbonate, $NaHCO_3$:

$$CO_2 + Na_2CO_3 + H_2O \underset{\text{hot}}{\overset{\text{cold}}{\rightleftharpoons}} 2NaHCO_3.$$

Upon heating this solution, carbon dioxide is obtained. The gas is also obtained from limestone kilns by the decomposition of calcium carbonate, $CaCO_3$.

$$CaCO_3 \longrightarrow CaO + CO_2$$

Less important sources are natural fissures in Mexico and the southwestern United States, and the brewing industry, in which it is a by-product of the fermentation of glucose. It may be prepared in the laboratory by the action of acid upon carbonates or bicarbonates. Calcium carbonate, for example, reacts with sulphuric acid, H_2SO_4, to produce calcium sulphate, $CaSO_4$, and carbonic acid, H_2CO_3, which decomposes into carbon dioxide and water.

$$CaCO_3 + H_2SO_4 \longrightarrow CaSO_4 + H_2O + CO_2$$

The gas is stored in cylinders at a pressure of 1,000 lb. per sq. in. or is solidified into "dry ice."

Properties. Carbon dioxide is a colorless gas, 1.529 times heavier than air. Concentrations of more than five per cent have a harmful effect on human beings, probably due more to a lack of oxygen than to the presence of CO_2. The gas is very stable, even at 2,000° C.; but, in the presence of oxygen in the blast furnace, an equilibrium mixture containing carbon dioxide, oxygen, and carbon monoxide (CO) is formed. Carbon dioxide readily combines with metallic oxides and with hydroxides to form carbonates; with excess CO_2, bicarbonates are formed. These reactions can be demonstrated by breathing into limewater or calcium hydroxide, $Ca(OH)_2$. A milky precipitate of calcium carbonate forms:

$$CO_2 + Ca(OH)_2 \longrightarrow CaCO_3 + H_2O.$$

Upon further breathing into the mixture, the precipitate dissolves as the bicarbonate, $Ca(HCO_3)_2$, forms:

$$CaCO_3 + CO_2 + H_2O \longrightarrow Ca(HCO_3)_2.$$

When this solution is heated, the carbonate reprecipitates.

Dry ice, or solid carbon dioxide, is obtained in cubes by rapidly evaporating liquid CO_2 into steel molds. Dry ice sublimes or evaporates without melting.

Uses. The principal use of CO_2 is in making carbonated beverages. It is also employed as a refrigerant. Because it is heavier than air and does not support combustion, carbon dioxide is useful in fire extinguishers. One type contains liquid carbon dioxide under pressure; the Foamite extinguisher employs a bicarbonate, licorice, and an acid salt, such as aluminum sulphate. The acid salt reacts with the bicarbonate to liberate carbon dioxide foam; the licorice keeps the foam suspended. Another type of extinguisher uses sulphuric acid and sodium bicarbonate solution.

The Oxygen-Carbon Dioxide Cycle. Plants absorb carbon dioxide from the atmosphere, and, by means of a series of reactions which also involve water, produce carbohydrates and give off oxygen. Animals take in oxygen and carbohydrate, giving off water and carbon dioxide.

AMERICAN MUSEUM OF NATURAL HISTORY

Graphite pencil tip pointing to a diamond embedded in rock

The air man inhales is about 21 per cent oxygen and 0.4 per cent carbon dioxide. He exhales a gas containing approx-

$$C_6H_{12}O_6 + 6O_2 \xrightleftharpoons[\text{plant}]{\text{animal}} 6CO_2 + 6H_2O$$
(A sugar)

imately 16 per cent oxygen and 4.0 per cent carbon dioxide. The remainder is nitrogen and inert gases which do not

an important intermediate in the industrial preparation of organic compounds. Carbon monoxide plays a vital role in the production of pig iron. It is the chief reducing agent acting on the iron oxides in the blast furnace. Carbon monoxide is extremely poisonous. Because of its ability to combine with the hemoglobin of the blood, forming carbonyl hemoglobin, it blocks off the supply of oxygen to the body and produces asphyxiation. One volume of carbon monoxide in 800 of air is fatal within thirty minutes. Since birds and mice are more sensitive to its action than human beings, they are used as warning signals in mines where carbon monoxide may be present.

Carbonates. Carbon dioxide reacts with water, produc-

Large electric furnace carbon electrode being extruded from hydraulic press

change during respiration. If the cycle did not exist, man's life upon this earth would be short, indeed, because the oxygen of the air would soon be depleted.

Carbon Monoxide. *Preparation.* Carbon monoxide, CO, is formed by the incomplete combustion of carbonaceous materials, as in automobile engines, stoves, and furnaces. In the laboratory, it is prepared by treating formic or oxalic acids with concentrated sulphuric acid. In industry, carbon monoxide is a component of important industrial gases: water gas, which is made by passing superheated steam over hot coke; and producer gas, formed when a limited supply of air is passed through coke or anthracite coal. The blue flame which is noticed above burning coal in an ordinary grate fire is due to burning of CO formed by the incomplete combustion of the coal beneath it.

Properties. Carbon monoxide is a colorless, practically odorless, and tasteless gas. It liquefies at 35.5 atmospheres pressure at $-140°$ C., boils (1 atm.) at $-190.0°$ C., and melts at $-211.0°$ C. It is 0.967 times as heavy as air. The physical properties of carbon monoxide strikingly resemble those of nitrogen. It combines with oxygen to form carbon dioxide; with members of the iron family it forms carbonyls, such as nickel carbonyl, $Ni(CO)_4$, and iron carbonyl, $Fe(CO)_5$. In sunlight or in the presence of active charcoal, carbon monoxide reacts with chlorine to form carbonyl chloride or phosgene, $COCl_2$, a deadly war-gas lung irritant and

ing carbonic acid, H_2CO_3. From this very weak acid come two related classes of salts, the carbonates and the bicarbonates. Examples of these salts are sodium carbonate or washing soda, Na_2CO_3, and sodium bicarbonate or baking soda, $NaHCO_3$. In limestone regions, such as in the Shenandoah Valley, calcium carbonate deposits are slowly acted upon by a water solution of carbon dioxide, forming soluble calcium bicarbonate. This in time eats the rock away, leaving a cave. If at the roof of the cave the above reaction is reversed and calcium bicarbonate loses carbon dioxide, calcium carbonate is deposited as a stony icicle, a stalactite; as water drips to the bottom of the cave and evaporation occurs, deposits of calcium carbonate build up, forming stalagmites.

Other Carbon Compounds. Carbon tetrachloride, CCl_4, is widely used as a solvent, dry cleaner, and fire extinguisher. It is obtained by heating carbon disulphide with chlorine in the presence of iodine catalyst. Cyanogen (C_2N_2), prussic acid (HCN), and cyanides made from them are useful as insecticides and fumigators, in silver and gold metallurgy, and in the electroplating industries; they are all poisonous.

Calcium carbide, which is produced by the reaction of pulverized lime and coke, reacts with water to form acetylene, C_2H_2, used in welding torches and in the preparation of vinyl plastics. Calcium cyanamide, $CaCN_2$, which was once an important fertilizer, is produced by the reaction of nitrogen with calcium carbide. Still more important today

JEAN ROUBIER FOR RAPHO-GUILLUMETTE

The ramparts of the old city in Carcassonne, France

is the formation of a plastics ingredient, melamine, a ring compound containing three cyanamide units. Silicon carbide, SiC, an important abrasive, is harder than corundum. Carbon disulphide, CS_2, a low-boiling liquid with a disagreeable odor, is used chiefly for "ripening" wood pulp in the viscose process for manufacturing rayon and as a solvent for fats and oils, sulphur, and iodine. Fluorocarbons, compounds of carbon and fluorine, are useful as plastics, refrigerants, and in a variety of other applications. *See also* FLUOROCARBONS.   H. N. A.

CARBONARI [kɑ'rbonɑ'ri], a secret society of Latin Europe active in the early part of the nineteenth century. The uncertain origin is ascribed to charcoal burners of Champagne, followers of St. Theobald. Lodges (*vendite*) appeared in Spain and Italy following Napoleon's campaigns. The greatest growth was in Murat's Kingdom of Naples (1808-1815), where an elaborate organization and ritual were developed. The organization served, after 1815, as a vehicle for liberal and nationalistic aspirations. The Carbonari, however, lacked a uniform doctrine and program. Some of its members were republicans, others constitutional monarchists. Thus, the society lacked the unity to throw its full weight behind a specific plan. However, the society played a part in the Spanish revolution of 1820 and the Piedmontese movement of 1821, but its greatest rôle was in Naples where it spread with great rapidity following the revolt of 1820. The direct effect of the society in these revolutions is easily exaggerated. Its indirect results are difficult to measure because of its great secrecy, but many an Italian nationalist received his first patriotic inspiration as a member of the society.
                    H. McG. S.

CARBONDALE, a city in Jackson Co., southwestern Illinois, is situated in an area of coal fields about 50 mi. north of Cairo. It was incorporated in 1852 and has the commission form of government. Carbondale is the seat of Southern Illinois University, founded in 1874. Gloves and clothing are among its manufactures. Pop. 1950, 10,921.

CARBONDALE, a city in northeastern Pennsylvania, is situated in Lackawanna Co. on the Lackawanna River, 16 mi. northeast of Scranton. Poultry, fruit, and truck crops are raised in the surrounding territory, and dairying is carried on. Lying within the great anthracite coal area of the state, the city is an important coal-shipping center. Founded about 1829, Carbondale was incorporated as a city in 1851 and is governed by a commission. It is the seat of the Carbondale Commercial Institute. Transportation is supplied by the Erie, the Delaware and Hudson, and the New York, Ontario and Western railroads. Manufactures include coal-mining machinery, silk, women's dresses, perforated metals, boilers, chemicals, and tanks. Pop. 1950, 16,296.

CARBON DIOXIDE. *See* CARBON; POISONS.
CARBONIC ACID. *See* ORGANIC CHEMISTRY.
CARBONYL GROUP. *See* ORGANIC CHEMISTRY.
CARBOXYLIC ACIDS. *See* ORGANIC CHEMISTRY.

CARBUNCLE, the old name given to a red variety of garnet. Chemically an iron aluminum silicate, Fe_3Al_2 $(SiO_4)_3$, the mineral has a hardness of 7.5 and a density of 4.00. It crystallizes in the isometric system, and its index of refraction varies from 1.75 to 1.83. Prior to the time of Christ, carbuncle was the name given to any dark red colored stone, such as the ruby or spinel. It ranks with pyrope garnet as being one of the more popular semiprecious red colored gem stones. A common mineral, carbuncle is found in Ceylon, India, and Brazil.   A. E. A.

CARBUNCLE. *See* SKIN AND SKIN DISEASES.
CARBURETOR. *See* MOTOR VEHICLES.

CARCASSONNE [ka'rka'sɔ'n], a city in southern France, the capital of the department of Aude, on the Aude River and Canal du Midi, about 55 mi. southeast of Toulouse. Two villages divided by the river constitute the city. The lower village on the plains, which is newer, contains the thirteenth-century Cathedral of St. Michel and the Gothic church of St. Vincent, dating from the fourteenth century and remarkable for the width (66 ft.) of its vault. The other village, the Cité, which is the more famous, contains intact one of the best surviving examples of a medieval walled city. The Cité, which celebrated its two thousandth anniversary in 1928, was settled by the Gauls, conquered and fortified by the Romans, Visigoths, and Saracens, refortified by feudal lords, and completed by the kings St. Louis and Philip the Hardy. It held a strategic position until the annexation of Roussillon in 1659. It was conquered after a siege by Simon de Montfort during the Albigensian Crusade in 1209, but, strengthened, it withstood the Black Prince, Edward, son of Edward III of England. In 1566 a massacre of Huguenots took place there. Carcassonne is a market town dealing principally in grains and wines. A very old textile industry still operates, and leather goods, paper, soap, iron ware, and pottery are manufactured. Pop. 1954, 37,035.

CARDAMOM [ka'rdəməm], *Elettaria cardamomum,* member of the ginger family native to India, is a perennial herb growing from 5 to 10 ft. tall with large leaves, purple striped flowers, and small fruiting capsules filled with pungent spicy seeds. The dried capsules are the true cardamoms used for flavoring in medicine and in cooking. The plant is cultivated in Jamaica.

CARDAMOM HILLS, a long, narrow chain of hills at the southern tip of peninsular India. The crest of the hills forms the boundary between Kerala State (formerly Travancore-Cochin), situated on the west, and Madras State, on the east. They extend a distance of about 175 mi. from the Palghat Gap on the north to a short distance north of Cape Comorin, the southern tip of India. The width of the range is only 20 mi. in the south, but broadens to 85 mi. in the north, where the Anaimalai Hills form a western branch and the Palni Hills an eastern branch of the range. The highest point is Apsimudi Peak, 8,841 ft. above sea level in the northern part of the hills. The Sheucottah Pass cuts across the southern part of the range and is utilized by a highway and a railroad that connects Quilon, on the west coast, and Tuticorin and Tiruchendur, on the east coast.

The Cardamom Hills act as a rainfall barrier and there are decided differences in temperature and precipitation within distances of a few miles. The major river in the hills is the Periyar, which flows north and west into the Indian Ocean; the river has been dammed, forming Periyar Lake. By means of tunnels driven through the mountains, water from the lake is carried under the divide to the eastern and drier side of the range and used for irrigation in Madras. The hills are sparsely settled. They are named after the herb cardamom, which grows in the region.   J. E. F.

CÁRDENAS, LÁZARO [kɑ'rthenɑs] (1895-   ), Mexican soldier and political leader, was born in Julquinpán de Juárez, Michoacán, May 21, 1895. After a public school

LÁZARO CÁRDENAS

INTERNATIONAL NEWS PHOTO

education, he operated a small printing shop. In 1913 he joined the Mexican revolutionary army and was a consistent adherent of its socialistic ideas. Cárdenas was appointed to his first political office in 1920, becoming provisional governor of Michoacán. In 1930 he became president of the executive committee of the National Revolutionary Party, the overwhelmingly dominant and official party of the nation. After that he rose rapidly, first as minister of the interior and later as minister of war. In 1934 he was elected president and his administration, from 1934 to 1940, witnessed the most vigorous application of the principles of the Mexican

Revolution since its beginning in 1910. More than 40,000,-000 acres of land were distributed to peasants, labor organizations were strengthened, rural and Indian education was enlarged, and foreign-owned oil properties were expropriated. On his retirement from the presidency, Cárdenas aided his successor, General Ávila Camacho, in Mexico's World War II effort and continued to be interested in national affairs and those of his home state, Michoacán.   S. G. I.

CÁRDENAS [kɑ'rdenɑs], a city on the northern coast of western Cuba in Matanzas Province, about 75 mi. east of Havana, at 23° 5′ N. lat. and 81° 5′ W. long. The city is just inland from the shallow, pouch-shaped Cárdenas Bay, and directly south of Cape Sable, Fla. One of the engagements of the Spanish-American War was fought near the city on May 11, 1898. Cárdenas is the center of a sugar-exporting region, and La Progresiva College is located there. The school was founded by the Reverend Robert H. Wharton, who also raised the money to pave the streets of Cárdenas and helped to improve the port. The city has broad streets and many squares, one of which, the Plaza Colón, contains a bronze statue of Columbus, donated by Queen Isabella of Spain and erected in 1862. Pop. 1953, 43,750.
    J. E. F.

CARD GAMES. Any game played with one or more packs of standard playing cards as the principal equipment may be classified as a card game. The ordinary pack of playing cards is divided into four suits—clubs, diamonds, hearts, and spades—and has fifty-two cards, thirteen in each suit; extra cards known as jokers are supplied for use in certain games that require more cards. The four suits are distinguished from each other by four symbols, and the thirteen cards in each suit have further distinguishing marks. Three cards of each suit are marked with faces and figures representing a king, a queen, and a jack respectively and are known as face cards. Nine other cards are marked with numerals and a corresponding number of spots in the form of the suit symbol; these cards range from the two up to the ten and are called pip cards. The thirteenth card in each suit is the ace, which is marked by one large symbol of the suit it represents and, depending upon the game played, may be either the highest or the lowest card in the suit. Some of the best-known card games, current and obsolete, are described below; not included in this classification are card games played with special types of cards, usually patented or copyrighted by their manufacturers.

ACCORDION

Accordion, one of the forms of Solitaire, may be played with either a full or partial pack of cards. The cards are dealt face up in a horizontal row, and whenever two adjacent cards match—being either the same value or the same suit—the right-hand card is placed on top of the left-hand card. During the game, the move of one card may uncover another which makes possible another move of a matching card from the right. Some players vary the game by matching and moving to the third card from the left instead of the adjacent card. Others move the entire pile with the top card when it matches and is moved to another card. The player wins the game if he succeeds in moving all of the cards into one pile.

BACCARAT

Formerly popular in the casinos of France but now generally supplanted by Chemin de Fer, Baccarat may be played by either a large or small group of players. Preparatory to playing, an auction determines which player will be the banker and dealer. Three to six packs of cards are shuffled together, and hands of two cards are dealt to the dealer, the player on his right, and the player on his left. The others then bet that the player at the right or the player at the left, or both, will beat the banker. The object is to hold a hand that totals or closely approaches a total of eight or nine, counting the pip cards and aces at face value and tens and

The oldest English King of Hearts extant, 1642, often erroneously believed to represent King Henry VIII

face cards nothing. If a player so desires, he may have one more card; then the hands are exposed, and the dealer pays all bets on a hand that is nearer nine than his own and collects all bets on a hand that is not as near as his own. The cards are not reshuffled until seven or fewer cards remain undealt or until the bank changes hands, either voluntarily or when the banker has lost all his funds.

BASSET

Somewhat similar to Baccarat and generally popular in Europe during the nineteenth century, Basset is played between a banker and four players instead of two. The banker's winning and losing depends upon the comparison of his cards with those exposed by the other players.

BELOTTE

Belotte is a French form of the game Klaberjass, the essential difference between the two games being in the relative ranking of various melds. Belotte is little known outside of France.

BEZIQUE

Of disputed French and Spanish origin, Bezique is the game from which Pinochle is supposed to have been derived. The game is seldom played in the United States, but it is popular with some people in England—Winston Churchill among them.

BIRITCH

A Russian game, Biritch is considered to be one of the precursors of Bridge and was played to a slight extent in England and Greece during the last decade of the nineteenth century.

BLACK JACK

Also known as Twenty-One and as *Vingt-et-un* in France, Black Jack has been popular among Americans, especially among the military personnel. Any number of people may play, but from five to nine players make the most interesting game. One player is designated dealer and banker, and

all other players bet against him. The object of the game is to hold a hand in which the sum of the card values totals twenty-one, with the pip cards counted at their face values, face cards counted ten, and aces counted either one or eleven. The holding must total twenty-one or less; when it exceeds twenty-one, the player is said to have "busted" and he loses. Small hands of two cards are dealt one at a time to each player and the dealer. Then if any player wants more cards to bring his total nearer twenty-one, the dealer obliges by giving him another card, or as many more as the player feels he needs, dealt one at a time. When the dealing is over, the hands are revealed, and all players whose hands total nearer twenty-one than the dealer's win; otherwise the dealer collects all bets.

BLACK LADY

In the United States, Black Lady is the most popular form of Hearts. Several innovations have been introduced to change the original game. In Black Lady, the queen of spades is counted as a penalty card in addition to all of the cards of the heart suit. However, the queen of spades, frequently called the Black Lady from which the game derives its name, counts thirteen penalty points and therefore assumes greater importance than each heart card, which carries a value of only one point. According to some rules, this card must be played on a trick the first time that a player holding it cannot follow suit, and under all rules the queen retains its value as a spade, the holder of it being forced to follow suit to a spade lead. The high penalty card, the queen of spades, although commonly known as the Black Lady, is sometimes known under several other names such as Lil, Calamity Jane, and Black Maria.

Another distinguishing feature of Black Lady is the pass. After the cards have been dealt and before the first lead is made, each player passes any three cards from his hand to the player at his left. Thus each player receives from the player on his right three cards which he incorporates in his own hand prior to the playing of the hands. When there are five or more players, only two cards are passed.

At the end of each hand the score is counted as it is in the straight game of Hearts.

BOSTON

Boston is a form of Whist invented by French officers stationed in the city of Boston, Mass., during the American Revolution. Because the scoring in the game involved a very complicated table of undertrick penalties, few people knew how to keep score, and the game was eventually abandoned.

CANFIELD

Canfield is probably the most familiar of all solitaire games and derives its name from the famous Saratoga gaming house of R. A. Canfield, where it was introduced in the last decades of the nineteenth century.

To lay out the cards for playing, a player deals thirteen cards face down in one pile and then turns the pile face up to form the stock. The next card, dealt face up to the right of the stock, is called the first foundation. Four more cards, which form the tableau, are dealt face up in a row below the foundation and to the right of the stock. During the course of play, the other foundation cards must be played when they appear. For example, if the first foundation card is a six, the three other sixes in the pack become the other foundation cards and are played in a row to the right of the first. Each foundation pile is thereafter built upon in ascending sequence of the same suit, with the sequence continuous "around the corner" from queen, to king, to ace, to deuce, and so on. To build each of the four foundations to its full thirteen cards is the object of the game, and with this in mind, cards are always played to the foundations whenever possible.

After the stock, the first foundation card, and the tableau have been dealt, the remainder of the pack is held face down in the hand. The player then starts to go through the pack, taking three cards at a time from the top of the pack and placing them face up in a pile that is known as the talon. The top card of the talon is always available for playing, and when it has been played, the card beneath it immediately becomes available.

As the play proceeds, cards are played either from the stock or talon to the foundation or the tableau. The tableau piles are built down in sequence, black on red and red on black, e.g., a six of spades on a seven of diamonds. Whenever possible, cards must be played to the foundation, and as a general rule, cards should be played from the stock instead of the talon when a player has a choice. If a card that can be played on a foundation is uncovered in the tableau, it must be played to the foundation. Cards within the tableau itself may also be moved. For example, when the highest card of a pile is of opposite color and immediately lower than the lowest card of some other pile, the entire lower pile may be transferred to the higher one. If a tableau pile is cleared off and a space remains, the space must be filled by a card from the stock pile, or from the talon if the stock pile has been exhausted.

Canfield is sometimes confused with Klondike, although the layout and play of the two games are different.

CASINO (CASSINO)

One of the most extensively played card games of relatively simple nature, Casino is of Italian origin, having been derived from Papillon, a game which is described in a book published in 1768. Casino is a game for two, three, or preferably, four players who play partners, two against two. A standard pack of fifty-two cards is used, face cards having no numerical value, aces one, and the others their pip values.

Hands of four cards are dealt to each player, and four cards are placed face up on the table. Then, in turn, each player tries to take as many cards as possible by matching the cards in his hand with those on the table. A combination may be taken in when a player holds a card in his hand of the same denomination as a card on the board; e.g., if there is an eight on the board and a player holds an eight in his hand, he may play it and take both cards, piling them face down in front of him. It is possible and more profitable to take combinations involving more cards. For instance, an eight played to the board will take all other eights and any other cards which in combination total eight, such as a seven and an ace or a six and a two. If a player prefers, he may build combinations instead of immediately taking in cards. That is, he may place a card from his hand on one or any number of cards on the table and announce the combination that he is building; if he says "building sevens," for instance, he may place a seven on top of a three and four, or an ace on two threes with the hope of taking in the pile on his next turn by playing another seven from his hand. Since the face cards have no numerical value, they cannot be built. A player takes a risk in building, because if an opponent holds a card of the same denomination as those being built, he may take in the cards himself. The original builder, or any other player, may continue the build or change it by adding other cards instead of taking the pile. When a player

can neither build nor take in any cards, he must discard from his hand by playing one card face up on the table.

Following disposal of the first deal of four cards apiece, the dealer deals four more cards to each player but none to the table, and play resumes as before. Upon making the deal of the last remaining cards, the dealer must announce that it is the final deal; on the last deal, the player who takes the last trick takes in all cards remaining on the table. When the last trick has been taken in, the cards are counted and scored according to the following point schedule:

Greatest number of cards	3
Greatest number of spades	1
Each ace	1
Big Casino, the 10 of diamonds	2
Little Casino, the 2 of spades	1

Normally, eleven points may be scored during each run through the pack, but if "sweeps" are counted, the scoring is higher. A sweep, for which one additional point is given, occurs when a player takes in all the remaining cards and leaves the board clean. If there is a tie for greatest number of cards, no points are awarded in this category. Game consists of twenty-one points, a score which can be attained in two runs through the deck but usually is not reached in fewer than three or four runs.

Royal Casino. Royal Casino is distinguished from Casino by the importance which the face cards assume in the former game. In Royal Casino, face cards have values and may be used for building, whereas in Casino the face cards have no building value. Jacks have a value of eleven; queens, twelve; kings, thirteen; and aces, either one or fourteen. Some players also assign a value of ten or sixteen, for building purposes, to Big Casino (ten of diamonds), and two or fifteen to Little Casino (two of spades).

Draw Casino. Draw Casino is basically the same game as Casino, but in the former the hands are replenished by drawing after each play, instead of by a series of deals. Following the initial deal to players and board, the pack is turned face down and becomes the stock from which the players draw after each play. Thus, each player always has four cards in his hand until the stock is exhausted.

Spade Casino. In Spade Casino, spades are scored individually instead of as a majority. Each spade taken in counts one, except the jack and deuce, each of which counts two. Since the scoring is higher than in Casino, game score is sixty-one instead of twenty-one. To facilitate scoring, some players use cribbage boards.

CHEMIN DE FER

Chemin de Fer is similar to Baccarat, a game which it has supplanted as the most popular card game of the French casinos; it is also popular among French and Russian émigrés. Chemin de Fer differs from Baccarat in that the dealer changes after each hand, and he plays against only one man instead of two. The first banker is selected by auction or lot, but thereafter the player to the dealer's right becomes the new dealer and banker after each hand. Before dealing, the banker announces the size of his bank, and the bettors may then cover any part or all of it. The cards are dealt only to the dealer and the player at his right, but all other players may bet with the dealer by betting that his opponent will beat him.

CINCH

Cinch is usually played by four people as a partnership game, but any number from two to seven people may play. A standard pack of fifty-two cards is used and the cards in each suit rank in the normal order from the ace (high) down to the two (low). The five of trumps is called "right Pedro," and the five of the other suit of the same color as the trump is the "left Pedro." Although the left Pedro is not of the trump suit, it is played as a trump and ranks just beneath the trump five. In scoring, each Pedro is worth five points to the hand which wins it in a trick. Other points are

 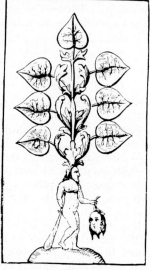

COURTESY OF THE NEW YORK PUBLIC LIBRARY

Old German Playing Cards: (left) Seven of Clubs; (right) Seven of Diamonds

scored by the cards known as "high," "low," "jack," and "game," each worth one point. "High" is the ace of trumps and naturally is scored by the player to whom it is dealt. "Low" is the two of trumps and scores one point for a player taking it in a trick. "Jack" is the jack of trumps, and "game," the ten of trumps, each scoring one point when taken in a trick. Thus, there are fourteen possible scoring points in each deal. Cards are dealt three at a time until each player has nine, and then the bidding is opened by the player on the dealer's left. The bidding proceeds clockwise around the table with each player bidding for the privilege to name the trump suit. A bidder estimates the number of points that he thinks he can take (when playing partners, the number of points that the partners' combined hands can take) and bids that number without naming the suit in which he intends to play the hand. If a player feels that his hand is not strong enough to bid, he may pass; but if he wants to bid, his bid must always be higher than that made by the previous bidder. Each player is allowed only one bid, and when the bidding is over, the highest bidder names the trump suit. In the event that all players pass, the dealer names the trump, but he is not obliged to bid.

When the trump suit has been named, the players discard face up all of the cards in their hands except trumps. The dealer then gives each player enough cards to bring his hand to six cards, and the dealer himself "robs the pack" by thumbing through the pack and taking the remaining trump cards to bring his own hand to six cards. If there are not enough trumps to fill his hand, the dealer has his choice of any other cards; but if more trumps remain in the pack than are needed to fill his hand, the dealer "faces" them in order that the other players may see which trumps are out of action; the dealer must also announce how many cards he took to fill his hand.

The player who named the trump suit opens the play by

leading any card. When a trump is led a player must always follow suit if able; if another suit is led, he must follow suit, or he may trump, even if able to follow suit; when unable to follow suit, he may play any card, trump or otherwise. A trick is won by the highest trump or, if no trumps are played, by the highest card of the suit led, and the winner of each trick makes the next lead. After the hands have been played, the points are counted and the partnership that made the most points scores the difference between its points and the opposition's only if the bidder was successful in making his bid. If the bidder fails to make his contract, the opposition scores all of its own points plus the bidder's contract. Game score is usually fifty-one, but if a Cribbage board is used for scoring, game is sixty-one.

Cinch has many variations which are known by other names such as High-Low-Jack, Pedro, and All-Fours.

Auction Cinch. A game for five or six players, Auction Cinch is played very much like Cinch, but it is not a partnership game. Only six cards are dealt, three at a time to each player, but the bidding, discarding, and restoring of the hands to six cards is performed as it is in Cinch. When the bidding has been completed, the highest bidder names some card—one that he does not hold—in the suit that will be trump, and the player who holds that card becomes his partner for the hand. The partners remain in the same seats, even though next to each other, and if the contract is made, each partner adds the partnership score to his own; if the contract is not made, each opponent gets his own points plus the amount of the bid.

CRIBBAGE

Cribbage is a popular two-handed game and one of the few card games whose invention is ascribed to a particular person. Sir John Suckling is said to have derived Cribbage from several earlier games and introduced it in London during the early part of the seventeenth century. There are several more modern variants of Cribbage for large numbers of players, but all are based on the standard two-player contest. A Cribbage board is usually employed to facilitate scoring, but it is in no sense essential; during World War II many American service men who became devotees of the game kept score with paper and pencil.

The Cribbage board which is generally made of plastic or wood, has four rows of holes, thirty in each, and one extra hole in the center of each end of the board. Each player has two pegs that fit into the holes and are used to score points as the play progresses. Game usually consists of sixty-one points, or once around the board and home—and first along the player's outer row, then back down his inside row for thirty points each way or a total of sixty, plus one to the center to make a game of sixty-one. The first time a player scores, he places one peg in its proper place by counting up the board, one hole for each point scored; the next time, he uses the second peg and counts from the first peg; thereafter the near peg is moved in order that a player and his opponents may see at a glance whether the correct number of points have been recorded.

At the start of the game, the player cutting the lowest card deals six cards, one at a time, to his opponent and himself. After the cards have been dealt, each player discards two cards from his hand, putting them face down on the table. These four cards form the "crib," which is used after the hands have been played. Since only the dealer can score points in the crib, his opponent tries to discard cards that will have no scoring value. After the crib has been established, the non-dealer cuts the pack and the dealer places the top card of the bottom portion face up on top of the reunited pack. This card is called the "starter" and is not used until after the hand has been played; but if the card is a jack, which is called "His Heels," the dealer scores two points immediately.

The non-dealer then begins the playing of the hands by laying a card from his hand face up in front of him and announcing its numerical value. All face cards and tens have a value of ten; the ace, one; and all other cards, their face value. The dealer follows up the play by placing a card in front of himself, adding its value to the non-dealer's card, and announcing the total; e.g., if the non-dealer played a queen and the dealer a four, the dealer would say, "fourteen," as he played his card. Play continues in this manner with each player alternately increasing the total, which can never exceed thirty-one. If a player is unable to play a card that will bring the total to thirty-one or less, he must say "go," and allow his opponent to score one point and continue playing until he too is unable to play. Whenever a player puts down a card that brings the total to exactly thirty-one, he scores two points instead of only one for having played the last card. After the count reaches thirty-one, or after a "go," the cards are turned face down and the player next in turn starts a new series. The procedure is repeated until thirty-one is reached, or a "go" is scored, or the hands are depleted; in the latter case, the player who lays down the last card scores a "go."

As play proceeds, the contestants can score other points in addition to those scored for "go" and thirty-one. When a card played makes the total exactly fifteen, two points are scored. For playing a card of identical rank with that just played by his opponent, a player scores two points for a pair; for adding immediately a third matching card to a pair, a player scores a pair royal, worth six points; and when the fourth card of the set is played, it is called a double pair royal, worth twelve. Pairs include only two cards of identical rank, not two different face cards of ten count each. Playing a card in immediate sequence with two or more played just before is worth one point for each card in the sequence. The cards need not be of the same suit, nor must they be played in ascending or descending order, e.g., nine-seven-eight is a valid sequence. Neither pairs nor sequences may be scored, however, if any intervening cards are played.

After all the cards of the hand have been played, the players turn the cards face up and count their hands, non-dealer counting first. The starter card is now used as a fifth card in each player's hand and is counted by both players. Each combination of cards totaling fifteen is worth two points; pairs also count two points; triplets, six; fours, twelve; three-card sequences, three; each additional card in a sequence, one; four-card flush (any four cards of the same suit), four; five-card flush, five; and "His Nobs," the jack of the same suit as the starter, one. The same card or cards may be scored in an unlimited number of ways; e.g., an eight, six, another six, and seven may be scored as two different sequences of six-seven-eight, a pair of sixes, and a fifteen. Some players use a scoring variation that they call Muggins; under this system, a player may take for his own score all points that his opponent fails to score in counting his own hand. When both hands have been counted, the dealer turns the cards in the crib face up and, using the starter as a fifth card, counts the crib exactly as he did his hand, with the one exception that a four-card flush may not be counted in the crib.

Game consists of either 61 or 121 points and terminates as soon as either player reaches that score. Even though a player's score might exceed his opponent's if he could count his hand after the opponent has reached game, the opponent would still be considered the winner because he was the first to reach game.

Three-Hand Cribbage. Instead of six cards, only five are dealt to each player in three-hand Cribbage and only one card is discarded by each player for the crib. To put four cards in the crib, one card is dealt to it after the players have received their hands. Play proceeds to the left, beginning with the player to the left of dealer. Three-player boards are made for convenience in scoring three-hand games.

Four-Hand Cribbage. Cards are drawn to determine partners in four-hand Cribbage. Five cards are dealt to each player and one is discarded by each into the crib. During the showing, or counting of the hands, the two partners pool their hands to be scored as one.

Five-Card Cribbage. The earliest form of Cribbage for two players was five-card Cribbage. Each player receives five cards, laying away two for the crib and keeping three. Thus, the crib contains more cards than a hand.

Seven-Card Cribbage. In seven-card Cribbage, seven cards are dealt to each player, and two cards are discarded for the crib.

Solitaire Cribbage. As the name implies, Solitaire Cribbage is a game for only one person. Three cards are dealt to the player's hand; two cards are then dealt to the crib, and finally three more cards to the hand. The player picks up his hand and, retaining the four best scoring cards, discards two for the crib. The starter is then turned, and the player first counts his hand and then the crib, scoring all the points for himself on the board. After each hand, the starter is placed at the bottom of the pack and, without shuffling, the cards are dealt again. Play is repeated until the pack is depleted, the object of the game being to score 121 points while going through the pack only once.

ÉCARTÉ

Écarté is a game that was formerly popular in Europe but seldom played in the United States. It is a game for two people that is always played as a gambling game with other people betting on the success or failure of either player. A short pack of thirty-two cards is used—all pip cards below the seven having been removed—and the cards rank in the following order: king (high), queen, jack, ace, ten, nine, eight, and seven (low).

Five cards are dealt to each player, and the eleventh card is faced, its suit becoming the trump. The dealer's opponent has the option of playing his hand or improving it by discarding any number of cards and drawing new ones. If he decides to play, he says, "I play," but if he wants to draw, he says, "I propose." The dealer then has the same option and may either accept the proposal to draw or force the play by refusing. If the dealer accepts the proposal to draw, he deals as many cards as he and his opponent discard. This procedure of discarding and drawing is repeated until one of the players elects to play. Then the dealer's opponent leads any card, and the dealer must follow suit; if unable to follow suit, he must trump; otherwise he may play any card. But a player must always take every trick that he can, i.e., he must top the card led or trump if unable to follow suit.

The object of the game is to take as many tricks as possible. If a player takes all five tricks, he scores two points; if he takes three or four, he scores one point. However, if the player who elected to play fails to take three or more tricks, his opponent scores two points. If the dealer turns up a king when he faces the eleventh card, he scores one point; and if a player is dealt the king of trumps, that player scores one point if he announces before the first lead that he is holding it. Game is five points.

EUCHRE

Euchre has undoubtedly been played in more different forms than any other card game still popular in the United States. Although Euchre is primarily a game for four

COURTESY OF THE NEW YORK PUBLIC LIBRARY

Tarot court cards, a type of unnumbered playing cards originating in Italy and used in Europe after the thirteenth century

players competing as partners, it has been adapted for two, three, five, six, and seven players, and special features have been added to lend variety to the original game.

In the standard game one pack of thirty-two cards is used, the rank in nontrump suits being ace (high), king, queen, jack, ten, nine, eight, and seven. In the trump suit, the jack is the highest card, called the right bower, and the second highest card is the left bower, being the jack of the other suit which is the same color as the trump; below them come the ace, king, queen, ten, nine, eight, and seven. Thus the trump suit contains nine cards, the nontrump suit of the same color as the trump contains only seven cards, and the other two nontrump suits, eight cards.

Five cards are dealt to each player, three each on the first round and two each on the second, or vice versa. The rest of the pack is then placed face down, except for the top card, which is faced. If the first player on the dealer's left wants to play the hand with the suit of the faced card as trump, he says, "I order it up." The card then becomes the dealer's, and he must discard some card from his hand, placing it crosswise beneath the pack. But if the player to the dealer's left passes and the dealer's partner favors the card, he may say, "I assist," whereupon the dealer picks up the card and discards. If the dealer's partner passes, the third player can order up, and if he passes, the dealer may accept the card by simply saying so and discarding. Custom requires that the dealer not actually pick up the faced card at any time, but leave it on the undealt cards until played. If all players pass, the faced card is put crosswise and still face up under the undealt cards. Proceeding around the table again, each player has the opportunity to name another

trump suit or pass. If all four players pass, the hands are thrown in, and the deal passes to the left. This continues until someone accepts the trump or dictates another. The namer of the trump then has the right to play the hand with his partner or, if he wishes, to play it alone. In the latter case, the partner puts his hand face down on the table and is out of action while the namer plays against the opponents.

When the namer plays alone, the first lead is made by the player at his left; at other times it is by the player to dealer's left regardless of where the namer sits. On each lead a player must follow suit if able to; when not able to, he may play any card. A trick is won by the highest trump, if a trump be in it; otherwise, by the highest card of the suit led, and the winner of a trick is the leader to the next.

The aim of each side is to win three tricks or more. When the naming side wins fewer than three tricks, it is euchred; if either side wins all five tricks, it scores a march. Points are recorded at the completion of a hand on the following basis:

If namer of trump wins 3 or 4 tricks	1 point
If namer of trump wins 5 tricks	2 points
If lone hand wins 3 or 4 tricks	1 point
If lone hand wins 5 tricks	4 points
If lone hand or partners are euchred, opponents score	2 points

The standard game is five points, but by consent it may be made seven or ten. To keep score, many players use the low pip cards from a standard pack, since they are not required for the game itself. Usually each side takes a three and a four from the deck and, by covering one card with another, exposes a number of spots equal to the total number of points scored at any point in the game. Other players use small chips or matches, starting with the same number of units as there are points in a game; they discard one every time a point is scored, and the number remaining shows how many points are still required for game. Many Euchre players keep score on the basis of rubbers, as in bridge or whist; as soon as a partnership wins two games, it wins the rubber, which produces a premium of two rubber points. In addition, the winners of the rubber score the difference between their points and those of their opponents in each game, plus another three points for each game in which opponents failed to score, two for a game in which opponents scored only one or two points, or one for a game in which opponents scored three or four.

Some players add the joker to the pack, ranking it higher than any other card, no matter what suit is trump, and treating it as a spade if it is the faced card.

Auction Euchre. Auction Euchre differs from Euchre in that no trump card is faced and the players bid the number of tricks that they anticipate taking, the highest bidder having the privilege of naming the trump suit. Five, six, or seven people can play: with five players, thirty-two cards are used; with six players, the sixes are put in the pack, making thirty-six cards; with seven players, the complete pack of fifty-two cards is used. In the five-hand and six-hand games, five cards are dealt to each player, and in the middle of the deal two cards are dealt to the "widow," which the eventual maker of the trump later takes into his hand, then discarding two of his cards. In the seven-hand game, each player gets seven cards, the rest going to the widow.

Two-Hand Euchre. Two-hand Euchre is the standard game of Euchre adapted for two players. A smaller pack of twenty-four cards is used, the sevens and eights having been removed.

Three-Hand Euchre. Called Cutthroat by many, Three-hand Euchre is identical with the lone-hand phase of the standard game; the player naming the trump always plays alone against the other two players, but there is no special score for this as there is in Euchre. The scoring is usually one point for maker taking three or four tricks, three points for all five tricks, and if the maker is euchred, two points for each opponent.

Railroad Euchre. Railroad Euchre has several novel features designed to make the game more exciting. One of these innovations is the use of a joker as the highest trump card. Another novelty is the practice of calling for a partner's best card. Under this rule, the player naming the trump and playing a lone hand can ask for and receives his partner's best card. This maneuver is not restricted to the maker of the trump suit, for either player of the opposing partnership may declare that he will defend alone and call for his partner's best card. In all cases, the player receiving his partner's best card must discard a card from his hand. If a lone hand is euchred by a lone opponent, the opponents score four points.

Two other variations present in Railroad Euchre are "laps," and "slams." Under the lap rule, all points scored in excess of game are carried over into the ensuing game. A slam is scored when a side wins a five-point game before its opponents have scored a point; this entitles the winning side to score two games instead of one.

Call-Ace Euchre. A unique method of determining the partnerships is employed in Call-Ace Euchre. Whether four, five, or six people are playing, the namer of the trump always has a partner, although it is not revealed who the partner is until after the play has begun. After the trump suit has been named, the maker names another suit, and the holder of the ace of that suit becomes his partner. But a player gives no indication that he might hold that ace, and thus the partnership is not disclosed until the card falls on a trick during the play.

FAN TAN

From three to eight people may play Fan Tan. A standard pack of cards is used, and the entire deck is dealt, one card at a time. Depending upon the number of players, the number of cards in each hand will vary, some players usually having fewer cards than others. Each player must ante one chip before the deal, and after the deal each player with fewer than maximum cards must ante a second chip.

The player on the dealer's left opens the play by putting a seven in the center of the table; if he has no seven, he must pay a chip to the pot. Thereafter, the play moves around the table to the left, each player putting out his sevens or building in sequence next to those already played. The four sevens are placed one above the other in the center of the table. To the left of a seven, the six of the same suit is played, and to the right the eight is played. Subsequent plays are made on top of the sixes and eights, building down to the ace on one and up to the king on the other, always in sequence and in the same suit. Every time a player is unable to play, he must pass and put a chip in the pot. If a player passes when he can play, he must pay three chips, but if he holds a seven and passes, he must pay five chips apiece to the holders of the six and eight of the suit.

A player's objective is to play all the cards in his hand as soon as possible and catch the other players still holding cards. For each card a player holds at the end of play, he must pay the pot one chip, and the winner collects the entire pot that has been built up as play progresses.

FARO

Faro is a gambling game that originated in Europe and became popular in the United States during pioneer days. The game was called Faro because one of the kings in an old French deck of cards resembled an Egyptian pharaoh. Any number of players bet against a single banker. Played strictly according to rule, Faro requires a dealing box, an elaborate contraption designed to eliminate cheating. The dealer's box had practically disappeared from use by the 1940's. Two cards drawn from the box constitute a turn. Using a standard deck of fifty-two cards, there are twenty-five turns, since the first and last cards are not counted. Bets against the bank are placed before each turn and are paid off immediately after it. Bets which are not decided by the turn are allowed to ride.

When Faro is played without professional supervision, players bid for the bank, which goes to the player who puts up the largest amount. The bank's advantage is apparently at least 4 per cent, but expert mathematicians believe it to be nearer 15 per cent. This advantage is one of the game's main appeals to professional gamblers. Another attractive feature is Faro's speed; bets are decided every time two cards are drawn.

Stuss, from the German and Yiddish *stuss*, meaning nonsense, is a game similar to Faro. The dealing is done from the banker's hand. In Stuss, when two cards of the same denomination are drawn within one turn, the player loses his entire bet, whereas in Faro he loses only half of it. Stuss is still played in gambling establishments.

FIVE HUNDRED

Five Hundred was derived by combining the popular features of Bridge and Euchre, and the rules were copyrighted in 1904 by the United States Playing Card Company. For a number of years before Auction Bridge became popular, Five Hundred was played in North America more extensively than any other bidding game.

In its original form, Five Hundred is a game for three players, and a pack of thirty-two cards, plus a joker, is used. The joker is always the highest card, other cards ranking as in Euchre: right bower (jack of the trump suit), left bower (jack of the other suit same color as trump), the ace, king, queen, ten, nine, eight, and seven. In nontrump suits and in all suits in no-trump, the rank is ace (high), king, queen, jack, ten, nine, eight, and seven. The suits have a relative rank in bidding as follows: hearts (high), diamonds, clubs, and spades, with no-trump outranking them all. Ten cards are dealt to each player in packets of three, four, and three, and after the first round of a deal, three cards are dealt to the table as a widow.

In bidding his hand, a player names the suit in which he wants to play as well as the number of tricks he thinks he can take. The minimum bid is six in any suit or no-trump, which is bid when a player desires to play without a trump suit. Having no bid, a player passes. Bidding begins at the dealer's left, each player having only one bid, which must always be higher than that of the preceding bidder. The same bid but in a higher-ranking suit is considered a higher bid. If all three players pass, the hands are thrown in, and the deal passes to the left; but under some rules, the hand is played at no-trump, each player scoring ten points for each trick he takes. The highest bidder gets the contract and takes the widow into his hand, discarding three cards to keep his holding to ten cards. The bidder then leads, and the other players must follow suit if able; otherwise they may trump or discard. The highest trump in any trick wins it, or the highest card of the suit led wins if a trump is not played. At no-trump, the joker will top any other card, but it may be played only when its holder is unable to follow suit. If a player leads the joker in no-trump, he may specify any suit to be played on it.

The bidder's objective is to make his contract; that of his opponents, to defeat it. The opponents combine their efforts against the bidder, but keep their tricks separately for scoring. Each opponent scores ten points for each trick he takes. If the bidder makes his contract, he scores points according to the following table.

Number of Tricks

Declaration	6	7	8	9	10
Spades..	40	140	240	340	440
Clubs	60	160	260	360	460
Diamonds	80	180	280	380	480
Hearts	100	200	300	400	500
No-trump	120	220	320	420	520

There is no bonus for tricks taken in excess of the bid, unless the bidder takes all ten tricks with a bid of less than 250, in which case he scores 250 instead of his bid's listed value. When he fails to fulfill his contract, or is set, the value of his bid is deducted from his score. It is therefore possible for a player to have a minus score, in which case a ring is usually drawn around it, and he is said to be "in the hole."

The game is five hundred points. If the bidder and an opponent go out on the same deal, the bidder wins, and if two of the bidder's opponents go out in the same deal, the first to reach five hundred wins; when an opponent goes out, play ceases unless the bidder by making his contract could also reach 500, in which event play continues until he makes it or is defeated.

Some players permit an irregular bid called "nullo," which is a bid to take no tricks whatsoever with the play at no-trump. A bid and made nullo scores 250, which places it between eight spades and eight clubs for bidding purposes; if this becomes the contract, the bidder loses when he takes even one trick, and each opponent then scores ten for each trick the bidder takes. Five Hundred is also played as a two-handed contest, with one hand dead, which makes it more speculative and less skillful. Others play it as a four-handed game between two pairs of partners. For this game forty-two cards are used so that each player may have ten and leave two for a widow, or three if the joker is used. There is also a form of the game for five or six players, a larger pack being utilized.

HEARTS

Unlike most games, Hearts is won by the lowest scorer, and the object of the game is to avoid taking the scoring cards, which are hearts. The game of Hearts had many antecedents, all of which have been rendered virtually obsolete by the more modern game that became popular during the 1920's.

There are still many different forms of the game, but the basic form is called simply "Hearts," while the variations are known by other names such as Domino Hearts, Joker Hearts, or Black Lady.

A standard pack of fifty-two cards is used, and any number from three to six people may play. Since each player must have the same number of cards, the pack is stripped when the number of players is other than four. When there are three players, the club two is discarded; five players, the club two and diamond two; six players, the club two and three, the diamond two, and the spade two.

The entire pack of cards is dealt, and the player on the dealer's left makes the opening lead. The other players must follow suit if they can; otherwise any discard may be made. In all suits, the ace is high, the other cards descending in their natural order, and the highest card of the suit led wins each trick. The objective of each player is to avoid taking any hearts in tricks and thereby keep his score low; each heart taken in a trick adds one point to the player's score. Since there is no standard number of points that constitutes game, each deal is a game in itself, but any number of deals may be played before a final score is tabulated. When the game is over, the totals of all the players are added into a grand total and divided by the number of players to determine the average score. Each player whose score is above the average pays into the pot the difference between the average score and his own, and each player whose score is below the average then collects the difference between his score and average.

Auction Hearts. Auction Hearts differs from the regular game in that hearts is not always the suit to be avoided. After the deal, each player may bid for the privilege of naming the penalty suit by bidding the number of chips he will put into the pot.

Beginning with the player on the dealer's left, each player may bid only once and most always bid higher than the preceding bidder. The suit eventually named is called the trump suit, although it has none of the privileges of trump suits in other games. Once the trump has been named, the play is the same as in Hearts, each player trying to avoid winning cards of the trump suit.

At the completion of the playing of a hand, each player puts a chip in the pot for each trump he took, and the player who was successful in not taking any trumps wins the entire pot. If two players take no trumps, they divide the pot; but if more than two players are without trumps, the pot is retained intact for the next deal and is called a jack pot. The same procedure is followed if one player takes all thirteen trumps. In the event of a jack pot, there is no bidding on the next deal, and the previous successful bidder names the trump again.

Omnibus Hearts. Omnibus Hearts is played exactly like Black Lady with one exception: a card scoring plus values is employed in addition to the negative scoring hearts and queen of spades. Usually the ten of diamonds is used as the plus card, but some players use the jack or eight of diamonds. In all cases, the plus card taken in a trick counts ten points.

KLABERJASS

Klaberjass is a two-handed game that was publicized by the late Damon Runyon in his stories of Broadway denizens, who call it by various names including Klaberjass, Clabber, Clabby, or Klob. A pack of thirty-two cards is used to play Klaberjass, and the cards rank jack (high), nine, ace, ten, king, queen, eight, and seven (low) in the trump suit; ten (high), king, queen, jack, nine, eight, and seven (low) in the other suits.

To begin the game, six cards are dealt in packets of three to both players. The thirteenth card is faced, and the rest of the pack is placed face down, partly covering the turned card. The dealer's opponent has the first option in naming the trump suit. He may accept the suit of the faced card, or pass, or "schmeiss," i.e., offer the dealer the opportunity either to throw in the hands or play with the faced card as trump. If the dealer accepts the schmeiss, the hands are thrown in and the cards are dealt again; but if the dealer refuses, play proceeds with the original trump. If the opponent passes, the dealer may accept the trump, pass, or schmeiss himself. When both players pass, the bidding is open for another round, each player having an opportunity to name one of the three other suits. If neither player names a suit, the hands are thrown in, and the cards are dealt again. Whenever either player accepts or names a trump, the bidding ends, and the dealer gives his opponent and himself three cards each. If either player holds the seven of trump, he may exchange it for the faced card; otherwise, the faced card is put on top of the pack out of play.

Prior to the playing of the first trick, both players meld the sequences in their hands. For melding purposes, the cards rank in their natural order: ace (high), king, queen, jack, ten, nine, eight, and seven (low). Sequences must be of the same suit and of adjacent rank, three-card sequences counting twenty points and four-card sequences, fifty. A four-card sequence will beat a three-card sequence, a higher sequence will beat a lower one, and a sequence in the trump suit will beat one of the same rank in any other suit; in the event that both players have sequences of the same rank, the non-dealer's beats the dealer's. If the non-dealer holds a sequence, he announces whether it is worth twenty or fifty, whereupon the dealer may say, "Good," or "Not good," depending upon his own holding. If the dealer has a sequence of the same value, he may ask his opponent how high his sequence runs in order to determine whose is the highest. The high sequence is not revealed until after the first trick has been played; then it is faced on the table along with any other sequences that the player might hold.

In playing a hand, the first lead is made by the non-dealer, and the dealer must always follow suit if able; otherwise he must trump if he can. When a trump is led, the dealer must

TAROT TRUMP CARDS

take the trick if possible by playing a higher trump. The winner of each trick leads to the next, the objective of each player being to take tricks in which there are counting cards. The counting cards are the trump jack (jasz) worth twenty points, the trump nine (menel) worth fourteen, any other jack worth two, any queen worth three, any king worth four, any ten worth ten, and any ace worth eleven. In addition to taking points in tricks, the player holding the king

and queen of trumps may, upon playing the second of those cards, say "Bella," and score twenty points. Ten more points are scored for taking the last trick of the hand. After the hand has been played, each player totals his score, including the melds, points in tricks, bella, and the last trick. When the trump maker has the higher score, each player records his full score, but in the case of a tie, the trump maker scores nothing, while his opponent scores his own total. If the non-maker has the higher score, he gets both his own and his opponent's score. The trump maker who holds bella and sees that his opponent is going to outscore him can strategically limit his losses by not claiming the bella score. Game is five hundred points and is usually played to the completion of each hand, for if both players reach five hundred in the same deal, the player with the higher total wins, not necessarily the one who reached five hundred first.

LOO

Loo is a game that was popular in England around the year 1800, but it has been played very little since then. It is a game for practically any number of players, cards being dealt until each has three. The play is for three tricks, each player following suit if able, otherwise trumping. No trump exists until some player is unable to follow suit; then after the player has discarded, the top card of the pack is turned and its suit becomes trump. Since the trump is retroactive, the card discarded on the preceding trick will take it if it happens to be a trump. The players who win the tricks take the pool of chips anted and contributed to the table by the several players under various circumstances.

MICHIGAN

A popular family game, Michigan is played by three to eight people using a standard pack of cards, chips, and four cards from another pack. The extra cards are called boodle cards and consist of an ace, a king, a queen, and a jack—each of a different suit. The boodle cards are placed face up on the table, and before every deal, each player except the dealer puts a chip on each card. The entire fifty-two cards are dealt one at a time, and depending upon the number of players, the hands vary in size, some hands having an extra card. An extra hand, which is dealt in turn on the dealer's left, may be taken by the dealer in exchange for his own hand, or may be auctioned off to the other players.

The player on the dealer's left opens the play by leading the lowest card of any suit in his hand, and if he has other cards of the same suit in sequence with his lead, he plays them also. Then the player who holds the next card in the sequence plays it, and the play proceeds in this manner until interrupted by the playing of the top card of a sequence (the ace) or by the absence of a card that is out of play in the dead hand. When the sequence is interrupted, the last person to play begins a new sequence by leading the lowest card of any other suit. If he has no other suit, the player must pass and the person on his left has an opportunity to lead.

Each player's objective is to play the cards that correspond to the boodle cards and to play all of his cards before any other player does. Each time a card identical with a boodle is played, the player collects the chips from that particular boodle on the table. Any chips that have not been collected at the end of a deal are retained on the same card for the next deal. When a player succeeds in playing all of his cards, he collects a chip for every card that each other player has in his hand.

NAPOLEON

At one time a popular game in England, Napoleon is similar to Euchre and Contract Bridge in that tricks are bid and played for. Two to six people may play, and five cards are dealt to each person. Each player has only one bid in which to name the number of tricks that he estimates he can take, and the highest bidder leads a card of the suit he wishes to play the hand in. The cards rank in the natural order from the ace (high) to the two (low), and tricks are won by either the highest trump or the highest card of the suit led if a trump is not played.

A bid of five, ordinarily the highest bid, is called Nap; an overcall of five is known as Wellington; and a second overcall is a Blucher. Although a bidder does not increase his scoring possibilities by bidding Wellington or Blucher, he does incur heavier penalties if his contract is defeated. When a bidder makes his contract, he collects from each other player, but when he loses he pays each other player according to the following table.

Bid	Won by Bidder	Lost by Bidder
Less than five	1 per trick	1 per trick
Nap	10 per trick	5 per trick
Wellington	10 per trick	10 per trick
Blucher	10 per trick	20 per trick

Payments are usually made with chips or counters, and game is any arbitrary number. Since there is no overtrick or undertrick scoring, the playing of a hand is terminated as soon as a bidder makes or loses his contract.

OKLAHOMA

A variation of Rummy, Oklahoma is a game for two people. Two standard packs are shuffled together, and thirteen cards are dealt to each player. The hands are melded as they are in Rummy, but deuces and jokers are used as wild cards. Each player's objective is to meld as many high cards as possible, for the scoring is based on a player's melded cards instead of his opponent's unmelded cards as in Rummy.

OLD MAID

A favorite game among children, Old Maid can be played by any number of people. Any one of the queens is removed, and the other fifty-one cards are dealt, one card at a time. Prior to the actual play, each player discards all pairs from his hand, but the third card of a set of three of a kind must be held. The player at the left then holds his hand so that the player on his left can draw an unknown card. The player who drew may then discard any pair formed by the newly acquired card. He in turn holds his hand for the player on his left to draw, and the play proceeds in this manner until all the cards except the odd queen have been paired. At the end of the hand, the player holding the queen is called "The Old Maid."

PANGUINGUI

Panguingui is a game that is little known outside of the American Southwest where it is played in gambling houses and sometimes called Pan. Eight packs of forty cards are shuffled together, and all eights, nines, and tens are discarded. Cards rank in the normal order with king high and ace low, and since the intervening cards have been removed, a jack and seven are considered to be in sequence.

Any number up to fifteen people may play, and each is dealt a hand of ten cards. The rest of the pack is placed on the table, and the top card is turned up. The player

on the dealer's left may take the turned card or draw another and discard. Thereafter, the play moves to the right, each player drawing and discarding in turn until all the cards have been drawn or until one player has melded eleven cards.

The object of each player is to meld his hand in various combinations, which he lays on the table as he acquires them in the process of drawing cards. The scoring combinations are three or more cards of the same denomination in different suits, unless they are aces or kings; three or more cards of the same suit and denomination; and three or more cards of the same suit in sequence. The value of each combination is arbitrary, but every time a player lays down a meld he collects from each other player. The player who first melds eleven cards is the winner and collects any predetermined amount from each other player.

PINOCHLE

Pinochle is played with a special pack of forty-eight cards; actually the Pinochle deck is two packs of twenty-four cards, because each card has a duplicate. The four standard suits each have six denominations that rank ace (high), ten, king, queen, jack, and nine (low). Although there are many variations of Pinochle, the basic game, which is sometimes called American Pinochle, is generally a two-handed game.

Twelve cards are dealt, three or four at a time, to each player, and then the next card is turned up to determine the trump suit. The play begins immediately with the non-dealer leading first; thereafter the winner of each trick leads. The higher trump card, or the higher card of the suit led when a trump is not played, wins the trick. If two identical cards fall on the same trick, the player making the lead wins the trick. There is no obligation to follow suit, and a player may discard, trump, or follow suit as he pleases. Every time a player takes a trick he may lay down one meld from his hand, and then both players draw one card apiece from the pack to replenish their hands, the trick winner drawing first. The card combinations and the scoring values of the various melds are shown in the following list.

Class A

Royal Sequence (A, K, Q, J, 10 of trumps)	150 points
Royal Marriage (K and Q of trumps)	40 points
Common Marriage (K and Q of any plain suit)	20 points
Dix (the 9 of trumps)	10 points

Class B

Four Aces (one of each suit)	100 points
Four Kings (one of each suit)	80 points
Four Queens (one of each suit)	60 points
Four Jacks (one of each suit)	40 points

Class C

Pinochle (Q of spades and J of diamonds)	40 points

Cards that have been scored in one meld may be used again in another, providing that the second meld is not of the same class. Having melded a Royal Marriage, however, a player may later add the ace, jack, and ten of trumps and score a Royal Sequence. Instead of playing a card from his hand, a player may lead or play one of his own melded cards on any trick, but once a card has been played on a trick, it cannot be used in a meld. The score for a meld should be recorded as soon as it is laid on the table. Only one meld may be laid down after each trick, and for each new meld, at least one card must be played from the hand.

In addition to scoring by melds, players also score by taking cards in tricks. For each ace a player takes he scores eleven points; each ten, ten points; each king, four points; each queen, three points; each jack, two points. At the beginning of the game, the dealer scores ten points if the card he turns for trump is a nine. At any time during the game, the player holding the nine of trumps may exchange it for the faced trump card. When the nine of trumps is played as a meld, another meld may be made at the same time.

After the twelfth trick has been taken, only one card remains to be drawn. This is drawn by the winner of the trick, who must show the card to his opponent, and the opponent takes the faced trump card for his hand. The remainder of the deal is played under altered rules and is called the play-off. During the play-off each player must follow suit and if a trump is led, play higher if he can. If he cannot follow a nontrump lead, he must play a trump. After playing the last trick, players count their respective trick points and add them to their meld scores. Each deal may be considered a complete game, but if a game score is decided upon, it is usually one thousand.

Auction Pinochle. One of the most popular forms of Pinochle, Auction Pinochle, may be played by as many as six people, but only three actively participate at one time. When four people play, the dealer receives no hand; when five play, the dealer and the second player on his left sit out; and with six, the former two and the player on the dealer's right do not play. During the playing of a hand, the inactive players are not permitted to give any advice or information to the others.

Fifteen cards are dealt to each of the active players, and the three remaining cards are placed face down on the table to comprise what is known as the "widow." Beginning with the player on the dealer's left, the players vie for the privilege of naming the trump by bidding the number of points that they estimate they can make. The minimum bid is usually 200, but under some rules it is 250 or 300. Bids are given in multiples of ten and always must be higher than the preceding bid. Bidding continues until two players pass, leaving the highest bidder with the contract. Once a player passes, he may not bid again. When the bidding is over, the successful bidder exposes the widow, then takes the cards into his hand and discards any three cards face down, without showing them.

After he discards, the bidder names the trump suit and lays down his melds to be counted and scored. Unlike American Pinochle, the bidder is the only player who melds, and all of his melds must be made before the first trick is played. The cards are melded and points in tricks are counted exactly as in American Pinochle (*see lists of combinations and values on preceding page*). When the melds have been counted, the bidder returns the cards to his hand and makes the first lead, playing alone against the other two players, who attempt to defeat his contract. Players must always follow suit if possible; being unable to follow suit, a player must trump if he can. If trump is led, a player must always play higher if possible than the highest card already on the trick. Tricks are taken as they are in American Pinochle, and the winner of a trick leads to the next one.

The bidder keeps the tricks that he wins in one pile with his three discarded cards, and the opponents keep their tricks combined in another pile. At the end of play, the bidder counts his trick points, including any points that might be in the three discarded cards, and adds them to his meld score. If the aggregate score is at least as much as his bid, the bidder scores his bid times the number of

players in the game, both active and inactive; but if the bidder's score falls below his bid, each of the active and inactive players scores twice the bid. Instead of scoring on paper, players may collect in chips, usually one chip for each one hundred points. Under some rules, the scoring is doubled if played in spades and tripled if played in hearts. If the score is kept on paper, game score is a thousand points.

Sixty-Four-Card Pinochle. A special Pinochle pack with eights and sevens added to the standard deck is used to play Sixty-four-card Pinochle. The seven instead of the nine of trump is the dix card, and sixteen instead of twelve cards are dealt to each player. Otherwise, the game is exactly like the two-handed American Pinochle.

Three-Hand Pinochle. Played with either the standard or enlarged Pinochle pack, Three-hand Pinochle is merely an adaptation of the American two-handed game for three people.

Partnership Pinochle. A game for four people playing two against two, Partnership Pinochle is played with the standard Pinochle pack of forty-eight cards. Twelve cards are dealt to each player except the dealer, whose twelfth card is placed face up on the table and becomes the trump card. Beginning with the first player on the dealer's left, any player who holds a trump nine may exchange it for the faced card and score for the dix meld. The player who holds the other trump nine melds it at this time and also scores it for his partnership. The dealer then takes the nine for his twelfth card, and each player lays all of his melds on the table. The cards are melded and scored as they are in American Pinochle, already described, and each partnership scores its combined total. In addition to the standard melds, some players also count a double pinochle worth 300 points; eight jacks, 400; eight queens, 600; eight kings, 800; eight aces, 1,000; and a double royal sequence, 1,500 points.

When the melds have been counted, the cards are taken back into the hands, and the player on the dealer's left makes the lead to the first trick. The other players must follow suit if able and must trump if possible when unable to follow suit. The winner of a trick leads to the next, and play continues until all the cards have been played. Points are scored for cards taken in tricks, but the card values differ from the standard scoring values. Each ace and each ten taken in tricks counts ten points, and each king and each queen is worth five points. If neither partner takes a trick, the points scored for melds by the partnership are nullified. Game score is one thousand points.

Partnership Auction Pinochle. As the name of the game implies, Partnership Auction Pinochle is the regular partnership game with the bidding features of Auction Pinochle (*see above*) added. Before the melds are shown, the players bid on the combined strength of the partnership hands. The minimum bid is one hundred, and the bidding partners score all points made if they make their contract; the opponents score all points that their own partnership makes. If the partners fail to make their contract, the opponents score the full amount of the bid, and there is no other scoring on the deal. Game score is one thousand, and in the event that both partnerships reach game on the same deal, the bidding side wins.

Check Pinochle. A partnership game for four people, Check Pinochle derives its name from the checks, or chips, that are used in scoring. It is a bidding game in which the minimum bid is two hundred, and in order to bid, a player must hold a marriage in his hand. An exception to the latter rule is made when all players up to the dealer pass: then the dealer must bid whether he has a marriage or not. Any player may overcall the preceding bid, providing that he has not passed on a previous round. Bidding continues in multiples of ten until no player is willing to bid higher; then the highest bidder names the trump suit.

Prior to the play for tricks, each player puts down all of his melds, which are made and scored in accordance with standard American Pinochle melds. The trick play is similar to that of Partnership Pinochle.

When the bidding partnership makes its contract, each side scores whatever points its players make, but if the contract is not made, the full amount of the bid is subtracted from the bidders' score and the opponents score their own points. As the play proceeds and at the end of the game, players collect chips, or checks, from their opponents for the following scores.

Melds

Round Trip (K's and Q's of all four suits)................ 4 checks
Trump Flush .... 2 checks
Four Aces (one of each suit)........................... 2 checks
Four Kings (one of each suit).......................... 1 check
Four Queens (one of each suit)......................... 1 check
Four Jacks (one of each suit).......................... 1 check
Double Pinochle (2 spade Q's and 2 diamond J's).......... 1 check

Contracts Bid and Made

Bid of 200-240.. 2 checks
Bid of 250-290.. 4 checks
Bid of 300-340.. 7 checks
Bid of 400-440...13 checks

In bids higher than 440, three additional checks are paid for each fifty points above 440. When contracts are defeated, the opponents collect twice the number of checks ordinarily paid for a successful bid. If a slam (all twelve tricks) is bid and made, the bidders collect a bonus of four checks. For each game of one thousand points, the winners collect seven checks plus one for each one hundred points or fraction thereof in the difference between the winners' and losers' totals. If the losers' net score is on the minus side, they must pay another bonus of four checks.

PIQUET

Piquet is a game of French origin that was played as early as the sixteenth century and has been referred to frequently in works of French literature. One of the oldest games currently played, Piquet is basically a two-handed game although it has been adapted for three and four players.

A standard pack of playing cards is used, but the deck is stripped to thirty-two cards by removing all pip cards below the seven; the remaining cards rank in the normal order from the ace (high) down to the seven (low). Cards are dealt two at a time until both players have hands of twelve. The eight remaining cards are known as the stock and are spread out face down on the table.

When a hand has no face cards, it is called a "carte blanche," and the nondealer may declare it immediately and score ten points; but if the dealer has a carte blanche, he must wait until his opponent has discarded and drawn before he declares it and scores. The nondealer has the first option of discarding one to five cards from his hand and replacing them by drawing from the first five cards of the stock. Although he does not draw all of the first five cards, the player can look at them without showing them to the dealer. The dealer then has the option of taking all, any, or none of the remaining cards in the stock and discarding from his hand the number of cards that he draws. If the dealer leaves some cards in the stock, he may look at them and decide whether

to face the cards or leave them face down and unseen by his opponent. The discarded cards are kept separately because during the play each player may look at his own discards.

After both players have drawn, the nondealer declares his scoring combinations, the dealer either conceding or contesting and scoring himself. The hands are compared in three categories: points, sequences, and sets (three or four of a kind). Without showing his hand, the non-dealer first states the number of cards in his longest suit. If the dealer does not have a longer suit, his opponent scores one point for each card he holds in the long suit, but if the dealer has a longer suit, he scores a point for each card he holds in his long suit. If both players have suits of equal length, the values of the cards are added—aces counting eleven, face cards ten, and pip cards their face values—and the player having the highest total wins the privilege of scoring one point for each card he holds in his long suit. If the totals are equal, neither player scores for points.

The nondealer next declares his best sequence, which must be at least three consecutive cards in the same suit. Only the player holding the longest sequence scores, but if both players have sequences of equal length, the player having the highest sequence scores. If the sequences are equal, neither player scores. One point is scored for each card in the sequence, but if the sequence is of five or more cards, an extra ten points is scored, e.g., a seven-card sequence is worth seventeen points. Only the holder of the highest sequence may score, but he may also score all other sequences he holds.

The sets are then scored, with the nondealer declaring any set of four or three cards of a kind that he may hold. The player holding the highest set of four wins the privilege of scoring, but if neither player has four of a kind, the highest triplet wins. Four of a kind are worth fourteen points, and triplets, three. Only the holder of the highest set may score, and he may score all other sets that he holds.

After the combinations have been counted, the nondealer leads to the first trick. If he is able, the dealer must follow suit, otherwise he may play any card. Tricks are won by the higher card of the suit led, and the winner leads to the next trick. The player who takes the majority of the tricks scores ten points, neither scoring in the event of a tie. One point is scored by the player taking the last trick. If a player takes all of the tricks, he scores a "capot" worth forty points, but no score is given for majority of tricks or for taking the last trick. Points are also scored for leads and individual tricks. Each time a player leads a card above a nine, he scores one point, and each time a player takes a trick with a card higher than nine he also scores a point. Since the scoring is rapid, each player is expected to announce his accumulated score whenever it is increased. If either player accumulates thirty points in declarations before his opponent has scored any points, the scoring player receives an additional sixty points for "repiquet." If a player scores thirty points in declarations and trick play before his opponent scores, only thirty addition points are awarded for "piquet."

A game is terminated at the end of either four or six deals or when either player has one hundred points. At the end of each game, the winner scores the difference between his and his opponent's score plus one hundred points for game.

When Piquet is played as a three-hand game, only ten cards are dealt to each player, but otherwise the game is the same. With four players, Piquet becomes a partnership game. All cards are dealt to the players, and, since there is no stock, discarding and drawing are eliminated. The play proceeds as it does in the two-hand game, but the scores of the individuals are combined to make a partnership score.

PITCH

Pitch is a game very similar to Cinch. At first six cards are dealt to each player, and the next card is faced to indicate the trump suit. Beginning with the player at the dealer's left, each player has the option of accepting or refusing to play the hand in the suit of the turned card. As soon as a player accepts the trump, the option is dropped and the play for tricks is begun. If the option is carried around the table to the dealer, he may also refuse or accept or name another suit for trump. If the dealer refuses the trump and doesn't elect to name another suit, three more cards are dealt to each player, and the procedure of refusing or accepting the trump is repeated. When the trump is finally fixed, each player discards, keeping only six cards in his hand. The player who is responsible for naming the trump then leads to the first trick. Trick play and scoring procedures are identical with those employed in the game of Cinch, except that in Pitch the pedro cards (five of trumps) have no scoring value and no unusual trump value. Instead, the five of trumps works in normal order as a trump card between the six and four, and the card which would be the left pedro has no trump value at all.

Auction Pitch. With one exception, Auction Pitch is similar to the regular Pitch game. Instead of turning a card to determine the trump suit, the players bid for the privilege of naming trumps. The minimum bid is usually one, although some players stipulate a minimum bid of two, and the maximum bid is four. Since no player may overcall a bid of four, the bidding is terminated and trick play is begun as soon as a player bids four. At the end of one round of bidding, the highest bidder gets the contract and leads to take first trick. His lead is called "the pitch," and its suit becomes the trump suit. Thereafter the play then proceeds as it does in Pitch and Cinch.

RED DOG

Red Dog is a comparatively simple gambling game that can be played by as many as ten people. A standard pack of fifty-two cards is used, and the cards rank in the normal order from ace (high) to deuce (low). Before every deal, each player pays the pot an ante, which may be one chip or any number previously agreed upon.

Five cards are dealt to each player—if there are nine or ten players in the game, only four cards are dealt to each— and the remainder of the pack, which is called the stock, is placed on the table. The player on the left of the dealer has the first opportunity to bet that he holds a card of the same suit but of higher denomination than the top card of the stock. The player may bet any number of chips as long as his bet does not exceed the number of chips in the pot. If he elects not to bet, he may pass and forfeit a chip to the pot. After the player has made his bet, the dealer turns the top card of the stock, and if the player has a higher card of the same suit, he shows it and collects from the pot. If he can't beat the turned card, the player must leave his bet in the pot, and the next player has an opportunity to make a similar bet. Play continues around the table until each player, including the dealer, has had his turn. Then the deal passes to the player at the dealer's left, and the cards are shuffled and dealt again for another round.

ROUGE ET NOIR

Rouge et Noir is a game very similar to Faro and Chemin de Fer. It is played with six packs of cards which are shuffled together as one large deck, and may be played by a large group of players. The game is seldom played outside of France, where it is popular at Monte Carlo and other French casinos. The house always deals, and the players bet on the turn of the cards, either that the next card will be red or that it will be black.

RUMMY

Rummy in its many forms has been a popular game in the United States since 1900, and by the middle of the twentieth century it had gained a following comparable to that of Poker and Bridge. Although Rummy evolved from an old Spanish game, its most popular variations are distinctively American in origin. Boathouse Rum, Gin Rummy, Oklahoma, Knock Rummy, Liverpool Rummy, and Persian Rummy are a few of the variations that have been derived from the straight, unadorned Rummy game.

Any number from two to six people may play. A standard pack of fifty-two cards is used, and the cards rank in normal sequence from the king (high) down to the ace (low). Ten cards are dealt to each player if two people are playing; seven cards, if there are three or four players; and five, if there are five or six players in the game. After the cards have been dealt, the dealer places the remainder of the pack in the center of the table and turns the top card face up to start the discard pile.

A player's objective in Rummy is to lay down the cards of his hand in sets of three or four cards of a kind and in sequences—sequences must have at least three cards of the same suit in consecutive order. The player on the left of the dealer has the first turn. He draws one card either from the stock or from the top of the discarded pile; then he may lay down in front of him any combinations that he has in his hand. However, it is not imperative that a player lay down a combination as soon as he makes it; he may hold all combinations in his hand until he is ready to lay down his complete hand or any part of it. After each draw, a player must discard a card face up to the discard pile whether he lays down combinations or not. The play moves to the left around the table, each player having a turn to draw, play, and discard. A player may draw either the top card of the stock or the top card of the discard pile. In addition to laying down new combinations from his own hand, a player may complete combinations that other players have laid down. If a player holds the fourth card of a set of three or the next card of a sequence that has been played by an opponent, he may lay down the additional cards in front of himself.

The first player to succeed in disposing of all the cards in his hand is said to have "gone rummy," and he is the winner of the hand. If a player can lay down the last card in his hand in a combination, he usually may do so, although under some rules he must also have a discard to go rummy. If the stock pile should be depleted before any player wins, the discard pile is turned over without shuffling and becomes the new stock. The winner adds to his score the total number of points remaining in each of his opponents' hands. Face cards are counted as ten, aces as one, and all other cards at their face value. Each deal may be considered a complete game, or the game may be continued until one player has scored one hundred points.

Boathouse Rum. The game known as Boathouse Rum may be played by two to six players. With a few exceptions, the cards are melded as they are in Rummy, but a player may not lay down his hand until his entire hand is matched in sets and sequences. In Boathouse Rum, a combination of two-ace-king is permissible and is known as an "around the corner" sequence. Another variant from Rummy is found in the play. If a player draws the card from the top of the discard pile, he must take another card, either the card immediately below it on the discard pile or the top card on the stock pile. But after drawing two cards, a player may discard only one, and thereby increases the number of cards in his hand. When a player has matched all his cards, he lays them down, and the other players pay the winner for each card in their own hands that they have not been able to meld.

Canasta. Developed in South America and introduced to the United States from Argentina, Canasta is also referred to as Argentine Rummy. The game was brought to the United States in 1948 and found immediate favor, supplanting in popularity gin rummy and even bridge among many card players. Two packs of standard playing cards and four jokers are shuffled together to comprise the 108-card playing pack. The four-handed game is the most popular, but two, three, four, or six people may play. Partners and the dealer are determined by cutting the cards, and eleven cards are dealt to each player when four people are playing the game; thirteen cards are dealt when two or three are playing.

The objective of each player is to acquire cards of three or more of a kind and meld them. Unlike many rummy games, sequences have no value in canasta. All jokers and deuces are wild cards to be used in melds with other cards, but may not be melded by themselves as such. Black treys may be melded only when calling, that is, when all other cards of the hand have been played and the player is going out of the game.

After the hands have been dealt, the dealer puts the remainder of the pack face down to form the stock. He then turns the top card and places it face up beside the stock to start the discard pile. If it is a red trey or a wild card, another card is turned and placed face up on top of it. After this, each player in turn, beginning at the left of the dealer, faces all red treys that he holds in his hand and draws from the stock to refill his hand to its original number. Regular play then proceeds in turn, with each player drawing either from the stock or discard pile, then melding if possible, and finally discarding.

In order to make the first meld of each deal for his partnership, a player must lay down cards totaling at least 50 points, counted as follows: jokers, 50; deuces or aces, 20; eight-spot through king, 10; black trey through seven-spot, 5. If, however, a partnership score has attained 1,500 points, its first meld must be of at least 90, and if its score is 3,000, its first meld must be of at least 120. When a side's score is minus, a count of 15 is sufficient for its first meld. After one player has put down his first meld, no minimum count is required for melds made by either partner thereafter. All melds must have at least two naturally matched cards and no more than three wild cards. Although a meld may be added to as the game progresses, it may never contain more than three wild cards. All melds are kept together in front of one or the other partners.

A player may draw from the discard pile only when he is able to meld the card that is on the top. He then is permitted to take the entire pile. If a player desires to use the up-card in making the first meld for his partnership, he must have two natural cards in his hand to match it. Thereafter the partnership may use a wild card in melding an up-card, unless the situation involves what is known as a "frozen" pack.

The discard pile becomes "frozen" whenever a wild card is discarded. Then the pile may not be drawn from or taken up until some player in his turn is able to match the current up-card with a natural pair from his hand. A discarded wild card is called a "stop card," since it prohibits the next player from drawing on the discard pile, forcing him to draw from the stock. Although a discarded black trey does not freeze the pack, it also is a stop card because it prohibits the player next in turn from drawing from the discard pile, since black treys may be melded only when calling.

When a meld has been built to contain seven cards, it is called a Canasta, which means "basket" in Spanish. If it has any wild card or cards (limited to three), it is a mixed Canasta, but if it consists of seven natural cards, it is a pure Canasta. As soon as a Canasta is made it is closed up, with a black card on top if it is mixed or a red card if pure.

Play proceeds until one player goes out by calling, all his cards being melded, or all except one, which may be discarded. In order to call, the partnership must have at least one Canasta. After a player has called, the value of the cards still held in his partner's hand are deducted from the score of the melds played. Similarly, all cards held by the opponents are deducted from their board score.

The basic scores consisting of the following are counted first: each red trey, 100; four red treys drawn by one partnership, 800 (unless the side has not made a Canasta by the time an opponent calls, in which case 800 is deducted from the score); calling, 100; calling with a concealed hand, that is, melding the entire hand at once without having previously played any cards to the board from that hand, 200; mixed Canastas, 300; pure Canastas, 500. Following this, all melded cards are counted at their respective values as listed above and added to the basic scores. The standard game score is 5,000 points.

Gin Rummy. Gin Rummy is the most popular form of all Rummy games and one that has warranted the formation of a committee of noted card game authorities to draw up rules governing the play of the game. Although two, three, or four people may play, Gin Rummy is essentially a two-handed game, the actual play being between only two players at one time. If three people play, one player must be inactive during each deal, the winner of one hand playing the inactive player on the next deal. Each player has a separate score and can make points only when he is an active player. When four people play, the game actually consists of two separate games played simultaneously. Two people play as partners, alternately opposing the two other players and keeping a partnership score.

The dealer deals his opponent and himself each ten cards and places the pack face down in the center of the table. The top card is turned face up alongside of the pack to start the discard pile. The non-dealer begins the play by drawing either the faced card or the top card from the stock. After he has drawn, he must discard, and then the dealer draws and discards, play alternating in this fashion until one of the players "knocks" or "gins." The "gin," which comprises the highest scoring, is accomplished when a player can lay down his entire hand replete with the regular Rummy combinations of sets and sequences. When a player gins, he scores twenty-five points plus the total value of all unmatched cards in his opponent's hand. Each face card counts ten points; aces, one point; and all others, their face value.

To knock, a player does not have to have all the cards in his hand matched, but the total count of the unmatched cards may not exceed ten. After a player has announced that he intends to knock, he lays down his hand, and his opponent may play any of his unmatched cards that will match with the knocker's combinations. Then the remaining unmatched cards are totaled and subtracted from the knocker's unmatched total. The knocker scores the difference in the totals. However, if the knocker's total is the same as or exceeds his opponent's, the opponent scores the difference plus twenty-five points and the knocker, nothing. Whether the deal ends in a gin or a knock, only the winning player scores. All combinations are held in the hand and are not laid down until one or the other player knocks or gins.

The score is kept in columns, one for each player, and each entry constitutes a box. The first player scoring one hundred points wins the game and scores the difference between his total score and his opponent's. A bonus of one hundred points is given for winning the game, and a bonus of twenty points is given each player for each box that he scores. If one player scores one hundred points before his opponent, he scores a "Schneider" and receives another bonus of one hundred points.

Knock Rummy. A game that employs the knocking feature of Gin Rummy, Knock Rummy is played by two to five players. If two people play, ten cards are dealt to each; if three or four play, seven cards; and for five players, six cards. The players draw and discard in turn, always attempting to improve their hands by building the standard Rummy combinations. No combinations are laid down on the table until a player is ready to knock; then all hands are shown and counted. Under some rules, a player may knock with any hand, but under others, his unmatched cards must not total more than fifteen. The hands are compared, and if the player who knocked has the lowest count in unmatched cards, he scores the difference between his total and that of each of his opponents. If some other player has the same or a lower count than the knocker, that player instead of the knocker does the scoring and receives a bonus of ten points from the knocker. If a player has matched his entire hand when he knocks, he scores a bonus of twenty-five points from each other player plus his regular score.

Liverpool Rummy. A game for three to eight players, Liverpool Rummy is played with two packs of cards shuffled together. The number of deals that will constitute a game (usually between four and eight) is decided upon prior to playing. Liverpool Rummy is sometimes called Contract Rummy because on each deal a player must make a certain contract before he can play out the rest of his cards. The contract determines the number and type of combinations to be laid down by the players, and it varies with each deal. On the first deal, the contract is two sets; on the second, it is one set and one run; on the third, two runs; fourth, three sets; fifth, two sets and one run; sixth, two runs and one set; and on the seventh, three runs. A set is three or more cards of a kind, and a run is a sequence of four or more cards in the same suit. After a player has laid down his contract, he may get rid of his other cards by adding to his own and his opponent's melds, but he may not lay down any new sets or runs. The combinations put down must never exceed the contract, and a player may not play to other melds until he has laid down his contract combinations.

Ten cards are dealt to each player on the first four deals, and twelve cards thereafter. The objective of each player is to get rid of all of his cards, and when he succeeds, the other players are penalized according to the cards they hold in their hands. Each player totals the cards remaining in his hand, counting aces fifteen, face cards ten, and all others their face values, and the total is added to his score. At the end of the game, the player with the lowest score is the winner.

RUSSIAN BANK

Russian Bank is a double solitaire game to be played by two people using two packs of standard playing cards. Each player takes a pack and deals a stock pile of twelve cards face down on his right. Four cards from each pack are then dealt face up in two rows extending from top to bottom between the two players, each player dealing his cards on his right in order to leave space between the two rows. These cards are called the tableau. Each player then places the remainder of the pack, which is called his hand, face down on his left.

Either player may start the game (usually determined by cutting the cards) by moving all the aces in the tableau to the center space between the two rows. These aces are used to start the foundation piles, which are built upon in suit and ascending sequence throughout the game. Whenever one of the eight aces or any other card that can be played on a foundation is uncovered, it must be played to the center. If a player neglects to play on a foundation when he can, his opponent may call, "Stop!" and then it becomes his turn to play. As soon as the player touches another card, the stop may be invoked.

After he has made all possible moves to the foundation, a player may then make changes in the tableau by building upon any card in descending sequence and in alternate colors; e.g., a black eight on a red nine. Only the top card of any tableau pile may be moved at one time. Having completed the moves he wishes to make in the tableau, a player turns the top card of his stock pile. If he can, he must play this card on the foundation; otherwise he plays it on the tableau when possible or leaves it turned face up on the stock pile. The player continues turning cards from the stock until he cannot play further. Then he goes to his hand, turns the top card of that pile, and plays until he has no further moves. The unplayed card from the hand must be left face up alongside of the hand and becomes the first card of the discard pile. Once a card is put into the discard pile, it may not be played again, and the player must turn a new card from his hand when he has another opportunity to play. When the hand is depleted, the discard pile is turned over, and the player begins anew. If a card played to the foundation or tableau makes possible a subsequent play from the stock pile, the player may resume play from the stock. A player's turn continues until he has no further plays from either pile; then his opponent has a turn to play in the same manner.

In addition to playing to the foundation and tableau, either player may put cards on his opponent's discard or stock pile; but he may play only cards of the same suit, either ascending or descending. For example, if the top card of the stock or discard pile is the six of hearts, either the five or seven of hearts may be played on it; and these cards may come from the stock, the hand, or the tableau.

The first player to successfully play out all of his cards, first from his stock and then his hand, is the winner of the game and scores thirty points. In addition to the game points, the winner scores two points for each card remaining in his opponent's stock, and one point for each card left in his opponent's hand.

SEVEN-UP

Seven-up is played in a manner very similar to Pitch, the principal difference being in the determination of the trump suit. After the cards have been dealt and the trump card turned, the player on the left of the dealer and the dealer himself look at their hands. If the player on the left of the dealer favors the trump suit, he "stands," and play begins immediately. If he does not like the trump, he "begs," in which case the dealer may either concede him one point and let the trump stand or discard the trump and deal three more cards to each player. A new trump card is turned, but if it is of the same suit as the original, it is discarded, and three more cards are dealt to each player. This procedure is repeated until a card of a different suit from the original is faced for the trump, and then the player on the dealer's left leads to the first trick.

Under some rules, the players discard all but six cards from their hands before playing; under other rules, play proceeds with the full hands. The trick play and the scoring is identical with that of Auction Pitch.

SHEEPSHEAD (SCHAFSKOPF)

Sheepshead has been played since the early eighteenth century, but in so many different ways that it is difficult to formulate any standardized set of regulations. However, Sheepshead is important because it was the forerunner of Skat.

SIXTY-SIX

Sixty-six is usually played as a two-handed game, but it has been adapted for three and four players. The two-handed game is very similar to the regular, two-handed Pinochle with a simplified playing and scoring system. Either a half of a Pinochle pack, or twenty-four cards from a standard playing card pack may be used to play Sixty-six. The twenty-four cards used are the ace, ten, king, queen, jack, and nine of each of the four suits, there being no duplicate of each card as in the standard Pinochle pack. Cards rank in the order listed above.

Six cards are dealt to each player, and the next card is turned face up to indicate the trump suit. The non-dealer makes the first lead, and his opponent need not follow suit. The higher card of the suit led, or the higher trump wins a trick, and the winner of a trick leads to the next. The only scoring melds in Sixty-six are marriages, which are shown when a lead is made and not after winning a trick as they are in Pinochle. To score a marriage, a player must lead one of the cards of the combination and show the other, and he must take at least one trick during the course of play. After each trick, both players draw a card from the pack to replenish their hands. At any point in the play when a player has the lead, he may "close" by turning the trump card face down. If this move is made, no more cards may be drawn by either player. After the pack has been exhausted or after a "close," a player must follow suit to a lead if he can, but he is not obligated to take the trick. At the end of the trick play, points taken in tricks are counted and added to the marriage scores. As in Pinochle, a marriage consists of the king and queen of the same suit. A marriage in the trump suit counts forty points, and any other marriage, twenty points. Cards taken in tricks are scored as follows: each ace, eleven points; each ten, ten points; each king, four points; each queen, three points; and each jack, two points. The winner of the last trick scores ten points unless a "close" had been employed during the hand. Sixty-six points constitute a game, and if a player scores sixty-six points before his opponent scores thirty-three, he scores two additional points; if the sixty-six points are won before his opponent takes a trick, he is entitled to three points. If a player "closes" and fails to make sixty-six points, his opponent scores two points. If he closes before his opponent has taken a trick and fails, his opponent scores three points.

SKAT

Skat was first played in 1811 at Altenburg, Germany, and in 1886 a group of players convened in the same city to codify a set of rules and regulations for the game. The American Skat League was organized in St. Louis, Mo., in 1898, and since the time of its founding the organization has sponsored numerous championship tournaments in the United States.

Although three, four, or five people may play Skat, only three players receive hands on each deal, and the others are inactive. A pack of thirty-two cards is used, all cards beneath the seven having been removed from a standard pack of playing cards. Ten cards are dealt to each of the three active players, and two cards are dealt face down in the center of the table to comprise the skat.

A hand may be played either as a trump declaration in which the player tries to take point cards totaling sixty-one points or as a nullo hand in which a player declares that he will take no tricks. No matter what suit is named in a trump declaration, all jacks (called bowers in Skat) become the highest trump cards, giving the trump suit eleven cards and the others seven. The club jack is high, followed by the spade, heart, and diamond jacks in that order. Below the bowers, the trumps rank ace, ten, king, queen, nine, eight, and seven, which is also the rank of cards in the three other suits. But if a nullo bid is declared, there is no trump suit, and the cards rank in the normal order: ace (high), king, queen, jack, ten, nine, and so on down to the two (low).

In bidding, a player calls out numbers that represent the various potential scores in his hand. No suit is revealed, although each player who is contemplating a trump declaration bids with some suit in mind. Each suit has a unit value (clubs, twelve; spades, eleven; hearts, ten; diamonds, nine) that is multiplied by the number of consecutive top trumps held in a hand plus one to determine a player's maximum bid. For example, if a player held the jack of clubs and the jack of spades, his maximum bid in clubs would be thirty-six. When a player does not have the highest trumps in his hand, his maximum bid is determined by multiplying the number of trump cards above his highest trump plus one times the unit value of the suit. For example, if a player wanted to name spades as the trump and held no trump cards above the spade ace, he would be without the four top trumps and would multiply five times eleven (the unit value of spades) to determine that his highest bid was fifty-five.

Instead of all players bidding consecutively around the table, only two players bid at a time. The holder of the second hand dealt bids to the holder of the first hand by naming some potential score in his own hand. The player to whom the bid is made either consents to meet a similar bid himself or passes. If he consents, the bidder makes a higher bid, and the process is continued until either the bidder is unwilling to bid higher or the receiver passes. This first phase of bidding having been completed, the holder of the third hand bids in the same manner to the survivor of the first bidding. The survivor of the second session is the successful bidder and has the privilege of naming the game.

The bidding over, the successful bidder picks up the two cards of the skat and discards two cards from his hand. He then names the game—either nullo or a suit for trump—which must always have a scoring value equal to or higher than the bid. The holder of the first hand dealt always makes the lead to the first trick, and thereafter the winner of a trick leads to the next. Players must follow suit if possible, and the high card of the suit led or the high trump wins each trick. No matter what a player has bid, he must always take at least sixty-one points (playing points, not to be confused with bidding points) in tricks to successfully make his contract and score the points of his bid. Points are made in trick play by taking the cards that have the following counting value: each ace, eleven points; each ten, ten points; each king, four; queen, three; and bower, two.

If a player successfully takes in sixty-one points, he scores his bid; if he takes in ninety-one points, he has made a little slam, and another unit value is added to the score. Should he take all of the tricks, he has made a bid slam, and still another unit value is added to his score. If a player leaves the cards of the skat hand on the table until after he has played his hand, his score is increased by another unit value for handplay. The score may be increased one more unit by announcing a little slam and still another by announcing a big slam. Thus, for a big slam announced and made as a handplay, a player increases his original bid by five units of value.

A nullo bid has no unit value, but it carries a fixed score of twenty-three points. A nullo hand may be played as an open hand with the declarer exposing his hand by laying it face up on the table after the first trick. A player who successfully plays an open nullo scores forty-six points, and if it is a handplay, he scores fifty-nine. Whenever a bidder fails in a handplay, he loses whatever score he would have made if he had won; if he fails on any other hand, he loses double his potential score. A running score for each player is kept in columns, and the final settlement is based on the differences in the totals.

SLAP JACK

A comparatively simple game to play, Slap Jack has become a popular game for children. There is no limit to the number of players or to the number of cards used in playing. The entire pack of cards is dealt, and each player arranges his hand in a small pile face down in front of him. The play begins immediately with the player on the left of the dealer turning the top card of his hand and putting it face up in the center of the table. In turning the card, the player turns it away from him in order that he won't have an advantage over the other players by being the first to see what the card is. If the card is a jack, each player hurries to slap the jack, or cover it with his hand. The first player to cover the card takes it into his own hand. If the card is not a jack, it is left on the table, and the next player on the left turns his top card. As the play proceeds around the table, the cards accumulate in the center of the table until a jack is turned. Then the successful slapper takes not only the jack but also the cards under it. The newly acquired cards are shuffled in with the rest of the player's hand, and play is resumed. If a player slaps any cards other than a jack, he must forfeit a card from his hand to the player turning the card. Each player's objective is to gain for his own hand all of the cards in the pack. When a player's hand is depleted, he does not have to retire from the game immediately. Instead, he may have one more opportunity to acquire some cards by successfully slapping a jack. If he fails then, he must withdraw from the game. The winner of each game is the player who first acquires all of the cards in his own hand.

SOLITAIRE

Any game that may be played by only one participant is called Solitaire, and of these games, there are many and various types. Solitaire games like Canfield, already described, may be played in gaming houses, and frequently players bet independently with each other on the outcome of their games, wagering that they can excel some self-imposed standard. In gaming houses the house usually establishes a standard against which an individual may play, and whenever a player's success equals or exceeds the house standard, the player is paid by the house according to the degree of his success. Some other Solitaire games such as Accordion are particularly popular among people who play cards alone. On occasions when no opponents are available, a game of Solitaire against chance or an imaginary opponent provides a satisfactory substitute for many enthusiastic card players. Since a player is accountable to nobody but himself and his conscience, some players are tempted to cheat their imaginary opponents in Solitaire.

Solitaire Cribbage. Based on the regular game of Cribbage, Solitaire Cribbage provides an excellent learning medium for Cribbage players. A player deals himself three cards, then deals two cards to the crib, and three more to himself. After looking at his hand, the player discards two cards to the crib and turns the starter. Using a board, the player first scores his hand and then the crib. The starter is then put on the bottom of the pack, and the deal and play are repeated until there are only four cards left in the pack. These are then faced and scored as a hand. The object is to score 121 points, or as many points as possible, while going through the pack once.

Klondike. Although the layout and play are different, the principles of Klondike and Canfield are similar, and the two games are frequently confused. Klondike is a popular game in the United States, where it is probably played more extensively than any other solitaire game.

Using a standard pack of cards, the player lays out the tableau by dealing one card face up and then six face down to the right, making a row of seven cards; next, he deals one card face up on top of the second card and then one face down on each of the other five cards to the right. Starting one pile farther to the right each time, the player repeats the process until the top card of each pile is face up. Then the seven piles of the tableau should have, reading from left to right, one, two, three, four, five, six, and seven cards respectively.

A player's object in Klondike is to get the aces out to the center and build on them in ascending sequence and in suit. After dealing the tableau, the player starts these foundation piles by putting in the center of the table all aces and other cards that can be built in sequence on them. Having done this, the player may make plays in the tableau itself by building in descending sequence and in alternate colors; e.g., a red ten on a black jack. Whenever some move leaves a vacant space in the tableau, a faced king may be put in the space. Although no other card except a king may be played in a blank space, all other cards that have been played on the king must be moved to the new space with it. Part or all of the faced cards in a tableau pile may be moved to some other pile as long as the bottom card of the pile being moved will form an uninterrupted descending sequence in alternate colors with the top card of the pile to which it is moved.

After a player has made his moves in the foundation or tableau, he takes the remainder of the pack and turns the top card. If he can, he plays this card on the foundation or tableau. Having no play, the player puts the card down alongside of the pack as the first card of the talon. The next card is then turned and played in the same manner. If at any time the playing of a card provides a move for the top card of the talon, the player may turn to the talon and play the top card and subsequent top cards as long as there is a move for each. Then he resumes turning cards of the pack one at a time. When all the cards of the pack have been turned once, and the player has made all possible moves to the foundation and tableau, the game is terminated.

In gaming houses, the house sells a player a pack of cards with which to play a game of Klondike, and pays the player in accordance with the number of cards he succeeds in playing to the foundation. The scale is usually such that if a player puts out eleven or more cards, he will win; if less than that, the house wins. The game may also be played as double solitaire by two players using two packs. Each may build on the other's foundations as well as his own, and the player who has more cards in the center is the winner.

Solitaire Poker. To lay out the cards for Solitaire Poker, a player deals five Poker hands face up on the table. The cards are then scored by totaling the points in each of the five hands. The various Poker combinations may be counted in several ways, but the system most frequently used in the United States is as follows: a royal flush, one hundred points; a straight flush, seventy-five; four of a kind, fifty; full house, twenty-five; flush, twenty; straight, fifteen; three of a kind, ten; two pairs, five; and one pair, two points.

Since there are five cards in each hand and five hands, the cards are laid down in a square, but no order is required in dealing. The only requirements are that there be no more than five cards in each row and that each card laid down be contiguous to some other card, either vertically, horizontally, or diagonally. Some skill in laying down the cards is necessary to build the best possible hands. Once a card is placed, it may not be moved to any other position.

The game described above is the standard form of Poker Solitaire, but there are many variations of this game. Under some rules, the hands are counted only horizontally, but other players count them both horizontally and vertically. Most players score the original hands, but some play a draw game similar to draw poker in which cards may be discarded from each hand and new ones drawn in an effort to improve the hands.

STUSS

Stuss is almost identically the same game as Faro. The principal difference in the two games is that Faro is always dealt from a box, but in Stuss, the dealer holds the pack in his hand to deal. Another difference appears in the collection of bets on splits. When two cards of the same denomination appear on the same turn, a split has been turned. In Faro, the banker takes half of a player's bet on a split; in Stuss, the banker collects the entire bet. Aside from these slight differences, the two games are identical.

TOWIE

Although more than three people may play the game, Towie is a three-handed variation of Contract Bridge. Only three players may be active on any one deal, but four hands are dealt. In dealing the fourth hand, which is the dummy, the dealer turns six of its thirteen cards face up. On the strength of his own hand and the six exposed cards in the dummy, each player bids against the others. The bidding proceeds as in Contract Bridge with the highest bidder becoming the declarer. The bidding completed, the cards of the dummy are arranged face up on the table opposite the declarer, and the other two players seat themselves on the right and left of the declarer. If, during the bidding, no player bids game, the hands are gathered up and without being shuffled are dealt again as a Goulash. The dealer deals four hands, giving each hand five cards on the first two rounds and three on the last. This results in freakish and unusually powerful hands that encourage the players to make high bids. When the four hands have been dealt, the

dealer shuffles the dummy hand and turns six of its cards face up. Then the bidding and trick play proceed as usual.

WHIST

The forerunner of Bridge Whist, Auction Bridge, and Contract Bridge, Whist is an English game of seventeenth-century origin. Thirteen cards are dealt to each of four players, but the dealer temporarily faces his last card in the center of the table. This card determines the trump suit and is left on the table until after the first trick has been played; then the dealer takes it into his hand. Since there is no bidding the player on the dealer's left leads immediately to the first trick. Since each player plays his own hand, there is no dummy as there is in Bridge. The partners combine strength in an attempt to win as many tricks as possible for their partnership. The highest card of the suit led or the highest trump card wins each trick. Unlike Bridge, every play at tricks has a trump suit because Whist does not provide for play at no-trump. In scoring, each trick is worth one point, but players may count only the tricks that their partnership takes in excess of six. Game score is seven. *See also* BRIDGE.

Bid Whist. In Bid Whist the trump is determined by the players and not by the turning of a card as in Whist. Thirteen cards are dealt to each of the four players, and the bidding is opened by the player on the dealer's left. No suits are mentioned, but each player bids the number of tricks that he estimates his side can take in excess of six, or he passes. Each bid must be higher than the preceding one. The player who makes the highest bid names the trump suit, and the play for tricks proceeds as in Whist. If the bidding partnership successfully makes its bid, it scores one point for each trick taken above six. When a bid is not made, the opponents score the bid plus one point for each trick by which the bid is defeated.

Contract Whist. Contract Whist is a natural combination of two games—Whist and Contract Bridge. The bidding and scoring are identical with that of Contract Bridge, and the play for tricks is exactly like the play in Whist, without a dummy hand.

Norwegian Whist. Norwegian Whist is a form of Whist in which play is always in no-trump. Like the other Whist games, it is a partnership game, and hands of thirteen cards are dealt to each of the four players. Beginning with the player on the dealer's left, each player has an opportunity to bid either a grand, a nullo, or pass. The former bid is a contract to take a majority of the thirteen tricks; the latter, to lose the majority. If the first three players pass, the dealer is obliged to bid, but as soon as a bid is made by any player, play begins.

When the bid is a grand, the player on the bidder's right makes the first lead; when it is a nullo, the player on the dealer's left leads first. When a grand is bid and made, the bidding partnership scores four points for each trick above six. If the bidders are unsuccessful, the opponents score eight points for each trick they take above six. In a nullo contract, there is no penalty for a bidder's failure; either partnership may score four points for each trick that its opponents take above six. The side first scoring fifty points wins the game. *See also* BRIDGE; POKER; PLAYING CARDS.   S. B.

CARDIFF [ka′rdɪf], the largest city in Wales, situated in an industrial region about a mile above the mouth of the river Taff. It is a county, municipal and parliamentary borough, seaport, railroad center and county town of Glamorganshire. About A.D. 75 the site was a Roman station to protect a ford on the Taff. Its most famous building, the Castle, begun in 1090 by Robert Fitzhamon, was the town's nucleus. Cardiff was a borough by prescription, and grants were made to it by many sovereigns. Its earliest known charter was granted by Robert, Earl of Gloucester, who married Fitzhamon's daughter. In 1608, James I confirmed earlier grants, speeding Cardiff's development. It was made a county borough in 1888, and a city in 1905. The Castle and its manors, from the Earl of Gloucester, passed through several families to the Crown. Edward VI, in 1551, granted them to Sir William Herbert, afterwards Baron Herbert of Cardiff, Earl of Pembroke. Through his descendants the estates passed to the first Marquis of Bute (Baron Cardiff, 1776), to whose descendants they belong. Development of near-by coal fields hastened Cardiff's growth, and, sponsored by the second Marquis of Bute, Cardiff docks were opened in 1839, creating an important port. The Marquis, who died in 1900, rebuilt the Castle, making the interior magnificent. In 1938, John Crichton-Stuart, Marquis of Bute, sold most of the docks, and about half of Cardiff, for £20,000,000 ($80,000,000). He died on Apr. 25, 1947, and was succeeded by his eldest son. In World War II, Cardiff was bombed several times, but few important places were hit, except historic Llandaff Cathedral. Cathays Park, a civic center, includes the University of South Wales and Monmouthshire, founded in 1883, one of four colleges forming the University of Wales, established in 1893. In Cardiff also are the Medical School of the University, a technical college, and denominational colleges. Great steel works constitute the chief industries; others include copper and smelting works, breweries, grain mills, cattle pens and abattoirs, and biscuit factories. Pop. 1952, 244,800.

CARDIGANSHIRE, a maritime county of western Wales, extending along Cardigan Bay from the estuary of the Dovey River in the north to a point somewhat beyond Port

Severn and the Wye rivers rise in Montgomery, about a mile from the Cardigan border, which is formed by tributaries of the Dovey, Wye, and Ystwyth. The Towy River forms the boundary with Brecknock. The Teifi River flows northeasterly-southwesterly within the county to Lampeter, then forms the Carmarthen and Pembroke boundaries. The Rheidol, Uptwyth, and Aeron rivers all flow northwest into Cardigan Bay, the mouths of the first two being about a mile apart. The coast line is relatively even and regular. Two small fragments of the county lie south and west of Port Cardigan. The area is 692.4 sq. mi.

Clay slate and shale are the prevalent rocks of the Cardiganshire mountains. The soil is either peaty or sandy loam. The January temperature is 41°-42° F., the July temperature 60°-61° F. May is the driest and November the wettest month; rainfall in the former month ranges from 2 to 4 in. and in the latter from 6 to 8 in. Annual rainfall is between 40 and 60 in. Lying just west of the upland pasture belt, the county is primarily a dairy region. Oats and barley are the principal crops. Lead, copper, zinc, and slate are worked. Lead-silver ores were mined and smelted at Swansea, particularly during the seventeenth century. Gloves, woolens, bricks, tile, and farming tools are manufactured. There is considerable export trade with Wexford and Rosslare, in Ireland, about 90 mi. west across the Irish Sea. Aberystwyth (pop. 1952, 10,240), on the northern coast between the mouths of the Rheidol and Ystwyth rivers, is a watering place, seat of the University College of Wales, and the commercial center of central Wales. Cardigan, the county town, is in the southwest at the mouth of the Teifi River. Its ruined castle dates from the reign of Henry II. St. Dogmael's Abbey, founded in the twelfth century, is one mile distant. Lampeter, on the Teifi at about the center of the Cardigan-Carmarthen boundary, is the assize town and the site of St. David's College. The county sends one member to Parliament. Cardiganshire has ample communications, being served by the Great Western Railway.

View of Cardigan, Wales, located on the Teifi River

Cardigan on the south. It is bounded on the north by Merioneth, northeast by Montgomery, east by Radnor, southeast by Brecknock, south by Carmarthen, and southwest by Pembroke. The southwest is low and fairly level, as is the northwest coastal area from the Dovey south to Aberystwyth, but the northeast and east are mountainous. The principal summits are Plynlymon (2,469 ft.) near the Montgomery border, Carngrow (1,776 ft.), and Moelyllyn (1,705 ft.). Both the

The county has few historical and architectural remains. Of all Welsh counties, Cardiganshire, the former lordship of Ceredigion, has remained the most Celtic, and Welsh is almost universally spoken. Pop. 1952, 53,240.

CARDINAL (Lat. *cardo,* a hinge, *cardinalis,* pivotal, important) is a member of the senate of the Roman pontiff and one of his councillors and assistants in the administration of the Roman Catholic Church. In recognition of the universal extent of these administrative responsibilities, Pius XII in 1945 selected his cardinals from all parts of the world. Hence they are generally the supreme directors of the congregations (Curia Romana) established at Rome to take care of Roman Catholic activities throughout the world, although a few of these congregations are under the presidency of the pope in person. The name cardinal, originally applied to a cleric attached to a determined church, later given only to clerics assisting the bishop in his church, and later still only to prominent clerics of large cities, is now reserved to those created such by the pope, who in selecting them is independent of governments, states and churches. A cardinal is created at the moment in which the pope declares one to be such. This declaration is made in a secret meeting (consistory) with the cardinals resident in Rome, the colorful ceremonies which take place after the naming of cardinals being mere incidentals. The pope may, when he informs the cardinals present that he has created a new cardinal, withhold the man's name; a cardinal thus created is a cardinal *in petto*, enjoying neither privileges nor precedence until his name is publicized.

The present body of cardinals originated in the 25 parish priests of Rome, the 7 (later 14) regional and 6 palatine deacons, and the 7 (later 6) bishops of the suburban dioceses of Rome. Since 1150 they have formed the Sacred College with a dean and camerlengo, or papal chamberlain, and since 1179 they have enjoyed the exclusive right of electing the pope, a right which they exercise in conclave. Their number, which is rarely reached, was fixed in 1586 at 70. This is divided into 6 cardinal bishops, corresponding to the bishops of the suburban dioceses; 50 cardinal priests, who are usually archbishops of important sees throughout the world; and 14 cardinal deacons, who are officials of the Vatican and often merely priests. The last cardinal not in priest's orders was Giacomo Antonelli, who died in 1876. *See also* CONCLAVE.

J. J. McL.

CARDINAL, any one of a number of songbirds of the genus *Richmondena* in the family Fringillidae. *R. cardinalis* occurs throughout the southern half of the United States and in Mexico; *R. phoenicea* is found on the coasts of Colombia and Venezuela. Males are bright red, with a black face patch and a conspicuous pointed crest; females are similarly crested, but are gray or brown, varied with red. Their powerful bills enable them to crack the shells of hard seeds, and they are valuable for their consumption of weed seeds and insects. In the southeastern United States, the eastern cardinal is a familiar inhabitant of gardens and parks; the clear, ringing whistled song made it formerly prized as a cage bird.   H. G. De.

CARDINAL FLOWER, *Lobelia cardinalis,* also called Indian pink, is a perennial herb of the lobelia family. It grows 2 to 4 ft. high, and is native to moist ground in eastern North America. In midsummer, slender upright spikes of intense scarlet blossoms make this one of our most spectacular wild flowers. It is sometimes cultivated as an ornamental.   J. C. Wis.

CARDOON [kardu′n], *Cynara cardunculus,* a coarse, 6-ft. thistlelike, perennial herb of the family Compositae, native to the Mediterranean regions. Closely related to the artichoke, it is cultivated as a vegetable in Europe and recently in North America. It was introduced to South America, where it has run wild on the pampas. The stalks, roots, and inner leaves are edible after blanching.   J. C. Wis.

CARDOZO, BENJAMIN NATHAN [kardo′zo] (1870-1938), American jurist, was born in New York City, May 24, 1870. He was educated at Columbia University, graduating in 1889 and becoming a master of arts in 1890. A year later he was admitted to the New York bar and practiced law in New York City until 1914. In 1913 he was elected a justice of the Supreme Court of New York for the

Benjamin Nathan Cardozo, American jurist and associate justice of the United States Supreme Court

INTERNATIONAL NEWS PHOTO

term to run from 1914 to 1928, but in February of the former year he was appointed an associate judge of the Court of Appeals, a position to which he was elected for a full term in 1918. In 1927 he was elected chief judge of the Court of Appeals. President Herbert Hoover appointed him to the United States Supreme Court in 1932 to fill the vacancy caused by the death of Justice Oliver Wendell Holmes. Cardozo was noted for his liberalism and for his high ideals of justice, which he expressed in his books, including *Jurisdiction of the New York Court of Appeals* (1909), *The Nature of the Judicial Processes* (1921), *The Growth of the Law* (1924), and *The Paradoxes of Legal Science* (1927). He died at Port Chester, N. Y., July 9, 1938.   R. T.

CARDSTON, a town on Lee Creek, in Alberta, Canada, 50 mi. southwest of Lethbridge and 17 mi. from the United States border, on the Canadian Pacific Railway. Founded by the Mormons in 1887, it is the Canadian center for this religious group. An impressive temple is situated in the town. Cardston is the distributing center of a farming and cattle-ranching district and is one of the gateways to Waterton Lakes and Glacier Parks. Pop. 1956, 2,607.

CARDUCCI, GIOSUÈ [kardu′ttshi] (1835-1907), Italian poet and educator, was born at Val di Castello, Tuscany, July 27, 1835. After studying in Florence and at the Scuola Normale in Pisa he taught for a year in San Miniato al Tedesco (1856-57), and published there a volume of poetry. He then returned to Florence and engaged in editorial work. Appointed professor in the University of Bologna in 1860, he lectured there until his retirement in 1904. Despite attacks on his republicanism and his opposition to the Roman Catholic Church, his reputation as poet, critic and orator brought him many honors, including the Nobel Prize for literature in 1906. Partly because of admiration for Queen Margherita, he modified his republican views and gave allegiance to the Savoy monarchy as the government best suited to Italy. At his death, Feb. 16, 1907, he was honored as a patriot and the foremost literary personage in Italy.

Carducci's early poems show the influence of Latin and Italian models. As *Juvenilia* they were republished in 1871 in *Poesie,* with *Levia gravia* (1868) and some political poems which later were included in *Giambi ed epodi* (1882). Typical of Carducci's attitude in the 1860's is the *Inno a Satana* (1863). This "hymn" exalts, under the name of Satan, reason and nature as opposed to the Christian asceticism that he despised. Polemics resulted, followed by a period of comparative serenity. The feeling for nature becomes a religion in *Nuove poesie* (1873), notably in *Il Bove* (The Ox), the finest among many admirable sonnets. The period from the appearance of *Odi barbare* in 1877 until 1890 marks the maturity of Carducci's poetic genius. *Rime nuove* appeared in 1887, and more *Odi barbare* in 1882 and 1889. These odes, his most original contribution to poetic art, represent a return to the metrical system of the Greek and Latin classics, which is based on syllabic quantity without rhyme, not on accent like modern poetry. He called them "barbarian" because their language would have seemed such to an ancient Roman; but they show complete devotion to Classical ideals. Carducci always condemned the Romantic attitude and gave it no place in his writing. Of course the merit of the odes depends on their poetic quality, not on any theory of composition; they include masterpieces. Typical is *Alle fonti del Clitunno,* in which the vivid description of the rural scene calls up memories of ancient Roman history. The *Canzone*

GIOSUÈ CARDUCCI

HISTORICAL PICTURES SERVICE

di Legnano, which recounts the defense of Milan against Barbarossa in 1176, was written in protest against the realists who limit the scope of literature to pictures of contemporary life. Carducci's last collection of poems, *Rime e ritmi* (1898), shows his interest in Irredentism, as in *Per il monumento di Dante a Trento.*

In his prose, as in his poetry, Carducci always had national ideals in mind. His polemics (*Confessioni e battaglie*) are now significant only as they throw light on his personality. His literary criticism, on the other hand, even though not based on a philosophy of esthetics, has permanent value. Noteworthy are his studies of many individual poets, and of the development of the national literature from its beginning to his own time, with bitter comment on the decadence of the mid-nineteenth century. His works were collected in twenty volumes (Bologna, 1889-1909); with later additions, in the Edizione Nazionale (Bologna, 1935-1940), they fill thirty volumes, of which the first four contain the poetry. Although with his critical and editorial work Carducci established for himself a permanent place in Italian culture, his reputation and renown rest primarily on his contribution to Italian poetry. K. McK.

CARE (Cooperative for American Remittances to Everywhere, Inc.), a nonprofit, nonsectarian, U.S. Government-approved agency for voluntary, person-to-person international assistance. Incorporated on Nov. 27, 1945, in Washington, D. C., it assembles needed supplies and delivers them to individuals and institutions abroad as gifts from American individuals or organizations. CARE gifts ranging from food and clothing textiles to educational, agricultural, industrial, and medical and scientific equipment, "to help people help themselves," were adapted to the local needs of war-depleted and underdeveloped countries, and now go to needy families and institutions in Europe, Asia, Latin America, and Africa. CARE also accepts gifts for its Food Crusade, which ships packages made up of U.S. farm surplus foods, and for its large-scale Refugee Aid program all over the free world. Deliveries are made to designated addresses and to those chosen on the basis of greatest need by CARE's American representatives abroad. The donor's name accompanies each gift and donors receive a delivery receipt bearing the name and address of the recipient. Since its inception, CARE aid has totaled more than $210,000,000. Sponsors of CARE are 26 major accredited American service, religious, and civic organizations serving as CARE member agencies. Headquarters are in New York City.

CAREW, RICHARD [kəru'] (1555-1620), English poet and antiquary, was born July 17, 1555, at East Antony, Cornwall. He is noted for his translations from Tasso and Huarte (1594) and for his *Survey of Cornwall* (1602), a delightful description of that region. Carew died on Nov. 6, 1620, at East Antony. W. R.

CAREW, THOMAS [kəru'] (1595-c.1639), English poet, was born in 1595 at West Wickham, Kent. Carew received a bachelor's degree from Oxford University and entered the Middle Temple in 1612. He was subsequently employed as secretary by Sir Dudley Carleton, English ambassador at Venice and The Hague, and in 1619 he went to France with another ambassador, Lord Herbert of Cherbury. Carew became a gentleman of the privy chamber in 1628, later holding the office of sewer, or taster, to Charles I. His masque, *Coelum Britannicum,* was produced by Inigo Jones at Whitehall in 1634, and his portrait was painted by Van Dyck. His *Poems* (1640) is a miscellaneous collection: an elegy on John Donne; ardent, vigorous poems in Donne's manner, a notable example being *A Rapture;* epistles to Ben Jonson and other friends; and songs, such as *Ask Me No More,* which gave Carew a high place among Cavalier lyric poets. The exact date of his death is unknown. M. E.

CAREX [ke'rɛks], a large genus of the sedge family with about 900 species native chiefly to swampy places in temperate regions; about 300 occur in North America. They are grasslike plants, generally less than 3 ft. tall, called sedges, usually with triangular stems and greenish flowers, the staminate and pistillate being usually borne on separate spikes either on the same or different plants. Hay is occasionally made from them but it is harsh and not nutritious. A few are used in the manufacture of grass rugs and some, such as *C. morrowi,* a native of Japan, are grown as ornamental pot plants; *C. intumescens* is cultivated for its stiff, effective foliage. *See also* SEDGE. J. C. Wis.

CAREY, HENRY (c.1687-1743), English poet, dramatist, and musician, was born probably in Yorkshire about 1687, probably the illegitimate son of Henry Savile, Marquis of Halifax. Coming to London about 1713, Carey made a precarious living from his plays, verses, and tunes. Though popular, his productions did not support his increasing family, and he ultimately committed suicide in London on Oct. 4, 1743. Of Carey's farces, parodies, and burlesques the best remembered is *Chrononhotonthologos* (1734), a burlesque of the contemporary theatre. Of his two volumes of verse, he set one, *The Musical Century* (1737), to music. Carey is famous for his ballad *Sally in Our Alley,* celebrating the love of a London apprentice, and for *Namby Pamby,* ridiculing Ambrose Philips. His poetry reveals genuine feeling, patriotism, and humor.　　　　　　　　　　　　T. B. S.

CAREY, HENRY CHARLES (1793-1879), American economist, was born in Philadelphia, Pa., Dec. 15, 1793. In 1814 he entered into partnership with his father, and after a successful career as a bookseller and publisher he retired from active business in 1835. Impressed by the rich resources of America, Carey could not accept the pessimistic implications of Classical economists. He rejected the Malthusian theory of population, criticized severely the Ricardian theory of rent, and was extremely optimistic regarding the economic future of the laboring classes. He was definitely nationalistic in his viewpoint, and advocated a protectionist policy for the United States. His most noted works are *The Principles of Political Economy* (3 vol. 1837-1840); *The Past, the Present, and the Future* (1848); *The Principles of Social Science* (3 vol. 1858-1859); and *The Unity of Law: as Exhibited in the Relations of Physical, Social, Mental and Moral Science* (1872). He died in Philadelphia, Pa., Oct. 13, 1879.　　　J. E. Mo.

CARGO SHIPS. *See* SHIPS, MERCHANT.

CARIA [kɛ'əriə], an ancient country in southwestern Asia Minor, bounded on the south and southwest by the Aegean Sea, on the north by Ionia and Lydia, and on the east by Lycia and Phrygia. The coastline is jagged, consisting of many deep inlets, promontories, and islands, including the islands of Rhodes and Cos. The interior is largely mountainous, though it contains a number of extensive and fertile valleys. Caria was inhabited by the Carians and Caunians, a people with a similar language but of widely differing customs. The latter were considered inferior and were not admitted to the temple of the Carian Zeus at Mylasa, which was open to the Carians, Lydians, and Mysians. According to Herodotus and other Greek writers, the Carians, then called Leleges, originally occupied the Aegean islands and were driven to the mainland by the invading Greeks. As proof of this assertion Thucydides states that over half the bodies found buried on the sacred island of Delos were those of Carians. They were regarded by the Greeks as a warlike race and often served as mercenary troops. The Phoenicians are known to have founded colonies in Caria. Later it was invaded by the Ionians and the Dorians, who settled on the seacoast and drove the Carians into the interior. Caria was incorporated into the kingdom of Lydia by Croesus, and passed under Persian dominion after he was overthrown by Cyrus the Great in 546 B.C. The Persians established native monarchs in Cairia; the best-known of these was Mausolus (died c. 353 B.C.), whose widow, Queen Artemisia, erected the renowned Mausoleum at Halicarnassus. Orontobalis, a Carian ruler of Persian blood, valiantly resisted Alexander the Great when he invaded Asia Minor in 334 B.C. Ada, a native princess who betrayed the city of Alinda into Alexander's hands, was rewarded by being made queen of the Carians. Shortly thereafter the country was absorbed into

the empire of the Seleucidae. Following the defeat of Antiochus III of Syria by the Romans in 190 B.C., Caria was divided between Pergamum and the Rhodians. In 133 B.C., Caria became part of the Roman province of Asia. Its subsequent history is part of that of Asia Minor; it is now included in the Republic of Turkey.　　　C. W. D.

CARIAN [kɛ'əriən], the language of the Carians of Asia Minor, mentioned by Homer and by several other Greek authors. Seventy-six Carian inscriptions are extant, most of them very short and written in a mixed script partly derived from a western Greek alphabet and partly from a syllabary. These inscriptions are more or less legible, but they have not yet been deciphered, and it is certain only that the language is not Indo-European. Most of the inscriptions were found in Egypt and were written by Carian mercenaries in the service of the Pharaoh Psammetichus I (663-609 B.C.) or II (593-588 B.C.).　　　G. B.

CARIB. *See* INDIAN TRIBES, SOUTH AMERICAN.

CARIBBEAN COMMISSION, a body formed to study and, when possible, to improve social and economic conditions in the Caribbean dependencies of Great Britain, the United States, France, and the Netherlands. It resulted from recommendations made in a report of the Royal Commission of Inquiry, set up in 1938. The United States officially accepted membership Mar. 5, 1948, and this was followed by similar action of the other members. The Caribbean Commission, with its affiliated West India Conference, a functioning body which also includes representatives from each of the colonial dependencies of the Commission membership, is possibly the first body of this nature in which, and before which, colonial dependencies can meet and discuss their various problems and needs.

CARIBBEAN SEA [kæ'rɪbi'ən; kərɪ'biən], a small and partly landlocked body of water in the Northern and Western hemispheres, formed by the southwestern extension of the North Atlantic Ocean, enclosed by the West Indian Islands on the north and east, South America and Panama on the south, and Central America on the west. The Channel of Yucatán, between Yucatán and Cuba, connects the Caribbean Sea and the Gulf of Mexico. The total area of the sea is about 750,000 sq. mi. and the coast line is varied and irregular. The western boundary, or east coast of Central America, is a swampy, low-lying region with a dense growth of vegetation and many mosquitoes and other insects, while the coast line of many of the West Indian Islands and parts of South America is cliffed or mountainous. There is a large number of small islets and reefs just off the shore line of the Caribbean. There are also thousands of small indentations of the sea, but the major gulfs and bays are the Gulf of Honduras, Mosquito Gulf (Panama), the Gulf of Darien (Panama and Colombia), the Gulf of Venezuela and its connection with Lake Maracaibo, the Gulf of Paria (Venezuela), the Gulf of Gonaives (Haiti), the Gulf of Guacanayabo (eastern Cuba), and the Gulf of Batabanó (western Cuba). The major passages or channels connecting the Caribbean with the other water bodies are the Channel of Yucatán; the Windward Passage between Cuba and Haiti, which is the major steamship lane between the eastern United States and the Canal Zone; and the Mona Passage between the Dominican Republic and Puerto Rico, which is frequently used by ships plying between Europe and the Panama Canal.

The Caribbean Sea has an average depth of approximately

7,270 ft., but is divided into a northwestern and a southeastern basin by a shallow area, or submarine plateau, that extends from the southern peninsula of Haiti to Jamaica and then to Nicaragua and southeastern Honduras. In places over this submarine plateau the water is less than 500 ft. deep. Most of the larger southern basin, as well as the northern basin, is over 10,000 ft. in depth. There are two known deeps in the Caribbean Sea, both descending 20,000 and 25,000 ft. One deep is immediately south of Grand Cayman Island and the other is between Cuba and Jamaica.

The sea was named after the Carib Indians. It was first explored by Columbus and from the sixteenth to eighteenth centuries was a battle zone for rival European colonial powers, as well as pirates who raided the convoys crossing from South America. When the Panama Canal was built and bananas and sugar became commercially important, the sea became an important route of trade. The Caribbean is sometimes referred to as the "Spanish Main" or "American Mediterranean." The sea is noted for its long periods of fair and calm weather, but from late August through September and October hurricanes cause tremendous waves and much damage.   J. E. F.

CARIBE, or **PIRANHA** [kɑri′be, pɪrɑ′nyə], mostly of the genus *Serrasalmus,* in the family Characinidae, is a ferocious fish of South American rivers. Many species are known and although rather small, the largest being about two feet long, they are fearless and voracious. These tropical pests have strong jaws armed with strong, rather short, but sharp teeth. Although normally feeding on fishes, they quickly cut to pieces any animal unlucky enough to fall into a stream which they inhabit. Blood apparently attracts many to a spot and the victim is torn up and devoured in short order. Many natives have been badly injured and some even killed by these fishes. There is an authentic account of a horse which, fording a stream, was attacked, killed, and torn apart in a short time. In many places fishing by rod and line is impossible, since caribes quickly devour any wounded fish, including one of their own kind.   E. C. R.

CARIBOU [kæ′rɪbu], a reindeer, *Rangifer caribou,* of North America. Wandering erratically in great herds across mountains and rivers, these animals are somewhat larger and much wilder than the reindeer of the Old World. Both sexes bear large, slightly flattened antlers having perhaps as many as 30 points. These antlers are shed each winter. Depending on the species, the bulls are 40 to 60 in. high at the withers, and weigh 200 to 700 lb. Cows are one-third smaller, and their antlers are less impressive. Both have brown summer coats and grayish brown winter ones, and both have a heavy yellowish-white ruff on the neck. The hairs of the fur are coarse and hollow. The large, cleft hoofs spread and help to support the animals in deep snow and spongy ground. Caribou browse on shrubs, herbs, and lichens. *See also* REINDEER.   V. H. C.

CARICATURE [kæ′rɪkətshʊr], exaggeration of the peculiarities of a person in order to create a grotesque or ridiculous effect. The word "caricature" is derived from the Italian *caricare,* "to load," and can be simply defined as overloaded representation. *Caricatura* does not appear as a term until about 1650 in Italy. The ancient Egyptian artist, however, was an inveterate caricaturist, and examples are frequently found in Egyptian papyri caricaturing human beings as animals. Here, as usual in the history of caricature, the art is used as an instrument against authority, its purpose being

generally malicious. The Greeks commonly burlesqued their gods in highly effective satire. There is much caricature in the comic art of Rome, clearly reflected in the humorous

COURTESY OF THE NEW YORK PUBLIC LIBRARY

"William Shakespeare, His Methods of Work" from **The Poet's Corner,** *1904, by Max Beerbohm*

drawings from Pompeii showing the war between the geese and the pigmies.

The Middle Ages reflect caricature in many phases of art, whether in the sculptured details of Romanesque capitals, in the grotesques and gargoyles of Gothic cathedrals, or in the elaborate woodcarvings of choir stalls. As early as 1233 this type of art appears in an English Receipt Roll, and from the fifteenth century on, secular caricature becomes increasingly popular throughout Europe. One of the greatest of the Renaissance caricaturists was Leonardo da Vinci. In the Orient the art of caricature has flourished, most effectively, perhaps, in the work of the Japanese artists Toba Sojo and Mitsunaga in the twelfth century and the Japanese print makers of the Ukiyoyé school of the eighteenth and nineteenth centuries.

In modern times, caricature and the satirical cartoon have become inextricably linked for political, social, economic, or purely humorous purposes. Eighteenth-century England produced one of the greatest of all caricaturists in William Hogarth. In the nineteenth century Honoré Daumier was notable among many in France; in England *Punch* carried outstanding caricatures, perhaps achieving its greatest fame for any single cartoon with Sir John Tenniel's *Dropping the Pilot* of 1890. Aubrey Beardsley and Max Beerbohm produced superb personal caricatures. In America Thomas Nast became the dominant figure in caricature and was famed for his attacks on Tammany Hall, which led to the overthrow of the Tweed ring.

Among the great examples of twentieth-century caricature few can excel the power of *Ecce Homo* by the German satirist, George Grosz, many of whose other bitter caricatures appeared in the German magazines *Fliegende Blätter* and *Simplizissimus.* Florencio Molina Campos has become rather widely known in the United States for his calendar caricatures of gaucho life on the Argentine pampas. Molina Campos is also a fine illustrator in the manner of caricature, as his *Fausto* illustrations published in Buenos Aires in 1942 show. During World War I, undoubtedly the most popular caricaturist was the Scotsman, Bruce Bairnsfather, whose "Old Bill" and "The Better 'Ole" became familiar to every household on the side of the Allies. Leaders in World War II caricature were David Low in England and Bill Mauldin in the United States. Among contemporary American political caricaturists are J. N. ("Ding") Darling of the *Des Moines Register,* Daniel Fitzpatrick of the *St. Louis Post-Dispatch,* and Edmund Duffy of the *Baltimore Sun.* In the nonpolitical field probably no one has more devastatingly caricatured human foibles than James Thurber of the *New Yorker.*   A. F. M.

CARIES. *See* MOUTH DISEASES.

CARILLON [kaʹriʹyɔ́; kæʹrɪlɒn], a series of vari-pitched bells with clappers, customarily hung in a church or munici-

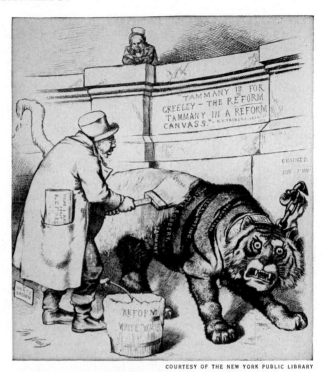

Caricature of Horace Greeley in a cartoon (c. 1872) by Thomas Nast attacking Greeley's support of Tammany Hall

pal tower and played by a manually-operated keyboard or an automatic mechanism. The bells are attuned to intervals of the chromatic scale, many in number and covering four octaves or more. The lowest in tone often weigh several tons; each succeeding bell is smaller and in the highest octaves they range in weight down to about 20 lb. They are hung fixed, except in the largest modern carillons, where some swing. By means of the keyboard the *carillonneur,* or bellmaster, causes their clappers to strike inside their sound bows, and a clockwork mechanism causes a hammer to strike the outside.

The fundamental difference between the carillon and the chime is that the carillon is essentially chromatic in its intervals, while the chime is diatonic. The chromatic scale proceeds by semitones, the diatonic by whole tones. A master of the carillon keyboard not only can play a wide variety of music, but he can interpret it and produce effects beyond the power of any other instrument. Carillons are played by an automatic device at the hour or other periods and by a *carillonneur* in a concert or recital. The device may be thought of as a gigantic music box, or *carillon à cylindre* or *carillon à tambour.* Before the hour strikes, and at certain other intervals, this cylinder or drum is moved by a mechanism of the great tower clock; it plays a few notes or a melody, as arranged. The drum, originally of wood, and now of metal, has rows of holes punched in its wall, and spikes or pegs, called notes, are placed in position by the *carillonneur.* As the cylinder revolves, the peg comes in contact with a tongue which pulls a wire connected with a hammer and lets it fall on the outside of the bell.

Even automatic playing of the carillon has charm, since its notes, coming from a great height, are modified by the currents of air. But when the *carillonneur* plays, as on a giant piano or organ, the music is more effective and the instrument may be called *carillon à clavier.* Each key of the *clavier* is connected by a lever and wire with the clapper of its corresponding bell. In what is known as the Belgian system, perfected by Josef Dendyn of Mechlin (Malines), one of the

DEEDS CARILLON, DAYTON, OHIO

greatest *carillonneurs* of all time, each clapper when at rest is held by a spring and guide wire in an exactly defined position close to the inner soundbow. The bells of the lowest octave and a half are connected also with a pedal clavier, since the larger bells require a forceful stroke to bring out their full tones. It also gives the *carillonneur* greater command of the resources of his instrument, allowing use of both hands and feet.

The Netherlands and Belgium boasted of more than one hundred carillons before World War II. They were chiefly municipally owned and the *carillonneur* was a municipal employee. While the carillons were often used for religious purposes, their prime use was and is for the daily pleasure of the people in their work and play. The carillon was developed some time in the fifteenth century. Today the difference between a carillon and a chime or peel, in number of bells, is that the carillon consists of twenty-three or more bells and a chime of fewer than twenty-three bells. In the past twenty-five years carillons have multiplied in the United States and Canada; they number over sixty in the United States. The Memorial Tower in Ottawa has a carillon of fifty-three bells, the same number that were in the Park Avenue Baptist Church, given as a memorial to his mother by John D. Rockefeller. When the new church was erected on Riverside Drive, the bells were increased to seventy-two, forming the largest carillon in the world. The Bok Singing Tower in Florida has sixty-one bells. The Riverside Church tower has swinging as well as fixed bells, and they were made in Croydon, England. Its bourdon bell, the largest and heaviest tuned bell in the world, weighs 40,926 lb.   W. Li.

CARINA [kərai′nə], the Keel, a long, irregular-shaped constellation, all of which lies south of declination —50°, and is therefore wholly invisible north of 40° N. lat. It extends from right ascension 6 hr. to 11 hr. 20 min. Carina is one of the modern subdivisions of the much larger ancient constellation Argo Navis. This group includes the splendid whitish-yellow star Canopus and is thickly sprinkled with stars of the second, third, and fourth magnitudes, thus making a striking appearance. Carina contains the fine globular cluster N.G.C. 2808. *See also* ARGO NAVIS; CANOPUS.
          J. H. P.

CARINTHIA (Ger. **KÄRNTEN**) [kərı′nthiə, kɛ′rntən], a province of southern Austria with an area of 3,680 sq. mi., bounded on the north by the province of Salzburg, on the east by Styria, on the south by Yugoslavia and Italy, and on the west by the Tirol. The north is very mountainous and has an abundant water-power supply; the south includes the forested Carnic and Karawanken Alps area, with its iron, lead, zinc, and small amounts of coal. Agriculture is mainly confined to the Drava River basin, where cereals and fruit are the leading crops. In the cities of Klagenfurt, Villach, and Spittal, the chief industrial products are machines, cables, matches, coarse woolens, steel, paper, leather, and cement; Klagenfurt, the provincial capital, has a machine-tool industry, first developed during World War II. The population of Carinthia, 474,764 in 1951, is predominantly German, with a small Slovene minority.

Under Augustus, Carinthia formed part of the province of Noricum. After the fall of the Roman Empire it was the nucleus of the Kingdom of Carentania. It was a margravate under Charlemagne and a duchy under Louis the German in 843. In 1335 it was bestowed by Louis the Bavarian on the Hapsburgs, becoming one of their crown lands after 1453. It formed part of the Austrian Empire from 1804 to 1918. In 1920 the province voted overwhelmingly to remain

DRAGON FOUNTAIN AT KLAGENFURT, AUSTRIA

in Austria rather than join Yugoslavia. It was part of Greater Germany in World War II, and after the war was in the British zone of occupation until 1955.   W. O. S.

CARLETON, GUY, BARON DORCHESTER (1724-1808), British soldier and administrator in Canada, was born at Strabane, County Tyrone, Ireland, Sept. 2, 1724. He was commissioned as an officer in the Twenty-fifth Foot at the age of eighteen, and by 1753 had become a lieutenant colonel commanding the Seventy-second Foot, later the Seaforth Highlanders. He sailed for Halifax in 1759 with General James Wolfe, under whom he served in the victorious attack on Quebec made in the same year. After the French ceded their Canadian empire to England in the next year, an act formalized in the Treaty of Paris signed in 1763, Carleton, in 1766, was appointed lieutenant governor, and in 1768 governor, of the Province of Quebec. As governor, he became convinced that the province would remain predominantly French Canadian and, discarding the program of anglicization which had prevailed since 1763, he instituted a policy of conciliation designed to win over the inhabitants to the new British regime. The Quebec Act passed by the House of Lords in 1774, which has been called the "Magna Carta of the French Canadians," expressed this new policy. In accordance with its terms, French Canadians became eligible for official posts; French forms of land law and land tenure were re-established; and the Roman Catholic Church was placed on a regularized basis.

In 1775 and 1776 much of the Province of Quebec was occupied by forces of the American Continental Congress. Carleton, however, was able to defend the city of Quebec until he was relieved in the spring of 1776 by vessels of the British navy. Difficulties for Carleton increased because of a change in colonial secretaries in England, and in 1778 he resigned all of his offices in Canada and returned to England. In 1782, however, he was sent to New York as commander in chief of all the royal forces there, with orders to evacuate all British troops and loyalists. He accomplished this mission by November 1783. Until 1786 he then lived quietly at his home in England; in that year he was created Baron Dorchester and was sent back to Canada as governor of the Province of Quebec. In 1791 he went to England on a two-year leave of absence, returning to Canada in 1793. Together with Chief Justice William Smith, a New York loyalist, Carleton drew up the Constitutional Act of 1791. Shortly thereafter he resigned, for the second time, as governor of Quebec and returned to England, where he died in Stubbings, Maidenhead, Nov. 10, 1808.   J. I. C.

CARLETON COLLEGE, an accredited, coeducational, privately controlled college of arts and sciences, is situated at Northfield, Minn., about 40 mi. south of the twin cities of Minneapolis and St. Paul. The college occupies 905 acres which include a farm of 419 acres and an arboretum of 360 acres. Carleton was founded as Northfield College in 1866 by a board of trustees nominated by the Minnesota Conference of Congregational Churches; instruction began in 1867. In 1872 the present name was adopted to honor William Carleton, an early benefactor. Affiliations were established with the Baptist Church in 1916 and with the Protestant Episcopal Church in 1923.

Carleton offers strong preparation in the humanities, in science, and in the social sciences. The A.B. degree is conferred, and all requirements for certification for high-school teaching can be met. Large gifts have been received to further studies in international relations and religious and spiritual education. Recent developments at Carleton include the introduction of comprehensive examinations in the major subjects of all seniors and individually adjusted programs of study for candidates seeking honors in a concentrated field.

The $1,500,000 library, dedicated in May 1956, contains the special collections of James E. Parker relating to international peace and of the Frank B. Kellogg Foundation of International Relations. Generous scholarship and student loan aid is available both to foreign and U. S. students. Students must live in dormitories unless they are living at home, and nonresident students are required to take one meal daily at college. *For statistics see* COLLEGES AND UNIVERSITIES.

CARLETON PLACE, a town in Lanark Co., Ontario, Canada, on the Mississippi River (not the same as the famed Mississippi River of the United States), 35 mi. southwest of Ottawa. It is a junction point on the Canadian Pacific Railway and is served by three provincial highways. It was incorporated as a town in 1890. Factories in Carleton Place produce woolen goods, stoves, electric ranges, and builders' supplies. The Mississippi Lakes which lie just above the town are favorite resorts for boating and fishing. Pop. 1956, 4,790.   D. F. P.

CARLISLE, JOHN GRIFFIN (1835-1910), American legislator, was born in Kenton Co., Kentucky, on Sept. 5, 1835. After obtaining a public school education, he studied law, was admitted to the bar at Covington, Ky., in 1858, and at twenty-four was elected to the Kentucky legislature, where he served in the lower house, 1859-1861, and in the upper house, 1866-1869. He was instrumental in keeping Kentucky from seceding during the Civil War. He was elected lieutenant-governor of Kentucky by the Democrats for the term 1871-1875, and to the United States House of Representatives in 1876; and in 1890, after serving six terms in the House, during which he was speaker for six years (1883-1889), he was elected to the Senate. In 1893, President Grover Cleveland appointed him secretary of the treasury. Carlisle supported a low tariff, and, during the 1896 presidential campaign, advocated "sound money" in opposition to the free-silver program of the Democratic nominee, William Jennings Bryan. In 1897, after the defeat of the Democrats, Carlisle went to New York City, where he practiced law until his death, July 31, 1910.   D. R.

CARLISLE [kɑrlai′l], a city, municipal and parliamentary borough, and county town of Cumberland, England, situated 299 mi. northwest of London, in an industrial district, near the joining of the Eden and Calder rivers. It is the chief railroad center near the Scottish border. It was the British *Caer Luel* and the Roman *Luguvallium*. As Luel, it is first mentioned in 685. In the ninth century the Danes destroyed it, and in 1092 William Rufus re-established it and built the castle as defense against the Scots. In 1566 Queen Elizabeth incorporated Carlisle, and in 1638 Charles I made it a city. Industries include lithography, iron working, brewing, tanning, and the manufacture of machinery, locomotives, and railroad cars. Pop. 1952, 67,900.

CARLISLE, a borough and the county seat of Cumberland Co., in southeast Pennsylvania, situated about 18 mi. southwest of Harrisburg. Carlisle was founded in 1751,

On South Street in Carlisle, Pennsylvania, is the grave of "Molly Pitcher" (Mary McCauley), American Revolutionary heroine who earned her nickname by carrying water to the soldiers at the Battle of Monmouth, June 28, 1778.

incorporated as a borough in 1782 and it now has the borough-manager type of government. During the French and Indian, and the Revolutionary wars, Carlisle became identified with many historic events. In 1757 General John Forbes marched from Carlisle to capture Ft. Duquesne (Pittsburgh), and in 1763 from the same city Colonel Henry Bouquet led two expeditions which crushed Pontiac's conspiracy. Carlisle Barracks, the oldest military post in the United States, was active during both wars, and from 1879 to 1918 it was the Carlisle Indian School. Later it became a United States Army medical field service school and has more recently been designated the Army War College. Molly Pitcher, who won fame for her heroic participation in the Battle of Monmouth in 1778 during the Revolutionary War, was a resident of Carlisle and is buried in the Old Grave Yard, where a monument was erected to her in 1876. Another site of historical interest is the old guardhouse built by the Hessian prisoners in 1777. During the Civil War, Carlisle was the most northern point reached by the Confederates, who occupied it for three days. It was then occupied by Union troops, when it was bombarded by the Confederates, who also set fire to the town. Carlisle is the seat of Dickinson College, founded in 1773. Transportation is supplied by the Pennsylvania and Reading railroads. The principal industries include the manufacture of carpets and rugs, ribbons, inner tubes, railroad track equipment, knitting yarns, radio parts, and textiles. Pop. 1950, 16,812.

CARLISLE CATHEDRAL, seat of the diocese of Carlisle, Cumberland, England, was formerly the church of a priory of the Augustinian canons, founded in 1102. The edifice was made the seat of a bishopric by Henry I in 1133. The choir, burned in 1292, was not replaced until about 1377. After a second fire in 1392, the central tower, 110 ft. high, and the north transept were rebuilt. The cathedral again was badly damaged during the Civil War, at which time a portion of the nave was pulled down to repair the fortifications of the town. Thus only two Norman bays remain. The structure, 204 ft. long and 121 ft. wide at the transepts, is the smallest cathedral in England. The choir has a large eastern window, 58 ft. high and 32 ft. broad, but only the upper portion is of ancient glass. The south transept contains a runic inscription. The eastern end presents a fine composition and the exterior sculptures are likewise good.   R. Ne.

CARLIST WARS, an intermittent series of campaigns in support of the following claimants to the Spanish throne: Don Carlos (1788-1855), his son Carlos (1818-1861), the latter's brother Juan (1822-1887), and his son Carlos (1848-1909). The basis of the claim was the Salic law which denied the rights of Isabella II, daughter of Ferdinand VII. Supporting the Carlists were the clerical party (*los apostólicos*) and the peasants of northern and eastern Spain. Victories in battle and the weaknesses of their opponents gave the Carlists many opportunities for success. But the claimants lacked adequate qualities of leadership. The greatest gains were made in 1873-1874. The armies of Alfonso XII crushed this last appeal to arms in 1876, although there were threats of trouble in 1885 and in 1902.   J. J. Van N.

CARLOVINGIAN DYNASTY. *See* CAROLINGIAN DYNASTY.

CARLOW [kɑ'rlo], a county in southeastern Eire, one of the few Irish counties with a large percentage of its area in cultivation. The region along the western boundary contains coal seams of the Leinster coal fields. The county has a small amount of rainfall and a large amount of sunshine in comparison with the bleak Galway and Mayo coasts to the west. Its towns are small and of little importance. It is enclosed by the Barrow and Slaney valleys and the Kilkenny Hills. Pop. 1951, 34,162.   S. Van V.

CARLSBAD. *See* KARLOVY VARY.

CARLSBAD [kɑ'rlzbæd], a city in southeastern New Mexico, the county seat of Eddy Co., located on the Pecos River, about 70 mi. southeast of Roswell. It is served by the Atchison, Topeka and Santa Fe Railway. Called Eddy originally, the city became Carlsbad in 1899, and was in-

corporated in 1918. The city is the center of an extensive potash region and is the gateway to Carlsbad Caverns National Park, 20 mi. southwest of the city. The surrounding, irrigated farm district produces livestock, cotton, alfalfa, corn, grain, sorghums, and truck crops. Pop. 1950, 17,975.

CARLSBAD CAVERNS NATIONAL PARK, a park approximately thirty miles southwest of Carlsbad, New Mexico, containing the largest explored series of underground caves in the world. These caves, the Carlsbad Caverns, were discovered in 1901 by Jim White, a cowboy. Reports of their size and beauty resulted in further exploration by government representatives in 1923 and 1924. Carlsbad Cave National Monument, with an area of 720 acres, was established by presidential proclamation on Oct. 25, 1923. Congress, by act of May 14, 1930, designated the area as Carlsbad Caverns National Park.

The caverns were formed by the action of water penetrating massive limestone formations. Myriads of beautifully sculptured, variously ornamented spires, known as stalactites, hang from the ceilings. Some are huge, some delicate growths resembling plant structures. Grotesque stalagmites rise from the floor. Some stalactites and stalagmites have joined to form great columns. The principal chamber, called the Big Room, 4,000 ft. long, 625 ft. wide, and 300 ft. high, contains Giant Dome, a stalagmite sixty million years old. Other scenic chambers in natural sequence are the King's Palace, Queen's Chamber, and Papoose's Chamber. Each evening during the summer months millions of bats fly through the entrance arch from a part of the caverns 180 ft. below the surface, causing a "smoke" of two or three hours' duration. They return before dawn, having consumed an estimated 11½ tons of insects nightly. The caverns are lighted by an ingenious electrical illumination system, artfully concealed behind rocks. Seven miles of trails had in 1946 been opened to visitors, whose numbers had reached 300,000 annually. Although over 37 mi. of underground caverns at three levels had been explored in 1946, their full extent was still unknown. Surface area of the park was extended to 49,568 acres on Feb. 3, 1939, thereby including other caves rich in decorative deposits and in archaeological remains which date back four thousand years. *See illustration on following page.*   A. Po.

CARLSBAD DECREES, the resolutions adopted by the ministers of the nine leading German states at a meeting called at Carlsbad, Germany, Aug. 6-31, 1819, by Austrian Foreign Minister Metternich, who had been created a hereditary Austrian prince three years earlier. Metternich, brought up in the courts of the Rhine electorates, where his father was ambassador, had witnessed in his late teens several acts of violence on the part of French revolutionaries. These incidents, perhaps more than anything else, provided the foundation for his strongly reactionary attitudes, which in turn led him to call the meeting of 1819, the purpose of which was to pass legislation curbing revolutionary activities. Anxious to take advantage of the murder of August von Kotzebue, a German writer and dramatist who, only a short time before, had been stabbed to death by a university student for ridiculing the *Burschenschaft* (Students' Union) movement, Metternich planned to enforce a system for suppressing Liberalism in Germany.

Originally intended to cover a five-year period, the Carlsbad Decrees were renewed many times and remained in force for nearly a generation. Although they included strict censorship of political opinion and of the press, they were

The Carlsbad Caverns, New Mexico, set aside as a National Monument in 1923, are spectacular underground wonders noted for their beauty of formations and color and a vast variety of stalagmites and stalactites.

directed chiefly at the universities. They provided for the suppression of the gymnastic societies founded by Friedrich Jahn, the "Father of Gymnastics," and the appointment at each university of a special officer to supervise instruction and to report on the conduct of students and professors alike. These officials were required, under the provisions of the Carlsbad Decrees, to turn in regular reports and to make special note of any deviation from the established doctrines. Students and instructors dismissed from one university were not permitted to enroll at another. The *Burschenschaft* was abolished and prohibitions were set up concerning its re-establishment. Johann Fichte's *Reden an die deutsche Nation* (1808), famous patriotic lectures, were forbidden re-publication; Ernst Arndt, German patriot and author, was dismissed from his professorship at the University of Bonn in 1820, and Friedrich Jahn, who had been of great service in training and drilling the youth of Germany for the struggle against Napoleon, was imprisoned for six years. The federal commission established at Carlsbad to study discontent and suppress organized plots tried 161 Germans and acquitted 44.

R. H. L.

CARLSRUHE. *See* Karlsruhe.

CARLSTADT, an industrial borough overlooking the Hackensack River in Bergen Co., northeastern New Jersey, is situated 5 mi. southeast of Passaic and 8 mi. west of New York City. The townsite was bought in the 1840's on a co-operative basis by a group of German exiles, liberals, and freethinkers who were seeking political liberty. It was first known as Tailor Town because many of the inhabitants worked for New York tailors, but it was later renamed in honor of the group's leader. Carlstadt was incorporated as a borough in 1894 and has the mayor-council form of government. The local industries include the manufacture of chemicals, textile piece-dyeing, and textbook printing. Transportation is supplied by the New Jersey and New York Railroad. Pop. 1950, 5,591.

CARLYLE, THOMAS (1795-1881), Scottish essayist, historian, and moralist, was born Dec. 4, 1795, in Ecclefechan, Scotland. From his father, James, an uneducated stone-mason and farmer, he received indelible convictions concerning the power of decisive religiousness and the importance of work; he also absorbed his father's admiration for intellectual force, his belief in authority, and his feeling that poetry and fiction, as opposed to more solid writings, were idle diversions. These convictions, reinforced by his wide reading, became fundamental principles in his books. From his father, too, he received the gift of vivid expression which, shaped by the study of German, made him one of the powerful, although eccentric, stylists of his century. His mother, Janet Carlyle, who was not able to read or write until she learned to do so in order to write to her son, also exerted a strong moral influence on him.

Carlyle received his early education in Ecclefechan and at Annan Academy. In 1809 he entered Edinburgh University, where he planned to study for the ministry; instead, he took a degree in mathematics and taught for the next several years, from 1814 to 1818, first at Annan Academy and then at Kirkcaldy. In 1818 he returned to Edinburgh to study law but gave more attention to German, history, and philosophy. Finally, in 1820, after abandoning all thought of the ministry, law, mathematics, or teaching as a means of livelihood, and giving up the idea of emigration, he resolved to earn his living by writing.

During the next fifteen years Carlyle served his literary apprenticeship. For a time he tutored and did hack work, but in 1824 he published a life of Schiller and translations of Adrien Legendre's *Geometry* and Goethe's *Wilhelm Meister*. In 1826 he married Jane Welsh, whom he had met through Edward Irving, and settled in Edinburgh, supporting himself by contributions to the *Edinburgh Review* and other magazines. In 1828 poor health and financial necessity caused him to remove to Craigenputtock, his wife's farm, and there he lived until 1834, writing occasionally for magazines but working mainly on his *Sartor Resartus*. In 1834, his long apprenticeship ended, Carlyle settled permanently in London with his wife at No. 5 Cheyne Row, where he produced a stream of books, essays, conversations, and letters which was rarely interrupted save for holiday trips to Scotland, two visits to Germany in 1852 and 1858, the Lord Rectorship of Edinburgh University (1865-1866), which did not require residence, and the death of his wife in 1866.

Sartor Resartus, the first work by Carlyle to gain much notice, was published in *Fraser's Magazine* in 1833 and 1834 and as a book in America in 1836 and in London in 1837. Herein appears in substance the basis of Carlyle's philosophy, that the modern world was out of joint because it had adopted the methods of scientific rationalism to solve its problems instead of revivifying spiritual truth. Also in 1837 appeared his *French Revolution,* an epical treatment of the fall of a decadent French aristocracy which had lost the power of leadership and was unable to save itself by granting needed reforms to the people.

In the meantime the Chartist movement, an agitation on the part of the masses for popular rights, was reducing the English ruling classes to terror. Carlyle, in *Chartism* (1839), urged the aristocrats to profit by the lessons of the French Revolution and to give the masses the wise leadership that was needed to restore prosperity and tranquillity. He enlarged upon this theme of leadership in *On Heroes, Hero Worship, and the Heroic in History* (1841), where he attempted to show that leadership should rest in the hands of heroes who are leaders by virtue of superior spiritual insight, and that the masses, unless misled by false heroes, are willing and contented to be governed by their superiors.

To this theme, by now an obsession with him, he returned in 1843 in *Past and Present.* Here he showed how a new, strong abbot had brought order into a twelfth-century monastery, which had fallen into anarchy during the weak leadership of an old monk, by eradicating immorality, clearing it of debt, and gaining for it new privileges and liberties. In like manner, he said, the moral and social deterioration of England could be remedied only by a wise, strong ruling class that was spiritually qualified to rule. The existing emphasis on temporal things—power for its own sake, money, pleasure, reform by law, popular suffrage, popular education, trust in machines—would have to give way to an emphasis on the eternal principles of obedience, reverence, veracity, sacrifice, the sacredness of work, the obligations of duty, and the eternal rightness of God-inspired authority.

Most of the subsequent books by Carlyle were attempts to show specifically that such leadership as he advocated was

Thomas Carlyle, Scottish essayist, historian, and philosopher

practical. *Oliver Cromwell* (1845) is a striking portrait of a strong leader in seventeenth-century England; *Latter Day Pamphlets* (1850) is a series of definite proposals for remedying specific social ills; *The Life of John Sterling* (1851) is the biography of a man who illustrated perfect veracity; and *Frederick the Great* (1858-1865) is an idealized portrait of a hero-king.

Carlyle died without issue on Feb. 4, 1881, in London. Within a few months of his death appeared what some critics think to be his finest book, *Reminiscences,* a series of vivid portraits of his wife, his father, and his friends Edward Irving and Lord Jeffrey, as well as sketches of Southey and Wordsworth. In later life, after fame had come to him, Carlyle consistently refused most of the honors offered him, among which were an English title and a pension. He did, however, in 1872, accept the Prussian Order of Merit established by Frederick the Great, and in 1875 he received an honorary degree from Harvard University. He is buried in Ecclefechan beside his parents.　　　N. MacM.

CARMARTHEN [karma'rthən], a municipal borough and the county town of Carmarthenshire, Wales, on the Towy River, about 80 mi. northwest of Cardiff. It is a railroad and highway center in a rural area. The castle, long a ruin, is on the site of the Roman station known as Maridunum. After the Romans departed Carmarthen was the center of activity of the south Wales chieftains. When the Normans invaded Carmarthen in 1123, they erected a castle, and the community was the subject of continuous attacks from the hills, which persisted throughout the Middle Ages. The castle and church, built in the twelfth century, were the nucleus of the medieval town which occupied a key position on the north-south roads. In the Middle Ages the town became renowned for its wool trade. On the east

Newcastle-in-Emlyn, Carmarthenshire, as seen from Carmarthen on the Towy River

side of the town was located the Benedictine priory noted for the *Black Book of Carmarthen,* and on the west side of the town were the Black Friars. In 1451 the first recorded eisteddfod, an assembly of Welsh bards and literati at which there are contests and prizes for poetry, prose, music, and art, was held at Carmarthen. The town's position at the highest navigable point of the Towy River stimulated its development after the sixteenth century as a river port. It became the region's social center as well as its printing and literary center. In 1747 the first iron-smelting works were established in the town, continuing as an important factor in its economic life until 1900. With the development of the Welsh seacoast and the advent of the industrial revolution the town declined. The revival of the eisteddfod in the nineteenth century again made Carmarthen the literary center of South Wales. Pop. 1952, 11,910.

CARMARTHENSHIRE [kərmɑ'rthənshir], a county of South Wales, bounded by the counties of Pembroke on the west, Cardigan on the southeast, Brecknock on the east, and Glamorgan on the southeast, and by Carmarthen Bay, an inlet of Bristol Channel, on the south. It is the largest county of Wales, with an area of 919.5 sq. mi. The hilly surface, rising to almost 2,500 ft. in the east, is dissected by the south-flowing Taff and Towy rivers, which merge into Carmarthen Bay; the Teifa River, flowing westward, separates Carmarthen and Cardigan counties.

Cattle and sheep are grazed on the highlands, and the county is rich in minerals, particularly coal, lead, tin, and copper. The county's largest town, Llanelly, has steel mills and chemical factories and, with nearby Burry Port, ships much of the county's coal.

The region of Carmarthenshire was occupied by the Romans, who had an outpost at Maridunum (Carmarthen). The Welsh princes dominated the region in the early medieval period, yielding the urban centers to the aggressive Normans in the twelfth century, and under Edward I the county was formed, although not with its present borders. The county was the center of a successful outbreak in 1847 against the imposition of tolls on public roads; the movement, taking its name from a passage in Genesis (xxiv:60), with leaders calling themselves "Rebeccas," became known as the Rebecca Riots. Pop. 1952, 170,700.   E. A.

CARMEL, a residential community and art center on the Pacific shore of Monterey Co., Calif., about 130 mi. south of San Francisco. It was chartered as a village in 1916 and is governed by a mayor and council. The settlement dates back to 1771, when Father Junípero Serra founded the Mission of San Carlos Borromeo de Carmel. The building still stands, and the natural beauty and seclusion of the site has drawn many artists and writers. Carmel has no cemetery, no jail, and no industry except handicrafts. However, it has many shops. The nearest railroad is six miles away, but adequate bus service from the village is provided. Carmel has several Little Theatre groups and is credited with the first open-air theatre in California. It has also had a yearly Shakespeare Festival since 1926. The Bach Festival is held annually in July. Pop. 1950, 4,351.

CARMEL, MOUNT, 1,932 ft. high, the northwestern spur of the Judean Hills in Israel, extending almost to the Mediterranean Sea at the Bay of Acre. The low ridge is composed of limestone and separates the Plain of Sharon from the Plain of Esdraelon. The city of Haifa is located at the foot of Mount Carmel, which is reputed to be the place where Elijah was confronted by fire in his contest with the prophets of Baal.

CARMELITES [kɑ'rmələits], members of a Roman Catholic religious order of four chief divisions, stemming from a common and much disputed origin. (1) The Order of Friars of the Blessed Virgin Mary of Mount Carmel (Carmelites, O. Carm.) traditionally ascribed its foundation to Elias. This attribution was acrimoniously debated, the disputants being silenced in 1698 by the Holy See. After migrating from Palestine to Europe, the order was approved in 1226, and under St. Simon Stock, general from 1247 to 1265, it shifted the emphasis from the solitary to communal life. The order spread rapidly, its general chapters uniting from 500 to 1,000 delegates. Irregularities not peculiar to the Carmelites, stemming from four sources (permanency of superiors, private property, acceptance of honors, and numerous small houses), occasioned a *chronique scandaleuse*. The accusations were of slight importance, in view of the average fifteenth-century membership of 20,000 friars, and they resulted in reform, notably that of Blessed John Soreth, general from 1451 to 1471. Of some 2,000 professed Carmelites, about 250 are in the United States. (2) The Order of Discalced (barefoot) Carmelite Friars sprang from the reform undertaken by St. Teresa and St. John of the Cross and stimulated a real rebirth of mystic theology. The order has about 3,000 members, with about 150 in the United States. (3) The Second Order of Carmelite Nuns, founded by St. Teresa, is famous for the extreme austerity of the life professed in its nunneries (Carmels), which are juridically independent units. There are some 35 convents in the United States, with some 475 professed members. (4) The Third Order, besides secular tertiaries, includes several groups of tertiaries regular, living in community and engaged in apostolic activities.   N. J. T.

CARMEN [kɑ'rme'n], the best-known of Prosper Mérimée's *nouvelles* (novelettes), appeared in 1845 in *La Revue des deux mondes* and was published in book form in 1847. The story portrays the gradual demoralization and downfall of a young Spanish-Basque corporal, José Navarro, when subjected to the wiles, passion, and cool viciousness of the gypsy cigarette-girl Carmen. With the inevitability of classical tragedy, José degenerates from an honorable but naïve soldier to smuggler, to highwayman, to murderer, in order to keep the love of the fickle girl. At last, tired of killing her lovers, he stabs her to death in fulfilment of a destiny which she had predicted, but fatalistically had made no effort to avoid. The story, though exceedingly violent and exotic in background, is related in a sober, concise style and with realistic detail.

The novelette served as basis for Georges Bizet's opera *Carmen,* first produced at the Opéra Comique in Paris in 1875 with libretto by Henri Meilhac and Ludovic Halévy.

R. A. P.

CARMEN, an opera in four acts by Georges Bizet with a libretto by Henri Meilhac and Ludovic Halévy based on the novel by Prosper Mérimée. It was first performed in Paris, Mar. 3, 1875, not long before Bizet's death. *Carmen* was not a success at first because, absurd though this charge may seem today, its sustained melodic line was accused of being Wagnerian. Actually, the vividness and clarity of the orchestration is French, some of the rhythms are superficially Spanish, and the general effect is closer to the folk music of southern France than to anything else. But this was all new and shocking in the Opéra Comique in 1875, and the work's present popularity was very gradually acquired. When Nietzsche turned his back on Wagner after years of veneration of the Wagnerian ideals, it was to the warmth and brightness of Bizet's *Carmen* that he looked to replace the chill of Wagner's misty North.

S. C.

CARMICHAEL, LEONARD (1898-   ), American psychologist, was born in Philadelphia on Nov. 9, 1898. He was educated at the Germantown Friends School and Tufts College, where, in 1923, he began his teaching career. In 1924 he received a Ph.D. from Harvard and did graduate work at the University of Berlin. Returning to the United States, he became an instructor of psychology in 1924 and an assistant professor in 1926 at Princeton University. In 1927, he joined the faculty of Brown University as an associate professor of psychology and, in 1928, was promoted to the rank of full professor in the same subject, a chair he held until 1936, when he became chairman of the department of psychology and dean of the faculty of arts and sciences at Rochester University. Two years later he returned to Tufts to act as president of the college and as director of the laboratory of sensory psychology and physiology. He was also a visiting professor at Harvard, Radcliffe, and other universities. During World War II, Carmichael held a number of public offices, including membership in an emergency committee in psychology for the National Research Council (1940), in a committee on selection and training of aircraft pilots, and in a committee on service personnel, selection, and training. He was chairman of the council's division of anthropology and psychology (1941-1945). On April 9, 1952, he resigned from the presidency of Tufts College to accept an appointment as secretary of the Smithsonian Institution in Washington, D.C. Carmichael acted as co-operating editor of the *Psychological Index* (1931-1936). He was the co-author of many studies and textbooks, and joint editor (with Leonard C. Mead) of *The Selection of Military Manpower* (1952).

D. R.

CARMONA, ANTONIO OSCAR DE FRAGOSO [kərmo'nə] (1869-1951), Portuguese general, was born in Lisbon, Nov. 24, 1869. He graduated from the Military College in Lisbon in 1888 and at once entered the army. His military training and experience earned him a general's insignia in 1922. In the following year he was appointed minister of war. Together with General da Costa, Carmona led the revolt of 1926 and was appointed minister of foreign affairs. A *coup d'état* on July 9, 1926, removed da Costa and placed Carmona in supreme power. He was president of the Council of Ministers; then under a revised constitution he was officially elected to the presidency in 1928 and continued to rule as a constitutional dictator. The change to a corporative state in 1933 marked the transfer of authority to Prime Minister Antonio de Oliveira Salazar. Carmona was re-elected to the presidency for seven-year terms in 1935, 1942, and 1949. He died in Lisbon on Apr. 18, 1951.

J. J. Van N.

CARNAC [ka'rna'k], the site of prehistoric alignments of upright megalithic blocks in Morbihan, France. The alignments, which extend for nearly two miles in an approximately east-west direction, vary in composition from ten to thirteen rows and fall into three groups interrupted by gaps in which the stones diminish in numbers and height. Many of the larger uprights are from eleven to thirteen feet in height. Associated with the alignments, of which other examples occur close by at Erdeven, are a number of burial sites, and the whole Carnac area abounds in megalithic structures of various kinds. Although the precise purpose of the alignments is obscure, there is no doubt that they relate to the megalithic cult which had spread widely in Atlantic Europe by 2000 B.C. *See also* MEGALITHIC MONUMENTS.

J. G. D. C.

CARNARVON, GEORGE EDWARD STANHOPE MOLYNEUX HERBERT, 5TH EARL OF [karna'r-vən] (1866-1923), British Egyptologist and collector of antiquities, was born at Highclere, Hampshire, June 26, 1866. He

George Edward Stanhope Molyneux Herbert, Earl of Carnarvon, British Egyptologist, sponsor for the opening of the tomb of Tutankhamen in the Valley of the Kings

INTERNATIONAL NEWS PHOTO

was educated at Eton and at Trinity College, Cambridge, and succeeded his father, the fourth earl, in 1890. He was a sportsman, a big-game hunter, turf enthusiast, and collector of rare items. When the British Egyptologist Sir Ernest Budge suggested that he take up the study of Egyptology, he made the acquaintance of the archaeologist Howard Carter, and in 1906 they began excavations in Egypt near Thebes and Der el-Bahari. There they discovered tombs of kings of the XII and XVIII Egyptian dynasties, which Carnarvon described in an account published in 1912, *Five Years' Explorations at Thebes.*

World War I put an end to these excavations, but they were resumed shortly thereafter. In November 1922 Carnarvon and Carter discovered, so concealed by fallen debris that it had never been touched by grave robbers, the tomb of Tutankhamen, the Amarnaage pharaoh of the fourteenth century B.C. The sepulcher chamber itself was opened in February 1923, and the sarcophagus was found in January 1924. So spectacular and costly were the items thus brought to light that magazines and newspapers everywhere gave much space to the work. The general public became aware, as perhaps through no other discovery, of the immense value to be derived from understanding the past.

Through all these years Lord Carnarvon was acquiring a priceless selection of Egyptian antiquities which were frequently on display at the best exhibitions. He died, however, without living to see some of the best results of his most famous discovery. An insect bite, presumably that of a mosquito, became infected; blood poisoning and pneumonia set in, and he died in Cairo on Apr. 5, 1923. Among the prolific writings on this discovery may be mentioned *The Tomb of Tut-ankh-amen* by Howard Carter (1923) and *Tutankhamen, and the Discovery of His Tomb* by Grafton Elliott Smith (1923).   G. D. Y.

CARNARVONSHIRE or CAERNARVONSHIRE

[karna'rvənshır], a maritime county in North Wales, bounded by the Irish Sea on the north, the Menai Strait, which separates it from the county of Anglesey, on the west, Cardigan Bay on the south, and the counties of Denbighshire and Merionethshire on the east. Carnarvonshire covers an area of 569 sq. mi. The surface is mountainous, and Snowdon, with an elevation of 3,560 ft., the highest peak in Wales and England, is in the eastern part of the county. The Conway River is on the eastern boundary. Lead, zinc, and ocher are mined and granite is quarried, but slate is the principal product. The Lleyn Peninsula in the southwest is 24 mi. long and 5 to 10 mi. wide. On Tre'r Ceiri, 1,591 ft. high, one of the triple peaks of The Rivals, is a fortified village built during the Iron Age of Wales. Carnarvon, the county town, near the southwestern end of the Menai Strait, has preserved almost all of its own town walls. There are slate quarries near Bethesda, Nantille, and Llanberis. The scenery near Bettws-y-coed is a tourist attraction. The University College of North Wales is at Bangor, at the north mouth of the Menai Strait. At Conway is a famous castle begun in 1285 during the reign of Edward I. Llandudno is a popular seaside resort. The county returns one member to Parliament. Pop. 1952, 122,500.

CARNATIC, THE

[karnæ'tık], a large section of southeast India, variously defined, including the southern part of Madras State. Its northern boundary region extends as far as the Guntur District, north of 16° N. lat., and its southern boundary is Cape Comorin, the southernmost tip of India. The region is bounded on the east by the Bay of Bengal, on the southwest by the crest of the Cardamom Hills, and on the northwest by the eastern edge of the Deccan Plateau near the Mysore boundary line. The Carnatic is about 500 mi. long from northeast to southwest and is approximately 210 mi. wide at its widest point, at about 11° N. lat.

The Carnatic is subdivided into a northern, a central, and a southern district. The northern boundary of the central district is the Penner River; its southern boundary is the Coleroon River, the major distributary of the Cauvery River. The Carnatic region may be subdivided into two general physical regions. On the east is the low, almost sea-level coastal plain, composed of unconsolidated sediments and alluvial material deposited by large rivers such as the Pallar, the Cheyair, the Ponnaiyar and the Cauvery. The coastal plain has a few low, flat-topped hills and some small but steep granite hills. The western part of the Carnatic region is composed of a hilly belt, most of which is between 500 and 2,000 ft. above sea level and, in some places on the eastern flanks of the Cardamom Hills, above 2,000 ft.

The climate varies, but in general the whole area has a high year-round temperature of from 76° F., in the coldest month, January, to about 90° F. average in July. The average annual rainfall for most of the Carnatic occurs in winter and is between 30 and 50 in. One area, just north of Cape Calimere, receives between 50 and 100 in., while another section just southwest of Cape Calimere receives only 10 to 30 in. of rainfall.

The Carnatic produces rice, cotton, sugar cane, coffee, tobacco, and peanuts, and, along the coast, coconuts. Because of the variation in amount of rainfall, irrigation is needed to ensure the crops, and the Cauvery River irrigation system is one of the largest in the area. Teak grows in the forest and is the most valuable wood of the region. There is some coal and iron in the area, and gold is mined in Mysore, just west of the Carnatic region.

The major cities of the Carnatic region are Nellore; Madras, the largest and a major port; Conjeeveram; Chingleput; Pondichéry, a port; Cuddalore; Salem; Coimbatore; Trichinopoly; Tanjore; Kumbakonam; Mayavaram; Tranquebar, a port; Karikal, a port; Negapatam, a port; Madura; Dhanushkodi, a port for Ceylon trade; Tuticorin, a port; and Tinnevelly. The rail network is adequate, and two lines connect the east and west coasts across the Carnatic. The region is densely populated by Tamils, a people whose civilization and history started considerably before the Christian Era. The three ancient Tamil kingdoms were Pandya, Chola, and Kerula, and there were many small, independent, and semi-independent kingdoms. The Chola Kingdom flourished in the fourth century B.C. and even carried on trade with the Romans. There were many struggles for power and control of the Carnatic region, and until 1801, when the British defeated Haidar Ali, Mohammedan prince who ruled Mysore, its history had been one of frequent wars and battles.

CARNATION

Dianthus caryophyllus, a member of the pink family, a perennial native to southern Europe, sometimes also called clove-pink because of its spicy fragrance. For over 2,000 years it has been popular in gardens. It hybridizes easily, and in the sixteenth century European gardeners produced many varieties, some of which were the forerunners of the present type. The perpetual flowering form is the one grown extensively in America for winter bloom. This was developed in France after 1840 but was not brought to America for almost thirty years. Frederick Dorner and other American florists made thousands of crosses which after twenty years produced great range of color (white, pink, red, yellow, and striped), easy growing habits, free blooming, and wide adaptability to commercial purposes. Size of flowers and strength of stem were among the improvements; some flowers are 4 in. across. The carnation ranks in America as a flower of great commercial value, second only to the rose. In 1891 the American Carnation Society was organized. Millions of plants are grown annually from cuttings. They are rooted in sand in winter, planted outdoors in summer, and when cool weather approaches, they are transferred to greenhouses. Flowering usually begins early in the autumn and continues until May or June of the following year. In Europe carnations are less popular in greenhouses but are more widely grown as outdoor flowers. Two types of carnations, Chaband and Marguerite carnations, which are largely grown as garden annuals, are low, intensely fragrant and long blooming, with many flowers on a stem and a wide range of color

J. C. Wis.

CARNEADES [kɑrni'ədiz] (c.214-129 B.C.), Greek philosopher, the founder of the New Academy, and an able skeptical opponent of the Stoics, was born at Cyrene. He studied with Diogenes the Stoic, and in 155 accompanied him and Critolaus the Peripatetic to Rome on a political mission. So great was the enthusiasm for speculation that he aroused among the Roman youth that Cato the Elder insisted upon his banishment from the city.

Carneades taught that neither sensation nor reason furnishes a criterion of truths, that there is no infallible distinction between a true and a mistaken idea. Some ideas, however, are more probable than others, and this fact saves skepticism from denying the possibility of reasonable conduct. Carneades' interest in morality is also seen in his attack on the Stoic doctrine of fate, for he argued that the denial of free will makes morality meaningless. His writings have not been preserved, and Cicero is our chief source of information.

G. H. Cl.

CARNEGIE, ANDREW (1835-1919), American industrialist and philanthropist, was born in Dunfermline, Scotland, Nov. 25, 1835. After the failure of his father's handloom weaving business the family came to the United States in 1848 and settled in Allegheny City, Pa. Carnegie started work as a bobbin-boy at $1.20 a week and soon became a clerk in the business. He then became a telegraph messenger boy in Pittsburgh and soon was promoted to operator, while he added to his income by serving as a newspaper reporter. He then joined the staff of the Pennsylvania Railroad as a telegraphic train dispatcher and eventually became secretary to the general superintendent, Colonel Thomas A. Scott. At the same time, he acquired an eighth share in the Woodruff Company, which owned the rights to the early Pullman cars. When Colonel Scott became vice-president of the company, in 1860, Carnegie was appointed superintendent of the western division, and on the outbreak of the Civil War, when Scott was appointed assistant secretary of war, Carnegie took control of the eastern military and telegraph lines. In 1862, recognizing that wooden bridges were becoming obsolete, Carnegie organized the Keystone Bridge Works, which built the first iron bridge over the Ohio River. To obtain supplies more easily, he entered the iron business, founding the Union Iron Mills, which in 1868 became the first American user of the Bessemer steel converter. From this time Carnegie's business expanded rapidly until, in 1888, he gained control of the rival Homestead Steel Works and seven other enterprises in the Pittsburgh vicinity. In 1899 all these companies were combined into the Carnegie Steel Company. In 1901 Carnegie retired from business, transferring his company, at a valuation of $500,000,000, to form a part of the United States Steel Corporation. Thereafter Carnegie devoted his energies to philanthropy, building libraries all over the world and endowing many worthy causes. It has been estimated that he gave away more than $300,000,000. Carnegie received honors from many countries. Among the books he wrote are *Triumphant Democracy* (1886), *The Gospel of Wealth* (1900), *The Empire of Business* (1902), and *Problems of To-day* (1909). He died at Lenox, Mass., Aug. 11, 1919. R. T.

CARNEGIE [kɑrnɛ'gi; kɑrne'gi], an industrial borough in southwestern Pennsylvania, situated in Allegheny Co., in the scenic Chartiers Valley, 6 mi. southwest of Pittsburgh, in an area of dairying and truck gardening. The region is rich in coal, for which the borough is a shipping point. The community includes the former boroughs of Chartiers and Mansfield, which were consolidated to form Carnegie when it was incorporated in 1894. The government is administered by a mayor and council. Transportation is provided by two railroads, the Pennsylvania and the Pittsburgh, Chartiers & Youghiogheny. Besides steel and iron manufactures, industrial products include diesel engines, enamel powder, wooden toys, water heaters, gas burners, lubricants, signs, stamp pads, and ink. Pop. 1950, 12,105.

CARNEGIE INSTITUTE OF TECHNOLOGY, at Pittsburgh, Pa., an accredited, privately controlled technological institute occupying 70 acres in an urban environment. The institute is the outgrowth of a gift by Andrew

PRESS BUREAU, CARNEGIE INSTITUTE OF TECHNOLOGY

Carnegie Institute of Technology, at Pittsburgh, Pennsylvania

Carnegie, the steel magnate and philanthropist, to the city of Pittsburgh for the Carnegie Technical Schools, which opened in 1905. The present name was adopted in 1912. The Carnegie Institute is coeducational in all divisions except for Margaret Morrison Carnegie College for women, which, with the Colleges of Fine Arts and Engineering and Science, was established in 1905; the Carnegie Library School was founded in 1930 and the Division of Humanistic and Social Studies still later. The Graduate School of Industrial Administration, W. L. Mellon, founder, was established in 1949, followed by the School of Printing Management in 1953.

Degrees conferred are the B.S. in engineering, science, and industrial and printing management and the B.F.A., M.F.A., M.S., M.Arch., M.A. and Ph.D.

More than 350 graduate students are enrolled in all colleges and divisions except the women's college. The College of Fine Arts offers courses in architecture, painting, design, sculpture, art education, music, and drama; the college for women has programs in the four main fields of biological science, home economics, secretarial studies, and general studies in liberal arts leading to the B.S.

A co-operative program in which 22 liberal-arts colleges are enrolled permits students of Carnegie Institute of Technology to earn two bachelor's degrees in five years.

The School of Printing Management was the first in the

country to offer instruction in the graphic arts leading to an academic degree. Courses dealing with basic production procedure and equipment in printing plants, in administration and management, and in general academic work are units of the program.

Generous scholarship and loan funds are available, and there are opportunities for earning part of the cost of tuition. Residence halls are provided. *For statistics see* Colleges and Universities.

CARNEGIE TRUSTS, a series of trusts, or foundations, established by Andrew Carnegie, manufacturer and philanthropist, who came to the United States in 1848 from Dunfermline, Fifeshire, Scotland, where he was born. These organizations include:

Carnegie Corporation of New York. Established by Andrew Carnegie in 1911 as the culmination of his philanthropic program, this corporation has a basic endowment of $135,000,000. Its assets total about $178,000,000. Income only is expendable for the advancement and diffusion of knowledge and understanding among the people of the United States and certain British Commonwealth areas. More than $250,000,000 has been appropriated since 1911.

The Carnegie Corporation has a continuing interest in improving higher education. Grants are made to colleges and universities, professional associations, and other educational organizations for specific programs. Such programs include basic research as well as more effective use of the results of research, increased understanding of international affairs, better preparation for teachers, and new teaching programs. Offices are in New York City.

Carnegie Foundation for the Advancement of Teaching. This organization was incorporated by act of Congress, on Mar. 10, 1906, "to provide retiring pensions, without regard to race, creed, sex, or color for teachers of universities, colleges and technical schools in the United States, the Dominion of Canada, and Newfoundland," and "in general, to do and perform all things necessary to encourage, uphold, and dignify the profession of the teacher and the cause of higher education. . . ." Andrew Carnegie, concluding that "the least rewarded of all the professions is that of the teacher in our higher educational institutions," had established the Foundation with $10,000,000 of endowment, later increased to $15,000,000. The Carnegie Corporation of New York has subsequently granted large additional sums for the Foundation's work. The trustees number 25. For retiring allowances and widows' pensions, the Foundation has disbursed more than $66,000,000 up to now. It has conducted numerous educational studies in the past, but at the present time its resources are almost entirely committed to the payment of pensions to retired college teachers. Offices of the organization are in New York City.

Carnegie Institute in Pittsburgh. The institute was established in 1896 as Carnegie's gift to the city in which he made his fortune. It includes a museum of natural history, a music hall, and a department of fine arts; closely related to it is the Carnegie Institute of Technology. The department of fine arts gives a variety of exhibitions. Loans from permanent collections are made to a number of art museums. The museum of natural history has conducted various expeditions in the field, has revised many exhibits, and has added to its collections. The music hall is widely used by various educational organizations for lectures, concerts, and meetings.

Carnegie Institution of Washington. Established in 1902, this foundation is devoted to scientific research. It has expended over $50,000,000 in its program of encouraging scientific investigation, research, and discovery, and the application of knowledge to the improvement of mankind. It has organized its own departments of research in astronomy, terrestrial science, the biological sciences, and archaeology. It is located in Washington, D.C.

Carnegie Hero Fund Commission. This fund was established in 1904 to recognize heroic acts performed in the United States, in Canada, including Newfoundland, and the waters thereof, by persons whose duties do not necessarily require them to perform such acts. The fund has made 58 awards of medals, or of funds, thus bringing the total number of awards since 1904 to more than 4,000, and the total in pecuniary awards to about $8,000,000. It is located in Pittsburgh, Pa.

Carnegie Endowment for International Peace. Established in 1910 to serve the purpose indicated by its name, this foundation expends its funds in efforts to further friendly understanding among the nations of the world. The work of the endowment consists of efforts to promote international understanding through research, publication, conferences, the distribution of books and pamphlets at strategic centers, lectures on international law, and the study of means of promoting the general cause of peace. The organization headquarters are at the United Nations Plaza in New York City. The endowment also has a European center at Geneva, Switzerland.

In addition, there are four separately endowed and locally administered Carnegie trusts in Great Britain.

Carnegie Trust for the Universities of Scotland. Edinburgh is the site of this trust, established in 1901. The trust has an endowment of £2,000,000, the income of which is used in improving and extending opportunities for scientific study and research in the universities of Scotland, and in aiding deserving and qualified youth in that country to attend and enjoy the advantages of those universities.

Carnegie Dunfermline Trust. An endowment of £750,000 was provided for this foundation, established in 1903, the income "to be used in attempts to bring into the monotonous lives of the toiling masses of Dunfermline more of sweetness and light." The Dunfermline Trust includes a school of handicraft, a youth center, a music institute, and operates general and dental clinics.

Carnegie Hero Fund Trust. For this trust, established in 1908, an endowment of £250,000 was provided. The income is used to recognize heroic acts "in Great Britain and Ireland and the adjacent islands pertaining thereto, including the Channel Islands, and the territorial waters surrounding said countries and islands." The trust's roll of heroes numbers more than 5,500.

Carnegie United Kingdom Trust. Dunfermline, Fife, Scotland, became the site of this trust in 1913. The trust has an endowment of £2,000,000, the income being used for improvement of the well-being of the masses of the people of Great Britain and Ireland by such means as are embraced within the meaning of the word "charitable." Its recent expenditures, amounting to more than £67,000, were devoted to the aid of music, drama, and the visual arts, museum services, education, and community services.   F. A.

CARNELIAN or **CORNELIAN,** a clear, red or brownish-red variety of chalcedony, a cryptocrystalline form of quartz, SiO_2. The hardness is 7, and the density is usually slightly less than 2.65. Being a dense mineral made up of very minute particles, the indices of refraction are not as definite as they are for pure quartz. A figure of 1.537 is given for carnelian. The gem stone's color is due to the presence of a trace of iron oxide. Like agate and onyx, it is sometimes subjected to heat to improve the color or impregnated with various stains or dyes to achieve the same result. Impregnation is possible because most cryptocrystalline varieties of silica are slightly porous, either in their entirety or from layer to layer if the mineral is banded or striated. Brazil, Arabia, and India are sources of this semiprecious gem stone, which is used for making intaglios for signet rings or beads for necklaces when rounded and highly polished. A. E. A.

CARNIC ALPS, a mountain system 60 mi. long in southern Austria, lying south of the Drava River, on the Austro-Italian border. To the south are the headwaters of the Piave and Tagliamento rivers flowing into the Adriatic Sea. The Carnic Alps contain several peaks above 8,000 ft., notably Parabla, 8,825 ft. In the west is the Toblach Pass (3,965 ft.), and in the east is the Tarvis Pass (2,615 ft.) between Carinthia and Trieste. The region is sparsely populated, but lemons, olives, and wheat are grown, and some cattle grazing is to be found in the valleys. The evergreen, oak, beech, ash, and sycamore trees grow to 4,000 ft., while pines are found as high as 6,000 ft. During World War I, the Carnic Alps were a theatre of operations of Gen. Cadorna opposing Austrian operations on the Italian front of the Allied Forces. Since World War II, the Carnic Alps lie in the British Occupation Zone. S. Van V.

CARNIOLA [karnyɔ'la], a former province of Austria, ceased to exist as a unit on being merged with Slovenia when the Serb, Croat, and Slovene State, which became Yugoslavia in January 1929, was created under the Treaty of Versailles in 1919. The former province of Carniola covered an area of 3,845 sq. mi. It was bounded on the northwest by the watershed of the Julian Alps; on the north by the Karawanken range, the Steiner Alps and the Sava River; the Uskok Mountains and the Kulpa River form part of its southern and eastern frontiers.

The Carni, a Celtic tribe, were the first recorded people of this area; they were followed by the Romans, who invaded and occupied the area next. The history of Carniola proper begins when the Slovenes invaded and occupied the upper valley of the Sava by the end of the sixth century. The Slovenes defended themselves against the encroaching Bavarian princes, as well as the Turko-Finnish Avars of the middle Danube, but Carniola was swallowed up by the empire of Charlemagne. In the tenth century the upper part of Carniola emerged as a separate country, and, under the House of Saxony, it formed part of the general system of Marches, or frontier districts, which guarded Bavaria. At this time Carniola consisted of two parts: the country proper and the March between the Gurk and the Kulpa rivers. During the thirteenth century the Hapsburgs began to push south, and in 1278 Carniola became a Hapsburg dominion, Rudolf IV of Austria taking the title of Duke of Carniola in 1365.

Between 1809 and 1813 Carniola was incorporated into the French Illyrian Provinces by Napleon; it was restored to Austria by the Congress of Vienna. In 1849 Carniola became an Austrian crownland or province, and it so remained until 1919, when it was merged with Slovenia. *See also* YUGO-SLAVIA.

CARNIVORE [ka'rnivɔr], a flesh-eating mammal of the order Carnivora, a well-marked group characterized by a dentition adapted for tearing and shearing flesh. The canines are large and pointed, projecting well beyond the other teeth. Most of the flesh eaters possess a specialized shearing tooth in the upper and lower jaw, known as the carnassial or sectorial tooth. The incisors are small. Usually five toes are present on each foot; these are invariably provided with claws, which are blunt in the dogs, but sharp and retractile in the cats. The carnivores include small to large mammals occupying a variety of habitats, terrestrial, arboreal, or aquatic in nature. Carnivores are native to all parts of the world except Australia. As their name implies, they are primarily flesh eaters, although many species, such as the bear, skunk, raccoon, fox, and many others eat large quantities of vegetation. Many are dependent upon the fast-breeding rodents for a large share of their diet. An annual litter of young is the rule, unlike the rodents, which may produce several litters in a single breeding season. Many carnivores are of considerable economic significance. Some, such as wolves and the larger cats, compete with man for food by destroying livestock, or actually threaten man's security. Others are important in the fur trade, providing pelts for wearing apparel. The order Carnivora has been generally divided into two major groups or suborders, the Fissipedia, or terrestrial Carnivora, and the Pinnipedia, or aquatic Carnivora.

Terrestrial Carnivora. The Fissipedia may readily be distinguished by the structure of the teeth. The incisors are nearly always six in number and rather feebly developed. The canines are always present, invariably large and strong. The number of molariform teeth may vary, but the presence of a sectorial or cutting tooth in each jaw separates the sharp-edged cutting teeth before and the broad, crowned, tuberculate teeth behind. Seven families of the Fissipedia are recognized:

(1) Canidae, the dog family, include wolves, jackals, foxes, and some less familiar forms. With the exception of Australia (the dingo is considered an introduced form) and some of the oceanic islands, the family has a world-wide distribution.

(2) Ursidae, the bear family, have occurred within historic times throughout Europe, Asia, North America, the East Indies, in the Atlas mountains of North Africa, and in the Andes of South America.

(3) Procyonidae, raccoon family, include the well-known Asiatic panda, the coati, the kinkajou, and the cacomistle. This family, with the exception of the panda, is confined to the New World.

(4) Mustelidae, the weasel family, which are important in the fur industry, include the mink, skunk, sea otter, badger, marten, and others. This large group is generally distributed except for Australia and some oceanic islands.

(5) Hyaenidae are restricted to Africa and Asia.

(6) Viverridae, the genets, civets, and their allies, are catlike or weasellike carnivores having partially retractile claws. Representatives occur in Africa, Madagascar, the Orient, and northern regions of the Old World.

(7) Felidae, the cat family, are world-wide in distribution except for Australia, the polar regions, and the oceanic islands. The cats are a rather uniform group, differing primarily in size, length of tail, and color pattern.

Aquatic Carnivora. The suborder Pinnipedia constitutes the seals, sea lions, and walruses. They differ from the Fissipedia principally in modification for an aquatic existence. They have to some extent developed a fishlike form, though not so completely as have the whales. Such modification is best observed in the seals, where the hind limbs have become soldered to the tail and are inefficient as walking legs, while the external ears have vanished and the form is tapering and fishlike. Such modification is not so great in walruses and sea lions. In sea lions the small external ear is persistent, and in both walruses and sea lions the hind limbs are capable of being used as organs of progression upon dry land. The teeth approach those of whales and porpoises in likeness to a homodont condition. The limbs and feet are partially or wholly enveloped in the general integument of the body, forming the prominent flippers characteristic of the group. Three families of the suborder Pinnipedia are recognized:

(1) Otariidae are the eared seals, sea lions, and fur seals. Members of the family occur in the subarctic, temperate, and warm shores of the Pacific, south Atlantic, Indian, and northern Antarctic oceans. This family includes the famous fur seal of the Pribilof Islands.

(2) Phocidae are true seals or hair seals, the most highly specialized of all seals. They are distributed over the ocean shores throughout the world, some forms occurring even in the Caspian Sea.

(3) Odobenidae are the walruses. These huge beasts are restricted to the Arctic Ocean, where they still occur in large numbers.   W. J. Ha.

CARNOT, LAZARE NICOLAS MARGUERITE

[ka'rno'] (1753-1823), French soldier and statesman, was born at Nolay, Côte d'Or, on May 13, 1753. He entered the corps of engineers and, following publication of his *Essai sur les machines en général* (1783), he was promoted to captain. At this time he was a supporter of the theories of Sébastien Le Prestre, marquis de Vauban, as regards the use of fortifications, but, as a result of conversations with Marc René, marquis de Montalembert, he became an opponent of these theories, which were acceptable to those in power. On the outbreak of the French Revolution he was elected deputy to the Legislative Assembly in 1791 for the Pas de Calais. He reorganized the republican army, abandoning the official method of defense at all points in favor of large masses of troops prepared to deal overwhelming blows at the enemy. The success of the army can be primarily credited to him. In 1793 he was made a member of the Committee of Public Safety and was in charge of the construction of new armies, creating fourteen in less than a year. He became a member of the Directory in 1795 and twice served as its president, but in 1797, just before the *coup d'état,* he fled to Switzerland. He returned to France in 1799, and became minister of war in the following year. He resigned later that year, and retired. As a member of the Tribunate, from 1802 to 1807, he was a consistent opponent of Napoleon's plans for self-aggrandisement, deploring the return of a monarchy against which he had worked, even to the extent of voting for the execution of Louis XVI. He received a pension from Napoleon in 1809 and was commissioned to write an account of the fortifications of Metz. In 1810 he published his greatest work, *De la défense de places fortes,* which quickly became a standard work throughout Europe. When events in 1814 seemed to threaten the safety of France he offered his services to Napoleon and was appointed governor of Antwerp, conducting a brilliant defense of the fortress. During the Hundred Days, in 1815, he served as minister of the interior, and later in the year was exiled by Louis XVIII. He went to Magdeburg, where he died on Aug. 2, 1823.   R. T.

CARNOT, (MARIE FRANÇOIS) SADI (1837-1894), fourth president of the French Republic, was born at Limoges on Aug. 11, 1837. He was the grandson of Lazare Nicolas Marguerite; the son of Lazare Hippolyte, political foe of Napoleon III; and nephew of the physicist Nicolas Léonard Sadi Carnot. Sadi Carnot studied civil engineering at the École Polytechnique after 1857. His most important engineering work was the tubular bridge at Colognes-sur-Rhône, near the Swiss frontier. He was stationed at Annecy as government engineer when the Franco-Prussian War broke out in 1870; and on Jan. 13, 1871, was appointed *commissaire extraordinaire* in charge of defense for the departments of Seine-Inférieure, Eure, and Calvados. He resigned the post after the fall of Paris. On Feb. 8, 1871, the department of Côte d'Or elected Carnot deputy to the National Assembly of the Provisional Republic. After the adoption, in 1875, of the constitution which established the Third Republic, he was re-elected to the new Chamber of Deputies, becoming its secretary in 1877. He was again elected to the Chamber after the *coup d'état* of May 18, 1877. In 1880-1881 Carnot held the post of Minister of Public Works and was re-appointed April 7, 1885. Two weeks later he became minister of finance, and held the post under two presidents. He resigned it in 1886. Carnot was elected president the following year and served from Dec. 2, 1887, to June 25, 1894. The Paris Exhibition of 1887, celebrating the centenary of the French Revolution, and the signing of an alliance with Russia in 1891 were the outstanding events of his term of office. While attending an exhibition at Lyons, Carnot was stabbed by Santo Jeronimo Caserio, an anarchist, and died June 25, 1894.   R. M. Br.

CARNOTITE [ka'rnotait], a soft, yellow, radioactive mineral which chemically is a hydrous vanadate of potassium and uranium. Its formula is $K_2O \cdot 2U_2O_3 \cdot V_2O_5 \cdot 3H_2O$; the water content actually varies with humidity. Carnotite was named after a French mining engineer and chemist, Marie-Adolph Carnot (1839-1920). In the United States it occurs disseminated through sandstone in Paradox Valley and other parts of the Colorado Plateau in Colorado, Utah, and Arizona. Carnotite is a source of vanadium and of uranium.   K. K. L.

CARO, JOSEPH [ka'ro] (1488-1575), Jewish codifier, Talmudic scholar, and Cabalist, was born, probably in Spain, in 1488. At the expulsion of the Jews from Spain in 1492, Caro's family sought refuge in Portugal, only to have to flee again in 1497. For some years they tarried in Turkey, and in 1523 Caro occupied the position of head of the academy at Nikopolis. In 1535, he settled permanently in Safed, Palestine, then a center of study of Cabala and mysticism.

Caro devoted twenty years, from 1522 to 1542, to the writing of a commentary, *Beth Yoseph* ("House of Joseph"), to Jacob ben Asher's great code *Arba'ah Turim* ("Four Pillars"). He then devoted twelve more years to the revision of his commentary and the compilation of his own monumental code, *Shulchan Aruch* ("The Prepared Table"), now known as *The Code of Jewish Law.* The *Shulchan Aruch* was first published in Venice in 1565. In this code Caro presented a compendium of Jewish religious practices and halakic decisions culled from earliest days up to and including his own time. It was based primarily on Sephardic usage and was opposed by German and Polish scholars. Within a short time, however, it became authoritative, and with the glosses of Moses Isserles, called "Mappah" (table cloth), soon became the standard Jewish code, used for all religious decisions and in preparation for ordination. Caro also wrote a commentary entitled *Keseph Mishneh* ("Double Money") on the Code of Maimonides, and was addressed as *maran* ("our master") by his contemporaries. He died in Safed, Mar. 24, 1575.   M. A. G.

CARO, MIGUEL ANTONIO [kɑ'ro] (1843-1909), Colombian statesman, linguist, and philologist, was born in Bogotá, Nov. 10, 1843. Son of José Ensebio Caro, the well-known Colombian writer, Caro had a distinguished career both in literature and in politics. He took an active and enduring part in the councils of the Conservative Party, served as vice-president under Rafael Núñez, and succeeded Núñez as president in 1894. His administration, lasting until 1898, was wise and moderate. Among his literary activities were excellent translations of Horace and Vergil, original poems, and essays on J. H. Groot, Diego Fallón, Menéndez y Pelayo, and Andrés Bello. Caro also published important linguistic works, among them *Tratado del participio* (1870), *Del uso en sus relaciones con el lenguaje* (1881), and a good Latin grammar, written in 1893 in collaboration with R. J. Cuervo. Caro died in Bogotá, Aug. 5, 1909.   G. B.

CAROB [kæ'rəb], *Ceratonia siliqua,* an evergreen tree of the pea family, also called St.-John's-bread or algarroba. It is a native of the eastern Mediterranean region, cultivated in such climates since ancient times for the edible pods. It has been planted in southern California experimentally as fodder, and as an ornamental and a sidewalk tree. It grows 40 to 50 ft. high, with sturdy branches forming a dense round head; shining dark-green leaves composed of 2 or 3 pairs of leaflets; flowers in small red clusters directly on the limb surface. The flat pods, 6 to 12 in. long and 1 in. broad, contain many seeds surrounded by a sweet, fleshy pulp that is edible. In various Mediterranean countries, the pods, rich in protein and sugar, constitute an important forage crop and are used to some extent for human food. Mature trees may yield 1,000 lb. of pods annually. Carob pods are probably the husks mentioned in the Biblical parable of the prodigal son; they sustained the mounts of Lord Allenby's cavalry in World War I and the Duke of Wellington's horses in Spain during the Peninsular Campaign. The small seeds, remarkably uniform in mass, are said to have been the original carat weight used by jewelers and goldsmiths.
                    R. S. Ho.

CAROL II (1893-1953), king of Romania, was born in Sinaia, Oct. 16, 1893, the son of King Ferdinand and Queen Marie. In 1917, when he was twenty-four, Carol eloped with Mme Zizi Lambrino, the daughter of a Romanian army officer. He divorced her, however, to marry Princess Helen of Greece in 1921. In 1925 Carol moved to Paris, where he established residence with Mme Magda Lupescu, and was known as Carol Caraiman. In December of that year he renounced his right to the Romanian throne. Upon Ferdinand's death, July 20, 1927, Michael, the young son of Carol and Helen (b. Oct. 25, 1921), became king. In 1928 Carol's marriage with Helen was dissolved. In 1930 he returned by plane to Romania, and on June 8 was proclaimed king in place of his son. His reign, which lasted ten years, was marked by confusion, for Carol tried to win the favor of both the Soviet Union and Germany. He broke with the National Peasant Party, which had previously supported him; then he tried unsuccessfully to become dictator. Finally, in 1940, German influence drove him from the throne and the country. Michael, then nineteen, became king under a Nazi-dominated regime. Accompanied by Mme Lupescu, Carol went to Spain. The following year he went to Cuba, then to Mexico, and from there to Brazil. When Mme Lupescu became seriously ill, apparently on her deathbed, Carol married her in Rio de Janeiro on July 6, 1947, asking for an exception to Brazilian divorce laws to legalize the ceremony. Upon her recovery, Carol and his bride, with the permission of the government, established themselves at Estoril, near Lisbon. They were married a second time, Aug. 20, 1949, in Lisbon. Carol died April 4, 1953, near Lisbon.

CAROL, in modern usage, a simple song of rejoicing, usually associated with a festive occasion, such as Christmas or Easter, and with social singing. Carols may be either religious or secular in subject matter and frequently mingle the devotional spirit with the convivial in a manner that sets them off from formal hymns on the one hand and from mere occasional or holiday verse on the other.

The derivation of the word from the Old French *carole*—a ring dance accompanied by song, popular both in England and on the Continent—gives the essential clue to the history of this type of lyric. In the later Middle Ages the English word "carol" denoted a song in a particular form, consisting of a number of metrically similar stanzas, sung to the same melody, and a chorus or burden sung at the beginning and repeated after every stanza. This form was required for the vocal accompaniment of the medieval *carole,* in which the leader of the dance sang the stanza as a solo while the ring of participants marked time, and then the ring circled about the leader while all together sang the burden. Most often the burden is a rhymed couplet and the stanza is of four lines, of which the first three rhyme with each other and the last rhymes with the burden, but there are many variations within this general pattern of burden and stanza. The medieval English carol thus corresponds to the French *chanson à carole* and the Italian *ballata,* both of similar origin.

The well-known *Boar's Head Carol,* current in the early sixteenth century and still sung annually at Queen's College, Oxford, preserves this typical form and also shows the macaronic mixture of Latin and English found in many early carols:

(Burden)
Caput apri defero,
Reddens laudes Domino.

(Stanza 1)
The boar's head in hand bear I,
Bedeck'd with bays and rosemary,
And I pray you, masters, be merry,
Quot estis in convivio.

(Burden repeated)
Caput apri defero,
Reddens laudes Domino.

The turning to religious use of a form of song originally worldly and frivolous was especially furthered in England by the Franciscan friars, one of whom, James Ryman, wrote some 119 carols that are still preserved. Most of the nearly five hundred English carols extant in pre-Reformation manuscripts or early printed books appear to have resulted from this process of composing religious or moralizing words in the verse forms and to the tunes of popular and secular songs. Although the content of some medieval English carols is political, humorous, or satirical, the story of the Nativity and the joy attending Christmas and its following feast days were well established in the fifteenth century as the principal themes of songs in the carol form. With the virtual disappearance of the medieval ring dance and the rise of new and more sophisticated fashions in music and poetry, the custom of singing the burden first, or indeed of requiring a burden at all, was lost, and the primary meaning of the word "carol" gradually became "a song about Christmas or for Christmas singing," like the French *noël.* In the seventeenth and eighteenth centuries the carol, like the ballad, was regarded as a socially inferior and rustic kind of poetry, and, like the ballad, it survived chiefly in penny broadsides sold by itinerant vendors, and in oral tradition among the uneducated. The singing of carols by bands of waits at Christmas was an annual custom, surviving in many English villages until recent decades.

The recognition of the artistic merit of the old carols and the conscious cultivation of carol singing as an aid to worship and to social enjoyment date from the mid-nineteenth century in England and are related to both the emphasis on medieval traditions accompanying the Oxford Movement in the Anglican Church and the interest in ballads and other folk songs fostered by the Romantic Movement in poetry. Interest in the collection and singing of carols has grown steadily in both England and the United States. Modern Christmas hymns, such as Phillips Brooks' *O Little Town of Bethlehem* (1868), and the English translation of Joseph Mohr's German verses (1818), *Silent Night, Holy Night,* are now generally thought of as "Christmas carols" and are valued equally with such more ancient and genuinely traditional pieces as *The First Nowell* and *God Rest You Merry, Gentlemen.*

R. L. G.

CAROLINE INCIDENT, an event in the Canadian Rebellion of 1837 which threatened to disrupt relations between the United States and Great Britain. In December 1837, a group of Canadian insurrectionists established themselves on Navy Island in the Niagara River. A small steamer, the *Caroline,* kept them supplied from the New York shore. On the night of December 30, a group of Canadian loyalists cut the *Caroline* loose from its moorings at Fort Schlosser, set it on fire, and sent it drifting downstream. It grounded and burned in the rapids above Niagara Falls. During the skirmish which began this operation, a United States citizen was killed, and this act of violence, along with the violation of United States territory, caused vigorous protest to be made. To maintain neutrality, the New York militia was mobilized at the border and General Winfield Scott was sent to the scene by President Martin Van Buren. The British government declined redress, with the result that the Caroline incident and the McLeod case, resulting later, served to envenom Anglo-American relations. In 1842, the British government made a tardy apology. *See also* McLeod Case.   **J. I. C.**

CAROLINE ISLANDS, a widely scattered group of small islands under United States trusteeship, in the west Pacific Ocean, north of the equator, and comprising much of what is known as Micronesia. They lie between 2° and 10° N. lat. and 131° and 164° E. long. and comprise some 48 island units, together with a number of reefs and shoals. The largest island units are, from west to east, Palau, Yap, Truk, Ponape, and Kusaie. The enclosing ocean zone has been estimated at close to 350,000 sq. mi., but the combined land area of the island units is only about 460 sq. mi. Most of the islands are of coral formation, either atolls with a series of islets around the rim of the lagoon, or low flat coral pancakes. Volcanic outcroppings occur on the five largest units, producing a cluster of high islands within an enclosing barrier reef. Maximum elevations are: Palau, 641 ft.; Yap, 585 ft.; Truk, 1,483 ft.; Ponape, 2,579 ft.; Kusaie, 2,064 ft. The Palaus and Yap form part of a great submarine arcuate ridge which also includes the Marianas and Bonins. The rest of the group emerges from a ridge system extending eastward toward the north-south arc on which the Marshall and Gilbert islands lie. The climate is oceanic and tropical, and vegetation is generally dense. The most notable anchorages are Malakal Harbor in the Palaus, Tomil Harbor at Yap, Ulithi lagoon (used in World War II by the U.S. Navy as a fleet base), Truk lagoon, and Ponape Harbor in Ponape.

There are airstrips at Palau, Truk, and Ponape and seaplanes can land at many points.

Early Spanish and Portuguese voyagers touched at various islands. In 1686 the Spanish Admiral Francisco Lezcano gave the name "Carolina" to Yap, and this was later extended to the group as a whole. Spain's sovereignty over the islands was disputed by expanding German commercial interests, and in 1885 the Pope adjudicated their sovereignty in favor of Spain. In 1899 these and other Spanish holdings in Micronesia were purchased by Germany. In 1914 the islands came under the control of Japan and in 1945 were assigned to the United States. The indigenous islanders are Micronesians, divided into a number of ethnic and linguistic groups. Commercial products are limited almost exclusively to copra and shell. Pop. 1955 est., 42,800.

F. M. K. and M. M. K.

CAROLINE OF ANSPACH (1683-1737), whose full name was Wilhelmina Carolina, Queen of Great Britain and Ireland as wife of George II, was born in Brandenburg on Mar. 1, 1683. She was the daughter of John Frederick, Margrave of Brandenburg-Ansbach. She was married to George Augustus, electoral Prince of Hanover, in September 1705, and accompanied him to England upon the accession of her father-in-law to the British throne in 1715 as George I. She did much to try to keep the peace between the Prince of Wales and his father, but from 1717 to 1720 there was complete disagreement among them. She encouraged many bril-

CAROLINE OF ANSPACH

liant men of her time, including Lord Hervey and Alexander Pope. She seems to have paid little attention to her husband's entanglement with Henrietta Howard. She was crowned queen in 1727 and used all her efforts to keep Sir Robert Walpole in power. Her appointments of bishops were remarkable for the time in that she preferred learning to orthodoxy. She served as regent when George II was out of England in 1729, 1732, 1735, and 1736. She bore eight children and quarreled bitterly with the eldest of these, Frederick. She died in London on Nov. 20, 1737.   **R. T.**

CAROLINE OF BRUNSWICK (1768-1821), whose full name was Amelia Elizabeth Caroline, Queen of Great Britain and Ireland as wife of George IV, was born on May 17, 1768. She was the daughter of Charles William Ferdinand, Duke of Brunswick-Wolfenbüttel. In 1795 she entered into a marriage of convenience with George, Prince of Wales, whose previous marriage to Mrs. Fitzherbert had been illegalized. From the very beginning there were acrimonious quarrels between husband and wife, and they were formally separated early in 1796. Popular sympathy was with the princess, for the immoralities of her husband were well known. About 1806, rumors concerning Caroline's conduct began to circulate, but a commission that investigated found her behavior merely unwise. When George became king in 1820, he refused to recognize Caroline as queen. At this time, after living on the Continent for six years, she returned to England to claim her rights. In reply the king had a bill introduced into the House of Lords to dissolve the marriage on the grounds of her adultery. Though she was probably guilty, public excitement was roused to a high pitch and the bill was withdrawn on November 10. She died in London on Aug. 7, 1821, less than three weeks after being excluded from the coronation of George IV at Westminster Abbey.

E. R. A.

CAROLINGIAN DYNASTY [kæˈrolɪˈnjən], the

second line of Frankish kings, which in 751 succeeded the Merovingians, descendants of Clovis. The family emerged in Austrasia in the early seventh century, when the daughter of Pepin of Landen, mayor of the palace and the real power in this kingdom, married the son of Arnulf, Bishop of Metz. In 687 their son, Pepin of Heristal, made himself supreme in both Austrasia and Neustria, thus combining the two main parts of the old Frankish kingdom. This unification was made permanent under Pepin's son, Charles Martel, who succeeded him as mayor of the palace in 714 and restored the kingdom to its original boundaries. Charles gained the acclaim of the Western world for his defeat of the Moslems at the Battle of Tours. His son, Pepin the Short, succeeded to his father's office in 741, and ten years later, with papal support, dethroned the last Merovingian puppet king and had himself proclaimed King of the Franks. Charlemagne, the greatest of the Carolingians, after sharing the kingdom three years with his brother Carloman, became sole king in 771 and conquered new territories within Germany and Italy and beyond the Pyrenees into Spain. In 800 he was crowned Emperor of the West by Pope Leo III. His son, Louis the Pious, ruled from 814 to 840, and after his death the empire was divided among his three sons. Lothair, the eldest, received the central portion, including Italy and Lorraine, with the title of emperor. Louis the German became king of the East Franks, and Charles the Bald king of the West Franks. With the extinction of the family of Lothair the central kingdom was broken into several fragments; but although weakened by the rising power of the feudal nobles, the other two kingdoms held together, becoming known as Germany and France. The direct Carolingian line in France ended in 987; thenceforth the Capetians, who had contested the throne with the Carolingians for a hundred years, gained undisputed control. In Germany the last Carolingian king was Arnulf, who died in 899.

F. C. H.

CARON, PIERRE AUGUSTIN. *See* BEAUMARCHAIS, DE.

CAROTHERS, WALLACE HUME [kərʌˈthərz]

(1896-1937), American chemist, inventor of nylon and coinventor of synthetic neoprene rubber, was born in Burlington, Iowa, Apr. 27, 1896. He studied in Tarkio College (1920) and the University of Illinois (Ph.D., 1924). Carothers taught in South Dakota (1921-1922), Illinois (1924-1926), and Harvard (1926-1928). He subsequently became associated with the Du Pont Company and directed their polymer research. Collaborating with J. A. Nieuwland, Carothers directed the production of synthetic neoprene rubber, announcing its successful production on Nov. 2, 1931.

He will be best remembered, however, for his series of investigations which led to the production of nylon, for which he was awarded patents, posthumously, in 1938. The series of research papers which preceded the development of nylon is concerned with the polymerization of proteinlike materials called polyamides, which are similar to proteins in natural silk. During the years 1933 to 1937 Carothers pursued his investigations on the polyamides, constantly modifying and improving his processes. He died in Philadelphia, Apr. 29, 1937.

H. N. A.

CARP, *Cyprinus carpio,* a minnow, native to fresh waters of Asia and widely introduced in Europe and North America. Distinguished by two long barbels on either side of

COURTESY OF THE U. S. FISH AND WILDLIFE SERVICE

CARP, CYPRINUS CARPIO

the mouth, the carp also has a long dorsal fin with a serrate spine in front. One variety, called leather carp, has no scales; another, the mirror carp, has relatively few, large scales. Selectively bred and cultivated in ponds, these fish are used for food both in the Orient and in Europe. Carp, successfully introduced into the United States in 1877, are found throughout the country. Many are shipped alive to the New York and Chicago markets; but because of the carp's strong odor and muddy taste it is not generally a popular food fish. Much effort is now expended annually in attempting to exterminate carp from certain lakes where sport fishing is the primary interest. They make the water turbid through their rooting in the mud and occupy space and eat food which might produce more desirable species. Carp usually weigh about 15 to 20 lb. However, a 42-in. carp weighing 42 lb. was taken on a rod in Virginia, and an 83.5-lb. fish is on record from South Africa.

E. C. R.

CARPACCIO, VITTORE [karpaˈttsho] (c. 1455-1526), Venetian painter, was born in Venice about 1455, but there is no documentary evidence of the exact date. It is probable that he spent his youth in Venice, where he came in contact with the art of the Bellinis, Antonello da Messina, Giorgione, and Andrea Mantegna. Most authorities believe that his first master was Lazzaro Bastiani. Carpaccio worked mainly in Venice, traveling to Capodistria during his later life. He died in Venice in 1526.

Carpaccio's major works are the several series of paintings done for the *scuole,* or confraternities, of Venice, dealing with the lives of their patron saints. These paintings afford vivid glimpses of the life and pageantry of the city in the artist's time. From 1490 to 1495 he painted, for the Scuola di Sant' Orsola, the series from the legend of St. Ursula that is now in the Academy, Venice. Commissions from other confraternities resulted in paintings from the lives of Saints George, Tryphonius, Jerome, and Stephen, and in the *Miracle of the Holy Cross,* in the Academy, Venice, done for the Scuola di San Giovanni Evangelista. Carpaccio's work in the Doge's Palace, done in 1501, was destroyed by fire. His single paintings include altarpieces, and such secular works as the *Courtesans* in the Correr Museum in Venice.

                                                                    B. C. G.

CARPATHIANS [karpe'thiənz], a mountain chain of south central Europe describing an 800-mi. arc from Bratislava on the Danube in Czechoslovakia, at about the latitude of Vienna, to Orsova at the Iron Gate in Romania. Its area exceeds 22,000 sq. mi., including territory in southern Poland and in the Soviet Union province of Carpatho-Ukraine. The Carpathians partially surround the Little Hungarian Plain, which lies south and west of them. The ranges, in order of occurrence from west to east, are the Black Carpathians and White Carpathians, both in Moravia; the West Beskids, between Poland and Moravia; the Oravska or Arva Magura

the Dukla, the Lupkow, and the Wysz Row. The Dukla Pass is on the Polish-Carpatho-Ukrainian border, the others farther east. In Romania are the Prislopul and Borgo passes.

Essentially an eastern continuation of the Alps, the Carpathians have as their backbone a core of resistant crystalline rock, but most of the chain is composed of folded sedimentaries, presenting a less spectacular landscape than is found in the Alps. The structure has been greatly complicated by volcanic action and by complex folding and faulting. The northern mountains are rugged. The rocks of the Carpathians are largely Tertiary, with considerable Cretaceous, but much Archean on the southern and western slopes and in Transylvania. Quaternary and Palaeozoic rocks occur, but only in limited areas.

The January temperature ranges from 10° to 20° F., and

Hikers in the High Tatra Mountains, chief group of the Central Carpathians, pause at the edge of a small lake near Štrbske Pleso (Csorbato), Czechoslovakia, not far from the Polish border.

in Slovakia; the High Tatra between Slovakia and Poland, and the Low Tatra to the south, in mid-Slovakia; and the East Beskids, on the Slovakian-Carpatho-Ukrainian-Polish frontier. Here the Carpathians, continued in the Rodnei and Calamanului Mountains, bend rather sharply to the south. The Transylvanian Alps extend west and east between the Iron Gate on the Danube and the Siret (Sereth), a major Danubian tributary. The Hategului Mountains are a western extension of the Transylvanian Alps. Bukovina and Moldavia are east of the Carpathians, Wallachia to the south, while Transylvania is bounded by them on the east and south. The highest peak is Gerlsdorfspitze (8,737 ft.) in the High Tatra, at 49° N. lat., 20° E. long. Other prominent peaks are Negoiul (8,320 ft.) in the Transylvanian Alps, Djumbir (6,700 ft.) in the Low Tatra, and Howerla (6,689 ft.) in the East Beskids. The majority of the summits, however, are below 5,000 ft. elevation and are heavily timbered, particularly in the northern sections. Mountain floras occur in a few small areas. In the Carpathians are the headwaters of some of the principal rivers of central Europe—the Vistula, Oder, San, Tisza, Dniester, and Prut—and there are numerous lakes and ponds, many of them noted for their picturesque settings. Among the more important passes are

far below 10° on the summits. In July, the crest temperatures are 50° F. or below and elsewhere 50° to 60°. January rainfall ranges from 2 to 4 in., dropping to but 1 or 2 in. southwest of the mountains. July rainfall is heavy, 4 in. and upwards.

An area of the rather inaccessible eastern Carpathians has a population under 26 per sq. mi. The population is densest toward the western extremity of the range. Cattle grazing is the chief occupation in the northern Carpathians. The mixed hardwood and coniferous forests have been exploited for centuries. In Romania, where the climate is milder and the terrain less rugged, sugar beets, barley, and oats are cultivated. Wheat and maize are grown up to the eastern fringe of the range. In the foothills are gold, silver, copper, lead, and coal. Salt is mined. The Transylvanian Alps of central Romania are an important source of petroleum; and there is an oil field on the northern Carpathian slopes of Poland. The large Romanian communities of Brașov, Sibiu, and Cluj are situated in the mountainous section of the country.

Railroads cross the Carpathians at Leluchow and Lupkow, both in Poland; through the Tizsa valley via Jasiňa and Rahovo; from Bistrita to Câmpu Lung; from Brașov to

Sinaia; through the Olt valley; and via Petrosani and the Jiul valley.

Among numerous small ethnic groups surviving in the Carpathians are the Podolians, the Gorales, the Tukholzes, the Boikes (Bojki) of Ruthenia, and the Huzuli, all located along the northern and northeastern slopes, principally in Poland, and the Zeklers of Transylvania. The Carpathians between Tarnów and Moddova were the scene of a costly and indecisive winter campaign, January-April 1915, between the Austrian and Russian armies on the Eastern Front. The siege of Przemyśl by the Russians was a dramatic episode in this conflict. S. Van V.

CARPEAUX, JEAN BAPTISTE [ka'rpo'] (1827-1875), French sculptor, was born at Valenciennes, May 14, 1827. He studied in Paris with Abelde Pujol, Francisque Joseph Duret, and François Rude, and in 1854 won the Prix de Rome, producing in Italy the *Neapolitan Fisher Boy* and *Ugolino.* Carpeaux became the leading sculptor of the Second Empire, recording its typical figures in a series of distinguished portraits. In such works as the *Pavilion de Flore* pediment, the *Dance* (Paris Opera) and the *Four Parts of the World* (Luxembourg Gardens), he captured the spirit of the period. Freedom of movement, open forms and bold manipulation of surfaces for contrasts of light and shade characterize Carpeaux's original, nonacademic style. He died at the Château Bécon near Counbevoie, Oct. 11, 1875, and left a prodigious amount of work, including 3,000 drawings.
E. D. B.

CARPENTARIA, GULF OF, a large indentation of the Arafura Sea into northeastern Australia. The gulf is about 480 mi. long as measured along the 140° east meridian, and about 410 mi. wide at its greatest width along the 15° south parallel. On the east the gulf is bordered by the Cape York Peninsula of Queensland, and the western side is formed by Arnhem Land, of North Australia. Cape York forms the most northeastern point of the gulf, and the most northwesterly point of land is Cape Arnhem. The gulf is believed to be the remnant of a much larger sea which covered a large area of north central Australia. The present body of water occupies the lowest part of a large but rather shallow basin and probably does not exceed 250 ft. in depth. There are numerous islands in the gulf, particularly along the western and southern coasts.

The coast line of the Gulf of Carpentaria is rather even and low, except for the northwestern part, where the drowning of the edge of the Arnhem Plateau has formed islands and irregularities. The coastal region is an almost flat plain of sediment that extends between 60 and 200 mi. inland before it attains an elevation of 500 ft. above sea level in the east and south, but in the northwest the plain is only about 30 to 50 mi. wide. This gulf plain has a hot year-round climate; July, the coolest month, averages from 65° to 70° F. The winters are dry, but large amounts of rain fall during the Australian summer. The average annual rainfall along the coast may be about 20 to 40 in., but around Cape York and Cape Arnhem the precipitation is much higher. Because of the alternate wet and dry seasons, the vegetation is primarily high grass, with occasional jungles of high bushes and low thorn trees.

Because of this climatic rhythm, the rivers and creeks which flow into the gulf almost all tend to dry up during the winter. These streams are not of much value because they cannot be used for irrigation, for power, or for navigation, but at the mouths of some of these rivers small towns are located. The total population along the Gulf of Carpentaria

averages two or less per square mile. Some alluvial gold mining is carried on in the creek beds near the coast line, and there is a short railroad line that connects the Croydon gold and silver fields with Glenore and Normanton. There are occasional small-boat connections with Kimberly, and air services to Clancurry. The gulf is noted for its tremendous number of crocodiles. J. E. F.

CARPENTER, JOHN ALDEN (1876-1951), American composer, was born at Park Ridge, Ill., Feb. 28, 1876. He received basic music training with John Knowles Paine at Harvard University (A.B. 1897, M.A. 1922). He also studied abroad a few months with Sir Edward Elgar and did further theoretical study with Bernard Ziehn in Chicago. After leaving Harvard in 1897 he entered his father's business and, like his contemporaries Charles Ives and Wallace Stevens, combined a successful business career with creative activity. He died in Chicago, Ill., Apr. 26, 1951.

Carpenter wrote symphonic and chamber music, ballets, many songs (the *Gitanjali* cycle is his best known group), and other choral and instrumental works. He is claimed as an "Americanist" composer. Such works as the ballets *Krazy Kat* (1921, based on the cartoon strip) and *Skyscrapers* (1924), the charming symphonic suite *Adventures in a Perambulator* (1914), and the *Concertino for Piano and Orchestra* (1915) with its "ragtime" echoes certainly exemplify this tendency. But the deepest impetus for his music came from France. A strongly conservative personality, he rejected experimentation and adapted the luminous harmonic and orchestral palette of the French School. J. N.

CARPENTER BEE, the name given to members of the family Xylocopidae, of the order Hymenoptera. These are large bees that resemble bumblebees but are less hairy. They are generally black or metallic dark blue or green, but a few are yellowish. The carpenter bees are remarkable because of the large tunnels they construct in dead wood. The tunnels may be a foot long, and may result in considerable damage to structural timbers. They are divided into cells filled with pollen honey, and an egg is laid in each. The adults may hibernate in the tunnels. The small carpenter bees of the family Ceratinidae build their nests in hollow stems of plants or in small twigs. C. H. Cu.

CARPETBAGGERS, adventurers, political and economic, who moved into the South during the Reconstruction Era in American history and gained control of state governments by exploiting the Negro vote. Some native Southerners, called Scalawags, and former Confederate army officers were appointed to local offices by military governors. Northerners who went South to operate businesses or to make devious arrangements with the corrupt governments of the region, however, were the real Carpetbaggers. The term originally characterized private bankers in frontier towns, some of whom, in fact, began business with no more personal property than the contents of a carpetbag. Rabid southerners applied the term indiscriminately to all northerners who held office in the South. In the west, the term was applied to federal appointees to territorial offices when those appointees came from outside the locality. W. B. H.

CARPET GRASS, *Axonopus compressus,* a prolific, perennial 2-ft. grass, common in the tropics and the southern United States. It has broad leaf blades, slender flowering spikes, and underground stems. In rich lowlands from Virginia south, it is the chief pasture grass. J. C. Wis.

CARPETS AND RUGS. Although the term carpet usually refers to a large woven floor covering, sometimes reaching from wall to wall and often tacked down, as distinguished from the smaller rug or mat, the terms carpet and rug are frequently used interchangeably.

Early History. The weaving of rugs and carpets is a craft so ancient that its origins are shrouded in the mystery of distant ages. A loom with its workers is depicted in an Egyptian fresco of about 3000 B.C., but crude hand-weaving antedates the earliest Egyptian dynasty. It probably began in Mesopotamia (Iraq). The first wool carpet may have been woven in Babylon or Ninevah as early as 5000 B.C. The Roman historian Pliny relates that the Babylonians were skilled in the weaver's art. The most ancient records, including the Bible, mention the use of carpets. Woven floor coverings were made at a very early period by the Assyrians, Arabs, and Persians, and in China and India. They were woven in Egypt for use in temples 1,500 years before the Christian Era. These were not, however, carpets as we know them today—that is, carpets having a "pile" or surface of wool yarn tufts—but floor coverings having a flat weave, in the tapestry style, worked on a woven linen fabric. The most ancient bit of tufted or pile fabric preserved today, a forerunner of the modern carpet, dates back to the second century of the Christian Era.

Persian Rug Weaving. After the Persian conquest of Babylon in 538 B.C., Persian rug weaving gained ascendancy. The matchless artistry of Persian carpets placed them among the treasures of the rich and powerful of ancient times. Both Greece and Rome prized such carpets highly. The armies of Alexander the Great returned with them from Eastern conquests, and when the Romans subjugated the same areas the products of Oriental looms found their way farther westward to Italy. Centuries later the seizure of Constantinople by the Turks drove many skilled artists and craftsmen to Italy and France, and thus Oriental carpets penetrated to still other parts of Europe.

Marco Polo, setting out from Venice in the thirteenth century on his fabled travels through Asia, was amazed by the beauty of the rugs he saw. These rugs were priceless works of art, inimitable in their coloring. In Richard Hakluyt's *Principall Navigations, Voiages, and Discoveries of the English Nation* (1589) a trader about to journey to Persia is told: "In Persia you shall find carpets of coarse thrummed wool, the best of the world, and excellently colored . . . and you must use means to learn all the order of the dyeing of those thrummes, which are so dyed as neither rain, wine, nor yet vinegar can stain."

European Developments. The Crusaders of the later Middle Ages brought home with them from the holy wars examples of the wondrous rugs of the Orient to spread upon the cold stone floors of baronial halls, on cathedral floors, and on the floors of palace rooms in France, Germany, and England. Louis IX of France brought back such carpets on his return from the Crusades in 1254. With the Crusaders came the Saracens, who are credited by some historians with introducing rug and carpet weaving into Italy and Spain during the fourteenth century. The French called the Oriental rugs *sarrasinois,* from their Saracen origin. Whether the Saracens, or the Moors in their invasion of Spain, actually set up in Europe the earliest carpet looms, the first official record still in existence recognizing the art is that of Henry IV of France, creating in the Louvre, in 1604, a workroom for weaving Oriental carpets. French rug making was an outgrowth of tapestry weaving at Aubusson and Paris. Aubusson gave its name to the rug weave which is the same as tap-

estry except that a coarser stitch is used, making the fabric of sufficient thickness and weight to serve as a floor covering. The rugs made at Paris were exquisitely woven by hand and were of a deep, rich pile, in contrast to the flat weave of Aubussons. They became known as Savonnerie, from the abandoned soap factory in which they were first made (*savon* being the French word for soap). The Savonnerie technique is essentially the same as that employed in the hand-loomed carpets of the Orient. The two French weaves, Aubusson and Savonnerie, are among the most famous carpet names in history. Designed by the greatest artists of the times, woven with infinite care, they were works of art executed at the command of kings for palace and castle. Their period of greatest glory was reached under Louis XIV. When this monarch in 1685 revoked the Edict of Nantes, the members of the weavers' guilds, most of whom were Protestants, were left without religious protection, and large numbers of French artisans fled to Germany, Belgium, and England. In Brussels these refugees made the type of loop-pile carpet which bears the city's name. In England the carpet-weaving industry sprang up in the towns of Wilton and Axminster, which gave their names to these types of weaves, under a charter granted by King William III. Scotch weavers established looms in Kidderminster, an important name in English carpet manufacturing. The Brussels weave was introduced into England in 1740 by additional weavers brought from France and Holland.

Early Looms. Early in the nineteenth century, Joseph Marie Jacquard, in France, perfected a mechanical device applicable to existing hand looms, using perforated cards, on the principle of the player-piano roll, to form patterns in woven fabrics. His silk-weaving neighbors stoned him out of the French city of Lyons, fearing that his labor-saving invention would rob them of employment. Instead, Jacquard's loom, by revolutionizing the weaving of Wilton and Brussels fabrics, lowered production costs and brought rug prices within the reach of many more consumers. The result was greater employment than before for the weaving trades. Six years after his death the people of Lyons raised a monument to the memory of Jacquard. Today all Wilton rugs are woven on Jacquard looms.

Two other important European inventions extended the scope of rug weaving and spurred development of the industry. In 1831 Richard Whytock of Edinburgh, Scotland, developed a process of printing yarns for tapestry weaving, permitting the use of a greater range of colors, and reducing production costs. This development was followed in 1839 by an invention of James Templeton, a Glasgow weaver: a "patent Axminster" or double-weaving chenille process, which allowed a great saving in wool. This step further reduced manufacturing expense, and again widened the market for the products of carpet looms.

Developments in the United States. Still lacking, however, was the secret indispensable to the large-scale industrial production of rugs and carpets: namely, the application of power to the mechanical looms fashioned by these inventors. This immense step forward was made in the United States. For more than a century and a half after the settlement of America, the United States had bought virtually all of its carpets from England. It was not until after the Revolution that carpets were manufactured on a commercial basis in the United States. The first American tariff, drafted by Alexander Hamilton, was designed to protect the carpet industry at its inception. In 1791 William P. Sprague began the manufacture of Axminsters in Philadelphia, one of the first designs being a representation of the coat of arms of the new republic.

However, it was not until fifty years later that the industry began to assume substantial proportions. It may be said to have had its real beginning in 1825 in the little town of Medway, Mass., where Henry S. Burdett started a small ingrain carpet mill, supervised and managed by Alexander Wright, who worked with hand looms brought from his native Scotland. In 1828 the Lowell Manufacturing Company bought the Medway Mills, and in the same year Orrin Thompson was granted a charter to manufacture ingrain carpets at Thompsonville, Conn., as the Hartford Manufacturing Company. The period 1827-1831 is notable in the development of the American carpet industry. As noted by Arthur H. Cole and Harold F. Williamson in *The American Carpet Manufacture, a History and an Analysis* (1941): "These four or five years saw launched enterprises which, under favorable auspices, survived the competition of subsequent decades, and from which may be traced in an unbroken line concerns important or predominant in the present American industry. These were the Thompsonville Carpet Manufacturing Company in Enfield, Conn.; the Lowell Manufacturing Company at Lowell, Mass.; and the Saxon mill at Saxonville, Mass. Of these, the Thompsonville concern . . . and the Lowell company have since become amalgamated with other similar units to form the Bigelow-Sanford Company of today; while the Saxon factory constituted the original unit of the present Roxbury Carpet Company."

The First Power Loom. The year 1839 marks the technical advance which made possible the modern large-scale industrial production of rugs and carpets. This was the invention of the power carpet loom by Erastus Brigham Bigelow. The first steam-driven loom was set up in the Lowell Manufacturing Company mill. Up to this time the product of a hard day's work of 10 to 12 hours for a weaver, including a boy to draw the wires, was 7 yd. of Brussels-type carpet. Bigelow's loom produced more than 25 yd. of far superior fabric in the same time. It was this invention which revolutionized the industry and brought fine wool floor coverings within the reach of millions. For thousands of years the art of weaving had fashioned beauty and comfort for floors, but only for those of great wealth or title. Even as late as 1800 only the more prosperous homes could afford carpets. Bigelow's invention enabled the American carpet industry, within two decades, to provide the average man with something more than primitive coverings for his floors.

The Axminster Loom. Equally important to the development of the industry was the perfection in 1876 of Halcyon Skinner's loom for a machine-made Axminster. Skinner developed his invention, originally known as the Moquette loom, with the financial backing of Alexander Smith, founder of the firm of Alexander Smith and Sons, Yonkers, N. Y. By the end of the century Axminster looms of this type were turning out 40 to 60 yd. of carpeting a day, compared with the 1½ yd. previously produced in a day by the hand labor of two men and a boy.

The Broadloom. The first power carpet loom produced narrow fabrics, usually 27 in. wide, which were sewn together to produce rugs of various sizes, or to cover floors completely from wall to wall. Then came the development of the wide looms, which again revolutionized methods of production, making it possible to weave large seamless rugs in one piece in widths from 9 to 18 ft., and to produce the fabrics later in universal use. These looms brought into use the term "broadloom," which, however, contrary to popular misconception, does not refer in any sense to the type, color, or construction of the fabric, but to any carpet, plain or figured, woven in one piece on a loom 4½ ft. wide or wider.

The introduction of the broadloom profoundly influenced decorative practices. Floor coverings as a purely utilitarian fixture in the home—tacked to the floor, and taken up only for an outdoor beating at housecleaning times—gave way to rugs and carpets of style, design, and texture forming an integral part of the decorating scheme of the home. Today all American carpet manufacturers maintain staffs of stylists, designers, and colorists. Since 1930 there has been a growing trend toward complete wall-to-wall carpeting. In the smaller homes and in apartments this carpeting has made the rooms look larger and has tended to make furniture arrangement simpler.

Types of Weaving. *Axminster.* Axminster weaving simulates the hand-tufted carpets of the Orient, in that each tuft of wool is inserted into the warp independently. This method offers the designer unlimited opportunity to color every tuft without any weaving limitation. Nearly all of the yarn appears on the face of the carpet, combining economy in the use of material and in manufacture with richness of texture and endless potentialities of design, color, and textured effects. The Axminster weave is produced in greater yardage than any other in America, and is woven in seamless broadloom widths up to 18 ft. Axminster, which took its name from the English town, is in reality a true American achievement because of the invention of the Skinner-Smith loom. The term Axminster is often associated in the public mind only with a figured, low-cost rug. Actually, some of the costliest "high style" solid-color carpets are woven on types of Axminster looms. It is a popular fallacy that the method of weaving necessarily determines the quality of the individual carpet.

An Axminster rug 9 by 12 ft. can be woven in minutes but it requires weeks to set yarns for the design. Each color of the yarn is wound on spools. Each spool represents a row of tufts in the carpet, and each strand of yarn on the spool represents a tuft in that row. The spools are assembled in a single tube frame, a fixture that guides each end of yarn into its proper place in weaving. By mounting the spools in proper sequence in an overhead-chain carrying device, the frames are presented to the loom in correct order to form the pattern desired. At the proper time two "arms" reach up from the loom, remove the spool from the chain, and lower it, tubes foremost, into the lengthwise cotton warps, so that each yarn end is in its allotted position. In a split-second action, the suspended yarn is both bound into place and wrapped around a "shot" of jute thread, which is placed in the weave by the transverse action of a needle. The yarn from the spool is then cut by a pair of long knives in one scissorlike motion at the surface of the carpet, leaving the newly formed tuft in place, and the spool is returned to the conveying chain. The chain moves into position to present the next spool for the next row of tufts, and the process is repeated. Axminster carpets are the only carpets that cannot be rolled crosswise because of the stiff jute construction of the back.

Jacquard, or Wilton. Jacquard weaving, introduced into the United States at the beginning of the nineteenth century, embodies an attachment to the plain weaving process which makes possible the raising of each yarn thread independently to form a pattern. Most complicated of all carpet weaves, the Jacquard, or Wilton (so called from the English town in which it was first made), is produced by a series of pattern cards punched with holes like player-piano rolls. More than 11,000 such cards, each 2⅜ in. wide and 19 in. long, may be required for a single rug, each card controlling a row of pile tufts. The thousands of holes, punched by skilled operators, correspond to the checks and colors on the design paper for the carpet. Laced together on an endless belt at the top of the loom, the cards pass one by one over the Jacquard mechanism, directing the operation of needles which deftly select and lift the strands of yarn of the right color for the surface pile. All other yarns are left buried beneath the surface, giving to Jacquard or Wilton the name of the "hidden value" weave. The Brussels weave is exactly the same as Wilton, except that the yarn is left in loops instead of being a cut pile.

Velvet. The velvet weave is the simplest of all carpet weaves. The pile is woven over wires and cut as the wires are withdrawn. The velvet loom, generally employed in the weaving of solid-color rugs, is responsible for the greatest volume of plain carpeting. Velvet in the better qualities resembles Wilton in appearance, but lacks the structural quality of the Wilton, since there is no buried wool: only one yarn is used, but this yarn must be of good quality and of the same grade throughout in order to absorb the various color dyes properly. The tapestry weave is the same as the velvet, except that the wires have no knife blades on the end and so, when withdrawn, leave loops instead of a cut pile.

Chenille. The Chenille weave originated in France. *Chenille* is French for "caterpillar," the weave being so named because its surface is composed of rows of fuzzy, V-shaped cord or fur, cut in strips from a blanket woven on the weft loom. These strips are attached, by means of strong linen or cotton catcher threads, to the coarse wool backing of the rug as it is being woven on the second or Chenille loom. It is woven up to 30 ft. wide on a power loom.

Lokweave. A type of carpeting requiring no binding is the Lokweave. It can be cut in any direction without raveling. A sealer and tape are used in joining pieces, thus eliminating sewn seams, and giving an almost seamless effect in the finished installation. Special patterns or designs can be executed in any desired color scheme. If such a rug is damaged in any way, as by a bad stain or a burn, the damaged spot may be cut out and a new piece inserted and sealed into place.

Ingrain. The ingrain carpet was of a type of early power-loom weave now obsolete. Ingrain carpet was woven like plain cloth from 2-ply or 3-ply yarn, and dyed before weaving. The warp, often made up of threads of various colors, was so handled that the ground color of the design on the face became the color of the figure on the reverse; an ingrain carpet could therefore be used on either side. The name "ingrain" came from the mixing and weaving of these threads of different colors. The heaviest ingrain lacked the resiliency now possessed by even the cheapest looped-pile carpet.

Design and Color. In a rug or carpet, design and color are produced by a proper placing of tiny tufts of wool pile, each dyed a specific color. Each tuft of exactly the right color must be placed by the great loom in exactly the right position. Simple as may be the design, or intricate as are those inspired by Oriental carpets—whether with few or many colors—that design has been created by an artist who painstakingly builds it color by color, tuft by tuft. Designs are made on large sheets of paper cross-ruled into tiny squares each representing a single tuft of wool pile in the surface of the finished rug. There may be as many as 128 tufts to a square inch of fabric. Artists draw inspiration from leaves, flowers, and other natural forms, from Oriental and other foreign carpets, from historic textiles and tapestries, and from paintings—in fact, from every form of artistic expression. Carpet styles and design may be roughly grouped in the following classifications:

Oriental. Reproductions of priceless Persian carpets are included in this category. Types of Oriental design vary with the demand. Chinese motifs, as well as motifs from India, Egypt, Syria, and from other Mohammedan countries contribute their richness of form and symbolic significance to modern Oriental rugs.

Self-Tone. Out of plain broadlooms, to enliven solid colors, grew the self-tone, or tone-on-tone patterns, which are all-over designs in conventional and natural leaf and fern forms. These patterns, ranging from delicate, muted forms to bold, strong forms, are versatile in their wide adaptability. They employ two or more tones of the same color, enlivened at times by the introduction of highlights in a third color.

Texture. Interest is created by variations in texture through different heights of pile; by the use of cut and uncut pile; by "sculpturing," real or simulated; and by the use of twisted or frieze yarns. Texture, a distinctly modern contribution, ushered in the great revival in rug and carpet interest which began in the United States in the 1930's. Wide variation in textures is achieved by ingenious adaptations made in conventional looms. The texture types of carpets are particularly significant in Modern decoration.

Floral. Floral designs of various types are perennially popular. Patterns may be gay, stylized bouquet forms, particularly interesting in some Georgian and most Victorian decorative schemes. They may be conventional, all-over designs, or self-tone effects. Together with the closely related leaf and fern patterns in self-tone effects, the florals comprise a substantial contribution.

Early American. Modern looms produce replicas of the old hand-hooked rugs which were so extensively produced in Colonial days, particularly in New England. Their rich variety of color is especially effective when used with Early American decorative schemes.

Modern. By "Modern" is meant solid color or tone-on-tone broadloom, the texture-interest carpets and the newer modern leaf creations which became increasingly popular for wall-to-wall installations in the period following World War II.

Raw Materials. Wool, cotton, and jute are the raw materials from which a rug is made. Jute from India and Pakistan and cotton from various countries are used for the backing. Wool for the pile surface or wearing face of the rug is, of course, most important. All carpet wool is imported because American wool, fine and soft and therefore ideal for clothing and blankets, lacks the toughness and resiliency indispensable in carpet making. Before World War II disrupted the world market, carpet wools were imported from forty countries. After the war the number of countries supplying wools was reduced to seventeen, the principal sources of supply being Argentina, India, Iraq, Syria, Turkey, China, and the British Isles. The best carpet wools come from rugged, mountainous areas where hardy sheep grow long, tough, coarse, protective fleeces.

The characteristics of fiber length, strength, and resiliency essential to a good grade of carpet yarn are attained only by mixing the different kinds of wool. At the carpet factory, predetermined amounts of each grade are fed into a wool opener, where the tightly packed wools are stripped apart and the various locks blended in this first operation of carpet making. The raw wool is then scoured in successive washing and rinsing operations to remove grease and dirt. Dyeing is the next step. There are more than 4,000 colors, representing a range of hue, value, and intensity of the primary colors, within the carpet dyeing range. The blended wools are carded, or combed, on large revolving cylinders closely studded with fine wire teeth. The wool emerges from this operation in a yarn-like form known as "roving," which is then delivered to the spinning room, where it is drawn out to reduce its diameter, and at the same time it is twisted or spun into yarn strong enough to be woven. The yarn is then ready for the loom.

Since World War II rug manufacturers have made steadily growing use of synthetic materials, e.g. nylon and Orlon.
J. L. B.

CARPI, GIROLAMO DA [ka'rpi] (1501-1556), Italian painter originally known as Girolamo de' Sellari was born at Ferrara in 1501 and studied under Benvenuto da Garofalo. Under Pope Paul III he directed the architectural work on the pontifical palaces. As a painter he shows the influence of Correggio, many of the copies of that master which he made passing as originals. Examples of his works are the *St. George* and the *St. Jerome* at Ferrara and the *Descent of the Holy Spirit* in the church of St. Francis, Rovigo. Da Carpi died at Ferrara in 1556.
R. T.

CARPI, UGO DA [ka'rpi] (c. 1455-c. 1523), Italian wood engraver, was born in Carpi, a town near Modena, probably in 1455. He improved the German technique of making shaded wood engravings by using several blocks, one for the outline and others for different shades. To this process he gave the name of *chiaroscuro,* and his earliest known print in the method dates from 1518. Examples of his works, the best being after Raphael and Parmigianino, can be seen in most comprehensive collections of engravings. He died, probably at Rome, about 1523.
R. T.

CARR, HARVEY (1873-1954), American experimental psychologist, was born at Morris, Ill., Apr. 30, 1873. He received his bachelor's and master's degrees at the University of Colorado and his doctorate at the University of Chicago in 1905. Carr taught at Pratt Institute and the University of Chicago, where he directed the experimental psychology laboratory and was chairman of the department from 1926 to 1938, when he became professor emeritus. In 1926 he was president of the American Psychological Association. His experimental works were in three fields: comparative psychology, systematic learning, and visual space perception. His writings include *Psychology, a Study of Mental Activity* (1925) and *Introduction to Space Perception* (1935). He died on June 27, 1954, in Culver, Ind.
F. A. K.

CARRACCI, ANNIBALE [karra'ttshi] (1560-1609), Italian painter, the most famous of the Bolognese Carracci,

Annibale Carracci, Italian painter and one of the founders of the eclectic school of painting

CULVER SERVICE

was born in Bologna on Nov. 3, 1560. After a trip to Parma and Venice, he returned to Bologna in 1582, and with his brother, Agostino (1557-1602), and cousin, Ludovico (1555-1617), founded the renowned Bolognese Academy, the teachings of which were based on systematic eclecticism and an attempted codification of the arts. In 1595 Annibale went with his brother to Rome, where he effected a fusion of North Italian and Venetian elements with Roman Classicism, establishing a new current of art which forms the basis of the seventeenth-century Classicistic trend. As a reform directed against the decorative complexity and the superficiality of Mannerism, he sought a more natural style, simpler and more ordered in design and more serious in expression. His great achievement, the frescoes of the Gallery of the Palazzo Farnese, established a formula for palace decoration in the succeeding century. The seventeenth-century tradition of Roman Classical landscape also stems from such tranquilly ordered and composed landscapes as Annibale's *Flight into Egypt,* originally painted for the Villa Aldobrandini and now in the Doria Gallery. Annibale died in Rome on July 15, 1609.
M. C.

CARRANZA, BARTOLOMÉ DE [karra'ntha] (1503-1576), Spanish churchman, was born in Miranda, Navarre, in 1503. He joined the Dominican order in 1520, became a professor of theology at Valladolid, and attended the Council of Trent as a theologian in 1546. The confidant of Charles V and later Philip II, he accompanied Philip to England, and became confessor to Queen Mary. In 1558 he was appointed archbishop of Toledo and in the same year published his *Comentarios sobre el catequismo cristiano,* which brought the charge of heresy upon him by the Inquisition and resulted in imprisonment for the rest of his life. He died in Rome, May 2, 1576.

CARRANZA, VENUSTIANO [karra'nsa] (1859-1920), political leader and president of Mexico, was born in Cuatro Ciénegas, Coahuila, on Dec. 29, 1859. He held various government offices in Coahuila before being elected to the Mexican Senate in 1901. As a senator, Carranza supported Francisco I. Madero in the revolt against President Díaz in 1910. After Madero became president in 1911, Carranza was elected governor of Coahuila. In 1913, when the Madero government was overthrown by Victoriano Huerta and Madero was killed, Carranza assumed the leadership of the Constitutionalist forces, a group that opposed President Huerta. Although Huerta was supported by the foreign oil companies, he was forced to resign in 1914, and after a year of civil war, Carranza was recognized as provisional president. An advocate of a new constitution, Carranza convoked the Querétaro convention to draft the present constitution, which, among other reforms, provided improved social and labor laws, reasserted the government's right to subsoil mineral and oil deposits, and brought foreign oil operations in Mexico directly under Mexican law. These restrictive measures, plus production and exportation taxes, drew the resentment of foreign oil companies against Carranza. During World War I, Carranza kept neutrality for Mexico but lost favor through his failure to procure promised agrarian reforms. In 1920, General Álvaro Obregón led a revolt against Carranza, who fled toward Veracruz to rally his forces and save the government. He was captured and killed at Tlaxcalaltongo, Puebla, May 21, 1920.
S. G. I.

CARRARA [karra'ra], a city in northwestern Tuscany, in north central Italy, famous for its marble. It lies about

TET BORSIG

Quarrying marble in Carrara, a city in Tuscany

60 mi. south of Genoa, in a narrow valley among the foot-hills of the Apuanian Alps, 4½ mi. from the Tyrrhenian Sea. The extraction and working of marble, in over 400 quarries, is the city's leading industry and normally employs a third of the working population. This stone has been exported all over the world for buildings and monuments. Michelangelo used Carrara marble, and at times supervised its cutting and transportation. The quarries are connected with the finishing mills and with the small port of Marina di Carrara by a special railway.

In 1938 the commune of Carrara, which includes the city, was amalgamated with those of Massa and Montignoso to form the new commune of Apuania. The three communes regained their separate status after World War II; Carrara and the nearby city of Massa remained the administrative center of the province of Massa e Carrara.

The city is surrounded on all sides by the steep marble-bearing mountains distinguished by their white "glaciers" of stone tailings from the quarries. There is a marble-working school and a fine arts academy founded in 1769. The cathedral, dating from the twelfth century, has a Pisan façade and combines the Gothic with the Romanesque style. Although Carrara marble was known to the Romans, the city was not founded until the tenth century, and until 1261 it was under the control of local bishops. Thereafter it was ruled first by Pisa and then by a series of noble families, concluding with the Malaspina, Cybo, and Este. The city was damaged during World War II. Pop. 1954, 63,300.

R. G. W.

CARREL, ALEXIS [kæ′rəl, ka′rɛ′l] (1873-1944), French-American physician, surgeon, and biologist, was born at Ste-Foy-lès-Lyon, France, on June 28, 1873. He received an L.B. degree from the University of Lyon in 1890, an Sc.D. from the University of Dijon in 1891, and an M.D. from Lyon in 1900, after his internship at the Hospital of Lyon. He was prosector (demonstrator of dissections) at the University of Lyon from 1900 to 1902. The university authorities were indifferent toward his contributions to surgical tech-

nique, notably his method of surgical stitching, in which he had trained himself from school days by arduous exercises, and Carrel emigrated to Canada in 1904 with the thought of taking up cattle raising. In 1905, however, he came to the United States and spent a year at the physiology laboratories of the University of Chicago. Thenceforth he was connected with the Rockefeller Institute for Medical Research, serving on its staff from 1906 to 1912, as member from 1912 to 1939, and then as member emeritus. During World War I, from 1914 to 1919, he was a major in the medical corps of the French army. At this time, with Henry D. Dakin, Carrel developed the invaluable Carrel-Dakin solution for the treatment of wounds and the prevention of gangrene.

Carrel was distinguished as a surgeon and biologist and was noted especially for the brilliance of his research and his work in the field of experimental surgery. His contributions in developing methods for suturing blood vessels (vascular ligature) and for transplanting arteries, veins, and organs won him the 1912 Nobel Prize for physiology and medicine. He studied the physiology of living tissues, succeeded in cultivating chicken-heart and other tissues outside the body, and performed other work in this field. With Charles A. Lindbergh, he invented the mechanical heart (perfusion pump) for the cultivation of organs. Among his awards, besides the Nobel Prize, were the United States Distinguished Service Medal (1922), the Nordhoff-Jung Cancer Prize (1931), and the Newman Foundation Award (1937).

Carrel wrote *Treatment of Infected Wounds* (with Georges Dehelly, 1917), *Man, the Unknown* (1935), *The Culture of Organs* (with Charles A. Lindbergh, 1938), and *The Prayer,* published posthumously. He also contributed many articles and reports on biological and surgical subjects to scientific journals. In *Man, the Unknown* he elaborated a system of world government by an intelligentsia, the High Council, to whose "thinking center" politicians would repair for advice. In June 1940, after the fall of France, the German-dominated

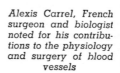

Alexis Carrel, French surgeon and biologist noted for his contributions to the physiology and surgery of blood vessels

CULVER SERVICE

Vichy government appointed Carrel director of the Foundation for the Study of Human Relations, to promote the mental and physical "reconstruction" of mankind in accordance with authoritarian ideas. In August 1944, after the liberation of Paris, he was dismissed from his post and charged with being a collaborationist with the Germans. He died in Paris on Nov. 5, 1944.

D. D. M.

CARRERA, RAFAEL [karrɛ′ra] (1814-1865), Central American soldier and conservative president of Guatemala.

He became known during the anticlerical Liberal revolt against President Morazán of the Central American Confederation in 1837. Ten years later, after Morazán was overthrown and the Confederation dissolved, Carrera imposed himself as president of Guatemala. He was twice elected, and in 1854 became perpetual president, serving until his death in 1865. Carrera was illiterate and gained a reputation for reaction and cruelty.   S. G. I.

CARRERA ANDRADE, JORGE

CARRERA ANDRADE, JORGE [karre′ra andra′the] (1903-   ), Ecuadorian poet, was born in Quito, Sept. 28, 1903. After studying literature in Spain at the Uni-

Jorge Carrera Andrade, Ecuadorian poet

COURTESY OF THE MACMILLAN COMPANY

versity of Barcelona and in France at Aix-en-Provence, he became secretary-general of the Ecuadorian Socialist Party (1927-1928) and later entered the diplomatic service, occupying posts in Europe, Asia, and South America.

Carrera Andrade and the Chilean Pablo Neruda have been called the greatest modern poets of Spanish America, but they have developed in opposite ways. Neruda began by writing poems of purely aesthetic value but turned later to social and political themes; Carrera Andrade, on the other hand, was an active revolutionary in his earlier years, but when he wrote poetry he was guided exclusively by aesthetic principles. He started writing when he was very young, and his first book, *El Estanque inefable* (*Secret Country,* 1946) dates from 1922, but the work that made him famous was *Boletines de mar y tierra* ("Bulletins of Sea and Land"), published with a prologue by Gabriela Mistral in 1930. His fame increased with *El Tiempo manual* (1935) ("Manual Time"); *Rol de la manzana* (1935) ("Catalogue of the Apple"), *Biografía para uso de los pájaros* (1937) ("Biography for the Birds"), and *La Hora de las ventanas iluminadas* (1937) ("Hour of the Lighted Windows"). In 1942 an anthology of his poetry was published whose title, *Registro del mundo* ("Census of the World"), reflects the artist's intent to examine the world, to know it step by step, and to prepare almost a catalogue of terrestrial beauty.

Carrera Andrade's poetry, taken in one aspect, is poetry of the restless traveler, and he confesses his feeling that his blood is "full of ships that come and go with each moment." A profusion of geographical names appears in his verses: the rivers, seas, and cities of three continents. The other basic aspect of his poetry is an inventory of material things, and in his poem *El Objecto y su sombra* ("The Object and Its Shadow") he expresses his feeling for them: "Things—that is to say, life." His ambition as a poet is to see these things limpidly and to clear the world "of the phantoms of the mind," but he does not hesitate to use metaphors for most of them, and this characteristic is responsible for much of his poetic power. Carrera Andrade is the greatest Ecuadorian writer, and one of the outstanding Hispanic poets of the twentieth century, a period which has been compared with the golden age of Spanish poetry.   J. A. L. M.

CARRÈRE, JOHN MERVEN [kəre′r] (1858-1911), American architect, was born in Rio de Janeiro, Brazil, on Nov. 9, 1858, of American parents. At the age of fourteen he was sent to school in Switzerland, and in 1882 he received a diploma from the École des Beaux-Arts, Paris. He was with the architectural firm of McKim, Mead and White in the year 1883-1884; then, after a two-year interval of private practice, he formed, with Thomas Hastings, the firm of Carrère and Hastings, with which he was associated the rest of his life. Prominent among their buildings are the Public Library, the Century Theatre, and the Thomas F. Ryan Art Gallery in New York; the United States Senate and House office buildings in Washington; and the Royal Bank of Canada in Montreal. The firm won wide acclaim for these correct but unfunctional Classical and Florentine re-creations and for the Ponce de Leon and Alcazar hotels in St. Augustine, Fla., which were in an eclectic Spanish-Moorish style. Carrère died in New York City on Mar. 1, 1911.   R. Ne.

CARRIÈRE, EUGÈNE [ka′rye′r] (1849-1906), French painter, was born in Gournay (Seine et Marne), Jan. 17, 1849. He developed a very personal technique by reducing his color scheme to tones of misty gray, using a strong division of planes, blurred outlines, and contrasts of black and white, thus conveying an atmosphere of mystery and simple poetry. Among his best-known works are *Portrait of the Poet Paul Verlaine* in the Luxembourg, Paris, and *Maternity.* He died Mar. 27, 1906, in Paris.   K. B.

CARRIER PIGEON, in popular usage the name applied to a pigeon trained to return home from a distance carrying a message, but such a bird is nowadays more properly called a homing pigeon. By releasing it at gradually increased distances from its loft, one can teach it to find its way back with some certainty from as far as 1,000 mi.
                                    H. G. De.

CARRION BEETLE is the name given to members of the family Silphidae of the order Coleoptera. Most of them feed on dead matter, but others are destructive to plants. The species of *Necrophorus* and some species of *Silpha* are notable for their habit of burying small dead animals to provide food for their young. If a dead mouse is found, these beetles will dig out the soil beneath it until the animal is below the surface of the ground. Eggs are laid on it, and it is covered over. Often, a single beetle will do the work, very frequently two will be present; less often, there are three or more. The species of *Necrophorus* are large (¾ in. to 1 in. or more), and usually have orange spots on the elytra. In *Silpha,* the length is usually about ½ in., the elytra blackish, the thorax usually more or less yellow.
                                    C. H. Cu.

CARRION FLOWER, *Stapelia,* about sixty species of low (2.5-12 in.), fleshy, cactuslike herbs of the milkweed family (Asclepiadaceae), native to arid parts of Africa. In spite of their fetid smell, several species are grown in greenhouses for their dull-purplish, variegated flowers, sometimes a foot across. The outer surface of the stem contains the green tissue, and the center is used for storing water, as with the cactus. In eastern North America a thornless, herbaceous species of greenbrier, *Smilax herbacea,* with small greenish ill-smelling flowers, is also called carrion flower. J. C. Wis.

CARROLL, CHARLES (1737-1832), United States senator, signer of the Declaration of Independence, who signed himself Charles Carroll of Carrollton. He was born at Annapolis, Md., Sept. 19, 1737, of a wealthy Roman Catholic family.

Upon attaining the age of twenty-eight, after an extensive education in church schools in Maryland and France, Carroll settled in his native province to manage one of the family estates. With the approach of the American Revolution, he began to take an interest in politics, writing and performing organizational work for the patriotic cause. His ability to speak French and his standing as a lay Catholic were factors in his selection by the Continental Congress in 1776 as one of three emissaries sent to Canada to make an effort to persuade that country to ally herself with the revolutionary cause. Upon his return, Carroll was elected to Congress and signed the Declaration of Independence. From 1776 to 1779 he served in the Continental Congress and from 1789 to 1792 as a United States senator, becoming a strong Federalist. Carroll devoted his later years to the development of his vast landholdings and to the affairs of internal improvement companies. He was reputed to be the wealthiest citizen of the United States when he died at the age of ninety-five in Baltimore, Nov. 14, 1832. He was the last surviving signer of the Declaration of Independence.

R. W.

CARROLL, JAMES (1854-1907), American bacteriologist and army surgeon, was born in Woolwich, England, June 5, 1854. He received his early education at Albion House Academy, Woolwich, and in 1869 emigrated to Canada. He then went to the United States and in January 1874 enlisted in the United States Army. In 1883, while serving as a sergeant in the Seventh United States Infantry at Fort Snelling, he became a hospital steward and gained permission to continue his medical studies elsewhere. He attended New York University from 1886 to 1887, the University of Maryland from 1889 to 1891, and Johns Hopkins University from 1891 to 1892. In 1895 he became an assistant to Major Walter Reed, then curator of the Army Medical Museum in Washington. In 1900, when Reed was made chairman of an army commission to study yellow fever, Carroll was the second in command in Cuba. In 1898 at Camp Alger he had studied the blood of fever patients and showed conclusively that the disease was typhoid, not malaria. With Reed, Aristides Agramonte, and Jesse W. Lazear, Carroll did epochal work in isolating the cause of yellow fever. In 1902 Carroll was appointed a first lieutenant and assistant surgeon in the army, and in 1903 he was made associate professor of bacteriology and pathology at George Washington University; in 1905 he became a full professor. Carroll was promoted to major in the army by special act of Congress in 1907. His greatest scientific contribution was to establish that the yellow fever virus is ultramicroscopic. He died Sept. 16, 1907, in Washington, D. C.

CARROLL, JOHN (1735-1815), proto-bishop of the Roman Catholic Church in America, was born at Upper Marlboro, Maryland, Jan. 8, 1735. His youth was affected by the social, educational, and political disabilities under which the Catholics of colonial America labored, and in his long priestly and episcopal career he did much to lessen them. Educated at St. Omer's, Louvain, Belgium, he entered the Jesuit Novitiate at Watten, Belgium, Sept. 8, 1753. The decree of Pope Clement XIV, suppressing the Society of Jesus (Aug. 16, 1773), found Carroll at Bruges an ordained and professed Jesuit priest. The following year he returned to Maryland as a secular priest and immediately aligned himself with the cause of the rebellious colonists. His appointment as Prefect-Apostolic by the Holy See in 1784, his consecration as Bishop of Baltimore at Lulworth, England, in 1790, and his subsequent elevation to Archbishop of Baltimore in 1808 mark the organization of the unsettled Catholic Church in America into a unified, learned, patriotic body of clergy and laity. Carroll surmounted the evils of trusteeism and nationalism among his subjects, established three seminaries for the training of his future clergy, drew up the first American code of discipline for clergy and laity at the first general synod at Baltimore in 1791, founded Georgetown College, and gave the initial impetus to the system of Roman Catholic primary and secondary education followed in America. He died at Baltimore, Dec. 3, 1815. W. C.

CARROLL, LEWIS. *See* Dodgson, Charles Lutwidge.

CARROLL, a city in west central Iowa, the county seat of Carroll Co., about 75 mi. northwest of Des Moines, situated in an agricultural area known for its corn. It was incorporated as a city in 1869 and has the mayor and council form of government. A site of interest is the Swan Lake State Park. Transportation is furnished by the Chicago and Northwestern and the Chicago Great Western railways. Local industries manufacture ladders and farm equipment. A cold-storage plant for poultry and eggs is located in the town. Pop. 1950, 6,231.

CARROLL COLLEGE, located on a 50-acre campus at Helena, Mont., is an accredited, privately controlled, coeducational college of arts and sciences affiliated with the Roman Catholic Church. Carroll was founded in 1909 as Mount Saint Charles College and opened for instruction in 1910. The name was changed to Carroll College in 1932 to honor the founder, the Most Reverend John Patrick Carroll. The department of nursing education for women was added in 1946. Degrees granted are the A.B. and the B.S. in liberal arts and business administration. Degrees in nursing education were to be granted beginning in 1950. Undergraduate scholarship aid is available. All students must reside in college dormitories or in approved homes. *For statistics see* Colleges and Universities.

CARROLL COLLEGE, an accredited, coeducational college of arts and sciences located on a 37-acre campus at Waukesha, Wis., about 18 mi. west of Milwaukee. It is affiliated with the Presbyterian Church. Carroll College was first known as Prairieville Academy, and instruction was begun in 1840. The present name was adopted in 1846, when the college was granted a charter. The degrees conferred are the A.B. and B.S. Carroll is affiliated with Illinois Institute of Technology in a five-year engineering program in which students spend three years at Carroll and two at Illinois. A number of field trips are given in connection with courses in biology, astronomy, geology, and psychology. A full teacher-training program is also offered. Limited scholarship and student-loan aid is available. Dormitory facilities are provided for men and women, and a Commons-Union houses the college dining halls, snack bar, student-activities offices, lounges, and ballroom. Out-of-town students must live in residence halls or in approved homes. *For statistics see* Colleges and Universities.

CARROLLTON [kæ'rəltən], the seat of Carroll Co. in northwestern Georgia, was named for Charles Carroll, a signer of the Declaration of Independence. It lies on the Little Tallapoosa River about 50 mi. southwest of Atlanta. As a trade center for a region which produces cotton, fruit, poultry, and livestock, it manufactures textiles, hosiery, fertilizer, lumber, and processed food. West Georgia College, a unit of the University System of Georgia, was established in Carrollton in 1933. The local government is headed by a mayor and council. Rail transportation is provided by the Central of Georgia. Pop. 1950, 7,753.

CARROT, *Daucus carota,* a member of the parsley family which often grows wild. Carrots were first introduced into England from Holland during the sixteenth century. The species, *D. c. sativa,* because of its flavor, nutritive value, and accessibility, is one of the most popular vegetables. When grown for stock feed, carrots are left in the ground until late fall to obtain large yields. Carrot seed may be sown in earliest spring and the roots left in the ground until late fall without danger. A well-limed sandy loam soil is most suitable. The seed is slow to germinate and radish seeds, about one to the inch, should be sown with it to mark the rows so that tillage may start promptly. The radishes are removed within four weeks. When the carrot plants are 3 to 4 in. tall they must be thinned to 2 to 4 in. apart. Early varieties require about ten weeks to reach edible size; late ones, including stock-feed varieties, from early spring until late fall. There are many excellent varieties available for garden and commercial culture.

CARRYING CHARGES, a term used loosely to refer to interest and other charges made on loans. Thus, the charges made by a broker for a loan to a customer to finance the purchase of securities are sometimes called carrying charges. Carrying charges on loans made by finance companies often include charges for credit investigation, and for insurance on property pledged as security. On real-estate mortgage loans, carrying charges may include payments for taxes as well as periodic repayments of principal. H. C. S.

CARSON, CHRISTOPHER ("KIT") (1809-1868), American trapper and guide, was born in Madison County Ky., Dec. 24, 1809, but was reared on the Missouri frontier. He worked as a saddler's apprentice and teamster in the Southwest, but in 1826 became a professional trapper, hunter, and guide in the Rocky Mountain region. He accompanied John C. Frémont on his various journeys of exploration from 1842 to 1846. In 1853 he took part in the Mexican War, and later he became Indian agent at Taos, N. M. He resigned this post when the Civil War began to help organize the First New Mexican Volunteer Infantry and was commissioned a lieutenant colonel, eventually becoming a brevet brigadier general. Illiterate, modest, and taciturn, he was remarkable for his exploits, but accounts of his life have often been glorified to suit fancy rather than fact. He died at Ft. Lyon, Colo., May 23, 1868.

CARSON LAKE and **LOWER CARSON LAKE,** in Churchill County, west central Nevada. Lower Carson Lake, the smaller of the two, is about 25 mi. north of Carson Lake. Both lakes are within the Carson Desert. During recent geologic history the region was under the waters of ancient Lake Lahontan. Lake Lahontan dried up and some small saline remnant lakes, among them the Carson Lakes, were left in the former lake bed. Carson Lake is fed by the Carson River, which flows down the eastern slope of the Sierra Nevada Mountains. In the early spring the melting snows of the Sierras cause the river to have a short high-water period which fills Carson Lake and makes it overflow. The excess water flows northward into Lower Carson Lake, which dries up during the summer. J. E. F.

CARSON CITY, the capital city of Nevada, the county seat of Ormsby Co., in the western part of the state, near the California state line. Carson City is 4,720 ft. above sea level, located about 25 mi. south of Reno and 12 mi. east of Lake Tahoe. In the vicinity are gold, silver, and copper mines; 16 mi. to the west is Virginia City, the site of the famous Comstock Lode. The city is named after Kit Carson, well-known scout and Indian fighter of the nineteenth century. It was designated as the capital in 1864 and made a city in 1874. The state museum at Carson City, a branch of the United States Mint from 1870 to 1893, contains a large collection of Indian relics, minerals, mastodon skeletons, and other fossils found in the vicinity. The state supreme court, library, and penitentiary are also located here. The area about the city is suitable for farming and livestock raising, and lumbering and mining are among the principal industries. Pop. 1950, 3,082.

CARSON-NEWMAN COLLEGE, at Jefferson City, Tenn., an accredited, coeducational, privately controlled college of liberal arts located on a 72-acre campus. It is affiliated with the Baptist Church and was chartered in 1851 as Mossy Creek Missionary Baptist Seminary. First instruction began in that year. In 1856 the name was changed to Mossy Creek Baptist College, and in 1880 to Carson College in honor of J. H. Carson, a benefactor. Upon its merger with Newman College for Women in 1899, the name was changed to Carson-Newman College. Degrees offered are the A.B. and B.S. in liberal arts and the B.S. in commerce. In addition to the newly added curriculum in business administration a major sequence in physical education and music has been established. Notable among the college buildings is the astronomical observatory equipped with an excellent telescope. A library, a fine arts building, a central heating plant, and eight apartments for married students are among others recently erected. A student-loan fund and a number of scholarships in small amounts are available. Women students are required to live either in the college residences or with relatives nearby. *For statistics see* COLLEGES AND UNIVERSITIES.

CARTAGENA [ka'rtahe'na; kartəji'nə], a seaport and the capital of Bolívar department on the Caribbean coast in northwest Colombia. One of the most picturesque cities in the Americas, Cartagena lies on an island within its excellent harbor and is reached by a causeway. The city has a hot climate, the temperature averaging 82° F.

Cartagena was founded on Jan. 21, 1533, by Pedro de Heredia, and soon ranked after Mexico City as the most important city of the New World. In spite of strong fortifications, including twenty-nine forts and bastions and walls 40 ft. thick, which remain in a remarkable state of preservation, the city was attacked by French forces in 1544. It was seized by the English buccaneer, Francis Drake, who exacted a heavy ransom in 1585, and was taken by French forces in 1697, a tribute of $5,000,000 being obtained on this occasion. Forces led by the English admiral Edward Vernon unsuccessfully attacked the city in 1741, and it remained under the rule of Spain until 1811, when it was the first city of New Granada

Cartagena, Colombia, once the scene of great yearly fairs and the departure of treasure-laden galleons, now harbors the local fishing and some larger vessels.

to declare its independence. It was one of the bases from which Bolívar launched his campaign to liberate Venezuela. The Barataria Pirates led by Jean Lafitte, who harassed Spanish and British shipping from their headquarters near New Orleans, held their commissions from the Republic of Cartagena. The city fell, after a siege of nearly a year, to the Spanish general Pablo Morillo; for its resistance and the savage punishment it endured, it was named the Heroic City. It was liberated and incorporated in the new state of Gran Colombia in 1821.

The new districts of the city are modern and attractive, but the old area within the walls remains the heart of the metropolis. Old buildings include the Palace of the Inquisi-

The old section of Cartagena, Colombia, with the spire of the sixteenth-century cathedral in the background.

PHILIP GENDREAU

tion and the cathedral dating from 1538, one of the three oldest ecclesiastical buildings in the Americas. The fortress of San Felipe, guarding the city, was one of the most elaborate fortifications of colonial Latin America; it was completed in 1657 after twenty-seven years of labor at great cost. The University of Cartagena, one of the republic's four departmental universities, and the Naval School of Colombia

are located in Cartagena. Knit goods, perfumes, chocolate, sugar, candles, leather, lard, soap, footwear, and beverages are among the local manufactures; the principal exports are oil, coffee, and hides. Cartagena is reached by rail as well as by sea, and air services connect it with other Latin American cities. Pop. 1951, 111,291.   S. G. I.

CARTAGENA, a historic port and naval base on the Mediterranean Sea, in the province of Murcia, in southeastern Spain, about 250 mi. southeast of Madrid. It is situated at the head of a magnificent natural harbor, deep and narrow, but spacious and commanded by high ground. The climate is mild, though occasionally in winter the city is exposed to chilly north winds. The annual rainfall at Cartagena averages 15 in.

Cartagena lives largely from its port, the finest belonging to Spain in the Mediterranean. It is strongly protected from seaward attack by forts on near-by hills, by various batteries, and other defensive works. The arsenal, dry and floating docks, warehouses, hospital, barracks, and other parts of the Spanish navy's extensive establishment employ many men. Since the later nineteenth century the government has invested large sums to improve and modernize the facilities of the naval base, and it was first in importance at the time of the Civil War of 1936-1939. The port also exports much of the agricultural produce and the mineral output (lead, silver, zinc, iron, copper, and sulphur) from near-by mining districts. Some of these ores are processed at local smelters. Cartagena has suffered in the twentieth century from the competition of such other ports as Alicante, Málaga, and Valencia. It is at the end of a rail line to Murcia, Albacete, and Madrid.

The city itself is of only moderate interest. Parts of the ancient walls remain as well as the Puerta de San José. The cathedral, a Gothic structure, was built in the thirteenth century. Overlooking the city are the castillos del Moro, de la Concepción, de las Galeras, and de San Julián. The suburb of Santa Lucia, adjacent to the harbor, is an industrial center. To the east is the mining district around La Unión, and beyond this lies the Mar Menor, a shallow lagoon (12 by 7 mi.) separated from the sea by a narrow isthmus north of Cape Palos.

The foundation of Cartagena is traced to Hasdrubal, son-in-law of Hamilcar Barca, about 243 B.C. The city soon became the greatest Carthaginian stronghold in Spain, known to the Romans as Carthago Nova, and provided Carthage with wealth from its gold and silver mines. Scipio Africanus captured the city in 209 B.C. This famous victory led eventually to the destruction of Carthaginian supremacy in Spain and still later to Carthage's downfall in Africa. The city became a fortress and one of the two chief Roman administrative centers in eastern Spain. The Romans likewise exploited the near-by mines with great labor gangs and eventually exhausted the silver veins.

The Visigoths largely destroyed the city in A.D. 425, but it seems to have revived somewhat under the Moors, who called it Kartadjanah. St. Ferdinand took it for Castile in 1243, but soon lost it. James I ("the Conqueror") of Aragon finally drove out the Moors in 1269. Thereafter it declined to a mere village until revived for naval purposes by Philip II in the sixteenth century. Favoring the Austrian claimant in the War of the Spanish Succession, it was first occupied by the English in 1706 and later by the French. It led the Andalusian revolt against the French in 1808 and took part in the insurrections of 1844 and 1873. The latter lasted several months, during which the city was besieged and bombarded from the sea. Though the government of the republic won, it fell into disrepute and was soon overthrown. Cartagena remained in Loyalist hands throughout the Civil War of 1936-1939,

still stand, among them the Basilica of Our Lady of the Angels. The Church of La Negrita enjoys widespread fame, drawing pilgrims from Mexico, Nicaragua, and other Central American countries. Cartago was the seat of the Central American Court of Justice during the years of the court's existence, from 1908 to 1918, and the organization occupied a building donated by Andrew Carnegie, the American philanthropist. Coffee is the chief product of the surrounding area, which is a fertile agricultural region; cattle raising is also important. Cartago is connected by rail with San José and the port of Limón. Pop. 1950, 12,944.   S. G. I.

CARTEL. *See* MONOPOLY AND COMPETITION.

CARTER, HOWARD (1873-1939), English Egyptologist, was born in Swaffham, Norfolk, in 1873, the son of Samuel John Carter, an animal painter. He was educated privately and in 1891 was sent to Egypt under the auspices of Lord Amherst of Hackney as a draftsman with the Egyptian Exploration Fund. The following year he obtained his first digging experience under Professor Flinders Petrie at Tel el Amarna. He remained with the Exploration Fund, on the staff of Professor Édouard Naville at Deir el-

Panorama of Cartagena, Spain

and served as base for that part of the fleet which did not go over to Franco. Pop. 1950 (city), 38,839; (metropolitan area), 72,000; (municipality), 110,979.   R. G. W.

CARTAGO [kɑrtɑ'go], the capital city of the province of the same name in central Costa Rica, situated about 12 mi. east of San José, at 9° 50′ N. lat. and 83° 50′ W. long. The city is 4,930 ft. above sea level and has a mean temperature of 78° F. The volcano of Irazú rises to a height of 11,260 ft. beside the city, and there are hot mineral springs at Agua Caliente, a suburb. Cartago was founded in 1563 by the Spanish conquistador Juan Vásquez de Coronado. It served as the capital city of the country until 1823, when the capital was moved to San José because of repeated seismic disturbances. The town was virtually destroyed by earthquakes in 1823 and 1910, and was substantially damaged by tremors on other occasions, notably in 1723 and 1841. In spite of the earthquakes, many of the old churches and other buildings

Bahari, until 1900, when he was appointed Inspector General for the Antiquities Department of the Egyptian Government. Working under Sir Gaston Maspero and Sir William Garstin, he installed electric lighting at Abu Simbel and the Tombs of the Kings at Thebes, and as assistant to Theodore M. Davis in excavation work in the Valley of Tombs was largely responsible for the discovery of the tombs of King Mentuhotep I, Queen Hatshepsut, and Thutmose IV. In 1903, shortly after being transferred to Sakkara as inspector for Lower and Middle Egypt, he was dismissed from the department as the result of an unfortunate incident with a group of disorderly French tourists, and for several years devoted his time to painting water colors of Egyptian scenes. In 1906 he became associated with the 5th Earl of Carnarvon in excavation work at the Theban Necropolis which resulted in the discovery of the tomb of Amenhotep I, the Valley Temple of Hatshepsut, the cemetery of the Eighteenth-Dynasty queens, and the cliff tomb of Princess Hatshepsut. Further digging was interrupted by World War I, but as soon as conditions permitted he persuaded Lord Carnarvon to continue exploration in the Valley of Tombs. Finally, in November 1922, he made what was possibly the most important archaeological discovery in Egypt, the tomb of Tutankhamen of the Eighteenth Dynasty. The tomb of the boy king, unopened for over three thousand years, yielded a wealth of art objects, furniture, and jewelry which Carter spent some ten years in packing, preserving, and recording for the National Museum at Cairo. He died in London on Mar. 2, 1939, and left several works which described his explorations in Egypt.   C. W. D.

CARTER, MRS. LESLIE (1862-1937), American actress, was born Caroline Louise Dudley, at Lexington, Ky., on June 10, 1862. After an unhappy marriage with Leslie Carter in 1880 and an obscure theatrical start she had her first great stage success under the management and tutelage of David Belasco as Maryland Calvert in his *The Heart of Maryland* in 1895. She played this part with great success both in New York and London for five years. Belasco starred her for over a decade in several shoddy plays and adaptations of his own, notably *Adrea, Zaza,* and *Du Barry.* In 1906 she married William L. Payne. Later, under her own management and then under David Cort's, she was for a decade before the public. After a brief retirement she made a triumphant return to the stage in 1921 as the frivolous Lady Kitty in W. Somerset Maugham's *The Circle.* Later she toured in *The Shanghai Gesture* and *Stella Dallas.* In her seventies she played in a motion picture, *The Vanishing Pioneer.* She died in California on Nov. 13, 1937.   D. T.

CARTER, NICK, the hero of a series of detective stories of the dime-novel genre, popular in the last decade of the nineteenth century. The character of Nick Carter was created in 1886 by John Russell Coryell (1848-1924), and his lurid adventures were continued by other writers, notably Thomas Chalmers Harbaugh (1849-1924) and Frederick Van Renssalaer Dey (1861-1922); often the writer used the pseudonym of Nick Carter. Some four million copies of the stories were sold, usually in pulp-magazine form. They represent the late and somewhat degenerate type of the so-called dime novel, produced by hack writers of the Civil War and Reconstruction eras, generally simple and romantic tales of the Far West with heroes like Daniel Boone and Davy Crockett and clear-cut villains inevitably foiled near the 120th page by a time-honored formula. The Nick Carter stories were less wholesome and related the operations of its sleuth-hero in an endless series, much in the manner of subsequent comic books.   E. A.

CARTERET, SIR GEORGE [kɑ'rtərɛt] (c. 1610-1680), English political leader, was born on Jersey, in the Channel Islands, about 1610. He became comptroller of the English navy in 1639, and was active on behalf of Charles I. He succeeded his uncle, Sir Philip de Carteret (1584-1643), as bailiff of Jersey, and proceeded to suppress the Parliamentary party on the island. For this service he was created vice-admiral of Jersey, and proceeded to harry such Parliamentary ships as came his way. Jersey became a refuge for the Royalists who had fled from England, including Prince Charles, later Charles II, who made Carteret a baronet in 1650. A year later, surrounded by overwhelming forces, he was forced to surrender the island to the Parliament and fled to France, where he served as a vice-admiral in the French navy. In 1660, at the

Restoration, he returned to England with Charles II. He was made a privy councilor and was member of Parliament for Portsmouth. He served as treasurer of the navy from 1661 to 1667, and in 1669 was severely censured by the House of Commons for the incompetence with which he had controlled the funds in his keeping. He was one of the eight persons to whom Charles II granted the colony of Carolina in 1663 and 1665; and in 1664 James, Duke of York, later James II, granted him and Lord John Berkeley the American territory between the Hudson and Delaware rivers. In honor of his defense of Jersey, this land was named New Jersey. He served as deputy treasurer of Ireland from 1667 to 1673, and sold his share of the New Jersey grant in 1674. Carteret died in London on Jan. 14, 1680.   R. T.

CARTERET, JOHN (EARL GRANVILLE) (1690-1763), English statesman, grandson of Sir George Carteret and great-grandson of Admiral Sir Richard Grenville, was born on Apr. 22, 1690, and educated at Westminster School and Christ Church, Oxford. He was best known as Lord Carteret after succeeding to a baronetcy in 1695. He was a strong supporter of the accession of George I to the British throne in 1714. From 1719 to 1720 he served as ambassador extraordinary to Sweden, a post he filled with great success. In 1721 he was made Secretary of State and soon found himself in opposition to Sir Robert Walpole, over whom he had the great advantage of being the only minister who could talk in German to the King who knew practically no English. From 1724 to 1730 he held the thankless post of Lord-Lieutenant of Ireland. Then followed twelve years of being in the opposition. His great chance came in 1742, with the retirement of Walpole, when he was made Secretary of State. In this position, which he retained for two years, he gave his full support to King George II's Hanoverian policy and England's participation in the War of the Austrian Succession. In 1751 he became Lord President of the Council, an office he held until his death at Bath on Jan. 2, 1763. Though Carteret had a great knowledge of foreign affairs, he never became a popular statesman.   E. R. A.

CARTERET [kɑ'rtərɛt], a borough in Middlesex Co., northeastern New Jersey, is situated about 12 mi. northeast of New Brunswick. It is a manufacturing community, incorporated in 1907, and is governed by a mayor and council. The borough was founded in 1906 and was first called Roosevelt. Its name was changed in honor of the Carteret family, who originally owned the district under British crown grants. Oil refining and storage are important activities. There are copper refining and detinning works and acid and creosoting plants. Other industries produce steel, chemicals, paints, varnishes, textiles, fertilizer, paper, and lumber. Pop. 1950, 13,030.

CARTERSVILLE, a city in northwestern Georgia, the county seat of Bartow Co., 41 mi. northeast of Atlanta. It is served by the Seaboard Air Line, Louisville and Nashville, and Nashville, Chattanooga & St. Louis railroads. The surrounding region is rich in gold, iron, graphite, manganese, ocher, and barite deposits. Local industries produce textiles, rugs, cottonseed oil, and fertilizer. Three miles southwest of the city is Etowah Mound, one of the largest of the prehistoric Indian mounds. Pop. 1950, 7,270.

CARTESIANISM, a term of classification applied to any philosophy following the main lines of thought in the system of René Descartes. The philosophies of Spinoza, Leib-

Ruins of a Roman theatre at Carthage, in the process of being excavated.

niz, Malebranche, and Locke are examples of Cartesianism. Their typical concern was with the nature of substance, the relation of mind and body, and proof of the existence of God. *See also* DUALISM; RATIONALISM; SUBSTANCE.   C. W. H.

CARTHAGE (*Gr.* Karchedon, *Lat.* Carthago), one of the wealthiest and most powerful cities of the ancient world, situated on a beautiful gulf on the coast of North Africa near the site of modern Tunis. It was founded, probably in the ninth century B.C., by Phoenician settlers from Tyre, or perhaps as a joint colony of Tyre and the older Phoenician settlement of Utica. The colony was named Kart Hadash, "New City." According to legend, the founder was Elissa, or Dido, who fled from Tyre after her husband Sychaeus had been assassinated by her brother Pygmalion, king of Tyre. The Carthaginians throughout their history were noted for their commercial astuteness, and cunning played its part in the traditional founding of the city: Dido, permitted to have only as much land as a cowhide (*byrsa*) would cover, acquired a large area by cutting the hide into very narrow strips, and the citadel which the encircling strips encompassed was thereafter known as the Byrsa. Dido owes her great fame to the Roman poet Vergil who told in the *Aeneid* of her tragic love for Trojan Aeneas; this poetic version has become one of the great love stories of world literature.

Geography and Topography. Carthage was located on low hills near the beach of a peninsula in a sheltered position on the Gulf of Tunis. The isthmus joining the peninsula to the mainland was narrow and enabled the Carthaginians to defend themselves against the natives with ease. Triple walls were erected across the neck of the peninsula, the main wall being described in antiquity as 21 mi. long, with stables inside the walls for 400 war-elephants and 4,000 horses. The original city grew up around the Byrsa, now the hill of St. Louis, with narrow streets and high, flat-roofed houses. The adjacent hills were occupied by residences and nearer the sea were more modern public buildings, including law courts and temples, erected under the influence of Hellenistic Greek architecture. Carthage had two harbors which are now represented by lagoons at Salammbô. Its position permitted the Carthaginians to control shipping along the coast of North Africa to the east and west, and when they gained possession of western Sicily they dominated the entire area of the western Mediterranean.

Society and Government. The Carthaginians were primarily traders who exchanged the products of Egypt, the Orient, and Greece for the raw materials from the west. Their ships brought tin from Britain, silver from Spain, slaves and gems from the south, and gold from the west coast of Africa. Their own exports were few: some agricultural products, such as wax, honey, and figs, and manufactured goods, especially textiles and pottery; these last had little originality, being copied from Oriental or Greek models. The great wealth of Carthage came not only from its extensive commerce, but also from tribute imposed on subject races and from the large estates. The agricultural skill of the Carthaginians was evaluated highly by the Romans; after the destruction of the city, the Roman Senate had the thirty-two books by Mago on agriculture translated into Latin, presumably for the use of Roman settlers in the province of Africa. As the large estates were worked by slave labor, so the armies were filled in large part by non-Carthaginian warriors, the Carthaginians themselves preferring to make money and let others fight for them, and this may have been an important factor in the many defeats which they suffered at the hands of both Greeks and Romans.

Punic (*Lat.* Punica or Poenica, "Phoenician") Carthage was an oligarchical republic, ostensibly governed by two executives known as *suffetes*, elected annually from the leading families, by a senate of 300, and by a popular assembly. But the conflict between the ruling oligarchy and outstanding individuals produced additional institutions and created a curious type of "mixed" constitution. To curtail the influence of members of leading families, a Court of 104 Judges was established, its function being to approve or punish public officials for their conduct during their term of office. Although nominally elected each year from men of senatorial rank, the members of the Court actually held office for life and had far-reaching powers over both the magistrates and the people. They were elected not by popular vote but by small committees, Boards of Five, who probably composed the Small Senate of 30 members. The Court of 104 Judges and the Boards of Five dominated the state and maintained the rights of the oligarchy against the lower classes and against ambitious members of the aristocracy. Bribery and corruption were widespread, but a certain amount of wise statesmanship was essential to build up and hold together so widespread an empire for hundreds of years.

Culture. The inhabitants of Punic Carthage spoke a Semitic tongue related to Hebrew. The language continued to be used in the area for centuries after the total destruction of the city in 146 B.C. The culture of the Carthaginians was predominantly Oriental. What is known of Carthaginian life and culture comes from two main sources: material remains, relatively slight with the exception of inscriptions, since the Romans were thorough in their devastation of the city and later built a Roman city on the same site; and descriptions of the Carthaginians by contemporary Greeks and Romans who in general looked upon them as a cruel, corrupt, and barbarous race, one which had but little appreciation of literature and art. Although the ancient writers were undoubtedly prejudiced, their unfavorable estimate is shared by modern historians.

Carthage could claim technical advances in shipbuilding, artillery, and agriculture, but it made no real contribution to ancient culture. Although hundreds of short inscriptions have been found, there is only one extant specimen of Punic literature, an account in Greek translation of the voyage of an explorer named Hanno about 500 B.C. along the west coast of Africa. Technical treatises and histories were composed, but there is no evidence that the Carthaginians produced works of poetry, drama, or philosophy. Their art was imitative and based upon imported products from Egypt and Greece which were often of inferior quality, unlike those brought from Greece to Rome. The imported objects thus provided less stimulus to artistic imitation among the Carthaginians than among the Romans. In architecture the original Oriental structures were superseded by temples and public buildings constructed in the style of Hellenistic Greek buildings.

The Punic religion seems typical of the fanatic and cruel nature of the people. Their chief deities were Tanit, goddess of the sky and fertility, Baal Hammon, Lord of Heaven, and Melkarth, god of the city. Archaeological evidence supports the statements of Roman writers that young children were offered as human sacrifices to Tanit and Baal Hammon, a practice which survived the destruction of the city and lasted in some areas as late as the first century of the Christian Era. The Romans considered the religion of the Carthaginians as unattractive and repulsive as the people themselves.

History. The history of Punic Carthage falls into three well-defined periods. The first stage of the city's growth was marked by the domination of other Phoenician settlements, and the subjugation of the native population, but by the middle of the sixth century B.C. Carthage had become the greatest commercial and trading center in the Mediterranean.

The second period was one of attempted conquest, which resulted in centuries of warfare with the Greeks of eastern Sicily. The first recorded naval engagement was that of 535 B.C. when the Carthaginians, allied with the Etruscans, defeated the Phocaeans off the coast of Corsica. By the end of the sixth century Carthage had gained control of Sardinia and western Sicily, and had planted settlements in Corsica

and along the Mediterranean coast of Spain and taken over Gadir (Cádiz), a Phoenician settlement in Spain antedating Carthage and called Gades by the Romans. In 509 B.C. Carthage concluded a treaty with the newly created Roman Republic. During the wars between the Greeks and the Persians, when the Sicilian Greeks could not look to Greece for assistance, the Carthaginians attempted to subdue eastern Sicily. But an invading army of 300,000, including Sardinians, Corsicans, and Ligurians, was defeated at Himera in 480 B.C. by Gelon of Syracuse.

Blocked in its advance eastward, Carthage expanded toward the interior of Africa, turning its attention in part to agriculture and the establishment of estates maintained by slave labor. Local industries were developed, but the Carthaginians continued as a commercial and importing nation. In 410 B.C., toward the end of the Greek Peloponnesian War, Carthage renewed the attempt to conquer eastern Sicily but was defeated in 405 B.C. by Dionysius I. The conflict continued for more than a century. Carthaginian armies were defeated by Timoleon in 344 B.C., and in 310 B.C. Agathocles of Syracuse landed in Africa and threatened Carthage; although the attack was unsuccessful it pointed the way to later invasions of Africa by the Romans. The attempt of Pyrrhus in 277 B.C. to drive the Carthaginians from Sicily failed, and the western part of the island remained under Punic control.

The third period of Carthaginian history extends from 264 to 146 B.C. and includes the three wars with Rome which ended with the total destruction of Carthage. Dissension between Syracuse and Messana led to the intervention of both Rome and Carthage and the accidental outbreak of war between the two great powers. This stage of Carthaginian history is also an important part of the history of ancient Rome and may be briefly outlined here. The First Punic War (264-241 B.C.) was primarily a series of naval engagements. The Romans, having constructed an enormous navy, were victorious at Mylae and Cape Ecnomus, but an army under Regulus which landed in Africa was defeated near Carthage. With the Roman naval victory at the Aegates Islands, Carthage accepted peace on the enemy's terms, paid a huge indemnity, and gave up all claim to Sicily. Shortly after the end of the war Rome also seized both Sardinia and Corsica, thus arousing in the Carthaginians a strong desire for revenge, and the Punic state, after quelling a serious revolt among the mercenaries in 240-238 B.C. (the background for Flaubert's *Salammbô*), spent twenty years in preparation for the next conflict. They strengthened their power in Spain, at first under Hamilcar Barca, a veteran of the First Punic War, then under his son-in-law Hasdrubal, who founded Nova Carthago (Cartagena). This city, near valuable gold and silver mines, became the chief Carthaginian center in Spain. In 219 B.C. the Carthaginians, endeavoring to expand their Spanish domain under its new governor, Hannibal, son of Hamilcar, attacked and captured Saguntum, a Spanish ally of Rome. The result was the Second Punic War (218-201 B.C.). Hannibal, a military genius, made a sensational and unprecedented march through southern France and over the Alps, invading Italy from the north. He won a series of brilliant victories, at the Trebia, at Lake Trasimenus, and at Cannae, but was unable to force Rome to surrender, although he controlled much of southern Italy for fifteen years. The invasion of Africa by Scipio Africanus resulted in the recall of Hannibal in 203 B.C. and the decisive battle of Zama the following year. Again the defeated Carthaginians paid a heavy indemnity, gave up all claim to Spain, and were required to pledge that they would consult Rome before taking up arms and to reduce their navy to ten warships.

During the next half century, although Carthage no longer had a monopoly on trade, it maintained its position as the mercantile capital of the western Mediterranean. The city at this time had a population of about 700,000 and was said by the Greek historian Polybius to be the richest city in the world. The Romans were envious of its increasing prosperity and fearful of a repetition of the Hannibalic invasion. Cato the Elder is said to have urged incessantly that Carthage be liquidated, ending each speech in the Senate with the theme: *Carthago delenda est.* The pretext for the accomplishment of this project was an unauthorized conflict between Carthage and Massinissa, king of Numidia, in 150 B.C. Rome made exorbitant demands which Carthage indignantly rejected, and the Third Punic War (149-146 B.C.) began. Carthage was besieged by the Romans and after its capture by Scipio Aemilianus, the surviving inhabitants, 50,000 in number, were sold into slavery and the city was razed. A plough was driven over the ruins, salt was sown in the furrows, and a solemn curse was pronounced on the site. The conquered territory became the Roman province of Africa; the residence of the Roman proconsul was located at Utica, 20 mi. northwest of Carthage.

Roman Carthage. The history of ancient Carthage is unique in that two cities flourished on the same site, each for a period of about 700 years, with a century of desolation intervening. Gaius Gracchus planned in 122 B.C. to establish a colony at Carthage and Julius Caesar considered restoring the city shortly before his assassination. It was finally rebuilt by Octavian (Augustus) after he rose to supreme power in the Roman state by defeating Mark Antony and Cleopatra at Actium in 31 B.C. Named the Colonia Julia Carthago, the new city replaced Utica as the headquarters of the proconsul of Africa and soon became the chief place for the export of oil and grain from North Africa. By the second century it was one of the most prosperous cities of the Roman Empire.

Many noted Romans were associated with Carthage and the surrounding region. The novelist, orator, and philosopher, Apuleius, studied in Carthage as a youth and later gained such fame there for his Greek and Latin orations that statues were erected in his honor. Marcus Cornelius Fronto, the tutor of the emperor Marcus Aurelius, was a native of North Africa, as was the emperor Septimius Severus; the extent to which Punic had survived as a language is attested by the statement that the sister of Septimius Severus could speak Latin only with difficulty.

The old Punic religion survived in a Romanized form, with Tanit worshipped as Juno Caelestis and Baal Hammon being assimilated to Cronus-Saturn; Melkarth was identified with Hercules. North Africa became, however, a stronghold of Christian belief and Carthage was famous in the early history of the Church. Cyprian was bishop of Carthage in the third century and Tertullian spent most of his life there. Augustine was educated at Carthage and returned to Africa in 388, becoming bishop of Hippo Regius. Donatism, the most important schism in the ancient church, had its origin at Carthage in the early fourth century.

In the fifth century the Vandals invaded Africa and their leader Genseric made Carthage the capital of the Vandal Kingdom in A.D. 439. Belisarius, the famous general of the emperor Justinian, recaptured the city in A.D. 533 and named it Colonia Justiniana Carthago. The Byzantine phase of the city lasted until A.D. 698, when it was completely destroyed by the Arabs under Hasan ibn-Noman. Although for some centuries small groups of natives lived among the ruins, the story of Carthage ends with its destruction by the Arabs.

Archaeological Remains. Ancient Carthage has been thoroughly excavated and numerous objects, both Punic and Roman, are now located at the Musée Lavigerie, on the hill of St. Louis, and in the Musée Bardo near Tunis. The architectural remains of Punic Carthage are represented only by tombs and a few foundations, as the destruction of the city by the Romans in 146 B.C. was thorough. Hundreds of inscriptions, however, have been found, as well as numerous temple offerings. The tombs have supplied much: lamps, imported vases, gold and silver objects, Egyptian scarabs, cinerary urns, and sarcophagi, either imported or made by Greeks at Carthage.

Of the Roman city, few monuments antedate the second century, when much of the city was burned and rebuilt under the Antonines and the Severi. The later Roman remains are extensive and include a theatre, an odeon, an amphitheatre, the Baths of Antoninus, and Roman villas with mosaic floors, many of the mosaics being now on display at the Bardo Museum. Other Roman objects are statues to Victory and Felicitas and altars of the imperial cult. Among the Christian monuments are a cemetery and several basilicas, one, perhaps that of Saint-Cyprien, on the hill of Sainte-Monique, another that of a large Christian basilica of the Byzantine period. *See also* PUNIC WARS; ROME.

G. E. D.

CARTHAGE, an industrial city in southwestern Missouri, the county seat of Jasper Co., situated on the Spring River, in a poultry and livestock area, for which it is a market and shipping center. The district is noted for the Holstein cattle bred by its farmers. Natural resources of the region are coal, lead, zinc, oak timber, and exceptionally fine marble and white limestone. Founded in 1833, Carthage was made the county seat in 1842 and was incorporated as a city in 1873. It has the mayor and council form of government. Carthage was the home of Belle Starr, leader of a Confederate guerrilla band during the Civil War, and the site of the Battle of Carthage (July 1861), described as the first serious engagement between the North and South. Memorial Hall is a museum of souvenirs of the wars in which the United States has fought, and the Carnegie Library contains a collection of relics from ancient Carthage. The College of Our Lady of the Ozarks is also located here. Manufactures include flour, clothing, explosives, caskets, dairy products, bedsprings, concrete products, commercial dynamite, wood products, and fluorescent fixtures. Pop. 1950, 11,188.

CARTHAGE COLLEGE, an accredited, coeducational, privately controlled liberal arts college, is located on a campus of 35 acres at Carthage, Ill. It is operated by the United Lutheran Church. Carthage was founded as Hillsboro College at Hillsboro, Ill., in 1846. It was rechartered under its present name in 1870, and the various departments were organized in 1873. Carthage College offers courses leading to three Bachelor degrees: arts, science, and music. There is also a five-year integrated course with Illinois Institute of Technology for the Institute's B.S. in engineering and the B.A. from Carthage, and a five-year nurse's training course in co-operation with approved hospitals. There are no graduate degrees. Scholarship and loan-fund assistance is available. Students must reside in college domitories or in approved student houses. *For statistics see* COLLEGES AND UNIVERSITIES.

CARTHAMIN. *See* SAFFLOWER.

CARTHUSIANS [kɑrthyu'zhənz] are the members of a monastic order founded in 1084 by St. Bruno of Cologne in the mountains of Chartreuse, near Grenoble, France. The name of the original establishment, La Grande Chartreuse, is the source of the Latin adjective *cartusianus* (*Carthusian* in English); the word "charterhouse," which denotes a Carthusian monastery, is a corruption of the French *chartreuse*.

The Carthusians combine the cenobitical with the eremitical life. Originally the monks lived without a formal rule, striving to emulate the founder. Later, however, with expansion of the order, their customs were embodied in written constitutions. An authoritative Carthusian rule was first printed in 1510 and confirmed by Pope Innocent XI in 1688. The Offices of the current day, of the Blessed Virgin, and of the dead occupy much of the Carthusian day and night, with the remainder given to mental prayer, study, manual labor, rest, and some recreation. The hair shirt is always worn and silence is broken only at specified times. Often but one meal is taken, meat is never eaten, and all fast once a week on bread and water. For nearly nine centuries this manner of life has had few variations, "never reformed because never deformed." Though practicing extreme poverty, the order is renowned for its libraries and for its printing press at Tournai. Following a similar rule, but with less stringent solitude and silence, a few convents of nuns have been affiliated with the order since the twelfth century. Their habit is white, like that of the monks, but with a black veil and linen wimple. The superiors of the charterhouses are priors, and the prior of the Grande Chartreuse is the order's head. The Carthusians flourished in France except for the period of the French Revolution and the last four decades of the Third Republic. Forced to abandon their eleven monasteries by the Law of 1901, they returned in 1940 to La Grande Chartreuse. They also have houses in Spain, Italy, one in England since 1833, and one at Whitingham, Vt., since 1951. They number about 500. The Carthusian Fathers are noted for the liqueur, Chartreuse, which provided much of their revenue after their lands were taken away in France early in the 19th century. The secret recipe was preserved through the years of exile, when the authentic liqueur was produced in Tarragona, Spain. A commercial firm obtained the right to the name and produced a similar liqueur called Chartreuse until 1929, but since 1941 all Chartreuse has been produced by the Carthusians in France according to the ancient recipe.

CARTIER, SIR GEORGE ÉTIENNE [ka'rtye'] (1814-1873), Canadian statesman, was born at St. Antoine, Lower Canada (modern Quebec), on Sept. 6, 1814. He was educated in Montreal for the law, but soon entered politics and became a leader of the French Canadian movement of 1837 to set up a French republic. When the rebellion collapsed he fled to Burlington, Vt., but in 1838 returned to Montreal, achieved success as a lawyer, became attorney general of Lower Canada in 1856, and co-premier in 1858. He represented Montreal in Parliament from 1861 until 1872, and was active in organizing Canada as a dominion. Cartier was knighted by Queen Victoria in 1868.

The Canadian federation was at first made up of the provinces of Quebec, Ontario, Nova Scotia, and New Brunswick, but Cartier saw that the country must expand, and the areas of Alberta, Manitoba, and Saskatchewan were secured by negotiation with the Hudson's Bay Company, with a payment of £300,000, in 1868. In the first federal cabinet, Cartier served as minister of militia, frequently acting as prime minister. When this responsibility impaired his health, he went to London, England, where he died May 20, 1873.

J. I. C.

CARTIER, JACQUES (1491-1557), French navigator and explorer, known as the discoverer of the St. Lawrence River, was born in St. Malo, Brittany, near the close of 1491.

Jacques Cartier, French navigator and explorer, the discoverer of the St. Lawrence River

There is little record of his early life, though he undoubtedly made a voyage to the New World prior to 1534, probably landing in Brazil. In 1534, he was given a grant by King Francis I of France to search for the Northwest Passage. Cartier explored the coast of Newfoundland, but finding no passage to the westward, he landed on the Gaspé Peninsula, claiming it for the French Crown, and returned to St. Malo. Though this expedition added little to the discoveries of Cabot and Verrazano, it did bring to light the existence of a country in the interior, named Saguenay, which the natives described as containing gold and precious stones, and in 1535 Cartier was commissioned to make a second voyage. Departing from St. Malo in three ships, he entered and named the Gulf of St. Lawrence, and, finding the entrance to the St. Lawrence River, proceeded to a point near the present site of Quebec. After wintering there, Cartier explored farther up the river, reaching an island which he named Mount Royal (Montreal), but his advance was then stopped by the Lachine rapids. He was again told of fabulous riches in the interior of the Saguenay country, but the presence of scurvy among his crew and trouble with natives forced a return to France in the spring of 1536.

The outbreak of war between Francis I of France and Charles V of Spain, together with the opposition of Admiral Chabot, prevented another expedition for several years, but in 1541 Cartier was again commissioned to lead an expedition to the New World in an effort to discover the treasures of the Saguenay country and to establish a French colony on the St. Lawrence. This expedition was on a more ambitious scale, and many colonizers were assembled, with François de Roberval as viceroy and commander in chief.

Cartier sailed in May 1541, leaving De Roberval to follow him later, and established a settlement at Cap Rouge, above Quebec, where he spent the winter. The following spring he again reached Montreal, but succeeded only in obtaining some illusory samples of the promised gold. The increasing hostility of the natives then forced him to return to Cap Rouge and abandon the settlement. Putting in at Newfoundland, he encountered De Roberval's ships, which had finally arrived from France, but Cartier refused to return to the settlement and sailed for Europe.

Cartier may have returned to Canada the following year in order to bring back De Roberval, but there is no reliable information regarding this last voyage. The remainder of his life was spent in St. Malo, where he occasionally served as advisor in nautical matters and as a Portuguese interpreter. He published an account of his voyages in 1545, which was translated into English by Richard Hakluyt in 1600. Cartier died at St. Malo, Sept. 1, 1557.   C. W. D.

CARTILAGE [kɑ'rtɪlɪj], a firm yet flexible supportive tissue of the body related to the connective tissues. It consists of rounded, unbranched cells (chondrocytes) embedded in a dense ground substance, or matrix. Three common types are hyalin cartilage, in which the matrix is clear; elastic cartilage, with yellow elastic fibers in the matrix; and fibrocartilage, in which cartilage elements permeate a mass of dense, white fibrous connective tissue. Hyalin cartilage forms much of the embryonic skeleton, but is replaced by bone except for remnants over joint surfaces, the articular cartilage. The cartilages of the nose, ribs, larynx (in part), trachea, and bronchi are also hyalin. Elastic cartilage is found in the external ear, Eustachian tube, epiglottis, and minor cartilages of the larynx. Fibrocartilage forms the intervertebral discs, the articular discs (menisci) of certain joints, and the articular cartilage of a few joints; it also occurs in the pubic symphysis, rims of joint sockets, and linings of tendinous grooves in bones.   S. W. C.

CARTOGRAPHY. *See* Maps and Charts.

CARTON, SIDNEY, dissipated but noble-hearted lawyer in Dickens' *Tale of Two Cities,* who for love of Lucie Manette goes to the guillotine in her husband's stead.

CARTOON, a term that was first used during the Renaissance to describe a large drawing made on paper, to be used as a model for a picture in fresco, oil, or tapestry and sometimes for statuary. The term has also been employed in connection with glass and mosaic work.

While this technical sense of the term is still in use, the more usual application is one which dates from about the middle of the nineteenth century, when the term also came to be applied to large drawings, usually caricatures, dealing with political or other questions in an attempt to correct abuses or to influence public opinion. At one time the cartoon was used as a weapon of venomous attack; gradually, however, the artist and the publisher came to realize that a subtler satirical or humorous approach could be more effective, which, with the proper title, or caption, carried a more powerful argument than one packed with rancor. English, French, and German artists, as well as those of other nations, have made notable contributions to the art of the cartoon. In the United States, since the time of Thomas Nast (1840-1902), who created the symbols of the elephant and the donkey to represent the Republican and Democratic parties (to say nothing of the tiger as the symbol of Tammany), the cartoon has become the "strong arm" of the editorial point of view. Today it may be compared to a leading editorial, but it graphically visualizes a thought quicker, and often with more force, than a whole column of words could do.

Toward the end of the nineteenth century, the cartoon was adapted to narrative use for purposes of sheer entertainment in the comic strips, and in the late 1920's the motion picture industry carried this development a step further in the animated cartoon. *See also* Caricature; Comics; Disney, Walter Elias; Motion Pictures.   A. N. Ho.

CARTOUCHE [kɑrtu'sh], a scroll-like design used in architectural ornamentations. Usually an inscription or design framed in a scroll and enclosed in an oval-shaped panel, the cartouche is used on capitals of columns or on entablatures. The figure is common in Egypt, the royal cartouche bearing the king's name in hieroglyphics. Cartouche designs enclosing coats of arms are characteristic of both Italian and English Renaissance architecture and the baroque styles of France, Austria, and Italy.   M. K.

CARTWRIGHT, ALEXANDER JOY (1820-1892), American sportsman, was born Apr. 17, 1820, in New York City. He was one of the first to take a serious interest in baseball, and the Knickerbocker Baseball Club, which he founded in 1842, issued a challenge to other early baseball enthusiasts. The Knickerbockers played the first organized game on June 19, 1846, at the Elysian Fields, Hoboken, N. J., against a club called the New Yorks. Cartwright himself revised many of Abner Doubleday's rules for the game, ending the practice of putting a man out by hitting him with a thrown ball and introducing the nine-man team, nine-inning game, and ninety-foot baseline. He also dressed his team in the game's first uniforms. Traveling west late in the 1840's, Cartwright popularized baseball in a large part of the country and in Hawaii, where he settled and where his family became one of the most prominent in the islands. Cartwright died in Honolulu, July 12, 1892. In 1939 his name was added to baseball's Hall of Fame at Cooperstown, N. Y.   R. E. Le.

CARTWRIGHT, EDMUND (1743-1823), English clergyman and inventor, was born at Marnham, Nottinghamshire, Apr. 24, 1743. He was educated at Oxford University, where he received his M.A. degree in 1766. He was rector of Goadby Marwood, Leicestershire, 1779-1786. In 1784 he met Richard Arkwright and began speculating on using machinery in cotton weaving. In 1785 he took out his first patent for a power loom and moved to Doncaster to start a spinning and weaving factory; the mill was claimed by his creditors, however, in 1793. Another mill, at Manchester, made use of his power looms but was destroyed, probably by arson, in 1791. Cartwright's wool-combing machine was first patented in 1789. The financial rewards of his inventions, however, did not suffice to prevent his bankruptcy in 1793. He patented a rope-making machine in 1792, and in 1797 constructed an engine employing alcohol as fuel. In 1801 the British parliament continued the patent on his wool-combing machine for another fourteen years, and in 1807 a memorial was presented to the government stating that his inventions had done much to increase the wealth of the country. The House of Commons voted Cartwright a grant of £10,000 in 1809 and he retired to a small farm at Hollander, near Sevenoaks, Kent, where he spent the remainder of his life and invented improvements on agricultural machinery. Cartwright died at Hastings, Oct. 30, 1823.   R. T.

CARTWRIGHT, JOHN (1740-1824), English parliamentary reformer, was born at Marnham, Nottinghamshire, on Sept. 17, 1740. He was the older brother of Edmund Cartwright. After receiving his education at Newark Grammar School and Heath Academy, he entered the navy about 1758, and was present at the capture of Cherbourg. He was chief magistrate of Newfoundland from 1765 until 1770, when ill-health led to his retirement. When the disputes about taxation began with the American colonies, Cartwright became a staunch supporter of their cause. When the Nottinghamshire Militia was founded in 1775, he was gazetted major and served till 1792. His first work on parliamentary reform, *Take Your Choice* (1776), was expanded in a second edition as *The Legislative Rights of the Commonalty Vindicated* (1777). In his writings he advocated universal suffrage, the abolition of slavery, annual parliaments, and, later, the emancipation of Greece. He was indicted for conspiracy in 1819 and fined. He died in London, Sept. 23, 1824.   R. T.

CARUSO, ENRICO [kɑru'zo; kəru'so] (1873-1921), Italian dramatic tenor, was born Feb. 27, 1873, in Naples. Despite the objections of his parents, who wanted him to be an engineer, he early embarked on a musical career. At the age of fifteen, after the death of his mother, he began to earn a living by singing at church festivals, and, during his subsequent term in the army, his major was sufficiently impressed by his voice to secure him the services of a singing teacher. Caruso made his operatic debut on Nov. 16, 1894, in Morelli's *L'Amico Francesco* at the Teatro Nuovo in Naples. After numerous appearances on the European continent, he made his debut in London in 1902 and followed this by his debut in New York, as Rigoletto at the Metropolitan Opera House, on Nov. 23, 1903. From that time until his death, Caruso was the leading figure at the Metropolitan Opera House. His extremely large repertory included the chief roles in Italian and French opera, and he came to typify all that is colorful and dramatic in opera. His last performance at the Metropolitan was on Dec. 24, 1920. He died in Naples on Aug. 2, 1921.   R. Mo.

CARUTHERSVILLE [kərʌ'thərzvɪl], a city in southeastern Missouri, the county seat of Pemiscot Co., situated on the border of Tennessee, and on the Mississippi River, 77 mi. northeast of Memphis, Tenn. It is in the cotton belt, in an area marked also by dairying and general farming. Oak, cottonwood, and gum timber are natural resources of the region. John Hardeman Walker founded Caruthersville in 1857 on a part of his plantation. It became the county seat about 1899, succeeding Gayoso, and is governed by a mayor and council. Manufactures include cotton products, boxes, and cartons. Pop. 1950, 8,614.

CARVER, GEORGE WASHINGTON (c. 1864-1943), American botanist, the son of Negro slaves, was born near Diamond Grove, Mo. With great tenacity he acquired a good education, receiving a B.S. in 1894 and a M.S. in 1896 from Iowa State College. From 1896 he taught and carried on research at Tuskegee Institute, especially in peanut and sweet-potato culture, his discoveries bringing him international fame. From peanuts alone he derived more than 300 products, and he synthesized over 100 products from the sweet potato. His ideas helped to diversify the crops of the Southern states and to extend the use of Southern agricultural products. In 1916 he was elected a fellow of the Royal Society of Arts in London. From 1935 Carver was attached to the U.S. Department of Agriculture, and in 1940 with his life savings of $33,000 he established the Carver Foundation. Having dedicated himself wholly to his work, Carver never married. He died Jan. 5, 1943, in Tuskegee, Ala. On July 14th of the same year Congress authorized the creation of the George Washington Carver National Monument at his birthplace in Newton County, Mo., and it was formally established in June 1951.   W. Lin.

CARVER, JOHN (c. 1576-1621), first governor of Plymouth Colony, Mass., was born in Nottinghamshire, or in Derbyshire, England. In 1608, he joined the English Separatist exiles at Leiden (Holland), and, in 1620, helped secure an American land patent from the Virginia Company. He later helped select and equip the *Mayflower*. He was elected governor of Plymouth Colony in November 1620 and was re-elected in March 1621. An able administrator, he is credited with negotiating a treaty with the Indians which was helpful in maintaining peace for many years. He died at Plymouth, Apr. 5, 1621.   D. R.

CARY, (ARTHUR) JOYCE (LUNEL) (1888-1957), British novelist, was born in Londonderry, County Donegal, Ireland, Dec. 7, 1888. He received A.B. and M.A. degrees at Trinity College, Oxford, and studied art at the University of Edinburgh and in Paris. Cary joined the Nigerian Political Service in 1913, fought with native Nigerian troops against the Germans during World War I, and continued to live in West Africa until his health failed and he was forced to return to England in 1920. His first novel *Aissa Saved* was published in 1932. Altogether he completed over 15 novels and several volumes of essays and poetry. He died Mar. 29, 1957, in Oxford, England.

In most of his novels Cary delineated men and women whose nonconformism affirms the dissenting spirit of the English character. For his exuberant comic sense and imaginative characterization he has been compared with Dickens and Fielding, for his realism and narrative force with Defoe and Kipling. His trilogy *Herself Surprised* (1941), *To Be a Pilgrim* (1942), and *The Horse's Mouth* (1944) contains notable portraits of the engaging amoralist Sara Monday, her eccentric lover Thomas Whilcher, and the reckless but talented artist Gulley Jimson. A second trilogy *Prisoner of Grace* (1952), *Except the Lord* (1953), and *Not Honor More* (1955) also has several memorable though unpleasant characterizations. Other novels are *The African Witch* (1936), *Mister Johnson* (1939), and *The Moonlight* (1946).   A. Wa.

CASABIANCA, LOUIS DE [ka'za'byɑ̃'ka'] (1755-1798), French naval hero, was born in Bastia, Corsica, in 1755. As a young naval officer he served with the French fleet under the Comte de Grasse during the American Revolution. In 1792, during the French Revolution, Casabianca became a member of the National Convention and of the Council of Five Hundred. At the expiration of his mandate he returned to naval service and became captain of the *Orient*, flagship of the French fleet in the Egyptian campaign. When the *Orient* caught fire during the Battle of Abu Qîr, Aug. 1, 1798, Casabianca, although seriously wounded, refused to leave his ship and he and his son Giacomo were killed when the vessel exploded.   W. Fr.

CASABLANCA (*Arab. Dar-el-Beida*) [ka'sabla'ŋka, dɑ'r ɛl be'dɑ], the largest city and chief port of Morocco, located in the northern part of the country, on the Atlantic Ocean, about 55 mi. southwest of Rabat. The city enjoys a temperate climate, favorably influenced by the ocean and by winds from the north. Its harbor, protected by extensive works, is one of the largest artificial ports in the world, handling all of the passenger traffic and most of the foreign trade of Morocco. Casablanca has rail and road connections with other points in Morocco and with Algeria and Tunisia to the east, and it has an international airport. The city's manufactures include food products, furniture, textiles, cement, bricks, tobacco, and glass.

Much of the city presents the appearance of a white, sparklingly new city of southern Europe. It was built in a semicircle around an old Moorish city that had been built on the site of a town founded by the Portuguese.

The Portuguese destroyed the original Berber village on the site of Casablanca in 1468, and in 1515 built a city of

poned for another year. This was also the occasion on which unconditional surrender was first agreed upon by the Allies as a condition for peace.   C. W. D.

CASA DE CONTRATACIÓN, LA [la ka'sa the ko'ntratathyo'n], a house of trade established at Cadiz in 1503

BUILDINGS OF MODERN DESIGN IN ANCIENT CASABLANCA, CHIEF SEAPORT AND LARGEST CITY OF FRENCH MOROCCO

COURTESY OF THE FRENCH EMBASSY
PRESS AND INFORMATION DIVISION

their own, which they later abandoned. In 1755 it was destroyed by an earthquake and was rebuilt only in the nineteenth century. Its period of rapid growth began only after the French military occupation in 1907, which resulted from the killing of several European workers by fanatical Moslems. The French soon made of Casablanca a base of operations, first for conquering, then for developing their zone in the Sherifian Empire.

During World War II when United States troops sought to land at Casablanca in November 1942, the local Vichy-controlled French forces put up a brief but spirited resistance, which resulted in a naval and aerial bombardment that considerably damaged the port. The famous Casablanca Conference was held in the suburb of Anfa in January 1943. Pop. 1951, 682,388.

CASABLANCA CONFERENCE, a historic World War II meeting of American, British, and French chiefs of state and military leaders, held at Anfa, a suburb of Casablanca, in West Morocco, Africa, between Jan. 14 and Jan. 24, 1943. President Franklin D. Roosevelt and Prime Minister Winston Churchill met to discuss the military and political phases of the war effort and, in particular, to settle the problem of French leadership. The Soviet Union and China were not represented, but General Henri Giraud and General Charles de Gaulle were invited to participate and to aid in the establishment of a satisfactory interim administration for free France. Considerable difficulty had been caused by the presence in Giraud's North African Imperial Council of collaborationist members, but the Casablanca talks led to a compromise solution which paved the way for a united French leadership. On the military side, the invasion of Sicily was decided upon and the invasion of France was post-

to supervise, regulate, and promote trade with the newly discovered Spanish colonies in the Western Hemisphere. Shortly after its creation, the Casa was moved to Seville where it remained until 1717, when it was again moved to Cadiz, where it was located permanently. Besides supervising and enforcing colonial trade regulations, the Casa controlled emigration to the colonies, organized and managed the fleets sent to the New World, and collected the government's share of all products brought back from the colonies. These activities were under the general supervision of the Council of the Indies. The Casa also developed a hydrographic bureau and a school of navigation.   J. F. R.

CASALS, PABLO (PAU) [kasa'ls] (1876-   ), Spanish cellist, conductor, and composer, was born Dec. 29, 1876, at Vendrell, Tarragona, Spain. By the age of twelve he had learned to play several instruments and decided to devote himself to the cello. He studied in Barcelona and Madrid, became solo cellist at the Paris Opéra in 1895, and taught at the Barcelona Conservatory in 1897. His career as a virtuoso cellist began in 1898, and he continued to tour the world with the highest acclaim for technical skill and artistry during the next three decades. Casals is also an accomplished pianist. He has composed music primarily for stringed instruments, orchestra, and chorus.

Since the Spanish Civil War Casals has been opposed to the Franco regime and in protest refused to perform publicly for a great many years. He left Spain in 1939 to live in Prades, France. Here since 1950 he has conducted the Prades Festivals and attracted distinguished musicians and innumerable music lovers throughout the world. On Apr. 16, 1957, he suffered a heart attack in San Juan, Puerto Rico, where he was to open the Casals Music Festival.   W. B.

CASANOVA, GIOVANNI JACOPO [kɑ'sanɔ'va] (1725-1798), Italian cosmopolitan adventurer whose candid self-revelation in his *Mémoires* has made his name synonymous with libertinism and roguery, was born at Venice Apr. 2, 1725. His parents, both of whom were actors, left his upbringing to others, and at an early age he showed precocious ability as a student and a remarkable aptitude for ingratiating himself in the dissolute society of Venice. After studying for the priesthood, serving in the Venetian army, and playing the violin at the San Samuele Theatre, he found his true vocation as a successful parasite, conducting amatory

GIOVANNI JACOPO
CASANOVA

FROM AN ENGRAVING
FROM A PAINTING BY
JACQUES CASANOVA

HISTORICAL PICTURES SERVICE

affairs, intriguing, gambling, cheating, and duping the gullible with his pretended magic powers.

In 1750 he went to France, then traveled in central Europe, and returned to Venice to resume his old ways. He was imprisoned July 26, 1755, in the Doge's Palace, allegedly for Freemasonry and other charges, having incurred the personal enmity of the new Inquisitor. After fifteen months Casanova escaped on Nov. 1, 1756, as he tells in the romantic *Histoire de ma fuite* ("Story of My Escape"), written in French in his old age and published at Prague in 1788.

He returned to France and resumed his intrigues and love affairs, amassing a fortune as director of a government lottery and in other ventures, and adopting the title "Chevalier de Seingalt." Thereafter he traveled across Europe from Spain and England to Poland and Russia, but his personal charms had begun to wane, and his dubious reputation preceded him. He was forced finally to return to Venice and seek employment as a police spy in 1774. A scandal forced him to leave in 1782, and he wandered again until given a sinecure by the Count of Waldstein as librarian in his castle at Dux, Bohemia, in 1785. He lived at Dux until his death on June 4, 1798, engaged in studies and, from 1791 onward, in the composition of his *Mémoires*.

Casanova's *Mémoires* were written in French and extend only to the year 1774. Though their authenticity was doubted at first, research has proved that they are usually correct as to historical events and persons, though shamelessly romanticized when it is a question of presenting their author as the "hero of libertinage and genius of erotic conquest."

G. R. S.

CASAUBON, ISAAC [ka'zo'bɔ̃'; kəsɔ'bən] (1559-1614), French humanist, was born in Geneva on Feb. 18, 1559, the son of a pastor of the Reformed Church. He studied at the Academy of Geneva and later married the daughter of Henri Estienne, the famous printer. Casaubon was professor of Greek at Geneva from 1592 to 1596 and subse-

quently at Montpellier, but was called to the court of France and attended the colloquy of Fontainebleau in 1600. Here the accuracy of patristic quotations in Duplessis-Mornay's treatise against the Mass was tested, and Reformed scholars blamed Casaubon for siding with the Catholic commissioners. Meanwhile, his refusal to be converted to Catholicism caused him to be denied a professor's chair in the Collège Royal, but he was nevertheless appointed assistant in the king's library in 1604. In 1610, he was invited to England by the Archbishop of Canterbury and welcomed by King James I. His moderation was not appreciated by the Puritans, however, and he shared in the growing unpopularity of his patrons. Casaubon died on July 1, 1614, in London, and was buried in Westminster Abbey. Casaubon's most ambitious work was his edition, with commentary, of Athenaeus (1600). He also wrote commentaries on Theophrastus (1592), Suetonius (1595), Persius (1605), and Polybius (1609-1617) and undertook a refutation of the *Church History* of Baronius for the Anglican bishops. His diary *Ephemerides* (begun in 1547, published in 1850) contains valuable historical and biographical material. His son Florence Étienne Méric (1599-1671) was also a Classical scholar.

G. A. B.

CASCADE RANGE, one of the major mountain chains of the northwestern United States. It extends from the general vicinity of Feather River in northeastern California, northward through Oregon and Washington to the Fraser River in British Columbia. The range is about 500 mi. long and about 60 mi. wide in the south and 120 mi. wide in the north. The Puget Sound-Willamette Valley trough is west of the Cascades, and the Columbia River Plateau is on the east. The Cascades have had a complicated geologic history involving several periods of uplift, folding, and peneplanation. During different geologic ages granite was intruded into the sedimentary rocks and then the surface at different times was covered or partly covered by gravel, lava, tuff, and volcanic ash. Subsequently, during the ice age, the continental as well as later and local glaciers scoured the surface and caused changes in the drainage.

The summit elevation of the northern and central parts of the Cascades is formed by an upraised peneplain. The general elevation is about 8,000 ft. above sea level. The surface slopes southward and is only about 4,000 ft. above sea level at the southern end. The southern section has been covered by lava flows. Rising above the general level are a series of conical-shaped volcanoes, formed in comparatively recent times. From north to south these peaks are Mount Baker, 10,778 ft.; Glacier Peak, 10,568; Mount Rainier, 14,410; Mount St. Helens, 9,671; and Mount Adams, 12,307, all in Washington. In Oregon are Mount Hood, 11,245 ft.; Mount Jefferson, 10,495; Mount Pitt, 9,700; and Mount Scott, 9,164. In California are Mount Shasta, 14,161 ft. and, near the southern end of the Cascades, Lassen Peak, 10,466 ft., which erupted in 1914 and 1915. The northern part of the Cascades is subdivided into three chains: the Skagit, Hozomeen, and Okanogan mountains. In British Columbia the Cascades are separated from the Coast Range by the Fraser River Valley.

Although the Cascades are not very high, they form an important climatic and economic barrier. The western side of the range receives more than 80 in. of precipitation a year and is almost always humid because it intercepts the moist winds from the north Pacific Ocean. The eastern or leeward side is dry, receiving from 10 to 25 in. of precipitation. This difference causes a significant contrast in vegetation and use of the two sides. The western slope is covered with a dense growth of huge Douglas fir and other conifers; grass, semiarid scrub plants, and yellow pine grow on the east. Cottonwoods flourish along the streams. On the western slope agriculture is hampered by too much moisture. On the eastern side there is too little; dry farming is practiced and fruits, particularly apples, are grown in small, irrigated valleys such as the Yakima and Wenatchee.

Lumbering is an important industry on the western slope, but a part of the Cascades has been set aside as national forest or national park regions. This is helping to protect the remaining big forests and the large game animals of the region. The Cascades are also a barrier to overland travel; although the wheatlands of eastern Washington are not far from the port of Seattle, the route over and through the Cascades is time-consuming and expensive. The Cascades are a source of water power and irrigation water, and have mineral deposits which have not been thoroughly prospected or developed. A few of the more noted scenic areas are Lake Chelan, on the eastern side, Crater Lake National Park, Mount Rainier National Park, the cascades of the Columbia River gorge, and the Lava Beds National Monument.

J. E. F.

CASCADE SHOWERS. *See* COSMIC RAYS.

CASCARA [kæskæ′rə], the dried bark obtained from *Rhamnus purshiana* a 20-ft. shrub of northwestern United States. It is used medicinally as a purgative. The berries are diuretic and laxative. It is also known as "sacred bark," and "chittem bark." J. A. Bo.

CASCARILLA [kæ′skərɪ′lə], also called sweet-wood bark, the dried, bitter, aromatic bark of *Croton eleuteria,* a small tree of the spurge family native to the West Indies. It is used in medicine as an aromatic stomachic tonic. An unofficial cinchona substitute, it has been used as an addition to smoking tobacco for flavoring. J. A. Bo.

CASCO BAY, an indentation of the Atlantic Ocean into the southern coast of Maine, located in the eastern part of Cumberland County, southwestern Maine. The central part of the bay is at 43° 45′ N. lat. and 70° 5′ W. long. Portland, the largest port and most important city on the bay, is on the southwestern side at 43° 40′ N. lat. and 70° 15′ W. long. The northeastern boundary of Casco Bay is Small Point, and the southwestern side is formed by Cape Elizabeth. The distance between these two points, marking the entrance to Casco Bay, is approximately 21 mi. The bay extends about 15 mi. inland, but has an extremely irregular coast line. There are many small points and bays, and some fiordlike formations along the coast, and there are some islands in the bay. Three of the larger islands are Orrs, Chebeague, and Bailey islands. The bay, which was formed by the subsidence and subsequent drowning of the coast, is deep, and is an excellent harbor. Although most of the shipping and commercial activity centers upon Portland, there are many small towns along the bay, including South Portland, Falmouth, Yarmouth, and East Harpswell.

J. E. F.

CASE, in grammar, any one of the inflectional forms of a noun, adjective, or pronoun, indicating the specific function of the word in relation to other words associated with it. Familiar examples of these inflectional forms are Latin *lupus, lupi, lupo;* German *der Hund, des Hundes, dem Hunde;* and English *I, my, me, he, his, him.* The word "case" is also used frequently, but inexactly, to designate the syntactic function itself, as in the expression *the use of the dative.*

In the Indo-European languages, the treatment of case is in keeping with the generally anomalous character of these languages. Thus, the same case may have a certain suffix in one declension and a different one in another: for example, Latin *lupi, familiae,* and *pedis* are all genitives, singular; *lupo, lunae, pedi,* and *cornu* are all datives, singular; and *amici, pedes, cornua* are all nominatives, plural. Furthermore, the same suffix may be the distinguishing mark of more than one case: for example, *lupis* is both a dative and an ablative, plural, and *familiae* is a genitive singular, a dative singular, and also a nominative plural. When, as in the latter group of examples, different cases have the same form, the distinction between cases may be inferred by a comparison with corresponding forms in other declensions. Thus, in the combinations *Iuliae anulum dare* and *cum Iulia errare,* it is clear that *Iuliae* and *Iulia* are two distinct cases, a dative and an ablative respectively; from this example it follows that, in the combinations *lupis carnem dare* and *cum lupis errare,* the form *lupis* is in the first instance a dative and in the second an ablative. Accordingly, despite the frequent insufficiency of formal case distinctions in the Indo-European languages, there is no doubt that the morphological categories of genitive, dative, and the rest were clearly perceived by the ancient Romans, just as they are, for example, by modern Germans and Russians.

Primitive Indo-European had probably eight cases, usually designated as nominative, genitive, dative, accusative, ablative, locative, instrumental, and vocative. The vocative, however, which closely resembles the interjection in function, should be definitely set apart from the others. It does not fit the usual definition of case, for it constitutes a sentence in itself and has therefore no syntactic relation whatever with other words; and when it occurs in the midst of a group of words, it is set apart between two pauses, usually indicated by two commas, as in *Now, John, I am going.* The vocative is usually identical with the pure stem and shows, accordingly, no characteristic ending; in fact, it is characterized by the absence of ending, as may be seen in Latin *lupe* and *luna* and Old Church Slavic *bože* and *ženo* (the so-called "zero" sign).

The functions of the various cases are extremely difficult to define, because the structure of language is neither logical nor rational. These functions, as Herman Paul observed as early as 1910, in *Zeitschrift für Psychologie,* do not correspond to constant logical and psychological relations. According to the usual definitions, which fall far short of covering all instances, the nominative expresses the grammatical relation of subject; the genitive expresses possession (though it may also express the grammatical relation of subject or object); the dative expresses the grammatical relation of indirect object; the accusative expresses the grammatical relation of direct object or indicates the aim of a movement in space; the ablative indicates the origin of a movement in space; the instrumental expresses the relation of instrument or agent; the locative indicates location at rest; and the vocative indicates the person or thing addressed.

A useful distinction may here be made, between the concrete cases (ablative, instrumental, and locative), which express simple, clear, visible, material functions, and the grammatical cases (nominative, genitive, and dative), which express abstract relationships. The functions of the accusative, which date back to Primitive Indo-European, give it a place in both categories. This distinction is important in the history of declension, for in those languages in which the Indo-European declension shows serious signs of weakening and decay, the concrete cases disappear much earlier than the grammatical ones and are replaced by prepositional peri-phrases (e.g., German *in dem Lande, in das Land, aus dem Lande, mit dem Hammer*), whereas the grammatical cases resist. With few exceptions, Old English, ancient Greek, spoken Latin (in Imperial times), and modern literary Ger-man have only the grammatical cases; the Baltic and Slavic languages, on the other hand, with the exception of Bul-garian, seem to preserve almost intact the old Indo-European case system.

Modern English may be said to preserve three of the four grammatical cases—nominative, genitive, and accusative—in most personal pronouns. Examples of these survivals are *I, my, mine, me; he, his, him; we, our, ours, us; they, their,* and *them,* although some scholars would classify *my, mine, our,* and *ours* as possessive adjectives rather than genitives. A more difficult question is whether a general category of the nominative case, distinct from the accusative, can be recog-nized in English and applied to substantives; for example, in a sentence such as *Peter loves Mary,* which is parallel to the sentence *he loves her,* can it be said properly that *Peter* is a nominative and *Mary* an accusative? The word order pro-vides the only formal distinction between the two words, and without its help the sentence *Peter loves Mary* could not be distinguished from *Mary loves Peter,* whereas there is a clear distinction in Latin between *Petrus amat Mariam* and *Maria amat Petrum.* Otto Jespersen, in his *Philosophy of Grammar,* denied outright the existence of such a distinction in English, but his reasons are not all convincing and the question re-mains open. As to the dative case, English certainly does not distinguish, as Latin does, between direct and indirect object even in the pronouns; thus *him* is an indirect object in *he gave him a book* and a direct object in *he saw him,* just as *book* is a direct object in *he gave him a book* and an indirect object in *he gave his book a new cover.* There is no doubt, on the other hand, that English has a real genitive, signalized by *'s,* although its use is now much restricted, being limited to the so-called possessive genitive (*Paul's book*), the sub-jective genitive (*Peter's departure*), and a few objective geni-tives (*she mourns her daughter's loss, he reported the army's defeat.*)

Jespersen inclined to the belief that English is tending to distinguish subject from predicate, as Russian does in part, by using the nominative for the former, the oblique (Latin accu-sative) for the latter; in support he cited the colloquial Eng-lish *it's me* (for *it is I*), comparing Danish *det er mig.* There is no serious basis for such a belief, for in English the oblique case of the pronoun is being increasingly employed to indi-cate the subject of the sentence whenever emphasis is wanted, except in the position immediately before the verb. Thus, the nominative case is still employed exclusively in *I say, he sees,* and *we go,* but the oblique is gaining ground in such expressions as "Who's that?" "Me"; "He's bigger than me"; and even "Me, I don't believe it." This trend, which is still opposed by English purists, has definitely triumphed in French, where *moi, toi,* and other oblique forms are regu-larly used in this way: *moi, je vous le répète!; l'État c'est moi; lui et moi, nous irons à la gare.* It is also gaining ground in Italian, and one finds, especially since the time of Manzoni, such expressions as *lui non viene; io e te; è bello come me; è vecchio quanto te; loro restano qui;* and *lui e me.* G. B.

CASEIN [ke'siɪn], the protein found in the milk of mammals, existing as a colloidal suspension or emulsion, not in the free state but in combination with calcium. Casein is present in cow's milk in the amount of about 3.5 per cent and constitutes 80 per cent of the entire protein content of milk.

In milk, casein acts as an emulsifying agent for the butterfat. Like all proteins, casein contains nitrogen (15.6 per cent). Small quantities of sulphur and phosphorus are also present in the casein molecule.

Precipitation. When treated with slight excesses of acid, the casein in milk is displaced from its union with calcium, and on gentle heating is precipitated as free casein that can be dried and ground. The enzyme, rennet, precipitates a curd from milk. This is not free casein but, as a result of the action of the enzyme, is a cleavage product of casein, called paracasein, which combines with calcium to form the precipi-tated curd. Casein is an amphoteric electrolyte, i.e., it can react with either acids or alkalies.

In the preparation of technical casein the removal of fats is a prerequisite. The milk, after centrifuging to remove the bulk of the cream (butterfat) is treated with a weak alkali solution. Following further centrifuging to eliminate the last traces of fat, it is treated with dilute sulphuric or hydro-chloric acid until all possible curd is precipitated. The curd is washed to remove any acid. Then it is dried, first by press-ing, then in a vacuum drier to remove final traces of water. Casein must be dried at low temperatures, since it is sensitive to heat.

In Cheese. When the enzyme rennet is employed as a precipitating agent, the modified casein obtained from milk is called a cheese and contains milk fat. Analyses of different cheeses follow, showing the casein content:

CHIEF CONSTITUENTS OF VARIOUS CHEESES
(Per Cent)

	Cheddar	Swiss	Cream
Water	34.3	35.8	±38.0
Casein	26.4	24.4	±25.3
Fat	32.2	37.4	30.0
Sugar	3.0	...	2.0
Ash	3.6	2.3	4.1

Industrial Applications. Besides its use in tremendous quantities as cheese, casein has many industrial applications: as a water-resistant adhesive, for sizing in the paper and leather industries, as a binder in cold-water paints, as a stabilizer for various commercial emulsions, and in the manu-facture of plastics formed from the reaction of casein and formaldehyde. In its preparation as an adhesive, the colloidal casein is treated with alkali (borax caustic alkali or sodium carbonate) in an amount not quite sufficient to dissolve the casein to form a true solution; otherwise the adhesive proper-ties characteristic of the colloid would be destroyed. These casein glues are marketed as a powder or a liquid, and have the advantage over many glues because they lack odor, and become insoluble in water when dry. Because of these fea-tures, casein glue is demanded for the plying operations in both the plywood and plyboard industries. E. S. F.

CASE INSTITUTE OF TECHNOLOGY, at Cleve-land, Ohio, is an accredited, privately controlled technologi-cal institute for men occupying a 20-acre campus in an urban environment. Case Institute was chartered as the Case School of Applied Science in 1880, and its first instruction was offered the following year. The graduate division was founded in 1930 and the evening division in 1934. The present name was adopted in 1947.

Degrees conferred are the B.S. in civil, mechanical, elec-trical, metallurgical, and chemical engineering, industrial chemistry, and engineering administration. Graduate de-grees are the M.S. and Ph.D. In addition to the customary eight semesters required for a degree, certain students must attend as many as three summer practice terms of one or two weeks each, depending on the curriculum. These are the surveying camp at the end of the freshman year, the practice term at the end of the sophomore year, and the inspection trip at the end of the junior year.

All curricula are professional and include a preponderance of prescribed work; the freshman year is identical in all curricula. Courses in mathematics, chemistry, physics, graphics, applied mechanics, English, democracy, and western civilization are required. Effective speaking and writing are emphasized in the freshman curricula.

Reference privileges are extended to students by such outstanding sources as the Cleveland Public Library, the Leonard Case Library, Western Reserve University, the Municipal Reference Library, the National Carbon Company, and the General Electric Company. A number of undergraduate scholarships are available, some being awarded on competitive examinations, some on scholarship and extracurricular records in high school, and some to outstanding men in Case classes. A loan fund is also available. Graduate fellowships in substantial amounts are awarded to outstanding candidates. Two modern dormitories provide on-campus housing for 600 undergraduate students. *For statistics see* COLLEGES AND UNIVERSITIES.

CASERTA [kɑzɛ'rtɑ], a province and its capital city in Campania, southern Italy.

The City. The city is located 17 mi. northeast of Naples, at the foot of a mountain near the entrance to one of the best trans-Apennine routes to Italy's east coast. It is an

century on a site 7 mi. northeast of the present city. It was taken by the Normans in 1057. In the twelfth century the inhabitants began to move down to the plain, where the modern city rises. In the old city in the hills, Caserta Vecchia, is an interesting cathedral, consecrated in 1153, which embodies diverse architectural styles. Pop. 1954 (city), 31,200; (commune), 45,900.

The Province. The province, with an area of 1,019 sq. mi., includes 100 communes. A farming and livestock region, it is drained by the Volturno River. Pop. (est. 1954), 623,400.

CASEWORK, SOCIAL, a method of helping persons, on an individual basis, to meet their personal and family difficulties. The difficulties may be a result of external forces or of personality factors, or a combination of both. The essential characteristic of casework is the concept of individualization, and of extending help that is appropriate to the person's particular needs. The help includes services in connection with financial need, the care of children, health, employment, budget management, vocational guidance, and with problems of family relationships and personality development.

Casework was developed in the first two decades of the twentieth century by social agencies in dealing with problems of poverty, illness, and neglect. Its basic principles, which have been enriched by the contributions of medicine, psychology, and psychiatry, are applied, not only to public assistance programs, family and children's agencies, protective agencies, hospitals, and mental hygiene clinics, but also to various vocational and industrial counselling programs, and

Palazzo Reale at Caserta, Italy, constructed in typical style of Italian Renaissance architecture, was built for Charles III by Vanvitelli.

important highway and rail center, as well as the market place and industrial center for the surrounding rich agricultural region. Caserta is famous for the vast palace and gardens designed by Vanvitelli for Charles III, and built between 1752 and 1774. The palace is rectangular, with four courtyards, a notable chapel, picture gallery, and theatre. Smaller buildings are around the palace, which is connected with Monte San Silvestro by a series of lagoons and fountains originating in a cascade almost 2 mi. away. The water is supplied by a 30-mi.-long aqueduct. The splendor and beauty of the establishment, which includes a notable botanical garden, have caused Caserta to be called the "Versailles of Naples." In 1926 the palace became the seat of the Italian Aeronautical Academy; parts of it were damaged in World War II. After the capture of Caserta in October 1943, it became the headquarters for the Allied forces in Italy and was the scene of the surrender of German troops in Italy on Oct. 29, 1945.

Caserta was originally built by the Lombards in the ninth

to military units and veteran services. Casework service, under various auspices, is also utilized in programs having a psychological orientation, such as marriage adjustment and child development. C. Ka.

CASH, an accounting term embracing currency, bank deposits subject to check, and checks in process of collection or not yet deposited. Foreign currencies and balances in foreign banks are cash and may be converted into domestic currency for financial-statement purposes at prevailing rates of exchange. Time deposits in banks are not considered to be cash, nor are funds deposited with or amounts owed by others than banks, even though these assets may be converted readily into cash. The word "cash" is also used as a term of sale to indicate that the buyer must pay for the goods upon receipt of the invoice, or within ten days thereafter. E. E. E.

CASHEW [kəshu'], *Anacardium occidentale,* a medium-sized 40-ft. evergreen tree with leathery leaves and panicles of small, yellow-pink flowers, native to tropical America, and bearing at the same time both the cashew nut and so-called cashew apple. The latter is the brilliant red or yellow swollen receptacle to which the kidney-shaped nut is attached and, being composed of pleasantly acid flesh, is eaten as a fruit. The nut is surrounded by a double shell, the inner one of which contains an acrid oil that is roasted out before the kernels are extracted for the market. Like other members of the large, chiefly tropical cashew family, which includes, in temperate regions, the sumacs and Japanese lacquer tree, the cashew stem is resinous and yields a varnish and a gum similar to gum arabic. The nuts have a very high fat content, and in addition to their sale as a dessert nut, are used to some extent as a source of a delicate table oil.   U. P. H.

CASHMERE. *See* Textile Fabrics.
CASHMERE GOAT. *See* Goats, Domestic.

CASH ON DELIVERY, a term, usually abbreviated C.O.D., used in the sale of goods to indicate that the seller must deliver the goods to the buyer, who, in turn, must pay the full amount of the sales price immediately upon receipt. When the seller makes delivery by parcel post or express, the post office or express company usually makes the collection and remits to the seller. If delivery is by freight, collection ordinarily must be made through banking channels. In the case of retail stores, delivery and collection frequently are made by the store employees.   E. E. E.

CASH REGISTER. *See* Business Machines and Equipment.

CASPER, the county seat of Natrona Co. in central Wyoming, is located on the North Platte River, about 165 air mi. northwest of Cheyenne. It was incorporated as a city in 1889. Casper is a busy transportation center served by the Chicago and North Western and the Chicago, Burlington & Quincy railroads and by the Frontier and Western airlines. Natural resources of the surrounding region are oil, gas, sodium, uranium, and asbestos, and the chief industry is the refining of oil from nearby fields, among which are the famed Teapot Dome and Salt Creek. Sheep raising is the principal agricultural occupation. Casper Junior College was organized in 1945. Pop. 1950, 23,673.

CASPER RANGE, a small mountainous district in Natrona County, east central Wyoming. The North Platte River flows around its western and northern sides. The Casper Range is the northwestern end of the Laramie Range and is formed by a fold in a sedimentary formation. It has gentle slopes and the highest elevation is Mount Casper (8,500 ft.), which overlooks the point where the pioneers crossed the North Platte River. A bridge was later built at this crossing and the city of Casper was developed. A small fort was constructed and the range, the mountain, the fort, and the city were named after Lieutenant Casper Collins, who was killed in an Indian attack in 1865.   J. E. F.

CASPIAN SEA, the largest body of inland water in the world (169,000 sq. mi.), in western Asia and occupying the deepest part of the Aralo-Caspian Depression, the most extensive on earth. It is a remnant of a vast inland sea of ancient geological times, which stretched from the Black Sea to the Arctic Ocean. The Caspian Sea is bounded on the north and northeast by the Kazakh Soviet Socialist Republic, on the southeast by the Turkmen Soviet Socialist Republic, on the

south by Iran, on the southwest by Azerbaidzhan Soviet Socialist Republic, and on the west by the Russian Soviet Federated Socialist Republic. It is about 770 mi. long and, at the northern end, where it is widest, it is 300 mi. wide. The surface is 92 ft. below sea level and receding. The northern portion, north of Fort Shevchenko, is shallow, nowhere more than 81 ft. deep. East of Derbent there is a depth of 2,496 ft., and east of Lenkoran, at about the middle of the southern Caspian, is the greatest depth, 3,072 ft. On the south the sea is bordered by the Elburz Mountains, the highest of which, Mount Demavend, is 18,934 ft. above sea level. The high Caucasus Mountains are on the west. The rest of the coast line is low, indented by the gulfs of Komsomolets on the northeast, Kara-Bogaz and Krasnovodsk on the east, and Gurgan Bay on the southeast. The Gulf of Kara-Bogaz, largest of these, is practically landlocked by narrow bars enclosing it on the west; it is about 120 mi. long, 90 mi. wide, and no more than 39 ft. deep. The peninsulas of Buzachi and Mangyshlak are prominent features of the northeast coast. The Volga delta begins a few miles above Astrakhan, about 50 mi. from the coast, and is some 70 mi. wide, having 200 mouths, of which the southernmost is the principal. There are numerous small islands along the northern and northwestern shores, particularly in the vicinity of the Volga delta. South of Krasnovodsk on the eastern shore are Ogurchinskiy and Cheleken islands, the latter over 18 mi. long.

Of the rivers entering the Caspian Sea, the Volga flows generally south, but flows southeast in its course of over 250 mi. from Stalingrad to the sea; the Kuma and the Terek, the latter a river of the Caucasus, flow east; the Sulak has first a northerly, last an easterly course; the Kura courses southeast through Azerbaidzhan; the Araks forms the Azerbaidzhan-Iran boundary to long. 48° E., then flows northeasterly in Soviet territory, emptying into the Kura and also directly into the Caspian; the Qizil Uzun, in Iran, trends first southeast, then northeast, entering the Caspian as the Sefid Rud; the Atrek, in the latter part of a course west and southwest, is the boundary between Iran and Turkmenistan; the Emba flows west; and the Ural, the second longest river in Europe after the Volga, flows south.

The Caspian has no perceptible tide, but differences of pressure and persistent north winds create differences of level, often of 4 and sometimes of 8 ft. The northern shores are icebound every winter, for 100 days in the coldest spots; Astrakhan is closed to navigation from mid-December to late March. The southern Caspian is open to navigation the year round, and is served by regular scheduled steamer routes. The annual rainfall varies from 2.75 in. near Guryev in the north to about 3 in. at Krasnovodsk 500 mi. farther south.

The waters near the mouth of the Volga River are excellent fish-breeding grounds, owing to their shallowness, lower salinity, and wealth of organic matter provided by the river. Pike, bream, perch, roach, herring, and various species of sturgeon flourish here. The Caspian yields one quarter of the annual production of Soviet fisheries. Astrakhan is the center of this industry and has modern fishing fleets, canneries, and refrigerating and preserving plants. The Ural is the only large river in the world devoted wholly to fishing; traffic is forbidden during the sturgeon breeding season.

Major seaport cities skirt the shores of the Caspian Sea. Astrakhan lies on the northwestern shore, at the mouth of the Volga. Makhachkala, Derbent, and Baku are located on the west coast; Lenkoran and Pahlavi on the southwest coast; Bandar Shah on the southeast coast; Krasnovodsk and Fort Shevchenko on the east coast; and Guryev on the north, at the mouth of the Ural. With respect to thousands of tons of freight handled, the chief Russian sea ports in 1935 were Baku, Astrakhan, and Makhachkala. Krasnovodsk ranked eleventh. Seventy per cent of Caspian freight is oil and petroleum products. Baku exports oil to Astrakhan and imports wheat and timber from the Volga. Krasnovodsk exports cotton from Central Asia. Makhachkala sends oil to Astrakhan and grain to Krasnovodsk. Astrakhan transfers the oil from Caspian ports to river tankers for the trip up the Volga to European Russia. In addition to its fishing industry, which includes the canning of caviar, Astrakhan also produces lumber, furniture, boats, barrels, glass, and salt.

A line of railroad follows the western and northern shores of the Caspian from Astara, south of Lenkoran, to Guryev, passing through Baku, Derbent, Makhachkala, and Astrakhan. There are lines from Tiflis to Baku, Groznyy to Makhachkala, and from Astrakhan to Moscow via Saratov. A railroad crossing the Turkmen Soviet Socialist Republic from Ashkhabad reaches the eastern Caspian shore at Krasnovodsk. From the three termini of Abadan, Bandar Shahpur, and Khorramshahr, near the head of the Persian Gulf, railroads unite at Ahwaz and proceed via Qum, Tehran, and Babul to Bandar Shah on the Caspian. J. E. F.

CASS, LEWIS (1782-1866), American lawyer and statesman, was born in Exeter, N.H., Oct. 9, 1782. He attended Phillips Exeter Academy, and, about 1799, went to Marietta,

Lewis Cass, American lawyer and statesman

CULVER SERVICE

Ohio, to join his father. After studying law with a Marietta lawyer, Cass was admitted to the bar in 1802 and, in 1806, was elected to the Ohio legislature. During the War of 1812, he rose from a colonel of a volunteer regiment to major general in the Ohio militia, and to brigadier general in the regular army. In 1813, he was appointed governor of the Michigan territory, a post he held until July 1831. In carrying out the United States expansionist policy during his administration of the territory, he negotiated twenty-two treaties with the Indians, in which land was sold to the United States equalling one-fourth of the area of the present states of Wisconsin, Michigan, Ohio, Indiana, and Illinois. President Andrew Jackson appointed Cass secretary of war in August 1831, and, in 1836, minister to France. Cass is accredited with dissuading France from ratifying the Quintuple Treaty—a measure being negotiated by England, Russia, Prussia, and Austria, designed to prevent American slave trade by establishing the right of search of American vessels. When the United States and England signed the Webster-

Ashburton Treaty, which did not prohibit England from searching American vessels, Cass resigned from his ambassadorial post (1842).

Elected by Michigan to the United States Senate in 1845, he was repeatedly re-elected until 1857, when he was defeated by Zachariah Chandler, Republican. During his career in the Senate, Cass supported the Oregon 54° 40′ line, the Mexican War, the Compromise Measures of 1850, and the Kansas-Nebraska bill of 1854. As Democratic presidential nominee, in 1848, he was defeated through the splitting of the party in New York by the "barnburners," who left the ranks of the Democrats to help form the Free Soil Party. In this campaign Cass enunciated a "squatter sovereignty" doctrine which would leave to inhabitants of territories the responsibility of slavery extension. His view was later incorporated in the 1854 Kansas-Nebraska bill.

Cass was appointed secretary of state by President James Buchanan in 1857, but he resigned in 1860 because of Buchanan's weak stand on the secession trend of Southern states. Until his death at Detroit, June 17, 1866, Cass devoted himself to writing. In addition to his contributions to periodicals, he wrote *Inquiries Concerning the History, Traditions, and Languages of Indians Living Within the United States* (1823) and *France: Its King, Court, and Government* (1840). D. R.

CASSABA [kəsɑ'bə], *Cucumis melo inodorus,* a smooth-skinned, golden-colored melon about 8 in. in diameter, having a sweet yellow flesh somewhat resembling that of the muskmelon, to which it is related; the cassaba is also called winter muskmelon. Cassabas were first introduced to California from Asia in 1878. They are grown chiefly in the San Fernando Valley. Harvested usually in November and December, they keep for many weeks under proper conditions. They do best under high temperatures, in dry climates. They will not develop satisfactorily in cool climates. *See also* MUSKMELON.

CASSANDRA [kəsa'ndrə], in Greek legend, the daughter of Priam and Hecuba of Troy. Beloved by Apollo, Cassandra received the gift of prophecy, but she refused to comply with his wishes, and as a punishment he decreed that no one should believe her prophecies. At the capture of Troy, she fled to the temple of Athena but was violated by Ajax the Lesser, son of Oileus. Agamemnon took her home to Mycenae as his captive; she warned him of his fate, but her prophecy was unheeded and both were slain by Clytemnestra. *See also* ILIAD, THE; ORESTEIA; TROJAN WAR. G. E. D.

CASSATT, MARY [kəsæ't] (1845-1926), American painter and printmaker, was born in Pittsburgh, Pa., May 22, 1845. In 1874 she settled permanently in Paris, where her highly original style, developed with almost no formal training, brought her into contact with Degas and the Impressionists. Exhibiting with this group, Mary Cassatt shared their early struggles for recognition and through her American contacts helped to make their work known in the United States. The majority of her paintings and pastels, remarkable for their brilliant draftsmanship and warm color, were based on the theme of mother and child. She was the master of many print techniques and is particularly noted for her color prints. Mary Cassatt died June 19, 1926, at Mesnil-Théribus, Oise, France. E. B. S.

CASSAVA [kəsɑ'və], *Manihot esculenta,* of the spurge family, native to Brazil, a perennial shrub-like plant growing to 9 ft., of great economic importance. It is also called manioc, mandioc, or bitter cassava. With large, deeply lobed leaves, small flowers in clusters, and globular seed capsules, it somewhat resembles the castor-oil plant. It is widely cultivated in tropical countries for its starch-bearing roots, which are a staple food and from which Brazilian arrowroot, tapioca, and other products are derived. These fleshy roots, which may be 3 ft. long and 9 in. in diameter, contain so much prussic (hydrocyanic) acid that when raw they are exceedingly poisonous; they are rendered harmless by cooking, or by having the juice pressed out. A related nonpoisonous species, *M. aipi*, known as sweet cassava, also native to Brazil, has a reddish root and is cultivated to a lesser extent. Cassava as a food is as important to the tropics as potatoes are to temperate regions.

CASSEL, GUSTAV [kas'səl] (1866-1945), Swedish economist, was born Oct. 20, 1866, at Stockholm. He graduated from Uppsala University and received his Ph.D. from the University of Stockholm. He became professor of economics at the latter in 1904 and professor emeritus in 1933. In 1920 he achieved international recognition for his *Memorandum on World Monetary Problems* and was invited by the League of Nations to submit a paper on the subject in 1921. In 1922 he was financial expert on the Swedish delegation to the International Economic Conference in Genoa. In the same year he was engaged by the Soviet Union as adviser to the newly created Russian State Bank. His Rhodes lectures at Oxford were published as *The Crisis in the World's Monetary System* (1932), in which he advocated a permanently managed currency. Later he advocated a controlled currency inflation. In 1928 he was invited by the Banking Committee of the United States House of Representatives to give his opinion on the stabilization of the dollar. He was appointed tax and financial expert for the Department of Finance in the Swedish government. Among his books, *The Nature and Necessity of Interest* (1903) emphasized the relationship between interest and the age-distribution of wealth; *Theoretische Sozialökonomie* (1918) pre-

sented the Neoclassical viewpoint on economic theory; *Money and Foreign Exchange After 1914* (1922) studied the contemporarily important problem of unbalanced foreign exchanges and offered the purchasing-power parity explanation of exchange rates, i.e., if two currencies have been inflated, the new normal rate of exchange will be equal to the old rate multiplied by the quotient between the degrees of inflation of the two countries. His *Downfall of the Gold Standard* (1936) held that gold had failed as a standard of value and a means of payment. Cassel died in Stockholm, Jan. 15, 1945.

E. W.

CASSEL. *See* KASSEL.
CASSE-NOISETTE, LE. *See* NUTCRACKER, THE.

CASSIA, shrubs and trees of the pea family with about 400 species, mostly from the tropics but a few extending into temperate regions. The extracts of many species, such as various sennas and the pudding-pipe tree (30 ft.), *C. fistula*, are used as purgatives. They are used as ornamentals for their rapid growth, handsome pinnate foliage, and abundant yellow or rose flowers. Among woody species in more common use as ornamentals are: showy cassia, *C. corymbosa* (10 ft.), from Argentina; the pink shower, *C. grandis* (50 ft.), from tropical America; and wormwood senna, *C. artemisioides*, a low greyish Australian shrub.

R. S. Ho.

CASSIMERE. *See* TEXTILE FABRICS (*Wool and Worsted Fabrics*).

CASSINO [kɑssi'no], a small city at the southeastern end of Latium, in the province of Frosinone, in central Italy. It is situated on the Rapido River, about 85 mi. southeast of Rome, at the foot of Monte Cassino, and is dominated by the abbey of Monte Cassino and at a lower level by a medieval castle. The city itself is without any particular historical or economic importance. A number of ruins, notably an amphitheatre, mark the site of Roman Cassinum.

The monastery, the most famous in Italy, was founded by St. Benedict in 529 on a commanding prominence some 1,400 ft. above the city. Before World War II it was connected with the town by a winding mule path and with the railroad station by an aerial cableway. The monastery, as well as the city itself, was almost completely destroyed by Allied artillery and air bombardment in the winter of 1944. Cassino and its nearby heights commanded the inland route to Rome (the Via Latina), and for several months Nazi forces entrenched along the Gustav Line held up the advance on Rome. The town finally fell on May 18 to British troops, while a Polish detachment took the ruins of the monastery. Part of the invaluable library had been saved, but the building, with its historic and artistic treasures, was reduced to rubble. After the war the Italian government decreed that the small community, which had been located on both sides of the mountain, would stand in complete ruin as a national monument, and the government started the erection of a new town on the flatlands around the foot of Monte Cassino. In 1954 the new city was completed with the inauguration of its civic buildings. The monastery also was restored, largely from the ruins of the original building. Pop. 1954 (city), 8,000; (commune), 20,900.

R. G. W.

CASSIO, MICHAEL [kæ'sio], a Florentine soldier in the Venetian army in Shakespeare's tragedy *Othello*. Promoted by Othello to a lieutenancy in preference to Iago, Cassio has aroused Iago's jealous resentment, and he becomes an

View of Cassino, with modern church in foreground and reconstruction of the famous mountain-top abbey at rear

ITALIAN STATE TOURIST OFFICE

unwitting instrument in Iago's vicious scheme to besmirch the character of Othello's wife, Desdemona. He learns of the fabricated charges against him after narrowly escaping an attempt on his life, but the revelation of his innocence comes too late to avert the tragedy that destroys both Desdemona and Othello.

CASSIODORUS, FLAVIUS MAGNUS [kæ'siodɔ'rəs]
(c. 480-575), Roman writer and statesman, held the high office of secretary under Theodoric and later Ostrogothic kings of Italy. He finally attained the office of prætorian prefect. After forty years of service, about A.D. 540, Cassiodorus retired to his estate at Squillace in southern Italy, where he founded two monasteries. For another thirty years he devoted himself to the collection and preservation of the learning of the past, by which he accomplished a great service for the future. He encouraged his monks to copy ancient manuscripts and to translate the Greek writings into Latin under his supervision, thus originating a function which became an important responsibility of the medieval monk. His own work of translation, compilation, and commentary did much to preserve the learning of the past and to make it available to the Middle Ages.   F. C. H.

CASSIOPEIA [kæ'siopi'ə], a conspicuous constellation in the northern celestial hemisphere. This W-shaped group, located on the opposite side of the North Star from the Big

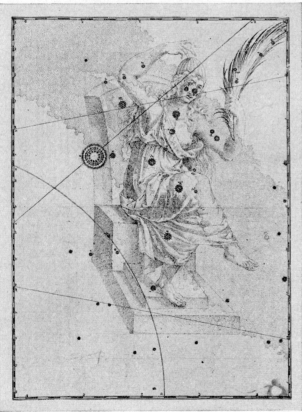

CASSIOPEIA, "THE LADY IN THE CHAIR"

Dipper, never sets for observers in middle north latitudes and higher, but daily makes a complete circuit in the northern heavens around the celestial pole. The five stars of the second and third magnitudes forming the W stand so apart that they attract instant attention. With its many fine

clusters and doubles, Cassiopeia furnishes a glorious field for owners of small telescopes. The Danish astronomer Tycho Brahe discovered and described a brilliant nova, named Tycho's star in his honor, that appeared in Cassiopeia in 1572. At its best, it rivaled Venus in brilliance and was visible in full sunlight, but after 16 months it faded into invisibility.

In Greek mythology, Cassiopeia was the wife of King Cepheus and the mother of Andromeda.   J. H. P.

CASSIRER, ERNST [kɑsi'rər] (1874-1945), German philosopher and historian of ideas, was born in Breslau, on July 28, 1874. After completing his preliminary education in that city, he entered the university of Berlin in 1892. In accordance with the European tradition which encouraged students to work in several institutions, he attended also the universities of Leipzig, Heidelberg, Munich, and Marburg. His first intention had been to study law, but his interests carried him to literature and humanistic studies; furthermore, in the course of his work in philosophy, he engaged in an intensive study of physical science and mathematics. At Marburg, where he received the doctorate of philosophy in 1899 with a dissertation on Descartes's *Critique of Mathematical and Scientific Knowledge,* he was a student of Hermann Cohen and Paul Natorp, leaders of the neo-Kantian school, who had returned to Kant's philosophical teaching in contrast to that of Hegel, which was then dominant. Cassirer remained especially close to Cohen both in his Kantianism and in his interest in Judaism, which was by no means fashionable in German academic circles. Though never a traditionalist with respect to the Jewish faith to which he was born, Cassirer retained a lifelong interest in the Jewish heritage.

His relation to neo-Kantianism was also marked by independent judgment. In his teaching and writing while at the University of Berlin, from 1906 to 1919, he was generally regarded as a member of the neo-Kantian group. His interests at this time were especially in the theory of knowledge and the philosophy of science, particularly with regard to mathematics and physics, fields which he later explored further, following Einstein's theories and writings about them. He also pursued his literary and historical interests with studies of the great figures of German literature, including Lessing, Goethe, and Schiller. To this period, also, belong his biography of Kant and his edition of Kant's writings.

In 1919 Cassirer was appointed professor of philosophy at the University of Hamburg, of which he became rector in 1930. He was also a director of the Warburg Institute in Hamburg, an institution devoted to studies in the history of culture, and he promoted a fruitful relationship between the institute and the university. Cassirer was engaged in these pursuits and in active literary production when Hitler took power in 1933. With his wife, Toni Bondy Cassirer of Vienna, whom he had married in 1902, Cassirer then left Germany for England. He carried on his teaching at All Souls College, Oxford, from 1933 to 1935, and was given the honorary degree of Doctor of Laws at Glasgow. From 1935 to 1941 he was a visiting professor at the University of Göteborg, in Sweden. He came to the United States in 1941 and was visiting professor at Yale University until 1944, and at Columbia University from then until his death on Apr. 13, 1945.

Cassirer's philosophy was expressed in a series of works which with single-minded devotion he continued to write despite all vicissitudes of fortune. He made a comprehensive study in three volumes entitled *Das Erkenntnisproblem in der Philosophie und Wissenschaft der neueren Zeit* (1906-1920) (*The Problem of Knowledge*), which treated the subject both systematically and historically from Greek times to the fourth decade of the twentieth century. Combining his cultural, scientific, and historical interests he published another three-volume work entitled *Philosophie der symbolischen Formen* (1923) (*The Philosophy of Symbolic Forms*).

In the above and other studies he analysed the functions of myth, language, and science as "symbolic forms" through which man gains understanding of his own nature and the natural order. In this endeavor Cassirer developed an aspect of philosophy largely neglected by his fellow neo-Kantians and which, following Kant, he called philosophical anthropology. Cassirer advanced these studies further in a series of publications on language and myth, and in works on science, religion, art, and history. Historical studies, especially of the Renaissance and the eighteenth century, marked Cassirer as a pioneer in those studies which have come to be known as the "history of ideas."   J. Gu.

CASSITERITE, or TINSTONE [kəsɪ'tərɑit], one of
the few tin-containing minerals, and the only ore of that metal. It is composed of tin dioxide, SnO_2. The word "cassiterite" comes from the Greek κασσίτερος, "tin." Both the mineral and the metal were described by Pliny the Elder (A.D. 23-79). Tin was brought to Italy from Cornwall, England, by the Roman invaders under Caesar and, thus, that part of Europe became known as the Cassiterides, or Tin Islands. The Cornish deposits are now exhausted.

Cassiterite is a black, heavy mineral. It may have a dull appearance or an adamantine luster, that is, like the diamond. Cassiterite has a hardness of six or seven on Mohs' scale and leaves a white streak when rubbed against a surface. The mineral occurs as tetragonal crystals which frequently are in the form of elbow-shaped twins with a characteristic notch (visor tin). When found in the form of rolled pebbles in placer deposits, cassiterite is known as stream tin. Another naturally occurring form is called wood tin because of its fibrous appearance.

Cassiterite is a typical high-temperature mineral. It may occur in hydrothermal veins (lode tin) or, more rarely, in pegmatites. The mother rock is invariably granite with essential potash feldspar. Cassiterite is often associated with the tungsten ore, wolframite. Although widely distributed, cassiterite is found in only a few places in quantities sufficient to be mined. In the United States, for example, it is present in pegmatites, but in such small amounts that mining is not commercially feasible. Most of the world's tin supply comes from Malaya, Indonesia, Bolivia, Belgian Congo, Thailand, and Nigeria.   K. K. L.

CASS LAKE, a body of water in north central Minnesota
located on the line between Beltram and Cass counties. It is noted as a summer resort, and the shores of the Lake and the surrounding area are included in the Chippewa National Forest. The lake is at 1,351 ft. above sea level and is dotted by a number of islands, among which Star Island is the largest. The town of Bemidji is northwest of Cass Lake and the town of Cass Lake is on the southwestern shore of the lake in Cass County. The upper Mississippi River flows through the lake. It was named after Lewis Cass, who explored the region between Detroit, Mich., and north central Minnesota as far northwest as Cass Lake and made treaties with Indian tribes in the region.   J. E. F.

CASSOCK [kæ'sək], sometimes called by the French
name *soutane,* is the distinctive ordinary dress of clerics, prescribed in the Roman Church since the sixth century under the name *vestis talaris* (ankle-length garment). In modern times it is generally close fitting, with standing collar, and fastened in front with many small buttons. The pope's cassock is always white. A cardinal's choir cassock is scarlet, a bishop's (and Roman prelate's) purple, their ordinary cassocks being black with colored trimmings. Other clerics wear black. The simar (It. *cimarra*) is a cassock with short cape and oversleeves.   N. J. T.

CASSON AND GALINÉE, EXPLORATIONS OF
[ka'sɔ̃', ga'li'ne']. François Dollier de Casson and René de Brehaut Galinée, two Sulpician missionaries, in an attempt to reach the Mississippi River and to determine the advisability of establishing missions among the western Indian tribes, carried out important explorations of the country north of Lake Erie and west to Sault Ste. Marie. They traveled with LaSalle as far as Lake Ontario, where they separated, LaSalle going on to the Ohio River, while Dollier de Casson and Galinée went west into Lake Erie.

They left Burlington Bay Oct. 1, 1669, and descended Grand River to Lake Erie. Traveling west along the shore, they reached Port Dover, where they established their camp for the winter and took possession of the region in the name of Louis XIV of France. In March 1670 they continued along the northern shore of Lake Erie and followed the Detroit River into Lake St. Clair and Lake Huron. They coasted along the eastern shore of Lake Huron and the southern side of Manitoulin Island to the Mackinac Islands, then up St. Mary's River to the Sault Ste. Marie, where they found Fathers Jacques Marquette and Claude Dablon. They returned to Montreal by way of Georgian Bay, French River, Lake Nipissing, and the Ottawa River. Galinée wrote a narrative of the journey and made a map of the Great Lakes before returning to France; Dollier de Casson became superior of the Seminary of Montreal.   S. Van V.

CASSOWARY [kæ'sowɛ'ri], any one of a number of
large, flightless birds with degenerate wings, allied to the emu and ostrich. They inhabit New Guinea and adjacent islands, and one form reaches northern Australia. The cassowary has a horny helmet and wing quills reduced to a few stout, barbless shafts. The inner toe has a long, straight claw capable of being used as a weapon. The head and upper neck are naked and bright-colored, and the dark feathers of the body are long and hairlike. Cassowaries inhabit dense forests and, despite their bulk, are able to run at great speed through what, to a man, would be impenetrable growth. The nest is a mass of vegetable matter, on which the dark green, rough-shelled eggs are incubated by the male.   H. G. De.

CASTAGNO, ANDREA DEL [kɑstaˈnyo] (1423-
1457) Florentine Renaissance painter, was born Andrea (or Andreino) de Bartolommeo at Castagno. Until Giorgio Vasari's date of 1390 for his birth was proved erroneous, Castagno was grouped with Masaccio and Paolo Uccello among the first generation of Florentine Renaissance painters. Brief as his career now appears to have been, he developed figure painting to almost Michelangelesque grandeur and carried portraiture to a point of vigorous and massive realism. He died in Florence, Aug. 19, 1457.

Many of Castagno's major works, all of them frescoes, are collected in the former convent of S. Apollonia, Florence: a Last Supper, two Crucifixions, and a series of heroic figures representing the great men of Florence and their legendary precursors. His equestrian portrait of Niccolò da Tolentino (1456), also in fresco, confronts Uccello's *Sir John Hawkwood* in the cathedral in Florence. Among the rare tempera paintings ascribed to Castagno, two of the most impressive are now in the National Gallery at Washington: a *David* painted on a leather shield, and a half-length male portrait. The latter is sometimes, but with less reason, attributed to Pollaiuolo. S. L. F.

CASTANETS [kaˈstənɛˈts], a musical instrument of indefinite pitch, comprising two small, shell-shaped clappers of hard wood which are clicked between the thumb and fingers of the dancer's hand, or, in modern orchestras and bands, between wooden handles. Castanets have accompanied popular dancing in the Mediterranean world, particularly in Spain, for some 2,000 years, and since the middle of the nineteenth century have provided Spanish color and rhythmic patterns in Occidental art music. W. Li.

CASTE, a principle of social organization whereby social status is inherited at birth from the parents and is fixed for life. The term originated from *casta,* which the Portuguese used to describe the caste groups in India. Indeed, India represents the most extreme and thorough embodiment of the caste principle to be found. In theory, the Hindu's membership in the caste group is inherited from his parents and, except for the possibility of being outcaste, is fixed for life. Choice of marriage partners is strictly within the caste. Contact with other castes is limited by restrictions on touching, associating with, dining with, or eating food cooked by outsiders. Consciousness of caste is emphasized by the caste name, by identification with the caste in the eyes of one's community, by conformity to the customs peculiar to one's caste, and by subjection to government by one's caste. The caste is united by a common traditional occupation, although it may be united also or instead by a common tribal or racial origin, by adherence to a common religious sect, or by some other common peculiarity. The relative prestige of the different castes in any locality is well established and jealously guarded. This is the theory, but in practice some modification occurs. India has never been able to restrain people from changing their occupation, or to prevent new caste groups from splitting off. Under Western influence caste rigidity has begun to crumble, especially in the cities. K. D.

CASTEL GANDOLFO [kɑsteˈlgɑndɔˈlfo], a small village, the summer residence of the popes, in the Alban Hills, about 20 mi. southeast of Rome. It is situated on a sharp rise at an elevation of 1,360 ft. above sea level, overlooking from the west Lake Albano, a volcanic lake also known as the Lake of Castel Gandolfo.

Village. Some hold that the village of Castel Gandolfo rests on the site of the ancient city of Alba Longa, supposedly founded by Ascanius. It owes its name to the Gandolfi family of Rome, which built a castle here in the twelfth century. It later belonged to the Savellis, but was purchased by Clement VIII in 1596, and in 1608 it was declared the inalienable property of the Holy See.

The village of Castel Gandolfo lies in a district noted for its wines, which are highly prized on the Roman market. Olives are grown and fish in some quantity are taken from the lake. Pop. 1954 (village), 2,600; (commune), 4,300.

Papal Palace and other Landmarks. The papal palace was begun in 1629 on the ruins of an older castle and has been enlarged on several occasions. However, during the period of the popes' "voluntary captivity" in the Vatican from 1870 to 1929, it was not occupied by the pontiffs. South of the village is the Villa Barberini, built on the site of a villa of Domitian, third of the Flavian emperors of Rome. This villa is also papal property and, with the papal palace, enjoys extraterritorial rights granted in the Law of Guarantees (1871) and the Lateran Treaty (1929). Notable also are the church of San Tomaso da Villanova, begun in 1661 and containing paintings by Giovanni Lorenzo Bernini (1598-1680), celebrated Italian sculptor, architect, and painter, and the palaces of several aristocratic Roman families which followed the pope in erecting summer residences here, where the altitude provided refuge from the heat, humidity, and former malaria of the Campagna. There is an astronomical observatory of the Vatican in the village, which is connected with Rome by a branch railway and a tramway. Castel Gandolfo was damaged during World War II. R. G. W.

CASTELLO-BRANCO, CAMILLO [kəshteˈlu bræˈŋku] (1825-1890), Portuguese author, was born in Lisbon Mar. 16, 1825. Until the age of eight, when he was orphaned, he lived in Lisbon; then his sister took him to a remote hamlet in Tras-os-Montes. His life here was erratic. By the age of sixteen he was married, but he soon left his wife, who died in neglect. His erratic schooling, continued after marriage, included terms at the polytechnical school and a wild period as a medical student in Oporto; he intrigued, quarreled, conducted spectacular love affairs, and suffered imprisonment for his indiscretions. Yet five years before his death he was honored by the king with the title of Viscount Correia-Botelho. In his last years he withdrew to the northern province of Minho where, blind and ill, he took his own life June 1, 1890.

Camillo, as he is affectionately known throughout the Portuguese world, produced a prodigious number of works embracing poetry, drama, criticism, translations, stories, romances, novels, and a voluminous personal correspondence; but it is as a novelist or romancer that he won his chief fame and popularity. His numerous fictional pieces display a variety of moods: passionate, sentimental, or satirical, in settings historical as well as contemporary, regional as well as urban. These fictional writings are imitative of other authors, and show the influence first of Romanticism, and later of literary Realism. Their distinctiveness lies in Camillo's style. As a romancer he is at his best when spinning with lively fancy a tale of loves, persecutions, and capricious changes of fortune, as in *Os mysterios de Lisboa* ("The Mysteries of Lisbon"). Typical of his creation of sentiment and passion is the novel *Amor de perdição* ("Doomed Love"). His many *Novelas do Minho* ("Stories of the Minho") depict vividly, and without sentimental benevolence, scenes of the life of the northernmost province of Portugal. In *Eusebio Macario* and *Brasileira de Prazim* he experimented with novelistic realism. Camillo lacked the creative power of a great novelist; but his gift for literary painting was lively, and he delights the reader with his sentiment and inventiveness. Above all he lives as a master of language, in his hands an instrument rich, varied, and plastic, and solidly rooted in the traditions of Portugal. R. S. Ws.

CASTELLÓN DE LA PLANA [kɑˈstɛlyoˈn de lɑ plɑˈnɑ], the capital of the province of Castellón on the eastern coast of Spain.

The City. Castellón de la Plana lies about 4 mi. inland from the Mediterranean Sea and about 40 mi. northeast of

Valencia. The city is on the Barcelona-Valencia railway and is connected with the harbor of El Grao de Castellón by a narrow-gauge railway. It is a market and shipping center for the province's agricultural products, and manufactures textiles, porcelain, paper, rope, and leather goods. Castellón is partly surrounded by ruins of walls, but in comparison with most Spanish cities it is regular, spacious, and fairly modern in appearance. Of interest are the Gothic church of Santa María (1378-1409), which has three naves and is flanked by an imposing tower approximately 150 ft. high; and a fourteenth-century church which contains a painting by Francisco de Ribalta, who, it is claimed, was born here about 1555. There are several ancient convents. The present city was founded 2 mi. from old Castellón, a Moorish town on a hill; hence the *de la Plana* (of the plain) after its name. The change was effected in 1251 by King James I of Aragon, who had taken the city from the Moors in 1233. During the Spanish Civil War Castellón was held by Loyalist forces until June 15, 1938. Pop. 1950 (city), 44,940; (municipality), 52,778.

The Province. The province of Castellón has an area of 2,579 sq. mi. The terrain is mountainous in the interior, rising to heights of nearly 6,000 ft. The climate is hot in summer and temperate in winter in the lowlands, but cold in winter in the hilly sections. The principal rivers, all short, are the Cenia, Vinaroz, Mijares, and Palencia. The coast in general is flat. The coastal plain, though not wide, is very fertile and, where irrigated, quite productive of citrus fruits, especially oranges, and of vegetables. Rice, cereals, olives, and hemp are also cultivated. Most of the water used for irrigation is brought from the Mijares River by means of an aqueduct built by the Moors. Produce is exported through the ports of El Grao de Castellón and Vinaroz. Most of the people depend on agriculture, there being little industry, although fishing is carried on along the coast. There is no harbor suitable for extensive commercial operations. The two cities of importance, other than the capital, are Villareal, a citrus-growing center on the lower Mijares River, and Burriana, a few miles away in the same district. Of interest is Segorbe, an ancient cathedral town on the upper Palencia River, which has Roman remains and various castles in the vicinity. Pop. 1950, 330,257.   R. G. W.

CASTELO BRANCO [kəshteʹlu braʹŋku], the capital of an administrative district of the same name, in the old province of Beira, in east central Portugal, situated on a plateau between the Ponsul and Ocreza rivers—northern tributaries of the Tagus—at an elevation of 1,570 ft. above sea level. The Spanish frontier is about 15 mi. southeast.

City. Castelo Branco is served by a branch railway running from Abrantes to the southwest (on the Lisbon-Madrid line), to Guarda to the northeast (on the Lisbon-Coimbra-Salamanca-Burgos line). The city's industries include the spinning and weaving of linen and woolen cloth, the processing of the cereals, grapes, and olives grown in the surrounding region, and the shipping of livestock. Several schools and other public institutions serve the district, which in general is sparsely populated. Castelo Branco consists of an upper—the older—town, with its narrow, winding streets, and the lower town which is relatively new, with wide, straight streets and modern public buildings, a former cathedral, and an episcopal palace. The older town, which is partly surrounded by walls and towers, is surmounted by a ruined castle the origin of which is disputed, some tracing it back to the Roman Castraleuca, and others only to the twelfth century, when it was given to the Templars by

Sancho II, King of Portugal from 1223 to 1248. After the Council of Vienne suppressed the Order of Templars in 1312, the castle passed to its successor, the Order of Christ. In 1701 a Spanish force captured the castle but was soon obliged by the Portuguese to relinquish it. From 1771 to 1882 Castelo Branco was a bishopric of the archbishopric of Lisbon. Pop. 1950, 13,056.

District. The administrative district of Castelo Branco comprises 2,588 sq. mi. It is bounded on the east and southeast by Spain (Estremadura); on the north by the district of Guarda; on the west by those of Coimbra, Leiria, and Santarem; and in the southwest by that of Portalegre. On the south it is marked by the Tagus River, and most of its western border is formed by the Zêzere. In the north it extends to the Serra das Mesas and nearly to the Serra da Estralla in the northwest. In the west central portion are located the Serras do Moradel and Guardunha. In general, the terrain is very hilly or mountainous, with elevations reaching 4,000 ft. The entire area lies within the basin of the Tagus, which flows through a deep, narrow gorge. Only about one third of the land is cultivated, the chief products being cereals, vegetables, fruits, wine, and vinegar. Pasturing is of minor importance, but industrial development has attained an appreciable level, principally woolen milling. Covilhã, the principal industrial center of the district, is set amphitheatrically in a rugged mountainous region above the upper Zêzere. Covilhã is noted for its thermal springs and for the manufacture of *saragoça,* a coarse brown cloth. Pop. 1950, 324,577.   R. G. W.

CASTERBRIDGE [kæʹstərbrɪj], Thomas Hardy's name for Dorchester, a town of Roman origin in Dorset, England. It is the scene of *The Mayor of Casterbridge* and the center of Hardy's fictional "Wessex." *See also* MAYOR OF CASTERBRIDGE, THE; WESSEX.   C. J. W.

CASTIGLIONE, COUNT BALDASSARE [kɑʹstilyoʹne] (1478-1529), Italian diplomat, soldier, and author, was born Dec. 6, 1478 in his family's ancient castle at Casatico, near Mantua. His education was completed at the University of Milan while he was being trained at Duke Ludovico Sforza's court in the customary accomplishments of the young nobleman. In 1496 he entered the Duke's service, remaining there until his father's death in 1499 recalled him to Mantua. For the next five years he served the Marquis of Mantua, sharing with him the dangers of the ill-fated French attack on Naples.

In 1504 Castiglione's services were sought by the Duke of Urbino, and he thus entered into one of the most renowned courts of Italy, where Duke Guidobaldo and his charming consort, Elisabetta Gonzaga, gave hospitality to some of the most brilliant men of the Italian Renaissance. Pietro Bembo spent there the six happiest years of his life; Giuliano de'Medici was a frequent visitor, along with Cardinal Bibiena and others. Castiglione was well received by this noble company, although he was constantly embarrassed by the financial difficulties that were to attend him all his life. Sent by the ailing Duke to England in 1506 to receive as proxy the Order of the Garter from Henry VII, he acquitted himself most honorably.

Guidobaldo's death in 1508 marked the end of an epoch for Castiglione as well as for Urbino. In the service of the new Duke, Francesco I, Castiglione spent much time in Rome. This duty was made pleasant for him, on the one hand, by the company of Bembo and others formerly at Urbino; and Castiglione, who had already composed a dramatic eclogue, *Tirsi* ("Thyrsis"), was inspired to write further lyrics in Latin and in Italian. On the other hand, his professional duties were arduous, as Duke Francesco's position became daily more precarious. These two influences combined to turn his attention to a treatise in dialogue form, *Il Cortegiano* (*The Courtier*), which he claimed to have begun soon after Guidobaldo's death. The first three books may indeed have existed then in rough form, but the fourth book definitely dates from the Roman period. Its tone indicates clearly that the recent changes had filled its author with a nostalgic appreciation of the old order at Urbino and a realization that it is harder to find the perfect prince than to train the perfect courtier.

In 1516 the machinations of the Medici finally drove Duke Francesco from Urbino, and Castiglione found himself back at Mantua where the Duke had taken refuge with the Gonzagas. Financial pressure had now increased to a point where Castiglione was forced into a marriage that proved unexpectedly happy. During these peaceful years *The Courtier* was completed, though its author's modesty kept it unpublished until 1528.

With the accession in 1519 of Federigo Gonzaga, Castiglione was again sent to Rome where he remained until "borrowed" in 1524 by Pope Clement VII as nuncio to the Emperor Charles V. He reached Spain, and the climax of his career, under most trying circumstances. Cordially received by Charles and his court, Castiglione was exasperated by Clement's vacillation and duplicity, which undid all his good services and led in 1527 to the sack of Rome. Although blameless and later absolved by Clement himself, Castiglione never recovered from the shock of this misfortune. He was taken seriously ill in January 1529, and he died in Toledo, Spain, on Feb. 7. The greatest of the many honors accorded him was Charles V's own tribute: "I tell you that there has died one of the world's finest gentlemen." His tomb in Mantua bears a monument by Giulio Romano and an epitaph by Bembo. Castiglione's own great monument is *The Courtier,* but his lyrics, both Latin and Italian, reveal him to have been a gifted and sensitive poet as well as the perfect embodiment of the courtier he so well described. *See also* CORTEGIANO, IL. A. T. MacA.

CASTILE [kæsti'l], an ancient kingdom of north central Spain, divided into the former provinces of Old Castile in the north and New Castile in the south. Castile had its beginning under García, King of León (ruled 910-914), who expanded his frontier on the east and built numerous castles, from which the name Castile was derived. Count Fernán González of Burgos, later Castile (ruled 932-970), allied himself with the Moors and made his expanded county autonomous. He was succeeded in 970 by Sancho the Great of Navarre, who united Castile and Navarre, and began the conquest of León which was completed by Ferdinand I of Castile (ruled 1035-1065). After a brief separation, León and Castile were again united, and were greatly extended again in wars against the Moorish invaders by Alfonso VI (ruled 1072-1109 as Alfonso I of Castile) and Alfonso VII (ruled 1126-1157). Again separated, the two kingdoms were finally reunited by Ferdinand III (ruled 1217-1252). Alfonso X, the Learned (ruled 1252-1284) who succeeded Ferdinand, was a distinguished scholar who helped to make Castile a center of culture. However, he was a weak monarch who neglected his kingdom while he engaged in futile foreign intrigues. His successors were not of great ability, and the authority of the crown was further weakened by frequent minority and dynastic struggles. Feudal anarchy reached its height under Henry IV (ruled 1454-1474). On his death, his step-sister and heiress, Isabella, who had married Ferdinand, the heir of the king of Aragon, succeeded to the throne after a period of civil war. A personal union of Aragon and Castile resulted. This union became complete under their grandson Charles, the heir to both kingdoms, in the early sixteenth century. *See also* NEW CASTILE; OLD CASTILE. F. C. H.

CASTILLA, RAMÓN [kɑsti'yɑ] (1797-1867), Peruvian soldier and statesman, was born in Tarapaca, Aug. 27, 1797. He spent his early life exploring the interior of South America, and he later served in the wars for independence and in subsequent revolutions. In 1845 he was elected president of Peru for a six-year term and succeeded in establishing peace in the country, which had undergone a long period of unrest. He stabilized finances, consolidated the national debt with the income from the guano deposits of the Chincha Islands, and promoted the development of telegraph communications, railroads, and other public works. In 1855 he began his second term as president, serving from 1855 to 1862, but internal disorders and trouble with Ecuador prevented progress; the Peruvian constitution was, however, promulgated in 1860. After Castilla retired he continued active in politics until his death at Tiviliche, Aug. 29, 1867. S. G. I.

CASTILLO DE SAN MARCOS, a national monument located on the northeastern coast of Florida in the city of St. Augustine. This monument preserves the oldest masonry fort within the borders of the United States. Construction of the fort was started by the Spanish in 1672; it was their northeasternmost fortification in the New World. The fort was built with coquina (shell rock) blocks cemented together by mortar made from oyster shells, and the walls in some places are 10 ft. thick. The structure is built around a patio 100 ft. square and is circled by a moat 40 ft. wide.

The fort, built to protect the Spanish settlement of St. Augustine from the British and from pirates, was attacked unsuccessfully in 1702 by Governor James Moore and his men from South Carolina. An attack in 1728 also failed. In 1740, Governor James E. Oglethorpe of Georgia besieged the fort for twenty-seven days without capturing it. When the United States acquired Florida the structure was named Fort Marion and was used as a prison. It was declared a national monument on Oct. 15, 1924. *See also* FLORIDA *for illustration.* J. E. F.

CASTILLO NÁJERA, FRANCISCO [kɑsti'yo nɑ'herɑ] (1886-1954), Mexican physician and diplomat, was born Nov. 25, 1886, in Durango. After graduating from the College of the State of Durango and receiving his medical degree at the University of Mexico, Castillo Nájera studied further in Paris, Berlin, Brussels, and New York City. From 1918 to 1919 he was director of the Juárez Hospital, Mexico City, and the following year he was appointed director of the Mexican Army Medical School.

An accomplished linguist as well as a surgeon, Castillo Nájera was called into the diplomatic service, and from 1922 to 1924 he was minister to China. For the next two years he studied in Europe. From 1927 to 1935 he was successively minister to Belgium, Holland, Sweden, France, and Austria. His longest appointment was as Mexican ambassador to the United States from 1935 to 1945, after which he returned to Mexico to become minister of foreign affairs. During the spring of 1945 he was Mexican delegate to the United Nations Conference on International Organization, and in 1947 was briefly president of the UN Security Council. He died in Mexico City on Dec. 20, 1954.   S. G. I.

CASTINGS. *See* Metal Castings.
CAST IRON. *See* Iron and Steel.
CAST-IRON PLANT. *See* Aspidistra.

CASTLE or **CHÂTEAU** [shæto']. The word "castle" is derived from the Latin *castellum,* diminutive of *castrum,* meaning "a fortified place." "Château" is the French form. The term is generally used to denote a fortified building or group of buildings, especially those of a chieftain, lord, noble, or king. Castles and castle architecture came to their completest development during the medieval period, although fortified buildings have been known from early times. Indeed, such features as thick, sheer walls, embattled towers, machicolations, and battlements were known as early as the days of the Assyrians and were features of the fortified palace of Sargon (eighth century B.C.), built in the mountains north of Nineveh at modern Khorsabad (Iraq).

Castles seem not to have figured widely in Egyptian and Greek architecture but reappear in Roman times, though largely as city walls or as protections of such country palaces as that which the emperor Diocletian built at Spalatum (Split) in Dalmatia. Fortified structures were not important in early Christian times in the West, but the Byzantine emperors built elaborate fortifications and fortified palaces at Constantinople.

With the feudal system, castles attained their greatest importance. Feudal society divided itself into three classes: the knights or nobles to defend society, the clergy to pray, and the peasants to till the soil and support the other classes. The knights lived in castles situated upon easily fortified hilltops or in the bends of rivers. From these military strongholds they managed their lands. Here they received their vassals,

Castle of Neuschwanstein, near Schwangau, Germany

EWING GALLOWAY, NEW YORK

held councils, and, upon occasion, defended themselves against their rivals.

Early western European castles seem to have been of timber, consisting of a circular palisade built atop a hill or mound that could be surrounded by a dry moat. Inside the palisade was built a citadel from which the surrounding country could be surveyed. In time these wooden structures were replaced by stone, and strongholds like the massive Tower of London (eleventh century) and the earlier parts of Kenilworth Castle (1120) were built. As the materials changed, so did the plan, which soon exhibited a whole group of structures, including the donjon (keep), an inner court with walls and towers, and a bailey or courtyard, with garden, gatehouse, stables, and all the necessities of a self-contained establishment, all surrounded by heavy walls and a moat with drawbridge.

Coucy Castle in northern France, blown up by the Germans in 1918, and the châteaux Pierrefonds and Gaillard, with their circular towers, heavy walls, and embattled parapets, are typical of the best French examples. With the Renaissance, châteaux became far less martial, as will be noted by an examination of many such noble residences in the valley of the Loire.

During the twelfth century, fortified residences were highly important in England, some thousand castles going up during the twenty-year reign of Stephen. This vogue kept up as long as petty chieftains carried on feudal wars and the power of the king remained weak. With the invention of gunpowder (1500) the moat and other defense features became useless and castles became less popular. However, in England as in France, features once functional and important in defense were long retained as decorative reminiscences. Such ensembles as Windsor Castle, a fortification and a seat of royalty since the eleventh century, have been added to or altered in every important period of their existence. Windsor Castle, as well as Carnarvon Castle in Wales are excellent British illustrations of the medieval castle.

Germany, Spain, Hungary, and lesser lands had feudal strongholds. The Kremlin in Moscow is such a structure. The strongholds of the Prussian lords were important, and in south Germany such castles as those at Heidelberg and Neuschwanstein are renowned, as are Drachenfels and other castles along the Rhine. A whole chain of fortresses was built in Spain during the reconquest of the country from the Moors. A Spanish stronghold is called a "castillo" or an "alcázar," the latter being the Moorish version of *castrum,* of which the Moors built a late equivalent, the Alhambra, on the hills above Granada.

The Crusaders, mainly from western Europe, built many castles in the Holy Land during the twelfth century. Here they had opportunity to study Byzantine fortifications and gained considerable experience in the erection of strongholds. Out of this experience came a system of defense which, carried home by the returning Crusaders, greatly influenced castle architecture in western Europe. The Crusaders learned (1) that a second line of defense must be erected within the main or outer *enceinte* (enclosure), (2) that within the second line a donjon, or keep, should form a third or last refuge, and (3) that walls must be flanked by projecting towers. These principles were carried out by Richard the Lion-Hearted in his Château Gaillard, where no less than three well-defined wards defended the donjon. By many this is considered one of the finest of feudal castles.

Aside from separate and distinct castles, the Middle Ages furnish examples of fortified or castle-like towns, such as Carcassonne in France. Other fortified residences were

Château of Fontainebleau near Paris, France

monastic castles and structures like the palaces of the popes at Avignon.   R. Ne.

CASTLE GARDEN, a circular building at the southernmost point of Manhattan, known as The Battery, was one of New York's most popular early playhouses. Originally the site of a seventeenth-century Dutch fort, and later turned into Castle Clinton for harbor defense during the War of 1812, it opened as a theatre in 1845. First to appear there was a troupe of minstrels headed by Charles White. The same year Castle Garden acquired a regular company of well-regarded actors, including George Holland and Charles M. Walcot, and grand opera was given there by a troupe of singers from Havana. Jenny Lind made her celebrated American debut there on Sept. 11, 1850, under P. T. Barnum's management. After this high point in its history, Castle Garden became an immigrant receiving station until the establishment of a receiving center on Ellis Island in 1892. The New York City Aquarium was located in the former theatre building from 1896 until 1941. Castle Garden was also used for receptions for the Marquis de Lafayette, Andrew Jackson, and John Tyler. Samuel F. B. Morse gave one of his first demonstrations of the telegraph there. The old fort, Castle Clinton, was established as a national monument in 1946 and is being restored.   J. Ga.

CASTLE GATE, a geological formation resembling a pair of castle towers, situated at the northern end of the Price River Canyon in east central Utah. This geological gateway is in Carbon Co., about 2 mi. north of the town of Castle Gate and 90 mi. southeast of Salt Lake City. The great gray sandstone pinnacles rise 450 to 500 ft. above the level of the Price River. The Denver and Rio Grande Western Railroad and a highway also pass through the gate.
                                                                      J. E. F.

CASTLE OF OTRANTO, THE [otrɑ′nto], a "Gothic" romance, pseudonymously published by the English writer Horace Walpole in 1764. The author's imagination created without restraint a wealth of incidents of supernatural horror. A monstrously large helmet, bedecked with "a mountain of sable plumes," crushes to death a bridegroom on his espousal day. A portrait heaves and sighs, and a statue bleeds at the nose; the earth quakes and enormous arms and legs ghoulishly appear amid the eerie recesses of the haunted castle. The influence of this epoch-making romance can be seen in "Gothic" qualities found in the works of later writers, among them Scott, the Brontës, Byron, and Poe.
                                                                      H. Dr.

CASTLE PINCKNEY NATIONAL MONUMENT, a historic site occupying an area of 3½ acres on an island in the harbor of Charleston, S. C. During the Revolutionary War a fort, Castle Pinckney, was built on the island. Castle Pinckney helped to protect Charleston from the British naval attacks in 1776 and 1779, but in May 1780 Sir Henry Clinton captured Charleston. The fort was eventually destroyed, but in 1810 was rebuilt and for a while was a United States buoy station. It was established as a national monument on Oct. 15, 1924.   J. E. F.

CASTLEREAGH, ROBERT STEWART, VISCOUNT (MARQUIS OF LONDONDERRY) [ka′sǝlre] (1769-1822), British statesman, was born in County Down, Ireland, on June 18, 1769. He was educated in a school at Armagh and at St. John's College, Cambridge, and traveled on the Continent during 1788 and 1789. Through the efforts of his father, a rich landowner, he was elected to the Irish House of Commons in 1790. Here he advocated parliamentary union with England and emancipation for the Irish Roman Catholics. From 1797 to 1799, during the absence of Thomas Pelham, Chief Secretary for Ireland, Castlereagh carried out the duties of that office, succeeding to it on Pelham's retirement in 1799; he was largely responsible for the vigorous measures taken to put down the revolt of the United Irishmen and to defeat the French invasion in 1798. It was chiefly through his skill in negotiation and bribery that the Act of Union was finally passed by the Irish parliament in 1800. Notwithstanding the strong views of Pitt and Castlereagh, King George III refused to agree to a bill for Catholic emancipation, whereupon both Pitt and Castlereagh resigned office. Since Viscount Castlereagh was a courtesy title, Stewart could be elected to the new Union House of Commons in London, where he represented English and Irish constituencies from 1801 to 1822. In 1802 he entered Addington's cabinet as President of the Board of Control for India. Here he occupied himself mainly with foreign policy, though he gave every support to the vigorous action of Lord Wellesley in India. From 1805 to 1806 he was Secretary of State for War and the Colonies, an office he resumed in March 1807. Both Castlereagh and Canning, the Foreign Secretary, supported the giving of aid to Portugal and the dispatch of an expedition to Spain, though Castlereagh had the chief share in planning it and placing his old friend Arthur Wellesley (later Duke of Wellington) in command. Castlereagh was the victim of all the unpopularity that followed the failure of the Walcheren expedition (1809), especially as it coincided with heavy losses in Spain. He blamed Canning for intrigues, and both resigned after a duel.

Castlereagh returned to the cabinet as Foreign Secretary and leader of the House of Commons in 1812, and it was largely through his diplomatic skill that the coalition against Napoleon was held together until the final victory at Waterloo (1815). He was mainly responsible for the generous terms given France and played an important role in the Congress of Vienna (1814). Moreover, though he was prepared to allow the intervention of Austria in Italy in support of her traditional claims there, he protested strongly against the general policy of intervention in favor of the *status quo* and was contemptuous of the Holy Alliance; in this respect his policy foreshadowed that of Canning, his successor. In his domestic policies, Castlereagh was bitterly attacked, notably by the poet Byron, for his opposition to social and economic reform, exemplified in 1819 by his share in the Peterloo Massacre, in which soldiers fired on a meeting of workers, and by the Six Acts, which restricted civil liberties. In 1822, a year after succeeding to the Irish title Marquis of Londonderry, he committed suicide on August 12 at North Cray in Kent.

Castlereagh had great ability in the conduct of foreign affairs. More than any other statesman, he contributed to Napoleon's final defeat and to the subsequent *Pax Britannica* in Europe. E. R. A.

CASTOR, also designated Alpha (α) Geminorum, in modern times the second star in brightness of the constellation Gemini. Centuries ago it probably exceeded Pollux, now the brighter of the two. Castor is white in color, approximately 45 light-years distant, and over 40 times more luminous than the sun. Telescopically, this star becomes a fine double, the components of which have magnitudes 2.0 and 2.8. The combination gives 1.6, or only slightly too faint to be classed as a first-magnitude star. The two stars revolve around their common center of gravity in about 350 yr. During this time their apparent separation varies from 1½″ to 6″. A ninth-magnitude star, 73″ distant, evidently belongs to the same system. The spectroscope reveals that each of the three stars is itself a double, making six in the system. The periods of revolution of the two brighter pairs are nine and three days, respectively. *See also* GEMINI. J. H. P.

CASTOR AND POLLUX [ka'stər, pɒ'ləks], heroes in Greek mythology, sometimes called the Dioscuri, or "sons of Zeus." The name Pollux is the Roman form of the Greek Polydeuces. In one version of the myth Castor was the son of Tyndareus and Leda, Pollux the son of Zeus and Leda; in another, they were the twin sons of Zeus and Leda and were worshiped as deities by sailors, to whom they appeared as St. Elmo's fire. Castor was famed for his ability to manage horses, Polydeuces for his skill as a boxer. They rescued Helen, their sister, when as a child she was carried off by Theseus; they also took part in the Calydonian hunt and, as members of the Argonautic expedition, captured Talus, the Cretan man of bronze. When Castor was killed in a fight with Idas and Lynceus, Polydeuces asked to die also, and Zeus allowed them to take turns in Hades, or to spend alternate days in Hades and Heaven. Later the twins were identified with the constellation Gemini. Castor and Pollux were said to have fought on the side of the Roman army at Lake Regillus in 496 B.C. and to have brought news of the victory to Rome. They had a temple in the Forum, usually known as the temple of Castor. *See also* CALYDONIAN HUNT; HELEN; JASON; TALUS. G. E. D.

CASTOR OIL, a pale yellow or almost colorless, transparent, viscid liquid having a faint, mild odor, and a bland, afterward slightly acrid and usually nauseating taste. It is a fixed oil obtained from the seeds of *Ricinis communis* and is an active cathartic. It is used externally as a demulcent in eye burns and in hair tonics and frequently used as a low temperature lubricant in airplanes. J. A. Bo.

CASTOR-OIL PLANT, *Ricinus communis,* also called *palma Christi,* a member of the spurge family, probably native to Africa, but since ancient times cultivated and widely naturalized in warm regions, where it is a tree-like perennial growing to 40 ft., and in temperate zones, where it is a stout herbaceous annual to 15 ft. The smooth stems bear large star-shaped leaves sometimes 2½ ft. across, numerous small flowers in clusters, and prickly seed pods which split when ripe into 3 parts, each containing a smooth grayish bean-like seed very rich in oil. It is in India that the plant is chiefly cultivated for oil; in North America it is planted as an ornamental and has become naturalized from Ottawa to Florida and in California. J. C. Wis.

CASTRATO [kɑstrɑ'to], a type of male soprano employed chiefly in Italian opera from the sixteenth to the nineteenth centuries. As the Italian name implies, this voice was achieved by castrating male singers before puberty so that the lengthening of their vocal chords and the consequent deepening of the voice at puberty was avoided. The adult *castrato* thus possessed an abnormally high and extended range to which his normal lungs and chest added a power not found in boy or female sopranos. One of the greatest of all *castrati* was Carlo Broschi, commonly called Farinelli; his life (1705-1782) spanned the greatest period of *castrato* singing, a period when the *castrato* was the supreme figure in opera, exceeding in popularity even the prima donna. W. Li.

CASTRÉN, MATTHIAS ALEXANDER [ka'stren] (1813-1852), Finnish linguist and ethnologist, was born Dec. 2, 1813, at Tervola. Stimulated by Finland's new national consciousness, he undertook four scientific journeys to various Finno-Ugric, Turkic, and Mongol peoples in Scandinavia, Russia, and Siberia. In 1838 he journeyed through Lapland and in the following year through Karelia. His third and fourth journeys form two of the best known episodes in Uralic and Altaic studies. Castrén went to Russia in 1841 and crossed the Urals to Obdursk in 1843, but because of ill health he returned to Finland in the following year; the fruits of this journey were his *Elementa grammatices Syrjaenae* and *Elementa grammatices Tscheremissiae.* In 1845 he returned to Siberia, working along the Irtysh and Yenisey rivers among the Samoyedes and the Ugric Ostyaks. Early in 1847 he went to Lake Baykal, near Mongolia, where, besides studying Tatar, Tungus, and Burjat, he investigated Kamassian, a dying Samoyed language. Returning to Finland in 1849, he published his *Versuch einer ostjakischen Sprachlehre* and *De affixis personalibus linguarum Altaicarum.* He died in Helsingfors on May 7, 1852.

Most of Castrén's material was still in manuscript form at the time of his death. His works were edited in Swedish in five volumes between 1852 and 1858. A German translation was published between 1853 and 1862 under the editorship of Anton Schiefner. A. N. N.

CASTRIES [ka'stris], the capital, largest city, and port of the island of St. Lucia, in the British West Indies, located on a beautiful and almost completely landlocked bay, on the northwest coast of St. Lucia, at 13° 59′ N. lat. and 61° 1′ W. long. The deep, mountain-encircled harbor is one of the best in the West Indies, and most of the history and economic development of St. Lucia center around it. The valuable port has changed back and forth from French to English control with the fortunes of war, but most of the time, after the original French settlement established in 1650, Castries has been English. Admiral Horatio Nelson used Castries Bay as a base, and later in history the town became a coaling station. Castries was a useful base during World War II. Castries suffered a disastrous fire in 1948, four-fifths of the city being destroyed by flames which broke out on June 20 and raged for two days. The mean annual temperature is 78.6° F.; the mean annual rainfall, 91 in. Sugar, limes and other fruits, cacao, cotton, and copra are exported. Pop. (est. 1955), 25,000. J. E. F.

CASTRO, CIPRIANO [ka'stro] (1856-1924), Venezuelan dictator, was born in Capacho in 1856. At an early age he became one of the local chiefs who divided the country among themselves and either followed or fought the national dictator, as best served their purposes. When General

Ignacio Andrade decided to extend his presidency for life, Castro led a "restoring revolution" to return the country to constitutional processes. Once he had seized power, however, he followed his own illegal course to dictatorship. A man of few abilities, Castro initiated one of the most cruel regimes in South American history. He was aided by an equally ruthless and ignorant neighbor, Juan Vicente Gómez, who later betrayed Castro and succeeded him. The outside world would have heard little of Castro if he had not chosen to defy foreign creditors. When he replied to their claims with insults, Great Britain, Holland, France, and Germany threatened to blockade Venezuelan ports. President Theodore Roosevelt of the United States notified Germany that such action would violate the Monroe Doctrine, and he threatened in 1902 to send Admiral George Dewey and his fleet to intervene. Kaiser Wilhelm II accepted peaceful arbitration of the claims. Castro went to Europe in 1908 for medical treatment, leaving his lieutenant, Gómez, in charge. Gómez immediately installed himself as dictator, and Castro was not permitted to return to Venezuela. After wandering from port to port in the Caribbean, a man without a country, he went into exile in Puerto Rico. He died in poverty in San Juan, Puerto Rico, Dec. 4, 1924.   S. G. I.

CASTRO, GUILLÉN DE (1569-1631), Spanish dramatist, was born in Valencia in 1569 and, until 1619, when he moved permanently to Madrid, made that city the scene of his literary career. As a young man he became a captain in the coastal militia and later accepted the post of governor of the fortress of Scigliano, in Spanish territory in southern Italy. His first marriage in 1595 appears, on the evidence of his dramatic treatment of the marriage theme, to have been not entirely happy. He married again in 1626 in Madrid, where he had obtained the literary patronage of the Marquis of Peñafiel. His death in 1631 found him impoverished.

As a dramatist Guillén de Castro belonged to that school which followed the precepts for the Spanish national theatre laid down by Lope de Vega. Many of his approximately fifty dramas follow traditional Spanish ballad themes, and there are three which dramatize various parts of Cervantes' works. His best known drama, *Las Mocedades del Cid* ("The Youthful Exploits of the Cid," 1618), however, does not employ Lope's technique of transmuting the essential spirit of a single ballad into an entirely new dramatic expression. Castro, instead, organized and incorporated into his play many of the original ballads themselves. It was a process which at once assured him of historical and poetic success and communicated a certain unwieldiness to his dramatic organization. The Cid ballads which he used derive from a late fourteenth-century epic and are historically without foundation. As the dramatist tells the traditional story, the young untried Rodrigo, not yet possessor of his soubriquet of Cid, is forced for the sake of his father's honor to kill Count Lozano, the father of his beloved Jimena. His exploits against the Moors and his ultimate reconciliation with Jimena make up the body of this drama of physical and emotional conflict. Pierre Corneille, in 1636, used *Las Mocedades* as the basis for the first outstandingly successful French drama, *Le Cid*. Other Castro plays which employ ballad material, according to this same formula, are *El Conde Alarcos, El Conde Dirlos,* and *Las Hazañas del Cid.*   S. G.

CASTRO ALVES, ANTONIO DE [ka'shtru a'lvəs] (1847-1871), Brazilian poet, was born in Muritiba, Bahia. He studied law in Pernambuco and São Paulo, but abandoned his studies because of poor health. Handsome, rich, and talented, he won literary acclaim at an early age, identifying himself with the idealistic causes of his day, and putting his art at their service. His name is particularly associated with the Brazilian abolitionist movement. His antislavery poems *Voices from Africa* and *The Slave-Traders' Ship* had an influence in Brazil comparable with that of *Uncle Tom's Cabin* in the United States. With them Castro Alves won over great sections of public opinion to the antislavery cause, which was finally to triumph some years after his death. In his writings Brazilian poetry laid aside its usual individualistic tone and became concerned with social ideals; it has been said that he personified the moral conscience of his country. The impetuous eloquence of his lyricism recalls that of Victor Hugo in *Les Châtiments* by virtue of its sound and color, its grandiose images, and its use of rich, warm, and stimulating adjectives. Castro Alves was one of the founders of the poetic school known in Brazil as the *escola condoreira* ("condor school"), and he occasionally indulged in the declamatory bombast characteristic of many of its adherents. His early death lent a certain tragic appeal to his later reputation, which places him in the forefront of Brazilian poets. Fifty editions of his works have been published. His verse is collected in the following volumes: *Espumas flutuantes (Floating Foams,* 1871), *A Cachoeira de Paulo Afonso (Paulo Afonso's Waterfall,* 1876), and *Obras Completas (Complete Works,* 1921).
          E. G. DaC.

CASTROP-RAUXEL [ka'strɔp rau'ksəl], an industrial and coal-mining town in North Rhine-Westphalia, in the (West) German Federal Republic, located 8 mi. northwest of Dortmund, on the Rhine-Herne and Dortmund-Ems canals. An important industrial city of the Ruhr Valley, Castrop-Rauxel has manufactures of chemicals, textiles, concrete, and cigarettes, as well as brickworks, sawmills, and distilleries. Extensive coal-mining operations are carried on in the immediate vicinity of the city. Castrop, which had been formed in 1902 by the union of Obercastrop and Behringhausen, merged with Rauxel and four other towns in 1926 to form Castrop-Rauxel. It was formerly in the Prussian province of Westphalia. Severely bombed during World War II, it was afterwards included in the British zone of occupation (1945-1955). Pop. 1953, 80,400.

CAST STEEL. *See* IRON AND STEEL.

CASUARINA [kæ'syuərai'nə], a genus of trees, with about twenty-five species, native to Australia and the islands of the Pacific. The name of the plant is derived from the vague resemblance of the twigs to the feathers of the cassowary, a bird native to the same region. In Australia the casuarina is commonly called oak, she-oak, and beefwood. The female flowers are borne in dense clusters; the male flowers in slender spikes. One species of casuarina, *C. equisetifolia,* which may reach a height of 150 ft., is much planted as a shade tree. Several species, including the above, are grown as ornamentals in Florida, California, and other warm regions of the United States.

CASUISTRY [kæ'zhuɪstri], the technique of applying moral principles to particular cases. When a system of ethics is set forth in general rules, there arises in any particular moral problem the question of which rule primarily applies to it; e.g., the question whether a householder is justified in killing a burglar is decided by inquiring whether it is a case of murder or a case of defense of property. Reasoning of this sort is obviously subject to abuse, since ethical terms are ambiguous enough, and actual cases are complicated enough, to permit an apparent justification of almost any action. Hence the odium which has become attached to the epithet "casuist."   M. C. Be.

CAT, any carnivorous mammal of the family Felidae, which includes the lions, tigers, leopards, wildcats, and lynx. Cats vary in size from wild species scarcely larger than the domestic cat to the large Siberian tiger, which may attain 14

EWING GALLOWAY, NEW YORK

The tabby cat, striped and varicolored common cat, is a familiar favorite.

feet in length. The cats all possess somewhat rounded, relatively short skulls, with highly inflated auditory bullae. The teeth are extremely specialized for a diet of meat, much more so than in dogs, bears, or other carnivores. The large molar teeth have compressed high crowns without crushing surfaces, the last upper premolar and the first lower molar presenting the extreme phase of carnassial modification. The last upper molar is narrow, the main axis of its crown transverse to the tooth row. Cats are usually slender animals, the legs being moderately long. Retractile claws are a distinctive feature of all true cats. Normally, the claws are drawn into a sheath preserving them from friction and undue wear; when in use for fighting, climbing, or other purposes, a set of muscles frees them from the sheath.

Cats are found throughout the world. They are most abundant in tropical or semitropical countries, although the Manchurian tiger and the Canada lynx are adapted for a boreal existence. Three well-defined groups may be recognized. The genus *Felis* includes the long-tailed cats, such as the domestic species, the lion, and the tiger. The genus *Lynx* comprises the bobcats and lynx, short-tailed cats of moderate size and prominent ear tufts. Hunting leopards, or cheetahs, of the genus *Acinonyx* (trained in southern Asia for use in hunting antelope and other game) lack the retractile claws of other cats and have somewhat longer legs.   W. J. Ha.

CAT, DOMESTIC (*Felis catus*), a small fur-bearing carnivore domesticated throughout the world as a household pet. The origin of the word "cat" is uncertain, but its presence in nearly every language, differently spelled but often similarly pronounced, attests to its antiquity and world-wide recognition. A traveler in almost any country will be understood if he refers to a "cat." The word, however, relates not only to the domestic breeds, but to cats of all sizes, such as the lion, tiger, cheetah, leopard, and the five American groups comprising the jaguar, puma or mountain lion, jaguarundi, ocelot, and lynx or bobcat.

Early History. The cat family evolved about 40,000,000 years before the advent of man on this planet, and among fifty extinct species some were fourteen feet long. Their fossils fall into two groups, the true cats and the saber-tooth tigers. Though remains of extinct felines of various sizes have been unearthed in North America and Europe, the question remains unsettled as to when and where small household cats came into existence. They were domesticated even by prehistoric man, and are known to have been tamed in earliest times in China, India, Syria, Nubia, Egypt, and other countries.

It has been thought that the dog was first domesticated by primitive man to accompany him in the hunt, and that the rodent-destroying cat was tamed by woman to protect grain stored for winter use; but sculptured decoration on Egyptian tombs shows that cats were also used to hunt birds; swimming cats were especially adapted to this purpose because they could leap from a boat and bring back the quarry. Cats were kept as pets not only on account of their helpfulness, but because of their beauty, intelligence and grace, and were associated with the gods by such widely separated races as Egyptians and Norsemen. In Egypt they were sacred to the chief god, Ra, who sometimes took the form of a cat, and Isis, the chief goddess, was portrayed with a cat's ears; moreover, the Egyptians revered a cat-headed goddess, Pasht, who was closely related to Isis and from whose name it is believed the word "puss" has been derived. Cat temples, and also cat cemeteries containing thousands of bodies of embalmed cats, have been excavated in different parts of Egypt. Many other animals were sacred to the Egyptians, but none except the bull was worshiped over the entire country like the cat, which they immortalized also in pyramid texts and in their jewelry, pottery, and furniture.

YLLA - GUILLUMETTE

The gray Persian cat, like the white Persian, is of unknown original habitat.

Early Norsemen reverenced the cat, and their Freya, a goddess of love like Pasht, traveled in a chariot drawn by two cats. Pasht and Freya were both linked with the sun and the moon. On its introduction into Europe the cat enjoyed high regard and legal protection, but its association with the witch superstition of the Middle Ages led to extremely cruel treatment, reversing the exalted position the cat had occupied in other lands. It is only during later centuries that it has been restored to favor.

Breeds. Domestic cats number more than thirty breeds, but are of only one genus and one species (the latter called variants and variations), with no subspecies (varieties). No wildcats in the Western Hemisphere are related to *F. catus,* and the ancestors of house cats of North and South America were introduced from foreign countries. Domestic animals gone wild frequently revert to original types, and Darwin took home from South America a cat closely resembling the Kaffir cat of Africa (*F. caffra*), which has been identified as one of the several species tamed by the ancient Egyptians and also as one of the various wild ancestors of the domestic breeds, which are believed to have included a mixture of Kaffir and other African wildcats with European wildcats (*F. sylvestris*). The domestic cat is willing to mate with these Old World related wildcats.

Angora and Persian. Among the long-haired breeds are the Angora and the so-called Persian, and the characteristics of the latter predominate when the two are mated. In foreign countries the two breeds are kept separate, but in the United States they have been fused until pure Angora cats seldom are found except in Maine and Massachusetts, where they are known as "coon cats." The Angora cat was introduced into New England by seafaring men from its home in Angora (Ankara), now the capital of Turkey. Later came the Persian breed, whose original habitat is unknown. It has long been exported from Afghanistan. The Angora cat is shaped like the short-haired breeds, with long body, legs, face, and ears; but cat fanciers prefer the Persian traits: a short ("cobby") body, short legs and ears, and a round face.

Siamese and Burmese. Foreign short-haired cats introduced subsequently to these two long-haired breeds, and attaining great popularity, are the Siamese, Burmese, Abyssinian, Manx, and Russian Blue. The Siamese, as the first to reach America, and because of its remarkable fertility, is most numerous. It is the common cat of Siam, and neither "royal" nor "sacred" as originally advertised. White at birth, with blue eyes, the body color after a few months changes to delicate fawn with seal brown "points," i.e., muzzle, ears, legs, and tail, or with blue points, the two then being known as seal-point and blue-point Siamese. In both breeds the eyes, which remain blue through life, may slant a little or be slightly crossed, while the tail occasionally carries a kink near the end. The Burmese cat resembles the Siamese except that the newborn kitten is a light milk chocolate; the

YLLA · GUILLUMETTE

The Abyssinian ticked cat's gray or brown coat of dark-tipped hair gives the ticked appearance of wild rabbit fur.

body color of the adult is walnut brown, with still darker brown points, and the eyes are round and range from turquoise to yellow.

Abyssinian Ticked Cat. The gray or brown coat of the Abyssinian ticked cat is like a wild rabbit's, its fur differing from the rabbit's only in that its upper coat overlies a rufous undercoat. Each hair is tipped with the darker color, which produces the ticking. This breed is believed to be similar to one which arose in the later Egyptian dynasties. The earlier cat of Egypt was apparently striped, and it is possible that by mutation it may have become a finely spotted cat, which, in turn, developed into the ticked cat.

Manx. Cats' tails differ considerably, and the Manx cat, to rank as a perfect specimen in American cat-show judging, must lack any vestige of a tail, exhibiting instead a depression or dimple, with a tuft of fur where the tail ordinarily begins. Many Manx cats, however, after generations of selective breeding, are born with tails. How the tailless cat reached the Isle of Man is an unsolved mystery. It occurs in several eastern countries and may have been introduced, or it may have become established by natural selection long ago. The hind legs are exceptionally long, the rump round, and the head large; the color varies, as in the common cat. In habit it differs from other cats in being a fast runner, and when running makes rabbitlike leaps, engages in keeping

YLLA

The Siamese cat, the common cat of Siam, has blue, often slightly crossed eyes. It is fawn-colored with blue or seal brown points.

strange dogs off the home grounds, and is not only agile but unusually well-balanced. It makes an even better turn in falling and landing on its feet than the tailed cat, this ability, which is marked also in wild felines, being due to the structure of the semicircular ear canals.

Common Cats. Fashions among cats, as among dogs, come and go. The Angora, once the favorite show cat in the United States, yielded to the Persian, and one breed of Persian may yield to another. The common cat, however, is unexcelled in beauty when properly cared for, and some breeders devote their attention exclusively to the rearing and exhibiting of such striking breeds as the blue-eyed white and the silver and brown.

The common cat may represent many other breeds, such as the wide-striped or narrow-striped specimens, generally called "tiger cats," with gray body, black vertical stripes, and a deeper stripe down the back, transverse lines on the cheeks and a letter M in the forehead, black necklaces and bracelets and barred tail, and green or hazel eyes. There is also the blotched type, such as the brown, with the same general markings as the striped cat but having three stripes down the back, side stripes not vertical but borne in wide spirals or whorls, and with orange or copper eyes. The silver cat has been specially bred for black whorls on a light silver background and blue-green eyes. Other types are the blue and the red, but the latter shows no black in its coat, the orange body being marked instead by whorls of rich red and the eyes matching the fur. Approved cats show no white in the coat. Cats of solid color may be black, white, blue, red (also called orange), cream, brown, or gray.

Colors. For centuries two of the most popular short-haired cats have been the black-and-white and the tortoise-shell-and-white, both with orange eyes. The tortoise-shell-and-white cat, commonly called tortoise-shell, is marked with the three colors of the much rarer tortoise-shell cat, black, red and cream, with considerable white in the coat and a white face. In the pure tortoise-shell there is no white, and the face reveals a nose half black and half orange. Darwin, noticing that a yellow coat invariably signified a male cat and a tortoise-shell coat a female, concluded that these two were natural pairs; but since his day the occurrence of yellow females and tortoise-shell males has been reported many times, though tortoise-shell males are apt to be sterile.

Colors of long-haired cats generally follow those of the short-haired breeds in black, white, blue, orange, tortoise-shell, and tabby, together with silver Persians, among which are numbered the chinchilla and shaded silver, and the smoke cat, in which the black hairs of the surface are silvery white beneath. The white cat and the Siamese are semialbinos. Full albinos (those having pink eyes) rarely occur among cats, but have been reported in the short-haired breeds, domestic and foreign.

New Breeds. Cats, in the course of the centuries, have not undergone the wide variation under domestication observable in dogs, and efforts to produce new breeds by artificial selection have been few and seldom enduring. In a peke-faced cat developed from the long-haired red and red tabby, the head resembled that of a Pekingese dog, with a short nose and wrinkled muzzle; and several experimenters have succeeded in evolving a long-haired Siamese cat, a breed which still survives in England. Sometimes a breed arises by natural selection, persists for a few decades, and then suddenly disappears, like the Mexican hairless cat.

Characteristics. The cat, from the beginning, has proved a serviceable and companionable friend of man. Among Semitic peoples there is a legend that the cat was given to Adam and Eve for comfort on their banishment from Eden. The purr, which is a characteristic of most cats, great and small, is considered soothing in the domestic cat. A poorly fed cat makes an indifferent mouser; efficiency in mousing and ratting requires strong, well-nourished muscles. Rodent hunters seldom prey on birds, and these constitute most farm cats. Almost all cats are omnivorous, i.e., they eat vegetables and fruits as well as meats, fish, and dairy products. They make friends with farm animals and sometimes with wild animals such as skunks and raccoons, but do not mate with these or other unrelated creatures. Cats possess powers of concentration higher than those of other animals. They are nocturnal and though unable to see in total darkness, have excellent vision in a dim light. Their fore paws are employed in a great variety of ways, such as embracing a kitten, grasping food, securing a rat, ringing a bell, and opening a door. Their hearing is acute and their memory good. They appear to possess a sense of humor, and the majority have a strongly developed homing instinct. Their neatness and good nature are proverbial.   I. M. M.

CAT SHOWS

History. Interest in the improvement of the breeding of cats as pets and for show purposes developed in the latter half of the nineteenth century. The first shows were held in Maine as early as 1870, but most of these were in the sporting interest and for prizes rather than for the development of a fine animal desirable as a pet. The first really big show was held at the Crystal Palace in London in 1871. In 1887 a larger exhibition was held in London, sponsored by British royalty and nobility, and the first cat society, the National Cat Club of London, was organized under like sponsorship. Then followed two other major organizations; the Scottish Cat Club in 1894, and the Cat Club in London in 1898.

In the United States the first shows, other than the informal ones held from time to time in Maine, were held in Boston, Philadelphia, and New York in the 1880's and early 1890's. But the cat fancy in America grew out of a big international cat exhibition, which was largely attended by persons of prominence, with many visitors and cats coming from England. This was held at Madison Square Garden in New York in 1895. The first organizations of cat fanciers and breeders for show purposes and for the promotion of public interest in the cat were the Chicago Cat Club and the Beresford Cat Club of Chicago, both formed in 1899. In 1900 the latter held the first championship cat show, which since has been repeated annually.

Beginning about 1900, other breeders' and fanciers' clubs were organized throughout the eastern and central United States, the largest of the earlier ones being the Atlantic Cat Club in New York, established in 1902. In 1901 shows were held in perhaps half a dozen of the larger cities from Boston to Chicago, and thereafter there was a rapid increase in the number of clubs and the number of shows held annually.

National Cat Associations. As cat fanciers increased, national organizations were formed for the affiliation of local clubs under general supervision and control, beginning with the American Cat Association in 1902. There are now four others: Cat Fanciers' Association, Cat Fanciers' Federation, United Cat Federation, and the American Cat Fanciers' Association. Operating widely across the country from the east and west coasts and the Gulf of Mexico, these five associations are generally classified as representing All-Western, All-Midwestern, and All-Eastern areas. They cover a total of more than one hundred and fifty affiliated clubs whose shows are regularly reported in pet magazines and cat journals. Canada and Hawaii are also represented. The parent association registers cats and also maintains studbooks. A small number of clubs operate independently of a parent association, such as the Central Maine Cat Club. Shows are held by member and nonmember clubs, the former operating under the rules of their respective associations, to which they must apply for show licenses and show dates and must submit a choice of three judges for approval. Printed rules of each association cover the duties of the show committee, the show managers, and the judges. The show rules, classification, and general standards of the national associations are substantially the same.

Show Procedure. The show classes recognized for each color of cat are: Grand Champion, Champion, Open, Novice, Kitten, Neuter, and Spay. The latter two classes consist of altered cats more than eight months old; the former is male and the latter female. The championship colors in both the long-hair and domestic short-hair breeds are: Blue-eyed White; Orange-eyed White; Black, Blue, Red, Cream, Chinchilla, Shaded Silver, Silver Tabby, Smoke, Red Tabby, Brown Tabby, Tortoiseshell, Blue-Cream. The Manx may have all colors, including Mackerel or Ticked Tabby and Parti-colored. The foreign breeds consist of the Manx, the Blue-Point, Chocolate-Point, Seal-Point Siamese, the Abyssinian, the Russian Blue, and the Burmese, all these being short-haired cats. Usually, the majority of cats in a show are long-haired or Persians. Competition is open to all cats, including the domestic short-hair, with or without a pedigree. The points of a show are competed for between the blue-ribbon winner in the Open class against the blue-ribbon winner in the Novice class in each color, breed, or sex. The winner in the contest between the Open and the Novice class receives the Winner's ribbon, which carries the points of the show. The number of points of the show is governed by the number of cats competing, exclusive of kittens under eight months old, neuters, spays, and household pets, the latter any color with white. Under C.F.A. rules, 40

competing cats constitute a one-point show; 60, two points; 80, three points; 100 and over, four points. To complete a championship, a cat must acquire ten points. To complete a Grand Championship, a champion competes for Best Champion in the show. Best Champion in a show acquires one Grand Championship point for every three champions

COURTESY OF ROLLIN A. CABLE

MANX CAT

competing, with a limit of points governed by the points of the show in which the winnings are made; 15 points to constitute a Grand Championship, to be won under three judges in as many shows.

Cats are benched individually in separate cages; they are taken to the judge's enclosure by stewards and placed in other individual cages provided for that purpose. Each cat is removed from the cage and is thoroughly examined by the judge. The cat is compared with the other cats of its

YLLA-GUILLUMETTE

The white Persian cat is typically long-haired, short-eared, and round-faced.

color and sex, and the ribbons are then awarded. By process of elimination, the best of each color is selected, and they in turn compete against each other for Best Cat and Best Cat of Opposite Sex.

The scale of points by which cats are judged is based upon standard requirements, which vary only slightly in the different associations. The scale of the Cat Fanciers' Association is as follows: color, 25 points; coat, 15; condition, 10; head, including size and shape of eyes, 20; type, including shape, size, bone, and length of tail, 20; color of eyes, 10; total, 100. This scale is applied to all breeds and colors except Siamese, Manx, Russian Blue, Abyssinian, and Burmese. Aside from ribbons denoting the winners, prizes at shows are cups or other trophies and, usually, a number of cash awards contributed by the exhibiting or other clubs and individual breeders and fanciers.

Most shows are given for the benefit of some local charity. Clubs usually hold shows annually or biennially during the late fall and winter, when the animals' coats are at their best. Generally shows are benched for two days, more than one day being required to complete the judging. In some of the larger shows, in which there are two hundred or more animals in competition, two judges may be required. In some shows there have been more than three hundred entries. Usually kittens, and sometimes adult cats, are on sale at the shows, the prices ranging from $10 up for kittens and from $25 up for adults. However, the most valuable cats for breeding purposes, for which the prices range up as high as $500 are sold privately. A few cats have sold at even higher prices.　O. H. S.

CATACOMBS [kæ'təkomz], subterranean burial places consisting of excavated galleries with recesses for tombs. Burial places hewn from solid rock have been used from remote times, those of the Etruscans being prominent early examples. Catacomb burial became popular during early Christian times, when the Christians, following Roman precedent, cut wall niches in underground caves for the urn burial of their dead. The niches, resembling rows of dovecots, were called *columbaria,* dovehouses. There were also recesses called *loculi* for the uncremated, and small chapels before Christian worship was permitted above ground.

By the year 313, when the emperor Constantine promulgated the Edict of Milan, giving Christianity an equal footing with other religions, the vicinity of Rome and some other Italian cities had been honeycombed with catacombs three or four feet wide with larger chambers at intervals. There are at least twenty-eight catacombs in the Province of Rome, and other noteworthy examples exist in Naples and on the islands of Sicily and Malta. The symbols and drawings found in catacombs furnish much of the information available on the earliest Christian art.

One of the largest of these labyrinthine burial places is that of St. Calixtus, on the Appian Way about a mile and a half from the Porta San Sebastiano, where nearly eleven miles of galleries have been excavated. This holy place, lighted by electricity, is easily visited under the guidance of the Trappists. The near-by Catacomb of St. Sebastian is held in particular reverence because of the tradition that the bodies of Peter and Paul were interred there before they were buried in the crypts of their respective basilicas.

R. Ne.

CATALAN [kæ'tələn], the language spoken in Catalonia, Spain, as well as in the Balearic islands, the Roussillon, which is politically French, and Andorra; it is also spoken in the provinces of Valencia, Castellón, and Alicante in Spain, and in the city of Alghero in Sardinia. Catalan is the native language of no more than 5,000,000 persons, about 185,000 of them in the Roussillon, and is attested, under the name of *parladura catalana,* as far back as the eleventh century in notary documents; it is used in the written agreements between Guitart Isarn, lord of Caboet, and Guillem and Mir Arnal, dating between 1080 and 1095.

Catalan can be considered as an intermediary dialect between Provençal and Castilian or Aragonese Spanish, but in general it is much closer to Provençal than to Castilian. The isoglosses connecting Catalan and Provençal are innumerable, and it will be more useful here to indicate only the few that unite Catalan with Castilian. Thus, Catalan has the change of Latin *au* to *o* and of *ai* to *a* that is found in Castilian but not in Provençal; and Catalan, like Castilian, has the change of *mb* to *m* and of *nn* to *n*. The change of initial *l-* to *ll-*, a palatalized *l*, is found in Catalan and partly in Aragonese, but not in Castilian. Several relatively late Provençal innovations, notably the change of *ū* to *ü*, and the use of *illui, illaei, illorum* and other forms, have not reached Catalonia, and for this reason the agreement between Catalan and Castilian on these points remains a purely negative one, having no bearing on the problem of kinship. Catalan has been in the past under the constant influence of neighboring Provençal. It once had the diphthongization of *ŏ* to *ue* and *ě* to *ie*, employed the Latin *ipse* as an article, and possessed other characteristics which have now more or less completely disappeared in imitation of Provençal. In more recent centuries, however, Castilian has penetrated Catalan more and more, and only recently has a strong Catalanist movement attempted, with fairly good success, a resurrection of the national language for scholarly use.

G. B.

CATALEPSY [kæ'tələɛ'psi], the pathological retention of physical attitudes or postures, usually synonymous with the psychiatric term *cerea flexibilitas* (waxy flexibility) commonly found in the catatonic form of schizophrenia. Catalepsy is generally regarded as the quintessence of suggestibility, and is often associated with such other suggestible situations as echopraxia (the repetition of movements seen), echolalia (the repetition of words heard), etc. Catalepsy can also be induced by hypnosis. Eugen Bleuler, describing cataleptics, wrote, "The patients make no movements of their own volition; but, if they are placed in no matter how uncomfortable an attitude they maintain it for a very long time." If the posture is rigid rather than waxy, it is called rigid catalepsy. Besides catatonic schizophrenia, catalepsy is seen in hysteria, and in certain cerebellar diseases where pathways between the cerebellum and the frontal lobes are blocked or impaired.

J. A. Br.

CATALINA IRONWOOD [kætəli'nə], *Lyonothamnus floribundus,* a rare, beautiful shrubby tree of the rose family, native only to the islands off southern California. *L. floribundus asplenifolius,* a variety cultivated in California, is a tree sometimes 50 ft. high, with reddish bark scaling in strips, leathery fernlike leaves, and white flowers in large, branched clusters. It is difficult to transplant. R. S. Ho.

CATALONIA [kætəlo'niə], a region, formerly a principality, in the northeastern corner of Spain, separated from France, on the north, by the Pyrenees. It is bounded on the west by Aragon, on the south by Valencia, and on the east by the Mediterranean Sea. The region is divided into the modern administrative provinces of Barcelona, with an area of 2,942 sq. mi.; Tarragona, 2,426 sq. mi.; Gerona, 2,264 sq. mi.; and Lérida, 4,659 sq. mi. The lower Pyrenees border the province on the north, and there are mountainous areas, with occasional plains, in the Gerona and Vich regions.

Like Aragon and Navarre, Catalonia has vast dry land areas underlaid with marble, gypsum, granite, limestone, and clay. The fertile soil produces excellent grapes, olives, and other fruits, and a very important output of cork. The hinterland is grim in contrast to the coastal areas, but with the aid of irrigation and the conservation of water supplies, it produces various grains. Catalonia also includes the valleys of the lower Pyrenees, which support herds of cattle and provide timber—rare in Spain—for local building. The rapidly flowing streams produce all the electrical power needed and operate the factories producing oil, textiles, paper, iron and steel, silk, flour, and chocolate. There are chemical factories, potash and coal mines, and other enterprises that together make Catalonia the most important industrial region of Spain. The Mediterranean ports are busy and productive, particularly Barcelona, where shipbuilding, fish canning, and other industries flourish.

The Catalans speak their own language, which is a dialect related to Provençal and Castilian. The peasant costume is characterized by the *barretina,* a red or purple stockinglike cap, now worn mostly by porters in the cities. The tendency of the people towards separatism has been evidenced by their espousal of Carlism, Republicanism, and Anarchism.

Barcelona, the capital of the administrative province of the same name and of the ancient principality of Catalonia, is the leading Spanish industrial and commercial center. It is the most prosperous city of the country and the most populous seaport of the Mediterranean. An important cultural center, Barcelona is the seat of one of Spain's twelve universities. It was in Barcelona, in 1923, that Gen. Primo de Rivera published his *pronunciamento* declaring the establishment of a military dictatorship. Tarragona, situated on a limestone rock above the Mediterranean Sea and the Fran-

A RIBBON OF PAVED MOUNTAIN ROAD SKIRTS THE TERRACED CATALONIAN GRAIN FIELDS NEAR VICH.

coli River, is noted for its wines, which are exported in substantial quantities. The city has a history of stubborn loyalty to the kings of Spain and resistance to insurgents and invaders. Lérida, the capital of the province of the same name, is the second largest city of the Catalonian region. Strategically located near the mouth of several valleys leading up into the Pyrenees, Lérida is an important trade and communications center. Gerona, another provincial capital, is situated at the confluence of the Oña and the Ter rivers and is noted for its Gothic cathedral.

History. The first roots of Roman civilization on the Iberian Peninsula were apparently planted in Catalonia, which, under the Emperor Augustus, had the status of a Roman colony. Later it was occupied first by the Visigoths and then by the Moors. In 874, under the rule of the counts of Barcelona, it gained independence. In 1149 the heiress to the throne of Catalonia was married to the King of Aragon, and the two provinces were united. By the middle of the fifteenth century the Catalans, in alliance with the Aragonese, had conquered the kingdoms of Naples and Sicily and were a power in the Mediterranean. Upon the marriage of Ferdinand and Isabella, Catalonia became part of the Spanish kingdom; Barcelona then vied with Venice and Genoa as one of the important trading centers of the Mediterranean. In 1640 the province rebelled against Philip IV and elected Louis XIII of France as Count of Barcelona. This independence lasted until 1652, when the province was again subjugated by Philip. But the spirit of independence was not crushed, and during the War of the Spanish Succession, Catalonia cast its lot with the Austrians. Again, in 1701, the province was subdued by the Duke of Berwick, who led the armies of the French allies of Philip V. It was not until Catalonia's freedom was threatened by Napoleon's armies

that the independent Catalans merged their loyalty with that of all Spain. Catalonia's striving for autonomy was successful in 1932 under the Republican government, which the Catalans later supported in the civil war of 1936-1939. Catalonian nationalists and anarchists, the latter being traditionally strong in the region, displayed sectional tendencies in the course of the war, and finally the Republican government took control of the province. In January 1939 General Francisco Franco began his offensive against Catalonia. Barcelona was taken and the Republic collapsed. The Catalonian privileges were suppressed by the victor and Spanish rule was re-established.   J. S. R.

CATALPA [kətæ′lpə], a genus of trees of the bignonia family; about 12 species grow in Asia and North America. The southern catalpa or Indian bean, *C. bignonioides,* of the southeastern United States grows to 50 ft. with broad, heart-shaped leaves and showy, upright clusters of white, spotted flowers in June. The hardier northern catalpa, *C. speciosa,* native from Indiana to Arkansas and Texas may reach 100 ft. It has larger, less spotted flowers and longer-pointed leaves, and is a desirable ornamental tree. The wood is soft but very durable in soil and is valued for fence posts and railroad ties. (*See illustration on following page.*)   J. C. Wis.

CATALYSIS [kətæ′lɪsɪs] (Gr. κατάλυσις, "a dissolving"), according to Wilhelm Ostwald's classical definition formulated in 1902, is a chemical reaction in which a substance (called the catalyst or catalytic agent) alters the velocity of a chemical change but does not itself appear in the end products. This emphasis on velocity of reaction, a measurable quantity, deflected chemists from the vague property of "catalytic force" which Jöns Jakob Berzelius had proposed in

PHOTO BY TET BORSIG

Catalpa tree in bloom, with detail of leaf and fruit

1836 in the first systematic examination of catalyzed reactions, which included the H^+ catalysis of starch to sugar (Antoine Auguste Parmentier, 1781), of spongy platinum on the combination of O_2 with H_2 (Sir Humphry Davy, 1817; Johann Wolfgang Döbereiner, 1823), and of metals on the decomposition of aqueous H_2O_2 (Baron Louis Jacques Thénard, 1818).

CHARACTERISTICS OF CATALYSTS

Catalysts and their action can best be defined by considering a variety of their properties.

Action. The catalyst may accelerate chemical action, as in the instances above (positive catalysts); or it may retard action, as in the inhibition by pyrogallol of the oxidation of sodium sulphite (negative catalysis or inhibition). Sometimes one of the products acts as a catalyst (autocatalyis).

Physical State. The catalyst may be in the same state of matter as the reactants, such as Fe^{++} catalyzing the decomposition of hydrogen peroxide solution (homogeneous catalysis); or in a different phase, as with solid platinum gauze catalyzing the gaseous reaction $2SO_2 + O_2 \rightarrow 2SO_3$ (heterogeneous catalysis).

Concentration of Catalyst. Since the catalyst is unchanged chemically, it is present at the end of the reaction. However, it may change in physical form, and secondary reactions may gradually destroy it. Thus the platinum gauze used commercially in the Ostwald process for the oxidation of ammonia noticeably deteriorates, physically, during use. Often, mere traces of catalyst suffice to accelerate noticeably: an expert chemist, while studying the oxidation of aqueous sodium sulphite, inadvertently washed out his reaction vessel with faucet water, thereby introducing sufficient Cu^{++} im-

purity (perhaps 10^{-10} mole) to alter the reaction rate noticeably. Catalytic effect is often proportional to the concentration of the catalyst, though not necessarily so. For instance, the oxidation of sodium sulphite is proportional to the Cu^{++} concentration up to a certain small concentration; beyond this point any more Cu^{++} inhibits. Again, the polymerization of methyl methacrylate is catalyzed by benzoyl peroxide, the catalytic effect being proportional to the square root of the peroxide concentration.

Mechanism of Reaction. The action of many catalysts is to be explained by intermediate compound formation. When the reaction

$$A + B \rightarrow AB \qquad \text{(slow)}$$

proceeds only slowly, it may be hastened by the presence of catalyst (Cat) if the reaction rates are as follows:

$$A + Cat \rightarrow ACat \qquad \text{(fast)},$$
$$ACat + B \rightarrow AB + Cat \qquad \text{(fast)},$$

in which the catalyst is regenerated at the end of the two-step reaction. Numerous examples substantiate this mechanism of reaction. Arthur T. Williamson showed in the preparation of ether from alcohol that sulphuric acid acts as an intermediate compound catalyst by forming ethyl sulphuric acid in the reacting mixture. The Friedel-Crafts syntheses with aluminum chloride involve formation of intermediate compounds. Nitrosyl sulphuric acid, $NO—O—SO_2—OH$, is formed in the chamber process for the oxidation of SO_2 in the presence of nitrogen oxide catalyst.

The catalyst may act in a more subtle manner. For the rate of reaction the expressions is $k = Z \cdot e^{-Q/RT}$, in which Z is the number of collisions, Q is the energy necessary for reaction to occur, R is the gas constant, and T is the absolute temperature. A tiny concentration of catalyst cannot affect Z but may alter the activation energy required for reaction. A small change in Q will have an exponential effect, and this the catalyst is able to bring about.

For heterogeneous catalysis, the mechanism is essentially the same: intermediate compounds such as hydrides of iron (FeH_2) or nickel $(NiH_2$ or $NiH_4)$ may contain hydrogen loosely bound, but they orient the reactant molecules sufficiently long to lower the activation energy of the subsequent reaction which is being catalyzed. Activity in this case involves adsorption of the reactants on the catalyst surface, as discussed later in this article under The Catalyst.

Effect on Equilibrium. The catalyst does not alter the position of equilibrium in a reversible reaction. For instance, the same equilibrium for the $2SO_2 + O_2 \rightarrow SO_3$ reaction is reached by using V_2O_5, Pt, or Fe_2O_3 catalyst. In a few cases the catalyst appears to shift the equilibrium; usually the effect can be ascribed to catalyst concentrations sufficiently large to alter the activity of the reactants. Also, the question of whether a catalyst has initiated a reaction which would not otherwise have taken place cannot easily be answered, because, in the absence of the catalyst, the reaction may have been occurring at an immeasurably slow pace. Since the catalyst does not shift the equilibrium, it must affect the forward and backward reactions to the same extent: Hence, iron not only catalyzes the combination of N_2 with H_2 but likewise accelerates the decomposition of NH_3, and Paul Sabatier has shown that hydrogenation catalysts are also efficient dehydrogenation catalysts.

HOMOGENEOUS CATALYSIS

VAPOR PHASE

Water. For many years it was believed that water vapor was essential for certain gaseous reactions, but recent work shows that water is not required for the combination of H_2

with Cl_2, for the dissociation of NH_4Cl and of Hg_2Cl_2, or for the combination of CO with O_2.

Iodine. The decomposition of ethers and aldehydes is markedly accelerated in the vapor phase by traces of iodine. The iodine lowers the energy of activation, as discussed above, the value of Q diminishing for methyl ethyl ether from 54,500 cal. for the uncatalyzed reaction to 38,000 cal. for the iodine-catalyzed reaction. The former reaction is unimolecular, the latter bimolecular involving the collision of an iodine molecule with the reactant. Similar values for diethyl ether range from 53,000 to 34,300 cal., and for diisopropyl ether from 61,000 to 28,500 cal.

Nitrogen Oxides. The lead-chamber process for manufacturing sulphuric acid involves a homogeneous reaction forming lead-chamber crystals, NO—O—SO_2—OH, an example of catalysis by intermediate compound formation in which the stepwise reaction regenerates the gaseous catalyst. Nitric oxide is also able to catalyze the combination of CO with O_2, perhaps first forming NO_2 which subsequently reacts with CO to regenerate NO.

LIQUID PHASE

Acid-Base Catalysis. By far the most important examples in the liquid phase are those included under acid-base catalysis. As early as 1883, Ostwald studied the action of various acids in catalyzing the hydrolysis of esters, and the inversion of sucrose. In his doctoral thesis, submitted in 1883, Svante A. Arrhenius showed that catalytic action is proportional to the hydrogen ion concentrations of these various acids. Hydroxyl ions, on the other hand, are known to catalyze the conversion of acetone to diacetone alcohol, the mutarotation of aqueous glucose, the decomposition of nitrosotriacetone-amine, and so on. Extensive research by Lowry in England and Johannes Nicolaus Brönsted in Denmark from 1923 onward has shown that not only hydrogen ions and hydroxyl ions but also any substance able to donate protons (H^+) or accept them (that is, acids and bases in the Brönsted sense) can catalyze many reactions. This category includes neutral salts, cations of weak bases, and anions of weak acids. It is known as general acid-base catalysis. This term distinguishes it from specific acid catalysis, exemplified by the hydrolysis of acetals, which are catalyzed much more by H^+ ions than by any other acid ions.

The mechanism of general acidbase catalysis can well be illustrated by the enolization of ketone, $(CH_3)_2CO$, to form $CH_3C(OH)=CH_2$. Essentially the change is

$$O=C-\overset{x}{C}-H \quad \text{to form} \quad HO\overset{x}{C}=C,$$

where x is H and y is CH_3. Enolization is affected by (a) removal of a proton, followed by internal electronic shifts and subsequent (b) addition of a proton. The basic catalyst removes the proton, the acid catalyst donates one. The steps involved are

$$O::\overset{x}{C}:\overset{x}{C}:H \xrightarrow{+H^-} \left[O::\overset{x}{C}:\overset{x}{C}:\right]^- \longrightarrow \left[:\overset{-}{O}:\overset{+}{C}\cdots\overset{x}{C}\right]^-$$

$$\longrightarrow :\overset{-}{O}:C::\overset{x}{C} \xrightarrow{+H^+} H:O:C::\overset{x}{C}.$$

Reactions such as these carried out in aqueous solution find the water acting in one of two roles: in the presence of acids (proton donors) the water acts as a proton acceptor, whereas in the presence of a base catalyst (proton acceptor) the water acts as a proton donor. Because of this dual role which water is able to play, many reactions are catalyzed in aqueous solutions by either acids or bases. In nonaqueous solutions both acid and base must be simultaneously present to catalyze the reaction.

Brönsted's work has led to an interesting correlation of catalytic activity with acid-base strength, a measure of the tendency of molecules to donate or accept protons.

The influence of salts on catalytic activity is ascribed to two effects. Many of the acid-base catalyzed reactions involve a univalent ion (H^+ or OH^-) and a neutral molecule (acetone, an ester, sucrose). The presence of foreign salts in sufficiently concentrated solutions will influence the ionic strength, by what is known as a primary salt effect. The rate of reaction, in turn, is a linear function of this ionic strength. Mathematical treatment and confirmation of this linearity has been achieved by Brönsted, Niels Janniksen Bjerrum, and others for ester hydrolysis, sucrose inversion, and the decomposition of nitramide. The secondary salt effect is a common-ion effect, in which an added salt suppresses the ionization of a weak-acid catalyst. It can often be deduced by classical mass-action treatment. For instance, the esterification of benzoic acid with ethyl alcohol is catalyzed by picric acid, which ionizes as $HPic \rightarrow H^+ + Pic^-$ to yield a certain amount of H^+ catalyst. The addition of a picrate, actually p-toluidine picrate, furnishes the common ion Pic^-, which drives the equilibrium to the left ($\longleftarrow$), represses the ionization, diminishes the H^+ concentration, and thereby retards esterification. Goldschmidt (1896) found that the rate of esterification with picric catalyst, which was 0.0187 in the absence of p-toluidine picrate, dropped to 0.0086 upon the addition of a 1 : 1 salt : acid, and to 0.0072 at a salt : acid ratio of 2 : 1.

Iodide Ion. With the iodide-ion catalysis of the decomposition of hydrogen peroxide and the iodide-ion catalysis of the hydrogen-peroxide-thiosulphate reaction, it has been possible to predict reaction velocities, by combining the rates of the separately determined step reactions.

Enzymes. Many biological processes are catalyzed by complex organic substances called enzymes. Thus the enzyme ptyalin, in the saliva, changes starch into sugar; and the enzymes pepsin and trypsin hasten the digestion of albumin. Their catalytic action is very specific. They are sensitive to traces of inhibitors, such as HCN, $HgCl_2$, and iodine. The kinetics of reactions with enzymes has been extensively studied by Richard Willstätter and his school. Kinetic studies with catalase, an enzyme found in the blood, on the decomposition of hydrogen peroxide have shown an analogy with the catalytic activity of colloidal platinum. By selective adsorption of enzymes on silica (acid) or alumina (basic) materials, Willstätter was able to separate lipase (a fat-splitting enzyme) from amylase (protein-splitting) from erepsin (peptide-splitting). Subsequently John Howard Northrop succeeded in preparing pure crystalline pepsin, for which, together with his work on proteinogen, he received a quarter share in the Nobel Prize in chemistry for 1946. The enzyme action is not entirely homogeneous, and the term "microheterogeneous" has been applied to catalysts of colloidal dimensions.

Esters. Historically, ester reactions played an important role in acid-base catalysis, in which Goldschmidt's work has been discussed. Both esterification and hydrolysis of esters were extensively studied.

Friedel-Crafts Reaction. The alkylation of benzene by alkyl halides in the presence of aluminum chloride is known as the Friedel-Crafts reaction:

$$C_6H_6 + RCOCl \xrightarrow{AlCl_3 \text{ catalyst}} RCOC_6H_5 + HCl.$$

Although the catalyst is added in the solid form, it goes into solution and exemplifies homogeneous catalysis. In 1907, Jakob Böesekin attacked the idea of an intermediate compound formation. Tracer studies (Meerwein, 1927; Fairbrother, 1937) with radioactive chlorine indicate that the ionized addition compound $(CH_3CO)^+ (AlCl_4)^-$ first forms the benzene and subsequently reacts with it, because the same products are obtained using either (a) normal $AlCl_3$ with radioactive $RCOCl^*$ or (b) radioactive $AlCl_3^*$ with normal $RCOCl$. This identity of end products indicates complete interchange of the Cl^* and is in agreement with the formation of $(AlCl_3Cl^*)^-$ as a first step.

Hydrogen Peroxide Decomposition. Several thousand papers have appeared on positive and negative catalytic effects on this decomposition in aqueous solution. During the 1920's, William C. Bray and John Jacob Abel investigated the catalytic effects of halide-halogen ions. A steady-state concentration of $Br^- + Br_2$ is soon reached, the catalyzed decomposition of the peroxide following this course:

$$2H^+ + 2Br^- + H_2O_2 \longrightarrow Br_2 + 2H_2O$$
$$Br_2 + H_2O_2$$
$$\longrightarrow O_2 + 2H^+ + 2Br^-.$$

Since the H^+ and Br^- are regenerated, once a steady concentration of Br^- and Br_2 is reached, the only apparent reaction becomes $2H_2O_2 \longrightarrow 2H_2O + O_2$. The two steps are themselves a result of several stage reactions involving HBrO. With chlorine, HClO is involved, but with iodine the intermediate stages go via IO^-. The mechanism of the decomposition, accelerated by Fe^{+2} and Cu^{+2}, was studied by Fritz Haber in 1931; and the influence of inhibitors on the thermal, photochemical, and catalyzed decomposition has been investigated extensively.

Inversion of Sucrose. The action of acids in this reaction is one of the classics in the field of catalysis. In 1889, Svante A. Arrhenius showed that with formic acid-sodium formate mixtures the inversion of sucrose is exactly proportional to the H^+ concentration. He also studied the effect of added salts on the reaction and found that sometimes they gave an enhanced effect. Eventually this discovery led to the concept of acid-base catalysis.

HETEROGENEOUS CATALYSIS

THE CATALYST

Most catalytic reactions are heterogeneous: the catalyst is to be found in one phase and the reactants in another. Thus, platinum gauze catalyzes the combination of gaseous sulphur dioxide and oxygen, whereas solid nickel assists in the hydrogenation of certain liquid hydrocarbons.

Varieties. All possible combinations of the physical states (gas, liquid, solid) are represented. In practice, by far the most numerous are gaseous or liquid reactions occurring at solid catalyst surfaces.

Adsorption. The fact that most catalytic reactions are gaseous or liquid focuses attention on the adsorption processes which precede catalytic action. In 1916, Irving Langmuir first emphasized that the adsorbed gases form what are virtually chemically bonds with the catalyst surface. In addition, there are loosely absorbed molecules, held by van der Waals forces of the order of a few kilocalories only; but these are not considered to be catalytically active. It is conjectured that the reactant molecules become absorbed on adjacent spaces on the catalyst surface, thereby forming an intermediate compound with the catalyst. This complex then decomposes at a definite rate, releasing the reaction products into the gas space. According to this theory, both gases must be absorbed on the catalytic surface.

The catalyst, then, (a) provides a large area for concentrating the reacting species and (b) lowers the activation energy of the homogeneous reaction.

Catalyst Area. The method of preparing a catalyst is often critical. Considerable catalyst surface must be achieved. Extremely porous materials are impregnated with solutions of salts, whose subsequent reduction to the metallic or oxide state will deposit enormous areas of catalyst. For instance, 1 cc. of silica gel may have an area of 5×10^6 sq. cm. (P. H. Emmett, 1937). Activated charcoal, asbestos, bentonite, fuller's earth, silica gel, and other porous supporting materials achieve this fineness of division of the catalyst, to give enormous surface upon which to concentrate the reacting species.

Chemical Types. Large area alone does not make a good catalyst. Its chemical nature is also important. For example, nickel catalyst at $300°$ C. dehydrogenates ethanol vapor to form acetaldehyde and hydrogen, whereas an alumina catalyst at the same temperature dehydrates it to form ethylene and water. Significantly, good dehydrogenation catalysts adsorb hydrogen strongly; these include zinc oxide, Cu, Ni, Co, and metals of the platinum family. On the other hand, dehydration catalysts adsorb water; these include metallic oxides such as alumina, ferric oxide, and thoria.

Energy of Activation. The specific efficiency of the catalyst is attributed to its ability to lower the energy of activation, Q, of the homogeneous reaction. For instance, the ratio of $Q_{heterogeneous} : Q_{homogeneous}$ as experimentally determined from temperature coefficients follows. For the decomposition of HI on Pt it is $14 : 44$; for the decomposition of N_2O on gold, $29.0 : 58.5$; for the decomposition of ammonia on tungsten, $39 : >80$. In each case the decrease in energy of activation is marked; the adsorption process involves a loosening of the bonds in other parts of the molecules and thereby facilitates reaction.

Poisons. Only a very small fraction of the solid surface is catalytically active. For instance, traces of carbon monoxide completely inhibit the hydrogenation of ethylene on copper (Pease, 1925). Incidentally, a platinum wire which has been poisoned for the ammonia decomposition is still active in the HI decomposition, indicating selective action on different parts of the catalyst. Again, when alcohol vapor is passed over copper, the aldehyde which is formed tends to decompose. Addition of water vapor to the gas stream poisons that portion of the catalyst responsible for the decomposition and thereby increases the yield of acetaldehyde. This ease of poisoning the solid catalyst has long been known in industry. In fact, the poisoning of platinum by arsenicals accounted for the early failures in the contact process for making SO_3. Mercury in such tiny quantities that it is even insufficient to form a unimolecular layer on the catalyst may markedly retard the hydrogenation of CO on copper; in this instance the mercury is obviously being adsorbed on the active portions of the catalyst.

Promoters. Small quantities of certain ingredients called promoters may markedly increase the efficiency of the catalyst. The addition of aluminum and potassium oxides to iron increases its efficiency in the ammonia synthesis. One per cent of ceria, CeO_2, in thoria makes a most active catalyst for the combination of hydrogen with oxygen. Most of the industrial catalysts today contain promoters, and "mixed catalysts" fill the patent literature to the extent of confusion. A mixture of zinc and chromium oxides is superior to either oxide alone in preparing methanol by the hydrogenation of water gas. An iron catalyst has its efficiency increased tenfold by the admixture of potassium-aluminum oxides; in this promoted condition 99.5 per cent of the surface is catalytically inert.

Active Centers. The concept that only certain portions of the catalyst are available was first developed by H. S. Taylor in 1925. Lines of discontinuity, crystal imperfections, grain boundaries, are all points of unsaturation or so-called active centers. A further advance in this concept is due to Robert E. Burk (1926) and Balandin (1929), who assumed that the molecule is active when it becomes adsorbed at more than one active center; supposedly this activity produces a strain on the bonds of the reacting molecule. This theory of "multiple adsorption" provides an interpretation of alternative modes of decomposition (as of methanol giving either acetaldehyde or ethylene) depending upon the relative spacings of the active centers and the resultant differences in strains set up.

Oriented Surfaces. In 1940, by sputtering nickel on glass, Beek, Smith, and Wheeler were able to orient crystals with the 110 plane parallel to the supporting material. Such films hydrogenated ethylene ten times more readily than randomly oriented crystals. The authors connect their results with the space considerations of the Ni—Ni bonds compared with those of the reactants.

Chain Reactions. Sometimes the walls of the reaction vessel may (a) initiate reaction chains which extend out into the gas phase away from the walls, or (b) terminate gaseous reaction chains. In these ways the wall is either accelerating or retarding in its action.

INDUSTRIAL REACTIONS

A few examples will illustrate the vast field of industrial catalysts.

Synthesis. The synthesis of ammonia by the Haber-Bosch process (1913) was a milestone in high-pressure catalysis. Previously all explosives came from Chile saltpeter; the ammonia process made Germany independent of this source and enabled her to fight World War I despite the Allied blockade. Haber used iron oxide catalyst promoted with about 1 per cent of alumina and potassium oxide at about 200 atmospheres pressure and $500°$ C. Recent industrial processes (Claude, Casale) use up to 1,000 atmospheres pressure. Hydrogen is obtained from water gas from which CO has been scrubbed; nitrogen is obtained from producer gas from which CO has been scrubbed, or from liquid air. During World War II the United States Government built ten synthetic ammonia plants at a cost of $200,000,000. These can fix 700,000 tons of nitrogen annually, and private companies can produce an additional 862,000 tons. The synthesis of methanol is a hydrogenation process ($CO + 2H_2$) employing a mixed catalyst of ZnO, Cr_2O_3 at 200 atmospheres and 200 to $400°$ C., and a space velocity of 3,000 volumes of gas per hour per 1 volume of catalyst. A copper lining prevents the catalytic formation of higher alcohols; the product is over 99 per cent pure methanol. Sulphur poisons the catalyst. Higher alcohols are sometimes manufactured, but there are complicating side reactions. Gasoline is synthesized by the direct combination of C and H in the Bergius process.

Decomposition. Industrial hydrogen is obtained by passing ammonia through heated iron at atmospheric pressure; this is a cheap source, since liquid ammonia can be transported easily. It is also obtained by cracking propane and other gaseous hydrocarbons. Petroleum hydrocarbons are catalytically cracked by using $AlCl_3$, alloys, and promoted aluminum silicate (Houdry process); by these processes a heavy oil ($C_{20}H_{18}$) can be broken down into a valuable gasoline (C_8H_{18}). A great many processes are involved: disproportionation ($C_{20}H_{42} \longrightarrow C_{10}H_{22} + C_{10}H_{20}$); aromatic hydrocarbons may split off their side chains (C_6H_5—

$C_3H_7 \longrightarrow C_6H_6 + C_3H_6$); naphthenes may lose hydrogen to form aromatic hydrocarbons ($C_6H_{12} \longrightarrow C_6H_6 + 3H_2$); isomers are formed by rearrangements; and so on. Sometimes the catalyst is so fine a powder that it flows, becoming a fluid catalyst, and the petroleum vapors are blown through the finely powdered catalyst. In these processes the catalyst has to be regenerated, since it becomes coated during its action, and continuous regenerative flow systems have been devised; for instance, ten minutes catalytic cracking of the crude oil, five minutes purge with nitrogen, ten minutes regeneration with air, five minutes purge, then back to the beginning of the cycle again.

Dehydration. Methanol is dehydrated over alumina; other alcohols are similarly treated.

Reduction. Higher alcohols and nitro compounds, including nitrobenzene, are catalytically reduced.

Oxidation. Ammonia prepared by the Haber process is oxidized by the Ostwald process at atmospheric pressure and $400°$ C. Reactions are:

$$3H_2 + N_2 \longrightarrow 2NH_3 \quad \text{(Haber-Bosch)},$$
$$4NH_3 + 5O_2 \longrightarrow 4NO + 6H_2O + 214,200 \text{ cal.}$$
$$2NO + 4NO + 3O_2 \xrightarrow{140° C.} 6NO_2$$
$$6NO_2 + 2H_2O \longrightarrow 2NO + 4HNO_3$$
$$\text{(hot)}$$
$$\text{(recirculated)} \qquad \text{(Ostwald)}.$$

One volume of ammonia and seven of air is passed through platinum rhodium gauze or fine platinum. About 95 per cent conversion occurs in the incredibly short contact time of five ten-thousandths of a second. The exothermic reaction keeps the gauze heated to between $800°$ and $900°$ C. As little as 20 parts of phosphine (PH_3) per 100,000,000 feed gas can ruin the catalyst. The nitric acid made by this process is this basis of nitrate fertilizers and explosives.

Sulphuric acid is made in catalytic processes. In 1740 Ward prepared it by heating sulphur with saltpeter in glass globes. Six years later, John Roebuck substituted a lead chamber into which iron carts containing sulphur and saltpeter were wheeled and the mixture was ignited. By 1870 a continuous process using sulphur dioxide + steam + air + oxides of nitrogen was in use, the nitric oxides functioning as a homogeneous catalyst. The Glover tower introduced the nitric oxide, and the Gay-Lussac removed it from the exit gases. The other catalytic process is heterogeneous: sulphur dioxide and air are passed over platinum or vanadium pentoxide catalyst at $400°$ to $500°$ C. Arsenic compounds poison the former especially, but with a clean feed gas the catalyst will operate continuously for a decade without replacement. During World War II there were about ninety chamber plants and an equal number of contact plants operating in the United States, producing, respectively, 3,200,000 and 5,300,000 tons of sulphuric acid each year.

Carbon monoxide can be oxidized to carbon dioxide by the use of Hopcallite (50 per cent MnO_2 + 30 CuO + 15 Co_2O_3 + 5 Ag_2O) or by 60 per cent MnO_2 + 40 CuO.

Methane is oxidized to $CO_2 + H_2$ by the use of metallic catalysts, chiefly iron and nickel. Ethanol is oxidized to acetaldehyde using a silver catalyst. In turn, acetaldehyde is oxidized to acetic acid by using Cu, Mn, and Ni oxides on silica gel. Naphthalene is oxidized to phthalic anhydride over vanadium pentoxide. The Gibbs and Conover process (1916) obtains an 85 per cent yield, whereas the old German process using Hg was only 25 per cent efficient. Since 1946 a fluid catalyst consisting of finely powdered vanadium pentoxide has also been used. Over 150,000,000 lb. each of phthalic anhydride and phenol are used each year in the plastics industry. An equal quantity of phenol is also used by the plastics industry. In the Raschig catalytic process for phenol, benzene, hydrochloric acid, and air are passed over an oxidation catalyst ($4HCl + O_2 \longrightarrow 2H_2O + Cl_2$; and $2Cl_2 + 2C_6H_6 \longrightarrow 2HCl + 2C_6H_5Cl$), and the chlorbenzene is hydrolyzed over a phosphate catalyst ($C_6H_5Cl + H_2O \longrightarrow C_6H_5OH + HCl$), the HCl being returned for step 1. The net result of these three steps is $2C_6H_6 + O_2 \longrightarrow 2C_6H_5OH$.

Hydrogenation. Around 1900, Sabatier and J. B. Senderens, and later V. N. Ipatieff, showed that nickel facilitates the hydrogenation of organic hydrocarbons at high pressures. A vast new industry grew up. Liquid animal and vegetable oils such as fish, wheat, cottonseed, soybean, and corn oil are hydrogenated to solid and semisolid fats for use in shortening, soap, and candles. In practice not all the double bonds are hydrogenated. The process is called the hardening of oils because the melting point is raised by the hydrogenation process. A mixture of liquid oil and finely powdered nickel suspended on diatomaceous earth is heated with hydrogen at 200 atmospheres and at 100° to 200° C. These synthetic fats, to which vitamins and color have been added, have virtually the same food value as natural butter. Synthetic gasoline by the hydrogenation of coal (Friedrich Bergius, 1912) or by the hydrogenation of water gas (Fischer-Tropsch, 1936) are other important catalytic processes.

Dehydrogenation. Many organic compounds are dehydrogenated in industry; for instance, ethanol is dehydrogenated to give acetaldehyde over Cu catalyst. But by far the largest tonnage catalytic dehydrogenations are devoted to producing butadiene and styrene for synthetic rubber. An annual production of over 800,000 tons of GR-S rubber (Government Rubber-Styrene) containing approximately 200,000 tons of styrene and 600,000 tons of butadiene comes from catalytic plants. The butadiene is made by dehydrogenating butylene from petroleum; a catalytic process from alcohol is too expensive in peacetime. The styrene comes from interaction of ethylene and benzene to form ethylbenzene followed by dehydrogenation to produce styrene, C_6H_5—CH=CH_2.

Biological Catalysts. Bacteria, molds, and enzymes have been used in industry for thousands of years. The fermentation of sugar to ethyl alcohol and to by-products such as glycerine, fusel oils, and succinic acid dates from Biblical times. The bacterium Clostridium acetobutylicum, first discovered by Chaim Weizmann, long afterward President of Israel, ferments starch to a mixture of acetone and butyl alcohol. In World War I this reaction enabled the British to manufacture acetone for smokeless powder at home; in World War II the Russians used the reaction to prepare butyl alcohol for making butadiene rubbers. Molds perform other industrial miracles: Penicillium purpurogenum oxidizes glucose to citric acid, and Mucor stalonifer oxidizes acetates to oxalates.

Miscellaneous. A host of other reactions which are catalyzed in industry include halogenations, nitrations, sulphonations, and the corresponding reverse reactions. Desulphurization has received especial attention by the petroleum industry in attempts to remove sulphur compounds. Also alkylation, condensation, polymerization, isomerization, and cyclization have been extensively employed in the petroleum field. Through such processes, low-grade petroleums and waste gases are converted into antiknock gasoline, plastics, and synthetic rubber. By cyclization of heptane to form toluene, a basic material was made, from which 5,000,000 tons of trinitrotoluene explosives were prepared for World War II.

NEGATIVE CATALYSIS

Homogeneous Reactions. Sometimes traces of impurities can markedly retard chemical reaction. The oxidization of sodium sulphite in aqueous solution has been repeatedly studied because of its sensitivity to impurities. In 1898, G. Lawrence Bigelow found that alcohols, amines, phenollics, and many other substances retarded the reaction. Five years later, Titoff observed that traces of cupric ion (about 10^{-6} molar) noticeably accelerate the oxidation and that equally small quantities of cyanide ion retard reaction. He concluded that the inhibitor acts by combining with positive catalyst already present; and since copper-cyanide complexes are well known, his example in this case is probably correct.

However, in 1924 Christiansen proposed another mechanism for inhibition. Photochemical chain reactions were already known. For instance, the hydrogen-chlorine combination, in which the initial step is the photochemical formation of chlorine atoms, proceeds by the following repeated chain step:

$$Cl + H_2 \longrightarrow HCl + H$$
$$H + Cl_2 \longrightarrow HCl + Cl.$$

Chapman had shown in 1923 that traces of oxygen inhibit this photochemical chain reaction by breaking the chain via the process $H + O_2 \longrightarrow HO_2$ (the HO_2 reacts further to form water), so that each time a chain is broken, one oxygen molecule is removed to form water. Christiansen proposed that thermal chain reactions also existed, and that inhibitors acted by breaking these thermal chains. This theory was given credence by Hans L. J. Bäckström, who showed in 1927 that a number of reactions known to be sensitive to poisons are also photochemical chain reactions, that is, give many molecules reactions per quantum of light. He found this to be true in the case of the oxidations of benzaldehyde, of heptaldehyde, and of aqueous sodium sulphite; and his discovery increased the likelihood of thermal chains for these reactions, with inhibitors acting by breaking the chains.

Such a mechanism was finally confirmed by H. N. Alyea and Bäckström in 1929. They showed that alcohols inhibit the oxidation of sodium sulphite by breaking thermal chains: in breaking a chain, one alcohol molecule oxidizes to aldehyde or ketone. On the basis of this chain-breaking mechanism they were able to account quantitatively for the amounts of various alcohols oxidized at different concentrations. Furthermore, the chain-breaking mechanism was the same whether the sulphite oxidization was initiated thermally, by light, or by copper catalyst.

Many other reactions are undoubtedly of this chain-breaking nature. In gasoline the antiknock action of tetraethyl lead, of iodine, and of aniline is undoubtedly of this type. Iodine and halogens inhibit the combination of hydrogen with oxygen, by breaking chains. Nitric acid inhibits the thermal decomposition of acetaldehyde, which proceeds via free radicals by combining with these free radicals.

Heterogeneous Reactions. Obviously, in contact catalysis an inhibitor can act by blanketing out the active centers. Only tiny quantities of poison are required, since the active centers are but a small fraction of total catalyst surface. (*See* section on POISONS earlier in this article.) If the reaction is initiated on the walls and extends into the gas or liquid phase, the inhibitor may (a) act by preventing the initiation of the reaction chains at the wall, (b) break reaction chains after they have left the wall, or (c) terminate the reaction at the wall. Each reaction is its own special case. *See also* ENZYMES; NITRIC ACID; PETROLEUM; PLASTICS; RUBBER; SULPHURIC ACID. H. N. A.

CATAMARCA [ka'tama'rka], a province and its capital in the Andean region of northwestern Argentina.

The City. An old colonial city, situated at an elevation of 1,600 ft., Catamarca was founded in 1683 when the former capital of the province, Chacra, was deemed unsuitable because of frequent floods. The city has remained rather isolated from the life of the nation, but it is a busy market and industrial center, with food-processing and meat-packing plants and tanneries, and is noted for its hand-woven rugs, shawls, and ponchos. There are thermal springs nearby, and the Church of the Virgin of the Valley is visited by pilgrims from all parts of Argentina. Pop. 1947, 31,067.

The Province. The province of Catamarca is a fertile region producing figs, alfalfa, wine, and cotton. The grazing of cattle and lumbering and mining are also important. Pop. 1947, 147,213. S. G. I.

CATANIA [kata'nya], a province and its capital on the eastern shore of Sicily. The province is one of the most densely populated in Sicily, and the city is the second largest on the island.

City. Catania, a port and archiepiscopal see, 102 mi. southeast of Palermo, is situated on a narrow coastal plain fronting the Gulf of Catania and on the lower slopes of Mount Etna, the summit of which overlooks the city from a distance of 15 mi. The climate is mild and one of the most healthful in Italy. Daily and seasonal temperature ranges are moderate in Catania, and the annual rainfall averages 18 in.

Catania is connected by highway and rail with the other important Sicilian cities and is the terminus of the railway around Etna. Its airport is served by domestic and foreign airlines. The port, one of the busiest in Italy, is artificial; it was first developed under the Bourbons and supplied with its breakwater, docks, and other modern facilities following the unification of Italy. Catania refines and exports a large part of Sicily's sulphur output. Numerous industries and the rich agricultural produce of the hinterland, especially fruit, also contribute to the port's activity. Catania has at times been invaded by lava flows from Etna, and in 1693 it was completely destroyed by an earthquake. The city was replanned with wide, straight streets and is one of the most progressive cities in southern Italy.

Despite the volcanic and seismic disturbances, Catania still has many interesting monuments, including a Roman amphitheatre, baths, and tombs. The city contains many Baroque churches, palaces, and public buildings. Connected with the university, founded about 1445, are institutes, museums, and libraries. Vincenzo Bellini, operatic composer, was born in Catania.

Catania rests on the site of a Greek colony founded in the latter part of the eighth century B.C. A city of secondary importance during the Greek period, it was captured during the First Punic War by the Romans, who called it Catina. The city later fell into decay, was occupied by the Byzantine Army under Belisarius in 546, fell prey to Moorish pillagers in 902, and in the eleventh century became part of the Norman domain. Catania was nearly obliterated by an earthquake in 1170, and Henry VI ordered it sacked in 1194. Thereafter it partook of the general political vicissitudes of Sicily under the rule of Aragon, Spain, and the Bourbons. In 1837, and more particularly in 1848 and 1849, Catania was the scene of organized fighting in favor of Sicilian autonomy. On May 31, 1860, the city threw off Bourbon rule and declared union with Italy. In World War II Catania suffered from Allied aerial bombardment and

EWING GALLOWAY. NEW YORK

Granite columns from an ancient theatre embellish the eighteenth-century façade of Catania's cathedral.

from operations of the British Eighth Army against the German forces who held out in the area until August 1943. Pop. 1954, 321,000.

Province. The province of Catania comprises 54 communes and has an area of 1,371 sq. mi. Although nine tenths of the population live in towns or cities, the province is primarily agricultural, producing cereals, grapes and other fruit, vegetables, and livestock. Geographically the province may be said to consist of three parts: Mount Etna and its vicinity, the marshy Plain of Catania south of Etna and the capital, and a mountainous section farther south in the region of Monti Iblei and Caltagirone. The Simeto is the chief river. The Sicilian land-reform program has as one of its aims the lowering and eventual elimination of the province's high illiteracy rate. Other important cities are Caltagirone, Paternò, Adrano, Acireale, Vizzini, and Grammichele. Pop. (est. 1954), 834,100. R. G. W.

CATANZARO [ka'tandza'ro], a province and its capital, which is also an episcopal see, is located in Calabria, southern Italy.

The City. The city of Catanzaro is situated on a rocky eminence 1,100 ft. above the Ionian Sea, 6 mi. to the south, and about 95 mi. northeast of Reggio Calabria. Because of its altitude, the city has cold winters, with snow and hail fairly common; and cool summers. Sala, its suburb, 600 ft. below, is the junction point for the branch line connecting Calabria's two main coastal railways. A line also runs to Cosenza. The port is Marina di Catanzaro. Gloves, damask, lace, and embroidery are made here, but the city's economic life depends primarily on its governmental, religious, and cultural activities. Among the schools that are located in Catanzaro is the Pius X Pontifical University of Theological Studies.

Catanzaro was founded in the ninth century as a Byzantine fortress and soon acquired fame for its silk-manufacturing industry. In the Middle Ages it became the seat of the Ruffo feudal domain, one of the largest in Calabria. In the modern era, particularly under Bourbon rule, the city decayed. It was bombed by the Allies in World War II and was later occupied by the British Eighth Army early in September 1943. Pop. 1954 (city), 40,300; (commune), 65,000.

The Province. The province of Catanzaro, with an area of 2,025 sq. mi., has 156 communes. Its principal rivers are the Neto and Savuto. Periodically many parts of the province have suffered from earthquakes. The terrain is largely hilly or mountainous, and for southern Italy there

COURTESY OF THE U.S. FISH AND WILDLIFE SERVICE

A catbird feeding its young

is a high percentage of forest zone. Most of the people live in rural towns, and about two thirds are engaged in agriculture and the grazing of cattle, horses, swine, sheep, and goats. Cereals, fruit, olives, grapes, and raw silk are the chief crops. Lumbering, fishing, and sulphur and zinc mining are also carried on.

Other towns of importance in the province are Crotone, a port on the Ionian Sea; Nicastro, an industrial center; and Vibo Valentia, an ancient Greek city which is now a busy industrial town. Pop. (est. 1954), 747,000.   R. G. W.

CATAPULT. *See* ENGINES OF WAR.
CATARACT. *See* EYE (*Eye Surgery*).

CATATONIA [kætəto′niə], literally, a breakdown of tension or tone, referring, in medical science, to the muscles when involved in psychopathologic conditions. While catatonia may be observed in various psychogenic states, it is predominantly a feature of schizophrenia (dementia praecox). It also has cataleptic manifestations. In schizophrenia, the patient, in addition to the basic symptoms of this mental illness, manifests his catatonia either as a stupor or as excitement. Catatonic stupor is characterized by mutism, negativism (active or passive), and by hypersuggestibility seen as echolalia (repetition of sounds heard), echopraxia (repetition of movements seen), or catalepsy. Negativism signifies that the patient, although aware of environmental stimuli, opposes them. Active negativism is evident when the patient does exactly the opposite of what he is asked to do; passive negativism is when the patient, without prompting, does not do what he is expected to do. The catatonic patient who maintains statue-like, grotesque attitudes which can be molded or changed, the patient continuing to maintain the new position, is called *cerea flexibilitas* (waxy mobility). Catatonic excitement is manifested by stereotypy (the constant repetition of an action) of movement, writing, or speech. In the latter condition repetitive speech is termed "verbigeration." Catatonic excitement is described as purposeless and impulsive; hence, the common finding of such patients in wards for the mentally disturbed, because of their assaultiveness and destructiveness. *See also* CATALEPSY; SCHIZOPHRENIA.
J. A. Br.

CATAWBA. *See* INDIAN TRIBES, NORTH AMERICAN.

CATAWBA COLLEGE, at Salisbury, N.C., an accredited, coeducational, privately controlled college of arts and

sciences affiliated with the Evangelical and Reformed Church. It has a campus of 198 acres. First instruction was offered in 1851, and in the following year the institution was granted a charter. The Bachelor of Arts degree is conferred. Candidates must complete a minimum core-curriculum and basic requirements in the field of specialization. Scholarship and student-loan aid is available, and dormitories and dining halls are provided for boarding students. *For statistics see* COLLEGES AND UNIVERSITIES.

CATBIRD, an American songbird, *Dumetella carolinensis,* allied to the thrashers and mockingbirds. It breeds in southern Canada and almost throughout the United States, except the Pacific Coast, and it winters as far south as Panama. The plumage in both sexes is slaty gray, with the crown and tail black and the under tail coverts reddish brown. The catbird is an inhabitant of hedgerows and thickets and will live in gardens where suitable cover is found. Its diet consists of insects and wild or cultivated fruits. The name derives from a common alarm call, by some thought to resemble the mew of a cat, but its vocal powers encompass also a great variety of other sounds; the protracted song is a mixture of fine phrases and harsh notes, without the definite pattern heard in the songs of its relatives.   H. G. De.

CATCHFLY, the name given to various plants of the pink family that trap insects by secretion of sticky substances. Among garden plants are the 2-ft. sweet William catchfly, *Silene armeria,* with glutinous stem joints; and the 1.5-ft. German catchfly, *Lychnis viscaria,* having sticky patches beneath the flower clusters. The sleepy catchfly, *S. antirrhina,* a 2.5-ft. plant, growing wild across North America, has a number of black, sticky bands around the stem which prevent crawling insects from reaching the flower pollen.

CATEAU-CAMBRÉSIS, TREATY OF [ka′to′ kã′-bre′zi′] (1559), the peace settlement ending the intermittent state of war which had existed since 1522 between the Valois dynasty of France and the Austrian and Spanish Hapsburgs. The treaty, concluded in 1559 between Henry II of France and Philip II of Spain, provided for the restoration of all territory which the two powers had taken from each other since 1551. England, which had been in alliance with Spain, lost Calais, the last English foothold on the Continent. France recognized the Hapsburg claims to Italy, although it was over this issue that Francis I had embarked upon the war almost forty years earlier. In return, France expanded eastward by annexing the bishoprics of Metz, Toul, and Verdun. The treaty was sealed by the marriage in 1560 of Philip II and Elizabeth, daughter of the French king.   M. K.

CATECHISM [kæ′təkɪzəm] (Gr. κατηχεῖν, "to sound down," "to din in"), an outline or digest of Christian doctrines arranged in question-and-answer form for the purpose of instructing children and those who are about to become members of the Church. A catechism differs from a creed or confession of faith by being mainly an oral means of religious education, while the latter is a written affirmation of religious convictions. Early in the Christian Church, converts became known as catechumens, a name signifying those who received catechetical instruction prior to baptism and Church membership. The various forms of the Apostles' Creed indicate that this may have been the basis of such doctrinal teaching. Many of the early Fathers wrote treatises on catechetics, among these being the *Catechetical Lectures* (A.D. 347) of Cyril of Jerusalem, *The Catechetical Oration* (A.D. 383) of Gregory of Nyssa, and the *Enchiridion* (A.D. 420) of Augustine. There are some examples of medieval catechisms, but the modern development dates from pre-Reformation times. The Waldenses of Italy, the Brothers of the Common Life in Germany, and the Unitas Fratrum of Bohemia all used a catechism dealing with the Creed, the Lord's Prayer, and the Ten Commandments.

The chief Protestant catechisms are: Luther's "Small Catechism" (1529); Calvin's "Genevan Catechism" (1541), the German Reformed or Calvinistic "Heidelberg Catechism" (1563), the "Anglican Catechisms" (1549, 1662), the Socinian or Unitarian "Racovian Catechism" (1605), the "Westminster Shorter Catechism" (1647). The Roman Catholic Church issued a catechism in 1566 as a summary of the doctrines defined at the Council of Trent; more widely circulated, however, was a private catechism (1603) of Robert Bellarmine, which was later sanctioned by the Vatican Council. Since 1885 the "Baltimore Catechism" has been the most widely used Roman Catholic catechism in America. The chief catechism of the Eastern Orthodox Church was prepared in 1642 by Mogilas and was given general authority by the Synod of Jerusalem in 1672. H. T. K.

CATECHUMEN [kætəkyu′mən], literally, "one taught by word of mouth," from the Greek word κατηχούμενος. In the early Christian Church the catechumens were taught according to a syllabus, which they memorized in the form of the Creed, and this became the mark of identification of a Christian. The full Creed and its order were the last part of the catechumen's instruction prior to baptism and admission to the sacrament of Communion. This first Communion usually took place on Easter Day, when the catechumen appeared in a white garment, which he wore for the festal week. The role of catechumen was also assigned to those who had lapsed from the faith, and by this means they were required to prove their repentance prior to readmission. F. W. B.

CATEGORY. *See* LOGIC.

CATERPILLAR, the common designation of the larvae of moths and butterflies. It has a distinct head, and thirteen body segments, the first three of which form the thorax and bear the three pairs of true legs. Most caterpillars have five pairs of false legs or prolegs, but the number varies; in the cankerworms there are two pairs of prolegs. In rare cases, only the posterior pair is present. Caterpillars may be smooth or hairy, or armed with spines; some, like the *Automeris io,* have poisonous spines; others, poisonous, barbed hairs. Most caterpillars are vegetarians, but a small number live on plant lice, and a very few in the nests of ants. C. H. Cu.

CATERPILLAR HUNTER, the name given to the various species of *Callosoma,* of the family Carabidae. They are large beetles, and are generally beautifully colored, iridescent green, copper, blue, or gold; but many of them are black or brown, often with the edge of the elytra of brighter color. They are nocturnal, hiding under cover or in the soil by day; once out of hiding, they run rapidly over the ground, and up and down trees and low plants, in search of caterpillars and other prey. The European *C. sycophanta,* metallic green, was introduced into America to prey upon the larvae of the gypsy and brown-tailed moths. *C. calidus,*

black with rows of coppery spots on the elytra (modified anterior wings), is a common American species. C. H. Cu.

CATFISH, an enormous cosmopolitan group of over 1,200 kinds found mostly in fresh waters. It is easily recognized by the barbels, or feelers, about the mouth, a body either naked or with bony plates, and a fleshy adipose fin on the back near the tail. Classified in twenty-eight families, they

COURTESY OF THE U.S. FISH AND WILDLIFE SERVICE

Catfish, or Channel Cat, Ictalurus punctatus

reach their greatest abundance in the Amazon region, and vary in size from a few inches to 6 ft. In many sea catfish, family Ariidae, of tropical waters, the pea-sized eggs are carried and cared for in the mouth of the male until hatched.

In North America, east of the Rocky Mountains, many varieties of catfish occur in the family Ictaluridae. Most are nocturnal, dwelling and feeding on or near the bottom. Channel cats, *Ictalurus,* are large, fork-tailed species. Individuals weighing over 150 lb. have been captured in the Mississippi River, where they constitute a substantial commercial fishery. The shovelhead catfish, *Pilodictis olivaris,* also reaches a great size. Other small kinds are: bullheads, or horned pout, *Ameiurus;* stone cats, *Noturus;* and mad toms, *Schilbeodes.* These build nests in the mud or under stones, and guard the eggs and young.

In Europe, the huge sheatfish, *Silurus glanis,* family Siluridae, reaches a weight of 400 lb. An electric catfish *Malapterus electricus* inhabits the Nile River. *See also* CANDIRU; BULLHEAD; MAD TOM. E. C. R.

CATHA [kæ′thə], *Catha edulis,* one of the staff tree family, an evergreen growing to 10 ft. in tropical Africa. It has small white flowers and oblong toothed leaves. It is also known as khat, cafta, or Arabian tea. The twigs and leaves are sold in Arabian markets. A beverage is made from them which has been used for centuries, with qualities similar to those of coffee and tea. J. C. Wis.

CATHARS, or **CATHARI** [kæ′thɑrz; kæ′thərai], adherents of a heretical movement that was widespread in southern France from the eleventh to the fourteenth centuries. The tenets of the Cathars go back to Manichaeism, to the Eastern Bogomiles, and to the Paulicians. Frequently they are designated Albigenses, from Albi, southwest of which, around Toulouse, their activity centered in the twelfth century. When their success threatened the life of the Church, Innocent III in 1209 inaugurated vigorous crusades against them. Holy wars and the Inquisition (formally established in 1232 by Gregory IX) all but extirpated the Cathars within a century and destroyed the Provençal civilization.

The Cathars were strongly dualistic, holding that an evil God created the visible world and ordained water baptism and marriage. For them this world was both purgatory and hell, the place where spirits are punished by being placed in bodies and reincarnated at death in other human or animal bodies. In place of the orthodox Christ, the eternal God who became true man, they affirmed that He was a kind of Archangel who was neither really incarnated nor actually raised from the dead.

In organization the Cathars copied the Church in having a Pope in Constantinople and bishops chosen from the Perfect, their highest order, with Believers and Hearers as the main body of members. One became a Perfect by receiving the *consolamentum,* a sacrament of the Spirit, in which the persecuting Church was renounced with all its rites and sacraments, and might then use the Lord's Prayer and bestow this sacrament upon others. The Perfect was obliged to refuse all meats (although fish was allowed), practice complete chastity, never kill anything, leave father and mother for the divine kinship and the kingdom of the inward man. Frequently members of the Perfect Order refused all food and starved themselves to death, in what they called the *endura,* lest they commit other sin. *See also* ALBIGENSES. W. C. Ro.

CATHER, WILLA SIBERT (1873-1947), American novelist, was born Dec. 7, 1873, at Back Creek Valley (now Gore), Va. In 1883 her parents moved to Webster County, Nebr., and in 1884 to Red Cloud, Nebr. She graduated from the University of Nebraska in 1895. From 1896 to 1905 she lived in Pittsburgh, Pa., first as editor and reporter, then as teacher. From 1905 to 1912 she worked for *McClure's Magazine,* the last five years as managing editor. After 1912 she devoted all her time to writing.

Her first book (poetry), *April Twilights* (1903), aroused little interest. Her second, *The Troll Garden* (1905), contained seven short stories, four of which were reprinted in *Youth and the Bright Medusa* (1920). Of these the best known is "Paul's Case" which embodies the theme, ever

WILLA CATHER

PHOTOGRAPHED BY STEICHEN

present in her work, of artistic man's disharmony with his environment. In 1912 she published her first novel, *Alexander's Bridge.* National recognition came with the publication of *O Pioneers!* (1913), a story from Miss Cather's prairie background, portraying a Swedish pioneer woman who buries all passion in love of the land. *The Song of the Lark* (1915) revealed the author's interest in the Southwest and emphasized her belief that singleness of purpose in an artist must cut away all nonessentials. *My Ántonia* (1918) is the story of a Bohemian girl in Nebraska who sublimates her artistic impulses in the creation of a home full of happy children. *One*

of Ours, a World War I story, won the Pulitzer Prize in 1922. *A Lost Lady* (1923) depicts a charming woman unable to withstand adverse circumstances.

The Cather protest against change, her identification of the past with the genuine and the present with the artificial, is crystallized in *The Professor's House* (1925). *My Mortal Enemy* (1926) was the first of three books contemplating the Catholic faith. *Death Comes for the Archbishop* (1927), considered by many to be her best work, told the life story of a French missionary priest in the Southwest. *Shadows on the Rock,* a picture of seventeenth-century Quebec, won the Prix Femina Américaine in 1931. Other books are *Obscure Destinies* (1932), three Nebraska stories; *Lucy Gayheart* (1935); *Not Under Forty* (1936), essays; and *Sapphira and the Slave Girl* (1940), a novel of pre-Civil War Virginia. *The Old Beauty and Others,* a volume of stories, appeared posthumously in 1948.

Miss Cather's writing is clear and her story patterns forceful. The beauty of her style, the depth of her vision, and her insistence on universal values make her one of the greatest American novelists of the twentieth century. In 1938 she was elected to the American Academy of Arts and Letters. She died on Apr. 24, 1947, in New York City. M. R. B.

CATHERINE II (1729-1796), Empress of Russia, known as Catherine the Great, was born Sophia Augusta Frederica of Anhalt-Zerbst at Stettin, in Prussian Pomerania on May 2, 1729. She was the daughter of Christian Augustus, ruler of the petty principality of Anhalt-Zerbst, and Johanna Elizabeth of Holstein-Gottorp.

Early Life. Though brought up in the simplest manner, she was well educated by French governesses and tutors. In 1744 she was betrothed to the Grand Duke Peter Feodorovich, nephew of the Empress Elizabeth of Russia and heir presumptive to the Russian throne. This match was arranged by the families of the betrothed but was particularly encouraged by Frederick the Great of Prussia, who saw in it a means of improving his relations with Russia and the weakening of Austrian influence. To ingratiate herself with Elizabeth, the young princess adopted the name Ekaterina (Catherine) Alekseevna before her marriage on Sept. 1, 1745, and renounced Lutheranism in favor of the Greek Orthodox religion.

Catherine soon became alienated from her husband, whose education had been neglected and who had a very limited knowledge of men and public affairs. After the birth of her son Paul in 1754 she became active in politics, opposing Peter's pro-Lutheran and pro-Prussian policy, and using to advantage the disaffection caused among the military caste by his introduction of Prussian tactics in the Russian army. The Grand Duke succeeded to the throne as Peter III on Jan. 5, 1762. He was impolitic enough to threaten Catherine with a divorce on the grounds of infidelity. Six months later, Peter was with his Holstein troops at the castle of Oranienbaum, thirty miles from St. Petersburg. On July 13 and 14, a group of conspirators led by Gregory Orlov, Catherine's current lover, took advantage of Peter's absence from court to issue a pronunciamento in the name of the regiments of the Imperial Guard, which removed Peter from the throne and made Catherine empress. She was crowned by the Archbishop of Novgorod. Peter was secluded in a country house at Ropcha, where he died on July 18, officially of apoplexy.

Foreign Policy. An able ruler, Catherine transformed Russia into a great power and gained for herself a place among the "enlightened despots" of the eighteenth century. Her foreign policy represents perhaps the most spectacular side of her reign. Catherine took an active part in the three partitions of Poland (1772-1773, 1793, and 1795) and brought within the fold of the Russian Empire millions of Orthodox and Russian-speaking subjects, thereby almost completing the dream of Ivan III of the reunion of all the Russian lands under the scepter of the tsar. The Russian share of Poland included Lithuania and Kurland, which established the extent of the Russian-controlled Baltic coast almost to the Niemen River. In her wars with Turkey (1769-1774 and 1787-1791) Catherine carried through the policy inherited from Peter the Great and obtained a firm hold on the Black Sea coast from the Kerch Straits to the Dniester River, giving Russia a natural frontier in the south and another outlet to the sea. The last remnant of the medieval Mongol Empire, once a powerful enemy of Russia, the Khanate of Crimea, became a Russian possession. During the reign of Catherine, Sweden attempted to reconquer the part of the Baltic coast which had been taken away from her by Peter the Great, but after the war (1788-1790) the Russo-Swedish frontier remained unchanged. Catherine played a conspicuous part in European affairs. In 1779 she acted as mediator between Prussia and Austria and became a guarantor of the Treaty of Teschen. In 1780 Catherine issued the "Act of Armed Neutrality" supported by many European states. In 1796 death interrupted her plans of intervention in France.

Internal Politics. *Proposed New Laws.* The internal policies of Catherine were a compromise between her "enlightened" inclinations and the necessity to appease the nobility which was her main support on the throne. Finding the state of governmental affairs in Russia in a rather disorderly condition, Catherine started her reign with an attempt to give the country new modernized laws. To prepare these laws, she convened in 1767 a legislative commission composed of 565 representatives of the nobility, towns, free peasants, and the government institutions. The enserfed peasants were not represented among the deputies. For the guidance of the commission, Catherine herself prepared an elaborate "Instruction," consisting of more than 500 articles and based on the ideas of Montesquieu, Beccaria, and other writers of that period. After a year and a half of deliberation, the commission was dismissed by Catherine without having accomplished any legislative work.

Administrative Reforms. Having failed in her grandiose plans to present Russia with a new code of laws, Catherine launched a number of administrative reforms. After making some slight changes in the central government, Catherine, in 1775, came forth with a reform of the provincial administration. The need of such a reform became apparent during the huge peasant rebellion led by Pugachev (1773-1774) when the local administration proved to be totally inefficient and impotent. Catherine changed the number of the *gubernias*—the large territorial units into which Russia was divided—from 20 to 51. The administrative machinery within each *gubernia* was reorganized and, in accordance with Western ideas, the administrative, financial, and judicial functions of the government were separated. On the lower level, separate courts for the nobility, the townsmen, and free peasants were introduced, whose judges were elected from the class over whom they had jurisdiction. The judges of the superior courts were appointed by the crown. On the whole, the reform greatly favored the nobility because all the high crown officers came from this class, and the local gentry acquired a complete control of the rural administration.

The Nobles' Charter. In addition to granting the nobles a large share of government functions, in 1785 Catherine granted the nobles a charter confirming and amplifying the privileges given to them by Peter III. This charter gave the nobles organization as a class enjoying special rights and represented before the throne by their elected marshals; it freed the nobles from their obligations to the state and definitely transformed the serfs into their private property.

CATHERINE II
(THE GREAT)
OF RUSSIA

Simultaneously Catherine issued a charter to the cities, granting them a degree of self-government, limited by the presence of an appointed crown officer with police and supervisory duties. Although Catherine defined the civic status of the noble and middle classes, she did nothing for the enserfed peasants whose position during her reign was worse than ever before. In the beginning of her reign she played with the idea of at least the gradual emancipation of the serfs. Faced with the hostile attitude of the nobility toward such projects, Catherine abandoned them and ended by enserfing more than a million hitherto free state peasants, who were distributed among her various favorites. She also legalized serfdom in the Ukraine.

Economic Measures. In her economic policies Catherine followed the tendencies of her age and adopted the doctrine of *laissez faire*. Without attempting any regulation, she was interested in the development of industry and trade, especially export trade. The Black Sea grain trade was made possible after the colonization of southern Russia, the building of several towns, and the foundation of the Russian naval base in Sevastopol. Among her economic measures were the establishment of the Loan Bank, the introduction of paper currency, the reduction of the burdensome salt tax, and the encouragement of the Free Economic Society, founded through private initiative for the dissemination of information about agriculture. During Catherine's reign the government brought potatoes from Ireland, and the people were taught how to cultivate and use them.

Cultural Innovations. The enlightened ideas of Catherine were particularly noticeable in her cultural activities and educational and humanitarian reforms. A friend, correspondent, and sometimes patron of many contemporary philosophers, Catherine encouraged the translation of their works into Russian. She permitted private printing of books, stimulated literary efforts among her subjects, and herself wrote articles and plays in which she introduced progressive ideas of Western culture to Russian readers. The results of Catherine's efforts soon became evident. A number of magazines made their appearance; in 1783 the Russian Academy of Letters was founded and the first private bookstore was opened. The Academy of Sciences started publication of Russian chronicles, and on private initiative twenty volumes of ancient Russian documents were published. Several scientific expeditions for the study of the Russian borderlands were organized, and the Scientific Society at the University of Moscow was started. Although Catherine failed to put through her plans for an extensive school system, many schools were opened during her reign, including the first schools for girls. In 1763 Catherine founded a medical commission to look after public health. She established many hospitals and asylums for foundlings and incurable mental cases. She tried to increase the number of physicians and pharmacists in the country and, as an example to her subjects, had herself and her son Paul inoculated against smallpox.

Evaluation of Catherine's Reign. During Catherine's reign, Russian national prestige as well as the fear of Russia greatly increased in Western Europe. The internal organization of the empire became improved and modernized, although chiefly in the interest of only one class of the Russian people. The social conditions, in so far as the tightening of serfdom was concerned, had a backward trend, making the solution of the peasant question more difficult for Catherine's successors. Culturally, Russia advanced considerably with the influx of new ideas, the growth of national literature, and the progress of science.   G. V. L.

CATHERINE DE MÉDICIS [ka'tri'n də me'di'si's] (1519-1589), queen of France, was born in Florence, Italy, daughter of Lorenzo II de' Medici and Madeleine de la Tour d'Auvergne, a French princess, in April 1519. In October 1533, she was married to the Duke of Orleans, later Henry II of France. As Henry's wife, she had little political influence, but later as a mother (one of her daughters, Elizabeth, became the third wife of Philip II of Spain), especially as a mother of kings (the last three Valois kings of France: Francis II, Charles IX, and Henry III), she had greater scope for her latent Medicean flair for power and influence.

During the French civil-religious wars, Catherine, herself a Catholic, vacillated among policies of compromise, conciliation, and immediate action, not hesitating, in the latter recourse, at assassination and massacre. Catherine's chief concern was always to maintain her own influence paramount, as against excessive Catholic influence, represented by François de Lorraine, duke of Guise, and Charles, cardinal and archbishop of Lorraine, and against the Protestant influence of Henry of Navarre (to whom she married her daughter Margaret) and of Gaspard de Coligny, the admiral and staunch Huguenot leader high in the esteem of Charles IX. It was this determination, rather than fanatic Catholicism, that caused her to instigate the Massacre of St. Bartholomew on Aug. 24, 1572. This massacre of some 50,000 Huguenots in the whole of France and the assassination of Coligny sprang from Catherine's fear of the strength of Coligny's influence on her son, Charles IX. Catherine's political and religious policies, however, ultimately met with little success.

It was rather as a patron of letters and art, especially architecture, that Catherine will be remembered. A lover of pomp and magnificence, she ordered the construction of a new wing of the Louvre and started the Tuileries. Outside Paris, she built the Château of Monceau. Her personal library, which contained many rare manuscripts, was one of the most noted in Renaissance France. Catherine died at Blois, Jan. 5, 1589.   R. J. K.

CATHERINE OF ALEXANDRIA, ST. (died c. 310), a virgin martyr of Alexandria, is venerated as the patroness of Christian philosophers. According to legend, she rebuked the Emperor Valerius Maximinus for persecuting the Christians and, though only eighteen, converted a number of the learned philosophers he assembled to dispute with her. When the spiked wheel on which she was sentenced to die broke in pieces, she was beheaded. The legend contends that her body was carried by angels to Mount Sinai. Her feast is November 25.   W. C.

CATHERINE OF ARAGON (1485-1536), first wife of Henry VIII, King of England, was born at Alcala, Spain, Dec. 15, 1485, the daughter of Ferdinand and Isabella of Spain. In 1501 she was sent to England as the bride of Prince Arthur, eldest son of Henry VII. Arthur died in 1502; but because of the rapacity of Henry VII, who did not want to forfeit Catherine's dowry, and the ambition of Ferdinand, who wanted Spanish influence to dominate England's foreign policy, Catherine was betrothed to Arthur's younger brother, Henry, nearly six years her junior. A papal dispensation was obtained for the marriage, which was solemnized on June 11, 1509. Catherine bore five children, all of whom except the youngest, Mary, born in 1516, died in infancy. By the early 1520's, when the alliance with Spain had cooled and it had become clear that Catherine would never provide a male heir, Henry began to find his wife tiresome. He asked for a declaration of nullity from Pope Clement VII, on the ground that the dispensation had been illegal. Catherine fought the suit bitterly, finally appealing the case from the legislative court in London to Rome (1529); the Pope, who was in the power of the Emperor Charles V, Catherine's nephew, refused Henry's request and in 1536 pronounced his marriage to Catherine valid. Meanwhile, in 1531, Henry had left Catherine at Windsor and set up a separate establishment. In 1533 her marriage was declared null and void by Archbishop Cranmer, and she was removed in semicustody to Buckden in Huntingdonshire. In 1534 she was transferred to more comfortable quarters at Kimbolton, where she died on Jan. 7, 1536.   E. R. A.

CATHERINE OF SIENA, ST. (1347-1380), Roman Catholic religious, was born in Siena, Italy. Practicing austerities and seeing visions from early childhood, she became at sixteen a Dominican Tertiary and in 1366 had the mystical experience of the "spiritual espousals." Suffering much, devoting herself to the plague-stricken, and preserving a cheerful disposition, she gathered disciples with whom she began in 1370 her great work of restoring peace to the Church. By journeys and extensive correspondence she reconciled factions, promoted a crusade, strove to settle the dispute between the pope and Florence, and (her great achievement) persuaded Gregory XI, seventh of the Avignon popes, to return to Rome in 1377. Urban VI, Gregory's successor, enlisted her help against the antipope in Avignon. She offered herself as a victim for unity and, after a mysterious agony of three months, died April 29, 1380. In addition to the *Dialogue* (a mystical treatise on the spiritual life) and a series of *Prayers,* nearly four hundred of St. Catherine's letters are preserved.   W. C.

CATHODE. *See* ELECTROLYTES; ELECTRON TUBES.
CATHODE-RAY TUBES. *See* ELECTRON TUBES.

CATHOLIC. The term "catholic" is derived through the Latin from the Greek καθ'ὅλου, meaning "wholly," "entirely." In common speech the adjective catholic means extensive, inclusive, or universal, in contrast to the narrow, restricted, or local; thus a man of catholic tastes or sympathies is a man of wide-reaching interests or affections. As applied to the Christian Church, the first use of the term is by St. Ignatius in his letter of about 110 A.D. to the Smyrnaeans: ἡ καθολικὴ ἐκκλησία, translated by Lightfoot, "the universal Church." That this is the primary meaning is shown by a letter from the Smyrnaeans on the martyrdom of St. Polycarp, written some fifty years later, in which the martyred saint is said to have prayed for "all the universal (catholic) Churches throughout the world" and Christ is called "the shepherd of the universal Church which is throughout the world." The Greek word οἰκουμένη, here translated as "world," means the inhabited world and is the source of the English word "ecumenical."

The meaning of the term "catholic" was naturally extended in course of time. What is taught in all parts of the world is assumed to be the truth, and accordingly "catholic" came to mean "orthodox" as opposed to what is taught only locally or by smaller sects. Unity of doctrine implied unity of authority, and thus the term was taken to exclude not only the heretical but also the schismatic. St. Cyril of Jerusalem (348) gave the marks of catholicity as extension in place, completeness of doctrine, universality of adaptation, and moral and spiritual perfection of aim. Vincent of Lerins (about 434) composed the famous formula, "*Quod ubique, quod semper, quod ab omnibus creditum est,*" distinguishing as truly catholic that which is believed at all times, in all places, and by all. Similarly John Pearson, in *On the Creed* (1650), speaks of the "Holy Catholick Church" as worldwide by the command of Christ: "to be extended to all places, to be propagated to all ages, to contain in it all truths necessary to be known, to exact absolute obedience from all men . . . . and to furnish us with all graces necessary . . . ."

In America and Great Britain the word "Catholic" as adjective and noun is used in a twofold ecclesiastical sense. As defined in the *Century Dictionary* it means "1. A member of the universal Christian Church. 2. A member of the Roman Catholic Church." Similarly Webster defines the noun as "1. A person who belongs to the universal Christian church. 2. (cap.) A member of a Catholic church, specif. of the Roman Catholic Church." The use of the term Catholic has thus become a matter of controversy between the Roman Catholics and the Protestants. The Roman Catholics claim exclusive right to the use of the adjective, believing their Church to be the one church founded by Christ. They may appeal also to the common use of language, which divides the Christian world between "Catholic" and "Protestant." But Protestants, Anglo-Catholics, and Eastern Orthodox believe that they are truly apostolic, since all in common accept and repeat the ecumenical Creeds formed before the separation from Rome, and in this light they also call themselves Catholic. All repeat with equal conviction, "I believe in one Holy Catholic and Apostolic Church" (Nicene Creed, formulated in 381), each believer being assured that his sense of the word "Catholic" is the correct one. Eastern Orthodox writers have maintained, furthermore, that their Church is the true and faithful continuation of the old and Catholic Church, and that it is the Roman Church which has made the innovations. Others who use the Catholic name, besides the Roman Catholic Church, are the Anglo-Catholics, who insist that they are "essentially Catholic, only incidentally national"; the Old Catholic Church, which after the Vatican Council of 1870 rejected the infallibility and universal jurisdiction of the Bishop of Rome; and a smaller sect, the Catholic Apostolic Church, associated with the name of Edward Irving. *See* Roman Catholic Church.   W. H. J.

CATHOLIC EMANCIPATION, in Irish history, refers to the passage through the British Parliament in 1829 of the Roman Catholic Relief Bill. Under it, Roman Catholics were admitted to the British Parliament without being forced to take oaths offensive to their religious principles, and they were to be allowed to hold all civil and political offices except those of king, regent, lord chancellor and lord lieutenant of Ireland. In 1801, Pitt had resigned as prime minister, because George III had refused to allow him to introduce Catholic Emancipation which he had promised the Irish in connection with the union of Great Britain and Ireland. It had been a burning question in Ireland and many bills in its favor had been introduced in the British House of Commons. The issue was precipitated by the election to Parliament in 1828 of the Catholic Irish leader Daniel O'Connell. To secure peace in Ireland, the English Tories finally gave way, the king and the House of Lords abandoned their opposition, and the bill was passed.   E. R. A.

CATHOLIC UNIVERSITY OF AMERICA, at Washington, D. C., an accredited institution, coeducational in all schools except canon law, engineering, architecture, and undergraduate philosophy and theology, controlled by the hierarchy of the Roman Catholic Church in the United States. It is located on 142 acres in a suburban section of the city. The university consists of the following schools: Sacred Theology, Canon Law, Philosophy, Law, Graduate School and College of Arts and Sciences, Engineering and Architecture, Social Service, Nursing Education, Social Science, and the Summer Session.

The university was incorporated in 1887 and chartered by Pope Leo XIII in 1889, when the School of Sacred Theology was founded. The School of Law was opened in 1895; the Catholic Sisters' College in 1911 (discontinued in 1950); the Summer Session in 1911; the School of Canon Law in 1923; the Graduate School of Arts and Sciences in 1930 (graduate work has been a part of the university program since 1889); the College of Arts and Sciences in 1930 (undergraduate work has been offered since 1904); the School of Social Work in 1934 (amalgamated with the National Catholic School of Social Service in 1947 under that name); the School of Nursing Education in 1935; the School of Philosophy in 1936 (graduate work since 1889); and the School of Social Service in 1937 (graduate work since 1889).

Degrees conferred are the A.B. in liberal arts, the bachelor's degree in engineering, and the bachelor's and master's degrees in law, social work, nursing, and music. Graduate degrees include the M.A., Ph.D., M.S., M.F.A., M.Mus., S.T.L., J.C.L., and J.C.O. There is also an Air Force R.O.T.C. program.

Special services include annual workshops in higher, secondary, and elementary education, music and art education, and in nursing and special education. Institutes are conducted annually in the Summer Session in the field of preaching and in the special fields of education. A program of affiliation which services Roman Catholic institutions of higher education, secondary schools, and nursing schools is also maintained. Field trips are used in connection with botany and geography courses.

The Catholic University of America Press issues numerous special publications and periodicals. Among these are educational, historical, and ecclesiastical reviews, educational research monographs, studies in economics and nursing education, and the proceedings of the annual workshops.

Scholarship and student loan aid is available. *For statistics see* Colleges and Universities.

CATILINE (LUCIUS SERGIUS CATILINA) [kæ′-tɪlaɪn] (108-62 B.C.), Roman politician, was a reckless and dissolute young noble. In his contest for political supremacy at Rome, Crassus supported Catiline for the consulship in the campaign of 64 B.C., but Catiline was not elected, partly because he was opposed by Cicero and partly because he was suspected of having been involved in a revolutionary plot two years earlier. Without the backing of Crassus, Catiline again ran for the consulship in 63. When he was not elected, he plotted the murder of the consuls and the seizure of the city, but the conspiracy was exposed by Cicero. Catiline was declared a traitor and died fighting against government forces in northern Italy in 62 B.C.   T. B. J.

CATION. *See* ELECTROLYTES.

CATLIN, GEORGE (1796-1872), American artist, writer, explorer, and student of the American Indian, was born in Wilkes-Barre, Pa.; a year later his parents settled in Broome County, N. Y. Young Catlin grew up on stories of Indian life and traditions; his mother had been captured by Indians, and the friends of his youth were frontiersmen, trappers, and Indian fighters. After a brief career at law, Catlin turned to painting and, in 1823, opened a studio in Philadelphia. At the Pennsylvania Academy of Fine Arts he befriended Thomas Sully, Rembrandt Peale, and other leading artists of his day, and during this period painted the great of Albany, Washington, and Richmond. But finding little satisfaction in portrait painting, Catlin determined to return to the Indian and to dedicate his life to making a pictorial record of the history and customs of the vanishing aborigines. From 1829 to his death he devoted himself to this project beyond the settled frontiers of the New World. Catlin spent eight years exploring the western Plains and returned with five hundred paintings and a large collection of Indian articles. These comprised the core of his Indian Gallery, which met with immediate success both in the United States and abroad. In Paris Catlin met Alexander von Humboldt, who urged the artist to go to South America to make similar studies, and for six years he explored and painted the South American continent, returning via Central America and Yucatan. The principal Catlin collections are housed in the Smithsonian Institution and in the American Museum of Natural History. His main literary contribution is entitled *Letters and Notes on the Manners, Customs, and Condition of the North American Indians* (1842).   H. T.

CATNIP, *Nepeta cataria*, also called catnep or catmint, a perennial of the mint family, native to Europe but widely naturalized in the United States. It is a branching herb growing to 4 ft., with downy leaves and terminal racemes of pale purplish flowers. All parts of the plant have an aromatic odor when crushed, and this odor is particularly attractive to cats.   J. C. Wis.

CATO, DIONYSIUS [ke′to], the name erroneously given to the unknown author (c. third century A.D.) of the *Dionysii Catonis disticha de moribus ad filium,* a collection of moral apothegms in four short books of hexameter couplets. The name of Cato seems to have become attached to the work through association with the wisdom of Cato the Elder, to whom the *Distichs* were formerly attributed, though they are now generally believed to be the work of some other author. The *Distichs* were first quoted, about A.D. 370, by Vindicianus in an epistle to Valentinian I,

and later had a considerable literary influence, being mentioned by Alcuin, Chaucer, and other writers. The work was widely used as a schoolbook in the Middle Ages and was translated into several languages. An English translation was put out in 1483 by William Caxton.   C. W. D.

CATO, MARCUS PORCIUS [ke′to], the name of two prominent Romans of the Republican period: Cato the Elder (234-149 B.C.), also known as Cato the Censor, and his great-grandson, Cato the Younger (95-46 B.C.).

1. The elder Cato was born in Tusculum in 234 B.C. His fundamental honesty, ability, and rugged individuality marked him as a Roman of the old school and won universal

MARCUS PORCIUS CATO, THE ELDER

FROM AN OLD ENGRAVING

CULVER SERVICE

respect. Although not a member of the senatorial aristocracy, Cato had a successful political career. He was quaestor in 204, aedile in 199, praetor in 198, and consul in 195. He conducted a notable military campaign in Spain in 196 and later helped Flamininus to halt the advance of Antiochus the Great in Greece. As censor in 184, Cato tried to combat the rising Greek influence and the trend toward luxury and ostentation which he felt was undermining the Roman character. His anti-Hellenism brought him into conflict with the powerful Scipio family, and he also had many a bitter political battle with them over their pro-Carthaginian policy. Cato resented and feared the renascence of commercial prosperity at Carthage; thus, he advocated harsh treatment for the Carthaginians, and it is said that he ended every speech he made in the Senate with the recommendation that Carthage should be destroyed. Cato is also remembered as the father of Latin prose. His treatise on agriculture has survived, but his history of Rome, the *Origines,* is not extant. As an orator and writer Cato's style was not polished, although it had directness and force.

2. The younger Cato, great-grandson of Cato the Elder, conducted himself as though he were the great censor reborn. Unfortunately, Romans of the old school were out of fashion in the days of Julius Caesar, and the rugged determination of the younger Cato to conform to an outmoded policy did more harm than good. A strict constitutionalist, he opposed the assumption of extraordinary powers by Pompey and Caesar and supported Cicero in that statesman's demand for the execution of the fellow conspirators of Catiline. Cato never learned the value of compromise; if he had, he might have supported Cicero in the great plan for the "concord of the orders" and thus delayed the rise of Caesar. As it was, when the final conflict between Caesar and the Senate took place, Cato finally had to side with Pompey, whom he liked no better than Caesar. After Pompey's defeat at Pharsalus in 48 B.C., Cato became the leader of the senatorial forces in Africa, where he was defeated by Caesar at Thapsus in 46

B.C. and besieged in Utica. There, he recognized the inevitable and committed suicide. T. B. J.

CATROUX, GEORGES [ka'tru'] (1879-   ), French soldier, was born at Limoges, Jan. 29, 1879. He attended the military academies at La Flèsche and Saint Cyr. In 1899 he entered the mounted company of the French Foreign Legion; and except for the years 1903-1905, spent in Indochina, Catroux served in North Africa until World War I. He was taken prisoner by the Germans in 1916, and in 1918, after his release, he became a military attaché at Constantinople. In 1939-1940 he was governor general of Indochina and became a five-star general. After the fall of France, he joined General de Gaulle's Free French forces; he was appointed a member of the French Council of Imperial Independence and delegated general plenipotentiary and commander in chief of Free French forces in the Levant, a position he held from 1941 to 1943. During 1943 and 1944 Catroux was made governor general of Algeria and commissioner for co-ordination of Moslem affairs. He served as French ambassador to the Soviet Union from 1945 to 1948. Among his many decorations is the Grand Cross of the Legion of Honor. D. R.

CATS, JACOB [ka'ts] (1577-1660), Dutch poet, was born in Zeeland on Nov. 10, 1577. He studied at Leyden and Orleans, began to practice law at Middleburg, and was called to a high official position at The Hague.

Cats was essentially a didactic poet. Contrary to the practice of most of the other poets of his time, he used the popular language, and this attracted to him a large audience unable to understand the refined writings of his literary colleagues. The most popular of his works are devoted to the joys of rural life, *Ouderdom en Buyten-leven* (1655), and to the blessings and troubles of marriage, *Houwelyck* (1625). A solid Calvinist, Cats pleased the rural population of Holland, who consulted his writings with as much fervor as they used their Bible. Although he was a verbose and often a careless writer, many of his verses sounded like proverbs and axioms and many have passed into the vernacular. At the end of his career his writing became surprisingly frank, as demonstrated in his autobiography, *Eighty-Two Years of My Life* (1734). He died on Sept. 12, 1660, at The Hague. J.-A. G.

CAT'S-CLAW, *Acacia greggi,* also known as Texas mimosa, a straggling shrub of the pea family found on dry lands from western Texas to California and Mexico. It grows from 4 to 15 ft. high, the branches armed with thick curved spines. The foliage is finely divided; the flowers are yellow in dense clusters, the pods long and contorted. This name is better applied to a deciduous vine, *Doxantha unguis-cati,* with yellow, short trumpet flowers, climbing 100 ft. into trees or on buildings. R. S. Ho.

CAT'S-EAR, *Hypochoeris radicata,* a perennial herb of the family Compositae with hairy leaves somewhat resembling a cat's ear. The slender stems, 12 in. or less, bear a rosette of basal leaves and long-stalked heads of bright yellow flowers, much like those of the dandelion. The plant, originally from Europe and Asia, is a troublesome lawn weed in North America, especially in California. R. S. Ho.

CAT'S EYE, the name applied to gems on the surface of which shifting bands of light seem to move when the stones are turned. This optical effect is called chatoyancy and is best observed in polished, rounded stones shaped like coffee beans. Cat's eye is frequently considered a synonym for the mineral chrysoberyl, but other minerals, such as quartz, tourmaline, scapolite, fibrolite, and diopside, may display chatoyancy. The effect is caused by the reflection of light from microscopic hollow channels arranged parallel to a given crystallographic axis in chrysoberyl. In certain varieties of the other minerals which also exhibit chatoyancy the effect is due to a closely knit fibrous structure like that of asbestos. Greenish yellow or honey-yellow are preferred colors of chrysoberyl cat's eye, although other less desirable shades of green and brown are found. A fine rare, honey-colored chrysoberyl cat's eye of average size commands a price comparable with the finest diamond or flawless emerald of similar size and weight. The superior hardness of the gem, 8.5 (Mohs' scale), makes this mineral a good wearing stone. The finest chrysoberyl cat's eyes are obtained from Ceylon. *See also* CHRYSOBERYL. A. E. A.

CATSKILL, the county seat of Greene Co. in eastern New York, is situated on the west bank of the Hudson River, 30 mi. south of Albany, in an area devoted to dairying, truck farming, and fruit raising. Catskill was founded about 1680 by the Dutch, under Derrick van Vechten, and incorporated in 1806. This residential and resort village is often referred to as the "gateway" to the Catskill Mountains. Transportation is supplied by the New York Central Railroad, and Rip Van Winkle Bridge connects with Hudson on the east bank of the river. Mushroom culture and the manufacture of cement, metalwork, dresses, and rayon underwear are the chief industries. The administration of the village government is in the hands of a mayor and council. Pop. 1950, 5,392.

CATSKILL MOUNTAINS, a highland region in southeastern New York State, situated mainly in Greene County but occupying adjoining sections of Albany, Schoharie, Delaware, and Ulster counties. The Hudson River valley forms the eastern boundary of the Catskills. These so-called mountains are actually a plateau surface that has been deeply dissected and eroded. The mountains are formed by almost horizontal beds of sandstone, shale, and limestone, and the more resistant areas remain as flat-topped mountains. The Catskills are not very high; the maximum elevation is Slide Mountain, 4,204 ft. above sea level.

In spite of their low elevations the Catskills are rather spectacular, inasmuch as the valley floors and the bases of the mountains are only a few hundred feet above sea level and there are many small, deep valleys. There is a steep descent to the Hudson River trough on the east. The Catskills are covered with thick forests, and 176,440 acres are in a New York State forest. The climate is cool and pleasant and there are many small streams and lakes for fishing and swimming. The area also provides a valuable water supply for New York City. In literature the region was made famous by Washington Irving in *Rip Van Winkle.* J. E. F.

CAT SQUIRREL. *See* CACOMISTLE.

CATT, CARRIE LANE CHAPMAN (1859-1947), American suffragist leader, was born Jan. 9, 1859, in Ripon, Wis., but when she was seven years old her family moved to a farm near Charles City, Iowa. She worked her way through Iowa State College, and was graduated in 1880. She studied law in a lawyer's office in Charles City, then left this position to accept the principalship of a Mason City, Iowa, high school, becoming superintendent of schools in 1883. She married Leo Chapman, a newspaper editor, in 1885, but he died a year later. In 1890 she became state organizer of the Iowa Woman Suffrage Association. She married George W. Catt in 1890 and soon afterwards in South Dakota participated in her first suffrage campaign. She was president of the National American Woman Suffrage Association (1900-1904 and 1915-1920), when the Nineteenth Amendment (equal suffrage) came into effect in 1920. She organized the International Woman Suffrage Alliance, was its president (1904-1923), and lectured in Europe for the movement. A zealous

CARRIE LANE CHAPMAN CATT

CULVER SERVICE

worker for peace, she served as chairman of the National Committee on the Cause and Cure of War (1925-1932). She died in New Rochelle, N. Y., Mar. 9, 1947.

CATTAIL, *Typha,* the only genus of the cattail family with about 10 species widely distributed in northern marshes of both hemispheres. They are hardy perennials with long flat leaves higher than the strong rounded stems, which bear terminal, dark brown, club-like spikes of minute flowers. The creeping root-stocks are rich in starch and a favorite food of muskrats, which usually abound in cattail swamps. The leaves are used for chair bottoms and mats and in Russia the young shoots are used as food. The dried fluffy seeds were used by the Indians in absorbent pads. Cattails are occasionally used as an aquatic ornamental. Two North American species are the common cattail, *T. latifolia,* and the narrow-leaved cattail, *T. angustifolia.* The narrow-leaved cattail grows 4 to 9 ft. high.   J. C. Wis.

CATTANEO, DANESE DI MICHELE [kɑttɑ'neo] (1509-1573), Italian sculptor, was born at Colonnata, near Carrara in 1509. He went to Rome where he studied under Jacopo Sansovino. He was captured three times during the sack of Rome in 1527, and then fled to Florence. Upon his return to Rome, about 1530, he accompanied his master to Venice where he carved the Apollo on the fountain in the Zecca, and St. Jerome, in San Salvatore. With his pupil, Gerolamo Campagna, he executed the tomb of Gian Fregoso in Sant' Anastasia, Verona. He also carved the bust on the tomb of Cardinal Pietro Bembo in Sant' Antonio, Padua. As a poet he wrote *Dell' amor di Marfisa,* 1562, which was much admired by Torquato Tasso. He died in Padua in 1573, leaving the reliefs for the Capella del Santo in Sant' Antonio to be finished by Campagna.   R. T.

CATTELL, JAMES McKEEN [kətɛ'l] (1860-1944), American psychologist, was born at Easton, Pa., May 25, 1860. A graduate of Lafayette College (1880), he took a Ph.D. at Leipzig in 1886 and later studied at Paris, Geneva, and Göttingen. For some time he was assistant to Professor Wilhelm Wundt at Leipzig. He held the position of lecturer at Cambridge University and Bryn Mawr College, as well as at the University of Pennsylvania, where as professor of psychology (1888-1891) he held the first chair of psychology in any university. In 1891 he accepted a call to Columbia University, where he was professor of experimental psychology (1891-1896); head of the department of anthropology (1896-1902); professor in the department of philosophy (1902-1905); and professor of psychology (1891-1917). Resigning in 1917, Cattell became first president of the Psychological Corporation. He investigated problems of human behavior, conducting research and writing reports on psychological measurements, education, scientific organization, and the various practical applications of psychological principles. He was president of the first American International Congress of Psychology; editor of many scientific publications, including the *Psychological Review, American Men of Science, Scientific Monthly,* and *Science,* and became a commander of the French Legion of Honor in 1937. Cattell died in Lancaster, Pa., Jan. 20, 1944. A. S. M.

CATTLE, domesticated bovines principally of two species, *Bos taurus* and *Bos indicus.* They are cud-chewing mammals (ruminants) with a four-compartment stomach, have split hoofs, are either naturally hornless or with nonshedding type of horns; and have no upper incisor or canine teeth. They have long contributed greatly to the welfare of mankind. Cattle furnish meat, milk and milk products, draft power, hides for leather, and numerous lesser materials.

History. Domesticated cattle are the descendants of wild species of the genus *Bos,* one of the largest genera of the family Bovidae. Both the ancestry of cattle and the time of their original domestication are obscure, and various writers on the subject differ in their interpretation of the existing information. Fossil remains of prehistoric wild cattle have been found only in Europe, Asia, and Africa. Numerous fossil remains of one important wild cattle species designated *Bos primigenius* have been found over a wide region in western Asia, northern Africa, and continental Europe. These cattle, being six or seven feet high at the shoulders, were much larger than present-day domesticated cattle. The first appearance of *Bos primigenius* was apparently in the Pleistocene Period, and some domestication by man of these cattle or a modified subspecies occurred in Neolithic times. Wild types apparently existed until the seventeenth century. These cattle were described in writings of Caesar and others, who referred to them as aurochs or uri. Another similarly distributed early species, *Bos longifrons,* is believed to be a remote ancestor of modern cattle. This type, commonly called Celtic Shorthorn, was much smaller than the urus. Fossil remains indicate that it was the most important European domesticated bovine of the Stone Age. However, certain authorities believe that these cattle were first domesticated in Asia and then were brought into Europe by Neolithic man in his migrations. Most modern breeds of cattle are believed to trace back to either the urus or the Celtic Shorthorn, or to both. The humped cattle of Asia and Africa, *Bos indicus* or zebu, are believed to be derived from native cattle of the East, with the banting or gayal the most probable ancestor.

Man, in early nomadic ages, probably hunted cattle much as he did other wild animals. Domestication followed as the need arose for a dependable supply of cattle near camps or settlements. The process of domestication must have been slow. For many centuries both domesticated and wild cattle served the needs of man, but with the former gradually increasing in importance. Cattle have played a prominent part throughout the process of civilization. In the early civilizations not only were they valued highly for work, but cattle in certain areas were held sacred. Also, cattle were commonly considered by man to be a symbol of wealth and well-being far above their actual utility value. They are mentioned prominently in the oldest written records of the Hindu and Hebrew peoples. Cattle or oxen for a long period were, and still are among many semicivilized peoples, a medium of exchange. As new areas of the world were settled, domesticated cattle were brought into them by settlers.

Wild cattle and the earliest domesticated cattle were used in a limited way for meat; but as man became dependent upon his own agricultural efforts, work was the most important benefit obtained from cattle, and for centuries the ox was the common draft animal. This is still true in many areas of the world.

Development of Breeds. For many centuries, cattle were raised with little systematic improvement by man, although they gradually became better adapted to the environment in which they were kept. Possibly the earliest attempt toward improving cattle through selection and breeding methods was by the Romans. However, the British, Dutch, French, and Swiss were most influential in producing the modern improved types of cattle. The British Isles and the Channel Islands, adjacent to continental Europe, were the areas in which the most noted improvement in cattle took place. The original ancestors of the cattle in these areas probably had the same or similar origins; but by the eighteenth century the cattle within each area were tending to become alike, especially in size and color, and different from cattle of other areas. Robert Bakewell of Leicestershire, England, started the most important era of livestock improvement. He began his work about 1760 and demonstrated that cattle and sheep could be markedly improved for a specific purpose through crossing, inbreeding, and selection for desired characteristics. His work attracted much interest and his methods were and are still followed widely by cattle breeders.

From the native cattle of various countries, or even the native cattle of a relatively small region, livestock farmers began to develop cattle of separate and distinct characteristics. This led to the origin of different breeds. A breed may be defined as a group of cattle having a common origin and possessing distinguishing characteristics not found in other cattle. Numerous breeds of cattle were developed and named in the British Isles, the Channel Islands, and adjacent continental Europe during the latter part of the eighteenth and the early part of the nineteenth centuries. Not only distinct breeds but also specialized types of cattle were developed during this period. For example, the breeders in certain areas of England and Scotland emphasized meat production rather than milk production. This situation gave rise to breeds of beef cattle. In other areas breeders stressed improvement of both meat production and milk production, developing breeds of cattle commonly referred to as dual-purpose. In the Channel Islands and adjacent continental Europe the major emphasis was on milk production. Most of the major dairy breeds originated in these areas.

To a lesser degree, cattle improvement was taking place at the same time in other areas of Europe, in Africa, and in Asia. Here, however, there was less progress in making cattle more useful to man. In most of these areas cattle still are used primarily for work, with milk and meat of much less importance. In comparison with the breeds developed in the areas mentioned previously, the breeds of cattle developed are less efficient for production of either meat or milk.

Since cattle were native only to western Asia, North Africa, and continental Europe, man is responsible for their introduction to all other parts of the world. The kind of cattle introduced originally in the various areas of the world was dependent largely upon the time of settlement and the race of people which migrated to these countries. This may be illustrated by the development of the cattle industry in the United States.

Introduction and Development in North America. The first cattle to reach the Western Hemisphere were brought by Christopher Columbus on his second voyage, made in 1493. These cattle, of Spanish stock, were used for work by the colonists on an island of the West Indies. Starting about 1521, the Spaniards introduced sizable numbers of cattle into Mexico and the southwestern range country. These cattle, called Spanish Longhorns, multiplied rapidly, especially in Mexico, the Rio Grande valley, and along the coastal plains. For a time, they became half wild; but starting from 1845, when Texas was admitted to the Union, cattle ranches were developed and the Spanish Longhorns served as foundation stock for the then-developing range cattle industry. Early settlers on the eastern coast of the United States also brought cattle with them, starting about 1624. These cattle were typical of the native cattle of the various areas from which the settlers came: mainly England but some from Holland. At first these cattle were used primarily for work, secondly for milk and butter production, and for meat only after the animals had passed their prime for work. However, as eastern areas favorable for cattle raising were settled and as cities were established, cattle raising for milk production and for slaughter became an important industry.

During the period from the first introduction of cattle by the Spaniards in the West and by the colonists in the East up to 1783, cattle increased greatly in numbers but improved relatively little in ability to produce milk or meat. During the century following 1783, however, many improved types and breeds of cattle were imported from the British Isles, Holland, and the Channel Islands. These importations established the present breeds of cattle in the United States, which country soon became a leader in cattle breeding and production. The early-maturing rapid-fattening beef animals and the high-producing dairy cattle of the twentieth century bear little resemblance to the cattle of the eighteenth century.

Distribution and Numbers. Cattle are raised wherever agriculture is possible, and are commonly recognized as the most important domesticated animal. There were roughly 600,000,000 head of cattle in the world at the middle of the twentieth century. Some of the leading countries in cattle numbers are India, United States, Brazil, Russia, Argentina, China, Germany, France, Australia, Canada, Mexico, Great Britain, and Union of South Africa. Certain other countries have larger cattle populations in relationship to land area than some of the countries mentioned.

United States. There were about 94,000,000 cattle in the United States on Jan. 1, 1958. The major breeds of beef cattle were Hereford, Aberdeen-Angus, Shorthorn, Polled Hereford, and Polled Shorthorns. The major breeds of dairy cattle were Holstein-Friesian, Guernsey, Jersey, Brown Swiss, and Ayrshire. The major breeds of dual-purpose cattle were Milking Shorthorn, Red Polled, and Devon.

BEEF CATTLE

Beef cattle are a specialized type of cattle raised for meat

AMERICAN SHORTHORN BREEDERS' ASSOCIATION

SHORTHORN COW

AMERICAN BRAHMAN BREEDERS' ASSOCIATION

BRAHMAN BULL

AMERICAN ANGUS ASSOCIATION

BLACK ANGUS BULL

AMERICAN HEREFORD ASSOCIATION

HEREFORD BULL

production. Modern beef-type cattle are the result of many years of constructive breeding aimed at the development of an animal that will convert pasture, hays, silages, other roughages, and grain with maximum efficiency into high-quality beef for human consumption. In the beef cattle breeds, milk production has been stressed only to ensure an ample amount for the proper rearing of the calves.

Beef, the flesh of the cattle, was probably utilized to some extent by man even before cattle had been domesticated. Domesticated cattle were first used primarily for work, with meat considered a by-product. It is not known when cattle were first raised especially for meat. The first important development of cattle for meat purposes occurred in Great Britain, starting in 1707. Farmers of Scotland had surplus cattle which they exported to England. The English quickly acquired a taste for good-quality beef, and to them is given credit for providing the incentive for breeding beef-type cattle. Other contributing factors of the period were the replacement of oxen by horses for work, the new knowledge of methods of livestock improvement, and more intensive crop production. The British developed several leading breeds of beef cattle, and these breeds were later extremely important in starting beef cattle production in other countries. These British breeds are still the major beef breeds

in the most important beef-producing countries of the world.

In general, beef production is most important in countries, or areas within countries, having large amounts of grazing lands, relatively light population, and soil or climatic conditions not suited to intensive types of agriculture. Some of the well-recognized beef-producing countries of the world are the United States, Argentina, Uruguay, Australia, New Zealand, Canada, South Africa, and Mexico. These countries generally export beef in chilled, frozen, cured, or canned form. Great Britain is the most important buyer.

PRODUCTION METHODS IN THE UNITED STATES

Beef production in the United States is more specialized than in most other countries. Also, production methods differ widely between areas and between farms in the same area, depending largely upon the feeds available. Producers may engage in only one phase of production, such as producing calves, growing young stock, or fattening for slaughter. Under usual conditions, beef herds are grazed on pasture as much of the year as possible. This period varies from a minimum of about five months in some sections to a full year in others. A wide variety of pastures, both native and seeded, are used, depending upon the area. Feeds used to supplement pastures or ranges during dormant or other periods of scanty feed include hays, silages, straw, stover, various protein-rich supplements, meadow or grain field aftermath, and various specially seeded forage crops. Mature beef cows are fed grain or other expensive feeds sparingly in order to keep down the cost of producing the calves. Those that are winter fed in barns or sheds generally receive mostly hay, silage, and other roughages.

Beef calves are allowed to remain with their mothers under usual conditions until they are weaned at about six to eight months of age. Male calves not intended for breeding use are castrated, usually before weaning time, since steers are more suitable for production of beef. Heifers that are fed for slaughter are seldom spayed. At weaning time the calves may be sold as feeders, for slaughter, or for breeding purposes. If not sold, they may be fed a growing ration consisting largely or entirely of roughages, depending upon feeds available. A limited amount of grain is fed if more rapid growth and development is desired. Calves may also be fed a fattening ration from weaning time until they are ready for market, to produce what is popularly called baby beef. Calves fed liberally on grain, but with limited roughage, will make high-class beef under typical feeding conditions of six to eight months. Calves that are not fattened but fed for growth may eventually be marketed off pasture as grass-fattened cattle; or, since beef of greater value results if cattle are fed some grain prior to slaughter, many yearling and older cattle are fed grain or fattening rations prior to marketing, especially in grain-producing areas. Corn, barley, grain sorghum and oats are the chief grains used. There has been a noticeable trend to market cattle at relatively young ages and at light weight. Steers or heifers under three years and weighing from 700 to 1,100 lb. best suit most consumer demands and make up the bulk of the high-quality beef supply of the country. This market trend has had great influence in establishing the preferred type in breeding animals, as emphasis has been toward developing cattle that have early maturity, or ability to fatten rapidly at young ages and light weights.

MAIN PRODUCING AREAS

The United States may be divided into four main areas on the basis of the feeds available for beef cattle and the beef production methods. These areas are the range area, the corn belt, the Appalachian and Great Lakes area, and the cotton belt. In other parts of the country, the raising of cattle is not a major enterprise or is concentrated in circumscribed areas.

Range Area. The range area consists roughly of the low-rainfall region lying west of the 90th meridian, which cuts through western Wisconsin and Illinois, as far as the foothills of the Rocky Mountains on the west. This is one of the most important beef-producing areas in the United States, with beef-cattle raising a major enterprise on most ranches. Much of the land is unsuited to cultivation because of rough topography, shallow soil, and low rainfall. Also, large areas are still under control of governmental agencies rather than private ownership. These conditions permit extensive grazing which is suited to beef production or sheep production but not to more intensive types of agriculture. Beef cattle herds are large. In general, the cattle are grazed throughout the year, with only a minimum of other feeds such as hay, silage, or protein-rich supplement provided as needed to supplement the winter range. Under these conditions ranchers sell most of their young market stock when they are calves, yearlings, or two-year-olds as feeder cattle suitable for further growing and fattening or directly for slaughter. In areas of fertile valleys or irrigated sections, grains are produced and cattle

fattening is practiced. Most of the beef cattle of the area are cattle of one of the major breeds, notably Hereford.

Corn Belt. The corn belt lies in the central part of the United States, east of the range area. With level fertile land and favorable rainfall and climate, the area is highly suitable for crop production. Much of the land is used for growing corn and other grains, but pastures and hay crops are very important. Many feeder cattle from the western range are brought to the corn belt for fattening entirely on grain and harvested roughages or with a relatively limited amount of grazing. The feeder cattle may be fed from three months to a year before being marketed for slaughter. The length of time they are fed depends upon the age and size of the cattle at the start of the feeding period, and upon the feed supply on the individual farm. Since corn grain is usually fed liberally, high-quality beef results. This area is the most important source of this kind of beef in the United States.

While the feeding of purchased feeder cattle has a dominant place in the corn-belt beef industry, other types of production are important. Many breeding herds of strictly beef-type cattle are found, especially on farms with considerable pasture. Although individual herds average smaller in size than in the range area, the total number of locally produced beef cattle is large. Also, many farmers of the area operate herds which are essentially dual-purpose in nature, with both beef and milk produced for market.

Appalachian and Great Lakes Area. The Appalachian and Great Lakes area extends from the western Great Lakes into Pennsylvania and Virginia. It has rainfall and climate favorable for production of feed crops, especially pasture and hays; but the land varies widely because of uneven topography, variable soil productivity, and relatively short growing seasons. In the heavily populated sections with their correspondingly high land values, intensive types of agriculture rather than beef production have been favored since about the beginning of the twentieth century. The number of beef cattle declined appreciably from 1920 until World War II. Since then there has been a considerable increase. All types of beef production are carried on. However, except in several well-defined grain and grass fattening regions, the trend has been toward increasing the number of herds rather than the feeding of shipped-in cattle. Small herds of beef cattle are found on many farms where the major enterprise, such as poultry raising or vegetable growing, may be more intensive.

Cotton Belt. Although the cotton belt, corresponding to the cotton-growing region in the Southeast, is traditionally a cash-crop area, its long growing season makes it well adapted to the raising of beef cattle. The industry has been slow to develop in this area. The cattle tick *Margaropus (Boophilus) annulatus,* an insect parasite that carries a protozoan (*Babesia bigemina*) causing tick fever or Texas fever in cattle, was not brought under control until the 1920's. Moreover, the early cattle of the area were of poor beef quality, and the industry was handicapped by poor feeding and management practices. Since the 1920's, there has been much more diversified farming, with livestock as a means of soil conservation, rather than the raising of a single cash crop such as cotton. In general, southern beef cattle are maintained and fattened on pasture, with a minimum of grain, or are fattened in relatively large feeding yards. Unlike the range area, where the length of grazing is similar, the cotton belt does not specialize in the production of feeder cattle.

BREEDS IN THE UNITED STATES

A high percentage of the beef cattle in the United States are grade cattle (that is, of mixed blood) that have the definite characteristics of one of the beef breeds. The beef breeds of most interest are Shorthorn, Polled Shorthorn, Hereford, Polled Hereford, Aberdeen-Angus, Brahman, Santa Gertrudis and Galloway.

Shorthorn. The Shorthorn breed had its origin in northeastern England, especially in York and Durham counties; its former name, "Teeswater cattle," was derived from the Tees River in the area. The foundation of the breed was the local native stock, which in earlier times may have been crossed with a Dutch dairy type. The herdbook established in 1822 for the recording of Shorthorns was the first for any breed of cattle. Early English breeders developed it for both meat and milk production. Later, certain breeders, especially in Scotland, stressed beef-producing qualities rather than milk, starting a true beef breed. Others improved milk production, originating the Milking Shorthorn breed.

Shorthorns were first imported from England to the United States in 1783. During the period of 1817 to 1860, Shorthorns were imported in sizable numbers and became the most numerous cattle at that time in the eastern United States. The Scottish beef Shorthorns became popular between 1880 and 1900, and modern beef-type Shorthorns trace mostly to Scottish breeding rather than to the cattle of England. The modern Shorthorn may be red, white, red and white, or roan in color. Shorthorn cattle are widely esteemed for their size, thickness of fleshing, fast rate of growth, and milking qualities. Cattle of this breed are found in all parts of the country but are most numerous in the central and corn belt states. The breed ranked third among the beef breeds in numbers of cattle registered in 1957.

Polled Shorthorn. Polled Shorthorns are a strain of Shorthorns that are naturally hornless. The first real attempt to breed naturally hornless purebred Shorthorn cattle started about 1890. The first registry association was the American Polled Durham Breeders Association. This organization at first permitted the registration of grade cattle that were hornless and had a high percentage of Shorthorn blood. The cattle were called Polled Durhams until 1919, when the name was changed to Polled Shorthorn. The original association was disbanded in 1923, and the registration since then has been in the *American Shorthorn Herd Book*. Only cattle having parents previously registered as purebred Shorthorns in the herd book are eligible for registration. Polled Shorthorns are well-established.

Hereford. The Hereford had its origin in Herefordshire, England, with the most marked development occurring in the years following 1750. The early improvers of the breed wanted cattle of good size and ruggedness for work and for meat, but gave little special regard to milk production. The early cattle had white faces, a characteristic color that soon marked the breed. The English herdbook was established in 1846.

The earliest well-known importation of Herefords to the United States was in 1817. Other importations in small numbers followed, and after about 1880 the breed became well established. Herefords became popular in all sections of the country but especially in the range area. In numbers, the Hereford ranged as the leading beef breed in the United States in 1957. Herefords have red bodies with white on the head, the neck, the underparts of the body, the legs, and the switch of the tail. The breed is noted especially for its good size, ruggedness, and grazing ability.

Polled Hereford. Polled Herefords are naturally hornless Herefords which were derived from hornless sports from the horned Hereford breed. The breed or strain was started in 1901 by Warren Gammon of Des Moines, Iowa, when he founded a small herd of polled cattle of pure Hereford breeding. From this small beginning Polled Herefords increased rapidly in numbers. Since 1907, Polled Herefords have been registered in the *American Hereford Record* and in the *American Polled Hereford Record*. Such cattle are called double-standard to distinguish them from the earlier single-standard cattle, largely of Hereford origin but not eligible for registration in the *American Hereford Record*. Polled Hereford breeders have made liberal use of horned Herefords in their breeding programs by having one of the animals in a mating polled, usually the sire. Both horned and polled calves are produced in most herds. The hornless calves are eligible for double-standard registration, (in either or both the *American Hereford Record* or the *American Polled Hereford Record*) while the horned calves are usually registered only in the *American Hereford Record*. Recently, horned calves with polled ancestry have been recorded as such in the *American Polled Hereford Record*.

Aberdeen-Angus. The Aberdeen-Angus breed originated in northeastern Scotland, in the Brechin district of Forfarshire and the Buchan district of Aberdeenshire. Two similar early strains of the area were combined, the "Angus doddies" and the "Buchan humlies." The true development of the breed started prior to 1800, but it was from this date to about 1875 that it became firmly established. The Scottish herdbook for the breed appeared in 1879.

The first importation of Aberdeen-Angus into the United States was in 1873, or 90 years after Shorthorns and 56 years after Herefords had been introduced. The breed soon had its supporters, and the American Aberdeen-Angus Breeders Association was formed in 1883. In 1957 this breed ranked second only to Herefords in numbers of purebred cattle registered. Aberdeen-Angus are naturally hornless and are solid black in color, except that some white is permissible on the underline behind the navel. They are especially noted for early maturity, good fleshing qualities, and general carcass qualities. The breed is widely distributed throughout the United States.

Galloway. The Galloway breed originated in southwestern Scotland, and the foundation stock was probably related to that of the Aberdeen-Angus. The Galloway was first imported into the United States in 1870. Galloway cattle are rather small in size, black in color, polled, and have long, thick hair coats. The breed has not been important in the United States.

Brahman. Brahman cattle, also called Brahma, Zebu, or Indian cattle, include the numerous breeds of humped cattle of India. While not of true beef type, they have been brought into the southern part of the United States because of their ability to withstand heat, various insect pests, and generally unfavorable range conditions. Their chief use in the United States has been in crossing with the British breeds to which they are inferior in beef conformation. However, the breed is used in the Coastal plains area for the production of heavy milk-fattened calves for slaughter.

Santa Gertrudis. This American breed with valuable traits was developed by Robert J. Kleberg, Jr., at the King Ranch, Kingsville, Texas, by crossing the Brahman with the Shorthorn. The first crossbreeding started about 1910 and was carried out extensively after 1920. These cattle are red or cherry in color, and are large and vigorous. The preferred breeding is three-eighths Brahman and five-eighths Shorthorn. This combination seems to give the proper size and carcass qualities along with resistance to heat and insect pests. The typical hump of the Brahman is practically eliminated in this cross.

Crosses of the Brahman with the Aberdeen-Angus and the Hereford breeds have also been made for the same purposes, but the resulting crossbreeds are not so well known.

Numbers in the United States. The total number of beef cattle in the United States on Jan. 1, 1958, was estimated to be about 60,300,000 head. Of this number there were about 24,000,000 cows two years old and over; 6,100,000 heifers one year old and under two years old; 9,500,000 steers

States in 1955 was 35,361,000, of which 23,462,000 were two or more years old (Agricultural Statistics 1956). This is a decrease in total population of 3,732,000 during the preceding ten years.

BREEDS AND CONFORMATION

Holstein-Friesian. The Holstein-Friesian breed originated in the Netherlands, mainly in North Holland and Fries-

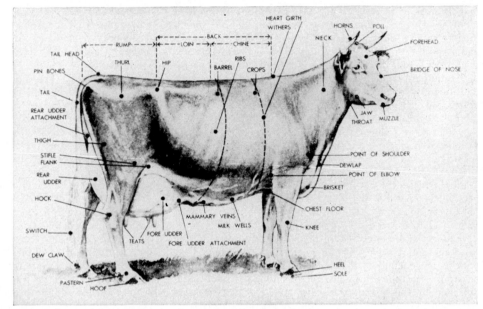

PARTS OF A DAIRY COW

one year old and older; 18,700,000 calves; and about 1,200,000 bulls. Numbers of beef cattle have increased and decreased in fairly regular cycles of about fourteen years in length, with approximately seven years of expansion. A recent peak in numbers occurred in 1956. During the decades following 1920, the human population in the United States increased relative to numbers of beef cattle. J. I. M.

DAIRY CATTLE

Dairy cattle, bred primarily for milk production, originated in Europe. Distinct breeds were developed in different countries and often were named for these countries or their provinces. Some breeds date back several hundred years, whereas others were developed as recently as the eighteenth century.

Development in the United States. Dairy cattle were introduced into the United States by the early settlers, with importations becoming more numerous during the nineteenth century. About 1850, importers and early breeders began keeping records of their animals and mated them only with others of the same breed. In this way different breeds of dairy cattle were established in the United States. Most descend from five major breeds originating in as many different countries. Some have been kept pure and are called purebred or registered cattle. Records of these animals are maintained by associations organized to preserve and promote the different breeds. According to the census of 1930, there were 1,280,161 registered dairy animals in the United States, or approximately 4 per cent of the total dairy cattle population. The remainder are classed as grades or scrubs. The grades resemble registered animals, but they have not been recorded or they carry the mixed blood of two or more breeds. This group comprises a large portion of American dairy cattle. The term "scrub" is applied to those animals of an inferior quality. The total dairy cattle population of the United

land, and in Oldenburg, Germany, where black-and-white piebald cattle predominated. Importations which formed the nucleus of the breed in the United States were made from 1850 to 1886. The color of Holstein-Friesian cattle makes them easily recognizable. They must be black and white. Some animals are nearly white, having only a few small black spots. Others are nearly black, but must have white under the body, on lower portions of the legs, and a white switch (long hairs at the tip of the tail). The association bars from registration all animals with one or more of the following color characteristics: (1) solid black; (2) solid white; (3) black in switch; (4) solid black belly; (5) one or more legs encircled with black touching the hoof; (6) black on one or more legs beginning at the hoof and extending to or above the knee or hock; (7) black and white intermixed to give grayish appearance; (8) color other than distinct black and white. Holstein-Friesian cattle have other distinctive characteristics. They are the largest of the dairy breeds; a few cows have weighed over 2,000 lb. and bulls over 3,000 lb. The desired weight for the breed, according to the Purebred Dairy Cattle score card, is 1,500 lb. for females and 2,000 lb. for males. Holstein-Friesians are docile. Because of their size, they consume large quantities of roughage, but they do not equal some breeds in grazing qualities. In quantity of milk production they rank first, but the percentage of fat content is lowest. The milk is generally white and the fat globules small.

Jersey. The native home of Jersey cattle is the island of Jersey, in the English Channel. It is assumed that this breed originated from cattle transported to Jersey from Brittany and Normandy. It is not known how long the breed has been kept pure, but as early as 1789 the island legislature passed an act prohibiting the importation of breeding stock. The first Jerseys to be registered in the United States were imported in 1850. From then through Mar. 31, 1948, according to a report from the American Jersey Cattle Club, 4,696 males and 22,660 females were imported from the island. The characteristic color of the Jersey is some shade of fawn as tan, or red, brown, gray, mulberry, or black. They may be all fawn, which is known as solid color, or they may be a broken color, which is fawn and white. Fawn-colored Jerseys are generally darker in the face, along the upper part of the body, and on the foreparts of the legs, shading to a lighter fawn on the lower portions of the body and the rear of the legs. They may have either a black or white switch or a mixture of the two. The desired weight for Jerseys, according to the score card, is 1,100 lb. for females and 1,500 lb. for males. Jerseys are alert, but very tractable if properly handled. They are good grazers and are popular in the southern United States because they withstand the heat. The quantity of milk produced is the lowest of the dairy breeds, but it has the highest fat percentage and is known as the richest milk. The fat globules in the milk are large and the color is a yellowish white. Because of the large fat globules, the cream rises rapidly and a distinct cream line is formed.

Guernsey. Guernsey cattle were developed on three islands: Alderney, Guernsey, and Sark, in the English Channel. They, as well as the Jersey, were often called Alderney, but Guernsey was adopted as the breed name in the United States. They are reddish or golden fawn and white in color. A majority of the animals are predominantly fawn, with a small amount of white. The pigment around the eye and the muzzle is generally flesh-colored or pinkish, but may be black. Females should weigh 1,100 lb. and males 1,700 lb., as indicated by the official score card. In general, Guernseys are docile. They are relatively good grazers, but hardly comparable to Jerseys. They produce a slightly greater quantity of milk than Jerseys, but the butterfat content is correspondingly lower. Guernsey milk is yellower than that from other breeds. The fat globules are larger, the cream rises rapidly, and the cream line is very distinct.

Ayrshire. The Shire of Ayr in Scotland is the native home of Ayrshire cattle. This breed was developed from cattle in England and Scotland during the eighteenth century; therefore the breed is not so old as the Holstein-Friesian, Jersey, and Guernsey. It is, however, the leading dairy breed in Scotland. Ayrshires were imported to Canada from Scotland during the nineteenth century, but relatively few came directly to the United States before 1900. The characteristic color is red and white, with the red color varying from a light or brownish shade to a very dark mahogany. During the first quarter of the twentieth century the preference was for nearly all-white animals, but the second quarter saw a growing demand for a higher proportion of red color. This breed is smaller in size than the Holstein-Friesian and larger than the Guernsey. The desired weight, according to the score card, is 1,150 lb. for females and 1,800 lb. for males. In disposition Ayrshires are alert, with a tendency toward nervousness in some strains. They are excellent grazers. The average milk production and the butterfat content of the milk lie between those of the Holstein-Friesian and the Guernseys. The milk is white and the fat globules are relatively small.

Brown Swiss. Brown Swiss are native to Switzerland and primarily to the canton of Schwyz, where they received the name of Braunvieh or Schwyz. They are a very old breed and were developed as beasts of burden as well as producers of milk and meat. Most of the Brown Swiss importations into the United States were made between 1869 and 1906. For many years the Brown Swiss was not considered a dairy breed in the United States because of its meat-producing

characteristics. It was improved in dairy qualities during the early part of the twentieth century, however, and then became recognized as one of the five main dairy breeds. As the name indicates, this breed is brown in color, the shade varying from light to dark seal. Most animals are a solid color, but a few may show some white. The darker animals usually have lighter hair around the muzzle, on the ears, and along the back. In size the Brown Swiss ranks next to the Holstein-Friesian; females are expected to weigh 1,400 lb. and males 1,900 lb. It is a very docile breed, sometimes almost sluggish. The cattle are good feeders and fair grazers. In quantity of milk produced, butterfat content, color of the milk, and fat-globule size, they are comparable to the Ayrshire.

Minor Breeds. The most important minor breeds in the United States are Devon, Dutch Belted, Milking Shorthorn, and the Red Polled.

Conformation. Heads of the Holstein-Friesian, Ayrshire, and Brown Swiss are relatively long and narrow, while those of the Guernsey and Jersey are shorter and broader. The horns of the Holstein-Friesian, Guernsey, Jersey, and Brown Swiss are medium in size and generally curve forward. The Ayrshire has the largest horns of the five breeds; they may curve forward or upward when growing naturally, but they are often trained to a graceful curve upward with the tips turned slightly backward.

Except for size and certain head and horn characteristics, cattle of the main dairy breeds are comparable in conformation. This accepted conformation is closely correlated with high milk and butterfat production, and therefore is sought by most breeders. The head should show strength, but at the same time indicate quality and temperament. Strength is indicated by a strong muzzle and jaw and a large nostril, while quality is expressed by clean-cut bones of the face and refined horns. Bright, prominent eyes indicate alertness. The neck should be long and slender. Body conformation should be angular and is obtained by having width at the shoulder points, refinement at the wither, with good width through the hips and rump. The ribs should be wide and long, with good spacing between them to indicate an open conformation. The loin should be broad, with the ribs well sprung to give plenty of room for feeding capacity and constitution. The pelvic region should be long and level, with refinement indicated about the tail and pin bones. It is necessary to have straight, strong legs and sound feet to withstand strain over a period of years. The mammary system or udder should be approximately the same length as the rump and should be firmly attached to the body both fore and rear. Quality of udder is important because it indicates glandular tissue for secretion and storage of milk.

Improvement. Groups of breeders interested in promoting the different breeds organized associations for the purpose of maintaining records of their animals and developing programs to improve them. Each established publications for the purpose of making these records available and useful in breed improvement. The names, dates of organizing, and locations in 1958 of the five leading American breed associations are: Holstein-Friesian Association of America, 1885, Brattleboro, Vt.; American Jersey Cattle Club, 1868, Columbus, Ohio; American Guernsey Cattle Club, 1877, Peterborough, N. H.; Ayrshire Breeders' Association, 1875, Brandon, Vt.; and Brown Swiss Cattle Breeders' Association of America, 1880, Beloit, Wis. Representatives of these associations formed the Purebred Dairy Cattle Association in 1940 to develop uniformity in the breed programs and to further the improvement of all dairy cattle in the United States.

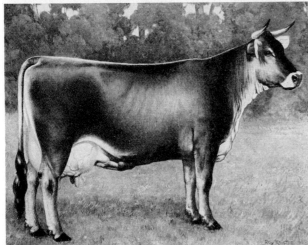

DAIRY CATTLE

(Above) *Guernsey Cow*

GUERNSEY BREEDERS' JOURNAL

(Above left) *Holstein Cow*

HOLSTEIN-FRIESIAN ASSOCIATION OF AMERICA

(Left) *Brown Swiss Cow*

THE BROWN SWISS CATTLE BREEDERS' ASSOCIATION

(Below left) *Jersey Cow*

AMERICAN JERSEY CATTLE CLUB

(Below) *Ayrshire Cow*

AYRSHIRE BREEDERS' ASSOCIATION

PRODUCTION AND CLASSIFICATION

Individual Records. As breeders began to improve their dairy cattle, it became necessary to have some measurement of production. The common system used before 1894 was to weigh the milk and to determine the butter produced by churning. This system was introduced by the Dutch-Friesian Association and later adopted by the Holstein-Friesian Association of America. Such records were called Advanced Register records, and the association established the *Advanced Register Year Book* ("Bluebook") for the purpose of publishing them. In 1894 the Babcock test was accepted by the Holstein-Friesian Association as a method of determining the butterfat content of milk, and became the standard system upon which the published records were based. This became commonly known as official testing. The American Jersey Cattle Club used the churn method of determining butter production of Jersey cows until 1903, when they adopted the Babcock test. Their production records were termed Register of Merit. The American Guernsey Cattle Club and the Ayrshire Breeders' Association, which adopted the system in 1901 and 1902 respectively, use the term "Advanced Register" for their records. This system of production testing was adopted in 1911 by the Brown Swiss Cattle Breeders' Association and called the Register of Production.

Herd Records. The breed associations established their testing for the purpose of determining the production of individual cows for such periods of time as 7, 305, or 365 days. These records were selective and did not give all the information needed by breeders to improve their herds properly. It became a recognized need to have complete lactation production records for every cow in the herd and where possible, to obtain cumulative lifetime records. Such a program of testing was adopted by the Ayrshire Breeders' Association in 1925. This herd test system, officially known as the Herd Improvement Registry or Herd Test, was adopted by the Holstein-Friesian, Jersey, Guernsey, and Brown Swiss associations in 1927, 1928, 1930, and 1932 respectively.

Testing of Grade Cattle. These record systems were applied only to registered cows. It was deemed equally important that owners of grade cattle have an opportunity to secure production records for their herds. To meet this need, a system of co-operative testing, known as Cow Testing Associations, was started in 1905. The name was later changed to Dairy Herd Improvement Associations (D.H.I.A.). The direction of this testing program became an activity of the United States Department of Agriculture, working with the agricultural extension services in the various states. On Jan. 1, 1956, there were 2,266 associations operating with 1,406,306 cows on test.

Computation of Records. Most cows are milked twice daily, but some, mostly registered animals, are milked three or four times daily. The increased number of milkings increases the yearly production, on an average, by approximately 20 to 25 per cent. The producing capacity of cows varies with age, generally increasing until they are 6 to 7 years old, and then gradually decreasing with the advance in years. Because of these variations, conversion factors have been determined whereby production records can be computed to a length of 305 days on a twice-per-day milking basis (2x) and to an age of maximum capacity commonly called mature equivalent (M.E.). Such factors have been published by the breed associations, the Department of Agriculture, and several investigators. Average production records for all cows in the United States, those in D.H.I.A., and the different breeds are given in the accompanying table. The average for all cows is approximately one-half of that for the different breeds, and indicates the possibility for improvement. The breed averages vary slightly because the figures furnished by the associations were not all computed on the same basis. As a rule, the five breeds should be considered comparable in their butterfat-producing ability.

MILK AND BUTTERFAT PRODUCTION IN THE UNITED STATES

Group	Number of Records	Length of Records	Lb. Milk	% Fat	Lb. Fat
All cows[1]	21,232,000	365 days or less	5,812	3.86	224
D.H.I.A[2]	1,333,866	365 days or less	9,502	3.90	375
Ayrshire[3]	5,976	305 days M.E. 2X	10,478	4.12	432
Brown Swiss[4] .	—	305 days actual 2X	9,834	4.11	404
Guernsey[5]	76,621	305 days M.E. 2X	8,839	4.90	430
Holstein-Friesian[6] . . .	63,426	305 days M.E. 2X	13,187	3.69	486
Jersey[7]	26,472	305 days actual 2X	7,558	5.33	403

[1] Agricultural Census 1955.
[2] Agricultural Statistics 1956.
[3] Ayrshire Breeders' Association 1957.
[4] Brown-Swiss Cattle Breeders' Association Annual Report 1957. Average of H.I.R. class records reported.
[5] American Guernsey Cattle Club.
[6] Holstein-Friesian Association Annual Report 1957.
[7] American Jersey Cattle Club Annual Report 1958-59.

Type has been considered in the improvement of dairy cattle. Most animals are selected upon this basis because production records are not available for them. A type classification program was started by the Holstein-Friesian Association of America in 1929. Similar programs were adopted by the other four breed associations: Jersey, 1932; Ayrshire, 1941; Brown Swiss, 1942; Guernsey, 1946.

MANAGEMENT AND FEEDING

Reproduction. Puberty occurs at 8 to 12 months of age, although it may be earlier or later. This may be influenced by environmental factors, especially feeding. Males are considered of serviceable age when one year old. The accepted breeding age for females is 15 to 21 months. Dairy cattle are polyoestrous; they breed at any time of the year. Oestrus (heat) lasts from 12 to 24 hours, and the oestrus cycle is approximately 21 days. The gestation period averages 283 days, with a range from 265 to 300 days. Parturition before 265 days of pregnancy should be considered premature or an abortion. The young are generally produced as singles, but twins appear on an average of once in 49 times. Triplets and quadruplets are rare. About 90 per cent of the females born twin to males will not breed and are called freemartins. The desirable age for heifers to freshen is from 24 to 30 months. The normal length of the lactation period is 10 months, although it may be 12 months or even more. Cows should be given a rest or dry period of 2 months and thus they produce their young about once a year. Some animals reach the age of 20 years or more, but many are disposed of when relatively young because of inefficient production, injury, or disease. This results in less than 5 years as the average useful age of dairy cattle.

Improvement. The average yearly milk production of dairy cows in the United States, according to census reports, has increased from 3,646 lb. in 1899 to 5,812 lb. in 1955. This has been due in part to improved practices of feeding and management and in part to improvement through better breeding. The registration and production record systems established by the breed associations during the last half of the nineteenth century formed a basis for selection and improved breeding and the science of genetics has made possible the development of modern systems of breeding.

Bulls. A means of rating the transmitting ability of bulls, known as bull indexes, was developed as a result of research undertaken by a number of men from 1915 to 1930. To compute this index they compared the average production of the daughters of a bull with that of their dams. If there was a decrease, that amount was subtracted from the daughters' production; while if an increase, it was added. Methods of calculating these indexes have been improved by more recent research, and they came into quite general use after 1935. This information makes possible the selection of sires with high production indexes for more general service. The term "proved sire" has been used to designate those bulls with enough tested daughters from tested dams to justify a comparison between the producing ability of the two groups. Five pairs of unselected daughter-dam comparisons have been considered sufficient for a proving. The Department of Agriculture brought the proved-sire program into general use in 1935, when it began publishing lists of all sires proved in the D.H.I.A. This Proved-Sire Program has been of immeasurable value in the selection of good, proved sires.

Artificial Insemination. Artificial insemination of dairy cattle in the United States was started in New Jersey in March 1938. This is a process whereby the semen is collected from a herd sire by use of an artificial vagina. During the early years, the semen was diluted with a mixture of egg yolk and citrate. This mixture stored at a temperature of 38° F. was used to inseminate cows. The best conception rates were obtained with diluted semen up to four days of age. Research developments have brought about improved methods of diluting and storing semen which lengthen the period of usefulness. Under modern methods, the useful period for fresh or liquid semen has been extended to one week. The most noticeable progress has been made through the discovery of a method used to freeze the diluted semen. The freezing and holding temperature must be —110° F. or lower. Through this process, semen has been stored and used successfully after one year. This has made possible the acquiring of several thousand offspring from each of the most valuable sires. In the United States during 1957 there were 6,055,301 cows in 946,500 herds being serviced by 2,671 herd sires through the use of artificial insemination.

Feeding. *Digestive Process.* Dairy cattle are ruminants, or cud-chewing animals. Their stomachs are divided into four compartments, namely, the rumen, reticulum, omasum, and abomasum. A mature dairy cow may have a capacity of 250 qt. or more in the four compartments. Therefore, large amounts of roughage, such as hay and silage, can be consumed. While the animal is eating, the feed is chewed only enough to be swallowed, and passes to the rumen. By regular action of the muscular walls of the rumen and reticulum, the food is moistened and mixed. Between periods of eating, the animal ruminates or "chews its cud." In this process, food is passed from the rumen and reticulum to the mouth, where it is thoroughly chewed and again swallowed. It is returned to the rumen, and from there passes through the other three compartments. The last compartment, or abomasum, empties into the small intestine, and it in turn empties into the large intestine. The small intestine is about 130 ft. long in mature cattle, while the large one is considerably shorter. Digestion and absorption take place in the intestine.

Requirements. Mature cows consume from 20 to 30 lb. of hay per day as the sole roughage, or from 15 to 20 lb. of hay and 30 to 50 lb. of silage when both roughages are fed. Some cows have consumed at least 70 lb. of grass silage per day. This amount of roughage, if of good quality, is more than sufficient to maintain the body weight, and the excess will be stored as body fat or be converted into milk. During the major part of the lactation period a cow must receive, in addition to the roughage, some concentrated feed or grain. The rate of feeding, for maximum production, should be about 1 lb. of grain daily for every 3 to 4 lb. of 4 per cent butterfat milk produced. On good pasture, cows may consume from 100 to 150 lb. of grass per day. In this case, other roughages need not be consumed and the ratio of feed grain to milk may be more nearly 1 to 5.

Diseases. Tuberculosis, brucellosis, and mastitis have caused heavy losses of dairy cattle. There are many other less important diseases and ailments.

Tuberculosis. The most serious losses from tuberculosis were realized before a definite program of eradication was instituted. The use of tuberculin was discovered in 1890 as a test to detect the disease. This test was used by individual herd owners before 1917, when a country-wide campaign was started under the Accredited Herd Plan. This campaign was supported by state and federal appropriations; testing was done on an area basis. The program called for prompt disposal of reactors, adequate disinfection, and regulations governing the movement of cattle. As the infection in an area was reduced to less than 0.5 per cent, that area became accredited. The entire United States became an accredited area

in 1940, but testing must be continued to prevent possible spreading of the disease.

Brucellosis. Brucellosis is often called Bang's disease, infectious or contagious abortion, or simply abortion. It is caused by the organism *Brucella abortus,* and is generally recognized by the premature birth of the fetus. The agglutination test (blood test) has been recognized as the most reliable method of detecting infected animals. With the use of this test an eradication program, known as the test-and-slaughter method, was started by the federal and state governments. As in the tuberculosis program, the infected animal was slaughtered and the owner was paid an indemnity. Calfhood vaccination has been in general use in the United States since 1925. Currently, some states require all calves, excepting steers, to be vaccinated. In 1958, eleven states and Puerto Rico were designated as brucellosis-free areas.

Mastitis. Mastitis, commonly called garget, is an infection of the mammary gland. It affects the secretory tissue, often causing it to harden and become inactive, thus generally reducing milk production. Some treatments have been developed, but none has proved very satisfactory. Mastitis can best be controlled by sanitation and proper methods of fast milking. *See also* DAIRY INDUSTRY, THE.   M. H. C.

CATULLUS, GAIUS VALERIUS [kətʌ'ləs] (c. 84-54 B.C.), Latin lyric poet, was born at Verona of a wealthy family; his father on one occasion received Julius Caesar as a guest. About 63 B.C. Catullus repaired to Rome, where he formed a close friendship with Gaius Cinna, Gaius Licinius Calvus, and several other poets who were, like himself, natives of northern Italy. These poets had an excessive admiration for the artifices of later Greek poetry, known as Alexandrian, and Catullus shared their views. But his passion for the notorious Clodia, wife of Q. Caecilius Metellus Celer, became the pivot of Catullus' life and drew from him verse of great naturalness, sincerity, and power. The course of his unhappy love cannot be traced precisely, but it appears that the death of Clodia's husband in 59 B.C., instead of furthering it, rather encouraged new rivals to solicit Clodia's favor. In 57 B.C. Catullus went to Bithynia on the staff of the governor Memmius and this change of scene is reflected in his verse; he visited his brother's grave in the Troad upon the return journey to Italy, and composed the farewell, outstanding for its dignity and intensity of feeling, which ends with the still familiar words: *Atque in perpetuum, frater, ave atque vale* ("And for eternity, brother, hail and farewell"). He had occasion to write happily when the mission came to an end, and he greeted his home, at Sirmio, on Lake Garda, with heartfelt joy. He died in Rome, probably in 54 B.C., at the age of thirty.

Whether or not Catullus so arranged them, his poems have come down to us in an order based not on chronology but on metric form. First come sixty short lyrics, then eight longer poems, and last forty-eight elegiac pieces. Two of the longer poems (61 and 62) are epithalamia, or bridal songs, in which a chorus of girls and a chorus of boys alternate gracefully in frank admonitions to bride and groom. The *Attis* (63) tells of the ecstasy, self-mutilation, and later repentance of a celebrant of Cybele, mother of the Gods. The longest poem, *The Marriage of Peleus and Thetis,* is an epyllion, or short epic, of 476 loosely knit lines containing many beautiful passages; of the other longer poems, one, *The Lock of Berenice,* is translated from the Alexandrian Greek Callimachus.

Many of the short lyrics of Catullus have a movement and tone agreeably resembling ordinary prose, while others have a musical flow of surpassing beauty. Catullus writes affectionately of his friends and scurrilously of his enemies; he praises or castigates the statesmen of his day; and he gives intimate expression to his love of Clodia, the "Lesbia" of his poems. In the famous *Vivamus, mea Lesbia, atque amemus* ("Let us live, my Lesbia, and let us love") Catullus writes in the first flush of a lover's happiness; in the poems that follow he sets down his first doubts of Lesbia's fidelity, his first quarrel with her, and in the elegies, his reconciliation, his recurrent doubts, his disillusionment, and his final prayer to be freed from the foul disease that his love finally appears to be.

In his elegiac pieces Catullus often seems to strive for effect, but when he records his reunion with Lesbia and his final renunciation of her, his sincerity is overwhelming. The lines in which he consoles Calvus for his wife's death and those in which he bids farewell to his own brother mark Catullus as one of the outstanding lyric poets of any age.

G. McL. H.

CAUCASIAN LANGUAGES [kɔke'shən; kɔke'zhən; kɔkæ'shən], the common name of many languages of neither Indo-European, Semitic, nor Ural-Altaic origin, spoken by some 4,000,000 people in the Caucasus. Intensive work in the field during the first decades of the twentieth century has made it possible to distinguish about forty distinct languages. Of these only Georgian is spoken by more than 1,000,000 persons; and only Mingrelian, Kabardian, Chechen, Avar, Dargwa and Lezghian are spoken by more than 100,000. Some are spoken in a few villages only.

The Caucasian languages are divided in two major groups with numerous subgroups and branches. Approximate estimates of the number of speakers, based mainly on the Soviet census of 1939, are given in brackets.

The southern group (2,250,000) is divided into three branches: Mingrelian (250,000) in Western Georgia and Laz (a few thousand) on either side of the Turkish border, these two being the modern representatives of the language of the Colchians, known from Greek sources like the legend of the Argonauts, some centuries before the Christian Era; Georgian (almost 2,000,000) in Central and Eastern Georgia, known to the ancient Greek geographers as Iberia, and in the adjacent mountain valleys; and Svanetian (20,000), the most archaic of the southern languages, in the mountain valleys north of Kutaisi in Western Georgia.

The northern group is also divided into three branches. The northwestern branch (310,000) comprises Abkhasian (59,000) on the Black Sea coast, in the Sukhumi region and in the hinterland and Abaza (8,000); Adyghe, which is spoken in two dialects, Circassian or Cherkess (88,000), north and east of Abkhasian around the Kuban River and in some villages near Tuapse; and Kabardian (164,000) in the inland region toward the Terek Basin. Other members of this branch, like Ubykh, are no longer spoken in the Caucasus because of the wholesale emigration of Caucasians to Turkey in 1864. The central branch (500,000), in the middle of the Terek district and in the eastern parts of Daghestan, until 1943 comprised Chechen (408,000), with Groznyy as its chief center; Ingush (92,000), spoken in and around Ordzhonikidze; and Batsbi, spoken in some scattered villages south of the mountain range in the region of Telav, Georgia. Most of those speaking these languages were deported at the height of World War II to the Kazakh S.S.R. or Siberia, and were not returned to the Caucasus until 1957.

The eastern branch (857,000) of the northern group of Caucasian languages is spoken in isolated villages and tribal communities of Daghestan, where it is represented by a great variety of distinct languages, only a few of which are well known. Their classification is hypothetical and therefore subject to modifications. The Avaro-Andi languages (300,000), Andi, Botlikh, Godoberi, Chamalal, Karata, Akhwakh, Bagulal, Tindil, Dido, Khwarsai, Kapucha, Khunzal, Ginukh, and Avar, are spoken in the basin of the Andi and Avar Koisu rivers. Of these languages only Avar is spoken by a considerable number. It is important because outside the Avar territory, the chief center of which is Gunib, it is used as a common language in most parts of Daghestan, where it competes with Russian and the Azerbaidzhan variety of Turkish. Other languages of the eastern branch include Lakk, or Kazi-Khumukh (100,000), in the basin of the Kazi-Khumukh Koisu River, and Archi, which is spoken in a single village on the upper Kara-Koisu River. Also in this branch are the Dargwa languages (200,000), Akusha, Tsudakhar, Kaitak, Kubuchi, and Dargwa proper, which are spoken east of Lakk. Of these languages only the most important, Dargwa proper, is known to any extent. Of the languages of the eastern branch in the Samur region (250,000), the best known members are Rutul, Agul, Lezghian, and Tabasaran; the other members are small languages, like Tsakhur, Budukh, Djek or Kryz, and Khinalugh, which are confined to isolated communities. Udi, isolated from the other languages of the eastern branch in Daghestan, is spoken in two villages near Nish and Vartashen, south of the Caucasus. Before the Arabic and Turkish invasions, it was an important language in Albania and was well known to Greek and Armenian historians.

In their entire structure, the Caucasian languages are clearly differentiated from all the other languages in their part of the world. Their sound system is characterized by the simplicity of the vowels and by the extraordinary variety of the consonants, as shown in Abaza, for example, where the consonants number about 70. Besides the common voiced and unvoiced, or aspirated, stops and affricates, they all have glottalized stops. The northern languages share a number of consonants in common, like complex labial-dental stops, lateral and laryngeal stops, labialized s- and š- sounds, and a number of whistling and hissing fricatives. In the morphology of certain Caucasian languages the number of cases in the noun rises to extraordinary heights, unparalleled in all other known languages; thus Tabasaran distinguishes more than 50 cases, compared with the 6 cases of classical Latin and the 21 of Hungarian. In most of the northern languages, the nouns are divided in classes which correspond to grammatical genders in Indo-European. The distinctions between animate and inanimate, human and non-human, masculine and feminine, sexually mature and sexually immature, and intricate combinations of these, are the most common. But the most complicated part of the grammar of these northern languages is the verb, which often expresses not only person, time, aspect, and mood but also the mutual relations and the class-relationships of the subject and the direct and indirect objects.

In modern times only one of the Caucasian languages has the status of a literary language with some standing, Georgian, the official language of the Georgian Soviet Republic, which has had an unbroken literary tradition from at least the fifth century A.D. In pre-Arabic times the so-called Albanian language, the ancestor of present-day Udi, was also a written language of some importance, and interesting remains of its alphabet were discovered by accident in 1937 in an Armenian manuscript of the fifteenth century.

The relationship between all the Caucasian languages has been supposed, and accepted as proven, by Georgian scholars in the 1930's. Tentative efforts have been made to relate these languages with other living languages, like Basque in the Pyrenees and Burushaski in the Karakoram in Central Asia, and with extinct languages, like Etruscan in Italy and Mitanni and the language of the Vannic inscription in Asia Minor, but no conclusive proof has been advanced. Since the Russian Revolution much work has been done to reduce many of the Caucasian languages to writing and to use them in the local schools and in community administration. But at the same time, twentieth-century conditions in the Caucasus, as modified by incipient industrialization, have reduced the isolation in which the inhabitants of the region have lived since the beginning of historical times. The knowledge of Russian is spreading and is threatening with rapid extinction many of the smaller linguistic units. Only a few of them have any chance of prolonged survival, with the exception of Georgian, which is firmly entrenched in a compact population of a much higher cultural and economic standard than that of other Caucasian peoples.   H. V.

CAUCASIAN PEOPLES. *See* Asiatic Tribes.
CAUCASOID RACE. *See* Races of Man.

CAUCASUS [kɔ′kəsəs], an extensive mountain range between the Sea of Azov and the Black Sea on the west and the Caspian Sea on the east. Traditionally the land boundary between Asia Minor and European Russia, the system occupies approximately 175,000 sq. mi. of the southeast European part of the Soviet Union. The main chain, beginning in the Crimean Peninsula and flanked by outlying ranges for much of its distance, extends in a northwest-southeast direction for over 900 mi. before it disappears under the Caspian Sea to reappear as the Kopet Dagh, part of the northern boundary of Iran. Although the Caucasus Range, like the Pyrenees, is well defined, it includes numerous subsidiary chains and peaks which result in a complex topography and structure. On the north is the Pre-Caucasus, rising gradually from the flat steppe lands around the Manych Depression and reaching its highest elevations, 2,000 to 2,600 ft., in the Stavropol Plateau around the city of Stavropol. Between it and the massif of the Greater Caucasus is the Pre-Caucasus Depression, a structural downfold complicated by two anticlinoria and drained to the west by the Kuban River, to the east by the Terek. The Greater Caucasus forms an exceptionally continuous watershed. No low passes break through the mountains as they do in the Alps, although the Dariel Pass at 7,800 ft. and the Mamison Pass at 9,000 ft. afford north-south routes for the Georgian and Ossetian military highways, respectively. Much of the range is from 10,000 to 12,000 ft. in elevation, with such well-known peaks as volcanic Mount Elbrus, 18,468 ft., the highest peak in all Europe; Mount Kazbek, 16,541 ft., also volcanic; Koshtan-tau, 16,880 ft.; and many others reaching more than 13,000 ft. The arid, treeless region of Daghestan, "Land of Mountains," in the east, is noteworthy for its extremely wild, irregular topography and great relief. In its eastern section, the Greater Caucasus gradually tapers down to the Caspian. There are no peaks higher than 9,000 ft., and the range is devoid of snow in the summer. South of the Greater Caucasus is the Kura-Rion Depression, a tectonic downwarp divided into two unequal parts by the Surami Mountains, a watershed for the Kura on the east and the Rion on the west. The transverse Surami Range acts as a link between the Greater Caucasus and the Little Caucasus, drained by the Araks River and rising in the center in the complicated Armenian Knot, which has the twin volcano Mount Ararat (16,946 ft.), in Turkish Armenia, as its culminating point.

Geology. Geologically, the Caucasus is part of the great alpine system of folding which extends from the Carpathians under the Black Sea to the Yaila Mountains of southern Crimea and then continues east of the Caspian Sea in the Kopet Dagh. The core of the Greater Caucasus is principally crystalline rock, especially granite; in the center and west this lies exposed, whereas in the east sedimentary layers are uppermost. Jurassic and Tertiary beds form the flanks. Extensive volcanic activity in the west is indicated by large numbers of hot springs and frequent earthquakes. Whereas the Lesser Caucasus is block-faulted, the Surami Range is a granite mass. Intruded igneous rocks are rich in minerals, yielding gold, silver, zinc, copper, tungsten, and molybdenum. The largest deposits of high-grade manganese known in the world are found in the Georgian Soviet Socialist Republic at Chiatura. Coal deposits have been mined at Tkvarcheli and Tkibuli. Petroleum, however, is the most valuable natural resource. The oilfields are at Baku on the Apsheron Peninsula, and at Groznyy and Maykop on the northern flanks.

Climate and Vegetation. Contrast is the keynote to Caucasian climate. Depending on elevation and relative exposure, there are deserts such as that of the eastern Kura Plain, subtropical gardens such as that of the Colchis lowland of the Rion Valley, and perennial snowfields such as that of any of the 1,400 glaciers. By blocking the path of the westerly-moving cyclonic storms, the Surami Range has a Mediterranean regime on its western slopes, with such crops as tea, grapes, cotton, corn, tung oil, flax, figs, olives, and citrus fruits. At higher elevations deciduous forests and temperate zone fruits appear, and these in turn are replaced by conifers and nutritious alpine meadows which are used extensively for summer pasturage. Inland, however, precipitation diminishes. Trees are absent from the upland valleys and mountain slopes, and bare rock outcrops to interrupt the expanse of grass. The winds blowing in from the steppes bring no moisture to freshen the northern slopes of the mountains. Consequently, much of the Caucasus region is a bleak and arid one.

Peoples. From an ethnographic standpoint, the Caucasus is a museum of peoples and languages. Scores of separate tribes dwell in isolated sections in the mountains where they withdrew for protection. Migrating peoples moving through the Dariel Pass and higher routes often left behind small groups who continued their existence in the wild, mountainous environment. A consideration of the peoples of the Caucasus is a complex chapter in human geography. Classification of the heterogeneous groups is usually made on a linguistic basis, yet even this method is extremely difficult because of the presence of villages in which languages heard nowhere else in the Soviet Union are spoken. Aleš Hrdlička has estimated that Slavs constitute the strongest element in Caucasian population (40 per cent of the total). Also important are the Turco-Tatars, the Georgians, and the Armenians. Diversity of language, occupation, and religion contribute to a lack of understanding among the various tribes. Politically, the Caucasus includes the Transcaucasian and Ciscaucasian units, whose largest cities are Baku, Tbilisi, and Yerevan. Other important cities are Batumi, Kislovodsk, and Makhachkala.   C. C. H.

CAUCA VALLEY [kɑu′kɑ], a rich valley of Colombia, lying between the central and western Cordillera and between Popayán, on the south, 32 mi. below the source of the Cauca River, and Cartago, where the river enters its mountain gorge. It is one of the most beautiful and fertile valleys in the New World, with soil that produces sugar cane, rice, corn, tobacco, bananas, and many other products. The subsoil contains coal, iron, and gold. The department of Valle del Cauca occupies the northern section of the valley and the department of Cauca occupies the south. The two chief cities in the valley are Cali and Popayán.   S. G. I.

CAUCUS, a term originating in pre-Revolutionary Boston referring to clandestine gatherings of parties or factions which decided on candidates and issues prior to the public meeting or election. Those who participated in the caucus were bound by the decision of the group. The caucus later was merely the designation given open party meetings at which candidates were selected. The Congressional caucus determined presidential candidates in the elections from 1800 until 1824; thereafter it gave way to the national party convention. The state caucus was also replaced by the convention and later by the direct primary as the instrument for selecting party nominees. The caucus remains the legally recognized party agency in the smaller towns of Connecticut and Rhode Island. Today the party caucuses of members of Congress or of state legislatures usually determine the general policies which the major parties will advocate. Most members of Congress usually feel bound by the decisions of the caucus, but state legislators follow caucus decisions more faithfully.   H. P.

CAUDATA. *See* AMPHIBIAN.

CAULIFLOWER, *Brassica oleracea botyritis,* one of several vegetables belonging to the cabbage family. The curd, the edible portion of the plant, is formed of immature stems and buds condensed into flattened, compact heads. Cauliflower seed is expensive and difficult to produce. A good loam soil well supplied with lime is necessary. Anything that stunts the young plants will cause them to form heads prematurely. When floral parts become overdeveloped, the flavor is impaired. In perfect heads the parts which form the curd seem to be almost homogeneous. A cold spring may cause much bolting or premature heading. The heads would normally become brown from exposure to the sun, but they are blanched by tying the flower head, when it is 3 or 4 in. in diameter, in its surrounding leaves, or by breaking and laying the leaves over it. The head will grow to its full diameter in a few days after being covered.

CAULKING, the sealing of joints in wood or steel structures against leakage of liquids or gases. The joints between planks on a wooden ship, for example, are caulked to prevent water from leaking into the ship, and riveted seams in steam boiler drums and air tanks are caulked to prevent the steam and hot water or air from leaking out. Caulking is done quite differently in these two cases. In caulking a wooden ship, strands of oakum are pounded into the seams; with the steel plates, the edge of one of the plates is compressed or "upset."

The planking of a wooden ship is made to allow space for the caulking material between adjacent pieces. This is usually done by cutting the edges of the planking so that the inside edges against the frames fit together nicely and the outer edges are a small distance apart. The wedge-shaped slot thus produced has an included angle of about 15°. In laying-out this angle prior to cutting the planking, two lines are drawn. They are 10 in. long, meet at one end, and are spaced ½ in. apart at the other. The thickness of the plank is then laid off along the lines, starting at the point where the lines meet. The spacing of the lines at the

plank thickness is then the opening to be left on the outside of the ship.

The materials used for caulking wooden ships are oakum and cotton, both being made in the form of loosely spun yarns. Oakum is made from old rope which has been untwisted and picked apart. White oakum is untreated; black oakum has been saturated with a tarry substance. The cotton material used is similar to lamp-wicking. Both the oakum and cotton are wound into bales, which generally weigh about 50 lbs.

In the caulking operation, the seam is first spread, using iron wedges which are driven into the slot at intervals. Next, a special iron tool is used to pound into the seam white oakum or cotton, followed by black oakum. The number of threads forced into the seam varies with the plank thickness. One authority states that one double-thread of black oakum is sufficient for bottom planking one in. thick and that five double-threads should be used for four-in. planking. Great care is exercised by the skilled caulker to be sure that there are no void spaces in the seam, since such cavities cause decay. When the seam has been caulked to within about ¾ in. of the outer surface, the spacing wedges are all removed. The oakum is hardened up by pounding, and the slot is filled with pitch or marine glue so that the filling of the seam is level with the outer surface of the planking.

Caulking riveted seams on steel drums and tanks or on ships is done after riveting is completed. If a seam is to be caulked, it must be designed for this purpose. The spacing of the rivets along the joint must be sufficiently close so that the outer plate will not bulge between rivets. Experience has shown that this condition will be satisfied if the spacing is not more than 3½ times the rivet diameter for seams to hold oil pressure and 4½ times the rivet diameter for those which must hold water pressure. The distance from the caulked edge to the first row of rivets must not be great enough to allow bulging in that direction. Experience has shown that a maximum width of twice the rivet diameter is indicated.

Use is made of special chisel-shaped tools operated with air hammers similar to those for riveting or chipping operations. A tool with two parallel edges first scores the edge of the outer plate and the face of the under one. Next, one or more passes along the scored grooves are made with a blunt or square-edged chisel. This operation should seal the joint. Water or air pressure is then applied to the inside of the tank and the joint examined for leaks, additional hammering of the joint being necessary if leaks are found. Some claim that both the inside edges and the outside edges of boiler drum seams should be caulked; others feel that caulking the outside edges alone is adequate.   E. D. H.

CAUSALGIA [kɔzæ'ljiə], a specific type of neuralgia (nerve plus pain) characterized by tenderness and localized burning pain over the distribution of a peripheral nerve, most commonly the median and ulnar nerves of the forearm. Chief causes include an incomplete severance of the nerve, the crushing of a sensory or a "mixed" (sensoro-motor) nerve, or the introduction of a toxic substance (usually by injection) around the nerve. Treatment is highly unsatisfactory. The average acute stage of causalgia may persist for as long as two years, and since the use of analgesics is indicated, the possibility of converting the patient into a drug addict is ever present. Surgery may be required, in which the offending nerve is removed or transplanted to a new bed. If it has been partially severed, surgical removal of the cut portion may be advisable. Novocaine injection gives temporary, not permanent, relief. Therapy must be directed also at complications, which include atrophied and stiff muscles due to disuse; and the stiff and faulty function of joints, resulting from the patient's maintenance of fixed postures as a means of avoiding exacerbations of pain. These latter conditions are usually treated by physiotherapy (baking, heat machines, massage, and manipulation).   J. A. Br.

CAUSALITY, the relation between a cause and its effect. Aristotle distinguished four causes: in a statue, for example, the material cause is the marble; the moving or efficient cause is the sculptor's carving; the formal cause is the shape of the statue; and the final cause is the purpose or end for which the statue exists.

Ordinarily in modern times, when one asks what caused the existence or occurence of something (E), what is sought is some preceding event (C), the occurrence of which, in the circumstances then existing, necessitated the occurrence of E, i.e., made E happen. Cause and effect are thus conceived essentially as events; whereas the things or substances, of which these events are changes, are rather agents and patients. A cause immediately preceding and adjoining its effect is called its proximate cause; whereas one causing a given effect through intermediary steps of causation is termed the remote cause of it. A statement of causation as between events of stated kinds (rather than as between individual events) is a causal law. Such a law is of the form: An event of kind C, occurring in a situation of kind S, always causes an effect of kind E.

Causation as between events is called transeunt causation and is contrasted with immanent causation. Immanent causation is the relation between an inner essence, or principle, and the outer facts which the essence is conceived as pervading. In particular, it is the relation between God and the world when God is regarded as pervading his creation rather than as dwelling outside or beyond it, i.e., as the immanent, rather than the transcendent cause of the world.

Hume's Theory. Modern discussions of causality have mainly stemmed from David Hume's contention (1739) that a cause cannot be said to necessitate its effect, because no contradiction is ever involved in supposing either event to occur without the other. Hume held that causation is therefore nothing but succession that happens to be regular, and that the "necessity" which we speak of as between cause and effect is nothing but the impulsion, which habit produces in us, to think of the second event when we observe the first. However, inconsistently with this conception of causation, as succession that has been in fact regular, Hume declares that it is sometimes possible to discover a causal connection by means of a single experiment. The rules he gives for discovering this connection are thus tacitly based on a different conception of causation. The chief of them are (1) that "where several different objects produce the same effect, it must be by means of some quality which we discover to be common amongst them"; and (2) that "the difference in the effects of two resembling objects must proceed from that particular in which they differ."

Mill's "Method of Difference." These two rules are the same in essence as those stated better by Sir John Herschel in 1830, and named by him the "Method of Agreement." In 1843 J. S. Mill formulated still another statement of the rules, under the name of the "method of difference." The last is the great method of scientific experimentation, which consists in making some single change (difference) in a given set of circumstances, and observing what other change in

them follows; the change that follows is identified as the effect, the first change as the cause. The causal relation thus always has three terms: a given set of circumstances; a single change in them, which is the cause; and the ensuing change in them, which is the effect. Mill, however, proposed to reckon the circumstances part of the cause, making causality a two-term relation; he gratuitously abolished, however, the useful and valid common-sense distinction between a condition of an event (something necessary but not sufficient to its occurrence) and a cause of an event (something sufficient but perhaps not necessary to its occurrence).

Kantian Theory. In Hume's view, there is only so much causation among objects as there is empirical regularity of succession. Immanuel Kant, on the other hand, maintained (1781) that all objects or events that one possibly can experience must have a cause; and that one knows this to be true and knows it *a priori*, i.e., independently of experience. This is so, he argues, because, although sensations are passively received, things and events are conceived as objective only through the activity of one's understanding, which synthesizes the sensations. This activity has certain specific forms, the categories of the understanding. Causality is one of them. And it is because one's understanding—conceptual faculty—thus contributes certain of the features of one's conception of the world of objects of experience, that one knows these features to be universal in that world, and knows it independently of observation of that world.   C. J. D.

CAUSSES [ko's], a flat plateau lying in the departments of Aveyron, Lozère, Gard, and Hérault, in south central France, between the Central Plateau and the Cévennes Mountains. Originally Jurassic limestone, the plateau's porous rock has been eroded by the Lot, Aveyron, Tarn, Jonte, and Dourbie rivers into several smaller areas: Causse Méjean, between the Tarn and the Jonte; Causse de Sauveterre, to the north; Causse de Sévérac, to the west; Causse Noir and Causse de Larzac to the south. The Causses reach an altitude of 4,000 ft. They are treeless and waterless because the calcareous and permeable surface of the rock has many chasms into which the rainfall quickly sinks, forming subterranean caverns with stalagmites and stalactites, and draining to lower terrains. The oak-, birch-, and pine-clad valleys of the Causses are fertile, particularly the gorge of the Tarn which is 37 mi. long, 1,650 ft. deep, and 1,500 to 2,000 yd. wide. Along the well-populated rivers, the inhabitants grow apples, pears, prunes, grapes, and vegetables. Sheep raising is the most important industry. Glove factories are situated at Le Rozier and Millau. Florac and Meyrueis are resort towns. The Causses have stormy weather throughout the year, particularly in the autumn. The annual rainfall is about 39 in. Pop. 1946, 74,415.   S. Van V.

CAUSTIC POTASH. *See* POTASSIUM.

CAUVERY [kɔ'vəri], an important river of southern India which supplies a large amount of water for irrigation and hydroelectric power. It rises in the western Ghats on the western border of Coorg, about 35 mi. east of the Arabian Sea at 12° 25′ N. lat. and 75° 34′ E. long., and flows east by south all the way across the peninsula of India, emptying into the Bay of Bengal near Negapatam, in the Tanjore district of Madras, at 10° 45′ N. lat. and 79° 53′ E. long. The River flows an air-line distance of about 300 mi., but its actual course runs about 475 mi. The Cauvery rises in a mountainous area that varies between 2,000 and 6,000 ft. above sea level and receives an annual rainfall of about 100 in. The river plunges eastward through a narrow and rocky course onto the Deccan Plateau of Mysore, where it has cut a narrow gorge, forming a 320-ft. fall, and has divided to form two islands. In its eastern or lower course, the river crosses the coastal plain of Madras and forms the division point between the Salem and Kumbakonam districts. In the Tanjore district it divides into two main distributaries; the northern or main branch is called the Coleroon River.

The Cauvery carries a large amount of silt, much of which has been deposited in a large delta. This fertile soil supports, with the aid of irrigation, a rice economy. The mouths of the Cauvery are rapidly building seaward and there is no good natural harbor, but at Negapatam a port has been built as an outlet for the Cauvery district. A railroad spur connects Negapatam with the Indian rail network and the Cauvery hinterland. The major tributaries of the Cauvery are the Nomanati, Kabbeni, Shamsha, Bhayani, and Noyil; some of the cities and towns on or near its banks are: Mysore, Seringapatam, Swansakudram, Erode, Karur, Trichinoply, Tanjore, and Negapatam. Immediately north of the mouth of the Cauvery is the city of Karikal, formerly a French possession.

CAVALCANTI, GUIDO [kɑˈvɑlkɑˈnti] (c. 1250-1300),

Italian lyric and philosophic poet, was born in Florence of a Guelph family about 1250. In his childhood he was affianced to Beatrice, daughter of Manente degli Uberti, called Farinata, the Ghibelline leader, as one of the moves made to restore peace between Ghibellines and Guelphs. When the Florentine Guelphs divided, Cavalcanti joined the Whites, Dante's party, against the Blacks, and played an active role in party strife. Dante had dedicated his *Vita nuova* to Cavalcanti, his "first friend"; in 1300, however, as one of the city priors, Dante joined in exiling him, along with others, from Florence. This move deprived both factions in the general city council of their leaders and attempted to reduce the strife between the parties. In exile at Sarzana, Cavalcanti fell ill with malaria; he was readmitted to Florence but died toward the end of August.

Cavalcanti's poetry, which Dante praises in the *Purgatorio* as surpassing the glory of Guinizelli, and which subsequent criticism considers second only to Dante's in its presentation of the *dolce stil nuovo,* may be considered as falling into two categories. Many of his lyrics, in the first place, are akin to traditional popular poetry, but they are characterized by a greater refinement of vocabulary than Guinizelli's, a tone of greater elevation, and sometimes a new life and vigor as compared with their conventional models. Other poems deal with love from the philosophical approach of the *dolce stil nuovo,* notably the doctrinal canzone, *Donna me prega,* which stands out with the authority of a manifesto among Cavalcanti's works. Cavalcanti here pretends that a lady begged him for answers to eight questions about the nature of love, which he answers dryly in scholastic and scientific fashion, using as his authority Albertus Magnus. Here the rationalizing Cavalcanti has made love an affair of the mind and regarded its object as an abstraction. Cavalcanti undoubtedly helped Dante to formulate his conception of Beatrice, but Beatrice remained a real person, with an essential part to play in the *Divina Commedia.* L. H. G.

CAVALIERS,

a term used to designate the supporters of King Charles I of England in the Civil War of the 1640's. The name, derived from the French *cavalier,* a horseman and therefore a man of good birth, was first applied contemptuously to the Royalists in 1641 by their opponents, who claimed to be solid middle-class citizens; the Royalists, however, adopted it and used it during the Civil War and on through the Restoration period. It was superseded by the term "Tory" at the end of the seventeenth century. E. R. A.

CAVALLA. *See* KAVALLA.

CAVALLERIA RUSTICANA [kɑˈvɑlleriˈɑ ruˈstikɑˈnɑ],

a one-act opera by Pietro Mascagni with a libretto by Giovanni Targioni-Tozzetti and Guido Menasci; the libretto is based on a short story by the Italian novelist Giovanni Verga, who later turned his tale into a play in which Eleanora Duse appeared. *Cavalleria Rusticana* ("Rustic Chivalry") was Mascagni's first opera. The composer was leading a difficult existence as an obscure music teacher in a small town when he hastily composed this short work for a competition announced in Milan by the music publisher Eduardo Sonzogno, but when it won the prize Mascagni became famous literally overnight. Its emphasis upon *verismo,* or realism, appealed strongly to audiences that were weary of Wagner, and the opera has been enormously popular since its first performance in Rome on May 17, 1890. Unfortunately, however, the success of *Cavalleria* was Mascagni's last as well as his first, though he wrote other operatic works.

The action of the opera is set in nineteenth-century Sicily, and its title is ironic, for far from behaving with "rustic chivalry," the characters show the most vengeful bitterness toward one another, and the occasional moments of tenderness or generosity are lost in the general passion and violence of the action. When Santuzza (soprano) finds that Turiddu (tenor) has left her for his old love Lola (mezzo-soprano), the wife of Alfio (baritone), she prepares bloody vengeance by convincing Alfio that his wife is unfaithful. Turiddu finds Alfio will not drink with him and places himself at the disposal of the man he has wronged. The two men embrace, Turiddu formally bites Alfio's ear in the Sicilian form of challenge to a duel with knives, and in the ensuing fight Turiddu meets death at Alfio's hands. S. C.

CAVALLINI, PIETRO [kɑˈvɑlliˈni] (fl. 1273-1308),

Italian painter and mosaicist, was born in Rome. In the brief revival of the mosaic school of church decoration, which lasted from about 1270 to the exile of the popes in Avignon in 1305, Cavallini seems to have been the most prolific artist. Of the many works attributed to him all that remain are the apse mosaics in Santa Maria in Trastevere, Rome, and most of a *Last Judgment* in Santa Cecilia in Trastevere, uncovered early in this century with much of its brilliant coloring still intact. The Santa Maria mosaics, dated c. 1291, consist of a *Virgin and Child Enthroned* and five scenes from the Virgin's life. There is also documentary proof that Cavallini worked in Naples in 1308, where most of the fresco decoration in Santa Maria Donna Regina is in a comparable style.

Cavallini's work is largely Byzantine in iconography but, as Vasari noted, "he delighted to give relief to his figures"; thus he may be thought of as intermediary between late Byzantine art and Giotto. But the simplified and blanket-like folds of his drapery, the inert gestures, and the puffed up faces are static and have little corporeal or schematic significance. The evidence of the Santa Cecilia fresco suggests that he was at his best as a charming colorist. A. N.

CAVALRY,

a mounted military arm which has been almost outmoded by mechanization. Armored units have largely replaced this arm in modern warfare, but horse cavalry, as formerly employed, will go down in history as one of the most versatile and effective of military forces, as well as the most colorful.

Development of Cavalry. A natural development as the military arms of nomadic herdsmen, cavalry scored initial successes against foot soldiers by spontaneous application of the principles of offensive action, mass, economy of force, movement, surprise, and simplicity. When it came to be opposed by other cavalry, specialization of the mounted arm and co-operation with infantry appeared.

Two major classifications of cavalry developed: light and heavy. Light cavalry was employed in reconnaissance, skirmishing, and for providing security for main bodies of troops, on point, flank, rear guard, or outpost duty. Heavy cavalry was used against other cavalry, as well as against foot troops, for shock effect. The distinction between the two was a matter of weight of arms and armor, and consequent variation in speed and size of mount. The hussar, with his sabre and carbine, was a light cavalryman. The cuirassier, with his body-armor, was a heavy cavalryman. Dragoons and lancers might be light or heavy cavalry. The American trooper was originally a light cavalryman, but in the Civil War developed along independent lines as a mounted rifleman. He did much of his fighting on foot, using his horse as a means of transportation.

Horse cavalry reached its highest point of development as a swiftly maneuvering and highly effective military force in the nineteenth century under such brilliant cavalry leaders as Blücher, Murat, Stuart, Forrest, and Sheridan.

Decline of Cavalry. The decline in importance of cavalry paralleled the development of modern automatic weapons for an obvious reason, i.e., a man on horseback is a much more vulnerable target than a man in a trench or foxhole. In the static warfare of World War I, cavalry was employed very little.

In World War II, generally a war of movement, the part of cavalry was played by armored divisions and smaller mechanized units. Originally adaptable to all sorts of terrain, horse cavalry was used only in mountainous regions impassable to tanks. The United States First Cavalry Division fought dismounted, as infantrymen, in the Pacific, and only one American cavalry regiment, the Mars Task Force, in Burma, remained mounted throughout the war. An additional consideration, logistics, also worked to the disadvantage of cavalry in World War II. With troops involved in unprecedented numbers, it was equally impossible for horses to live off the land, or for feed and forage to be transported to them. Furthermore, to ship one horse overseas, with feed and tack, required as much shipping space as was necessary for one tank. K. K. H.

CAVAN [kæ'vən], or **AN CABHAN,** an inland county in Eire, with an area of 477,399 acres, of which 238,883 acres are water. It is bounded by the counties of Leitrim and Longford on the west, Westmeath and Meath on the south, Meath and Monaghan on the east, and Leitrim and Fermanagh in the north. The principal rivers are the Shannon, which rises in Cavan under Cuilcagh Mountain, and the River Erne. The largest lake, which is on the Erne, is Lough Orter, 4 mi. long and 3 mi. wide. The northwestern part of the county is bleak and mountainous. Over the rest of the county the surface is undulating, and there are good fishing lakes. Cavan, in the center of the county, is the county town. Jonathan Swift finished *Gulliver's Travels* at Cuilcagh House. Pop. 1951, 66,377. S. Van V.

CAVATINA. *See* MUSICAL TERMS.

CAVE, a natural hollow under the surface of the earth or in a mountain or hill, usually in rock formations, with an opening to the surface. A cave of large or indefinite extent is often called a cavern. Caves are formed in various ways in various types of rock, but they are commonly associated with underground drainage of limestone formations in humid areas. Water, containing carbon dioxide, which is obtained from the air and the soil, seeps into the rock and along pores and joints. The soluble limestone is dissolved by the water and the pores and fissures are enlarged to form caves. Some caves formed in this manner are unusually large and contain miles of passages and gallerylike rooms. Frequently, mineral-charged water seeps into the cave and is evaporated, leaving limestone ($CaCO_3$) growths called stalactites (hanging from the roof) and stalagmites (growing up from the floor). Some of these formations are highly spectacular. Carlsbad Caverns in New Mexico, Mammoth Cave in Kentucky, Luray Cave in Virginia, Crystal Cave in Pennsylvania, and Wyandotte in Indiana are all of this type. The Karst region of Yugoslavia and the Causses district in southern France are also rich in caves.

Caves also occur in volcanic formations caused by the rapid cooling of the surface of the flow, while the molten lava underneath flows away. Also, gas chambers or pockets form in the lava, leaving caves, as does ice melting underneath the lava. Sometimes earthquakes cause caves. Another common form of cave is the sea cave, which is formed by the action of waves on the base of a cliff or headland. Fingal's Cave on the island of Staffa in the Hebrides, off the coast of Scotland, is a famous cave of this type. Sometimes river currents form caves in cliffs in a somewhat similar fashion. Some caves, usually in arid regions, may be formed by wind carrying fine particles of sand against a weak rock surface. Caves have been a source of legend and wonder to mankind and have served as homes for man and animals. Unusual species of blind animals are found in some caves. *See also* DRIPSTONE. J. E. F.

CAVE ART. The earliest documents of human art are those from the caves of the Upper Paleolithic period of western Europe. The art products fall into two main groups: namely, engravings, paintings, and bas-reliefs on the walls and ceilings of caves, and engraved or sculptured objects from the cave deposits.

The art comprises naturalistic representations, representations of a more or less schematic or conventionalized character, and more or less geometrical patterns, some of which can be shown to be final outcomes of conventionalization. The great majority of the subjects are wild animals, particularly the chief game animals of the period, reindeer, bison, wild horses, and mammoths, but carnivores, like the cave lion and bear, and a few fish and birds are also found. Plant forms are very rare, and when human figures occur, they are usually badly drawn.

Most prehistorians believe that the principal motive behind the art on the cave walls was the desire to influence fertility and hunting luck. With the exception of pairs, the animals are generally drawn as separate entities; unlike the rock-shelter art of eastern Spain or southern Africa, there was no attempt to render scenes, and where several drawings are found together on the same rock-surface, they normally bear no relation to one another and in fact often intersect. Again, many of the finest works are hidden in the innermost recesses far from the light of day and can only have been executed by firelight. It is obvious that the engravings and paintings were not designed for mere decoration; the act of delineating a figure was evidently intended to secure some magical control over the species. Representations of human beings dancing and wearing animal masks suggest that miming may have played some part in the magical rites. This is further supported by the indications of missiles commonly shown in the flanks of the animals and by the actual spearmarks visible on the clay models of bears from Montespan, France.

Although love of decoration probably played some part in the engraving of bone and antler objects of daily use, it is likely that considerations of hunting luck played some part;

BETTMANN ARCHIVE

BISON STRUCK BY ARROWS
FROM THE CAVE DRAWINGS AT NIAUX, FRANCE

at least it is significant that the objects most lavishly decorated were spear throwers and shaft straighteners. In the case of the female figurines associated with the Aurignacian culture, it is likely that we have to do with a fertility cult.

Study of palimpsests and analysis of the engravings covered by deposits of different ages has shown that there were definite sequences of art styles in different regions. This, and the fact that numerous trial pieces in the shape of engraved stone plaques are often found in the cave deposits, suggests that there were definite canons of art and that these were transmitted from one artist to another.

As regards technique, the principal tool for engraving was evidently the flint burin or graving tool, many forms of which have been recognized in the equipment of Upper Paleolithic man. Pigments used for painting included ochres ranging in color from yellow to chocolate and red, and oxide of manganese and burnt bone for black; they were evidently applied, mixed with fat, by brushes or stamps, and in powdered form may have been blown on.   J. G. D. C.

CAVEAT EMPTOR [keʹviæt ɛʹmptɔr] (Lat., "Let the buyer beware"), at common law, an ancient rule and maxim signifying that the purchaser must abide the loss from any defect in the thing purchased in the absence of relevant express warranty by the seller. However, the principle that sales are thus made caveat emptor was not without its exceptions, even prior to the enactment of the modern legislation, particularly the Uniform Sales Act, designed in general to increase the buyer's protection.

Thus, upon a sale of products manufactured by the seller, the law implied a warranty by the seller to the buyer, against undisclosed latent defects resulting from faulty workmanship, and to a limited extent for like defects resulting from improper selection of raw material by the manufacturer-seller. An analogous implied warranty was held to prevail in the matter of sales of produce by the grower. In addition there prevailed in most American jurisdictions, and in England, as a further limitation upon the dominance of caveat emptor, the rule that accompanying all sales by a retail dealer of articles of food for immediate use, there was an implied warranty that the food was fit for human consumption.

The Uniform Sales Act excludes from the scope of caveat emptor sales made to buyers who, expressly or by implication, make known to the seller the particular purpose for which the goods are required, and rely upon his skill and judgment to the extent of imposing an implied warranty that the goods shall be reasonably fit for such purpose. This act further provides that where goods are bought by description from a dealer in such goods, there is an implied warranty that the goods shall be of merchantable quality. However, if the buyer has examined the goods there is no implied warranty as regards defects which such examination ought to have revealed.

Although the Uniform Sales Act, generally, has accorded greater protection to the buyer than existed under common-law concept of implied warranty, and has thereby restricted the operation of the rule of caveat emptor, a New York court has observed that in the case of sales of food for immediate use the common law implied warranty in most states may have afforded greater protection to the consumer than the new Uniform Sales Act, which renders the implied warranty effective only upon the buyer's reliance on the skill and judgment of the seller.   H. Si.

CAVE DWELLINGS. From the earliest times men have sought shelter in natural caves or under overhanging rocks, and it is by exploring these that archaeologists have learned most about the Paleolithic Age. Each successive group of occupants left behind fireplaces, discarded meat bones, and objects of material equipment, and so, by taking out the deposits layer by layer, it is often possible to obtain a correct sequence from which the development of early culture can be deduced. Since early man quite often buried his dead in caves, much information is available about his burial rites, about the physical characteristics of the various groups, and about personal adornment. Again, it was on the walls and ceilings of caves that Upper Paleolithic man executed the engravings and paintings which give us so much insight into his aesthetic and spiritual life.

Caves continued in use to a greater or less degree in different localities throughout prehistoric times, and in parts of Europe they are still used, often with the front walled in, for habitation.   J. G. D. C.

CAVE FISHES, fishes found in subterranean waters and cave pools. Some twenty totally blind species are known. These are whitish in color, and usually have some compensating organs such as sensory cavities on the head, or fleshy sensory barbels on the head and body. In addition, there are about twenty other known species with the defective eyes usually associated with animals found in caves or cavelike environments.

Blind cave fishes have evolved in all parts of the world and represent 16 genera in 9 families and 7 orders. Seven species are found in the limestone caves of Illinois, Indiana, Kentucky, south to Missouri, Arkansas and Alabama. These all belong to the family Amblyopsidae, which is closely related to the killifish. They have been derived from a form much like the modern ricefish, *Chologaster,* which inhabits the Atlantic Coastal Plain area. The caves of Yucatan and Cuba are noted for their blindfishes. An almost blind cave catfish, *Gronias nigrilabris,* occurs in eastern Pennsylvania. *See also* BLINDFISHES. E. C. R.

CAVENDISH, GEORGE [kæ'vəndɪʃ] (1500-c.1562), English biographer, was a member of Cardinal Wolsey's household for several years, accompanying him on an embassy to France. When Wolsey lost royal favor, Cavendish remained with him; shortly after Wolsey's death (1530) he retired to his home at Glemsford in Suffolk. About 1557 he wrote a sympathetic *Life of Cardinal Wolsey* (printed imperfectly in 1641 and more accurately in 1810 and later), one of the best of early English biographies and a primary historical source. W. R.

CAVENDISH, SIR HENRY [kæ'vəndɪʃ] (1731-1810), English physicist and chemist, was born at Nice (Savoy), Oct. 10, 1731. A son of Lord Charles Cavendish, he attended school at Hackney in 1742 and later went to Peterhouse, Cambridge, from 1749 to 1753 but left without graduating. There is no record of his activities during the next decade, although it may be assumed that he was active in science, his only great interest. In 1766 he published his first important chemical paper, "Factitious Air," concerning his discovery of hydrogen, or inflammable air. His two vital reports, "Experiments on Air," were published in the *Philosophical Transactions* of 1784 and 1785. The first report describes the use of the electric spark to burn five parts of common air with two parts of hydrogen to form water, thus establishing the compound nature of water. The second report is based on an experiment by which an electric spark caused the combination of nitrogen and oxygen over water, the product reacting to form nitric acid. In the second of these papers, Cavendish noted that 1/120 part of the air was unreactive, an observation which foreshadowed the presence of the inert gas, argon, to be discovered by Sir William Ramsay 100 years later. Cavendish also investigated latent and specific heats from 1796 to 1798, invented the eudiometer tube and introduced the use of drying agents. He anticipated many of the nineteenth century discoveries in electricity, but his writings on these subjects remained in the Devonshire family until 1879, when Clerk Maxwell edited *Chemical Research of the Hon. Henry Cavendish.* He conceived the possibility of electrical potential and anticipated Ohm's law in his measurements of conductance of electrical charge, and measured inductive capacity. Although Cavendish was an adherent of the phlogiston theory, he did not oppose his contemporary, Antoine Laurent Lavoisier, and admitted that the latter's theory might be as satisfactory as the phlogiston theory. Among his publications were "Phenomena of Electricity," published in the *Philosophical Transactions* (1771); *Discovery of the Composition of Water* (1784); *Discovery of the Composition of Nitric Acid* (1785); *Freezing Point of Mercury* (1783); *Experiments to Determine the Density of the Earth* (1798); and *An Improved Method for Graduating Astronomical Instruments* (1809). In 1851 George Wilson published a *Life of Honorable Henry C. Cavendish;* and in 1921 the Royal Society published the history of his scientific researches in two well-known volumes.

Although he was a scientist of high rank, Cavendish's retiring manner kept him and his work from publicity. He had peculiarities of dress and diet and a speech defect. He avoided meeting people, and even his domestics were forbidden to appear in his presence. He never married and, despite the inheritance of a large fortune, he lived simply. Cavendish has been described as the richest of the wise, and

the wisest of the rich, having been one of the largest shareholders of the Bank of England in his time. Cavendish found his sole social enjoyment in the meetings of the Royal Society, of which he became a fellow in 1760. He also became a foreign associate of the Institute of France in 1803. Upon his death at Clapham, Feb. 24, 1810, he left £700,000 of funded property, £50,000 at his bankers, and a landed estate of £8,000 a year. He was buried in the

Sir Henry Cavendish, English chemist and physicist

FROM AN OLD ENGRAVING FROM AN OLD PRINT

COURTESY OF THE NEW YORK PUBLIC LIBRARY

family vault at All Saint's church, Derby, and in 1927 a monument was erected there to his memory. In 1874 the Cavendish Physical Laboratory was dedicated at Cambridge University. H. N. A.

CAVITE [kɑvi'te], a province and the capital city of that province, in the west central portion of Luzon Island, in the Philippine Republic, in the western Pacific Ocean.

The City. Cavite is an important port and naval base. It lies on a small peninsula 1¼ mi. long which projects into Manila Bay from its southern shore, 8 mi. southwest of Manila. A native town preceded Spanish occupation of Manila in 1571, but life in the community has revolved around the Spanish and later the United States naval installations that have helped to guard entrance into the bay. The Dutch bombarded Cavite in 1647. In 1872 it was the site of a military insurrection and in 1896 the site of an execution of thirteen insurgents to whom a monument was erected by their Filipino sympathizers in 1906. Commander George Dewey of the United States Navy defeated the Spanish fleet in Manila Bay and captured Cavite on May 1, 1898. Japanese forces bombed the Cavite naval installations on Dec. 7, 1941 (New York time), and largely destroyed them in another raid two days later, but most of the Pacific Fleet at the base was evacuated. Cavite was captured and held by Japanese ground troops as Manila was declared an open city (December 24), and American forces retired to the Bataan Peninsula and the Island of Corregidor in Manila Bay, starting December 30. The Japanese were driven from Cavite at the time of the recapture of Manila in February 1945. Before its recapture the port installations were subjected to concentrated bombings by huge forces of United States aircraft.

From 1898 until 1941 Cavite was the chief naval base and coaling station for the United States' fleet in Asiatic waters. The coaling docks were at Sangley Point near the northern edge of the municipality. Sangley Point is one of four naval installations which the United States may maintain in the Philippine Islands as a result of a ninety-nine-year agreement with the new republic in 1946. The community is a walled town and most of the buildings are of stone. There are a parochial school, two convents, a hospital, and several small manufacturing industries. The home of Emilio Aguinaldo, Filipino insurrection leader first against Spain and later against the United States, was at Cavite Viejo, the adjacent municipality. There are rail and highway connections from Cavite to Manila. Pop. 1948, 35,052.   A. Cu.

The Province. Cavite province is in southern Luzon, Philippine Islands, in the western Pacific Ocean, 14° 16′ N. lat.; 120° 50′ E. long., with an area of 498 sq. mi., across the bay from Bataan peninsula and Corregidor island. The region is of volcanic origin and the soils, derived from soft volcanic ash, are especially productive. The crops of the area are rice, sugar cane, abacá, coconuts, and corn. Pop. 1948, 262,550.

CAVOUR, COUNT CAMILLO BENSO DI [kɑvu′r] (1810-1861), Italian statesman, was born at Turin, Aug. 1, 1810. A son of the Marchese Michele Benso di Cavour, he served as a page from 1824 to 1826 in the court of the heir apparent, Charles Albert. He was trained at the Turin military academy, graduating in 1826. He was commissioned a lieutenant, but his unhappy military career terminated as a result of his too freely-expressed sympathy for the French revolution of 1830. His great passion was politics. He visited France and England in 1835 and gained impressions of constitutional government which strengthened his own view of constitutional monarchy as the best middle course between republicanism and absolutism. During the next five years he gained business experience by managing the family estate at Leri. In the 1840's he began writing about such problems of the day as the Irish situation, the English corn laws, the Italian railways, and the influence on Italy of the new English commercial policy.

In 1847, with the reforms of Charles Albert, King of Sardinia, Cavour founded the newspaper, *Il Risorgimento,* and urged the king to grant a constitution. He assisted in drafting the suffrage decree-law which accompanied the *Statuto.* He passionately advocated war against Austria when the first hostilities, lasting from March 23 to Aug. 9, 1848, broke out. However, he was dismayed by Charles Albert's uncertain strategy and dilatory tactics and regarded the direct exercise of command by the king as unsound and contrary to constitutional practice. Cavour was defeated in the first election to the Chamber in April 1848 but won a seat in the supplementary election of June. He was cautious regarding the resumption of hostilities demanded by the Democrats and lost his seat when the chamber was dissolved in January 1849. After the disastrous defeat at Novara on March 23, 1849, he favored making peace with Austria and, on returning to parliament in July of the same year, supported D'Azeglio's policy of ratification of the Treaty of Milan.

Cavour entered the D'Azeglio cabinet in 1850 as Minister of Agriculture and in 1851 also held the Ministry of Finance. In 1852, as a result of an arrangement with Urbano Rattazzi, leader of the Left Center, a "connubio" (marriage) was made with the Right Center, giving a parliamentary majority to Cavour, who became prime minister. He was continuously in power from Nov. 3, 1852, to July 12, 1859, and effected a series of extensive reforms in tariffs, finance, the army, and relations with the Church. Constitutional Piedmont prepared for resumption of the struggle against Austria, but Cavour, recognizing the need of French and British support, first brought Piedmont into the Crimean War on their side in 1855. At the Congress of Paris in 1856, which terminated that war, he was unable to secure any territorial changes in Italy, but placed the Italian question on the agenda and publicly denounced Austrian misrule in the peninsula. In 1858, Cavour secretly met Napoleon III at Plombières and the verbal agreement was made for a Franco-Sardinian alliance to drive Austria completely out of Italy. A definite treaty, signed the following January, proposed annexation of Parma, Modena, Lombardy, and Venetia to Piedmont, and promised Italian independence if not unity through the projected Italian federation, dominated by the constitutional Kingdom of North Italy. To make sure of the alliance, Cavour persuaded the King to offer his daughter, Clotilde, in marriage to Prince Jerome Napoleon of France. Cavour guaranteed to provoke Austria to attack and thereby enable Napoleon III to maintain his diplomatic understanding with Alexander II of Russia. Nice and Savoy were promised as compensation to France, which would furnish 200,000 troops. Through the National Society, Cavour was able to draw many nationalists away from Mazzini to the banner of the monarchy. British diplomatic efforts to avert the conflict were an obstacle to Cavour, but an Austrian ultimatum precipitated the war. Napoleon III, however, faltered in his pledged course after the bloody battle of Solferino and on July 11, 1859, arranged the preliminary peace of Villafranca, which left Venetia an Austrian province, proposed restoration of the princes in Modena and Tuscany, and would have made the Austrian emperor a member of an Italian federation. As a result, Cavour burst into a violent rage and resigned.

After his successors had marked time for six months, Cavour was called back to power Jan. 20, 1860, somewhat against the wishes of Victor Emmanuel II. He recognized opportunity in the uncertain situation which found Parma, Modena, Tuscany, and the Romagna under provisional governments barring the restoration of the former régimes and demanding union with the House of Savoy. Since Napoleon III did not dare permit a situation which would restore Austrian predominance, Cavour secretly negotiated the treaties of March 1860, which promised the transfer of Nice and Savoy to France. The emperor acquiesced in the annexation of the central states to Piedmont. Plebiscites accompanied all of the changes of sovereignty. Cavour gave little opportunity to the opponents of change on either side of the Alps, with the result that the pro-French vote in Nice was believed suspect and provoked Garibaldi's indignation.

When Garibaldi undertook his filibustering expedition of "The Thousand" against the Kingdom of Naples, Cavour maintained a diplomatic position, secretly giving some encouragement and aid, but ready to disavow the expedition if necessary. After Garibaldi had conquered Sicily and crossed to the mainland, Cavour felt that intervention by the regular army was necessary. Napoleon III was consulted at Chambéry on Aug. 28, 1860, and the royal army was sent south to complete the defeat of Francis II and to occupy Naples. On its way under Cialdini, it shattered the papal army at Castelfidardo, with the result that Umbria and the Marches were annexed along with Sicily and Naples. In March 1861, Cavour saw Victor Emmanuel II proclaimed King of Italy. Only Venetia, still an Austrian province, and Rome, the last remnant of papal territory, remained unredeemed. Cavour, favoring a free church in a free state, attempted to negotiate with the Vatican on that basis but failed. He had Rome almost within his grasp at the time of his death, for Napoleon

III had promised the withdrawal of the French garrison at the Vatican. Overwork, illness, and a brief falling-out with Garibaldi hastened Cavour's death. He died at Turin, June 6, 1861.   H. McG. S.

CAVY, or GUINEA PIG, a small rodent about ten inches long, belonging to the family Caviidae. Cavies are stocky animals, with large heads, short snouts, short legs and no tails. Various breeds of domestic cavies present a variety of colors. Cavies are native to most of South America, and related forms were present in Argentina from the Oligocene epoch. The wild species from which the domestic cavy was derived is undetermined. Its food includes many different kinds of plants, including leaves, tubers, and fruits. Cavies are exceedingly fertile, having two or three litters a year. In cool climates there are two to five young in a litter; in warmer climates, six to seven. Cavies are sexually mature in about nine months. They are commonly used as laboratory animals, and, together with white rats and white mice, have served as the basis for most experimental work on mammals.   A. E. W.

CAWNPORE [kɔnpɔ'r], now officially Kanpur, a manufacturing city of north central India and the administrative center of Cawnpore District. The city is the largest in the state of Uttar Pradesh and is located about 45 mi. southwest of Lucknow, the state capital, on the southwestern bank of the Ganges River. Built on the river's flat alluvial plain, about 416 ft. above sea level, Cawnpore has an annual average temperature of 77° F. The winters are cool, sunny, and dry; January has an average temperature of 59° F. Summers are hot and dry, May and June having a maximum temperature of 118° F. About 32 in. of rain falls yearly, most of it during July and August. The rich surrounding region produces wheat, barley, rice, gram, rape, mustard, and sugar cane. Cawnpore is a railroad center, and there is a bridge across the Ganges at this point. The city employs over 100,000 workers in over 200 factories, including cotton, woolen, and jute mills and production centers for metals, foods, beverages, chemicals, leather goods, and paper. Cawnpore's educational institutions include an agricultural college, a leather-working school, and a technological institute. There are also many federal and state government offices. The city was the site of the Cawnpore Massacre during the Sepoy Mutiny of 1857. Pop. 1951, 636,443 (metropolitan area, 705,383).

CAWNPORE MASSACRE. Commanding the road across the Ganges between Delhi and Lucknow, the military station of Cawnpore was one of the East India Company's strategic centers when in the summer of 1857 a mutiny of Sepoy mercenaries at Delhi and popular discontent over changes in government introduced by Lord Dalhousie, governor-general from 1848 to 1856, threatened to disaffect the civilian population. On June 6, the loyal garrison at Cawnpore, with a small contingent of British troops, attempted to defend an improvised entrenchment against a superior force of insurgents commanded by Nana Sahib, who resented the cancellation of a pension previously granted to his father. On June 27, General Sir H. M. Wheeler, the British commander, accepted an offer, made without material guarantees, to provide safe conduct to Allahabad for the besieged garrison and civilians. The next day, as the British garrison was leaving the place in boats, murderous fire was opened on them and all but four were massacred at the Ganges river bank. Two hundred and eleven women and children, captured by the

mutineers, were put to death on July 15 and cast into the well of Cawnpore, later marked by a memorial which was moved to a museum in London when India became independent in 1947.   B. La.

CAXTON, WILLIAM [kæ'kstən] (c. 1422-1491), first English printer, was born in Tenterden, Kent, about 1422. He was apprenticed in 1438 to the London mercer, Robert Large, and resided from about 1445 to 1476 in the Low Countries, mainly at Bruges, where from 1463 to 1471 he served as governor of the Merchant Adventurers, an asso-

WILLIAM CAXTON

ciation of English merchants at home and abroad. During 1471 and 1472 he learned the new art of printing in Cologne; thereafter he set up a press in Bruges and there produced *Recuyell of the Historyes of Troye* (c. 1475), the first book to be printed in English. In 1476 Caxton returned to England, established himself at Westminster, and by December produced an *Indulgence*, the first known specimen of printing in England. The first English book to bear a date, *Dictes and Sayings of the Philosophres*, appeared Nov. 18, 1477.

Caxton's literary work, consisting of twenty-four translations and produced over a period of twenty-three years, was designed for the leisure classes and is chiefly significant for its standardizing effect upon the literary language. His book production, mostly in English, totaled one hundred items; this output included religious and liturgical works but no scientific or Classical texts. After Caxton's death in 1491, the press was continued by his foreman, Wynkyn de Worde. Many of Caxton's books have been reprinted in modern editions.   C. F. Bu.

CAYENNE [kɑi'ε'n], the capital, chief port, and most important city of French Guiana, an overseas department of France. Cayenne is located at 5° N. lat. and 52° 20' W. long., on an island at the mouth of the Cayenne River. Since the harbor has a depth of only 14 ft., large steamers must anchor a few miles offshore. The annual temperature averages 80° F., with slight variation between the months and seasons. The average annual humidity ranges between 80 and 90 per cent, and the annual rainfall is approximately 130 in. February and March are the two least wet months. Besides the climate, there have been other hindrances to development. For a century and a half after its foundation by well-to-do Norman emigrants in 1635, the history of Cayenne is one of struggle against disease, Carib Indians, and raiders, of internal dissension, and of wars against the Dutch, Portuguese, and English. Slavery, until its abolishment in 1848, brought only an illusory prosperity to planters of the region. A penal colony for French criminals and political offenders, established in 1851 and not abandoned until 1946, also retarded the development of the city. Poverty is still general. The newer section of the town has broad macadamized streets, and there are many open squares, among them the spacious Place d'Armes. Gold, tropical woods, sugar, rum, coffee, cacao, hides, and spices are exported. Cayenne is connected by air with both North and South America, and there is a monthly steamship service with France. Pop. 1954, 13,346.   J. E. F.

CAYENNE PEPPER, also called long pepper, a variety, *Capsicum frutescens* var. *longum,* developed by cultivation from the red pepper. It is a tropical perennial of the nightshade family. The fully matured fruits, sometimes a foot long, are dried and ground to make a hot, strong seasoning for food. *Capsicum* is also used in medicine as a counterirritant and local stimulant.   J. A. Bo.

CAYES, LES [ke'], or Aux Cayes, a seaport on the southwest coast of Haiti, located at 18° 12' N. lat. and 73° 46' W. long. on the south side of the southern peninsula, 50 mi. east of Pointe à Gravois, the southernmost tip of Haiti. Port-au-Prince, the capital of Haiti, is about 95 air-mi. northeast of Les Cayes. The city is situated on a low but narrow coastal plain immediately south of the La Hotte Mountains, which form the backbone of the southwestern peninsula. Les Cayes has a humid, warm climate, and the temperature for January, the coolest month, averages about 68° F., while July may average 80° F. The average annual rainfall is between 40 and 60 in., and during the fall Les Cayes may be struck by hurricanes, which bring a large amount of rain and sometimes do considerable damage. The natural vegetation around Les Cayes is of a tropical, savannah type, and there are acacia, sugar cane, coffee, coconut, and palm trees; in the wetter hill areas behind the city there is mahogany and a rainforest type of vegetation. Les Cayes was settled in 1503 by Spanish colonists. Nearly destroyed by fire in 1908, it has been largely rebuilt with concrete. Les Cayes is an active commercial center and is connected with the rest of Haiti by an all-weather road. Small boats carry part of the trade of Les Cayes. Coffee, cotton, bananas, and logwood are the chief exports. Pop. (prelim. 1950), 11,608.

CAYLEY, ARTHUR (1821-1895), English mathematician, was born at Richmond, Surrey, Aug. 16, 1821. He was educated at Trinity College, Cambridge University, where he became a fellow in 1842 and was advanced to major fellow in 1845. He entered Lincoln's Inn in 1846 and was admitted to the bar three years later. Cayley practiced as a solicitor, but much of his time was taken up with mathematical research and in 1863 he was elected to the newly founded Sadlerian chair of pure mathematics at Cambridge University. Cayley wrote more than eight hundred papers on pure mathematics which were collected in thirteen quarto volumes. In his papers on quantics he developed the theory of algebraic invariants. He founded the study of the geometry of *n*-dimensional space and that of matrices, and devised the abbreviated hyperdeterminant notation for invariants. A theorem and curve are named after him. Cayley received almost every important honor which it was possible for a scientist to receive. He died in Cambridge, Jan. 26, 1895.   R. T.

CAYLEY, SIR GEORGE (1773-1857), English inventor, called "Father of British Aeronautics," was born Dec. 27, 1773, at Brompton Hall, Scarborough, England. After receiving his early education in schools at York and Nottingham, he went to Southgate in 1792 to study electricity and chemistry under the tutelage of George Cadogan Morgan. In the same year his father, Sir Thomas Cayley, died, and he succeeded to the baronetcy. In 1833 he was elected to Parliament and served two years.

Cayley first experimented with aeronautics at Southgate in 1792, using a Chinese "flying top," a toy helicopter demonstrated by Launoy and Bienvenu about 1784. The next evidence of his interest in aeronautics, discovered in 1935, was a silver disk dated 1799 and bearing a design of an aircraft with a fixed wing, rudder, and elevator, and two large oars extending from a boat-shaped body suspended from the wing. For several years after 1800 his notebook contains observations and theoretical studies on the flight of many species of birds. In 1804 he began experiments in aerodynamics with a crude whirling arm, and during this period built his first model glider, consisting of a plane inclined at 6°, connected by a rod to two smaller planes crossing each other at right angles and adjustable to any angle. Cayley considered the problem of heavier-than-air flight to depend upon research on the behavior of the inclined plane against air and upon the development of a suitable engine—the same approach that the Wright brothers used nearly one hundred years later. Cayley's researches along both lines continued until about 1810. In 1807 he published his first article, on his "expansion air engine," a hot-air mechanism using a pump which forced air through a connected air-tight furnace and into a working cylinder at alternate ends. In 1807 he experimented with an engine utilizing the heat of exploding gunpowder. In 1808 he built a number of fixed-wing gliders, some of such size that he invented the tension or bicycle wheel for use as a launching device. His articles in Nicholson's *Journal of Natural Philosophy* in 1809 and 1810, widely reprinted in later years, summarized his thoughts and the results of his experiments; he discussed the relation of velocity to lift, wing loading, stresses, weight saving, and the principle of the internal-combustion engine. He recommended streamlining, stating that every pound of direct resistance which could be avoided would support 30 lb. of additional weight without requiring additional power. Cayley's biplane glider, built with a total wing area of 300 sq. ft., could carry a man several yards.

About 1815 Cayley became interested in navigable balloons, and his writings of that period discuss the relations of size to weights lifted, the desirable shape of the balloon for minimum air resistance, and the need for internal bracing. He recommended division of the gas containers into sections and waterproofing of the outside envelope; he also discussed the merits of hot air and hydrogen as lifting gases and methods of preventing fires in balloons. Cayley patented his hotair engine in 1837 and proposed a twin-rotor, steam-powered helicopter in 1840. In 1853 he recommended the use of the screw propeller for power and suggested a hydrogen-powered engine as a possibility. There is evidence that he was still experimenting with gliders as late as 1850 to 1853, and in 1855 he described an improvement on the aerial top with which he had experimented more than sixty years before. He died in Scarborough, Dec. 15, 1857. Although best known for his aeronautical work, Cayley is credited with experimental work on automatic signaling for railways, safety lifeboats, rifled shot, and an artificial hand, and with the invention of the caterpillar tractor.   M. H. Sm.

CAYMAN ISLANDS [kaimɑ'n], a group of three small islands in the Caribbean Sea, 150 mi. northwest of Jamaica. The islands—Grand Cayman, Little Cayman, and Cayman Brac—have a total area of 93 sq. mi. The Cayman Islands became part of the West Indies Federation in 1957 as a dependency of Jamaica, but in February 1958 a permissive act was signed providing for separation from Jamaica and the future status of the islands as a component colony and territory of the Federation. The islanders build small ships for trading goods in their area. The exports include green turtles (after which the islands were once called Tortugas) and turtle shells, shark skins, coconuts, and dyewood. Georgetown on Grand Cayman is the principal city. Pop. (est. 1955), 8,266. **J. E. F. and G. Con.**

CAYUGA LAKE [keyu'ga; kɑyu'gə], one of the Finger Lakes of upper New York State. The boundary between Cayuga and Seneca counties runs through the lake, and it extends into Tompkins Co. Cayuga Lake, with an area of 75 sq. mi., is about 38 mi. long, 1-3 mi. wide, and about 400 ft. deep, with a surface elevation of 381 ft. Taughannock Creek and its 210-ft. cataract flow into the lake, which is drained to the north by the Seneca River, which joins the Oswego River and flows into Lake Ontario. Cayuga Lake is connected by canal with Seneca Lake on the west and with the Erie Canal on the north. The city of Ithaca, N. Y., seat of Cornell University, is located at the southern end of the lake. The Cayuga Indians, a branch of the Iroquois, lived around the lake. **J. E. F.**

CEANOTHUS [siəno'thəs], a large genus of the buckthorn family, with about fifty North American species, chiefly on the Pacific coast. They are shrubs and small trees, from 2 to 20 ft. tall, some with varieties of ornamental value. Many hybrids have been developed in Europe. About thirty species are native to California, being abundant in the chaparral, among which are the whitehorn, *C. leucodermis,* and *C. thyrsiflorus,* native from Oregon south, with beautiful blue, freely borne flowers. *C. sanguineus* is sometimes called the Oregon tea tree, while *C. americanus,* native to the east coast, is known as New Jersey tea. The redroot, *C. ovatus,* is native from New England west and south to Colorado and Alabama. *See also* CALIFORNIA LILAC. **J. C. Wis.**

CEBU [sebu'], an island, a province virtually coextensive with that island, and the capital city of that province, in the Republic of the Philippines.

The Island and Province. Cebu is a long, narrow island of the Visayan group in the central Philippine Islands, with an area of 1,702 sq. mi. Mactán and other small islands nearby account for the total area of the province, 1,884 sq. mi. Southeast of the province, across Bohol Strait, lies the island of Bohol; to the west, across Tañon Strait, is Negros Island; and to the northeast, across the Camotes Sea, is Leyte Island. The island of Cebu is mountainous, attaining an elevation of 3,324 ft. on Mt. Cabalasan. The dense population of Cebu, over 800 per sq. mi., consists largely of small-scale farmers. Cebu has a limestone base and a porous, infertile soil in which the sparse rainfall dries quickly. It is suited to the raising of corn, the staple diet of the islanders. The most important export items are copra, sugar, hemp, lumber, and iron and chrome ore. Pop. 1948 (province), 1,123,107.

The City. The city of Cebu lies on the eastern side of the island, 375 mi. southeast of Manila and 100 mi. east of Iloilo. It is the second city of the republic and an archdiocesan headquarters of the Roman Catholic Church. A regular port of call for both interisland and foreign ships, Cebu is the market center for all the Visayans, with branch offices of numerous foreign import firms. The city is one of the most historic points in the Philippine Islands. A native village occupied the site of the present city when Magellan landed there on Apr. 7, 1521. Across the strait lies Mactán Island. Here Magellan met the native chieftain Sicatuan and each sealed a truce with his own blood. However, despite

Thatched cottages, clustered together over the water on pile-supported foundations, border a canal which serves Cebu's harbor in the Philippines.

the compact, the famous explorer later lost his life in a skirmish with the natives of the island. In 1565 Miguel López de Legaspi arrived with some Augustinian friars and established a Spanish colony at Cebu, from which, for the next six years, he ruled whatever portion of the archipelago the Spaniards were able to subjugate; later he moved the capital to a site on Panay and then on to Manila.

Situated on a peninsula somewhat semicircular in shape, Cebu occupies a small plain at the base of the central mountain range which extends the length of the narrow island. It consists of four districts, each functionally apart from the others. The business and commercial area adjacent to the harbor contains the commercial firms and warehouses, hotels, and municipal buildings. In this district the city's industries produce pottery, sugar sacks, and salt, the latter by evaporation from salt pans. In Lahug, between the railway and the hills behind the city, is the largest and least congested district. It is the administrative center and a residential district with the beautiful provincial capitol and Osmeña fountain, both prominent landmarks. The smaller San Nicolás District, at the southwestern edge of the city, is an extension of the older section and separated from the business area by the Guadalupe River. Mabolo, in the northwestern part of the city, is a small barrio of native homes with a small church and convent. Cebu has an all-weather airport 3 mi. north of the business district, two local radio stations broadcasting in the English and Visayan languages, and three local daily newspapers. The languages spoken are English, Cebuano (a Visayan dialect), and Spanish.

During World War II Cebu was severely damaged. It was largely rebuilt after the war, but the typhoons of 1949 and 1951 destroyed much of this hasty construction. Permanent concrete structures are gradually being built. Prominent buildings besides the provincial capitol, include the city hall, San Carlos College and Church, Cebu Normal School, Cebu High School, Southern Islands Hospital, the cathedral, San Nicolás Church, the customshouse, and the bank. Newly established commercial firms include a manufacturing plant for rubber shoes, another for corn products, and several soft-drink bottling works. Cebu is the birthplace and residence of Sergio Osmeña, the independence leader and second president of the Philippine Commonwealth, whose term of office extended from 1944 to 1946. Pop. 1948, 77,411.

ČECH, SVATOPLUK [tsh3′k] (1846-1908), Czech poet, was born Feb. 21, 1846. He was the most popular Czech poet of the nineteenth century and the last poet of the regeneration period, influenced by Russian and Polish Byronism and Czech Romanticism. His nationalism, deep Slavonic feeling, and inner inclination toward the East were the main reasons for his popularity. As head of the nationalist school in literature, with his brother Vladimir he founded his own periodical *Kvety* ("Blossoms") in 1879 to report on cultural, political, and social movements in Czech lands. He achieved popularity in long epic poems, mostly from Czech history, among the most important of which are *The Adamites* (1874) and *Václav z Michalovic* (1882). These works are philosophical in character and lay special emphasis on the humanitarian and democratic ideals. He also drew subjects from contemporary Czech life in the social story, *The Blacksmith of Lešetín* (1884) and the idyllic story, *In the Shade of the Linden-tree* (1880). His satirical novels, *Excursion of Mr. Brouček to the Moon* (1888) and *Excursion of Mr. Brouček to the Fifteenth Century,* were very popular, and his collections of eloquent lyrics, such as *Morning Songs* (1886) and *New Songs* (1888), in which he expressed the social and national sentiments, are of great artistic and historical value. In all his works, but especially in his great symbolic *Songs of the Slave* (1895), he expressed the Czech political and social convictions and defended the Czech cause during the Austrian oppression of his nation. He died on Feb. 23, 1908.   E. Mi.

CECIL, ROBERT, 1st EARL OF SALISBURY [sɛ′səl] (c. 1563-1612), English statesman, third son of William Cecil, Lord Burghley, was born at Westminster sometime between 1563 and 1565, and was educated at St. John's College, Cambridge. From 1584 to 1588 he was probably employed abroad; he was also a member of the House of Commons in all the Parliaments from 1584 to the end of Elizabeth's reign in 1603. In 1591 he was knighted and started doing the work of Secretary of State, to which office he was finally appointed in 1596. In 1598 he went on a special mission to Henry IV of France. On his father's death in the same year there was a bitter conflict between Cecil and the Earl of Essex for the position as chief adviser to the Crown. Because of his great administrative ability, in this conflict the hunchbacked and crippled Cecil was victorious over Elizabeth's handsome but reckless favorite. It was largely Cecil's influence that secured a peaceful succession for James I, whose chief minister he then became; in 1604 he was made Viscount Cranborne and in 1605 Earl of Salisbury. In 1608 he became Lord Treasurer and applied his skill to the management of the king's tangled finances. Although desiring peace with Spain and France, and a balance between them, he aimed at making England the leading Protestant power; to this end, in 1612 he married James's daughter Elizabeth to the Elector of the Palatinate. He died at Marlborough on May 24, 1612. Though he did not attain the stature of a great statesman he was a careful, cautious, and orderly administrator.   E. R. A.

CECIL, WILLIAM, BARON BURGHLEY or **BURLEIGH** (1520-1598), English statesman, was born at Bourne, Lincolnshire, on Sept. 13, 1520. Educated at St. John's College, Cambridge, he was brought into contact with the greatest English scholars of his day. He attached himself to the Protector, Somerset, and shared his downfall in 1550, but his real ability made him a secretary of state later in the year. In 1551 he was knighted. Under Mary he lost his office, but conformed to the Catholic faith and kept out of trouble, and with Elizabeth's accession in 1558, he became her chief secretary of state and most trusted adviser. Preeminently cautious, he agreed with the Queen on the necessity of a middle way in religion between Papists and Puritans, though in later years he became more Protestant than Elizabeth and more inclined to aid Protestants abroad. At home, he preached moderation and prosperity, and finding himself, on the whole, in accord with the Queen, was able to put his policies into effect. In 1559 he was made Chancellor of the University of Cambridge, and in 1571 he was raised to the peerage as Baron Burghley; in the following year he became Lord High Treasurer, though he still remained Elizabeth's chief adviser on all matters, foreign and domestic. He died in London on Aug. 4, 1598. Honest, cautious and moderate, of blameless private life, he was almost ideally suited to guide England in the tempestuous years of the late sixteenth century.   E. R. A.

CECILIA, ST. (second or third century), a Christian virgin martyr, who has been greatly venerated for over a thousand years. Her cult as patroness of musicians is probably to be ascribed to a medieval misreading of a statement in her *Acts,* taken to imply that she played the organ.

According to the same fifth-century *Acts,* she was a patrician of Rome and was brought up a Christian. Her father gave her in marriage to a patrician named Valerian, but she had determined to remain a virgin, dedicated to God, and told Valerian that she had an angel of God as her spouse; Valerian, upon believing and being baptized, saw the angel at her side and respected her virginity. The story ends with the marytrdom of Cecilia and Valerian.

Of Cecilia and Valerian nothing is certain beyond their marytrdom and their burial in Rome. Cecilia was buried in the crypt of the Cecilii at the catacomb of St. Callistus, and Valerian in the cemetery of Praetextatus. St. Cecilia's Feast is November 22.   W. C.

CECROPIA [sikro′piə], the common name of the largest North American moth (*Samia cecropia*), of the family Saturnidae. It has dusky wings with "eye spots" and paler markings on the margins; the body is red with white bands. Its wing expanse is from 5 to 7 in. The caterpillar is about 4 in. long when full grown, and bears six rows of stout, thorny tubercles. It feeds on a wide variety of trees and shrubs. The cocoons are large, tapering at both ends, and light brownish in color.   C. H. Cu.

CEDAR, a name widely used for many kinds of cone-bearing evergreen trees. The true cedar, *Cedrus,* has 3 species native to Asia and Africa: the very handsome wide-branched cedar of Lebanon, *C. libani,* mentioned in the Bible and valued through many centuries for its durable red wood; the deodar, *C. deodara,* native to the Himalayas;

and an African cedar, *C. atlantica,* a native of the Atlas Mountains. All these are grown in this country as ornamentals. In the United States, cedar is the common name of various trees, such as the white cedar, an 80-ft. tree, *Chamaecyparis thyoides,* of the southern states; the yellow cedar, *C. nootkatensis,* a 120-ft. tree of the northern Pacific coast; and the very beautiful Port Orford cedar, *C. lawsoniana,* a 200-ft. tree, native to Oregon and California. The common arborvitae, *Thuja occidentalis,* native to the northeast is also called white cedar and the giant arborvitae, *T. plicata,* of the Pacific northwest is known as western red cedar or canoe cedar. In addition, it is the common name of many junipers, the red cedar, *Juniperus virginiana,* and the desert white cedar, *J. californica.* A rare yew-like tree, *Torreya taxifolia,* of the southern states is called stinking cedar. Spanish cedar, *Cedrela odorata,* is not a conifer but belongs to the mahogany family. Its name is derived from the fact that its fragrant wood, much used for making cigar boxes, resembles that of the true cedar.   J. C. Wis.

CEDAR CITY, a city in Iron Co., in southwestern Utah, about 230 air mi. southwest of Salt Lake City. It is located at 5,800 ft. above sea level at the base of the Wasatch Mountains in an agricultural region which contains one of the largest open-pit iron mines in the United States. Founded in 1851, it was incorporated as a city in 1868 and is governed by a mayor and council. Cedar Breaks National Monument and Kolob Canyon are only a short distance from the city, which is a conveniently located rail point giving

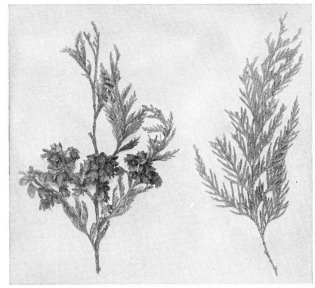

COURTESY OF THE U. S. FOREST SERVICE

Branches of White Cedar, Thuja occidentalis, *showing (left) woody, scaled cones, and (right) flat, opposite leaves closely pressed to twigs*

access to Zion, Bryce Canyon, and Grand Canyon national parks. It is also a trade and shipping center for the farm produce and ranch livestock of a widespread area. Cedar City's economy is based primarily on iron, coal, and uranium mines, seed nurseries, meat-packing and poultry-processing plants, feed mills, a cannery, and a bottle works. Plaster, wool products, lumber, and excelsior are other manufactures. Cedar City is the seat of the College of Southern Utah, a branch of the Utah State Agricultural College. Transportation is provided by the Union Pacific Railroad and Western Air Lines. Pop. 1950, 6,106.

CEDAR CREEK, BATTLE OF (Oct. 19, 1864), an engagement in the Shenandoah Valley of Virginia during the Civil War. General Philip H. Sheridan, having devastated the Shenandoah Valley and defeated the Confederate army under General Jubal A. Early at Fisher's Hill, left his army of 30,000 encamped at Cedar Creek, 15 mi. from Winchester, Va., while he proceeded to Washington for consultation. Returning promptly, he spent the night of October 18 in Winchester. In the early morning of October 19, taking advantage of the darkness and fog, the Confederates attacked, driving the Union troops from their camps, taking about 1,500 prisoners, and capturing supplies. General Horatio G. Wright, commanding in Sheridan's absence, rallied part of his forces and withstood the Confederate attack. Meantime, Sheridan riding from Winchester, met the fleeing soldiers and wagon trains. Riding swiftly to the front and rallying his men, Sheridan arrived in time to turn the tide of battle. By nightfall the Federal troops had driven the Confederates from the field. The Union loss, in addition to Early's first prisoners, was 4,070; the Confederate loss about 3,000. Sheridan's ride from Winchester was immortalized in a famous poem by Thomas Buchanan Read.   W. B. H.

CEDAR CREST COLLEGE, an accredited, privately controlled college of arts and sciences for women affiliated with the Evangelical and Reformed Church, located on a campus of 104 acres at Allentown, Pa. It was chartered in 1867 as Allentown Female College, and the name was

LYNWOOD M. CHACE—C. P. CUSHING

Samia cecropia, a large silkworm moth, native to the eastern United States. Its larvae feed on the leaves of many fruit and forest trees.

changed in 1926 to Cedar Crest. The curriculums offered include liberal arts, home economics, business education, co-operative nursing (a five-year course), elementary education, and medical technology. Degrees awarded are the A.B. and the B.S. There are a limited number of scholarships available to students on the basis of high grades and financial need. Residence halls are available for all students. *For statistics see* COLLEGES AND UNIVERSITIES.

CEDARHURST, a village in the southern part of Nassau Co., Long Island, in southeastern New York, is 21 mi. from New York City. Its business section adjoins that of Lawrence on the southwest. A residential community, it is served by the Long Island Railroad. Pop. 1950, 6,051.

CEDAR MOUNTAIN, BATTLE OF (Aug. 9, 1862), an engagement of the Civil War in Virginia. Confederate troops under Gen. T. J. ("Stonewall") Jackson moved out of Richmond toward the line of the Rappahannock River, and the remainder of Gen. Robert E. Lee's forces prepared to follow. Two brigades of the Federal Army of the Potomac, which was under the command of Gen. John Pope, advanced across the Rappahannock and met Jackson's force at the foot of Cedar or Slaughter's Mountain. Federal Gen. Nathaniel P. Banks ill-advisedly attacked as commanded by Pope, although he had barely half as many men as his opponent. The battle lasted well into the night, the Confederates pushing the Union troops back several miles. The Union forces lost 2,381 men; the Confederates, 1,276. Several days later, the bulk of Lee's army having come up, the northward advance was resumed. W. B. H.

CEDAR RAPIDS, the county seat of Linn Co. in eastern Iowa, is situated on the Cedar River, about 27 mi. north of Iowa City and 115 mi. northeast of Des Moines. The city was first settled in 1838, and named Rapids City in 1841. The name was changed to Cedar Rapids in 1848, and the city was incorporated in 1856. It has the commission type of government. The history of Cedar Rapids is linked with the notorious Shepard gang of horse thieves which, until 1851, made its rendezvous on what was later Municipal Island, located in the Cedar River channel between the east and west business districts. The Cedar River provides ample water power for the city's industrial establishments, the principal ones being machine shops, packing houses, and grain mills. One of the most important buildings is the Memorial

Cedar Rapids Municipal Island situated in the Cedar River, Linn Co., Iowa, houses the city commission in its million-dollar Memorial Building. The city of Cedar Rapids, through which the river flows, is connected with the island by three pairs of bridges.

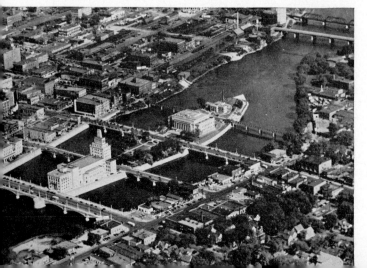

Building, erected at a cost of $1,000,000 and dedicated to those men and women of the nation who have served in its wars. Cedar Rapids is the seat of Coe College and Mount Mercy Junior College. The city is served by the Chicago and North Western, the Chicago, Rock Island and Pacific, the Illinois Central, the Chicago, Milwaukee, St. Paul and Pacific, the Cedar Rapids & Iowa City, and the Waterloo, Cedar Falls & Northern railroads, and by the United Air Lines. Pop. 1950, 72,296.

CEDARTOWN, the seat of Polk Co., in northwestern Georgia, is situated 62 mi. northwest of Atlanta. It was incorporated in 1850. The Central of Georgia and the Seaboard Air Line railroads furnish transportation. Textiles, plows, paper products, furniture, and other lumber products comprise the local manufactures. Pop. 1950, 9,470.

CEFALÙ [tshe'falu'], a small port on the northern coast of Sicily, in Palermo province, on the railway to Messina. Located on a narrow coastal plain at the foot of a peak rising nearly 1,000 ft. out of the sea, Cefalù is the center of a fertile agricultural region. The city's cathedral, one of the most beautiful examples of the Norman style in Italy, was begun in 1131 by King Roger II and completed in 1148. Pop. 1954 (city), 10,700; (commune), 12,300. R. G. W.

CELANDINE [sɛ'lɔɾ.dain] *Chelidonium majus,* a loosely branching European herb of the poppy family, 2 to 4 ft. high, with finely cut leaves and bright yellow flowers, and poisonous, orange-colored juice, sometimes used as a purgative or mild narcotic. It is found in some old gardens and has run wild west and south from Maine. The figwort buttercup, *Ranunculus ficaria,* is called the lesser celandine.
J. C. Wis.

CELAYA [sɛla'ʃa], a city in the state of Guanajuato, in central Mexico, situated about 180 mi. northwest of Mexico City. Located 5,673 ft. above sea level, it has a temperate climate. Celaya is at the junction point of two important railroads. It is noted for a special confection, *cajeta de Celaya,* which is known throughout Mexico. The candy has the consistency of a heavy jam. Local manufactures also include saddles, candles, soap, and textiles. The city has an interesting market place; the surrounding country is very attractive. Francisco Eduardo Tresguerras, the great architect, sculptor, and painter, was born in Celaya. His masterpiece, the Church of Our Lady of Carmen, with a Corinthian portico, is in the city. Celaya was founded in 1570 by 16 Biscayan families and named "Zalaya," meaning "level land" in Basque. It became a city in 1655 and was sacked by revolutionists in 1810. Pop. 1950, 34,426. S. G. I.

CELEBES [sɛ'ləbiz], an island, known officially as Sulawesi, in the Republic of Indonesia, situated east of Borneo between about 1° 45' N. lat. and 5° 37' S. lat. and about 118° 49' and 125° 5' E. long. Celebes is bounded on the north by the Celebes Sea, on the northeast by Molucca Sea, on the east by the Banda Sea, on the south by the Flores Sea, and on the west by Macassar Strait. The island consists of four long peninsulas; in outline it somewhat resembles an octopus with four tentacles missing on the western side. The peninsulas partly enclose three great gulfs: Tomini in the northeast, Tolo in the east, and Bone in the south. Although its length is about 800 mi., no part of the island is more than 70 mi. from the sea. Celebes covers slightly less than 70,000 sq. mi., but adjacent small islands, included for administrative purposes, raise this figure to 83,810 sq. mi., or about the same size as Kansas. The island is mountainous, with peaks rising to more than 10,000 ft. in the center and south. There are at least ten large lakes of great scenic beauty occupying structural basins in the mountains, some of them several miles long and more than 1,000 ft. deep. The rivers of Celebes are short and steep, with many rapids and picturesque waterfalls. The best natural harbors are situated for the most part well out toward the extremities of the four peninsulas.

The climate of Celebes is warm and humid in the lower elevations and appreciably cooler above 2,000 ft. The average annual rainfall varies within short distances from about 21 in. to more than 120 in., depending primarily on elevation and exposure to the monsoon winds rather than on differences in latitude or distance from the sea. The flora and fauna, on the whole, are more Asiatic than Australian in character and origin.

The chief food crops are rice, maize, fruits, vegetables, and coconuts. Exports include rubber, coffee, kapok, nutmeg, copra, corn, rattan, hides, ebony, sandalwood, nickel, gold, and pearl shell. Iron, copper, lead, and coal have been found on the island but have not been mined to any extent.

The population consists of many peoples and tribes, who differ widely in language, culture, and religion. The northeastern tip of the island is inhabited by about 255,000 Minahassians or Menadonese, most of whom are Christian. West of them live about 204,000 Muslim Gorontalese. In the center of the island are a large number of pagan (now in part Christian) tribes, usually grouped together under the term of Toradja, who number about 800,000. Among the tribes of eastern Celebes, the approximately 100,000 Tolaki are the most numerous. The southwestern peninsula is inhabited by Muslim peoples, its southern end by about 900,-000 Macasserese, and the rest by about 1,800,000 Bugi. The Muslim Mandarese on the west coast of central Celebes, numbering about 175,000, are frequently classed with the Bugi. The natives are primarily farmers, but some are seminomadic hunters and others are coastal fishermen.

Celebes was known to Portuguese traders at least as early as 1512, when Portugal had a monopoly of the Molucca Islands spice trade. Portuguese influence on the island was supplanted by Dutch early in the seventeenth century. Celebes was occupied by the Japanese in January 1942 and was used chiefly as an air base during World War II. Returned to the Netherlands at the end of the war, it was included in the State of East Indonesia, formed Dec. 24, 1946. It is now one of the 10 provinces of the Republic of Indonesia, with Makassar as its capital. Pop. (est. 1955), 5,500,000.

R. G. B.

CELEBES APE, or black ape, *Cynopithecus niger,* is related to the macaques of Asia and to the baboons of Africa; but, unlike typical members of those groups, has no tail and is generally of an amiable disposition.

CELEBES SEA, a large, tropical, body of water between the southern Philippine Islands and the northern Netherlands East Indies, enclosed by the Sulu Archipelago and Mindanao on the north, the Sangihe and Talaud (Talaur) islands on the east, Celebes on the south, and Borneo on the west, at 3° N. lat. and 123° E. long. R. G. B.

CELERE. *See* MUSICAL TERMS.

CELERY, a temperate climate vegetable, developed from European wild celery, *Apium graveolens,* a biennial of the parsley family. Two types, "turnip-rooted" (Hamburg) celery or "celeriac," *A.g. rapaceum,* and true celery, *A.g.*

BLACK STAR

The burial grounds on the outskirts of the village of Lemo in Turajaland are typical of south central Celebes. On a decorative platform directly below the roof of this tiered and elaborately thatched burial house lie two cylindrically wrapped bodies.

dulce, are frequently grown for northeastern markets here, and largely grown in Europe. The green or blanched stems are used in salads, as a cooked vegetable, as a savory seasoning, or are eaten raw. Seed is sown in hotbeds for the early crop and in the open for late celery. The seedlings are transplanted once or twice before being planted in permanent quarters. In the new celery culture, rows are made 12 in. or less apart so that the plants will blanch themselves without being hilled or boarded. This method is more popular for early than for late celery. Blanching is otherwise achieved by excluding the light by means of boards, tile, paper, or hilled-up earth. Under the still popular method for home use, the late crop is dug and the plants set close together in moist earth in cellars until blanched. Much celery is now sold green; tender varieties for this purpose are available in heights ranging from 1 to 3 ft. Although still grown in home gardens, the difficulties involved, together with the constant commercial supply available, have made celery growing less popular than formerly. Commercial plantations are mostly on wet but artificially drained peaty areas, where a supply of water is obtained when necessary by closing the drains and allowing water to rise in the soil. Soil to be used for celery should be well supplied with magnesium limestone and an abundance of plant food. It should have been well cultivated for several years before celery is attempted.

The commercial production of celery in the United States started around Kalamazoo, Mich., somewhere in the 1880's, but its rapid popularity soon spread its production to many more states, of which about 15 rank it as an important industry. Among some of the chief growers of celery in the United States are California, Florida, Michigan, New York, and New Jersey. It ranks about fifteenth from the standpoint of acreage devoted to it, and production usually is in excess of 25 million crates.

The various consuming markets show particular preferences for different types of celery, and special sizes and this is determined largely by local tastes. V. A. T.

CELESTIAL MECHANICS, the division of astronomy which treats of positions, velocities, shapes, masses, and sizes of the heavenly bodies. Of primary importance are Newton's laws of motion:

(1) Every body continues in its state of rest or of uniform motion in a straight line, unless impelled by external force to change that state.

(2) Rate of change of momentum is proportional to the force acting, and the change takes place in the direction in which the force acts.

(3) To every action there is an equal and opposite reaction.

For centuries it was believed that rest was a more natural state than motion, but in accordance with the first law, this notion is false and motion alone implies no acting force present. Momentum, in the second law, is the product of mass by velocity. This law implies that whether or not a body is in motion, and whether or not other forces are acting, a certain force causes the same change of momentum that it would if this force alone were acting on the body at rest.

Calculations of Motion. By means of the laws of motion, celestial mechanics can determine the entire circumstance of a body's motion; for when the force is given, the manner of change of velocity of the object from time to time can be found. Newton derived important applications to astronomy from Kepler's laws. Kepler's first law shows that the attraction of the sun on a planet momentarily varies inversely as the square of the planet's distance from the sun. According to the second law, the law of areas, a planet moves so that the radius vector (line from sun to planet) sweeps over equal areas in equal times. From the third law Newton found that the sun's attraction depends only on distance and not on physical properties of the planets. This law allows the establishment of the distance of the planets from the sun in terms of the distance of any of them, after the planets' sidereal periods of revolution have been observed.

Calculations of Gravity. Newton's law of gravitation has a leading part in celestial mechanics: Every particle of matter in the universe attracts every other particle with a force that varies inversely as the square of the distance between them, and directly as the product of their masses.

This law appears to be applicable to all parts of the universe even, for example, to the orbits of far-distant binary stars. Gravitation is thus a universal attraction, whereas gravity is the resultant — at the surface of the earth — of the earth's gravitation and the centrifugal force due to rotation of the globe. Newton demonstrated that the moon, while traveling in its orbit, "falls" toward the earth by the same law that pulls an apple toward the ground. In 1 sec. the moon deviates from a straight line, or falls toward the earth, by about 0.05 in., and the earth deviates about 0.11 in. in its orbit in falling toward the sun.

Determination of the constant of gravitation, the earth's mass, the surface gravity of any planet, and many other problems are of interest to celestial mechanics. For example, the surface gravity on another planet, compared to that on the earth's surface, is given by

$$\frac{M}{r^2}$$

where M is the planet's mass and r is the planet's radius, both compared to the earth's. For Jupiter the ratio is

$$318.35/(10.97)^2$$

or 2.64; hence a 200-lb. object would weigh 528 lb. on Jupiter.

Problem of Two Bodies. In the problem of two bodies, if the masses of two spheres which are subject to their mutual gravitation are known, and their positions and velocities are given for a certain moment, it is possible to determine their motions at any time. The two bodies move in orbits around their center of mass, and the size and shape of the two orbits are governed by the velocities and masses of the two bodies. The orbits are always some form of the conic sections (circle, ellipse, parabola, or hyperbola).

Calculation of Positions. The calculation of positions of a planet or other heavenly body can be effected when the dimensions of the orbit are known, together with the velocity of the object and time of perihelion passage; and when the positions are known, together with the earth's positions, an ephemeris can be constructed that shows the places for various times in the future. Such a problem may be complex, because a planet's motion is not simple but is disturbed by the action of all the other planets, and for precise work these attractions or perturbations must be taken into account. The orbits themselves are not invariable but slowly change their "elements" over long periods of time. Many of the perturbations are periodic, and some are "secular"—running on for ages—but secular perturbations may be periodic with respect to vast lapses of time. Only minor changes are occurring in the planets' orbits, and according to authorities in celestial mechanics the stability of the planetary system is assured for millions of years at least. *See also* EPHEMERIS; GRAVITATION; HARMONIC LAW; ORBIT; PERIHELION; PERTURBATIONS.　　　　　　　　　　　　　　　　H. S. R.

CELESTIAL SPHERE, the imaginary sphere upon which all heavenly objects appear to be placed. Its radius is generally assumed to be infinite and its center is commonly taken as the earth's center; but on account of its tremendous size, the center may be considered at the observer or at the sun. Because of the rotation of the earth, the celestial objects seem to rotate daily around it. The sphere is simply the empty background against which the stars, planets, and other bodies are in continuous motion.

Applications. The sphere is of immense aid in astronomy, for it assists in measurement of distances on the sky and in locating objects. Although all the objects actually are at various distances from the earth, to the student of spherical astronomy all such objects are said to lie on the surface of the celestial sphere. The apparent position of such a body is described by the location of its projection on the sphere, and often only the direction of the object from the observer is of importance. Distances on the celestial sphere cannot be expressed in ordinary units, such as miles, but only in angular measurement, either in degrees, minutes, and seconds of arc (° ′ ″) or in hours, minutes, and seconds of "time" (hr., min., sec.; h m s), or sometimes in radians. Distances in absolute space between two bodies, however, may be known in miles, light-years, and so on. The apparent or angular diameter of an object is the angle subtended by the actual linear diameter (say in miles) at the observer, and for the same sized object the apparent diameter evidently depends on the distance from the spectator, the greater distance giving a smaller angular diameter.

Systems of Co-ordinates. Positions of points on the celestial sphere are described by numbers called co-ordinates. On the celestial sphere four systems of co-ordinates are in use: the horizon, the equator, the ecliptic, and the galactic systems. Circles composing these systems form imaginary networks on the sky, and the networks are offset against each other.

Horizon System. The horizon system is used to locate a point in the heavens with respect only to the observer, without regard to the objects's place in the constellation regions of the sky. The fundamental circle is the astronomical horizon, and its poles are the zenith and the nadir. Secondary great circles are called vertical circles. Any point on the sphere has a vertical circle, which is a great circle passing through the observer's zenith and nadir, and cutting the horizon at right angles. The spectator's meridian is the vertical circle passing through the celestial poles and his north and south points of the horizon. At right angles to the meridian is the prime vertical, the vertical circle going through the east and west points. Parallels in this system are called parallels of altitude, circles of equal altitude, or almucantars; they are small circles parallel to the horizon. Co-ordinates are azimuth (A) and altitude (h). Because of the apparent rotation of all objects in the sky, an object's azimuth and altitude are constantly changing with time. The system is of use particularly in navigation and in geodesy, and also is applied in astronomy.

Equator System. The equator system is of value primarily to locate objects in their more or less permanent position in the stellar background. With relatively fixed bodies such as a star, the equatorial co-ordinates remain practically unaltered for long periods of time. The fundamental circle is the celestial equator, whose poles are the celestial poles. Secondary circles are the hour circles, and the parallels are small circles parallel to the equator and known as parallels of declination. The co-ordinates are right ascension (α or R.A.) and declination (δ or dec.). These co-ordinates are used more than any others on the sky. The standard method of locating heavenly objects is by their R.A. and dec. Such co-ordinates are always referred to a given equinox, inasmuch as precession shifts the origin (the vernal equinox) through the years, against the starry background. For certain purposes which concern the diurnal rotation of stars and planets on the sphere, the pair of co-ordinates called hour angle and declination is also in use, and here the hour angle is perpetually changing with time. This last set of values is of use especially with the equatorial telescope. Right ascension and declination correspond to the geographic co-ordinates of longitude and latitude, respectively.

Ecliptic System. The ecliptic system has for its primary circle the ecliptic, and for its poles the north and south ecliptic poles. Secondaries are circles of latitude, and the parallels are parallels of latitude. Co-ordinates are celestial longitude and latitude. Symbols are λ and β, respectively. (These refer to geocentric longitude and latitude; heliocentric co-ordinates, referred to the sun, are l and b.) Ecliptic co-ordinates have their network offset with respect to the equatorial system by the amount of the obliquity of the ecliptic; hence the ecliptic poles are about $23° 27'$ from the poles of the equator. The ecliptic system is used especially in the study of planetary and other solar-system bodies.

Galactic System. The galactic system, of extremely limited use, is important in stellar statistics and galactic problems of research. The primary circle is the galactic circle, in the plane of the Milky Way; its poles are the north and south galactic poles; secondaries are secondaries to the galactic circle; and parallels are parallels of galactic latitude. Co-ordinates are galactic longitude (G) and galactic latitude (g). The north galactic pole is at $\alpha = 12$ hr. 40 min. and $\delta + 28°$. Galactic longitude is measured in degrees from the intersection of the galactic circle with the celestial equator, at $\alpha = 18$ hr. 40 min., and galactic latitude is measured at right angles to the galactic circle. *See also* ALTITUDE; AZIMUTH; CELESTIAL MECHANICS; DECLINATION; HORIZON; HOUR ANGLE; HOUR CIRCLE; LATITUDE, CELESTIAL; LONGITUDE, CELESTIAL; NADIR; RIGHT ASCENSION; SEASONS; ZENITH.   H. S. R.

CELESTINA, LA. *See* ROJAS, FERNANDO DE; SPANISH LITERATURE.

CELESTINE I, ST. [sɛ'ləstain] (c.360-432), deacon of the Roman Church, was elected pope in 422. He espoused the cause of St. Cyril of Alexandria against Nestorius of Constantinople, threatening Nestorius with excommunication unless he retracted within ten days his errors in regard to relationship of personality and natures in Christ. At the Council of Ephesus (431), which was called to decide the controversy, Celestine was represented by legates. Nestorius was condemned by the majority of the council, but because of political rivalry between Alexandria and Constantinople the discussion continued. Celestine sent St. Germanus of Auxerre to Brittany to combat Pelagianism, and during his pontificate St. Palladius and St. Patrick began the evangelization of the Irish.   E. A. R.

CELESTINE V, ST. (c. 1215-1296), was pope for some five months in 1294. Named Pietro, and called also di Morrone because he led an eremitical life on Monte Morrone, he was the son of peasants in the Abruzzi. He became a Benedictine, famed for his penitential practices, and founded a special congregation that was later known as the Celestines. The conclave following the death of Pope Nicholas IV had lasted two years when Charles II, King of Naples, caused Pietro to be elected pope, July 5, 1294. Totally unprepared for the high office, Celestine allowed Charles to keep him at Naples and exploit him. In addition, his generous concessions of privileges to designing persons seemed to threaten the Church with anarchy. Celestine was aware of his unfitness and feared its consequences. Upon learning that he could resign, he did so, Dec. 13, 1294, after issuing decrees which insured a speedy election of a new pope. His successor, Boniface VIII, fearing a schism should the inexperienced old man fall into the hands of intriguers, kept him in protective captivity until his death more than a year later. Celestine was canonized by Pope Clement V in 1313.   E. A. R.

CELESTINES [sɛ'ləstɪnz; sɛ'ləstainz], the members of two Roman Catholic orders named for Pope St. Celestine V. (1) Many disciples gathered around the austere and saintly hermit, Pietro di Morrone (Celestine V), who formed them into a community in 1250; at his death in 1296 they numbered six hundred in thirty-six monasteries, and followed a rule based on that of St. Benedict. During his brief pontificate (July to December, 1294) the founder approved their constitutions and imposed them on the Benedictines of Monte Cassino, an arrangement rescinded by the next pope, Boniface VIII. The order eventually numbered nearly 150 houses, the last of which was suppressed in 1785. (2) Certain of the extreme Spirituals, on the occasion of the Franciscan dispute concerning poverty, obtained Pope Celestine's permission to live in hermitages independent of the Franciscan jurisdiction. This group was suppressed in 1302 by Celestine's successor, Boniface VIII, the legitimacy of whose election they contested; the survivors became in 1308 the Minorites of Narbonne.   N. J. T.

CELESTITE [sɛ′ləstɑit], the most abundant strontium-containing mineral. It is composed of strontium sulphate, SrSO₄. Like the barium sulphate, barite, celestite is heavy, nonmetallic, and crystallizes in the orthorhombic system with perfect cleavage parallel to the base and the two prism faces. Its hardness (Mohs scale) is 3-3.5. Its color is usually white, but may be bluish, which gives the mineral its name. Celestite was in unusual demand during World War II for use in tracer bullets and signal flares. Peacetime uses include increasing the weight of rotary-drilling mud, in fireworks, and in the manufacture of strontium chemicals. Commonest occurrence of celestite is in pockets, veins, and cavity linings in limestone. Leading producing countries are Mexico, England, and Spain. Notable deposits of celestite in the United States occur in Put-in-Bay, Ohio; Mineral County, West Virginia, and certain localities in Texas and California. *See also* BARITE.   K. K. L.

CELIA, daughter of Frederick, the usurping duke, in Shakespeare's comedy *As You Like It*. When her cousin Rosalind, daughter of the rightful duke, is banished from court, Celia accompanies her into exile, disguising herself and taking the name of Aliena. The exiles join Rosalind's father in the Forest of Arden, where Celia becomes betrothed to Oliver de Boys, whose brother, Orlando, is to marry Rosalind.

CELIBACY [sɛ′lɪbəsi] (Latin *caelibatus*) is in general the single or unmarried state of life and has been variously evaluated in different cultural and social environments. More particularly it connotes the single state adopted for religious motives in various times and places and is perhaps most frequently associated with the renunciation of marriage among Christian clergy. In the early Church celibacy was widely practiced by the clergy of the East and West, although there was no written legislation to compel it. Influenced no doubt by the personal example of their founder Jesus Christ, and mindful of the rich promises held out to those who would sever all domestic ties for the sake of the kingdom of God (Matt. xix:10-11; Luke xviii:29), aspirants to holy orders sensed an inner compulsion to forego marriage or its use if they were already married. Again, St. Paul in his Epistle to the Corinthians had extolled the excellence of the virginal or celibate state, and his rather practical observation that marriage had a tendency to divide the interests of a man's heart, making him more solicitous to please his wife, unquestionably influenced those whose vocation called for a devoted and undistracted service of the Lord (I Cor. vii:32-35). Gradually what was a matter of counsel for the clergy was imposed first by custom and finally by written legislation. Broadly speaking, the legislation for the Church of the West was fixed by the time of Gregory the Great (Pope 590-604), and for the East by the Council in Trullo (692), although subsequent centuries were to witness not a few declinations from the spirit and even the letter of the law.

At the present time, in the Latin Church the law of celibacy affects all clerics in major orders. It imposes the obligation of perfect chastity, any violation of which becomes a sacrilege; it prohibits the contracting of marriage or the use of marriage already contracted; it renders null and void a marriage attempted after ordination to the subdiaconate. In the Eastern Church marriage and the use of marriage are permitted provided the marriage has taken place prior to the diaconate. Candidates for the episcopate, however, are drawn from the celibate or unmarried clergy. The Eastern Churches in union with Rome are drawing closer to the more demanding ideal of the Latin Church. By others clerical celibacy is praised and practiced. By yet others it has been often denounced as an impossible ideal or as a reflection on the divine vocation of marriage. Its advocates in reply point to the many priests and religious who, with God's grace, have actually realized the ideal, and contend further that its repudiation would lead inevitably to a weakening of the Christian ideal of marriage, which always demands pre-marital continence and not rarely periodic, and even perpetual, continence in those actually married.   P. F. J. P.

CELL. A cell is a definite organized unit of living substance. It typically consists of a small mass of cytoplasm with a nucleus (together, the protoplasm) and a cell membrane or plasma membrane surrounding the protoplasm. Animal cells may possess additional coats or may adhere to each other by means of intercellular cement which covers them on the outside in the form of a very fine layer; a rigid membrane of cellulose, the cell wall, typically surrounds plant cells which are also held together by a mutual cementing layer called the middle lamella.

General Characteristics of Cells. The bodies of typical higher or more complex plants and animals consist of cells and their products. Cells are usually arranged in groups, the tissues, which in turn make up the various organs of the body. A simple method of studying typical living cells is to place a few scrapings from the inside of the cheek in a small drop of water on a piece of flat glass known as a glass slide, covering this preparation with a thinner piece of glass, the coverslip. Normally some cells are always sloughed off from the lining of the mouth and a few may be also present in the saliva. Similarly, a preparation for microscopic study may be made from a very thin surface layer of a scale of an onion bulb. The stripped "onion skin" is placed in a drop of water on a slide under a coverslip. Such preparations are called temporary wet mounts and must be examined immediately; if allowed to stand too long, the water evaporates and the cells undergo irreversible changes and die. The cells may be readily observed under a lens with a magnification of 100 times, and by properly adjusting the intensity of the light the limits of the cell membrane in the mouth cells, the cell wall in the onion cells, as well as nuclei and various cytoplasmic granules in both, may be recognized. Such simple observations extend far beyond those presented in 1665 by Robert Hooke. In describing "the texture of cork by means of magnifying lenses," Hooke left to us the term "cell" (from the Greek *kytos,* meaning hollow space), although he had only seen cell walls and not the living protoplasts.

Size. Cells, because of their size, are usually studied under the microscope and are measured in microscopic units known as microns; each micron unit represents 1/1000 of a millimeter. The yolk of a hen's egg is a familiar example of a very large single cell, but the majority of the cells, for example those of the human body, do not measure more than 10 microns in length.

Shape. Single animal cells, separated from a tissue mass and suspended in an appropriate solution of a concentration similar to that of the fluids by which the cells were ordinarily surrounded, usually assume a spherical shape. The proximity of other cells, on the other hand, affects the shape of the cells, many cells possessing fourteen sides or more. Plant cells, due to the presence of the outer rigid wall which they produce, are more limited in the shape they may assume, and shape is determined by the growth pattern typical of the plant or plant tissue.

Differentiation. All higher plants and animals contain a great number of different cell types. During the growth and development of the individual the large number of cells produced by rapid multiplication, that is, by cell division or mitosis, undergo various changes. These changes make certain cells different in appearance and in function from the others and are referred to as the process of cellular differentiation. Differentiated cells usually lose their capacity to continue multiplying by cell division. Mitosis is a property typical of younger, undifferentiated, and embryonic

Cell Constituents. *Plasma Membrane.* The plasma membrane has been demonstrated under the electron microscope, but it is invisible under the light microscope, since its thickness, estimated at about 0.010 microns is too far below the limits of resolution of the ordinary microscope. When the plasma membrane of a cell is injured in an irreparable way, the cell disintegrates or undergoes cytolysis. Cells, however, are able to survive expert micromanipulation and surgery (micrurgy) even when the cell membrane is pierced for the removal of the nucleus or cut across to separate the

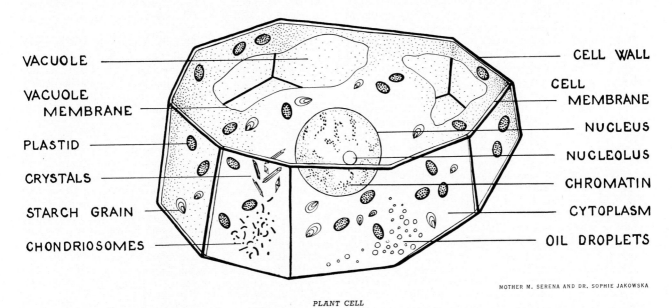

VACUOLE — CELL WALL

VACUOLE MEMBRANE — CELL MEMBRANE

PLASTID — NUCLEUS

CRYSTALS — NUCLEOLUS

STARCH GRAIN — CHROMATIN

— CYTOPLASM

CHONDRIOSOMES — OIL DROPLETS

MOTHER M. SERENA AND DR. SOPHIE JAKOWSKA

PLANT CELL

cells. Differentiated cells assume their specific functions, such as protection of various outer and inner body surfaces, binding, connecting and supporting of various body parts, storage of materials taken in or produced by the body, production of specialized substances to be used by the organism, as well as such specialized functions as contractility or conduction of stimuli, which are peculiar to muscle and nerve cells respectively.

Aging. In a normally functioning body some of the differentiated cells become worn out. Replacement is possible, with few exceptions, from certain cells, set aside in the body, which retain their ability to multiply and to transform into the cell types requiring replacements. Youth, maturity, and senility are normal stages in the life cycle of plant and animal cells, the functions of which usually end shortly before death. In some exceptional instances differentiation and full function are achieved when the protoplast is no longer alive, as in the case of some plant tissues (xylem), specialized for the transport of water. The age of a cell may often be judged from the appearance of its constituent parts, the cytoplasm and the nucleus. For example, a plant cell shows fewer but larger vacuoles in the cytoplasm and its nucleus changes in appearance and becomes shifted to the side from its original central position as the cell becomes older. While it is difficult to determine the actual moment of death for an individual cell, certain phenomena are associated with impending death; these include the rounding up of cells, loss of distinct boundaries between adjoining cells, abnormal granularity of the cytoplasm, change in the texture of the nucleus, and dissolution of various cytoplasmic granules.

cell into two parts. The ability of the cell membrane to undergo repair after such treatment depends on its chemical and physical composition; it is believed that this fine protoplasmic film or membrane, which regulates the passage of substances in and out of the cell, consists of a flat network of elongated protein molecules to which lipid (fat) molecules are intimately bound.

Nucleus. The nucleus is the most conspicuous structure in a typical cell, although in a commonly known cell such as the mammalian red blood cell it is absent in the final stage of development. The nucleus is usually a spherical or ovoid body located in the midst of the cytoplasm. It is bounded externally by a nuclear membrane, a true membrane which opposes resistance during micromanipulation. The interior of the nucleus is filled with a liquid material, the nuclear sap or karyolymph, and with material of a granular or reticular nature. In living unstained cells the nuclear contents often appear homogeneous except for one (nucleolus) or more spherical refractile bodies (nucleoli). When cells are dyed, the granular or network pattern becomes colored, hence the substance has been given the name of chromatin. The nucleoli also stain with certain dyes, often in a specific way, indicating that they differ in chemical composition from the chromatin material.

The nucleus of a non-dividing cell or one which is fully differentiated retains the granular or network pattern. When the cell enters mitosis or cell division, the chromatin material condenses into a definite number of strands (chromosomes), which proceed to shorten and thicken as the process of mitosis advances. The nuclei of degenerating cells may exhibit a dark staining reaction, often accompanied by a shrinkage and disappearance of structural details; this phenomenon is called pycnosis. The nucleus may also undergo fragmentation (karyorrhexis) or lose its stainability and dissolve (karyolysis).

Cytoplasm. The cytoplasm does not contain structures as striking as the nuclear chromosomes. Most of the structures present, except for the plastids of plants, are not large enough to be seen under the ordinary microscope and they do not undergo marked changes or cyclical modifications. While classical cytology contributed chiefly to our knowledge of the nucleus, it is through the use of the most modern instruments and techniques that an understanding of the cytoplasmic components is being obtained.

The cytoplasm consists of a cytoplasmic matrix and of inclusions (organoids) which are embedded in it. The cytoplasm itself has been shown in some cells to possess a very elaborate structure composed of closely folded parallel membranes, which separate the protoplasm proper from a watery substance that fills part of the cell. Among the cytoplasmic inclusions, some are common to both plant and animal cells, such as drops of fat, carbohydrates, granules of protein, salt crystals, secretion granules, chondriosomes, and vacuoles. Others are known to appear only in animal cells—centrioles, yolk globules, pigment granules, and the Golgi apparatus. Centrioles of animal cells divide in the early stage of mitosis and are associated in some unknown way with the formation of the structure known as the spindle or achromatic figure. Inclusions found only in plant cells are plastids, especially chloroplasts or chlorophyll-containing plastids, and starch granules.

The chondriosomes, also called mitochondria, have been known for about 50 years. They appear as minute spherical or rod-shaped cytoplasmic bodies about the size of bacteria, with which they have been confused by some investigators. Combined cytological and biochemical approaches in investigations have shown that they are the chief centers of respiration, or regions where most of the enzymes are situated and where they bring about the liberation of energy needed by the protoplasm. The electron microscope reveals that they have a layered structure.

Microsomes are bodies still smaller than chondriosomes recently isolated by ultracentrifugation. They are visible at times, but generally are of submicroscopical dimensions.

Plastids are found in cells of all plants, with the possible exception of bacteria, certain algae, and fungi. In young developing cells they are usually colorless, while in differentiated cells they contain pigments (chlorophyll or carotenoids) and are known as chromoplasts or colored plastids. Chloroplasts are a special type of chromoplasts, containing the green pigment chlorophyll. Plastids also have the capacity for synthesizing several reserve substances such as starch, fats, and proteins. The size, shape, and distribution of chloroplasts may vary in different cells and species, but they are relatively constant within the same tissue. The plastids most familiar to students are those found in the living cells of leaves of the common aquarium plant *Elodea* where these ovoid bodies undergo a cyclic motion around the periphery of the cell; their motion reveals the characteristic protoplasmic streaming or cyclosis. Another both familiar and interesting plastid is the ribbon-shaped, spirally wound chloroplast of the cells of the aquatic filamentous alga, *Spirogyra*. It has been established that plastids are inherited from the egg through the maternal line and that their mode of expression, that is, the type of pigment or substance which they synthesize, depends on the various types of genes present in the cell. The chloroplasts are composed of granules

or "grana," which under the electron microscope show a layered appearance.

The vacuoles of fluid content, surrounded by a membrane (tonoplast), may be seen in plant and animal cells. In older cells they often show a tendency to coalesce into fewer and larger vacuoles. The contents of the vacuoles of plant and animal cells have been investigated by means of various micromanipulation procedures. In some specialized cells, capable of phagocytosis, the contents may consist of ingested matter such as food particles, bacteria, and broken down cellular fragments. Vacuoles, plastids, and mitochondria have been isolated from cells and found to react to changes in osmotic pressure.

The Golgi apparatus, also called Golgi substance or Golgi complex, discovered by Camillo Golgi in 1898 in animal cells by means of a silver staining method, appears, after fixation and staining, as a net-like inclusion. It cannot be demonstrated in living cells even with the use of phase microscopy and so still awaits a definitive interpretation of its nature and functional significance.

Another type of cytoplasmic inclusion of interest to students of heredity are the minute particles known as kappa-particles, found in the cytoplasm of certain strains of the ciliated protozoan, *Paramecium aurelia*. These kappa-particles apparently reproduce from pre-existing kappa-particles only in those paramecia, carrying a gene known as the K gene. Animals, with this gene, produce a substance which diffuses into the surrounding water in which they live and which kills other "sensitive" paramecia.

Special Cell Types. *Unicellular Animals and Plants.* Unicellular or one-celled animals (protozoans), and one-celled plants (certain algae) represent a very special type of cells. Often considered as simple or primitive animals and plants, they are far from being such, both in structure and in function. Each single cell constitutes a whole individual, containing within the boundaries of a single protoplasmic unit the most elaborate system of highly specialized cellular structures (organelles), and is capable of displaying the most complex functions, actually comparable to those of higher animals and plants. In all the multicellular forms of life capable of sexual reproduction, including man, the new individual begins its existence as a single cell (the zygote), resulting from the fusion of the egg and the sperm. It is only through the cleavage of the zygote and later development that organisms acquire the immense number and variety of cellular types that are found in the mature, more highly evolved plants and animals.

Cancer Cells. The cancer cell is a very much modified cell, usually one which has reverted from a differentiated state to an embryonic mode of existence. It multiplies rapidly by cell division, which is often abnormal in nature. The cancer cell frequently displays nuclear and cytoplasmic characteristics conspicuously different from those of the surrounding normal cells, and all the metabolic functions of such a cell are considerably altered. *See also* CELL DIVISION; CELL PHYSIOLOGY; CYTOLOGY.   S. J.

CELL DIVISION. Cells of plants and animals including man do not originate from a mere aggregation of protoplasmic particles, but are derived from other cells. R. Virchow aptly summarized this in a brief Latin aphorism *"omnis cellula e cellula"* (every cell originates from a cell). Early microscopic observations lead many to suspect that cells do not merely split in half, but that the various strange configurations seen in the cells of actively growing tissues represent stages in the process of cellular division. The chromosomes, which appear as the most striking structures in the cell during division were seen for the first time in the 1840's, but it was only between 1873 and 1887 that they were described in accurate detail. Three major types of cellular division were recognized soon thereafter in the great variety of biological material under observation: direct division or amitosis; indirect division or mitosis (also referred to as karyokinesis by some authors); and a specialized process, involving two modified nuclear divisions, known as meiosis.

Amitosis. Amitosis occurs in primitive plants, such as bacteria and blue-green algae, and in certain animal cells. The division occurs in a seemingly simple fashion, with the nucleus and the cytoplasm pinching off through the middle or becoming separated into two approximately equal parts by a cross wall. With the use of special highly magnifying equipment, such as the electron microscope, scientists have become aware that the division of even such primitive organisms is not so simple and that the process involves a rather orderly separation of cellular components. However, the existence of such direct cellular division cannot be totally denied. Amitotic nuclear division, sometimes not accompanied by cytoplasmic division, seems also to occur in abnormal diseased plant and animal tissues and under certain exceptional conditions in normal organisms.

Mitosis. Mitosis is responsible for the development of embryos from dividing fertilized eggs (egg cleavage), for the growth of roots, stems, and leaves from growing regions (meristematic regions), and for the usual replacement of worn-out cells in plants and animals. Normally, only young or embryonic cells are capable of undergoing mitosis. Such cells usually exhibit a certain nucleo-cytoplasmic ratio, that is, the nucleus is relatively large in comparison to the total volume of the cytoplasm. As the cells change in volume and become highly specialized (differentiated), they lose their ability to undergo repeated divisions. Mitosis may show up, however, among highly differentiated cells in regenerating organs or in abnormal growths, as for example in cancer tissues.

The complete details of the mitotic process awaited the production of better optical equipment and the formulation of various staining techniques. In view of the fact that various plants and animals are composed of cells which differ greatly in size from species to species, some of those forms composed of relatively large cells became the classical cytological materials. Among such especially favorable materials for the study of cell division are the cells of the growing onion root tip, the developing fertilized eggs of the parasitic roundworm *Ascaris,* salamander epidermis, grasshopper testis, as well as those plants in which the chromosomes are considerably larger than in other plants, such as the wake robin (*Trillium*) and spiderwort (*Tradescantia*). The giant chromosomes, which appear during the development of the fly maggots (especially in the fruitfly, *Drosophila melanogaster*) were discovered much later, but they have contributed tremendously to our understanding of chromosomal structure.

It has not always been possible to observe all the details of the mitotic process in a living cell, although W. Flemming described it very completely from living material as early as 1882. Under the phase microscope which highly emphasizes the slightest differences in optical density of the various cell components, the stages of cellular division can be observed and recorded in form of moving pictures. This is of particular value for an understanding of the process as a continuous one. The stages usually described are arbitrarily based on a characteristic appearance assumed by the cell as mitosis proceeds. The stages may be listed in the following order: "resting stage," prophase, metaphase, anaphase, and telophase, with the final production of two daughter cells. If a mass of cells from an actively growing tissue, such as an onion root tip, or the skin of a salamander tadpole, is properly fixed (killed and preserved) and stained, all of these stages may be seen, as well as intermediate conditions, as cells do not usually enter and complete division at the same time.

"Resting Stage." The term "resting stage" used to describe a cell which is about to enter mitosis is somewhat of a misnomer. From various sources there is sufficient information to indicate that although the appearance of the cell does not reveal any activity, numerous chemical as well as physical submicroscopic changes take place in such cells. These changes concern molecular phenomena, in which materials needed for the production of certain components of the cell are formed; these cannot be detected with the ordinary optical equipment. Thus, the name "resting stage" simply implies that at this time the cell, and especially its nucleus, resembles a typical non-dividing cell. In this stage the nuclear membrane is clearly visible and the nuclear contents consist of chromatin in the form of delicate strands (chromatin reticulum or network) or in form of a more or less specific number of chromatin clumps of varying shape and size (heterochromatic bodies or prochromosomes). One or more nucleoli may be seen in such cells; they do not participate in the visible phase of active mitotic division and are usually omitted from the discussion of this process until their reappearance in late telophase, prior to the reconstruction of the daughter cell nuclei.

Prophase. In the initial active stage, or prophase, certain characteristic changes appear in the nucleus and in the cytoplasm. The nuclear chromatin assumes a more distinct shape of thin threads which gradually shorten and thicken. They are spoken of as prophase chromosomes and it may be seen that each is composed of two distinct strands or chromatids. Early and late prophase may be differentiated on the basis of relative thickness and length of the chromosomes. The cytoplasm surrounding the nucleus also undergoes changes in early and late prophase: a number of delicate fibers begins to form in the close proximity of the nucleus at the two poles of the cell. These fibers represent the precursors of a structure known as the spindle, sometimes referred to as the achromatic figure, because of the obvious indifference of the component fibers to dyes which succeed in coloring the chromatin material, including the chromosomes. This structure does not become fully formed until metaphase and it originates in a somewhat different fashion in plant and animal cells. In a plant cell the fibers become arranged in the shape of conical caps (polar caps) of fibers running from the two opposite surfaces of the nucleus and converging in each case at the pole. One polar cap of fibers is separated from the other polar cap by the spherical nucleus. In an animal cell there is a minute cytoplasmic body, known as the centriole, usually located near the surface of the nucleus. The centriole divides in two and one of the pair formed migrates around the nucleus until the two parts of the divided centriole become located at the opposite ends of the cell. It is from the region directly surrounding the divided centriole that the fibers appear to radiate in all directions, some reaching the surface of the nucleus. These structures, corresponding to the polar caps in the plant cells, are called asters and are precursors of the spindle.

PLANT CELL	CELL DIVISION – MITOSIS	ANIMAL CELL
	CELL MEMBRANE CELL WALL CENTRIOLE NUCLEUS (NUCLEAR MEMBRANE) NUCLEOLUS CHROMATIN CYTOPLASM **RESTING CELL**	
	DIVIDED CENTRIOLE CHROMOSOME NUCLEAR MEMBRANE **EARLY PROPHASE**	
	POLAR CAP ASTER { ASTRAL RAY CENTRIOLE PROPHASE CHROMOSOME NUCLEAR MEMBRANE POLAR CAP ASTER **LATE PROPHASE**	
	} SPINDLE FIBERS { EQUATORIAL PLATE METAPHASE CHROMOSOME TWO CHROMATIDS JOINED AT THE SPINDLE ATTACHMENT REGION **METAPHASE**	
	CHROMOSOMAL FIBER ANAPHASE CHROMOSOME COMPOSED OF ONE CHROMATID CONTINUOUS FIBER **ANAPHASE**	
	CHROMOSOMES GROUPED AT THE POLE BEGINNING OF CYTOPLASMIC DIVISION CELL PLATE FURROW **TELOPHASE**	
	NUCLEAR MEMBRANE OF DAUGHTER CELL NUCLEOLUS OF DAUGHTER CELL CELL MEMBRANE OF DAUGHTER CELL WALLS SEPARATING PLANT DAUGHTER CELLS **DAUGHTER CELLS**	

Metaphase. The onset of metaphase is marked by the disappearance of the nuclear membrane and the completion of the spindle, with fibers reaching across the span previously occupied by the nucleus. The spindle fibers are definite structures and micromanipulation has shown that they possess a certain tensile strength and elasticity. The chromosomes in the meantime reach their shortest and thickest condition. In this condition each chomosome can be seen to consist of two strands or chromatids, held together at a constriction known as the spindle attachment region or centromere. Careful study with the highest magnifications available further indicates the presence of two half-chromatid strands in each chromatid and a very fine spiral structure of the strand. At a region of the spindle which would correspond to the geographic concept of the equator, the metaphase chromosomes become attached individually to separate spindle fibers. All the chromosomes of each cell are found at this stage attached by their spindle attachment regions to individual fibers at the equatorial plate, an imaginary plane perpendicular to the long axis of the cell. The spindle fibers on which the chromosomes are located are known as chromosomal fibers; others, which run directly from pole to pole, are called continuous fibers.

Anaphase. The next stage, which anticipates an orderly separation of the chromatin material into two parts, is known as anaphase. It begins with the longitudinal separation (splitting) of the spindle attachment region of each chromosome which permits the separation of the two chromatids and their subsequent movement along the chromosomal fiber towards the opposite poles. While the number of chromosomes moving in the opposite direction is the same per group as it was originally at metaphase on the equatorial plate, each chromosome (anaphase chromosome) differs now in consisting of only one chromatid, instead of two. The movement of the two groups of anaphase chromosomes proceeds until they reach the poles. Nothing definite is known about the forces involved.

Telophase. The telophase stage, with the arrival of the chromosomes at the poles, is characterized by changes in the cytoplasm, anticipating the final cellular separation. The latter is achieved differently in plant and in animal cells. In a plant cell a deposition of fine granules may be observed in the region which at the metaphase stage was referred to as the equatorial plate. At this stage these granules begin to coalesce and form a structural cross-plane, known as the cell plate. The cell plate marks the separation of the original mother cell into two daughter cells. Final individuality is achieved by each cell with the formation of the cell wall. In the animal cell the separation takes place by means of a furrow which deepens while the spindle fibers become less distinct. A form of cleavage completes the separation into two distinct cells.

Each chromosome group in the daughter cells loses its identity and becomes reconstituted into the daughter nucleus with an arrangement of chromatin material similar to that originally found in the nucleus of the mother cell. The nucleolus or nucleoli usually reappear at this stage. Following a brief growth period, the cells are ready to divide again or become differentiated.

The process of mitosis described above is not carried out in steps but represents a continuous sequence of events, the changing nature of which requires the use of specific terms to indicate structures that are only temporary. Thus the term "polar cap" is no longer employed when the spindle is completed in a plant cell, while the term equatorial plate applies only to an imaginary plate on which chromosomes aggregate at metaphase. The latter does not correspond to the "cell plate," a real structure separating the plant mother cell into two daughter cells during late telophase. For the same reason the metaphase chromosome and anaphase chromosome are not identical, since the latter represents only one chromatid of the original chromosome. The basic composition of both is the same, however, as the two chromatids which separate during anaphase were originally the product of chromatin reduplication during the "resting stage." Thus, in the "resting stage," which follows the production of the daughter cells after mitosis, the single thread of each individual chromosome received by each daughter cell during division becomes again reduplicated. This process cannot be demonstrated optically, until a certain point in prophase reveals the double condition of the chromatin strands. In cells which undergo repeated divisions, the "resting stage" between divisions is sometimes referred to as interphase.

The duration of mitosis is of interest. It varies in different kinds of plants and animals and is influenced by a number of factors, including temperature. In pea roots at 59° F. the mitotic process takes 25.6 hours, with 3 hours of active division (prophase through telophase). Metaphase lasts 24 minutes and anaphase only 5 minutes. At 77° F. the entire process takes place in 15.9 hours.

Meiosis. Meiosis is a special process involving two modified nuclear divisions as a result of which the number of chromosomes is reduced to one half the original number. For this reason the process is sometimes called "reductional division," in contrast to mitosis or equational division. The latter produces daughter cells with chromosomes exactly equal in number and kind to those of the mother cell. Meiosis occurs in the formation of germ cells or gametes—the eggs (female gametes) and sperms (male gametes) in animals. It also occurs in plants during the process of gametophyte formation or after a zygote is formed as a result of sexual reproduction (fusion of gametes) as in the common green alga *Spirogyra*. Because of the peculiar nature of the reductional division in meiosis, the chromosomes are not divided into equally corresponding groups as in mitosis. They are segregated or sorted out in an orderly fashion, usually in the first meiotic division. In such case the division is reductional, that is, it gives rise to two daughter cells each of which has only one half the number of chromosomes found in the mother cell. This division involves a temporary association or synapsis of the corresponding (homologous) chromosomes, which attach themselves as pairs (or bivalent chromosomes) to the spindle fibers and terminate their association by the movement of each partner towards the opposite pole on the same chromosomal fiber. In this fashion the reduction to one half the number of chromosomes is accomplished in the daughter cells. The second division of meiosis is equational in nature, resembling mitosis, with the exception of the lack of reduplication of chromatin during the period intervening between the two meiotic divisions. Meiosis gives rise, therefore, to four male or female germ cells.

The number of chromosomes is generally constant in all the cells of an individual or in individuals belonging to the same species, although exceptions are known. Cytologists, through a careful search of dividing cells, have determined the number of chromosomes typical of body cells in plants and animals representing practically every major group. The smallest number of chromosomes was reported from the parasitic roundworm, *Ascaris,* and some of the highest numbers from certain arthropods.

The parallelism of the behavior of chromosomes at meiosis and of the hereditary particles or genes responsible for the transmission of characteristic traits, recognized in 1903, makes studies of meiosis an important phase of cytogenetics. *See also* CELL; CELL PHYSIOLOGY; CYTOLOGY.　　S. J.

CELLE [tsɛ′lə], a town in the state of Lower Saxony, in north central Germany, on the left bank of the Aller River, 23 mi. northeast of Hannover. Celle is a rail junction and manufactures industrial chemicals, metal wares, leather, and textiles. Extensive kalium-mining operations are carried on in the vicinity of the city, which is also an oil supply and refining center. A city since 1292, Celle was the residence of the dukes of Lüneburg from 1371 until 1705. In the old city are many medieval buildings, including the thirteenth-century ducal palace. Pop. 1950, 59,800.　　H. Rob.

CELLINI, BENVENUTO [tshɛlli′ni] (1500-1571), Italian goldsmith and sculptor, was born in Florence Nov. 1, 1500. His fame rests less on his merit as an artist than on his *Autobiography,* an important source for the cultural history of the Renaissance.

Against the desire of his father, who wished him to study music, Benvenuto at fifteen had himself apprenticed to a goldsmith. Characteristically, he was soon banished from his native city for sword play. Thus began a thirty-year period of wandering from city to city, working under Michelangelo and other masters and on his own. About 1524 Pope Clement VII recognized his ability and took him under his protection. Cellini boasts that during the sack of Rome in 1527 he himself killed the Duke of Bourbon and wounded the Prince of Orange. During this time, until the beginning of his second sojourn in France in 1540, Cellini was essentially a goldsmith, although he made medals and dies for coins. Of all the ambitious works in precious metals and stones which he describes, only one, the golden salt cellar of Francis I (in Vienna), has survived. This, and his first important sculpture, the bronze relief called the *Nymph of Fontainebleau,* are replete with ornament and fine detail.

In 1545 Cellini returned to Florence to spend the rest of his days in the service of Duke Cosimo de′Medici, of whom he immediately made a colossal bronze bust, and for whom he modeled and cast the famous *Perseus with the Head of Medusa* (1545-1554) in the Loggia dei Lanzi. Cellini also restored antique statues for the duke, and began to carve marble. Of this material he made the large *Crucifix,* originally intended for his own tomb, which is now in the Escorial. He died in Florence, Feb. 14, 1571.　　G. H. H.

CELLO. *See* VIOLONCELLO.

CELLOPHANE PLANT, *Echinodorus cordifolius,* a very beautiful aquatic plant with knife-like, transparent green, cellophane-like leaves which grow from a central crown. It is a member of the water plantain family. An attractive plant when grown in bright light, it should be planted in good soil, not sand. It is a native of Central America, Mexico, and the southern United States.　　A. Gr.

CELL PHYSIOLOGY, a branch of biology concerned with the fundamental biological activities of plants, animals, and man. It is a study of cellular metabolism, the sum total of physical and chemical functions in the cell. Complex organs, such as those found in the familiar higher plants and animals, are not essential to their performance. For example, nutritional phenomena of a complex nature occur even in the smallest unicellular organisms which have no specialized systems for food intake and digestion, and respiration occurs in all forms of life, even in those living things such as bacteria and viruses that are without known respiratory structures or organelles of any kind. The cell is the basic functional and structural unit for all living things in their various activities—the intake (animals) or synthesis (plants) of food, utilization of oxygen, release of energy, elimination of wastes, responses to the changes in the environment, growth, and reproduction.

The science of cell physiology is a little more than one hundred years old. Following an exploratory period, beginning with the formulation of the cell theory, it entered an analytical stage at the beginning of the twentieth century. From the earliest times interest centered on protoplasmic structures only as a means of interpreting cellular functions. Observations were made on the types of organelles in the cells of various plants and animals, on the properties and behavior of protoplasm under various conditions, and the types of substances which enter and leave the cells. The characteristic of irritability of the cell and the nature of cell division, essential features of living organisms, were studied.

In recent years, the invention of the phase microscope has permitted the study of living unstained cells and the cyclic changes they exhibit; the micromanipulator has made it possible to determine that many structures appearing in stained dead cellular material actually exist in the living cell; the oscilloscope has been used in the investigation of certain features of nerve impulses not previously known; and radioisotopes, introduced into cells as part of essential chemical substances such as nutrient salts or sugars, have made possible research on many fundamental problems of metabolism. The application of biochemical methods has led to an elucidation of the problems of the breakdown of nutrients in cells and the mode of energy liberation related to the enzyme and protein chemistry of the cell. Some of the stepping stones include, for example, the discovery of an enzyme called cytochrome oxidase and the identification of other enzymes concerned with most stages in the decomposition of cell nutrients. Biochemical genetics has made it possible to determine the steps by which cells make certain amino acids and many vitamins and some of the steps in the formation of other important cellular constituents such as the purines and pyrimidines.

The latest approach to cellular physiology, promising to uncover many new aspects of living matter, is a field known as molecular biology. It attempts to analyze the operation of each cellular structure down to the molecular level in terms of physical and chemical principles.　　S. J.

PHYSIOLOGY OF THE CELL

Organic Content. The organic constituents of the cell are proteins, carbohydrates, and fats. Cells are made up largely of proteins, fats, and related compounds, most of which are organized into large, complex molecules, with considerable amounts of water, partially free and partly combined with other substances. There is some carbohydrate, but relatively small quantities of inorganic salts.

Proteins make up the framework of protoplasm. They are essential in the building of new tissue and in the repair of old tissues. They may also be utilized to produce energy. Lipids, or fats, are a source of energy, and they play an important role in the exchanges between cells.

Since it has not been possible to construct protoplasm in the laboratory, it is evident that it is not a mere admixture of these materials, but a unique organization of substances of many types.

Protoplasm is colloidal in nature. Since the particles of a colloid substance are too large to pass through the pores of membranes of plant and animal cells, cell organization and the integrity of cell substances is maintained, and cell individuality, therefore, is preserved.

Inorganic Content. Inorganic substances formed in the cell are water and compounds of iron, phosphorus, sodium, calcium, and magnesium. Other elements present in certain forms are silicon, sulphur, chlorine, copper, bromine, potassium, iodine, and aluminum. Approximately 99 per cent of the body of all living organisms is composed of the six common ingredients: oxygen, hydrogen, carbon, nitrogen, calcium, and phosphorus.

About 75 per cent of the protoplasm in most animal cells is composed of water; plant cells have an even higher water content. Water is of first importance in all chemical reactions, and because of its unique physical and chemical properties, it plays an important role in all vital biological processes. It is an almost universal solvent; many substances, when in solution in water, separate into electrically charged particles, called ions. Water carries food and oxygen to the tissues and serves as the vehicle for processes of exchange, secretion, excretion, and absorption.

Although only minute amounts of inorganic salts are present in cells, usually less than 1 per cent of these salts are extremely important. They help in the maintenance of osmotic pressure, in the transport of oxygen and carbon dioxide, in maintaining the necessary alkaline reaction of blood and tissue fluids, in blood-clotting, in the development of bones in animals, and of the walls of plant cells in all organisms. Many kinds of salts are found in body fluids as well as in cells. They influence the irritability, conductivity, and contractility of tissue, which are basic attributes of protoplasm.

Dynamic Equilibrium. The constant chemical activity of a cell necessitates the continuous entrance and exit of materials. While the amount of any one substance within a cell remains remarkably constant, the same particles of that substance do not remain in the cell indefinitely. Small quantities of a number of substances are continually leaving the cell, while similar quantities of identical materials are entering it. Since the composition of the cell is in general constant, despite the fact that certain particles of substances are always entering and leaving it, the cell is spoken of as being in a condition of dynamic equilibrium. Cell constituents are arranged in such a way that the surface film of cytoplasm acts like a membrane. This membrane is rich in lipid material. In its physical processes filtration, diffusion, and osmosis, frequently encountered in nonliving systems, occur. These processes are responsible for much molecular exchange.

Filtration. The passage of water and dissolved substances across a membrane, caused by differences in pressure on the two sides of the membrane, is called filtration. Materials passed through the membrane depend on the size of the particles and on the fineness of the filter-like membrane. In the animal body, filtration occurs in the walls of capillaries, which serve as membranes. Much of the fluid content of the blood, with certain dissolved substances in it, filters through this membrane because of the blood pressure produced by the pumping action of the heart.

Diffusion. The tendency of substances to extend uniformly throughout a space, depending on the fact that particles of substances are in constant motion, is called diffusion. Gases diffuse rapidly from a point of high pressure to points of low pressure until they are uniformly distributed in the area which confines them. If a mixture of gases is concerned, each gas acts independently, each gas becoming evenly distributed throughout the space. The separation of two gases in solution by means of living membranes, as in the capillaries or air sacs, does not interfere with diffusion. Carbon dioxide passes from the site of high pressure, in lung capillaries, to a point of low pressure in the air sacs. Similarly, since oxygen pressure is greater in the air sacs than in capillaries, dissolved oxygen passes from the air sacs into the blood stream.

Other substances in solution behave much like gases, but the diffusion occurs much more slowly. Here molecules or ions of dissolved substances are surrounded by a solvent. If two identical solutions of different concentration are separated by a membrane which will permit the dissolved substances and water to pass, the dissolved substances will pass from the side of high concentration into the solution of lower concentration, while water will pass in the opposite direction, until the solutions are of the same strength. This is another example of diffusion. Here the membrane actually speeds up the process of distribution of the dissolved materials.

Mixtures of substances in solution behave similarly. If two solutions contain substances that will pass through a membrane, as well as molecules too large to pass through it, a modified diffusion results. One solute diffuses, while the other, to which the membrane is impermeable, will not. This type of diffusion is known as dialysis. The process by which water passes from the less concentrated to the more concentrated solution is called osmosis. In osmosis, water molecules penetrate the membrane in both directions depending upon the osmotic pressure of the solution.

Osmosis. Osmotic pressure is an inherent property of a solution in contact with a particular membrane. Since molecules are in constant motion, the molecules of any two solutions would be constantly hitting any membrane separating them. However, the number of water molecules striking a given area per unit of time would determine the exchange of water molecules between the two solutions. Particles of dissolved substance in the more concentrated solution would occupy a part of the area on the membrane in contact with the solution and would thus prevent water particles from striking and penetrating the membrane in that region. More molecules of water in the less concentrated solution, therefore, would be able to contact and pass through the membrane during any given period of time. Although water passes in both directions through the membrane, there is a "tendency" to dilute the more concentrated solution.

Red blood cells exhibit this process of osmosis well. In blood, the concentration of inorganic salts (sodium chloride) inside the blood cell is the same as that of salts in the surrounding blood plasma. However, if these cells are put into a dilute salt solution, water will flow into the cells, causing them to swell and finally to burst (hemolysis). Water passes through the semipermeable membrane (cell membrane) of the red blood corpuscles into a more highly concentrated medium within the cell. On the other hand, if red blood cells are placed in a medium of greater salt concentration than that inside of them, the cell water will leave the cell and pass into the surrounding fluid. Under this condition the cells would shrink (crenate).

Considerable investigation has been carried out in an attempt to understand the factors that regulate cell-membrane permeability. The size of the molecules plays an important part, but this is apparently only one factor in cell permeability. A semipermeable membrane is regarded as having minute pores large enough to admit water, but too small to admit many larger particles. It has also been suggested that fat-soluble particles enter the cell by dissolving in the fatty portions of a cell membrane. Since electrical charges are commonly found on cell surfaces, it may be that a cell whose surface is positively charged will repel positively charged particles, while negatively charged particles can easily enter the cell. While there are some instances of this kind of selective permeability, all instances of permeability cannot be explained upon a purely physical basis.

Functional Characteristics. In addition to possessing many physical features in common, cells also tend to behave alike. Certain activities are common to all cells and are called the functional characteristics of protoplasm. While it is difficult to separate these attributes, as they depend one upon another, they may be said to include growth, irritability, secretion and excretion, and reproduction.

Growth. This property permits cells to increase in size by absorbing food and incorporating it within their cytoplasm. All cells release energy from food, usually by oxidizing it. The process by which foods and other materials are physically and chemically changed within cells is called metabolism. Metabolism consists of the sum of all chemical and physical changes taking place within an organism, such as the preparation and assimilation of foodstuffs for their normal role in the growth and repair of the cell. Nutrient substances are taken into the cell and manufactured into new protoplasm. This synthetic process is known as anabolism. However, in any building process, wastes are formed. This refuse must be eliminated in order to assure continued progress. The process here is called catabolism. During the youth of an organism, anabolism exceeds catabolism, and the cells grow. At maturity, the two processes continue at approximately equal rates, permitting no great amount of growth. During old age, catabolism surpasses anabolism, with the result that the cells undergo a decline.

Irritability. This is the property that enables protoplasm to respond to changes in its surrounding environment. All cells react in some manner to sudden changes (stimuli) in their neighborhood, and the effect of stimulation at any one point may be transmitted to other parts of the cell. The one-celled animal known as the paramecium may be observed swimming away from some irritating chemical substance. Electrical, thermal, mechanical, and chemical changes in the cell environment may produce such a response. When a cell is young, the response is stronger and quicker than after it has become aged. After death, this ability of the cell to respond to a stimulus is lost.

Secretion and Excretion. Every cell possesses the ability to eliminate fluid wastes through its cell membrane. These waste materials formed by the cell are discharged into its environment. Some of these cellular products, however, are useful to other organs in the body. Such fluids, known as secretions, play very important roles in the functioning of the body. It is only when the fluid product is discharged from the organism that its loss is known as excretion.

Reproduction. Most cells in the body keep themselves in repair, or are replaced. The essential factor in replacement or reproduction is cell multiplication. Living cells can reproduce cells like themselves by cell division. Only in this way are living organisms capable of reproducing their kind, and of assuring continuation of the species. *See also* CELL; CELL DIVISION; CYTOLOGY.   J. H. Van D.

CELLULOSE, the fundamental compound forming cell walls of plants and trees. It is the main structural material of the vegetable kingdom, and is one of man's most basic and useful raw materials. Since the dawn of history, it has fur-

nished him with the essential articles of clothing in the form of vegetable fibers such as cotton and flax, and with shelter in the form of lumber. Although these materials may be considered cellulose derivatives in the widest sense of the term, this article will be primarily concerned with newer adaptations of cellulose such as chemical fibers and plastics which have been developed by means of special chemical manufacturing methods.

History. With the Egyptians' discovery of the process by which papyrus could be transformed to a writing material, about 2500 B.C., and with the invention of paper by the Chinese at the beginning of the Christian Era, there came the realization that cellulosic materials could be adapted to fit a special purpose by other than purely mechanical means such as shaping wood or spinning cotton. Although paper cannot be considered an actual chemical derivative of cellulose, its process of manufacture involves chemical principles such as the tendency of cellulose to swell in water because of association with water molecules (hydration). This concept of cellulose as a material which could be chemically treated in a solution is fundamental to later inventions which actually involve the chemical reaction of the cellulose molecules.

The first chemical derivative of cellulose to be discovered was nitrocellulose, a product of the reaction of cellulose with nitric acid. This reaction was studied by German and French scientists in the 1830's, and by 1850 two of its major industrial uses, explosives and protective coatings, had been foreshadowed. The highly nitrated form of cellulose had been suggested for use in explosives, and the soluble type had been proposed for use as a protective coating in the form of an ether-alcohol solution—since known as collodion. About 1866, the English scientist, Sir Frederick A. Abel, succeeded in eliminating impurities and retained nitric acid in nitrocellulose or guncotton, by washing and beating methods similar to those used in papermaking. Thus he produced a stable and reliable explosive which has been widely used ever since.

The next step came in 1870 when the American inventor, John Wesley Hyatt, searching for a substitute for ivory in the manufacture of billiard balls, found that by combining nitrocellulose with camphor and certain fillers to give color, a material having many useful properties could be obtained. It could be softened by heat and molded to desired shapes, which upon cooling had strength, rigidity and hardness. He named this new material celluloid, and it became known as the first plastic. It was still being manufactured in large volume in 1952.

As early as 1664, the English physicist Robert Hooke suggested that some means might be found to make an artificial fiber analogous to that formed naturally by the silkworm. It was almost two centuries later before an appropriate raw material, in the form of cellulose nitrate solutions, was available. The first experiments in spinning a fiber from this material in 1850 and 1860 were unsuccessful due to mechanical problems, but these were finally surmounted by Count Hilaire de Chardonnet in France in 1884. In 1890, commercial manufacture of "artificial silk" or rayon based on his process was begun. This process involves squirting a thin stream of cellulose nitrate solution into air, which evaporates the solvent, leaving a thin cellulose filament.

Because of certain undesirable characteristics of cellulose nitrate, notably its instability and inflammability, investigators began to study the technology of other cellulose derivatives in hopes that these disadvantages could be eliminated. Within fifteen years after 1890, three other processes were discovered for the manufacture of artificial filaments from cellulose. These were responsible for over 93 per cent of world chemical fiber production in 1951. The first two, the viscose and cuprammonium processes, produce regenerated cellulose filaments. Here the cellulose, after chemical treatment, is returned to its original chemical state, although it is in filament form. The third discovery, the acetate process, on the other hand, involves the use of a true chemical derivative of cellulose. According to the revised Federal Trade Commission Rules, acetate must not be labeled rayon.

Investigations before 1900 had led to the manufacture of transparent films from the cellulose derivatives. Cellulose nitrate film became important in photography, and French production of a thin film of regenerated cellulose, so-called cellophane, by the viscose process, was established in 1905.

The twentieth century has seen a vast expansion in the application and use of these cellulose derivatives in the form of textile filaments, films for photography and packaging,

E. I. DU PONT DE NEMOURS & CO.

FINISHED CELLOPHANE SHEETING

plastic structural materials, and protective coatings such as lacquers. In 1900, world rayon and acetate production was slightly over 2,000,000 lb.; by 1951, this figure had risen to the astronomical total of 3.9 billion pounds, with production in the United States alone at 1.3 billion pounds per year. Similar increases have taken place in other fields, aided by many notable technological advances. Among these can be included the development of low-viscosity nitrocellulose lacquer and its resultant adoption in major industrial uses such as automobile finishes; invention of the injection molding machine, which allows simple fabrication of small articles from plastics at very high production speeds; improvement of cellophane by use of a wax coating to increase water resistance; development of other cellulose derivatives such as ethyl cellulose and cellulose propionate, which have improved properties for special plastic or coating applications; and improvement in techniques for spinning short lengths of rayon and acetate filament into so-called staple fiber, which can be used to replace

spun woolen or cotton fibers in various applications not suitable for continuous-filament yarn.

Chemical Nature of Cellulose. The technology and commercial application of cellulose have preceded detailed theoretical explanations of its chemical nature and structure, as has been the case with many other industrial raw materials. However, many examples have shown that industrial uses can progress only a limited distance ahead of basic knowledge and understanding, after which further fundamental research is always necessary to provide ideas and inspiration. A brief review of knowledge regarding the structure and chemistry of cellulose will provide an excellent basis for consideration of its commercial derivatives.

A cellulose molecule is a very long threadlike shape made up of carbon, hydrogen, and oxygen atoms. This long molecule is formed of many successive identical units or groups of atoms, one of which can be represented by the chemical formula shown, in which H stands for hydrogen atoms, O for oxygen atoms, and C for carbon atoms.

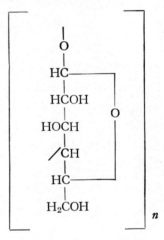

This formula can also be written as $C_6H_{10}O_5$. This latter formula also describes starch and glucose, a type of sugar, but these compounds have a different structure than that given for cellulose in the diagrammatic formula. Cellulose, starch, and sugar are all members of the carbohydrate family.

As was previously mentioned, the above structural formula for cellulose covers only one unit in the chain; cellulose molecules are made of many such units linked to each other at the open bond positions. Long-chain molecules of this kind consisting of many recurring units are known as polymers. This concept of the polymeric structure of cellulose, accepted since 1930, helps to explain why rayon and acetate can be made from cellulose, although manufactured for 40 years without this understanding.

The hydroxy, or alcohol groups in the structural formula, which contain hydrogen, and oxygen, give cellulose its chemical reactivity, to react with a wide variety of other chemicals. Since there are hydroxy groups in other simple compounds whose reactions are well known, it is possible partially to predict the reactions of cellulose by analogy with such compounds.

The long-chain structure of cellulose modifies the chemical properties which would be expected from the simple formula of one chain unit. In their original state in vegetable matter, these chains are held closely together by so-called secondary forces, giving strength and rigidity to the structure. However, in this form it would be possible to secure chemical reaction only with cellulose molecules on the outer surface. This limitation accounts for the necessity of swelling cellulose aggregates in water and subjecting them to mechanical and chemical forces in order to separate the long chains and to form pulp before chemical derivatives can be made. These forces not only separate the chains from each other but also partially break down individual chains. Table I shows the approximate number (*n* in the structural formula) of indivi-

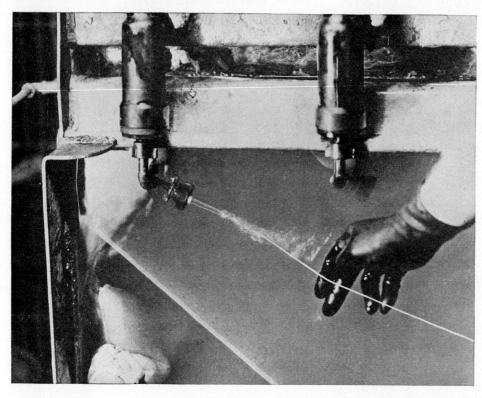

PROCESSING OF LIQUID VISCOSE INTO RAYON THREAD

Liquid viscose is forced through minute openings in the spinneret into hardening bath where first filaments, then thread, are formed.

dual units which make up cellulose molecules after various types of treatment or after the formation of certain well-known derivatives.

TABLE I. DEGREE OF POLYMERIZATION OF CELLULOSE AND DERIVATIVES

Material	Approx. Number of Units in Chain
Native cellulose	3,500
Bleached cotton linters	1,000–3,000
Guncotton (cellulose nitrate)	3,000–3,500
Wood pulps	600–1,000
Cellulose nitrate plastics	500– 600
Cellulose acetate or plastics	175– 360
Regenerated cellulose (viscose rayon)	200– 600
Ethyl cellulose	300

Adapted from E. O. Kraemer, *Industrial and Engineering Chemistry*, Vol. 30, p. 1200 (1940). Revised (1952).

After cellulose is broken down into pulp and the derivative is formed, the cellulose chains can again be precipitated in a desired structural form by removal of water or other solvents. Close association of the long chains then occurs again, giving the properties of strength, hardness or rigidity desired in rayon, plastics, or protective coatings.

Sources of Cellulose. *Vegetable Fibers.* Cellulose occurs in all vegetable matter to some extent. For use as an industrial raw material, however, it must be processed into a pure state; therefore, it is desirable to find sources containing the least amount of other compounds such as oils, tannins, and lignins which also occur in plant life. Cellulose was required in large volume for paper manufacture long before other cellulose

derivatives were discovered, and cotton or linen rags were primary sources of cellulose pulp for paper until the invention of various wood-pulping methods in the middle of the nineteenth century.

Early work on the chemical derivatives of cellulose was carried out by using pulp from cotton fibers, since these contain only 3 to 15 per cent of noncellulosic impurities, the lowest proportion found in any readily available source. The resultant ease of purification necessary for chemical use thus makes cotton fibers a very desirable commercial source of cellulose.

The first commercial production of the various cellulose derivatives was carried out by using raw cotton or linen rags as a raw material. The search for cheaper materials, however, led to the discovery that certain short cotton fibers, called linters, which were not ordinarily usable in textile applications, made a very satisfactory source of cellulose for chemical treatment. These cotton linters are not removed from the seed during the ordinary ginning processes, but are recovered later in the cottonseed-oil mill by special techniques developed to handle the short fiber length ⅛ to ¼ in. Recovery of cotton linters was given a great impetus during World War I because of the large requirements for nitrocellulose explosives. By 1920, a very large proportion of all chemical derivatives of cellulose used cotton linters as a raw material.

Experiments have been carried out on many other types of plants in the hope of finding other valuable sources of pure cellulose. Yields are usually low, however, because of the large amount of undesirable impurities present. Despite this fact, purified pulp from straw has been used in Germany for rayon production since 1935.

Wood Pulp. Tremendous expansion of production in this field required development of additional raw-material sources, and various attempts were made to purify wood pulps sufficiently for use in chemical manufacturing processes. Viscose-type rayon was first manufactured by using wood pulps made by the sulphite process from needle-leaf trees. By World War II, wood pulps of sufficient purity were available to produce other derivatives such as cellulose nitrate and cellulose acetate. Despite increased consumption of wood pulp in the manufacture of chemical derivatives, this use is still rather insignificant compared to that of paper production. In 1944, slightly over 400,000 tones of wood pulp was used in the United States to manufacture cellulose derivatives, whereas paper production took over 10,400,000 tons, more than 25 times as much.

The increasing importance of wood pulp as a source of raw material for rayon and other derivatives is shown in Table II.

TABLE II. CONSUMPTION OF CELLULOSE BY UNITED STATES RAYON AND ACETATE INDUSTRY
(Figures in Tons)

Year	Rayon and Acetate Production	Total Pulp	Wood Pulp		Linters Pulp	
			Tons	%	Tons	%
1930	63,842	72,000	45,000	62	27,000	38
1935	131,077	137,000	86,000	63	51,000	37
1940	235,585	238,000	178,000	75	60,000	25
1945	396,000	400,000	297,000	74	103,000	26
1950	630,000	590,600	456,200	77	134,400	23
1951	647,100	616,300	515,500	84	100,800	16

Textile Organon.

Manufacture of Purified Cellulose. Since the manufacture of derivatives from cellulose involves critical chemical and mechanical processes, it is necessary to utilize very pure and uniform grades of cellulose pulp to ensure smooth plant operation. Preparation of these pure grades of cellulose has been the object of much research and investigation, particularly from the point of view of using cheaper raw materials in pulp preparation.

Alpha Cellulose. For use in chemical processes, it is desirable to eliminate from the cellulose all impurities found in

E. I. DU PONT DE NEMOURS & CO.

Shredded cotton linters and wood pulp in early stage of plastics manufacture

the original plant form, such as lignins and waxes. In addition, it is preferable to have as high a content as possible of so-called alpha cellulose, which has not been degraded or broken down by the pulping process. Alpha cellulose is defined as cellulose which is insoluble in 17.5 per cent caustic soda solution after a 30-min. treatment; other forms, such as the beta and gamma types, dissolve under these conditions. Alpha cellulose content is used as a measure of pulp quality, since the higher the alpha content, the better the quality of the cellulose derivative. The best grades of pulp made from cotton linters are over 99 per cent alpha cellulose. Wood pulps made by the sulphite process used in viscose rayon manufacture about 1920 had alpha contents around 86 per cent. By 1934, however, chemical research by pulp manufacturers had resulted in the large scale production of 90 per cent alpha pulps. In the early 1940's, production of several specially purified grades of wood pulp was started for use in the manufacture of nitrocellulose and cellulose acetate, which previously had been limited to the use of cotton linters pulp because of critical purity requirements. These latter grades have alpha contents above 95 per cent.

Chemical Cotton. Production of "chemical cotton," which is the raw material made from linters for manufacture of cellulose derivatives, starts with a mechanical cleaning of the lint fibers to remove particles of cottonseed hull, dirt, and sand. The linters are then digested for several hours in large pressure vessels at around 130° C. in the presence of weak caustic soda solution, which dissolves other undesirable impurities such as waxes and fatty acids. The mass of linters pulp is then discharged, washed thoroughly with water, and sent to the bleaching stage. Here treatment with various chemicals such as chlorine or peroxides serves to destroy color bodies. During both the digestion and bleaching stages very careful control is exercised in order to destroy the maximum

E. I. DU PONT DE NEMOURS & CO.

Spinning rayon thread from rayon filaments

amount of impurities and yet avoid degradation of the cellulose itself, which would lower the alpha cellulose content.

The bleached cellulose is then blended in large tanks after analysis of the various chemical and physical properties important in its subsequent processing. If intended for rayon manufacture, the pulp is put through a beater as in paper manufacture and then sheeted out on a Fourdrinier paper machine, dried, and finally cut into sheets and baled. Pulp for acetate or nitrocellulose is dried in uncompacted form to a uniform moisture content and baled.

Sulphite Process. The production of wood pulp to be used in cellulose derivative manufacture is similar in its first stages to one of the processes used to produce pulp for paper making. The method used is the so-called sulphite process, which involves digestion of the wood chips in a solution of chemicals that dissolve the unwanted impurities, leaving a fairly pure cellulose pulp. Quality demands are much more stringent than in the case of pulp for paper, however, and the process must be more carefully controlled in the manufacture of pulp for chemical processing. In addition, special bleaching treatments using chlorine are carried out followed by further digestion with caustic soda to remove the chlorinated impurities. Special washing and drying methods are also used to prepare pulp of unusual uniformity and quality. Pulps produced with a very high alpha content for use in acetate or other special derivatives command a premium price over viscose pulps because of the extra processing involved.

PRODUCTS FROM CELLULOSE

The family of products derived from cellulose by chemical means has grown manyfold since its first crude beginnings about 1850. It provides textiles for clothing and other uses, decorative structural materials, good-looking finishes of ex-

TABLE III. CONSUMPTION OF REFINED CELLULOSE
IN THE UNITED STATES, 1933-1943

Type of Product	% Cellulose Consumed
Viscose rayon, cellophane	77
Acetate	12
Plastics (cellulose acetate, ethyl cellulose, etc.)	3
Nitrocellulose (including lacquers)	7
Cuprammonium rayon	1
	100

Adapted from G. D. Bieber, *Chemical Industries,* July 1944, pp. 97-99.

cellent quality and durability, and transparent coverings, as well as explosives. This industry was producing materials in the United States valued at approximately a billion dollars in 1947, and so represented quite an appreciable factor in the nation's economy.

TABLE IV. UNITED STATES PRODUCTION OF CELLULOSE
DERIVATIVES IN 1943
(*Millions of Pounds*)

Derivative	Amount
Viscose rayon	440
Acetate fiber	220
Cellophane	79.4
Ethyl cellulose	3.9
Cellulose acetate and acetate butyrate	60.2
Nitrocellulose	85.2
Total	888.7

(War Production Board; *Textile Organon.*)

These products may be considered in four main groups. The first group includes fibers such as viscose, acetate, and other rayon types; the second, plastics, such as cellulose nitrate, acetate, ethyl cellulose and cellophane, or regenerated cellulose film; the third group includes protective coatings and lacquers; and the fourth, explosives or nitrocellulose. The relative importance of these groups on a volume basis is made apparent in Table III. These figures do not include nitrocellulose for explosives, which during peacetime is a relatively insignificant quantity.

Synthetic Fibers. Although the four methods of production—viscose, cuprammonium, acetate, and nitrate—were discovered betweeen 1890 and 1905, the tremendous growth of this industry did not really get under way until the end of World War I. During the next 25 years, however, rayon and acetate grew from high-cost, low-volume specialty materials into inexpensive high-quality fiber produced in very large volume and finding general use throughout the textile field. By 1938, rayon and acetate had surpassed wool in volume of consumption in the United States and thereby became second only to cotton as a textile raw material. Figures on the growth of production in the United States and the world are given in Table V.

TABLE V. RAYON AND ACETATE PRODUCTION
(*Thousands of Pounds*)

Year	United States	World
1911	365	18,700
1916	5,780	23,400
1921	14,990	48,200
1926	62,695	211,860
1931	150,880	499,740
1936	277,625	1,004,300
1941	560,000	2,825,395
1947	975,000	1,978,000
1951	1,294,000	3,957,000

Textile Organon.

Coincident with this tremendous growth was a steady reduction in rayon and acetate prices, from over $4 a pound in 1920 to approximately 70¢ in 1951.

Two major factors have aided the growth of rayon and acetate consumption in the United States since 1935. The first of these has been the adoption of rayon cord in the manufacture of heavy-duty truck and bus tires. This factor became particularly important in the United States during World War II because of the superior strength and durability obtainable by using rayon instead of cotton cord in synthetic rubber tires. Only 10,000,000 lb. of rayon went to this use in 1939, in comparison to 333,000,000 lb. by 1951—half the total United States viscose rayon filament yarn production. The second factor has been a large increase in staple-fiber production. This material is made by spinning short lengths of rayon staple in the same way in which cotton or wool are spun into yarn. Before 1935, United States rayon and acetate production had been entirely continuous rayon filaments twisted together into one strand. Availability of textiles from staple fiber widened the applications of rayon and acetate considerably, and by 1951 almost one-third of the total United States rayon and acetate was produced in this form.

All four methods of rayon and acetate production are similar in general outline. The purified cellulose pulp is put into solution by chemical means, and a very fine strand of the solution is drawn or extruded through a minute hole or orifice called a spinneret into some medium, either liquid or vapor, which serves to precipitate the cellulose and remove the solvent, thus forming a fine filament. A number of these filaments are then spun or twisted together into yarn or fiber of appropriate thickness. In all processes the very closest control must be exercised over chemical and mechanical variables because of the critical nature of the various steps. Even the slightest trace of dust in the solution is enough to cause clogging of the spinnerets, and small variations in uniformity of the spinning solution are sufficient to cause breakage of the filaments.

Plastics. As has been mentioned, cellulose nitrate (celluloid) was the first material to be produced among the large family since known as plastics. Other types of plastics made

Use of sheets and films of the various cellulose derivatives has increased greatly during this same period, particularly for the attractive packaging of consumer items. In this use the plastic types mentioned above meet competition from cellophane, which is regenerated cellulose produced by the viscose process and coated with wax against water absorption.

Cellulose nitrate production, beginning on a very small scale in 1870, had reached a volume of over 20,000,000 lb. per year in the United States in 1919. Since that time, with the exception of a few isolated years, its production has been declining somewhat because of competition with other plas-

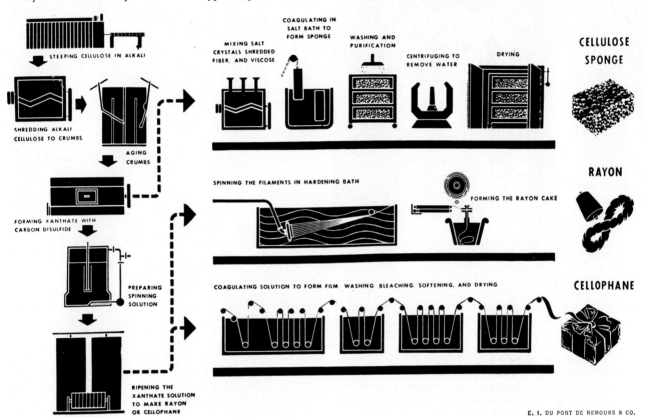

STEEPING CELLULOSE IN ALKALI

SHREDDING ALKALI CELLULOSE TO CRUMBS

AGING CRUMBS

FORMING XANTHATE WITH CARBON DISULFIDE

PREPARING SPINNING SOLUTION

RIPENING THE XANTHATE SOLUTION TO MAKE RAYON OR CELLOPHANE

MIXING SALT CRYSTALS SHREDDED FIBER, AND VISCOSE

COAGULATING IN SALT BATH TO FORM SPONGE

WASHING AND PURIFICATION

CENTRIFUGING TO REMOVE WATER

DRYING

CELLULOSE SPONGE

SPINNING THE FILAMENTS IN HARDENING BATH

FORMING THE RAYON CAKE

RAYON

COAGULATING SOLUTION TO FORM FILM WASHING BLEACHING, SOFTENING, AND DRYING

CELLOPHANE

E. I. DU PONT DE NEMOURS & CO.

STEPS IN THE MANUFACTURING OF VARIOUS PLASTIC PRODUCTS

from cellulose include cellulose acetate, mixed cellulose esters such as cellulose acetate-butyrate, and other derivatives such as methyl and ethyl cellulose, benzyl cellulose, and carboxymethyl cellulose. Most of these plastics can be produced in any desired shape, form, and color, and have found wide application for useful and decorative articles such as fountain pens, spectacle frames, decorative hardware, handles for tools or tableware, packaging materials, and a thousand and one novel, decorative, or utilitarian items.

Cellulose plastics are normally produced in four forms—molding powder, sheets, films, and rods and tubes. All types are thermoplastic, i.e., soften at high temperatures, and this quality is utilized effectively in molding. Cellulose nitrate, because of its inflammability, cannot be molded at high temperatures. Other types, however, are produced in powder form for use in injection molding machines. These machines heat a charge of powder until it is liquid and then force it under high pressures into a mold of the desired shape. Very rapid cycles of operation can be obtained and a large number of duplicate articles produced at very low cost. This injection molding process has been responsible for much of the growth in production of acetate and mixed-ester cellulosics since 1930.

tics. Cellulose acetate production for plastics was started on a commercial basis in this country in 1931, and has expanded greatly since that time. Cellulose acetate-butyrate molding powder followed in 1938, and production of ethyl cellulose was begun around the same time. Benzyl cellulose and

TABLE VI.
UNITED STATES PRODUCTION OF CELLULOSE PLASTICS

Year	Cellulose Nitrate	Cellulose Acetate	Total
1951	7,611,086	109,368,118	116,979,204
1943	14,042,348	54,386,181	68,428,529
1942	15,128,826	48,245,825	63,374,651
1941	16,499,019	36,934,768	53,433,787
1940	11,915,290	23,850,050	35,765,340
1939	13,373,172	20,795,835	34,169,007
1938	9,487,926	14,224,797	23,712,723
1937	17,722,309	13,235,062	30,957,371
1936	16,934,850	13,036,497	29,971,347
1935	16,205,413	10,504,003	26,709,416
1934	12,000,000	5,000,000	17,000,000

Modern Plastics Encyclopedia.

E. I. DU PONT DE NEMOURS & CO.

EXTRUDED PLASTIC RODS
Formed by being squeezed under pressure through openings of desired diameter

methyl cellulose have been produced commercially in Europe, but their production in the United States in 1946 was still on a very small scale. Carboxy-methyl cellulose, the newest member of the family, was introduced during 1946 in small quantities for experimental evaluation, and is now manufactured in large volume for use as a thickening agent.

Ethyl cellulose production expanded from small experimental quantities in the years 1937 through 1940 to over 12,000,000 lb. in 1944, almost equivalent to cellulose nitrate in volume, but its use has decreased since 1947.

Protective Coatings. Chemical derivatives of cellulose such as cellulose nitrate, cellulose acetate, and ethyl cellulose, whose wide usage as plastics has been discussed above, also find major application as protective coatings. Although an ether-alcohol solution of nitrocellulose, or collodion, found some early use in medical applications as a protective coating, it was not until the discovery of other solvents such as amyl acetate that industrial applications of nitrocellulose in this field began.

The lacquer industry underwent its major expansion during the years immediately following World War I, when it was stimulated by extensive supplies and facilities for manufacture of nitrocellulose and new types of lacquer solvents, principally ethyl and butyl acetate. In 1922 and 1923, modern cellulosic lacquers found their first major industrial application in automobile manufacturing. These finishes, applied by spraying and with a very rapid drying time, were a great step forward from older types of slow-drying paints or enamels.

Nitrocellulose dopes were used during World War I to stiffen and protect the fabric covering of aircraft wings and bodies. Because of their high flammability, attempts were made to substitute cellulose acetate for cellulose nitrate, and by the end of the war most aircraft were made with this relatively nonflammable coating.

Modern cellulosic lacquers are compounded primarily from a cellulose nitrate base, although both cellulose acetate and ethyl cellulose find some use in specialty lacquers. To dissolve the cellulosic, various so-called primary solvents may be used, such as ethyl, propyl, or butyl acetate. Latent solvents of the alcohol type and extenders, such as petroleum naphtha or toluene, are added in order to reduce cost and obtain desirable coating and drying characteristics. Various pigments are incorporated in the solution to give color, and other resins and also plasticizers are added to increase the hardness, gloss, and flexibility of the dry film. By adjusting the proportion and types of these various ingredients, the lacquer compounder is able to produce a variety of finishes suitable for a wide range of industrial and home uses. Automobile finishing still remains one of the largest markets open to cellulosic lacquers, but these are also used as protective coatings on furniture, hardware, airplanes, toys and novelties, and many other mass-produced consumer items.

Explosives. Cellulose nitrate, or nitrocellulose, has found major uses in the explosives industry since the middle of the nineteenth century. For explosive use, nitration of the purified cotton or wood pulp is carried farther—i.e., more nitro groups are added to the cellulose molecule—than is the case in the manufacture of cellulose nitrate for plastics or lacquers. The most highly nitrated form, so-called guncotton, containing over 13 per cent nitrogen, is a major ingredient in smokeless powders. Proportions of this material are usually blended with nitrocellulose containing 12.6 per cent nitrogen to give powders the desired explosive characteristics. In peacetime, several million pounds of such powders are sold each year for sporting and small-game use; in wartime, production is greatly expanded.

Nitrocellulose is also mixed with trinitrotoluene, or TNT, to make one form of dynamite, called blasting gelatin, which is preferred for critical blasting work because of its insensitiveness to shock, its water resistance, and very high explosive power. *See also* PLASTICS; SYNTHETIC FIBERS.

R. W. KixM.

CELSUS, AULUS CORNELIUS [sɛ'lsəs], Latin writer who probably lived about the time of Tiberius (B.C. 42-37 A.D.). Celsus is believed to have been a Roman patrician; whether he was a physician is uncertain. An encyclopedist, he wrote a series of technical works on agriculture, law, philosophy, military science, and medicine. Of these, only the last is extant; as *De medicina* it was first printed at Florence in 1476. It passed through many editions and was for a long time a standard treatise. Celsus professed to be a follower of Asclepiades of Bithynia, although he was really a follower of Hippocrates and his methods. The ethical tone of *De medicina* is lofty and the line of treatment humane and sensible. It is notable for a classic description of inflammation: redness, swelling, heat, and pain. It deals with diet, therapeutics, pathology, internal and external diseases, and surgery. The standard edition is that of Daremberg (1859), and there is an English translation by Grieve (1856).

D. D. M.

CELTIC [sɛ'ltik; kɛ'ltɪk], an Indo-European language now spoken in the Highlands of Scotland, in the Hebrides, in parts of Ireland, in Wales and Brittany, and in Nova Scotia. Continental Celtic is chiefly represented by Gaulish; insular Celtic falls into two groups: Brythonic, which includes Welsh, Cornish, and Breton; and Goidelic, which includes Irish, Scottish Gaelic, and Manx. Celtic is recognized most easily by features of phonology. Celtic shares with Latin and Italic some features of sound and form, and these members of the Indo-European family are thus closely akin, but it also has distinct features in common with Indo-Iranian, Hittite, and Tocharian, and is therefore of considerable importance for the study of Indo-European grammar.

The term Gaulish is commonly used for all the remains of Celtic speech on the Continent, for most of the material is from Gaul and there is not enough from other Continental regions to establish separate dialects. Some sixty Gaulish inscriptions have been discovered, the earliest, from Northern Italy, dating from the third or second century B.C., the latest from the third century of the Christian Era. Ancient Latin and Greek writers give us many proper names and some other words which they say are Gaulish, but very little is known about this language. The name *Ver-cingeto-rix* ("king of great warriors") illustrates the loss of *p*, *ver-* being equivalent to the Greek ὑπέρ ("above"), and the change of *ē* to *i*, *-rix* being comparable to the Latin *rēx* ("king"). The name *Epo-so-gnātus* ("knowing horses well"), which echoes the Homeric epithet ἱππόδαμος, illustrates the change of *ō* to *ā*, Greek having the form γνωτός. The place name *Novio-dūnum* means "new fortress." The sum of our knowledge of Gaulish amounts to a list of proper names and other words, the etymology of which is often clear, with good evidence for the sounds of the language and some fragments of evidence for the grammatical forms.

Brythonic is first known to us as Old British and Goidelic as Old Irish; these may have been dialects of the same language, and thus mutually intelligible in some degree as late as the fourth century of the Christian Era. At this time the chief differences were in the treatment of the Indo-European *k^w*, which remained as *q* in Irish and had become *p* in British, and in the stress, which was on the first syllable in Irish and on the penult in British. But Old British is known to us only from names in the Latin inscriptions of Britain. The earliest Welsh documents date from the eighth century, and by that time a great many changes had taken place. Thus the Welsh *pump* ("five") contrasts with the Irish *cóic*, *brawd* ("brother") with *bráthir*, *rhin* ("secret") with *rún*, *gwir* ("true") with *fír*, *ieuanc* ("young") with *oäc*, *newydd* ("new") with *nuae*, *chwedl* ("story") with *scél*, *cant* ("100") with *cét*, and *tywysog* ("chieftain") with *toísech*.

The most striking feature of Brythonic and Goidelic alike is the system of initial mutations, by which the beginning of a word may be altered by the preceding word. Thus the Welsh *pen* ("head"), which corresponds to Irish *cenn*, mutates variously to *fy mhen* ("my head"), *ei ben* ("his head"), and *ei phen* ("her head"); and Irish has a similar system. A notable feature of Celtic is the formation of singulatives from collective nouns, by means of a suffix *-inio-*; thus in Irish *grán* ("corn") becomes *gráinne* ("a single grain") while in Welsh the forms are *grawn* and *gronyn* and in Breton *greun* and *greunenn*. Similarly the Irish *folt* ("hair") becomes *foiltne* ("a single hair"), the Welsh *gwallt* ("hair") becomes *gwelltyn* ("blade of grass"), and the Welsh *adar* ("birds") becomes *ederyn* ("a single bird"). *See also* Breton; Cornish; Irish; Manx; Scottish Gaelic; Welsh.

M. Di.

CELTIC LITERATURE. *See* Breton Literature; Irish Literature; Scottish Gaelic Literature; Welsh Literature.

CELTS, the name of a warlike people originating in south-eastern Germany between the Rhine and the Upper Danube in the Bronze Age, who buried their dead in round barrows, fought with a heavy slashing sword, and spoke a common Celtic language. The great age of the Celts was the La Tène period of the Iron Age, which lasted through-

out the last five centuries before Christ. About the beginning of the fifth century B.C. they began to expand in all directions from their homeland in the northern Alps and on the Danube. They occupied Gaul, northern Italy, and the Spanish peninsula, where they mingled with the native Iberians and became known as the Celtiberians. Other waves of invaders moved into the British Isles, where earlier Celts had established themselves two or three centuries before. Shortly before 400 B.C. an army of Celts, known to the Romans as Gauls, marched southward into Italy and destroyed the Etruscan power. Under their leader Brennus they defeated the Roman army in 390 B.C. and sacked Rome. Bought off after an occupation of seven months they withdrew from Rome, but continued to hold a great part of northern Italy. At the same time other Celts advanced down the Danube and into the Balkans. About the year 280 B.C. a large army overran Macedonia, as well as Thessaly and Phocis in Greece, before being repulsed by the Aetolians and their allies in 279 B.C. These and other Celts then conquered Thrace, crossed the Hellespont, and occupied most of Asia Minor. In 232 B.C. Attalus I of Pergamum defeated them in a series of battles and confined them to the interior area of Asia Minor known as Galatia. Other Celts had, meanwhile, moved into southern Russia.

The ancients described the Celts as a fair haired, blue or grey eyed people of great stature; and they called all the northern invaders by this name if they answered to the general description and spoke a Celtic dialect. Their culture during the La Tène period is remarkable artistically for a love of decoration, which included geometrical devices and a flamboyant treatment of plant and animal forms. Celtic literature shows similar richness of imagination. F. C. H.

CEMBALO. *See* Musical Terms.
CEMENT. *See* Engineering Materials; Highway Engineering.

CENCI, THE [tshe′ntshi], a tragedy in blank verse by Percy Bysshe Shelley, first published in 1819. The play, set in Rome, concerns the wealthy and noble family of the Cenci. The debauched and malign Count Francesco Cenci rapes his only daughter, Beatrice, who, with her step-mother, Lucretia, and her brother, Bernardo, brings about his murder. Suspected, the Cenci are tortured into confession and sentenced to death. In spite of Beatrice's plea, Pope Clement VIII refuses to pardon them, and the sentence is carried out. Although the play is inclined to be declamatory, it has the terror and power of Jacobean drama. H. M. J.

CENOBITES. *See* Monasticism.
CENSER. *See* Thurible.

CENSORS, Roman magistrates. Two censors, usually ex-consuls, were elected by the Romans every five years. The first task of the censors was to assess the property of the citizens as a basis for assigning individuals to the proper tribes and classes. The censors also revised the lists of equestrians and senators. This was a most important function, because the censors could thus materially affect the composition of the senate by adding new members and dropping others from the rolls. The censors were also in charge of the public finances. They farmed out the taxes, sold or rented the public lands, and let the contracts for public works. As guardians of the public morals, censors might degrade in class a person guilty of cowardice, misuse of public funds, or cruelty in private life. T. B. J.

CENSORSHIP. No society has ever existed, so far as we know, which has not exercised some censorship over the conduct and opinions of its members. In primitive societies, censorship is ordinarily the work of taboo, traditional prohibitions upon certain acts and attitudes; and those taboos are so thoroughly imprinted upon the minds of the young by the tribal elders that they become almost a part of the nature of all members of the group, without much later necessity for enforcing conformity to these commandments. In more civilized societies, censorship assumes elaborate forms, now enforced by political authority; again by private or voluntary agencies.

The word "censorship" is of Roman origin, referring to the office and duties of the two magistrates who presided over the taking of the census in the Republic and the Empire, and with whose function of enumeration was joined the responsibility of assigning burdens and duties to the various classes and groups in Roman society. The censors, in short, were expected to determine the responsibilities of Roman citizens, and to see that those responsibilities were properly executed. They were the guardians of "the high old Roman virtue," and their powers were very great—indeed, once elected (they were chosen every eighteen months, beginning in 443 B.C.), they were responsible to no superior, being held accountable only to Roman traditions and to their own consciences. Election to the censorship was the crown of a political career. The most famous of the censors was the elder Cato; his great-grandson, Cato of Utica, also celebrated as a censor, took his own life in 46 B.C., rather than yield to Caesar. Through the stern integrity of such magistrates, the office became associated historically with the defense of traditional ways, and the memory of it has exerted a considerable influence upon later thought, particularly in the Renaissance. The old censorship finally expired about the middle of the third century.

It is the function of the Roman censors as arbiters of public morality which has given the word "censorship" its modern meaning. The Roman censors could exclude citizens from public functions on moral grounds; and in their scrutiny of the conduct of knights and plebeians, they came to publish edicts detailing the moral precepts by which they were governed in the execution of office. They looked into family life and private conduct, and into the exercise of political duties; they reproved certain occupations and criminal records; and their sentences of disapproval, which carried the punishment of exclusion from political life, were called *in-famia*—the disclosure of infamous acts. Moral worth, in the view of the censors, was the quality which made a man great and a society just; moral worth took precedence even over intellectual power. As R. H. Barrow, in *The Romans,* writes of the elder Cato, "It is not intellect which Cato despises, but the contemporary use of intellect to undermine character. His ideal is the citizen of high moral principle, based on tradition, realizing himself in the commonwealth and its business, and so creating a triumphant government pre-eminent for enlightened policy and massive integrity." To enforce respect for such principles, the censors were empowered to look into bad cultivation of land, to restrict the spread of luxury, to inquire into sexual conduct, and generally to see that manliness and probity should not decline in the Roman state.

The office of the Roman censors, then, became the agency for preserving the morality and the established ways of life of Roman society. Such an agency, in one form or another, has existed in every coherent society, with brief and partial exceptions (the period of the Directory in France may be cited as one of these), down to the present time. No society has tolerated moral anarchy for long—unless certain states in the twentieth century succeed in refuting this rule; and therefore every society has had its censors, intended to oversee private and public conduct in certain grave matters and to hold in check the persons and factions which rebel against established moral order. Every society, usually in theory and invariably in practice, down to the present century, has asserted its right to restrain those who would destroy the foundations of that society. Ordinarily a society has considered morally subversive those persons who would overthrow the predominant religion, or the accepted view of the nature of human personality, or the established system of justice and order, or prescriptive rights, including private liberties and the prescriptive system of property-holding. In every society, censors—though often called by some other name—have existed to guard against the undermining of this received moral and social order. Sometimes the function of censorship has been undertaken by the priesthood, sometimes by the state, sometimes by unofficial groups. The members of the Athenian assembly acted as censors in condemning Socrates for corrupting the youth of Athens, though their judgment in that particular case was influenced by a misapprehension of Socrates' actual ends and influence; Robespierre fulfilled such a function in endeavoring to purge revolutionary France of corruption, though he exalted his private judgment above the old rules of justice and moderation. The medieval Church, in extirpating the Albigensians, was assuming the role of moral and social censor; Luther, in denouncing the errors of the Anabaptists, similarly was speaking as the censor of his age and country. A harsh and imprudent censorship ordinarily has provoked a reaction of license and defiance; while the decay of just and prudent censorship usually has led to moral and political confusion, and ultimately to a regime of repression, by way of antidote. In every age there has been some conflict between the censorship, the constituted authority for obtaining conformity to the accepted ways of a people, and the forces of personal rebellion against the established moral and social order, who take for their maxim Rabelais' motto of the Abbey of Thélème, "do as you will," or Ben Jonson's "every man in his own humour."

From the beginning of the civil social order, then, censorship has been a prudential conservative device. Much discussed in the present century, and often denounced without an understanding of its historical origins or underlying purpose, censorship is at present in a state of flux throughout most of the world. In the majority of modern states, censorships of a rigor and efficiency impossible in earlier times are now in force; in a few nations, as in Sweden, censorship has virtually ceased to exist.

Whether any modern society will long remain without effectual censorship is in question. Soviet Russia, in its first years, announced the abolition of restraints upon private life but, after studying certain consequences of this emancipation, established a rigorous censorship of personal conduct, extending to marital relationships and enforced by an elaborate system of positive law and state propaganda. Modern revolutionary regimes, after a brief period of license, commonly adopt a "puritanical" policy, in reaction: as in the French Revolution, and in the attitudes of the radical factions during the Spanish Civil War.

The concept of censorship, therefore, is to be regarded neither as a "god-term" nor a "devil-term," but as a social policy and phenomenon of very ancient and widespread origins, sometimes resulting in a beneficial conservation of human character and society, sometimes resulting in a leaden repression which provokes a disastrous reaction. The three principal forms in which censorship has been exercised within historic time may be distinguished as church censorship, state censorship, and private censorship.

Church Censorship. As the body of laws of every civilized society has grown from a root of religious law (ordinarily interpreted and administered by a priestly class), so the earlier manifestations of censorship commonly have been concerned with religious questions, and priests, or priest-rulers, or the hierarchy of a highly-developed church, or the body of ministers and deacons (under various names) have long exercised censorial powers. Except in such states as have suppressed organized religion, some such view and administration of censorship survives, in great or small degree, to the present day. Religion being concerned with the whole purpose of human existence, any dispute over first principles has involved religious assumptions, tempers have been excited accordingly, and intensity of censorship, or reaction against it, has varied directly in proportion to the sincerity of religious feeling among a people. Some of the greatest excesses of censorial policy occurred during the Reformation and Counter-Reformation, when both Catholics and Protestants were compelled to review their first principles and to realize the threat that their opponents' doctrines, equally sincere, presented to their concept of a good morality and a good society. Frederick the Great of Prussia, on the other hand, contemptuous of all religious faiths and reared in the latitudinarian atmosphere of the eighteenth century, chose to indulge within his dominions every variety of religious doctrine, so long as his political security was not imperilled; his was the toleration of indifference.

Of church or religious censorships, perhaps the most generally known examples are the several Roman censures and expulsions of Greek philosophers, Constantine's and Justinian's suppression of heretical writings, the *Index Librorum Prohibitorum,* Savonarola's purgation of Renaissance Florence, the Tudor and Stuart presecutions of Catholics and Dissenters, Calvin's ascendancy in Geneva, the Cromwellian restrictions upon the printing of books, the policies of Puritan New England, and the antireligious censorships of Soviet Russia and China. Other examples could be cited from Chinese and Indian history, and from Moslem lands— although the most celebrated instance of the last, the alleged burning of the Alexandrian Library by the Arab conquerors of Egypt, rests upon scanty evidence. Of all these censorships, probably the most interesting and important is the Catholic Index.

From the days of the primitive Church, a high degree of watchfulness over heretical books has been exercised by ecclesiastics. Despite the confinement of literacy to a small minority of the population until the eighteenth century, books exerted an influence during late classical and medieval times out of all proportion to their circulation. The very scarcity of manuscripts and books gave the written word— and later the printed word—an authority over men's minds which has now passed, in part, to radio, motion-pictures, and other media; to find a positive statement set down on parchment was almost to give it credence without criticism; and writings were communicated rapidly to the mass of men by innumerable preachers and clerks, through sermons and lectures. Accordingly, the ecclesiastical authorities always scrutinized new writings for error, and took measures to ensure that Christianity should not be corrupted by heretical or reckless books. Pope Gelasius, in 494, issued what was probably the first regular list of prohibited books; many others

followed; and when the Inquisition took form in the thirteenth century, to that institution passed the duty of guarding against heretical publications. Among the many celebrated actions of the medieval Church in the matter of censorships, the fate of the writings of the great Schoolman Pierre Abélard is conspicuous. A provincial synod forced Abélard to burn his *Introduction to Theology* in 1120; Innocent II ordered the burning of all his works in 1140; and in 1559 and 1564, all of Abélard's books were placed upon the Catholic Index.

It should not be supposed, however, that the suppression of such literature was consistent during the Middle Ages, or often very rigorous. A toleration of various opinions on theological questions prevailed in most European countries most of the time, and often quasi-heretical or clearly heretical opinions were indulged so long as they did not appear to have any bearing upon the security of established society. The social principals of the Albigensians, more than the purely theological doctrines of the Cathari, brought the wrath of the Church upon them; and when the Church in Scotland put down the Lollard preachers, at the beginning of the fifteenth century, it was because of their insistence upon social levelling, and their denunciations of the economic basis of the Church, rather than their theological speculation. The invention and diffusion of printing, late in the fifteenth century, caused the Roman Catholic Church to increase greatly its censorial inspection of books; the Lateran Council of 1515 pronounced that no book should be printed without previous examination by ecclesiastical authority, lest the laity be deluded.

Not until the Counter-Reformation, nevertheless, did the *Index Librorum Prohibitorum* take regular form. Dismayed at the insistence of the Reformers upon translating the Bible into the vernacular, and at the flood of Protestant tracts, Paul IV, through the Roman Inquisition, instituted the Index which has continued to the present day, publishing lists of prohibited books in 1557 and 1559; the work was regularized at the twenty-fifth session of the Council of Trent, in 1564. The Index was reformed by Leo XIII, in 1897, and the latest edition is that of 1948. This Index is a list of books which Catholics are forbidden to read, under ultimate penalty of excommunication: heretical works, obscene writings, works of superstition and magic, books inimical to society, and immoral and irreligious newspapers. An elaborate machinery of censorship determines what books shall be listed in this Index. Although sometimes—especially in the age of the Counter-Reformation—supported by the secular arm in Southern Europe, generally the Index has exerted its influence through the voluntary acquiescence of clergy and laity; and though many Roman Catholics wink at certain of its prohibitions, and others are ignorant of its details, it has probably been the most successful censorial device of modern times. Dr. Margaret Mead, an influential cultural anthropologist, in her article "Sex and Censorship," published in *New World Writing* (1953), touched upon this form of censorship with some sympathy: "The Index performs a very important function: it makes Catholic readers aware of the kind of books they are reading. They may read them, but as they read, a persistent sense of alertness to sin protects them from a loss of values."

The Catholic Index, intended to shelter religion, has its twentieth-century imitations and opposites in official lists of books published by Communist regimes and intended to make the study of religion impossible; and the powers of the militant atheists to enforce such censorship ordinarily are much greater, today, than the power of the Catholic Church to prevent the reading of books upon its Index. A directive of the Russian Supreme Soviet in 1926 ordered libraries to ensure that "the section on religion must contain solely anti-religious books. Religiously dogmatic books such as the *Gospels*, the *Koran*, the *Talmud*, must be left in the large libraries, but removed from the smaller ones." Such prohibitions were relaxed somewhat when the Soviet regime tolerated some degree of religious observance during the Second World War; but the general policy of "dialectical materialism" remains in force to discourage general reading or discussion of theological topics.

What with the intensity of the present contest between religious faith and varieties of "Marxist dialectic" throughout a great part of the world, the twentieth-century problem of religious censorship is as urgent as was the sixteenth-century problem. In Eastern Europe and in most of Asia, however, the question today is not whether censorship will tolerate dissent from religious orthodoxy, but whether any form of religious belief can endure under a political censorship fiercely hostile toward either a church establishment or private religious convictions—and that a censorship infinitely more pervasive than any which prevailed during the Wars of Religion.

State Censorship. In recent usage, "censorship" has come principally to mean any system for examining important items of information, opinion, dramatic representation, pictures and works of art, and similar matters touching upon public opinion or taste—but especially supervision by a political authority over questions of political belief and social morality. This narrowing of the term is the result of the secularization of the censorial function which followed hard upon Reformation and Counter-Reformation. In Protestant Europe, the national monarchies undertook the censorial function eagerly, as the Catholic Church was forced to abandon it; while in Catholic Europe, though the Church retained its censorial powers, the nation-states generally supplemented or superseded these by separate political censorships. Thorough censorship or licensing of publications continued in force in England until 1694, in France until 1789, in Sapin until 1808, in most of Italy until 1848, and in Russia until 1905. Although some of these censorships later were restored in part, generally the "liberal era" was characterized by a progressive decline of state censorship. No official general censorship was ever established in the United States of America, though in actuality a variety of particular censorships has long existed in the United States: a customs censorship over the importation of obscene literature, a post-office censorship over the use of the mails to distribute improper writings or pictures, and a variety of state and local bodies to censor immoral or seditious publications. Until the Civil War, any endeavor in this country to censor political expression was intensely unpopular, the Federalists' Alien and Sedition Acts being the most conspicuous example; but since 1861 there have been repeated wartime censorships of political opinions as well as of military information, especially the precedents set by President Woodrow Wilson during the first World War. The provisions for freedom of the press and of speech in the "Bill of Rights" of the American Constitution, however, and similar provisions in most of the state constitutions, have served to prevent any thoroughgoing censorship of political writings and utterances in the United States, except in time of war. Recent decisions of the United States Supreme Court have extended, rather than contracted, the application of the "Bill of Rights," so that the lawfulness of certain state and local censorships over taste and morals is now in question,

The state censorships which prevailed from the middle of the sixteenth century until the later years of the nineteenth century were often harsh, but rarely were they efficient enough to secure enduring conformity. The most eloquent appeal against such censorship—concerned both with religion and politics—was John Milton's *Areopagitica* (1644); but it needs to be read in the context of its times; Milton was not really urging complete freedom of expression, but only a reasonable toleration of varieties of Protestant opinion—he had no intention of tolerating Catholics. Before the influence of liberal ideas of the eighteenth and nineteenth centuries, and as the

An old cartoon, showing the devil of censorship trying to get hold of the free press

powers of the European monarchs were diminished, these state censorships rapidly gave ground—first in England, last in Russia. The most intelligent of these censorial systems, that of Austria as devised by Metternich after 1815, collapsed with the fall and flight of that statesman during the revolutionary upheavals of 1848.

Despite the existence of state censorships for four centuries, those centuries constituted one of the most remarkable periods of human achievement in the works of philosophy and imaginative literature. A censorship, however bigoted in intention, may serve actually as a stimulant to thought and writing, if the censors are not powerful enough to make their decisions thoroughly obeyed. So it was with the political censors of this age. Since European governments were not sufficiently ruthless or efficient to suppress criticism utterly, their censors awakened dissent more often than they suppressed it, so that politicians of the opposition and dissenting authors had their wits sharpened and their talents brought to the fore by this disapproval—which, however, was not a disapproval effectual enough to cow them. Restrained by Christian ethics or the remnants of Christian ethics, the state could not put these dissidents to death; many of them had friends at court, and all of them had a considerable following in the nation; so, in the end, they often triumphed over the state censors.

During the greater part of the nineteenth century, when liberal political doctrines were in the ascendant, it was believed by the leaders of liberalism that no censorship of any sort was endurable; that surviving censorships were vestiges of medievalism; and that future generations would enjoy perfect freedom of expression. John Stuart Mill and his school assumed that every man is the best judge of his own actions and welfare, competent to choose for himself what he will read or hear, to be restrained only by his own enlightened self-interest (reinforced by universal education) from indulging depraved tastes or entertaining fallacious notions. Mill's only important qualification was the remark that a man does not have the right to shout "Fire!" in a crowded theatre; he was convinced that if truth and falsity are allowed to compete in the modern market place, truth is sure to prevail. Until the inception of the twentieth century, it seemed that these liberals were true prophets, for almost everywhere censorship receded and every manner of freedom was indulged. Then, however, the catastrophes of the twentieth-century time of trouble began to dissipate the liberal dream; liberty, too often, turned into license, and then into anarchy, and at length into tyranny, over a great part of the world; nearly everywhere, censorship returned, but this time censorship of a malignant nature, scarcely conceivable in earlier years, employing the immense powers of the modern state for its enforcement. The twentieth-century censorships, for the most part, were unrestrained by moral considerations. By the mid-twentieth century, only the United States, Britain, France, one or two Latin-American states, Belgium, Luxembourg, the Netherlands, the Scandinavian states, Western Germany, Switzerland, and Italy were free from a general censorship; and even in several of these countries, partial censorships exist.

In Communist China, as the culmination of this grim process, appeared the most thorough form of censorship known; "brainwashing," or indoctrination of the suspected dissident by repeated interrogation until he should be not merely silenced, but dazed into acquiescence. The method had been employed earlier, though not to thoroughly or extensively, by the Nazis and by the Russian Communists. The lengths to which it may be carried in the future are suggested by George Orwell in his novel *1984,* in which, by means of "Doublethink" and "Newspeak" and techniques of shock, men are severed from the past, from personality, and from any ability to discern objective truth from falsehood.

Private Censorship. In many societies, a high degree of censorship has been exerted by private associations. In the twentieth century, the recrudescence of state censorship appears to coincide with an ominous extension of private censorship, or the suppression of opinion by a conscious or unconscious conspiracy of silence among persons substantially in control of publishing and publicizing. Such apprehensions have been frequently expressed in Britain in recent years, particularly in connection with the increased power of quasi-public corporations and great industrial concerns over what shall be expressed in the press. In both Britain and the United States, serious surveys of this problem have been made. In America, through the concentration in New York City of the publishing industry, the book-reviewing journals, the great national newspapers, and the headquarters of radio networks—a process of consolidation at work for many years—a curious kind of censorship of ideas and imagination has become possible. This private censorship does not seem ordinarily to have been deliberate or conspiratorial; rather,

it has been a kind of contagion of opinion within a comparatively small set of people living a highly artificial life in a city with few roots in the past—persons sometimes with small faith in traditional values, and therefore the more anxious for the approval of other people in their coterie of publicists, writers, or entertainers. Many of them were what David Riesman, in *The Lonely Crowd,* calls "other-directed persons"—that is, men and women who depend upon the approbation of their neighbors and their little group for a sanction to their own actions. In such a set, certain words or concepts take on what Richard Weaver, in *The Ethics of Rhetoric,* calls "charismatic terms" or "god terms"; words almost divorced from their original meanings and become abstract symbols summoning forth approving or disapproving responses almost automatically, regardless of particular circumstances.

Many publishers, reviewers, radio employees, writers, and others engaged in satisfying the public's taste for awareness, had for their charismatic terms such words as "liberal," "progressive," "pragmatic," "ambivalent," and the like, and corresponding terms of an unpleasant charismatic power, devil-terms, like "traditional," "religionist," "value-judgment," and "authoritarian." Being anxious for the approval of their associates (who themselves were often governed by the same desire and the same word-tags), many of these persons ignored or sneered at any work of literature, political opinion, or artistic accomplishment which did not conform to these fashionable prejudices. Thus they tended to exercise a censorship, sometimes vociferous, sometimes silent, over a variety of publications—a tyranny of the other-directed mind over the old-fashioned mind, and often over the truly independent mind.

The opinions of the people who tend to control publishing and publicizing are not necessarily those of the majority of Americans; often, indeed, they are at sharp variance; but the majority which these people court is the majority within their own circle, "the little platoon they belong to in society," and American opinion, from the peculiar concentration of publishing and publicizing in one or two cities, is often censored according to whatever may be the fad of the month or the year within the charmed circle of cognoscenti. These fads, and even ideologies, alter from time to time, with the drift of events; but a simple change to another set of prejudices does not ordinarily solve the problem of private censorship; it merely changes its current application.

Current Problems. In the light of the history of censorship and of the fact that no society has long existed without some such control upon forces opposed to established morality and society, it has come to appear that the twentieth-century attitude toward the whole problem must differ considerably from the nineteenth-century hope that censorship would disappear altogether. It is possible that persons who take a stand that nothing should be censored, all opinions being equally valuable, and all books equally deserving, whether holy or obscene, may come to find themselves saddled with a censorship more inflexible than anything they ever dreamt of. If even voluntary censorship by well-intentioned groups is condemned, then the way may be left open for rigorous state censorship which will leave no activity of the mind unrestricted. Out of this realization has come, in recent years, widespread discussion of the proper limits and methods of censorship: principally in relation to political censorship, in connection with the dissemination of Communist doctrines, and moral censorship, in connection with the increasing circulation of pornographic and psychopathic publications.

R. K.

CENSUS, the enumerating of the population. In modern times information concerning the social status of the people and commercial and other data are also collected. Censuses were taken in ancient China, Persia, and Babylonia, and over a period of several centuries in Rome. After the cessation of the Roman census, there was no systematic enumeration of populations until the middle of the eighteenth century. Modern periodical censuses date from about 1800 and now include most populous areas of the world except China. The first census of the United States was taken in 1790 by United States marshals in accordance with the provisions of the Constitution apportioning representatives in Congress according to the population of the states. Subsequently there has been a census every decade, each in general more extensive and detailed than the preceding one. With the increase in the volume of information gathered, the task of tabulating and publishing the results became ultimately so great that it was necessary in 1902 to establish a permanent organization. The Bureau of the Census, now functioning continuously, takes many partial censuses, such as those of agriculture and manufacturing, in addition to the regular decennial enumeration. Several of the states and nearly all school districts regularly take censuses to meet their special requirements. The information usually obtained with respect to individuals includes age, sex, race, marital status, education, and occupation. Sometimes it includes income, housing, and various other facts pertaining to standards of living. Errors in the census occur because of ignorance, faulty memory, or reluctance to answer truthfully, but they are difficult to correct because there are few sources against which to check results. Census information has proved of inestimable value in legislation, commerce, and sociological research.   C. M. R.

CENSUS, BUREAU OF THE, the chief statistical agency of the United States Government, a part of the Department of Commerce. A population census has been taken every ten years in the United States since 1790 in order to meet the Constitutional requirement for such an "enumeration" in order to apportion Congressional representation. As early as 1810 the census began to include other subjects, and the fact-gathering program of the federal government has grown steadily since. In 1902 the Bureau of the Census was formally established, and today it gathers, tabulates, and correlates statistics on a very wide range of subjects, making this information available to the government and, through publication, to private persons. Its fact-gathering program includes, but is not limited to, vital statistics, population distribution and composition, agriculture, business and manufactures, geography, natural resources, housing, and United States territories and possessions.   D. W.

CENTAUR [sɛ'ntɔr], in Greek mythology, a creature shaped like a horse, with a man's torso and head in place of the horse's neck and head. The centaurs were said to be the offspring of Ixion and Nephele and dwelt in the mountains of Thessaly and Arcadia; with the exception of Chiron and Pholus, they were wild and lawless beings. Their most famous exploit was an attempt to carry off Hippodamia, bride of Pirithous, king of the Lapithae, but in a battle with the Lapithae, the centaurs were defeated. *See also* CHIRON; HERACLES; PIRITHOUS.   G. E. D.

CENTAUREA [sɛ'ntɔri'ə; sɛntɔ'riə], a very large genus of the family Compositae. The genus *Centaurea* contains about 500 species, chiefly native to the Old World; only one occurs in North America. They are mostly annuals

or half-hardy perennials with showy heads of blue, purple, white, or yellow flowers. Many are grown as ornamentals, among which are bachelors button, *C. cyanus,* also called cornflower, ragged robin, or bluet; the sweet sultan, *C. moschata;* the dusty-miller, *C. cineraria;* and the basket flower, *C. americana.* Several Old World species have become weeds in this country. The yellow star thistle, *C. solstitialis,* and the napa thistle, *C. melitensis,* are pests in California. They average about two to three feet tall.   G. M. Sm.

CENTAURUS [sɛntɔ'rəs], the Centaur, an ancient, irregular-shaped southern constellation, supposed to depict the mythical creature with the body and legs of a horse and the torso, arms, and head of a man. It extends in right

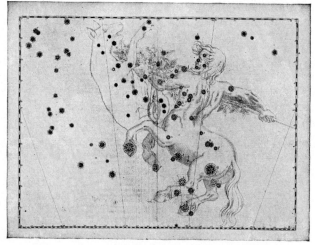

COURTESY OF THE AMERICAN MUSEUM OF NATURAL HISTORY
CENTAURUS, "THE CENTAUR"

ascension from 11 hr. to 15 hr.; in declination from —30° to —64°. A great deal of it is visible from the middle north latitudes. It includes the noted first-magnitude star Alpha (α) Centauri, which shares with Proxima Centauri the title of nearest of all known stars, though 270,000 times more distant than the sun. Alpha is approaching us at a rate of 22 mi. a second. Not far from this star in angular measurement is Beta (β) Centauri, of somewhat lesser brightness yet rated as of the first magnitude. It is approximately 200 light-years distant.

From the tropics and the southern hemisphere, Centaurus presents a splendid sight. Besides the stars just mentioned, there are several of the second and third magnitudes within its wide boundaries. Of special interest is the brightest of the distant globular clusters, Omega (ω) Centauri. To the naked eye this is a hazy circular spot of light of somewhat more than half the apparent diameter of the full moon. Through good telescopes it is resolved into thousands of stars of the twelfth magnitude and fainter. It is one of the nearer globular clusters, only about 20,000 light-years distant. Numerous variable stars have been found in this cluster; and in 1895, a temporary star, or nova, was observed. The southern part of the Milky Way borders the lower part of Centaurus. *See also* ALPHA CENTAURI; BETA CENTAURI; PROXIMA CENTAURI.   J. H. P.

CENTENARY COLLEGE OF LOUISIANA, an accredited, coeducational, privately controlled college of arts and science operated by the Methodist Church at Shreveport, La. It is located on a campus of eighty acres in the residential section of the city. Chartered in 1825 as the College of Louisiana, it moved from Jackson to Shreveport in 1907. The name was changed to Centenary College of Louisiana when the Methodists gave funds to the college on the one-hundredth anniversary of the founding of Methodism. Degrees conferred are the A.B., B.S., and the B.Mus. Interdivisional and interdepartmental seminars entitled Great Issues of Today, Arts and Aesthetics, and Science in Modern Life are required of all seniors. Scholarships and grants-in-aid are available to high school honor graduates, to those preparing for full-time Christian work, and to children of faculty members. Resident women must live on the campus. *For statistics see* COLLEGES AND UNIVERSITIES.

CENTER PARTY, a term which originally referred exclusively to the Zentrumspartei, which was organized after the unification of Germany in 1871 in order to assert the position of the Catholic minority within the predominantly Protestant Reich. Its united and determined front often enabled the minority party to outweigh the divided and indifferent majority, as was indicated in the so-called Kulturkampf, the struggle which resulted in Germany between the Old Catholics, who refused to accept the dogma of the infallibility of the pope, decreed by the Vatican in 1870, and those Catholics who supported the decree. The latter demanded dismissal from state posts of all Old Catholics, a demand that Bismarck interpreted as inteference in matters of state. The struggle broke out in 1873, when Bismarck, supported by the Liberals, with whom he formed a temporary alliance, issued decrees against political agitation from the pulpits and later took more drastic steps, including expulsion of the Jesuits from the state. Within six years, however, Bismarck found it necessary to come to terms with the Vatican, largely because of the alarming growth in strength made by the Socialists. Through this victory over Bismarck's aggressive statism the Zentrum gained so enormously in strength as to acquire a key position, which was, in part, conditioned by the fact that, in contrast to all other German parties, it was heterogeneous both in ideological basis and social composition, recruiting followers from divergent classes and political groups. This intermediate position gave the Center Party a decisive power, far beyond its numerical strength, in the balance of political forces in the Second Empire and in the Weimar Republic, and thus allowed for a rare political flexibility and for coalition with either the Right or Left.

The Center Party concept was later used in a wider sense for the bloc of parties in the center, fighting for preservation and predominance in view of rising threats from right-wing reactionism and left-wing radicalism. In this respect all the parties of the middle ground may be classified under that heading, especially the different Christian Democratic movements in western Europe, such as the Mouvement Républicain Populaire (MRP) in France, Italy's Democrazia Cristiana, under the leadership of Prime Minister Alcide de Gasperi (successor to Luigi Sturzo's pre-Fascist Popolari), and Belgium's Catholic Christian Social Party. Furthermore the ideological shifts in the period following World War II moved the formerly "leftist" liberal and even Socialist parties into a center position in the face of increasing pressure from the Communists. Thus, the French Radical-Socialist Party, formerly the leading leftist group of the Third Republic, became the right wing of the political center, and the Socialist Party of Léon Blum made itself the spokesman for a "Third Force" against Fascist and Communist dictatorship. In this capacity, center parties stand for moderate policies, constitutional development, and peaceful change in opposition to radical transformation and extraparliamentarian in-

tervention by militant minority groups. A bipolarization of political forces has endangered the position of the center parties in a period of revolutionary upheaval. Their strength or weakness thus easily reflects the degree of stability in twentieth century politics. S. N.

CENTERVILLE, the seat of Appanoose Co. in southeastern Iowa, is located on the Chariton River, about 80 mi. southeast of Des Moines. It was founded in 1846 as Chaldea and incorporated as Centerville in 1855. It is the seat of Centerville Community College, founded in 1930. Although there are coal and gypsum deposits nearby, Centerville is primarily a livestock market. Local crops are soybeans, corn, alfalfa, and hay. Castings, bricks, buttons, beverages, boxes, and stationery supplies are among the city's products. Pop. 1950, 7,625.

CENTERVILLE, a borough in Washington Co., southwestern Pennsylvania, situated about 23 mi. south of Pittsburgh. It is in a farming and mining region. Centerville was settled in 1766, laid out and incorporated as a town in 1821, and is governed by a mayor and council. Two miles distant is a statue known as The Madonna of the Trail, which is dedicated to the pioneer mothers of covered wagon days. Pop. 1950, 5,845.

CENTIGRADE SCALE. *See* MEASUREMENTS, STANDARDS AND UNITS OF.

CENTIPEDE [sɛ'ntɪpid], an animal of the class Chilopoda of the phylum Arthropoda, related to the insects. The body is elongate, segmented, and bears many pairs of legs. The head region is distinct, but the rest of the body is fairly uniform throughout its length, except for minor modifications at the hind end. The head bears a pair of long, many-jointed antennae. The eyes are simple or sometimes absent, except, in the common house centipede, *Scutigera,* in which the eyes are compound as in insects. There are four pairs of mouth parts, including the stout poison claws. The number of legs varies greatly in the different orders, in some being many less than the hundred that the name "centipede" implies, and in others many more. The segments of the body are covered with chitinous plates, and each segment bears one pair of jointed legs. The sexes are separate; the reproductive organs open at the rear end of the body.

There are many species of centipedes, found on all continents. They are usually found living on or near the ground in more or less damp situations, as under stones, trash, or leaves, and in loose soil. They feed on insects or other small animals. Most centipedes are only 1 or 2 in. in length, but some large tropical forms may exceed 6 in. Although all centipedes have poison fangs, most of them are harmless. W. I.

CENTLIVRE, SUSANNAH [sɛntlɪ'vər; sɛntli'vər] (c. 1667-1723), dramatist and actress, was born in 1667, probably in Ireland. The details of her youth are uncertain, but it was rumored that she ran away from home because of ill treatment, and that at one time she lived in Cambridge dressed as a boy. She later formed several amorous connections and numbered among her friends Sir Richard Steele, George Farquhar, and Nicholas Rowe. As an actress she met, and later married, Joseph Centlivre, a cook at Court.

Her first play was *The Perjured Husband* (1700), and she appeared for the first time on the stage in her play *Love at a Venture* (1706). Her best-known works are *The Gamester* (1705) and *The Busy Body* (1709); in her *Bold Stroke for a*

Wife (1718), she gave the English language the expression "Simon Pure," which was the name of one of her characters. One of the most successful of women dramatists, Mrs. Centlivre enjoyed some fame abroad as well as in England. She drew heavily on Molière and others for her materials. Besides her plays, she also wrote miscellaneous pieces of verse and may have had a hand in *The Female Spectator,* a periodical. She died Dec. 1, 1723, in London.   R. C. B.

CENTRAL AMERICA, the long narrow isthmus connecting North America and South America. In terms of geologic structure the boundary between North and Central America is the volcanic zone which extends from northwest to southeast across the southern part of the Mexican plateau just south of Mexico City. The two thirds of Mexico north

formed a continuous chain connecting the Rocky Mountains of North America and the Andes of South America. Actually, Central America is composed of two distinct geologic units, separated by the continuous belt of lowland which crosses the isthmus diagonally through Nicaragua.

From the Chiapas highland of Mexico, southeast of the Istmo de Tehuantepec, to the Nicaraguan lowland the geologic structures have a predominant trend from west to east, paralleling the Pacific coast line, and belong to the same Central American-Antillean geologic region as Cuba, Jamaica, Hispaniola (Haiti and the Dominican Republic), Puerto Rico, and the Virgin Islands. Along the Pacific coast there extends a belt of lowland, 25 to 30 mi. wide at the border of Mexico and Guatemala and gradually becoming narrower toward the south until it is pinched out

Both the Atlantic and Pacific Oceans can be seen on a clear day from the lip of the huge, smoking crater of the Irazu volcano in Costa Rica.

of this zone form part of the North American continent. In terms of political units Central America includes Guatemala, British Honduras, Honduras, El Salvador, Nicaragua, and Costa Rica. Panama, which belonged to Colombia until 1903, is geographically but not historically a part of Central America. It has usually refused to enter into a full-fledged partnership with the Central American republics.

Topography. The Central American isthmus, largely mountainous, extends from northwest to southeast from the Istmo de Tehuantepec, at approximately 95° W. long., 16° N. lat., to the eastern boundary of Panama, at 77° W. long., 8° N. lat. The principal gulfs and peninsulas formed along the curving coast lines are: on the Caribbean side, the Golfo de Campeche, the Yucatán peninsula, the Gulf of Honduras, the Bahía de San Juan del Norte, and the Golfo de los Mosquitos; on the Pacific side, the Golfo de Tehuantepec, the Golfo de Fonseca, the Golfo del Papagayo, the Península de Nicoya, the Golfo de Nicoya, the Bahía de Coronado, the Península de Osa, the Golfo de Chiriquí, the Península de Azuero, and the Gulf of Panama. It was once incorrectly believed, following the interpretation of Alexander von Humboldt, that the mountains of Mexico and Central America

by spurs of the highland in El Salvador north of the Golfo de Fonseca. The mountains which rise abruptly from the inner margin of this lowland constitute the highest part of the highland, since they are covered with a thick accumulation of volcanic materials. They are surmounted by volcanoes which are frequently active and destructive. This southern highland volcanic zone reaches its greatest elevations in Guatemala, where the general level is between 8,000 and 10,000 ft. and the highest volcanoes are over 13,000 ft. In El Salvador, the much lower volcanic zone is divided into two parallel sections by the deep structural valley of the Río Lempa, a depression which continues southeastward until it is invaded by the Golfo de Fonseca. Within the volcanic zone there are numerous large and small intermont basins. The cover of lava and ash thins out north and east across the highlands toward the Caribbean, and the underlying crystalline rock appears in a rugged surface of folded and faulted, steep-sided ranges, separated by deep longitudinal valleys. As the highlands descend in elevation toward the Caribbean the valleys become deeper and wider, forming small patches of coastal lowland. The largest of the Caribbean-facing valleys are those of the Río Sarstun, in Guatemala and British Honduras; Lago de Izabal and the Río Motagua in Guatemala; the Río Ulúa, Río Aguán, and Río Patuca, in Honduras; the Río Coco (formerly Segovia), which forms much of the border between Honduras and Nicaragua; and the Río Tuma and the Río Grande in Nicaragua. The most extensive area of plain along the Caribbean is the Yucatán Peninsula, a limestone platform related geologically to Cuba, the Bahamas, and Florida. Most of it is in Mexico, but northern Guatemala and northern British Honduras occupy part of it. South of Yucatán the widest area of plain is the 40- to 75-mile wide Caribbean coastal lowland of Nicaragua, the thickly-forested Mosquito Coast, which merges at its southern end with the trans-isthmian Nicaragua lowland and is finally pinched off by highlands south of Limón, Costa Rica. The Nicaraguan lowland is a long narrow structural depression with its northwestern extremity in the Lempa Valley of El Salvador and its southeastern end on the Caribbean. The deepest part of the depression has been invaded by the Golfo de Fonseca. Within the lowland are Lago de Managua, 560 sq. mi., and Lago de Nicaragua, 3,089 sq. mi., which are drained to the Caribbean through the Río San Juan.

The Costa Rica-Panama section of the Central American highlands is composed of northwest-southeast extending mountain structures, largely of volcanic origin. The northwestern end is in the chain of more than twenty volcanoes which begins at Mount Coseguina at the entrance to the Golfo de Fonseca and extends southeastward separating Lago de Nicaragua from the Pacific Ocean. The highland backbone reaches its greatest elevations in the Cordillera de Talamanca between the volcanoes Poás (8,930 ft.), Barba (9,657 ft.), Irazú (11,260 ft.), and Turrialba (10,974 ft.) in central Costa Rica and Chiriquí (11,410 ft.) in western Panama. Between the four Costa Rican volcanoes and the main crest of the mountains there has been formed a large intermont basin, the Meseta Central, in which most of Costa Rica's population is concentrated. The streams draining the highland area have cut deep, narrow canyons in which little flat land is found. The highland backbone continues eastward into Panama as the Serranía de Tabasará, becoming lower and narrower until it comes to an abrupt ending just northeast of Antón and southwest of the city of Panama. A second mountain system, the 3,000-ft. Cordillera de San Blas, begins east of Colón and runs southeastward, as the Serranía del Darién, along the Caribbean coast for a short distance into Colombia. Along the Pacific coast south of the Golfo de San Miguel, the Serranía de Baudó also extends across the border from Panama into Colombia. Except for the extension into Costa Rica of the southern end of the Nicaraguan lowland, areas of coastal plain are small and discontinuous. A narrow fringe of swampy lowland extends along the Caribbean coast south of Limón, widening slightly around the Laguna de Chiriquí in Panama. On the Pacific coast there are lowland areas at the head of the Golfo de Nicoya and at the mouth of the Río Diquis. There are extensive low-lying areas around the Gulf of Panama, but they are composed largely of low hills rather than of flat land.

There are four principal crossings of the Central American isthmus. The most northerly is the Istmo de Tehuantepec in southern Mexico. The distance from north to south is 130 mi., and it requires a climb of only 800 ft. A railroad was built across it, but lost its importance with the decline of the banana trade. Another route, used during the period of early Spanish settlement, is formed by a north-south rift across Honduras from the mouth of the Río Motagua to the Golfo de Fonseca. The distance from ocean to ocean is about 175 mi. and the highest point on the mountain divide is only

Woman obtaining water from a village fountain in the Guatemalan highlands

3,100 ft. The Nicaraguan lowland, already mentioned, has long been under consideration for a possible trans-isthmian canal. With a cut through the narrow border of hills between Lago de Nicaragua and the Pacific, the distance would be about 180 mi. The off-set gap between the eastern end of the Serranía de Tabasará and the western end of the Cordillera de San Blas in Panama has provided a route across the isthmus since 1519. The distance from Caribbean to Pacific is only 42 mi., and the highest elevation under 285 ft. This was the location chosen for the Panama Canal.

Oxen supply power for the grinding of sugar cane near San Vicente, El Salvador.

Steamship passing eastward from the Atlantic to the Pacific through the Panama Canal's Pedro Miguel Locks into Miraflores Lake. In the background is the Gaillard Cut.

Climate and Natural Vegetation. Central America, although entirely within the tropics, has a variety of climates. Among the several factors affecting the climate are the temperature of the bordering seas, the direction of prevailing winds, and the elevation of the highlands. The water temperature increases southward along the Pacific coast, reaching a maximum (average: 80° F.) in the Gulf of Panama. The waters of the Caribbean are likewise very warm. As air passes over these warm waters, it becomes saturated with water vapor which is released as rainfall as the air is forced to rise by the highlands. Along the Pacific coast from southern Mexico to the Panama Canal, the wind is monsoonlike, in that it seasonally blows offshore during the winter months and onshore during the summer months. The west coast of Central America, therefore, receives rain principally during the summer months when the onshore winds are blowing. Along the Caribbean coast the prevailing winds blowing onshore from the east and northeast bring rain throughout the year, averaging well over 100 in. a year in many places. The high rainfall of the Caribbean coast is reflected in the thick tropical rain forest, while the relatively drier Pacific slopes with about 70 in. of rain annually support a tropical semideciduous forest which is interspersed with patches of savanna, or treeless plain.

As in other tropical mountain regions, decreases in temperature and changes in vegetation occur as elevation above sea level increases. Three vertical zones are generally recognized. Lowest and hottest of the zones is the *tierra caliente* ("hot country") in which average temperatures are over 75°. Above this is the *tierra templada* ("temperate country") with average temperatures between 65° and 75°. The *tierra fría* ("cold country") has annual temperatures averaging between 55° and 65°. Above the *tierra fría* are continuously cool mountaintops. The upper temperature limits of the three zones are higher on the wetter eastern side of the highlands than on the drier western side. The altitude limits of the zones become lower as the distance from the equator increases. In Costa Rica, on the Caribbean side, the *tierra caliente* extends to 2,100 ft. and the *tierra templada* up to 5,900 ft., while on the Pacific side the respective limits are only 1,475 ft. and 4,900 ft. These high-altitude climates are unlike the middle-latitude climates of the United States, for seasonal differences in temperature are slight and with increased elevation the differences become less and less. In San José, Costa Rica, for instance, the difference between summer and winter is a matter of only about 3°. Each vertical zone possesses a distinctive type of vegetation. In the *tierra caliente* a heavy tropical rain forest is found where rainfall is heavy. A semideciduous forest occurs in areas of lighter rainfall. This is also a zone in which bananas and cacao are grown. In the *tierra templada* oaks and other middle-latitude species appear. Here are located most of the coffee plantations. In the upper part of the *tierra fría* pines are found, but only as far south as northern Nicaragua, the southern limit of North American conifers.

Population. The six Central American republics, Guatemala, Honduras, El Salvador, Nicaragua, Costa Rica, and Panama, together with British Honduras and the Canal Zone, have an area of 207,689 sq. mi. and a population of nearly 10,000,000. The pattern of population distribution is one of clusters isolated by sparsely populated territory, a fact which accounts for the division into a number of small countries. The principal concentrations of population are found in the intermontane basins of Guatemala, El Salvador, and Honduras, around Lago de Managua and Lago de Nicaragua, in the Meseta Central of Costa Rica, and in the Canal Zone and adjacent area. The interior highlands and the Caribbean coastal areas, which make up three quarters to seven eighths of the territory of most of the countries, have hardly been occupied. There are only four cities of over 100,000 population in Central America: Guatemala, San Salvador, Panama, and Managua.

The people of Central America are Indian, European (descendants of early Spanish settlers), or *mestizo* (produced by the intermingling of Indian and European). In Guatemala, where the Indian population was relatively dense before the conquest, the Indian and the *mestizo* make up 97 per cent of the population. In the other countries the preconquest Indian population was scanty, and the Indian makes up a much smaller proportion of the modern population. A relatively large proportion of the scanty population of the Caribbean coast, particularly in British Honduras and the banana lands of Nicaragua, Costa Rica, and Panama, is composed of Negroes, as is the civilian population of the Canal Zone. The population of highland Costa Rica, on the other hand, is of unmixed European ancestry.

Products. Bananas and coffee are the two leading exports of Central America. United Fruit Company plantations in Honduras, Guatemala, Costa Rica, and Panama account for most of the bananas. Sigatoka disease forced the transfer of some of the plantations from the Caribbean to the Pacific coast. Abandoned lands were planted in cacao and abacá, a fiber used in Manila hemp. Coffee, grown in the highlands, is the leading export of Guatemala, El Salvador, and Costa Rica. Other products of Central America are chicle, gathered in the forests of northern Guatemala and British Honduras, rice, sugar, coconuts, honey, and lumber. Gold is exported in small quantities from most of the countries, and Honduras exports silver. The crop which occupies the largest area is maize, raised on a subsistence basis and forming the basic item of diet of most of the rural people.

Transportation. There is no continuous system of railroads throughout Central America. A railroad from Mexico City extends to the cities of Guatemala and San Salvador. The principal lowland towns of Nicaragua are connected by railroad with the two tiny Pacific ports Corinto and Puerto Morazán. A railroad extends across Costa Rica from Limón on the Caribbean to Puntarenas on the Pacific. The Panama Railroad parallels the Canal across the isthmus. Other railroad lines are short spurs from the banana plantations to the company ports.

The first land route binding the Central American countries together is the Pan-American Highway, which extends from the northern border of Guatemala to San José, Costa Rica. Completion of the highway will provide a route from the United States to the Canal Zone.

Airlines have done much to facilitate travel between the Central American republics, and several Central American lines exist in addition to such major international companies as Pan American World Airways.

History. During its colonial period Central America was organized for administrative purposes as the Captaincy General of Guatemala under New Spain. In 1821 the province declared its independence from Spain and until 1823 was under the jurisdiction of the Mexican empire of Agustín de Iturbide. With the downfall of Iturbide's empire the confederation of the United Provinces of Central America was organized. The foremost advocate of unification of the republics was Francisco Morazán who was president of the confederation from 1830 until its dissolution in 1839, at which time the five constituent states became independent republics. Repeated attempts at unification have since been unsuccessful. However, the most recent attempt, the Organización de Estados Centroamericanos (ODECA), founded in 1951 with headquarters in El Salvador, has been moderately successful. *See also* LATIN AMERICA; GUATEMALA; EL SALVADOR; HONDURAS; NICARAGUA; COSTA RICA.

P. E. J. and R. Hi.

CENTRAL AMERICAN COURT OF JUSTICE, a tribunal formed in 1907 by the governments of Costa Rica, El Salvador, Guatemala, Honduras, and Nicaragua to settle controversies among them. Each state was represented by a judge elected by its legislature, and jurisdiction covered disputes which had gone beyond diplomatic control. From its seat in Costa Rica the court, with the strong moral support of the United States, prevented international wars in Central America from 1910 to 1917. Called upon by Costa Rica and El Salvador to uphold their territorial claims to the San Juan River and the Gulf of Fonseca, threatened by the Bryan-Chamorro Treaty of 1913 between Nicaragua and the United States, the court found the treaty in violation of the rights of the two states. However, both Nicaragua and the United States ignored the decision, thereby so weakening the position of the court that it discontinued its sessions on Mar. 17, 1918.

W. L. G.

CENTRAL COLLEGE, an accredited, coeducational college of liberal arts owned and controlled by three conferences of the Methodist Church in Fayette, Mo. It has a forty-two acre campus. Central College was chartered in 1855, and first instruction was offered in 1857. Between 1922 and 1925 it absorbed Howard-Payne College, Central College for Women, Scarritt-Morrisville College, and Marvin College, becoming the only Methodist college in Missouri. Degrees offered are the A.B., B.S. in education, B.Mus., and the B.Mus.Ed. Courses in journalism have been added to the curriculum. Recently acquired audio-visual aids are used in connection with music and language instruction. Undergraduate scholarship and loan aid is available to qualifying students. Women must live on the campus or at home. Men must live on the campus or in approved quarters. *For statistics see* COLLEGES AND UNIVERSITIES.

J. R. To.

CENTRAL FALLS, a city in Providence Co., in northeastern Rhode Island, situated on the Blackstone River. On the south it adjoins Providence and on the east, Pawtucket. Central Falls is an industrial center. In 1730 it was a part of Smithfield town. A man named Wheat began the manufacture of chocolate in 1790, and for a time the place was known as Chocolate Mill. In 1847 it was incorporated as Central Falls Fire District of Smithfield, and in 1871 it became a part of the new town of Lincoln. Central Falls became a separate city in 1895 and has the mayor and council form of government. The New York, New Haven and Hartford Railroad provides transportation. Textiles, thread, rayon cloth, and glass are the leading commodities manufactured in Central Falls. Pop. 1950, 23,550.

CENTRALIA [sɛntre′liə], a city in south central Illinois, situated in Clinton and Marion Cos., about 60 mi. southeast of East St. Louis. Natural resources of the region are coal and oil. The surrounding area is noted for its dairying and fruit raising. The city was founded in 1856 by the Illinois Central Railroad Company and has the commission form of government. It is the seat of Centralia Township Junior College, founded in 1940. Transportation is supplied by the Illinois Central, the Chicago, Burlington & Quincy, the Southern, and the Missouri Pacific railroads. Centralia has railroad shops and foundry works. Its manufactures include enameled ranges, women's dresses, candy, and paper products. Pop. 1950, 13,863.

CENTRALIA [sɛntre′liə], a city in Lewis Co., in southwestern Washington, located 45 mi. southwest of Tacoma.

Centralia was founded in 1875 and incorporated in 1890 and has the commission form of government. An old blockhouse, built in 1856, stands in Borst Park, which adjoins the city. Centralia is in the center of a rich timber and coal-mining region, and its farms supply poultry, dairy products, and berries. Its manufactures include gloves, lumber, logging shoes, and beverages. The city is the seat of Centralia Junior College, founded in 1925. The Chicago, Milwaukee, St. Paul and Pacific, the Great Northern, the Northern Pacific, and the Union Pacific railroads, and the West Coast Airlines serve the city. Pop. 1950, 8,657.

CENTRALIZATION, a term employed to describe both political and administrative systems. As a result, considerable ambiguity exists as to its real meaning. In the political sense, centralization implies the location of power in a single instrument, such as a despot, a monarch, or a legislative body. Modern totalitarian governments illustrate political centralization in an extreme form. But democracy may also employ centralized governments.

Military organizations are good examples of centralized control. Orders in the form of directives flow from the general staff to all commissioned and noncommissioned officers and to the common soldiers as well. These orders embrace not only military subjects; in addition, matters of an extremely private nature, such as the types of haircuts, may be minutely regulated.

Central Park, New York City. (Top) A quiet spot is the little lake in the southeast corner of the park, backdropped by some of New York's finest hotels. (Bottom) Bethesda Fountain taken from the park's broad terrace. Boating on the lake beyond is a popular pastime.

CHARLES PHELPS CUSHING

Modern Examples. The government of Great Britain exists as a classic example of centralization in a democratic state. All governmental power is lodged in the parliament. That this parliament has, for its own convenience, seen fit to delegate authority in local affairs to county and municipal councils is no denial of power, for power so delegated may be recalled at the will of the delegating authority. As exemplified in the United States, federal government illustrates the decentralized type. Legislative power is divided, under the Constitution, between the national and state governments. Neither is superior to the other. They function as co-ordinate constitutional authorities. Contemporary examples of centralized political systems, besides that of Great Britain, are the governments of France, Spain, Chile, Turkey, the Soviet Union and the Netherlands.

Soviet Union. The Soviet Union offers a curious contradiction; its constitution provides for a federal system, yet the thoroughgoing centralization is apparently achieved through the dominance of the Communist Party; and, as a result, though each of the republics has constitutional discretion in the formulation of policy in specific fields, the unanimity of party programs in the sixteen republics achieves a practical centralization.

France. In administration the line of authority in a centralized system runs from the top official or committee to the lowliest employee of the state. The system in the Third French Republic represented administrative centralization in its highest modern development. The curriculum in every public school in France was rigidly prescribed by the ministry of education. Thus, at a particular time of day, all children in, for example, the fifth grade would be studying the same subject and probably the same page of the same textbook.

United States. Administration may be centralized in a federal system. In the United States, the development of administrative services, largely the product of the last half century, was in the framework of centralized organization. The congestion deriving from the employment of increasing numbers of government employees in the national capital forced the creation of branch offices in administrative districts. But this was only a decentralization of the physical, and not of the legal aspects of the administration. The government was merely following the practice of large economic corporations which had found it profitable to create a decentralized structure.   C. A. M. E.

CENTRAL PARK, a famous municipal park in the center of the borough of Manhattan, New York City. It extends about 2½ mi. north from 59th Street to 110th Street (Cathedral Parkway), and ½ mi. east from Central Park West (Eighth Avenue) to Fifth Avenue. Its 840 acres, acquired chiefly in the 1850's and 1860's for more than $7,000,000, are enclosed by a low, stone wall, with entrances and gates at convenient intervals. The park offers varied scenery, with numerous small rocky hills, beautifully wooded slopes, lawns and grassy areas, three lakes, two ponds, a "loch" and a pool. There are approximately 9 mi. of driveways, some 5½ mi. of bridle paths, about 3¼ mi. of specially built bicycle paths, and 28½ mi. of walks. To assure the uninterrupted flow of crosstown traffic, avenues on the east and west of the park are connected by three transverse roads below the level of the park. In the park are also the Metropolitan Museum of Art, an Egyptian obelisk popularly known as Cleopatra's Needle, many portrait statues, a menagerie usually called the Central Park Zoo, a bird sanctuary, a former arsenal now the headquarters of the Park Department, a formal garden, a meteorological observatory in the Belvedere, a police station, a reservoir, a paved mall used for free summer concerts and for public occasions, a fashionable restaurant, and a cafeteria. Facilities are provided for boating, ice skating, roller skating, baseball, softball, football, bowling, croquet, and horseshoe pitching. There are twenty-two children's playgrounds and a merry-go-round.

The idea of a large park for the city was advanced separately by the poet-editor William Cullen Bryant and the landscape architect Andrew Jackson Downing, and was adopted after it was an issue in the 1850 mayoralty campaign. In 1857 Frederick Law Olmsted and Calvert Vaux won a contest for the best design for the park, and their plan has since been followed in its general outline. Park development and maintenance suffered at times from political graft, notably around 1870 during the ascendancy of the Tweed Ring. In 1934, under the administration of Mayor Fiorello H. La Guardia, with Robert Moses as Parks Commissioner, essential improvements were made in the park, which had been allowed to deteriorate; and the prevailing concept of the use of the park for active rather than passive purposes was established. J. E. F.

CENTRAL POWERS, the name given to the allied states of Austria-Hungary and Germany while they fought together during World War I. These two powers, along with Italy, had made up the Triple Alliance. Italy, however, refused to enter the war on their side, and later fought against them. Turkey and Bulgaria joined the Central Powers. After a hard-fought war, the Central Powers finally were defeated in 1918. M. K.

CENTRAL PROVINCES AND BERAR [berɑ'r], a former state in central India which forms the core of the present state of Madhya Pradesh. The political entity which became the Central Provinces had its beginning in the Maratha kingdom of Nagpur, which came under British administration in 1853. In 1861, in the reorganization which followed the Indian Mutiny, the Narbada territories were united with Nagpur to form the Central Provinces, and in 1902 Berar, which since 1853 had been administered by the British under agreement with the Nizam of Hyderabad, was also attached. In 1937 the Central Provinces and Berar became an autonomous province with its capital at Nagpur, and in 1948 fourteen Chhattisgarh states were merged with the province. In 1950 the province was reconstituted as the state of Madhya Pradesh.

The Central Provinces was a transitional zone between north and south India; it was the meeting place of the Dravidian languages of the south and the northern Indo-Aryan languages. In its hills dwelt several million tribesmen (Gonds, Mundas, and Bhils), while the plains and river valleys were occupied by Hindu cultivators of both northern and southern cultural tradition. During the late Middle Ages the northern part of this area was ruled by Rajputs. The rest of the area, known as Gondwana, was held by Gond dynasties. These latter maintained virtual autonomy under the Moguls, but in the eighteenth century the Gond rajas fell before invading Marathas, and by 1751 Maratha chiefs had conquered the great Gond kingdoms of Nagpur, Chanda, and Chhattisgarh. It was the Maratha kingdom of Nagpur that became the nucleus of the Central Provinces.

Berar, which lies on the Deccan Plateau, was part of a succession of southern kingdoms until the late thirteenth century, when it was conquered by Moslem invaders from northwest India; in the sixteenth and seventeenth centuries it was governed alternately by Mogul and independent Moslem rulers. Toward the end of the seventeenth century Berar, like the Gond kingdom of Nagpur, fell prey to Maratha invaders, and during the eighteenth century it was contested by both Maratha chiefs and the Nizam of Hyderabad. It was still an object of contention in 1853 when the British, although recognizing the Nizam's claims, took over the administration of this rich territory. *See also* ASIATIC TRIBES. E. E. B.

CENTRE COLLEGE OF KENTUCKY, an accredited and privately controlled college operated under the auspices of the Presbyterian Church. Its co-ordinate divisions for men and women, with campuses a mile apart, are located in Danville, Ky. The college received its charter in 1819 and began instruction in 1820. In 1901 Central University of Kentucky, founded in 1873, was absorbed by merger. In 1926 Kentucky College for Women, founded in 1854, was similarly absorbed. The A.B. degree is conferred. The curriculum includes pre-professional training courses, general education requirements, and the usual major fields. The freshman and sophomore years are primarily devoted to general education. Small classes are maintained, and the low student-faculty ratio is favorable to an effective counseling program. The college also maintains a vocational guidance clinic. Scholarships and financial aid are available. Competitive honor scholarships are granted to outstanding students. The Scholastic Aptitude Test of the College Entrance Examination Board is an entrance requirement. *For statistics see* COLLEGES AND UNIVERSITIES.

CENTRIFUGE. *See* ANALYTICAL CHEMISTRY (*Physical Methods*); COLLOID CHEMISTRY; DAIRY INDUSTRY, THE; LUBRICATION; PETROLEUM (*Lubricating Oils*).

CENTUM LANGUAGES [kɛ'ntəm], a name used to designate those Indo-European languages which show a velar (k, kh, g, gh) in such words as Latin *centum* and Greek ἑκατόν, meaning "one hundred," as opposed to the sibilants s, $š$, $ś$, z, or $ž$, which occur in the corresponding words of the so-called *satem*-languages, such as Lithuanian *šim̃tas*, Russion *sto*, Avestan *satem* (whence the name of the *satem*-languages), and Sanskrit *śatám*. Since the velar articulation is certainly the older of the two, the centum characteristic constitutes not an innovation but merely a preserved archaism; it is improper, therefore, to speak of a centum group of Indo-European languages, whereas it is entirely proper to speak of a satem group, owing its existence to a common innovation. This distinction between archaism and innovation is further confirmed by the areal distribution of the centum and satem languages. While the satem languages are all contiguous to each other and thus show the spread of a common innovation (k becoming s, for example, and g becoming z), the centum languages (Latin, Italic, Greek, Celtic, Germanic, Hittite, and Tocharian) are widely separated from each other and evidently are the remainder of a once united area later broken by the satem innovation. In addition to those mentioned above, Palaic, Luwian, Lydian, and probably Illyrian were centum languages. G. B.

CENTURY PLANT, *Agave americana,* a striking plant of the amaryllis family native to arid sections of Mexico and tropical America. Its name comes from the erroneous idea that it does not bloom until it is 100 years old, whereas in reality it blooms when about 10 years old. The plant bears a rosette of thick spiny leaves from 3 to 6 ft. long. From its center the flower stalk grows very fast, sometimes

5 in. a day, to a height of 20 to 40 ft. The lily-like yellowish flowers are borne on branches near the top. When the seed has ripened the plant dies. The plant, also called agave and American aloe, is grown in Mexico for the fibers obtained from its leaves, called pita flax and sisal. A beverage, pulque,

COURTESY OF THE J. HORACE MC FARLAND COMPANY

Century plant before growing stalk and in bloom

is made from the fermented sap. The century plant is often grown as a pot plant, especially those varieties having striped leaves. 　　　　　　　　　　　　　　　　J. C. Wis.

CEPHALIC INDEX [səfæ′lɪk], the percentile relationship of the maximum width of the head (taken generally just above the ears) to head length (measured in the midline of the head from the glabella, the most projecting point above the root of the nose, to the most projecting point on the occiput). This index, obtained by dividing the head breadth by the head length and multiplying by 100, was first suggested by A. A. Retzius, a Swedish anthropologist, as a useful criterion for the differentiation of various types and races of man. Heads with widths 77 per cent or less of the lengths are classified as dolichocephalic (long heads or narrow heads); those 82 per cent or over as brachycephalic (broad heads). The intermediate form is grouped as mesocephalic. On the dry skull the dividing points are placed at 75 and 80. With the somewhat uncritical use of this device, it became in time symbolic of racial differences, and more emphasis than was warranted was placed upon its significance. There is no doubt that mankind differs in this measure, individuals varying from indices as low as 60 to those over 100 with group averages falling within these limits. Its value as a taxonomic criterion, however, has been considerably diminished as the result of studies showing that this relationship is affected to some degree by environment. 　　　　　　　　　H. L. Sh.

CEPHALONIA [sɛfəlo′niə] (Kephallēnia), Greek island of the Ionian Sea, off the western coast of Greece. The largest of the Ionian Islands, Cephalonia has an area of 290 sq. mi.; it is 27 mi. long and varies in width from 2 to 19 mi. It is located 60 mi. west of Patrai, major port of the Peloponnesus. A mountainous island, the highest point is Mount Nero, or Elato (ancient Aenus), with an elevation of 5,218 ft., near the southern end of the island. There are about 78 towns and villages on the island. Argostolion, situated on the west coast, is the capital and chief port. The chief exports of the island are currants, oil, wine, and melons.

Homer referred to the island as Samos, but he called its inhabitants Cephallenes. The name Cephalonia is sup-

posedly derived from the mythological Cephalus, who became master of the island with the aid of Amphitryon, King of Tiryns. In ancient times the city states of Same and Proni existed on the eastern part of the island, and those of Pale and Crannii on the western part. The island was conquered by Rome in 189 B.C. After the division of the Roman Empire, Cephalonia was under rule until the twelfth century when it was seized by the Normans. In the thirteenth century Cephalonia was taken over by the Venetians. It was held by Venice until the fall of the Venetian republic in 1797, except for the years 1479-1500, when it was conquered by the Turks. It was ruled by Great Britain from 1809 to 1863. Cephalonia has been a portion of the Greek kingdom since 1864. Points of interest are the castle of St. George, the ruins of Cranii, and the site of the ancient town of Samos. Pop. 1951, 47,369. 　　　　　　　　　　　　　　　W. S. V.

CEPHALOPODA. *See* MOLLUSKS.

CEPHALUS [sɛ′fələs], in Greek mythology, the husband of Procris. He was beloved by Eos, goddess of the dawn, but returned to Procris, loving her more than he did the goddess. Having received from Procris a spear, given her by Artemis, which never missed its object, he hurled the spear into a bush in which he had heard a noise and accidentally killed his wife, who had been jealously watching him as he rested from the chase. The son of Eos and Cephalus was Phosphorus, the morning star. 　　　　G. E. D.

CEPHEUS [si′fyus], a constellation which extends from near the North Star for over 30° in the direction away from the Big Dipper. The center of its principal area is at approximately right ascension, 22 hr. 30 min. It includes no star as bright as the second magnitude. Its configuration resembles a church steeple. Among its stars is Delta (δ) Cephei, the first found to vary in the regular manner characteristic of the large class of yellow giants known as Cepheid variables. In Greek mythology, Cepheus was a king of Ethiopia, husband of Cassiopeia and father of Andromeda. *See also* DELTA CEPHEI, V. V. CEPHEI. 　　　　　　J. H. P.

CEPHISODOTUS [sɛ′fɪsɒ′dətəs], Greek sculptor, flourished in Athens in the early part of the fourth century B.C. He was probably the son of an older Praxiteles and the father of the famous sculptor, Praxiteles. The art of Cephisodotus marks the transition from the first to the second classical period of Greek art.

His most celebrated work is a statue of Eirene carrying the boy Plutos, an allegory of peace nourishing the young god of wealth. It was commissioned by the Athenians after the conclusion of peace with Sparta in 375 and expressed their hope for a new prosperity. A copy of the whole statue is in Munich; a copy of the torso is in the Metropolitan Museum of New York, and copies of the child are in Dresden and in Athens. The style is reminiscent of the fifth century, but the soft tenderness in the face of the Eirene bent down to the child on her arm is an early expression of the spirit of the fourth century.

Cephisodotus is a forerunner of Praxiteles in the practice of combining a child with an adult in sculptural subjects, not only in the Eirene, but also in a group representing Hermes with the little Dionysos. This group is known from coins, a drawing by I. B. de Cavalleriis of the sixteenth century, a statue in Madrid, and a fragment found in the Agora of Athens. The Agora fragment is in the style of the Hermes of Alcamenes, the pupil of Phidias. 　　　　　　M. Bi.

CERAM [sərɑ'm], an island in the Molucca or Spice Island group, now belonging to the Republic of Indonesia. Ceram lies west of the Vogelkop, or Bird's Head, of Netherlands New Guinea at 3° S. lat. and 130° E. long. The island is about 215 mi. long and from 30 to 50 mi. wide, with an area, including the adjacent small islands, of slightly more than 6,600 sq. mi. Much of the island is mountainous, with peaks in the central part rising to about 10,000 ft.; swampy lowlands occupy parts of the north coast. The climate is hot and humid. Earthquakes occur at frequent intervals. The dense, tropical forests that cover much of the island yield valuable timber, oil of cajuput (used in treating skin diseases), dammar (a resin), and wild nutmegs. The swamp forests of the lowlands supply sago, an important starch food in many tropical countries. There is little animal life other than the cassowary, a large, ostrichlike bird; the cuscus, a small, possumlike animal; deer; pigs; shrews; fish; and a few large, colorful birds such as the cockatoo and bird of paradise. The population is concentrated for the most part near the coast, and consists mainly of Mohammedan Malays and remnants of the primitive Melanesian people. The natives depend mainly on subsistence agriculture and fishing. Leading crops include sago, rice (introduced by the Malays), and maize, sugar cane, coconuts, and tobacco. Arabs and Chinese handle a large share of the trade of the island. There are coconut, spice, and other plantations which were formerly under European management. Copra and resin are the chief exports. There is a small oil field near Boela on the east coast. The island remained under Dutch authority from the middle of the seventeenth century until February 1942, when it was occupied by the Japanese, who used it during the latter part of World War II as an advance air base. After World War II it reverted to Dutch rule until the Republic of Indonesia was established in 1949. Wahai on the north coast is the chief port. Pop. (est. 1949), 100,000. R. G. B.

CERAMICS [səræ'mɪks], the art and science of manufacturing silicate and oxide articles, such as pottery, dinnerware, porcelain for electrical and chemical apparatus, glass, porcelain enamels, refractories, structural clay products,

abrasives, and cements. The many different kinds of clays, feldspars, limestones, silica sands, and other minerals are the important raw materials. The materials of manufacture are generally silicates or oxides and combinations of them. These ceramic products are made by the applications of heat, which produces fusion (melting), crystallization, and high-temperature chemical and physical changes. Structurally, ceramic products are made up of crystals and glass, the latter often constituting the bond which cements the crystals together.

The history of ceramics in most of its phases dates back to the activities of man when he first learned to build a fire and develop heat. Because of the resistance of ceramic products to weather and time, the archaeologist depends largely on relics of pottery, glass, enamels, and brick to study the early development of civilization.

Ceramic Industries. The ceramic industries as a group represent over a billion dollars' worth of production per year in the United States alone, where about 5,500 plants employ over a quarter of a million people. The raw materials are plentiful and low-priced, the value being increased on an average of about 200 per cent by the manufacture. Many of these plants are modern mass-production units utilizing the latest automatic equipment and scientific control.

An outline of the branches of the industry and its products follows:

Abrasives	Grinding wheels, sharpeners, abrasive sands and papers, and special tools
Cements	Portland, dental, refractory, and magnesia cements
Glass	Bottles, window sheet, light bulbs, art glass, chemical glass, plate glass, tableware, optical glass, and lighting fixtures
Porcelain enamels	Kitchen utensils, stoves, refrigerator linings, signs, sanitary ware, reflectors, architectural enamels, water heaters, tanks, and chemical ware
Pottery	Vases, bowls, flowerpots, and figurines
Refractories	Firebrick, flue linings, refractory cements, and special shapes
Terra cotta	Architectural shapes, garden pottery, art tile, and floor tile
Whiteware	Dinnerware, electrical porcelain, chemical porcelain, vitreous sanitary ware, floor and wall tile, and refractory ware
Structural-clay products	Face brick, common brick, drain tile, roofing tile, hollow building block, glazed brick, floor tile, and paving brick.

A. I. A.

CERARGYRITE [sərɑ'rjərait] or horn silver, a pearl gray or colorless mineral which becomes violet-brown on exposure to the light. Its name is derived from its characteristic waxy luster. Chemically cerargyrite is silver chloride, $AgCl$. It is one of the few minerals that can be smoothly cut with a knife (sectile). It has a hardness (Mohs scale) of 2-3. The occurrence of cerargyrite is confined to the oxidized zones of deposits of silver ore. The mineral is formed when primary silver minerals, or argentiferous galena, are oxidized and altered by chlorine-containing waters to silver chloride. Cerargyrite has been mined at Leadville, Colo., and the Comstock lode in Nevada. It also occurs in Mexico and parts of South America. K. K. L.

CERBERUS [s3'rbərəs], in Greek mythology, the dog who guarded the entrance to the underworld. Cerberus was usually described as three-headed and serpent-tailed; according to Hesiod, he had fifty heads. One of the labors of Heracles was to bring Cerberus to the upper world. *See also* HERACLES. G. E. D.

CEREALS. *See* GRAIN.

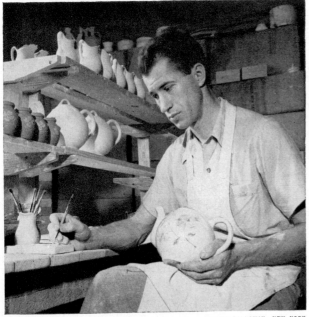

EWING GALLOWAY, NEW YORK

PAINTING CLAY POTTERY BEFORE FIRING

CEREBELLUM. *See* Brain.
CEREBRAL PALSY. *See* Paralysis.
CEREBRUM. *See* Brain.

CERES [sɪ′əriz], an old Italian goddess of agriculture, whom the Romans identified with the Greek goddess Demeter. Her festival, the Cerealia, was celebrated annually at Rome on April 12-19. *See also* Demeter.   G.E.D.

CEREUS, NIGHT-BLOOMING [sɪ′əriəs], the common name of several members of several genera of the cactus family. They are trailing or climbing plants usually

Night-blooming cereus (Selenicereus grandiflorus), a semi-tropical, climbing cactus. Its huge ten-inch fragrant white flowers, which open about midnight, are framed in a circle of spike-like bracts.

with three-angled, slightly spiny stems. About 18 species are native from southwestern United States to South America. Some species are cultivated in tropical countries for hedges. *Selenicereus grandiflorus* is one of three or four widely grown as a conservatory plant for the sake of its foot-long, intensely fragrant, many-petalled white flowers which bloom only at night, opening but once and collapsing in strong light. In the Harvard Botanic Garden a very large plant of *Hylocereus undatus,* another conservatory species, has often had 65 to 70 flowers open in one night.   J. C. Wis.

CERIMAN [sɛ′rɪmən], *Monstera deliciosa,* a strong, long, straggling vine of the arum family, native to Mexico and Central America. It is grown in greenhouses and warm regions as an ornamental. Its leaves are thick, round, 2 to 3 ft. across, with deep indentations and perforations. There are many hanging, cordlike, aerial roots. The white flowering spathe surrounds a spadix reaching 10 in., which forms a conelike, fleshy fruit with a luscious pineapple flavor. *See also* Arum.   J. C. Wis.

CERINTHUS [sərɪ′nthəs], heresiarch of the first century A.D., lived probably in Syria. He taught that the universe was not the work of the First God, but of some inferior angelic power. His belief was that Jesus, son of Mary and Joseph, received the divine power, or Christos, upon baptism, the spirit of God departing from him before the Passion. The members of the sect which Cerinthus founded were known as Cerinthians.   R. T.

CERIUM. *See* Rare Earths.
CERNĂUȚI. *See* Chernovtsy.

CERRO DE PASCO [sɛ′rro de pɑ′sko], a mining town in central Peru, the capital city of the department of Pasco, situated approximately 14,000 ft. above sea level on a wide plateau between the cordilleras. It is about 228 mi. northeast of Callao, at 10° 41′ S. lat. and 76° 16′ W. long. The mountains surrounding Cerro de Pasco contain vast deposits of gold, silver, copper, vanadium, and other metals. Because of its altitude the area about the town has a cold, harsh climate and is without foliage. Located in the town are the headquarters of one of the largest mining companies in the world. Pop. 1940, 19,187.   S. G. I.

CERRO GORDO, BATTLE OF [sɛ′ro gɔ′rdo] (April 17-18, 1847), a military engagement in the Mexican War. It was fought along the route of the Mexican national highway, at a narrow defile in rugged foothills fifty miles northwest of Veracruz, between General Winfield Scott's invading army of 8,500 and Mexican defenders numbering 12,000 under Santa Anna. Fearful of the yellow fever season after the capture of Veracruz, Scott hurried his men toward the highlands and Mexico City. Santa Anna prepared defenses at a pass just below Cerro Gordo. At the suggestion of Captain Robert E. Lee, Brigadier General David E. Twiggs's division left the highway some distance from the Mexican position and struck out in a flanking movement over rough terrain. On April 17, Twiggs's men occupied one defended height, and the next day Colonel W. S. Harney's command stormed the main defensive bastion. Simultaneously, Brigadier General James Shields's brigade emerged from the thick brush and struck hard against the extreme left flank of the Mexican army as it fled down narrow paths into the canyon of Río del Plan. The Mexican loss was 1,200 men. The cost to the Americans was 30 officers and 387 men (64 killed). This was Scott's last important battle before he reached the Valley of Mexico.   G. W. S.

CERTIORARI [sɜ′rshiorɛ′əri], a common law discretionary writ used in both civil and criminal cases as a mode of review of the proceedings of an inferior court or other tribunal, board, or officer exercising a judicial function. The object of the writ is primarily to give relief whenever it is shown that the inferior court or other body has exceeded its jurisdiction or has proceeded illegally, and no other mode of review has been provided. The writ is now regulated by statute in virtually every jurisdiction where it is used, with the result that its scope and the procedure for obtaining it vary. In some jurisdictions the writ has been extended to proceedings ordinarily subject to review by writ of error or appeal. Also in some jurisdictions, as in federal practice, the writ is used to take the judgment of an intermediate court to the ultimate court of review, thus enabling the latter to determine whether in its discretion the judgment shall be reviewed.   E. O. B.

CERULLI, ENRICO [tsheru′lli] (1898-   ), Italian orientalist and public administrator, was born in Naples, on Feb. 15, 1898. After rising in the Italian colonial service and being especially active in Somaliland and Ethiopia, he resigned the vice-governorship general of Italian East Africa in 1937 because his sympathetic attitude towards the demands of the African natives ran contrary to the policy of the Fascist Government. One of the greatest living authorities on East Africa, he has produced a great number of highly significant books and articles on linguistics, geography, anthropology, history, and literature in the Somali and Ethiopian areas. Among these are *The Folk-literature of the Galla,* in *Harvard African Studies, III; Etiopia occidentale* (1933); *Studi etiopici* (1936-1938); and *Etiopi in Palestina* (1943-1947). He has also considered the problem of the mutual relations between Oriental and European literatures in the Middle Ages in *Il Libro etiopico dei miracoli di Maria* (1943), and again in *Il Libro della Scala* (1949).   G. B.

CERUSSITE [sɪ'ərəsait], a colorless to gray mineral which chemically is lead carbonate, $PbCO_3$. It occurs in orthorhombic crystals, frequently twinned. It has a specific gravity of 6.5, which is high for a mineral with nonmetallic luster, and a hardness of 3-3½ on Mohs' scale. Cerussite, an ore of lead, is widely distributed and is associated with galena, lead sulphide, which is altered to cerussite by percolating waters containing carbon dioxide. An intermediate substance in this change is the mineral anglesite.   K. K. L.

CERVANTES SAAVEDRA, MIGUEL DE [therva'ntes sa'ave'thra; sərvæ'ntiz] (1547-1616), Spanish writer, was born at Alcalá de Henares in the province of Madrid. His father, Rodrigo de Cervantes, was a modest surgeon, and the numerous family lived in the constant penury familiar to the younger Cervantes throughout his unhappy life. Very little is known about his early years except that he was baptized on Oct. 9, 1547; in the next record of his life, some twenty years later, he is named as the author of a sonnet addressed to Queen Isabel of Valois, the third wife of Philip II, before her death on Oct. 3, 1568. Shortly afterward we find him as a student in the College of the City of Madrid, the principal of which was a fine humanist, Juan López de Hoyos. López de Hoyos was commissioned by the city to prepare a book reviewing all the solemnities that marked the death of the Queen, and in this volume Cervantes, designated by the editor as his "beloved and cherished pupil," figured as the author of several poems written in the name of the entire college. Thus, although these poems in no way foreshadow the future author of *Don Quixote,* Cervantes had already developed at the age of twenty-one a personality that attracted attention.

Cervantes' studies were probably too irregular and fragmentary to bring him within reach of an academic degree. In any case, finding no means of livelihood in Spain, he went to Italy, and in 1570 he emerges as an attendant, or *camarero,* to Cardinal Giulio Acquaviva. But we know nothing further of his Italian sojourn except that in 1571 he enlisted as a soldier in the naval expedition that the King of Spain, the Pope, and the Seigniory of Venice were preparing to send against the Turks. Cervantes fought with courage at Lepanto (Oct. 7, 1571), although he was ill and had a high fever, and one of the two wounds he received left his left arm and hand crippled and useless. He returned to Sicily to convalesce and remained in southern Italy until 1575 but then decided to return to Spain, thinking that he might be rewarded for his services by being given the captaincy of a company in the army. Fate was against him, however, for on Sept. 26, 1575, the ship he was on was overpowered by Turkish pirates. Cervantes was taken to

Algiers as a captive and remained there until Sept. 19, 1580. During those five bitter years his qualities as a leader came into sharp relief and he showed great daring and heroism in organizing several unsuccessful schemes of escape for himself and many of his fellow prisoners. The Bey of Algiers considered him a very dangerous person, but in

Miguel de Cervantes Saavedra

PORTRAIT ATTRIBUTED TO JUAN DE JÁUREGUI, NOW IN THE ROYAL SPANISH ACADEMY, MADRID

spite of this, and incomprehensible as it may seem in view of the well-known cruelty of the Turks, Cervantes was never severely punished. His powerful and ingenious imagination, later revealed in *Don Quixote,* probably helped to preserve his life.

Eventually, the Trinitarian friars, with the help of money collected by Cervantes' family, managed to ransom him. He expected worthy rewards when he returned home, but actually he obtained almost nothing. Spanish officialdom took no notice of his existence, and, like many other Spaniards, Cervantes found himself at odds with the society in which he lived. Nevertheless, it was out of his experience in this very conflict that he was later to create *Don Quixote.*

In 1584, at the age of thirty-seven, Cervantes was married in Esquivias, in the province of Toledo, to a nineteen-year-old girl, Catalina de Palacios. But family life, like everything else touching Cervantes, was irregular for him, and he spent long years separated from his wife. Indeed, it was an illicit love affair that gave him his only child, his daughter Isabel de Saavedra.

In 1585 Cervantes took a strange job: he became an agent of the crown charged with the requisitioning of wheat, barley, and olive oil in Andalusia to supply Philip II's Invincible Armada. From the heroic dream of Lepanto Cervantes thus awakened to work at a task as undistinguished as it was difficult and perilous. The crop owners yielded their goods only with ill will, since they hoped to sell them at a higher price than the royal administration paid. Moreover, on two occasions Cervantes had to requisition wheat that belonged to ecclesiastics, and, in spite of the fact that he was carrying out orders of the king, he was excommunicated. As a final misfortune, he was tried and imprisoned because his accounts appeared to be irregular. Another disappointment (1590) was his unsuccessful application for a position in the Spanish American colonies.

It seems safe to assume that it was during one of his periods of imprisonment that Cervantes began to write his immortal book, but in 1602 judges and courts had done with annoying him about his alleged debts to the crown and in 1604 he moved to Valladolid where the King was then residing. In 1608, however, he established himself in Madrid for good and there devoted himself exclusively to writing and publishing his books. During these last years he was able to subsist chiefly by means of the pensions he received from the Count of Lemos and the Archbishop of Toledo. Cervantes died in Madrid on Apr. 23, 1616.

The foregoing facts afford only a fragmentary and hardly an intimate view of Cervantes' life, but in his life the greatest events were, after all, the works that brought him immortality. The very nature of the personality of Cervantes, a man who was reserved and cautious though at times aggressive, is reflected in the scarcity of documents concerning him, whereas there is an abundance of information about persons of minor significance. Sixteen years after his college verses were printed, there appeared *La primera parte de la Galatea* (1585), a pastoral novel based upon the genre introduced into Spain by Jorge de Montemayor's *Diana* (1559). Its theme is the fortunes and misfortunes in love of a number of idealized shepherds and shepherdesses, who spend their life "singing and playing musical instruments" after a fashion in which no real shepherds have ever indulged. This, indeed, Cervantes admits in his tale *Coloquio de los perros* (*The Dogs' Colloquy*), in which he observes that pastorals are merely "things of the imagination, well-written," or in other words poetic works that do not depict the reality of actual experience. In the *Galatea* prose alternates with poetry; it possesses no central character nor action, and the incidents are linked together only by means of the simple device of shepherds meeting other shepherds and relating their joys and sorrows. The action has a conventionalized natural setting of woods, springs, or clear streams which are always the same, and takes place in an eternal springtime that makes living out-of-doors possible.

Pastorals of this type charmed readers of both sexes, but especially women, throughout Europe in the second half of the sixteenth century, and many of them were much moved by the sentimental discourses of these tormented and spectral characters. Such prose narration seems to have stirred the emotions of the reader more effectively than did lyric poetry, by giving the illusion of being more probable; since the exchange of amorous confidences arose out of familiar minor happenings, and in addition strong emphasis was placed upon the feelings of the heart. The *Galatea* fulfilled these conditions, for although it frequently takes the form of a dialogue, it is really a collection of monologues revealing what the heart experiences in solitude:

> With this thought, and with the many that his love caused in him, after leaving his herd in a place of safety, he went from his hut, as was his wont at other times, and by the light of the beauteous Diana, who showed herself resplendent in the sky, he entered the denseness of a dense wood beyond, seeking some solitary spot where, in the silence of the night, with greater peace he might give rein to his amorous fancies: for it is an assured fact that to sad, fanciful hearts, there is no greater joy than solitude, the awakener of sad or happy memories.

Inspired by the Neoplatonic ideas of the Renaissance, which were the basis of this literary genre, Cervantes derives the outpouring of feelings from the spirit of love, which transcends them and from which they seem to be an emanation:

> Though rustic, he was, like a true lover, so discreet in things of love, that whenever he discoursed thereon, it seemed that Love himself revealed them to him, and by his tongue uttered them.

The pastoral novel, with its meditations, torments, uncertainty, and sublime joys, thus appears as a secularized version of mystical literature. The notion of divine grace, sanctifier of the souls of the elect, is here humanized, and love comes to be like a divinity which the enamoured one adores and from which he receives quickening faith and the will to live. A faith arising from human desires was thus set up alongside religious belief, and to this fact may be ascribed the constant attacks of Catholic moralists against the pastoral novel, which flourished and died out in the second half of the sixteenth century. Tears and sighs were more perceptible than murmurs of joy in the ideal forms that peopled these works, and although spotless chastity characterized the love that animated them, this circumstance was not sufficient to protect the pastoral novel from church censure. Cervantes, Lope de Vega, and several other writers had tried to make the artistic evaluation of purely human feelings compatible with the rigorous discipline introduced by the Council of Trent, but they had tried in vain.

In more than one sense, the *Galatea* is a forerunner of the novelistic technique of *Don Quixote,* for the characters are endowed with an inner life based upon the desires of the individual and not merely on generic abstractions. As occurs later in *Quixote,* so here, too, even the animals possess the consciousness of being individual creatures:

> Erastro came accompanied by his mastiffs, the faithful guardians of the simple sheep. He made sport with them, and called them by their names, giving to each the title that its disposition and spirit deserved. One he would call Lion, another Hawk, one Sturdy and another Spot; and they, as if they were endowed with understanding, came up to him and, by the movement of their heads, expressed the pleasure which they felt at his pleasure.

The *Galatea* is a book which is undeservedly forgotten, for the conception of life and of the world possessed by the author of *Don Quixote* was already sketched in this, his first important work. Repeatedly its author promised a second part that he said he had finished in his touching letter addressed to the Count of Lemos a few days before his death, but this continuation seems never to have appeared.

Prior to 1600, Cervantes cultivated only such literary genres as the pastoral novel, poetry, and the drama. Fifty years of his life had thus already passed when he began to discover his novelistic capacity to narrate and describe human incidents in prose and to animate them with a new interest. The ideas of the author upon Spanish life and man in general, the projections of his fantasy and disillusionment, were to make themselves apparent in the masterworks written between 1600 to 1615, and although Cervantes had now come to the sunset of his physical life, this was the great period of dawning for his genius. In 1605 the first part of *El ingenioso hidalgo Don Quixote de la Mancha (The Ingenious Gentleman Don Quixote de la Mancha)* was published, and in 1615 the second part, *Segunda tomo del ingenioso hidalgo Don Quixote de la Mancha,* appeared. In 1613 came the *Novelas exemplares (Exemplary Novels)*; in 1614 the *Viaje del Parnaso (Voyage to Parnassus)* appeared; and in 1615 *Ocho comedias y ocho entremeses nuevos* ("Eight Comedies and Eight New Interludes") was published. *Los Trabajos de Persiles y Sigismunda* ("The Labors of Persiles and Sigismunda") appeared as a posthumous work in 1617. Cervantes also mentions the titles of several of his works that have not come down to us: the second part of *Galatea, Las Semanas del jardín* ("Garden Weeks"), *El Engaño á los ojos* ("Deception to the Eyes"), and some others.

The *Exemplary Novels* are twelve short stories of varied types, but the "exemplary" of the title refers to the moral significance which the author consciously injected into all of them. Four of them are perhaps of less interest than the rest: *El Amante liberal (The Liberal Lover), La Señora Cornelia (The Lady Cornelia), Las dos donzellas (The Two Maidens),* and *La Española inglesa (The Spanish-English*

Lady). The theme common to these is basically the traditional one of the Byzantine novel: pairs of lovers separated by lamentable and complicated happenings are finally reunited and find the happiness they have longed for. The heroines are all of most perfect beauty and of sublime morality; they and their lovers are capable of the highest sacrifices, and they exert their souls in the effort to elevate themselves to the ideal of moral and aristocratic distinction which illuminates their lives. In *The Liberal Lover,* to cite an example, the beautiful Leonisa and her lover Ricardo are carried off by Turkish pirates; both fight against serious material and moral dangers; Ricardo conquers all obstacles, returns to his homeland with Leonisa, and is ready to renounce his passion and to hand Leonisa over to her former lover in an outburst of generosity; but Leonisa's preference naturally settles on Ricardo in the end.

Another group of "exemplary" novels is formed by *La Fuerza de la sangre* (*The Force of Blood*), *La ilustre fregona* (*The Illustrious Kitchen-maid*), *La Gitanilla* (*The Little Gypsy*), and *El celoso estremeño* (*The Jealous Estremaduran*). The first three offer examples of love and adventure happily resolved, while the last unravels itself tragically. Its plot deals with the old Felipe Carrizales, who, after traveling widely and becoming rich in America, decides to marry, taking all the precautions necessary to forestall being deceived. He weds a very young girl and isolates her from the world by having her live in a house with no windows facing the street; but in spite of his defensive measures, a bold youth succeeds in penetrating the fortress of conjugal honor, and one day Carrizales surprises his wife in the arms of her seducer. Surprisingly enough, he pardons the adulterers, recognizing that he is more to blame than they, and dies of sorrow over the grievous error he has committed. Cervantes here deviated from the literary tradition observed in the plays of Lope de Vega and Calderón, which demanded the death of the adulterers, but he transformed the punishment inspired by the social ideal of honor into a criticism of the responsibility of the individual.

Rinconete y Cortadillo, El Casamiento engañoso (*The Deceitful Marriage*), *El Licenciado vidriera* (*The Licentiate of Glass*), and *The Dogs' Colloquy,* four works of art which are concerned more with the personalities of the characters who figure in them than with the subject matter, form the final group of these stories. The protagonists are two young vagabonds, Rincón and Cortado; Lieutenant Campuzano; a student, Tomás Rodaja, who goes mad and believes himself to have been changed into a man of glass; and finally two dogs, Cipión and Berganza, whose wandering existence serves as a mirror for the most varied aspects of Spanish life. *Rinconete y Cortadillo* is one of the most delightful of Cervantes' works. Its two young vagabonds come to Seville attracted by the riches and disorder that the sixteenth-century commerce with the Americas had brought to that metropolis. There they come into contact with a brotherhood of thieves led by the unforgettable Monipodio, whose house is the headquarters of the Sevillian underworld. Cervantes presents his tale with great effect. Under the bright Andalusian sky persons and objects take form with the brilliance and subtle drama of a Velázquez, and a distant and discreet irony endows the figures, insignificant in themselves, as they move within a ritual pomp that is in sharp contrast with their morally deflated lives. When Monipodio appears, serious and solemn among his silent subordinates, "all who were looking at him performed a deep, protracted bow." Rincón and Cortado had initiated their mutual friendship beforehand "with saintly and praiseworthy ceremonies." The solemn ritual of this band of ruffians produces an impression of comedy which is all the more effective for being concealed in Cervantes' drily humorous style.

Cervantes' greatest work, *Don Quixote,* is a unique book of multiple dimensions. From the moment of its appearance it has amused readers or caused them to think, and its influence has extended in literature not only to works of secondary value but also to those which have universal importance. Don Quixote is a country gentleman, an enthusiastic visionary crazed by his reading of romances of chivalry, who rides forth to defend the oppressed and to right wrongs; so vividly was he presented by Cervantes that many languages have borrowed the name of the hero as the common term to designate a person inspired by lofty and impractical ideals.

The theme of the book, in brief, concerns Hidalgo Alonso Quijana, who, because of his reading in books about chivalry, comes to believe that everything they say is true and decides to become a knight-errant himself. He assumes the name of Don Quixote de la Mancha and, accompanied by a peasant, Sancho Panza, who serves him as a squire, sets forth in search of adventures. Don Quixote interprets all that he encounters in accordance with his readings and thus imagines himself to be living in a world quite different from the one familiar to the ordinary men he meets. Windmills are thus transformed into giants, and this illusion, together with many others, is the basis for the beatings and misadventures suffered by the intrepid hero. After the knight's second sally in search of adventure, friends and neighbors in his village decide to force him to forget his wild fancy and to reintegrate himself into his former life. The "knight" insists upon following his calling, but at the end of the first part of the book they make him return to his home by means of a sly stratagem. In the second part the hidalgo leaves for the third time and alternately gives indication of folly and of wisdom in a dazzling array of artistic inventions. But now even his enemies force him to abandon his endeavors. Don Quixote finally recognizes that romances of chivalry are mere lying inventions, but upon recovering the clarity of his mind, he loses his life.

The idea that Don Quixote is a symbol of the noblest generosity, dedicated to the purpose of doing good disinterestedly, suggests the moral common denominator to be found in Cervantes' creation. But in addition to furnishing a moral type capable of being recognized and accepted as a symbol of values in any time or place, *Don Quixote* is a work of art with as many aspects and reflections as it has readers to seek them. Considerations of general morality thus become intermingled with the psychological and aesthetic experience of each individual reader in a way that vastly stimulated the development of the literary genre later known as the novel, and Fielding, Dickens, Flaubert, Stendhal, Dostoyevsky, and many others have thus been inspired by Cervantes. In *Madame Bovary,* by Gustave Flaubert, for example, the heroine changes the orientation of her life because she, like Don Quixote, has read her romances of chivalry, the romantic novels of the nineteenth century.

Cervantes demonstrated to the Western world how poetry and fantasy could coexist with the experience of reality which is perceptible to the senses. He did this by presenting poetic reality, which previously had been confined to the ideal region of dream, as something experienced by a real person, and the dream thus became the reality of any man living his dream. Therefore, the trivial fact that a poor hidalgo loses his reason for one cause or another is of little importance. The innovation is that Don Quixote's madness is converted into the theme of his life and into a theme for the life of other people, who are influenced as much by the madness of the hidalgo as is he himself. Some want him to revert to his condition of a peaceful and sedentary hidalgo; others would like him to keep on amusing or stupefying people with his deeds, insane and wise at the same time.

Before Cervantes, literature was, as occasion offered, fantastic, idealistic, naturalistic, moralistic, or didactic. After his time, literature continued to exploit all these types, but with them it was inclined to incorporate, as well, some reader's experience of them. Romances of chivalry could now attain a significance beyond that of mere books and could become what people felt or thought about them, thus growing to be part of the dynamic substance of living persons. In *Don Quixote,* for example, the hero takes them for the gospel; the priest believes them to be false; the innkeeper admires the tremendous blows delivered by the knights; his daughter is taken by the sentimental aspect of the love affairs which they describe; and so on. But the reality of the literary work is the ideal integration of all possible experience which all of the possible readers undergo. This point can be further illustrated by taking proverbs as an example. Before *Don Quixote,* many collections of sayings and proverbs had been published, but when Sancho interspersed these proverbs helter-skelter in his conversation and thus brought his master to despair, the proverbs became the living experiences which Sancho and Don Quixote derived from them. In this manner, everything in *Don Quixote* can be either real or ideal, either fantastic or possible, according to the manner in which it affects the variety of readers, whether they be creators of beautiful and comforting illusions or dispassionate demolishers of dreams. To live, for Cervantes, is to let loose the extensive capacity of all that is human; it may also be to remain deaf and inert before the attractions of love, faith, and enthusiasm. All who live in the human universe of the greatest book of Spanish literature succeed or destroy themselves, according to one of these opposing trends.

When compared with such a prodigious book, all of Cervantes' works which have not previously been mentioned, no matter what their value, must be relegated to a lower level. Among his dramatic works, *La Numancia,* a description of the heroic defense of that Iberian city during the Roman conquest of Spain in the second century B.C., and the amusing *Interludes,* such as *El Juez de los divorcios* ("The Judge of Divorces") and *El Retablo de las maravillas* ("The Picture of Marvels"), are outstanding. Also worth mentioning is the verse *Voyage to Parnassus* (1614), in which almost all of the Spanish writers of the period are lauded, and *Persiles y Sigismunda,* published posthumously in 1617. In this last named work the author returns to the theme of the Byzantine novel and relates the ideal love and unbelievable vicissitudes of a couple who, starting from the Arctic regions, arrive in Rome, where they find a happy ending for their complicated adventures. A. C.

CERVERA Y TOPETE, PASCUAL [thɛrveˈra i topeˈte] (1833-1909), Spanish naval officer, was born in Medina Sidonia, Spain, Feb. 18, 1833. He entered a naval cadet school at the age of twelve and became an officer of honesty, skill, and bravery. In the Spanish-American War he commanded the Spanish fleet operating in Cuban waters. He took refuge in the harbor of Santiago, but on orders from his government he steamed out and engaged the blockading American forces, far superior to his own. His small fleet was destroyed. Cervera was court-martialed by his government, but was honorably acquitted. In 1901 he was made a vice-admiral and the next year became chief of staff of the Spanish navy. In 1903 he was made a senator for life. Cervera died in Puerto Real, Spain, Apr. 3, 1909. J. J. Van N.

CESIUM [siˈziəm], symbol Cs, a metallic chemical element. It is one of the alkali metals and is found near the bottom of Group I-A in the periodic table. It is the most active metal known, and the most electropositive. Cesium compounds are widely distributed in nature, usually in small amounts with those of the other alkali metals. Pollucite is a silicate mineral containing 34 per cent of cesium oxide, Cs_2O. The element was discovered by Bunsen and Kirchhoff in 1860. It is prepared by heating cesium chloride with calcium. It is a silvery white liquid in a warm room; it burns in air and reacts vigorously with water. Cesium compounds are similar to those of potassium. Cesium hydroxide, $CsOH$, is the most basic hydroxide known. The element is univalent, but forms a number of interesting stable complex salts, such as CsI_3 and $CsCl_2I$. Cesium metal has been used in the manufacture of photoelectric cells and radio tubes.

PROPERTIES OF CESIUM

Atomic number	55
Atomic weight	132.91
Stable isotopes	133
Density (g./ml.) 20°C.	1.90
Melting point, °C.	28.5
Boiling point, °C.	670
Specific heat (cal./g.) 20°C.	0.052
Hardness (Mohs' scale)	0.2

B. S. H.

ČESKÉ BUDĚJOVICE [tshɛˈske buˈdyeyɔˈvitsɛ] (Ger. Budweis), the principal city of southwestern Bohemia, in Czechoslovakia and the capital of the province of the same name. An important manufacturing and communications center, it is located about 80 mi. south of Prague, near the headwaters of the Vltava River. The city lies at the foot of the heavily forested Böhmer Wald, bordering a fertile Bohemian agricultural district where hops, potatoes, and grain are raised. The city's industries include breweries, food processing plants, and trade in lumber; there are manufactures of pencils, enamelware, and furniture. The eighteenth-century town hall fronts on a beautiful square surrounded by arcades.

Founded in the thirteenth century, České Budějovice was a royal town under early Czech kings and figured prominently in Bohemian politics during the Hussite Wars of the fourteenth and fifteenth centuries. It was strongly Germanized during the seventeenth and eighteenth centuries. Included in Czechoslovakia after World War I, it was occupied by Germany in 1939 and, soon after, was made a Reich city. Following World War II, it was included in the re-established Czech republic. Pop. 1947, 38,194.

CESTRUM [sɛˈstrəm], a tropical American genus of woody shrubs or small (15 ft.) trees, of the solanum family. The flowers, which occur in clusters, are tubular, about an inch long, and often fragrant. The species most commonly seen in cultivation are *C. aurantiacum,* with large clusters of orange flowers, *C. nocturnum,* called night-blooming jessamine, with greenish white flowers and a fragrance at night, *C. parqui,* Chilean cestrum, or willow-leaved jessamine, with whitish flowers and a fragrance, and *C. elegans,* with large clusters of red flowers. E. McCl.

CETACEA [səteˈshiə], an order of exclusively aquatic mammals, fishlike in form, including whales, dolphins, and porpoises. Cetacea breathe atmospheric air, bear their young alive after placental intrauterine development, suckle their young with milk, and have warm blood and the remnants of body hair. In these characteristics, and some others, they resemble all mammals, and their fusiform body has evolved on a true mammalian basic anatomy. The tail fins, flukes, of Cetacea, are horizontal instead of vertical as in the fish, and are unsupported by a bony skeleton; the external hind legs have disappeared completely. The fore flippers correspond with the pectoral fins of the fish. The nostrils of most are situated on top of the head, and the neck is extremely short, the usual seven mammalian cervical vertebrae being compressed into plates totaling about 6 in. in length.

Physical Characteristics. *Blubber.* A characteristic structure of whales and other marine mammals is blubber, which may attain a foot or more in thickness in some species (sperm and bowhead whales), but only an inch or so in porpoises and dolphins. It is a tough, elastic layer of fiber and fat just below the skin. Its exact function is not known, but it stores an immense amount of oil when the whale is "fat," and is the principal source of whale and sperm oil. Generally blubber is said to act as an insulator against the loss of body heat, but it undoubtedly also serves as a storage for food.

Stomach. The stomachs of all Cetacea are complex, and the intestines long. The beaked whales (ziphoids) have fourteen distinct compartments in the stomach, and the baleen whales have four. The "stomachs" of one large blue whale held a ton of shrimp, and the "stomachs" of a captured specimen of killer whale have revealed the remains of several porpoises and as many as eighteen to twenty-four seal pups.

Baleen. The whalebone, or baleen, of the baleen whales is an interesting structure and adaptation enabling the whale to feed upon small particles of food. It is found nowhere else in the animal kingdom. It resembles a long knife-blade, and is horny, fibrous, and elastic. Each blade hangs down from a row on either side of the roof of the mouth, transversely and close together; as many as three hundred blades may be situated in each row. The outer edge of each blade is straight but the inner is gradually curved to meet the outer in a sharp point and is heavily fringed with fibrous hairs. This fringe of hairs forms a dense mat, through which the water is squeezed in the manner of a sieve to retain shrimp taken as food. Whalebone once had a high value to the dress trade, and the right and bowhead whales were practically exterminated for their extra-long baleen of 7 to 14 ft. Other whalebone whales, although larger, have shorter baleen, for which there is no current market. Sperm and other toothed whales and porpoises and dolphins do not have baleen.

Liver. The liver is large, and in the blue whale may weigh a ton. The oil content is small but the amount of vitamin A in the oil is high. Vitamin D is practically absent.

Digestive Tract and Kidneys. Excretion of liquids is done both by the intestines of the digestive tract and by the kidneys. There is practically no solid matter in the feces. The kidneys are huge and made up of thousands of smaller complete kidneys (renculi) about the size of golf balls. Whales undoubtedly take a certain amount of salt water into their systems, requiring elimination. The physiology of their water-balance is little understood, but it is certain that they drink no fresh water.

Blood. Whales have red blood in large quantities—perhaps more in proportion to their weight than terrestrial mammals. The blood is salty and warm, the temperature of a whale being about 95° F., or slightly higher (35° to 37° C.). Peculiarly, the blood of the blue whale has proportionately less hemoglobin, or oxygen-holding substance, than that of man. The blood of the blue whale, according to Laurie, also has strange "X-organisms" to which he ascribed the function of nitrogen-fixation as an aid in the physiology of deep diving. Other peculiar structures are the *retia mirabilia,* knots of capillaries scattered through the circulatory system; their function is not definitely known.

Nervous System. The nervous system of whales is specialized. The brain is relatively small, but the parts associated with co-ordinated involuntary muscular movement (the parafloccular lobes of the cerebellum) and with the reception of acoustic vibrations and spacial reflexes (the acoustic and vestibular tracts, especially the inferior colliculus) are well developed. The ears lack outer pinna, although remnants persist in some porpoises. The bones of the middle ear and the tympanic membrane are degenerate, but the ear-drum has developed into a large, dense, resonating, vibratory chamber. The auditory tube leading from the external ear slit is small and clogged with wax. However, whales can detect vibrations in the water and perhaps communicate with each other, although their vocal powers are rudimentary or absent. The eyes are relatively small and heavily armored with a rigid sclera behind and around the optic nerve, and vision is not acute. The sense of smell is probably also inefficient; certainly it does not function through the nostrils for detecting odors under water. However, there are two pits inside the front of the mouth, "organs of Jacobsen," which may function to detect odors in the water. These pits are blind, about ½ in. deep, and connect with sensory nerve fibers. The sense of taste may be good. Touch undoubtedly is a well-developed or retained sense. Any part of the body is probably sensitive to contact, but particularly the snout, where the remnants of hairs are said to be tactile and hydrostatic in function. Each small, stiff hair ends in a blood-sinus surrounded by many nerve endings, the "Pacinian corpuscles." The sinus magnifies the area of sensitivity at the base of the hair, and the bunch of nerves should transmit the faintest stimulus.

Locomotion. In Cetacea, locomotion is done almost entirely by the horizontally expanded flukes (tail fins), which are sculled up and down and with a slight twisting motion of terrific power. The front flippers do no more than balance and steer. The propulsive power of a whale or porpoise can drive the body through the water at speeds up to twenty or twenty-five knots. Their immense swimming powers can be realized by considering the ability of a harpooned whale to pull a 100-ton whaleboat through the water at an appreciable rate, even with the motors going full speed astern. It has been estimated that 520 horse power would be generated by a 90-ft. blue whale swimming at 20 knots if the water-resistance were equal to that of a like-sized rigid body, or 4.35 hp. per ton of weight. A porpoise of the same speed would generate about 87 hp. per ton, although less in total, according to Gray. Both Gray and Parry indicated that such horse power output is too high and means greater efficiency for the cetacean body.

Feeding. The food of all Cetacea consists of fish, squid, or small organisms like shrimp. Ordinarily, one kind is preferred, and the digestive mechanism of a species is adapted to the taking of that one kind. All food is swallowed whole; none is chewed, and none of the teeth found in any species is designed for cutting or grinding. The fish-eating species are the dolphins and porpoises; their teeth are numerous, sharp, and conical, and their mouths and tongues are small, but their throats are relatively large. Fish are "run down," grasped and swallowed whole, but great depths are not attained in diving for the prey. The squid-eaters are the sperm, beaked, and bottlenose whales, as well as some of the smaller species. These have a reduced number of teeth, sometimes only two, and all are normally in the lower jaw only. The mouths and tongues are relatively small, and the throats large, and great depths are reached in hunting for food. The shrimp-eaters are the baleen (whalebone) whales. These species gulp masses of hundreds or thousands of their tiny prey by cruising slowly and at no great depth through a school, or shoal, with their mouths wide open. They fill their enormous mouths, squeeze the water out through the baleen plates with the aid of huge tongues, and swallow the quantity of shrimp in a fine stream down narrow throats. The throats of all baleen whales, large or small, as well as of all fish- and squid-eaters, except the killer whale and sperm, are too small to admit a man.

Diving. Diving is a function of locomotion and feeding, and most Cetacea must dive to obtain food, sometimes to considerable depths. The baleen whales which feed almost exclusively upon schooling shrimp and other macroplanktonic animals, and the fish-eating porpoises and dolphins, probably can dive to 500 or 600 ft., but the sperm whale and bottlenose whales dive much deeper in quest of squid. The sperm is known to go as deep as 3,240 ft., where it must resist pressures of 1,400 lbs. per sq. in., or 100 tons per sq. ft., and presumably they can go deeper. Diving involves ability to withstand terrific pressures, to produce continuous energy without continual breathing, and to avoid the "bends" or "caisson disease" on suddenly rising to the surface. How whales accomplish these things is not known and is one of the interesting problems of cetacean physiology. Many theories have been advanced, but none is completely satisfactory, and some are actually conflicting. These speculations revolve about points such as the ability to keep air in the lungs, and water out, by means of nasal plugs and valves; the ability to resist pressure, or to collapse the lungs and thorax; the ability to store oxygen in the blood, in the capillary knots (retia mirabilia), or in fat; the ability to store the nitrogen from the last breath of air in some part of the blood, or in fat, if it is fully absorbed by collapse of the lungs, and to release it slowly so that there is no effervescence to cause the bends; and the ability to store excess carbon dioxide (a waste product), or to have lack of sensitivity to its presence in excess in the blood by the respiratory center of the brain. Scholander and Irving have shown that probably the heart slows down markedly (brachicardia) during diving, and that there is a restriction of peripheral circulation which keeps the blood in the internal organs.

Respiration. In whales and porpoises, which breathe air like those of humans, respiration is entirely by lungs. All Cetacea come to the surface to breathe at regular intervals when traveling, or at intermittent periods when diving deeply and seeking food. A sperm may blow gustily 20 or 30 times in from 3 to 5 minutes after a dive of 40 minutes or so. The baleen whales generally blow 3 to 5 times in a minute or so after a dive of from 4 to 10 minutes. The suddenly expired air may condense in a geyser-like spout, especially in the larger species, and the spout may be characteristic of the species. No water is included in the spout unless some slopping of sea-water into the blow-holes occurs in rough weather. Nostrils are situated on top of the head and are paired in the baleen whales; they are a bit farther forward and fused into a single outlet in the porpoises, dolphins, and bottlenose whales; and they are at the tip of the blunt snout on the left side in a single S-shaped blowhole in the sperm. Connected with the respiration is the production of sound.

Some whales and porpoises can sigh gustily by forcible expulsion of air out of the nostrils, which perhaps are semiconstructed at the time, and the normal blows of the larger species can be heard for long distances over calm water. In addition, some porpoises and dolphins are said to chuckle, squeak, click, and so forth. However, no vocal cords have been found, so the manner of production of the latter sounds is not known. The expired air is often fetid. The inspired air rushes in quickly through massive cartilagenous trachea into large lungs where there are thousands of alveoli which have thick septa and can be shut off from the bronchioles by sphincter muscles. In the baleen whales, the nostrils open for the blow like huge buckets, the constricting muscles raising in distinct ridges forward and laterally; they remain open for the quick exhalation and inhalation which together may take two seconds. The nostrils, whether paired or single at the outlet, are paired into two passages in the head, and often have diverticula (chambers) and plug-valves for specialized functions of holding reservoirs of air, or preventing water from entering under high pressure.

General Behavior. In general behavior, whales apparently have some intelligence and this is expressed in their wariness after hunting and their playful social tendencies. Most are timid, but the male sperm has a streak of belligerency which makes him a fighter and dangerous adversary. The killer whale also has such pugnacious and aggressive tendencies. Whales are not known to sleep soundly, although they rest at the surface for periods of time and perhaps accomplish the same purpose as sleep by such reduced activity. Generally, they are active by day or night as the demands of feeding or traveling dictate.

Reproduction. The process of reproduction in Cetacea follows the mammalian pattern, the embryo being developed in utero with placenta and surrounding membranes. The offspring is born alive, and is suckled with milk. The milk is rich in fats, but low in sugars, and has an ascorbic acid (vitamin C) content in the pregnant finback of about twice that of the cow and about the same as that of the human. Smaller Cetacea probably bear once a year, a single young at a time, while the larger species have a single young every other year as a rule. Gestation is not definitely known, but appears to be from 10 to 11 months in the larger baleen whales, and slightly less in the porpoises and dolphins. The sperm may have a longer gestation. The baby whale is relatively large at birth, being from 13 to 14 ft. long in the 30- to 35-ft. female sperm; 15 to 17 ft. in the 40- to 45-ft. female humpback; 21 to 22 ft. in the 60- to 75-ft. finback; and about 23 to 24 ft. in the blue whale female of from 80 to 90 ft. Growth is extremely rapid, and after nursing for about 7 months, a young blue whale is from 50 to 55 ft. long; at two years it is from 74 to 77 ft. long and ready to breed. Longevity for most species of Cetacea is unknown, but is presumed to be from 10 to 20 years, depending on the species.

Enemies. The enemies of whales and porpoises are primarily man (in recent times), the killer whale, and perhaps disease. The toll of large species by the killer whale is small, but the toll of smaller porpoises by this wolf of the sea is undoubtedly larger. Disease is an unknown factor. Man is the greatest enemy, and when he singles out a species for exploitation, that species is doomed unless the catch is carefully regulated. Parasites exist, both external and internal, but their morbid effect is probably small. External parasites consist of barnacles, found regularly on the humpback and gray whale; small crablike lice (copepods) on the humpback and gray whale; a plantlike growth on many whales called a pennelid (really an animal, a crustacean, like the copepods); and certain microscopic diatoms which cling to the skin of some species and give a yellowish brown color. Internal parasites are mainly round worms (nematodes), spiny-headed worms (acanthocephala), and flukes (tremadotes). An ulcerous condition of unknown cause affects some whales, and apparently is contracted in warm waters and heals in cold waters, leaving an oblong scar of several inches.

Geographical Distribution. In geographic distribution, Cetacea cover the world's oceans and some of its fresh waters. Most marine species are almost cosmopolitan, although some are limited in their range to a certain part of the sea. Some baleen whales migrate annually over great distances in their hemisphere, going from warmer waters, where they breed in the winter season, to colder waters, where in summer they fatten on the enormous quantities of available shrimp and related organisms. Many other whales make less extensive migrations.

Fossil History of Whales. The fossil history of whales is extensive, but it is as yet by no means complete; some critical stages in evolution are unknown. All living whales are highly specialized for aquatic life, but whales are definitely mammals and undoubtedly rose from terrestrial stock. Consequently, the paleontologists look to the fossil record to reveal any forms which may link the two habits with corresponding structures. But they look in vain, since all fossil whales are true whales. There were many primitive genera and species, but all were clearly baleen or toothed whales (suborders Mysticeti and Odontoceti), or members of the extinct suborder Archaeoceti (zeuglodonts), and no fossils bridge the gap between these distinct main groups. The zeuglodonts were long, snaky-bodied Cetacea with teeth differentiated into a back series with serrated edge, and front teeth of simple conical shape. There is a vague resemblance in this to the typical mammalian condition of heterodont dentition (molars, canines, incisors). Cetotheres, an extinct group, were primitive whalebone whales.

All fossil Cetacea are found in Tertiary beds, Eocene to Recent, but their full development by the Eocene indicates that they originated far back in the Mesozoic.

Scientific Study. Scientific knowledge of whales was, until recently, based on the examination of a few stranded specimens, and on the observations of a few intelligent men in the whaling industry. These data were mixed with a large amount of fantasy originating in the accounts of sailors and whalers plus some wild hypotheses and speculations. Within the last 40 or 50 years, however, scientists from the United States, England, Norway, Germany, the Soviet Union, and Japan have made special efforts to utilize the industry to gain a larger knowledge of whales. The principal species studied have been the finback and the blue whale, with the humpback, sei, sperm, and right whales receiving less attention. The bowhead had been depleted and the right whale almost so by this time.

The large amount of routine data taken on whales by the industry as to species, length, sex, and length and sex of fetus if present, with products, are summarized in the reports of the International Bureau of Whaling Statistics, Oslo, Norway. The other special studies have appeared in technical journals, in the reports of the British Discovery Committee, the Norwegian *Hvalrädets Skrifter* (the Norwegian *Whaling Gazette*), and the Japanese *Bulletin of Scientific Fisheries*. These reports include such studies as those on the technology of the industry, the morphology and physiology of whales, and the oceanographic conditions of their existence.

As the whale is not subject to direct experimentation in a tank when alive, much information must be obtained indirectly. Some ingenious methods have been adopted. One involves the examination of ovaries of females to determine from the count of scars of corpora lutea, the number of ovulations and thus the probable age of the individual. Another method involves the chopping of vertebral edges with an axe to determine from the amount or the absence of open cartilagenous unions of epiphyses (terminal growing portions) the state of physical maturity. Still another technique employs the shooting of aluminum tubes into whales so that they are marked and thus, when picked up later, will give information as to movements and age. Some American scientists recently succeeded in obtaining some physiological information from a captive porpoise in a tank, but so far the data is meager. *See also* DOLPHINS AND PORPOISES; WHALES; WHALING. R. M. G.

CETINJE [tsɛ'tinye], a town in southeastern Yugoslavia, about 10 mi. from Kotor, or Cattaro, its seaport on the Adriatic, at 42° N. lat. and about 11° E. long. Cetinje, the capital

Cetinje, Yugoslavia, once the capital of Montenegro, high in the Black Mountains. A townsman, in native Montenegran costume, stands on a rocky point overlooking the town, which sprang up around a monastery founded in 1478.

of the former kingdom of Montenegro, lies on a narrow limestone plateau 2,068 ft. high, reached from Kotor by means of a steep, zigzagging highway rounding Mount Lovcen. The town was founded in 1484 by Ivan the Black, ruler of Montenegro, when he was forced by invading Turkish forces to retreat from his former capital, Zhabliak. Ivan successfully defended the new site against the invaders, but in 1683, 1714, and 1785, Turkish forces pillaged and burned the town. In 1918, at the conclusion of World War I, Cetinje was included in Yugoslavia. During World War II the town was occupied from 1941 to 1945 by Italian troops, and in 1945 Cetinje was returned to Yugoslavia. The palace of Nicholas I, king of Montenegro, the old monastery around which the town grew, the foreign legations, and the old schools and seminaries are largely in ruins. The remains of Peter II, the poet-king, are buried in the town. There is a tower in Cetinje that was once adorned with the heads of Turks. Pop. 1948, 9,109.   F. Sc.

CETUS [si'təs], the Whale, a large constellation extending irregularly from about right ascension 0 hr. to 3 hr. 20 min.; from declination, +10° to −25°. Although only one

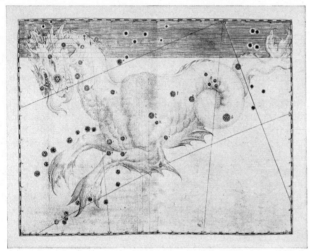

CETUS, "THE WHALE"

star in the group is constantly as bright as the second magnitude, the configuration is quite striking. This region includes many beautiful and interesting colored doubles. The best-known star is Mira, a long-period variable. In Greek mythology, Cetus was the monster sent by Poseidon to devour Andromeda, but was slain by Perseus. *See also* MIRA.
                                                      J. H. P.

CEUTA [syu'tə; the'uta], a city in northwestern Africa located on the peninsula forming the southern "Pillar of Hercules" guarding the eastern entrance to the Strait of Gibraltar. It is an enclave in Morocco, constituting a municipality belonging to metropolitan Spain. The city occupies a low, narrow isthmus connecting the promontory, crowned by Mt. Hacho (636 ft. in elevation), with the African mainland. At this point the Strait of Gibraltar has a width of 14 mi. The Arabic name for the city is Sebta. Ceuta is almost wholly European in its appearance and population. The climate is equable, showing strong marine influences. The harbor, protected by breakwaters, lies on the northern side of the city, facing the strait. It is spacious, and its installations permit large ships to moor at the principal pier. There are facilities for providing ships with bunker coal and fuel

oil. Ceuta is connected with Tetuán, Morocco, by a narrow-gauge railway (25 mi.).

Ceuta is administered as part of the province of Cádiz. The Spanish have fortified the promontory and maintain a garrison there. The city contains no public buildings of outstanding historical or artistic value. The cathedral has been partly reconstructed from an old Moorish mosque.

Ceuta appears to have been the site of the Phoenician-Carthaginian Abyla and the Roman Septem Fratres. After being held by the Vandals, it passed to the Byzantine Empire under Justinian. At the end of the seventh century the local governor, Count Julian, asserted his independence but later encouraged the Berber leader Tarik to invade Visigothic Spain in 711. Thereafter Ceuta was under Moslem rule, sometimes subject to Córdoba, more often to successive dynasties in Morocco. The city reached its height under the Merinids in the fourteenth century. In August 1415 King John I of Portugal took Ceuta, which became the first Portuguese possession in Africa. Spain assumed control in 1580 on the annexation of Portugal by Philip II, and in 1688 this transfer became definitive. Several sieges by the Moroccans, including one that lasted from 1694 to 1720, were unsuccessful. Ceuta was the base of Spanish operations in the "African War" of 1859-1860, which resulted in a modest expansion of Spain's holdings in Morocco. Only after the effective occupation of the interior by Spanish forces following World War I did Ceuta acquire a hinterland and thereby a certain amount of commerce. Since Morocco achieved independence in 1956, pressure for the removal of European troops from North Africa has tended to threaten continued Spanish sovereignty over Ceuta and the other four *presidios* of the region. Pop. 1950, 56,909.   R. G. W.

CÉVENNES [se've'n], a mountain chain of south central France extending, in its widest sense, in an arc of some 300 mi. from the west bank of the Saône near Chalon southward along the Rhône toward the Mediterranean, then to the southeast and east to the vicinity of Castelnaudary on the Canal du Midi. Except for the northern quarter, this is the area which, with the adjacent Mediterranean lowland, formed the historic province of Languedoc. Its inhabitants, the Cévenols, were noted for their independence, especially in matters of religion. The southwestern Cévennes were the center of the Albigensian sect, which, after flourishing for a century, was exterminated by 1229. Calvinism later secured a stronghold here and, after the revocation of the Edict of Nantes in 1685, flared up into the bitter revolt of the Camisards (1702-1704). After this revolt was crushed, the Huguenot faith continued to be practiced secretly in the wilder parts of the Cévennes.

At present this region is one of the most sparsely settled of France. Except for coal in the vicinity of Alès, there is no mineral wealth. Mulberry trees flourish along the gentle southeast slopes, and silkworm culture is the basis of an important textile industry in neighboring cities. The chestnuts of the Cévennes are also famous, and a fine wine is grown in the northern mountains of Beaujolais. A large part of the terrain provides good pasturage for sheep and cattle. The climate is cold in the winters, with heavy rains causing the rivers to rush precipitously through the gorges for which much of the region is famous. Tourists frequent the picturesque Causses district, with its caverns and subterranean rivers, and there are resort hotels such as the one on Mont Aigoual. Probably the most famous literary account of the region is that of Robert Louis Stevenson, *Travels With a Donkey in the Cévennes* (1879).

Physical Characteristics. The Cévennes, constituting the east and southeast fringe of the Massif Central, are a major watershed between the Atlantic and Mediterranean. The Loire and Allier rivers flow toward the north; the Tarn, Lot, and Aveyron (Garonne tributaries) toward the west; the Ardèche and Gard eastward to the Rhone; the Hérault southward to the Golfe du Lion.

Geology. Like the Massif Central, the Cévennes were formed during the late Paleozoic Era (Hercynian mountain-building) by the folding of formations of early Paleozoic origin, resulting in a core of metamorphic rock (mainly gneiss and schist). Later depositions include the limestone layers of Jurassic origin in the Causses; there was also much volcanism throughout the region.

Ranges and Heights. The Cévennes as a whole have a general elevation of 3,000-4,000 ft. Principal subranges (from north to southwest):

Mountains of Charolais, Beaujolais, and Lyonnais, all north of Lyon, maximum height 3,200 ft.

Mountains of Velay (west) and Vivarais: the former, of volcanic origin, separating the upper Loire and Allier valleys, maximum elevation 4,669 ft.; the latter, also largely volcanic, reaching 5,089 ft. at Mont Gerbier de Jonc and 5,750 ft. (highest in Cévennes) at Mont Mézanc.

Cévennes proper: principal heights, Pic de Finiels in Mont Lozère massif, 5,584 ft., and Mont Aigoual, 5,141 ft.

The Causses: semicircular limestone plateau, 3,000-4,000 ft. in elevation, separating the Cévennes proper (on the east) from the Massif Central; gorges cut by Lot, Aveyron, and Tarn.

Garrigues, Espinouse, and Montagne Noire: southwestern extremities of Cévennes system, the last a subrange of granite, maximum height 3,970 ft., Pic de Nore.   E. A.

CEYLON [siln′n], a large island, a dominion of the British Commonwealth, is located in the Indian Ocean, to the east of the southern tip of India. A low, narrow sandbar once connected the island with the mainland, but in modern times the central portion of this bar, known as Adam's Bridge, has become partly submerged. The extreme northern tip of the island is separated from India by Palk Strait. In shape, Ceylon somewhat resembles a pear, and in local legend has been called "India's teardrop." The Dominion is slightly smaller than Eire, having an area of 25,332 sq. mi.

Geology and Relief. In the north the land is flat and low-lying, with swamps toward the coast and an underlying rock formation which is mostly limestone. The southern region consists for the most part of a mountain core, with surrounding foothills; the formation is pre-Cambrian crystalline rock. The highest peak is Pidurutalagala, 8,281 ft.; others, including Adam's Peak, are over 7,000 ft.

Minerals. Ceylon has some iron deposits, largely undeveloped, but no coal. It was once famous for its precious and semiprecious gem stones, such as rubies, sapphires, amethysts, cat's eyes, moon-stones, alexandrites, and garnets, but these resources have been largely depleted, as have pearl resources due to bad economic planning and natural causes. Plumbago (graphite) has become more important as a resource than all of the island's gem stones.

Climate. Ceylon lies between 5 and 10° N. of the equator and, except in the mountain region, the climate is tropical, with year-round temperatures of about 80° F. Like the Indian mainland, Ceylon receives rain in the summer from the southwest monsoons, but unlike India, it also has rainfall in the winter during the northeast monsoons.

Precipitation varies from about 25 in. on some parts of the coast to almost 100 in. in some sections of the mountain region, but because of the alternation between wet and dry seasons, agriculture in the northern, north central, and eastern plains (Dry Zone) is dependent upon irrigation.

Flora. The native plant life of Ceylon naturally bears a close resemblance to that of southern India. However, the island's strategic trade location in the Indian Ocean has resulted in the importation through the centuries of many exotic plants, some of which now dominate the economy. The rice plant, cinnamon tree, and areca (betel) nut are probably indigenous, while the coconut palm seems to have been an early import. The coffee plant was introduced by the Portuguese, and the currently important tea plant and rubber tree by the British. The island produces cinnamon bark, cinchona bark (quinine), and other drugs and spices, but not to the same extent as formerly.

Population. The population of Ceylon in the census of 1953 was 8,098,637, an increase of 21.7 per cent since 1946.

By 1958 the number was estimated to be over 9,000,000. A successful antimalaria campaign greatly reduced the death rate after World War II.

At the time of the census the predominant Sinhalese numbered 5,621,332. Indian Tamils, mostly noncitizens, were the second largest ethnic group, numbering 983,304. The remainder of the population was divided as follows: Ceylon Tamils, 908,705; Ceylon Moors (Moslems), 468,146; Burghers (of partly European ancestry, chiefly Dutch and Portuguese), 43,916; Malays, 28,736; Europeans (chiefly British), 6,909; Pakistanis, 5,749; others, 31,840. The aboriginal Veddahs now number less than 3,000.

In Ceylon, as elsewhere in the East, there is a high correlation between religious and ethnic groups. Buddhism is the religion of about 64 per cent of the population, and most Ceylonese Buddhists are Sinhalese. Other religions are represented as follows: Hinduism, about 20 per cent, almost wholly Tamil; Islam, about 7 per cent; and Christianity, about 9 per cent. The last two groups are ethnically the most mixed. Among the Sinhalese, Catholics vastly outnumber Protestants, largely because of the missionary zeal of the early Portuguese; but a high percentage of Burghers are Protestants. Animism is represented by Veddahs clinging to old ways.

About 15 per cent of Ceylon's inhabitants are urban; the rest live in small towns, on plantations, and in rural areas divided into "villages." Colombo, the capital and commercial center, had a population of 423,481 in 1953. A densely populated chain of towns extends southward from Colombo along the coast for many miles. The other leading cities are Jaffna, the Ceylon Tamil center in the extreme north; Galle, once the island's leading seaport, in the extreme southwest; and Kandy, before 1815 the capital of the Sinhalese kingdom, in the south-central highlands.

Economic Activities. Ceylon's economy is heavily dependent on agricultural exports, chiefly tea, rubber, and coconut products, in that order. Although only about one third of the labor force works on these products, the government and most of the commercial sector of the economy derive the bulk of their income directly or indirectly from the three exports. Peasant agriculture, which encompassed almost the entire economy before the days of European rule, is a second major area. Rice is the peasant sector's principal crop; but the surplus which the paddy farmers produce beyond their own needs does not nearly satisfy the demands of the urban and plantation population, which import large quantities of rice from south and east Asia. In recent years the government has made ambitious attempts to reclaim irrigable Dry Zone acreage which supported the bulk of the island's population until about 700 years ago.

Ceylonese attempts to develop manufacturing industry other than the tea factories, crude-rubber factories, and coconut-product mills closely associated with the plantations have so far accomplished little. Government and private enterprise have, however, in recent years provided the island with a somewhat greater variety and volume of domestic manufactures. The growth of such white-collar activities as trade, banking, medicine, education, and government services has been much more pronounced.

The Ceylon Government Railway connects the island's leading cities, and in recent years paved highways have opened most districts to automobiles. Much traffic, however, is via bullock cart, bicycle, and foot. There are international airports near Colombo and Jaffna. Urban and plantation Ceylon are comparatively well supplied with electric power from hydroelectric projects such as that at Watawala.

In Western terms most Ceylonese are extremely poor, but income per capita is higher than in the surrounding countries. A fairly large class of small-scale planters, merchants,

government employees, professional men, teachers, and other white-collar workers form a middle stratum between a few wealthy landlords and capitalists and the very poor masses. Average income is highest among Europeans, Burghers, and Sinhalese Christians. In recent years rapid population growth has brought about increasing landlessness, division of farms into uneconomically small sizes, and underemployment of labor.

Caste and feudal obligation dominated the precolonial economy. Remnants of a caste system remain and, especially among the rural population, play an important role in marriage and social life but are of only small and dwindling importance in economic affairs.

Education and Cultural Life. Ceylon has been and is better supplied with schools than most Asian countries. In 1954 the Department of Education supervised 6,894 schools having an enrollment of 1,625,742 students. Govern-

Ceylonese dancer, arrayed in an intricately worked, beaded and studded dress, with bejeweled coronet and girdle, performing ceremonial dance rites unchanged in 2,000 years.

ment schools, government-assisted church schools, and privately financed church schools provide elementary and secondary education in Sinhalese, Tamil, and English. Instruction at the University of Ceylon (about 2,500 students), now solely in English, will soon be in Sinhalese and Tamil as well. Other higher educational institutions include teacher-training institutes and the Technical College.

Partly because of the English-language education received by upper-income Ceylonese, a wide cultural gulf exists between them and the island's peasantry and proletariat. Ceylon's leading newspapers, periodicals, and books are published in English, and upper-income Ceylonese have in large part adopted Western ways, including male dress. The Nationalist revival has, however, influenced costume and the arts as well as politics and education. Sinhalese leaders especially have attempted to revive and promote national culture. Among outstanding Sinhalese arts are Kandyan dancing and drumming and brasswork. Ayurvedic medicine, now officially supported (along with Western), derives from ancient Ceylonese sources.

Government. Since Feb. 4, 1948, Ceylon has been a self-governing nation with dominion status in the British Commonwealth. Its government is similar to those of other dominions in the Commonwealth, with administration centered in a cabinet functioning under a prime minister, and chosen from the two chambers of a parliament. Most legislative power is concentrated in the House of Representatives. The governor general officially representing the British crown is only the ceremonial head of state and for several years has been a native Ceylonese. The prime minister elected in 1956 has announced his intention to follow the lead of India and Pakistan by changing Ceylon from a dominion to a republic while remaining within the British Commonwealth.

The island is divided into nine provinces, each in charge of a centrally appointed Government Agent. The provinces are:

Province	Capital	Area (sq. mi.)	Pop. (1953)
Western	Colombo	1,432	2,231,189
Central	Kandy	2,290	1,368,409
Southern	Galle	2,146	1,132,956
Northern	Jaffna	3,429	571,306
Eastern	Batticaloa	3,840	355,021
North-Western	Kurunegala	3,016	857,063
North-Central	Anuradhapura	4,009	228,792
Uva	Badulla	3,277	465,337
Sabaragamuwa	Ratnapura	1,839	893,608

The provinces are further subdivided for administrative purposes into a total of twenty districts. Village, town, and city government is in the hands of locally elected committees and councils. Citizenship derives primarily from Ceylonese ancestry rather than from residence or birth on the island.

Cabinets and Political Parties. Ceylon's first prime minister was Don Stephen Senanayake, who entered the Legislative Council in 1924 and became the Council's official leader in 1942. His United National Party, although receiving only a plurality in the 1947 election, was able to form a cabinet by forming a coalition with smaller parties and independent legislators. In 1948 a Citizenship Act deprived most Indian Tamils of the right to vote, and in the 1952 election the United National Party won a sweeping victory under the leadership of Dudley Senanayake, son of the first prime minister. In 1953 Dudley Senanayake resigned and was replaced by his cousin, John Lionel Kotelawala.

Although led by wealthy planters and generally regarded as the most conservative Ceylonese party, the United National Party in its early years announced a program of "practical socialism," embodying welfare-state measures and government ownership of "basic" manufacturing industries. A leading slogan concerned the island's transition "from colonial to national economy": i.e., from one dominated by foreign trade and British capital to one better balanced and characterized chiefly by local ownership and management. By 1953, however, foreign-exchange difficulties and the poor record of government industrial enterprise led the party to abandon much of its "practical socialism." In both foreign and domestic affairs the United National Party is strongly anti-Communist, although certain grievances caused it to negotiate rice-rubber pacts with Communist China. At the Bandung conference of 1955 Prime Minister Kotelawala incurred Nehru's wrath and won the West's applause by attacking Communism.

PHILIP GENDREAU

A beach on the Indian Ocean near Colombo, capital of Ceylon

Before 1951 the leading opposition party was the Trotskyite (anti-Stalin) Lanka Sama Samaja Party, which had been outlawed during World War II because of its opposition to the war effort. Its supporters included many young intellectuals, ardent Asianists, and non-Marxist social democrats. Also in opposition were the much less numerous Communists (pro-Stalin) and parties representing ethnic minorities. In 1951 Solomon West Ridgway Diaz Bandaranaike left the United National Party cabinet to form the Sri Lanka Freedom Party, which quickly surpassed the Lanka Sama Samaja in size. The new party's announced program included welfare-state and socialistic measures earlier stressed by the United National Party, but its leading features appeared to be Ceylonization of foreign-held jobs and foreign-owned properties, displacement of English by native tongues (especially Sinhalese) in government service, the courts, and the schools, and emphasis upon Sinhalese culture.

In 1956 an election coalition (People's United Front) composed of the Sri Lanka Freedom Party and certain former leaders of the Lanka Sama Samaja Party elected a substantial majority of the new Parliament and Bandanaraike became prime minister. Although the United National Party was a strong second in the popular vote, it elected so few candidates that in Parliament it shrank to third in size, behind both the winning coalition and the Lanka Sama Samaja Party.

Ceylonese workers harvesting salt at Elephant Pass

UNITED NATIONS

HISTORY

Precolonial Period. Much of Ceylon's early history is obscure. The now dominant Sinhalese people migrated from India to the island in about the sixth century B.C., settling chiefly in the irrigable plains of north-central Ceylon and establishing their capital at Anuradhapura. During the third century B.C. they were converted to Buddhism. Tamils, also from India, were the next major invaders. During the thirteenth century A.D. a series of wars between Tamils and Sinhalese destroyed Anuradhapura and the more recent capital Polonnaruwa, wrecked the irrigation system, turned the north-central plains into a malarial jungle, and drove the surviving Sinhalese to the central highlands and Wet Zone plains along the southern and western coasts. When the Portuguese arrived early in the sixteenth century, Ceylon was divided into three kingdoms: two Sinhalese, with capitals at Kotte (near Colombo) and Kandy, and one Tamil, with Jaffna as its chief city.

Precolonial Ceylon had an almost self-sufficient agricultural economy organized along caste and feudal lines. Arabs dominated the island's small volume of foreign trade. In the Sinhalese area Buddhist monks played a role roughly comparable to that of the Christian priesthood in medieval Europe.

Colonial Period. The period of European dominance falls into three almost equal parts: Portuguese, Dutch, and British. Until 1815, however, European rule was restricted to the coastal lowlands. Sinhalese kings in Kandy continued to rule the central highlands.

Although the Portuguese rulers expanded trade in spices and other products, their chief impact was not economic but rather religious. The Dutch, who gradually superseded the Portuguese during the seventeenth century, introduced new plants, increased the volume of production for export, and in some areas restored and developed irrigation, but did not fundamentally transform the island's economy. Perhaps their more lasting contributions were Roman-Dutch law, still the most important basis of Ceylonese law, and the ethnic group of Dutch Burghers, whose European traditions and superior education made them an important administrative and clerical class during the 152 years of British rule over the island.

Great Britain seized the island in 1796 after French Republican armies occupied the Netherlands. After a few years of administration by the East India Company, Ceylon became a crown colony in 1802, and in 1815 a British expedition, aided by rebel Sinhalese chiefs, overthrew the King of Kandy, thus uniting the island under one rule for the first time in many centuries. The British governors encouraged plantation and other export agriculture, and during the nineteenth century seized vast quantities of "waste" lands in the central highlands which were utilized first for coffee and later for tea and rubber plantations. These plantations were owned and managed very largely by the British, manned principally by Tamil labor imported from south India. Coconut growing and processing was largely developed by Ceylonese enterprise. Other economic growth was largely dependent on the plantations.

Local participation in the government of the colony through nominated members of the Governor's Legislative Council began in 1833, and the number of Ceylonese Council members continued to grow during the century following this innovation. British officials remained a majority of the Council, however, and elected members were not introduced until 1920. Even then, the electorate was only a small part of the population. Not until 1931 did a new constitution make the Council mainly elective, on a basis of universal adult suffrage. Most of the civil administration was centered in executive committees of Council members. Although Great Britain retained the right to veto or impose any measure, the governor usually concerned himself only with defense, external affairs, and the rights of minorities.

Independence. Ceylonese leaders began their campaign for independence during World War I and began to expect independence during World War II. Unlike the Indian Congress Party, however, most Ceylonese politicians co-operated with the British war effort. In 1946 the British government granted Ceylon a new constitution as a step toward dominion status. The election of a bicameral Parliament in 1947 and the formal grant of independence on Feb. 4, 1948, made Ceylon a fully self-governing member of the British Commonwealth. For some years thereafter Great Britain retained, by treaty, military bases on the island, but these bases were turned over to Ceylon after the 1956 election.

During its first two years in power the new cabinet reversed the post-1952 trend to the Right, but did not nationalize foreign-owned properties. Steps were taken to replace English with Ceylonese languages, but after bitter argument and some rioting Parliament did not subordinate Tamil to Sinhalese as fully as election speeches had proclaimed. Although Sinhalese became the sole official language in 1956, the government attempted to placate the Tamil Federal Party by extending the period of transition to allow Tamil-speaking citizens an opportunity to become proficient in Sinhalese. The more zealous Sinhalese professed to fear a movement favoring the establishment of a separatist Tamil state, weakening the unity of Ceylon. New disturbances arose in the first months of 1958, culminating in serious riots in May.

In foreign policy Prime Minister Bandaranaike generally followed Nehru's "neutralist" line. In February and March of 1958 loans were accepted from the Soviet and Chinese governments, the former involving credit for the construction of hydroelectric plants and the latter intended to finance relief for flood disasters.   W. M. W. and H. M. O.

CÉZANNE, PAUL [se′za′n] (1839-1906), French Postimpressionist painter, was born at Aix-en-Provence, Jan. 19, 1839, the son of a successful banker. When he showed no interest in business or law his father reluctantly permitted

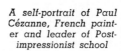
A self-portrait of Paul Cézanne, French painter and leader of Postimpressionist school

him to go to Paris in 1863 with his schoolfriend, Émile Zola. Cézanne prepared for the École des Beaux Arts, but failed to qualify. His first works were dramatic in content and Baroque in design, influenced by Gustave Courbet and Honoré Daumier. Although his intentionally antiacademic approach was vigorous, his immature technique was inadequate for the projection of his fervid emotions. Through Camille Pissarro he met the younger painters of Edouard Manet's circle and became interested in the new methods of painting landscape subjects out of doors.

Cézanne spent the summers of 1872 and 1873 at Auvers-sur-Oise with Pissarro, who taught him the use of a brighter palette and more disciplined brushwork. At the first Impressionist exhibition in 1874, Cézanne's *Maison du Pendu* (the Louvre) resembled his comrade's paintings in its commonplace landscape motif, but already looked beyond the typical Impressionist preoccupation with the infinitesimal facts of atmospheric coloration toward a more rigorous design and bolder three-dimensional structure. Until the end of the 1870's Cézanne continued to perfect his version of Impressionism in landscapes of the Île-de-France, but he also studied earlier painting in the Louvre in an effort to discover a more substantial basis for his art by reconciling the brilliance of Impressionist color with the permanence of three-dimensional design. This intention, which lay behind all his subsequent work, he defined as his ambition to do the paintings of Nicolas Poussin over again after nature.

After the third Impressionist exhibition in 1877, to which he contributed seventeen paintings, Cézanne withdrew from the group and in 1879 retired to Aix, where he passed the rest of his life. In these years his technique matured, and the masterpieces of his later years were created. In his attempt, as he described it, "to realize his sensations" of nature, Cézanne proceeded with infinite caution to construct on the picture plane the illusion of deep space in combination with the most vibrant colors, painstakingly accounting for every shift in plane and perspective by the subtlest variations of color rather than of value. For the fugitive vision of the Impressionists Cézanne substituted prolonged contemplation of the object. For this purpose the unvarying light and climate of Provence were more suitable than the ever-changing atmospheric effects of northern France.

Possibly Cézanne's greatest achievement was his realization of the immutable majesty of his beloved Mont Sainte-Victoire near Aix, where he sought the permanent unity of spatial order underlying the transient temporal data of light and color. Although still-lifes and landscapes were his preferred subjects, he painted a number of portraits and figure compositions, the grandiosely monumental results of which are like landscapes of humanity. In his last years Cézanne experienced a revival of the passionate emotion of his youth, which he delineated in a series of large figure compositions of the female nude. He was handicapped by his reluctance to draw from the model, and his greatest paintings, such as his *Baigneuses* (Philadelphia Museum) remained unfinished; but his attempt to revive the European tradition of monumental design was of incalculable importance in the Post-impressionist transformation of Impressionism. Toward the end of his solitary life Cézanne was almost forgotten by the Parisian art world until a retrospective exhibition of his work at the Salon d'Automne in 1904 and a larger posthumous exhibition in 1907 revealed his work to a younger generation. The study of his exhaustive analytical procedure and elaborate formal structure was an important factor in the subsequent development of Cubism. Cézanne died at Aix, Oct. 22, 1906. (*See color plate in article* PAINTING.)   G. H. H.

THE THEME OF THE END PAPERS

1. The early use of fire; 2. The use of the wheel; 3. The development of weaving; 4. The building of the pyramids of Egypt; 5. Moses receives the Ten Commandments; 6. Confucius, one of the great moral philosophers; 7. Hippocrates, the father of scientific medicine; 8. Athens, the cradle of Western culture; 9. Early exploration; 10. The birth of Christ; 11. Medieval culture in Europe; 12. King John signing the Magna Carta; 13. The introduction of gunpowder to European warfare; 14. Gutenberg and the invention of printing by movable type; 15. Copernicus and the modern concept of the universe; 16. The discovery of the new world by Columbus; 17. William Shakespeare; 18. The Declaration of Independence; 19. The Industrial Revolution; 20. Samuel F. B. Morse, inventor of the telegraph; 21. Thomas A. Edison and the first electric light; 22. The Wright brothers at Kitty Hawk; 23. The development of radio communication; 24. The coming of the Atomic Age.

HOW TO USE THE BIBLIOGRAPHY

HOW TO USE THE INDEX

NOTE ON THE PRONUNCIATION SYSTEM

See table of contents, Page v, Volume 20

The pronunciation of the symbols given below is indicated by the italicized letters in the words that immediately follow them:

ɑ	f*a*ther, c*a*r	ə	m*a*k*e*r, *a*go	ŋ	si*ng*i*ng*	t	*t*ro*t*
ɑ̃	(Fr.) él*an*, *en**	ɜ	f*i*rst, b*u*rn	o	n*o*te, *o*ld	th	*th*irty-*th*ree
ɒ	wh*a*t, n*o*t	f	*f*or*f*eit	õ	(Fr.) b*on*, r*om*pre	t͟h	*o*th*er* *th*an *th*is
a	*a*sk, *a*nswer;	g	*g*a*g*	ö	(Ger.) sch*ö*n, b*ö*se	u	r*u*le, pr*u*ne
	(Fr.) *a*ttacher	h	*h*ot*h*ouse	ɔ	*o*rb, *a*ll	ü	(Fr.) cr*u*;
æ	h*a*t, b*a*ck	i	*e*ve, benz*i*ne	œ	(Fr.) l*eu*r;		(Ger.) gr*ü*n*
æ̃	(Fr.) v*in*, m*ain**	ɪ	*i*f, st*i*ng		(Ger.) k*ö*nnen*	ʊ	b*u*ll, b*u*sh
ai	cr*y*, sp*i*ne	j	*j*u*dg*e	œ̃	(Fr.) br*un*, l*un*di*	ʌ	b*u*t, s*o*n
au	pr*ow*, l*ou*d	k	*c*a*k*e	ɔi	t*oy*, p*oin*t	v	*v*i*v*id
b	*b*o*b*	χ	(Ger.) i*ch*, a*ch**	p	*p*ro*p*	w	*w*ood*w*ork
d	*d*i*d*	l	*l*oya*l*	r	*r*oa*r*	y	*y*esteryear
e	f*a*te, *e*lite	m	*m*i*m*e	s	*s*au*c*e	z	pri*z*e*s*
ɛ	*y*et, sp*e*ll	n	*n*o*n*e	sh	ha*sh*i*sh*	zh	plea*s*ure, a*z*ure

*All symbols marked with a tilde (~) represent nasalized vowels. Thus the French vowels ɑ̃, æ̃, and õ are somewhat like a nasal American pronunciation of the vowels in *pon*(d), *an*(d), and *lon*(g); by pronouncing these words while holding the nose one may approximate the French sounds.

The symbol ö is roughly equivalent to the vowel of *cu*(r) or *fi*(r), but with the r silent, as in Southern speech. The symbol œ represents the same sound, but shortened, as in *cu*(r)*tain*, *pu*(r)*ple*. The nasalized vowel, æ̃, resembles the vowel of *u*(r)*n*, *chu*(r)*n*.

The symbol ü represents the sound of *ee* in *fee* pronounced with the lips rounded as for the *oo* in *goose*.

The symbol χ represents the sound of *ch* in Scottish *loch*; it is like the *ck* in *lock*, except that the sound continues.

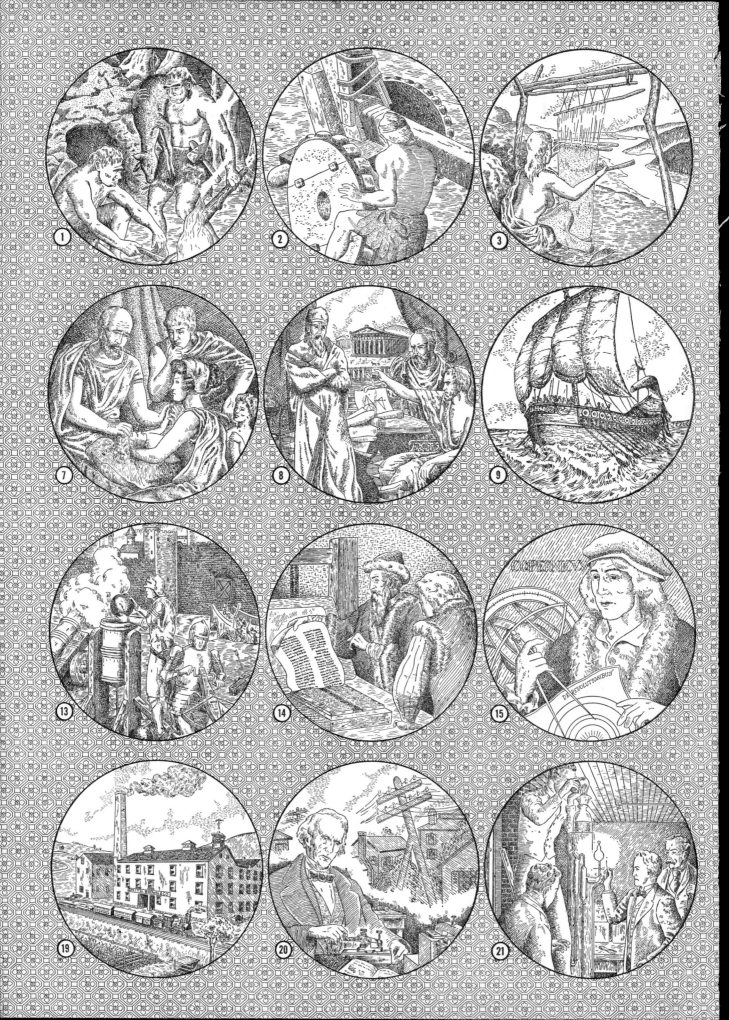